ATLAS

HAMMOND INCORPORATED   MAPLEWOOD, NEW JERSEY 07040

Hammond Publications Advisory Board

Library of Congress Cataloging-in-Publication Data
Hammond Incorporated.
    Citation world atlas.
        p. cm.
    At head of title: Hammond.
    Includes indexes.
    1. Atlases.   I. Title   II. Title: Hammond citation world atlas.
III. Title: World atlas.
G1021.H2446   1991   [G&M]
912—dc20   91-7719
ISBN 0-8437-1258-9 (thumb-indexed) $29.95   CIP
ISBN 0-8437-1253-8 (paperback)   MAP

Contents

Introduction to the World Atlas

The current edition of the Hammond World Atlas features an outstanding new section devoted to THE PHYSICAL WORLD — a series of terrain maps of land forms and ocean floors. These physical maps were originally produced as sculptured terrain models, thus simulating the earth's surface in a highly realistic manner. The three-dimensional effect is both instructive and pleasing to the eye.

As in previous editions, the atlas is organized to make the retrieval of information as simple and quick as possible. The guiding principle in organizing the atlas material has been to present separate subjects on *separate* maps. In this way, each individual map topic is shown with the greatest degree of clarity, unencumbered with extraneous information that is best revealed on separate maps. Of equal importance from the standpoint of good atlas design is the treatment of all current information on a given country or state as a single atlas unit. Thus, the basic reference map of an area is accompanied on adjacent pages by all supplementary information pertaining to that area. For example, the detailed index for a given map always appears on the same page as, or on the pages immediately following, the reference map. This same map index provides population data for the many cities, towns and villages shown on the map. Highlight information on the area, i.e., the total population and area, the capital, the highest point, is listed in the summary fact listings accompanying each unit. An adjacent locator map relates the subject area to the larger world beyond. A three-dimensional picture of the area is exhibited by means of the accompanying full-color topographic map. A separate economic map defines the vital agricultural, industrial and mineral resources of the area. In the case of the foreign maps, the flag of each independent nation appears on the appropriate page. Finally, certain country units contain special subject maps dealing with the history, climate, demography and vegetation of the area.

An important feature of the atlas is the addition of ZIP codes to the index entries for each of the legion of communities shown on the state maps. With the exception of the U.S. Postal Service directories of limited availability, the ZIP code listings herein are the most extensive published.

The back of the book contains a second type of index. This is a multi-paged "A-to-Z" index of places that appear on the maps. The use of this map index is essential when the name of a place is known but its country, state, or province is unknown.

Of course, the maps have been thoroughly updated. These revisions echo the new nations, shifting boundaries and the fluid internal divisions of many countries. New communities generated by the opening up of resources in the developing nations are also noted. Up-to-date geographical information, both foreign and domestic, is received daily by the atlas editors. A worldwide correspondence and thorough research brings to the atlas user the latest geographical and demographic information obtainable.

In closing it may be said that the atlas has truly been designed for contemporary use. Just as the information presented on the following pages is as current and up to date as the editors and cartographers could issue it, so the design and organization has been as well planned as possible to create a work useful to present generations.

President
HAMMOND INCORPORATED

Introduction to the Maps and Indexes

The following notes have been added to aid the reader in making the best use of this atlas. Though the reader may be familiar with maps and map indexes, the publisher believes that a quick review of the material below will add to his enjoyment of this reference work.

Arrangement—The Plan of the Atlas. The atlas has been designed with maximum convenience for the user as its objective. Part I of the atlas is devoted to the physical world—terrain maps of land forms and the sea floor. Part II contains the general political reference maps, area by area. All geographically related information pertaining to a country or region appears on adjacent pages, eliminating the task of searching throughout the entire volume for data on a given area. Thus, the reader will find, conveniently assembled, political, topographic, economic and special maps of a political area or region, accompanied by detailed map indexes, statistical data, and illustrations of the national flags of the area.

The sequence of country units in this American-designed atlas is international in arrangement. Units on the world as a whole are followed by a section on the polar regions which, in turn, is followed by pages devoted to Europe and its countries. Every continent map is accompanied by special population distribution, climatic and vegetation maps of that continent. Following the maps of the European continent and its countries, the geographic sequence plan proceeds as follows: Asia, the Pacific and Australia, Africa, South America, North America, and ends with detailed coverage on the United States.

Political Maps—The Primary Reference Tool. The most detailed maps in each country unit are the *political maps.* It is our feeling that the reader is likely to refer to these maps more often than to any other in the book when confronted by such questions as—Where? How big? What is it near? Answering these common queries is the function of the political maps. Each political map stresses *political* phenomena—countries, internal political divisions, boundaries, cities and towns. The major political unit or units, shown on the map, are banded in distinctive colors for easy identification and delineation. First-order political subdivisions (states, provinces, counties on the state maps) are shown, scale permitting.

The reader is advised to make use of the *legend* appearing under the title on each political map. Map *symbols,* the special "language" of maps, are explained in the legend. Each variety of dot, circle, star or interrupted line has a special meaning which should be clearly understood by the user so that he may interpret the map data correctly.

Each country has been portrayed at a *scale* commensurate with its political, areal, economic or tourist importance. In certain cases, a whole map unit may be devoted to a single nation if that nation is considered to be of prime interest to most atlas users. In other cases, several nations will be shown on a single map if, as separate entities, they are of lesser relative importance. Areas of dense settlement and important significance within a country have been enlarged and portrayed in inset maps inserted on the margins of the main map. The scale of each map is indicated as a fractional representation (1:1,000,000). The reader is advised to refer to the linear or "bar" scale appearing on each map or map inset in order to determine the distance between points.

The *projection* system used for each map is noted near the title of the map. Map projections are the special graphic systems used by cartographers to render the curved three-dimensional surface of the globe on a flat surface. Optimum map projections determined by the attributes of the area have been used by the publishers for each map in the atlas.

A word here as to the choice of place names on the maps. Throughout the atlas names appear, with a few exceptions, in their local official spellings. However, conventional Anglicized spellings are used for major geographical divisions and for towns and topographic features for which English forms exist; i.e., "Spain" instead of "España" or "Munich" instead of "München." Names of this type are normally followed by the local official spelling in parentheses. As an aid to the user the indexes are cross-referenced for all current and most former spellings of such names.

Names of cities and towns in the United States follow the forms listed in the *Post Office Directory* of the United States Postal Service. Domestic physical names follow the decisions of the Board on Geographic Names, U.S. Department of the Interior, and of various state geographic name boards.

It is the belief of the publishers that the boundaries shown in a general reference atlas should reflect current geographic and political realities. This policy has been followed consistently in the atlas. The presentation of *de facto* boundaries in cases of territorial dispute between various nations does not imply the political endorsement of such boundaries by the publisher, but simply the honest representation of boundaries as they exist at the time of the printing of the atlas maps.

Indexes—Pinpointing a Location. Each political map is accompanied by a comprehensive index of the place names appearing on the map. If you are unfamiliar with the location of a particular geographical place and wish to find its position within the confines of the subject area of the map, consult the map index as your first step. The name of the feature sought will be found in its proper alphabetical sequence with a key reference letter-number combination corresponding to its location on the map. After noting the key reference letter-number combination for the place name, turn to the map. The place name will be found within the square formed by the two lines of latitude and the two lines of longitude which enclose the coordinates—i.e., the marginal letters and numbers. The diagram below illustrates the system of indexing.

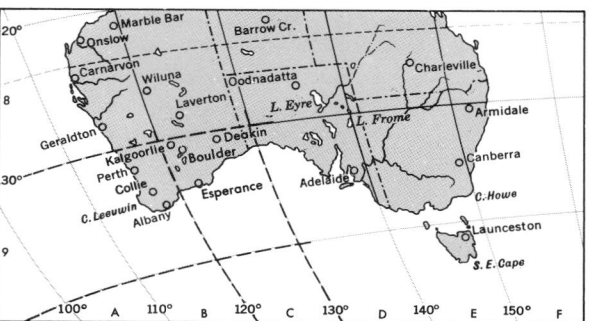

In the case of maps consisting entirely of insets, the place name is found near the intersection point of the imaginary lines connecting the coordinates at right angles. See below.

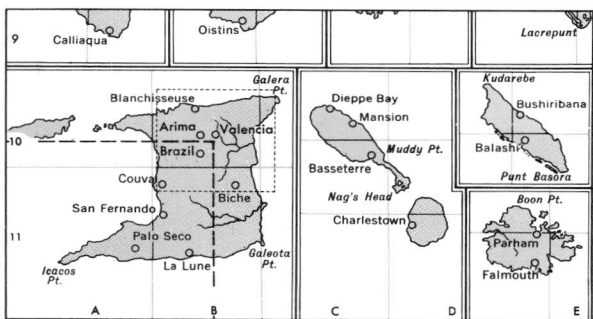

Where space on the map has not permitted giving the complete form of the place name, the complete form is shown in the index. Where a place is known by more than one name or by various spellings of the same name, the different forms have been included in the index. Physical features are listed under their proper names and not according to their generic terms; that is to say, Rio Negro will be found under Negro and not under Rio Negro. On the other hand, Rio Grande will be found under Rio Grande. Accompanying most index entries for cities and towns, and for other political units, are *population figures* for the particular entries. The large number of population figures in the atlas makes this work one of the most comprehensive statistical sources available to the public today. The population figures have been taken from the latest official censuses and estimates of the various nations. Dates and sources for the population figures are listed in the Gazetteer-Index of the World following this section.

Population and area figures for countries and major political units are listed in bold type *fact lists* on the margins of the indexes. In addition, the capital, largest city, highest point, monetary unit, principal languages and the prevailing religions of the country concerned are also listed. The Gazetteer-Index of the World on the following pages provides a quick reference index for countries and other important areas. Though population and area figures for each major unit are also found in the map section, the Gazetteer-Index provides a conveniently arranged statistical comparison contained in five pages. As mentioned, dates and sources of the population figures appearing in the country indexes are also listed in this section.

All index entries for cities and towns in the indexes accompanying individual state maps for the United States are preceded by a five-digit postal ZIP code number applying to the community. A dagger (†) designates those places that do not possess a post office. The ZIP code number listed in such cases refers to that of the nearest post office. An asterisk (*) marks those larger cities which are divided into multiple ZIP code areas. Using the single ZIP code number listed in such cases will direct your letter to the proper city with dispatch. However, if the precise ZIP code number of the address within the city is needed, it is suggested that the reader refer to the latest National ZIP Code Directory at his local post office. This detailed guide lists every street in a multiple ZIP code city with the proper ZIP code for the street.

Relief Maps. Accompanying each political map is a relief map of the area. These are in addition to the terrain maps of land forms in Part I of the atlas. The purpose of the relief map is to illustrate the surface configuration (TOPOGRAPHY) of the region. A shading technique in color simulates the relative ruggedness of the terrain—plains, plateaus, valleys, hills and mountains. Graded colors, ranging from greens for lowlands, yellows for intermediate evaluations to brown in the highlands, indicate the height above sea level of each part of the land. A vertical scale at the margin of the map shows the approximate height in meters and feet represented by each color.

Economic Maps—Agriculture, Industry and Resources. One of the most interesting features that will be found in each country unit is the economic map. From this map one can determine the basic activities of a nation as expressed through its economy. A perusal of the map yields a full understanding of the area's economic geography and natural resources.

The agricultural economy is manifested in two ways: color bands and commodity names. The color bands express broad categories of *dominant land use,* such as cereal belts, forest lands, livestock range lands or nonagricultural wastes. The red commodity names, on the other hand, pinpoint the areas of production of *specific* crops, i.e., wheat, cotton, sugar beets, etc.

Major mineral occurrences are denoted by standard letter symbols appearing in blue. The relative size of the letter symbols signifies the relative importance of the deposit.

The manufacturing sector of the economy is presented by means of diagonal line patterns expressing the various *industrial* areas of consequence within a country.

The fishing industry is represented by names of commercial fish species appearing offshore in blue letters. Major waterpower sites are designated by blue symbols.

The publishers have tried to make this work the most comprehensive and useful atlas available, and it is hoped that it will prove a valuable reference work. Any constructive suggestions from the reader will be welcomed.

Sources and Acknowledgements

A multitude of sources goes into the making of a large-scale reference work such as this. To list them all would take many pages and would consume space better devoted to the maps and reference materials themselves. However, certain general sources were very useful in preparing this work and are listed below.

STATISTICAL OFFICE OF THE UNITED NATIONS.
Demographic Yearbook. New York. Issued annually.

STATISTICAL OFFICE OF THE UNITED NATIONS.
Statistical Yearbook. New York. Issued annually.

THE GEOGRAPHER, U.S. DEPARTMENT OF STATE.
International Boundary Study papers. Washington. Various dates.

THE GEOGRAPHER, U.S. DEPARTMENT OF STATE.
Geographic Notes. Washington. Various dates.

UNITED STATES BOARD ON GEOGRAPHIC NAMES.
Decisions on Geographic Names in the United States. Washington. Various dates.

UNITED STATES BOARD ON GEOGRAPHIC NAMES.
Official Standard Names Gazetteers. Washington. Various dates.

CANADIAN PERMANENT COMMITTEE ON GEOGRAPHICAL NAMES.
Gazetteer of Canada series. Ottawa. Various dates.

UNITED STATES POSTAL SERVICE.
National Five Digit ZIP Code and Post Office Directory. Washington. Issued annually.

UNITED STATES POSTAL SERVICE.
Postal Bulletin. Washington. Issued weekly.

UNITED STATES DEPARTMENT OF THE INTERIOR. BUREAU OF MINES.
Minerals Yearbook. 4 vols. Washington. Various dates.

UNITED STATES GEOLOGICAL SURVEY.
Elevations and distances in the United States. Reston, Va. 1980.

CARTACTUAL.
Cartactual—Topical Map Service. Budapest. Issues bi-monthly.

AMERICAN GEOGRAPHICAL SOCIETY.
Focus. New York. Issued ten times a year.

THE AMERICAN UNIVERSITY.
Foreign Area Studies. Washington. Various dates.

CENTRAL INTELLIGENCE AGENCY.
General reference maps. Washington. Various dates.

A sample list of sources used for specific countries follows:

Afghanistan
CENTRAL STATISTICS OFFICE.
Preliminary Results of the First Afghan Population Census 1979. Kabul.

Albania
DREJTORIA E STATISTIKES.
1979 Census. Tiranë.

Argentina
INSTITUTO NACIONAL DE ESTADISTICA Y CENSOS.
Censo Nacional de Población y Vivienda 1980. Buenos Aires.

Australia
AUSTRALIAN BUREAU OF STATISTICS.
Census of Population and Housing 1981. Canberra.

Brazil
FUNDACAO INSTITUTO BRASILEIRO DE GEOGRAFIA E ESTATISTICA.
IX Recenseamento Geral do Brasil 1980. Rio de Janeiro.

Canada
STATISTICS CANADA.
1981 Census of Canada. Ottawa.

Cuba
COMITE ESTATAL DE ESTADISTICAS.
Censo de Población y Viviendas 1981. Havana.

Hungary
HUNGARIAN CENTRAL STATISTICAL OFFICE.
1980 Census. Budapest.

Indonesia
BIRO PUSAT STATISTIK.
Sensus Penduduk 1980. Jakarta.

Kuwait
CENTRAL OFFICE OF STATISTICS.
1980 Census. Al Kuwait.

New Zealand
DEPARTMENT OF STATISTICS.
New Zealand Census of Population and Dwellings 1981. Wellington.

Panama
DIRECCIÓN DE ESTADISTICA Y CENSO.
Censos Nacionales de 1980. Panamá.

Papua New Guinea
BUREAU OF STATISTICS.
National Population Census 1980. Port Moresby.

Philippines
NATIONAL CENSUS AND STATISTICS OFFICE.
1980 Census of Population. Manila.

Saint Lucia
CENSUS OFFICE.
1980 Population Census. Castries.

Singapore.
DEPARTMENT OF STATISTICS.
Census of Population 1980. Singapore.

U.S.S.R.
CENTRAL STATISTICAL ADMINISTRATION.
1979 Census. Moscow.

United States
BUREAU OF THE CENSUS.
1980 Census of Population. Washington.

Vanuatu
CENSUS OFFICE.
1979 Population Census. Port Vila.

Zambia
CENTRAL STATISTICAL OFFICE.
1980 Census of Population and Housing. Lusaka.

Gazetteer-Index of the World

This alphabetical list of continents, countries, states, possessions and other major geographical areas provides a quick reference to their area in square miles and square kilometers, population, capital or chief town, map page number and an alpha-numeric index reference. The index reference indicates the square on the respective page in which the name may be found. An indication of the population sources used is also included, and refers both to the total figures given in this Gazetteer-Index.

populations appearing in greater detail with the maps throughout the atlas. The population figures used in each case are the latest reliable figures obtainable. A glance at the sources will show that the dates vary considerably throughout the world. In certain areas where no census has ever been taken, we must rely on official estimates. In other areas where censuses have been taken at infrequent intervals, we again rely on estimates. The key to the abbreviations used in the Gazetteer-Index follows:

aut = autonomous	est = estimates	reg = regions	
boro = boroughs	excl = excluding	rep = republics	
cap = capital	FC = final census	S.S.R. = Soviet Socialist Republic	
CE = census (undetermined)	gov = governorates	terr = territories; territory	
CIA = U.S. Central Intelligence Agency	incl = including	TP = total population	
	isl = islands	U.K. = United Kingdon	
cit = cities	met = metropolitan	UN = United Nations	
co = counties	OE = official estimate	U.S.A. = United States of America	
com = communes	oth = other populations	U.S.S.R. = Union of Soviet Socialist Republics	
dist = departments	par = parishes		
dist = districts	PC = preliminary census	ws = with suburbs	
div = divisions	prov = provinces; provincial		

Country	Area Square Miles	Area Square Kilometers	Population	Capital or Chief Town	Page and Index Ref.	Sources of Population Data
*Afghanistan	250,775	649,507	15,540,000	Kabul	68/A 2	79 PC
Africa	11,707,000	30,321,130	469,000,000	....	102/.......	80 UN est
Alabama, U.S.A.	51,705	133,916	3,893,888	Montgomery	195/.......	80 FC & OE
Alaska, U.S.A.	591,004	1,530,700	401,851	Juneau	196/.......	80 FC & OE
*Albania	11,100	28,749	2,590,600	Tiranë	45/E 5	TP—79 PC; cit over 6,000—70 OE; oth—63 OE
Alberta, Canada	255,285	661,185	2,237,724	Edmonton	182/.......	81 FC
*Algeria	919,591	2,381,740	17,422,000	Algiers	106/D 3	77 PC
American Samoa	77	199	32,297	Pago Pago	87/J 7; 86/.......	80 FC
Andorra	188	487	31,000	Andorra la Vella	33/G 1	TP—79 OE; cap—75 OE
*Angola	481,351	1,246,700	7,078,000	Luanda	114/C 6	TP—80 UN est; oth—70 FC
Anguilla, U.K.	35	91	6,519	The Valley	156/F 3	74 FC
Antarctica	5,500,000	14,245,000	....	....	5/.......	....
*Antigua and Barbuda	171	443	75,000	St. John's	161/E 11; 156/G 3	TP—80 OE; oth—70 FC
*Argentina	1,072,070	2,776,661	28,438,000	Buenos Aires	143/.......	TP—82 OE; oth—80 PC
Arizona, U.S.A.	114,000	295,260	2,718,425	Phoenix	198/.......	80 FC & OE
Arkansas, U.S.A.	53,187	137,754	2,286,435	Little Rock	202/.......	80 FC & OE
Armenian S.S.R., U.S.S.R.	11,506	29,800	3,031,000	Erivan	52/F 6	TP, cit over 50,000—79 PC; oth—70 FC
Aruba, Netherlands	75	193	66,790	Oranjestad	161/E 9	TP—86 OE; cap—72 est
Ascension Island, St. Helena	34	88	719	Georgetown	102/A 5	76 FC
Ashmore & Cartier Islands, Australia	61	159	....	(Canberra, Austr.)	88/C 2	....
Asia	17,128,500	44,362,815	2,633,000,000	....	54/.......	80 est
*Australia	2,966,136	7,682,300	14,576,330	Canberra	88/.......	81 FC
Australian Capital Territory	927	2,400	221,609	Canberra	96/E 4	81 FC
*Austria	32,375	83,851	7,507,000	Vienna	40/B 3	TP—80 OE; cap, cit over 100,000—73 OE; oth—71 FC
Azerbaidzhan S.S.R., U.S.S.R.	33,436	86,600	6,028,000	Baku	52/G 6	TP, cit over 50,000—79 PC; oth—70 FC
Azores, Portugal	902	2,335	264,400	Ponta Delgada	32/.......	TP—77 OE; oth—70 FC & PC
*Bahamas	5,382	13,939	209,505	Nassau	156/C 1	80 PC
*Bahrain	240	622	358,857	Manama	58/F 4	TP—81 PC; oth—71 FC
Baker Island, U.S.A.	1	2.6	....	....	87/J 5	....
Balearic Islands, Spain	1,936	5,014	558,287	Palma	33/H 3	70 FC
*Bangladesh	55,126	142,776	87,052,024	Dhaka	68/G 4	TP—81 PC; oth—74 FC
*Barbados	166	430	248,983	Bridgetown	161/B 8	80 PC
*Belgium	11,781	30,513	9,855,110	Brussels	27/E 7	TP—80 OE; oth—70 FC (com)
*Belize	8,867	22,966	144,857	Belmopan	154/C 2	TP, cap, cit over 1,000—80 PC; oth—70 PC
*Benin	43,483	112,620	3,338,240	Porto-Novo	106/E 6	TP—79 PC; cap, Cotonou—75 OE; oth—73 OE
Bermuda, U.K.	21	54	67,761	Hamilton	156/H 3	80 PC
*Bhutan	18,147	47,000	1,298,000	Thimphu	68/G 3	TP—80 UN est; oth—70 OE
*Bolivia	424,163	1,098,582	5,600,000	La Paz; Sucre	136/.......	TP—80 OE; cap, dept, dept cap—76 FC; oth—50 FC
Bonaire, Neth. Antilles	112	291	8,087	Kralendijk	161/E 9	TP—71 FC; cap—72 est
Bophuthatswana, South Africa	15,570	40,326	1,200,000	Mmabatho	119/D 5	TP—78 est; oth—70 FC
*Botswana	224,764	582,139	819,000	Gaborone	119/C 4	TP—80 OE; cap, Francistown—74 OE; Selebi-Pikwe—75 FC; oth—71 FC
Bouvet Island, Norway	22	57	....	....	5/D 1	....
*Brazil	3,284,426	8,506,663	119,098,992	Brasília	132/.......	80 PC
British Columbia, Canada	366,253	948,596	2,744,467	Victoria	184/.......	81 FC
British Indian Ocean Terr.	29	75	2,000	(London, U.K.)	54/L 10	78 est
British Virgin Islands	59	153	11,006	Road Town	157/H 1	TP—80 FC; oth—70 FC
*Brunei	2,226	5,765	192,832	Bandar Seri Begawan	85/E 4	81 PC
*Bulgaria	42,823	110,912	8,862,000	Sofia	45/F 4	TP—80 OE; oth—75 PC
*Burkina Faso	105,869	274,200	6,908,000	Ouagadougou	106/D 6	TP—80 UN est; oth—75 FC, 73 OE
*Burma (Myanmar)	261,789	678,034	32,913,000	Rangoon	72/B 2	TP—79 OE; states, div. cit over 100,000—73 PC; oth—53 FC
*Burundi	10,747	27,835	4,021,910	Bujumbura	114/E 4	79 PC
*Byelorussian S.S.R. (White Russian S.S.R.), U.S.S.R.	80,154	207,600	9,560,000	Minsk	52/C 4	TP, cit over 50,000—79 PC; oth—70 FC
California, U.S.A.	158,706	411,049	23,667,565	Sacramento	204/.......	80 FC & OE
*Cambodia (Kampuchea)	69,898	181,036	5,200,000	Phnom Penh	72/E 4	TP—79 CIA est; cap—80 est
*Cameroon	183,568	475,441	8,503,000	Yaoundé	114/B 2	TP—80 OE; cit over 21,000—76 FC; Ebolowa, oth—70 OE
*Canada	3,851,787	9,976,139	24,343,181	Ottawa	162/.......	81 FC
Canary Islands, Spain	2,808	7,273	1,170,224	Las Palmas; Santa Cruz	32/B 4	70 FC
Cape Province, South Africa	261,705	677,816	5,543,506	Cape Town	118/C 6	TP—80 PC; oth—70 PC
*Cape Verde	1,557	4,033	324,000	Praia	106/B 8	TP—80 UN est; oth—70 PC
Cayman Islands, U.K.	100	259	18,000	Georgetown	156/B 3	TP—81 OE; oth—79 FC
Celebes, Indonesia	72,986	189,034	7,732,383	Ujung Pandang	85/G 6	71 PC
*Central African Republic	242,000	626,780	2,284,000	Bangui	114/C 2	TP—79 est; oth—75 FC

*Member of the United Nations

Gazetteer-Index of the World

Country	Area Square Miles	Square Kilometers	Population	Capital or Chief Town	Page and Index Ref.	Sources of Population Data
Central America	197,480	511,475	21,000,000	....	154/.......	79 OE
*Chad	495,752	1,283,998	4,309,000	N'Djamena	111/C 4	TP—78 OE; oth—72 OE
Channel Islands, U.K.	75	194	133,000	St. Helier; St. Peter Port	13/E 8	TP—81 OE; oth—71 FC
*Chile	292,257	756,946	11,275,440	Santiago	138/.......	TP—82 PC; cit (part)—79 OE; oth—70 FC & PC
*China, People's Rep. of	3,691,000	9,559,690	958,090,000	Beijing	77/.......	TP, prov, Beijing, Shanghai, Tianjin—78 OE; oth—70 est
China, Republic of (Taiwan)	13,971	36,185	16,609,961	Taipei	77/K 7	TP, cap, Penghu Isl., cit over 300,000—77 OE; oth—70 OE
Christmas Island, Australia	52	135	3,184	Flying Fish Cove	54/M 11	80 OE
Ciskei, S. Africa	2,988	7,740	635,631	Bisho	119/D 6	80 PC
Clipperton Island, France	2	5.2	....	....	146/H 8	....
Cocos (Keeling) Islands, Australia	5.4	14	555	West Island	54/N 11	81 PC
*Colombia	439,513	1,138,339	27,520,000	Bogotá	126/.......	TP—80 OE; oth—73 PC
Colorado, U.S.A.	104,091	269,596	2,889,735	Denver	208/.......	80 FC & OE
*Comoros	719	1,862	290,000	Moroni	119/G 2	TP—78 est; cap—75 OE; oth—66 FC
*Congo	132,046	342,000	1,537,000	Brazzaville	114/B 4	TP—80 UN est; cap—74 FC; oth—74 PC
Connecticut, U.S.A.	5,018	12,997	3,107,576	Hartford	210/.......	80 FC & OE
Cook Islands, New Zealand	91	236	17,695	Avarua	87/K 7	81 PC
Coral Sea Islands, Australia	8.5	22	....	....	88/J 3	....
Corsica, France	3,352	8,682	289,842	Ajaccio; Bastia	28/B 6	75 FC
*Costa Rica	19,575	50,700	2,245,000	San José	154/E 5	TP—80 OE; oth—73 FC
*Cuba	44,206	114,494	9,706,369	Havana	158/.......	TP—81 PC; prov, cap—81 PC; oth—81 & 70 PC
Curaçao, Neth. Antilles	178	462	145,430	Willemstad	161/G 7	TP—71 FC; cap—75 OE
*Cyprus	3,473	8,995	629,000	Nicosia	62/E 5	TP—80 OE; oth—73 FC, 72 OE
*Czechoslovakia	49,373	127,876	15,276,799	Prague	41/C 2	TP—80 PC; cap, cit over 100,000—75 OE; rep, reg—74 OE; oth—75 OE, 70 FC
Delaware, U.S.A.	2,044	5,294	594,317	Dover	245/R 3	80 FC & OE
*Denmark	16,629	43,069	5,124,000	Copenhagen	21/.......	TP—80 OE; oth—75 OE, 71 OE, 70 FC
District of Columbia, U.S.A.	69	179	638,432	Washington	244/F 5	80 FC
*Djibouti	8,880	23,000	386,000	Djibouti	111/H 5	TP—79 est; cap—73 OE
*Dominica	290	751	74,089	Roseau	161/E 7	TP—80 PC; oth—70 FC
*Dominican Republic	18,704	48,443	5,647,977	Santo Domingo	158/D 6	81 PC
*Ecuador	109,483	283,561	8,644,000	Quito	128/C 3	TP—81 OE; oth—74 FC
*Egypt	386,659	1,001,447	41,572,000	Cairo	110/E 2	TP—79 OE; oth—76 PC
*El Salvador	8,260	21,393	4,813,000	San Salvador	154/C 4	TP—80 OE; oth—71 FC
England, U.K.	50,516	130,836	46,220,955	London	13/.......	TP—81 PC; co, cap (boro & ws)—76 OE; cit—76 & 73 OE; oth—71 FC
*Equatorial Guinea	10,831	28,052	244,000	Malabo	114/A 3	TP—79 est; terr—68 OE; oth—60 FC
Estonian S.S.R., U.S.S.R.	17,413	45,100	1,466,000	Tallinn	52/C 3; 53/.......	TP, cit over 50,000—79 PC; oth—70 FC
*Ethiopia	471,776	1,221,900	31,065,000	Addis Ababa	110/G 5	TP—80 OE; cap, Asmara—78 OE; prov—72 OE; oth—72 & 71 OE
Europe	4,057,000	10,507,630	676.000.000	....	7/.......	80 est
Faeroe Islands, Denmark	540	1,399	41.969	Tórshavn	21/B 2	77 FC
Falkland Islands & Dependencies, U.K.	6,198	16,053	1,813	Stanley	120/E 8; 143/D 7	76 FC
*Fiji	7,055	18,272	588,068	Suva	87/H 8; 86/.......	80 FC
*Finland	130,128	337,032	4,788,000	Helsinki	18/O 6	TP—80 OE; prov—75 OE; oth—75 OE, 70 FC
Florida, U.S.A.	58,664	151,940	9,746,342	Tallahassee	212/.......	80 FC & OE
*France	210,038	543,998	53,788,000	Paris	28/.......	TP—80 OE; oth—75 FC
French Guiana	35,135	91,000	73,022	Cayenne	131/E 3	82 FC
French Polynesia	1,544	4,000	137,382	Papeete	87/L 8	77 FC
*Gabon	103,346	267,666	551,000	Libreville	114/B 4	TP—80 UN est; oth—70 FC
*Gambia	4,127	10,689	601,000	Banjul	106/A 6	TP—80 OE; oth—73 FC
Gaza Strip	139	360	400,000	Gaza	65/A 4	TP—76 OE; oth—67 CE
Georgia, U.S.A.	58,910	152,577	5,463,105	Atlanta	217/.......	80 FC & OE
Georgian S.S.R., U.S.S.R.	26,911	69,700	5,015,000	Tbilisi	52/F 6	TP, cit over 50,000—79 PC; oth—70 FC
*Germany	137,753	356,780	78,395,000	Berlin	22/.......	TP—80 OE; states, cap—76 OE; oth—75 OE, 76 OE, 70 FC
*Ghana	92,099	238,536	11,450,000	Accra	106/D 7	TP—80 OE; oth—70 FC
Gibraltar, U.K.	2.28	5.91	29,760	Gibraltar	33/D 4	79 OE
*Great Britain & Northern Ireland (United Kingdom)	94,399	244,493	55,672,000	London	10/.......	TP—81 OE (see England, Wales, Scotland, Northern Ireland)
*Greece	50,944	131,945	9,599,000	Athens	45/F 6	TP—80 OE; oth—71 FC
Greenland, Denmark	840,000	2,175,600	49,773	Nuuk (Godthåb)	4/B 12	TP—80 OE
*Grenada	133	344	103,103	St. George's	161/D 9; 156/G 4	TP, cap—81 OE; oth—70 FC
Guadeloupe & Dependencies, France	687	1,779	328,400	Basse-Terre	161/A 5; 156/F 4	82 FC
Guam, U.S.A.	209	541	105,979	Agaña	87/E 4; 86/.......	80 FC
*Guatemala	42,042	108,889	7,262,419	Guatemala	154/B 3	TP—80 OE; oth—73 FC
*Guinea	94,925	245,856	5,143,284	Conakry	106/B 6	TP, cap (ws), Kankan, Kindia, Labé—72 FC; oth—67 OE
*Guinea-Bissau	13,948	36,125	777,214	Bissau	106/A 6	79 PC
*Guyana	83,000	214,970	793,000	Georgetown	131/B 3	TP—80 OE; cap, cit over 10,000—70 FC; oth—60 FC
*Haiti	10,694	27,697	5,053,792	Port-au-Prince	158/C 5	82 PC
Hawaii, U.S.A.	6,471	16,760	964,691	Honolulu	218/.......	80 FC & OE
Heard & McDonald Islands, Australia	113	293	....	....	2/N 8	....
Holland, see Netherlands						
*Honduras	43,277	112,087	3,691,000	Tegucigalpa	154/D 3	TP—80 OE; oth—74 FC
Hong Kong, U.K.	403	1,044	5,022,000	Victoria	77/H 7; 78/.......	TP—81 PC; oth—76 FC
Howland Island, U.S.A.	1	2.6	....	....	87/J 5	....
*Hungary	35,919	93,030	10,709,536	Budapest	41/D 3	TP, cap, co—80 PC; oth—80 PC, 70 FC
*Iceland	39,768	103,000	228,785	Reykjavík	21/B 1	TP—80 PC; oth—70 FC
Idaho, U.S.A.	83,564	216,431	944,038	Boise	220/.......	80 FC & OE
Illinois, U.S.A.	56,345	145,934	11,426,596	Springfield	222/.......	80 FC & OE

Gazetteer-Index of the World

Country	Area Square Miles	Square Kilometers	Population	Capital or Chief Town	Page and Index Ref.	Sources of Population Data
*India	1,269,339	3,287,588	683,810,051	New Delhi	68/D 4	TP & states—81 PC; oth—71 FC
Indiana, U.S.A.	36,185	93,719	5,490,260	Indianapolis	227/......	80 FC & OE
*Indonesia	788,430	2,042,034	147,490,298	Jakarta	85/D 7	TP—80 PC; cit—80 PC & 71 PC; isls.—71 PC
Iowa, U.S.A.	56,275	145,752	2,913,808	Des Moines	229/......	80 FC & OE
*Iran	636,293	1,648,000	37,447,000	Tehran	66/F 4	TP—80 OE; div, cit over 50,000—76 PC; oth—66 FC & PC, 56 FC
*Iraq	172,476	446,713	12,767,000	Baghdad	66/C 4	TP—79 OE; oth—65 & 57 FC
*Ireland	27,136	70,282	3,440,427	Dublin	17/......	TP—81 PC: oth—71 FC
Ireland, Northern, U.K.	5,452	14,121	1,543,000	Belfast	17/F 2	TP—81 OE; dist—76 OE; cap, Londonderry—73 OE; oth—71 FC
Isle of Man, U.K.	227	588	64,000	Douglas	13/C 3	TP—80 OE; oth—71 FC
*Israel	7,847	20,324	3,878,000	Jerusalem	65/B 4	TP—80 OE; cap, cit over 100,000—77 OE; dist, cit over 5,000—72 PC; oth—61 FC
*Italy	116,303	301,225	57,140,000	Rome	34/......	TP—80 PC; oth—71 FC
*Ivory Coast (Côte d'Ivoire)	124,504	322,465	7,920,000	Yamoussoukro	106/C 7	TP—79 OE; oth—75 PC
*Jamaica	4,411	11,424	2,184,000	Kingston	158/......	TP—80 OE; oth—70 & 60 FC
Jan Mayen, Norway	144	373	....	....	6/D 1	....
*Japan	145,730	377,441	117,057,485	Tokyo	81/......	TP—80 PC; oth—75 FC
Jarvis Island, U.S.A.	1	2.6	....	....	87/K 6	....
Java, Indonesia	48,842	126,500	73,712,411	Jakarta	85/J 2	71 PC
Johnston Atoll, U.S.A.	.91	2.4	327	....	87/K 4	80 FC
*Jordan	35,000	90,650	2,152,273	Amman	65/D 3	TP—79 PC; cap, cit over 100,000—77 OE; gov, cit 9,000-100,000—73 OE; oth—61 FC
*Kampuchea (Cambodia)	69,898	181,036	5,200,000	Phnom Penh	72/E 4	TP—79 CIA est; cap—80 est
Kansas, U.S.A.	82,277	213,097	2,364,236	Topeka	232/......	80 FC & OE
Kazakh S.S.R., U.S.S.R.	1,048,300	2,715,100	14,684,000	Alma-Ata	48/G 5	TP, cit over 50,000—79 PC; oth—70 FC
Kentucky, U.S.A.	40,409	104,659	3,660,257	Frankfort	237/......	80 FC & OE
*Kenya	224,960	582,646	15,327,061	Nairobi	115/G 3	TP—79 PC; oth—69 FC
Kermadec Islands, New Zealand	13	33	5	....	87/J 9	81 FC
Kingman Reef, U.S.A.	0.1	0.26	....	....	87/K 5	....
Kirgiz S.S.R., U.S.S.R.	76,641	198,500	3,529,000	Frunze	48/H 5	TP, cit over 50,000—79 PC; oth—70 FC
Kiribati	291	754	56,213	Bairiki	87/J 6	TP—78 FC; oth—73 FC
Korea, North	46,540	120,539	17,914,000	P'yŏngyang	80/D 3	TP—80 UN est; cap—76 OE; Hamhŭng—72 OE; oth—70 OE
Korea, South	38,175	98,873	37,448,836	Seoul	80/D 5	TP—80 PC; oth—75 FC & PC
*Kuwait	6,532	16,918	1,355,827	Al Kuwait	58/E 4	80 PC
*Laos	91,428	236,800	3,721,000	Vientiane	72/D 3	TP—80 UN est; cap—66 FC; oth—58 OE
Latvian S.S.R., U.S.S.R	24,595	63,700	2,521,000	Riga	52/B 3; 53/......	TP, cit over 50,000—79 PC; oth—70 FC
*Lebanon	4,015	10,399	3,161,000	Beirut	62/F 6	TP—80 UN est; cap—70 FC; Tarabulus—64 OE; oth—61 OE
*Lesotho	11,720	30,355	1,339,000	Maseru	119/D 5	TP—80 OE; oth—80 est
*Liberia	43,000	111,370	1,873,000	Monrovia	106/C 7	TP—80 OE; oth—74 FC
*Libya	679,358	1,759,537	2,856,000	Tripoli	110/B 2	TP—79 OE; oth—73 FC & PC
*Liechtenstein	61	158	25,220	Vaduz	39/J 2	80 PC
Lithuanian S.S.R., U.S.S.R.	25,174	65,200	3,398,000	Vilnius	52/B 3; 53/......	TP, cit over 50,000—79 PC; oth—70 FC
Louisiana, U.S.A.	47,752	123,678	4,206,312	Baton Rouge	238/......	80 FC & OE
*Luxembourg	999	2,587	364,000	Luxembourg	27/J 9	TP—79 OE; cap—74 OE; oth—70 FC
Macau, Portugal	6	16	271,000	Macau	77/H 7	TP—78 OE; cap—70 FC
*Madagascar	226,657	587,041	8,742,000	Antananarivo	119/H 3	TP—80 UN est; prov, cap, cit over 40,000—75 PC; oth—71 OE
Madeira Islands, Portugal	307	796	262,800	Funchal	32/A 2	TP—77 OE; oth—70 FC & PC
Maine, U.S.A.	33,265	86,156	1,125,027	Augusta	243/......	80 FC & OE
*Malawi	45,747	118,485	5,968,000	Lilongwe	114/F 6	TP—80 OE; oth—77 PC
Malaya, Malaysia	50,806	131,588	11,138,227	Kuala Lumpur	72/D 6	TP, states, Kuala Lumpur—80 PC; cit over 100,000—70 FC; oth—70 PC
*Malaysia	128,308	332,318	13,435,588	Kuala Lumpur	72/D 6; 85/E 4	TP, states, Kuala Lumpur—80 PC; Kuching, Kota Kinabalu, cit over 100,000—70 FC; oth—70 PC
*Maldives	115	298	143,046	Male	54/L 9	78 FC
*Mali	464,873	1,204,021	6,906,000	Bamako	106/C 6	TP—80 OE; oth—76 PC
*Malta	122	316	343,970	Valletta	34/E 7	TP, cit—79 OE; oth—73 OE
Manitoba, Canada	250,999	650,087	1,026,241	Winnipeg	179/......	81 FC
Marquesas Islands, French Polynesia	492	1,274	5,419	Atuona	87/N 6	77 FC
Marshall Islands	70	181	30,873	Majuro	87/G 4	80 FC
Martinique, France	425	1,101	328,566	Fort-de-France	161/D 5	82 FC
Maryland, U.S.A.	10,460	27,091	4,216,975	Annapolis	245/......	80 FC & OE
Massachusetts, U.S.A.	8,284	21,456	5,737,037	Boston	249/......	80 FC & OE
*Mauritania	419,229	1,085,803	1,634,000	Nouakchott	106/B 5	TP—80 UN est; oth—76 PC
*Mauritius	790	2,046	959,000	Port Louis	119/G 5	TP—80 OE; cap—77 OE; Curepipe, Quatre Bornes—74 OE; oth—72 PC
Mayotte, France	144	373	47,300	Dzaoudzi	119/G 2	TP—78 CE; cap—66 FC
*Mexico	761,601	1,972,546	67,395,826	Mexico City	150/......	TP, states, cap—80 PC; cap (ws), Guadalajara (ws), Monterrey (ws)—78 OE; oth—70 FC
Michigan, U.S.A.	58,527	151,585	9,262,078	Lansing	250/......	80 FC & OE
Micronesia, Federated States of	1.9	4.9	73,160	Kolonia	87/E 5	TP—80 FC
Midway Islands, U.S.A.	1.9	4.9	453	....	87/J 3	80 FC
Minnesota, U.S.A.	84,402	218,601	4,075,970	St. Paul	255/......	80 FC & OE
Mississippi, U.S.A.	47,689	123,515	2,520,638	Jackson	256/......	80 FC & OE
Missouri, U.S.A.	69,697	180,515	4,916,759	Jefferson City	261/......	80 FC & OE
Moldavian S.S.R., U.S.S.R.	13,012	33,700	3,947,000	Kishinev	52/C 5	TP, cit over 50,000—79 PC; oth—70 FC
Monaco	368 acres	149 hectares	25,029	....	28/G 6	75 FC
*Mongolia	606,163	1,569,962	1,594,800	Ulaanbaatar	77/E 2	TP—79 PC; prov, cap, Darhan—77 OE; oth—69 FC
Montana, U.S.A.	147,046	380,849	786,690	Helena	262/......	80 FC & OE
Montserrat, U.K.	40	104	12,073	Plymouth	157/G 3	80 PC
*Morocco	172,414	446,550	20,242,000	Rabat	106/C 2	TP—80 OE; oth—71 FC
*Mozambique	303,769	786,762	12,130,000	Maputo	119/E 4	TP, prov, cap—80 PC; oth—70 FC
*Namibia	317,827	823,172	1,200,000	Windhoek	118/B 3	TP—74 est; oth—70 PC
Natal, South Africa	33,578	86,967	5,722,215	Pietermaritzburg	119/E 5	TP—80 PC; oth—70 FC
Nauru	7.7	20	7,254	Yaren (district)	87/G 6	77 FC
Navassa Island, U.S.A.	2	5	....	....	156/C 3	....
Nebraska, U.S.A.	77,355	200,349	1,569,825	Lincoln	264/......	80 FC & OE
*Nepal	54,663	141,577	14,179,301	Kathmandu	68/E 3	TP—81 PC; oth—71 FC
*Netherlands	15,892	41,160	14,227,000	The Hague; Amsterdam	27/F 5	TP—81 OE; oth—76 OE (com)

Gazetteer-Index of the World

Country	Area Square Miles	Square Kilometers	Population	Capital or Chief Town	Page and Index Ref.	Sources of Population Data
Netherlands Antilles	390	1,010	246,000	Willemstad	156/E 4	TP—78 OE; Willemstad—75 OE; oth—72 est.
Nevada, U.S.A.	110,561	286,353	800,493	Carson City	266/......	80 FC & OE
New Brunswick, Canada	28,354	73,437	696,403	Fredericton	170/......	81 FC
New Caledonia & Dependencies, France	7,335	18,998	133,233	Nouméa	87/G 8	76 FC
Newfoundland, Canada	156,184	404,517	567,681	St. John's	166/......	81 FC
New Hampshire, U.S.A.	9,279	24,033	920,610	Concord	268/......	80 FC & OE
New Jersey, U.S.A.	7,787	20,168	7,364,823	Trenton	273/......	80 FC & OE
New Mexico, U.S.A.	121,593	314,926	1,302,981	Santa Fe	274/......	80 FC & OE
New South Wales, Australia	309,498	801,600	5,126,217	Sydney	96/B 2	81 FC
New York, U.S.A.	49,108	127,190	17,558,072	Albany	276/......	80 FC & OE
*New Zealand	103,736	268,676	3,175,737	Wellington	100/......	TP, inc. places, isls.—81 FC; oth—76 FC
*Nicaragua	45,698	118,358	2,703,000	Managua	154/D 4	TP—80 OE; oth—71 PC
*Niger	489,189	1,267,000	5,098,427	Niamey	106/F 5	TP, cap, Maradi, Tahoua, Zinder—77 PC; oth—72 OE
*Nigeria	357,000	924,630	82,643,000	Lagos	106/F 6	TP—79 OE; prov—63 FC; oth—75 & 71 OE
Niue, New Zealand	100	259	3,578	Alofi	87/K 7	79 OE
Norfolk Island, Australia	13.4	34.6	2,175	Kingston	88/L 5	81 FC
North America	9,363,000	24,250,170	370,000,000	....	146/......	80 UN est
North Carolina, U.S.A.	52,669	136,413	5,881,813	Raleigh	281/......	80 FC & OE
North Dakota, U.S.A.	70,702	183,118	652,717	Bismarck	282/......	80 FC & OE
Northern Ireland, U.K.	5,452	14,121	1,543,000	Belfast	17/F 2	TP—81 OE; dist—76 OE; cap, Londonderry—73 OE; oth—71 PC
Northern Marianas, U.S.A.	184	477	16,780	Capitol Hill	87/E 4	80 FC
Northern Territory, Australia	519,768	1,346,200	123,324	Darwin	93/......	81 FC
North Korea	46,540	120,539	17,914,000	P'yŏngyang	80/D 3	TP—80 UN est; cap—76 OE; Hamhŭng—72 OE; oth—70 OE
Northwest Territories, Canada	1,304,896	3,379,683	45,741	Yellowknife	187/G 3	81 FC
*Norway	125,053	323,887	4,092,000	Oslo	18/F 7	TP—80 OE; co, Svalbard—76 OE; oth—76 OE, 70 FC
Nova Scotia, Canada	21,425	55,491	847,442	Halifax	168/......	81 FC
Oceania	3,292,000	8,526,280	23,000,000	....	87/......	80 UN est
Ohio, U.S.A.	41,330	107,045	10,797,624	Columbus	284/......	80 FC & OE
Oklahoma, U.S.A.	69,956	181,186	3,025,290	Oklahoma City	288/......	80 FC & OE
*Oman	120,000	310,800	891,000	Muscat	58/G 6	TP—80 UN est; cap, Matrah—66 OE; Salala—68 OE
Ontario, Canada	412,580	1,068,582	8,625,107	Toronto	175, 177/....	81 FC
Orange Free State, South Africa	49,866	129,153	1,833,216	Bloemfontein	119/D 5	TP—80 PC; oth—70 FC
Oregon, U.S.A.	97,073	251,419	2,633,149	Salem	291/......	80 FC & OE
Orkney Islands, Scotland	376	974	17,675	Kirkwall	15/E 1	TP—76 OE; oth—71 FC
*Pakistan	310,403	803,944	83,782,000	Islamabad	68/B 3	TP—81 PC; Abbottabad, Bannu, cit over 50,000—72 PC; oth—61 FC
Palau	188	487	12,116	Koror	86/D 5	80 FC
Palmyra Atoll, U.S.A.	3.85	1	....	....	87/K 5	....
*Panama	29,761	77,082	1,830,175	Panamá	154/G 6	TP, cit over 1,600—80 PC; oth—70 FC
*Papua New Guinea	183,540	475,369	3,010,727	Port Moresby	85/B 7; 87/E 6	80 PC
Paracel Islands, China	....	....	....	....	85/E 2	....
*Paraguay	157,047	406,752	2,973,000	Asunción	144/......	TP—79 OE; oth—72 PC
Pennsylvania, U.S.A.	45,308	117,348	11,863,895	Harrisburg	294/......	80 FC & OE
*Philippines	115,707	299,681	48,098,460	Manila	82/......	80 FC
Pitcairn Islands, U.K.	18	47	54	Adamstown	87/O 8	81 FC
*Poland	120,725	312,678	35,815,000	Warsaw	47/......	TP—81 OE; prov, cap, Cracow, Łódź—75 OE; oth—70 FC
*Portugal	35,549	92,072	9,933,000	Lisbon	32/B 3	TP—80 OE; cap (ws)—76 OE; oth—70 FC & PC
Prince Edward Island, Canada	2,184	5,657	122,506	Charlottetown	168/E 2	81 FC
Puerto Rico, U.S.A.	3,515	9,104	3,196,520	San Juan	161/......	80 FC
*Qatar	4,247	11,000	220,000	Doha	58/F 4	TP—80 UN est; cap—79 OE
Québec, Canada	594,857	1,540,680	6,438,403	Québec	172, 174/....	81 FC
Queensland, Australia	666,872	1,727,200	2,295,123	Brisbane	95/......	81 FC
Réunion, France	969	2,510	491,000	St-Denis	119/F 5	TP—80 OE; oth—74 FC
Rhode Island, U.S.A.	1,212	3,139	947,154	Providence	249/H 5	80 FC & OE
*Romania	91,699	237,500	22,048,305	Bucharest	45/F 3	79 OE
Russian S.F.S.R., U.S.S.R.	6,592,812	17,075,400	137,551,000	Moscow	48/D 4	TP, cit over 50,000—79 PC; oth—70 FC
*Rwanda	10,169	26,337	4,819,317	Kigali	114/E 4	78 PC
Sabah, Malaysia	29,300	75,887	1,002,608	Kota Kinabalu	85/F 4	TP—80 PC; Kota Kinabalu—70 FC; oth—70 PC
Saint Helena & Dependencies, U.K.	162	420	5,147	Jamestown	102/B 6	76 FC
*Saint Kitts and Nevis	104	269	44,404	Basseterre	156/F 3; 161/C 11	TP, isl, cap—80 PC; oth—70 FC
*Saint Lucia	238	616	115,783	Castries	161/G 6	80 PC
Saint Pierre & Miquelon, France	93.5	242	6,034	Saint-Pierre	166/C 4	82 FC
*Saint Vincent & the Grenadines	150	388	124,000	Kingstown	161/A 8; 157/G 4	TP—80 OE; oth—70 FC
Sakhalin, U.S.S.R.	29,500	76,405	655,000	Yuzhno-Sakhalinsk	48/P 4	TP, cit over 50,000—79 PC; oth—70 FC
San Marino	23.4	60.6	19,149	San Marino	34/D 3	TP—76 FC; oth—77 OE
*São Tomé and Príncipe	372	963	85,000	São Tomé	106/F 8	TP—80 UN est; oth—70 PC
Sarawak, Malaysia	48,202	124,843	1,294,753	Kuching	85/E 5	TP—80 PC; Kuching—70 FC; oth—70 PC
Sardinia, Italy	9,301	24,090	1,450,483	Cagliari	34/B 4	71 FC
Saskatchewan, Canada	251,699	651,900	968,313	Regina	181/......	81 FC
*Saudi Arabia	829,995	2,149,687	8,367,000	Riyadh	58/D 4	TP—80 UN est; oth—74 PC
Scotland, U.K.	30,414	78,772	5,117,146	Edinburgh	15/......	TP—81 PC; reg—75 OE; cit—75 & 73 OE, 71 FC; oth—71 FC
*Senegal	75,954	196,720	5,508,000	Dakar	106/A 5	TP—79 OE; oth—76 FC
*Seychelles	145	375	63,000	Victoria	119/H 5	TP—79 OE; oth—77 FC
Shetland Islands, Scotland	552	1,430	18,494	Lerwick	15/G 2	TP—76 OE; oth—73 OE & 71 FC
Siam, see Thailand						
Sicily, Italy	9,926	25,708	4,628,918	Palermo	34/D 6	71 FC
*Sierra Leone	27,925	72,325	3,470,000	Freetown	106/B 7	TP—80 UN est; cap, Bo, Kenema, Makeni—74 PC; oth—63 FC
*Singapore	226	585	2,413,945	Singapore	72/F 6	80 FC
Society Islands, French Polynesia	677	1,753	117,703	Papeete	87/L 7	77 FC
*Solomon Islands	11,500	29,785	221,000	Honiara	87/G 6; 86/......	TP—79 OE; oth—76 FC
*Somalia	246,200	637,658	3,645,000	Mogadishu	115/H 3	TP—80 UN est; prov, cap—75 PC; oth—69, 68, 67, 63 & 62 OE
*South Africa	455,318	1,179,274	23,771,970	Cape Town; Pretoria	118/C 5	TP (excl Transkei, Bophuthatswana, Venda), prov—80 PC; Transkei, Bophuthatswana—78 est; Venda—79 est; oth—70 FC

Gazetteer-Index of the World

Country	Area Square Miles	Square Kilometers	Population	Capital or Chief Town	Page and Index Ref.	Sources of Population Data
South America	6,875,000	17,806,250	245,000,000	....	120/.......	80 UN est
South Australia, Australia	379,922	984,000	1,285,033	Adelaide	94/.......	81 FC
South Carolina, U.S.A.	31,113	80,583	3,121,833	Columbia	296/.......	80 FC & OE
South Dakota, U.S.A.	77,116	199,730	690,768	Pierre	298/.......	80 FC & OE
South Korea	38,175	98,873	37,448,836	Seoul	80/D 5	TP—80 PC; oth—75 FC & PC
*Spain	194,881	504,742	37,430,000	Madrid	33/.......	TP—80 OE; met areas—75 OE; oth—70 FC
Spratly Islands	....	....	....	....	85/E 4	....
*Sri Lanka	25,332	65,610	14,850,001	Colombo	68/E 7	TP—81 PC; cap, Jaffna—73 OE; oth—71 FC
*Sudan	967,494	2,505,809	18,691,000	Khartoum	110/E 4	TP—80 OE; cap, prov, prov cap—73 PC; oth—73 PC, 72 OE
Sumatra, Indonesia	164,000	424,760	19,360,400	Medan	84/B 5	71 PC
*Suriname	55,144	142,823	354,860	Paramaribo	131/C 3	TP, cap—80 PC; dist—71 PC; oth—64 FC
Svalbard, Norway	23,957	62,049	3,431	Longyearbyen	18/C 2	76 OE
*Swaziland	6,705	17,366	547,000	Mbabane	119/E 5	TP—80 OE; oth—76 FC
*Sweden	173,665	449,792	8,320,000	Stockholm	18/J 8	TP—81 OE; oth—75 FC
Switzerland	15,943	41,292	6,365,960	Bern	39/.......	TP—80 FC; cantons—78 OE; cap, cit over 100,000 (& ws)—74 OE; cit (com) over 30,000 (& ws)—73 OE; oth—70 FC
*Syria	71,498	185,180	8,979,000	Damascus	62/G 5	TP—80 OE; oth—70 FC
Tadzhik S.S.R., U.S.S.R.	55,251	143,100	3,801,000	Dushanbe	48/G 6	TP, cit over 50,000—79 PC; oth—70 FC
Tahiti, French Polynesia	402	1,041	95,604	Papeete	87/L 7	77 FC
Taiwan	13,971	36,185	16,609,961	Taipei	77/K 7	TP, cap, Penghu Isl., cit over 300,000—77 OE; oth—70 OE
*Tanzania	363,708	942,003	17,527,560	Dar es Salaam	114/F 5	TP—78 PC; div, cap, cit over 17,000—78 PC; oth—67 FC
Tasmania, Australia	26,178	67,800	418,957	Hobart	99/.......	81 FC
Tennessee, U.S.A.	42,144	109,153	4,591,120	Nashville	237/.......	80 FC & OE
Texas, U.S.A.	266,807	691,030	14,229,288	Austin	303/.......	80 FC & OE
*Thailand	198,455	513,998	46,455,000	Bangkok	72/D 3	TP—80 OE; oth—70 FC
Tibet, China	463,320	1,200,000	1,790,000	Lhasa	76/C 5	TP—78 OE; oth—70 est
*Togo	21,622	56,000	2,472,000	Lomé	106/E 7	TP—79 OE; oth—70 FC
Tokelau, New Zealand	3.9	10	1,575	Fakaofo	87/J 6	TP—76 FC; oth—72 FC
Tonga	270	699	90,128	Nuku'alofa	87/J 8	76 PC
Transkei, South Africa	16,910	43,797	2,000,000	Umtata	119/D 6	TP—80 est; oth—70 FC
Transvaal, South Africa	109,621	283,918	10,673,033	Pretoria	119/D 4	TP—80 PC; oth—70 FC
*Trinidad and Tobago	1,980	5,128	1,067,108	Port-of-Spain	157/G 5; 161/A 10	80 PC
Tristan da Cunha, St. Helena	38	98	251	Edinburgh	2/J 7	79 OE
Tuamotu Archipelago, French Polynesia	341	883	9,052	Apataki	87/M 7	77 FC
*Tunisia	63,378	164,149	6,367,000	Tunis	106/F 1	TP—79 OE; oth—75 FC
*Turkey	300,946	779,450	45,217,556	Ankara	62/D 3	TP—80 PC; oth—75 FC
Turkmen S.S.R., U.S.S.R.	188,455	488,100	2,759,000	Ashkhabad	48/F 6	TP, cit over 50,000—79 PC; oth—70 FC
Turks and Caicos Islands, U.K.	166	430	7,436	Cockburn Town, Grand Turk	156/D 2	80 PC
Tuvalu	9.78	25.33	7,349	Fongafale, Funafuti	87/H 6	79 FC
*Uganda	91,076	235,887	12,630,076	Kampala	114/F 3	TP, cap—80 PC; oth—69 FC
*Ukrainian S.S.R., U.S.S.R.	233,089	603,700	49,755,000	Kiev	52/D 5	TP, cit over 50,000—79 PC; oth—70 FC
*Union of Soviet Socialist Republics	8,649,490	22,402,179	262,436,227	Moscow	48/.......	TP, S.S.R., cit over 50,000—79 PC; oth—70 FC
*United Arab Emirates	32,278	83,600	1,040,275	Abu Dhabi	58/F 5	TP—80 PC; oth—79 OE
*United Kingdom	94,399	244,493	55,672,000	London	10/.......	TP—81 OE (see England, Wales, Scotland, Northern Ireland)
*United States of America	3,623,420	9,384,658	226,504,825	Washington	188/.......	80 FC & OE
*Uruguay	72,172	186,925	2,899,000	Montevideo	145/.......	TP—80 OE; oth—75 PC
Utah, U.S.A.	84,899	219,888	1,461,037	Salt Lake City	304/.......	80 FC & OE
Uzbek S.S.R., U.S.S.R.	173,591	449,600	15,391,000	Tashkent	48/G 5	TP, cit over 50,000—79 PC; oth—70 FC
*Vanuatu	5,700	14,763	112,596	Vila	87/G 7	79 FC
Vatican City	108.7 acres	44 hectares	728	....	34/B 6	78 OE
Venda, South Africa	2,510	6,501	450,000	Thohoyandou	119/E 4	79 est
*Venezuela	352,143	912,050	14,313,000	Caracas	124/.......	TP—81 OE; oth—71 FC
Vermont, U.S.A.	9,614	24,900	511,456	Montpelier	268/.......	80 FC & OE
Victoria, Australia	87,876	227,600	3,832,443	Melbourne	96/B 5	81 FC
*Vietnam	128,405	332,569	52,741,766	Hanoi	72/E 3	TP—79 FC; cap, Haiphong, Ho Chi Minh City—79 PC; oth cit over 100,000 (north)—70 est, (south)—73 & 71 OE; oth—69 OE, 60 FC
Virginia, U.S.A.	40,767	105,587	5,346,818	Richmond	307/.......	80 FC & OE
Virgin Islands, British	59	153	11,006	Road Town	157/H 1	TP—80 FC; oth—70 FC
Virgin Islands, U.S.A.	132	342	96,569	Charlotte Amalie	161/A 4	80 FC
Wake Island, U.S.A.	2.5	6.5	302	Wake Islet	87/G 4	80 FC
Wales, U.K.	8,017	20,764	2,790,462	Cardiff	13/D 5	TP—81 PC; co—76 OE; cit—76 & 73 OE; par—71 FC
Wallis and Futuna, France	106	275	9,192	Mata Utu	87/J 7	80 FC
Washington, U.S.A.	68,139	176,480	4,132,180	Olympia	310/.......	80 FC & OE
West Bank	2,100	5,439	c. 800,000	....	65/C 3	TP—81 est; oth—67 CE & 61 FC
Western Australia, Australia	975,096	2,525,500	1,273,624	Perth	92/.......	81 FC
Western Sahara	102,703	266,000	76,425	....	106/B 3	70 FC
*Western Samoa	1,133	2,934	158,130	Apia	87/J 7	81 PC
West Virginia, U.S.A.	24,231	62,758	1,950,279	Charleston	312/.......	80 FC & OE
*White Russian S.S.R. (Byelorussian S.S.R.), U.S.S.R.	80,154	207,600	9,560,000	Minsk	52/C 4	TP, cit over 50,000—79 PC; oth—70 FC
Wisconsin, U.S.A.	56,153	145,436	4,705,521	Madison	317/.......	80 FC & OE
World	(land) 57,970,000	150,142,300	4,415,000,000	....	1,2/.......	80 UN est
Wyoming, U.S.A.	97,809	253,325	469,557	Cheyenne	319/.......	80 FC & OE
*Yemen	188,321	487,752	8,425,189	San'a	58/D 7	TP—80 OE; 81 PC, Mukalla, Seiyun—76 OE; cap—73 OE; Saihut—60 OE; Oth-75FC
*Yugoslavia	98,766	255,804	22,471,000	Belgrade	45/C 3	TP—81 OE; oth—71 FC
Yukon Territory, Canada	207,075	536,324	23,153	Whitehorse	186/E 3	81 FC
*Zaire	905,063	2,344,113	28,291,000	Kinshasa	114/D 4	TP—80 OE; prov, cap—70 FC; oth—70 FC & PC
*Zambia	290,586	752,618	5,679,808	Lusaka	114/E 7	80 PC
*Zimbabwe	150,803	390,580	7,360,000	Harare	119/D 3	TP—80 OE; cap, cit over 12,000—77 OE; oth—69 FC

Glossary of Abbreviations

A

A. A. F. — Army Air Field
Acad. — Academy
A. C. T. — Australian Capital Territory
adm. — administration; administrative
A. F. B. — Air Force Base
Afgh., Afghan. — Afghanistan
Afr. — Africa
Ala. — Alabama
Alb. — Albania
Alg. — Algeria
Alta. — Alberta
Amer. — American
Amer. Samoa — American Samoa
And. — Andorra
Ant., Antarc. — Antarctica
Ant. & Bar. — Antigua and Barbuda
Ar. — Arabia
arch. — archipelago
Arg. — Argentina
Ariz. — Arizona
Ark. — Arkansas
A. S. S. R. — Autonomous Soviet
 Socialist Republic
Aust. — Austria
Aust. Cap. Terr. — Australian Capital
 Territory
Austr., Austral. — Australian, Australia
aut. — autonomous
Aut. Obl. — Autonomous Oblast

B

B. — bay
Bah. — Bahamas
Barb. — Barbados
Battlef. — Battlefield
Bch. — Beach
Belg. — Belgium
Berm. — Bermuda
Bol. — Bolivia
Bots. — Botswana
Br. — Branch
Br. — British
Braz. — Brazil
Br. Col. — British Columbia
Br. Ind. Oc. Terr. — British Indian
 Ocean Territory
Bulg. — Bulgaria

C

C. — cape
Calif. — California
Can. — Canada
can. — canal
cap. — capital
Cent. Afr. Rep. — Central African
 Republic
Cent. Amer. — Central America
C. G. Sta. — Coast Guard Station
C. H. — Court House
chan. — channel
Chan. Is. — Channel Islands
Chem. Ctr. — Chemical Center
co. — county
C. of G. H. — Cape of Good Hope
Col. — Colombia
Colo. — Colorado
comm. — commissary
Conn. — Connecticut
cont. — continent
cord. — cordillera (mountain range)
C. Rica — Costa Rica
C. S. — County Seat
C. Verde — Cape Verde
Czech. — Czechoslovakia

D

D. C. — District of Columbia
Del. — Delaware
Dem. — Democratic
Den. — Denmark
depr. — depression
dept. — department
des. — desert
dist., dist's — district, districts
div. — division
Dom. Rep. — Dominican Republic

E

E. — East
Ec., Ecua. — Ecuador
elec. div. — electoral division
El Salv. — El Salvador
Eng. — England
Equat. Guinea, Eq. Guin — Equatorial
 Guinea

escarp. — escarpment
est. — estuary
Eth. — Ethiopia

F

Falk. Is. — Falkland Islands
Fin. — Finland
Fk., Fks. — Fork, Forks
Fla. — Florida
for. — forest
Fr. — France, French
Fr. Gui. — French Guiana
Fr. Poly. — French Polynesia
Ft. — Fort

G

G. — gulf
Ga. — Georgia
Game Res. — Game Reserve
Ger. — Germany
geys. — geyser
Gibr. — Gibraltar
glac. — glacier
gov. — governorate
Gr. — Group
Greenl. — Greenland
Gren. — Grenada
Gt. Brit. — Great Britain
Guad. — Guadeloupe
Guat. — Guatemala
Guinea-Biss. — Guinea-Bissau
Guy. — Guyana

H

har., harb., hbr. — harbor
hd. — head
highl. — highland, highlands
Hist. — Historic, Historical
Hond. — Honduras
Hts. — Heights
Hung. — Hungary

I

i., isl. — island, isle
I. C. — independent city
Ice., Icel. — Iceland
Ida. — Idaho
Ill. — Illinois
Ind. — Indiana
ind. city — independent city
Indon. — Indonesia
Ind. Res. — Indian Reservation
int. div. — internal division
inten. — intendency
Int'l — International
Ire. — Ireland
is., isls. — islands
Isr. — Israel
isth. — isthmus
Iv. Coast — Ivory Coast

J

Jam. — Jamaica
Jct. — Junction

K

Kans. — Kansas
Ky. — Kentucky

L

L. — Lake, Loch, Lough
La. — Louisiana
Lab. — Laboratory
lag. — lagoon
Ld. — Land
Leb. — Lebanon
Les. — Lesotho
Liecht. — Liechtenstein
Lux. — Luxembourg

M

Mad., Madag. — Madagascar
Man. — Manitoba
Mart. — Martinique
Mass. — Massachusetts
Maur. — Mauritania
Md. — Maryland
met. area — metropolitan area
Mex. — Mexico
Mich. — Michigan
Minn. — Minnesota
Miss. — Mississippi
Mo. — Missouri
Mon. — Monument
Mong. — Mongolia
Mont. — Montana

Mor. — Morocco
Moz., Mozamb. — Mozambique
mt. — mount
mtn. — mountain

N

N., No., North. — North, Northern
N. Amer. — North America
Nam., Namib. — Namibia
N. A. S. — Naval Air Station
Nat'l — National
Nat'l Cem. — National Cemetery
Nat'l Mem. Park — National Memorial
 Park
Nat'l Mil. Park — National Military
 Park
Nat'l Pkwy. — National Parkway
Nav. Base — Naval Base
Nav. Sta. — Naval Station
N. B., N. Br. — New Brunswick
N. C. — North Carolina
N. Dak. — North Dakota
Nebr. — Nebraska
Neth. — Netherlands
Neth. Ant. — Netherlands Antilles
Nev. — Nevada
New Bruns. — New Brunswick
New Cal., New Caled. — New Caledonia
Newf. — Newfoundland
New Hebr. — New Hebrides
N. H. — New Hampshire
Nic. — Nicaragua
N. Ire. — Northern Ireland
N. J. — New Jersey
N. Mex. — New Mexico
Nor. — Norway, Norwegian
North. — Northern
North. Terr., No. Terr. — Northern
 Territory
 (Australia)
N. S. — Nova Scotia
N. S. W., N.S. Wales — New South Wales
N. W. T., N. W. Terrs. — Northwest
 Territories
 (Canada)
N. Y. — New York
N. Z., N. Zealand — New Zealand

O

Obl. — Oblast
O. F. S. — Orange Free State
Okla. — Oklahoma
Okr. — Okrug
Ont. — Ontario
Ord. Depot — Ordnance Depot
Oreg. — Oregon

P

Pa. — Pennsylvania
Pak. — Pakistan
Pan. — Panama
Papua N. G. —Papua New Guinea
Par. — Paraguay
par. — parish
passg. — passage
P. E. I. — Prince Edward Island
pen. — peninsula
Phil., Phil. Is. — Philippines
Pk. — Park
pk. — peak
plat. — plateau
P. N. G. — Papua New Guinea
Pol. — Poland
Port. — Portugal, Portuguese
Pr. Edward I. — Prince Edward Island
pref. — prefecture
P. Rico — Puerto Rico
prom. — promontory
prov. — province, provincial
pt. — point

Q

Que. — Québec
Queens. — Queensland

R

R. — River
ra. — range
Rec., Recr. — Recreation, Recreational
reg. — region
Rep. — Republic
res. — reservoir
Res. — Reservation, Reserve
R. I. — Rhode Island
riv. — river
Rom. — Romania

S

S. — South
Sa. — Sierra, Serra
S. Afr., S. Africa — South Africa
salt dep. — salt deposit
salt des. — salt desert
S. Amer. — South America
São T. & Pr. — São Tomé
 and Príncipe
Sask. — Saskatchewan
Saudi Ar. — Saudi Arabia
S. Aust., S. Austral. — South Australia
S. C. — South Carolina
Scot. — Scotland
Sd. — Sound
S. Dak. — South Dakota
Sen. — Senegal
sen. dist. — senatorial district
Seych. — Seychelles
S. F. S. R. — Soviet Federated Socialist
 Republic
Sing. — Singapore
S. Leone — Sierra Leone
S. Marino — San Marino
Sol. Is. — Solomon Islands
Sp. — Spanish
Spr., Sprs. — Spring, Springs
S. S. R. — Soviet Socialist Republic
St., Ste. — Saint, Sainte
Sta. — Station
St. P. & M. — Saint Pierre and
 Miquelon
St. Vin. & Grens. — St. Vincent & The
 Grenadines
str., strs. — strait, straits
Sur. — Suriname
S. W. Afr. — South-West Africa
Swaz. — Swaziland
Switz. — Switzerland

T

Tanz. — Tanzania
Tas. — Tasmania
Tenn. — Tennessee
terr., terrs. — territory, territories
Tex. — Texas
Thai. — Thailand
trad. — traditional
Trin. & Tob. — Trinidad and Tobago
Tun. — Tunisia
twp. — township

U

U. A. E. — United
 Arab Emirates
U. K. — United Kingdom
Upp. Volta — Upper Volta
urb. area — urban area
Urug. — Uruguay
U. S. — United States
U. S. S. R. — Union of Soviet Socialist
 Republics

V

Va. — Virginia
Ven., Venez. — Venezuela
V. I. (Br.) — Virgin Islands (British)
V. I. (U. S.) — Virgin Islands (U. S.)
Vic. — Victoria
Viet. — Vietnam
Vill. — Village
vol. — volcano
Vt. — Vermont

W

W. — West, Western
Wash. — Washington
W. Aust., W. Austral. — Western
 Australia
W. Indies — West Indies
Wis. — Wisconsin
W. Samoa — Western Samoa
W. Va. — West Virginia
Wyo. — Wyoming

Y

Yugo. — Yugoslavia
Yukon — Yukon Territory

Z

Zim. — Zimbabwe

Index to Terrain Maps
on pages X through XXXII

This index contains only names of land and ocean physical features. Names of towns, internal divisions and countries are not included. The entry name is followed by a letter-number combination which refers to the area on the map in which the name will be found. The number following the map reference for the entry refers, not to the page on which the entry will be found, but to the map plate number.

Index continued

HAMMOND®

THE PHYSICAL WORLD
Terrain Maps of Land Forms and Ocean Floors

CONTENTS

RELIEF MODELS BY ERNST G. HOFMANN, ASSISTED BY RAFAEL MARTINEZ

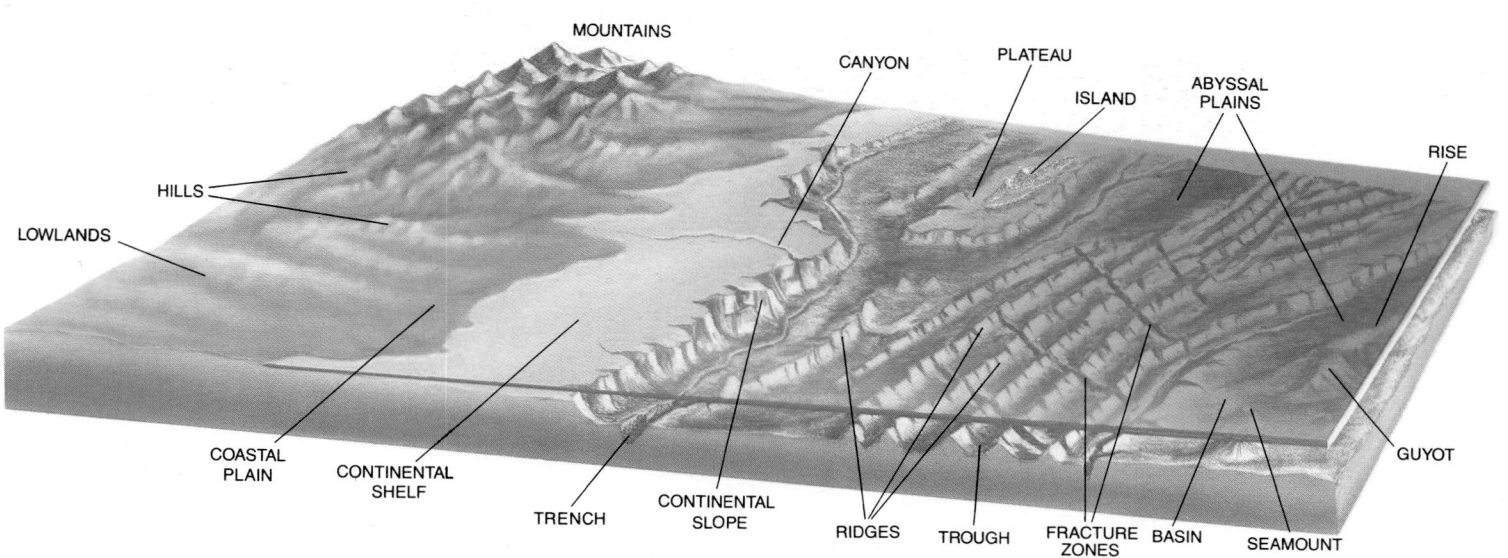

The oblique view diagram above is designed to provide a detailed view of the ocean floor as if seen through the depth of the sea. Graduating blue tones are used to contrast ocean floor depths: from light blue to represent shallow continental shelves to dark blues in the greater depths. Land relief is shown in conventional hypsometric tints.

In this dramatic collection of topographic maps of continents, oceans and major regions of the world, Hammond introduces a revolutionary new technique in cartography.

While most maps depicting terrain are created from painted artwork that is then photographed, Hammond now premiers the use of a remarkable sculptured model mapping technique created by one of our master cartographers.

The process begins with the sculpting of large scale three-dimensional models. Once physical details have been etched on the models and refinements completed, relief work is checked for accurate elevation based on a vertical scale exaggerated for visual effect.

Finished models are airbrushed and painted, then photographed using a single northwesterly light source to achieve a striking three-dimensional effect. The result is the dynamic presentation of mountain ranges and peaks on land, and canyons, trenches and seamounts on the ocean floor. Never before have maps conveyed such rich beauty while providing a realistic representation of the world as we know it.

ARCTIC OCEAN

QUEEN ELIZABETH
ISLANDS

Ellesmere

CANADA
BASIN

GREENLAND

Devon I.

Baffin

Beaufort Sea

Banks
I.

Pt. Barrow

Wrangel
I.

Chukchi
Sea

Baffin
Island

Victoria
I.

Bay

Arctic Circle

Iceland

Yukon

Mackenzie

ROCKY

Great Bear
L.

LABRADOR
BASIN

IRMINGER BASIN

Denmark Str.

Great
Britain

Mt. McKinley

Great Slave
L.

NORTH

Hudson

Bering Sea

ALEUTIAN
BASIN

ALEUTIAN ISLANDS

Gulf of Alaska

Peace

MOUNTAINS

AMERICA

Bay

Newfoundland

Ireland

ALEUTIAN TRENCH

Great Plains

Great
Lakes

C. Race

CHARLIE-GIBBS
FRACTURE ZONE

ICELAND BASIN

Missouri

MENDOCINO FRACTURE ZONE

C. Mendocino

Ohio

Appalachian Mts.

Colorado

Mississippi

C. Hatteras

ATLANTIC

HAWAIIAN

Lower

Rio
Grande

Gulf of
Mexico

HAWAIIAN RIDGE

MOLOKAI FRACTURE ZONE

Tropic of Cancer

California

MID-ATLANTIC RIDGE

OCEAN

ISLANDS

Cuba

WEST

Azores

Sea

Caribbean
Sea

INDIES

C. Verde

A

CENTRAL

PACIFIC

CLIPPERTON FRACTURE ZONE

GUATEMALA
BASIN

Orinoco

PACIFIC

Equator

 Madeira

Amazon

ROMANCHE FRACTURE ZONE

BASIN

Negro

Andes

Negro

SOUTH

BRAZIL

OCEA

PERU
BASIN

PERU-CHILE TRENCH

AMERICA

São Francisco

C. de São Roque

BASIN

TONGA
TRENCH

OCEAN

EAST PACIFIC RISE

NAZCA RIDGE

Tropic of Capricorn

MID-ATLANTIC RIDGE

KERMADEC
TRENCH

CHILE
BASIN

Mountains

Paraná

Cerro
Aconcagua

ARGENTINE
BASIN

SOUTHWEST

PACIFIC

BASIN

Falkland Is.

Tierra del Fuego

C. Horn

SOUTH
SANDWICH
TRENCH

Drake Passage

PACIFIC-ANTARCTIC RIDGE

Antarctic
Peninsula

WEDDELL

AMUNDSEN ABYSSAL PLAIN

Antarctic Circle

ABYSSAL PLAIN

W e d d e l l

Bellingshausen
Sea

S e a

Ross Sea

ANTARCTICA

Edith Ronne

Ross Ice Shelf

Ice Shelf

0   500   1000   1500   2000   2500   3000 MILES at Equator
0   500 1000 1500 2000 2500   3000 KILOMETERS at Equator

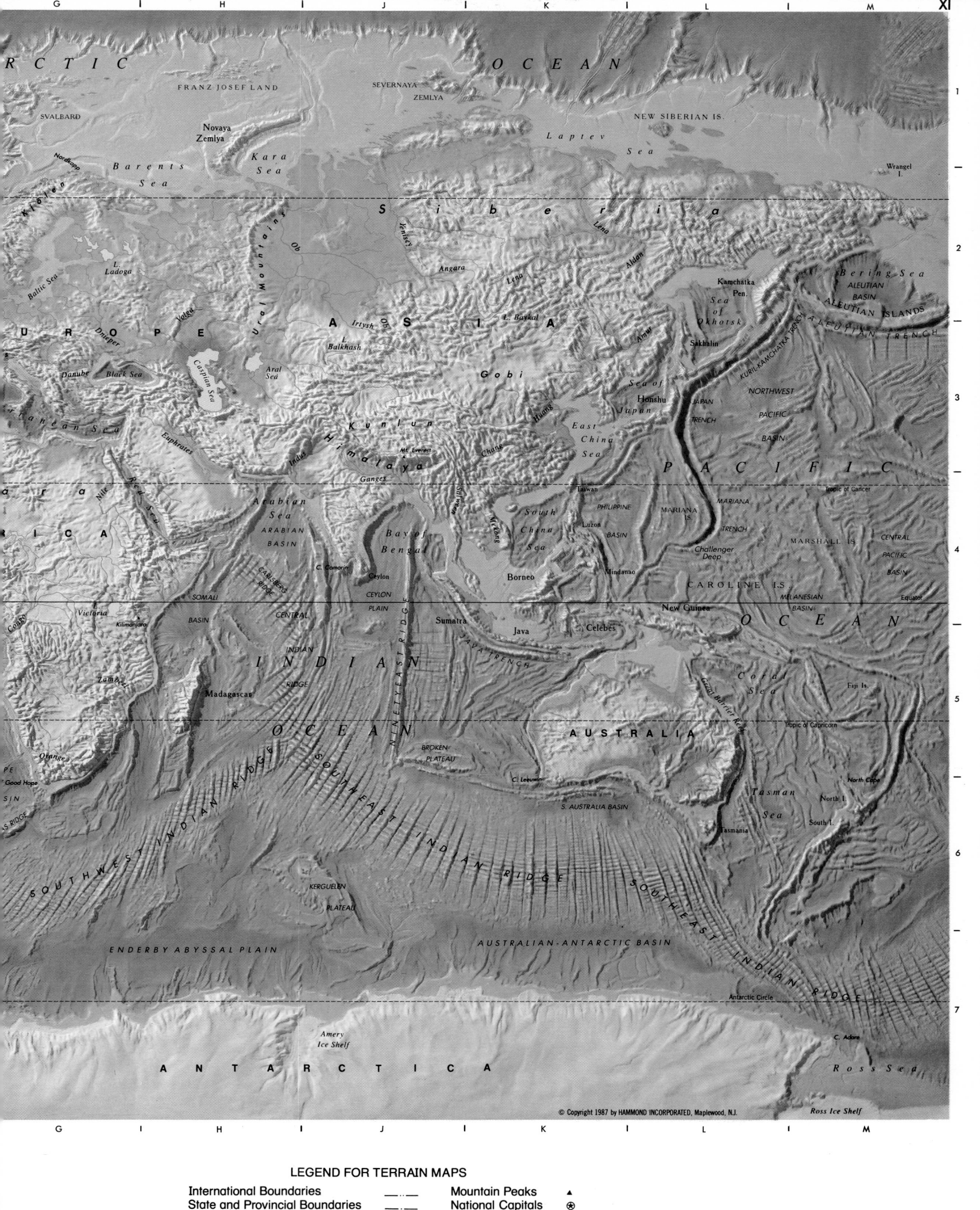

LEGEND FOR TERRAIN MAPS

International Boundaries	_.._
State and Provincial Boundaries	_._
Other Boundaries	_._
Boundaries Along Rivers	_ _ _

Mountain Peaks	▲
National Capitals	⊛
Other Capitals	⊙
Canals	

© Copyright 1987 by HAMMOND INCORPORATED, Maplewood, N.J.

WORLD | Plate 1

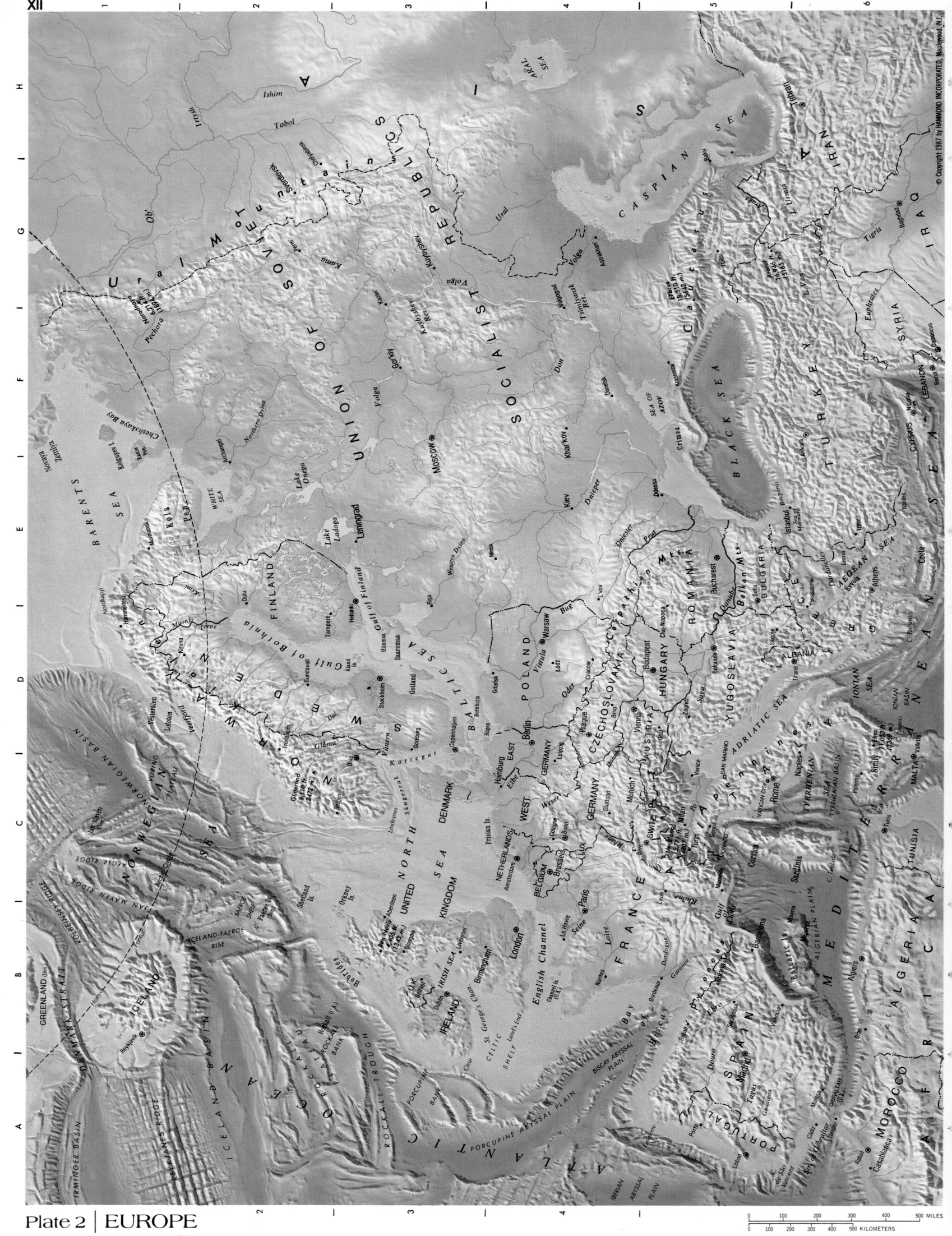

Plate 2 | EUROPE

0   100   200   300   400   500 MILES
0   100   200   300   400   500 KILOMETERS

WESTERN EUROPE | Plate 3

© Copyright 1987 by HAMMOND INCORPORATED, Maplewood, N.J.

Plate 4 | ASIA

| 0 | 300 | 600 | 900 | 1200 | 1500 MILES |
| 0 | 300 | 600 | 900 | 1200 | 1500 KILOMETERS |

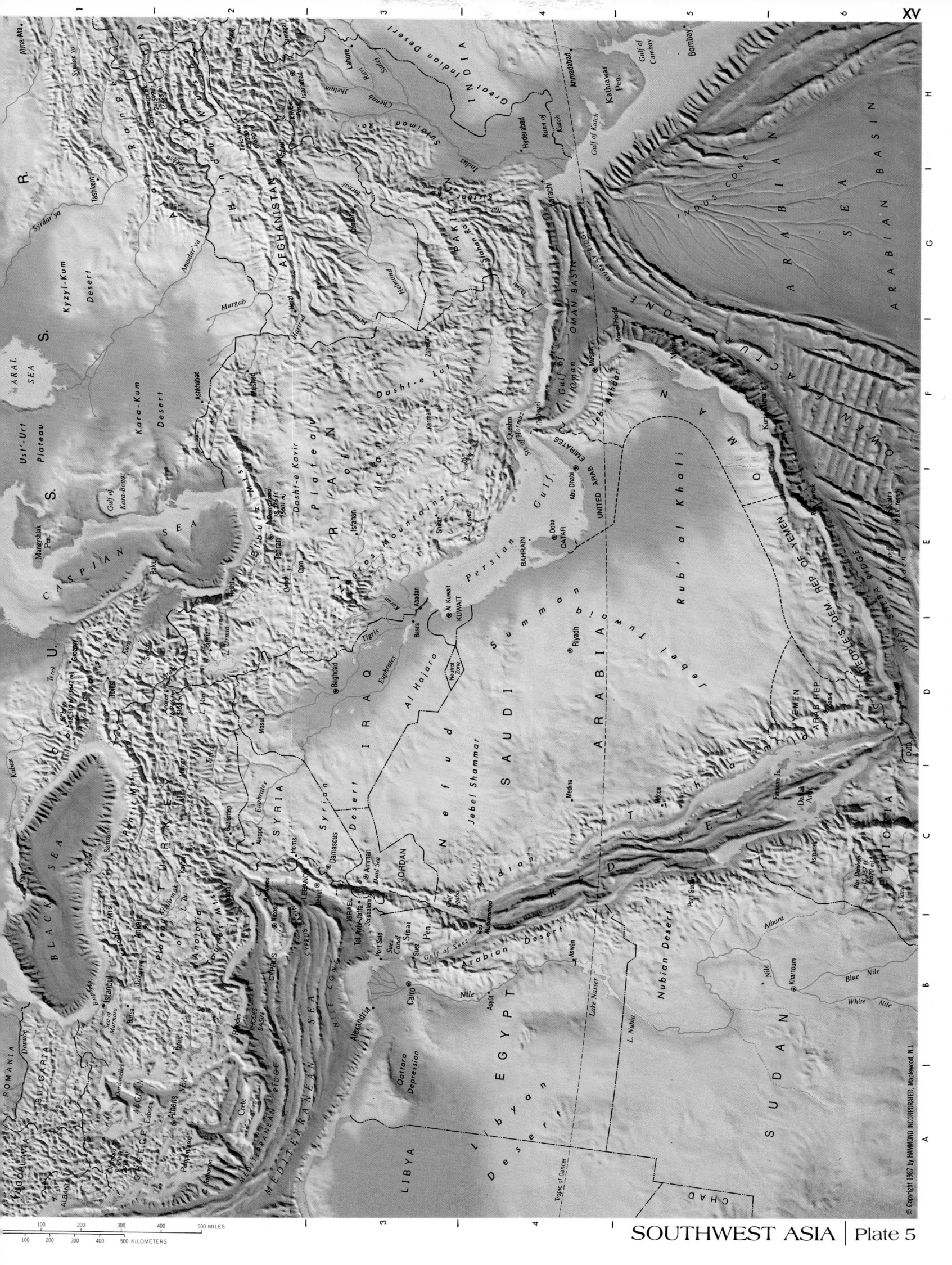

SOUTHWEST ASIA | Plate 5

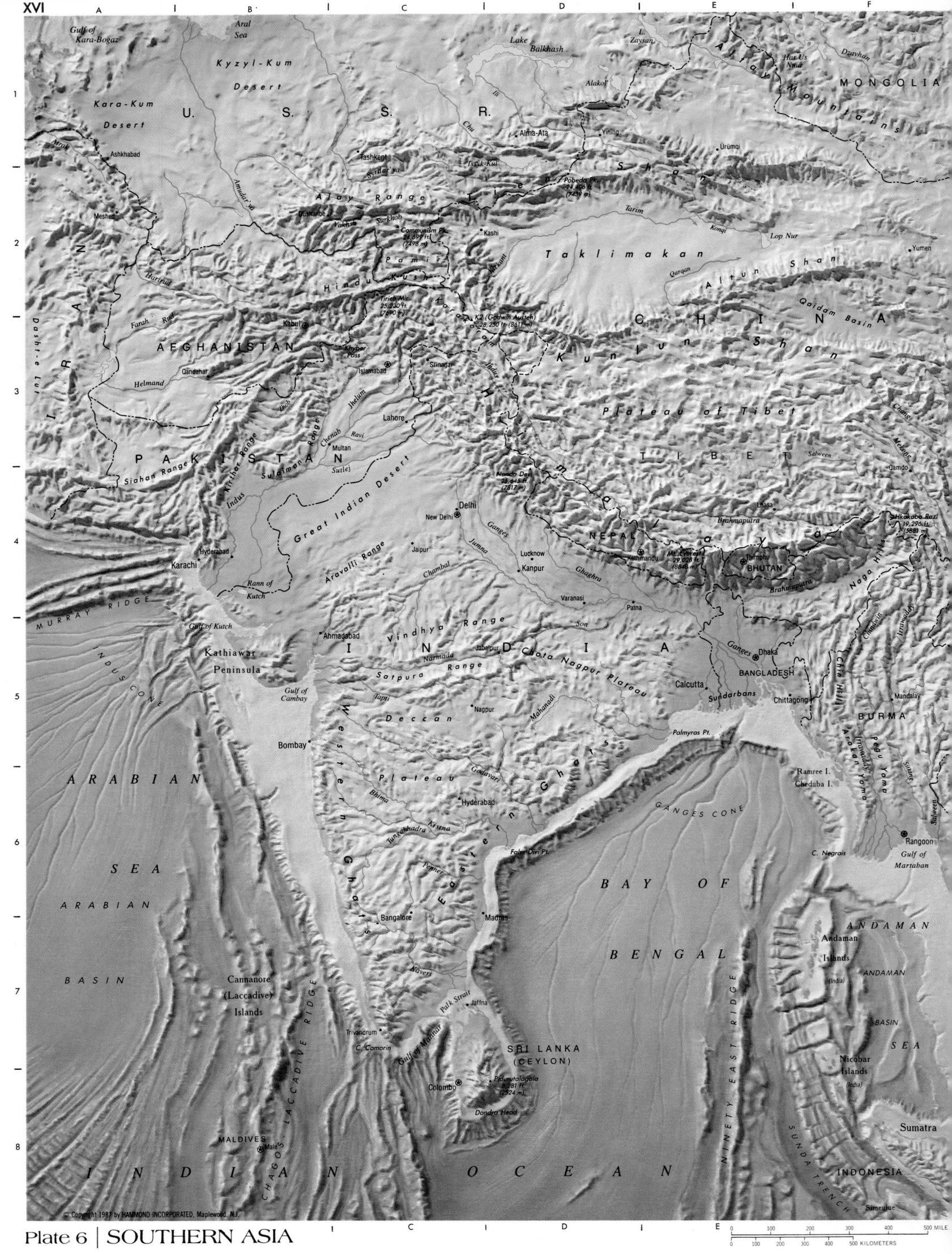

XVI

Gulf of
Kara-Bogaz

Aral
Sea

*Kyzyl-Kum
Desert*

Lake
Balkhash

L. Zaysan

Dzhalhan

Hor Us
Nuur

MONGOLIA

1

*Kara-Kum
Desert*

U. S. S. R.

Alakol

Ili

Tien
Shan

Altay Mountains

Ashkhabad

Tashkent

Syrdar'ya

Issyk-Kul

Alma-Ata

Yining

Ürümqi

Meshed

Alay Range

Dushanbe

Vakhsh

Surkhob

Communism Pk.
24,599 ft
(7498 m)

Kashi

Pobeda Pk.
24,406 ft
(7439 m)

Tarim

Konqi

Lop Nur

Yumen

2

IRAN

Hari Rud

Pamir

Hindu Kush

Tirich Mir
25,230 ft
(7690 m)

Yarkant

Taklimakan

Qarqan

Altun Shan

Qaidam Basin

Farah

Rud

Kabul

K2 (Godwin Austen)
28,250 ft
(8611 m)

CHINA

Kunlun Shan

Chang

Dashl-e Lut

AFGHANISTAN

Khyber
Pass

Srinagar

Indus

Plateau of Tibet

TIBET

Qamdo

3

Qandahar

Helmand

Islamabad

Jhelum

Lahore

T

I

B

E

T

Salween

Mekong

Zhob

Chenab

Ravi

Nanda Devi
25,645 ft
(7817 m)

Lhasa

Hkakabo Razi
19,296 ft
(5881 m)

PAKISTAN

Kirthar Range

Sulaiman Range

Multan

Sutlej

Great Indian Desert

Delhi

Ganges

Brahmaputra

NEPAL

Kathmandu

Mt. Everest
29,028 ft
(8848 m)

Thimphu

BHUTAN

Naga Hills

4

Siahan Range

New Delhi

Jaipur

Jumna

Lucknow

Ghaghra

Kanpur

Chambal

Brahmaputra

Chindwin

Irrawaddy

Hyderabad

Karachi

*Rann of
Kutch*

Aravalli Range

Varanasi

Son

Patna

Ganges

Dhaka

MURRAY RIDGE

INDUS CONE

Gulf of Kutch

Ahmadabad

Vindhya Range

INDIA

Chota Nagpur Plateau

BANGLADESH

Chin Hills

5

Kathiawar
Peninsula

Gulf of
Cambay

Narmada

Jabalpur

Calcutta

Sundarbans

Chittagong

Mandalay

BURMA

Satpura

Range

Tapti

Nagpur

Mahanadi

Western

Deccan

Palmyras Pt.

Pegu Yoma

Arakan Yoma

ARABIAN

Bombay

Plateau

Godavari

Ramree I.

Cheduba I.

Irrawaddy

Bhima

Krishna

Hyderabad

GANGES CONE

6

SEA

Eastern

Tungabhadra

Pennar

False Divi Pt.

ARABIAN

Ghats

BAY OF

C. Negrais

Rangoon

Gulf of
Martaban

BASIN

Bangalore

Madras

BENGAL

ANDAMAN

7

Cannanore
(Laccadive)
Islands

Kaveri

Andaman
Islands
(India)

ANDAMAN

LACCADIVE RIDGE

Palk Strait

Jaffna

NINETY EAST RIDGE

BASIN

Trivandrum

C. Comorin

Gulf of Mannar

SRI LANKA
(CEYLON)

Pidurutalagala
8,281 ft
(2524 m)

SEA

Nicobar
Islands
(India)

CHAGOS

Colombo

Dondra Head

8

MALDIVES

Male

Sumatra

SUNDA TRENCH

INDONESIA

I N D I A N   O C E A N

Simeulue

© Copyright 1987 by HAMMOND INCORPORATED, Maplewood, N.J.

Plate 6 | SOUTHERN ASIA

0   100   200   300   400   500 MILE

0   100   200   300   400   500 KILOMETERS

EAST ASIA | Plate 7

KYUSHU-PALAU RIDGE

PACIFIC

JAPAN TRENCH

OCEAN

KURIL BASIN

Sakhalin

Hokkaido

La Perouse Str.

Sapporo

N

A

P

A

J

SEA OF

JAPAN BASIN

Honshu

Tokyo

Nagoya

Osaka

Shikoku

Kyushu

Fukuoka

PHILIPPINE BASIN

PHILIPPINE SEA

Babuyan Is.

C. Engaño

Luzon

PHILIPPINES

Manila

C. Bolinao

SOUTH

CHINA

BASIN

RYUKYU TRENCH

Ryukyu Islands

Okinawa

TAIWAN

Taiwan (Formosa)

Taipei

C. Olwanpi

Taiwan Strait

EAST CHINA SEA

SOUTH CHINA SEA

CONTINENTAL SHELF

Leizhou Bandao

Hainan

Gulf of Tonkin

Haiphong

DaNang

VIETNAM

U. S. S. R.

Amur

Khabarovsk

Ussuri

Blagoveshchensk

L. Khanka

Vladivostok

Songhua

NORTH KOREA

P'yongyang

Pusan

SOUTH KOREA

Seoul

Korea

Korea Bay

Cheju

SEA

YELLOW

Shandong Bandao

Qingdao

Dalian

Bo Hai

Shanghai

Nanjing

Xuzhou

Hongze Hu

Huai

Wuhan

Poyang Hu

Nanchang

Xiamen

Fuzhou

Changsha

Guangzhou

HONG KONG (U.K.)

Macau (Port.)

Hanoi

Red

Kunming

LAOS

Vientiane

THAILAND

Bangkok

Korat Plateau

CAMBODIA

Amur

Gan

Nen

Qiqihar

Harbin

Changchun

Shenyang

Anshan

Luo

Beijing

Tianjin

Baotou

Jinan

Taiyuan

Zhengzhou

Xi'an

Wei

Huang

Chang

Han

Chang

Jiuling

Chongqing

Chengdu

Kunming

U. S. S. R.

Angara

Irkutsk

L. Baikal

Selenge

Onon

Ulaanbaatar

Kerulen

Hulun Nur

Hentiyn Mts.

MONGOLIA

Gobi

Khangai Mountains

Orhon

Alakol

Balkhash

Ili

Tarim

Taklimakan

Kunlun Shan

Altun Shan

Qaidam Basin

Qinghai Hu

Lop Nur

Yumen

Lanzhou

Huang

Yalong

Mekong

Salween

Gamdo

Tanggula Shan

Chamdo

TIBET

Plateau of Tibet

Lhasa

NEPAL

Kathmandu

Mt. Everest

BHUTAN

Thimphu

BANGLADESH

Dhaka

Chittagong

BURMA

Irrawaddy

Rangoon

ANDAMAN SEA

Andaman Is. (India)

C. Negrais

INDIA

Calcutta

Ganges

Patna

New Delhi

Delhi

Jumna

Jaipur

Nagpur

Kanpur

BAY OF BENGAL

GANGES CONE

Eastern Ghats

Lake Balkhash

Syrdar'ya

Tashkent

Alma-Ata

Semipalatinsk

C

H

I

N

A

Ordos

Gobi

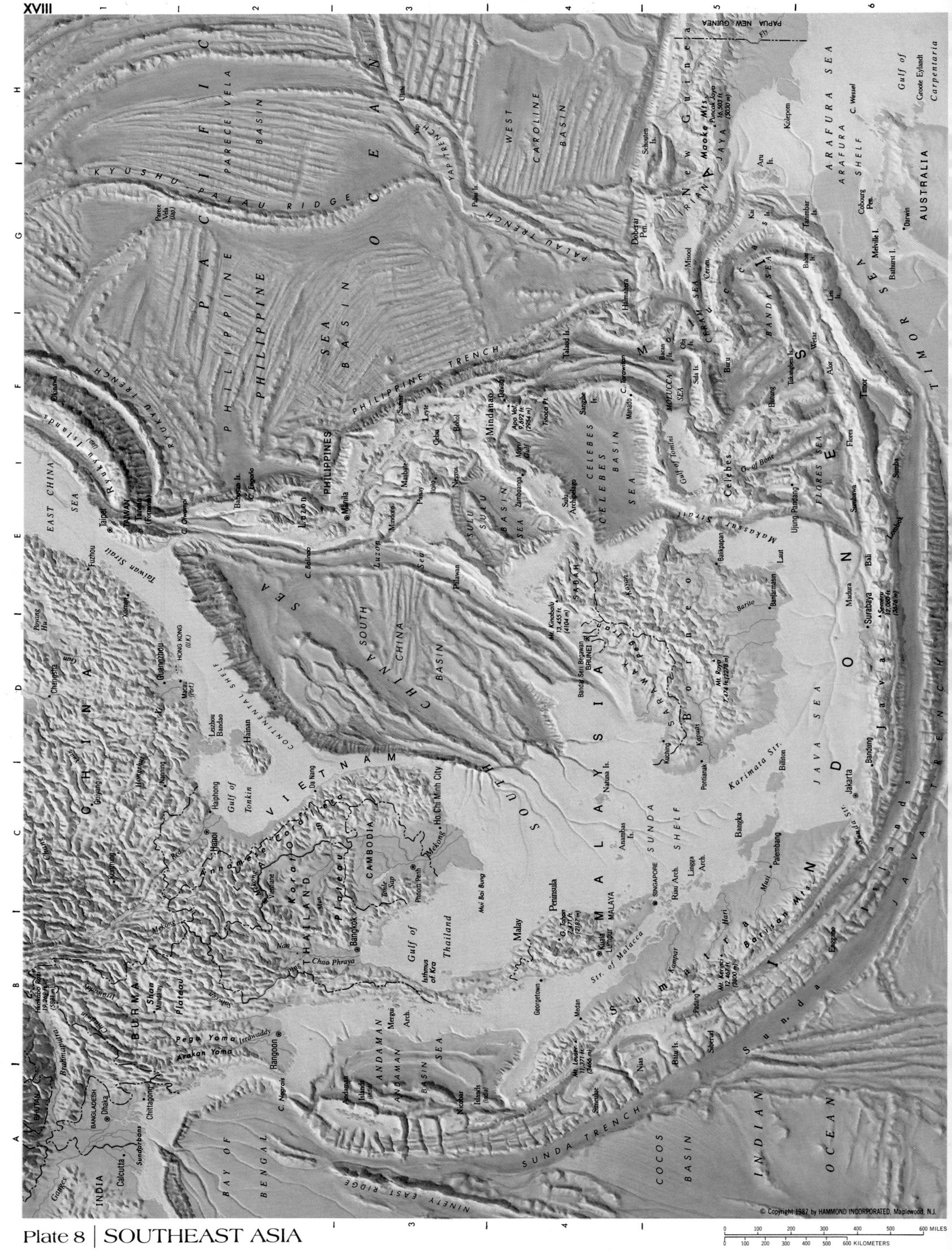

Plate 8 | SOUTHEAST ASIA

© Copyright 1987 by HAMMOND INCORPORATED, Maplewood, N.J.

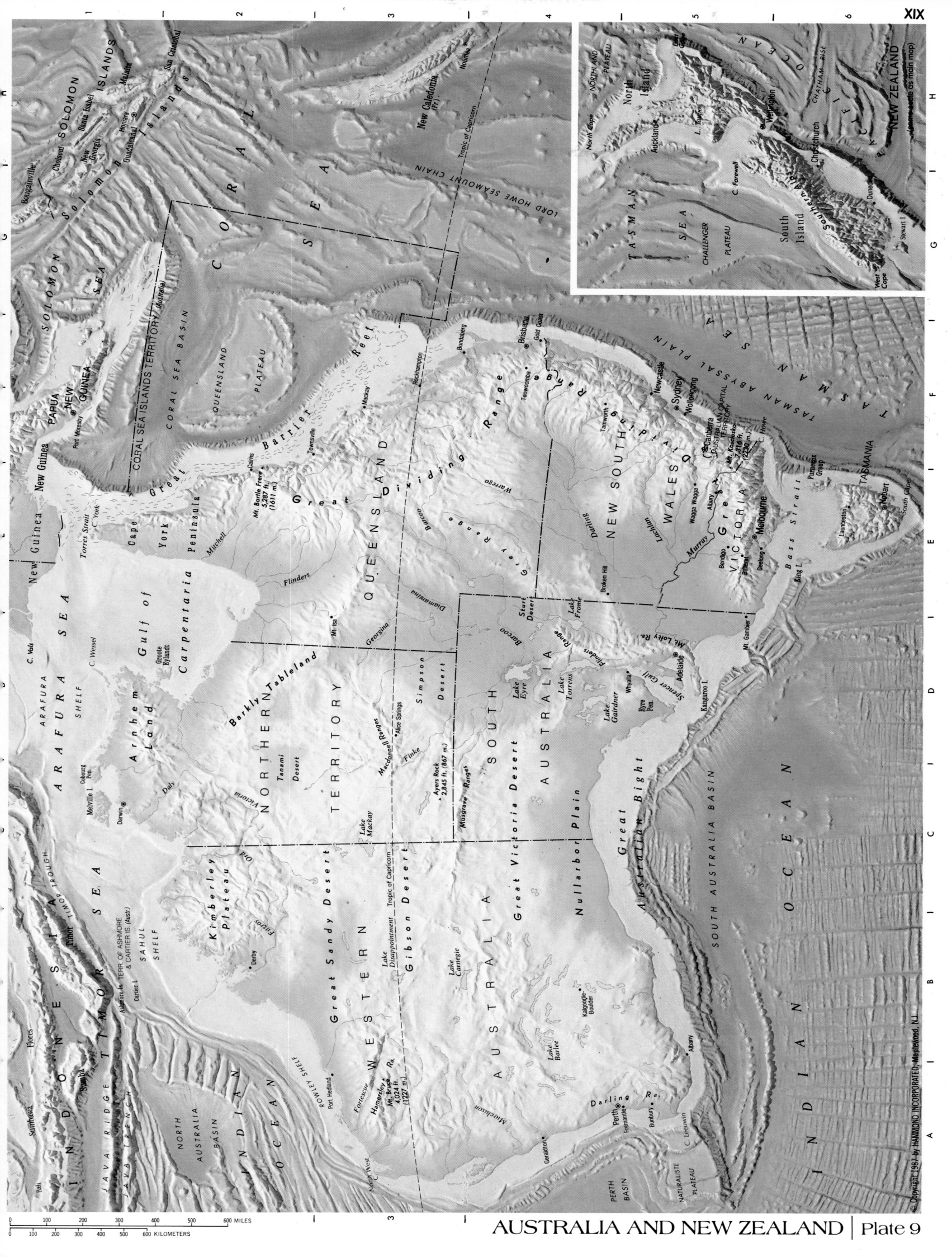

AUSTRALIA AND NEW ZEALAND | Plate 9

© Copyright 1987 by HAMMOND INCORPORATED · Maplewood, N.J.

0 100 200 300 400 500 600 MILES
0 100 200 300 400 500 600 KILOMETERS

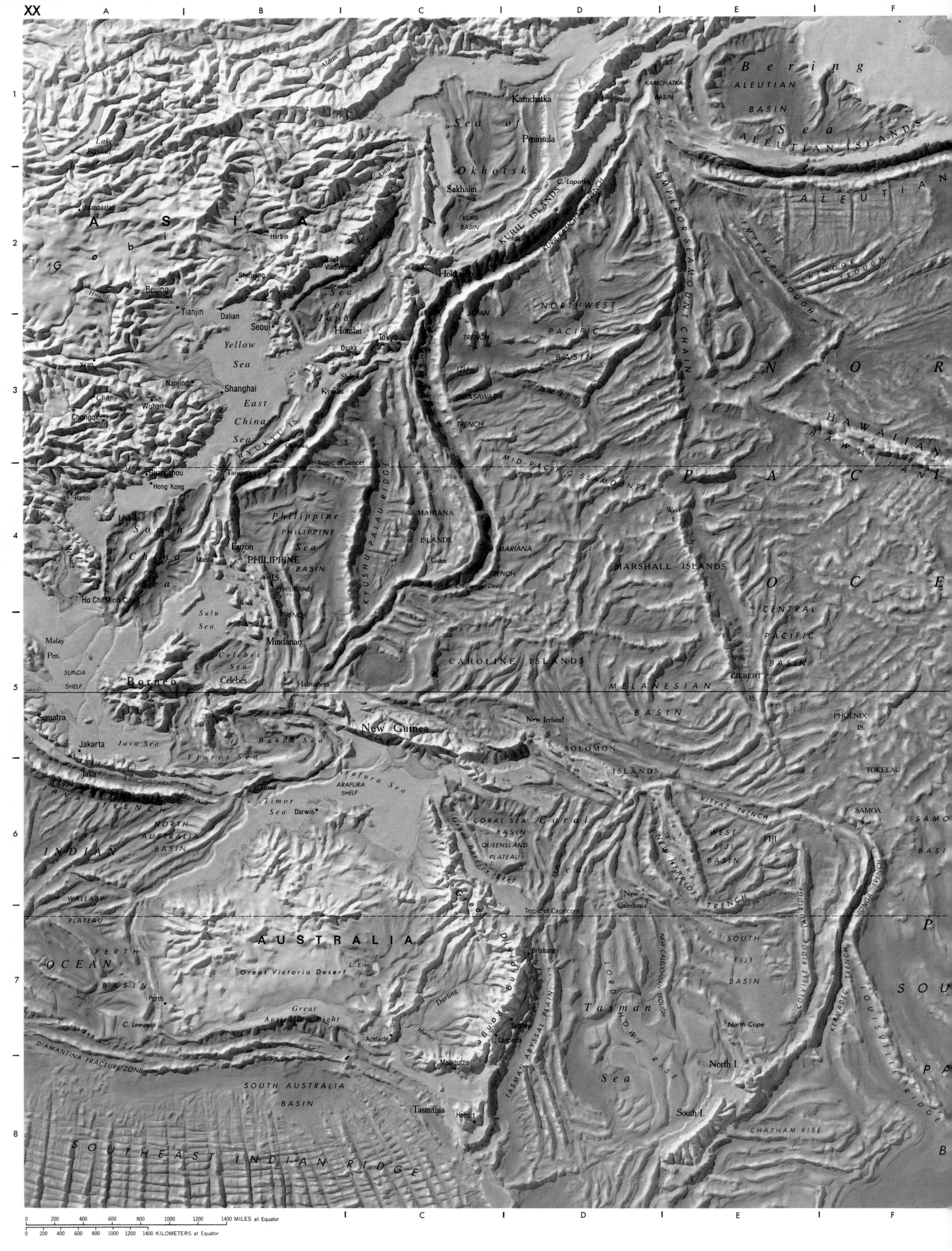

A A I B I B I C I D I E I E I F

1

ASIA

Lena

Aldan

Kamchatka

Sea of
Okhotsk

Peninsula

Bering

Kamchatka
Basin

ALEUTIAN

BASIN

Sea

ALEUTIAN ISLANDS

ALEUTIAN

2

Ulanbaatar

Gobi

Harbin

Amur

Sakhalin

C. Lopatka

KURIL
BASIN

KURIL ISLANDS

KURIL-KAMCHATKA TRENCH

EMPEROR SEAMOUNT CHAIN

EMPEROR TROUGH

CHINOOK TROUGH

Shenyang

Vladivostok

Hokkaido

JAPAN

TRENCH

NORTHWEST

PACIFIC

BASIN

N O R

Beijing

Huang

Sea
of
Japan

Honshu

Tokyo

Osaka

3

Tianjin

Dalian

Seoul

Shikoku

IZU

BONIN TRENCH

HAWAIIAN

HAWAIIAN

Xian

Yellow

Sea

Kyushu

OGASAWARA

Nanjing

Shanghai

East

China

Sea

RYUKYU IS.

TRENCH

Chang

Wuhan

Chongqing

Tropic of Cancer

MID-PACIFIC SEAMOUNTS

P A C I

4

Guangzhou

Taiwan

Philippine

Sea

MARIANA

Wake
I.

Hong Kong

PHILIPPINE

ISLANDS

Hanoi

South

Hainan

KYUSHU-PALAU RIDGE

Luzon

MARIANA

MARSHALL ISLANDS

O C E

China

Manila

PHILIPPINE

Guam

TRENCH

PHILIPPINE

IS.

BASIN

Challenger Deep

Mekong

Ho Chi Minh City

PHILIPPINE

CENTRAL

Sea

Sulu
Sea

TRENCH

PACIFIC

Malay
Pen.

Mindanao

BASIN

GILBERT

SUNDA
SHELF

Celebes
Sea

Celebes

Halmahera

CAROLINE   ISLANDS

MELANESIAN

IS.

5

Borneo

Equator

BASIN

PHOENIX
IS.

Sumatra

New Ireland

Jakarta

Java Sea

Banda Sea

New Guinea

SOLOMON

TOKELAU

Java

Flores Sea

ISLANDS

VITYAZ TRENCH

SAMOA

SAMO

JAVA

Arafura Sea

ARAFURA

SHELF

Timor

CORAL SEA
BASIN

Coral

WEST

FIJI

BASIN

FIJI

BASI

6

TRENCH

NORTH
AUSTRALIA
BASIN

Timor
Sea

Darwin

QUEENSLAND

PLATEAU

Sea

NEW HEBRIDES TRENCH

INDIAN

Great Barrier Reef

New
Caledonia

WALLABY

PLATEAU

Tropic of Capricorn

NEW CALEDONIAN TROUGH

LORD

HOWE

RISE

COLVILLE RIDGE

LAU RIDGE

TONGA TRENCH

P

7

OCEAN

PERTH

BASIN

AUSTRALIA

Great Victoria Desert

L. Eyre

Great
Dividing
Range

Brisbane

SOUTH

FIJI

BASIN

North Cape

SOU

Perth

Darling

Sydney

Canberra

TASMAN ABYSSAL PLAIN

Tasman

KERMADEC TRENCH

LOUISVILLE RIDGE

PA

C. Leeuwin

Great
Australian Bight

Adelaide

Murray

Melbourne

North I.

8

DIAMANTINA FRACTURE ZONE

SOUTH AUSTRALIA

BASIN

Tasmania

Hobart

Sea

South I.

CHATHAM RISE

S O U T H E A S T   I N D I A N   R I D G E

A I A I B I B I C I D I E I E I F

0   200   400   600   800   1000   1200   1400 MILES at Equator

0   200   400   600   800   1000   1200   1400 KILOMETERS at Equator

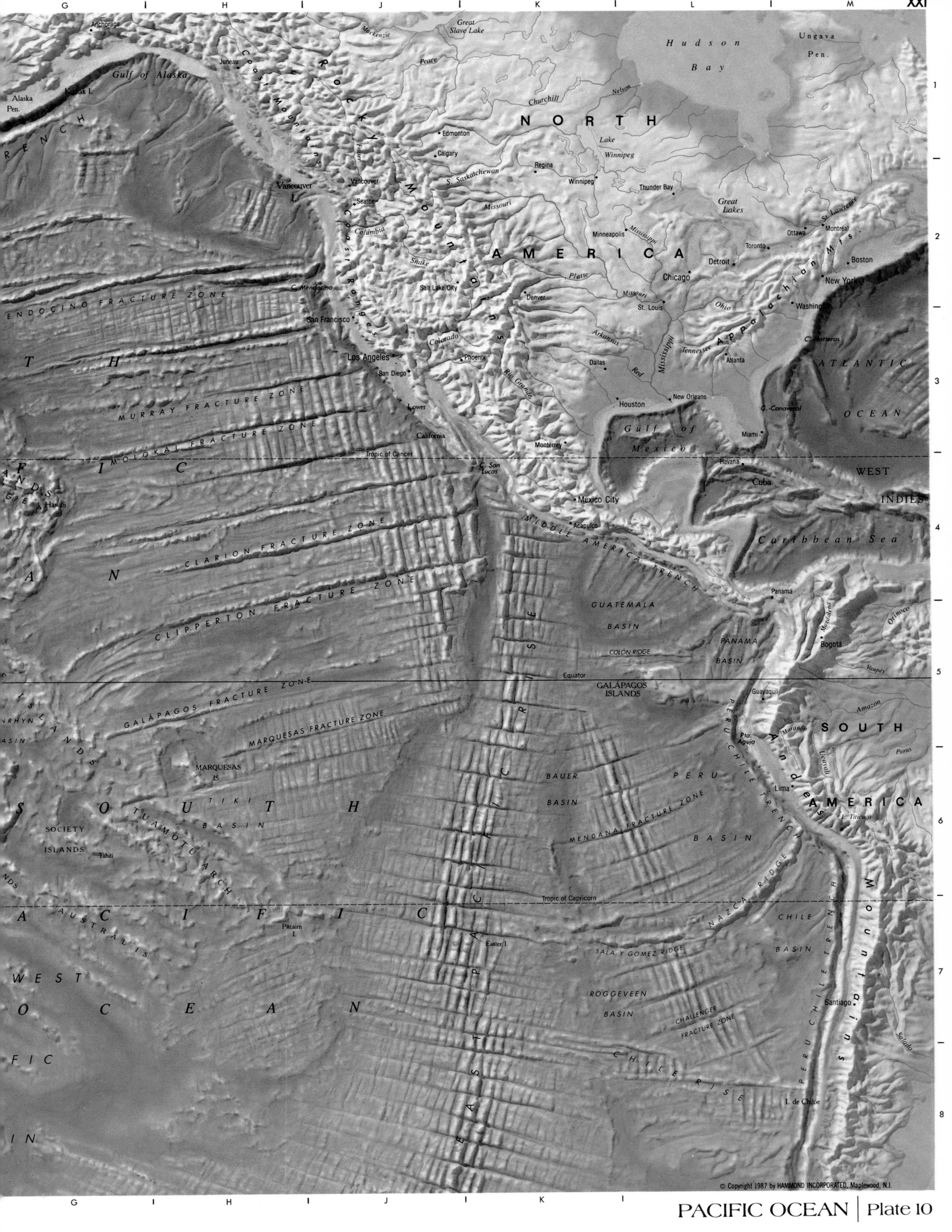

PACIFIC OCEAN | Plate 10

© Copyright 1987 by HAMMOND INCORPORATED, Maplewood, N.J.

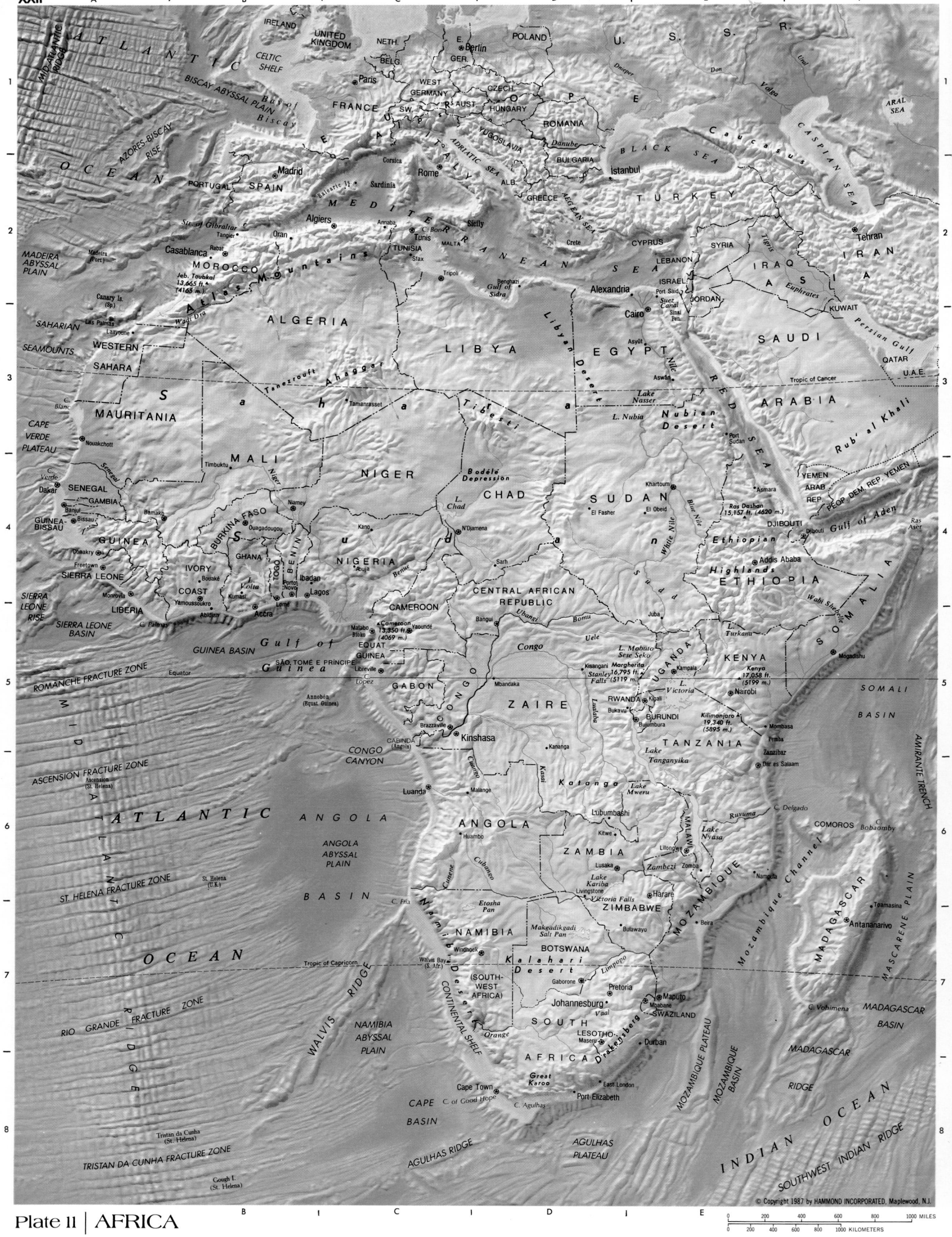

Plate 11 | AFRICA

© Copyright 1987 by HAMMOND INCORPORATED, Maplewood, N.J.

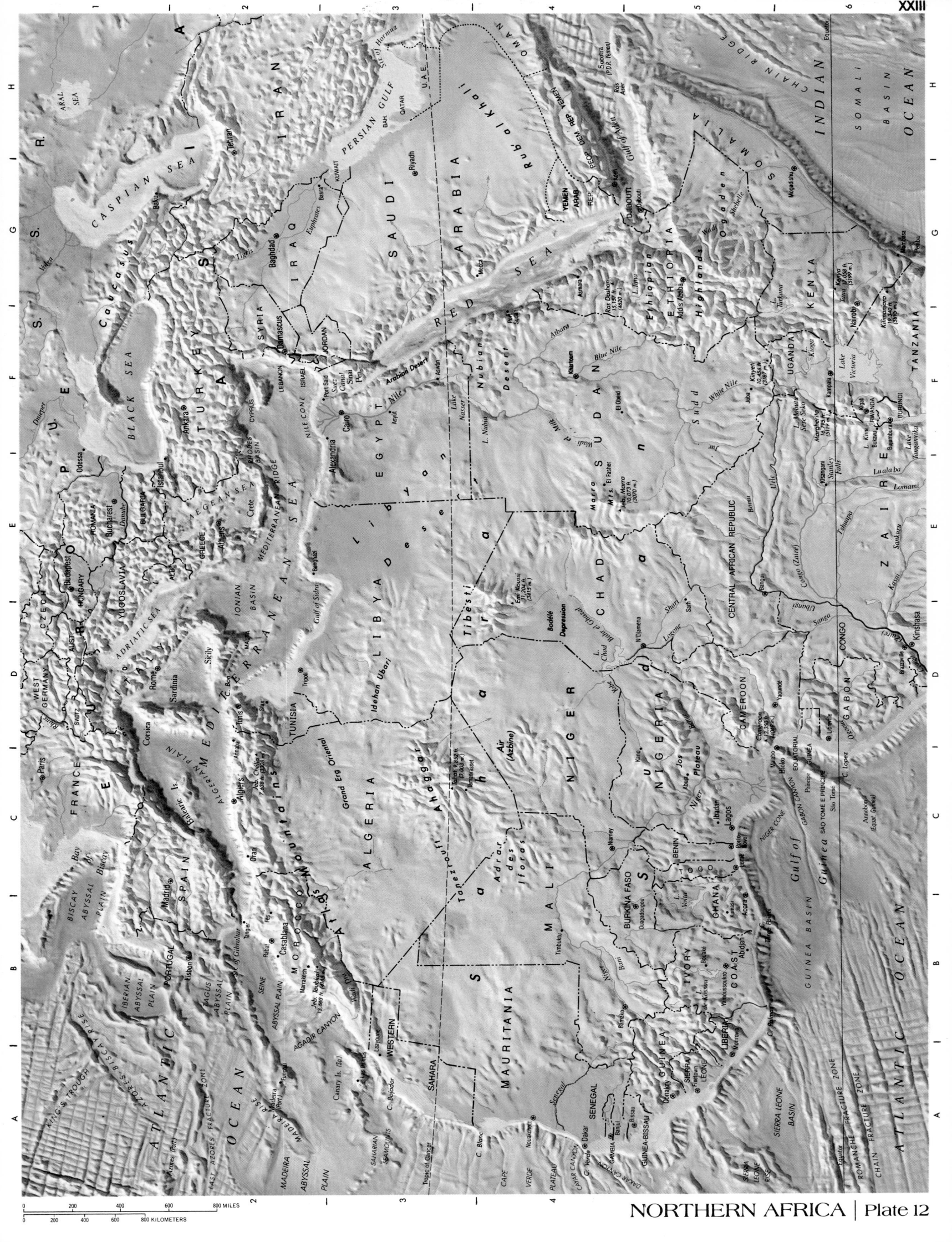

NORTHERN AFRICA | Plate 12

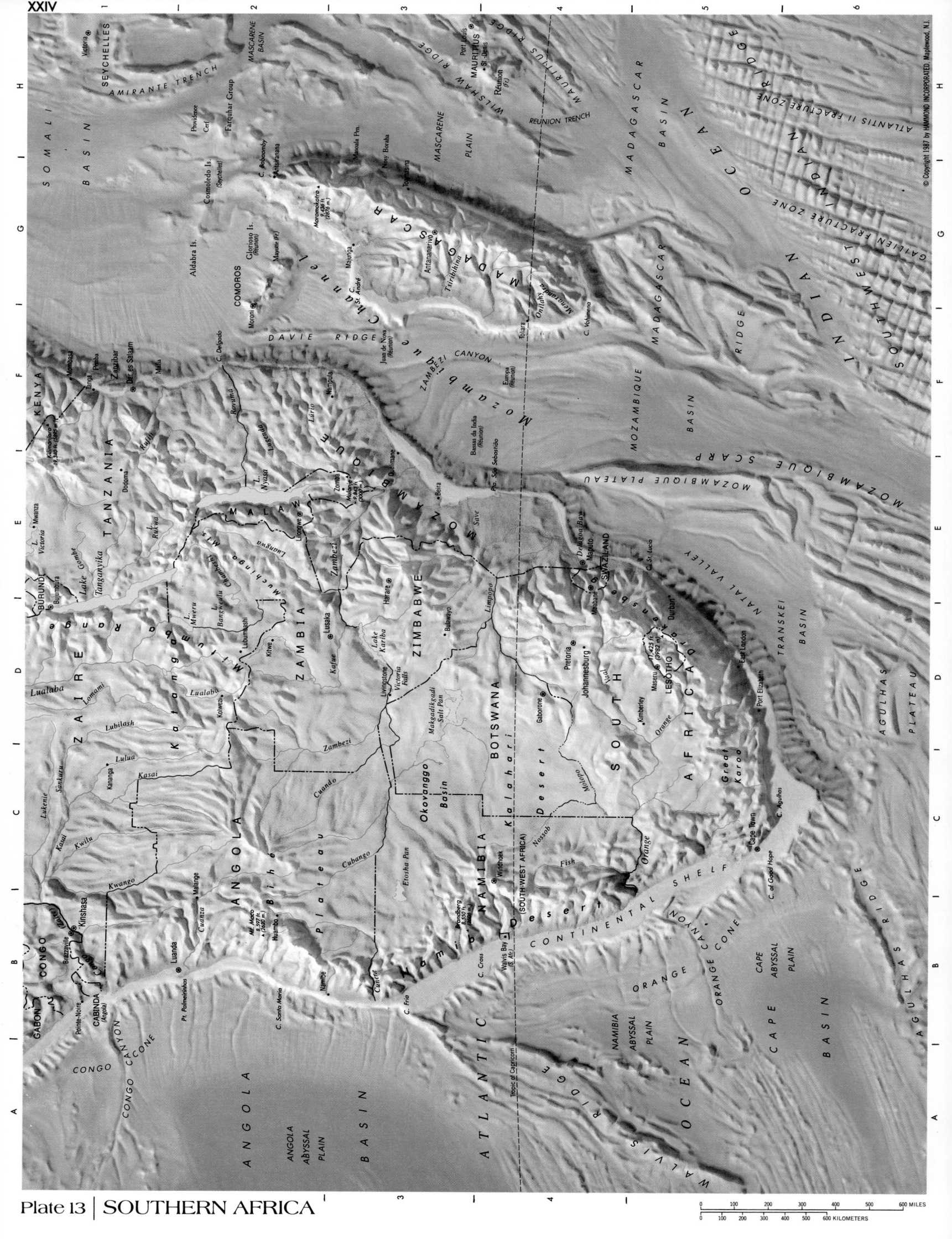

Plate 13 | SOUTHERN AFRICA

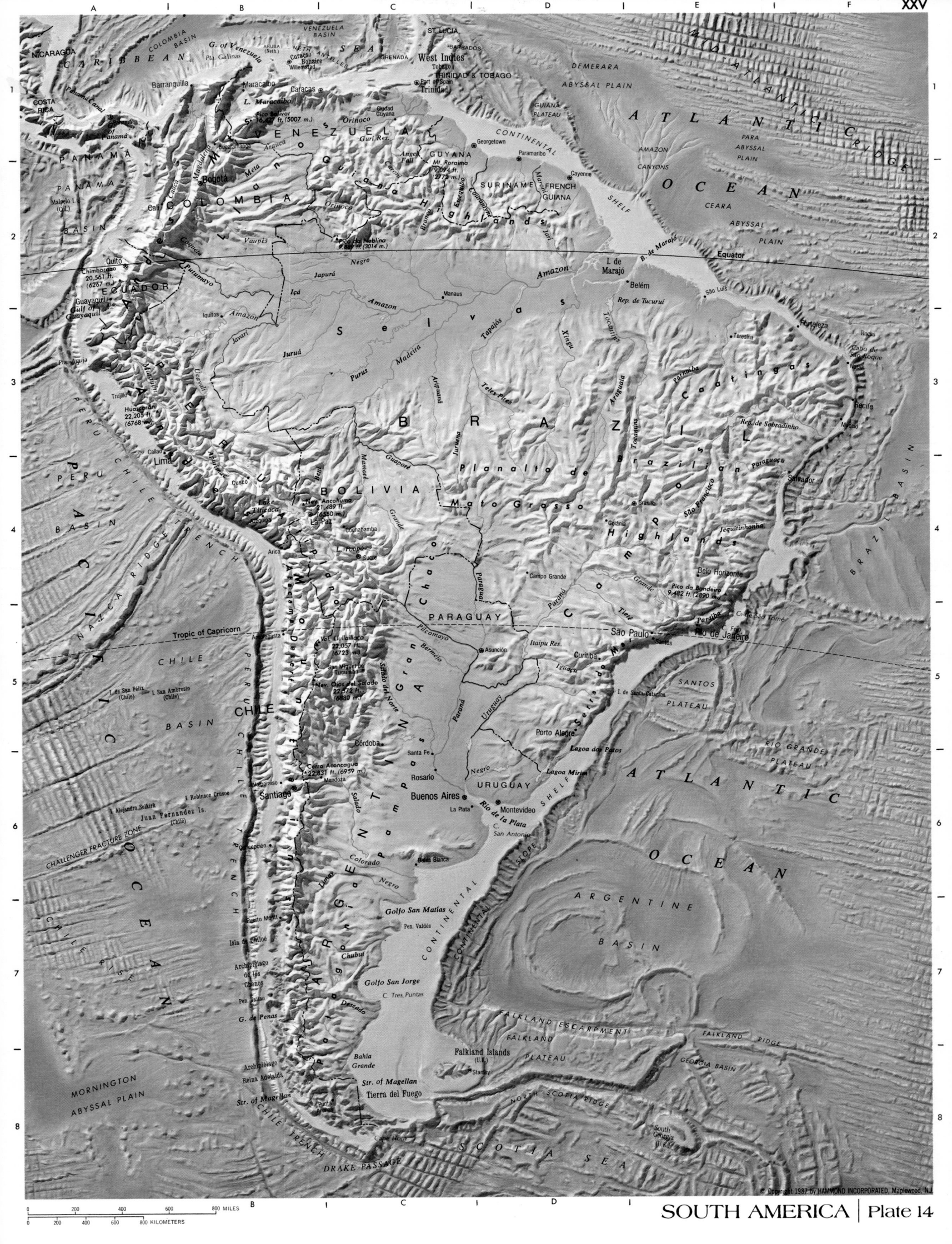

SOUTH AMERICA | Plate 14

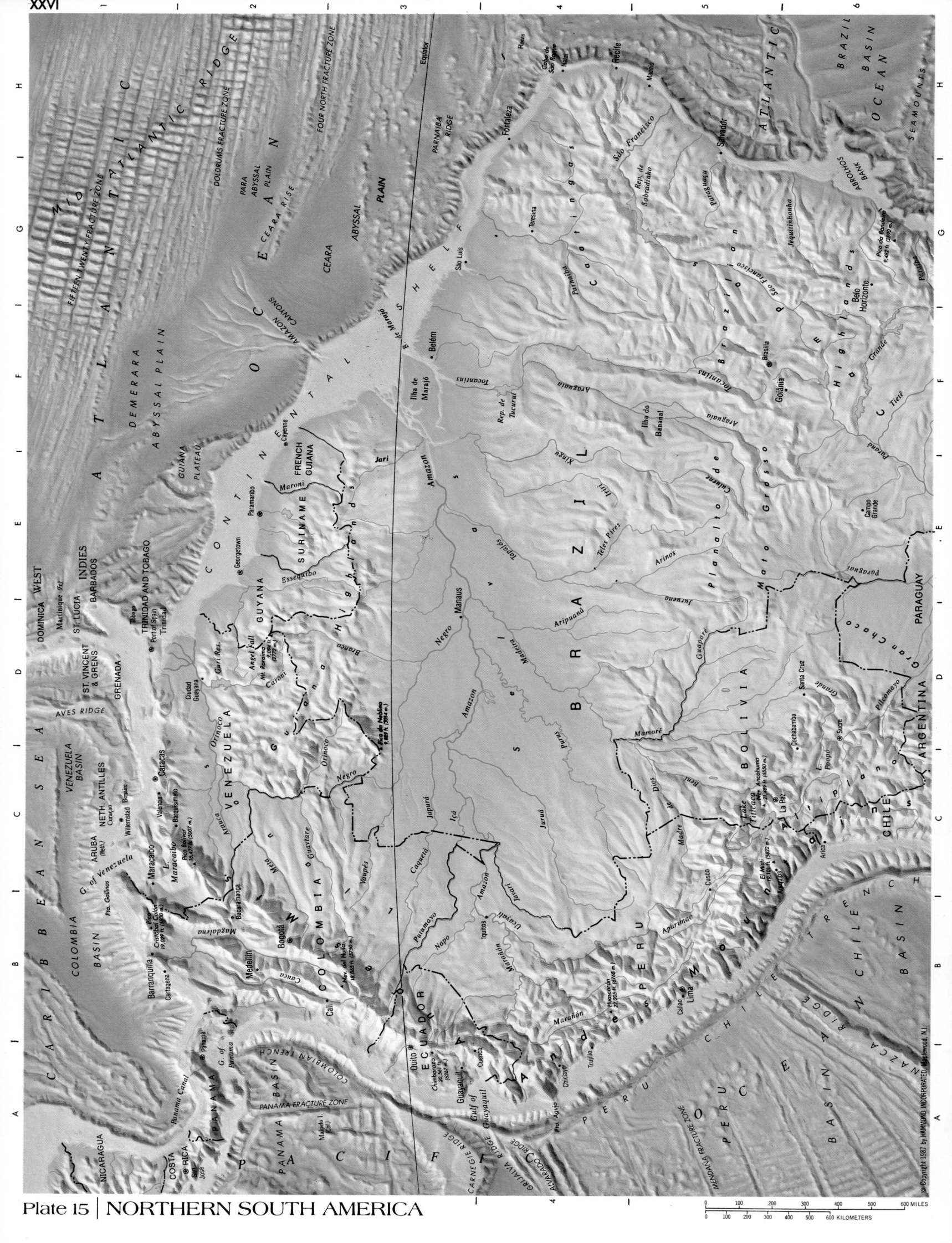

Plate 15 | NORTHERN SOUTH AMERICA

| 0 | 100 | 200 | 300 | 400 | 500 | 600 MILES |
| 0 | 100 | 200 | 300 | 400 | 500 | 600 KILOMETERS |

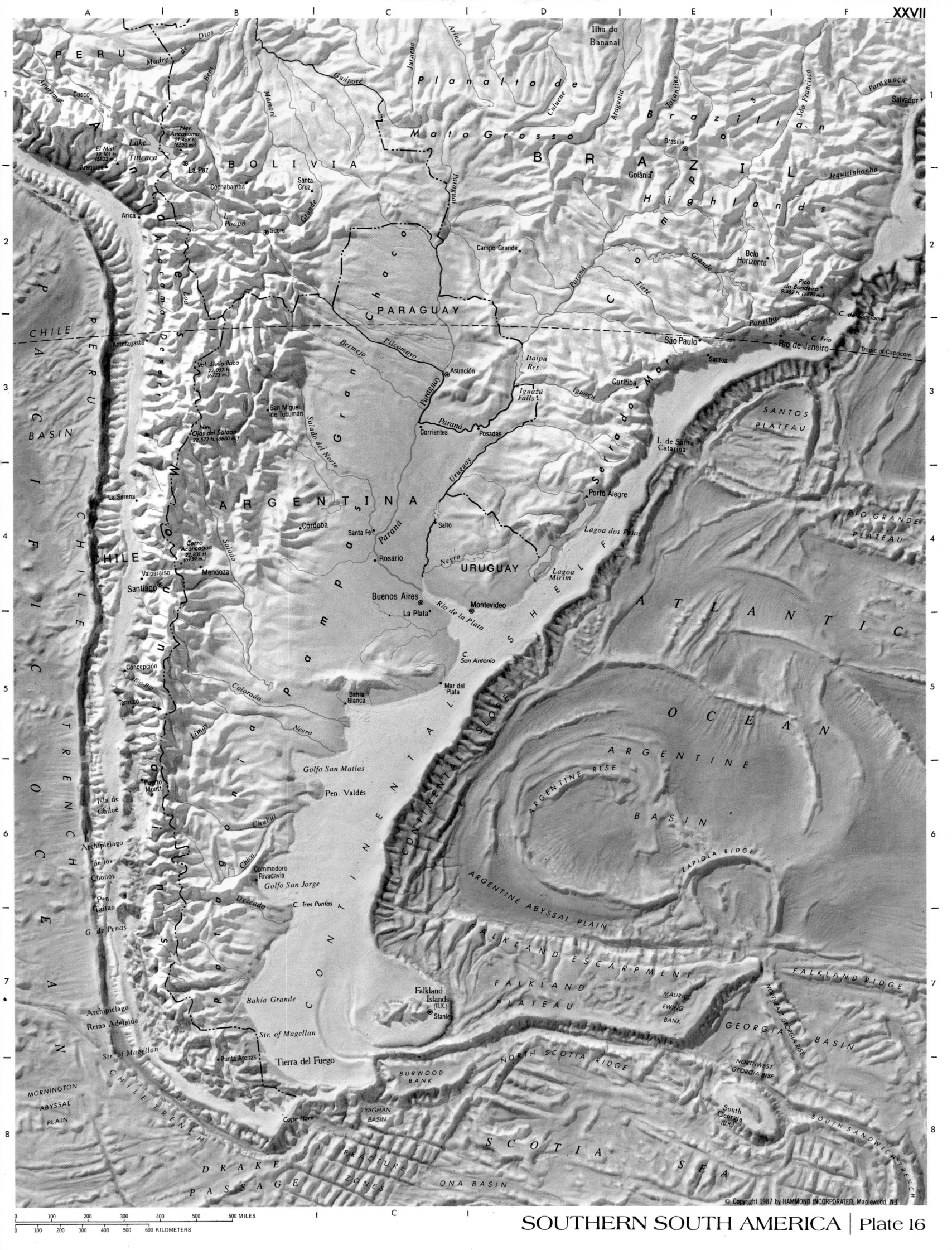

SOUTHERN SOUTH AMERICA | Plate 16

Plate 17 | NORTH AMERICA

0   200   400   600   800   1000 MILES
0   200 400 600 800 1000 KILOMETERS

© Copyright 1982 by HAMMOND INCORPORATED, Maplewood, N.J.

0 100 200 300 400 500 600 MILES
0 100 200 300 400 500 600 KILOMETERS

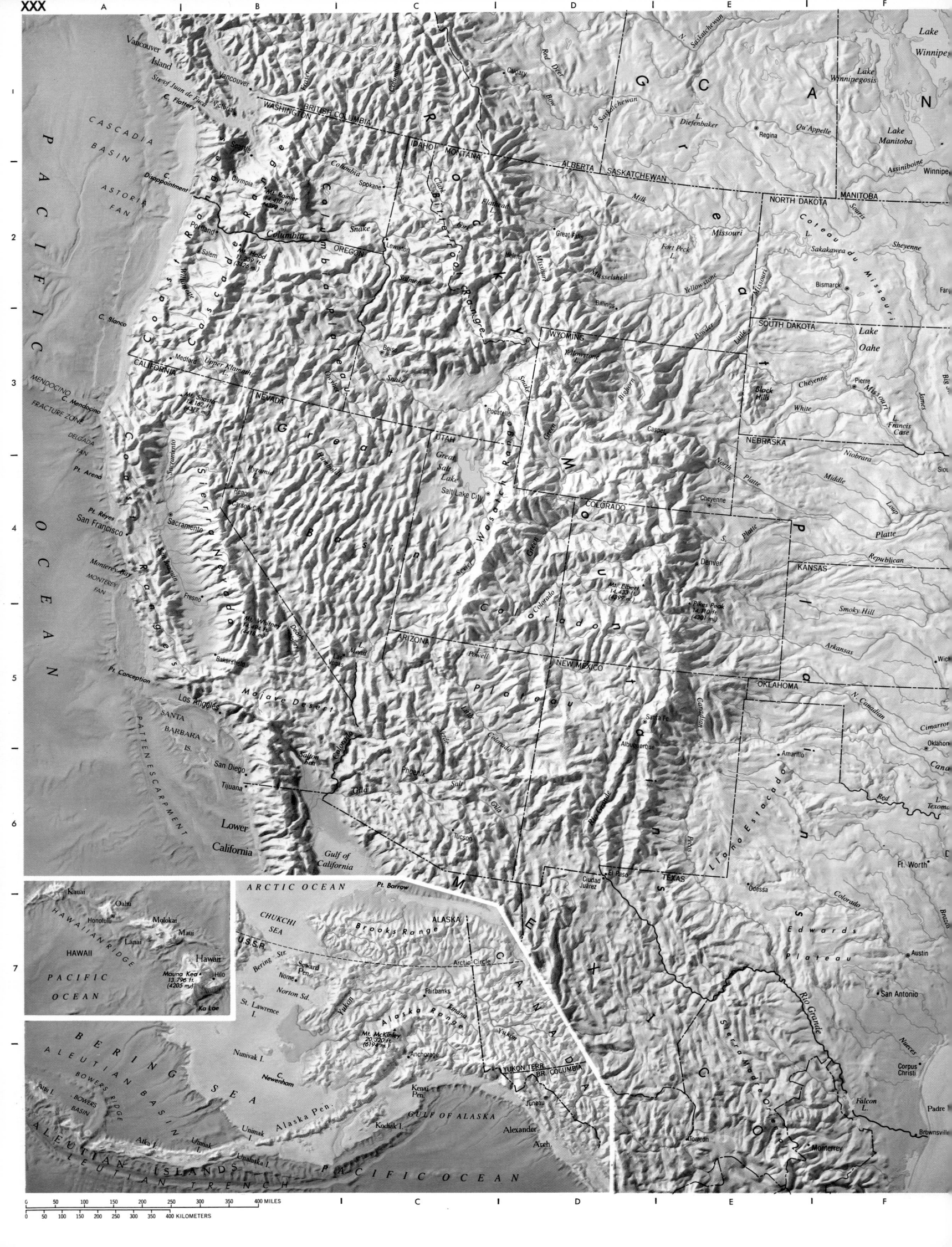

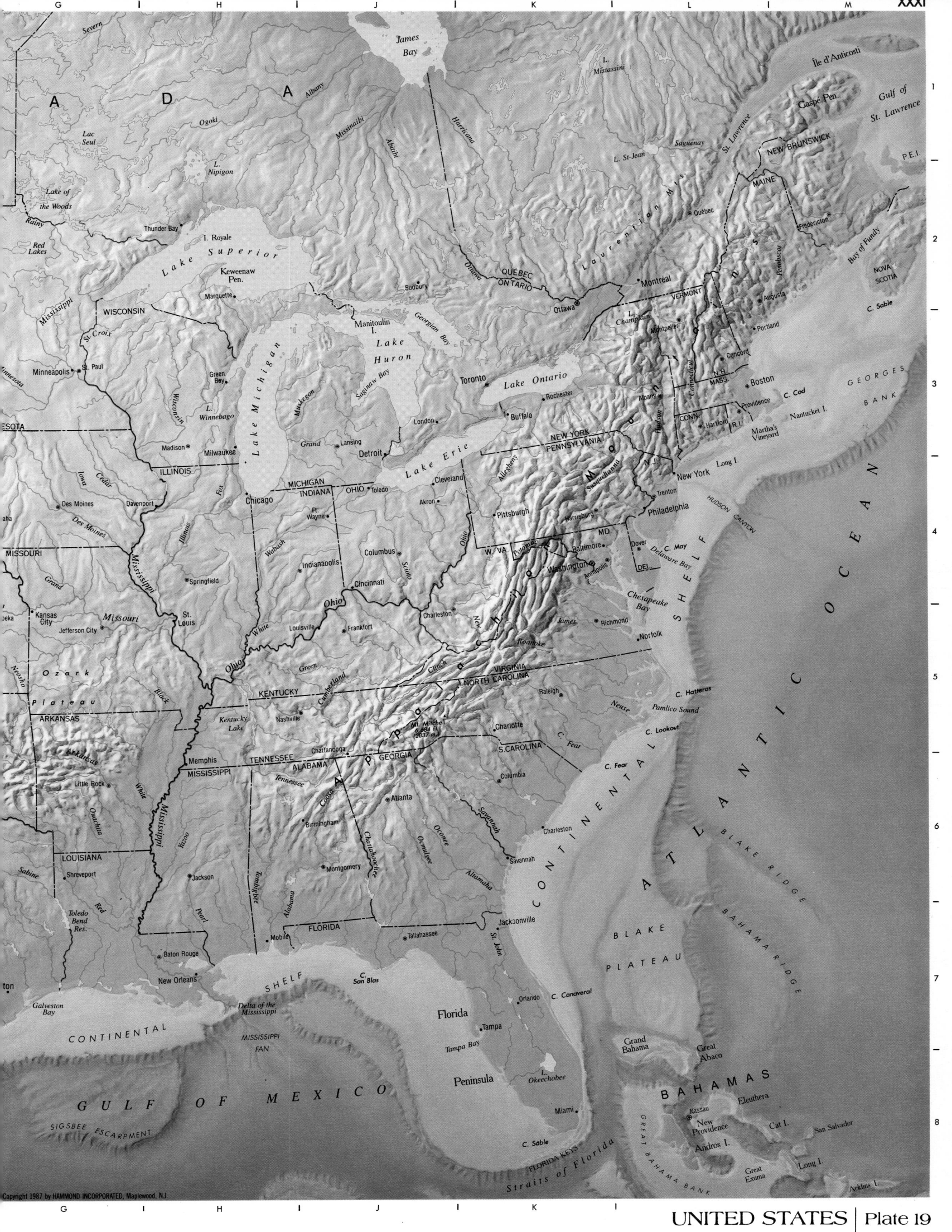

Plate 20 | MIDDLE AMERICA

| 0 | 100 | 200 | 300 | 400 | 500 | 600 MILES |
| 0 | 100 | 200 | 300 | 400 | 500 | 600 KILOMETERS |

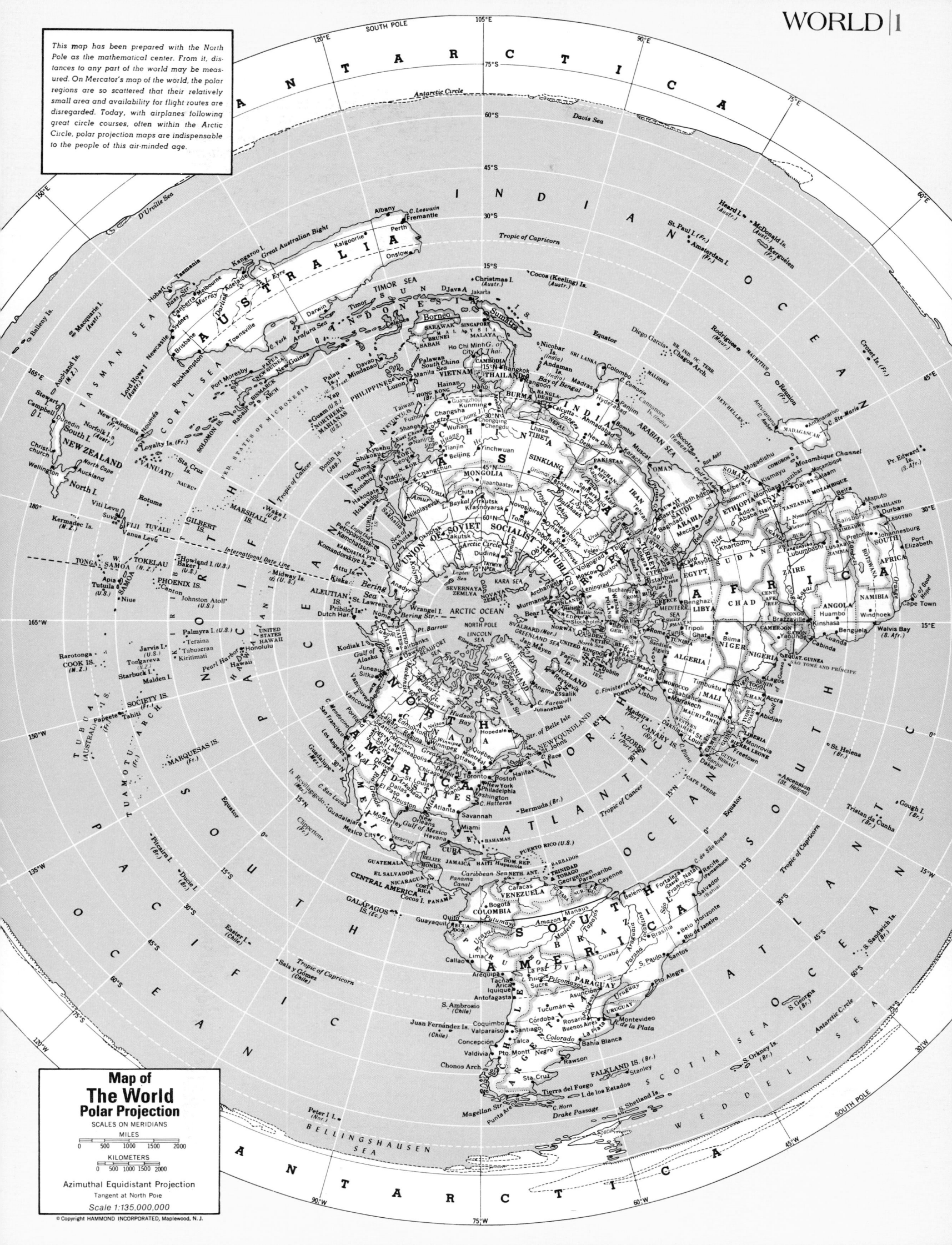

This map has been prepared with the North Pole as the mathematical center. From it, distances to any part of the world may be measured. On Mercator's map of the world, the polar regions are so scattered that their relatively small area and availability for flight routes are disregarded. Today, with airplanes following great circle courses, often within the Arctic Circle, polar projection maps are indispensable to the people of this air-minded age.

Map of
The World
Polar Projection

SCALES ON MERIDIANS

MILES

0   500   1000   1500   2000

KILOMETERS

0   500   1000   1500   2000

Azimuthal Equidistant Projection
Tangent at North Pole
Scale 1:135,000,000

© Copyright HAMMOND INCORPORATED, Maplewood, N.J.

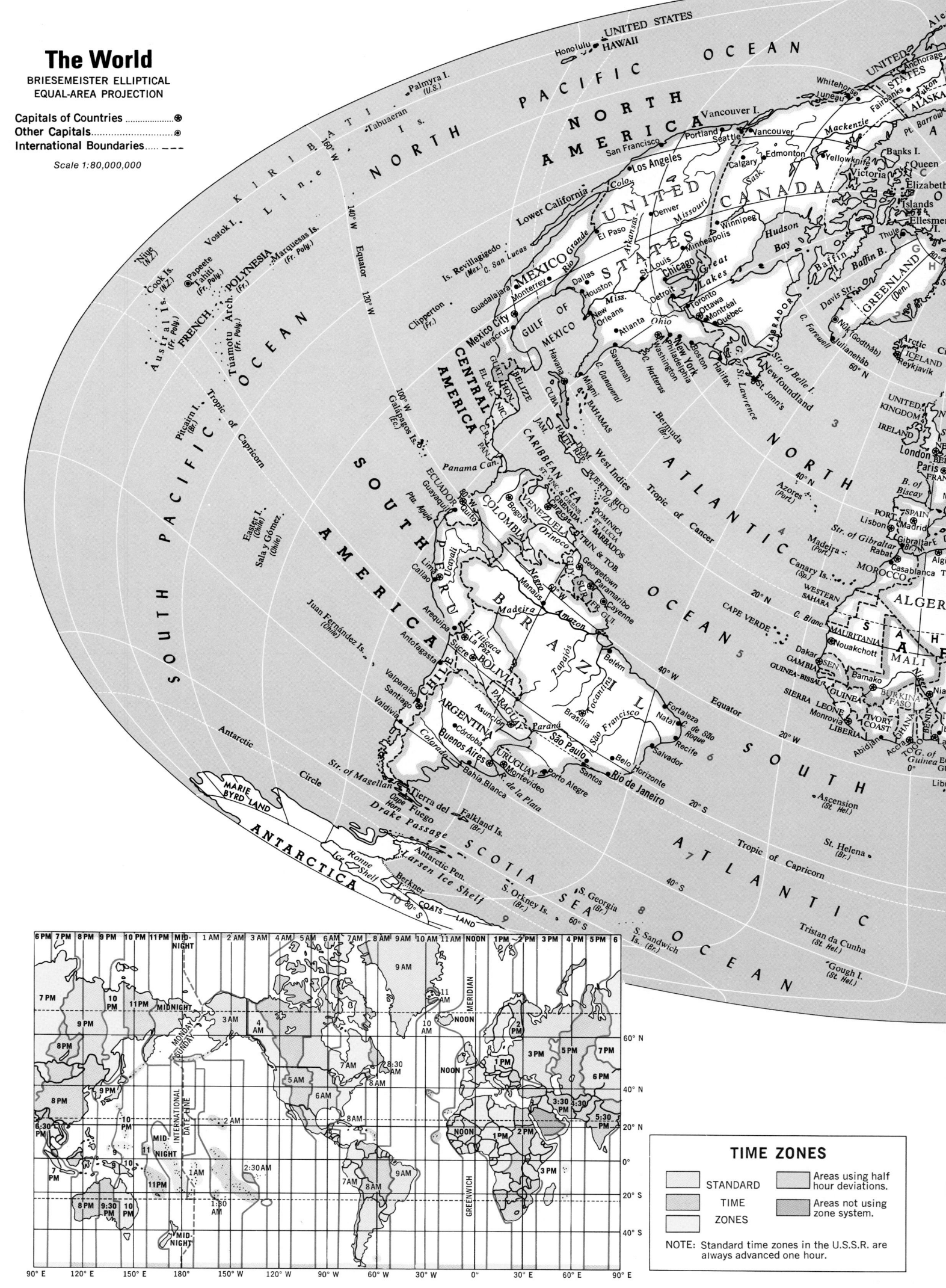

The World

**BRIESEMEISTER ELLIPTICAL
EQUAL-AREA PROJECTION**

Capitals of Countries .... ⊛
Other Capitals .... ⊛
International Boundaries ..... ‑ ‑ ‑

Scale 1:80,000,000

TIME ZONES

☐ STANDARD
☐ TIME
☐ ZONES

☐ Areas using half hour deviations.
☐ Areas not using zone system.

NOTE: Standard time zones in the U.S.S.R. are always advanced one hour.

LAND AREA   57,970,000 sq. mi.
(150,142,300 sq. km.)
WATER AREA   139,781,000 sq. mi.
(362,032,790 sq. km.)
TOTAL SURFACE AREA   197,751,000 sq.mi.
(512,175,090 sq. km.)
POPULATION   4,415,000,000

Antarctica

AZIMUTHAL EQUIDISTANT PROJECTION

Scale 1:62,000,000

© Copyright HAMMOND INCORPORATED, Maplewood, N.J.

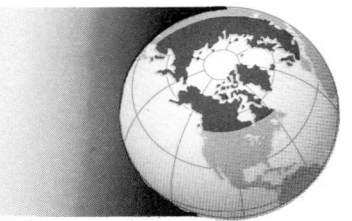

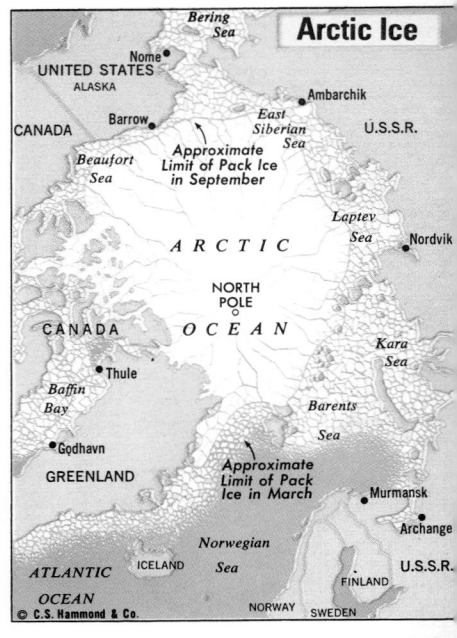

Arctic Ice
Bering Sea
Nome
UNITED STATES
ALASKA
Barrow
Ambarchik
CANADA
East Siberian Sea
U.S.S.R.
Approximate Limit of Pack Ice in September
Beaufort Sea
Laptev Sea
Nordvik
ARCTIC OCEAN
NORTH POLE
CANADA
Kara Sea
Thule
Baffin Bay
Barents Sea
Godhavn
GREENLAND
Approximate Limit of Pack Ice in March
Murmansk
Archange
Norwegian Sea
ICELAND
ATLANTIC OCEAN
FINLAND
U.S.S.R.
NORWAY
SWEDEN
© C.S. Hammond & Co.

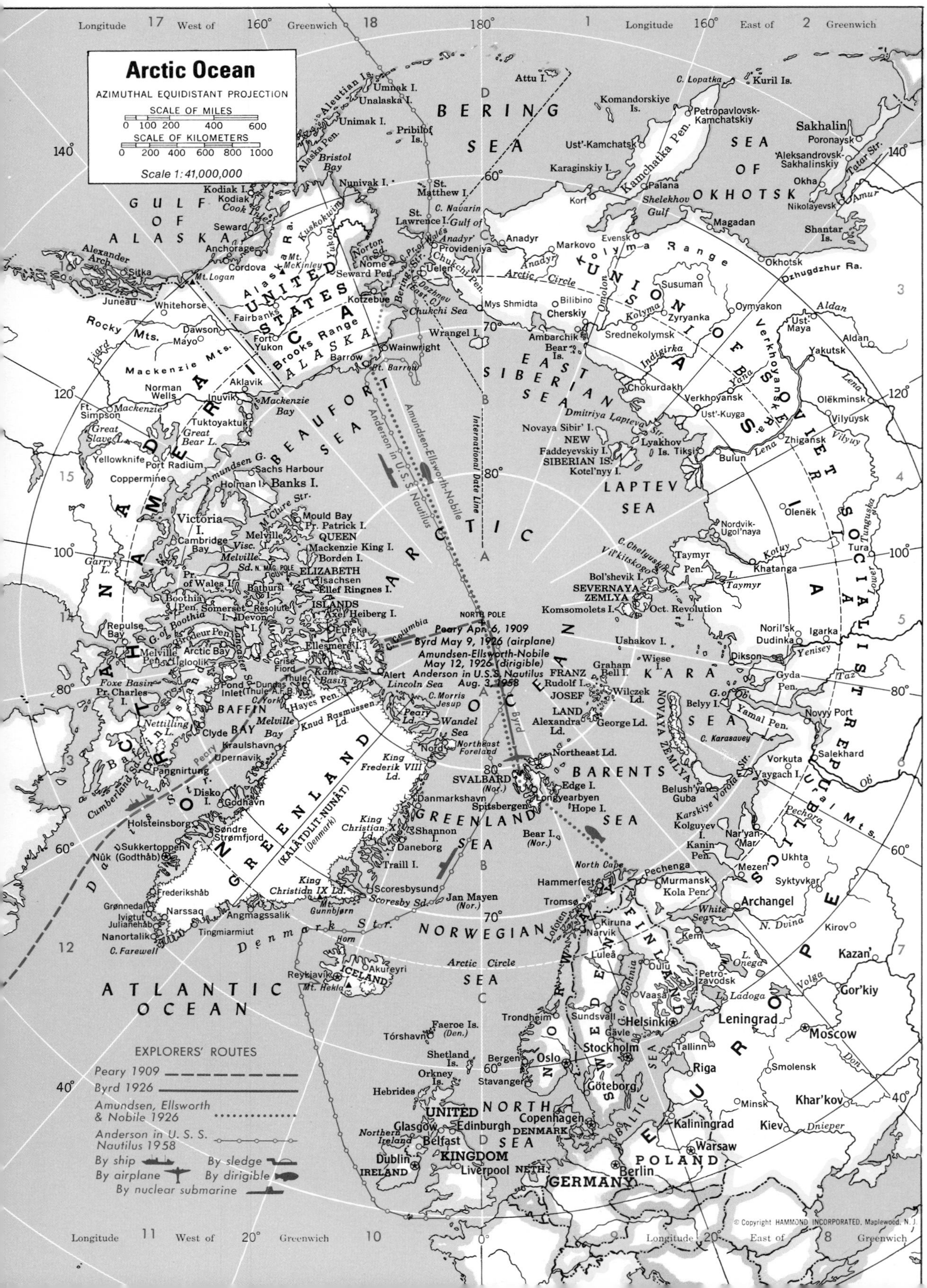

Arctic Ocean
AZIMUTHAL EQUIDISTANT PROJECTION
SCALE OF MILES
0 100 200 400 600
SCALE OF KILOMETERS
0 200 400 600 800 1000
Scale 1:41,000,000
Longitude 17 West of 160° Greenwich 18 180° 1 Longitude 160° East of 2 Greenwich
BERING SEA
SEA OF OKHOTSK
GULF OF ALASKA
EAST SIBERIAN SEA
BEAUFORT SEA
LAPTEV SEA
ARCTIC OCEAN
KARA SEA
BARENTS SEA
GREENLAND SEA
NORWEGIAN SEA
ATLANTIC OCEAN
NORTH SEA
UNITED STATES
UNION OF SOVIET SOCIALIST REPUBLICS
NORTH AMERICA
GREENLAND (KALÂTDLIT-NUNÂT) (Denmark)
EUROPE
NORTH POLE
Peary Apr. 6, 1909
Byrd May 9, 1926 (airplane)
Amundsen-Ellsworth-Nobile May 12, 1926 (dirigible)
Anderson in U.S.S. Nautilus Aug. 3, 1958
International Date Line
Arctic Circle
EXPLORERS' ROUTES
Peary 1909
Byrd 1926
Amundsen, Ellsworth & Nobile 1926
Anderson in U. S. S. Nautilus 1958
By ship
By sledge
By airplane
By dirigible
By nuclear submarine
Longitude 11 West of 20° Greenwich 10 0° Longitude 20° East of 8 Greenwich
© Copyright HAMMOND INCORPORATED, Maplewood, N.J.

Antarctica
AZIMUTHAL EQUIDISTANT PROJECTION

SCALE OF MILES
0 200 400 600 800

KILOMETERS
0 200 400 600 800 1000

© Copyright HAMMOND INCORPORATED, Maplewood, N.J

EXPLORERS' ROUTES

Palmer 1820
Amundsen 1910-12
Scott 1910-13
Byrd 1928-30
Fuchs 1957- 58
By ship   By sledge   By airplane
By snow tractor

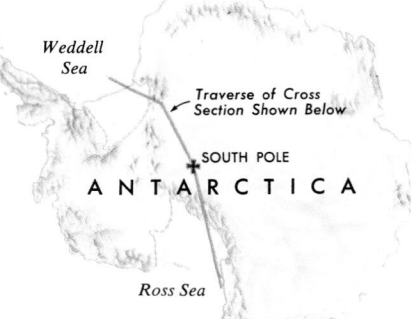

Weddell Sea

Traverse of Cross Section Shown Below

SOUTH POLE

ANTARCTICA

Ross Sea

Antarctic Cross Section: Weddell Sea to Ross Sea

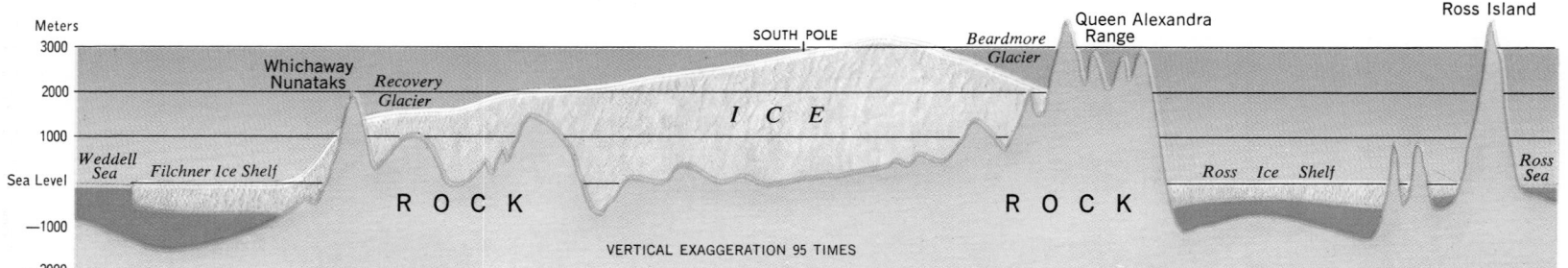

VERTICAL EXAGGERATION 95 TIMES

Information Based on American Geographical Society's "Antarctic Map Folio Series"

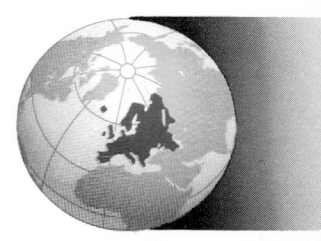

AREA   4,057,000 sq. mi.
        (10,507,630 sq. km.)
POPULATION   676,000,000
LARGEST CITY   Paris
HIGHEST POINT   El'brus 18,510 ft.
        (5,642 m.)
LOWEST POINT   Caspian Sea -92 ft.
        (-28 m.)

Population Distribution

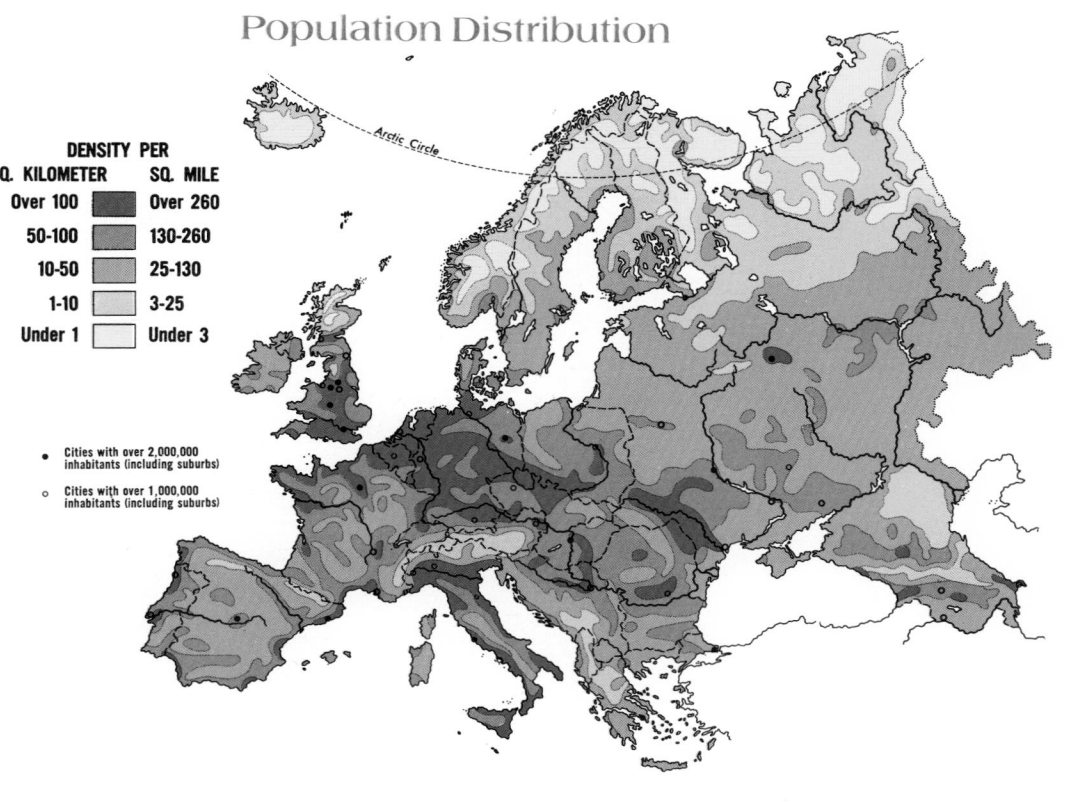

DENSITY PER

SQ. KILOMETER		SQ. MILE
Over 100		Over 260
50-100		130-260
10-50		25-130
1-10		3-25
Under 1		Under 3

• Cities with over 2,000,000 inhabitants (including suburbs)

○ Cities with over 1,000,000 inhabitants (including suburbs)

Vegetation

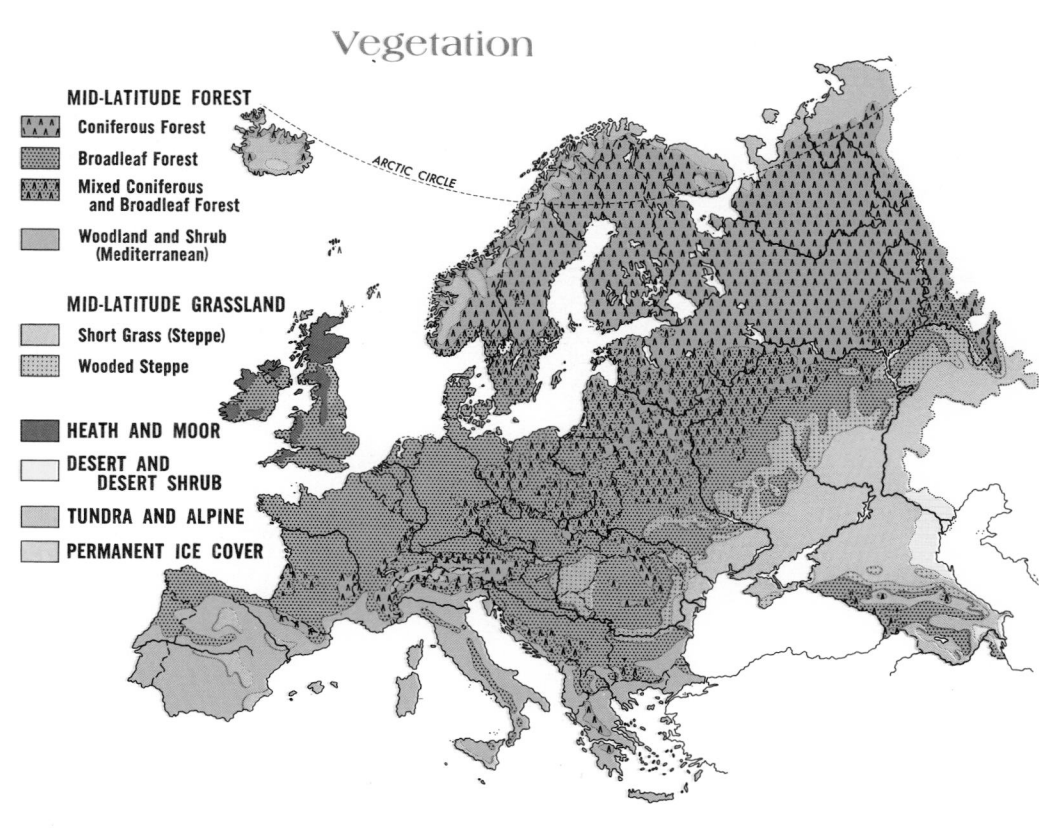

MID-LATITUDE FOREST

- Coniferous Forest
- Broadleaf Forest
- Mixed Coniferous and Broadleaf Forest
- Woodland and Shrub (Mediterranean)

MID-LATITUDE GRASSLAND

- Short Grass (Steppe)
- Wooded Steppe

HEATH AND MOOR

DESERT AND DESERT SHRUB

TUNDRA AND ALPINE

PERMANENT ICE COVER

© Copyright HAMMOND INCORPORATED, Maplewood, N.J.

Vegetation / Relief

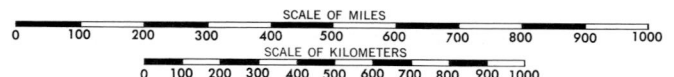

SCALE OF MILES
0 100 200 300 400 500 600 700 800 900 1000

SCALE OF KILOMETERS
0 100 200 300 400 500 600 700 800 900 1000

Capitals of Countries .... ⊛
International Boundaries .... –·–·–
Canals ....

Depths in Fathoms

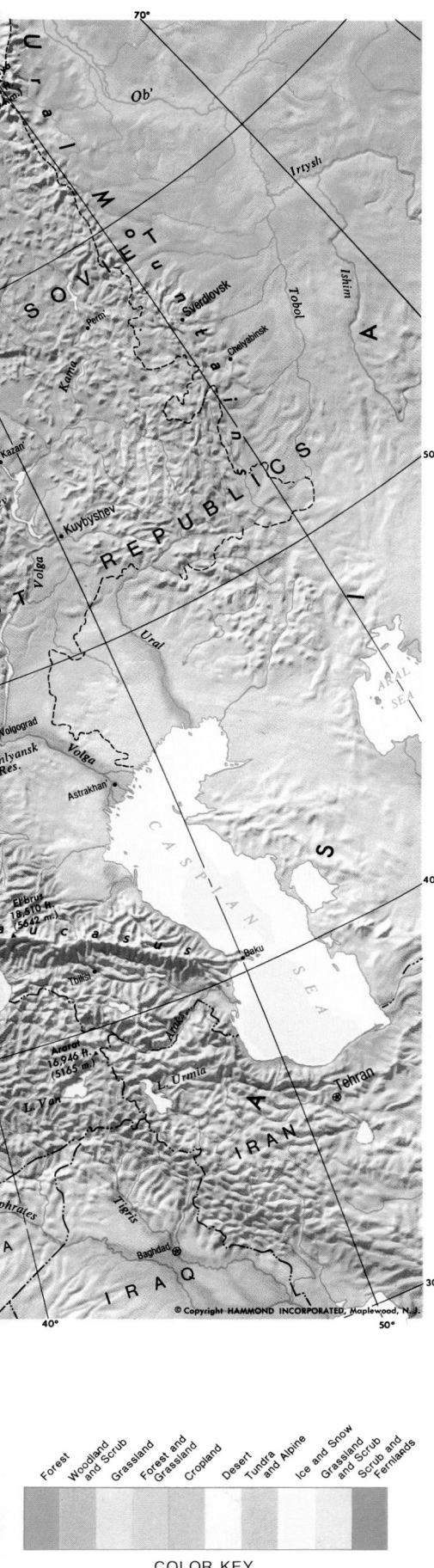

Forest | Woodland and Scrub | Grassland | Forest and Grassland | Cropland | Desert | Tundra and Alpine | Ice and Snow | Grassland and Scrub | Scrub and Fernlands

COLOR KEY

Rainfall

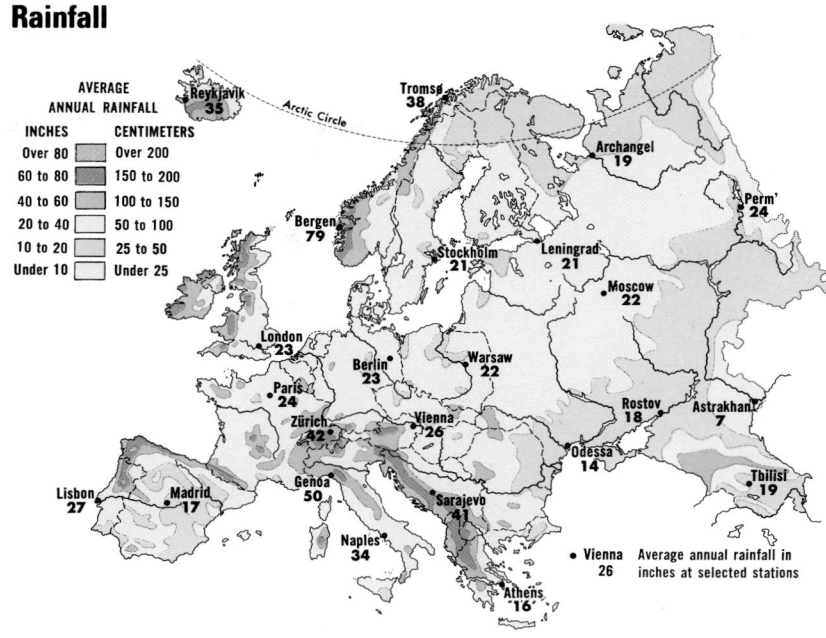

AVERAGE ANNUAL RAINFALL

INCHES	CENTIMETERS
Over 80	Over 200
60 to 80	150 to 200
40 to 60	100 to 150
20 to 40	50 to 100
10 to 20	25 to 50
Under 10	Under 25

• Vienna   Average annual rainfall in
  26   inches at selected stations

Average January Temperature

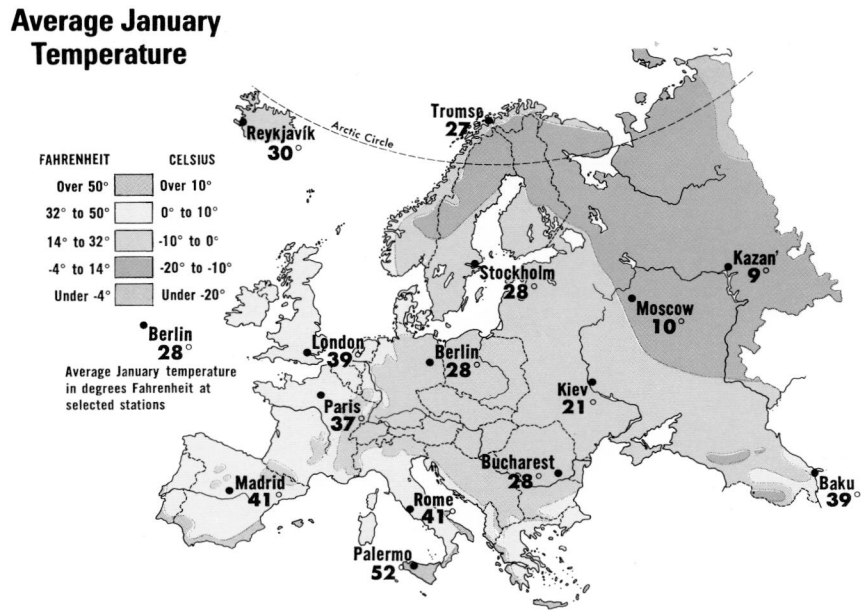

FAHRENHEIT	CELSIUS
Over 50°	Over 10°
32° to 50°	0° to 10°
14° to 32°	-10° to 0°
-4° to 14°	-20° to -10°
Under -4°	Under -20°

Average January temperature
in degrees Fahrenheit at
selected stations

Average July Temperature

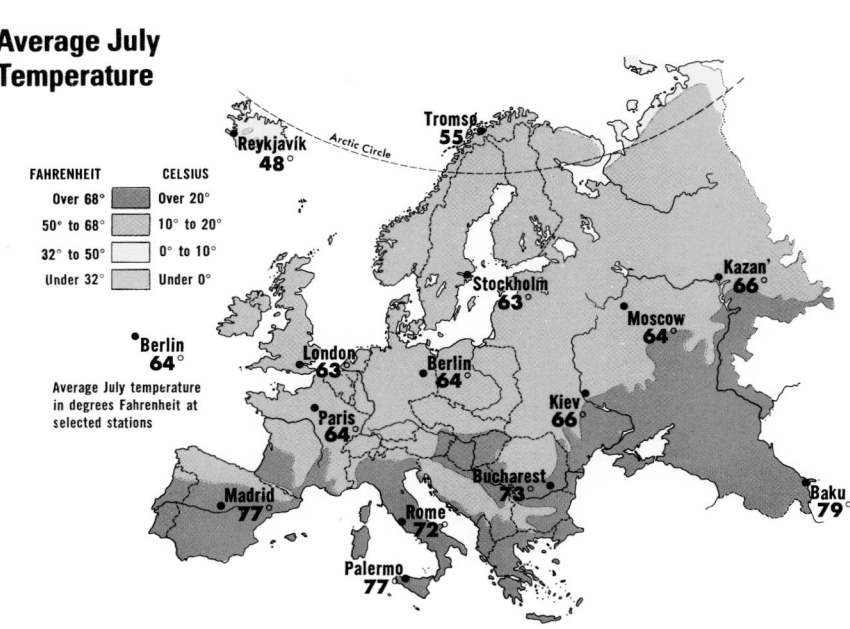

FAHRENHEIT	CELSIUS
Over 68°	Over 20°
50° to 68°	10° to 20°
32° to 50°	0° to 10°
Under 32°	Under 0°

Average July temperature
in degrees Fahrenheit at
selected stations

United Kingdom and Ireland

BONNE PROJECTION

SCALE OF MILES

SCALE OF KILOMETERS

Capitals of Countries..........★
International Boundaries........
Other Boundaries...............
Canals.........................

Scale 1: 4,200,000

Shetland Islands

Same scale as main map.

UNITED KINGDOM

AREA 94,399 sq. mi. (244,493 sq. km.)
POPULATION 55,672,000
CAPITAL London
LARGEST CITY London
HIGHEST POINT Ben Nevis 4,406 ft. (1,343 m.)
MONETARY UNIT pound sterling
MAJOR LANGUAGES English, Gaelic, Welsh
MAJOR RELIGIONS Protestantism, Roman Catholicism

IRELAND

AREA 27,136 sq. mi. (70,282 sq. km.)
POPULATION 3,440,427
CAPITAL Dublin
LARGEST CITY Dublin
HIGHEST POINT Carrantuohill 3,415 ft. (1,041 m.)
MONETARY UNIT Irish pound
MAJOR LANGUAGES English, Gaelic (Irish)
MAJOR RELIGION Roman Catholicism

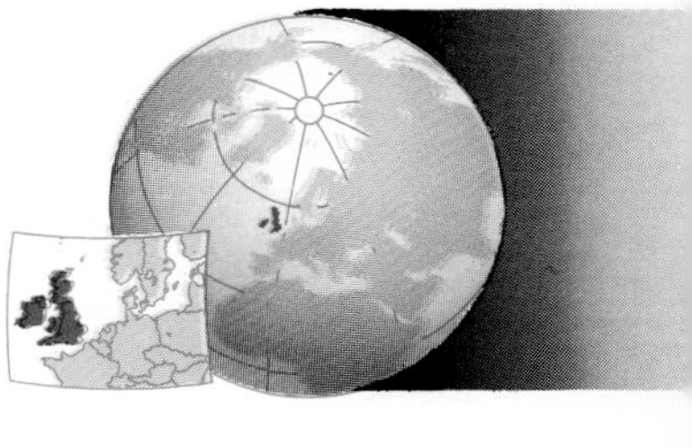

ENGLAND

COUNTIES

Avon, 920,200 . . . E 6
Bedfordshire, 491,700 . . . G 5
Berkshire, 659,000 . . . F 6
Buckinghamshire, 512,000 . . . G 6
Cambridgeshire, 563,000 . . . G 5
Cheshire, 916,400 . . . E 4
Cleveland, 567,900 . . . F 3
Cornwall, 405,200 . . . C 7
Cumbria, 473,600 . . . D 3
Derbyshire, 887,600 . . . F 5
Devon, 942,100 . . . D 7
Dorset, 575,800 . . . E 7
Durham, 610,400 . . . F 3
East Sussex, 655,600 . . . H 7
Essex, 1,426,200 . . . H 6
Gloucestershire, 491,500 . . . E 6
Greater London, 7,028,200 . . . H 8
Greater Manchester, 2,684,100 . . . H 2
Hampshire, 1,456,100 . . . F 6
Hereford and Worcester, 594,200 . . . E 5
Hertfordshire, 937,300 . . . G 6
Humberside, 848,600 . . . G 4
Isle of Wight, 111,300 . . . F 7
Isles of Scilly, 1,900 . . . A 7
Kent, 1,448,100 . . . H 6
Lancashire, 1,375,500 . . . E 4
Leicestershire, 837,900 . . . F 5
Lincolnshire, 524,500 . . . G 4
London, Greater, 7,028,200 . . . H 8
Manchester, Greater, 2,684,100 . . . H 2
Merseyside, 1,578,000 . . . G 2
Norfolk, 662,500 . . . H 5
Northamptonshire, 505,900 . . . G 5
Northumberland, 287,300 . . . E 2
North Yorkshire, 653,000 . . . F 3
Nottinghamshire, 977,500 . . . F 4
Oxfordshire 541,800 . . . F6
Shropshire (Salop) 359,000 . . . E5
Somerset 404,400 . . . E6
South Yorkshire 1,318,300 . . . F4
Staffordshire 997,600 . . . E5
Suffolk 577,600 . . . H5
Surrey 1,002,900 . . . G6
Sussex, East 655,600 . . . H7
Sussex, West 623,400 . . . G7
Tyne and Wear 1,182,900 . . . H3
Warwickshire 471,000 . . . F5
West Midlands 2,743,300 . . . F5
West Sussex 623,400 . . . G7
West Yorkshire 2,072,500 . . . J1
Wiltshire 512,800 . . . E6
Yorkshire, North 653,000 . . . F3
Yorkshire, South 1,318,300 . . . F4
Yorkshire, West 2,072,500 . . . J1

CITIES and TOWNS

Abingdon, 20,130 . . . F 6
Accrington, 36,470 . . . H 1
Adwick le Street, 17,650 . . . K 2
Aldeburgh, 2,750 . . . J 5
Aldershot, 33,750 . . . G 8
Aldridge Brownhills, 89,370 . . . E 5
Alfreton, 21,560 . . . F 4
Alnwick, 7,300 . . . F 2
Altrincham, 40,800 . . . H 2
Amersham, ⊙17,254 . . . G 7
Andover, 27,620 . . . F 6
Appleby, 2,240 . . . E 3
Arnold, 35,090 . . . F 4
Arundel, 2,390 . . . G 7
Ashford, 36,380 . . . H 6
Ashington, 24,720 . . . F 2
Ashton-under-Lyne, 48,500 . . . H 2
Axminster, ⊙4,515 . . . D 7
Aycliffe, ⊙20,203 . . . F 3
Aylesbury, 41,420 . . . G 7
Bacup, 14,990 . . . H 1
Bakewell, 4,100 . . . J 2
Banbury, 31,060 . . . F 5
Banstead, 44,100 . . . H 8
Barking, 153,800 . . . H 8
Barnet, 305,200 . . . H 7
Barnsley, 74,730 . . . J 2
Barnstaple, 17,820 . . . D 6
Barrow-in-Furness, 73,400 . . . D 3
Barton-upon-Humber, 7,750 . . . G 4
Basildon, 135,720 . . . J 8
Basingstoke, 60,910 . . . F 6
Bath, 83,100 . . . E 6
Batley, 41,630 . . . J 1
Battle, ⊙4,987 . . . H 7
Bebington, 62,500 . . . G 2
Bedford, 74,390 . . . G 5
Bedlington, 27,200 . . . F 2
Bedworth, 41,600 . . . F 5
Beeston and Stapleford, 65,360 . . . F 5
Benfleet, 49,180 . . . J 8
Bentley with Arksey, 22,320 . . . F 4
Berkhamsted, 15,920 . . . G 7
Beverley, 16,920 . . . G 4
Bexhill, 34,680 . . . H 7
Bexley, 213,500 . . . H 8
Biddulph, 18,720 . . . H 2
Birkenhead, 135,750 . . . G 2
Birmingham, 1,058,800 . . . F 5
Bishop Auckland, 32,940 . . . E 3
Bishop's Stortford, 21,720 . . . H 6
Blackburn, 101,670 . . . H 1
Blackpool, 149,000 . . . G 1
Blaydon, 31,940 . . . H 3
Blyth, 35,390 . . . F 2
Bodmin, 10,430 . . . C 7
Bognor Regis, 34,620 . . . G 7
Boldon, 24,430 . . . J 3
Bolton, 154,480 . . . H 2
Bootle 71,160 . . . G2
Boston 26,700 . . . G5
Bournemouth 144,100 . . . F7
Bracknell† 34,067 . . . G8
Bradford 458,900 . . . J1
Braintree and Bocking 26,300 . . . H6
Brent 256,500 . . . H8
Brentwood 58,690 . . . J8
Bridgwater 26,700 . . . E6
Bridlington 26,920 . . . G3
Bridport 6,660 . . . E7
Brigg 4,870 . . . G4
Brighouse 35,320 . . . J1
Brightlingsea 7,170 . . . J6
Brighton 156,500 . . . G7
Bristol 416,300 . . . E6
Broadstairs and Saint Peter's 21,670 . . . J6
Bromley 299,100 . . . H8
Bromsgrove 41,430 . . . E5
Buckfastleigh 2,870 . . . C7
Buckingham 5,290 . . . G6
Bude-Stratton 5,750 . . . C7
Bungay 4,120 . . . J5
Burgess Hill 20,030 . . . G7
Burnham-on-Crouch 4,920 . . . H6
Burnley 74,300 . . . H1
Burntwood† 23,088 . . . F5
Burton upon Trent 49,480 . . . F5
Bury 69,550 . . . H2
Bury Saint Edmunds 26,800 . . . H5
Bushey 24,500 . . . H7
Buxton 20,050 . . . J2
Caister-on-Sea† 6,287 . . . J5
Camborne-Redruth 43,970 . . . B7
Cambridge 106,400 . . . G5
Camden 185,800 . . . H8
Cannock 56,440 . . . E5
Canterbury 115,600 . . . H6
Canvey Island 29,550 . . . J8
Carlisle, 99,600 . . . D 3
Carlton, 46,690 . . . F 5
Caterham and Warlingham, 35,840 . H 8
Chatham, 59,550 . . . J 8
Cheadle and Gatley, 62,460 . . . H 2
Chelmsford, 58,320 . . . J 7
Cheltenham, 75,910 . . . E 6
Chertsey, 45,070 . . . G 8
Chesham, 20,830 . . . G 7
Cheshunt, 45,750 . . . H 7
Chester, 117,200 . . . G 2
Chesterfield, 69,480 . . . J 2
Chester-le-Street, 20,720 . . . J 3
Chichester, 20,940 . . . G 7
Chigwell, 54,220 . . . H 8
Chippenham, 18,550 . . . E 6
Chorley, 31,800 . . . G 2
Christchurch, 31,610 . . . F 7
Cirencester, 14,500 . . . E 6
Clacton, 39,380 . . . J 6
Clay Cross, 9,630 . . . J 2
Cleator Moor, ⊙7,686 . . . D 3
Cleethorpes, 37,200 . . . H 4
Clevedon, 15,140 . . . D 6
Clun, ⊙1,261 . . . D 6
Coalville, 28,740 . . . F 5
Cockermouth, 6,480 . . . D 3
Colchester, 79,600 . . . H 6
Colne, 19,030 . . . H 1
Colne Valley, 21,190 . . . J 2
Congleton, 21,500 . . . H 2
Consett, 35,080 . . . H 3
Corby, 48,850 . . . G 5
Coventry, 336,800 . . . F 5
Cowes, 19,190 . . . F 7
Crawley, 72,600 . . . G 6
Crewe and Nantwich, 98,100 . . . E 4
Cromer, 5,720 . . . J 5
Crook and Willington, 21,120 . . . E 3
Crosby, 56,750 . . . G 2
Croydon, 330,600 . . . H 8
Cuckfield, 26,500 . . . G 6
Darlington, 85,120 . . . F 3
Dartford, 44,130 . . . J 8
Darton, 15,710 . . . J 2
Darwen, 29,290 . . . H 1
Deal, 26,840 . . . J 6
Dearne, 24,780 . . . K 2
Denton, 38,110 . . . H 2
Derby, 213,700 . . . F 5
Dewsbury, 50,560 . . . J 1
Didcot, ⊙14,277 . . . F 6
Doncaster, 81,530 . . . F 4
Dorking, 22,410 . . . G 8
Dover, 34,160 . . . J 6
Downham Market, 4,120 . . . H 5
Droitwich, 13,950 . . . E 5
Dronfield, 20,000 . . . J 2
Dudley, 187,110 . . . E 5
Dunstable, 32,090 . . . G 6
Durham, 88,800 . . . J 3
Ealing, 293,800 . . . H 8
Eastbourne, 73,200 . . . H 7
East Grinstead, 19,420 . . . G 6
Eastleigh, 46,340 . . . F 7
East Retford, 18,260 . . . G 4
Egham, 30,320 . . . G 8
Egremont, ⊙7,253 . . . D 3
Eling, ⊙20,006 . . . F 7
Ellesmere, ⊙2,630 . . . E 5
Ellesmere Port, 63,870 . . . G 2
Enfield, 260,900 . . . H 7
Epsom and Ewell, 70,700 . . . G 8
Esher, 63,970 . . . H 8
Eston, ⊙46,219 . . . F 3
Eton, 4,950 . . . G 8
Evesham, 14,090 . . . F 5
Exeter, 93,300 . . . D 7
Exminster, ⊙3,181 . . . D 7
Exmouth, 26,840 . . . D 7
Falmouth, 17,530 . . . B 7
Fareham, 86,300 . . . F 7
Farnborough, 43,520 . . . G 8
Farnham, 33,140 . . . G 8
Farnworth, 26,110 . . . H 2
Faversham, 15,010 . . . H 6
Felixstowe, 19,460 . . . J 6
Felling, 38,990 . . . J 3
Filey, 5,660 . . . G 3
Fleet, 22,930 . . . G 8
Fleetwood, 30,070 . . . D 4
Folkestone, 45,610 . . . J 6
Formby, 24,850 . . . G 2
Framlingham, ⊙2,258 . . . J 5
Frimley and Camberley, 47,390 . . . G 8
Fulwood, 22,910 . . . G 1
Gainsborough, 17,440 . . . G 4
Gateshead, 91,230 . . . J 3
Gillingham, Dorset, ⊙4,050 . . . E 6
Gillingham, Kent, 93,900 . . . J 8
Glastonbury, 6,580 . . . E 6
Glossop, 24,820 . . . J 2
Gloucester, 91,600 . . . E 6
Godalming, 18,840 . . . G 8
Golborne, 28,720 . . . G 2
Goole, 17,920 . . . G 4
Gosport, 82,300 . . . F 7
Grange, 3,520 . . . E 3
Grantham 27,830 . . . G5
Gravesend 53,500 . . . J8
Great Grimsby 93,800 . . . G4
Great Torrington 3,430 . . . C7
Great Yarmouth 49,410 . . . J5
Greenwich 207,200 . . . H8
Guildford 58,470 . . . G8
Guisborough 14,860 . . . F3
Hackney 192,500 . . . H8
Hale 17,080 . . . H2
Halesowen 54,120 . . . E5
Halifax 88,580 . . . J1
Haltemprice 54,850 . . . G4
Haltwhistle† 3,511 . . . E2
Hammersmith 170,000 . . . H8
Haringey 228,200 . . . H8
Harlow 79,160 . . . H7
Harrogate 64,620 . . . F4
Harrow 200,200 . . . B5
Hartlepool 97,100 . . . F3
Harwich 15,280 . . . J6
Haslingden 15,140 . . . H1
Hastings 74,600 . . . H7
Hatfield† 25,359 . . . H7
Havant and Waterloo 112,430 . . . G7
Haverhill 14,550 . . . H5
Havering 239,200 . . . J8
Hayle† 5,378 . . . B7
Hazel Grove and Bramhall 40,400 . . . H2
Heanor 24,590 . . . F4
Hebburn 23,150 . . . J3
Hedon 3,010 . . . G4
Hemel Hempstead 71,150 . . . G7
Hereford 47,800 . . . E5
Hertford 20,760 . . . H7
Hetton 16,810 . . . J3
Hexham 9,820 . . . E3
Heywood 31,720 . . . H2
High Wycombe 61,190 . . . G8
Hillingdon 230,800 . . . G8
Hinckley 49,310 . . . F5
Hinderwell† 2,551 . . . G3
Hitchin 29,190 . . . G6
Hoddesdon 27,510 . . . H7
Holmfirth 19,790 . . . J2
Horley† 18,593 . . . H8
Hornsea 7,280 . . . G4
Horsham 26,770 . . . G6
Horwich 16,670 . . . G2
Houghton-le-Spring 33,150 . . . J3
Hounslow, 199,100 . . . G 8
Hove, 72,000 . . . G 7
Hoylake, 32,000 . . . G 2
Hoyland Nether, 15,500 . . . J 2
Hucknall, 27,110 . . . F 4
Huddersfield, 130,060 . . . J 2
Hugh Town, ⊙1,958 . . . A 8
Hull, 276,600 . . . G 4
Hunstanton, 4,140 . . . H 5
Huntingdon and Godmanchester, 17,200 . . . G 5
Huyton-with-Roby, 65,950 . . . G 2
Hyde, 37,040 . . . H 2
Ilfracombe, 9,350 . . . C 6
Ilkeston, 33,690 . . . F 5
Immingham, ⊙10,259 . . . G 4
Ipswich, 121,500 . . . J 5
Islington, 171,600 . . . H 8
Jarrow, 28,510 . . . J 3
Kendal, 22,440 . . . E 3
Kenilworth, 19,730 . . . F 5
Kensington and Chelsea, 161,400 . G 8
Keswick, 4,790 . . . D 3
Kettering, 44,480 . . . G 5
Keynsham, 18,970 . . . E 6
Kidderminster, 49,960 . . . E 5
Kidsgrove, 22,690 . . . E 4
King's Lynn, 29,990 . . . H 5
Kingston upon Thames, 135,600 . . H 8
Kingswood, 30,450 . . . E 6
Kirkburton, 20,320 . . . J 2
Kirkby, 59,100 . . . G 2
Kirkby Lonsdale, ⊙1,506 . . . E 3
Kirkby Stephen, ⊙1,539 . . . E 3
Knutsford, 14,840 . . . H 2
Lambeth, 290,300 . . . H 8
Lancaster, 126,300 . . . E 3
Leatherhead, 40,830 . . . G 8
Leeds, 744,500 . . . J 1
Leek, 19,460 . . . H 2
Leicester, 289,400 . . . F 5
Leigh, 46,390 . . . H 2
Leighton-Linslade, 22,590 . . . F 7
Letchworth, 31,520 . . . G 6
Lewes, 14,170 . . . H 7
Lewisham, 237,300 . . . H 8
Leyland, 23,690 . . . G 1
Lichfield, 23,690 . . . F 5
Lincoln, 73,700 . . . G 4
Liskeard, 5,360 . . . C 7
Litherland, 23,530 . . . G 2
Littlehampton, 20,320 . . . G 7

(continued on following page)

UNITED KINGDOM

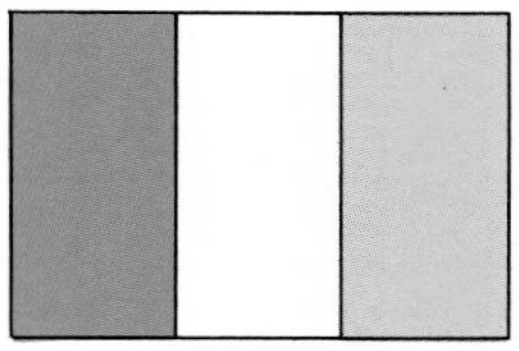
IRELAND

ENGLAND

AREA 50,516 sq. mi. (130,836 sq. km.)
POPULATION 46,220,955
CAPITAL London
LARGEST CITY London
HIGHEST POINT Scafell Pike 3,210 ft. (978 m.)

WALES

AREA 8,017 sq. mi. (20,764 sq. km.)
POPULATION 2,790,462
CAPITAL Cardiff
LARGEST CITY Cardiff
HIGHEST POINT Snowdon 3,560 ft. (1,085 m.)

SCOTLAND

AREA 30,414 sq. mi. (78,772 sq. km.)
POPULATION 5,117,146
CAPITAL Edinburgh
LARGEST CITY Glasgow
HIGHEST POINT Ben Nevis 4,406 ft. (1,343 m.)

NORTHERN IRELAND

AREA 5,452 sq. mi. (14,121 sq. km.)
POPULATION 1,543,000
CAPITAL Belfast
LARGEST CITY Belfast
HIGHEST POINT Slieve Donard 2,796 ft. (852 m.)

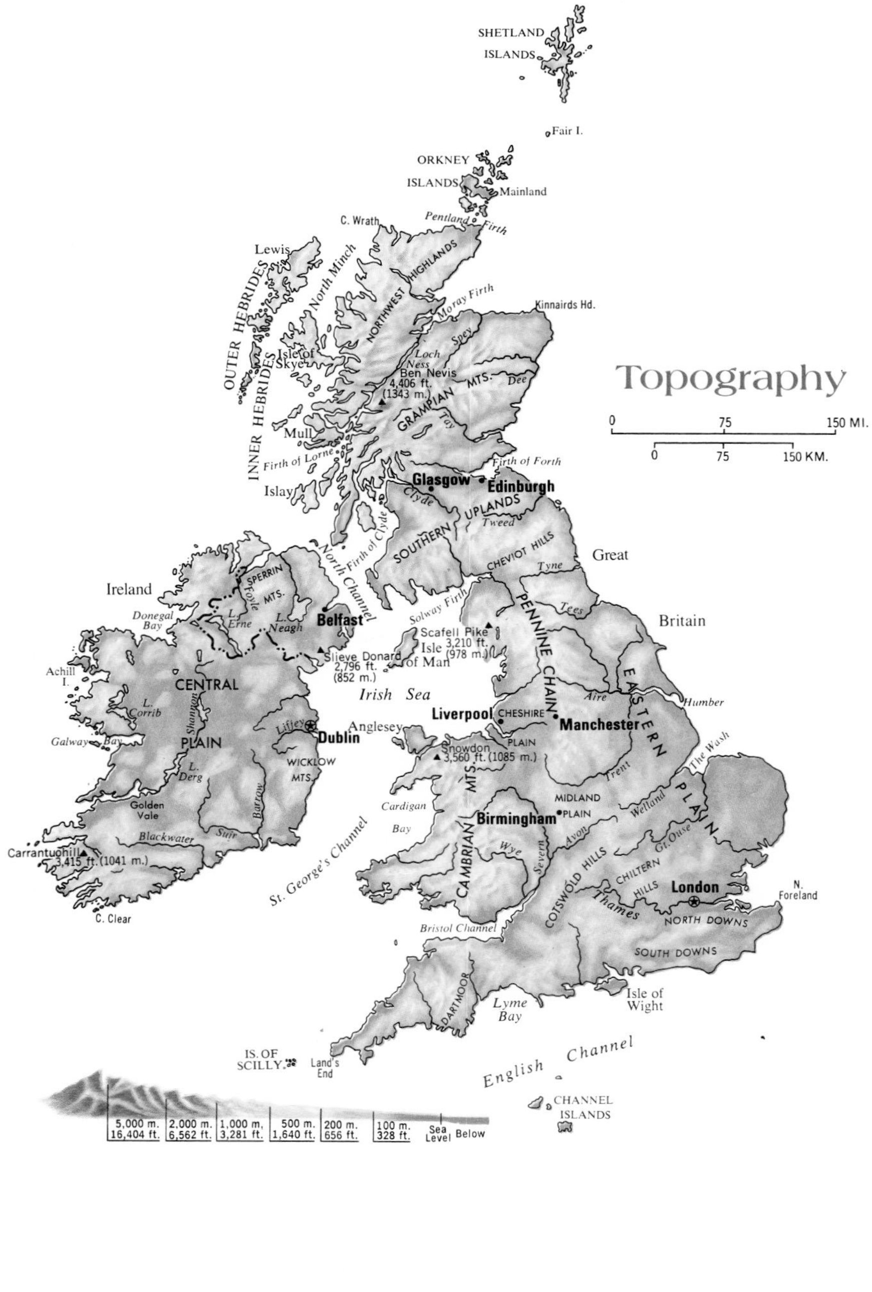
Topography
0 75 150 MI.
0 75 150 KM.
SHETLAND ISLANDS
Fair I.
ORKNEY ISLANDS
Mainland
C. Wrath
Pentland Firth
Lewis
OUTER HEBRIDES
North Minch
NORTHWEST HIGHLANDS
Moray Firth
Kinnairds Hd.
Isle of Skye
INNER HEBRIDES
Loch Ness
Spey
Ben Nevis 4,406 ft. (1343 m.)
GRAMPIAN MTS.
Dee
Tay
Mull
Firth of Lorne
Firth of Forth
Islay
Glasgow
Edinburgh
Clyde
SOUTHERN UPLANDS
Tweed
Firth of Clyde
North Channel
CHEVIOT HILLS
Tyne
Great Britain
Ireland
SPERRIN MTS.
Donegal Bay
L. Erne
L. Neagh
Belfast
Solway Firth
Scafell Pike 3,210 ft. (978 m.)
Isle of Man
Tees
PENNINE CHAIN
Slieve Donard 2,796 ft. (852 m.)
Achill I.
CENTRAL PLAIN
L. Corrib
Shannon
Irish Sea
Liverpool
CHESHIRE PLAIN
Manchester
EASTERN PLAIN
Aire
Humber
Galway Bay
Liffey
Dublin
Anglesey
WICKLOW MTS.
Snowdon 3,560 ft. (1085 m.)
Trent
The Wash
L. Derg
Barrow
Golden Vale
Blackwater
Suir
Cardigan Bay
CAMBRIAN MTS.
MIDLAND PLAIN
Birmingham
Welland
Ouse
Carrantuohill 3,415 ft. (1041 m.)
St. George's Channel
Wye
Severn
Avon
COTSWOLD HILLS
CHILTERN HILLS
London
Thames
N. Foreland
NORTH DOWNS
C. Clear
Bristol Channel
SOUTH DOWNS
DARTMOOR
Lyme Bay
Isle of Wight
IS. OF SCILLY
Land's End
English Channel
CHANNEL ISLANDS
5,000 m. 16,404 ft.
2,000 m. 6,562 ft.
1,000 m. 3,281 ft.
500 m. 1,640 ft.
200 m. 656 ft.
100 m. 328 ft.
Sea Level
Below

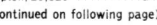

Liverpool, 539,700 . . . G 2
Loftus, 7,850 . . . G 3
London (cap.), 7,028,200 . . . H 8
London, ★12,332,900 . . . H 8
Long Eaton, 33,560 . . . F 5
Longbenton, 50,120 . . . J 3
Looe, 4,060 . . . C 7
Loughborough, 49,010 . . . F 5
Lowestoft, 53,260 . . . J 5
Ludlow, ⊙7,466 . . . E 5
Luton, 164,500 . . . G 6
Lydd, 4,670 . . . H 7
Lyme Regis, 3,460 . . . E 7
Lymington, 36,780 . . . F 7
Lynton, 1,770 . . . D 6
Lytham Saint Anne's, 42,120 . . . G 1
Mablethorpe and Sutton, 6,750 . . . H 4
Macclesfield, 45,420 . . . H 2
Maidenhead, 48,210 . . . G 8
Maidstone, 72,110 . . . J 8
Maldon, 14,350 . . . H 6
Malmesbury, 2,550 . . . E 6
Malton, 4,010 . . . G 3
Malvern, 30,420 . . . E 5
Manchester, 490,000 . . . H 2
Mangotsfield, 23,000 . . . E 6
Mansfield, 58,450 . . . K 2
Mansfield Woodhouse, 25,400 . . . F 4
March, 14,560 . . . H 5
Margate, 50,290 . . . J 6
Market Harborough, 15,230 . . . G 5
Marlborough, 6,370 . . . F 6
Matlock, 20,300 . . . J 2
Melton Mowbray, 20,680 . . . G 5
Merton, 169,400 . . . H 8
Middlesbrough, 153,900 . . . F 3
Middleton, 53,340 . . . H 2
Middlewich, 7,600 . . . H 2
Mildenhall, ⊙9,269 . . . H 5
Millom, ⊙7,101 . . . D 3
Milton Keynes, 89,900 . . . F 5
Minehead, 8,230 . . . D 6
Moretonhampstead, ⊙1,440 . . . C 7
Morpeth, 14,450 . . . F 2
Mundesley, ⊙1,536 . . . J 5
Nelson, 31,220 . . . H 1
Neston, 18,210 . . . G 2
Newark, 24,760 . . . G 4
Newbury, 24,850 . . . F 6
Newcastle upon Tyne, 295,800 . . . H 3
Newcastle-under-Lyme, 75,940 . . . E 4
Newham, 228,900 . . . H 8
Newhaven, 9,970 . . . H 7
Newport, 22,430 . . . F 7
New Romney, 3,830 . . . J 7
Newton Abbot, 19,940 . . . D 7
Newton-le-Willows, 21,780 . . . H 2
New Windsor, 29,660 . . . G 8
Northallerton . . . F 3
Northam, 8,310 . . . C 6
Northampton, 128,290 . . . F 5
Northfleet, 27,150 . . . J 8
North Sunderland, ⊙1,725 . . . F 2
Northwich, 17,710 . . . H 2
Norton, 5,580 . . . G 3
Norton-Radstock, 15,900 . . . E 6
Norwich, 119,200 . . . J 5
Nottingham, 280,300 . . . F 5
Nuneaton, 69,210 . . . F 5
Oadby, 20,700 . . . F 5
Oakham, 7,280 . . . G 5
Okehampton, 4,000 . . . D 7
Oldham, 103,690 . . . H 2
Ormskirk, 28,860 . . . G 2
Oswaldtwistle, 14,270 . . . H 1
Oxford, 117,400 . . . F 6
Padstow, ⊙2,802 . . . B 7
Penryn, 5,660 . . . B 7
Penzance, 19,360 . . . B 7
Peterborough, 118,900 . . . G 5
Peterlee, ⊙21,846 . . . J 3
Plymouth, 259,100 . . . C 7
Polperro, ⊙1,491 . . . C 7
Poole, 110,600 . . . E 7
Porlock, ⊙1,290 . . . D 6
Portishead, 9,680 . . . E 6
Portland, 14,860 . . . E 7
Portslade-by-Sea, 18,040 . . . G 7
Portsmouth, 198,500 . . . F 7
Potters Bar, 24,670 . . . H 7
Poulton-le-Fylde, 16,340 . . . G 1
Preston, 94,760 . . . G 1
Prestwich, 32,850 . . . H 2
Queenborough, 31,550 . . . H 6
Radcliffe, 29,630 . . . H 2
Ramsbottom, 16,710 . . . H 2
Ramsgate, 40,090 . . . J 6
Rawtenstall, 20,950 . . . H 1
Rayleigh, 26,740 . . . J 8
Reading, 131,200 . . . G 8
Redbridge, 231,600 . . . H 8
Redcar, ⊙46,325 . . . F 3
Redditch, 44,750 . . . E 5
Reigate, 55,600 . . . H 8
Richmond upon Thames, 166,800 . . . H 8
Rickmansworth, 29,030 . . . G 8
Ripley, 18,060 . . . F 4
Rochdale, 93,780 . . . H 2
Rochester, 56,030 . . . J 8
Rothbury, ⊙1,818 . . . E 2
Rotherham, 84,770 . . . K 2
Royal Leamington Spa, 44,950 . . . F 5
Royal Tunbridge Wells, 44,800 . . . H 6
Rugby, 60,380 . . . F 5
Rugeley, 24,440 . . . E 5
Runcorn, 42,730 . . . G 2
Rushden, 21,840 . . . G 5
Ryde, 23,170 . . . F 7
Rye, 4,530 . . . H 7
Ryton, 15,170 . . . H 3
Saddleworth, 21,340 . . . J 2
Saint Agnes, ⊙4,747 . . . B 7
Saint Albans, 123,800 . . . H 7
Saint Austell-with-Fowey, 32,710 . . . C 7
Saint Columb Major, ⊙3,953 . . . B 7
Saint Helens, 104,890 . . . G 2
Saint Ives, Cornwall, 9,760 . . . B 7
Saint Neots, 17,940 . . . G 5
Salcombe, 2,370 . . . D 7
Sale, 59,060 . . . H 2
Salford, 261,100 . . . H 2
Salisbury, 35,460 . . . F 6
Saltburn and Marske-by-the-Sea, 21,170 . . . G 3
Sandbach, 14,280 . . . H 2
Sandown-Shanklin, 14,800 . . . F 7
Sandwich, 4,420 . . . J 6
Saxmundham, 1,820 . . . J 5
Scarborough, 43,300 . . . G 3
Scunthorpe, 68,100 . . . G 4
Seaford, 18,020 . . . H 7
Seaham, 22,470 . . . J 3
Seascale, ⊙2,106 . . . D 3
Seaton, 4,500 . . . D 7
Seaton Valley, 35,880 . . . J 3
Sedbergh, ⊙2,741 . . . E 3
Selsey, ⊙6,491 . . . G 7
Sevenoaks, 18,160 . . . J 8
Shaftesbury, 4,180 . . . E 7
Sheffield, 558,000 . . . J 2
Sherborne, 9,230 . . . E 7
Sheringham, 4,940 . . . J 5
Shildon, 15,360 . . . F 3
Shoreham-by-Sea, 19,620 . . . G 7
Shrewsbury, 56,120 . . . E 5
Silloth, ⊙2,662 . . . D 3
Sittingbourne and Milton, 32,830 . . . H 6
Skelmersdale, 35,850 . . . G 2
Skelton and Brotton, 15,930 . . . G 3
Sleaford, 8,050 . . . G 5
Slough, 89,060 . . . G 8
Solihull, 108,230 . . . F 5
Southampton, 213,700 . . . F 7
Southend-on-Sea, 159,300 . . . H 6
Southport, 86,030 . . . G 1
South Shields, 96,900 . . . J 3
Southwark, 224,900 . . . H 8
Southwold, 1,960 . . . J 5
Sowerby Bridge, 15,700 . . . H 1
Spalding, 17,040 . . . G 5
Spenborough, 41,460 . . . J 1
Spennymoor, 19,050 . . . F 3
Stafford, 54,860 . . . E 5
Staines, 56,380 . . . G 8
Stamford, 14,980 . . . G 5
Stanley, 42,280 . . . H 3
Staveley, 17,620 . . . K 2
Stevenage, 72,600 . . . G 6
Stockport, 138,350 . . . H 2
Stockton-on-Tees, 165,400 . . . F 3
Stoke-on-Trent, 256,200 . . . E 4
Stourbridge, 56,530 . . . E 5
Stourport-on-Severn, 19,430 . . . E 5
Stowmarket, 9,020 . . . J 5
Stratford-upon-Avon, 20,080 . . . F 5
Stretford, 52,450 . . . H 2
Stroud, 19,600 . . . E 6
Sudbury, 8,860 . . . H 5
Sunbury-on-Thames, 40,070 . . . G 8
Sunderland, 214,820 . . . J 3
Sutton, 166,700 . . . H 8
Sutton Bridge, ⊙3,113 . . . H 5
Sutton in Ashfield, 40,330 . . . K 2
Swadlincote, 21,060 . . . F 5
Swanage, 8,000 . . . E 7
Swindon, 90,680 . . . F 6
Tamworth, 46,960 . . . F 5
Taunton, 37,570 . . . D 6
Tavistock, ⊙7,620 . . . C 7
Telford, ⊙79,451 . . . E 5
Tenbury, ⊙2,151 . . . E 5
Tewkesbury, 9,210 . . . E 6
Thetford, 15,690 . . . H 5
Thirsk, ⊙2,884 . . . F 3
Thornaby-on-Tees, ⊙42,385 . . . F 3
Thorne, ⊙16,694 . . . F 4
Thornton Cleveleys, 27,090 . . . G 1
Thurrock, 127,700 . . . J 8
Tiverton, 16,190 . . . D 7
Todmorden, 14,540 . . . H 1
Tonbridge, 31,410 . . . H 8
Torbay, 109,900 . . . D 7
Torpoint, 6,840 . . . C 7
Tower Hamlets, 146,100 . . . H 8
Tow Law, 2,460 . . . H 4
Trowbridge, 20,120 . . . E 6
Truro, 15,690 . . . B 7
Turton, 22,800 . . . H 2
Tynemouth, 67,090 . . . J 3
Upton upon Severn, ⊙2,048 . . . E 5
Urmston, 44,130 . . . H 2
Uttoxeter, 9,100 . . . E 5
Ventnor, 6,980 . . . F 7
Wainfleet All Saints, ⊙1,116 . . . H 4
Wakefield, 306,500 . . . J 2
Wallasey, 94,520 . . . G 2
Wallsend, 45,490 . . . J 3
Walsall, 182,430 . . . E 5
Waltham Forest, 223,700 . . . H 8
Waltham Holy Cross, 14,810 . . . H 7
Walton and Weybridge, 51,270 . . . G 8
Walton-le-Dale, 27,660 . . . G 1
Wandsworth, 284,600 . . . H 8
Wantage, 8,490 . . . F 6
Ware, 14,900 . . . H 7
Wareham, 4,630 . . . E 7
Warley, 161,260 . . . E 5
Warminster, 14,440 . . . E 6
Warrington, 65,320 . . . G 2
Warwick, 17,870 . . . F 5
Washington, 27,720 . . . J 3
Watchet, 2,980 . . . D 6
Watford, 77,000 . . . H 7
Wellingborough, 39,570 . . . G 5
Wells, 8,960 . . . E 6
Wells-next-the-Sea, 2,450 . . . H 5
Welwyn, 39,900 . . . H 7
Wem, ⊙3,411 . . . E 5
West Bridgford, 28,340 . . . F 5
West Bromwich, 162,740 . . . F 5
West Mersea, 4,730 . . . H 6
Westminster, 216,100 . . . H 8
Weston-super-Mare, 51,960 . . . D 6
Weymouth and Melcombe Regis, 41,080 . . . E 7
Whickham, 29,710 . . . J 3
Whitchurch, ⊙7,142 . . . E 5
Whitehaven, 26,260 . . . D 3
Whitley Bay, 37,010 . . . J 3
Widnes, 58,330 . . . G 2
Wigan, 80,920 . . . G 2
Wigston, 31,650 . . . F 5
Wilmslow, 31,250 . . . H 2
Wilton, 4,090 . . . F 6
Winchester, 88,900 . . . F 6
Windermere, 7,860 . . . E 3
Winsford, 26,920 . . . G 2
Wirral, 27,510 . . . G 2
Wisbech, 16,990 . . . H 5
Witham, 19,730 . . . H 6
Withernsea, 6,300 . . . H 4
Wivenhoe, 5,630 . . . J 6
Woking, 79,300 . . . G 8
Wokingham, 22,390 . . . G 8
Wolverhampton, 266,400 . . . E 5
Wombwell, 17,850 . . . K 2
Woodhall Spa, 2,420 . . . G 4
Woodley and Sandford, ⊙24,581 . . . G 8
Woodstock, 2,070 . . . F 6
Wooler, ⊙1,833 . . . F 2
Worcester, 73,900 . . . E 5
Workington, 28,260 . . . D 3
Worksop, 36,590 . . . F 4
Worsbrough, 15,180 . . . J 2
Worsley, 49,530 . . . H 2
Worthing, 89,100 . . . G 7
Wymondham, 9,390 . . . J 5
Yateley, ⊙16,505 . . . G 8
Yeovil, 26,180 . . . E 7
York, 101,900 . . . F 4

OTHER FEATURES

Aire (riv.) . . . F 4
Atlantic Ocean . . . A 7
Avon (riv.) . . . F 5
Avon (riv.) . . . F 7
Axe Edge (mt.) . . . H 2
Barnstaple (bay) . . . C 6
Beachy (head) . . . H 7
Bigbury (bay) . . . C 7
Blackwater (riv.) . . . H 6
Bristol (chan.) . . . C 6
Brown Willy (mt.) . . . C 7
Cheviot (hills) . . . E 2
Cheviot, The (mt.) . . . E 2
Chiltern (hills) . . . G 6
Cleveland (hills) . . . F 3
Colne (riv.) . . . G 8
Cornwall (cape) . . . B 7
Cotswold (hills) . . . E 6
Cross Fell (mt.) . . . E 3
Cumbrian (mts.) . . . D 3
Dart (riv.) . . . D 7
Dartmoor National Park . . . C 7
Dee (riv.) . . . D 4
Derwent (riv.) . . . G 3
Derwent (riv.) . . . H 3
Don (riv.) . . . F 4
Dorset Heights (hills) . . . E 7
Dove (riv.) . . . J 2
Dover (str.) . . . J 7
Dungeness (prom.) . . . J 7
Dunkery (hill) . . . D 6
Eddystone (rocks) . . . C 7
Eden (riv.) . . . E 3
English (chan.) . . . D 8
Esk (riv.) . . . D 2
Exe (riv.) . . . D 7
Exmoor National Park . . . D 6
Fens, The (reg.) . . . G 5
Flamborough (head) . . . G 3
Formby (head) . . . G 2
Foulness Island (pen.) . . . J 6
Gibraltar (pt.) . . . H 4
Great Ouse (riv.) . . . H 5
Hartland (pt.) . . . C 6
High Willhays (mt.) . . . C 7
Hodder (riv.) . . . H 1
Holderness (pen.), 43,900 . . . G 4
Holy (isl.), 189 . . . F 2
Humber (riv.) . . . G 4
Irish (sea) . . . B 4
Kennet (riv.) . . . F 6
Lake District National Park . . . D 3
Land's End (prom.) . . . B 7
Lea (riv.) . . . G 6
Lincoln Wolds (hills) . . . G 4
Lindisfarne (Holy) (isl.), 189 . . . F 2
Liverpool (bay) . . . D 4
Lizard, The (pen.), 7,371 . . . B 8
Lundy (isl.), 49 . . . C 6
Lune (riv.) . . . E 3
Lyme (bay) . . . D 7
Manacle (pt.) . . . C 7
Medway (riv.) . . . H 6
Mendip (hills) . . . E 6
Mersea (isl.), 4,423 . . . J 6
Mersey (riv.) . . . G 2
Morecambe (bay) . . . D 3
Mounts (bay) . . . B 7
Naze, The (prom.) . . . J 6
Nene (riv.) . . . H 5
New (for.) . . . F 6
North (sea) . . . J 4
North Downs (hills) . . . G 6
North Foreland (prom.) . . . J 6
Northumberland National Park . . . E 2
North York Moors National Park . . . G 3
Orford Ness (prom.) . . . J 5
Ouse (riv.) . . . G 4
Ouse (riv.) . . . G 6
Parrett (riv.) . . . E 6
Peak District National Park . . . F 4
Peak, The (mt.) . . . J 2
Peel Fell (mt.) . . . E 2
Pennine Chain (range) . . . E 3
Plymouth (sound) . . . C 7
Portland, Bill of (pt.) . . . E 7
Prawle (pt.) . . . D 7
Purbeck, Isle of (pen.), 39,500 . . . F 7
Ribble (riv.) . . . E 4
Saint Alban's (head) . . . F 7
Saint Bees (head) . . . D 3
Saint Martin's (isl.), 106 . . . A 8
Saint Mary's (isl.), 1,958 . . . A 8
Scafell Pike (mt.) . . . D 3
Scilly (isls.), 1,900 . . . A 7
Selsey Bill (prom.) . . . G 7
Severn (riv.) . . . E 6
Sheppey (isl.), 31,550 . . . J 6
Sherwood (for.) . . . F 4
Skiddaw (mt.) . . . D 3
Solent (chan.) . . . F 7
Solway (firth) . . . D 3
South Downs (hills) . . . G 7
Spithead (chan.) . . . F 7
Spurn (head) . . . H 4
Stonehenge (ruins) . . . F 6
Stour (riv.) . . . E 7
Stour (riv.) . . . H 6
Stour (riv.) . . . J 6
Swale (riv.) . . . F 3
Tamar (riv.) . . . C 7
Taw (riv.) . . . D 7
Tees (riv.) . . . F 3
Test (riv.) . . . F 6
Thames (riv.) . . . H 6
Tintagel (head) . . . C 7
Torridge (riv.) . . . C 7
Trent (riv.) . . . G 4
Tresco (isl.), 246 . . . A 8
Tweed (riv.) . . . E 2
Tyne (riv.) . . . F 3
Ure (riv.) . . . F 3
Ver (riv.) . . . H 7
Walney, Isle of (isl.), 11,241 . . . D 3
Wash, The (bay) . . . H 5
Weald, The (reg.) . . . H 6
Wear (riv.) . . . F 3
Weaver (riv.) . . . G 2
Welland (riv.) . . . G 5
Wey (riv.) . . . G 6
Wharfe (riv.) . . . E 3
Wirral (pen.), 432,900 . . . G 2
Witham (riv.) . . . G 4
Wolds, The (hills) . . . G 4
Wye (riv.) . . . D 5
Wyre (riv.) . . . G 1
Yare (riv.) . . . J 5
Yorkshire Dales National Park . . . E 3

CHANNEL ISLANDS

CITIES and TOWNS

Saint Anne . . . E 8
Saint Helier (cap.), Jersey, ⊙28,135 . . . E 8
Saint Peter Port (cap.), Guernsey, ⊙16,303 . . . E 8
Saint Sampson's, ⊙6,534 . . . E 8

OTHER FEATURES

Alderney (isl.), 1,686 . . . E 8
Guernsey (isl.), 51,351 . . . E 8
Herm (isl.), 96 . . . E 8
Jersey (isl.), 72,629 . . . E 8
Sark (isl.), 590 . . . E 8

ISLE of MAN

CITIES and TOWNS

Castletown, 2,620 . . . C 3
Douglas (cap.), 20,389 . . . C 3
Laxey, 1,170 . . . C 3
Michael, 408 . . . C 3
Onchan, 4,807 . . . C 3
Peel, 3,081 . . . C 3
Port Erin, 1,714 . . . C 3
Port Saint Mary, 1,508 . . . C 3
Ramsey, 5,048 . . . C 3

OTHER FEATURES

Ayre (pt.) . . . C 3
Calf of Man (isl.) . . . C 3
Langness (prom.) . . . C 3
Snaefell (mt.) . . . C 3
Spanish (head) . . . C 3

WALES

COUNTIES

Clwyd, 376,000 . . . D 4
Dyfed, 323,100 . . . C 6
Gwent, 439,600 . . . D 6
Gwynedd, 225,100 . . . C 4
Mid Glamorgan, 540,400 . . . D 6
Powys, 101,500 . . . D 5
South Glamorgan, 389,200 . . . A 7
West Glamorgan, 371,900 . . . D 6

CITIES and TOWNS

Aberaeron, 1,340 . . . C 5
Abercarn, 18,370 . . . B 6
Aberdare, 38,030 . . . A 6
Abertillery, 20,550 . . . B 6
Amlwch, 3,630 . . . C 4
Bala, 1,650 . . . D 5
Bangor, 16,030 . . . C 4
Barmouth, 2,070 . . . C 5
Barry, 42,780 . . . B 7
Beaumaris, 2,090 . . . C 4
Bedwellty, 25,460 . . . B 6
Bethesda, 4,180 . . . D 4
Betws-y-Coed, 720 . . . D 4
Brecknock (Brecon), 6,460 . . . D 6
Brecon, 6,460 . . . D 6
Bridgend, 14,690 . . . A 7
Brynmawr, 5,970 . . . B 6
Builth Wells, 1,480 . . . D 5
Burry Port, 5,990 . . . C 6
Caernarfon, 8,840 . . . C 4
Caerphilly, 42,190 . . . B 6
Cardiff, 281,500 . . . B 7
Cardigan, 3,830 . . . C 5
Chepstow, 8,260 . . . E 6
Chirk, ⊙3,564 . . . D 5
Colwyn Bay, 25,370 . . . D 4
Criccieth, 1,590 . . . C 5
Cwmamman, 3,950 . . . D 6
Cwmbran, 32,980 . . . B 6
Denbigh, 8,420 . . . D 4
Dolgellau, 2,430 . . . D 5
Ebbw Vale, 25,670 . . . B 6
Ffestiniog, 5,510 . . . D 5
Fishguard and Goodwick, 5,020 . . . B 5
Flint, 15,070 . . . G 2
Gelligaer, 33,820 . . . A 6
Harlech, ⊙332 . . . C 5
Haverfordwest, 8,930 . . . B 6
Hawarden, ⊙20,389 . . . G 2
Hay, 1,200 . . . D 5
Holywell, 8,570 . . . G 2
Kidwelly, 3,090 . . . C 6
Knighton, 2,190 . . . D 5
Llandeilo, 1,780 . . . C 6
Llandovery, 2,040 . . . D 5
Llandrindod Wells, 3,460 . . . D 5
Llandudno, 17,700 . . . D 4
Llanelli, 25,870 . . . C 6
Llanfairfechan, 3,800 . . . D 4
Llangefni, 4,070 . . . C 4
Llangollen, 3,050 . . . D 5
Llanguicke, ⊙15,029 . . . D 6
Llanidloes, 2,390 . . . D 5
Llantrisant, ⊙27,490 . . . A 7
Llanwrtyd Wells, 460 . . . D 5
Llwchwr, 27,530 . . . D 6
Machynlleth, 1,830 . . . D 5
Maesteg, 21,100 . . . D 6
Menai Bridge, 2,730 . . . C 4
Merthyr Tydfil, 61,500 . . . A 6
Milford Haven, 13,960 . . . B 6
Mold, 8,700 . . . G 2
Montgomery, 1,000 . . . D 5
Mountain Ash, 27,710 . . . A 6
Mynyddislwyn, 15,590 . . . B 6
Narberth, 970 . . . C 6
Neath, 27,280 . . . D 6
Nefyn, ⊙2,086 . . . C 5
Newcastle Emlyn, 690 . . . C 5
Newport, Dyfed, ⊙1,062 . . . C 5
Newport, Gwent, 110,090 . . . B 6
New Quay, 760 . . . C 5
Newtown, 6,400 . . . D 5
Neyland, 2,690 . . . B 6
Ogmore and Garw, 19,680 . . . A 6
Pembroke, 14,570 . . . C 6
Penarth, 24,180 . . . B 7
Penmaenmawr, 4,050 . . . C 4
Pontypool, 36,710 . . . B 6
Pontypridd, 34,180 . . . A 6
Porthcawl, 14,980 . . . D 6
Porthmadog, 3,900 . . . C 5
Port Talbot, 58,200 . . . D 6
Prestatyn, 15,480 . . . D 4
Presteigne, 1,330 . . . D 5
Pwllheli, 4,020 . . . C 5
Rhondda, 85,400 . . . A 6
Rhyl, 22,150 . . . D 4
Risca, 15,780 . . . B 6
Ruthin, 4,780 . . . D 4
Saint David's, ⊙1,638 . . . B 6
Swansea, 190,800 . . . C 6
Tenby, 4,930 . . . C 6
Tredegar, 17,450 . . . B 6
Tywyn, 3,850 . . . C 5
Welshpool, 7,370 . . . D 5
Wrexham, 39,530 . . . E 4

OTHER FEATURES

Anglesey (isl.), 64,500 . . . C 4
Aran Fawddwy (mt.) . . . C 5
Bardsey (isl.), 9 . . . C 5
Berwyn (mts.) . . . D 5
Black (mts.) . . . D 6
Braich-y-Pwll (prom.) . . . C 5
Brecon Beacons (mt.) . . . D 6
Brecon Beacons National Park . . . D 6
Caldy (isl.), 70 . . . C 6
Cambrian (mts.) . . . D 5
Cardigan (bay) . . . C 5
Carmarthen (bay) . . . C 6
Cemmaes (head) . . . C 5
Dee (riv.) . . . D 4
Dovey (riv.) . . . D 5
Ely (riv.) . . . B 7
Gower (pen.), 17,220 . . . C 6
Great Ormes (head) . . . C 4
Holy (isl.), 13,715 . . . C 4
Lleyn (pen.), 25,800 . . . C 5
Menai (str.) . . . C 4
Milford Haven (inlet) . . . B 6
Pembrokeshire Coast National Park . . . C 6
Plynlimon (mt.) . . . D 5
Preseli (mts.) . . . C 6
Radnor (for.) . . . D 5
Rhymney (riv.) . . . B 6
Saint Brides (bay) . . . B 6
Saint David's (head) . . . B 6
Saint George's (chan.) . . . B 5
Saint Gowans (head) . . . C 6
Severn (riv.) . . . E 5
Snowdon (mt.) . . . D 4
Snowdonia National Park . . . D 4
Taff (riv.) . . . B 7
Teifi (riv.) . . . C 5
Towy (riv.) . . . D 6
Tremadoc (bay) . . . C 5
Usk (riv.) . . . B 6
Wye (riv.) . . . D 5
Ynys Môn (Anglesey) (isl.), 64,500 . . . C 4

★Population of met. area.
⊙Population of parish.

SCOTLAND

(map on page 15)

REGIONS

Borders, 99,409 . . . E 5
Central, 269,281 . . . D 4
Dumfries and Galloway, 143,667 . . . E 5
Fife, 336,339 . . . E 4
Grampian, 448,772 . . . F 3
Highland, 182,044 . . . D 3
Lothian, 754,008 . . . E 5
Orkney (islands area), 17,675 . . . E 1
Shetland (islands area), 18,494 . . . F 2
Strathclyde, 2,504,909 . . . C 4
Tayside, 401,987 . . . E 4
Western Isles (islands area), 29,615 . . . A 3

CITIES and TOWNS

Aberchirder, 877 . . . F 3
Aberdeen, 210,362 . . . F 3
Aberdour, 1,576 . . . D 1
Aberfeldy, 1,552 . . . E 4
Aberfoyle, 793 . . . D 4
Aberlady, 737 . . . F 4
Aberlour, 842 . . . E 3
Abernethy, 776 . . . E 4
Aboyne, 1,040 . . . F 3
Acharacle, ⊙764 . . . C 4
Achiltibuie, ⊙1,564 . . . C 3
Achnasheen, ⊙1,078 . . . C 3
Ae, 239 . . . E 5
Airdrie, 38,491 . . . C 2
Alexandria, 9,758 . . . A 1
Alford, 764 . . . F 3
Alloa, 13,558 . . . C 1
Alness, 2,560 . . . D 3
Altnaharra, ⊙1,227 . . . D 2
Alva, 4,593 . . . C 1
Alyth, 1,738 . . . E 4
Ancrum, 266 . . . F 5
Annan, 6,250 . . . E 6
Annat, ⊙550 . . . C 3
Annbank Station, 2,530 . . . D 5
Applecross, ⊙550 . . . C 3
Arbroath, 22,706 . . . F 4
Ardavasar, ⊙449 . . . B 3
Ardersier, 942 . . . E 3
Ardgay, 193 . . . D 3
Ardrishaig, 946 . . . C 4
Ardrossan, 11,072 . . . D 5
Armadale, 7,200 . . . C 2
Arrochar, 543 . . . D 4
Ascog, 230 . . . A 2
Auchenblae, 339 . . . F 4
Auchencairn, 215 . . . E 6
Auchinleck, 4,883 . . . D 5
Auchterarder, 1,738 . . . E 4
Auchtermuchty, 1,426 . . . E 4
Auldearn, 405 . . . E 3
Aviemore, 1,224 . . . E 3
Avoch, 776 . . . D 3
Ayr, 47,990 . . . D 5
Ayton, 410 . . . F 5
Bailivanish, 347 . . . A 3
Baillieston, 7,671 . . . B 2
Balallan, 283 . . . B 2
Balerno, 3,576 . . . D 2
Balfron, 1,149 . . . B 1
Ballantrae, 262 . . . C 5
Ballater, 981 . . . F 3
Ballingry, 4,332 . . . D 1
Ballinluig, 188 . . . E 4
Balloch, Highland, 572 . . . D 3
Balloch, Strathclyde, 1,484 . . . B 1
Baltasound, 246 . . . G 2
Banchory, 2,435 . . . F 3
Banff, 3,832 . . . F 3
Bankfoot, 868 . . . E 4
Bankhead, 1,492 . . . F 3
Bannockburn, 5,889 . . . C 1
Barrhead, 18,736 . . . B 2
Barrhill, 236 . . . D 5
Barvas, 279 . . . B 2
Bathgate, 14,038 . . . C 2
Bayble, 543 . . . B 2
Bearsden, 25,128 . . . B 2
Beattock, 309 . . . E 5
Beauly, 1,141 . . . D 3
Beith, 5,859 . . . D 5
Bellsbank, 3,066 . . . D 5
Bellshill, 18,166 . . . C 2
Berriedale, ⊙1,927 . . . E 2
Bieldside, 1,137 . . . F 3
Biggar, 1,718 . . . E 5
Birnam, 659 . . . E 4
Bishopbriggs, 21,570 . . . B 2
Bishopton, 2,931 . . . B 2
Blackburn, 7,636 . . . C 2
Blackford, 529 . . . E 4
Blair Atholl, 437 . . . E 4
Blairgowrie and Rattray, 5,681 . . . E 4
Blanefield, 835 . . . B 1
Blantyre, 13,992 . . . B 2
Blyth Bridge, ⊙441 . . . E 5
Bo'ness, 12,959 . . . C 1
Boat of Garten, 406 . . . E 3
Boddam, 1,429 . . . G 3
Bonar Bridge, 519 . . . D 3
Bonhill, 4,385 . . . B 1
Bonnybridge, 5,701 . . . C 1
Bonnyrigg and Lasswade, 7,429 . . . D 2
Bowmore, 947 . . . B 5
Braemar, 394 . . . E 3
Breasclete, 234 . . . B 2
Brechin, 6,759 . . . F 4
Bridge of Allan, 4,638 . . . C 1
Bridge of Don, 4,086 . . . F 3
Bridge of Weir, 4,724 . . . A 2
Brightons, 3,106 . . . C 1
Broadford, 310 . . . B 3
Brodick, 630 . . . C 5
Brora, 1,436 . . . E 2
Broxburn, 7,776 . . . D 1
Buchlyvie, 412 . . . B 1
Buckhaven and Methil, 17,930 . . . F 4
Buckie, 8,145 . . . E 3
Bucksburn, 6,567 . . . F 3
Bunessan, ⊙585 . . . B 4
Burghead, 1,321 . . . E 3
Burnmouth, 300 . . . F 5
Burntisland, 5,626 . . . D 1
Cairndow, ⊙874 . . . D 4
Cairnryan, 199 . . . D 6
Callander, 1,805 . . . D 4
Cambuslang, 14,607 . . . B 2
Campbeltown, 6,428 . . . C 5
Cannich, 203 . . . D 3
Canonbie, 234 . . . F 5
Caol, 3,719 . . . C 4
Carbost, ⊙772 . . . B 3
Cardenden, 6,802 . . . D 1
Carloway, 178 . . . B 2
Carluke, 8,864 . . . E 5
Carnoustie, 6,838 . . . F 4
Carnwath, 1,246 . . . E 5
Carradale, 262 . . . C 5
Carrbridge, 416 . . . E 3
Carron, 2,626 . . . C 1
Carsphairn, 186 . . . D 5
Castlebay, 284 . . . A 4
Castle Douglas, 3,384 . . . E 6
Castle Kennedy, 307 . . . D 6
Castletown, 902 . . . E 2
Catrine, 2,681 . . . D 5
Cawdor, 111 . . . E 3
Chirnside, 888 . . . F 5
Chryston, 8,322 . . . C 2
Clackmannan, 3,248 . . . C 1
Clarkston, 8,404 . . . B 2
Closeburn, 225 . . . E 5
Clovulin, ⊙315 . . . C 4
Clydebank, 47,538 . . . B 2
Coalburn, 1,460 . . . E 5
Coatbridge, 50,806 . . . C 2
Cockburnspath, 233 . . . F 5
Cockenzie and Port Seton, 3,539 . . . D 1
Coldingham, 423 . . . F 5
Coldstream, 1,393 . . . F 5
Coll, 305 . . . B 2
Colmonell, 218 . . . D 5
Comrie, 1,119 . . . E 4
Connel, 300 . . . C 4
Cononbridge, 914 . . . D 3
Corpach, 1,296 . . . C 4
Coupar Angus, 2,010 . . . E 4
Cove and Kilcreggan, 1,402 . . . A 1
Cove Bay, 765 . . . F 3
Cowdenbeath, 10,215 . . . D 1
Cowie, 2,751 . . . C 1
Craigellachie, 382 . . . E 3
Craignure, ⊙544 . . . C 4
Crail, 1,033 . . . F 4
Crawford, 384 . . . E 5
Creetown, 769 . . . D 6
Crieff, 5,718 . . . E 4
Crimond, 313 . . . G 3
Crinan, ⊙462 . . . C 4
Cromarty, 492 . . . E 3
Crosshill, 535 . . . D 5
Crossmichael, 317 . . . D 6
Cruden Bay, 528 . . . G 3
Cullen, 1,199 . . . F 3
Culross, 504 . . . C 1
Cults, 3,336 . . . F 3
Cumbernauld, 41,200 . . . C 1
Cumnock and Holmhead, 6,298 . . . D 5
Cupar, 6,607 . . . E 4
Currie, 6,764 . . . D 2
Dailly, 1,258 . . . D 5
Dalbeattie, 3,659 . . . E 6
Daliburgh, 261 . . . A 3
Dalkeith, 9,713 . . . D 2
Dalmally, 283 . . . D 4
Dalmellington, 1,949 . . . D 5
Dalry, 5,833 . . . D 5
Dalrymple, 1,336 . . . D 5
Darvel, 3,177 . . . D 5
Daviot, ⊙513 . . . D 3
Denholm, 581 . . . F 5
Denny and Dunipace, 10,424 . . . C 1
Dervaig, ⊙1,081 . . . B 4
Dingwall, 4,275 . . . D 3
Dollar, 2,573 . . . E 4
Dornoch, 880 . . . D 3
Douglas, 1,843 . . . E 5
Doune, 859 . . . D 4
Drongan, 3,609 . . . D 5
Drumbeg, ⊙833 . . . C 2
Drummore, 336 . . . D 6
Drumnadrochit, 359 . . . D 3
Drymen, 659 . . . B 1
Dufftown, 1,481 . . . E 3
Dumbarton, 25,469 . . . B 1
Dumfries, 29,259 . . . E 5
Dunbar, 4,609 . . . F 4
Dunbeath, 161 . . . E 2
Dunbeg, 939 . . . C 4
Dunblane, 5,222 . . . E 4
Dundee, 194,732 . . . F 4
Dundonald, 2,256 . . . D 5
Dunfermline, 52,098 . . . D 1
Dunkeld, 273 . . . E 4
Dunning, 564 . . . E 4
Dunoon, 8,759 . . . A 2
Dunragit, 323 . . . D 6
Duns, 1,812 . . . F 5
Duntochter, 3,532 . . . B 2
Dunure, 452 . . . D 5
Dunvegan, 301 . . . B 3
Dyce, 2,733 . . . F 3
Eaglesfield, 581 . . . E 5
Eaglesham, 2,788 . . . D 5
Earlston, 1,415 . . . F 5
East Calder, 2,690 . . . D 2
East Kilbride, 71,200 . . . B 2
East Linton, 882 . . . F 5
Eastriggs, 1,455 . . . E 5
Ecclefechan, 844 . . . E 5
Edinburgh (cap.), 470,085 . . . D 1
Edzell, 658 . . . F 4
Elderslie, 5,204 . . . B 2
Elgin, 17,042 . . . E 3
Elie and Earlsferry, 807 . . . F 4
Ellon, 2,855 . . . F 3
Embo, 260 . . . E 3
Errol, 762 . . . E 4
Evanton, 562 . . . D 3
Eyemouth, 2,704 . . . F 5
Fairlie, 1,029 . . . D 5
Falkirk, 36,901 . . . C 1
Falkland, 998 . . . E 4
Fallin, 3,159 . . . C 1
Fauldhouse, 5,247 . . . C 2
Ferness, ⊙287 . . . E 3
Ferryden, 740 . . . F 4
Findhorn, 664 . . . E 3
Findochty, 1,229 . . . E 3
Fintry, 296 . . . B 1
Fochabers, 1,238 . . . E 3
Forfar, 11,179 . . . F 4
Forres, 5,317 . . . E 3
Fort Augustus, 670 . . . D 3
Forth, 2,929 . . . C 2
Fortrose, 1,150 . . . D 3
Fort William, 4,370 . . . C 4
Foyers, 276 . . . D 3
Fraserburgh, 10,930 . . . G 3
Friockheim, 807 . . . F 4
Furnace, 220 . . . C 4
Fyvie, 405 . . . F 3
Gairloch, 125 . . . C 3
Galashiels, 12,808 . . . F 5
Galston, 4,256 . . . D 5
Gardenstown, 892 . . . F 3
Garelochhead, 1,552 . . . A 1
Gargunnock, 457 . . . B 1
Garlieston, 385 . . . D 6
Garmouth, 352 . . . E 3
Garrabost, 307 . . . B 2
Gartmore, 253 . . . B 1
Gatehouse-of-Fleet, 835 . . . D 6
Giffnock, 10,987 . . . B 2
Gifford, 575 . . . F 5
Girvan, 7,597 . . . D 5
Glamis, 190 . . . F 4
Glasgow, 880,617 . . . B 2
Glasgow, ★1,674,789 . . . B 2
Glenbarr, ⊙691 . . . C 5
Glencaple, 275 . . . E 5
Glencoe, 195 . . . C 4
Glenelg, ⊙1,468 . . . C 3
Glenluce, 725 . . . D 6
Glenrothes, 31,400 . . . E 4
Golspie, 1,374 . . . E 3
Gordon, 320 . . . F 5
Gorebridge, 3,426 . . . D 2
Gourock, 11,192 . . . A 1
Grangemouth, 24,430 . . . C 1
Grantown-on-Spey, 1,578 . . . E 3
Greenlaw, 574 . . . F 5
Greenock, 67,275 . . . A 2
Gretna, 1,907 . . . E 5
Gullane, 1,701 . . . F 4
Haddington, 6,767 . . . F 5
Halkirk, 679 . . . E 2
Hamilton, 45,495 . . . C 2
Hamnavoe, 307 . . . G 2
Harthill, 4,712 . . . C 2
Hatton, 315 . . . G 3
Hawick, 16,484 . . . F 5
Heathhall, 1,365 . . . E 5
Helensburgh, 13,327 . . . A 1
Helmsdale, 727 . . . E 2
Hill of Fearn, 233 . . . D 3
Hillside, 692 . . . F 4
Hillswick, ⊙696 . . . G 2
Hopeman, 1,248 . . . E 3
Huntly, 4,078 . . . F 3
Hurlford, 4,294 . . . D 5
Inchnadamph, ⊙833 . . . D 2
Innellan, 922 . . . A 2
Innerleithen, 2,293 . . . E 5
Insch, 881 . . . F 3
Inveraray, 473 . . . C 4
Inverbervie, 853 . . . F 4
Invercassley, ⊙1,067 . . . D 3
Invergordon, 2,385 . . . D 3
Invergowrie, 1,389 . . . E 4
Inverie, ⊙1,468 . . . C 3
Inverkeithing, 6,102 . . . D 1
Inverness, 35,801 . . . D 3
Inverurie, 5,534 . . . F 3
Irvine, 48,500 . . . D 5
Isle of Whithorn, 222 . . . D 6
Jedburgh, 3,953 . . . F 5
John O'Groats, 195 . . . E 2
Johnshaven, 544 . . . F 4
Johnstone, 23,251 . . . B 2
Kames, 230 . . . C 5
Keiss, 344 . . . E 2
Keith, 4,192 . . . F 3
Kelso, 4,934 . . . F 5
Kelty, 6,573 . . . D 1
Kemnay, 1,042 . . . F 3
Kenmore, 211 . . . E 4
Kilbarchan, 2,669 . . . A 2
Kilbirnie, 8,259 . . . A 2
Kilchoan, ⊙764 . . . B 4
Kildonan, ⊙1,105 . . . E 2
Killearn, 1,086 . . . B 1
Killin, 600 . . . D 4
Kilmacolm, 3,348 . . . A 2
Kilmarnock, 50,175 . . . D 5
Kilmaurs, 2,518 . . . D 5
Kilninver, ⊙247 . . . C 4
Kilrenny and Anstruther, 2,951 . . . F 4
Kilsyth, 10,210 . . . B 1
Kilwinning, 8,460 . . . D 5
Kinbrace, ⊙1,105 . . . E 2
Kincardine, 3,278 . . . C 1
Kinghorn, 2,163 . . . D 1
Kingussie, 1,036 . . . D 3
Kinlochewe, ⊙1,794 . . . C 3
Kinlochleven, 1,243 . . . D 4
Kinloch Rannoch, 241 . . . D 4
Kinloss, 2,378 . . . E 3
Kinross, 2,829 . . . E 4
Kintore, 970 . . . F 3
Kippen, 529 . . . B 1
Kirkcaldy, 50,207 . . . D 1
Kirkcolm, 346 . . . C 6
Kirkconnel, 3,318 . . . E 5
Kirkcowan, 354 . . . D 6
Kirkcudbright, 2,690 . . . E 6
Kirkhill, 210 . . . D 3
Kirkintilloch, 26,664 . . . B 2
Kirkmuirhill, 2,575 . . . E 5
Kirkton of Glenisla, ⊙331 . . . E 4
Kirkwall, 4,777 . . . E 2
Kirriemuir, 4,295 . . . E 4
Kyleakin, 268 . . . C 3
Kyle of Lochalsh, 687 . . . C 3
Kylestrome, ⊙745 . . . D 2
Ladybank, 1,216 . . . E 4
Laggan, 393 . . . D 3
Lairg, 572 . . . D 2
Lamlash, 613 . . . C 5
Lanark, 8,842 . . . E 5
Langholm, 2,509 . . . E 5
Larbert, 4,922 . . . C 1
Largs, 9,461 . . . A 2
Larkhall, 15,926 . . . E 5
Lauder, 639 . . . F 5
Laurencekirk, 1,416 . . . F 4

(continued)

England and Wales

CONIC PROJECTION

MILES

KILOMETERS

Capitals of Countries............ ⊛
Administrative Centers.......... ◉
Other Capitals.................. ⊚
Canals.........................

International Boundaries....___
County Boundaries....___ ___
Other Boundaries....___ . ___

Scale 1:2,886,000

© Copyright HAMMOND INCORPORATED, Maplewood, N.J.

The administrative centers for MID GLAMORGAN, NORTHUMBERLAND and SURREY are Cardiff, Newcastle upon Tyne and Kingston upon Thames, respectively.

Longitude West of Greenwich 0° Longitude East of Greenwich

Lennoxtown, 3,070 . . . B 1
Lerwick, 6,195 . . . G 2
Leslie, 3,303 . . . E 4
Lesmahagow, 3,906 . . . E 5
Leswalt, 237 . . . C 6
Letham, 804 . . . F 4
Leuchars, 2,482 . . . F 4
Leurbost, 461 . . . B 2
Leven, 9,507 . . . F 4
Leverburgh, 223 . . . B 3
Lhanbryde, 1,184 . . . E 3
Lilliesleaf, 212 . . . F 5
Limekilns, 812 . . . D 1
Linlithgow, 6,098 . . . C 1
Linwood, 10,510 . . . B 2
Lionel, 187 . . . B 2
Livingston, 21,900 . . . C 2
Loanhead, 5,971 . . . D 2
Lochailort, ⊙673 . . . C 4
Lochaline, 213 . . . C 4
Lochans, 355 . . . D 6
Locharbriggs, 2,561 . . . E 5
Lochawe, 200 . . . C 4
Lochboisdale, 382 . . . A 3
Lochcarron, 204 . . . C 3
Lochgelly, 7,754 . . . D 1
Lochgilphead, 1,217 . . . C 4
Lochgoilhead, 216 . . . D 4
Lochinver, 283 . . . C 2
Lochmaben, 1,304 . . . E 5
Lochmaddy, 307 . . . A 3
Lochore, 2,994 . . . D 1
Lochwinnoch, 2,064 . . . A 2
Lockerbie, 3,135 . . . E 5
Lossiemouth and Branderburgh, 5,817 . . . E 3
Lumsden, 248 . . . F 3
Luncarty, 584 . . . E 4
Lybster, 554 . . . E 2
Lyness, ⊙454 . . . E 2
Macduff, 3,682 . . . F 3
Machrihanish, 212 . . . C 5
Maidens, 536 . . . D 5
Mallaig, 903 . . . C 4
Markinch, 2,366 . . . E 4
Mauchline, 3,612 . . . D 5
Maud, 634 . . . F 3
Maybole, 4,703 . . . D 5
Mayfield, 8,232 . . . D 2
Meigle, 357 . . . E 4
Melrose, 2,197 . . . F 5
Melvaig, ⊙1,794 . . . C 3
Methlick, 315 . . . F 3
Methven, 806 . . . E 4
Mid Yell, 220 . . . G 2
Millport, 1,161 . . . A 2
Milnathort, 1,099 . . . E 4
Milngavie, 10,846 . . . B 1
Minnigaff, 658 . . . D 6
Mintlaw, 657 . . . F 3
Moffat, 2,041 . . . E 5
Moniaive, 342 . . . E 5
Monifieth, 7,100 . . . F 4
Montrose, 4,704 . . . F 4
Morar, 184 . . . C 4
Motherwell and Wishaw, 72,991 . . . C 2
Muirkirk, 2,607 . . . E 5
Muir of Ord, 1,339 . . . D 3
Musselburgh, 17,045 . . . D 2
Muthill, 672 . . . E 4
Nairn, 5,821 . . . E 3
Neilston, 4,358 . . . B 2
Nethy Bridge, 431 . . . E 3
New Abbey, 339 . . . E 6
Newarthill, 7,003 . . . C 2
Newburgh, Fife, 2,124 . . . E 4
Newburgh, Grampian, 447 . . . G 3
Newcastleton, 903 . . . F 5
New Cumnock, 5,077 . . . D 5
New Deer, 601 . . . F 3
New Galloway, 337 . . . D 5
Newmains, 6,847 . . . C 2
Newmarket, 613 . . . B 2
Newmill, 449 . . . E 3
Newmilns and Greenholm, 3,509 . . . D 5
New Pitsligo, 1,125 . . . F 3
Newport-on-Tay, 3,762 . . . F 4
New Scone, 3,830 . . . E 4
Newtongrange, 4,555 . . . D 2
Newton Mearns, 6,901 . . . B 2
Newtonmore, 894 . . . D 3
Newton Stewart, 1,983 . . . D 6
Newtown Saint Boswells, 1,101 . . . F 5
Newtyle, 664 . . . E 4
North Berwick, 4,317 . . . F 4
North Tolsta, 527 . . . B 2
Oakley, 3,499 . . . C 1
Oban, 6,515 . . . C 4
Old Kilpatrick, 3,256 . . . B 2
Oldmeldrum, 1,103 . . . F 3
Oykel Bridge, ⊙742 . . . D 3
Paisley, 94,833 . . . B 2
Palnackie, 225 . . . E 6
Patna, 2,867 . . . D 5
Peebles, 6,049 . . . E 5
Penicuik, 10,476 . . . D 2
Penpont, 364 . . . E 5
Perth, 43,098 . . . E 4
Peterculter, 3,226 . . . F 3
Peterhead, 14,846 . . . G 3
Pierowall, ⊙735 . . . E 1
Pitlochry, 2,468 . . . E 4
Pitmedden, 313 . . . F 3
Pittenweem, 1,548 . . . F 4
Plockton, 288 . . . C 3
Poolewe, ⊙1,794 . . . C 3
Port Appin, ⊙2,172 . . . C 4
Port Askaig, ⊙1,795 . . . B 5
Port Bannatyne, 730 . . . A 2
Port Charlotte, 240 . . . B 5
Port Ellen, 932 . . . B 5
Port Glasgow, 22,189 . . . A 2
Portgordon, 814 . . . F 3
Portknockie, 1,217 . . . F 3
Portmahomack, 226 . . . E 3
Portpatrick, 643 . . . C 6
Portree, 1,374 . . . B 3
Portsoy, 1,717 . . . F 3
Port William, 517 . . . D 6
Prestonpans, 3,272 . . . D 1
Prestwick, 13,218 . . . D 5
Queensferry, 5,339 . . . D 1
Reay, 283 . . . E 2
Renfrew, 18,880 . . . B 2
Renton, 3,443 . . . A 1
Rhu, 1,540 . . . A 1
Rhynie, 333 . . . F 3
Rigside, 1,195 . . . E 5
Rosehearty, 1,220 . . . F 3
Rosneath, 946 . . . A 1
Rothes, 1,240 . . . E 3
Rothesay, 6,285 . . . A 2
Rutherglen, 24,091 . . . B 2
Saint Abbs, 203 . . . F 5
Saint Andrews, 12,837 . . . F 4
Saint Combs, 738 . . . G 3
Saint Cyrus, 340 . . . F 4
Saint Margaret's Hope, 210 . . . F 2
Saint Monance, 1,205 . . . F 4
Saline, 831 . . . C 1
Saltcoats, 14,861 . . . D 5
Sandbank, 850 . . . A 1
Sandhead, 248 . . . D 6
Sandwick, 603 . . . B 2
Sanquhar, 2,030 . . . D 5
Sauchie, 6,082 . . . C 1
Scalasaig, ⊙137 . . . B 4
Scalloway, 896 . . . G 2
Scarinish, ⊙875 . . . B 4
Scourie, ⊙745 . . . C 2
Scrabster, 273 . . . E 2
Selkirk, 5,635 . . . F 5
Shader, 258 . . . B 2
Shawbost, 458 . . . B 2
Shieldaig, ⊙550 . . . C 3
Shotts, 9,512 . . . C 2
Skateraw, 674 . . . F 3
Skelmorlie, 1,535 . . . A 2
Skipness, ⊙765 . . . C 5
Slamannan, 1,584 . . . C 2
Spean Bridge, 235 . . . D 4
Springholm, 340 . . . E 5
Stanley, 1,385 . . . E 4
Stenhousemuir, 8,203 . . . C 1
Stevenston, 11,786 . . . D 5
Stewarton, 5,165 . . . D 5
Stirling, 29,799 . . . C 1
Stonehaven, 4,837 . . . F 4
Stonehouse, 7,900 . . . D 5
Stornoway, 5,371 . . . B 2
Stow, 485 . . . F 5
Strachan, ⊙390 . . . F 3
Strachur Bay, ⊙678 . . . C 4
Stranraer, 10,174 . . . C 6
Strathaven, 5,464 . . . D 5
Strathpeffer, 874 . . . D 3
Strichen, 962 . . . F 3
Stromeferry, ⊙1,724 . . . C 3
Stromness, 1,680 . . . E 2
Strontian, ⊙764 . . . C 4
Struan, ⊙772 . . . B 3
Swinton, 235 . . . F 5
Tain, 2,057 . . . D 3
Tarbert, Strathclyde, 1,391 . . . C 5
Tarbert, W. Isles, 479 . . . B 3
Tarbolton, 2,224 . . . D 5
Tarland, 452 . . . F 3
Tayport, 2,848 . . . F 4
Thornhill, Central, 443 . . . D 4
Thornhill, Dumf. & Gall., 1,510 . . . E 5
Thurso, 9,113 . . . E 2
Tillicoultry, 4,320 . . . C 1
Tobermory, 652 . . . B 4
Tolob, ⊙2,033 . . . G 2
Tomatin, 214 . . . D 3
Tomintoul, 306 . . . E 3
Torphins, 499 . . . F 3
Tradespark, 425 . . . E 3
Tranent, 7,212 . . . F 5
Troon, 11,656 . . . D 5
Tullibody, 6,082 . . . C 1
Turriff, 3,051 . . . F 3
Tweedsmuir, ⊙105 . . . E 5
Twynholm, 274 . . . D 6
Tyndrum, ⊙1,153 . . . D 4
Uddingston, 5,278 . . . B 2
Uig, Highland, 103 . . . B 3
Uig, W. Isles, ⊙1,948 . . . A 2
Ullapool, 807 . . . C 3
Uphall, 3,035 . . . C 1
Viewpark, 9,812 . . . C 2
Walkerburn, 842 . . . F 5
Watten, 347 . . . E 2
Wemyss Bay, 323 . . . A 2
West Barns, 659 . . . F 5
West Calder, 2,005 . . . C 2
West Kilbride, 3,883 . . . D 5
West Linton, 705 . . . D 2
Whitburn, 11,647 . . . C 2
Whitehills, 875 . . . F 3
Whithorn, 990 . . . D 6
Whiting Bay, 352 . . . C 5
Wick, 7,804 . . . E 2
Wigtown, 1,118 . . . D 6
Winchburgh, 2,409 . . . D 1
Yetholm, 435 . . . F 5

OTHER FEATURES

A'Chralaig (mt.) . . . C 3
Ailsa Craig (isl.), 3 . . . C 5
Almond (riv.) . . . E 4
Annan (riv.) . . . E 5
Appin (dist.), 2,006 . . . C 4
Ardgour (dist.), 315 . . . C 4
Ardle (riv.) . . . E 4
Ardnamurchan (pen.), 764 . . . B 4
Argyll (dist.), 4,940 . . . C 4
Arkaig, Loch (lake) . . . C 4
Arran (isl.), 3,564 . . . C 5
Askival (mt.) . . . B 4
Assynt (dist.), 833 . . . C 2
Athol (dist.), 1,082 . . . D 4
Atlantic Ocean . . . B 2
Avon (riv.) . . . C 1
Avon (riv.) . . . E 3
Awe, Loch (lake) . . . C 4
Ayr (riv.) . . . D 5
Ayr, Heads of (cape) . . . D 5
Badenoch (dist.), 2,717 . . . D 4
Baleshare (isl.), 64 . . . A 3
Balmoral Castle . . . E 3
Barra (sound) . . . A 3
Barra (isl.), 1,005 . . . A 4
Barra (head) . . . A 4
Barra Isles (isls.), 1,092 . . . A 4
Battock (mt.) . . . F 4
Beauly (riv.) . . . D 3
Beinn Dearg (mt.) . . . D 3
Beinn a Ghlo (mt.) . . . E 4
Bell Rock (isl.), 3 . . . F 4
Ben Alder (mt.) . . . D 4
Ben Avon (mt.) . . . E 3
Benbecula (isl.), 1,355 . . . A 3
Ben Cruachan (mt.) . . . C 4
Ben Lawers (mt.) . . . D 4
Ben Lui (mt.) . . . D 4
Ben Macdhui (mt.) . . . E 3
Ben Mhor (mt.) . . . A 3
Ben More (mt.) . . . B 4
Ben More (mt.) . . . D 4
Ben More Assynt (mt.) . . . D 2
Ben Nevis (mt.) . . . D 4
Bernera (isl.), 276 . . . B 2
Berneray (isl.), 131 . . . A 3
Berneray (isl.), 6 . . . A 4
Bidean nam Bian (mt.) . . . D 4
Black Isle (pen.), 7,209 . . . D 3
Blackwater (res.) . . . D 4
Boisdale, Loch (inlet) . . . A 3
Bracadale, Loch (inlet) . . . B 3
Braemar (dist.), 7,624 . . . E 3
Breadalbane (dist.), 3,649 . . . D 4
Bressay (isl.), 248 . . . G 2
Broad (bay) . . . B 2
Broad Law (mt.) . . . E 5
Broom, Loch (inlet) . . . C 3
Brough Ness (prom.) . . . F 2
Buchan (dist.), 40,089 . . . F 3
Buddon Ness (prom.) . . . F 4
Burray (isl.), 209 . . . F 2
Burrow (head) . . . D 6
Bute (isl.), 8,423 . . . C 5
Bute (sound) . . . C 5
Butt of Lewis (prom.) . . . B 2
Cairn Gorm (mt.) . . . E 3
Cairngorm (mts.) . . . E 3
Cairn Toul (mt.) . . . E 3
Caledonian (canal) . . . D 3
Canna (isl.), 22 . . . B 3
Carn Ban (mt.) . . . D 3
Carn Eige (mt.) . . . C 3
Carrick (dist.), 21,425 . . . D 5
Carron (riv.) . . . C 1
Carron (riv.) . . . C 3
Cheviot (hills) . . . F 5
Cheviot, The (mt.) . . . F 5
Clisham (mt.) . . . B 3
Clyde (riv.) . . . D 5
Clyde (firth) . . . D 5
Coll (isl.), 144 . . . B 4
Colonsay (isl.), 137 . . . B 4
Copinsay (isl.), 3 . . . F 2
Cowal (dist.), 15,548 . . . C 4
Creag Meagaidh (mt.) . . . D 4
Cromarty (firth) . . . D 3
Cuillin (hills) . . . B 3
Cuillin (sound) . . . B 3
Dee (riv.) . . . D 5
Dee (riv.) . . . F 3
Dennis (head) . . . F 1
Deveron (riv.) . . . F 3
Don (riv.) . . . F 3
Doon (riv.) . . . D 5
Dornoch (firth) . . . E 3
Duirinish (dist.), 1,085 . . . B 3
Duncansby (head) . . . F 2
Dunnet (head) . . . E 2
Earn (riv.) . . . E 4
Earn, Loch (lake) . . . D 4
Eday (isl.), 179 . . . F 1
Eddrachillis (bay) . . . C 2
Eden (riv.) . . . F 4
Egilsay (isl.), 39 . . . F 1
Eigg (isl.), 69 . . . B 4
Eil, Loch (lake) . . . C 4
Eishort, Loch (inlet) . . . B 3
Enard (bay) . . . C 2
Eriboll, Loch (inlet) . . . D 2
Ericht, Loch (lake) . . . D 4
Eriskay (isl.), 219 . . . A 3
Erisort, Loch (inlet) . . . B 2
Esk (riv.) . . . F 5
Etive, Loch (inlet) . . . C 4
Ewe, Loch (inlet) . . . C 3
Eye (pen.), 850 . . . B 2
Fair Isle (isl.), 65 . . . F 3
Fetlar (isl.), 88 . . . G 2
Fife Ness (prom.) . . . F 4
Findhorn (riv.) . . . E 3
Flannan (isls.), 3 . . . A 2
Formartine (dist.), 10,768 . . . F 3
Forth (riv.) . . . B 1
Forth (firth) . . . F 4
Forth and Clyde (canal) . . . B 2
Foula (isl.), 33 . . . F 2
Fyne, Loch (inlet) . . . C 5
Galloway (dist.), 54,972 . . . D 5
Galloway, Mull of (prom.) . . . D 6
Gare Loch (inlet) . . . A 1
Garioch (dist.), 6,863 . . . F 3
Garry, Loch (lake) . . . D 3
Gigha (isl.), 174 . . . C 5
Girdle Ness (prom.) . . . G 3
Glass (riv.) . . . D 3
Glen More (dist.), 55,035 . . . D 3
Goat Fell (mt.) . . . C 5
Gometra (isl.), 10 . . . B 4
Grampian (mts.) . . . D 4
Great Cumbrae (isl.), 1,296 . . . A 2
Gruinard (bay) . . . C 3
Hallandale (riv.) . . . E 2
Harris (sound) . . . A 3
Harris (dist.), 2,175 . . . B 3
Hebrides (sea) . . . B 3
Hebrides, Inner (isls.), 14,881 . . . B 4
Hebrides, Outer (isls.), 29,615 . . . A 3
Helmsdale (riv.) . . . E 2
Herma Ness (prom.) . . . G 2
Holy (isl.), 10 . . . C 5
Holy Loch (inlet) . . . A 1
Hoy (isl.), 419 . . . E 2
Inchcape (Bell Rock) (isl.), 3 . . . F 4
Inchkeith (isl.), 3 . . . D 1
Indaal, Loch (inlet) . . . B 5
Inner (sound) . . . C 3
Inner Hebrides (isls.), 14,881 . . . B 4
Iona (isl.), 145 . . . B 4
Isla (riv.) . . . E 4
Islay (isl.), 3,816 . . . B 5
Jura (isl.), 210 . . . C 5
Jura (sound) . . . C 5
Katrine, Loch (lake) . . . D 4
Kerrera (isl.), 27 . . . C 4
Kilbrannan (sound) . . . C 5
Kinnairds (head) . . . G 3
Kintyre (pen.), 10,077 . . . C 5
Kintyre, Mull of (prom.) . . . C 5
Knapdale (dist.), 4,082 . . . C 5
Kyle of Tongue (inlet) . . . D 2
Laggan (bay) . . . B 5
Lammermuir (hills) . . . F 5
Lennox (hills) . . . B 1
Leven (lake) . . . E 4
Leven, Loch (inlet) . . . D 4
Lewis (dist.), 20,047 . . . B 2
Liddel Water (riv.) . . . F 5
Linnhe, Loch (inlet) . . . C 4
Lismore (isl.), 166 . . . C 4
Little Minch (sound) . . . B 3
Lochaber (dist.), 13,813 . . . D 4
Lochnagar (mt.) . . . E 4
Lochy, Loch (lake) . . . D 3
Lomond, Loch (lake) . . . D 4
Long, Loch (inlet) . . . D 4
Lorne (dist.), 12,162 . . . C 4
Lorne (firth) . . . C 4
Loyal, Loch (lake) . . . D 2
Luce (bay) . . . D 6
Luing (isl.), 151 . . . C 4
Lyon (riv.) . . . D 4
Machers, The (pen.), 6,192 . . . D 6
Mainland (isl.), 12,747 . . . E 1
Mainland (isl.), 12,944 . . . G 2
Mar (dist.), 23,931 . . . F 3
Maree, Loch (lake) . . . C 3
May, Isle of (isl.), 10 . . . F 4
Merrick (mt.) . . . D 5
Minginish (dist.), 772 . . . B 3
Moidart (dist.), 155 . . . C 4
Monach (sound) . . . A 3
Monadhliath (mts.) . . . D 3
Moorfoot (hills) . . . E 5
Moray (firth) . . . E 3
Moriston (riv.) . . . D 3
Morven (dist.), 398 . . . C 4
Morven (mt.) . . . E 2
Muck (isl.), 24 . . . B 4
Muckle Flugga (isl.), 3 . . . G 2
Mull (isl.), 2,024 . . . C 4
Mull (head) . . . F 1
Mull (sound) . . . C 4
Nairn (riv.) . . . D 3
na Keal, Loch (inlet) . . . B 4
Naver (riv.) . . . D 2
Ness, Loch (lake) . . . D 3
Nevis, Loch (inlet) . . . C 3
Nith (riv.) . . . E 5
North (chan.) . . . C 5
North (sound) . . . F 1
North (sound) . . . G 4
North Esk (riv.) . . . F 4
North Minch (sound) . . . B 3
North Ronaldsay (isl.), 134 . . . F 1
North Uist (isl.), 1,469 . . . A 3
Oa, Mull of (prom.) . . . B 5
Ochil (hills) . . . E 4
Oich (riv.) . . . D 3
Orchy (riv.) . . . D 4
Orkney (isls.), 17,675 . . . F 1
Oronsay (isl.), 2 . . . B 4
Outer Hebrides (isls.), 29,615 . . . A 3
Oykel (riv.) . . . D 3
Pabbay (isl.), 4 . . . A 3
Papa Stour (isl.), 24 . . . F 2
Papa Westray (isl.), 106 . . . F 1
Paps of Jura (mt.) . . . C 5
Park (dist.), 210 . . . B 2
Peel Fell (mt.) . . . F 5
Pentland (hills) . . . D 2
Pentland (firth) . . . E 2
Pladda (isl.), 2 . . . C 5
Quoich, Loch (lake) . . . C 3
Raasay (isl.), 163 . . . C 3
Rannoch (dist.), 1,177 . . . D 4
Rannoch, Loch (lake) . . . D 4
Rhinns, The (pen.), 8,295 . . . C 6
Roag, Loch (inlet) . . . B 2
Rona (isl.), 3 . . . B 3
Ross of Mull (pen.), 585 . . . B 4
Rousay (isl.), 181 . . . E 1
Rudha Hunish (cape) . . . B 3
Rudh Re (cape) . . . C 3
Rum (isl.), 40 . . . B 3
Ryan, Loch (inlet) . . . C 5
Saint Kilda (isl.), 65 . . . A 2
Saint Magnus (bay) . . . F 2
Sanda (isl.), 9 . . . C 5
Sanday (isl.), 11 . . . B 3
Sanday (isl.), 592 . . . F 1
Scalpay (isl.), 483 . . . B 3
Scalpay (isl.), 5 . . . C 3
Scapa Flow (chan.) . . . E 2
Scarp (isl.), 12 . . . A 2
Scridain, Loch (inlet) . . . B 4
Scurdie Ness (prom.) . . . F 4
Seaforth, Loch (inlet) . . . B 3
Seil (isl.), 326 . . . C 4
Sgurr a Choire Ghlais (mt.) . . . D 3
Sgurr Alasdair (mt.) . . . B 3
Sgurr Mor (mt.) . . . C 3
Sgurr na Lapaich (mt.) . . . C 3
Shapinsay (isl.), 346 . . . F 1
Shetland (isls.), 18,494 . . . G 2
Shiant (sound) . . . B 3
Shiel, Loch (lake) . . . C 4
Shin (falls) . . . D 3
Shin, Loch (lake) . . . D 2
Shona (isl.), 17 . . . C 4
Sidlaw (hills) . . . E 4
Sinclair's (bay) . . . E 2
Skye, Isle of (isl.), 7,183 . . . B 3
Sleat (pt.) . . . B 4
Sleat (dist.), 449 . . . C 3
Small Isles (isls.), 171 . . . B 4
Snizort, Loch (inlet) . . . B 3
Soay (isl.), 5 . . . B 3
Solway (firth) . . . E 6
South Esk (riv.) . . . F 4
South Ronaldsay (isl.), 776 . . . F 2
South Uist (isl.), 2,281 . . . A 3
Spean (riv.) . . . D 4
Spey (riv.) . . . E 3
Start (pt.) . . . F 1
Stinchar (riv.) . . . D 5
Strathbogie (dist.), 7,959 . . . F 3
Strathmore (valley) . . . E 4
Strathspey (dist.), 6,668 . . . E 3
Strathy (pt.) . . . E 2
Stroma (isl.), 8 . . . E 2
Stronsay (isl.), 436 . . . F 1
Sumburgh (head) . . . G 2
Sunart, Loch (inlet) . . . C 4
Swona (isl.), 3 . . . E 2
Taransay (isl.), 5 . . . A 3
Tarbat Ness (prom.) . . . E 3
Tarbert, East Loch (inlet) . . . B 3
Tarbert, Loch (inlet) . . . B 5
Tarbert, West Loch (inlet) . . . A 3
Tay (riv.) . . . E 4
Tay (firth) . . . F 4
Tay, Loch (lake) . . . D 4
Teith (riv.) . . . D 4
Teviot (riv.) . . . F 5
Thurso (riv.) . . . E 2
Tiree (isl.), 875 . . . B 4
Tolsta (head) . . . B 2
Tor Ness (prom.) . . . E 2
Torridon, Loch (inlet) . . . C 3
Trossachs, The (valley) . . . D 4
Trotternish (dist.), 1,948 . . . B 3
Tweed (riv.) . . . F 5
Tyne (riv.) . . . F 5
Ulva (isl.), 23 . . . B 4
Unst (isl.), 1,124 . . . G 2
Vaternish (dist.), 162 . . . B 3
Vatersay (isl.), 77 . . . A 4
West Burra (isl.), 501 . . . G 2
Westray (firth) . . . E 1
Westray (isl.), 735 . . . E 1
Whalsay (isl.), 870 . . . G 2
White Coomb (mt.) . . . E 5
Wigtown (bay) . . . D 6
Wrath (cape) . . . C 2
Wyre (isl.), 36 . . . F 1
Yarrow (riv.) . . . E 5
Yell (isl.), 1,143 . . . G 2
Ythan (riv.) . . . F 3

★Population of met. area
⊙Population of parish.

Agriculture, Industry and Resources

DOMINANT LAND USE

- Cereals (chiefly oats, barley)
- Truck Farming, Horticulture
- Dairy, Mixed Farming
- Livestock, Mixed Farming
- Pasture Livestock

MAJOR MINERAL OCCURRENCES

Ba	Barite	Na	Salt
C	Coal	O	Petroleum
F	Fluorspar	Pb	Lead
Fe	Iron Ore	Pe	Peat
G	Natural Gas	Sn	Tin
K	Potash	Zn	Zinc
Ka	Kaolin (china clay)		

Water Power

Major Industrial Areas

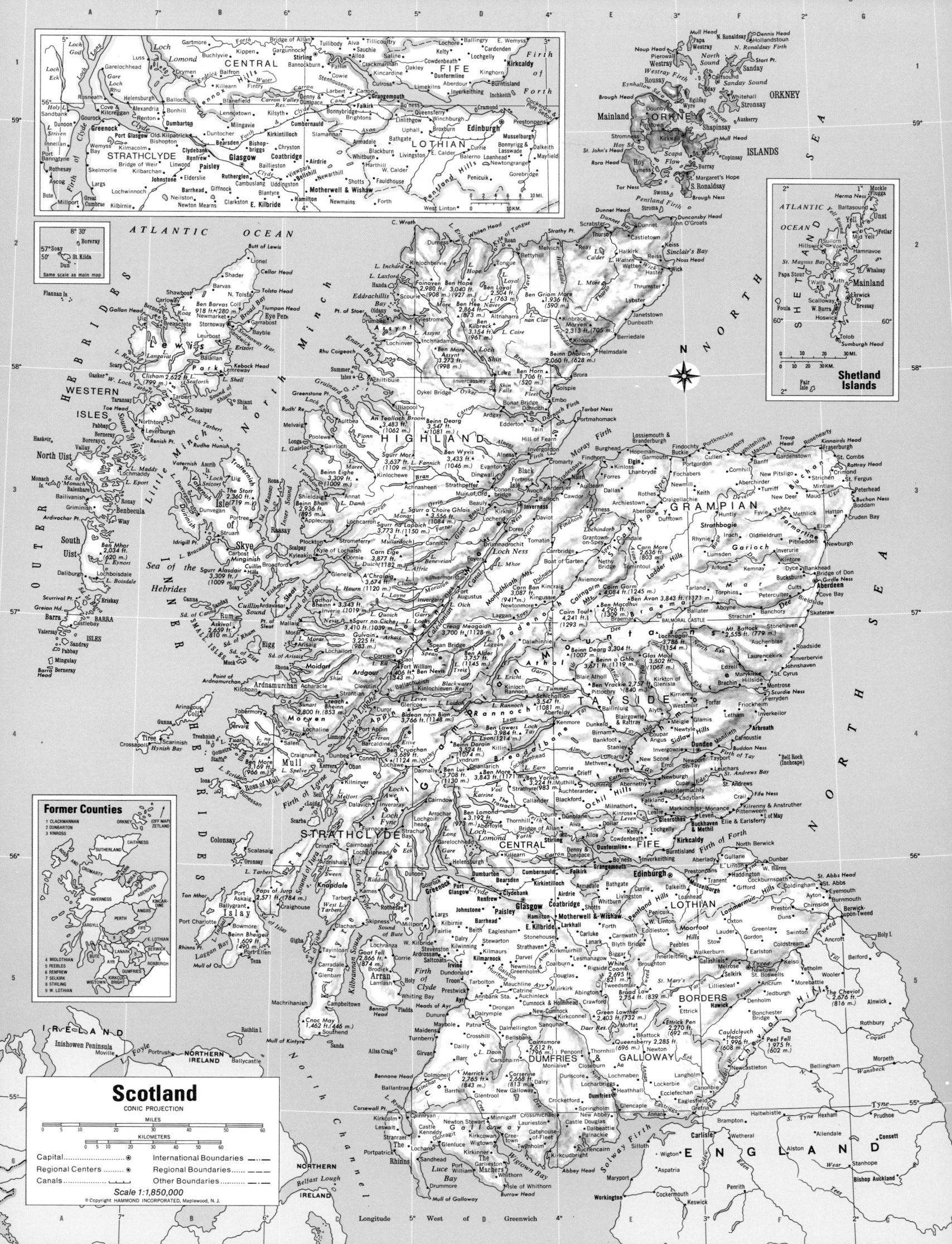

Scotland

CONIC PROJECTION

MILES

KILOMETERS

Capital................................ ⊛
Regional Centers.................. ●
Canals.................................. ────
International Boundaries....... ─·─·─
Regional Boundaries............ ─ ─ ─
Other Boundaries................. ·······

Scale 1:1,850,000

© Copyright HAMMOND INCORPORATED, Maplewood, N.J.

Former Counties

IRELAND

Carlow 34,237 H6
Cavan 52,618 G4
Clare 75,008 D6
Cork 352,883 D7
Donegal 108,344 K2
Dublin 852,219 J5
Galway 149,223 D5
Kerry 112,772 B7
Kildare 71,977 H5
Kilkenny 61,473 G6
Laois 45,259 G6
Leitrim 28,360 E3
Leix (Laois) 45,259 G6
Limerick 140,459 D7
Longford 28,250 F4
Louth 74,951 J4
Mayo 109,525 C4
Meath 71,729 H4
Monaghan 46,242 H3
Offaly 51,829 F5
Roscommon 53,519 E4
Sligo 50,275 D3
Tipperary 123,565 F6
Waterford 77,315 F7
Westmeath 53,570 G5
Wexford 86,351 H7
Wicklow 66,295 J5

CITIES and TOWNS

Abbeydorney, 188 B 7
Abbeyfeale, 1,337 C 7
Abbeylara, ‡290 F 4
Abbeyleix, 1,033 G 6
Achill Sound, ‡1,163 B 4
Aclare, ‡336 D 3
Adare, 545 D 6
Aghada-Farsid-Rostellan, 461 E 8
Aghadoe, ‡497 B 7
Aghagower, ‡693 C 4
Ahascragh, 221 E 5
Annagry, 201 E 1
Annascaul, 236 B 7
An Uaimh, 4,605 H 4
An Uaimh, *6,665 H 4
Ardagh, Limerick, 213 C 7
Ardagh, Longford, ‡974 F 4
Ardara, 683 E 2
Ardee, *3,183 H 4
Ardee, 3,096 H 4
Ardfert, 286 B 7
Ardfinnan, 510 F 7
Ardmore, 233 F 8
Ardrahan, ‡239 D 5
Arklow, 6,948 J 6
Arthurstown, 1,188 H 7
Arva, 370 F 4
Ashford, 341 J 5
Askeaton, 844 D 6
Athboy, 705 H 4
Athea, 328 C 7
Athenry, 1,240 D 5
Athleague, ‡955 E 4
Athlone, 9,825 F 5
Athlone, *11,611 F 5
Athy, 4,270 H 6
Athy, *4,654 H 6
Aughrim, 451 J 6
Avoca, ‡620 J 6
Bagenalstown (Muinebeag), 2,321 H 6
Baile Átha Cliath (Dublin) (cap.), 567,866 K 5
Bailieborough, 1,293 G 4
Balbriggan, 3,741 J 4
Balla, 293 C 4
Ballaghaderreen, 1,121 E 4
Ballina, Mayo, 6,063 C 3
Ballina, *6,369 C 3
Ballina, Tipperary, 336 E 6
Ballinagh, 459 G 4
Ballinakill, 300 G 6
Ballineen D 8
Ballinamore, 808 F 3
Ballinasloe, 5,969 E 5
Ballincollig-Carrigrohane, 2,110 D 8
Ballindine, 232 C 4
Ballingarry, Limerick, 422 D 7
Ballingarry, Tipperary, ‡574 F 6
Ballinlough, 242 D 4
Ballinrobe, 1,272 C 4
Ballintober, ‡867 E 4
Ballintra, 197 E 2
Ballisodare, 486 E 3
Ballivor, 287 H 4
Ballybay, 754 G 3
Ballybay, *1,159 G 3
Ballybofey-Stranorlar, 2,214 F 2
Ballybunion, 1,287 B 7
Ballycanew, ‡460 J 6
Ballycarney, ‡294 J 6
Ballycastle, ‡724 C 3
Ballyconnell, 421 F 3
Ballycotton, 389 F 8
Ballydehob, 253 C 8
Ballyduff, 406 B 7
Ballygar, 359 E 4
Ballygeary, 725 J 7
Ballyhaise, 274 G 3
Ballyhaunis, 1,093 D 4
Ballyheigue, 450 B 7
Ballyjamesduff, 673 G 4
Ballylanders, 266 E 7
Ballylongford, 504 B 6
Ballymahon, 707 F 4
Ballymakeery, 272 C 8
Ballymore, ‡447 F 5
Ballymore Eustace, 433 J 5
Ballymote, 952 D 3
Ballyporeen, ‡810 E 7
Ballyragget, 519 G 6
Ballyroan, ‡478 G 6
Ballyshannon, 2,325 E 3
Ballytore, ‡580 H 5
Baltimore, 200 C 9
Baltinglass, 909 H 6
Baltray, 236 J 4
Banagher, 1,052 F 5
Bandon, 2,257 D 8
Bandon, *4,071 D 8
Bannow, ‡798 H 7
Bansha, 184 E 7
Bantry, 2,579 C 8
Barna, ‡1,734 C 5
Belmullet, 744 B 3
Belturbet, 1,092 G 3
Bennettsbridge, 367 G 6
Birr, 3,319 F 5
Birr, *3,881 F 5
Blanchardstown, 3,279 H 5
Blarney, 1,128 D 8
Blessington, 637 J 5
Boherbue, 372 C 7
Borris, 430 H 6
Borris-in-Ossory, 276 F 6
Borrisokane, 769 E 6
Borrisoleigh, 471 E 6
Boyle, 1,727 E 4
Boyle, *1,939 E 4
Bray, 14,467 K 5
Bray, *15,841 K 5
Bri Chualann (Bray), 14,467 K 5
Broadford, 226 C 7
Brosna, 250 C 7
Bruff, 547 D 7
Bruree, 243 D 7
Bunbeg-Derrybeg, 878 E 1
Bunclody-Carrickduff, 929 H 6
Buncrana, 2,955 G 1
Buncrana, *3,334 G 1
Bundoran, 1,337 E 3
Burtonport, ‡1,288 E 2
Buttevant, 1,045 D 7
Cahir, 1,747 F 7
Cahirciveen, 1,547 A 8
Callan, 1,283 G 7
Camolin, 306 J 6
Campile, 231 H 7
Cappamore, 567 E 6
Cappawhite, 305 E 6
Cappoquin, 872 F 7
Carbury, ‡894 H 5
Carlingford, 559 J 3
Carlow, 9,588 H 6
Carlow, *10,399 H 6
Carndonagh, 1,146 G 1
Carnew, 570 H 6
Carrickmacross, 2,100 H 4
Carrickmacross, *2,475 H 4
Carrick-on-Shannon, 1,854 F 4
Carrick-on-Suir, 5,006 F 7
Carrigaholt, ‡493 B 6
Carrigaline, 951 E 8
Carrigallen, 230 F 4
Carrigart, ‡753 F 1
Carrigtwohill, 622 E 8
Carrowkeel, ‡326 G 1
Cashel, 2,692 F 7
Castlebar, 5,979 C 4
Castlebar, *6,476 C 4
Castlebellingham, 407 J 4
Castleblayney, 2,118 H 3
Castleblayney, *2,395 H 3
Castlecomer-Donaguile, 1,244 G 6
Castledermot, 583 H 6
Castlefin, 610 F 2
Castlegregory, 216 A 7
Castleisland, 1,929 B 7
Castlemartyr, 491 E 8
Castlepollard, 693 G 4
Castlerea, 1,752 D 4
Castletown, ‡504 F 6
Castletownbere, 812 B 8
Castletownroche, 399 D 7
Castletownshend, 170 C 9
Causeway, 215 B 7
Cavan, 3,273 G 3
Cavan, *4,312 G 3
Ceanannus Mór, 2,391 G 4
Ceanannus Mór, *2,653 G 4
Celbridge, 1,568 H 5
Charlestown-Bellahy, 677 D 4
Charleville (Rathluirc), 2,232 D 7
Clara, 2,156 F 5
Claregalway, ‡594 D 5
Claremorris, 1,718 C 4
Clashmore, ‡379 F 8
Clifden, 790 B 5
Cloghan, 404 F 5
Clogh-Chatsworth, 324 G 6
Clogheen, 530 F 7
Clogherhead, 649 J 4
Clonakilty, 2,430 D 8
Clonaslee, 285 F 5
Clondalkin, 7,009 J 5
Clonegal, 202 H 6
Clones, 2,164 G 3
Clonfert, ‡430 E 5
Clonmany, ‡936 G 1
Clonmel, 11,622 F 7
Clonmel, *12,291 F 7
Clonmellon, 328 H 4
Clonroche, 222 H 7
Clontuskert, 351 E 4
Cloone, ‡460 F 4
Cloughjordan, 480 E 6
Cloyne, 654 E 8
Coachford, 290 D 8
Cóbh, 6,076 E 8
Cóbh, *7,141 E 8
Coill Dubh, 920 H 5
Collon, 262 J 4
Collooney, 546 E 3
Cong, 233 C 4
Convoy, 654 F 2
Coolaney, ‡352 D 3
Coolgreany, ‡603 J 6
Cootehill, 1,415 G 3
Cootehill, *1,542 G 3
Cork, 128,645 E 8
Cork, *134,430 E 8
Corofin, 342 C 6
Courtmacsherry, 210 D 8
Courtown Harbour, 291 J 6
Creeslough, 269 F 1
Crookhaven, ‡400 B 9
Croom, 756 D 6
Crosshaven, 1,222 E 8
Crossmolina, 1,077 C 3
Crusheen, ‡405 D 6
Culdaff, ‡621 G 1
Daingean, 492 G 5
Delvin, 223 G 4
Dingle, 1,401 A 7
Doaghbeg, ‡701 F 1
Donabate, 426 J 5
Donegal, 1,725 F 2
Doneraile, 799 D 7
Dooagh-Keel, 649 A 4
Doon, 387 E 6
Douglas, ‡4,448 D 8
Drimoleague, 415 C 8
Drishane, ‡1,548 C 7
Drogheda, 19,762 J 4
Drogheda, *20,095 J 4
Droichead Nua, 5,053 H 5
Droichead Nua, *6,444 H 5
Dromahair, 177 E 3
Drumcar, ‡1,215 J 4
Drumconrath, ‡1,044 H 4
Drumkeerin, ‡467 E 3
Drumlish, 205 F 4
Drumshanbo, 576 E 3
Dublin (cap.), 567,866 K 5
Dublin, *679,748 K 5
Duleek, 658 J 4
Duncannon, 228 H 7
Dundalk, 21,672 H 3
Dundalk, *23,816 H 3
Dunfanaghy, 303 F 1
Dungarvan, 5,583 F 7
Dungloe, 940 E 2
Dunkineely, 288 E 2
Dún Laoghaire, 53,171 K 5
Dún Laoghaire, *98,379 K 5
Dunlavin, 423 H 5
Dunleer 855 J4
Dunmanway 1,392 C8
Dunmore 522 D4
Dunmore East 656 G7
Dunshaughlin⊙ 283 H5
Durrow, Laois 596 G6
Durrow, Offaly⊙ 441 F5
Easky 184 D3
Edenderry 2,953 G5
Edenderry* 3,116 G5
Elphin 489 E4
Emyvale 281 G3
Ennis 5,972 D6
Ennis* 10,840 D6
Enniscorthy 5,704 J7
Enniscorthy* 6,642 J7
Enniskerry 772 J5
Ennistymon 1,013 C6
Eyrecourt 314 E5
Fahan⊙ 1,023 G1
Falcarragh 506 E1
Feakle⊙ 398 D6
Fenit 360 B7
Ferbane 1,064 F5
Fermoy 3,237 E7
Fermoy* 4,033 E7
Ferns 712 J6
Fethard, Tipperary 1,064 F7
Fethard, Wexford⊙ 637 H7
Foxford 868 C4
Foynes 624 C6
Frankford (Kilcormac) 1,089 F5
Frenchpark⊙ 693 E4
Freshford 585 G6
Galbally 258 E7
Galway 27,726 C5
Galway* 29,375 C5
Geashill⊙ 751 G5
Glandore⊙ 695 C8
Glanmire-Riverstown 1,113 E8
Glanworth 335 E7
Glenamaddy 315 D4
Glenbeigh 266 B7
Glencolumbkille⊙ 787 D2
Glengarriff 244 C8
Glenties 734 E2
Glenville⊙ 264 D7
Glin 623 C6
Golden⊙ 640 F7
Gorey 2,946 J6
Gorey* 3,024 J6
Gormanston⊙ 1,384 J4
Gort 975 D5
Gowran 402 G6
Graiguenamanagh-Tinnahinch 1,303 H6
Granard 1,054 F4
Greencastle 322 H1
Greenore 882 J4
Greystones-Delgany 4,517 K5
Gurteen 165 D3
Hacketstown 574 H6
Headford 673 C5
Holycross⊙ 902 F6
Hospital 525 E7
Inchigeelagh⊙ 516 C8
Inishannon 190 D8
Inistioge 179 G7
Inniscrone 582 C3
Johnstown 303 G6
Kanturk 2,063 D7
Keel-Dooagh 649 A4
Kells⊙ 423 G6
Kells (Ceanannus Mór) 2,391 G4
Kenmare 903 B8
Kilbaha⊙ 471 B6
Kilbeggan 635 G5
Kilcar 273 D2
Kilcock 827 H5
Kilconnell⊙ 629 E5
Kilcoole 679 K5
Kilcormac 1,089 F5
Kilcullen 880 H5
Kildare 3,137 H5
Kildysart 239 C6
Kilfenora⊙ 441 C6
Kilfinane 561 D7
Kilgarvan 228 B8
Kilkee 1,287 B6
Kilkelly 225 D4
Kilkenny 9,838 G6
Kilkenny* 13,306 G6
Killala 368 C3
Killaloe 871 D6
Killarney 7,184 C7
Killarney* 7,541 C7
Killavullen 221 D7
Killenaule 592 F6
Killeshandra 432 F3
Killimor 221 E5
Killinaboy⊙ 297 C6
Killorglin 1,150 B7
Killucan-Rathwire 290 G4
Killybegs 1,094 E2
Kilmacrennan 274 F1
Kilmacthomas 396 G7
Kilmallock 1,170 D7
Kilmeadan⊙ 262 G7
Kilmihill 284 C6
Kilmoganny 181 G7
Kilmore Quay 273 H7
Kilmurry⊙ 387 C6
Kilnaleck 273 G4
Kilronan 243 B5
Kilrush 2,671 C6
Kilsheelan⊙ 665 F7
Kiltimagh 978 C4
Kilworth 360 E7
Kingscourt 1,016 H4
Kingstown (Dún Laoghaire) 53,171 K5
Kinlough 160 E3
Kinnegad 362 G5
Kinnitty⊙ 420 F5
Kinsale 1,622 D8
Kinsale* 1,989 D8
Kinvara 293 D5
Knightstown 236 A8
Knock⊙ 1,202 D4
Knocklong 248 D7
Knocknagashel 168 C7
Labasheeda⊙ 468 C6
Laghy⊙ 625 E2
Lahinch 455 C6
Lanesborough-Ballyleague 906 E4
Laracor⊙ 404 H4
Laytown-Bettystown-Mornington 1,882 J4
Leenane⊙ 271 B4
Leighlindridge 379 H6
Leitrim⊙ 544 F3
Leixlip 2,402 H5
Letterkenny 4,930 F2
Letterkenny* 5,207 F2
Lifford 1,121 F2
Limerick 57,161 D6
Limerick* 63,002 D6
Liscarroll 231 D7
Lisdoonvarna 459 C5
Lismore 884 F7
Lismore⊙ 1,041 F7
Listowel 3,021 C7
Littleton 322 F6
Longford 3,876 F4
Longford* 4,791 F4
Lorrha⊙ 685 E5
Loughrea 3,075 E5
Louisburgh 310 B4
Louth 208 J4
Lucan-Doddsborough 4,245 J5
Luimneach (Limerick) 57,161 D6
Lusk 553 J4
Macroom 2,256 C8
Malahide 3,834 J5
Malin⊙ 552 G1
Mallow 5,901 D7
Mallow* 6,506 D7
Manorhamilton 858 E3
Manulla⊙ 660 C4
Maryborough (Portlaoise) 3,902 G5
Maynooth 1,296 H5
Meathas Truim 546 G4
Midleton 3,075 E8
Midleton* 4,666 E8
Milford 763 F1
Millstreet 1,319 D7
Milltown 260 A7
Miltown-Malbay 677 C6
Minard⊙ 397 A7
Mitchelstown 2,783 E7
Moate 1,378 F5
Mohill 868 F4
Monaghan 5,256 G3
Monasterevan 1,619 H5
Moneygall 282 F6
Monivea⊙ 405 D5
Mooncoin 413 G7
Mount Bellew 275 D5
Mountcharles 445 E2
Mountmellick 2,595 G5
Mountmellick* 2,864 G5
Mountrath 1,098 F5
Moville 1,089 G1
Moycullen⊙ 498 C5
Moynalty⊙ 583 H4
Muff 240 G1
Muinebeag 2,321 H6
Mullagh 293 H4
Mullaghmore⊙ 629 D3
Mullinahone 262 F7
Mullinavat 343 G7
Mullingar 6,790 G4
Mullingar* 9,245 G4
Naas 5,078 H5
Navan (An Uaimh) 4,605 H4
Nenagh 5,085 E6
Nenagh* 5,174 E6
Newbliss⊙ 547 G3
Newbridge (Droichead Nua) 5,053 H5
Newcastle 2,549 D7
Newcastle* 2,680 D7
Newmarket 886 C7
Newmarket-on-Fergus 1,052 D6
New Pallas⊙ 1,271 E6
Newport, Mayo 420 C4
Newport, Tipperary 582 E6
New Ross 4,775 H7
New Ross* 5,153 H7
Newtown Forbes⊙ 495 F4
Newtownmountkennedy 882 J5
Newtownsandes 268 C6
O'Briensbridge-Montpelier 237 D6
Oldcastle 759 G4
Old Leighlin⊙ 309 G6
Oola 348 E6
Oranmore 440 D5
Oughterard 628 C5
Passage East 408 G7
Passage West 2,709 E8
Patrickswell 415 D6
Pettigo 332 F2
Piltown 456 G7
Portarlington 3,117 G5
Portlaoise 3,902 G5
Portlaoise* 6,470 G5
Portlaw 1,166 G7
Portmarnock 1,726 J5
Portumna 913 E5
Queenstown (Cóbh) 6,076 E8
Rahan⊙ 531 F5
Ramelton 807 F1
Raphoe 945 F2
Rathangan 868 G5
Rathcoole 1,740 J5
Rathcormac 191 E7
Rathdowney 892 F6
Rathdrum 1,141 J6
Rathgormuck⊙ 231 F7
Rathkeale 1,543 D7
Rathluirc 2,232 D7
Rathmore 437 J5
Rathmullen 486 F1
Rathnew-Merrymeeting 954 J6
Rathowen⊙ 294 F4
Rathvilly 230 H6
Ratoath 300 J5
Riverstown 236 E3
Rockcorry 233 H3
Rosapenna⊙ 822 F1
Roscommon 1,556 E4
Roscommon* 2,821 E4
Roscrea 3,855 F6
Rosscarbery 309 C8
Rosses Point 464 D3
Rosslare 588 J7
Rosslare Harbour (Ballygeary) 725 J7
Roundstone 204 A5
Roundwood 260 J5
Rush 2,633 J4
Saint Johnston 463 F2
Scarriff 619 E6
Schull 457 B8
Scotstown 264 H3
Shanagolden 231 C6
Shannon Airport 3,657 D6
Shannon Bridge 188 F5
Shercock 313 G4
Shillelagh 246 J6
Shinrone 365 F5
Shrule 288 C4
Sixmilebridge 567 D6
Skerries 3,044 J4
Skibbereen 2,104 C8
Slane 483 H4
Sligo 14,080 E3
Sligo* 14,456 E3
Sneem 285 B8
Spiddal⊙ 819 C5
Stepaside 748 J5
Stradbally, Laois 891 G5
Stradbally, Waterford 158 F7
Strokestown 563 E4
Swanlinbar 257 F3
Swinford 1,105 C4
Swords 4,133 J5
Taghmon 369 H7
Tallaght 6,174 J5
Tallow, 883 F 7
Tarbert, 485 C 6
Teltown, ‡739 H 4
Templemore, 2,174 F 6
Templetuohy, 197 F 6
Termonfeckin, 328 J 4
Thomastown, 1,270 G 7
Thurles, 6,840 F 6
Thurles, *7,087 F 6
Timoleague, 257 D 8
Tinahely, 450 H 6
Tipperary, 4,631 E 7
Tipperary, *4,717 E 7
Toomevara, 272 E 6
Tralee, 12,287 B 7
Tralee, *13,263 B 7
Tramore, 3,792 G 7
Trim, 1,700 H 4
Trim, *2,255 H 4
Tuam, 3,808 D 4
Tuam, *4,952 D 4
Tubbercurry, 959 D 3
Tulla, 415 D 6
Tullamore, 6,809 G 5
Tullamore, *7,474 G 5
Tullaroan, ‡301 G 6
Tullow, 1,838 H 6
Tullow, *1,945 H 6
Tynagh, ‡452 E 5
Tyrrellspass, 289 G 5
Urlingford, 652 F 6
Virginia, 583 G 4
Waterford, 31,968 G 7
Waterford, *33,676 G 7
Waterville, 547 A 8
Westport, 3,023 C 4
Wexford, 11,849 H 7
Wexford, *13,293 H 7
Whitegate, 370 E 8
Wicklow, 3,786 K 6
Wicklow, *3,915 K 6
Woodenbridge, ‡620 J 6
Woodford, 198 E 5
Youghal, 5,445 F 8
Youghal, *5,626 F 8

OTHER FEATURES

Achill (isl.), 3,129 A 4
Allen (lake) E 3
Allen, Bog of (marsh) H 5
Aran (isl.), 773 D 2
Aran (isls.), 1,499 B 5
Arklow (bank) K 6
Arrow (lake) E 3
Awbeg (riv.) D 7
Ballinskelligs (bay) A 8
Ballycotton (bay) F 8
Ballyheige (bay) B 7
Ballyhoura (hills) E 7
Ballyteige (bay) H 7
Bandon (riv.) D 8
Bann (riv.) J 6
Bantry (bay) B 8
Barrow (riv.) H 7
Baurtregaum (mt.) A 7
Bear (isl.), 288 B 8
Blacksod (bay) A 3
Blackstairs (mt.) H 6
Blackwater (riv.) D 7
Blackwater (riv.) H 4
Blasket (isls.) A 7
Bloody Foreland (prom.) E 1
Blue Stack (mts.) E 2
Boderg (lake) E 4
Boggeragh (mts.) D 7
Boyne (riv.) J 4
Brandon (head) A 7
Bride (riv.) E 7
Broad Haven (harb.) B 3
Brosna (riv.) F 5
Bull, The (isl.), 5 A 8
Caha (mts.) B 8
Carlingford (inlet) J 3
Carnsore (pt.) J 7
Carrantuohill (mt.) B 7
Clare (riv.) D 5
Clare (isls.), 168 A 4
Clear (cape) B 9
Clear (isl.), 192 C 9
Clew (bay) B 4
Comeragh (mts.) F 7
Conn (lake) C 3
Connacht (prov.), 390,902 C 4
Connemara (dist.), 7,599 B 5
Cork (harb.) E 8
Corrib (lake) C 5
Courtmacsherry (bay) D 8
Curragh, The H 5
Dee (riv.) H 4
Deel (riv.) D 7
Deele (riv.) F 2
Derg (lake) E 6
Derravaragh (lake) G 4
Derryveagh (mts.) E 2
Dingle (bay) A 7
Donegal (bay) D 3
Drum (hills) F 7
Dublin (bay) J 5
Dundalk (bay) J 4
Dunmanus (bay) B 8
Dursey (isl.), 38 A 8
Ennell (lake) G 5
Erne (riv.) E 3
Errigal (mt.) E 1
Erris (head) A 3
Fanad (head) F 1
Fastnet Rock (isl.), 3 B 9
Feale (riv.) C 7
Fergus (riv.) D 6
Finn (riv.) F 2
Finn (riv.) G 3
Flesk (riv.) C 7
Foyle (inlet) G 1
Foyle (riv.) G 2
Galley (head) D 9
Galtee (mts.) E 7
Galtymore (mt.) E 7
Galway (bay) C 5
Gara (lake) D 4
Garadice (lake) F 3
Gill (lake) E 3
Glyde (riv.) H 4
Golden Vale (plain) E 7
Gorumna (isl.), 1,108 B 5
Gowna (lake) G 4
Grand (canal) G 5
Greenore (pt.) J 7
Gweebarra (bay) D 2
Hags (head) B 6
Helvick (head) G 7
Hook (head) H 7
Horn (head) E 1
Iar Connacht (dist.), 10,774 C 5
Inishbofin (isl.), 236 A 4
Inishbofin (isl.), 103 E 1
Inisheer (isl.), 313 B 5
Inishmaan (isl.), 319 C 5
Inishmore (isl.), 864 B 5
Inishowen (head) H 1
Inishowen (pen.), 24,109 G 1
Inishtrahull (isl.), 3 G 1
Inishturk (isls.), 83 A 4
Inny (riv.) A 8
Inny (riv.) F 4
Inver (bay) E 2
Ireland's Eye (isl.) K 5
Irish (sea) K 4
Joyce's Country (dist.), 2,021 B 4
Kenmare (riv.) A 8
Kerry (head) A 7
Key (lake) E 3
Kilkieran (bay) B 5
Killala (bay) C 3
Killary (harb.) A 4
Kinsale (harb.) E 8
Kippure (mt.) J 5
Knockboy (mt.) B 8
Knockmealdown (mts.) F 7
Lady's Island Lake (inlet) J 7
Lambay (isl.), 24 K 4
Laune (riv.) B 7
Leane (lake) B 7
Leane (lake) G 4
Lee (riv.) D 8
Leinster (mt.) H 6
Leinster (prov.), 1,498,140 G 5
Lettermullan (isl.), 221 B 5
Liffey (riv.) H 5
Liscannor (bay) B 6
Long Island (bay) B 9
Loop (head) A 6
Lugnaquillia (mt.) J 5
Macgillicuddy's Reeks (mts.) B 7
Macnean (lake) F 3
Maigue (riv.) D 6
Maine (riv.) C 7
Malin (head) F 1
Mask (lake) C 4
Maumturk (mts.) B 5
Melvin (lake) E 3
Mizen (head) B 9
Moher (cliffs) B 6
Monavullagh (mts.) F 7
Moy (riv.) C 3
Mulkear (riv.) E 6
Mullaghareirk (mts.) C 7
Mulroy (bay) F 1
Munster (prov.), 882,002 D 7
Mweelrea (mt.) B 4
Mweenish (isl.), 198 B 5
Nagles (mts.) E 7
Nenagh (riv.) E 6
Nephin (mt.) C 3
Nore (riv.) G 7
North (sound) B 5
Omey (isl.), 34 A 5
Oughter (lake) G 3
Ovoca (riv.) J 6
Owenmore (riv.) D 3
Owey (isl.), 51 D 1
Paps, The (mt.) C 7
Partry (mts.) C 4
Pollaphuca (res.) J 5
Punchestown H 5
Rathlin O'Birne (isl.), 3 C 2
Ree (lake) F 5
Roaringwater (bay) B 9
Rosses (bay) D 1
Rosskeeragh (pt.) D 3
Royal (canal) G 4
Saint Finan's (bay) A 8
Saint George's (chan.) K 7
Saint John's (pt.) D 2
Saltee (isls.) H 7
Seven (heads) D 8
Seven Hogs, The (isls.) A 7
Shannon (riv.) E 6
Sheeffry (hills) B 4
Sheelin (lake) G 4
Sheep Haven (harb.) F 1
Sheeps (head) B 8
Sherkin (isl.), 82 C 9
Silvermine (mts.) E 6
Slaney (riv.) H 7
Slieve Aughty (mts.) D 5
Slieve Bloom (mts.) F 5
Slieve Gamph (mts.) D 3
Slievenaman (mt.) F 7
Sligo (bay) D 3
Slyne (head) A 5
South (sound) C 5
Stacks (mts.) B 7
Suck (riv.) E 5
Suir (riv.) G 7
Swilly (inlet) F 1
Tara (hill) H 4
Tory (isl.), 273 E 1
Tory (sound) E 1
Tralee (bay) B 7
Trawbreaga (bay) F 1
Ulster (part) (prov.), 207,204 G 2
Valencia (Valentia) (isl.), 770 A 8
Valentia (isl.), 770 A 8
Waterford (harb.) G 7
Wexford (bay) J 7
Wicklow (head) K 6
Wicklow (mts.) J 6
Youghal (bay) F 8

NORTHERN IRELAND

DISTRICTS

Antrim, 37,600 J 2
Ards, 52,100 K 2
Armagh, 47,500 H 3
Ballymena, 52,200 J 2
Ballymoney, 22,700 J 1
Bainbridge, 28,800 J 3
Belfast, 368,200 J 2
Carrickfergus, 27,500 K 2
Castlereagh, 63,600 K 2
Coleraine, 44,900 H 1
Cookstown, 27,500 H 2
Craigavon, 71,200 J 3
Down, 48,800 K 3
Dungannon, 43,000 H 3
Fermanagh, 50,900 F 3
Larne, 29,000 K 2
Limavady, 25,000 H 1
Lisburn, 80,800 J 2
Londonderry, 86,600 G 2
Magherafelt, 32,200 H 2
Mourne (Newry and Mourne), 75,300 J 3
Moyle, 13,400 J 1
Newtownabbey, 71,500 J 2
North Down, 59,600 K 2
Omagh, 41,800 G 2
Strabane, 35,500 G 2

CITIES and TOWNS

Ahoghill, ‡1,929 J 2
Annalong, 1,001 K 3
Antrim, 8,351 J 2
Ardglass, 1,052 K 3
Armagh, 13,606 H 3
Armoy, ‡1,051 J 1
Augher, ‡1,986 G 3
Aughnacloy, ‡1,885 H 3
Ballycastle, 2,899 J 1
Ballyclare, 5,155 J 2
Ballygawley, ‡2,165 G 3
Ballykelly, 1,116 G 1
Ballymena, 23,386 J 2
Ballymoney, 5,697 J 1
Ballynahinch, 3,485 J 3
Banbridge, 7,968 J 3
Bangor, 35,260 K 2
Belfast (cap.), 353,700 J 2
Belfast, *551,940 J 2
Bellaghy, ‡2,265 H 2
Belleek, ‡2,487 E 3
Beragh, ‡2,137 G 2
Bessbrook, 2,619 J 3
Brookeborough, ‡2,534 G 3
Broughshane, 1,288 J 2
Bushmills, 1,288 J 1
Caledon, ‡1,828 H 3
Carnlough, 1,416 J 2
Carrickfergus, 16,603 K 2
Carrowdore, 2,548 K 2
Castledawson, 1,162 H 2
Castlederg, 1,766 F 2
Castlewellan, 1,488 K 3
Claudy, ‡2,507 G 2
Clogher, ‡1,888 G 3
Coalisland, 3,614 H 2
Coleraine, 16,354 H 1
Comber, 5,575 K 2
Cookstown, 6,965 H 2
Craigavon, 12,740 J 3
Crossgar, 1,098 K 3
Crossmaglen, 1,085 H 3
Crumlin, 1,450 J 2
Cullybackey, 1,649 J 2
Derrygonnelly, ‡2,539 F 3
Dervock, ‡1,191 J 1
Donaghadee, 4,008 K 2
Downpatrick, 7,918 K 3
Draperstown, ‡2,247 H 2
Dromore, Bainbridge, 2,848 J 3
Dromore, Omagh, ‡2,224 G 3
Drumquin, ‡1,982 F 2
Dundrum, ‡2,245 K 3
Dungannon, 8,190 H 3
Dungiven, 1,536 H 2
Dunnamanagh, ‡2,242 G 2
Ederny and Kesh, ‡2,497 F 2
Enniskillen, 9,679 F 3
Feeny, ‡1,459 H 2
Fintona, 1,190 G 3
Fivemiletown, ‡1,649 G 3
Garvagh, ‡2,363 H 2
Gilford, 1,592 J 3
Glenarm, ‡1,728 J 2
Glenavy, ‡2,360 J 2
Glynn, ‡1,872 K 2
Gortin, ‡2,033 G 2
Greyabbey, ‡2,646 K 2
Hillsborough, 1,021 J 3
Holywood, 9,892 K 2
Irvinestown, 1,457 F 3
Keady, 2,145 H 3
Kells, ‡2,560 J 2
Kesh, ‡2,497 F 3
Kilkeel, 4,090 K 3
Killough, ‡3,295 K 3
Killyleagh, 2,359 K 3
Kilrea, 1,196 H 2
Kircubbin, 1,075 K 3
Larne, 18,482 K 2
Limavady, 6,004 H 1
Lisburn, 31,836 J 2
Lisnaskea, 1,443 G 3
Londonderry, 51,200 G 2
Loughbrickland, ‡2,056 J 3
Maghera, 2,085 H 2
Magherafelt, 4,704 H 2
Markethill, ‡2,352 H 3
Millisle, 1,172 K 2
Moneymore, 1,178 H 2
Moy, ‡2,349 H 3
Moygashel, 1,086 H 3
Newcastle, 4,647 J 3
Newry, 20,279 J 3
Newtownabbey, 58,114 K 2
Newtownards, 15,484 K 2
Newtownbutler, ‡2,663 G 3
Newtownhamilton, ‡1,936 H 3
Newtownstewart, 1,433 G 2
Omagh, 14,594 G 2
Pomeroy, ‡1,786 H 2
Portaferry, 1,730 K 3
Portavogie, 1,310 K 3
Portglenone, ‡2,061 H 2
Portrush, 5,376 H 1
Portstewart, 5,085 H 1
Randalstown, 2,799 J 2
Rathfriland, 1,886 J 3
Rostrevor, 1,617 J 3
Saintfield, ‡2,198 K 3
Sion Mills, 1,588 G 2
Sixmilecross, ‡1,980 G 2
Stewartstown, ‡1,759 H 2
Strabane, 9,413 G 2
Strangford, ‡1,987 K 3
Tandragee, 1,725 J 3
Tempo, ‡2,282 G 3
Trillick, ‡2,167 G 3
Warrenpoint, 4,291 J 3
Whitehead, 2,642 K 2

OTHER FEATURES

Bann (riv.) H 2
Belfast (inlet) K 2
Blackwater (riv.) H 3
Bush (riv.) H 1
Derg (riv.) F 2
Divis (mt.) J 2
Dundrum (bay) K 3
Erne (lake) F 3
Foyle (inlet) G 1
Foyle (riv.) G 2
Giant's Causeway H 1
Lagan (riv.) K 2
Larne (inlet) K 2
Magee, Island (pen.), 1,581 K 2
Magilligan (pt.) H 1
Main (riv.) J 2
Mourne (mts.) J 3
Mourne (riv.) G 2
Neagh (lake) J 2
North (chan.) K 1
Rathlin (isl.), 109 J 1
Red (bay) K 1
Roe (riv.) H 1
Saint John's (pt.) K 3
Slieve Donard (mt.) K 3
Sperrin (mts.) G 2
Strangford (inlet) K 3
Torr (head) K 1
Ulster (part) (prov.), 1,537,200 G 2
Upper Lough Erne (lake) F 3

*City and suburbs.
‡Population of district.

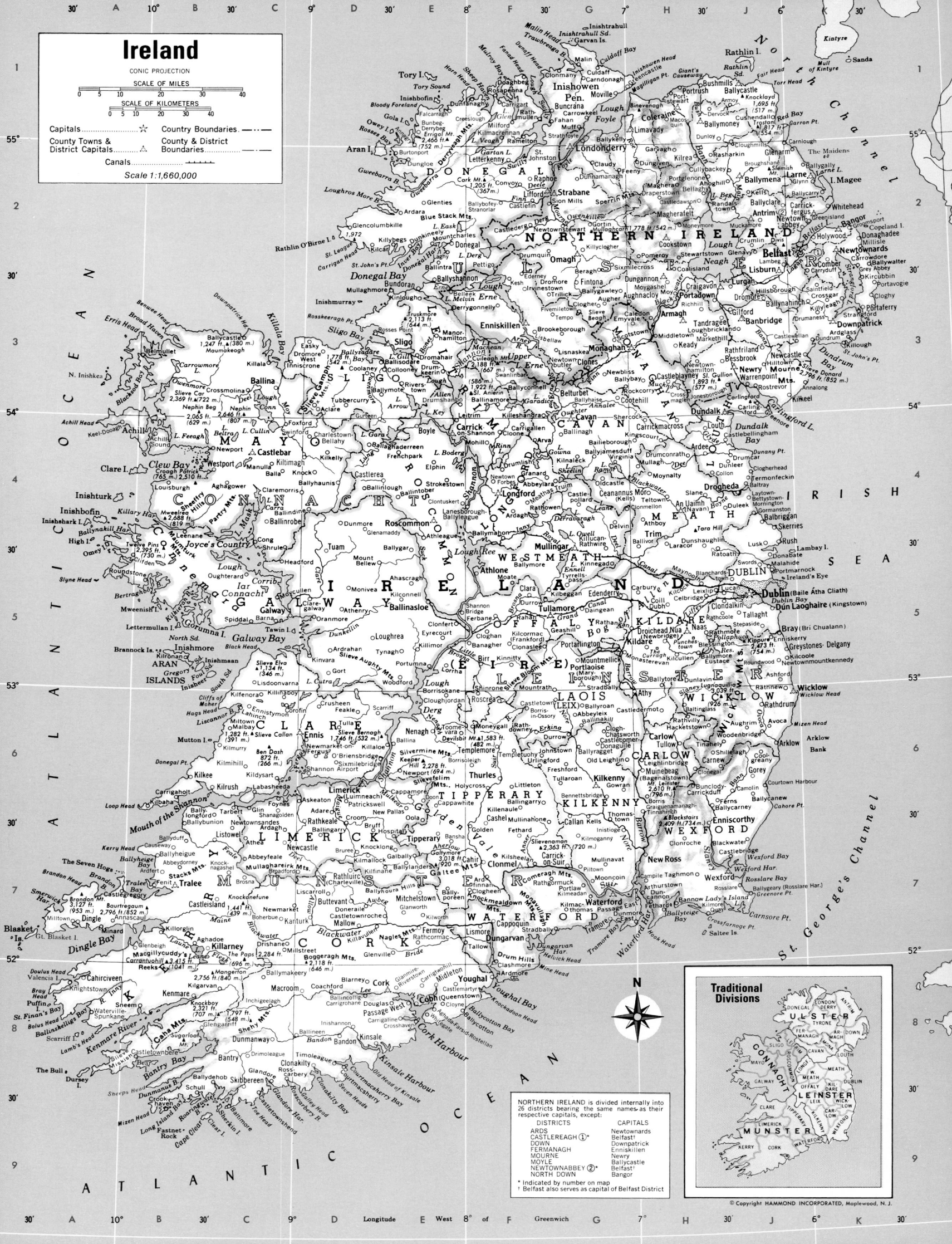

Ireland

CONIC PROJECTION

SCALE OF MILES

SCALE OF KILOMETERS

Capitals .... ☆   Country Boundaries. — · · —
County Towns &
District Capitals .... △   County & District
                                    Boundaries. — — —
Canals ....

Scale 1:1,660,000

Traditional Divisions

NORTHERN IRELAND is divided internally into 26 districts bearing the same names as their respective capitals, except:

DISTRICTS	CAPITALS
ARDS	Newtownards
CASTLEREAGH ① *	Belfast†
DOWN	Downpatrick
FERMANAGH	Enniskillen
MOURNE	Newry
MOYLE	Ballycastle
NEWTOWNABBEY ② *	Belfast†
NORTH DOWN	Bangor

* Indicated by number on map
† Belfast also serves as capital of Belfast District

© Copyright HAMMOND INCORPORATED, Maplewood, N.J.

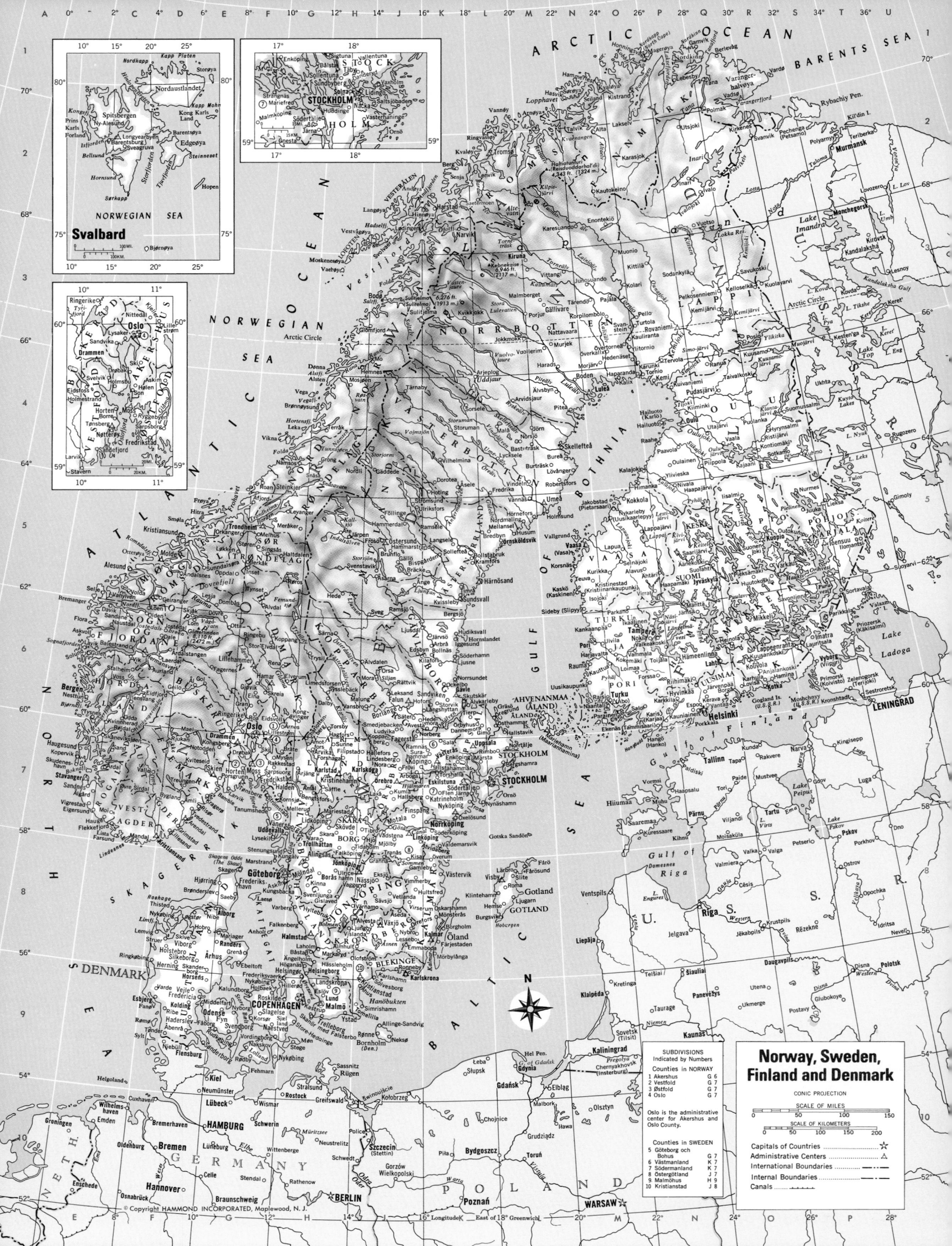

Svalbard

NORWEGIAN SEA

Norway, Sweden, Finland and Denmark

CONIC PROJECTION

SCALE OF MILES
0   50   100   150

SCALE OF KILOMETERS
0   50   100   150   200

Capitals of Countries .... ☆
Administrative Centers .... △
International Boundaries .... ·—·—·
Internal Boundaries ....
Canals ....

SUBDIVISIONS
Indicated by Numbers

Counties in NORWAY
1 Akershus   G 6
2 Vestfold   G 7
3 Østfold   G 7
4 Oslo   G 7

Oslo is the administrative
center for Akershus and
Oslo County.

Counties in SWEDEN
5 Göteborg och
  Bohus   G 7
6 Västmanland   K 7
7 Södermanland   K 7
8 Östergötland   J 7
9 Malmöhus   H 9
10 Kristianstad   J 8

© Copyright HAMMOND INCORPORATED, Maplewood, N.J.

AREA 125,053 sq. mi. (323,887 sq. km.)
POPULATION 4,092,000
CAPITAL Oslo
LARGEST CITY Oslo
HIGHEST POINT Glittertinden 8,110 ft. (2,472 m.)
MONETARY UNIT krone
MAJOR LANGUAGE Norwegian
MAJOR RELIGION Protestantism

AREA 173,665 sq. mi. (449,792 sq. km.)
POPULATION 8,320,000
CAPITAL Stockholm
LARGEST CITY Stockholm
HIGHEST POINT Kebnekaise 6,946 ft. (2,117 m.)
MONETARY UNIT krona
MAJOR LANGUAGE Swedish
MAJOR RELIGION Protestantism

AREA 130,128 sq. mi. (337,032 sq. km.)
POPULATION 4,788,000
CAPITAL Helsinki
LARGEST CITY Helsinki
HIGHEST POINT Haltiatunturi 4,343 ft. (1,324 m.)
MONETARY UNIT markka
MAJOR LANGUAGES Finnish, Swedish
MAJOR RELIGION Protestantism

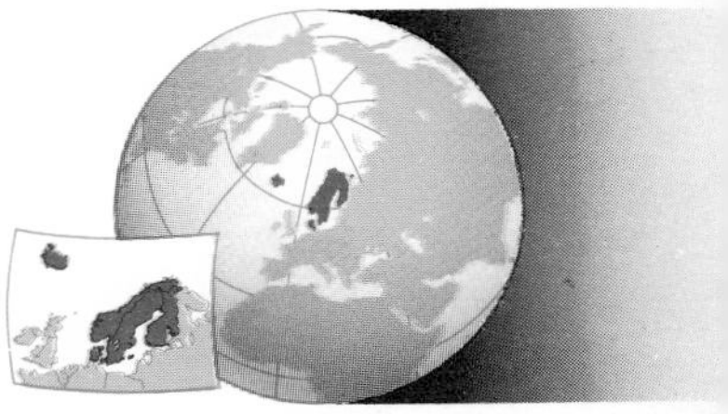

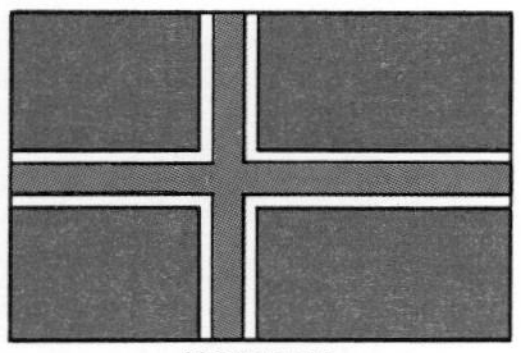

NORWAY

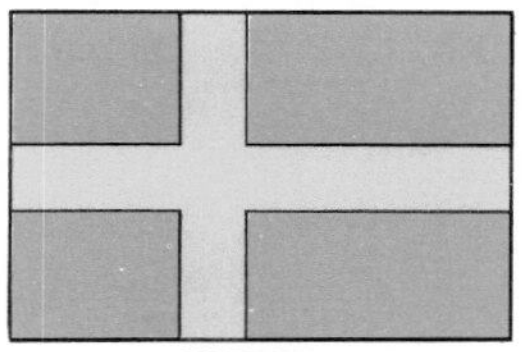

SWEDEN

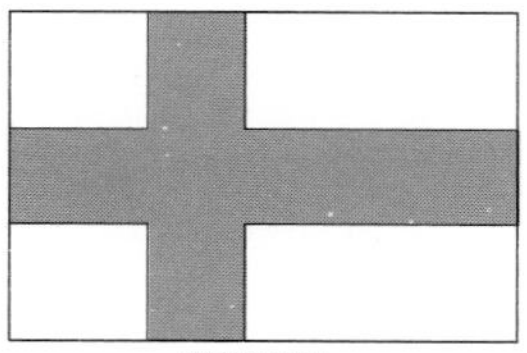

FINLAND

FINLAND

PROVINCES

Ahvenanmaa 22,380 ... L6
Åland (Ahvenanmaa) 22,380 ... L6
Häme 662,500 ... O6
Keski-Suomi 241,770 ... O5
Kuopio 252,023 ... P5
Kymi 346,478 ... Q6
Lappi 196,792 ... P3
Mikkeli 211,453 ... P6
Oulu 406,309 ... P4
Pohjois-Karjala 179,065 ... Q5
Turku ja Pori 697,988 ... N6
Uusimaa 1,085,625 ... O6
Vaasa 425,283 ... N5

CITIES and TOWNS

Äänekoski 10,725 ... O5
Åbo (Turku) 164,857 ... N6
Alavus 10,285 ... N5
Borgaå 18,740 ... O6
Ekenäs 7,391 ... N6
Espoo 117,090 ... O6
Forssa 18,442 ... N6
Haapajärvi 7,791 ... O5
Hämeenlinna 40,761 ... O6
Hamina 11,055 ... P6
Hangö 10,374 ... N7
Hanko (Hangö) 10,374 ... N7
Harjavalta 8,445 ... M6
Heinola 15,350 ... P6
Helsinki (cap.) 502,961 ... O6
Helsinki* 794,746 ... O6
Huutokoski† 6,458 ... P5
Hyvinkää 35,865 ... O6
Iisalmi 21,159 ... P5
Ikaalinen 8,364 ... N6
Imatra 35,590 ... Q6
Ivalo 2,661 ... P2
Jakobstad 20,397 ... N5
Jämsä 12,526 ... O6
Järvenpää 16,259 ... O6
Joensuu 41,429 ... R5
Jyväskylä 61,209 ... O5
Jyväskylä* 84,185 ... O5
Kajaani 20,583 ... P4
Kalajoki 3,624 ... N4
Kankaanpää 12,564 ... M6
Karhula 21,834 ... P6
Karis 8,152 ... N6
Karjaa (Karis) 8,152 ... N6
Karkkila 8,678 ... N6
Kauniainien 6,219 ... O6
Kauttua 3,297 ... M6
Kelloselkä† 8,200 ... Q3
Kemi 27,893 ... O4
Kemijärvi 12,951 ... P3
Kerava 19,966 ... O6
Kokemäki 10,188 ... N6
Kokkola 22,096 ... N5
Kotka 34,026 ... P6
Kotka* 60,235 ... P6
Kouvola 29,383 ... P6
Kouvola* 59,507 ... P6
Kristiinankaupunki (Kristinestad) 9,331 ... N5
Kristinestad 9,331 ... N5
Kuhmo 4,150 ... Q4
Kuopio 71,684 ... Q5
Kurikka 11,177 ... M5
Kuusamo 4,449 ... Q4
Kuusankoski 22,342 ... P6
Lahti 94,864 ... O6
Lahti* 112,129 ... O6
Lappeenranta 52,682 ... P6
Lapua 15,189 ... N5
Lieksa 20,274 ... R5
Loimaa 6,575 ... N6
Lovisa 8,674 ... P6
Maarianhamina (Mariehamn) 9,574 ... M7
Mänttä 7,910 ... O6
Mariehamn 9,574 ... M7
Mikkeli 27,112 ... P6
Naantali 7,814 ... M6
Nokia 22,308 ... N6
Nurmes 11,721 ... Q5
Nykarleby 7,408 ... N5
Oulainen 7,322 ... O4
Oulu 93,707 ... O4
Oulu* 103,044 ... O4
Outokumpu 10,736 ... Q5
Parainen 10,170 ... M6
Parkano 8,518 ... N6
Pieksämäki 12,923 ... P5
Pietarsaari (Jakobstad) 20,397 ... N5
Pori 80,343 ... M6
Pori* 86,635 ... M6
Posio† 6,205 ... Q3
Pudasjärvi† 12,594 ... P4
Raahe 15,379 ... O4
Raisio 14,271 ... M6
Rauma 29,081 ... M6
Riihimäki 24,106 ... O6
Rovaniemi 28,411 ... O3
Saarijärvi 2,714 ... O5
Salo 19,176 ... N6
Savonlinna 28,336 ... Q6
Seinäjoki 22,123 ... N5
Sodankylä 3,304 ... P3
Sotkamo 2,316 ... Q4
Suolahti 5,936 ... O5
Suonenjoki 9,286 ... P5
Tammisaari (Ekenäs) 7,391 ... N6
Tampere 168,118 ... N6
Tampere* 220,920 ... N6
Toijala 8,080 ... N6
Tornio 19,971 ... O4
Turku 164,857 ... N6
Turku* 217,423 ... N6
Turtola† 5,852 ... O3
Ulvila† 8,040 ... N6
Uusikaarlepyy (Nykarleby) 7,408 ... N5
Uusikaupunki 11,915 ... M6
Vaasa 54,402 ... M5
Vaasa* 58,224 ... M5
Valkeakoski 22,588 ... N6
Vammala 16,363 ... N6
Varkaus 24,450 ... Q5
Vasa (Vaasa) 54,402 ... M5
Vuotso† 10,186 ... P2
Ylivieska 10,827 ... O4

OTHER FEATURES

Åland (isls.) ... L6
Baltic (sea) ... K9
Bothnia (gulf) ... M5
Finland (gulf) ... P7
Hailuoto (isl.) ... O4
Haltiatunturi (mt.) ... M2
Hangöudd (prom.) ... N7
Haukivesi (lake) ... Q5
Iijoki (riv.) ... O4
Inari (lake) ... P2
Ivalojoki (riv.) ... P2
Juojärvi (lake) ... Q5
Kalajoki (riv.) ... O4
Kallavesi (lake) ... P5
Karlö (Hailuoto) (isl.) ... O4
Keitele (lake) ... O5
Kemijärvi (lake) ... Q3
Kemijcki (riv.) ... O3
Kiantajärvi (lake) ... Q4
Kilpisjärvi (lake) ... M2
Kitinen (riv.) ... P3
Kivijärvi (lake) ... O5
Koitere (lake) ... R5
Kuusamojärvi (lake) ... Q4
Längelmävesi (lake) ... O6
Lapland (reg.) ... O2
Lappajärvi (lake) ... O5
Lapuanjoki (riv.) ... N5
Lestijärvi (lake) ... O5
Lokka (res.) ... Q3
Muojärvi (lake) ... R4
Muonio (riv.) ... M2
Näsijärvi (lake) ... O6
Onkivesi (lake) ... P5
Orihvesi (lake) ... Q5
Oulujärvi (lake) ... P4
Oulujoki (riv.) ... O4
Ounasjoki (riv.) ... O3
Päijänne (lake) ... O6
Pielinen (lake) ... Q5
Puruvesi (lake) ... Q6
Puulavesi (lake) ... P5
Pyhäjärvi (lake) ... O5
Pyhäjärvi (lake) ... M6
Saimaa (lake) ... Q6
Siikajoki (riv.) ... O4
Simojärvi (lake) ... P3
Simojoki (riv.) ... O4
Tana (riv.) ... P2
Tornio (riv.) ... O3
Vallgrund (isl.) ... M5
Ylikitka (lake) ... Q3

NORWAY

COUNTIES

Akershus 355,196 ... G6
Aust-Agder 86,216 ... E7
Buskerud 209,684 ... F6
Finnmark 79,373 ... O2
Hedmark 183,465 ... G6
Hordaland 386,492 ... E6
Møre og Romsdal 231,944 ... E5
Nordland 243,233 ... J3
Nord-Trøndelag 122,886 ... H4
Oppland 178,259 ... F6
Oslo (city) 462,732 ... D3
Østfold 228,546 ... G7
Rogaland 287,653 ... E7
Sogn og Fjordane 103,135 ... E6
Sør-Trøndelag 241,361 ... G5
Telemark 158,853 ... F7
Troms 144,111 ... L2
Vest-Agder 131,659 ... E7
Vestfold 182,433 ... G7

CITIES and TOWNS

Ålesund 40,868 ... D5
Ålgård 2,322 ... D7
Alta 5,582 ... N2
Åndalsnes 2,574 ... F5
Årdalstangen 2,360 ... F6
Arendal 11,701 ... F7
Arendal* 21,228 ... F7
Årnes 2,267 ... G6
Askim 8,413 ... E4
Bamble† 7,031 ... F7
Barentsburg ... C2
Bergen 213,434 ... D6
Bodø 31,077 ... J3
Borge† 3,294 ... H2
Brønnøysund 3,130 ... G4
Dombås 1,114 ... F5
Drammen 50,777 ... C4
Drammen* 56,521 ... C4
Drøbak 4,538 ... D4
Eidsvoll 2,906 ... G6
Eigersund 11,379 ... D7
Elverum 7,391 ... G6
Farsund 8,908 ... E7
Flekkefjord 8,750 ... E7
Flora 8,822 ... D6
Fredrikstad 29,024 ... D4
Fredrikstad* 51,141 ... D4
Gjøvik 25,963 ... G6
Grimstad 13,091 ... F7
Halden 27,087 ... G7
Hamar 16,418 ... G6
Hamar* 25,138 ... G6
Hammerfest 7,610 ... N1
Hammerfest* 8,005 ... N1
Harstad 21,125 ... K2
Haugesund 27,386 ... D7
Haugesund* 29,277 ... D7
Hermansverk 706 ... E6
Holmestrand 8,246 ... C4
Holmsbu 273 ... D4
Honningsvag 3,780 ... O1
Horten 13,746 ... D4
Horten* 17,246 ... D4
Kirkenes 4,466 ... Q2
Kongsberg 19,854 ... F7
Kongsvinger 16,146 ... H6
Kopervik 4,221 ... D7
Kornsjø† 6,079 ... G7
Kragerø 5,249 ... F7
Kristiansand 59,488 ... F8
Kristiansund 18,847 ... E5
Kvinnherad† 2,898 ... E6
Larvik 9,097 ... C4
Larvik* 19,202 ... C4
Lenvik† 11,098 ... L2
Levanger 5,066 ... G5
Lillehammer 21,248 ... F6
Lillesand 3,028 ... F7
Lillestrøm† 11,550 ... E3
Longyearbyen ... D2
Lysaker† 81,612 ... D3
Mandal 11,579 ... E7
Meråker† 2,907 ... G5
Mo 21,033 ... J3
Molde 20,334 ... E5
Mosjøen 9,341 ... H4
Moss 25,786 ... D4
Moss* 27,430 ... D4
Mysen 3,760 ... G7
Namsos 11,452 ... G4
Narvik 19,582 ... K2
Nesttun† 11,519 ... D6
Nittedal† 8,889 ... D3
Notodden 12,970 ... F7
Nøtterøy 11,944 ... D4
Ny-Ålesund ... C2
Odda 7,401 ... E6
Oppdal 2,173 ... F5
Orkanger 3,685 ... F5
Oslo (cap.) 462,732 ... D3
Oslo* 645,413 ... D3
Porsgrunn 31,709 ... G7
Rakkestad 2,392 ... G7
Ringerike 30,156 ... C3
Risør 6,560 ... F7
Rjukan 5,334 ... F7
Røros 3,041 ... G5
Sandefjord 33,350 ... C4
Sandnes 33,934 ... D7
Sandvika† 34,337 ... C3
Sarpsborg 12,889 ... D4
Sarpsborg* 36,449 ... D4
Selje† 3,386 ... D5
Ski 9,081 ... D4
Skien 47,105 ... F7
Stavanger 86,639 ... D7
Stavern 2,604 ... D4
Steinkjer 20,553 ... G4
Stor-Elvdal† 2,993 ... G6
Sunndalsøra 5,114 ... F5
Sveagruva ... D2
Svolvaer 3,942 ... J2
Tønsberg 9,964 ... D4
Tønsberg* 36,374 ... D4
Tromsø 43,830 ... L2
Trondheim 134,910 ... F5
Ullensvang† 2,326 ... E6
Vadsø 6,019 ... Q1
Vardø 3,875 ... R1
Vik 1,019 ... E6
Volda 3,511 ... E5
Voss 5,944 ... E6

OTHER FEATURES

Alsten (isl.) ... H4
Andøya (isl.) ... J2
Barduelv (riv.) ... L2
Bellsund ... C2
Bjørnafjorden (fjord) ... D6
Bjornøya (isl.) ... D3
Boknafjord (fjord) ... D7
Bremanger (isl.) ... D6
Dønna (isl.) ... H3
Dovrefjell (hills) ... F5
Edgeøya (isl.) ... E2
Femundsjø (lake) ... G5
Folda (fjord) ... G4
Folda (fjord) ... J3
Frohavet (bay) ... F5
Frøya (isl.) ... F5
Glittertinden (mt.) ... F6
Hardangervidda (plat.) ... E6
Hardangerfjord (fjord) ... D7
Hinlopenstreten (str.) ... C1
Hinnøya (isl.) ... K2
Hitra (isl.) ... F5
Hopen (isl.) ... E2
Isfjorden (fjord) ... C2
Jostedalsbreen (glac.) ... E6
Kjölen (mts.) ... K3
Kongsfjorden (fjord) ... B2
Kvaløya (isl.) ... O1
Lågen (riv.) ... G6
Laksefjorden (fjord) ... P1
Langøy (isl.) ... J2
Lapland (reg.) ... K2
Leka (isl.) ... G4
Lindesnes (cape) ... E8
Lista (pen.) ... E7
Lofoten (isls.) ... H2
Lopphavet (bay) ... M1
Magerøya (isl.) ... P1
Moskenesøya (isl.) ... H3
Namsen (riv.) ... H4
Nordaustlandet (isl.) ... D1
Nordfjord (fjord) ... E6
Nordkapp (pt.) ... C1
Nordkinn (headland) ... Q1
Nordkinn (pen.) ... P1
North Cape (Nordkapp) (pt.) ... P1
Norwegian (sea) ... F3
Ofotfjorden (fjord) ... K2
Oslofjord (fjord) ... D4
Otra (riv.) ... E7
Otterøya (isl.) ... E5
Pasvikelv (riv.) ... Q2
Platen, Kapp (pt.) ... D1
Porsangen (fjord) ... O1
Rana (fjord) ... H3
Rauma (riv.) ... F5
Ringvassøy (isl.) ... L2
Romsdalsfjorden (fjord) ... E5
Saltfjorden (fjord) ... J3
Seiland (isl.) ... N1
Senja (isl.) ... K2
Skagerrak (str.) ... F8
Smøla (isl.) ... E5
Sognafjorden (fjord) ... D6
Sørkapp (pt.) ... C2
Sorøya (isl.) ... N1
Spitsbergen (isl.) ... C2
Storfjorden (fjord) ... D2
Sulitjelma (mt.) ... J3
Svalbard (isls.) ... C3
Tana (riv.) ... P1
Tanafjord (fjord) ... Q1
Tokke (riv.) ... F7
Trondheimsfjorden (fjord) ... G5
Tyrifjord (lake) ... C3
Vaerøy (isl.) ... H3
Vagåvatn (lake) ... F6
Vannøy (isl.) ... L1
Varangerhalvøya (pen.) ... Q1
Varangerfjord (fjord) ... Q2
Vega (isl.) ... G4
Vesterålen (isls.) ... J2
Vestfjord (fjord) ... H3
Vestvågøya (isl.) ... H3
Vikna (isls.) ... G4

SWEDEN

COUNTIES

Älvsborg 418,150 ... H7
Blekinge 155,391 ... J8
Gävleborg 294,595 ... K6
Göteborg och Bohus 714,660 ... G7
Gotland 54,447 ... L8
Halland 219,767 ... H8
Jämtland 133,559 ... J5
Jönköping 301,905 ... H8
Kalmar 240,768 ... K8
Kopparberg 281,082 ... J6
Kristianstad 272,090 ... J8

(continued on following page)

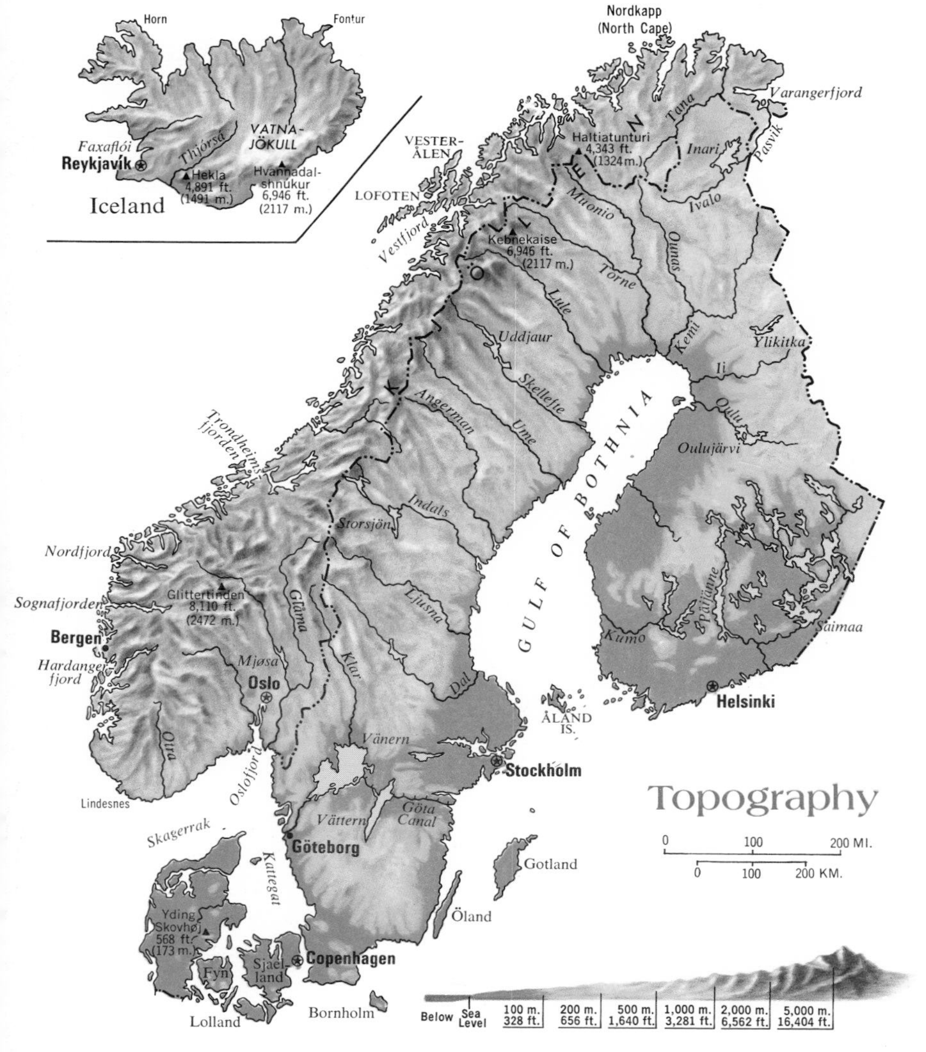
Horn
Fontur
Faxaflói
Reykjavík
Thjórsá
VATNA-JÖKULL
Hekla 4,891 ft. (1491 m.)
Hvannadal-shnúkur 6,946 ft. (2117 m.)
Iceland
Nordkapp (North Cape)
Varangerfjord
VESTER-ÅLEN
LOFOTEN
Vestfjord
Haltiatunturi 4,343 ft. (1324 m.)
Kebnekaise 6,946 ft. (2117 m.)
Inari
Ivalo
Muonio
Ounas
Torne
Lule
Uddjaur
Kemi
Ylikitka
Skellefte
Ume
Ångerman
Trondheimsfjorden
Oulujärvi
Storsjön
Indals
Nordfjord
Sognafjorden
Bergen
Glittertinden 8,110 ft. (2472 m.)
Glåma
Ljusna
Hardangerfjord
Mjøsa
Oslo
Klar
Dal
Saimaa
Kumo
Helsinki
ÅLAND IS.
Otra
Vänern
Stockholm
Lindesnes
Oslofjord
Vättern
Göta Canal
Skagerrak
Kattegat
Göteborg
Gotland
Öland
Yding Skovhøj 568 ft. (173 m.)
Sjælland
Fyn
Copenhagen
Lolland
Bornholm
Topography
0 100 200 MI.
0 100 200 KM.
Below Sea Level
100 m. 328 ft.
200 m. 656 ft.
500 m. 1,640 ft.
1,000 m. 3,281 ft.
2,000 m. 6,562 ft.
5,000 m. 16,404 ft.

Kronoberg 169,454 ... J8
Malmöhus 740,137 ... H9
Norrbotten 264,215 ... L3
Örebro 273,994 ... J7
Östergötland 387,104 ... J7
Skaraborg 263,382 ... H7
Södermanland 252,030 ... K7
Stockholm 1,493,052 ... L7
Uppsala 229,879 ... K7
Värmland 284,442 ... H7
Västerbotten 236,367 ... K4
Västernorrland 268,202 ... K5
Västmanland 259,872 ... K7

CITIES and TOWNS

Åhus 6,125 ... J9
Alingsås 18,892 ... H8
Almhult 7,390 ... H8
Alvesta 7,261 ... J8
Älvsbyn 4,707 ... M4
Åmål 9,556 ... H7
Ånge 3,760 ... J5
Angelholm 16,016 ... H8
Arboga 11,819 ... J7
Arbrå 2,734 ... K6
Årjäng 2,596 ... H7
Arvidsjaur 4,194 ... L4
Arvika 13,934 ... H7
Åseda 2,465 ... J8
Askim 17,609 ... G8
Åtvidaberg 8,436 ... K7
Avesta 19,095 ... J6
Bålsta 8,243 ... G1
Båstad 2,452 ... H8
Bengtsfors 3,535 ... H7
Boden 19,590 ... M4
Bollnäs 13,305 ... K6
Bollstabruk 3,548 ... L5
Borås 67,537 ... H8
Borås* 187,710 ... H8
Borgholm 2,789 ... K8
Borlänge 40,158 ... J6
Brunflo 3,460 ... J5
Dalby† 4,013 ... H6
Danderyd† 36,596 ... H1
Dannemora 291 ... K6
Edsbyn 4,388 ... J6
Eksjö 9,686 ... J8
Emmaboda 5,652 ... J8
Enköping 18,541 ... G1
Eskilstuna 66,409 ... K7
Eslöv 13,629 ... H9
Fagersta 14,778 ... J6
Falkenberg 14,148 ... H8
Falköping 15,126 ... H7
Falun 30,073 ... J6
Färjestaden 2,995 ... K8
Filipstad 7,835 ... H7
Finspång 16,346 ... K7
Flen 6,770 ... K7
Forshaga 6,000 ... H7
Fröso 10,274 ... J5
Frövi 2,583 ... J7
Gällivare 8,669 ... M3
Gamleby 3,666 ... J8
Gävle 67,454 ... K6

Gimo 3,154 ... K6
Gislaved 8,564 ... H8
Gnesta 3,835 ... G2
Göteborg 444,540 ... G8
Göteborg* 690,767 ... G8
Hagfors 8,060 ... H6
Hällefors 7,862 ... J6
Hallsberg 6,799 ... J7
Hallstahammar 13,583 ... J7
Hällstavik 5,162 ... L6
Hallstad 49,558 ... H8
Haparanda 5,031 ... N4
Härnösand 18,971 ... K5
Hässleholm 16,813 ... H8
Hedemora 7,039 ... J6
Helsingborg 80,986 ... H8
Helsingborg* 215,894 ... H8
Hjo 4,615 ... J7
Hofors 11,459 ... K6
Höganäs 10,866 ... H8
Holmsund 5,467 ... M5
Hörnefors 2,441 ... L5
Hudiksvall 15,004 ... K6
Hultsfred 5,763 ... J8
Husum 2,517 ... L5
Hyltebruk 3,469 ... H8
Iggesund 4,448 ... K6
Järna 6,237 ... G2
Jokkmokk 3,186 ... L3
Jönköping 78,650 ... H8
Jönköping* 131,499 ... H8
Kalix 7,668 ... N4
Kalmar 32,049 ... K8
Karlshamn 17,447 ... J8
Karlskoga 35,425 ... J7
Karlskrona 33,414 ... J8
Karlstad 51,243 ... H7
Katrineholm 22,884 ... K7
Kinna 13,676 ... H8
Kiruna 25,410 ... L3
Kisa 4,323 ... J7
Köping 20,059 ... J7
Kopparberg 3,942 ... J7
Kramfors 7,719 ... L5
Kristianstad 30,780 ... J8
Kristinehamn 21,146 ... H7
Kumla 11,451 ... J7
Kungälv 12,764 ... G8
Kungsbacka† 11,986 ... G8
Kvissleby 3,413 ... K5
Laholm 3,898 ... H8
Landskrona 29,486 ... H9
Långshyttan 2,744 ... K6
Laxå 5,166 ... J7
Leksand 4,410 ... J6
Lessebo 2,991 ... J8
Lidingö 30,086 ... H1
Lidköping 21,001 ... H7
Lindesberg 8,247 ... J7
Linköping 80,274 ... K7
Linköping† 132,839 ... K7
Ljungby 12,969 ... H8
Ljusdal 7,075 ... J6
Ljusne 3,578 ... K6
Ludvika 18,217 ... J6
Luleå 42,139 ... N4
Lund 55,047 ... H9

Lycksele 8,586 ... L4
Lysekil 7,815 ... G7
Malmberget 10,239 ... M3
Malmö 241,191 ... H9
Malmö* 453,339 ... H9
Malung 6,211 ... H6
Mariefred 2,553 ... F1
Mariestad 16,454 ... H7
Markaryd 4,266 ... H8
Märsta 17,066 ... K7
Marstrand 1,168 ... G8
Mellerud 3,579 ... H7
Mjölby 12,488 ... J7
Mölndal 47,248 ... H8
Monsterås 5,005 ... K8
Mora 8,772 ... J6
Motala 29,454 ... J7
Nacka 16,370 ... H1
Nässjö 18,634 ... J8
Nora 5,515 ... J7
Norberg 5,438 ... K6
Norrköping 85,244 ... K7
Norrköping* 163,206 ... K7
Norrtälje 12,784 ... L7
Nybro 13,010 ... J8
Nyköping 30,352 ... K7
Nynäshamn 11,070 ... L7
Ockelbo 2,810 ... K6
Olofström 10,096 ... J8
Örebro 117,877 ... J7
Örebro* 171,440 ... J7
Örnsköldsvik 29,514 ... L5
Orrefors 919 ... J8
Orsa 5,099 ... J6
Oskarshamn 19,021 ... K8
Östersund 40,056 ... J5
Östhammar 1,783 ... L6
Oxelösund 13,862 ... K7
Piteå 16,169 ... M4
Rättvik 4,087 ... J6
Rimbo 3,404 ... L7
Ronneby 12,086 ... J8
Saffle 11,428 ... H7
Sala 11,216 ... K7
Saltsjöbaden 8,113 ... J1
Sandviken 27,994 ... K6
Säter 4,297 ... J6
Sävsjö 4,913 ... J8
Sigtuna 4,780 ... H1
Simrishamn 5,834 ... J9
Skänör med Falsterbo 4,909 ... H9
Skara 10,138 ... H7
Skellefteå 29,353 ... M4
Skövde 29,945 ... H7
Skutskär 7,174 ... K6
Smedjebacken 8,418 ... J6
Söderhamn 14,673 ... K6
Söderköping 5,310 ... K7
Södertälje 58,408 ... G1
Sollefteå 8,923 ... K5
Sollentuna† 40,905 ... H1
Sölvesborg 7,292 ... J8
Stenungsund 8,361 ... G8
Stockholm (cap.) 665,550 ... G1
Stockholm* 1,357,183 ... G1
Storuman 2,587 ... K4
Storvik 2,748 ... K6

Strängnäs 10,255 ... F1
Strömstad 4,735 ... G7
Strömsund 4,119 ... K5
Sundbyberg† 27,058 ... K7
Sundsvall 52,268 ... K5
Sunne 4,273 ... H7
Surahammar 6,509 ... J7
Sveg 2,608 ... J5
Svenljunga 3,189 ... H8
Täby† 41,285 ... J7
Tibro 8,476 ... J7
Tidaholm 8,039 ... J7
Tierp 5,005 ... K6
Timrå 11,416 ... K5
Tomelilla 5,371 ... J9
Torsby 3,632 ... H6
Torshälla 8,231 ... K7
Tranås 14,854 ... J7
Trelleborg 22,559 ... H9
Trollhättan 42,499 ... H7
Trosa 3,128 ... K7
Uddevalla 32,700 ... G7
Ulricehamn 7,827 ... H8
Umeå 49,715 ... M5
Uppsala 101,850 ... K7
Uppsala* 157,202 ... K7
Vadstena 5,294 ... J7
Vaggeryd 3,974 ... J8
Valdemarsvik 3,558 ... K7
Vallentuna 9,037 ... H1
Vänersborg 20,510 ... G7
Vännäs 3,876 ... L5
Vansbro 2,708 ... H6
Vara 3,049 ... H7
Varberg 19,467 ... G8
Värnamo 15,726 ... H8
Västerås 98,858 ... K7
Västerås* 147,508 ... K7
Västerhaninge 14,125 ... H1
Västervik 21,239 ... K8
Vaxholm† 3,744 ... J1
Växjö 40,328 ... J8
Vetlanda 12,358 ... J8
Vilhelmina 4,060 ... K4
Vimmerby 7,405 ... J8
Virserum 2,495 ... J8
Visby 19,886 ... L8
Ystad 14,286 ... H9

OTHER FEATURES

Ångermanälven (riv.) ... K5
Åsnen (lake) ... J8
Baltic (sea) ... K9
Bolmen (lake) ... H8
Bothnia (gulf) ... N4
Dalälven (riv.) ... K6
Fårö (isl.) ... L7
Göta (canal) ... J7
Göta (riv.) ... H7
Gotland (isl.) ... L8
Gråsö (isl.) ... L6
Handöbukten (bay) ... J9
Hjälmaren (lake) ... K7
Hoburgen (cliff) ... K8
Hornslandet (pen.) ... K6
Indalsälven (riv.) ... H5
Kalixälv (riv.) ... N3

Kalmarsund (sound) ... K8
Kattegat (str.) ... G8
Kebnekaise (mt.) ... L3
Kölen (mts.) ... K3
Klarälv (riv.) ... H6
Lapland (reg.) ... M2
Ljusnan (riv.) ... H5
Luleälv (riv.) ... L4
Mälaren (lake) ... G1
Muonioälv (riv.) ... M2
Öland (isl.) ... K8
Öresund (sound) ... H9
Orrö (isl.) ... J2
Österdalälven (riv.) ... M4
Piteälv (riv.) ... L3
Siljan (lake) ... J6
Skagerrak (str.) ... F8
Sommen (lake) ... J8
Stora Lulevatten (lake) ... L3
Storsjön (lake) ... J5
Sulitelma (mt.) ... K3
Tornealv (riv.) ... M3
Torneälv (riv.) ... L4
Umeälv (riv.) ... L4
Vänern (lake) ... H7
Västerdalälven (riv.) ... H6
Vättern (lake) ... J7

*City and suburbs
†Population of commune
‡Population of parish

DENMARK
COUNTIES

Århus 534,333 ... D5
Bornholm 47,241 ... F6
Copenhagen (commune) 622,612 ... F6
Faerøe Islands 41,969 ... B2
Frederiksberg (commune) 101,874 ... F6
Frederiksborg 260,825 ... E5
Fyn 433,765 ... D7
København (Copenhagen) (commune) 622,612 ... F6
København 616,571 ... F6
Nordjylland 457,165 ... D4
Ribe 198,153 ... B7
Ringkøbing 242,006 ... B5
Roskilde 154,314 ... E6
Sønderjylland 238,502 ... C7
Storstrøm 252,780 ... E7
Vejle 306,809 ... C6
Vestsjaelland 259,484 ... E6
Viborg 221,002 ... C4

CITIES and TOWNS

Åbenrå 15,196 ... C7
Åbybro 2,897 ... C3
Åkirkeby 2,001 ... F9
Ålborg 154,582 ... D4
Ålestrup 1,926 ... C4

Århus 245,941 ... D5
Års 4,266 ... C4
Årup 1,675 ... D7
Æröskøbing 1,223 ... D8
Agerbaek 935 ... B6
Allinge 1,385 ... D5
Allinge-Sandvig 1,991 ... F8
Ansager 1,157 ... B6
Arden 1,303 ... C4
Aså 1,344 ... D3
Askov 904 ... C7
Asnaes 1,413 ... E6
Assens, Århus 1,341 ... D4
Assens, Fyn 5,139 ... D7
Augustenborg 2,628 ... D8
Auning 1,516 ... D5
Avlum 1,729 ... B5
Baelum 1,169 ... D4
Bagenkop 776 ... D8
Ballerup 50,673 ... F6
Bandholm 693 ... E7
Bedsted 965 ... B4
Birkerød 13,663 ... F6
Bjerringbro 4,761 ... C5
Bjerringbro 6,495 ... C7
Boldersclev 774 ... C8
Børkøp 1,410 ... C6
Borup 1,591 ...
Braedstrup 2,163 ... C6
Bramming 3,678 ... B7
Brande 4,784 ... B6
Bredebro 1,173 ... B7
Broager 2,143 ... C8
Brønderslev 10,247 ... C3
Brørup 2,584 ... C7
Brovst 4,200 ... C3
Bryrup 579 ... C5
Christiansfeld 1,994 ... C7
Copenhagen (cap.) 603,368 ... F6
Copenhagen* 1,327,940 ... F6
Dronningmål 4,661 ... D3
Dybvad 805 ... D3
Ebeltoft 3,017 ... D5
Egernsund 1,323 ... C8
Egtved 1,311 ... C6
Ejby 1,372 ... C7
Esbjerg 68,097 ... B7
Fåborg 6,495 ... D7
Fakse 2,720 ... F7
Fakse Ladeplads 1,799 ... F7
Farsø 2,437 ... C4
Farum 9,936 ... F6
Fjerritslev 2,134 ... C3
Fredensborg 4,709 ... F6
Fredericia 36,157 ... C6
Frederikshavn 24,846 ... D3
Frederikssund 11,272 ... E6
Frederiksvaerk 8,903 ... E6
Fuglebjerg 1,094 ... E7
Gedser 1,200 ...
Gedsted 1,006 ... C4
Gelsted 1,307 ... C7
Gentofte 77,744 ... F6
Gilleleje 2,943 ... F5
Give 2,366 ... C6
Glamsbjerg 2,226 ... D7
Glostrup 28,326 ... F6
Glumsø 1,027 ... E7
Glyngøre 1,071 ... C4
Gørding 1,261 ... B7
Gørlev 1,542 ... E7
Graested 1,654 ... F5
Gram 2,061 ... C7
Gråsten 2,947 ... C8
Grenå 12,569 ... D5
Grindsted 7,558 ... B6
Hårby 1,506 ... D7

Haderslev 20,042 ... C7
Hadsten 3,914 ... C5
Hadsund 3,652 ... D4
Hals 1,654 ... D3
Hammel 3,247 ... C5
Hammerum 3,227 ... C5
Hanstholm 1,716 ... B3
Harboør 1,359 ... B4
Hårlev 1,228 ... F7
Hasle 18 ...
Haslev 6,925 ... E7
Havdrup 1,833 ...
Hedensted 2,659 ... C6
Hellebaek 2,911 ... F5
Helsinge 3,613 ...
Helsingør 42,425 ... F5
Herning 32,973 ... B5
Hirtshals 6,861 ... C2
Hjallerup 1,573 ... D3
Hobro 8,737 ... C4
Højer 1,416 ... B8
Højerup 19,485 ... C6
Holeby 1,434 ... E8
Holstebro 25,006 ... B5
Holsted 1,390 ... B6
Høng 2,488 ... E7
Hornslet 2,561 ... D5
Horsens 44,120 ... C6
Hørsholm 19,346 ... F6
Hørve 1,139 ... E6
Hov 635 ... D6
Humlum 546 ... B4
Hundested 5,443 ... E6
Hurup 2,287 ... B4
Hvide Sande 2,129 ... A5
Hvidbjerg 994 ... B4
Ikast 9,222 ... B5
Jelling 1,540 ... C6
Jerslev 798 ... D3
Juelsminde 1,991 ... D6
Jyderup 2,901 ... E6
Kalundborg 12,248 ... E6
Karise 1,184 ... F7
Karup 1,694 ... C5
Kastrup† 17,391 ... F6
Kerteminde 5,007 ... D7
Kibaek 1,279 ... B5
Kjellerup 3,245 ... C5
Klitmøller 542 ... B3
Køge 18,608 ... F7
Kolding 41,602 ... C7
Kolind 1,036 ... D5
Korsør 15,502 ... E7
Kvaerndrup 891 ... D7
Langaa 2,320 ... C5
Lem 1,203 ... B5
Lemvig 6,448 ... B4
Løgstør 3,633 ... C4
Løgumkloster 2,091 ... B7
Lohals 580 ... D7
Løt Kirkeby 1,203 ... C7
Løkken 1,345 ... C3
Løsning 1,467 ... C6
Lundby 747 ... D7
Lunderskov 1,494 ... C7
Lyngby 61,516 ... F6
Malling 1,584 ... D5
Manager 1,692 ... D4
Maribo 5,287 ... E8
Marstal 4,124 ... D8
Middelfart 13,315 ... C7

Agriculture, Industry and Resources

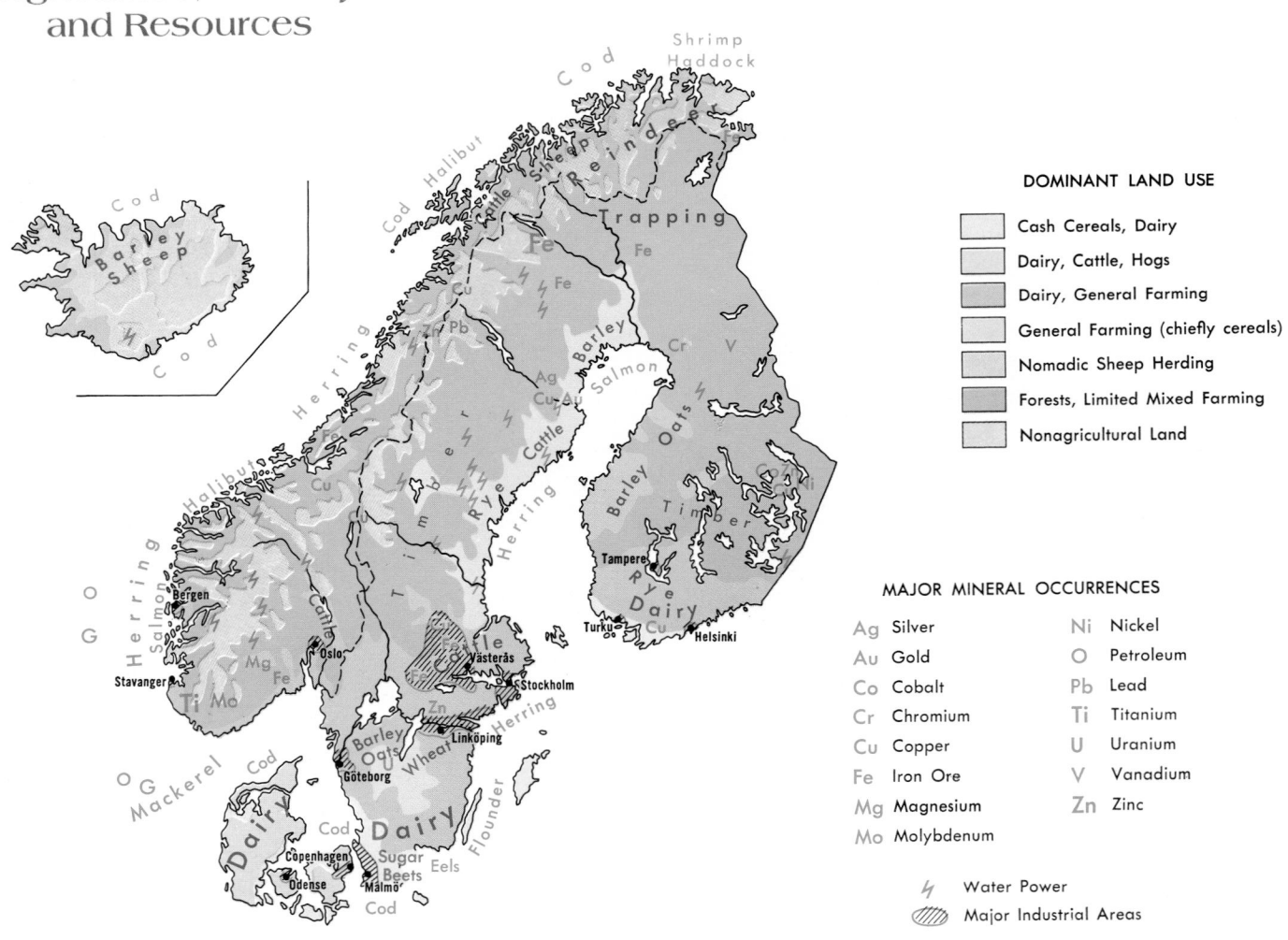

DOMINANT LAND USE

Cash Cereals, Dairy
Dairy, Cattle, Hogs
Dairy, General Farming
General Farming (chiefly cereals)
Nomadic Sheep Herding
Forests, Limited Mixed Farming
Nonagricultural Land

MAJOR MINERAL OCCURRENCES

Ag Silver
Au Gold
Co Cobalt
Cr Chromium
Cu Copper
Fe Iron Ore
Mg Magnesium
Mo Molybdenum

Ni Nickel
O Petroleum
Pb Lead
Ti Titanium
U Uranium
V Vanadium
Zn Zinc

⚡ Water Power
▨ Major Industrial Areas

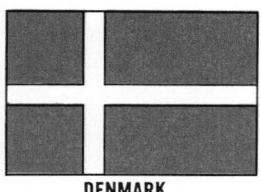

DENMARK

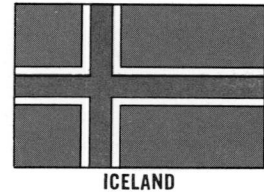

ICELAND

DENMARK
AREA 16,629 sq. mi. (43,069 sq. km.)
POPULATION 5,124,000
CAPITAL Copenhagen
LARGEST CITY Copenhagen
HIGHEST POINT Yding Skovhøj
568 ft. (173 m.)
MONETARY UNIT krone
MAJOR LANGUAGE Danish
MAJOR RELIGION Protestantism

ICELAND
AREA 39,768 sq. mi. (103,000 sq. km.)
POPULATION 228,785
CAPITAL Reykjavík
LARGEST CITY Reykjavík
HIGHEST POINT Hvannadalshnúkur
6,952 ft. (2,119 m.)
MONETARY UNIT króna
MAJOR LANGUAGE Icelandic
MAJOR RELIGION Protestantism

Møgeltønder 711 .... B8
Næstved 35,011 .... E7
Nakskov 16,393 .... E8
Neksø 3,527 .... F9
Nibe 2,796 .... C4
Nordborg 4,132 .... C7
Nordby, Ribe 2,084 .... C7
Nørre Åby 2,165 .... C7
Nørre Alslev 1,338 .... E8
Nørre Nebel 901 .... B6
Nørre Snede 1,461 .... C6
Nørre Voruper 644 .... B4
Nyborg 14,181 .... D7
Nørre Voruper 644 .... B4
Nykøbing, Storstrøm 20,059 .... F8
Nykøbing,
Vestsjælland 4,996 ....
Nykøbing, Viborg 9,066 .... B4
Nysted 1,229 .... E8
Odder 6,617 .... D6
Odense 168,178 .... D7
Ølgod 2,258 .... B6
Ørsted 1,093 .... D5
Øster Vrå 906 .... D3
Otterup 2,673 .... D7
Ovtrup 602 .... B6
Pandrup 1,525 .... C3
Præstø 2,789 .... F7
Ramme 506 .... B4
Randers 58,409 .... C5
Ranum 1,472 .... C4
Ribe 8,254 .... B7
Ringe 3,584 .... D7
Ringkøbing 6,298 .... A5
Ringsted 14,076 .... E7
Rødby 5,296 .... E8
Rødding 2,102 .... B7
Rødekro 2,246 .... C7
Rødkaersbro 1,098 .... C5
Rødvig 1,115 .... F7
Rømø 816 .... B7
Rønde 1,523 .... D5
Rønne 14,736 .... F8
Roskilde 44,248 .... E6
Roslev 1,058 .... C4
Rudkøbing 4,080 .... D8
Ruds Vedby 1,071 .... E7
Ry 2,699 .... C5
Ryomgård 1,000 .... D5
Saeby 5,430 .... D3
Sakskøbing 4,102 .... E8
Silkeborg 29,015 .... C5
Sindal 2,406 .... D3
Skælskør 4,585 .... E7
Skaerbaek 2,483 .... B7
Skagen 11,620 .... D2
Skals 960 .... C4
Skanderborg 11,344 .... D5
Skårup 1,216 .... C6
Skibby 1,549 .... E6
Skive 17,015 .... B4
Skjern 6,056 .... B6
Skodborg 935 .... C7
Skørping 1,675 .... C4
Slagelse 26,851 .... E7
Slangerup 3,036 .... E6
Snedsted 1,105 .... B4
Snedsted 1,105 .... B4
Sollested 960 .... E8
Sønderborg 24,526 .... C8
Sønder Omme 1,393 .... B6
Søndersø 885 .... D7
Sorø 8,683 .... E7
Støge 3,869 .... E6
Stenlille 1,014 .... E6
Stenstrup 1,245 .... D7
Stoholm 1,224 .... C4
Store Heddinge 2,630 .... F7
Støvring 2,366 .... C4
Strandby 1,017 .... D3
Struer 10,848 .... B5
Stubbekøbing 2,031 .... E8
Svaneke 1,193 .... F8
Svendborg 24,203 .... D7
Svinninge 1,797 .... E6
Tarm 3,150 .... B6
Tårnby 45,661 .... F6
Tåstrup 30,608 .... F6
Them 511 .... C5
Thisted 11,252 .... B4
Thyborøn 2,425 .... A4
Thyregod 1,001 .... C6
Tim 553 .... B5
Tinglev 1,531 .... C8
Tistrup 762 .... B6
Toftlund 2,147 .... B7
Tinglev 1,982 .... E6
Tønder 7,469 .... B8
Terring 1,537 .... C6
Tranebjerg 657 .... D6
Troense 771 .... D7
Trustrup 794 .... D5
Uldum 885 .... C6
Ulfborg 1,357 .... B5
Vamdrup 3,111 .... C7
Varde 11,615 .... B6
Vejen 6,213 .... C7
Vejle 43,976 .... C6
Vemb 989 .... B5
Vester Skerninge 603 .... D7
Vestervig 747 .... B4
Vester 27,441 .... C5
Vig 1,549 .... E6
Videbaek 2,248 .... B5
Vildbjerg 1,500 .... B5
Vinderup 2,284 .... B5
Vojens 5,595 .... C7
Vorbasse 796 .... B6
Vordingborg 11,639 .... E7

Vraá 2,652 .... C3

OTHER FEATURES

AErø (isl.) D8
Als (isl.) C8
Amager (isl.) F6
Anholt (isl.) E4
Arø (isl.) C7
Baagø (isl.) C7
Baltic (sea) E9
Bornholm (isl.) F9
Endelave (isl.) D6
Falster (isl.) E8
Fanø (isl.) B7
Fehmarn (str.) E8
Fejø (isl.) E8
Femø (isl.) E8
Frisian, North (isls.) B7
Fyn (isl.) D7
Gelsaa (riv.) C5
Gudenaa (riv.) C5
Isefjord (fjord) E6
Jutland (pen.) C5
Jylland (Jutland)
(pen.) C5
Kattegat (str.) E4
Laesø (isl.) D3
Langeland (isl.) D8
Lille Baelt (chan.) C7
Limfjorden (fjord) A4
Løgstør Bredning (fjord) C4
Lolland (isl.) E8
Møn (isl.) F7
Mors (isl.) B4
North (sea) B9
North Frisian (isls.) B7
Ømø (isl.) E7
Øresund (sound) F6
Rømø (isl.) B7
Samsø (isl.) D6
Sejerø (isl.) E6
Sjaelland (isl.) E6
Skagens Odde (cape) D2
Skagerrak (str.) C2
Skaw, The (Skagens Odde)
(cape) D2
Storaa (riv.) B5
Store Baelt (chan.) D6
Susaá (riv.) E7
The Skaw (Skagens Odde)
(cape) D2
Tranebjerg (pt.) C6
Yding Skovhøj (mt.) C6

FÆRØE ISLANDS

CITIES and TOWNS

Klaksvik 4,536 .... B2
Tórshavn (cap.), Faerøe
Is. 11,618 .... A3

OTHER FEATURES

Faerøe (isls.) B2
Sandoy (isl.) B3
Streymoy (isl.) B3
Sudhuroy (isl.) B3

ICELAND

CITIES and TOWNS

Akranes 4,253 .... B1
Akureyri 10,755 .... C1
Hafnarfjørdhur 9,696 .... B2
Húsavík 1,993 .... C1
Isafjørdhur 2,680 .... B1
Keflavík 5,663 .... B1
Kópavogur 11,165 .... B1
Nes (Neskaupstadhur) 1,552 .... D1
Neskaupstadhur 1,552 .... D1
Ólafsfjørdhur 1,086 .... C1
Reykjavík (cap.) 81,693 .... B1
Saudhárkrókur 1,600 .... C1
Seydhisfjørdhur 884 .... D1
Siglufjørdhur 2,161 .... C1
Vestmannaeyjar 5,186 .... B2

OTHER FEATURES

Bjargtangar (pt.) A1
Breidhafjørdhur (fjord) B1
Faxaflói (bay) B1
Fontur (pt.) D1
Gerpir (cape) D1
Grímsey (isl.) C1
Hekla (vol.) B1
Horn (cape) B1
Húnaflói (bay) B1
Hvannadalshnúkur (mt.) C1
North (Horn) (cape) B1
Reykjanes (cape) A2
Surtsey (isl.) B2
Thjórsá (riv.) C1
Vatnajökull (glac.) C1

*City and suburbs.

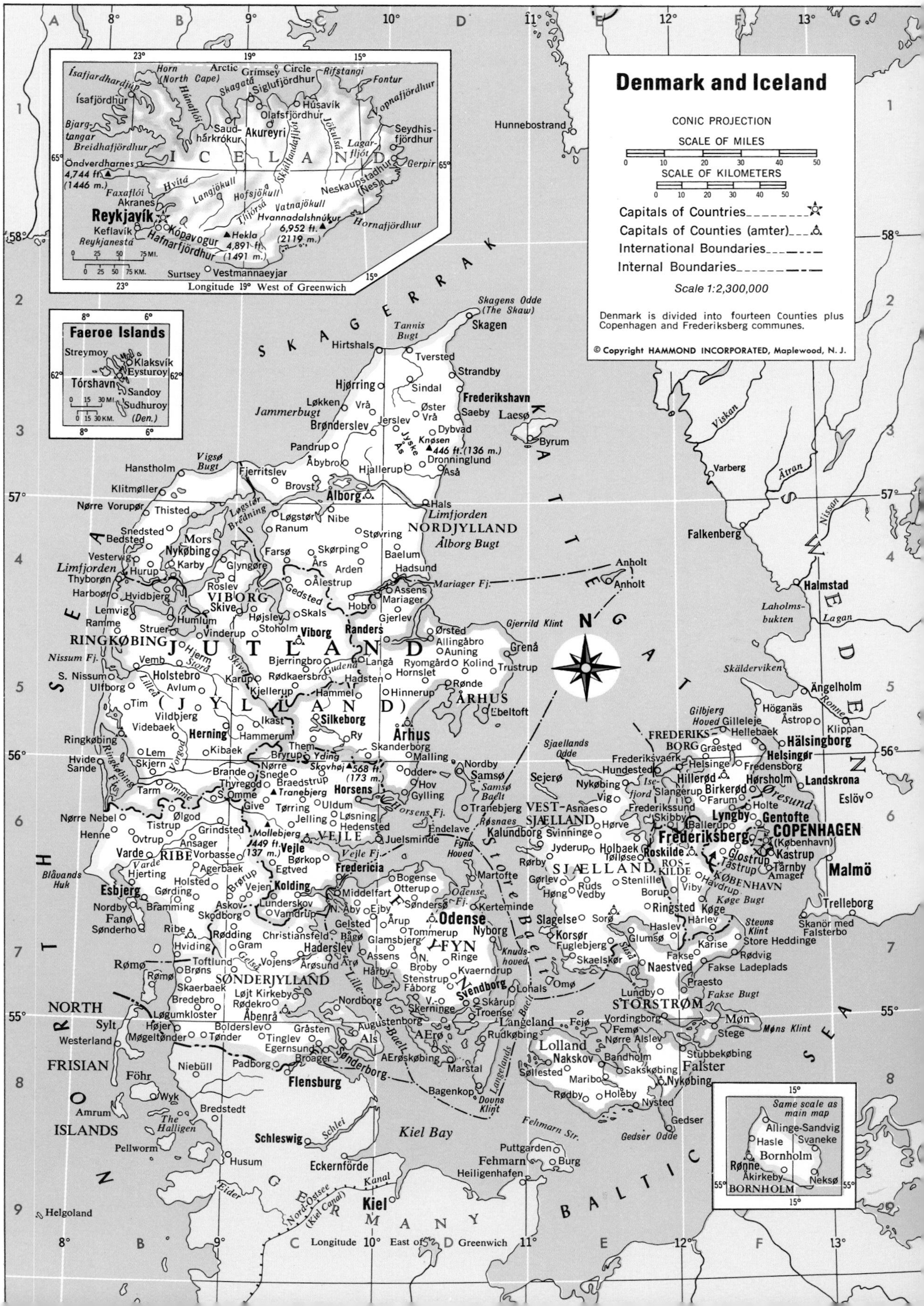

Denmark and Iceland

CONIC PROJECTION

SCALE OF MILES
0 10 20 30 40 50

SCALE OF KILOMETERS
0 10 20 30 40 50

Capitals of Countries _____ ☆
Capitals of Counties (amter) ____ ⌂
International Boundaries _____
Internal Boundaries ____ _ ____

Scale 1:2,300,000

Denmark is divided into fourteen Counties plus
Copenhagen and Frederiksberg communes.

© Copyright HAMMOND INCORPORATED, Maplewood, N. J.

Faeroe Islands
Streymoy
Klaksvík
Eysturoy
Tórshavn
Sandoy
Sudhuroy
(Den.)
0 15 30 MI.
0 15 30 KM.

BORNHOLM
Allinge-Sandvig
Hasle Svaneke
Rønne Bornholm
Åkirkeby Neksø
Same scale as main map

Germany

CONIC PROJECTION
SCALE OF MILES

SCALE OF KILOMETERS

Capitals of Countries .... ★
State Capitals .... ◉
International Boundaries ....
State Boundaries ....
Canals ....

Scale 1:3,040,000

Berlin

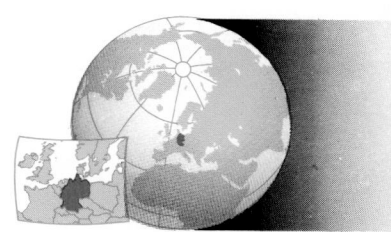

AREA 137,753 sq. mi. (356,780 sq. km.)
POPULATION 78,395,000
CAPITAL Berlin
LARGEST CITY Berlin
HIGHEST POINT Zugspitze 9,718 ft. (2,962 m.)
MONETARY UNIT Deutsche mark
MAJOR LANGUAGE German
MAJOR RELIGIONS Protestantism, Roman
Catholicism

GERMANY

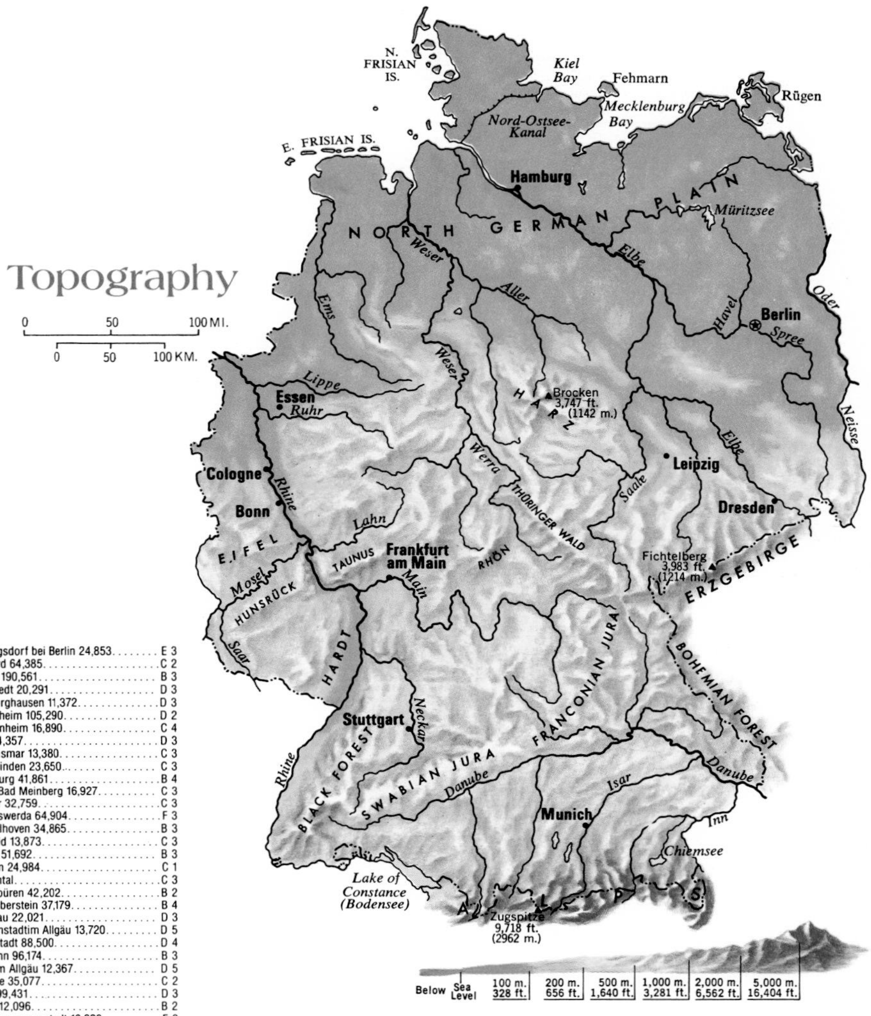

Topography

0   50   100 MI.

0   50   100 KM.

N. FRISIAN IS.
Kiel Bay
Fehmarn
E. FRISIAN IS.
Nord-Ostsee-Kanal
Mecklenburg Bay
Rügen
NORTH GERMAN PLAIN
Müritzsee
Hamburg
Weser
Aller
Elbe
Oder
Berlin
Spree
Ems
Lippe
Essen
Ruhr
Weser
Werra
Havel
Neisse
Cologne
Rhine
Leipzig
Bonn
Lahn
THÜRINGER WALD
Elbe
Dresden
EIFEL
Mosel
TAUNUS
Brocken 3,747 ft. (1142 m.)
HUNSRÜCK
Main
RHÖN
Frankfurt am Main
Fichtelberg 3,983 ft. (1214 m.)
ERZGEBIRGE
HARDT
Saar
Neckar
FRANCONIAN JURA
BOHEMIAN FOREST
Stuttgart
BLACK FOREST
Danube
SWABIAN JURA
Danube
Isar
Munich
Inn
Lake of Constance (Bodensee)
Iller
Chiemsee
Zugspitze 9,718 ft. (2962 m.)

| Below Sea Level | 100 m. 328 ft. | 200 m. 656 ft. | 500 m. 1,640 ft. | 1,000 m. 3,281 ft. | 2,000 m. 6,562 ft. | 5,000 m. 16,404 ft. |

(continued on following page)

Germany Before World War I 1871-1914

Germany Between Wars 1919-1937
SAAR (To Germany 1935)

Occupied Germany 1945-1949
BRITISH ZONE · RUSSIAN ZONE · FRENCH ZONE · AMERICAN ZONE

Rastatt 38,030....C 4
Rastede 16,905....C 2
Rathenow 32,011....E 2
Ratingen 86,028....B 3
Ratzeburg 12,189....D 2
Ravensburg 42,725....C 5
Recklinghausen 122,437....B 3
Regensburg 131,886....E 4
Reichenbach 27,440....E 3
Remagen 14,627....B 3
Remscheid 133,145....B 3
Rendsburg 34,407....C 1
Reutlingen 95,289....C 4
Rheda-Wiedenbrück 37,371....C 3
Rheine 71,539....B 2
Rheinfelden 27,500....B 5
Ribnitz-Damgarten 17,254....E 1
Riesa 49,989....E 3
Rietberg 22,421....C 3
Rinteln 25,595....C 2
Rosenheim 38,419....D 5
Rosslau 16,520....E 3
Rostock 210,167....E 1
Rotenburg 19,155....C 2
Rotenburg an der Fulda 14,438....C 3
Roth bei Nürnberg 17,782....D 4
Rothenburg ob der Tauber 11,609....D 4
Rottenburg am Neckar 30,583....C 4
Rottweil 24,534....C 4
Rudolstadt 31,698....D 3
Rüsselsheim 62,067....C 4
Säckingen 13,956....C 5
Saalfeld 33,648....D 3
Saarbrücken 205,336....B 4
Saarlouis 39,974....B 4
Salzgitter 117,341....D 2
Salzwedel 21,741....D 2
Sangerhausen 32,721....D 3
Sankt Goar 3,511....B 3
Sankt Ingbert 43,263....B 4
Sankt Wendel 27,558....B 4
Sassnitz 13,857....E 1
Saulgau 15,403....C 5
Schkeuditz 15,585....E 3

Schleswig 30,974....C 1
Schlüchtern 13,801....C 3
Schmalkalden 15,017....D 3
Schmölln 13,406....E 3
Schneeberg 20,376....E 3
Schönebeck 45,197....D 2
Schöneberg 169,835....E 4
Schöningen 16,348....D 2
Schramberg 19,677....C 4
Schwabach 33,136....D 4
Schwäbisch Gmünd 56,422....C 4
Schwäbisch Hall 32,129....C 4
Schwalmstadt 17,800....C 3
Schwandorf im Bayern 22,547....E 4
Schwedt 45,729....F 2
Schweinfurt 56,164....D 3
Schwelm 31,850....B 3
Schwerin 104,984....D 2
Schwetzingen 18,286....C 4
Sebnitz 13,470....F 3
Seesen 23,577....D 3
Selb 16,723....E 3
Senftenberg 29,953....F 3
Sennestadt....C 3
Siegburg 34,943....B 3
Siegen 116,552....C 3
Sigmaringen 15,437....C 4
Sindelfingen 54,134....C 4
Singen 45,566....C 5
Soest 40,308....C 3
Solingen 171,810....B 3
Soltau 19,949....C 2
Sömmerda 20,712....D 3
Sondershausen 23,383....D 3
Sonneberg 29,193....D 3
Sonthofen 17,821....D 5
Spandau....E 3
Speyer 44,471....C 4
Spremberg 22,862....F 3
Springe 30,968....C 2
Stade 42,097....C 2
Stadthagen 23,003....C 2
Stassfurt 26,225....D 3
Stendal 39,647....D 2
Stolberg 57,379....B 3
Stralsund 72,167....E 1

Straubing 43,774....E 4
Strausberg 21,334....F 2
Stuttgart 600,421....C 4
Suhl 36,642....D 3
Sulzbach 22,133....B 4
Sulzbach-Rosenberg 18,596....D 4
Taifingen 17,278....C 4
Tangermünde 12,898....D 2
Tegel....E 3
Telgte 15,165....B 3
Teltow 16,171....E 4
Tempelhof....F 4
Templin 11,718....E 2
Thale 17,248....D 3
Thomas-Müntzer-Stadt 44,106....D 3
Timmendorfer Strand 10,690....D 1
Torgau 21,613....E 3
Torgelow 14,320....F 2
Traunstein 14,088....E 5
Treptow 127,448....F 4
Treuchtlingen 11,939....D 4
Trier 100,338....B 4
Troisdorf 56,402....B 3
Tübingen 71,348....C 4
Tuttlingen 32,342....C 5
Ubach-Palenberg 22,403....B 3
Überlingen 17,735....C 5
Ueckermünde 11,423....F 2
Uelzen 37,550....D 2
Uetersen 16,330....C 2
Ulm 98,237....C 4
Uslar 17,251....C 3
Varel 24,435....C 2
Vechta 21,786....C 2
Verden 24,247....C 2
Viersen 84,220....B 3
Villingen-Schwenningen 80,646....C 5
Völklingen 47,271....B 4
Waldheim 11,925....E 3
Waldkirch 19,009....B 4
Waldkraiburg 20,140....E 4
Waldshut-Tiengen 22,046....C 5
Walsrode 23,423....C 2
Waltershausen 13,893....D 3
Wangen im Allgäu 23,127....C 5
Warburg 22,150....C 3

Waren 22,921....E 2
Warendorf 32,273....B 3
Wedel 30,045....C 2
Weida 11,816....D 3
Weiden in der Oberpfalz 42,697....D 4
Weilburg 12,652....C 3
Weilheim im Oberbayern 15,347....D 5
Weimar 63,144....D 3
Weingarten 21,143....C 5
Weinheim 41,005....C 4
Weisenburg im Bayern 16,083....D 4
Weissenfels 43,191....D 3
Weissensee 78,451....F 3
Weisswasser 25,910....F 3
Werdau 22,249....E 3
Wernigerode 34,658....D 3
Wertheim 20,942....C 4
Westerstede 16,977....B 2
Wesel 56,584....B 3
Westerland 9,652....C 1
Wetzlar 37,729....C 3
Wiehl 19,004....B 3
Wiesbaden 250,592....C 3
Wildbad im Schwarzwald 11,611....C 4
Wildeshausen 12,055....C 2
Wilhelm-Pieck-Stadt 32,731....F 3
Wilhelmshaven 103,417....C 2
Wismar 56,765....D 2
Witten 108,771....B 3
Wittenberg 51,364....E 3
Wittenberge 32,907....D 2
Wittingen 12,189....D 2
Wittlich 15,321....B 3
Witzenhausen 16,877....C 3
Wolfen 27,570....E 3
Wolfenbüttel 51,386....D 2
Wolfsburg 126,298....D 2
Wolgast 16,384....E 1
Worms 75,732....C 4
Wunstorf 36,795....C 2
Wuppertal 405,369....B 3
Würzburg 112,584....C 4
Xanten 15,688....B 3
Zehdenick 12,651....E 2
Zeitz 44,582....E 3
Zella-Mehlis 16,301....D 3

Zerbst 19,356....E 3
Zeulenroda 13,452....D 3
Zirndorf 13,661....D 4
Zittau 42,298....F 3
Zülpich 16,171....B 3
Zweibrücken 35,978....B 4
Zwickau 123,069....E 3
Zwischenahn 22,581....B 2

OTHER FEATURES

Aller (riv.)....C 2
Allgäu (reg.)....D 5
Altmark 267,229 (reg.)....D 2
Altmühl (riv.)....D 4
Ammersee (lake)....D 4
Amrum (isl.)....E 1
Arkona (cape)....E 1
Baltic (sea)....E 1
Baltrum 661 (isl.)....B 2
Bavarian (for.)....D 4
Bavarian Alps (range)....D 5
Bayerischer Wald Nat'l Park....E 4
Black (for.)....C 4
Black Elster (riv.)....E 3
Bodensee (Constance) (lake)....C 5
Bohemian (for.)....E 4
Borkum 8,495 (isl.)....B 2
Brandenburg 7,130,055 (reg.)....E 2
Breisgau (reg.)....B 4
Chiemsee (lake)....E 5
Constance (lake)....C 5
Danube (riv.)....C 4
Donau (Danube) (riv.)....C 4
East Friesland (reg.)....B 2
East Frisian (isls.)....B 2
Eder (res.)....C 3
Elbe (riv.)....C-D 2
Elde (riv.)....D 2
Elster, Black (riv.)....E 3
Elster, White (riv.)....D 3
Ems (riv.)....B 2
Erzgebirge (mts.)....E 3
Fehmarn 12,455 (isl.)....D 1
Feldberg (mt.)....C 5
Fichtelberg (mt.)....E 3

Fichtelgebirge (range)....D 3
Föhr (isl.)....C 1
Franconian Jura (range)....D 4
Frisian, East (isls.)....B 2
Frisian, North (isls.)....B 1
Grosser Arber (mt.)....E 4
Halligen (isls.)....C 1
Hardt (mts.)....C 4
Harz (mts.)....D 3
Hase (riv.)....B 2
Havel (riv.)....E 2
Hegau (reg.)....C 5
Helgoland (bay)....C 1
Helgoland 2,377 (isl.)....B 1
Hunsrück (mts.)....B 4
Hunte (riv.)....C 2
Iller (riv.)....D 4
Inn (riv.)....E 5
Isar (riv.)....E 4
Juist 2,228 (isl.)....B 2
Kaiserstuhl (mt.)....B 4
Kiel (bay)....D 1
Kiel (Nord-Ostsee) (canal)....C 1
Königssee (lake)....E 5
Lahn (riv.)....C 3
Langeoog 2,535 (isl.)....B 2
Lech (riv.)....D 4
Leine (riv.)....C 2
Lippe (riv.)....B 3
Lüneburger Heide (dist.)....D 2
Lusatia 594,784 (reg.)....F 3
Main (riv.)....C 3
Mecklenburg (bay)....D 1
Mecklenburg 1,925,669 (reg.)....D 2
Mosel (riv.)....B 3
Mulde (riv.)....E 3
Naab (riv.)....D 4
Neckar (riv.)....C 4
Neisse (riv.)....F 3
Nord-Ostsee (canal)....C 1
Norderney 8,307 (isl.)....B 2
Nordstrand 2,729 (isl.)....C 1
North (sea)....B 1
North Friesland (reg.)....C 1
North Frisian (isls.)....B 1
Odenwald (for.)....C 4

Oder (riv.)....F 2
Oker (riv.)....D 2
Peene (riv.)....E 2
Pellworm 1,261 (isl.)....C 1
Pomerania 630,524 (reg.)....E 1
Pomerania (bay)....F 1
Regen (riv.)....E 4
Regnitz (riv.)....D 4
Rhine (riv.)....B 3
Rhön (mts.)....D 3
Ruhr (riv.)....B 3
Saale (riv.)....D 3
Saar (riv.)....B 4
Sauer (riv.)....B 4
Sauerland (reg.)....C 3
Saxony 5,148,714 (reg.)....E 3
Schneeberg (mt.)....D 3
Schwarzwald (Black) (for.)....C 4
Spessart (range)....C 4
Spiekeroog 732 (isl.)....B 2
Spree (riv.)....F 3
Spreewald (for.)....F 3
Starnbergersee (lake)....D 5
Swabian Jura (range)....C 4
Sylt 20,875 (isl.)....C 1
Tauber (riv.)....C 4
Taunus (range)....C 3
Tegernsee (lake)....D 5
Teutoburger Wald (for.)....C 2
Thüringer Wald (for.)....D 3
Thuringia (reg.)....D 3
Ücker (riv.)....E 2
Unstrut (riv.)....D 3
Usedom (isl.)....F 1
Vogelsberg (mts.)....C 3
Walchensee (lake)....D 5
Wangerooge 1,700 (isl.)....B 1
Warnow (riv.)....D 1
Watzmann (mt.)....E 5
Werra (riv.)....D 3
Weser (riv.)....C 2
Westerwald (for.)....B 3
White Elster (riv.)....D 3
Würmsee (Starnbergersee) (lake)....D 5
Zugspitze (mt.)....D 5

Agriculture, Industry and Resources

DOMINANT LAND USE
- Wheat, Sugar Beets
- Cereals (chiefly rye, oats, barley)
- Potatoes, Rye
- Dairy, Livestock
- Mixed Cereals, Dairy
- Truck Farming
- Grapes, Fruit
- Forests

MAJOR MINERAL OCCURRENCES

Ag	Silver	K	Potash
Ba	Barite	Lg	Lignite
C	Coal	Na	Salt
Cu	Copper	O	Petroleum
Fe	Iron Ore	Pb	Lead
G	Natural Gas	U	Uranium
Gr	Graphite	Zn	Zinc

⚡ Water Power
/// Major Industrial Areas

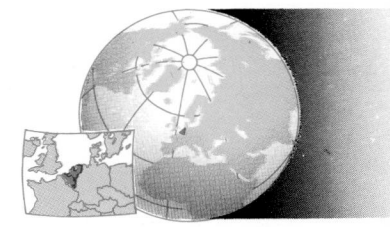

AREA 15,892 sq. mi. (41,160 sq. km.)
POPULATION 14,227,000
CAPITALS The Hague, Amsterdam
LARGEST CITY Amsterdam
HIGHEST POINT Vaalserberg 1,056 ft. (322 m.)
MONETARY UNIT guilder (florin)
MAJOR LANGUAGE Dutch
MAJOR RELIGIONS Protestantism, Roman
Catholicism

AREA 11,781 sq. mi. (30,513 sq. km.)
POPULATION 9,855,110
CAPITAL Brussels
LARGEST CITY Brussels (greater)
HIGHEST POINT Botrange 2,277 ft. (694 m.)
MONETARY UNIT Belgian franc
MAJOR LANGUAGES French (Walloon), Flemish
MAJOR RELIGION Roman Catholicism

AREA 999 sq. mi. (2,587 sq. km.)
POPULATION 364,000
CAPITAL Luxembourg
LARGEST CITY Luxembourg
HIGHEST POINT Ardennes Plateau 1,825 ft. (556 m.)
MONETARY UNIT Luxembourg franc
MAJOR LANGUAGES Luxembourgeois (Letzeburgisch), French, German
MAJOR RELIGION Roman Catholicism

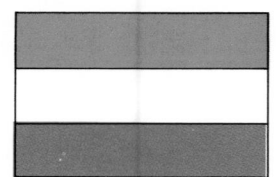

NETHERLANDS

BELGIUM

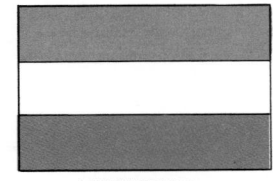

LUXEMBOURG

Agriculture, Industry and Resources

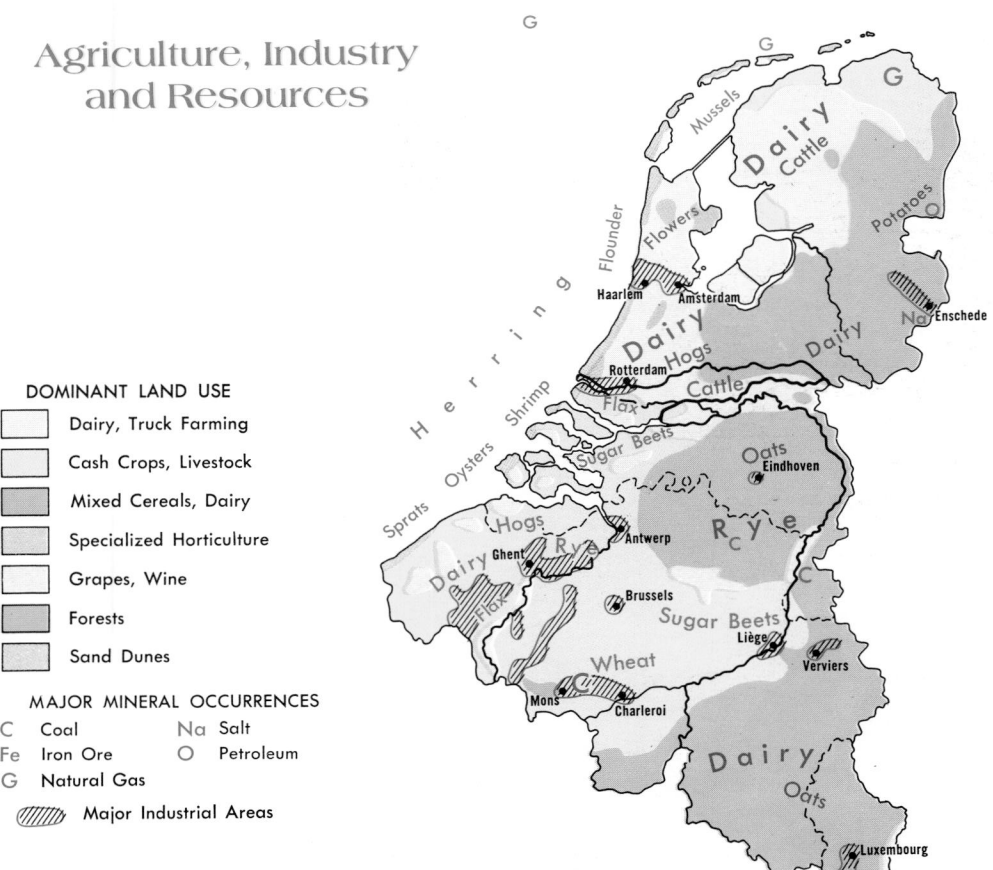

DOMINANT LAND USE

- Dairy, Truck Farming
- Cash Crops, Livestock
- Mixed Cereals, Dairy
- Specialized Horticulture
- Grapes, Wine
- Forests
- Sand Dunes

MAJOR MINERAL OCCURRENCES

C	Coal	Na	Salt
Fe	Iron Ore	O	Petroleum
G	Natural Gas		

Major Industrial Areas

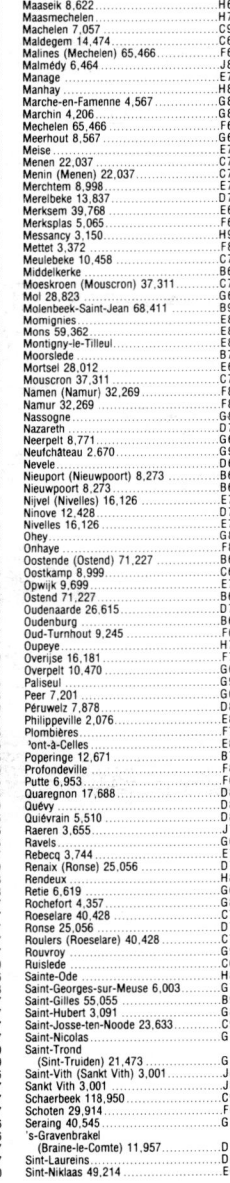

BELGIUM

PROVINCES

Antwerp 1,533,249	F6
Brabant 2,176,373	F7
East Flanders 1,310,117	D7
Hainaut 1,317,453	D7
Liège 1,008,905	H7
Limburg 652,547	G7
Luxembourg 217,310	G9
Namur 380,561	F8
West Flanders 1,054,429	B7

CITIES and TOWNS†

Aalst 46,659	D7
Aalter 9,173	C6
Aarlen (Arlon) 13,745	H9
Aarschot 12,474	F7
Aat (Ath) 11,842	D7
Aiken 8,677	G7
Alost (Aalst) 46,659	D7
Amay 7,617	G7
Andenne 8,091	G8
Anderlecht 103,796	B9
Anderlues 12,176	E8
Ans	H7
Antoing 3,426	C7
Antwerp 224,543	E6
Antwerp* 928,000	E6
Antwerpen (Antwerp) 224,543	E6
Ardooie 7,081	C7
Arendonk 9,919	G6
Arlon 13,745	H9
As 5,496	H6
Asse 6,583	E7
Ath 11,842	D7
Attert	H9
Aubange 3,761	H9
Audenarde (Oudenaarde) 26,615	D7
Auderghem 34,546	C9
Auvelais 8,287	F8
Aywaille 3,850	H8
Baarle-Hertog	F6
Balen 15,110	G6
Basse-Sambre	F8
Bastenaken (Bastogne) 6,816	H9
Bastogne 6,816	H9
Beernem	C6
Beloeil	D7
Berchem 50,241	F6
Berchem-Sainte-Agathe 19,087	B9
Bergen (Mons) 59,362	E8
Beringen	G6
Bertogne	H8
Bertrix 4,562	G8
Beveren 15,913	E6
Bilzen 7,178	G7
Binche 10,098	E8
Blankenberge 13,969	C6
Bocholt 6,497	H6
Boom 16,584	E6
Borgerhout 49,002	E6
Borgloon 3,412	G7
Borgworm (Waremme) 10,956	G7
Bourg-Léopold (Leopoldsburg) 9,593	G6
Boussu 11,474	D8
Braine-l'Alleud 18,531	E7
Braine-le-Comte 11,957	D7
Brecht	F6
Bredene 9,244	B6
Bree 10,389	H6
Bruges 117,220	C6
Brugge (Bruges) 117,220	C6
Brussels (cap.)* 1,054,970	C9
Bruxelles (Brussels)	
(cap.)* 1,054,970	C9
Cerfontaine	E8
Charleroi 23,689	E8
Charleroi* 458,000	E8
Chastre	F8
Châtelet 14,752	F8
Chièvres 3,283	D7
Chimay 3,288	D8
Chiny 7,536	G9
Ciney 7,536	F8
Comblain-au-Pont 3,582	G8
Comines 8,192	B7
Courcelles 17,015	E8
Courtrai (Kortrijk) 44,961	C7
Couvin 4,234	F8
Damme	C6
De Haan	C6
Deinze 16,711	C7
Denderleeuw 9,925	E7
Dendermonde 22,119	E6
De Panne 6,985	B6
Dessel 7,505	G6
Destelbergen	D6
Deurne 80,766	E6
Diest 10,799	F7
Diksmuide 6,669	B6
Dilbeek 15,108	B9
Dilsen	H6
Dinant 9,747	G8
Dison 8,466	H7
Dixmude (Diksmuide) 6,669	B6
Doische	E8
Doornik (Tournai) 32,794	C7
Dour 10,059	D8
Drogenbos 4,840	B10
Duffel 13,802	F6
Durbuy	H8
Ecaussinnes 6,630	E7
Edingen (Enghien) 4,115	D7
Eeklo 19,144	D6
Eghezée	F7
Eigenbrakel (Braine-l'Alleud) 18,531	E7
Ekeren 27,648	E6
Ellezelles 3,556	D7
Enghien 4,115	D7
Erezée	G8
Erquelinnes 4,471	E8
Esneux 6,183	H7
Essen 10,795	F6
Estampuis	C7
Etterbeek 51,030	B9
Eupen 14,879	J7
Evere 26,957	C9
Evergem 12,886	D6
Farciennes	E8
Fernelmont	F7
Ferrières	H8
Flémalle 8,135	G7
Fleurus 8,523	E8
Florennes 4,107	F8
Forest 55,135	B9
Fosses-La-Ville 3,972	F8
Frameries 11,224	D8
Froidchapelle	E8
Furnes (Veurne) 9,496	B6
Ganshoren 21,147	B9
Geel 29,346	F6
Geldenaken (Jodoigne) 4,132	F7
Gembloux-sur-Orneau 11,249	F7
Genk 57,913	H7
Gent (Ghent) 148,860	D6
Geraardsbergen 17,533	D7
Gerpinnes	F8
Ghent 148,860	D6
Ghent* 477,000	D6
Gistel	B6
Gooik	C9
Gouvy	H8
Grammont (Geraardsbergen) 17,533	D7
Grez-Doiceau	F7
Grimbergen	F7
Haacht 4,436	F7
Habay	H9
Hal (Halle) 20,017	E7
Halen 5,322	G7
Halle 20,017	E7
Hamme 17,559	E6
Hamois	G8
Hamont-Achel 6,893	H6
Hannut (Hannut) 7,232	G7
Hannut 7,232	G7
Harelbeke 18,498	C7
Hasselt 39,663	G7
Hastière	F8
Heist-Knokke 27,582	C6
Heist-op-den-Berg 13,472	F6
Hensies	D8
Herentals 18,639	F6
Herne	E7
Herselt 7,412	F6
Herstal 29,600	H7
Herve 4,118	H7
Heuvelland	B7
Hoboken 33,693	E6
Hoei (Huy) 12,736	G7
Hoeselt 6,884	G7
Honnelles	D8
Hoogstraten 4,381	F6
Hotton	G8
Huy 12,736	G7
Ichtegem	B6
Ieper 20,825	B7
Ingelmunster 10,245	C7
Ittre	E7
Ixelles 86,450	C9
Izegem 22,928	C7
Jabbeke	C6
Jemappes 18,632	D8
Jette 40,013	B9
Jodoigne 4,132	F7
Kalmthout 12,724	F6
Kapellen 13,352	E6
Kasterlee	F6
Kinrooi	H6
Knokke-Heist 27,582	C6
Koekelare 7,807	B6
Koekelberg 17,570	B9
Koksijde	B6
Kontich 14,432	E6
Kortemark 5,904	C6
Kortrijk 44,961	C7
Kraainem 11,390	C9
La Louvière 23,310	E8
La Louvière* 113,259	E8
Landen 8,659	H7
Langemark-Poelkapelle 5,457	B7
Lasne	F7
Lede 10,316	D7
Léglise	H9
Leopoldsburg 9,593	G6
Le Roeulx	E8
Lessen (Lessines) 8,906	D7
Lessines 8,906	D7
Leuven 30,623	F7
Leuze-en-Hainaut 7,185	D7
Libin	G9
Libramont-Chevigny 2,975	G9
Lichtervelde 7,459	C6
Liedekerke 10,482	D7
Liège 145,573	H7
Liège* 622,000	H7
Lier 28,416	F6
Lierre (Lier) 28,416	F6
Limbourg 3,762	J7
Limburg (Limbourg) 3,762	J7
Linkebeek 4,265	C10
Linter	G7
Lochristi	D6
Lokeren 26,740	D6
Lommel 21,984	G6
Lontzen	H9
Looz (Borgloon) 3,412	G7
Lo-Reninge	B7
Louvain (Leuven) 30,623	F7
Luik (Liège) 145,573	H7
Lummen	G7
Maaseik 8,622	H6
Maasmechelen	H7
Machelen 7,057	C9
Maldegem 14,474	C6
Malines (Mechelen) 65,466	F6
Malmédy 6,464	J8
Manage	E7
Manhay	H8
Marche-en-Famenne 4,567	G8
Marchin 4,206	G7
Mechelen 65,466	F6
Meerhout 8,567	G6
Meise	E7
Menen 22,037	C7
Menin (Menen) 22,037	C7
Merchtem 8,998	E7
Meréibeke 13,837	D7
Merksem 39,768	E6
Merksplas 5,065	F6
Messancy 3,150	H9
Mettet 3,372	F8
Meulebeke 10,458	C7
Middelkerke	B6
Moeskroen (Mouscron) 37,311	C7
Mol 26,823	G6
Molenbeek-Saint-Jean 68,411	B9
Momignies	E8
Mons 59,362	E8
Montigny-le-Tilleul	E8
Moorslede	B7
Mortsel 28,012	E6
Mouscron 37,311	C7
Namen (Namur) 32,269	F8
Namur 32,269	F8
Nassogne	G8
Nazareth	D7
Neerpelt 8,771	G6
Neufchâteau 2,670	G9
Nevele	D6
Nieuport (Nieuwpoort) 8,273	B6
Nieuwpoort 8,273	B6
Nijvel (Nivelles) 16,126	E7
Ninove 12,428	D7
Nivelles 16,126	E7
Ohey	G8
Onhaye	F8
Oostende (Ostend) 71,227	B6
Oostkamp 8,999	C6
Opwijk 9,699	E7
Ostend 71,227	B6
Oudenaarde 26,615	D7
Oudenburg	B6
Oud-Turnhout 9,245	F6
Oupeye	H7
Overijse 16,181	F7
Overpelt 10,470	G6
Paliseul	G9
Peer 7,201	G6
Péruwelz 7,878	D8
Philippeville 2,076	E8
Plombières	F7
Pont-à-Celles	E8
Poperinge 12,671	B7
Profondeville	F8
Putte 6,953	F6
Quaregnon 17,688	D8
Quévy	D8
Quiévrain 5,510	D8
Raeren 3,655	J7
Ravels	G6
Rebecq 3,744	E7
Renaix (Ronse) 25,056	D7
Rendeux	H8
Retie 6,619	G6
Rochefort 4,357	G8
Roeselare 40,428	C7
Ronse 25,056	D7
Roulers (Roeselare) 40,428	C7
Rouvroy	G9
Ruislede	H8
Sainte-Ode	
Saint-Georges-sur-Meuse 6,003	G7
Saint-Gilles 55,055	B9
Saint-Hubert 3,091	G8
Saint-Josse-ten-Noode 23,633	C9
Saint-Nicolas	G7
Saint-Trond (Sint-Truiden) 21,473	G7
Saint-Vith (Sankt Vith) 3,001	J8
Sankt Vith 3,001	J8
Schaerbeek 118,950	C9
Schoten 29,914	F6
Seraing 40,545	G7
's-Gravenbrakel (Braine-le-Comte) 11,957	D7
Sint-Laureins	D6
Sint-Niklaas 49,214	E6

(continued on following page)

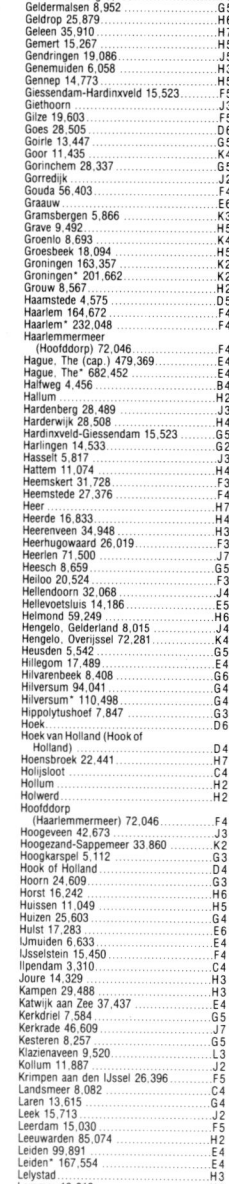

Land from the Sea

Reclaimed Land and Dates of Completion

Future Polders

□ = 10 Square Miles

For centuries the Dutch have been renowned for the drainage of marshes and the construction of polders, i.e., arable land reclaimed from the sea. Future projects will convert much of the present IJsselmeer to agricultural land.

Topography

5,000 m.	2,000 m.	1,000 m.	500 m.	200 m.	100 m.	Sea Level	Below
16,404 ft.	6,562 ft.	3,281 ft.	1,640 ft.	656 ft.	328 ft.		

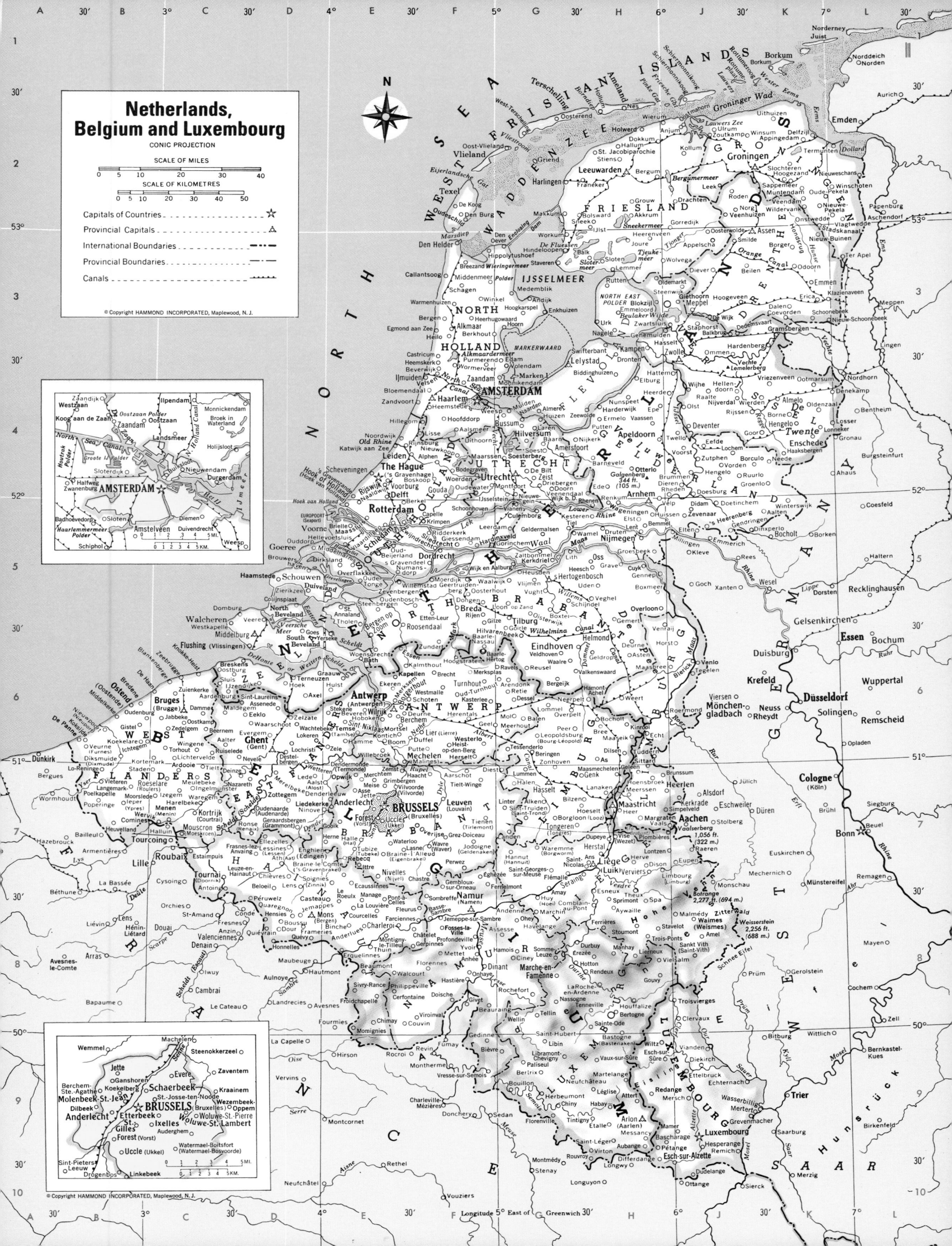

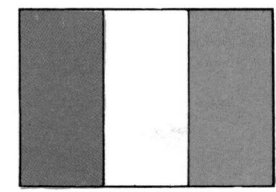

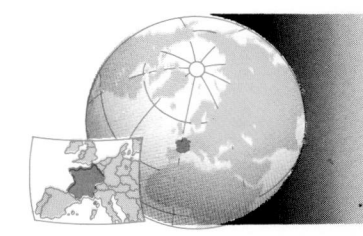

DEPARTMENTS

Ain 418,516............F 4
Aisne 533,970............E 3
Allier 369,580............E 4
Alpes-de-Haute-
  Provence 119,068.....G 5
Alpes-Maritimes
  881,198.............G 6
Ardèche 267,970......F 5
Ardennes 302,338......F 3
Ariège 135,725........D 6
Aube 289,300..........E 3
Aude 280,686..........E 6
Aveyron 278,654.......E 5
Bas-Rhin 915,676......G 3
Belfort 131,999........G 4
Bouches-du-Rhône
  1,724,199............F 6
Calvados 589,559.....C 3
Cantal 162,838........E 5
Charente 340,770......D 5
Charente-Maritime
  513,220.............C 5
Cher 320,174..........E 4
Corrèze 241,448.......D 5
Corse du Sud
  108,604.............B 6
Côte-d'Or 473,548.....F 4
Côtes-du-Nord
  538,869.............B 3
Creuse 139,968........D 4
Deux-Sèvres
  342,812.............C 4
Dordogne 377,356......D 5
Doubs 477,163........G 4
Drôme 389,781........F 5
Essonne 988,000......E 3
Eure 462,323..........D 3
Eure-et-Loir 362,813....D 3
Finistère 828,364......A 3
Gard 530,478..........F 6
Gers 174,154..........D 6
Gironde 1,127,546.....C 5
Haute-Corse
  131,574.............B 6
Haute-Garonne
  824,501.............D 6
Haute-Loire 205,895....E 5
Haute-Marne
  210,670.............F 3
Hautes-Alpes
  105,070.............G 5
Haute-Saône
  231,962.............G 4
Haute-Savoie
  494,505.............G 5
Hautes-Pyrénées
  227,922.............D 6
Haute-Vienne
  355,737.............D 5
Haut-Rhin 650,372.....G 4
Hauts-de-Seine
  1,387,039...........A 2
Hérault 706,499.......E 6
Ille-et-Vilaine
  749,764.............C 3
Indre 243,191.........D 4
Indre-et-Loire
  506,097.............D 4
Isère 936,771.........F 5
Jura 242,925..........F 4
Landes 297,424.......C 5

Loire 739,521............F 5
Loire-Atlantique
  995,498.............C 4
Loiret 535,669..........E 4
Loir-et-Cher 296,220....D 4
Lot 154,533...........D 5
Lot-et-Garonne
  298,522.............D 5
Lozère 74,294.........E 5
Maine-et-Loire
  675,321.............C 4
Manche 465,948.......C 3
Marne 543,627.........F 3
Mayenne 271,784......C 3
Meurthe-et-Moselle
  716,846.............G 3
Meuse 200,101........F 3
Morbihan 590,889......B 4
Moselle 1,007,189.....G 3
Nièvre 239,635........E 4
Nord 2,520,526.......E 2
Oise 661,781..........E 3
Orne 295,472..........C 3
Paris 2,188,918.......B 2
Pas-de-Calais
  1,412,413...........E 2
Puy-de-Dôme
  594,365.............E 5
Pyrénées-Atlantiques
  555,696.............C 6
Pyrénées-Orientales
  334,557.............E 6
Rhône 1,445,208......F 5
Saône-et-Loire
  571,852.............F 4
Sarthe 504,768........D 3
Savoie 323,675........G 5
Seine-et-Marne
  887,112.............E 3
Seine-Maritime
  1,324,301...........D 3
Seine-Saint-Denis
  1,324,301...........C 1
Somme 544,570........E 3
Tarn 339,345..........E 6
Tarn-et-Garonne
  190,485.............D 5
Val-de-Marne
  1,193,655...........C 1
Val-d'Oise 920,598.....E 3
Var 708,331..........G 6
Vaucluse 427,343......F 6
Vendée 483,027.......C 4
Vienne 371,428........D 4
Vosges 395,769.......G 3
Yonne 311,019........E 4
Yvelines 1,196,111....D 3

CITIES and TOWNS

Aigues-Mortes 4,106....F 6
Aix-en-Provence
  100,221.............F 6
Aix-les-Bains 22,331....G 5
Ajaccio 48,324.........B 7
Alençon 30,952........D 3
Amboise 10,823........D 4
Amiens 130,302.......E 3
Angers 135,293.......C 4
Angoulême 45,495......D 5
Annecy 49,753.........G 5
Antibes 62,427........G 6
Argenteuil 94,826......A 1

Arles 37,554............F 6
Armentières 22,849......E 2
Arras 41,376............E 2
Asnières-sur-Seine
  71,058.............A 1
Aubervilliers 67,684.....B 1
Aubusson 5,326........E 4
Aulnay-sous-Bois
  75,543.............B 1
Aurignac 772..........D 6
Avignon 75,178.........F 6
Ax-les-Thermes
  1,283.............D 6
Bagnolet 32,556........B 2
Barbizon 478..........E 3
Barcelonnette 2,674.....G 5
Barfleur 617..........C 3
Bastia 43,502.........B 6
Bayeux 14,568.........C 3
Bayonne 40,088.......C 6
Beaucaire 10,622......F 6
Beaune 19,110........F 4
Beauvais 51,542.......E 3
Belfort 51,034........G 4
Bergerac 24,604.......D 5
Besançon 112,023.....G 4
Bessèges 4,352.......F 5
Béziers 74,114........E 6
Biarritz 26,579........C 6
Blois 46,925.........D 4
Bobigny 42,630........B 1
Bonifacio 1,727.......B 7
Bordeaux 201,965.....C 5
Boulogne-Billancourt
  102,582.............A 2
Boulogne-sur-Mer
  47,482.............D 2
Bourg-en-Bresse
  37,582.............F 4
Bourges 74,622.......E 4
Brest 154,110.........A 3
Brignoles 8,529.......G 6
Brive-la-Gaillarde
  50,898.............D 5
Bruay-en-Artois
  22,502.............E 2
Caen 112,332.........C 3
Calais 76,206.........D 2
Caluire-et-Cuire
  41,864.............F 5
Cambrai 35,070.......E 2
Cannes 71,888.........G 6
Carcassonne
  38,379.............E 6
Castres 39,216........E 6
Chalons-sur-Marne
  49,941.............F 3

AREA 210,038 sq. mi. (543,998 sq. km.)
POPULATION 53,788,000
CAPITAL Paris
LARGEST CITY Paris
HIGHEST POINT Mont Blanc 15,771 ft.
  (4,807 m.)
MONETARY UNIT franc
MAJOR LANGUAGE French
MAJOR RELIGION Roman Catholicism

Topography

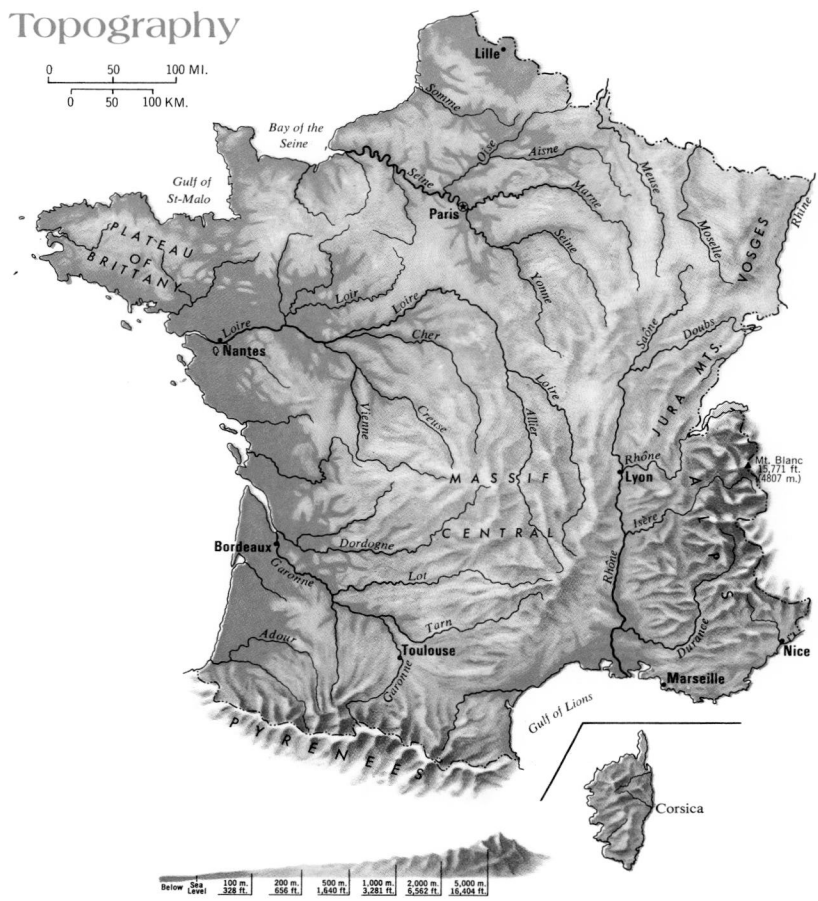

Historic Provinces

A resident of the city of Caen thinks of himself as a Norman rather than as a citizen of the modern department of Calvados. In spite of the passing of nearly two centuries, the historic provinces which existed before 1790 command the local patriotism of most Frenchmen.

Chalon-sur-Saône
  53,893.............F 4
Chambéry 49,465......F 5
Chambord 159........D 4
Chamonix-Mont-Blanc
  7,406.............G 5
Champigny-sur-Marne
  76,039.............C 2
Chantilly 10,065.......E 3
Charleville-Mézières
  7,814.............F 3
Chartres 36,706.......D 3
Châteaudun 15,905....D 3
Châteauneuf-sur-Loire
  5,630.............E 4
Châteauroux 51,744....D 4
Château-Thierry
  14,427.............E 3
Chatou 28,435........A 1
Cherbourg 28,324......C 3
Chinon 6,030.........D 4
Choisy-le-Roi 35,443....B 2
Cholet 51,620........C 4
Clamart 48,210........A 2
Clermont-Ferrand
  145,901............E 5
Clichy 46,830.........B 1
Cluny 4,133..........F 4
Cognac 20,247........C 5
Colmar 61,560........G 3
Colombes 78,485......A 1
Compiègne 39,909......E 3
Courbevoie 59,821......A 1
Creil 34,332..........E 3
Créteil 71,559........B 2
Deauville 4,682.......C 3
Dieppe 35,659........D 3
Digne 12,540.........G 5
Dijon 139,188.........F 4
Dinard 9,562.........B 3
Domrémy-la-Pucelle
  162.............F 3
Douai 41,576.........E 2
Drancy 60,122........B 1
Dunkirk 71,756........E 2

Ernée 5,253..........C 3
Évreux 45,215........D 3
Falaise 8,424.........C 3
Fécamp 21,212........D 3
Foix 9,212...........D 6
Fontainebleau
  14,687.............E 3
Fontenay-sous-Bois
  52,397.............C 2
Gex 4,776...........G 4
Grasse 24,257........G 6
Grenoble 156,437......F 5
Guise 6,179.........E 3
Harfleur 9,470........D 3
Hazebrouck 19,266.....E 2
Hendaye 10,492......C 6
Héricourt 9,239........G 4
Honfleur 8,125........D 3
Issy-les-Moulineaux
  45,702.............A 2
Istres 21,286.........F 6
Ivry-sur-Seine
  55,682.............B 2
La Baule-Escoublac
  13,151.............B 4
La Courneuve
  33,525.............B 1
Langres 9,718.........F 4
Lapalisse 3,173.......E 4
La Rochelle 74,728.....C 4
La Roche-sur-Yon
  42,026.............C 4
Laval 53,582.........C 3
Le Bourget 11,020......B 1
Le Creusot 32,013......F 4
Le Havre 198,700......D 3
Le Mans 145,976......C 3
Le Puy 22,806.........F 5
Le Tréport 6,330.......D 2
Levallois-Perret
  53,485.............B 1
Lille 167,791.........E 2
Limoges 137,809......D 5
Lisieux 24,454........D 3
Lorient 62,207........B 4

Lourdes 17,252........C 6
Lunéville 21,200........G 3
Lyon 410,455.........F 5
Mâcon 36,517........F 4
Maisons-Alfort
  51,041.............B 2
Maisons-Laffitte
  22,565.............A 1
Mantes-la-Jolie
  43,551.............D 3
Marmande 14,264......C 5
Marseille 868,435......F 6
Maubeuge 35,424......F 2
Mayenne 12,156......C 3
Meaux 44,386........E 3
Melun 34,379.........E 3
Mende 10,520.........E 5
Menton 22,234........G 6
Metz 113,236.........G 3
Meudon 29,356........A 2
Montauban 36,122.....D 5
Montbéliard 31,174.....G 4
Montceau-les-Mines
  26,877.............F 4
Mont-de-Marsan
  25,896.............C 6
Mont-Dore 2,091.......E 5
Montfort 8,020.........C 3
Montluçon 49,737......E 4
Montmédy 1,880.......F 3
Montpellier 190,423.....E 6
Montreuil 96,441......B 2
Mont-Saint-Michel
  65.............C 3
Mulhouse 111,742.....G 4
Nancy 95,654.........G 3
Nanterre 88,567.......A 1
Nantes 237,789.......C 4
Narbonne 38,222......E 6
Nemours 11,624......E 3
Neufchâtel-en-Bray
  5,452.............D 3
Neuilly-sur-Seine
  64,093.............A 1
Nice 331,165.........G 6

Nîmes 120,515.........F 6
Niort 56,256..........C 4
Nogent-le-Rotrou
  11,963.............D 3
Noisy-le-Sec 36,821....B 1
Nontron 3,407........D 5
Noyon 13,949........E 3
Nyons 5,219.........F 5
Orléans 81,615........D 3
Orly 23,729..........B 2
Oyonnax 22,516......F 4
Paris (cap.)
  2,165,892...........B 2
Paris *10,073,059.....B 2
Pau 82,186..........C 6
Périgueux 33,032......D 5
Perpignan 107,812.....E 6
Pessac 49,019........C 5
Poitiers 76,793.......D 4
Pontoise 27,885.......E 3
Port-Vendres 4,871.....E 6
Privas 9,253.........F 5
Quimper 52,335.......A 4
Rambouillet 21,136.....D 3
Redon 9,071.........C 4
Reims 176,419........E 3
Rennes 190,861.......C 3
Roanne 48,574........E 4
Rochefort 25,392......C 4
Roubaix 101,488......E 2
Rouen 100,696........D 3
Rueil-Malmaison
  63,310.............A 2
Saint-Brieuc 48,259.....B 3
Saint-Cloud 28,561.....A 2
Saint-Denis 90,686.....B 1
Saint-Dizier 34,074.....F 3
Sainte-Mère-Église
  1,205.............C 3
Saint-Étienne
  193,938............F 5
Saint-Germain-en-Laye
  36,585.............D 3
Saint-Jean-d'Angély
  8,268.............C 4

(continued on following page)

Wine Regions

Climate, soil and variety of grape planted determine the quality of wine. Long, hot and fairly dry summers with cool, humid nights constitute an ideal climate. The nature of the soil is such a determining influence that identical grapes planted in Bordeaux, Burgundy and Champagne, will yield wines of widely different types.

Agriculture, Industry and Resources

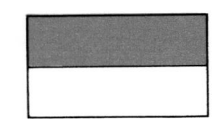

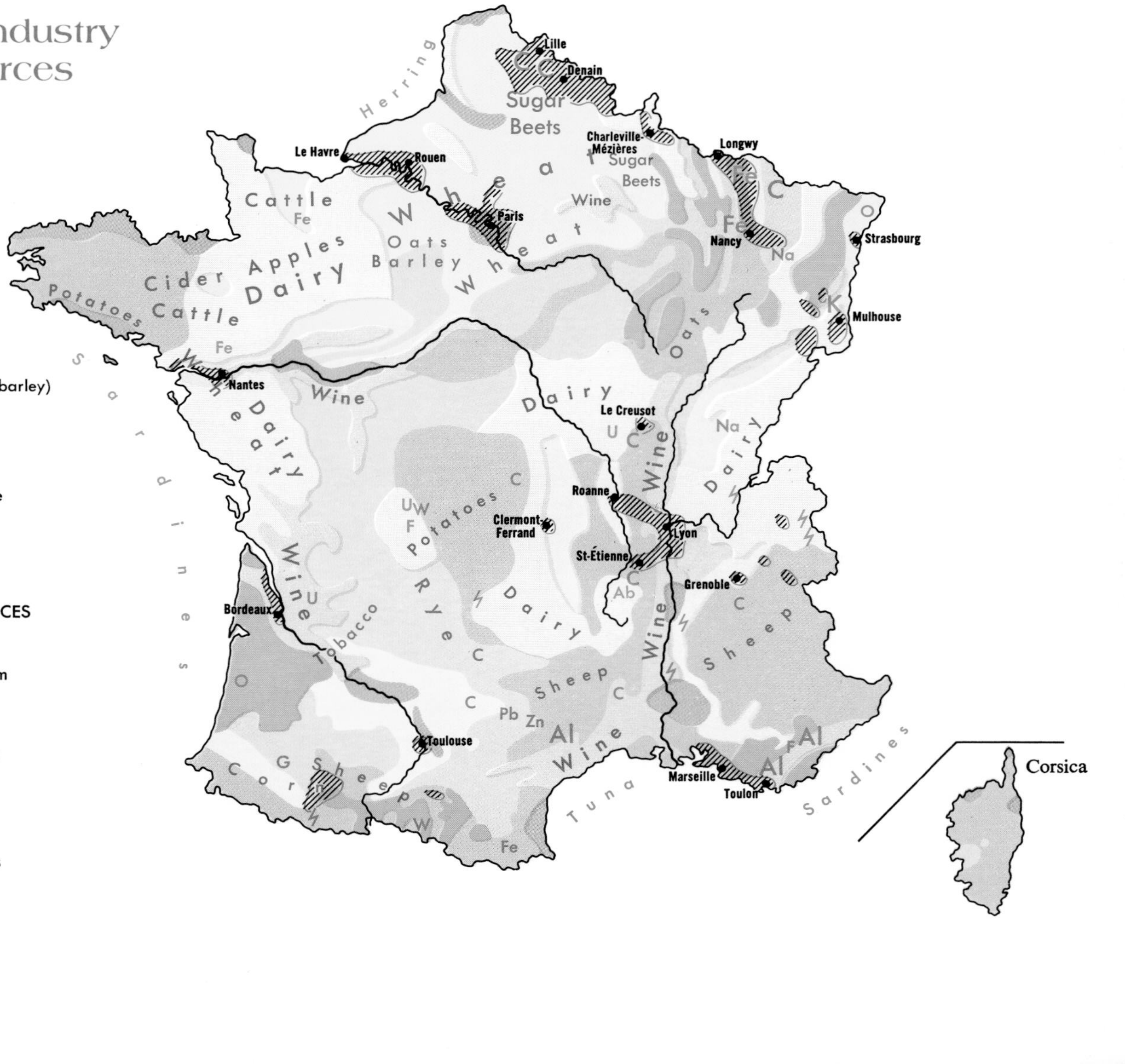

DOMINANT LAND USE

- Cereals (chiefly wheat)
- Cereals (chiefly rye, oats, barley)
- Dairy
- Pasture Livestock
- Truck Farming, Horticulture
- Grapes, Wine
- Forests

MAJOR MINERAL OCCURRENCES

Ab	Asbestos	Na	Salt
Al	Bauxite	O	Petroleum
C	Coal	Pb	Lead
F	Fluorspar	U	Uranium
Fe	Iron Ore	W	Tungsten
G	Natural Gas	Zn	Zinc
K	Potash		

⚡ Water Power

▨ Major Industrial Areas

Corsica

ANDORRA

SPAIN

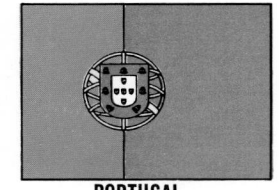
PORTUGAL

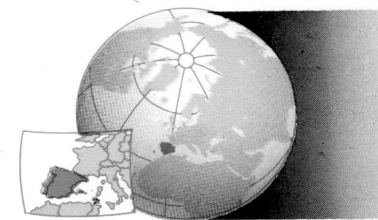

SPAIN

AREA 194,881 sq. mi. (504,742 sq. km.)
POPULATION 37,430,000
CAPITAL Madrid
LARGEST CITY Madrid
HIGHEST POINT Pico de Teide 12,172 ft. (3,710 m.)
(Canary Is.); Mulhacén 11,411 ft. (3,478 m.)
(mainland)
MONETARY UNIT peseta
MAJOR LANGUAGES Spanish, Catalan, Basque,
Galician, Valencian
MAJOR RELIGION Roman Catholicism

ANDORRA

AREA 188 sq. mi. (487 sq. km.)
POPULATION 31,000
CAPITAL Andorra la Vella
MONETARY UNITS French franc, Spanish peseta
MAJOR LANGUAGE Catalan
MAJOR RELIGION Roman Catholicism

PORTUGAL

AREA 35,549 sq. mi. (92,072 sq. km.)
POPULATION 9,933,000
CAPITAL Lisbon
LARGEST CITY Lisbon
HIGHEST POINT Malhão da Estrela
6,532 ft. (1,991 m.)
MONETARY UNIT escudo
MAJOR LANGUAGE Portuguese
MAJOR RELIGION Roman Catholicism

GIBRALTAR

AREA 2.28 sq. mi. (5.91 sq. km.)
POPULATION 29,760
CAPITAL Gibraltar
MONETARY UNIT pound sterling
MAJOR LANGUAGES English, Spanish
MAJOR RELIGION Roman Catholicism

Agriculture, Industry and Resources

DOMINANT LAND USE

Cereals (chiefly wheat)

Livestock (chiefly sheep, goats)

Mixed Cereals, Livestock

Olives, Fruit

Grapes, Fruit, Nuts, Mixed Cereals

Forests

Nonagricultural Land

MAJOR MINERAL OCCURRENCES

Ag Silver
C Coal
Cu Copper
Fe Iron Ore
G Natural Gas
Hg Mercury
K Potash
Lg Lignite
Mg Magnesium

Na Salt
O Petroleum
Pb Lead
Py Pyrites
Sb Antimony
Sn Tin
U Uranium
W Tungsten
Zn Zinc

⚡ Water Power
▨ Major Industrial Areas

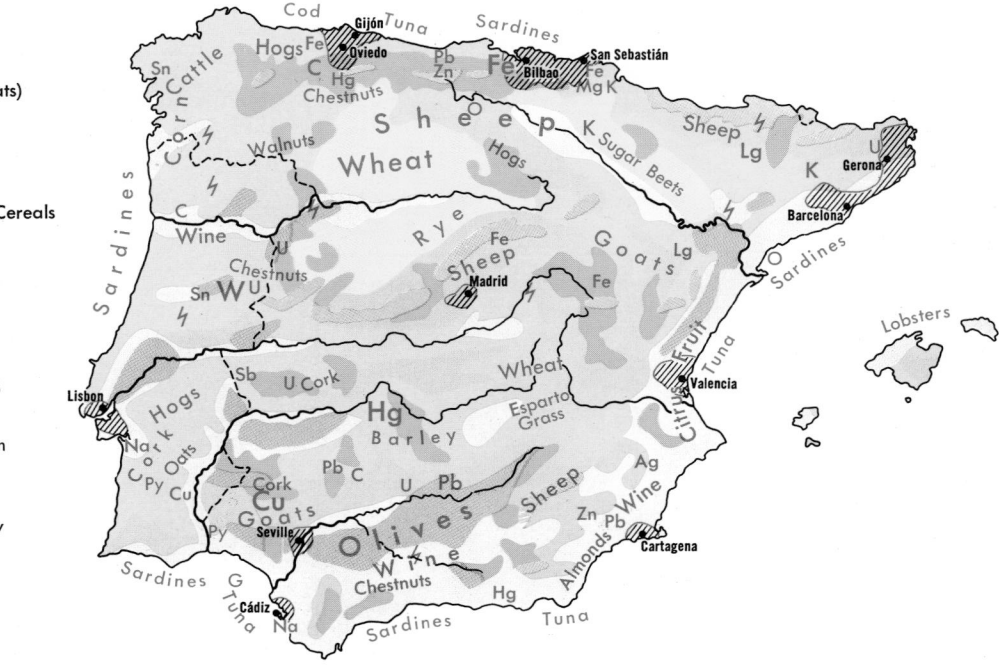

(continued on following page)

San Lorenzo de El Escorial 8.098 . . . . E2
Sanlúcar de Barrameda 29.483 . . . . C4
Sanlúcar la Mayor 6.121 . . . . C4
San Roque 8.224 . . . . D4
San Sebastián 159.557 . . . . E1
Santa Cruz de la Palma 10.393 . . . . B4
Santa Cruz de Mudela 6.354 . . . . E3
Santa Cruz de Tenerife 74.910 . . . . B4
Santa Eugenia 5.946 . . . . B1
Santa Fé 8.990 . . . . E4
Santander 130.019 . . . . D1
Santiago 51.620 . . . . B1
Santo Domingo de la Calzada 5.638 . . . . E1
Santoña 9.546 . . . . E1
San Vicente de Alcántara 7.006 . . . . C3
Saragossa 449.319 . . . . F2
Saragossa1 500.000 . . . . F2
Segorbe 6.962 . . . . F3
Segovia 41.880 . . . . D2
Seo de Urgel 6.604 . . . . G1
Seville 511.447 . . . . D4
Seville1 560.000 . . . . D4
Sitges 8.906 . . . . G2
Socuéllamos 12.610 . . . . E3
Sóller 6.470 . . . . H3
Solsona 5.346 . . . . G2
Sonseca 6.594 . . . . D3
Soria 24.744 . . . . E2
Sotrondio 5.914 . . . . D1
Sueca 20.019 . . . . F3
Tabernes de Valldigna 13.962 . . . . G3
Tafalla 8.858 . . . . F1
Talavera de la Reina 39.889 . . . . D2
Tarancón 8.238 . . . . E3
Tarazona 11.067 . . . . E2
Tarazona de la Mancha 5.952 . . . . F3
Tarifa 9.201 . . . . D4
Tarragona 53.548 . . . . G2
Tarrasa 134.481 . . . . G2
Tárrega 9.036 . . . . G2
Tauste 6.832 . . . . F2
Telde 13.257 . . . . B5
Teruel 20.614 . . . . F2

Tobarra 5.887 . . . . F3
Toledo 43.905 . . . . D3
Tolosa 15.164 . . . . F1
Tomelloso 26.041 . . . . E3
Tordesillas 5.815 . . . . D2
Toro 8.455 . . . . D2
Torredonjimeno 12.507 . . . . D4
Torrejón de Ardoz 21.081 . . . . F4
Torrelavega 19.933 . . . . D1
Torremolinos 20.484 . . . . D4
Torrente 38.397 . . . . F3
Torrevieja 9.431 . . . . F4
Torrijos 6.362 . . . . F4
Torrox 5.583 . . . . E4
Tortosa 20.030 . . . . G2
Totana 12.714 . . . . F4
Trigueros 6.280 . . . . C4
Trujillo 9.024 . . . . D3
Tudela 20.942 . . . . F1
Úbeda 28.306 . . . . E3
Ubrique 13.166 . . . . D4
Utiel 9.168 . . . . F3
Utrera 28.287 . . . . D4
Valdemoro 6.263 . . . . F4
Valdepeñas 24.018 . . . . E3
Valencia 626.675 . . . . F3
Valencia1 700.000 . . . . F3
Vall de Uxó 23.976 . . . . F3
Vallecas G4
Valls 14.189 . . . . G2
Valverde del Camino 10.566 . . . . C4
Vejer de la Frontera 6.184 . . . . D4
Vélez-Málaga 20.794 . . . . E4
Vendrell 7.951 . . . . G2
Vera 4.903 . . . . F4
Vergara 11.541 . . . . E1
Vicálvaro . . . .
Vich 23.449 . . . . H2
Vilafranca del Penedés 16.875 . . . . G2
Villacañas 9.883 . . . . E3
Villacarrillo 9.452 . . . . E3
Villafranca de los

Barros 12.610 . . . . C3
Villagarcía 6.601 . . . . B1
Villajoyosa 12.573 . . . . F3
Villanueva de Córdoba 11.270 . . . . D3
Villanueva del Arzobispo 8.076 . . . . E3
Villanueva de la Serena 16.687 . . . . D3
Villanueva de los Infantes1 8.154 . . . . E3
Villanueva y Geltrú 35.714 . . . . G2
Villarreal de los Infantes 29.482 . . . . G3
Villarrobledo 19.698 . . . . E3
Villarrubia de los Ojos 9.144 . . . . E3
Villaverde F4
Villena 23.483 . . . . F3
Vinaroz 13.727 . . . . G2
Vitoria 124.791 . . . . E1
Yecla 19.352 . . . . F3
Zafra 11.583 . . . . C3
Zalamea de la Serena 6.017 . . . . D3
Zamora 48.791 . . . . D2
Zaragoza (Saragossa) 449.319 . . . . F2

OTHER FEATURES

Alborán (isl.) E5
Alcaraz, Sierra de (range) E3
Alcudia (bay) H3
Almanzor (mt.) D3
Almanzora (riv.) F4
Andalusia (reg.) C4
Aneto (peak) G1
Aragón (reg.) F2
Arosa, Ría de (est.) B1
Asturias (reg.) C1
Balearic (Baleares) (isls.) H3
Barbate (riv.) D4
Biscay (bay) D1
Cabrera (isl.) H3
Cádiz (gulf) C4
Cala Burras (pt.) D4
Canary (isls.) B4
Cantabrian (range) C1
Catalonia (reg.) G2

Cinca (riv.) G2
Columbretes (isls.) G3
Costa Brava (reg.) H2
Costa de Sola (Costa del Sol) (reg.) D4
Creus (cape) H1
Cuenca, Sierra de (range) F3
Demanda, Sierra de la (range) E1
Douro (riv.) C2
Duero (Douro) (riv.) C2
Ebro (riv.) G2
Eresma (riv.) D2
Esla (riv.) D1
Estats (peak) G1
Estremadura (reg.) C3
Finisterre (cape) B1
Formentera (isl.) G4
Formentor (cape) H2
Fuerteventura (isl.) C4
Galicia (reg.) B1
Gata (cape) F4
Gata (mts.) C2
Genil (riv.) D4
Gibraltar (str.) D5
Gomera (isl.) B5
Gran Canaria (isl.) B5
Gredos, Sierra de (range) D2
Guadalimar (riv.) E3
Guadalquivir (riv.) C4
Guadarrama, Sierra de (range) E2
Guadarrama (riv.) E2
Guadiana (riv.) D3
Güdar, Sierra de (range) F2
Henares (riv.) G4
Hierro (isl.) A5
Ibiza (isl.) G4
Jalón (riv.) E2
Jarama (riv.) D2
Júcar (riv.) F3
Lanzarote (isl.) C4
La Palma (isl.) A4
León (reg.) C1
Llobregat (riv.) G2
Majorca (isl.) H3
Mallorca (Majorca) (isl.) H3

Mancha, La (reg.) E3
Manzanares (riv.) F4
Marismas, Las (marsh) C4
Mar Menor (lag.) F4
Mayor (cape) E1
Menorca (Minorca) (isl.) J2
Miño (riv.) B1
Minorca (isl.) J2
Moncayo, Sierra de (range) E2
Montserrat (mt.) G2
Morena, Sierra (range) E3
Mulhacén (mt.) E4
Murcia (reg.) F4
Nao (cape) G3
Navia (riv.) C1
Nevada, Sierra (mts.) E4
New Castile (reg.) E3
Odiel (riv.) C4
Old Castile (reg.) D1
Órbigo (riv.) D1
Palos (cape) F4
Peñalara (mt.) D2
Peñas (cape) D1
Peña Vieja (mt.) D1
Peníbética, Sistema (range) E4
Perdido (mt.) G1
Pyrenees (range) F1

Rosas (gulf) H1
San Jorge (gulf) G2
Segre (riv.) G2
Segura (riv.) F3
Sil (riv.) C1
Tagus (riv.) D3
Tajo (Tagus) (riv.) D3
Teide, Pico de (peak) B5
Tenerife (isl.) B5
Ter (riv.) H1
Tinto (riv.) C4
Toledo (mts.) D3
Tortosa (cape) G2
Trafalgar (cape) C4
Turia (riv.) F3
Ulla (riv.) B1
Urgel, Llanos de (plain) G2
Valencia (gulf) G3
Valencia (reg.) F3
Valencia, Albufera de (lag.) G3
Vascongadas (reg.) E1

PORTUGAL

DISTRICTS

Aveiro 545.230 . . . . B2

Beja 204.440 . . . . B3
Braga 609.415 . . . . B2
Bragança 180.395 . . . . C2
Castelo Branco 254.355 . . . . C2
Coimbra 399.380 . . . . B2
Évora 178.415 . . . . C3
Faro 268.040 . . . . B3
Guarda 210.720 . . . . C2
Leiria 376.940 . . . . A1
Lisbon 1.568.020 . . . . A1
Oporto (Porto) 1.309.560 . . . . B2
Portalegre 145.545 . . . . C3
Porto 1.309.560 . . . . B2
Santarém 427.995 . . . . B3
Setúbal 469.555 . . . . B3
Viana do Castelo 250.510 . . . . B2
Vila Real 265.605 . . . . C2
Viseu 410.795 . . . . C2

CITIES and TOWNS
Abrantes 11.775 . . . . B3
Águeda 9.343 . . . . B2
Albufeira 7.479 . . . . B3
Alcácer do Sal 13.187 . . . . B3
Alcántara 23.699 . . . . A1

Topography

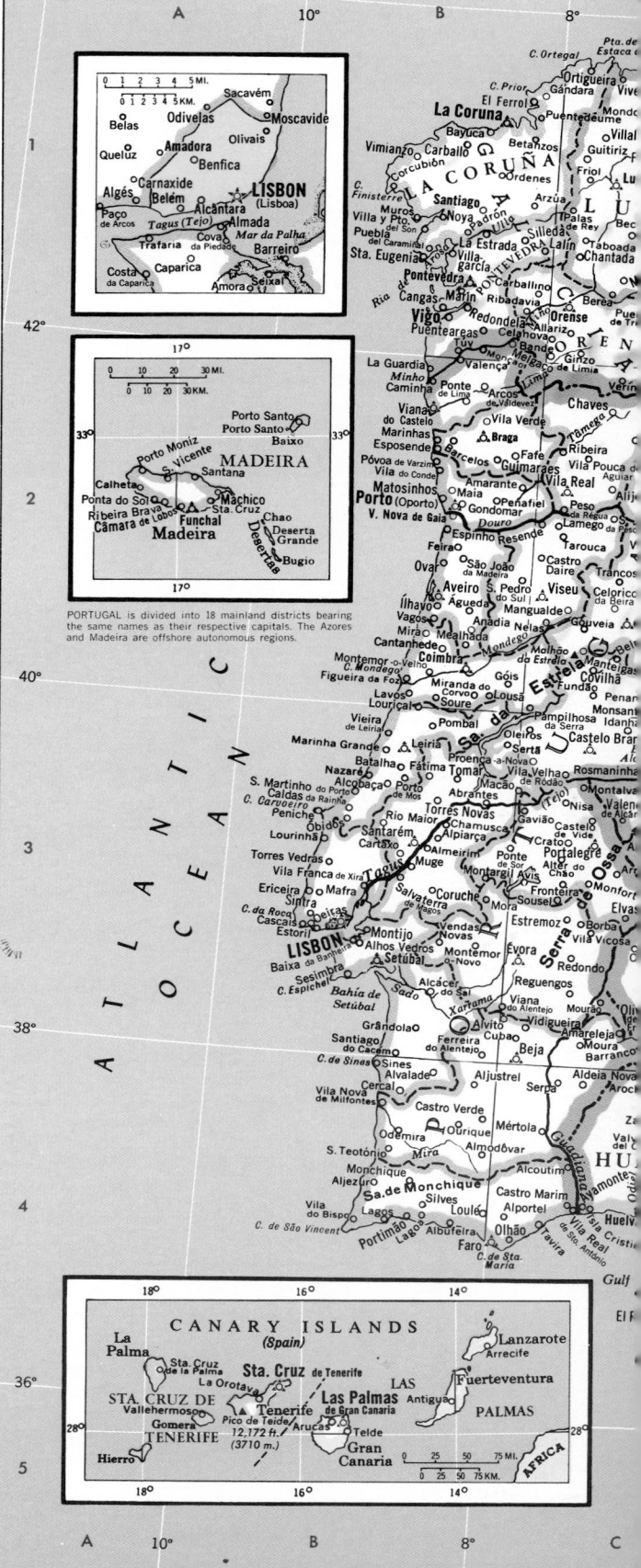

PORTUGAL is divided into 18 mainland districts bearing the same names as their respective capitals. The Azores and Madeira are offshore autonomous regions.

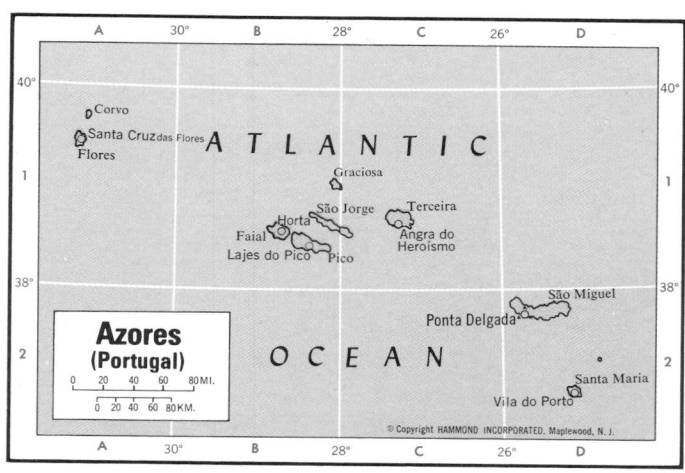

Azores
(Portugal)

© Copyright HAMMOND INCORPORATED, Maplewood, N. J.

AZORES

INTERNAL DIVISIONS

Angra do Heroísmo (dist.) 83.500 . . . . C1
Horta (dist.) 38.700 . . . . A1
Ponta Delgada (dist.) 153.700 . . . . D2

CITIES and TOWNS

Angra do Heroísmo 13.795 . . . . C1
Horta 6.145 . . . . B1
Lajes do Pico 2.147 . . . . B1
Ponta Delgada 20.195 . . . . C2
Santa Cruz das Flores 1.880 . . . . A1
Vila do Porto 4.149 . . . . D2

OTHER FEATURES

Azores (isls.) A2
Corvo (isl.) A1
Faial (isl.) B1
Flores (isl.) A1
Graciosa (isl.) C1
Pico (isl.) C2
Santa Maria (isl.) D2
São Jorge (isl.) B1
São Miguel (isl.) D2
Terceira (isl.) C1

Italy

CONIC PROJECTION

SCALE OF MILES

SCALE OF KILOMETERS

Capitals of Countries .... ☆
Regional Capitals .... ⬡
Provincial Capitals .... △
International Boundaries .... —·—·—
Regional Boundaries .... —··—··—

Scale 1: 4,710,000

The regions are subdivided into provinces bearing the same names as their respective capitals, except:

PROVINCE	CAPITAL
MASSA-CARRARA	Massa
PESARO-URBINO	Pesaro

Vatican City

SCALE

Rome and Environs

© Copyright HAMMOND INCORPORATED, Maplewood, N.J.

VATICAN CITY

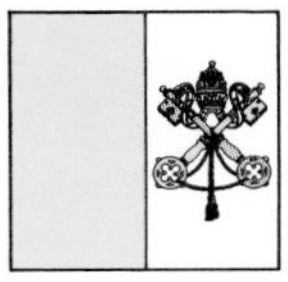

AREA 108.7 acres (44 hectares)
POPULATION 728

SAN MARINO

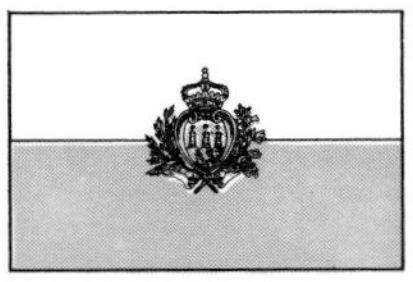

AREA 23.4 sq. mi. (60.6 sq. km.)
POPULATION 19,149

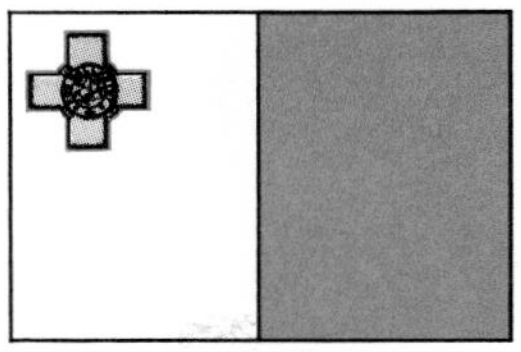

MALTA

AREA 122 sq. mi. (316 sq. km.)
POPULATION 343,970
CAPITAL Valletta
LARGEST CITY Sliema
HIGHEST POINT 787 ft. (240 m.)
MONETARY UNIT Maltese lira
MAJOR LANGUAGES Maltese, English
MAJOR RELIGION Roman Catholicism

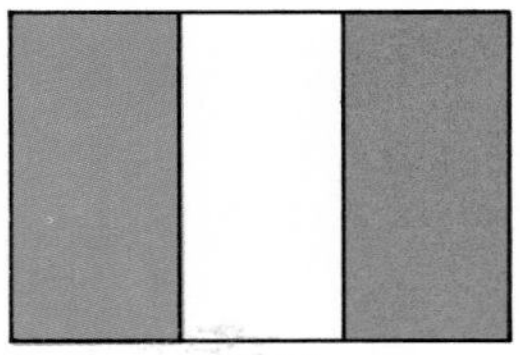

ITALY

AREA 116,303 sq. mi. (301,225 sq. km.)
POPULATION 57,140,000
CAPITAL Rome
LARGEST CITY Rome
HIGHEST POINT Dufourspitze (Mte. Rosa) 15,203 ft. (4,634 m.)
MONETARY UNIT lira
MAJOR LANGUAGE Italian
MAJOR RELIGION Roman Catholicism

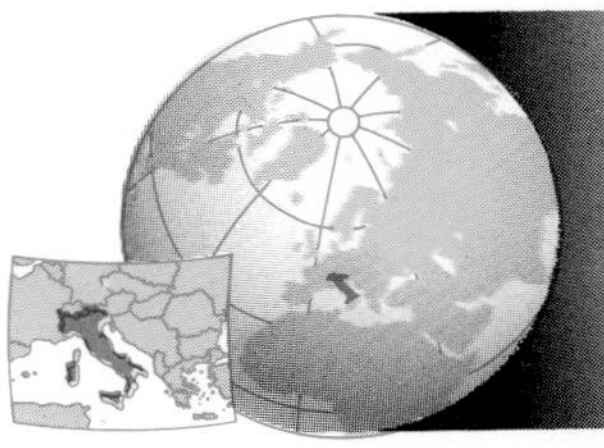

ITALY

REGIONS

Abruzzi 1,166,664 .... D3
Aosta 109,150 .... A2
Apulia (Puglia) 3,582,787 .... F4
Basilicata 603,064 .... F4
Calabria 1,988,051 .... F5
Campania 5,059,348 .... E4
Emilia-Romagna 3,846,755 .... C2
Friuli-Venezia Giulia 1,213,532 .... D1
Latium (Lazio) 4,689,482 .... D3
Liguria 1,853,578 .... B2
Lombardy 8,543,657 .... B2
Marche 1,359,907 .... D3
Molise 319,807 .... E4
Piedmont 4,432,313 .... A2
Sardinia 1,473,800 .... B4
Sicily 4,680,715 .... D6
Trentino-Alto Adige 841,886 .... C1
Tuscany 3,473,097 .... C3
Umbria 775,783 .... D3
Veneto 2,109,502 .... D3

PROVINCES

Agrigento 454,045 .... D6
Alessandria 483,183 .... B2
Ancona 416,611 .... D3
Aosta 109,150 .... A2
Arezzo 306,340 .... C3
Ascoli Piceno 340,758 .... D3
Asti 218,547 .... B2
Avellino 427,509 .... E4
Bari 1,351,288 .... F4
Belluno 221,155 .... D1
Benevento 286,499 .... E4
Bergamo 829,019 .... B2
Bologna 918,844 .... C2
Bolzano-Bozen 414,041 .... C1
Brescia 957,686 .... C2
Brindisi 366,027 .... G4
Cagliari 802,888 .... B5
Caltanissetta 282,069 .... D6
Campobasso 227,641 .... E4
Caserta 677,959 .... E4
Catania 938,273 .... E6
Catanzaro 718,069 .... F5
Chieti 351,567 .... E3
Como 720,463 .... B2
Cosenza 691,659 .... F5
Cremona 334,281 .... B2
Cuneo 540,504 .... A2
Enna 202,131 .... E6
Ferrara 383,639 .... C2
Florence 1,146,367 .... C3
Foggia 657,292 .... E4
Forlì 565,470 .... D2
Frosinone 422,630 .... D4
Genoa 1,087,973 .... B2
Gorizia 142,412 .... D2
Grosseto 216,315 .... C3
Imperia 225,127 .... B3
Isernia 92,166 .... E4
L'Aquila 293,066 .... D3
La Spezia 244,435 .... B2
Latina 376,238 .... D4
Lecce 696,503 .... G4
Leghorn 335,265 .... C3
Lucca 380,356 .... C3
Macerata 286,155 .... D3
Mantua 376,892 .... C2
Massa-Carrara 200,955 .... C2
Matera 194,629 .... F4
Messina 654,703 .... E5
Milan 3,903,685 .... B2
Modena 553,852 .... C2
Naples 2,709,929 .... E4
Novara 496,811 .... B2
Nuoro 273,021 .... B4
Padua 762,998 .... C2
Palermo 1,124,015 .... D5
Parma 395,497 .... C2
Pavia 526,389 .... B2
Perugia 552,936 .... D3
Pesaro e Urbino 316,383 .... D3
Pescara 264,981 .... E3
Piacenza 284,881 .... B2
Pisa 375,933 .... C3
Pistoia 254,335 .... C2
Pordenone 253,906 .... D2
Potenza 408,435 .... E4
Ragusa 255,047 .... E6
Ravenna 351,876 .... D2
Reggio di Calabria 578,323 .... E5
Reggio nell'Emilia 392,696 .... C2
Rieti 143,162 .... D3
Rome 3,490,377 .... F6
Rovigo 251,908 .... C2
Salerno 957,452 .... E4
Sassari 397,891 .... B4
Savona 296,043 .... B2
Siena 257,221 .... C3
Sondrio 169,149 .... B1
Syracuse 365,039 .... E6
Taranto 511,677 .... F4
Teramo 257,080 .... D3
Terni 222,847 .... D3
Trapani 405,393 .... D5
Trento 427,845 .... C1
Treviso 668,620 .... D2
Trieste 300,304 .... E2
Turin 2,287,016 .... A2
Udine 516,910 .... D1
Varese 725,823 .... B2
Venice 807,251 .... D2
Vercelli 406,252 .... B2
Verona 733,595 .... C2
Vicenza 677,884 .... C2
Viterbo 257,075 .... C3

CITIES and TOWNS

Acireale 34,081 .... E6
Acqui Terme 20,099 .... B2
Acri 8,150 .... F5
Adrano 31,988 .... E6
Adria 11,951 .... D2
Agira 11,262 .... E6
Agnone 3,965 .... E4
Agrigento 40,513 .... D6
Agropoli 9,413 .... E4
Alassio 13,512 .... A2
Alatri 5,710 .... D4
Alba 23,522 .... B2
Albano Laziale 15,561 .... F7
Albenga 13,397 .... B3
Albino 8,837 .... B2
Alcamo 41,448 .... D6
Alessandria 78,644 .... B2
Alghero 28,454 .... B4
Altamura 44,879 .... F4
Amalfi 4,205 .... E4
Amantea 6,132 .... E5
Amelia 4,331 .... D3
Ancona 88,427 .... D3
Andria 76,405 .... F4
Anguillara Sabazia 3,241 .... F6
Anzio 14,966 .... D4
Aosta 35,053 .... A2
Aprilia 18,412 .... D4
Aragona 11,213 .... D6
Arezzo 56,693 .... C3
Argenta 6,682 .... D2
Ariano Irpino 9,796 .... E4
Ariccia 7,287 .... F7
Artena 5,034 .... F7
Ascoli Piceno 43,041 .... D3
Assisi 4,630 .... D3
Asti 62,277 .... B2
Atessa 3,079 .... E3
Atri 4,686 .... D3
Augusta 32,501 .... E6
Avellino 44,750 .... E4
Aversa 46,536 .... E4
Avezzano 26,456 .... D3
Avigliano 5,400 .... E4
Avola 29,089 .... E6
Bagheria 32,465 .... D5
Barcellona Pozzo di Gotto 25,280 .... E5
Bari 339,110 .... F4
Barletta 75,116 .... F4
Bassano del Grappa 33,002 .... C2
Bellagio 3,258 .... B2
Belluno 22,180 .... D1
Benevento 48,523 .... E4
Bergamo 127,553 .... B2
Biancavilla 18,743 .... E6
Biella 46,453 .... B2
Bisceglie 45,014 .... F4
Bitonto 39,714 .... F4
Bitti 4,606 .... B4
Bologna 493,282 .... C2
Bolzano (Bolzen) 102,806 .... C1
Bondeno 7,451 .... C2
Bonorva 5,232 .... B4
Bordighera 8,994 .... A3
Borgo 4,013 .... C1
Borgomanero 16,655 .... B2
Bòrgo San Lorenzo 7,699 .... C2
Bosa 8,045 .... B4
Boves 3,896 .... A2
Bra 18,399 .... A2
Bracciano 7,681 .... C3
Brescia 189,092 .... C2
Bressanone 12,261 .... C1
Brindisi 76,612 .... G4
Bronte 17,823 .... E6
Brunico 5,175 .... D1
Budrio 5,635 .... C2
Busto Arsizio 72,400 .... B2
Cagli 4,356 .... D3
Cagliari 211,015 .... B5
Caltagirone 34,444 .... E6
Caltanissetta 52,838 .... D6
Camaiore 8,578 .... C3
Camerino 4,644 .... D3
Campobasso 35,551 .... E4
Campo Tures 1,325 .... C1
Canicatti 28,761 .... E6
Canosa di Puglia 30,263 .... E4
Cantù 28,617 .... B2
Capua 13,938 .... E4
Caravaggio 11,298 .... B2
Carbonia 23,031 .... B5
Carini 14,255 .... D5
Carloforte 6,671 .... B5
Carmagnola 16,469 .... A2
Carpi 41,789 .... C2
Carrara 56,236 .... C2
Casale Monferrato 35,156 .... B2
Casalmaggiore 6,374 .... C2
Cascina-Navacchio 28,263 .... C3
Caserta 51,621 .... E4
Cassano allo Ionio 9,661 .... F5
Cassino 14,747 .... D4
Castelfranco Veneto 16,042 .... D2
Castel Gandolfo 2,965 .... F7
Castellammare del Golfo 13,144 .... D5
Castellammare di Stabia 64,341 .... E4
Castel San Pietro Terme 6,985 .... C2
Castelvetrano 29,167 .... D6
Castiglion Fiorentino 3,797 .... C3
Castrovillari 15,207 .... F5
Catania 403,390 .... E6
Catanzaro 52,054 .... F5
Caulonia 3,402 .... F5
Cava de'Tirreni 33,868 .... E4
Cavarzere 7,917 .... D2
Cecina 19,415 .... C3
Cefalù 11,043 .... E5
Ceglie Messapico 17,512 .... F4
Celano 9,531 .... D3
Cerignola 44,648 .... E4
Cernobbio 8,026 .... B2
Cerveteri 5,239 .... E6
Cesano 2,883 .... F6
Cesena 49,915 .... D2
Cesenatico 12,805 .... D2
Chiari 12,017 .... C2
Chiavari 29,950 .... B2
Chieri 27,548 .... A2
Chieti 31,895 .... E3
Chioggia 24,044 .... D2
Chivasso 21,369 .... A2
Ciampino 36,728 .... F7
Cittadella 9,321 .... C2
Città di Castello 18,880 .... C3
Cittanova 11,045 .... F5
Cividale del Friuli 8,345 .... D1
Civitavecchia 41,305 .... C3
Clusone-Fiorine 6,428 .... C2
Codroipo 6,117 .... D2
Colle di Val d'Elsa 8,657 .... C3
Comacchio 10,437 .... D2
Comiso 24,508 .... E6
Como 73,257 .... B2
Conegliano 28,635 .... D2
Conversano 16,805 .... F4
Corato 38,163 .... F4
Cori 6,829 .... F7
Corigliano Calabro 14,518 .... F5
Corleone 11,057 .... D6
Correggio 11,415 .... C2
Cortina d'Ampezzo 7,285 .... D1
Cortona 3,482 .... C3
Cosenza 94,565 .... F5
Courmayeur 1,401 .... A2
Crema 26,061 .... B2
Cremona 75,988 .... B2
Crotone 44,081 .... F5
Cuneo 41,633 .... A2
Cuorgnè 6,752 .... A2
Desenzano del Garda 14,624 .... C2
Diano Marina 6,001 .... B3
Domodossola 18,562 .... A1
Dorgali 6,714 .... B4
Eboli 19,787 .... E4
Edolo 3,707 .... C1
Empoli 30,526 .... C3
Enna 27,351 .... E6
Este 12,992 .... C2
Fabriano 18,355 .... D3
Faenza 36,241 .... D2
Fano 31,238 .... D3
Fasano 21,247 .... F4
Favara 27,940 .... D6
Feltre 11,806 .... C1
Fermo 17,521 .... D3
Ferrandina 8,372 .... F4
Ferrara 97,507 .... C2
Fidenza 18,064 .... B2
Fiesole 3,772 .... C3
Finale Emilia 7,474 .... C2
Finale Ligure 11,461 .... B2
Firenze (Florence) 441,654 .... C3
Fiumicino 13,180 .... F7
Florence 441,654 .... C3
Floridia 16,562 .... E6
Foggia 136,436 .... E4
Foligno 26,887 .... D3
Fondi 16,472 .... D4
Forlì 83,303 .... D2
Formia 18,978 .... D4
Fossano 15,857 .... A2
Fossombrone 5,882 .... D3
Francavilla Fontana 30,347 .... F4
Frascati 14,217 .... F7
Frosinone 34,066 .... D4
Gaeta 21,973 .... D4
Galatina 22,137 .... G4
Galatone 13,880 .... F4
Gallarate 43,773 .... B2
Gallipoli 16,878 .... F4
Garessio 3,359 .... A2
Gela 66,845 .... E6
Gemona 6,863 .... D1
Genoa 787,011 .... B2
Genova (Genoa) 787,011 .... B2
Genzano di Roma 14,147 .... F7
Giarre 18,233 .... E6
Gioia del Colle 23,299 .... F4
Gioiosa Ionica 3,811 .... F5
Giovinazzo 17,768 .... F4
Giulianova 17,926 .... E3
Gorizia 35,912 .... D2
Gravina in Puglia 32,006 .... F4
Grosseto 48,309 .... C3
Grottaferrata 10,639 .... F7
Grottaglie 23,556 .... F4
Guardiagrele 4,122 .... E3
Guastalla 7,639 .... C2
Gubbio 12,371 .... D3
Guidonia 8,413 .... F6
Iglesias 24,472 .... B5
Imola 42,111 .... C2
Imperia 37,585 .... B3
Isernia 12,290 .... E4
Ivrea 26,530 .... B2
Jesi 33,011 .... D3
Ladispoli 6,625 .... E6
Lagonegro 5,613 .... E4
La Maddalena 10,405 .... B4
Lanciano 19,652 .... E3
Lanusei 5,508 .... B5
Lanuvio 2,970 .... F7
L'Aquila 36,233 .... D3
Larino 5,166 .... E4
La Spezia 121,254 .... B2
Latina 53,003 .... D4
Lauria 4,927 .... E4
Lavello 11,486 .... E4
Lecce 80,114 .... G4
Lecco 53,165 .... B2
Leghorn 170,369 .... C3
Legnago 15,534 .... C2
Lendinara 7,079 .... C2
Lentini 31,429 .... E6
Leonforte 16,317 .... E6
Lerici 5,407 .... B2
Licata 40,997 .... D6
Lido di Ostia 61,492 .... F7
Lido di Venezia 18,794 .... D2
Lipari 3,886 .... E5
Livigno 2,135 .... C1
Livorno (Leghorn) 170,369 .... C3
Lodi 42,489 .... B2
Lonigo 6,368 .... C2
Lucca 54,280 .... C3
Lucera 29,355 .... E4
Lugo 19,497 .... D2
Macerata 33,470 .... D3
Macomer 9,433 .... B4
Maglie 13,326 .... G4
Manduria 25,194 .... F4
Manfredonia 44,463 .... F4
Mantua 59,529 .... C2
Marino 12,135 .... F7
Marsala 34,150 .... D6
Marsciano 5,372 .... D3
Martina Franca 31,811 .... F4
Massa 56,591 .... C2
Massafra 22,610 .... F4
Massa Marittima 6,438 .... C3
Matera 43,026 .... F4
Mazara del Vallo 37,441 .... D6
Mazzarino 14,981 .... E6
Melfi 13,355 .... E4
Menfi 12,386 .... D6
Merano 30,951 .... C1
Mesagne 26,955 .... G4
Messina 203,937 .... E5
Mestre 184,818 .... D2
Milan 1,724,557 .... B2
Milazzo 18,576 .... E5
Minturno 2,428 .... D4
Mirandola 11,551 .... C2
Mira Taglio 10,194 .... D2
Mistretta 6,631 .... E6
Modena 149,029 .... C2
Modica 31,074 .... E6
Mola di Bari 23,778 .... F4
Molfetta 63,250 .... F4
Moncalieri 49,953 .... A2
Mondovì Breo 12,524 .... A2
Monfalcone 29,589 .... D2
Monopoli 29,776 .... F4
Monreale 19,348 .... D5
Monselice 9,047 .... C2
Montalto Uffugo 3,173 .... E5
Montebelluna 9,573 .... D2
Montefiascone 6,885 .... D3
Montepulciano 4,069 .... C3
Monterotondo 15,869 .... F6
Monte Sant'Angelo 17,756 .... F4
Montevarchi 16,849 .... C3
Monza 110,735 .... B2
Mortara 13,929 .... B2
Naples 1,214,775 .... E4
Nardò 24,142 .... F4
Narni 6,213 .... D3
Naro 13,171 .... D6
Nettuno 20,927 .... D4
Nicastro 27,206 .... F5
Nicosia 13,982 .... E6
Niscemi 23,925 .... E6
Nizza Monferrato 7,532 .... B2
Nocera Inferiore 44,415 .... E4
Noto 21,606 .... E6
Novara 92,634 .... B2
Novi Ligure 29,944 .... B2
Nuoro 30,551 .... B4
Olbia 20,998 .... B4
Oliena 7,030 .... B4
Orbetello 6,884 .... C3
Oristano 20,966 .... B5
Ortona 11,966 .... E3
Orvieto 8,813 .... D3
Osimo 12,034 .... D3
Ostia Antica 2,583 .... F7
Ostuni 27,241 .... F4
Otranto 3,707 .... G4
Ozieri 9,149 .... B4
Pachino 20,427 .... E6
Padua 210,950 .... C2
Palazzolo Acreide 8,981 .... E6
Palermo 556,374 .... D5
Palestrina 9,239 .... F7
Palma di Montechiaro 22,381 .... D6
Palmi 14,405 .... E5
Palombara Sabina 5,292 .... F6
Pantelleria 3,116 .... C6
Paola 11,330 .... E5
Parma 151,967 .... C2
Partanna 10,303 .... D6
Partinico 25,447 .... D6
Paterno 41,504 .... E6
Patti 7,500 .... E5
Pavia 80,639 .... B2
Pavullo nel Frignano 5,026 .... C2
Penne 5,889 .... D3
Pergine Valsugana 6,248 .... C1
Pergola 3,866 .... D3
Perugia 65,975 .... D3
Pesaro 72,104 .... D3
Pescara 125,391 .... E3
Pescia 9,918 .... C3
Piacenza 100,001 .... B2
Piazza Armerina 21,754 .... E6
Pietrasanta 6,620 .... B3
Pinerolo 33,935 .... A2
Piombino 35,641 .... C3
Piove di Sacco 7,035 .... C2
Pisa 91,156 .... C3
Pisticci 11,239 .... F4
Pistoia 55,403 .... C2
Poggibonsi 21,271 .... C3
Pomezia 11,915 .... F7
Pont Canavese 4,075 .... A2
Pontecorvo 5,986 .... D4
Pontinia 3,166 .... D4
Pontremoli 5,222 .... B2
Popoli 5,372 .... E3
Pordenone 43,230 .... D2
Portocivitanova 25,773 .... D3
Porto Empedocle 15,986 .... D6
Portoferraio 7,579 .... C3
Portofino 720 .... B2
Portogruaro 12,258 .... D2
Portomaggiore 6,343 .... C2
Porto Recanati 5,389 .... D3
Porto Torres 15,422 .... B4
Potenza 46,869 .... E4
Pozzallo 12,199 .... E6
Pozzuoli 53,546 .... D4
Prato 108,385 .... C3
Prima Porta 11,393 .... F6
Priverno 9,950 .... D4
Putignano 19,290 .... F4
Quartu Sant'Elena 29,715 .... B5
Ragusa 55,751 .... E6
Rapallo 22,272 .... B2
Ravenna 75,153 .... D2
Recanati 10,176 .... D3
Reggio di Calabria 110,291 .... E5
Reggio nell'Emilia 102,337 .... C2
Rho 39,206 .... B2
Riesi 15,855 .... E6
Rieti 26,775 .... D3
Rimini 101,579 .... D2
Rionero in Vulture 11,230 .... E4
Riva del Garda 8,513 .... C2
Roccastrada 2,629 .... C3
Rome (cap.) 2,535,018 .... F6
Ronciglione 5,900 .... C3
Rossano 12,119 .... F5
Rovereto 26,827 .... C2
Rovigo 31,124 .... C2
Ruvo di Puglia 23,133 .... F4

(continued on following page)

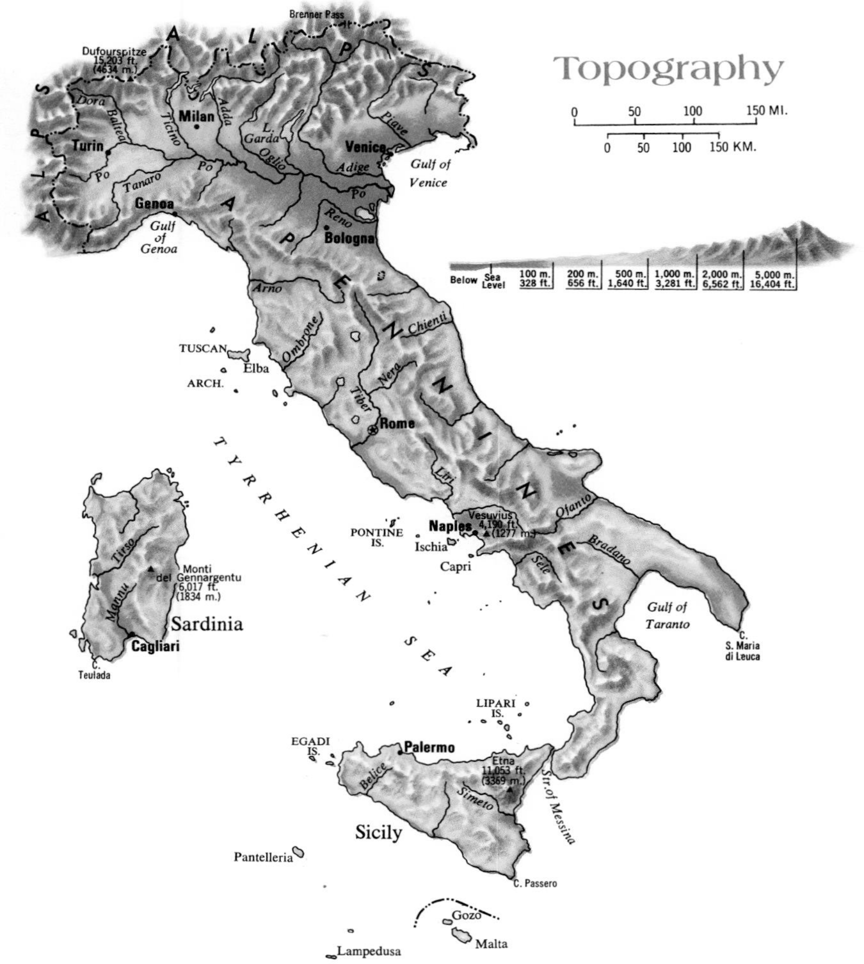
Topography
0 50 100 150 MI.
0 50 100 150 KM.
Below Sea Level
100 m. 328 ft.
200 m. 656 ft.
500 m. 1,640 ft.
1,000 m. 3,281 ft.
2,000 m. 6,562 ft.
5,000 m. 16,404 ft.
Brenner Pass
Dufourspitze 15,203 ft. (4634 m.)
A L P S
Dora Baltea
Ticino
Adda
Garda
Oglio
Piave
Adige
Milan
Turin
Po
Tanaro
Venice
Gulf of Venice
Genoa
Gulf of Genoa
Reno
Bologna
A P E N N I N E S
Arno
Ombrone
Chienti
Nera
Tiber
TUSCAN ARCH.
Elba
Rome
T Y R R H E N I A N S E A
PONTINE IS.
Ischia
Naples
Vesuvius 4,190 ft. (1277 m.)
Capri
Liri
Ofanto
Bradano
Sele
Gulf of Taranto
S. Maria di Leuca
Sardinia
Tirso
Mannu
Monti del Gennargentu 6,017 ft. (1834 m.)
Cagliari
C. Teulada
LIPARI IS.
EGADI IS.
Palermo
Etna 11,053 ft. (3369 m.)
Belice
Simeto
Str. of Messina
Sicily
C. Passero
Pantelleria
Gozo
Malta
Lampedusa

Agriculture, Industry and Resources

DOMINANT LAND USE

Wheat, Rice, Dairy

Pasture Livestock

Cereals, Livestock

Fruit, Truck and Mixed Farming

Grapes, Wine

Forests

Nonagricultural Land

MAJOR MINERAL OCCURRENCES

Ab	Asbestos	K	Potash	Pb	Lead
Al	Bauxite	Lg	Lignite	Py	Pyrites
C	Coal	Mr	Marble	S	Sulfur
Fe	Iron Ore	Na	Salt	Sb	Antimony
G	Natural Gas	O	Petroleum	Zn	Zinc
Hg	Mercury				

⚡ Water Power

Major Industrial Areas

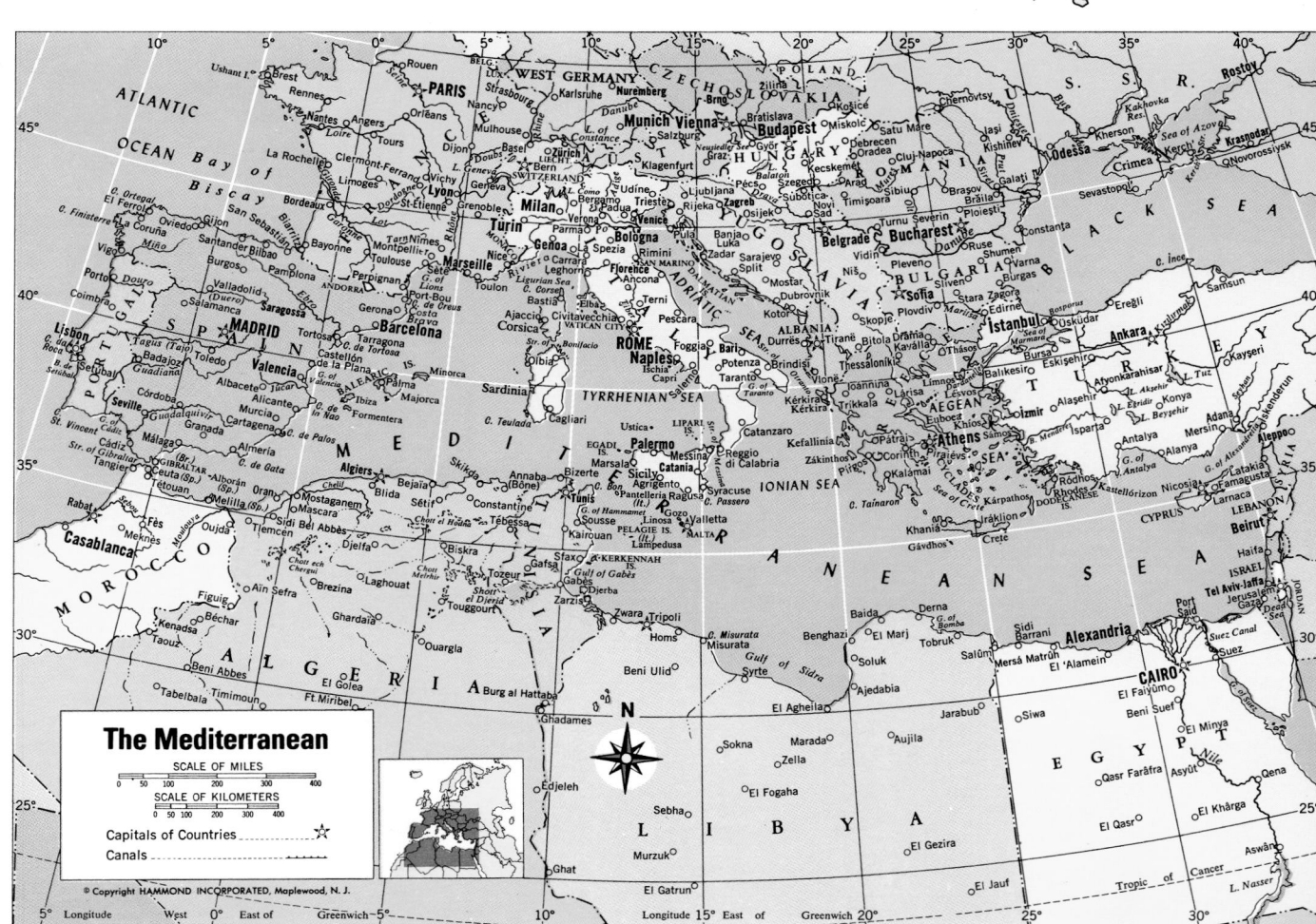

The Mediterranean

SCALE OF MILES
0 50 100 200 300 400

SCALE OF KILOMETERS
0 50 100 200 300 400

Capitals of Countries .... ☆
Canals ....

® Copyright HAMMOND INCORPORATED, Maplewood, N.J.

SWITZERLAND

AREA 15,943 sq. mi. (41,292 sq. km.)
POPULATION 6,365,960
CAPITAL Bern
LARGEST CITY Zürich
HIGHEST POINT Dufourspitze
   (Mte. Rosa) 15,203 ft. (4,634 m.)
MONETARY UNIT Swiss franc
MAJOR LANGUAGES German, French,
   Italian, Romansch
MAJOR RELIGIONS Protestantism,
   Roman Catholicism

LIECHTENSTEIN

AREA 61 sq. mi. (158 sq. km.)
POPULATION 25,220
CAPITAL Vaduz
LARGEST CITY Vaduz
HIGHEST POINT Grauspitze 8,527 ft.
   (2,599 m.)
MONETARY UNIT Swiss franc
MAJOR LANGUAGE German
MAJOR RELIGION Roman Catholicism

SWITZERLAND

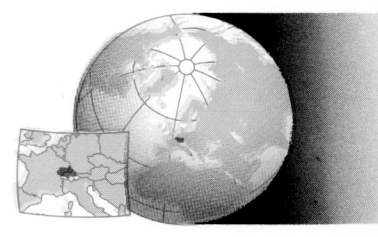

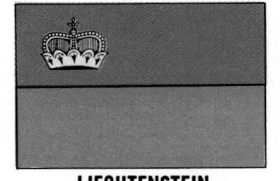

LIECHTENSTEIN

Languages

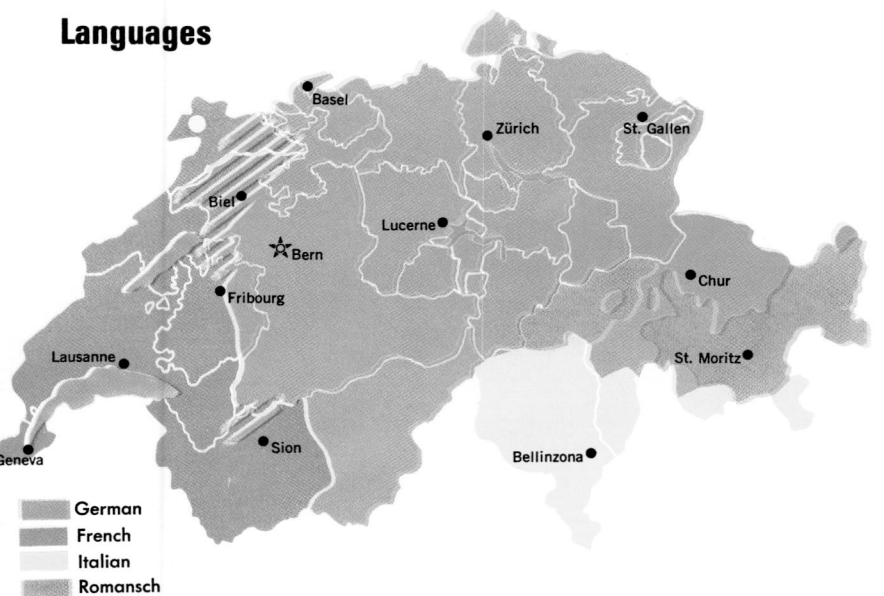

- German
- French
- Italian
- Romansch

Switzerland is a multilingual nation with four official languages. 70% of the people speak German, 19% French, 10% Italian and 1% Romansch.

SWITZERLAND

CANTONS

Aargau 442,400	F2
Appenzell, Ausser Rhoden 46,700	H2
Appenzell, Inner Rhoden 13,500	H2
Baselland 219,500	E2
Baselstadt 209,700	E1
Bern 920,900	D2
Fribourg 181,600	D3
Geneva (Genève) 338,600	B4
Glarus 35,700	H3
Graubünden (Grisons) 164,300	H3
Grisons (Graubünden) 164,300	H3
Jura 67,200	D2
Lucerne (Luzern) 292,900	F2
Luzern 292,900	F2
Neuchâtel 162,200	C3
Nidwalden 26,900	F3
Obwalden 25,400	F3
Sankt Gallen 385,000	H2
Schaffhausen 69,300	G1
Schwyz 93,100	G2
Soleure (Solothurn) 221,800	E2
Solothurn 221,800	E2
Thurgau 183,500	H1
Ticino 264,400	G4
Uri 34,000	G3
Valais 214,000	D4
Vaud 523,500	B3
Zug 73,600	G2
Zürich 1,117,300	G2

CITIES and TOWNS

Aadorf 3,022	G2
Aarau 16,881	F2
Aarau* 51,800	F2
Aarberg 3,122	D2
Aarburg 5,943	E2
Adelboden 3,326	E3
Adliswil 15,920	F2
Aeschi bei Spiez 1,402	E3
Affoltern am Albis 7,363	F2
Affoltern im Emmental 1,223	E2
Aigle 6,532	C4
Airolo 2,140	G3
Alle 1,615	D2
Allschwil 17,638	D1
Alpnach 3,277	F3
Altdorf 8,647	G3
Altstätten 9,084	J2
Amriswil 7,601	H1
Andelfingen 1,453	G1
Andermatt 1,589	G3
Appenzell 5,217	H2
Arbedo-Castione 2,456	G4
Arbon 12,227	H1
Arbon* 15,400	H1
Ardon 1,498	D4
Arosa 2,717	J3
Arth 7,580	F2
Ascona 4,086	G4
Attalens 1,116	C3
Au 4,944	J2
Aubonne 1,983	B4
Avenches 2,235	D3
Baar 14,074	F2
Baden 14,115	F2
Baden* 66,800	F2
Bad Ragaz 3,713	H2
Balerna 3,885	G5
Balsthal 5,607	E2
Baretswil 2,733	G2
Basel 199,600	E1
Basel* 379,700	E1
Bassecourt 2,985	D2
Bätterkinden 1,757	E2

Bauma 3,159	G2
Beatenberg 1,263	E3
Beinwil am See 2,520	F2
Belfaux 1,075	D3
Bellinzona 16,979	H4
Bellinzona* 31,000	H4
Belp 6,981	D3
Berg 1,039	H1
Bern (cap.) 154,700	D3
Bern* 285,300	D3
Beromünster 1,552	F2
Bettlach 4,046	D2
Bex 5,069	C4
Biasca 4,696	H4
Biberist 7,769	D2
Biel 63,400	D2
Biel*89,900	D2
Bière 1,252	B3
Binningen 15,344	D1
Bischofszell 4,233	H1
Blumenstein 1,049	E3
Bodio 1,425	G4
Bolligen 26,121	E3
Boltigen 1,519	D3
Bonaduz 1,289	H3
Boncourt 1,528	C2
Bönigen 1,738	E3
Boswil 1,904	F2
Boudry 4,372	C3
Bourg Saint-Pierre 236	D5
Breil-Brigels 1,215	H3
Breitenbach 2,455	E2
Bremgarten 4,873	F2
Brienz 2,796	F3
Brig 5,191	F4
Brissago 2,120	G4
Brittnau 2,888	E2
Broc 1,842	D3
Brugg 8,635	F2
Brusio 1,344	K4
Bubendorf 2,070	E2
Bubikon 3,244	G2
Buchs 8,454	H2
Büchs 11,043	G1
Bülle 7,556	D3
Buochs 3,232	F3
Büren an der Aare 3,085	D2
Burgdorf 15,888	E2
Burgdorf* 18,400	E2
Bürglen, Thurgau 1,920	H1
Bürglen, Uri 3,401	G3
Bussigny-près-Lausanne 4,509	B3
Bütschwil 3,270	H2
Carouge 14,055	B4
Castagnola 4,430	G4
Cazis 1,687	H3
Cernier 1,717	C2
Chalais 1,651	E4
Cham 8,209	F2
Chamoson 2,049	D4
Charmey 1,155	D3
Château-d'Oex 3,203	D4
Châtel-Saint-Denis 2,842	C3
Chêne-Bougeries 8,670	B4
Chavornay 1,521	C3
Chexbres 1,607	C3
Chiasso 8,868	G5
Chippis 1,561	E4
Chur 32,400	J3
Churwalden 1,052	J3
Claro 1,143	G4
Collombey-Muraz 2,279	C4
Collonge-Bellerive 3,541	B4
Conthey 4,259	D4
Coppet 1,097	B4
Corcelles-pres-Payerne 1,256	C3
Corgémont 1,645	D2
Cossonay 1,529	B3
Courgenay 1,954	D2
Courrendlin 2,656	D2
Courroux 1,788	D2
Courtelary 1,462	D2
Courtételle 1,864	D2
Couvet 3,481	C3
Cully 1,535	C4
Davos 10,238	J3
Degersheim 3,400	H2
Delémont 11,797	D2
Derendingen 4,917	E2
Dielsdorf 2,691	F1
Diemtigen 1,913	D3
Diepoldsau 3,311	J2
Diessenhofen 2,532	G1
Dietikon 22,705	F2
Disentis-Muster 2,319	G3
Domat-Ems 5,701	H3
Dombresson 1,109	C2
Dornach 5,258	E2
Döttingen 3,380	F1
Dübendorf 19,639	G2
Düdingen 4,932	D3
Dürnten 4,820	G2
Dürrenroth 1,084	E2
Ebnat-Kappel 5,131	H2
Echallens 1,643	C3
Ecublens 6,379	B3
Egg 5,250	G2
Eggiwil 2,391	E3
Eglisau 2,160	G1
Egnach 3,466	H1

(continued on following page)

Agriculture, Industry and Resources

DOMINANT LAND USE

- Cereals, Dairy
- Pasture Livestock
- General Farming, Livestock
- Fruit, Truck, Mixed Farming
- Forests
- Nonagricultural Land

⚡ Water Power
▨ Major Industrial Areas

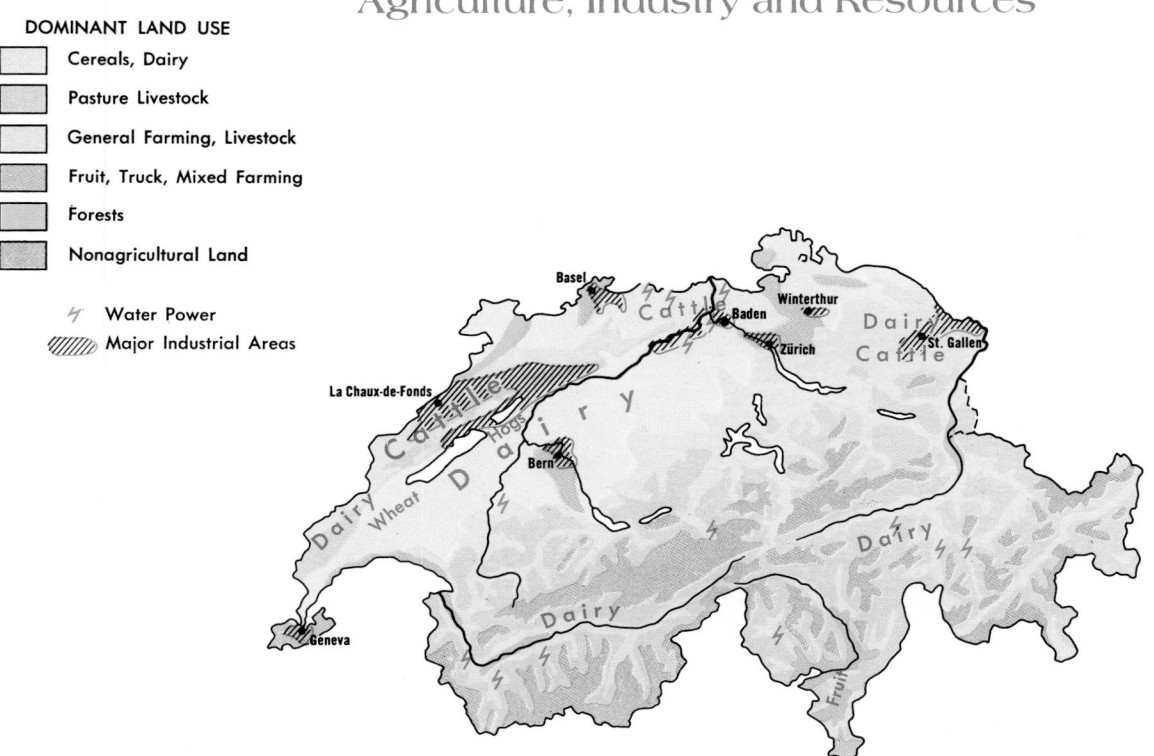

Topography

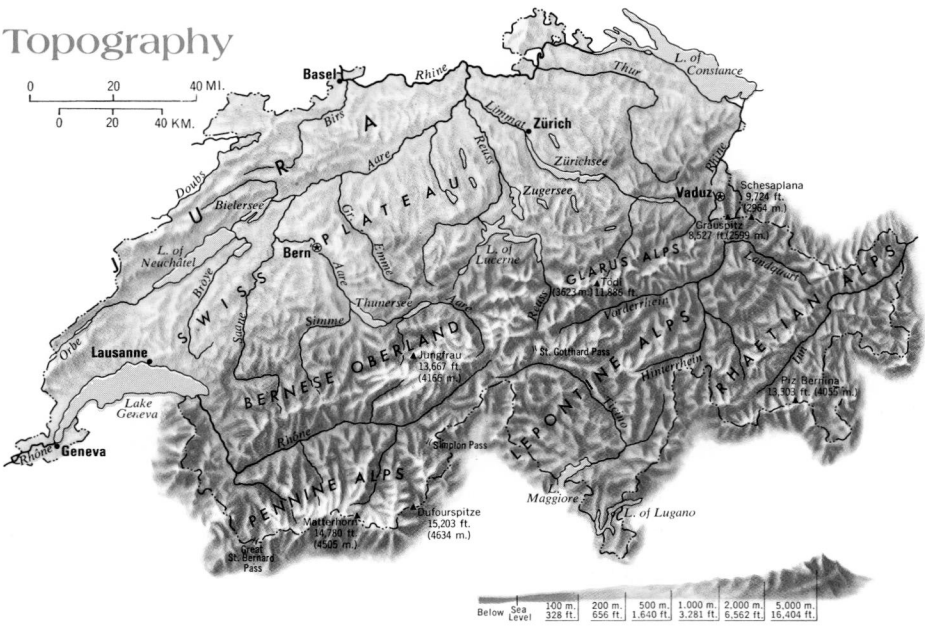

Below Sea Level | 100 m. 328 ft. | 200 m. 656 ft. | 500 m. 1,640 ft. | 1,000 m. 3,281 ft. | 2,000 m. 6,562 ft. | 5,000 m. 16,404 ft.

Einsiedeln 10,020 ...G2
Elgg 2,970 ...G2
Emmen 22,040 ...F2
Engelberg 2,841 ...F3
Ennenda 2,762 ...H2
Entlebuch 3,310 ...F3
Erlach 1,052 ...D2
Erlenbach im Simmental 1,436 ...E3
Ermatingen 1,787 ...H1
Erstfeld 4,516 ...F3
Eschenbach 3,387 ...G2
Escholzmatt 3,161 ...E3
Estavayer-le-Lac 3,439 ...C3
Evolène 1,403 ...D4
Faido 1,866 ...F3
Felsberg 1,321 ...H3
Feuerthalen 3,118 ...G1
Flawil 8,474 ...H2
Fleurier 4,124 ...C3
Flims 3,452 ...H3
Flüelen 1,731 ...F3
Flums 4,474 ...H2
Frauenfeld 17,576 ...G1
Freienbach 8,429 ...G2
Fribourg 41,600 ...D3
Fribourg* 53,500 ...D3
Frick 3,112 ...E1
Frutigen 5,796 ...D4
Fully 3,643 ...D4
Gais 2,344 ...H2
Gelterkinden 5,157 ...E2
Geneva (Genève) 163,100 ...B4
Geneva (Genève)* 320,200 ...B4
Gersau 1,753 ...F3
Gimel 1,205 ...B3
Giornico 1,389 ...G4
Giswil 2,760 ...F3
Giubiasco 5,796 ...H4
Gland 2,404 ...B4
Glarus 6,189 ...H2
Glattfelden 2,857 ...F1
Glis 3,389 ...E4
Gordola 2,586 ...G4
Gossau 12,793 ...H2
Grabs 4,245 ...H2
Grachen 1,063 ...E4
Grandson 2,135 ...C3
Grenchen 20,051 ...D2
Grenchen* 28,300 ...D2
Grindelwald 3,511 ...E3
Grosswangen 2,213 ...F2
Gruyères 1,234 ...D3
Gstaad 865 ...D4
Gsteig 865 ...D4
Guggisberg 1,739 ...D3
Gurtnellen 1,048 ...G3
Guttingen 1,060 ...H1
Hallau 1,836 ...F1
Heiden 3,716 ...H2
Heimberg 3,046 ...E3
Hérémence 1,484 ...D4
Hergiswil 4,364 ...F3
Herisau 14,597 ...H2
Herzogenbuchsee 5,140 ...E2
Hilterfingen 3,647 ...E3
Hinwil 6,547 ...G2
Hitzkirch 1,468 ...F2
Hochdorf 5,222 ...F2
Horgen 15,691 ...G2
Huttwil 4,800 ...E2
Igis 5,283 ...J3
Ilanz 1,783 ...H3
Illnau 13,693 ...G2
Ingenbohl 5,111 ...G2
Innertkirchen 1,064 ...F3
Ins 2,435 ...D2
Interlaken 4,735 ...E3
Jegenstorf 2,858 ...D2
Jenaz 1,312 ...J3
Jona 9,286 ...G2
Jungfraujoch ...E3
Kaltbrunn 2,751 ...H2
Kandersteg 957 ...E4
Kerns 3,807 ...F3
Kerzers 2,688 ...D2
Kirchberg, Bern 3,595 ...E2
Kirchberg, St. Gallen 6,309 ...H2
Kleinlützel 1,271 ...D2
Klingnau 2,545 ...F1
Klosters Dorf 3,534 ...J3
Kloten 16,388 ...G1
Kollbrunn 1,439 ...F1
Koblenz 3,219 ...F1
Köniz 33,800 ...D3
Konolfingen 4,137 ...E3
Kreuzlingen 15,760 ...H1
Kriens 20,409 ...F2
Krummenau 1,904 ...H2
Küsnacht 12,193 ...G2
Küssnacht am Rigi 7,956 ...F2

Küttigen 4,181 ...F2
Küblis 1,319 ...B3
La Chaux-de-Fonds 42,500 ...C2
Lachen 4,914 ...G2
Lancy 20,523 ...B4
La Neuveville 3,917 ...D2
Langenthal 13,077 ...E2
Langenthal* 22,100 ...E2
Langnau am Albis 4,879 ...G2
Langnau im Emmental 8,950 ...E3
La Roche 1,069 ...D3
La Sarraz 1,190 ...C3
Läufelfingen 1,243 ...D2
Laufen 4,723 ...D2
Laufenburg 2,128 ...F1
Laupen 2,139 ...D3
Lauperswil 2,542 ...E3
Lausanne 136,100 ...C3
Lausanne* 228,700 ...C3
Lauterbrunnen 3,431 ...E3
Le Brassus 5,465 ...B3
Le Châble 4,541 ...D4
Le Chenit (Le Brassus) 5,465 ...B3
Le Landeron 2,768 ...D2
Le Locle 14,452 ...C2
Le Mont-sur-Lausanne 2,692 ...C3
Lengau 4,785 ...D4
Lenk 1,876 ...D4
Le Noirmont 1,516 ...C2
Lens 2,052 ...D4
Lenzburg 7,594 ...F2
Les Bois 1,110 ...C2
Les Ponts-de-Martel 1,327 ...C2
Leuk 2,796 ...E4
Leukerbad 1,056 ...E4
Leysin 2,752 ...D4
Liechtensteig 2,131 ...H2
Liestal 12,500 ...E2
Liestal-Sissach* 40,800 ...E2
Linthal 1,458 ...H3
Littau 13,495 ...F2
Locarno 14,143 ...G4
Locarno* 39,200 ...G4
Lodrino 1,075 ...G4
Lotzwil 2,323 ...E2
Lucens 2,144 ...C3
Lucerne 70,200 ...F2
Lucerne* 158,600 ...F2
Lugano 22,280 ...G4
Lugano* 64,200 ...G4
Lungern 1,813 ...F3
Luthern 1,706 ...E2
Lutry 4,994 ...C4
Lützelflüh 3,842 ...E2
Lyss 8,131 ...D2
Maienfeld 1,542 ...J3
Malans 1,294 ...J3
Malleray 1,969 ...D2
Malters 5,100 ...F2
Malvaglia 1,099 ...H4
Männedorf 7,419 ...G2
Marbach 1,265 ...E3
Martigny 10,478 ...D4
Meilen 9,881 ...G2
Meiringen 3,759 ...F3
Melide 1,315 ...G5
Mellingen 3,211 ...F2
Mels 5,969 ...H2
Mendrisio 6,223 ...G5
Menziken 3,483 ...F2
Menznau 2,185 ...E2
Mesocco 1,376 ...H4
Meyrin 14,255 ...B4
Minusio 5,027 ...G4
Möhlin 6,003 ...E1
Mollis 2,628 ...H2
Montana 1,725 ...D4
Monthey 10,114 ...C4
Montreux 20,421 ...C4
Morges 11,931 ...B3
Morges* 17,200 ...B3
Moudon 2,751 ...C3
Moutier 8,794 ...D2
Mülheim 1,620 ...G1
Mümliswil-Ramiswil 2,702 ...E2
Münchenbuchsee 6,459 ...E2
Münsingen 8,350 ...E3
Muotathal 2,763 ...G3
Muri 4,853 ...F2
Muri bei Bern 3,057 ...E3
Mürren 1,936 ...E3
Murten 4,256 ...D3
Muttenz 15,518 ...E1
Naters 5,517 ...E4
Nebikon 1,378 ...F2
Nendaz 4,051 ...D4
Nesslau 1,934 ...H2

Netstal 2,771 ...H2
Neuchâtel 38,400 ...C3
Neuchâtel* 61,700 ...C3
Neuenegg 3,452 ...D3
Neuhausen am Rheinfall 12,103 ...G1
Neunkirch 1,239 ...F1
Nidau 7,962 ...D2
Niederbipp 3,293 ...E2
Niederurnen 3,354 ...H2
Nunningen 1,450 ...E2
Nyon 11,424 ...B4
Oberägeri 2,992 ...G2
Oberburg 3,015 ...E2
Oberdiessbach 2,145 ...E3
Oberdorf 1,953 ...E2
Oberriet 6,123 ...J2
Obersiggenthal 6,623 ...F1
Oberwil 4,659 ...H2
Oensingen 3,387 ...E2
Oftringen 9,189 ...E2
Ollon 4,470 ...D4
Olten 21,209 ...E2
Olten* 49,000 ...E2
Opfikon 11,115 ...G2
Orbe 4,522 ...C3
Orsières 2,470 ...D4
Ouchy ...C4
Paradiso 3,101 ...G5
Payerne 6,899 ...C3
Penthalaz 1,701 ...C3
Péry 1,486 ...D2
Peseux 5,578 ...C3
Pfaffnau 2,584 ...E2
Pfäffikon 3,485 ...G2
Plaffeien 1,448 ...D3
Pontresina 1,646 ...J3
Porrentruy 7,827 ...C2
Port-Valais 1,363 ...C4
Pratteln 15,127 ...E1
Prangins 1,466 ...B4
Pully 15,917 ...C4
Quinto 1,490 ...G3
Rafz 2,215 ...G1
Ramsen 1,217 ...G1
Rapperswil 8,713 ...G2
Raron 1,257 ...E4
Regensdorf 8,566 ...F2
Reichenbach im Kandertal 2,900 ...E3
Reiden 3,275 ...E2
Reinach in Aargau 5,862 ...F2
Reinach in Baselland 13,419 ...E1
Renan 1,094 ...C2
Renens 17,391 ...C3
Rheinau 2,075 ...G1
Rheineck 3,275 ...J2
Rheinfelden 6,866 ...E1
Richterswil 7,380 ...G2
Rieden 21,026 ...E1
Riggisberg 2,193 ...E3
Riva San Vitale 1,607 ...G5
Rivera 1,146 ...G4
Roggwil 3,403 ...E2
Rolle 3,658 ...B4
Romanshorn 8,329 ...H1
Romont 3,276 ...C3
Rorschach 11,963 ...H2
Rorschach* 24,200 ...H2
Rosenlaui ...F3
Rothrist 5,883 ...E2
Roveredo 2,037 ...H4
Rüeggisberg 1,857 ...E3
Rumlang 5,677 ...
Rüschegg 1,346 ...D3
Ruswil 4,756 ...F2
Rüthi 1,493 ...J2
Rüti 9,546 ...G2
Saanen 5,840 ...D4
Sachseln 3,059 ...F3
Saignelégier 1,745 ...C2
Saint-Aubin-Sauges 2,058 ...C3
Saint-Blaise 2,586 ...D2
Sainte-Croix 6,240 ...C3
Saint-Imier 6,740 ...C2
Saint-Légier-La Chiésaz 2,230 ...C4
Saint-Martin 1,120 ...D4
Saint-Maurice 3,808 ...C4
Saint Niklaus 2,043 ...E4
Saint Prex 2,306 ...B4
Saint Stephan 1,213 ...D3
Saint-Ursanne 1,073 ...C2
Samedan 1,287 ...J3
Sankt Gallen 81,900 ...H2
Sankt Gallen* 90,400 ...H2
Sankt Margrethen 5,101 ...J2
Sargans 4,058 ...H3
Sarnen 6,952 ...F3
Satigny 1,877 ...A4

Savièse 3,585 ...D4
Saxon 2,409 ...D4
Schaffhausen 36,800 ...G1
Schaffhausen* 55,800 ...G1
Schänis 2,355 ...H2
Schattdorf 3,292 ...G3
Scherzingen 1,420 ...H1
Schiers 2,342 ...J3
Schinznach-Dorf 1,154 ...F2
Schleitheim 1,544 ...G1
Schlieren 11,869 ...G2
Schönenwerd 4,793 ...E2
Schübelbach 4,395 ...G2
Schüpfheim 3,773 ...E3
Schwanden 2,823 ...H2
Schwyz 12,194 ...G2
Scuol 1,686 ...K3
Sempach 1,619 ...F2
Seon 3,628 ...F2
Seuzach 3,258 ...G1
Sevelen 2,742 ...H2
Sierre 11,017 ...D4
Signau 2,642 ...E3
Sigriswil 3,540 ...E3
Silenen 2,338 ...G3
Sils im Domleschg 762 ...H3
Silvaplana 714 ...J4
Sins 2,435 ...F2
Sion 21,925 ...D4
Sirnach 3,706 ...G2
Sissach 4,938 ...E2
Solothurn (Soleure) 17,708 ...E2
Solothurn* 35,600 ...E2
Somvix 1,555 ...G3
Sonvico 1,129 ...G4
Spiez 9,911 ...E3
Stäfa 9,937 ...G2
Stalden 1,121 ...E4
Stans 5,370 ...F3
Steckborn 3,252 ...G1
Steffisburg 12,621 ...E3
Stein 1,763 ...E1
Stein am Rhein 2,751 ...G1
Suhr 7,223 ...F2
Sulgen 1,834 ...H1
Sumiswald 5,334 ...E2
Sursee 7,052 ...F2
Tafers 2,021 ...D3
Täuffelen 1,761 ...D2
Tavannes 3,869 ...D2
Tavetsch 1,273 ...G3
Teufen 5,300 ...H2
Thal 4,919 ...J2
Thalwil 13,591 ...G2
Thayngen 3,640 ...G1
Therwil 5,412 ...E1
Thun 37,000 ...E3
Thun* 63,600 ...E3
Thunstetten 2,483 ...E2
Thusis 2,381 ...H3
Trachselwald 1,199 ...E2
Tramelan 5,549 ...D2
Trimmis 1,109 ...J3
Troistorrents 2,208 ...C4
Trub 1,833 ...E3
Trun 1,607 ...G3
Turbenthal 2,939 ...G2
Uetendorf 3,132 ...E3
Unterägeri 4,671 ...G2
Unterkulm 2,596 ...F2
Unterseen 4,192 ...E3
Untervaz 1,230 ...J3
Urnäsch 2,313 ...H2
Uster 21,819 ...G2
Utzenstorf 3,193 ...E2
Uznach 3,984 ...H2
Uzwil 9,133 ...H2
Vallorbe 4,028 ...B3
Vaz-Obervaz 2,003 ...J3
Vechigen 3,595 ...E3
Vernayaz 1,356 ...D4
Versoix 5,627 ...B4
Vevey 15,957 ...C4
Vevey-Montreux* 62,300 ...C4
Villeneuve 3,705 ...C4
Visp 5,252 ...E4
Vouvry 1,851 ...C4
Vuadens 1,278 ...D3
Wädenswil 15,695 ...G2
Wahlern 4,832 ...D3
Wald 8,185 ...G2
Waldenburg 1,449 ...E2
Waldkirch 2,641 ...H2
Walenstadt 3,446 ...H2
Wallisellen 10,415 ...G2
Walzenhausen 2,082 ...J2
Wangen an der Aare 2,013 ...E2
Wangen 2,730 ...H2
Wartau 3,604 ...H2

Wattwil 8,566 ...H2
Weesen 1,308 ...H2
Weggis 2,517 ...F2
Weinfelden 8,621 ...H1
Wettingen 19,900 ...F2
Wetzikon 13,469 ...G2
Wil 14,646 ...H2
Wil* 20,500 ...H2
Wilchingen 1,066 ...F1
Wilderswil 1,666 ...E3
Wildhaus 1,104 ...H2
Willisau 2,728 ...F2
Wimmis 1,833 ...E3
Windisch 7,444 ...F1
Winterthur 93,500 ...G1
Winterthur* 110,100 ...G1
Wohlen 12,024 ...F2
Wohlen* 16,000 ...F2
Wohlen bei Bern 4,190 ...D3
Wolfenschiessen 1,470 ...F3
Wolhusen 3,556 ...F2
Worb 9,526 ...E3
Wünnewil 3,652 ...D3
Wynigen 1,986 ...E2
Yverdon 20,538 ...C3
Yvonand 1,321 ...C3

Zell, Luzern 1,590 ...E2
Zell, Zürich 4,008 ...G2
Zernez 1,913 ...K3
Zizers 1,913 ...J3
Zofingen 9,292 ...E2
Zollikofen 9,069 ...D3
Zollikon 12,117 ...G2
Zug 22,972 ...G2
Zug* 51,300 ...G2
Zuoz 1,165 ...J3
Zürich 401,600 ...G2
Zürich* 718,100 ...G2
Zurzach 3,098 ...F1
Zweisimmen 2,738 ...D3

OTHER FEATURES

Aa (riv.) ...F3
Aare (riv.) ...E3
Agerisee (lake) ...G2
Aiguille d'Argentière (mt.) ...C5
Aletschhorn (mt.) ...E4
Aroser Rothorn (mt.) ...H3
Ault (peak) ...D5
Balmhorn (mt.) ...E4
Bernese Oberland (reg.) ...E3

Bernina (peak) ...J4
Bernina (pass) ...K4
Bielersee (lake) ...D2
Bietschhorn (mt.) ...E4
Birs (riv.) ...D2
Blinnenhorn (mt.) ...F4
Blümlisalp (mt.) ...E3
Bodensee (Constance) (lake) ...H1
Borgne (riv.) ...D4
Breithorn (mt.) ...F3
Breithorn (mt.) ...E4
Brienzer Rothorn (mt.) ...F3
Brienzersee (lake) ...E3
Broye (riv.) ...C3
Buchegg (mts.) ...E2
Bürn (peak) ...G4
Campo Tencia (peak) ...G4
Chasseron (mt.) ...C3
Churfirsten (mts.) ...H2
Clariden (mt.) ...G3
Constance (lake) ...H1
Cornettes de Bise (mts.) ...C4
Davos (valley) ...J3
Dent Blanche (mt.) ...D4
Dent de Lys (mt.) ...D3

Switzerland and Liechtenstein

CONIC PROJECTION

SCALE OF MILES
0   5   10   20   30

SCALE OF KILOMETERS
0 5 10   20   30   40   50

Capitals of Countries .... ☆
Capitals of Cantons .... ◉
International Boundaries .... ▄▄ ▪ ▄▄ ▪
Canals ....

Scale 1:1,140,000

© Copyright HAMMOND INCORPORATED, Maplewood, N.J.

AUSTRIA

PROVINCES

Burgenland 272,119 ....D3
Carinthia 525,728 ....B3
Lower Austria 1,414,161 ....C2
Salzburg 401,766 ....B3
Styria 1,192,442 ....C3
Tirol 540,771 ....A3
Upper Austria 1,223,444 ....B2
Vienna (city) 1,614,841 ....D2
Vorarlberg 271,473 ....A3

CITIES and TOWNS†

Admont 3,126 ....C3
Allentsteig 2,783 ....C2
Altheim 4,766 ....B2
Althofen 3,886 ....B3
Amstetten 13,330 ....C2
Andau 3,058 ....D3
Arnoldstein 6,740 ....B3
Aspang Markt 2,316 ....D3
Attnang-Puchheim 7,837 ....B2
Bad Aussee 5,039 ....B3
Baden 22,631 ....D2
Badgastein 5,228 ....B3
Bad Goisern 6,360 ....B3
Bad Hofgastein 5,525 ....B3
Bad Ischl 12,740 ....B3
Bad Leonfelden 2,712 ....C2
Bad Sankt-Leonhard im
  Lavanttal 4,882 ....C3
Berndorf 8,371 ....D2
Bischofshofen 9,417 ....B3
Bludenz 12,050 ....A3
Bramberg am Wildkogel 3,129 ....B3
Braunau am Inn 16,432 ....B2
Bregenz 22,839 ....A3
Bruck an der Leitha 7,506 ....D2
Bruck an der Mur 16,359 ....C3
Deutsch Feistritz 3,820 ....C3
Deutschkreutz 3,673 ....D3
Deutsch Landsberg 6,614 ....C3
Deutsch Wagram 4,481 ....D2
Dornbirn 33,810 ....A3
Ebenfurth 2,272 ....D3
Ebensee 9,413 ....B3
Eferding 3,014 ....B2
Eggenburg 3,730 ....C2
Ehrwald 2,198 ....A3

Eisenerz 11,563 ....C3
Eisenkappel-Vellach 3,761 ....C3
Eisenstadt 10,059 ....D3
Enns 9,622 ....C2
Feldbach 3,887 ....C3
Feldkirch 21,214 ....A3
Feldkirchen in
  Kärnten 11,188 ....B3
Ferlach 7,621 ....B3
Fieberbrunn 3,651 ....B3
Fohnsdorf 11,169 ....C3
Frankenmarkt 2,960 ....B2
Frauenkirchen 2,749 ....D3
Freistadt 5,956 ....C2
Freidberg 2,504 ....D3
Friesach 7,257 ....C3
Frohnleiten 5,081 ....C3
Fulpmes 2,553 ....A3
Fürstenfeld 6,054 ....D3
Gaming 4,181 ....C3
Gänserndorf 4,211 ....D2
Gleisdorf 4,921 ....C3
Gloggnitz 7,078 ....D3
Gmünd, Carinthia 2,267 ....B3
Gmünd, Lower Austria 6,323 ....C2
Gmunden 12,270 ....B3
Golling an der Salzach 3,089 ....B3
Götzis 7,931 ....A3
Gratwein 2,747 ....C3
Graz 251,900 ....C3
Graz* 314,200 ....C3
Grein 2,767 ....C2
f21Grieskirchen 4,519 ....B2
Grosssieghards 3,288 ....C2
Grünburg 3,775 ....C3
Güssing 3,675 ....D3
Haag 5,060 ....C2
Hainburg an der Donau 6,009 ....D2
Hainfeld 3,897 ....D3
Hallein 14,371 ....B3
Hallstatt 1,303 ....B3
Hartberg 5,702 ....D3
Haslach an der Mühl 2,636 ....C2
Heidenreichstein 4,340 ....C2
Heiligenblut 1,324 ....B3
Hermagor-Presseggersee 7,531 .....B3
Herzogenburg 7,299 ....C2
Hohenau an der March 3,591 ....D2
Hohenberg 2,016 ....D3
Hohenems 11,487 ....A3
Hollabrunn 6,563 ....C2
Hopfgarten in Nordtirol 4,784 ......A3

Horn 6,264 ....C2
Hüttenberg 3,251 ....C3
Imst 5,855 ....A3
Innsbruck 115,800 ....A3
Innsbruck* 167,200 ....A3
Jenbach 5,868 ....A3
Jennersdorf 4,210 ....D3
Judenburg 11,346 ....C3
Kapfenberg 26,001 ....C3
Kappl 2,156 ....A3
Kaprun 2,604 ....B3
Kindberg 6,128 ....C3
Kirchdorf an der Krems 3,471 ....B3
Kitzbühel 7,995 ....B3
Klagenfurt 74,326 ....C3
Klagenfurt* 112,600 ....C3
Klosterneuburg 21,912 ....D2
Knittelfeld 14,517 ....C3
Koflach 12,612 ....C3
Königswiesen 2,921 ....C2
Korneuburg 8,892 ....D2
Kösen 2,764 ....B3
Kötschach-Mauthen 3,740 ....B3
Krems an der Donau 21,733 ....C2
Kufstein 12,766 ....A3
Kundl 3,020 ....A3
Laa an der Thaya 5,455 ....D2
Laakirchen 7,664 ....B3
Lambach 3,301 ....C2
Landeck 7,388 ....A3
Langenlebld 2,838 ....A3
Langenlois 4,957 ....C2
Langenwang 4,071 ....C3
Lavamünd 4,120 ....C3
Leibnitz 6,646 ....C3
Lenzing 5,385 ....B3
Leoben 35,153 ....C3
Leonfelden 1,696 ....B3
Liezen 6,244 ....C3
Lilienfeld 3,126 ....C3
Linz 205,700 ....C2
Linz* 356,500 ....C2
Lustenau 15,239 ....A3
Mannersdorf am
  Leithagebirge 4,012 ....D3
Marchegg 2,678 ....D2
Mariazell 2,298 ....C3
Matrei in Osttirol 4,003 ....B3
Mattersburg 5,417 ....D3
Mattighofen 4,344 ....B2
Mauerkirchen 2,237 ....B2
Mautern in Steiermark 2,536 ....C3

Mauthausen 4,419 ....C2
Mauthen-Kötschach 3,750 ....B3
Mayrhofen 3,174 ....A3
Melk 5,108 ....C2
Mistelbach an der Zaya 6,306 ....D2
Mittersill 4,361 ....B3
Mödling 18,712 ....D2
Mondsee 2,141 ....B3
Murau 2,710 ....C3
Mürzzuschlag 11,564 ....C3
Neuberg an der Mürz 2,183 ....C3
Neumarkt am Wallersee 3,267 ......B3
Neunkirchen 10,922 ....D3
Neusiedl am See 3,999 ....D3
Neustift im Stubaital 2,581 ....A3
Ober Grafendorf 4,109 ....C2
Oberndorf bei Salzburg 3,293 ....B3
Obervellach 2,420 ....B3
Oberwart 5,661 ....D3
Paternion 5,805 ....B3
Perg 4,872 ....C2
Peuerbach 2,161 ....B2
Pfunds 2,043 ....A3
Pinkafeld 4,610 ....D3
Pöchlarn 3,199 ....C2
Pörtschach am
  Wörthersee 2,511 ....C3
Poysdorf 5,774 ....D2
Pregarten 3,249 ....C2
Raabs an der Thaya 4,194 ....C2
Radenthein 6,847 ....B3
Radkersburg 2,000 ....C3
Radstadt 3,585 ....B3
Rankweil 8,440 ....A3
Rechnitz 3,412 ....D3
Reichenau an der Rax 4,053 ....D3
Retz 4,780 ....C2
Ried im Innkreis 10,534 ....B2
Rottenmann 4,781 ....C3
Saalfelden am Steinernen
  Meer 10,172 ....B3
Salzburg 122,100 ....B3
Salzburg* 213,430 ....B3
Sankt Aegyd am Neuwalde 3,165 ..C3
Sankt Anton am Arlberg 2,086 ......A3
Sankt Johann in Tirol 5,942 ....B3
Sankt Michael im Lungau 2,839 ....B3
Sankt Michael in
  Obersteiermark 3,717 ....C3
Sankt Michael im Lungau 2,839 ....B3
Sankt Paul im Lavanttal 6,721 ....C3
Sankt Pölten 43,300 ....C2

Sankt Valentin 8,715 ....C2
Sankt Veit an der Glan 11,047 ....C3
Sankt Wolfgang im
  Salzkammergut 2,746 ....B3
Schärding 5,874 ....B2
Scheibbs 4,419 ....C2
Schladming 3,460 ....B3
Schrems 3,393 ....C2
Schruns 3,607 ....A3
Schwarzach im Pongau 3,616 ....B3
Schwaz 10,253 ....A3
Schwechat 14,997 ....D2
Schwertberg 3,881 ....C2
Sierning 8,162 ....C2
Sillian 1,988 ....B3
Solbad Hall in Tirol 12,335 ....A3
Spital am Pyhrn 2,315 ....C3
Spittal an der Drau 13,690 ....B3
Steinach 2,698 ....A3
Steyr 40,578 ....C2
Stockerau 12,634 ....D2
Strassburg 2,850 ....B3
Tamsweg 5,060 ....B3
Telfs 6,589 ....A3
Traiskirchen 8,878 ....C2
Traun 20,843 ....C2
Trieben 4,639 ....C3
Trofaiach 8,731 ....C3
Tulln 7,705 ....C2
Velden am Wörthersee 7,306 ....C3
Vienna (cap.) 1,700,000 ....D2
Vienna* 1,858,700 ....D2
Villach 50,979 ....B3
Vöcklabruck 10,627 ....B2
Voitsberg 11,094 ....C3
Völkermarkt 10,772 ....C3
Vordernberg 2,506 ....C3
Waidhofen an der Thaya 4,200 .....C2
Waidhofen an der Ybbs 5,218 ....C2
Weitensfeld-Flattnitz 5,206 ....B3
Weitra 3,250 ....C2
Weiz 8,241 ....C3
Wells 47,279 ....C2
Weyer Markt 2,518 ....C2
Wien (Vienna) (cap.) 1,700,000 .....D2
Wiener Neustadt 34,774 ....D3
Wildon 2,002 ....C3
Wilhelmsburg 6,307 ....C2
Wolfsberg 31,176 ....C3
Wörgl 7,811 ....A3
Ybbs an der Donau 6,422 ....C2

Zams 3,120 ....A3
Zell am See 7,456 ....B3
Zell am Ziller 1,882 ....A3
Zeltweg 8,431 ....C3
Zirl 4,157 ....A3
Zistersdorf 3,412 ....D2
Zwettl-Niederösterreich 11,624 ....C2

OTHER FEATURES

Allgäu Alps (mts.) A3
Bavarian Alps (mts.) A3
Bodensee (Constance) (lake) A3
Brenner (pass) A3
Carnic Alps (mts.) B3
Constance (lake) A3
Danube (riv.) C2
Donau (Danube) (riv.) C3
Drau (riv.) C3
Enns (riv.) C3
Grossglockner (mt.) B3
Hohe Tauern (range) B3
Inn (riv.) B2
Karawanken (range) C3
March (riv.) D2
Mühlviertel (reg.) C2
Neusiedler See (lake) D3
Niedere Tauern (range) B3
Ötztal Alps (mts.) A3
Raab (riv.) D3
Rhine (riv.) A3
Salzach (riv.) B2
Salzkammergut (reg.) C3
Semmering (pass) C3
Thaya (riv.) C2
Traun (riv.) C2
Wildspitze (mt.) A3
Zugspitze (mt.) A3

CZECHOSLOVAKIA

REPUBLICS

Czech Socialist Rep. 9,964,338 ....B1
Slovak Socialist Rep. 4,670,409 ...E2
REGIONS

Bratislava (city) 333,000 ....D2
Jihočeský 662,002 ....D2
Jihomoravský 1,966,850 ....D2
Praha (city) 1,161,200 ....C1

Severočeský 1,122,035 ....C1
Severomoravský 1,849,286 ....D2
Středočeský 1,193,041 ....D2
Středoslovenský 1,436,351 ....E2
Východočeský 1,214,581 ....D2
Východoslovenský 1,298,481 ....F2
Západočeský 865,094 ....B2
Západoslovenský 1,610,542 ....D2

CITIES and TOWNS

Aš 120,000 ....B1
Austerlitz (Slavkov) D2
Bánovce nad Bebravou 11,400 .....E2
Banská Bystrica 53,000 ....E2
Banská Štiavnica 7,486 ....E2
Bardejov 17,400 ....F2
Benešov 11,100 ....C2
Beroun 17,600 ....B1
Bílina 17,800 ....B1
Blansko 13,800 ....D2
Boskovice 8,531 ....D2
Brandýs nad Labem-Stará
  Boleslav 333,000 ....C1
Bratislava 333,000 ....D2
Břeclav 21,100 ....D2
Brezno 14,800 ....E2
Brno 335,700 ....D2
Broumov 7,782 ....D1
Bruntál 12,300 ....D2
Bystřice nad
  Pernštejnem 6,471 ....D2
Bystřice pod
  Hostýnem 6,681 ....D2
Frýdlant v
  Čechách 5,948 ....C1

Čadca 16,800 ....E2
Čalovo 6,591 ....D3
Čáslav 10,200 ....C2
Česká Lípa 18,600 ....C1
Česká Třebová 14,700 ....D2
České Budějovice 80,800 ....C2
Český Brod 6,640 ....C1
Český Krumlov 12,000 ....C2
Český Těšín 17,200 ....E2
Děčín 46,500 ....B1
Detva 13,100 ....E2
Dobříš 6,378 ....C2
Dobruška 5,779 ....D1
Dolný Kubín 9,900 ....E2
Domažlice 9,100 ....B2
Dubnica nad Váhom 11,300 ....E2
Duchcov 9,712 ....B1
Dunajská Streda 13,000 ....D3
Dvory nad Žitavou 5,847 ....E3
Dvůr Králové nad
  Labem 16,800 ....C1
Falknov (Sokolov) 23,900 ....B1
Fil akovo 7,822 ....E2
Frenštát pod
  Radhoštěm 8,516 ....E2
Frýdek-Místek 43,800 ....E2

Frýdlant nad
  Ostravicí 6,250 ....E2
Galanta 12,300 ....D2
Gottwaldov 84,300 ....D2
Handlová 16,200 ....E2
Havířov 85,000 ....E2
Havlíčkův Brod 19,200 ....D2
Hlinsko 8,890 ....D2
Hlohovec 15,200 ....D2
Hlučín 15,300 ....E2
Hnúšť a-Likier E2
Hodonín 22,600 ....D2
Holešov 9,091 ....D2
Holíč 7,602 ....D2
Holice 6,151 ....C2
Horažd ovice C2
Hořice v
  Podkrkonoší 7,715 ....C1
Horná Štubňa E2
Horní Benešov D2
Horní Libina D2
Hofovice 5,665 ....C2
Horovský Týn B2
Hostinné C1
Hradec Králové 85,600 ....C1
Hranice 13,300 ....D2
Hrinova 7,800 ....E2
Hronov 9,767 ....D1
Hrušovany D2
Humenné 22,200 ....F2
Humpolec 7,810 ....C2
Hurbanovo E3
Hustopeče D2
Ilava E2
Ivančice 7,314 ....D2

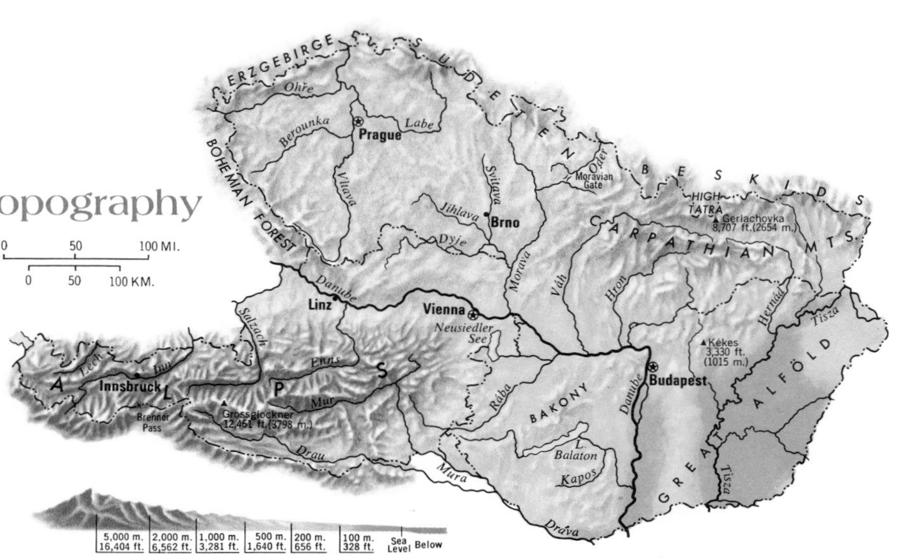

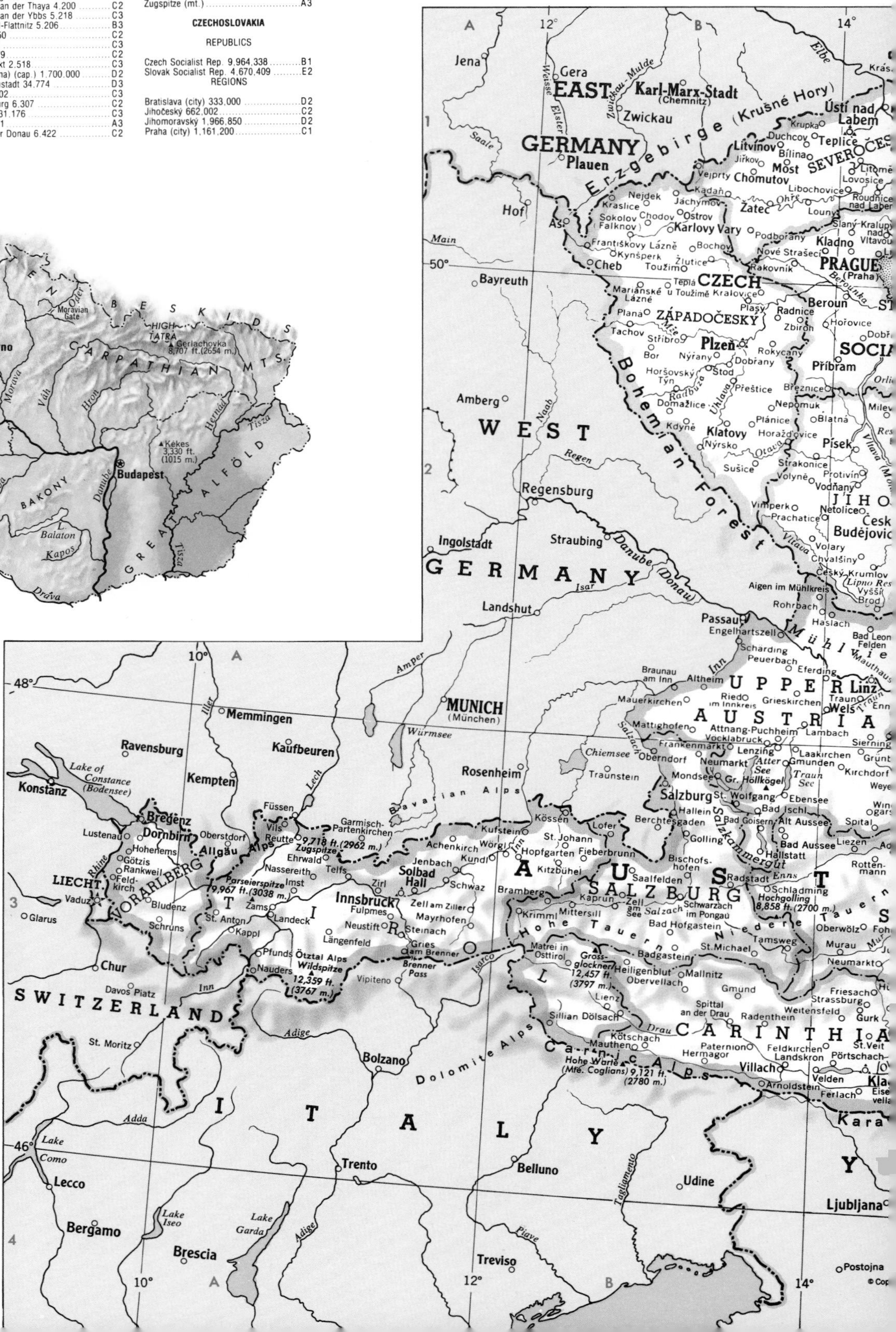

AREA 32,375 sq. mi. (83,851 sq. km.)
POPULATION 7,507,000
CAPITAL Vienna
LARGEST CITY Vienna
HIGHEST POINT Grossglockner
12,457 ft. (3,797 m.)
MONETARY UNIT schilling
MAJOR LANGUAGE German
MAJOR RELIGION Roman Catholicism

AREA 49,373 sq. mi. (127,876 sq. km.)
POPULATION 15,276,799
CAPITAL Prague
LARGEST CITY Prague
HIGHEST POINT Gerlachovka 8,707 ft.
(2,654 m.)
MONETARY UNIT koruna
MAJOR LANGUAGES Czech, Slovak
MAJOR RELIGIONS Roman Catholicism,
Protestantism

AREA 35,919 sq. mi. (93,030 sq. km.)
POPULATION 10,709,536
CAPITAL Budapest
LARGEST CITY Budapest
HIGHEST POINT Kékes 3,330 ft.
(1,015 m.)
MONETARY UNIT forint
MAJOR LANGUAGE Hungarian
MAJOR RELIGIONS Roman Catholicism,
Protestantism

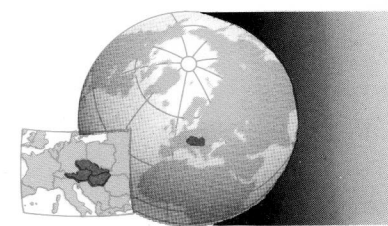

AUSTRIA

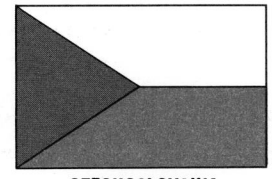

CZECHOSLOVAKIA

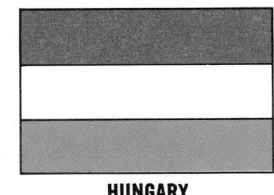

HUNGARY

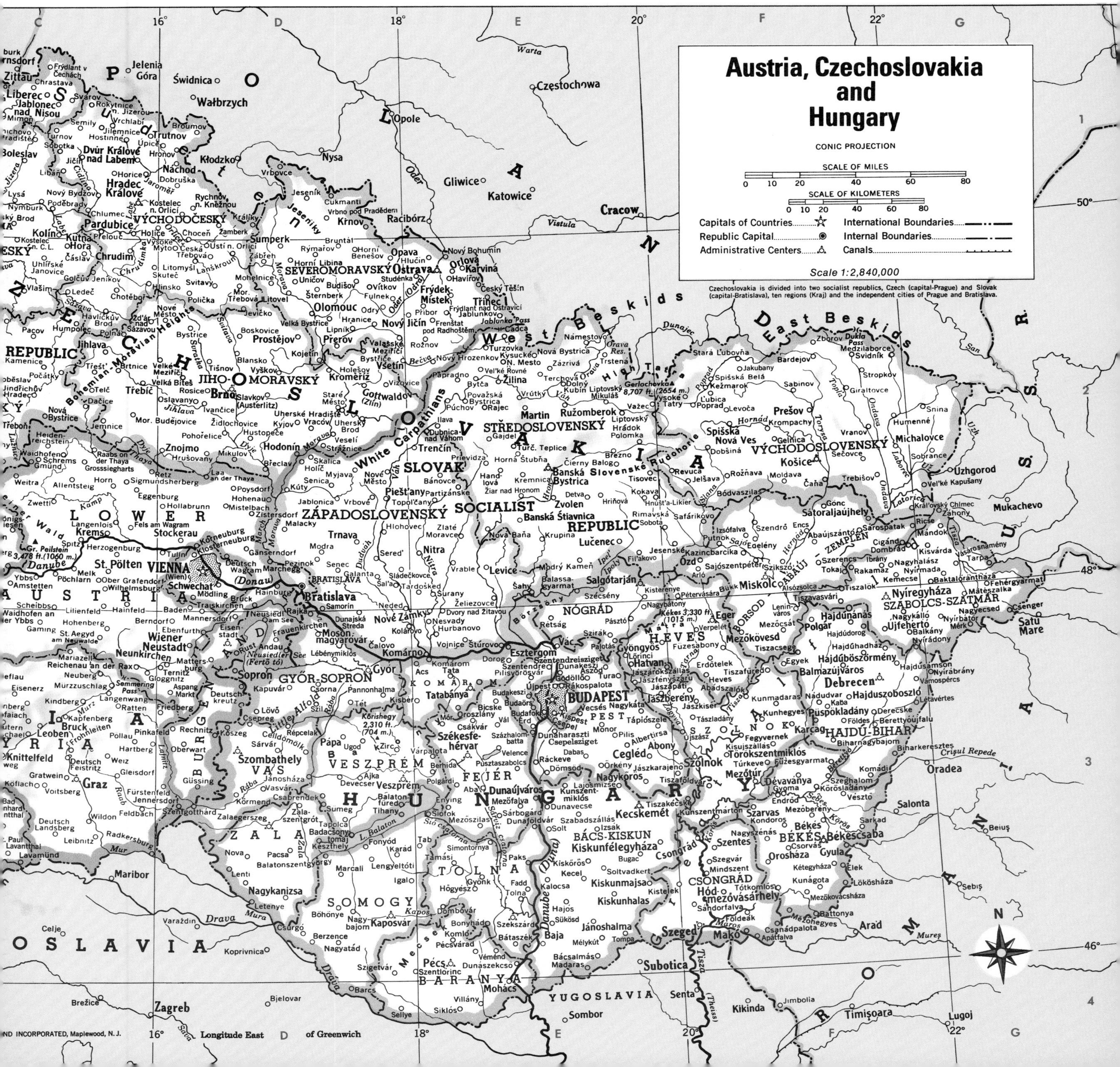

Austria, Czechoslovakia and Hungary

CONIC PROJECTION

SCALE OF MILES
0 10 20 40 60 80

SCALE OF KILOMETERS
0 10 20 40 60 80

Capitals of Countries..........☆   International Boundaries......
Republic Capital..................◉   Internal Boundaries..........
Administrative Centers.........△   Canals.............................

Scale 1:2,840,000

Czechoslovakia is divided into two socialist republics, Czech (capital-Prague) and Slovak (capital-Bratislava), ten regions (Kraj) and the independent cities of Prague and Bratislava.

Agriculture, Industry and Resources

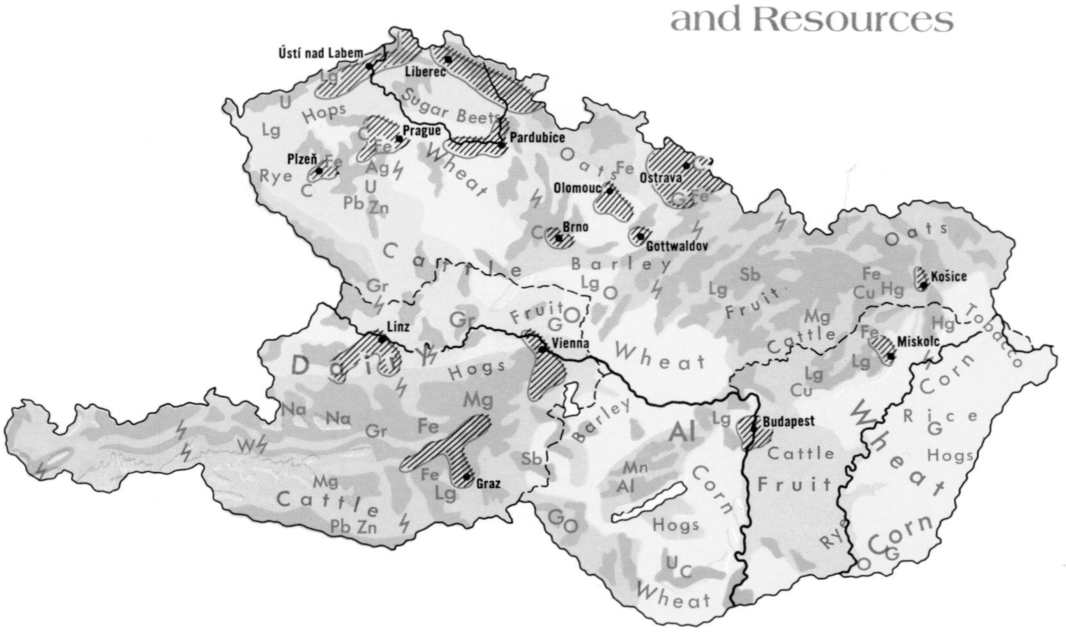

DOMINANT LAND USE

- Cereals (chiefly wheat, corn)
- Other Cereals, Livestock, Dairy
- General Farming, Livestock
- General Farming, Truck Farming
- Pasture Livestock
- Grapes, Wine
- Forests
- Nonagricultural Land

MAJOR MINERAL OCCURRENCES

Ag	Silver	Mg	Magnesium
Al	Bauxite	Mn	Manganese
C	Coal	Na	Salt
Cu	Copper	O	Petroleum
Fe	Iron Ore	Pb	Lead
G	Natural Gas	Sb	Antimony
Gr	Graphite	U	Uranium
Hg	Mercury	W	Tungsten
Lg	Lignite	Zn	Zinc

ϟ Water Power

Major Industrial Areas

Jablonec nad Nisou 36,300 C1
Jablonica D2
Jablunkov 9,405 E2
Jáchymov B1
Jakubany F2
Jaroměř 11,600 C1
Jelšava F2
Jemnice C2
Jeseník 10,900 D1
Jesenské F2
Jevíčko D2
Jičín 13,200 C1
Jihlava 44,500 C2
Jilemnice C1
Jindřichův Hradec 15,700 C2
Jirkov 11,400 B1
Kadaň 18,100 B1
Kamenice C2
Kaplice C2
Karlovy Vary 43,300 B1
Karviná 79,100 E2
Kdyně B2
Kežmarok 11,000 F2
Kladno 61,200 B1
Klatovy 18,500 B2
Kojetín 5,852 D2
Kokava nad Rimavicou 5,391 E2
Kolárovo 10,500 D3
Kolín 29,100 C1
Komárno 28,200 D3
Košice 169,100 F2
Kostelec nad Orlicí 5,575 D1
Král'ovský Chlmec 5,329 G2
Kralupy nad Vltavou 16,900 C1
Kraslice 6,733 B1
Kremnica 5,941 E2
Krnov 25,000 D1
Kroměříž 23,200 D2
Krompachy 6,332 F2
Krupina 6,627 E2
Krupka 8,301 B1
Kutná Hora 19,200 C2
Kyjov 10,700 D2
Kynšperk 5,524 B1
Kysucké Nové Mesto 11,700 E2
Lanškroun 8,683 D2
Levice 19,000 E2
Levoča 10,100 F2
Libáň C1
Liberec 75,600 C1
Lidice C1
Lipník nad Bečvou 7,358 D2
Liptovský Mikuláš 19,400 E2
Litoměřice 19,700 C1
Litomyšl 8,112 D2
Litovel 5,805 D2
Litvínov 23,300 B1
Lomnice C2
Louny 15,200 B1
Lovosice 9,323 C1
L'ubica F2
Lučenec 23,300 E2
Lysá nad Labem 9,920 C1
Malacky 13,200 D2
Mariánské Lázně 14,600 B2
Martin 47,800 E2
Medzilaborce F2
Mělník 17,800 C1
Michalovce 23,600 G2
Mikulov 6,267 D2
Milevsko 7,091 C2
Mimoň 6,773 C1
Mladá Boleslav 36,900 C1
Mladá Vožice C2
Mnichovo Hradiště 5,239 C1
Modra 7,219 D2
Modrý Kameň 6,200 E2
Mohelnice 6,050 D2
Moldava nad Bodvou 5,397 F2
Moravská Třebová 9,052 D2
Moravské Budějovice 5,576 D2
Most 59,400 B1
Myjava 6,657 D2
Náchod 19,300 D1
Námestovo E2
Neded D2
Nejdek 8,187 B1
Nepomuk B2
Nesvady 5,453 E3
Netolice C2
Nitra 50,000 E2
Nová Baňa 6,218 E2
Nová Bystrica E2
Nová Bystřice C2
Nové Hrady C2
Nové Město na Moravě 6,581 D2
Nové Město nad Váhom 15,900 D2
Nové Strašecí B1
Nové Zámky 27,300 D3
Nový Bohumín 16,700 E2
Nový Bor 7,621 C1
Nový Bydžov 6,824 C1
Nový Hrozenkov E2
Nový Jičín 21,400 E2
Nymburk 13,600 C1
Nýřany 6,204 B2
Nýrsko B2
Odry D2
Olomouc 82,800 D2
Opava 53,800 E2
Orlová 25,500 E2
Ostrava 293,500 E2
Ostrov 18,200 B1
Pardubice 78,500 C1
Partizánske 15,100 E2
Pelhřimov 11,900 C2
Pezinok 13,100 D2
Piešt'any 25,400 D2
Písek 25,100 C2
Plzeň 155,000 B2
Počátky C2
Podbořany B1
Poděbrady 13,400 C1
Pohořelice D2
Polička 6,529 D2
Polná C2
Polomka E2
Poprad 25,800 F2
Považská Bystrica 19,300 E2
Prachatice 7,900 B2
Prague (Praha) (cap.) 1,161,200 C1
Přelouč 6,251 C1
Přerov 43,500 D2
Prešov 61,000 F2
Přeštice B2
Příbor 7,726 E2
Příbram 31,300 B2
Prievidza 30,900 E2
Prostějov 44,200 D2
Protivín C2
Púchov 9,306 E2
Radnice B2
Rajec E2
Rakovník 14,200 B1
Revúca 5,901 F2
Říčany u Prahy 8,407 C2
Rimavská Sobota 5,800 E2
Rokycany 12,800 B2
Rokytnice nad Jizerou C1
Rosice D2
Roudnice nad Labem 11,800 C1
Rožňava 12,400 F2
Rožnov pod Radhoštěm 11,600 E2
Rumburk C1
Ružomberok 22,600 E2
Rychnov nad Kněžnou 7,500 D1
Rýmařov 7,522 D2
Sabinov 5,473 F2
Šafárikovo F2
Šahy 5,049 E2
Šal'a 15,200 D2
Šamorín 8,287 D2
Sečovce 5,744 F2
Sedlčany C2
Semily 8,200 C1
Senec 8,544 D2
Senica 12,300 D2
Sereď 12,500 D2
Skalica 11,100 D2
Skuteč D2
Sládečkovce 5,598 D2
Slaný 13,200 C1
Slavkov D2
Snina 10,900 G2
Soběslav 6,140 C2
Sobotka C1
Sobrance G2
Sokolov 23,900 B1
Spišská Belá F2
Spišská Nová Ves 26,100 F2
Stará L'ubovňa 5,800 F2
Staré Město 6,293 D2
Šternberk 13,700 D2
Stod B2
Strakonice 19,000 B2
Strážnice 5,482 D2
Stříbro B2
Stropkov 5,645 F2
Studénka 9,744 D2
Štúrovo 8,287 E3
Šumperk 25,900 D1
Šurany 6,693 E2
Sušice 10,300 B2
Svárov C1
Svidník 4,600 F2
Svitavy 15,000 D2
Tábor 28,100 C2
Tachov 11,400 B2
Telč 5,285 C2
Teplice 52,300 B1
Tišnov 8,263 D2
Topol'čany 17,500 D2
Třebíč 23,900 C2
Trebišov 13,700 F2
Třeboň 6,068 C2
Trenčín 38,800 E2
Třešť 5,053 C2
Třinec 32,000 E2
Trnava 48,600 D2
Trutnov 24,500 D1
Turnov 13,600 C1
Turzovka 6,107 E2
Uherské Hradiště 32,100 D2
Uherský Brod 12,800 D2
Uničov 10,800 D2
Úpice 6,323 C1
Ústí nad Labem 74,900 C1
Ústí nad Orlicí 13,700 D2
Valašské Meziříčí 19,400 D2
Varnsdorf 14,700 C1
Važec E2
Vejprty B1
Velká Bíteš D2
Velká Bystřice D2
Vel'ké Kapušany G2
Velké Meziříčí 7,590 D2
Vel'ké Rovné E2
Veselí nad Lužnicí C2
Veselí nad Moravou 11,500 D2
Vimperk 5,749 B2
Vítkov 5,138 D2
Vizovice D2
Vlašim 8,873 C2
Vodňany 5,620 C2
Vojnice E3
Volary B2
Volyně B2
Votice C2
Vráble E2
Vracov D2
Vranov nad Teplou 14,700 F2
Vrbno pod Pradědem 5,594 D1
Vrbovce D1
Vrbové D2
Vrchlabí 11,700 C1
Vrútky 5,756 E2
Vsetín 24,100 D2
Vyškov 15,100 D2
Vysoké Mýto 8,830 D2
Vysoké Tatry F2
Vyšší Brod C2
Zábřeh 11,300 D2
Žamberk 5,040 D1
Žatec 17,400 B1
Zázrivá E2
Zbiroh B2
Zborov F2
Žd'ár nad Sázavou 17,800 C2
Želiezovce 5,478 E2
Žiar nad Hronom 14,800 E2
Židlochovice D2
Žilina 56,000 E2
Zlaté Moravce 10,300 E2
Zlín (Gottwaldov) 84,300 D2
Žlutice B1
Znojmo 28,500 D2
Zvolen 29,000 E2

OTHER FEATURES

Berounka (riv.) C2
Beskids, East (mts.) F1
Beskids, West (mts.) E2
Bohemian (for.) B2
Bohemian-Moravian Heights (hills) C2
Danube (riv.) C2
Dunajec (riv.) F2
Dyje (riv.) D2
Erzgebirge (mts.) B1
Gerlachovka (mt.) E2
Hornád (riv.) F2
Hron (riv.) E2
Ipel' (riv.) E2
Jablunka (pass) E2
Jeseníky (mts.) D1
Jihlava (riv.) D2
Krušné Hory (Erzgebirge) (mts.) B1
Labe (riv.) C1
Lipno (res.) C2
Lužnice (riv.) C2
Moldau (Vltava) (riv.) C2
Morava (riv.) D2
Nitra (riv.) E2
Oder (Odra) (riv.) D2
Ohře (riv.) B1
Ondava (riv.) F2
Orava (riv.) E2
Orlická (res.) C2
Sázava (riv.) C2
Slovenské Rudohorie (mts.) E2
Sudeten (mts.) C1
Svitava (riv.) D2
Svratka (riv.) D2
Tatra, High (mts.) E2
Torysa (riv.) F2
Úhlava (riv.) B2
Váh (riv.) D2
Vltava (riv.) C2
White Carpathians (mts.) E2

HUNGARY

COUNTIES

Bács-Kiskun 568,532 E3
Baranya 434,030 E4
Békés 436,987 F3
Borsod-Abaúj-Zemplén 808,924 F2
Budapest (city) 2,060,170 E3
Csongrád 456,862 F3
Fejér 421,568 E3
Győr-Sopron 428,476 D3
Hajdú-Bihar 552,417 F3
Heves 350,874 F3
Komárom 321,579 E3
Nógrád 239,907 E3
Pest 973,486 E3
Somogy 360,308 D3
Szabolcs-Szatmár 593,746 G3
Szolnok 446,379 F3
Tolna 266,414 E3
Vas 285,527 D3
Veszprém 386,740 D3
Zala 316,610 D3

CITIES and TOWNS

Aba 4,271 E3
Abádszalók 6,386 F3
Abaújszántó 4,209 F2
Abony 15,624 E3
Ács 8,423 E3
Ajka 29,601 D3
Albertirsa 11,252 E3
Alsózsolca 5,045 F2
Arló 4,203 F2
Aszód 6,218 E3
Bácsalmás 9,025 E3
Badacsonytomaj 2,933 D3
Baja 38,456 E3
Baktalórántháza 3,736 G2
Balassagyarmat 18,534 E2
Balatonfüred 12,599 D3
Balkány 7,667 G3
Balmazújváros 17,371 F3
Barcs 11,448 D4
Bátaszék 7,274 E3
Battonya 9,324 F3
Békés 22,287 F3
Békéscsaba 67,266 F3
Berettyóújfalu 16,406 F3
Berzence 3,406 D3
Bicske 10,720 E3
Biharkeresztes 4,788 F3
Biharnagybajom 4,093 F3
Böhönye 3,215 D3
Bonyhád 14,841 E3
Budafok 40,623 E3
Budaörs 13,958 E3
Budakeszi 10,429 E3
Budapest (cap.) 2,060,170 E3
Bugak 4,989 E3
Cegléd 40,567 E3
Celldömölk 12,533 D3
Cigánd 4,767 F2
Csabrendek 3,045 D3
Csákvár 5,238 E3
Csanádpalota 4,642 F3
Csenger 4,792 G3
Csepel 71,693 E3
Csepreg 4,079 D3
Csongrád 22,202 E3
Csorna 12,131 D3
Csorvás 6,826 F3
Csurgó 5,463 D3
Dabas 13,075 E3
Debrecen 192,484 F3
Derecske 9,579 F3
Dévaványa 11,208 F3
Devecser 5,482 D3
Dombóvár 19,917 E3
Dombrád 6,328 F2
Dömsöd 6,545 E3
Dorog 10,754 E3
Dunaföldvár 10,318 E3
Dunaharaszti 15,788 E3
Dunakeszi 25,187 E3
Dunaszekcső 2,999 E3
Dunaújváros 60,694 E3
Dunavecse 4,521 E3
Edelény 9,559 F2
Eger 61,283 F3
Egyek 7,956 F3
Elek 6,032 F3
Enes 2,565 F2
Endrőd 8,136 F3
Enying 7,518 E3
Érd 41,210 E3
Erdőtelek 4,250 F3
Esztergom 30,476 E3
Fadd 4,805 E3
Fegyvernek 8,421 F3
Fehérgyarmat 6,729 G3
Földeák 3,855 F3
Földes 5,293 F2
Fonyód 3,957 D3
Füzesabony 6,965 F3
Füzesgyarmat 7,097 F3
Gödöllő 28,057 E3
Gönc 2,875 F2
Gyoma 10,392 F3
Gyöngyös 36,927 E3
Gyönk 2,507 E3
Győr 123,618 D3
Gyula 34,514 F3
Hajdúböszörmény 32,145 F3
Hajdúdorog 10,118 F3
Hajdúhadház 13,626 F3
Hajdúnánás 18,146 F3
Hajdúsámson 7,492 F3
Hajdúszoboszló 23,374 F3
Hajós 5,113 E3
Hatvan 24,790 E3
Heves 10,943 F3
Hódmezővásárhely 54,481 F3
Hőgyész 3,534 E3
Ibrány 7,037 F2
Izsák 7,686 E3
Izsófalva 6,816 F2
Jánoshalma 12,534 E3
Jánosháza 3,274 D3
Jászapáti 10,424 E3
Jászárokszállás 10,139 E3
Jászberény 31,347 E3
Jászfényszaru 6,869 E3
Jászkarajenő 4,101 E3
Jászkisér 6,816 F3
Jászladány 7,823 F3
Kaba 6,654 F2
Kalocsa 18,613 E3
Kaposvár 72,330 D3
Kapuvár 11,243 D3
Karád 2,754 D3
Karcag 25,264 F3
Kazincbarcika 37,481 F2
Kecel 10,493 E3
Kecskemét 91,929 E3
Kemecse 4,583 F2
Keszthely 21,671 D3
Kétegyháza 4,728 F3
Kisbér 4,562 D3
Kiskőrös 15,499 E3
Kiskunfélegyháza 35,339 E3
Kiskunhalas 30,552 E3
Kiskunmajsa 14,439 E3
Kispest 65,106 E3
Kistelek 8,544 E3
Kisterenye 6,844 E2
Kisújszállás 13,699 F3
Kisvárda 17,828 G2
Komádi 8,765 F3
Komárom 19,955 E3
Komló 30,301 E3
Kondoros 7,319 F3
Körmend 11,787 D3
Körösladány 6,565 F3
Kőszeg 12,705 D3
Kunágota 4,622 F3
Kunhegyes 10,116 F3
Kunmadaras 7,343 F3
Kunszentmárton 11,103 F3
Kunszentmiklós 7,952 E3
Lajosmizse 12,872 E3
Lébénymiklós 6,190 D3
Lengyeltóti 3,389 D3
Leninváros 18,667 F3
Lenti 8,106 D3
Létavértes 9,106 G3
Letenye 4,395 D3
Lőkösháza 2,514 F3
Lőrinci 10,679 E3
Madaras 4,519 E3
Makó 29,943 F3
Mándok 5,093 G2
Marcali 12,485 D3
Mátészalka 17,709 G3
Mélykút 7,640 E3
Mérk 3,211 G3
Mezőberény 12,702 F3
Mezőcsát 6,729 F3
Mezőfalva 5,008 E3
Mezőhegyes 8,631 F3
Mezőkovácsháza 7,473 F3
Mezőkövesd 18,435 F3
Mezőszilas 2,792 E3
Mezőtúr 22,018 F3
Mindszent 8,730 F3
Miskolc 206,727 F2
Mohács 21,385 E4
Monor 16,838 E3
Mór 12,066 E3
Mosonmagyaróvár 29,732 D3
Nádudvar 9,447 F3
Nagyatád 12,946 D3
Nagybajom 4,402 D3
Nagyecsed 8,225 G3
Nagyhalász 6,437 F2
Nagykálló 11,282 F3
Nagykanizsa 48,494 D3
Nagykáta 11,922 E3
Nagykőrös 27,900 E3
Nagyszénás 7,124 F3
Nyírábrány 4,509 G3
Nyíradony 7,146 G3
Nyírbátor 13,388 G3
Nyíregyháza 108,156 F3
Nyírmada 4,744 F2
Örkény 5,013 E3
Orosháza 36,243 F3
Oroszlány 20,604 E3
Ózd 48,521 F2
Pacsa 1,984 D3
Paks 19,514 E3
Pannonhalma 3,731 D3
Pápa 32,202 D3
Pásztó 7,962 E3
Pécs 168,788 E3
Pécsvárad 3,672 E3
Pétervására 2,753 F3
Pilis 9,055 E3
Pilisvörösvár 10,217 E3
Polgár 9,429 F3
Polgárdi 5,767 E3
Püspökladány 15,730 F3
Pusztaszabolcs 5,794 E3
Putnok 7,103 F2
Ráckeve 7,534 E3
Rajka 2,448 D3
Rakamaz 5,407 F2
Rákospalota 60,983 E3
Répcelak 1,997 D3
Ricse 2,992 G2
Sajószentpéter 13,992 F2
Salgótarján 49,320 E2
Sándorfalva 5,949 F3
Sárbogárd 11,178 E3
Sarkad 11,937 F3
Sárospatak 15,316 F2
Sárvár 15,126 D3
Sátoraljaújhely 19,252 F2
Sellye 2,804 D4
Siklós 10,567 E4
Simontornya 4,892 E3
Siófok 20,084 E3
Solt 6,911 E3
Soltvadkert 7,934 E3
Sopron 53,930 D3
Sükösd 4,430 E3
Sümeg 6,229 D3
Szabadszállás 8,223 E3
Szarvas 20,598 F3
Szécsény 5,690 E2
Százhalombatta 13,963 E3
Szeged 171,342 E3
Szeghalom 9,736 F3
Szegvár 6,395 F3
Székesfehérvár 103,197 E3
Szekszárd 34,592 E3
Szendrő 4,098 F2
Szentendre 16,844 E3
Szentes 35,326 F3
Szentgotthárd 5,837 D3
Szentlőrinc 3,926 E3
Szerencs 8,612 F2
Szigetvár 12,114 D3
Szikszó 6,419 F2
Szil 2,073 D3
Szolnok 75,203 F3
Szombathely 82,830 D3
Tab 3,922 E3
Tamási 7,602 E3
Tápiószele 5,575 E3
Tapolca 17,161 D3
Tarpa 3,436 G2
Tata 24,114 E3
Tatabánya 75,942 E3
Tét 4,441 D3
Tiszacsege 6,263 F3
Tiszaföldvár 12,560 F3
Tiszafüred 12,259 F3
Tiszakécske 12,378 E3
Tiszalök 6,230 F2
Tiszavasvári 13,292 F3
Tokaj 4,845 F2
Tolna 8,997 E3
Tompa 5,365 E3
Törökszentmiklós 25,551 F3
Tótkomlós 8,803 F3
Tura 8,235 E3
Túrkeve 11,393 F3
Újfehértó 14,412 F3
Újpest 80,384 E3
Újszász 7,098 F2
Vác 34,837 E3
Vál 2,488 E3
Vámospércs 5,213 F3
Várpalota 28,293 E3
Vásárosnamény 8,637 G2
Vasvár 4,275 D3
Vecsés 19,193 E3
Velence 3,463 E3
Véménd 2,293 E3
Verpelét 4,622 F2
Veszprém 54,898 D3
Vésztő 9,815 F3
Villány 2,764 E4
Záhony 3,049 G2
Zalaegerszeg 39,671 D3
Zalaszentgrót 5,346 D3
Zirc 5,980 D3

OTHER FEATURES

Bakony (mts.) D3
Balaton (lake) D3
Berettyó (riv.) F3
Bükk (mts.) F2
Csepelsziget (isl.) E3
Danube (riv.) E3
Dráva (riv.) D3
Duna (Danube) (riv.) E3
Fertő tó (Neusiedler See) (lake) D3
Great Alföld (plain) F3
Hernád (riv.) F2
Kapos (riv.) D3
Kékes (mt.) E3
Körös (riv.) F3
Maros (riv.) F3
Mátra (mts.) E3
Mecsek (mts.) D3
Mura (riv.) D3
Rába (riv.) D3
Sajó (riv.) F2
Sárviz csatorna (canal) E3
Sió csatorna (canal) E3
Szentendreisziget (isl.) E3
Tisza (riv.) F3
Zala (riv.) D3

*City and suburbs.
†Population of Austrian cities are communes.

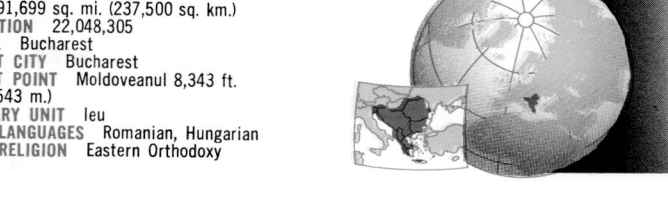

YUGOSLAVIA

AREA 98,766 sq. mi. (255,804 sq. km.)
POPULATION 22,471,000
CAPITAL Belgrade
LARGEST CITY Belgrade
HIGHEST POINT Triglav 9,393 ft. (2,863 m.)
MONETARY UNIT Yugoslav dinar
MAJOR LANGUAGES Serbo-Croatian, Slovenian, Macedonian, Montenegrin, Albanian
MAJOR RELIGIONS Eastern Orthodoxy, Roman Catholicism, Islam

ALBANIA

AREA 11,100 sq. mi. (28,749 sq. km.)
POPULATION 2,590,600
CAPITAL Tiranë
LARGEST CITY Tiranë
HIGHEST POINT Korab 9,026 ft. (2,751 m.)
MONETARY UNIT lek
MAJOR LANGUAGE Albanian
MAJOR RELIGIONS Islam, Eastern Orthodoxy, Roman Catholicism

ROMANIA

AREA 91,699 sq. mi. (237,500 sq. km.)
POPULATION 22,048,305
CAPITAL Bucharest
LARGEST CITY Bucharest
HIGHEST POINT Moldoveanul 8,343 ft. (2,543 m.)
MONETARY UNIT leu
MAJOR LANGUAGES Romanian, Hungarian
MAJOR RELIGION Eastern Orthodoxy

BULGARIA

AREA 42,823 sq. mi. (110,912 sq. km.)
POPULATION 8,862,000
CAPITAL Sofia
LARGEST CITY Sofia
HIGHEST POINT Musala 9,597 ft. (2,925 m.)
MONETARY UNIT lev
MAJOR LANGUAGE Bulgarian
MAJOR RELIGION Eastern Orthodoxy

GREECE

AREA 50,944 sq. mi. (131,945 sq. km.)
POPULATION 9,599,000
CAPITAL Athens
LARGEST CITY Athens
HIGHEST POINT Olympus 9,570 ft. (2,917 m.)
MONETARY UNIT drachma
MAJOR LANGUAGE Greek
MAJOR RELIGION Eastern (Greek) Orthodoxy

BULGARIA

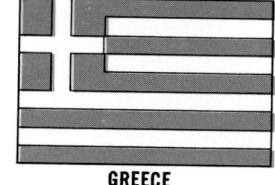

GREECE

YUGOSLAVIA

ALBANIA

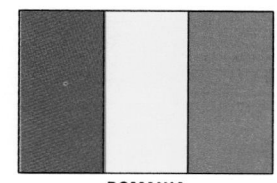

ROMANIA

Agriculture, Industry and Resources

DOMINANT LAND USE

- Cereals (chiefly wheat, corn)
- Mixed Farming, Horticulture
- Pasture Livestock
- Tobacco, Cotton
- Grapes, Wine
- Forests
- Nonagricultural Land

MAJOR MINERAL OCCURRENCES

Ab	Asbestos	Mg	Magnesium
Ag	Silver	Mn	Manganese
Al	Bauxite	Mr	Marble
C	Coal	Na	Salt
Cr	Chromium	Ni	Nickel
Cu	Copper	O	Petroleum
Fe	Iron Ore	Pb	Lead
G	Natural Gas	Sb	Antimony
Hg	Mercury	U	Uranium
Lg	Lignite	Zn	Zinc

⚡ Water Power
▨ Major Industrial Areas

ALBANIA

CITIES and TOWNS

Berat 25.700 .... D5
Çorovodë E5
Burrel D5
Delvinë 6.000 .... D6
Durrës (Durazzo) 53.800 .... D5
Elbasan 41.700 .... E5
Ersekë E5
Fier 23.000 .... D5
Gjirokastër 17.100 .... D5
Kavajë 18.700 .... D5
Korçë 47.300 .... E5
Krujë 7.900 .... D5
Kuçovë (Stalin) 14.000 .... D5
Kukës 6.100 .... E5
Leskovik E5
Lezhë D5
Lushnjë 18.900 .... D5
Memaliaj D5
Peqin D5
Përmet E5
Peshkopi 6.600 .... E5
Pogradec 10.100 .... E5
Pukë E4
Sarandë 8.700 .... E6
Shëngin D5
Shijak 6.200 .... D5
Shkodër 55.300 .... D5
Stalin 14.000 .... D5
Tepelenë D5
Tiranë (Tirana) (cap.) 171.300 .... E5
Vlorë 50.000 .... D5

OTHER FEATURES

Adriatic (sea) B4
Drin (riv.) E4
Korab (mt.) E5
Ohrid (lake) E5
Otranto (str.) D5
Prespa (lake) E5
Sazan (isl.) D5
Scutari (lake) D4
Vijosë (riv.) D5

BULGARIA

CITIES and TOWNS

Akhtopol 938 .... H4
Alfatar 3.249 .... H4
Ardino 5.080 .... G5
Asenovgrad 43.049 .... G5
Aytos 20.967 .... H4
Balchik 11.070 .... J4
Bansko 10.011 .... F5
Belogradchik 6.892 .... F4
Berkovitsa 16.253 .... F4
Blagoevgrad 50.043 .... F5
Botevgrad 17.789 .... F4
Bregovo 5.567 .... F3
Breznik 4.699 .... F4
Burgas 144.449 .... H4
Byala 10.564 .... G4
Byala Slatina 15.788 .... G4
Chirpan 20.595 .... G4
Devin 7.120 .... G5
Dimitrovgrad 45.596 .... G4
Dobrich (Tolbukhin) 86.184 .... H4
Dryanovo 9.804 .... G4
Elena 7.008 .... H4
Elin Pelin 5.499 .... F4
Elkhovo 12.397 .... H4
Gabrovo 75.034 .... G4
General-Toshevo 8.928 .... H4
Godech 5.225 .... F4
Gorna Oryakhovitsa 34.157 .... G4
Gotse Delchev 17.015 .... F5
Grudovo 9.871 .... H4
Ikhtiman 11.482 .... F4
Isperikh 10.500 .... H4
Ivaylovgrad 3.900 .... H5
Karapelit H4
Karlovo 25.472 .... G4
Karnobat 21.480 .... H4
Kavarna 10.872 .... J4
Kazanlŭk 53.607 .... G4
Kharmanli 19.240 .... H5
Khaskovo 75.031 .... G4
Kotel 8.229 .... H4
Krumovgrad 5.211 .... G5
Kubrat 9.826 .... H4
Kula 5.667 .... F4
Kŭrdzhali 47.757 .... G5
Kyustendil 48.239 .... F4
Lom 30.538 .... F4
Lovech 43.858 .... G4

Lukovit 10.400 .... G4
Malko Tŭrnovo 4.233 .... H4
Maritsa 8.664 .... H4
Michurin 4.434 .... H4
Mikhaylovgrad 40.064 .... F4
Momchilgrad 8.185 .... G5
Nesebŭr 6.768 .... H4
Nikopol 5.563 .... G4
Nova Zagora 21.872 .... H4
Novi Pazar 15.751 .... H4
Omurtag 9.067 .... H4
Oryakhovo 14.012 .... F4
Panagyurishte 20.649 .... G4
Pazardzhik 65.577 .... G4
Pernik 87.432 .... F4
Peshtera 16.882 .... G4
Petrich 24.381 .... F5
Pirdop 8.248 .... G4
Pleven 107.567 .... G4
Plovdiv 300.242 .... G4
Pomorie 11.960 .... H4
Popina H3
Popovo 19.428 .... H4
Provadiya 15.143 .... H4
Radomir 10.436 .... F4
Razgrad 42.486 .... H4
Razlog 13.690 .... F5
Rositsa H4
Ruse 160.351 .... H4
Samokov 25.763 .... F4
Sandanski 19.003 .... F5
Sevlievo 24.421 .... G4
Shabla 4.471 .... J4
Shumen 83.525 .... H4
Silistra 58.270 .... H3
Simeonovgrad (Maritsa) 8.664 .... H4
Sliven 90.137 .... H4
Smolyan 29.032 .... G5
Smyadovo 5.020 .... H4
Sofia (cap.) 965.728 .... F4
Sozopol 3.877 .... H4
Stanke Dimitrov 42.034 .... F4
Stara Zagora 122.200 .... G4
Svilengrad 15.150 .... G5
Svishtov 29.412 .... G4
Teteven 12.555 .... G4
Tolbukhin 86.184 .... H4
Topolovgrad 7.230 .... H4
Troyan 23.692 .... G4
Trŭn 2.381 .... F4
Tŭrgovishte 38.796 .... H4
Tŭtrakan 11.447 .... H4
Varna 251.654 .... J4
Veliko Tŭrnovo 56.497 .... G4
Vidin 53.030 .... F4
Vratsa 61.265 .... F4
Yambol 75.861 .... H4
Zimnitsa H4
Zlatograd 7.732 .... G5

OTHER FEATURES

Balkan (mts.) G4
Black (sea) J4
Danube (riv.) H4
Dunav (Danube) (riv.) H4
Emine (cape) H4
Iskŭr (riv.) G4
Kaliakra (cape) J4
Maritsa (riv.) F5
Mesta (riv.) F5
Midzhur (mt.) F4
Musala (mt.) F4
Osŭm (riv.) G4
Rhodope (mts.) G5
Rujen (mt.) F4
Struma (riv.) F4
Timok (riv.) F3
Tundzha (riv.) G4
Vit (riv.) G4

GREECE

REGIONS

Aegean Islands 417.813 .... G6
Athens, Greater 2.566.775 .... F7
Áyion Óros (aut. dist.) 1.732 .... G5
Central Greece and Euboea 986.543 .... F6
Crete 456.642 .... G8
Epirus 310.334 .... E6
Ionian Islands 184.443 .... D6
Macedonia 1.888.952 .... F5
Pelopónnisos 986.912 .... F7
Thessaly 659.913 .... F6
Thrace 329.582 .... G5

CITIES and TOWNS

Agrínion 30.973 .... E6
Aiyina 5.704 .... F7

Aíyion 18.829 .... F6
Alexandroúpolis 22.995 .... H5
Alivérion 4.414 .... G7
Almirós 5.680 .... F6
Amaliás 14.177 .... E7
Amfilokhía 4.668 .... E6
Ámfissa 6.605 .... F6
Andíssa 1.762 .... H6
Andravídha 3.046 .... E6
Ándros 1.827 .... G7
Áno Viánnos 1.431 .... G8
Anóyia 2.750 .... G8
Ardhéa 3.555 .... F5
Areópolis 674 .... F7
Argalastí 1.621 .... F6
Árgos 18.890 .... F7
Argostólion 7.060 .... E6
Arkhángelos 3.016 .... J7
Arnaía 2.424 .... F5
Árta 19.498 .... E6
Astipálaia 787 .... H7
Atalándi 4.581 .... F6
Athens (cap.) 867.023 .... F7
Athens* 2.566.775 .... F7
Ayiá 5.241 .... F6
Ayíos Kírikos 1.083 .... H7
Ayíos Matthaíos 1.596 .... D6
Ayíos Nikólaos 5.002 .... G8
Candia (Iráklion) 77.506 .... G8
Canea (Khania) 40.564 .... G8
Corinth 20.773 .... F7
Corinth 20.773 .... F7
Delfí 1.185 .... F6
Delvinákion 1.067 .... E6
Dhidhimótikhon 8.388 .... H5
Dhíkaia 1.222 .... H5
Dhimitsána 996 .... F7
Dhonoúsis 1.991 .... H6
Dráma 29.692 .... G5
Édhessa 13.967 .... F5
Elassón 7.200 .... F6
Elevtheroúpolis 4.888 .... G5
Ermoúpolis 13.502 .... G7
Fársala 6.967 .... F6
Filiátes 2.923 .... E6
Fílatra 5.919 .... E7
Fílippias 3.248 .... E6
Flórina 11.164 .... E5
Gargaliánoi 5.888 .... E7
Grevená 8.106 .... E5
Ídhra 2.381 .... F7
Ierápetra 7.055 .... G8
Igoumenítsa 4.109 .... E6
Ioánnina 40.130 .... E6
Íos 1.270 .... G7
Iráklion 77.506 .... G8
Istíaia 4.059 .... F6
Itháki 2.293 .... E6
Kalamai 39.133 .... F7
Kalampáka 5.453 .... E6
Kalávrita 1.948 .... F6
Kálimnos 6.492 .... H7
Kándanos 403 .... F8
Kardhítsa 25.685 .... F6
Kariá 1.350 .... E6
Karíaí 301 .... G5
Káristos 3.550 .... G6
Kárpathos 1.363 .... H8
Karpenísion 4.414 .... E6
Kastéllion (Kíssamos) 2.996 .... F8
Kastéllíota 1.152 .... F7
Kastoría 15.407 .... E5
Katákolon 690 .... E7
Kateríni 28.808 .... F5
Kavála 46.234 .... G5
Kéa 693 .... G7
Kérkira 28.630 .... D6
Khalkís 36.300 .... F6
Khaniá 40.564 .... G8
Khíos 24.084 .... G6
Khóra Sfakíon 246 .... G8
Kiáton 7.392 .... F6
Kilkís 10.538 .... F5
Kími 2.772 .... G6
Kiparissía 3.882 .... E7
Kíssamos 2.996 .... F8
Klíthira 349 .... F7
Komotiní 28.896 .... G5
Kónitsa 3.150 .... E5
Kóropi 9.367 .... F7
Kós 7.828 .... H7
Kozáni 23.240 .... E5
Kranídhion 3.657 .... F7
Lagkadía 1.350 .... F7
Lamía 37.872 .... F6
Langadhás 6.707 .... F5
Langadhía F7
Lárisa 72.336 .... F6
Lávrion 8.283 .... G7
Leonídhion 3.181 .... F7
Levádhia 15.445 .... F6
Lévkas 8.573 .... E6
Limenária 1.507 .... G5

(continued on following page)

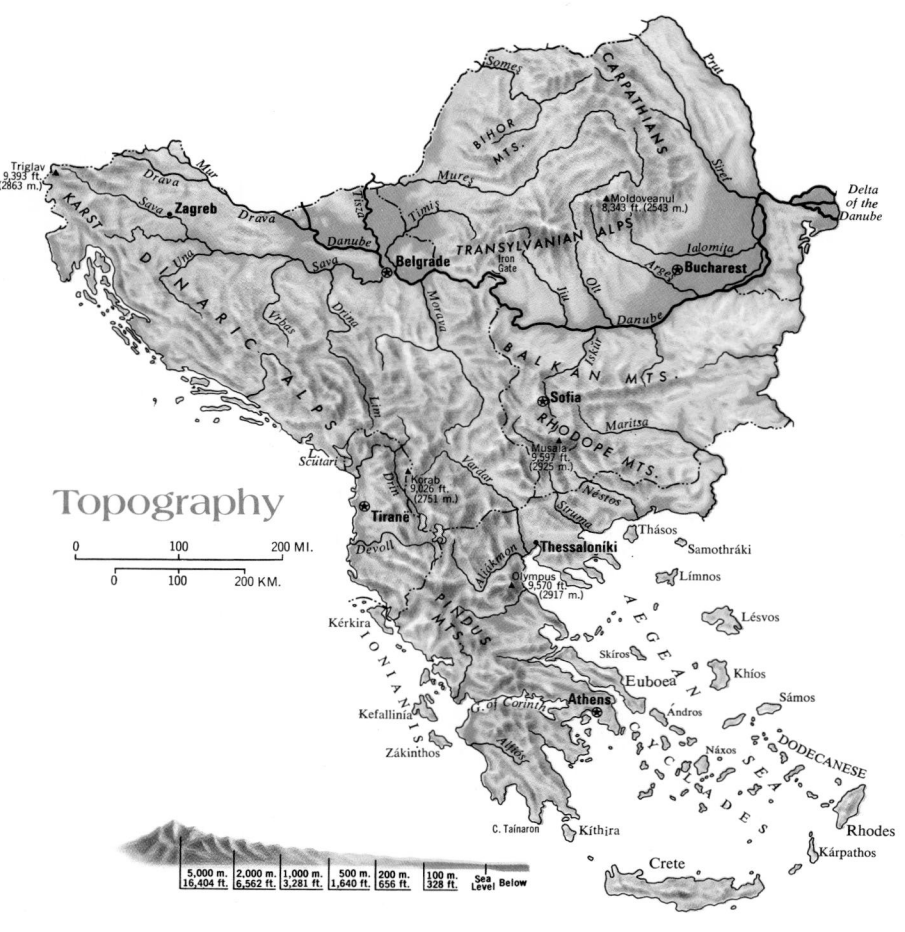

Topography

Triglav 9,393 ft. (2,863 m.)

Moldoveanul 8,343 ft. (2543 m.)

Delta of the Danube

Zagreb

Belgrade

Bucharest

Iron Gate

Sofia

Musala 9,597 ft. (2925 m.)

Tirane

Korab 9,026 ft. (2751 m.)

Olympus 9,570 ft. (2917 m.)

Thessaloniki

Thásos
Samothráki

Límnos

Kérkira

Lésvos

Skíros

Khíos

Euboea

Sámos

Athens

Ándros

Kefallinía

Náxos

DODECANESE

Zákinthos

Rhodes

C. Taínaron
Kíthira

Kárpathos

Crete

0 100 200 MI.

0 100 200 KM.

| 5,000 m. 16,404 ft. | 2,000 m. 6,562 ft. | 1,000 m. 3,281 ft. | 500 m. 1,640 ft. | 200 m. 656 ft. | 100 m. 328 ft. | Sea Level | Below |

The Balkan States

CONIC PROJECTION

SCALE OF MILES

0   25   50   75   100   125   150   175

SCALE OF KILOMETERS

0   25   50   75   100   125   150   175

Capitals of Countries .... ☆

Administrative Centers .... △

International Boundaries _____

Major Internal Boundaries _ _ _ _ _

Minor Internal Boundaries _ . _ . _

Canals ....

Scale 1: 6,150,000

BULGARIA and GREECE are divided into counties and departments, respectively. Because of the scale no attempt has been made to delimit and name these subdivisions; their administrative centers have, however, been designated.

The larger divisions named in Greece are well-known geographical regions, without administrative function.

ROMANIA consists of thirty-nine counties and three cities of regional status, Bucharest, Constanța and Petroșeni. Scale does not permit delimiting these counties.

ALBANIA is divided into twenty-seven districts. Scale does not permit the delimitation of these divisions.

YUGOSLAVIA is a federation of six republics. The Serbian republic includes an autonomous province (Vojvodina), and an autonomous region (Kosovo).

© Copyright HAMMOND INCORPORATED, Maplewood, N.J.

Topography

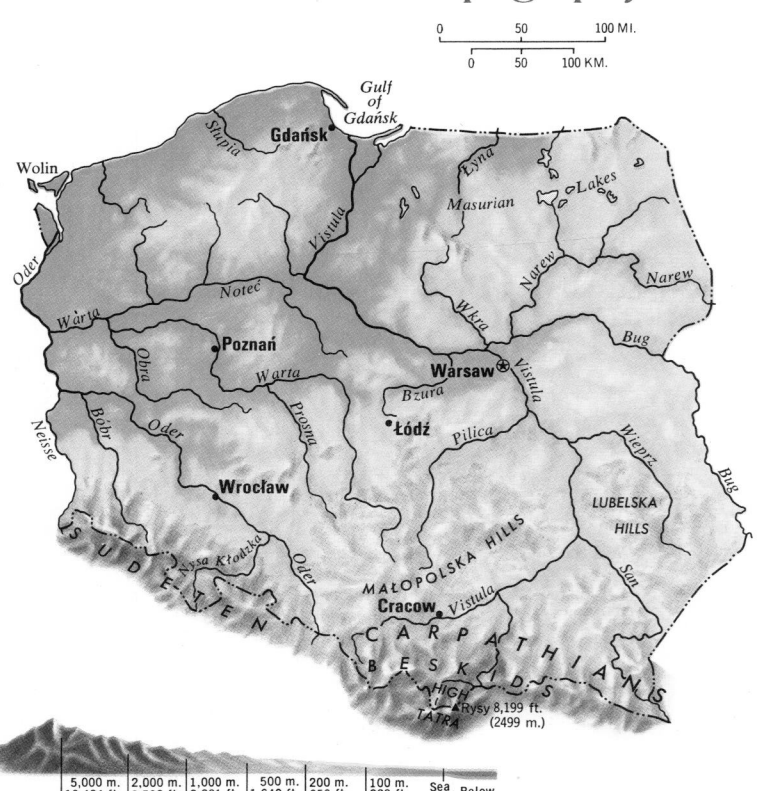

0 50 100 MI.
0 50 100 KM.

Gulf of Gdańsk

Wolin
Gdańsk
Słupia
Łyna
Masurian
Lakes
Vistula
Oder
Bo
Notec
Narew
Narew
Warta
Obra
Poznań
Oder
Warta
Prosna
Wkra
Warsaw
Bzura
Bug
Neisse
Bóbr
Oder
Łódź
Pilica
Wieprz
Wrocław
Nysa Kłodzko
LUBELSKA HILLS
Oder
San
SUDETEN
MAŁOPOLSKA HILLS
Cracow
Vistula
CARPATHIANS
B E S K I D S
HIGH
TATRA
Rysy 8,199 ft.
(2499 m.)

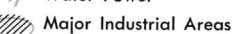

5,000 m. | 2,000 m. | 1,000 m. | 500 m. | 200 m. | 100 m. | Sea | Below
16,404 ft. | 6,562 ft. | 3,281 ft. | 1,640 ft. | 656 ft. | 328 ft. | Level

Agriculture, Industry and Resources

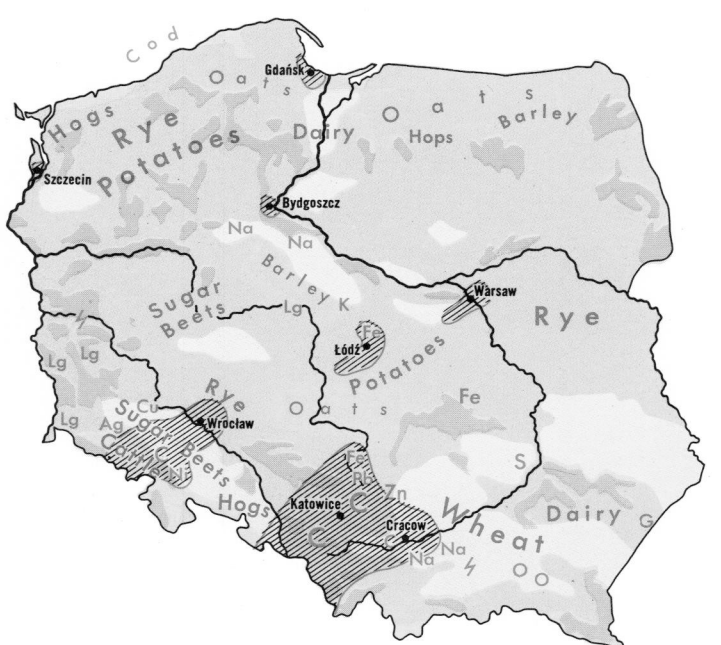

Cod
Gdańsk
Hogs
Rye
Oats
Oats
Barley
Potatoes
Dairy
Hops
Szczecin
Na
Bydgoszcz
Na
Barley
K
Sugar
Beets
Lg
Warsaw
Lg
Łódź
Potatoes
Rye
Lg
Rye
Fe
Lg
Oats
Su
Ag Cu
Sugar
Beets
Wrocław
S
Hogs
Katowice
Zn
Cracow
Dairy
G
Wheat
Na
Oo

MAJOR MINERAL OCCURRENCES

Ag	Silver	Na	Salt
C	Coal	Ni	Nickel
Cu	Copper	O	Petroleum
Fe	Iron Ore	Pb	Lead
G	Natural Gas	S	Sulfur
K	Potash	Zn	Zinc
Lg	Lignite		

⚡ Water Power
▨ Major Industrial Areas

DOMINANT LAND USE

▢ Cereals (chiefly wheat)

▢ Rye, Oats, Barley, Potatoes

▢ General Farming, Livestock

▢ Forests

Poland 1938

0 50 100 MILES

BALTIC SEA
LITHUANIA
Niemen
DANZIG
GERMANY
Vilna
Oder
Stettin
U.S.S.R.
Berlin
Poznań
Vistula
Warsaw
Bug
Brest
Pinsk
Warta
GERMANY
Breslau
Oder
Cracow
Lwów
Dniester
CZECHOSLOVAKIA
HUNGARY
ROMANIA

Poland 1945

0 50 100 MILES

BALTIC SEA
Niemen
U.
Gdańsk
(Danzig)
Vilna
Oder
Szczecin
(Stettin)
S.
Berlin
Poznań
Vistula
Warsaw
Bug
Brest
Pinsk
S.
GERMANY
Warta
R.
Neisse
Wrocław
(Breslau)
Oder
Cracow
L'vov
(Lwów)
Dniester
CZECHOSLOVAKIA
HUNGARY
ROMANIA

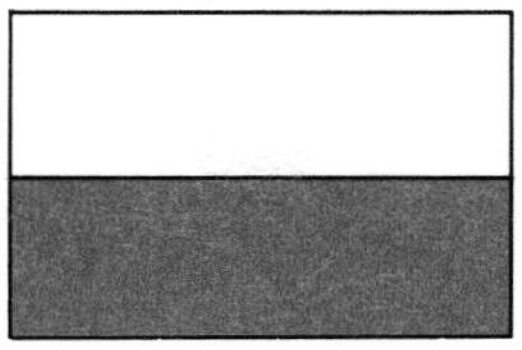

AREA 120,725 sq. mi. (312,678 sq. km.)
POPULATION 35,815,000
CAPITAL Warsaw
LARGEST CITY Warsaw
HIGHEST POINT Rysy 8,199 ft.
(2,499 m.)
MONETARY UNIT zloty
MAJOR LANGUAGE Polish
MAJOR RELIGION Roman Catholicism

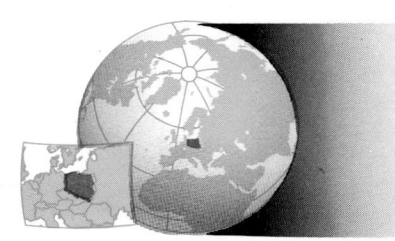

raniewo 12.100	D1
reslau (Wrocław) 461.900	C3
rieg (Brzeg) 30.780	D2
rodnica 17.300	D2
rzeg 30.780	C3
rzeg Dolny 10.800	C3
rzesko 9.701	E3
usko Zdrój 11.100	E4
ydgoszcz 280.460	C2
ytom 186.993	A3
ytów 10.642	C1
hełm 38.789	F3
hełmno 17.906	D2
hełmża 14.200	D2
hodzież 14.100	C2
hojnice 23.500	C2
hojnów 11.000	B3
horzów 151.338	B2
hoszczno 9.800	B2
hrzanów 29.300	A4
iechanów 28.500	E2
ieplice	
Śląskie-Zdrój 15.400	B3
ieszyn 25.234	E4
zechowice-Dziedzice 25.400	C4
zeladż 31.843	B3
zęstochowa 187.613	D3
ąbrowa Górnicza 61.660	B3
anzig (Gdańsk) 364.285	C1
arłowo 11.200	C1
ebica 22.961	E3
eblin 14.600	E3
ęblin 10.700	E2
ziałdowo 10.100	E2
zierzoniów 32.800	C3
łding (Elbląg) 89.835	D1
łk 27.188	F2
ansk 364.285	C1
dynia 190.125	D1
iwice (Gliwice) 170.912	A3
łogów (Głogów) 20.226	C3
ubczyce 11.300	C2
ubchołazy 13.200	C3
niezno 50.643	C2
odawa 14.600	E3
orlice 15.200	E4
órzów Wielkopolski 74.267	B2
ostyń 13.000	C3
ostynin 12.000	E2
rodzisk Mazowiecki 20.400	E2
rodzisk Wielkopolski 20.400	B2
rudziądz 75.511	D2
rünberg (Zielona	
Góra) 59.700	B3
yfice 13.200	B1
ajnówka m4.345	F2
indenburg (Zabrze) 199.400	A3
irschberg (Jelenia	
Góra) 55.720	B3
rubieszów 14.999	F3
wa 16.400	D2
nowrocław 54.817	D2

Jarocin 18.100	C3
Jarosław 29.000	F4
Jasło 17.025	E4
Jastrzębie Zdrój 34.400	D3
Jaworzno 63.271	B4
Jędrzejów 18.244	E3
Jelenia Góra 55.720	B3
Kalisz 81.227	D3
Kamienna Góra 21.000	B3
Kartuzy 10.558	C1
Katowice 303.264	B4
Kędzierzyn-Koźle 45.600	C3
Kępno 10.151	C3
Kętrzyn 19.300	E1
Kielce 125.952	E3
Kłobuck 12.600	C3
Kłodzko 26.000	C3
Kluczbork 18.000	C3
Knurów 28.400	A4
Kolberg (Kołobrzeg) 25.419	B1
Koło 13.100	D2
Kołobrzeg 25.419	B1
Konin 40.600	D2
Końskie 13.100	E3
Konstantynów	
Łódzki 12.800	D3
Kościan 18.700	C3
Kościerzyna 18.914	C1
Koślin (Koszalin) 64.414	C1
Kostrzyń 11.200	B2
Koszalin 64.414	C1
Kraków (Cracow) 651.300	E4
Krapkowice 13.800	C3
Kraśnik Fabryczny 14.600	F3
Krasnystaw 12.495	F3
Krosno 26.500	E4
Krotoszyn 21.900	C3
Krynica 10.200	E4
Kûstrin 31.837	B2
Kutno 30.000	D2
Kwidzin 23.104	D2
Łańcut 12.049	F3
Landsberg (Gorzów	
Wielkopolski) 74.267	B2
Łaziska Górne 10.800	A4
Łębork 25.000	C1
Łęczyca 13.900	D2
Legionowo 20.800	E2
Legnica 75.843	C3
Leszczyn 12.200	A4
Leszno 33.890	C3
Libiąż 10.600	D3
Lidzbark Warmiński 12.900	E1
Liegnitz (Legnica) 75.843	C3
Lipno 10.600	D2
Łódź 777.800	D3
Łomża 25.500	F2
Łowicz 20.400	D2
Lubań 17.200	B3
Lubartów 10.600	F3
Lubin 16.400	C3
Lublin 235.937	F3
Lubliniec 19.800	D3
Lubon 16.400	C2
Lubsko 12.600	B3
Łuków 15.500	F3
Malbork (Marienburg) 30.900	D1

Międzyrzec Podlaski 13.500	F3
Międzyrzecz 14.900	B2
Mielec 26.800	E3
Mików 21.300	B4
Mińsk Mazowiecki 24.200	E2
Mława 20.007	E2
Mogilno 9.560	D2
Morag 9.681	D2
Mrągowo 13.400	E2
Myślenice 12.100	E4
Mysłowice 44.737	B4
Myszków 18.000	D3
Nakło nad Notecią 16.800	C2
Namysłów 11.076	C3
Neisse (Nysa) 31.837	C3
Nidzica 9.642	E2
Nisko 10.000	F3
Nowa Ruda 18.100	C3
Nowa Sól 33.300	B3
Nowy Dwór Mazowiecki 16.900	E2
Nowy Sącz 41.103	E4
Nowy Targ 21.900	E4
Nysa 31.837	C3
Oborniki 10.200	C2
Oława 17.600	C3
Oleśnica 27.500	C3
Olkusz 15.800	D3
Olsztyn 94.119	E2
Opoczno 12.168	E3
Opole 86.510	C3
Oppeln 86.510	C3
Orzesze 9.600	A4
Ostróda 21.300	D2
Ostrołęka 27.981	E2
Ostrów Mazowiecka 15.000	E2
Ostrów Wielkopolski 49.530	C3
Ostrowiec	
Świętokrzyski 49.958	E3
Ostrzeszów 9.600	C3
Otwock 39.663	E2
Ozorków 18.200	D3
Pabianice 62.275	D3
Piekary Śląskie 36.300	A3
Piła 43.778	C2

Pionki 13.600	E3
Piotrków Trybunalski 59.683	D3
Pisz 11.100	E2
Pleszew 13.348	C3
Płock 71.727	D2
Płońsk 11.619	E2
Police 12.700	B2
Poznań 469.085	C2
Prudnik 20.300	C3
Pruszcz Gdański 13.000	D1
Pruszków 42.961	E2
Przasnysz 11.100	E2
Przemyśl 53.228	F4
Puck 9.540	D1
Puławy 34.800	F3
Pułtusk 12.800	E2
Rabka 10.700	D4
Racibórz 40.418	D3
Radom 158.640	E3
Radomsko 31.179	D3
Ratibor (Racibórz) 40.418	D3
Rawa Mazowiecka 9.800	E3
Rawicz 14.100	C3
Ruda Śląska 142.407	B4
Rumia 25.800	D1
Rybnik 43.415	D3
Rypin 10.029	D2
Rzeszów 82.192	F4
Sandomierz 16.800	E3
Sanok 21.600	F4
Schneidemühl (Piła) 36.600	C2
Schweidnitz	
(Świdnica) 47.542	C3
Siedlce 38.983	F2
Siemianowice	
Śląskie 67.278	B4
Sieradz 38.500	D3
Sierpc 12.700	D2
Skarżysko-Kamienna 39.194	E3
Skawina 15.900	D4
Skierniewice 25.590	E2
Sławno 10.200	C1
Słubice 12.000	A2
Słupsk 68.311	C1

Sochaczew 20.500	E2
Sokołów 10.023	F2
Sokołów Podlaski 9.569	F2
Sopot 47.573	D1
Sosnowiec 144.652	B4
Śrem 15.600	C2
Środa Śląska 10.259	C3
Środa Wielkopolska 14.800	C2
Stalowa Wola 29.768	F3
Starachowice 42.807	E3
Stargard Szczeciński 44.400	B2
Starogard Gdański 33.400	D2
Stary Sącz 57.400	E4
Stettin (Szczecin) 337.294	B2
Stolp (Słupsk) 68.311	C1
Strzegom 14.000	C3
Strzelce Opolskie 14.700	D3
Strzelin 9.800	C3
Sulechów 10.200	B2
Suwałki 25.360	F1
Swarżędz 12.100	C2
Świdnica 47.542	C3
Świdnik 31.900	F3
Świdwin 12.500	B2
Świebodzice 18.500	C3
Świebodzin 14.900	B2
Świecie 17.900	D2
Świętochłowice 57.633	A4
Świnoujście	
(Swinemünde) 27.900	B1
Szamotuły 14.600	C2
Szczecin 337.204	B2
Szczecinek 28.600	C2
Szczytno 17.371	E2
Szprotawa 11.200	B3
Tarnobrzeg 18.800	E3
Tarnów 85.514	E4
Tarnowskie Góry 34.200	A3
Tczew 40.794	D1
Tomaszów Lubelski 12.329	F3
Tomaszów Mazowiecki 54.911	E3
Toruń 85.120	D2
Trzcianka 10.900	C2
Trzebinia-Siersza	C4

Turek 18.500	D2
Tychy 71.384	B4
Ustka 9.900	C1
Wabrzeźno 11.800	D2
Wadowice 11.700	D4
Wągrowiec 15.600	C2
Wałbrzych 125.048	C3
Wałcz 18.900	C2
Waldenburg	
(Wałbrzych) 125.048	C3
Warsaw (Warszawa)	
(cap.) 1.377.100	E2
Wejherowo 33.400	D1
Wieliczka 13.600	E3
Wieluń 14.300	D3
Wiślo 9.800	D4
Włocławek 77.169	D2
Wodzisław Śląski 25.600	D3
Wolin 35.458	B2
Wołomin 24.000	E2
Wołów 10.500	C3
Wrocław 523.318	C3
Września 17.800	C2
Wschowa 8.900	C3
Wyszków	E2
Ząbki 16.000	E2
Ząbkowice Śląskie 13.800	C3
Zabrze 197.214	A4
Zagań 21.400	B3
Zakopane 27.039	D4
Zambrów 14.082	F2
Zamość 34.734	F3
Żary 28.300	B3
Zawiercie 39.410	D3
Zduńska Wola 29.066	D3
Zgierz 42.838	D3
Zgorzelec 28.400	B3
Zięhce 9.700	C3
Zielona Góra 73.156	B3
Złocieniec 10.100	C2
Złotoryja 12.200	C3
Złotów 11.600	C2
Znin 9.600	C2
Żyrardów 33.196	E2

Żywiec 22.400	D4

OTHER FEATURES

Baltic (sea)	B1
Beskids (range)	D4
Brda (riv.)	C2
Brynica (riv.)	B4
Bug (riv.)	F3
Danzig (Gdańsk) (gulf)	D1
Dukla (pass)	E4
Dunajec (riv.)	E4
Gwda (riv.)	C2
Hel (pen.)	D1
High Tatra (range)	D4
Łyna (riv.)	E1
Mamry, Jezioro (lake)	E1
Masurian (lkes)	E2
Narew (riv.)	E2
Neisse (riv.)	B3
Notec (riv.)	B2
Nysa Kłodzka (riv.)	C3
Nysa Łużycka (Neisse)	
(riv.)	B3
Oder (riv.)	B2
Orava (res.)	D4
Pilica (riv.)	D3
Pomeranian (bay)	B1
Prosna (riv.)	C3
Przemsza (riv.)	B4
Rysy (mt.)	D4
San (riv.)	F3
Słupia (riv.)	C1
Śniardwy, Jezioro (lake)	E2
Sudeten (range)	B3
Uznam (Usedom) (isl.)	B1
Vistula (riv.)	D2
Warmia (reg.)	D1
Warta (riv.)	D2
Wieprz (riv.)	F3
Wisła (Vistula) (riv.)	D2
Wkra (riv.)	E2
Wolin (Wollin) (isl.)	B2

Poland

CONIC PROJECTION

SCALE OF MILES
0 10 20   40   60   80

SCALE OF KILOMETERS
0 10 20   40   60   80

Capitals of Countries..........⍟
Other Capitals....................⊛
International Boundaries ____
Internal Boundaries _____
Canals_____

Scale 1:4,500,000

Poland is divided into 49 provinces (bearing the same name as their capitals) and the autonomous cities of Warsaw, Łódź and Cracow.

UNION REPUBLICS

Armenian S.S.R.	3,031,000	E6
Azerbaidzhan S.S.R.	6,028,000	E5
Estonian S.S.R.	1,466,000	C4
Georgian S.S.R.	5,015,000	E5
Kazakh S.S.R.	14,684,000	G5
Kirgiz S.S.R.	3,529,000	H5
Latvian S.S.R.	2,521,000	C4
Lithuanian S.S.R.	3,398,000	C4
Moldavian S.S.R.	3,947,000	D5
Russian S.F.S.R.	137,551,000	D4
Tadzhik S.S.R.	3,801,000	G6
Turkmen S.S.R.	2,759,000	F6
Ukrainian S.S.R.	49,755,000	D5
Uzbek S.S.R.	15,391,000	G5
White Russian S.S.R.	9,560,000	C4

INTERNAL DIVISIONS

Abkhaz A.S.S.R.	505,000	E5
Adygey Aut. Obl.	405,000	D5
Adzhar A.S.S.R.	354,000	E5
Aginsk Buryat Aut. Okr.	69,000	M4
Bashkir A.S.S.R.	3,849,000	F4
Buryat A.S.S.R.	900,000	M4
Chechen-Ingush A.S.S.R.	1,154,000	E5
Chukchi Aut. Okr.	133,000	D3
Chuvash A.S.S.R.	1,292,000	E4
Dagestan A.S.S.R.	1,628,000	E5
Evenki Aut. Okr.	16,000	K3
Gorno-Altay Aut. Obl.	172,000	J4
Gorno-Badakhshan Aut. Obl.	127,000	H6
Jewish Aut. Obl.	190,000	O5
Kabardin-Balkar		

A.S.S.R.	674,000	E5
Kalmuck A.S.S.R.	294,000	E5
Karachay-Cherkess Aut. Obl.	368,000	E5
Karakalpak A.S.S.R.	904,000	G5
Karelian A.S.S.R.	736,000	D3
Khakass Aut. Obl.	500,000	J4
Khanty-Mansi Aut. Okr.	569,000	H3
Komi A.S.S.R.	1,119,000	F3
Komi-Permyak Aut. Okr.	173,000	F4
Koryak Aut. Okr.	34,000	R3
Mari A.S.S.R.	703,000	E4
Mordvinian A.S.S.R.	991,000	E4
Nagorno-Karabakh Aut. Obl.	161,000	E6
Nakhichevan' A.S.S.R.	239,000	E6
Nenets Aut. Okr.	47,000	F3
North Ossetian A.S.S.R.	597,000	E5
South Ossetian Aut. Obl.	98,000	E5
Tatar A.S.S.R.	3,436,000	E4
Taymyr Aut. Okr.	44,000	K2
Tuvinian A.S.S.R.	267,000	K4
Udmurt A.S.S.R.	1,494,000	F4
Ust'-Ordynskiy Buryat Aut. Okr.	133,000	L4
Yakut A.S.S.R.	839,000	N3
Yamal-Nenets Aut. Okr.	158,000	H3

CITIES and TOWNS

Abakan	128,000	K4
Abay	34,245	H5
Abaza	15,202	J4
Achinsk	117,000	K4
Agata		K3
Aginskoye	7,922	M4
Akmolinsk (Tselinograd)	234,000	H4
Aksay	10,010	J4
Aktas		G5
Aktash		J5
Aktyubinsk	191,000	F4
Aldan	17,689	N4
Aleksandrovsk-Sakhalinskiy	20,342	P5
Aleksin	18,041	H4
Aleysk	32,487	J4
Alga	12,000	F4
Aliskerovo		R3
Allakh-Yun'		N4
Alma-Ata	910,000	H5
Almaznyy		M3
Amarchik		R3
Amderma		E3
Amursk	24,010	O4
Anadyr'	7,703	S3
Andizhan	230,000	H5
Andropov	239,000	E4
Angarsk	239,000	L4
Angren		H5
Anzhero-Sudzhensk	105,000	J4
Aral'sk	37,722	G5
Archangel (Arkhangel'sk)	385,000	E3
Arkalyk	15,108	G4
Armavir	162,000	E5
Arsen'yev	60,000	O5
Artem	69,000	O5
Artemovskiy		M4
Arys	26,414	G5
Arzamas	93,000	E4
Asbest	79,000	G4

Ashkhabad	312,000	F6
Asino	29,395	J4
Astrakhan'	461,000	F5
Atbasar	37,228	G4
Atka		Q3
Ayaguz	35,827	J5
Ayan		P4
Aykhal		M3
Bagdarin		M4
Baku	1,022,000	F5
Baku'	1,550,000	F5
Balakovo	152,000	F4
Balashov	93,000	E4
Baley	27,215	M4
Balkhash	78,000	H5
Balykshi	22,397	F5
Bam		N5
Barabinsk	37,274	H4
Baranovichi	131,000	C4
Barnaul	533,000	J4
Batagay	10,000	N3
Batumi	123,000	E5
Baykit		K3
Baykonyr		H5
Bayram-Ali	31,987	G6
Belgorod	240,000	D4
Belogorsk	63,000	O4
Belomorsk	16,595	D3
Beloretsk	71,000	F4
Belovo	112,000	J4
Berdichev	80,000	D5
Berdsk	67,000	J4
Berezniki	185,000	F4
Berezovo	6,000	G3
Beringovskiy		S3
Bikin	17,473	O5
Bira		O5

Birobidzhan	69,000	O5
Biruni		G5
Biysk	212,000	J4
Blagoveshchensk	172,000	O4
Bobruysk	192,000	C4
Bodaybo	14,000	M4
Borisoglebsk	68,000	E4
Borzya	27,815	M4
Bratsk	214,000	L4
Brindakit		N4
Bryansk	394,000	D4
Bugul'ma	89,000	F4
Bukachacha	10,000	M4
Bukhara	185,000	G5
Bulun		N2
Buzuluk	76,000	F4
Chadan		K4
Chapayevsk	85,000	F4
Chara		M4
Chardzhou	140,000	G6
Chegdomyn	16,499	O4
Chelkar	19,377	G5
Chelyabinsk	1,030,000	G4
Cheremkhovo	77,000	L4
Cherepovets	266,000	D4
Cherkessk	91,000	E5
Chernenko		E4
Chernigov	238,000	D4
Chernogorsk	71,000	J4
Chernyshevsk	10,000	M4
Cherskiy		S3
Chimkent	322,000	G5
Chirchik	132,000	G5

Chita	303,000	M4
Chokurdakh		P2
Chukmani		O4
Chulman		O4
Dal'negorsk	33,506	O5
Dal'nerechensk	28,224	O5
Daugavpils	116,000	C4
Denau		G6
Dimitrovgrad	106,000	F4
Dnepropetrovsk	1,066,000	D5
Donetsk	1,021,000	D5
Drogobych	66,000	C5
Druzhba		J5
Dudinka	19,701	J3
Dushanbe	494,000	G6
Dzerzhinsk	257,000	E4
Dzhalil-Abad	55,000	H5
Dzhambul	264,000	H5
Dzhankoy		D5
Dzhetygara	32,169	G4
Dzhezkazgan	89,000	G5
Dzhusaly	20,658	G5
Egvekinot		S3
Ekibastuz	66,000	H4
Ekimchan		O4
El'dikan		N4
Elista	70,000	E5
Emba	17,820	F5
Engel's	161,000	E4
Erivan	1,019,000	E6
Evensk		Q3
Fergana	176,000	H5
Fort-Shevchenko	12,000	F5
Frolovo	33,398	E4
Frunze	533,000	H5

Gasan-Kuli		F6
Gol'chikha		J2
Gomel'	383,000	D4
Gor'kiy	1,344,000	E4
Gorno-Altaysk	34,413	J4
Gornyak	16,643	J4
Grodno	195,000	C4
Groznyy	375,000	E5
Gubakha	33,243	F4
Gulistan	30,879	G5
Gusinoozersk	10,000	L4
Gyda		H2
Igarka	15,624	J3
Igrim		G3
Ilanskiy	22,852	K4
Indiga		F3
Inta	51,000	G3
Iolotan'	10,000	G6
Irkutsk	550,000	L4
Ishim	63,000	G4
Isil'kul'	25,958	H4
Iul'tin		T3
Ivano-Frankovsk	150,000	C5
Ivanovo	465,000	E4
Izhevsk (Ustinov)	549,000	F4
Izmail	83,000	D5
Kachug		M4
Kalachinsk	20,809	H4
Kalinin	412,000	D4
Kaliningrad	355,000	B4
Kalmykovo		F5
Kaluga	265,000	D4
Kamen'-na-Obi	35,604	J4

Union of Soviet Socialist Republics

CONIC PROJECTION

SCALE OF MILES
0   100   200   300   400   500   600

SCALE OF KILOMETERS
0   100   200   300   400   500   600

Scale 1:30,400,000

Capitals		Boundaries
★ National		
☆ Union Republic		
◉ A.S.S.R.		
◎ Autonomous Oblast		
◉ Autonomous Okrug		

ADMINISTRATIVE DIVISIONS NOT NAMED ON MAP

Division	Ref.	Division	Ref.
1. Abkhaz A.S.S.R.	E5	13. Khakass Aut. Oblast	J4
2. Adygey Aut. Oblast	D5	14. Komi-Permyak Aut Okrug	F4
3. Adzhar A.S.S.R.	E5	15. Mari A.S.S.R.	E4
4. Aginsk Buryat Autonomous Okrug	M4	16. Mordvinian A.S.S.R.	E4
5. Chechen-Ingush A.S.S.R.	E5	17. Nagorno-Karabakh Aut. Oblast.	E5
6. Chuvash A.S.S.R.	E4	18. Nakhichevan' A.S.S.R.	E6
7. Gorno-Altay Aut. Oblast	J4	19. North Ossetian Aut. Oblast	E5
8. Gorno-Badakhshan Aut. Oblast	H6	20. South Ossetian Aut. Oblast	E5
9. Jewish Aut. Oblast	O5	21. Tatar A.S.S.R.	F4
10. Kabardin-Balkar A.S.S.R.	E5	22. Tuvinian A.S.S.R.	K4
11. Karachay-Cherkess Aut. Oblast.	G5	23. Udmurt A.S.S.R.	F4
12. Karakalpak A.S.S.R.		24. Ust-Ordynsk Buryat Autonomous Okrug	L4

AREA 8,649,490 sq. mi. (22,402,179 sq. km.)
POPULATION 262,436,227
CAPITAL Moscow
LARGEST CITY Moscow
HIGHEST POINT Communism Peak 24,599 ft. (7,498 m.)
MONETARY UNIT ruble
MAJOR LANGUAGES Russian, Ukrainian, White Russian, Uzbek, Azerbaidzhani, Tatar, Georgian, Lithuanian, Armenian, Yiddish, Latvian, Mordvinian, Kirgiz, Tadzhik, Estonian, Kazakh, Moldavian (Romanian), German, Chuvash, Turkmenian, Bashkir
MAJOR RELIGIONS Eastern (Russian) Orthodoxy, Islam, Judaism, Protestantism (Baltic States)

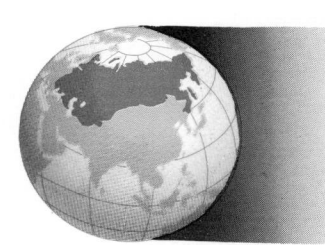

Kamenskoye	R3	Kavalerovo 16,415	O5
Kamensk-Ural'skiy 187,000	G4	Kazan' 993,000	F4
Kamyshin 112,000	E4	Kem' 21,025	D3
Kandalaksha 42,656	C3	Kemerovo 471,000	J4
Kansk 101,000	J4	Kentau 52,000	G5
Kapchagay	H5	Kerki 10,000	G6
Kara	G3	Khabarovsk 528,000	O5
Karaganda 572,000	H5	Khandyga	O3
Karasuk 22,637	H4	Khanty-Mansiysk 24,754	H3
Karatau 26,962	H5	Khar'kov 1,444,000	D4
Karazhal 17,702	H5	Khatanga	L2
Kargasok	J4	Kherson 319,000	D5
Karpinsk	F4	Khilok 17,000	M4
Karshi 108,000	G6	Khiva 24,139	F5
Kartaly 42,801	G4	Khodzheyli 36,435	F5
Katangli	P4	Kholmsk 37,412	P5
Kattakurgan 53,000	G5	Khorog 12,295	H6
Kaunas 370,000	C4	Kiev 2,144,000	D4

UNION REPUBLICS

	AREA (sq. mi.)	AREA (sq. km.)	POPULATION	CAPITAL and LARGEST CITY
RUSSIAN S.F.S.R.	6,592,812	17,075,400	137,551,000	Moscow 7,831,000
KAZAKH S.S.R.	1,048,300	2,715,100	14,684,000	Alma-Ata 910,000
UKRAINIAN S.S.R.	233,089	603,700	49,755,000	Kiev 2,144,000
TURKMEN S.S.R.	188,455	488,100	2,759,000	Ashkhabad 312,000
UZBEK S.S.R.	173,591	449,600	15,391,000	Tashkent 1,780,000
WHITE RUSSIAN S.S.R.	80,154	207,600	9,560,000	Minsk 1,262,000
KIRGIZ S.S.R.	76,641	198,500	3,529,000	Frunze 533,000
TADZHIK S.S.R.	55,251	143,100	3,801,000	Dushanbe 494,000
AZERBAIDZHAN S.S.R.	33,436	86,600	6,028,000	Baku 1,022,000
GEORGIAN S.S.R.	26,911	69,700	5,015,000	Tbilisi 1,066,000
LITHUANIAN S.S.R.	25,174	65,200	3,398,000	Vilnius 582,000
LATVIAN S.S.R.	24,595	63,700	2,521,000	Riga 835,000
ESTONIAN S.S.R.	17,413	45,100	1,466,000	Tallinn 430,000
MOLDAVIAN S.S.R.	13,012	33,700	3,947,000	Kishinev 503,000
ARMENIAN S.S.R.	11,506	29,800	3,031,000	Erivan 1,019,000

Kirensk 10,000	L4	Krasnokamsk 56,000	F4	Leninakan 207,000	E5	Miass 150,000	G4	Nazyvayevsk 15,792	H4
Kirov 390,000	E4	Krasnotur'insk 61,000	G3	Leningrad 4,073,000	D4	Michurinsk 101,000	E4	Nebit-Dag 71,000	F6
Kirovabad 232,000	E5	Krasnoural'sk 39,743	G4	Leningrad* 4,588,000	D4	Millerovo 34,627	E5	Nefteyugansk 52,000	H3
Kirovograd 237,000	D5	Krasnovodsk 53,000	F5	Leningorsk 54,000	J5	Minsk 1,262,000	C4	Nel'kan	O4
Kirovskiy	H5	Krasnoyarsk 796,000	K4	Leninsk	G5	Minsk* 1,276,000	C4	Nepa	L4
Kiselevsk 122,000	J4	Kremenchug 210,000	D5	Leninsk-Kuznetskiy 132,000	J4	Minusinsk 56,000	K4	Neryungri	N4
Kishinev 503,000	C5	Krivoy Rog 650,000	D5	Leninskoye	E6	Mirnyy 23,826	M3	Nevel'sk 20,726	P5
Kizel 46,264	F4	Kudymkar 26,350	F4	Lenkoran' 35,505	E6	Mogilev 290,000	D4	Nikolayev 440,000	D5
Kizyl-Arvat 21,671	F6	Kul'sary 16,427	F5	Lensk 16,758	M3	Mogocha 17,884	N4	Nikolayevsk-na-Amure 30,082	P4
Klaipeda 176,000	B4	Kulunda 15,264	H4	Lesosibirsk	K4	Molodechno 73,000	C4	Nikol'skoye	R4
Kokand 153,000	H5	Kulyab 55,000	H6	Lesozavodsk 34,957	O5	Monchegorsk 51,000	C3	Nizhneudinsk 39,743	K4
Kokchetav 103,000	H4	Kum-Dag 10,000	F6	Liepaja 108,000	B4	Moscow (cap.) 7,831,000	D4	Nizhnevartovsk 109,000	H3
Kolomna 147,000	E4	Kungur 80,000	F4	Lipetsk 396,000	E4	Moscow* 8,011,000	D4	Nizhneyansk	O3
Kolpashevo 24,911	J4	Kupino 20,799	H4	Lisichansk	E4	Motygino 10,000	K4	Nizhniy Tagil 398,000	F4
Komsomol'sk 15,385	G4	Kurgan 310,000	G4	Lutsk 137,000	C4	Mozyr' 73,000	D4	Nordvik-Ugol'naya	M2
Komsomol'sk-na-Amure 264,000	O4	Kurgan-Tyube 34,620	G6	L'vov 667,000	C4	Murgab	H6	Noril'sk 180,000	J3
Kondopoga 27,908	D3	Kursk 375,000	D4	Lys'va 75,000	F4	Murmansk 381,000	D3	Novaya Kazanka	F5
Kopeysk 146,000	G4	Kushka	G6	Magadan 121,000	P4	Muynak 12,000	F5	Novgorod 186,000	D4
Korf	R3	Kustanay 165,000	G4	Magdagachi 15,059	N4	Mys Shmidta	T3	Novokazalinsk 34,815	G5
Korsakov 38,210	P5	Kutaisi 194,000	E5	Magnitogorsk 406,000	G4	Nadym	H3	Novokuznetsk 541,000	J4
Koslan	E3	Kuybyshev 1,216,000	F4	Makhachkala 251,000	E5	Nagornyy	N4	Novomoskovsk 147,000	E4
Kostroma 255,000	E4	Kuybyshev 40,166	H4	Makinsk 22,850	H4	Nakhichevan' 33,279	E6	Novorossiysk 159,000	D5
Kotlas 61,000	E3	Kyakhta 15,316	L4	Mama	M4	Nakhodka 133,000	O5	Novosibirsk 1,312,000	J4
Kovel' 33,351	C4	Kyusyur	N2	Markovo	S3	Nal'chik 207,000	E5	Novozybkov 34,433	D4
Kovrov 143,000	E4	Kyzyl 66,000	K4	Mary (Merv) 74,000	G6	Namangan 227,000	H5	Novyy Port	H3
Kozhevnikovo	L2	Kyzyl-Orda 156,000	G5	Maykop 128,000	D5	Naminga	M4	Novyy Uzen' 18,073	F5
Krasino	F2	Labytnangi	G3	Mednogorsk 38,024	F4	Nar'yan-Mar 16,864	F3	Novyy Urengoy	H3
Krasnodar 560,000	E5	Lebedinyy	N4	Medvezh'yegorsk 17,465	D3	Naryn 21,098	H5	Nukus 109,000	G5
Krasnokamensk 51,000	M4	Leninabad 130,000	G5	Mezen'	E3	Navoi 84,000	G6		

Topography

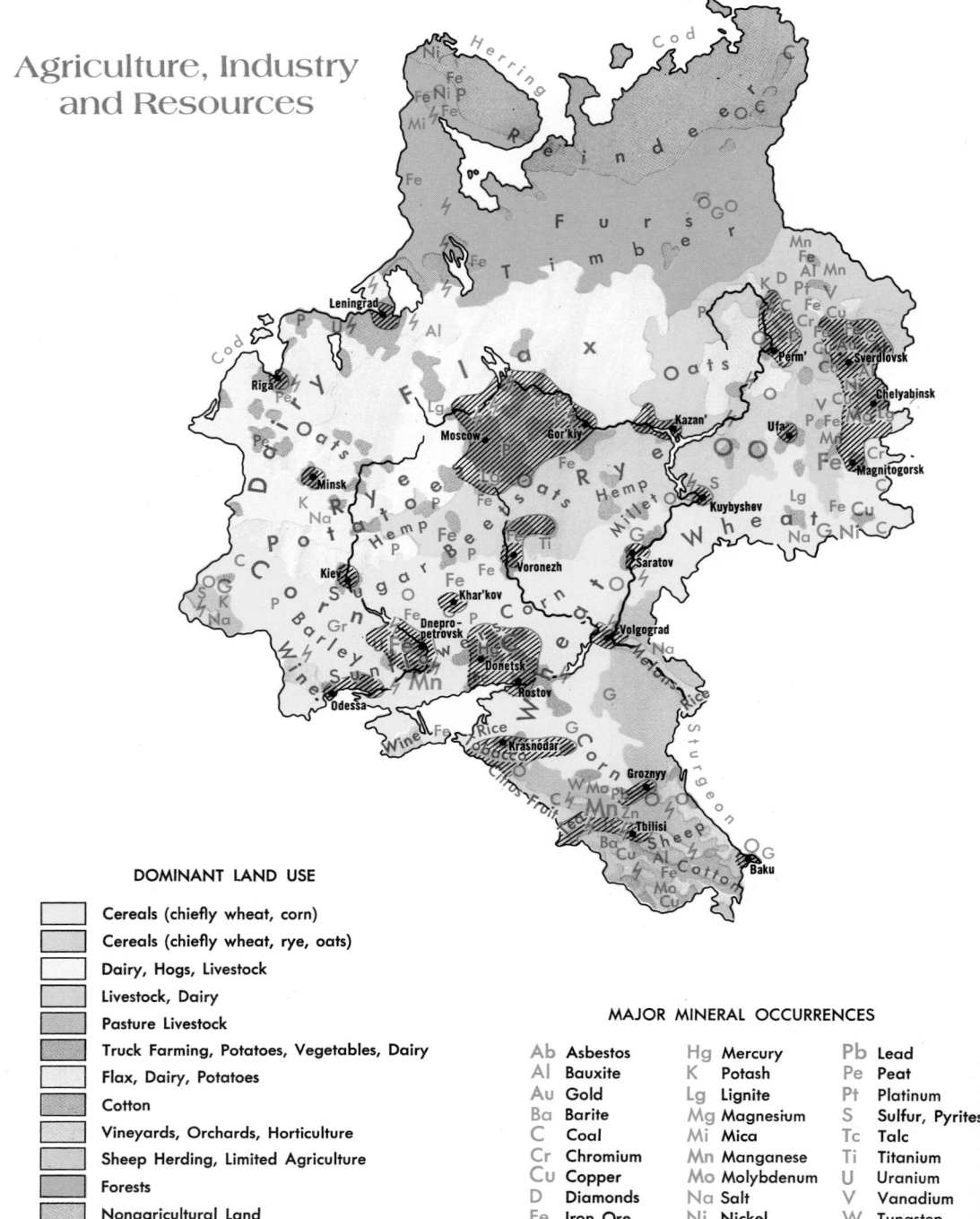

Agriculture, Industry and Resources

DOMINANT LAND USE

- Cereals (chiefly wheat, corn)
- Cereals (chiefly wheat, rye, oats)
- Dairy, Hogs, Livestock
- Livestock, Dairy
- Pasture Livestock
- Truck Farming, Potatoes, Vegetables, Dairy
- Flax, Dairy, Potatoes
- Cotton
- Vineyards, Orchards, Horticulture
- Sheep Herding, Limited Agriculture
- Forests
- Nonagricultural Land

MAJOR MINERAL OCCURRENCES

Ab	Asbestos	Hg	Mercury	Pb	Lead
Al	Bauxite	K	Potash	Pe	Peat
Au	Gold	Lg	Lignite	Pt	Platinum
Ba	Barite	Mg	Magnesium	S	Sulfur, Pyrites
C	Coal	Mi	Mica	Tc	Talc
Cr	Chromium	Mn	Manganese	Ti	Titanium
Cu	Copper	Mo	Molybdenum	U	Uranium
D	Diamonds	Na	Salt	V	Vanadium
Fe	Iron Ore	Ni	Nickel	W	Tungsten
G	Natural Gas	O	Petroleum	Zn	Zinc
Gr	Graphite	P	Phosphates		

⚡ Water Power ▨ Major Industrial Areas

Agriculture, Industry and Resources

DOMINANT LAND USE

- Cereals (chiefly wheat, corn)
- Livestock, Dairy
- Truck Farming, Potatoes, Vegetables, Dairy
- Cotton
- Sheep Herding, Limited Agriculture
- Forests
- Nonagricultural Land

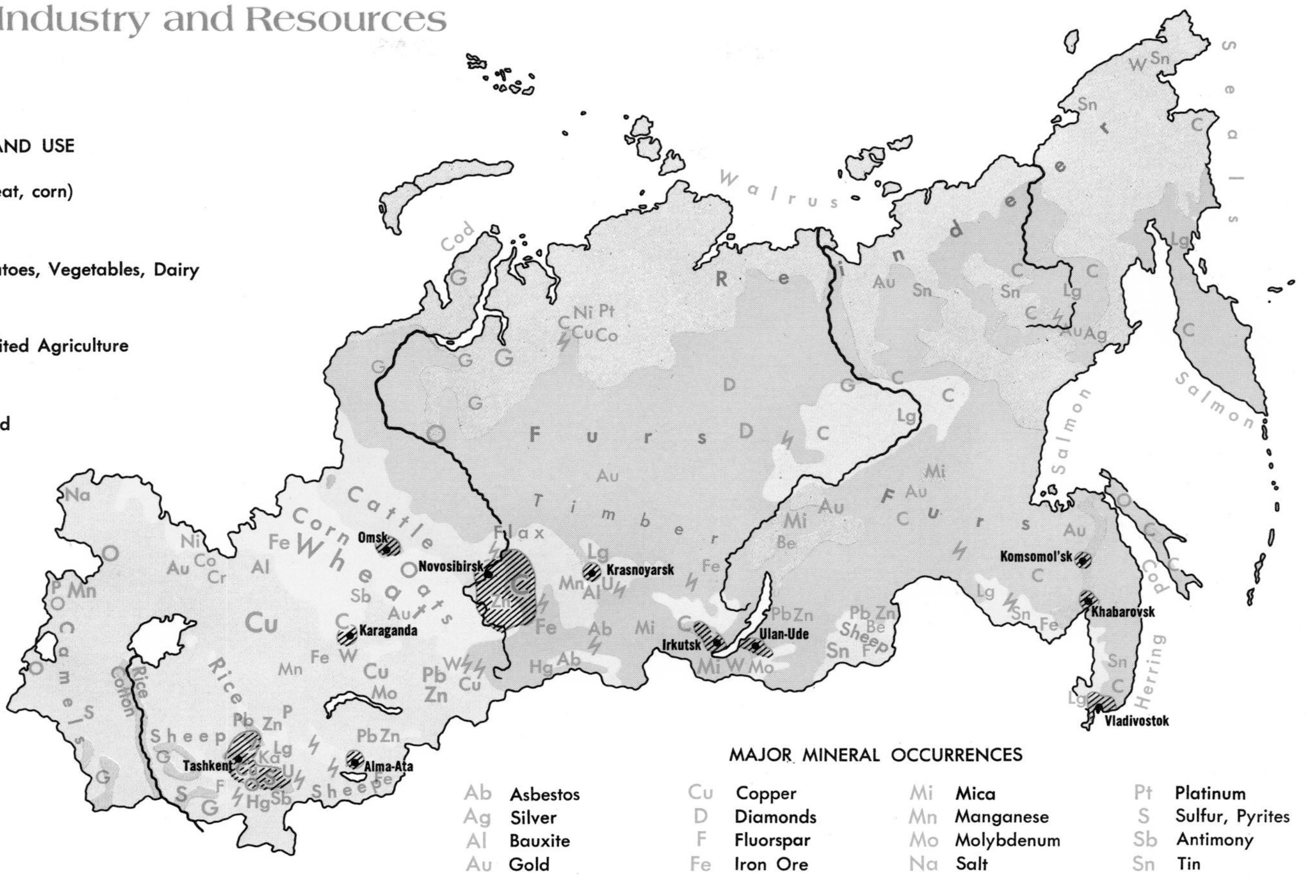

MAJOR MINERAL OCCURRENCES

Ab	Asbestos	Cu	Copper	Mi	Mica	Pt	Platinum
Ag	Silver	D	Diamonds	Mn	Manganese	S	Sulfur, Pyrites
Al	Bauxite	F	Fluorspar	Mo	Molybdenum	Sb	Antimony
Au	Gold	Fe	Iron Ore	Na	Salt	Sn	Tin
Be	Beryl	G	Natural Gas	Ni	Nickel	U	Uranium
C	Coal	Hg	Mercury	O	Petroleum	W	Tungsten
Co	Cobalt	Ka	Kaolin	P	Phosphates	Zn	Zinc
Cr	Chromium	Lg	Lignite	Pb	Lead		

⚡ Water Power   ▧ Major Industrial Areas

U.S.S.R.—Railroads and Navigation

- Principal Railroads
- Navigable Rivers
- Canals
- Main Sea Routes
- Major Russian Ports

SCALE OF MILES
0   500   1000

SCALE OF KILOMETERS
0   500   1000

© Copyright HAMMOND INCORPORATED, Maplewood, N.J.

(continued on following page)

Union of Soviet Socialist Republics
European Part

CONIC PROJECTION

SCALE OF MILES
0   100   200   300

SCALE OF KILOMETERS
0   50 100   200   300

National Capitals .... ★
Capitals of Union Republics .... ✪
Administrative Centers .... △
International boundaries .... —··—··—
Union Republic boundaries .... —·—·—
A.S.S.R., Oblast, Kray boundaries ... —··—··—
Autonomous Oblast boundaries .... ·········
Autonomous Okrug boundaries .... ·········

Scale 1:13,250,000

The government of the United States has not recognized the
incorporation of Estonia, Latvia and Lithuania into the Soviet
Union, nor does it recognize as final the de facto western limit
of Polish administration in Germany (the Oder-Neisse line).

Administrative Divisions bear same
names as their respective Capitals
or Centers, except:

Abkhaz A.S.S.R.	Sukhumi	F6
Adygey Aut. Oblast	Maykop	F6
Adzhar A.S.S.R.	Batumi	F6
Bashkir A.S.S.R.	Ufa	J4
Chechen-Ingush A.S.S.R.	Groznyy	G6
Chuvash A.S.S.R.	Cheboksary	G3
Crimean Oblast	Simferopol'	D6
Dagestan A.S.S.R.	Makhachkala	G6
Kabardin-Balkar A.S.S.R.	Nal'chik	F6
Kalmuck A.S.S.R.	Elista	F5
Karachay-Cherkess Aut. Obl.	Cherkessk	F6
Karelian A.S.S.R.	Petrozavodsk	D2
Komi A.S.S.R.	Syktyvkar	H2
Komi-Permyak Aut. Okrug	Kudymkar	H3
Mari A.S.S.R.	Yoshkar-Ola	G3
Mordvinian A.S.S.R.	Saransk	G4
Nagorno-Karabakh Aut. Obl.	Stepanakert	G7
Nenets Aut. Okrug	Nar'yan-Mar	H1
North Ossetian A.S.S.R.	Ordzhonikidze	F6
South Ossetian Aut. Obl.	Tskhinvali	F6
Tatar A.S.S.R.	Kazan'	G3
Trans-Carpathian Oblast	Uzhgorod	B5
Udmurt A.S.S.R.	Izhevsk	H3
Volyn Oblast	Lutsk	C4

® Copyright HAMMOND INCORPORATED, Maplewood, N.J.

U.S.S.R. — EUROPEAN

UNION REPUBLICS

Armenian A.S.S.R. 3,031,000	F6
Azerbaidzhan S.S.R. 6,028,000	G6
Estonian S.S.R 1,466,000	F6
Georgian S.S.R. 5,015,000	F6
Latvian S.S.R. 2,521,000	B3
Lithuanian S.S.R. 3,398,000	B3
Moldavian S.S.R. 3,947,000	C5
Russian S.F.S.R. 137,551,000	F3
Ukrainian S.S.R. 49,755,000	D5
White Russian S.S.R. 9,560,000	C4

INTERNAL DIVISIONS

Abkhaz A.S.S.R. 505,000	F6
Adygey Aut. Obl. 405,000	F6
Adzhar A.S.S.R. 354,000	F6
Bashkir A.S.S.R. 3,849,000	J4
Chechen-Ingush A.S.S.R. 1,154,000	G6
Chuvash A.S.S.R. 1,292,000	G3
Crimean Oblast 2,183,000	D6
Dagestan A.S.S.R. 1,628,000	G6
Kabardin-Balkar A.S.S.R. 674,000	F6
Kalmuck A.S.S.R. 294,000	F5
Karachay-Cherkess Aut. Obl. 368,000	F6
Karelian A.S.S.R. 736,000	D2
Komi A.S.S.R. 1,119,000	H2
Komi-Permyak Aut. Okr. 173,000	H3
Mari A.S.S.R. 703,000	G3
Mordvinian A.S.S.R. 991,000	G4
Nagorno-Karabakh Aut. Obl. 161,000	G7
Nakhichevan` A.S.S.R. 239,000	F7
Nenets Aut. Okr. 47,000	H1
North Ossetian A.S.S.R. 597,000	F6
South Ossetian Aut. Obl. 98,000	F6
Tatar A.S.S.R. 3,436,000	G3
Trans-Carpathian Oblast 1,155,000	B5
Udmurt A.S.S.R. 1,494,000	H3
Volyn Oblast 1,015,000	C4

CITIES and TOWNS

Abdulino 26,010	H4
Agdam 21,277	G6
Agryz 19,267	H3
Akhaltsikhe 18,972	F6
Akhtubinsk 43,466	G5
Akhty	G6
Akhtyrka 41,354	E4
Akkerman (Belgorod-Dnestrovskiy) 32,928	D5
Alagir 18,161	F6
Alatyr` 43,499	G4
Alaverdi 21,311	F6
Aleksandriya 82,000	D5
Aleksandrovsk 18,286	J3
Alekseyevka 25,562	E4
Aleksin 67,000	E4
Ali-Bayramly 33,828	G7
Al`met`yevsk 110,000	H3
Alushta 22,016	D6
Amderma	K1
Anapa 29,900	E6
Andropov 239,000	E3
Apatity 62,000	D1
Apsheronsk 32,867	F6
Archangel (Arkhangel`sk) 385,800	F2
Armavir 162,000	F6
Arzamas 93,000	F4
Astara	G7
Astrakhan` 461,000	G5
Atkarsk 28,881	F4
Azov 75,000	E5
Bakhchisaray 15,912	D6
Baku 1,022,000	H6
Balakhna 36,542	F3
Balakleya	D6
Balakovo 152,000	G4
Balashov 93,000	F4
Baltiysk 20,300	A4
Baranovichi 131,000	C4
Barysh 20,792	G4
Bataysk 90,000	E5
Batumi 123,000	F6
Belaya Tserkov` 151,000	D4
Beleboy 32,460	H4
Belev 17,733	E4
Belgorod 240,000	E4
Belgorod-Dnestrovskiy 32,928	D5
Belomorsk 16,595	D2
Belorechensk 35,970	F6
Beloretsk 71,000	J4
Belozersk	E3
Bel`tsy 125,000	C5
Belush`ya Guba	H1
Bendery 101,000	C5
Berdichev 80,000	C4
Berdyansk 122,000	E5
Berezniki 185,000	J3
Beslan 26,893	F6
Bezhetsk 30,030	E3
Birsk 29,607	J3
Bobrov 17,977	F4
Bobruysk 192,000	C4
Bologoye 33,949	F3
Bor 63,000	F3
Borislav 33,869	B5
Borisoglebsk 68,000	F4
Borisov 112,000	C4
Borovichi 60,000	D3
Brest 177,000	B4
Brezhnev 301,000	H3
Bryansk 394,000	D4
Bugul`ma 80,000	H4
Buguruslan 54,000	H4
Buturlinovka 21,643	F4
Buy 29,946	F3
Buynaksk 37,946	G6
Buzuluk 76,000	H4
Bykhov 17,371	C4
Cēsis 17,696	C3
Chadyr-Lunga 20,474	C5
Chapayevsk 85,000	G4
Chaykovskiy 48,034	H3
Cheboksary 308,000	G3
Cherepovets 266,000	E3
Cherkassy 228,000	D5
Cherkessk 91,000	F6
Chernigov 238,000	D4
Chernovtsy 219,000	C5
Chernushka 21,106	H3
Chervonograd 55,000	B4
Chiatura 25,474	F6
Chistopol` 64,000	H3
Chortkov 19,183	C5
Chudovo	D3
Dankov 20,030	E4
Daugavpils 116,000	C3
Davlekanovo 20,123	H4
Derbent 70,000	G6
Dimitrovgrad 106,000	G4
Dneprodzerzhinsk 250,000	D5
Dnepropetrovsk	D5
Dobrush 16,809	D4
Dobryanka 18,349	J3
Donetsk 1,021,000	E5
Drogobych 66,000	B5
Dubna 55,000	E3
Dubna	E4

Dubno 25,442	C4
Dvinsk (Daugavpils) 116,000	C3
Dyat`kovo 26,825	D4
Dzerzhinsk 257,000	F3
Dzhankoy 43,459	D5
Dzhul`fa	G7
Echmiadzin 31,819	F6
Elektrostal` 139,000	E3
Elista 70,000	F5
El`ton	G5
Engel`s 161,000	G4
Erivan 1,019,000	F6
Fastov 51,000	D4
Feodosiya 76,000	D5
Frolovo 33,398	F4
Furmanov 40,155	F3
Gagra 23,025	E6
Galich 23,374	F3
Gandzha (Kirovabad) 232,000	G6
Gatchina 75,000	D3
Gay 28,250	J4
Gaysin 23,741	C5
Gdov	D3
Gelendzhik 29,086	E6
Genichesk 20,031	E5
Georgiu-Dezh 52,000	E4
Glazov 81,000	H3
Gluboloye	C3
Glukhov 27,096	D4
Gomel` 383,000	D4
Gori 56,000	F6
Gorki 22,117	D4
Gor`kiy 1,344,000	F3
Gorlovka 336,000	E5
Gorodets 34,229	F3
Gremikha	E1
Gremyachinsk 29,975	J3
Grodno 195,000	B4
Groznyy 375,000	G6
Gryazi 41,292	F4
Gubakha 33,243	J3
Gubkin 65,000	E4
Gudauta	F6
Gudermes 32,445	G6
Gukovo 68,000	E5
Gus`-Khrustal`nyy 72,000	F3
Imishli 17,839	G7
Inta 51,000	K1
Inza 19,060	G4
Ishimbay 57,000	J4
Ivano-Frankovsk 150,000	B5
Ivanovo 465,000	F3
Izberbash 17,299	G6
Izhevsk (Ustinov) 549,000	H3
Izmail 83,000	C5
Izyum 61,000	E5
Jēkabpils 22,440	C3
Jelgava 68,000	B3
Jurmala 61,000	B3
Kadiyevka (Stakhanov) 108,000	E5
Kafan 29,916	G7
Kagul 26,249	C5
Kakhovka 28,472	D5
Kalach 18,475	F4
Kalach-na-Donu 20,795	F4
Kalinin 412,000	E3
Kaliningrad, Kaliningrad 355,000	B4
Kaliningrad, Moscow Oblast 133,000	E3
Kalinkovichi 23,918	C4
Kaluga 265,000	E4
Kalush 60,000	B5
Kamenets-Podol`skiy 81,000	C5
Kamenka 30,067	F4
Kamensk-Shakhtinskiy 72,000	F5
Kamyshin 112,000	F4
Kanash 40,682	G3
Kandalaksha 42,656	D1
Kapsukas 28,763	B4
Karachayevsk	F6
Karachev 15,397	E4
Kashin 17,678	E3
Kasimov 33,066	F4
Kaspiysk 38,990	G6
Kaunas 370,000	B4
Kazan` 993,000	G3
Kazatin 26,649	C5
Kem` 21,025	D2
Kerch` 157,000	E5
Keret`	D1
Khachmas 22,313	G6
Khadyzhensk 17,856	F6
Khar`kov 1,444,000	E4
Khashuyuri 65,000	F6
Khashuri 24,469	F6
Kherson 319,000	D5
Khmel`nitskiy 172,000	C5
Khotin 10,319	C5
Khust 23,810	B5
Khvalynsk 16,249	G4
Kiev 2,144,000	D4
Kiliya 24,276	C5
Kimovsk 44,490	E4
Kimry 58,000	E3
Kinel` 39,373	H4
Kineshma 101,000	F3
Kirishi 27,252	D3
Kirov, Kaluga 29,355	D4
Kirov, Kirov 390,000	G3
Kirovabad 232,000	G6
Kirovakan 146,000	F6
Kirovo-Chepetsk 71,000	H3
Kirovograd 237,000	D5
Kirqsk 38,484	D1
Kirsanov 21,795	F4
Kishinev 503,000	C5
Kislovodsk 101,000	F6
Kizel 46,264	J3
Kizlyar 29,745	G6
Klaipeda 176,000	B3
Klintsy 67,000	D4
Kobrin 24,935	B4
Kobuleti 18,051	F6
Kohtla-Järve 73,000	C3
Kolomiya 52,000	C5
Kolomna 147,000	E4
Kolpino 114,000	D3
Kommunarsk 120,000	E5
Komrat 21,369	C5
Konakovo 24,796 17,078	K1
Kondopoga 27,908	D2
Königsberg (Kaliningrad) 355,000	B4
Konotop 82,000	D4
Konstantinovka 112,000	E5
Korenovsk 26,323	F6
Korosten` 65,000	C4
Korostyshev 21,153	C4
Koryazhma 33,230	G2
Kostopol` 17,548	C4
Kostroma 255,000	F3
Kotel`nich 29,196	G3
Kotel`nikovo 19,063	F5
Kotlas 61,000	G2
Kotovsk 20,553	C5
Kotovsk, Odessa 36,463	C5
Kovel` 33,351	C4
Kovrov 143,000	F3
Kovylkino 17,300	F4
Kramatorsk 178,000	E5
Krasnoarmeysk 60,000	G4
Krasnodar 560,000	F6
Krasnograd 18,386	E5
Krasnokamsk 56,000	H3
Krasnoslobodsk 17,749	G5
Krasnovishersk	J2
Krasnyy Kut 17,087	G4

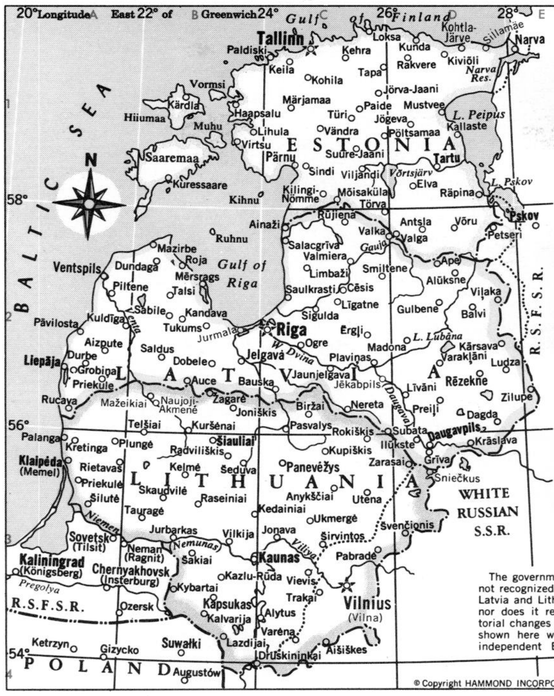

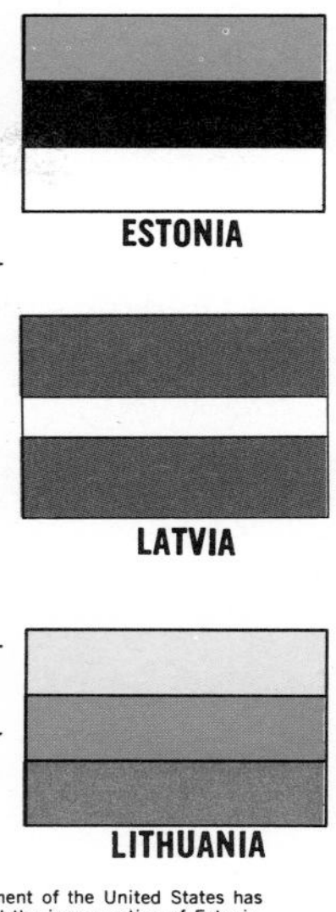

Krasnyy Luch 106,000	E5
Krasnyy Sulin 41,684	F5
Kremenchug 210,000	D4
Krichev 25,682	D4
Krivoy Rog 650,000	D5
Krolevets 18,307	D4
Kronshtadt 39,477	C3
Kropotkin 78,000	F5
Krymsk 41,430	F5
Kuba 18,871	G6
Kudymkar 26,350	H3
Kulebaki 46,252	F3
Kumertau 52,000	J4
Kunda	C3
Kungur 80,000	J3
Kupyansk 30,055	E5
Kuressaare 12,140	B3
Kursk 375,000	E4
Kutaisi 194,000	F6
Kuvandyk 22,914	J4
Kuybyshev 1,216,000	H4
Kuznetsk 94,000	G4
Kuzomen`	E1
Labinsk 54,000	F6
Lakhdenpokh`ya	D2
Lebedin 29,240	B4
Leninakan 207,000	F6
Leningrad 4,073,000	C3
Leningrad` 4,588,000	C3
Leningorsk 54,000	H4
Lenkoran` 35,505	G7
L`gov 25,110	E4
Lida 66,000	C4
Liepāja 108,000	B3
Likhoslavl`	E3
Lipetsk 396,000	E4
Lisichansk 119,000	E5
Livny 37,290	E4
Lodeynoye Pole 19,632	D2
Lozovaya 53,000	E5
Lubny 54,000	D4
Luga 31,905	D3
Lutsk 137,000	C4
L`vov (Lwów) 667,000	B5
Lys`va 75,000	J3
Lyubertsy 160,000	E3
Lyudinovo 33,324	D4
Makeyevka 436,000	E5
Makhachkala 251,000	G6
Makharadze 21,679	F6
Malaya Vishera 15,381	D3
Maglobek 20,548	F6
Manturovo 21,510	F3
Margarets 50,000	D2
Mariupol` (Zhdanov) 503,000	E5
Marks 17,132	G4
Maykop 147,000	F6
Mednogorsk 38,024	J4
Melenki 18,545	F3
Meleuz 24,851	J4
Melitopol` 161,000	E5
Memel (Klaipeda) 176,000	B3
Merefa 29,985	E5
Mezen`	F1
Michurinsk 101,000	F4
Mikhaylovka 58,000	F4
Millerovo 34,627	F5
Mineral`nye Vody 67,000	F6
Mingechaur 60,000	G6
Minsk 1,262,000	C4
Minsk` 1,276,000	C4
Mogilev 290,000	C4
Mogilev-Podol`skiy 26,051	C5
Molodechno 73,000	C4
Molotov (Perm`) 999,000	J3
Monchegorsk 51,000	D1
Morshansk 44,245	F4
Moscow (Moskva) (cap.) 7,831,000	E3
Moscow* 8,011,000	E3
Mozhaysk 20,321	E3
Mozhga 38,900	H3
Mtsensk 27,833	E4
Mukachevo 72,000	B5
Murmansk 381,000	D1
Murom 114,000	F3
Mytishchi 141,000	E3
Nakhichevan` 33,279	F7
Nal`chik 207,000	F6
Narva 73,000	C3
Narva-Jam-Mar 16,864	H1
Neftekamsk 70,000	H3
Nelidovo 29,813	D3
Nerekhta 25,722	F3
Nevel` 17,804	D3
Nevinnomyssk 104,000	F6

Nezhin 70,000	D4
Nikel` 21,299	C1
Nikolayev 440,000	D5
Nikol`sk 20,740	G4
Nikopol` 146,000	D5
Nizhnekamsk 134,000	H3
Nizhniy Lomov 17,460	F4
Nizhniy Novgorod 934,000	F3
Nosovka 19,430	D4
Novaya Kakhovka 52,000	D5
Novgorod 186,000	D3
Novgorod-Severskiy	D4
Novoaninskiy 20,461	F4
Novocherkassk 183,000	F5
Novograd-Volynskiy 41,194	C4
Novokubyshevsk 109,000	G4
Novomoskovsk 147,000	E4
Novopolotsk 67,000	C3
Novorossiysk 159,000	E6
Novoshakhtinsk 104,000	E5
Novotroitsk 95,000	J4
Novoukrainka 19,554	D5
Novouzensk	G4
Novovolynsk 41,187	B4
Novovyaznik 26,408	F3
Novozybkov 34,433	D4
Nurlat 17,533	H4
Nyandoma 23,366	F2
Nytva 17,491	H3
Nyuvchim	E3
Obninsk 73,000	E3
Ochamchira 18,718	F6
Odessa 1,046,000	D5
Oktyabr`sk 33,981	G4
Oktyabr`skiy 88,000	H4
Okulovka 19,194	D3
Olenegorsk 21,485	D1
Olonets	D2
Omutninsk 28,777	H3
Onega 25,047	E2
Ordzhonikidze 279,000	F6
Orel 305,000	E4
Orenburg 459,000	J4
Orgeyev 25,798	C5
Orsha 112,000	C4
Orsk 247,000	J4
Osa 15,038	J3
Osipenko (Berdyansk) 122,000	E5
Osipovichi 19,705	C4
Ostrogozhsk 29,921	E4
Ostrov 22,369	C3
Otradnyy 44,426	H4
Panevėžys 102,000	B3
Pärnu 51,000	C3
Pavlograd 107,000	E5
Pavlovsk 25,573	C4
Pechenga	D1
Pechora 56,000	J1
Penza 483,000	G4
Perm` 999,000	J3
Pervomaysk 72,000	D5
Petrokrepost`	D3
Petrozavodsk 234,000	D2
Petsamo (Pechenga)	D1
Pinsk 90,000	C4
Podol`sk 202,000	E3
Podporozh`ye 21,545	D2
Pokhvistnevo 26,125	H4
Polotsk 71,000	C3
Poltava 279,000	D5
Polyarnyy 15,321	D1
Ponoy	F1
Povenets	E2
Povorino 20,591	F4
Prikumsk 35,768	F6
Priluki 65,000	D4
Primorsk	C3
Primorsko-Akhtarsk 25,981	F5
Priozersk 18,632	D2
Privolzhskiy 23,041	H4
Priyutnovo 21,051	F6
Prokhladnyy 40,074	F6
Pskov 176,000	C3
Pugachev 33,963	G4
Pushkin 90,000	C3
Pyatigorsk 110,000	F6
Rabocheostrov	C2
Rakhov	B5
Rakvere 17,891	C3
Rasskazovo 40,038	F4
Razdan 26,833	F6
Rechitsa 60,000	D4
Reni 16,325	C5
Revel (Tallinn) 430,000	B3

Rēzekne 30,803	C3
Riga 835,000	B3
Romny 53,000	D4
Roslavl` 56,000	D4
Rossosh` 36,438	E4
Rostov 30,815	E3
Rostov-na-Donu 934,000	F5
Tikhoretsk 64,000	F5
Tikhvin 59,000	D3
Tilsit (Sovetsk) 38,456	B4
Timashevsk 29,055	F5
Tiraspol` 139,000	D5
Togliatti (Tol`yatti) 502,000	G4
Tokmak 59,000	E5
Toropets 16,863	D3
Tskhinvali 30,311	F6
Tuapse 60,000	E6
Tula 514,000	E4
Tutayev 16,839	E3
Tuymazy 37,021	H4
Tver (Kalinin) 412,000	E3
Tyrnyauz 18,253	F6
Uchaly 21,808	J4
Ufa 969,000	J4
Uglich 35,463	E3
Ukmerge 21,663	C3
Ul`yanovsk 464,000	G4
Uman` 79,000	D5
Ungeny 17,228	C5
Uryupinsk 38,192	F4
Usinsk	J1
Usman` 20,150	E4
Ust`-Kut 64,000	E4
Uzhgorod 91,000	B5
Uzlovaya 65,000	E4
Valga 16,795	C3
Valmiera 20,331	C3
Vasil`kov 26,741	D4
Velikiye Luki 102,000	D3
Veliky Ustyug 36,737	F2
Vel`sk 21,890	F2
Ventspils 40,467	B3
Vereshchagino 23,585	H3
Vichuga 52,000	F3
Vilyuy (Vyborg) 76,000	C3
Vilyeyka	C4
Vilnius (Vilna) 582,000	C4
Vinnitsa 314,000	C5
Vinogradov 20,580	B5
Vitebsk 297,000	C3
Vladimir 296,000	F3
Vladimir-Volynskiy 28,412	B4
Volgograd 929,000	F5
Volkhov 47,025	D3
Volkovysk 28,266	B4
Vologda 237,000	E3
Volozhin 52,000	C4
Volzhskiy 209,000	F5
Vorkuta 100,000	K1
Voronezh 783,000	E4
Voroshilovgrad 463,000	E5
Voskresensk 76,000	E3
Votkinsk 90,000	H3
Voznesensk 36,457	D5
Vsevolozhsk	D3
Vyatskiye Polyany 33,820	H3
Vyaz`ma 52,000	D3
Vyborg 76,000	C3
Vyksa 54,000	F3
Vyshniy Volochek 70,000	D3
Sovetsk (Tilsit) 38,456	B4
Svetsk 17,027	D4
Stakhanov 108,000	E5
Yalta 80,000	D6
Yanaul 20,115	J3
Yaroslavl` 597,000	E3
Yartsevo 36,662	D3
Yefremov 53,000	E4
Yelabuga 31,728	H3
Yelets 112,000	E4
Yenakiyevo 114,000	E5
Yeniseisk 21,731	E4
Yessentuki 78,000	F6
Yevlakh 29,462	G6
Yevpatoria 93,000	D5
Yeysk 71,000	F5
Yoshkar-Ola 201,000	G3
Yur`yevets 20,144	F3
Zagorsk 107,000	E3
Zaporozh`ye 781,000	E5
Zaporozh`ye 22,084	E5
Zavolzh`ye 40,000	F3
Zelenodol`sk 84,000	G3
Zelenokumsk 29,691	F6
Zernograd 20,324	F5
Zheleznodorozhnyy 76,000	H2
Zheleznogorsk 65,000	E4
Zhigulevsk 52,130	G4

Telšiai 20,220	B3
Temryuk 23,172	E5
Ternopol` 144,000	C5
Teykovo 41,607	E3
Tiflis (Tbilisi) 1,066,000	F6
Tighina (Bendery) 101,000	C5
Tobol`sk 64,000	D3

Zhitomir 244,000	C4
Zhlobin 25,359	C4
Zhmerinka 36,195	C5
Zhodino 22,083	C4
Zhovtnevoye 31,102	D5
Znamenka 27,393	D5
Zolotonosha 27,639	D5
Zugdidi 39,896	F6
Zuyevka 17,001	H3

OTHER FEATURES

Apsheron (pen.)	H6
Araks (riv.)	G7
Azov (sea)	E5
Baltic (sea)	B3
Barents (sea)	E1
Belaya (riv.)	H3
Beloye (lake)	E2
Black (sea)	D6
Bug (riv.)	C5
Caspian (sea)	G6
Caucasus (mts.)	F6
Crimea (pen.)	D5
Desna (riv.)	D4
Dnieper (riv.)	D5
Dniester (riv.)	C5
Donets (riv.)	E5
Dvina (bay)	E1
Dvina, Northern (riv.)	F2
Dvina, Western (riv.)	C3
Dykh-Tau (mt.)	F6
El`brus (mt.)	F6
Finland (gulf)	C3
Hiiumaa (isl.)	B3
Il`men` (lake)	D3
Imandra (lake)	D1
Kakhovka (res.)	D5
Kama (riv.)	H3
Kandalaksha (gulf)	D1
Kanin (pen.)	G1
Kara (sea)	K1
Karskiye Vorota (str.)	J1
Kazbek (mt.)	F6
Khoper (riv.)	F4
Kola (pen.)	E1
Kolguyev (isl.)	G1
Kuban` (riv.)	F6
Kuybyshev (res.)	G4
Ladoga (lake)	D2
Lapland (reg.)	D1
Mezen` (riv.)	G1
Moksha (riv.)	F4
Narodnaya (mt.)	J4
Niemen (riv.)	B4
Novaya Zemlya (isls.)	H1
Oka (riv.)	F4
Onega (bay)	E2
Onega (lake)	D2
Onega (riv.)	E2
Pechora (riv.)	H1
Peipus (lake)	C3
Pripet (marshes)	C4
Pripyat` (riv.)	C4
Prut (riv.)	C5
Riga (gulf)	B3
Rybachiy (pen.)	D1
Rybinsk (res.)	E3
Saaremaa (isl.)	B3
Samara (riv.)	H4
Selenge (lake)	D3
Seym (riv.)	D4
Svir` (riv.)	D2
Timan (ridge)	G1
Tsil`ma (riv.)	G1
Tsimlyansk (res.)	F5
Ural (mts.)	J3
Ural (riv.)	J4
Usa (riv.)	K1
Valday (hills)	D3
Vashka (riv.)	G2
Velikaya (riv.)	C3
Volga (riv.)	G4
Volga-Don (canal)	F5
Volkhov (riv.)	D3
Vorskla (riv.)	D4
Vyatka (riv.)	H3
Vychegda (riv.)	G2
White (sea)	E1
Yugorskiy (pen.)	K1

The Baltic States

SCALE OF MILES
0 — 25 — 50 — 75 — 100

SCALE OF KILOMETERS
0 — 30 — 60 — 90 — 120 — 150 — 180

Capitals	☆
International Boundaries	——·——·——
Union Republic Boundaries	——·——·——
Prewar boundaries of the Baltic States where divergent from present boundaries	———————

ESTONIA (flag)

LATVIA (flag)

LITHUANIA (flag)

The government of the United States has not recognized the incorporation of Estonia, Latvia and Lithuania into the Soviet Union, nor does it recognize other post-war territorial changes shown on this map. The flags shown here were the official flags of the independent Baltic States prior to 1939.

© Copyright HAMMOND INCORPORATED, Maplewood, N.J.

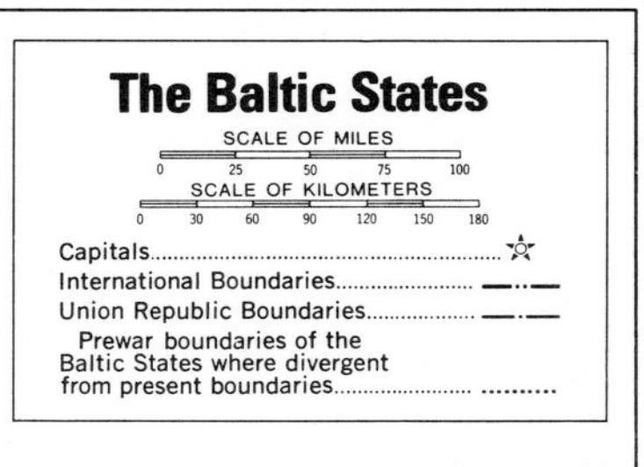

BALTIC STATES

Alytus 55,000	C3
Biržai 11,400	C2
Cēsis 17,696	C2
Daugava (Western Dvina) (riv.)	D2
Daugavpils 127,000	D3
Dobele 10,100	B2
Druskininkai 11,200	C3
Dvina, Western (riv.)	D1
Finland (gulf)	D1
Gauja (riv.)	C2
Haapsalu 11,483	B2
Hiiumaa (isl.)	B2
Jēkabpils 22,440	C2
Jelgava 68,000	B2
Jonava 14,400	C3
Jūrmala 61,000	B2
Kapsukas 28,763	B3
Kaunas 423,000	C3
Kedainiai 19,677	C3
Kihnu (isl.)	B1
Kingisepp (Kuressaare) 12,140	B1
Kiviōli 11,153	D1
Kuldiga 12,300	A2
Kuressaare 12,140	B1
Kuršenai 11,500	B2
Liepāja 114,000	A2
Lubāna (lake)	D2
Mažeikiai 13,400	A2
Memel (Klaipėda) 204,000	A3
Muhu (isl.)	B1
Narva 73,000	E1
Naujoji-Akmene 10,200	B2

Niemen (riv.)	A3
Ogre 15,708	C2
Panevėžys 126,000	C2
Pärnu 51,000	C2
Peipus (lake)	D1
Plunge 13,600	B3
Radviliškis 16,841	B3
Rakvere 17,891	D1
Rēzekne 30,803	D2
Riga (cap.): Latvia 915,000	C2
Riga (gulf)	B2
Saaremaa (isl.)	B1
Saldus 10,000	B2
Šiauliai 145,000	B3
Sillamäe 13,505	D1
Šilute 12,400	A3
Tallinn (cap.): Estonia 482,000	C1
Tapa 10,037	C1
Tartu 114,000	D1
Taurage 19,461	B3
Telšiai 20,220	B2
Tukums 14,800	B2
Ukmerge 21,663	C3
Utena 13,300	C3
Valga 16,795	D1
Valmiera 20,331	C2
Venta (riv.)	B2
Ventspils 40,467	A2
Vilnius (cap.): Lithuania 582,000	C3
Vilniys 20,814	C1
Võru 15,398	D2
Western Dvina (riv.)	C2

*City and suburbs.

Asia

LAMBERT AZIMUTHAL EQUAL-AREA PROJECTION

SCALE OF MILES

0 100 200   400   600   800   1000   1200

SCALE OF KILOMETERS

0 200 400 600 800 1000 1200

Capitals of Countries .... ⊛
Other Capitals .... ⊛
International Boundaries .... —·—·—
Other Boundaries...................... —··—··—
Canals ....

Scale 1:46,500,000

© Copyright HAMMOND INCORPORATED, Maplewood, N.J.

Population Distribution

AREA 17,128,500 sq. mi.
(44,362,815 sq. km.)
POPULATION 2,633,000,000
LARGEST CITY Tokyo
HIGHEST POINT Mt. Everest 29,028 ft.
(8,848 m.)
LOWEST POINT Dead Sea -1,296 ft.
(-395 m.)

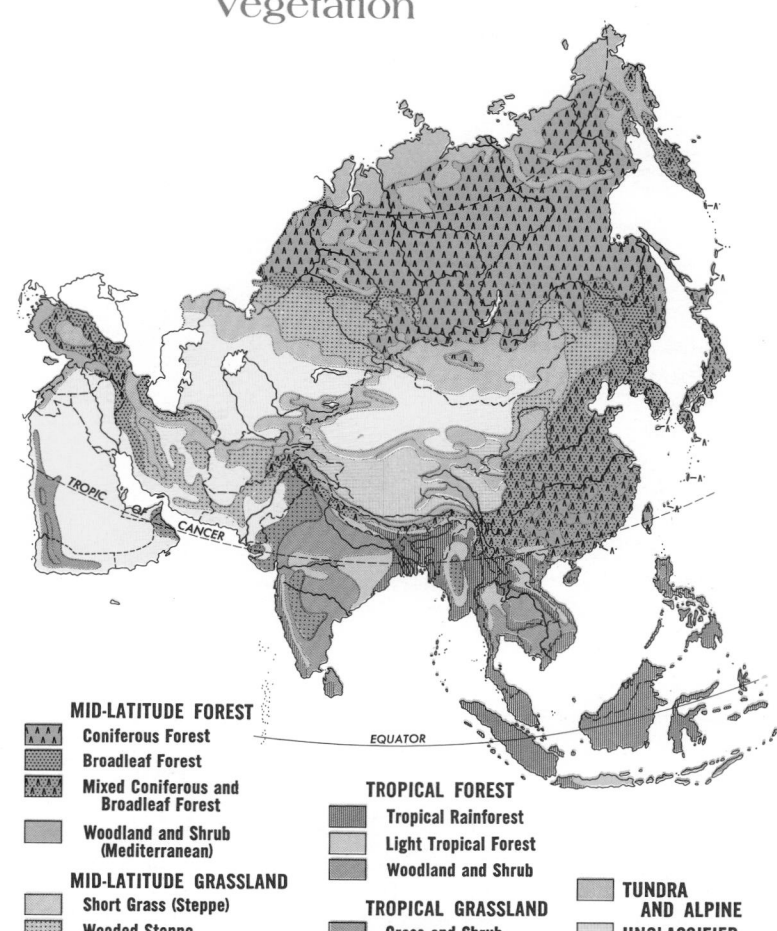

Vegetation

DENSITY PER

SQ. KILOMETER	SQ. MILE
Over 100	Over 260
50-100	130-260
10-50	25-130
1-10	3-25
Under 1	Under 3

● Cities with over 2,000,000 inhabitants (including suburbs)

○ Cities with over 1,000,000 inhabitants (including suburbs)

MID-LATITUDE FOREST

- Coniferous Forest
- Broadleaf Forest
- Mixed Coniferous and Broadleaf Forest
- Woodland and Shrub (Mediterranean)

MID-LATITUDE GRASSLAND

- Short Grass (Steppe)
- Wooded Steppe

DESERT AND DESERT SHRUB

TROPICAL FOREST

- Tropical Rainforest
- Light Tropical Forest
- Woodland and Shrub

TROPICAL GRASSLAND

- Grass and Shrub (Savanna)
- Wooded Savanna

TUNDRA AND ALPINE

UNCLASSIFIED HIGHLANDS

Average January Temperature

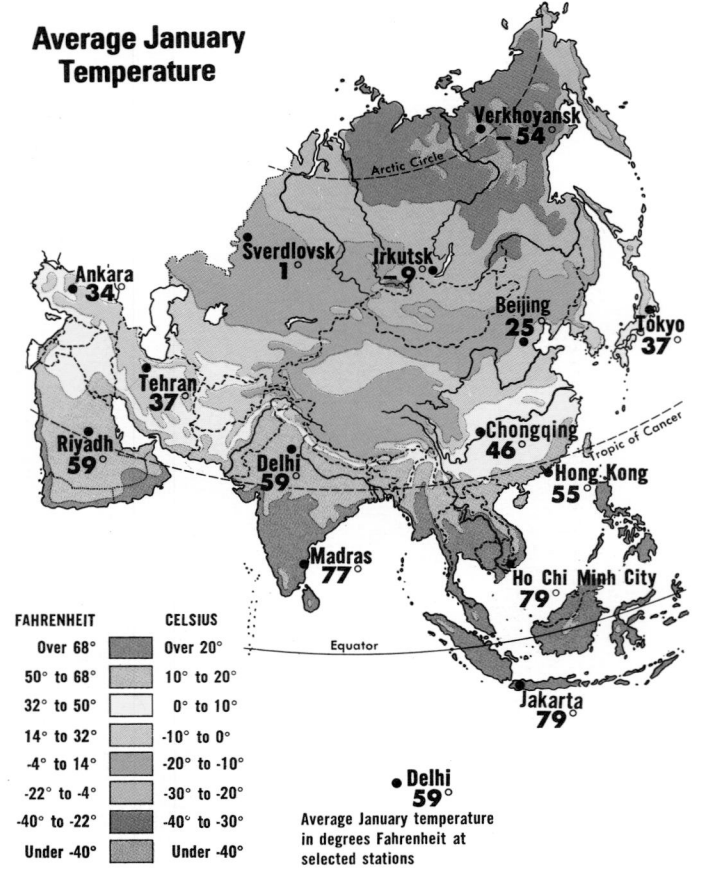

FAHRENHEIT	CELSIUS
Over 68°	Over 20°
50° to 68°	10° to 20°
32° to 50°	0° to 10°
14° to 32°	-10° to 0°
-4° to 14°	-20° to -10°
-22° to -4°	-30° to -20°
-40° to -22°	-40° to -30°
Under -40°	Under -40°

● Delhi
59°
Average January temperature
in degrees Fahrenheit at
selected stations

Average July Temperature

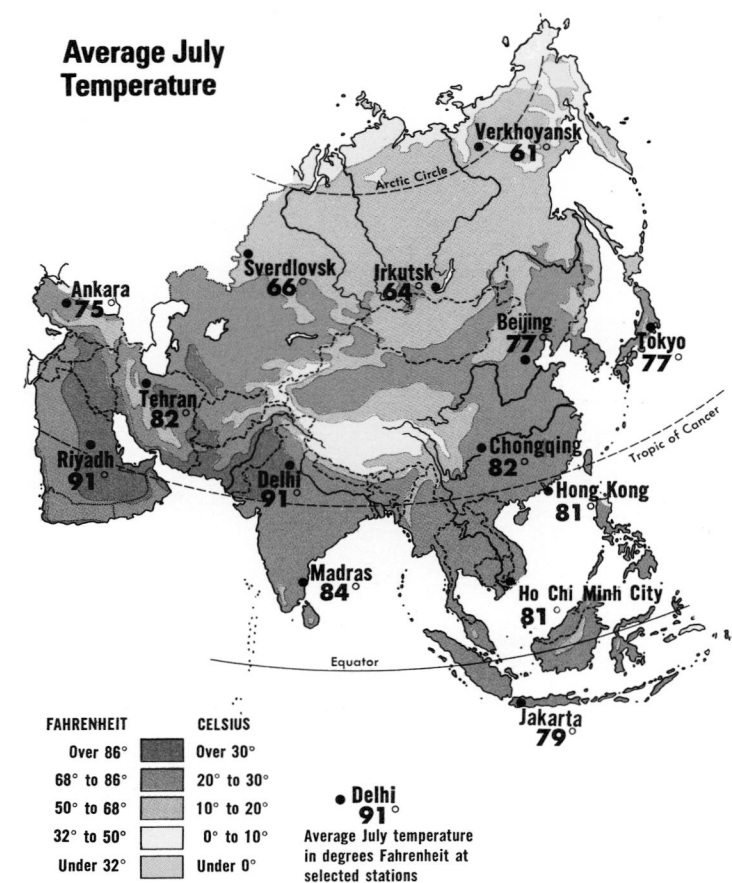

FAHRENHEIT	CELSIUS
Over 86°	Over 30°
68° to 86°	20° to 30°
50° to 68°	10° to 20°
32° to 50°	0° to 10°
Under 32°	Under 0°

● Delhi
91°
Average July temperature
in degrees Fahrenheit at
selected stations

Rainfall

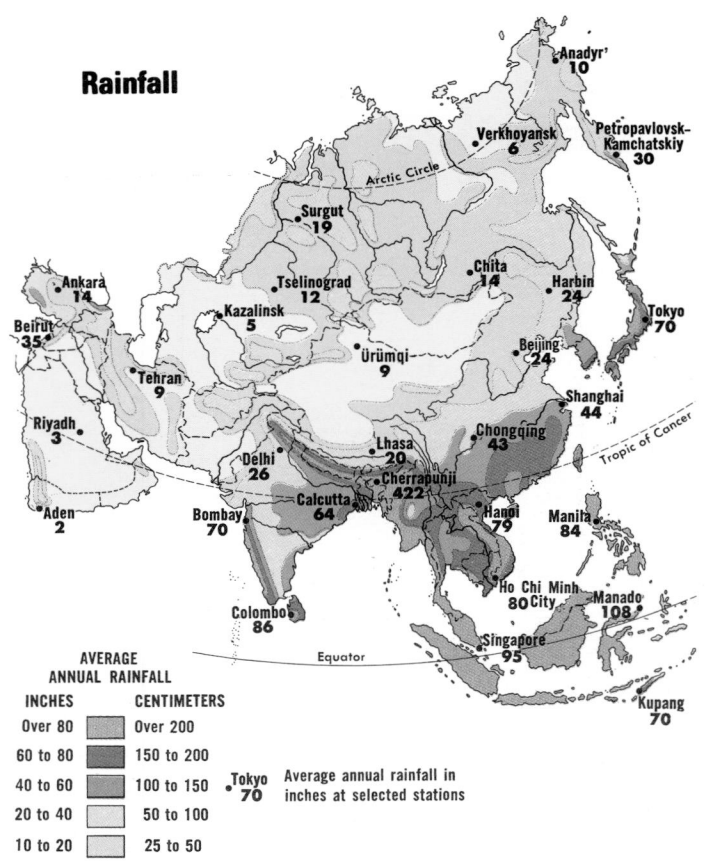

AVERAGE
ANNUAL RAINFALL

INCHES	CENTIMETERS
Over 80	Over 200
60 to 80	150 to 200
40 to 60	100 to 150
20 to 40	50 to 100
10 to 20	25 to 50
Under 10	Under 25

Tokyo
70
Average annual rainfall in
inches at selected stations

Vegetation / Relief

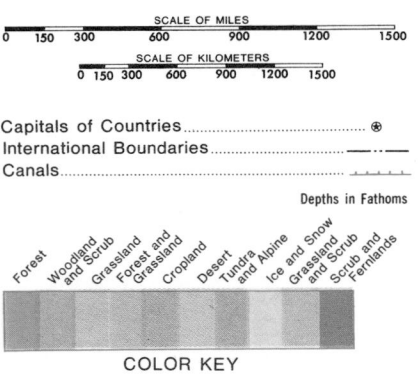

SCALE OF MILES
0 150 300 600 900 1200 1500

SCALE OF KILOMETERS
0 150 300 600 900 1200 1500

Capitals of Countries..............................⊛
International Boundaries......................
Canals...

Depths in Fathoms

Forest | Woodland and Scrub | Grassland | Forest and Grassland | Cropland | Desert | Tundra and Alpine | Ice and Snow | Grassland and Scrub | Scrub and Fernlands

COLOR KEY

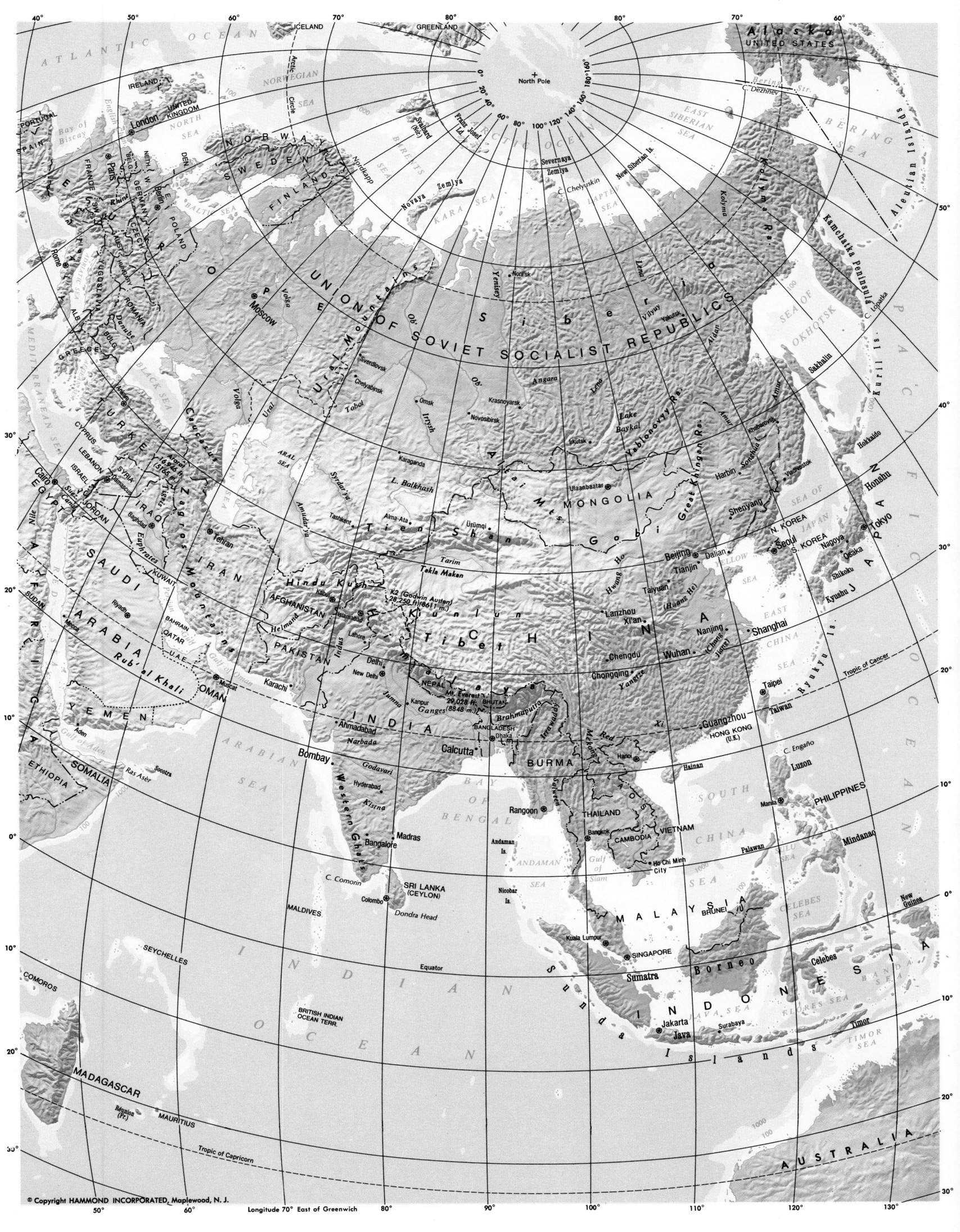

Longitude 70° East of Greenwich

SAUDI ARABIA

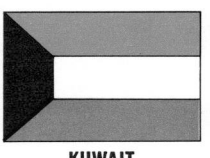
KUWAIT

YEMEN

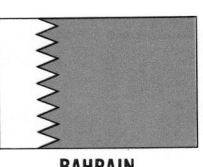
BAHRAIN

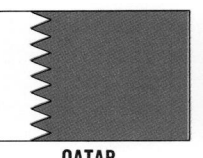
QATAR

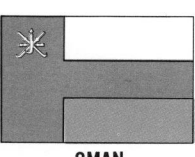
OMAN

AFGHANISTAN

CITIES and TOWNS

Anar Darreh	H3	Balkh	J2	Farsi	H3	Jorm	K2	Lashkar Gah 26.646	H3	Qalat 5.946	J3	Sheberghan 54.870	H2
Andkhvoy	H2	Bamian 7.355	J3	Feyzabad 10.142	K2	Kabul (cap.) 905.108	J3	Mar uf	J3	Qale h-ye Now 5.340	H3	Shindand	H3
Aqcheh	J2	Baraki Barak	J3	Gardez 11.415	J3	Kalat (Qalat) 5.946	J3	Mazar-e Sharif 122.567	J2	Qale h-ye Panjeh	K2	Spin Buldak	K3
Aybak 33.016	J2	Belcheragh	J2	Gereshk	H3	Kandahar (Qandahar) 178.409	J3	Meymaneh 54.954	H2	Qandahar 178.409	J3	Tagab	K2
Baghlan 75.130	J2	Chahar Boriak	H3	Ghazni 30.425	J3	Khanabad	J2	Mirabad	H3	Qonduz 107.191	J2	Talogan 46.202	J2
		Charikar 25.093	J3	Ghurian	H3	Khugiani	J3	Mogor	J3	Rostaq	J2	Teyvareh	H3
		Dowlat Yar	J3	Gizab	J3	Kowst	J3	Now Zad	H3	Rudbar	J3	Tulak	H3
		Dowlatabad	H3	Hazar Qadam	J3	Kuhestan	H3	Owbeh	H3	Sakhar	J3	Zaranj 6.477	H3
		Dowshi	J2	Herat 163.960	H3	Landay	J3	Panjab	J3	Sar-e Pol	J2	Zibak	K2
		Farah 18.797	H3	Jalalabad 56.384	K3	Lash-e Joveyn	H3	Pol-e Khomri	J2	Shah Juy	J3		

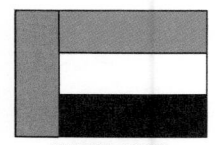

UNITED ARAB EMIRATES

OTHER FEATURES

Farah Rud (riv.)	H3
Gowd-e Zerreh (depr.)	H4
Harirud (riv.)	H3
Helmand (riv.)	J3
Hindu Kush (mts.)	J2
Kabul (riv.)	K3
Konar (riv.)	K2
Lurah (riv.)	J3

Margow, Dasht-e (des.)	H3
Murghab (riv.)	H2
Namaksar (salt lake)	H3
Paropamisus (mts.)	H3
Rigestan (reg.)	H3

BAHRAIN

CITIES and TOWNS

Manama (cap.) 88,785	F4
Muharraq 37,732	F4

GAZA STRIP

CITIES and TOWNS

Gaza* 118,272	B3

IRAN

CITIES and TOWNS

Abadan 296,081	E3
Abadeh 16,000	F3
Abarqu 8,000	F3
Ahvaz 329,006	E3

Amol 68,782	F2
Anar 463	G3
Anarak 2,038	F3
Arak 114,507	E3
Ardabil 147,404	E2
Ardestan 5,868	F3
Asterabad (Gorgan) 88,348	F2
Babol 67,790	F2
Bafq 5,000	G3
Baft 6,000	G4

(continued on following page)

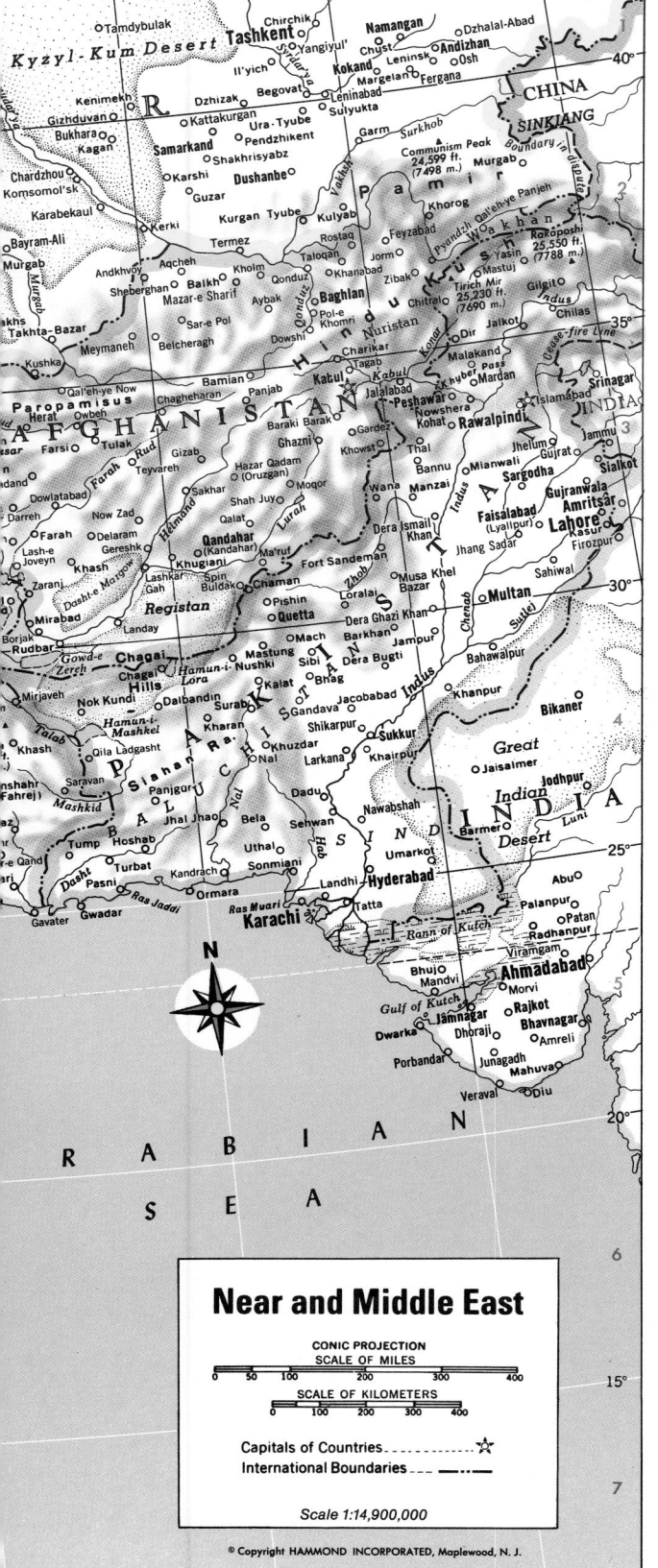

SAUDI ARABIA

AREA 829,995 sq. mi.
(2,149,687 sq. km.)
POPULATION 8,367,000
CAPITAL Riyadh
MONETARY UNIT Saudi riyal
MAJOR LANGUAGE Arabic
MAJOR RELIGION Islam

YEMEN

AREA 188,321 sq. mi. (487,792 sq. km.)
POPULATION 8,425,189
CAPITAL San'a
MONETARY UNIT Yemeni rial
MAJOR LANGUAGE Arabic
MAJOR RELIGION Islam

QATAR

AREA 4,247 sq. mi. (11,000 sq. km.)
POPULATION 220,000
CAPITAL Doha
MONETARY UNIT Qatari riyal
MAJOR LANGUAGE Arabic
MAJOR RELIGION Islam

KUWAIT

AREA 6,532 sq. mi. (16,918 sq. km.)
POPULATION 1,355,827
CAPITAL Al Kuwait
MONETARY UNIT Kuwaiti dinar
MAJOR LANGUAGE Arabic
MAJOR RELIGION Islam

BAHRAIN

AREA 240 sq. mi. (622 sq. km.)
POPULATION 358,857
CAPITAL Manama
MONETARY UNIT Bahraini dinar
MAJOR LANGUAGE Arabic
MAJOR RELIGION Islam

OMAN

AREA 120,000 sq. mi. (310,800 sq. km.)
POPULATION 891,000
CAPITAL Muscat
MONETARY UNIT Omani rial
MAJOR LANGUAGE Arabic
MAJOR RELIGION Islam

UNITED ARAB EMIRATES

AREA 32,278 sq. mi. (83,600 sq. km.)
POPULATION 1,040,275
CAPITAL Abu Dhabi
MONETARY UNIT dirham
MAJOR LANGUAGE Arabic
MAJOR RELIGION Islam

Near and Middle East

CONIC PROJECTION
SCALE OF MILES
0 50 100 200 300 400

SCALE OF KILOMETERS
0 100 200 300 400

Capitals of Countries .... ☆
International Boundaries ___ ___

Scale 1:14,900,000

® Copyright HAMMOND INCORPORATED, Maplewood, N.J.

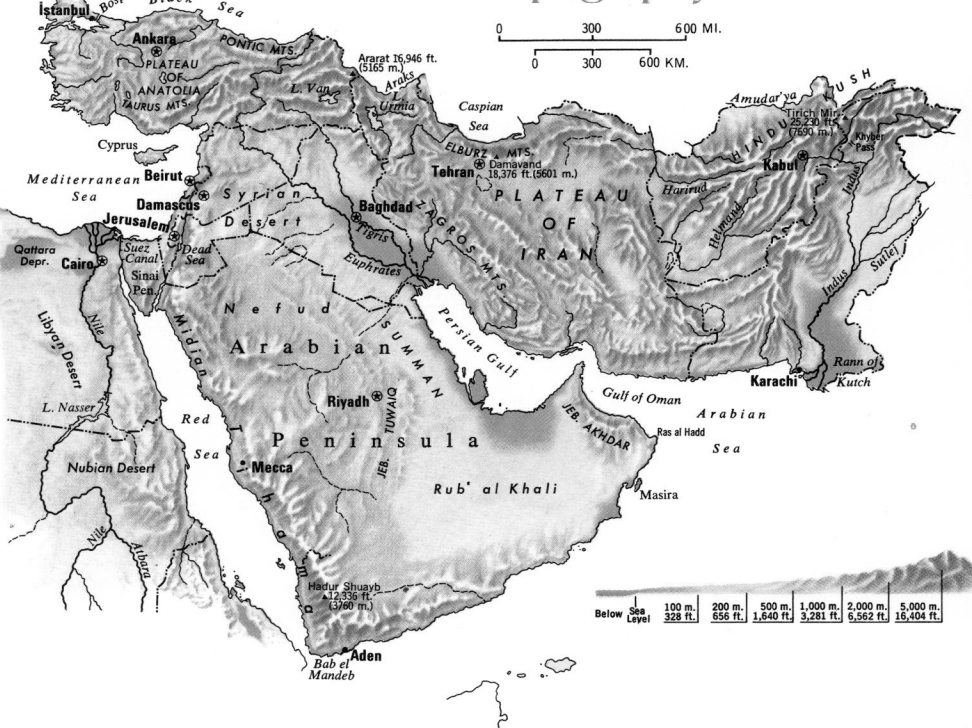

Topography

Below Sea Level	100 m. 328 ft.	200 m. 656 ft.	500 m. 1,640 ft.	1,000 m. 3,281 ft.	2,000 m. 6,562 ft.	5,000 m. 16,404 ft.

- Bakhtaran 290,861 E3
- Bam 22,000 G4
- Bampur 1,585 H4
- Bandar 'Abbas 89,103 G4
- Bandar-e Anzali (Enzeli) 55,978 E2
- Bandar-e Khomeyni 6,000 E3
- Bandar-e Lengeh 4,920 F4
- Bandar-e Rig 1,889 F4
- Bandar-e Torkeman 13,000 F2
- Bejestan 3,823 G3
- Birjand 25,854 G3
- Bojnurd 31,248 G2
- Borazjan 20,000 F4
- Borujerd 100,103 E3
- Bushehr 57,681 F4
- Chah Bahar 1,800 H4
- Chalus 15,000 F2
- Damghan 13,000 F2
- Darab 13,000 G4
- Dasht-e Azadegan 21,000 E3
- Dashtiari H4
- Dezful 110,287 E3
- Dezh Shahpur 1,384 E2
- Emamshahr 30,767 G2
- Enzeli 55,978 E2
- Estahbanat 18,187 F4
- Fahrej (Iranshahr) 5,000 H4
- Fasa 19,000 F4
- Ferdows 11,000 G3
- Gach Saran F3
- Garmsar 4,723 F2
- Golpayegan 20,515 F3
- Gonabad 8,000 G3
- Gorgan 88,348 F2
- Hamadan 155,846 E3
- Iranshahr 5,000 H4
- Isfahan 671,825 F3
- Jahrom 38,236 F4
- Kangan 2,682 F4
- Kangavar 9,414 E3
- Kashan 84,545 F3
- Kashmar 17,000 G2
- Kazerun 51,309 F4
- Kerman 140,309 G3
- Khash 7,439 H4
- Khorramabad 104,928 E3
- Khorramshahr 146,709 E3
- Khvoy 70,040 E2
- Lar 22,000 F4
- Mahabad 28,610 E2
- Maragheh 60,820 E2
- Marand 24,000 E2
- Meshed 670,180 H2
- Mianeh 28,447 E2
- Minab 4,228 G2
- Mirjaveh 11,000 H4
- Nahavand 24,000 E3
- Na'in 5,925 F3
- Najafabad 76,236 F3
- Nasratabad (Zabol) 20,000 H3
- Natanz 4,370 F3
- Nehbandan 2,130 G3
- Neyshabur 59,101 G2
- Nikshahr H4
- Pahlevi (Enzeli) 55,978 E2
- Qasr-e Qand 1,879 H4
- Qayen 6,000 G3
- Qazvin 138,527 E2
- Qom 246,831 F3
- Quchan 29,133 G2
- Qum (Qom) 246,831 F3
- Rafsanjan 21,000 G3
- Rasht 187,203 E2
- Ravar 5,074 G3
- Rey 102,825 F2
- Reza'iyeh (Urmia) 163,991 D2
- Sabzevar 69,174 G2
- Sabzvaran 7,000 G4
- Sai'dabad 20,000 G4
- Sanandaj 95,834 E2
- Saqqez 17,000 E2
- Saravan H4
- Sari 70,936 F2
- Saveh 17,565 F2
- Semnan 31,058 F2
- Shahdad 2,777 G3
- Shahreza 34,220 F3
- Shiraz 416,408 F4
- Shirvan 11,000 G2
- Shustar 24,000 E3
- Sirjan (Sai'dabad) 20,000 G4
- Tabas 10,000 G3
- Tabas-Masina (Tabas) 466 H3
- Tabriz 598,576 E2
- Tarom 394 G4
- Tehran (cap.) 4,496,159 F2
- Tonekabon 12,000 F2
- Torbat-e Heydariyeh 30,106 G2
- Torbat-e Jam 13,000 H2
- Torud 721 F2
- Turan G2
- Turbat-i-Shaikh Jam 13,000 H2
- Urmia 163,991 D2
- Yazd 135,978 F3
- Yazdan H3
- Zabol 20,000 H3
- Zahedan 92,628 H4
- Zanjan 99,967 E2
- Zarand 5,000 G3

OTHER FEATURES

- Araks (riv.) E2
- Atrek (riv.) G2
- Bazman, Kuh-e (mt.) H4
- Damavand (mt.) F2
- Dez (riv.) E3
- Elburz (mts.) F2
- Gavkhuni (lake) F3
- Gorgan (riv.) F2
- Halil (riv.) G4
- Jaz Murian, Hamun-e (marsh) G4
- Karun (riv.) E3
- Kavir, Dasht-e (salt des.) G3
- Kavir-e Namak (salt des.) G3
- Lut, Dasht-e (des.) G3
- Maidani, Ras (cape) G4
- Mand Rud (riv.) F4
- Mashkid (riv.) H4
- Mehran (riv.) F4
- Namak, Daryacheh-ye (salt lake) F3
- Namaksar (salt lake) H3
- Namakzar-e Shahdad (salt lake) G3
- Oman (gulf) G5
- Persian (gulf) F4
- Qeys (isl.) F4
- Qezel Owzan (riv.) E2
- Qeshm (isl.) G4
- Safidar, Kuh-e (mt.) F4
- Shaikh Shua'ib (isl.) F4
- Shir Kuh (mt.) F3
- Taftan, Kuh-e (mt.) H4
- Talab (riv.) H4
- Tashk (lake) F4
- Urmia (lake) E2
- Zagros (mts.) E3

IRAQ

CITIES and TOWNS

- Al 'Aziziya 7,450 E3
- Al Falluja 38,072 D3
- Al Fathat 15,329 D2
- Al Musaiyib 15,955 D3
- Al Qurna 5,638 E3
- 'Amadiya 2,578 D2
- 'Amara 64,847 E3
- 'Ana 15,729 D3
- An Najaf 128,096 D3
- An Nasiriya 60,405 E3
- Arbela (Erbil) 90,320 D2
- Ar Rahhaliya 1,579 D3
- As Salman 3,584 E3
- Baghdad (cap.) 502,503 E3
- Baghdad* 1,745,328 E3
- Baq'uba 34,575 D3
- Basra 313,327 E3
- Erbil 90,320 D2
- Habbaniya 14,405 D3
- Haditha 6,870 D3
- Hai 16,988 E3
- Hilla 84,717 D3
- Hit 9,131 D3
- Karbal'a 83,301 D3
- Khanaqin 23,522 D3
- Kirkuk 167,413 D2
- Kirkuk* 176,794 D2
- Kut 42,116 E3
- Maidan 354 E3
- Mosul 315,157 D2
- Qala' Sharqat 2,434 D2
- Ramadi 28,723 D3
- Rutba 5,091 D3
- Samarra 24,746 D3
- Samawa 33,473 D3
- Shithatha 2,326 D3
- Sulaimaniya 86,822 E2
- Tikrit 9,921 D3

OTHER FEATURES

- 'Aneiza, Jebel (mt.) C3
- 'Ara'r, Wadi (dry riv.) D3
- Batin, Wadi al (dry riv.) E4
- Euphrates (riv.) E3
- Hauran, Wadi (dry riv.) D3
- Mesopotamia (reg.) D3
- Syrian (El Hamad) (des.) D3
- Tigris (riv.) E3

KUWAIT

CITIES and TOWNS

- Al Kuwait (cap.) 181,774 E4
- Mina al Ahmadi E4
- Mina Saud E4

OTHER FEATURES

- Bubiyan (isl.) E4
- Persian (gulf) F4

OMAN

CITIES and TOWNS

- Adam G5
- Buraimi G5
- Dhank G5
- Ibra G5
- I'bri G5
- Juwara G6
- Kamil G5
- Khaluf G5
- Khasab G4
- Manah G5
- Masqat (Muscat) (cap.) 7,500 G5
- Matrah 15,000 G5
- Mina al Fahal G5
- Murbat G6
- Muscat (cap.) 7,500 G5
- Nizwa G5
- Quryat G5
- Raysut (Risut) F6
- Salala 4,000 F6
- Sarur G5
- Shinas G5
- Sohar G5
- Sur G5
- Suwaiq G5

OTHER FEATURES

- Akhdar, Jebel (range) G5
- Batina (reg.) G5
- Dhofar (reg.) F6
- Hadd, Ras al (cape) G5
- Jibsh, Ras (cape) G5
- Kuria Muria (isls.) G6
- Madraka, Ras (cape) G6
- Masira (gulf) G6
- Masira (isl.) G5
- Musandam, Ras (cape) G4
- Nus, Ras (cape) G6
- Oman (gulf) G5
- Oman (reg.) G5
- Ruus al Jibal (dist.) G4
- Sauqira (bay) G6
- Sauqira, Ras (cape) G6
- Sham, Jebel (mt.) G5
- Sharbatat, Ras (cape) G6

QATAR

CITIES and TOWNS

- Doha (cap.) 150,000 F4
- Dukhan F4
- Umm Sai'd F5

OTHER FEATURES

- Persian (gulf) F4
- Rakan, Ras (cape) F4

SAUDI ARABIA

CITIES and TOWNS

- Aba as Sau'd 47,501 D6
- 'Abaila F5
- Abha 30,150 D6
- Abqaiq E4
- Abu 'Arish D6
- Abu Hadriya E4
- 'Ain al Mubarrak C5
- Al 'Ain C4
- Al 'Ala C4
- Al 'Auda E4
- Al Birk D6
- Al Hilla E5
- Al Lidam D5
- Al Lith C5
- Al Muadhdam C4
- 'Anaiza D4
- Artawiya E4
- 'Ashaira D5
- Ayun D4
- Badr C5
- Buraida 69,940 D4
- Dam D5
- Dammam 127,844 F4
- Dar al Hamra C4
- Dhaba C4
- Dhahran E4
- Dharma E5
- Dilam E5
- Doqa D6
- Duwadami D5
- Er Ras D4
- Faid D4
- Gail E5
- Haddar E5
- Hadiya C4
- Hafar al Batin E4
- Hail 40,502 D4
- Hamar E5
- Hamda D6
- Hanakiya D5
- Haql C4
- Harad E5
- Haraja D6
- Hariq E5
- Hofuf 101,271 E4
- Jabrin E5
- Jauf C4
- Jidda 561,104 C5
- Jizan (Qizan) 32,812 D6
- Jubail F4
- Jubba D4
- Junaina D5
- Kaf C3
- Khaibar, 'Asir D5
- Khaibar, Hejaz C4
- Khamis Mushait 49,581 D6
- Khay D6
- Khurma D5
- Laila E5
- Majmaa' D4
- Maqna C4
- Marib E6
- Mastaba C5
- Mastura C5
- Mecca 366,801 C5
- Medain Salih C4
- Medina 198,186 D5
- Mendak D5
- Mina Sau'd E4
- Mubarraz 54,325 E4
- Mudhnib D4
- Muwailih C4
- Najran (Aba as Sau'd) 47,501 D6
- Nisab D4
- O'qair E4
- Qadhima C5
- Qafar D4
- Qasr al Haiyanya D4
- Qatif E4
- Qizan 32,812 D6
- Qunfidha D6
- Qusaiba D4
- Rabigh C5
- Ra's al Khafji E4
- Ras Tanura F4
- Riyadh (cap.) 666,840 E5
- Rumah E4
- Sabya D6
- Sakaka D4
- Salwa F5
- Shaqra D4
- Shuqaiq D6
- Sufeina D5
- Sulaiyil E5
- Taif 204,857 D5
- Taima C4
- Tamra E5
- Tathlith D6
- Tebuk (Tabuk) 74,825 C4
- Truba D4
- Turaba D5
- Umm Lajj C4
- Wejh C4
- Yamama E5
- Yenbo C5
- Zahran D6
- Zalim D5
- Zilfi E4

OTHER FEATURES

- Abu-Mad, Ras (cape) C5
- 'Aneiza, Jebel (mt.) C3
- Aqaba (gulf) C4
- Arafat, Jebel (mt.) D5
- 'Ara'r, Wadi (dry riv.) D3
- Arma (plat.) E4
- Aswad, Ras al (cape) C5
- Bahr es Safi (des.) E6
- Barida, Ras (cape) C5
- Bisha, Wadi (dry riv.) D5
- Dahana (des.) E4
- Dawasir, Wadi (dry riv.) E5
- Dawasir, Hadhb (range) D5
- Farasan (isls.) D6
- Hatiba, Ras (cape) C5
- Jafura (des.) F5
- Mashabi (isl.) C4
- Midian (dist.) C4
- Mishaa'b, Ras (cape) E4
- Nefud (des.) D4
- Nefud Dahi (des.) D5
- Persian (gulf) F4
- Ranya, Wadi (dry riv.) D5
- Red (sea) C5
- Rima, Wadi (dry riv.) D4
- Rimal, Ar (des.) F5
- Rub al Khali (des.) F5
- Safaniya, Ras (cape) E4
- Salma, Jebel (mts.) D4
- Shaibara (isl.) C4
- Shammar, Jebel (plat.) D4
- Sirhan, Wadi (dry riv.) C3
- Subh, Jebel (mt.) C5
- Summan (plat.) E4
- Tihama (reg.) C5
- Tiran (isl.) C4
- Tiran (str.) C4
- Tuwaiq, Jebel (range) E5

UNITED ARAB EMIRATES

CITIES and TOWNS

- Abu Dhabi (cap.) 347,000 F5
- 'AJman G4
- 'Aradah F5
- Buraimi G5
- Dubai F4
- Fujairah G4
- Jebel Dhanna F5
- Ras al Khaimah G4
- Ruwais F5
- Sharjah F4
- Umm al Qaiwain G4

OTHER FEATURES

- Das (isl.) F4
- Oman (gulf) G5
- Yas (isl.) F5
- Zirko (isl.) F5

WEST BANK

CITIES and TOWNS

- Hebron 38,309 C3

OTHER FEATURES

- Dead (sea) C3

YEMEN

CITIES and TOWNS

- Aden 240,370 E7
- Ahwar E7
- 'Amran D6
- Bait al Faqih D7
- Balhaf E7
- Bir 'Ali E7
- Damqut F6
- Dhamar 19,467 D7
- El Beida 5,975 E7
- Ghaida F6
- Habban E7
- Hadibu F7
- Hajarain E6
- Hajja 5,814 D6
- Harib E7
- Haura E7
- Hodeida 80,314 D7
- Hureidha E6
- Huth D6
- Ibb 19,066 D7
- 'Irqa E7
- Lahej D7
- Leijun E6
- Lodar E7
- Luhaiya D6
- Madinat ash Sha'b E7
- Marib 292 E6
- Meifa E7
- Mocha D7
- Mukalla 45,000 E7
- Nisab E7
- Nuqub E6
- Qishn F6
- Riyan E7
- Sa'ada 4,252 D6
- Saihut F6
- San'a (cap.) 134,588 D6
- Seiyun 20,000 E6
- Shabwa E6
- Sheikh Sa'id D7
- Shibam E6
- Shihr E7
- Shuqra E7
- Ta'izz 78,642 D7
- Tarim E6
- Yarim D7
- Yeshbum E7
- Zabid D7
- Zinjibar E7

OTHER FEATURES

- Bab el Mandeb (str.) D7
- Fartak, Ras (cape) F6
- Hadhramaut (dist.) E7
- Hadhramaut, Wadi (dry riv.) F7
- Hanish (isls.) D7
- Jebel Manar (mt.) D7
- Jebel Sabir (mt.) D7
- Kamaran (isl.) D6
- Manar, Jebel (mt.) D7
- Mandeb, Bab el (str.) D7
- Perim (isl.) D7
- Ras Fartak (cape) F6
- Red (sea) C5
- Sabir, Jebel (mt.) D7
- Socotra (isl.) F7
- Tihama (reg.) C5
- Wadi Hadhramaut (dry riv.) F7
- Zuqar (isl.) D7

*City and suburbs.

Agriculture, Industry and Resources

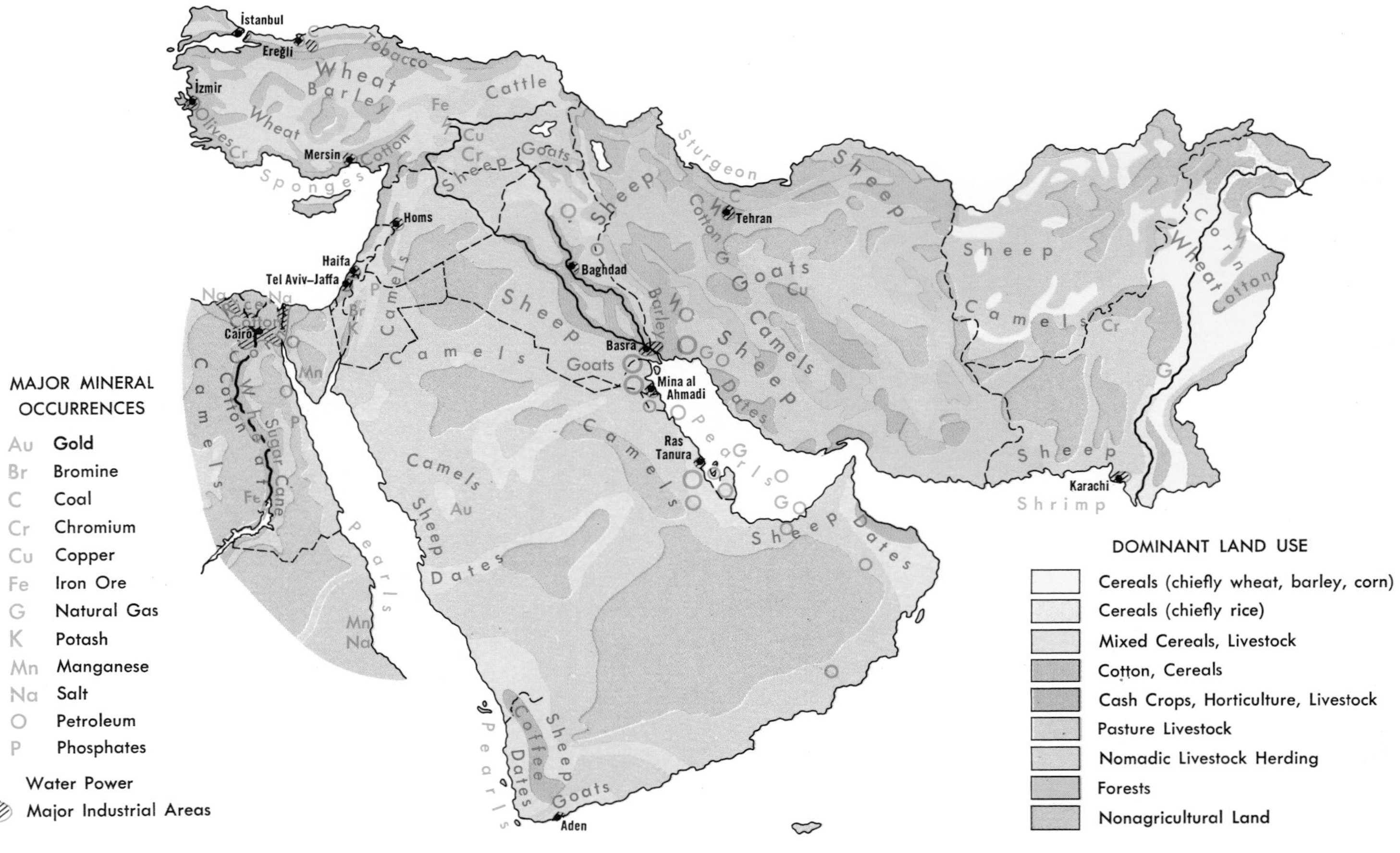

İstanbul
Ereğli
İzmir
Mersin
Homs
Haifa
Tel Aviv–Jaffa
Cairo
Baghdad
Tehran
Basra
Mina al Ahmadi
Ras Tanura
Karachi
Aden
Wheat
Barley
Tobacco
Cattle
Olives
Cotton
Sponges
Sheep
Goats
Camels
Sturgeon
Dates
Pearls
Shrimp
Coffee
Corn
Sugar Cane
MAJOR MINERAL OCCURRENCES
Au Gold
Br Bromine
C Coal
Cr Chromium
Cu Copper
Fe Iron Ore
G Natural Gas
K Potash
Mn Manganese
Na Salt
O Petroleum
P Phosphates
Water Power
Major Industrial Areas
DOMINANT LAND USE
Cereals (chiefly wheat, barley, corn)
Cereals (chiefly rice)
Mixed Cereals, Livestock
Cotton, Cereals
Cash Crops, Horticulture, Livestock
Pasture Livestock
Nomadic Livestock Herding
Forests
Nonagricultural Land

TURKEY

SYRIA

LEBANON

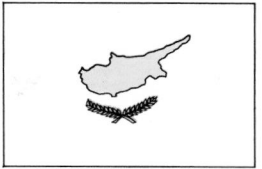
CYPRUS

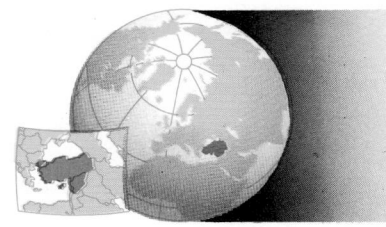

TURKEY

AREA 300,946 sq. mi.
(779,450 sq. km.)
POPULATION 45,217,556
CAPITAL Ankara
LARGEST CITY Istanbul
HIGHEST POINT Ararat 16,946 ft.
(5,165 m.)
MONETARY UNIT Turkish lira
MAJOR LANGUAGE Turkish
MAJOR RELIGION Islam

SYRIA

AREA 71,498 sq. mi. (185,180 sq. km.)
POPULATION 8,979,000
CAPITAL Damascus
LARGEST CITY Damascus
HIGHEST POINT Hermon 9,232 ft.
(2,814 m.)
MONETARY UNIT Syrian pound
MAJOR LANGUAGES Arabic, French,
Kurdish, Armenian
MAJOR RELIGIONS Islam, Christianity

LEBANON

AREA 4,015 sq. mi. (10,399 sq. km.)
POPULATION 3,161,000
CAPITAL Beirut
LARGEST CITY Beirut
HIGHEST POINT Qurnet es Sauda
10,131 ft. (3,088 m.)
MONETARY UNIT Lebanese pound
MAJOR LANGUAGES Arabic, French
MAJOR RELIGIONS Christianity, Islam

CYPRUS

AREA 3,473 sq. mi. (8,995 sq. km.)
POPULATION 629,000
CAPITAL Nicosia
LARGEST CITY Nicosia
HIGHEST POINT Troödos 6,406 ft. (1,953 m.)
MONETARY UNIT Cypriot pound
MAJOR LANGUAGES Greek, Turkish, English
MAJOR RELIGIONS Eastern (Greek) Orthodoxy,
Islam

Agriculture, Industry and Resources

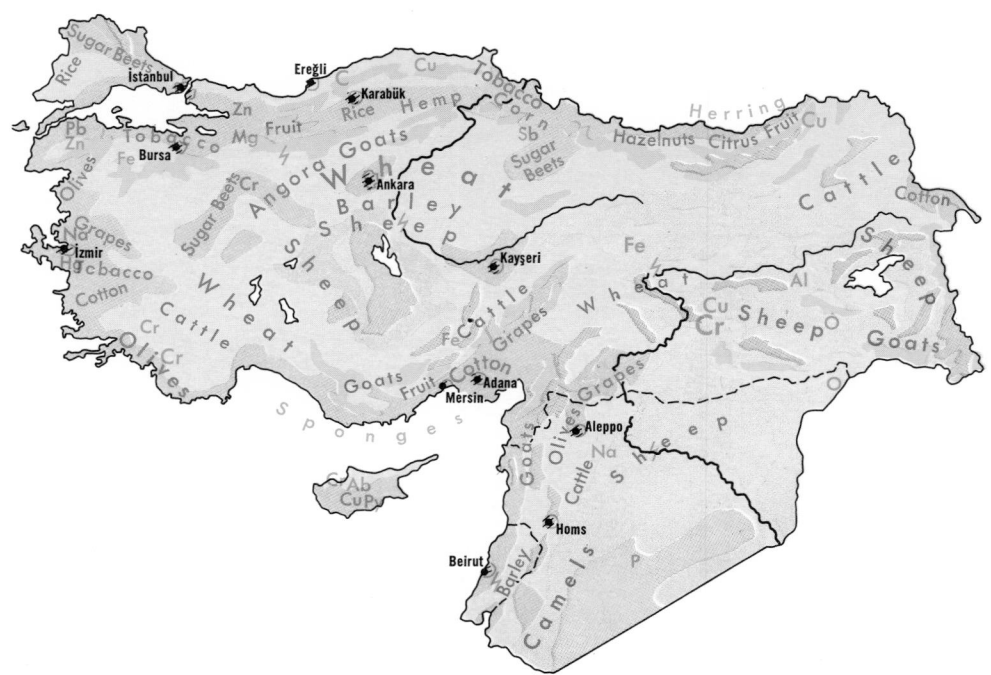

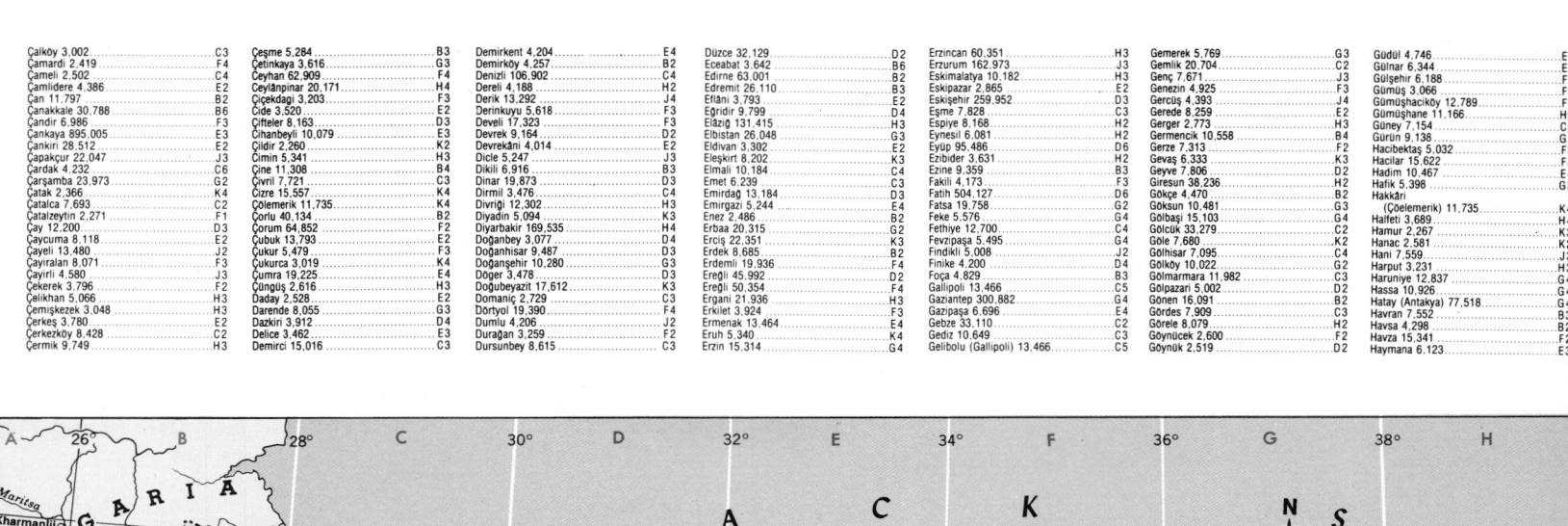

Turkey is divided into provinces bearing the same names as their capital towns, except:

Province	Capital	
AĞRI	Karaköse	K3
BİNGÖL	Çapakçur	J3
HAKKÂRİ	Çölemerik	K4
HATAY	Antakya	G4
İÇEL	Mersin	F4
KOCAELİ	İzmit	C2
SAKARYA	Adapazarı	D2
TUNCELİ	Kalan	H3

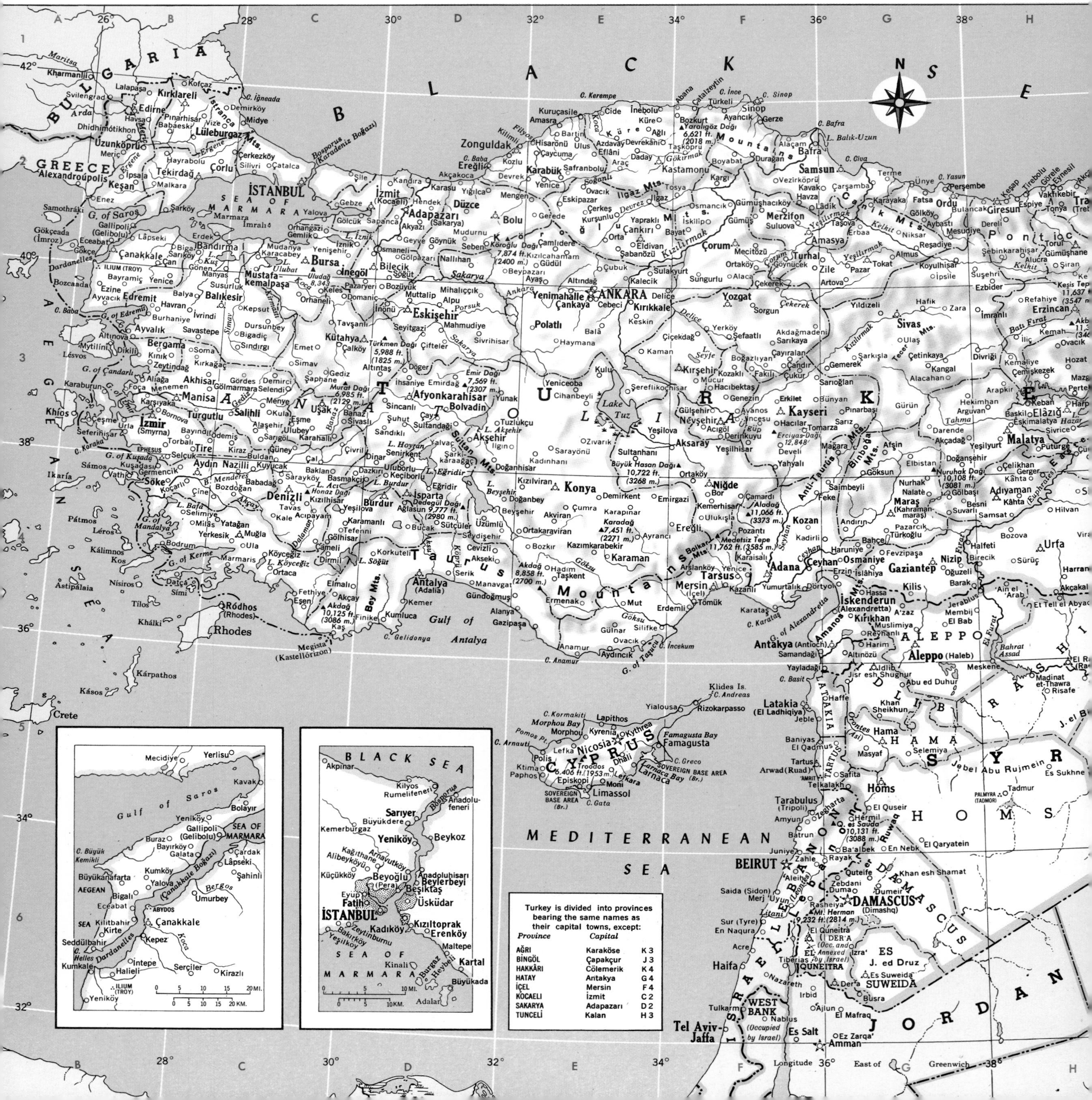

Hayrabolu 12.331	B2	Islahiye 20.683	G4
Hazro 4.896	J3	Isparta 62.870	D4
Hekimhan 11.818	G3	Ispir 3.929	J2
Hendek 15.291	D2	Istanbul 2.547.364	D6
Hilvan 6.473	H4	Ivrindi 3.730	B3
Hınıs 10.226	J3	Izmir 636.834	B3
Hisarönü 4.485	E2	Izmit 165.483	D2
Hizan 2.545	K3	Iznik 11.614	C2
Hopa 9.089	J2	Kadıköy 354.957	D6
Horasan 7.724	K2	Kadınhanı 11.802	E3
Hozat 5.796	H3	Kadirli 34.779	F4
İçel (Mersin) 152.236	F4	Kağıthane 164.448	D6
İdil 4.862	J4	Kağızman 11.517	K2
Iğdır 29.542	K3	Kâhta 15.602	H4
Ilgaz 6.624	E2	Kale 11.637	H3
İliğin 11.830	D3	Kale 3.399	C4
İmranlı 5.667	J3	Kalecik 4.707	E2
İncesu 7.089	F3	Kaman 16.516	E2
İnebolu 6.824	E2	Kandıra 10.187	D2
İnegöl 37.805	C2	Kangal 5.937	G3
İnönü 4.152	D3	Karabük 69.182	E2
İpsala 6.829	B2	Karacabey 21.648	C2
İpsile 2.328	J4	Karaali 5.539	E2
İskenderun 107.437	G4	Karaisali 2.316	F4
İskilip 16.588	F2	Karaköçan 5.604	H3
		Karaköse (Ağrı) 35.284	K3

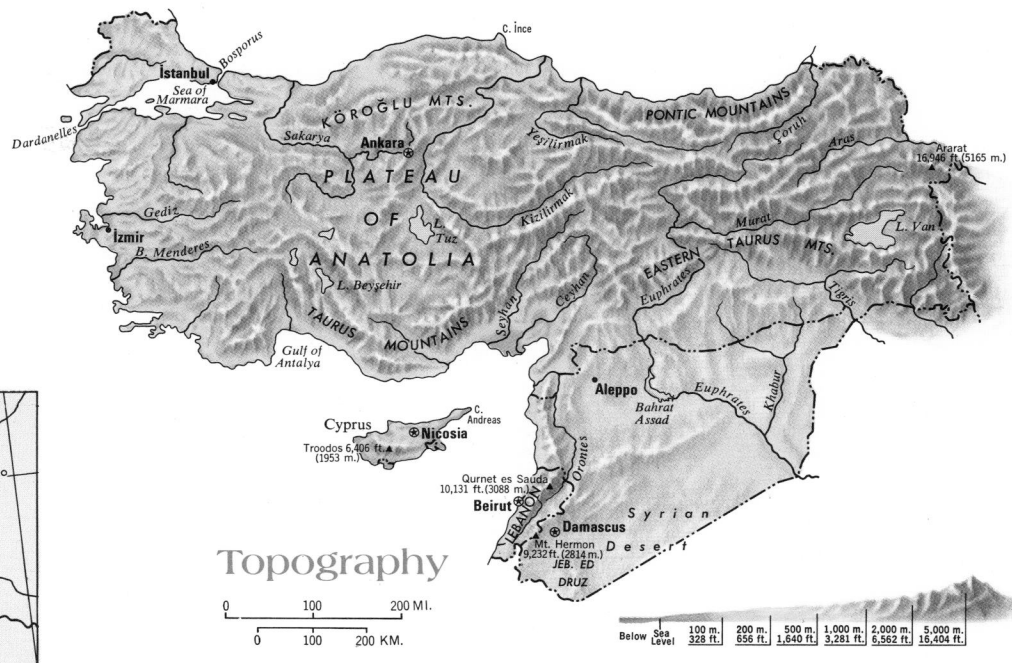

Topography

0   100   200 MI.
0   100   200 KM.

Below Sea Level	100 m. 328 ft.	200 m. 656 ft.	500 m. 1,640 ft.	1,000 m. 3,281 ft.	2,000 m. 6,562 ft.	5,000 m. 16,404 ft.

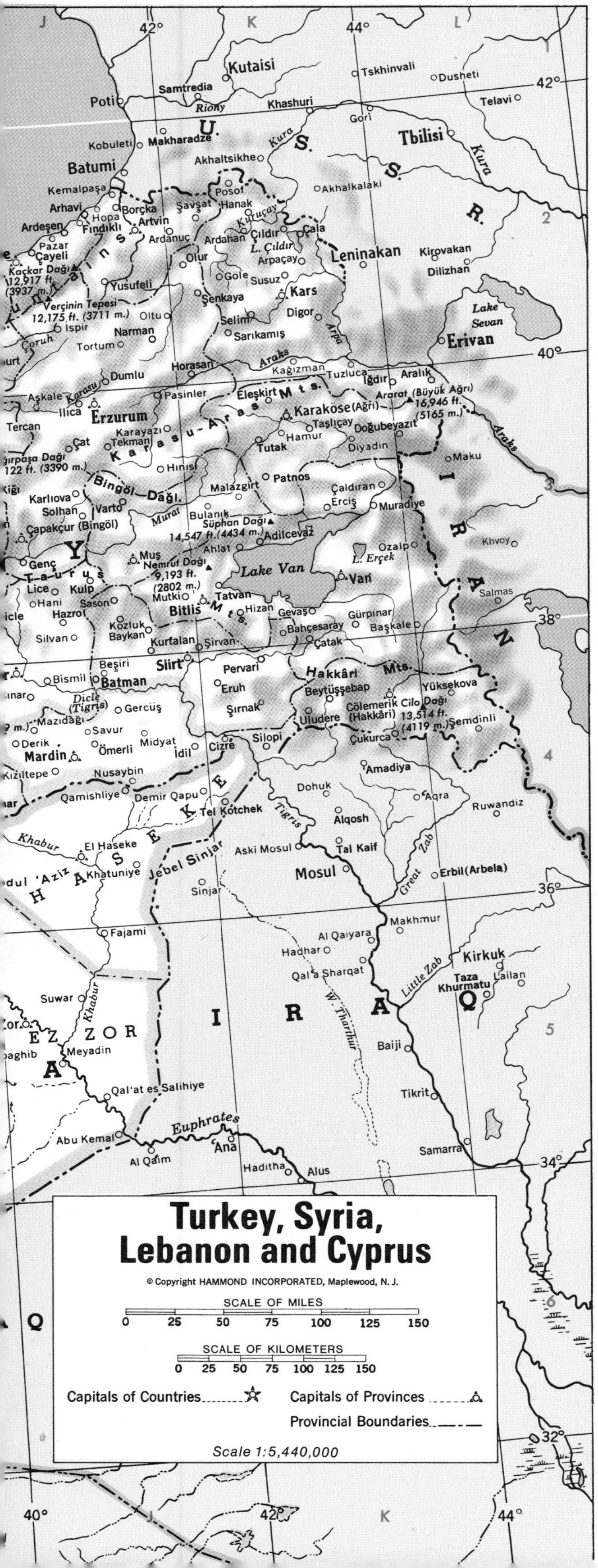

Turkey, Syria, Lebanon and Cyprus

© Copyright HAMMOND INCORPORATED, Maplewood, N.J.

SCALE OF MILES
0   25   50   75   100   125   150

SCALE OF KILOMETERS
0   25   50   75   100   125   150

Capitals of Countries .... ✪   Capitals of Provinces .... ⊕

Provincial Boundaries ....

Scale 1:5,440,000

Karaman 43.759	E4	Muğla 24.178	C4	Silvan 29.599	J3	Yeşilyurt 7.451	H3
Karamanlı 5.904	C4	Muradiye 6.334	K3	Simav 11.601	C3	Yıldızeli 7.043	G3
Karapınar 19.589	E4	Muş 27.761	J3	Sincanlı 3.847	D3	Yozgat 32.501	F3
Karasu 11.600	D2	Mustafakemalpaşa 27.706	C3	Sındırgı 7.818	C3	Yüksekova 7.329	L4
Karataş 5.598	F4	Mut 11.466	E4	Sinop 16.098	F2	Yumurtalık 2.442	F4
Karayaka 4.242	G2	Mutki 2.815	J3	Şiran 5.048	H2	Yunak 6.187	D3
Karayazı 3.595	J3	Muttalip 3.917	D3	Şırnak 10.587	J4	Yusufeli 3.050	J2
Kargı 5.021	F2	Nallıhan 7.883	D2	Şırvan 5.166	K3	Zara 10.376	G3
Karlıova 3.631	J3	Narman 4.607	J2	Sivas 149.201	G3	Zeytinburnu 123.548	D6
Kars 54.892	K2	Nazilli 52.176	C4	Sivaşlı 4.394	C3	Zeytindağ 3.517	B3
Karşıyaka 171.600	B3	Nevşehir 30.203	F3	Siverek 40.990	H4	Zile 32.157	G2
Kartal 53.073	D6	Niğde 31.844	F4	Sivrihisar 8.713	D3	Zivarik 2.703	E3
Kaş 2.493	C4	Niksar 19.156	G2	Smyrna (İzmir) 636.834	B3	Zonguldak 90.221	D2
Kastamonu 29.993	F2	Nizip 36.190	G4	Söğüt 5.329	D3	
Kavak, Çanakkale 3.932	C5	Nurhak 5.330	G4	Söke 35.407	B4	**OTHER FEATURES**
Kavak, Samsun 3.964	F2	Nusaybin 23.684	J4	Solhan 7.014	J3	
Kayseri 207.037	F3	Ödemiş 37.364	C3	Soma 23.713	B3	Abydos (ruins)	B6
Kazanlı 4.461	F4	Of 10.376	J2	Sorgun 14.081	F3	Acı (lake)	C4
Kazımkarabekir 4.086	E4	Oğuzeli 7.194	G4	Şuhut 8.154	D3	Adalar (isl.)	D6
Keban 5.800	H3	Oltu 10.093	J2	Sulakyurt 4.311	E2	Aegean (sea)	A3
Keçiborlu 7.096	D4	Ömerli 4.738	J4	Sultandağı 4.017	D3	Ağrı, Büyük (Ararat)	
Keles 2.423	C3	Ordu 47.481	G2	Sultanhanı 5.112	E3	(mt.)	L3
Kelkit 6.928	H2	Orhaneli 3.335	C3	Suluova 21.278	F2	Akdağ (mt.)	C4
Kemah 3.038	H3	Orhangazi 12.181	C2	Sungurlu 21.641	F2	Aladağ (mt.)	F4
Kemaliye 3.014	H3	Orta 3.596	E2	Sürmene 8.096	J2	Amanos (mts.)	G4
Kemalpaşa 7.572	J2	Ortaca 8.604	C4	Sürüç 20.395	H4	Amanur (cape)	E5
Kemerburgaz 7.234	D5	Ortakaraviran 3.856	E4	Suşehri 10.863	H2	Anatolia (reg.)	D3
Kemirhisar 6.205	F4	Ortaköy, Çorum 2.657	F2	Susurluk 14.000	C3	Ankara (riv.)	D3
Kepsut 4.704	C3	Ortaköy, Niğde 6.371	F3	Susuz 5.006	K2	Antalya (gulf)	D4
Keşan 27.088	B2	Osmancık 11.921	F2	Taşkent 7.098	E4	Anti-Taurus (mts.)	G3
Keşap 5.264	H2	Osmaneli 4.789	D2	Taşköprü 8.146	F2	Araks (riv.)	K2
Keşkin 10.540	E3	Osmaniye 61.581	G4	Tarsus 102.186	F4	Ararat (mt.)	L3
Kiği 5.598	J3	Ovacık, Tunceli 2.248	H3	Tatvan 29.271	K3	Arpa (riv.)	K2
Kilimli 26.649	D2	Özalp 4.188	L3	Taşlıçay 3.684	K3	Baba (cape)	A3
Kilis 54.055	G4	Palu 5.489	H3	Taşova 6.516	F4	Bati Fırat (riv.)	H3
Kınık 11.785	B3	Pasinler 14.267	J3	Tatvan 29.271	K3	Beyşehir (lake)	D4
Kiraz 5.284	C3	Patnos 15.918	K3	Tavas 9.728	C4	Black (sea)	E1
Kırıkhan 38.118	G4	Pazar, Rize 8.856	J2	Tavşanlı 19.575	C3	Bosporus (str.)	C2
Kırıkkale 137.874	E2	Pazar, Tokat 4.337	G2	Tefenni 4.385	C4	Bozcaada (isl.)	A3
Kırkağaç 15.078	B3	Pazarcık 15.943	G4	Tekirdağ 41.257	B2	Burgaz (isl.)	D6
Kırklareli 33.265	B2	Pazaryeri 5.633	C2	Tercan 6.068	H3	
Kırşehir 41.415	F3	Pera (Beyoğlu) 230.532	D6	Tire 30.694	B3	Büyük Ağrı (Ararat)	
Kızılcamamam 7.050	E2	Perşembe 6.701	G2	Tirebolu 7.385	H2	(mt.)	L3
Kızılhisar 11.119	C4	Pertek 4.176	H3	Tokat 48.588	G2	Çanakkale Boğazı (Dardanelles) (str.)	B6
Kızıltepe 21.531	J4	Pervari 4.126	K4	Tomarza 6.548	F3	Candarli (gulf)	B3
Kızılviran 3.260	E3	Pınarbaşı 9.503	G3	Tömük 7.660	F4	Canik (riv.)	G2
Kocaeli (İzmit) 165.483	D2	Pınarhisar 10.523	B2	Tonya 10.544	H2	Ceyhan (riv.)	F4
Koçarlı 5.182	B4	Polatlı 35.267	E3	Torbalı 17.237	B3	Cilo Daği (mt.)	K4
Konya 246.727	E4	Posof 2.209	K2	Tortum 4.110	J2	Çoruh (riv.)	J2
Korkuteli 10.334	D4	Pozantı 5.408	F4	Torul 3.221	H2	Dardanelles (str.)	A3
Köyceğiz 4.612	C4	Pülümür 3.442	H3	Tosya 17.515	F2	Dicle (riv.)	J3
Koyulhisar 3.861	G2	Putürge 4.878	H3	Trabzon 97.210	H2	Eastern Taurus (mts.)	J3
Kozaklı 6.200	F3	Refahiye 6.570	H3	Tunceli (lake) 11.637	H3	Ephesus (ruins)	B3
Kozan 32.045	F4	Reşadiye 9.022	G2	Turgutlu 47.009	B3	Erciyas Daği (mt.)	F3
Kozlu 27.322	D2	Reyhanlı 25.749	G4	Turhal 39.170	G2	Ergene (riv.)	B2
Kozluk 6.197	J3	Rize 36.044	J2	Türkeli 2.194	E2	Euphrates (Fırat) (riv.)	H3
Küçükköy 56.411	C6	Sabanözü 3.442	E2	Türkoğlu 9.207	G4	Gediz (riv.)	C3
Kula 10.807	C3	Safranbolu 14.793	E2	Tutak 4.325	K3	Gelidonya (cape)	D4
Kulp 4.474	J3	Saimbeyli 3.622	G4	Tuzluca 5.209	K3	Gökçeada (isl.)	A2
Kulu 11.707	E3	Sakarya (Adapazarı) 114.130	D2	Tuzluku 4.613	D3	Göksu (riv.)	E4
Kumkale 1.752	B6	Salihli 45.514	C3	Ula 5.117	C4	Helles (cape)	B6
Kumluca 2.704	D4	Samandağ 22.540	F4	Ulaş 2.469	G3	Heybeli (isl.)	D6
Küre 2.378	F2	Samsat 2.083	H4	Ulubey 4.214	C3	Ilium (ruins)	B6
Kurşunlu 6.562	E2	Samsun 168.478	F2	Uluborlu 10.016	D3	
Kurtalan 7.001	J3	Sandıklı 13.181	D3	Uludere 4.050	J4	Imroz (Gökçeada)	
Kurtalan 7.001	J3	Sapanca 9.040	D2	Ulukışla 6.336	F4	(isl.)	A2
Kuşadası 10.269	B4	Sarayköy 10.513	C4	Umurbey 2.754	C2	İnce (cape)	F1
Kütahya 82.442	C3	Şaphane 3.919	C3	Ünye 23.366	G2	Istrancа (mts.)	B2
Kuyucak 6.039	C4	Sarayönü 8.946	E3	Urfa 132.934	H4	Kaçkar Daği (mt.)	J2
Lâdik 6.785	C6	Sarıgöl 6.979	C3	Ürgüp 6.758	F3	
Lâpseki 3.727	A3	Sarıkamış 21.262	K2	Urla 13.903	B3	Karadeniz Boğazı (Bosporus)	
Lice 8.625	J3	Sarıkaya 5.160	F3	Uşak 58.578	C3	(str.)	C2
Lüleburgaz 32.401	B2	Sarıköy 4.695	B2	Üsküdar 202.957	D6	Karasu-Aras (mts.)	J3
Maden 15.151	H3	Sarıoğlan 3.245	F3	Üzümlü 4.365	C3	Kelkit (riv.)	G2
Mağara 4.314	G4	Sarıyer 79.329	D5	Uzunköprü 27.005	B2	Kerme (gulf)	B4
Mahmudiye 5.240	D3	Sariz 3.591	G3	Vakfıkebir 12.556	H2	Keşiş Tepesi (mt.)	C3
Malatya 154.505	H3	Sarkaraağaç 4.772	D3	Van 63.663	L3	Kızılırmak (riv.)	F2
Malazgirt 13.094	K3	Şarkışla 12.763	G3	Varto 5.572	J3	Koca (riv.)	C2
Malkara 14.399	B2	Şarköy 5.396	B2	Vize 8.203	C2	Küre (mts.)	E2
Maltepe 66.343	D6	Sason 3.211	J3	Vezirköprü 11.705	F2	Mandalya (gulf)	B4
Manavgat 10.804	D4	Savaştepe 7.179	B3	Viranşehir 26.244	H4	Marmara (isl.)	B2
Manisa 78.114	B3	Şavşat 3.078	K2	Yahşihan 13.738	E2	Marmara (sea)	C2
Manyas 4.410	B3	Savur 4.983	J4	Yalova, İstanbul 27.289	C2	Menderes, Büyük (riv.)	C4
Maraş		Seben 2.471	D2	Yalvaç 18.305	D3	Meriç (riv.)	B2
(Kahramanmaraş) 135.782	G4	Şebinkarahisar 10.214	H2	Yaprakli 3.020	E2	Murat (riv.)	H3
Mardin 36.629	J4	Şefaatli 6.769	F3	Yatağan 4.903	C4	Pontic (mts.)	F2
Marmaris 5.596	C4	Seferihisar 6.484	B3	Yayladağı 4.471	F5	Porsuk (riv.)	D3
Mazgirt 3.141	H3	Selçuk 12.251	B4	Yenice 4.457	C2	Prinkipo (Adalar) (isl.)	D6
Mazıdağı 4.842	J4	Selendi 4.857	C3	Yenice, Çanakkale 4.004	B3	Sakarya (riv.)	D2
Mecitözü 6.066	F2	Selim 3.569	K2	Yenice, İçel 4.161	F4	Saros (gulf)	B2
Menemen 18.464	B3	Selimiye 2.989	B4	Yenice, Zonguldak 5.791	E2	Seyhan (riv.)	F3
Mengen 2.459	D2	Senirkent 8.247	D3	Yeniceoba 5.740	E3	Simav (riv.)	C3
Meriç 3.922	B2	Şenkaya 3.190	K2	Yeniköy, İstanbul	D6	Sinop (cape)	F1
Mersin 152.236	F4	Şereflikoçhisar 20.523	E3	Yenimahalle 198.643	D3	Sultan (mts.)	D3
Merzifon 30.801	F2	Serik 14.161	D4	Yenişehir 15.188	C2	Süphan Daği (mt.)	K3
Mesudiye 4.294	G2	Seydişehir 25.651	D4	Yerkesik 2.381	C4	Taurus (mts.)	D4
Midilli 26.905	G2	Seyitgazi 2.819	D3	Yerköy 19.877	F3	Tigris (Dicle)	J3
Midye 2.003	C2	Siirt 35.654	J4	Yeşilhisar 10.409	F3	Troy (Ilium) (ruins)	B6
Milâs 17.929	B4	Silifke 19.257	E4	Yeşilköy	D6	Tuz (lake)	E3
Mucur 9.398	F3	Silifke 19.257	E4	Yeşilova, Burdur 3.685	C4	Van (lake)	K3
Mudanya 8.399	C2	Silivri 8.525	C2	Yeşilova, Niğde 5.237	E3	Yeşilırmak (riv.)	G2
Mudurnu 3.905	D2	Silopi 4.460	K4			

* City and suburbs

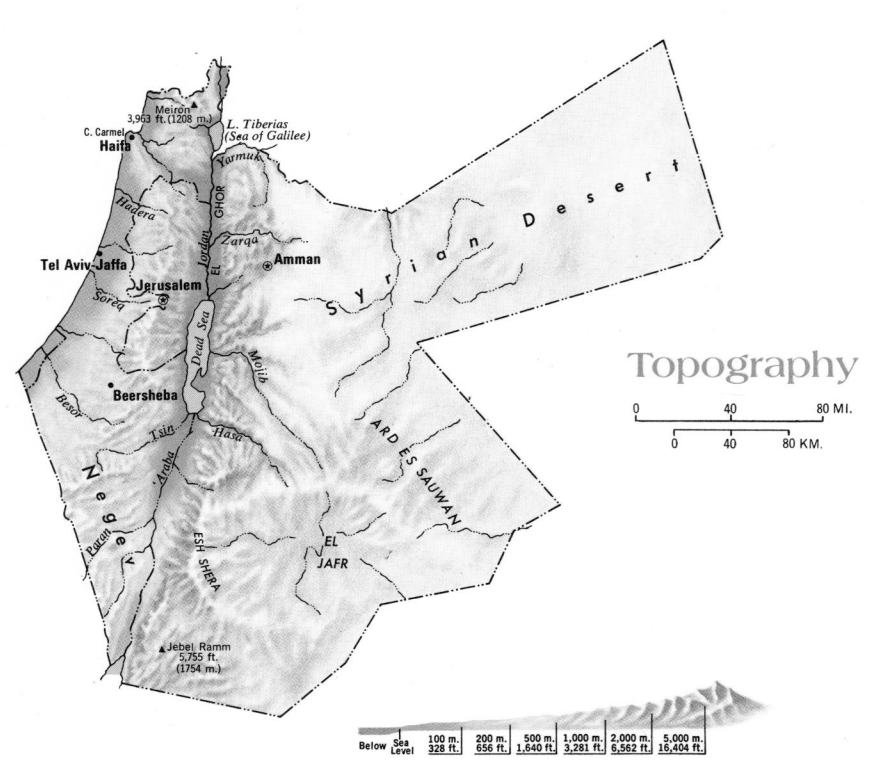

Topography

100 m. 200 m. 500 m. 1,000 m. 2,000 m. 5,000 m.
Below Sea 328 ft. 656 ft. 1,640 ft. 3,281 ft. 6,562 ft. 16,404 ft.
Level

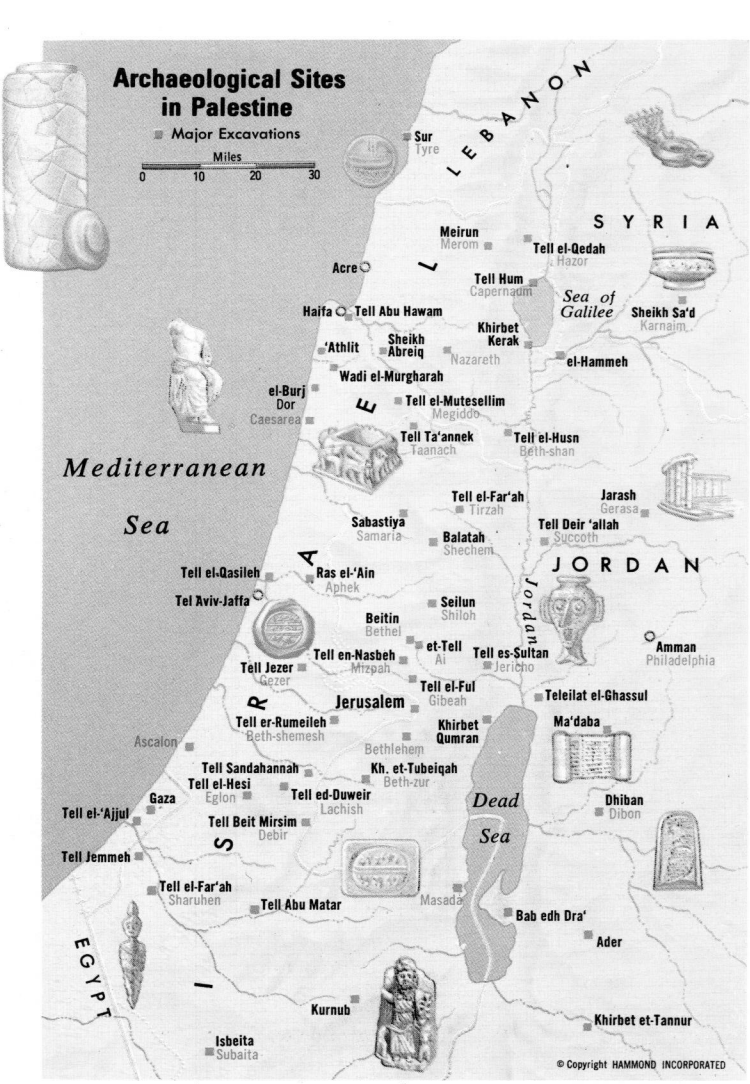

Archaeological Sites in Palestine

■ Major Excavations

Miles
0 10 20 30

© Copyright HAMMOND INCORPORATED

Agriculture, Industry and Resources

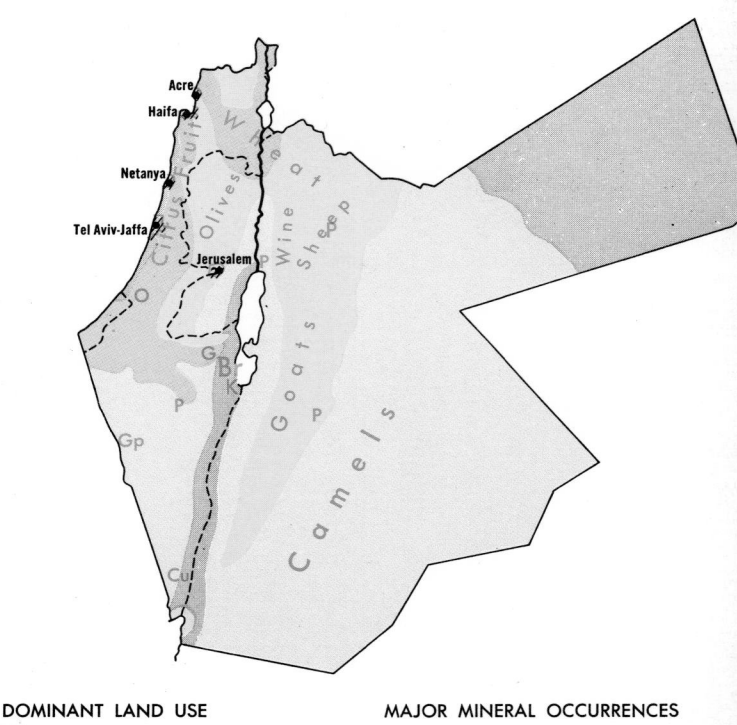

DOMINANT LAND USE

- Cereals, Livestock
- Cash Crops, Horticulture
- Nomadic Livestock Herding
- Nonagricultural Land

MAJOR MINERAL OCCURRENCES

Br	Bromine	K	Potash
Cu	Copper	O	Petroleum
G	Natural Gas	P	Phosphates
Gp	Gypsum		

▨ Major Industrial Areas

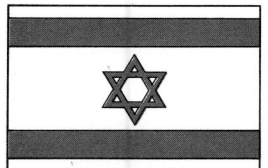

ISRAEL

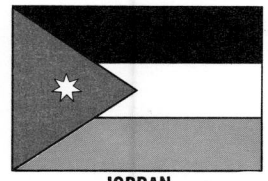

JORDAN

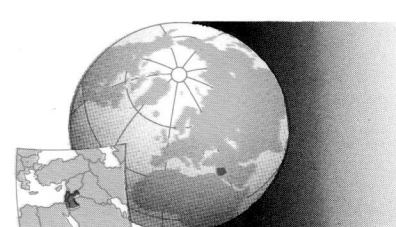

ISRAEL

AREA 7,847 sq. mi. (20,324 sq. km.)
POPULATION 3,878,000
CAPITAL Jerusalem
LARGEST CITY Tel Aviv-Jaffa
HIGHEST POINT Meiran 3,963 ft. (1,208 m.)
MONETARY UNIT shekel
MAJOR LANGUAGES Hebrew, Arabic
MAJOR RELIGIONS Judaism, Islam, Christianity

JORDAN

AREA 35,000 sq. mi. (90,650 sq. km.)
POPULATION 2,152,273
CAPITAL Amman
LARGEST CITY Amman
HIGHEST POINT Jeb. Ramm 5,755 ft. (1,754 m.)
MONETARY UNIT Jordanian dinar
MAJOR LANGUAGE Arabic
MAJOR RELIGION Islam

shon (riv.) C2
mon (mt.) D5
bin (dry riv.) B4
bor (mt.) C2
berias (lake) D2
rmuk (riv.) D2
rqon (riv.) B3

GAZA STRIP

CITIES and TOWNS

basan 1,481 A5
ni Suheila 7,561 A5
it Hanun 4,756 A4
ir el Balah 10,854 A5
ir el Balah* 18,118 A5
za 87,793 A5
za* 118,272 A5
baliya 10,508 A4
baliya* 43,604 A4
an Yunis 29,522 A5
an Yunis* 52,997 A5
fah 10,812 A5
fah* 49,812 A5

WEST BANK

CITIES AND TOWNS

ja 1,322 C3
nabta 3,426 C3
in 914 C2
nza 807 C3
qqaba 1,127 C3
qraba 2,501 C3
iha (Jericho) 5,312 C4
raba 4,231 C3
rura 849 C3
til 3,808 C3
it Fajjar 2,474 C4
it Hanina 1,177 C4
it Jala 6,041 C4
it Lahm (Bethlehem) 14,439 C4
it Nuba 1,350 C4
it Sahur 5,380 C4
thlehem 14,439 C4
ddu 1,259 C4
qin 2,036 C3
Zeit 2,311 C4
rqa 2,477 C3
ir Ballut 1,058 C3
ir Sharaf 973 C3
ahiriya 4,875 B5
ma 524 C3
ra 4,954 C4
Bira 9,674 C4
Bira* 13,037 C4
Khalil (Hebron) 38,309 C4
Rihiya 679 C5
Zababida 1,474 C3
lama 162 C3
lhul 6,041 C4
ris 641 C3
bron 38,309 C4
na 3,713 B4
nwas 1,955 B4
ba 2,817 C3
ama 784 C3
bun 914 C3
ud 221 C3
nin 8,346 C3
nin* 13,365 C3
richo 5,312 C4
richo* 6,931 C4
na 655 C4
aras 1,364 C4
blus (Nabulus) 41,799 C3
hhalin 1,109 C4
in 1,227 C4
balan 1,970 C3
batiya 6,005 C3
ffin 2,480 C3
lqiliya 8,926 C3
bya 926 C4
fidiya 1,123 C3
mallah 12,134 C4
mmun 1,198 C4
ntis 897 C3
lfit 3,201 C3
mu 3,784 C5
uf'at 14,000 C4
uweika 2,332 C3
at Dhahr 2,104 C3
jil 1,823 C3
is 1,285 C3
mmun 2,952 C3
rqumiya 2,412 C4
bas 5,262 C3
karm 10,255 C3
karm* 15,275 C3
12,200 C4
b'ad 4,857 C3
brud 277 C4
mun 4,384 C3
ta 7,281 C5
buba 633 C2

OTHER FEATURES

Golan Heights D1
West Bank C3

JORDAN

GOVERNORATES

El Asima 1,000,000 D4
El Balqa 113,000 D4
El Karak 93,000 E5
Irbid 506,000 D3
Ma'an 62,000 D5

CITIES and TOWNS

'Ajlun⊙ 42,000 D3
Amman (cap.) 711,850 D4
'Anjara 3,163 D3
'Aqaba 15,000 D6
Bala'ma 769 E3
Baqura 3,042 D2
Damiya 483 D3
Dana 844 E5
Deir Abu Sai'd 1,927 D3
Dhira' D5
El 'Al 492 D4
El Husn 3,728 D3
El Karak 10,000 E4
El Kitta 987 D3
El Madwar 164 E3
El Mafraq 15,500 E3
El Majdal 259 D3
El Quweira 268 E5
El Yaduda 251 D4
Er Rafid 787 D2
Er Ramtha 19,000 E2
Er Rumman 293 D3
Er Ruseifa 6,200 E3
Esh Shaubak 01 D5
Es Sahab 2,580 E4
Es Salt 24,000 D3
Es Sukhna 649 E3
Et Tafila⊙ 17,000 E5
Et Taiyiba 2,606 D2
Ez Zarqa' 263,400 E3
Harima 635 D2
Hawara 2,342 D2
Hisban 718 D4
I'bbin 1,364 D3
Irbid 136,770 D2
Jabir 132 E2
Jarash⊙ 29,000 D3
Kitim 1,026 D3
Kufrinja 3,922 D3
Kuraiyima D3
Maa'd 125 D2
Maa'n 9,500 E5
Ma'daba 22,600 D4
Mai'n 1,271 D4
Manja 353 D4
Mazra' C5
Nau'r 2,382 D4
Nitil 348 D4
Qumeim 955 D2
Ra's en Naqb 225 E5
Safi E5
Safut 4,210 D3
Samar 716 D2
Sarih 3,390 D2
Shunat Nimrin 109 D4
Subeihi 514 D3
Suf D3
Suweilih 3,457 D3
Suweima 315 D4
Um Jauza 582 D3
Wadi es Sir 4,455 D4
Wadi Musa 654 E5
Waqqas 2,321 D2
Zuweiza 126 D4

OTHER FEATURES

Ajlun (range) D3
Aqaba (gulf) D6
'Araba, Wadi (valley) D5
Dead (sea) C4
Ebal (mt.) C3
El Ghor (reg.) C6
El Lisan (pen.) C5
Hasa, Wadi el (dry riv.) E5
Jordan (riv.) D3
Judaea (reg.) C4
Khirbet Qumran (site) D4
Mashash, Wadi (dry riv.) C4
Nebo (mt.) D4
Petra (ruins) D5
Ramm, Jebel (mt.) D5
Samaria (reg.) C3
Shallala, Wadi esh (dry riv.) D2
Shu'eib, Wadi (dry riv.) D4
Tell 'Asur (mt.) C4
Yabis, Wadi el (dry riv.) D3
Zarqa' (riv.) D3

*City and suburbs.
⊙Population of subdivision.

Israel and Jordan
CYLINDRICAL PROJECTION
© Copyright HAMMOND INCORPORATED, Maplewood, N. J.
SCALE OF MILES
SCALE OF KILOMETERS
Capitals of Countries
Internal Capitals
International Boundaries
Internal Boundaries
Scale 1:1,325,000
MEDITERRANEAN SEA
SYRIA
JORDAN
EGYPT
GAZA STRIP (Occupied by Israel)
DEAD SEA
Jerusalem
Tel Aviv - Jaffa
Haifa
Amman
Beersheba
Nablus (Nabulus)
Hebron (El Khalil)
Jericho
Irbid
Elat (Elath)
Aqaba
SOUTHERN
Longitude East of Greenwich

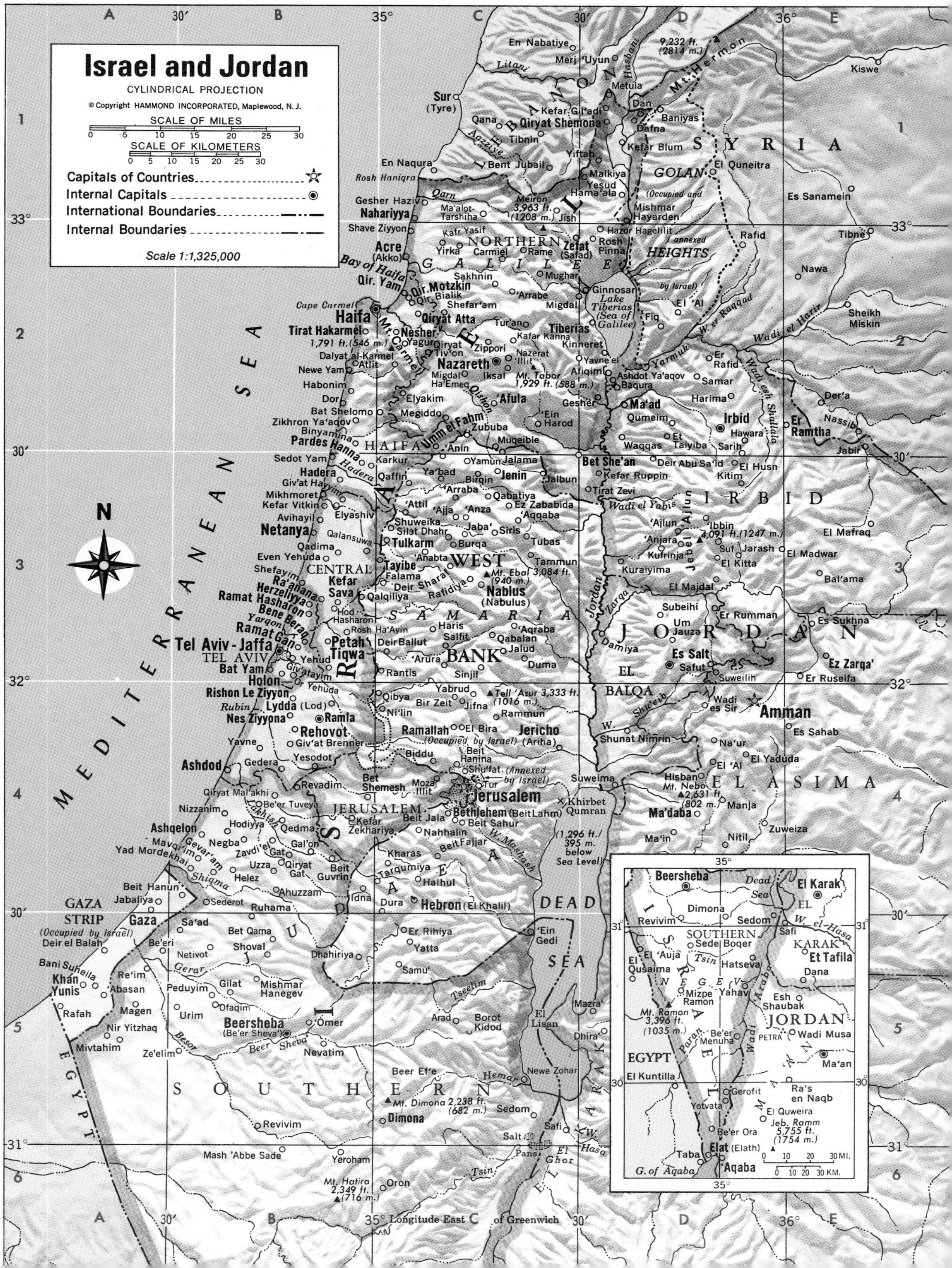

IRAN

INTERNAL DIVISIONS

Azerbaijan, East
  (prov.) 3,194,543 .... E1
Azerbaijan, West
  (prov.) 1,404,875 .... D1
Bakhtaran (prov.) 1,016,199 ..... E3
Bakhtaran
  (governorate) 394,300 .... F4
Boyer Ahmediyeh and Kohkiluyeh
  (governorate) 244,750 .... G5
Bushehr (prov.) 345,427 .... G6
Central (Markazi)
  (prov.) 6,921,283 .... G3
Esfahan (Isfahan)
  (prov.) 1,974,938 .... H4
Fars (prov.) 2,020,947 .... H6
Gilan (prov.) 1,577,800 .... F2
Hamadan (governorate) 1,086,512 . F3
Hormozgan (prov.) 463,419 .... J7
Ilam (governorate) 244,222 ...... F4
Isfahan (prov.) 1,974,938 .... H4
Kerman (prov.) 1,088,045 .... K6
Khorasan (prov.) 3,266,650 .... K3
Khuzestan (prov.) 2,176,612 ...... F5
Kordestan (Kurdistan)
  (prov.) 781,889 .... E3
Lorestan (Luristan)
  (governorate) 924,848 .... F4
Mazandaran (prov.) 2,384,226 ..... H2
Semnan (governorate) 485,875 .... J3
Sistan and Baluchestan
  (prov.) 659,297 .... M6
Yazd (governorate) 356,218 .... J5
Zanjan (governorate) 579,000 ..... F2

CITIES and TOWNS

Abadan 296,081 .... F5
Abadeh 16,000 .... H5
Abarqu 8,000 .... H5
Abhar 24,000 .... F2
Agha Jari 24,195 .... F5
Ahar 24,000 .... E1
Ahvaz (Ahwaz) 329,006 .... F5
Amol 68,782 .... H2
Anarak 2,038 .... H4
Andimeshk 16,000 .... F4
Aradan 8,978 .... H3
Arak 114,507 .... G3
Ardabil 147,404 .... F1
Ardestan 5,868 .... H3
Asadabad 7,000 .... F3
Asterabad (Gorgan) 88,348 .... J2
Babol 67,790 .... H2
Babol Sar 7,237 .... H2
Baft 6,000 .... K6
Bakhtaran 290,861 .... E3
Bam 22,000 .... L6
Bandar-e Abbas 89,103 .... J7
Bandar-e Anzali
  (Enzeli) 55,978 .... F2
Bandar-e Deylam 3,691 .... G5
Bandar-e Khomeyni 6,000 .... F5
Bandar-e Lengeh 4,920 .... J7
Bandar-e Mas hur 17,000 .... F5
Bandar-e Rig 1,889 .... G6
Bandar-e Torkeman 13,000 .... H2
Bandar Shahpur 6,000 .... F5
Bastak 2,473 .... J7
Bastam 3,296 .... J2
Behbehan 39,874 .... G5
Behshahr 26,032 .... H2

Bejestan 3,823 .... K3
Bijar 12,000 .... E3
Birjand 25,854 .... L4
Bojnurd 31,248 .... K2
Borazjan 20,000 .... G6
Borujerd 100,103 .... F4
Bostan 4,619 .... F4
Bowkan 9,000 .... E2
Bushehr (Bushire) 57,681 .... G6
Chalus 15,000 .... G2
Damavand 5,319 .... H3
Damghan 13,000 .... J2
Darab 13,000 .... J6
Daran 4,609 .... G4
Darreh Gaz 11,000 .... L2
Dasht-e Azadegan 21,000 .... F5
Dehkhwareqan 6,000 .... F3
Delijan 6,000 .... G4
Dezful 110,287 .... F4
Dizful (Dezful) 110,287 .... F4
Duzdab (Zahedan) 92,628 .... M6
Emamshahr 30,767 .... J2
Enzeli 55,978 .... F2
Esfahan (Isfahan) 671,820 .... G4
Eslamabad 12,000 .... E3
Estahabad 18,187 .... H6
Ezna 6,064 .... J7
Ezna 5,000 .... G4
Fahrej (Iranshahr) 5,000 .... M7
Fariman 8,000 .... L3
Farrashband 3,532 .... G6
Fasa 19,000 .... H6
Ferdows 11,000 .... K3
Firuzabad 8,718 .... H6
Firuzkuh 4,684 .... H3
Fowman 9,000 .... F2
Gach Saran G5

Ganaveh 9,000 .... G6
Garmsar 4,723 .... H3
Gavater M8
Ghaemshahr 63,289 .... H2
Golpayegan 20,515 .... G4
Golshan (Tabas) 10,000 .... K4
Gomishan 6,000 .... J2
Gonabad 8,000 .... L3
Gonbad-e Kavus 59,868 .... J2
Gonbadli 531 .... M2
Gorgan (Gurgan) 88,348 .... J2
Haft Gel 10,000 .... F5
Hamadan 155,846 .... F3
Hashtpar 5,000 .... F2
Hormoz 2,569 .... J7
Huzgan 4,032 .... F4
Ilam 15,000 .... E4
Iranshahr 5,000 .... M7
Isfahan 671,825 .... G4
Jahrom 38,236 .... H6
Jajarm 3,641 .... J2
Jask 1,078 .... K8
Kakhk 4,000 .... L3
Kangan 2,682 .... G7
Kangavar 9,414 .... F3
Karaj 138,774 .... G3
Kashan 84,545 .... G3
Kashmar 17,000 .... L3
Kazerun 51,309 .... H6
Kazvin (Qazvin) 138,527 .... F2
Kerman 140,309 .... K5
Khaf 5,000 .... L3
Khalkhal 5,422 .... F2
Khash 7,439 .... M6
Khiyav 9,000 .... E1
Khoman 3,054 .... F2
Khomeinishar 46,836 .... G4

Khorramabad 104,928 .... F4
Khorramshahr 146,709 .... F5
Khvonsar 10,947 .... G4
Khvor 2,912 .... J4
Khvoy (Khoi) 70,040 .... D1
Kord Kuy 9,855 .... J2
Lahijan 25,725 .... G2
Lar 22,000 .... J7
Mahabad 28,610 .... D2
Mahallat 12,000 .... G4
Mahan 8,000 .... K5
Mako 7,000 .... D1
Malamir (Izeh) 1,983 .... F5
Malayer 28,434 .... F3
Maragheh 60,820 .... D1
Marand 24,000 .... D1
Marv Dasht 25,498 .... H6
Mashhad (Meshed) 670,180 .... L2
Masjed Soleyman 77,161 .... F5
Medishahr 9,000 .... H3
Mehran 664 .... E4
Meshed 670,180 .... L2
Meshed-i-Sar (Babol
  Sar) 12,000 .... H2
Meybod 15,000 .... J4
Miandowab 19,000 .... E2
Mianeh 28,447 .... E2
Minab 4,240 .... K7
Mirjaveh 11,000 .... M5
Naft-e Shah 3,043 .... F4
Nahavand 24,000 .... F3
Nain 5,925 .... H4
Najafabad 76,236 .... G4
Naqab 4,012 .... N7
Naraq 2,725 .... G4
Natanz 4,370 .... H4
Neyriz 16,114 .... J6
Neyshabur 59,101 .... L2

Nishapur (Neyshabur) 59,101 ...... L2
Nosratabad 20,000 .... L6
Now Shahr 8,000 .... G2
Orumiyeh (Urmia) 163,991 .... D2
Oshnoviyeh 5,000 .... D2
Pahlevi (Enzeli) 55,978 .... F2
Pazanan 81 .... F5
Qayen 6,000 .... L4
Qasr-e-Shirin 15,094 .... E3
Qazvin 138,527 .... F2
Qom 246,831 .... G3
Qorveh 2,929 .... E3
Quchan 29,133 .... L2
Qum (Qom) 246,831 .... G3
Rafsanjan 21,000 .... K5
Ramhormoz 9,000 .... F5
Rasht 187,203 .... F2
Ravar 5,074 .... K5
Resht (Rasht) 187,203 .... F2
Reza'iyeh (Urmia) 163,991 .... D2
Rigan 8,255 .... L6
Rud Sar 7,460 .... G2
Sabzevar 69,174 .... L2
Saeendey 4,195 .... E2
Sai'dabad 20,000 .... J6
Sakht-Sar 12,000 .... D1
Salmas 13,161 .... D1
Sanandaj 95,834 .... E3
Saqqez 17,000 .... E3
Saravan 4,012 .... N7
Sar Dasht 6,000 .... D2
Sari 70,936 .... H2
Sarakhs 3,461 .... M2
Saravan 4,012 .... N7
Sari 70,936 .... H2
Savanat (Estahabanat) 18,187 ..... J6
Saveh 17,565 .... G3
Semnan 31,058 .... H3

Shadegan 6,000 .... F5
Shahdad 2,777 .... K5
Shahistan (Saravan) 4,012 .... N7
Shahreza 34,220 .... G4
Shahr Kord 24,000 .... G4
Shahrud (Emamshahr) 30,767 .... J2
Sharafkhaneh 1,260 .... D1
Shiraz 416,408 .... H6
Shirvan 11,000 .... L2
Shush 1,433 .... F4
Shushtar 24,000 .... F4
Sinneh (Sanandaj) 95,834 .... E3
Sirjan (Sai'dabad) 20,000 .... J6
Sivand 1,811 .... H6
Sofian 2,914 .... D1
Sultanabad (Kashmar) 17,000 ...... L3
Tabas 10,000 .... K4
Tabriz 598,576 .... D2
Taft 7,000 .... J5
Tajrish 157,486 .... G3
Takestan 13,485 .... F2
Tehran (cap.) 4,496,159 .... G3
Tonekabon 12,000 .... G2
Torbat-e-Heydariyeh 30,106 .... L3
Torbat-e-Jam 13,000 .... M3
Tun (Ferdows) 11,000 .... K3
Turbat-i-Shaikh Jam 13,000 .... M3
Tuysarkan 12,000 .... F3
Urmia 163,991 .... D2
Varamin 11,183 .... G3
Yazd (Yezd) 135,978 .... J5
Yazd-e-Khvast 3,544 .... H5
Zabol 16,000 .... M5
Zahedan 92,628 .... M6
Zanjan 99,967 .... F2
Zarand 11,000 .... K5
Zarand 7,000 .... H6
Zarqam 7,000 .... H6
Zenjan (Zanjan) 99,967 .... F2

Iran and Iraq

CONIC PROJECTION

SCALE OF MILES
0 25 50 100 200

SCALE OF KILOMETERS
0 25 50 100 150 200

Capitals of Countries .... ★
Capitals of Provinces .... △
Capitals of Governorates .... ◉
International Boundaries .... ——
Provincial Boundaries .... —·—
Governorate Boundaries .... ·····

Scale 1:8,160,000

© Copyright HAMMOND INCORPORATED, Maplewood, N.J.

Iran consists of fifteen provinces
called ostans. Attached to seven of
these provinces are eight governorates.

IRAN

IRAQ

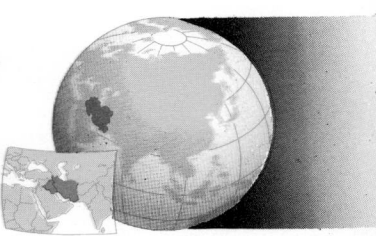

AREA 636,293 sq. mi. (1,648,000 sq. km.)
POPULATION 37,447,000
CAPITAL Tehran
LARGEST CITY Tehran
HIGHEST POINT Damavand 18,376 ft. (5,601 m.)
MONETARY UNIT Iranian rial
MAJOR LANGUAGES Persian, Azerbaijani, Kurdish
MAJOR RELIGION Islam

AREA 172,476 sq. mi. (446,713 sq. km.)
POPULATION 12,767,000
CAPITAL Baghdad
LARGEST CITY Baghdad
HIGHEST POINT Haji Ibrahim 11,811 ft. (3,600 m.)
MONETARY UNIT Iraqi dinar
MAJOR LANGUAGES Arabic, Kurdish
MAJOR RELIGION Islam

Topography

0   200   400 MI.
0   200   400 KM.

5,000 m. 2,000 m. 1,000 m. 500 m. 200 m. 100 m. Sea Below
16,404 ft. 6,562 ft. 3,281 ft. 1,640 ft. 656 ft. 328 ft. Level

Agriculture, Industry and Resources

DOMINANT LAND USE

Cereals, Livestock
Cash Crops, Horticulture, Livestock
Pasture Livestock
Nomadic Livestock Herding
Forests
Nonagricultural Land

MAJOR MINERAL OCCURRENCES

C	Coal
Cr	Chromium
Cu	Copper
Fe	Iron Ore
G	Natural Gas
Mn	Manganese
Na	Salt
O	Petroleum
Pb	Lead
S	Sulfur, Pyrites
Zn	Zinc

Water Power
Major Industrial Areas

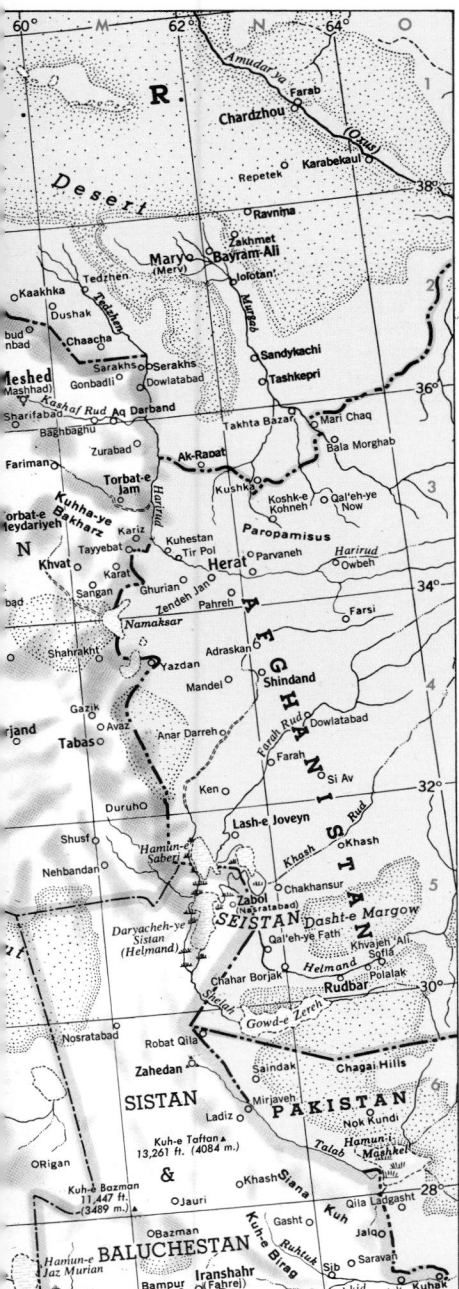

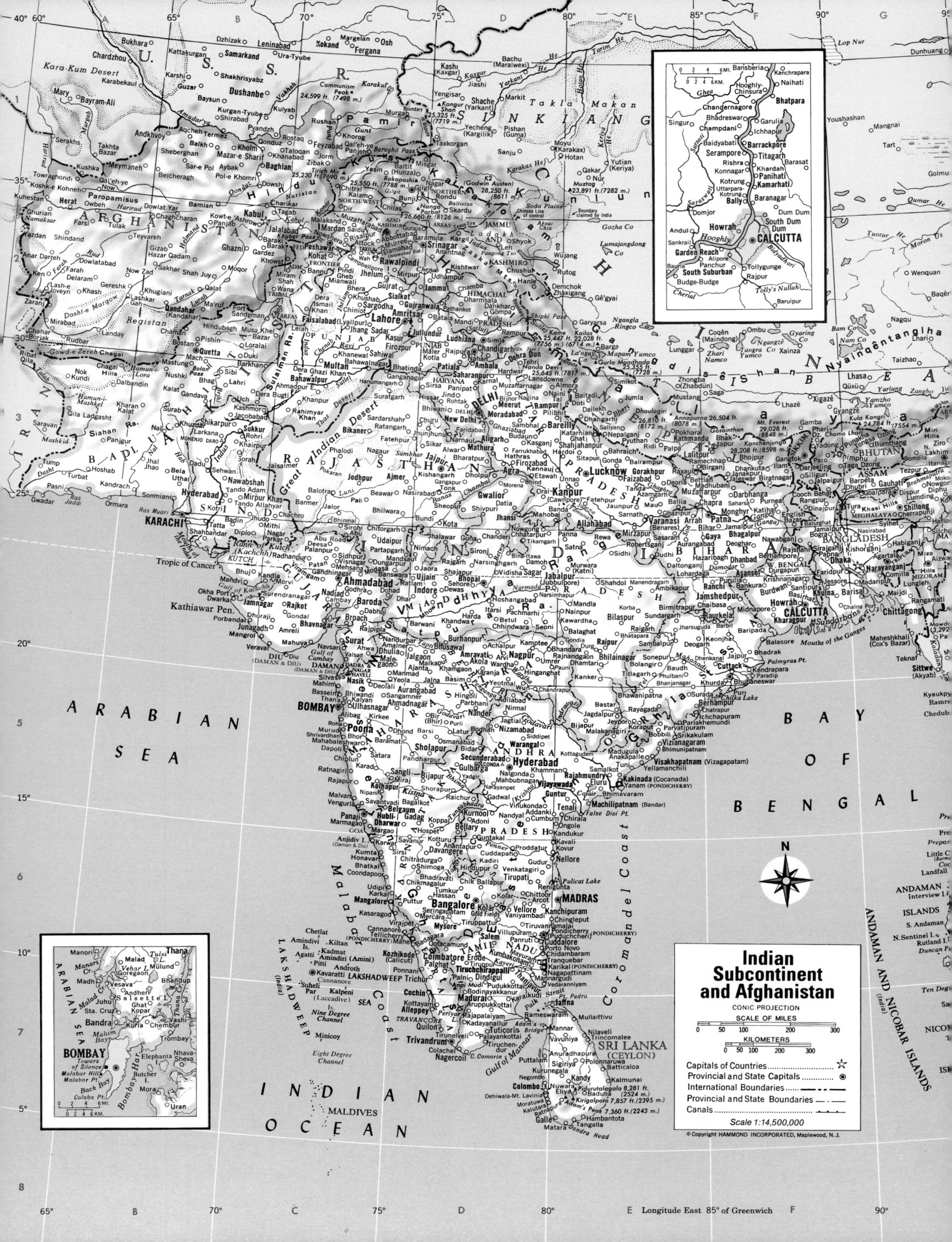

Indian Subcontinent and Afghanistan

CONIC PROJECTION

SCALE OF MILES

0   100   200   300

KILOMETERS

0   100   200   300

Capitals of Countries ....☆
Provincial and State Capitals ....⊙
International Boundaries ....– – – – – –
Provincial and State Boundaries .....– – – – –
Canals ....

Scale 1:14,500,000

© Copyright HAMMOND INCORPORATED, Maplewood, N.J.

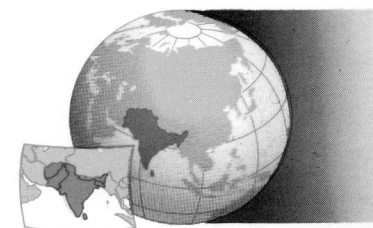

INDIA

AREA   1,269,339 sq. mi. (3,287,588 sq. km.)
POPULATION   683,810,051
CAPITAL   New Delhi
LARGEST CITY   Calcutta (greater)
HIGHEST POINT   Nanda Devi 25,645 ft. (7,817 m.)
MONETARY UNIT   Indian rupee
MAJOR LANGUAGES   Hindi, English, Bengali,
   Telugu, Marathi, Tamil, Urdu, Gujarati,
   Malayalam, Kannada, Oriya, Punjabi,
   Assamese, Kashmiri, Sindhi
MAJOR RELIGIONS   Hinduism, Islam, Christianity,
   Sikhism, Buddhism, Jainism, Zoroastrianism, Animism

PAKISTAN

AREA   310,403 sq. mi. (803,944 sq. km.)
POPULATION   83,782,000
CAPITAL   Islamabad
LARGEST CITY   Karachi
HIGHEST POINT   K2 (Godwin Austen)
   28,250 ft. (8,611 m.)
MONETARY UNIT   Pakistani rupee
MAJOR LANGUAGES   Urdu, English, Punjabi,
   Pushtu, Sindhi, Baluchi, Brahui
MAJOR RELIGIONS   Islam, Hinduism, Sikhism,
   Christianity, Buddhism

SRI LANKA (CEYLON)

AREA   25,332 sq. mi.
   (65,610 sq. km.)
POPULATION   14,850,001
CAPITAL   Colombo
LARGEST CITY   Colombo
HIGHEST POINT   Pidurutalagala
   8,281 ft. (2,524 m.)
MONETARY UNIT   Sri Lanka rupee
MAJOR LANGUAGES   Sinhala, Tamil,
   English
MAJOR RELIGIONS   Buddhism,
   Hinduism, Christianity, Islam

AFGHANISTAN

AREA   250,775 sq. mi.
   (649,507 sq. km.)
POPULATION   15,540,000
CAPITAL   Kabul
LARGEST CITY   Kabul
HIGHEST POINT   Nowshak
   24,557 ft. (7,485 m.)
MONETARY UNIT   afghani
MAJOR LANGUAGES   Pushtu, Dari,
   Uzbek
MAJOR RELIGION   Islam

NEPAL

AREA   54,663 sq. mi.
   (141,577 sq. km.)
POPULATION   14,179,301
CAPITAL   Kathmandu
LARGEST CITY   Kathmandu
HIGHEST POINT   Mt. Everest
   29,028 ft. (8,848 m.)
MONETARY UNIT   Nepalese rupee
MAJOR LANGUAGES   Nepali,
   Maithili, Tamang, Newari, Tharu
MAJOR RELIGIONS   Hinduism,
   Buddhism

MALDIVES

AREA   115 sq. mi. (298 sq. km.)
POPULATION   143,046
CAPITAL   Male
LARGEST CITY   Male
HIGHEST POINT   20 ft. (6 m.)
MONETARY UNIT   Maldivian rufiyaa
MAJOR LANGUAGE   Divehi
MAJOR RELIGION   Islam

BHUTAN

AREA   18,147 sq. mi.
   (47,000 sq. km.)
POPULATION   1,298,000
CAPITAL   Thimphu
LARGEST CITY   Thimphu
HIGHEST POINT   Kula Kangri
   24,784 ft. (7,554 m.)
MONETARY UNIT   ngultrum
MAJOR LANGUAGES   Dzongka,
   Nepali
MAJOR RELIGIONS   Buddhism,
   Hinduism

BANGLADESH

AREA   55,126 sq. mi.
   (142,776 sq. km.)
POPULATION   87,052,024
CAPITAL   Dhaka
LARGEST CITY   Dhaka
HIGHEST POINT   Keokradong
   4,034 ft. (1,230 m.)
MONETARY UNIT   taka
MAJOR LANGUAGES   Bengali,
   English
MAJOR RELIGIONS   Islam,
   Hinduism Christianity

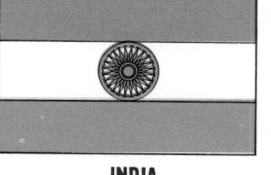
INDIA

PAKISTAN

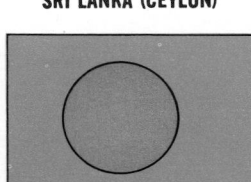
SRI LANKA (CEYLON)

BHUTAN

AFGHANISTAN

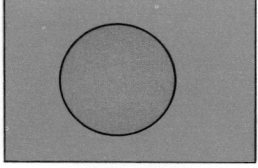
MALDIVES

BANGLADESH

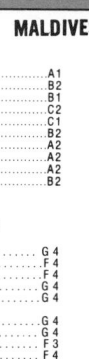
NEPAL

AFGHANISTAN

CITIES and TOWNS

Andkhvoy	A1
Aqcheh	B1
Aybak 33,016	B1
Baghlan 75,130	B1
Balkh	B1
Bamian 7,355	B2
Belcheragh	B1
Chaghcharan 2,974	B2
Chahar Borjak	A2
Charikar 25,093	B1
Delaram	A2
Dowlatabad	A2
Dowlat Yar	A2
Dowshi	B1
Farah 18,797	A2
Farsi	A2
Feyzabad 10,142	C1
Gardez 11,415	B2
Gereshk	A2
Ghazni 30,425	B2
Ghurian	A2
Gizab	B2
Hazar Qadam	B2
Herat 163,960	A2
Jalalabad 56,384	B2
Jorm	C1
Kabul (cap.) 905,108	B2
Kalat (Qalat) 5,946	B2
Kandahar (Qandahar) 178,409	B2
Ken	A2
Khanabad	B1
Khash	A2
Kholm	B1
Khowst	B2
Khugiani	B2
Koshke-e Kohneh	A2
Kowt-e 'Ashrow	B2
Kuhestan	A2
Landay	A2
Lash-e Joveyn	A2
Lashkar Gah 26,646	A2
Mar'uf	B2
Mazar-e Sharif 122,567	B1
Meymaneh 54,954	A1
Mirabad	A2
Moqor	A2
Now Zad	A2
Oruzgan (Hazar Qadam)	B2
Owbeh	A2
Panjab	B2
Pol-e Khomri	B1
Qalat 5,946	B2
Qale'h-ye Now 5,340	A1
Qale'h-ye Panjeh	C1
Qandahar 178,409	B2
Qonduz 107,191	B1
Rostaq	B1
Rudbar	A2
Sakhar	B2
Sar-e Pol	B1
Shay Juy	B2
Sheberghan 54,870	A2
Shindand	A2
Spin Buldak	B2
Tagab	B2
Taloqan 46,202	B1
Teyvareh	A2
Towraghondi	A1
Tulak	A2
Zaranj 6,477	A2
Zibak	C1

OTHER FEATURES

Farah Rud (riv.)	A2
Harirud (riv.)	A1
Helmand (riv.)	B2
Hindu Kush (mts.)	B1
Kabul (riv.)	C2
Konar (riv.)	C1
Lurah (riv.)	B2
Margow, Dasht-e (des.)	A2
Namaksar (salt lake)	A2
Paropamisus (range)	A2
Tarnak (riv.)	B2

BANGLADESH

CITIES and TOWNS

Barisal 98,127	G 4
Bogra 47,154	F 4
Chalna Port 14,590	G 4
Chittagong 889,760	G 4
Comilla 86,446	G 4
Cox's Bazar (Maheshkhali) 15,720	G 4
Dhaka (cap.) 1,679,572	G 4
Dinajpur 61,866	F 3
Faridpur 46,232	F 4
Habiganj 16,281	G 4
Jamalpur 60,261	F 4
Jessore 76,168	F 4
Khulna 437,304	F 4
Kishorganj 35,605	G 4
Madaripur 32,488	G 4
Maheshkhali 15,720	G 4
Mymensingh (Nasirabad) 182,153	G 4
Narayanganj 270,680	G 4
Nasiabad 182,153	G 4
Nawabganj 46,059	F 4
Noakhali 32,490	G 4
Pabna 62,254	F 4
Rajshahi 132,909	F 4
Rangmati 20,473	G 4
Rangpur 72,829	F 3
Sirajganj 74,457	G 4
Sylhet 59,546	G 4
Teknaf	F 4

OTHER FEATURES

Bengal, Bay of (sea)	F 5
Brahmaputra (riv.)	G 3
Ganges (riv.)	F 3
Sundarbans (reg.)	F 4

BHUTAN

CITIES and TOWNS

Bumthang 10,000	G3
Paro 35,000	F3
Punakha 12,000	G3
Taga Dzong 18,000	G3
Thimphu (cap.) 50,000	G3
Tongsa Dzong 2,500	G3

OTHER FEATURES

Chomo Lhari (mt.)	F3
Himalaya (mts.)	E2
Kula Kangri (mt.)	G3

INDIA

INTERNAL DIVISIONS

Andaman and Nicobar Isls. (terr.) 188,254	G 6
Andhra Pradesh (state) 53,403,619	D 5
Arunachal Pradesh (state) 628,050	G 3

(continued on following page)

Topography

0   200   400 MI.

0   200   400 KM.

Assam (state) 19,902,826 G 3
Bihar (state) 69,823,154 F 4
Chandigarh (terr.) 450,061 D 2
Dadra and Nagar Haveli
(terr.) 103,677 C 4
Daman and Diu (state) C 4
Delhi (terr.) 6,196,414 D 3
Goa (state) C 4
Gujarat (state) 33,960,905 C 4
Haryana (state) 12,850,902 D 3
Himachal Pradesh
(state) 4,237,569 D 2
Jammu and Kashmir
(state) 5,981,600 D 2
Karnataka (state) 37,043,451 D 6
Kerala (state) 25,403,217 D 6
Lakshadweep (terr.) 40,237 C 6
Madhya Pradesh
(state) 52,131,717 D 4
Maharashtra (state) 62,693,898 C 5
Manipur (state) 1,433,691 G 4
Meghalaya (state) 1,327,874 G 3
Mizoram (state) 487,774 G 4
Nagaland (state) 773,281 G 3
Orissa (state) 26,272,054 E 5
Pondicherry (terr.) 604,136 E 6
Punjab (state) 16,669,755 D 2
Rajasthan (state) 34,102,912 C 3
S.kkim (state) 315,682 F 3
Tamil Nadu (state) 48,297,456 D 6
Tripura (state) 2,060,189 G 4
Uttar Pradesh
(state) 110,858,019 D 3
West Bengal (state) 54,485,560 F 4

CITIES and TOWNS

Abu 9,840 C4
Abu Road 25,331 C4
Achalpur 42,326 D4
Addanki 10,223 D5
Adilabad 30,368 D5
Adoni 85,311 D5
Agartala 59,625 G4
Agartala□ 100,264 G4
Agra 591,917 D3
Agra□ 634,622 D3
Ahmadabad 1,591,832 C4
Ahmadabad□ 1,741,522 C4
Ahmadnagar 118,236 C5
Ahmadnagar□ 148,405 C5
Aizwal 31,740 G4
Ajanta D4
Ajmer 262,851 C3
Akola 168,438 D4
Alibag 11,913 C5
Aligarh 252,314 D3
Alipore F2
Allahabad 490,622 E3
Allahabad□ 513,036 E3
Alleppey-Cochin 160,166 D7
Almora 19,671 D3
Along 3,524 G3
Alwar 100,378 D3
Amalner 55,544 C4
Ambala 83,633 D2
Ambala□ 186,168 D2
Ambikapur 23,087 E4
Amravati 193,800 D4
Amreli 39,520 C4
Amritsar 407,628 C2
Amritsar□ 458,029 C2
Anakapalle 57,273 E5
Anantapur 80,069 D6
Anantnag 27,643 D2
Andheri B7
Andul 3,602 F2
Arcot 30,230 D6
Arrah 92,919 E3
Aruppukkottai 62,223 D7
Arvi 26,494 D4
Asansol 155,968 F4
Asansol□ 241,792 F4
Aurangabad, Bihar 18,714 E4
Aurangabad,
Maharashtra 150,483 D5
Aurangabad□ 165,253 D5
Azamgarh 40,963 E3
Badagara 53,938 D6
Bagalkot 51,746 D5
Bahraich 73,931 E3
Baidyabati 54,130 F1
Balaghat 27,872 E4
Balasore 46,239 F4
Ballia 47,101 E3
Bally 38,892 F1
Balotra 17,595 C3
Balrampur 36,191 E3
Balurghat 67,088 F3
Banda 50,575 D3
Bandar (Machilipatnam) 112,612 E5
Bandra B7
Bangalore 1,540,741 D6
Bangalore□ 1,653,779 D6
Bankura 79,129 F4
Bansberia 61,748 F1
Banswara 27,363 C4
Baramati 27,912 C5
Baramula 26,334 C2
Baranagar 136,842 F1
Barasat 42,642 F1
Barbil 24,342 F4
Bareilly 296,248 D3
Bareilly□ 326,106 D3
Baripada 28,725 F4
Barmer 38,630 C3
Baroda (Vadodara) 466,696 C4
Barpeta 26,479 G3
Barrackpore 96,889 F1
Barrackpore□ 198,255 F1
Barsi 62,374 D5
Baruipur 20,501 F2
Barwani 22,099 D4
Basim 32,496 D4
Basirhat 63,816 F4
Bassein 30,594 C5
Bastar E5
Batala 58,200 D2
Baudh 8,891 E4
Bauria 10,610 E2
Beawar 66,114 C3
Belgaum 192,427 C5
Belgaum□ 213,872 C5
Bellary 125,183 D5
Benares (Varanasi) 583,856 E3
Berhampore 72,605 F4
Berhampur 117,662 F5
Bettiah 51,018 E3
Betul 30,862 D4
Bhadrak 40,487 F4
Bhadravati 40,203 D6
Bhadravati□ 101,358 D6
Bhadreswar 45,586 F1
Bhagalpur 172,202 F4
Bhandara 39,423 E4
Bhandup B7
Bhanjanagar 12,353 E4
Bharatpur 68,036 D3
Bharuch 91,589 C4
Bhatapara 20,980 E4
Bhatinda 53,684 C2
Bhatkal 18,732 C6
Bhatpara 204,750 F1
Bhavnagar 225,358 C4
Bhavnagar□ 225,974 C4
Bhawanipatna 22,808 E5
Bhilai 157,173 E4
Bhilwara 82,155 C3
Bhimavaram 63,762 E5
Bhimunipatnam 14,291 E5
Bhind 42,371 D3
Bhinmal 14,050 C3
Bhir (Bir) 49,965 D5
Bhiwandi 79,576 C5
Bhiwani 73,086 D3
Bhopal 298,022 D4
Bhor 10,708 C5
Bhubaneswar 105,491 F4
Bhuj 52,177 B4
Bhusawal 96,800 D4
Bhusawal□ 104,708 D4
Bidar 50,670 D5
Bihar 100,046 F3
Bijapur, Karnataka 103,931 D5
Bijapur, Madhya Pradesh 5,289 E5
Bijnor 43,290 D3
Bikaner 188,518 C3
Bikaner□ 208,894 C3
Bilaspur 98,410 E4
Bina-Itawa 33,106 D4
Bir 49,965 D5
Birmitrapur 28,063 E4
Bobbili 30,649 E5
Bodhan 37,589 D5
Bodinayakkanur 54,176 D6
Bolangir 35,748 E4
Bombay (Greater)* 5,970,575 B7
Bomdila 2,264 G3
Broach (Bharuch) 91,589 C4
Budaun 72,204 D3
Budge-Budge 51,039 F2
Bundi 34,279 D3
Burdwan 143,318 F4
Burhanpur 105,246 D4
Calcutta 3,148,746 F2
Calcutta□ 7,031,382 F2
Calicut (Kozhikode) 333,979 D6
Cambay 62,097 C4
Cannanore 55,162 C6
Cawnpore (Kanpur) 1,154,388 E3
Chaibasa 35,386 F4
Chamba 11,814 D2
Champdani 58,596 F1
Chanderi 10,294 D4
Chandernagore 75,238 F1
Chandigarh 218,743 D2
Chandigarh□ 232,940 D2
Chandrapur 75,134 D5
Chapra 83,101 F3
Chatrapur 10,835 F5
Chembur B7
Cherrapunji⊙ 83,987 G3
Chhatarpur 32,271 D4
Chhindwara 53,492 D4
Chidambaram 48,811 E6
Chik Ballapur 29,227 D6
Chikmagalur 41,639 D6
Chingleput 38,419 E6
Chiplun 20,942 C5
Chirala 54,487 E5
Chitorgarh 25,917 C4
Chitradurga 50,254 D6
Chittoor 63,035 D6
Churachandpur 8,706 G4
Churu 52,502 D3
Chushul D2
Cocanada (Kakinada) 164,200 E5
Cochin-Alleppey 439,066 D6
Coimbatore 356,368 D6
Coimbatore□ 736,203 D6
Colachel 18,819 D7
Cooch Behar 53,684 F3
Coondapoor 23,831 C6
Cuddalore 101,335 E6
Cuddapah 66,195 D6
Cumbum 9,745 D5
Cuttack 194,068 F4
Cuttack□ 205,759 F4
Dabhoi 37,892 C4
Daltonganj 32,367 E4
Damoh 59,489 D4
Dapoli 6,296 C5
Darbhanga 132,059 F3
Darjeeling 42,873 F3
Datia 36,439 D3
Davangere 121,110 D6
Deesa 28,324 C4
Dehra Dun 166,073 D2
Dehra Dun□ 203,464 D2
Delhi 3,287,883 D3
Delhi□ 3,647,023 D3
Demchok D2
Deogarh, Orissa 8,906 E4
Deoghar, Bihar 40,356 F4
Deolali 55,436 C5
Deoria 38,161 E3
Dewas 51,545 D4
Dhamtari 34,546 E4
Dhanbad 79,838 F4
Dhanbad□ 434,031 F4
Dhar 36,172 C4
Dharmsala 10,939 D2
Dharwar-Hubli 379,166 C5
Dhenkanal 19,615 E4
Dholpur 31,865 D3
Dhond 16,583 C5
Dhoraji 59,773 C4
Dhubri 36,503 G3
Dhulia 137,129 C4
Dibrugarh 80,348 G3
Digboi 16,538 H3
Dindigul 128,429 D6
Diphu 10,200 G3
Dispur 1,725 G3
Diu 6,214 C4
Dohad 44,506 C4
Domjor 10,896 F1
Dudhi 5,084 E4
Dum Dum 31,363 F1
Dum Dum□ 273,812 F1
Dungarpur 19,773 C4
Durg 67,892 E4
Durgapur 206,638 F4
Dwarka 17,801 B4
Eluru 127,023 E5
English Bazar 61,335 F3
Erode 105,111 D6
Etawah 85,894 D3
Faizabad-cum-Ayodhya 102,835 E3
Faridabad 85,762 D3
Farrukhabad-cum-Fatehgarh 102,768 D3
Farrukhabad-cum-Fatehgarh□ 110,835 D3
Fatehpur, Rajasthan 34,929 C3
Fatehpur, Uttar Pradesh 54,665 E3
Firozabad 133,863 D3
Firozpur 49,545 C2
Gadag-Betgeri 95,426 D5
Gadwal 21,828 D5
Gandhinagar 24,055 C4
Ganganagar 90,042 C3
Gangapur 27,453 D3
Gangtok 12,000 F3
Garden Reach 154,913 F2
Garulia 44,271 F1
Gauhati 123,783 G3
Gauhati□ 200,377 G3
Gaya 179,884 F4
Ghat Kopar 34,256 B7
Ghaziabad 118,836 D3
Ghaziabad□ 127,700 D3
Ghazipur 45,635 E3
Goalpara 16,703 G3
Godhra 66,403 C4
Gonda 52,662 E3
Gondal 54,928 C4
Gondia 77,992 E4
Gorakhpur 230,911 E3
Goregaon B7
Gudur 33,778 D6
Gulbarga 145,588 D5
Guna 40,006 D4
Guntakal 66,320 D5
Guntur 269,991 D5
Gurais D2
Gwalior 384,772 D3
Gwalior□ 406,140 D3
Haflong 5,197 G3
Hanle D2
Hanumangarh 30,017 C3
Harda 28,504 D4
Hardoi 46,639 E3
Hardwar 77,864 D2
Hassan 51,325 D6
Hathras 74,349 D3
Hazaribagh 54,818 F4
Hindupur 42,959 D6
Hinganghat 44,349 D4
Hingoli 31,948 D5
Hissar 89,437 D3
Honavar 12,444 C6
Hooghly-Chinsura 105,241 F1
Hoshangabad 27,011 D4
Hospet 65,196 D5
Howrah 737,877 F2
Hubli-Dharwar 379,166 C5
Hyderabad 1,607,396 D5
Hyderabad□ 1,796,339 D5
Ichchapuram 15,850 F5
Ichhapur 11,975 F1
Imphal 100,366 G4
Indore 543,381 D4
Indore□ 560,936 D4
Itanagar⊙ 18,787 G3
Itarsi 44,191 D4
Jabalpur 426,224 D4
Jabalpur□ 534,845 D4
Jagdalpur 31,344 E5
Jagtial 30,900 D5
Jaipur 615,258 D3
Jaipur□ 636,768 D3
Jaisalmer 16,578 C3
Jajpur 16,707 F4
Jalgaon 106,711 D4
Jalna 91,099 D4
Jalor 15,478 C3
Jalpaiguri 55,159 F3
Jamalpur 61,731 F3
Jammu 155,338 D2
Jammu□ 164,207 D2
Jamnagar 214,816 B4
Jamnagar□ 227,640 B4
Jamshedpur 341,576 F4
Jamshedpur□ 456,146 F4
Jaora 37,235 D4
Jaunpur 80,737 E3
Jeypore 34,319 E5
Jhalawar 20,035 D4
Jhansi 173,292 D3
Jhansi□ 198,135 D3
Jharsuguda 24,727 E4
Jhunjhunu 32,024 D3
Jind 38,161 D3
Jodhpur 317,612 C3
Jorhat 30,247 G3
Jubbulpore (Jabalpur) 426,224 D4
Juhu B7
Jullundur 296,106 D2
Jullundur□ 329,830 D2
Junagadh 95,485 B4
Kadayanallur 50,295 D7
Kadiri 33,810 D6
Kakinada 164,200 E5
Kalyan 99,547 C5
Kamarhati 169,404 F1
Kamptee 53,412 D4
Kanchipuram 110,657 E6
Kanchrapara 78,768 F1
Kandla 17,995 C4
Kandukur 16,654 E5
Kanker 9,278 E4
Kannauj 28,187 D3
Kanpur 1,154,388 E3
Kanpur□ 1,275,242 E3
Karad 42,329 C5
Karaikudi 55,449 D7
Karanja 31,150 D4
Kargil 2,390 D2
Karikal 26,080 E6
Karkal 18,593 C6
Karnal 92,784 D3
Karwar 27,770 C6
Kasaragod 34,984 C6
Kasganj 46,467 D3
Katarnian Ghat E3
Katihar 67,014 F3
Katni (Murwara) 54,864 E4
Kavali 29,616 E6
Kavaratti 4,420 C6
Kawardha 11,226 E4
Kendrapara 20,079 F4
Keonjhar 19,340 F4
Khamgaon 53,692 D4
Khamman 56,919 D5
Khandwa 84,517 D4
Kharagpur 61,783 F4
Khardah 32,302 F1
Khurda 15,879 F4
Kirkee 65,497 C5
Kishangarh 37,405 D3
Kishtwar 5,276 D2
Kohima 21,545 G3
Kolar 43,418 D6
Kolar Gold Fields 76,112 D6
Kolhapur 259,050 C5
Konnagar 34,424 F1
Koppal 27,277 D5
Koraput 21,505 E5
Korba 30,963 E4
Kota 212,991 D3
Kottaguden 75,542 E5
Kottayam 59,714 D7
Kotturu 12,873 D6
Kovur 16,846 E6
Kozhikode 333,979 D6
Krishnanagar 85,923 F4
Kulu 8,958 D2
Kumbakonam 113,130 D6
Kumta 19,112 C6
Kurla B7
Kurnool 136,710 D5
Laful⊙ 8,161 G7
Lansdowne 6,670 D3
Latur 70,156 D5
Leh 5,519 D2
Lohardaga 17,087 E4
Lucknow 749,239 E3
Lucknow□ 813,982 E3
Ludhiana 397,850 D2
Ludhiana□ 401,176 D2
Lumding 29,253 G3
Lungleh 6,019 G4
Machilipatnam 112,612 E5
Madh B7
Madhubani 32,919 F3
Madras 2,469,449 E6
Madras□ 3,169,930 E6
Madugula 8,376 E5
Madurai 549,114 D7
Madurai□ 711,501 D7
Mahabaleshwar 7,318 C5
Mahbubnagar 51,756 D5
Mahe 8,972 D6
Mahim 11,344 C5
Mahoba 29,707 D3
Mahuva 39,497
Malad
Malakanagiri 7,494
Malegaon 191,847
Maler Kotla 48,536
Malkapur 35,476
Malvan 17,579
Mandi 16,849
Mandla 24,406
Mandsaur 52,347
Mandvi 27,849
Manendragarh 11,936
Mangalore 165,174
Mangrol 27,183
Manmad 29,571
Mannargudi 42,783
Manori
Margao 41,655
Marmagao 44,065
Mathura 132,028
Mau 64,058
Mayuram 60,195
Meerut 270,993
Mehsana 51,598
Mercara 19,357
Mhow 59,037
Midnapore 71,326
Miraj 77,606
Mirzapur-cum-Vindhyachal 105,939
Modasa 22,483
Mokokchung 17,423
Monghyr 102,474
Mora
Moradabad 258,590
Morena 44,901
Morvi 60,976
Mulund
Murud 11,210
Murwara 54,864
Muzaffarnagar 114,783
Muzaffarpur 126,379
Mysore 355,685
Nadiad 108,269
Nagapattinam 68,026
Nagaur 36,448
Nagercoil 141,288
Nagina 37,066
Nagpur 866,076
Nagpur□ 930,459
Nahan 16,017
Naihati 82,080
Naini Tal 23,986
Nainpur 14,683
Nalgonda 33,126
Nander 126,538
Nandurbar 54,070
Nandyal 63,193
Narayanpet 21,744
Narnaul 31,875
Narsimhapur 25,552
Narsinghgarh 13,814
Nasik 176,091
Nasirabad 25,732
Navsari 72,979
Nellore 133,590
New Delhi (cap.) 301,801
Nhava-Sheva
Nimach 47,113
Nipani 35,116
Nirmal 28,529
Nizamabad 115,640
North Lakhimpur 20,094
Nova Goa (Panaji) 34,953
Nowgong, Assam 56,537
Nowgong, Madhya Pradesh 10,248
Okha Port 10,687
Ongole 53,330
Ootacamund 63,310
Orai 42,513
Osmanabad 27,279
Pachmarhi 1,212
Palanpur 42,114
Palayankottai 70,070
Palghat 95,788
Pali 49,834
Palni 49,575
Panaji 34,953
Panchur 59,021
Pandharpur 53,638
Panihati 148,046
Panipat 87,981
Panna 22,316
Panruti 34,065
Paradip
Parbhani 61,570
Parlakhemundi 26,917
Partapgarh 17,402
Parvatipuram 30,025
Pasighat 5,116
Patan 64,519
Pathankot 76,355
Patiala 148,686
Patiala□
Patna 473,001
Patna□
Pauni 17,781
Phalodi 17,379
Phulbani 10,677
Pilibhit 68,273
Pokaran 7,769
Pondicherry 90,537
Ponnani 35,723
Poona (Pune)□
Porbandar 96,881
Porbandar□
Port Blair 26,218
Porto Novo 17,412
Proddatur 70,822
Puduchcheri
(Pondicherry) 90,537
Pudukkottai 66,384
Pune 856,105
Puri 72,674
Purli 31,078
Purnea 56,484
Purulia 57,708
Puttur 17,483
Quilon 124,208
Radhanpur 18,360
Raichur 79,831
Raigarh 46,745
Raipur 174,518
Raipur□
Rajahmundry 165,912
Rajahmundry□
Rajapalaiyam 86,952
Rajapur 9,017
Rajgarh 11,475
Rajkot 300,612
Rajnandgaon 41,183
Rajpipla 25,769
Rajpur 34,393
Rajpura 14,840
Rameswarem 16,755
Rampur, Him. Pradesh 2,623
Rampur, Uttar Pradesh 161,417
Ranchi 175,934
Ratangarh 31,506
Ratlam 106,666
Ratnagiri 37,551
Raurkela 47,076
Raxaul 12,064
Rayagada 25,064
Renigunta 8,567
Rewa 69,182
Rishra 63,486
Robertsganj 7,093
Roha 8,631
Rohtak 124,783
Sadiya⊙ 64,252

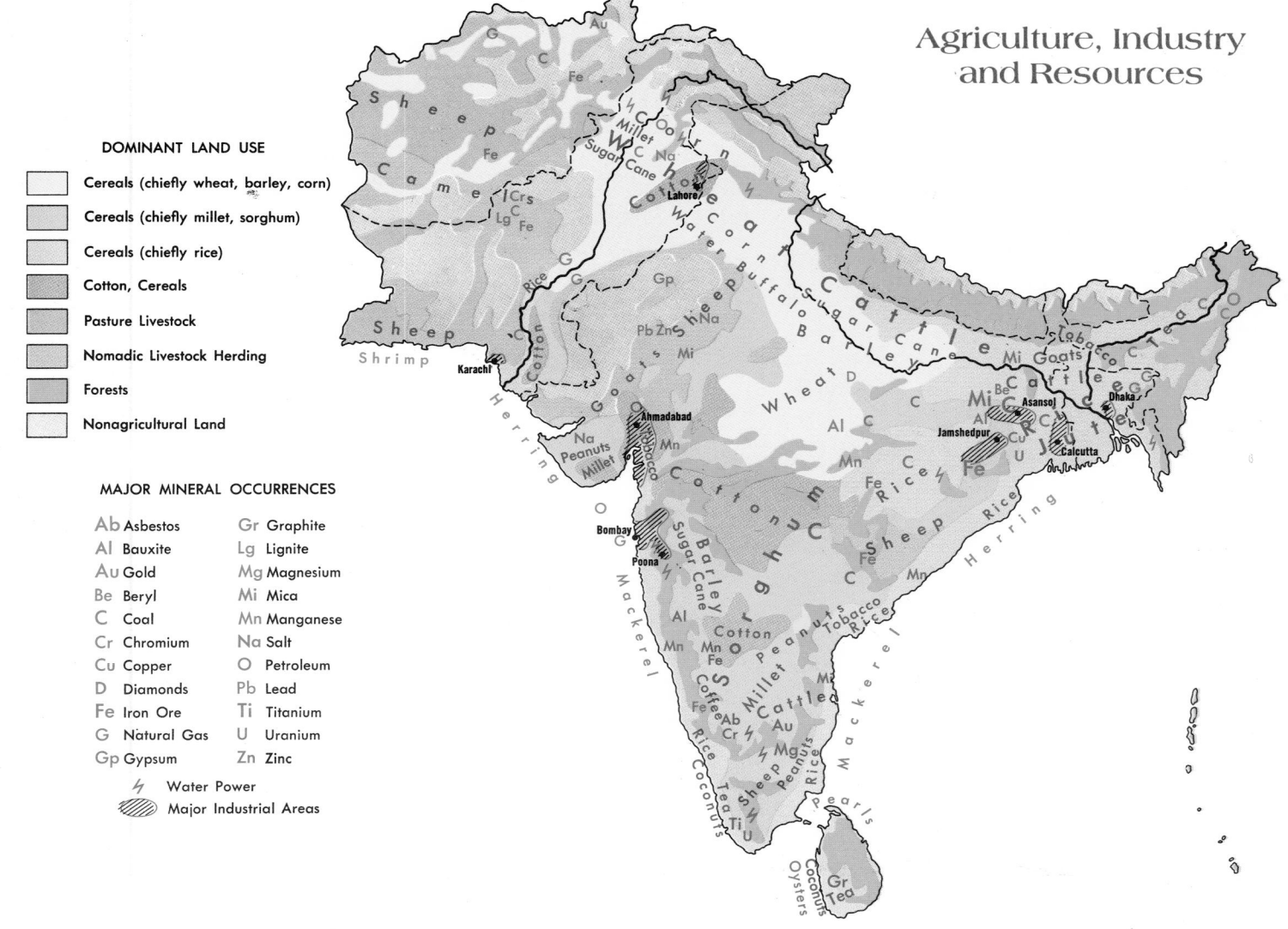

Agriculture, Industry and Resources

DOMINANT LAND USE

- Cereals (chiefly wheat, barley, corn)
- Cereals (chiefly millet, sorghum)
- Cereals (chiefly rice)
- Cotton, Cereals
- Pasture Livestock
- Nomadic Livestock Herding
- Forests
- Nonagricultural Land

MAJOR MINERAL OCCURRENCES

Ab	Asbestos	Gr	Graphite
Al	Bauxite	Lg	Lignite
Au	Gold	Mg	Magnesium
Be	Beryl	Mi	Mica
C	Coal	Mn	Manganese
Cr	Chromium	Na	Salt
Cu	Copper	O	Petroleum
D	Diamonds	Pb	Lead
Fe	Iron Ore	Ti	Titanium
G	Natural Gas	U	Uranium
Gp	Gypsum	Zn	Zinc

Water Power
Major Industrial Areas

Burma, Thailand, Indochina and Malaya

CONIC PROJECTION

SCALE OF MILES

50   100   150   200

SCALE OF KILOMETERS

50   100   150   200   300

International Boundaries ....
Division and State Boundaries ......
Capitals of Countries ....☆
Division and State Capitals ....◉

Scale 1:10,000,000

© Copyright HAMMOND INCORPORATED, Maplewood, N.J.

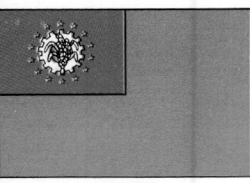

BURMA

THAILAND

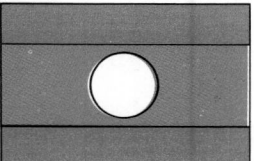

LAOS

CAMBODIA

VIETNAM

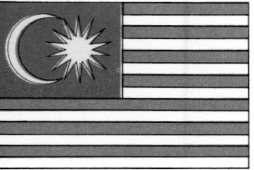

MALAYSIA

SINGAPORE

BURMA

AREA 261,789 sq. mi. (678,034 sq. km.)
POPULATION 32,913,000
CAPITAL Rangoon
LARGEST CITY Rangoon
HIGHEST POINT Hkakabo Razi 19,296 ft. (5,881 m.)
MONETARY UNIT kyat
MAJOR LANGUAGES Burmese, Karen, Shan, Kachin, Chin, Kayah, English
MAJOR RELIGIONS Buddhism, tribal religions

THAILAND

AREA 198,455 sq. mi. (513,998 sq. km.)
POPULATION 46,455,000
CAPITAL Bangkok
LARGEST CITY Bangkok
HIGHEST POINT Doi Inthanon 8,452 ft. (2,576 m.)
MONETARY UNIT baht
MAJOR LANGUAGES Thai, Lao, Chinese, Khmer, Malay
MAJOR RELIGIONS Buddhism, tribal religions

LAOS

AREA 91,428 sq. mi. (236,800 sq. km.)
POPULATION 3,721,000
CAPITAL Vientiane
LARGEST CITY Vientiane
HIGHEST POINT Phou Bia 9,252 ft. (2,820 m.)
MONETARY UNIT kip
MAJOR LANGUAGE Lao
MAJOR RELIGIONS Buddhism, tribal religions

CAMBODIA

AREA 69,898 sq. mi. (181,036 sq. km.)
POPULATION 5,200,000
CAPITAL Phnom Penh
LARGEST CITY Phnom Penh
HIGHEST POINT 5,948 ft. (1,813 m.)
MONETARY UNIT riel
MAJOR LANGUAGE Khmer (Cambodian)
MAJOR RELIGION Buddhism

VIETNAM

AREA 128,405 sq. mi. (332,569 sq. km.)
POPULATION 52,741,766
CAPITAL Hanoi
LARGEST CITY Ho Chi Minh City (Saigon)
HIGHEST POINT Fan Si Pan 10,308 ft. (3,142 m.)
MONETARY UNIT dong
MAJOR LANGUAGES Vietnamese, Thai, Muong, Meo, Yao, Khmer, French, Chinese, Cham
MAJOR RELIGIONS Buddhism, Taoism, Confucianism, Roman Catholicism, Cao-Dai

MALAYSIA

AREA 128,308 sq. mi. (332,318 sq. km.)
POPULATION 13,435,588
CAPITAL Kuala Lumpur
LARGEST CITY Kuala Lumpur
HIGHEST POINT Mt. Kinabalu 13,455 ft. (4,101 m.)
MONETARY UNIT ringgit
MAJOR LANGUAGES Malay, Chinese, English, Tamil, Dayak, Kadazan
MAJOR RELIGIONS Islam, Confucianism, Buddhism, tribal religions, Hinduism, Taoism, Christianity, Sikhism

SINGAPORE

AREA 226 sq. mi. (585 sq. km.)
POPULATION 2,413,945
CAPITAL Singapore
LARGEST CITY Singapore
HIGHEST POINT Bukit Timah 581 ft. (177 m.)
MONETARY UNIT Singapore dollar
MAJOR LANGUAGES Chinese, Malay, Tamil, English, Hindi
MAJOR RELIGIONS Confucianism, Buddhism, Taoism, Hinduism, Islam, Christianity

Topography

0 200 400 MI.
0 200 400 KM.

5,000 m. 2,000 m. 1,000 m. 500 m. 200 m. 100 m. Sea Level Below
16,404 ft. 6,562 ft. 3,281 ft. 1,640 ft. 656 ft. 328 ft.

BURMA

INTERNAL DIVISIONS

Arakan (state) 1,710,913	B3
Chin (state) 323,094	B2
Irrawaddy (div.) 4,152,521	B3
Kachin (state) 735,144	C1
Karen (state) 865,218	C3
Kayah (state) 126,492	C3
Magwe (div.) 2,632,144	B2
Mandalay (div.) 3,662,312	B2
Mon (state) 1,313,111	C3
Pegu (div.) 3,174,109	C3
Rangoon (div.) 3,186,886	C3
Sagaing (div.) 3,115,502	B1
Shan (state) 3,178,214	C2
Tenasserim (div.) 717,607	C4

CITIES and TOWNS

Akyab (Sittwe) 42,329	B2
Allanmyo 15,580	B3
Amarapura 11,268	B2
Amherst 6,000	C3
An	B3
Anin	C4
Bassein 126,045	B3
Bhamo 9,821	C1
Chauk 24,466	B2
Danubyu	B3
Falam	B2
Fort Hertz (Putao)	C1
Gawai	C1
Gokteik	C2
Gwa	B3
Gyobingauk 9,922	B3
Haka	B2
Henzada 61,972	B3
Hmawbi 23,032	C3
Homalin	B1
Hsenwi	C2
Hsipaw	C2
Htawgaw	C1
Insein 143,625	C3
Kamaing	C1
Karathpri	C5
Katha 7,648	C1
Kawludo	C3
Kawthaung 1,520	C5
Keng Hkam	C2
Keng Tung	C2
Koma	C4
Kunlong	C2
Kyaikto 13,154	C3
Kya-in Seikkyi	C3
Kyangin 6,073	B3
Kyaukme	C2
Kyaukpadaung 5,480	B2
Kyaukpyu 7,335	B3
Kyaukse 8,659	C2
Labutta 12,982	B3
Lai-hka	C2
Lamu	B3
Lashio	C2
Lenya	C5
Letpadan 15,896	C3
Lewe	B3
Loi-kaw	C3
Lonton	B1
Magwe 13,270	B2
Maingkwan	C1
Maliwun	C5
Mandalay 418,008	C2
Man Hpang	C2
Martaban 5,661	C3
Ma-ubin 23,362	B3
Maungdaw 3,772	B2
Mawkmai	C2
Mawlaik 2,993	B2
Mawlu	C1
Maymyo 22,287	C2
Meiktila 19,474	B2
Mergui 33,697	C4
Minbu 9,096	B2

Minhla 6,470	B3
Mogaung 2,920	C1
Mogok 8,334	C2
Mohnyin	C1
Möng Hsat	C2
Möng Mau	C3
Möng Mit	C2
Möng Pan	C2
Möng Si	C2
Möng Ton	C2
Möng Tung	C2
Monywa 26,279	B2
Moulmein 171,977	C3
Mudon 20,136	C3
Myanaung 11,155	B3
Myaungmya 24,532	B3
Myingyan 36,439	B2
Myitkyina 12,382	C1
Myohaung 6,534	B2
Naba	B1
Namhkam	C2
Namlan	C2
Namtu	C2
Natmauk	B2
Okkan 14,443	B3
Okpo 12,155	C3
Pakokku 30,943	B2
Palaw 5,596	C4
Paletwa	B2
Pantha	B2
Papun	C3
Pasawng	C3
Paungde 17,286	B3
Pegu 47,378	C3
Prome (Pye) 36,997	B3
Putao	C1
Pyapon 19,174	B3
Pye 36,997	B3
Pyinmana 22,025	C3
Pyu 10,443	C3
Rangoon (cap.) 1,586,422	C3
Rangoon* 2,055,365	C3
Rathedaung 2,969	B2
Sadon	C1
Sagaing 15,382	B2
Samka	C2
Sandoway 5,172	B3
Shingbwiyang	B1
Shwebo 17,827	B2
Shwenyaung	C2
Singkaling Hkamti	B1
Singu 4,027	C2
Sinlumkaba	C1
Sittwe 42,329	B2
Sumprabum	C1
Syriam 15,296	C3
Taungdwingyi 16,233	C2
Taunggyi	C2
Tavoy 40,312	C4
Tharrawaddy 8,977	C3
Thaton 38,047	C3
Thaungdut	B1
Thayetmyo 11,649	B3
Thazi 7,531	C2
Thongwa 10,829	C3
Toungoo 31,589	C3
Wakema 20,716	B3
Yamethin 11,167	C2
Yandoon 15,245	B3
Ye 12,852	C4
Yenangyaung 24,416	B2
Yesagyo 7,880	B2
Ye-u 5,307	B2
Ywathit	C3
Zadi	C4
Zalun 899	B3

OTHER FEATURES

Amya (pass)	C4
Andaman (sea)	B4
Arakan Yoma (mts.)	B3
Ataran (riv.)	C4
Bengal, Bay of (sea)	B3
Bentinck (isl.)	C5

(continued on following page)

Agriculture, Industry and Resources

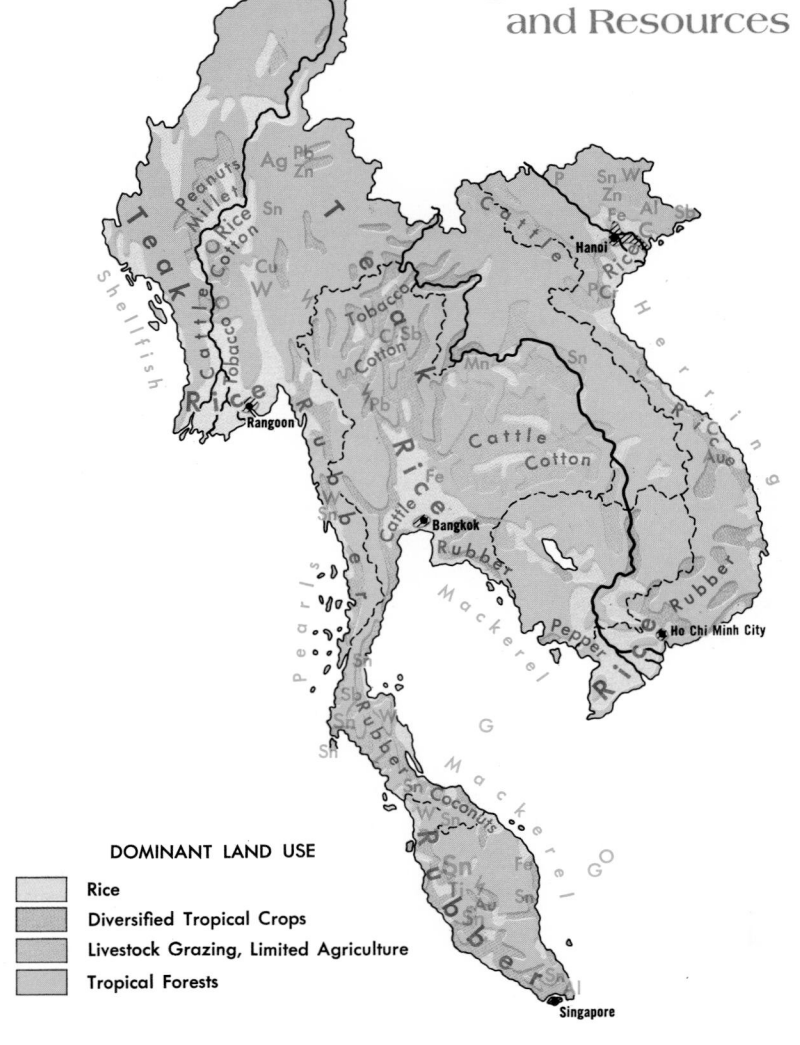

DOMINANT LAND USE

Rice

Diversified Tropical Crops

Livestock Grazing, Limited Agriculture

Tropical Forests

MAJOR MINERAL OCCURRENCES

Ag	Silver	Cu	Copper	O	Petroleum	Sn	Tin
Al	Bauxite	Fe	Iron Ore	P	Phosphates	Ti	Titanium
Au	Gold	G	Natural Gas	Pb	Lead	W	Tungsten
C	Coal	Mn	Manganese	Sb	Antimony	Zn	Zinc
Cr	Chromium					

⚡ Water Power   Major Industrial Areas

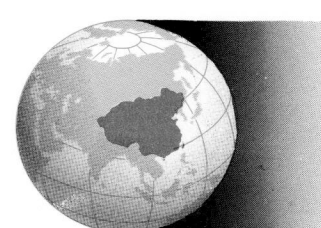

CHINA (MAINLAND)

AREA 3,691,000 sq. mi. (9,559,690 sq. km.)
POPULATION 958,090,000
CAPITAL Beijing
LARGEST CITY Shanghai
HIGHEST POINT Mt. Everest 29,028 ft. (8,848 m.)
MONETARY UNIT yuan
MAJOR LANGUAGES Chinese, Chuang, Uigur, Yi, Tibetan, Miao, Mongol, Kazakh
MAJOR RELIGIONS Confucianism, Buddhism, Taoism, Islam

CHINA (TAIWAN)

AREA 13,971 sq. mi. (36,185 sq. km.)
POPULATION 16,609,961
CAPITAL Taipei
LARGEST CITY Taipei
HIGHEST POINT Yü Shan 13,113 ft. (3,997 m.)
MONETARY UNIT new Taiwan yüan (dollar)
MAJOR LANGUAGES Chinese, Formosan
MAJOR RELIGIONS Confucianism, Buddhism, Taoism, Christianity, tribal religions

MONGOLIA

AREA 606,163 sq. mi. (1,569,962 sq. km.)
POPULATION 1,594,800
CAPITAL Ulaanbaatar
LARGEST CITY Ulaanbaatar
HIGHEST POINT Tabun Bogdo 14,288 ft. (4,355 m.)
MONETARY UNIT tughrik
MAJOR LANGUAGES Khalkha Mongolian, Kazakh (Turkic)
MAJOR RELIGION Buddhism

HONG KONG

AREA 403 sq. mi. (1,044 sq. km.)
POPULATION 5,022,000
CAPITAL Victoria
MONETARY UNIT Hong Kong dollar
MAJOR LANGUAGES Chinese, English
MAJOR RELIGIONS Confucianism, Buddhism, Christianity

MACAU

AREA 6 sq. mi. (16 sq. km.)
POPULATION 271,000
CAPITAL Macau
MONETARY UNIT pataca
MAJOR LANGUAGES Chinese, Portuguese
MAJOR RELIGIONS Confucianism, Buddhism, Taoism, Christianity

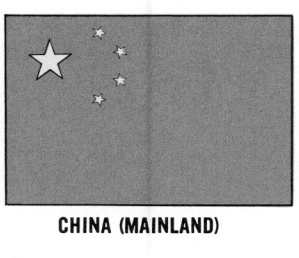

CHINA (MAINLAND)

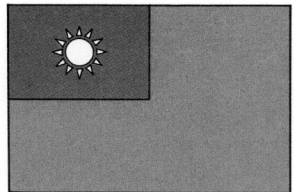

CHINA (TAIWAN)

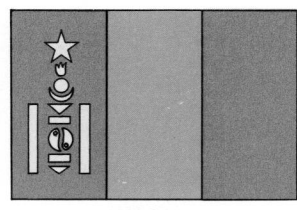

MONGOLIA

CHINA

PROVINCES

Anhui (Anhwei) 47,130,000	J 5
Chekiang (Zhejiang) 37,510,000	K 6
Fujian (Fukien) 24,500,000	J 6
Gansu (Kansu) 18,730,000	E 3
Guangdong (Kwangtung) 55,930,000	H 7
Guangxi Zhuangzu (Kwangsi Chuang Aut. Reg.) 34,020,000	G 7
Guizhou (Kweichow) 26,860,000	G 6
Hainan	H 8
Heilongjiang (Heilungkiang) 33,760,000	K 2
Hebei (Hopei) 50,570,000	J 4
Henan (Honan) 70,660,000	H 5
Hubei (Hupei) 45,750,000	H 5
Hunan 51,660,000	H 6
Inner Mongolian Aut. Reg. (Nei Monggol) 8,900,000	H 3
Jiangsu (Kiangsu) 58,340,000	J 5
Jiangxi (Kiangsi) 31,830,000	J 6
Jilin (Kirin) 24,740,000	L 3
Kansu (Gansu) 18,730,000	E 3
Kiangsi (Jiangxi) 31,830,000	J 6
Kiangsu (Jiangsu) 58,340,000	K 5
Kirin (Jilin) 24,740,000	L 3
Kwangsi Chuang Aut. Reg. (Guangxi Zhuang) 34,020,000	G 7
Kwangtung (Guangdong) 55,930,000	H 7
Kweichow (Guizhou) 26,860,000	G 6
Liaoning 37,430,000	K 3
Nei Monggol (Inner Mongolian Aut. Reg.) 8,900,000	H 3
Ningxia Huizu (Ningsia Hui Aut. Reg.) 3,660,000	H 3
Qinghai (Tsinghai) 3,650,000	E 4
Shaanxi (Shensi) 27,790,000	G 5
Shandong (Shantung) 71,600,000	J 4
Shanxi (Shansi) 24,340,000	H 4
Sichuan (Szechwan) 97,070,000	F 5
Sinkiang-Uigur Aut. Reg. (Xinjiang Uygur) 12,330,000	B 3
Taiwan 16,609,961	K 7
Tibet Aut. Reg. (Xizang) 1,790,000	B 5
Tsinghai (Qinghai) 3,650,000	E 4
Xinjiang Uygur (Sinkiang-Uigur Aut. Reg.) 12,330,000	B 3
Xizang (Tibet Aut. Reg.) 1,790,000	B 5
Yunnan 30,920,000	F 7
Zhejiang (Chekiang) 37,510,000	K 6

CITIES and TOWNS†

Aba	F 5
Abagnar (Silinhot)	J 3
Aihui (Aigun) (Heihe)	L 1
Aksu (Aqsu)	B 3
Altay	C 2
Alxa Youqi	F 4
Alxa Zuoqi	F 4
Amoy (Xiamen) 400,000	J 7
Ankang	G 5
Anqing (Anking) 160,000	J 5
Anshan 1,500,000	K 3
Anshun	G 6
Antu	L 3
Anxi	E 3
Anyang 225,000	H 4
Aqsu (Aksu)	B 3
Aratürük (Yiwu)	D 3
Ar Horqin	K 3
Arixang (Wenquan)	B 3
Artux (Atushi)	A 4
Bachu (Maralwexi)	A 4
Baicheng, Jilin	K 2
Baicheng (Bay), Xinjiang Uygur	B 3
Bairin Zuoqi	J 3
Baoding (Paoting) 350,000	J 4
Baoji (Paoki) 275,000	G 5
Baoshan	E 7
Baoting	G 8
Baotou (Paotow) 800,000	G 3
Bargrax (Bohu)	C 3
Batang	E 5
Bay (Baicheng)	B 3
Bayan Obo	G 3
Ba Xian	J 4
Bei'an (Pehan) 130,000	L 2
Beihai (Pakhoi) 175,000	G 7
Beijing (Peking) (cap.) •8,000,000	J 3
Bengbu (Pengpu) 400,000	J 5
Benxi (Penki) 750,000	K 3
Bohu (Bagrax)	C 3
Bole	B 3
Bortala (Bole)	B 3
Boshan	J 4
Bo Xian (Pohsien)	J 5
Butha	K 2
Cangzhou (Tsangchow)	J 4
Chamdo (Gamdo)	E 5
Changchih (Changzhi)	H 4
Changchow (Changzhou) 400,000	J 5
Changchow (Zhangzhou)	J 7
Changchun 1,500,000	K 3
Changde (Changteh) 225,000	H 6
Changhua 137,236	K 7
Changji	C 3
Changjiang	G 8
Changsha 850,000	H 6
Changteh (Changde) 225,000	H 6
Changyeh (Zhangye)	F 4
Changzhi (Changchih)	H 4
Changzhou (Changchow) 400,000	K 5
Chankiang (Zhanjiang) 220,000	H 7
Chao'an (Chaochow)	J 7
Chaotung (Zhaotung)	F 6
Chaoyang, Liaoning	J 3
Chaoyang, Guangdong	J 7
Charkhlia (Ruoqiang)	C 4
Chefoo (Yantai) 180,000	K 4
Chengchow (Zhengzhou) 1,500,000	H 5
Chengde (Chengteh) 200,000	J 3
Chengdu (Chengtu) 2,000,000	F 5
Chen Xian	H 6
Cherchen (Qiemo)	C 4
Chiai 238,713	K 7
Chifeng	J 3
Chinchow (Jinzhou) 750,000	K 3
Chindu	E 5
Chinkiang (Zhenjiang) 250,000	J 5
Chinsi (Jinxi)	K 3
Chinwangtao (Qinhuangdao) 400,000	K 4
Chishui	G 6
Chongqing (Chungking) 3,500,000	G 6
Chüanchow (Quanzhou) 130,000	J 7
Chuchow (Zhuzhou) 350,000	H 6
Chuguchak (Tacheng)	B 2
Chumatien (Zhumadian)	H 5
Chunghsing	K 7
Chungking (Chongqing) 3,500,000	G 6
Chungshan (Zhongshan) 135,000	H 7
Da'an (Talai)	K 2
Dali	E 6
Dalian 1,480,240	K 4
Danba	F 5
Dandong (Tantung) 450,000	K 3
Dan Xian	G 8
Da Qaidam	E 4
Daqing 758,430	L 2
Datong, Qinghai	F 4
Datong (Tatung), Shanxi 300,000	H 3
Da Xian	G 5
Dazhai	H 4
Dengkou	G 3
Deyang	F 5
Dezhou (Tehchow)	J 4
Dingxing	H 4
Dongchuan	F 6
Dongfang	G 8
Dongsheng	H 4
Dongtai	K 5
Dorbiljin (Emin)	B 2
Dukou	E 4
Dulan	F 4
Dunhua (Tunhwa)	L 3
Dunhuang	E 3
Duolun	J 3
Dushan	G 6
Duyun (Tuyün)	G 6
Ejin	F 3
Emin (Dorbiljin)	B 2
Erenhot	H 3
Ergun Youqi	K 1
Ergun Zuoqi	K 1
Ertai	C 2
Fatshan (Foshan)	H 7

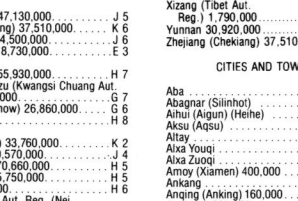

China and Mongolia Transportation

Railroads	——
Under Construction	-----
Connecting Roads	——
Navigable Rivers	～～
Canals	——
Major Seaports	‡

© Copyright HAMMOND INCORPORATED, Maplewood, N.J.

(continued on following page)

Foochow (Fuzhou) 900,000 ..... J6
Foshan (Fatshan) H7
Fowyang (Fuyang) J5
Fushun 1,700,000 ..... K3
Fusingchen (Simao) F7
Fu Xian, Liaoning K4
Fu Xian, Shaanxi G4
Fuxin (Fusin) 350,000 ..... K3
Fuyang (Fowyang) J5
Fuyu, Heilongjiang K2
Fuyu, Jilin L2
Fuyuan, Heilongjiang M2
Fuyuan, Yunnan F6
Fuyun C2
Fuzhou (Foochow), Fujian 900,000 ..... J6
Fuzhou, Jiangxi J6
Ganzhou (Kanchow) 135,000 ..... H6
Garyarsa (Gartok) B5
Gejiu (Kokiu) 250,000 ..... F7
Golmud (Golmo) D4
Gonghe F4
Guangyuan G5
Guan Xian F5
Guangzhou (Canton) 2,300,000 ..... H7
Guilin (Kweilin) 225,000 ..... G6
Guiyang (Kweiyang), Guizhou 1,500,000 ..... G6
Guiyang, Hunan H6
Gulja (Yining) 160,000 ..... B3
Guma (Pishan) A4
Guyang G3
Guyuan G4
Gyaca D6
Gyangzê C6
Habahe C2
Haikou (Hoihow) 500,000 ..... H7
Hailar J2
Hami (Kumul) D3
Hancheng H4
Hanchung (Hanzhong) 120,000 ..... G5
Handan (Hantan) 500,000 ..... H4
Hangzhou (Hangchow) 1,100,000 ..... J5
Hantan (Handan) 500,000 ..... H4
Hanzhong (Hanchung) 120,000 ..... G5
Harbin 2,750,000 ..... L2
Hebi H4
Hechuan (Hochwan) G5
Hefei (Hofei) 400,000 ..... J5
Hegang (Hokang) 350,000 ..... L2
Heihe (Aihui) (Aigun) L1
Hekou F7
Hengchun K7
Hengshan G4
Hengyang 310,000 ..... H6
Hepu (Hoppo) G7
Hexigten J3
Hezuo F5
Hochwan (Hechuan) G5
Hofei (Hefei) 400,000 ..... J5
Hohhot (Huhehot) 700,000 ..... H3
Hoihow (Haikou) 500,000 ..... H7
Hokang (Hegang) 350,000 ..... L2
Hoppo (Hepu) G7
Horqin Youyi Qianqi (Ulanhot) 100,000 ..... K2
Hotan B4
Houma H4
Hsüchang (Xuchang) H5
Huadian L3
Huaibei J5
Huaide (Hwaiteh) K3
Huainan 350,000 ..... J5
Hualien K7
Huangling G4
Huangshi 200,000 ..... J5
Huangzhong F4
Huhehot (Hohhot) 700,000 ..... H3
Huizhou H7
Hulin M2
Hunchun M3
Hunjiang L3
Hwainan (Huainan) 350,000 ..... J5
Hwaiteh (Huaide) K3
Hwangshih (Huangshi) 200,000 ..... J5
Ichang (Yichang) 150,000 ..... H5
Ichun (Yichun) 200,000 ..... L2
Ilan K7
Ipin (Yibin) 275,000 ..... F6
Jeminay C2
Jiamusi (Kiamusze) 275,000 ..... M2
Ji'an (Kian) 100,000 ..... J6
Jiangmen (Kongmoon) 150,000 ..... H7
Jian'ou J6
Jiaozuo (Tsiaotso) 300,000 ..... H4
Jiaxing (Kashing) K5
Jiayuguan E4
Jieyang J7
Jilin (Kirin) 1,200,000 ..... L3
Jinan (Tsinan) 1,500,000 ..... J4
Jingdezhen (Kingtehchen) 300,000 ..... J6
Jinghong F7
Jingxi G7
Jing Xian, Anhui J5
Jing Xian, Hunan H6
Jingyuan F4
Jinhua (Kinhwa) J6
Jining (Tsining), Nei Monggol 160,000 ..... H3
Jining (Tsining), Shandong J4
Jinshi (Tsingshih) 100,000 ..... H6
Jinxi (Chinsi) K3
Jinzhou (Chinchow) 750,000 ..... K3
Jiujiang (Kiukiang) 120,000 ..... J6
Jiuquan (Kiuchüan) E4
Jixi (Kisi) 350,000 ..... M2
Juichin (Ruijin) J6
Jun Xian H5
Kaba (Habahe) C2
Kaifeng 330,000 ..... H5
Kailu K3
Kaiyuan, Liaoning K3
Kaiyuan, Yunnan F7
Kalgan (Zhangjiakou) 1,000,000 ..... J3
Kanchow (Ganzhou) 135,000 ..... H6
Kangding F5
Kaohsiung 1,028,334 ..... J7
Karakax (Kara Kash) (Moyu) A4
Karamay B2
Karghalik (Yecheng) A4
Kashi (Kashgar) 175,000 ..... A4
Kashing (Jiaxing) K5
Kaxgar (Kashi) 175,000 ..... A4
Keelung 342,604 ..... K6
Kenli J4
Keriya (Yutian) B4
Khotan (Hotan) B4
Kiamusze (Jiamusi) 275,000 ..... M2
Kian (Ji'an) 100,000 ..... J6
Kienyang (Qianyang) H6
Kingtehchen (Jingdezhen) 300,000 ..... J6
Kinhwa (Jinhua) J6
Kirin (Jilin) 1,200,000 ..... L3
Kisi (Jixi) 350,000 ..... M2
Kiuchüan (Jiuquan) E4
Kiukiang (Jiujiang) 120,000 ..... J6
Kokiu (Gejiu) 250,000 ..... F7
Kongmoon (Jiangmen) 150,000 ..... H7
Korla C3
Kuldja (Yining) 160,000 ..... B3
Kumul (Hami) D3
Künes (Xinyuan) B3
Kunming 1,700,000 ..... F6
Kuqa B3
Kuytun C3
Kwangchow (Canton) 2,300,000 ..... H7
Kweilin (Guilin) 225,000 ..... G6
Kweisui (Hohhot) 700,000 ..... H3
Kweiyang (Guiyang) 1,500,000 ..... G6
Lanzhou (Lanchow) i,500,000 ..... F4
Lenghu D4
Lengshuijiang H6
Leshan (Loshan) 250,000 ..... F6
Lhasa 175,000 ..... D6
Lhazê (Lhatse) C6
Lianyungang (Lienyünkang) 300,000 ..... J5
Liaoyang 250,000 ..... K3
Liaoyuan 300,000 ..... K3
Lijiang F6
Linfen H4
Lingling H6
Linhe G3
Linqing (Lintsing) J4
Linxi J3
Linxia (Linsia) F4
Liuzhou (Liuchow) 250,000 ..... G7
Loho (Luohe) H5
Longjiang K2
Lopnur (Yuli) C3
Loshan (Leshan) 250,000 ..... F6
Loyang (Luoyang) 750,000 ..... H5
Lu'an J5
Luchow (Luzhou) 225,000 ..... G6
Lüda (Dalian) 1,480,240 ..... K4
Luohe H5
Luoyang (Loyang) 750,000 ..... H5
Lüshun K4
Luxi F7
Luzhou (Luchow) 225,000 ..... G6
Ma'anshan J5
Manas C3
Manchouli (Manzhouli) J2
Maoming (Mowming) H7
Maralwexi (Bachu) A4
Mengcheng J5
Mengzi F7
Mianyang, Hubei H5
Mianyang, Sichuan G5
Minfeng (Niya) B4
Mingshui, Gansu E3
Mingshui, Heilongjiang L2
Minle F4
Mowming (Maoming) H7
Moyu (Karakax) A4
Mudanjiang (Mutankiang) 400,000 ..... M3
Mukden (Shenyang) 3,750,000 ..... K3
Muli F6
Nagqu D5
Nanchang 900,000 ..... J6
Nanchong (Nanchung) 275,000 ..... G5
Nanjing (Nanking) 2,000,000 ..... J5
Nanning 375,000 ..... G7
Nanping J6
Nantong 300,000 ..... K5
Nanyang H5
Napo G7
Neijiang (Neikiang) 240,000 ..... G6
Nenjiang L2
Ningbo (Ningpo) 350,000 ..... K6
Ningpo (Ningbo) 350,000 ..... K6
Ningsia (Yinchuan, Yinchwan) 175,000 ..... G4
Niya (Minfeng) B4
Ongniud J3
Oroqen K1
Paicheng (Baicheng) K2
Pakhoi (Beihai) 175,000 ..... G7
Paoki (Baoji) 275,000 ..... G5
Paoting (Baoding) 350,000 ..... J4
Paotow (Baotou) 800,000 ..... G3
Pehan (Bei'an) 130,000 ..... L2
Peking (Beijing) (cap.)● 8,500,000 ..... J3
Pengpu (Bengbu) 400,000 ..... J5
Penki (Benxi) 750,000 ..... K3
Pingdingshan H5
Pingliang G4
Pingtung 165,360 ..... K7
Pingxiang, Guangxi Zhuangzu G7
Pingxiang, Jiangxi H6
Piqan (Shanshan) D3
Pishan (Guma) A4
Pohsien (Bo Xian) J5
Qamdo E5
Qarkilik (Ruoqiang) C4
Qarqan (Qiemo) C4
Qianyang (Kienyang) H6
Qiemo (Qarqan) C4
Qingdao (Tsingtao) 1,900,000 ..... K4
Qingjiang, Jiangxi J6
Qingjiang 110,000 ..... J5
Qinhuangdao (Chinwangtao) 400,000 ..... K4
Qionghai H8
Qiqihar (Tsitsihar) 1,500,000 ..... K2
Qitai C3
Qog G3
Qoqek (Tacheng) B2
Quanzhou (Chüanchow) 130,000 ..... J7
Qu Xian, Sichuan G5
Qu Xian, Zhejiang J6
Qüxü D6
Ruijin (Juichin) J6
Ruoqiang (Qarkilik) C4
Rutog A5
Sanmenxia H5
Sanming J6
Sêrxü E5
Shache (Yarkand) A4
Shandan F4
Shangdu H3
Shanghai● 10,980,000 ..... K5
Shangqiu (Shangkiu) 250,000 ..... J5
Shangrao (Shangjao) 100,000 ..... J6
Shangshui 100,000 ..... J5
Shanshan (Piqan) D3
Shantou (Swatow) 400,000 ..... J7
Shaoguan (Shiukwan) 125,000 ..... H7
Shaoxing (Shaohing) 225,000 ..... K5
Shaoyang 275,000 ..... H6
Shashi 125,000 ..... H5
Shenyang (Mukden) 3,750,000 ..... K3
Shigatse (Xigazê) C6
Shihezi (Shihhotzu) C3
Shijiazhuang (Shihkiachwang) 1,500,000 ..... J4
Shiquanhe A5
Shiukwan (Shaoyuan) 125,000 ..... H7
Shiyan H5
Shizuishan (Shihsuishan) G4
Shuangcheng L2
Shuangyashan 150,000 ..... M2
Shuo Xian H4
Siakwan (Xiaguan) E6
Sian (Xi'an) 1,900,000 ..... G5
Siangfan (Xiangfan) 150,000 ..... H5
Siangtan (Xiangtan) 300,000 ..... H6
Sienyang (Xianyang) 125,000 ..... G5
Silinhot (Abnagar) J3
Simao (Fusingchen) F7
Sinchu 208,038 ..... K7
Singtai (Xingtai) H4
Sining (Xining) 250,000 ..... F4
Sinsiang (Xinxiang) 300,000 ..... H4
Sinyang (Xinyang) 125,000 ..... H5
Siping (Szeping) 180,000 ..... K3
Soche (Shache) A4
Soochow (Suzhou) 1,300,000 ..... K5
Suao K7
Süchow (Xuzhou) 1,500,000 ..... J5
Suifenhe M3
Suihua L2
Suining G5
Suzhou (Soochow) 1,300,000 ..... K5
Swatow (Shantou) 400,000 ..... J7
Szeping (Siping) 180,000 ..... K3
Tacheng (Qoqek) B2
Tai'an J4
Taibus J3
Taichow (Taizhou) 275,000 ..... K5
Taichung 565,255 ..... K7
Taigu H4
Tainan 541,390 ..... J7
Taipei 2,108,193 ..... K7
Taitung K7
Taiyuan 2,725,000 ..... H4
Taizhou (Taichow) 275,000 ..... K5
Talai (Da'an, Dalai) K2
Tali (Dali) E6
Tangshan 1,200,000 ..... J4
Tantung (Dandong) 450,000 ..... K3
Tao'an K2
Taoyuan 105,841 ..... K6
Tart D4
Tatung (Datong) 300,000 ..... H3
Taxkorgan A4
Tehchow (Dezhou) J4
Tengchong E6
Tianjin (Tientsin)● 7,210,000 ..... J4
Tianjun E4
Tianshui 100,000 ..... F5
Tieling K3
Tienshui (Tianshui) 100,000 ..... F5
Tientsin (Tianjin)● 7,210,000 ..... J4
Tingri C6
Togtoh H3
Toksu (Xinhe) B3
Toksun C3
Tongchuan (Tungchwan) G5
Tonghua (Tunghwa) 275,000 ..... L3
Tongjiang (Tungkiang) M2
Tongliao K3
Tongling J5
Tongxin G4
Tongyu K3
Tsangchow (Cangzhou) J4
Tsiaotso (Jiaozuo) 300,000 ..... H4
Tsinan (Jinan) 1,500,000 ..... J4
Tsingkiang (Qingjiang) 110,000 ..... J5
Tsingshih (Jinshi) 100,000 ..... H6
Tsingtao (Qingdao) 1,900,000 ..... K4
Tsining (Jining), Nei Monggol 160,000 ..... H3

Topography

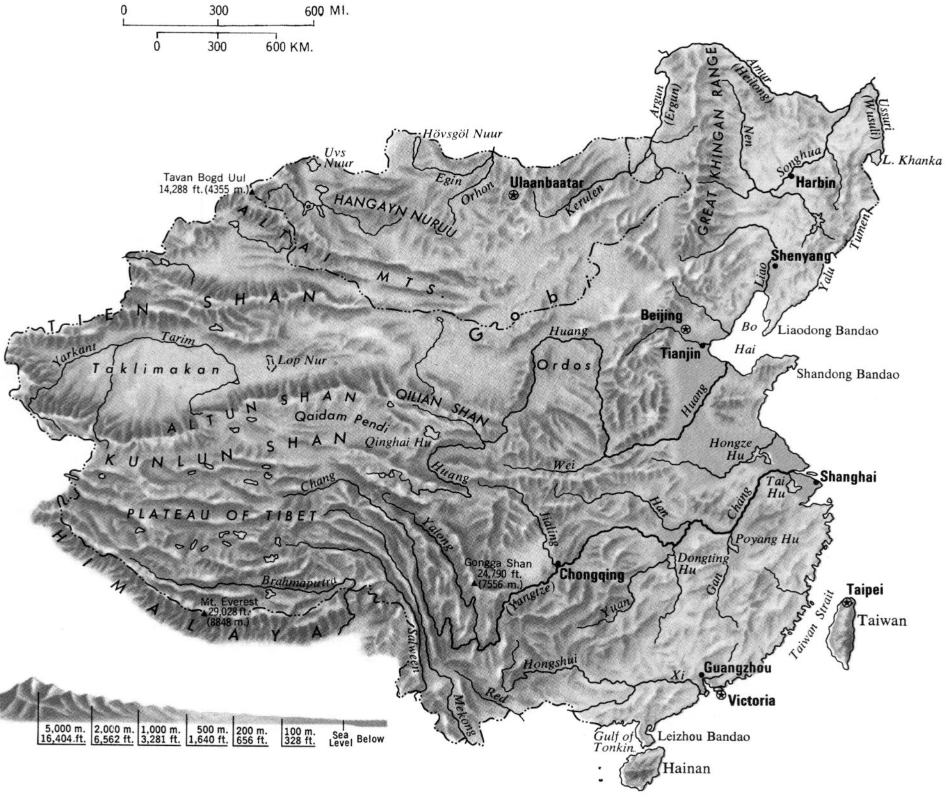

0 300 600 MI.
0 300 600 KM.
Hövsgöl Nuur
Uvs Nuur
Tavan Bogd Uul 14,288 ft. (4355 m.)
Ulaanbaatar
HANGAYN NURUU
Egiin
Orhon
Kerulen
GREAT KHINGAN RANGE
Argun (Ergun)
Amur (Heilong)
Nen
Songhua
Ussuri (Wusuli)
L. Khanka
Harbin
Tumen
Yalu
Liao
Shenyang
A L T A I M T S.
G o b i
T I E N S H A N
Beijing
Tianjin
Bo Hai
Liaodong Bandao
Shandong Bandao
Yarkant
Tarim
Taklimakan
Lop Nur
Ordos
Huang
A L T U N S H A N
QILIAN SHAN
Qaidam Pendi
Qinghai Hu
K U N L U N S H A N
Wei
Hongze Hu
Shanghai
Tai Hu
Chang
Han
PLATEAU OF TIBET
H I M A L A Y A
Yalong
Jialing
Gongga Shan 24,790 ft. (7556 m.)
Chongqing
Poyang Hu
Dongting Hu
Gan
Brahmaputra
Mt. Everest 29,028 ft. (8848 m.)
Chang (Yangtze)
Yuan
Taipei
Taiwan
Taiwan Strait
Salween
Hongshui
Guangzhou
Xi
Victoria
Red
Mekong
Gulf of Tonkin
Leizhou Bandao
Hainan
5,000 m. 16,404 ft.
2,000 m. 6,562 ft.
1,000 m. 3,281 ft.
500 m. 1,640 ft.
200 m. 656 ft.
100 m. 328 ft.
Sea Level
Below

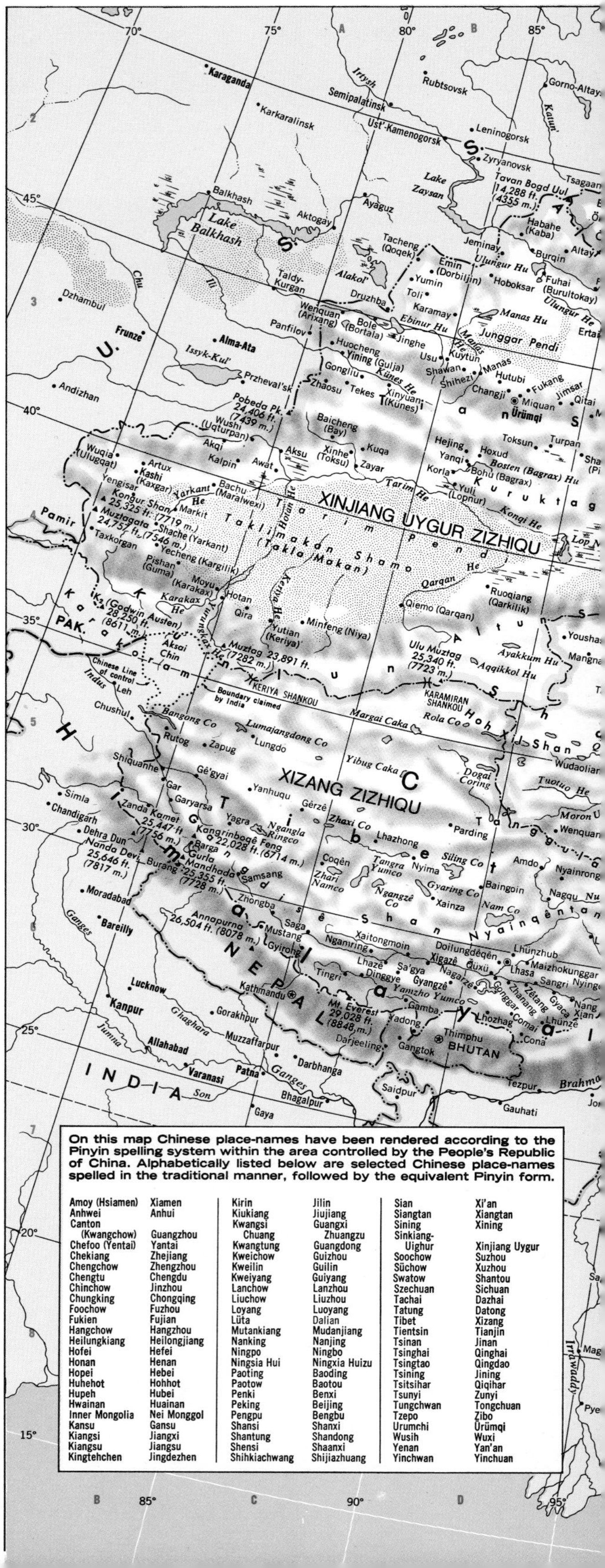

70°
75°
80°
85°
A
B
C
D
45°
40°
35°
30°
25°
20°
15°
90°
95°
Karaganda
Semipalatinsk
Rubtsovsk
Gorno-Altaysk
Karkaralinsk
Ust'-Kamenogorsk
Leninogorsk
Zyryanovsk
Irtysh
Lake Zaysan
Tavan Bogd Uul 14,288 ft. (4355 m.)
Balkhash
Lake Balkhash
Ayaguz
Aktogay
Habahe (Kaba)
Burqin
Altay
Tacheng (Qoqek)
Jeminay
Emin (Dorbiljin)
Yumin
Hoboksar
Fuhai (Burultokay)
Ulungur Hu
Taldy-Kurgan
Alakol'
Toli
Dzhambul
Chu
Ili
Druzhba
Karamay
Manas Hu
Junggar Pendi
Frunze
Alma-Ata
Wenquan (Arixang)
Bole (Bortala)
Panfilov
Ebinur Hu
Jinghe
Huocheng
Yining (Gulja)
Usu
Kuytun
Shawan
Manas
Shihezi
Hutubi
Issyk-Kul'
Gongliu
Künes He
Przheval'sk
Zhaosu
Tekes
Xinyuan (Künes)
Changji
Fukang
Jimsar
Ürümqi
Qitai
Andizhan
Pobeda Pk. 24,406 ft. (7439 m.)
Wushi (Uqturpan)
Baicheng (Bay)
Toksun
Turpan
Akqi
Kalpin
Aksu
Awat
Xinhe (Toksu)
Kuqa
Zayar
Hejing
Hoxud
Yanqi
Bosten (Bagrax) Hu
Bohu (Bagrax)
Korla
Kuruktag
Wuqia (Ulugqat)
Artux
Kashi (Kaxgar)
Yengisar
Bachu (Maralwexi)
Yarkant He
Tarim He
Yuli (Lopnur)
Konqi He
XINJIANG UYGUR ZIZHIQU
Kongur Shan 25,325 ft. (7719 m.)
Markit
Muztagata 24,757 ft. (7546 m.)
Shache (Yarkant)
Taklimakan Shamo
Tarim Pendi
Pamir
Taxkorgan
Yecheng (Kargilik)
Pishan (Guma)
Moyu (Karakax)
Hotan
Qira
Keriya He
Yutian (Keriya)
Minfeng (Niya)
Qarqan
Qiemo (Qarqan)
Ruoqiang (Qarkilik)
K2 (Godwin Austen) 28,250 ft. (8611 m.)
Aksai Chin
Muztag 23,891 ft. (7282 m.)
Ulu Muztag 25,340 ft. (7723 m.)
Ayakkum Hu
Aqqikkol Hu
Chinese Line of control
Leh
Indus
Boundary claimed by India
KERIYA SHANKOU
KARAMIRAN SHANKOU
Chushul
Bangong Co
Lumajangdong Co
Margai Caka
Rola Co
Rutog
Zapug
Lungdo
Yibug Caka
Dogai Coring
Shiquanhe
Gê'gyai
XIZANG ZIZHIQU
Gar
Yanhuqu
Gêrzê
Garyarsa
Yagra
Zhaxi Co
Simla
Chandigarh
Zanda Kamet 25,447 ft. (7756 m.)
Kangrinboqê Feng 22,028 ft. (6714 m.)
Ngangla Ringco
Lhazhong
Parding
Dehra Dun
Nanda Devi 25,646 ft. (7817 m.)
Burang
Mandhata 25,355 ft. (7728 m.)
Coqên
Tangra Yumco
Nyima
Siling Co
Moradabad
Zhari Namco
Ngangzê Co
Baingoin
Gyaring Co
Xainza
Nam Co
Samsang
Zhongba
Saga
Xaitongmoin
Bareilly
Annapurna 26,504 ft. (8078 m.)
Ngamring
Lhunzhub
Maizhokunggar
Lucknow
Mustang
Gyirong
Lhazê
Sa'gya
Xigazê
Qüxü
Lhasa
Tingri
Gyangzê
Yamzho Yumco
Kathmandu
NEPAL
Mt. Everest 29,028 ft. (8848 m.)
Kanpur
Gorakhpur
Gamba
Nagarzê
Lhünzê
Yadong
Thimphu
BHUTAN
Cona
Ghaghara
Allahabad
Muzzaffarpur
Darjeeling
Gangtok
Darbhanga
I N D I A
Varanasi
Patna
Ganges
Son
Saidpur
Tezpur
Brahmaputra
Gauhati
Bhagalpur
Gaya
Irrawaddy

On this map Chinese place-names have been rendered according to the Pinyin spelling system within the area controlled by the People's Republic of China. Alphabetically listed below are selected Chinese place-names spelled in the traditional manner, followed by the equivalent Pinyin form.

Amoy (Hsiamen)	Xiamen	Kirin	Jilin	Sian	Xi'an
Anhwei	Anhui	Kiukiang	Jiujiang	Siangtan	Xiangtan
Canton (Kwangchow)	Guangzhou	Kwangsi Chuang	Guangxi Zhuangzu	Sining	Xining
Chefoo (Yentai)	Yantai	Kwangtung	Guangdong	Sinkiang-Uighur	Xinjiang Uygur
Chekiang	Zhejiang	Kweichow	Guizhou	Soochow	Suzhou
Chengchow	Zhengzhou	Kweilin	Guilin	Süchow	Xuzhou
Chengtu	Chengdu	Kweiyang	Guiyang	Swatow	Shantou
Chinchow	Jinzhou	Lanchow	Lanzhou	Szechuan	Sichuan
Chungking	Chongqing	Liuchow	Liuzhou	Tachai	Dazhai
Foochow	Fuzhou	Loyang	Luoyang	Tatung	Datong
Fukien	Fujian	Lüta	Dalian	Tibet	Xizang
Hangchow	Hangzhou	Mutankiang	Mudanjiang	Tientsin	Tianjin
Heilungkiang	Heilongjiang	Nanking	Nanjing	Tsinan	Jinan
Hofei	Hefei	Ningpo	Ningbo	Tsinghai	Qinghai
Honan	Henan	Ningsia Hui	Ningxia Huizu	Tsingtao	Qingdao
Hopei	Hebei	Paoting	Baoding	Tsining	Jining
Huhehot	Hohhot	Paotow	Baotou	Tsitsihar	Qiqihar
Hupeh	Hubei	Penki	Benxi	Tsunyi	Zunyi
Hwainan	Huainan	Peking	Beijing	Tungchwan	Tongchuan
Inner Mongolia	Nei Monggol	Pengpu	Bengbu	Tzepo	Zibo
Kansu	Gansu	Shansi	Shanxi	Urumchi	Ürümqi
Kiangsi	Jiangxi	Shantung	Shandong	Wusih	Wuxi
Kiangsu	Jiangsu	Shensi	Shaanxi	Yenan	Yan'an
Kingtehchen	Jingdezhen	Shihkiachwang	Shijiazhuang	Yinchwan	Yinchuan

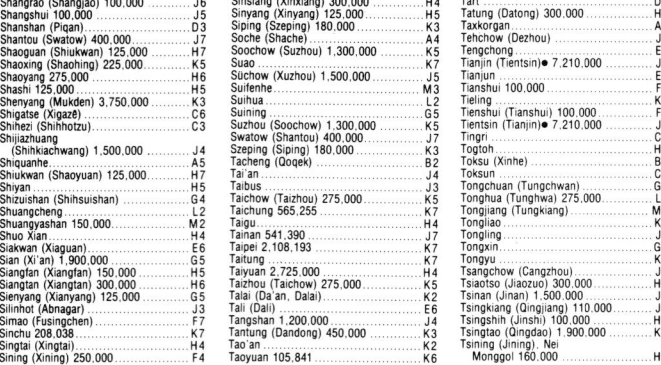

Tsining (Jining), Shandong J4	Wenzhou 250,000 .... J6	Xigazê (Shigatse) C6	Yichang (Ichang) 150,000 .... H5	Zhangzhou (Changchow) J7
Tsitsihar (Qiqihar) 1,500,000 .... K2	Wuchow (Wuzhou) 150,000 .... H7	Ximiao F3	Yichun, Jiangxi H6	Zhanjiang (Chankiang) 220,000 .... H7
Tumen M3	Wuchuan, Guizhou G6	Xin Barag Zuoqi K2	Yichun, Heilongjiang 200,000 .... L2	Zhaodong K2
Tungchwan (Tongchuan) G5	Wuchuan, Nei Monggol H3	Xinhe (Toksu) B3	Yidu, Hubei H5	Zhaoqing H7
Tunghwa (Tonghua) 275,000 .... L3	Wuchung (Wuzhong) G4	Xining (Sining) 250,000 .... F4	Yidu, Shandong J4	Zhaosu B3
Tungliao (Tongliao) K3	Wuda G4	Xinxiang (Sinsiang) 300,000 .... H4	Yinchuan (Ningsia) 175,000 .... G4	Zhaotong (Chaotung) F6
Tunhwa (Dunhua) L3	Wuhan 4,250,000 .... H5	Xinyang (Sinyang) 125,000 .... H5	Yingkou 215,000 .... K3	Zhengzhou (Chengchow) 1,500,000 .... H5
Tunxi (Tunki) J6	Wuhing (Wuxing) 160,000 .... K5	Xinyu (Künes) B3	Yining 160,000 .... B3	Zhenjiang (Chinkiang) 250,000 .... J5
Turpan (Turfan) C3	Wuhu 300,000 .... J5	Xuanhua H3	Yitan, Hebei J4	Zhenyuan G6
Tüyün (Duyun) G6	Wuqi A4	Xuchang H5	Yitulihe K2	Zhongba B6
Tzekung (Zigong) 350,000 .... F6	Wuqia A4	Xugdit K2	Yiwu (Aratürük) D3	Zhongshan (Chungshan) 135,000 .... H7
Tzepo (Zibo) 1,750,000 .... J4	Wushi A3	Ya'an (Yenan) F6	Yuanping H4	Zhongwei F4
Uch Turfan (Wushi) A3	Wushih (Wuxi) 900,000 .... A3	Yadong C6	Yueyang H6	Zhumadian (Chumatien) H5
Ulanhot (Horguin Youyi	Wutai H4	Yan'an (Yenan) G4	Yuli (Lopnur) C3	Zhushan G5
Qianqi) 100,000 .... K2	Wuwei F4	Yangchow (Yangzhou) 210,000 .... J5	Yulin, Guangxi Zhuangzu G7	Zhuzhou (Chuchow) 350,000 .... H6
Uluqchat (Wuqia) A4	Wuxi (Wusih) 900,000 .... K5	Yangchuan (Yangquan) 350,000 .... H4	Yulin, Shanxi G4	Zibo (Tzepo) 1,750,000 .... J4
Ürümqi (Urumchi) 500,000 .... C3	Wuxing (Wuhing) 160,000 .... K5	Yangjiang H7	Yumen 325,000 .... E4	Zigong (Tzekung) 350,000 .... F6
Usu B3	Wuyuan G4	Yanji (Yenki) L3	Yungkia (Wenzhou) 250,000 .... J6	Zinhui H7
Wanning H8	Wuzhong (Wuchung) G4	Yanjiang (Yangchuan) 350,000 .... H4	Yushu, Jilin L3	Zunhua J3
Wanxian (Wanhsien) 175,000 .... G5	Wuzhou (Wuchow) 150,000 .... H7	Yangquan (Yangchuan) 210,000 .... H4	Yushu, Qinghai E5	Zunyi (Tsunyi) 275,000 .... G6
Weichang J3	Xiaguan (Siakwan) E6	Yanqi C3	Yütze (Yuci) H4	
Weifang 260,000 .... J4	Xiamen (Amoy) 400,000 .... J7	Yantai (Chefoo) 180,000 .... K4		**OTHER FEATURES**
Weihai (Weihaiwei) K4	Xi'an (Sian) 1,900,000 .... G5	Yarkant (Shache) A4	Zaozhuang J5	
Weixi E6	Xiangfan (Siangfan) 150,000 .... H5	Ya Xian G8	Zayü E6	Altun Shan (range) C4
Weixin F6	Xiangtan (Siangtan) 300,000 .... H6	Yecheng A4	Zetang D6	Alxa Shamo (des.) F4
Wenchow (Wenzhou) 250,000 .... J6	Xianyang (Sienyang) 125,000 .... G5	Yenan (Yan'an) G4	Zhanghei J3	A'nyêmaqên Shan (mts.) E5
Wenquan, Qinghai D5	Xiapu (Siapu) K6	Yenki (Yanji) 130,000 .... L3	Zhangjiakou (Kalgan) 1,000,000 .... J3	Aqqikkol Hu (lake) C4
Wenquan, Xinjiang Uygur B3	Xichang (Sichang) F6	Yibin (Ipin) 275,000 .... F6	Zhangye (Changye) F4	Argun' (Ergun He) (riv.) K1

Bagrax (Bosten Hu) (lake) C3	Hangzhou Wan (bay) K5
Bangong Co (lake) A5	Han Shui (riv.) H5
Bashi (chan.) K7	Heilong Jiang (Amur) (riv.) L2
Bayan Har Shan (range) E5	Himalaya (mts.) C6
Bo Hai (gulf) J4	Hongshui He (riv.) G7
Bosten (Bagrax) Hu (lake) C3	Hongze Hu (lake) J5
Chang Jiang (Yangtze) (riv.) K5	Hotan He (riv.) B4
Da Hingan Ling (range) J3	Huang He (Yellow) (riv.) J4
Dian Chi (lake) F7	Hulun Nur (lake) J2
Dongsha (isl.) J7	Hungtow (isl.) K7
Dongting Hu (lake) H6	Inner Mongolia (reg.) H3
East China (sea) L6	Jinmen (Quemoy) (isl.) J7
Ebinur Hu (lake) B2	Jinsha Jiang (Yangtze) (riv.) E5
Ergun He (Argun') (riv.) K1	Junggar Pendi (desert basin) C2
Er Hai (lake) F6	Kangrinboqê Feng (mt.) B5
Everest (mt.) C6	Karakhoto (ruins) F4
Fen He (riv.) H4	Keriya Shankou (pass) C4
Formosa (Taiwan) (str.) J7	Keriya Shankou (pass) C4
Formosa (Taiwan)	Khanka (lake) M3
(isl.) K7	Kongur Shan (mt.) A4
Gangdisê Shan (range) B5	Künes (riv.) B3
Gaoyou Hu (lake) J5	Kunlun Shan (range) B4
Gob (des.) G3	Kuruktag Shan (range) C3
Gongga Shan (mt.) F6	Lancang Jiang (riv.) F7
Grand (canal) J4	Leizhou Bandao (pen.) G7
Great Wall (ruins) G4,J	Liaodong Bandao (pen.) K3
Ghenghis Khan Wall (ruin) J2	Liao He (riv.) K3
Gurla Mandhada (mt.) B5	Lop Nor (Lop Nur) (lake) D3
Hailar He (riv.) K2	Manas He (riv.) C3
Hainan (isl.) H8	Manas Hu (lake) C2

(continued on following page)

China and Mongolia

SCALE OF MILES
0 · 100 · 200 · 300 · 400 · 500

SCALE OF KILOMETERS
0 · 100 · 200 · 300 · 400 · 500

Capitals of Countries ...... ⊛   International Boundaries _____

Provincial Capitals ...... ⊛   Provincial Boundaries _ _ _ _

Canals ......   Walls ...... ∿∿∿∿∿

Scale 1:19,100,000

© Copyright HAMMOND INCORPORATED, Maplewood, N.J.

Mazu (Matsu) (isl.) K6
Mekong (Lancang Jiang) (riv.) F7
Min Jiang (riv.) J6
Mudan Jiang (riv.) L3
Muztag (mt.) B4
Muztagata (mt.) A4
Nam Co (lake) E6
Namzha Parwa (mt.) H6
Nan Ling (mts.) H6
Nen Jiang (riv.) K2
Ngangzê Co (lake) C5
Ngoring Hu (lake) E5
Nu Jiang (riv.) E6
Nyainqêntanglha Shan
(range) D5
Olwampi (cape) K7
Ordos (reg.) G4
Penghu (Pescadores)
(isls.) 113,397 .... J7
Pingtan (isl.) J6
Pobeda (peak) A3
Poyang Hu (lake) J6
Pratas (Dongsha) (isl.) J7
Qaidam Pendi (basin) (swamp) D4
Qarqan He (riv.) C4
Qinghai Hu (lake) E4
Qilian Shan (range) E4
Qiongzhou Haixia (str.) G7
Quemoy (Jinmen) (isl.) J7
Qumar He (riv.) D4
Salween (Nu Jiang) (riv.) E6
Siling Co (lake) C5
Songhua Hu (lake) L3
Songhua Jiang (Sungari)
(riv.) M2
South China (sea) J7
Tachen (Taizhou) (isls.) K6
Tai Hu (lake) J5
Taiwan (Formosa)
(isl.) 16,609,961 .... K7
Taiwan (Formosa) (str.) J7
Taizhou (Tachen) (isls.) K6
Takla Makan (Taklimakan Shamo)
(des.) .... B
Tanggula Shan (range) D5
Tangra Yumco (lake) C5
Tarim He (riv.) B3
Tarim Pendi (basin) B4
Tian Shan (range) C3
Tibet (reg.) B5
Tongtian He (Zhi Qu) (riv.) E5
Tonkin (gulf) G7

Tumen (riv.) L3
Ulu Muztag (mt.) C4
Ulungur He (riv.) C2
Ulungur Hu (lake) C2
Ussuri (Wusuli Jiang) (riv.) M2
Wei He (riv.) G5
Wu Jiang (riv.) G6
Wusuli Jiang (Ussuri) (riv.) M2
Xiang Jiang (riv.) H6
Xi Jiang (riv.) H7
Yagradagzê Shan (mt.) D4
Yalong Jiang (riv.) F6
Yalu (riv.) L3
Yangtze (Chang Jiang) (riv.) K5
Yarkant He (riv.) A4
Yellow (Huang He) (riv.) K4
Yellow (sea) K4
Yin Shan (mts.) F3
Yuhuan (isl.) K6
Yu Shan (mt.) K7
Yushan (isls.) K6
Zhoushan (arch.) K5

HONG KONG
CITIES and TOWNS
Kowloon* 2,378,480 .... H7
Victoria (cap.)* 1,026,870 .... H7

MACAU (MACAO)
CITIES and TOWNS
Macau (Macao) (cap.) 226,880 .... H7

MONGOLIA
PROVINCES
Arhangay 90,500 .... F2
Bayamhongor 64,900 .... E2
Bayan-Ölgiy 73,300 .... C2
Bulgan 45,700 .... F2
Dornod 51,100 .... G3
Dornogovĭ 36,400 .... G3
Dundgovĭ 37,800 .... G2
Dzavhan 87,600 .... E2
Govĭ-Altay 59,200 .... E3
Hentiy 49,900 .... H2

Hovd 68,300 .... D2
Hövsgöl 89,600 .... E1
Ömnögovĭ 32,200 .... F3
Övörhangay 84,100 .... F2
Selenge 53,700 .... G2
Sühbaatar 44,100 .... H2
Töv 74,900 .... G2
Uvs 76,300 .... D2

CITIES AND TOWNS
Altay 10,000 .... E2
Arvayheer 9,100 .... F2
Baatsagaan 800 .... E2
Baruun-Urt 8,200 .... H2
Bayanbaraat 400 .... F2
Bayandalay 500 .... F3
Bayangovĭ 400 .... E2
Bayanhongor 11,300 .... E2
Bayan-Öndör 300 .... E3
Bayan-Uul 1,200 .... H2
Beger 800 .... E2
Bulgan, Bulgan 9,800 .... F2
Bulgan, Hovd 3,100 .... D2
Bulgan, Ömnögovĭ 700 .... F3
Bürentsogt 3,000 .... H2
Chandmań 700 .... D2
Choybalsan 20,500 .... H2
Dalandzadgad 6,600 .... G3
Darhan (Darkhan) 32,900 .... G2
Dashbalbar 1,100 .... H2
Dashinchilen 600 .... F2
Delgertsogt 500 .... G2
Dzamiń Üüd 1,500 .... H3
Dzüünharaa 8,100 .... G2
Dzuunmod 7,200 .... G2
Erdenesagaan 1,500 .... H2
Ereen 700 .... H2
Hanbogd 300 .... G3
Hanh 500 .... F1
Hatgal 5,000 .... E1
Hongor H2

Mönhhaan 400 .... H2
Mörön (Muren) 10,700 .... F2
Nalayh (Nalaikha) 14,000 .... G2
Nomgon 500 .... G3
Noyon 300 .... F3
Öndörhaan (Undur
Khan) 7,900 .... G2
Onon 2,600 .... H2
Sayhan-Ovoo 400 .... F2
Saynshand 10,000 .... H3
Selenge 1,300 .... F2
Sühbaatar (Sukhe
Bator) 10,000 .... G1
Sulanheer 300 .... G3
Tamsagbulag J2
Tsagaannuur 2,000 .... C2
Tsagaan-Ovoo 900 .... H2
Tsagaan-Uul 1,700 .... E2
Tsetseg 700 .... D2
Tsetserleg 12,400 .... F2

OTHER FEATURES
Altai (mts.) C2
Dörgön Nuur (lake) D2
Dzavhan Gol (riv.) D2
Ghenghis Khan Wall (ruins) H2
Gobi (des.) G3
Hangayn Nuruu (mts.) E2
Har Us Nuur (lake) D2
Herlen Gol (Kerulen) (riv.) H2
Hovd Gol (riv.) D2
Hövsgöl Nuur (lake) F1
Hyargas Nuur (lake) D2
Ider Gol (riv.) E2
Karakorum (ruins) F2
Kerulen (riv.) H2
Munku-Sardyk (mt.) F1
Orhon Gol (riv.) F2
Selenge Mörön (riv.) G2
Tannu-Ola (range) D1
Tavan Bogd Uul (mt.) C2
Uvs Nuur (lake) D1

• Population of municipality
* City and suburbs

† Populations of mainland cities, excluding Peking (Beijing), Shanghai and Tianjin (Tientsin), courtesy of Kingsley Davis, Office of Int'l Pop. and Research, Inst. of Int'l Studies Univ. of California.

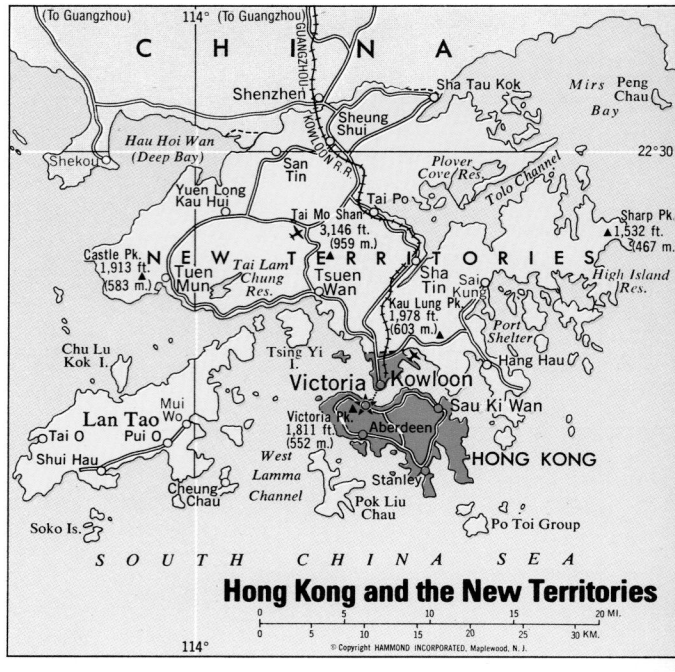

Hong Kong and the New Territories

© Copyright HAMMOND INCORPORATED, Maplewood, N.J.

Agriculture, Industry and Resources

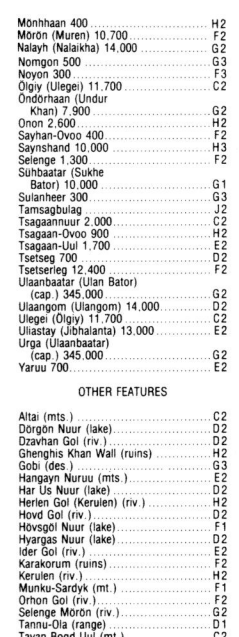

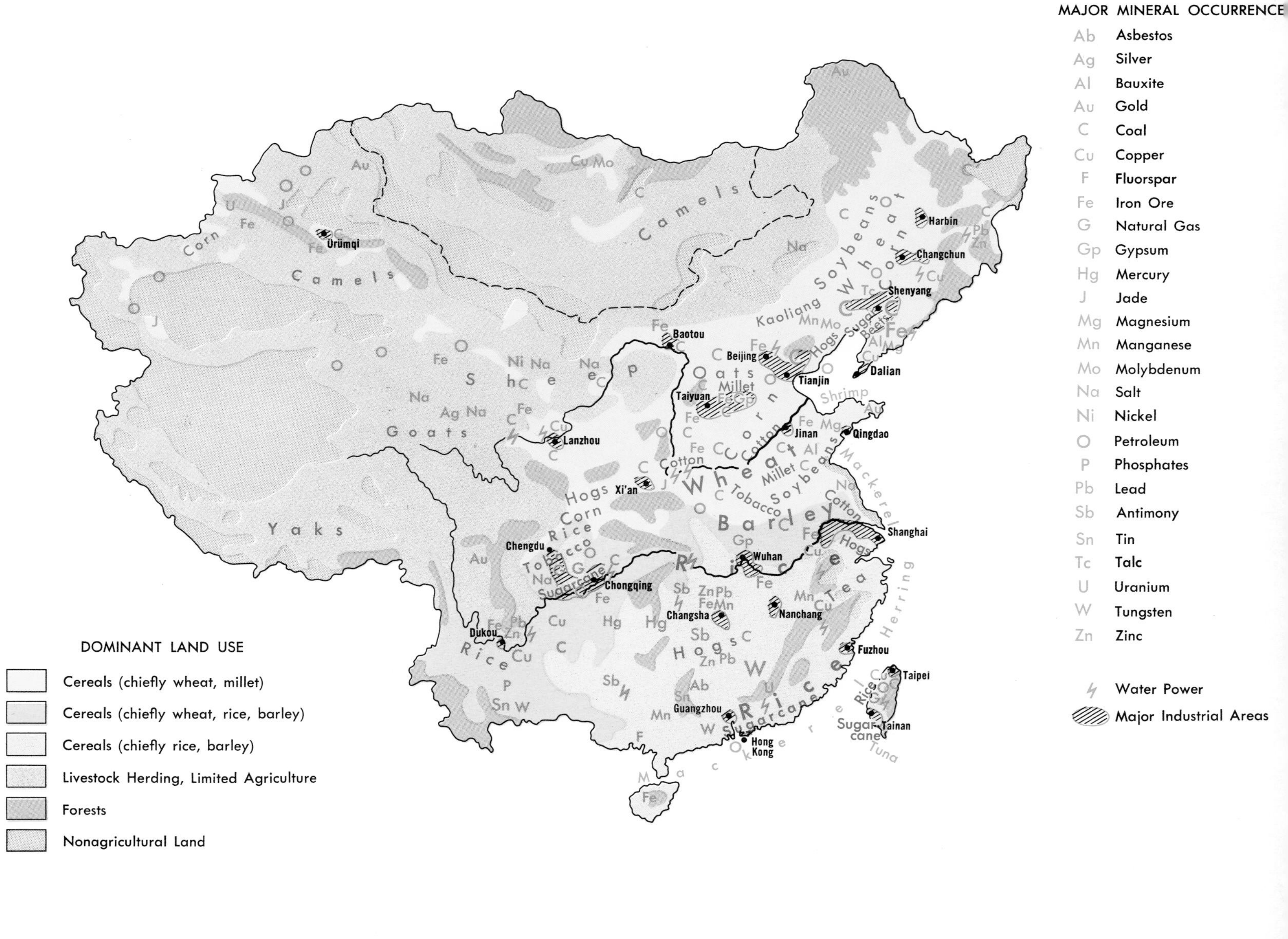

DOMINANT LAND USE

- Cereals (chiefly wheat, millet)
- Cereals (chiefly wheat, rice, barley)
- Cereals (chiefly rice, barley)
- Livestock Herding, Limited Agriculture
- Forests
- Nonagricultural Land

MAJOR MINERAL OCCURRENCE

Ab	Asbestos
Ag	Silver
Al	Bauxite
Au	Gold
C	Coal
Cu	Copper
F	Fluorspar
Fe	Iron Ore
G	Natural Gas
Gp	Gypsum
Hg	Mercury
J	Jade
Mg	Magnesium
Mn	Manganese
Mo	Molybdenum
Na	Salt
Ni	Nickel
O	Petroleum
P	Phosphates
Pb	Lead
Sb	Antimony
Sn	Tin
Tc	Talc
U	Uranium
W	Tungsten
Zn	Zinc

⚡ Water Power

▨ Major Industrial Areas

AREA 145,730 sq. mi. (377,441 sq. km.)
POPULATION 117,057,485
CAPITAL Tokyo
LARGEST CITY Tokyo
HIGHEST POINT Fuji 12,389 ft. (3,776 m.)
MONETARY UNIT yen
MAJOR LANGUAGE Japanese
MAJOR RELIGIONS Buddhism, Shintoism

AREA 46,540 sq. mi. (120,539 sq. km.)
POPULATION 17,914,000
CAPITAL P'yŏngyang
LARGEST CITY P'yŏngyang
HIGHEST POINT Paektu 9,003 ft. (2,744 m.)
MONETARY UNIT won
MAJOR LANGUAGE Korean
MAJOR RELIGIONS Confucianism, Buddhism, Ch'ondogyo

AREA 38,175 sq. mi. (98,873 sq. km.)
POPULATION 37,448,836
CAPITAL Seoul
LARGEST CITY Seoul
HIGHEST POINT Halla 6,398 ft. (1,950 m.)
MONETARY UNIT won
MAJOR LANGUAGE Korean
MAJOR RELIGIONS Confucianism, Buddhism, Ch'ondogyo, Christianity

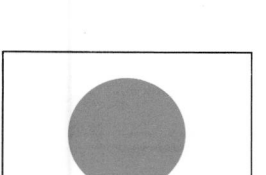

JAPAN

NORTH KOREA

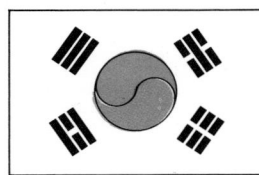

SOUTH KOREA

JAPAN

PREFECTURES

Aichi 5,923,569	H6
Akita 1,232,481	J4
Aomori 1,468,646	K3
Chiba 4,149,147	P2
Ehime 1,465,215	F7
Fukui 773,599	G5
Fukuoka 4,292,963	D7
Fukushima 1,970,616	K5
Gifu 1,867,978	H6
Gumma 1,756,480	J5
Hiroshima 2,646,324	E6
Hokkaido 5,338,206	K2
Hyogo 4,992,140	H7
Ibaraki 2,342,198	K5
Ishikawa 1,069,872	H5
Iwate 1,385,563	K4
Kagawa 961,292	G6
Kagoshima 1,723,902	E8
Kanagawa 6,397,748	O2
Kochi 808,397	F7
Kumamoto 1,715,273	E7
Kyoto 2,424,856	J7
Mie 1,626,002	H6
Miyagi 1,955,267	K4
Miyazaki 1,085,055	E8
Nagano 2,017,564	J5
Nagasaki 1,571,912	D7
Nara 1,077,491	J8
Niigata 2,391,938	J5
Oita 1,190,314	E7
Okayama 1,814,305	F6
Okinawa 1,042,572	N6
Osaka 8,278,925	J8
Saga 837,674	E7

Saitama 4,821,340	O2
Shiga 985,621	J7
Shimane 768,886	F6
Shizuoka 3,308,799	H6
Tochigi 1,698,003	K5
Tokushima 805,166	G7
Tokyo 11,673,554	O2
Tottori 581,311	G6
Toyama 1,070,791	H5
Wakayama 1,072,118	G6
Yamagata 1,220,302	K4
Yamaguchi 1,555,218	E6
Yamanashi 783,050	J6

CITIES and TOWNS

Abashiri 43,825	M1
Agea 146,358	O2
Aikawa 13,546	H4
Aizuwakamatsu 108,650	J5
Ajigasawa 18,086	J3
Akashi 234,905	H8
Aki 24,480	F7
Akita 261,246	J4
Akkeshi 16,778	M2
Akune 30,295	E7
Amagasaki 545,783	H8
Amagi 42,725	E7
Anan 60,439	G7
Aomori 264,222	K3
Asahi 34,028	K6
Asahikawa 320,526	L2
Ashibetsu 36,520	L2
Ashikaga 162,359	J5
Ashiya 76,211	H8
Atami 51,437	J6
Atsugi 108,955	O2
Awaji 9,623	H8

Ayabe 43,490	G6
Beppu 133,894	E7
Bibai 38,416	L2
Biratori 9,331	L2
Chiba 659,356	P2
Chichibu 61,798	J5
Chigasaki 152,023	O3
Chitose 61,031	K2
Chofu 175,924	O2
Choshi 90,374	K6
Daito 110,829	J8
Ebetsu 77,624	K2
Eniwa 39,884	K2
Esashi, Hokkaido 10,172	L1
Esashi, Hokkaido 14,409	J3
Esashi, Iwate 36,336	K4
Fuchu, Hiroshima 50,217	F6
Fuchu, Tokyo 182,474	O2
Fuji 199,195	J6
Fujieda 90,358	J6
Fujisawa 265,975	O3
Fukagawa 36,000	L2
Fukuchiyama 60,003	G6
Fukue 32,018	D7
Fukui 231,364	G5
Fukuoka 1,002,201	D7
Fukushima 246,531	K5
Fukuyama 329,714	F6
Funabashi 423,101	P2
Furukawa 54,356	K4
Gifu 408,707	H6
Gobo 30,272	G7
Gose 37,554	J8
Gosen 39,376	J5
Goshogawara 49,040	K3
Gotsu 27,992	F6
Habikino 94,160	J8
Haboro 13,624	K1

Hachinohe 224,366	K3
Hachioji 322,580	O2
Hadano 103,663	O3
Hagi 52,724	E6
Hakodate 307,453	K3
Hakui 28,726	H5
Hamada 50,316	E6
Hamamatsu 468,884	H6
Hanamaki 65,826	K4
Hanno 55,926	O2
Haramachi 43,483	K5
Hayama 24,026	O3
Higashiosaka 524,750	J8
Hikone 85,066	H6
Himeji 436,086	G6
Himi 61,789	H5
Hino 126,847	O2
Hirakata 297,618	J7
Hirara 29,301	L7
Hirata 30,942	F6
Hiratsuka 195,635	O3
Hiroo 11,399	L2
Hirosaki 164,911	K3
Hiroshima 852,611	E6
Hitachi 202,383	K5
Hitachiota 35,322	K5
Hitoyoshi 41,118	E7
Hofu 105,540	E6
Hondo 40,432	E7
Honjo 40,488	J4
Hyuga 53,448	E7
Ibaraki 210,286	J7
Ibusuki 32,339	E8
Ichihara 194,068	P3
Ichikawa 319,291	P2
Ichinohe 21,433	K3
Ichinomiya 238,463	H6
Ichinoseki 59,122	K4

Ide 9,112	J7
Iida 77,112	H6
Iizuka 75,417	E7
Ikeda, Hokkaido 12,306	L2
Ikeda, Osaka 100,268	H7
Ikoma 48,848	J8
Ikuno 6,658	G6
Imabari 119,726	F6
Imari 60,913	D7
Imazu 11,519	G6
Ina 54,468	H6
Isahaya 73,341	D7
Ise 107,887	H6
Ishigaki 34,657	L7
Ishige 19,220	P2
Ishinomaki 115,085	K4
Ishioka 43,679	K5
Itami 151,978	H7
Ito 68,072	J6
Itoigawa 36,646	H5
Iwaizumi 20,219	K4
Iwaki 330,213	K5
Iwakuni 111,069	E6
Iwami 16,063	J6
Iwamizawa 72,305	L2
Iwanai 25,823	K2
Iwasaki 4,437	J3
Iwata 67,665	H6
Iwatsuki 83,825	O2
Iyo 27,805	F7
Izuhara 18,460	D6
Izumi 118,237	J8
Izumiotsu 66,250	J8
Izumisano 86,139	G6
Izumo 71,568	F6
Joetsu 123,418	H5
Joyo 57,221	J7

Kadoma 143,238	J7
Kaga 61,599	H5
Kaizuka 75,644	J8
Kaizuka 79,506	H8
Kakogawa 169,293	G6
Kamaishi 88,880	L4
Kamakura 165,552	O3
Kameoka 58,184	J7
Kamiisco 27,229	K3
Kaminoyama 37,858	J4
Kamiyaku 8,668	E8
Kamo 8,953	J5
Kanazawa 395,263	H5
Kanonji 44,131	F6
Kanoya 67,951	E8
Kanuma 81,799	J5
Karatsu 75,224	D7
Kaseda 24,969	J8
Kashihara 95,701	J8
Kashiwa 203,065	P2
Kashiwara 63,586	J8
Kashiwazaki 80,351	J5
Kasugai 213,857	H6
Kasukabe 121,639	O2
Katsuta 79,996	K5
Katsuura 26,755	K6
Kawachinagano 66,936	J8
Kawagoe 225,465	O2
Kawaguchi 345,538	O2
Kawanishi 115,773	H7
Kawasaki 1,014,951	O2
Kesennuma 66,616	K4
Kikonai 10,034	K3
Kimitsu 76,016	P3
Kiryu 134,239	J5
Kisarazu 96,840	P3
Kishiwada 174,952	J8
Kitaibaraki 44,332	K5

Kitakami 48,759	K4
Kitakata 37,471	J5
Kitakyushu 1,058,058	E8
Kitami 91,519	L2
Kizu 11,890	J7
Kobayashi 38,325	E8
Kobe 1,360,605	H7
Kochi 280,962	F7
Kodaira 156,181	O2
Kofu 193,879	J6
Koga 55,973	J5
Koganei 102,714	O2
Kokubu 31,660	E8
Komagane 30,318	H6
Komatsu 100,273	H5
Koriyama 264,628	K5
Koshigaya 195,917	P2
Koyama 16,394	E8
Kubohama 17,817	F7
Kuji 38,122	K3
Kuki 45,797	O2
Kumagaya 131,485	J5
Kumamoto 488,166	E7
Kumano 27,026	G7
Kumiyama 11,540	J7
Kurashiki 392,755	F6
Kurayoshi 50,785	F6
Kure 242,655	F6
Kuroiso 42,349	K5
Kurume 204,474	E7
Kushikino 30,456	E8
Kushima 30,038	E8
Kushiro 206,840	M2
Kushimoto 18,997	G7
Kusatsu 24,269	J7
Kyoto 1,461,059	J7
Machida 255,305	O2
Maebashi 250,241	J5
Maihara 12,845	G6
Maizuru 97,780	G6
Makubetsu 18,444	L2
Makurazaki 29,685	O3
Mashike 9,312	K2
Masuda 50,734	E6
Matsubara 132,662	H8
Matsue 177,440	F6
Matsumae 18,307	J3
Matsumoto 185,595	K5
Matsusaka 108,893	H6
Matsuto 36,170	H5
Matsuyama 367,323	F7
Mihara 83,679	F6
Miki 53,731	H7
Mikuni 21,602	H5
Minamata 36,782	E7
Minobu 10,345	J6
Minoo 79,621	J7
Misawa 37,437	K3
Mitaka 164,950	O2
Mito 197,953	K5
Mitsukaido 38,820	P2
Miura 47,888	O3
Miyako 61,912	L4
Miyakonojo 118,289	E8
Miyazaki 234,347	E8
Miyazu 30,194	J7
Miyoshi 37,193	F6
Mizusawa 52,266	K4
Mobara 64,942	K6
Mombetsu 32,825	L1
Monbetsu 15,029	L2
Mooka 47,345	K5
Mori 17,030	K2
Moriguchi 178,383	J7
Morioka 216,223	K4
Motobu 17,823	N6
Muko 45,886	J7
Murakami 32,939	J4
Muroran 158,715	K2
Muroto 26,660	G7
Musashino 139,508	O2
Mutsu 44,646	K3
Nachikatsuura 23,596	H7
Nagahama, Ehime 13,144	F7
Nagahama, Shiga 54,064	H6
Nagano 306,637	J5
Nagaoka, Kyoto 65,557	J7
Nagaoka, Niigata 171,742	J5
Nagaokakyo 65,557	J7
Nagasaki 450,194	D7
Nagato 27,327	E6
Nago 45,210	N6
Nagoya 2,079,740	H6
Naha 295,006	N6
Nakaminato 33,147	K5
Nakamura 34,437	F7
Nakasato 14,248	K3
Nakatsu 59,111	E7
Nanao 49,493	H5
Nankoku 42,832	F7
Nara 257,538	J8
Narashino 117,852	P2
Nayoro 35,145	L1
Naze 46,359	O5
Nemuro 45,817	M2
Neyagawa 254,311	J7
Nichinan 52,171	E8
Niigata 423,188	J5
Niihama 131,712	F6
Niimi 30,014	F6
Niitsu 58,970	J5
Nishinomiya 400,622	H8

(continued on following page)

Agriculture, Industry and Resources

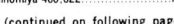

DOMINANT LAND USE

- Cereals, Cash Crops
- Truck Farming, Horticulture
- Mixed Farming, Dairy
- Rice
- Forests, Scrub

MAJOR MINERAL OCCURRENCES

Ag	Silver	Mn	Manganese
Au	Gold	Mo	Molybdenum
C	Coal	O	Petroleum
Cu	Copper	Pb	Lead
Fe	Iron Ore	Py	Pyrites
G	Natural Gas	U	Uranium
Gr	Graphite	W	Tungsten
Mg	Magnesium	Zn	Zinc

⚡ Water Power

▨ Major Industrial Areas

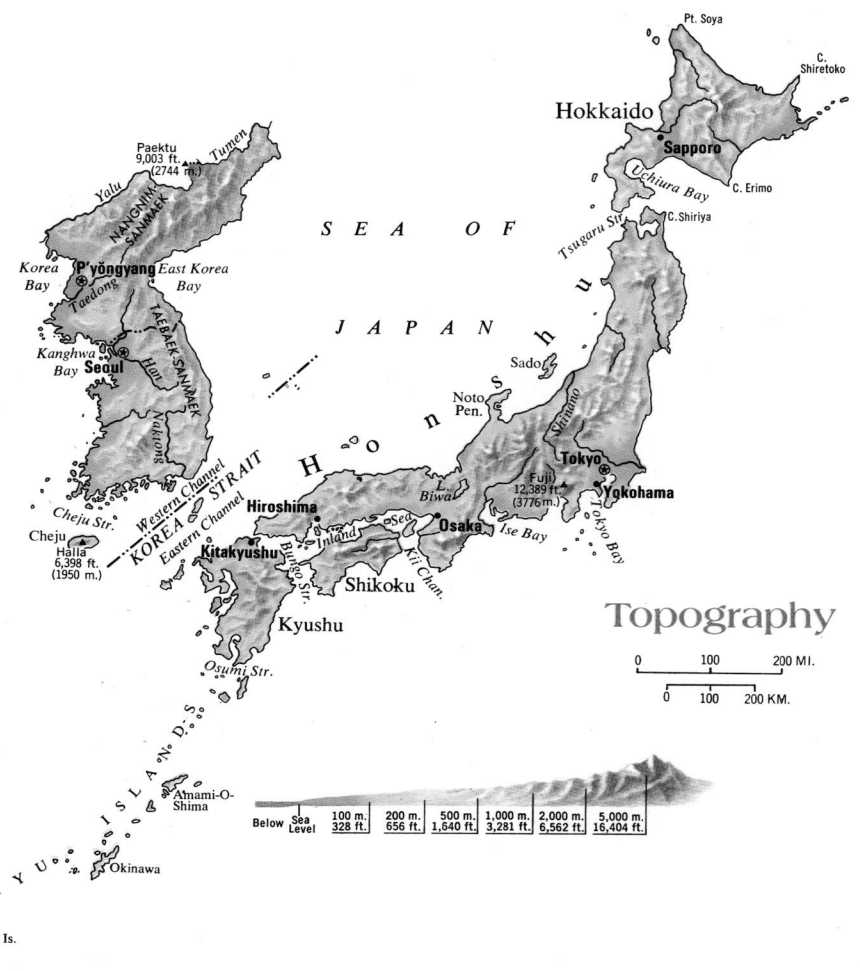

Topography

JAPAN is divided into prefectures bearing the same names as their capitals except:

Prefecture	Capital	Ref.
AICHI	NAGOYA	H 6
EHIME	MATSUYAMA	F 7
GUMMA	MAEBASHI	J 5
HOKKAIDO	SAPPORO	K 2
HYOGO	KOBE	H 7
IBARAKI	MITO	K 5
ISHIKAWA	KANAZAWA	H 5
IWATE	MORIOKA	K 4
KAGAWA	TAKAMATSU	G 6
KANAGAWA	YOKOHAMA	O 3
MIE	TSU	H 6
MIYAGI	SENDAI	K 4
OKINAWA	NAHA	N 6
SAITAMA	URAWA	O 2
SHIGA	OTSU	J 7
SHIMANE	MATSUE	F 6
TOCHIGI	UTSUNOMIYA	K 5
YAMANASHI	KOFU	J 6

Tarama (isl.) ... L7
Tazawa (lake) ... K4
Teshio (mt.) ... L1
Teshio (riv.) ... L1
Tobi (isl.) ... J4
Tokachi (mt.) ... L2
Tokachi (riv.) ... L2
Tokara (isls.) ... O5
Tokuno (isl.) ... D7
Tokyo ... O2
Tone (riv.) ... O2
Tosa (bay) ... F7
Towada (lake) ... K3
Towada-Hachimantai National Park ... K2
Toya (lake) ... K2
Toyama (bay) ... H5
Tsu (isls.) ... D6
Tsugaru (str.) ... K3
Tsurugi (mt.) ... G7
Tsushima (isl.) ... K2
Uchiura (bay) ... K2
Unzen (mt.) ... D7
Unzen-Amakusa National Park ... M4
Volcano (isls.) ... M5
Wakasa (bay) ... G6

Yaeyama (isls.) ... K7
Yaku (isl.) ... E8
Yodo (riv.) ... J7
Yonaguni (isl.) ... K7
Yoron (isl.) ... N6
Yoshino (riv.) ... G7
Yoshino-Kumano National Park ... H7
Zao (mt.) ... K5

KOREA (NORTH)

CITIES and TOWNS

Ch'ŏngjin 306.000 ... E3
Chŏngju ... B4
Haeju 140.000 ... B4
Hamhŭng 484.000 ... C4
Heijo (P'yŏngyang)
  (cap.) 1.250.000 ... C4
Hongwŏn ... C3
Huch'ang ... C3
Hŭich'ŏn ... C3
Hyesan ... D3
Iwŏn ... D3

Kaech'ŏn ... B4
Kaesŏng 175.000 ... C4
Kangye ... C3
Kapsan ... C3
Kilchu ... D3
Kimch'aek 100.000 ... D3
Najin ... E2
Namp'o 140.000 ... B4
Onsŏng ... D2
P'anmunjŏm ... C4
P'yŏngyang (cap.) 1.250.000 ... C4
Sariwŏn ... B4
Sinŭiju 300.000 ... B3
Songnim ... C4
Wŏnsan 275.000 ... C4

OTHER FEATURES

Baktu (Paektu) (mt.) ... C3
Changjin (riv.) ... C3
East Korea (bay) ... D4
Japan (sea) ... B5
Kanghwa (bay) ... C4
Changsong 26.266 ... C5
Chech'ŏn 74.239 ... C5
Cheju 135.081 ... C7
Kangnŭng 84.981 ... D4
Kŭmgang (mt.) ... D4

Kwanmo (mt.) ... D3
Myohyang (mt.) ... C3
Nangnim-sanmaek (range) ... C3
Paektu (mt.) ... C3
Puksubaek (mt.) ... C3
Sasu (mt.) ... B3
Supung (res.) ... B3
Taedong (riv.) ... C4
Tumen (riv.) ... D2
Tuun (mt.) ... C3
Yalu (riv.) ... C3
Yellow (sea) ... B6

KOREA (SOUTH)

CITIES and TOWNS

Andong 95.364 ... D5
Ansŏng 27.723 ... C5
Changhŭng 22.227 ... C6

Chinju 154.646 ... D6
Choch'iwŏn 29.198 ... C5
Ch'ŏnan 96.766 ... C5
Ch'ŏngju 192.707 ... C5
Chŏngŭp 54.864 ... C6
Chŏnju 311.393 ... C6
Ch'ŏrwŏn 8.180 ... C4
Ch'unch'ŏn 140.530 ... D4
Chunju 105.274 ... C5
Hongch'ŏn 29.499 ... D4
Hŭngnam 26.995 ... C5
Inch'ŏn 800.007 ... C5
Iri 117.155 ... C6
Kimch'ŏn 67.078 ... D5
Kimje 221.414 ... C6
Kimhae 203.428 ... D6
Koch'ang 23.721 ... C6
Kŏhŭng 217.446 ... C6
Kongju 59.263 ... C5
Kunsan 154.780 ... C6
Kwangju 607.011 ... C6
Kyŏngju 108.431 ... D6
Masan 371.917 ... D6
Miryang 42.951 ... D6

Mokp'o 192.958 ... C6
Muju 18.130 ... C5
Namwŏn 50.857 ... C6
Nonsan 226.429 ... C5
P'ohang 134.418 ... D5
Posŏng 20.256 ... C6
Pusan 2.453.173 ... D6
Samch'ŏk 42.526 ... D5
Samnangjin 19.374 ... D6
Sangju 52.839 ... D5
Seoul (cap.) 6.889.502 ... C5
Sŏch'ŏn 71.387 ... C6
Sŏsan 38.081 ... C5
Sokch'o 108.063 ... D4
Suwŏn 224.145 ... C5
Taegu 1.310.768 ... D6
Taejŏn 506.708 ... C5
Tamyang 15.494 ... C6
Ŭisŏng 26.480 ... D5
Ulchin 27.607 ... D5
Ulsan 252.570 ... D6
Wŏnju 120.276 ... C5
Yanggu 277.986 ... C4
Yangyang 10.819 ... D4

Yŏngch'ŏn 50.765 ... D6
Yŏngdŏk 18.671 ... D5
Yŏngju 70.793 ... D5
Yŏsu 130.623 ... C6

OTHER FEATURES

Cheju (isl.) ... C7
Cheju (str.) ... C7
Chiri (mt.) ... C6
Dagelet (Ullŏng) (isl.) ... E5
East China (sea) ... C8
Halla (mt.) ... C7
Han (riv.) ... C5
Japan (sea) ... D4
Kanghwa (bay) ... C4
Kebang (mt.) ... D5
Kŏje (isl.) ... D6
Korea (str.) ... D7
Kŭm (riv.) ... C6
Naktong (riv.) ... D5
Port Hamilton (So.) (isl.) ... C7
Quelpart (Cheju) (isl.) ... C7
So (isl.) ... C6

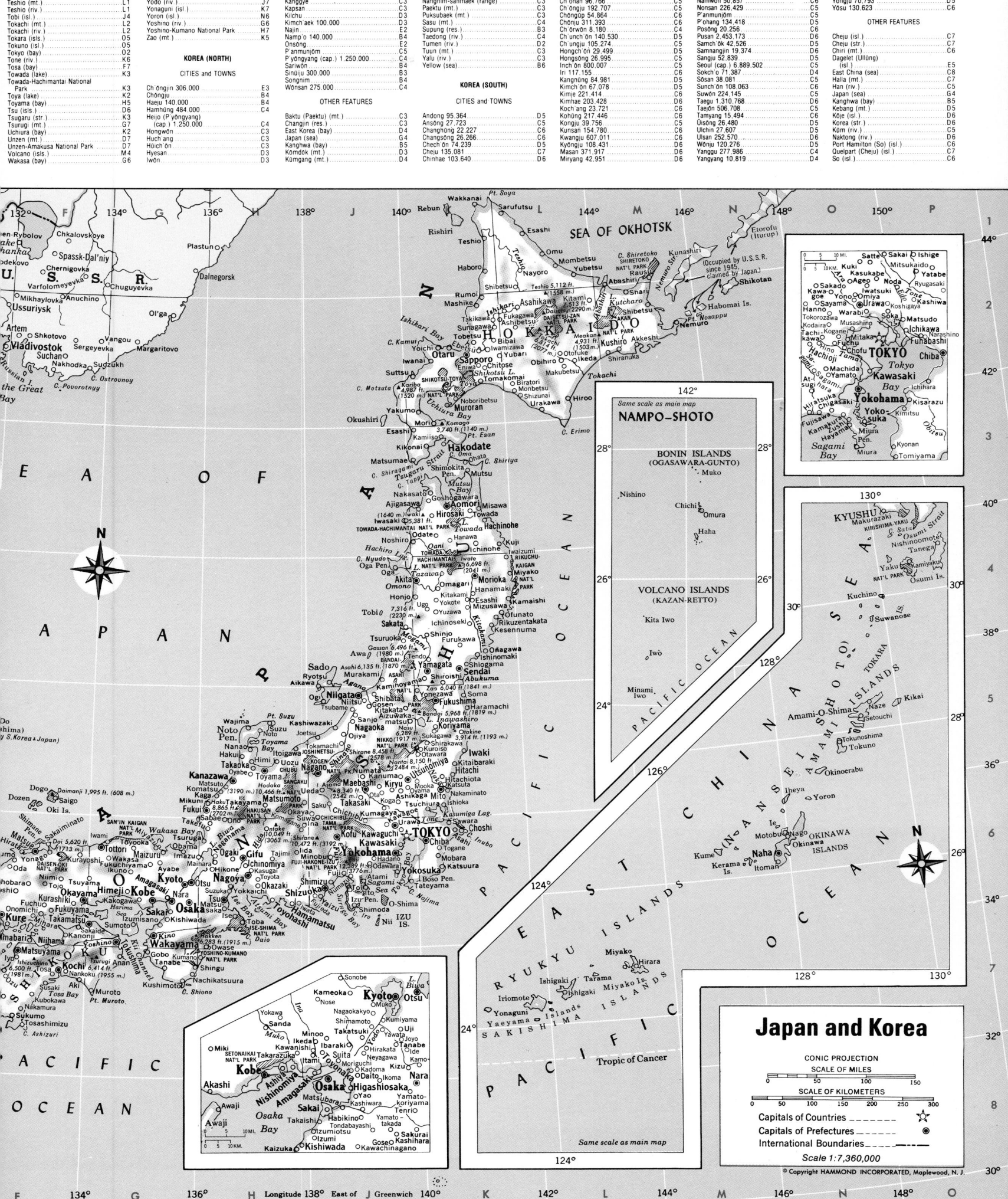

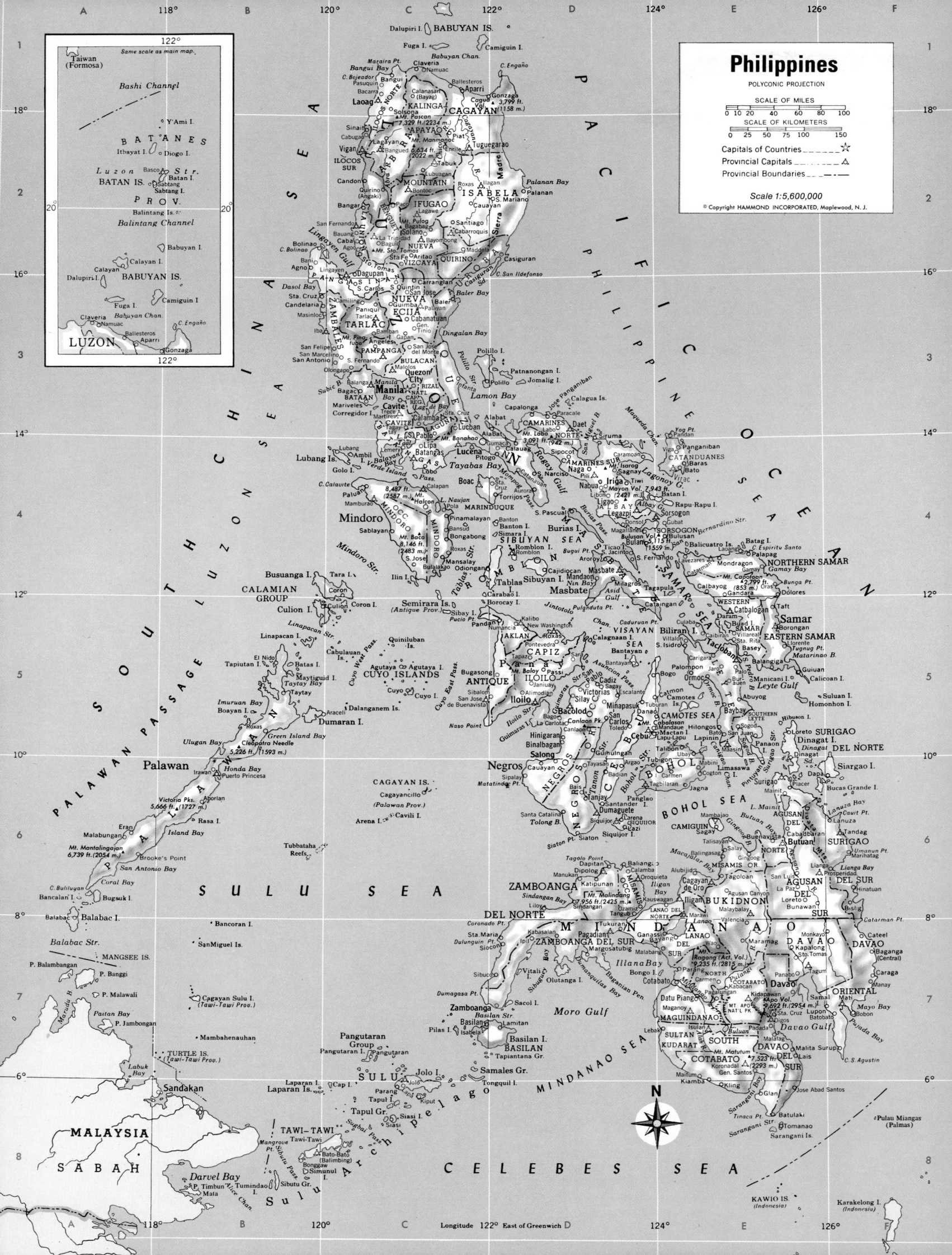

Philippines

POLYCONIC PROJECTION

SCALE OF MILES

SCALE OF KILOMETERS

Capitals of Countries _____ ☆
Provincial Capitals _____ △
Provincial Boundaries _ _ _ _

Scale 1:5,600,000

© Copyright HAMMOND INCORPORATED, Maplewood, N.J.

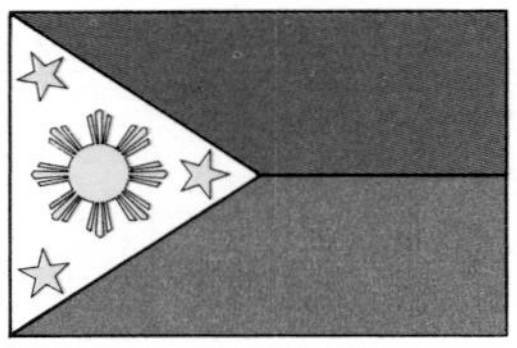

AREA 115,707 sq. mi. (299,681 sq. km.)
POPULATION 48,098,460
CAPITAL Manila
LARGEST CITY Manila
HIGHEST POINT Apo 9,692 ft. (2,954 m.)
MONETARY UNIT peso
MAJOR LANGUAGES Pilipino (Tagalog), English, Spanish, Bisayan, Ilocano, Bikol
MAJOR RELIGIONS Roman Catholicism, Islam, Protestantism, tribal religions

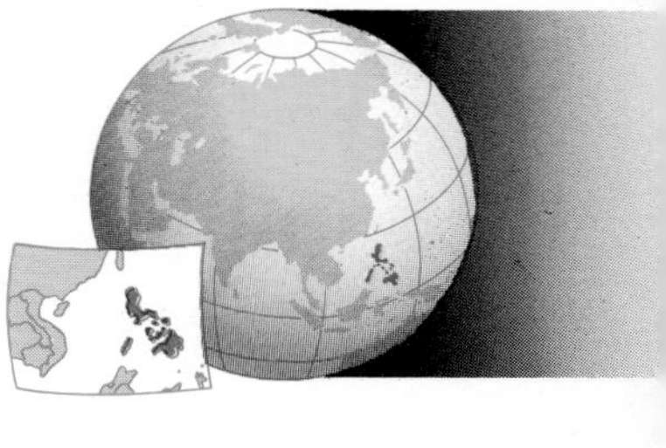

PROVINCES

Abra 160,198 . . . C2
Agusan del Norte 365,421 . . E6
Agusan del Sur 631,634 . . E6
Aklan 324,563 . . . D5
Albay 809,177 . . . D4
Antique 344,879 . . . D5
Aurora 107,145 . . . C3
Basilan 201,407 . . . D7
Bataan 323,254 . . . C3
Batanes 12,091 . . . A2
Batangas 1,174,201 . . . C4
Benguet 354,751 . . . C2
Bohol 806,031 . . . E6
Bukidnon 631,634 . . . E6
Bulacan 1,098,046 . . . C3
Cagayan 711,476 . . . C1
Camarines Norte 368,007 . . D3
Camarines Sur 1,099,346 . . D4
Camiguin 57,126 . . . E6
Capiz 492,231 . . . D5
Catanduanes 175,247 . . . E4
Cavite 771,320 . . . C3
Cebu 2,091,602 . . . D5
Davao 725,153 . . . E7
Davao del Sur 1,133,599 . . E7
Davao Oriental 339,931 . . . F7
Eastern Samar 320,637 . . . E5
Ifugao 111,368 . . . C2
Ilocos Norte 390,666 . . . C1
Ilocos Sur 443,591 . . . C2
Iloilo 1,433,641 . . . D5
Isabela 870,604 . . . C2
Kalinga-Apayao 185,063 . . . C1
Laguna 973,104 . . . C3
Lanao del Norte 461,049 . . . E6
Lanao del Sur 404,971 . . . E7
La Union 452,578 . . . C2
Leyte 1,302,648 . . . E5
Maguindanao 536,546 . . . E7
Manila 5,925,884 . . . C3
Marinduque 173,715 . . . C4
Masbate 584,526 . . . D4
Misamis Occidental 386,328 D6
Misamis Oriental 690,032 . . E6
Mountain 103,052 . . . C2
National Capital Region (Manila) 5,925,884 . . . C3
Negros Occidental 1,930,301 . . . D6
Negros Oriental 819,399 . . . D6
North Cotabato 564,599 . . . E7
Northern Samar 378,516 . . . E4
Nueva Ecija 1,069,409 . . . C3
Nueva Vizcaya 241,690 . . . C2
Occidental Mindoro 222,431 C4
Oriental Mindoro 448,938 . . C4
Palawan 371,782 . . . B6
Pampanga 1,181,590 . . . C3
Pangasinan 1,636,057 . . . C3
Quezon 1,129,277 . . . C3
Quirino 83,230 . . . C2
Rizal 555,533 . . . C3
Romblon 193,174 . . . D4
Siquijor 70,300 . . . D6
Sorsogon 500,685 . . . E4
South Cotabato 770,473 . . . E7
Southern Leyte 298,294 . . . E5
Sultan Kudarat 303,784 . . . E7
Sulu 360,588 . . . C7
Surigao del Norte 363,414 . . F5
Surigao del Sur 377,647 . . . F6
Tarlac 638,457 . . . C3
Tawi-Tawi 194,651 . . . B8
Western Samar 501,439 . . . E5
Zambales 444,037 . . . C3
Zamboanga del Norte 588,015 . . . D6
Zamboanga del Sur 1,183,845 . . . D7

CITIES and TOWNS

Angeles 188,834 . . . C3
Aparri 45,070 . . . C1
Bacolod 262,415 . . . D5
Bagac 13,109 . . . C3
Bago 99,631 . . . D5
Baguio 119,009 . . . C2
Balanga 39,132 . . . C3
Baler 18,349 . . . C3
Balimbing (Bato-Bato) 22,189 . . . C8
Bamban 26,072 . . . C3
Basco 4,341 . . . A2
Batangas 143,570 . . . C4
Bato-Bato 22,189 . . . C8
Baybay 74,640 . . . E5
Bislig 81,615 . . . F6
Boac 37,005 . . . C4
Bontoc 17,091 . . . C2
Burauen 48,058 . . . E5
Butuan 172,489 . . . E6
Cabanatuan 138,298 . . . C3
Cabarroquis 17,450 . . . C2
Cadiz 129,632 . . . D5
Cagayan de Oro 227,312 . . . E6
Calamba 121,175 . . . C3
Calbayog 106,719 . . . E4
Carigara 34,377 . . . E5
Cauayan 70,017 . . . D6
Cavite 87,666 . . . C3
Cebu 490,281 . . . D5
Cotabato 83,871 . . . D7
Dagupan 98,344 . . . C2
Davao 610,375 . . . E7
Digos 70,065 . . . E7
Escalante 71,293 . . . D5
General Santos 149,396 . . . E7
Gingoog 79,937 . . . E6
Guihulngan 84,156 . . . D5
Guimba 58,847 . . . C3
Iba 22,791 . . . B3
Ilagan 79,336 . . . C2
Iligan 167,358 . . . E6
Iloilo 244,827 . . . D5
Infanta 27,914 . . . C3
Jaro 29,739 . . . E5
Jolo 52,429 . . . C8
Koronadal 80,566 . . . E7
Lagawe 15,075 . . . C2
Lapu-Lapu 98,723 . . . E5
Legazpi 99,766 . . . D4
Ligao 69,860 . . . D4
Lingayen 65,187 . . . C2
Lipa 121,166 . . . C4
Lucena 107,880 . . . C4
Maganoy 45,845 . . . E7
Mainit 18,078 . . . E6
Malabang 18,955 . . . D7
Malolos 95,699 . . . C3
Mandaue 110,590 . . . E5
Manila (cap.) 1,630,485 . . . C3
Mariveles 48,594 . . . C3
Mati 78,178 . . . F7
Naga 90,712 . . . D4
Olongapo 156,430 . . . C3
Ormoc 104,978 . . . E5
Ozamiz 77,832 . . . D6
Pagadian 80,861 . . . D7
Palo 31,124 . . . E5
Palompon 40,242 . . . E5
Panabo 71,098 . . . E7
Prosperidad 33,824 . . . F6
Puerto Princesa 60,234 . . . B6
Quezon City 1,165,865 . . . C3
Romblon 24,251 . . . D4
Roxas 81,183 . . . D5
Sagay 99,118 . . . D5
San Antonio 42,969 . . . B3
San Carlos, Negros Occ. 91,627 . . . D5
San Carlos, Pangasinan 101,243 . . . C3
San Fernando, La Union 68,410 . . . C2
San Fernando, Pampanga 110,891 . . . C3
San Jose 64,254 . . . C3
San Jose del Monte 90,732 . . C3
San Pablo 131,655 . . . C3
Santa Fe 6,338 . . . C2
Santiago 69,877 . . . C2
Silay 111,131 . . . D5
Siquijor 17,533 . . . D6
Surigao 79,745 . . . E6
Tacloban 102,523 . . . E5
Tagaytay 16,322 . . . C3
Tagum 86,201 . . . E7
Tarlac 175,691 . . . C3
Toledo 91,668 . . . D5
Tuguegarao 73,507 . . . C2
Zamboanga 343,722 . . . C7

OTHER FEATURES

Agusan (riv.) . . . E6
Alabat (isl.) . . . D3
Apo (vol.) . . . E7
Babuyan (isl.) . . . B2
Balabac (isl.) . . . A7
Balayan (bay) . . . C4
Balintang (chan.) . . . A2
Baloy (mt.) . . . D5
Bantayan (isl.) . . . D5
Banton (isl.) . . . D4
Bashi (chan.) . . . A1
Basilan (isl.) . . . D7
Batan, Albay (isl.) . . . E4
Batan, Batanes (isl.) . . . B2
Batan (isls.) . . . A2
Bay, Laguna de (lake) . . . C3
Biliran (isl.) . . . E5
Bohol (isl.) . . . E6
Bojeador (cape) . . . C1
Borocay (isl.) . . . D5
Bucas Grande (isl.) . . . F6
Bugsuk (isl.) . . . A6
Buliluyan (cape) . . . A6
Bunga (pt.) . . . E4
Burias (isl.) . . . D4
Busuanga (isl.) . . . B4
Cabalasan (mt.) . . . E5
Cabulauan (isls.) . . . C5
Cagayan (isls.) . . . C6
Cagayan (riv.) . . . C2
Cagayan Sulu (isl.) . . . B7
Cagua (vol.) . . . D1
Calagua (isls.) . . . D3
Calamian Group (isls.) . . . B4
Calayan (isl.) . . . A2
Calicoan (isl.) . . . E5
Camiguin, Cagayan (isl.) . . . B3
Camiguin, Camiguin (isl.) . . . E6
Camotes (isls.) . . . E5
Camotes (sea) . . . E5
Canigao (chan.) . . . E5
Canlaon (peak) . . . D5
Capotoan (mt.) . . . E4
Carabao (isl.) . . . D4
Catanduanes (isl.) . . . E4
Cebu (isl.) . . . D5
Celebes (sea) . . . D8
Cleopatra Needle (mt.) . . . B5
Coron (isl.) . . . C5
Corregidor (isl.) . . . C3
Culion (isl.) . . . B5
Cuyo (isl.) . . . C5
Cuyo (isls.) . . . C5
Daram (isl.) . . . E5
Davao (gulf) . . . E7
Dinagat (isl.) . . . E5
Diuata (mts.) . . . E6
Dumanquilas (bay) . . . D7
Dumaran (isl.) . . . C5
Engaño (cape) . . . D1
Espiritu Santo (cape) . . . E4
Fuga (isl.) . . . A3
Guimaras (isl.) . . . D5
Halcon (mt.) . . . C4
Hibuson (isl.) . . . E5
Homonhon (isl.) . . . E5
Honda (bay) . . . B6
Iligan (bay) . . . E6
Ilin (isl.) . . . C4
Illana (bay) . . . D7
Imuruan (bay) . . . B5
Island (bay) . . . B6
Itbayat (isl.) . . . A2
Jintotolo (chan.) . . . D5
Jolo (isl.) . . . C7
Jomalig (isl.) . . . D3
Lagonoy (gulf) . . . E4
Lamon (bay) . . . C3
Lanao (lake) . . . E7
Laparan (isls.) . . . B8
Lapinin (isl.) . . . E5
Leyte (gulf) . . . E5
Leyte (isl.) . . . E5
Limasawa (isl.) . . . E6
Linapacan (isl.) . . . B5
Lingayen (gulf) . . . C2
Lubang (isls.) . . . B4
Luzon (isl.) . . . C3
Luzon (str.) . . . A2
Macajalar (bay) . . . E6
Malindang (mt.) . . . D6
Mangsee (isls.) . . . A7
Manila (bay) . . . C3
Mantalingajan (mt.) . . . A6
Maqueda (chan.) . . . D3
Maraira (pt.) . . . C1
Marinduque (isl.) . . . C4
Masbate (isl.) . . . D4
Mayon (vol.) . . . D4
Maytiguid (isl.) . . . B5
Mindanao (isl.) . . . D7
Mindanao (riv.) . . . E7
Mindoro (isl.) . . . C4
Mindoro (str.) . . . C4
Mompog (passg.) . . . D4
Moro (gulf) . . . D7
Mount Apo National Park . . . E7
Naso (pt.) . . . C5
Negros (isl.) . . . D6
Olutanga (isl.) . . . D7
Pacsan (mt.) . . . C2
Palawan (isl.) . . . B6
Palawan (passg.) . . . A6
Panaon (isl.) . . . E5
Panay (isl.) . . . D5
Panglao (isl.) . . . D6
Pangutaran (isl.) . . . C7
Pangutaran Group (isls.) . . . C7
Patnanongan (isl.) . . . D3
Philippine (sea) . . . D3
Pilas (isl.) . . . C7
Pinatubo (mt.) . . . C3
Polillo (isl.) . . . C3
Pujada (bay) . . . F7
Pulangi (riv.) . . . E7
Ragang (vol.) . . . E7
Ragay (gulf) . . . D4
Rapu-Rapu (isl.) . . . E4
Romblon (isl.) . . . D4
Sabtang (isl.) . . . B2
Sacol (isl.) . . . D7
Samal (isl.) . . . E7
Samales Group (isls.) . . . D7
Samar (isl.) . . . E5
Samar (sea) . . . E4
San Agustin (cape) . . . F7
San Bernardino (str.) . . . E4
San Miguel (bay) . . . D3
San Pedro (bay) . . . E5
Santo Tomas (mt.) . . . C2
Semirara (isls.) . . . C5
Siargao (isl.) . . . F6
Sibay (isl.) . . . C5
Sibuguey (bay) . . . D7
Sibutu Group (isls.) . . . B8
Sibuyan (isl.) . . . D4
Sibuyan (sea) . . . D4
Sierra Madre (mt.) . . . D2
Simunul (isl.) . . . B8
Siquijor (isl.) . . . D6
South China (sea) . . . B3
Subic (bay) . . . C3
Sulu (arch.) . . . B8
Sulu (sea) . . . B6
Suluan (isl.) . . . F5
Surigao (str.) . . . E6
Taal (lake) . . . C4
Tablas (isl.) . . . D4
Tablas (str.) . . . C4
Tagapula (isl.) . . . E4
Tagolo (pt.) . . . D6
Tanon (str.) . . . D6
Tapul (isl.) . . . C8
Tapul Group (isls.) . . . C8
Tara (isl.) . . . C4
Tawi-Tawi (isl.) . . . B8
Tayabas (bay) . . . C4
Ticao (isl.) . . . D4
Tinaca (pt.) . . . E8
Tongquil (isl.) . . . D8
Tumindao (isl.) . . . B8
Turtle (isls.) . . . B7
Verde Island (passg.) . . . C4
Victoria (peaks) . . . B6
Visayan (sea) . . . D5

Topography

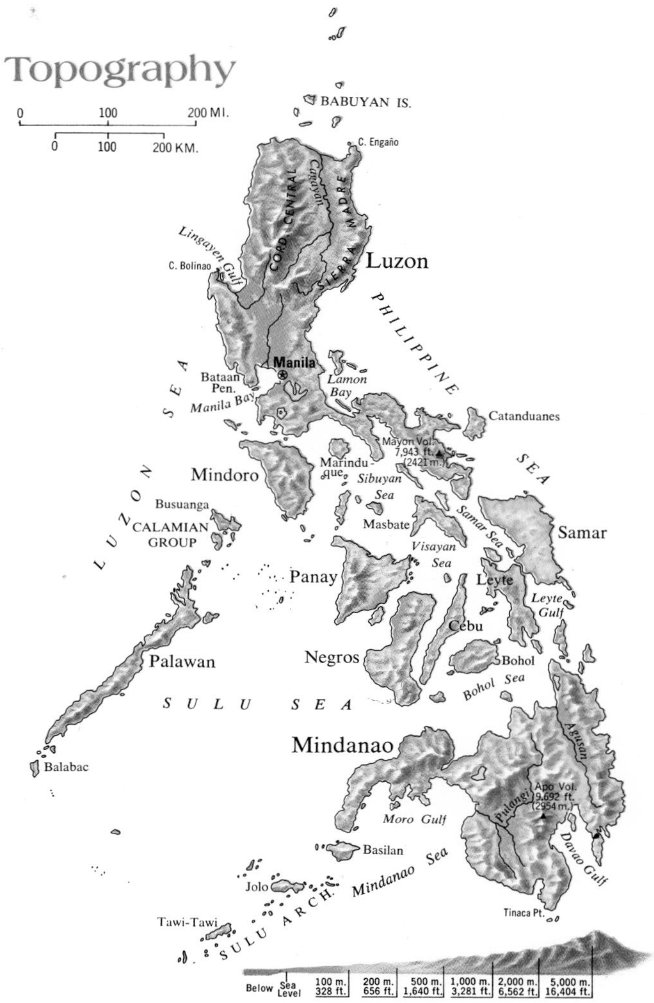

0 100 200 MI.
0 100 200 KM.
BABUYAN IS.
C. Engaño
Luzon
C. Bolinao
Lingayen Gulf
CORD. CENTRAL
SIERRA MADRE
PHILIPPINE
SEA
Manila
Bataan Pen.
Manila Bay
Lamon Bay
Catanduanes
Mayon Vol. 7,943 ft. (2421 m.)
Mindoro
Marinduque
Sibuyan Sea
Busuanga
CALAMIAN GROUP
Masbate
Samar Sea
Samar
LUZON
Visayan Sea
Panay
Leyte
Leyte Gulf
Cebu
Palawan
Negros
Bohol
Bohol Sea
SULU SEA
Mindanao
Agusan
Apo Vol. 9,692 ft. (2954 m.)
Pulangi
Moro Gulf
Davao Gulf
Balabac
Basilan
Jolo
Mindanao Sea
Tawi-Tawi
SULU ARCH.
Tinaca Pt.
Below Sea Level
100 m. 328 ft.
200 m. 656 ft.
500 m. 1,640 ft.
1,000 m. 3,281 ft.
2,000 m. 6,562 ft.
5,000 m. 16,404 ft.

Agriculture, Industry and Resources

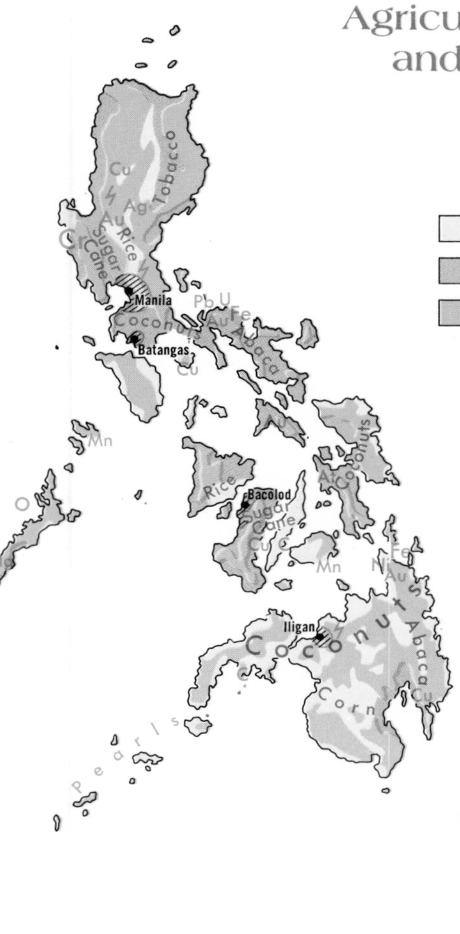

Tobacco
Rice
Sugar Cane
Manila
Batangas
Coconuts
Abaca
Bacolod
Iligan
Corn
Pearls

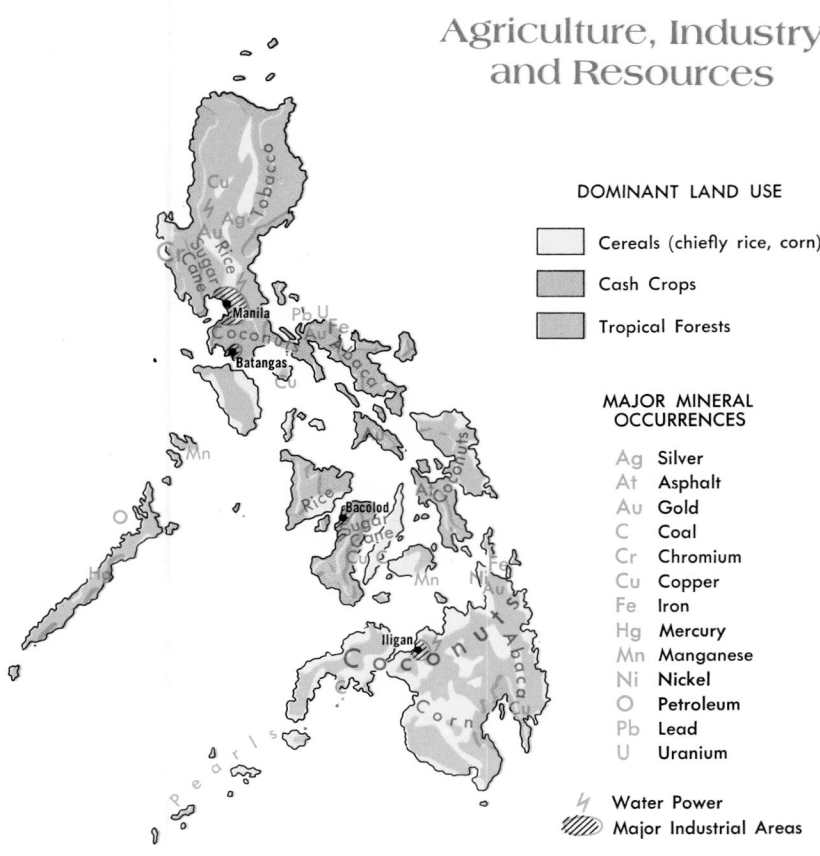

DOMINANT LAND USE

Cereals (chiefly rice, corn)
Cash Crops
Tropical Forests

MAJOR MINERAL OCCURRENCES

Ag Silver
At Asphalt
Au Gold
C Coal
Cr Chromium
Cu Copper
Fe Iron
Hg Mercury
Mn Manganese
Ni Nickel
O Petroleum
Pb Lead
U Uranium

Water Power
Major Industrial Areas

BRUNEI

CITIES and TOWNS

Bandar Seri Begawan 63,868 E4
Seria 23,511 .... E5

INDONESIA

CITIES and TOWNS

Adaut.............J7
Agats.............K7
Ambon (Amboina) 208,898 .. H6
Amuntai F6
Amurang G5
Atambua G7
Aubā H7
Baa G8
Bagansiapiapi C5
Balikpapan 280,675 ..F6
Banda Aceh 72,090 ..A4
Bandanaira H6
Bandung 1,462,637 ..H2
Banggai G6
Banjarmasin 381,286 ..E6
Banyumas J2
Batang J2
Batavia (Jakarta) (cap.)
  6,503,449 ....H1
Baukau H7
Bekasi H2
Belawan B5
Bengkulu 64,783 ..C6
Beo H5
Biak K6
Binjai 76,464 .....B5
Bintuhan C6
Blitar 78,503 .....K2
Bogor 247,409 ....H2
Bojonegoro J2
Bukittinggi 70,771 ..B6
Bula J6
Bulukumba G7
Buntok F6
Cianjur H2
Cimahi H2
Cirebon 223,776 ..H2
Demta L6
Denpasar E7
Dili H7
Djambi (Jambi) 230,373 ..C6
Djokjakarta (Yogyakarta)
  398,727 ....J2
Dobo J7
Donggala F6
Enaratoli K6
Ende G7
Fakfak J6
Garut H2

Gorontalo 97,628 ....G5
Hollandia (Jayapura) K6
Indramayu H2
Jailolo H5
Jakarta (cap.) 6,503,449 ..H1
Jambi 230,373 ...C6
Jayapura (Hollandia) K6
Jogjakarta (Yogyakarta)
  398,727 ....J2
Jombang K2
Kaimana J6
Kampung Baru (Tolitoli) ..G5
Kediri 221,820 ..K2
Kendari G6
Kepi K7
Ketapang E6
Kokonau K6
Kolonodale G6
Kotabaharu E6
Kotabaru F6
Kotawaringin E6
Kragen K2
Kupang G8
Kutaraja (Banda Aceh)
  72,090 ....A4
Labuha H6
Labuhan G2
Laiwui H6
Larantuka G7
Lekitobi G6
Longiram F5
Madiun 150,562 ..K2
Magelang 123,484 ..J2
Majalengka H2
Makassar (Ujung Pandang)
  709,038 ....F7
Malang 511,780 ..K2
Malili G6
Manado 217,159 ..G5
Manokwari J6
Maumere G7
Medan 1,378,955 ..B5
Menggala D6
Merauke K7
Mindiptana L7
Mojokerto 68,849 ..K2
Muarasiberut B6
Nangatayap E6
Pacitan J2
Padang 480,922 ..B6
Padangpanjang 34,517 ..B6
Padangsidempuan ..B5
Pakanbaru 186,262 ..C5
Palangkaraya 60,447 ..E6
Palembang 787,187 ..D6
Pangkalanbuun ...E6
Pangkalpinang 90,096 ..D6
Parepare 86,450 ..F6
Pasangkayu F6
Pasuruan 95,864 ..K2

Payakumbuh 78,836 ....C6
Pekalongan 132,558 ....J2
Pemalang J2
Pematangsiantar 150,376 ..B5
Pinrang F6
Plaju D6
Pontianak 304,778 ..D6
Probolinggo 100,296 ..K2
Purbolinggo J2
Raha G6
Rantauprapat C5
Rembang K2
Sabang, Celebes ..F5
Sabang, Weh 23,821 ..B4
Salatiga 85,849 ..J2
Samarinda 264,718 ..F6
Sampit E6
Sarmi K6
Sawahlunto 13,561 ..C6
Seba G8
Semarang 1,026,671 ..J2
Semitau E5
Serui K6
Sibolga 59,897 ...B5
Sigli B4
Sinabang B5
Singaraja F7
Solo (Surakarta) 469,888 ..J2
Solok 31,724 ....C6
Sorong J6
Sragen J2
Subang H2
Sukabumi 109,994 ..H2
Sumbawa Besar ..F7
Sumedang H2
Surabaya 2,027,913 ..K2
Surakarta 469,888 ..J2
Tanahmerah K7
Tanjungbalai 41,894 ..C5
Tanjungkarang 284,275 ..D7
Tanjungpinang ...C5
Tanjungselor F5
Tarakan F5
Tebingtinggi 92,087 ..B5
Tegal 131,728 ...H2
Telukbayur C6
Tepa H7
Terempa D5
Tjilatjap (Cilacap) ..J2
Tjirebon (Cirebon) 223,776 ..H2
Tolitoli G5
Tuban K2
Ujung Pandang 709,038 ..F7
Vikeke H7
Wahai H6
Waigama H6
Wajabula H5
Waren K6
Weda H5
Wonreli H7

Yogyakarta 398,727 ....J2

OTHER FEATURES

Anambas (isls.) 29,572 ..D5
Arafura (sea) J8
Aru (isls.) 34,195 ..K7
Babar (isl.) H7
Bali (isl.) 2,074,438 ..F7
Banda (sea) H7
Banggai (arch.) 169,025 ..G6
Bangka (isl.) 298,017 ..D6
Banyak (isls.) 1,980 ..B5
Barisan (mts.) ...C6
Barito (riv.) E6
Batu (isls.) 16,390 ..B6
Bawean (isl.) 64,551 ..K1
Belitung (Billiton) (isl.)
  128,694 ....D6
Berau (bay) J6
Biak (isl.) K6
Billiton (isl.) 128,694 ..D6
Binongko (isl.) 11,549 ..G7
Bone (gulf) G7
Borneo (isl.) E5
Bosch, van den (cape) ..J6
Bunguran (Great Natuna)
  (isl.) D5
Buru (isl.) 23,034 ..H6
Butung (isl.) 188,173 ..G6
Celebes (Sulawesi) (isl.)
  7,732,383 ....G6
Celebes (sea) ...G5
Cenderawasih (bay) ..K6
Dampier (str.) ...J6
Digul (riv.) K7
Doberai (pen.) ...J6
Enggano (isl.) 1,082 ..C7
Ewab (Kai) (isls.) 108,328 ..J7
Flores (isl.) 860,328 ..G7
Flores (sea) F7
Frederik Hendrik (Kolepom)
  (isl.) K7
Geelvink (Cenderawasih)
  (bay) K6
Great Kai (isl.) 38,748 ..J7
Halmahera (isl.) 122,521 ..H5
Irian Jaya (reg.) 923,440 ..K6
Jambuair (cape) ..B4
Jamursba (cape) ..J5
Java (head) C7
Java (isl.) 73,712,411 ..J2
Java (sea) D6
Jaya, Puncak (mt.) ..K6
Jayawijaya (range) ..K6
Jemaja (isl.) 5,628 ..D5
Kabaena (isl.) ...G7
Kai (isls.) 108,328 ..J7
Kalao (isl.) G7
Kalaotoa (isl.) ...G5

Kalimantan (reg.) 4,956,865 ..E5
Kangean (isls.) ..F7
Kapuas (riv.) D6
Karakelong (isl.) ..H5
Karimata (arch.) 9,398 ..D5
Karimunjawa (isls.) 5,025 ..J1
Kerinci (mt.) C6
Kisar (isl.) H7
Komodo (isl.) 30,407 ..F7
Krakatau (Rakata) (isl.) ..C7
Laut (isl.) 55,711 ..F6
Leuser (mt.) B5
Lingga (arch.) 46,658 ..D5
Lingga (isl.) 18,027 ..D6
Lombok (isl.) 1,581,193 ..F7
Madura (isl.) 1,509,774 ..K2
Mahakam (riv.) ..F6
Makassar (str.) ..F6
Malacca (str.) ...C5
Mamberamo (riv.) ..K6
Maoke (mts.) K6
Mapia (isls.) J5
Mentawai (isls.) 30,107 ..B6
Misool (isl.) J6
Molucca (sea) ...H6
Moluccas (isls.) 944,240 ..H6
Morotai (isl.) 27,333 ..H5
Muli (str.) K6
Müller (mts.) E5
Muna (isl.) 156,186 ..G7
Musi (riv.) C6
Natuna (isls.) 23,893 ..D5
Ngunju (cape) ...G7
Nias (isl.) 356,093 ..B5
Numfoor (isl.) ...J6
Obi (isls.) 12,437 ..H6
Ombai (str.) H7
Pantar (isl.) 28,259 ..G7
Perkam (cape) ...K6
Puting, Borneo (cape) ..E6
Puting, Sumatra (cape) ..C7
Raja Ampat Group (isls.) ..H6
Rakata (isl.) C7
Rantekombola (mt.) ..G6
Raya (mt.) E6
Riau (arch.) 483,230 ..C5
Rokan (riv.) C5
Roti (isl.) 76,270 ..G8
Salawati (isl.) ...J6
Sangihe (isl.) H5
Sangihe (isls.) 183,000 ..G5
Sawu (isls.) 51,002 ..G8
Sawu (sea) G8
Schouten (isls.) 110,148 ..K6
Schwaner (mts.) ..E6
Sebuku (bay) F5
Selatan (cape) ...G7
Selayar (isl.) 92,342 ..G7
Semeru (mt.) K2
Siau (isl.) 46,801 ..H5

Siberut (str.) B6
Simeulue 29,147 ..A5
Singkep (isl.) 28,631 ..D6
Sipura (isl.) 6,051 ..B6
Slamet (mt.) J2
Sorikmerapi (mt.) ..B5
South Natuna (isls.) ..D5
Sula (isls.) 36,922 ..H6
Sulawesi (isl.) 7,732,383 ..G6
Sumatra (isl.) 19,360,400 ..B5
Sumba (isl.) 291,190 ..F7
Sumba (str.) F7
Sumbawa (isl.) 621,140 ..F7
Sunda (str.) C7
Tahulandang (isl.) 21,493 ..H5
Talaud (isls.) 46,395 ..H5
Taliabu (isl.) 18,303 ..G6
Tambelan (isls.) 4,032 ..D5
Tanimbar (isls.) 55,405 ..J7
Tariku (riv.) K6
Tidore (isl.) 28,655 ..H5
Timor (reg.) 1,435,527 ..H7
Timor (sea) G8
Toba (lake) B5
Tolo (gulf) G6
Tomini (gulf) G6
Tukangbesi (isls.) 73,106 ..G7
Vals (cape) K7
Vogelkop (Doberai) (pen.) ..J6
Waigeo (isl.) J5

Wakde (isl.) K6
Wangiwangi (isl.) 28,469 ..G7
We (isl.) B4
Wetar (isl.) H7
Yapen (isl.) 50,888 ..K6

MALAYSIA

STATES

North Borneo (Sabah)
  1,002,608 ....F3
Sarawak 1,294,753 ..E5

CITIES and TOWNS

Beaufort 2,709 ....F4
Bintulu 4,424 ....E5
Kabong E5
Kampong Sibuti ..E5
Kapit 1,929 .....E5
Keningau 2,037 ..F4
Kota Kinabalu 40,939 ..F4
Kuching 63,535 ..E5
Kudat 5,089 .....F4
Labuan 7,216 ....F4
Lahad Datu 5,169 ..F4
Lamag F4
Marudi 4,700 ....E5
Miri 35,702 .....E5
Mukah 1,717 ....E5

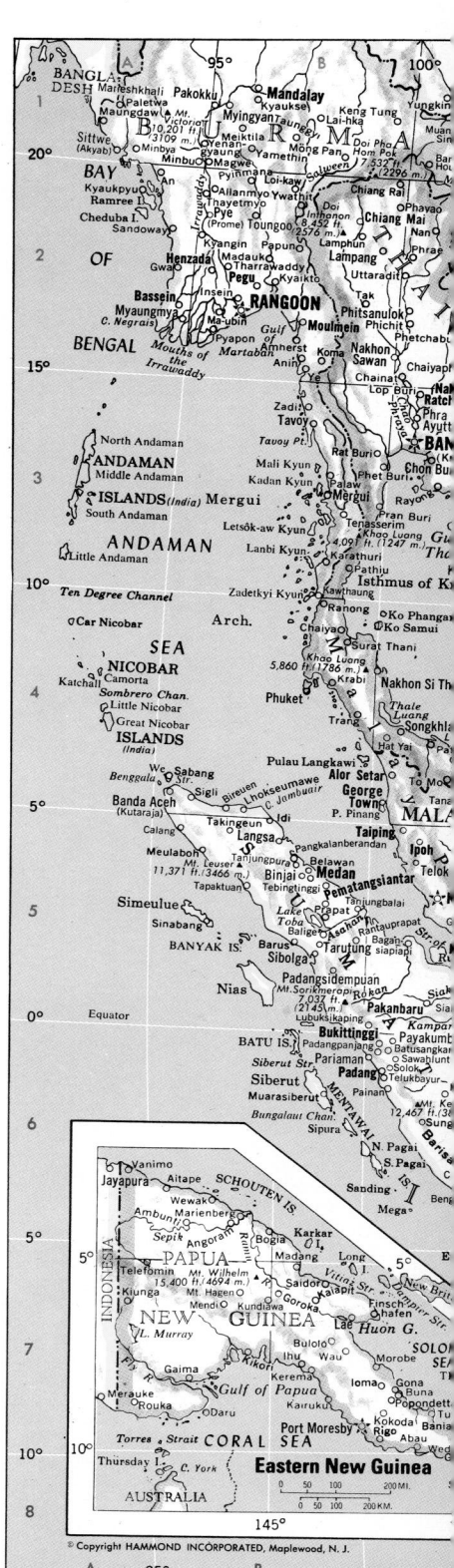

© Copyright HAMMOND INCORPORATED, Maplewood, N.J.

Topography

0   300   600 MI.
0   300   600 KM.

| Below Sea Level | 100 m. 328 ft. | 200 m. 656 ft. | 500 m. 1,640 ft. | 1,000 m. 3,281 ft. | 2,000 m. 6,562 ft. | 5,000 m. 16,404 ft. |

Agriculture, Industry and Resources

DOMINANT LAND USE

Cereals (chiefly rice, corn)

Diversified Tropical Crops

Forests

MAJOR MINERAL OCCURRENCES

Al Bauxite   Cu Copper   Mn Manganese   O Petroleum
Au Gold   Fe Iron Ore   Ni Nickel   Sn Tin
C Coal   G Natural Gas

Major Industrial Areas

Papar 1,855 ....F4
Ranau 2,024 ....F4
Sandakan 42,413 ......F4
Sematan D5
Semporna 3,371 ......F5
Serian 2,209 ....E5
Sibu 50,635 ....E5
Simanggang 8,445 ....E5
Suai E5
Tawau 24,247 ....F4
Weston F4

OTHER FEATURES

Balambangan (isl.) F4
Banggi (isl.) F4
Iran (mts.) E5
Kinabalu (mt.) F4
Labuan (isl.) 17,189 ..F4
Labuk (bay) F4
Rajang (riv.) E5
Sirik (cape) E5

PAPUA NEW GUINEA
CITIES and TOWNS

Abau C7
Aitape 3,368 ....B6
Ambunti 1,035 ....B6
Angoram 1,846 ....B6

Baniara C7
Bogia 755 ....B6
Bulolo 6,730 ....B7
Buna C7
Daru 7,127 ....B7
Finschhaffen 756. ....C7
Gaima B7
Gehua C8
Gona C7
Goroka 18,511 ....B7
Ihu 541 ....C7
Ioma C7
Kaiapit 515 ....B7
Kairuku C7
Kerema 3,389 ....B7
Kikori 763 ....B7
Kiunga 1,407 ....B7
Kokoda C7
Kundiawa 4,299 ......B7
Lae 61,617 ....B7
Madang 21,335 ......B7
Marienberg B6
Mendi 4,130 ....C7
Morobe C7
Mount Hagen 13,441 ..B7
Popondetta 6,429 ....C7
Port Moresby
(cap.) 123,624 ......B7
Rouka B7
Saidor 500 ....B7
Samarai 864 ....C8

Telefomin B7
Vanimo 3,071 ....B6
Wau 2,349 ....B7
Wedau C7
Wewak 19,890 ......B6

OTHER FEATURES

Dampier (str.) C7
D'Entrecasteaux (isls.) ..C7
Fly (riv.) A7
Huon (gulf) C7
Karkar (isl.) B6
Kiriwina (isl.) C7
Long (isl.) B7
Louisiade (arch.) D8
Milne (bay) C8
Misima (isl.) C8
New Britain (isl.) 148,773 ..C7
Ramu (riv.) B7
Rossel (isl.) D8
Schouten (isls.) B6
Sepik (riv.) B6
Solomon (sea) C7
Tagula (isl.) C8
Torres (str.) A7
Trobriand (isls.) C7
Vitiaz (str.) B7
Woodlark (isl.) C7

★See page 74 for other Malaysian entries.

INDONESIA

AREA 788,430 sq. mi. (2,042,034 sq. km.)
POPULATION 147,490,298
CAPITAL Jakarta
LARGEST CITY Jakarta
HIGHEST POINT Puncak Jaya 16,503 ft. (5,030 m.)
MONETARY UNIT rupiah
MAJOR LANGUAGES Bahasa Indonesia, Indonesian and Papuan languages, English
MAJOR RELIGIONS Islam, tribal religions, Christianity, Hinduism

PAPUA NEW GUINEA

AREA 183,540 sq. mi. (475,369 sq. km.)
POPULATION 3,010,727
CAPITAL Port Moresby
LARGEST CITY Port Moresby
HIGHEST POINT Mt. Wilhelm 15,400 ft. (4,694 m.)
MONETARY UNIT kina
MAJOR LANGUAGES pidgin English, Hiri Motu, English
MAJOR RELIGIONS Tribal religions, Christianity

BRUNEI

AREA 2,226 sq. mi. (5,765 sq. km.)
POPULATION 192,832
CAPITAL Bandar Seri Begawan
LARGEST CITY Bandar Seri Begawan
HIGHEST POINT Pagon 6,070 ft. (1,850 m.)
MONETARY UNIT Brunei Dollar
MAJOR LANGUAGES Malay, English, Chinese
MAJOR RELIGIONS Islam, Buddhism, Christianity, tribal religions

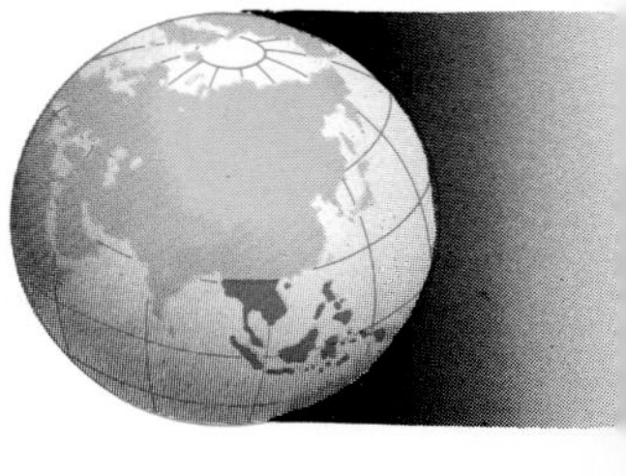

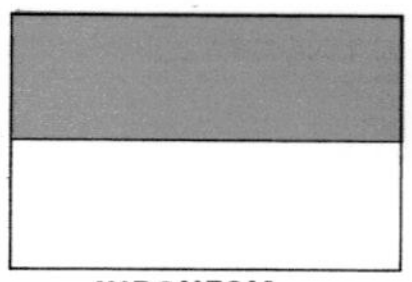

INDONESIA    PAPUA NEW GUINEA    BRUNEI

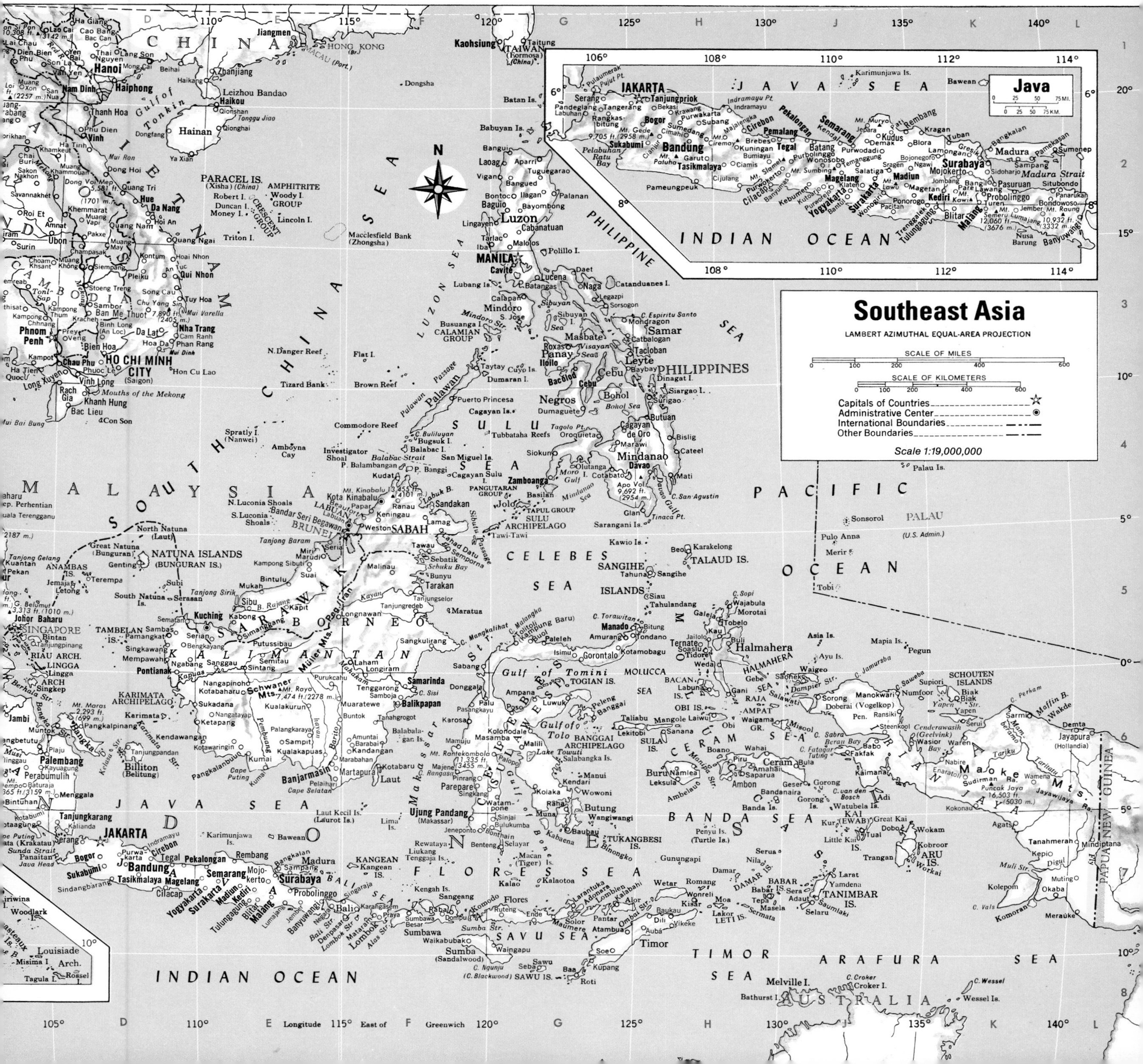

FIJI

AREA 7,055 sq. mi. (18,272 sq. km.)
POPULATION 588,068
CAPITAL Suva
LARGEST CITY Suva
HIGHEST POINT Tomaniivi 4,341 ft. (1,323 m.)
MONETARY UNIT Fijian dollar
MAJOR LANGUAGES Fijian, Hindi, English
MAJOR RELIGIONS Protestantism, Hinduism

KIRIBATI

AREA 291 sq. mi. (754 sq. km.)
POPULATION 56,213
CAPITAL Bairiki (Tarawa)
HIGHEST POINT (on Banaba I.) 285 ft. (87 m.)
MONETARY UNIT Australian dollar
MAJOR LANGUAGES I-Kiribati, English
MAJOR RELIGIONS Protestantism, Roman Catholicism

NAURU

AREA 7.7 sq. mi. (20 sq. km.)
POPULATION 7,254
CAPITAL Yaren (district)
MONETARY UNIT Australian dollar
MAJOR LANGUAGES Nauruan, English
MAJOR RELIGION Protestantism

SOLOMON ISLANDS

AREA 11,500 sq. mi. (29,785 sq. km.)
POPULATION 221,000
CAPITAL Honiara
HIGHEST POINT Mount Popomanatseu 7,647 ft. (2,331 m.)
MONETARY UNIT Solomon Islands dollar
MAJOR LANGUAGES English, pidgin English, Melanesian dialects
MAJOR RELIGIONS Tribal religions, Protestantism, Roman Catholicism

TONGA

AREA 270 sq. mi. (699 sq. km.)
POPULATION 90,128
CAPITAL Nuku'alofa
LARGEST CITY Nuku'alofa
HIGHEST POINT 3,389 ft. (1,033 m.)
MONETARY UNIT pa'anga
MAJOR LANGUAGES Tongan, English
MAJOR RELIGION Protestantism

TUVALU

AREA 9.78 sq. mi. (25.33 sq. km.)
POPULATION 7,349
CAPITAL Fongafale (Funafuti)
HIGHEST POINT 15 ft. (4.6 m.)
MONETARY UNIT Australian dollar
MAJOR LANGUAGES English, Tuvaluan
MAJOR RELIGION Protestantism

Abaiang (atoll) 3,296..........H 5
Abemama (atoll) 2,300..........H 5
Adamstown (cap.), Pitcairn Is. 54..........N 8
Admiralty (isls.)..........E 6
Agaña (cap.), Guam 896..........E 4
Agrihan (isl.)..........E 4
Ailinglapalap (atoll) 1,385..........G 5
Ailuk (atoll) 413..........H 4
Aitutaki (atoll) 2,348..........K 7
Alofi (cap.), Niue 960..........K 7
Alotau 4,310..........E 7
Ambrym (isl.) 6,324..........G 7
American Samoa 32,297..........J 7
Anaa (atoll) 444..........M 7
Angaur (isl.) 243..........D 5
Apataki (atoll)..........M 7
Apia (cap.), W. Samoa 33,100..........J 7
Arno (atoll) 1,487..........H 5
Arorae (atoll) 1,626..........H 6
Atafu (atoll) 577..........J 6
Atiu (isl.) 1,225..........L 8
Austral (isls.) 5,208..........L 8
Avarua (cap.), Cook Is...........L 8
Babelthuap (isl.) 10,391..........D 5
Bairiki (cap.), Kiribati 1,777..........H 5
Baker (isl.)..........J 5
Banaba (isl.) 2,314..........G 6
Banks (isls.) 3,158..........G 7
Belep (isls.) 624..........G 7
Bellona (reefs)..........G 8
Beru (atoll) 2,318..........H 6
Bikini (atoll)..........G 4
Bismarck (arch.) 218,339..........E 6
Bonin (isls.) 1,879..........E 3
Bora-Bora (isl.) 2,572..........L 7
Bougainville (isl.) 71,761..........F 6
Bounty (isls.)..........H 10
Bourail 3,149..........G 8
Butaritari (atoll) 2,971..........H 5
Capitol Hill (cap.), No. Marianas 592..........E 4
Caroline (isl.)..........M 7
Caroline (isls.)..........E 5
Chichi (isl.) 1,879..........E 3
Choiseul (isl.) 10,349..........F 6
Christmas (Kiritimati) (isl.) 674..........L 6
Cook (isls.) 17,695..........K 7
Coral (sea)..........F 7
Danger (Pukapuka) (atoll) 797..........K 7
Daru 7,127..........E 6
Disappointment (isls.) 373..........N 7
Ducie (isl.)..........O 8
Easter (isl.) 1,598..........Q 8
Ebon (atoll) 887..........G 5
Efate (isl.) 18,038..........G 7
Enderbury (isl.)..........J 6
Enewetak (Eniwetok) (atoll) 542..........G 4
Erromanga (isl.) 945..........H 7
Espiritu Santo (isl.) 16,220..........G 7
Fais (isl.) 207..........E 5
Fakaofo (atoll) 654..........J 6
Fanning (Tabuaeran) (isl.) 340..........L 5
Faraulep (atoll) 132..........E 5
Fatuhiva (isl.) 386..........N 7
Fiji 588,068..........H 8
Flint (isl.)..........L 7
Fly (riv.)..........E 6
Fongafale (cap.), Tuvalu..........H 6
French Polynesia 137,382..........L 8
Funafuti (atoll) 2,120..........H 6
Futuna (Hoorn) (isls.) 3,173..........J 7
Gambier (isls.) 556..........N 8
Gardner (Nukumaroro)(isl.)..........J 6
Gilbert (isls.) 47,711..........H 6
Greenwich (Kapingamarangi) (atoll) 508..........F 5
Guadalcanal (isl.) 46,619..........F 7
Guam (isl.) 105,979..........E 4
Hall (isls.) 647..........F 5
Hawaiian (isls.) 964,691..........J 3
Henderson (isl.)..........O 8
Hivaoa (isl.) 1,159..........N 6
Honiara (cap.), Solomon Is. 14,942..........F 6
Hoorn (isls.) 3,173..........J 7
Howland (isl.)..........J 5
Huahine (isl.) 3,140..........L 7
Hull (Orona)(isl.)..........J 6
Huon (gulf)..........E 6
Ifalik (atoll) 389..........E 5
Iwo (isl.)..........E 3
Jaluit (atoll) 1,450..........G 5
Jarvis (isl.)..........K 6
Johnston (atoll) 327..........K 4
Kadavu (Kandavu) (isl.) 8,699..........H 7
Kanton (isl.)..........K 6
Kapingamarangi (atoll) 508..........F 5
Kavieng 4,633..........E 6
Kermadec (isls.) 5..........J 9
Kieta 3,491..........F 6
Kimbe 4,662..........F 6
Kingman (reef)..........K 5
Kiribati 57,500..........J 6
Kiritimati (isl.) 674..........L 5
Kolonia (cap.), Micronesia 5,549..........F 5
Koror (cap.), Belau 6,222..........D 5
Kosrae (isl.) 5,491..........G 5
Kwajalein (atoll) 6,624..........G 5
Lae 61,617..........E 6
Lau Group (isls.) 14,452..........J 7
Lavongai (isl.)..........F 6
Lifu (isl.) 7,585..........G 8
Line (isls.)..........K 5
Little Makin (atoll) 1,445..........H 5
Lord Howe (Ontong Java) (isl.) 1,082..........G 6
Lord Howe (isl.) 287..........H 9
Lorengau 3,986..........E 6
Louisiade (arch.)..........F 7
Loyalty (isls.) 14,518..........G 8
Luganville 4,935..........G 7
Madang 21,335..........E 6

Majuro (atoll) (cap.), Marshall Is. 8,583..........H 5
Makin (Butaritari) 2,971..........H 5
Malaita (isl.) 50,912..........G 6
Malden (isl.)..........L 6
Malekula (isl.) 15,931..........G 7
Maloelap (atoll) 763..........H 5
Mangaia (isl.) 1,364..........L 8
Mangareva (isl.) 556..........N 8
Manihiki (atoll) 405..........K 7
Manua (isls.) 1,459..........K 7
Manus (isl.) 25,844..........E 6
Marcus (isl.)..........F 3
Maré (isl.) 4,156..........G 8
Marianas, Northern 16,780..........E 4
Mariana Trench..........E 4
Marquesas (isls.) 5,419..........N 6
Marshall Islands 30,873..........J 4
Marutea (atoll)..........N 8
Mata Utu (cap.), Wallis and Futuna 558..........J 7
Mauke (isl.) 684..........L 8
Melanesia (reg.)..........E 5
Micronesia (reg.)..........E 4
Micronesia, Federated States of 73,160..........F 5
Midway (isls.) 453..........J 3
Mili (atoll) 763..........H 5
Moen (isl.) 10,351..........F 5
Moorea (isl.) 5,788..........L 7

Mururoa (isl.)..........M 8
Nadi 6,938..........H 7
Namonuito (atoll) 783..........E 5
Namorik (atoll) 617..........G 5
Nanumea (atoll) 844..........H 6
Nauru 7,254..........G 6
Ndeni (isl.) 4,854..........G 7
New Britain (isl.) 148,773..........F 6
New Caledonia 133,233..........G 8
New Caledonia (isl.) 118,715..........G 8
New Georgia (isls.) 16,472..........F 6
New Guinea (isl.)..........E 6
New Ireland (isl.) 65,657..........F 6
Ngatik (atoll) 560..........F 5
Ngulu (atoll) 21..........D 5
Niuatoputapu (isl.) 1,650..........J 7
Niue (isl.) 3,578..........K 7
Niutao (atoll) 866..........H 6
Nomoi (isls.) 1,879..........F 5
Nonouti (atoll) 2,223..........H 6
Norfolk Island (terr.) 2,175..........G 8
Northern Marianas 116,780..........E 4
Nouméa (cap.), New Caled. 56,078..........G 8
Nouméa *74,335..........G 8
Nui (atoll) 603..........H 6
Nuku'alofa (cap.), Tonga 18,356..........J 8
Nukuhiva (isl.) 1,484..........M 6

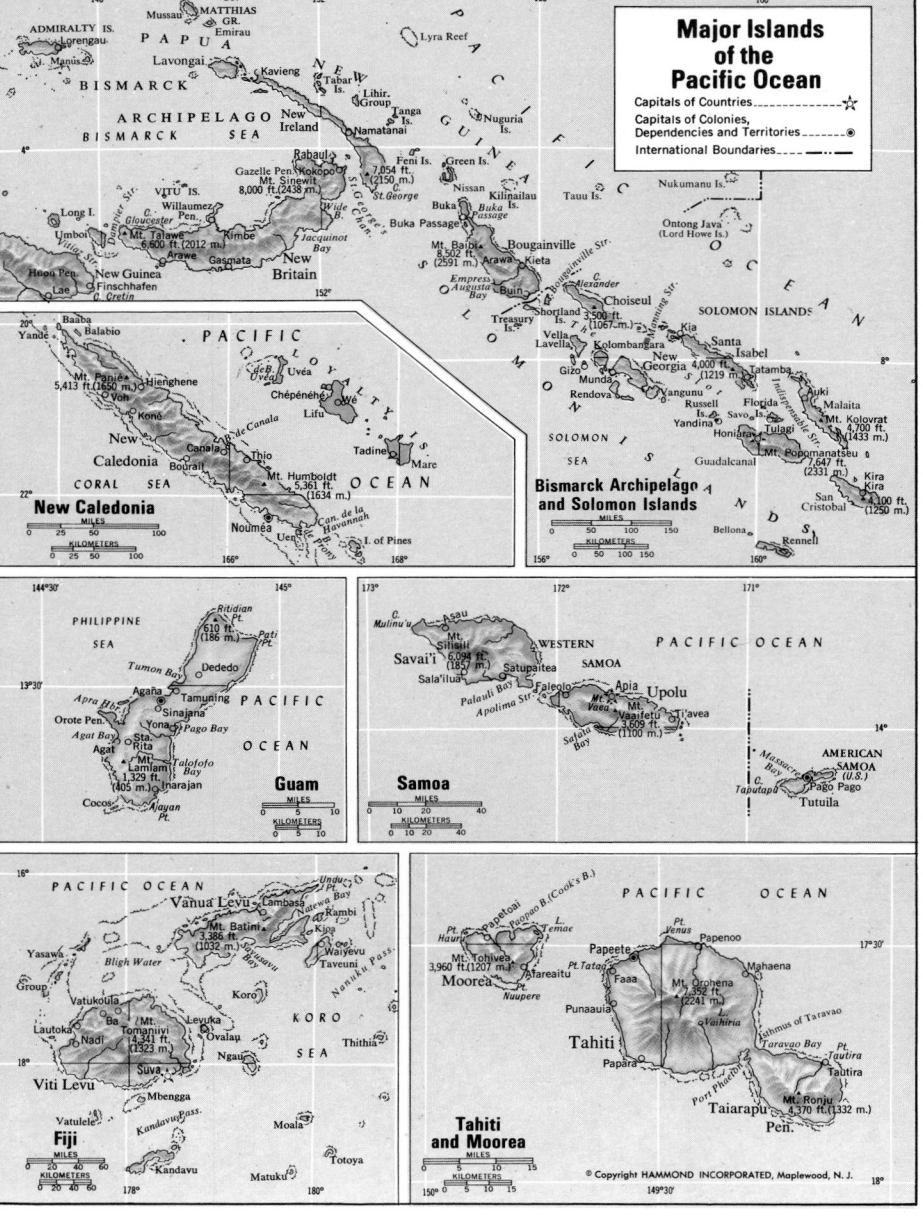

Major Islands of the Pacific Ocean
Capitals of Countries...........☆
Capitals of Colonies, Dependencies and Territories.........◉
International Boundaries.......

New Caledonia

Bismarck Archipelago and Solomon Islands

Guam

Samoa

Fiji

Tahiti and Moorea

© Copyright HAMMOND INCORPORATED, Maplewood, N.J.

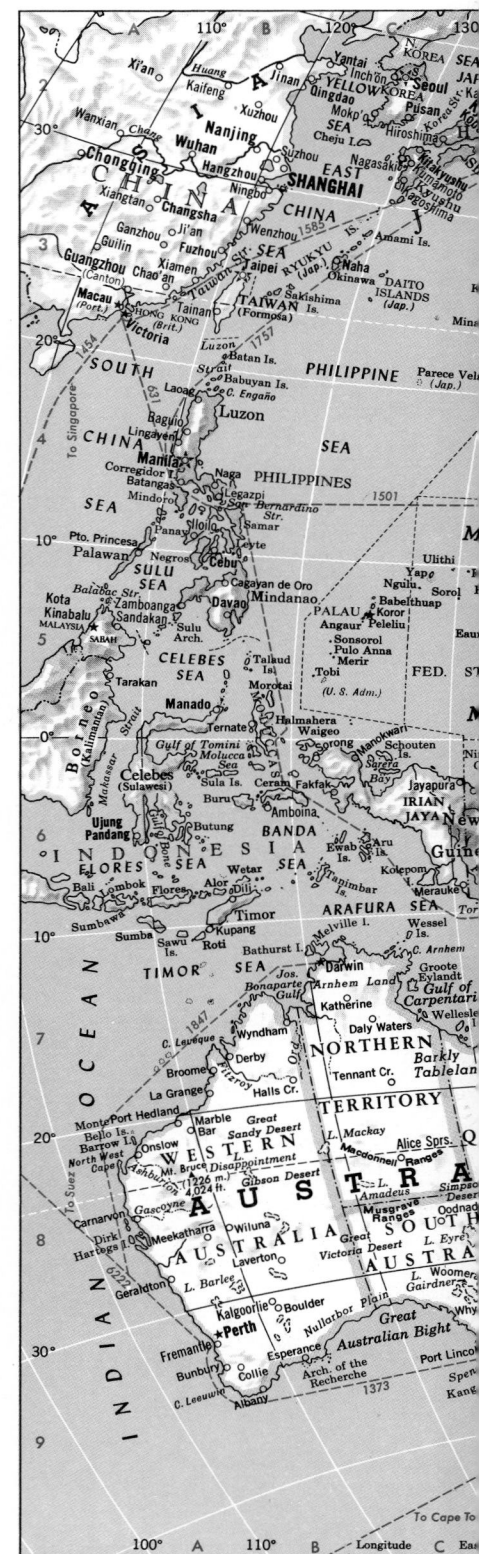

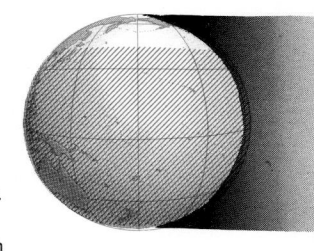

VANUATU

AREA 5,700 sq. mi. (14,763 sq. km.)
POPULATION 112,596
CAPITAL Vila
HIGHEST POINT Mt. Tabwemasana 6,165 ft. (1,879 m.)
MONETARY UNIT vatu
MAJOR LANGUAGES Bislama, English, French
MAJOR RELIGIONS Christian, animist

WESTERN SAMOA

AREA 1,133 sq. mi. (2,934 sq. km.)
POPULATION 158,130
CAPITAL Apia
LARGEST CITY Apia
HIGHEST POINT Mt. Silisili 6,094 ft. (1,857 m.)
MONETARY UNIT tala
MAJOR LANGUAGES Samoan, English
MAJOR RELIGIONS Protestantism, Roman Catholicism

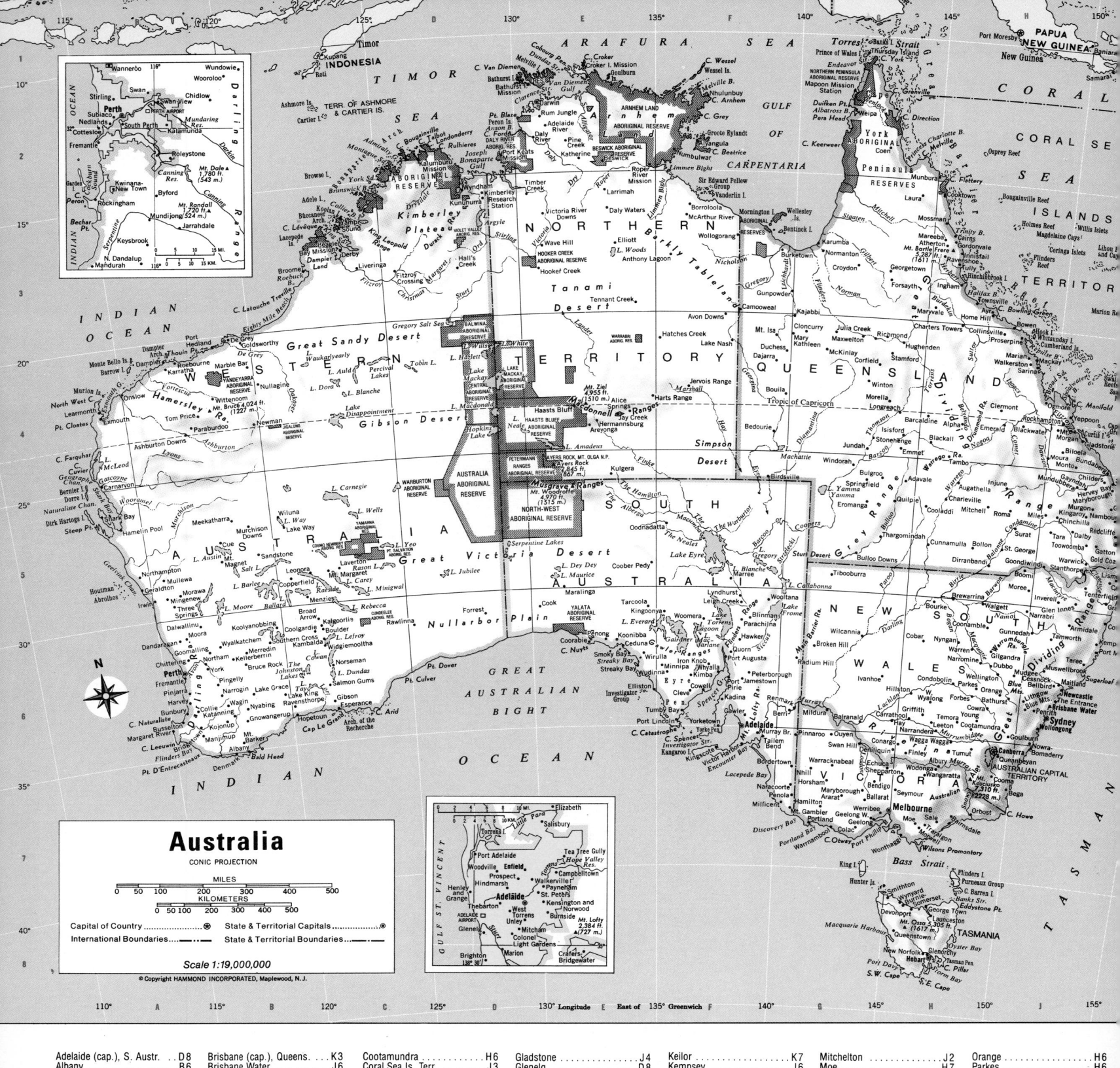

Australia

CONIC PROJECTION

MILES

KILOMETERS

Capital of Country ....⊛ State & Territorial Capitals ....⊛

International Boundaries....... State & Territorial Boundaries........

Scale 1:19,000,000

© Copyright HAMMOND INCORPORATED, Maplewood, N.J.

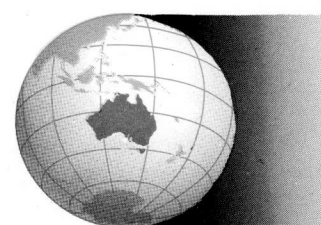

AREA 2,966,136 sq. mi. (7,682,300 sq. km.)
POPULATION 14,576,330
CAPITAL Canberra
LARGEST CITY Sydney
HIGHEST POINT Mt. Kosciusko 7,310 ft.
  (2,228 m.)
LOWEST POINT Lake Eyre -39 ft. (-12 m.)
MONETARY UNIT Australian dollar
MAJOR LANGUAGE English
MAJOR RELIGIONS Protestantism,
  Roman Catholicism

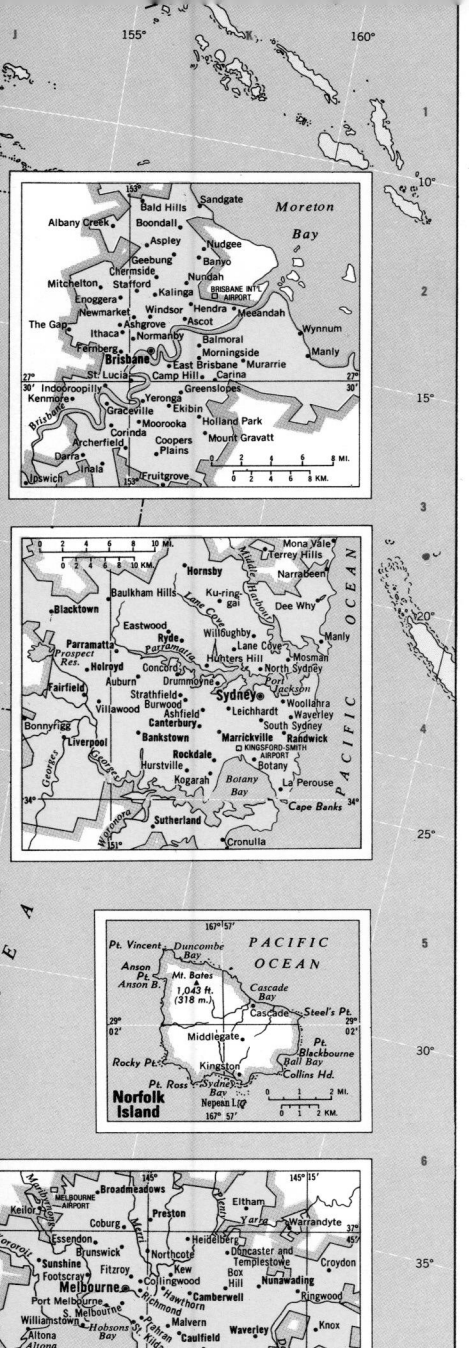

Population Distribution

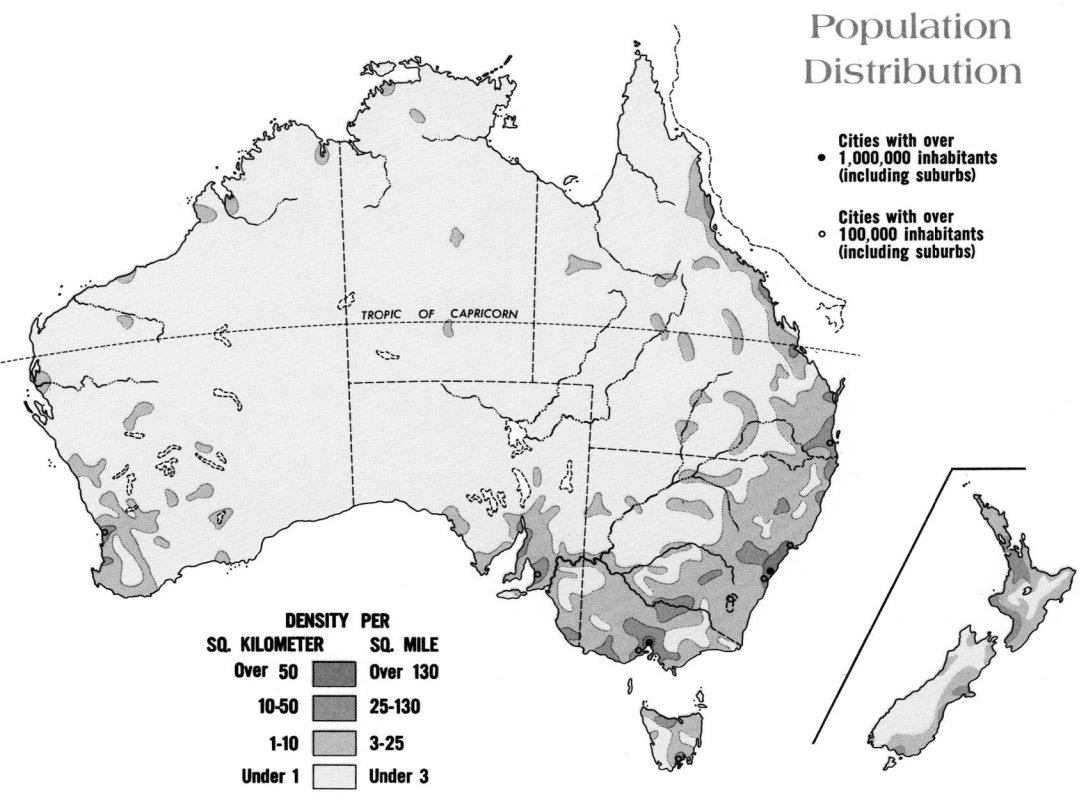

● Cities with over
  1,000,000 inhabitants
  (including suburbs)

○ Cities with over
  100,000 inhabitants
  (including suburbs)

DENSITY PER

SQ. KILOMETER	SQ. MILE
Over 50	Over 130
10-50	25-130
1-10	3-25
Under 1	Under 3

Vegetation

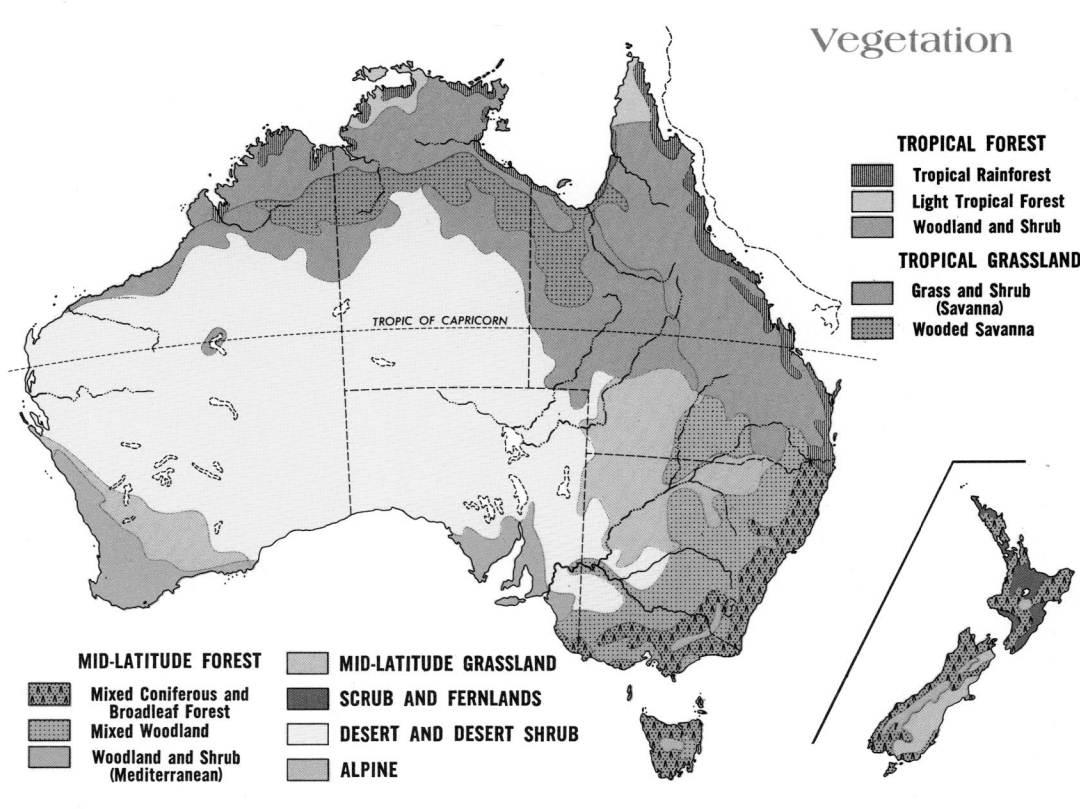

TROPICAL FOREST
Tropical Rainforest
Light Tropical Forest
Woodland and Shrub

TROPICAL GRASSLAND
Grass and Shrub
(Savanna)
Wooded Savanna

MID-LATITUDE FOREST
Mixed Coniferous and
Broadleaf Forest
Mixed Woodland
Woodland and Shrub
(Mediterranean)

MID-LATITUDE GRASSLAND
SCRUB AND FERNLANDS
DESERT AND DESERT SHRUB
ALPINE

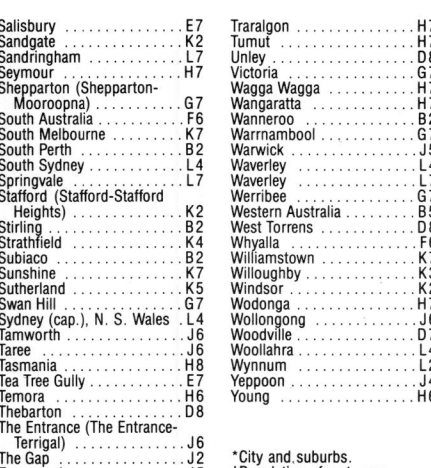

Average January Temperature

FAHRENHEIT	CELSIUS
Over 86°	Over 30°
68° to 86°	20° to 30°
50° to 68°	10° to 20°
32° to 50°	0° to 10°
Under 32°	Under 0°

Darwin 83°
Derby 88°
Onslow 85°
Cairns 81°
Alice Springs 82°
Brisbane 77°
Kalgoorlie 78°
Broken Hill 79°
Adelaide 72°
Perth 74°
Sydney 70°
Albany 63°
Melbourne 67°
Hobart 62°
Auckland 66°
Dunedin 60°

• Sydney 70° Average January temperature in degrees Fahrenheit at selected stations

Average July Temperature

FAHRENHEIT	CELSIUS
Over 68°	20° to 30°
50° to 68°	10° to 20°
32° to 50°	0° to 10°
Under 32°	Under 0°

Darwin 76°
Derby 72°
Onslow 63°
Cairns 70°
Alice Springs 52°
Brisbane 59°
Kalgoorlie 52°
Broken Hill 51°
Adelaide 52°
Perth 55°
Sydney 54°
Albany 53°
Melbourne 49°
Hobart 46°
Auckland 52°
Dunedin 43°

• Sydney 54° Average July temperature in degrees Fahrenheit at selected stations

Rainfall

AVERAGE ANNUAL RAINFALL

INCHES	CENTIMETERS
Over 80	Over 200
60 to 80	150 to 200
40 to 60	100 to 150
20 to 40	50 to 100
10 to 20	25 to 50
Under 10	Under 25

Darwin 60
Thursday Island 66
Derby 23
Cairns 86
Tennant Creek 15
Cloncurry 19
Mackay 63
Onslow 12
Alice Springs 12
William Creek 5
Brisbane 45
Geraldton 19
Kalgoorlie 9
Broken Hill 9
Perth 36
Adelaide 20
Albury 28
Sydney 47
Albany 37
Melbourne 26
Hobart 25
Auckland 48
Hokitika 116
Wellington 48
Dunedin 36

• Sydney 47 Average annual rainfall in inches at selected stations

DOMINANT LAND USE

- Cereals (chiefly wheat), Livestock
- Dairy, Truck Farming
- Cash Crops, Horticulture, Fruit
- Pasture Livestock
- Range Livestock
- Forests
- Nonagricultural Land

MAJOR MINERAL OCCURRENCES

Ab	Asbestos	Na	Salt
Ag	Silver	Ni	Nickel
Al	Bauxite	O	Petroleum
Au	Gold	Op	Opals
C	Coal	P	Phosphates
Cu	Copper	Pb	Lead
D	Diamonds	S	Sulfur, Pyrites
Fe	Iron Ore	Sb	Antimony
G	Natural Gas	Sn	Tin
Gp	Gypsum	Ti	Titanium
Lg	Lignite	U	Uranium
Ls	Limestone	W	Tungsten
Mg	Magnesium	Zn	Zinc
Mi	Mica	Zr	Zirconium
Mn	Manganese		

⚡ Water Power
▨ Major Industrial Areas

Agriculture, Industry and Resources

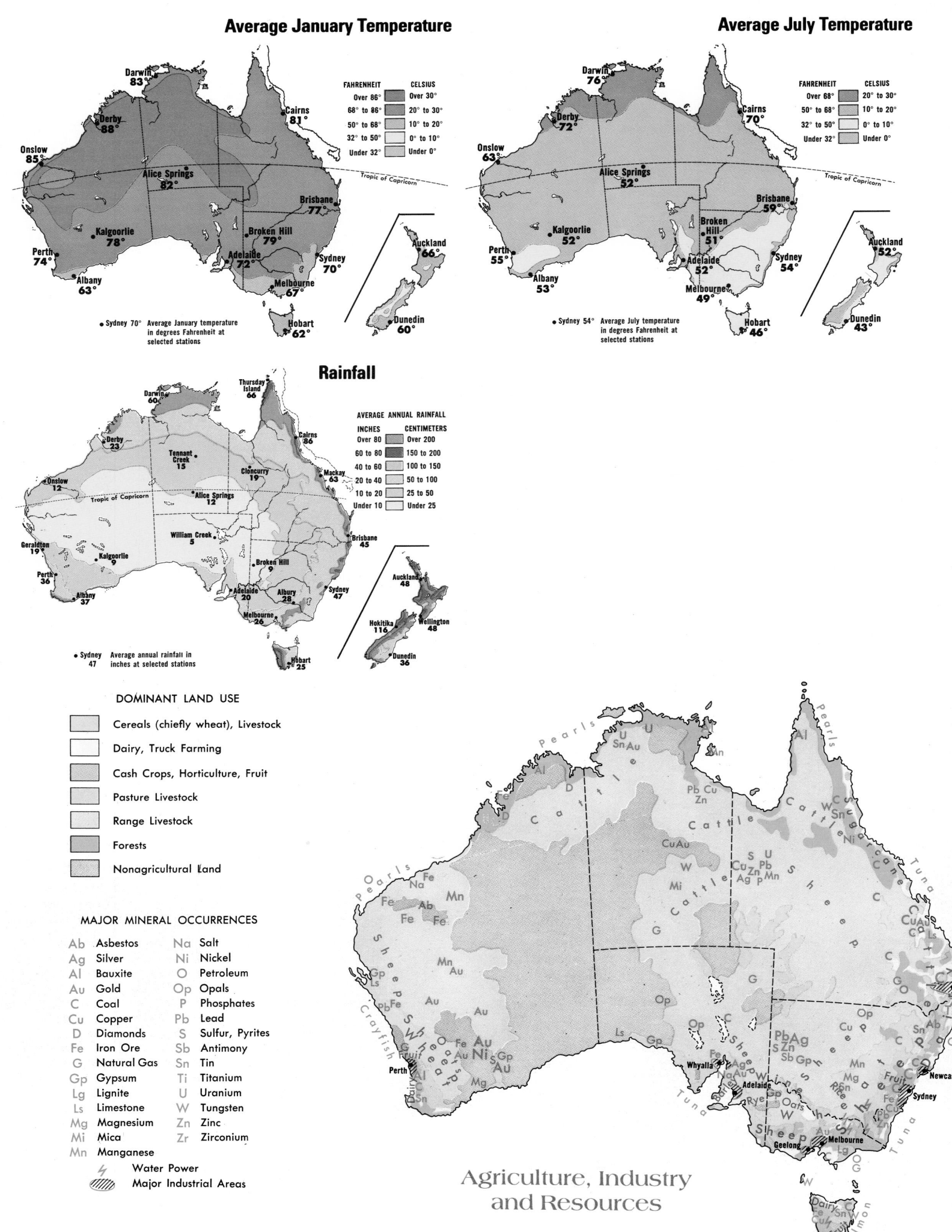

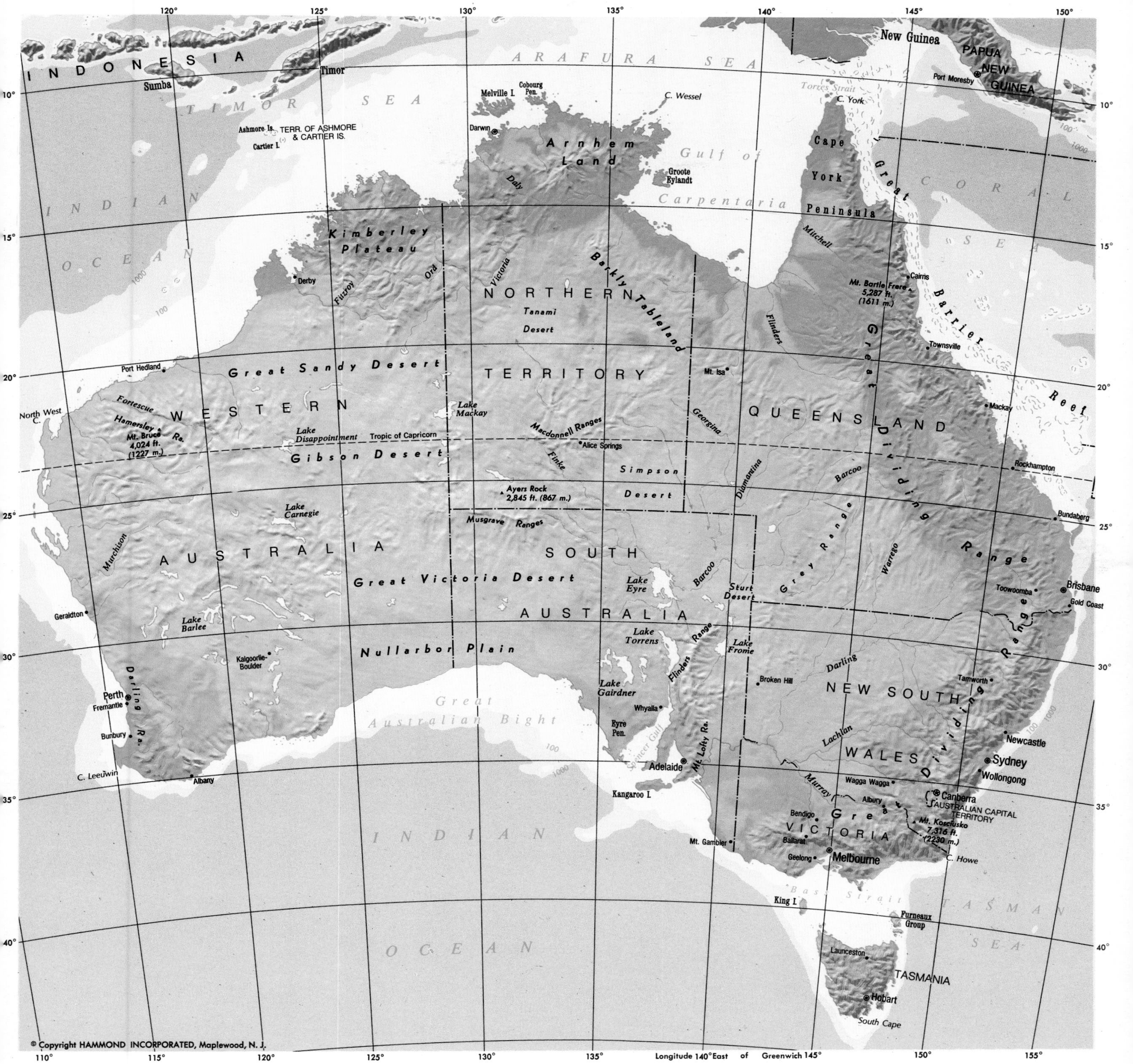

110° 115° 120° 125° 130° 135° 140° 145° 150°

INDONESIA

Sumba   Timor

T I M O R   S E A

A R A F U R A   S E A

New Guinea   **PAPUA**
Port Moresby   **NEW**
GUINEA

Ashmore Is. TERR. OF ASHMORE
Cartier I.   & CARTIER IS.

Melville I.   C. Wessel
Cobourg Pen.

Darwin

Arnhem Land

Groote Eylandt

Gulf of

Carpentaria

C. York

Cape York Peninsula

Torres Strait

C O R A L

I N D I A N

O C E A N

Derby

Kimberley Plateau

Fitzroy   Ord

Victoria   Daly

NORTHERN

Tanami Desert

Mitchell

Mt. Bartle Frere
5,287 ft.
(1611 m.)

Cairns

Great

S E A

Barrier

Townsville

Port Hedland

Great Sandy Desert

T E R R I T O R Y

Backly Tableland

Flinders

Mt. Isa

QUEENSLAND

Mackay

Reef

North West C.

Fortescue

Hamersley Ra.
Mt. Bruce
4,024 ft.
(1227 m.)

W E S T E R N

Lake
Disappointment

Lake Mackay

Macdonnell Ranges

Tropic of Capricorn

Alice Springs

Finke

Georgina

Barcoo

Dividing

Rockhampton

Gibson Desert

Simpson

Desert

Djamantina

Great

Grey

Warrego

Bundaberg

Lake
Carnegie

A U S T R A L I A

Ayers Rock
2,845 ft. (867 m.)

Musgrave   Ranges

S O U T H

Barcoo

Sturt
Desert

Range

Brisbane
Toowoomba
Gold Coast

Murchison

Lake
Barlee

Great Victoria Desert

Lake
Eyre

A U S T R A L I A

Lake
Torrens

Broken Hill

Darling

Tamworth

NEW SOUTH

Geraldton

Kalgoorlie-
Boulder

Nullarbor Plain

Lake
Gairdner

Flinders Range

Lake
Frome

WALES

Newcastle

Perth
Fremantle

Darling Ra.

Great

Whyalla

Eyre
Pen.

Lachlan

Sydney

Wollongong

Bunbury

Australian Bight

100

Spencer Gulf

Adelaide

Mt. Lofty Ra.

Murray

Wagga Wagga

Albury

Canberra
AUSTRALIAN CAPITAL
TERRITORY

C. Leeuwin

Albany

Kangaroo I.

Bendigo

Gre

VICTORIA

Mt. Kosciusko
7,316 ft.
(2230 m.)

I N D I A N

Mt. Gambier

Ballarat

Geelong

Melbourne

C. Howe

O C E A N

Mt. Gambier

King I.

Bass Strait

T A S M A N

Furneaux
Group

S E A

Launceston

TASMANIA

Hobart

South Cape

© Copyright HAMMOND INCORPORATED, Maplewood, N. J.

110° 115° 120° 125° 130° 135° Longitude 140° East of Greenwich 145° 150° 155°

Vegetation / Relief

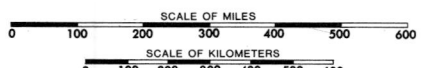
SCALE OF MILES
0 100 200 300 400 500 600

SCALE OF KILOMETERS
0 100 200 300 400 500 600

Capital of Country...................................⊛
State and Territorial Capitals................◉
International Boundaries.........................————
State and Territorial Boundaries.............— — —

Depths in Fathoms

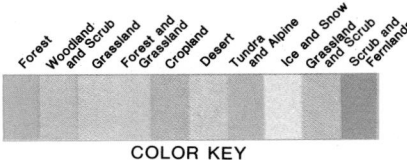

Forest
Woodland and Scrub
Grassland
Forest and Grassland
Cropland
Desert
Tundra and Alpine
Ice and Snow
Grassland and Scrub
Scrub and Fernlands

COLOR KEY

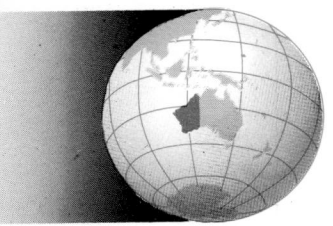

AREA 975,096 sq. mi.
(2,525,500 sq. km.)
POPULATION 1,273,624
CAPITAL Perth
LARGEST CITY Perth
HIGHEST POINT Mt. Bruce 4,024 ft.
(1,227 m.)

Topography

Below Sea Level	100 m. 328 ft.	200 m. 656 ft.	500 m. 1,640 ft.	1,000 m. 3,281 ft.	2,000 m. 6,562 ft.	5,000 m. 16,404 ft.

CITIES and TOWNS

Albany 15,222 .... B6
Augusta 588 .... A6
Australind 1,681 ...... A2
Balladonia D6
Beverley 756 .... B1
Boddington 367 ...... B2
Boulder-Kalgoorlie 19,848 .. C5
Boyanup 365 .... A2
Bridgetown 1,521 .... B6
Brookton 595 .... B2
Broome 3,666 .... C2
Bruce Rock 565 ...... B5
Brunswick Junction 889 .. A2
Bunbury 21,749 ...... A2
Busselton 6,463 ..... A6
Canning 52,816 ...... A1
Capel 680 .... A2
Carnamah 422 .... A5
Carnarvon 5,053 ..... A4
Collie 7,667 .... B2
Coolgardie 891 ...... C5

Coorow 226 .... B5
Corrigin 841 .... B6
Cranbrook 316 ...... B6
Cuballing ○647 ..... B2
Cue 320 .... B4
Cunderdin 731 ...... B5
Dalwallinu 639 ...... B5
Dampier 2,471 ...... B3
Dandaragan ○1,748 .. A5
Darkan 242 .... B2
Denham 402 .... A4
Denmark 985 .... B6
Derby 2,933 .... C2
Dongara-Port Denison 1,155 .. A5
Donnybrook 1,197 ... A2
Dwellingup 453 ..... B2
Esperance 6,375 .... C6
Eucla E5
Exmouth 2,583 ..... A3
Fitzroy Crossing D2
Fremantle 22,484 ... A1
Geraldton 20,895 ... A5
Gingin 382 .... A1
Gnowangerup 872 .. B6

Goldsworthy 923 .... B3
Goomalling 600 ..... B1
Halls Creek 966 .... D2
Harvey 2,479 .... A2
Hopetoun C6
Hyden B6
Jarrahdale 315 ..... B2
Kalbarri 820 .... A4
Kalgoorlie 9,145 ... C5
Kalgoorlie-Boulder 19,848 .. C5
Kambalda 4,463 .... C5
Karratha 8,341 ..... B3
Katanning 4,413 .... B6
Kellerberrin 1,091 .. B5
Kojonup 544 .... B6
Koolyanobbing 277 .. B5
Kununurra 2,081 ... E2
Kwinana New Town 12,355 . A1
Lake Grace 575 .... B6
Laverton 872 ...... C5
Learmonth A3
Leonora 524 .... C5
Madura D5
Mandurah 10,978 .. A2

Manjimup 4,150 ..... B6
Marble Bar 357 ..... C3
Margaret River 798 .. A6
Meekatharra 989 .... B4
Melville 61,211 ..... A1
Menzies 232 .... C5
Merredin 3,520 ..... B5
Mingenew 368 ...... A5
Moora 1,677 .... B5
Morawa 694 .... B5
Mount Barker 1,519 .. B6
Mount Magnet 618 .. B5
Mukinbudin 370 .... B5
Mullewa 918 .... A5
Mundijong 356 ..... A2
Nannup 552 .... B6
Narrogin 4,969 ..... B2
Nedlands 20,257 ... A1
Newman 5,466 ...... B3
New Norcia A5
Norseman 1,895 .... C6
Northam 6,791 ..... B1
Northampton 750 ... A5
Northcliffe B6
Nungarin ○332 .... B5
Onslow 594 .... A3
Pannawonica 1,170 .. B3
Paraburdoo 2,357 .. B3
Pardoo B3
Pemberton 871 ..... A6
Perenjori 257 ...... B5
Perth (cap.) 809,035 .. A1
Perth *898,918 ..... A1
Pingelly 937 .... B2
Pinjarra 1,336 ..... A2
Port Denison-Dongara 1,155 A5
Port Hedland 12,948 .. B3
Quairading 741 .... B1
Ravensthorpe 327 .. B6
Rockingham 24,932 . A2
Roebourne 1,688 ... B3

Sandstone ○133 ..... B4
Shay Gap 853 ...... C3
Southern Cross 798 .. B5
South Perth 31,524 .. A1
Stirling 161,858 .... A1
Three Springs 638 .. A5
Tom Price 3,540 .... B3
Toodyay 560 .... B1
Turkey Creek 212 ... E2
Wagin 1,488 .... B2
Walpole 291 .... B6
Wandering ○470 ... B2
Wanneroo 6,745 ... A1
Waroona 1,462 .... A2
Wickepin 267 ...... B2
Wickham 2,387 .... B3
Williams 453 ...... B2
Wiluna 221 .... C4
Wittenoom 247 .... B3
Wongan Hills 947 .. B5
Wundowie 720 ..... B1
Wyalkatchem 453 .. B5
Wyndham 1,509 ... E1
Yalgoo ○315 ...... B5
Yampi Sound C2
York 1,136 .... B1

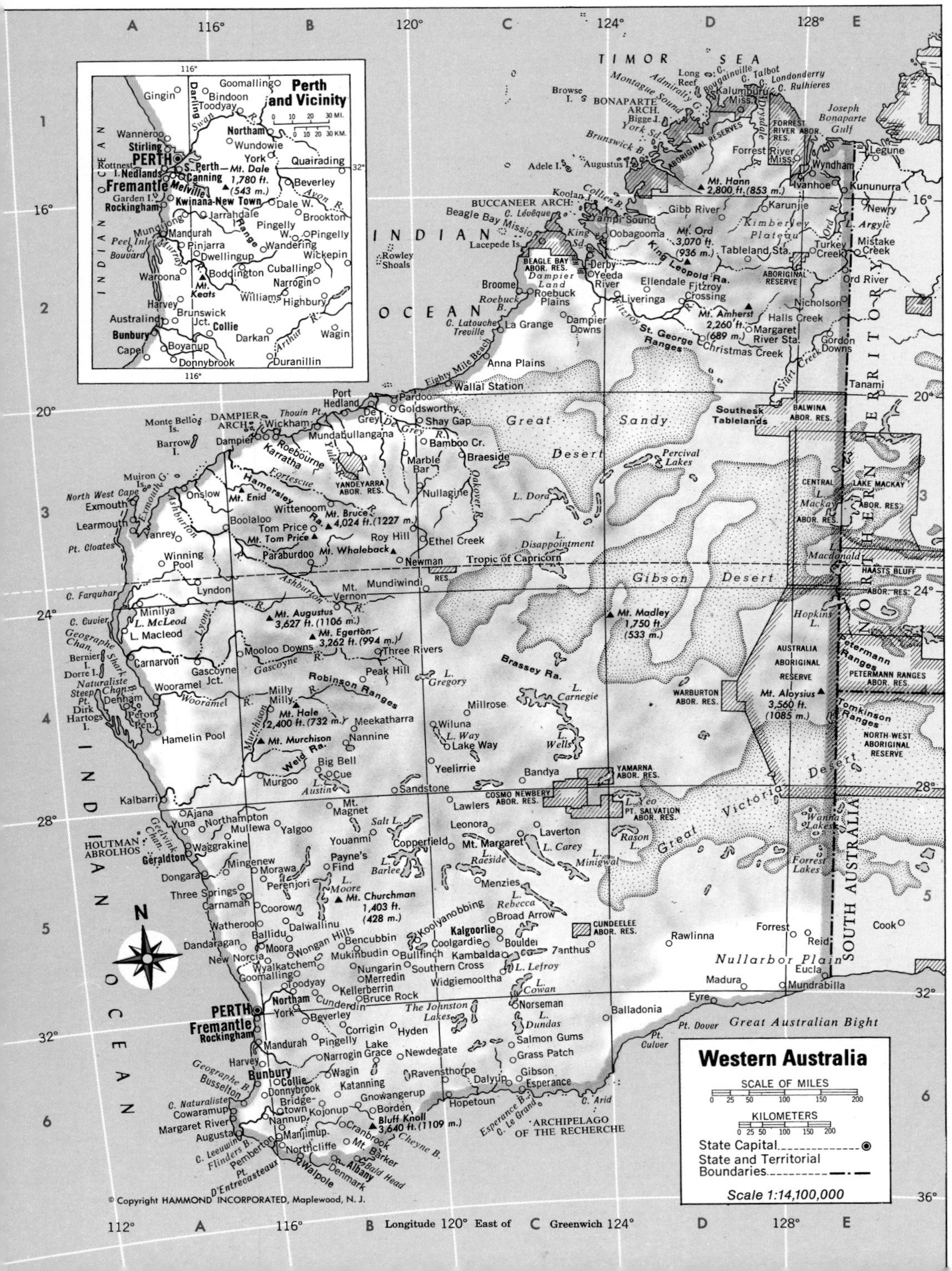

OTHER FEATURES

Adele (isl.) C1
Admiralty (gulf) D1
Aloysius (mt.) E4
Argyle (lake) E2
Arid (cape) C6
Ashburton (riv.) A3
Augustus (mt.) B4
Austin (lake) B4
Australia Aboriginal Res. E4
Bald (head) B6
Balwina Aboriginal Res. E3
Barlee (lake) B5
Barrow (isl.) A3
Beaglebay Aboriginal Res. C2
Bluff Knoll (mt.) ... B6
Bonaparte (arch.) .. D1
Bougainville (cape) . D1
Brassey (range) C4
Bruce (mt.) B3
Brunswick (bay) ... D1
Buccaneer (arch.) .. C2
Carey (lake) C5
Carnegie (lake) C4
Central Aboriginal Res. E3
Churchman (mt.) ... B5
Collier (bay) C1
Cosmo Newbery Aboriginal Res. .. C5
Cowan (lake) C5
Cundeelee Aboriginal Res. C5
Dale (mt.) B1
Dampier (arch.) B3
Dampier Land (reg.) . C2
Darling (range) A1
De Grey (riv.) B3
D'Entrecasteaux (pt.) A6
Dirk Hartogs (isl.) .. A4
Disappointment (lake) C3
Drysdale (riv.) D1
Dundas (lake) C6
Egerton (mt.) B4
Eighty Mile (beach) . C2
Enid (mt.) B3
Esperance (bay) C6

Exmouth (gulf) A3
Fitzroy (riv.) D2
Flinders (bay) A6
Forrest River Aboriginal Res. D1
Fortescue (riv.) B3
Garden (isl) A1
Gascoyne (riv.) A4
Geelvink (chan.) ... A5
Geographe (bay) ... A6
Geographe (chan.) . A4
Gibson (des.) D3
Great Australian (bight) E6
Great Sandy (des.) .. C3
Great Victoria (des.) D5
Hamersley (range) .. B3
Hann (mt.) E4
Hopkins (lake) E4
Houtman Abrolhos (isls.) A5
Indian Ocean A5
Johnston, The (lakes) C6
Joseph Bonaparte (gulf) E1
Kimberley (plat.) .. D2
King (sound) C2
King Leopold (range) D2
Koolan (isl.) C1
Leeuwin (cape) A6
Le Grand (cape) ... C6
Lévêque (cape) C2
Londonderry (cape) . D1
Lyons (riv.) A4
Macdonald (lake) .. E3
Mackay (lake) E3
McLeod (lake) A4
Minigwal (lake) C5
Monte Bello (isls.) . A3
Moore (lake) B5
Murchison (riv.) ... A4
Murray (riv.) A2
Naturaliste (cape) .. A6
Naturaliste (chan.) . A4
North West (cape) . A3
North-West Aboriginal Res. E4
Nullarbor (plain) ... D5
Oakover (riv.) C3
Ord (mt.) D2
Ord (riv.) E2
Percival (lakes) D3
Peron (pen.) A4
Petermann (ranges) . E4
Rason (lake) D5
Rebecca (lake) C5
Recherche (arch.) .. C6
Robinson (ranges) .. B4
Roebuck (bay) C2
Rottnest (isl.) A1
Saint George (ranges) C3
Shark (bay) A4
Southesk Tablelands D3
Sturt (creek) D2
Swan (riv.) A1
Timor (sea) D1
Tomkinson (ranges) . E4
Wanna (lake) C5
Warburton Aboriginal Res. D4
Way (lake) C5
Weld (range) B4
Wells (lake) C4
Whaleback (mt.) ... B3
Wooramel (riv.) ... A4
York (sound) C2

○ Population of district.
*Population of met. area.

Perth and Vicinity

Western Australia

SCALE OF MILES

KILOMETERS

State Capital .... ◉
State and Territorial Boundaries ------ -- ·· --

Scale 1:14,100,000

© Copyright HAMMOND INCORPORATED, Maplewood, N.J.

Longitude 120° East of Greenwich

CITIES and TOWNS

Adelaide River B2
Aileron C7
Alice Springs 18,395 . . . . D7
Alyangula 1,181 . . . . E2
Angurugu 597 . . . . E3
Anthony Lagoon D4
Areyonga C8
Arltunga D7
Avon Downs E5
Bamyili-Beswick 685 . . . . C3
Banka Banka C5
Barrow Creek D6
Batchelor B2
Bathurst Island 1,032 . . . . B1
Birdum C3
Birrimbah C3
Birrindudu A5
Borroloola 420 . . . . E4
Bundooma D8
Burramurra E6
Charlotte Waters D8
Claravale B3
Coniston C7
Coolibah B3
Creswell Downs E4
Croker Island Mission C1
Daly River B2
Daly Waters C3
Darwin (cap.) 56,482 . . . . B2
Docker River 217 . . . . A8
Elliott C4
Epenarra D6
Erldunda C8
Eva Downs D5

Ewaninga D7
Goulburn Island 277 . . . . C1
Gove (Nhulunbuy) 3,879 . . . . E2
Harts Range D7
Hatches Creek D6
Helen Springs C5
Henbury C8
Hermannsburg 541 . . . . C7
Hooker Creek 671 . . . . B5
Humpty Doo B2
Katherine 3,737 . . . . B3
Kildurk A4
Koolpinyah B2
Kulgera C8
Kurundi D6
Lake Nash E6
Larrimah C3
Legune A3
Limbunya B4
Lucy Creek E7
Mainoru C3
Maningrida 702 . . . . C2
Mataranka C3
Milingimbi 564 . . . . D2
Mistake Creek A4
Montejinnie C4
Mount Cavenagh C8
Mount Doreen B7
Murray Downs D6
Napperby C7
Newcastle Waters C4
Nhulunbuy 3,879 . . . . E2
Numbulwar 422 . . . . D3
Oenpelli 452 . . . . C2
O. T. Downs D4
Papunya 635 . . . . B7
Pine Creek 214 . . . . B2

Plenty River Mine D7
Port Keats 819 . . . . A3
Powell Creek C5
Rankine Store E5
Robinson River E4
Rockhampton Downs D5
Rodinga D8
Rum Jungle B2
Santa Teresa 479 . . . . D8
Soudan E6
Stirling Station C6
Tanami A5
Tarlton Downs E7
Tea Tree Well C7
Tempe Downs C8
Tennant Creek 3,118 . . . . C5
The Granites B6
Top Springs C4
Ucharonidge D4
Umbakumba 247 . . . . E3
Umbeara C8
Urapunga D3
Utopia D7
Victoria River Downs B4
Warrabri 459 . . . . D6
Wave Hill B4
White Quartz Hill D7
Willeroo B3
Willowra C6
Wollogorang F4
Yambah C7
Yirrkala 543 . . . . E2
Yuendumu 687 . . . . B7

OTHER FEATURES

Amadeus (lake) B8

Arafura (sea) D1
Arnhem (cape) E2
Arnhem Land (reg.) D2
Arnhem Land Aboriginal
Res. C2
Arnold (riv.) D3
Ayers Rock Nat'l Park B8
Barkly Tableland D4
Bathurst (isl.) A1
Beagle (gulf) A2
Beatrice (cape) E3
Bennett (lake) B7
Beswick Aboriginal Res. C3
Bickerton (isl.) E2
Blaze (pt.) A2
Carpentaria (gulf) E3
Central Wedge (mt.) C7
Clarence (str.) B2
Cobourg (pen.) C1
Conner (mt.) B8
Croker (cape) C1
Daly (riv.) B2
Daly River Aboriginal Res. B2
Davenport (mt.) B7
Dundas (str.) B1
East Alligator (riv.) C2
Ehrenberg (range) B7
Elcho (isl.) D1
Finke (riv.) C8
Fitzmaurice (riv.) B3
Ford (cape) A2
Georgina (riv.) E6
Goulburn (isls.) C1
Goyder (riv.) D2
Groote Eylandt (isl.) 2,230 . . . . E3
Haasts Bluff Aboriginal Res. B7
Hale (riv.) D8

Hanson (riv.) C6
Hay (dry riv.) E7
Hogarth (mt.) E6
Hopkins (lake) A8
Joseph Bonaparte (gulf) A3
Katherine (riv.) C3
Lake MacKay Aboriginal
Res. A6
Lander (riv.) C6
Leisler (mt.) A7
Limmen (bight) D3
Limmen Bight (riv.) D4
Macdonald (lake) B7
Macdonnell (ranges) C7
MacKay (lake) A7
Mann (riv.) D2
Marshall (riv.) D7
Melville (bay) E2
Melville (isl.) B1
Mount Olga Nat'l Park B8

Murchison (range) D6
Napier (mt.) A4
Neale (lake) A8
Newcastle (creek) C4
Nicholson (riv.) E5
Olga (mt.) B8
Peron (isls.) A2
Petermann (ranges) A8
Petermann Ranges
Aboriginal Res. A8
Port Darwin (inlet) B2
Ranken (riv.) E6
Robinson (riv.) E4
Roper (riv.) D3
Sandover (riv.) D6
Simpson (des.) E8
Singleton (mt.) B6
Sir Edward Pellew Group
(isls.) E3
South Alligator (riv.) C2

Stanley (mt.) B7
Stewart (cape) D1
Stirling (creek) A4
Sturt (plain) C4
Tanami (des.) C5
Timor (sea) A1
Todd (riv.) D8
Vanderlin (isl.) E3
Van Diemen (cape) A1
Van Diemen (gulf) B1
Victoria (riv.) B3
Wagait Aboriginal Res. E3
Warwick (chan.) E3
Wessel (cape) E1
Wessel (isls.) E1
West Baines (riv.) A4
White (lake) A6
Woods (lake) C4
Young (mt.) D3
Ziel (mt.) C7

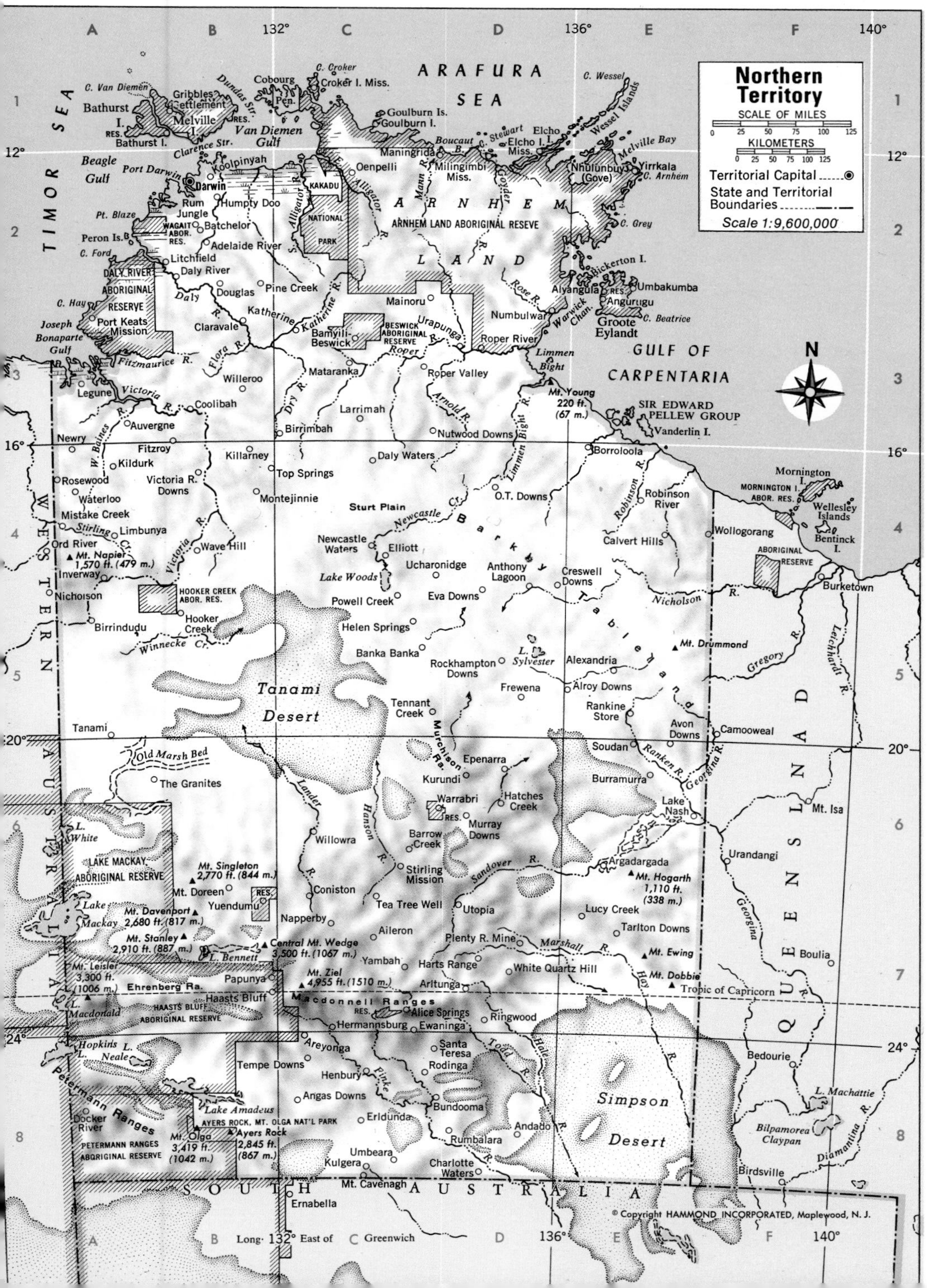

AREA 519,768 sq. mi.
(1,346,200 sq. km.)
POPULATION 123,324
CAPITAL Darwin
LARGEST CITY Darwin
HIGHEST POINT Mt. Ziel 4,955 ft.
(1,510 m.)

Northern Territory

SCALE OF MILES
0 25 50 75 100 125
KILOMETERS
0 25 50 75 100 125

Territorial Capital . . . . ◉
State and Territorial
Boundaries . . . .

Scale 1:9,600,000

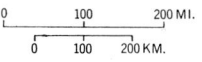

Topography

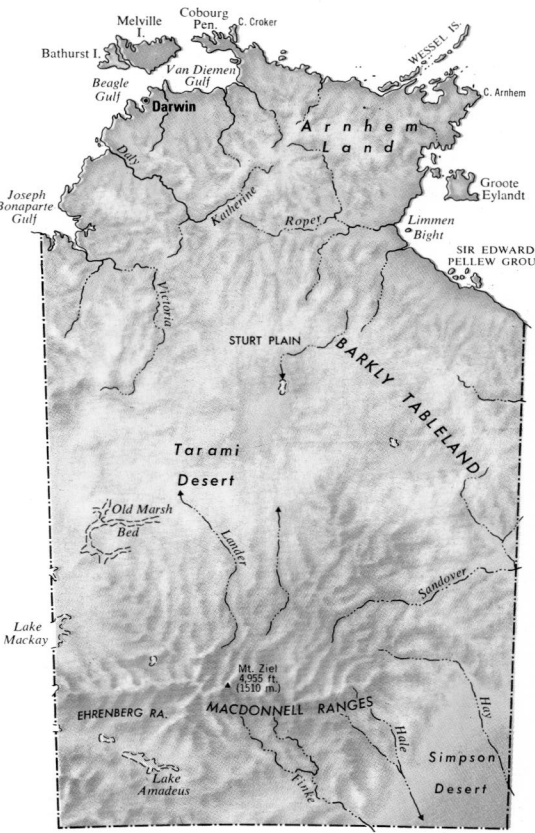

5,000 m. 2,000 m. 1,000 m. 500 m. 200 m. 100 m. Sea
16,404 ft. 6,562 ft. 3,281 ft. 1,640 ft. 656 ft. 328 ft. Level Below

© Copyright HAMMOND INCORPORATED, Maplewood, N.J.

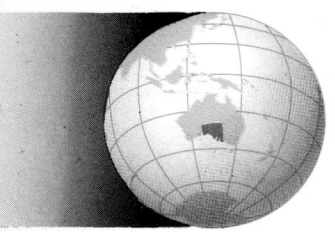

AREA 379,922 sq. mi. (984,000 sq. km.)
POPULATION 1,285,033
CAPITAL Adelaide
LARGEST CITY Adelaide
HIGHEST POINT Mt. Woodroffe 4,970 ft.
(1,515 m.)

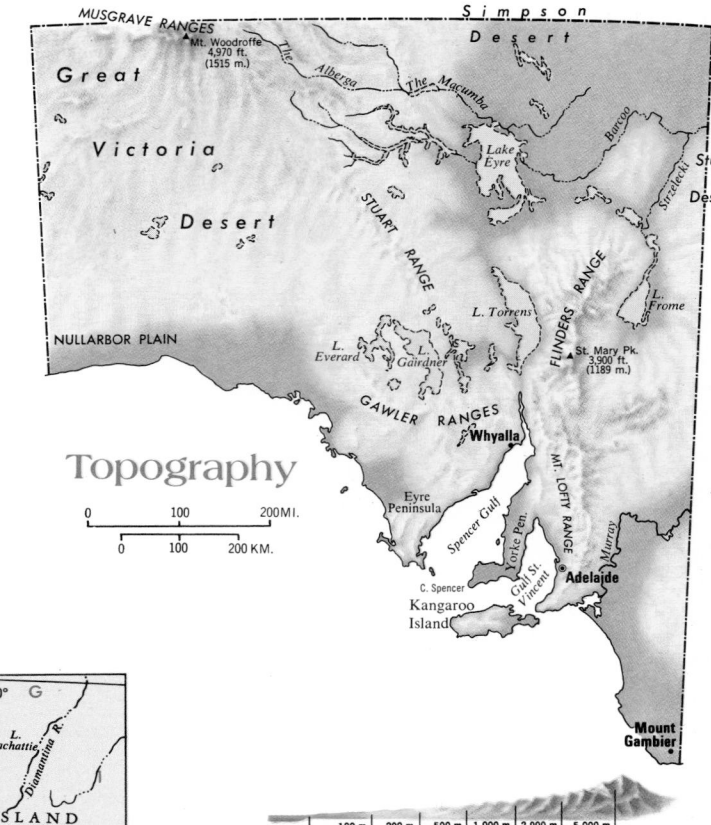

Topography

CITIES and TOWNS

Adelaide (cap.) 882,520	B6
Adelaide *931,886	B6
Andamooka 402	E4
Angaston 1,753	F6
Balaklava 1,306	F6
Barmera 2,014	G6
Beachport 357	F7
Berri 3,419	G6
Birdwood 397	C7
Blinman	F4
Bordertown 2,138	G7
Brighton 19,441	A8
Burnside 37,593	B8
Burra 1,222	F5
Campbelltown 43,084	B7
Ceduna 2,794	F5
Clare 2,381	F5
Cleve 827	E5
Coober Pedy 2,078	D3
Cowell 626	E5
Crafters-Bridgewater 9,764	B8
Crystal Brook 1,240	E5
Cummins 767	D6
Edithburgh 359	E6
Elizabeth 32,608	B7
Elliston ○1,345	D5
Enfield 66,797	B7
Gawler 9,433	B6
Gladstone 680	F5
Glenelg 13,306	A8
Gumeracha 387	C7
Hahndorf 1,274	C8
Hawker 351	F4
Hindmarsh 7,593	A7
Iron Knob 398	E5
Jamestown 1,384	F5
Kadina 2,943	E5
Kapunda 1,340	F6
Keith 1,147	G7
Kensington and Norwood 8,950	B8
Kimba 862	E5
Kingscote 1,236	E6
Kingston 1,325	G7
Lameroo 599	G6
Laura 504	F5
Leigh Creek 1,635	F4
Lobethal 1,522	C7
Lock 213	D5
Loxton 3,100	G6
Lyndoch 539	C6
Maitland 1,085	E6
Mannum 1,984	F6
Marion 66,580	A8
Marree	E3
Meadows 388	B8
Meningie 807	F6
Millicent 5,255	F7
Minlaton 865	E6
Mitcham 60,309	B8
Moonta 1,751	E5
Mount Barker 4,190	C8
Mount Gambier 18,193	G7
Murray Bridge 8,664	F6
Nairne 706	C8
Nangwarry 758	G7

Naracoorte 4,758	G7
Noarlunga 60,928	A8
Nuriootpa 2,851	F6
Oodnadatta	D2
Orroroo 604	F5
Payneham 16,502	B7
Penola 1,205	G7
Peterborough 2,575	F5
Pinnaroo 731	G6
Port Adelaide 35,407	A7
Port Augusta 15,566	E5
Port Broughton 587	F5
Port Lincoln 9,846	E6
Port Pirie 14,695	E5
Prospect 18,591	B7
Quorn 1,049	F5
Renmark 3,475	G5
Robe 590	F7
Salisbury 86,451	B7
Snowtown 492	E5
Strathalbyn 1,756	F6
Streaky Bay 985	D5
Tailem Bend 1,677	F6
Tanunda 2,621	C6
Tea Tree Gully 67,237	B7
Thebarton 9,208	A7
Tumby Bay 933	E6
Unley 35,844	B8
Uraidla 303	B8
Victor Harbor 4,522	F6
Virginia 353	B7
Waikerie 1,629	F6
Wallaroo 2,043	E5
West Torrens 45,099	A8
Whyalla 30,518	E5
Williamstown 495	C7
Willunga 667	F6
Wilmington 227	F6
Woodside 724	C8
Woodville 77,634	A7
Woomera 1,658	E4
Wudinna 572	D5
Yorketown 713	E6

Flinders (range)	F4
Frome (lake)	G4
Gairdner (lake)	D4
Gawler (ranges)	E5
Gawler (riv.)	B6
Gilles (lake)	E5
Goyders (lag.)	F2
Great Australian (bight)	A5
Great Victoria (des.)	B3
Gregory (lake)	F3
Hack (mt.)	F4
Hamilton, The (riv.)	D2
Harris (lake)	D4
Head of Bight (bay)	B4
Indian Ocean	E6
Investigator (str.)	E6
Investigator Group (isls.)	D5
Island (lag.)	E4
Jaffa (cape)	F7
Kangaroo (isl.) 3,515	E7
Lacepede (bay)	F7
Lofty (mt.)	B8
Macfarlane (lake)	E5
Macumba, The (riv.)	E2
Maurice (lake)	B3
Meramangye (lake)	C3
Morris (mt.)	A2
Murray (res.)	F6
Musgrave (ranges)	A2
Neales, The (riv.)	E2
Northumberland (cape)	F7
Nukey Bluff (mt.)	D5
Nullarbor (plain)	A4
Nuyts (arch.)	C5
Nuyts (cape)	C5
Peera Peera Poolanna (lake)	F2
Saint Mary (peak)	F4
Saint Vincent (gulf)	E6
Serpentine (lakes)	A3
Simpson (des.)	E1
Sir Joseph Banks Group (isls.)	E6
Spencer (cape)	E6
Spencer (gulf)	E5
Stevenson, The (riv.)	D2
Streaky (bay)	D5
Strzelecki (creek)	G3
Stuart (range)	D3
Sturt (des.)	G2
The Alberga (riv.)	D2
The Coorong (lag.)	F6
The Hamilton (riv.)	D2
The Macumba (riv.)	E2
The Neales (riv.)	E3
The Stevenson (riv.)	D2
The Warburton (riv.)	E2
Thistle (isl.)	E6
Torrens (lake)	E4
Torrens (riv.)	B8
Warburton, The (riv.)	E2
Wilkinson (lakes)	B4
Woodroffe (mt.)	A2
Yalata Aboriginal Res.	B4
Yarle (lakes)	B4
Yorke (pen.)	E6

OTHER FEATURES

Acraman (lake)	D5
Alberga, The (riv.)	D2
Alexandrina (lake)	F6
Anxious (bay)	D5
Arckaringa (creek)	D2
Barcoo (creek)	F3
Birksgate (range)	A2
Blanche (lake)	F3
Brady (mt.)	D3
Cadibarrawirracanna (lake)	D3
Callabonna (lake)	F3
Catastrophe (cape)	D6
Coffin (bay)	D6
Coffin Bay (pen.)	D6
Coopers (Barcoo) (creek)	F3
Coorong, The (lag.)	F6
Dey Dey (lake)	B3
Encounter (bay)	F6
Everard (lake)	D4
Everard (ranges)	C2
Eyre (pen.)	D5
Eyre North (lake)	E3
Eyre South (lake)	E3
Finke (riv.)	C1

○ Population of district.
*Population of met. area.

Adelaide and Vicinity

South Australia
SCALE OF MILES
KILOMETERS
State Capital
State and Territorial Boundaries
Scale 1:9,790,000

Longitude D East 136° of E Greenwich F 140° G

AREA 666,872 sq. mi. (1,727,200 sq. km.)
POPULATION 2,295,123
CAPITAL Brisbane
LARGEST CITY Brisbane
HIGHEST POINT Mt. Bartle Frere 5,287 ft. (1,611 m.)

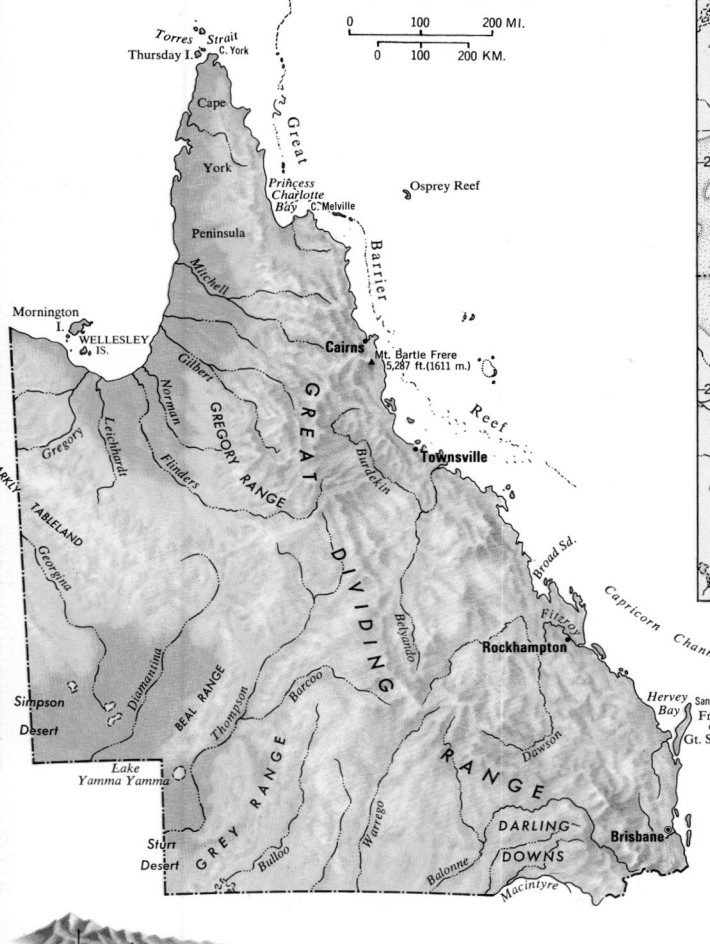

Topography

5,000 m. 16,404 ft.	2,000 m. 6,562 ft.	1,000 m. 3,281 ft.	500 m. 1,640 ft.	200 m. 656 ft.	100 m. 328 ft.	Sea Level	Below

© Copyright HAMMOND INCORPORATED, Maplewood, N.J.

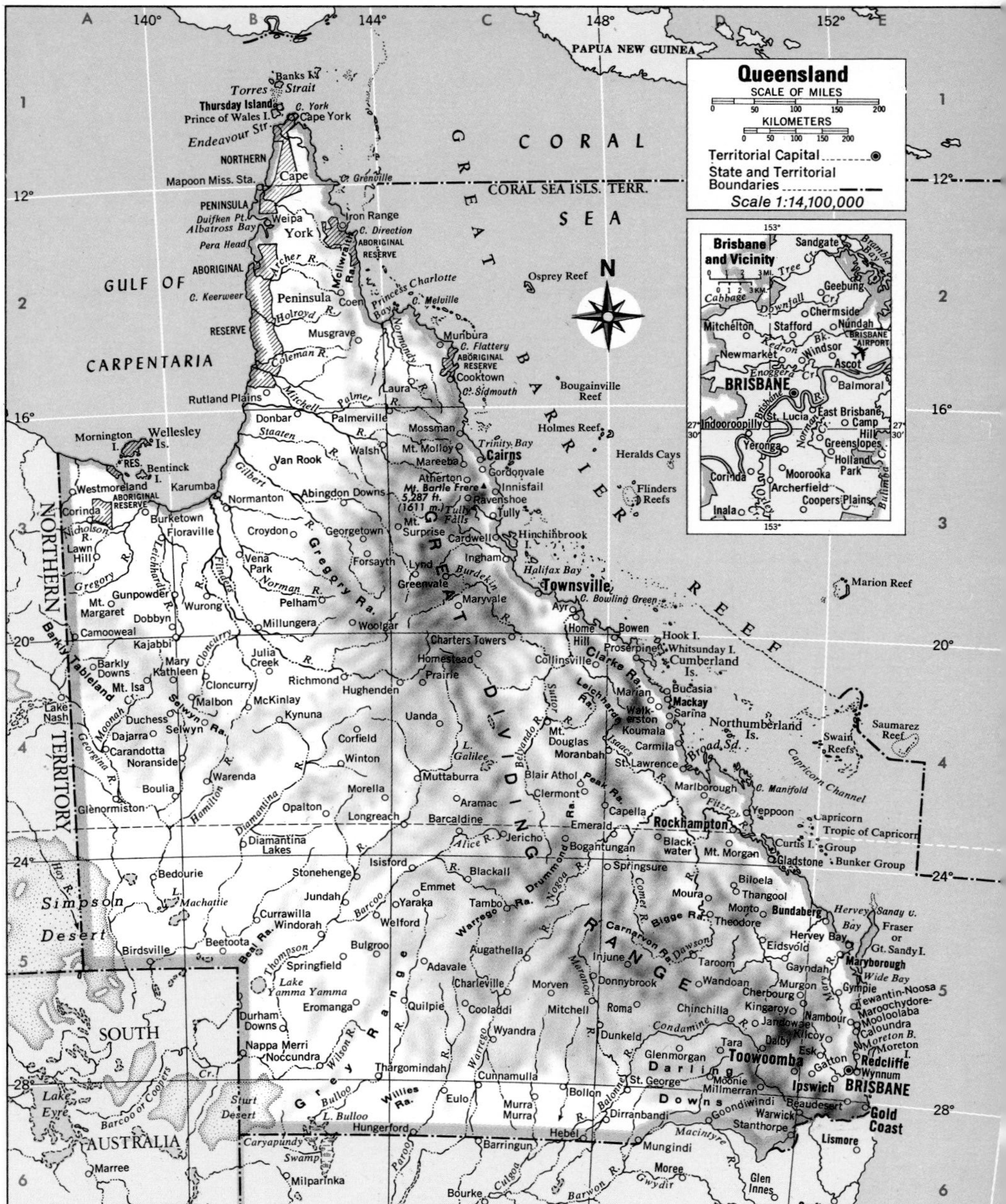

© Copyright HAMMOND INCORPORATED, Maplewood, N.J.

NEW SOUTH WALES

AREA 309,498 sq. mi.
(801,600 sq. km.)
POPULATION 5,126,217
CAPITAL Sydney
LARGEST CITY Sydney
HIGHEST POINT Mt. Kosciusko
7,310 ft. (2,228 m.)

VICTORIA

AREA 87,876 sq. mi.
(227,600 sq. km.)
POPULATION 3,832,443
CAPITAL Melbourne
LARGEST CITY Melbourne
HIGHEST POINT Mt. Bogong
6,508 ft. (1,984 m.)

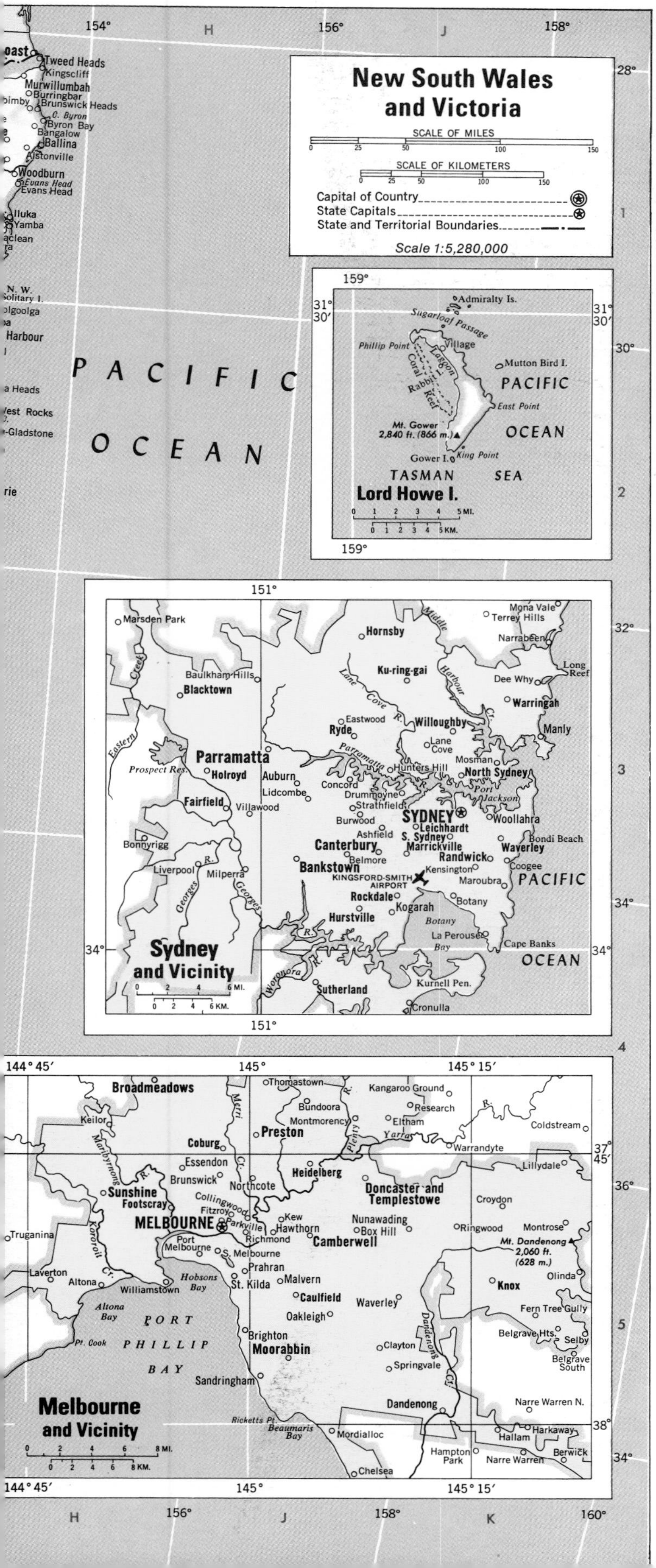

Topography

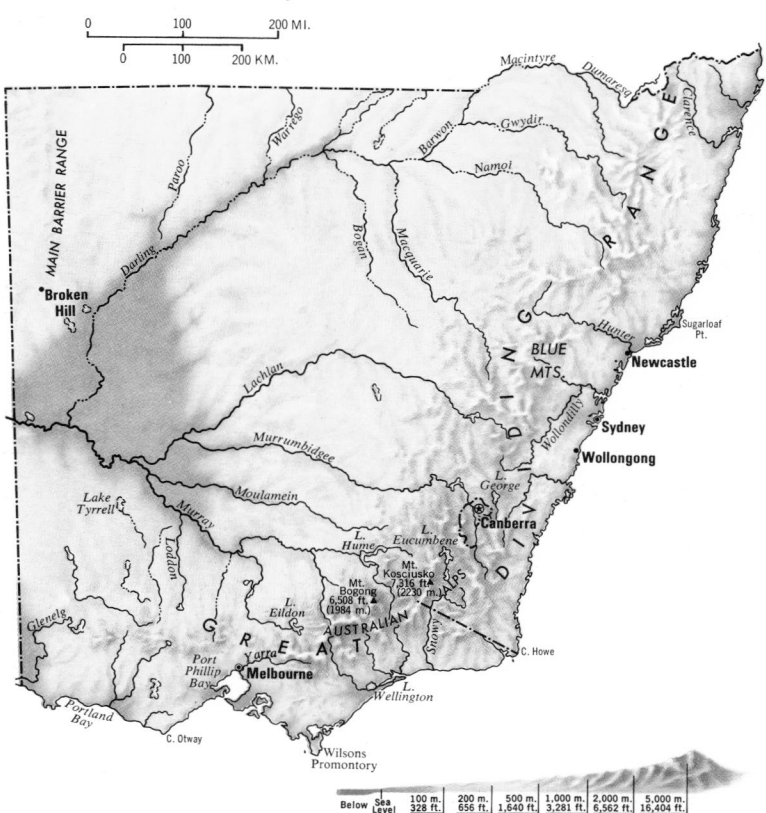

Below Sea Level	100 m. 328 ft.	200 m. 656 ft.	500 m. 1,640 ft.	1,000 m. 3,281 ft.	2,000 m. 6,562 ft.	5,000 m. 16,404 ft.

(continued on following page)

Map labels: New South Wales and Victoria

New South Wales and Victoria

SCALE OF MILES
0 25 50 100 150
SCALE OF KILOMETERS
0 25 50 100 150

Capital of Country .... ⊛
State Capitals .... ⊛
State and Territorial Boundaries .... ▬ ▬

Scale 1:5,280,000

Lord Howe I.

Admiralty Is., Sugarloaf Passage, Village, Phillip Point, Rabbit I., Coral Reef, Lagoon, Mt. Gower 2,840 ft. (866 m.), Mutton Bird I., East Point, King Point, Gower I.

PACIFIC OCEAN
TASMAN SEA
0 1 2 3 4 5 MI.
0 1 2 3 4 5 KM.

Sydney and Vicinity

Marsden Park, Hornsby, Terrey Hills, Mona Vale, Baulkham Hills, Ku-ring-gai, Narrabeen, Long Reef, Blacktown, Dee Why, Eastwood, Willoughby, Warringah, Ryde, Lane Cove, Manly, Parramatta, Holroyd, Auburn, Hunters Hill, North Sydney, Mosman, Fairfield, Lidcombe, Concord, Drummoyne, Villawood, Strathfield, Burwood, SYDNEY, Leichhardt, Woollahra, Bonnyrigg, Ashfield, S. Sydney, Liverpool, Belmore, Canterbury, Marrickville, Randwick, Waverley, Milperra, Bankstown, KINGSFORD-SMITH AIRPORT, Kensington, Coogee, Rockdale, Kogarah, Maroubra, Hurstville, Botany, La Perouse Bay, Cape Banks, Sutherland, Kurnell Pen., Cronulla

PACIFIC OCEAN
0 2 4 6 MI.
0 2 4 6 KM.

Melbourne and Vicinity

Broadmeadows, Thomastown, Kangaroo Ground, Keilor, Bundoora, Research, Coburg, Montmorency, Eltham, Coldstream, Preston, Yarra, Warrandyte, Sunshine, Brunswick, Heidelberg, Lillydale, Footscray, Northcote, Collingwood, Doncaster and Templestowe, Croydon, Fitzroy, Kew, Nunawading, Ringwood, Montrose, MELBOURNE, Hawthorn, Box Hill, Mt. Dandenong 2,060 ft. (628 m.), Port Melbourne, Richmond, Camberwell, Prahran, Malvern, Olinda, St. Kilda, Knox, Fern Tree Gully, Williamstown, Hobsons Bay, Caulfield, Waverley, Belgrave Hts., Altona Bay, Oakleigh, Selby, Brighton, Moorabbin, Clayton, Springvale, Belgrave South, Sandringham, PORT PHILLIP BAY, Narre Warren N., Pt. Cook, Ricketts Pt., Beaumaris Bay, Mordialloc, Hallam, Harkaway, Hampton Park, Narre Warren, Berwick, Chelsea

0 2 4 6 8 MI.
0 2 4 6 8 KM.

Ryde 88,948 J3
Rylstone 651 E3
Salisbury Downs B1
Sawtell 5,970 G2
Scone 3,949 F3
Shellharbour 41,790 F4
Singleton 9,572 F3
Smithtown-Gladstone 953 G2
South Sydney 30,776 J3
South West Rocks 1,314 G2
Stephen's Creek A2
Strathfield 25,882 J3
Stroud 522 G3
Sussex Inlet 1,293 F4
Sutherland 165,336 J4
Sydney (cap.) 2,876,508 J3
Sydney †3,204,696 J3
Talbingo 481 E4
Tamworth 29,657 F2
Taralga 272 E4
Tarcutta 263 D4
Taree 14,697 G2
Tathra 1,077 F5
Temora 4,350 D4
Tenterfield 3,402 G1
Terrigal-The Entrance 37,891 F3
The Rock 693 D4
Thurloo Downs B1
Tibbita C4
Tibooburra B1
Tiltagara C2
Tingha 886 F1
Tocumwal 1,174 C4
Tongo B2
Torrowangee A2
Tottenham 366 D3
Trangie 977 D3
Trundle 515 D3
Tullamore 324 D3
Tumbarumba 1,536 D4
Tumut 5,816 E4
Tweed Heads G1
Ulladulla 6,018 F4
Ulmarra 395 G1
Ungarie 428 D3
Uralla 2,090 F2
Urana 419 D4
Urbenville 282 G1
Urunga 2,045 G2
Villawood H3
Wagga Wagga 36,837 D4
Wakool 278 C4
Walcha 1,674 F2
Walgett 2,157 E2
Walla Walla 593 D4
Wallerawang 1,855 F3
Wangi-Rathmines 5,106 F3
Warialda 1,340 F1
Warragamba 1,406 F3
Warren 2,153 D2
Warringah ○172,653 K3
Wauchope 3,645 G2
Waverley 61,575 K3
Waverley Downs B1
Wee Waa 1,904 E2
Wellington 5,280 E3
Wentworth 1,180 B4
Werris Creek 1,924 F2
West Wyalong 3,778 D3
Wetuppa B4
White Cliffs B2
Whitton 344 D4
Whyjonta B1
Wilcannia 982 B2
Willoughby 52,120 J3
Willow Tree 258 F2
Wingham 3,937 G2
Wollongong 169,381 F4
Wollongong †222,539 F4
Woodburn 647 G1
Woodenbong 409 G1
Woodstock 266 E3
Woolgoolga 2,081 G2
Wooli 457 G1
Woollahra 51,659 K3
Wyong 3,902 F3
Yallock C3
Yalpunga A1
Yamba 2,528 G1
Yancannia B2
Yanco 415 D4
Yantara B1
Yass 4,283 E4
Yenda 697 D4
Yeoval 288 E3
Young 6,906 E4

OTHER FEATURES

Ana Branch, Darling (riv.) A3
Australian Alps (mts.) D5
Barrington Tops (mt.) F2
Barwon (riv.) D2
Blue (mts.) F3
Bogan (riv.) D2
Bondi (beach) K3
Botany (bay) J4
Broken (bay) F3
Burrinjuck (res.) E4
Byron (cape) G1
Caryapundy (swamp) B1
Castlereagh (riv.) E2
Cawndilla (lake) A3
Clarence (riv.) G1
Colo (riv.) F3
Cowal (lake) D3
Culgoa (riv.) D1
Cuttaburra (creek) C1
Darling (riv.) B3
Dumaresq (riv.) F1
Eucumbene (lake) E5
George (lake) E4
Georges (riv.) H4
Gower (mt.) J2
Great Dividing (range) E3
Green (cape) F5
Gunderbooka (ranges) C2
Gwydir (riv.) E1
Howe (cape) F5
Hume (res.) D4
Hunter (riv.) F3
Kosciusko (mt.) E5
Kurnell (pen.) J4
Lachlan (range) C3
Lachlan (riv.) C3
Liverpool (range) F2
Lord Howe (isl.) 287 J2
Macintyre (riv.) E1
Macquarie (lake) F3
Macquarie (riv.) D2
Main Barrier (range) A2
Manning (riv.) F2
Marthaguy (creek) D2
McPherson (range) G1
Menindee (lake) B3
Monaro (range) E5
Moonie (riv.) E1
Moulamein (creek) C4
Mount Royal (range) F2
Murray (riv.) A4
Murrumbidgee (riv.) C4
Myall (lake) G3
Namoi (riv.) E2
Narran (lake) D1
New England (range) F1
Paroo (riv.) C1
Parramatta (riv.) J3
Poopeloe (lake) C2
Port Jackson (inlet) J3
Port Stephens (inlet) G3
Richmond (range) G1
Richmond (riv.) G1
Riverina (reg.) C4
Robe (mt.) A2
Round, The (mt.) G2
Salt, The (lake) B2
Shoalhaven (riv.) E4
Smoky (cape) G2
Snowy (mts.) E5
Snowy (riv.) E5
Stony (ranges) B2
Sturt (mt.) A1
Sugarloaf (pt.) G3
Talyawalka (creek) B2
Tandou (lake) A3
Tasman (sea) F5
The Round (mts.) G2
The Salt (lake) B2
Timbarra (riv.) G1
Tuggerah (lake) F3
Victoria (lake) A3
Warrego (riv.) C1
Willandra Billabong (creek) C3
Wollondilly (riv.) F4

VICTORIA

CITIES and TOWNS

Alexandra 1,756 C5
Altona 30,909 H5
Apollo Bay 921 B6
Ararat 8,336 B5
Avoca 1,032 B5
Bacchus Marsh 6,224 C5
Bairnsdale 9,459 D5
Ballarat 35,681 C5
Ballarat †71,930 C5
Balmoral 257 A5
Beaufort 1,214 B5
Beechworth 3,154 D5
Belgrave Heights J5
Belgrave South K5
Benalla 8,151 D5
Bendigo 31,841 C5
Bendigo †58,818 C5
Berwick 36,181 K6
Beulah 290 B4
Birchip 895 B4
Birregurra 416 B6
Boort 863 B5
Box Hill 47,579 J5
Bright 1,545 D5
Brighton 33,697 J5
Broadford 1,580 C5
Broadmeadows 103,540 H4
Brunswick 44,464 H5
Bruthen 449 D5
Bundoora J4
Camberwell 85,883 J5
Camperdown 3,545 C6
Cann River 345 E5
Casterton 1,945 A5
Castlemaine 7,583 C5
Caulfield 69,922 J5
Charlton 1,377 B5
Chelsea 26,034 J6
Churchill 4,796 D6
Clunes 761 B5
Cobden 1,453 B6
Cobram 3,817 C4
Coburg 55,035 H5
Cohuna 2,178 C4
Colac 10,587 B6
Coldstream 1,395 K4
Coleraine 1,232 A5
Collingwood 15,089 J5
Corryong 1,320 D5
Craigieburn 4,296 C5
Cranbourne 9,400 C6
Creswick 2,036 B5
Croydon 36,210 K5
Dandenong 54,962 K5
Darby D6
Dartmoor 349 A5
Daylesford 2,883 C5
Derrinallum 287 B5
Dimboola 1,675 B5
Donald 1,609 B5
Doncaster and Templestowe 90,660 J5
Drouin 3,492 C6
Dunkeld 402 B5
Dunolly 621 B5
Eaglehawk 7,355 C5
Echuca 7,943 C5
Edenhope 827 A5
Eildon 737 C5
Eltham 34,648 J4
Erica 236 D5
Essendon 56,380 H5
Euroa 2,640 C5
Fitzroy 19,112 H5
Footscray 49,756 H5
Geelong 14,471 C6
Geelong †137,173 C6
Geelong West 14,823 C6
Goroke 370 A5
Gunbower 259 C4
Hamilton 9,751 B5
Hawthorn 30,689 J5
Healesville 4,526 C5
Heathcote 1,213 C5
Heidelberg 64,757 J5
Heyfield 1,635 D6
Heywood 1,266 A6
Hopetoun 1,832 B4
Horsham 12,034 B5
Inglewood 674 B5
Inverloch 1,523 C6
Kaniva 956 A5
Keilor 81,762 H5
Kerang 4,049 B4
Kew 28,870 J5
Kilmore 1,728 C5
Knox 88,902 K5
Koroit 1,988 B6
Korumburra 2,798 D6
Kyabram 5,414 C5
Kyneton 3,185 C5
Lake Boga 502 B4
Lake Bolac 211 B5
Lakes Entrance 3,414 E5
Lara 4,231 C6
Leongatha 3,736 C6
Lillydale 62,077 J4
Macarthur 322 A6
Maffra 3,822 D5
Maldon 1,009 C5
Mallacoota 726 E5
Malvern 43,211 J5
Mansfield 1,920 D5
Maryborough 7,858 B5
Melbourne (cap.) 2,578,759 H5
Melbourne †2,722,817 H5
Melton 20,599 C5
Merbein 1,735 A4
Merino 298 A5
Mildura 15,763 A4
Minyip 567 B5
Moe 16,649 D6
Montmorency J4
Montrose K5
Moorabbin 97,810 J5
Mooroopna C5
Mordialloc 27,869 J6
Morea A5
Mornington 23,512 C6
Mortlake 1,056 B6
Morwell 16,491 D5
Mount Beauty 1,509 D5
Murrayville 313 A4
Murtoa 946 B5
Myrtleford 2,815 D5
Nagambie 1,102 C5
Narre Warren North 761 K5
Nathalia 1,222 C5
Natimuk 482 A5
Newtown 10,210 C6
Nhill 1,567 A5
Northcote 51,235 J5
Numurkah 2,713 C5
Nunawading 97,052 J5
Nyah 351 B4
Nyah West 535 B4
Oakleigh 55,612 J5
Omeo 272 D5
Orbost 2,586 E5
Ouyen 1,527 B4
Penshurst 558 B5
Porepunkah 268 D5
Port Albert 267 D6
Port Fairy 2,276 B6
Portland 9,353 A6
Port Melbourne 8,585 H5
Prahran 45,018 J5
Preston 84,519 J4
Quambatook 359 B4
Queenscliff 3,420 C6
Rainbow 700 A4
Red Cliffs 2,409 B4
Richmond 24,506 J5
Ringwood 38,665 K5
Robinvale 1,751 B4
Rochester 2,399 C5
Rushworth 994 C5
Rutherglen 1,454 D5
Saint Arnaud 2,721 B5
Saint Kilda 49,366 J5
Sale 12,968 D6
Sandringham 31,175 J5
Sea Lake 943 B4
Sebastopol 6,462 B5
Seymour 6,494 C5
Shepparton-Mooroopna ‡28,373 C5
South Barwon 35,307 C6
South Melbourne 19,955 J5
Springvale 80,186 J5
Stawell 6,160 B5
Sunbury 11,085 C5
Sunshine 94,419 H5
Swan Hill 8,398 B4
Swifts Creek 288 D5
Tallangatta 950 D5
Tatura 2,697 C5
Templestowe and Doncaster 90,660 J5
Terang 2,111 B6
Tongala 994 C5
Traralgon 18,057 D6
Underbool 274 A4
Wangaratta 16,202 D5
Warburton 2,009 C5
Warracknabeal 2,735 B5
Warragul 7,712 D6
Warrnambool 21,414 B6
Waverley 122,471 J5
Wedderburn 868 B5
Werrimull A4
Whittlesea 65,657 C5
Willaura 377 B5
Williamstown 25,554 H5
Winchelsea 825 B6
Wodonga 19,208 D5
Wonthaggi 4,797 C6
Woodend 1,785 C5
Wycheproof 938 B5
Yallourn 26 D6
Yarram 2,085 D6
Yarrawonga 3,442 C5
Yea 996 C5

OTHER FEATURES

Australian Alps (mts.) D5
Avoca (riv.) B5
Barry (mts.) D5
Bogong (mt.) D5
Bridgewater (cape) A6
Buller (mt.) D5
Campaspe (riv.) C5
Corangamite (lake) B6
Corner (inlet) D6
Dandenong (mt.) K5
Difficult (mt.) B5
Discovery (bay) A6
Eildon (lake) C5
French (isl.) 123 C6
Gippsland (reg.) D6
Glenelg (riv.) A5
Goulburn (riv.) C5
Hindmarsh (lake) A5
Hobsons (bay) H5
Hopkins (riv.) B5
Hume (lake) D4
Indian Ocean B6
Loddon (riv.) B5
Mitchell (riv.) D5
Mitta Mitta (riv.) D5
Mornington (pen.) C6
Mount Emu (creek) B5
Murray (riv.) A4
Nelson (cape) A6
Ninety Mile (beach) D6
Otway (cape) B6
Ovens (riv.) D5
Phillip (isl.) 2,832 C6
Portland (bay) A6
Port Phillip (bay) C6
Rocklands (res.) B5
Snowy (riv.) E5
South East (pt.) D6
Tasman (sea) F5
Tyrrell (lake) B4
Waratah (bay) C6
Wellington (lake) D6
Western Port (inlet) C6
Wilsons (prom.) D6
Wimmera (riv.) A5
Yarra (riv.) C5

*City and suburbs.
○ Population of district.
†Population of met. area.
‡Population of urban area.

Irrigation Areas and Artesian Basins in Australia

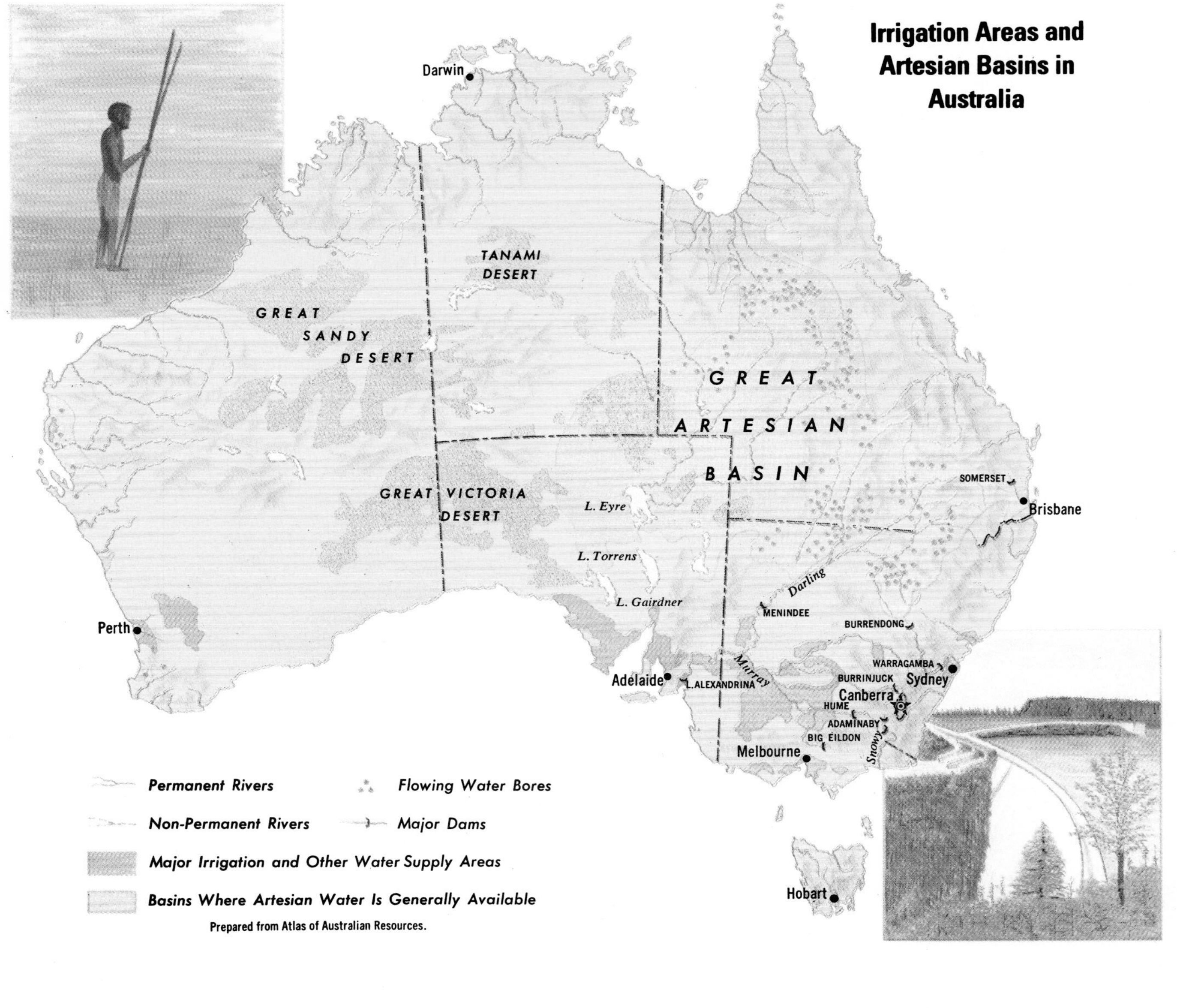
Darwin
TANAMI DESERT
GREAT SANDY DESERT
GREAT VICTORIA DESERT
L. Eyre
L. Torrens
L. Gairdner
GREAT ARTESIAN BASIN
SOMERSET
Brisbane
Darling
MENINDEE
BURRENDONG
Murray
WARRAGAMBA
BURRINJUCK
Sydney
Canberra
HUME
ADAMINABY
BIG EILDON
Snowy
Melbourne
Adelaide
L. ALEXANDRINA
Perth
Hobart
Permanent Rivers
Flowing Water Bores
Non-Permanent Rivers
Major Dams
Major Irrigation and Other Water Supply Areas
Basins Where Artesian Water Is Generally Available

Prepared from Atlas of Australian Resources.

Topography

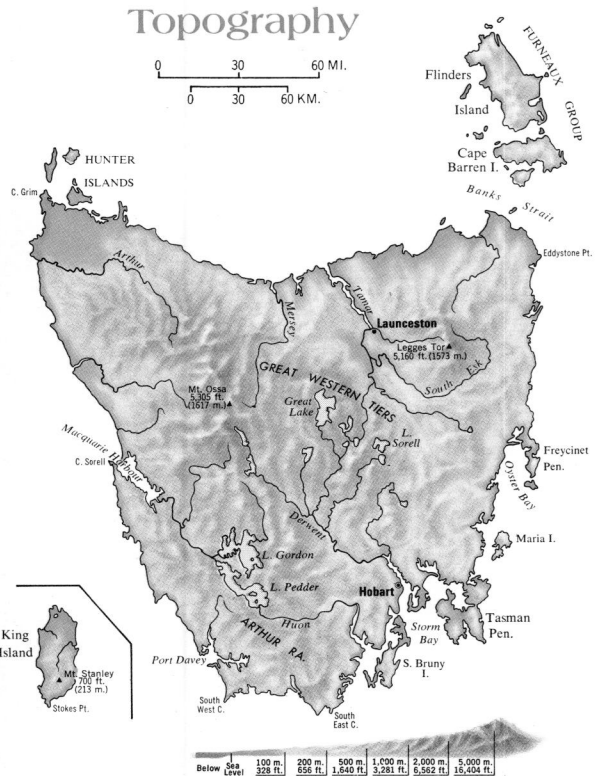

0   30   60 MI.

0   30   60 KM.

Below Sea Level | 100 m. 328 ft. | 200 m. 656 ft. | 500 m. 1,640 ft. | 1,000 m. 3,281 ft. | 2,000 m. 6,562 ft. | 5,000 m. 16,404 ft.

TASMANIA

AREA 26,178 sq. mi. (67,800 sq. km.)
POPULATION 418,957
CAPITAL Hobart
LARGEST CITY Hobart
HIGHEST POINT Mt. Ossa 5,305 ft. (1,617 m.)

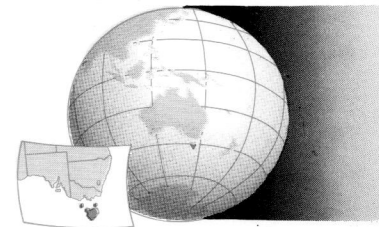

CITIES and TOWNS

Adventure Bay............D5
Avoca...................D3
Bagdad..................D4
Beaconsfield 898.........C3
Beauty Point 998.........C3
Bell Bay................C3
Bicheno 674.............E3
Boat Harbour.............B2
Bothwell 356............C4
Bracknell 347............C3
Branxholm 273...........D3
Bridgewater 6,880........D4
Bridport 885............D3
Brighton 9,441...........D4
Burnie 19,994...........B3
Campbell Town 879........D3
Chudleigh...............C3
Colebrook...............D4
Cressy 640..............C3
Currie 859..............A1
Cygnet 715..............C5
Deloraine 1,923..........C3
Derwent Bridge..........C4
Devonport 21,424........C3
Dover 570...............C5
Dunalley 203............D4
Evandale 614............D3
Exeter 353..............C3
Fingal 424..............E3
Forth 273...............C3
Franklin 479............C5
Geeveston 860...........C5
George Town 5,592........C3
Glenorchy 41,019........D4
Gormanston 126..........B4
Gowrie Park.............C3
Grassy 780..............B1
Gravelly Beach 535.......C3
Hadspen 908............C3
Hagley 232..............C3
Hamilton 2,488..........C4
Heybridge 395...........C3
Hobart (cap.) 128,603....D4
Hobart *168,359.........D4
Huonville-Ranelagh 1,347..C5
Kettering 288...........D5
Kingston 8,556..........D4
Latrobe 2,401...........C3
Lauderdale 2,117........D4
Launceston 31,273.......C3
Launceston *64,555.......C3
Legana 964..............C3
Lilydale 308............D3
Longford 2,027..........C3
Luina 522...............B3
Margate 476.............D4
Maydena 461.............C4
Meander.................C3
Mole Creek 303..........C3
New Norfolk 6,243........C4
Nubeena 225.............D5
Oatlands 545............D4
Orford 378..............D4
Penguin 2,616...........C3
Perth 1,229.............D3
Poatina.................C3
Port Sorell 859.........C3
Queenstown 3,714........B4
Railton 857.............C3
Richmond 587............D4
Ridgley 452.............B3

Ringarooma 223..........D3
Rosebery 2,675..........B3
Ross 289................D4
Rossarden 365...........D3
Saint Helens 1,005......E3
Saint Marys 653.........E3
Sassafras...............C3
Savage River 1,141......B3
Scottsdale 2,002........D3
Sheffield 945...........C3
Smithton 3,378..........A2
Snug 684................D5
Sorell-Midway Point 2,544..D4
Stanley 603.............B2
Storeys Creek...........D3
Strahan 402.............B4
Strathgordon............C4
Sulphur Creek 367.......C3
Swansea 428.............D4
Tarraleah 498...........C4
Temma...................A3
Triabunna 924...........D4
Tullah 1,894............B3
Ulverstone 9,413........C3
Waratah 342.............B3
Wesley Vale.............C3
Westbury 1,161..........C3
Whitemark...............D2
Woodbridge 259..........D5
Wynyard 4,582...........B3
Zeehan 1,750............B3

OTHER FEATURES

Anderson (bay)..........D2
Anne (mt.)..............C4
Anser Group (isls.).....C1
Arthur (lake)...........D4
Arthur (range)..........C5
Arthur (riv.)...........B3
Babel (isl.)............E1
Banks (str.)............D2
Barn Bluff (mt.)........B3
Barren (cape)...........E2
Bass (str.).............C1
Bathurst (gulf).........C5
Cape Barren (isl.)......E2
Chappell (isls.)........D2
Circular (gulf).........B2
Clarke (isl.)...........E2
Clyde (riv.)............D4
Cox (bight).............C5
Cradle (mt.)............B3
Cradle Mt. Lake St. Clair Nat'l Park....B3
Crescent (lake).........D4
Curtis Group (isls.)....C1
D'Aguilar (range).......B4
Davey (riv.)............B4
Deal (isl.).............D1
Dee (riv.)..............C4
Denison (range).........C4
D'Entrecasteaux (chan.)..D5
Derwent (riv.)..........C4
East Sister (isl.)......E1
Echo (lake).............C4
Eddystone (pt.).........E2
Elliott (bay)...........B5
Fires (bay).............E3
Flinders (isl.) 2,150...D1
Florence (riv.).........C4
Forestier (chan.).......E4
Forestier (pen.)........E4

Forth (riv.)............C3
Frankland (cape)........D1
Frankland (range).......B4
Franklin (riv.).........B4
Frenchmans Cap (mt.)....B4
Freycinet (pen.)........E4
Furneaux Group (isls.) 1,039..E1
Gordon (lake)...........B4
Gordon (riv.)...........B4
Great (lake)............C3
Great Western Tiers (mts.)..C3
Grim (cape).............A2
Hartz (mt.).............C5
Hibbs (pt.).............B4
Hogan Group (isl.)......D1
Hummock (isl.)..........D2
Hunter (isl.)...........A2
Hunter (isls.)..........B2
Huon (riv.).............C5
Indian Ocean............A4
Kent Group (isls.)......D1
King (isl.) 2,592........A1

King (riv.).............B4
King William (lake).....C4
Lake (riv.).............C4
Legges Tor (mt.)........D3
Leven (riv.)............B3
Lofty (range)...........B3
Low Rocky (pt.).........B4
Lyell (mt.).............B4
Maatsuyker (isls.)......C5
Macquarie (harb.).......B4
Macquarie (riv.)........D3
Maria (isl.)............E4
Marion (bay)............E4
Mersey (riv.)...........C3
Munro (mt.).............E2
Naturaliste (cape)......E2
Nive (riv.).............C4
Norfolk (bay)...........D4
North (pt.).............E1
North Bruny (isl.)......D5
North Esk (riv.)........D3
Ossa (mt.)..............C3

Ouse (riv.).............C4
Oyster (bay)............E4
Pedder (lake)...........B4
Phoques (bay)...........A1
Picton (mt.)............C5
Pieman (riv.)...........B3
Pillar (cape)...........E5
Port Davey (inlet)......B5
Portland (cape).........D2
Ramsey (riv.)...........B3
Raoul (cape)............D5
Reid (rapid)............B1
Ringarooma (bay)........D2
Robbins (isl.)..........B2
Saint Clair (lake)......C4
Saint Helens (pt.)......E3
Saint Vincent (cape)....B5
Savage (riv.)...........B3
Schouten (isl.).........E4
Sorell (isl.)...........E4
Sorell (lake)...........D4
South (cape)............C5

South Bruny (isl.)......D5
South East (cape).......C5
South Esk (riv.)........D3
South West (cape).......B5
Stanley (mt.)...........A1
Stokes (pt.)............A1
Storm (bay).............D5
Strzelecki (mt.)........D2
Tamar (riv.)............D3
Tasman (head)...........D5
Tasman (pen.)...........E5
Tasman (sea)............E4
Three Hummock (isl.)....B2
Vansittart (isl.).......E2
West (pt.)..............A2
West Sister (isl.)......D1
Wickham (cape)..........A1

○ Population of district.
*Population of met. area.

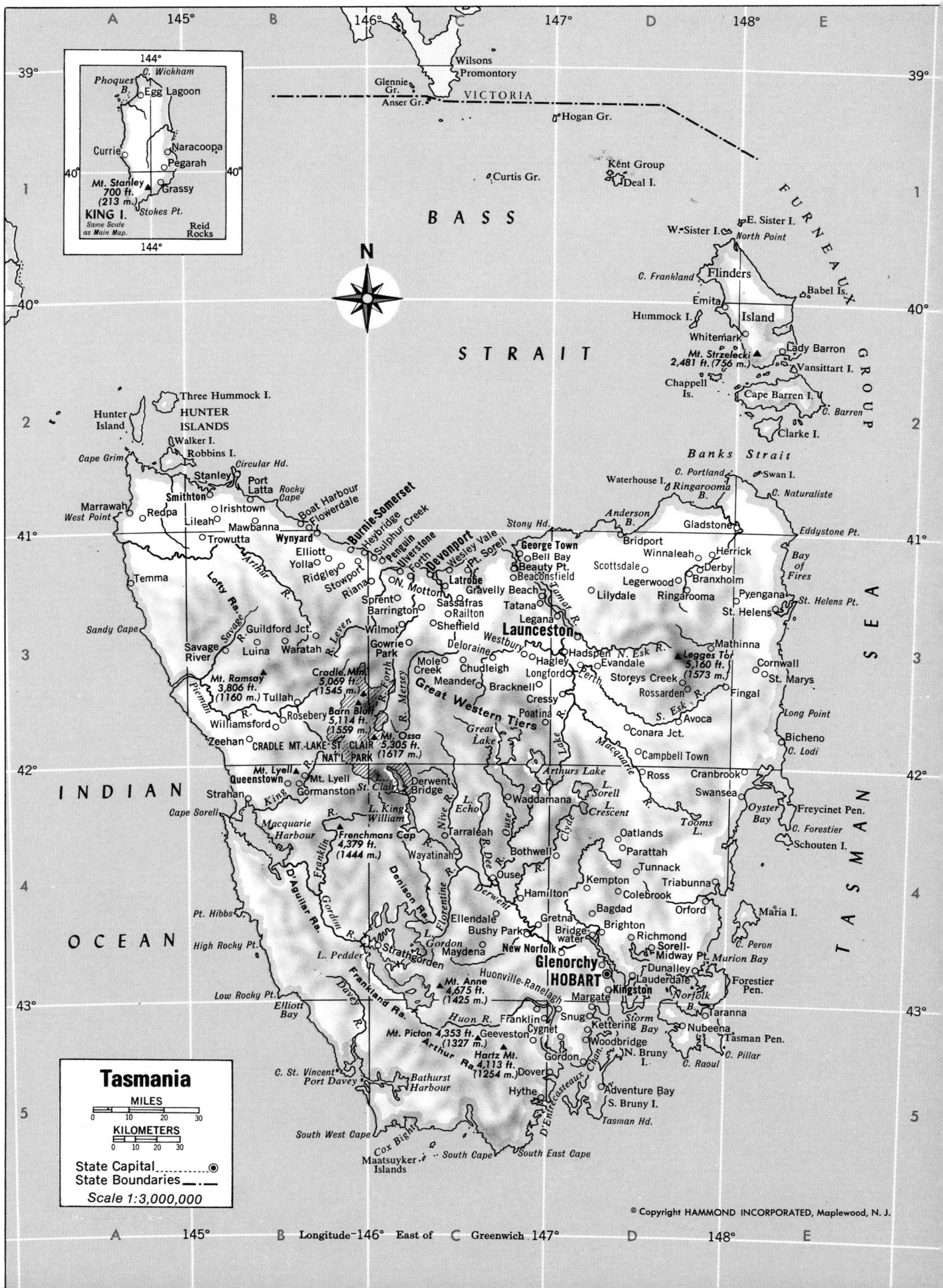

Tasmania

MILES
0   10   20   30

KILOMETERS
0 10 20 30

State Capital............◉
State Boundaries____
Scale 1:3,000,000

© Copyright HAMMOND INCORPORATED, Maplewood, N.J.

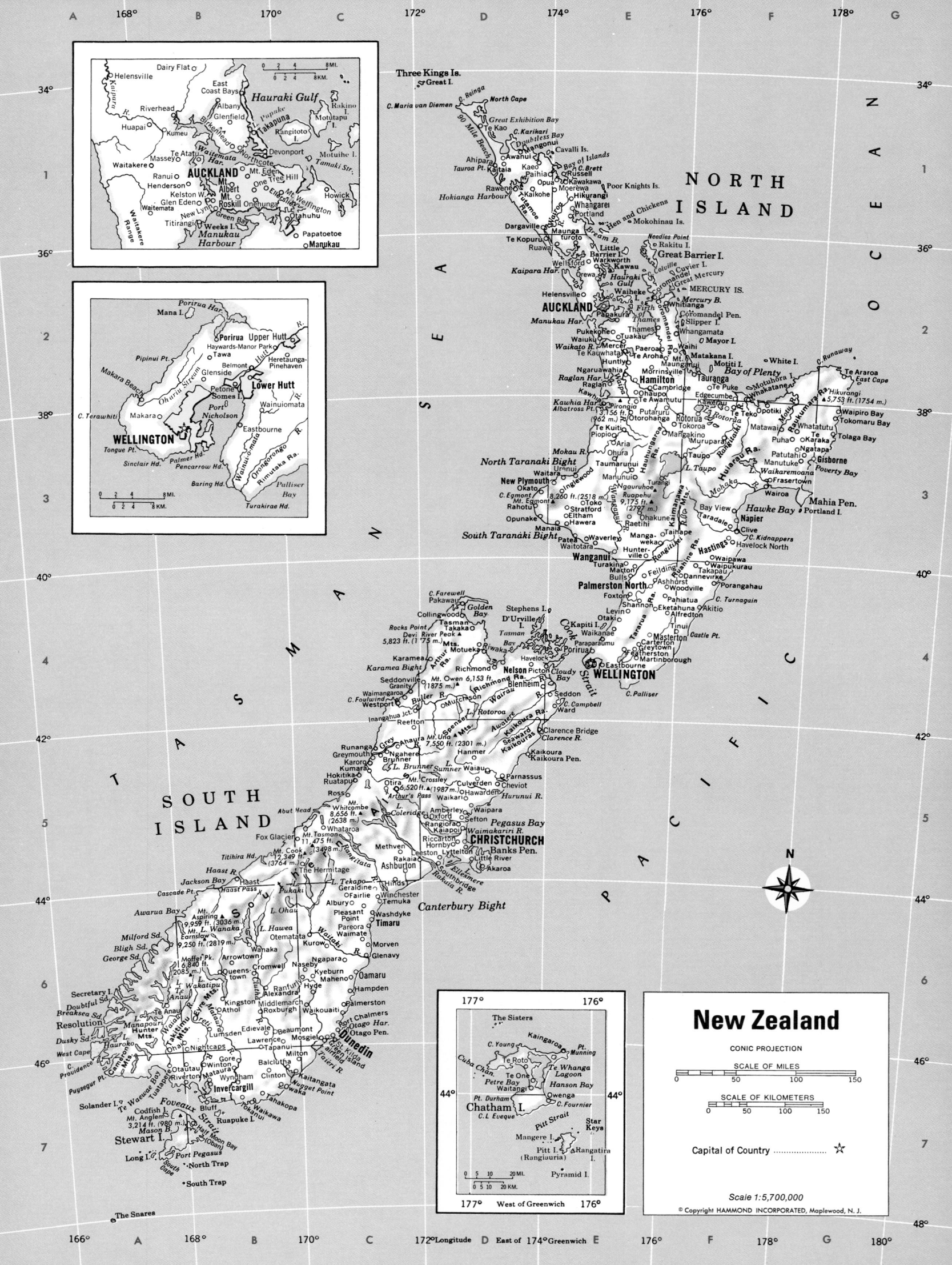

New Zealand

CONIC PROJECTION

SCALE OF MILES

0   50   100   150

SCALE OF KILOMETERS

0   50   100   150

Capital of Country .... ☆

Scale 1:5,700,000

© Copyright HAMMOND INCORPORATED, Maplewood, N.J.

Topography

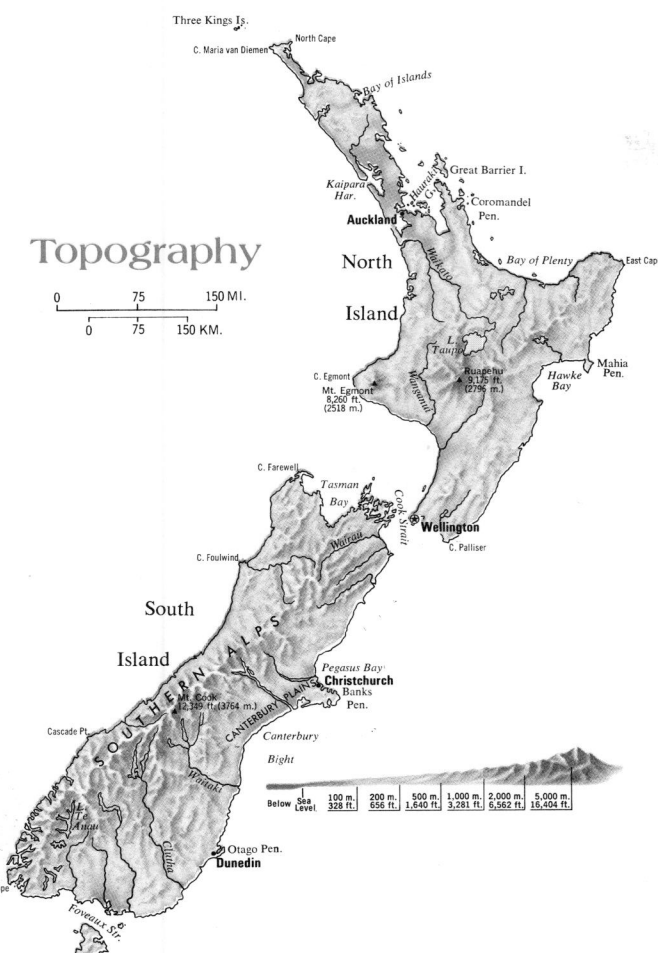

Three Kings Is.
North Cape
C. Maria van Diemen
Bay of Islands
Kaipara Har.
Great Barrier I.
Coromandel Pen.
Auckland
North
Island
Bay of Plenty
East Cape
C. Egmont
Mt. Egmont 8,260 ft. (2518 m.)
Ruapehu 9,175 ft. (2796 m.)
Mahia Pen.
Hawke Bay
C. Farewell
Tasman Bay
Cook Strait
C. Foulwind
Wellington
C. Palliser
South
Island
SOUTHERN ALPS
Mt. Cook 12,349 ft. (3764 m.)
CANTERBURY PLAINS
Pegasus Bay
Christchurch
Banks Pen.
Canterbury
Bight
Cascade Pt.
West Cape
Otago Pen.
Dunedin
Foveaux Str.
Stewart I.

Scale bars: 0 75 150 MI. / 0 75 150 KM.

Elevation legend: Below Sea Level | 100 m. 328 ft. | 200 m. 656 ft. | 500 m. 1,640 ft. | 1,000 m. 3,281 ft. | 2,000 m. 6,562 ft. | 5,000 m. 16,404 ft.

AREA 103,736 sq. mi. (268,676 sq. km.)
POPULATION 3,175,737
CAPITAL Wellington
LARGEST CITY Auckland
HIGHEST POINT Mt. Cook 12,349 ft. (3,764 m.)
MONETARY UNIT New Zealand dollar
MAJOR LANGUAGES English, Maori
MAJOR RELIGIONS Protestantism, Roman Catholicism

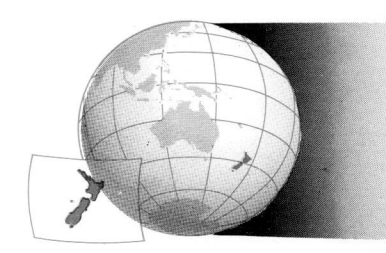

Wellington †321,004	A3
Wellsford 1,621	E2
Westport 4,686	C4
Whakatane 12,286	F2
Whangamata 1,566	F2
Whangarei 36,550	E1
Whangarei †40,212	E1
Whitianga 1,960	E2
Winton 2,035	B7
Woodville 1,647	F4

OTHER FEATURES

Arthur's (pass)	C5
Aspiring (mt.)	B6
Banks (pen.)	D5
Bream (bay)	E1
Brett (cape)	E1
Buller (riv.)	D4
Campbell (cape)	E4
Canterbury (bight)	D6
Cascade (pt.)	B6
Chatham (isls.) 751	D7
Cloudy (bay)	E4
Clutha (riv.)	B6
Coleridge (lake)	C5
Colville (cape)	E2
Cook (mt.)	C5
Cook (str.)	E4
Coromandel (pen.)	F2
Devil River (peak)	D4
D'Urville (isl.)	D4
Dusky (sound)	A6
East (cape)	G2
Egmont (cape)	D3
Egmont (mt.)	D3
Ellesmere (lake)	D5
Farewell (cape)	D4
Foulwind (cape)	C4
Fournier (cape)	E7
Foveaaux (str.)	A7
Golden (bay)	D4
Great Barrier (isl.) 572	E2
Haast (pass)	B6
Hauraki (gulf)	C1
Hawke (bay)	F3
Hikurangi (mt.)	G2
Hokianga (harb.)	D1
Huiarau (range)	F3
Hutt (riv.)	C2
Islands (bay)	E1
Jackson (bay)	B5
Kaikoura (range)	D5
Kaimanawa (range)	E3
Kaipara (harb.)	D2
Karamea (bight)	C4
Kawhia (harb.)	E3
Kidnappers (cape)	F3
Mahia (pen.)	G3
Manapouri (lake)	A6
Manukau (harb.)	B1
Maria van Diemen (cape)	D1
Mataura (riv.)	B6
Mercury (isls.)	F2
Milford (sound)	A6
Needles (pt.)	E2
Nicholson, Port (inlet)	B3
Ninety Mile (beach)	D1
North (cape)	D1
North (isl.) 2,322,989	F1
Otago (pen.)	C6
Owen (mt.)	D4
Palliser (cape)	E4
Pegasus (bay)	D5
Pitt (isl.)	E7
Plenty (bay)	F2
Port Nicholson (inlet)	B3
Port Pegasus (inlet)	B7
Pukaki (lake)	B6
Puysegur (pt.)	A7
Rakaia (riv.)	C5
Rangitata (riv.)	C5
Rangitikei (riv.)	E3
Raukumara (range)	F3
Reinga (cape)	D1
Resolution (isl.)	A6
Richmond (range)	D4
Rocks (pt.)	C4
Rotorua (lake)	F3
Ruahine (range)	F4
Ruapehu (mt.)	E3
Ruapuke (isl.)	B7
South (cape)	A7
South (isl.) 852,748	B5
Southern Alps (range)	C5
South Taranaki (bight)	D3
Spenser (mts.)	C5
Stewart (isl.) 600	A7
Tararua (range)	E4
Tasman (bay)	D4
Tasman (mt.)	C5
Tasman (mts.)	D4
Tasman (sea)	B4
Taupo (lake)	F3
Tauroa (pt.)	D1
Te Anau (lake)	A6
Tekapo (lake)	C5
Terawhiti (cape)	A3
Thames (firth)	E2
Three Kings (isls.)	D1
Turakirae (head)	B3
Una (mt.)	D5
Waiheke (isl.) 3,223	E2
Waikato (riv.)	E2
Waimakariri (riv.)	D5
Waipa (riv.)	E2
Wairau (riv.)	D4
Waitaki (riv.)	C6
Waitemata (harb.)	B1
Wakatipu (lake)	B6
Wanaka (lake)	B6
Wanganui (riv.)	E3
West (cape)	A6
Whitcombe (mt.)	C5

†Population of urban area.

Agriculture, Industry and Resources

CITIES and TOWNS

Albany 2,001	B1
Alexandra 4,348	B6
Ashburton 14,151	C5
Ashhurst 1,906	E4
Auckland 144,963	B1
Auckland †769,558	B1
Balclutha 4,495	B7
Belmont 2,402	B2
Birkenhead 21,324	B1
Blenheim 17,849	D4
Bluff 2,720	B7
Bulls 1,839	E4
Cambridge 8,514	E2
Carterton 3,971	E4
Christchurch 164,680	D5
Christchurch †289,959	D5
Cromwell 2,364	B6
Dannevirke 5,663	F4
Dargaville 4,747	D1
Devonport 10,410	C1
Dunedin 77,176	C6
Dunedin †107,445	C6
Eastbourne 4,561	B3
East Coast Bays 28,866	B1
Edgecumbe 1,929	F2
Ellerslie 5,404	C1
Eltham 2,411	E3
Fairfield 1,849	C6
Featherston 2,458	E4
Feilding 11,522	E4
Foxton 2,719	E4
Geraldine 2,128	C6
Gisborne 29,986	G3
Gisborne †32,062	G3
Glen Eden 9,406	B1
Glenfield 3,691	B1
Gore 9,185	B7
Green Bay 3,035	B1
Green Island 6,899	C7
Greymouth 8,103	C5
Greytown 1,797	E4
Half Moon Bay (Oban) 2,448	B7
Hamilton 91,109	E2
Hamilton †97,907	E2
Hastings 36,083	F3
Hastings †52,563	F3
Havelock North 8,507	F3
Hawera 8,400	E3
Helensville 1,360	B1
Henderson 6,645	B1
Heretaunga-Pinehaven 6,171	C2
Hokitika 3,414	C5
Hornby 8,215	D5
Howick 13,866	C1
Huntly 6,534	E2
Hutt (Upper and Lower) †131,257	B2
Inglewood 2,839	E3
Invercargill 49,446	B7
Invercargill †53,868	B7
Kaiapoi 4,894	D5
Kaikohe 3,663	D1
Kaikoura 2,180	D5
Kaitaia 4,737	D1
Kawerau 8,593	F3
Kumeu 3,414	B1
Levin 14,652	E4
Lower Hutt 63,245	B2
Lyttelton 3,184	D5
Manukau 159,362	C1
Marton 4,858	E4
Masterton 18,785	E4
Mataura 2,345	B7
Milton 2,193	B7
Morrinsville 5,080	E2
Mosgiel 9,264	C6
Motueka 4,693	D4
Mount Albert 26,462	B1
Mount Eden 18,305	B1
Mount Maunganui 11,391	F2
Mount Roskill 33,577	B1
Mount Wellington 19,528	C1
Murupara 2,964	F3
Napier 48,314	F3
Napier †51,330	F3
Nelson 33,304	D4
Nelson †43,121	D4
New Lynn 10,445	B1
New Plymouth 36,048	D3
New Plymouth †44,095	D3
Ngaruawahia 4,435	E2
Northcote 10,061	B1
Oamaru 13,043	C6
Oban (Half Moon Bay) 2,448	B7
Onehunga 15,386	B1
One Tree Hill 11,078	B1
Opotiki 3,388	F3
Orewa 5,552	E2
Otahuhu 10,298	C1
Otaki 4,301	C5
Otorohanga 2,574	E3
Paeroa 3,702	E2
Pahiatua 2,599	F4
Paihia 1,740	E1
Palmerston North 60,105	E4
Palmerston North †66,691	E4
Papakura 22,473	C1
Papatoetoe 21,700	C1
Patea 1,938	E3
Petone 8,113	B2
Picton 3,220	D4
Pinehaven (Heretaunga-Pinehaven) 6,171	C2
Porirua 41,104	B2
Port Chalmers 2,917	C6
Pukekohe 9,070	E2
Putaruru 4,222	E3
Queenstown 3,367	B6
Raetihi 1,247	E3
Raglan 1,414	E2
Rangiora 6,385	D5
Reefton 1,200	C5
Riccarton 6,709	D5
Richmond 6,847	D4
Riverton 1,479	B7
Rotorua 38,157	F3
Rotorua †48,314	F3
Runanga 1,264	C5
Russell 932	E1
Saint Kilda 6,147	C7
Shannon 1,465	E4
Stratford 5,518	E3
Taihape 2,586	E3
Takapuna 64,844	B1
Tapanui 1,042	B6
Taradale 4,681	F3
Taumarunui 6,541	E3
Taupo 13,651	F3
Tauranga 37,099	F2
Tauranga †53,097	F2
Tawa 12,216	B2
Te Anau 2,610	A6
Te Aroha 3,331	E2
Te Atatu 14,713	B1
Te Awamutu 7,922	E3
Te Kauwhata 842	E2
Te Kuiti 4,795	E3
Temuka 3,771	C6
Te Puke 4,577	F2
Thames 6,456	E2
The Hermitage	C5
Timaru 28,412	C6
Timaru †29,225	C6
Titirangi 8,426	B1
Tokoroa 18,713	E3
Tuakau 1,982	E2
Tuatapere 884	A7
Turangi 5,517	E3
Upper Hutt 31,405	B2
Waihi 3,538	E2
Waikanae 4,818	E4
Waikouaiti 858	C6
Waimate 3,393	C6
Wainuiomata 19,192	B3
Waipawa 1,732	F3
Waipukurau 3,648	F4
Wairoa 5,439	F3
Waitangi	D7
Waitara 6,012	E3
Waitemata 87,452	B1
Waiuku 3,654	E2
Waanaka 1,155	B6
Wanganui 37,012	E3
Wanganui †39,595	E3
Warkworth 1,734	E2
Washdyke 949	C6
Waverley 1,239	E3
Wellington (cap.) 135,688	A3

DOMINANT LAND USE

- Mixed Farming, Livestock
- Dairy
- Truck Farming, Horticulture
- Pasture Livestock (chiefly sheep)
- Livestock Herding
- Forests
- Nonagricultural Land

MAJOR MINERAL OCCURRENCES

- C Coal
- G Natural Gas
- J Jade
- Ka Kaolin
- Lg Lignite
- O Petroleum
- U Uranium

⚡ Water Power
▨ Major Industrial Areas

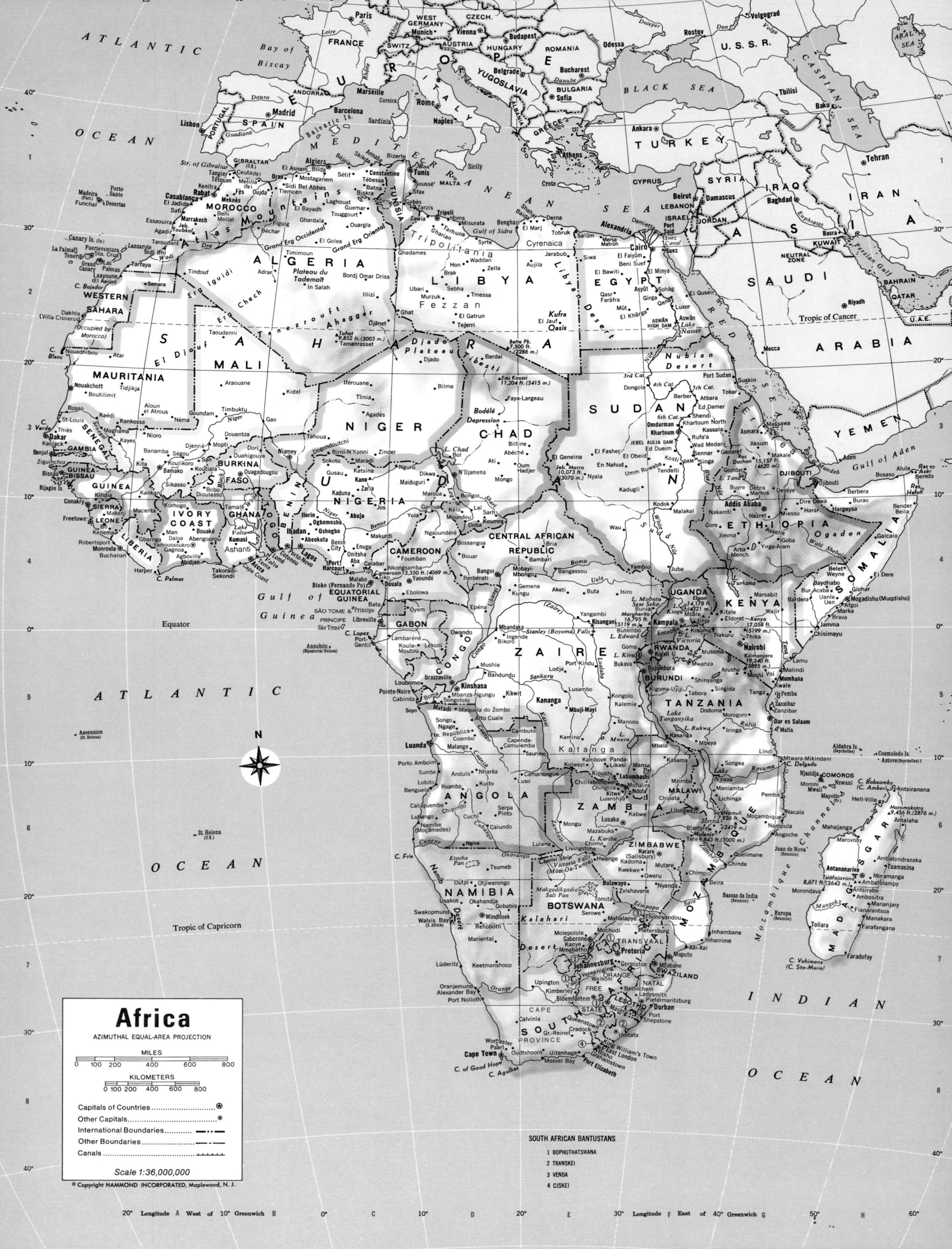

Africa

AZIMUTHAL EQUAL-AREA PROJECTION

MILES

0 100 200   400   600   800

KILOMETERS

0 100 200   400   600   800

Capitals of Countries .... ⊛

Other Capitals .... ⊛

International Boundaries .... ▪▪▪▪

Other Boundaries .... ▪▪▪▪

Canals .... ▪▪▪▪

Scale 1:36,000,000

® Copyright HAMMOND INCORPORATED, Maplewood, N.J.

SOUTH AFRICAN BANTUSTANS

1 BOPHUTHATSWANA

2 TRANSKEI

3 VENDA

4 CISKEI

AREA 11,707,000 sq. mi. (30,321,130 sq. km.)
POPULATION 469,000,000
LARGEST CITY Cairo
HIGHEST POINT Kilimanjaro 19,340 ft.
(5,895 m.)
LOWEST POINT Lake Assal, Djibouti -512 ft.
(-156 m.)

Population Distribution

Vegetation

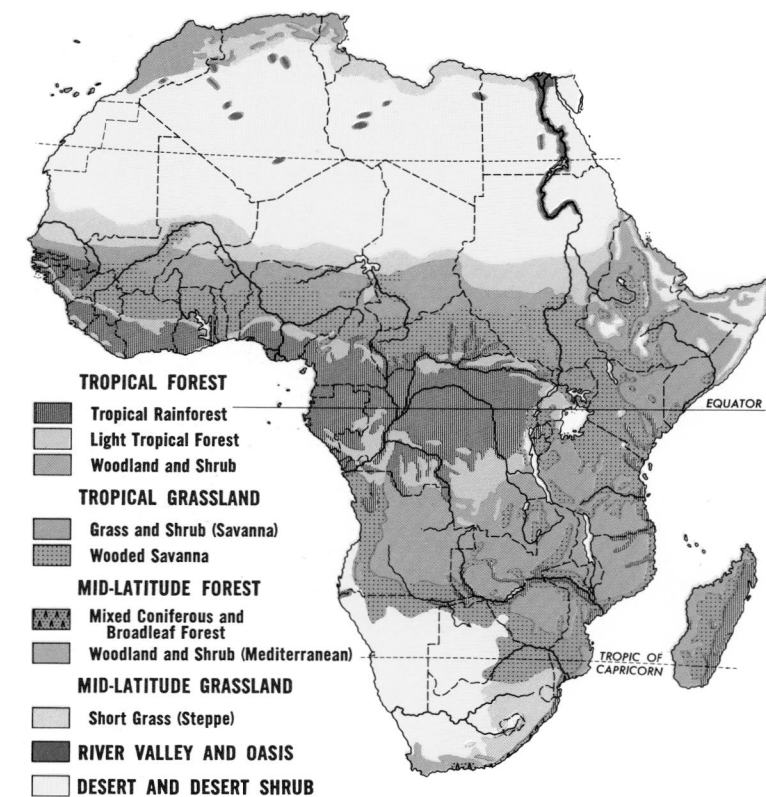

DENSITY PER

SQ. KILOMETER	SQ. MILE
Over 100	Over 260
50-100	130-260
10-50	25-130
1-10	3-25
Under 1	Under 3

• Cities with over 1,000,000
inhabitants (including suburbs)

○ Cities with over 350,000
inhabitants (including suburbs)

TROPICAL FOREST
- Tropical Rainforest
- Light Tropical Forest
- Woodland and Shrub

TROPICAL GRASSLAND
- Grass and Shrub (Savanna)
- Wooded Savanna

MID-LATITUDE FOREST
- Mixed Coniferous and Broadleaf Forest
- Woodland and Shrub (Mediterranean)

MID-LATITUDE GRASSLAND
- Short Grass (Steppe)

RIVER VALLEY AND OASIS

DESERT AND DESERT SHRUB

UNCLASSIFIED HIGHLANDS

Average January Temperature

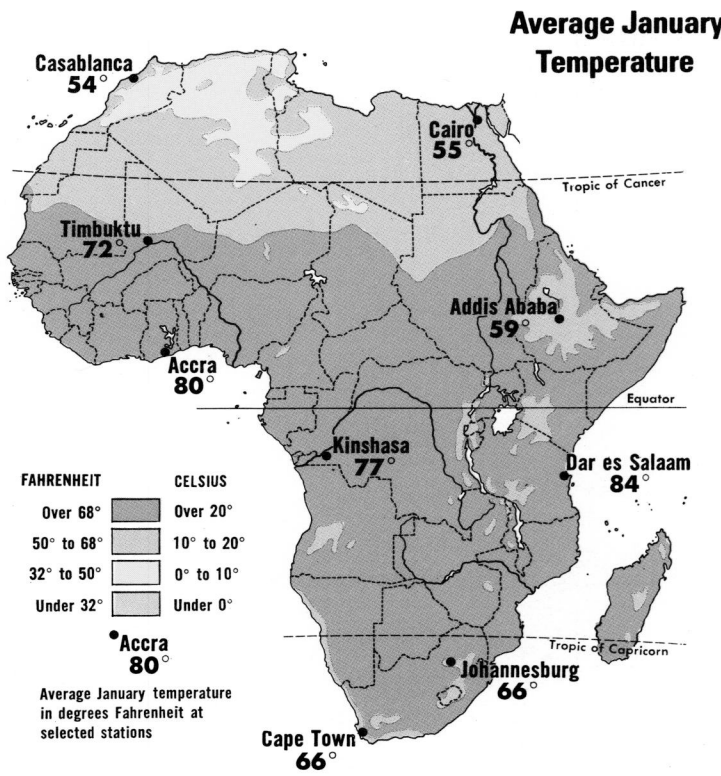

Casablanca 54°
Cairo 55°
Timbuktu 72°
Addis Ababa 59°
Accra 80°
Kinshasa 77°
Dar es Salaam 84°

FAHRENHEIT

Over 68°
50° to 68°
32° to 50°
Under 32°

CELSIUS

Over 20°
10° to 20°
0° to 10°
Under 0°

● Accra 80°

Average January temperature in degrees Fahrenheit at selected stations

●Johannesburg 66°
Cape Town 66°

Tropic of Cancer
Equator
Tropic of Capricorn

Average July Temperature

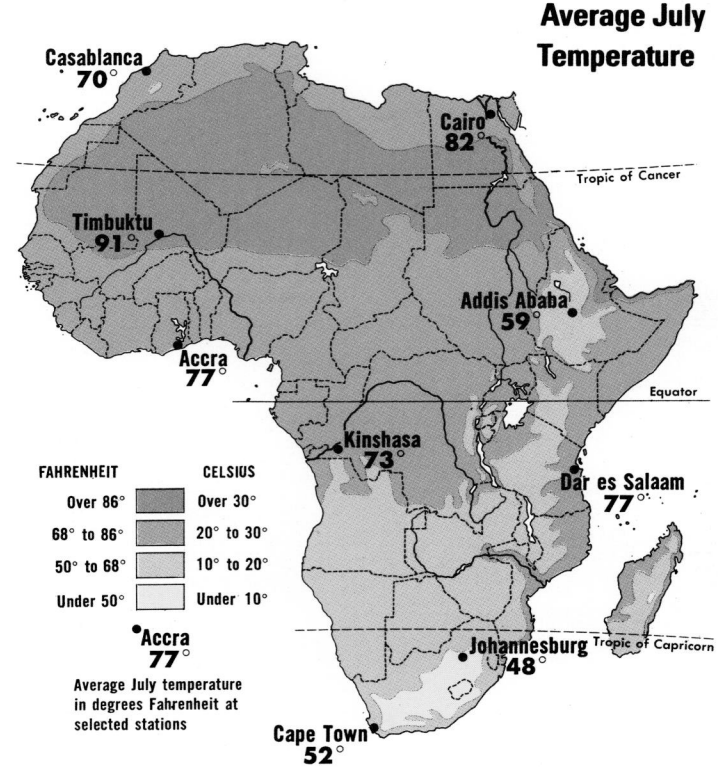

Casablanca 70°
Cairo 82°
Timbuktu 91°
Addis Ababa 59°
Accra 77°
Kinshasa 73°
Dar es Salaam 77°

FAHRENHEIT

Over 86°
68° to 86°
50° to 68°
Under 50°

CELSIUS

Over 30°
20° to 30°
10° to 20°
Under 10°

● Accra 77°

Average July temperature in degrees Fahrenheit at selected stations

●Johannesburg 48°
Cape Town 52°

Tropic of Cancer
Equator
Tropic of Capricorn

Rainfall

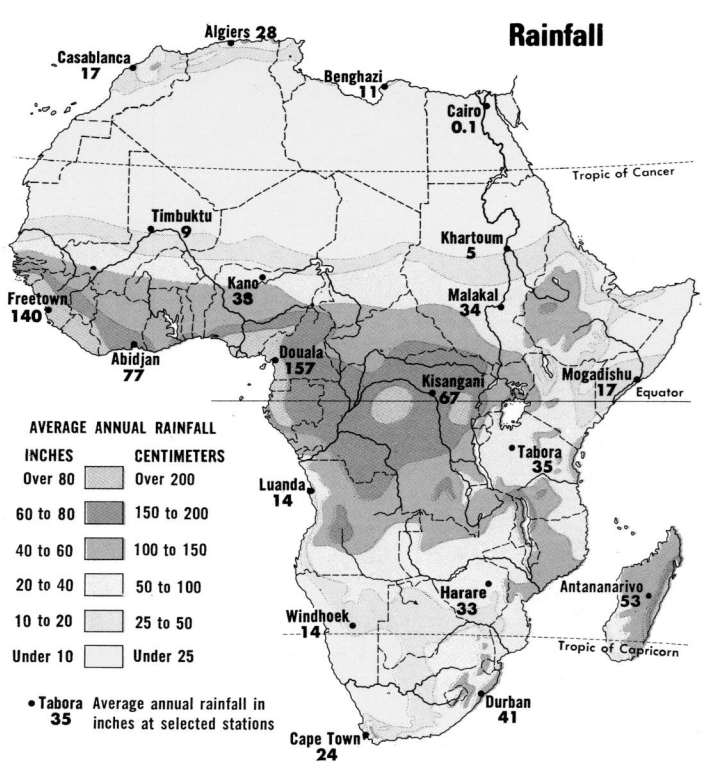

Algiers 28
Casablanca 17
Benghazi 11
Cairo 0.1
Timbuktu
Khartoum 5
Kano 35
Malakal 34
Freetown 140
Douala 157
Abidjan 77
Kisangani 67
Mogadishu 17
Tabora 35
Luanda 14
Harare 33
Antananarivo 53
Windhoek 14
Durban 41
Cape Town 24

Tropic of Cancer
Equator
Tropic of Capricorn

AVERAGE ANNUAL RAINFALL

INCHES	CENTIMETERS
Over 80	Over 200
60 to 80	150 to 200
40 to 60	100 to 150
20 to 40	50 to 100
10 to 20	25 to 50
Under 10	Under 25

● Tabora 35 Average annual rainfall in inches at selected stations

Vegetation / Relief

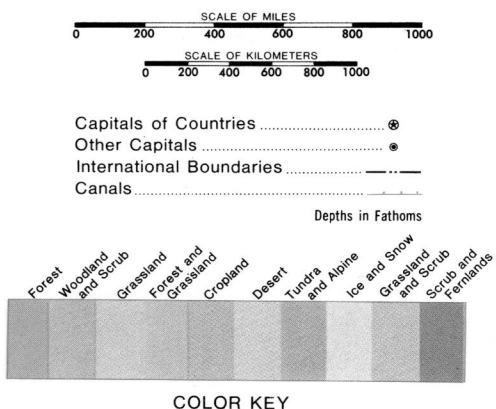

SCALE OF MILES
0 200 400 600 800 1000

SCALE OF KILOMETERS
0 200 400 600 800 1000

Capitals of Countries .... ⊛
Other Capitals .... ⊛
International Boundaries .... ▬ ▬
Canals ....

Depths in Fathoms

Forest
Woodland and Scrub
Grassland
Forest and Grassland
Cropland
Desert
Tundra and Alpine
Ice and Snow
Grassland and Scrub
Scrub and Fernlands

COLOR KEY

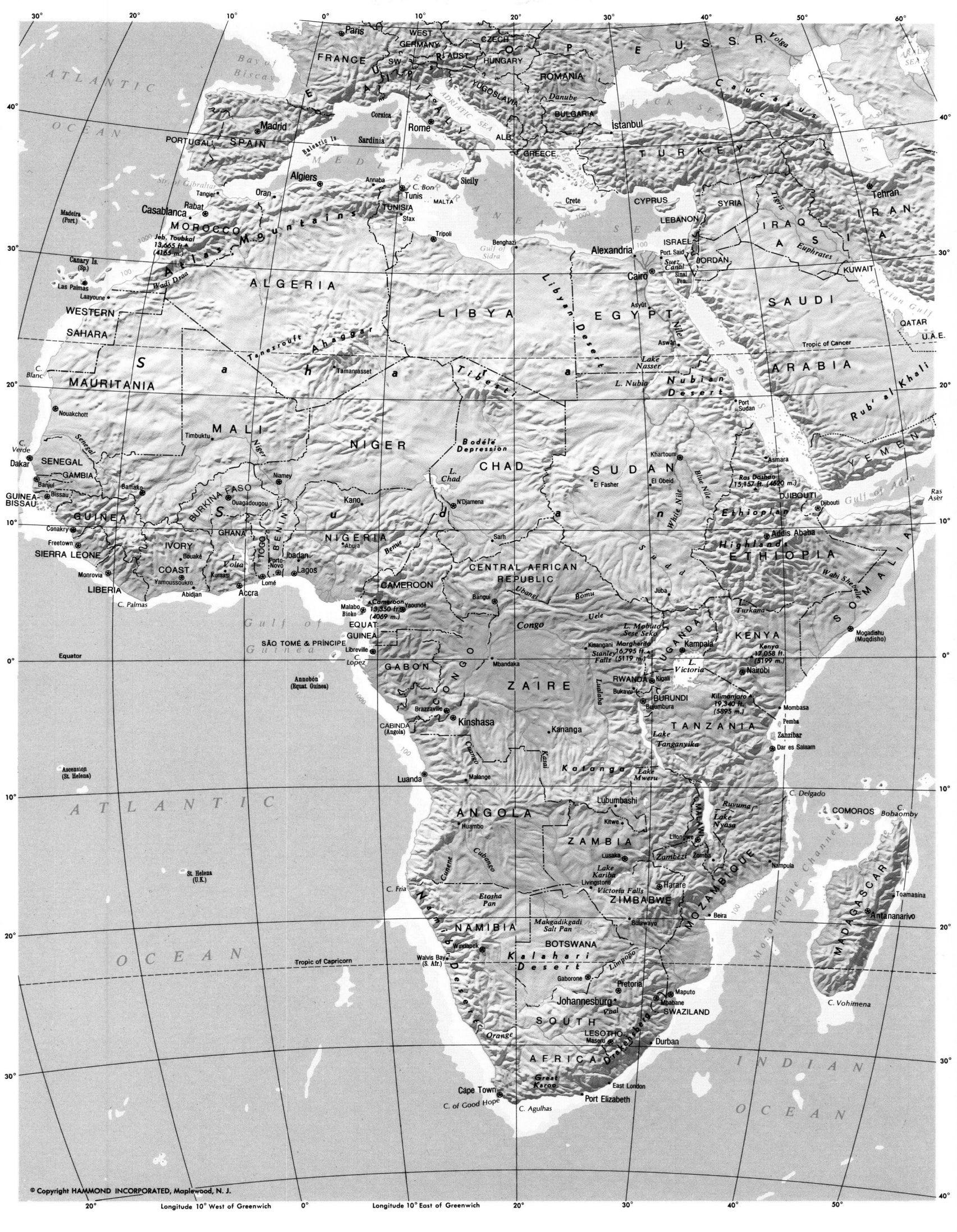

Western Africa

CONIC EQUAL-AREA PROJECTION

SCALE OF MILES

0   100   200   400

SCALE OF KILOMETERS

0   100   200   400

Capitals of Countries ___ ★   International Boundaries ___ ___

Other Capitals ___ ◉   Internal Boundaries ___ ___

Scale 1:15,200,000

© Copyright HAMMOND INCORPORATED, Maplewood, N.J.

Cape Verde

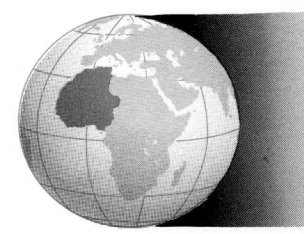

ALGERIA

AREA 919,591 sq. mi. (2,381,740 sq. km.)
POPULATION 17,422,000
CAPITAL Algiers
LARGEST CITY Algiers
HIGHEST POINT Tahat 9,852 ft. (3,003 m.)
MONETARY UNIT Algerian dinar
MAJOR LANGUAGES Arabic, Berber,
  French
MAJOR RELIGION Islam

BENIN

AREA 43,483 sq. mi. (112,620 sq. km.)
POPULATION 3,338,240
CAPITAL Porto-Novo
LARGEST CITY Cotonou
HIGHEST POINT Atakora Mts. 2,083 ft.
  (635 m.)
MONETARY UNIT CFA franc
MAJOR LANGUAGES Fon, Somba, Yoruba,
  Bariba, French, Mina, Dendi
MAJOR RELIGIONS Tribal religions, Islam,
  Roman Catholicism

CAPE VERDE

AREA 1,557 sq. mi. (4,033 sq. km.)
POPULATION 324,000
CAPITAL Praia
LARGEST CITY Praia
HIGHEST POINT 9,281 ft. (2,829 m.)
MONETARY UNIT Cape Verde escudo
MAJOR LANGUAGE Portuguese
MAJOR RELIGION Roman Catholicism

GAMBIA

AREA 4,127 sq. mi. (10,689 sq. km.)
POPULATION 601,000
CAPITAL Banjul
LARGEST CITY Banjul
HIGHEST POINT 100 ft. (30 m.)
MONETARY UNIT dalasi
MAJOR LANGUAGES Mandingo, Fulani,
  Wolof, English, Malinke
MAJOR RELIGIONS Islam, tribal religions,
  Christianity

GHANA

AREA 92,099 sq. mi. (238,536 sq. km.)
POPULATION 11,450,000
CAPITAL Accra
LARGEST CITY Accra
HIGHEST POINT Togo Hills 2,900 ft.
  (884 m.)
MONETARY UNIT cedi
MAJOR LANGUAGES Twi, Fante, Dagbani,
  Ewe, Ga, English, Hausa, Akan
MAJOR RELIGIONS Tribal religions,
  Christianity, Islam

GUINEA

AREA 94,925 sq. mi. (245,856 sq. km.)
POPULATION 5,143,284
CAPITAL Conakry
LARGEST CITY Conakry
HIGHEST POINT Nimba Mts. 6,070 ft.
  (1,850 m.)
MONETARY UNIT syli
MAJOR LANGUAGES Fulani, Mandingo,
  Susu, French
MAJOR RELIGIONS Islam, tribal religions

GUINEA-BISSAU

AREA 13,948 sq. mi. (36,125 sq. km.)
POPULATION 777,214
CAPITAL Bissau
LARGEST CITY Bissau
HIGHEST POINT 689 ft. (210 m.)
MONETARY UNIT Guinea-Bissau peso
MAJOR LANGUAGES Balante, Fulani,
  Crioulo, Mandingo, Portuguese
MAJOR RELIGIONS Islam, tribal religions,
  Roman Catholicism

IVORY COAST

AREA 124,504 sq. mi. (322,465 sq. km.)
POPULATION 7,920,000
CAPITAL Yamoussoukro
LARGEST CITY Abidjan
HIGHEST POINT 5,745 ft. (1,751 m.)
MONETARY UNIT CFA franc
MAJOR LANGUAGES Bale, Bete, Senufu,
  French, Dioula
MAJOR RELIGIONS Tribal religions, Islam

LIBERIA

AREA 43,000 sq. mi. (111,370 sq. km.)
POPULATION 1,873,000
CAPITAL Monrovia
LARGEST CITY Monrovia
HIGHEST POINT Wutivi 5,584 ft.
  (1,702 m.)
MONETARY UNIT Liberian dollar
MAJOR LANGUAGES Kru, Kpelle, Bassa,
  Vai, English
MAJOR RELIGIONS Christianity, tribal
  religions, Islam

MALI

AREA 464,873 sq. mi. (1,204,021 sq. km.)
POPULATION 6,906,000
CAPITAL Bamako
LARGEST CITY Bamako
HIGHEST POINT Hombori Mts. 3,789 ft.
  (1,155 m.)
MONETARY UNIT CFA franc
MAJOR LANGUAGES Bambara, Senufu,
  Fulani, Soninke, French
MAJOR RELIGIONS Islam, tribal religions

MAURITANIA

AREA 419,229 sq. mi. (1,085,803 sq. km.)
POPULATION 1,634,000
CAPITAL Nouakchott
LARGEST CITY Nouakchott
HIGHEST POINT 2,972 ft. (906 m.)
MONETARY UNIT ouguiya
MAJOR LANGUAGES Arabic, Wolof,
  Tukolor, French
MAJOR RELIGION Islam

MOROCCO

AREA 172,414 sq. mi. (446,550 sq. km.)
POPULATION 20,242,000
CAPITAL Rabat
LARGEST CITY Casablanca
HIGHEST POINT Jeb. Toubkal 13,665 ft.
  (4,165 m.)
MONETARY UNIT dirham
MAJOR LANGUAGES Arabic, Berber, French
MAJOR RELIGIONS Islam, Judaism,
  Christianity

NIGER

AREA 489,189 sq. mi. (1,267,000 sq. km.)
POPULATION 5,098,427
CAPITAL Niamey
LARGEST CITY Niamey
HIGHEST POINT Banguezane 6,234 ft.
  (1,900 m.)
MONETARY UNIT CFA franc
MAJOR LANGUAGES Hausa, Songhai, Fulani,
  French, Tamashek, Djerma
MAJOR RELIGIONS Islam, tribal religions

NIGERIA

AREA 357,000 sq. mi. (924,630 sq. km.)
POPULATION 82,643,000
CAPITAL Lagos
LARGEST CITY Lagos
HIGHEST POINT Dimlang 6,700 ft. (2,042 m.)
MONETARY UNIT naira
MAJOR LANGUAGES Hausa, Yoruba, Ibo, Ijaw,
  Fulani, Tiv, Kanuri, Ibibio, English, Edo
MAJOR RELIGIONS Islam, Christianity,
  tribal religions

SÃO TOMÉ AND PRÍNCIPE

AREA 372 sq. mi. (963 sq. km.)
POPULATION 85,000
CAPITAL São Tomé
LARGEST CITY São Tomé
HIGHEST POINT Pico 6,640 ft. (2,024 m.)
MONETARY UNIT dobra
MAJOR LANGUAGES Bantu languages,
  Portuguese
MAJOR RELIGIONS Tribal religions,
  Roman Catholicism

SENEGAL

AREA 75,954 sq. mi. (196,720 sq. km.)
POPULATION 5,508,000
CAPITAL Dakar
LARGEST CITY Dakar
HIGHEST POINT Futa Jallon 1,640 ft. (500 m.)
MONETARY UNIT CFA franc
MAJOR LANGUAGES Wolof, Peul (Fulani),
  French, Mende, Mandingo, Dida
MAJOR RELIGIONS Islam, tribal religions,
  Roman Catholicism

SIERRA LEONE

AREA 27,925 sq. mi. (72,325 sq. km.)
POPULATION 3,470,000
CAPITAL Freetown
LARGEST CITY Freetown
HIGHEST POINT Loma Mts. 6,390 ft.
  (1,947 m.)
MONETARY UNIT leone
MAJOR LANGUAGES Mende, Temne, Vai,
  English, Krio (pidgin)
MAJOR RELIGIONS Tribal religions, Islam,
  Christianity

TOGO

AREA 21,622 sq. mi. (56,000 sq. km.)
POPULATION 2,472,000
CAPITAL Lomé
LARGEST CITY Lomé
HIGHEST POINT Agou 3,445 ft. (1,050 m.)
MONETARY UNIT CFA franc
MAJOR LANGUAGES Ewe, French, Twi,
  Hausa
MAJOR RELIGIONS Tribal religions,
  Roman Catholicism, Islam

TUNISIA

AREA 63,378 sq. mi. (164,149 sq. km.)
POPULATION 6,367,000
CAPITAL Tunis
LARGEST CITY Tunis
HIGHEST POINT Jeb. Chambi 5,066 ft.
  (1,544 m.)
MONETARY UNIT Tunisian dinar
MAJOR LANGUAGES Arabic, French
MAJOR RELIGION Islam

BURKINA FASO
(UPPER VOLTA)

AREA 105,869 sq. mi. (274,200 sq. km.)
POPULATION 6,908,000
CAPITAL Ouagadougou
LARGEST CITY Ouagadougou
HIGHEST POINT 2,352 ft. (717 m.)
MONETARY UNIT CFA franc
MAJOR LANGUAGES Mossi, Lobi, French,
  Samo, Gourounsi
MAJOR RELIGIONS Islam, tribal religions,
  Roman Catholicism

WESTERN SAHARA

AREA 102,703 sq. mi.
  (266,000 sq. km.)
POPULATION 76,425
HIGHEST POINT 2,700 ft. (823 m.)
MAJOR LANGUAGE Arabic
MAJOR RELIGION Islam

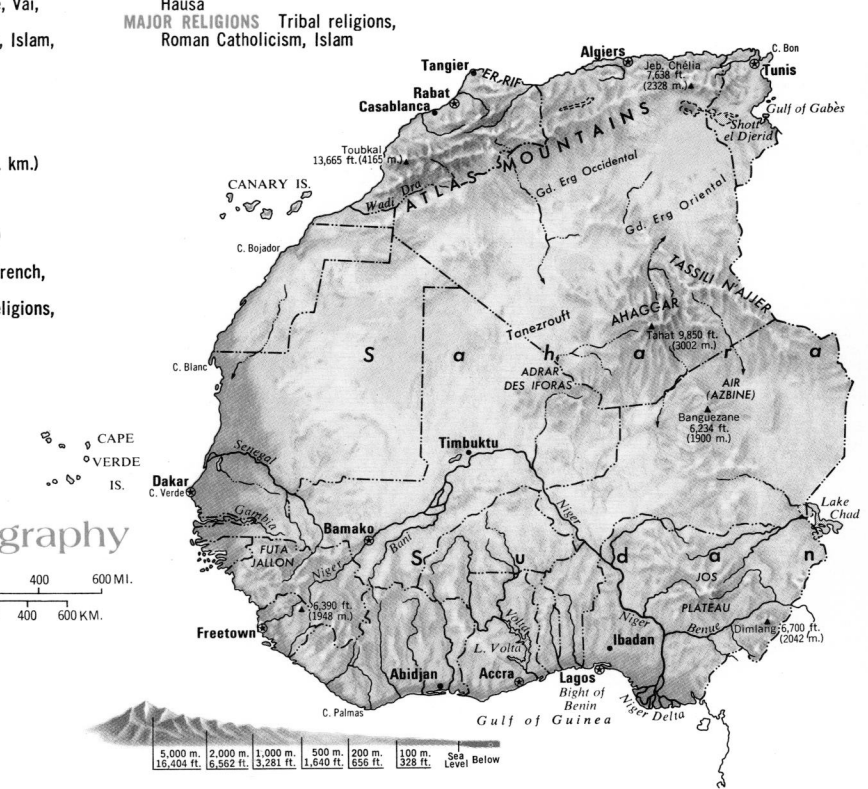

Topography

0   200   400   600 MI.
0   200   400   600 KM.

5,000 m. 2,000 m. 1,000 m. 500 m. 200 m. 100 m. Sea
16,404 ft. 6,562 ft. 3,281 ft. 1,640 ft. 656 ft. 328 ft. Level Below

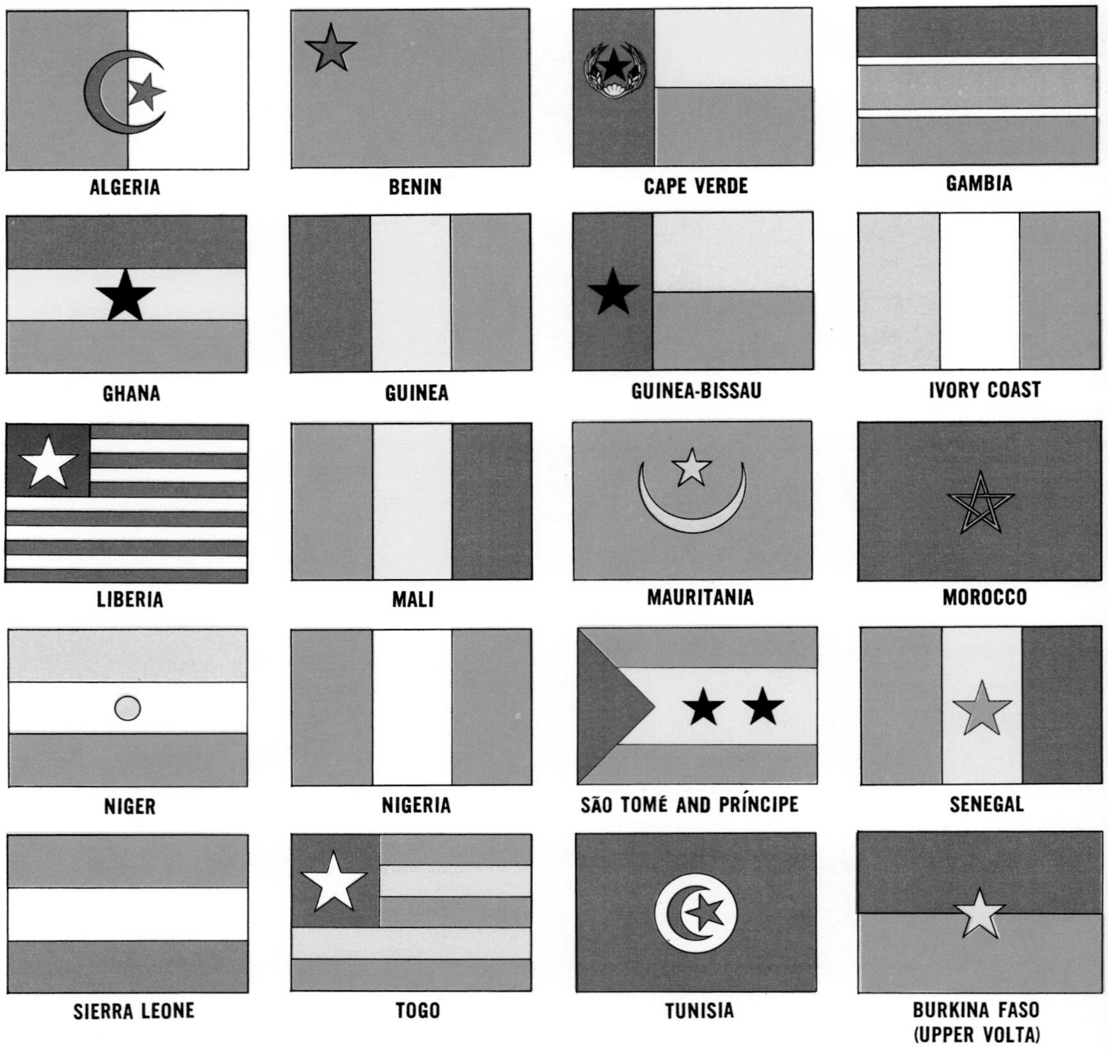
ALGERIA
BENIN
CAPE VERDE
GAMBIA
GHANA
GUINEA
GUINEA-BISSAU
IVORY COAST
LIBERIA
MALI
MAURITANIA
MOROCCO
NIGER
NIGERIA
SÃO TOMÉ AND PRÍNCIPE
SENEGAL
SIERRA LEONE
TOGO
TUNISIA
BURKINA FASO (UPPER VOLTA)

ALGERIA

CITIES and TOWNS

Abadla 12,200	D2
Adrar 22,800	D3
Aïn Beïda 26,976	F1
Aïn Sefra 22,400	D2
Aïn Temouchent 42,000	D1
Algiers (cap.) 1,365,400	E1
Amguid	F3
Annaba 255,900	F1
Aoulef 17,200	E3
Arak	E3
Batna 112,100	F1
Béchar 72,800	D2
Bejaïa 89,500	F1
Beni Abbès 5,000	D2
Beni Ounif 7,500	D2
Beni Saf 30,700	D1
Berga	E3
Bidon 5 (Poste Maurice Cordier)	E4
Biskra 90,500	F2
Blida 160,900	E1
Bône (Annaba) 255,900	F1
Bordj Bou Arreridj 65,000	E1
Bordj Fly Sainte Marie	D3
Bordj Omar Driss 1,900	F3
Boufarik 50,000	E1
Bougie (Béjaïa) 89,500	F1
Bou Saâda 50,000	E1
Brezina 10,000	E2
Charouine	D3
Chenachane	D3
Cherchell 36,800	E1
Constantine 335,100	F1
Deldoul	E3
Dellys 29,700	E1
Djanet 5,300	F4
Djelfa 51,000	E2
Djemaa 34,600	F2
Edjeleh	F3
El Abiod Sidi Cheikh 15,300	E2
El Asnam 106,100	E1
El Bayadh 38,500	E2
El Djezair (Algiers) (cap.) 1,365,400	E1
El Goléa 24,400	E2
El Oued 72,100	F2
Fort Lallemand	F2
Fort MacMahon	E3
Fort Miribel	E3
Fort Tarat	F3
Ghardaïa 70,500	E2
Ghazaouet 25,900	D2
Guelma 60,100	F1
Guemar	F2
Guerara 22,300	E2
Guerzim	D3
Hassi Messaoud	F2
Hassi R'Mel	E2
Idelès	F4
Igli 3,400	D2
Illizi 4,600	F3
In Amenas 4,200	F3
In Amguel	E4
In Eker	F4
In Guezzam	F5
In Rhar	E3
In Salah 18,800	E3
Jijel 49,800	F1
Kenadsa 7,600	D2
Kerzaz 2,900	D3
Khemis Miliana 57,800	E1
Ksar el Boukhari 41,200	E1
Laghouat 59,200	E2
Mascara 62,300	D1
Mecheria 22,600	D2
Médéa 72,300	E1
Metlili Chaamba 21,300	E2
Miliana 36,400	E1
Mohammadia 53,700	D1
Mostaganem 101,600	D1
M'Sila 49,100	E1
Oran 491,900	D1
Orléansville (El Asnam) 106,100	E1
Ouallene	E4
Ouargla 77,400	F2
Ouled Djellal 22,700	F2
Philippeville (Skikda) 107,700	F1
Poste Maurice Cortier	E4
Poste Weygand	D4
Reggane 11,300	D3
Relizane 60,000	E1
Saïda 62,100	E2
Sbaa	D3
Sétif 144,200	F1
Sidi Bel-Abbes 116,000	D1
Silet	E4
Skikda 107,700	F1
Souk Ahras 60,200	F1
Tabelbala 3,100	D3
Taghit 3,500	D2
Tamanrasset 23,200	F4
Tamentit	D3
Taourirt	E3
Tébessa 67,200	F1
Temacine	F2
Ténès 30,100	E1
Tiaret 62,900	E1
Tiguentourine	F3
Timgad 9,800	F1
Timimoun 20,500	E3
Tindouf 6,500	C3
Tinjoub	C3
Tin-Zaouatene	E5
Tizi Ouzou 73,100	E1
Tlemcen 109,400	D2
Touggourt 75,600	F2
Zaouiet Kounta 13,800	D3

OTHER FEATURES

Adrar des Iforas (plat.)	E5
Ahaggar (range)	F4
Anaï (well)	G4
Aouinet Bel Egrâ (well)	C3
Atlas (mts.)	E2
Aurès (lag.)	F1
Azzel Mati, Sebkha (lake)	E3
Bougaroun (cape)	F1
Chech, Erg (des.)	D3
Chelia (mt.)	F1
Chelif (riv.)	E1
Chergui, Chott Ech (salt lake)	E2
Gourara (oasis)	E3
Grand Erg Occidental (des.)	E2
Grand Erg Oriental (des.)	F2
Guir Hamada (des.)	D2
High Plateaus (ranges)	D2
Iguidi, Erg (des.)	C3
In Ezzane (well)	G4
Irharhar, Wadi (dry riv.)	F3
Issaouane Erg (des.)	F3
Kabylia (reg.)	E1
Mediterranean (sea)	E1
Medjerda (riv.)	F1
Melrhir, Chott (salt lake)	F2
Mouydir (mts.)	E3
Mya, Wadi (dry riv.)	E2
M'zab (oasis)	E2
Raoui, Erg er (des.)	D3
Rhir, Wadi (dry riv.)	F2
Sahara (des.)	E4
Saharan Atlas (ranges)	E2
Saoura, Wadi (dry riv.)	D3
Souf (oasis)	F2
Tademaït, Plateau du (plat.)	E3
Tafassasset, Wadi (dry riv.)	F4
Tahat (mt.)	F4
Tamanrasset, Wadi (dry riv.)	E4
Tanezrouft (des.)	E4
Tassili N'Ahagger (plat.)	E4
Tassili N'Ajjer (plat.)	F3
Tidikelt (oasis)	E3
Timmissao (well)	E4
Tindouf, Sebkha de (salt lake)	C3
Tinrhert, Hamada de (des.)	F3
Tni Haïa (well)	D4
Touat (oasis)	E3
Touila (well)	C3

BENIN

CITIES and TOWNS

Abomey 38,000	E7
Cotonou 178,000	E7
Djougou	E7
Grand-Popo	E7
Kandi	E6
Lokossa 6,000	E7
Malanville	E6
Natitingou 49,000	E6
Nikki	E7
Ouidah	E7
Parakou 21,000	E7
Porto-Novo (cap.) 104,000	E7
Savalou	E7
Savé	E7

OTHER FEATURES

Atakora (mts.)	E6
Benin (bight)	E8
Guinea (gulf)	E8
Mono (riv.)	E7
Niger (riv.)	E6
Ouémé (riv.)	E7
Slave Coast (reg.)	E7
Sudan (reg.)	E6

CAPE VERDE

CITIES and TOWNS

Mindelo 28,797	A7
Praia (cap.) 21,494	B8
Ribeira Grande 1,892	B7
Sal Rei 1,296	B8
Santa Maria 956	B8

OTHER FEATURES

Boa Vista (isl.)	B8
Brava (isl.)	B8
Fogo (isl.)	B8
Maio (isl.)	B8
Sal (isl.)	B7
Santa Luzia (isl.)	B8
Santo Antão (isl.)	A7
São Nicolau (isl.)	B8
São Tiago (isl.)	B8
São Vicente (isl.)	B7

GAMBIA

CITIES and TOWNS

Banjul (cap.) 39,476	A6
Basse Santa Su 2,899	B6
Brikama 9,483	A6
Georgetown 2,510	A6

GHANA

CITIES and TOWNS

Accra (cap.) 564,194	D7
Accra* 738,498	D7
Ada 4,285	E7
Akuse 3,791	E7
Attebubu 6,630	D7
Awaso 5,449	D7
Axim 8,107	D8
Bawku 20,567	D6
Bekwai 11,287	D7
Berekum 14,296	D7
Bole 4,772	D7
Bolgatanga 18,896	D6
Cape Coast 51,653	D7
Daboya 1,872	D7
Damongo 7,760	D7
Dunkwa 15,437	D7
Elmina 11,401	D8
Enchi 4,382	D7
Gambaga 3,730	D6
Gyasikan 6,403	D7
Half Assini 5,429	D8
Ho 24,199	E7
Keta 14,446	E7
Kete Krachi 5,097	E7
Kintampo 7,149	D7
Koforidua 46,235	D7
Kpandu 12,842	D7
Kumasi 260,286	D7
Kumasi* 345,117	D7
Lawra 2,709	D6
Mampong 13,895	D7
Mpraeso 5,908	D7
Navrongo	D6
Nsawam 25,518	D7
Nsuta 3,854	D7
Obuasi 31,005	D7
Oda 20,957	D7
Prestea 15,143	D7
Salaga 6,413	D7
Sekondi 33,713	D8
Sekondi-Takoradi* 160,868	D8
Sunyani 23,780	D7
Takoradi 58,161	D8
Tamale 83,653	D7
Tarkwa 14,702	D7
Tema 60,767	E7
Tumu 4,366	D6
Wa 21,374	D6
Wenchi 13,836	D7
Wiawso 5,558	D7
Winneba 30,778	D7
Yapei 1,203	D7
Yendi 22,072	D7

OTHER FEATURES

Ashanti (reg.)	D7
Benin (bight)	E8
Black Volta (riv.)	D6
Gold Coast (reg.)	D8
Guinea (gulf)	E8
Oti (riv.)	E7
Red Volta (riv.)	D6
Saint Paul (cape)	E7
Three Points (cape)	D8
Volta (lake)	D7
Volta (riv.)	E7
White Volta (riv.)	D6

GUINEA

CITIES and TOWNS

Beyla	C7
Boffa	B6
Boké	B6
Conakry (cap.)* 525,671	B7
Dabola	B6
Dalaba	B6
Dinguiraye	B6
Dubréka	B7
Faranah	B6
Forécariah	B7
Fria	B6
Gaoual	B6
Guéckédou	B7
Kamsar	B6
Kankan 85,310	C6
Kérouané	C7
Kindia 79,861	B6
Kissidougou	B7
Koundara 6,000	B6
Kouroussa	C6
Labé 79,670	B6
Macenta	C7
Mali	B6
Mamou	B6
N'Zérékoré 23,000	C7
Sangaredyi	B6
Siguiri	C6
Télimélé 12,000	B6
Tougué	B6
Victoria	B6

OTHER FEATURES

Bafing (riv.)	B6
Bakoy (riv.)	B6
Futa Jallon (lag.)	B6
Los (isls.)	B7
Milo (riv.)	C7
Moa (riv.)	B7
Niger (riv.)	C6
Nimba (lag.)	C7
Verga (cape)	B6

GUINEA-BISSAU

CITIES and TOWNS

Bissau (cap.) 109,486	A6
Bolama○ 9,133	A6
Buba○ 6,706	B6
Bubaque○ 8,441	A6
Cacheu○ 15,194	A6

OTHER FEATURES

Bijagós (isls.)	A6

IVORY COAST

CITIES and TOWNS

Abengourou 31,239	D7
Abidjan 685,828	D7
Aboisso 14,272	D7
Agboville 27,192	D7
Bingerville 18,218	D7
Bondoukou 19,111	D7
Bouaflé 15,917	C7
Bouaké 173,248	D7
Bouna 5,787	D7
Boundiali 9,869	C7
Dabakala 3,272	D7
Dabou 23,870	D7
Daloa 60,958	C7
Danané 19,872	C7
Dimbokro 30,986	D7
Divo 37,896	C7
Ferkessédougou 25,307	D7
Fresco 1,865	C7
Gagnoa 42,362	C7
Grand-Bassam 25,808	D7
Grand-Lahou 4,070	C8
Guiglo 10,441	C7
Issia 11,143	C7
Katiola 21,559	C7
Kong 2,551	D7
Korhogo 47,657	C7
Man 50,315	C7
Mankono 6,570	C7
Odienné 13,864	C7
Port-Bouet 72,616	D7
San Pedro 27,616	C8
Sassandra 9,404	C8
Séguéla 12,587	C7
Sinfra 16,399	C7
Tabou 7,255	C8
Touba 5,256	C7
Toumodi 12,983	D7
Yamoussoukro (cap.) 50,000	C7

OTHER FEATURES

Aby (lag.)	D8
Bagoé (riv.)	C6
Bandama (riv.)	C7
Baoulé (riv.)	C6
Black Volta (riv.)	D6
Cavally (riv.)	C7
Comoé (riv.)	D7
Ebrié (lag.)	D8
Guinea (gulf)	E8
Ivory Coast (reg.)	C8
Kossou, Lac de (lake)	C7
Nimba (lag.)	C7
Sassandra (riv.)	C7

LIBERIA

CITIES and TOWNS

Buchanan 23,999	B7
Gbarnga 6,896	C7
Grand Cess	C8
Greenville 8,462	C8
Harbel 11,445	B7
Harper 10,627	C8
Kolahun	C7
Marshall	B7
Monrovia (cap.) 166,507	B7
Plahn	C7
River Cess 2,041	C7
Robertsport 2,562	B7
Sasstown	C8
Tapeta 3,927	C7
Tchien 6,094	C7
Tubmanburg 14,089	B7

OTHER FEATURES

Bong (range)	B7
Cavalla (riv.)	C7
Cestos (riv.)	C7
Grain Coast (reg.)	B8
Kru Coast (reg.)	C8
Mano (riv.)	B7
Mount (cape)	B7
Nimba (lag.)	C7
Palmas (cape)	C8
Roberts Field Int'l Airport	C7

MALI

CITIES and TOWNS

Anéfis	E5
Ansongo 3,485	E5
Araouane	D5
Bafoulabé 2,163	B6
Bamako (cap.) 404,022	C6
Bamba	D5
Banamba 6,776	C6
Bandiagara 8,920	D6
Bankass 3,229	D6
Bou Djebeha	D5
Bougouni 17,246	C6
Bourem 4,538	E5
Dioila 4,953	C6
Dire 8,941	D5
Djenné 10,251	D6
Douentza 6,746	D6
Gao 30,714	E5
Goundam 10,262	D5
Gourma-Rharous 4,671	D5
Hombori	D5
Kadiolo 3,991	C6
Kangaba 3,184	C6
Kati 24,991	C6
Kayes 44,736	B6
Ké-Macina 5,426	C6
Kéniéba 4,510	B6
Kerchoual	E5
Kidal 3,308	E5
Kita 17,538	C6
Kolokani 8,923	C6
Kolondiéba 5,882	C6
Koulikoro 16,376	C6
Kourouba	B6
Koutiala 27,497	C6
Mabrouk	D5
Ménaka 3,693	E5
Mopti 53,885	D6
Nampala	C5
Nara 6,091	C5
Niafunké 6,399	D5
Niono 12,290	C6
Nioro 11,617	C5
San 22,962	D6
Satadougou	B6
Ségou 64,890	C6
Sikasso 47,030	C6
Sokolo	C6
Taoudenni	D4
Ténenkou 4,708	C6
Tessalit	E4
Timbuktu (Tombouctou) 20,483	D5
Toukoto	C6
Yanfolila 3,809	C6
Yelimané 1,481	B5
Yorosso 2,390	C6

OTHER FEATURES

Achourat (well)	D4
Adrar des Iforas (plat.)	E5
Asselar (well)	D5
Azaouad (reg.)	D5
Azaouak (dry riv.)	E5
Bafing (riv.)	B6
Bagoé (riv.)	C6
Bakoy (riv.)	B6
Bani (riv.)	C6
Baoulé (dry riv.)	C6
Baoulé (riv.)	C6
Bir Ounane (well)	D4
Chech, Erg (des.)	D4
Debo (lake)	D5
El Mraiti (well)	D5
Faguibine (lake)	D5
Falémé (riv.)	B6
Haricha Hamada (des.)	D4
Hombori (mts.)	D5
In Dagouber (well)	D4
Macina (depr.)	D6
Niger (riv.)	D5
Oum el Asel (well)	D4
Sahara (des.)	D4
Sekkane, Erg (des.)	D4
Senegal (riv.)	B5
Sudan (reg.)	D6
Tadjnout Hagguerete (well)	D4
Terhazza (ruins)	C4
Tilemsi (valley)	E5
Toufourine (well)	C4

MAURITANIA

CITIES and TOWNS

Aïoun el Atrous	C5
Akjoujt 8,044	B5
Akreïjit	C5
Aleg 6,415	B5
Atar 16,326	B4
Bassikounou	C5
Bir Mogreïn	B3
Boutilimit 7,261	B5
Bogué 8,056	B5
Chinguetti	B4
Fderik (Fort-Gouraud) 2,160	B4
Kaédi 20,848	B5
Kankossa	B5
Kiffa 10,629	B5
Maghama	B5
M'Bout	B5
Méderdra	A5
Néma 8,232	C5
Nouakchott (cap.) 134,986	A5
Nouadhibou 21,961	A4
Ouadane	B4
Oualata	C5
Oujaf	C5
Oujeft	B4
Rosso 16,466	A5
Sélibaby 5,994	B5
Tamchakett	B5
Tamsagout	C4
Tazadit	B4
Tichitt	C5
Tidjikja 7,870	B5
Timbédra 5,317	C5
Zouîrât 17,474	B4

OTHER FEATURES

Adafer (reg.)	B5
Adrar (reg.)	B4
Affolé (reg.)	B5
Agueraktem (well)	C4
Aïn ben Tili (well)	C3
Arguin (bay)	A4
Assaba (reg.)	B5
Atoui, Wadi (dry riv.)	B4
Ben Guerdane (well)	B3
Bir el Khzaim (well)	C4
Blanc (cape)	A4
Brakna (reg.)	B5
Chegga (well)	C3
Djouf, El (des.)	C4
El Mrayer (well)	C4
El Mreïti (well)	C4
Gorgol (reg.)	B5
Hodh (reg.)	C5
Iguidi, Erg (des.)	C3
Inchiri (reg.)	A5
Koumbi Saleh (ruins)	C5
Lévrier (bay)	A4
Makteïr (des.)	B4
Meraia (reg.)	C5
Mirik (Timiris) (cape)	A5
Ouarane (reg.)	B4
Sahara (des.)	C4
Senegal (riv.)	B5
Tagant (reg.)	B5
Tidra (isl.)	A5
Timiris (cape)	A5
Touila (well)	C3
Trarza (reg.)	A5

MOROCCO

CITIES and TOWNS

Agadir 61,192	C2
Al Hoceima 18,686	D1
Asilah 14,074	C1
Azemmour 17,182	C2
Azrou 20,756	C2
Beni Mellal 53,826	C2
Berguent 3,356	D2
Bou Arfa	D2
Bou Izakarn 2,342	C3
Boujad 18,838	C2
Casablanca 1,506,373	C2
Chechaouene 15,362	D1
Dar-el-Beida (Casablanca) 1,506,373	C2
El Jadida 55,501	C2
El Kelaa des Srarhna 17,163	C2
Erfoud 5,400	D2
Er Rachidia 16,775	D2
Essaouira 30,061	B2
Fédala (Mohammedia) 70,392	C2
Fès (Fez) 325,327	D2
Figuig 13,660	D2
Goulmima 4,056	C2
Inezgane 11,495	C2

- Jerada 30,633 .... D2
- Kenitra 139,206 .... C2
- Khenifra 25,526 .... C2
- Khouribga 73,667 .... C2
- Ksar el Kebir 48,262 .... C2
- Larache 45,710 .... C1
- Marrakech 332,741 .... C2
- Mazagan (El Jadida) 55,501 .... C2
- Meknès 248,369 .... C2
- Mogador (Essaouira) 30,061 .... B2
- Mohammedia 70,392 .... C2
- Nador 32,490 .... D1
- Ouarzazate 11,142 .... C2
- Oued Zem 33,323 .... C2
- Ouezzane 33,267 .... C2
- Oujda 175,532 .... D2
- Petitjean (Sidi Kacem) 26,831 .... C2
- Port-Lyautey (Kénitra) 139,206 .... C2
- Rabat (cap.) 367,620 .... C2
- Safi 129,113 .... C2
- Saïdia D2
- Salé 155,557 .... C2
- Sefrou 28,607 .... D2
- Settat 42,325 .... C2
- Sidi Ifni 13,650 .... B3
- Sidi Kacem 26,831 .... C2
- Tagounite C3
- Tangier (Tanger) 187,894 .... C1
- Tan-Tan 10,772 .... B3
- Taourirt 15,580 .... D2
- Taouz D2
- Tarfaya 1,104 .... B3
- Taroudant 22,272 .... C2
- Taza 55,157 .... D2
- Tendrara D2
- Tétouan 139,105 .... C1
- Tiznit 11,391 .... B3
- Youssoufia 22,435 .... C2
- Zagora 5,306 .... C2

OTHER FEATURES

- Anti-Atlas (ranges) C3
- Atlas (mts.) C2
- Bani, Jebel (mts.) C3
- Beddouza, Ras (cape) C2
- Dra, Wadi (dry riv.) C3
- Er Rif (range) D2
- Gibraltar (str.) C1
- High Atlas (ranges) C2
- Juby (cape) B3
- Mediterranean (sea) D1
- Middle Atlas (ranges) C2
- Moulouya (riv.) D2
- Rhéris, Wadi (dry riv.) D2
- Rhir (cape) B2
- Rif, Er (range) D2
- Sarhro, Jebel (mts.) C2
- Sebou (riv.) C2
- Sim (cape) B2
- Toubkal, Jebel (mt.) C2
- Ziz, Wadi (dry riv.) D2

NIGER

CITIES and TOWNS

- Agadès 11,000 .... F5
- Arhli (Arlit) F4
- Bilma G5
- Birni-N'Konni 10,000 .... E6
- Bosso G6
- Chirfa G4
- Dakoro F6
- Dessa E6
- Diffa G6
- Djado G4
- Dogondoutchi 9,000 .... E6
- Dosso E6
- Fachi G5
- Filingué 10,000 .... E6
- Gangara F6
- Gaya 5,000 .... E6
- Gouré G6
- Iférouane F5
- Illéla 9,000 .... F6
- In-Gall F5
- Madama G4
- Madaoua F6
- Magaria F6
- Mainé-Soroa G6
- Maradi 45,852 .... F6
- N'Guigmi G6
- Niamey (cap.) 225,314 .... E6
- Quallam E6
- Say E6
- Tahoua 31,265 .... F6
- Tanout F6
- Téra 8,000 .... E6
- Tessaoua 5,000 .... F6
- Tillabéry E6
- Tîmia F4
- Zinder 58,436 .... F6

OTHER FEATURES

- Achégour (well) G5
- Agadem (well) G5
- Air (mts.) F5
- Anaye (well) G5
- Assakarai (dry riv.) F5
- Azaoua (reg.) E5
- Azbine (Air) (mts.) F5
- Bagam (well) F5
- Banguezane (mt.) F5
- Bedouaram (well) G5
- Chad (lake) G6
- Dallol Bosso (dry riv.) E6
- Dillia (dry riv.) G5
- Djado (plat.) G4
- El War (well) G4
- In Azaoua (well) F4
- Komadugu Yobe (riv.) G6
- Mantas (well) E5
- Niger (riv.) E6
- Sahara (des.) F4
- Sudan (reg.) F6
- Tafassasset, Wadi (dry riv.) F4
- Talak (reg.) E5
- Ténér´ (des.) G5
- Timboulaga (well) F5
- Tummo (El War) (well) G4
- Zoo Baba (well) G5

NIGERIA

STATES

- Anambra 2,300,000 .... F7
- Bauchi 2,496,329 .... F6
- Bendel 2,336,000 .... F7
- Benue 2,641,496 .... F7
- Borno 2,853,553 .... G6
- Cross River 3,633,582 .... F7
- Gongola 1,585,200 .... G7
- Imo 5,000,000 .... F7
- Kaduna 4,098,303 .... F6
- Kano 5,775,000 .... F6
- Kwara 1,600,600 .... E7
- Lagos 1,100,000 .... E7
- Niger 2,900,000 .... F7
- Ogun 1,448,966 .... E7
- Ondo 2,727,676 .... F7
- Oyo 5,208,884 .... E7
- Plateau 1,367,450 .... F7
- Rivers 1,544,314 .... F8
- Sokoto 1,367,450 .... F6

CITIES and TOWNS

- Aba 177,000 .... F7
- Abeokuta 253,000 .... E7
- Abuja F7
- Ado 213,000 .... E7
- Afikpo F7
- Aku F7
- Akure F7
- Argungu E6
- Asaba F7
- Azare G6
- Baga G6
- Bama G6
- Baro F7
- Bauchi F6
- Benin City 136,000 .... F7
- Bida F7
- Birnin Kebbi E6
- Biu G6
- Bonny F8
- Brass F8
- Burutu F7
- Calabar 103,000 .... F7
- Deba Habe G6
- Degema F8
- Dikwa G6
- Donga G7
- Ede 182,000 .... E7
- Eha Amufu F7
- Enugu 187,000 .... F7
- Forcados E7
- Funtua F6
- Gashaka G7
- Gbogo F7
- Geidam G6
- Gombe G6
- Gumel F6
- Gummi F6
- Gusau F6
- Gwadabawa F6
- Hadejia G6
- Ibadan 847,000 .... E7
- Ibi F7
- Ife 176,000 .... E7
- Ijebu-Ode E7
- Ikeja E7
- Ikom F7
- Ilesha 224,000 .... F7
- Ilorin 282,000 .... E7
- Isa F6
- Iseyin 115,083 .... E7
- Iwo 214,000 .... E7
- Jalingo G7
- Jebba E7
- Jega E6
- Jos F7
- Kabba F7
- Kaduna 202,000 .... F6
- Kaiama E7
- Kalmalo F6
- Kano 399,000 .... F6
- Katsina 109,424 .... F6
- Katsina Ala F7
- Kaura Namoda F6
- Keffi F7
- Koko F7
- Kontagora F6
- Kukawa G6
- Kumo G7
- Kuta F7
- Lafia F7
- Lafiagi F7
- Lagos (cap.) 1,060,848 .... E7
- Laro E7
- Lere F7
- Lokoja F7
- Maiduguri 189,000 .... G6
- Maigatari F6
- Makurdi F7
- Minna F7
- Mubi G6
- Nasarawa F7
- New Bussa E6
- Nguru G6
- Nnewi F7
- Nsukka F7
- Offa E7
- Ogbomosho 432,000 .... E7
- Ogoja F7
- Okene F7
- Ondo F7
- Onitsha 220,000 .... F7
- Oron F8
- Oshogbo 282,000 .... F7
- Owerri F7
- Owo F7
- Oyo 152,000 .... E7
- Pankshin F7
- Panyam F7
- Port Harcourt 242,000 .... F8
- Ringim F6
- Sapele F7
- Shaki E7
- Shendam F7
- Sokoto F6
- Toungo G7
- Uromi F7
- Vom F7
- Wamba F7
- Warri F7
- Wukari F7
- Yan G7
- Yelwa F6
- Yola G7
- Zaria 224,000 .... F6
- Zungeru F7

OTHER FEATURES

- Adamawa (reg.) G7
- Benin (bight) E8
- Benue (riv.) F7
- Biafra (bight) F8
- Biu (plat.) G6
- Bonny (bight) F8
- Chad (lake) G6
- Cross (riv.) F7
- Dimlang (mt.) G7
- Donga (riv.) G7
- Foge (isl.) E6
- Gongola (riv.) G6
- Guinea (gulf) E8
- Hadejia (riv.) F6
- Jos (plat.) F7
- Kaduna (riv.) F7
- Kainji (res.) E6
- Kebbi (riv.) E6
- Komadugu Yobe (riv.) G6
- Niger (delta) F8
- Niger (riv.) F7
- Osse (riv.) F7
- Slave Coast (reg.) E7
- Sokoto (riv.) F6
- Sudan (reg.) F6

PORTUGAL-Madeira

CITIES and TOWNS

- Funchal (cap.) 38,340 .... A2

OTHER FEATURES

- Desertas (isls.) A2
- Madeira (isl.) A2
- Pôrto Santo (isl.) A2
- Salvage (isls.) A2

SÃO TOMÉ AND PRINCIPE

CITIES and TOWNS

- Santo António 1,618 .... F8
- São Tomé (cap.) 7,681 .... F8

OTHER FEATURES

- Guinea (gulf) E8
- Príncipe (isl.) F8
- São Tomé (isl.) F8

SENEGAL

CITIES and TOWNS

- Bakel 6,339 .... B6
- Bignona 14,537 .... A6
- Dagana 10,506 .... A5
- Dakar (cap.) 798,792 .... A6
- Diourbel 50,618 .... A6
- Kaolack 106,899 .... A6
- Kédougou 7,575 .... B6
- Kaffrine 11,211 .... A6
- Kolda 19,302 .... B6
- Linguère 7,890 .... B5
- Louga 35,063 .... A5
- Matam 10,002 .... B5
- M'Bour 37,663 .... A6
- Nioro-du-Rip 7,824 .... A6
- Podor 6,914 .... B5
- Richard Toll A5
- Rufisque A6
- Saint-Louis 88,404 .... A5
- Sedhiou 9,421 .... A6
- Tambacounda 25,147 .... B6
- Thiès 117,333 .... A5
- Tivaouane 17,351 .... A5
- Touba A6
- Yarboutenda B6
- Ziguinchor 72,726 .... A6

OTHER FEATURES

- Casamance (riv.) A6
- Falémé (riv.) B6
- Ferlo (reg.) B6
- Gambia (riv.) B6
- Senegal (riv.) B5
- Verde (cape) A6

SIERRA LEONE

CITIES and TOWNS

- Bo 42,216 .... B7
- Bonthe 6,230 .... B7
- Freetown (cap.) 274,000 .... B7
- Kabala 4,610 .... B7
- Kambia 3,700 .... B7
- Kenema 33,880 .... B7
- Lungi 2,170 .... B7
- Marampa B7
- Makeni 28,684 .... B7
- Moyamba 4,564 .... B7
- Pendembu 2,696 .... B7
- Pepel 3,793 .... B7
- Port Loko 5,809 .... B7
- Pujehun 1 .... B7

OTHER FEATURES

- Loma, Mansa (lag.) B7
- Mano (riv.) B7
- Moa (riv.) B7
- Sherbro (isl.) B7
- Yawri (bay) B7

SPAIN-Canary Islands, Ceuta and Melilla

CITIES and TOWNS

- Arrecife 21,310 .... B3
- Ceuta 60,639 .... C1
- La Laguna A3
- Las Palmas de Gran Canaria 260,368 .... B3
- Melilla 64,942 .... D1
- Santa Cruz de la Palma 10,393 .... A3
- Santa Cruz de Tenerife 74,910 .... A3

OTHER FEATURES

- Canary (isls.) A3
- Fuerteventura (isl.) B3
- Gomera (isl.) A3
- Grand Canary (isl.) A3
- Hierro (isl.) A3
- Lanzarote (isl.) B3
- La Palma (isl.) A3
- Tenerife (isl.) A3

TOGO

CITIES and TOWNS

- Aného (Anécho) 10,889 .... E7
- Atakpamé 17,440 .... E7
- Dapaong 10,100 .... E6
- Kpalimé 19,801 .... E7
- Kpémé 3,600 .... E7
- Lama-Kara 9,400 .... E7
- Lomé (cap.) 148,443 .... E7
- Mango 9,600 .... E6
- Sokodé 29,623 .... E7

OTHER FEATURES

- Benin (bight) E8
- Guinea (gulf) E8
- Mono (riv.) E7
- Oti (riv.) E7
- Slave Coast (reg.) E7

TUNISIA

CITIES and TOWNS

- Béja 39,226 .... F1
- Ben Gardane 6,593 .... G2
- Bizerte 62,856 .... F1
- Burj al Hattaba F2
- El Borma F2
- El Djem 10,666 .... G1
- El Kef 27,939 .... F1
- Gabès 40,585 .... F2
- Gafsa 42,225 .... F2
- Halq el Oued 41,912 .... G1
- Jendouba 18,127 .... F1
- Kairouan 54,546 .... F1
- Kalaa-Kebira 23,508 .... F1
- Kasserine 22,594 .... F1
- La Goulette (Halq el Oued) 41,912 .... G1
- La Skhirra 4,565 .... G2
- Le Kef (El Kef) 27,939 .... F1
- Mahdia 25,711 .... G1
- Mareth 2,185 .... F2
- Mateur 19,645 .... F1
- Médenine 15,826 .... F2
- Menzel Bourguiba 42,111 .... F1
- Menzel Temime 18,857 .... G1
- Moknine 26,035 .... G1
- Monastir 26,759 .... G1
- Msaken 33,559 .... G1
- Nabeul 30,476 .... G1
- Nefta 12,476 .... F2
- Remada 6,100 .... F2
- Sbeitla 8,039 .... F1
- Sfax 171,297 .... G2
- Sousse 69,530 .... G1
- Tabarka 3,140 .... F1
- Tatahouine 10,399 .... G2
- Tozeur 16,772 .... F2
- Tunis (cap.) 550,404 .... G1
- Tunis* 873,515 .... G1
- Zarzis 14,420 .... G2

OTHER FEATURES

- Abiad, Ras el (Blanc) (cape) G1
- Blanc (cape) G1
- Bon (cape) G1
- Chambi, Jebel (mt.) F2
- Djerba (isl.) G2
- Djerid, Shott el (salt lake) F2
- Gabès (gulf) G2
- Grand Erg Oriental (des.) F2
- Hammamet (gulf) G1
- Jefara (reg.) G2
- Kerkennah (isls.) G2
- Mediterranean (sea) F1
- Medjerda (riv.) F1
- Tib, Ras el (Bon) (cape) G1
- Tunis (gulf) G1

BURKINA FASO (UPPER VOLTA)

CITIES and TOWNS

- Aribinda D6
- Banfora 12,358 .... D6
- Batié D7
- Bobo Dioulasso 115,063 .... D6
- Bogandé E6
- Dédougou D6
- Diapaga E6
- Diébougou D6
- Djibo D6
- Dori D6
- Fada-N'Gourma 12,000 .... E6
- Gaoua D6
- Houndé D6
- Kaya 18,000 .... D6
- Koudougou 36,838 .... D6
- Koupela D6
- Léo D6
- Ouagadougou (cap.) 172,661 .... D6
- Ouahigouya 25,690 .... D6
- Pama E6
- Po D6
- Tenkodogo E6
- Tougan D6
- Yako D6
- Zabré D6

OTHER FEATURES

- Black Volta (riv.) D6
- Comoé (riv.) D7
- Oti (riv.) E7
- Red Volta (riv.) D6
- Sudan (reg.) D6
- White Volta (riv.) D6

WESTERN SAHARA

CITIES and TOWNS

- Dakhla 6,554 .... A4
- El Aaiún (Laayoune) 24,519 .... B3
- Semara 2,655 .... B3
- Villa Cisneros (Dakhla) 6,554 .... A4

OTHER FEATURES

- Atoui, Wadi (dry riv.) B4
- Ausert (well) B4
- Barbas (cape) A4
- Bir Ganduz (well) A4
- Bir Nzaran (well) B4
- Blanc (cape) A4
- Bojador (cape) B3
- Durnford (pt.) A4
- Guelta de Zemmur (well) B3
- Saguia el Hamra (dry riv.) B3
- Tichlá (well) B4

*City and suburbs.
○Population of sub-district or division.

Agriculture, Industry and Resources

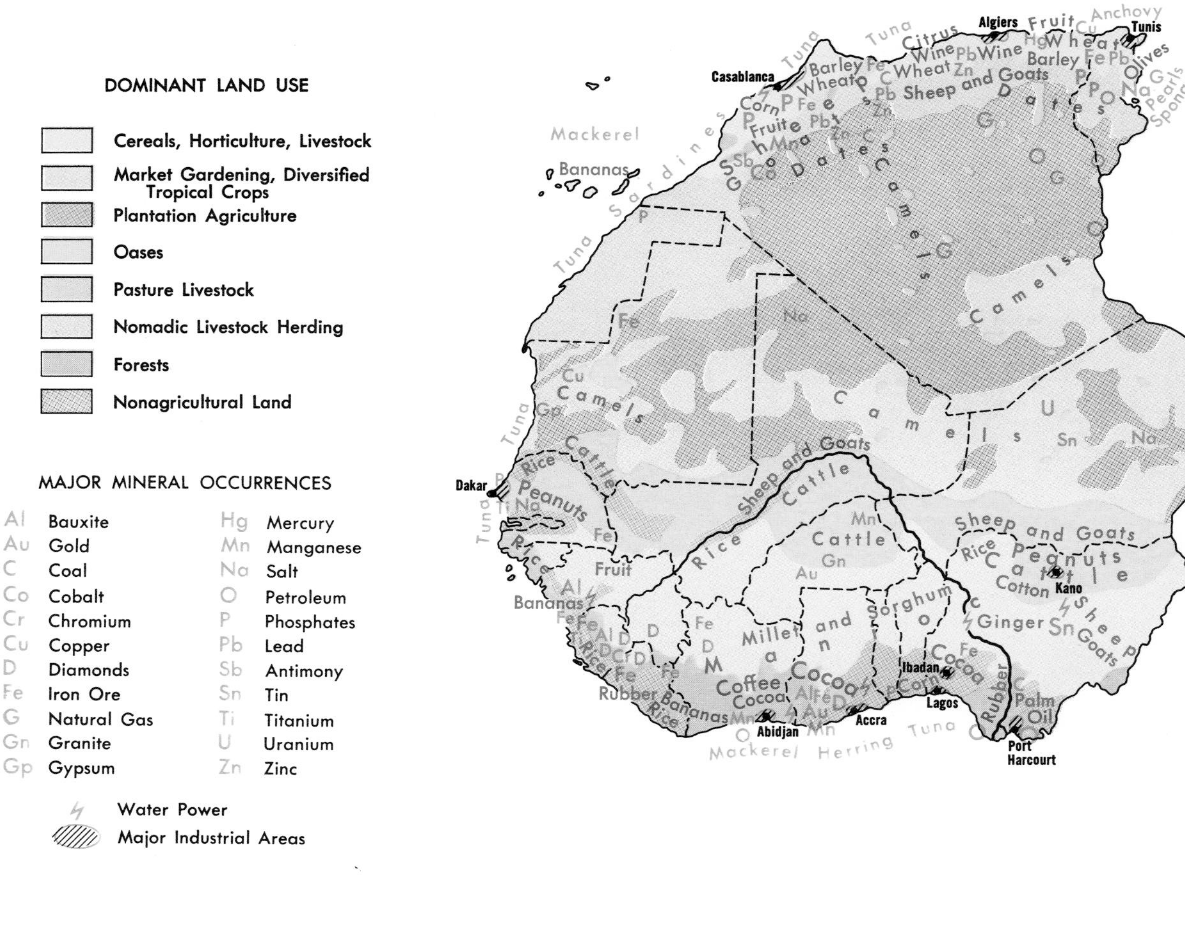
DOMINANT LAND USE
Cereals, Horticulture, Livestock
Market Gardening, Diversified Tropical Crops
Plantation Agriculture
Oases
Pasture Livestock
Nomadic Livestock Herding
Forests
Nonagricultural Land
MAJOR MINERAL OCCURRENCES
Al Bauxite
Au Gold
C Coal
Co Cobalt
Cr Chromium
Cu Copper
D Diamonds
Fe Iron Ore
G Natural Gas
Gn Granite
Gp Gypsum
Hg Mercury
Mn Manganese
Na Salt
O Petroleum
P Phosphates
Pb Lead
Sb Antimony
Sn Tin
Ti Titanium
U Uranium
Zn Zinc
Water Power
Major Industrial Areas
Algiers
Tunis
Casablanca
Dakar
Kano
Ibadan
Lagos
Accra
Abidjan
Port Harcourt
Mackerel
Bananas
Tuna
Sardines
Anchovy
Citrus
Wine
Wheat
Barley
Olives
Fruit
Sheep and Goats
Dates
Corn
Camels
Sponges
Pearls
Cattle
Rice
Peanuts
Millet and Sorghum
Cotton
Ginger
Coffee
Cocoa
Rubber
Palm Oil
Herring

LIBYA EGYPT CHAD SUDAN ETHIOPIA

DJIBOUTI

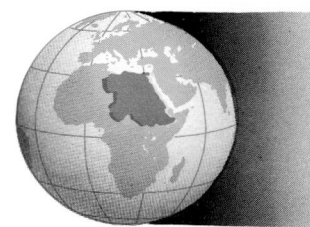

LIBYA

AREA 679,358 sq. mi. (1,759,537 sq. km.)
POPULATION 2,856,000
CAPITAL Tripoli
LARGEST CITY Tripoli
HIGHEST POINT Bette Pk. 7,500 ft. (2,286 m.)
MONETARY UNIT Libyan dinar
MAJOR LANGUAGES Arabic, Berber
MAJOR RELIGION Islam

EGYPT

AREA 386,659 sq. mi. (1,001,447 sq. km.)
POPULATION 41,572,000
CAPITAL Cairo
LARGEST CITY Cairo
HIGHEST POINT Jeb. Katherina 8,651 ft.
(2,637 m.)
MONETARY UNIT Egyptian pound
MAJOR LANGUAGE Arabic
MAJOR RELIGIONS Islam, Coptic Christianity

CHAD

AREA 495,752 sq. mi. (1,283,998 sq. km.)
POPULATION 4,309,000
CAPITAL N'Djamena
LARGEST CITY N'Djamena
HIGHEST POINT Emi Koussi 11,204 ft.
(3,415 m.)
MONETARY UNIT CFA franc
MAJOR LANGUAGES Arabic, Bagirmi, French,
Sara, Massa, Moudang
MAJOR RELIGIONS Islam, tribal religions

SUDAN

AREA 967,494 sq. mi. (2,505,809 sq. km.)
POPULATION 18,691,000
CAPITAL Khartoum
LARGEST CITY Khartoum
HIGHEST POINT Jeb. Marra 10,073 ft.
(3,070 m.)
MONETARY UNIT Sudanese pound
MAJOR LANGUAGES Arabic, Dinka, Nubian,
Beja, Nuer
MAJOR RELIGIONS Islam, tribal religions

ETHIOPIA

AREA 471,776 sq. mi. (1,221,900 sq. km.)
POPULATION 31,065,000
CAPITAL Addis Ababa
LARGEST CITY Addis Ababa
HIGHEST POINT Ras Dashan 15,157 ft.
(4,620 m.)
MONETARY UNIT birr
MAJOR LANGUAGES Amharic, Gallinya,
Tigrinya, Somali, Sidamo, Arabic, Ge'ez
MAJOR RELIGIONS Coptic Christianity, Islam

DJIBOUTI

AREA 8,880 sq. mi. (23,000 sq. km.)
POPULATION 386,000
CAPITAL Djibouti
LARGEST CITY Djibouti
HIGHEST POINT Moussa Ali 6,768 ft.
(2,063 m.)
MONETARY UNIT Djibouti franc
MAJOR LANGUAGES Arabic, Somali,
Afar, French
MAJOR RELIGIONS Islam,
Roman Catholicism

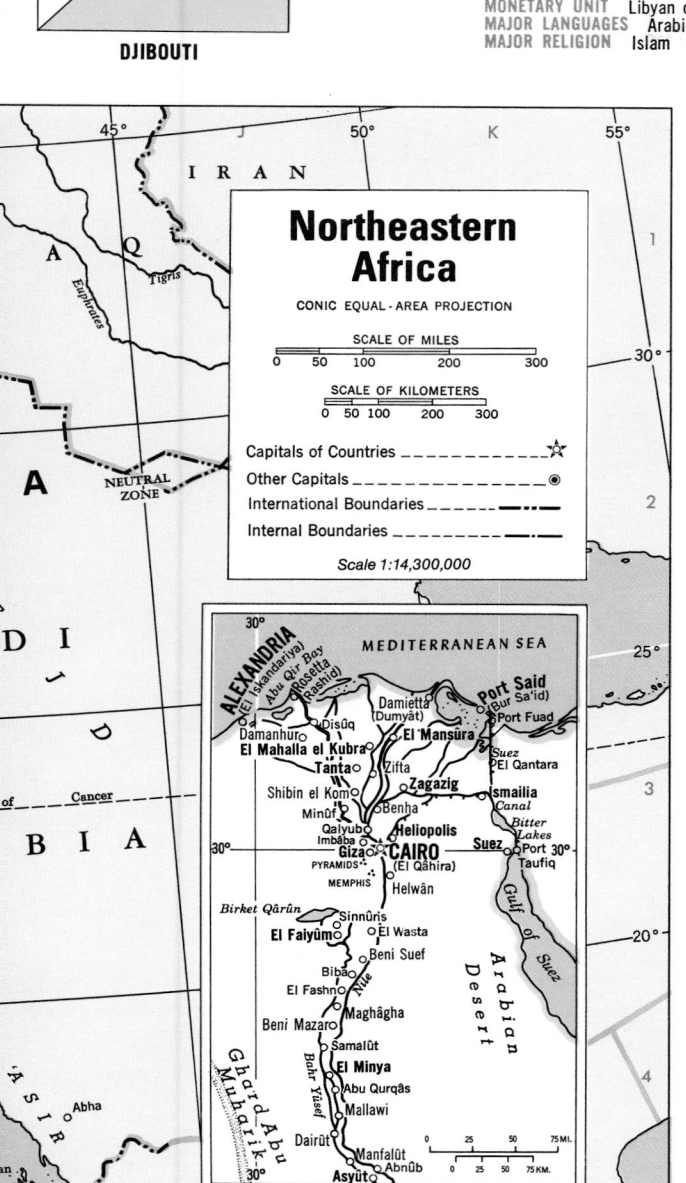

Northeastern Africa

CONIC EQUAL-AREA PROJECTION

SCALE OF MILES
0 50 100 300

SCALE OF KILOMETERS
0 50 100 200 300

Capitals of Countries _____ ☆
Other Capitals _____ ◉
International Boundaries _____
Internal Boundaries _____

Scale 1:14,300,000

© Copyright HAMMOND INCORPORATED, Maplewood, N.J.

CHAD

CITIES and TOWNS

Abéché 28,100	D5
Abou Dela	D5
Adré	D5
Ain-Galakka	C4
Am-Dam	D5
Am-Timan 4,200	D5
Arada	D4
Ati 7,500	C5
Baibokoum 5,500	C6
Biltine 3,900	D5
Bitkine 5,000	C5
Bokoro 6,500	C5
Bol 2,500	B5
Bongor 14,300	C6
Bousso 4,500	C6
Doba 13,300	C6
Fada	D4
Faya-Largeau 6,800	C3
Fianga 10,000	C6
Goré	C6
Gouro	C4
Goz Beïda	D5
Guéréda	D4
Ham	C5

Haraz	C5
Iriba	D4
Kélo 16,800	C6
Koro Toro	C4
Koumra 17,000	C6
Kouno	C6
Kyabé 5,000	C6
Lal 10,400	C6
Léré	B6
Madadi	D4
Mangueigne	D5
Mao 4,900	C5
Massakory	C5
Massénya	C5
Melfi	C5
Mogororo	C5
Moïssala 5,100	C6
Mongo 8,300	C5
Moundou 39,600	C6
Moussoro 7,700	C5
N'Djamena (cap.) 179,000	C5
Nokou	B5
Oum Chalouba	D4
Oum Hadjer 5,600	D5
Ounianga-Kébir	D4
Pala 13,200	B6
Rig Rig	B5
Sarh 43,700	C6
Wour	C3
Yarda	C4

Yebbi-Bou	C3
Ziguei	C5
Zouar	C3

OTHER FEATURES

Azoum, Bahr	D5
Baguirmi (reg.)	C5
Bahr el Ghazal (dry riv.)	C5
Batha (riv.)	C5
Bodélé (depr.)	C4
Borku 72	C4
Chad (lake)	C5
Domar (dry riv.)	C4
Emi Koussi (mt.)	D4
Ennedi (plat.)	D4
Fittri (lake)	C5
Haouach, Wadi (dry riv.)	C4
Jef Jef es Seghin (plat.)	D3
Kanem (reg.)	C5
Logone (riv.)	C6
Maro (dry riv.)	C4
Mbéré (riv.)	C6
Mourdi (depr.)	D4
Ouham (riv.)	C6
Pendé (riv.)	C6
Sahara (des.)	C3
Salamat, Bahr (riv.)	C6
Sara (riv.)	C6
Shari (riv.)	C5

Sudan (reg.)	C5
Tibesti (mts.)	C3
Wadaï (reg.)	D5

DJIBOUTI

CITIES and TOWNS

Ali Sabieh	H5
Dikhil	H5
Djibouti (cap.) 96,000	H5
Obock	H5
Tadjoura	H5

OTHER FEATURES

Abbe (lake)	H5
Aden (gulf)	J5
Bab el Mandeb (str.)	H5

EGYPT

CITIES and TOWNS

Abnûb 39,343	J4
Abu Qurqâs	J4
Akhmim 53,234	F2
Alexandria 2,318,655	J2

(continued on following page)

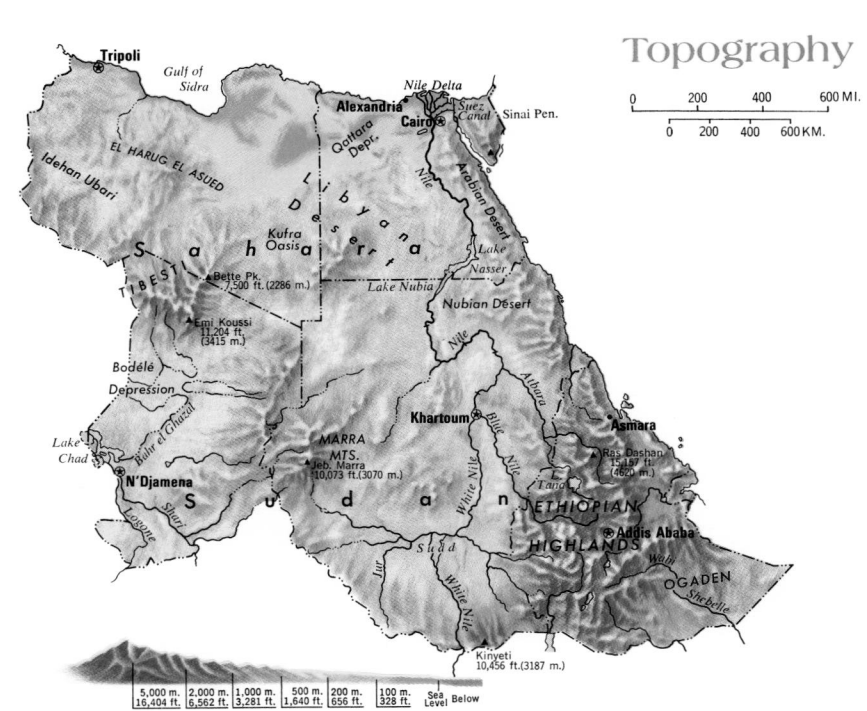

Topography

(continued on following page)

Aswân 144,377 F3
Asyût 213,983 J4
Bâris F3
Benha 88,992 J3
Beni Mazar 39,373 J4
Beni Suef 118,148 J3
Biba 33,074 J4
Bûlaq F2
Bur Sai'd (Port Said) 262,620 K2
Cairo (cap.) 5,084,463 J3
Dahab F2
Dairût 31,624 J4
Damanhur 188,927 J3
Damietta 93,546 J3
Disûq 58,650 J3
Dumyât (Damietta) 93,546 J3
Dûsh F3
El A'lamein E1
El A'rish F1
El Bawiti E2
El Faiyûm 167,081 J3
El Fashn 33,506 J4
El Hammam 6,588 E1
El Iskandariya (Alexandria) 2,318,655 J2
El Karnak F2
El Khârga 26,375 F2
El Mahalla el Kubra 292,853 J3
El Mansûra 257,866 K3
El Minya 146,423 J4
El Qâhira (Cairo) (cap.) 5,084,463 J3
El Qantara 919 K3
El Qasr E2
El Quseir 12,297 F2
El Tûr F2
El Wasta 17,659 J3
Gemsa F2
Girga 51,110 F2
Giza 1,246,713 J3
Heliopolis J3
Helwân J3
Hurghada F2
Idfu 34,858 F3
Imbâba J3
Ismailia 145,978 K3
Isna 34,186 F2
Karnak (El Karnak) F2
Kôm Ombo 44,531 F3
Luxor 92,748 F2
Maghâgha 40,802 J4
Mallawi 74,256 J4
Manfalût 41,126 J4
Mersá Matrûh 27,857 E1
Minûf 55,131 J3
Mût 8,032 E2
Nuweiba F2
Port Fuad K3
Port Safâga F2
Port Said 262,620 K2
Port Taufiq K3
Qalyub 62,739 J3
Qasr Farâfra E2
Qena 94,013 F2
Ras Ghârib F2
Rashid (Rosetta) 42,962 J2
Rudeis F2
Salûm 4,161 E1
Samalût 48,146 J4
Shibin el Kom 102,844 J3
Sidi Barrani 1,574 E1
Sinnûris 42,022 J3
Siwa 4,999 E2
Sohâg 101,758 F2
Suez 194,001 K3
Tahta 45,242 F2
Tanta 284,636 J3
Zagazig 202,637 K3
Zifta 50,410 J3

OTHER FEATURES

Abu Qir (bay) J2
Abydos (ruins) F2
A'llaqi, Wadi (dry riv.) F3
A'qaba (gulf) G2
Arabian (des.) F2
Aswân (dam) F3
Aswân High (dam) F3
Bahariya (oasis) E2
Bahr Yusef (stream) J4
Bânâs, Ras (cape) G3
Berenice (ruins) F3
Birket Qârûn (lake) J3
Bir Taba (well) F2
Bitter (lkes) K3
Dakhla (oasis) E2
Eastern (Arabian) (des.) F2
El Sollum (gulf) E1
Farâfra (oasis) E2
Foul (bay) G3
Ghard Abu Muharik (des.) J4
Gilf Kebir (plat.) E3
Great Sand Sea (des.) D2
Katherina, Jebel (mt.) F2
Khârga (oasis) F2
Libyan (des.) E2
Libyan (plat.) E1
Mediterranean (sea) E1
Memphis (ruins) J3
Muhammad, Ras (cape) F2
Nasser (lake) F3
Nile (riv.) F2
Pyramids (ruins) J3
Qattara (depr.) E2
Red (sea) G3
Sahara (des.) E3
Sinai (mt.) F2
Sinai (pen.) F2
Siwa (oasis) E2
Suez (canal) K3
Suez (gulf) F2
Tiran (str.) F2
U'weinat, Jebel (mt.) E3

ETHIOPIA

PROVINCES

Arusi 852,900 G6
Bale 707,800 H6
Eritrea 1,947,600 G4
Gamu-Gofa 698,800 G6
Gojjam 1,750,100 G5
Gondar 1,355,800 G5
Harar 3,359,200 H6
Ilubabor 688,800 F6
Kaffa 1,693,000 G6
Shoa 5,369,500 G6
Sidamo 2,479,800 G7
Tigre 1,828,900 H5
Wallaga 1,269,100 G6
Wallo 2,459,900 H5

CITIES and TOWNS

Addis Ababa (cap.) 1,196,300 G6
Addis Alam 5,500 G6
Adigrat 9,400 G5
Adi Ugri 12,800 G5
Adwa 16,400 G5
Afdem H6
Agordat G4
Aksum 12,800 G5
Ankober H6
Arba Mench 7,660 G6
Asmara 393,800 G4
Asosa F5
Assab 16,000 H5
Asselle 19,390 G6
Awareh H6
Awasa 16,790 G6
Awash H6
Axum (Aksum) 12,800 G5
Bahir Dar 25,100 G5
Burye G5
Callafo H6
Chilga G5
Dagabur H6
Dallol G5
Dangila G5
Debra Birhan 16,700 G6
Debra Markos 30,260 G5
Debra Tabor 8,700 G5
Dembidollo 7,600 F6
Dessye 49,750 G5
Dilla 13,800 G6
Dire Dawa 63,700 H6
Dolo H7
Domo J6
Edd H5
El Carre H6
El Der H6
Filtu H6
Gabredarre H6
Galadi J6
Gambela F6
Gardula 5,800 G6
Gedo G6
Gerlogubi H6
Ghimbi 8,300 G6
Ginir H6
Goba 13,500 H6
Gondar 38,600 G5
Gore 8,500 G6
Gorrahei H6
Harar 48,440 H6
Harkiko G4
Hosseina 8,500 G6
Imi H6
Jijiga 8,000 H6
Jimma 47,360 G6
Jiran G6
Karkabat G4
Keren G4
Kibre Mengist 8,300 G6
Lalibela G5
Magdala G5
Maji G6
Makale 30,780 G5
Massawa 19,800 G4
Mega G7
Mendi G6
Mersa Fatma H5
Metamma G5
Metu G6
Miesso H6
Mizan Teferi G6
Moyale G7
Murle G6
Mustahil H6
Nakamti 18,310 G6
Nakfa G4
Nazret 42,900 G6
Negelli 8,800 G6
Nejo G6
Saio (Dembidollo) 7,600 F6
Soddu 11,900 G6
Sokota G5
Tessenei G4
Thio H5
Tori F6
Umm Hajar G5
Waka G6
Waldia 9,600 G5
Wardere J6
Wolta G6
Yaballo G6
Zula G4

OTHER FEATURES

Abay (riv.) G5
Abaya (lake) G6
Akobo (riv.) F6
Assale (lake) H5
Atbara (riv.) G4
Awash (riv.) H5
Bale (mt.) G6
Baraka (riv.) G4
Baro (riv.) G6
Billate (riv.) G6
Blue Nile (Abay) (riv.) G5
Buri (pen.) H4
Chamo (lake) G6
Dahlak (arch.) H4
Dahlak (isl.) H4
Danakil (reg.) H5
Dawa (riv.) G7
Fafan (riv.) H6
Ganale Dorya (riv.) H6
Gash Mareb (riv.) G5
Gughe (mt.) G6
Haud (reg.) J6
Kasar, Ras (cape) G4
Ogaden (reg.) H6
Omo (riv.) G6
Ras Dashan (mt.) G5
Red (sea) H4
Rudolf (Turkana) (lake) G7
Simen (mts.) G5
Stefanie (lake) G7
Takkaze (riv.) G5
Tana (lake) G5
Tisisat (fall) G5
Turkana (lake) G7
Wabi (riv.) H6
Wabi Shebelle (riv.) H6
Zwai (lake) G6

LIBYA

CITIES and TOWNS

Ajedabia○ 53,170 D1
Aujila○ 6,695 D2
Baida○ 59,765 D1
Barce (El Marj)○ 55,444 D1
Benghazi (cap.)○ 286,943 C1
Beni Ulid○ 19,113 B1
Berken B2
Brak○ 12,507 B2
Bu Ngem C1
Cyrene (Shahat)○ 17,157 D1
Derj○ 2,152 B1
Derna○ 44,145 D1
Edri B2
El Abiar○ 17,685 D1
El Agheila C1
El Azizia○ 34,077 B1
El Bardi○ 4,330 D1
El Barkat○ 2,139 B3
El Fogaha C2
El Gatrun B3
El Gezira D2
El Jauf○ 6,481 D3
El Marj○ 55,444 D1
El' Uweinat B2
Es Sidr○ 706 C1
Ez Zuetina○ 7,256 D1
Ghadames○ 6,172 A2
Gharlan○ 65,224 B1
Ghat○ 6,924 B3
Ghemines○ 4,313 C1
Homs○ 66,890 B1
Hon○ 2,766 C2
Jaghbub (Jarabub)○ 1,436 D2
Jalo D2
Jarabub○ 1,436 D2
Marada○ 3,201 C2
Marsa el Brega○ 2,618 D1
Marsa el Hariga○ 5,043 D1
Mekili D1
Misurata○ 102,439 C1
Mizda○ 11,472 B1
Murzuk○ 22,185 B2
Nalut○ 23,535 B1
Ras Lanuf○ 1,990 C1
Sabrathaa○ 30,836 B1
Sebha○ 35,879 B2
Shahat○ 17,157 D1
Sinawen○ 1,549 B1
Sokna○ 3,757 C2
Soluk○ 6,501 D1
Susa D1
Syrte○ 22,797 C1
Tarhuna○ 52,657 B1
Tejerri B3
Tesawa B2
Tmessa C2
Tobruk○ 58,384 D1
Tokra○ 10,714 D1
Traghen B2
Tripoli (cap.)○ 550,438 B1
Ubari○ 19,132 B2
Umm el Abid C2
Waddan○ 5,347 C2
Wau el Kebir C2
Zawia○ 72,092 B1
Zella○ 4,835 C2
Zliten○ 58,981 C1
Zuila C2
Zwara○ 15,078 B1

OTHER FEATURES

Ain Zueiya (well) D3
Akhdar, Jebel (mts.) D1
A'mir, Ras (cape) D1
Barqa (Cyrenaica) (reg.) D1
Ben Ghnema, Jebel (mts.) C2
Bette (peak) C3
Bey el Kebir, Wadi (dry riv.) B1
Bir Hakeim (ruins) D1
Bishiara (well) D3
Bomba (gulf) D1
Buzeima (well) D3
Calansho Sand Sea (des.) D2
Calansho, Serir (des.) D2
Cyrenaica (reg.) D1
Fezzan (reg.) B2
Great Sand Sea (des.) D2
Harug el Asued, El (mts.) C2
Homra, Hamada el (des.) B2
Hosenofu (well) D3
Idehan Ubari (des.) B2
Idehan Murzuk (des.) B2
Jalo (oasis) D2
Jefara (reg.) B1
Jef Jef es Seghin (plat.) D3
Jofra (oasis) C2
Kufra (oasis) D3
Leptis Magna (ruins) B1
Libyan (des.) D2
Libyan (plat.) D1
Mediterranean (sea) C1
Nefusa, Jebel (mts.) B1
Rebiana○ (oasis) D3
Rebiana Sand Sea (des.) D3
Sahara (des.) C3
Sarra (well) D3
Shati, Wadi esh (dry riv.) B2
Sidra (gulf) C1
Soda, Jebel es (mts.) C2
Tazerbo○ (oasis) D2
Tibesti, Serir (des.) C3
Tinghert Hamada (Tinrhert) (des.) B2
Tripolitania (reg.) B1
U'weinat, Jebel (mt.) E3
Zelten, Jebel (mts.) D2

SUDAN

PROVINCES

Central F5
Darfur D5
Eastern G4
Khartoum F4
Kordofan E5
Northern E3
Southern E6

CITIES and TOWNS

A'bri F3
Abu Hamed F4
Abu Matariq E5
Abu Zabad E5
Abwong F6
Abyei E6
Adarama G4
Adok F6
Akasha F3
Akobo F6
Amadi F6
A'qiq G4
Argo F4
Aroma G4
Atbara 66,000 F4
Aweil E6
Ayod F6
Babanusa E5
Bara F5
Bentiu E6
Berber F4
Bor F6
Bo River Post E6
Buram E5
Damazin (Ed Damazin) 12,000 F5
Deim Zubeir E6
Delgo F3
Derudeb G4
Dilling E5
Dongola 6,000 F4
Dungunab G3
Ed Dae'in E5
Ed Damer 17,000 F4
Ed Damazin 12,000 F5
Ed Debba F4
Ed Dueim 27,000 F5
El Abbasiya F5
El Fasher 52,000 E5
El Fifi D5
El Geneina 33,000 D5
El Geteina F5
El Hilla E5
El Khandaq E4
El Managil F5
El Obeid 90,000 E5
El Odaiya E5
En Nahud 23,000 E5
Er Rahad F5
Er Roseires F5
Famaka F5
Fangak F6
Fashoda (Kodok) F6
Gabras E5
Gallabat G5
Gebeit Mine G3
Gedaref 92,000 G5
Gogrial E6
Goz Regeb G4
Haiya Junction G4
Halaib G3
Heiban F5
Jonglei F6
Juba 57,000 F7
Kadugli 18,000 E5
Kafia Kingi D6
Kajok E6
Kaka F5
Kapoeta F7
Karima F4
Karora G4
Kassala 99,000 G4
Kerma F4
Khartoum (cap.) 334,000 F4
Khartoum North 151,000 F4
Khashm el Girba G5
Kodok F6
Kongor F6
Korti F4
Kosti 57,000 F5
Kubbum D5
Kurmuk F5
Kutum D5
Lado F6
Loka F7
Malakal 35,000 F6
Maridi E7
Marsa Oseif G3
Melut F5
Merowe F4
Meshra er Req E6
Mongalla F6
Muglad E5
Muhammad Qol G3
Musmar G4
Nagishot F7
Nasir F6
Nimule F7
Nyala 60,000 E5
Nyamlell E6
Nyerol F6
Omdurman 299,000 F4
Opari F7
Pibor Post F6
Port Sudan 133,000 G4
Qalae'n Nahl F5
Raga E6
Rashad F5
Rejaf F7
Renk F5
Rufaa' F5
Rumbek 17,000 E6
Sennar F5
Shambe F6
Shendi F4
Shereik F4
Showak G5
Singa F5
Sinkat G4
Sodiri E5
Suakin G4
Suki F5
Tali Post F6
Talodi F5
Tambura E6
Tendelti F5
Tokar G4
Tombe F6
Tonga F6
Tonj E6
Torit F7
Towot F6
Trinkitat G4
Umm Keddada E5
Umm Ruwaba F5
Wadi Halfa F3
Wad Medani 107,000 F5
Wankai E6
Wau 53,000 E6
Yambio 7,000 E7
Yei F7
Yirol F6
Zalingei D5

OTHER FEATURES

Abu Dara, Ras (cape) G3
Abu Habl, Wadi (dry riv.) F5
Abu Shagara, Ras (cape) G3
Abu Tabari (well) E4
Adda (riv.) D6
Akobo (riv.) F6
A'mur, Wadi (dry riv.) G4
Asoteriba, Jebel (mt.) G3
Atbara (riv.) G4
Bahr Azoum (riv.) D5
Bahr el A'rab (riv.) E6
Bahr ez Zeraf (riv.) F6
Baraka (riv.) G4
Blue Nile (riv.) F5
Dar Hamid (reg.) F5
Dar Masalit (reg.) D5
Dinder (riv.) F5
El A'trun (oasis) E4
Fifth Cataract F4
Fourth Cataract F4
Gabgaba, Wadi (dry riv.) F3
Gezira, El (reg.) F5
Ghalla, Wadi el (dry riv.) E5
Hadarba, Ras (cape) G3
Howar, Wadi (dry riv.) E4
Ibra, Wadi (dry riv.) D5
Jebel Abyad (plat.) E4
Jebel Aulia (dam) F4
Jur (riv.) E6
Kasar, Ras (cape) G4
Kinyeti (mt.) F7
Laqiya U'mran (well) E3
Libyan (des.) E3
Lol (dry riv.) E6
Lotagipi Swamp (plain) F6
Marra, Jebel (mt.) D5
Meroe (ruins) F4
Milk, Wadi el (dry riv.) E4
Muqaddam, Wadi (dry riv.) F4
Napata (ruins) F4
Naqa (ruins) F4
Nile (riv.) F4
Nuba (mts.) E5
Nubia (lake) F3
Nubian (des.) F3
Nukheila (oasis) E4
Nuri (ruins) F4
Oda, Jebel (mt.) G3
Pibor (riv.) F6
Red (sea) G3
Sahara (des.) E3
Second Cataract F3
Selima (oasis) E3
Sennar (dam) F5
Setit (riv.) G5
Sixth Cataract F4
Sobat (riv.) F6
Suakin (arch.) G4
Sudan (reg.) E5
Sudd (swamp) F6
Sue (riv.) E6
Third Cataract E4
U'weinat, Jebel (mt.) E3
White Nile (riv.) F5

○Population of sub-district or division.

Agriculture, Industry and Resources

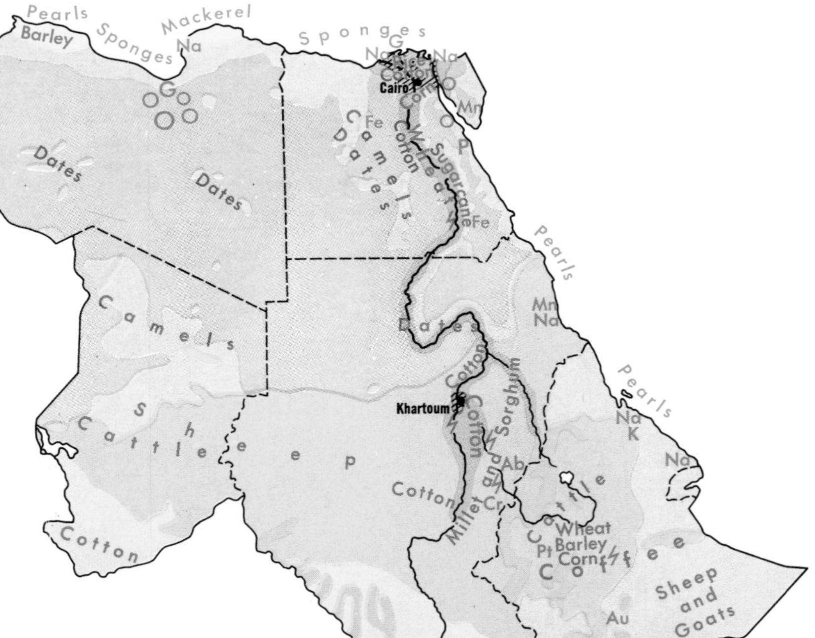

DOMINANT LAND USE

- Cereals, Horticulture, Livestock
- Cash Crops, Mixed Cereals
- Cotton, Cereals
- Market Gardening, Diversified Tropical Crops
- Plantation Agriculture
- Oases
- Pasture Livestock
- Nomadic Livestock Herding
- Forests
- Nonagricultural Land

MAJOR MINERAL OCCURRENCES

Ab	Asbestos	Mn	Manganese
Au	Gold	Na	Salt
Cr	Chromium	O	Petroleum
Fe	Iron Ore	P	Phosphates
G	Natural Gas	Pt	Platinum
K	Potash		

Water Power
Major Industrial Areas

ANGOLA
AREA 481,351 sq. mi. (1,246,700 sq. km.)
POPULATION 7,078,000
CAPITAL Luanda
LARGEST CITY Luanda
HIGHEST POINT Mt. Moco 8,593 ft. (2,620 m.)
MONETARY UNIT kwanza
MAJOR LANGUAGES Mbundu, Kongo, Lunda,
  Portuguese
MAJOR RELIGIONS Tribal religions, Roman
  Catholicism

BURUNDI
AREA 10,747 sq. mi. (27,835 sq. km.)
POPULATION 4,021,910
CAPITAL Bujumbura
LARGEST CITY Bujumbura
HIGHEST POINT 8,858 ft. (2,700 m.)
MONETARY UNIT Burundi franc
MAJOR LANGUAGES Kirundi, French, Swahili
MAJOR RELIGIONS Tribal religions, Roman
  Catholicism, Islam

CAMEROON
AREA 183,568 sq. mi.
  (475,441 sq. km.)
POPULATION 8,503,000
CAPITAL Yaoundé
LARGEST CITY Douala
HIGHEST POINT Cameroon 13,350 ft. (4,069 m.)
MONETARY UNIT CFA tranc
MAJOR LANGUAGFS Fang, Bamileke, Fulani,
  Duala, French, English
MAJOR RELIGIONS Tribal religions, Christianity, Islam

CENTRAL AFRICAN REP.
AREA 242,000 sq. mi. (626,780 sq. km.)
POPULATION 2,284,000
CAPITAL Bangui
LARGEST CITY Bangui
HIGHEST POINT Gao 4,659 ft. (1,420 m.)
MONETARY UNIT CFA franc
MAJOR LANGUAGES Banda, Gbaya, Sangho,
  French
MAJOR RELIGIONS Tribal religions,
  Christianity, Islam

CONGO
AREA 132,046 sq. mi. (342,000 sq. km.)
POPULATION 1,537,000
CAPITAL Brazzaville
LARGEST CITY Brazzaville
HIGHEST POINT Leketi Mts. 3,412 ft.
  (1,040 m.)
MONETARY UNIT CFA franc
MAJOR LANGUAGES Kikongo, Bateke,
  Lingala, French
MAJOR RELIGIONS Christianity, tribal
  religions, Islam

EQUATORIAL GUINEA
AREA 10,831 sq. mi. (28,052 sq. km.)
POPULATION 244,000
CAPITAL Malabo
LARGEST CITY Malabo
HIGHEST POINT 9,868 ft. (3,008 m.)
MONETARY UNIT CFA franc
MAJOR LANGUAGES Fang, Bubi, Spanish
MAJOR RELIGIONS Tribal religions,
  Christianity

GABON
AREA 103,346 sq. mi. (267,666 sq. km.)
POPULATION 551,000
CAPITAL Libreville
LARGEST CITY Libreville
HIGHEST POINT Ibounzi 5,165 ft. (1,574 m.)
MONETARY UNIT CFA franc
MAJOR LANGUAGES Fang and other Bantu
  languages, French
MAJOR RELIGIONS Tribal religions,
  Christianity, Islam

KENYA
AREA 224,960 sq. mi. (582,646 sq. km.)
POPULATION 15,327,061
CAPITAL Nairobi
LARGEST CITY Nairobi
HIGHEST POINT Kenya 17,058 ft. (5,199 m.)
MONETARY UNIT Kenya shilling
MAJOR LANGUAGES Kikuyu, Luo, Kavirondo,
  Kamba, Swahili, English
MAJOR RELIGIONS Tribal religions,
  Christianity, Hinduism, Islam

MALAWI
AREA 45,747 sq. mi. (118,485 sq. km.)
POPULATION 5,968,000
CAPITAL Lilongwe
LARGEST CITY Blantyre
HIGHEST POINT Mulanje 9,843 ft. (3,000 m.)
MONETARY UNIT Malawi kwacha
MAJOR LANGUAGES Chichewa, Yao,
  English, Nyanja, Tumbuka, Tonga,
  Ngoni
MAJOR RELIGIONS Tribal religions, Islam,
  Christianity

RWANDA
AREA 10,169 sq. mi. (26,337 sq. km.)
POPULATION 4,819,317
CAPITAL Kigali
LARGEST CITY Kigali
HIGHEST POINT Karisimbi 14,780 ft.
  (4,505 m.)
MONETARY UNIT Rwanda franc
MAJOR LANGUAGES Kinyarwanda, French,
  Swahili
MAJOR RELIGIONS Tribal religions,
  Roman Catholicism, Islam

SOMALIA
AREA 246,200 sq. mi. (637,658 sq. km.)
POPULATION 3,645,000
CAPITAL Mogadishu
LARGEST CITY Mogadishu
HIGHEST POINT Surud Ad 7,900 ft.
  (2,408 m.)
MONETARY UNIT Somali shilling
MAJOR LANGUAGES Somali, Arabic,
  Italian, English
MAJOR RELIGION Islam

TANZANIA
AREA 363,708 sq. mi. (942,003 sq. km.)
POPULATION 17,527,560
CAPITAL Dar es Salaam
LARGEST CITY Dar es Salaam
HIGHEST POINT Kilimanjaro 19,340 ft.
  (5,895 m.)
MONETARY UNIT Tanzanian shilling
MAJOR LANGUAGES Nyamwezi-Sukuma,
  Swahili, English
MAJOR RELIGIONS Tribal religions,
  Christianity, Islam

UGANDA
AREA 91,076 sq. mi. (235,887 sq. km.)
POPULATION 12,630,076
CAPITAL Kampala
LARGEST CITY Kampala
HIGHEST POINT Margherita 16,795 ft.
  (5,119 m.)
MONETARY UNIT Ugandan shilling
MAJOR LANGUAGES Luganda, Acholi, Teso,
  Nyoro, Soga, Nkole, English, Swahili
MAJOR RELIGIONS Tribal religions,
  Christianity, Islam

ZAIRE
AREA 905,063 sq. mi. (2,344,113 sq. km.)
POPULATION 28,291,000
CAPITAL Kinshasa
LARGEST CITY Kinshasa
HIGHEST POINT Margherita 16,795 ft.
  (5,119 m.)
MONETARY UNIT zaire
MAJOR LANGUAGES Tshiluba, Mongo, Kikongo,
  Kingwana, Zande, Lingala, Swahili,
  French
MAJOR RELIGIONS Tribal religions,
  Christianity

ZAMBIA
AREA 290,586 sq. mi. (752,618 sq. km.)
POPULATION 5,679,808
CAPITAL Lusaka
LARGEST CITY Lusaka
HIGHEST POINT Sunzu 6,782 ft.
  (2,067 m.)
MONETARY UNIT Zambian kwacha
MAJOR LANGUAGES Bemba, Tonga,
  Lozi, Luvale, Nyanja, English
MAJOR RELIGIONS Tribal religions

ANGOLA

DISTRICTS

...ngo 68,885	B5
...nguela 474,897	B6
...e 650,337	C6
...abinda 80,857	B5
...wando Cubango 112,073	C7
...uanza-Norte 298,062	B5
...uanza-Sul 458,592	C6
...unene 147,394	C7
...uambo 837,627	C6
...ulla 497,470	B7
...uanda 491,704	B5
...unda Norte 210,000	C5
...unda Sul 98,000	D5
...alange 558,630	C6
...oxico 213,119	D6
...amibe 53,058	B7
...ge 386,037	B5
...aire 41,766	B5

CITIES and TOWNS

...to Chicapa	C6
...to Cuale	C5
...mbriz	B5
...ndulo	C6
...ala dos Tigres	B7
...aia Farta	B6
...ela Vista	B6
...embe	B5
...enguela 40,996	B6
...aala 8,894	C5
...abinda 21,124	B5
...aconda	B6
...acuso	C7
...aiundo	C6
...alulo	C6
...aluquembe	C6
...amacupa 5,740	D6
...amanongue	D6
...ambulo	D5
...angamba	C6
...apelonga	C6
...apenda-Camulemba	C5
...assai	D6
...assamba	D6
...atete	B5
...atumbela	B6
...auingula	C5
...axito	B5
...azombo	D6
...ela 2,784	B7
...hiange	C6
...hinguar	C6
...hitado	B7
...hitembo	C6
...oambo	C6
...cuango	C5
...uchi	C7
...uilo	C6
...uito-Cuanavale	C7
...uma	B6
...amba	B5
...irico	D7
...ombe Grande	B6
...ondo	B5
...olgares	D5
...orte República	C5

Foz do Cunene	B7
Gabela 6,930	B6
Gambos	B6
Golungo Alto	B5
Huambo 61,885	C6
Iona	B7
Kalandula	B6
Kassinga	C7
Kuito 18,941	C6
Lobito 59,528	B6
Lóvua	C5
Longa	C6
Luacano	D6
Luachimo	D5
Luanda (cap.) 475,328	B5
Lubango 31,674	B6
Lucira	C6
Luiana	D7
Lukapa	D5
Macondo	D6

Malange 31,599	C5
Maquela do Zombo	C5
Massango (Forte República)	C5
Mavinga	D7
Mbanza Congo 4,002	B5
Menongue 3,023	C6
Moçâmedes (Namibe) 12,076	B7
Muconda	D6
Mucope	C7
Mucusso	D7
Munhango	C6
Muxima	B5
Namibe 12,076	B7
Nana Candundo	D6
Ndalatando 7,342	B5
N'gage 2,548	C5
Ngiva	C7
Ngunza (Sumbe) 7,911	B6
Nharêa	C6
Nóqui	B5

Nova Gaia	C5
Nzeto	B5
Oncócua	B7
Porto Alexandre 8,235	B7
Porto Amboim	B6
Quela	C6
Quibala	C6
Quibaxe	B5
Quinzau	C5
Sanza Pombo	C5
São Nicolau	B6
Saurimo 12,901	D5
Songo	C5
Soyo	B5
Sumbe 7,911	B6
Uíge 11,972	C5
Vila Guilherme Capelo	B5
Xangongo	C7

OTHER FEATURES

Bero (riv.)	B7
Chicapa (riv.)	D5
Chiumbe (riv.)	D5
Congo (riv.)	C4
Coporolo (riv.)	C7
Cuando (riv.)	C7
Cuango (riv.)	C7
Cuanza (riv.)	C5
Cubango (riv.)	C7
Cuito (riv.)	C7
Cunene (riv.)	B7
Cunene (dam)	C7
Cuvo (riv.)	B6
Kasai (riv.)	D5
Kwilu (riv.)	C5
Loange (riv.)	C5
Loge (riv.)	B5
Lungwebungu (riv.)	D6
Matala (dam)	B6

M'Bridge (riv.)	B5
Moco (mt.)	C6
Negro (cape)	B7
Palmeirinhas (pt.)	B5
Ruacana Falls (dam)	B6
Santa Maria (cape)	B6
Zambezi (riv.)	D6

BURUNDI

CITIES and TOWNS

Bujumbura (cap.) 141,040	E4
Bururi 7,800	F4
Gitega 19,500	F4

OTHER FEATURES

Ruzizi (riv.)	E4

Tanganyika (lake)	E5

CAMEROON

CITIES and TOWNS

Abong-Mbang 6,000	B3
Ambam 4,000	B3
Bafia 12,000	B3
Bafoussam 62,239	B2
Bali	A2
Bamenda 48,111	B2
Banyo	B2
Batouri 7,000	B3
Bélabo	B3
Bengbis	B3
Bertoua 10,000	B3
Bétaré-Oya	B2
Bonabéri	A3

(continued on following page)

ANGOLA

EQUATORIAL GUINEA

SOMALIA

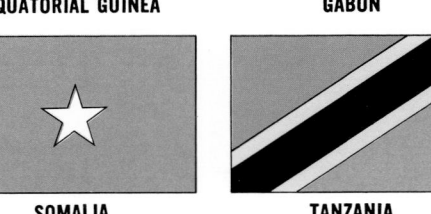
TANZANIA

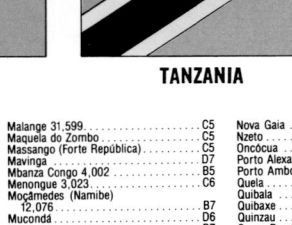
UGANDA

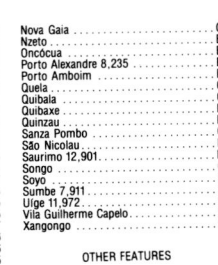
ZAIRE

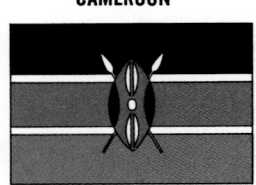
GABON

KENYA

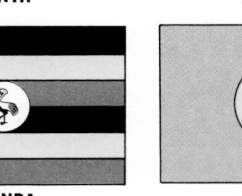
MALAWI

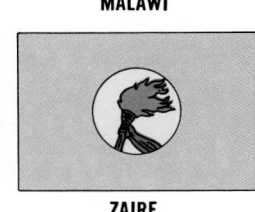
RWANDA

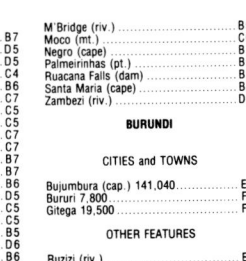
ZAMBIA

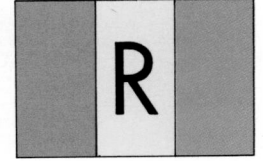
CONGO

Kounde ... B2
Mbalki 12,346 ... C3
Mbres 2,622 ... D3
Mobaye 4,220 ... D3
Mouka ... D2
Ndele 5,858 ... D2
Ngouru ... D2
Nola 6,703 ... C3
Obo 3,978 ... E2
Ouadda 3,009 ... D2
Paoua 7,052 ... C2
Posse ... C2
Sibut 13,341 ... C2
Zako ... D2
Zemio 3,259 ... D2

Zemongo ... E2

OTHER FEATURES

Bamingui (riv.) ... C2
Bomu (riv.) ... D2
Dar Rounga (reg.) ... D2
Gao (mt.) ... C2
Kadei (riv.) ... C3
Kotto (riv.) ... D2
Lobaye (riv.) ... C3
Mbéré (riv.) ... B2
Ouham (riv.) ... C2
Pende (riv.) ... C2
Sanga (riv.) ... C3

Sara (riv.) ... C2
Shari (riv.) ... C2
Shinko (riv.) ... D2
Ubàngi (riv.) ... C3

CONGO

CITIES and TOWNS

Abala ... C4
Boko ... B4
Brazzaville (cap.) 298,967 ... B4
Boundji ... B4
Djambala ... B4

Dongou ... C3
Enyellé ... C3
Epéna ... C3
Etoumbi ... B3
Ewo ... C4
Gamboma ... C4
Ikelemba ... C3
Impfondo ... C3
Kellé ... C4
Kindamba ... B4
Kinkala ... B4
Komono ... B4
Loubomo 29,600 ... B4
Loudima ... B4

Madingo-Kayes ... B4
Madingou ... B4
Makoua ... C3
Mbinda ... B4
Mindouli ... C4
Mossaka ... C4
Mossendjo ... B3
M'Pouya ... C4
Nkayi 30,600 ... B4
Okoyo ... C4
Ouesso ... C3
Owando ... C4
Oyo ... C4
Pangala ... B4
Pointe-Noire 141,700 ... B4
Sembé ... B3
Sibiti ... B4
Souanké ... B3
Zanaga ... B4

Tchibanga 14,001 ... B4

OTHER FEATURES

Crystal (mts.) ... B4
Ibounzi (mt.) ... B4
Ivindo (riv.) ... B3
Lopez (cape) ... A4
Mayumba ... B4
M'Pouya ... C4
M'Vouti ... B4
N'Dogo (lag.) ... B4
N'Gounié (riv.) ... B4
N'Komi (lag.) ... A4
Ogooué (riv.) ... A4
Onangué (lake) ... A4
Pongara (pt.) ... A3

KENYA

PROVINCES

Central 1,675,647 ... G4
Coast 944,082 ... G4
Eastern 1,907,301 ... G4
Nairobi 509,286 ... G4
North-Eastern 245,757 ... G3
Nyanza 2,122,045 ... F4
Rift Valley 2,210,289 ... G3
Western 1,328,298 ... G3

CITIES and TOWNS

Buna ... G3
Bunyala ... H4
Bura ... H4
Eldoret 18,196 ... G4
El Wak ... H3
Embu 3,928 ... G4
Fort Hall 4,750 ... G4
Galole 3,609 ... G4
Garba Tula ... G3
Garissa ... G4
Garsen ... G4
Gilgil 4,178 ... G4
Isiolo 8,201 ... F3
Kakamega 6,244 ... F3
Kericho 10,144 ... F4
Kiambu 2,776 ... G4
Kilifi 2,662 ... G4
Kipini ... H4
Kisii 6,080 ... F4
Kisumu 32,431 ... F3
Kitale 11,573 ... F3
Kitui 3,071 ... G4
Kolbio ... H4
Konza ... G4
Laisamis ... G3
Lamu 7,403 ... H4
Lodwar ... G3
Lokitaung 4,090 ... G3
Lolgorien ... F4
Machakos 6,312 ... G4
Magadi ... G4
Malindi 10,757 ... H4
Mambrui ... H4
Maralal 3,878 ... G3
Marsabit 6,635 ... G3
Meru 4,475 ... G4
Mombasa 247,073 ... G4
Moyale ... G3
Nairobi (cap.) 509,286 ... G4
Naivasha 6,920 ... G4
Nakuru 47,151 ... G4
Namanga ... G4
Nanyuki 11,624 ... G3
Narok 2,608 ... G4
North Horr ... G3
South Horr ... G3
Taveta ... G4
Thika 18,387 ... G4
Thomson's Falls 7,602 ... G3
Todenyang ... G3
Tsavo ... G4
Vanga ... G4
Voi 5,313 ... G4
Wajir ... H3
Wamba 2,650 ... G4

OTHER FEATURES

Daua (riv.) ... H3
Elgon (mt.) ... F3
Formosa (bay) ... H4
Galana (riv.) ... G4
Gedi (ruins) ... H4
Kavirondo (gulf) ... F4
Kenya (mt.) ... G4
Lak Dera (dry riv.) ... H3
Lorian (swamp) ... H3
Natron (lake) ... G3
Nyiru (mt.) ... G3
Patta (isl.) ... H4

EQUATORIAL GUINEA

TERRITORIES

Bioko 78,000 ... A3
Rio Muni 203,000 ... B3

CITIES and TOWNS

Bata 27,024 ... B3
Luba 19,933 ... A3
Malabo (cap.) 37,237 ... A3
Mbini 14,503 ... A3

OTHER FEATURES

Biafra (bight) ... A3
Bioko (isl.) ... A3
Corisco (isl.) ... A3
Elobey (isls.) ... A3
Fernando Po (Bioko) (isl.) ... A3

GABON

CITIES and TOWNS

Banda ... B4
Bitam 5,936 ... B3
Booué ... B3
Chinchoua ... B3
Cocobeach ... A3
Fougamou ... B4
Franceville 9,345 ... B4
Iguéla ... A4
Kango ... B3
Kembama ... B3
Koula-Moutou 8,032 ... B4
Lalara ... B3
Lambaréné 17,770 ... B4
Lastoursville ... B4
Lekoni ... B4
Libreville (cap.) 105,080 ... A3
Makokou 5,005 ... B3
Mayumba ... B4
M'Bigou ... B4
Médouneu ... B3
Mekambo ... B3
Mimongo ... B4
Minvoul ... B3
Mitzic ... B3
Moanda 10,709 ... B4
Mouila 15,016 ... B4
Mounana 4,000 ... B4
N'Dendé ... B4
N'Djolé ... B4
Nyanga ... B4
Okondja ... B4
Omboué ... A4
Owendo ... A3
Oyem 12,455 ... B3
Port-Gentil 48,190 ... A4
Setté-Cama ... A4

Rudolf (Turkana) (lake) ... G3
Tana (riv.) ... G4
Tsavo Nat'l Park ... G4
Turkana (lake) ... G3
Victoria (lake) ... F4
Winam (bay) ... F4

MALAWI

CITIES and TOWNS

Bandawe ... F6
Blantyre 222,153 ... F7
Chilumba ... F6
Chipoka ... F6
Chiromo ... F7
Chitipa 3,079 ... F5
Dedza 5,448 ... F6
Karonga 11,873 ... F6
Kasungu ... F6
Lilongwe (cap.) 102,924 ... F6
Livingstonia ... F6
Mangochi 3,341 ... G6
Mzimba 4,962 ... F6
Nkhata Bay 4,024 ... F6
Nkhotakota 10,312 ... F6
Nsanje 6,091 ... G7
Rumphi 3,998 ... F6
Salima 4,646 ... F6
Thyolo 4,186 ... F7
Zomba 21,000 ... G7

OTHER FEATURES

Chilwa (lake) ... G7
Malawi (Nyasa) (lake) ... F6
Mulanje (mts.) ... G7
Nyasa (lake) ... F6
Shire (riv.) ... G7

RWANDA

CITIES and TOWNS

Butare 21,691 ... E4
Cyangugu 7,042 ... E4
Gisenyi 12,436 ... E4
Kigali (cap.) 117,749 ... E4
Nyabisindu 8,587 ... E4

OTHER FEATURES

Kagera Nat'l Park ... F4
Karisimbi (mt.) ... E4
Kivu (lake) ... E4
Ruzizi (riv.) ... E4
Virunga (range) ... E4

SOMALIA

PROVINCES

Bakool 100,000 ... H3
Bari 155,000 ... J1
Galguduud 182,000 ... H3
Gedo 212,000 ... H3
Hiiraan 147,000 ... J3
Jubbada Hoose 246,000 ... H3
Mogadiscio 371,000 ... J2
Mudug 215,000 ... J2
Nugaal 85,000 ... J2
Sanaag 146,000 ... J2
Shabeellaha Dhexe 237,000 ... J3
Shabeellaha Hoose 398,000 ... H3
Togdheer 258,000 ... J2
Woqooyi Galbeed 440,000 ... H1

CITIES and TOWNS

Adadle ... H2
Afgoi ... J3
Afmadu 2,580 ... H3
Alula ... K1
Ankhor ... J3
Audegle ... J3
Baduen ... J2
Barawa (Brava) ... H3
Bardera ... H3
Bargal ... K1
Baydhabo 14,962 ... H3
Belet Weyne 11,426 ... J3
Bender Beila ... K2
Bender Cassim (Bosaso) ... J1
Berbera 12,219 ... H1
Bereda ... K1
Bircao ... H4
Bohodleh ... J2
Borama 3,244 ... H1

(continued on following page)

Central Africa

CYLINDRICAL EQUAL-AREA PROJECTION

SCALE OF MILES
0 50 100   200   300

SCALE OF KILOMETERS
0 50 100   200   300

Capitals of Countries _ _ _ _ _ _ ☆
Other Capitals _ _ _ _ _ _ _ ◉
International Boundaries _ _ _ _
Internal Boundaries _ _ _ _ _ _

Scale 1:13,800,000

© Copyright HAMMOND INCORPORATED, Maplewood, N.J.

Topography

SCALE
0   200   400   600 MI.
0   200   400   600 KM.

	Below Sea Level	100 m. 328 ft.	200 m. 656 ft.	500 m. 1,640 ft.	1,000 m. 3,281 ft.	2,000 m. 6,562 ft.	5,000 m. 16,404 ft.

Bosaso	J1
Brava 6,167	H3
Bulhar	H1
Bulo Burti 5,247	J3
Bur Acaba	H3
Burao 12,617	J2
Callis	J2
Candala	J1
Chisimayu 17,872	H4
Chiambone	H4
Coriole 4,341	H3
Dante (Hafun)	K1
Dif	H3
Dinsor	H3
Dusa Marreb	J2
Eil	J2
El Athale (Itala)	J3
El Bur	J3
El Dere	J3
El Hamurre	J2
Erigabo 4,279	J1
Ferfer	J2
Galcaio	J2
Garad	J2
Garbahaarrey	H3
Gardo	J2
Garoe	J2
Giohar 13,156	J3
Gobwen	H4
Hafun	K1
Halin	J2
Harardera	J3
Hargeysa 40,254	H2
Hordio	K1
Iddan	J2
Iet	H3
Itala	J3
Jamama 5,408	H3
Jilib 3,232	H3
Karin	J1
Kismayu (Chisimayu) 17,872	H4
Las Dureh	J1
Luuq	H3
Margherita (Jamama)	H3
Marka (Merka) 17,708	H3
Mogadishu (cap.) 371,000	J3
Muqdisho (Mogadishu) (cap.) 371,000	J3
Obbia	J2
Oddur	H3
Taleh	J2
Uanle Uen	H3
Upper Sheikh	J2
Villabruzzi (Johar)	J3
Zeila 1,226	H1

OTHER FEATURES

Aden (gulf)	J1
Asèr, Ras (cape)	K1
Giuba (riv.)	H3
Guban (reg.)	H1
Hafun, Ras (cape)	K1
Haud (plat.)	J2
Lak Dera (dry riv.)	H3
Negro (bay)	J2
Nogal (reg.)	J2
Shimbir Berris (mt.)	J1
Sura, Ras (cape)	J1
Surud Ad (mt.)	J1
Webi Shabelle (riv.)	H3

TANZANIA

REGIONS

Arusha 928,478	G4
Dar es Salaam 851,222	G5
Dodoma 971,921	G5
Iringa 922,801	G5
Kagera 1,009,379	F4
Kigoma 648,950	F4
Kilimanjaro 902,394	G4
Lindi 527,902	G5
Mara 723,295	F4
Mbeya 1,080,241	F5
Morogoro 939,190	G5
Mtwara 771,726	G5
Mwanza 1,443,418	F4
Pemba 205,870	H5
Pwani (Coast) 516,949	G5
Rukwa 451,897	F5
Ruvuma 564,113	G6
Shinyanga 1,323,482	F4
Singida 614,030	F5
Tabora 818,049	F5
Tanga 1,088,592	G5
Zanzibar Mjini 143,616	G5
Zanzibar Shambani North 77,424	G5
Zanzibar Shambani South 52,325	G5

CITIES and TOWNS

Arusha 55,281	G4
Babati	G4
Bagamoyo 5,112	G5
Bukoba 20,430	F4
Chake Chake 4,862	H5
Dar es Salaam (cap.) 757,346	G5
Dodoma 45,703	G5
Geita 3,066	F4
Handeni	G5
Ifakara	G5
Iringa 57,182	G5
Itigi	F5
Kahama 3,211	F4
Kaliua	F5
Kanga	G5
Karema	F5
Kasanga	F5
Kasulu	F4
Kibara	F4
Kibaya	G5
Kibondo	F4
Kigoma-Ujiji 50,044	E4
Kilosa 4,458	G5
Kilwa Kivinje 2,790	G5
Kilwa Masoko	G5
Kinyangiri	G4
Kipili	F5
Kisiju	G5
Kitunda	F5
Kizimkazi	G5
Kondoa 4,514	G4
Kongwa	G5
Korogwe 6,675	G5
Lindi 27,308	G5
Liuli	F6
Liwale	G5
Longido	G4
Mahenge	G5
Makumbako	G5
Manda	F6
Manyoni	G5
Masasi	G6
Mbamba Bay	G6
Mbeya 76,606	F5
Mbulu	G4
Mchinga	H5
Mohoro	G5
Mombo	G4
Morogoro 61,890	G5
Moshi 52,223	G4
Mpanda	F5
Mtakuja	F5
Mtwara-Mikindani 48,510	H6
Murongo	F4
Musoma 32,658	F4
Muwale	F5
Mwadui 7,383	F4
Mwanza 110,611	F4
Mwaya	F5
Mwesi	F5
Nachingwea 3,751	G6
Newala	G6
Ngara	F4
Njombe	F5
Pangani 2,955	G5
Rungwa	F5
Sadani	G5
Same	G4
Sekenke	F4
Shinyanga 21,703	F4
Singida 29,252	F4
Songea 17,954	G6
Sumbawanga 28,586	F5
Tabora 67,392	F5
Tanga 103,409	G4
Tukuyu 4,089	F5
Tunduru	G6
Urambo	F4
Utete	G5
Uvinza	F5
Wete 8,469	G4
Zanzibar 110,669	G5

OTHER FEATURES

Eyasi (lake)	F4
Great Ruaha (riv.)	G5
Juani (isl.)	G5
Kalambo (falls)	F5
Kanzi (cape)	G5
Kilimanjaro (mt.)	G4
Kilombero (riv.)	G5
Mafia (isl.)	H5
Manyara (lake)	G4
Masai (steppe)	G4
Mbarangandu (riv.)	G5
Mbemkuru (riv.)	G5
Meru (mt.)	G4
Mikumi Nat'l Park	G5
Natron (lake)	G4
Ngorongoro (crater)	F4
Njombe (riv.)	F5
Nyasa (lake)	F6
Olduvai Gorge (canyon)	G4
Pangani (riv.)	G4
Pemba (isl.)	H5
Rovuma (riv.)	G6
Rufiji (riv.)	G5
Ruaha Nat'l Park	F5
Rukwa (lake)	F5
Rungwa (riv.)	F5
Rungwe (mt.)	F5
Serengeti Nat'l Park	F4
Tanganyika (lake)	E5
Tarangire Nat'l Park	G4
Victoria (lake)	F4
Wami (riv.)	G5
Wembere (riv.)	F4
Zanzibar (isl.)	G5

UGANDA

CITIES and TOWNS

Arua 10,837	F3
Atura	F3
Butiaba 261	F3
Entebbe 21,096	F4
Fort Portal 7,947	F3
Gulu 18,170	F3
Hoima 2,339	F3
Jinja 52,509	F3
Kabale 8,234	E4
Kampala (cap.) 478,895	F3
Kasese 7,213	F3
Kilembe	F3
Kitgum 3,242	F3
Lira 7,340	F3
Masaka 12,987	F4
Masindi 2,100	F3
Mbale 23,544	F3
Mbarara 16,078	F4
Moroto 5,488	F3
Moyo 2,656	F3
Mubende 6,004	F3
Rhino Camp 198	F3
Soroti 8,130	F3
Tororo 15,977	F3

OTHER FEATURES

Albert (Mobuto Sese Seko) (lake)	F3
Edward (lake)	E4
Elgon (mt.)	F3
George (lake)	F4
Kabalega (falls)	F3
Kagalega Nat'l Park	F3
Kidepo Nat'l Park	F3
Kioga (lake)	F3
Margherita (mt.)	E3
Mobuto Sese Seko (lake)	F3
Owen Falls (dam)	F3
Ruwenzori (range)	E3
Sese (isls.)	F4
Victoria (lake)	F4
Virunga (range)	E4
Virunga Nat'l Park	F4

ZAIRE

PROVINCES

Bandundu 2,600,556	C4
Bas-Zaîre 1,504,361	B4
Equateur 2,431,812	D3
Haut-Zaîre 3,356,419	E3
Kasai-Occidental 2,433,861	D4
Kasai-Oriental 1,872,231	D5
Kinshasa 1,323,039	C4
Kivu 3,361,883	E4
Shaba 2,753,714	E5

CITIES and TOWNS

Aba 7,600	F3
Abumombazi	D3
Aketi 17,200	D3
Andoma	E3
Ango	E3
Ankoro	E5
Bagata	C4
Balangala	D3
Bambesa	E3
Bambili	E3
Banalia	E3
Banana	B5
Bandundu 74,467	C4
Baraka	E4
Basankusu	C3
Basoko 9,100	D3
Basongo	D4
Befale	D3
Bena-Dibele	D4
Beni 22,800	E3
Bikoro	C4
Boende 12,800	D4
Bokote	D4
Bokungu	D4
Bolobo 10,300	C4
Bolomba 7,200	C3
Boma 61,100	B5
Bomboma	C3
Bomongo	C3
Bondo 10,000	D3
Bongandanga 12,900	D3
Bosobolo 11,100	D3
Budjala	C3
Bukama	E5
Bukavu 134,861	E4
Bulungu 16,300	C4
Bumba 34,700	D3
Bunia 28,800	E3
Bunkeya 5,100	E6
Businga 11,000	D3
Busu-Djanoa	D3
Buta 19,800	D3
Butembo 27,800	E3
Dekese	D4
Demba 22,000	D5
Dibaya 11,400	D5
Dibaya-Lubue 7,900	C4
Dilolo 14,000	D6
Dimbelenge	D5
Djolu	D3
Djugu	F3
Dongo	C3
Doruma	E3
Dungu 9,100	E3
Etoile	E6
Faradje 10,400	E3
Feshi	C5
Fizi	E4
Gandajika 60,100	D5
Gemena 37,300	D3
Goma 48,600	E4
Gungu	C5
Idiofa	C4
Ikela	D4
Ilebo 32,200	D4
Imese	C3
Ingende	C4
Inongo 14,800	C4
Irumu 9,300	E3
Isangi	D3
Isiro 49,300	E3
Kabalo 22,600	E5
Kabambare	E4
Kabare 12,600	E4
Kabinda 60,500	D5
Kabongo 6,500	E5
Kahemba	C5
Kalehe	E4
Kalemie 62,300	E5
Kalima 27,500	E4
Kama 17,700	E4
Kambove 18,900	E6
Kamina 56,300	D5
Kampene 14,600	E4
Kananga 428,960	D5
Kanda-Kanda	D5
Kaniama	D5
Kapanga	D5
Kasaji	D6
Kasangulu 11,900	C4
Kasenga	E6
Kasenyi	E3
Kasese	E4
Kasongo 37,800	E4
Kasongo-Lunda	C5
Katako-Kombe	D4
Katenga	E5
Kazumba	D5
Kenge 17,500	C4
Kiambi	E5
Kibombo	E4
Kikwit 111,960	C5
Kilembe	C5
Kilwa	E5
Kilo	E3
Kinda	D5
Kiniama	E6
Kinshasa (cap.) 1,323,039	C4
Kipushi 32,900	E6
Kiri	C4
Kirundu	E4
Kisangani 229,596	E3
Kole, Kasai-Oriental	D4
Kole, Haut-Zaîre	E3
Kolwezi 81,600	E6
Komba	D3
Kongolo 14,800	E5
Kungu	C3
Kutu 10,000	C4
Kwamouth	C4
Libenge 12,500	C3
Likasi, Panda- 146,394	E6
Likati	D3
Lisala	D3
Lodja 20,300	D4
Lokolama	D4
Lomela	D4
Loto	D4
Luashi	D6
Lubefu	D4
Lubero	E4
Lubudi 6,000	E5
Lubumbashi 318,000	E6
Lubutu	E4
Luebo 21,800	D5
Luishia	E6
Luiza	D5
Lukolela, Equateur	C4
Lukolela, Kasai-Oriental	D5
Lukula 9,400	B5
Luozi 7,000	B5
Lusambo 13,100	D4
Makanza	C3
Malemba-Nkulu	E5
Mambasa 7,400	E3
Mangai 15,200	C4
Manono 44,500	E5
Masi-Manimba 6,300	C4
Masisi	E4
Matadi 110,436	B5
Mbandaka 107,910	C3
Mbanza-Ngungu 55,800	C5
Mbuji-Mayi 256,154	D5
Mitwaba	E5
Moanda 6,400	B5
Mobayi-Mbongo	D3
Moliro	E5
Monga	D3
Monkoto	D4
Mulongo	E5
Mungbere	E3
Mushie 13,700	C4
Mutshatsha	D6
Muyumba	E5
Mwadingusha	E6
Mwanza	E5
Mweka 24,900	D4
Mwene-Ditu 71,200	D5
Mwenga	E4
Niangara 9,200	E3
Niemba	E5
Nyunzu 11,300	E5
Opala	D4
Oshwe	C4
Panda-Likasi 146,394	E6
Pangi	E4
Penge	D5
Poko	E3
Popokabaka	C5
Port Kindu 42,800	E4
Punia	E4
Pweto	E5
Rutshuru	E4
Sakania	E6
Sampwe	E5
Sandoa	D5
Seke-Banza	B5
Sentery 24,300	E5
Shabunda 6,900	E4
Songololo 4,600	B5
Tenke	E6
Titule	E3
Tshela 10,700	B4
Tshikapa 38,900	D5
Tshofa	D5
Ubundu 6,300	E4
Uvira 15,900	E4
Virunga 21,900	E5
Waka	D3
Walikale	E4
Wamba 11,500	E3
Watsa 21,300	E3
Yahuma	D3
Yakoma	D3
Yangambi 22,600	D3
Zongo	C3

OTHER FEATURES

Albert (Mobuto Sese Seko) (lake)	F3
Aruwimi (riv.)	E3
Bomu (riv.)	D3
Boyoma (Stanley) (falls)	D3
Chicapa (riv.)	D5
Congo (riv.)	C4
Edward (lake)	E4
Elila (riv.)	E4
Fimi (riv.)	C4
Garamba Nat'l Park	E3
Giri (riv.)	C3
Itimbiri (riv.)	D3
Ituri (for.)	E3
Karisimbi (mt.)	E4
Kasai (riv.)	C4
Kivu (lake)	E4
Kwa (riv.)	C4
Kwango (riv.)	C5
Kwilu (riv.)	C5
Lindi (riv.)	E3
Livingstone (falls)	B5
Loange (riv.)	C5
Lokoro (riv.)	C4
Lomami (riv.)	D4
Lomela (riv.)	D4
Lowa (riv.)	E4
Lua (riv.)	C3
Lualaba (riv.)	E4
Luapula (riv.)	E6
Lubilash (riv.)	D5
Lufira (riv.)	E5
Luilaka (riv.)	C4
Lukenie (riv.)	D4
Lukuga (riv.)	E5
Lulua (riv.)	D5
Luvua (riv.)	E5
Mai-Ndombe (lake)	C4
Malebo (Stanley Pool) (lake)	C4
Margherita (mt.)	E3
Marungu (mts.)	E5
Mobuto Sese Seko (lake)	F3
Mweru (lake)	E5
Ruwenzori (range)	E3
Ruzizi (riv.)	E4
Salonga Nat'l Park	D4
Sankuru (riv.)	D4
Stanley (falls)	D3
Stanley Pool (lake)	C4
Tanganyika (lake)	E5
Tshuapa (riv.)	D4
Tumba (lake)	C4
Ubangi (riv.)	C3
Uele (riv.)	E3
Ulindi (riv.)	E4
Upemba (lake)	E5
Upemba Nat'l Park	E5
Virunga (range)	E4
Virunga Nat'l Park	E4
Zaire (Congo) (riv.)	C4

ZAMBIA

CITIES and TOWNS

Abercorn (Mbala) 11,179	F
Bancroft (Chililabombwe) 61,928	E
Broken Hill (Kabwe) 143,635	E
Chibwe	E
Chilanga 12,503	E
Chililabombwe 61,928	E
Chingola 145,869	E
Chinsali 4,211	F
Chipata 32,291	F
Choma 17,943	E
Fort Rosebery (Mansa) 34,801	E
Isoka 6,832	F
Kabompo 5,357	D
Kabwe 143,635	E
Kafue 29,794	E
Kalabo 7,398	D
Kalomo 5,878	E
Kaoma 6,731	D
Kapiri Mposhi 13,677	E
Kasama 38,093	F
Kasempa 3,063	E
Kataba	D
Kawambwa 7,235	E
Kitwe 314,794	E
Lealui	D
Livingstone 71,987	E
Luanshya 132,164	E
Lundazi 4,083	F
Lusaka (cap.) 538,469	E
Luwingu 3,763	E
Mansa 34,801	E
Mazabuka 29,602	E
Mbala 11,179	F
Mkushi 4,104	E
Mongu 24,919	D
Monze 13,141	E
Mpika 25,880	F
Mporokoso 6,008	F
Mpulungu 6,354	F
Mufulira 149,778	E
Mulobezi 2,589	E
Mumbwa 7,570	E
Mwinilunga 3,169	D
Nakonde 4,599	F
Namwala 3,008	E
Ndola 282,439	E
Petauke 7,531	F
Senanga 7,204	D
Serenje 6,008	F
Sesheke 3,500	D
Solwezi 15,032	E
Zambezi 8,166	D

OTHER FEATURES

Bangweulu (lake)	F
Barotseland (reg.)	D
Chambeshi (riv.)	F
Cuando (riv.)	D
Dongwe (riv.)	D
Kabompo (riv.)	D
Kafue (riv.)	E
Kafue Nat'l Park	E
Kalambo (falls)	F
Kariba (dam)	E
Kariba (lake)	E
Luangwa (riv.)	F
Luapula (riv.)	E
Lungwebungu (riv.)	D
Mosi-Oa-Tunya (Victoria) (falls)	E
Mulungushi (dam)	E
Mweru (lake)	E
Sunzu (mt.)	F
Tanganyika (lake)	E
Victoria (falls)	E
Zambezi (riv.)	D

Agriculture, Industry and Resources

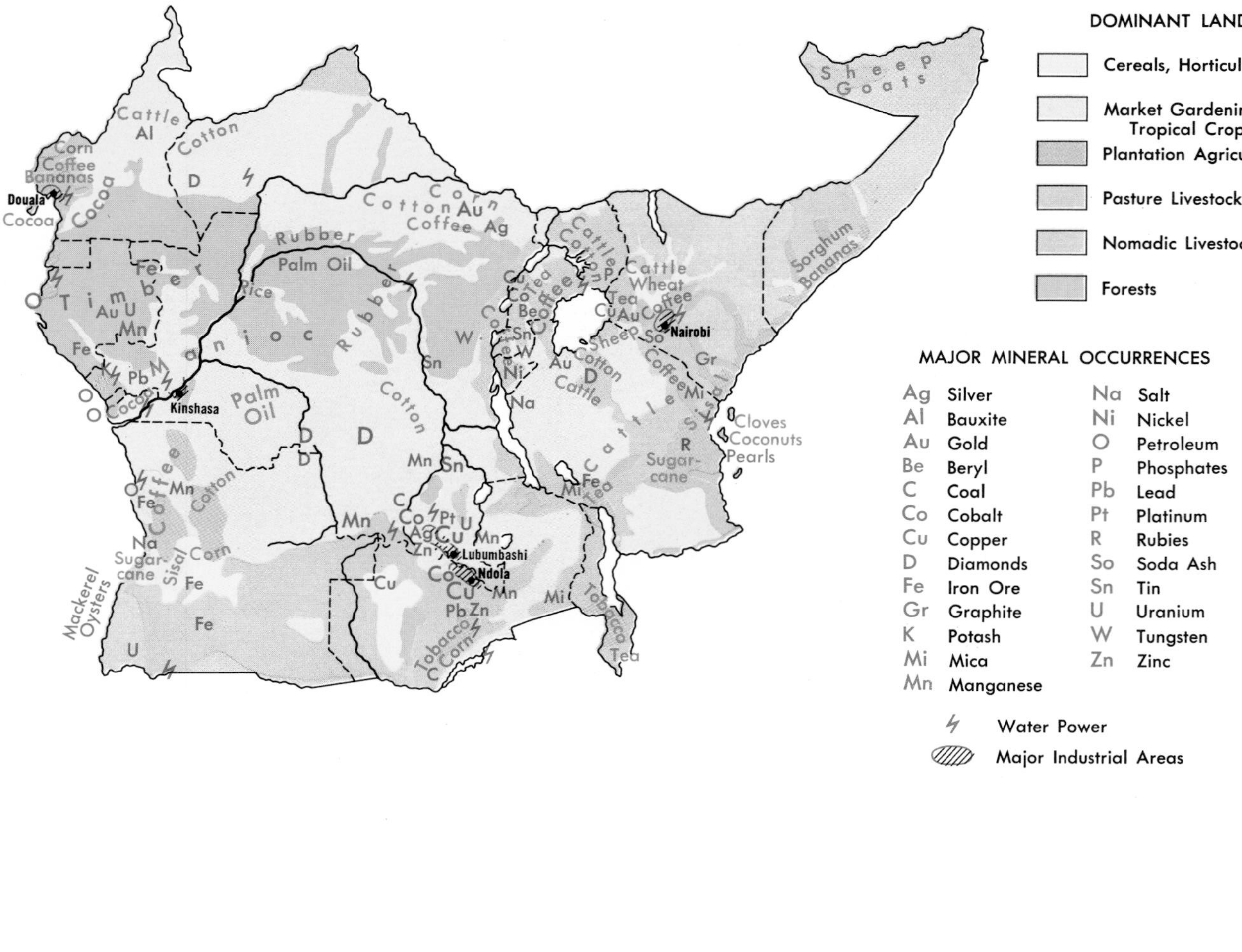
DOMINANT LAND USE
Cereals, Horticulture, Livestock
Market Gardening, Diversified Tropical Crops
Plantation Agriculture
Pasture Livestock
Nomadic Livestock Herding
Forests
MAJOR MINERAL OCCURRENCES
Ag Silver
Al Bauxite
Au Gold
Be Beryl
C Coal
Co Cobalt
Cu Copper
D Diamonds
Fe Iron Ore
Gr Graphite
K Potash
Mi Mica
Mn Manganese
Na Salt
Ni Nickel
O Petroleum
P Phosphates
Pb Lead
Pt Platinum
R Rubies
So Soda Ash
Sn Tin
U Uranium
W Tungsten
Zn Zinc
Water Power
Major Industrial Areas
Douala
Kinshasa
Nairobi
Lubumbashi
Ndola

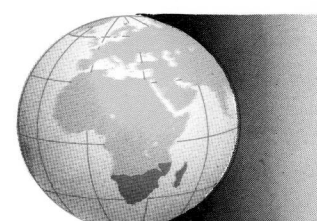

NAMIBIA

AREA 317,827 sq. mi. (823,172 sq. km.)
POPULATION 1,200,000
CAPITAL Windhoek
LARGEST CITY Windhoek
HIGHEST POINT Brandberg 8,550 ft. (2,606 m.)
MONETARY UNIT rand
MAJOR LANGUAGES Ovambo, Hottentot, Herero, Afrikaans, English
MAJOR RELIGIONS Tribal religions, Protestantism

BOTSWANA

AREA 224,764 sq. mi. (582,139 sq. km.)
POPULATION 819,000
CAPITAL Gaborone
LARGEST CITY Francistown
HIGHEST POINT Tsodilo Hill 5,922 ft. (1,805 m.)
MONETARY UNIT pula
MAJOR LANGUAGES Setswana, Shona, Bushman, English, Afrikaans
MAJOR RELIGIONS Tribal religions, Protestantism

ZIMBABWE

AREA 150,803 sq. mi. (390,580 sq. km.)
POPULATION 7,360,000
CAPITAL Harare
LARGEST CITY Harare
HIGHEST POINT Mt. Inyangani 8,517 ft. (2,596 m.)
MONETARY UNIT Zimbabwe dollar
MAJOR LANGUAGES English, Shona, Ndebele
MAJOR RELIGIONS Tribal religions, Protestantism

SOUTH AFRICA

AREA 455,318 sq. mi. (1,179,274 sq. km.)
POPULATION 23,771,970
CAPITALS Cape Town, Pretoria
LARGEST CITY Johannesburg
HIGHEST POINT Injasuti 11,182 ft. (3,408 m.)
MONETARY UNIT rand
MAJOR LANGUAGES Afrikaans, English, Xhosa, Zulu, Sesotho
MAJOR RELIGIONS Protestantism, Roman Catholicism, Islam, Hinduism, tribal religions

MOZAMBIQUE

AREA 303,769 sq. mi. (786,762 sq. km.)
POPULATION 12,130,000
CAPITAL Maputo
LARGEST CITY Maputo
HIGHEST POINT Mt. Binga 7,992 ft. (2,436 m.)
MONETARY UNIT metical
MAJOR LANGUAGES Makua, Thonga, Shona, Portuguese
MAJOR RELIGIONS Tribal religions, Roman Catholicism, Islam

MADAGASCAR

AREA 226,657 sq. mi. (587,041 sq. km.)
POPULATION 8,742,000
CAPITAL Antananarivo
LARGEST CITY Antananarivo
HIGHEST POINT Maromokotro 9,436 ft. (2,876 m.)
MONETARY UNIT Madagascar franc
MAJOR LANGUAGES Malagasy, French
MAJOR RELIGIONS Tribal religions, Roman Catholicism, Protestantism

MAURITIUS

AREA 790 sq. mi. (2,046 sq. km.)
POPULATION 959,000
CAPITAL Port Louis
LARGEST CITY Port Louis
HIGHEST POINT 2,711 ft. (826 m.)
MONETARY UNIT Mauritian rupee
MAJOR LANGUAGES English, French, French Creole, Hindi, Urdu
MAJOR RELIGIONS Hinduism, Christianity, Islam

LESOTHO

AREA 11,720 sq. mi. (30,355 sq. km.)
POPULATION 1,339,000
CAPITAL Maseru
LARGEST CITY Maseru
HIGHEST POINT 11,425 ft. (3,482 m.)
MONETARY UNIT loti
MAJOR LANGUAGES Sesotho, English
MAJOR RELIGIONS Tribal religions, Christianity

SWAZILAND

AREA 6,705 sq. mi. (17,366 sq. km.)
POPULATION 547,000
CAPITAL Mbabane
LARGEST CITY Manzini
HIGHEST POINT Emlembe 6,109 ft. (1,862 m.)
MONETARY UNIT lilangeni
MAJOR LANGUAGES siSwati, English
MAJOR RELIGIONS Tribal religions, Christianity

COMOROS

AREA 719 sq. mi. (1,862 sq. km.)
POPULATION 290,000
CAPITAL Moroni
LARGEST CITY Moroni
HIGHEST POINT Karthala 7,746 ft. (2,361 m.)
MONETARY UNIT CFA franc
MAJOR LANGUAGES Arabic, French, Swahili
MAJOR RELIGION Islam

SEYCHELLES

AREA 145 sq. mi. (375 sq. km.)
POPULATION 63,000
CAPITAL Victoria
LARGEST CITY Victoria
HIGHEST POINT Morne Seychellois 2,993 ft. (912 m.)
MONETARY UNIT Seychellois rupee
MAJOR LANGUAGES English, French, Creole
MAJOR RELIGION Roman Catholicism

RÉUNION

AREA 969 sq. mi. (2,510 sq. km.)
POPULATION 491,000
CAPITAL St-Denis

MAYOTTE

AREA 144 sq. mi. (373 sq. km.)
POPULATION 47,300
CAPITAL Dzaoudzi

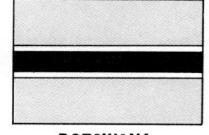
ZIMBABWE

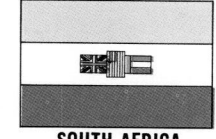
BOTSWANA

SOUTH AFRICA

LESOTHO

SWAZILAND

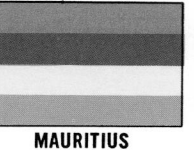
MOZAMBIQUE

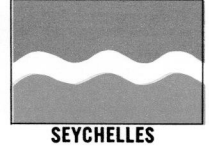
COMOROS

MADAGASCAR

MAURITIUS

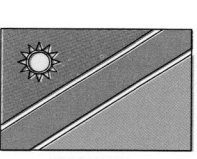
SEYCHELLES

NAMIBIA

Agriculture, Industry and Resources

DOMINANT LAND USE

- Cereals, Horticulture, Livestock
- Market Gardening, Diversified Tropical Crops
- Plantation Agriculture
- Pasture Livestock
- Nomadic Livestock Herding
- Forests
- Nonagricultural Land

⚡ Water Power
▨ Major Industrial Areas

MAJOR MINERAL OCCURRENCES

Ab	Asbestos	Cu	Copper	Mn	Manganese	Sb	Antimony
Ag	Silver	D	Diamonds	Na	Salt	Sn	Tin
Al	Bauxite	Fe	Iron Ore	Ni	Nickel	U	Uranium
Au	Gold	Gr	Graphite	P	Phosphates	V	Vanadium
Be	Beryl	Lt	Lithium	Pb	Lead	W	Tungsten
C	Coal	Mg	Magnesium	Pt	Platinum	Zn	Zinc
Cr	Chromium	Mi	Mica				

BOTSWANA

CITIES and TOWNS

Bobonong 2,184	D4
Dibete 1,599	D4
Dinokwe 560	D4
Francistown 22,000	D4
Gaborone (cap.) 21,000	C4
Ghanzi 1,198	C4
Gumare 689	C3
Kalkfontein 1,532	C4
Kang 1,151	C4
Kanye 10,664	C5
Kasane 1,476	D3
Lehututu 988	C4
Lephepe 1,355	D4
Lobatse 11,936	D5
Machaneng 725	D4
Mahalapye 12,056	D4
Maun 9,614	C4
Mochudi 6,945	D4
Molepolole 9,448	C4
Nata 873	D4
Orapa 1,269	D4
Palapye 5,217	D4
Ramotswa 7,991	C4
Selebi-Pikwe 20,572	D4
Serowe 15,723	D4
Serule 1,718	D4
Shakawe 1,767	C3
Shashe 1,337	D4
Shoshong 3,132	D4
Tonota 4,494	D4
Tsau 427	C4
Tshabong 983	C5
Tshane 604	C4

OTHER FEATURES

Chobe (riv.)	C3
Kalahari (des.)	C4
Limpopo (riv.)	D4
Makgadikgadi (salt pan)	D3
Molopo (riv.)	C5
Ngami (lake)	C4
Ngamiland (reg.)	C3
Nossob (riv.)	B4
Okovango (swamps)	C3
Orange (riv.)	B5
Shashe (riv.)	D4
Tati (riv.)	D4

COMOROS

CITIES and TOWNS

Fomboni 3,229	G2
Mitsamiouli 3,196	G2
Moroni (cap.) 12,000	G2
Mutsamudu 7,652	G2

OTHER FEATURES

Anjouan (Nzwani) (isl.) 83,486	G2
Grand Comoro (Njazidja) (isl.) 118,443	G2
Mohéli (Mwali) (isl.) 9,525	G2

LESOTHO

CITIES and TOWNS

Leribe 5,200	D5
Mafeteng 4,600	D5
Maseru (cap.) 71,500	D5
Mohaleshoek 3,600	D6

MADAGASCAR

PROVINCES

Antananarivo 2,167,973	H3
Antsiranana 597,982	H2
Fianarantsoa 1,804,365	H4
Mahajanga 819,750	H3
Toamasina 1,179,660	H3
Toliara 1,034,114	G4

CITIES and TOWNS

Ambalavao 6,988	H4
Ambanja 12,258	H2
Ambato Boeny 3,317	H3
Ambatofinandrahana 2,161	H4
Ambatolampy 11,539	H3
Ambatomainty 1,276	H3
Ambatondrazaka 18,044	H3
Ambilobe 9,415	H2
Amboasary 2,420	H4
Ambodifototra 1,112	J3
Ambohimahasoa 5,851	H4
Ambositra 16,780	H4
Ambovombe 1,375	H5
Ampanihy 2,262	G4
Analalava 5,184	H2
Andapa 6,275	H2
Andilamena 3,512	H3
Androka 1,068	G5
Ankazoabo 1,677	G4
Antalaha 17,541	J2
Antananarivo (cap.) 451,808	H3
Antsalova 2,202	G3
Antsirabe 32,979	H3
Antsiranana 40,443	H2
Antsohihy 8,721	H2
Arivonimamo 8,497	H3
Bealanana 2,299	H2
Befandriana 3,004	H3
Bekily 1,933	G4
Belo-Tsiribihina 4,403	G3
Beroroha 1,742	G4
Besalampy 2,874	G3
Betioky 3,964	G4
Betroka 3,943	H4
Brickaville (Vohibinany) 1,741	H3
Diégo-Suarez (Antsiranana) 40,443	H2
Fandriana 4,139	H4
Faradofay 13,805	H5
Farafangana 10,817	H4
Fenoarivo, Toamasina 7,696	H3
Fianarantsoa 68,054	H4
Fort-Dauphin (Faradofay) 13,805	H5
Foulpointe	H3
Hell-Ville 6,183	H2
Ifanadiana 1,111	H4
Ihosy 4,521	H4
Ivohibe 1,254	H4
Madirovalo 3,991	H3
Maevatanana 7,197	H3
Mahabo 4,941	G4
Mahanoro 5,041	H3
Maintirano 6,375	G3
Majunga 65,864	H3
Manakara 19,768	H4
Mananara 3,253	J3
Mananjary 14,638	H4
Mandabe 1,757	G4
Mandritsara 6,826	H3
Manja 4,151	G4
Manombo 2,908	G4
Maroantsetra 6,645	H3
Marovoay 20,253	H3

(continued on following page)

Topography

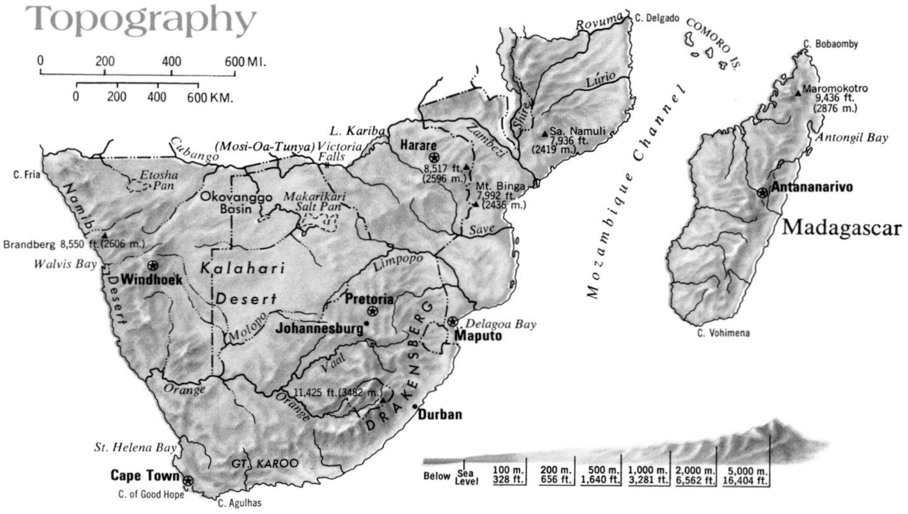
0 200 400 600 MI.
0 200 400 600 KM.
Rovuma
C. Delgado
COMORO IS.
C. Bobaomby
Lúrio
Maromokotro 9,436 ft. (2876 m.)
Antongil Bay
L. Kariba
(Mosi-Oa-Tunya) Victoria Falls
Harare
Sa. Namuli 7,936 ft. (2419 m.)
Cubango
C. Fria
Etosha Pan
Okovanggo Basin
Makarikari Salt Pan
8,517 ft. (2596 m.)
Mt. Binga 7,992 ft. (2436 m.)
Mozambique Channel
Antananarivo
Madagascar
Save
Brandberg 8,550 ft. (2606 m.)
Walvis Bay
Windhoek
Kalahari
Desert
Limpopo
Namib Desert
Pretoria
Johannesburg
Molopo
Delagoa Bay
Maputo
C. Vohimena
Vaal
Orange
DRAKENSBERG
11,425 ft. (3482 m.)
Durban
St. Helena Bay
GT. KAROO
Cape Town
C. of Good Hope
C. Agulhas
Below Sea Level
100 m. 328 ft.
200 m. 656 ft.
500 m. 1,640 ft.
1,000 m. 3,281 ft.
2,000 m. 6,562 ft.
5,000 m. 16,404 ft.

Miandrivazo 2,371 .... G3
Midongy Atsimo 1,068 .... H4
Mitsinjo 3,118 .... H3
Moramanga 10,806 .... H3
Morombe 6,967 .... G4
Morondava 19,061 .... G3
Nosy-Varika 1,252 .... H4
Port-Bergé 4,734 .... H3
Sambava 6,215 .... J2
Soanierana-Ivongo 2,876 .... H3
Sosumav 10,946 .... H2
Tamatave (Toamasina) 77,395 .... H3
Tambohorano 1,383 .... G3
Tananarive (Antananarivo) (cap.) 451,808 .... H3
Tangainony 6,952 .... H4
Toamasina 77,395 .... H3
Toliara (Tuléar) 45,676 .... G4
Tsihombe 1,008 .... H5
Tsiroanomandidy 11,444 .... H3
Tsivory 1,036 .... H4
Vangaindrano 3,249 .... H4
Vatomandry 4,202 .... H3
Vohibinany 1,741 .... H3
Vohimarina (Vohémar) 4,289 .... J2
Vohipeno 2,736 .... H4

OTHER FEATURES

Alaotra (lake) H3
Amber (Bobaomby) (cape) H2
Antongil (bay) J3
Betsiboka (riv.) H3
Bobaomby (Amber) (cape) H2
Mangoky (riv.) G4
Mangoro (riv.) H3
Maromokotro (mt.) H2
Masoala (pen.) J3
Mozambique (chan.) G3
Nosy Be (isl.) H2
Nosy Boraha (isl.) J3
Onilahy (riv.) G4
Saint-André (cape) G3
Sainte-Marie (Vohimena) (cape) G5
Sainte-Marie (Nosy Boraha) (isl.) J3
Tsiafajavona (mt.) H3
Tsiribihina (riv.) G3
Vohimena (cape) G5

MAURITIUS

CITIES and TOWNS

Curepipe 52,709 .... G5
Mahébourg 15,463 .... G5
Port Louis (cap.) 141,022 .... G5
Poudre d'Or 1,799 .... G5
Quatre Bornes 51,638 .... G5
Souillac 3,361 .... G5

OTHER FEATURES

Mascarene (isls.) F5

MAYOTTE

CITIES and TOWNS

Dzaoudzi (cap.) 196 .... H2

MOZAMBIQUE

PROVINCES

Cabo Delgado 940,000 .... F2
Gaza 999,900 .... E4
Inhambane 977,000 .... E4
Manica 541,200 .... E4
Maputo 491,800 .... E5
Maputo (city) 755,300 .... E5
Nampula 2,402,700 .... F2
Niassa 514,100 .... F2
Sofala 1,055,200 .... E3
Tete 831,000 .... E3
Zambézia 2,500,000 .... F3

CITIES and TOWNS

Alto Molócuè 415 .... F3
Angoche 1,714 .... G3
Bartolomeu Dias○ 6,102 .... F4
Beira 46,293 .... F3
Beira* 130,398 .... F3
Bela Vista 851 .... E5
Benga 1,398 .... E3
Caia 1,363 .... E3
Catandica 663 .... E3
Chemba 588 .... E3
Chibuto 23,763 .... E4
Chicualacuala 2,050 .... E4
Chimoio 4,507 .... E3
Chinde 742 .... F3
Cóbuè○ 770 .... F2
Cuamba 1,416 .... F2
Dona Ana (Mutarara) 686 .... F3
Dondo 2,112 .... F3
Errego 418 .... F3
Espungabera 405 .... E4
Fíngoè 1,137 .... E2
Funhalouro○ 42,366 .... E4
Gorongoza 435 .... E3
Guija 530 .... E4
Homoíne 1,122 .... E4
Ibo 1,015 .... G2
Inhambane 4,975 .... F4
Inhaminga 1,607 .... F3
Inharrime 856 .... F4
Lichinga 3,011 .... F2
Lumbo○ 11,080 .... G3
Lúrio○ 13,417 .... G2
Mabalane○ 13,158 .... E4
Mabote○ 28,970 .... E4
Machanga○ 15,754 .... F4
Machaze○ 42,255 .... E4
Macia 1,203 .... E4
Macomia 730 .... F2
Magude 1,502 .... E5
Malema 430 .... F2
Mandié○ 24,382 .... E3
Mandimba○ 7,634 .... F2
Manhiça 1,680 .... E5
Maniamba○ 2,045 .... F2
Manica 1,529 .... E3
Manjacaze 641 .... E5
Maputo (cap.) 755,300 .... E5
Marracuene 1,342 .... E5
Marromeu 1,330 .... F3
Marrupa 824 .... F2
Massangena○ 3,301 .... E4
Massinga 517 .... F4
Maxixe 902 .... F4
Meconta 1,051 .... F3
Memba 379 .... G2
Metangula 1,502 .... F2
Milanje 1,048 .... F3
Moamba 643 .... E5
Moçambique 1,730 .... G3
Mocímboa da Praia 935 .... G2
Mocuba 2,293 .... F3
Moma 433 .... F3
Monapo 902 .... G2
Montepuez 2,837 .... F2
Morrumbala 415 .... F3
Morrumbene 1,121 .... F4
Mualama○ 34,992 .... F3
Mucojo○ 15,867 .... G2
Mueda 1,583 .... F2
Murrupula 444 .... F3
Mutarara (Dona Ana) 686 .... F3
Nacala 4,601 .... G2
Namacurra 399 .... F3
Namapa 440 .... F2
Nametil 453 .... F3
Nampula 23,072 .... F3
Negomane○ 656 .... F2
Nova Lusitânia 1,363 .... E3
Nova Mambone 883 .... F4
Nova Sofala 274 .... F4
Pafúri○ 2,599 .... E4
Pemba 3,629 .... G2
Quelimane 10,522 .... F3
Quionga○ 3,181 .... G2
Quissico 2,615 .... F4
Ribáuè 437 .... F3
Songo 1,350 .... E3
Tete 4,549 .... E3
Ulongue 451 .... E2
Vila de Sena○ 21,074 .... E3
Vilanculos 887 .... E4
Xai-Xai 5,234 .... E5

OTHER FEATURES

Angoche (isl.) G3
Bazaruto, Ilha do (isl.) F4
Binga (mt.) E3
Changane (riv.) E4
Chilwa (lake) F3
Delagoa (bay) E5
Delgado (cape) G2
Ligonha (riv.) F3
Limpopo (riv.) E4
Lugenda (riv.) F2
Lúrio (riv.) F2
Mazoe (riv.) E3
Mozambique (chan.) G3
Namuli, Serra (mt.) F3
Nyasa (lake) E2
Olifants (riv.) D4
Rovuma (riv.) F2
São Sebastião (pt.) F4
Save (riv.) E4
Shire (riv.) E3
Zambezi (riv.) E3

NAMIBIA (SOUTH-WEST AFRICA)

CITIES and TOWNS

Aroab 783 .... B5
Aus 767 .... B5
Berseba B5
Bethanie 1,207 .... B5
Gibeon B5
Gobabis 4,428 .... B4
Grootfontein 4,627 .... B3
Kalkfeld 587 .... B4
Kamanjab 713 .... A3
Karasburg 2,693 .... B5
Karibib 1,653 .... B4
Katima Mulilo C3
Keetmanshoop 10,297 .... B5
Khorixas 1,299 .... A4
Koes 514 .... B5
Lüderitz 6,642 .... A5
Maltahöhe 1,313 .... B4
Mariental 4,629 .... B4
Ohopoho A3
Okahandja 1,688 .... B4
Omaruru 2,783 .... B4
Ondangua B3
Ongwediva B3
Oranjemund 2,594 .... B5
Otavi 1,814 .... B3
Otjiwarongo 8,018 .... B4
Outjo 2,545 .... B4
Rehoboth 5,363 .... B4
Runtu 521 .... B3
Stampriet 271 .... B4
Swakopmund 5,681 .... A4
Tsumeb 12,338 .... B3
Usakos 2,334 .... B4
Warmbad 810 .... B5
Windhoek (cap.) 61,369 .... B4
Witvlei 303 .... B4

OTHER FEATURES

Brandberg (mt.) A4
Caprivi Strip (reg.) C3
Chobe (riv.) C3
Cubango (riv.) B3
Damaraland (reg.) B4
Diamond Coast (reg.) A5
Elephant (riv.) B5
Etosha Pan (salt pan) B3
Fish (riv.) B5
Great Namaland (reg.) B4
Hottentot (bay) A5
Kalahari (des.) C4
Kaokoveld (reg.) A3
Kaukauveld (mts.) C3
Namib (des.) A3
Nossob (riv.) B4
Okovango (riv.) C3
Ovamboland (reg.) B3
Skeleton Coast (reg.) A3
Swakop (riv.) B4
Zambezi (riv.) C3

REUNION

CITIES and TOWNS

Le Port 21,564 .... F5
Saint-André 6,584 .... G5
Saint-Benoît 7,778 .... G5
Saint-Denis (cap.) 80,075 .... F5
Saint-Denis* 104,603 .... F5
Saint-Joseph 8,928 .... G6
Saint-Louis 10,252 .... F5
Saint-Pierre 21,817 .... F6

OTHER FEATURES

Bassas da India (isl.) F4
Europa (isl.) G4
Glorioso (isls.) H2
Juan de Nova (isl.) G3
Piton des Neiges (mt.) G5

SEYCHELLES

CITIES and TOWNS

Anse Boileau† 3,420 .... H5
Anse Royale† 3,182 .... H5
Cascade† 2,600 .... H5
Victoria (cap.) 15,559 .... H5
Victoria* 23,012 .... H5

OTHER FEATURES

Aldabra (isls.) H1
Assumption (isl.) H1
Astove (isl.) H2
Cosmoledo (isls.) H1
Frigate (isl.) J5
La Digue (isl.) J5
Mahé (isl.) H5
North (isl.) H5
Praslin (isl.) H5
Silhouette (isl.) H5

SOUTH AFRICA

PROVINCES

Cape Province 5,543,506 .... C6
Natal 5,722,215 .... E5
Orange Free State 1,833,216 .... D5
Transvaal 10,673,033 .... D4

AUTONOMOUS REPUBLICS

Bophuthatswana 1,200,000 .... D5
Ciskei 345,191 .... D6
Transkei 2,000,000 .... D6
Venda 450,000 .... E4

CITIES and TOWNS

Aberdeen 4,968 .... C6
Adelaide 7,227 .... D6
Alberton 23,988 .... H6
Alexandra 57,040 .... H6
Alexander Bay 2,675 .... B5
Aliwal North 12,311 .... D6
Barberton 12,382 .... E5
Barkly East 4,023 .... D6
Beaufort West 17,862 .... C6
Bellville 49,026 .... F6
Benoni 151,294 .... J6
Benoni□ 164,543 .... J6
Bethlehem 29,918 .... D5
Bethulie 4,918 .... D6
Bloemfontein 149,836 .... C5
Bloemfontein□ 182,329 .... C5
Bloubergstrand 378 .... E6
Boksburg 106,126 .... J6
Botrivier 743 .... F7
Brakpan 73,210 .... J6
Brandvlei 1,337 .... B6
Bredasdorp 5,264 .... B6
Brentwood Park 5,296 .... J6
Brits 12,182 .... D5
Britstown 3,039 .... C6
Burgersdorp 8,340 .... D6
Butterworth (Gcuwa) 2,769 .... D6
Caledon 5,406 .... G7
Calvinia 6,386 .... B6
Cape Town (cap.) 697,514 .... E6
Cape Town□ 833,731 .... E6
Carltonville 40,641 .... G7
Carnarvon 5,199 .... C6
Ceres 9,230 .... B6
Christiana 6,882 .... D5
Clanwilliam 2,724 .... B6
Clayville 3,994 .... H6
Colesberg 7,088 .... D6
Constantia 7,220 .... E6
Cradock 20,822 .... D6
De Aar 18,057 .... C6
Delmas 6,424 .... J6
Dibeng 945 .... C5
Douglas 4,335 .... C5
Dundee 17,162 .... E5
Dunnottar 3,089 .... J6
Durban 736,852 .... E5
Durban□ 975,494 .... E5
Durbanville 7,438 .... F6
East London 119,727 .... D6
East London□ 126,671 .... D6
Edenburg 3,710 .... D5
Edendale 41,194 .... D5
Edenvale 25,126 .... H6
Eersterivier 1,459 .... F6
Elliot 3,739 .... D6
Eloff 1,134 .... J6
Elsburg 3,501 .... H6
Elsiesrivier 63,706 .... F6
Empangeni 7,532 .... E5
Ermelo 19,036 .... E5
Eshowe 4,552 .... E5
Estcourt 10,922 .... D5
Ficksburg 9,504 .... D5
Firgrove 2,551 .... F6
Fort Beaufort 11,640 .... D6
Franschhoek 1,216 .... F6
Garies 1,339 .... B6
Gcuwa 2,769 .... D6
George 24,625 .... C6
Germiston 221,972 .... H6
Germiston□ 293,257 .... H6
Glencoe 10,513 .... E5
Goodwood 31,592 .... F6
Gordon's Bay 1,112 .... F7
Graaff-Reinet 22,392 .... C6
Grabouw 4,286 .... F7
Grahamstown 41,302 .... D6
Grassy Park 32,709 .... E6
Greytown 9,028 .... E5
Griquatown 2,996 .... C5
Halfway House 3,639 .... H6
Harrismith 16,082 .... D5
Hawston 2,501 .... G7
Heidelberg 12,521 .... J7
Heilbron 8,258 .... D5
Hermanus 4,956 .... G7
Hopetown 3,273 .... C5
Houtbaai 5,691 .... E6
Howick 12,429 .... E5
Humansdorp 4,215 .... C6
Ingwavuma 718 .... E5
Jagersfontein 4,142 .... D5
Jameson Park 2,280 .... J7
Johannesburg 654,232 .... H6
Johannesburg□ 1,417,818 .... H6
Keimoes 4,534 .... C5
Kempton Park 37,205 .... J6
Kenhardt 3,230 .... C5
Kimberley 105,258 .... C5
Kimberley□ 108,609 .... C5
King William's Town 15,798 .... D6
Kirkwood 5,151 .... D6
Kleinmond 1,115 .... F7
Klerksdorp 63,558 .... D5
Knysna 13,479 .... C6
Koffiefontein 3,672 .... D5
Kokstad 10,227 .... D6
Kraaifontein 10,286 .... F6
Kroonstad 51,988 .... D5
Krugersdorp 92,725 .... H6
Kuilsrivier 8,132 .... F6
Kuruman 5,758 .... C5
Ladybrand 8,757 .... D5
Ladysmith 28,920 .... D5
Lambert's Bay 3,247 .... B6
Lombardy 3,395 .... H6
Louis Trichardt 8,906 .... E4
Lydenburg 7,427 .... E4
Macassar 882 .... F6
Maclear 3,279 .... D6
Mafikeng (Mafeking) 6,515 .... C5
Malmesbury 9,314 .... B6
Margate 4,410 .... E6
Matatiele 3,853 .... D6
Melkbosstrand 453 .... E6
Messina 12,121 .... D4
Meyerton 8,654 .... H7
Middelburg, C. of Good Hope 11,121 .... D6
Middelburg, Transvaal 26,942 .... D5
Milnerton 10,893 .... F6
Modderfontein 8,538 .... H6
Molteno 5,825 .... D6
Montagu 5,504 .... C6
Moorreesburg 4,945 .... B6
Mossel Bay 17,574 .... C6
Nababeep 8,293 .... B5
Nelspruit 25,092 .... E5
Newcastle 14,407 .... E5
Nigel 41,179 .... J7
Noupoort 7,403 .... C6
Nyanga 15,655 .... F6
Nylstroom 6,906 .... D4
Odendaalsrus 15,603 .... D5
Okiep 4,983 .... B5
Oudtshoorn 26,907 .... C6
Paarl 49,244 .... F6
Parow 60,768 .... F6
Parys 17,447 .... D5
Phalaborwa 7,543 .... E4
Pietermaritzburg 114,822 .... E5
Pietermaritzburg□ 174,179 .... E5
Pietersburg 27,174 .... D4
Piet Retief 10,056 .... D5
Piketberg 3,638 .... B6
Pinelands 11,769 .... F6
Pinetown 22,721 .... E6
Pniel 1,596 .... F6
Port Alfred 8,640 .... D6
Port Elizabeth 392,231 .... D6
Port Elizabeth□ 413,961 .... D6
Port Nolloth 2,893 .... B5
Port Saint Johns (Umzimbuvu) 1,817 .... D6
Port Shepstone 5,581 .... E6
Postmasburg 9,020 .... C5

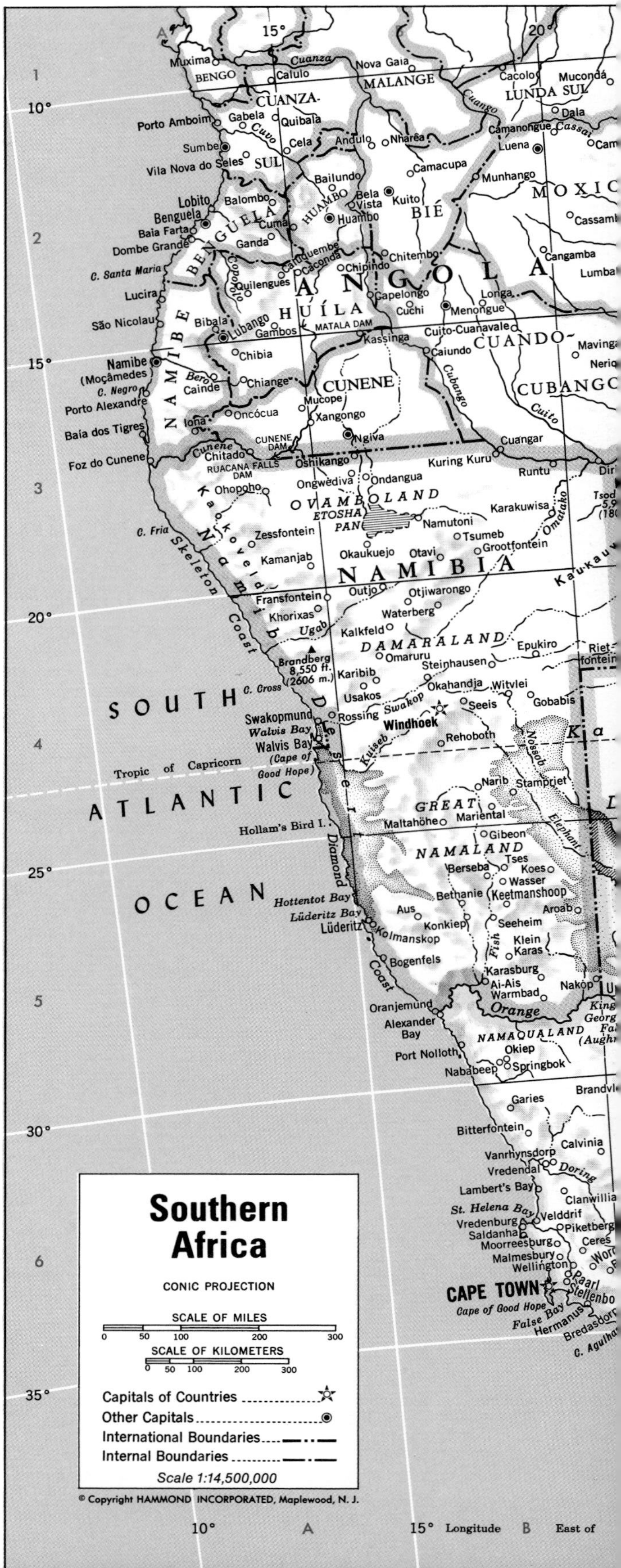
Southern Africa
CONIC PROJECTION
SCALE OF MILES
0 50 100 200 300
SCALE OF KILOMETERS
0 50 100 200 300
Capitals of Countries
Other Capitals
International Boundaries
Internal Boundaries
Scale 1:14,500,000
© Copyright HAMMOND INCORPORATED, Maplewood, N. J.
ANGOLA
NAMIBIA
SOUTH ATLANTIC OCEAN
Tropic of Capricorn
Windhoek
Walvis Bay
Swakopmund
Lüderitz
CAPE TOWN
Cape of Good Hope
10° A 15° Longitude B East of

Potchefstroom 57,443 .....D5
Potgietersrus 6,667 .....D4
Pretoria (cap.) 545,450 .....D5
Pretoria□ 573,283 .....D5
Prieska 8,521 .....C6
Prince Albert 3,346 .....C6
Queenstown 39,304 .....D6
Randburg 43,257 .....H6
Randfontein 50,481 .....G6
Reitz 5,650 .....D5
Rensburg 2,042 .....J7
Richards Bay 598 .....E5
Richmond 3,185 .....D5
Riversdale 6,165 .....C6
Robertson 10,237 .....C6
Roodepoort 115,366 .....H6
Rustenburg 22,303 .....D5
Saldanha 4,994 .....B6
Senekal 9,124 .....D5
Sesfontein 2,731 .....J6
Sishen 2,692 .....C5
Somerset East 10,383 .....D6
Somerset West 11,828 .....J6
Soweto 602,043 .....H6
Springbok 4,357 .....B5
Springs 142,812 .....J6
Springs□ 146,831 .....J6

Standerton 21,038 .....D5
Stanger 11,064 .....E5
Stellenbosch 29,955 .....F6
Strand 24,503 .....F7
Stutterheim 12,077 .....D6
Sundra 2,088 .....J6
Swellendam 6,423 .....C6
Taung 1,316 .....C5
Tembisa 81,821 .....H6
Thabazimbi 6,711 .....D4
Thohoyandou E5
Tzaneen 4,331 .....E5
Ubombo□ 3,697 .....E5
Ulundi E5
Umtata 25,216 .....D6
Umzimkuvu 1,817 .....D6
Umzinto 5,272 .....D6
Upington 28,632 .....C5
Vaalsdrop 5,699 .....C5
Vanderbijl Park 78,754 .....H7
Vanrhynsdorp 2,279 .....B6
Veldrif 3,361 .....B6
Ventersdorp G6
Vereeniging 172,549 .....H6
Vereeniging□ 200,078 .....J6
Victoria West 3,949 .....C6
Villiersdorp 2,349 .....G6

Vishoek 6,721 .....E7
Volksrust 10,238 .....D5
Vrede 6,309 .....D5
Vredenburg 6,094 .....B6
Vredendal 5,377 .....B6
Vryburg 16,916 .....C5
Vryheid 16,992 .....E5
Walvis Bay 21,725 .....A4
Warmbad 8,343 .....D5
Warrenton 9,614 .....C5
Waterval-Bo 6,951 .....D5
Welkom 67,472 .....D5
Wellington 17,092 .....B6
Westonaria 36,253 .....H7
Willowmore 3,740 .....C6
Winburg 6,761 .....D5
Witbank 37,456 .....D5
Wolmaransstad 7,219 .....D5
Worcester 41,198 .....B6
Zastron 4,483 .....D6
Zeerust 6,972 .....D5
Zwelitsha 22,131 .....D6

OTHER FEATURES

Addo Nat'l Park D6
Agulhas (cape) B6
Bot (riv.) G7

Bredasdorp Nat'l Park C6
Cape (pen.) E7
Crocodile (riv.) H6
Drakensberg (range) D5
False (bay) F7
Good Hope (cape) B6
Great Fish (riv.) D6
Great Karoo (reg.) C6
Great Kei (riv.) D6
Griqualand West (reg.) C5
Groote (riv.) C5
Hartbees (riv.) C5
King George's (falls) C5
Klip (riv.) H6
Kruger Nat'l Park E4
Limpopo (riv.) D4
Molopo (riv.) C5
Mountain Zebra Nat'l Park D6
Olifants (riv.) B5
Orange (riv.) C5
Palmiet (riv.) B5
Plettenberg (bay) C6
Pondoland (reg.) D6
Robben (isl.) E7
Royal Natal Nat'l Park D5
Saint Helena (bay) B6
Saint Lucia (lake) E5

Sak (riv.) C6
Sand (riv.) D4
Slangkop (pt.) E7
Sneeuwkop (mt.) F6
Table (bay) B6
Table (mt.) B6
Vaal (riv.) D5
Walvis (bay) A4
Witwatersberg (range) A4
Witwatersrand (reg.) H7
Zonderend (riv.) G6
Zululand (reg.) E5

SWAZILAND
CITIES and TOWNS

Manzini 28,837 .....E5
Mbabane (cap.) 23,109 .....E5
Siteki 1,362 .....E5

ZIMBABWE
CITIES and TOWNS

Beitbridge 1,986 .....E4
Bindura 17,000 .....E3

Bulawayo 359,000 .....D3
Chegutu 12,000 .....E3
Chimanimani 667 .....E3
Chinhoyi 25,000 .....D3
Chipinge 2,350 .....E4
Chivhu 1,669 .....E3
Dete 2,473 .....D3
Gwaai□ 2,710 .....D3
Gwanda 2,049 .....D3
Gweru 68,000 .....D3
Harare (Salisbury) (cap.) 601,000 .....E3
Hwange 33,000 .....D3
Inyanga 733 .....E3
Kadoma 32,000 .....D3
Kariba 3,943 .....D3
Kwekwe 54,000 .....D3
Marondera 23,000 .....E3
Masvingo 22,000 .....E3
Matopos 11,330 .....D3
Mount Darwin 904 .....E3
Mutare 61,000 .....E3
Mvuma 1,525 .....D3
Mwenezi 7,830 .....D4
Plumtree 2,041 .....D3
Rusape 5,286 .....E3
Salisbury (Harare) (cap.) 601,000 .....E3
Shamva 785 .....E3
Shurugwi 8,387 .....E3

Tuilo 340 .....D4
West Nicholson 1,929 .....D4
Zvishavane 20,000 .....E4

OTHER FEATURES

Inyanga Nat'l Park E3
Kariba (lake) D3
Lundi (riv.) D4
Masoala (reg.) E3
Mashonaland (reg.) 1,875,700 .....E3
Matabeleland (reg.) 969,220 .....D3
Mazoe (riv.) E3
Mushandike Nat'l Park D3
Sabi (riv.) D3
Shangani (riv.) D3
Shashe (riv.) D4
Umvukwe (range) D3
Victoria (falls) D3
Zambezi (riv.) D3
Zimbabwe Nat'l Park E4

*City and suburbs.
†Population of parish.
oPopulation of subdivision.
□Population of urban area.

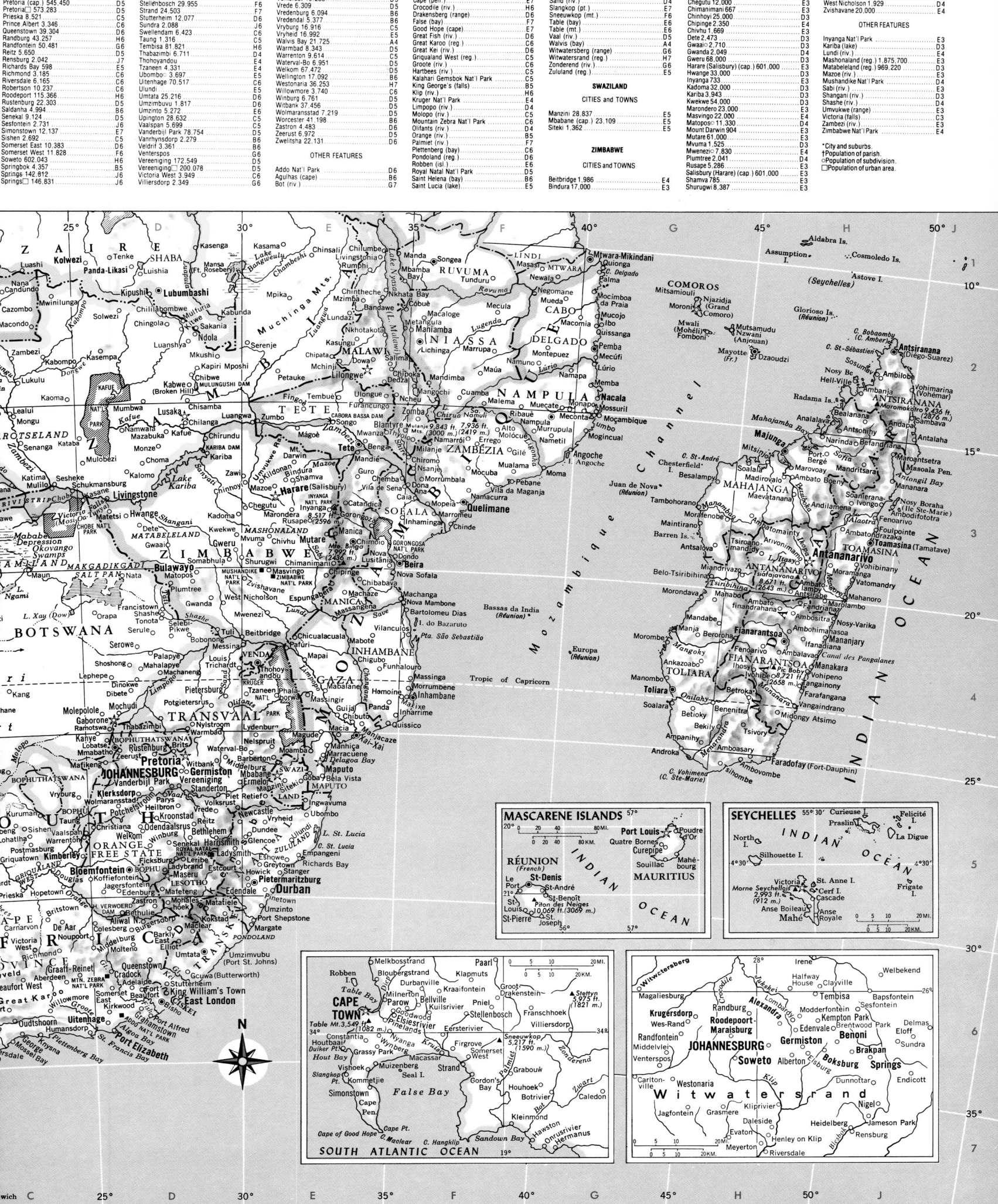

South America

AZIMUTHAL EQUAL-AREA PROJECTION

MILES
0   100   200   400   600

KILOMETERS
0   100 200   400   600

Capitals of Countries .... ⊛
Other Capitals .... ⊛
International Boundaries ....
Canals ....

Scale 1:27,000,000

© Copyright HAMMOND INCORPORATED, Maplewood, N.J.

Population Distribution

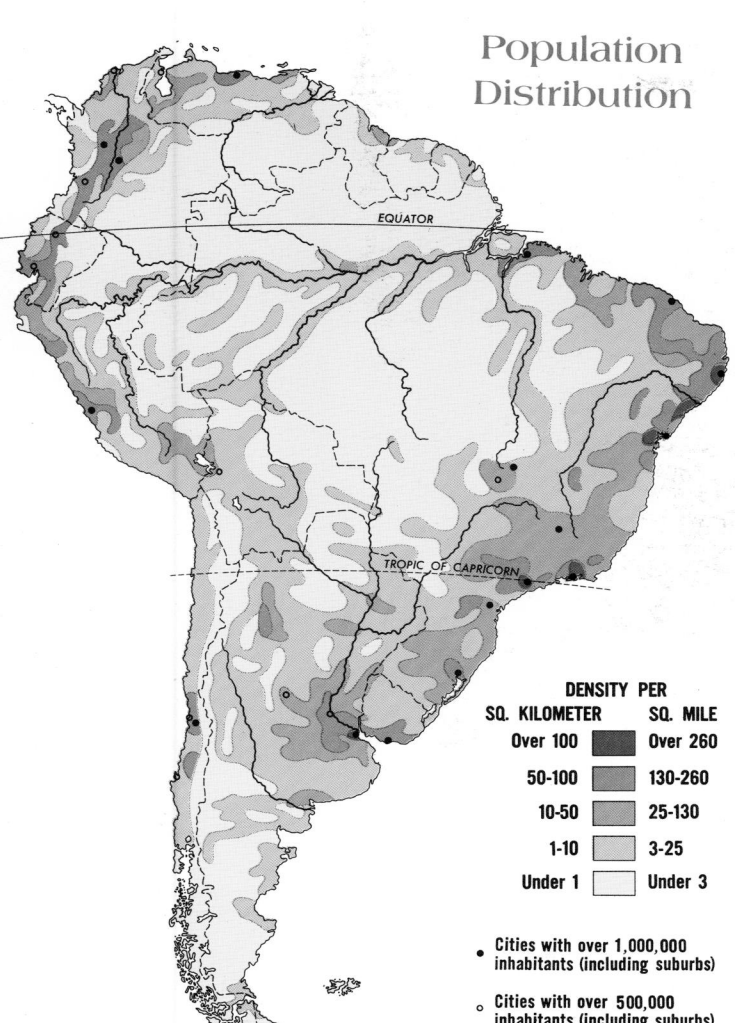

AREA 6,875,000 sq. mi. (17,806,250 sq. km.)
POPULATION 245,000,000
LARGEST CITY São Paulo
HIGHEST POINT Cerro Aconcagua 22,831 ft. (6,959 m.)
LOWEST POINT Salina Grande -131 ft. (-40 m.)

Vegetation

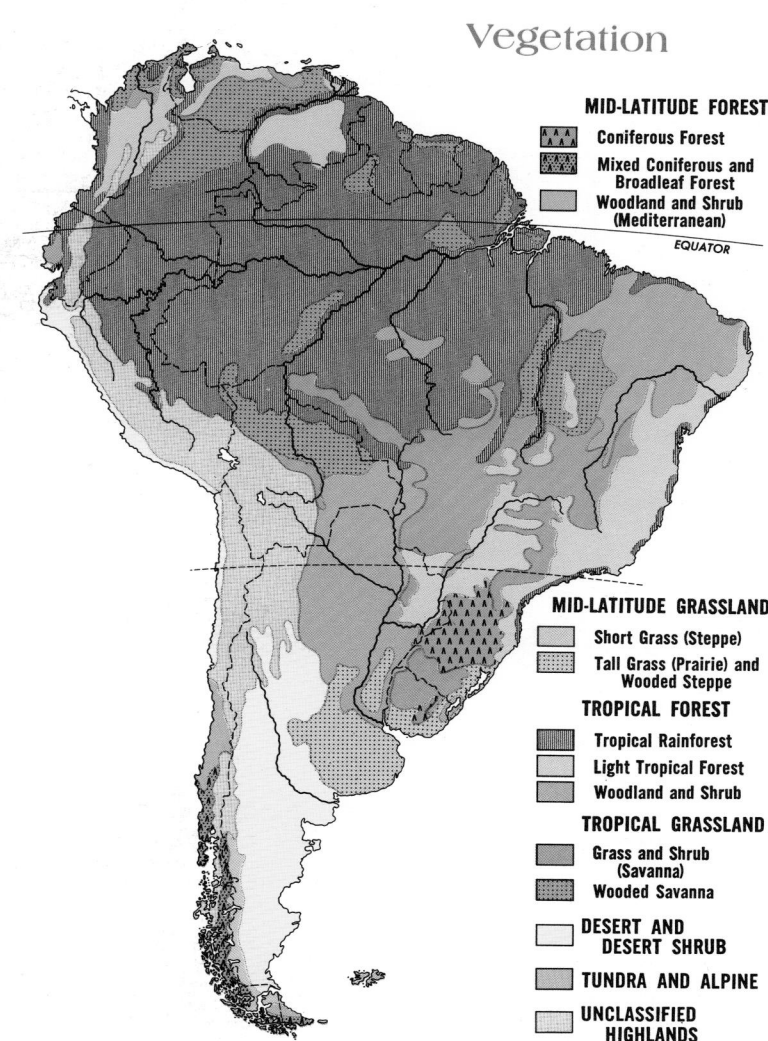

DENSITY PER

SQ. KILOMETER	SQ. MILE
Over 100	Over 260
50-100	130-260
10-50	25-130
1-10	3-25
Under 1	Under 3

● Cities with over 1,000,000 inhabitants (including suburbs)

○ Cities with over 500,000 inhabitants (including suburbs)

MID-LATITUDE FOREST
- Coniferous Forest
- Mixed Coniferous and Broadleaf Forest
- Woodland and Shrub (Mediterranean)

MID-LATITUDE GRASSLAND
- Short Grass (Steppe)
- Tall Grass (Prairie) and Wooded Steppe

TROPICAL FOREST
- Tropical Rainforest
- Light Tropical Forest
- Woodland and Shrub

TROPICAL GRASSLAND
- Grass and Shrub (Savanna)
- Wooded Savanna

DESERT AND DESERT SHRUB

TUNDRA AND ALPINE

UNCLASSIFIED HIGHLANDS

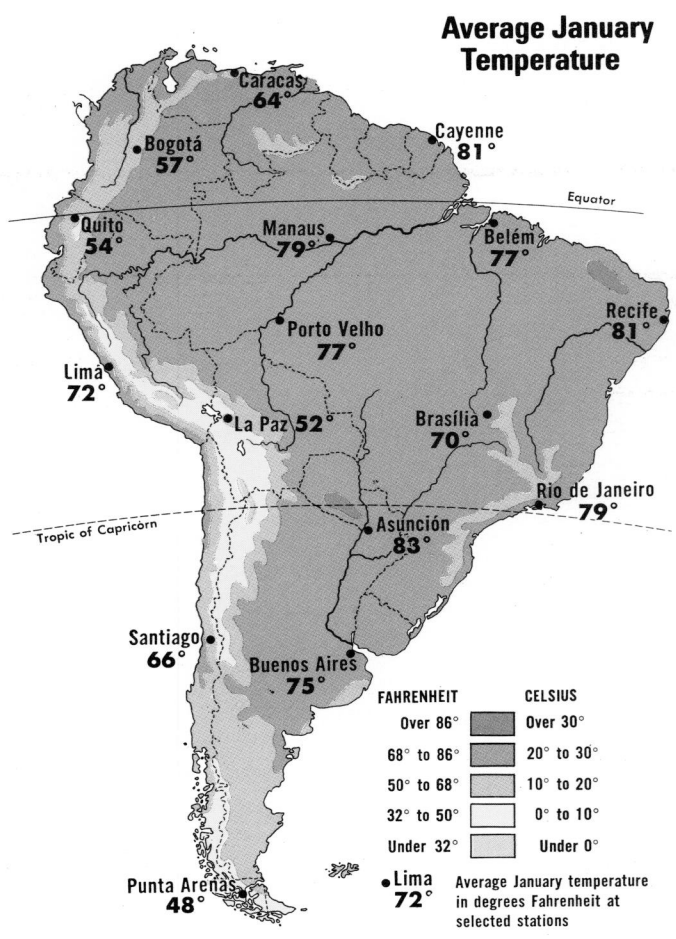

Average January Temperature

Caracas 64°
Cayenne 81°
Bogotá 57°
Equator
Quito 54°
Manaus 79°
Belém 77°
Recife 81°
Porto Velho 77°
Lima 72°
La Paz 52°
Brasília 70°
Rio de Janeiro 79°
Tropic of Capricorn
Asunción 83°
Santiago 66°
Buenos Aires 75°
Punta Arenas 48°

FAHRENHEIT	CELSIUS
Over 86°	Over 30°
68° to 86°	20° to 30°
50° to 68°	10° to 20°
32° to 50°	0° to 10°
Under 32°	Under 0°

• Lima 72° Average January temperature in degrees Fahrenheit at selected stations

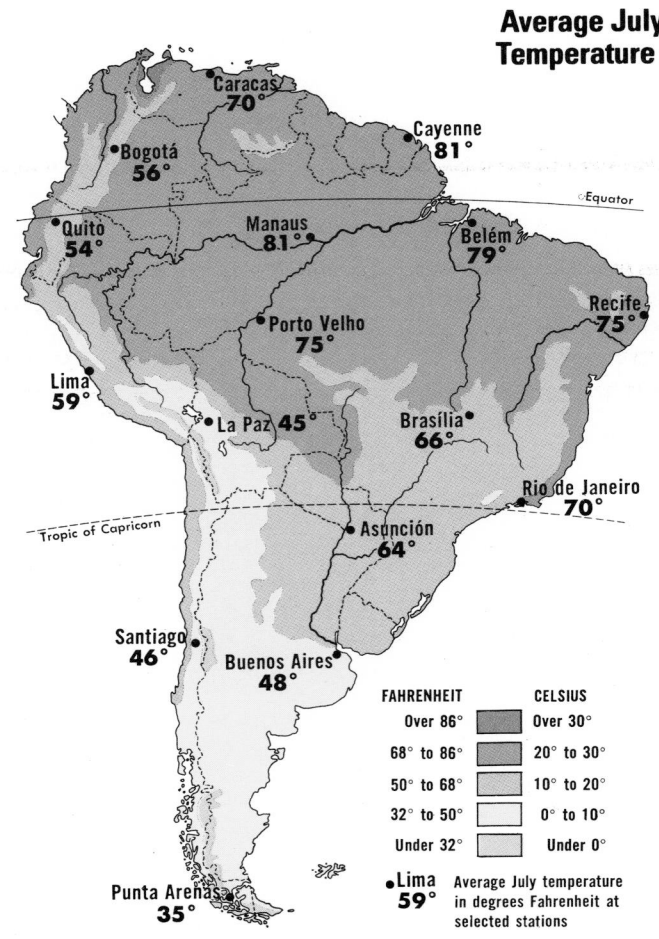

Average July Temperature

Caracas 70°
Cayenne 81°
Bogotá 56°
Equator
Quito 54°
Manaus 81°
Belém 79°
Recife 75°
Porto Velho 75°
Lima 59°
La Paz 45°
Brasília 66°
Rio de Janeiro 70°
Tropic of Capricorn
Asunción 64°
Santiago 46°
Buenos Aires 48°
Punta Arenas 35°

FAHRENHEIT	CELSIUS
Over 86°	Over 30°
68° to 86°	20° to 30°
50° to 68°	10° to 20°
32° to 50°	0° to 10°
Under 32°	Under 0°

• Lima 59° Average July temperature in degrees Fahrenheit at selected stations

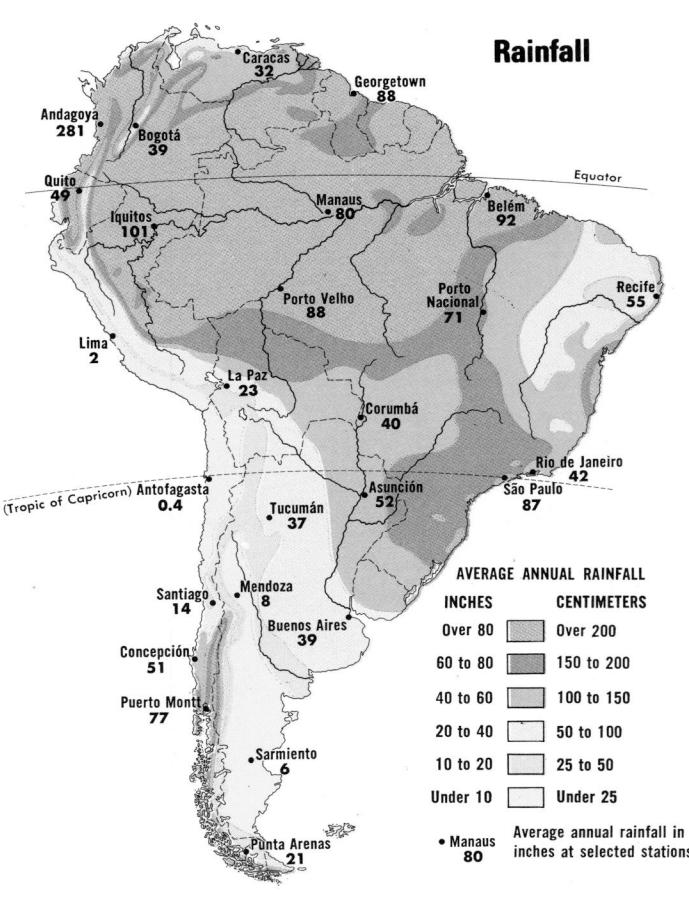

Rainfall

Caracas 32
Georgetown 88
Andagoyá 281
Bogotá 39
Quito 49
Equator
Iquitos 101
Manaus 80
Belém 92
Porto Velho 88
Porto Nacional 71
Recife 55
Lima 2
La Paz 23
Corumbá 40
Rio de Janeiro 42
Antofagasta 0.4 (Tropic of Capricorn)
Asunción 52
São Paulo 87
Tucumán 37
Santiago 14
Mendoza 8
Buenos Aires 39
Concepción 51
Puerto Montt 77
Sarmiento 6
Punta Arenas 21

AVERAGE ANNUAL RAINFALL

INCHES	CENTIMETERS
Over 80	Over 200
60 to 80	150 to 200
40 to 60	100 to 150
20 to 40	50 to 100
10 to 20	25 to 50
Under 10	Under 25

• Manaus 80 Average annual rainfall in inches at selected stations

Vegetation / Relief

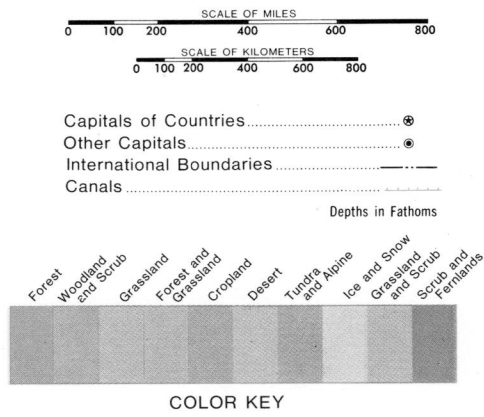

SCALE OF MILES
0 100 200 400 600 800

SCALE OF KILOMETERS
0 100 200 400 600 800

Capitals of Countries .... ⊛
Other Capitals .... ◉
International Boundaries .... —··—
Canals ....

Depths in Fathoms

Forest | Woodland and Scrub | Grassland | Forest and Grassland | Cropland | Desert | Tundra and Alpine | Ice and Snow | Grassland and Scrub | Scrub and Fernlands

COLOR KEY

STATES

Amazonas (terr.) 21,696 ....E5
Anzoátegui 506,297 ....F3
Apure 164,705 ....D4
Aragua 543,170 ....D3
Barinas 231,046 ....D3
Bolívar 391,665 ....F7
Carabobo 659,339 ....D2
Cojedes 94,351 ....D3
Delta Amacuro (terr.) 48,139 ....H3
Dependencias Federales (terr.) 463 ....E2
Distrito Federal 1,860,637 ....E2
Falcón 407,957 ....D2
Guárico 318,905 ....E3
Lara 671,410 ....D2
Mérida 347,095 ....C3
Miranda 856,272 ....E2
Monagas 298,239 ....G3
Nueva Esparta 118,830 ....G2
Portuguesa 297,047 ....D3
Sucre 469,004 ....G2
Táchira 511,346 ....C3
Trujillo 381,334 ....C2
Yaracuy 223,545 ....D2
Zulia 1,299,030 ....B2

CITIES and TOWNS

Acarigua 56,743 ....D3
Achaguas 4,633 ....D4

Adícora 707 ....D2
Aguada Grande 2,901 ....D2
Agua Fría D2
Agua Linda E5
Aguaray 1,752 ....G3
Altagracia 11,116 ....C3
Altagracia de Orituco 18,717 ....E3
Amuay D2
Anaco 29,487 ....G3
Aparurén G5
Apurito 740 ....D4
Arabopó H5
Aragua de Barcelona 9,107 ....F3
Aragua de Maturín 4,051 ....G3
Aricagua 231 ....C3
Arichuna 1,204 ....E4
Aripao 296 ....F4
Arismendi 1,257 ....D3
Aroa 5,418 ....D2
Atapirire 337 ....F4
Bachaquero C2
Baragua 659 ....D2
Barbacoas 2,513 ....E3
Barcelona 78,201 ....F2
Barinas 56,329 ....D3
Barinitas 9,644 ....C3
Barrancas, Monagas 5,738 ....G3
Barrancas, Barinas 4,489 ....D3
Betijoque 5,851 ....C2
Biruaca 2,266 ....E4

Biscucuy 6,114 ....D3
Bobare 1,204 ....D2
Bobures 2,468 ....C3
Boca de Aroa 2,756 ....D2
Boca del Mangle F3
Boca del Pao 403 ....F3
Bocono 15,915 ....C3
Borbón F4
Borojó 423 ....C2
Bruzual 941 ....D4
Buena Vista, Anzoátegui F3
Buena Vista, Apure D4
Cabimas 118,037 ....C2
Cabruta 1,927 ....E4
Cabudare 14,593 ....D2
Cabure 1,673 ....D2
Cacuri F5
Cagua 29,601 ....E2
Caica 6,092 ....D3
Caicara de Orinoco 6,867 ....E4
Calabozo 37,282 ....E3
Calderas 1,195 ....C3
Camaguán 4,143 ....E3
Camatagua 3,335 ....E3
Campo Claro 1,832 ....G2
Candelaria F4
Cantaura 15,839 ....G3
Capatárida 1,375 ....C2
Capibara E6
Carabobo, Bolívar H4

Carabobo, Carabobo D3
Carache 3,966 ....C3
Carapa 119 ....D3
Caracas* 2,183,935 ....E2
Caracas (cap.) 1,035,499 ....E2
Caribén E4
Caripe 4,729 ....F4
Caripito 19,053 ....G2
Carirubana 15,701 ....C2
Carmelo 2,556 ....C2
Carora 36,115 ....C2
Carrasquero 2,193 ....C2
Carúpano 50,935 ....G2
Casanay 4,985 ....G2
Casigua, Falcón 463 ....D2
Casigua, Zulia 3,665 ....B3
Caucagua 6,218 ....E2
Cazorla 700 ....E3
Chaguaramas 2,748 ....E3
Chichiriviche 3,236 ....D2
Chivacoa 19,210 ....D2
Choroní 534 ....D2
Churuguara 6,636 ....D2
Ciudad Bolívar 103,728 ....G4
Ciudad Bolivia 4,864 ....C3
Ciudad Guayana 143,540 ....G3
Ciudad de Nutrias 769 ....D3
Ciudad Ojeda 83,083 ....C2
Ciudad Piar 3,965 ....G4
Clarines 2,099 ....F3
Cojoro C2

Colón E6
Comunidad E7
Coporito H3
Coro 68,701 ....D2
Corozo Pando E3
Cúa 9,953 ....E2
Cubiro 1,988 ....D3
Cuchivero F4
Cumaná 119,751 ....F2
Cumanacoa 9,179 ....F2
Cunaviche 795 ....E4
Curiapo H3
Dabajuro 4,516 ....C2
Delicias 1,616 ....B3
Democracia E6
Dolores 1,454 ....D3
Duaca 7,519 ....D2
Ejido 11,170 ....C3
El Almacén F4
El Amparo de Apure 2,015 ....C4
El Baúl 1,715 ....D3
El Callao 4,270 ....G4
El Calvario 384 ....E3
El Chaparro 3,768 ....F3
El Cristo G2
El Dorado 1,888 ....H4
El Empedrado 1,788 ....C2
El Guapo 1,231 ....E2
El Manteco 1,962 ....G4
El Miamo 335 ....H4
Elorza 3,184 ....D4
El Oso H5

El Palmar 2,758 ....G4
El Pao, Anzoátegui 761 ....F3
El Pao, Bolívar 1,259 ....G4
El Pao, Cojedes 1,715 ....D3
El Perú H4
El Pilar 3,278 ....G2
El Rastro 903 ....E3
El Roque F2
El Saman de Apure 1,399 ....D4
El Socorro E3
El Sombrero 8,373 ....E3
El Tigre 49,801 ....F3
El Tocuyo 19,351 ....D3
El Toro H3
El Vigía 20,970 ....C3
El Vínculo D1
El Yagual 699 ....D4
Encontrados 5,607 ....B3
Esperanza E6
Espino 559 ....F3
Garcitas C3
Guacara 35,111 ....D2
Guachara 577 ....C4
Guadarrama 334 ....D3
Guaina G5
Guana G5
Guanare 34,148 ....D3
Guanarito 3,150 ....D3
Guanoco G2
Guanta 9,017 ....F2
Guardatinajas 1,206 ....E3
Guarero B2

Guárico 3,259 ....D3
Guariquén 619 ....G2
Guasdualito 7,793 ....C4
Guasimal 582 ....D4
Guasipati 4,807 ....H4
Guayabal, Amazonas E6
Guayabal, Guárico 1,403 ....E3
Guiria 13,905 ....G2
Guri G4
Guzmán Blanco E6
Higuerote 5,008 ....E2
Icabarú H4
Independencia 4,897 ....B4
Irapa 4,470 ....G2
Irapa 8,134 ....G2
Juangriego 6,062 ....G2
Judibana D1
Jusepín G3
Kavanayen H5
La Aduana D3
La Asunción 6,381 ....G2
La Canoa G3
La Ceiba, Apure C2
La Ceiba, Trujillo 212 ....C2
La Concepción B2
La Concepción 13,885 ....F6
La Esmeralda F6
La Esperanza H3
La Fría 8,134 ....B3
La Grita 9,954 ....C3
La Guaira 20,344 ....E2
Lagunetas C3
Lagunillas C2

Venezuela

MERCATOR PROJECTION

SCALE OF MILES

Capitals of Countries ....☆
State Capitals ....◉
International Boundaries
State Boundaries
Canals

Scale 1:6,120,000

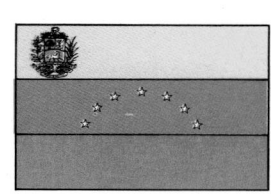

AREA 352,143 sq. mi. (912,050 sq. km.)
POPULATION 14,313,000
CAPITAL Caracas
LARGEST CITY Caracas
HIGHEST POINT Pico Bolívar 16,427 ft.
(5,007 m.)
MONETARY UNIT Bolívar
MAJOR LANGUAGE Spanish
MAJOR RELIGION Roman Catholicism

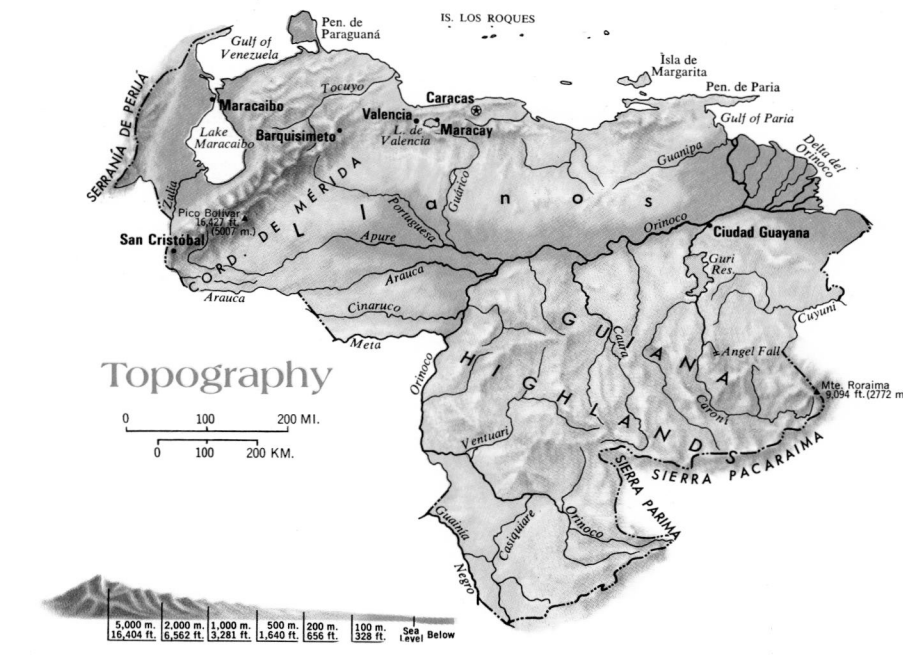

Topography

0   100   200 MI.
0   100   200 KM.

5,000 m. | 2,000 m. | 1,000 m. | 500 m. | 200 m. | 100 m. | Sea
16,404 ft. | 6,562 ft. | 3,281 ft. | 1,640 ft. | 656 ft. | 328 ft. | level / Below

Agriculture, Industry and Resources

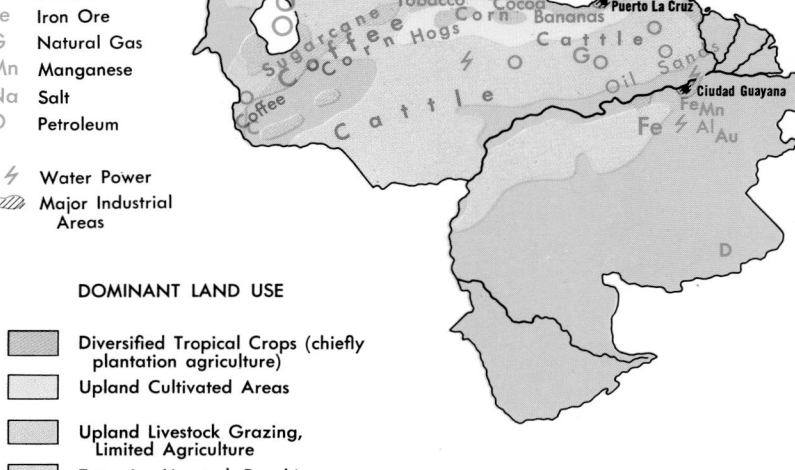

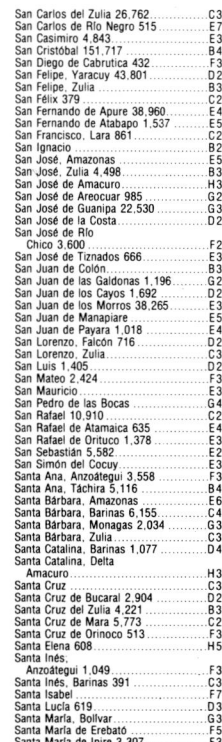

MAJOR MINERAL OCCURRENCES

Al Bauxite
Au Gold
C   Coal
D   Diamonds
Fe Iron Ore
G   Natural Gas
Mn Manganese
Na Salt
O   Petroleum

⚡ Water Power
▨ Major Industrial Areas

DOMINANT LAND USE

Diversified Tropical Crops (chiefly plantation agriculture)
Upland Cultivated Areas
Upland Livestock Grazing, Limited Agriculture
Extensive Livestock Ranching
Forests

HAMMOND INCORPORATED, Maplewood, N.J.

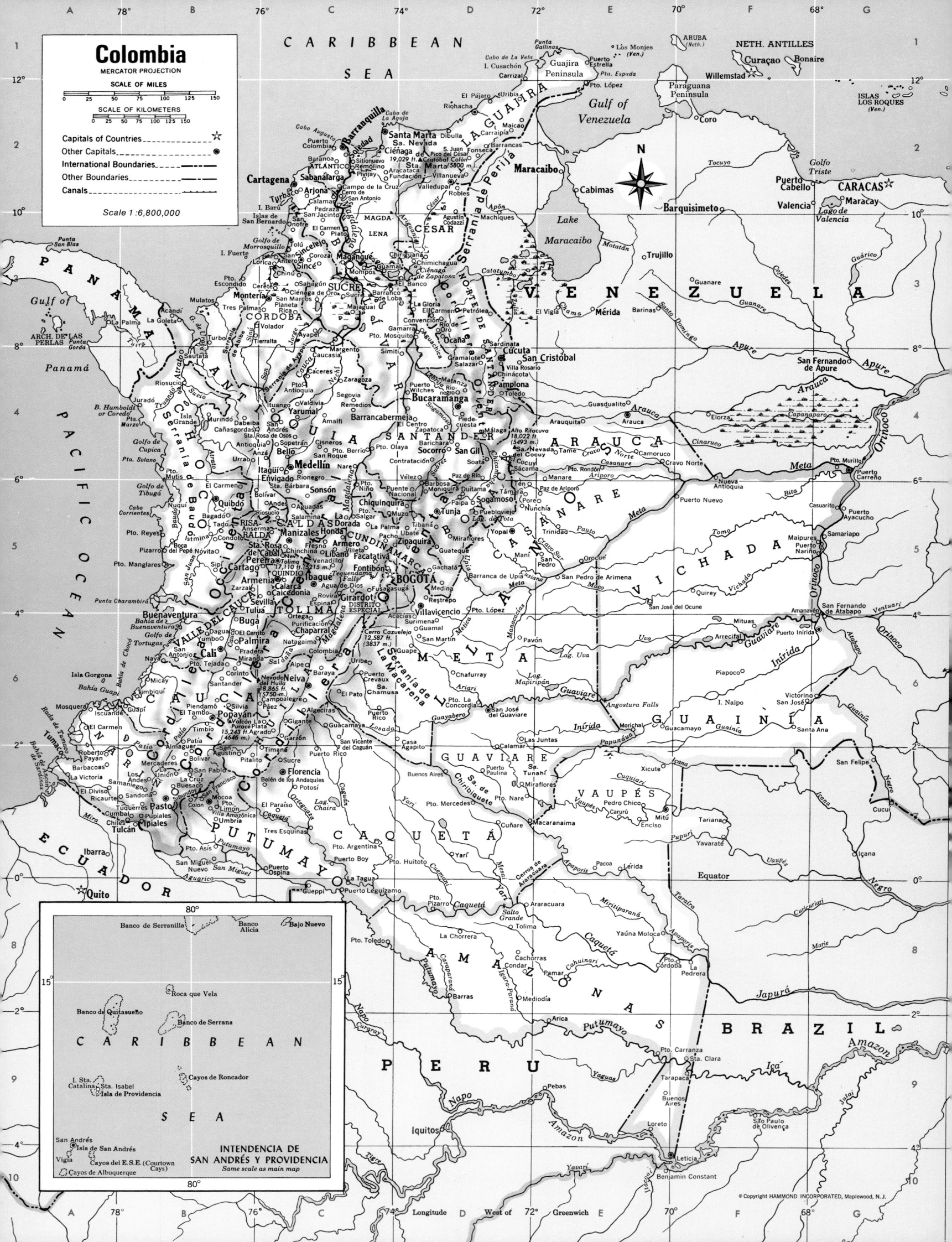

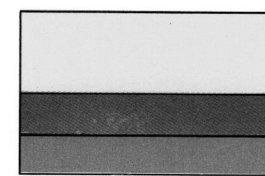

AREA 439,513 sq. mi. (1,138,339 sq. km.)
POPULATION 27,520,000
CAPITAL Bogotá
LARGEST CITY Bogotá
HIGHEST POINT Pico Cristóbal Colón 19,029 ft. (5,800 m.)
MONETARY UNIT Colombian peso
MAJOR LANGUAGE Spanish
MAJOR RELIGION Roman Catholicism

Agriculture, Industry and Resources

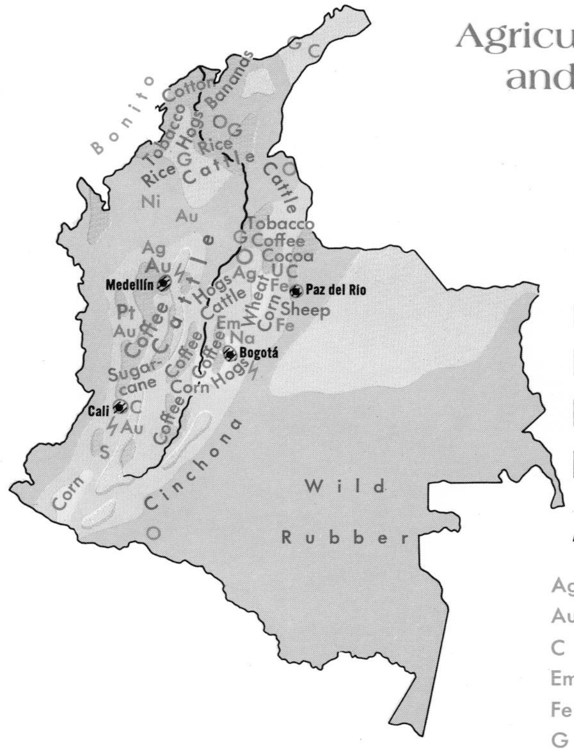
Bonito
Tobacco
Cotton
Bananas
Hogs
Rice
Cattle
Coffee
Cocoa
Wheat
Corn
Sheep
Sugar-cane
Cinchona
Wild Rubber
Medellín
Paz del Rio
Bogotá
Cali

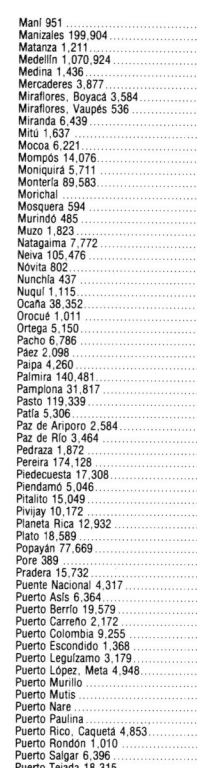

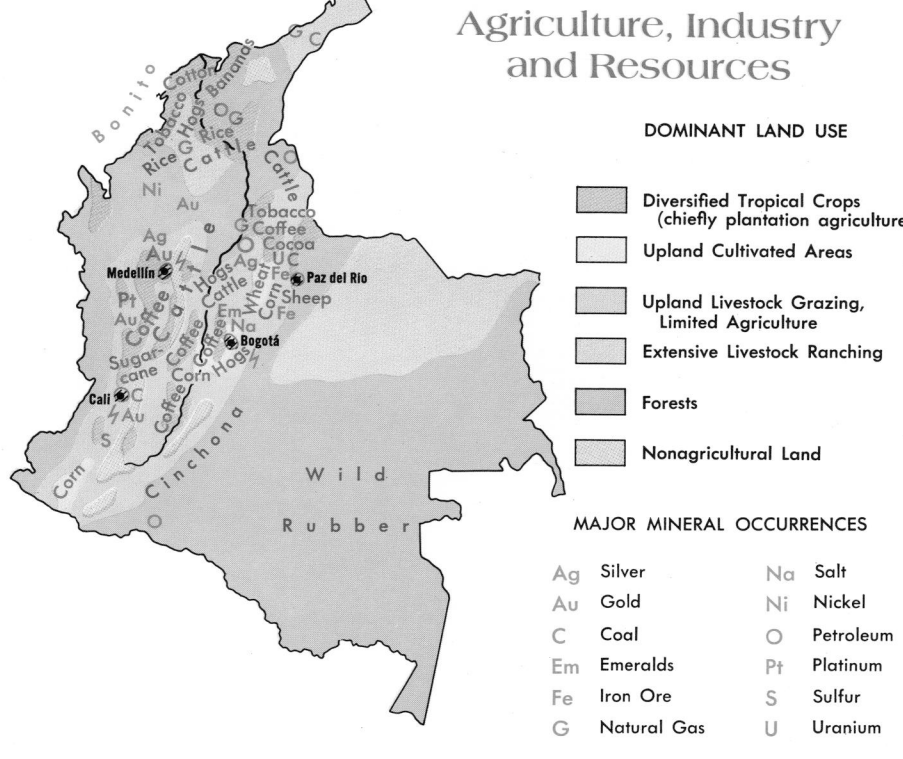

DOMINANT LAND USE

Diversified Tropical Crops (chiefly plantation agriculture)
Upland Cultivated Areas
Upland Livestock Grazing, Limited Agriculture
Extensive Livestock Ranching
Forests
Nonagricultural Land

MAJOR MINERAL OCCURRENCES

Ag Silver
Au Gold
C Coal
Em Emeralds
Fe Iron Ore
G Natural Gas
Na Salt
Ni Nickel
O Petroleum
Pt Platinum
S Sulfur
U Uranium

Water Power
Major Industrial Areas

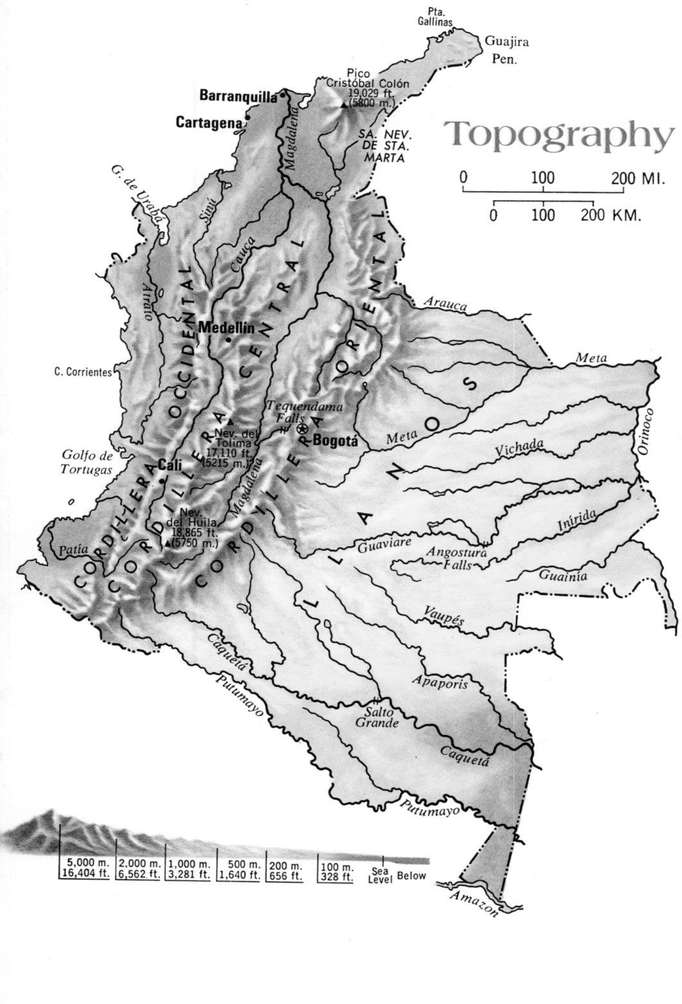
Topography
0 100 200 MI.
0 100 200 KM.
Pta. Gallinas
Guajira Pen.
Barranquilla
Cartagena
Pico Cristóbal Colón 19,029 ft. (5800 m.)
SA. NEV. DE STA. MARTA
G. de Urabá
Medellín
C. Corrientes
Bogotá
Tequendama Falls
Nev. del Tolima 17,110 ft. (5215 m.)
Cali
Golfo de Tortugas
Nev. del Huila 18,865 ft. (5750 m.)
CORDILLERA OCCIDENTAL
CORDILLERA CENTRAL
CORDILLERA ORIENTAL
LLANOS
Arauca
Meta
Vichada
Orinoco
Guaviare
Inírida
Guainía
Angostura Falls
Vaupés
Apaporis
Caquetá
Putumayo
Salto Grande
Amazon
Patía
Magdalena
Cauca
Sinú
Atrato
5,000 m. 16,404 ft.
2,000 m. 6,562 ft.
1,000 m. 3,281 ft.
500 m. 1,640 ft.
200 m. 656 ft.
100 m. 328 ft.
Sea Level
Below

INTERNAL DIVISIONS

Amazonas (comm.) 6,825 D8
Antioquia (dept.) 2,976,153 B4
Arauca (inten.) 19,884 E4
Atlántico (dept.) 958,560 C2
Bolívar (dept.) 802,407 C3
Boyacá (dept.) 1,084,766 D5
Caldas (dept.) 700,954 C5
Caquetá (inten.) 57,103 C7
Casanare (inten.) B3
Cauca (dept.) 603,894 B6
César (dept.) 339,843 D3
Chocó (dept.) 201,915 B4
Córdoba (dept.) 645,478 C3
Cundinamarca (dept.) 1,106,626 C5
Distrito Especial 2,855,065 C5
Guainía (comm.) 1,792 F6
Guajira, La (dept.) 180,520 D2
Guaviare (comm.) D7
Huila (dept.) 469,834 C6
La Guajira (dept.) 180,520 D2
Magdalena (dept.) 536,122 C3
Meta (dept.) 245,176 D6
Nariño (dept.) 807,112 B7
Norte de Santander (dept.) 693,298 D3
Putumayo (inten.) 22,916 C7
Quindío (dept.) 321,677 C5
Risaralda (dept.) 452,626 B5
San Andrés y Providencia (inten.) 22,719 B10
Santander (dept.) 1,130,977 D4
Sucre (dept.) 354,412 C3
Tolima (dept.) 903,520 C5
Valle del Cauca (dept.) 2,204,722 B6
Vaupés (comm.) 6,923 E7
Vichada (comm.) 2,172 F5

CITIES and TOWNS

Acacías 9,238 D6
Acandí 2,358 B3
Agrado 2,771 C6
Aguachica 16,771 D3
Aguadas 9,995 C5
Agua de Dios 9,689 C5
Agustín Codazzi 21,932 D3
Aipe 3,794 C6
Algeciras 5,022 C6
Almaguer 1,518 B7
Amalfi 6,494 C4
Andes 14,957 C5
Anserma 15,559 B5
Antioquia 6,841 B4
Anzá 647 C4
Aracataca 7,511 D2
Arauca 7,613 E4
Arauquita 1,096 E4
Arjona 20,571 C2
Armenia 135,615 B5
Armero 19,567 C5
Ayapel 7,475 C3
Bagadó 1,575 B5
Baranoa 18,397 C2
Baraya 2,581 C6
Barbacoas 4,653 A7
Barbosa 7,960 D5
Barichara 2,548 D4
Barrancabermeja 87,191 C4
Barrancas 2,979 D2
Barranco de Loba 2,215 C3
Barranquilla 661,009 C2
Belén de los Andaquíes 2,190 C7
Bello 115,119 C4
Bogotá (cap.) 2,696,270 D5
Bogotá* 2,855,065 D5
Bolívar, Antioquia 13,259 C5
Bucaramanga 291,661 D4
Buenaventura 115,770 B6
Buesaco 2,763 B7
Buga 71,016 B6
Cáceres 7,154 C4
Caicedonia 23,567 C5
Calamar, Bolívar 5,867 C2
Calarcá 29,349 C5
Cali 898,253 B6
Campoalegre 11,799 C6
Campo de la Cruz 13,137 C2
Cañasgordas 3,900 B4
Cartagena 292,512 C2
Cartago 69,154 B5
Caucasia 19,348 C4
Cereté 18,788 C3
Cerro de San Antonio 3,394 C2
Chaparral 14,546 C6
Chimichagua 6,382 D3
Chinácota 4,478 D4
Chinchiná 24,891 C5
Chinú 10,023 C3
Chiquinquirá 21,727 C5
Chiriguaná 6,611 D3
Ciénaga 42,546 C2
Ciénaga de Oro 10,607 C3
Cisneros 7,226 C4
Colombia 2,903 C6
Colón 1,306 B7
Condoto 4,798 B5
Contratación 3,057 D4
Convención 7,545 D3
Corinto 6,933 B6
Corozal 17,419 C3
Cravo Norte 771 F4
Cúcuta 219,772 D4
Cumbal 2,891 B7
Dabeiba 7,600 B4
Dagua 5,392 B6
Duitama 36,551 D5
El Banco 20,756 D3
El Carmen, Chocó 1,879 B5
El Carmen, Norte de Santander 2,362 D3
El Carmen de Bolívar 23,392 C3
El Cerrito 17,357 B6
El Cocuy 2,740 D4
El Tambo 2,179 B6
Envigado 63,584 C4
Espinal 32,475 C5
Facatativá 27,892 C6
Florencia 31,817 C7
Fonseca 9,988 D2
Fresno 8,141 C5
Fundación 17,497 C2
Fusagasugá 25,456 C5
Gachalá 1,364 D5
Gamarra 5,071 D3
Garzón 13,783 C6
Gigante 4,880 C6
Girardot 59,165 C5
Gramalote 2,880 D4
Guamal, Magdalena 4,986 C3
Guamal, Meta 2,854 D6
Guapí 5,005 B6
Guateque 6,032 D5
Honda 21,506 C5
Ibagué 176,223 C5
Inírida 1,792 F6
Ipiales 30,871 B7
Iscuandé 561 A6
Istmina 5,575 B5
Itagüí 96,972 C4
Ituango 5,561 C4
Juradó 935 B4
La Cruz 4,353 B7
La Dorada 30,962 C5
La Gloria 2,632 D3
La Palma 5,430 C5
La Plata 8,047 C6
La Unión 5,392 B7
Leticia 6,285 F10
Líbano 19,132 C5
Lorica 18,251 C3
Los Andes 1,414 B7
Magangué 34,396 C3
Maicao 21,645 D2
Majagual 2,329 C3
Málaga 10,645 D4
Maní 951 D5
Manizales 199,904 C5
Matanza 1,211 D4
Medellín 1,070,924 C4
Medina 1,436 D5
Mercaderes 3,877 B7
Miraflores, Boyacá 3,584 D5
Miraflores, Vaupés 536 D7
Miranda 6,439 B6
Mitú 1,637 E7
Mocoa 6,221 B7
Mompós 14,076 C3
Moniquirá 5,711 D5
Montería 89,583 B3
Morichal E6
Mosquera 594 A6
Murindó 485 B4
Muzo 1,823 D5
Natagaima 7,772 C6
Neiva 105,476 C6
Nóvita 802 B5
Nunchía 437 D5
Nuquí 1,115 B5
Ocaña 38,352 D3
Orocué 1,011 E5
Ortega 5,150 C6
Pacho 6,786 C5
Páez 2,098 C6
Paipa 4,260 D5
Palmira 140,481 B6
Pamplona 31,817 D4
Pasto 119,339 B7
Patía 5,306 B6
Paz de Ariporo 2,584 E5
Paz de Río 3,464 D4
Pedraza 1,872 C2
Pereira 174,128 C5
Piedecuesta 17,308 D4
Piendamó 5,046 B6
Pitalito 15,049 B7
Pivijay 10,172 C2
Planeta Rica 12,932 C3
Plato 18,589 C3
Popayán 77,669 B6
Pore 389 D5
Pradera 15,732 B6
Puente Nacional 4,317 D5
Puerto Asís 6,364 B7
Puerto Berrío 19,579 C4
Puerto Carreño 2,172 G4
Puerto Colombia 9,255 C2
Puerto Escondido 1,368 B3
Puerto Leguízamo 3,179 C8
Puerto López, Meta 4,948 D5
Puerto Murillo G4
Puerto Mutis B4
Puerto Nare D7
Puerto Paulina D7
Puerto Rico, Caquetá 4,853 C7
Puerto Rondón 1,010 E4
Puerto Salgar 6,396 C5
Puerto Tejada 18,315 B6
Puerto Wilches 5,282 D4
Pupiales 2,723 B7
Purificación 8,164 C6
Quibdó 28,040 B5
Remedios 4,681 C4
Remolino 3,408 C2
Restrepo 2,704 D5
Ricaurte 1,205 A7
Río de Oro 2,985 D3
Riohacha 19,604 D2
Rionegro, Antioquia 22,654 C4
Rionegro, Santander 3,491 D4
Riosucio, Caldas 11,619 C5
Riosucio, Chocó 2,184 B4
Roberto Payán 445 A7
Robles 5,422 D2
Rovira 5,105 C5
Sabanalarga 26,542 C2
Sácama 69 D4
Sahagún 18,717 C3
Salamina 12,136 C5
Salazar 2,791 D4
Samaniego 4,790 B7
San Agustín 4,532 B7
San Andrés, Antioquia 2,003 C4
San Andrés, San Andrés y Providencia 14,428 A9
San Antero 7,129 C3
Sandoná 7,222 B7
San Francisco 1,654 B7
San Gil 21,679 D4
San Jacinto 13,459 C3
San José del Guaviare 4,138 D6
San Juan del César 9,468 D2
San Marcos 10,415 C3
San Martín 8,281 D6
San Onofre 7,899 C3
San Pablo 3,662 B7
San Roque 4,972 C4
Santa Bárbara 11,848 C5
Santa Marta 102,484 D2
Santander 13,625 B6
Santa Rosa de Cabal 28,368 C5
Santa Rosa de Osos 8,593 C4
San Vicente del Caguán 3,182 C6
Sardinata 3,726 D3
Segovia 10,000 C4
Sevilla 31,143 C5
Sibundoy 2,853 B7
Silvia 3,045 B6
Simití 3,062 C4
Sincé 11,909 C3
Sincelejo 68,797 C3
Sipí 153 B5
Sitionuevo 5,919 C2
Soatá 4,294 D4
Socorro 15,596 D4
Sogamoso 48,891 D5
Soledad 64,469 C2
Sonsón 15,990 C5
Sopetrán 5,223 C4
Tadó 3,102 B5
Támara 947 D5
Tame 4,811 E4
Tibaná 1,100 D5
Tierralta 7,950 C3
Timaná 4,262 C7
Timbío 4,755 B6
Timbiquí 1,048 B6
Toledo 2,942 D4
Tolú 9,118 C3
Trinidad 729 E5
Tuluá 86,736 B5
Tumaco 38,742 A7
Tunja 51,620 D5
Túquerres 12,058 B7
Turbaco 19,360 C2
Turbo 16,070 B3
Ubaté 7,716 D5
Uribia 2,193 D2
Urrao 8,577 B4
Valdivia 4,318 C4
Valledupar 87,425 D2
Vélez 8,241 D4
Venadillo 8,383 C5
Villanueva 9,836 D2
Villa Rosario 8,668 D4
Villavicencio 82,869 D5
Villeta 6,507 C5
Yarumal 21,333 C4
Yopal 5,851 D5
Yumbo 28,011 B6
Zapatoca 6,258 D4
Zaragoza 9,660 C4
Zarzal 21,370 B5
Zipaquirá 25,413 D5

OTHER FEATURES

Abibe, Serranía de, (mts.) B3
Aguarico, (riv.) B7
Aguja, La, (cape) C2
Albuquerque, (cays) A10
Alicia, (bank) B8
Alto Ritacuva, (mt.) D4
Amazon, (riv.) E9
Ancón de Sardinas, (bay) A7
Angostura, (falls) E6
Apaporis, (riv.) F8
Araracuara, Cerros de, (mts.) E7
Arauca, (riv.) E4
Ariari, (riv.) D6
Ariguaní, (riv.) D3
Ariporo, (riv.) E4
Atabapo, (riv.) G6
Atrato, (riv.) B4
Augusta, (cape) C2
Ayapel, Serranía de, (mts.) C4
Bajo Nuevo, (shoal) C8
Barú, (isl.) C2
Baudó, Serranía de, (mts.) B5
Baudó, (riv.) B5
Bita, (riv.) F5
Buenaventura, (bay) B6
Caguán, (riv.) C7
Cahuinari, (riv.) E8
Caquetá, (riv.) E8
Caraparaná, (riv.) D8
Casanare, (riv.) E4
Catatumbo, (riv.) D3
Cauca, (riv.) C4
Cazueleja, Cerro, (mt.) C6
Central, Cordillera, (range) C5
César, (riv.) D2
Chaira, Laguna, (lake) C7
Chamusa, Sierra, (mts.) C6
Charambirá, (pt.) B5
Chicamocha, (riv.) D4
Chiribiquete, Sierra de, (mts.) D7
Cinaruco, (riv.) F4
Chocó, (bay) B6
Cocuy, Sierra Nevada del, (mts.) D4
Coredó (Humboldt), (bay) B4
Corrientes, (cape) B5
Courtown (Este Sudeste), (cays) A10
Cravo Norte, (riv.) E4
Cravo Sur, (riv.) E5
Cristóbal Colón, Pico, (peak) D2
Cuemaní, (riv.) D7
Cupica, (gulf) B4
Cuquiari, (riv.) E7
Cusachón, (isl.) D1
Cusiana, (riv.) D5
Espada, (pt.) E1
Este Sudeste, (cays) A10
Fuerte, (isl.) B3
Gallinas, (pt.) E1
Gorgona, (isl.) A6
Grande, (isl.) B4
Grande, Salto, (falls) D8
Guainía, (riv.) F6
Guajira, (pen.) E1
Guapi, (bay) A6
Guaviare, (riv.) F6
Guayabero, (riv.) D6
Huila, Nevado del, (mt.) C6
Humboldt, (bay) B4
Igara-Paraná, (riv.) D8
Inírida, (riv.) F6
Isana, (riv.) F7
La Aguja, (cape) C2
La Macarena, Serranía de, (mts.) D6
La Vela, (cape) D1
Lebrija, (riv.) D4
Llanos, (plains) D5
Losada, (riv.) C6
Macarena, Serranía de La, (mts.) D6
Magdalena, (riv.) C3
Manacacías, (riv.) D6
Mapiripán, Laguna, (lake) E6
Marzo, (pt.) B4
Mesai, (riv.) D7
Meta, (riv.) E5
Metica, (riv.) D6
Mira, (riv.) A7
Miritiparaná, (riv.) E8
Morrosquillo, (gulf) C3
Muco, (riv.) E5
Naipo, (isl.) F6
Nechí, (riv.) C4
Negro, (riv.) G7
Occidental, Cordillera, (range) B5
Oriental, Cordillera, (range) D5
Orinoco, (riv.) G5
Orteguaza, (riv.) C7
Papunáua, (riv.) E6
Papurí, (riv.) F7
Patía, (riv.) B6
Pauto, (riv.) E5
Perijá, Serranía de, (mts.) D2
Providencia, (isl.) B9
Puracé, (vol.) B6
Putumayo, (riv.) E9
Quitasueño, (bank) A8
Roca que Vela, (cay) B8
Roncador, (cays) B9
Saldaña, (riv.) C6
Salto Grande, (falls) D8
San Andrés, (isl.) A10
San Bernardo, (isls.) C3
San Jorge, (riv.) C3
San Juan, (riv.) B5
San Miguel, (riv.) B7
Santa Catalina, (isl.) A9
Santa Marta, Sierra Nevada de, (range) D2
Serrana, (bank) B9
Serranilla, (bank) B8
Sinú, (riv.) B3
Sogamoso, (riv.) D4
Solano, (pt.) B4
Suárez, (riv.) D4
Sucio, (riv.) B4
Taraira, (riv.) F8
Tequendama, (falls) C5
Tibugá, (gulf) B5
Tolima, Nevada del, (mt.) C5
Tomo, (riv.) F5
Tortugas, (gulf) B6
Tota, Laguna de, (lake) D5
Truandó, (riv.) B4
Tumaco, Rada de, (bay) A6
Tunahí, Sierra, (mts.) E7
Upía, (riv.) D5
Urabá, (gulf) B3
Uva, Laguna, (lake) E6
Uva, (riv.) E6
Vaupés, (riv.) E7
Vela, La, (cape) D1
Vela, Roca que, (cay) B8
Vichada, (riv.) F5
Vigía, (cay) A10
Yarí, (riv.) D8
Zapatosa, Ciénaga de, (swamp) D3

*City and suburbs.

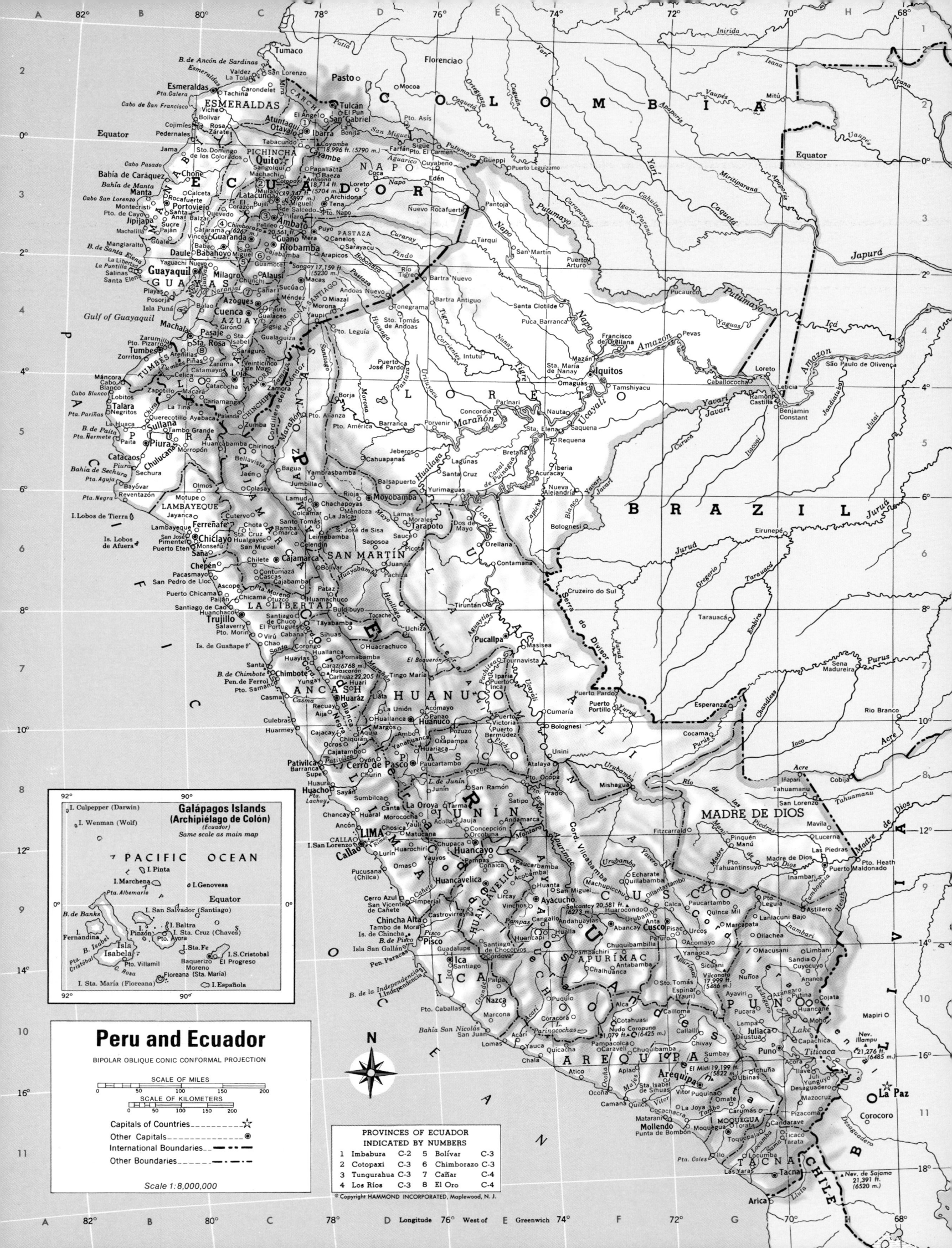

Galápagos Islands
(Archipiélago de Colón)
(Ecuador)
Same scale as main map

PACIFIC OCEAN

Peru and Ecuador

BIPOLAR OBLIQUE CONIC CONFORMAL PROJECTION

SCALE OF MILES
0   50   100   150   200

SCALE OF KILOMETERS
0   50   100   150   200

Capitals of Countries .... ☆
Other Capitals ....
International Boundaries ......
Other Boundaries ......

Scale 1:8,000,000

PROVINCES OF ECUADOR
INDICATED BY NUMBERS
1	Imbabura	C-2	5 Bolívar	C-3
2	Cotopaxi	C-3	6 Chimborazo	C-3
3	Tungurahua	C-3	7 Cañar	C-4
4	Los Ríos	C-3	8 El Oro	C-4

® Copyright HAMMOND INCORPORATED, Maplewood, N.J.

PERU

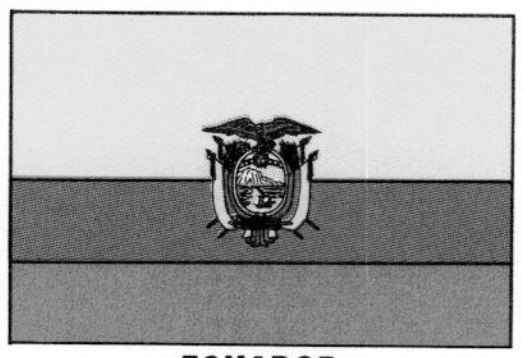

ECUADOR

PERU

AREA 496,222 sq. mi. (1,285,215 sq. km.)
POPULATION 17,031,221
CAPITAL Lima
LARGEST CITY Lima
HIGHEST POINT Huascarán 22,205 ft. (6,768 m.)
MONETARY UNIT inti
MAJOR LANGUAGES Spanish, Quechua, Aymara
MAJOR RELIGION Roman Catholicism

ECUADOR

AREA 109,483 sq. mi. (283,561 sq. km.)
POPULATION 8,644,000
CAPITAL Quito
LARGEST CITY Guayaquil
HIGHEST POINT Chimborazo 20,561 ft. (6,267 m.)
MONETARY UNIT sucre
MAJOR LANGUAGES Spanish, Quechua
MAJOR RELIGION Roman Catholicism

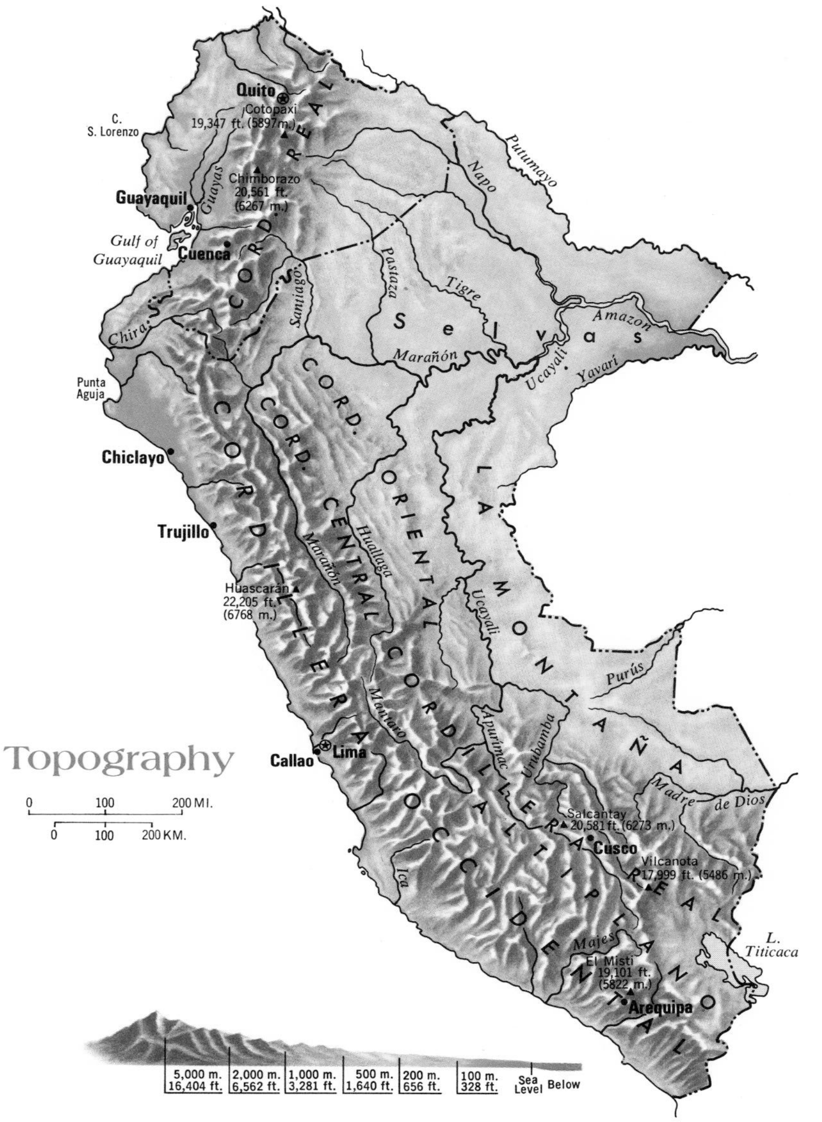
Topography
Quito
Cotopaxi 19,347 ft. (5897 m.)
C. S. Lorenzo
Chimborazo 20,561 ft. (6267 m.)
Guayaquil
Gulf of Guayaquil
Cuenca
Guayas
Putumayo
Napo
Pastaza
Tigre
Santiago
Chira
Marañón
Amazon
Yavari
Ucayali
S e l v a s
Punta Aguja
Chiclayo
Trujillo
Huascarán 22,205 ft. (6768 m.)
Huallaga
Marañón
Ucayali
Purús
Apurímac
Urubamba
Mantaro
Callao
Lima
Madre de Dios
Salcantay 20,581 ft. (6273 m.)
Cusco
Vilcanota 17,999 ft. (5486 m.)
Ica
Majes
El Misti 19,101 ft. (5822 m.)
Arequipa
L. Titicaca
CORD. REAL
CORD. CENTRAL
CORD. ORIENTAL
CORDILLERA OCCIDENTAL
CORDILLERA REAL
ALTIPLANO
LA MONTAÑA
0 100 200 MI.
0 100 200 KM.
5,000 m. 16,404 ft.
2,000 m. 6,562 ft.
1,000 m. 3,281 ft.
500 m. 1,640 ft.
200 m. 656 ft.
100 m. 328 ft.
Sea Level
Below

PERU

DEPARTMENTS

Amazonas 256,460 ... C5
Ancash 815,646 ... D7
Apurímac 321,936 ... F10
Arequipa 702,308 ... F10
Ayacucho 500,732 ... E9
Cajamarca 1,044,689 ... C6
Callao (prov.) 446,730 ... D9
Cusco 829,294 ... F9
Huancavelica 346,460 ... E9
Huánuco 481,924 ... D7
Ica 431,442 ... E10
Junín 848,993 ... E8
La Libertad 960,537 ... C6
Lambayeque 683,425 ... B6
Lima 4,738,266 ... D8
Loreto 446,316 ... E5
Madre de Dios 36,555 ... G8
Moquegua 99,287 ... G11
Pasco 221,219 ... E8
Piura 1,168,442 ... B5
Puno 893,586 ... G10
San Martín 319,670 ... D6
Tacna 133,240 ... G11
Tumbes 103,979 ... B4
Ucayali 200,085 ... E6

CITIES and TOWNS

Abancay 19,807 ... F9
Acarí 4,907 ... E10
Acobamba 2,156 ... E9
Acolla 5,717 ... E8
Acomayo, Cusco 1,419 ... G9
Acomayo, Huánuco 2,883 ... E7
Acora 1,910 ... H11
Acuracay 1,282 ... F5
Aija 1,843 ... D7
Alca 755 ... F10
Ambo 3,060 ... D8
Ananea 668 ... H10
Ancón 8,610 ... D8
Andahuaylas 7,654 ... F9
Andamarca 470 ... E8
Anta 3,703 ... F9
Antabamba 2,223 ... F10
Aplao 1,941 ... F11
Aquia 970 ... D8
Arequipa 107,858 ... G11
Arequipa* 447,431 ... G11
Ascope 12,070 ... C6
Astillero ... H9
Atalaya 2,229 ... E8
Atico 2,316 ... F11
Ayabaca 4,543 ... C5
Ayacucho 68,535 ... F9
Ayaviri 11,067 ... G10
Azángaro 7,658 ... H10
Bagua 9,735 ... C5
Balsapuerto 164 ... D5
Bambamarca 6,867 ... C6
Barranca, Lima 31,312 ... C8
Barranca, Loreto 1,351 ... D5
Bartra Antiguo ... E4
Bartra Nuevo ... E4
Bayóvar ... B5
Bellavista 4,906 ... C5
Bolívar 1,106 ... D6
Bolognesi ... F6
Bolognesi 661 ... F8
Borja 215 ... D5
Bretaña 1,035 ... E5
Buldibuyo 582 ... D7
Cabana 1,804 ... C7
Cabo Blanco ... B5
Cahuapanas 304 ... D5
Cailloma 1,187 ... G10
Cajabamba 7,282 ... C6
Cajacay 668 ... D8
Cajamarca 60,280 ... C6
Cajatambo 1,721 ... D8
Calca 6,112 ... G9
Callalli 819 ... G10
Callao 260,581 ... D9
Callao* 441,374 ... D9
Camaná 11,386 ... F11
Candarave 1,207 ... G11
Cangallo 1,584 ... E9
Canta 3,431 ... D8
Capachica 307 ... H10
Caraz 6,376 ... D7
Caravelí 1,827 ... F10
Carhuás 3,147 ... D7
Carumás 1,031 ... G11
Cascas 2,638 ... C6
Casma 12,725 ... C7
Castrovirreyna 1,749 ... E9
Catacaos 30,927 ... B5
Celendín 8,538 ... D6
Cerro Azul 2,314 ... D9
Cerro de Pasco 71,558 ... D8
Chachapoyas 11,919 ... D6
Chala 1,646 ... E10
Chalhuanca 3,071 ... F10
Chancay 18,993 ... D8
Chao ... C7
Chepén 29,919 ... C6
Chicama 11,160 ... C6
Chiclayo 280,244 ... C6
Chilca (Pucusana) 3,329 ... D9
Chilete 2,537 ... C6
Chimbote 216,406 ... C7
Chincha Alta 237,475 ... D9
Chiquián 3,521 ... D8
Chirinos 1,061 ... C5
Chivay 3,296 ... G10
Chosica ... D8
Chota 8,299 ... C6
Chulucanas 34,977 ... B5
Chupaca 5,422 ... E9
Chuquibamba 2,630 ... F10
Chuquibambilla 2,147 ... F9
Churín 1,801 ... D8
Cocachacra 5,985 ... G11
Cocama ... G8
Cojata 888 ... H10
Colasay 721 ... C5
Colcamar 1,216 ... D6
Conaica 1,154 ... E9
Concepción 7,129 ... E8
Concordia 1,372 ... E5
Contamana 5,718 ... E6
Contumazá 2,491 ... C6
Coracora 4,598 ... F10
Córdova 453 ... E10
Corongo 1,762 ... D7
Cotahuasi 1,301 ... F10
Culebras ... C7
Cumaría ... F7
Cusco (Cuzco) 85,044 ... F9
Cusco* 181,604 ... F9
Cutervo 6,890 ... C6
Cuyocuyo 1,101 ... H10
Desaguadero 2,682 ... H11
Deustua 544 ... G10
Dos de Mayo 574 ... E6
Echarate 1,071 ... F9
El Portugués ... C7
Esperanza 375 ... G7
Espinar 6,381 ... G10
Ferreñafe 22,200 ... C6
Francisco de Orellana 445 ... F4
Guadalupe 7,613 ... E9
Güeppi ... E3
Huacho 43,402 ... D8
Huacrachuco 1,210 ... D7
Hualgayoc 1,691 ... C6
Hualla 4,042 ... F9
Huallanca, Ancash 930 ... D7
Huallanca, Huánuco 4,806 ... D7
Huamachuco 8,273 ... D6
Huancabamba 4,393 ... C5
Huancané 5,227 ... H10
Huancapi 2,539 ... E9
Huancavelica 20,889 ... E9
Huancayo 165,132 ... E9
Huanchaco 6,005 ... C7
Huanta 11,213 ... E9
Huánuco 52,628 ... E7
Huaral 34,235 ... D8
Huaráz 45,116 ... D7
Huari 2,344 ... D7
Huariaca 2,671 ... E8
Huarmey 11,094 ... C8
Huarochirí 1,828 ... D9
Huarocondo 2,498 ... F9
Huaura 9,338 ... D8
Huaylas 1,344 ... C7
Iberia 2,307 ... F5
Ica 111,087 ... E10
Ichuña 277 ... G11
Ilave 9,891 ... H11
Ilo 31,549 ... G11
Imperial 20,894 ... D9
Iñapari 188 ... H8
Intutu 746 ... E4
Iparia 278 ... E7
Iquitos 173,629 ... F4
Jaén 24,356 ... C5
Jauja 14,630 ... E8
Jayanca 6,401 ... B6
Jeberos 1,493 ... D5
Juanjuí 9,324 ... D6
Juli 5,575 ... H11
Juliaca 77,976 ... G10
Jumbilla 1,035 ... C5
Junín 8,988 ... E8
Lagunas 4,601 ... E5
La Huaca 5,161 ... B5
La Jalca 1,769 ... D6
La Joya 5,000 ... G11
Lamas 8,937 ... D6
Lambayeque 23,746 ... B6
Lampa 4,319 ... G10
Lamud 2,405 ... C6
Lanlacuni Bajo 405 ... G9
La Oroya 33,305 ... D8
Las Piedras ... H9
Las Yaras 759 ... G11
La Unión 2,828 ... D7
Leimebamba 1,957 ... D6
Lima (cap.) 375,957 ... D8
Lima* 3,968,972 ... D8
Limbani 728 ... H10
Lircay 5,213 ... E9
Llata 2,922 ... D7
Lobitos 2,975 ... B5
Locumba 369 ... G11
Lomas 287 ... E10
Lucerna ... H9
Lurín 14,405 ... D9
Machupicchu 544 ... F9
Macusani 3,389 ... G10
Madre de Dios 660 ... G9
Máncora 5,358 ... B5
Manú 234 ... G9
Marcapata 369 ... G9
Marcona 25,962 ... E10
Margos 1,622 ... D8
Masisea 1,586 ... E7
Matarani ... F11
Matucana 4,196 ... D8
Mavila ... H8
Mazán 281 ... F4
Mazocruz 1,580 ... H11
Mendoza 1,902 ... D6
Mishagua ... F8
Moho 2,560 ... H10
Mollendo 21,206 ... F11
Monsefú 17,186 ... C6
Moquegua 21,488 ... G11
Morales 4,370 ... D6
Morococha 11,234 ... D8
Morropón 7,611 ... C5
Motupe 3,411 ... C6
Moyobamba 14,319 ... D6
Nauta 4,083 ... F5
Nazca 22,756 ... E10
Negritos 12,476 ... B5
Nuñoa 3,613 ... G10
Ocoña 1,062 ... F11
Ocros 1,037 ... D8
Ollachea 1,308 ... G9
Ollantaytambo 1,500 ... F9
Olmos 7,946 ... C5
Omaguas ... F5
Omas 249 ... D9
Omate 1,131 ... G11
Orcotuna 3,359 ... E8
Orellana 2,886 ... E6
Otuzco 5,765 ... C6
Oxapampa 5,233 ... E8
Oyón 6,279 ... D8
Pacasmayo 17,588 ... C6
Pachiza 889 ... D6
Paiján 12,699 ... C6
Paita 18,749 ... B5
Palpa 3,393 ... E10
Pampachiri 428 ... F10
Pampacolca 2,010 ... F10
Pampas 3,850 ... E9
Panao 1,363 ... E7
Pantoja 457 ... E3
Parinari 375 ... E5
Paruro 1,727 ... F9
Pataz 759 ... D6
Paucarbamba 534 ... E9
Paucartambo, Cusco 1,620 ... G9
Paucartambo, Pasco 3,497 ... E8
Pevas 1,325 ... G4
Picota 2,288 ... D6
Pimentel 9,129 ... B6
Pinquén ... G9
Pisac 1,566 ... G9
Pisco 53,414 ... D9
Piura 186,354 ... B5
Pizacoma 400 ... H11
Pomabamba 2,489 ... D7
Porvenir ... E5
Pozuzo 326 ... E8
Puca Barranca ... E4
Pucallpa 91,953 ... E7
Pucará 2,268 ... G10
Pucaurco 628 ... G4
Pucusana 3,329 ... D9
Puerto Alianza ... D5
Puerto América 240 ... D5
Puerto Arturo ... F3
Puerto Bermúdez 1,133 ... E8
Puerto Caballas ... E10
Puerto Chicama 3,136 ... C6
Puerto Eten 2,575 ... B6
Puerto Inca 1,286 ... E7
Puerto José Pardo ... D4
Puerto Leguía, Loreto ... D4
Puerto Leguía, Puno ... G9
Puerto Maldonado 12,609 ... H9
Puerto Morín ... C7
Puerto Ocopa 1,088 ... E8
Puerto Pardo ... F7
Puerto Pizarro ... B4
Puerto Portillo 86 ... F7
Puerto Prado 328 ... E8
Puerto Samanco 1,435 ... C7
Puerto Tahuantinsuyo ... G9
Puerto Victoria ... E7
Puno 66,477 ... G10
Punta de Bombón 4,647 ... F11
Punta Moreno ... C6
Puquina 1,026 ... G11
Puquio 8,099 ... F10
Putina 5,414 ... H10
Querecotillo 10,637 ... B5
Quicacha 255 ... F10
Quilca 235 ... F11
Quillabamba 16,837 ... F9
Quince Mil ... G9
Ramón Castilla 1,811 ... G5
Recuay 2,764 ... D7
Requena 8,270 ... F5
Reventazón ... B6
Rioja 9,876 ... D6
Salaverry 5,539 ... C7
Saña 40,144 ... C6
Sandia 1,682 ... H10
San José 4,070 ... B6
San José de Sisa 3,782 ... D6
San Juan ... E10
San Lorenzo 124 ... H8
San Martín ... E3
San Miguel, Ayacucho 1,440 ... F9
San Miguel, Cajamarca 1,798 ... C6
San Pedro de Lloc 11,463 ... C6
San Ramón 7,145 ... E8
Santa 20,490 ... C7
Santa Clotilde 1,068 ... E4
Santa Cruz, Cajamarca 2,739 ... C6
Santa Cruz, Loreto 449 ... E5
Santa Elena 368 ... F5
Santa María de Nanay 294 ... F4
Santiago 5,092 ... E10
Santiago de Cao 22,119 ... C6
Santiago de Chocorvos 525 ... E9
Santiago de Chuco 5,189 ... C7
Santo Tomás, Amazonas 1,093 ... C6
Santo Tomás, Cusco 2,755 ... G10
Santo Tomás de Andoas 272 ... D4
San Vicente de Cañete 15,277 ... D9
Saposoa 4,541 ... D6
Saquena 2,755 ... F5
Satipo 9,208 ... E8
Sauce 2,263 ... D6
Sayán 5,129 ... D8
Sechura 11,724 ... B5
Sicuani 21,176 ... G10
Sihuas 2,178 ... D7
Sullana 80,947 ... B5
Sumbay ... G10
Sumbilca 1,155 ... D8
Supe 10,061 ... D8
Tacna 92,640 ... G11
Tahuamanu 2,619 ... H8
Talara 55,122 ... B5
Tambo de Mora 2,790 ... D9
Tambo Grande 10,087 ... B5
Tamshiyacu 2,040 ... F5
Tarapoto 33,429 ... D6
Tarata 2,624 ... H11
Tarma 34,369 ... E8
Tarqui ... E3
Tayabamba 1,649 ... D7
Ticaco 781 ... H11
Tingo María 25,030 ... D7
Tiruntán 723 ... E6
Tocache 5,940 ... D7
Tonegrama ... D4
Topará ... D9
Toquepala ... G11
Torata 6,320 ... G11
Tournavista ... E7
Trujillo 354,557 ... C7
Tumbes 48,187 ... B4
Ubinas 422 ... G11
Uchiza 2,471 ... D7
Unini ... F8
Urcos 4,155 ... G9
Urubamba 4,686 ... F9
Vinchos 735 ... E9
Virú 6,587 ... C7
Vitor 416 ... G11
Yambrasbamba 277 ... D5
Yanahuanca 5,109 ... D8
Yanaoca 1,152 ... G10
Yauca 1,805 ... E10
Yauli 1,020 ... D8
Yauyos 1,296 ... E9
Yunguyo 7,253 ... H11
Yurimaguas 22,858 ... E5
Zarumilla 9,713 ... B4
Zorritos 4,497 ... B4

OTHER FEATURES

Acarí (riv.) ... E10
Aguaytía (riv.) ... E7
Aguja (pt.) ... B5
Amazon (riv.) ... F4
Andes, Cordillera de los (mts.) ... F10
Apurímac (riv.) ... F9
Azángaro (riv.) ... G10
Azul, Cordillera (mts.) ... E7
Blanca, Cordillera (mts.) ... D7
Blanco (cape) ... B5
Blanco (riv.) ... F6
Boquerón, El (pass) ... E7
Cañete (riv.) ... D9
Casma (riv.) ... C7
Chimbote (bay) ... C7
Chincha (isls.) ... D9
Coles (pt.) ... G11
Cóndor, Cordillera del (range) ... C5
Coropuna, Nudo (mt.) ... F10
Corrientes (riv.) ... E4
El Boquerón (pass) ... E7
El Misti (mt.) ... G11
Ene (riv.) ... E8
Ferrol (pen.) ... C7
Grande (riv.) ... E10
Guañape (isls.) ... C7
Heath (riv.) ... H9
Huallaga (riv.) ... D5
Huasaga (riv.) ... D4
Huascarán (mt.) ... D7
Huayabamba (riv.) ... D6
Ica (riv.) ... E10
Inambari (riv.) ... H9
Independencia (bay) ... D10
Independencia (isl.) ... D10
Junín (lake) ... E8
Juruá (riv.) ... F7
Lachay (pt.) ... D8
Lobos de Afuera (isls.) ... B6
Lobos de Tierra (isl.) ... B6
Locumba (riv.) ... G11
Madre de Dios (riv.) ... G9
Majes (riv.) ... F11
Mantaro (riv.) ... E8
Manú (riv.) ... G8
Marañón (riv.) ... E5
Mayo (riv.) ... D6
Misti, El (mt.) ... G11
Montaña, La (reg.) ... F8
Morona (riv.) ... D5
Nanay (riv.) ... E4
Napo (riv.) ... F4
Negra, Cordillera (mts.) ... D7
Negra (pt.) ... B6
Ñermete (pt.) ... B5
Occidental, Cordillera (range) ... F10
Ocoña (riv.) ... F11
Oriental, Cordillera (range) ... H10
Pachitea (riv.) ... E7
Paita (bay) ... B5
Pampas (riv.) ... E9
Paracas (pen.) ... D9
Parinacochas (lake) ... F10
Pariñas (pt.) ... B5
Pastaza (riv.) ... D5
Pativilca (riv.) ... D8
Perené (riv.) ... E8
Pichis (riv.) ... E8
Piedras, Las (riv.) ... G8
Pisco (bay) ... D9
Pisco (riv.) ... D9
Piura (riv.) ... B5
Puinagua, Canal de (riv.) ... E5
Purús (riv.) ... G8
Putumayo (riv.) ... G4
Rímac (riv.) ... D9
Salcantay (mt.) ... F9
Sama (riv.) ... G11
San Gallán (isl.) ... D9
San Lorenzo (isl.) ... D9
San Nicolás (bay) ... E10
Santa (riv.) ... C7
Santiago (riv.) ... D4
Sechura (bay) ... B5
Tahuamanu (riv.) ... H8
Tambo (riv.) ... G11
Tambopata (riv.) ... H9
Tapiche (riv.) ... E6
Tigre (riv.) ... E4
Titicaca (lake) ... H10
Tumbes (riv.) ... B4
Ucayali (riv.) ... F5

(continued on following page)

Agriculture, Industry and Resources

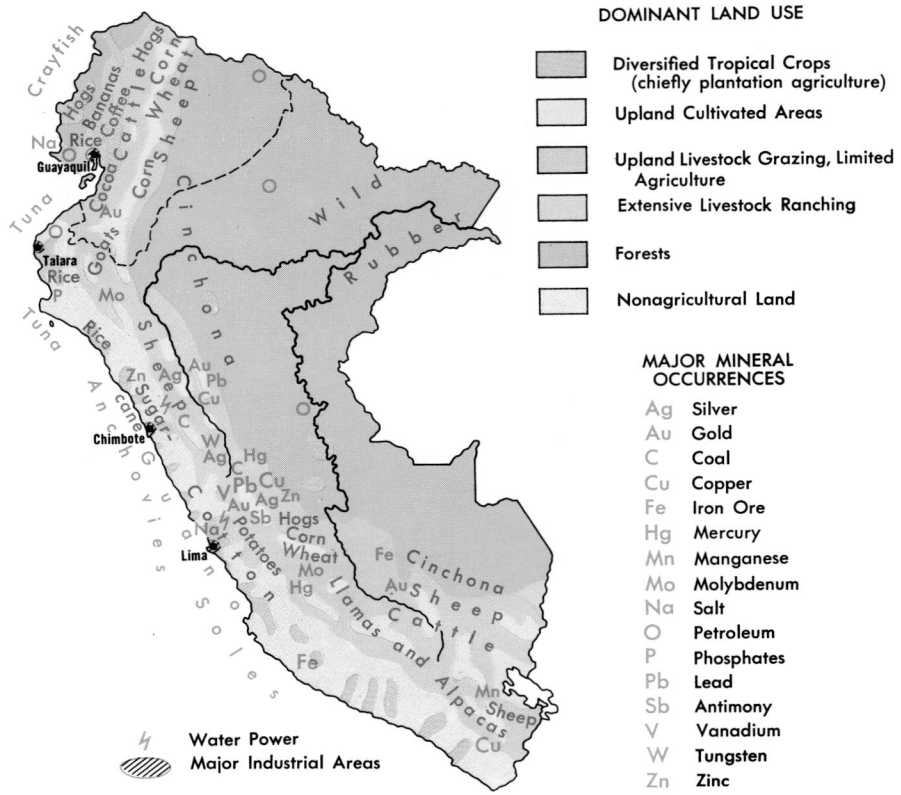

DOMINANT LAND USE

- Diversified Tropical Crops (chiefly plantation agriculture)
- Upland Cultivated Areas
- Upland Livestock Grazing, Limited Agriculture
- Extensive Livestock Ranching
- Forests
- Nonagricultural Land

MAJOR MINERAL OCCURRENCES

Ag	Silver
Au	Gold
C	Coal
Cu	Copper
Fe	Iron Ore
Hg	Mercury
Mn	Manganese
Mo	Molybdenum
Na	Salt
O	Petroleum
P	Phosphates
Pb	Lead
Sb	Antimony
V	Vanadium
W	Tungsten
Zn	Zinc

Water Power
Major Industrial Areas

Agriculture, Industry and Resources

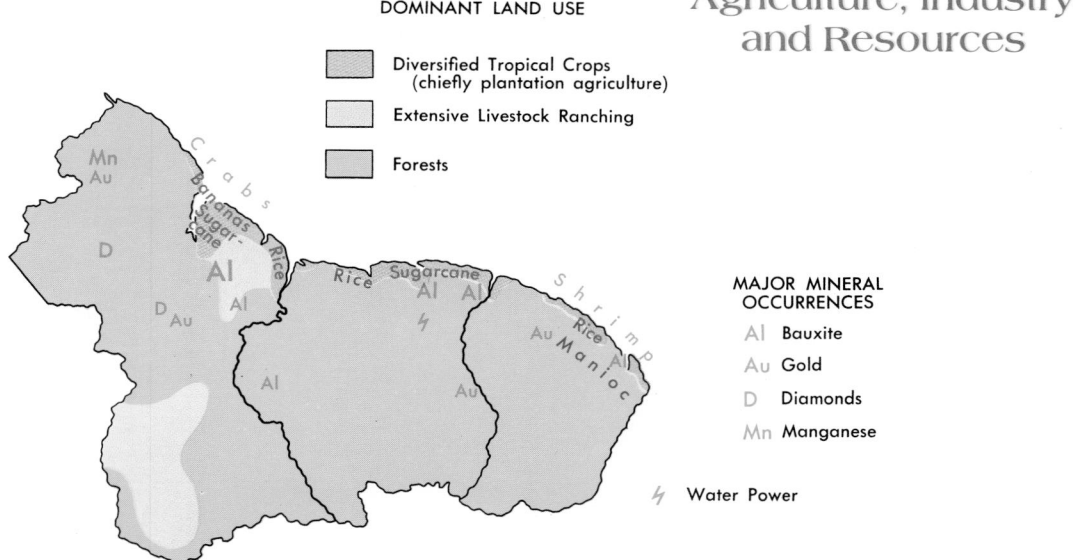

DOMINANT LAND USE

- Diversified Tropical Crops (chiefly plantation agriculture)
- Extensive Livestock Ranching
- Forests

MAJOR MINERAL OCCURRENCES

Al	Bauxite
Au	Gold
D	Diamonds
Mn	Manganese

Water Power

* City and suburbs
○ Population of district.

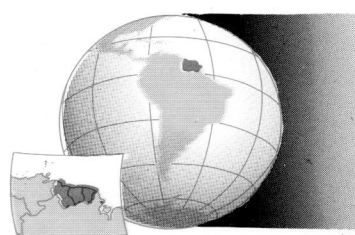

GUYANA

AREA 83,000 sq. mi. (214,970 sq. km.)
POPULATION 793,000
CAPITAL Georgetown
LARGEST CITY Georgetown
HIGHEST POINT Mt. Roraima 9,094 ft. (2,772 m.)
MONETARY UNIT Guyana dollar
MAJOR LANGUAGES English, Hindi
MAJOR RELIGIONS Christianity, Hinduism, Islam

SURINAME

AREA 55,144 sq. mi. (142,823 sq. km.)
POPULATION 354,860
CAPITAL Paramaribo
LARGEST CITY Paramaribo
HIGHEST POINT Julianatop 4,200 ft. (1,280 m.)
MONETARY UNIT Suriname guilder
MAJOR LANGUAGES Dutch, Hindi, Indonesian
MAJOR RELIGIONS Christianity, Islam, Hinduism

FRENCH GUIANA

AREA 35,135 sq. mi. (91,000 sq. km.)
POPULATION 73,022
CAPITAL Cayenne
LARGEST CITY Cayenne
HIGHEST POINT 2,723 ft. (830 m.)
MONETARY UNIT French franc
MAJOR LANGUAGE French
MAJOR RELIGIONS Roman Catholicism, Protestantism

Courantyne (riv.)	C3
Cuyuni (riv.)	B2
Demerara (riv.)	B3
Enwarak (mt.)	B3
Essequibo (riv.)	B3
Great (fall)	B3
Ireng (riv.)	B3
Kaieteur (fall)	B3
Kamaria (falls)	B2
Kuyuwini (riv.)	B4
Kwitaro (riv.)	B4
Leguan (isl.)	B2
Marudi (mts.)	B5
Mazaruni (riv.)	A2
Moruka (riv.)	B2
New (riv.)	C4
Pakaraima (mts.)	A3
Playa (pt.)	B1
Pomeroon (riv.)	B2
Potaro (riv.)	B3
Puruni (riv.)	A3
Roraima (mt.)	A3
Rupununi (riv.)	B4
Sororieng (mt.)	A2
Surwakwima (fall)	B4
Takutu (riv.)	B4
Venamo (mt.)	A3
Waini (riv.)	B2
Wenamu (riv.)	A2

SURINAME

DISTRICTS

Brokopondo 17,763	D4
Commewijne 18,740	D3
Coronie 3,251	C3
Marowijne 25,911	D4
Nickerie 35,178	C3
Para 16,635	D3
Paramaribo 102,297	D2
Saramacca 13,554	C3
Suriname 151,585	D3

CITIES and TOWNS

Ajoewa	C4
Alalapadu	C4

Albina 1,000	D3
Asidonhoppo	D4
Berg en Dal	D3
Bitagron	C3
Brokopondo	D3
Burnside	D2
Calcutta 1,100	C3
Cottica	D4
Domburg 1,200	D3
Groningen 600	D2
Huwelijkszorg	D3
Kwakoegron	D3
Lelydorp 300	D3
Majoli	D4
Marienburg 3,500	D3
Moengo 2,100	D3
Nieuw-Amsterdam 1,400	D2
Nieuw-Nickerie 7,400	C3
Paramaribo (cap.) ⊙ 167,905	D2
Paranam	D3
Totness 1,300	C3
Uitkijk	D3
Wageningen 800	C3
Zanderij	D3

OTHER FEATURES

Bakhuys (mts.)	C3
Coeroeni (riv.)	C4
Commewijne (riv.)	D3
Coppename (riv.)	C3
Corantijn (riv.)	C3
Cottica (riv.)	D3
Eilerts de Haan (mts.)	C4
Frederik Willem IV (falls)	C4
Julianatop (mts.)	C4
Kayser (mts.)	D4
Lely (mts.)	D3
Litani (riv.)	D4
Marowijne (riv.)	D3
Nickerie (riv.)	C3
Orange (mts.) j.	D4
Saramacca (riv.)	D3
Sipliwini (riv.)	C3
Suriname (riv.)	D3
Tapanahoni (riv.)	D4
Toekomstig (res.)	D3
Van Blommestein (lake)	D3
Wilhelmina (mts.)	C4

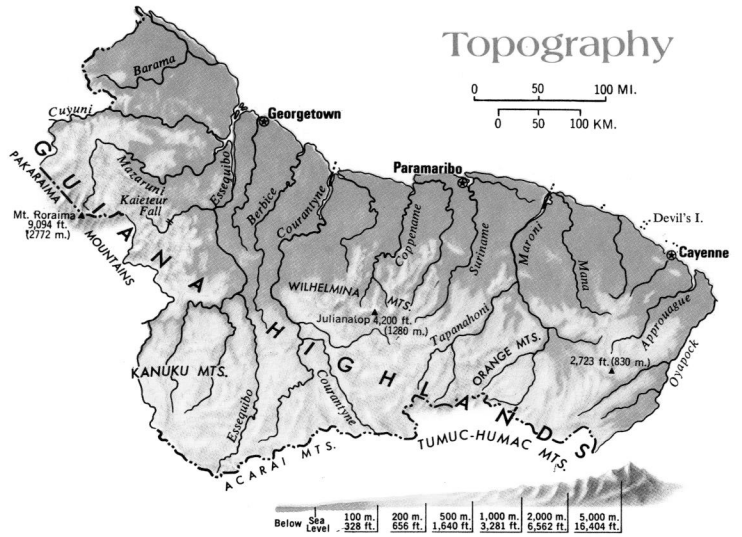

Topography

0   50   100 MI.
0   50   100 KM.

Below Sea Level | 100 m. 328 ft. | 200 m. 656 ft. | 500 m. 1,640 ft. | 1,000 m. 3,281 ft. | 2,000 m. 6,562 ft. | 5,000 m. 16,404 ft.

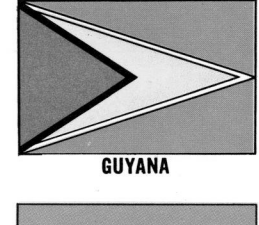

GUYANA

SURINAME

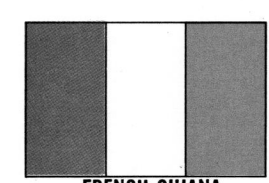

FRENCH GUIANA

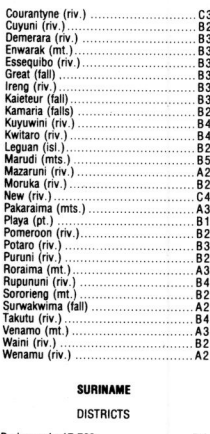

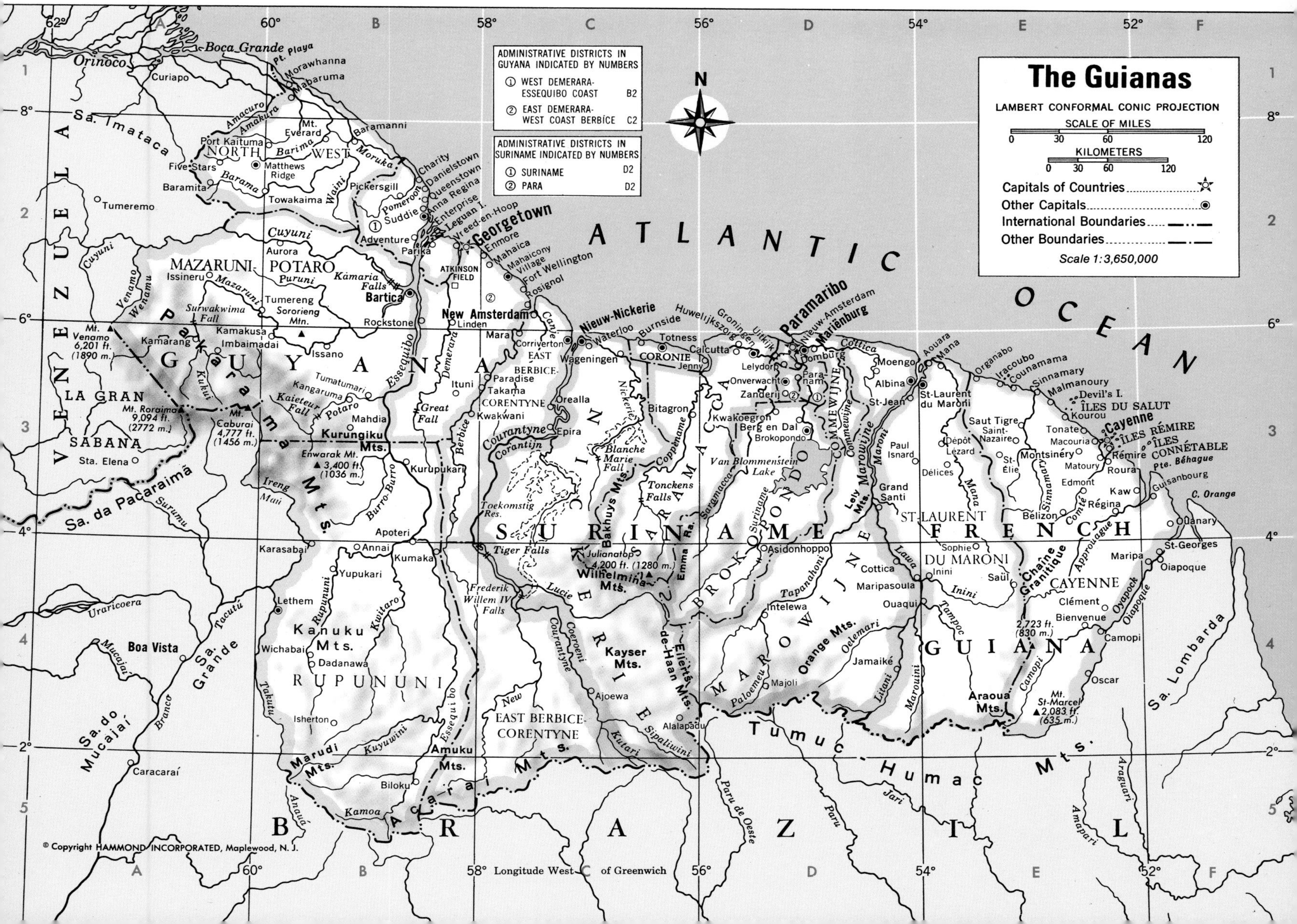

The Guianas

LAMBERT CONFORMAL CONIC PROJECTION
SCALE OF MILES
0   30   60   120
KILOMETERS
0   30   60   120

Capitals of Countries .... ☆
Other Capitals .... ⊙
International Boundaries ..... _ _ _
Other Boundaries .... _ . _ .

Scale 1:3,650,000

ADMINISTRATIVE DISTRICTS IN GUYANA INDICATED BY NUMBERS
① WEST DEMERARA-ESSEQUIBO COAST B2
② EAST DEMERARA-WEST COAST BERBICE C2

ADMINISTRATIVE DISTRICTS IN SURINAME INDICATED BY NUMBERS
① SURINAME D2
② PARA D2

© Copyright HAMMOND INCORPORATED, Maplewood, N.J.

58° Longitude West of Greenwich

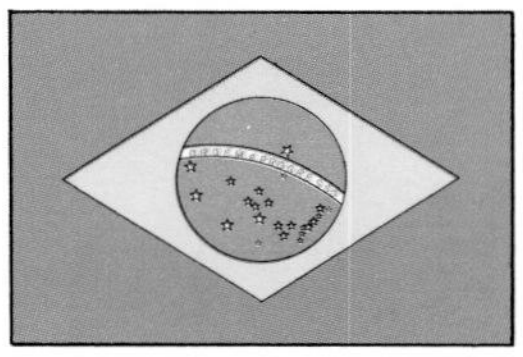

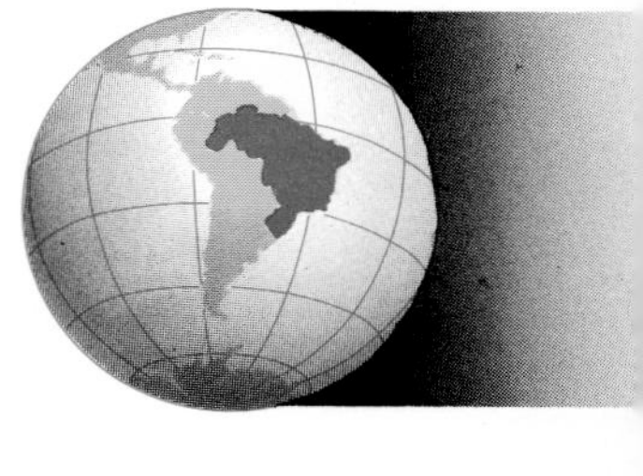

AREA 3,284,426 sq. mi. (8,506,663 sq. km.)
POPULATION 119,098,992
CAPITAL Brasília
LARGEST CITY São Paulo (greater)
HIGHEST POINT Pico da Neblina 9,889 ft. (3,014 m.)
MONETARY UNIT cruzado
MAJOR LANGUAGE Portuguese
MAJOR RELIGION Roman Catholicism

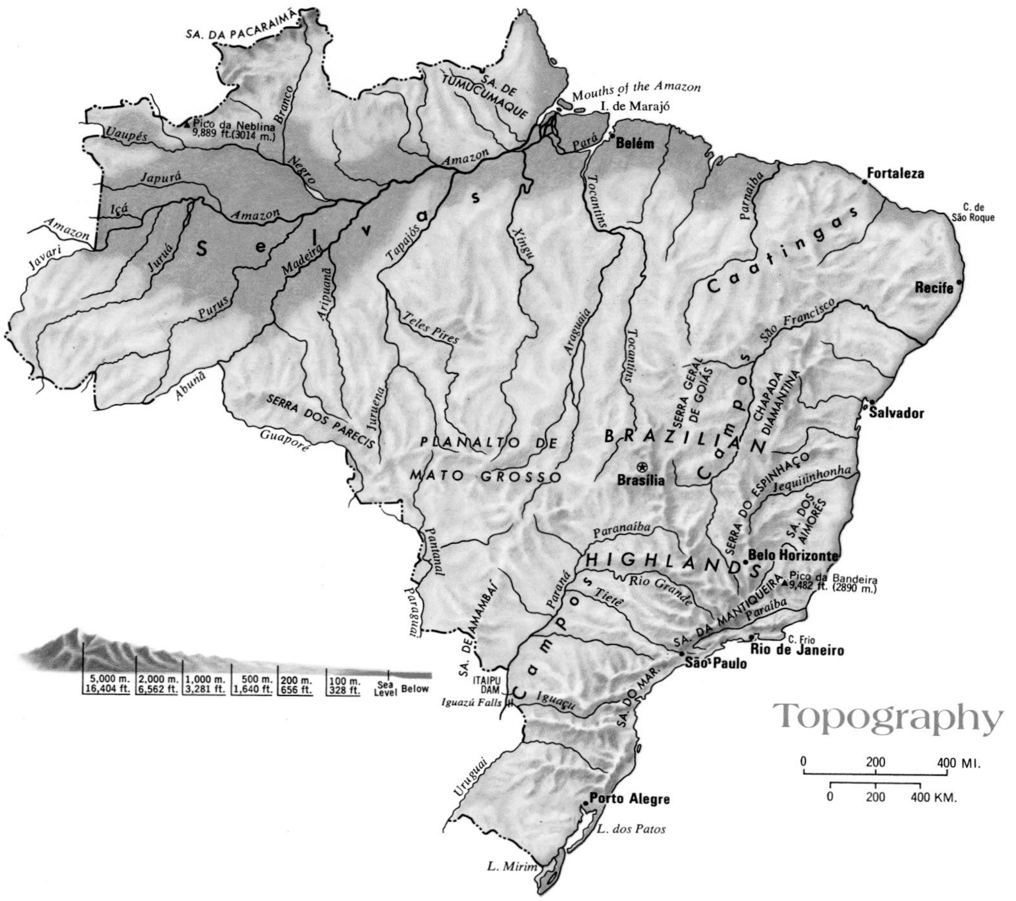

Topography

STATES and TERRITORIES

Acre 301,605 . . . . . G10
Alagoas 1,987,581 . . . . . G5
Amapá (terr.) 175,634 . . . . . D2
Amazonas 1,432,066 . . . . . G9
Bahia 9,474,263 . . . . . F6
Ceará 5,294,876 . . . . . G4
Espírito Santo 2,023,821 . . . F7
Federal District 1,177,393 . . . E6
Goiás 3,865,482 . . . . . D6
Maranhão 4,002,599 . . . . . E4
Mato Grosso 1,141,661 . . . . . B6
Mato Grosso do Sul 1,370,333 . . . . . C7
Minas Gerais 13,390,805 . . . . E7
Pará 3,411,868 . . . . . C4
Paraíba 2,772,600 . . . . . G4
Paraná 7,630,466 . . . . . D9
Pernambuco 6,147,102 . . . . . G5
Piauí 2,140,066 . . . . . F4
Rio de Janeiro 11,297,327 . . . F8
Rio Grande do Norte 1,899,720 . . . . . G4
Rio Grande do Sul 7,777,212 . . . . . C10
Rondônia (terr.) 492,810 . . . H10
Roraima (terr.) 79,153 . . . . . H8
Santa Catarina 3,628,751 . . . D9
São Paulo 25,040,698 . . . . . D8
Sergipe 1,141,834 . . . . . G5
Tocantins D5

CITIES and TOWNS

Abaeté 12,861 . . . . . E7
Abaetetuba 33,031 . . . . . D3
Acaraú 7,144 . . . . . F3
Acopiara 10,747 . . . . . G4
Açu 20,544 . . . . . G4
Agudos 18,790 . . . . . *B3
Alagoa Grande 14,204 . . . . . H4
Alagoinhas 76,377 . . . . . G6
Alcobaça 3,430 . . . . . G7
Alegre 9,441 . . . . . *F2
Alegrete 54,786 . . . . . B10
Além Paraíba 23,028 . . . . . *E2
Alenquer 16,477 . . . . . C3
Alfenas 31,815 . . . . . *D2
Altamira 24,846 . . . . . C3
Altos 13,621 . . . . . F4
Amambaí 12,507 . . . . . C8
Amapá 2,676 . . . . . D2
Amarante 6,848 . . . . . F4
Amargosa 11,118 . . . . . F6
Americana 121,794 . . . . . *C3
Amparo 26,970 . . . . . *C3
Anápolis 160,520 . . . . . D7
Anchieta 5,741 . . . . . F8
Andaraí 2,476 . . . . . F6
Andradina 42,036 . . . . . D8
Andrelândia 8,737 . . . . . *D2
Angra dos Reis 24,894 . . . . *D3
Antonina 11,950 . . . . . *B4
Aparecida 27,265 . . . . . *D3
Apiaí 7,809 . . . . . *B4
Aquidauana 21,514 . . . . . C8
Aracaju 288,106 . . . . . G5
Aracati 20,282 . . . . . G4
Araçatuba 113,486 . . . . . *A2
Araçuaí 12,292 . . . . . F7
Araguari 73,302 . . . . . D7
Araranguá 22,468 . . . . . D10
Araraquara 77,202 . . . . . *B2
Araras 54,323 . . . . . *C3
Araxá 51,339 . . . . . E7
Arcoverde 40,646 . . . . . G5
Areia Branca 12,979 . . . . . G4
Assis 57,217 . . . . . *A3
Avaré 40,716 . . . . . *B3
Bacabal 43,229 . . . . . E4
Bagé 66,743 . . . . . C10
Bahia (Salvador) 1,496,276 . . G6
Baixo Guandu 13,714 . . . . . F7
Balsas 13,566 . . . . . E4
Bambuí 14,172 . . . . . *C2
Barão de Cocais 11,950 . . . *E1
Barbacena 69,675 . . . . . *E2
Bariri 15,372 . . . . . *B3
Barra 10,809 . . . . . F5
Barra do Corda 19,280 . . . . . E4
Barra do Piraí 51,214 . . . . . *E3
Barra Mansa 123,421 . . . . . *D3
Barras 8,904 . . . . . F4
Barreiras 30,355 . . . . . E6
Barreiros 19,419 . . . . . H5
Barretos 65,294 . . . . . *B2
Batatais 30,478 . . . . . *C2
Baturité 12,388 . . . . . G4
Bauru 178,861 . . . . . *B3
Bebedouro 39,070 . . . . . *B2
Bela Vista 11,936 . . . . . C8
Belém 758,117 . . . . . E3
Belém †1,000,349 . . . . . E3
Belo Horizonte 1,442,483 . . *D1
Belo Horizonte †2,541,788 . *D1
Benjamin Constant 6,563 . . . G9
Bento Gonçalves 40,323 . . . C10
Betim 71,599 . . . . . *D2
Bicas 8,611 . . . . . *E2
Birigui 45,348 . . . . . *A2
Blumenau 144,819 . . . . . D9
Boa Esperança 17,394 . . . . *D2
Boa Vista 43,131 . . . . . H8
Bocaiúva 16,616 . . . . . E7
Bom Conselho 13,196 . . . . . G5
Bom Despacho 22,941 . . . . *D1
Bom Jesus da Lapa 19,978 . . F6
Bom Sucesso 10,331 . . . . . *D2
Borba 5,366 . . . . . H9
Bragança Paulista 61,021 . . *C3
Brasiléia 4,835 . . . . . G10
Brasília (cap.) 411,305 . . . . . E6
Brasília de Minas 10,171 . . . . F7
Brejo 5,859 . . . . . F3
Breves 31,452 . . . . . D3
Brumado 24,663 . . . . . F6
Brusque 37,898 . . . . . D9
Cabedolo 18,581 . . . . . H4
Cabo Frio 40,668 . . . . . *F3
Caçador 25,287 . . . . . D9
Caçapava 45,258 . . . . . *D3
Caçapava do Sul 15,180 . . . . C10
Cáceres 33,472 . . . . . B7
Cachoeira 11,520 . . . . . G6
Cachoeira do Sul 59,967 . . . C10
Cachoeiro de Itapemirim 84,994 . . . . . G8
Caeté 23,331 . . . . . *E1
Caetité 8,823 . . . . . F6
Caiaponia 9,358 . . . . . C7
Caicó 30,777 . . . . . G4
Cajazeiras 30,834 . . . . . G4
Cajuru 9,670 . . . . . *C2
Camaquã 28,078 . . . . . C10
Cambará 13,218 . . . . . *A3
Cambuí 8,552 . . . . . *C3
Cametá 15,539 . . . . . D3
Camocim 19,921 . . . . . F3
Campina Grande 222,229 . . . G4
Campinas 566,517 . . . . . *C3
Campo Belo 30,392 . . . . . *D2
Campo Formoso 10,324 . . . . F5
Campo Grand 282,844 . . . . . C8
Campo Largo 34,506 . . . . . *B4
Campo Major 24,009 . . . . . F4
Campos 174,218 . . . . . *F2
Cananéia 5,581 . . . . . *C4
Canavieiras 14,076 . . . . . G6
Canindé 18,573 . . . . . G4
Canoas 214,115 . . . . . D10
Canoinhas 25,880 . . . . . D9
Capanema 28,272 . . . . . E3
Capão Bonito 24,081 . . . . . *B4
Caraguatatuba 22,932 . . . . . *D3
Carangola 15,621 . . . . . *E2
Caratinga 39,621 . . . . . *E1
Caravelas 3,704 . . . . . G7
Carazinho 41,913 . . . . . C10
Carolina 10,136 . . . . . E4
Caruaru 137,636 . . . . . G5
Casa Banca 13,739 . . . . . *C2
Cascavel 16,238 . . . . . G4
Cássia 10,701 . . . . . *C2
Castanhal 51,797 . . . . . E3
Castelo 9,162 . . . . . F8
Castro 21,079 . . . . . *B4
Castro Alves 11,286 . . . . . G6
Cataguases 40,659 . . . . . *E2
Catalão 30,516 . . . . . E7
Catanduva 64,813 . . . . . *B2
Catolé do Rocha 12,165 . . . . G4
Caxambu 16,221 . . . . . *D2
Caxias 56,755 . . . . . F4
Caxias do Sul 198,824 . . . . . D10
Ceará (Fortaleza) 648,815 . . . G3
Ceará-Mirim 17,097 . . . . . H4
Ceres 13,671 . . . . . D6
Chapecó 53,198 . . . . . C9
Coari 14,841 . . . . . H9
Codajás 4,923 . . . . . H9
Codó 11,593 . . . . . E4
Colatina 61,057 . . . . . F7
Conceição do Araguaia 18,143 . . . . . D5
Concórdia 17,973 . . . . . D9
Conselheiro Lafaiete 66,262 E2
Corinto 17,056 . . . . . E7
Cornélio Procópio 31,201 . . . D8
Coroatá 16,070 . . . . . F3
coromandel 11,604 . . . . . F7
Corumbá 66,014 . . . . . B7
Coxim 14,876 . . . . . C7
Crateús 29,905 . . . . . F4
Crato 49,244 . . . . . G4
Criciúma 74,003 . . . . . D10
Cristalina 10,521 . . . . . E7
Cruz Alta 53,315 . . . . . C10
Cruzeiro 55,175 . . . . . *D3
Cruzeiro do Sul 11,189 . . . . . G10
Cubatão 78,327 . . . . . *C3
Cuiabá 167,894 . . . . . C6
Curitiba 843,733 . . . . . *B4
Curitiba †1,441,743 . . . . . *B4
Currais Novos 25,663 . . . . . G4
Cururupu 10,358 . . . . . E3
Curvelo 37,734 . . . . . E7
Diamantina 20,197 . . . . . F7
Divinópolis 108,344 . . . . . *D2
Dois Córregos 11,811 . . . . . *B3
Dom Pedrito 25,773 . . . . . C10
Dores do Indaiá 13,058 . . . . . E7
Dourados 76,838 . . . . . C8
Duque de Caxias 306,057 . . *E3
Erexim 46,927 . . . . . C9
Esperanca 12,964 . . . . . G4
Esplanada 9,822 . . . . . G5
Estancia 28,250 . . . . . G5
Feira de Santana 225,003 . . . G5
Fernandópolis 39,737 . . . . *A2
Floriano 35,761 . . . . . F4
Florianópolis 153,547 . . . . . E9
Fonte Boa 3,278 . . . . . G9
Formiga 36,681 . . . . . *D2
Formosa 29,304 . . . . . E6
Fortaleza 648,815 . . . . . G3
Fortaleza †1,581,588 . . . . . G3
Foz do Iguaçu 93,619 . . . . . C9
Franca 143,630 . . . . . *C2
Frutal 22,955 . . . . . *B2
Garanhuns 64,854 . . . . . G5
Garca 26,527 . . . . . *B3
Goiana 30,108 . . . . . H4
Goiania 703,263 . . . . . D7
Goiás 15,768 . . . . . D6
Governador Valadares 173,699 . . . . . F7
Grajaú 11,147 . . . . . E4
Guacul 12,715 . . . . . *F2
Guajará-Mirim 19,992 . . . . . H10
Guarapuava 17,189 . . . . . C9
Guarantiguetá 68,370 . . . . . *D3
Guarujá 67,730 . . . . . *C4
Guarulhos 395,117 . . . . . *C3
Guaxupé 23,637 . . . . . *C2
Guirantinga 8,981 . . . . . C7
Gurupi 27,39 . . . . . D5
Humaitá 10,004 . . . . . H10
Ibaiti 11,352 . . . . . *A3
Ibiá 11,161 . . . . . E7
Ibicaraí 18,202 . . . . . G6
Ibitinga 23,359 . . . . . *B2
Icó 13,007 . . . . . G4
Igarapava 15,342 . . . . . C2
Igarapé-Miri 12,172 . . . . . D3
Iguape 16,827 . . . . . *C4
Iguatu 39,611 . . . . . G4
Ijuí 51,925 . . . . . C10
Ilhéus 71,240 . . . . . G6
Imbituba 9,998 . . . . . D10
Imperatiz 111,818 . . . . . E4
Inhumas 23,455 . . . . . D7
Ipameri 14,163 . . . . . E7
Ipu 12,787 . . . . . F4
Irati 21,956 . . . . . *A4
Itabaiana, Paraiba 17,843 . . . H4
Itabaiana, Sergipe 26,055 . . . G5
Itaberaba 27,590 . . . . . F6
Itabira 57,691 . . . . . F7
Itabirito 22,978 . . . . . *E2
Itabuna 129,938 . . . . . G6
Itacoatiara 26,737 . . . . . B3
Itaituba 19,644 . . . . . C4
Itajai 78,867 . . . . . D9
Itajubá 53,506 . . . . . *D3
Itanhaem 26,181 . . . . . C4
Itapecerica 10,234 . . . . . *D2
Itapecuru-Mirim 12,216 . . . . F3
Itapemirim 16,829 . . . . . F8
Itaperuna 34,644 . . . . . *F2
Itapetinga 36,897 . . . . . G6
Itapetininga 61,344 . . . . . *B3
Itapeva 36,551 . . . . . *B3
Itapipoca 19,463 . . . . . G3
Itapira 36,308 . . . . . *C3
Itápolis 13,750 . . . . . *B2
Itaporanga 8,988 . . . . . G4
Itaqui 23,136 . . . . . B10
Itararé 24,368 . . . . . *B4
Itatiba 35,537 . . . . . *C3
Itaúna 49,372 . . . . . *D2
Itu 62,221 . . . . . *C3
Ituacu 1,749 . . . . . F6
Ituiutaba 65,178 . . . . . D7
Itumbiara 56,602 . . . . . D7
Iturama 12,363 . . . . . *A1
Ituverava 21,323 . . . . . *C2
Jaboatao 67,129 . . . . . H5
Jaboticabal 40,276 . . . . . *B2
Jacarel 103,652 . . . . . *D3
Jacarezinho 23,684 . . . . . *A3
Jacobina 26,723 . . . . . F5
Jacupiranga 7,044 . . . . . B4
Jaguaquara 11,336 . . . . . F6
Jaguarao 18,165 . . . . . C11
Jaguariaiva 8,566 . . . . . *B4
Januária 20,484 . . . . . E6
Jataí 40,957 . . . . . D7
Jaú 59,522 . . . . . *B3
Jequié 84,792 . . . . . F6
Jequitinhonha 10,900 . . . . . F7
Ji-Paraná 31,724 . . . . . H10
Joacaba 16,195 . . . . . D9
Joao Pessoa 290,424 . . . . . H4
Joao Pinheiro 17,013 . . . . . E7
Joinvile 217,074 . . . . . D9
Juazeiro 60,940 . . . . . G5
Juazeiro do Norte 125,248 . . F4
Juiz de Fora 299,728 . . . . . *E2
Jundiaí 210,015 . . . . . *C3
Lages 108,768 . . . . . D9
Laguna 27,743 . . . . . D10
Lambari 9,722 . . . . . *D2
Lapa 13,314 . . . . . D9
Laranjeiras do Sul 19,329 . . . C9
Lavras 35,345 . . . . . *D2
Leme 40,155 . . . . . *C3
Leopoldina 28,554 . . . . . *E2
Limeira 137,812 . . . . . *C3
Limoeiro 36,088 . . . . . H4
Limoeiro do Norte 13,112 . . . G4
Linhares 51,575 . . . . . F7
Lins 44,633 . . . . . *B2
Londrina 258,054 . . . . . D8
Lorena 51,276 . . . . . *D3
Luis Correia 3,576 . . . . . F3
Luz 10,068 . . . . . *D1
Luziania 67,284 . . . . . E7
Macaé 39,644 . . . . . *F3
Macalba 17,036 . . . . . H4
Macapá 89,081 . . . . . D2
Macau 17,543 . . . . . G4
Maceio 376,479 . . . . . H5
Machado 16,164 . . . . . *C2
Mafra 26,226 . . . . . D9
Magé 37,597 . . . . . *E3
Mamanguape 16,321 . . . . . H4
Manacapuru 17,016 . . . . . H9
Manaus 613,068 . . . . . H9
Manhuacu 22,678 . . . . . *E2
Manhumirim 11,085 . . . . . *E2
Manicoré 9,532 . . . . . H9
Marabá 41,564 . . . . . D4
Maracaju 9,699 . . . . . C8
Maragogipe 13,512 . . . . . G6
Maranguape 20,098 . . . . . G3
Marechal Deodoro 9,400 . . . . H5
Mariana 11,785 . . . . . *E2
Marilia 103,904 . . . . . *A3
Maringá 158,047 . . . . . D8
Mata de São João 23,741 . . . G6
Mato Grosso (Vila Bela da Santissima Trindade) 1,401 . . . . . B6
Maués 10,846 . . . . . B3
Mineiros 16,844 . . . . . C7
Miracema 15,545 . . . . . *E2
Miracema do Norte D5
Mirassol 25,173 . . . . . *B2
Mococa 33,682 . . . . . *C2
Mogi das Cruzes 122,265 . . *C3
Mogi-Mirim 41,827 . . . . . *C3
Monte Alegre 10,646 . . . . . C3
Monte Aprazivel 9,767 . . . . . *A2
Monteiro 11,051 . . . . . G4
Montenegro 27,246 . . . . . D10
Montes Claros 151,881 . . . . . E7
Morrinhos 20,154 . . . . . D7
Mossoró 118,007 . . . . . G4
Muriaé 50,040 . . . . . *E2
Muzambinho 8,803 . . . . . *C2
Nanuque 34,445 . . . . . F7
Natal 376,552 . . . . . H4
Nazaré 18,068 . . . . . G6
Niquelandia 8,828 . . . . . D6
Niterói 386,185 . . . . . *E3
Nova Cruz 12,824 . . . . . H4
Nova Era 11,126 . . . . . *E1
Nova Friburgo 88,943 . . . . . *E3
Nova Iguaçu 491,802 . . . . . *E3
Nova Lima 35,035 . . . . . *E2
Nova Russas 10,021 . . . . . F4
Novo Hamburgo 132,066 . . . D10
Novo Horizonte 18,439 . . . . *B2
Óbidos 17,143 . . . . . C3
Oeiras 12,406 . . . . . F4
Olimpia 24,376 . . . . . *B2
Olinda 266,392 . . . . . H4
Oliveira 22,642 . . . . . *D2
Oriximiná 12,078 . . . . . C3
Orlândia 22,924 . . . . . *C2
Osasco 376,689 . . . . . *C3
Ourinhos 52,698 . . . . . *B3
Ouro Preto 27,821 . . . . . *E2
Palmares 40,624 . . . . . H5
Palmas 15,823 . . . . . C9
Palmeira 11,521 . . . . . *B4
Palmeira das Missões 23,943 . . . . . C9
Pará (Belém) 758,117 . . . . . E3
Paracatu 29,911 . . . . . E7
Pará de Minas 37,127 . . . . *D1
Paraguaçu Paulista 17,399 . . . . . D8
Paraíba do Sul 13,510 . . . . *E3
Paranalba 21,305 . . . . . D7
Paranaguá 68,366 . . . . . *B4
Parati 8,684 . . . . . *D3
Parintins 29,369 . . . . . B3
Parnalba 78,718 . . . . . F3
Passo Fundo 103,121 . . . . . D10
Passos 56,998 . . . . . *C2
Patos 58,735 . . . . . G4
Patos de Minas 59,896 . . . . . E7
Patrocínio 29,520 . . . . . E7
Pau dos Ferros 12,985 . . . . . G4
Paulo Afonso 62,066 . . . . . G5
Pederneiras 18,864 . . . . . *B3
Pedra Azul 13,615 . . . . . F6
Pedreiras 30,843 . . . . . E4
Pedro Segundo 9,693 . . . . . F4
Pelotas 197,092 . . . . . C10
Penápolis 32,168 . . . . . *A2
Penedo 27,064 . . . . . G5
Pernambuco (Recife) 1,184,215 . . . . . H5
Petrolina 73,436 . . . . . G5
Petrópolis 149,427 . . . . . *E3
Picos 33,098 . . . . . F4
Piedade 13,054 . . . . . *C3
Pilar 14,778 . . . . . H5
Pindamonhangaba 51,174 . *D3

(continued on following page)

Pinhal (Espírito Santo do
  Pinhal) 23,235 ....*C3
Pinheiro 19,556 ....E3
Piquete 10,316 ....*D3
Piracanjuba 11,151 ....D7
Piracicaba 179,395 ......*C3
Piracuruca 9,419 ....F3
Piral do Sul 13,709 ......*B4
Piraju 16,288 ....*B3
Pirapora 31,533 ....E7
Pirassununga 32,510 ....*C2
Pires do Rio 16,659 ......D7
Piripiri 29,497 ....F4
Pitangui 12,116 ....*D1
Piuí 17,327 ....*D2
Poções 16,036 ....F6
Poconé 12,960 ....B7
Poços de Caldas 81,448 .*C2
Pombal 14,831 ....G4
Pompéia 11,282 ....*A3
Ponta Grossa 171,111 ....F6
Ponta Porã 25,807 ....C8
Ponte Nova 34,807 ......*E2
Porangatu 21,192 ....D6
Porto Alegre 1,108,883 ..D10
Porto Alegre †2,232,370 .D10
Porto Feliz 19,680 ....*C3
Porto Nacional 19,052 ....E5
Porto Seguro 5,007 ....G7
Porto União 19,426 ....D9
Porto Velho 101,644 .....H10
Pouso Alegre 50,517 .....*D3
Presidente Dutra 14,506 ..E4
Presidente Prudente
  127,623 ....D8
Presidente Venceslau 26,720 D8
Propriá 19,034 ....G5
Promissão 15,333 ....*B2
Prudentópolis 8,645 ......D9
Quaral 15,091 ....C10
Quixadá 25,149 ....G4
Quixeramobim 14,387 .....F4
Raposos 11,078 ....*E2
Raul Soares 10,055 ......*E2
Recife 1,184,215 ....H5
Recife †2,348,362 ....H5
Registro 28,702 ....*C4
Remanso 13,067 ....F5
Resende 36,633 ....*D3
Ribamar (São José de
  Ribamar) 17,560 ....F3
Ribeirão Prêto 300,704 ..*C2
Rio Bonito 20,561 ....E3
Rio Branco 87,462 ....G10
Rio Claro 103,174 ....*C3
Rio de Janeiro 5,093,237 .*E3
Rio de Janeiro †9,018,637 .*E3
Rio do Sul 33,408 ....D9
Rio Grande 124,706 .....D11
Rio Negro 15,851 ....D9
Rio Pardo 18,370 ....C10
Rio Pomba 9,319 ....*E2
Rio Tinto 12,511 ....H4
Rio Verde 47,639 ....D7
Rio Verde de Mato Grosso
  10,001 ....C7
Rosário 11,669 ....F3
Rosário do Sul 30,753 ....C10
Russas 16,259 ....G4
Sabará 22,883 ....*E1
Sacramento 10,524 ......*C1
Salgueiro 25,915 ....G5
Salinas 12,613 ....F7
Salinópolis 10,395 ....E3
Salto 42,351 ....*C3
Salvador 1,496,276 ......G6
Salvador †1,772,018 .....G6
Santa Cruz 13,172 ....G4
Santa Cruz do Rio Pardo
  20,507 ....*B3
Santa Cruz do Sul 52,050 .C10
Santa Helena de Goiás
  20,067 ....D7
Santa Leopoldina 1,217 ...G7
Santa Maria 151,202 .....C10
Santa Maria da Vitória
  16,294 ....F6
Santana do Ipanema 15,311 .G5
Santana do Livramento
  58,165 ....C10
Santarém 101,534 ....C3
Santa Rita do Sapucaí
  15,005 ....*D3
Santa Vitória do Palmar
  14,758 ....C11
Santiago 30,406 ....C10
Santo Amaro 29,627 .....G6
Santo Ângelo 50,161 .....C10
Santo André 549,278 ....*C3
Santo Antônio da Platina
  21,284 ....*A3
Santos 411,023 ....*C3
Santos Dumont 31,053 ...*E2
São Bento 9,607 ....E3
São Bernardo do Campo
  381,261 ....*C3
São Borja 41,598 ....C10
São Carlos 109,231 .....*C3
São Cristóvão 11,720 ....G5
São Fidélis 11,713 ......*F2
São Francisco 12,011 ....E6
São Francisco do Sul
  13,914 ....E9
São Gabriel 40,497 ......C10
São Gonçalo 221,278 ....F8
São João da Boa Vista
  45,712 ....*C2
São João del Rei 53,401 .*D2
São João dos Patos 12,848 .F4
São João Nepomuceno
  12,752 ....*E2
São Joaquim da Barra
  26,273 ....*C2

São José 37,562 ....D9
São José do Rio Pardo
  21,914 ....*C2
São José do Rio Preto
  171,982 ....*B2
São José dos Campos
  268,073 ....*D3
São José dos Pinhais
  53,422 ....D9
São Leopoldo 94,864 ....D10
São Lourenço 23,047 ....*D3
São Lourenço do Sul
  13,251 ....C10
São Luís 182,466 ....F3
São Luís Gonzaga 29,188 .C10
São Manuel 17,028 ......*B3
São Mateus 22,522 ......G7
São Miguel do Guamá 9,929 E3
São Miguel dos Campos
  18,495 ....G5
São Paulo 7,033,529 ....*C3
São Paulo †12,588,439 ..*C3
São Paulo de Olivença 3,102 G9
São Raimundo Nonato 8,574 F5
São Roque 26,118 ....*C3
São Sebastião 11,065 ...*C3
São Sebastião do Paraíso
  28,482 ....*C2
São Vicente 192,770 ....*C4
Senador Pompeu 10,109 ..G4
Senhor do Bonfim 33,811 .F5
Sena Madureira 6,668 ...G10
Serra do Navio 415 ......C2
Serra Talhada 28,912 ....G4
Serrinha 23,920 ....G5
Sertânia 11,410 ....G5
Sete Lagoas 94,502 ......E7
Sobral 69,072 ....G3
Socorro 12,111 ....*C3
Sorocaba 254,718 ....*C3
Soure 11,306 ....D3
Taguatinga 480,109 .....D6
Taquaritinga 28,018 .....*B2
Tarauacá 6,889 ....G10
Tatuí 44,816 ....*C3
Taubaté 155,371 ....E8
Tefé 14,670 ....G9
Teófilo Otoni 83,108 ....F7
Teresina 339,264 ....F4
Teresópolis 78,782 ......*E3
Tijucas 8,979 ....D9
Timon 55,318 ....F4
Tocantinópolis 8,427 ....D4
Touros H4

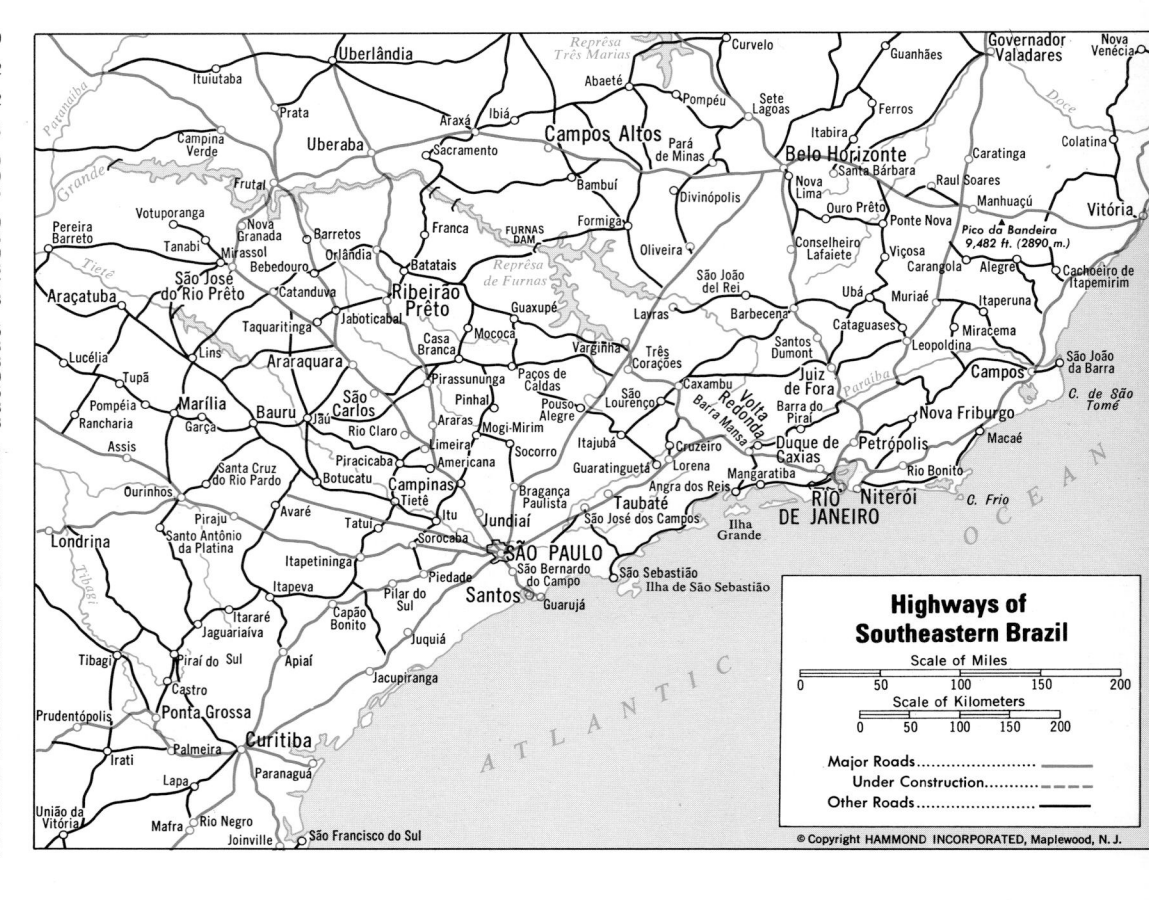

Highways of Southeastern Brazil

Scale of Miles

| 0 | 50 | 100 | 150 | 200 |

Scale of Kilometers

| 0 | 50 | 100 | 150 | 200 |

Major Roads ....
Under Construction ....
Other Roads ....

© Copyright HAMMOND INCORPORATED, Maplewood, N.J.

Agriculture, Industry and Resources

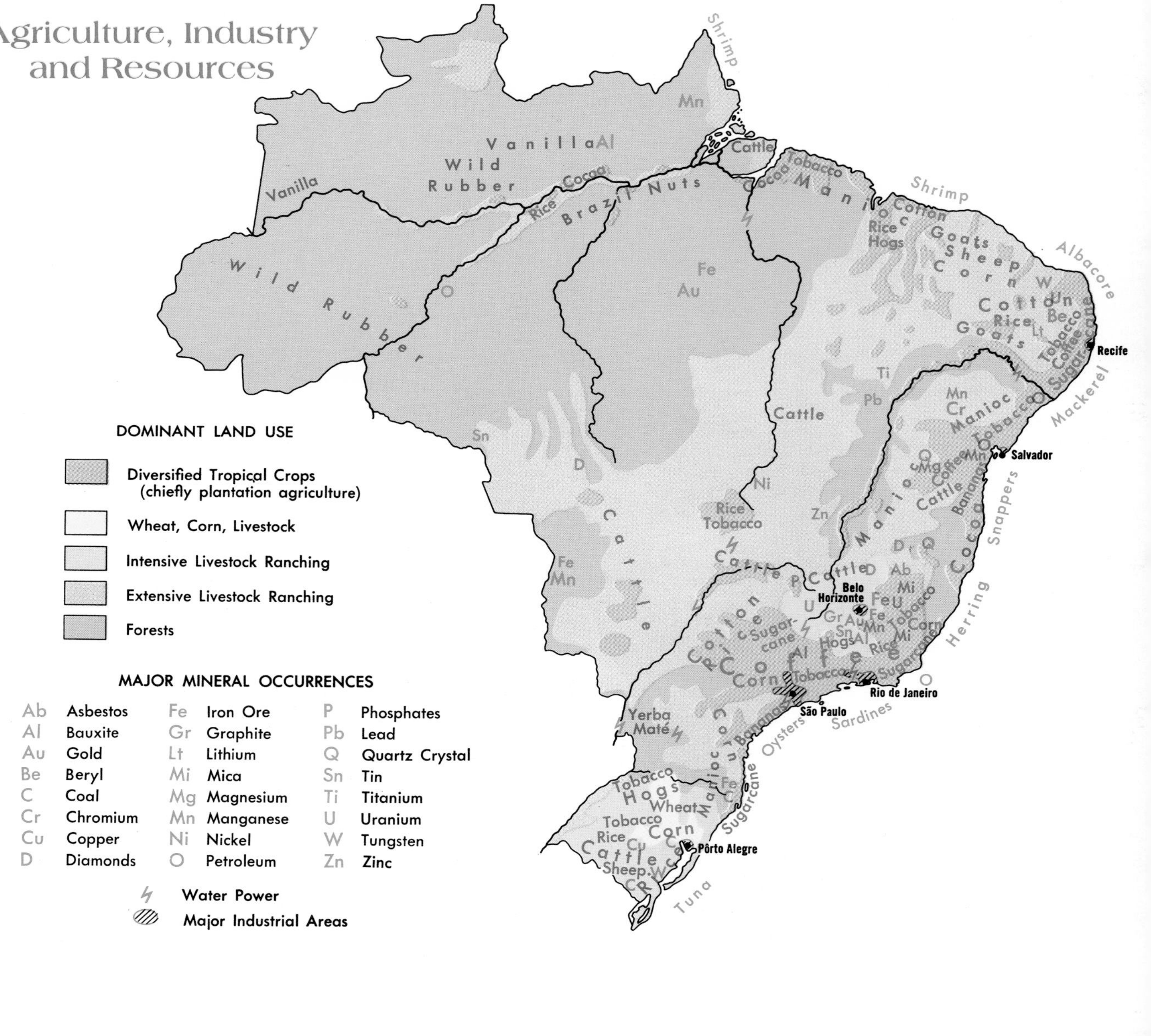

DOMINANT LAND USE

Diversified Tropical Crops
(chiefly plantation agriculture)

Wheat, Corn, Livestock

Intensive Livestock Ranching

Extensive Livestock Ranching

Forests

MAJOR MINERAL OCCURRENCES

Ab	Asbestos	Fe	Iron Ore	P	Phosphates
Al	Bauxite	Gr	Graphite	Pb	Lead
Au	Gold	Lt	Lithium	Q	Quartz Crystal
Be	Beryl	Mi	Mica	Sn	Tin
C	Coal	Mg	Magnesium	Ti	Titanium
Cr	Chromium	Mn	Manganese	U	Uranium
Cu	Copper	Ni	Nickel	W	Tungsten
D	Diamonds	O	Petroleum	Zn	Zinc

⚡ Water Power

▨ Major Industrial Areas

Três Corações 36,179.... *D2
Três Lagoas 45,171 .... C8
Três Pontas 24,225 .... *D2
Três Rios 47,497 ..... *E3
Trindade 22,321 ...... D7
Tubarão 64,585 .... D10
Tucuruí 27,209 .... A4
Tupã 44,450 .... *A2
Tupancireta 13,103 .... C10
Tutóia 4,766 .... F3
Ubá 43,080 .... D5
Ubaitaba 9,413 ...... G6
Ubatuba 23,078 ...... *D3
Uberaba 180,296 ..... *C1
Uberlândia 230,400.... E7
Una 28,148 .... E7
União 9,396 .... F4
União da Vitória 22,682 .. D9
Uruaçu 19,607 .... D6
Uruçuí 6,047 .... E5
Uruguaiana 79,059 .... B10
Vacaria 37,370 .... D10
Valença 34,231 ...... *E3
Varginha 57,448 ..... *D2
Viana 9,753 .... E3
Viçosa 9,843 .... G5
Viçosa 29,198 .... *E2
Vigia 14,749 .... E3
Vila Velha Argolas 74,166 .. F8
Vilhena 12,565 ...... H10
Viscondé dos Rio Branco
    17,295 .... G8
Vitória 144,143 ...... G8
Vitória da Conquista 125,717 F6
Vitória de Santo Antão
    62,890 .... G4
Volta Redonda 177,772 .. *D3
Votuporanga 44,169 ... *B2
Xapuri 3,122 .... G10
Xique-Xique 17,625 .... F5

OTHER FEATURES

Abacaxis (riv.) B4
Abunã (riv.) G10
Acaraí, Serra do (range) .. B2
Acre (riv.) G10
Aiama (lake) H9
Amambaí, Serra de (range) . C7
Amapari (riv.) C2
Amazon (riv.) C3

Anauá (riv.) B2
Aporé (riv.) D7
Araguaia (riv.) D4
Araguari (riv.) D2
Ararauama (lake) *E3
Arinos (riv.) B5
Aripuanã (riv.) A4
Armando Laydner (res.) . *B3
Balique (isl.) D2
Balsas (riv.) E5
Bananal (isl.) D5
Bandeira, Pico da (mt.) . *E2, F8
Braço Maior do Araguaia
    (riv.) D5
Braço Menor do Araguaia
    (riv.) D6
Branco (riv.) H8
Buzios (cape) *F3
Canumã (riv.) B4
Capim (riv.) D3
Carajás, Serra dos (range) . C4
Cardoso (isl.) *C4
Cassiporé (cape) D2
Caviana (isl.) D2
Chavantes, Serra dos
    (range) D5
Claro (riv.) D7
Comprida (isl.) *C4
Cuiabá (riv.) B7
Culuene (riv.) C6
Curuá (riv.) C4
Doce (riv.) *E2, F7
Dois Irmãos, Serra (range) . F5
Espigão Mestre (Geral
    de Goiás) (range) E6
Espinhaço, Serra do (range) F7
Estrondo, Serra do (range) . D4
Feia (lake) *F3
Feio (riv.) *B2
Formosa, Serra (range) . C5
Frio (cape) *F3
Furnas (dam) *C2
Geral de Goiás, Serra
    (range) E6
Gi-Paraná (riv.) H10
Gradaús, Serra dos (range) . D4
Grajaú (riv.) E4
Grande (isl.) *D3
Grande (riv.) *B2, E8
Guanabara (bay) *E3
Guaporé (riv.) H10

Gurguéia (riv.) E5
Gurupi, Serra do (range) . E4
Gurupi (riv.) E3
Ibicuí (riv.) C10
Içá (riv.) G9
Iguaçu (riv.) C9
Iguaçu (falls) C9
Ilha Grande (bay) *D3
Itaipu (dam) C9
Itaipu (riv.) C9
Itapecuru (riv.) F4
Itapi (riv.) B3
Itapicuru (riv.) G5
Itararé (riv.) *B3
Ival (riv.) C8
Jaculpe (riv.) F5
Jaguaribe (riv.) G4
Jamanxim (riv.) C4
Japurá (riv.) G9
Jari (riv.) C3
Jauari, Serra (mts.) ... C3
Javari (riv.) F9
Jequitinhonha (riv.) ... F7
Juruá (riv.) G10
Juruena (riv.) B5
Jutaí (riv.) G9
Lombarda, Serra (mts.) . D2
Madeira (riv.) A4
Mangueira (lag.) D11
Manso (riv.) C6
Mantiqueira (range) .. *D3
Mapuera (riv.) B3
Mar, Serra do (range) . *C4, E9
Maracá (isl.) D2
Marajó (bay) E2
Marajó (isl.) 147,895 .. D3
Mato Grosso, Planalto de
    (plat.) B6
Maués-Açú (riv.) B4
Mearim (riv.) E4
Mexiana (isl.) D2
Mirim (riv.) C11
Miranda (riv.) B8
Mogi Guaçu (riv.) *C2
Mortes (Manso) (riv.) . D6
Mucuri (riv.) D2
Negro (riv.) H9
Nhamundá (riv.) B3
Norte, Serra do (range) . B5
Oiapoque (Oyapock) (riv.) . C2

Orange (cape) D1
Órgãos (range) *E3
Oyapock (riv.) C2
Pacajá Grande (riv.) .. D4
Pacaraimã, Serra da (mts.) . H8
Papagaio (riv.) B6
Pará (riv.) D3
Paracatu (riv.) E7
Paraguai (riv.) F6
Paraguai (riv.) B8
Paraíba (riv.) *E2
Paraná (riv.) C8
Paraná (riv.) E6
Paranapanema (riv.) .. *B3, D8
Paranapiacaba (range) . *B4
Paranatinga (riv.) C6
Pardo (riv.) *B2, D8
Pardo (riv.) D5
Pardo (riv.) F6
Parecis, Serra dos (range) . A5
Parnaíba (riv.) F3
Paru (riv.) C3
Patos (lag.) D10
Penitente, Serra do (range) . E5
Piauí, Serra do (range) . F5
Piauí (riv.) F5
Purus (riv.) H9
Ribeira (riv.) *B4
Roncador, Serra do (range) . D5
Ronuro (riv.) C6
Roosevelt (riv.) A5
Santa Catarina (isl.) 138,556 E9
São Lourenço (riv.) .. C7
São Marcos (bay) F3
São Roque (cape) F3
São Francisco (riv.) .. *D2, G5
São Sebastião (isl.) 5,724. *D3, E8
São Tomé (cape) F8
Sapucaí (riv.) *D2
Sepetiba (bay) *D3
Sete Quedas (falls) ... C9
Sete Quedas (Grande) (isl.) . C8
Sobradino (res.) F5
Sono (riv.) E5
Sul (chan.) D2
Tacutu (riv.) B2
Tapajós (riv.) B4
Taquari (riv.) C7
Tefé (riv.) G9
Teles Pires (riv.) B5

Tibagi (riv.) *A4
Tietê (riv.) *B2, D8
Tiracambu, Serra (range) . E3
Tocantins (riv.) D3
Tombador, Serra do (range) B6
Trombetas (riv.) B3
Tucuruí (res.) D4
Tumucumaque, Serra de
    (range) C2

Turvo (riv.) *B2
Uaupés (riv.) G9
Uraricoera (riv.) H8
Urubu (riv.) A3
Urubupungá (dam) C8
Urucún, Morro do (mt.) . B7
Uruguai (riv.) C9
Vasa Barris (riv.) G5
Velhas (riv.) E7

Verde (riv.) C7
Verdinho (riv.) D7
Xavantes (res.) *B3
Xingu (riv.) C3

†Population of met. area.
*preceding reference indicates
that the name will be found on
S.E. Brazil map, page 135.

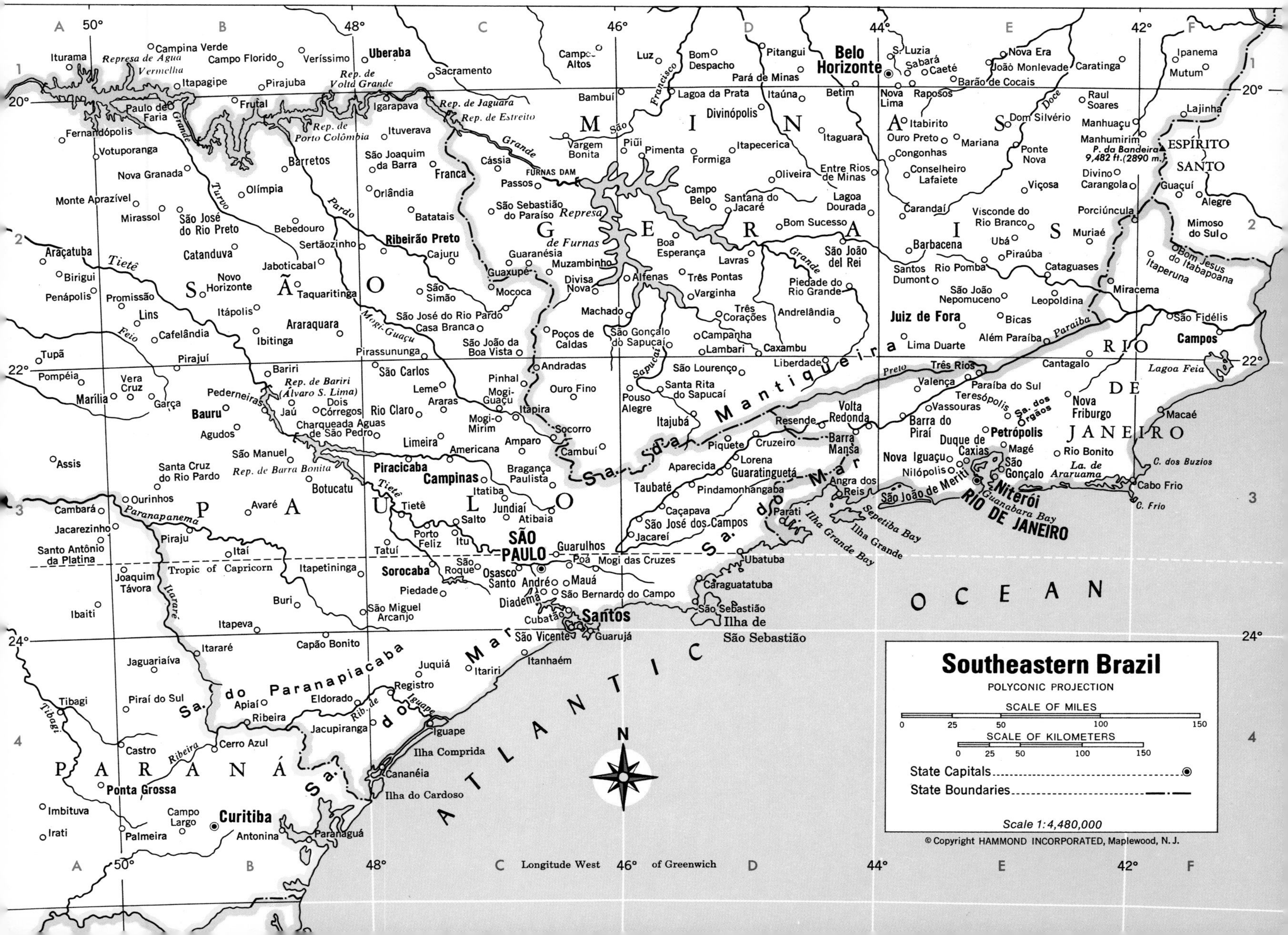

Brasilia

Botanical Garden
Individual Residences
Residential Superblocks
R.R. Station
Meteorological Observatory
Industrial Area
Cemetery
Residential Superblocks
Embassies & Legations
Novacap
Zoo
Bandeirante
Airport
Suburban Homes
Stadium
T.V. Tower
University
Plaza of the Three Powers
Presidential Palace
Golf Club
Yacht Club
Lago de
Hotel
Hydroelectric Station
Falls
Paranoá
Brasilia
Monastery
Individual Residences

0   5 MI.
0 5 KM.

© Copyright HAMMOND INCORPORATED, Maplewood, N.J.

Southeastern Brazil

POLYCONIC PROJECTION

SCALE OF MILES
0   25   50   100   150

SCALE OF KILOMETERS
0 25 50   100   150

State Capitals .... ◉
State Boundaries ....

Scale 1:4,480,000

© Copyright HAMMOND INCORPORATED, Maplewood, N.J.

DEPARTMENTS

Beni, El 168,367 .... C3
Chuquisaca 358,516 ..... C6
Cochabamba 720,952 ... C5
El Beni 168,367 .... C3
La Paz 1,465,078 .... A4
Oruro 310,409 .... A6
Pando 34,493 .... B2
Potosí 657,743 .... B7
Santa Cruz 710,724 ..... E5
Tarija 187,204 .... D7

CITIES and TOWNS

Abapó 466 .... D6
Acchilla 208 .... C7
Achacachi 3,621 ...... A5
Aiquile 3,465 .... C6
Alcalá 236 .... C6
Alejandría‡ 198 ...... C3
Alto Seco‡ 3,414 ..... D6
Amarete 992 .... A4
Ananea 302 .... A4
Ancoraimes 769 ...... A4
Andamarca‡ 5,187 .... B6
Añimbo 443 .... C7
Anzaldo 1,056 .... C5

Apolo 1,043 .... A4
Aracá 3,537 .... B5
Arampampa 829 .... D3
Arani 2,200 .... C5
Arcopongo‡ 2,223 .... B5
Aromat 873 .... A5
Arque 1,254 .... B5
Ascención (Añez) A2
Asunción B2
Asunta 45 .... B5
Atén 199 .... A4
Atocha‡ 3,964 .... B7
Ayacucho 729 .... D5
Ayata 479 .... C5

Azurduy 1,234 .... C6
Barrera B3
Baures 592 .... D3
Bella Flor A2
Bella Vista E3
Berenguela‡ 2,412 .... A5
Betanzos 1,097 .... C6
Bolívar B3
Bolpebra A2
Boyuibe 537 .... D7
Buena Vista, Santa Cruz . D5
Cabezas 298 .... D6
Cachuela Esperanza 1,073 . C2
Caiza 838 .... C7
Cajuata 447 .... B5

Calacoto 415 .... A5
Calamarca 802 .... A5
Callapa 636 .... A5
Camacho‡ 875 .... C7
Camargo 1,609 .... C7
Camatindi‡ 297 .... D7
Camiri 4,969 .... D7
Candelaria‡ 468 .... F5
Canquella 148 .... A7
Capinota 1,734 .... B5
Capirenda A5
Caquiaviri 760 .... A5
Carabuco 626 .... A5
Caracollo 909 .... B5
Caranaví‡ 525 .... B4

Carandaiti 1,403 .... D7
Caraparí 351 .... D7
Carmen 845 .... B2
Cataricahua 3,240 ...... A5
Cavari 249 .... B5
Cavinas‡ 1,011 .... B3
Chachacomani 159 ...... A6
Chacoma‡ 330 .... A6
Chaguaya 643 .... C7
Challacollo 284 .... B6
Challana 1,206 .... A4
Challapata 2,529 ...... B6
Chapacura‡ 152 .... B2
Chaquí 291 .... C6
Charagua 1,185 .... D6

Charaña 794 .... A5
Chayanta 1,272 .... A7
Chiguana 154 .... A7
Chiñijo 27 .... A5
Chivet 336 .... B5
Chocaya 444 .... C7
Choquecota‡ 1,976 ..... A6
Chulumani 2,362 .... A4
Chuma 931 .... C7
Chuquichambi‡ 1,094 ... A6
Chuquisaca‡ 1,892 ..... C6
Cliza 3,121 .... C5
Cobija 3,650 .... A2
Cocani 658 .... D6
Cocapata‡ 2,855 .... C5

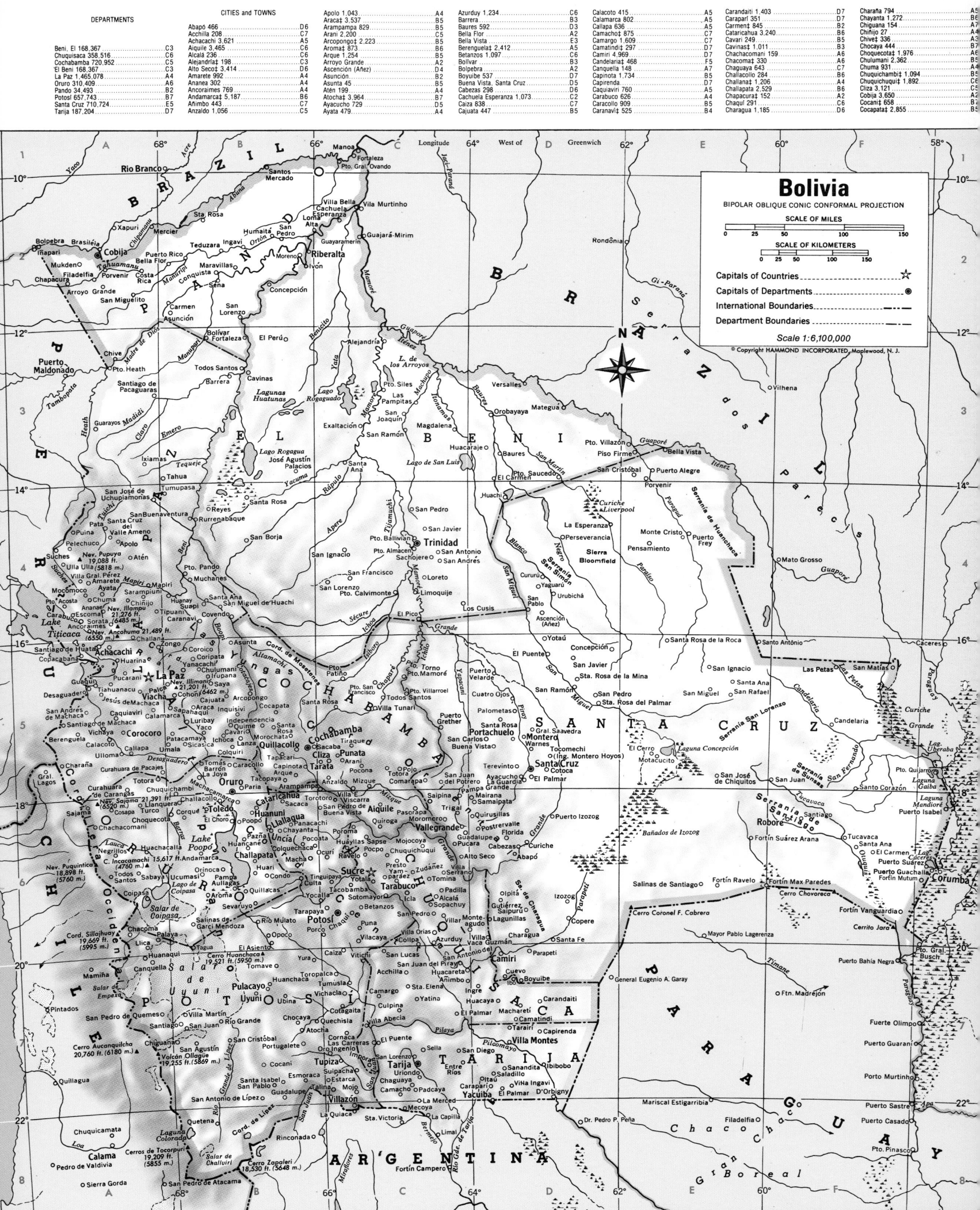

Cochabamba 204,684 .... C5
Cohoni 890 .... B5
Coipasa‡ 202 .... A6
Collpa 481 .... C6
Colquechaca 1,070 .... B6
Colquiri 806 .... B5
Comarapa 1,096 .... C5
Concepción, El Beni‡ 61 .... B2
Concepción, Santa Cruz 1,056 .... D5
Condo‡ 5,525 .... B6
Conquista‡ 1,162 .... B2
Copacabana 1,981 .... A5
Copere D6
Coripata 1,647 .... B5
Cornaca 264 .... C7
Corocoro 4,431 .... A5
Coroico 2,235 .... B5
Corque 423 .... B6
Cosapa 297 .... A6
Costa Rica‡ 43 .... A2
Cotagaita 1,353 .... C7
Cotoca 915 .... D5
Covendo 71 .... B4
Cuatro Ojos‡ 465 .... D5
Cuevo 902 .... D7
Culpina 981 .... C7
Culta‡ 4,412 .... B6
Curahuara de Carangas 235 .... A5
Curahuara de Pacajes 510 .... A5
Curiche 257 .... D6
Cururú D4
Desaguadero 201 .... A5
D'Orbigny‡ 214 .... D7
El Asiento B6
El Carmen, El Beni 232 .... D3
El Carmen, Santa Cruz F6
El Cerro 117 .... E5
El Choro 224 .... B6
El Palmar, Chuquisaca‡ 772 .... D7
El Palmar, Santa Cruz 437 .... D5
El Palmar, Tarija 832 .... D7
El Perú B3
El Pico C4
El Puente, Santa Cruz‡ 1,185 .... D5
El Puente, Tarija‡ 1,310 .... C7
Entre Ríos 1,011 .... C7
Escoma 220 .... A4
Esmoraca‡ 1,137 .... B7
Estarca‡ 2,331 .... C7
Exaltación, El Beni 405 .... C3
Filadelfia‡ 942 .... A2
Florida, Santa Cruz 128 .... D6
Fortaleza‡ 765 .... B3
Fortaleza C1
Fortín Campero‡ 87 .... C8
Fortín Max Paredes F6
Fortín Mutum F6
Fortín Ravelo E6
Fortín Suárez Arana F6
Fortín Vanguardia F6
General Saavedra 1,006 .... D5
Guadalupe, Potosí 71 .... B7
Guadalupe, Santa Cruz 2,355 .... C6
Guaqui 2,266 .... A5
Guayaramerín 1,470 .... C2
Huacaraje 673 .... D3
Huacareta 239 .... C7
Huacaya 229 .... D7
Huachacalla 801 .... A6
Huachi D4
Huanaqui 359 .... A7
Huanay 574 .... B4
Huancané 148 .... B6
Huanchaca B7
Huanuni 5,696 .... B6
Huari 1,070 .... B6
Huarina 1,151 .... A5
Huayllas 206 .... C6
Humaitá‡ 429 .... B2
Ibibobo D7
Ibo D7
Ichoca 591 .... B5
Icla 196 .... C6
Impora 274 .... C7
Independencia 1,742 .... B5
Ingavi‡ 111 .... B2
Ingeniero Montero Hoyos (Tocomechi) 575 .... D5
Ingre 162 .... D7
Inquisivi 530 .... B5
Irupana 1,937 .... B5
Itaú 102 .... D7
Ivón‡ 772 .... C2
Ixiamas 292 .... A3
Izozog‡ 2,759 .... D6
Jesús de Machaca 529 .... A5
José Agustín Palacios‡ 2,273 .... B3
La Capilla‡ 1,870 .... C8
La Esmeralda D8
La Esperanza D4
La Guardia 470 .... D5
Lagunillas 840 .... D6
La Joya 401 .... B5
La Merced‡ 688 .... C8
Lanza 526 .... B5
La Paz (cap.) 635,283 .... B5
Las Carreras 155 .... C7
Las Pampitas‡ 71 .... C3
Las Petas‡ 383 .... F5
Limal‡ 524 .... C8
Limoquije C4
Llallagua 6,719 .... B6
Llanquera 613 .... A6
Llica 560 .... A6
Loma Alta B2
Loreto 589 .... C4
Los Cusis D4
Luribay 392 .... B5
Macha 1,050 .... B6
Machacamarca 1,746 .... B5
Macharetí‡ 1,164 .... D7
Magdalena 1,724 .... C3
Mairana 508 .... D6
Manoa C1
Mapiri 289 .... B4
Maravillas B2
Mateguá 38 .... D3
Mecoya‡ 585 .... C8
Mercier‡ 272 .... B2
Mizque 870 .... C5
Mocomoco 977 .... A4
Mojo 469 .... C7
Mojocoya 498 .... C6
Monteagudo 971 .... D6
Monte Cristo E4
Montero 2,713 .... D5
Moreno B2
Morochata 461 .... B5
Moromoro 556 .... C6
Motacucito‡ 585 .... E5
Muchanes B4
Mukden‡ 84 .... A2
Negrillos 85 .... A6
Ocurí 1,531 .... C6
Opoco B6
Orinoca‡ 2,380 .... B6
Orobayaya‡ 1,132 .... D3
Oro Ingenio‡ 945 .... C7
Oruro 124,213 .... B5
Padcaya 324 .... C7
Padilla 2,462 .... C6
Palaya 300 .... A6
Palca 887 .... A5
Palometas‡ 3,453 .... D5
Pampa Aullagas‡ 1,834 .... B6
Pampa Grande 727 .... D5
Panacachi 952 .... B6
Paria 335 .... B5
Pasorapa 1,016 .... C6
Pata 122 .... A4
Patacamaya 1,278 .... B5
Pazña 671 .... B6
Pelechuco 873 .... A4
Pensamiento E4
Perseverancia D4
Piso Firme D3
Pocoata 859 .... B6
Pocona 518 .... C5
Pocpo‡ 2,791 .... C6
Pojo 1,047 .... C5
Poopó 736 .... B6
Porco 817 .... B6
Poroma 171 .... C6
Portachuelo 2,456 .... D5
Portugalete‡ 1,590 .... B7
Porvenir, Pando‡ 846 .... A2
Porvenir, Santa Cruz E4
Postrervalle 750 .... D6
Potosí 77,397 .... C6
Presto 725 .... C6
Pucara 762 .... C6
Pucarani 1,041 .... A5
Puerto Acosta 1,302 .... A4
Puerto Alegre E3
Puerto Almacen 358 .... C4
Puerto Ballivián C4
Puerto Calvimonte C4
Puerto Frey E4
Puerto General Ovando 50
Puerto Grether C5
Puerto Guachalla F6
Puerto Heath‡ 570 .... A3
Puerto Isabel F6
Puerto Izozog D6
Puerto Mamoré C5
Puerto Pando B4
Puerto Patiño C5
Puerto Quijarro G5
Puerto Rico‡ 539 .... B2
Puerto San Francisco C5
Puerto Saucedo D3
Puerto Siles 357 .... C3
Puerto Suárez 1,159 .... F6
Puerto Torno C5
Puerto Velarde D5
Puerto Villarroel C5
Puerto Villazón D3
Puina A4
Pulacayo 7,984 .... B7
Puna 852 .... C6
Punata 5,014 .... C5
Quechisla 171 .... C7
Queteña 183 .... B8
Quillacas 1,170 .... B6
Quillacollo 9,123 .... B5
Quime 1,256 .... B5
Quiroga‡ 3,467 .... C6
Quirusillas 433 .... D6
Ravelo 907 .... C6
Reyes 1,404 .... B4
Riberalta 6,549 .... C2
Río Grande 281 .... B7
Río Mulato 381 .... B6
Roboré 3,715 .... F6
Rurrenabaque 1,225 .... B4
Sabaya 649 .... A6
Sacaba 2,752 .... C5
Sacaca 1,778 .... B6
Sachojere 401 .... C4
Saipina 573 .... C6
Sajama 231 .... A6
Saladillo‡ 1,315 .... D7
Salinas de Garci Mendoza 335 .... B6
Salinas de Santiago E6
Samaipata 1,656 .... D6
San Agustín‡ 810 .... B7
Sanandita 379 .... D7
San Andrés 399 .... C4
San Andrés de Machaca 101 .... A5
San Antonio, El Beni 436 .... C4
San Antonio de Lípez‡ 177 .... B7
San Antonio del Parapetí 497 .... D7
San Borja 708 .... B4
San Buenaventura 307 .... A4
San Carlos 570 .... D5
San Cristóbal, Potosí‡ 1,200 .... B7
San Cristóbal, Santa Cruz E3
San Diego‡ 773 .... D7
San Francisco, El Beni 185 .... C4
San Ignacio, El Beni 1,757 .... C4
San Ignacio, Santa Cruz 1,819 .... E5
San Javier, El Beni 233 .... C4
San Javier, Santa Cruz 564 .... D5
San Joaquín 1,959 .... C3
San José de Chiquitos 1,933 .... E5
San José de Uchupiamonas 277 .... A4
San Juan, Potosí 131 .... B7
San Juan, Santa Cruz‡ 1,482 .... F5
San Juan del Piray 541 .... C7
San Juan del Potrero 263 .... C5
San Lorenzo, El Beni 496 .... C4
San Lorenzo, Pando‡ 317 .... B2
San Lorenzo, Tarija 785 .... C7
San Lucas 925 .... C7
San Matías 887 .... F5
San Miguel 502 .... E5
San Miguel de Huachi 25 .... B4
San Miguelito A2
San Pablo, Potosí 11 .... B7
San Pablo, Santa Cruz D4
San Pedro, Chuquisaca 182 .... C6
San Pedro, El Beni 262 .... C4
San Pedro, Pando‡ 312 .... B2
San Pedro, Santa Cruz 80 .... D5
San Pedro de Buena Vista 1,094 .... C6
San Pedro de Quemes‡ 290 .... A7
San Rafael‡ 1,282 .... E5
San Ramón, El Beni 1,161 .... C3
San Ramón, Santa Cruz 379 .... D5
Santa Ana, El Beni 2,225 .... C3
Santa Ana, La Paz 171 .... B4
Santa Ana, Santa Cruz 275 .... E5
Santa Ana, Santa Cruz 663 .... F6
Santa Cruz, Santa Cruz 254,682 .... D5
Santa Cruz del Valle Ameno 442 .... A4
Santa Elena‡ 4,474 .... C7
Santa Fe D6
Santa Isabel‡ 323 .... B7
Santa Rosa, Cochabamba‡ 942 .... B5
Santa Rosa, Cochabamba‡ 276 .... C5
Santa Rosa, El Beni 765 .... B4
Santa Rosa, Pando‡ 105 .... B2
Santa Rosa, Santa Cruz 995 .... D5
Santa Rosa de la Mina 99 .... D5
Santa Rosa de la Roca 101 .... E5
Santa Rosa del Palmar 441 .... E5
Santiago, Potosí 172 .... A7
Santiago, Santa Cruz 765 .... F6
Santiago de Huata 948 .... A5
Santiago de Machaca 218 .... A5
Santiago de Pacaguaras A3
Santo Corazón‡ 963 .... F5
Santos Mercado B1
Sapahaqui 55 .... B5
Sapse‡ 89 .... C6
Sarampiuni 138 .... A4
Saya 339 .... B5
Sella C7
Sena‡ 660 .... B2
Sevaruyo 475 .... B6
Sicasica 1,486 .... B5
Sopachuy 713 .... C6
Sorata 2,087 .... A4
Sotomayor 510 .... C6
Suapi‡ 1,750 .... B4
Suches‡ 231 .... A4
Sucre (cap.) 63,625 .... C6
Suipacha‡ 2,701 .... C7
Tacobamba‡ 6,933 .... C6
Tacopaya 795 .... B5
Tagua B6
Tahua B3
Talina 122 .... B7
Tapacarí 980 .... B5
Tarabuco 2,833 .... C6
Tarairí‡ 394 .... D7
Tarapaya 357 .... B6
Tarata 3,016 .... C5
Tarija 38,916 .... C7
Teduzara‡ 271 .... B2
Terevinto‡ 3,790 .... D5
Tiahuanacu 1,227 .... A5
Tinguipaya 766 .... C6
Tipuani‡ 1,216 .... B4
Tiraque 1,390 .... C5
Tocomechi 575 .... D5
Todos Santos, Cochabamba 408 .... C5
Todos Santos, La Paz B3
Todos Santos, Oruro 68 .... A6
Toledo 3,273 .... B6
Tomás Barrón 1,852 .... B5
Tomave 201 .... B7
Tomina 708 .... C6
Toropalca‡ 199 .... B7
Torotoro 1,233 .... C6
Totora, Cochabamba C5
Totora, Oruro A5
Trigal 749 .... C6
Trinidad, El Beni 27,487 .... C4
Trinidad, Pando‡ 332 .... B2
Tucavaca F6
Tumupasa 349 .... B4
Tumusla‡ 526 .... C7
Tupiza 8,248 .... C7
Turco 131 .... A6
Ubina‡ 462 .... B7
Ucumasi‡ 1,040 .... B6
Ulla Ulla 52 .... A4
Ulloma 116 .... A5
Umala 481 .... B5
Uncla 4,507 .... B6
Uriondo 860 .... C7
Urubichá 1,369 .... D4
Uyuni 6,968 .... B7
Vallegrande 5,094 .... C6
Versalles 83 .... D3
Viacha 6,607 .... A5
Vichacla 317 .... C7
Vichaya 422 .... A5
Vilacaya 200 .... C6
Villa Abecia 539 .... C7
Villa Bella 88 .... C2
Villa E. Viscarra 658 .... C6
Villa General Pérez 802 .... A4
Villa Ingavi 122 .... D7
Villa Martín 543 .... B7
Villa Montes 3,105 .... D7
Villa Orías 404 .... C6
Villar 322 .... C6
Villa Serrano 1,570 .... C6
Villa Tunari 510 .... C5
Villa Vaca Guzmán 699 .... D6
Villazón 6,261 .... C7
Vitichi 1,515 .... C7
Warnes 1,571 .... D5
Yaco 835 .... B5
Yacuiba 5,027 .... D7
Yaguarú D4
Yamparaéz 725 .... C6
Yanacachi‡ 1,964 .... B5
Yatina‡ 1,850 .... C7
Yocalla‡ 1,814 .... B6
Yotala 1,554 .... C6
Yotaú D5
Yura 136 .... B7
Zongo 141 .... B5
Zudáñez 1,868 .... C6

AREA 424,163 sq. mi. (1,098,582 sq. km.)
POPULATION 5,600,000
CAPITALS La Paz, Sucre
LARGEST CITY La Paz
HIGHEST POINT Nevada Ancohuma 21,489 ft. (6,550 m.)
MONETARY UNIT Bolivian peso
MAJOR LANGUAGES Spanish, Quechua, Aymara
MAJOR RELIGION Roman Catholicism

Topography

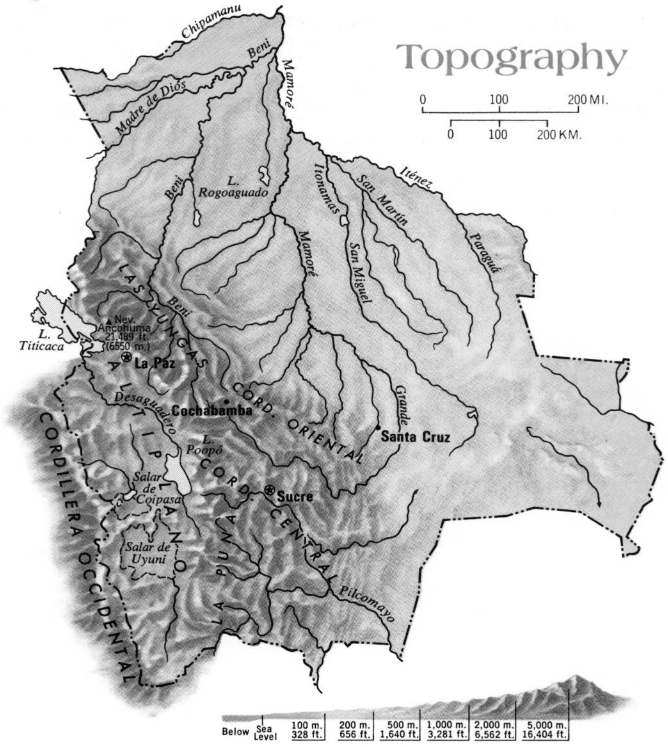

0 100 200 MI.
0 100 200 KM.
Chipamanu
Beni
Mamoré
Madre de Diós
L. Rogoaguado
Iténez
Itonamas
San Martín
Paraguá
San Miguel
LAS YUNGAS
Nev. Ancohuma 21,489 ft. (6550 m.)
L. Titicaca
La Paz
Cochabamba
CORD. ORIENTAL
Desaguadero
L. Poopó
Salar de Coipasa
ALTIPLANO
CORD. CENTRAL
Sucre
Santa Cruz
Grande
Salar de Uyuni
PUNA
CORDILLERA OCCIDENTAL
Pilcomayo
Below Sea Level
100 m. 328 ft.
200 m. 656 ft.
500 m. 1,640 ft.
1,000 m. 3,281 ft.
2,000 m. 6,562 ft.
5,000 m. 16,404 ft.

OTHER FEATURES

Abuná (riv.) B2
Altamachi (riv.) B5
Ancohuma, Nevada (mt.) A4
Apere (riv.) C4
Arroyas, Los (lake) C3
Barras (riv.) B6
Baures (riv.) D3
Beni (riv.) B2
Benicito (riv.) C3
Bermejo (riv.) C8
Blanco (riv.) D4
Bloomfield, Sierra (mts.) D4
Boopi (riv.) B4
Cáceres (lag.) G6
Candelaria (riv.) F5
Capitán Ustarés, Cerro (mt.) E6
Central, Cordillera (range) C6
Challviri (salt dep.) B8
Chaparé (riv.) C5
Charagua, Sierra de (mts.) D6
Chipamanu (riv.) A2
Chovoreca, Cerro (mt.) F6
Claro (riv.) A3
Coipasa (lake) B6
Coipasa (salt dep.) A6
Colorada (lag.) A8
Concepción (lag.) E5
Coronel F. Gabrera E6
Cotacajes (riv.) B5
Desaguadero (riv.) B5
Emero (riv.) B3
Empexa (salt dep.) A7
Gaiba (lag.) F5
Grande (marsh) F5
Grande (riv.) C4
Grande (riv.) C6
Grande de Lípez (riv.) B7
Guaporé (riv.) C3
Heath (riv.) A3
Huanchaca, Cerro (mt.) B7
Huanchaca, Serranía de (mts.) E4
Huatunas (lag.) B3
Ichilo (riv.) C5
Ichoa (riv.) C4
Illampu, Nevada (mt.) A4
Illimani, Nevada (mt.) B5
Incacamachi, Cerro (mt.) A6
Isiboro (riv.) C5
Iténez (Guaporé) (riv.) C3
Itonamas (riv.) C3
Izozog (swamp) E6
Jara, Cerrito (mt.) F6
Las Yungas (reg.) B5
Lauca (riv.) A6
Lípez, Cordillera de (range) B8
Liverpool (swamp) D4
Machupo (riv.) C3
Madidi (riv.) A3
Madre de Diós (riv.) A3
Mamoré (riv.) C2
Mandioré (lag.) F6
Manuripi (riv.) B2
Mizque (riv.) C6
Mosetenes, Cordillera de (range) B5
Negro (riv.) D4
Occidental, Cordillera (range) A6
Ollagüe (vol.) B7
Oriental, Cordillera (range) C5
Ortón (riv.) B2
Otuquis (riv.) F6
Paraguá (riv.) E4
Paraguay (riv.) F7
Parapetí (riv.) D6
Petas, Las (riv.) F5
Pilaya (riv.) C7
Pilcomayo (riv.) D7
Piray (riv.) D5
Poopó (lake) B6
Pupuya, Nevada (mt.) A4
Puquintica, Nevado (mt.) A6
Rápulo (riv.) C4
Real, Cordillera (range) A5
Rogagua (lake) B3
Rogaguado (lake) C3
Sajama, Nevada (mt.) A6
San Fernando (riv.) F5
San Juan (riv.) C7
San Lorenzo, Serranía (mts.) E5
San Luis (lake) C3
San Martín (riv.) D3
San Miguel (riv.) D4
San Simón, Serranía (mts.) D4
Santiago, Serranía de (mts.) F6
Sécure (riv.) C4
Sillajhuay, Cordillera (mt.) A6
Suches (riv.) A4
Sunsas, Serranía de (mts.) F5
Tahuamanu (riv.) A2
Tarija, Rio Grande de (riv.) C8
Tequeje (riv.) B3
Tijamuchi (riv.) C4
Titicaca (lake) A4
Tocorpuri, Cerros de (mt.) A8
Tucavaca (riv.) F6
Tuichi (riv.) A4
Uberaba (lag.) G5
Uyuni (salt dep.) B7
Yacuma (riv.) B3
Yapacani (riv.) C5
Yata (riv.) C3
Yungas, Las (reg.) B5
Zapaleri, Cerro (mt.) B8

‡Population of canton.

Agriculture, Industry and Resources

Cinchona
Au
Sheep
Corn
Potatoes
Cu
Hogs
Corn
Sugarcane
Rice
Cattle
Ag Sb W Cu Sn
Goats
Fe
Ag Sn W Pb
S
O G
Sb Zn Pb Fruit
S Cu
O

DOMINANT LAND USE

- Diversified Tropical Crops (chiefly plantation agriculture)
- Upland Cultivated Areas
- Upland Livestock Grazing, Limited Agriculture
- Extensive Livestock Ranching
- Forests
- Nonagricultural Land

MAJOR MINERAL OCCURRENCES

Ag	Silver	G	Natural Gas	Sb	Antimony
Au	Gold	O	Petroleum	Sn	Tin
Cu	Copper	Pb	Lead	W	Tungsten
Fe	Iron Ore	S	Sulfur	Zn	Zinc

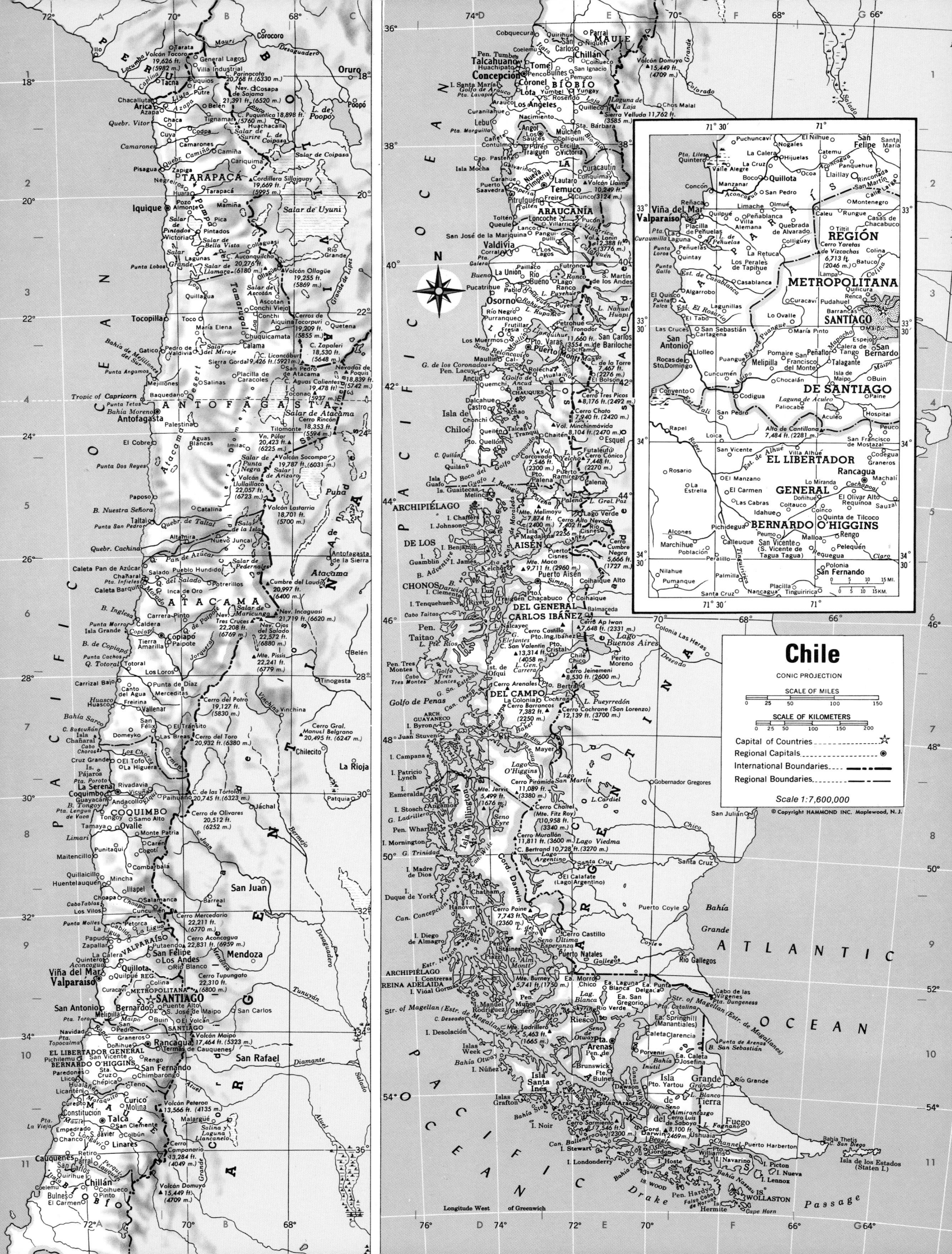

Chile

CONIC PROJECTION

SCALE OF MILES

0 25 50 100 150

SCALE OF KILOMETERS

0 25 50 100 150 200

Capital of Countries .... ☆
Regional Capitals .... ◉
International Boundaries .... ─ ─ ─
Regional Boundaries .... ─ ── ─

Scale 1:7,600,000

© Copyright HAMMOND INC. Maplewood, N.J.

AREA 292,257 sq. mi. (756,946 sq. km.)
POPULATION 11,275,440
CAPITAL Santiago
LARGEST CITY Santiago
HIGHEST POINT Ojos del Salado 22,572 ft. (6,880 m.)
MONETARY UNIT Chilean peso
MAJOR LANGUAGE Spanish
MAJOR RELIGION Roman Catholicism

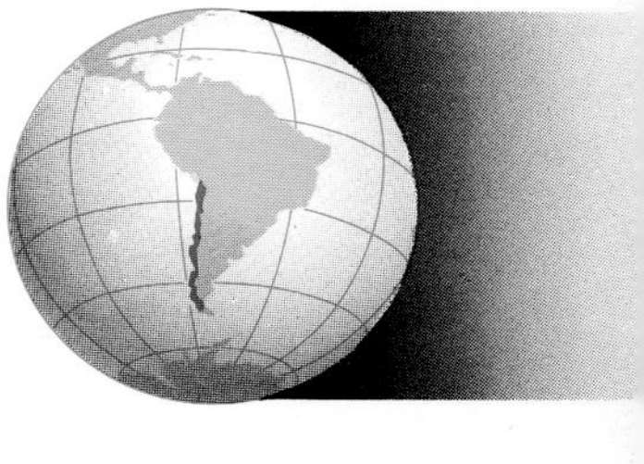

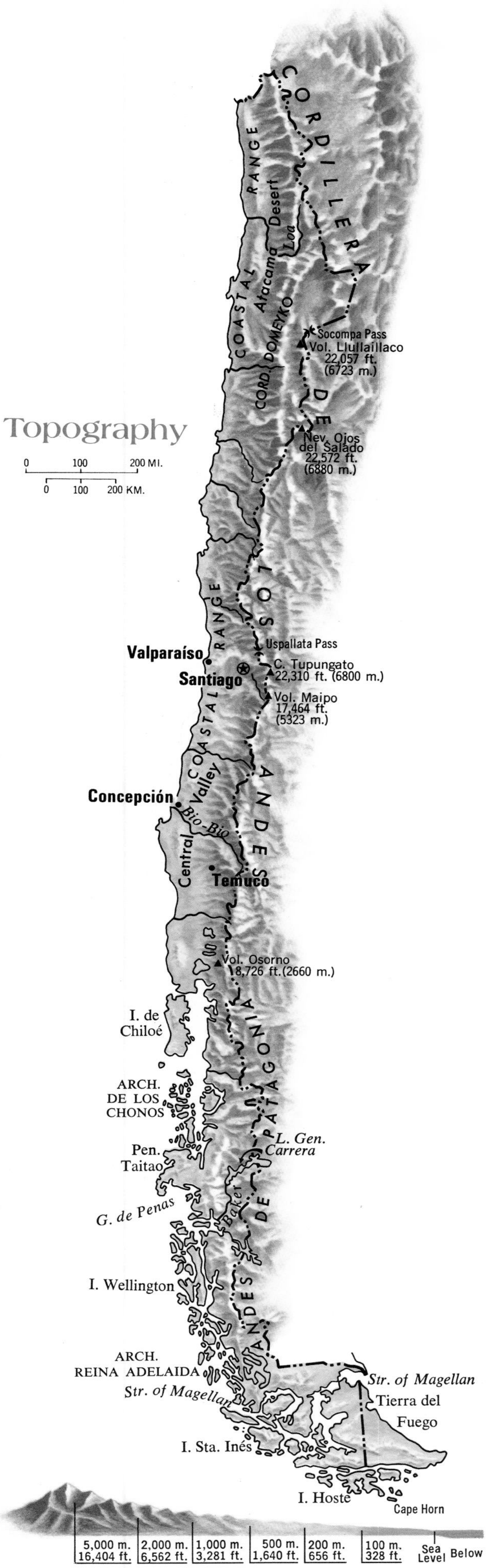

Topography
0 100 200 MI.
0 100 200 KM.
CORDILLERA DE LOS ANDES
COASTAL RANGE
Atacama Desert
Loa
CORD. DOMEYKO
Socompa Pass
Vol. Llullaillaco 22,057 ft. (6723 m.)
Nev. Ojos del Salado 22,572 ft. (6880 m.)
Valparaíso
Santiago
Uspallata Pass
C. Tupungato 22,310 ft. (6800 m.)
Vol. Maipo 17,464 ft. (5323 m.)
Concepción
Central Valley
Bío-Bío
Temuco
Vol. Osorno 8,726 ft. (2660 m.)
I. de Chiloé
ARCH. DE LOS CHONOS
PATAGONIA
Pen. Taitao
L. Gen. Carrera
G. de Penas
Baker
ANDES DE PATAGONIA
I. Wellington
ARCH. REINA ADELAIDA
Str. of Magellan
Str. of Magellan
Tierra del Fuego
I. Sta. Inés
I. Hoste
Cape Horn
5,000 m. 16,404 ft.
2,000 m. 6,562 ft.
1,000 m. 3,281 ft.
500 m. 1,640 ft.
200 m. 656 ft.
100 m. 328 ft.
Sea Level
Below

REGIONS

Aisén del General Carlos Ibáñez del Campo 65,478 .... E6
Antofagasta 341,203 .... B4
Atacama 183,071 .... B6
Bíobío 1,516,552 .... E1
Coquimbo 419,178 .... A8
El Libertador General Bernardo O'Higgins 584,989 .... A10
La Araucanía 692,924 .... E2
Los Lagos 843,430 .... D3
Magallanes 132,333 .... E10
Maule 723,224 .... A11
Santiago, Región Metropolitana de (Santiago Metropolitan Region) 4,294,938 .... A9
Tarapacá 273,427 .... B2
Valparaíso 1,204,693 .... A9

CITIES and TOWNS

Achao ○11,501 .... D4
Aguas Blancas ○203 .... B4
Algarrobo ○3,941 .... F3
Ancud 11,900 .... D4
Andacollo 6,000 .... A8
Angol 42,670 .... D1
Antofagasta 125,100 .... A4
Arauco 5,400 .... D1
Arica 87,700 .... A1
Ascotán B3
Barrancas ○184,241 .... G3
Belén ○925 .... B1
Buin 11,800 .... G4
Bulnes 6,900 .... E1
Cabildo 5,800 .... A9
Calama 45,900 .... B3
Calbuco ○21,673 .... D4
Caldera ○3,268 .... A6
Calera de Tango ○6,198 .... G4
Calle Larga ○7,172 .... G2
Cañete 7,900 .... D2
Carahue ○12,733 .... D2
Cartagena ○7,124 .... F3
Casablanca 5,500 .... F3
Casas de Chacabuco G2
Castro 11,200 .... D4
Catalina ○1,637 .... B5
Catemu ○8,728 .... G2
Cauquenes 20,200 .... A11
Cerro Castillo ○537 .... E9
Cerro Manantiales F10
Chaitén ○4,067 .... E4
Chañaral ○36,949 .... A6
Chanco ○12,433 .... A11
Chépica ○11,199 .... A10
Chillán 128,515 .... A11
Chimbarongo 5,300 .... A10
Chonchi ○8,911 .... D4
Chuquicamata 22,100 .... B3
Cobquecura ○6,298 .... D1
Cochamó ○5,042 .... E3
Codegua ○6,757 .... G4
Codpa ○950 .... B1
Coelemu 5,400 .... D1
Coihaique 32,129 .... E6
Coihueco ○17,276 .... A11
Coinco ○4,942 .... G5
Colbún ○12,924 .... A11
Colina 7,400 .... G3
Collipulli 7,200 .... E2
Coltauco ○11,857 .... F5
Combarbalá ○17,332 .... A8
Concepción 206,226 .... D1
Constitución 11,500 .... A11
Contulmo ○13,987 .... D2
Copiapó 45,200 .... B6
Coquimbo 73,953 .... A8
Coronel 37,300 .... D1
Corral ○5,533 .... D3
Cunco ○18,836 .... E2
Curacautín 9,800 .... E2
Curacaví 5,800 .... G3
Curanilahue 13,200 .... D1
Curepto ○13,020 .... A10
Curicó 41,300 .... A10
Dalcahue ○7,084 .... D4
Domeiko A7
Doñihue ○8,837 .... G5
El Carmen ○13,226 .... A11
El Monte 7,000 .... G4
El Quisco ○2,152 .... E3
El Tabo ○2,180 .... F3
El Tofo A7
Empedrado ○7,887 .... A11
Ercilla ○8,061 .... E2
Estancia Caleta Josefina ○1,042 .... F10
Estancia Morro Chico ○785 .... E9
Estancia San Gregorio ○1,156 .... E9
Estancia Springhill (Cerro Manantiales) F10
Freire ○23,313 .... E2
Freirina ○5,523 .... A7
Fresia ○15,359 .... D3
Frutillar ○12,721 .... D3
Futaleufú ○2,366 .... E4
Futrono ○7,109 .... E3
Galvarino ○9,495 .... D2
General Lagos ○810 .... B1
Graneros 8,900 .... G5
Guayacán A8
Hijuelas ○7,128 .... F2
Hualañé ○6,912 .... A10
Huara ○1,934 .... B2
Huasco ○4,971 .... A7
Illapel 12,200 .... A8
Inca de Oro 1,406 .... B6
Iquique 64,500 .... A2
Isla de Maipo ○12,903 .... G4
La Calera 24,600 .... F2
La Cruz ○8,907 .... F2
La Estrella ○3,707 .... F5
Lago Ranco ○12,767 .... E3
Lagunas ○5,653 .... B3
La Higuera ○6,991 .... A7
La Ligua 7,500 .... A9
Lampa ○10,220 .... G3
Lanco 5,200 .... D2
Las Cabras ○12,119 .... F5
La Serena 99,908 .... A8
La Unión 15,200 .... D3
Lautaro 11,900 .... E2
Lebu 12,500 .... D1
Licantén ○6,354 .... A10
Limache 15,200 .... F2
Linares 37,900 .... A11
Llay-Llay 9,700 .... G2
Loica F4
Loncoche ○17,539 .... D2
Longaví ○15,909 .... A11
Lonquimay ○9,524 .... E2
Los Andes 23,500 .... B9
Los Ángeles 49,500 .... D1
Los Lagos ○14,934 .... D3
Los Muermos ○9,296 .... D3
Los Sauces ○7,613 .... D2
Los Vilos ○10,453 .... A9
Lota 48,100 .... D1
Machali 5,800 .... G5
Maipú ○117,872 .... G3
Malloa ○9,742 .... G5
Marchigüe ○4,451 .... F5
María Elena 5,900 .... B3
María Pinto ○5,980 .... G3
Maullín ○14,544 .... D4
Mejillones ○3,333 .... A4
Melipilla 23,900 .... F4
Mincha ○11,329 .... A8
Molina 9,400 .... A10
Monte Patria ○18,927 .... A8
Mulchén 13,700 .... E1
Nacimiento ○17,651 .... D1
Nancagua ○11,076 .... F6
Navidad ○6,618 .... A10
Negreiros ○1,144 .... B2
Ñiquén ○13,640 .... E1
Nogales ○18,529 .... F2
Nueva Imperial 8,000 .... D2
Olivar Alto ○5,414 .... G5
Ollagüe B3
Olmué ○8,804 .... F2
Osorno 68,800 .... D3
Ovalle 31,700 .... A8
Paihuano ○6,048 .... B8
Paillaco 5,200 .... D3
Paine ○21,876 .... G4
Palena ○2,508 .... E5
Palmilla ○7,965 .... F6
Panguipulli 5,700 .... E2
Panquehue ○4,230 .... G2
Papudo ○2,594 .... A9
Paredones ○7,404 .... A10
Parral 17,000 .... A11
Pedro de Valdivia 6,200 .... B4
Pemuco ○7,577 .... E1
Peñaflor 15,500 .... G4
Penco ○33,962 .... D1
Peñuelas F3
Petorca ○8,343 .... A9
Petrohué E3
Peumo ○11,308 .... F5
Pica ○1,487 .... B2
Pichidegua ○13,550 .... F5
Pichilemu ○8,042 .... A10
Pinto ○8,687 .... A11
Pisagua ○1,880 .... A2
Pitrufquén 7,800 .... D2
Placilla ○6,441 .... F6
Porvenir ○4,000 .... E10
Potrerillos 5,800 .... B6
Pozo Almonte ○1,798 .... B2
Puchuncaví ○7,542 .... F2
Pucón 18,000 .... E2
Pudahuel G3
Pueblo Hundido 6,200 .... B6
Puente Alto 65,100 .... B10
Puerto Aisén 17,848 .... E6
Puerto Cisnes ○2,800 .... E5
Puerto Ingeniero Ibáñez ○1,900 .... E6
Puerto Montt 119,059 .... E4
Puerto Natales 17,280 .... E9
Puerto Quellón ○7,734 .... D4
Puerto Varas 10,900 .... E3
Puerto Williams ○949 .... F11
Pumanque ○3,137 .... F6
Punitaqui ○16,167 .... A8
Punta Arenas 2,140 .... E10
Purén ○11,604 .... D2
Purranque 5,900 .... D3
Putaendo ○12,806 .... A9
Putre ○855 .... B1
Puyehue E3
Queilén ○6,055 .... D4
Quemchi ○6,707 .... D4
Quilicura 8,100 .... G3
Quillagua B3
Quilleco ○16,043 .... E1
Quillota 36,500 .... F2
Quilpué 40,600 .... F2
Quinta de Tilcoco ○6,513 .... G5
Quintero 9,900 .... F2
Quirihue ○11,178 .... E1
Rancagua 140,589 .... G5
Renca ○67,168 .... G3
Rengo 12,400 .... G5
Requínoa ○10,730 .... G5
Retiro ○15,146 .... A11
Rinconada San Martín ○4,118 .... G2
Río Blanco B9
Río Bueno 9,600 .... D3
Río Negro 5,100 .... D3
Río Verde ○554 .... E10
Rocas de Santo Domingo ○4,114 .... F4
Rosario ○3,383 .... F5
Salamanca ○18,741 .... A9
Samo Alto ○5,689 .... A8
San Antonio 46,700 .... F3
San Bernardo ○117,766 .... G4
San Carlos 17,000 .... E1
San Clemente ○23,273 .... A11
San Felipe 26,100 .... G2
San Fernando 23,600 .... G6
San Francisco de Mostazal ○11,439 .... G4
San Ignacio ○13,523 .... E1
San Javier 10,800 .... A11
San José de Maipo ○9,601 .... B10
San Pablo ○7,978 .... D3
San Pedro ○8,255 .... F4
San Pedro de Atacama C4
San Rosendo ○14,337 .... E1
Santa Bárbara ○14,345 .... E1
Santa Cruz 8,600 .... F6
Santa María ○8,162 .... G2
Santiago (cap.) 3,614,947 .... G3
Santiago *3,672,374 .... G3
San Vicente F4
San Vicente (San Vicente de Tagua Tagua) ○28,333 F5
Sierra Gorda ○8,805 .... B4
Talagante 16,500 .... G4
Talca 133,160 .... A11
Talcahuano 148,300 .... D1
Taltal 6,400 .... A5
Tamaya A8
Tarapacá B2
Temuco 197,232 .... E2
Teno ○17,675 .... A10
Termas de Cauquenes B10
Tierra Amarilla ○7,899 .... A6
Tiltil ○9,198 .... G2
Toco ○8,734 .... B3
Toconao C4
Tocopilla 22,000 .... A3
Toltén ○16,265 .... D2
Tomé 29,600 .... D1
Traiguén 11,400 .... E2
Valdivia 115,536 .... D3
Vallenar 26,800 .... A7
Valparaíso 271,580 .... E2
Victoria 16,500 .... D2
Vicuña 5,100 .... A8
Villa Alemana 29,600 .... F2
Villa Alhué ○5,078 .... G4
Villarrica 25,091 .... E2
Viña del Mar 281,361 .... F2
Yumbel ○21,858 .... E1
Yungay ○10,725 .... E1
Zapallar ○2,894 .... A9
Zapiga B2

OTHER FEATURES

Aconcagua (riv.) F2
Aculeo (lag.) G4
Adventure (bay) D5
Aguas Calientes, Cerro (mt.) C4
Almirantazgo (bay) F11
Almirante Montt (gulf) D9
Ancud (gulf) D4
Angamos (isl.) D8
Angamos (pt.) A4
Ap Iwan, Cerro (mt.) E6
Arauco (gulf) D1
Arenales, Cerro (mt.) D7
Atacama (des.) B4
Atacama, Salar de (salt dep.) C4
Aucanquilcha, Cerro (mt.) B3
Azapa, Quebrada (riv.) B1
Baker (riv.) D7
Ballenero (chan.) E11
Bascuñán (cape) A7
Beagle (chan.) E11
Bella Vista, Salar de (salt dep.) B3
Benjamín (isl.) D5
Bío-Bío (riv.) E2
Blanca (lag.) E10
Blanco (lake) F10
Bravo (riv.) D7
Brunswick (pen.) E10
Bueno (riv.) D3
Buenos Aires (lake) E6
Byron (isl.) D7
Cachapoal (riv.) G5
Cachina, Quebrada (riv.) A5
Cachos (pt.) A6
Calafquén (lake) E3
Camarones (riv.) A2
Camiña, Quebrada (riv.) B2
Campana (isl.) D7
Campanario, Cerro (mt.) A10
Capitán Aracena (isl.) E10
Carmen (riv.) B7
Castillo, Cerro (mt.) E6
Catalina (pt.) F10
Chaffers (isl.) D5
Chaltel, Cerro (mt.) E8
Chañaral (isl.) A7
Chatham (isl.) D9
Chauques (isls.) D4
Cheap (chan.) D7
Chiloé (isl.) 119,286 .... D4
Choapa (riv.) A9
Chonos (arch.) D6
Choros (cape) A7
Cisnes (riv.) E5
Clarence (isl.) E10
Clemente (isl.) D6
Cochrane (lake) E7
Cochrane, Cerro (mt.) E7
Cockburn (chan.) E11
Concepción (chan.) D9
Cónico, Cerro (mt.) E4
Contreras (isl.) D9
Cook (bay) E11
Copiapó (bay) A6
Copiapó (riv.) A6
Corcovado (gulf) D4
Corcovado (vol.) D5
Coronados (gulf) D4
Curaumilla (pt.) E2
Darwin (bay) D6
Darwin, Cordillera (mts.) D8
Darwin, Cordillera (mts.) E11

(continued on following page)

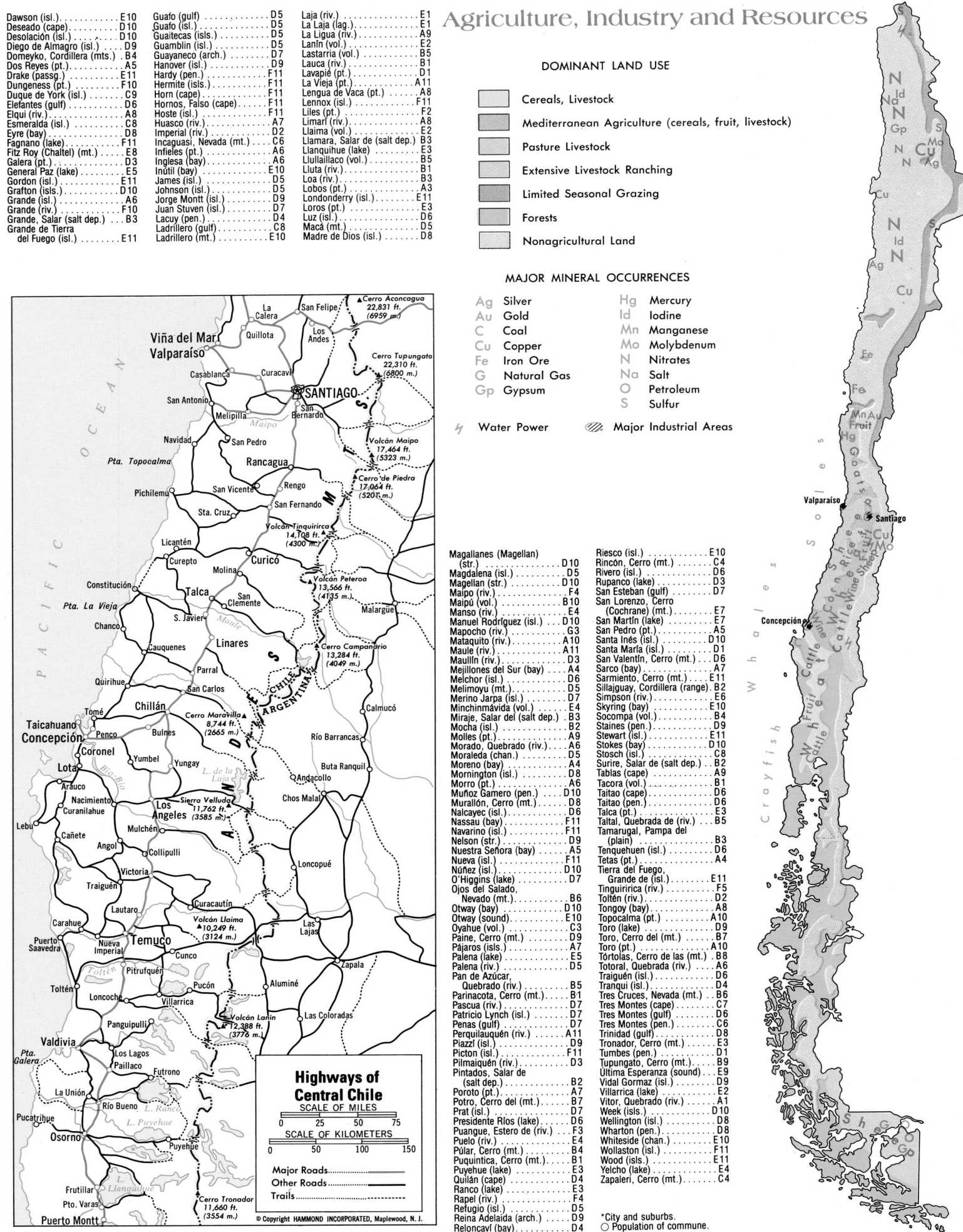

Agriculture, Industry and Resources

DOMINANT LAND USE

- Cereals, Livestock
- Mediterranean Agriculture (cereals, fruit, livestock)
- Pasture Livestock
- Extensive Livestock Ranching
- Limited Seasonal Grazing
- Forests
- Nonagricultural Land

MAJOR MINERAL OCCURRENCES

Ag	Silver	Hg	Mercury
Au	Gold	Id	Iodine
C	Coal	Mn	Manganese
Cu	Copper	Mo	Molybdenum
Fe	Iron Ore	N	Nitrates
G	Natural Gas	Na	Salt
Gp	Gypsum	O	Petroleum
		S	Sulfur

⚡ Water Power   ▨ Major Industrial Areas

Highways of Central Chile

SCALE OF MILES

0   25   50   75

SCALE OF KILOMETERS

0   50   100   150

Major Roads ————
Other Roads ------
Trails ....

© Copyright HAMMOND INCORPORATED, Maplewood, N.J.

*City and suburbs.
○ Population of commune.

PROVINCES

Buenos Aires 10,796,036 . . . D4
Catamarca 206,204 . . . . C2
Chaco 692,410 . . . . D2
Chubut 262,196 . . . . C5
Córdoba 2,407,135 . . . . D3
Corrientes 657,716 . . . . E2
Distrito Federal 2,908,001 . . H7
Entre Ríos 902,241 . . . . E3
Formosa 292,479 . . . . D1
Jujuy 408,514 . . . . C1
La Pampa 207,132 . . . . C4
La Rioja 163,342 . . . . C2
Mendoza 1,187,305 . . . . . . C4
Misiones 579,579 . . . . F2
Neuquén 241,904 . . . . C4
Río Negro 383,896 . . . . C5
Salta 662,369 . . . . D1
San Juan 469,973 . . . . C3
San Luis 212,837 . . . . C3
Santa Cruz 114,479 . . . . C6
Santa Fe 2,457,188 . . . . D3
Santiago del Estero 652,318 . . C2
Tierra del Fuego, Antártida,
 e Islas del Atlántico
 Sur 29,451 . . . . C7
Tucumán 968,066 . . . . C2

CITIES and TOWNS

Abra Pampa 2,929 . . . . C1
Adolfo Alsina 7,707 . . . . . . D4
Aguaray 4,802 . . . . D1
Aguilares 20,286 . . . . C2
Aimogasta 4,640 . . . . C2
Alberti 6,440 . . . . G7
Alcorta 5,818 . . . . F6
Algarrobo del Águila C4
Allen 14,041 . . . . C4
Alpachiri 1,657 . . . . D4
Alta Gracia 30,628 . . . . D3
Aluminé 1,560 . . . . B4
Alvear 5,419 . . . . E2
Ameghino 2,775 . . . . D3
Añatuya 15,025 . . . . D2
Andalgalá 6,853 . . . . C2
Antofagasta de la Sierra C2
Apóstoles 11,252 . . . . E2
Arrecifes 17,719 . . . . F7
Arroyo Seco 12,886 . . . . . . F6
Ascensión 3,031 . . . . F7
Avellaneda 330,654 . . . . . . G7
Ayacucho 12,363 . . . . E4
Azul 43,582 . . . . E4
Bahía Blanca 220,765 . . . . . D4
Bahía Bustamante C6
Bahía Thetis C7
Balcarce 28,985 . . . . E4
Balnearia 4,531 . . . . D3
Baradero 20,103 . . . . G6
Barrancas 3,602 . . . . F6
Barranqueras E2
Barreal 2,739 . . . . C3
Basavilbaso 7,657 . . . . G6
Belén 7,411 . . . . C2
Bella Vista, Corrientes
 14,229 . . . . E2
Bella Vista, Tucuman 9,177 . . D2
Bell Ville 26,559 . . . . D3
Bolívar 16,382 . . . . D4
Bovril 4,735 . . . . G5
Bragado 27,101 . . . . F7
Buenos Aires (cap.)
 2,908,001 . . . . H7
Buenos Aires *9,927,404 . . . H7
Cafayate 5,048 . . . . C2
Calafate B7
Calchaquí 5,958 . . . . F5
Caleta Olivia 20,141 . . . . . . C6
Camarones C5
Campana 51,498 . . . . G6
Cañada de Gómez 24,706 . . F6
Canals 6,627 . . . . D3
Cañuelas 14,831 . . . . G7
Carcarañá 11,121 . . . . F6
Carlos Casares 13,286 . . . . . F7
Carlos Tejedor 4,421 . . . . . . D4
Carmen de Areco 7,882 . . . . F7
Carmen de Patagones
 13,981 . . . . D5
Casilda 23,492 . . . . F6
Castelli 4,507 . . . . H7
Catamarca 88,432 . . . . C2
Caucete 14,512 . . . . C3
Ceres 10,743 . . . . D2
Chabás 5,156 . . . . F6
Chacabuco 26,492 . . . . F7
Chajarí 15,242 . . . . G5
Chamical 6,333 . . . . C3
Charadai 1,078 . . . . D2
Charata 13,070 . . . . D2
Chascomús 21,864 . . . . H7
Chepes 4,775 . . . . C3
Chicoana 1,844 . . . . C2
Chilecito 14,010 . . . . C2
Chivilcoy 43,779 . . . . F7
Choele-Choel 6,191 . . . . . . C4
Chos-Malal 4,823 . . . . C4
Cinco Saltos 15,094 . . . . . . C4
Cipolletti 40,123 . . . . C4
Clorinda 21,008 . . . . D1
Colón, Buenos Aires 16,070 . . F6
Colón, Entre Ríos 11,648 . . . G6
Colonia Las Heras 3,176 . . . . C6
Comandante Fontana 4,468 . . D2
Comandante Luis Piedrabuena
 2,492 . . . . C6
Comodoro Rivadavia 96,865 . . C6
Concepción 29,359 . . . . C2
Concepción de
 la Sierra 2,778 . . . . E2
Concepción del
 Uruguay 46,065 . . . . G6
Concordia 93,618 . . . . G5
Constanza 1,313 . . . . G6
Córdoba 982,018 . . . . D3
Coronda 11,554 . . . . F6
Coronel Brandsen 10,484 . . . H7
Coronel Dorrego 10,661 . . . . D4
Coronel Pringles 16,592 . . . . D4
Coronel Suárez 16,359 . . . . . D4

AREA 1,072,070 sq. mi. (2,776,661 sq. km.)
POPULATION 28,438,000
CAPITAL Buenos Aires
LARGEST CITY Buenos Aires
HIGHEST POINT Cerro Aconcagua 22,831 ft.
 (6,959 m.)
MONETARY UNIT austral
MAJOR LANGUAGE Spanish
MAJOR RELIGION Roman Catholicism

Agriculture, Industry and Resources

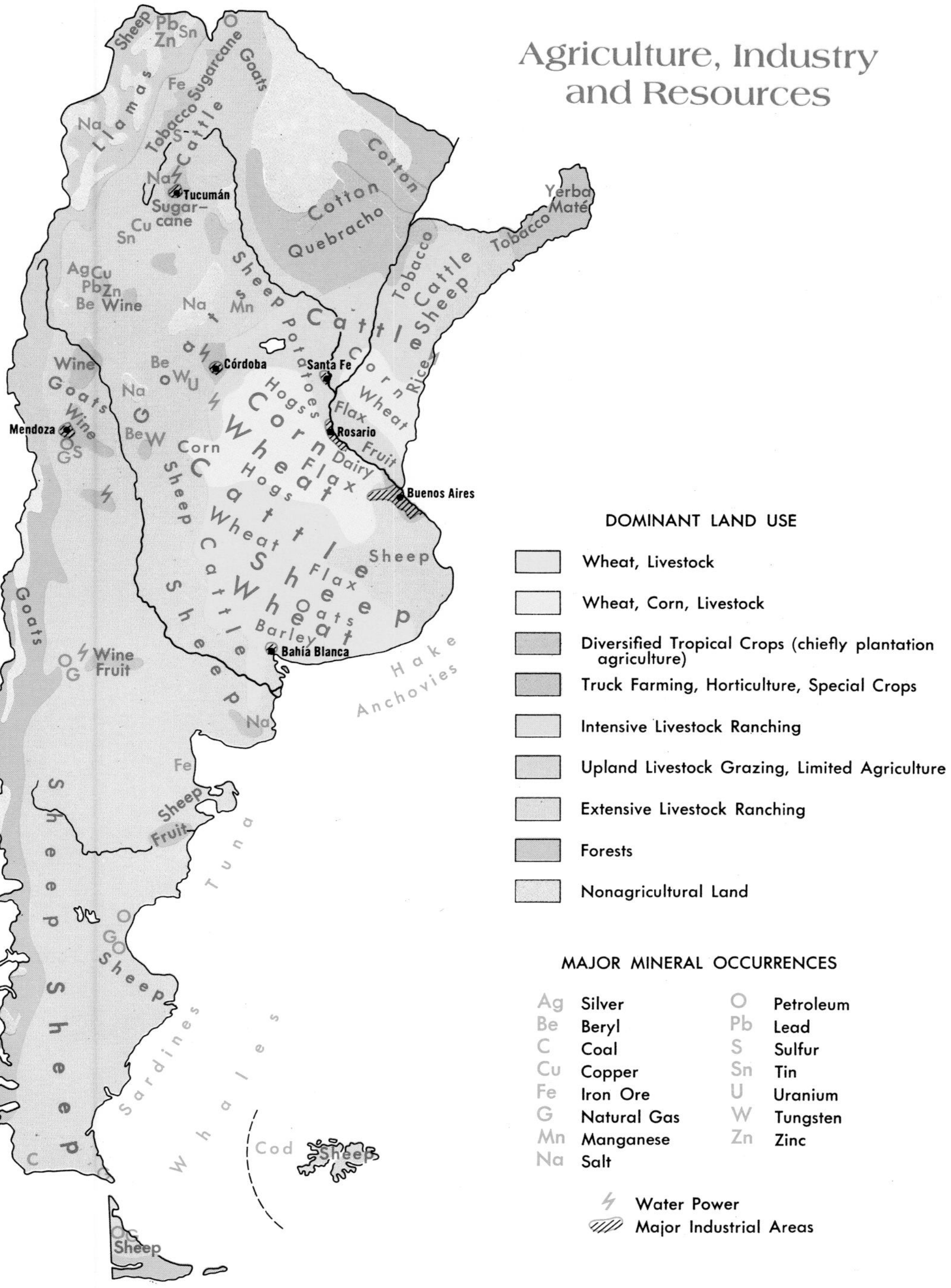

DOMINANT LAND USE

- Wheat, Livestock
- Wheat, Corn, Livestock
- Diversified Tropical Crops (chiefly plantation agriculture)
- Truck Farming, Horticulture, Special Crops
- Intensive Livestock Ranching
- Upland Livestock Grazing, Limited Agriculture
- Extensive Livestock Ranching
- Forests
- Nonagricultural Land

MAJOR MINERAL OCCURRENCES

Ag	Silver	O	Petroleum
Be	Beryl	Pb	Lead
C	Coal	S	Sulfur
Cu	Copper	Sn	Tin
Fe	Iron Ore	U	Uranium
G	Natural Gas	W	Tungsten
Mn	Manganese	Zn	Zinc
Na	Salt		

⚡ Water Power
▨ Major Industrial Areas

Coronel Vidal 4,774 . . . . E4
Corral de Bustos 8,613 . . . . D3
Corrientes 179,590 . . . . E2
Cosquín 13,929 . . . . D3
Crespo 10,668 . . . . F6
Cruz del Eje 23,473 . . . . . . C3
Curuzú Cuatiá 24,955 . . . . . G5
Cutral-Có 25,870 . . . . C4
Daireaux 8,150 . . . . D4
Deán Funes 16,306 . . . . D3
Diamante 13,464 . . . . F6
Dolavon 1,778 . . . . C5
Dolores 19,307 . . . . E4
Eduardo Castex 5,397 . . . . . D4
El Bolsón 5,001 . . . . B5
Eldorado 22,821 . . . . F2
El Maitén 2,350 . . . . B5
Elortondo 4,939 . . . . F6
El Quebrachal 2,202 . . . . . . D2
Embarcación 9,016 . . . . D1
Empedrado 4,732 . . . . E2
Escobar 70,829 . . . . G7
Esperanza 22,838 . . . . F5
Esquel 17,228 . . . . B5
Esquina 10,380 . . . . G5
Famatina 1,237 . . . . C2
Federación 7,259 . . . . G5
Felipe Yofré 1,140 . . . . G4
Fernández 6,062 . . . . D2
Fiambalá 1,201 . . . . C2
Firmat 13,588 . . . . F6
Formosa 95,067 . . . . E2
Fortín Olmos 1,101 . . . . F4
Frías 20,901 . . . . D2
Gaiman 2,651 . . . . C5
Gálvez 14,711 . . . . F6
General Acha 7,647 . . . . C4
General Alvear, Buenos Aires
 5,481 . . . . F7
General Alvear,
 Mendoza 21,250 . . . . C3
General Arenales 3,332 . . . . F7
General Belgrano 10,909 . . . G7
General Conesa 3,566 . . . . . C5
General Galarza 3,057 . . . . . G6
General Güemes 15,534 . . . . D1
General José de
 San Martín 16,296 . . . . . . E2
General Juan Madariaga
 13,409 . . . . E4
General La Madrid 5,154 . . . . D4
General Las Heras 6,005 . . . . G7
General Paz 5,127 . . . . H7
General Pico 30,180 . . . . . . D4
General Ramírez 5,393 . . . . . F6
General Roca 38,296 . . . . . . C4
General San Martín, Buenos
 Aires 384,306 . . . . G7
General San Martín,
 La Pampa 2,168 . . . . D4
General Viamonte 10,112 . . . F7
General Villegas 11,307 . . . . D4
Gobernador Crespo 2,972 . . . F5
Godoy Cruz 141,553 . . . . . . C3
Goya 47,357 . . . . G4
Gualeguay 24,883 . . . . G6
Gualeguaychú 51,057 . . . . . G6
Guandacol 1,351 . . . . C2
Hasenkamp 2,804 . . . . F5
Helvecia 3,927 . . . . F5
Hernandarias 3,002 . . . . F5
Hernando 8,619 . . . . D3
Huinca Renancó 7,187 . . . . . D3
Humahuaca 3,963 . . . . C1
Humberto (Humberto
 Primo) 4,163 . . . . F5
Ibarreta 5,262 . . . . D2
Ibicuy 3,082 . . . . G6
Ingeniero Huergo 3,385 . . . . C4
Ingeniero Jacobacci 4,045 . . . C5
Ingeniero Luiggi 3,002 . . . . . D4
Intendente Alvear 3,640 . . . . D4
Itatí 3,269 . . . . E2
Ituzaingó 8,687 . . . . E2
Jáchal 8,832 . . . . C3
Jesús María 17,594 . . . . D3
Joaquín V. González 6,054 . . D2
Juárez 11,798 . . . . E4
Jujuy 124,487 . . . . C1
Junín 62,080 . . . . F7
Junín de los Andes 5,638 . . . B4
La Banda 46,994 . . . . D2
Laboulaye 16,883 . . . . D3
La Carlota 8,614 . . . . D3
La Cruz 4,132 . . . . E2
La Cumbre 6,110 . . . . C3
La Falda 12,502 . . . . D3
Laguna Paiva 11,129 . . . . . . F5
Lanús 465,891 . . . . H7
La Paz, Entre Ríos 14,920 . . . G5
La Paz, Mendoza 4,604 . . . . C3
La Plata 560,341 . . . . H7
Laprida 6,495 . . . . D4
La Quiaca 8,289 . . . . C1
La Rioja 66,826 . . . . C2
Larroque 3,147 . . . . F5
Las Flores 18,287 . . . . E4
Las Lomitas 4,047 . . . . D1
Las Palmas 5,061 . . . . E2
Las Parejas 7,430 . . . . F6
Las Rosas 9,725 . . . . F6
Las Varillas 10,605 . . . . D3
La Toma 4,325 . . . . C3
Lincoln 19,009 . . . . F7
Lobería 8,898 . . . . E4
Lobos 20,798 . . . . G7
Lomas de Zamora 508,620 . . H7
Lucas González 3,015 . . . . . G6
Luján 38,919 . . . . G7
Lules 11,391 . . . . C2
Maciel 4,066 . . . . F6
Magdalena 7,135 . . . . H7
Maipú 7,289 . . . . E4
Malabrigo 3,294 . . . . F4
Malargüe 9,496 . . . . C4
Maquinchao 1,299 . . . . C5
Marcos Juárez 19,827 . . . . . D3
Mar del Plata 407,024 . . . . . E4
Máximo Paz 3,216 . . . . F6
Mburucuya 3,044 . . . . E2
Médanos 4,511 . . . . D4
Mendoza 596,796 . . . . C3
Mercedes, Buenos Aires
 46,581 . . . . G7
Mercedes, Corrientes
 20,603 . . . . G4
Mercedes, San Luis 50,856 . . C3
Merlo 293,059 . . . . G7
Metán 18,928 . . . . D2
Miramar 15,473 . . . . E4
Monte Caseros 18,247 . . . . . G5
Monte Quemado 4,707 . . . . . D2
Monteros 15,832 . . . . C2
Morón 596,769 . . . . G7
Morteros 11,456 . . . . D3
Navarro 7,176 . . . . G7
Necochea 50,939 . . . . E4
Neuquén 90,037 . . . . C4
Nogoyá 15,862 . . . . F6
Norquincó B5
Nueve de Julio 26,608 . . . . . F7
Oberá 27,311 . . . . F2
Olavarría 63,686 . . . . D4
Oliva 9,231 . . . . D3
Palo Santo 3,088 . . . . E2
Paraná 159,581 . . . . F5
Paso de Los Libres 24,112 . . E2
Pedro Luro 3,142 . . . . D4
Pehuajó 25,613 . . . . D4
Pellegrini 3,940 . . . . D4
Pergamino 68,989 . . . . F6
Pico Truncado 9,626 . . . . . . C6
Pigüé 10,793 . . . . D4
Pilar 3,805 . . . . F5
Pirané 9,039 . . . . D2
Plaza Huincul 7,988 . . . . . . B4

(continued on following page)

Posadas 139,941 . . . . E2
Presidencia de
la Plaza 4,904 . . . . D2
Presidencia Roque
Sáenz Peña 49,261 . . . . . D2
Puán 4,148 . . . . D4
Puerto Deseado 4,017 . . . . D6
Puerto Harberton C7
Puerto Iguazú 10,250 . . . . . F2
Puerto Madryn 20,709 . . . . C5
Puerto Rico 8,195 . . . . D1
Punta Alta 54,375 . . . . D4
Quequén 11,737 . . . . E4
Quimili 8,972 . . . . D2
Quines 3,352 . . . . C3
Quitilipi 9,937 . . . . D2
Rafaela 53,132 . . . . F5
Ramallo 8,248 . . . . F6
Rauch 8,348 . . . . E4
Rawson 12,981 . . . . D5
Reconquista 32,442 . . . . . . F4
Recreo 3,502 . . . . C2
Resistencia 218,438 . . . . . . E2
Rinconada C1
Río Colorado 7,361 . . . . . . D4
Río Cuarto 110,148 . . . . . . D3
Río Gallegos 43,479 . . . . . C7
Río Grande 13,271 . . . . . . C7
Río Segundo 12,839 . . . . . D3
Río Tercero 34,735 . . . . . . D3
Rivadavia 10,953 . . . . C3
Rojas 14,247 . . . . F7
Romang 4,017 . . . . F4
Roque Pérez 5,434 . . . . . . G7
Rosario 954,606 . . . . F6
Rosario de la
Frontera 13,531 . . . . D2
Rosario de Lerma 9,540 . . . C1
Rufino 15,306 . . . . D3
Saladas 7,345 . . . . E2
Saladillo 14,806 . . . . G7
Salliqueló 5,479 . . . . D4
Salta 260,323 . . . . C1
Salto 18,462 . . . . F7
San Antonio de
Areco 12,932 . . . . G7
San Antonio de
los Cobres 2,357 . . . . . . C1
San Antonio Oeste 8,690 . . C5
San Carlos 7,613 . . . . F6
San Carlos de
Bariloche 48,222 . . . . . . B5
San Cayetano 5,960 . . . . . E4

San Cristóbal 13,345 . . . . . F5
San Fernando 128,939 . . . . G7
San Francisco, Córdoba
58,616 . . . . D3
San Francisco, San Luis
2,448 . . . . C3
San Genaro 2,977 . . . . F6
San Ignacio 3,437 . . . . E2
San Jaime de la
Frontera 2,811 . . . . G5
San Javier 7,557 . . . . F5
San José de Feliciano 4,986 . G5
San Juan 290,479 . . . . C3
San Julián 4,278 . . . . C6
San Justo 14,135 . . . . F5
San Luis 70,632 . . . . C3
San Martín 29,746 . . . . . . C3
San Martín de
los Andes 9,507 . . . . . . C5
San Miguel del Monte 8,414 G7
San Miguel de
Tucumán 496,914 . . . . . D2
San Nicolás 96,313 . . . . . . F6
San Pedro, Buenos Aires
27,058 . . . . F6
San Pedro, Jujuy 36,907 . . . D1
San Rafael 70,477 . . . . C3
San Ramón de la
Nva. Orán 32,955 . . . . . D1
San Salvador 4,342 . . . . . . G5
San Sebastián C7
Santa Cruz 2,353 . . . . C7
Santa Elena 14,655 . . . . . . F5
Santa Fe 287,240 . . . . F5
Santa Lucía 4,452 . . . . E2
Santa María 5,380 . . . . C2
Santa Rosa, Córdoba 4,306 . D3
Santa Rosa, La Pampa
51,689 . . . . C4
Santa Rosa, San Luis 2,878 . C3
Santa Victoria D1
Santiago del Estero 148,357 D2
Santo Tomé, Corrientes
14,352 . . . . E2
Santo Tomé, Santa Fe
35,363 . . . . F5
Sarmiento 6,313 . . . . B6
Sauce 4,677 . . . . G5
Sierra Grande 9,585 . . . . . C5
Suipacha 4,505 . . . . G7
Sunchales 12,493 . . . . F5
Suncho Corral 3,837 . . . . . D2
Tafí Viejo 26,625 . . . . C2
Tandil 78,821 . . . . E4

Tapalquén 5,356 . . . . E4
Tartagal 31,367 . . . . D1
Tigre 199,366 . . . . G7
Tinogasta 7,829 . . . . C2
Toay 3,617 . . . . D4
Tornquist 4,696 . . . . D4
Tostado 10,492 . . . . D2
Trelew 52,073 . . . . C5
Trenque Lauquen 22,504 . . D4
Tres Arroyos 42,118 . . . . . D4
Trevelin 2,935 . . . . B5
Tunuyán 14,665 . . . . C3
Urdinarrain 5,472 . . . . G6
Valcheta 2,994 . . . . C5
Vedia 6.273 . . . . F6
Veinticinco de Mayo 18,936 . F7
Venado Tuerto 46,775 . . . . D3
Vera 13,555 . . . . F5
Verónica 5,657 . . . . H7
Viale 5,635 . . . . F5
Vicente López 289,815 . . . . G7
Victoria 18,883 . . . . F6
Victorica 3,895 . . . . C4
Vicuña Mackenna 5,665 . . . D3
Viedma 24,338 . . . . D5
Villa Ángela 25,586 . . . . . . D2
Villa Atuel 2,774 . . . . C3
Villa Cañas 7,303 . . . . F6
Villa Constitución 36,157 . . F6
Villa del Rosario 10,133 . . . D3
Villa Dolores 21,508 . . . . . C3
Villa Elisa 4,106 . . . . G6
Villa Federal 9,222 . . . . . . G5
Villaguay 18,699 . . . . G5
Villa Guillermina 2,971 . . . D2
Villa Huidobro 4,154 . . . . . D3
Villa María 67,490 . . . . . . D3
Villa María Grande 4,517 . . F5
Villa Nueva 4,604 . . . . C3
Villa Ocampo 9,162 . . . . . . D2
Villa Regina 14,017 . . . . . . C4
Villa San José 6,800 . . . . . G6
Villa San Martín 6,237 . . . . D2
Vinchina 1,070 . . . . C2
Zapala 18,293 . . . . B4
Zárate 65,504 . . . . G6
Zavalla 3,800 . . . . F6

OTHER FEATURES

Aconcagua, Cerro (mt.) . . . C3
Andes, Cordillera
de los (mts.) C2

Argentino (lake) B7
Arizaro, Salar de (salt dep.) . C2
Atacama, Puna de (reg.) . . . C2
Atuel (riv.) C4
Bermejo (riv.) E2
Blanca (bay) D4
Brazo Sur, Pilcomayo (riv.) . . E1
Buenos Aires (lake) B6
Campanario, Cerro (mt.) . . . C4
Chaco Austral (reg.) D2
Chaco Central (reg.) D1
Chico (riv.) C5
Chico (riv.) C6
Chubut (riv.) C5
Colhué Huapi (lake) C6
Colorado (riv.) D4
Cónico, Cerro (mt.) B5
Corrientes (riv.) E2
Coyle (riv.) B7
Delgada (pt.) D5
Desaguadero (riv.) C3
Deseado (riv.) C6
Diamante (riv.) C3
Domuyo (vol.) B4
Dos Bahías (cape) D5
Dulce (riv.) D2
Dungeness (pt.) C7
El Chocón (res.) C4
Estados, Los (isl.) D7
Fagnano (lake) C7
Famatina, Sierra de (mts.) . . C2
Feliciano (riv.) G5
Gallegos (riv.) B7
General Manuel Belgrano,
Cerro (mt.) C2
Gran Chaco (reg.) D1
Grande (bay) C7
Grande (falls) E3
Grande de Tierra del
Fuego (isl.) C7
Gualeguay (riv.) G5
Guayaquilaró (riv.) C3
Iguazú (falls) F2
Iguazú Nat'l Park E2
Lanín (vol.) B4
Lanín Nat'l Park B4
Lechiguanas (isls.) G6
Lennox (isl.) C8
Limay (riv.) C4
Llancanelo, Salina y
Laguna (salt lake) C4
Llullaillaco (vol.) C1
Magallanes (Magellan) (str.) . C7

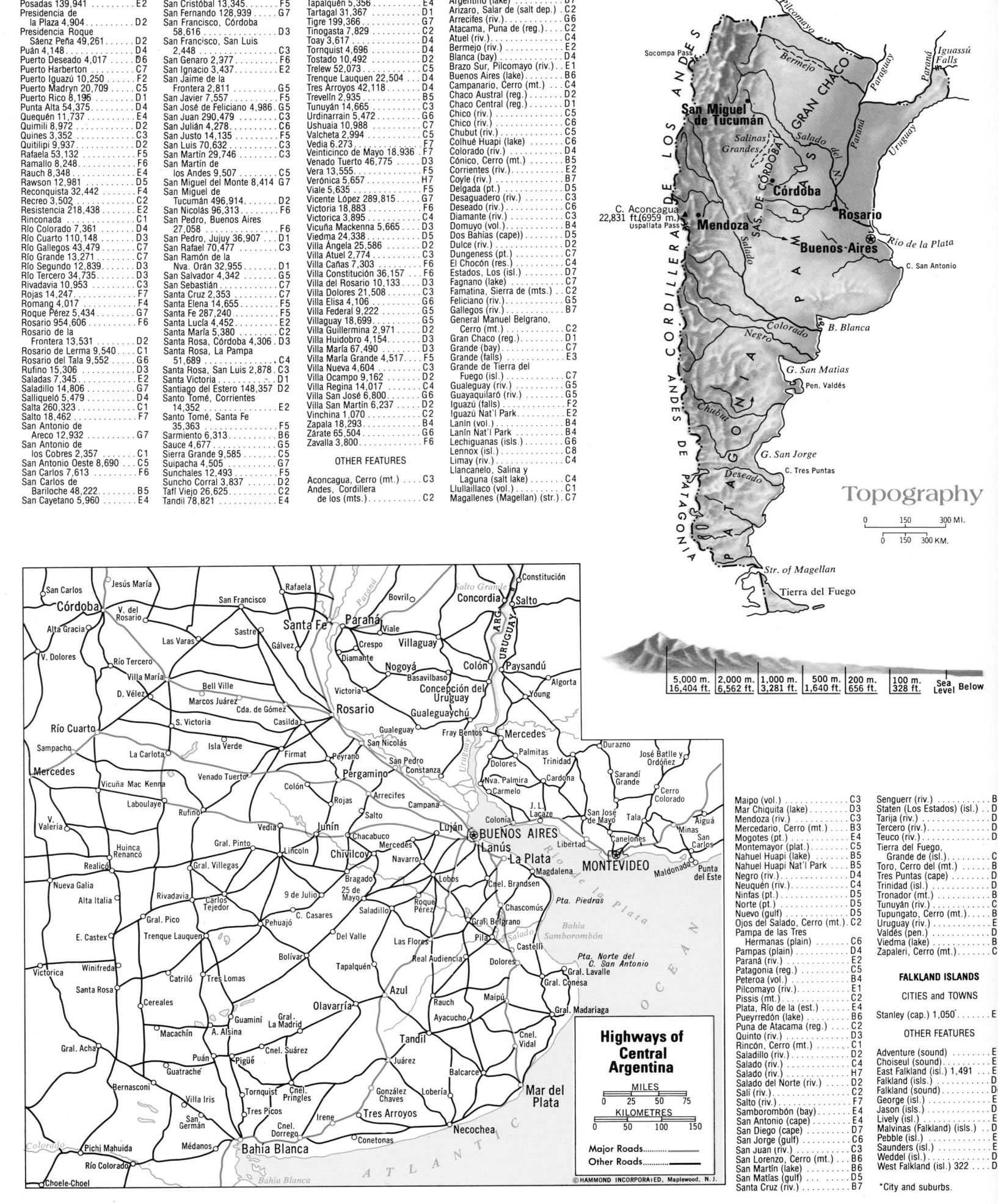

Topography

0   150   300 MI.
0   150   300 KM.

Socompa Pass
Uspallata Pass
C. Aconcagua
22,831 ft (6959 m.)
San Miguel de Tucumán
Salinas Grandes
Córdoba
Mendoza
Rosario
Buenos Aires
Río de la Plata
C. San Antonio
B. Blanca
G. San Matías
Pen. Valdés
G. San Jorge
C. Tres Puntas
Str. of Magellan
Tierra del Fuego

5,000 m. / 16,404 ft. | 2,000 m. / 6,562 ft. | 1,000 m. / 3,281 ft. | 500 m. / 1,640 ft. | 200 m. / 656 ft. | 100 m. / 328 ft. | Sea Level | Below

Highways of Central Argentina

MILES
0   25   50   75

KILOMETRES
0   50   100   150

Major Roads
Other Roads

© HAMMOND INCORPORATED, Maplewood, N.J.

Maipo (vol.) C3
Mar Chiquita (lake) D3
Mendoza (riv.) C3
Mercedario, Cerro (mt.) . . . B3
Mogotes (pt.) E4
Montemayor (plat.) C5
Nahuel Huapi (lake) B5
Nahuel Huapi Nat'l Park . . . B5
Negro (riv.) D4
Neuquén (riv.) C4
Ninfas (pt.) D5
Norte (pt.) D5
Nuevo (gulf) D5
Ojos del Salado, Cerro (mt.) . C2
Pampa de las Tres
Hermanas (plain) C6
Pampas (plain) D4
Paraná (riv.) E2
Patagonia (reg.) C5
Peteroa (vol.) B4
Pilcomayo (riv.) E1
Pissis (mt.) C2
Plata, Río de la (est.) E4
Pueyrredón (lake) B6
Puna de Atacama (reg.) . . . C2
Quinto (riv.) D3
Rincón, Cerro (mt.) C1
Saladillo (riv.) D2
Salado (riv.) C4
Salado (riv.) H7
Salado del Norte (riv.) D2
Salí (riv.) C2
Salto (riv.) F7
Samborombón (bay) E4
San Antonio (cape) E4
San Jorge (gulf) C6
San Juan (riv.) C3
San Lorenzo, Cerro (mt.) . . B6
San Martín (lake) B6
San Matías (gulf) D5
Santa Cruz (riv.) B7

Senguerr (riv.) . . . . B
Staten (Los Estados) (isl.) . . D
Tarija (riv.) . . . . D
Tercero (riv.) . . . . D
Teuco (riv.) . . . . D
Tierra del Fuego,
Grande de (isl.) C
Toro, Cerro del (mt.) . . . . . B
Tres Puntas (cape) . . . . . . D
Trinidad (isl.) . . . . D
Tronador (mt.) . . . . B
Tunuyán (riv.) . . . . B
Tupungato, Cerro (mt.) . . . B
Uruguay (riv.) . . . . E
Valdés (pen.) . . . . B
Viedma (lake) . . . . B
Zapaleri, Cerro (mt.) . . . . . B

FALKLAND ISLANDS

CITIES and TOWNS

Stanley (cap.) 1,050 . . . . . E

OTHER FEATURES

Adventure (sound) . . . . . . E
Choiseul (sound) . . . . E
East Falkland (isl.) 1,491 . . E
Falkland (isl.) . . . . D
Falkland (sound) . . . . D
George (isl.) . . . . D
Jason (isls.) . . . . D
Lively (isl.) . . . . E
Malvinas (Falkland) (isls.) . . D
Pebble (isl.) . . . . D
Saunders (isl.) . . . . D
Weddel (isl.) . . . . D
West Falkland (isl.) 322 . . . D

*City and suburbs

Argentina

CONIC PROJECTION

SCALE OF MILES

SCALE OF KILOMETERS

Capitals of Countries ⭐
Capitals of Provinces ◉
International Boundaries
Boundaries of Provinces

Scale 1:13,000,000

® Copyright HAMMOND INCORPORATED, Maplewood, N.J.

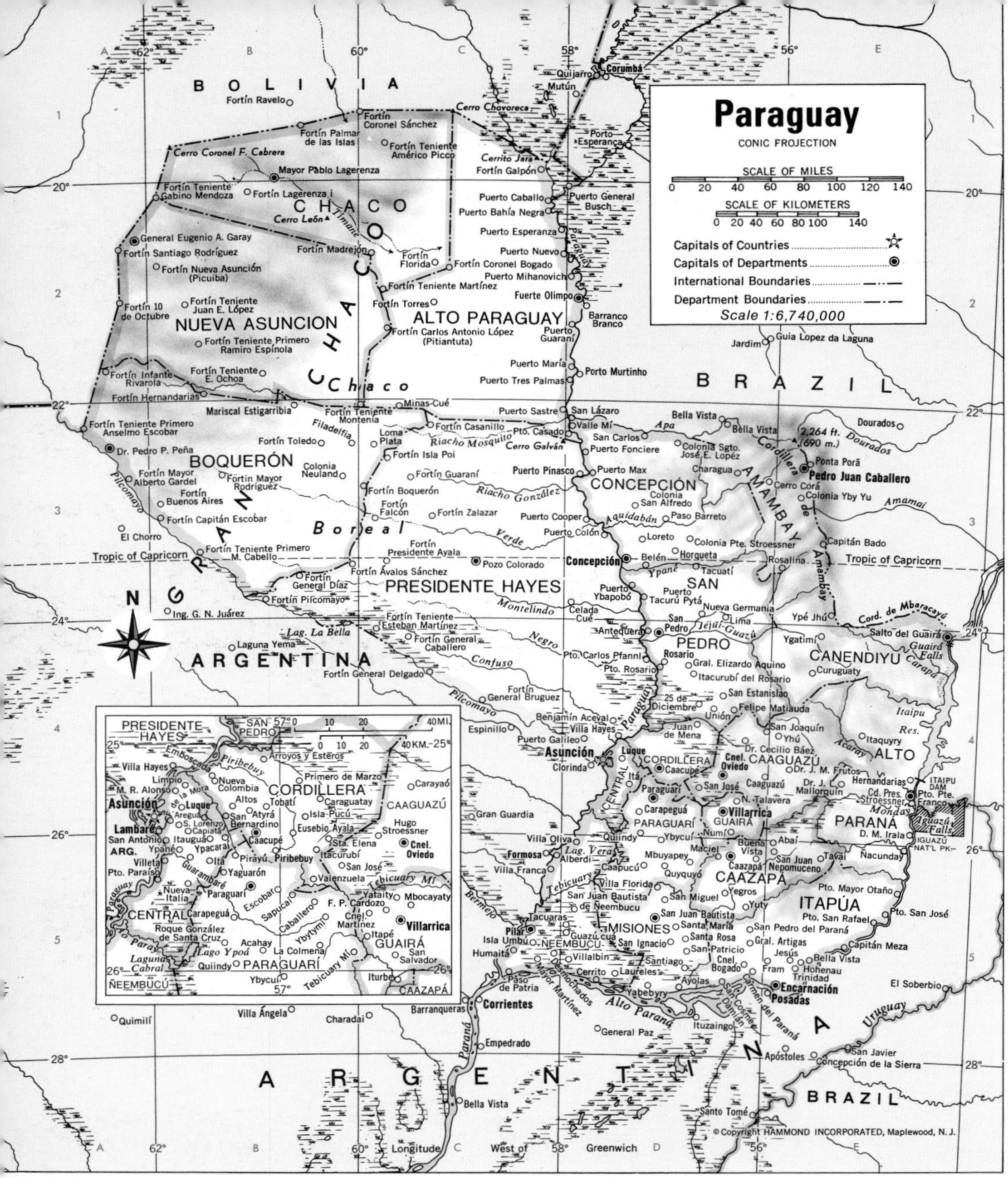

Paraguay

CONIC PROJECTION

SCALE OF MILES
0 20 40 60 80 100 120 140

SCALE OF KILOMETERS
0 20 40 60 80 100 120 140

Capitals of Countries .... ★
Capitals of Departments .... ◉
International Boundaries .... ——
Department Boundaries .... ——

Scale 1:6,740,000

PARAGUAY

DEPARTMENTS

Alto Paraguay	C2
Alto Paraná	E4
Amambay	D3
Asunción	A4
Boquerón	B3
Caaguazú	D-E4
Caazapá	D-E5
Canendiyu	E4
Central	D4
Chaco	B-C2
Concepción	D3
Cordillera	D4
Guaira	D4
Itapúa	E5
Misiones	D5
Ñeembucú	C-D5
Nueva Asunción	B2
Paraguarí	D4-5
Presidente Hayes	C3
San Pedro	D4-5

CITIES and TOWNS

Abaí 1,507	E4
Acahay 1,937	D5
Alberdi 2,346	D5
Altos 1,441	D4
Antequera 1,281	D4
Aregua 3,941	B4
Arroyos y Esteros 1,253	D4
Asunción (cap.) 387,676	A4
Atyrá 1,427	D4
Ayolas 309	D5
Belén 1,219	D3
Bella Vista 3,101	D3
Bella Vista 1,421	E5
Benjamín Aceval 2,877	C4
Buena Vista 1,353	D5
Caacupé 7,276	D4
Caaguazú 7,950	D4
Caapucú 1,400	D5
Caazapá 3,132	D5
Caballero 1,222	D4
Capiatá 2,827	B4
Capitán Bado 915	E3
Capitán Meza 375	E5
Caraguatay 1,439	D4
Carapegua 3,416	D5
Carayaó 1,190	C4
Carmen del Paraná 1,980	E5
Cerrito 958	D5
Ciudad Presidente Stroessner 7,085	E4
Concepción 19,392	D3
Coronel Bogado 3,973	D5
Coronel Martínez 1,598	B5
Coronel Oviedo 13,786	D4
Curuguaty 1,112	E4
Desmochados 551	C5
Doctor Cecilio Báez 1,300	D4
Doctor Juan L. Mallorquín 1,913	E4
Doctor Juan Manuel Frutos 1,494	E4
Doctor M. Irala 468	E4
Emboscada 1,222	D4
Encarnación 23,343	E5
Escobar 548	B5
Eusebio Ayala 4,328	B4
Fernando de la Mora 36,834	B4
Filadelfia 1,438	B3
Fram 1,090	E5
Fuerte Olimpo 3,063	C3
General Artigas 3,542	D5
General Elizardo Aquino 1,304	D4
General Eugenio A. Garay 740	A2
Guarambaré 3,640	B5
Hernandarias 3,898	E4
Hohenau 1,121	E5
Horqueta 4,328	D3
Hugo Stroessner 536	C4
Humaitá 938	C5
Isla Pucú 1,766	B4
Isla Umbú 236	C5
Itá 7,041	B5
Itacurubí 1,997	B5
Itacurubí del Rosario 2,467	D4
Itapé 1,376	C5
Itaquyry 1	E4
Itaugua 3,767	B5
Iturbe 3,413	C5
Jesús 1,495	E5
Juan de Mena 1,027	D4
La Colmena 1,804	B5
Lambaré 31,656	A4
Laureles 435	D5
Lima 1,098	D3
Limpio 2,219	B4
Loreto 1,258	D3
Luque 13,921	B4
Maciel 376	D5
Mariano Roque Alonso 1,492	A4
Mariscal Estigarribia 3,150	B3
Mayor Martínez 324	C5

Mayor Pablo Lagerenza	B1
Mbocayaty 925	D5
Mbuyapey 1,560	D5
Nacunday 380	E5
Natalicio Talavera 1,228	D4
Nueva Germania 572	D4
Nueva Italia 1,517	B5
Numí 941	D5
Paraguarí 5,036	D5
Paso de Patria 698	C5
Pedro Juan Caballero 21,033	E3
Pilar 12,506	C5
Pirayú 2,698	B5
Piribebuy 4,497	D4
Primero de Marzo 696	D4
Puerto Casado 4,078	C3
Puerto Guaraní 302	C3
Puerto Pinasco 5,477	C3
Puerto Presidente Franco 4,152	E4
Puerto Sastre 160	C3
Quiindy 2,664	D5
Quyquyó 928	D5
Roque González de Santa Cruz 4,165	B5
Rosario 4,165	D4
Salto del Guairá	E4
San Antonio 4,906	B5
San Bernardino 949	D4
San Cosme y Damián 602	D5
San Estanislao 4,753	D4
San Ignacio 6,116	D5
San Joaquín 536	D4
San José 3,102	D5
San Juan Bautista 6,457	D5
San Juan Bautista de Ñeembucú 688	C5
San Juan Nepomuceno 2,974	E5
San Lázaro 1,767	D2
San Lorenzo 11,616	B4
San Miguel 1,030	D5
San Patricio 1,130	D5
San Pedro 3,186	D4
San Pedro del Paraná 2,723	E5
San Salvador 1,393	D4
Santa Elena 1,439	B5
Santa María 793	D5
Santa Rosa 3,736	D5
Santiago 1,265	D5
Sapucaí 1,864	B5
Tacuaras 193	C5
Tacuatí 836	D4
Tavaí 472	E5
Tebicuary Mí 183	D5
Tobatí 4,983	D4
Trinidad 837	E5
Unión 1,286	D4
Valenzuela 1,108	D4
Valle Mí 1,318	C2
25 de Diciembre 439	D4
Villa Florida 1,261	D5
Villa Franca 359	C5
Villa Hayes 4,749	B4
Villa Oliva 564	C5
Villarrica 17,687	D5
Villeta 3,156	B5
Yabebyry 797	C5
Yaguarón 3,368	B5
Yataity 1,159	D5
Ybycuí 1,736	D5
Ybytymí 816	D5
Yegros 1,051	D5
Ygatimí 396	E4
Yhú 964	D4
Ypacaraí 5,195	B5
Ypané 1,474	B5
Ypé Jhú 645	E3
Yuty 2,392	D5

OTHER FEATURES

Acaray (riv.)	E4
Alto Paraná (riv.)	D5
Amambay, Cordillera de (mts.)	D-E3
Apa (riv.)	D3
Aquidabán (riv.)	D3
Chaco Boreal (reg.)	B2-3
Chovoreca (mt.)	C1
Confuso (riv.)	C4
Coronel F. Cabrera (mt.)	B1
González, Riacho (riv.)	C3
Gran Chaco (reg.)	B2-3
Iguazú (falls)	E4
Itaipú (res.)	E4
Jara (riv.)	C1
Mbaracayú, Cordillera de (mts.)	E3
Monday (riv.)	E4
Montelindo (riv.)	C3
Mosquito, Riacho (riv.)	C3
Negro (riv.)	C4
Paraguay (riv.)	C4
Pilcomayo (riv.)	C4
Tebicuary (riv.)	D5
Timane (riv.)	B2
Vera (lag.)	D4
Verde (riv.)	C3

Agriculture, Industry and Resources

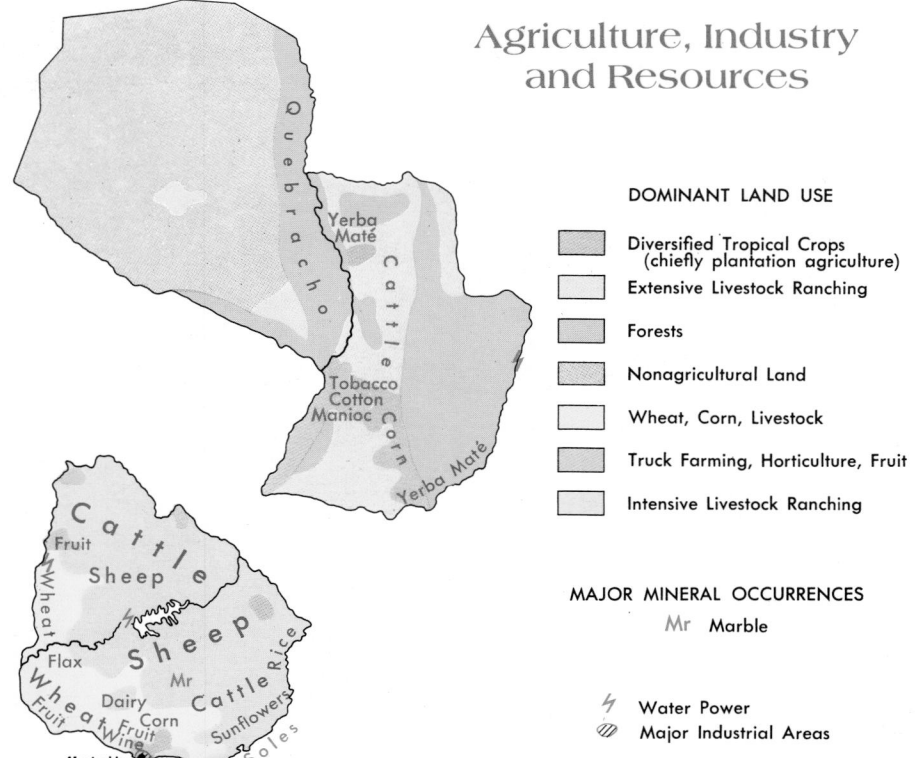

DOMINANT LAND USE

- Diversified Tropical Crops (chiefly plantation agriculture)
- Extensive Livestock Ranching
- Forests
- Nonagricultural Land
- Wheat, Corn, Livestock
- Truck Farming, Horticulture, Fruit
- Intensive Livestock Ranching

MAJOR MINERAL OCCURRENCES

Mr Marble

⚡ Water Power
▨ Major Industrial Areas

Topography

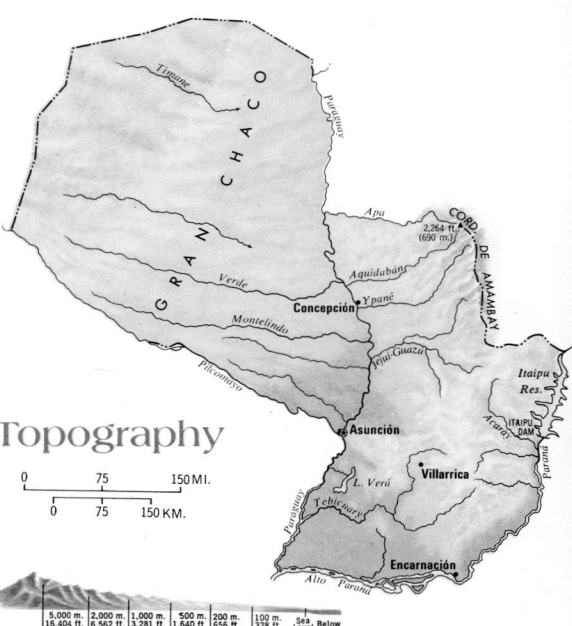

0   75   150 MI.
0   75   150 KM.

5,000 m. / 2,000 m. / 1,000 m. / 500 m. / 200 m. / 100 m. / Sea Level / Below
16,404 ft. / 6,562 ft. / 3,281 ft. / 1,640 ft. / 656 ft. / 328 ft.

Copyright HAMMOND INCORPORATED, Maplewood, N.J.

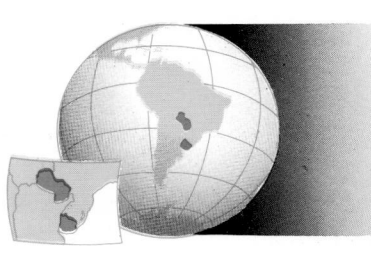

PARAGUAY

AREA 157,047 sq. mi. (406,752 sq. km.)
POPULATION 2,973,000
CAPITAL Asunción
LARGEST CITY Asunción
HIGHEST POINT Amambay Range
  2,264 ft. (690 m.)
MONETARY UNIT guaraní
MAJOR LANGUAGES Spanish, Guaraní
MAJOR RELIGION Roman Catholicism

URUGUAY

AREA 72,172 sq. mi. (186,925 sq. km.)
POPULATION 2,899,000
CAPITAL Montevideo
LARGEST CITY Montevideo
HIGHEST POINT Mirador Nacional 1,644 ft.
  (501 m.)
MONETARY UNIT Uruguayan peso
MAJOR LANGUAGE Spanish
MAJOR RELIGION Roman Catholicism

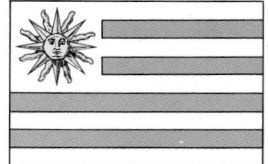

PARAGUAY   **URUGUAY**

Topography

0   50   100 MI.
0   50   100 KM.

Salto Grande · Salto
Rivera CUCH. DE SANTA ANA
Arapey Grande
Cuareim
Paysandú
Trinidad Hito 1,237 ft. (377 m.)
CUCH. DE HAEDO
Negro
Yaguarón
Uruguay
Embalse del R. Negro
Mercedes
Yí
CUCHILLA GRANDE
Cebollatí
Negro
Río de la Plata
Sta. Lucía
Lag. Merín
Mirador Nacional 1,644 ft. (501 m.)
Montevideo
Pta. Brava
Pta. del Este

Below Sea Level | Sea Level | 100 m. 328 ft. | 200 m. 656 ft. | 500 m. 1,640 ft. | 1,000 m. 3,281 ft. | 2,000 m. 6,562 ft. | 5,000 m. 16,404 ft.

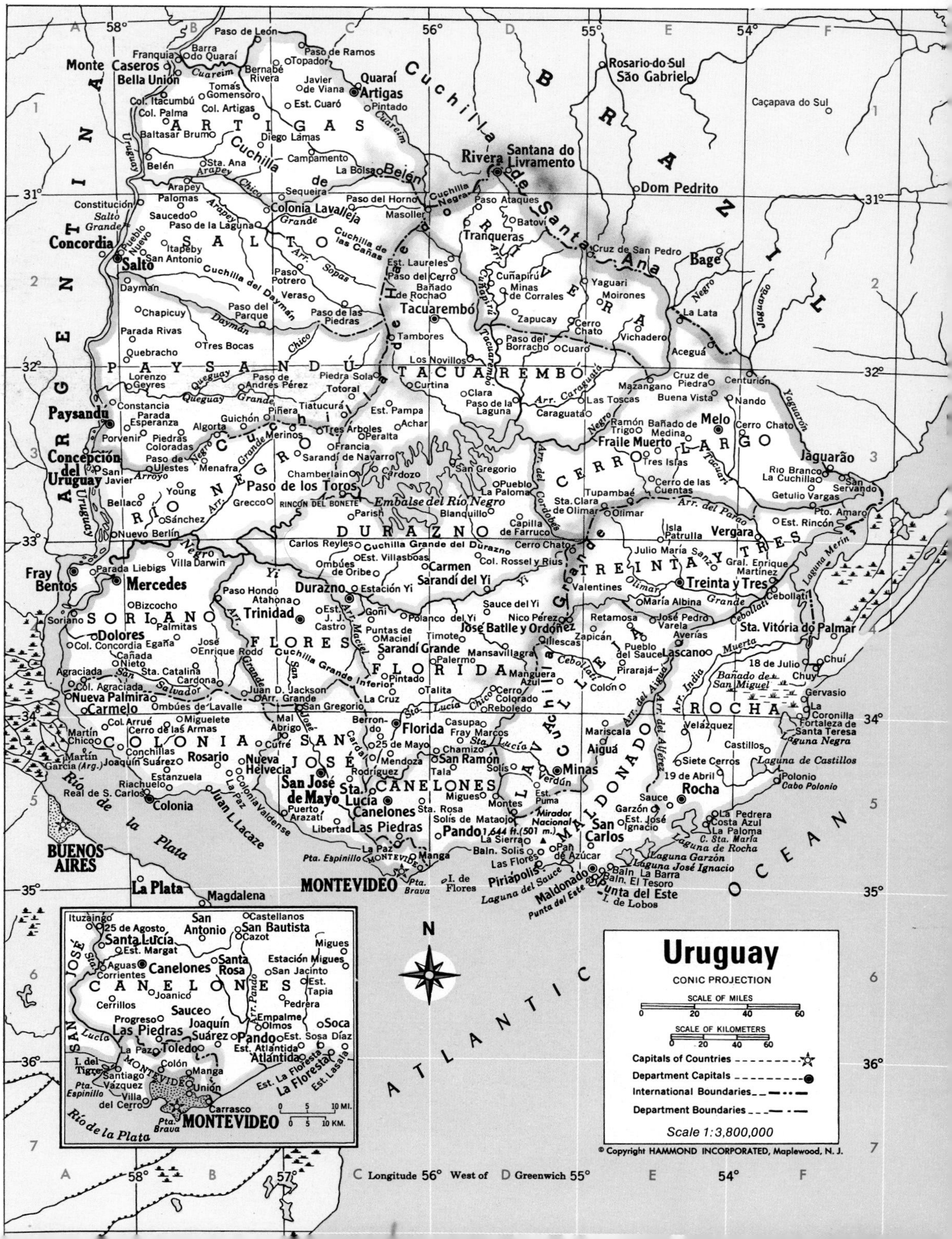

Uruguay

CONIC PROJECTION

SCALE OF MILES
0   20   40   60
SCALE OF KILOMETERS
0   20   40   60

Capitals of Countries .... ⭐
Department Capitals .... ●
International Boundaries ....
Department Boundaries ....

Scale 1:3,800,000

© Copyright HAMMOND INCORPORATED, Maplewood, N.J.

C Longitude 56° West of   D Greenwich 55°

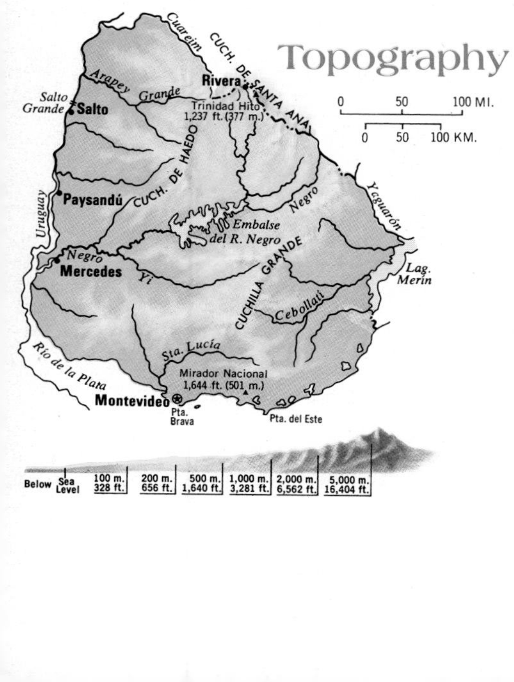

North America

LAMBERT AZIMUTHAL EQUAL-AREA PROJECTION

MILES

0   100 200   400   600   800

KILOMETERS

0 100 200   400   600   800

Capitals of Countries .... ⊛
Other Capitals .... ⊙
International Boundaries .... —·—·—
Other Boundaries .... — — —

Scale 1:36,600,000

© Copyright HAMMOND INCORPORATED, Maplewood, N.J.

Population Distribution

ARCTIC CIRCLE

TROPIC OF CANCER

AREA 9,363,000 sq. mi.
(24,250,170 sq. km.)
POPULATION 370,000,000
LARGEST CITY New York
HIGHEST POINT Mt. McKinley 20,320 ft.
(6,194 m.)
LOWEST POINT Death Valley -282 ft.
(-86 m.)

Vegetation

ARCTIC CIRCLE

TROPIC OF CANCER

DENSITY PER

SQ. KILOMETER	SQ. MILE
Over 100	Over 260
50-100	130-260
10-50	25-130
1-10	3-25
Under 1	Under 3

• Cities with over 2,000,000 inhabitants (including suburbs)

○ Cities with over 1,000,000 inhabitants (including suburbs)

MID-LATITUDE FOREST
- Coniferous Forest
- Broadleaf Forest
- Mixed Coniferous and Broadleaf Forest
- Woodland and Shrub (Mediterranean)

MID-LATITUDE GRASSLAND
- Short Grass (Steppe)
- Tall Grass (Prairie)

TROPICAL FOREST
- Tropical Rainforest
- Light Tropical Forest

TROPICAL GRASSLAND
- Wooded Savanna

DESERT AND DESERT SHRUB

TUNDRA AND ALPINE

PERMANENT ICE

Average January Temperature

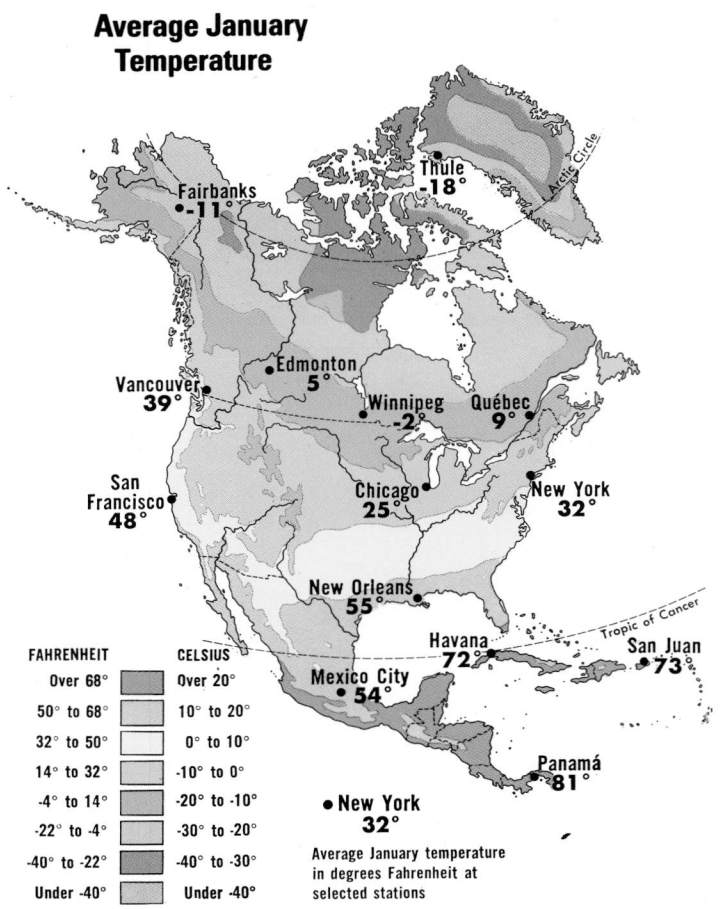

FAHRENHEIT		CELSIUS
Over 68°		Over 20°
50° to 68°		10° to 20°
32° to 50°		0° to 10°
14° to 32°		-10° to 0°
-4° to 14°		-20° to -10°
-22° to -4°		-30° to -20°
-40° to -22°		-40° to -30°
Under -40°		Under -40°

• New York
32°

Average January temperature
in degrees Fahrenheit at
selected stations

Average July Temperature

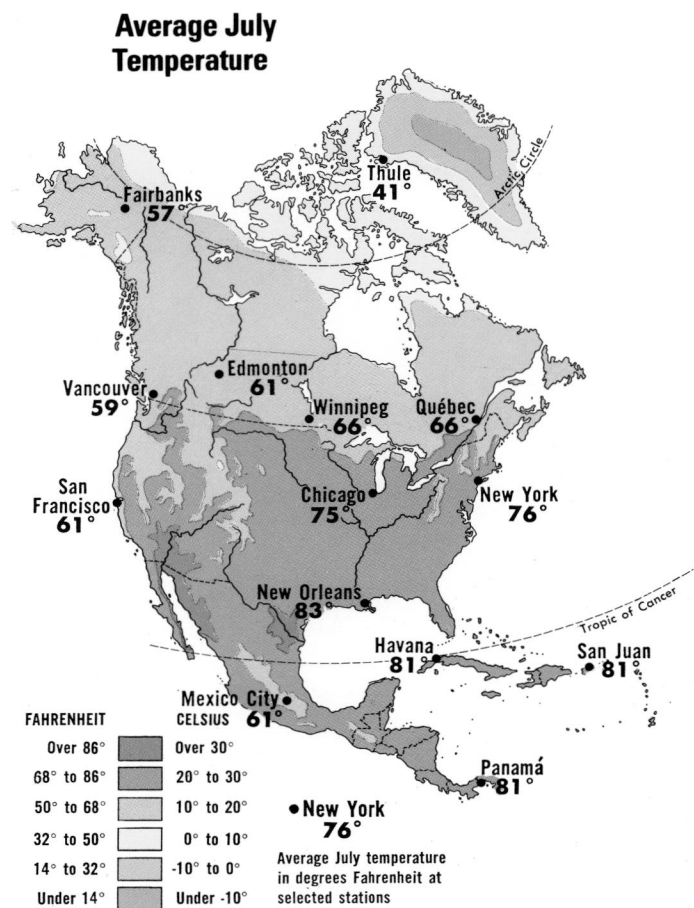

FAHRENHEIT		CELSIUS
Over 86°		Over 30°
68° to 86°		20° to 30°
50° to 68°		10° to 20°
32° to 50°		0° to 10°
14° to 32°		-10° to 0°
Under 14°		Under -10°

• New York
76°

Average July temperature
in degrees Fahrenheit at
selected stations

Rainfall

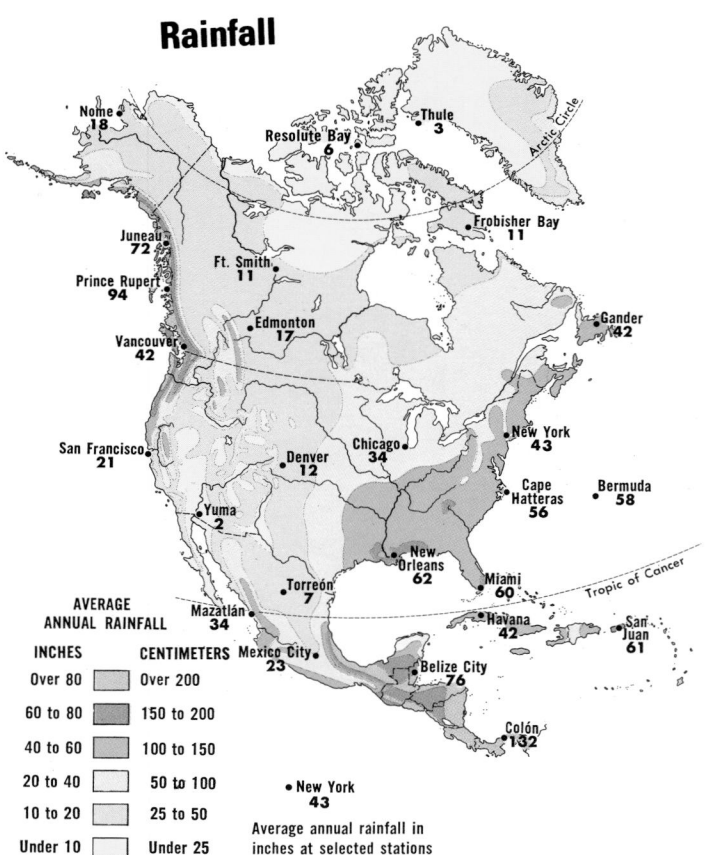

AVERAGE ANNUAL RAINFALL		
INCHES		CENTIMETERS
Over 80		Over 200
60 to 80		150 to 200
40 to 60		100 to 150
20 to 40		50 to 100
10 to 20		25 to 50
Under 10		Under 25

• New York
43

Average annual rainfall in
inches at selected stations

Vegetation / Relief

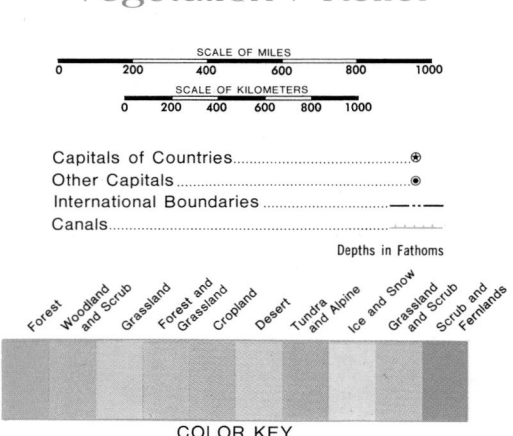

SCALE OF MILES
0   200   400   600   800   1000

SCALE OF KILOMETERS
0   200   400   600   800   1000

Capitals of Countries.....................................⊛
Other Capitals..⊚
International Boundaries.................... — —
Canals...

Depths in Fathoms

Forest | Woodland and Scrub | Grassland | Forest and Grassland | Cropland | Desert | Tundra and Alpine | Ice and Snow | Grassland and Scrub | Scrub and Fernlands

COLOR KEY

Longitude 90° West of Greenwich

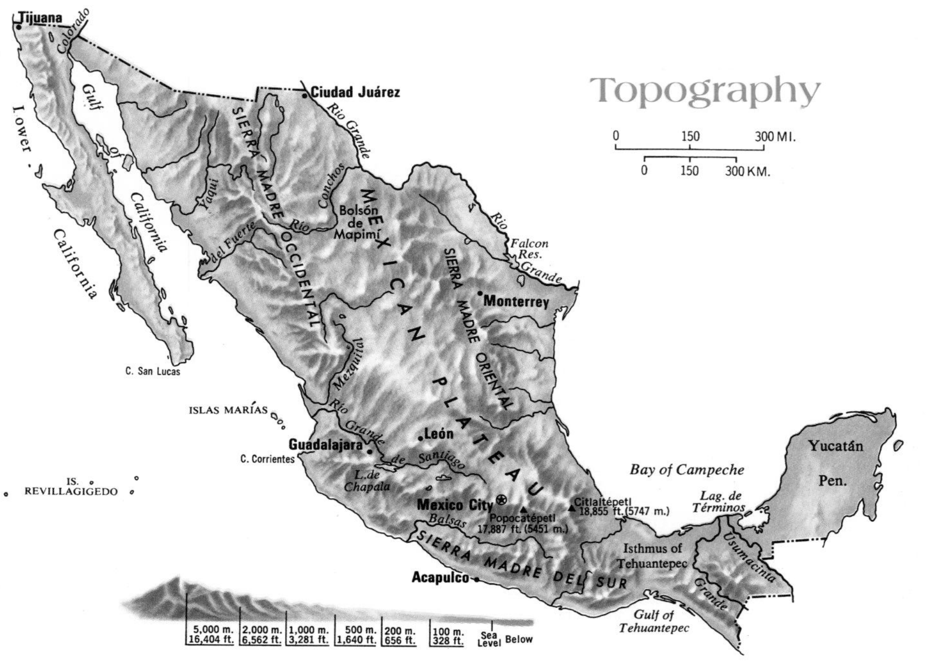
Topography
0 150 300 MI.
0 150 300 KM.
Tijuana
Ciudad Juárez
Colorado
Gulf of California
Lower California
Rio Grande
SIERRA MADRE OCCIDENTAL
MEXICAN PLATEAU
Bolsón de Mapimí
Conchos
Yaqui
Del Fuerte
Falcon Res.
Monterrey
SIERRA MADRE ORIENTAL
C. San Lucas
ISLAS MARÍAS
IS. REVILLAGIGEDO
Guadalajara
C. Corrientes
L. de Chapala
León
Rio Grande de Santiago
Mexico City
Balsas
Popocatépetl 17,887 ft. (5451 m.)
Citlaltépetl 18,855 ft. (5747 m.)
Bay of Campeche
Lag. de Términos
Yucatán Pen.
Isthmus of Tehuantepec
SIERRA MADRE DEL SUR
Acapulco
Usumacinta
Grande
Gulf of Tehuantepec
5,000 m. 16,404 ft.
2,000 m. 6,562 ft.
1,000 m. 3,281 ft.
500 m. 1,640 ft.
200 m. 656 ft.
100 m. 328 ft.
Sea Level
Below

STATES

Aguascalientes 504,300 .... H6
Baja California 1,227,400 .... B1
Baja California Sur 221,000 .... C3
Campeche 371,800 .... O7
Chiapas 2,097,500 .... N8
Chihuahua 1,935,100 .... F2
Coahuila 1,561,000 .... H3
Colima 339,400 .... G7
Distrito Federal 9,377,300 .... L1
Durango 1,160,300 .... G4
Guanajuato 3,045,600 .... J6
Guerrero 2,174,200 .... J8
Hidalgo 1,518,200 .... K6
Jalisco 4,296,500 .... H6
México 7,542,300 .... K7
Michoacán 3,049,400 .... H7
Morelos 931,400 .... K7
Nayarit 729,500 .... G6
Nuevo León 2,463,500 .... K4
Oaxaca 2,517,500 .... L8
Puebla 3,285,300 .... L7
Querétaro 730,900 .... J6
Quintana Roo 209,900 .... P7
San Luis Potosí 1,669,900 .... J5
Sinaloa 1,882,200 .... F4
Sonora 1,498,100 .... D2
Tabasco 1,150,000 .... N7
Tamaulipas 1,924,900 .... K4
Tlaxcala 548,500 .... N1
Veracruz 5,263,800 .... L7
Yucatán 1,034,300 .... P6
Zacatecas 1,144,700 .... H5

CITIES and TOWNS

Acala 11,483 .... N8
Acámbaro 32,257 .... J7
Acaponeta 11,844 .... G5
Acapulco de Juárez 309,254 .... K8
Acatlán de Osorio 7,624 .... K7
Acatzingo de Hidalgo 6,905 .... N2
Acayucan 21,173 .... M8
Aconchi 1,596 .... D2
Actopan, Hidalgo 11,037 .... K6
Actopan, Veracruz 2,265 .... Q1
Agua Dulce 21,060 .... M7
Agualeguas 2,502 .... J3
Agua Prieta 20,754 .... E1
Aguascalientes 181,277 .... H6
Aguililla 5,715 .... H7
Ahome 4,182 .... E4
Ahuacatitlán 6,436 .... L1
Ahuacatlán 5,350 .... G6
Ahumada 6,466 .... F1
Ajalpan 8,238 .... L7
Alamo 9,954 .... L6
Álamos 4,269 .... E3
Aldama, Chihuahua 6,047 .... G2
Aldama, Tamaulipas 3,033 .... L5
Aljojuca 3,204 .... O1
Allende, Coahuila 11,076 .... J2
Allende, Nuevo León 9,914 .... J4
Almoloya del Río 3,714 .... K1
Altamira 6,053 .... L5
Altar 2,519 .... D1
Altepexi 6,661 .... L7
Alto Lucero 3,698 .... P1
Altotonga 6,754 .... P1
Alvarado 15,592 .... M7
Amatlán de los Reyes 3,664 .... P2
Amealco 2,960 .... K6
Ameca 21,018 .... H6
Amecameca de Juárez 16,276 .... L1
Amozoc de Mota 9,203 .... N2
Anáhuac, Chihuahua 10,886 .... F2
Anáhuac, Nuevo León 8,168 .... J3
Angostura 2,663 .... E4
Antiguo Morelos 1,569 .... K5
Apan 13,705 .... M1
Apatzingán de la
Constitución 44,849 .... H7
Apizaco 21,189 .... N1
Aquiles Serdán 2,565 .... G2
Aramberri 1,786 .... J5
Arandas 18,934 .... H6
Arcelia 10,024 .... J7
Ario de Rosales 8,774 .... J7
Arizpe 1,736 .... D1
Armería 10,616 .... G7
Arriaga 13,193 .... N8
Arteaga 5,324 .... H7
Ascensión 4,104 .... E1
Asunción Nochixtlán 3,235 .... L8
Atlixco 41,967 .... M2
Atotonilco el Alto 16,271 .... H6
Atoyac de Álvarez 8,874 .... J8
Autlán de Navarro 20,398 .... G7
Axochiapan 8,283 .... M2
Ayutla de los Libres 3,618 .... K8
Azcapotzalco 534,554 .... L1
Azoyú 3,446 .... K8
Bacadéhuachi 1,514 .... E2
Bacalar 2,121 .... P7
Bachíniva 1,809 .... F2
Bácum 2,668 .... D3
Bahía Tortugas 1,457 .... B3
Balancán de
Domínguez 3,669 .... O8
Bamoa 5,866 .... E4
Banderilla 3,488 .... P1
Baviácora 2,049 .... E2
Benjamín Hill 5,366 .... D1
Bernardino de Sahagún 12,327 .... M1
Boca del Río 2,354 .... Q2
Bolonchén de Rejón 2,342 .... O7
Buenaventura 3,924 .... F2
Burgos 673 .... K4
Cabo San Lucas 1,534 .... E5
Cacahoatán 5,079 .... N9
Cadereyta Jiménez 13,586 .... K4
Calkiní 6,870 .... O6
Calnali 3,318 .... K6
Calpulálpan 8,659 .... M1
Calvillo 6,453 .... H6
Campeche 69,506 .... O7
Cananea 17,518 .... D1
Canatlán 5,983 .... G4
Cancún 326 .... Q6
Candela 1,689 .... J3
Candelaria 1,982 .... O7
Cañitas de Felipe
Pescador 4,885 .... H5
Capulhuac de Mirafuentes 8,289 .... K1
Carbo 2,804 .... D2
Cárdenas, San Luis
Potosí 12,020 .... K6
Cárdenas, Tabasco 15,643 .... N8
Carichic 1,520 .... F2
Castaños 8,996 .... J3
Catemaco 11,786 .... M7
Ceballos 2,937 .... H3
Cedral 4,057 .... J5
Celaya 79,977 .... J6
Celestún 1,490 .... O6
Cerritos 10,421 .... J5
Cerro Azul 20,259 .... L6
Chahuites 5,218 .... M8
Chalchihuites 1,894 .... G5
Chalco de Díaz
Covarrubias 12,172 .... M1
Champotón 6,606 .... O7
Charcas 10,491 .... J5
Chetumal 23,685 .... Q7
Chiapa de Corzo 8,571 .... N8
Chiautempan 12,327 .... N1
Chietla 4,602 .... M2
Chignahuapan 3,805 .... N1
Chihuahua 327,313 .... F2
Chilapa de Álvarez 9,204 .... K8
Chilpancingo de los
Bravos 36,193 .... K8
China, Nuevo León 4,958 .... K4
Chocomán 5,114 .... P2
Choix 2,503 .... E3
Cholula de Rivadavia 15,399 .... M1
Cihuatlán 9,451 .... G7
Cintalapa de Figueroa 12,036 .... N8
Ciudad Acuña (Villa
Acuña) 30,276 .... J2
Ciudad Altamirano 8,694 .... J7
Ciudad Camargo,
Chihuahua 24,030 .... G3
Ciudad Camargo,
Tamaulipas 5,953 .... K3
Ciudad del Carmen 34,656 .... N7
Ciudad Delicias 52,446 .... G2
Ciudad del Maíz 5,241 .... K5
Ciudad de Río Grande 11,651 .... H5
Ciudad Guerrero 3,110 .... F2
Ciudad Guzmán 48,166 .... H7
Ciudad Hidalgo, Chiapas 4,105 .... N9
Ciudad Hidalgo,
Michoacán 24,692 .... J7
Ciudad Juárez 424,135 .... F1
Ciudad Lerdo 19,803 .... H4
Ciudad Madero 115,302 .... L5
Ciudad Mante 51,247 .... K5
Ciudad Mendoza 18,696 .... O2
Ciudad Miguel Alemán 11,259 .... K3
Ciudad Obregón 144,795 .... E3
Ciudad Río Bravo 39,018 .... K4
Ciudad Satélite 35,083 .... L1
Ciudad Serdán 9,581 .... O2
Ciudad Valles 47,587 .... K5
Ciudad Victoria 83,897 .... K5
Coalcomán de Matamoros 4,875 .... H7
Coatepec 21,542 .... P1
Coatetelco 5,268 .... L2
Coatzacoalcos 69,753 .... M7
Coatzingo 3,038 .... N2
Cocorit 4,478 .... E3
Colima 58,450 .... H7
Colón 3,346 .... K6
Colotlán 6,135 .... H5
Comala 5,592 .... H7
Comalcalco 14,963 .... N7
Comitán de
Domínguez 21,249 .... O8
Compostela 9,801 .... G6
Concepción del Oro 8,144 .... J4
Concordia 3,947 .... G5
Contla 7,517 .... N1
Copala 3,783 .... K8
Coquimatlán 6,212 .... G7
Córdoba 78,495 .... P2
Cosalá 2,279 .... F4
Cosamaloapan de Carpio 19,766 .... M7
Cosautlán de Carvajal 2,039 .... P1
Coscomatepec de Bravo 6,023 .... P2
Cosío 2,680 .... H5
Costa Rica 11,795 .... F4
Cotija de la Paz 9,178 .... H7
Coyoacán 339,446 .... L1
Coyotepec 8,888 .... L1
Coyuca de Benítez 6,328 .... J8
Coyuca de Catalán 2,926 .... J7
Coyutla 3,726 .... L6
Cozumel 5,858 .... Q6
Creel 2,449 .... E3
Cuatrociénagas de
Carranza 5,523 .... H3
Cuauhtémoc 26,598 .... F2
Cuautepec de Hinojosa 5,501 .... K6
Cuautitlán de Romero
Rubio 11,439 .... L1
Cuautla Morelos 13,946 .... L2
Cuencamé de Ceniceros 3,774 .... H4
Cuernavaca 239,813 .... L2
Cuicatlán 2,733 .... L8
Cuitlahuac 4,813 .... P2
Culiacán 228,001 .... F4
Cumpas 2,395 .... E1
Cunduacán 4,397 .... N7
Dimas 2,194 .... F5
Doctor Arroyo 4,290 .... K5
Dolores Hidalgo de la Independencia
Naci 16,849 .... J6
Durango 182,633 .... G1
Dzibalchén 1,917 .... P7
Dzidzantún 7,064 .... P6
Dzitbalché 4,393 .... P6
Ebano 17,489 .... K5
Ecatepec de Morelos 11,899 .... L1
Ejutla de Crespo 5,263 .... L8
Eldorado 8,115 .... E4
El Fuerte 7,179 .... E3
El Porvenir 3,030 .... G1
El Potosí 2,032 .... J4
El Salto 7,818 .... G5
El Zacatón 2,686 .... J5
Empalme 24,927 .... D2
Encarnación de Díaz 10,474 .... H6
Ensenada 77,687 .... A1
Escalón 2,998 .... G3
Escarcega 7,248 .... O7
Escuinapa de Hidalgo 16,442 .... G5
Escuintla 4,111 .... N9
Esperanza, Puebla 4,258 .... O2
Esperanza, Sonora 11,762 .... E3
Espita 5,394 .... Q6
Esqueda 1,458 .... E1
Etchojoa 4,398 .... E3
Ezequiel Montes 3,139 .... K6
Fortín de las Flores 9,358 .... P2
Francisco I. Madero 12,613 .... H4
Fresnillo de González
Echererría 44,475 .... H5
Frontera 10,066 .... N7
Galeana, Nuevo León 3,429 .... J4
General Bravo 2,894 .... K4
General Cepeda 3,486 .... J4
General Terán 5,354 .... K4
Gómez Farías 3,030 .... F2
Gómez Palacio 79,650 .... G4
González 6,440 .... K5
Guadalajara 1,478,383 .... H6
Guadalajara* 2,343,034 .... H6
Guadalupe, Nuevo León 51,899 .... K4
Guadalupe, Zacatecas 13,246 .... H5
Guadalupe Bravo 3,333 .... F1
Guadalupe Victoria,
Durango 7,931 .... H4
Guadalupe Victoria,
Puebla 3,946 .... O1
Guamúchil 17,151 .... E4
Guanajuato 36,809 .... J6
Guasave 26,080 .... E4
Guaymas 57,492 .... D3
Gustavo Díaz Ordaz 10,154 .... K3
Gutiérrez Zamora 9,099 .... L6
Halachó 4,804 .... O6
Hecelchakán 4,279 .... O6
Hermosillo 232,691 .... D2
Heroica Caborca 20,771 .... C1
Heroica Nogales 52,108 .... D1
Hidalgo, Tamaulipas 2,450 .... K4
Hidalgo del Parral
(Parral) 57,619 .... G3
Hopelchén 3,699 .... P7
Huajuapan de León 13,822 .... L8
Huamantla 15,565 .... N1
Huaquechula 2,294 .... M2
Huatabampo 18,506 .... D3
Huatusco de Chicuellar 9,501 .... P2
Huauchinango 16,826 .... L6
Huautla de Jiménez 6,132 .... L7
Huehuetlán el Chico 2,667 .... M2
Huejotzingo 8,552 .... M1
Huejutla 6,854 .... K6
Huetamo 9,333 .... J7
Hueyotlipan de Hidalgo 2,353 .... M1
Huimanguillo 7,075 .... N8
Huitzilán 3,573 .... O1
Huitzuco de los Figueroa 9,406 .... K7
Huixcolotla 4,039 .... N2
Huixtepec 5,927 .... L8
Huixtla 15,737 .... N9
Hunucmá 8,020 .... O6
Ignacio de la Llave 3,962 .... Q2
Iguala de la
Independencia 45,355 .... K7
Imuris 1,958 .... D1
Irapuato 135,596 .... J6
Isla Mujeres 2,663 .... Q6
Isla, Veracruz 8,075 .... M7
Ixmiquilpan 6,048 .... K6
Ixtapa J8
Ixtapalapa 522,095 .... L1
Ixtenco 5,035 .... N1
Ixtepec 14,025 .... M8
Ixtlán del Río 10,986 .... G6
Izamal 9,749 .... P6
Izúcar de Matamoros 21,164 .... M2
Jala 4,535 .... G6
Jalacingo 3,427 .... P1
Jalapa Enríquez 161,352 .... P1
Jalpa 9,904 .... H6
Jalpa de Méndez 4,785 .... N7
Jalpan 1,878 .... K6
Jáltipan de Morelos 15,170 .... M8
Jantetelco 2,015 .... L2
Jaumave 3,072 .... K5
Jerez de García
Salinas 20,325 .... H5
Jico 7,269 .... P1
Jilotepec de Abasolo 4,252 .... K7
Jiménez, Chihuahua 18,095 .... G3
Joachín 3,918 .... Q2
Jojutla de Juárez 14,438 .... L2
Jonacatepec 3,868 .... M2
Jonuta 2,746 .... N7
José Cardel 5,396 .... Q1
Juan Aldama 9,667 .... H4
Juchipila 6,328 .... H6
Juchitán de Zaragoza 30,218 .... M8
Kantunilkin 1,970 .... Q6
La Barca 18,055 .... H6
La Barra de Navidad 1,829 .... G7
La Concordia 3,559 .... N9
La Cruz, Sinaloa 4,218 .... F5
Lagos de Moreno 33,782 .... J6
La Huerta 4,328 .... G7
La Paz, Baja California
Sur 46,011 .... D5
La Paz, San Luis
Potosí 3,735 .... J5
La Piedad Cavadas 34,963 .... H6
Las Choapas 20,166 .... M7
Las Hadas G7
Las Nieves 2,262 .... G3
Las Rosas 7,658 .... N8
León 468,887 .... J6
Lerdo de Tejada 11,628 .... M8
Lerma 4,158 .... O7
Libres 4,830 .... O1
Linares 24,456 .... K4
Llera de Canales 3,564 .... K5
Loma Bonita 15,804 .... M7
Loreto, Baja California 2,570 .... D4
Loreto, Zacatecas 7,132 .... J5
Los Mochis 67,953 .... E4
Los Reyes de Salgado 19,452 .... H7
Macuspana 12,293 .... N8
Madera 9,759 .... F2
Magdalena de Kino 10,281 .... D1
Maltrata 5,457 .... O2
Manzanillo 20,777 .... G7
Mapastepec 5,907 .... N9
Mapimí 2,737 .... G4
Martínez de la Torre 17,203 .... L6
Mascota 5,674 .... G6
Matamoros, Coahuila 15,125 .... H4
Matamoros, Tamaulipas 165,124 .... L4
Matehuala 28,799 .... J5
Matías Romero 13,200 .... M8
Maxcanú 6,505 .... O6
Mazatlán 147,010 .... F5
Melchor Múzquiz 18,868 .... H3
Melchor Ocampo del
Balsas 4,766 .... H8
Meoquí 12,308 .... G2
Mérida 233,912 .... P6
Metepec 4,625 .... M2
Metlatonoc 1,870 .... K8
Mexicali 317,228 .... B1
Mexico City (cap.) 9,377,300 .... L1
Mexico City* 13,993,866 .... L1
Miacatlán 3,980 .... K2
Mier 5,636 .... K3
Miguel Auza 9,303 .... H4
Minatitlán 68,397 .... M8
Mineral del Monte 8,887 .... K6
Miquihuana 1,971 .... J5
Misantla 8,799 .... P1
Miahuatlán de Porfirio
Díaz 5,714 .... L8
Mocorito 3,993 .... F4
Moctezuma, San Luis
Potosí 1,734 .... J5
Moctezuma, Sonora 2,700 .... E2
Monclova 78,134 .... J3
Montemorelos 18,642 .... K4
Monterrey 1,006,221 .... J4
Monterrey* 1,923,402 .... J4
Morelia 199,099 .... J7
Morelos 4,241 .... J2
Morelos Cañada 2,288 .... O2
Moroleón 25,620 .... J6
Motozintla de Mendoza 4,682 .... N9
Motul de Felipe Carillo
Puerto 12,949 .... P6
Muna 5,491 .... P6
Naco 3,580 .... D1
Nacozari 2,976 .... E1
Nadadores 2,461 .... H3
Naica 7,190 .... G2
Namiquipa 4,875 .... F2
Nanacamilpa 6,356 .... M1
Naolinco de Victoria 4,365 .... P1
Naranjos 14,732 .... L6
Naucalpan de Juárez 9,425 .... L1
Nautla 1,935 .... L6
Nava 4,097 .... J2
Navojoa 43,817 .... E3
Navolato 12,799 .... E4
Nazas 2,881 .... G4
Netzahualcóyotl 580,436 .... L1
Nieves 3,966 .... H5
Nochistlán 8,780 .... H6
Nogales 14,254 .... P2
Nombre de Dios 3,188 .... G5
Nopalucan de la Granja 3,002 .... O1
Nueva Casas Grandes 20,023 .... F1
Nueva Ciudad Guerrero 3,300 .... K3
Nueva Italia de Ruiz 14,718 .... J7
Nueva Rosita 34,706 .... J2
Nuevo Ideal 5,252 .... G4
Nuevo Laredo 184,622 .... J3
Oaxaca de Juárez 114,948 .... L8
Ocampo, Coahuila 1,613 .... H3
Ocampo, Tamaulipas 4,801 .... K5
Ocosingo 2,946 .... O8
Ocotlán 35,361 .... H6
Ocotlán de Morelos 5,882 .... L8
Ojinaga 12,757 .... G2
Ojocaliente 7,582 .... H5
Ometepec 7,342 .... K8
Oriental 6,009 .... O1
Orizaba 105,150 .... P2
Otumba de Gómez
Farías 3,198 .... M1
Oxkutzcab 8,182 .... P6
Ozuluama 2,851 .... L6
Ozumba de Alzate 6,876 .... M1
Pachuca de Soto 83,892 .... K6
Padilla 4,581 .... K5
Palenque 2,595 .... O8
Palizada 2,332 .... O7
Palomas 2,129 .... F1

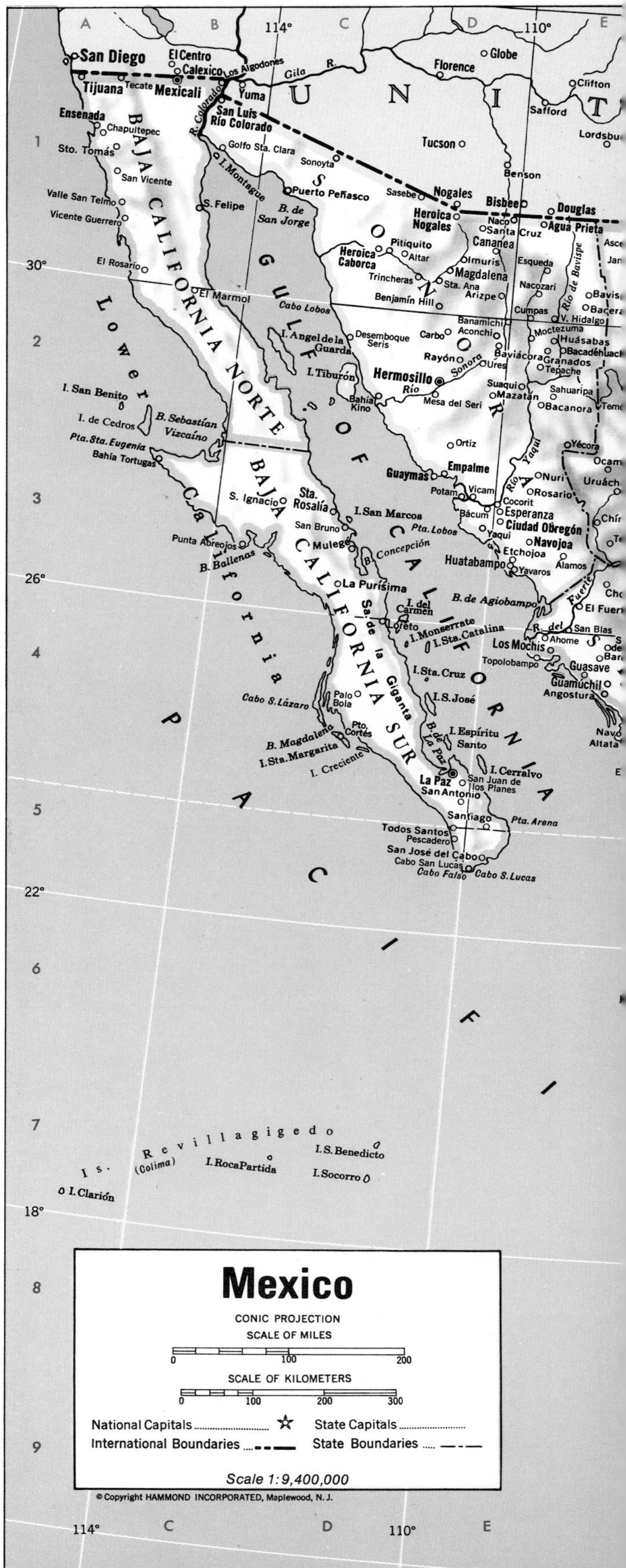
Mexico
CONIC PROJECTION
SCALE OF MILES
0 100 200
SCALE OF KILOMETERS
0 100 200 300
National Capitals
State Capitals
International Boundaries
State Boundaries
Scale 1:9,400,000
© Copyright HAMMOND INCORPORATED, Maplewood, N. J.
San Diego
El Centro
Calexico
Tijuana
Tecate
Mexicali
Yuma
San Luis Río Colorado
Ensenada
Tucson
Nogales
Heroica Nogales
Bisbee
Douglas
Agua Prieta
Cananea
Heroica Caborca
Magdalena
Hermosillo
Guaymas
Empalme
Ciudad Obregón
Navojoa
Huatabampo
Los Mochis
Guasave
Guamúchil
Sta. Rosalía
Mulegé
Loreto
La Paz
Todos Santos
San José del Cabo
Cabo San Lucas
BAJA CALIFORNIA NORTE
BAJA CALIFORNIA SUR
GULF OF CALIFORNIA
Lower California
PACIFIC
Is. Revillagigedo
I. Clarión
I. Roca Partida
I. Socorro
I. S. Benedicto

Panabá 3,056	P6	Profesor Rafael	
Pánuco 14,277	K6	Ramírez 5,338	O1
Papanoa 3,033	J8	Progreso 17,518	P6
Papantla de Olarte 26,773	L6	Puebla de Zaragoza 465,985	N2
Paraíso 7,561	N7	Puente de Ixtla 10,435	K2
Parral 57,619	G3	Puerto Ángel 1,489	L9
Parras de la Fuente 18,207	H4	Puerto Escondido 3,845	L9
Paso de Ovejas 4,371	Q2	Puerto Juárez 100	Q6
Pátzcuaro 17,299	J7	Puerto Madero 1,908	N9
Pedro Montoya 4,563	K6	Puerto Peñasco 8,452	C1
Pénjamo 9,245	J6	Puerto Vallarta 24,155	G6
Peñón Blanco 2,726	H4	Purificación 3,311	G7
Pericos 4,445	F4	Puruándiro 9,956	J7
Perote 12,742	L7	Putla de Guerrero 3,572	L8
Petatlán 9,419	J8	Quecholac 3,374	L2
Peto 8,362	P6	Querétaro 142,448	J6
Pichucalco 4,615	N8	Ramos Arizpe 6,205	J4
Piedras Negras,		Rayón, San Luis	
Coahuila 41,033	J2	Potosí 4,451	K6
Piedras Negras, Veracruz 4,099	Q2	Rayón, Sonora	D2
Pijijiapan 5,053	N9	Reynosa 181,646	K3
Pitiquito 2,268	D1	Rincón de Romos 8,348	H5
Potam 2,825	D3	Ríoverde 16,804	J6
Poza Rica de Hidalgo 152,276	L6	Rodeo 2,584	G4
Praxedis G. Guerrero 2,399	G1	Rosamorada 2,635	G5

(continued on following page)

AREA 761,601 sq. mi. (1,972,546 sq. km.)
POPULATION 67,395,826
CAPITAL Mexico City
LARGEST CITY Mexico City
HIGHEST POINT Citlaltépetl 18,855 ft. (5,747 m.)
MONETARY UNIT Mexican peso
MAJOR LANGUAGE Spanish
MAJOR RELIGION Roman Catholicism

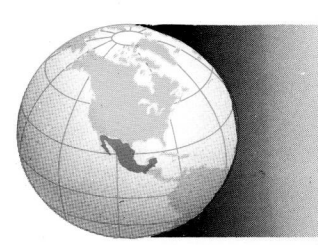

States Indicated by Numbers

1	Tlaxcala	6	Querétaro
2	Morelos	7	Guanajuato
3	Distrito Federal	8	Aguascalientes
4	México	9	Nayarit
5	Hidalgo	10	Colima

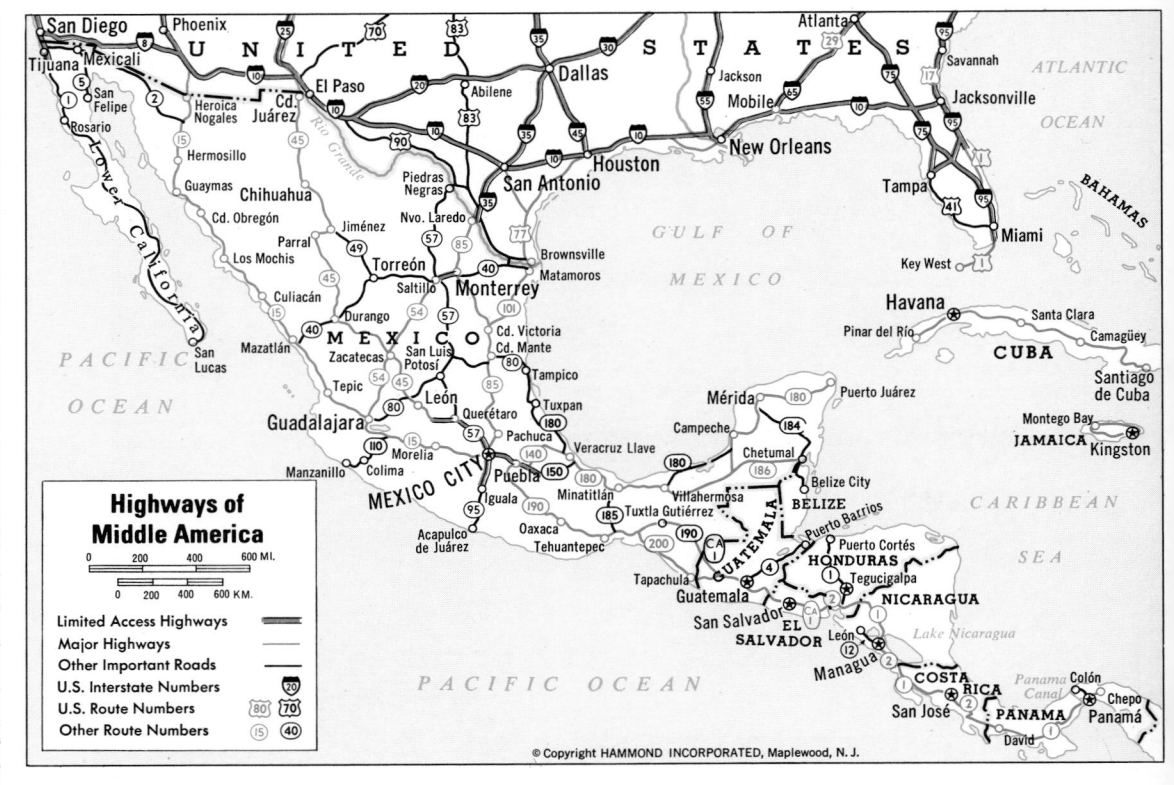

Highways of Middle America

0	200	400	600 MI.
0	200	400	600 KM.

Limited Access Highways
Major Highways
Other Important Roads
U.S. Interstate Numbers
U.S. Route Numbers
Other Route Numbers

© Copyright HAMMOND INCORPORATED, Maplewood, N.J.

Agriculture, Industry
and Resources

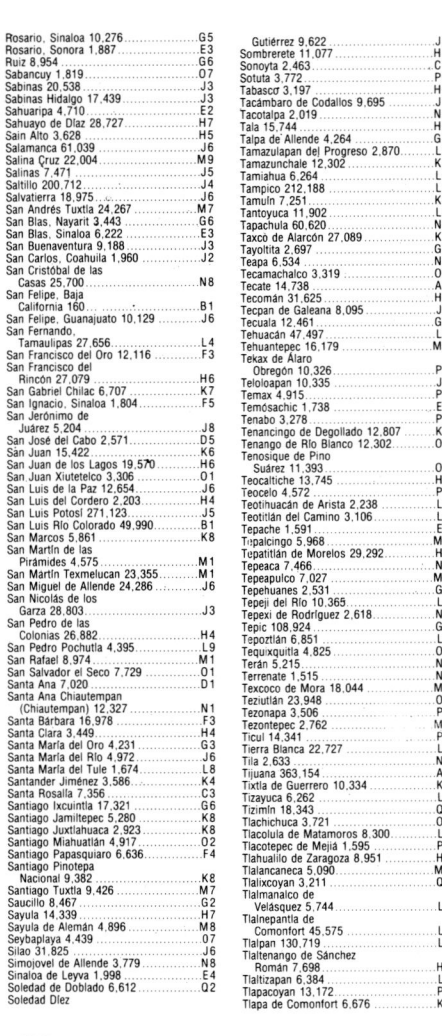

DOMINANT LAND USE

Wheat, Livestock

Cereals (chiefly corn), Livestock

Diversified Tropical Cash Crops

Cotton, Mixed Cereals

Livestock, Limited Agriculture

Range Livestock

Forests

Nonagricultural Land

Water Power

Major Industrial Areas

MAJOR MINERAL OCCURRENCES

Ag	Silver	G	Natural Gas	O	Petroleum
Au	Gold	Gr	Graphite	Pb	Lead
C	Coal	Hg	Mercury	S	Sulfur
Cu	Copper	Mn	Manganese	Sb	Antimony
F	Fluorspar	Mo	Molybdenum	Sn	Tin
Fe	Iron Ore	Na	Salt	W	Tungsten
				Zn	Zinc

*City and suburbs.

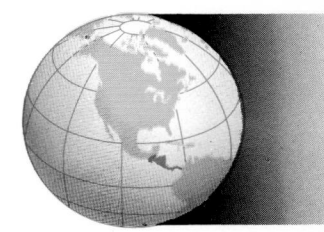

GUATEMALA

AREA 42,042 sq. mi. (108,889 sq. km.)
POPULATION 7,262,419
CAPITAL Guatemala
LARGEST CITY Guatemala
HIGHEST POINT Tajumulco 13,845 ft.
(4,220 m.)
MONETARY UNIT quetzal
MAJOR LANGUAGES Spanish, Quiché
MAJOR RELIGION Roman Catholicism

BELIZE

AREA 8,867 sq. mi. (22,966 sq. km.)
POPULATION 144,857
CAPITAL Belmopan
LARGEST CITY Belize City
HIGHEST POINT Victoria Peak 3,681 ft. (1,122 m.)
MONETARY UNIT Belize dollar
MAJOR LANGUAGES English, Spanish, Mayan
MAJOR RELIGIONS Roman Catholicism, Protestantism

EL SALVADOR

AREA 8,260 sq. mi. (21,393 sq. km.)
POPULATION 4,813,000
CAPITAL San Salvador
LARGEST CITY San Salvador
HIGHEST POINT Santa Ana 7,825 ft.
(2,385 m.)
MONETARY UNIT colón
MAJOR LANGUAGE Spanish
MAJOR RELIGION Roman Catholicism

HONDURAS

AREA 43,277 sq. mi. (112,087 sq. km.)
POPULATION 3,691,000
CAPITAL Tegucigalpa
LARGEST CITY Tegucigalpa
HIGHEST POINT Las Minas 9,347 ft.
(2,849 m.)
MONETARY UNIT lempira
MAJOR LANGUAGE Spanish
MAJOR RELIGION Roman Catholicism

NICARAGUA

AREA 45,698 sq. mi. (118,358 sq. km.)
POPULATION 2,703,000
CAPITAL Managua
LARGEST CITY Managua
HIGHEST POINT Cerro Mocotón 6,913 ft.
(2,107 m.)
MONETARY UNIT córdoba
MAJOR LANGUAGE Spanish
MAJOR RELIGION Roman Catholicism

COSTA RICA

AREA 19,575 sq. mi. (50,700 sq. km.)
POPULATION 2,245,000
CAPITAL San José
LARGEST CITY San José
HIGHEST POINT Chirripó Grande
12,530 ft. (3,819 m.)
MONETARY UNIT colón
MAJOR LANGUAGE Spanish
MAJOR RELIGION Roman Catholicism

PANAMA

AREA 29,761 sq. mi. (77,082 sq. km.)
POPULATION 1,830,175
CAPITAL Panamá
LARGEST CITY Panamá
HIGHEST POINT Vol. Baru 11,401 ft.
(3,475 m.)
MONETARY UNIT balboa
MAJOR LANGUAGE Spanish
MAJOR RELIGION Roman Catholicism

Agriculture, Industry and Resources

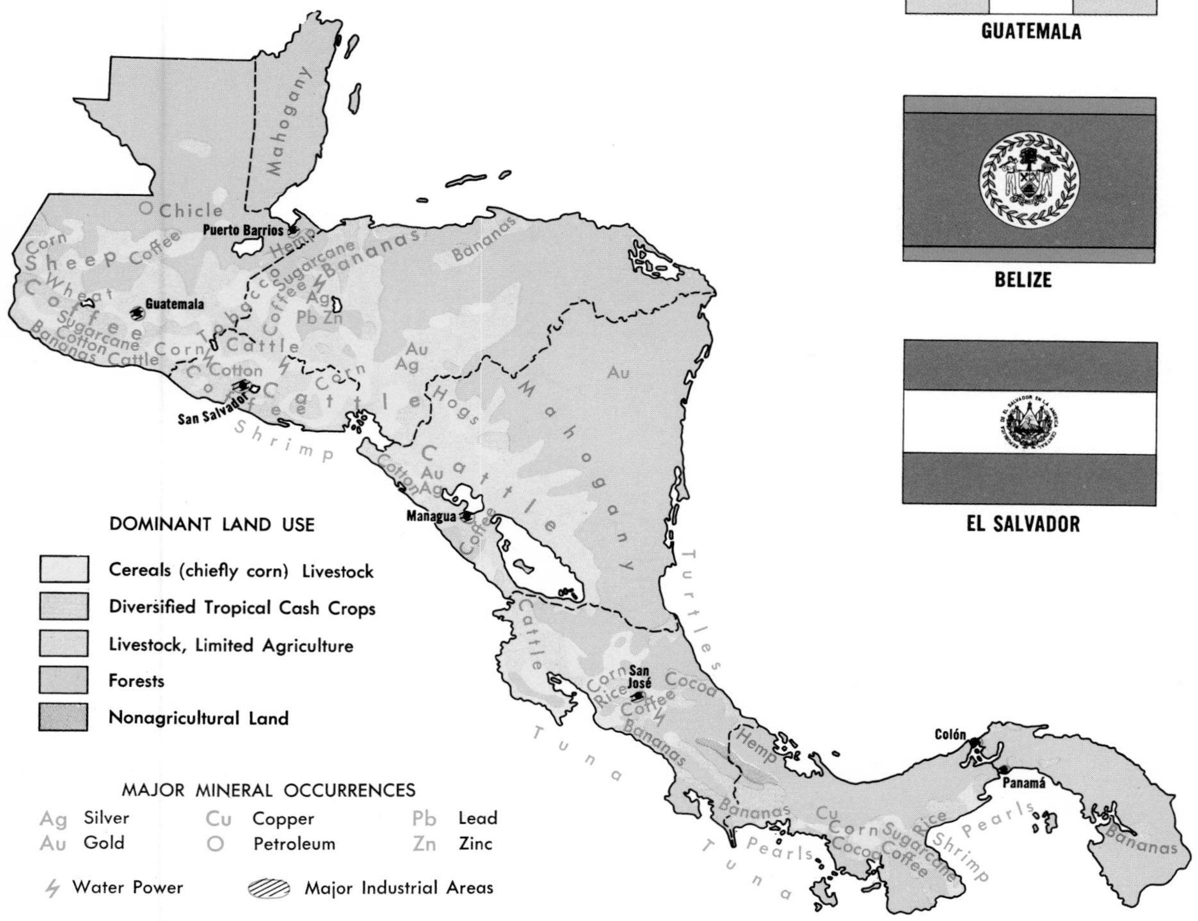

GUATEMALA

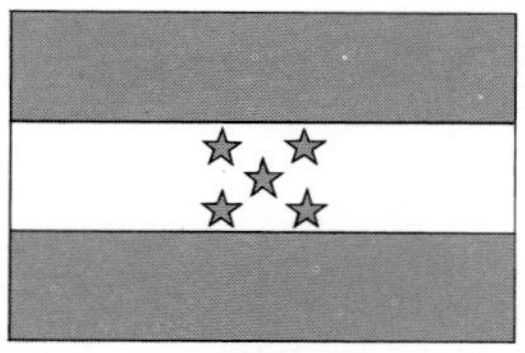

BELIZE

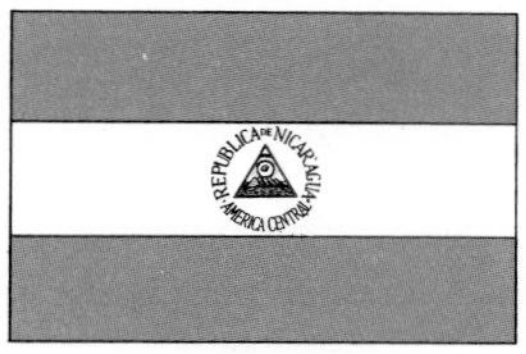

EL SALVADOR

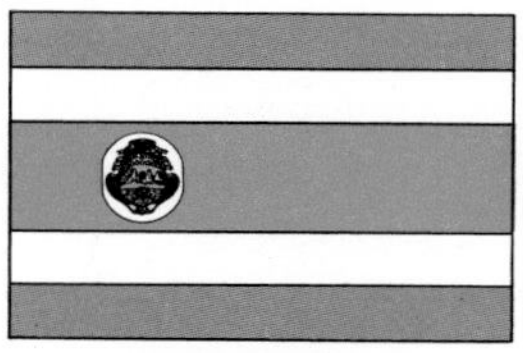

HONDURAS

NICARAGUA

COSTA RICA

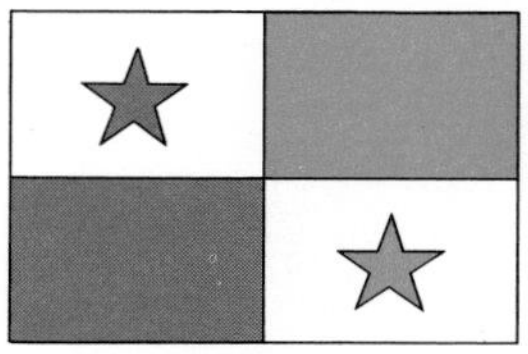

PANAMA

DOMINANT LAND USE

Cereals (chiefly corn) Livestock

Diversified Tropical Cash Crops

Livestock, Limited Agriculture

Forests

Nonagricultural Land

MAJOR MINERAL OCCURRENCES

Ag Silver   Cu Copper   Pb Lead
Au Gold   O Petroleum   Zn Zinc

⚡ Water Power   ⬚ Major Industrial Areas

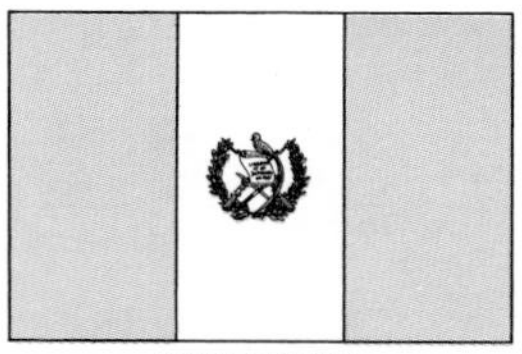

(continued on following page)

Central America

CONIC PROJECTION

SCALE OF MILES

0   25   50   100   150

SCALE OF KILOMETERS

0   25   50   100   150

Capitals of Countries .... ☆
International Boundaries ....
Canals ....

Scale 1:5,780,000

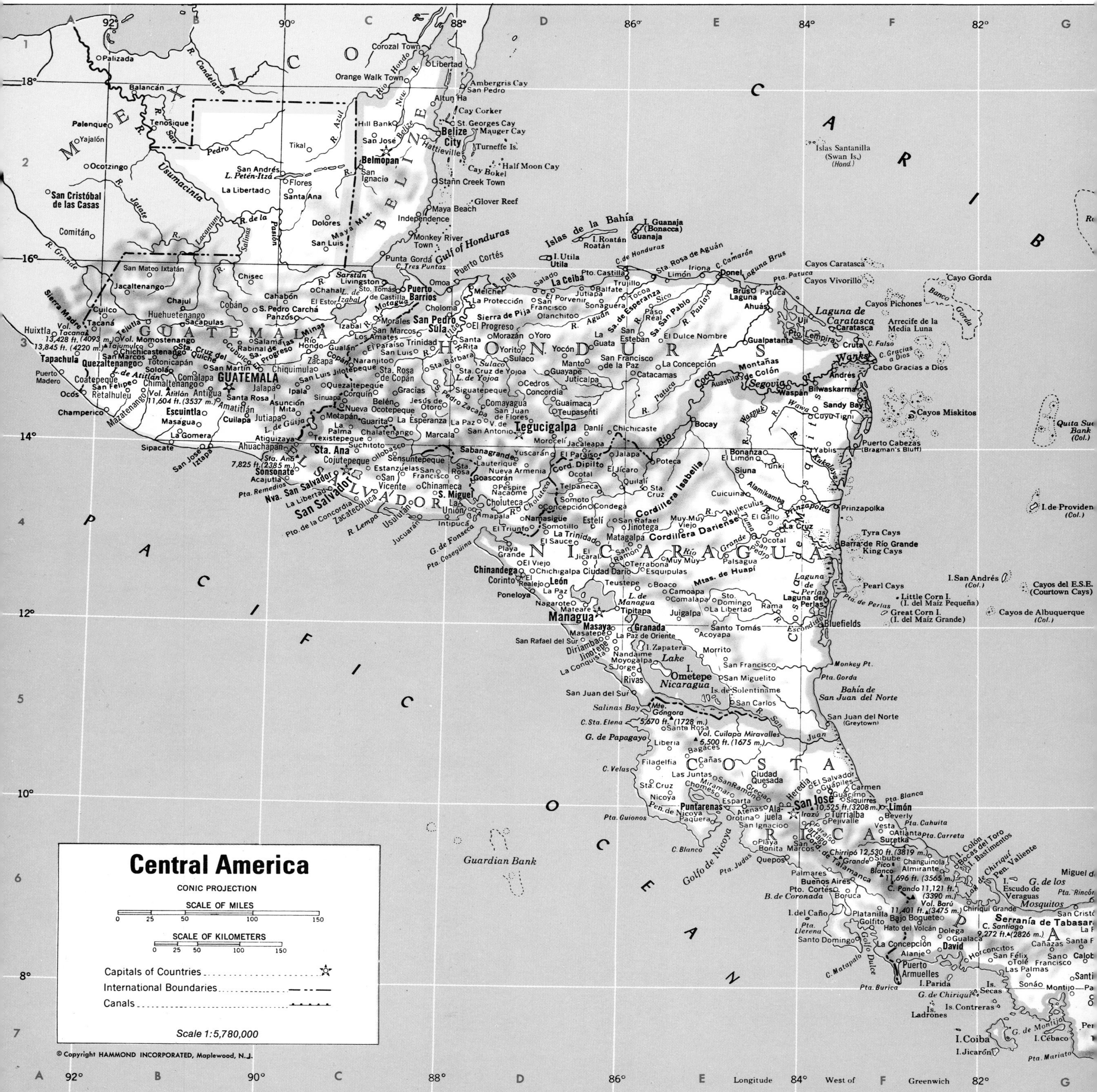

© Copyright HAMMOND INCORPORATED, Maplewood, N.J.

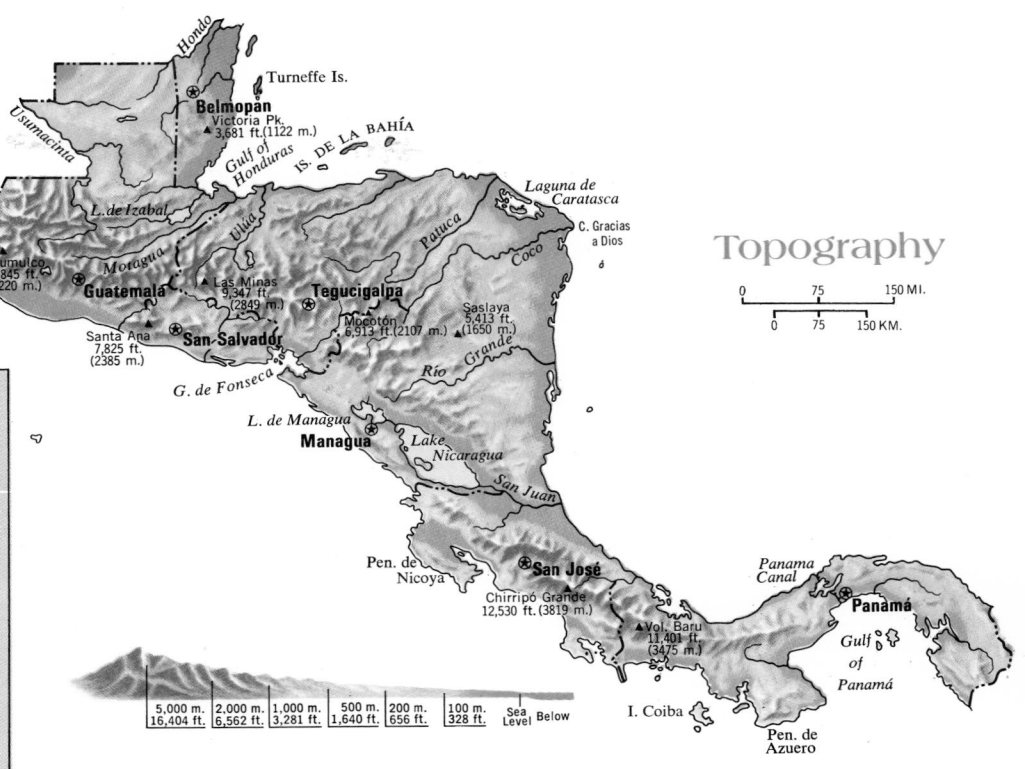

Topography

0   75   150 MI.

0   75   150 KM.

5,000 m.	2,000 m.	1,000 m.	500 m.	200 m.	100 m.	Sea
16,404 ft.	6,562 ft.	3,281 ft.	1,640 ft.	656 ft.	328 ft.	Level Below

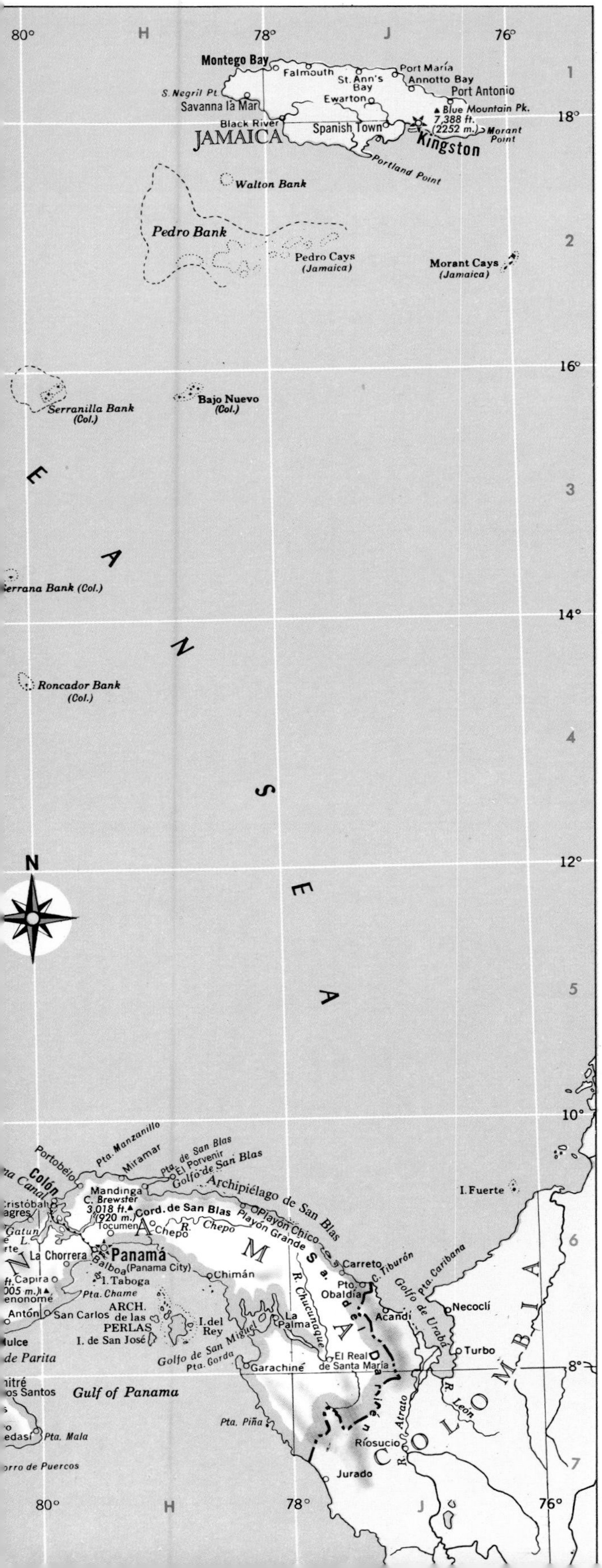

City and suburbs.
⊙Population of sub-district or division.
⊙Population of district.

CUBA

HAITI

DOMINICAN REPUBLIC

JAMAICA

TRINIDAD AND TOBAGO

BARBADOS

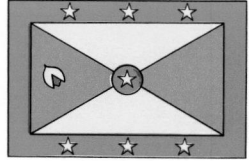
GRENADA

BAHAMAS

DOMINICA

ST. LUCIA

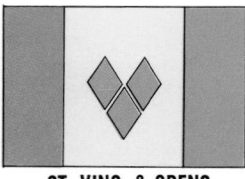
ST. VINC. & GRENS.

ANTIGUA AND BARBUDA

CUBA
AREA 44,206 sq. mi. (114,494 sq. km.)
POPULATION 9,706,369
CAPITAL Havana
LARGEST CITY Havana
HIGHEST POINT Pico Turquino
6,561 ft. (2,000 m.)
MONETARY UNIT Cuban peso
MAJOR LANGUAGE Spanish
MAJOR RELIGION Roman Catholicism

HAITI
AREA 10,694 sq. mi. (27,697 sq. km.)
POPULATION 5,053,792
CAPITAL Port-au-Prince
LARGEST CITY Port-au-Prince
HIGHEST POINT Pic La Selle 8,793 ft. (2,680 m.)
MONETARY UNIT gourde
MAJOR LANGUAGES Creole French, French
MAJOR RELIGION Roman Catholicism

DOMINICAN REPUBLIC
AREA 18,704 sq. mi. (48,443 sq. km.)
POPULATION 5,647,977
CAPITAL Santo Domingo
LARGEST CITY Santo Domingo
HIGHEST POINT Pico Duarte
10,417 ft. (3,175 m.)
MONETARY UNIT Dominican peso
MAJOR LANGUAGE Spanish
MAJOR RELIGION Roman Catholicism

JAMAICA
AREA 4,411 sq. mi. (11,424 sq. km.)
POPULATION 2,184,000
CAPITAL Kingston
LARGEST CITY Kingston
HIGHEST POINT Blue Mountain Peak
7,402 ft. (2,256 m.)
MONETARY UNIT Jamaican dollar
MAJOR LANGUAGE English
MAJOR RELIGIONS Protestantism,
Roman Catholicism

PUERTO RICO
AREA 3,515 sq. mi. (9,104 sq. km.)
POPULATION 3,196,520
CAPITAL San Juan
MONETARY UNIT U.S. dollar
MAJOR LANGUAGES Spanish, English
MAJOR RELIGION Roman Catholicism

NETHERLANDS ANTILLES
AREA 390 sq. mi. (1,010 sq. km.)
POPULATION 246,000
CAPITAL Willemstad
MONETARY UNIT Antilles guilder
MAJOR LANGUAGES Dutch, Papiamento, English
MAJOR RELIGIONS Roman Catholicism,
Protestantism

BERMUDA
AREA 21 sq. mi. (54 sq. km.)
POPULATION 67,761
CAPITAL Hamilton
MONETARY UNIT Bermuda dollar
MAJOR LANGUAGE English
MAJOR RELIGION Protestantism

ARUBA
AREA 75 sq. mi (193 sq. km.)
POPULATION 66,790
CAPITAL Oranjestad
MONETARY UNIT Aruba guilder
MAJOR LANGUAGES Dutch, Papiamento
MAJOR RELIGION Roman Catholic

ANGUILLA

Anguilla (isl.) 6,519 . . . . F3

ANTIGUA and BARBUDA

Antigua (isl.) 76,213 . . . . G3
Barbuda (isl.) 1,071 . . . . G3
Caribbean (sea) B4
Codrington 1,071 . . . . G3
Falmouth 1,134 . . . . F3
Redonda (isl.) F3
Saint John's (cap.) 21,814 . . . . . . G3

ARUBA

Aruba (isl.) 66,790 . . . . E4

BAHAMAS

Acklins (isl.) 616 . . . . C2
Andros (isl.) 8,397 . . . . B1
Atwood (Samana) (cay) D2
Berry (isls.) 509 . . . . B1
Biminis, The (isls.) 1,432 . . . . . . B1
Caicos (passg.) D2
Cat (isl.) 2,143 . . . . C1
Cay Sal (bank) B2
Crooked (isl.) 517 . . . . D2
Eleuthera (isl.) 8,326 . . . . C1
Exuma (cays) C1
Flamingo (cay) C2
Freeport 22,301 . . . . B1
Grand Bahama (isl.) 33,102 . . . . . . B1
Great Abaco (isl.) 7,324 . . . . C1
Great Bahama (bank) B1
Great Exuma (isl.) C2
Great Inagua (isl.) 939 . . . . D2
Great Isaac (isl.) B1

Gun (cay) B1
Harbour (isl.) C1
Little Inagua (isl.) D2
Long (cay) 33 . . . . C2
Long (isl.) 3,353 . . . . C2
Mayaguana (isl.) 476 . . . . D2
Mira Por Vos (cays) C2
Nassau (cap.) 135,437 . . . . C1
New Providence (isl.) 135,437 . . . . C1
Old Bahama (chan.) B2
Plana (cays) D2
Ragged (isl.) 146 . . . . C2
Rum (cay) C2
Samana (cay) D2
San Salvador (isl.) D1
Santarén (chan.) B1
Tongue of the Ocean (chan.) C1
Verde (cay) C2
Watling (San Salvador) (isl.) C1

BARBADOS

Bridgetown (cap.) 7,552 . . . . G4
Speightstown G4

BERMUDA

Bermuda (isl.) H3
Castle (harb.) H2
Great (sound) G3
Hamilton (cap.) 1,617 . . . . G3
Harrington (sound) G3
Ireland (isl.) G3
North (rapid) H2
Saint Davids (isl.) H2
Saint George 1,647 . . . . H2
Saint George's (isl.) H2
Somerset (isl.) G3

CAYMAN ISLANDS

Bartlett Deep B3
Cayman Brac (isl.) 1,603 . . . . B3
George Town (cap.) 7,617 . . . . B3
Grand Cayman (isl.) 15,000 . . . . . . B3
Little Cayman (isl.) 74 . . . . B3
Misteriosa (bank) A3

CUBA

Bayamo 109,201 . . . . C2
Camagüey 245,235 . . . . B2
Cienfuegos 107,396 . . . . B2
Florida (str.) B1
Guanabacoa 89,741 . . . . B2
Guantánamo 178,129 . . . . C2
Havana (cap.) 1,924,886 . . . . A2
Holguín 190,155 . . . . C2
Juventud (Pines) (isl.) 57,879 . . . . A2
Manzanillo 95,420 . . . . C2
Marianao ○127,563 . . . . A2
Matanzas 103,302 . . . . B2
Pinar del Río 104,598 . . . . A2
San Felipe (cays) A2
Santa Clara 175,113 . . . . B2
Santiago de Cuba 362,432 . . . . . . C3
Windward (passg.) C3

DOMINICA

Portsmouth 2,329 . . . . G4
Roseau 9,968 . . . . G4

DOMINICAN REPUBLIC

La Romana 91,571 . . . . E3
San Francisco de Macorís 64,906 . . E3
San Pedro de Macorís 78,562 . . . . E3
Santiago 278,638 . . . . D3
Santo Domingo (cap.) 1,313,172 . . E3

GRENADA

Carriacou (isl.) 6,052 . . . . G4
Gouyave 2,498 . . . . F4
Grenadines (isls.) G4
Saint George's (cap.) 6,463 . . . . . . F5

GUADELOUPE

Basse-Terre (cap.) 13,397 . . . . . . F4
Saint-Barthélemy (isl.) 3,059 . . . . F3
Saint Martin (isl.) 8,072 . . . . F3

HAITI

Cap-Haïtien 64,406 . . . . D3
Gonaïves 34,209 . . . . D3
Port-au-Prince (cap.) 449,831 . . . . D3
Gonâve (isl.) D3
Jamaica (chan.) C3
Tortuga (isl.) D2

JAMAICA

Blue Mountain (peak) C3
Jamaica (chan.) C3
Kingston (cap.) 106,791 . . . . C3
Montego Bay 43,521 . . . . B3
Pedro (cays) C3
Savanna-la-Mar 11,759 . . . . B3

MARTINIQUE

Fort-de-France (cap.) 96,649 . . . . G4
Saint-Pierre 4,923 . . . . G4
Pelée (vol.) G4

MONTSERRAT

Plymouth (cap.) 1,623 . . . . F3

NETHERLANDS ANTILLES

Bonaire (isl.) E4
Curaçao (isl.) E4
Oranjestad 10,100 . . . . D4
Saba (isl.) F3
Saint Eustatius (isl.) F3
Saint Martin (Sint Maarten) (isl.) . . F3
Willemstad (cap.) 95,000 . . . . E4

PUERTO RICO

Bayamón 185,087 . . . . G1
Caguas 87,214 . . . . G1
Culebra (isl.) 1,265 . . . . G1
Mayagüez 82,968 . . . . F1
Mona (passg.) E3
Ponce 161,739 . . . . F1

San Juan (cap.) 424,600 . . . . G1
Vieques (isl.) 7,662 . . . . G1

SAINT KITTS and NEVIS

Basseterre (cap.) 14,725 . . . . F3
Nevis (isl.) 9,300 . . . . F3
Saint Christopher (isl.) 35,104 . . . . F3

SAINT LUCIA

Castries (cap.) •42,770 . . . . G4
Vieux Fort •10,675 . . . . G4

**SAINT VINCENT and
THE GRENADINES**

Bequia (isl.) G4
Georgetown 1,100 . . . . G4
Grenadines (isls.) 8,371 . . . . G4
Kingstown (cap.) 17,117 . . . . G4

TRINIDAD and TOBAGO

Port-of-Spain (cap.) 67,978 . . . . . . G5
Scarborough 6,057 . . . . G5
Tobago (isl.) 39,695 . . . . G5
Trinidad (isl.) 1,020,130 . . . . G5

TURKS and CAICOS ISLANDS

Caicos (isls.) 4,008 . . . . D2
Cockburn Harbour D2
Grand Caicos (isl.) 371 . . . . D2
Grand Turk (isl.) 3,146 . . . . D2
Providenciales (isl.) 979 . . . . D2
Turks (isls.) 3,348 . . . . D2

VIRGIN ISLANDS (British)

Anegada (isl.) 89 . . . . H1
Jost Van Dyke (isl.) 135 . . . . G1
Road Town (cap.) 2,200 . . . . H1
Tortola (isl.) 9,257 . . . . H1
Virgin Gorda (isl.) 1,443 . . . . H1

VIRGIN ISLANDS (U.S.)

Charlotte Amalie (cap.) 11,842 . . . . H1
Christiansted 2,914 . . . . H2
Fredriksted 1,046 . . . . G2
Saint Croix (isl.) 49,725 . . . . H2
Saint John (isl.) 2,472 . . . . H1
Saint Thomas (isl.) 44,372 . . . . . . G1

WEST INDIES

Antilles, Greater (isls.) B2
Antilles, Lesser (isls.) E4
Aves (Bird) (isl.) F4
Hispaniola (isl.) D2
Leeward (isls.) F3
Navassa (isl.) C3
Windward (isls.) G4

• Population of district.
○ Population of municipality.

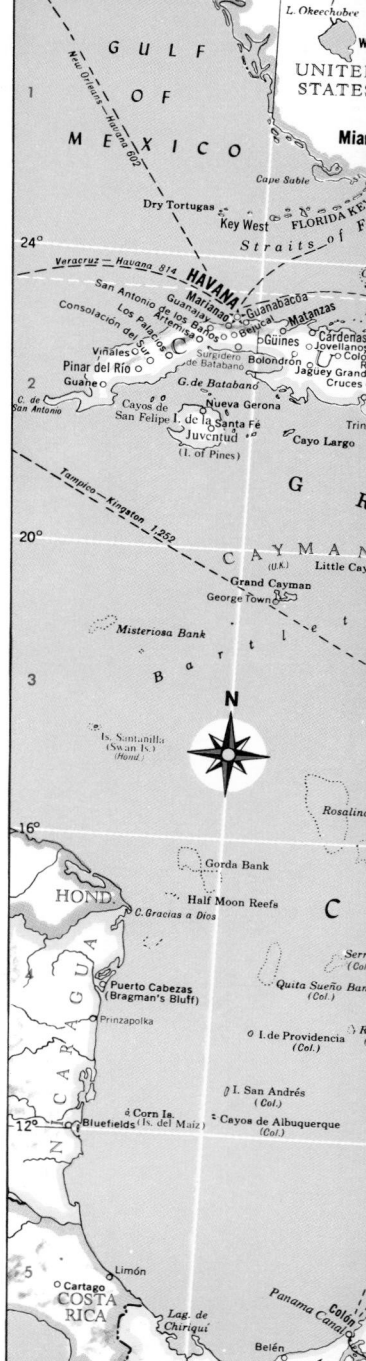

Topography

0   100   200 Mi.
0   100   200 KM.

TRINIDAD AND TUBAGO

AREA 1,980 sq. mi. (5,128 sq. km.)
POPULATION 1,067,108
CAPITAL Port of Spain
LARGEST CITY Port of Spain
HIGHEST POINT Mt. Aripo 3,084 ft. (940 m.)
MONETARY UNIT Trinidad and Tobago dollar
MAJOR LANGUAGES English, Hindi
MAJOR RELIGIONS Roman Catholicism,
Protestantism, Hinduism, Islam

SAINT KITTS AND NEVIS

SAINT LUCIA

AREA 238 sq. mi. (616 sq. km.)
POPULATION 115,783
CAPITAL Castries
HIGHEST POINT Mt. Gimie 3,117 ft. (950 m.)
MONETARY UNIT East Caribbean dollar
MAJOR LANGUAGES English, French patois
MAJOR RELIGIONS Roman Catholicism,
Protestantism

BARBADOS

AREA 166 sq. mi. (430 sq. km.)
POPULATION 248,983
CAPITAL Bridgetown
LARGEST CITY Bridgetown
HIGHEST POINT Mt. Hillaby 1,104 ft.
(336 m.)
MONETARY UNIT Barbadian dollar
MAJOR LANGUAGE English
MAJOR RELIGION Protestantism

BAHAMAS

AREA 5,382 sq. mi. (13,939 sq. km.)
POPULATION 209,505
CAPITAL Nassau
LARGEST CITY Nassau
HIGHEST POINT Mt. Alvernia 206 ft. (63 m.)
MONETARY UNIT Bahamian dollar
MAJOR LANGUAGE English
MAJOR RELIGIONS Roman Catholicism,
Protestantism

SAINT VINCENT AND THE GRENADINES

AREA 150 sq. mi. (388 sq. km.)
POPULATION 124,000
CAPITAL Kingstown
HIGHEST POINT Soufrière 4,000 ft. (1,219 m.)
MONETARY UNIT East Caribbean dollar
MAJOR LANGUAGE English
MAJOR RELIGIONS Protestantism,
Roman Catholicism

GRENADA

AREA 133 sq. mi. (344 sq. km.)
POPULATION 103,103
CAPITAL St. George's
LARGEST CITY St. George's
HIGHEST POINT Mt. St. Catherine
2,757 ft. (840 m.)
MONETARY UNIT East Caribbean dollar
MAJOR LANGUAGES English, French patois
MAJOR RELIGIONS Roman Catholicism,
Protestantism

DOMINICA

AREA 290 sq. mi. (751 sq. km.)
POPULATION 74,089
CAPITAL Roseau
HIGHEST POINT Morne Diablotin
4,747 ft. (1,447 m.)
MONETARY UNIT Dominican dollar
MAJOR LANGUAGES English, French patois
MAJOR RELIGIONS Roman Catholicism,
Protestantism

ANTIGUA AND BARBUDA

AREA 171 sq. mi. (443 sq. km.)
POPULATION 75,000
CAPITAL St. John's
HIGHEST POINT Boggy Peak 1,319 ft. (402 m.)
MONETARY UNIT East Caribbean dollar
MAJOR LANGUAGE English
MAJOR RELIGION Protestantism

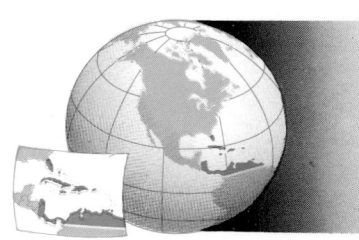

SAINT KITTS & NEVIS

AREA 104 sq. mi. (269 sq. km.)
POPULATION 44,404
CAPITAL Basseterre
HIGHEST POINT Mt. Misery 4,314 ft.
(1,315 m.)
MONETARY UNIT East Caribbean dollar
MAJOR LANGUAGE English
MAJOR RELIGIONS Protestantism,
Roman Catholicism

The West Indies

CONIC PROJECTION

SCALE OF MILES
0 50 100 150 200

SCALE OF KILOMETERS
0 100 200 300

Capitals .... ☆

Scale 1:11,200,000
Distances are given in Nautical Miles

Puerto Rico

Bermuda Islands

© Copyright HAMMOND INCORPORATED, Maplewood, N. J.

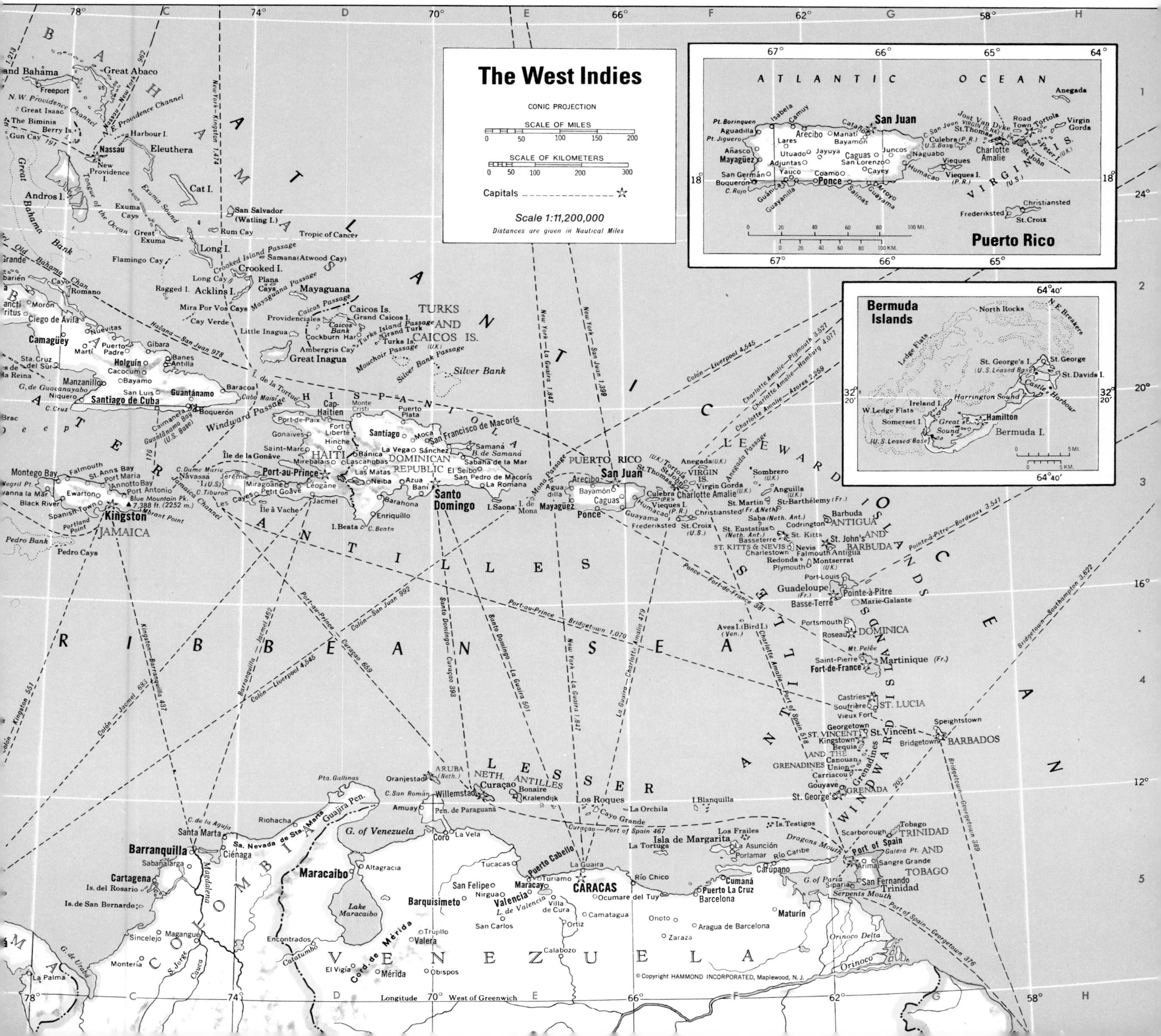

CUBA

PROVINCES

Camagüey 664,566 . . . . G2
Ciego de Ávila 320,961 . . . . F2
Cienfuegos 326,412 . . . . . . E2
Granma 739,335 . . . . H4
Guantánamo 466,609 . . . . . K4
Habana 1,924,886 . . . . C1
Habana, La (Havana)
586,029 . . . . C1
Holguín 911,034 . . . . J3
Juventud (municipio
especial) 57,879 . . . . . . C2
Las Tunas 436,341 . . . . . . H4
Matanzas 557,628 . . . . D1
Pinar del Río 640,740 . . . . A2
Sancti Spíritus 399,700 . . . F2
Santiago de Cuba 909,506 . . J4
Villa Clara 764,743 . . . . . . E1

CITIES and TOWNS

Abreus 14,267 . . . . D2
Agramonte 4,603 . . . . D2
Aguada de Pasajeros 20,219 D2
Alacranes 4,959 . . . . D1
Alonso Rojas 1,427 . . . . . . B2
Alquízar 12,691 . . . . C1
Altagracia 1,722 . . . . G3
Alto Songo-La Maya 25,188 . J4
Amarillas 2,767 . . . . D2
Amazonas 1,066 . . . . F2
Antilla 10,052 . . . . J3
Arroyo Blanco 1,431 . . . . . F2
Artemisa 45,689 . . . . B1
Báez 4,178 . . . . E2
Báguanos 12,678 . . . . J3
Bahía Honda 16,901 . . . . . B1
Baire 4,879 . . . . H4
Banao 803 . . . . F2
Banes 38,905 . . . . J3
Baracoa 36,702 . . . . K4
Baraguá 12,633 . . . . F2
Bauta 26,826 . . . . C1
Bayamo 109,201 . . . . H4
Bejucal 15,649 . . . . C1
Bolondrón 5,840 . . . . D1
Buenaventura 4,711 . . . . . H3
Buenavista 1,303 . . . . F2
Buey Arriba 8,017 . . . . . . H4
Cabaiguán 36,544 . . . . . . F2
Cabañas 4,897 . . . . B1
Cabezas 5,262 . . . . D1
Cacocum 14,145 . . . . H3
Caibarién 32,094 . . . . E1
Caimanera 6,664 . . . . J4
Calabazar de Sagua 9,023 . . E1
Calimete 19,925 . . . . D1
Camagüey 245,235 . . . . . . G3
Camajuaní 26,653 . . . . . . E1
Campechuela 20,743 . . . . . G4
Canasí 1,637 . . . . C1
Candelaria 10,810 . . . . . . B1
Cárdenas 65,585 . . . . D1
Cartagena 2,166 . . . . D2
Cascajal 3,530 . . . . E1
Cauto del Embarcadero 949 . H4
Cauto el Cristo 1,626 . . . . . J4
Central Amancio Rodríguez
22,506 . . . . G3
Central Bolivia 6,301 . . . . . F3
Central Brasil 4,904 . . . . . G2
Central Cándido González
3,414 . . . . G3
Central Colombia 16,799 . . . G3
Central Frank País 9,066 . . . K3
Central Guatemala 5,584 . . . J4
Central Haití 3,649 . . . . . . J4
Central Los Reynaldos 3,997 J4
Central Loynaz Echevarría
3,245 . . . . J3
Central Manuel Tames 7,864 K4
Céspedes 6,634 . . . . G2
Chambas 19,877 . . . . F2
Chaparra 8,428 . . . . H4
Cidra 3,567 . . . . D1
Ciego de Ávila 80,010 . . . . F2
Cienfuegos 107,396 . . . . . E2
Colón 47,010 . . . . D1
Condado 33,115 . . . . F2
Consolación del Norte 4,681 B1
Consolación del Sur 34,334 . B2
Contramaestre 44,991 . . . . H4
Corralillo 15,822 . . . . D1
Cruces 20,324 . . . . E2
Cueto 23,183 . . . . J3
Cumanayagua 25,338 . . . . . E2
Daiquirí J4
Delicias 10,562 . . . . H3
Dos Caminos 3,772 . . . . . . J4
Dos Ríos 1,786 . . . . J4
El Caney 3,921 . . . . J4
El Cobre 3,952 . . . . J4
El Santo 2,473 . . . . E1
Encrucijada 23,029 . . . . . . E1
Esmeralda 17,205 . . . . G1
Esperanza 9,241 . . . . D1
Florencia 6,979 . . . . F2
Florida 43,881 . . . . G3
Fomento 17,310 . . . . F2
Gaspar 2,682 . . . . F2
Gibara 23,137 . . . . J3
Guáimaro 29,712 . . . . G3
Guanabacoa 89,741 . . . . . . C1
Guanajay 21,042 . . . . B1
Guane 14,126 . . . . A2
Guantánamo 178,129 . . . . . K4
Guaro 3,086 . . . . J4
Guasimal 3,057 . . . . E2
Guayabal 3,703 . . . . G3
Guayos 6,753 . . . . F2
Güines 51,691 . . . . C1
Güira de Melena 19,851 . . . C1
Guisa 15,182 . . . . H4
Havana (cap.) 1,924,886 . . . C1
Herradura 3,762 . . . . B1
Holguín 190,155 . . . . J3
Ignacio Agramonte 1,487 . . G3
Imías 4,491 . . . . K4
Isabela de Sagua 3,721 . . . E1
Jagüey Grande 30,205 . . . . D2
Jamaica 5,128 . . . . K4
Jaruco 16,844 . . . . C1
Jatibonico 17,047 . . . . F2
Jíbaro 1,263 . . . . F2
Jiguaní 25,069 . . . . H4
Jobabo 14,899 . . . . H4
Jovellanos 35,043 . . . . D1
La Coloma 3,462 . . . . A2
La Maya-Alto Songo 25,188 . J4
Las Martinas 4,511 . . . . . . A2
Limonar 8,923 . . . . D1
Los Arabos 10,664 . . . . . . D1
Los Palacios 21,884 . . . . . B1
Lugareño 4,396 . . . . G3
Mabay 6,176 . . . . H4
Maceo 2,739 . . . . H3
Majagua 9,110 . . . . F2
Manacas 5,914 . . . . E1
Manatí 11,054 . . . . H3
Manguito 2,739 . . . . D1
Manicaragua 33,900 . . . . . E2
Mantua 9,165 . . . . A2
Mapos (Amazonas) 1,066 . . F2
Manzanillo 95,420 . . . . . . H4
Mariano ○127,563 . . . . . . C1
Mariel 24,115 . . . . B1
Martí 11,474 . . . . D1
Matanzas 103,302 . . . . . . C1
Máximo Gómez, Ciego
de Ávila 5,116 . . . . G3
Máximo Gómez, Matanzas
4,970 . . . . D1
Mayajigua 4,425 . . . . F2
Mayarí 54,699 . . . . J3
Mayarí Arriba 2,302 . . . . . J4
Media Luna 13,794 . . . . . . G4
Mendoza 2,914 . . . . A2
Meneses 4,768 . . . . F2
Minas 17,675 . . . . G2
Minas de Matahambre
14,976 . . . . A1
Moa 28,696 . . . . K3
Morón 40,396 . . . . F2
Nicaro 9,506 . . . . J3
Niquero 15,544 . . . . G4
Nueva Gerona 17,175 . . . . . B2
Nuevitas 35,103 . . . . G2
Orozco 4,256 . . . . B1
Palma Soriano 66,222 . . . . J4
Palmira 19,680 . . . . E2
Pedro Betancourt 22,915 . . D1
Perico 20,633 . . . . D1
Pilón 10,194 . . . . H4
Pinar del Río 104,598 . . . . B2
Placetas 46,038 . . . . E1
Primero Enero 14,807 . . . . F2
Puerto Esperanza 3,499 . . . A1
Puerto Padre 46,806 . . . . . H3
Quemado de Güines 11,208 E1
Rancho Veloz 3,966 . . . . . D1
Ranchuelo 34,255 . . . . E2
Regla 38,491 . . . . C1
Remedios 27,722 . . . . E2
República Dominicana
2,540 . . . . F2
Río Cauto 19,550 . . . . H4
Rodas 16,350 . . . . E2
Sagua de Tánamo 15,327 . . K3
Sagua la Grande 52,315 . . . E1
San Andrés 2,127 . . . . J3
San Antonio de los Baños
28,137 . . . . C1
San Cristóbal 30,769 . . . . . B1
San Diego de los Baños
1,430 . . . . B1
San Germán 12,362 . . . . . . J3
San José de las Lajas
37,149 . . . . C1
San José de los Ramos
1,726 . . . . D1
San Juan y Martínez 13,227 . B2
San Luis, Pinar del Río
5,677 . . . . B2
San Luis, Santiago de Cuba
32,826 . . . . J4
San Nicolás 12,368 . . . . . . C1
San Ramón 2,676 . . . . H4
Santa Clara 175,113 . . . . . E2
Santa Cruz del Norte
15,239 . . . . C1

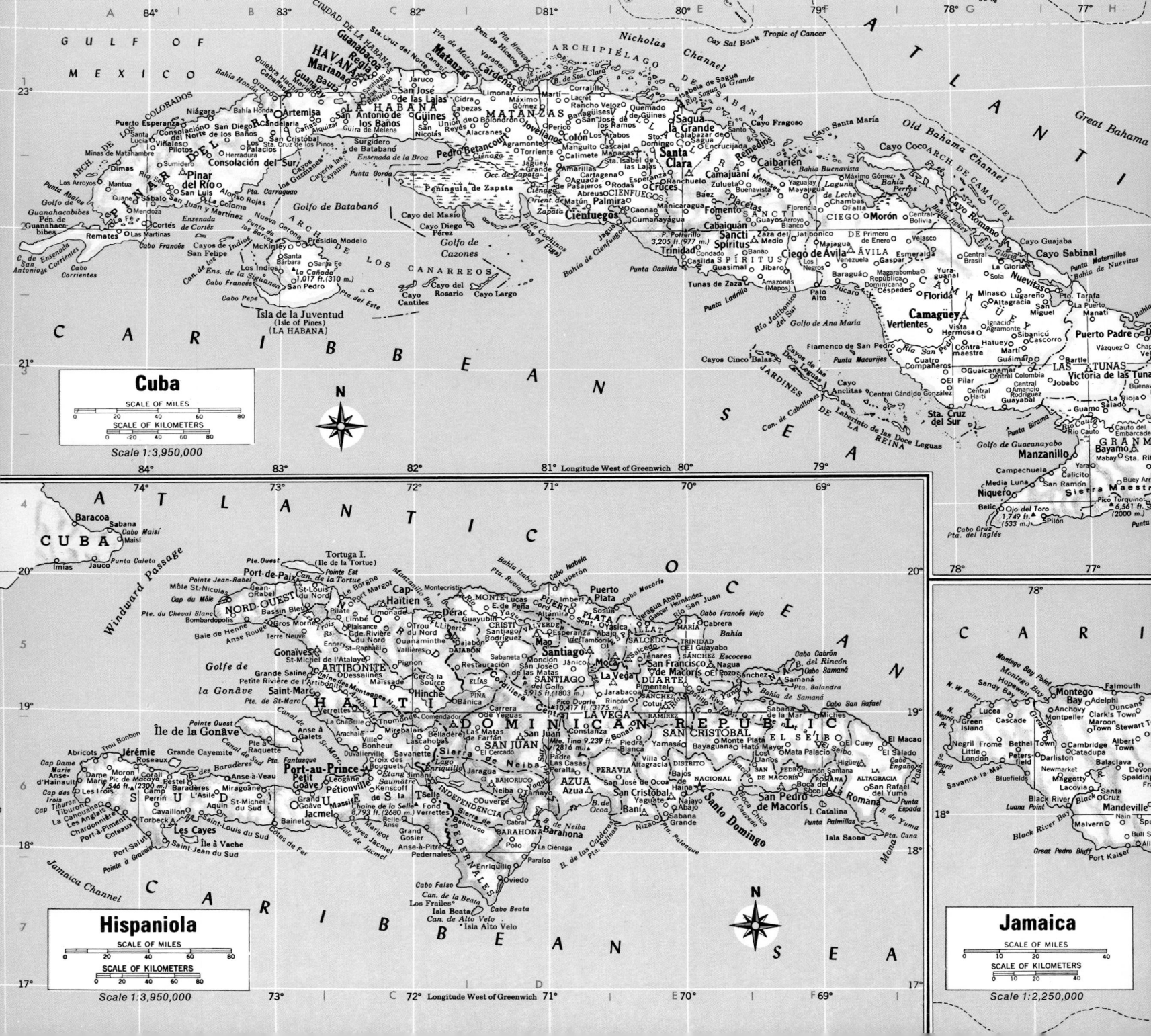

Santa Cruz de los Pinos 3,545 . . . . . . B1
Santa Cruz del Sur 27,142 . G3
Santa Fe 3,925 . . . . B2
Santa Isabel de las Lajas 7,279 . . . . E2
Santa Lucía 3,734 . . . . J3
Santa Rita 6,358 . . . . . H4
Santiago de Cuba 362,432 . J4
Santiago de las Vegas 29,325 . . . . C1
Santo Domingo 32,950 . . . C1
Sibanicú 14,252 . . . . . G3
Sola 2,436 . . . . G2
Sumidero 980 . . . . . . A2
Surgidero de Batabanó 11,533 . . . . C1
Tacajó 4,469 . . . . . . J3
Torriente 1,759 . . . . . D11
Trinidad 42,080 . . . . . E2
Unión de Reyes 28,422 . . C1
Varadero 14,737 . . . . . D1
Vázquez 3,851 . . . . . . H3
Velasco 5,618 . . . . . . H3
Venezuela 13,744 . . . . F2
Vertientes 25,178 . . . . G3
Victoria de las Tunas 87,522 H3
Viñales 2,049 . . . . . . A1
Yaguajay 30,720 . . . . F2
Yara 238,879 . . . . . . H4
Zaza del Medio 7,495 . . F2
Zulueta 5,425 . . . . . . E2

OTHER FEATURES

Abalos (pt.) A2
Ana María (gulf) F3
Anclitas (cay) F3
Batabanó (gulf) C2
Birama (pt.) G4
Broa (inlet) C1
Buenavista (bay) F2
Caballones (chan.) . . . G3
Camagüey (arch.) . . . G2
Cantiles (cay) F3
Cárdenas (bay) D1
Carraguao (pt.) D1
Casilda (pt.) E2
Cauto (riv.) H3
Cayamas (cays) C1
Cazones (gulf) D2
Cienfuegos (bay) D2
Cinco Balas (cays) . . . E3
Cochinos (bay) D2
Coco (cay) G1
Corrientes (cape) A2
Corrientes (inlet) A2
Cortés (inlet) A2
Cristal, Sierra del (mts.) . J3
Cruz (cape) G4
Diego Pérez (cay) C2
Doce Leguas (cays) . . . F3
Este (pt.) C3
Fragoso (cay) F1
Francés (cape) A2

Gorda (pt.) C2
Gran Piedra (mt.) J4
Guacanayabo (gulf) . . . G4
Guajaba (cay) G2
Guanahacabibes (gulf) . A2
Guanahacabibes (pen.) . A2
Guantánamo (bay) . . . J4
Guantánamo Bay U.S. Nav. Reserve K4
Guarico (pt.) K3
Guzmanes (cays) B2
Hicacos (pen.) D1
Hicacos (pt.) D1
Honda (bay) B1
Indios (chan.) B2
Inglés (pt.) G4
Jardines de la Reina (arch.) . F3
Jatibonico del Sur (riv.) . . F3
Jigüey (bay) G2
Juventud, Isla de la (Pines) (isl.) 57,879 . . . . . B3
Laberinto de las Doce Leguas (cays) F3
Ladrillo (pt.) E3
Largo (cay) D2
Leche (lag.) F2
Los Barcos (pt.) B2
Los Canarreos (arch.) . . B2
Los Colorados (arch.) . . A1
Lucrecia (cape) J3
Macurijes (pt.) F3
Maestra, Sierra (mts.) . . H4
Maisí (cape) K4
Mangle (pt.) J3
Maslo (cay) C2
Matanzas (bay) D1
Nicholas (chan.) E1
Nipe (bay) J3
Nuevitas (bay) H2
Ojo del Toro (mt.) . . . H4
Old Bahama (chan.) . . . G1
Pepe (cay) B3
Perros (bay) G2
Pigs (Cochinos) (bay) . . D2
Pines (Isla de la Juventud) (isl.) 7,879 . . . . . B3
Potrerillo (peak) E2
Quemado (pt.) K4
Romano (cay) G2
Rosario (cay) C2
Sabana (arch.) E1
Sabinal (cay) H2
Sagua la Grande (riv.) . . E1
San Antonio (cape) . . . A2
San Felipe (cays) B2
San Pedro (riv.) G3
Santa Clara (bay) D1
Santa María (cay) F1
Siguanea (bay) B2
Tabacal (pt.) H4
Toa, Cuchillas de (mts.) . K4
Tortuguilla (pt.) K4
Turquino (peak) H4
Zapata (pt.) C2
Zapata Occidental (swamp) . D2
Zapata Oriental (swamp) . D2

DOMINICAN REPUBLIC

PROVINCES

Azua 142,770 . . . . . . D6

Bahoruco 78,636 . . . . D6
Barahona 137,160 . . . . D6
Dajabón 57,709 . . . . . D5
Distrito Nacional 1,550,739 . E6
Duarte 235,544 . . . . . E5
Elías Piña 65,384 . . . . C5
El Seíbo 157,866 . . . . F6
Espaillat 164,017 . . . . E5
Independencia 38,768 . . D6
La Altagracia 100,112 . . F6
La Romana 109,769 . . . F6
La Vega 385,043 . . . . . D5
María Trinidad Sánchez 112,629 . . . . E5
Monte Cristi 83,407 . . . D5
Pedernales 17,006 . . . . D7
Peravia 168,123 . . . . . E6
Puerto Plata 206,757 . . . D5
Salcedo 99,191 . . . . . E5
Samaná 65,699 . . . . . F5
Sánchez Ramírez 126,567 . E5
San Cristóbal 446,132 . . E6
San Juan 239,957 . . . . D6
Santiago 550,372 . . . . D5
Santiago Rodríguez 55,411 . D5
Valverde 100,319 . . . . D5

CITIES and TOWNS

Altamira 2,759 . . . . . D5
Azua 31,481 . . . . . . D6
Bajos de Haina 33,135 . . E6
Baní 36,705 . . . . . . E6
Barahona 49,334 . . . . D6
Bonao 44,486 . . . . . . E5
Cabrera 2,542 . . . . . E5
Comendador 5,962 . . . D5
Constanza 15,141 . . . . D5
Cotuí 16,688 . . . . . . E5
Dajabón 8,808 . . . . . D5
El Seíbo 13,511 . . . . . F6
Hato Mayor 17,859 . . . F6
Higüey 33,501 . . . . . F6
Imbert 5,315 . . . . . . D5
Jarabacoa 13,416 . . . . E5
Jimaní 3,327 . . . . . . C6
La Romana 91,571 . . . . F6
La Vega 52,432 . . . . . E5
Luperón 2,500 . . . . . D5
Mao 33,527 . . . . D5
Moca 31,176 . . . . . . D5
Monción 3,344 . . . . . D5
Nagua 20,912 . . . . . . E5
Puerto Plata 45,348 . . . D5
Sabana de la Mar 9,983 . . F5
Sabaneta 9,170 . . . . . D5
Samaná 5,023 . . . . . . F5
Sánchez 7,919 . . . . . E5
San Cristóbal 58,520 . . . E6
San Francisco de Macorís 64,906 . . . . E5
San Juan 49,764 . . . . . D6
San Pedro de Macorís 78,562 . . . . F6
Santiago 278,638 . . . . D5
Santo Domingo (cap.) 1,313,172 . . . . E6
Tenares 4,065 . . . . . . E5
Villa Altagracia 20,890 . . E6

OTHER FEATURES

Alto Velo (chan.) C7
Alto Velo (isl.) D7
Balandra (pt.) F5
Beata (cape) D7
Beata (chan.) C7
Beata (isl.) C7
Cabrón (cape) F5
Calderas (bay) D6
Cana (pt.) F6
Catalina (isl.) F6
Caucedo (cape) E6
Central, Cordillera (range) . D5
Duarte (peak) D5
Engaño (cape) F6
Enriquillo (lake) C6
Escocesa (bay) E5
Espada (pt.) F6
Falso (cape) C7
Francés Viejo (cape) . . . E5
Gallo (mt.) D5
Isabela (bay) D5
Isabela (cape) D5
Los Frailes (isl.) C7
Macorís (cape) E5
Manzanillo (bay) C5
Mona (passg.) F6
Neiba (bay) D6
Neiba, Sierra de (mts.) . . D6
Ocoa (bay) D6
Oriental, Cordillera (range) . F6
Palenque (pt.) E6
Palmillas (pt.) F5
Rincón (bay) F5
Rucia (pt.) D5
Salinas (pt.) E6
Samaná (bay) F5
Samaná (cape) F5
San Rafael (cape) F5
Saona (isl.) F6
Septentrional, Cordillera (range) D5
Tina (mt.) D6
Yaque del Norte (riv.) . . . D5
Yaque del Sur (riv.) D6
Yuma (bay) F6
Yuna (riv.) E5

HAITI

DEPARTMENTS

Artibonite C5
Nord C5
Nord-Ouest B5
Ouest C6
Sud A6

CITIES and TOWNS

Anse-à-Galets 3,623 . . . B6
Anse-d'Hainault 5,220 . . A6
Aquin 3,820 . . . . . . B6
Cap-Haïtien 64,406 . . . C5
Croix des Bouquets 4,365 . C6
Dame Marie 4,320 . . . . A6
Dérac 1,300 . . . . C5

Dessalines 7,984 . . . . C5
Fort Liberté 5,012 . . . . C5
Gonaïves 34,209 . . . . B5
Grande Rivière du Nord 6,007 . . . . C5
Gros Morne 4,739 . . . . B5
Hinche 10,070 . . . . . C5
Jacmel 13,730 . . . . . C6
Jérémie 18,493 . . . . . A6
Kenscoff 2,605 . . . . . C6
Lascahobas 3,805 . . . . C6
Léogâne 5,782 . . . . . C6
Les Cayes 34,090 . . . . B6
Limbé 10,476 . . . . . . C5
Miragoâne 4,327 . . . . B6
Mirebalais 6,069 . . . . C6
Ouanaminthe 7,276 . . . C5
Pétionville 35,333 . . . . C6
Petite Rivière de l'Artibonite 10,099 . . . . . . B5
Petit Goâve 7,310 . . . . B6
Pignon 4,576 . . . . . . C5
Port-au-Prince (cap.) 449,831 . . . . C6
Port-de-Paix 15,540 . . . B5
Saint-Louis du Nord 7,203 . B5
Saint-Marc 24,165 . . . . B5
Saint-Michel de l'Atalaye 7,559 . . . . C5
Saint-Raaphaël 3,889 . . . C5
Trou du Nord 7,637 . . . C5
Verrettes 3,670 . . . . . C5

OTHER FEATURES

Artibonite (riv.) C5
Baradères (bay) B6
Cheval Blanc (pt.) B5
Dame Marie (cape) A6
Est (pt.) C4
Fantasque (pt.) B6
Gonâve (gulf) B5
Gonâve (isl.) B6
Grande Cayemite (isl.) . . B6
Gravois (pt.) A7
Irois (pt.) A6
Jean-Rabel (pt.) B5
Macaya (mt.) A6
Manzanillo (bay) C5
Môle (pt.) B5
Noires (mts.) C5
Ouest (pt.) B4
Ouest (pt.) B6
Saint-Marc (chan.) B5
Saint-Marc (bay) B5
Saumâtre (lake) C6
Selle (peak) C6
Sud (chan.) B6
Tortue (chan.) C5
Tortue (Tortuga) (isl.) . . . C4
Tortuga (isl.) C4
Trois-Rivières (riv.) B5
Vache (isl.) B6
Windward (passg.) A5

JAMAICA

CITIES and TOWNS

Alley J7

Alligator Pond H6
Anchovy 2,558 . . . . . H5
Annotto Bay K6
Bamboo 2,971 . . . . . J6
Bath K6
Black River 2,701 . . . . H6
Bog Walk J6
Bowden K6
Browns Town 5,479 . . . J6
Bull Savanna-Junction 5,110 . . . . H6
Cambridge 2,449 . . . . H5
Catadupa H5
Christiana J6
Discovery Bay 1,814 . . . J5
Falmouth 3,937 . . . . . H5
Green Island G6
Hope Bay K6
Kingston (cap.) 106,791 . . K6
Kingston *516,865 . . . . J7
Linstead J6
Lucea 3,635 . . . . . . G5
Mandeville 14,421 . . . . J6
Maroon Town 2,717 . . . H6
May Pen 26,074 . . . . . J6
Montego Bay 43,521 . . . H5
Montpelier H5
Morant Bay 7,465 . . . . K7
Negril G6
Ocho Rios 5,851 . . . . J6
Oracabessa J5
Port Antonio 10,538 . . . K6
Port Kaiser H7
Port Maria 5,259 . . . . J6
Port Morant K6
Saint Ann's Bay 7,101 . . J5
Saint Margaret's Bay . . . K6
Savanna-la-Mar 11,759 . . G6
Spanish Town 40,731 . . . J6
Williamsfield H6

OTHER FEATURES

Black (riv.) H6
Black River (bay) G6
Blue (mts.) J6
Blue Mountain (peak) . . K6
Galina (pt.) J6
Grande (riv.) K6
Great (riv.) H6
Great Pedro Bluff (prom.) . H7
Long (bay) H7
Luana (pt.) G6
Minho (riv.) J6
Montego (bay) G5
Montego Bay ((pt.) G5
North East (pt.) K6
North Negril (pt.) G6
North West (pt.) G5
Old Harbour (bay) J6
Portland (pt.) J7
Sir John's (peak) K6
South East (pt.) K6
South Negril (pt.) G6

*City and Suburbs.
○ Population of municipality.

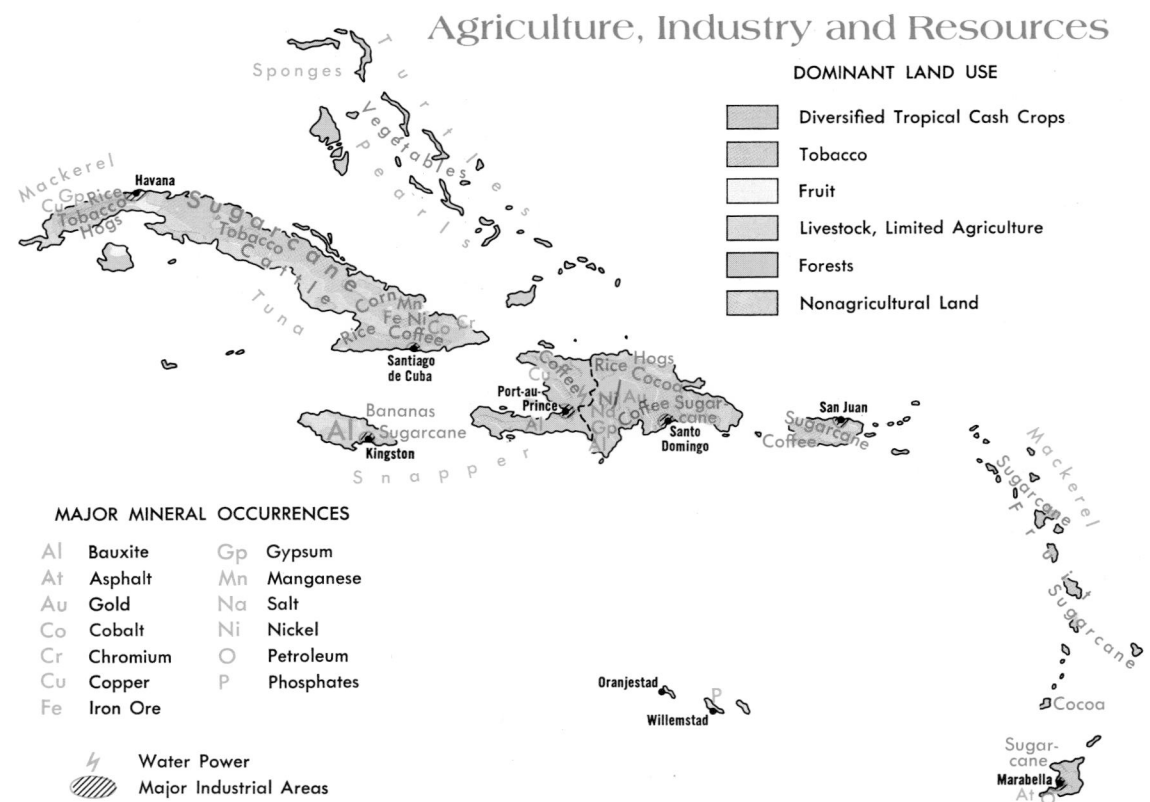

Agriculture, Industry and Resources

DOMINANT LAND USE

Diversified Tropical Cash Crops
Tobacco
Fruit
Livestock, Limited Agriculture
Forests
Nonagricultural Land

MAJOR MINERAL OCCURRENCES

Al Bauxite
At Asphalt
Au Gold
Co Cobalt
Cr Chromium
Cu Copper
Fe Iron Ore

Gp Gypsum
Mn Manganese
Na Salt
Ni Nickel
O   Petroleum
P   Phosphates

Water Power
Major Industrial Areas

PUERTO RICO

DISTRICTS

Aguadilla A1
Arecibo C1
Bayamón D1
Guayama D2
Humacao E2
Mayagüez B2
Ponce C2
San Juan D1

CITIES and TOWNS

Adjuntas 5,239 B2
Aguada 5,025 A1
Aguadilla 22,039 A1
Aguas Buenas 3,766 E2
Aibonito 9,331 D2
Añasco 5,646 A1
Ángeles ○2,817 B2
Arecibo 48,779 B1
Arroyo 8,435 E3
Bahomamey A1
Bajadero 3,678 C1
Barceloneta 4,502 C1
Barranquitas 3,618 D2
Bayamón 185,087 D1
Boquerón ○3,675 A3
Cabo Rojo 10,292 A2
Caguas 87,214 E2
Caguas †156,819 E2
Camuy 3,834 B1
Carolina 147,835 E1
Cataño 26,243 D1
Cayey 23,305 D2
Ceiba 4,973 F2
Central Aguirre 1,049 D3
Ciales 3,582 C1
Cidra 6,069 D2
Coamo 12,851 D2
Comerío 5,736 D2
Coquí 3,018 D3
Corozal 5,889 D1
Coto Laurel ○5,192 C2
Culebra (Dewey) 938 G1
Dorado 10,203 D1
Ensenada B3
Esperanza 1,130 G2
Fajardo 26,928 F1
Florida 3,641 C1
Guánica 9,628 B3
Guayama 21,097 E3
Guayanilla 6,163 B3
Guaynabo 65,075 D1
Gurabo 7,645 E2
Hatillo 5,019 B1
Hato Rey E1
Hormigüeros 12,031 A2
Humacao 19,147 E2
Isabela 12,087 A1
Isabel Segunda 2,330 G2
Jayuya 3,588 C2
Jobos 4,194 D3
Juana Díaz 10,469 C2
Juncos 7,851 E2
Lajas 4,275 A2
Lares 5,224 B2
Las Piedras 4,857 E2
Levittown 31,613 D1
Loíza 3,932 E1
Loíza Aldea E1
Luquillo 4,531 F1
Manatí 17,347 C1
Maricao 1,390 B2
Mayagüez 82,968 A2
Mayagüez †98,155 A2
Moca 3,960 A1
Naguabo 4,135 F2
Naranjito 2,849 D1
Palmer 1,566 F1
Palo Seco 1,172 D1
Parguera A3
Patillas 3,172 E2
Peñuelas 4,235 B2
Playa de Fajardo F1
Playa de Humacao ○5,573 F2
Ponce 161,739 C3
Ponce †168,272 C3
Puerto Nuevo D1
Puerto Real 2,390 A2
Puerto Real (Playa de Fajardo) F1
Punta Santiago (Playa de Humacao) ○5,573 F2
Quebradillas 3,770 B1
Río Blanco 1,433 F2
Río Grande 12,047 E1
Río Piedras E1
Rosario A2
Sabana Grande 7,435 B2
Sabana Seca 11,431 D1
Salinas 6,220 D3
San Antonio 2,681 A1
San Germán 13,054 A2
San Juan (cap.) 424,600 E1
San Juan †1,081,193 E1
San Lorenzo 8,880 E2
San Sebastián 10,619 B1
Santa Isabel 6,948 C3
Santurce E1
Tallaboa 1,059 B3
Toa Alta 4,427 D1
Toa Baja 1,992 D1
Trujillo Alto 41,141 E1
Utuado 11,113 B2
Vega Alta 10,582 D1
Vega Baja 18,233 D1
Vieques (Isabel Segunda) 2,330 G2
Villalba 3,469 C2
Yabucoa 6,797 E2
Yauco 14,594 B2

OTHER FEATURES

Aguadilla (bay) A1
Algarrobo (pt.) A2
Añasco (bay) A1
Arenas (pt.) F2
Bauta (riv.) C2
Bayamón (riv.) D1
Boquerón (bay) A3
Borinquen (pt.) A1
Cabullones (pt.) C3
Caja de Muertos (isl.) C3
Camuy (riv.) B1
Canovanas (riv.) E1
Caonillas (lake) C2
Carite (lake) E2
Carraízo (lake) E1
Cayey, Sierra de (mts.) D2
Central, Cordillera (range) C2
Cerro Gordo (pt.) D1
Coamo (res.) D3
Coamo (riv.) D3
Culebra (isl.) 1,265 G1
Culebrinas (riv.) A1
Culebrita (isl.) G2
El Toro (mt.) F2
El Yunque (mt.) F1
Este (pt.) G2
Fajardo (riv.) F1
Figuras (pt.) E3
Fosforescente (bay) A3
Grande de Añasco (riv.) B2
Grande de Arecibo (riv.) C1
Grande de Loíza (riv.) E1
Grande de Manatí (riv.) C1
Guajataca (lake) B1
Guanajibo (pt.) A2
Guanajibo (riv.) A2
Guánica (lake) B3
Guaniquilla (pt.) A2
Guayabal (lake) C2
Guayanés (pt.) F2
Guayanés (riv.) E2
Guayanilla (bay) B3
Guayo (lake) B2
Guilarte (mt.) B2
Honda (bay) F2
Jacaguas (riv.) C2
Jaicoa, Cordillera (mts.) B1
Jiguero (pt.) A1
Jobos (bay) D3
Lima (pt.) F2
Luquillo, Sierra de (mts.) E2
Manglillo (pt.) B3
Mayagüez (bay) A2
Miquillo (pt.) F1
Molinos (pt.) G1
Mona (passg.) A2
Negra (pt.) G2
Nigua (riv.) D2
Ola Grande (pt.) D3
Palmas Altas (pt.) C1
Patillas (lake) E2
Petrona (pt.) D3
Pirata (mt.) F2
Plata (riv.) D2
Puerca (pt.) F2
Puerto Medio Mundo (bay) F2
Punta, Cerro de (mt.) C2
Ramey A.F.B. A1
Rincón (bay) D3
Rojo (cape) A3
Roosevelt Road Naval Res. F2
Salinas (pt.) D1
San José (lag.) E1
San Juan, Cabezas de (prom.) F1
San Juan Nat'l Hist. Site D1
Soldado (pt.) G2
Sucia (bay) A3
Tanamá (riv.) B1
Toro, El (mt.) F2
Torrecilla (lag.) E1
Tortuguero (lag.) D1
Tuna (pt.) E3
Vacía Talega (pt.) E1
Vieques (isl.) 7,662 G2
Vieques (passg.) F2
Vieques (sound) G2
Yagüez (riv.) A2
Yauco (lake) B2
Yeguas ((pt.) F3

ANTIGUA

CITIES and TOWNS

All Saints 1,796 E11
Cedar Grove 1,460 E11
Falmouth 1,134 E11
Freetown 1,250 E11
Jennings 1,370 D11
Liberta 2,394 E11
Old Road 1,244 D11
Parham 1,570 E11
Saint John's (cap.) 21,814 E11
Willikies 1,843 E11

OTHER FEATURES

Antigua (isl.) 76,213 E11
Boggy (peak) D11
Boon (pt.) E11
Green (isl.) E11
Guiana (isl.) E11
Long (isl.) E11
Saint John's (harb.) C11
Standfast (pt.) E11
Willoughby (bay) E11

ARUBA

CITIES and TOWNS

Aresji D9
Balashi E10
Bubati D10
Bushiribana E10
Druif D1
Oranjestad (cap.) Aruba 10,100 D10
Sint Nicolaas E10
Westpunt D10

OTHER FEATURES

Aruba (isl.) 66,790 E9
Basora (pt.) E10
Jamanota (mt.) E10
Paarden (bay) D10
Palm (beach) D10

BARBADOS

CITIES and TOWNS

Bathsheba B8
Belleplaine B8
Bridgetown (cap.) 7,552 B9
Carlton B8
Cave Hill B9
Checker Hall B8
Codrington B8
Crab Hill B8
Crane C9
Drax Hall B8
Ellerton B9
Greenland B8
Holetown B8
Kendal B8
Lodge Hill B8
Marchfield B9
Mount Standfast B8
Oistins B9
Rose Hill B8
Rouen B9
Saint Lawrence B9
Saint Martins C9
Scarboro B9
Seawell B9
Six Mens B8
Speightstown B8
Spring Hall B8
Welchman Hall B8

OTHER FEATURES

Carlisle (bay) B9
Hillaby (mt.) B8
Long (bay) B9
North (pt.) B8
Oistins (bay) B9
Pelican (isl.) B9
Ragged (pt.) C8
Sam Lord's Castle C9
South (pt.) B9

DOMINICA

CITIES and TOWNS

Barroui 1,480 E6
Castle Bruce 1,975 F6
Coulihaut 1,735 E6
Delice F7
Grand Bay 3,152 F7
Hampstead E5
La Plaine F6
Mahout 2,095 E6
Marigot 3,183 F6
Petit Soufrière F6
Portsmouth 2,329 E5
Rosalie F6
Roseau (cap.) 9,968 E7
Roseau *16,035 E7
Saint Joseph 2,643 E6
Salybia F6
Soufrière E7
Vieille Case E5
Wesley 2,002 F5

OTHER FEATURES

Capuchin (cape) E5
Carib Reserve F6
Clyde (riv.) F6
Crumpton (pt.) F5
Diablotin, Morne (mt.) E6
Dominica (passg.) E5
Douglas (bay) E5
Grand (bay) F7
Jaquet (pt.) E5
Layou (riv.) E6
Martinique (passg.) E7
Micotrin (mt.) F6
Pagoua (bay) F6
Prince Rupert (bay) E5
Scotts (head) E7
Soufrière (bay) E7
Trois Pitons, Morne (mt.) E6

GRENADA

CITIES and TOWNS

Gouyave 2,498 C8
Grand Roy C8
Grenville 1,723 D8
Hermitage D8
La Taste D8
Marquis D8
Mount Tivoli D8
Saint George's (cap.) 6,463 C9
Saint George's *34,624 C9
Sauteurs 605 D8
Victoria 1,673 D8
Woodford C8

OTHER FEATURES

Bedford (pt.) D8
David (pt.) D8
Great Bacolet (pt.) D8
Green (isl.) D8
Grenville (bay) D8
Gros (pt.) C8
Halifax (harb.) C8
Irvin's (bay) D8
Les Tantes (isls.) D7
Molinière (pt.) C8
Prickly (pt.) C9
Ronde (isl.) D7
Saint Catherine (mt.) D8
Saline (pt.) C9
Sinai (mt.) D8
Telescope (pt.) D8

GUADELOUPE

Total Population 329,017

CITIES and TOWNS

Anse-Bertrand 1,921 A5
Baie-Mahault 5,874 A6
Baillif 3,844 A7
Bananier A7
Basse-Terre (cap.) 13,397 A7
Bouillante 1,821 A6
Bourg-des-Saintes 907 A7
Capesterre 7,541 A7
Ferry A6
Gosier 13,741 B6
Gourbeyre 5,637 A7
Goyave 1,709 A6
Grand-Bourg 3,249 B7
Lamentin 2,319 A6
Les Abymes 51,837 B6
Morne-à-l'Eau 9,457 A6
Moule 9,800 B6
Petit-Bourg 5,097 A6
Petit-Canal 1,581 A6
Pigeon A6
Pointe-à-Pitre 25,151 B6
Pointe-Noire 2,180 A6
Port-Louis 4,517 B5
Saint-Claude 6,755 A7
Sainte-Anne 11,527 B6
Sainte-Marguerite B6
Sainte-Marie A6
Sainte-Rose 4,805 A6
Saint-François 3,141 B6
Trois-Rivières 7,881 A7
Vieux-Fort 1,073 B7
Vieux-Habitants 4,065 A7

OTHER FEATURES

Allègre (pt.) A6
Antigues (pt.) A5
Basse-Terre (isl.) 138,777 A6
Châteaux (pt.) B6
Constant, Morne (hill) B7
Désirade, La (isl.) 1,602 B6
Fajou (isl.) A6
Grand Cul-de-Sac Marin (bay) A6
Grande-Terre (isl.) B6
Grande Vigie (pt.) B5
Grand-Îlet (isl.) A7
Guadeloupe (isl.) 167,896 B6
Guadeloupe (passg.) A5
Guadeloupe Nat'l Park A6
Kahouanne (isl.) A6
Marie-Galante (isl.) 13,757 B7
Nord (pt.) B7
Nord-Est (bay) B6
Petit Cul-de-Sac Marin (bay) A6
Petite-Terre (isls.) B6
Saintes (chan.) A7
Saintes (isls.) 2,901 A7
Salée (riv.) A6
Sans Toucher (mt.) A6
Soufrière (mt.) A7
Terre-de-Bas (isl.) 1,427 A7
Terre-de-Haut (isl.) 1,453 A7
Vieux-Fort (pt.) A7

MARTINIQUE

Total Population 330,220

CITIES and TOWNS

Ajoupa-Bouillon 1,569 C5
Basse-Pointe 2,163 C5
Bellefontaine 818 C6
Case-Pilote 1,776 C6
Ducos 4,429 D6
Fond-Saint-Denis 962 C6
Fort-de-France (cap.) 96,649 C6
Grand' Rivière 1,053 C5
Gros-Morne 1,976 D6
La Trinité 3,380 D6
Le Carbet 2,321 C6
Le François 2,940 D6
Le Lamentin 6,872 D6
Le Lorrain 2,024 D6
Le Marin 2,651 D7
Le Morne-Rouge 2,650 C5
Le Prêcheur 1,350 C5
Le Robert 3,610 D6
Le Saint-Esprit 3,947 D6
Les Trois-Îlets 1,484 D6
Le Vauclin 3,054 D6
Macouba 1,142 C5
Marigot 1,765 D5
Rivière-Pilote 1,587 D7
Rivière-Salée 1,859 D7
Sainte-Luce 1,502 D7
Sainte-Marie 3,966 D5
Saint-Joseph 2,052 D6
Saint-Pierre 4,923 C6
Schoelcher 16,412 C6

OTHER FEATURES

Cabet, Pitons du (mt.) C6
Cabrits (isl.) D7
Caravelle (pen.) D6
Cul-de-Sac du Marin (bay) D7
Diable (pt.) D5
Ferré (cape) E7
Fort-de-France (bay) C6
Galion (bay) D6
Lézarde (riv.) D6
Long (isl.) D6
Lorrain (riv.) D5
Martinique (passg.) C5
Pelée (vol.) C5
Pilote (riv.) D7
Ramiers (isl.) C6
Ramville (isl.) D6
Robert (harb.) D6
Rose (pt.) D6
Saint-Martin (cape) C5
Saint-Pierre (bay) C6
Salines (pt.) D7
Salomon (pt.) C7
Vauclin (mt.) D6

NETHERLANDS ANTILLES

CITIES and TOWNS

Ascension F8
Bacuna E8
Boven Bolivia E8
Dokterstuin F8
Emmastad F9
Entrejo E8
Fontein E8
Groot Sint Joris G9
Hato G8
Kralendijk (cap.), Bonaire 2,500 E8
Lagoen F8
Montanja di Reij G9
New Port G9
Noord di Salinja E8
Onima E8
Otrabanda F9
Patrick F8
Rincon E8
Rooi E8
Santa Barbara G9
Santa Catharina G9
Savonet F8
Sint Kruis F8
Sint Martha F8
Sint Michiel F9
Sint Willebrordus F8
Terra Corra E8
Westpunt F8
Willemstad (cap.) 95,000 F9
Willemstad *130,000 F9

OTHER FEATURES

Bonaire (isl.) 8,087 E9
Bullen (bay) F8
Caracas (bay) G9
Curaçao (isl.) 145,430 G7
Goto (lake) D8
Kanon (pt.) G9
Klein Bonaire (isl.) E8
Kudarebe (pt.) D9
Lac (bay) D9
Lacre (pt.) E9
Malmok (mt.) E8
Noord (pt.) D8
Noord (pt.) F8
Pekelmeer (lake) E9
Piscadera (bay) F9
Schottegat (bay) G9
Sint Anna (bay) F9
Sint Christoffel (mt.) F8
Sint Joris (bay) G9
Slag (bay) D8
Vierkant (pt.) E8

SAINT KITTS and NEVIS

CITIES and TOWNS

Basseterre (cap.) 14,725 C10
Cayon C10
Charlestown 1,326 C11
Cotton Ground 471 C11
Dieppe Bay C10
Frigate Bay C10
Gingerland D11
Golden Rock C10
Newcastle D11
Old Road Town C10
Sadlers Village C10
Sandy Point 862 C10
Tabernacle C10
Zion Hill D11

OTHER FEATURES

Brimstone (hill) C10
Dogwood (pt.) D11
Fort (pt.) C11
Great Salt (pond) D10
Heldens (pt.) C10
Horse Shoe (pt.) C11
Misery (mt.) C10
Monkey (hill) C10
Narrows, The (str.) D11
Nevis (isl.) 9,300 D11
Nevis (peak) D11
North Friars (bay) D10
Pinney's (beach) D11
Saint Christopher (Saint Kitts) (isl.) 35,104 D10
South Friars (bay) C10

SAINT LUCIA

CITIES and TOWNS

Anse la Raye •5,007 F6
Canaries •2,075 G6
Castries (cap.) •42,770 G6
Choc G5
Choiseul •6,382 F7
Dauphin G5
Dennery •9,654 G6
Gros Islet •10,329 G5
Laborie •6,944 G7
Marigot G6
Marquis G6
Micoud •12,264 G6
Preslin G6
Soufrière •7,456 F6
Vieux Fort •10,675 G7

OTHER FEATURES

Beaumont (pt.) F6
Canaries, Piton (mt.) G6
Cannelles (pt.) G7
Cannelles (riv.) G6
Cap (pt.) G5
Choc (bay) G5
Fond d'Or (bay) G6
Gimie (mt.) G6
Grand Caille (pt.) F6
Grand Cul de Sac (riv.) G6
Gros Islet (bay) G5
Gros Piton (mt.) G6
La Sorcière (mt.) G6
Maria (isls.) G7
Ministre (pt.) G7
Moule-à-Chique (cape) G7
Petit Piton (mt.) G6
Pigeon (isl.) G5
Port Castries (harb.) G6
Port Praslin (bay) G6
Roseau (riv.) G6
Saint Lucia (chan.) G5
Saint Vincent (chan.) G7
Savannes (bay) G7
Sorcière, La (mt.) G6
Soufrière (bay) F6
Vierge (pt.) G6

SAINT VINCENT and THE GRENADINES

CITIES and TOWNS

Barrouallie 1,298 A9
Calliaqua 627 A9
Camden Park A9
Colonarie A9
Georgetown 1,100 A8
Kingstown (cap.) 17,117 A9
Kingstown *23,330 A9
Layou 1,147 A9
Wallibu A8

OTHER FEATURES

Colonarie (pt.) A9
Cumberland (bay) A8
Dark (head) A8
De Volet (pt.) A8
Espagnol (pt.) A8
Greathead (bay) A9
Kingstown (bay) A9
Owia (bay) A8
Porter (pt.) A8
Richmond (peak) A8
Saint Andrew (mt.) A9
Saint Vincent (passg.) A8
Soufrière (mt.) A8
Yambou (head) A9

TRINIDAD and TOBAGO

CITIES and TOWNS

Arima 11,390 B10
Arouca B10
Basse Terre B11
Biche B10
Blanchisseuse B10
California A11
Carapichaima B10
Caroni B10
Cedros A11
Chaguanas 6,122 B10
Chaguaramas A10
Couva 3,635 B10
Cunapo B10
Flanagin Town B10
Fullarton A11
Fyzabad 1,564 A11
Grande Rivière B10
Guaico B10
Guayaguayare B11
La Brea 1,487 A11
Marabella 18,158 A11
Matelot B10
Matura B10
Mayaro 2,638 B11
Moruga B11
Mucurapo A10
Palo Seco A11
Peñal 3,606 B11
Point Fortin 6,538 A11
Port-of-Spain (cap.) 67,978 A10
Princes Town 8,288 B11
Redhead B10
Rio Claro 2,423 B11
Saint Joseph 4,132 B10
Saint Joseph B11
San Fernando 33,490 A11
San Francique A11
Sangre Grande 8,948 B1
San Juan A10
Sans Souci B10
Siparia 5,773 B11
Tabaquite 2,309 B11
Talparo B10
Toco 1,287 B10
Tunapuna 10,251 B10
Upper Manzanilla B1
Valencia B10
Waterloo A10

OTHER FEATURES

Aripo, El Cerro del (mt.) B10
Boca Grande (passg.) A10
Chacachacare (isl.) A10
Chupara (pt.) B10
Cocos (bay) B10
Dragons Mouth (str.) A10
El Tucuche (mt.) B10
Erin (bay) A11
Galeota (pt.) B11
Galera (pt.) C10
Guapo (bay) A11
Guatuaro (pt.) B11
Icacos (pt.) A11
Maracas (bay) C10
Pitch (lake) A11

VIRGIN ISLANDS (Br.)

CITIES and TOWNS

Road Town (cap.) 2,200 D3
West End C4

OTHER FEATURES

Flanagan (passg.) D4
Frenchman (cay) C4
Great Thatch (isl.) C4
Great Tobago (isl.) B3
Jost Van Dyke (isl.) 135 C3
Little Tobago (isl.) B3
Narrows, The (str.) C4
Norman (isl.) D4
Peter (isl.) D4
Road (bay) D3
Sage (mt.) D4
Sir Francis Drake (chan.) D4
Tortola (isl.) 9,257 D3

VIRGIN ISLANDS (U.S.)

CITIES and TOWNS

Bethlehem E4
Canebay E3
Charlotte Amalie (cap.) 11,842 B4
Christiansted 2,914 F4
Cruz Bay 1,928 C4
Diamond F4
Eastend D4
Emmaus C4
Fredensdal F4
Frederiksted 1,046 E4
Grove Place 3,599 E4
Kingshill F4
Longford F4
Negro Bay E4

OTHER FEATURES

Altona (lag.) F4
Annaly (bay) E3
Baron Bluff (prom.) E3
Bordeaux (mt.) C4
Brass (isls.) A4
Buck (isl.) G3
Buck Island (chan.) F3
Buck Island Reef Nat'l Mon. G3
Butler (bay) E4
Caneel (bay) B4
Capella (isls.) B5
Christiansted Nat'l Hist. Site F4
Coral (bay) C4
Crown (mt.) A4
Dutch Cap (cay) A4
Eagle (mt.) E4
East (pt.) G4
Flanagan (passg.) D4
Flat (cays) A4
Grass (pt.) G4
Great (pond) F4
Great Pond (bay) F4
Green (cay) F4
Hams Bluff (prom.) E3
Hans Lollik (isls.) B4
Hassel (isl.) B4
Jersey (bay) B4
Krause Lagoon (chan.) F4
Leeward (passg.) B4
Long (pt.) B4
Long (pt.) E4
Lovango (cay) C4
Magens (bay) B4
Maho (bay) C4
Narrows, The (str.) C4
Nulliberg (mt.) B4
Perseverance (bay) A4
Picara (pt.) B4
Pillsbury (sound) B4
Privateer (pt.) D4
Pull (pt.) F3
Ram (head) C5
Red (pt.) D4
Reef (bay) C4
Saba (isl.) A4
Saint Croix (isl.) 49,725 G4
Saint James (isls.) B4
Saint John (isl.) 2,472 C4
Saint Thomas (harb.) B4
Saint Thomas (isl.) 44,372 A4
Salt (cay) A4
Salt (riv.) F4
Salt River (bay) F3
Sandy (pt.) D4
Savana (isl.) A4
Southwest (cape) E4
Tague (bay) G4
Thatch (cay) B4
Turner Hole (bay) G4
U.S. Nav. Air Sta. A4
Virgin (str.) A4
Virgin Isls. Nat'l Park C4
Water (isl.) A4
Westend Saltpond (lag.) E4

*City and suburbs.
• Population of district.
†Population of met. area.
○ Population of municipality.

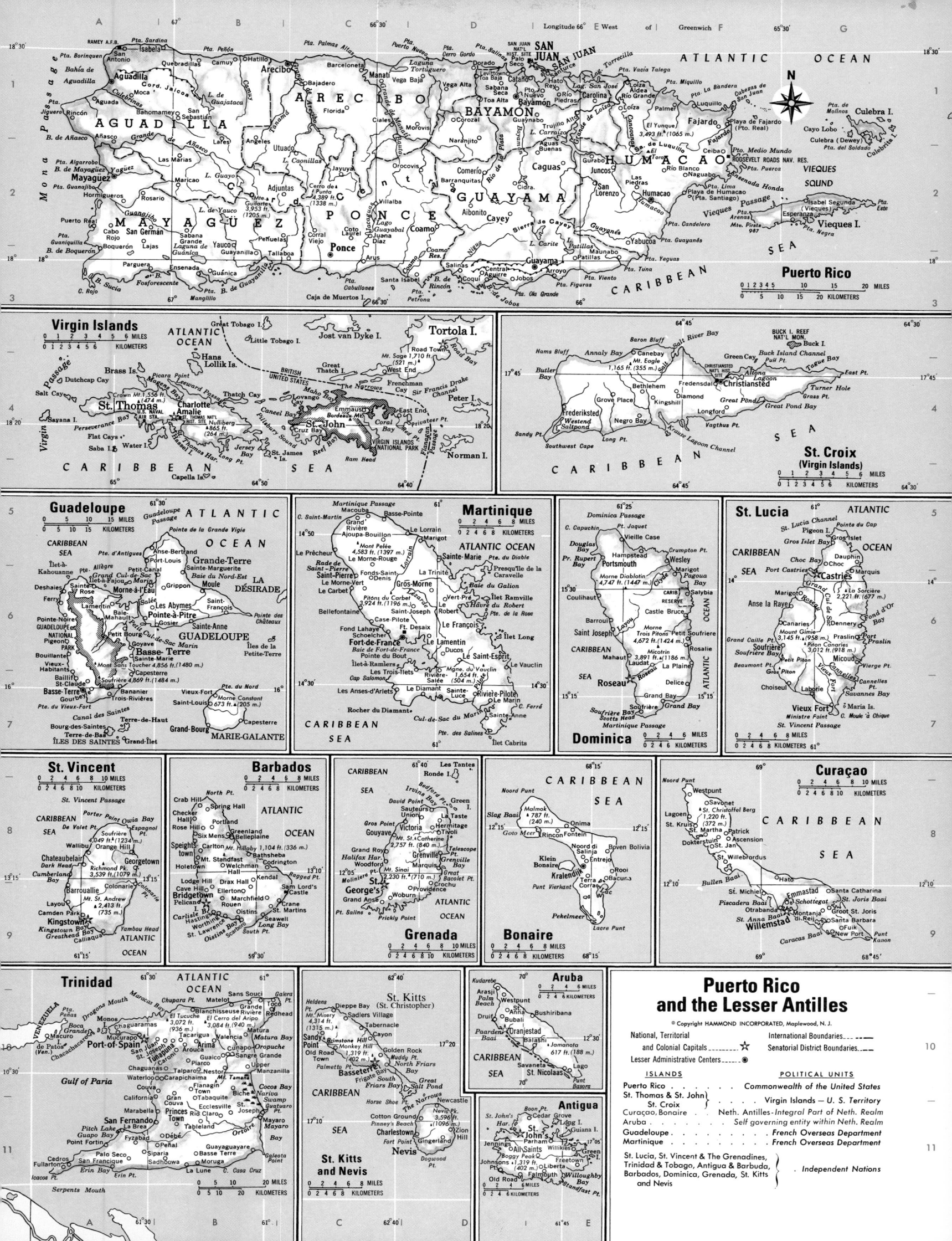

Puerto Rico and the Lesser Antilles

© Copyright HAMMOND INCORPORATED, Maplewood, N.J.

National, Territorial and Colonial Capitals .... ☆
Lesser Administrative Centers .... ◉

International Boundaries .... ───
Senatorial District Boundaries .... ───

ISLANDS — POLITICAL UNITS

ISLANDS	POLITICAL UNITS
Puerto Rico	Commonwealth of the United States
St. Thomas & St. John	Virgin Islands — U. S. Territory
St. Croix	
Curaçao, Bonaire	Neth. Antilles - Integral Part of Neth. Realm
Aruba	Self governing entity within Neth. Realm
Guadeloupe	French Overseas Department
Martinique	French Overseas Department
St. Lucia, St. Vincent & The Grenadines, Trinidad & Tobago, Antigua & Barbuda, Barbados, Dominica, Grenada, St. Kitts and Nevis	Independent Nations

Maps: Virgin Islands, St. Croix (Virgin Islands), Guadeloupe, Martinique, Dominica, St. Lucia, St. Vincent, Barbados, Grenada, Bonaire, Curaçao, Trinidad, St. Kitts and Nevis, Aruba, Antigua.

Canada

CONIC PROJECTION

SCALE OF MILES
0 50 100 200 300

SCALE OF KILOMETERS
0 50 100 200 300 400 500

Capitals of Countries .... ☆
Provincial & Territorial Capitals .... △
Administrative Centers .... ⊙
International Boundaries .... ▬ ▪ ▬ ▪
Provincial Boundaries .... ▬ ▪▪ ▬
Regional Boundaries .... ▬ ▪ ▪ ▪

Scale 1:19,600,000

© Copyright HAMMOND INCORPORATED, Maplewood, N. J.

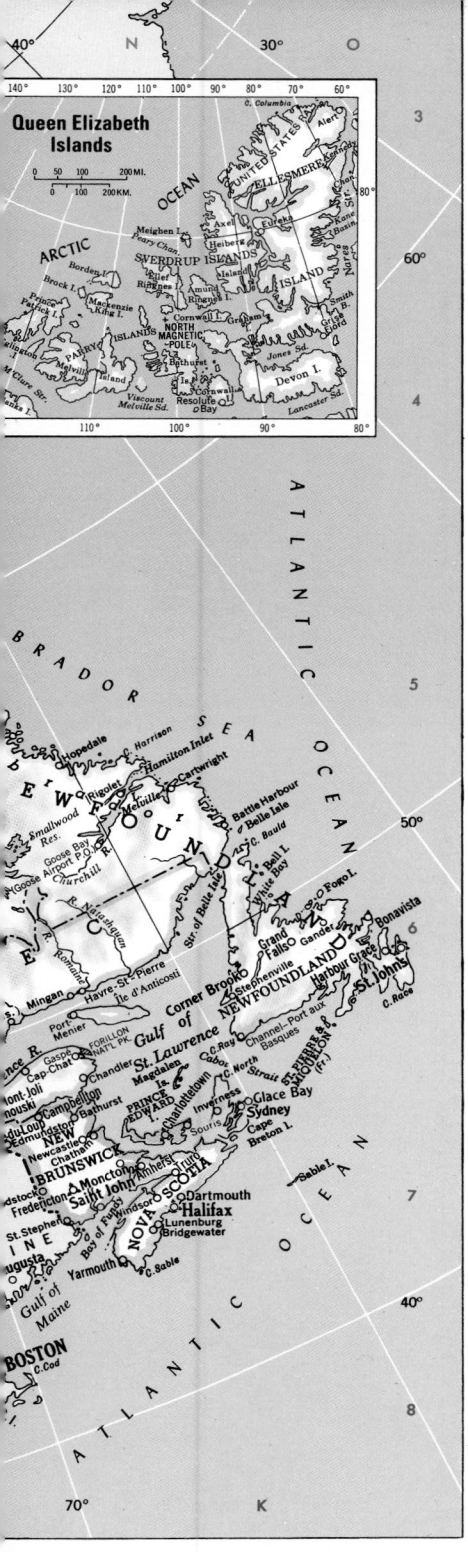

Queen Elizabeth Islands

AREA 3,851,787 sq. mi. (9,976,139 sq. km.)
POPULATION 24,343,181
CAPITAL Ottawa
LARGEST CITY Montréal
HIGHEST POINT Mt. Logan 19,524 ft. (5,951 m.)
MONETARY UNIT Canadian dollar
MAJOR LANGUAGES English, French
MAJOR RELIGIONS Protestantism, Roman Catholicism

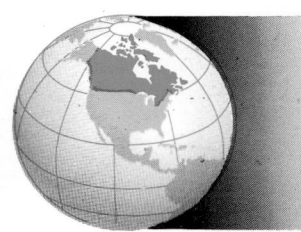

Population Distribution

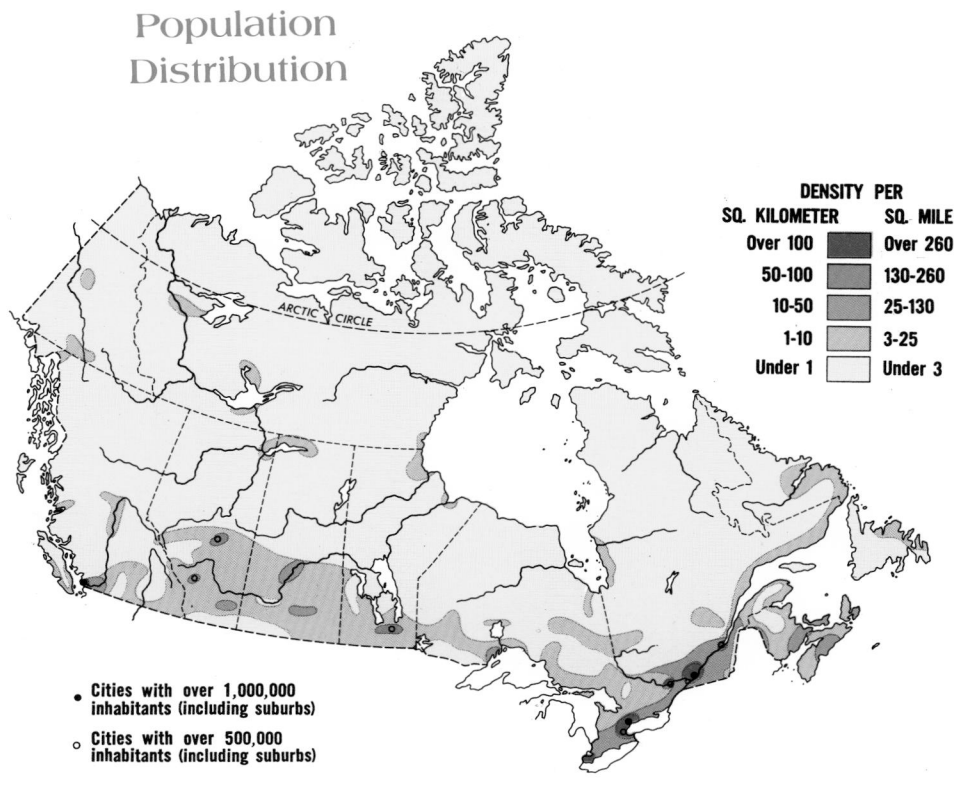

DENSITY PER

SQ. KILOMETER	SQ. MILE
Over 100	Over 260
50-100	130-260
10-50	25-130
1-10	3-25
Under 1	Under 3

• Cities with over 1,000,000 inhabitants (including suburbs)

○ Cities with over 500,000 inhabitants (including suburbs)

Vegetation

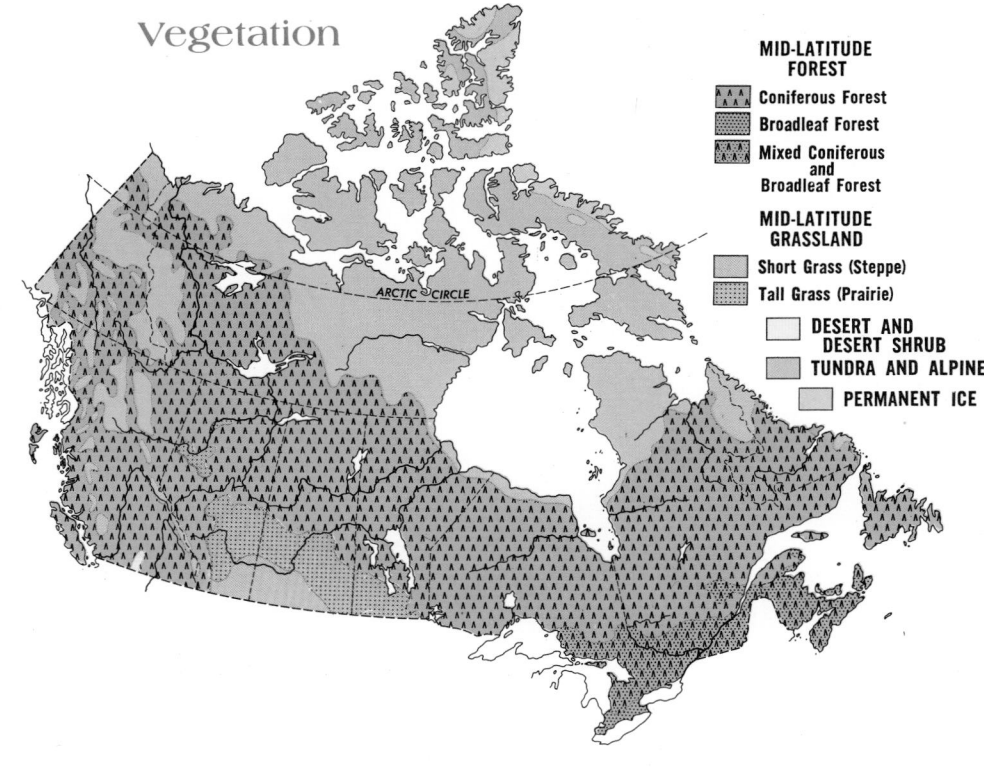

MID-LATITUDE FOREST
Coniferous Forest
Broadleaf Forest
Mixed Coniferous and Broadleaf Forest

MID-LATITUDE GRASSLAND
Short Grass (Steppe)
Tall Grass (Prairie)

DESERT AND DESERT SHRUB
TUNDRA AND ALPINE
PERMANENT ICE

Average January Temperature

FAHRENHEIT CELSIUS
Over 32° Over 0°
14° to 32° -10° to 0°
-4° to 14° -20° to -10°
-22° to -4° -30° to -20°
Under -22° Under -30°
Winnipeg -2
Average January temperature in degrees Fahrenheit at selected stations
ARCTIC CIRCLE
Resolute Bay -26°
Dawson -18°
Baker Lake -27°
Frobisher Bay -16°
Inoucdjouac -13°
Edmonton 5°
Vancouver 39°
Kamloops 21°
Winnipeg -2°
Thunder Bay 7°
Québec 9°
Gander 21°
Montréal 16°
Toronto 25°

Average July Temperature

FAHRENHEIT CELSIUS
Over 68° Over 20°
50° to 68° 10° to 20°
Under 50° Under 10°
Winnipeg 66°
Average July temperature in degrees Fahrenheit at selected stations
ARCTIC CIRCLE
Resolute Bay 40°
Dawson 60°
Baker Lake 51°
Frobisher Bay 46°
Inoucdjouac 48°
Edmonton 61°
Vancouver 59°
Kamloops 70°
Winnipeg 66°
Thunder Bay 64°
Québec 66°
Gander 62°
Montréal 71°
Toronto 72°

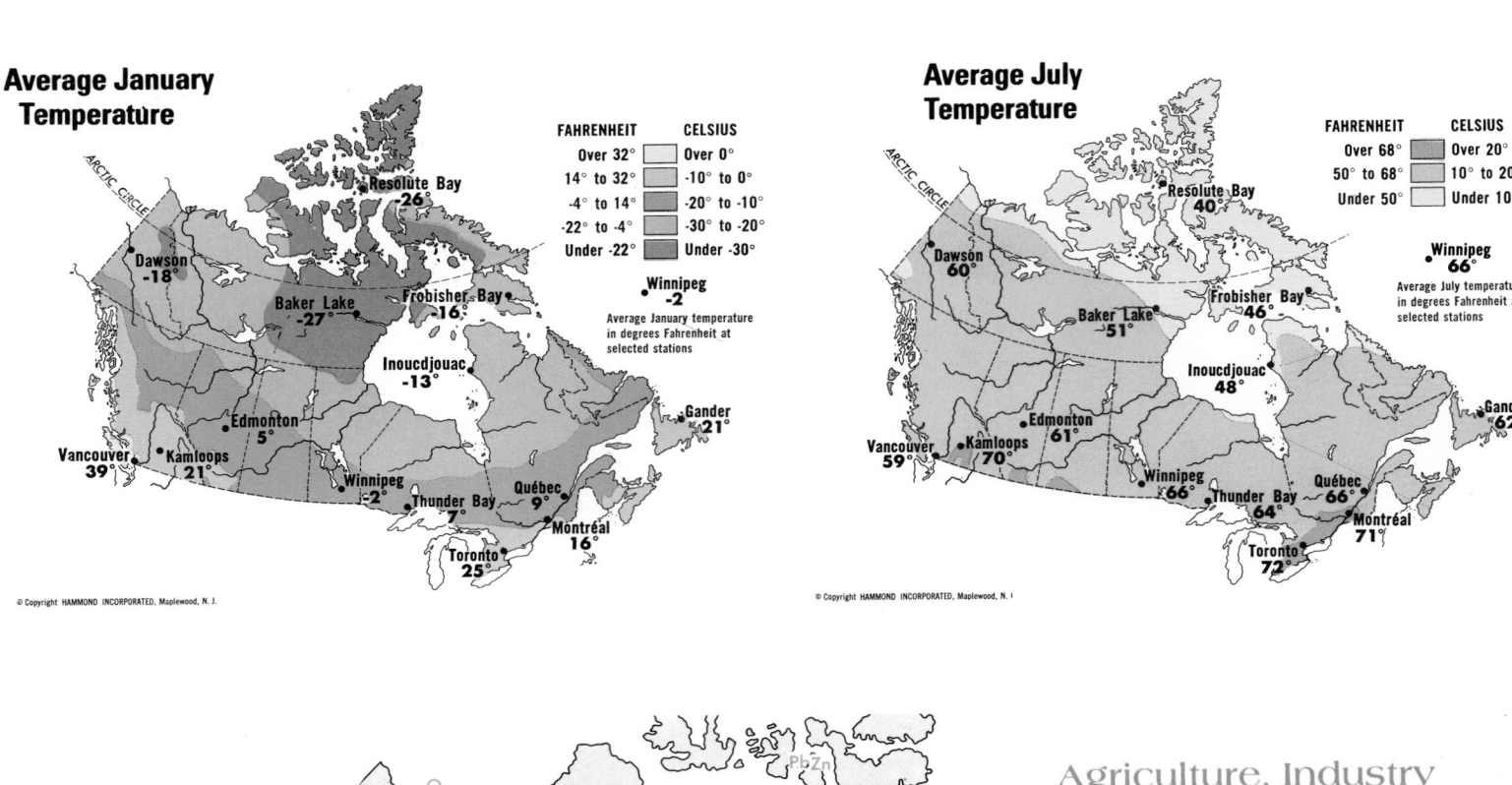

Agriculture, Industry and Resources

Salmon
Herring
Whales
Seals
Cod
Sheep
Wheat
Oats
Rye
Flax
Furs
Timber
Cattle
Dairy
Vancouver
Edmonton
Calgary
Winnipeg
Québec
Montréal
Toronto
Windsor

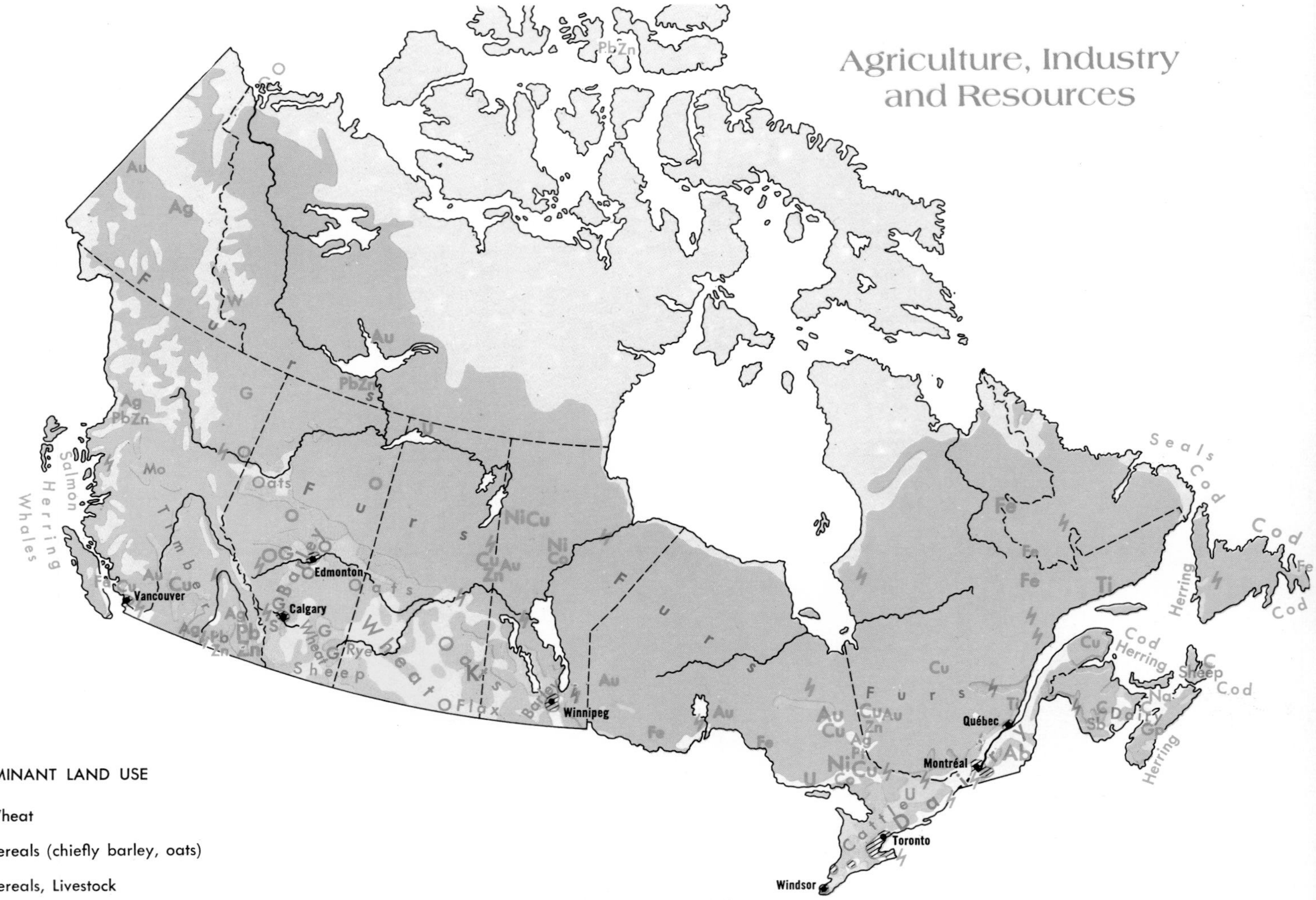

DOMINANT LAND USE

- Wheat
- Cereals (chiefly barley, oats)
- Cereals, Livestock
- General Farming, Livestock
- Dairy
- Fruit, Vegetables
- Pasture Livestock
- Range Livestock
- Forests
- Nonagricultural Land

MAJOR MINERAL OCCURRENCES

Ab	Asbestos	Fe	Iron Ore	Ni	Nickel	Sb	Antimony
Ag	Silver	G	Natural Gas	O	Petroleum	Ti	Titanium
Au	Gold	Gp	Gypsum	Pb	Lead	U	Uranium
C	Coal	K	Potash	Pt	Platinum	W	Tungsten
Co	Cobalt	Mo	Molybdenum	S	Sulfur	Zn	Zinc
Cu	Copper	Na	Salt				

- Water Power
- Major Industrial Areas

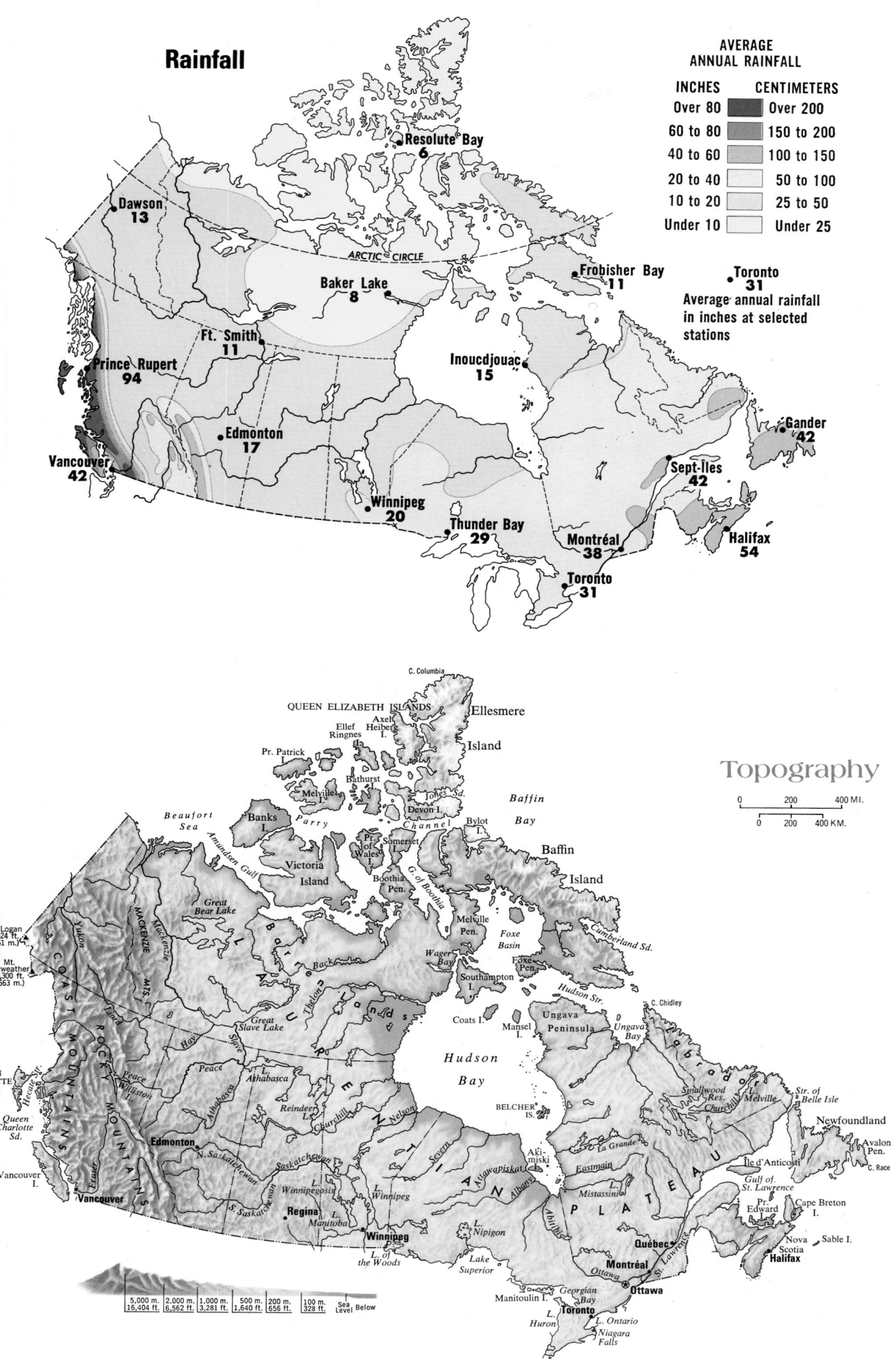

Rainfall

Resolute Bay
6

Dawson
13

ARCTIC CIRCLE

Frobisher Bay
11

Toronto
31
Average annual rainfall
in inches at selected
stations

Baker Lake
8

Ft. Smith
11

Prince Rupert
94

Inoucdjouac
15

Gander
42

Edmonton
17

Vancouver
42

Sept-Îles
42

Winnipeg
20

Thunder Bay
29

Montréal
38

Halifax
54

Toronto
31

Topography

0   200   400 MI.

0   200   400 KM.

C. Columbia

QUEEN ELIZABETH ISLANDS

Ellesmere

Axel
Heiberg
I.

Ellef
Ringnes

Island

Pr. Patrick
I.

Bathurst

Baffin

Melville
I.

Jones Sd.
Devon I.

Bay

Beaufort
Sea

Banks
I.

Parry   Channel

Bylot
I.

Amundsen Gulf

Pr.
of
Wales I.

Somerset
I.

Baffin

Victoria

Island

Boothia
Pen.

Island

Mt. Logan
19,524 ft.
(5951 m.)

Great
Bear Lake

G. of Boothia

Melville
Pen.

Foxe
Basin

Cumberland Sd.

Mt.
Fairweather
15,300 ft.
(4663 m.)

MACKENZIE MTS.

Back

Wager
Bay

Foxe
Pen.

Great
Slave Lake

Southampton
I.

Hudson Str.

C. Chidley

QUEEN
CHARLOTTE
IS.

Peace
Williston

Peace

Athabasca

Coats I.

Mansel
I.

Ungava
Peninsula

Ungava
Bay

Queen
Charlotte
Sd.

Reindeer

Athabasca

Churchill

Nelson

Hudson

Bay

Smallwood
Res.

L.
Melville

Str. of
Belle Isle

Newfoundland

Edmonton

N. Saskatchewan

Seven

BELCHER
IS.

La Grande

Churchill

Avalon
Pen.

Vancouver
I.

Saskatchewan

Akimiski
I.

Eastmain

C. Race

Vancouver

Winnipegosis

Attawapiskat

Albany

Mistassini

Gulf of
St. Lawrence

Île d'Anticosti

Regina
Manitoba

L.
Winnipeg

Pr.
Edward
I.

Cape Breton
I.

Winnipeg

L. of
the Woods

L.
Nipigon

Abitibi

PLATEAU

Québec

St. Lawrence

Nova
Scotia

Sable I.

Montréal

Halifax

Lake
Superior

Georgian
Bay

Ottawa

Ottawa

Manitoulin I.

Toronto

L. Ontario

L.
Huron

Niagara
Falls

5,000 m.
16,404 ft. | 2,000 m.
6,562 ft. | 1,000 m.
3,281 ft. | 500 m.
1,640 ft. | 200 m.
656 ft. | 100 m.
328 ft. | Sea
Level | Below

Newfoundland
including Labrador

SCALE
0 25 50 100 150 MI.
0 25 50 100 150 KM.

Capitals of Provinces .... ⊛
Provincial Boundaries ....
Provincial Boundary according to
Imperial Privy Council decision, 1927 ....

Scale 1:5,200,000

NEWFOUNDLAND

CITIES and TOWNS

Admiral's Beach 362 D2
Admiral's Cove 99 D2
Anchor Point 368 C3
Aquaforte 200 D2
Argentia 93 C2
Arnold's Cove 1,124 C2
Avondale 890 D2
Badger 1,090 C4
Badger's Quay-Valleyfield-Pool's Island 1,566 D4
Baie Verte 2,491 C4
Battle Harbour C3
Bauline 423 D2
Bay Bulls 1,081 D2
Bay de Verde 786 D2
Bay L'Argent 483 D4
Bay Roberts 4,512 D2
Bellburns 147 C3
Belleoram 565 C4
Bellevue 286 D2
Bide Arm 339 C3
Big Pond 167 D2
Birchy Bay 707 D4
Bird Cove 400 C3
Bishop's Falls 4,395 C4
Black Tickle 194 C3
Blackhead Road 1,855 D2
Blaketown 617 D2
Bloomfield 715 D2
Bonavista 4,460 D2
Botwood 4,074 C4
Branch 462 D2
Brigus 898 D2
Broad Cove 198 D2
Brooklyn 197 D2
Brownsdale 199 D2
Buchans 1,655 C4
Bunyan's Cove 590 C4
Burgeo 2,504 C4
Burin 2,904 C4
Burnt Islands 991 C4
Burnt Point 260 D2
Calvert 482 D2
Campbellton 703 D4
Cape Broyle 698 D2
Cape Ray 484 C4
Caplin Cove 150 D2
Carbonear 5,335 D2
Carmanville 966 D4
Cartwright 658 C3
Catalina 1,162 D2
Cavendish 343 D2
Champney's West 141 D2
Chance Cove 498 D2
Change Islands 580 D4
Channel-Port aux Basques 5,988 C4
Chapel Arm 689 D2
Charlottetown 330 D2
Charlottetown 250 C3
Churchill Falls 936 B3
Clarenville 2,878 C2
Clarke's Beach 1,009 D2
Codroy 346 C4
Colinet 318 D2
Colliers 819 D2
Come By Chance 337 C2
Conception Harbour 917 D2
Conche 464 C3
Cook's Harbour 388 C3
Corner Brook 24,339 C4
Cow Head 695 C4
Cox's Cove 980 C4
Cupids 706 D2
Daniell's Harbour 614 C3
Dark Cove 1,344 D4
Davis Inlet 240 B2
Deep Bight 243 C2
Deer Lake 4,348 C4
Dildo 877 D2
Dunville 1,817 D2
Durrell 1,145 D4
Eastport 597 D1
Elliston 527 D2
Embree 846 C4
Englee 998 C3
English Harbour 118 D2
English Harbour West 327 C4
Fermeuse 584 D2
Ferryland 795 D2
Flat Bay 322 C4
Flat Rock 808 D2
Fleur de Lys 616 C3
Flowers Cove 459 C3
Fogo 1,105 D4
Forteau 520 C3
Fortune 2,473 C4
Fox Harbour 280 C3
Fox Harbour 538 D2
François 219 C4
Freshwater 1,276 C2
Freshwater 209 D2
Gambo 2,932 D4
Gander 10,404 D4
Garnish 761 C4
Gaskiers-Point la Haye 505 D2
Gaultois 558 C4
Georges Brook 356 D2
Glenwood 1,129 D4
Glovertown 2,165 C1
Goobies 185 D2
Goose Bay-Happy Valley 7,103 B3
Gooseberry Cove 195 C2
Goose Cove 134 C2
Goose Cove 368 C3
Goulds 4,242 D2
Grand Bank 3,901 C4
Grand Falls 8,765 C4
Grates Cove 275 D2
Green Island Cove 222 C3
Green's Harbour 785 D2
Greenspond 423 D4
Grey River 234 C4
Gull Island 362 D2
Hampden 838 C4
Hant's Harbour 542 D2
Happy Adventure 352 D2
Happy Valley-Goose Bay 7,103 B3
Harbour Breton 2,464 C4
Harbour Deep 278 C3
Harbour Grace 2,988 D2
Harbour Main-Chapel Cove-Lakeview 1,303 D2
Hare Bay 1,520 D4
Hawke's Bay 553 C3
Head of Bay d'Espoir 586 C4
Heart's Content 625 D2
Heart's Delight-Islington 899 D2
Heart's Desire 416 D2
Heatherton 328 C4
Hermitage 863 C4
Hickman's Harbour 479 D2
Hillview 295 D2
Hodge's Cove 438 D2
Holyrood 1,789 D2
Hopedale 425 B2
Howley 456 C4
Isle aux Morts 1,238 C4
Jackson's Arm 623 C4
Jeffrey's 276 C4
Jerseyside 641 B3
Job's Cove 201 D2
Joe Batt's Arm-Barr'd Islands 1,155 D4
Keels 129 D1
Kelligrews (Foxtrap-Greeleytown-Peachtown-Kelligrews) 2,292 D2
Kilbride 5,014 D2
King's Cove 253 D1
King's Point 825 C4
Kippens 1,219 C4
Labrador City 11,538 A3
Lamaline 548 C4
L'Anse-au-Clair 267 C3
L'Anse-au-Loup 589 C3
L'Anse au Meadow 66 C3
La Poile 186 C4
Lark Harbour 783 C4
La Scie 1,422 C4
Lawn 999 C4
Lethbridge 686 D2
Lewisporte 3,963 C4
Little Bay Islands 407 C4
Little Catalina 750 D2
Little Heart's Ease 467 D2
Lodge Bay 124 C3
Long Harbour-Mount Arlington Heights 660 D2
Lourdes 932 C4
Lower Island Cove 415 D2
Lumsden 645 D4
Main Brook 514 C3
Makkovik 347 C2
Markland 344 D2
Mary's Harbour 408 C3
Marystown 6,299 D4
McCallum 243 C4
Melrose 416 D2
Middle Arm, Green Bay 575 C4
Millertown 228 C4
Milltown-Head of Bay d'Espoir 1,376 C4
Milton 258 C2
Mobile 171 D2
Mount Carmel-Mitchell's Brook-St. Catherine's 699 D2
Mount Pearl 11,543 D2
Musgrave Harbour 1,554 D4
Musgravetown 635 C2
Nain 938 B2
New Bonaventure 106 D2
New Chelsea 144 D2
New Harbour 777 D2
Newmans Cove 231 D2
New Perlican 350 D2
Newtown 511 D4
Nippers Harbour 259 C4
Norman's Cove-Long Cove 1,152 D2
Norris Arm 1,216 C4
Norris Point 1,033 C4
North Harbour 151 D2
North River 245 D2
North West Brook 279 C2
North West River 515 B3
O'Donnells 280 D2
Old Bonaventure 111 D2
Old Perlican 709 D2
Paradise 2,861 D2
Parkers Cove 424 D4
Parson's Pond 605 C3
Pasadena 2,685 C4
Patrick's Cove 155 C2
Perry's Cove 141 D2
Peterview 1,119 C4
Petites 108 C4
Petley 147 D2
Petty Harbour-Maddox Cove 853 D2
Picadilly 524 C4
Pinware River 201 C3
Placentia 2,204 C2
Plate Cove 474 D2
Point La Haye 195 D2
Point Lance 141 C2
Point Leamington 848 C4
Point Verde 296 C2
Pollards Point 502 C4
Port au Bras 366 D4
Port au Choix 1,311 C3
Port au Port 603 C4
Port Blandford 702 C2
Port Hope Simpson 581 C3
Port Kirwan 164 D2
Port Rexton 489 D2
Port Saunders 769 C3
Portugal Cove 2,361 D2
Portugal Cove South 371 D2
Port Union 671 D2
Postville 223 B3
Pouch Cove 1,522 D2
Princeton 204 D2
Raleigh 373 C3
Ramea 1,386 C4
Red Bay 316 C3
Red Head Cove 225 D2
Rencontre East 230 C4
Renews-Cappahayden 578 D2
Rigolet 271 C3
Riverhead 431 D2
River of Ponds 304 C3
Robert's Arm 1,005 C4
Rocky Harbour 1,273 C4
Roddickton 1,142 C3
Rose Blanche-Harbour le Cou 975 C4
Rushoon 520 D4
Saint Alban's 1,968 C4
Saint Andrew's 262 C4
Saint Anthony 3,107 C3
Saint Brendan's 468 D4
Saint Bride's 599 C2
Saint George's 1,756 C4
St. John's (cap.) 83,770 D2
Saint Joseph's 262 D2
Saint Lawrence 2,012 C4
Saint Lunaire-Griquet 1,010 C3
Saint Mary's 701 D2
Saint Paul's 454 C4
Saint Phillips 1,365 D2
Saint Shotts 239 D2
Saint Vincent's-Saint Stephens-Peter's River 796 D2
Sally's Cove 100 C4
Salmon Cove 786 D2
Seal Cove 751 C3
Seal Cove-White Bay 498 C4
Seldom-Little Seldom 560 D4
Ship Harbour 265 D2
Shoal Cove 223 C3
Shoal Harbour 1,000 C2
South Branch 264 C4
South Brook, Hall's Bay Dist. 786 C4
South Brook, Humber Dist. 477 C4
Southern Harbour 772 C2
South River 645 D2
Spaniard's Bay 2,125 D2
Springdale 3,501 C4
Stephenville 8,876 C4
Stephenville Crossing 2,172 C4
Summerford 1,198 C4
Summerville 346 D2
Sunnyside 703 D2
Sweet Bay 204 D2
Swift Current 329 C2
Terrenceville 796 D4
Tilting 427 D4
Torbay 3,394 D2
Tors Cove 355 D2
Traytown 383 D1
Trepassey 1,473 D2
Trinity 522 D2
Trinity 375 D4
Trout River 759 C4
Twillingate 1,506 C4
Upper Island Cove 2,025 D2
Victoria 1,870 D2
Wabana 4,254 D2
Wabush 3,155 A3
Wesleyville 1,125 D4
Western Bay 463 D2
West Saint Modeste 273 C3
Whitbourne 1,233 D2
Wild Cove 152 C3
Windsor 5,747 C4
Winterton 753 D2
Witless Bay 907 D2

OTHER FEATURES

Alexis (riv.) C3
Anguille (cape) C4
Annieopscotch (mts.) C4
Ashuanipi (lake) A3
Ashuanipi (riv.) A3
Atikonak (lake) B3
Attikamagen (lake) A3
Avalon (pen.) D2
Barachois Pond Prov. Park C4
Bauld (cape) C3
Bell (isl.) C3
Bell (isl.) D2
Belle Isle (isl.) C3
Belle Isle (str.) C3
Blackhead (bay) D2
Bonavista (bay) D1
Bonavista (cape) D1
Bonne (bay) C4
Branch (riv.) C2
Broyle (cape) D2
Bull Arm (inlet) D2
Burin (pen.) C4
Butter Pot Prov. Park D2
Cabot (str.) B4
Canada (bay) C3
Chidley (cape) B1
Churchill (falls) B3
Churchill (riv.) B3
Cirque (mt.) B2
Clode (sound) D2
Conception (bay) D2
Deep (inlet) B2
Double Mer (lake) C3
Dyke (lake) A3
Eagle (riv.) C3
Espoir (bay) C4
Exploits (riv.) C4
Fogo (isl.) D4
Fortune (bay) C4
Freels (cape) D3
Gander (lake) D4
Gander (riv.) D4
Glover (isl.) C4
Goose (riv.) B3
Grand (lake) B3
Grand (lake) C4
Grates (pt.) D2
Great Colinet (isl.) D2
Grey (isls.) C3
Groais (isl.) C3
Gros Morne (mt.) C4
Gros Morne Nat'l Park C4
Groswater (bay) C3
Hamilton (inlet) C3
Hamilton (sound) D4
Hare (bay) C3
Hawke (hills) D2
Hebron (fjord) B2
Hermitage (bay) C4
Holyrood (bay) D2
Horse (isls.) C3
Horse Chops (head) D2
Humber (riv.) C4
Ingornachoix (bay) C3
Ireland's Eye (isl.) D2
Islands (bay) C4
Kaipokok (bay) B2
Kanairiktok (riv.) B3
Kaumajet (mts.) B2
Kingurutik (mesa) B2
Labrador (reg.) B2
Labrador (sea) C2
La Manche Valley Prov. Park D2
La Poile (bay) C4
Little Mecatina (riv.) B3
Long (isl.) C4
Long (lake) A3
Long (pt.) C4
Long Range (mts.) C4
Main Topsail (mt.) C4
Makkovik (cape) C2
McLelan (str.) B1
Mealy (lake) C3
Meelpaeg (lake) C4
Melville (lake) C3
Menihek (lakes) A3
Merasheen (isl.) C2
Mistaken (pt.) D2
Mistastin (lake) B2
Nachvak (fjord) B2
Naskaupi (riv.) B3
Newfoundland (isl.) C4
Newman (sound) D2
New World (isl.) C4
Norman (cape) C3
North Aulatsivik (isl.) B2
Notre Dame (bay) C4
Okak (bay) B2
Ossokmanuan (res.) B3
Petitsikapau (lake) A3
Pine (cape) D2
Pinware (riv.) C3
Pistolet (bay) C3
Placentia (bay) C2
Ponds (isl.) C3
Port au Port (bay) C4
Port au Port (pen.) C4
Port Manvers (harb.) B2
Race (cape) D2
Ramah (bay) B2
Ramea (isls.) C4
Random (isl.) D2
Random (sound) D2
Ray (cape) C4
Red (isl.) C2
Red Indian (lake) C4
Red Wine (riv.) B3
Rocky (riv.) D2
Round (pond) C4
Saglek (bay) B2
Saint Francis (cape) D2
Saint George (cape) C4
Saint George's (bay) C4
Saint John (bay) C3
Saint John (cape) C3
Saint Lawrence (gulf) B4
Saint Lewis (cape) C3
Saint Mary's (bay) C2
Saint Mary's (cape) C2
Saint Michaels (bay) C3
Salmonier (riv.) D2
Sandwich (bay) C3
Shabogamo (lake) A3
Shoal (bay) D2
Smallwood (res.) B3
Smith (sound) D2
South Aulatsivik (isl.) B2
Spear (cape) D2
Squires Mem. Park C4
Swale (isl.) D1
Terra Nova (riv.) C2
Terra Nova Nat'l Park D2
Territok (cape) B2
Thoresby (mt.) B2
Torbay (pt.) D2
Torngat (mts.) B2
Trespassey (bay) D2
Trinity (bay) D2
Tunungayualok (isl.) B2
Ukasiksalik (isl.) B2
Victoria (lake) C4
White (bay) C3
White Bear (lake) C4
White Handkerchief (cape) B2

SAINT PIERRE and MIQUELON

CITIES and TOWNS

Saint-Pierre (cap.) 5,415 C4

OTHER FEATURES

Miquelon (isl.) 626 C4
Saint Pierre (isl.) 5,415 C4

AREA 156,184 sq. mi. (404,517 sq. km.)
POPULATION 567,681
CAPITAL St. John's
LARGEST CITY St. John's
HIGHEST POINT in Torngat Mountains 5,420 ft. (1,652 m.)
SETTLED IN 1610
ADMITTED TO CONFEDERATION 1949
PROVINCIAL FLOWER Pitcher Plant

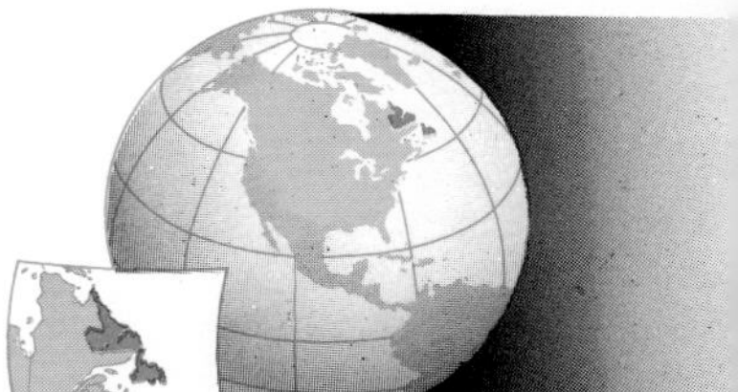

Agriculture, Industry and Resources

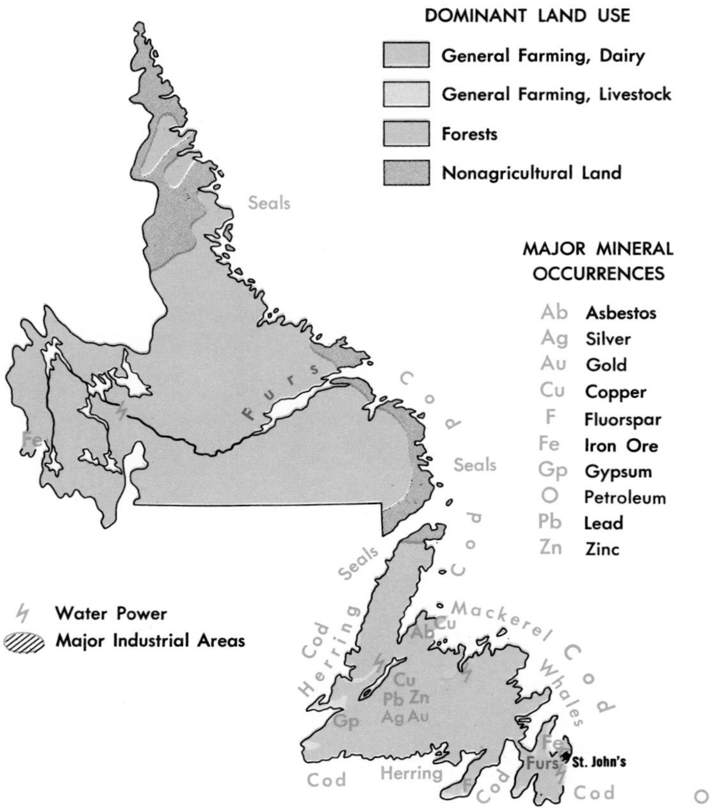
DOMINANT LAND USE
General Farming, Dairy
General Farming, Livestock
Forests
Nonagricultural Land
MAJOR MINERAL OCCURRENCES
Ab Asbestos
Ag Silver
Au Gold
Cu Copper
F Fluorspar
Fe Iron Ore
Gp Gypsum
O Petroleum
Pb Lead
Zn Zinc
Water Power
Major Industrial Areas
Seals
Furs
Fe
Cod
Seals
Seals
Cod
Mackerel
Herring
Whales
Ab
Cu
Cu
Pb Zn
Ag Au
Gp
Fe
Furs
St. John's
Herring
Cod
O

Topography

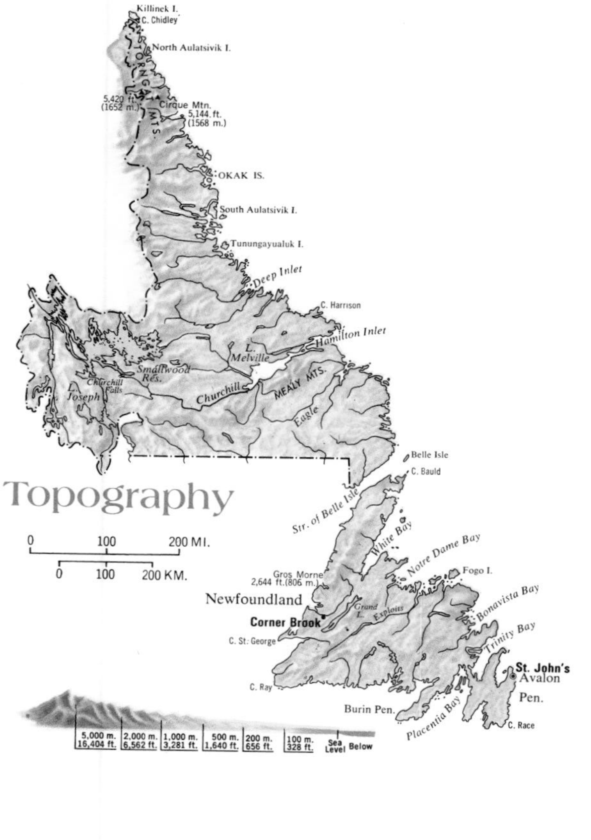
Killinek I.
C. Chidley
North Aulatsivik I.
5,420 ft. (1652 m.)
Cirque Mtn. 5,144 ft. (1568 m.)
OKAK IS.
South Aulatsivik I.
Tunungayualuk I.
Deep Inlet
C. Harrison
Hamilton Inlet
L. Melville
Smallwood Res.
Churchill Falls
MEALY MTS.
Churchill
Eagle
Belle Isle
C. Bauld
Str. of Belle Isle
White Bay
Notre Dame Bay
Fogo I.
Gros Morne 2,644 ft. (806 m.)
Newfoundland
Corner Brook
C. St. George
Bonavista Bay
Trinity Bay
St. John's
Avalon Pen.
C. Ray
Burin Pen.
Placentia Bay
C. Race
0 100 200 MI.
0 100 200 KM.
5,000 m. 16,404 ft.
2,000 m. 6,562 ft.
1,000 m. 3,281 ft.
500 m. 1,640 ft.
200 m. 656 ft.
100 m. 328 ft.
Sea Level
Below

NOVA SCOTIA

COUNTIES

Annapolis 22,522	C 4
Antigonish 18,110	F 3
Cape Breton 127,035	H 3
Colchester 43,224	D 3
Cumberland 35,231	D 3
Digby 21,689	C 4
Guysborough 12,752	F 3
Halifax 288,126	E 4
Hants 33,121	D 4
Inverness 22,337	G 2
Kings 49,739	D 4
Lunenburg 45,746	D 4
Pictou 50,350	F 3
Queens 13,126	D 4
Richmond 12,284	H 3
Shelburne 17,328	C 5
Victoria 8,432	H 2
Yarmouth 26,290	C 5

CITIES and TOWNS

Alder Point 651	H 2
Aldershot	D 3
Amherst⊛ 9,684	D 3
Annapolis Royal⊛ 631	C 4
Antigonish⊛ 5,205	F 3
Arichat 824	H 3
Aylesford 744	D 3
Baddeck⊛ 972	H 2
Barrington Passage 722	C 5
Bear River-Sissiboo 854	C 4
Beaverbank 1,322	E 4
Berwick 1,699	D 4
Bridgetown 1,047	C 4
Bridgewater 6,669	D 4
Brookfield 619	E 3
Brooklyn 1,269	C 4
Cambridge Station 799	D 3
Canning 763	D 3
Canso 1,255	H 3
Centreville 765	D 3
Chéticamp 1,022	G 2

Chester 1,131	D 4
Chester Basin 639	D 4
Church Point 318	B 4
Clark's Harbour 1,059	C 5
Coldbrook Station 617	D 3
Cow Bay 670	E 4
Dartmouth 62,277	E 4
Debert 618	E 3
Digby⊛ 2,558	C 4
Dominion 2,856	J 2
Donkin 873	J 2
Ellershouse-Hartville 662	D 4
Elmsdale 1,172	E 4
Enfield 1,510	E 4
Fall River 1,897	E 4
Falmouth 1,110	D 3
Glace Bay 21,466	J 2
Guysborough⊛ 496	G 3
Halifax (cap.)⊛ 114,594	E 4
Halifax *277,727	E 4
Hantsport 1,395	D 3
Herring Cove 1,323	E 4
Hilden 1,262	E 3

Ingonish 471	H 2
Inverness 2,013	G 2
Judique 925	G 3
Kentville⊛ 4,974	D 3
Kingston 1,612	D 4
Lakeside 936	E 4
Lantz 1,172	E 4
Liverpool⊛ 3,304	D 4
Lockeport 929	C 5
Louisbourg 1,410	J 2
Louisdale 979	G 3
Lower West Pubnico 790	C 5
Lunenburg⊛ 3,014	D 4
Mahone Bay 1,228	D 4
Meteghan 890	B 4
Middleton 1,834	C 4
Milford Station 748	E 3
Milton 1,678	D 4
Mount Uniacke 1,145	E 4
Mulgrave 1,099	G 3
Musquodoboit Harbour 936	E 4
New Glasgow 10,464	F 3
New Victoria 1,374	H 2

New Waterford 8,808	J 2
North Sydney 7,820	H 2
Oxford 1,470	E 3
Parrsboro 1,799	D 3
Pictou⊛ 4,628	F 3
Porters Lake 893	E 4
Port Hastings 312	G 3
Port Hawkesbury 3,850	G 3
Port Hood⊛ 701	G 2
Port Morien 717	J 2
Port Williams 1,227	D 3
Prospect 693	E 4
Pugwash 648	E 3
Reserve Mines 2,472	J 2
River Hébert 835	D 3
Saint Peters 669	H 3
Sandy Point 691	C 5
Scotchtown 2,037	J 2
Sheet Harbour 819	F 4
Shelburne⊛ 2,303	C 5
Shubenacadie 984	E 3
Springhill 4,896	E 3
Stellarton 5,435	F 3

Stewiacke 1,174	E 3
Sydney⊛ 29,444	H 2
Sydney Mines 8,501	H 2
Terence Bay 960	E 4
Thorburn 1,014	F 3
Three Mile Plains 1,355	D 4
Timberlea 1,159	E 4
Trenton 3,154	F 3
Truro⊛ 12,552	E 3
Waterville 687	D 3
Waverley 1,699	E 4
Wedgeport 827	C 5
Western Shore 1,712	D 4
Westmount 3,097	H 2
Westville 4,522	F 3
Wileville 746	D 4
Windsor⊛ 3,646	D 3
Wolfville 3,235	D 3
Yarmouth⊛ 7,475	B 5

OTHER FEATURES

Advocate (bay)	D 3

Ainslie (lake)	G 2
Amet (sound)	E 3
Andrew (isl.)	H 3
Annapolis (basin)	C 4
Annapolis (riv.)	C 4
Antigonish (harb.)	G 3
Argos (cape)	G 3
Aspy (bay)	H 2
Avon (riv.)	D 4
Baccaro (pt.)	C 5
Baddeck (riv.)	H 2
Barachois (pt.)	E 4
Barren (isl.)	C 5
Barren (pt.)	D 4
Barrington (bay)	C 5
Bedford (basin)	E 4
Berry (head)	G 3
Boularderie (isl.)	H 2
Bras d'Or (lake)	H 3
Breton (cape)	J 3
Brier (isl.)	B 4
Canso (cape)	H 3
Canso (str.)	G 3
Cap d'Or (cape)	D 3

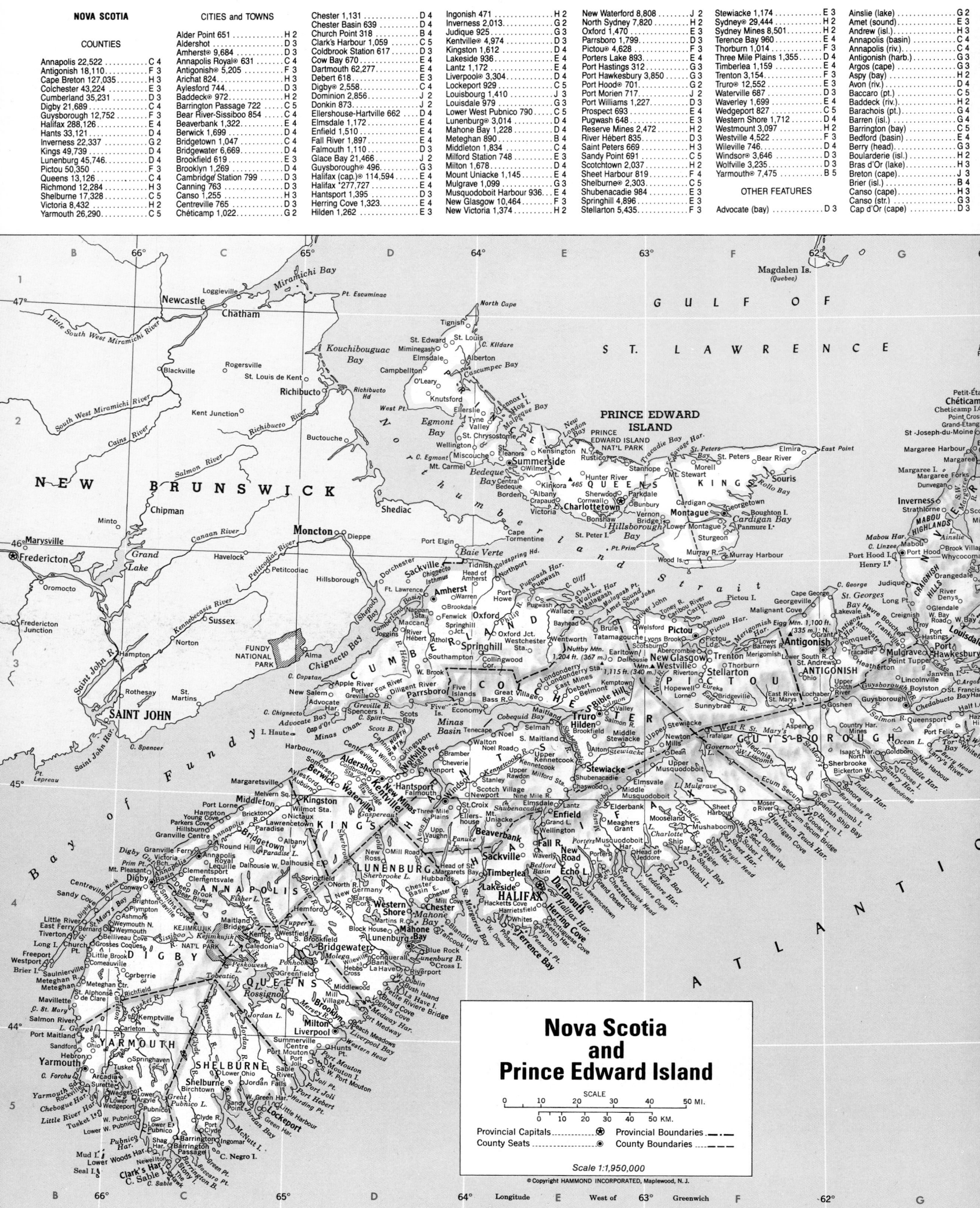

Nova Scotia and Prince Edward Island

SCALE

0 10 20 30 40 50 MI.

0 10 20 30 40 50 KM.

Provincial Capitals ⊛ Provincial Boundaries _·_·_

County Seats ⊙ County Boundaries _ _ _ _

Scale 1:1,950,000

© Copyright HAMMOND INCORPORATED, Maplewood, N. J.

PRINCE EDWARD ISLAND

AREA 2,184 sq. mi. (5,657 sq. km.)
POPULATION 122,506
CAPITAL Charlottetown
LARGEST CITY Charlottetown
HIGHEST POINT 465 ft. (142 m.)
SETTLED IN 1720
ADMITTED TO CONFEDERATION 1873
PROVINCIAL FLOWER Lady's Slipper

NOVA SCOTIA

AREA 21,425 sq. mi. (55,491 sq. km.)
POPULATION 847,442
CAPITAL Halifax
LARGEST CITY Halifax
HIGHEST POINT Cape Breton Highlands
  1,747 ft. (532 m.)
SETTLED IN 1605
ADMITTED TO CONFEDERATION 1867
PROVINCIAL FLOWER Trailing Arbutus or
  Mayflower

Topography

0 30 60 MI.
0 30 60 KM.

Below Sea 100 m. 200 m. 500 m. 1,000 m. 2,000 m. 5,000 m.
Level 328 ft. 656 ft. 1,640 ft. 3,281 ft. 6,562 ft. 16,404 ft.

Agriculture, Industry and Resources

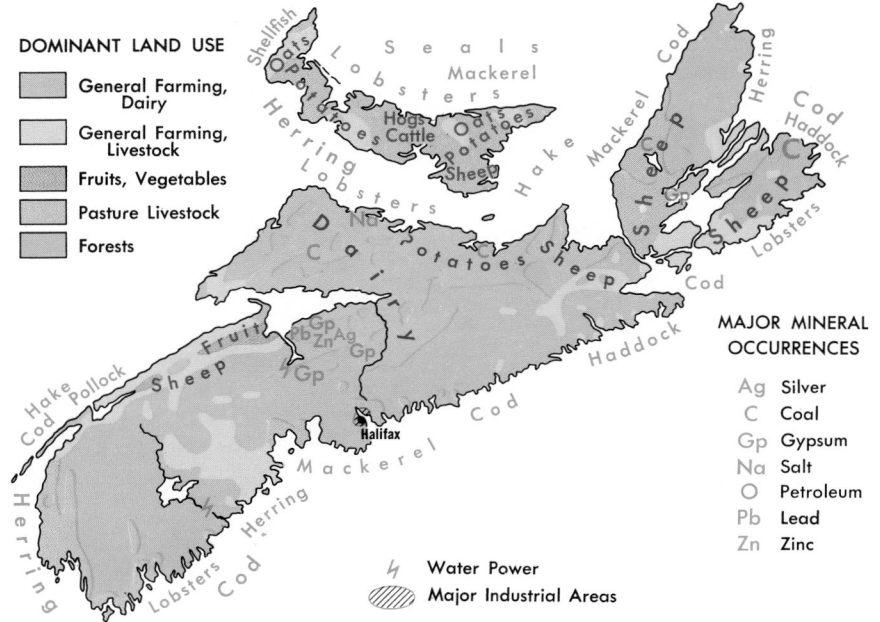

DOMINANT LAND USE

- General Farming, Dairy
- General Farming, Livestock
- Fruits, Vegetables
- Pasture Livestock
- Forests

MAJOR MINERAL OCCURRENCES

Ag Silver
C   Coal
Gp Gypsum
Na Salt
O   Petroleum
Pb Lead
Zn Zinc

⚡ Water Power
▨ Major Industrial Areas

COUNTIES

Albert 23,632	....	F 3
Carleton 24,659	....	C 2
Charlotte 26,571	....	C 3
Gloucester 86,156	....	E 1
Kent 30,799	....	E 2
King's 51,114	....	E 3
Madawaska 34,892	....	B 1
Northumberland 54,134	....	D 2
Queen's 12,485	....	D 3
Restigouche 40,593	....	C 1
Saint John 86,148	....	E 3
Sunbury 21,012	....	D 3
Victoria 20,815	....	C 1
Westmorland 107,640	....	F 2
York 74,213	....	C 3

CITIES and TOWNS

Acadie Siding 64	....	E 2
Acadieville 176	....	E 2
Adamsville 94	....	E 2
Albert Mines 120	....	F 3
Alcida 174	....	E 1
Aldouane 64	....	E 2
Allardville 478	....	E 1
Alma 329	....	F 3
Anagance 114	....	E 3
Anse-Bleue 562	....	E 1

Apohaqui 341	....	E 3
Argyle 63	....	C 2
Armstrong Brook 191	....	E 1
Aroostook 403	....	C 2
Arthurette 178	....	D 2
Astle 201	....	D 1
Atholville 1,694	....	D 1
Aulac 113	....	F 3
Back River 794	....	D 3
Baie-Sainte-Anne 709	....	F 1
Baie-Verte 175	....	F 2
Bairdsville 81	....	C 2
Baker Brook 527	....	B 1
Balmoral 1,823	....	D 1
Barachois 686	....	F 2
Barnaby River 38	....	E 2
Barnettville 117	....	E 2
Bartibog Bridge 122	....	E 1
Bas-Caraquet 1,859	....	F 1
Bass River 112	....	E 2
Bath 794	....	C 2
Bathurst⊙ 15,705	....	E 1
Bayfield 81	....	G 2
Bayside	....	C 3
Beaubois 211	....	F 2
Beaver Brook Station 95	....	E 1
Beaver Harbour 316	....	D 3
Beechwood 111	....	C 2
Beersville 52	....	E 2
Belledune 690	....	E 1

Bellefleur 83	....	C 1
Bellefond 243	....	E 1
Belleisle Creek 145	....	E 3
Benjamin River 171	....	D 1
Ben Lomond	....	E 3
Benton 101	....	C 3
Beresford 3,652	....	E 1
Berry Mills 238	....	E 2
Bertrand 1,268	....	E 1
Berwick 129	....	E 3
Black Point 131	....	D 1
Black River 150	....	E 3
Blacks Harbour 1,356	....	D 3
Blackville 892	....	E 2
Blissfield 119	....	D 2
Bloomfield Ridge 153	....	D 2
Bloomfield Station 62	....	E 3
Bocabec 34	....	C 3
Boiestown 299	....	D 2
Bonny River 153	....	D 3
Bossé 193	....	B 1
Bourgeois 215	....	F 2
Brantville 1,066	....	E 1
Breau-Village 293	....	F 2
Brest 343	....	E 1
Brewers Mills 199	....	C 2
Briggs Corner 89	....	D 3
Bristol 824	....	C 2
Brockway (Lower Brockway-Brockway) 97	....	C 3

Browns Flat 295	....	D 3
Buctouche 2,476	....	F 2
Burnsville 156	....	E 1
Burton⊙ 291	....	D 3
Burtts Corner 484	....	D 2
Cambridge-Narrows 433	....	E 3
Campbellton 9,818	....	D 1
Canaan 115	....	E 2
Canaan Forks 78	....	E 2
Canaan Road 86	....	E 2
Canterbury 474	....	C 3
Cap-Bateau 417	....	F 1
Cape Tormentine 229	....	G 2
Cap Lumière 262	....	F 2
Cap-Pelé 2,199	....	F 2
Caraquet 4,315	....	E 1
Carlingford 229	....	C 2
Carlisle 75	....	C 2
Caron Brook 171	....	B 1
Carrolls Crossing 119	....	D 2
Castalia 145	....	D 4
Central Blissville 155	....	D 3
Centre-Saint-Simon (St. Simon) 991	....	E 1
Centreville 577	....	C 2
Chance Harbour 63	....	D 3
Charlo 1,603	....	D 1
Chatham 6,779	....	E 1
Chatham Head	....	E 1
Chipman 1,829	....	E 2

Clair 915	....	B 1
Clarendon 80	....	D 3
Cliffordvale (Limestone-Cliffordvale) 69	....	C 2
Clifton 194	....	E 2
Coal Branch 90	....	E 2
Coal Creek 61	....	E 2
Cocagne Cape 278	....	F 2
Cocagne-Cocagne Sud 600	....	F 2
Codys 125	....	E 3
Coldstream 217	....	C 2
Coles Island 150	....	E 3
College Bridge 536	....	F 3
Collette 198	....	E 2
Connell 58	....	C 2
Connors 96	....	B 1
Cork 54	....	D 3
Cornhill 193	....	E 3
Coughlan 181	....	D 2
Cross Creek 192	....	D 2
Cumberland Bay 231	....	E 3
Dalhousie⊙ 4,958	....	D 1
Dalhousie Junction 105	....	D 1
Darlington 749	....	D 1
Daulnay 398	....	F 2
Dawsonville 278	....	C 1
Debec 200	....	C 2
Dieppe 8,511	....	F 2
Dipper Harbour 166	....	D 3
Doaktown 1,009	....	D 2

Dorchester⊙ 1,101	....	F 3
Dorchester Crossing 605	....	F 2
Douglastown 1,091	....	E 1
Drummond 849	....	C 1
Duguayville 337	....	E 1
Dumfries 150	....	C 3
Dupuis Corner 303	....	F 2
Durham Bridge 255	....	D 2
East Riverside-Kingshurst 989	....	E 3
Edmundston⊙ 12,044	....	B 1
Eel River Bridge 377	....	D 1
Eel River Crossing 1,431	....	D 1
Elgin 301	....	E 3
Enniskillen 63	....	D 3
Escuminac 194	....	F 1
Evandale 58	....	D 3
Evangeline 356	....	E 1
Everett 48	....	C 1
Fairfield 250	....	E 3
Fairhaven 142	....	C 4
Fairisle 415	....	E 1
Fairvale 3,960	....	E 3
Ferry Road 325	....	E 1
Fielding 197	....	C 2
Five Fingers 189	....	C 1
Flatlands 249	....	D 1
Florenceville 709	....	C 2
Forest City 25	....	C 3
Fosterville 58	....	C 3

Four Falls 69	....	C 2
Fredericton (cap.)⊛ 43,723	....	D 3
Fredericton Junction 711	....	D 3
Gagetown⊙ 618	....	E 3
Gardner Creek 56	....	E 3
Geary 654	....	D 3
Germantown 62	....	F 3
Gillespie 96	....	D 1
Glassville 147	....	C 2
Glencoe 147	....	D 1
Glenlivet 284	....	D 1
Gloucester Junction 36	....	E 1
Gondola Point 3,076	....	E 3
Grafton 385	....	C 2
Grand Bay 3,173	....	D 3
Grande-Anse 817	....	E 1
Grand Falls 6,203	....	C 1
Grand Falls Hill 152	....	C 1
Grand Harbour 614	....	D 4
Gray Rapids 266	....	E 2
Hammondvale 72	....	E 3
Hampstead 87	....	D 3
Hampton⊙ 3,141	....	E 3
Harcourt 127	....	E 2
Hardwicke 114	....	E 1
Hardwood Ridge 191	....	D 2
Hartland 846	....	C 2
Harvey, Albert 58	....	F 3
Harvey, York 356	....	D 3
Hatfield Point 176	....	E 3

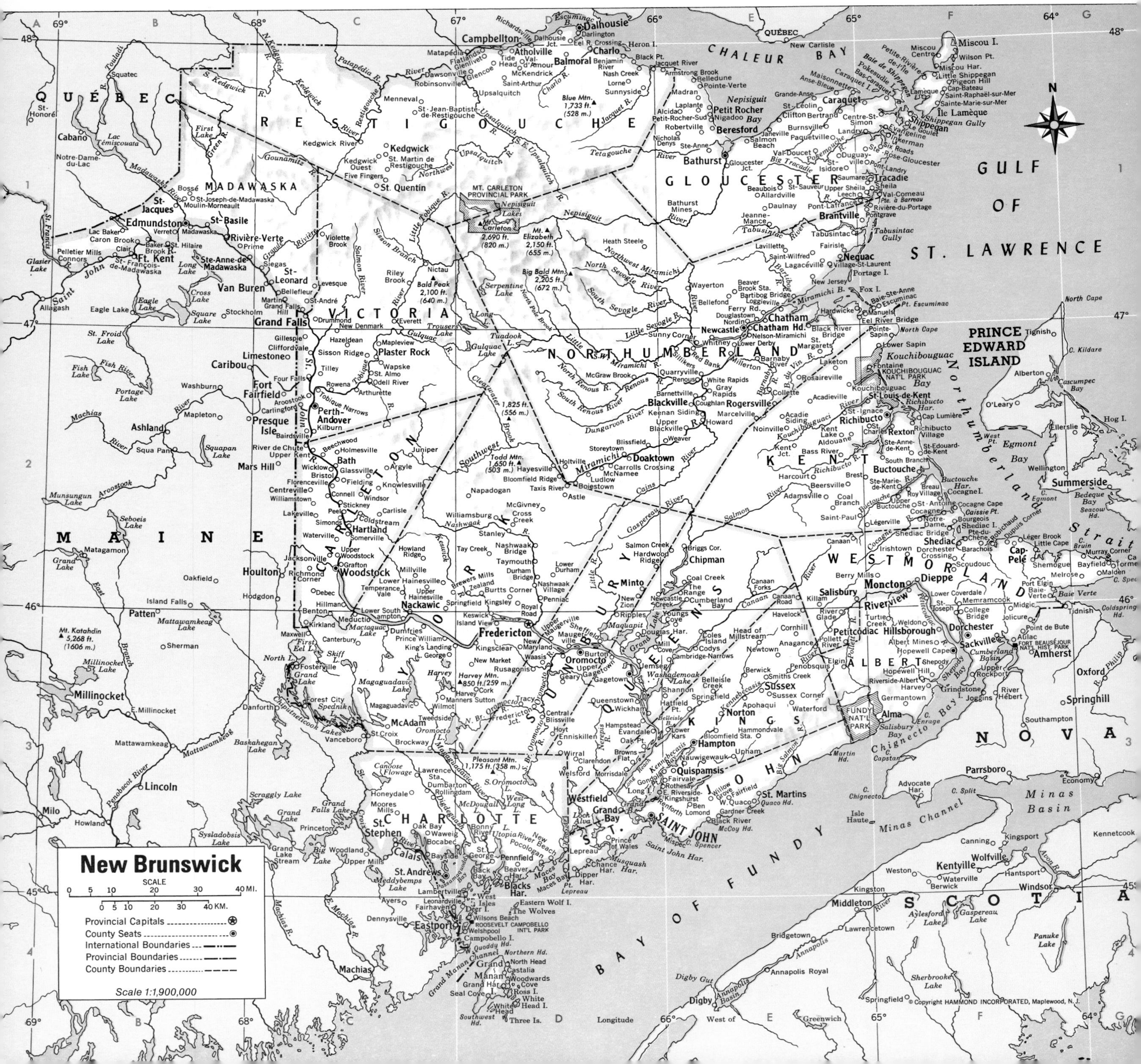

New Brunswick

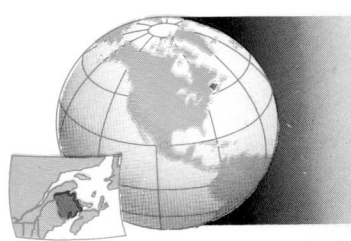

AREA 28,354 sq. mi. (73,437 sq. km.)
POPULATION 696,403
CAPITAL Fredericton
LARGEST CITY Saint John
HIGHEST POINT Mt. Carleton 2,690 ft.
(820 m.)
SETTLED IN 1611
ADMITTED TO CONFEDERATION 1867
PROVINCIAL FLOWER Purple Violet

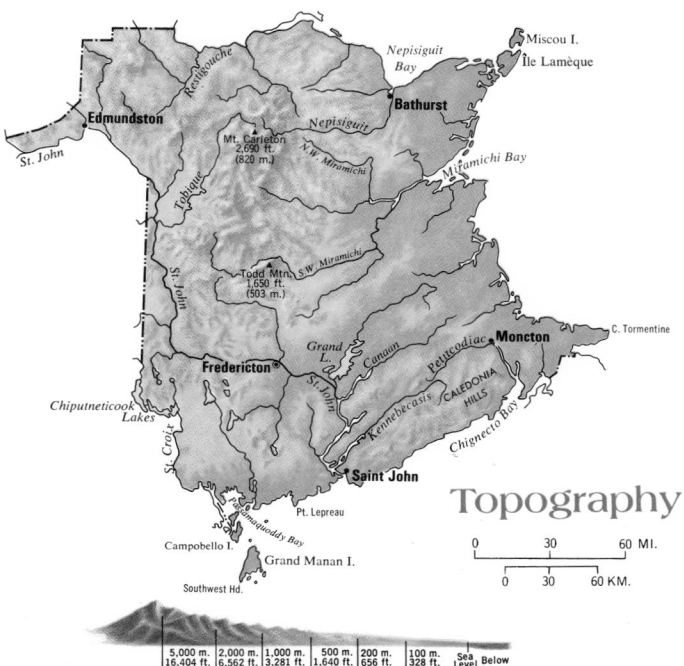

Topography

0   30   60 MI.

0   30   60 KM.

| 5,000 m. | 2,000 m. | 1,000 m. | 500 m. | 200 m. | 100 m. | Sea | Below |
| 16,404 ft. | 6,562 ft. | 3,281 ft. | 1,640 ft. | 656 ft. | 328 ft. | Level | |

Agriculture, Industry and Resources

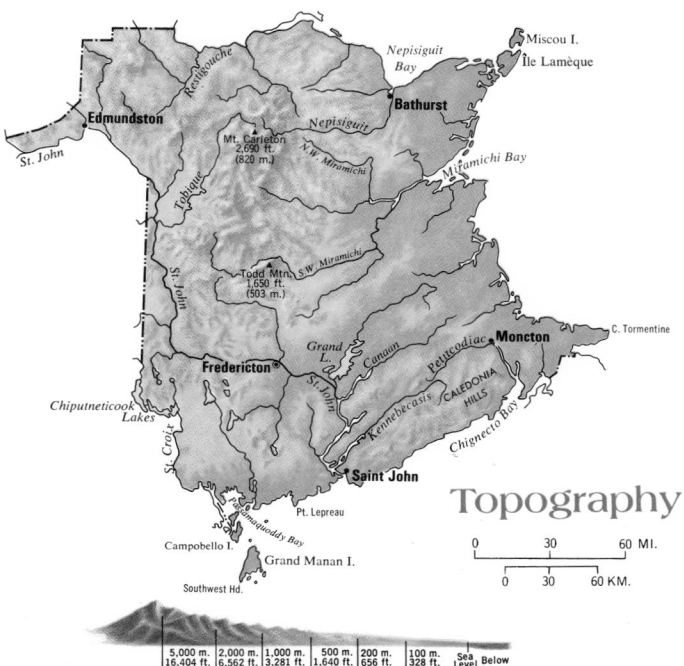

DOMINANT LAND USE

Cereals, Livestock
Dairy
Potatoes
General Farming, Livestock
Pasture Livestock
Forests

MAJOR MINERAL OCCURRENCES

Ag Silver   Pb Lead
C Coal   Sb Antimony
Cu Copper   Zn Zinc

⚡ Water Power
▨ Major Industrial Areas

Topography

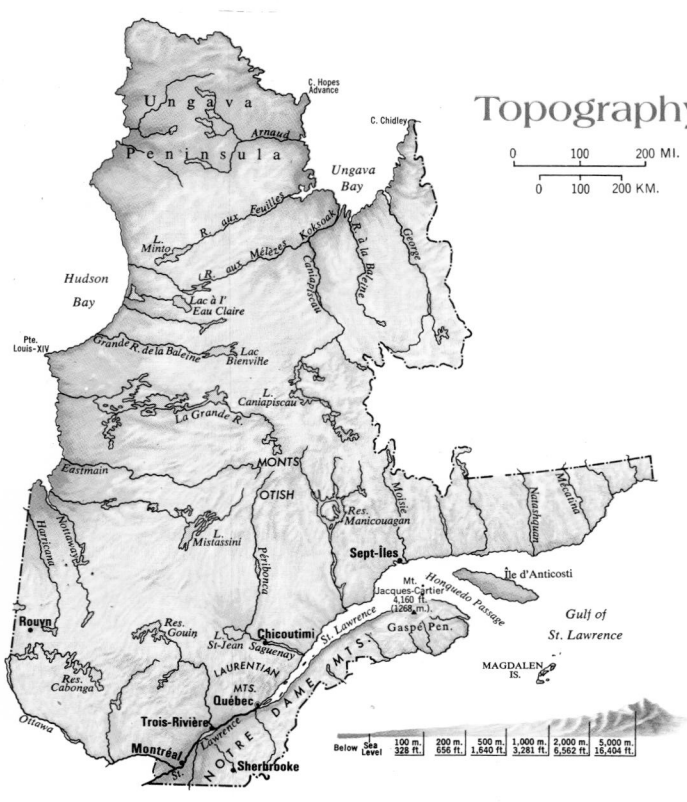

0 100 200 MI.
0 100 200 KM.

Below Sea Level | 100 m. 328 ft. | 200 m. 656 ft. | 500 m. 1,640 ft. | 1,000 m. 3,281 ft. | 2,000 m. 6,562 ft. | 5,000 m. 16,404 ft.

CITIES and TOWNS

Acton Vale 4,371 . . . . E 4
Albanel 992 . . . . E 1
Alma⊛ 26,322 . . . . F 1
Amqui⊛ 4,048 . . . . B 2
Ancienne-Lorette 12,935 . . . H 3
Angers . . . . B 4
Anjou 37,346 . . . . H 4
Annaville 712 . . . . E 3
Armagh 878 . . . . G 3
Arthabaska⊛ 6,827 . . . . . . F 3
Arvida . . . . F 1
Asbestos 7,967 . . . . F 4
Ascot Corner 847 . . . . . . F 4
Audet 760 . . . . G 4
Ayer's Cliff⊛ 810 . . . . . . E 4
Aylmer 26,695 . . . . B 4
Baie-Comeau 12,866 . . . . A 1
Baie-d'Urfé 3,674 . . . . . . G 4
Baie-Saint-Paul⊛ 3,961 . . G 2
Baie-Trinité 749 . . . . . . B 1
Beaconsfield 19,613 . . . . H 4
Beauceville 4,302 . . . . . . G 3
Beauharnois⊛ 7,025 . . . . D 4
Beaumont 791 . . . . F 3
Beauport 60,447 . . . . J 3
Beaupré 2,740 . . . . G 2
Bécancour⊛ 10,247 . . . . . E 3
Bedford⊛ 2,832 . . . . E 4
Beebe Plain 1,072 . . . . . . E 4
Bélair (Val-Bélair) 12,695 . H 3
Beloeil 17,540 . . . . D 4
Bernierville 2,120 . . . . . . F 3
Berthier-en-Bas 562 . . . . G 3
Berthierville⊛ 4,049 . . . . D 3
Bic 2,994 . . . . J 1
Biencourt 824 . . . . J 2
Black Lake 5,148 . . . . . . F 3
Blainville 14,682 . . . . . . H 4
Boischatel 3,345 . . . . . . J 3
Bois-des-Filion 4,943 . . . . H 4
Bolduc 1,565 . . . . G 4
Bonaventure 1,371 . . . . . C 2
Boucherville 29,704 . . . . J 4
Bromont 2,731 . . . . E 4
Bromptonville 3,035 . . . . F 4
Brossard 52,232 . . . . H 4
Brownsburg 2,875 . . . . . C 4
Buckingham 7,992 . . . . . B 4
Cabano 3,291 . . . . J 2
Cacouna 1,160 . . . . H 2
Calumet 729 . . . . C 4
Candiac 8,502 . . . . J 4
Cap-à-l'Aigle 819 . . . . . . G 2
Cap-Chat 3,464 . . . . B 1
Cap-de-la-Madeleine 32,626 E 3
Caplan-Rivière Caplan 1,139 . C 2
Cap-Saint-Ignace 1,485 . . G 2
Cap-Santé⊛ 671 . . . . F 3
Carignan 4,544 . . . . J 4
Carleton 2,710 . . . . C 2
Causapscal 2,501 . . . . . . B 2
Chambly 12,190 . . . . . . J 4
Chambord 961 . . . . E 1
Chandler 3,946 . . . . D 2
Charlemagne 4,827 . . . . . H 4
Charlesbourg 68,326 . . . . J 3
Charny 8,240 . . . . H 4
Châteauguay 36,928 . . . . H 4
Château-Richer⊛ 3,628 . . F 3
Chénéville 633 . . . . B 4
Chicoutimi⊛ 60,064 . . . . G 1
Chicoutimi-Jonquière
*135,172 . . . . G 1
Chute-aux-Outardes 2,280 . A 1
Clermont 3,621 . . . . G 2
Coaticook 6,271 . . . . F 4
Coleraine 1,660 . . . . F 4
Compton 728 . . . . F 4
Contrecoeur 5,449 . . . . . D 4
Cookshire⊛ 1,480 . . . . . . F 4
Coteau-du-Lac 1,247 . . . . C 4
Coteau-Landing⊛ 1,386 . . C 4
Côte-Saint-Luc 27,531 . . . H 4
Courcelles 608 . . . . G 4
Courville . . . . J 3
Cowansville 12,240 . . . . . E 4
Crabtree 1,950 . . . . D 4
Danville 2,200 . . . . E 4
Daveluyville 1,257 . . . . . E 3
Deauville 942 . . . . E 4
Dégelis 3,477 . . . . J 2
Delisle 4,011 . . . . F 1
Delson 4,935 . . . . H 4
Desbiens 1,541 . . . . E 1
Deschaillons-sur-Saint-
Laurent 950 . . . . E 3
Deschambault 977 . . . . . E 3
Deschênes . . . . B 4
Deux-Montagnes 9,944 . . H 4
Didyme 667 . . . . E 1
Disraëli 3,181 . . . . F 4
Dolbeau 8,766 . . . . E 1
Dollard-des-Ormeaux 39,940 . H 4
Donnacona 5,731 . . . . . . F 3
Dorion 5,749 . . . . C 4
Dorval 17,727 . . . . H 4
Dosquet 703 . . . . F 3
Douville . . . . D 4
Drummondville⊛ 27,347 . . E 4
Drummondville-Sud 9,220 . E 4
Dunham 2,887 . . . . E 4
Durham-Sud 1,045 . . . . . E 4
East Angus 4,016 . . . . . . F 4
East Broughton 1,397 . . . F 3
East Broughton Station 1,302 . F 3
Eastman 612 . . . . E 4
Entrelacs 1,735 . . . . C 3
Farnham 6,498 . . . . E 4
Ferme-Neuve 2,266 . . . . B 3
Forestville 4,271 . . . . . . H 1
Frampton 684 . . . . G 3
Francoeur 1,422 . . . . . . F 3
Gaspé 17,261 . . . . D 1
Gatineau 74,988 . . . . . . B 4
Giffard . . . . J 3
Girardville 1,128 . . . . . . E 1
Gracefield 869 . . . . A 3
Granby 38,069 . . . . E 4
Grand'Mère 15,442 . . . . . E 3
Grande-Rivière 4,420 . . . . D 2
Grandes-Bergeronnes 748 . H 1
Grande-Vallée 700 . . . . . D 1
Greenfield Park 18,527 . . J 4
Grenville 1,417 . . . . C 4
Gros-Morne 672 . . . . . . C 1
Hampstead 7,598 . . . . . . H 4
Ham-Sud⊛ 62 . . . . F 4
Hauterive 13,995 . . . . . . A 1
Hébertville 2,515 . . . . . . F 1
Hébertville-Station 1,442 . F 1
Hemmingford 737 . . . . . D 4
Henryville 595 . . . . D 4
Howick 639 . . . . D 4
Hudson 4,414 . . . . C 4
Hull⊛ 56,225 . . . . B 4
Huntingdon⊛ 3,018 . . . . . C 4
Île-Perrot 5,945 . . . . G 4
Iberville⊛ 8,587 . . . . D 4
Inverness⊛ 329 . . . . F 3
Joliette⊛ 16,987 . . . . D 3
Jonquière 60,354 . . . . . . F 1
Jonquière-Chicoutimi
*135,172 . . . . F 1
Kingsey Falls 818 . . . . . . E 4
Kirkland 10,476 . . . . H 4
Knowlton (Lac-Brome)⊛
4,316 . . . . E 4
La Baie 20,935 . . . . G 1
Labelle 1,534 . . . . C 3
Lac-à-la-Croix 1,017 . . . . F 1
Lac-Alouette-Lac-Brière 1,356 D 4
Lac-au-Saumon 1,332 . . . B 2
Lac-aux-Sables 838 . . . . E 3
Lac-Beaufort 717 . . . . . . F 3
Lac-Bouchette 1,703 . . . . E 1
Lac-Carré 717 . . . . C 3
Lac-des-Écorces 766 . . . . B 3
Lac-Drolet 1,120 . . . . . . G 4
Lac-Etchemin 2,729 . . . . G 3
Lachenaie 8,631 . . . . . . D 4
Lachine 37,521 . . . . H 4
Lachute⊛ 11,729 . . . . . . C 4
Lac-Mégantic⊛ 6,119 . . . . G 4
Lacolle 1,319 . . . . D 4
Lac-Saint-Charles 5,837 . . H 3
Lafontaine 4,799 . . . . . . C 4
La Guadeloupe 1,692 . . . F 4
La Malbaie⊛ 4,030 . . . . . G 2
Lambton 1,559 . . . . F 4
L'Annonciation 2,384 . . . . C 3
Lanoraie (Lanoraie-d'Autry)
1,613 . . . . D 4
La Pêche 4,977 . . . . B 4
La Pérade 1,039 . . . . . . E 3
La Pocatière 4,560 . . . . . H 2

La Prairie⊛ 10,627 . . . . . J 4
La Providence . . . . E 4
Larouche 662 . . . . F 1
La Salle 76,299 . . . . H 4
L'Ascension 1,287 . . . . . F 1
L'Assomption⊛ 4,844 . . . . D 4
La Station-du-Coteau 892 . C 4
Laterrière 788 . . . . F 1
La Tuque 11,556 . . . . . . E 2
Laurentides 1,947 . . . . . . D 4
Laurierville 939 . . . . F 3
Lauzon 13,362 . . . . J 3
Lavaltrie 2,053 . . . . D 4
L'Avenir 1,116 . . . . E 4
Lawrenceville 562 . . . . . E 4
Le Moyne 6,137 . . . . J 4
L'Épiphanie 2,971 . . . . . D 4
Léry 2,239 . . . . H 4
Lévis 17,895 . . . . J 3
Lennoxville 3,922 . . . . . . F 4
Les Méchins 803 . . . . . . B 1
Linière 1,168 . . . . G 3
L'Islet 1,070 . . . . G 2
L'Islet-sur-Mer 774 . . . . . G 2
L'Isle-Verte 1,142 . . . . . . G 1
Longueuil 124,320 . . . . . J 4
Loretteville 15,060 . . . . . H 3
Lorraine 6,881 . . . . H 4
Louiseville⊛ 3,735 . . . . . E 3
Luceville 1,524 . . . . J 1
Lyster 830 . . . . F 3
Magog 13,604 . . . . E 4

Maniwaki⊛ 5,424 . . . . . . B 3
Manseau 626 . . . . E 3
Maple Grove 2,009 . . . . . H 4
Maria 1,178 . . . . C 2
Marieville⊛ 4,877 . . . . . . D 4
Mascouche 20,345 . . . . . H 4
Maskinongé 1,005 . . . . . E 3
Masson 4,264 . . . . B 4
Massueville 671 . . . . . . D 4
Matane⊛ 13,612 . . . . . . B 1
Matapédia 586 . . . . C 2
Melocheville 1,892 . . . . . H 4
Mercier 6,352 . . . . H 4
Metabetchouan 3,406 . . . F 1
Mirabel⊛ 14,080 . . . . . . H 4
Mistassini 6,682 . . . . . . E 1
Montauban 557 . . . . E 3
Mont-Carmel 807 . . . . . . H 2
Montcerf 570 . . . . A 3
Montebello 1,229 . . . . . . B 4
Mont-Joli 6,359 . . . . J 1
Mont-Laurier⊛ 8,405 . . . . B 3
Mont-Louis 756 . . . . C 1
Montmagny⊛ 12,405 . . . . G 3
Montréal⊛ 980,354 . . . . . H 4
Montréal *2,828,349 . . . . H 4
Montréal-Est 3,778 . . . . . J 4
Montréal-Nord 94,914 . . . H 4
Mont-Rolland 1,517 . . . . C 4
Mont-Royal 19,247 . . . . . H 4
Mont-Saint-Hilaire 10,066 . D 4
Morin Heights 592 . . . . . C 4
Murdochville 3,396 . . . . . C 1
Nantes 1,167 . . . . F 4

Soulanges 15,429 . . . . . . C 4
Stanstead 38,186 . . . . . . F 4
Témiscouata 52,570 . . . . J 2
Terrebonne 193,865 . . . . H 4
Vaudreuil 50,043 . . . . . . C 4
Verchères 63,353 . . . . . . J 4
Wolfe 15,635 . . . . F 4
Yamaska 14,797 . . . . . . E 3

COUNTIES

Argenteuil 32,454 . . . . . . C 4
Arthabaska 59,277 . . . . . E 4
Bagot 26,840 . . . . E 4
Beauce 73,427 . . . . G 3
Beauharnois 54,034 . . . . C 4
Bellechasse 23,559 . . . . . G 3
Berthier 31,096 . . . . C 3
Bonaventure 40,487 . . . . C 2
Brome 17,436 . . . . E 4
Chambly 307,090 . . . . . . J 4
Champlain 119,595 . . . . . E 2
Charlevoix-Est 17,448 . . . G 2
Charlevoix-Ouest 14,172 . . G 2
Châteauguay 59,968 . . . . D 4
Chicoutimi 174,441 . . . . . F 1
Compton 20,536 . . . . . . F 4
Deux-Montagnes 71,252 . . C 4
Dorchester 33,949 . . . . . C 3
Drummond 69,770 . . . . . D 4
Frontenac 26,814 . . . . . . G 4

Gaspé-Est 41,173 . . . . . . D 1
Gaspé-Ouest 18,943 . . . . C 1
Gatineau 54,229 . . . . . . B 3
Hull 131,213 . . . . B 4
Iberville 23,180 . . . . D 4
Huntingdon 16,953 . . . . . C 4
Île-de-Montréal 1,760,122 . H 4
Île-Jésus 268,335 . . . . . . H 4
Joliette 60,384 . . . . C 3
Kamouraska 28,642 . . . . H 2
Labelle 34,395 . . . . B 3
Lac-Saint-Jean-Est 47,891 . F 1
Lac-Saint-Jean-Ouest 62,952 E 1
Laprairie 105,962 . . . . . . H 4
L'Assomption 109,705 . . . D 4
Lévis 94,104 . . . . J 3
L'Islet 22,062 . . . . G 2
Lotbinière 29,653 . . . . . . F 3
Maskinongé 20,763 . . . . . D 3
Matane 29,955 . . . . B 1
Matapédia 23,715 . . . . . . B 2
Mégantic 57,892 . . . . . . F 3

Missisquoi 36,161 . . . . . . D 4
Montcalm 27,557 . . . . . . C 3
Montmagny 25,622 . . . . . G 3
Montmorency No. 1 23,048 . F 2
Montmorency No. 2 6,436 . . G 3
Napierville 13,562 . . . . . D 4
Nicolet 33,513 . . . . E 3
Papineau 37,975 . . . . . . B 4
Pontiac 20,283 . . . . A 3
Portneuf 58,843 . . . . E 3
Québec 458,980 . . . . . . F 3
Richelieu 53,058 . . . . . . D 4
Richmond 40,871 . . . . . . E 4
Rimouski 69,099 . . . . . . J 1
Rivière-du-Loup 41,250 . . H 2
Rouville 42,391 . . . . D 4
Saguenay 115,881 . . . . . H 1
Saint-Hyacinthe 55,888 . . D 4
Saint-Jean 55,576 . . . . . D 4
Saint-Maurice 107,703 . . . D 3
Shefford 70,733 . . . . E 4
Sherbrooke 115,983 . . . . E 4

Agriculture, Industry and Resources

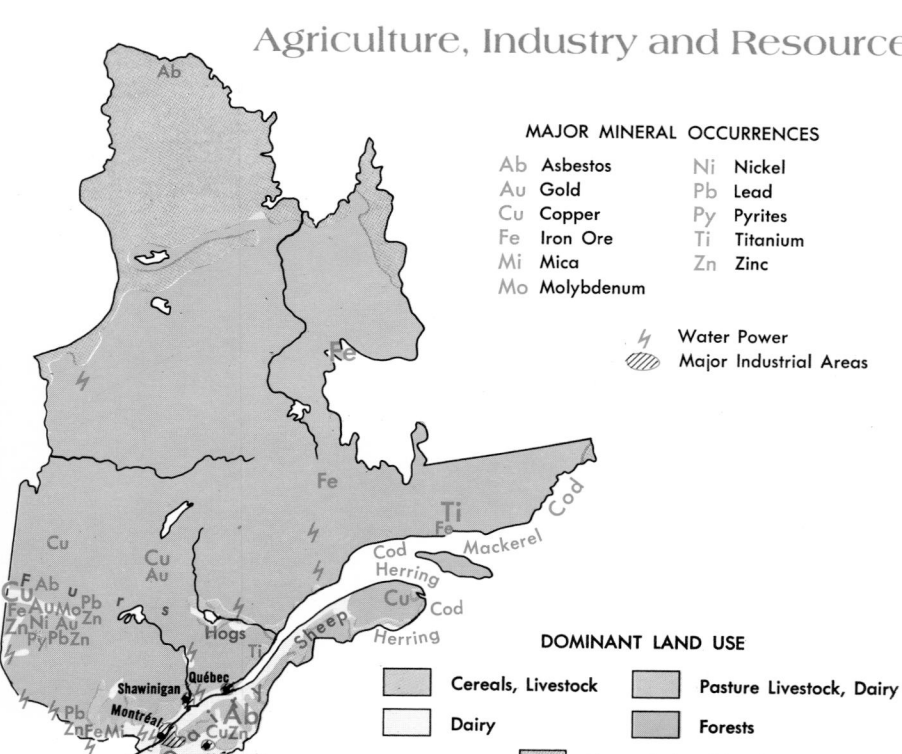

MAJOR MINERAL OCCURRENCES

Ab Asbestos
Au Gold
Cu Copper
Fe Iron Ore
Mi Mica
Mo Molybdenum

Ni Nickel
Pb Lead
Py Pyrites
Ti Titanium
Zn Zinc

⚡ Water Power
▨ Major Industrial Areas

DOMINANT LAND USE

▨ Cereals, Livestock
☐ Dairy
▨ Pasture Livestock, Dairy
▨ Forests
▨ Nonagricultural Land

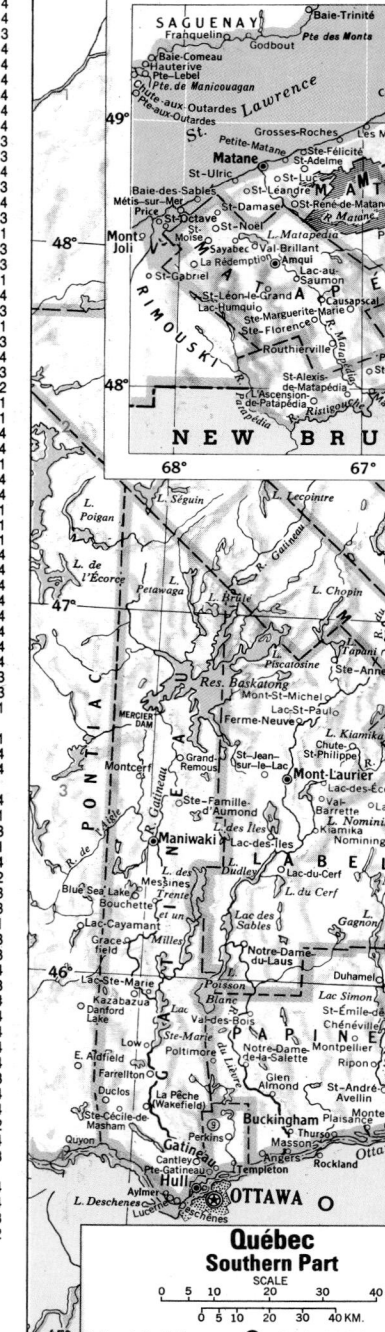

Québec
Southern Part

SCALE
0 5 10 20 30 40 MI.
0 5 10 20 30 40 KM.

National Capital — ⊛
Provincial Capital — ⊛
County Seats — ⊛
International Boundaries —
Provincial & State Boundaries —
County Boundaries —

Scale 1:2,250,000

...pierville® 2,343 .... D 4	Pincourt 8,750 .... D 4
...uville 996 .... F 3	Pintendre 1,849 .... J 3
...w Carlisle 1,292 .... D 2	Plaisance 748 .... B 4
...w Richmond 4,257 .... C 2	Plessisville 7,249 .... F 3
...colet 4,880 .... E 3	Pohénégamooke 3,702 .... H 2
...miningue 881 .... B 3	Pointe-à-la-Croix 1,481 ... C 2
...rmandin 4,041 .... E 1	Pointe-au-Père 796 .... J 1
...rth Hatley 689 .... F 4	Pointe-au-Pic 1,054 .... G 2
...tre-Dame-de-la-Doré 1,064 E 1	Pointe-aux-Outardes 1,056 . A 1
...tre-Dame-des-Laurentides H 3	Pointe-aux-Trembles 36,270 . H 4
...tre-Dame-des-Prairies D 3	Pointe-Calumet 2,935 .... H 4
...6,150 .... D 3	Pointe-Claire 24,571 .... H 4
...tre-Dame-du-Bon-Conseil E 4	Pointe-du-Lac 5,359 .... E 3
...1,089 .... E 4	Pointe-Gatineau .... B 4
...tre-Dame-du-Lac® 2,258 . J 2	Pointe-Lebel 1,573 .... A 1
...uvelle 669 .... C 2	Pont-Rouge 3,580 .... F 3
...1,538 .... C 4	Port-Alfred 8,621 .... G 1
...herville 1,398 .... E 4	Portneuf 1,333 .... F 3
...mstown 1,659 .... H 4	Portneuf-sur-Mer (Rivière-
...s 673 .... H 3	Portneuf-sur-Mer) 1,255 . H 1
...s 673 .... G 1	Price 2,273 .... A 1
...tremont 24,338 .... H 4	Princeville 4,023 .... F 3
...erburn Park 4,268 .... D 4	Proulxville 588 .... E 3
...bos 1,295 .... D 2	Québec (cap.) 166,474 ... H 3
...bos-Mills 1,565 .... D 1	Québec ®576,075 .... H 3
...pineauville 1,481 .... C 4	Quyon 744 .... A 4
...spébiac 1,914 .... D 2	Rawdon 2,958 .... D 3
...rcé® 4,839 .... D 1	Repentigny 34,419 .... J 4
...tite-Matane 1,065 .... D 1	Richelieu 1,832 .... D 4
...tit-Cap 1,023 .... D 1	Richmond® 3,568 .... E 4
...tit-Saguenay (Saint-	Rigaud 2,268 .... C 4
...François-d'Assise) 804 . G 1	Rimouski® 29,120 .... J 1
...rrefonds 38,390 .... H 4	Rimouski-Est 2,506 .... J 1
...erreville 1,212 .... E 3	Ripon 620 .... B 4

Rivière-à-Pierre 615 .... E 3	Saint-Anselme 1,808 .... F 3
Rivière-au-Renard 2,211 .. D 1	Saint-Antoine 7,012 .... H 4
Rivière-Bleue 1,690 .... J 2	Saint-Antonin 941 .... H 2
Rivière-Bois-Clair 604 ... F 3	Saint-Aubert 884 .... G 2
Rivière-du-Loup® 13,459 .. H 2	Saint-Augustin-de-Québec
Rivière-du-Moulin .... G 1	2,475 .... E 3
Rivière-Éternité 659 .... J 1	Saint-Basile-Sud 1,719 .. H 3
Rivière-Portneuf-Portneuf-sur-	Saint-Basile-le-Grand 7,658 . J 4
Mer 1,255 .... H 1	Saint-Benjamin 1,027 .... G 3
Robertsonville 1,987 .... F 3	Saint-Bernard 585 .... G 3
Roberval® 11,429 .... E 1	Saint-Bernard-sur-Mer 711 . G 2
Rock Island 1,179 .... E 4	Saint-Boniface-de-Shawinigan
Rosemère 7,778 .... H 4	3,164 .... D 3
Rougemont 972 .... D 4	Saint-Bruno 2,580 .... F 1
Roxboro 6,292 .... H 4	Saint-Bruno-de-Montarville
Roxton Falls 1,245 .... E 4	22,880 .... J 4
Sacré-Coeur-de-Saguenay	Saint-Camille-de-Bellechasse
1,678 .... H 1	1,744 .... G 3
Saint-Adelme 618 .... B 1	Saint-Casimir 1,133 .... E 3
Saint-Adelphe 1,159 .... E 3	Saint-Césaire 2,935 .... D 4
Saint-Adolphe-d'Howard	Saint-Charles 1,019 .... G 3
1,686 .... C 4	Saint-Charles-de-Mandeville
Saint-Adrien 597 .... F 4	1,392 .... D 3
Saint-Agapitville 2,954 .. F 3	Saint-Chrysostome 1,018 .. D 4
Saint-Aimé-des-Lacs 861 .. G 2	Saint-Côme 660 .... D 3
Saint-Alban 673 .... E 3	Saint-Constant 9,938 .... J 4
Saint-Alexandre-de-	Saint-Cyprien 860 .... J 2
Kamouraska 1,048 .... H 2	Saint-Cyrille 1,041 .... D 4
Saint-Alexis-des-Monts 1,984 . D 3	Saint-David-de-Buckland
Saint-Amable 2,424 .... J 4	1,522 .... G 3
Saint-Ambroise 3,606 .... F 1	Saint-David 5,380 .... D 4
Saint-Anaclet 1,377 .... J 1	Saint-David-de-Falardeau
Saint-André-Avellin 1,312 . B 4	1,876 .... F 1
Saint-André-Est 1,293 .... C 4	Saint-Denis 861 .... D 4

Saint-Dominique 2,068 .... E 4	Saint-Donat-de-Montcalm
1,521 .... C 3
Sainte-Adèle 4,675 .... C 4
Saint-Charles-de-Mandeville

Sainte-Catherine 1,474 .... F 3	Sainte-Martine® 2,196 .... D 4
Sainte-Claire 1,566 .... G 3	Saint-Émile 5,216 .... H 3
Sainte-Croix 1,814 .... F 3	Sainte-Monique 705 .... F 1
Sainte-Félicité 711 .... G 3	Sainte-Pétronille 982 .... J 3
Sainte-Foy 68,883 .... H 3	Sainte-Perpétue-de-l'Islet
Sainte-Geneviève 2,573 .. H 4	1,232 .... H 2
Sainte-Geneviève-de-	Saint-Éphrem-de-Tring 973 . G 3
Batiscan® 356 .... F 2	Sainte-Épiphane 647 .... H 2
Sainte-Hélène-de-Bagot	Sainte-Pudentienne 866 .... E 4
1,328 .... E 4	Sainte-Rosalie 2,862 .... E 4
Sainte-Hénédine® 639 .... F 3	Saint-Esprit 1,068 .... D 4
Sainte-Julie-de-Verchères	Sainte-Thérèse 18,750 .... H 4
14,243 .... J 4	Sainte-Thérèse-Ouest
Sainte-Julienne® 750 .... D 4	(Boisbriand) 13,471 .... H 4
Sainte-Justine 1,080 .... G 3	Sainte-Thècle 1,703 .... E 3
Saint-Élie 639 .... E 3	Saint-Étienne-de-Grès 845 . E 3
Saint-Elzéar 743 .... G 3	Saint-Étienne-de-Lauzon
Sainte-Marie 8,937 .... G 3	1,218 .... J 3

AREA 594,857 sq. mi. (1,540,680 sq. km.)
POPULATION 6,438,403
CAPITAL Québec
LARGEST CITY Montréal
HIGHEST POINT Mont D'Iberville 5,420 ft. (1,652 m.)
SETTLED IN 1608
ADMITTED TO CONFEDERATION 1867
PROVINCIAL FLOWER White Garden Lily

Gaspé Peninsula

COUNTIES (indicated by numbers):
1 Iberville ... D4
2 Napierville ... D4
3 Rouville ... D4
4 St-Hyacinthe ... D4
5 Île-de-Montréal ... D4
6 Deux-Montagnes ... D4
7 Soulanges ... C4
8 Beauharnois ... B4
9 Hull ... B4
10 Laprairie ... D4
11 Richelieu ... D4
12 Vaudreuil ... C4

Internal divisions represent Municipal Counties

© Copyright HAMMOND INCORPORATED, Maplewood, N.J.

Northern Québec

SCALE
0 50 100 150 200 MI.
0 50 100 150 200 KM.

Provincial Capital............® Provincial Boundaries ____
County Seats..................◉ County Boundaries _____
International Boundaries ___ Territorial Boundaries ....

Scale 1:8,400,000

© Copyright HAMMOND INCORPORATED, Maplewood, N.J.

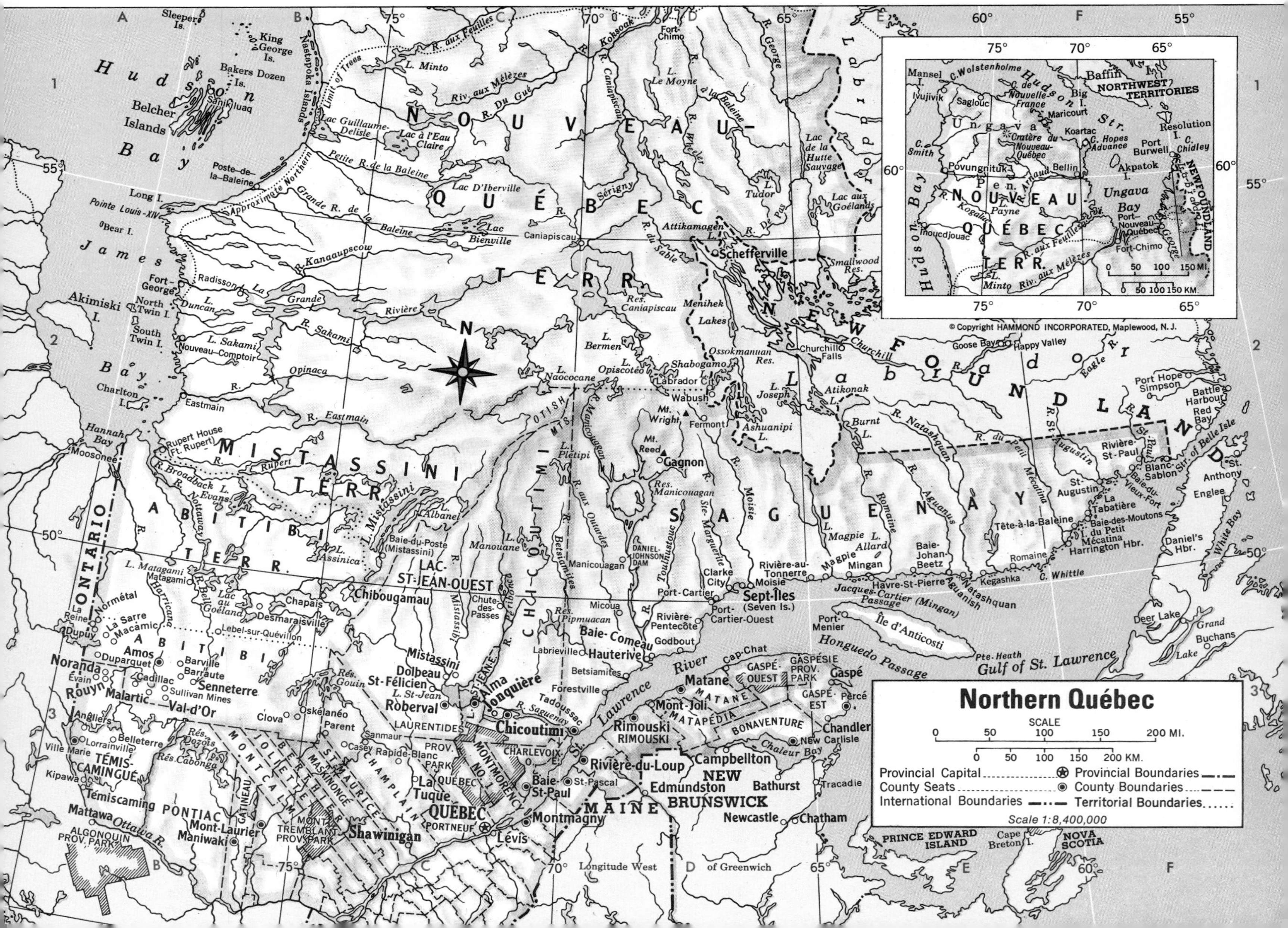

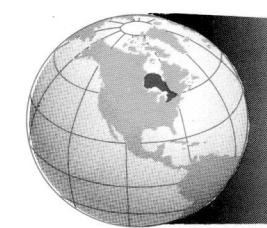

ONTARIO, NORTHERN

INTERNAL DIVISIONS

Algoma (terr. dist.) 133,553...D 3
Cochrane (terr. dist.) 96,875...D 2
Kenora (terr. dist.) 59,421...C 2
Manitoulin (terr. dist.) 11,001...D 3
Nipissing (terr. dist.) 80,268...E 3
Parry Sound (terr. dist.)
  33,528...E 3
Rainy River (terr. dist.) 22,798...D 3
Renfrew (county) 87,484...E 3
Sudbury (reg. munic.)
  159,779...D 3
Sudbury (terr. dist.) 27,068...D 3
Thunder Bay (terr. dist.)
  153,997...C 3
Timiskaming (terr. dist.)
  41,288...D 3

CITIES and TOWNS

Chalk River 1,010...E 3
Elliot Lake 16,723...D 3
Fort Albany 482...D 2
Fort Frances⊚ 8,906...B 3
Kapuskasing 12,014...D 3
Kenora⊚ 9,817...B 3
Kirkland Lake 12,219...D 3
Moose Factory 1,452...D 2
Moosonee 1,433...D 2
Nickel Centre 12,318...D 3
North Bay 51,268...E 3
Pembroke⊚ 14,026...E 3
Sault Sainte Marie⊚ 82,697...D 3
Sudbury 91,829...D 3
Thunder Bay 112,486...C 3
Timmins 46,114...D 3
Valley East 20,433...D 3

OTHER FEATURES

Abitibi (lake)...E 3
Abitibi (riv.)...D 2
Albany (riv.)...C 2
Algonquin Prov. Park...E 3
Asheweig (riv.)...C 2
Attawapiskat (lake)...C 2
Attawapiskat (riv.)...C 2
Basswood (lake)...B 3
Berens (riv.)...A 2
Big Trout (lake)...B 2
Black Duck (riv.)...C 1
Bloodvein (riv.)...A 2
Caribou (isl.)...C 3

Cobham (riv.)...A 2
Eabamet (lake)...C 2
Ekwan (riv.)...C 2
English (riv.)...B 2
Fawn (riv.)...C 2
Finger (lake)...B 2
Georgian (bay)...D 3
Hannah (bay)...D 2
Henrietta Maria (cape)...D 1
Hudson (bay)...D 1
Huron (lake)...D 3
James (bay)...D 2
Kapiskau (riv.)...D 2
Kapuskasing (riv.)...D 3
Kenogami (riv.)...C 2
Kesagami (lake)...E 2
Lake of the Woods (lake)...B 3
Lake Superior Prov. Park...D 3
Little Current (riv.)...C 2
Long (lake)...C 3
Manitoulin (isl.)...D 3
Mattagami (riv.)...D 3
Mille Lacs (lake)...B 3
Missinaibi (lake)...C 3
Missinaibi (riv.)...D 2
Missisa (lake)...C 2
Nipigon (lake)...C 3
Nipissing (lake)...E 3
North (chan.)...D 3
North Caribou (lake)...B 2
Nungesser (lake)...B 2
Ogidaki (mt.)...D 3
Ogoki (riv.)...C 2
Opazatika (riv.)...D 2
Opinnagau (riv.)...D 2
Otoskwin (riv.)...B 2
Ottawa (riv.)...E 3
Pipestone (riv.)...B 2
Polar Bear Prov. Park...D 2
Pukaskwa Prov. Park...C 3
Quetico Prov. Park...B 3
Rainy (lake)...B 3
Red (lake)...B 2
Sachigo (lake)...B 2
Saganaga (lake)...B 3
Saint Ignace (isl.)...C 3
Saint Joseph (lake)...B 2
Sandy (lake)...B 2
Savant (lake)...B 2
Seine (riv.)...B 3
Seul (lake)...B 2
Severn (lake)...B 2
Severn (riv.)...C 2
Shamattawa (riv.)...C 2
Shibogama (lake)...C 2

Sibley Prov. Park...C 3
Slate (isls.)...C 3
Stout (lake)...B 2
Superior (lake)...C 3
Sutton (lake)...D 2
Sutton (riv.)...D 2
Timagami (lake)...D 3
Timiskaming (lake)...E 3
Trout (lake)...B 2
Wabuk (pt.)...D 1
Winisk (lake)...C 2
Winisk (riv.)...C 2
Winnipeg (riv.)...A 2
Woods (lake)...B 3

ONTARIO

INTERNAL DIVISIONS

Algoma (terr. dist.) 133,553...J 5
Brant (county) 104,427...D 4
Bruce (county) 60,020...C 3
Cochrane (terr. dist.) 96,875...J 4
Dufferin (county) 31,145...D 3
Dundas (county) 18,946...J 2
Durham (reg. munic.) 283,639...F 3
Elgin (county) 69,707...C 5
Essex (county) 312,467...B 5
Frontenac (county) 108,133...H 3
Glengarry (county) 20,254...K 2
Grenville (county) 27,176...J 3
Grey (county) 73,824...D 3
Haldimand-Norfolk (reg.
  munic.) 89,456...E 5
Haliburton (county) 11,361...F 2
Halton (reg. munic.) 253,883...E 4
Hamilton-Wentworth (reg.
  munic.) 411,445...D 4
Hastings (county) 106,883...G 3
Huron (county) 56,127...C 4
Kenora (terr. dist.) 59,421...G 5
Kent (county) 107,022...B 5
Lambton (county) 123,445...B 5
Lanark (county) 45,676...H 3
Leeds (county) 53,765...H 3
Lennox and Addington
  (county) 33,040...G 3
Manitoulin (terr. dist.) 11,001...B 2
Middlesex (county) 318,184...C 4
Muskoka (dist. munic.)
  38,370...E 3
Niagara (reg. munic.) 368,288...E 4
Nipissing (terr. dist.) 80,268...F 2
Northumberland (county)
  64,966...G 3

Ottawa-Carleton (reg. munic.)
  546,849...J 2
Oxford (county) 85,920...D 4
Parry Sound (terr. dist.)
  33,528...D 2
Peel (reg. munic.) 490,731...E 4
Perth (county) 66,096...C 4
Peterborough (county)
  102,452...F 3
Prescott (county) 30,365...K 2
Prince Edward (county)
  22,336...G 4
Rainy River (terr. dist.) 22,798...G 5
Renfrew (county) 87,484...E 3
Russell (county) 22,412...J 2
Simcoe (county) 225,071...E 3
Stormont (county) 61,927...K 2
Sudbury (reg. munic.)
  159,779...K 6
Sudbury (terr. dist.) 27,068...J 5
Thunder Bay (terr. dist.)
  153,997...H 5
Timiskaming (terr. dist.)
  41,288...K 5
Toronto (metro. munic.)
  2,137,395...K 4
Victoria (county) 47,854...F 3
Waterloo (reg. munic.)
  305,496...D 4
Wellington (county) 129,432...D 4
York (reg. munic.) 252,053...E 4

CITIES and TOWNS

Ailsa Craig 765...C 4
Ajax 25,475...E 4
Alban 342...D 1
Alexandria 3,271...K 2
Alfred 1,057...K 2
Alliston 4,712...E 3
Almonte 3,855...H 2
Alvinston 736...B 5
Amherstburg 5,685...A 5
Amherst View 6,110...H 3
Ancaster 14,428...D 4
Angus 3,085...E 3
Apsley 264...F 3
Arkona 473...C 4
Armstrong 378...H 4
Arnprior 5,828...H 2
Aroland 291...H 4
Arthur 1,700...D 4
Astorville 340...E 1
Athens 948...J 3
Atherley 366...E 3
Atikokan 4,452...G 5

Atwood 723...D 4
Aurora 16,267...J 3
Avonmore 273...K 2
Aylmer 5,254...C 5
Ayr 1,295...D 4
Ayton 424...D 3
Baden 945...D 4
Bala 577...E 2
Bancroft 2,329...G 2
Barrie⊚ 38,423...E 3
Barry's Bay 1,216...G 2
Batawa 430...G 3
Bath 1,071...H 3
Bayfield 649...C 4
Beachburg 682...H 2
Beachville 917...D 4
Beardmore 583...H 5
Beaverton 1,952...E 3
Beeton 1,989...E 3
Belle River 3,568...B 5
Belleville⊚ 34,881...G 3
Belmont 831...C 5
Bethany 365...F 3
Bewdley 501...F 3
Binbrook 306...E 4
Blackstock 720...F 3
Blenheim 4,044...C 5
Blind River 3,444...J 5
Bloomfield 718...G 4
Blyth 926...C 4
Bobcaygeon 1,625...F 3
Bonfield 540...E 1
Bothwell 915...C 5
Bourget 1,057...J 2
Bracebridge⊚ 9,063...E 2
Bradford 7,370...E 3
Braeside 492...H 2
Brampton⊚ 149,030...J 4
Brantford⊚ 74,315...D 4
Bridgenorth 1,633...F 3

Brigden 635...B 5
Brighton 3,147...G 3
Britt 419...D 2
Brockville⊚ 19,896...J 3
Bruce Mines 635...J 5
Brussels 962...C 4
Burford 1,461...D 4
Burgessville 302...D 4
Burk's Falls 922...E 2
Burlington 114,853...E 4
Cache Bay 665...D 1
Caesarea 551...F 3
Calabogie 286...H 2
Caledon 26,645...E 4
Callander 1,158...E 1
Cambridge 77,183...D 4
Campbellford 3,409...G 3
Cannington 1,623...E 3
Capreol 3,845...K 5
Caramat 265...H 5
Cardinal 1,753...J 3
Carleton Place 5,626...H 2
Carlisle 781...D 4
Carlsbad Springs 616...J 2
Carp 707...H 2
Cartier 590...J 5
Casselman 1,675...J 2
Castleton 346...F 3
Chalk River 1,010...G 1
Chapleau 3,243...J 5
Charing Cross 443...B 5
Chatham⊚ 40,952...B 5
Chatsworth 383...D 3
Cherry Valley 289...G 4
Chesley 1,840...C 3
Chesterville 1,430...J 2
Chute-à-Blondeau 365...K 2
City View...J 2
Clarence Creek 796...J 2
Clarksburg 508...D 3

Clifford 645...D 4
Clinton 3,081...C 4
Cobalt 1,759...K 5
Cobden 997...H 2
Coboconk 426...F 3
Cobourg⊚ 11,385...F 4
Cochrane⊚ 4,848...J 4
Colborne 1,796...G 4
Colchester 711...B 6
Coldwater 964...E 3
Collingwood 12,064...D 3
Comber 667...B 5
Consecon 295...G 4
Cookstown 918...E 3
Cornwall⊚ 46,144...K 2
Cottam 404...B 5
Courtland 647...D 5
Courtright 1,024...B 5
Crediton 370...C 4
Creemore 1,182...D 3
Crysler 540...J 2
Cumberland 518...J 2
Cumberland Beach-Bramshot-
  Buena Vista 679...E 3
Dashwood 426...C 4
Deep River 5,095...G 1
Delaware 481...D 4
Delhi 4,043...D 5
Delta 360...H 3
Deseronto 1,740...G 3
Douglas 303...H 2
Drayton 809...D 4
Dresden 2,550...B 5
Drumbo 476...D 4
Dryden 6,640...G 5
Dublin 295...C 4
Dubreuilville △988...J 5
Dundalk 1,250...D 3
Dundas 19,586...D 4
Dungannon 284...C 4
Dunnville 11,353...E 5
Durham 2,458...D 3
Dutton 1,115...C 5
Earlton 1,028...K 5
East York 101,974...J 4
Echo Bay 786...J 5
Eden Mills 318...D 4
Eganville 1,245...G 2
Egmondville 465...C 4
Elgin 327...H 3
Elk Lake 526...K 5
Elliot Lake 16,723...B 1
Elmira 7,063...D 4
Elmvale 1,183...E 3
Elmwood 364...C 3
Elora 2,666...D 4
Embro 727...C 4
Embrun 1,883...J 2
Emeryville-Puce 1,611...B 5
Emo 762...F 5
Englehart 1,689...K 5
Enterprise 357...H 3
Erieau 430...C 5
Erin 2,313...D 4
Espanola 5,836...J 5
Essex 6,295...B 5
Etobicoke 298,713...J 4
Everett 570...E 3
Exeter 3,732...C 4
Fauquier 561...J 5
Fenelon Falls 1,701...F 3
Fergus 6,064...D 4
Field 462...J 2
Finch 353...J 2
Fingal 380...C 5
Fitzroy Harbour 446...H 2
Flesherton 565...D 3
Foleyet 484...J 5
Fordwich 365...C 4
Forest 2,671...C 4
Formosa 393...C 3
Fort Erie 24,096...E 5
Fort Frances⊚ 8,906...F 5
Foxboro 597...G 3
Frankford 1,919...G 3
Fraserdale 303...J 4
Freelton 307...D 4
Gananoque 4,863...H 3
Garden Village 270...E 1
Geraldton 2,956...H 5
Glencoe 1,694...C 5
Glen Miller 639...G 3
Glen Robertson 378...K 2
Glen Walter 710...K 2
Goderich⊚ 7,322...C 4
Gogama 652...J 5
Goodwood 335...E 3
Gore Bay 777...B 2
Gorrie 468...C 4
Grafton 409...G 4
Grand Bend 680...C 4
Grand Valley 1,226...D 3
Granton 315...C 4
Gravenhurst 8,532...E 3
Greely 567...J 2
Green Valley 459...K 2
Grimsby 15,797...E 4
Guelph⊚ 71,207...D 4

(continued on following page)

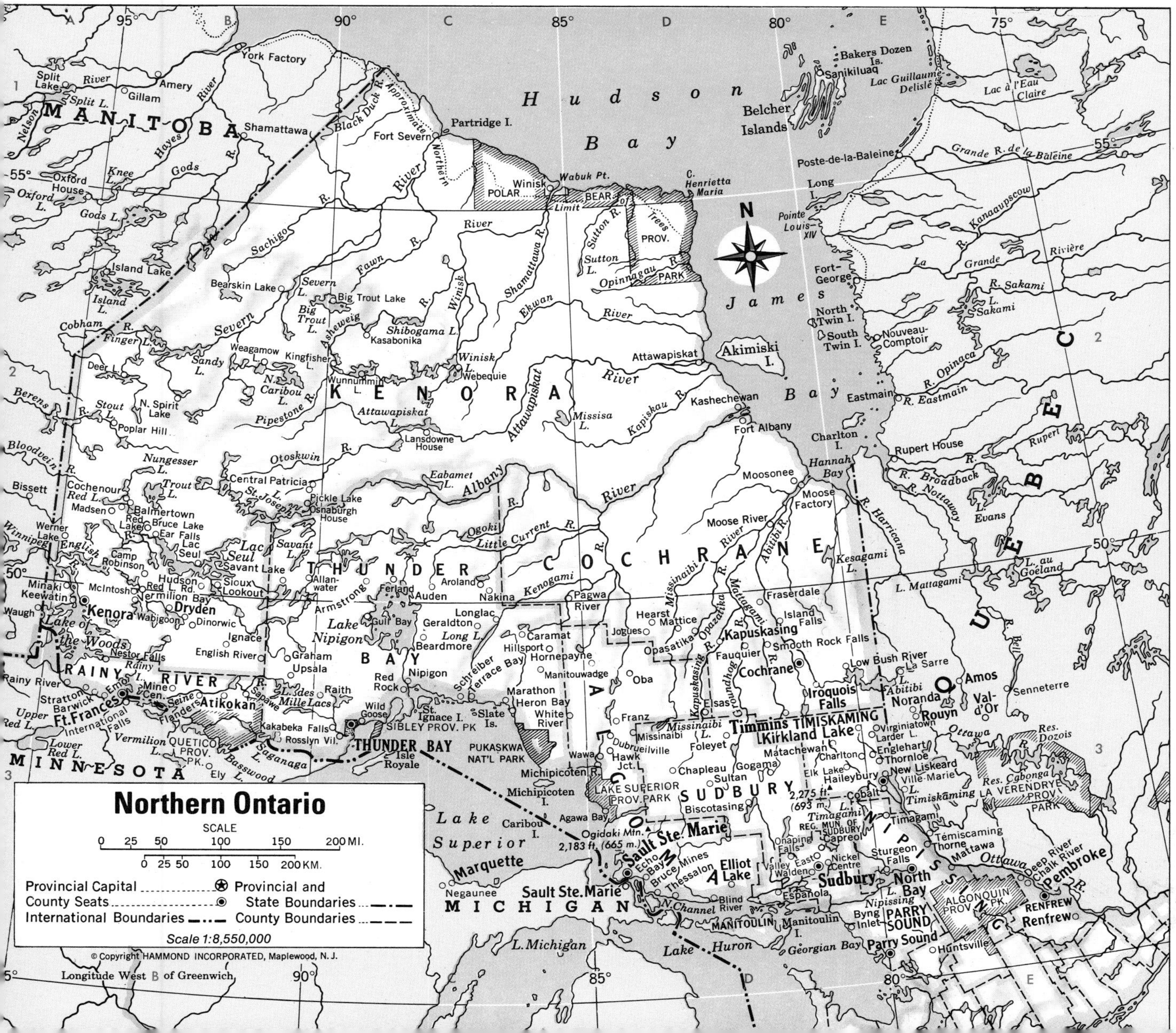

[Map]

AREA 412,580 sq. mi. (1,068,582 sq. km.)
POPULATION 8,625,107
CAPITAL Toronto
LARGEST CITY Toronto
HIGHEST POINT in Timiskaming Dist.
  2,275 ft. (693 m.)
SETTLED IN 1749
ADMITTED TO CONFEDERATION 1867
PROVINCIAL FLOWER White Trillium

Northern Ontario

SCALE
0 25 50 100 150 200 MI.
0 25 50 100 150 200 KM.

Provincial Capital ....⊛ Provincial and
County Seats ....⊚ State Boundaries —··—
International Boundaries ....— County Boundaries —···—

Scale 1:8,550,000

© Copyright HAMMOND INCORPORATED, Maplewood, N.J.

Longitude West B of Greenwich

Haileybury 4,925 .... K 5
Haldimand 16,866 .... E 5
Haliburton 1,443 .... F 2
Halton Hills 35,190 .... E 4
Hamilton® 306,434 .... E 4
Hamilton *542,095 .... E 4
Hanover 6,316 .... C 4
Harriston 1,954 .... D 4
Harrow 2,274 .... B 5
Harrowsmith 599 .... H 3
Harwood 332 .... F 3
Hastings 975 .... G 3
Havelock 1,385 .... G 3
Hawkesbury 9,877 .... K 2
Hawkestone 275 .... E 3
Hawk Junction 349 .... J 5
Hearst 5,533 .... J 5
Hensall 973 .... C 3
Hepworth 393 .... C 3
Hickson 263 .... D 4
Highgate 435 .... B 5
Hillsburgh 1,065 .... D 4
Hillsdale 370 .... E 3
Holland Landing 2,771 .... E 3
Honey Harbour 505 .... E 2
Hornepayne 1,848 .... J 5
Hudson 515 .... G 4
Huntsville 11,467 .... E 2
Huron Park 1,104 .... C 3
Ignace 2,499 .... G 5
Ilderton 301 .... C 4
Ingersoll 8,494 .... C 4
Ingleside 1,400 .... J 2
Innerkip 715 .... D 4
Inverhuron 438 .... C 3
Iron Bridge 821 .... A 1

Iroquois 1,211 .... J 3
Iroquois Falls 6,339 .... J 5
Johnstown 789 .... J 3
Kakabeka Falls 300 .... G 5
Kanata 19,728 .... J 2
Kapuskasing 12,014 .... J 5
Kars 449 .... J 2
Kearney 538 .... F 2
Keene 353 .... F 3
Keewatin 1,863 .... F 5
Kemptville 2,362 .... J 2
Kenora® 9,817 .... F 4
Killaloe Station 634 .... G 2
Killarney 433 .... C 2
Kincardine 5,778 .... C 3
Kingston® 52,616 .... H 3
Kingsville 5,134 .... B 5
Kinmount 262 .... F 3
Kirkland Lake 12,219 .... K 5
Kitchener 139,734 .... D 4
Kitchener *287,801 .... D 4
Komoka 1,152 .... C 4
Lakefield 2,374 .... F 3
Lanark 753 .... H 2
Lancaster 637 .... K 2
Langton 348 .... D 5
Lansdowne 540 .... H 3
Larder Lake 1,084 .... K 5
Latchford 397 .... K 5
Leamington 12,528 .... B 5
Limoges 930 .... K 2
Lincoln 14,196 .... E 4
Linden Beach 579 .... B 6
Lindsay® 13,596 .... F 3
Linwood 450 .... D 4
Lion's Head 467 .... C 2

Lisle 265 .... E 3
Listowel 5,026 .... D 4
Little Britain 265 .... F 3
Little Current 1,507 .... B 2
London 254,280 .... C 5
London *283,668 .... C 5
Longlac 2,431 .... H 5
Long Sault 1,227 .... K 2
L'Orignal® 1,819 .... K 2
Lucan 1,616 .... C 4
Lucknow 1,088 .... C 4
Lyn 518 .... J 3
Lynden 451 .... D 4
Lynhurst 685 .... C 5
MacGregor's Bay 861 .... G 2
MacTier 647 .... E 2
Madawaska 264 .... F 2
Madoc 1,249 .... G 3
Maitland 667 .... J 3
Mallorytown 368 .... J 3
Manitouwadge 3,155 .... H 5
Manitowaning 518 .... C 2
Manotick-Hillside Gardens
  2,694 .... J 2
Marathon 2,271 .... H 5
Markdale 1,289 .... D 3
Markham 77,037 .... K 4
Markstay 444 .... D 1
Marmora 1,304 .... G 3
Martintown 388 .... K 2
Massey 1,673 .... C 1
Matachewan 444 .... J 5
Matheson 965 .... K 5
Mattawa 2,652 .... F 1
Mattice 803 .... J 5
Maxville 836 .... K 2

Maynooth 277 .... G 2
McGregor 1,145 .... B 5
McKerrow 260 .... C 1
Meaford 4,367 .... D 3
Melbourne 346 .... C 5
Merlin 745 .... B 5
Merrickville 984 .... J 3
Metcalfe 687 .... J 2
Midhurst 1,457 .... E 3
Midland 12,132 .... E 3
Mildmay 928 .... C 3
Milford Bay 401 .... E 2
Millbank 337 .... D 4
Millbrook 927 .... F 3
Milton® 28,067 .... E 4
Milverton 1,463 .... D 4
Minaki 319 .... F 4
Mindemoya 376 .... B 2
Minden® 838 .... F 3
Mississauga 315,056 .... J 4
Mitchell 2,777 .... C 4
Monkton 520 .... C 4
Moonbeam 838 .... J 5
Moorefield 308 .... D 4
Mooretown 344 .... B 5
Moose Creek 393 .... K 2
Morewood 264 .... J 2
Morpeth 284 .... C 5
Morrisburg 2,308 .... J 3
Mount Albert 1,165 .... E 3
Mount Brydges 1,557 .... C 5
Mount Forest 3,474 .... D 4
Mount Hope 557 .... E 4
Munster 1,531 .... J 2
Nakina 936 .... H 4
Nanticoke® 19,816 .... E 5

Napanee® 4,803 .... G 3
Navan 419 .... J 2
Neustadt 511 .... D 3
Newboro 260 .... H 3
Newburgh 617 .... H 3
Newbury 441 .... C 5
Newcastle 32,229 .... F 4
New Hamburg 3,923 .... D 4
New Liskeard 5,551 .... K 5
Newmarket® 29,753 .... E 3
Niagara Falls 70,960 .... E 4
Niagara-on-the-Lake 12,186 .... E 4
Nickel Centre 12,318 .... D 1
Nipigon 2,377 .... H 5
Nobel 386 .... D 2
Nobleton 1,861 .... J 3
Noelville 702 .... D 1
North Bay® 51,268 .... E 1
North Gower 818 .... J 2
North York 559,521 .... J 4
Norwich 2,117 .... D 5
Norwood 1,278 .... F 3
Nottawa 360 .... E 3
Oakville 75,773 .... E 4
Oakwood 404 .... F 3
Odessa 849 .... H 3
Oil City 266 .... B 5
Oil Springs 627 .... B 5
Omemee 819 .... F 3
Onaping Falls 6,198 .... J 5
Opasatika 413 .... J 5
Orangeville® 13,740 .... D 4
Orillia 23,955 .... E 3
Osgoode 1,138 .... J 2
Oshawa 117,519 .... F 4
Oshawa *154,217 .... F 4

Ottawa® (cap.), Canada
  295,163 .... J 2
Ottawa-Hull *717,978 .... J 2
Otterville 776 .... D 5
Owen Sound® 19,883 .... D 3
Paincourt 414 .... B 5
Paisley 1,039 .... C 3
Pakenham 367 .... H 2
Palmerston 1,989 .... D 4
Paris 7,485 .... D 4
Parkhill 1,358 .... C 4
Parry Sound® 6,124 .... E 2
Pefferlaw 857 .... E 3
Pelham 11,104 .... E 4
Pembroke® 14,026 .... G 2
Penetanguishene 5,315 .... D 3
Perth® 5,655 .... H 3
Petawawa 5,520 .... G 2
Peterborough® 60,620 .... F 3
Petrolia 4,234 .... B 5
Pickering 37,754 .... K 4
Picton® 4,361 .... G 3
Plantagenet 870 .... K 2
Plattsville 495 .... D 4
Point Edward 2,383 .... B 4
Pontypool 759 .... F 3
Port Burwell 655 .... D 5
Port Carling 629 .... E 2
Port Colborne 19,225 .... E 5
Port Elgin 6,131 .... C 3
Port Franks 547 .... C 4
Port Hope 9,992 .... F 4
Port Lambton 921 .... B 5
Portland 271 .... H 3
Port McNicoll 1,883 .... E 3
Port Perry 4,712 .... F 3

Port Rowan 811 .... D 5
Port Stanley 1,891 .... C 5
Pottageville 286 .... J 3
Powassan 1,169 .... E 1
Prescott 4,670 .... J 3
Princeton 462 .... D 4
Puce-Emeryville 1,611 .... B 5
Rainy River 1,061 .... F 5
Ramore 382 .... K 5
Rayside-Balfour 15,017 .... J 5
Red Rock 1,260 .... H 5
Renfrew® 8,283 .... G 2
Richards Landing 405 .... A 1
Richmond 2,880 .... J 2
Richmond Hill 37,778 .... J 3
Ridgetown 3,062 .... C 5
Ripley 591 .... C 3
River Valley 275 .... D 1
Rockcliffe Park 1,869 .... J 2
Rockland 3,961 .... J 2
Rockwood 1,068 .... D 4
Rodney 1,007 .... C 5
Rosslyn Village 362 .... G 5
Round Lake Centre 255 .... G 2
Russell 1,099 .... J 2
Ruthven 649 .... B 6
Saint Albert 254 .... J 2
Saint Catharines® 124,018 .... E 4
Saint Catharines-Niagara
  *304,353 .... E 4
Saint Charles 382 .... D 1
Saint Clair Beach 2,845 .... B 5
Saint Clements 890 .... D 4
Saint-Eugène 470 .... K 2
Saint George 865 .... D 4
Saint Isidore de Prescott 746 . K 2

Ontario
Central Part
0 25 50 75 100 125 MI.
0 25 50 75 100 125 KM.

© Copyright HAMMOND INCORPORATED, Maplewood, N.J.

Longitude 80° West of 79° Greenwich

Saint Jacobs 1,189 . . . . D 4
Saint Mary's 4,883 . . . . C 4
Saint Thomas⊛ 28,165 . . . . C 5
Saint Williams 442 . . . . D 5
Salem 825 . . . . D 4
Sarnia⊛ 50,892 . . . . B 5
Sauble Beach 729 . . . . C 3
Sault Sainte Marie⊛ 82,697 . . . J 5
Scarborough 443,353 . . . . K 4
Schomberg 923 . . . . D 4
Schreiber 1,968 . . . . H 5
Scotland 307 . . . . D 4
Seaforth 2,114 . . . . C 4
Searchmont 384 . . . . J 5
Sebringville 579 . . . . C 4
Seeleys Bay 503 . . . . H 3
Shakespeare 602 . . . . C 4
Shallow Lake 418 . . . . C 3
Shannonville 314 . . . . G 3
Shanty Bay 358 . . . . E 3
Sharbot Lake 495 . . . . H 3
Shedden 292 . . . . C 5
Shelburne 2,862 . . . . D 3
Simcoe⊛ 14,326 . . . . D 5
Sioux Lookout 3,074 . . . . J 4
Sioux Narrows 394 . . . . F 5
Smithfield 349 . . . . G 3
Smiths Falls 8,831 . . . . H 3
Smithville 1,936 . . . . E 4
Smooth Rock Falls 2,352 . . . . . J 5
Sombra 420 . . . . B 5
Southampton 2,830 . . . . C 3
South Mountain 285 . . . . J 3
South River 1,109 . . . . E 2
Spanish 1,063 . . . . J 5
Sparta 283 . . . . C 5

Spencerville 438 . . . . J 3
Springfield 555 . . . . C 5
Springford 309 . . . . D 5
Stayner 2,530 . . . . E 3
Stirling 1,638 . . . . G 3
Stittsville 2,652 . . . . J 2
Stoney Creek 36,762 . . . . E 4
Stoney Point 1,090 . . . . B 5
Straffordville 752 . . . . D 5
Stratford⊛ 26,262 . . . . C 4
Strathroy 8,748 . . . . C 5
Sturgeon Falls 6,045 . . . . E 1
Sudbury⊛ 91,829 . . . . K 5
Sudbury *149,923 . . . . K 5
Sunderland 703 . . . . E 3
Sundridge 734 . . . . E 2
Sydenham 595 . . . . H 3
Tamworth 402 . . . . H 3
Tara 687 . . . . C 3
Tavistock 1,885 . . . . D 4
Tecumseh 6,364 . . . . B 5
Teeswater 1,026 . . . . C 3
Terrace Bay 2,639 . . . . H 5
Thamesford 1,920 . . . . C 4
Thamesville 961 . . . . C 5
Thedford 694 . . . . C 4
Thessalon 1,620 . . . . J 5
Thornbury 1,435 . . . . D 3
Thorndale 581 . . . . C 4
Thornton 414 . . . . E 3
Thorold 15,412 . . . . E 4
Thunder Bay⊛ 112,486 . . . . . . H 5
Thunder Bay *121,379 . . . . . . H 5
Tilbury 4,298 . . . . B 5
Tillsonburg 10,487 . . . . D 5
Timmins 46,114 . . . . J 5

Tiverton 806 . . . . C 3
Tobermory 282 . . . . C 2
Toronto (cap.)⊛ 599,217 . . . . . K 4
Toronto *2,998,947 . . . . K 4
Tottenham 3,022 . . . . E 3
Trenton 15,085 . . . . G 3
Trout Creek 652 . . . . E 2
Turkey Point 407 . . . . D 5
Tweed 1,574 . . . . G 3
Udora 375 . . . . E 3
Union 485 . . . . C 5
Uxbridge 4,209 . . . . E 3
Valley East 20,433 . . . . J 5
Vanier 18,792 . . . . J 2
Vankleek Hill 1,774 . . . . K 2
Vars 527 . . . . J 2
Vaughan 29,674 . . . . J 4
Vermilion Bay 505 . . . . G 4
Verner 1,076 . . . . D 1
Vernon 303 . . . . J 2
Verona 754 . . . . H 3
Victoria Harbour 1,125 . . . . . . E 3
Vienna 369 . . . . D 5
Virginiatown 1,010 . . . . K 5
Vittoria 350 . . . . D 5
Wabigoon 268 . . . . G 5
Walden 10,139 . . . . J 5
Walkerton⊛ 4,682 . . . . C 3
Wallaceburg 11,506 . . . . B 5
Wardsville 450 . . . . C 5
Warkworth 618 . . . . G 3
Warren 579 . . . . D 1
Warsaw 314 . . . . F 3
Wasaga Beach 4,705 . . . . D 3
Washago 569 . . . . E 3
Watches 49,428 . . . . D 4
Watford 1,402 . . . . C 5
Waubaushene 878 . . . . E 3
Wawa 4,206 . . . . J 5
Webbwood 519 . . . . C 1
Welcome 293 . . . . F 4
Welland 454,448 . . . . E 5
Wellesley 997 . . . . D 4
Wellington 1,082 . . . . G 4
Wendover 326 . . . . J 2
West Lorne 1,258 . . . . C 5
Westmeath 262 . . . . H 2
Westport 621 . . . . H 3
Wheatley 1,638 . . . . B 5
Whitby⊛ 36,698 . . . . F 4
Whitchurch-Stouffville 13,557 . J 3
White River △1,006 . . . . J 5
Whitney 766 . . . . F 2
Wiarton 2,074 . . . . C 3
Wikwemikong 1,030 . . . . C 2
Williamsburg 407 . . . . J 3
Williamsford 256 . . . . D 3
Williamstown 328 . . . . K 2
Winchester 2,001 . . . . J 2
Windsor⊛ 192,083 . . . . B 5
Windsor *246,110 . . . . B 5
Wingham 2,897 . . . . C 4
Wolfe Island 271 . . . . H 3
Woodstock⊛ 26,603 . . . . D 4
Woodville 575 . . . . F 3
Wroxeter 350 . . . . C 4
Wyoming 1,682 . . . . B 5
Yarker 319 . . . . H 3
York 134,617 . . . . J 4
Zephyr 330 . . . . E 3
Zurich 795 . . . . C 4

OTHER FEATURES

Abitibi (riv.) . . . . J 5
Algonquin Prov. Park . . . . F 2
Amherst (isl.) . . . . H 3
Balsam (lake) . . . . F 3
Barrie (isl.) . . . . B 1
Bays (lake) . . . . F 2
Big Rideau (lake) . . . . H 3
Black (riv.) . . . . E 3
Bruce (pen.) . . . . C 2
Buckhorn (lake) . . . . F 3
Cabot (head) . . . . C 2
Charleston (lake) . . . . J 3
Christian (isl.) . . . . D 3
Clear (lake) . . . . F 3
Cockburn (isl.) . . . . A 2
Couchiching (lake) . . . . E 3
Croker (cape) . . . . D 3

Don (riv.) . . . . J 4
Doré (lake) . . . . G 2
Douglas (pt.) . . . . C 3
Erie (lake) . . . . E 5
Flowerpot (isl.) . . . . C 2
French (riv.) . . . . D 1
Georgian (bay) . . . . D 2
Georgian Bay Is.
  Nat'l Park . . . . C 2, D 3
Georgina (isl.) . . . . E 3
Grand (riv.) . . . . D 4
Humber (riv.) . . . . J 3
Hurd (cape) . . . . C 2
Huron (lake) . . . . B 3
Ipperwash Prov. Park . . . . C 4
Joseph (lake) . . . . E 2
Killarney Prov. Park . . . . C 1
Killbear Point Prov. Park . . . . . D 2
Lake of the Woods (lake) . . . . . F 5

Lake Superior Prov. Park . . . . . J 5
Lonely (isl.) . . . . C 2
Long (pt.) . . . . D 5
Long Point (bay) . . . . D 5
Madawaska (riv.) . . . . G 2
Magnetawan (riv.) . . . . D 2
Main (chan.) . . . . C 2
Manitou (lake) . . . . C 2
Manitoulin (isl.) . . . . B 2
Mattagami (riv.) . . . . J 5
Michipicoten (isl.) . . . . H 5
Missinaibi (riv.) . . . . J 5
Mississagi (riv.) . . . . A 1
Mississippi (lake) . . . . H 2
Muskoka (lake) . . . . E 2
Niagara (riv.) . . . . E 4
Nipigon (lake) . . . . H 5
Nipissing (lake) . . . . E 1
North (chan.) . . . . A 1
Nottawasaga (bay) . . . . D 3
Ogidaki (mt.) . . . . J 5
Ontario (lake) . . . . G 4
Opeongo (lake) . . . . F 2
Ottawa (riv.) . . . . H 2
Owen (sound) . . . . D 3
Panache (lake) . . . . C 1
Parry (isl.) . . . . D 2
Parry (sound) . . . . D 2
Petre (pt.) . . . . G 4
Point Pelee Nat'l Park . . . . B 5
Presqu'ile Prov. Park . . . . G 4
Pukaskwa Prov. Park . . . . H 5
Quetico Prov. Park . . . . G 5

Rainy (lake) . . . . G 5
Rice (lake) . . . . F 3
Rideau (lake) . . . . H 3
Rondeau Prov. Park . . . . C 5
Rosseau (lake) . . . . E 2
Saint Clair (lake) . . . . B 5
Saint Clair (riv.) . . . . B 5
Saint Lawrence . . . . K 3
Saint Lawrence (riv.) . . . . J 3
Saint Lawrence Is. Nat'l Park . . J 3
Saugeen (riv.) . . . . C 3
Scugog (lake) . . . . F 3
Seul (lake) . . . . G 4
Severn (riv.) . . . . H 5
Sibley Prov. Park . . . . H 5
Simcoe (lake) . . . . E 3
South (bay) . . . . C 2
Spanish (riv.) . . . . C 1
Stony (lake) . . . . G 3
Superior (lake) . . . . H 5
Sydenham (riv.) . . . . B 5
Thames (riv.) . . . . B 5
Theano (pt.) . . . . J 5
Thousand (isls.) . . . . H 3
Timagami (lake) . . . . K 5
Trout (lake) . . . . E 1
Vernon (lake) . . . . E 2
Walpole (isl.) . . . . B 5
Welland (canal) . . . . E 5
Woods (lake) . . . . F 5

⊛County seat.
*Population of metropolitan area.
△Population of town or township.

Topography

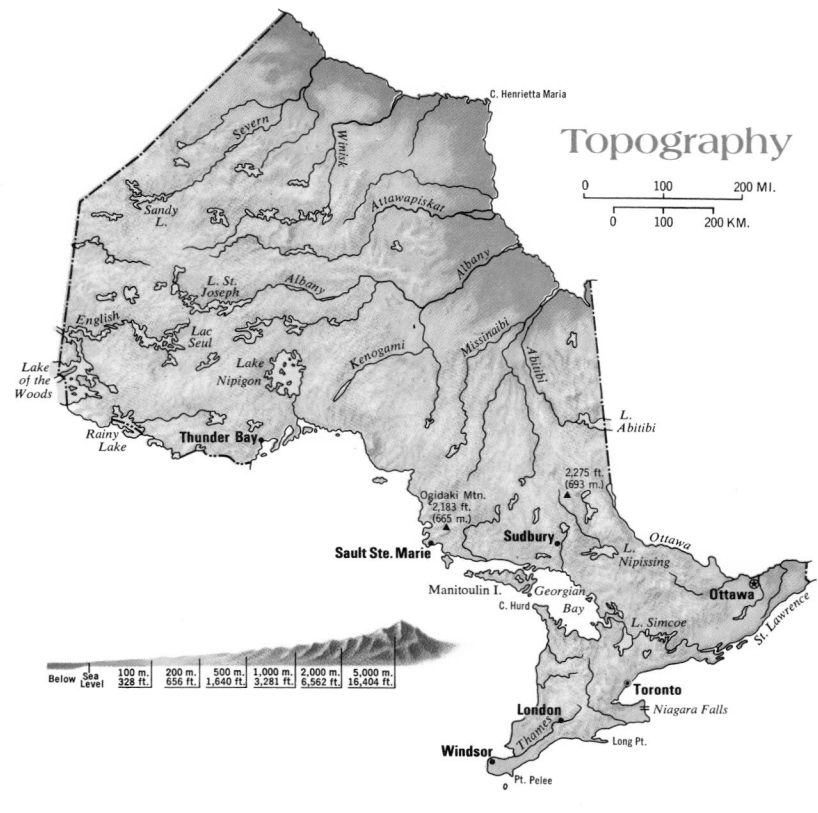

0   100   200 MI.
0   100   200 KM.

Below Sea Level | 100 m. 328 ft. | 200 m. 656 ft. | 500 m. 1,640 ft. | 1,000 m. 3,281 ft. | 2,000 m. 6,562 ft. | 5,000 m. 16,404 ft.

Ontario
Southern Part

SCALE
0   10   20   30   40   50 MI.
0   10   20   30   40   50 KM.

National Capital . . . . ⊛   Provincial & State
Provincial Capital . . . . ⊛   Boundaries
County Seats . . . . ⊙   County Boundaries ─ ─ ─ ─
International   Canals
  Boundaries . . . . ▬▬▬

Scale 1:2,620,000

Agriculture, Industry and Resources

DOMINANT LAND USE

Cereals, Cash Crops, Livestock
Dairy
General Farming, Livestock
Fruits, Vegetables
Pasture Livestock
Forests
Nonagricultural Land

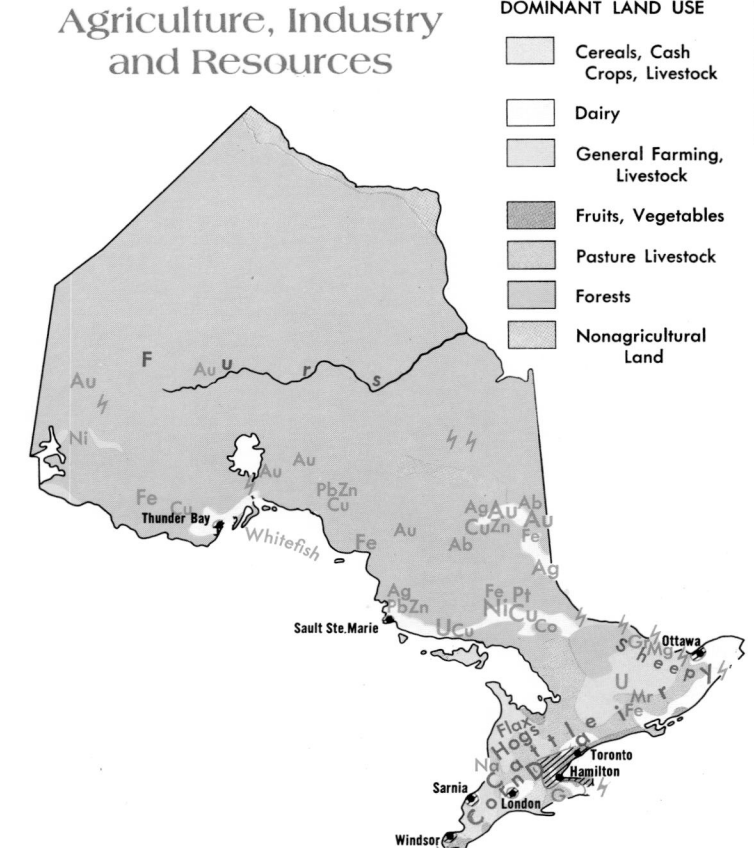

MAJOR MINERAL OCCURRENCES

Ab Asbestos   Mg Magnesium
Ag Silver   Mr Marble
Au Gold   Na Salt
Co Cobalt   Ni Nickel
Cu Copper   Pb Lead
Fe Iron Ore   Pt Platinum
G   Natural Gas   U   Uranium
Gr Graphite   Zn Zinc

⚡ Water Power
▨ Major Industrial Areas

Manitoba
Northern Part

0 40 80 120 MI.
0 40 80 120 KM.

Manitoba
Southern Part

SCALE

0 5 10 20   40   60 MI.
0 5 10 20   40   60 KM.

Provincial Capital .... ⊛
International Boundaries ⎯ ⋅ ⎯ ⋅
Provincial Boundaries ⎯ ⋅⋅ ⎯

Scale 1:2,340,000

© Copyright HAMMOND INCORPORATED, Maplewood, N.J.

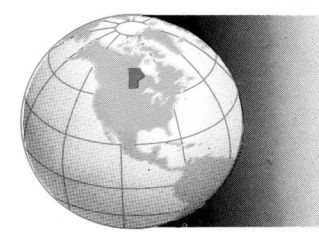

AREA 250,999 sq. mi. (650,087 sq. km.)
POPULATION 1,026,241
CAPITAL Winnipeg
LARGEST CITY Winnipeg
HIGHEST POINT Baldy Mtn. 2,729 ft.
 (832 m.)
SETTLED IN 1812
ADMITTED TO CONFEDERATION 1870
PROVINCIAL FLOWER Prairie Crocus

The Pas 6,390 .... H 3
Thicket Portage 195 .... J 3
Thompson 14,288 .... J 2
Treherne 743 .... D 5
Tyndall 421 .... F 4
Virden 2,940 .... A 5
Vita 364 .... F 5
Wabowden 655 .... J 3
Wallace Lake ●2,044 .... G 3
Wanless 193 .... H 3
Warren 459 .... E 4
Waskada 239 .... B 5
Wawanesa 492 .... C 5
Whitemouth 320 .... D 4
Whitewater ●856 .... B 5
Winkler 5,046 .... E 5
Winnipeg (cap.) 564,473 ...... E 5
Winnipeg *584,842 .... E 5
Winnipeg Beach 565 .... F 4
Winnipegosis 855 .... B 3
Woodlands 185 .... E 4
Wooodridge 170 .... G 5
York Landing 229 .... J 2

OTHER FEATURES

Aikens (lake) .... G 3
Anderson (lake) .... D 2
Anderson (pt.) .... F 3
Armit (lake) .... A 2
Assapan (riv.) .... G 2
Assiniboine (riv.) .... C 5
Assinika (lake) .... G 2
Assinika (riv.) .... G 2
Atim (lake) .... C 2
Baldy (mt.) .... B 3
Basket (lake) .... C 3
Beaverhill (lake) .... J 3
Berens (isl.) .... E 2
Berens (riv.) .... F 2
Bernic (lake) .... G 4
Big Sand (lake) .... H 2
Bigstone (lake) .... J 3
Bigstone (pt.) .... E 2
Bigstone (riv.) .... J 3
Birch (lake) .... C 2
Black (isl.) .... F 3
Black (lake) .... F 4
Bloodvein (riv.) .... F 3
Bonnet (lake) .... G 4
Buffalo (bay) .... G 5
Burntwood (riv.) .... J 2
Caribou (riv.) .... J 1
Carroll (lake) .... G 3
Cedar (lake) .... B 1
Channel (isl.) .... B 2
Charron (lake) .... G 2
Childs (lake) .... A 3
Chitek (lake) .... C 2
Churchill (cape) .... K 2
Churchill (riv.) .... J 2
Clear (lake) .... C 4
Clearwater Lake Prov. Park .. H 3
Cobham (riv.) .... G 1
Cochrane (riv.) .... H 2
Commissioner (isl.) .... E 2
Cormorant (lake) .... H 3
Cross (bay) .... C 1
Cross (lake) .... J 3
Crowduck (lake) .... G 4
Dancing (pt.) .... D 2
Dauphin (lake) .... C 3
Dauphin (riv.) .... D 3
Dawson (bay) .... B 2
Dog (lake) .... D 3
Dogskin (lake) .... G 3
Duck Mountain Prov. Park ... B 3
Eardley (lake) .... F 2

East Shoal (lake) .... E 4
Ebb and Flow (lake) .... C 3
Egg (isl.) .... E 3
Elbow (lake) .... G 4
Elk (isl.) .... F 4
Elliot (lake) .... G 2
Etawney (lake) .... J 2
Etomami (riv.) .... F 2
Falcon (lake) .... G 5
Family (lake) .... G 3
Fisher (bay) .... E 3
Fisher (riv.) .... E 3
Fishing (lake) .... G 2
Flintstone (lake) .... G 4
Fox (riv.) .... K 2
Gammon (riv.) .... G 3
Garner (lake) .... G 4
Gem (lake) .... G 4
George (isl.) .... E 2
George (lake) .... G 4
Gilchrist (creek) .... F 2
Gilchrist (lake) .... G 2
Gods (lake) .... K 3
Gods (riv.) .... K 3
Granville (lake) .... H 2
Grass (riv.) .... J 3
Grass River Prov. Park ...... H 3
Grindstone Prov. Rec. Park .. F 3
Gunisao (lake) .... J 3
Gypsum (lake) .... D 3
Harrop (lake) .... G 2
Harte (mt.) .... A 2
Hayes (riv.) .... K 3
Hecla (isl.) .... F 3
Hecla Prov. Park .... F 3
Hobbs (lake) .... G 3
Horseshoe (lake) .... G 2
Hubbart (pt.) .... K 2
Hudson (bay) .... K 2
Hudwin (lake) .... G 1
International Peace Garden .. B 5
Island (lake) .... K 3
Katimik (lake) .... C 2
Kawinaw (lake) .... C 2
Kinwow (bay) .... E 2
Kississing (lake) .... H 2
Knee (lake) .... J 3
Lake of the Woods (lake) .... H 5
La Salle (riv.) .... E 5
Laurie (lake) .... A 3
Leaf (riv.) .... F 2
Lewis (lake) .... G 2
Leyond (riv.) .... F 3
Little Birch (lake) .... E 3
Lonely (lake) .... C 3
Long (lake) .... G 4
Long (pt.) .... D 1
Long (pt.) .... D 4
Manigotagan (lake) .... G 4

Manigotagan (riv.) .... G 3
Manitoba (lake) .... D 4
Mantagao (riv.) .... E 3
Marshy (lake) .... B 5
McKay (lake) .... C 2
McPhail (riv.) .... F 2
Minnedosa (riv.) .... B 4
Moar (lake) .... G 2
Molson (lake) .... J 3
Moose (lake) .... E 3
Morrison (lake) .... C 1
Mossy (riv.) .... C 3
Mukutawa (lake) .... G 2
Mukutawa (riv.) .... E 1
Muskeg (bay) .... G 6
Nejanilini (lake) .... J 1
Nelson (riv.) .... J 2
Nopiming Prov. Park .... G 4
Northern Indian (lake) ...... J 2
North Knife (lake) .... J 2
North Seal (riv.) .... H 2
North Shoal (lake) .... E 4
Nueltin (lake) .... H 1
Oak (lake) .... B 5
Obukowin (lake) .... G 3
Oiseau (lake) .... G 4
Oiseau (riv.) .... G 4
Overflow (bay) .... A 1
Overflowing (riv.) .... A 1
Owl (riv.) .... K 2
Oxford (lake) .... J 3
Paint (lake) .... J 2
Palsen (riv.) .... G 2
Pelican (bay) .... B 2
Pelican (lake) .... B 2
Pelican (lake) .... C 5
Pembina (hills) .... D 5
Pembina (riv.) .... C 5
Peonan (pt.) .... D 3
Pickerel (lake) .... C 2
Pigeon (riv.) .... F 2
Pipestone (creek) .... A 5
Plum (creek) .... B 5
Plum (lake) .... B 5
Poplar (riv.) .... E 2
Porcupine (hills) .... A 2
Portage (bay) .... D 3
Punk (isl.) .... F 3
Quesnel (lake) .... G 4
Rat (riv.) .... F 5
Red (riv.) .... F 4
Red Deer (lake) .... A 2
Red Deer (riv.) .... A 2
Reindeer (isl.) .... E 2
Reindeer (lake) .... H 2
Riding (mt.) .... B 4
Riding Mountain Nat'l Park .. B 4
Rock (lake) .... C 5
Ross (isl.) .... J 3
Sagemace (bay) .... B 3

Saint Andrew (lake) .... E 3
Saint George (lake) .... E 3
Saint Martin (lake) .... D 3
Saint Patrick (lake) .... B 5
Sale (riv.) .... E 5
Sandy (isls.) .... D 2
Sasaginnigak (lake) .... G 3
Seal (riv.) .... J 2
Selkirk (isl.) .... C 1
Setting (lake) .... H 3
Shoal (lake) .... G 5
Shoal (lake) .... B 2
Sipiwesk (lake) .... J 3
Sisib (lake) .... C 2
Sleeve (lake) .... E 3
Slemon (lake) .... G 1
Snowshoe (lake) .... G 4
Soul (lake) .... C 2
Souris (riv.) .... B 5
Southern Indian (lake) ...... H 2
South Knife (riv.) .... J 2
South Seal (riv.) .... J 2
Split (lake) .... J 2
Spruce (isl.) .... B 1
Spruce Woods Prov. Park ... C 5
Stevenson (lake) .... J 3
Sturgeon (bay) .... E 3
Swan (lake) .... B 2
Swan (lake) .... D 5
Swan (riv.) .... A 3
Tadoule (lake) .... J 2
Tamarack (isl.) .... F 3
Tatnam (cape) .... K 2
Traverse (bay) .... F 4
Turtle (mts.) .... B 5
Turtle (riv.) .... C 3
Turtle Mountain Prov. Park .. B 5
Valley (lake) .... B 3
Vickers (lake) .... F 3
Viking (lake) .... G 3
Wanipigow (riv.) .... G 3
Washow (bay) .... F 3
Waterhen (lake) .... C 2
Weaver (lake) .... F 2
Wellman (lake) .... B 3
West Hawk (lake) .... G 5
West Shoal (lake) .... E 4
Whitemouth (lake) .... G 5
Whitemouth (riv.) .... G 5
Whiteshell Prov. Park .... G 4
Whitewater (lake) .... B 5
Wicked (pt.) .... D 2
Winnipeg (lake) .... E 2
Winnipeg (riv.) .... G 4
Winnipegosis (lake) .... C 2
Woods (lake) .... H 5
Wrong (lake) .... F 2

*Population of metropolitan area.
●Population of rural municipality.

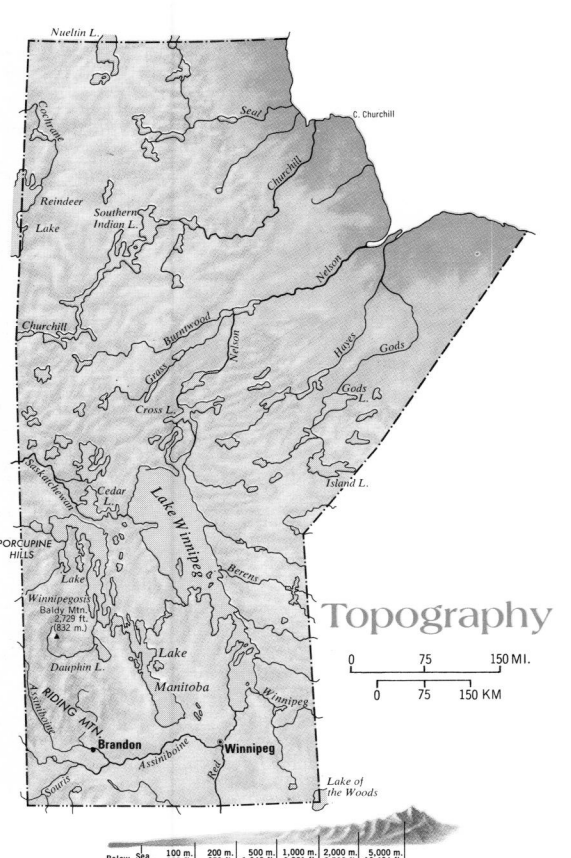

Topography

0   75   150 MI.
0   75   150 KM

Below Sea Level | 100 m. 328 ft. | 200 m. 656 ft. | 500 m. 1,640 ft. | 1,000 m. 3,281 ft. | 2,000 m. 6,562 ft. | 5,000 m. 16,404 ft.

Agriculture, Industry and Resources

DOMINANT LAND USE

- Cereals (chiefly barley, oats)
- Cereals, Livestock
- Dairy
- Livestock
- Forests
- Nonagricultural Land

MAJOR MINERAL OCCURRENCES

Au Gold
Co Cobalt
Cu Copper
Na Salt

Ni Nickel
O   Petroleum
Pb Lead
Pt Platinum
Zn Zinc

⚡ Water Power
▨ Major Industrial Areas

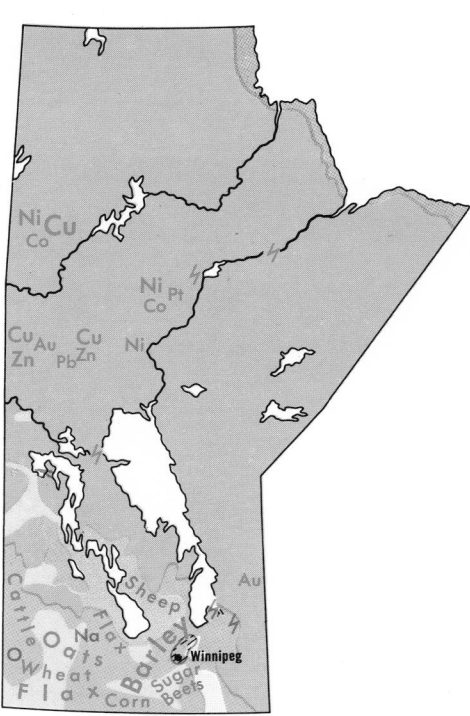

Topography

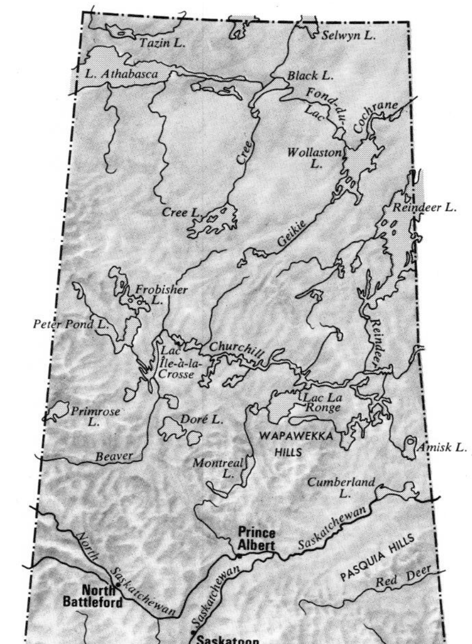
0 60 120 MI.
0 60 120 KM.
Tazin L.
Selwyn L.
L. Athabasca
Black L.
Fond-du-Lac
Cochrane
Wollaston L.
Cree
Cree L.
Geikie
Reindeer L.
Frobisher L.
Peter Pond L.
Churchill
Lac Île-à-la-Crosse
Reindeer
Lac La Ronge
Primrose L.
Doré L.
WAPAWEKKA HILLS
Amisk L.
Beaver
Montreal L.
Cumberland L.
Prince Albert
Saskatchewan
North Saskatchewan
PASQUIA HILLS
Red Deer
North Battleford
Saskatoon
Quill Lakes
Assiniboine
Last Mountain L.
GREAT SAND HILLS
South
COTEAU HILLS
Moose Jaw
Regina
Qu'Appelle
Swift Current
Old Wives L.
1392 m. 4,567 ft.
CYPRESS HILLS
Souris
5,000 m. 16,404 ft.
2,000 m. 6,562 ft.
1,000 m. 3,281 ft.
500 m. 1,640 ft.
200 m. 656 ft.
100 m. 328 ft.
Sea Level
Below

CITIES and TOWNS

Abbey 218	C 5
Aberdeen 496	E 3
Abernethy 300	H 5
Air Ronge 557	M 3
Alameda 318	J 6
Alida 169	K 6
Allan 871	E 4
Alsask 652	B 4
Annaheim 209	G 3
Antelope •231	C 5
Arborfield 439	H 2
Archerwill 286	H 3
Arcola 493	J 6
Arlington Beach •432	F 4
Asquith 507	D 3
Assiniboia 2,924	E 6
Avonlea 442	G 5
Baildon •799	F 5
Balcarres 739	H 5
Balgonie 777	G 5
Batoche	E 3
Battleford 3,565	C 3
Beauval 606	L 3
Beechy 279	D 5
Bengough 536	F 6
Bethune 369	F 5
Bienfait 835	J 6
Biggar 2,561	C 3
Big River 819	D 2
Birch Hills 957	F 3
Bjorkdale 269	H 3
Blaine Lake 653	D 3
Borden 197	D 3
Brabant Lake 245	M 3
Bradwell 168	E 4
Bredenbury 467	K 5
Briercrest 151	F 5
Broadview 840	J 5
Brock 184	C 4
Browning •687	J 6
Bruno 772	F 3
Buchanan 392	J 4
Buffalo Gap •598	F 6
Buffalo Narrows 1,088	L 3
Burstall 550	B 5
Cabri 632	C 5
Cadillac 173	D 6
Calder 164	K 4
Cana •1,238	J 5
Candle Lake 219	F 2
Cando 163	C 3
Canoe Lake 182	L 3
Canora 2,667	J 4
Canwood 340	E 2
Carievale 246	K 6
Carlyle 1,074	J 6
Carnduff 1,043	K 6
Carrot River 1,169	H 2
Central Butte 548	E 5
Ceylon 184	G 6
Chaplin 389	E 5
Chitek Lake 170	D 2
Choiceland 543	G 2
Christopher Lake 227	F 2
Churchbridge 972	J 5
Clavet 234	E 4
Climax 293	C 6
Cochin 221	C 2
Codette 236	H 2
Coleville 383	B 4
Colonsay 594	F 4
Connaught Heights •982	G 3
Conquest 256	D 4
Consul 153	B 6
Coronach 1,032	F 6
Craik 565	F 4
Craven 206	G 5
Creelman 184	H 6
Creighton 1,636	N 4
Cudworth 947	F 3
Cumberland House 831	J 2
Cupar 669	G 5
Cut Knife 624	B 3
Dalmeny 1,064	E 3
Davidson 1,166	E 4
Debden 403	E 2
Delisle 980	D 4
Denare Beach 592	M 4
Denzil 199	B 3
Deschambault Lake 386	M 3
Dinsmore 398	D 4
Dodsland 272	C 4
Domremy 209	F 3
Drake 211	G 4
Duck Lake 699	E 3
Dundurn 531	E 4
Dysart 275	H 5
Earl Grey 303	G 5
Eastend 723	C 6
Eatonia 528	B 4
Ebenezer 164	J 4
Edam 384	C 2
Edenwold 143	G 5
Elbow 313	E 4
Eldorado 229	L 2
Elfros 199	H 4
Elrose 624	D 4
Elstow 143	E 4
Endeavour 199	J 3
Englefeld 271	G 3
Erwood 149	J 3
Esterhazy 3,065	K 5
Estevan 9,174	J 6
Eston 1,413	C 4
Eyebrow 168	E 5
Fillmore 396	H 6
Fleming 141	K 5
Flin Flon 367	N 4
Foam Lake 1,452	H 4
Fond du Lac 494	L 2
Fort Qu'Appelle 1,827	H 5
Fox Valley 380	B 5
Francis 182	H 5
Frobisher 166	J 6
Frontier 619	C 6
Gainsborough 308	K 6
Gerald 197	K 5
Glaslyn 430	C 2
Glenavon 284	J 5
Glen Ewen 168	K 6
Goodsoil 263	L 4
Govan 394	G 4
Grand Coulee 208	G 5
Gravelbourg 1,338	E 6
Grayson 264	J 5
Green Acres 139	F 2
Green Lake 634	L 4
Grenfell 1,307	J 5
Guernsey 198	F 4
Gull Lake 1,095	C 5
Hafford 557	D 3
Hague 625	E 3
Hanley 484	E 4
Harris 259	D 4
Hawarden 137	E 4
Hearts Hill •552	B 3
Hepburn 411	E 3
Herbert 1,019	D 5
Hodgeville 329	E 5
Holdfast 297	F 5
Hudson Bay 2,361	J 3
Humboldt 4,705	F 3
Hyas 165	J 4
Île-à-la-Crosse 1,035	L 3
Imperial 501	F 4
Indian Head 1,889	H 5
Invermay 353	J 4
Ituna 870	H 4
Jansen 223	G 4
Jasmin •14	H 4
Kamsack 2,688	K 4
Kelliher 397	H 4
Kelvington 1,054	H 3
Kenaston 345	E 4
Kennedy 275	J 5
Kerrobert 1,141	C 4
Kincaid 256	D 6
Kindersley 3,969	B 4
Kinistino 783	F 3
Kipling 1,016	J 5
Kisbey 228	J 6
Kronau 154	G 5
Kyle 516	C 5
Lac Pelletier •586	C 6
Lafleche 583	E 6
Laird 233	E 3
Lake Lenore 361	G 3
La Loche 1,632	L 3
Lampman 651	J 6
Lancer 156	C 5
Landis 277	C 3
Lang 219	G 6
Langenburg 1,324	K 5
Langham 1,151	E 3
Lanigan 1,732	F 4
La Ronge 2,579	L 3
Lashburn 813	B 2
Leader 1,108	B 5
Leask 478	E 2
Lebret 274	H 5
Lemberg 414	H 5
Leoville 393	D 2
Leroy 504	G 4
Lestock 402	G 4
Limerick 164	E 6
Lintlaw 234	H 3
Lipton 364	H 5
Lloydminster 6,034	A 2
Loon Lake 369	B 1
Loreburn 201	E 4
Lucky Lake 333	D 5
Lumsden 1,303	G 5
Luseland 704	B 3
Macdowall 171	E 2
Macklin 976	A 3
Macoun 190	H 6
Maidstone 1,001	B 2
Mankota 375	D 6
Manor 368	K 6
Maple Creek 2,470	B 6
Marcelin 238	E 3
Margo 153	H 4
Marriott •627	D 4
Marsden 229	B 3
Marshall 453	B 2
Martensville 1,966	E 3
Maryfield 431	K 6
Maymont 212	D 3
McLean 189	G 5
Meacham 178	F 3
Meadow Lake 3,857	C 1
Meath Park 262	F 2
Medstead 163	C 2
Melfort 6,010	G 3
Melville 5,092	J 5
Meota 235	C 2
Mervin 155	C 2
Midale 564	H 6
Middle Lake 275	F 3
Milden 251	D 4
Milestone 602	G 5
Montmartre 544	H 5
Montreal Lake 448	F 1
Moose Jaw 33,941	F 5
Moose Range •679	H 2
Moosomin 2,579	K 5
Morse 416	D 5
Mortlach 293	E 5
Mossbank 464	E 6
Muenster 385	F 3
Naicam 886	G 3
Neilburg 354	B 3
Neuanlage 144	E 3
Neudorf 425	J 5
Neuhorst 146	E 3
Nipawin 4,376	H 2
Nokomis 524	F 4
Norquay 552	J 4
North Battleford 14,030	C 3
North Portal 164	J 6
Odessa 232	H 5
Ogema 441	G 6
Osler 527	E 3
Outlook 1,976	E 4
Oxbow 1,191	J 6
Paddockwood 211	F 2
Pangman 227	G 6
Paradise Hill 421	B 2
Patuanak 173	L 3
Paynton 210	B 2
Pelican Narrows 331	N 3
Pelly 391	K 4
Pennant 202	C 5
Pense 472	G 5
Perdue 407	D 3
Pierceland 425	K 4
Pilger 150	F 3
Pilot Butte 1,255	G 5
Pine House 612	M 3
Plenty 175	C 4
Plunkett 150	F 4
Ponteix 769	D 6
Porcupine Plain 937	H 3
Preeceville 1,243	J 4
Prelate 317	B 5
Prince Albert 31,380	F 2
Prud'homme 222	F 3
Punnichy 394	G 4
Qu'Appelle 653	H 5
Quill Lake 514	G 3
Quinton 169	G 4
Rabbit Lake 159	D 2
Radisson 439	D 3
Radville 1,012	G 6
Rama 133	H 4
Raymore 635	G 4
Redvers 859	K 6
Regina (cap.) 162,613	G 5
Regina *164,313	G 5
Regina Beach 603	F 5
Rhein 271	J 4
Richmound 188	B 5
Riverhurst 193	E 5
Rocanville 934	K 5
Roche Percé 142	J 6
Rockglen 511	F 6
Rosetown 2,664	D 4
Rose Valley 538	H 3
Rosthern 1,609	E 3
Rouleau 443	G 5
Saint Benedict 157	F 3
Saint Brieux 401	G 3
Saint Louis 448	F 3
Saint Philips •538	K 4
Saint Walburg 802	B 2
Saltcoats 549	J 4
Sandy Bay 756	N 3
Saskatoon 154,210	E 3
Saskatoon *154,210	E 3
Sceptre 169	B 5
Scott 203	C 3
Sedley 373	H 5
Semans 344	G 4
Shaunavon 2,112	C 6
Sheho 285	H 4
Shell Lake 220	D 2
Shellbrook 1,228	E 2
Simpson 231	F 4
Sintaluta 215	H 5
Smeaton 246	G 2
Southey 697	G 5
Spalding 337	G 3
Spiritwood 926	D 2
Springside 533	J 4
Spy Hill 354	K 5
Star City 527	G 3
Stenen 143	J 4
Stockholm 391	J 5
Stonehenge •701	F 6
Storthoaks 142	K 6
Stoughton 716	J 6
Strasbourg 842	G 4
Sturgis 789	J 4
Swift Current 14,747	D 5
Tantallon 196	K 5
Theodore 473	J 4
Timber Bay 152	F 1
Tisdale 3,107	H 3
Togo 181	K 4
Tompkins 275	C 5
Torch River •2,440	G 2
Torquay 311	H 6
Tramping Lake 178	B 3
Tugaske 175	E 5
Turnor Lake 166	L 3
Turtleford 505	B 2
Unity 2,408	B 3
Uranium City 2,507	L 2
Val Marie 236	D 6
Vanguard 292	D 6
Vanscoy 298	D 4
Vibank 369	H 5
Viscount 386	F 4
Vonda 313	F 3
Wadena 1,495	H 4
Wakaw 1,030	F 3
Waldeck 292	D 5
Waldheim 758	E 3
Walpole •711	K 6
Wapella 487	K 5
Warman 2,076	E 3
Waseca 169	B 2
Waskesiu Lake 176	E 2
Watrous 1,830	F 4
Watson 901	G 3
Wawota 622	J 6
Weldon 279	F 2
Welwyn 170	K 5
Weyburn 9,523	H 6
White City 602	G 5
White Fox 394	H 2
Whitewood 1,003	J 5
Wilcox 202	G 5
Wilkie 1,501	C 3
Willow Bunch 494	F 6
Willow Creek •1,218	B 6
Windthorst 254	J 5
Wiseton 195	D 4
Wishart 212	H 4
Wollaston Lake 248	N 2
Wolseley 904	H 5
Wymark 162	D 5
Wynyard 2,147	G 4
Yarbo 158	K 5
Yellow Grass 477	H 6
Yorkton 15,339	J 4
Young 456	F 4
Zenon Park 273	H 2

OTHER FEATURES

Allan (hills)	E 4
Amisk (lake)	M 4
Antelope (lake)	C 5
Antler (riv.)	K 6
Arm (riv.)	F 5
Assiniboine (riv.)	J 3
Athabasca (lake)	L 2
Bad (lake)	C 4
Bad (hills)	C 4
Basin (lake)	F 3
Batoche Nat'l Hist. Site	E 3
Battle (creek)	B 6
Battle (riv.)	B 3
Bear (hills)	C 4
Beaver (hills)	H 4
Beaver (riv.)	L 4
Beaverlodge (lake)	L 2
Big Muddy (lake)	G 6
Bigstick (lake)	B 5
Birch (lake)	C 2
Bitter (lake)	B 5
Black (lake)	M 2
Boundary (plat.)	B 6
Brightsand (lake)	B 2
Bronson (lake)	B 2

Agriculture, Industry and Resources

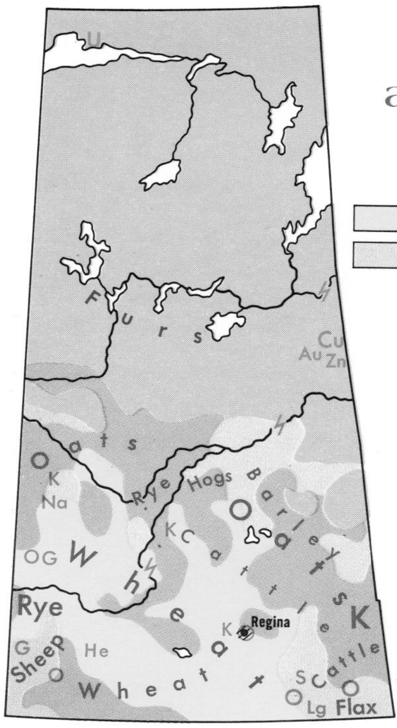
Furs
Cu
Au Zn
Oats
Rye
Hogs
Barley
Oats
OK
Na
OG
Wheat
Cattle
Rye
Regina
K
G
He
Sheep
Wheat
Oats
Cattle
Lg
Flax
K

DOMINANT LAND USE

- Wheat
- Cereals (chiefly barley, oats)
- Cereals, Livestock
- Livestock
- Forests

MAJOR MINERAL OCCURRENCES

Au	Gold	Na	Salt
Cu	Copper	O	Petroleum
G	Natural Gas	S	Sulfur
He	Helium	U	Uranium
K	Potash	Zn	Zinc
Lg	Lignite		

- Water Power
- Major Industrial Areas

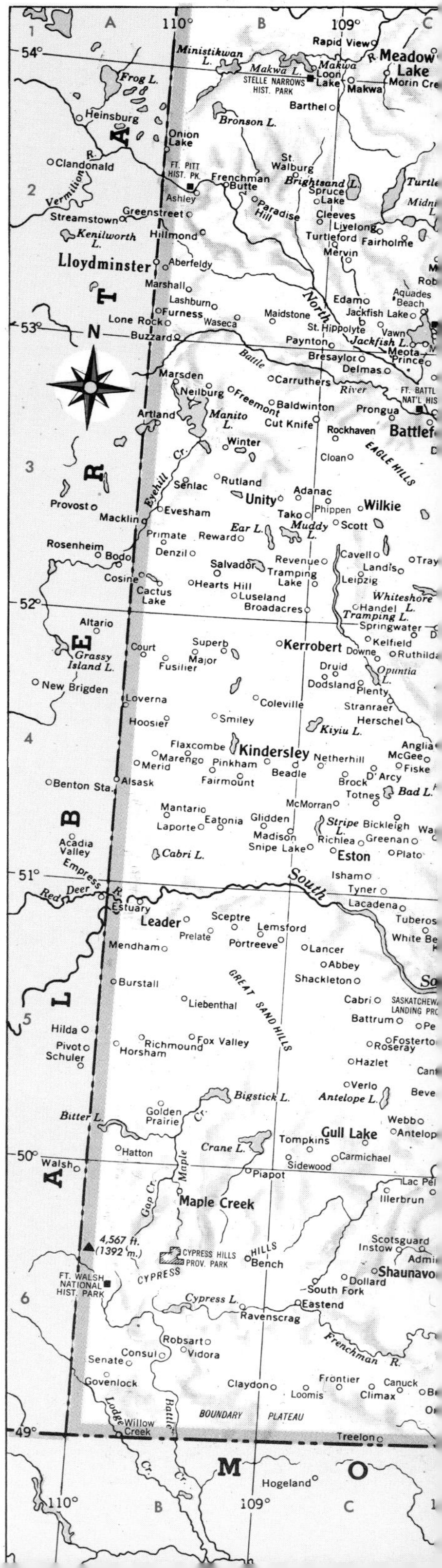
A
B
C
110°
109°
54°
53°
52°
51°
50°
49°
ALBERTA
MO
Meadow Lake
Ministikwan L.
Makwa L.
Makwa
Loon Lake
STELLE NARROWS HIST. PARK
Frog L.
Heinsburg
Barthel
Bronson L.
Onion Lake
Clandonald
FT. PITT HIST. PK.
Frenchman Butte
St. Walburg
Brightsand L.
Turtle
Vermilion
Ashley
Spruce Lake
Paradise Hill
Cleeves
Streamstown
Greenstreet
Turtleford
Liyelong
Fairholme
Kenilworth L.
Hillmond
Mervin
Lloydminster
Aberfeldy
Marshall
Lashburn
Edam
Aquadeo Beach
Jackfish Lake
Maidstone
Furness
Waseca
Lone Rock
Buzzard
St. Hippolyte
Vawn
Jackfish L.
Paynton
Meota
Bresaylor
Prince
Delmas
North
Battle
Marsden
Neilburg
Freemont
Carruthers
River
FT. BATTLEFORD NAT'L HIST. PK.
Baldwinton
Prongua
Artland
Manito L.
Cut Knife
Rockhaven
Battleford
Winter
Cloan
EAGLE HILLS
Eyehill Cr.
Senlac
Rutland
Adanac
Provost
Macklin
Unity
Wilkie
Evesham
Phippen
Tako
Muddy L.
Scott
Primate
Reward
Ear L.
Rosenheim
Bodo
Denzil
Salvador
Revenue
Cavell
Landis
Tramping Lake
Leipzig
Cosine
Cactus Lake
Hearts Hill
Luseland
Broadacres
Whiteshore
Handel
Tramping L.
Springwater
Altario
Court
Superb
Major
Kerrobert
Kelfield
Downe
Ruthilda
Grassy Island L.
Fusilier
Druid
Opuntia
New Brigden
Dodsland
Plenty
Loverna
Coleville
Stranraer
Hoosier
Smiley
Herschel
Kiyiu L.
Flaxcombe
Kindersley
Anglia
Marengo
Pinkham
Netherhill
McGee
Merid
Beadle
Fiske
Benton Sta.
Alsask
Fairmount
Brock
D'Arcy
Totnes
Bad L.
McMorran
Mantario
Eatonia
Glidden
Stripe
Bickleigh
Laporte
Madison
Richlea
Greenan
Acadia Valley
Snipe Lake
Eston
Plato
Cabri L.
Empress
Isham
Red Deer R.
South
Tyner
Lacadena
Estuary
Leader
Sceptre
Lemsford
Tuberose
Prelate
Portreeve
White Bear
Mendham
Lancer
Abbey
Shackleton
Burstall
GREAT SAND HILLS
Liebenthal
Cabri
SASKATCHEWAN LANDING PROV. PARK
Battrum
Hilda
Fosterton
Pivot
Richmound
Fox Valley
Roseray
Schuler
Horsham
Hazlet
Verlo
Bigstick L.
Antelope L.
Beverley
Bitter L.
Golden Prairie
Webb
Gull Lake
Antelope
Tompkins
Hatton
Crane L.
Carmichael
Walsh
Sidewood
Piapot
Lac Pelletier
Maple Creek
Illerbrun
Gap Cr.
Maple
4,567 ft. (1392 m.)
Scotsguard
Instow
CYPRESS HILLS PROV. PARK
Bench
Admiral
Shaunavon
FT. WALSH NATIONAL HIST. PARK
CYPRESS
Dollard
South Fork
Cypress L.
Eastend
Ravenscrag
Frenchman R.
Robsart
Consul
Vidora
Senate
Claydon
Frontier
Canuck
Govenlock
Loomis
Climax
Lodge
Hattie
BOUNDARY PLATEAU
Willow Creek
Treelon
Hogeland

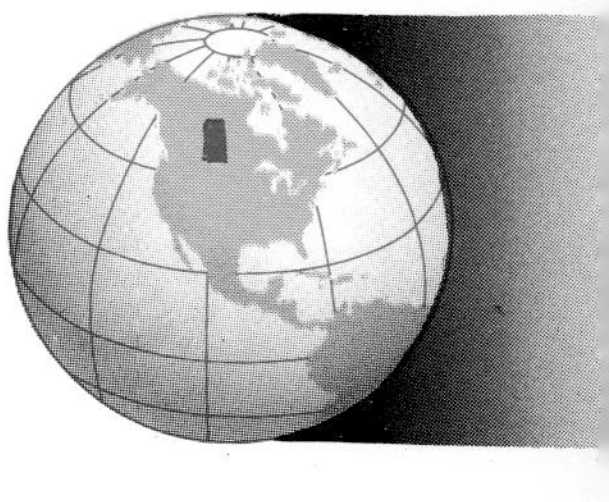

AREA 251,699 sq. mi. (651,900 sq. km.)
POPULATION 968,313
CAPITAL Regina
LARGEST CITY Regina
HIGHEST POINT Cypress Hills 4,567 ft. (1,392 m.)
SETTLED IN 1774
ADMITTED TO CONFEDERATION 1905
PROVINCIAL FLOWER Prairie Lily

*Population of metropolitan area.
●Population of rural municipality.

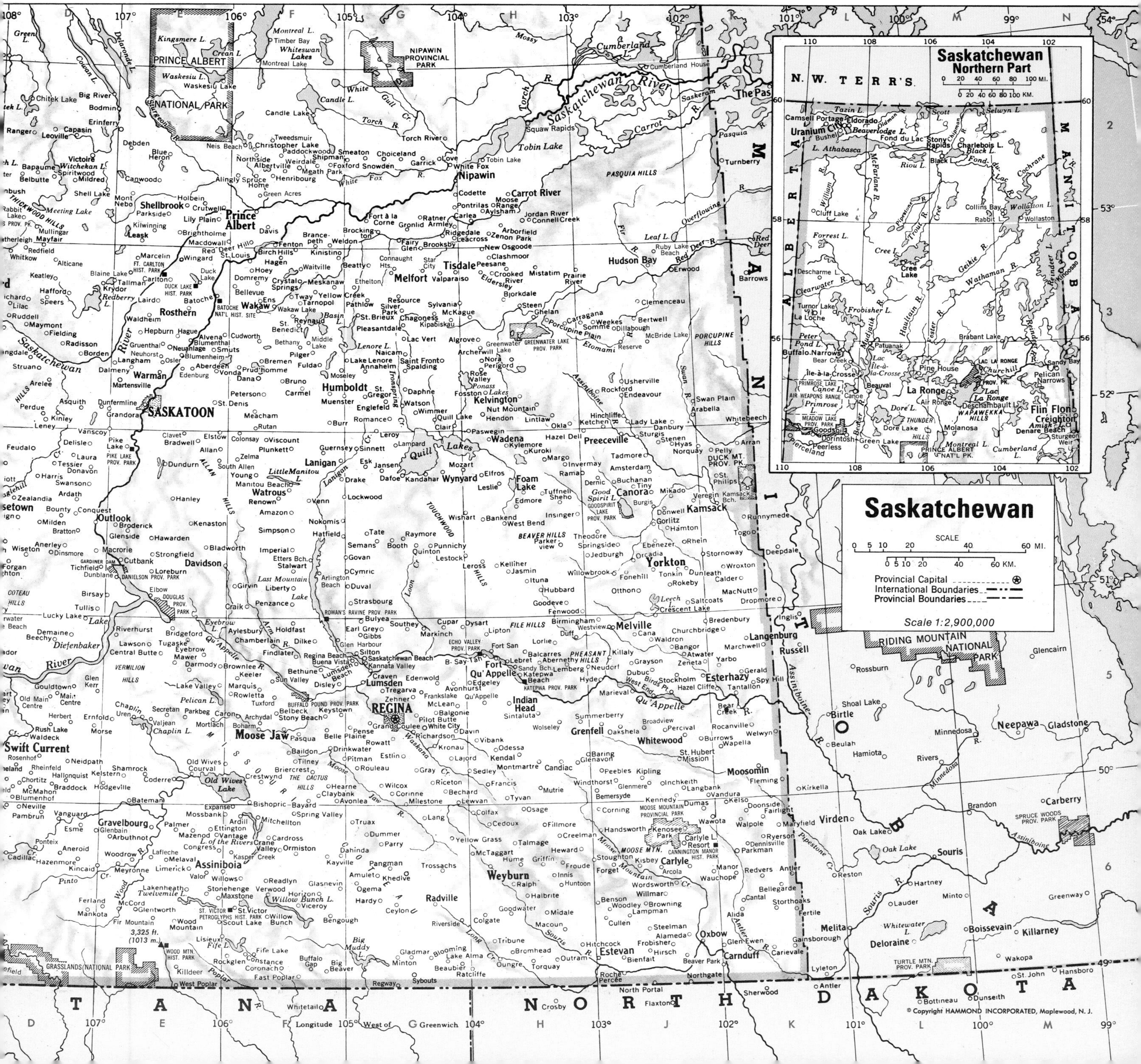

Saskatchewan

SCALE
0 5 10 20 40 60 MI.
0 5 10 20 40 60 KM.

Provincial Capital ⊛
International Boundaries
Provincial Boundaries

Scale 1:2,900,000

Saskatchewan Northern Part

0 20 40 60 80 100 MI.
0 20 40 60 80 100 KM.

© Copyright HAMMOND INCORPORATED, Maplewood, N.J.

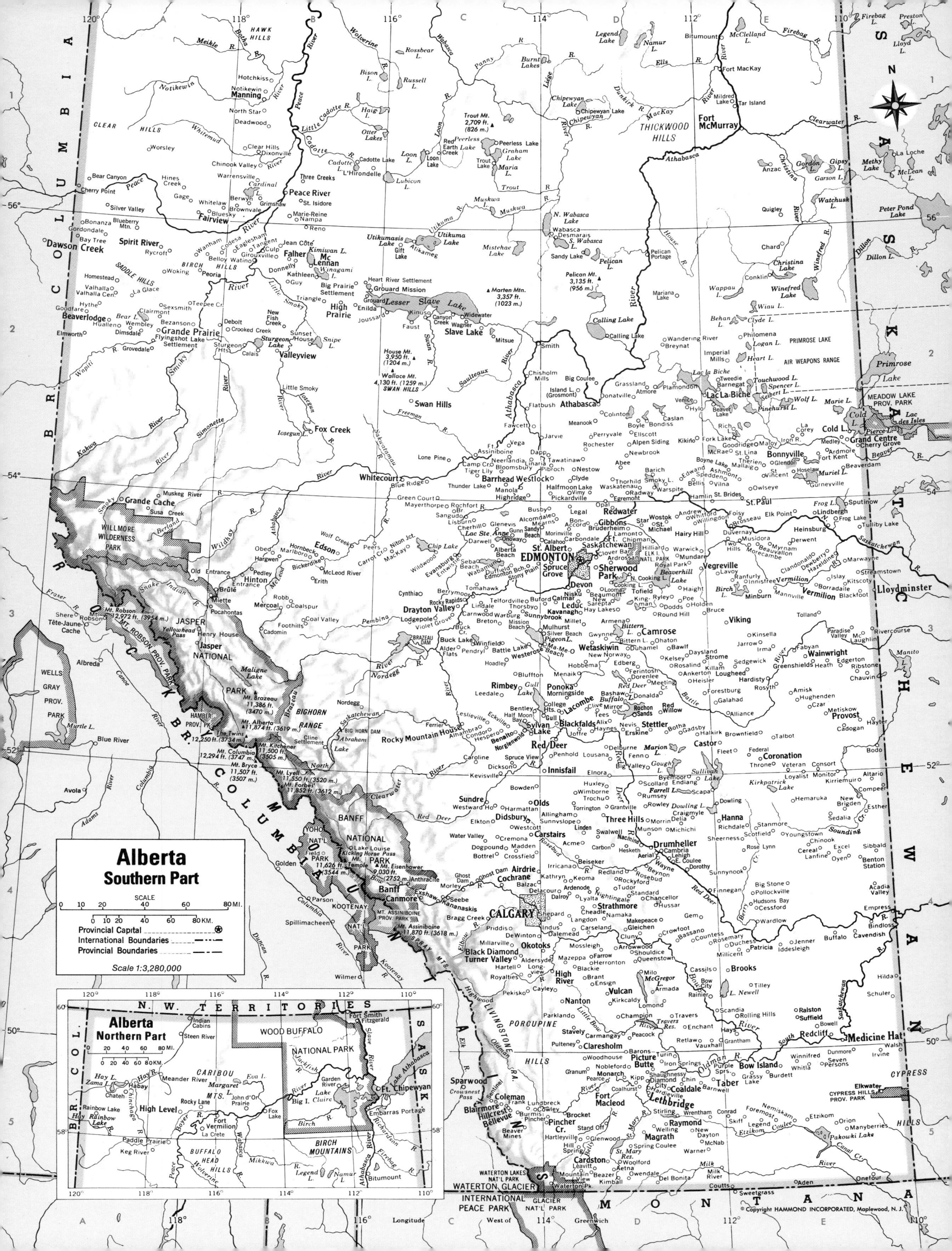

Alberta
Southern Part

SCALE

0 10 20 40 60 80 MI.

0 10 20 40 60 80 KM.

Provincial Capital .... ⊛
International Boundaries —·—·—·—
Provincial Boundaries —————

Scale 1:3,280,000

Alberta
Northern Part

0 20 40 60 80 MI.

0 20 40 60 80KM.

CALGARY

EDMONTON

® Copyright HAMMOND INCORPORATED, Maplewood, N.J.

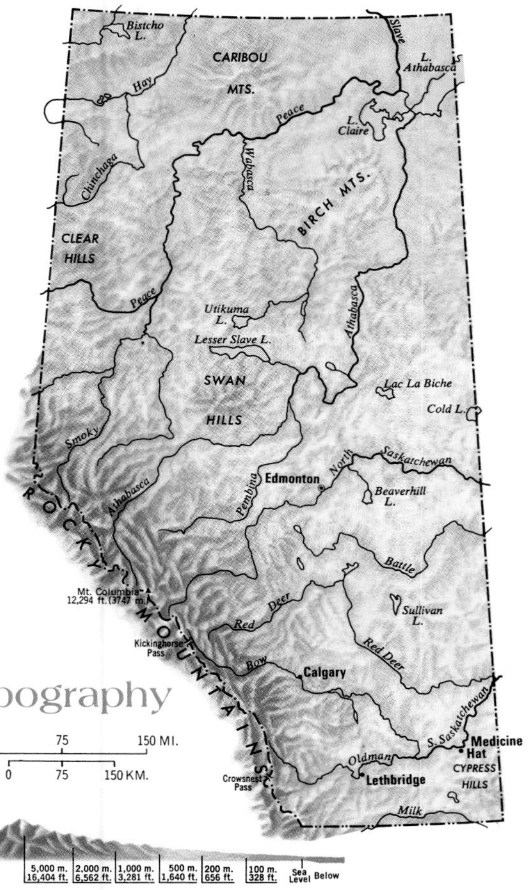

Bistcho L.
CARIBOU MTS.
Slave
L. Athabasca
Hay
Peace
L. Claire
Wabasca
Chinchaga
BIRCH MTS.
CLEAR HILLS
Peace
Utikuma L.
Lesser Slave L.
Athabasca
SWAN HILLS
Lac La Biche
Cold L.
Smoky
North Saskatchewan
Edmonton
Beaverhill L.
Athabasca
Pembina
ROCKY MOUNTAINS
Battle
Mt. Columbia 12,294 ft. (3747 m.)
Sullivan L.
Red Deer
Red
Kicking Horse Pass
Red Deer
Bow
Calgary
S. Saskatchewan
Medicine Hat
Oldman
CYPRESS HILLS
Crowsnest Pass
Lethbridge
Milk
0 75 150 MI.
0 75 150 KM.
5,000 m. 16,404 ft.
2,000 m. 6,562 ft.
1,000 m. 3,281 ft.
500 m. 1,640 ft.
200 m. 656 ft.
100 m. 328 ft.
Sea Level
Below

Topography

AREA 255,285 sq. mi. (661,185 sq. km.)
POPULATION 2,237,724
CAPITAL Edmonton
LARGEST CITY Edmonton
HIGHEST POINT Mt. Columbia 12,294 ft. (3,747 m.)
SETTLED IN 1861
ADMITTED TO CONFEDERATION 1905
PROVINCIAL FLOWER Wild Rose

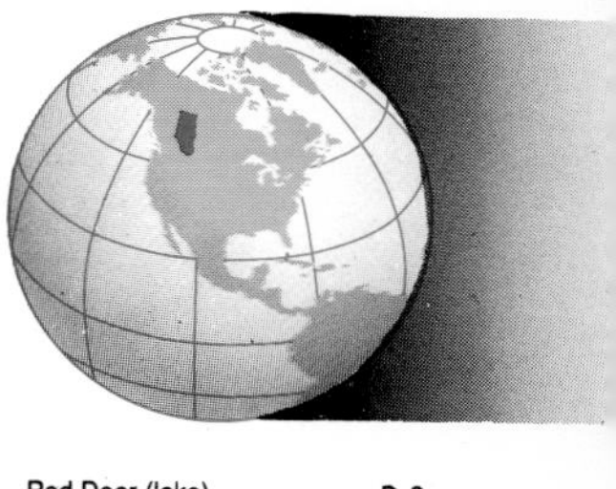

CITIES and TOWNS

Acme 457	D 4
Airdrie 8,414	C 4
Alberta Beach 485	C 3
Alix 837	D 3
Andrew 548	D 3
Antler Lake 334	D 3
Ardmore 224	E 2
Arrowwood 156	D 4
Athabasca 1,731	D 2
Banff 4,208	C 4
Barnwell 359	D 5
Barons 315	D 4
Barrhead 3,736	C 2
Bashaw 875	D 3
Bassano 1,200	D 4
Bawlf 350	D 3
Beaumont 2,638	D 3
Beaverlodge 1,937	A 2
Beiseker 580	D 4
Bentley 823	C 3
Berwyn 557	B 1
Big Valley 360	D 3
Black Diamond 1,444	C 4
Blackfalds 1,488	D 3
Blackfoot 220	E 3
Blackie 298	D 4
Bon Accord 1,376	D 3
Bonnyville 4,454	E 2
Bowden 989	C 4
Bow Island 1,491	E 5
Boyle 638	D 2
Bragg Creek 505	C 4
Breton 552	C 3
Brooks 9,421	E 4
Bruce 88	E 3
Bruderheim 1,136	D 3
Burdett 220	E 5
Calgary 592,743	C 4
Calgary *592,743	C 4
Calmar 1,003	D 3
Camrose 12,570	D 3
Canmore 3,484	C 4
Carbon 434	D 4
Cardston 3,267	D 5
Carmangay 266	D 4
Caroline 436	C 3
Carseland 484	D 4
Carstairs 1,587	D 4
Castor 1,123	D 3
Cereal 249	E 4
Champion 339	D 4
Chauvin 298	E 3
Chipman 266	D 3
Clairmont 469	A 2
Claresholm 3,493	D 4
Clive 364	D 3
Clyde 364	D 2
Coaldale 4,579	D 5
Coalhurst 882	D 5
Cochrane 3,544	C 4
Cold Lake 2,110	E 2
College Heights 267	D 3
Consort 632	E 3
Cooking Lake 218	D 3
Coronation 1,309	E 3
Coutts 400	D 5
Cowley 304	D 5
Cremona 382	C 4
Crossfield 1,217	C 4
Daysland 679	D 3
Delburne 574	D 3
Desmarais 260	D 2
Devon 3,885	D 3
Didsbury 3,095	C 4
Donalda 280	D 3
Donnelly 336	B 2
Drayton Valley 5,042	C 3
Drumheller 6,508	D 4
Duchess 429	E 4
East Coulee 218	D 4
Eckville 870	C 3
Edgerton 387	E 3
Edmonton (cap.) 532,246	D 3
Edmonton *657,057	D 3
Edmonton Beach 280	C 3
Edson 5,835	B 3
Elk Point 1,022	E 3
Elnora 249	D 3
Entwistle 462	C 3
Erskine 259	D 3
Evansburg 779	C 3
Exshaw 353	C 4
Fairview 2,869	A 1
Falher 1,102	B 2
Faust 399	C 2
Foremost 568	E 5
Forestburg 924	E 3
Fort Assiniboine 207	C 2
Fort Chipewyan 944	C 5
Fort Macleod 3,139	D 5
Fort McKay 267	E 1
Fort McMurray 31,000	E 1
Fort Saskatchewan 12,169	D 3
Fort Vermilion 752	B 5
Fox Creek 1,978	B 2
Fox Lake 634	B 5
Gibbons 2,276	D 3
Gift Lake 428	C 2
Girouxville 325	B 2
Gleichen 381	D 4
Glendon 430	E 2
Glenwood 259	D 5
Grand Centre 3,146	E 2
Grande Cache 4,523	A 3
Grande Prairie 24,263	A 2
Granum 399	D 5
Grimshaw 2,316	B 1
Grouard Mission 221	C 2
Hanna 2,806	E 4
Hardisty 641	E 3
Hay Lakes 302	D 3
Heisler 212	D 3
High Level 2,194	A 5
High Prairie 2,506	B 2
High River 4,792	D 4
Hines Creek 575	A 1
Hinton 8,342	B 3
Holden 430	D 3
Hughenden 267	E 3
Hythe 639	A 2
Innisfail 5,247	D 3
Innisfree 255	E 3
Irma 474	E 3
Irricana 558	D 4
Irvine 360	E 5
Jasper 3,269	B 3
John d'Or Prairie 437	B 5
Joussard 330	B 2
Killam 1,005	E 3
Kinuso 285	C 2
Kitscoty 497	E 3
Lac La Biche 2,007	E 2
Lacombe 5,591	D 3
La Crete 479	B 5
Lake Louise 355	B 4
Lamont 1,563	D 3
Leduc 12,471	D 3
Legal 1,022	D 3
Lethbridge 54,072	D 5
Linden 407	D 4
Little Buffalo Lake 253	B 1
Lloydminster 8,997	E 3
Longview 301	C 4
Lougheed 226	E 3
Lundbreck 244	C 5
Magrath 1,576	D 5
Manning 1,173	B 1
Mannville 788	E 3
Marlboro 211	B 3
Marwayne 500	E 3
Mayerthorpe 1,475	C 3
McLennan 1,125	B 2
Medicine Hat 40,380	E 4
Milk River 894	D 5
Millet 1,120	D 3
Mirror 507	D 3
Monarch 212	D 5
Morinville 4,657	D 3
Morrin 244	D 4
Mundare 604	D 3
Myrnam 397	E 3
Nacmine 369	D 4
Nampa 334	B 1
Nanton 1,641	D 4
New Norway 291	D 3
New Sarepta 417	D 3
Nobleford 534	D 5
North Calling Lake 234	D 2
Okotoks 3,847	C 4
Olds 4,813	D 4
Onoway 621	C 3
Oyen 975	E 4
Peace River 5,907	B 1
Penhold 1,531	D 3
Picture Butte 1,404	D 5
Pincher Creek 3,757	D 5
Plamondon 259	D 2
Pollockville 19	E 4
Ponoka 5,221	D 3
Provost 1,645	E 3
Rainbow Lake 504	A 5
Ralston 357	E 4
Raymond 2,837	D 5
Redcliff 3,876	E 4
Red Deer 46,393	D 3
Redwater 1,932	D 3
Rimbey 1,685	C 3
Robb 230	B 3
Rockyford 329	D 4
Rocky Mountain House 4,698	C 3
Rosemary 328	E 4
Rycroft 649	A 2
Ryley 483	D 3
Saint Albert 31,996	D 3
Saint Paul 4,884	E 3
Sangudo 398	C 3
Sedgewick 879	E 3
Sexsmith 1,180	A 2
Shaughnessy 270	D 5
Sherwood Park 29,285	D 3
Slave Lake 4,506	C 2
Smith 216	D 2
Smoky Lake 1,074	D 2
Spirit River 1,104	A 2
Spruce Grove 10,326	D 3
Standard 379	D 4
Stavely 504	D 4
Stettler 5,136	D 3
Stirling 688	D 5
Stony Plain 4,839	C 3
Strathmore 2,986	D 4
Strome 281	E 3
Sundre 1,742	C 4
Swan Hills 2,497	C 2
Sylvan Lake 3,779	C 3
Taber 5,988	E 5
Thorhild 576	D 2
Thorsby 737	C 3
Three Hills 1,787	D 4
Tilley 345	E 4
Tofield 1,504	D 3
Trochu 880	D 4
Turner Valley 1,311	C 4
Two Hills 1,193	E 3
Valleyview 2,061	B 2
Vauxhall 1,049	D 4
Vegreville 5,251	E 3
Vermilion 3,766	E 3
Veteran 314	E 3
Viking 1,232	E 3
Vilna 345	E 2
Vulcan 1,489	D 4
Wabamun 662	C 3
Wabasca 701	D 2
Wainwright 4,266	E 3
Warburg 501	C 3
Warner 477	D 5
Waskatenau 290	D 2
Wembley 1,169	A 2
Westlock 4,424	C 2
Wetaskiwin 9,597	D 3
Whitecourt 5,585	C 2
Wildwood 441	C 3
Willingdon 366	E 3
Youngstown 297	E 4

OTHER FEATURES

Abraham (lake)	B 3
Alberta (mt.)	B 3
Assiniboine (mt.)	C 4
Athabasca (lake)	C 5
Athabasca (riv.)	D 1
Banff Nat'l Park	B 4
Battle (riv.)	D 3
Bear (lake)	A 2
Beaver (riv.)	E 2
Beaverhill (lake)	D 3
Behan (lake)	E 2
Belly (riv.)	D 5
Berland (riv.)	A 3
Berry (creek)	E 4
Biche (lake)	E 2
Big (isl.)	B 5
Big Horn (dam)	B 3
Bighorn (range)	B 3
Birch (hills)	A 2
Birch (lake)	E 3
Birch (mts.)	B 5
Birch (riv.)	B 5
Bison (lake)	B 1
Bittern (lake)	D 3
Botha (riv.)	B 1
Bow (riv.)	D 4
Boyer (riv.)	A 5
Brazeau (mt.)	B 3
Brazeau (riv.)	B 3
Buffalo (lake)	D 3
Buffalo Head (hills)	B 5
Burnt (lakes)	C 1
Cadotte (lake)	B 1
Cadotte (riv.)	B 1
Calling (lake)	D 2
Canal (creek)	E 5
Cardinal (lake)	B 1
Caribou (mts.)	B 5
Chinchaga (riv.)	A 5
Chip (lake)	C 3
Chipewyan (lake)	D 1
Chipewyan (riv.)	D 1
Christina (lake)	E 2
Christina (riv.)	E 1
Claire (lake)	B 5
Clear (hills)	A 1
Clearwater (riv.)	C 4
Clearwater (riv.)	E 1
Clyde (lake)	E 2
Cold (lake)	E 2
Columbia (mt.)	B 3
Crowsnest (pass)	C 5
Cypress (hills)	E 5
Cypress Hills Prov. Park	E 5
Dillon (riv.)	E 2
Dowling (lake)	D 4
Dunkirk (riv.)	D 1
Eisenhower (mt.)	C 4
Elbow (riv.)	C 4
Elk Island Nat'l Park	D 3
Ells (riv.)	D 1
Etzikom Coulee (riv.)	E 5
Eva (lake)	B 5
Farrell (lake)	D 4
Firebag (riv.)	E 1
Forbes (mt.)	B 4
Freeman (riv.)	C 2
Frog (lake)	E 3
Garson (lake)	E 1
Gipsy (lake)	E 1
Gordon (lake)	E 1
Gough (lake)	D 3
Graham (lake)	C 1
Gull (lake)	C 3
Haig (lake)	B 1
Hawk (hills)	B 1
Hay (lake)	A 5
Hay (riv.)	A 5
Heart (lake)	E 2
Highwood (riv.)	C 4
House (mt.)	C 2
House (riv.)	D 2
Iosegun (lake)	B 2
Iosegun (riv.)	B 2
Jackfish (riv.)	B 5
Jasper Nat'l Park	A 3
Kakwa (riv.)	A 2
Kickinghorse (pass)	B 4
Kimiwan (lake)	B 2
Kirkpatrick (lake)	E 4
Kitchener (mt.)	B 3
Legend (lake)	D 1
Lesser Slave (lake)	C 2
Liége (riv.)	D 1
Little Bow (riv.)	D 4
Little Cadotte (riv.)	B 1
Little Smoky (riv.)	B 2
Livingstone (range)	C 4
Logan (lake)	E 2
Loon (lake)	C 1
Loon (riv.)	C 1
Lubicon (lake)	C 1
Lyell (mt.)	B 4
MacKay (riv.)	D 1
Maligne (lake)	B 3
Margaret (lake)	B 5
Marie (lake)	E 2
Marion (lake)	D 3
Marten (mt.)	C 2
McClelland (lake)	E 1
McGregor (lake)	D 4
McLeod (riv.)	B 3
Meikle (riv.)	A 1
Mikkwa (riv.)	B 5
Milk (riv.)	D 5
Mistehae (lake)	C 2
Muriel (lake)	E 2
Muskwa (lake)	C 1
Muskwa (riv.)	C 1
Namur (lake)	D 1
Newell (lake)	E 4
Nordegg (riv.)	C 3
North Saskatchewan (riv.)	E 3
North Wabasca (lake)	D 1
Notikewin (riv.)	A 1
Oldman (riv.)	D 5
Otter (lakes)	B 1
Pakowki (lake)	E 5
Panny (riv.)	C 1
Peace (riv.)	B 1
Peerless (lake)	C 1
Pelican (lake)	D 2
Pelican (mts.)	D 2
Pembina (riv.)	C 3
Pigeon (lake)	D 3
Pinehurst (lake)	E 2
Porcupine (hills)	C 4
Primrose (lake)	E 2
Rainbow (lake)	A 5
Red Deer (lake)	D 3
Red Deer (riv.)	D 4
Richardson (riv.)	C 5
Rocky (mts.)	B-C 4
Rosebud (riv.)	D 4
Russell (lake)	C 1
Saddle (hills)	A 2
Sainte Anne (lake)	C 3
Saint Mary (res.)	D 5
Saint Mary (riv.)	D 5
Saulteaux (riv.)	C 2
Seibert (lake)	E 2
Simonette (riv.)	A 2
Slave (riv.)	C 5
Smoky (riv.)	A 2
Snake Indian (riv.)	A 3
Snipe (lake)	B 2
Sounding (creek)	E 4
South Saskatchewan (riv.)	E 4
South Wabasca (lake)	D 2
Spencer (lake)	E 2
Spray (mts.)	C 4
Sturgeon (lake)	B 2
Sullivan (lake)	D 3
Swan (hills)	C 2
Swan (riv.)	C 2
Temple (mt.)	B 4
The Twins (mt.)	B 3
Thickwood (hills)	D 1
Touchwood (lake)	E 2
Travers (res.)	D 4
Trout (mt.)	C 1
Trout (riv.)	C 1
Utikuma (lake)	C 2
Utikuma (riv.)	C 1
Utikumasis (lake)	C 2
Vermilion (riv.)	E 3
Wabasca (riv.)	C 1
Wallace (mt.)	C 2
Wapiti (riv.)	A 2
Wappau (lake)	E 2
Watchusk (lake)	E 1
Waterton-Glacier Int'l Peace Park	C 5
Waterton Lakes Nat'l Park	C 5
Whitemud (riv.)	A 1
Wildhay (riv.)	B 3
Willmore Wilderness Prov. Park	A 3
Winagami (lake)	B 2
Winefred (lake)	E 2
Winefred (riv.)	E 2
Wolf (lake)	E 2
Wolverine (riv.)	B 1
Wood Buffalo Nat'l Park	B 5
Yellowhead (pass)	A 3
Zama (lake)	A 5

*Population of metropolitan area.

Agriculture, Industry and Resources

DOMINANT LAND USE

- Wheat
- Cereals (chiefly barley, oats)
- Cereals, Livestock
- Dairy
- Pasture Livestock
- Range Livestock
- Forests
- Nonagricultural Land

MAJOR MINERAL OCCURRENCES

- C Coal
- G Natural Gas
- Na Salt
- O Petroleum
- S Sulfur

Water Power
Major Industrial Areas

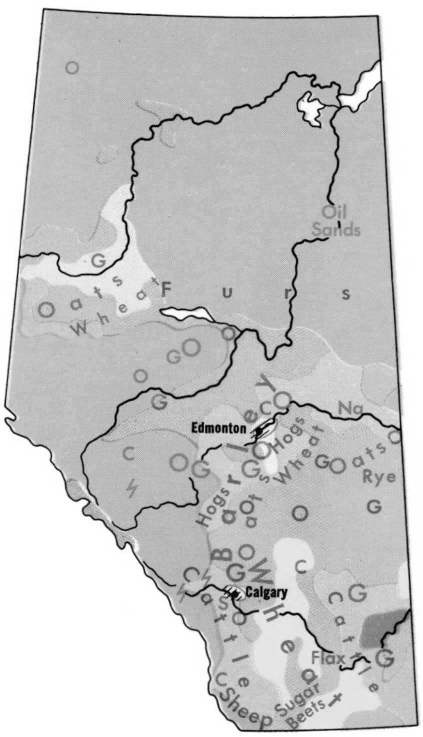

Oil Sands
Oats
Wheat
Furs
Edmonton
Na
Hogs
Wheat
Oats
Rye
Dairy
Calgary
Cattle
Flax
Sheep
Sugar Beets

Topography

0   100   200 MI.

0   100   200 KM.

Below Sea Level | 100 m. 328 ft. | 200 m. 656 ft. | 500 m. 1,640 ft. | 1,000 m. 3,281 ft. | 2,000 m. 6,562 ft. | 5,000 m. 16,404 ft.

Agriculture, Industry and Resources

DOMINANT LAND USE

- Cereals, Livestock
- Dairy
- Fruits, Vegetables
- Pasture Livestock
- Forests
- Nonagricultural Land

MAJOR MINERAL OCCURRENCES

Ab	Asbestos	Gp	Gypsum
Ag	Silver	Mo	Molybdenum
Au	Gold	Ni	Nickel
C	Coal	O	Petroleum
Cu	Copper	Pb	Lead
Fe	Iron Ore	S	Sulfur
G	Natural Gas	Sn	Tin
		Zn	Zinc

⚡ Water Power

▨ Major Industrial Areas

CITIES and TOWNS

Abbotsford 12,745 .... L 3
Alert Bay 626 .... D 5
Armstrong 2,683 .... H 5
Ashcroft 2,156 .... G 5
Ashton Creek 452 .... H 5
Balfour 472 .... J 5
Barlow 441 .... F 3
Barrière 1,370 .... H 4
Blueberry Creek 635 .... J 5
Blue River 384 .... G 4
Boston Bar 498 .... G 5
Bowen Island 1,125 .... K 3
Brackendale 1,719 .... F 5
Burnaby ○136,494 .... K 3
Burns Lake 1,777 .... D 3
Cache Creek 1,308 .... G 5
Campbell River 15,370 .... E 5
Canal Flats 919 .... K 5
Canyon 698 .... J 5
Cassiar 1,045 .... K 2
Castlegar 6,902 .... J 5
Cawston 785 .... H 5
Central Saanich ○9,890 .... K 3
Chase 1,777 .... H 5
Chemainus 2,069 .... J 3
Cherry Creek 450 .... G 5
Chetwynd 2,553 .... G 2
Chilliwack ○40,642 .... M 3
Clearwater 1,461 .... G 4
Clinton 804 .... G 4
Coldstream ○6,450 .... H 5
Comox 6,607 .... H 2
Coquitlam ○61,077 .... K 3
Courtenay 4,190 .... E 5
Cranbrook 15,915 .... K 5
Creston 4,190 .... J 5
Crofton 1,303 .... J 3
Cultus Lake 481 .... M 3
Cumberland 1,947 .... E 5
Dawson Creek 11,373 .... G 2
Delta ○74,692 .... K 3
Duncan 4,228 .... J 3
Elkford 3,126 .... K 5
Enderby 1,816 .... H 5
Erickson 972 .... J 5
Errington 609 .... J 3
Esquimalt ○15,870 .... K 4
Falkland 478 .... H 5
Fernie 5,444 .... K 5
Forest Grove 444 .... G 4
Fort Fraser 574 .... E 3
Fort Langley 2,326 .... L 3
Fort Nelson 3,724 .... M 2
Fort Saint James 2,284 .... E 3
Fort Saint John 13,891 .... G 2
Fraser Lake 1,543 .... E 3
Fruitvale 1,904 .... J 5
Gabriola 1,627 .... J 3
Galiano 669 .... K 3
Ganges 1,118 .... K 3
Gibsons 2,594 .... K 3
Gold River 2,225 .... D 5
Golden 3,476 .... J 4
Grand Forks 3,486 .... H 6
Granisle 1,430 .... D 3
Greenwood 856 .... H 5
Hagensborg 350 .... D 4
Harrison Hot Springs 569 .... M 3
Hatzic 1,055 .... L 3

Hazelton 393 .... D 2
Hedley 426 .... G 5
Holberg 444 .... C 5
Honeymoon Bay 474 .... J 3
Hope 3,205 .... M 3
Hornby Island 474 .... H 2
Horsefly 430 .... G 4
Houston 3,205 .... D 3
Hudson Hope 984 .... F 2
Invermere 1,969 .... J 5
Kaleden 998 .... H 5
Kamloops 64,048 .... G 5
Kaslo 854 .... J 5
Kelowna 59,196 .... H 5
Kent ○3,394 .... M 3
Keremeos 830 .... G 5
Kimberley 7,375 .... K 5
Kitimat 12,462 .... C 3
Kitsault 554 .... C 2
Kitwanga 369 .... D 2
Lac La Hache 647 .... G 4
Ladysmith 4,558 .... J 3
Lake Cowichan 2,391 .... J 3
Langley 15,124 .... L 3
Lantzville 969 .... J 3
Likely 425 .... G 4
Lillooet 1,725 .... G 5
Lion's Bay 1,078 .... K 3
Logan Lake 2,637 .... G 5
Lumby 1,266 .... H 5
Lytton 428 .... G 5
Mackenzie 5,797 .... F 2
Mackenzie ○5,890 .... F 2
Malakwa 392 .... H 5
Maple Bay 393 .... K 3
Maple Ridge ○32,232 .... L 3
Masset 1,569 .... B 3
Matsqui ○42,001 .... L 3
Mayne 546 .... K 3
McBride 641 .... G 3
Merritt 6,110 .... G 5
Midway 633 .... H 6
Mill Bay 583 .... K 3
Mission ○20,056 .... L 3
Mission City 9,948 .... L 3
Montrose 1,229 .... J 5
Nakusp 1,495 .... J 5
Nanaimo 47,069 .... J 3
Naramata 876 .... H 5
Nelson 9,143 .... J 5
New Denver 642 .... J 5
New Hazelton 792 .... D 2
New Westminster 38,550 .... K 3
Nicomen Island 360 .... L 3
Nootka .... D 5
North Cowichan ○18,210 .... J 3
North Pender Island 906 .... K 3
North Saanich ○6,117 .... K 3
North Vancouver 33,952 .... K 3
North Vancouver ○65,367 .... K 3
Oak Bay ○16,990 .... K 4
Okanagan Falls 1,030 .... H 5
Okanagan Landing 834 .... H 5
Okanagan Mission .... H 5
Old Barkerville 11 .... G 3
One Hundred Mile House
  1,925 .... G 4
Osoyoos 2,738 .... H 5
Oyama 430 .... H 5
Parksville 5,216 .... J 3

Penticton 23,181 .... H 5
Pitt Meadows ○6,209 .... L 3
Port Alberni 19,892 .... H 3
Port Alice 1,668 .... D 5
Port Clements 380 .... B 3
Port Coquitlam 27,535 .... L 3
Port Edward 989 .... B 3
Port Hardy ○3,778 .... D 5
Port McNeill 2,474 .... D 5
Port Moody 14,917 .... L 3
Pouce-Coupé 821 .... G 2
Powell River ○13,423 .... E 5
Prince George 67,559 .... F 3
Prince Rupert 16,197 .... B 3
Princeton 3,051 .... G 5
Qualicum Beach 2,844 .... J 3
Queen Charlotte 1,070 .... A 3
Quesnel 8,240 .... F 4
Radium Hot Springs 419 .... J 5
Revelstoke 5,544 .... J 5
Richmond ○96,154 .... J 5
Roberts Creek 926 .... J 3
Robson 1,008 .... J 5
Rossland 3,967 .... H 6
Royston 754 .... H 2
Saanich ○78,710 .... K 3
Salmo 1,169 .... J 5
Salmon Arm 1,946 .... H 5
Salmon Arm ○10,780 .... H 5
Saltair 1,356 .... J 3
Sandspit 794 .... B 3
Sayward 482 .... D 5
Sechelt 1,096 .... J 2
Shawnigan Lake 419 .... J 3
Shoreacres 555 .... J 5
Sicamous 1,057 .... H 5
Sidney 7,946 .... K 3
Slocan 351 .... J 5
Slocan Park 414 .... J 5
Smithers 4,570 .... D 3
Sointula 567 .... D 5
Sooke 852 .... J 4
Sorrento 659 .... H 5
South Hazelton 500 .... D 2
South Wellington 620 .... J 3
Spallumcheen 4,213 .... H 5
Sparwood 3,267 .... K 5
Sproat Lake 440 .... H 2
Squamish 1,590 .... F 5
Stewart ○1,456 .... C 2
Summerland ○7,473 .... G 5
Surrey ○147,138 .... K 3
Tahsis 1,739 .... D 5
Taylor 966 .... G 2
Telkwa 840 .... D 3
Terrace 8,893 .... C 3
Terrace ○10,914 .... C 3
Thornhill 4,281 .... C 3
Thrums 360 .... J 5
Tofino 705 .... E 5
Trail 9,599 .... J 5
Ucluelet 1,593 .... E 6
Union Bay 601 .... H 2
Valemount 1,130 .... H 4
Vancouver 414,281 .... K 3
Vancouver (Greater)
  *1,169,831 .... K 3
Vanderhoof 2,323 .... E 3
Vavenby 479 .... H 4
Vernon 19,987 .... H 5
Victoria (cap.) 64,379 .... K 4
Victoria *233,481 .... K 4
Warfield 1,969 .... J 5
Wasa 345 .... K 5
Wells 417 .... G 3
Westbank 1,271 .... H 5
West Vancouver ○35,728 .... K 3
Westwold 409 .... G 5
Whistler ○1,365 .... F 5
White Rock 13,550 .... K 3
Williams Lake 8,362 .... F 4
Wilson Creek 611 .... J 2
Windermere 611 .... K 5
Winlaw 435 .... J 5
Woss Lake 395 .... D 5
Wynndel 566 .... J 5
Yarrow 1,201 .... M 3
Youbou 965 .... J 3

OTHER FEATURES

Adams (lake) .... H 4
Adams (riv.) .... H 4
Alberni (inlet) .... H 3
Alsek (riv.) .... H 1
Aristazabal (isl.) .... C 4
Assiniboine (mt.) .... K 5
Atlin (lake) .... J 1
Azure (lake) .... G 4
Babine (lake) .... E 3
Babine (riv.) .... D 2
Banks (isl.) .... B 3
Barkley (sound) .... E 6
Beale (cape) .... E 6
Beatton (riv.) .... G 1
Bella Coola (riv.) .... D 4
Bennett, W.A.C. (dam) .... F 2
Birkenhead Lake Prov. Park .. F 5
Bowron Lake Prov. Park .... G 3
Bowser (lake) .... C 2
Brooks (pen.) .... D 5
Browning Entrance (str.) .... B 3
Bryce (mt.) .... J 4
Bugaboo Glacier Prov. Park .. J 5
Bulkley (riv.) .... D 3
Burke (chan.) .... D 4
Burnaby (isl.) .... B 4
Bute (inlet) .... E 5
Caamaño (sound) .... C 4
Calvert (isl.) .... C 4
Canim (lake) .... G 4
Canoe (riv.) .... H 4
Cariboo (mts.) .... G 3
Carpenter (lake) .... F 5
Carp Lake Prov. Park .... F 3
Cassiar (mts.) .... K 2
Castle (mt.) .... A 2

Cathedral Prov. Park .... H 5
Charlotte (lake) .... E 4
Chatham (sound) .... B 3
Chehalis (lake) .... L 3
Chilcotin (riv.) .... E 4
Chilko (lake) .... F 4
Chilko (riv.) .... F 4
Chilkoot (pass) .... J 1
Chuchi (lake) .... E 2
Churchill (peak) .... L 2
Clayoquot (sound) .... D 5
Clearwater (lake) .... G 4
Clearwater (riv.) .... G 4
Coast (mts.) .... D 3
Columbia (lake) .... K 5
Columbia (mt.) .... J 4
Columbia (riv.) .... H 4
Cook (cape) .... C 5
Cowichan (lake) .... J 3
Crowsnest (pass) .... K 5
Cypress Prov. Park .... K 3
Dean (chan.) .... D 4
Dean (riv.) .... D 4
Dease (lake) .... K 2
Dease (riv.) .... K 2
Devils Thumb (mt.) .... A 1
Dixon Entrance (chan.) .... A 3
Douglas (chan.) .... C 3
Duncan (riv.) .... J 5
Dundas (isl.) .... B 3
Elk (riv.) .... K 5
Elk Lakes Prov. Park .... K 5
Eutsuk (lake) .... D 3

Fairweather (mt.) .... H 1
Finlay (riv.) .... E 1
Fitzhugh (sound) .... D 4
Flathead (riv.) .... K 6
Flores (isl.) .... D 5
Fontas (riv.) .... M 2
Forbes (mt.) .... J 4
Fort Nelson (riv.) .... M 2
François (lake) .... D 3
Fraser (lake) .... D 3
Fraser (riv.) .... J 4
Fraser Reach (chan.) .... C 3
Galiano (isl.) .... K 3
Gardner (canal) .... C 3
Garibaldi Prov. Park .... F 5
Georgia (str.) .... J 3
Germansen (lake) .... E 2
Gil (isl.) .... C 3
Glacier Nat'l Park .... J 4
Golden Ears Prov. Park .... L 3
Gordon (isl.) .... H 3
Graham (isl.) .... A 3
Graham Reach (chan.) .... C 3
Grenville (chan.) .... C 3
Halfway (riv.) .... F 2
Hamber Prov. Park .... H 4
Harrison (lake) .... M 2
Hawkesbury (isl.) .... C 3
Hazelton (mts.) .... C 2
Hecate (str.) .... B 3
Hobson (lake) .... H 4
Homathko (riv.) .... E 4
Horsefly (lake) .... G 4

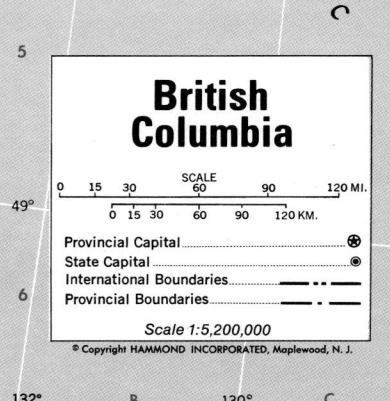

British Columbia

SCALE

0   15   30   60   90   120 MI.

0   15   30   60   90   120 KM.

Provincial Capital .... ⊛
State Capital .... ◉
International Boundaries .... —
Provincial Boundaries .... —

Scale 1:5,200,000

® Copyright HAMMOND INCORPORATED, Maplewood, N.J.

AREA 366,253 sq. mi. (948,596 sq. km.)
POPULATION 2,744,467
CAPITAL Victoria
LARGEST CITY Vancouver
HIGHEST POINT Mt. Fairweather 15,300 ft.
  (4,663 m.)
SETTLED IN 1806
ADMITTED TO CONFEDERATION 1871
PROVINCIAL FLOWER Dogwood

*Population of metropolitan area.
○Population of municipality.

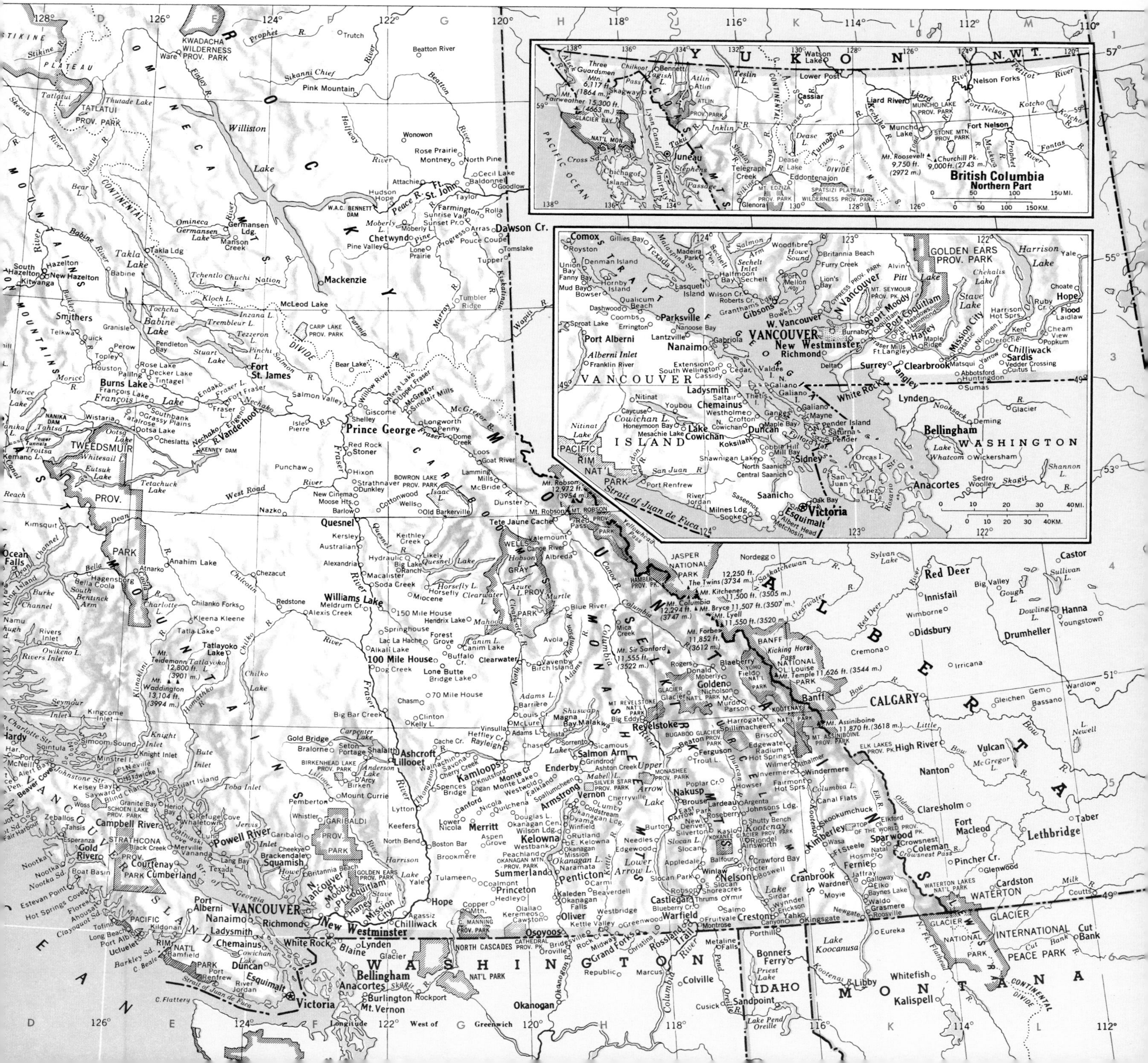

British Columbia
Northern Part

British Columbia

NORTHWEST TERRITORIES

DISTRICTS

Baffin 8,300 . . . . .J2
Fort Smith 22,384 . . . . . .G3
Inuvik 7,485 . . . . .F3
Keewatin 4,327 . . . . .J3
Kitikmeot 3,245 . . . . .G2

CITIES and TOWNS

Aklavik 721 . . . . .E3
Alert M1
Amadjuak L3
Arctic Bay 375 . . . . .K2
Arctic Red River 120 . . . .E3
Baker Lake 954 . . . . .J3
Bathurst Inlet 20 . . . . . . .H3
Bay Chimo 60 . . . . .H3
Bell Rock G3
Broughton Island 378 . . . .M3
Buffalo River Junction. . . .G3
Cambridge Bay 815 . . . . .H3
Cape Dorset 784 . . . . . . .L3
Cape Dyer M3
Cape Smith L3
Chesterfield Inlet 249 . . . .K3
Clyde (Clyde River) 443 . .M2
Colville Lake 57 . . . . .F3
Coppermine 809 . . . . . . .G3
Coral Harbour 429 . . . . . .K3
Detah 143 . . . . .G3
Dory Point G3
Enterprise 46 . . . . .G3
Eskimo Point 1,022. . . . . .J3
Eureka K2
Fort Franklin 521 . . . . . . .F3
Fort Good Hope 463 . . . . .F3
Fort Liard 405 . . . . .F3
Fort McPherson 632 . . . . .E3
Fort Norman 286. . . . . . . .F3
Fort Providence 605 . . . . .G3
Fort Resolution 480 . . . . .G3
Fort Simpson 980 . . . . . . .F3
Fort Smith 2,298 . . . . .G4
Frobisher Bay 2,333. . . . . .M3
Gjoa Haven 523 . . . . .J3
Grise Fiord 106 . . . . .K2
Hall Beach 349 . . . . .K3
Hay River 2,863 . . . . .G3
Holman Island 300 . . . . . .G2
Igloolik 746 . . . . .K3
Inuvik 3,147 . . . . .E3
Isachsen H2
Jean-Marie River 69 . . . . .F3
Kakisa 36 . . . . .G3
Kipisa 43 . . . . .M3
Lac la Martre 268 . . . . . . .G3
Lake Harbour 252 . . . . . . .L3
Mould Bay F2
Nahanni Butte 85. . . . . . . .F3
Nanisivik 261 . . . . .K2
Norman Wells 420. . . . . . .F3
Pangnirtung 839 . . . . .M3
Paulatuk 174 . . . . .F3
Pelly Bay 257 . . . . .K3
Pine Point 1,861. . . . . .G3
Pond Inlet 705 . . . . .L2
Port Burwell M3
Port Radium 56 . . . . .G3
Rae-Edzo 1,378 . . . . .G3
Rae Lakes 200 . . . . .G3
Rankin Inlet 1,109 . . . . . . .G3
Reliance 15 . . . . .H3
Repulse Bay 352. . . . . . . .K3
Resolute Bay 168 . . . . . . .J2

Resolution Island M3
Rocher River. G3
Sachs Harbour 161 . . . . . .F2
Salt River G3
Sawmill Bay G3
Snare Lake 69. . . . . .G3
Snowdrift 253. . . . . .G3
Spence Bay 431 . . . . .J3
Trout Lake 59 . . . . .F3
Tuktoyaktuk 772 . . . . .E3
Tungsten 320 . . . . .F3
Whale Cove 188 . . . . .J3
Wrigley 137. . . . . .F3
Yellowknife (cap.) 9,483. . . .G3

OTHER FEATURES

Adelaide (pen.) J3
Admiralty (inlet) K2
Air Force (isl.) L3
Akpatok (isl.) M3
Amadjuak (lake) L3
Amund Ringnes (isl.) J2
Amundsen (gulf) F2
Anderson (riv.) F3
Arctic Red (riv.) E3
Artillery (lake) H3
Axel Heiberg (isl.) J2
Aylmer (lake) H3
Back (riv.) J3
Baffin (bay) M2
Baffin (isl.) L2
Baker (lake) J3
Banks (isl.) F2
Barbeau (peak) L1
Barrow (str.) J2
Bathurst (cape) F2
Bathurst (inlet) H3
Bathurst (isl.) H2
Beaufort (sea) D2
Bellot (str.) J2
Boothia (gulf) K3
Boothia (pen.) J2
Borden (isl.) G2
Borden (pen.) K2
Brodeur (pen.) K2
Bruce (mts.) L2
Buchan (gulf) L2
Burnside (riv.) G3
Byam Martin (chan.) H2
Byam Martin (isl.) H2
Bylot (isl.) L2
Camsell (riv.) G3
Challenger (mts.) L1
Chantrey (inlet) J3
Chesterfield (inlet) J3
Chidley (cape) M3
Clinton-Colden (lake) H3
Clyde (inlet) M2
Coats (isl.) K3
Coburg (isl.) L2
Columbia (cape) M1
Colville (lake) F3
Committee (bay) K3
Contwoyto (lake) H3
Coppermine (riv.) G3
Cornwall (isl.) J2
Cornwallis (isl.) J2
Coronation (gulf) G3
Croker (bay) K2
Crown Prince Frederik (isl.) . .K3
Cumberland (pen.) M3
Cumberland (sound) M3
Dalhousie (cape) E2
Davis (str.) M3
Dease (str.) H3

Denmark (bay) H2
Devon (isl.) K2
Dolphin and Union (str.) G3
Dubawnt (lake) H3
Dubawnt (riv.) H3
Dundas (pen.) G2
Dyer (cape) M3
Eclipse (sound) L2
Eglinton (isl.) F2
Ellef Ringnes (isl.) H2
Ellesmere (isl.) K2
Ennadai (lake) H3
Eskimo (lakes) E3
Eureka (sound) K2
Evans (str.) K3
Exeter (sound) M3
Fisher (str.) K3
Fosheim (pen.) K1
Foxe (basin) L3
Foxe (chan.) K3
Foxe (pen.) L3
Franklin (bay) F2
Franklin (mts.) F3
Franklin (str.) J2
Frobisher (bay) M3
Frozen (str.) K3
Fury and Hecla (str.) K3
Gabriel (str.) M3
Garry (lake) H3
Gods Mercy (bay) K3
Great Bear (lake) F3
Great Bear (riv.) F3
Great Slave (lake) G3
Greely (fjord) K1
Grinnell (pen.) J2
Hadley (bay) H2
Hall (basin) M1
Hall (pen.) M3
Hayes (riv.) J3
Hazen (lake) L1
Hazen (str.) G2
Henik (lakes) J3
Henry Kater (cape) M3
Home (bay) M3
Hood (riv.) G3
Horn (mts.) G3
Hornaday (riv.) F3
Horton (riv.) F3
Hottah (lake) G3
Hudson (bay) K3
Hudson (str.) L3
Isachsen (cape) H2
James Ross (str.) J3
Jenny Lind (isl.) H3
Jens Munk (isl.) K3
Jones (sound) K2
Kaminuriak (lake) J3
Kane (basin) L2
Kasba (lake) H3
Kazan (riv.) H3
Keele (riv.) F3
Keith Arm (inlet) F3
Kellett (cape) F2
Kellett (str.) G2
Kennedy (chan.) M1
Kent (inlet) H3
King Christian (isl.) H2
King William (isl.) J3
Lady Ann (str.) K2
La Martre (lake) G3
Lancaster (sound) K2
Lands End (cape) F2
Larsen (sound) J2
Liard (riv.) F4
Lincoln (sea) M1
Liverpool (bay) E2
Lockhart (riv.) H3

Lougheed (isl.) H2
Lyon (inlet) K3
MacKay (lake) G3
Mackenzie (bay) E3
Mackenzie (mts.) E3
Mackenzie (riv.) F3
Mackenzie King (isl.) G2
Macmillan (pass) F3
Maguse (lake) J3
Makinson (inlet) L2
Mansel (isl.) K3
Marian (lake) G3
Markham (inlet) L1
McLeod (bay) G3
M'Clintock (chan.) H2
M'Clure (str.) G2
McTavish Arm (inlet) G3
Meighen (isl.) H1
Melville (isl.) G2
Melville (pen.) K3
Mercy (cape) M3
Mills (lake) G3
Minto (inlet) G2
Mistake (bay) J3
Nahanni Nat'l Park F3
Nansen (sound) J1
Nares (str.) L2
Navy Board (inlet) K2
Nelson Head (prom.) F2
Nettilling (lake) L3

Nonacho (lake) H3
North Arm (inlet) G3
North Magnetic Pole H2
Norwegian (bay) J2
Nottingham (isl.) L3
Nueltin (lake) H3
Ommanney (bay) H2
Padloping (isl.) M3
Parry (bay) K3
Parry (chan.) G2
Parry (isls.) G2
Parry (pen.) F2
Peary (chan.) H1
Peel (sound) J2
Pelly (bay) J3
Penny (str.) J2
Point (lake) G3
Pond (inlet) L2
Prince Albert (pen.) G2
Prince Albert (sound) G2
Prince Charles (isl.) L3
Prince Gustav Adolf (sea) . . .H2
Prince of Wales (isl.) J2
Prince of Wales (str.) G2
Prince Patrick (isl.) F2
Prince Regent (inlet) J2
Queen Elizabeth (isls.) H1
Queen Maud (gulf) H3
Queens (chan.) J2
Raanes (pen.) K2

Topography

QUEEN ELIZABETH
ISLANDS

Barbeau Peak
8,584 ft.
(2616 m.)
Axel Heiberg I.
Ellesmere
Island

Pr. Patrick I.
Melville I.
Devon I.
Banks I.
Parry Channel
Somerset I.
Baffin
Island

Amundsen Gulf
Victoria I.
Pr. of Wales I.
Boothia Pen.
Gulf of Boothia

Peel
Stewart
Melville Pen.
Foxe Basin

Mt. Logan
19,524 ft.
(5951 m.)
MACKENZIE MTS.
Great Bear Lake

Whitehorse
Mt. Sir James MacBrien
9,062 ft.
(2762 m.)
Yellowknife
Great Slave Lake

Southampton I.

Hudson Bay

0 200 400 MI.
0 200 400 KM.

5,000 m. 2,000 m. 1,000 m. 500 m. 200 m. 100 m. Sea Level Below
16,404 ft. 6,562 ft. 3,281 ft. 1,640 ft. 656 ft. 328 ft.

Agriculture, Industry and Resources

DOMINANT LAND USE

Forests

Nonagricultural Land

MAJOR MINERAL OCCURRENCES

Ab Asbestos
Ag Silver
Au Gold
C   Coal
Cu Copper
Fe Iron Ore
G   Natural Gas
O   Petroleum
Pb Lead
W   Tungsten
Zn Zinc

UNITED STATES

ALASKA
BROOKS RANGE

YUKON TERRITORY

Fairbanks

Whitehorse

BRITISH COLUMBIA

YUKON TERRITORY
AREA 207,075 sq. mi. (536,324 sq. km.)
POPULATION 23,153
CAPITAL Whitehorse
LARGEST CITY Whitehorse
HIGHEST POINT Mt. Logan 19,524 ft. (5,951 m.)
SETTLED IN 1897
ADMITTED TO CONFEDERATION 1898
PROVINCIAL FLOWER Fireweed

NORTHWEST TERRITORIES
AREA 1,304,896 sq. mi. (3,379,683 sq. km.)
POPULATION 45,741
CAPITAL Yellowknife
LARGEST CITY Yellowknife
HIGHEST POINT Mt. Sir James MacBrien 9,062 ft. (2,762 m.)
SETTLED IN 1800
ADMITTED TO CONFEDERATION 1870
PROVINCIAL FLOWER Mountain Avens

Map: Yukon and Northwest Territories. Scale 1:14,000,000.

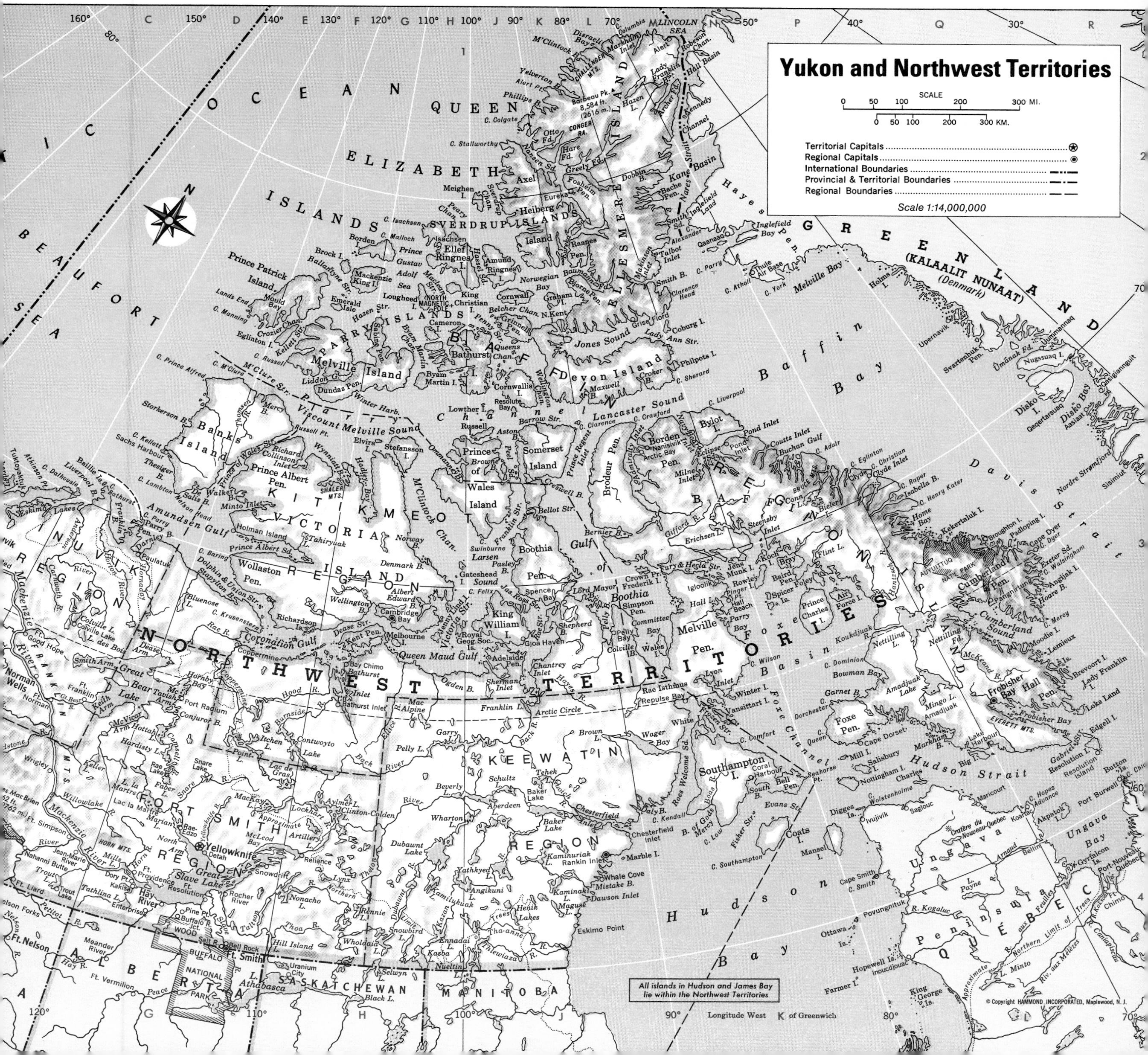

United States

POLYCONIC PROJECTION

SCALE OF MILES

SCALE OF KILOMETERS

Capitals of Countries .... ★
State Capitals .... △
International Boundaries .... ——

Scale 1:17,400,000

© Copyright HAMMOND INCORPORATED, Maplewood, N.J.

AREA 3,623,420 sq. mi.
(9,384,658 sq. km.)
POPULATION 226,504,825
CAPITAL Washington
LARGEST CITY New York
HIGHEST POINT Mt. McKinley 20,320 ft.
(6,194 m.)
MONETARY UNIT U.S. dollar
MAJOR LANGUAGE English
MAJOR RELIGIONS Protestantism,
Roman Catholicism, Judaism

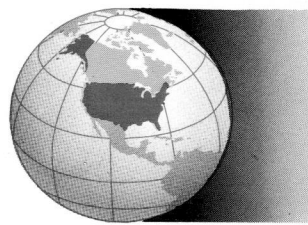

Population Distribution

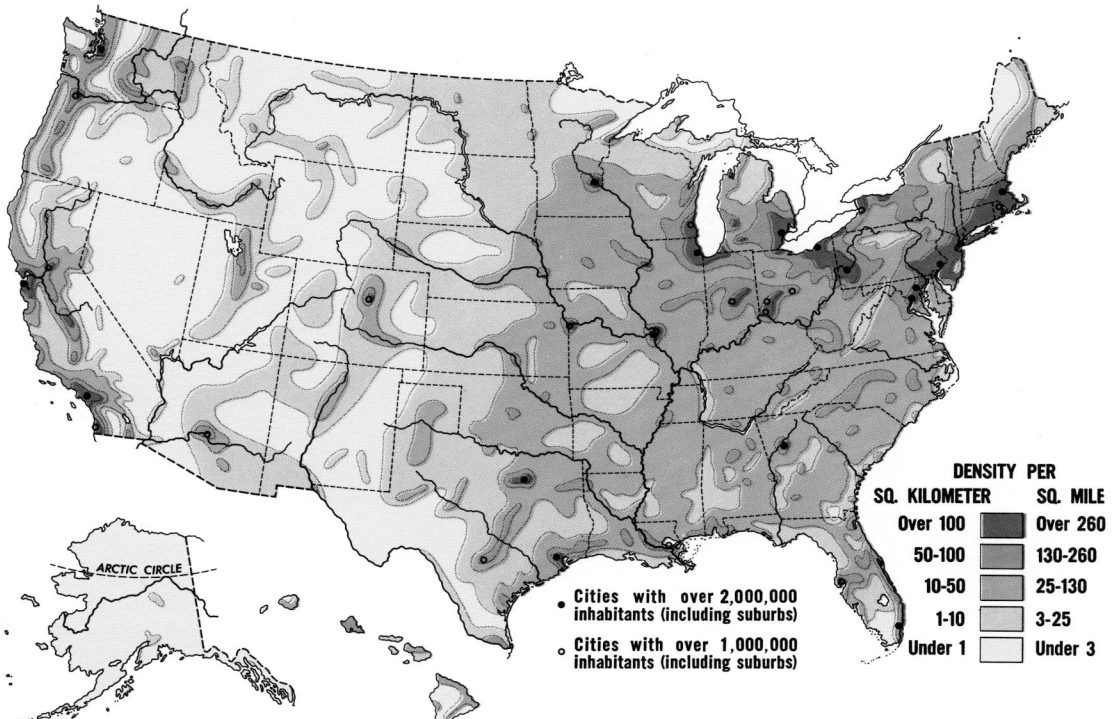

DENSITY PER	
SQ. KILOMETER	SQ. MILE
Over 100	Over 260
50-100	130-260
10-50	25-130
1-10	3-25
Under 1	Under 3

• Cities with over 2,000,000
inhabitants (including suburbs)

○ Cities with over 1,000,000
inhabitants (including suburbs)

Vegetation

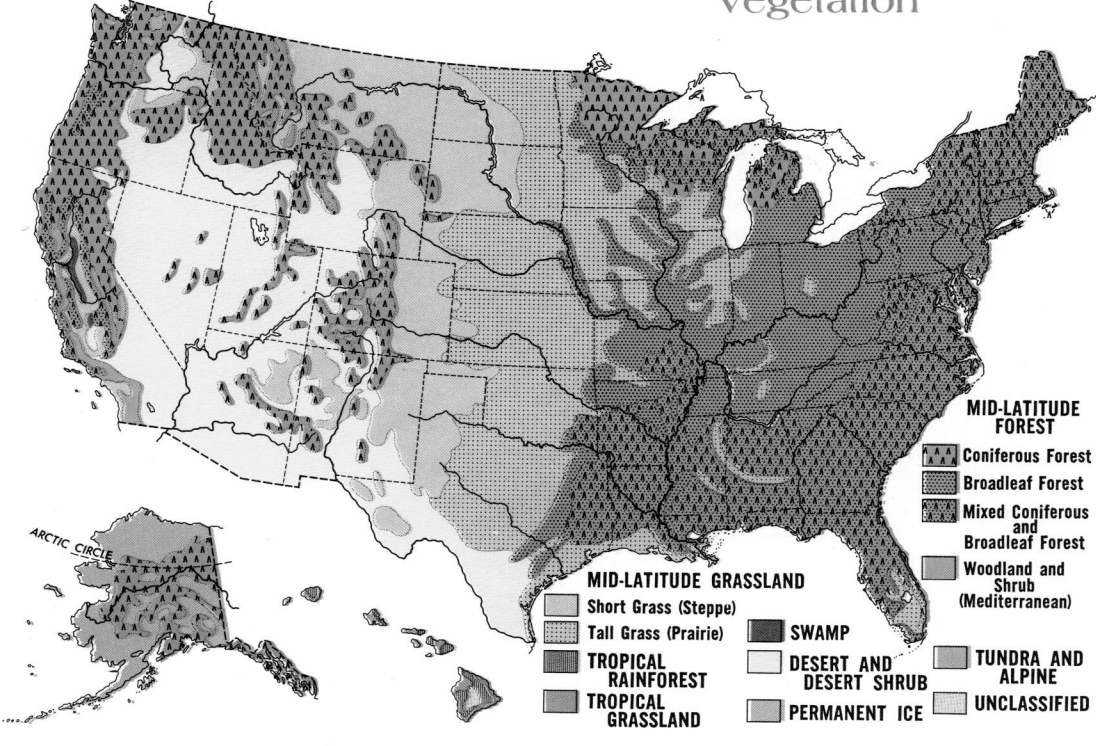

MID-LATITUDE FOREST

▲▲ Coniferous Forest

Broadleaf Forest

Mixed Coniferous
and
Broadleaf Forest

Woodland and
Shrub
(Mediterranean)

MID-LATITUDE GRASSLAND

Short Grass (Steppe)

Tall Grass (Prairie)   SWAMP

**TROPICAL
RAINFOREST**   DESERT AND
DESERT SHRUB   TUNDRA AND
ALPINE

**TROPICAL
GRASSLAND**   PERMANENT ICE   UNCLASSIFIED

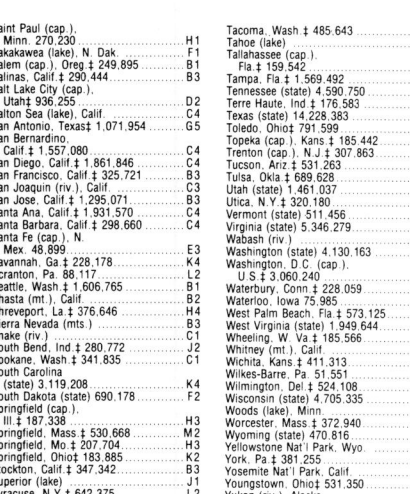

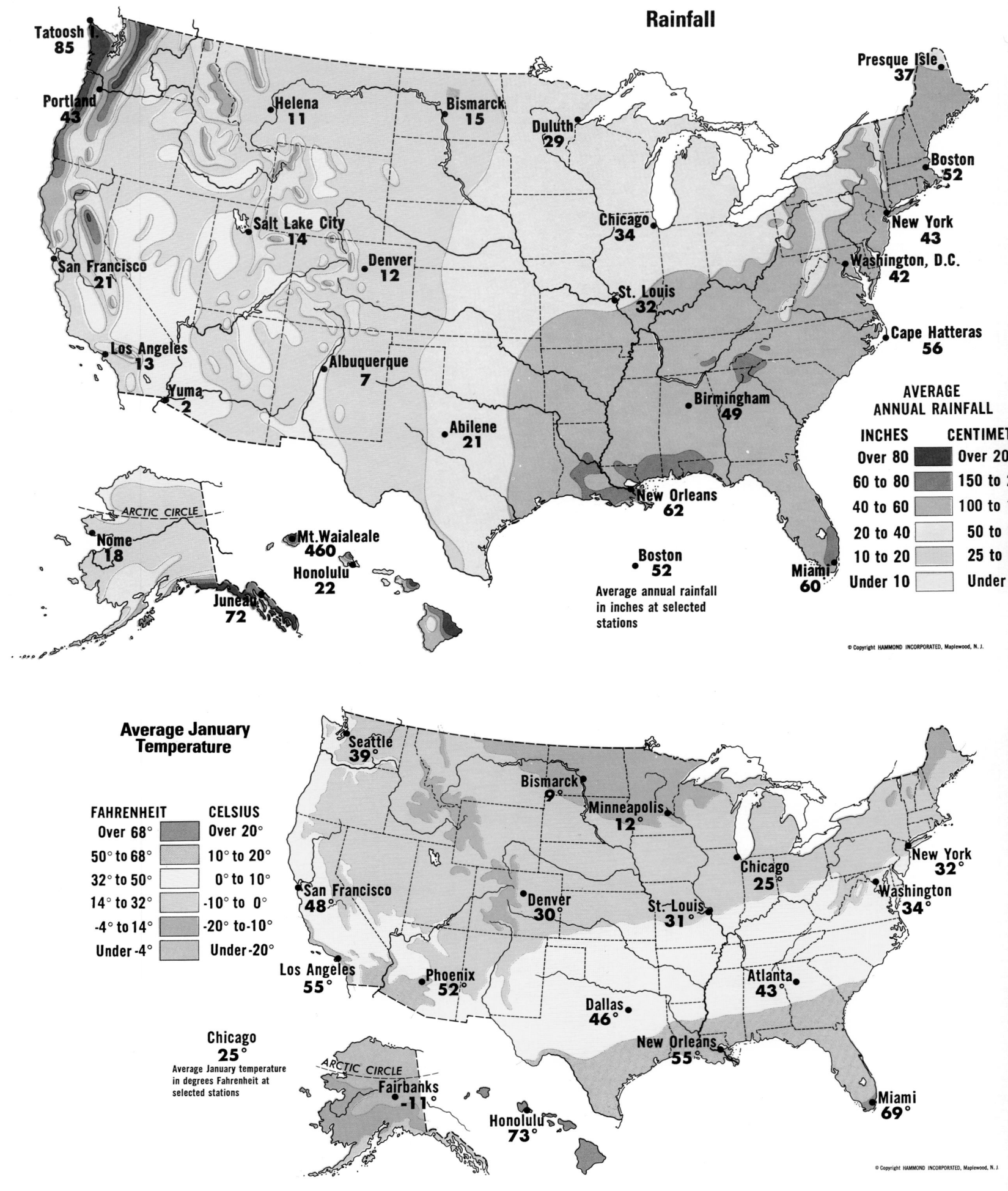

Rainfall

Tatoosh I. 85
Portland 43
Helena 11
Bismarck 15
Duluth 29
Presque Isle 37
Boston 52
San Francisco 21
Salt Lake City 14
Denver 12
Chicago 34
New York 43
Washington, D.C. 42
Los Angeles 13
Yuma 2
Albuquerque 7
St. Louis 32
Cape Hatteras 56
Abilene 21
Birmingham 49
New Orleans 62
Miami 60
Nome 18
Mt.Waialeale 460
Honolulu 22
Juneau 72

ARCTIC CIRCLE

Boston 52
Average annual rainfall in inches at selected stations

AVERAGE ANNUAL RAINFALL

INCHES	CENTIMET
Over 80	Over 20
60 to 80	150 to 2
40 to 60	100 to 1
20 to 40	50 to 1
10 to 20	25 to 5
Under 10	Under

© Copyright HAMMOND INCORPORATED, Maplewood, N.J.

Average January Temperature

FAHRENHEIT	CELSIUS
Over 68°	Over 20°
50° to 68°	10° to 20°
32° to 50°	0° to 10°
14° to 32°	-10° to 0°
-4° to 14°	-20° to -10°
Under -4°	Under -20°

Seattle 39°
Bismarck 9°
Minneapolis 12°
New York 32°
Chicago 25°
Washington 34°
San Francisco 48°
Denver 30°
St. Louis 31°
Los Angeles 55°
Phoenix 52°
Dallas 46°
Atlanta 43°
New Orleans 55°
Miami 69°
Chicago 25°
Average January temperature in degrees Fahrenheit at selected stations

ARCTIC CIRCLE
Fairbanks -11°
Honolulu 73°

© Copyright HAMMOND INCORPORATED, Maplewood, N.J.

Topography

0   200   400 MI.
0   200   400 KM.

C. Flattery
Seattle
Mt. St. Helens 8,364 ft.
(2,549 m.)
Mt. Rainier 14,410 ft.
(4392 m.)
CASCADE RANGE
BITTERROOT RANGE
COLUMBIA PLATEAU
Columbia
Snake
ROCKY
GREAT
Missouri
Fort Peck Lake
Yellowstone
Lake Sakakawea
Red
Rainy
Lake Superior
Keweenaw Pen.
St. Lawrence
L. Champlain
Gulf of Maine
Boston
C. Cod
COAST RANGES
Great
Basin
SIERRA NEVADA
Central Valley
Sacramento
San Francisco
Great Salt Lake
COLORADO
Lake Oahe
James
Missouri
Minneapolis
Wisconsin
Lake Michigan
Milwaukee
Chicago
Lake Huron
Detroit
Lake Erie
Cleveland
Lake Ontario
Niagara Falls
Long Island
New York
Philadelphia
ATLANTIC
MOUNTAINS
Mt. Whitney 14,494 ft. (4418 m.)
Pt. Conception
Mojave Desert
Los Angeles
San Diego
SANTA BARBARA IS.
Lake Mead
Lake Powell
Grand Canyon
PLATEAU
Colorado
Phoenix
Gila
Rio Grande
Denver
Mt. Elbert 14,431 ft. (4399 m.)
N. Platte
Platte
Arkansas
Des Moines
Illinois
Kansas City
Missouri
St. Louis
Indianapolis
Ohio
Wabash
Washington
APPALACHIAN MOUNTAINS
ALLEGHENY MTS.
OZARK PLATEAU
Tennessee
Ohio
ATLANTIC
OCEAN
Chesapeake Bay
C. Hatteras
LLANO ESTACADO
Canadian
Red
Arkansas
Wheeler L.
Memphis
Chattahoochee
Atlanta
Mt. Mitchell 6,684 ft. (2037 m.)
COASTAL PLAIN
C. Fear
Pecos
Dallas
Red
Savannah
Jacksonville
EDWARDS PLATEAU
Brazos
Colorado
Houston
New Orleans
Mississippi Delta
Gulf of Mexico
GULF COASTAL PLAIN
C. Canaveral
L. Okeechobee
The Everglades
Miami
FLORIDA KEYS

ARCTIC OCEAN
0   200   400 MI.
0   200   400 KM.
BROOKS RA.
Tanana
Yukon
St. Lawrence I.
BERING SEA
ALASKA RA.
Mt. McKinley 20,320 ft. (6194 m.)
Anchorage
Alaska Pen.
Gulf of Alaska
Kodiak I.
ALEXANDER ARCHIPELAGO
Aleutian Islands
Bering Str.

Kauai
Oahu
Honolulu
Molokai
Maui
HAWAIIAN ISLANDS
PACIFIC OCEAN
Mauna Kea 13,796 ft. (4205 m.)
Hawaii
0   50   100 MI.
0   50   100 KM.

5,000 m. 16,404 ft. | 2,000 m. 6,562 ft. | 1,000 m. 3,281 ft. | 500 m. 1,640 ft. | 200 m. 656 ft. | 100 m. 328 ft. | Sea Level | Below

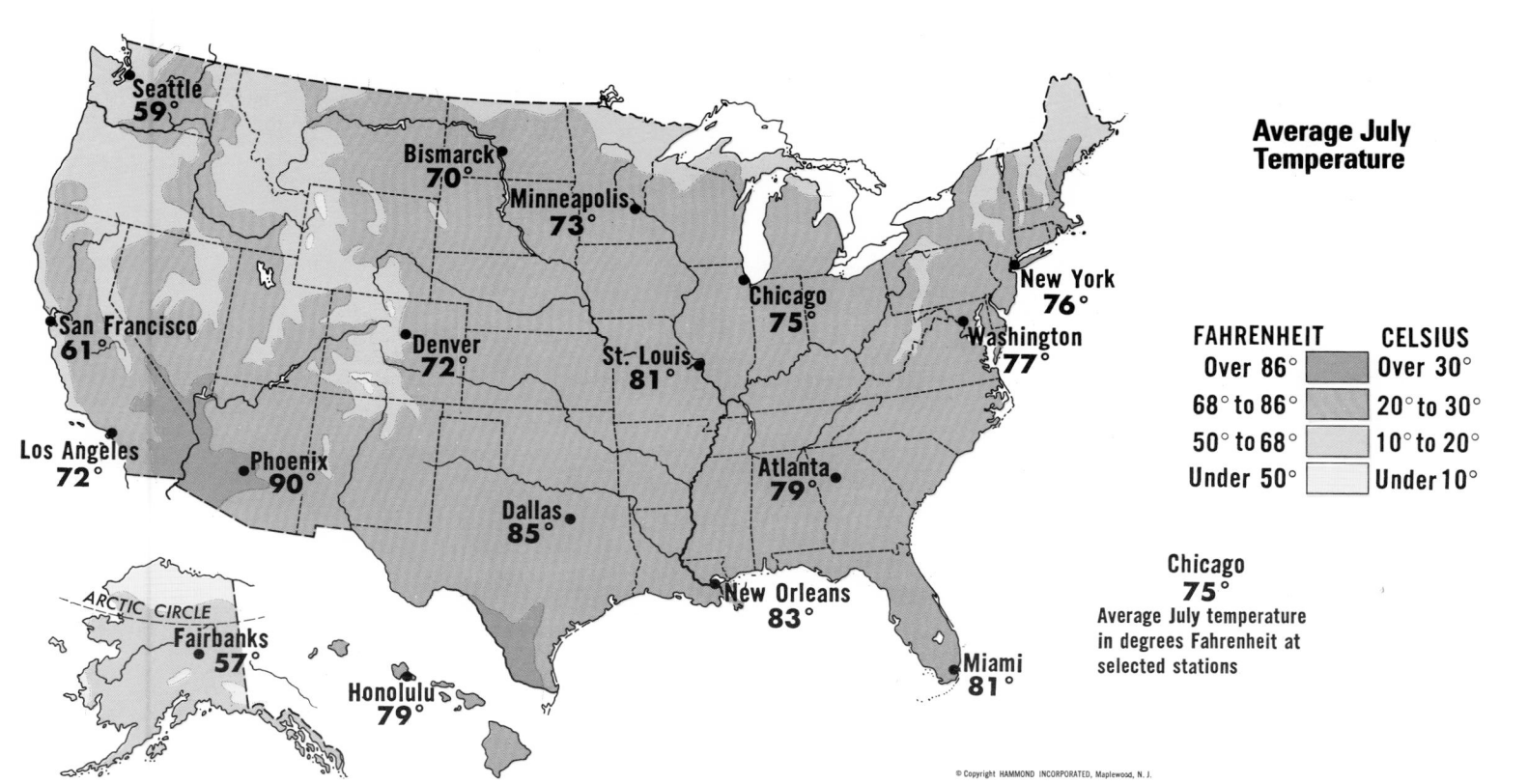

Average July Temperature

Seattle **59°**
Bismarck **70°**
Minneapolis **73°**
Chicago **75**
New York **76°**
San Francisco **61°**
Denver **72°**
St. Louis **81°**
Washington **77°**
Los Angeles **72°**
Phoenix **90°**
Atlanta **79°**
Dallas **85°**
New Orleans **83°**
Miami **81°**
ARCTIC CIRCLE
Fairbanks **57°**
Honolulu **79°**

FAHRENHEIT	CELSIUS
Over 86°	Over 30°
68° to 86°	20° to 30°
50° to 68°	10° to 20°
Under 50°	Under 10°

Chicago
75°
Average July temperature
in degrees Fahrenheit at
selected stations

United States Standard Time Zones

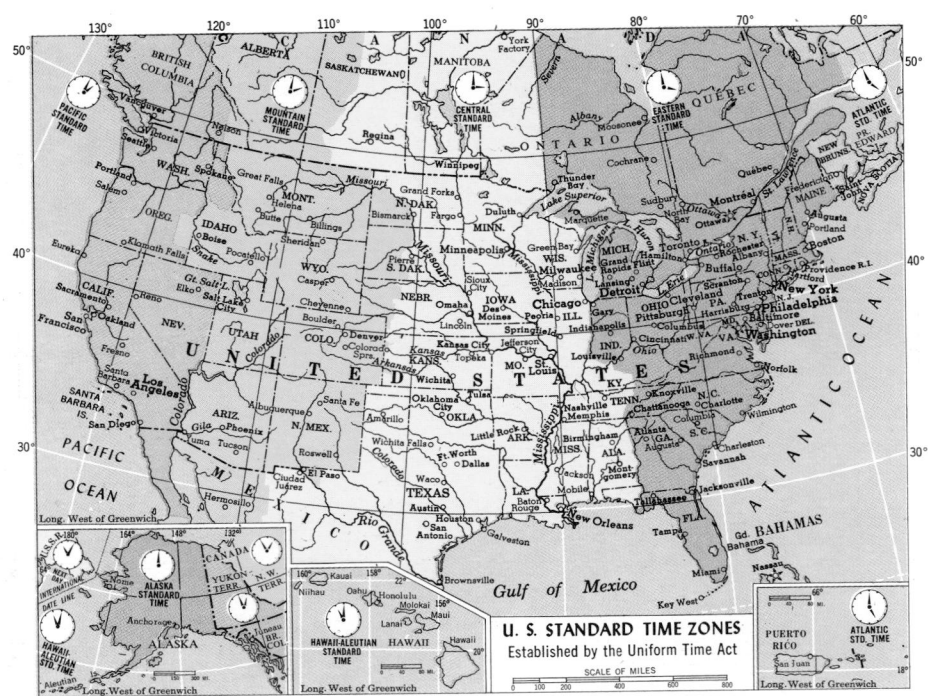

U. S. STANDARD TIME ZONES
Established by the Uniform Time Act
SCALE OF MILES
0   100   200   400   600   800

Agriculture, Industry and Resources

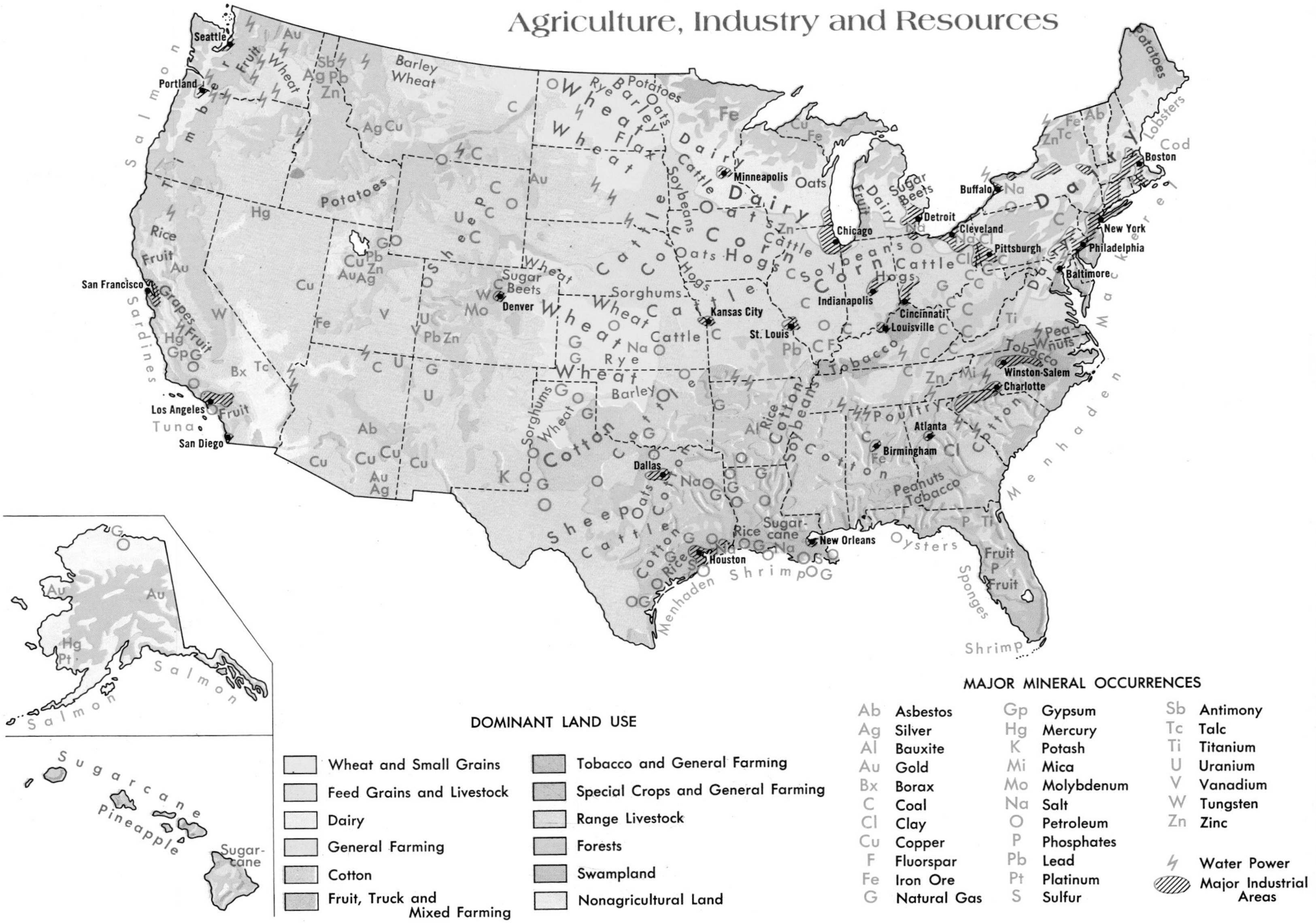

DOMINANT LAND USE

- Wheat and Small Grains
- Feed Grains and Livestock
- Dairy
- General Farming
- Cotton
- Fruit, Truck and Mixed Farming
- Tobacco and General Farming
- Special Crops and General Farming
- Range Livestock
- Forests
- Swampland
- Nonagricultural Land

MAJOR MINERAL OCCURRENCES

Ab	Asbestos	Gp	Gypsum	Sb	Antimony
Ag	Silver	Hg	Mercury	Tc	Talc
Al	Bauxite	K	Potash	Ti	Titanium
Au	Gold	Mi	Mica	U	Uranium
Bx	Borax	Mo	Molybdenum	V	Vanadium
C	Coal	Na	Salt	W	Tungsten
Cl	Clay	O	Petroleum	Zn	Zinc
Cu	Copper	P	Phosphates		
F	Fluorspar	Pb	Lead	⚡	Water Power
Fe	Iron Ore	Pt	Platinum	▨	Major Industrial Areas
G	Natural Gas	S	Sulfur		

AREA 51,705 sq. mi. (133,916 sq. km.)
POPULATION 3,893,888
CAPITAL Montgomery
LARGEST CITY Birmingham
HIGHEST POINT Cheaha Mtn. 2,407 ft. (734 m.)
SETTLED IN 1702
ADMITTED TO UNION December 14, 1819
POPULAR NAME Heart of Dixie; Cotton State; Yellowhammer State
STATE FLOWER Camellia
STATE BIRD Yellowhammer

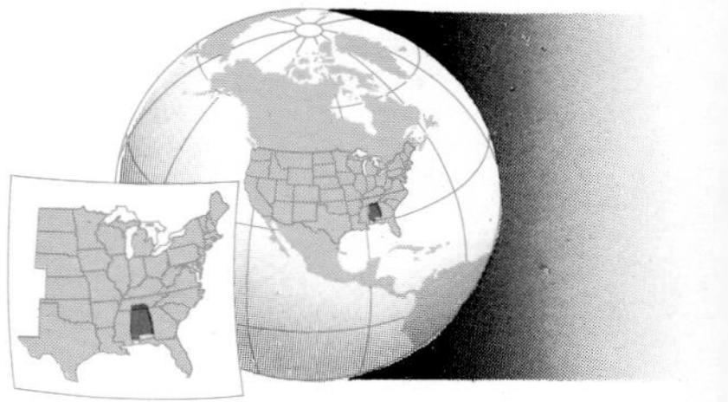

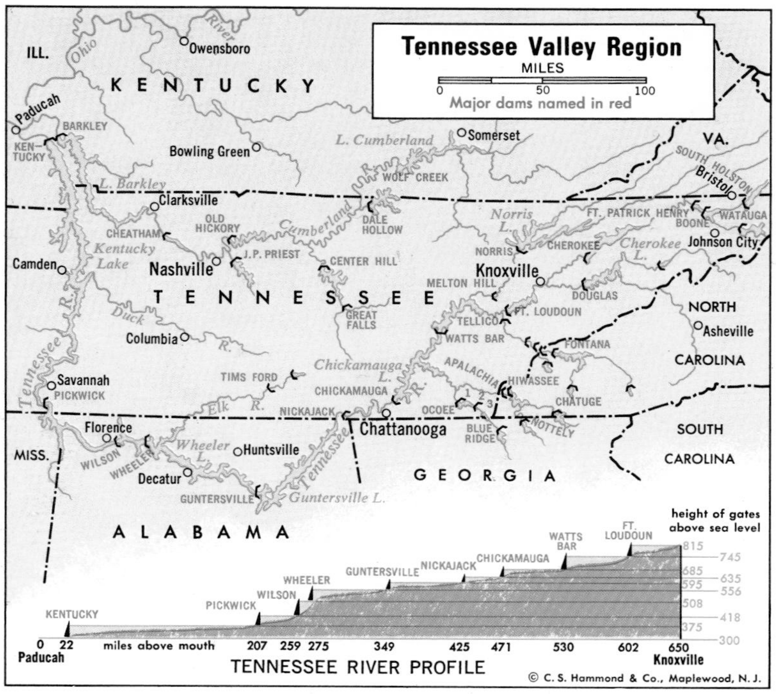

COUNTIES

utauga 32,259 E5
aldwin 78,556 C9
arbour 24,756 H7
ibb 15,723 D5
lount 36,459 E2
ullock 10,596 G6
utler 21,680 E7
alhoun 119,761 G3
hambers 39,191 H5
herokee 18,760 G2
hilton 30,612 E5
hoctaw 16,839 B6
larke 27,702 C7
lay 13,703 G4
leburne 12,595 G3
offee 38,533 G8
olbert 54,519 C1
onecuh 15,884 E8
oosa 11,377 F5
ovington 36,850 F8
renshaw 14,110 F7
ullman 61,642 E2
ale 47,821 G8
allas 53,981 D6
e Kalb 53,658 G2
more 43,390 F5
scambia 38,440 D8
towah 103,057 F2
ayette 18,809 C3
ranklin 28,350 C2
eneva 24,253 G8
reene 11,021 C5
ale 15,604 C5
enry 15,302 H7
ouston 74,632 H8
ackson 51,407 F1
efferson 671,324 E3
amar 16,453 B3
auderdale 80,546 C1
awrence 30,170 D1
ee 76,283 H5
imestone 46,005 E1
owndes 13,253 E6
lacon 26,829 G6
ladison 196,966 E1
larengo 25,047 C6
larion 30,041 C2
larshall 65,622 F2
lobile 364,980 B9
lonroe 22,651 D7
lontgomery 197,038 F6
lorgan 90,231 E2
erry 15,012 D5
ickens 21,481 B4
ike 28,050 G7
andolph 20,075 H4
ussell 47,356 H6
aint Clair 41,205 F3
helby 66,298 E4
umter 16,908 B5
alladega 73,826 F4
allapoosa 38,676 G5
uscaloosa 137,541 C4
/alker 68,660 D3
/ashington 16,821 B8
/ilcox 14,755 D7
/inston 21,953 D2

CITIES and TOWNS

ip Name/Pop. Key

36310 Abbeville⊙ 3,155 H7
35440 Abernant 405 D4
35005 Adamsville 2,498 D3
35540 Addison 746 D2
35006 Adger 400 D4
35441 Akron 604 C5
35007 Alabaster 7,079 E4
35950 Albertville 12,039 F2
35115 Aldrich 500 E4
35010 Alexander City 13,807 G5
36250 Alexandria 600 G3
35442 Aliceville 3,207 B4
35013 Allgood 387 F3
36501 Alma 500 C8
35952 Altoona 928 F2
36420 Andalusia⊙ 10,415 E8
35610 Anderson 405 D1
36201 Anniston⊙ 29,523 G3
Anniston‡ 116,936 G3
35016 Arab 5,967 E2
35805 Ardmore 1,096 E1
35173 Argo 600 E3
36311 Ariton 844 G7
35033 Arkadelphia 150 E3
35541 Arley 276 D2
35035 Ashby 500 E4
36312 Ashford 2,165 H8
36251 Ashland⊙ 2,052 G4
35953 Ashville⊙ 1,489 F3
35611 Athens⊙ 14,558 E1
36503 Atmore 8,789 C8
35954 Attalla 7,737 F2
36830 Auburn 28,471 H5
36003 Autaugaville 843 E6
†36312 Avon 433 H8
36505 Axis 500 B9
†36420 Babbie 553 F8
35019 Baileyton 396 E2
36005 Banks 160 G7
†36532 Barnwell 700 C10
36507 Bay Minette⊙ 7,455 C9
36509 Bayou La Batre 2,005 B10
35543 Bear Creek 353 C2
36425 Beatrice 558 D7
35544 Beaverton 360 B3
†35653 Belgreen 500 C2
35545 Belk 308 C3
36901 Bellamy 700 B6
35615 Belle Mina 675 E1
36313 Bellwood 400 G8
36785 Benton 74 E6
35546 Berry 916 C3
35020 Bessemer 31,729 D4
†36872 Beulah 500 H5
36006 Billingsley 106 E5
*35201 Birmingham⊙ 284,413 D3
Birmingham‡ 847,360 D3
36314 Black 156 G8
35031 Blountsville 1,509 E2
36201 Blue Mountain 284 G3
†36017 Blue Springs 112 G7
35957 Boaz 7,151 F2
35443 Boligee 164 C5
35032 Bon Air 118 F4
36511 Bon Secour 850 C10
†35120 Branchville 365 F3
36009 Brantley 1,151 F7
35034 Brent 2,862 D5
36426 Brewton⊙ 6,680 D8
35740 Bridgeport 2,974 G1
35020 Brighton 5,308 D4
35548 Brilliant 871 C2
35036 Brookside 1,409 E3
35444 Brookwood 492 D4
36010 Brundidge 3,213 G7
36725 Burkville 250 E6
36431 Burnt Corn 60 D7
36904 Butler⊙ 1,882 B6
†36767 Cahaba 75 D6
35040 Calera 2,035 E4
†36047 Calhoun 950 F6
36513 Calvert 600 B8
36726 Camden⊙ 2,406 D7
36850 Camp Hill 1,628 G5
†36502 Canoe 560 D8
†36726 Canton Bend 300 D6
35549 Carbon Hill 2,452 D3
35041 Cardiff 140 E3
†36420 Carolina 203 E8
35447 Carrollton⊙ 1,104 B4
†36023 Carrville 820 G5
†36548 Carson 400 C8
36432 Castleberry 847 D8
35959 Cedar Bluff 1,129 G2
35960 Centre⊙ 2,351 G2
35042 Centreville⊙ 2,504 D5
36518 Chatom⊙ 1,122 B8
35043 Chelsea 600 E4
35616 Cherokee 1,589 C1
36611 Chickasaw 7,402 B9
35044 Childersburg 5,084 F4
36254 Choccolocco 500 G3
36905 Choctaw 600 B6
†36550 Chrysler 400 C8
36521 Chunchula 700 B9
36522 Citronelle 2,841 B8
35045 Clanton⊙ 5,832 E5
†36322 Clayhatchee 560 G8
36015 Clayton⊙ 1,589 G7
35049 Cleveland 487 E3
36017 Clio 1,224 G7
35449 Coaling 400 D4
36523 Coden 800 B10
36318 Coffee Springs 339 G8
36524 Coffeeville 448 B7
35452 Coker 800 C4
35961 Collinsville 1,383 G2
36319 Columbia 881 H8
35051 Columbiana⊙ 2,655 E4
36020 Coosada 980 F5
35550 Cordova 3,123 D3
35453 Cottondale 500 D4
36320 Cottonwood 1,352 H8
†35172 County Line 199 E3
†36467 County Line 124 F8
35618 Courtland 456 D1
36321 Cowarts 418 H8
36435 Coy 950 D7
36525 Creola 1,652 B9
36906 Cromwell 650 B6
35962 Crossville 1,222 G2
36907 Cuba 486 B6
35055 Cullman⊙ 13,084 E2
36852 Cusseta 650 H5
36853 Dadeville⊙ 3,263 G5
36322 Daleville 4,250 G8
36526 Daphne 3,406 C9
36528 Dauphin Island 950 B10
36256 Daviston 334 G4
36731 Dayton 113 C6
*35601 Decatur⊙ 42,002 D1
36257 De Armanville 350 G3
36732 Demopolis 7,678 C6
35552 Detroit 326 B2
35062 Dora 2,327 D3
*36303 Dothan⊙ 48,750 H8
35553 Double Springs⊙ 1,057 D2
35964 Douglas 116 F2
36028 Dozier 494 F7
35744 Dutton 276 G1
36426 East Brewton 3,012 E8
36024 Eclectic 1,124 F5
36261 Edwardsville 207 H3
36323 Elba⊙ 4,355 F8
36530 Elberta 491 C10
35554 Eldridge 230 C3
35620 Elkmont 429 E1
36025 Elmore 600 F5
35458 Elrod 746 C4
35063 Empire 600 D3
36330 Enterprise 18,033 G8
35460 Epes 399 B5
35461 Ethelsville 95 B4
36027 Eufaula 12,097 H7
†36340 Eunola 169 G8
35462 Eutaw⊙ 2,444 C5
35621 Eva 185 E2
36401 Evergreen⊙ 4,171 E8
36439 Excel 385 D8
35746 Fackler 250 G1
36854 Fairfax 3,776 H5
35064 Fairfield 13,242 E4
36532 Fairhope 7,286 C10
35208 Fairview 450 E2
35622 Falkville 1,310 E2
36738 Faunsdale 174 C6
35555 Fayette⊙ 5,287 C3
36855 Five Points 197 H4
35966 Flat Rock 750 G1
†35601 Flint City 673 D1
36441 Flomaton 1,882 D8
36442 Florala 2,165 F8
*35630 Florence⊙ 37,029 C1
Florence‡ 135,023 C1
36535 Foley 4,003 C10
35214 Forestdale 10,814 E3
36740 Forkland 429 C5
36031 Fort Davis 500 G6
36032 Fort Deposit 1,519 E7
36856 Fort Mitchell 900 H6
35967 Fort Payne⊙ 11,485 G2
35463 Fosters 400 C4
36444 Franklin 133 G6
36445 Frisco City 1,424 D8
36539 Fruitdale 500 B8
36262 Fruithurst 239 G3
36446 Fulton 606 C7
35068 Fultondale 6,217 E3
35971 Fyffe 1,305 G2
*35901 Gadsden⊙ 47,565 G2
Gadsden‡ 103,057 G2
35464 Gainesville 207 B5
35972 Gallant 475 F2
36038 Gantt 314 E8
35070 Garden City 655 E2
35071 Gardendale 7,928 E3
35973 Gaylesville 192 G2
†35459 Geiger 200 B5
36340 Geneva⊙ 4,866 G8
36033 Georgiana 1,993 E7
35974 Geraldine 911 G2
36908 Gilbertown 218 B7
35559 Glen Allen 312 C3
35905 Glencoe 4,648 G3
36034 Glenwood 341 F7
†35010 Goldville 89 G4
†36024 Good Hope 1,442 E2
35072 Goodwater 1,895 F4
35466 Gordo 2,112 C4
36343 Gordon 362 H8
†35580 Gorgas 500 D3
36035 Goshen 365 F7
†36482 Gosport 500 C7
36541 Grand Bay 3,185 B10
35747 Grant 632 F1
35073 Graysville 2,642 D3
35074 Green Pond 750 D4
36744 Greensboro⊙ 3,248 C5
36037 Greenville⊙ 7,807 E7
†36350 Grimes 298 H8
36451 Grove Hill⊙ 1,912 C7
35563 Guin 2,418 C3
36542 Gulf Shores 1,349 C10
35976 Guntersville⊙ 7,041 F2
35748 Gurley 735 F1
†35563 Gu-Win 266 C3
35564 Hackleburg 883 C2
†36319 Haleburg 106 H8
35565 Haleyville 5,306 C2
35570 Hamilton⊙ 5,093 C2
†35989 Hammondville 369 G1
35077 Hanceville 2,220 E2
36039 Hardaway 600 G6
35078 Harpersville 934 F4
36344 Hartford 2,647 G8
35640 Hartselle 8,858 E2
36858 Hatchechubbee 840 H6
†35672 Hatton 950 D1
35079 Hayden 268 E3
36040 Hayneville⊙ 592 E6
35750 Hazel Green 1,503 E1
36345 Headland 3,327 H8
†36558 Healing Springs 100 B7
†36420 Heath 354 F8
36264 Heflin⊙ 3,014 G3
35080 Helena 2,130 E4
35978 Henagar 1,188 G1
35979 Higdon 925 G1
†35013 Highland Lake 210 F3
35643 Hillsboro 278 D1
†36201 Hobson City 1,268 G3
35571 Hodges 250 C2
35903 Hokes Bluff 3,216 G3
35082 Hollins 500 F4
35083 Holly Pond 493 E2
35752 Hollywood 1,110 G1
35209 Homewood 21,412 E4
†35216 Hoover 19,792 E4
36043 Hope Hull 975 F6
†36467 Horn Hill 186 F8
35020 Hueytown 13,478 D4
*35801 Huntsville⊙ 142,513 E1
Huntsville‡ 308,593 E1
36860 Hurtsboro 752 H6
35981 Ider 698 G1
35210 Irondale 6,510 E3
36545 Jackson 6,073 C8
36861 Jacksons Gap 800 G5
36265 Jacksonville 9,735 G3
35501 Jasper⊙ 11,894 D3
35085 Jemison 1,828 E5
35573 Kansas 267 C3
35574 Kennedy 604 B3
35645 Killen 747 D1
35091 Kimberly 1,043 E3
†36301 Kinsey 1,239 H8
36453 Kinston 604 F8
36862 Lafayette⊙ 3,647 H5
†35986 Lakeview 441 G2
36863 Lanett 6,897 H5
36864 Langdale 2,034 H5
†35768 Larkinsville 425 F1
36911 Lavaca 500 B6
35094 Leeds 8,638 E3
35983 Leesburg 116 G2
35646 Leighton 1,218 D1
36548 Leroy 699 B8
35647 Lester 117 D1
†36322 Level Plains 867 G8
35648 Lexington 884 D1
†36420 Libertyville 141 F8
35096 Lincoln 2,081 F3
36748 Linden⊙ 2,773 C6
36266 Lineville 2,257 G4
35020 Lipscomb 3,741 E4
36912 Lisman 638 B6
†36876 Little Shawmut 2,793 H5
†35653 Littleville 1,262 C1
35470 Livingston⊙ 3,187 B5
36865 Loachapoka 335 G5
36455 Lockhart 547 F8
35097 Locust Fork 488 E3
†35137 Longview 475 E4
36048 Louisville 791 G7
36751 Lower Peach Tree 926 C7
36752 Lowndesboro 207 E6
36551 Loxley 840 C9
36049 Luverne⊙ 2,639 F7
35575 Lynn 554 C2
35758 Madison 4,057 E1
36348 Madrid 172 H8
36555 Magnolia Springs 800 C10
36349 Malvern 558 G8
36750 Maplesville 754 E5
35112 Margaret 757 F3
36756 Marion⊙ 4,467 D5
35114 Maylene 500 E4
35111 McCalla 657 E4
36552 McCullough 500 D8
36553 McIntosh 319 B8
36456 McKenzie 605 E7
†35442 Memphis 95 B4
35984 Mentone 476 G1
35759 Meridianville 1,403 F1
35228 Midfield 6,203 E4
36350 Midland City 1,903 H8
36053 Midway 593 H6
†35150 Mignon 2,054 F4
36054 Millbrook 3,101 F6
35576 Millport 1,287 B3
36558 Millry 956 B7
36761 Minter 450 D6
*36601 Mobile⊙ 200,452 B9
Mobile‡ 442,819 B9
36460 Monroeville⊙ 5,674 D7
†35804 Monrovia 500 E1
35115 Montevallo 3,965 E4
*36101 Montgomery (cap.)⊙ 178,857 F6
Montgomery‡ 272,687 F6
36559 Montrose 750 C9
†35125 Moody 1,840 F3
35649 Mooresville 58 E1
35116 Morris 623 E3
35650 Moulton⊙ 3,197 D2
35474 Moundville 1,310 C5
†35957 Mountainboro 500 F2
35223 Mountain Brook 19,718 E4
36560 Mount Vernon 1,038 B8
36268 Munford 700 F3
35660 Muscle Shoals 8,911 C1
36763 Myrtlewood 252 C6
36764 Nanafalia 500 B6
36303 Napier Field 493 H8
35578 Nauvoo 259 D3
†35049 Nectar 367 E3
36765 Newbern 307 C5
36351 New Brockton 1,392 G8
35760 New Hope 1,546 F1
35761 New Market 680 F1
†35010 New Site 340 G4
36352 Newton 1,540 G8
36353 Newville 814 H8
35086 North Johns 243 D4
35476 Northport 14,291 C4
36866 Notasulga 876 G5
35006 Oak Grove 638 F4
36766 Oak Hill 63 D7
35579 Oakman 770 D3
35120 Odenville 724 F3
36271 Ohatchee 860 G3
35121 Oneonta⊙ 4,824 E3
†36467 Onycha 147 F8
36801 Opelika⊙ 21,896 H5
36467 Opp 7,204 F8
36561 Orange Beach 600 C10
36767 Orrville 349 D6
35763 Owens Cross Roads 804 E1
36203 Oxford 8,939 G3
36360 Ozark⊙ 13,188 G8
35764 Paint Rock 221 F1
35580 Parrish 1,583 D3
35124 Pelham 6,759 E4
35125 Pell City⊙ 6,616 F3
36916 Pennington 355 B6
36562 Perdido 500 C8
36471 Peterman 600 D7
36062 Petrey 93 F7
36867 Phenix City⊙ 26,928 H6
35581 Phil Campbell 1,549 C2
†35447 Pickensville 132 B4
36272 Piedmont 5,544 G3
36371 Pinckard 771 G8
36768 Pine Apple 298 E7
36769 Pine Hill 510 C7
35765 Pisgah 699 G1
36758 Plantersville 650 E5
35127 Pleasant Grove 7,102 D4
36564 Point Clear 1,812 C10
†36441 Pollard 144 D8

(continued on following page)

Agriculture, Industry and Resources

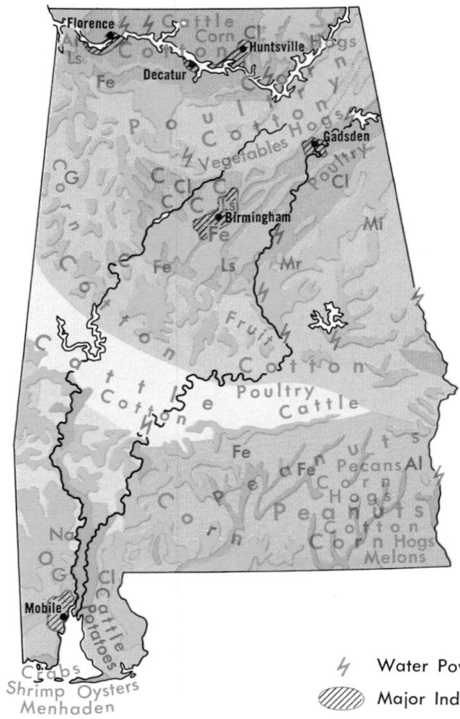

DOMINANT LAND USE

- Specialized Cotton
- Cotton, Livestock
- Cotton, General Farming
- Cotton, Hogs, Peanuts
- Cotton, Forest Products
- Peanuts, General Farming
- Truck and Mixed Farming
- Forests
- Swampland, Limited Agriculture

MAJOR MINERAL OCCURRENCES

Al	Bauxite	Ls	Limestone
At	Asphalt	Mi	Mica
C	Coal	Mr	Marble
Cl	Clay	Na	Salt
Fe	Iron Ore	O	Petroleum
G	Natural Gas		

Water Power

Major Industrial Areas

Topography

0 30 60 MI.
0 30 60 KM.

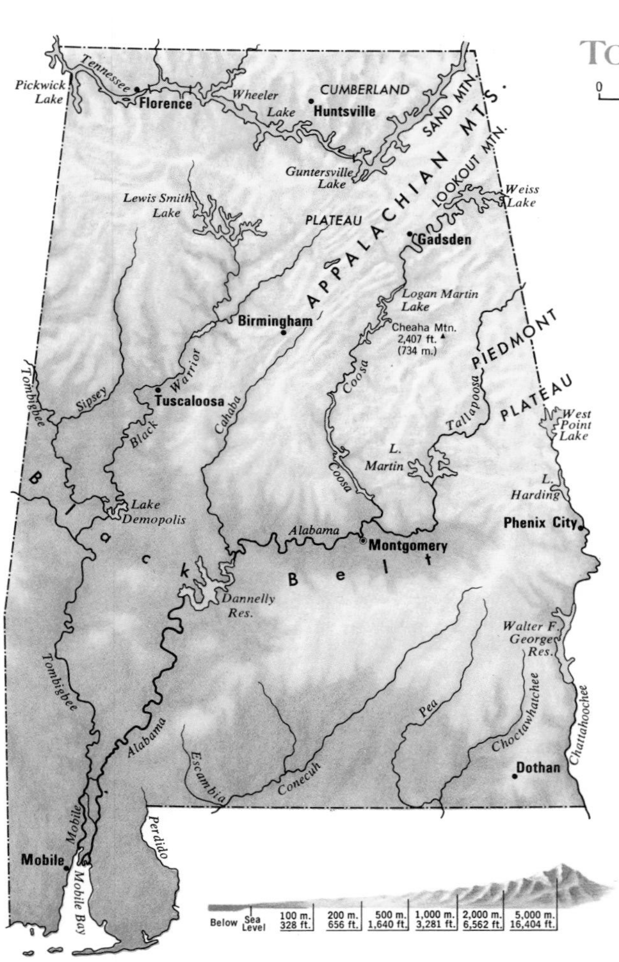

†35986 Powell's Crossroads 636 ... G1
36067 Prattville⊙ 18,647 ... E6
†35601 Priceville 966 ... E1
36610 Prichard 39,541 ... B9
†36748 Providence 363 ... C6
35131 Ragland 1,860 ... F3
35901 Rainbow City 6,299 ... F3
35986 Rainsville 3,907 ... G2
36069 Ramer 680 ... F6
36273 Ranburne 417 ... H3
35582 Red Bay 3,232 ... B2
36474 Red Level 504 ... E8
†35954 Reece City 718 ... G2
35481 Reform 2,245 ... C4
35133 Remlap 800 ... E3
36475 Repton 313 ... D8
†35203 Republic 500 ... E3
36476 River Falls 669 ... E8
35135 Riverside 849 ... F3
†36426 Riverview 132 ... D8
36274 Roanoke 5,896 ... H4
36567 Robertsdale 2,306 ... C9
35136 Rockford⊙ 494 ... F5
36274 Rock Mills 600 ... H4
35652 Rogersville 1,224 ... D1
35020 Roosevelt City 3,352 ... E4
†35049 Rosa 204 ... E3
35653 Russellville⊙ 8,195 ... C2
35228 Rutledge 496 ... F7
35137 Saginaw 475 ... E4
36568 Saint Elmo 700 ... B10
†35630 Saint Florian 305 ... C1
36569 Saint Stephens 700 ... B7
36570 Salitpa 550 ... C7
36477 Samson 2,402 ... F8
†36420 Sanford 250 ... F8
36571 Saraland 9,833 ... B9
†35957 Sardis 883 ... F2
36572 Satsuma 3,822 ... B9
35139 Sayre 700 ... E3
35768 Scottsboro⊙ 14,758 ... F1
35771 Section 821 ... G1
36701 Selma⊙ 26,684 ... E6
†36701 Selmont-West Selmont 5,255 ... E6
36876 Shawmut 2,284 ... H5
35660 Sheffield 11,903 ... C1
35143 Shelby 500 ... E4
†35979 Shiloh 297 ... G2
36919 Silas 343 ... B7
36576 Silverhill 624 ... C9
35584 Sipsey 678 ... D3
36375 Slocomb 2,153 ... G8
36877 Smiths 950 ... H5
35952 Snead 667 ... F2
35670 Somerville 140 ... E2
†35901 Southside 5,141 ... F3
36527 Spanish Fort 3,415 ... C9
†35674 Spring Valley 600 ... C1
35146 Springville 1,476 ... E3
36578 Stapleton 975 ... C9
35987 Steele 795 ... F3
35772 Stevenson 2,568 ... G1
35484 Stewart 450 ... C5
36579 Stockton 500 ... C9
35586 Sulligent 2,130 ... B3
35148 Sumiton 2,815 ... D3
36580 Summerdale 546 ... C10
36581 Sunflower 100 ... B8
36782 Sweet Water 253 ... C6
35149 Sycamore 800 ... F4
35150 Sylacauga 12,708 ... F4
35988 Sylvania 1,156 ... G1
35160 Talladega⊙ 19,128 ... F4
†35150 Talladega Springs 196 ... F4
36078 Tallassee 4,763 ... G5
35671 Tanner 600 ... E1
35217 Tarrant City 8,148 ... E3
†36301 Taylor 1,003 ... H8
36582 Theodore 6,392 ... B9
36783 Thomaston 679 ... C6
36784 Thomasville 4,387 ... C7
35171 Thorsby 1,422 ... E5
36583 Tibbie 675 ... B8
35672 Town Creek 1,201 ... D1
35587 Townley 500 ... D3
36921 Toxey 265 ... B7
35172 Trafford 673 ... E3
†35758 Triana 285 ... E1
35673 Trinity 1,328 ... D1
36081 Troy⊙ 12,945 ... G7
35173 Trussville 3,507 ... E3
*35401 Tuscaloosa⊙ 75,211 ... C4
Tuscaloosa‡ 137,473 ... C4
35674 Tuscumbia⊙ 9,137 ... C1
36083 Tuskegee⊙ 13,327 ... G6
36088 Tuskegee Institute ... G6
†35462 Union 358 ... C5
35175 Union Grove 127 ... E2
36089 Union Springs⊙ 4,431 ... G6
36786 Uniontown 2,112 ... D6
36480 Uriah 450 ... D8
35775 Valhermoso Springs 500 ... E2
35989 Valley Head 609 ... G1
35490 Vance 254 ... D4
35176 Vandiver 700 ... F4
36091 Verbena 500 ... E5
35592 Vernon⊙ 2,609 ... B3
35216 Vestavia Hills 15,722 ... E4
35593 Vina 346 ... B2
35178 Vincent 1,652 ... F4
35179 Vinemont ... E2
36481 Vredenburgh 433 ... D7
36276 Wadley 532 ... G4
†36022 Wadsworth 500 ... E5
36585 Wagarville 550 ... B8
†35150 Waldo 231 ... F4
36586 Walker Springs 500 ... C7
35990 Walnut Grove 510 ... F2
35180 Warrior 3,260 ... E3
35677 Waterloo 260 ... B1
35182 Wattsville 550 ... F3
36879 Waverly 228 ... G5
36277 Weaver 2,765 ... G3
36376 Webb 448 ... H8
36278 Wedowee⊙ 908 ... H4
35183 Weogufka 500 ... F4
35184 West Blocton 1,147 ... D4
†36201 West End-Cobb Town 5,189 ... G3
†35005 West Jefferson 357 ... D4
†35570 Weston 350 ... B2
35185 Westover 500 ... E4
†35179 West Point 248 ... D2
36092 Wetumpka⊙ 4,341 ... F5
36482 Whatley 800 ... C7
†36040 White Hall 195 ... E6
†35094 Whites Chapel 336 ... F3
36587 Wilmer 581 ... B9
35186 Wilsonville 914 ... E4
35187 Wilton 642 ... E4
35594 Winfield 3,781 ... C3
36280 Woodland 192 ... H4
35776 Woodville 609 ... F1
36924 Yantley 500 ... B6
36925 York 3,392 ... B6

OTHER FEATURES

Alabama (riv.) ... C8
Aliceville (dam) ... B4
Anniston Army Depot ... F3
Bankhead (lake) ... D4
Bartletts Ferry (dam) ... H5
Big Canoe (creek) ... F3
Big Creek (lake) ... B9
Black Warrior (riv.) ... C5
Bon Secour (bay) ... C10
Brookley Air Force Base ... B9
Buttahatchee (riv.) ... B3
Cahaba (riv.) ... D5
Cedar (pt.) ... B10
Chattahoochee (riv.) ... H8
Chattooga (riv.) ... H2
Cheaha (mt.) ... G4
Choctawhatchee (riv.) ... H8
Coffeeville (dam) ... B7
Conecuh (riv.) ... D8
Coosa (riv.) ... F4
Cowikee, North Fork (creek) ... H6
Cumberland (plat.) ... F1
Dannelly (res.) ... D6
Demopolis (dam) ... C5
Elk (riv.) ... D1
Escambia (creek) ... D8
Escambia (riv.) ... D8
Escatawpa (riv.) ... B9
Eufaula (Walter F. George Res.) (lake) ... H7
Fort Gaines ... B10
Fort McClellan Mil. Res. 7,605 ... G3
Fort Morgan ... C10
Fort Rucker 8,932 ... G8
Gainesville (dam) ... B5
Goat Rock (dam) ... H5
Goat Rock (lake) ... H5
Grants Pass (chan.) ... B10
Gunter Air Force Base ... F6
Guntersville (dam) ... F2
Guntersville (lake) ... F2
Harding (lake) ... H5
Herbes (isl.) ... B10
Holt (dam) ... D4
Horseshoe Bend Nat'l Mil. Park ... G5
Inland (lake) ... E3
Jordan (dam) ... F5
Jordan (lake) ... F5
Lay (lake) ... F4
Lewis Smith (dam) ... D3
Lewis Smith (lake) ... D2
Little (riv.) ... C8
Little (riv.) ... G2
Locust Fork (riv.) ... E3
Logan Martin (lake) ... F4
Lookout (mt.) ... G2
Martin (dam) ... G5
Martin (lake) ... G5
Maxwell Air Force Base ... F6
Mexico (gulf) ... E10
Mississippi (sound) ... B10
Mitchell (lake) ... F5
Mobile (bay) ... B10
Mobile (pt.) ... B10
Mobile (riv.) ... C9
Mulberry (creek) ... E5
Mulberry Fork (riv.) ... E3
Neely Henry (lake) ... F3
Oakmulgee (creek) ... D5
Oliver (dam) ... J5
Paint Rock (riv.) ... F1
Patsaliga (creek) ... F7
Pea (riv.) ... F8
Perdido (bay) ... D10
Perdido (riv.) ... C9
Pickwick (lake) ... B1
Pigeon (creek) ... E7
Redstone Arsenal 5,728 ... E1
Russell Cave Nat'l Mon. ... G1
Sand (mt.) ... G1
Sandy (creek) ... H7
Sepulga (riv.) ... E7
Sipsey (riv.) ... B4
Sipsey Fork (riv.) ... D2
Tallapoosa (riv.) ... G4
Tennessee (riv.) ... C1
Tennessee-Tombigbee Waterway ... B4
Tensaw (riv.) ... C9
Thurlow (dam) ... G6
Tombigbee (riv.) ... B7
Town (creek) ... C1
Tuscaloosa (lake) ... D4
Tuskegee Institute Nat'l Hist. Park ... G6
Walter F. George (dam) ... H7
Walter F. George (res.) ... H7
Warrior (dam) ... C5
Weiss (lake) ... G2
West Point (lake) ... H4
Wheeler (dam) ... D1
Wheeler (lake) ... D1
Wilson (dam) ... C1
Yates (dam) ... G5

⊙County seat.
‡Population of metropolitan area.
† Zip of nearest p.o. * Multiple zips

Alabama

SCALE

0 5 10   20   30   40 MI.

0 5 10   20   30   40 KM.

State Capitals .... ⊛

County Seats .... ◉

Major Limited Access Hwys. _____

Scale 1:1,930,000

© Copyright Hammond Incorporated, Maplewood, N.J.

Agriculture, Industry and Resources

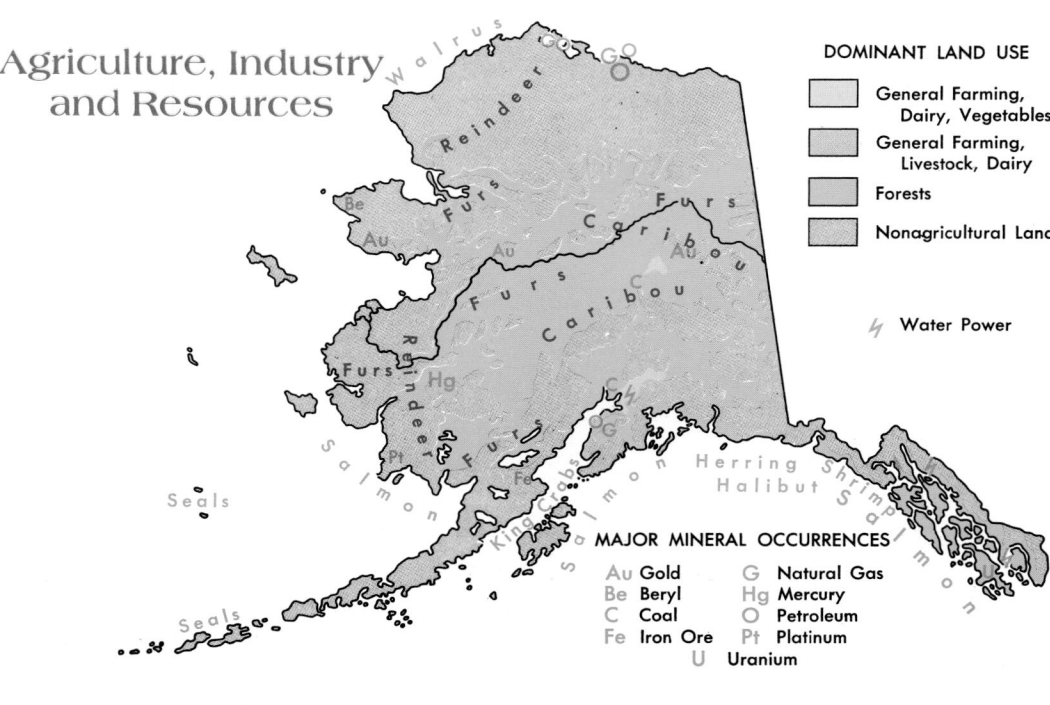

DOMINANT LAND USE

- General Farming, Dairy, Vegetables
- General Farming, Livestock, Dairy
- Forests
- Nonagricultural Land

⚡ Water Power

MAJOR MINERAL OCCURRENCES

Au Gold   G Natural Gas
Be Beryl   Hg Mercury
C Coal   O Petroleum
Fe Iron Ore   Pt Platinum
U Uranium

Topography

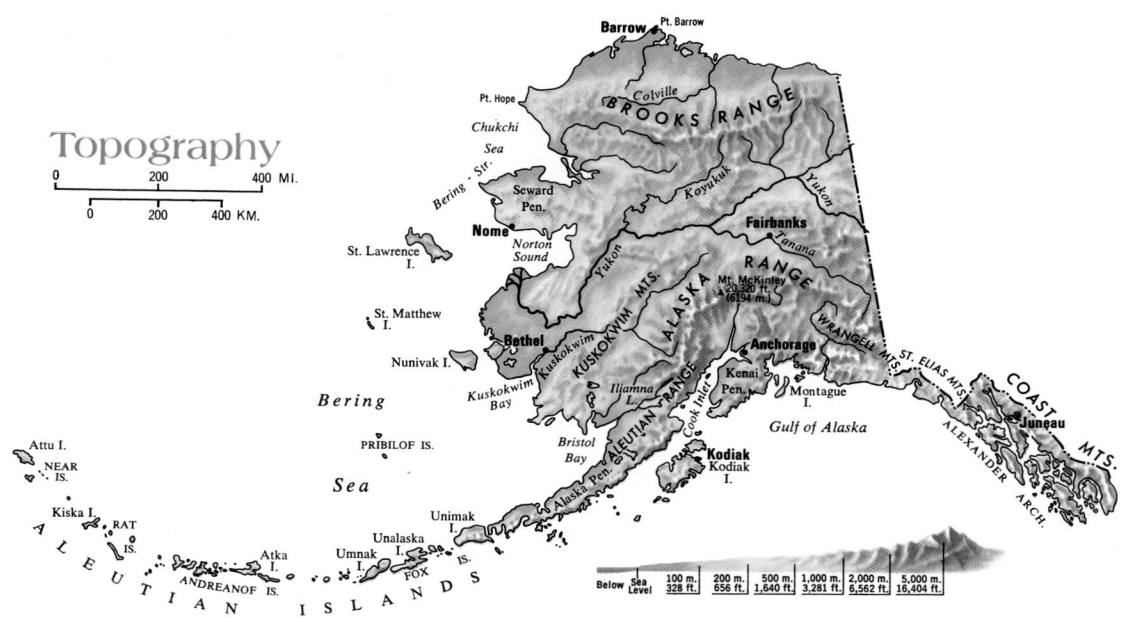

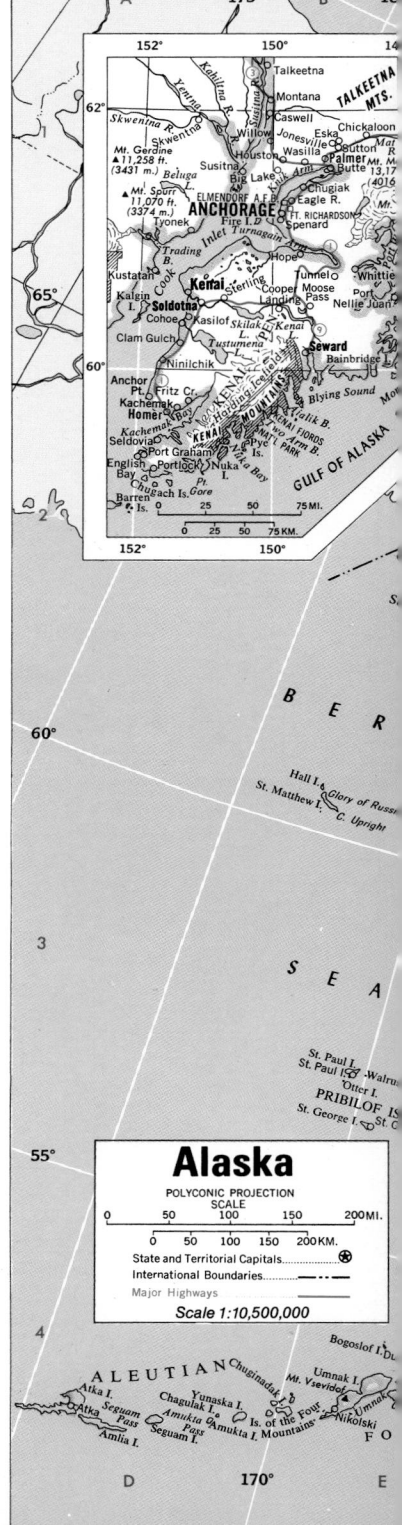

Alaska

POLYCONIC PROJECTION

SCALE
0   50   100   150   200MI.
0   50   100   150   200KM.

State and Territorial Capitals .... ⊛
International Boundaries ....
Major Highways ....

Scale 1:10,500,000

McKinley (mt.) H2
Meade (riv.) G1
Mendenhall (cape) E3
Mentasta (pass) K2
Merrill (pass) H2
Michelson (mt.) K1
Middleton (isl.) J3
Misty Fjords Nat'l Mon. N2
Mitkof (isl.) N2
Montague (isl.) D1
Muir (glac.) M1
Mulchatna (riv.) G2
Muzon (cape) M2
Naknek (lake) G3
Near (isls.) H3
Nelson (isl.) E2
Newenham (cape) F3
Noatak (riv.) F1
Norton (bay) F2
Norton (sound) E2
Nowitna (riv.) H2
Nuka (bay) C2
Nunivak (isl.) E3
Nushagak (riv.) G2
Nuyakuk (lake) F3
Ommaney (cape) M2
Otter (isl.) D3
Pastol (bay) F2
Pavlof (bay) F3
Pavlof (vol.) F3
Philip Smith (mts.) J1
Porcupine (riv.) K1
Port Clarence (inlet) E1
Port Heiden (inlet) G3
Portland Canal (inlet) N2
Port Moller (inlet) F3
Port Wells (inlet) C1
Pribilof (isls.) D3
Prince of Wales (cape) E1
Prince of Wales (isl.) N2
Prince William (sound) D1
Prudhoe (bay) J1
Rat (isls.) K4
Redoubt (vol.) H2
Revillagigedo (chan.) N2
Revillagigedo (isl.) N2
Romanzof (cape) E2
Sagavanirktok (riv.) J1
Saint Elias (cape) K3
Saint Elias (mts.) L2
Saint George (isl.) D3
Saint Lawrence (isl.) D2
Saint Matthew (isl.) D2
Saint Paul (isl.) D3
Salisbury (sound) M1
Sanak (isl.) F4
Sanford (mt.) K2
Schwatka (mts.) G1
Seguam (isl.) D4
Selawik (lake) F1
Semichi (isls.) J3
Semidi (isls.) G3
Semisopochnoi (isl.) K4
Seward (pen.) E1
Seymour (canal) N1
Sheenjek (riv.) K1
Shelikof (str.) H3
Shemya (isl.) J3
Shishaldin (vol.) E4
Shumagin (isls.) G4
Shuyak (isl.) H3
Sitka (sound) M1
Sitka Nat'l Hist. Park M1
Sitkinak (str.) H3
Skilak (lake) C1
Skwentna (riv.) A1
Smith (bay) H1
Spencer (cape) L1
Stephens (passage) N1
Stevenson Entrance (str.) H3
Stikine (riv.) N2
Stikine (str.) N2
Stony (riv.) G2
Stuart (isl.) F2
Suemez (isl.) M2
Sumner (str.) M2
Susitna (riv.) B1
Sutwik (isl.) G3
Taku (glac.) N1
Taku (riv.) N1
Talkeetna (mts.) J2
Tanaga (isl.) K4
Tanaga (vol.) K4
Tanana (riv.) J2
Taylor (mts.) G2
Tazlina (lake) D1
Tazlina (riv.) D1
Teshekpuk (lake) H1
Tigalda (isl.) F4
Tikchik (lkes) G2
Togiak (bay) F3
Tugidak (isl.) G3
Turnagain Arm (inlet) B1
Tustumena (lake) C1
Two Arm (bay) C2
Ugashik (lkes) G3
Umnak (isl.) E4
Umnak (passage) E4
Unalaska (isl.) E4
Unga (isl.) F3
Unimak (isl.) E4
Unimak (passage) F4
Utukok (riv.) F1
Valley of Ten Thousand Smokes G3
Vancouver (mt.) L2
Veniaminof (crater) F3
Vsevidof (mt.) E4
Walrus (isl.) E3
Walrus (isls.) F3
Waring (mts.) G1
West Point (mt.) K2
White (pass) N1
White (riv.) K2
White Mountains Nat'l Rec. Area J1
Witherspoon (mt.) C1
Wrangell (cape) H3
Wrangell (isl.) N2
Wrangell (mts.) K2
Wrangell-St. Elias Nat'l Park K2
Yakobi (isl.) M1
Yakutat (bay) K3
Yentna (riv.) A1
Yukon (riv.) F2

⊙Court House
‡Population of metropolitan area.
† Zip of nearest p.o.
* Multiple zips.

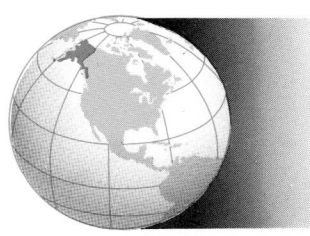

AREA 591,004 sq. mi. (1,530,700 sq. km.)
POPULATION 401,851
CAPITAL Juneau
LARGEST CITY Anchorage
HIGHEST POINT Mt. McKinley 20,320 ft. (6194 m.)
SETTLED IN 1801
ADMITTED TO UNION January 3, 1959
POPULAR NAME Great Land; Last Frontier
STATE FLOWER Forget-me-not
STATE BIRD Willow Ptarmigan

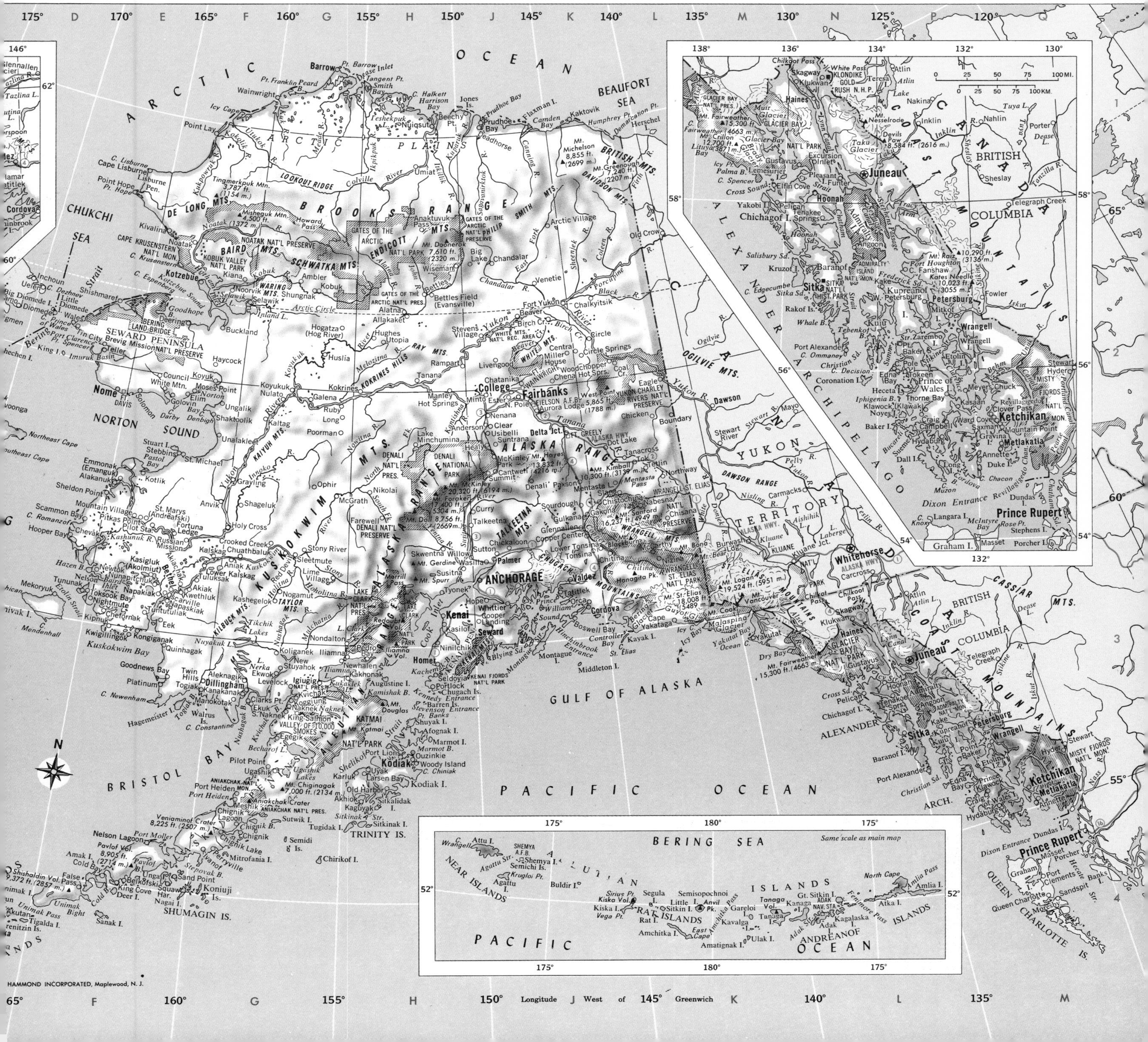

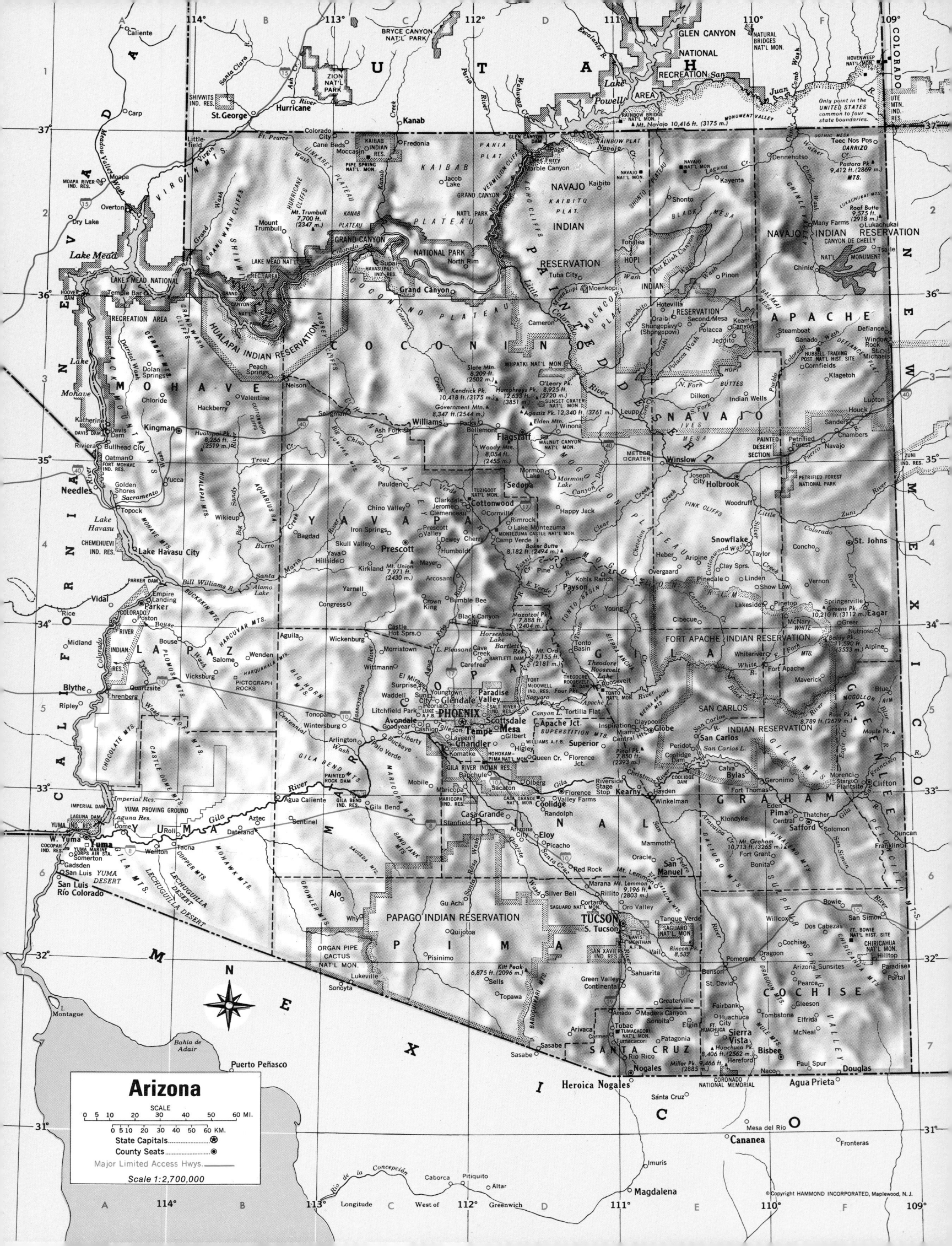

Arizona

SCALE

0 5 10   20   30   40   50   60 MI.

0 5 10 20 30 40 50 60 KM.

State Capitals.............⊛

County Seats.............◉

Major Limited Access Hwys.

Scale 1:2,700,000

© Copyright HAMMOND INCORPORATED, Maplewood, N.J.

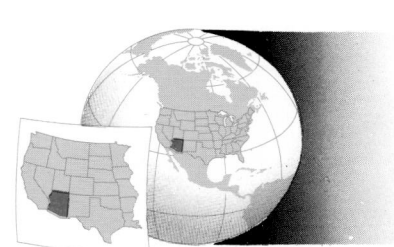

AREA 114,000 sq. mi. (295,260 sq. km.)
POPULATION 2,718,425
CAPITAL Phoenix
LARGEST CITY Phoenix
HIGHEST POINT Humphreys Pk. 12,633 ft.
 (3851 m.)
SETTLED IN 1752
ADMITTED TO UNION February 14, 1912
POPULAR NAME Grand Canyon State
STATE FLOWER Saguaro Cactus Blossom
STATE BIRD Cactus Wren

Agriculture, Industry and Resources

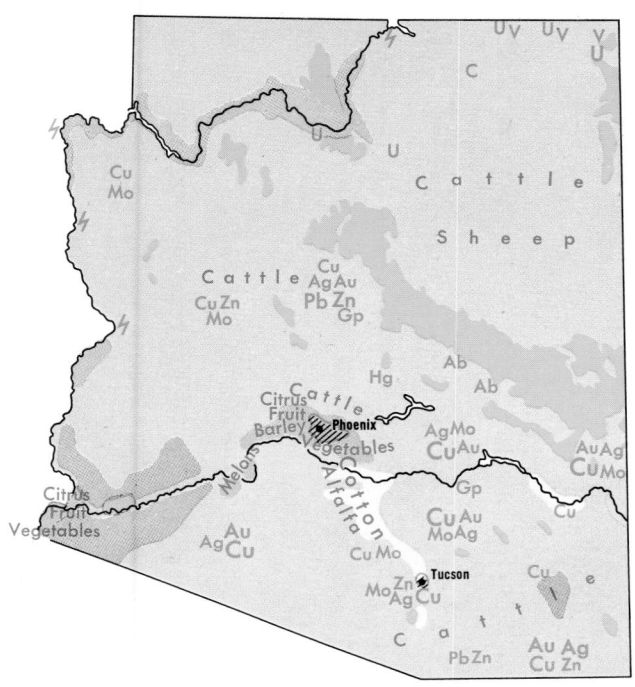

MAJOR MINERAL OCCURRENCES

Ab	Asbestos	Cu	Copper	Pb	Lead
Ag	Silver	Gp	Gypsum	U	Uranium
Au	Gold	Hg	Mercury	V	Vanadium
C	Coal	Mo	Molybdenum	Zn	Zinc

DOMINANT LAND USE

- Fruit, Truck and Mixed Farming
- Cotton and Alfalfa
- General Farming, Livestock, Special Crops
- Range Livestock
- Forests
- Nonagricultural Land

⚡ Water Power
▨ Major Industrial Areas

COUNTIES

Apache 52,108		F3
Cochise 85,686		F7
Coconino 75,008		C3
Gila 37,080		E5
Graham 22,862		E6
Greenlee 11,406		F5
La Paz• 13,100		A5
Maricopa 1,509,052		C5
Mohave 55,865		A3
Navajo 67,629		E3
Pima 531,443		D6
Pinal 90,918		D6
Santa Cruz 20,459		E7
Yavapai 68,145		C4
Yuma• 81,800		A6

•1982 official estimate.

CITIES and TOWNS

Zip	Name/Pop.	Key
†85333	Agua Caliente 60	B6
85320	Aguila 900	B5
85321	Ajo 5,189	C6
85920	Alpine 450	F5
85640	Amado 75	D7
85220	Apache Junction 9,935	D5
†85901	Aripine 25	E4
85601	Arivaca 400	D7
85223	Arizona City 825	D6
85625	Arizona Sunsites 825	F7
85322	Arlington 950	C5
85320	Ash Fork 800	C3
85323	Avondale 8,168	C5
†85333	Aztec 20	B6
86321	Bagdad 2,331	B4
85221	Bapchule 400	D5
86015	Bellemont 210	D3
85602	Benson 4,190	E7
85603	Bisbee⊙ 7,154	F7
85324	Black Canyon City 600	C4
85922	Blue 50	F5
†85643	Bonita 20	E6
85325	Bouse 500	A5
85605	Bowie 600	F6
85326	Buckeye 3,434	C5
86430	Bullhead City-Riviera 10,364	A3
†86301	Bumble Bee 15	C4
85530	Bylas 1,175	E5
†85530	Calva 10	E5
86020	Cameron 600	D3
86322	Camp Verde 1,125	D4
†86022	Cane Beds 30	B2
85222	Casa Grande 14,971	D6
85329	Cashion 3,014	C5
†85342	Castle Hot Springs 50	C5
85331	Cave Creek 1,589	D5
85531	Central 300	F6
†85501	Central Heights-Midland City 2,791	E5
86502	Chambers 500	F3
85224	Chandler 29,673	D5
†86327	Cherry 20	C4
86503	Chinle 2,815	F2
86323	Chino Valley 2,858	C4
86431	Chloride 225	A3
†85292	Christmas 201	E5
85911	Cibecue 100	E4
86324	Clarkdale 1,512	C4
85532	Claypool 2,362	E5
†85934	Clay Springs 500	E4
†86326	Clemenceau 300	C4
85533	Clifton⊙ 4,245	F5
85606	Cochise 150	F6
86021	Colorado City 350	B2
85924	Concho 100	F4
85332	Congress 800	C4
†85640	Continental 250	D7
85228	Coolidge 6,851	D6
†85542	Coolidge Dam 42	E5
†86505	Cornfields 200	F3
86325	Cornville 425	D4
85230	Cortaro 375	D6
86326	Cottonwood 4,550	D4
86333	Crown King 100	C4
86327	Dewey 100	C4
†86430	Davis Dam 125	A3
85331	Dateland 100	B6
†86047	Dilkon 90	E3
86441	Dolan Springs 870	A3
†85364	Dome 48	A6
†85643	Dos Cabezas 30	F6
85607	Douglas 13,058	F7
85609	Dragoon 150	F6
85534	Duncan 603	F6
85925	Eagar 2,791	F4
85535	Eden 89	F6
85334	Ehrenburg 93	A5

(continued on following page)

Topography

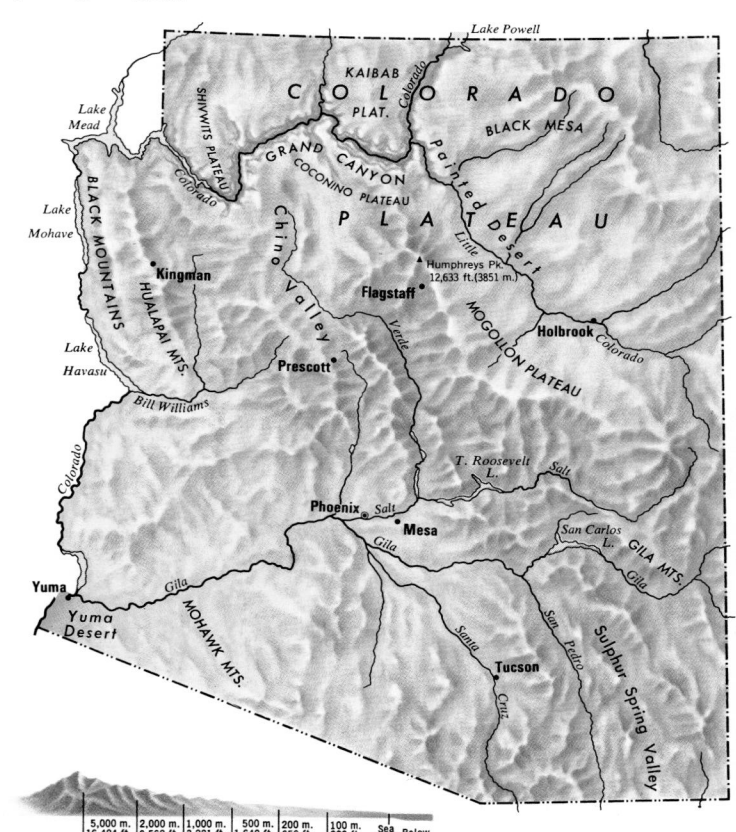

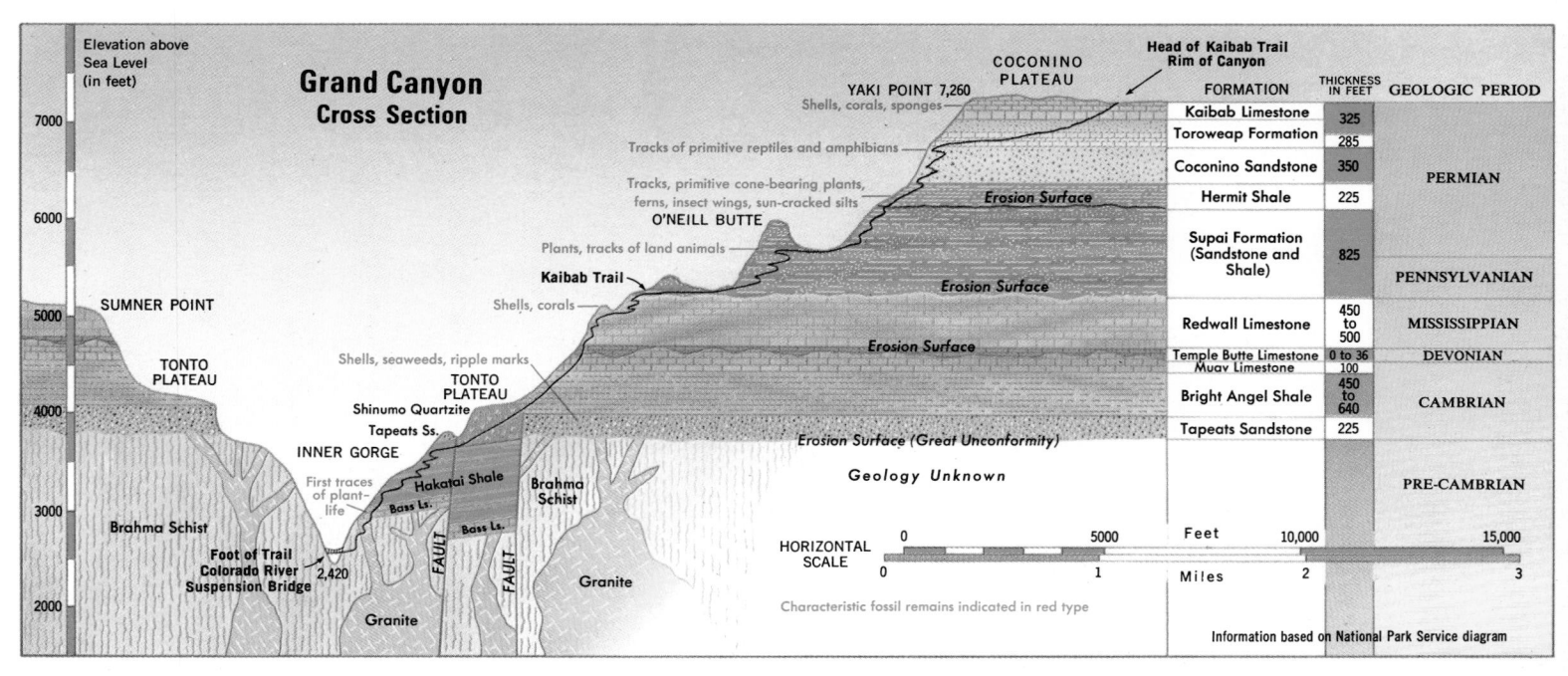

Grand Canyon Cross Section

Elevation above Sea Level (in feet)

Information based on National Park Service diagram

FORMATION	THICKNESS IN FEET	GEOLOGIC PERIOD
Kaibab Limestone	325	PERMIAN
Toroweap Formation	285	PERMIAN
Coconino Sandstone	350	PERMIAN
Hermit Shale	225	PERMIAN
Supai Formation (Sandstone and Shale)	825	PENNSYLVANIAN
Redwall Limestone	450 to 500	MISSISSIPPIAN
Temple Butte Limestone	0 to 36	DEVONIAN
Muav Limestone	100	
Bright Angel Shale	450 to 640	CAMBRIAN
Tapeats Sandstone	225	
		PRE-CAMBRIAN

Characteristic fossil remains indicated in red type

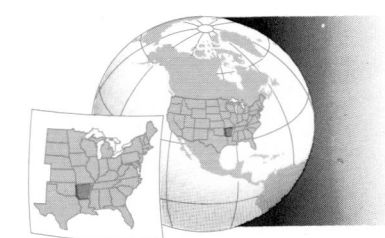

AREA 53,187 sq. mi. (137,754 sq. km.)
POPULATION 2,286,435
CAPITAL Little Rock
LARGEST CITY Little Rock
HIGHEST POINT Magazine Mtn. 2,753 ft. (839 m.)
SETTLED IN 1685
ADMITTED TO UNION June 15, 1836
POPULAR NAME Land of Opportunity
STATE FLOWER Apple Blossom
STATE BIRD Mockingbird

Agriculture, Industry and Resources

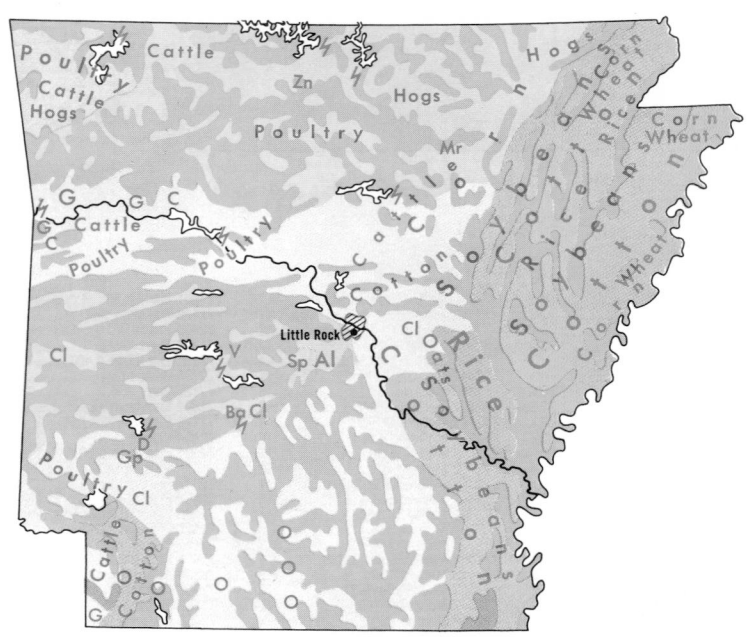

COUNTIES

Arkansas 24,175 ....H5
Ashley 26,538 ....G7
Baxter 27,409 ....F1
Benton 78,115 ....B1
Boone 26,067 ....D1
Bradley 13,803 ....F7
Calhoun 6,079 ....E6
Carroll 16,203 ....C1
Chicot 17,793 ....H7
Clark 23,326 ....D5
Clay 20,616 ....K1
Cleburne 16,909 ....F2
Cleveland 7,868 ....F6
Columbia 26,644 ....D7
Conway 19,505 ....E3
Craighead 63,239 ....J2
Crawford 36,892 ....B2
Crittenden 49,499 ....K3
Cross 20,434 ....J3
Dallas 10,515 ....E6
Desha 19,760 ....H6
Drew 17,910 ....G6
Faulkner 46,192 ....F3
Franklin 14,705 ....C2
Fulton 9,975 ....G1
Garland 70,531 ....D4
Grant 13,008 ....F5
Greene 30,744 ....J1
Hempstead 23,635 ....C6
Hot Spring 26,819 ....E5
Howard 13,459 ....C5
Independence 30,147 ....G2
Izard 10,768 ....G1
Jackson 21,646 ....H2
Jefferson 90,718 ....G5
Johnson 17,423 ....C2
Lafayette 10,213 ....C7
Lawrence 18,447 ....H1
Lee 15,539 ....J4
Lincoln 13,369 ....G6
Little River 13,952 ....B6
Logan 20,144 ....C3
Lonoke 34,518 ....G4
Madison 11,373 ....C1
Marion 11,334 ....E1
Miller 37,766 ....C7
Mississippi 59,517 ....K2
Monroe 14,052 ....H4
Montgomery 7,771 ....C4
Nevada 11,097 ....D6
Newton 7,756 ....D2
Ouachita 30,541 ....E6
Perry 7,266 ....E4
Phillips 34,772 ....J5
Pike 10,373 ....C5
Poinsett 27,032 ....J2
Polk 17,007 ....B5
Pope 39,021 ....D3
Prairie 10,140 ....G4
Pulaski 340,613 ....F4
Randolph 16,834 ....H1
Saint Francis 30,858 ....J3
Saline 53,161 ....E4
Scott 9,685 ....B4
Searcy 8,847 ....E2
Sebastian 95,172 ....B3
Sevier 14,060 ....B6
Sharp 14,607 ....G1
Stone 9,022 ....F2
Union 48,573 ....E7
Van Buren 13,357 ....E2
Washington 100,494 ....B2
White 50,835 ....G3
Woodruff 11,222 ....H3
Yell 17,026 ....D3

CITIES and TOWNS

Zip	Name/Pop.	Key
72001	Adona 230	E3
72002	Alexander 223	F4
72410	Alicia 246	H2
72820	Alix 225	C3
†72046	Allport 295	G4
72921	Alma 2,755	B3
72003	Almyra 294	H5
72004	Altheimer 1,231	G5
72821	Altus 441	C3
72005	Amagon 126	H2
71921	Amity 859	D5
71922	Antoine 194	D5
71923	Arkadelphia⊙ 10,005	D5
71630	Arkansas City⊙ 668	H6
72310	Armorel 500	L2
71822	Ashdown⊙ 4,218	B6
72513	Ash Flat⊙ 524	G1
72823	Atkins 3,002	E3
72311	Aubrey 267	J4
72006	Augusta⊙ 3,496	H3
72007	Austin 269	G4
72711	Avoca 256	B1
72010	Bald Knob 2,756	G3
71631	Banks 216	F6
72922	Barber 35	B3
72923	Barling 3,761	B3
72313	Bassett 243	K2
72924	Bates	B4
72501	Batesville⊙ 8,263	G2
72411	Bay 1,605	J2
71720	Bearden 1,191	E6
72613	Beaver	C1
72012	Beebe 3,599	G3
72014	Beedeville 183	H3
†72712	Bella Vista 2,589	B1
†72601	Bellefonte 393	D1
72824	Belleville 571	D3
71823	Ben Lomond 155	B6
72015	Benton⊙ 17,717	E4
72712	Bentonville⊙ 8,756	B1
72615	Bergman 320	E1
72616	Berryville⊙ 2,966	C1
†72764	Bethel Heights 296	B1
72016	Bigelow 373	E3
72617	Big Flat 150	F1
72413	Biggers 363	J1
72017	Biscoe 486	H4
72414	Black Oak 309	K2
72415	Black Rock 848	H1
†71960	Black Springs 92	C5
71825	Blevins 314	C6
65611	Blue Eye 43	D1
72826	Blue Mountain 112	C3
71722	Bluff City 292	D6
72315	Blytheville⊙ 23,844	L2
†71858	Bodcaw 197	D6
†72901	Bonanza 553	B3
72416	Bono 967	J2
72927	Booneville⊙ 3,718	C3
72020	Bradford 950	G3
71826	Bradley 790	C7
72928	Branch 353	C3
72021	Brinkley 4,909	H4
72417	Brookland 840	J2
72022	Bryant 2,682	F4
71827	Buckner 436	D7
72619	Bull Shoals 1,312	E1
72321	Burdette 328	L2
72023	Cabot 4,806	F4
72322	Caldwell 283	J3
71828	Cale 110	D6
72519	Calico Rock 1,046	F1
71724	Calion 638	E7
71701	Camden⊙ 15,356	E6
†72201	Cammack Village 920	E4
†72473	Campbell Station 297	G1
72419	Caraway 1,165	K2
72024	Carlisle 2,567	G4
71725	Carthage 568	E5
72025	Casa 179	D3
72421	Cash 285	J2
72026	Casscoe 297	H4
†72951	Caulksville 234	C3
72521	Cave City 1,634	G2
72718	Cave Springs 429	B1
72932	Cedarville 375	B2
72719	Centerton 425	B1
72829	Centerville 300	D3
†72923	Central City 339	B3
72933	Charleston⊙ 1,748	B3
†72525	Cherokee Village-Hidden Valley 4,058	G1
72324	Cherry Valley 729	J3
72934	Chester 139	B2
71726	Chidester 342	D6
72029	Clarendon⊙ 2,361	H4
72325	Clarkedale 300	K3
72830	Clarksville⊙ 5,237	D3
72031	Clinton⊙ 1,284	F2
72832	Coal Hill 859	C3
72476	College City 432	J1
72326	Colt 378	J3
71831	Columbus 265	C6
72523	Concord 234	G2
72032	Conway⊙ 20,375	F3
72524	Cord 250	H2
72422	Corning⊙ 3,650	J1
72626	Cotter 920	E1
72036	Cotton Plant 1,323	H3
71937	Cove 391	B5
72037	Coy 183	G4
72327	Crawfordsville 685	K3
71635	Crossett 6,706	G7
71728	Curtis 300	D6
72526	Cushman 556	G2
†71950	Daisy 177	C5
72039	Damascus 307	F3
72833	Danville⊙ 1,698	D3
72834	Dardanelle⊙ 3,621	D3
72722	Decatur 1,013	A1
72425	Delaplaine 161	J1
71940	Delight 431	C5
72426	Dell 310	K2
†72821	Denning 238	C3
71832	De Queen⊙ 4,594	B5
71638	Dermott 4,731	H7
72040	Des Arc⊙ 2,001	G4
72041	De Valls Bluff⊙ 738	H4
72042	De Witt⊙ 3,928	H5
72644	Diamond City 650	E1
72043	Diaz 1,192	H2
71833	Dierks 1,249	B5
71941	Donaldson 300	E5
72837	Dover 948	D3
71639	Dumas 6,091	H6
72935	Dyer 608	B3
72330	Dyess 446	K2
72331	Earle 3,517	K3
71701	East Camden 632	E6
72332	Edmondson 344	K3
72333	Elaine 991	J5
71730	El Dorado⊙ 25,270	E7
72727	Elkins 579	C1
72728	Elm Springs 781	B1
71740	Emerson 444	D7
71835	Emmet 475	D6
72046	England 3,081	G4
72047	Enola 186	F3
71640	Eudora 3,840	H7
72632	Eureka Springs⊙ 1,989	C1
72532	Evening Shade 397	G1
72633	Everton 134	E1
72730	Farmington 1,283	B1
72701	Fayetteville⊙ 36,608	B1
	Fayetteville-Springdale 07	B1
†71747	Felsenthal 220	F7
72429	Fisher 302	J2
72634	Flippin 1,072	E1
71742	Fordyce⊙ 5,175	F6
71836	Foreman 1,377	B6
72335	Forrest City⊙ 13,803	J3
*72901	Fort Smith⊙ 71,626	B3
	Fort Smith‡ 203,269	B3
71837	Fouke 614	C7
71642	Fountain Hill 352	G7
†72016	Fourche 51	E4
72536	Franklin 253	G1
72017	Fredonia (Biscoe) 486	H4
71942	Friendship 163	E5
71838	Fulton 326	C6
72732	Garfield 187	C1
71839	Garland 660	C7
72052	Garner 216	G3
72635	Gassville 859	F1
72733	Gateway 75	B1
71840	Genoa 350	C7
72734	Gentry 1,468	A1
72636	Gilbert 43	E2
72055	Gillett 927	H5
71841	Gillham 252	B5
72339	Gilmore 503	K3
71943	Glenwood 1,402	C5
72340	Goodwin 225	J4
†72315	Gosnell 3,215	K2
71643	Gould 1,671	G6
71644	Grady 488	G5
71944	Grannis 349	B5
72838	Gravelly 300	C4
72736	Gravette 1,218	B1
72058	Greenbrier 1,423	F3
72638	Green Forest 1,609	D1
72737	Greenland 622	B1
72430	Greenway 317	K1
72936	Greenwood⊙ 3,317	B3
†72067	Greers Ferry 558	F2
72060	Griffithville 254	G3
72431	Grubbs 546	H2
72540	Guion 177	G2
†71923	Gum Springs 255	D5
71743	Gurdon 2,707	D6
72061	Guy 209	F3
72937	Hackett 505	B3
†71638	Halley	H6
71646	Hamburg⊙ 3,394	G7
71744	Hampton⊙ 1,627	F6
72542	Hardy 643	H1
71745	Harrell 302	F7
72432	Harrisburg⊙ 1,921	J2
72601	Harrison⊙ 9,567	D1
72938	Hartford 613	B3
72840	Hartman 517	C3
†72015	Haskell 1,074	E4
71945	Hatfield 410	B5
72842	Havana 352	D3
72341	Haynes 359	J4
72064	Hazen 1,636	G4
72543	Heber Springs⊙ 4,589	G2
72843	Hector 449	E3
72342	Helena⊙ 9,598	J4
72065	Hensley 500	F4
71647	Hermitage 378	F7
72347	Hickory Ridge 478	J3
72067	Higden 45	F2
72068	Higginson 333	G3
†72734	Highfill 92	B1
72738	Hindsville 1	C1
72069	Holly Grove 754	H4
†72958	Hon 250	B4
71801	Hope⊙ 10,290	C6
71842	Horatio 989	B3
72512	Horseshoe Bend 1,909	G1
71901	Hot Springs National Park⊙ 35,781	D4
72070	Houston 183	E3

(continued on following page)

DOMINANT LAND USE

- Fruit and Mixed Farming
- Specialized Cotton
- Cotton, General Farming
- Rice, General Farming
- General Farming, Livestock, Truck Farming, Cotton
- Forests
- Swampland, Limited Agriculture

MAJOR MINERAL OCCURRENCES

Al	Bauxite	Gp	Gypsum
Ba	Barite	Mr	Marble
C	Coal	O	Petroleum
Cl	Clay	Sp	Soapstone
D	Diamonds	V	Vanadium
G	Natural Gas	Zn	Zinc
⚡	Water Power		Major Industrial Areas

Agriculture, Industry and Resources

DOMINANT LAND USE

- Wheat, Small Grains
- Specialized Dairy
- Fruit and Mixed Farming
- Fruit, Truck and Mixed Farming
- General Farming, Livestock, Special Crops
- Cotton, Alfalfa
- Potatoes, General Farming
- Range Livestock
- Forests
- Urban Areas
- Nonagricultural Land

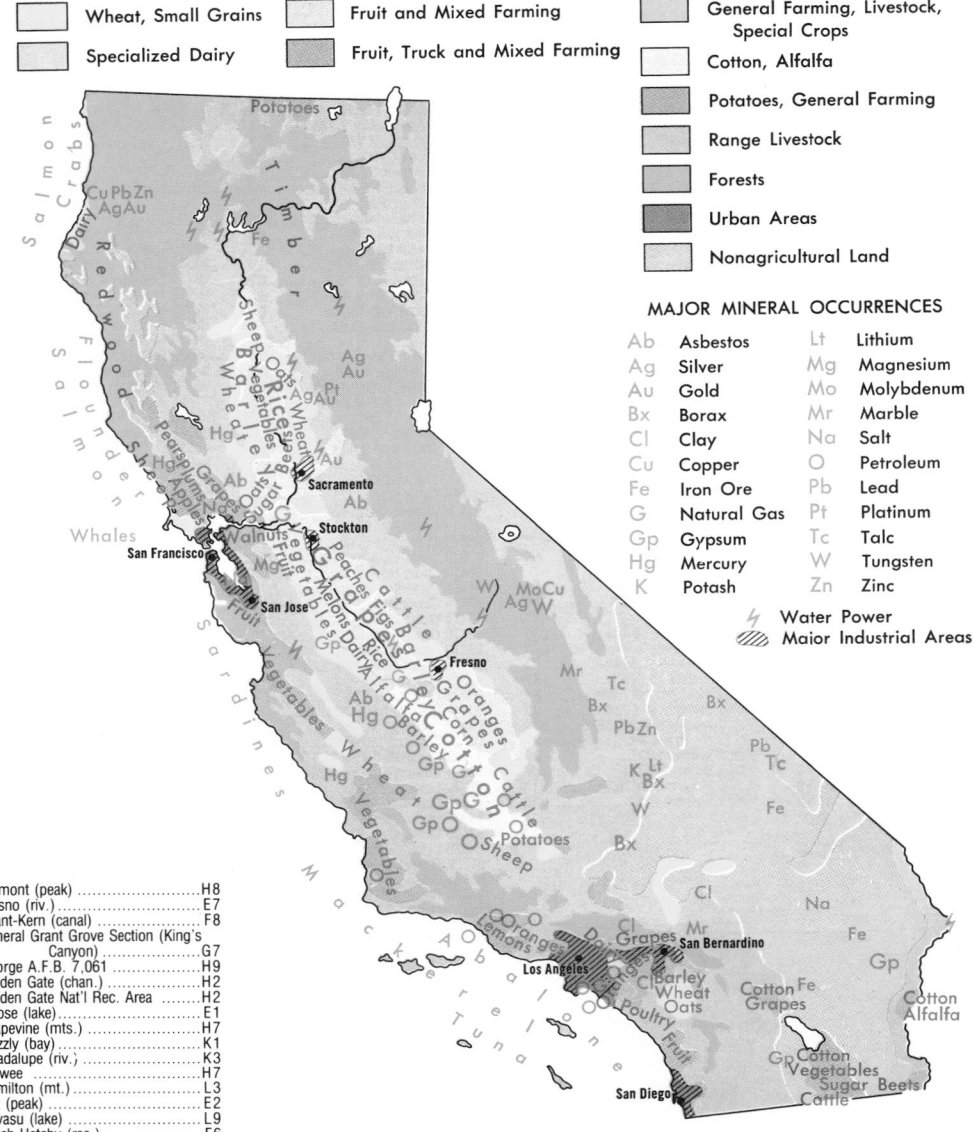

MAJOR MINERAL OCCURRENCES

Ab	Asbestos	Lt	Lithium
Ag	Silver	Mg	Magnesium
Au	Gold	Mo	Molybdenum
Bx	Borax	Mr	Marble
Cl	Clay	Na	Salt
Cu	Copper	O	Petroleum
Fe	Iron Ore	Pb	Lead
G	Natural Gas	Pt	Platinum
Gp	Gypsum	Tc	Talc
Hg	Mercury	W	Tungsten
K	Potash	Zn	Zinc

⚡ Water Power
▨ Major Industrial Areas

⊙County seat.
‡Population of metropolitan area.
† Zip of nearest p.o. * Multiple zips.

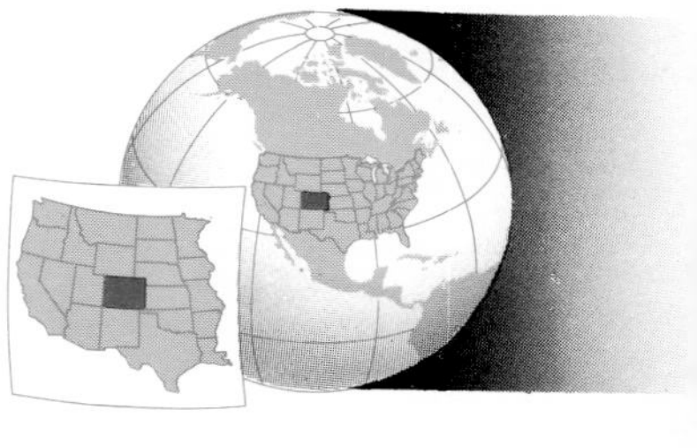

AREA 104,091 sq. mi. (269,596 sq. km.)
POPULATION 2,889,735
CAPITAL Denver
LARGEST CITY Denver
HIGHEST POINT Mt. Elbert 14,433 ft. (4399 m.)
SETTLED IN 1858
ADMITTED TO UNION August 1, 1876
POPULAR NAME Centennial State
STATE FLOWER Rocky Mountain Columbine
STATE BIRD Lark Bunting

COUNTIES

County	Key
Adams 245,944	L3
Alamosa 11,799	H7
Arapahoe 293,621	L3
Archuleta 3,664	E8
Baca 5,419	O8
Bent 5,945	N7
Boulder 189,625	J2
Chaffee 13,227	G5
Cheyenne 2,153	O5
Clear Creek 7,308	H3
Conejos 7,794	G8
Costilla 3,071	J8
Crowley 2,988	M6
Custer 1,528	J6
Delta 21,225	D5
Denver 492,365	K3
Dolores 1,658	C7
Douglas 25,153	K4
Eagle 13,320	F3
Elbert 6,850	L4
El Paso 309,424	K5
Fremont 28,676	J5
Garfield 22,514	C3
Gilpin 2,441	H3
Grand 7,475	G2
Gunnison 10,689	E5
Hinsdale 408	E7
Huerfano 6,440	K7
Jackson 1,863	G1
Jefferson 371,741	J3
Kiowa 1,936	O6
Kit Carson 7,599	O4
Lake 8,830	G4
La Plata 27,195	D8
Larimer 149,184	H1
Las Animas 14,897	L8
Lincoln 4,663	M5
Logan 19,800	N1
Mesa 81,530	B5
Mineral 804	F7
Moffat 13,133	C1
Montezuma 16,510	B8
Montrose 24,352	C6
Morgan 22,513	M2
Otero 22,567	M7
Ouray 1,925	D6
Park 5,333	H4
Phillips 4,542	P1
Pitkin 10,338	F4
Prowers 13,070	P7
Pueblo 125,972	K6
Rio Blanco 6,255	C3
Rio Grande 10,511	G7
Routt 13,404	E1
Saguache 3,935	G6
San Juan 833	D7
San Miguel 3,192	C6
Sedgwick 3,266	P1
Summit 8,848	G3
Teller 8,034	J5
Washington 5,304	N3
Weld 123,438	L1
Yuma 9,682	P2

CITIES and TOWNS

Zip	Name/Pop.	Key
80101	Agate 90	M4
81020	Aguilar 624	K8
80720	Akron⊙ 1,716	N2
81101	Alamosa⊙ 6,830	H8
80510	Allenspark 200	J2
80420	Alma 132	G4
81210	Almont 135	F5
80721	Amherst 85	P1
80801	Anton 55	N3
81120	Antonito 1,103	H8
80802	Arapahoe 300	P5
81021	Arlington 37	N6
80804	Arriba 236	N4
†81323	Arriola 56	B8
*80001	Arvada 84,576	J3
81611	Aspen⊙ 3,678	F4
80722	Atwood 100	N1
80610	Ault 1,056	K1
*80010	Aurora 158,588	K3
81410	Austin	D5
81620	Avon 640	F3
81022	Avondale 750	L6
80421	Bailey 150	H4
†80624	Barnesville 20	L2
81621	Basalt 529	E4
81122	Bayfield 724	D8
81411	Bedrock 45	B6
†80758	Beecher Island 5	P3
80512	Bellvue 250	J1
80102	Bennett 942	L3
80513	Berthoud 2,362	J2
†80438	Berthoud Pass 40	H3
80805	Bethune 149	P4
81023	Beulah 650	K6
80908	Black Forest 3,372	K4
80422	Black Hawk 232	J3
81123	Blanca 252	H8
†80424	Blue River 230	G4
†81155	Bonanza 8	G6
81024	Boncarbo 200	K8
80423	Bond 65	F3
81025	Boone 431	L6
*80301	Boulder⊙ 76,685	J2
†81428	Bowie 18	D5
80821	Boyero 12	N5
81026	Brandon 30	P6
81027	Branson 73	M8
80424	Breckenridge⊙ 818	G4
80611	Briggsdale 85	L1
80601	Brighton⊙ 12,773	K3
81028	Bristol 200	P6
†81212	Brookside 178	J6
80020	Broomfield 20,730	J3
80723	Brush 4,082	M2
†80742	Buckingham 5	L1
81211	Buena Vista 2,075	G5
80425	Buffalo Creek 150	J4
80807	Burlington⊙ 3,107	P4
80426	Burns 100	F3
80103	Byers 490	L3
81320	Cahone 200	B7
80808	Calhan 541	L4
81029	Campo 185	O8
81212	Canon City⊙ 13,037	J6
81124	Capulin 600	G8
81623	Carbondale 2,084	E4
80612	Carr 49	K1
80909	Cascade 950	K5
80104	Castle Rock⊙ 3,921	K4
81413	Cedaredge 1,184	D5
81125	Center 1,630	G7
80427	Central City⊙ 329	J3
81126	Chama 239	J8
81030	Cheraw 233	N6
80810	Cheyenne Wells⊙ 950	P5
81127	Chimney Rock 76	E8
81031	Chivington 20	O6
81128	Chromo 115	F8
81220	Cimarron 50	D6
80428	Clark 20	F1
81520	Clifton 5,223	C4
80429	Climax 975	G4
81221	Coal Creek 190	J6
81222	Coaldale 153	H6
80430	Coalmont 50	F1
81032	Cokedale 90	K8
81624	Collbran 344	C4
†81401	Colona 54	D6
81019	Colorado City 411	K6
*80901	Colorado Springs⊙ 214,821	K5
	Colorado Springs‡ 317,458	K5
†80428	Columbine 12	E1
80022	Commerce City 16,234	K3
80432	Como 30	H4
81129	Conejos⊙ 200	G8
80812	Cope 110	O3
†80611	Cornish 15	L2
81321	Cortez⊙ 7,095	B8
81223	Cotopaxi 250	H6
80434	Cowdrey 80	G1
81625	Craig⊙ 8,133	D2
81415	Crawford 268	D5
81130	Creede⊙ 610	E7
81224	Crested Butte 959	E5
81131	Crestone 54	H7
80813	Cripple Creek⊙ 655	J5
80726	Crook 177	O1
81033	Crowley 192	M6
81055	Cuchara 43	J8
80514	Dacono 2,321	K2
†80728	Dailey 20	O1
81630	De Beque 279	C4
†80135	Deckers 4	J4
80105	Deer Trail 463	M3
†81059	Delhi 10	M7
81132	Del Norte⊙ 1,709	G7
81416	Delta⊙ 3,931	D5
*80201	Denver (cap.)⊙ 492,365	K3
	Denver‡ 1,619,921	K3
†81054	Deora 2	O7
80435	Dillon 337	H3
81610	Dinosaur 313	B2
80814	Divide 700	J5
81323	Dolores 802	C8
81324	Dove Creek⊙ 826	A7
†81239	Doyleville 75	F6
80515	Drake 300	J2
81301	Durango⊙ 11,649	D8
81036	Eads⊙ 878	O6
81631	Eagle⊙ 950	F3
80615	Eaton 1,932	K1
80727	Eckley 262	P2
80214	Edgewater 4,766	J3
81632	Edwards 250	F3
81325	Egnar 50	B7
80106	Elbert 200	L4
†80466	Eldora 100	H3
80107	Elizabeth 789	K4
81633	Elk Springs 18	C2
80438	Empire 423	H3
†80110	Englewood 30,021	K3
80516	Erie 1,254	K2
80517	Estes Park 2,703	J2
†81433	Eureka 25	D7
80620	Evans 5,063	K2
80439	Evergreen 6,376	J3
80440	Fairplay⊙ 421	H4
81037	Farisita 116	J7
†80221	Federal Heights 7,846	J3
80520	Firestone 1,204	K2
†80810	Firstview 6	O5
80815	Flagler 550	N4
80728	Fleming 388	O1
81226	Florence 2,987	J6
80816	Florissant 130	J5
80521	Fort Collins⊙ 65,092	J1
	Fort Collins‡ 149,184	J1
81133	Fort Garland 700	J8
80621	Fort Lupton 4,251	K2
81038	Fort Lyon 500	N6
80701	Fort Morgan⊙ 8,768	M2
80817	Fountain 8,324	K5
81039	Fowler 1,227	L6
80441	Foxton 12	J4
80116	Franktown 200	K4
80442	Fraser 470	H3
80530	Frederick 855	K2
80820	Freshwater (Guffey) 24	H5
80443	Frisco 1,221	G3
81521	Fruita 2,810	B4
80622	Galeton 200	K1
81134	Garcia 75	J8
81040	Gardner 100	J7
81227	Garfield 30	G5
81522	Gateway 350	B5
80818	Genoa 165	N4
80444	Georgetown⊙ 830	H3
80623	Gilcrest 1,025	K2
80624	Gill 250	L2
81634	Gilman 160	G3
81523	Glade Park 100	B5
†80485	Glendevey 50	H1
80532	Glen Haven 110	H2
81601	Glenwood Springs⊙ 4,637	E4
80401	Golden⊙ 12,237	J3
†80653	Goodrich 85	M2
†80480	Gould 12	G2
81041	Granada 557	P6
80446	Granby 963	H2
81501	Grand Junction⊙ 27,956	B4
80447	Grand Lake 382	H2
81228	Granite 47	G4
80448	Grant 50	H4
80631	Greeley⊙ 53,006	K2
	Greeley‡ 123,438	K2
†80118	Greenland 21	K4
80819	Green Mountain Falls 607	K5
†81640	Greystone 2	B1
80729	Grover 158	L1
80820	Guffey 24	H5
81042	Gulnare 6	K8
81230	Gunnison⊙ 5,785	E5
81637	Gypsum 743	F3
80730	Hale 4	P3
81638	Hamilton 100	D2
81043	Hartman 122	P6
80449	Hartsel 69	H4
81044	Hasty 150	O6
81045	Haswell 126	N6
80731	Haxtun 1,014	O1
81639	Hayden 1,720	E2
80732	Hereford 50	L1
81326	Hesperus 250	C8
80733	Hillrose 213	N2
81232	Hillside 79	H6
81046	Hoehne 400	L8
81047	Holly 969	P6
80734	Holyoke⊙ 2,092	P1
81136	Hooper 71	H7
81419	Hotchkiss 849	D5
80451	Hot Sulphur Springs⊙ 405	H2
81233	Howard 200	H6
80641	Hoyt 60	L2
80642	Hudson 698	K2
80821	Hugo⊙ 776	N4
80533	Hygiene 450	J2
80452	Idaho Springs 2,077	H3
80735	Idalia 125	P3
81137	Ignacio 667	D8
80736	Iliff 218	N1
80455	Jamestown 223	J2
†81082	Jansen 267	K8
81138	Jaroso 50	H8
80456	Jefferson 50	H4
80822	Joes 100	O3
80534	Johnstown 1,535	K2
80737	Julesburg⊙ 1,528	P1
80823	Karval 51	N5
80643	Keenesburg 541	L2
†80729	Keota 4	L1
80644	Kersey 913	L2
81049	Kim 100	N8
80117	Kiowa⊙ 206	L4
80824	Kirk 30	P3
80825	Kit Carson 278	O5
80459	Kremmling 1,296	G2
†80832	Kutch 2	M5
80026	Lafayette 8,935	K3
†81132	La Garita 10	G7
80739	Laird 105	P2
81140	La Jara 858	H8
81050	La Junta⊙ 8,388	M7
81235	Lake City⊙ 206	E6
80827	Lake George 500	J5
80215	Lakewood 113,808	J3
81052	Lamar⊙ 7,713	O6
80535	Laporte 950	J1
80118	Larkspur 141	K4
80645	La Salle 1,929	K2
81054	Las Animas⊙ 2,818	N6
†81151	Lasauces 150	H8
†81153	Lavalley 237	J8
81055	La Veta 611	J8
†80452	Lawson 108	H3
†81625	Lay 40	D2
81420	Lazear 60	D5
80461	Leadville⊙ 3,879	G4
†81323	Lebanon 50	B8
81327	Lewis 150	B8
80828	Limon 1,805	M4
†81212	Lincoln Park 2,984	J6
80740	Lindon 60	N3
*80120	Littleton⊙ 28,631	K3
80536	Livermore 150	J1
†80601	Lochbuie 895	K2
†80701	Log Lane Village 709	M2
81524	Loma 265	B4
80501	Longmont 42,942	J2
†80135	Longview 10	J4
80027	Louisville 5,593	J3
80131	Louviers 300	K4
80537	Loveland 30,244	J2
80646	Lucerne 135	K2
†81054	Lycan 4	P7
80540	Lyons 1,137	J2
81525	Mack 380	B4
81421	Maher 75	D5
†80461	Malta 200	G4
81141	Manassa 945	H8
81328	Mancos 870	C8
80829	Manitou Springs 4,475	J5
81058	Manzanola 459	M6
†81623	Marble 30	E4
81329	Marvel 176	C8
80541	Masonville 200	J2
†80649	Masters 50	L2
80830	Matheson 120	M4
81640	Maybell 130	C2
81057	McClave 125	O6
80463	McCoy 62	F3
80542	Mead 356	K2
81641	Meeker⊙ 2,356	D2
81642	Meredith 47	F4
80741	Merino 255	N2
81005	Mesa 120	C4
81330	Mesa Verde National Park 45	C8
81142	Mesita 70	H8
80543	Milliken 1,506	K2
80477	Milner 196	F2
81645	Minturn 1,060	G3

(continued on following page)

Agriculture, Industry and Resources

DOMINANT LAND USE

- Specialized Wheat
- Wheat, Range Livestock
- Wheat, Grain Sorghums, Range Livestock
- Dry Beans, General Farming
- Sugar Beets, Dry Beans, Livestock, General Farming
- Fruit, Mixed Farming
- General Farming, Livestock, Special Crops
- Range Livestock
- Forests
- Urban Areas
- Nonagricultural Land

MAJOR MINERAL OCCURRENCES

Ag	Silver	Mi	Mica
Au	Gold	Mo	Molybdenum
Be	Beryl	Mr	Marble
C	Coal	O	Petroleum
Cl	Clay	Pb	Lead
Cu	Copper	U	Uranium
F	Fluorspar	V	Vanadium
Fe	Iron Ore	W	Tungsten
G	Natural Gas	Zn	Zinc

Water Power
Major Industrial Areas

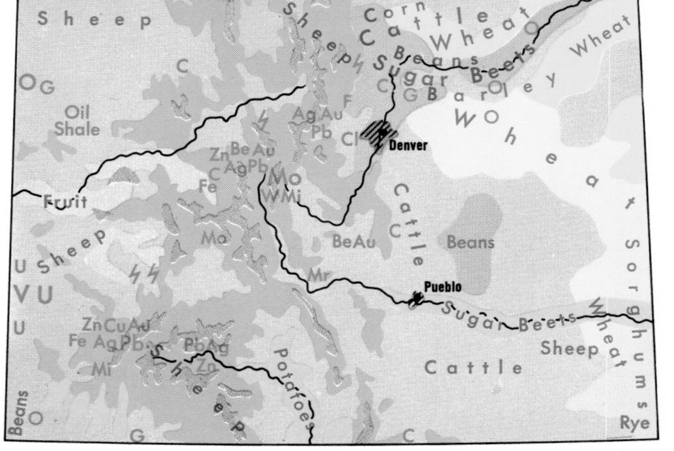

Topography

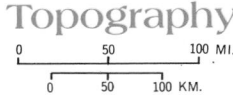

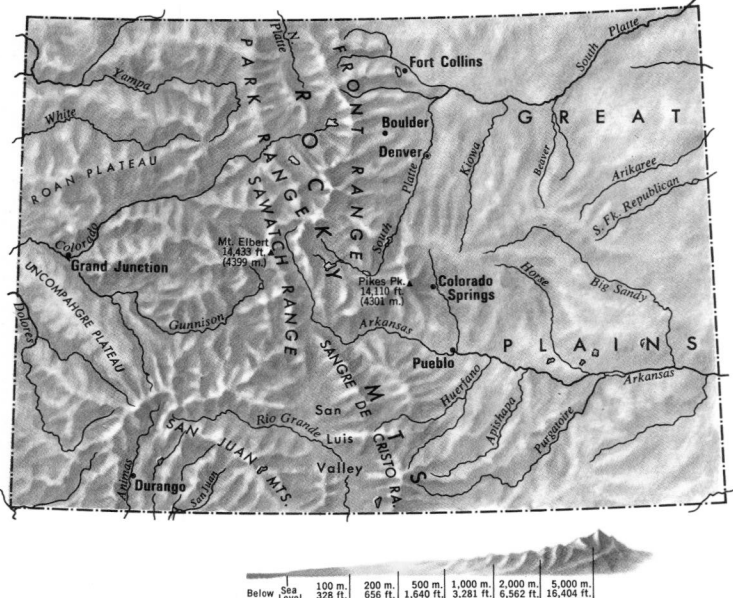

Below Sea Level | 100 m. 328 ft. | 200 m. 656 ft. | 500 m. 1,640 ft. | 1,000 m. 3,281 ft. | 2,000 m. 6,562 ft. | 5,000 m. 16,404 ft.

81646 Molina 200 ....D4	80473 Rand 50 ....G2	81334 Towaoc 300 ....B8
81144 Monte Vista 3,902 ....G7	81648 Rangely 2,113 ....B2	81080 Towner 61 ....P6
†80435 Montezuma 6 ....H3	80742 Raymer (New Raymer) 80 ....M1	81081 Trinchera 30 ....M8
81401 Montrose⊙ 8,722 ....D6	81649 Red Cliff 409 ....G4	81082 Trinidad⊙ 9,663 ....L8
80132 Monument 690 ....K4	80545 Red Feather Lakes 150 ....H1	†80864 Truckton 10 ....L5
80465 Morrison 478 ....J3	†81326 Red Mesa 100 ....C8	81251 Twin Lakes 40 ....G4
81146 Mosca 100 ....H7	81623 Redstone 115 ....E4	81084 Two Buttes 84 ....P7
81236 Nathrop 150 ....H5	81431 Redvale 300 ....B6	†81069 Tyrone 9 ....L8
81422 Naturita 819 ....B6	81066 Red Wing 200 ....J7	81436 Uravan 500 ....B6
80466 Nederland 1,212 ....H3	81332 Rico 76 ....C7	†81064 Utleyville 2 ....O8
81647 New Castle 563 ....E3	81432 Ridgway 369 ....D6	81657 Vail 2,261 ....G3
80742 New Raymer 80 ....M1	81650 Rifle 3,215 ....D3	†81082 Valdez 12 ....K8
†81054 Ninaview 2 ....N7	81650 Rio Blanco 4 ....C3	80755 Vernon 50 ....P3
80544 Niwot 500 ....J2	81244 Rockvale 338 ....J6	80860 Victor 265 ....J5
†81022 North Avondale 110 ....L6	81067 Rocky Ford 4,804 ....M6	81087 Vilas 118 ....P8
80233 Northglenn 29,847 ....K3	80652 Roggen 100 ....L2	81155 Villa Grove 37 ....G6
†81050 North La Junta 1,076 ....N7	81148 Romeo 308 ....G8	81088 Villegreen 6 ....M8
81424 Norwood 478 ....C6	80833 Rush 40 ....L5	81001 Vineland 100 ....K6
80648 Nunn 295 ....K1	81069 Rye 232 ....K7	80548 Virginia Dale 2 ....J1
80467 Oak Creek 929 ....F2	81149 Saguache⊙ 656 ....G6	80861 Vona 94 ....O4
81237 Ohio 100 ....F5	†81236 Saint Elmo 75 ....G5	†81130 Wagon Wheel Gap 20 ....F7
81425 Olathe 1,262 ....D5	81201 Salida⊙ 44,870 ....H6	80480 Walden⊙ 947 ....G1
81062 Olney Springs 253 ....M6	81150 San Acacio 50 ....J8	81089 Walsenburg⊙ 3,945 ....K7
81426 Ophir 38 ....D7	81151 Sanford 687 ....H8	81090 Walsh 884 ....P8
80649 Orchard 79 ....L2	†81069 San Isabel 8 ....K7	80481 Ward 129 ....H2
†81501 Orchard Mesa 4,876 ....C4	81152 San Luis⊙ 842 ....J8	80653 Weldona 200 ....M2
81063 Ordway⊙ 1,135 ....M6	81153 San Pablo 150 ....J8	80549 Wellington 1,215 ....K1
†81120 Ortiz 163 ....H8	81248 Sargents 31 ....F6	81252 Westcliffe⊙ 324 ....H6
80743 Otis 534 ....O2	†81430 Sawpit 41 ....D7	80135 Westcreek 2 ....J4
81427 Ouray⊙ 684 ....D6	80911 Security-Widefield 18,768 ....K5	80030 Westminster 50,211 ....J3
80744 Ovid 439 ....P1	80135 Sedalia 200 ....K4	81091 Weston 150 ....K8
80745 Padroni 100 ....N1	80749 Sedgwick 258 ....O1	81253 Wetmore 150 ....J6
†81147 Pagosa Junction 15 ....E8	81070 Segundo 200 ....K8	80033 Wheat Ridge 30,293 ....J3
81147 Pagosa Springs⊙ 1,331 ....E8	80834 Seibert 180 ....O4	81527 Whitewater 300 ....C5
81526 Palisade 1,551 ....C4	80546 Severance 102 ....H2	80654 Wiggins 531 ....L2
80133 Palmer Lake 1,130 ....J4	80475 Shawnee 100 ....H4	80862 Wild Horse 13 ....N5
80746 Paoli 81 ....P1	†80110 Sheridan 5,377 ....J3	81092 Wiley 425 ....O6
81428 Paonia 1,425 ....D5	81071 Sheridan Lake 87 ....P6	†81226 Williamsburg 72 ....J6
81635 Parachute 338 ....C4	81652 Silt 923 ....D4	80550 Windsor 4,277 ....J2
81429 Paradox 250 ....B6	81249 Silver Cliff 280 ....J6	80482 Winter Park 480 ....H3
†81212 Parkdale 21 ....H6	80476 Silver Plume 140 ....H3	81655 Wolcott 30 ....F3
80134 Parker 200 ....K4	80498 Silverthorne 989 ....G3	80863 Woodland Park 2,634 ....J4
81239 Parlin 60 ....F6	81433 Silverton⊙ 794 ....D7	80757 Woodrow 24 ....M3
80468 Parshall 80 ....G2	80835 Simla 494 ....M4	81656 Woody Creek 400 ....F4
80747 Peetz 220 ....N1	81653 Slater 10 ....E1	80758 Wray⊙ 2,131 ....P2
81240 Penrose 500 ....K6	81654 Snowmass 999 ....E4	80483 Yampa 472 ....F2
80831 Peyton 250 ....K4	80750 Snyder 200 ....M2	81335 Yellow Jacket 115 ....B7
80469 Phippsburg 300 ....F2	81434 Somerset 200 ....E5	80864 Yoder 25 ....L5
80650 Pierce 878 ....K1	81154 South Fork 500 ....F7	80759 Yuma 2,824 ....O2
80470 Pine 100 ....J4	81073 Springfield⊙ 1,657 ....O8	
80471 Pinecliffe 375 ....J3	81074 Starkville 127 ....L8	**OTHER FEATURES**
†81001 Pinon 50 ....K6	80477 Steamboat Springs⊙ 5,098 ....F2	
81241 Pitkin 59 ....F5	80751 Sterling⊙ 11,385 ....N1	Adams (mt.) H6
81430 Placerville 50 ....D6	80754 Stoneham 35 ....M1	Adobe Creek (res.) N6
†81624 Plateau City 35 ....D4	81075 Stonington 27 ....P8	Air Force Academy 8,655 ....K5
†80743 Platner 30 ....N2	80136 Strasburg 1,005 ....L3	Alamosa (riv.) G8
80651 Platteville 1,662 ....K2	80836 Stratton 705 ....O4	Alva B. Adams (tunnel) H2
81331 Pleasant View 300 ....B7	81076 Sugar City 306 ....M6	Animas (riv.) D8
81242 Poncha Springs 321 ....G6	†81640 Sunbeam 19 ....C1	Antero (mt.) G5
†81226 Portland 17 ....K6	†80027 Superior 208 ....J3	Antero (res.) H5
81247 Portland D6	81077 Swink 668 ....M7	Antora (peak) G6
81243 Powderhorn 100 ....E6	80478 Tabernash 250 ....H3	Apishapa (riv.) L8
81064 Pritchett 183 ....O8	81435 Telluride⊙ 1,047 ....D7	Arapaho Nat'l Rec. Area G2
†80736 Proctor 25 ....N1	†80461 Tennessee Pass 5 ....G4	Arapahoe (peak) H2
81065 Pryor 70 ....K8	81250 Texas Creek 80 ....H6	Arikaree (riv.) O3
*81001 Pueblo⊙ 101,686 ....K6	†81082 Thatcher 500 ....L7	Arkansas (riv.) P6
Pueblo‡ 125,972 ....K6	80229 Thornton 40,343 ....K3	Arkansas Divide (mts.) L4
80472 Radium 22 ....G3	†81137 Tiffany 24 ....D8	Baker (mt.) H2
80832 Ramah 119 ....L4	80547 Timnath 185 ....J2	Bald (mt.) H4
80473 Rand 50 ....G2	†81034 Timpas 25 ....M7	Bear (creek) P8
81648 Rangely 2,113 ....B2	†81210 Tincup 8 ....F5	Beaver (creek) M3
	80479 Toponas 55 ....F2	Bennett (peak) G7

Bent's Old Fort Nat'l Hist. Site M6	Cochetopa (creek) F6	Evans (mt.) H3
Big Grizzly (creek) G1	Colorado (riv.) A5	Florissant Fossil Beds Nat'l Mon. J5
Big Sandy (creek) N4	Colorado Nat'l Mon. B4	Fort Carson 19,399 ....K5
Big Thompson (riv.) H2	Conejos (peak) G8	Fountain (creek) K5
Bijou (creek) L3	Conejos (riv.) G8	Frenchman (creek) P1
Black Canyon of the Gunnison Nat'l Mon. D5	Crestone (peak) H7	Frenchman, North Fork (creek) O1
Black Squirrel (creek) L5	Crow (creek) L1	Frenchman, South Fork (creek) O1
Blanca (peak) H7	Culebra (creek) H8	Front (range) H1
Blue (mt.) B2	Culebra (peak) J8	Gore (range) G3
Blue (riv.) G3	Curecanti Nat'l Rec. Area F6	Graham (peak) G3
Blue Mesa (res.) E5	Del Norte (peak) F7	Granby (lake) G2
Bonny (res.) P3	De Weese (plat.) J6	Great Sand Dunes Nat'l Mon. H7
Box Elder (creek) K4	Dinosaur Nat'l Mon. B2	Green (riv.) A1
Cache la Poudre (riv.) H1	Disappointment (creek) B7	Green Mountain (res.) G3
Cameron (peak) H1	Dolores (riv.) B5	Gunnison (riv.) D5
Camp Hale G4	Douglas (creek) B3	Gunnison (tunnel) D6
Carbon (peak) E5	Eagle (riv.) E3	Gunnison, North Fork (riv.) D4
Castle (peak) F5	Elbert (mt.) G4	Hale, Camp G4
Cebolla (creek) E6	El Diente (peak) C7	Handies (peak) E6
Chacuaco (creek) M8	Eleven Mile Canyon (res.) H5	Harvard (mt.) G5
Cheesman (lake) J4	Elk (riv.) F1	Hermosa (peak) D7
Clay (creek) O7	Ent A.F.B. K5	Hesperus (mt.) C8
	Ethel (mt.) F1	Holy Cross (mt.) F4

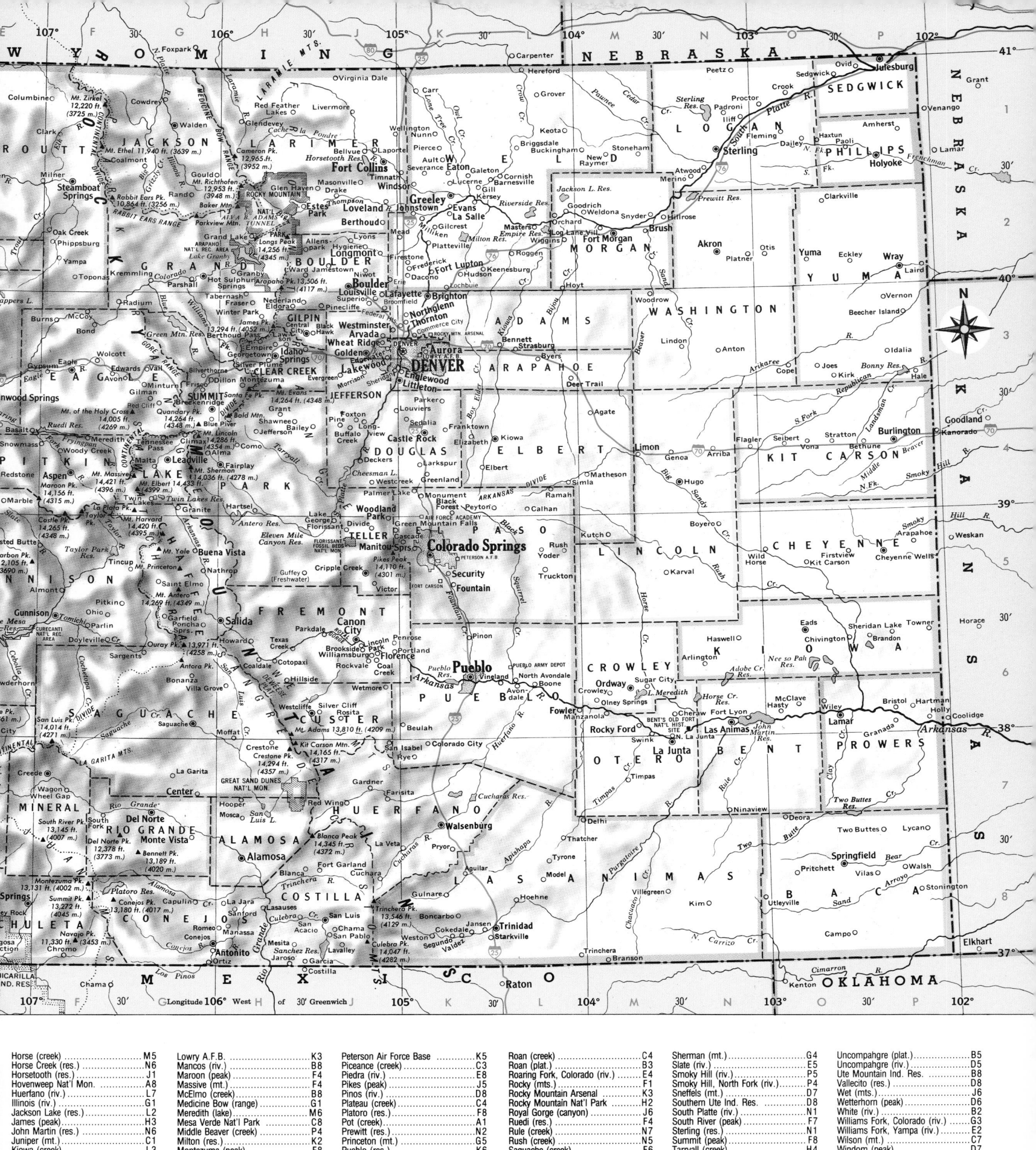

Horse (creek) M5	Lowry A.F.B. K3	Peterson Air Force Base K5	Roan (creek) C4	Sherman (mt.) G4	Uncompahgre (plat.) B5
Horse Creek (res.) N6	Mancos (riv.) B8	Piceance (creek) C3	Roan (plat.) B3	Slate (riv.) E5	Uncompahgre (riv.) D5
Horsetooth (res.) J1	Maroon (peak) F4	Piedra (riv.) E8	Roaring Fork, Colorado (riv.) E4	Smoky Hill (riv.) P5	Ute Mountain Ind. Res. B8
Hovenweep Nat'l Mon. A8	Massive (mt.) F4	Pikes (peak) J5	Rocky (mts.) F1	Smoky Hill, North Fork (riv.) ...P4	Vallecito (res.) D8
Huerfano (riv.) L7	McElmo (riv.) B8	Pinos (riv.) D8	Rocky Mountain Arsenal ...K3	Sneffels (mt.) D7	Wet (mts.) J6
Illinois (riv.) G1	Medicine Bow (range) G1	Plateau (creek) C3	Rocky Mountain Nat'l Park .H2	Southern Ute Ind. Res. ..D8	Wetterhorn (peak) D6
James (peak) H3	Meredith (lake) M6	Platoro (res.) E8	Royal Gorge (canyon) J6	South Platte (riv.) N1	White (riv.) B2
John Martin (res.) N6	Mesa Verde Nat'l Park C8	Pot (creek) A1	Ruedi (res.) F4	South River (peak) F7	Williams Fork, Colorado (riv.) ..G3
Juniper (mt.) C1	Middle Beaver (creek) P4	Prewitt (res.) N2	Rule (creek) N7	Sterling (res.) N1	Williams Fork, Yampa (riv.) E2
Kiowa (creek) L3	Milton (res.) K2	Princeton (mt.) G5	Rush (creek) N5	Summit (peak) F8	Wilson (mt.) C7
Kit Carson (mt.) H7	Montezuma (peak) F8	Pueblo (res.) K6	Saguache (creek) F6	Tarryall (creek) H4	Windom (peak) D7
La Garita (mts.) F7	Morrow Point (res.) E6	Pueblo Army Depot L6	San Juan (mts.) F7	Taylor (peak) F5	Yale (mt.) G5
Lake Fork, Gunnison (riv.) .E6	Muddy (creek) E4	Purgatoire (riv.) M8	San Juan (riv.) E8	Taylor (riv.) F5	Yampa (riv.) B2
Landsman (creek) P4	Navajo (peak) E8	Quandary (peak) G4	San Luis (creek) H6	Taylor Park (res.) F5	Yellow (creek) C3
La Plata (peak) G4	Navajo (res.) E8	Rabbit Ears (peak) F2	San Luis (lake) H7	Timpas (creek) M7	Yucca House Nat'l Mon. B8
La Plata (riv.) C8	Nee so Pah (res.) O8	Rabbit Ears (range) F2	San Luis (riv.) H6	Tomichi (creek) E6	Zenobia (peak) B1
Laramie (mts.) H1	North Carrizo (creek) N8	Redcloud (peak) E6	San Miguel (mts.) C7	Trappers (lake) E3	Zirkel (mt.) F1
Laramie (riv.) G1	North Platte (riv.) G1	Republican (riv.) P3	San Miguel (riv.) B6	Trinchera (creek) J8	
Lincoln (mt.) H4	Owl (creek) K1	Richthofen (mt.) F1	Santa Fe (riv.) H4	Trinchera (riv.) J8	⊙County seat.
Lone Cone (mt.) C7	Ouray (peak) G6	Rifle (creek) D3	Sawatch (range) G4	Trout (creek) E2	‡Population of metropolitan area.
Lone Tree (creek) K1	Pagoda (peak) E2	Rio Grande (res.) E7	Sheep (mt.) E6	Twin Lakes (res.) G4	
Longs (peak) H2	Park (range) F1	Rio Grande (riv.) H8		Two Butte (creek) N7	† Zip of nearest p.o. * Multiple zips.
Los Pinos (riv.) G8	Parkview (mt.) G2	Rio Grande Pyramid (mt.) .E7		Two Buttes (res.) O7	
	Pawnee (creek) M1	Riverside (res.) L2	Uncompahgre (peak) E6		

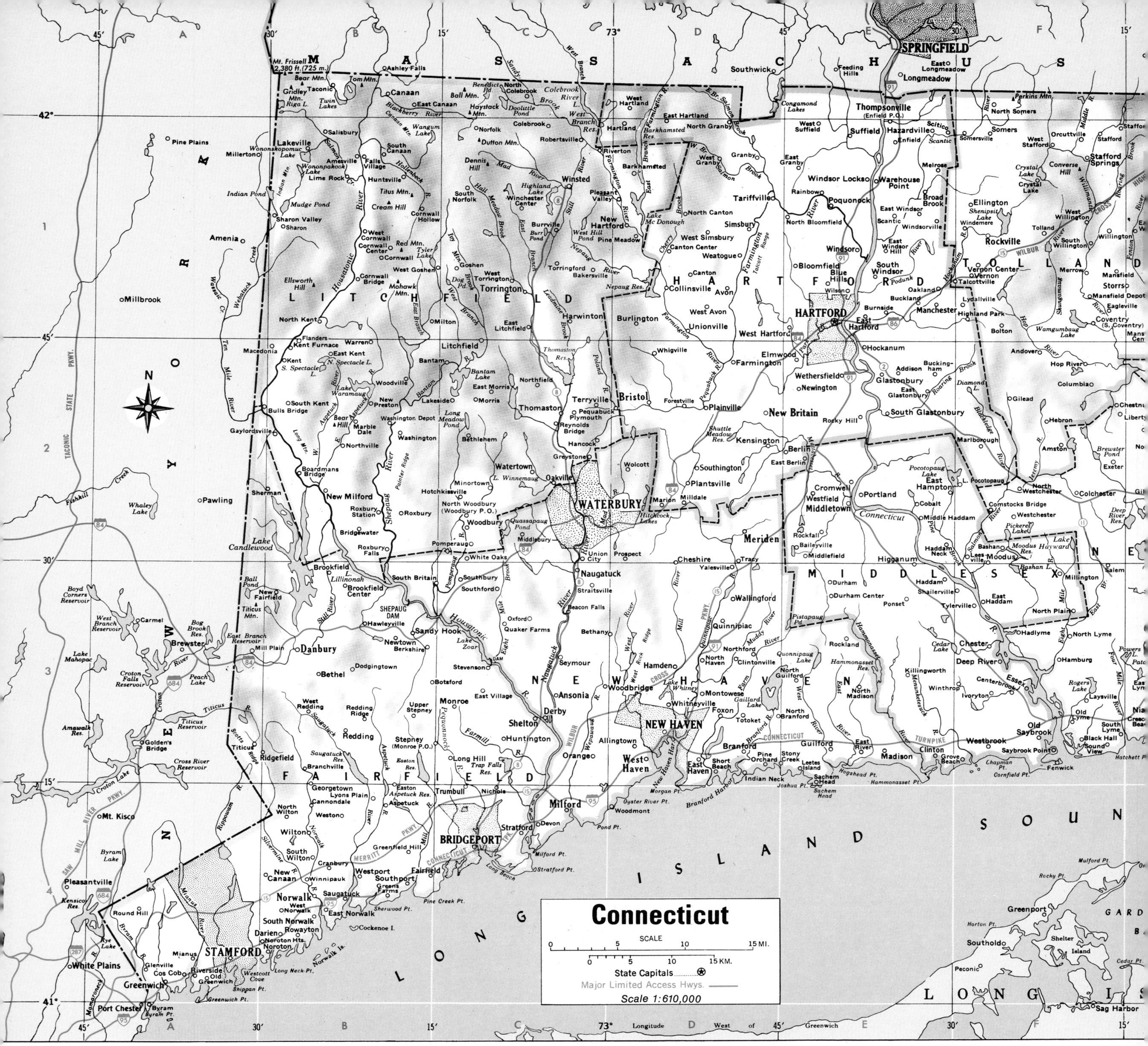

Connecticut
SCALE
0 5 10 15 MI.
0 5 10 15 KM.
State Capitals
Major Limited Access Hwys.
Scale 1:610,000
73° Longitude West of Greenwich
LITCHFIELD
HARTFORD
TOLLAND
FAIRFIELD
NEW HAVEN
MIDDLESEX
MASSACHUSETTS
NEW YORK
LONG ISLAND SOUND
HARTFORD
SPRINGFIELD
WATERBURY
NEW HAVEN
BRIDGEPORT
STAMFORD
Mt. Frissell 2,380 ft. (725 m.)
Lake Candlewood

Topography
0 15 30 MI.
0 15 30 KM.
Mt. Frissell
2,380 ft. (725 m.)
Housatonic
Shepaug
Farmington
Hartford
Connecticut
Willimantic
Natchaug
Quinebaug
Shetucket
Waterbury
Naugatuck
Quinnipiac
Lake Candlewood
Norwich
Thames
New Haven
New London
Stamford
Bridgeport
Below Sea Level
Sea Level
100 m. 328 ft.
200 m. 656 ft.
500 m. 1,640 ft.
1,000 m. 3,281 ft.
2,000 m. 6,562 ft.
5,000 m. 16,404 ft.

COUNTIES

Fairfield 807,143	B3
Hartford 807,766	D1
Litchfield 156,769	B1
Middlesex 129,017	E3
New Haven 761,337	D3
New London 238,409	G2
Tolland 114,823	F1
Windham 92,312	H1

CITIES and TOWNS

Zip	Name/Pop.	Key
06230	Abington 600	G1
06231	Amston 900	F2
06232	Andover○ 2,144	F2
06401	Ansonia 19,039	C3
06278	Ashford○ 3,221	G1
06278	Ashford P.O. (Warrenville) 500	G1
†06241	Attawaugan 400	H1
06001	Avon○ 11,201	D1
06001	Avon 1,434	D1
06233	Ballouville 800	H1
06330	Baltic	G2
06750	Bantam 860	B2
†06063	Barkhamsted○ 2,935	D1
†06423	Bashan 90	F2
06403	Beacon Falls○ 3,995	C3
06037	Berlin○ 15,121	E2
†06501	Bethany○ 4,330	C3
06801	Bethel○ 16,004	B3
06801	Bethel 8,755	B3
06751	Bethlehem○ 2,573	C2
06751	Bethlehem 1,762	C2
06002	Bloomfield○ 18,608	E1
06112	Blue Hills	E1
06040	Bolton○ 3,951	F1
06404	Botsford 400	C3
†06829	Branchville 600	B3
06405	Branford○ 23,363	D3
06405	Branford 5,438	D3
*06601	Bridgeport 142,546	C4
	Bridgeport‡ 395,455	C4
06752	Bridgewater○ 1,563	B2
06010	Bristol 57,370	D2
	Bristol‡ 73,762	D2
06016	Broad Brook	E1
06804	Brookfield○ 12,872	B3
06234	Brooklyn○ 5,691	H1
06013	Burlington○ 5,660	D1
06830	Byram	A4
06018	Canaan○ 1,002	B1
06018	Canaan 1,160	B1
†06897	Cannondale 400	B4
06331	Canterbury○ 3,426	H2
06019	Canton○ 7,635	D1
06019	Canton 1,680	D1
06409	Centerbrook 800	F3
06332	Central Village 950	H2
06235	Chaplin○ 1,793	G1
06410	Cheshire○ 21,788	D2
06410	Cheshire 5,722	D2
06412	Chester○ 3,068	F3
06412	Chester 1,388	F3
06413	Clinton○ 11,195	E3
06413	Clinton 3,168	E3
06414	Cobalt 700	E2
06415	Colchester○ 7,761	F2
06415	Colchester 3,190	F2
06021	Colebrook○ 1,221	C1
06022	Collinsville 2,555	D1
06237	Columbia○ 3,386	F2
06753	Cornwall○ 1,288	B1
06807	Cos Cob	A4
06238	Coventry○ 8,895	F1
06416	Cromwell○ 10,265	E2
06810	Danbury 60,470	B3
	Danbury‡ 146,405	B3
06239	Danielson 4,553	H1
06820	Darien○ 18,892	B4
06241	Dayville	H1
06417	Deep River○ 3,994	F3
06417	Deep River 2,495	F3
06418	Derby 12,346	C3
06422	Durham○ 5,143	E3
06422	Durham 2,641	E3
06023	East Berlin 950	E2
†06239	East Brooklyn 1,251	H1
06024	East Canaan 800	B1
06242	Eastford○ 1,028	G1
06025	East Glastonbury 300	E2
06026	East Granby○ 4,102	E1
06423	East Haddam○ 5,621	F3
06424	East Hampton○ 8,572	E2

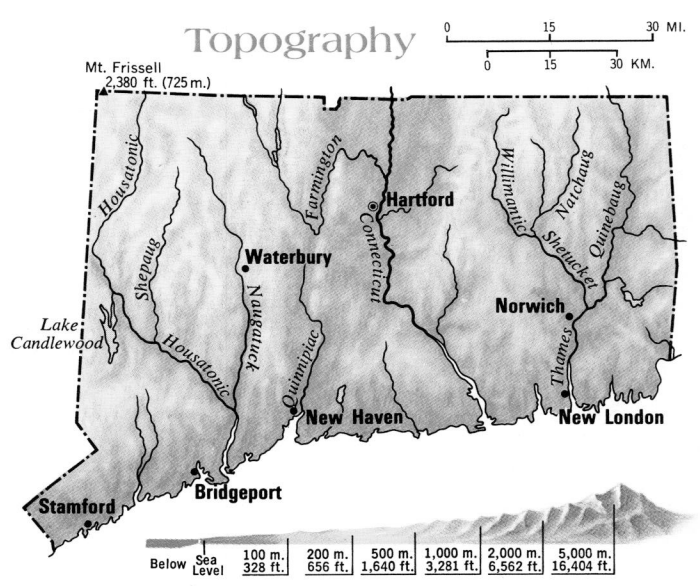

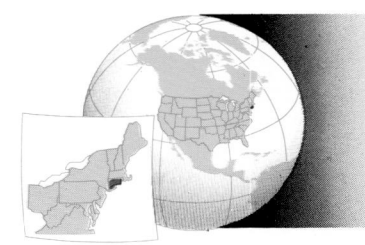

AREA 5,018 sq. mi. (12,997 sq. km.)
POPULATION 3,107,576
CAPITAL Hartford
LARGEST CITY Bridgeport
HIGHEST POINT Mt. Frissell (S. Slope) 2,380 ft. (725 m.)
SETTLED IN 1635
ADMITTED TO UNION January 9, 1788
POPULAR NAME Constitution State; Nutmeg State
STATE FLOWER Mountain Laurel
STATE BIRD Robin

06351 Lisbon○ 3,279	G2
06759 Litchfield 7,605	C2
06759 Litchfield 1,489	C2
†06378 Lords Point 500	H3
06443 Madison 14,031	E3
06443 Madison 2,069	E3
06040 Manchester○ 49,761	E1
06040 Manchester 31,058	E1
†06250 Mansfield○ 20,634	F1
06250 Mansfield Center 1,043	G1
06777 Marble Dale 300	B2
06444 Marion 900	D2
06447 Marlborough○ 4,746	F2
06447 Marlborough 1,039	F2
†06382 Massapeag 350	G3
06252 Mechanicsville 425	H1
06450 Meriden 57,118	D2
Meriden‡ 57,118	D2
06762 Middlebury○ 5,995	C2
06455 Middlefield○ 3,796	E2
06456 Middle Haddam 325	E2
06457 Middletown 39,040	E2
06460 Milford 49,101	C4
06467 Milldale 975	D2
†06759 Milton 600	C1
06468 Monroe 14,010	C3
06468 Monroe P.O. (Stepney)	B3
06353 Montville 16,455	G3
06353 Montville 1,711	G3
06469 Moodus 1,179	F2
06354 Moosup 3,308	H2
06763 Morris 1,899	C2
06355 Mystic 2,333	H3
06770 Naugatuck 26,456	C3
*06050 New Britain 73,840	E2
New Britain‡ 142,241	E2
06840 New Canaan○ 17,931	B4
06810 New Fairfield○ 11,260	B3
06057 New Hartford○ 4,884	C1
06057 New Hartford 1,310	C1
*06501 New Haven 126,109	D3
New Haven-West Haven‡ 417,592	D3
06111 Newington 28,841	E2
06320 New London 28,842	G3
New London-Norwich‡ 248,554	G3
06776 New Milford○ 19,420	B2
06776 New Milford 5,186	B2
06777 New Preston 1,209	B2
06470 Newtown○ 19,107	B3
06470 Newtown 2,022	B3
06357 Niantic 3,151	G3
06340 Noank 1,406	G3
06058 Norfolk○ 2,156	C1
06471 North Branford○ 11,554	E3
06778 Northfield 600	C2
06254 North Franklin 500	G2
06060 North Granby 450	D1
06255 North Grosvenor Dale 1,856	H1
†06437 North Guilford	E3
06473 North Haven○ 22,080	D3
06359 North Stonington 4,219	H3
06256 North Windham 200	G1
*06850 Norwalk 77,767	B4
06360 Norwich 38,074	G2
06370 Oakdale 608	G2
06779 Oakville 8,737	C2
06371 Old Lyme○ 6,159	F3

06372 Old Mystic 600	H3
06475 Old Saybrook 9,287	F3
06475 Old Saybrook 1,857	F3
06373 Oneco 550	H2
06477 Orange○ 13,237	C3
06483 Oxford○ 6,634	C3
06379 Pawcatuck 5,216	H3
06781 Pequabuck 642	C2
06061 Pine Meadow 400	D1
†06405 Pine Orchard 300	D3
06374 Plainfield○ 12,774	H2
06374 Plainfield 2,799	H2
06062 Plainville○ 16,401	D2
06063 Pleasant Valley 300	C1
06782 Plymouth○ 10,732	C2
06258 Pomfret○ 2,775	H1
†06340 Poquonock Bridge 2,549	G3
06480 Portland○ 8,383	E2
06480 Portland 5,914	E2
06712 Prospect○ 6,807	D2
06260 Putnam○ 8,580	H1
06260 Putnam 6,855	H1
06375 Quaker Hill 2,052	G3
06262 Quinebaug 1,088	H1
06875 Redding○ 7,272	B3
06876 Redding Ridge 550	B3
06877 Ridgefield○ 20,120	B3
06877 Ridgefield 6,066	B3
06065 Riverton 250	D1
06481 Rockfall 900	E2
†06066 Rockville	F1
06067 Rocky Hill 14,559	E2
06263 Rogers 650	H1
06875 Roxbury 1,400	B2
†06415 Salem○ 2,335	F3
06068 Salisbury○ 3,896	B1
06264 Scotland○ 1,072	G2
06483 Seymour○ 13,434	C3
06069 Sharon○ 2,623	B1
06484 Shelton 31,314	C3
06784 Sherman○ 2,281	B2
06070 Simsbury○ 21,161	D1
06070 Simsbury 5,488	D1
06071 Somers○ 8,473	F1
06071 Somers 1,643	F1
06072 Somersville 750	F1
06487 South Britain 390	B3
06488 Southbury○ 14,156	C3
†06238 South Coventry (Coventry) 3,769	F1
06073 South Glastonbury 500	E2
06489 Southington○ 36,879	D2
06785 South Kent 450	B2
06265 South Willington 450	F1
06266 South Windham 1,399	G2
06074 South Windsor○ 17,198	E1
06267 South Woodstock 1,319	G1
06075 Stafford○ 9,268	F1
06076 Stafford Springs 3,392	F1
06077 Staffordville 500	G1
*06901 Stamford 102,453	A4
Stamford‡ 198,854	A4
†06468 Stepney	B3
06377 Sterling○ 1,791	H2
06491 Stevenson 300	C3
06378 Stonington○ 16,220	H3
06378 Stonington 1,228	H3
06268 Storrs 11,394	F1
06497 Stratford 50,541	C4

06078 Suffield○ 9,294	E1
06078 Suffield 1,122	E1
06079 Taconic 400	B1
06380 Taftville	G2
06081 Tariffville 1,324	D1
06786 Terryville 5,234	C2
06787 Thomaston○ 6,276	C2
06277 Thompson○ 8,141	H1
†06082 Thompsonville	E1
06084 Tolland○ 9,694	F1
06611 Trumbull○ 32,989	C4
06382 Uncasville 1,597	G3
†06076 Union○ 546	G1
06066 Vernon○ 27,974	F1
06383 Versailles 540	G2
06384 Voluntown○ 1,637	H2
06492 Wallingford○ 37,274	D3
06492 Wallingford 17,821	D3
06754 Warren○ 1,027	B2
†06278 Warrenville 500	G1
06793 Washington○ 3,657	B2
06794 Washington Depot 900	B2
*06701 Waterbury 103,266	C2
Waterbury‡ 228,178	C2
06385 Waterford○ 17,843	G3
06385 Waterford 2,736	G3
06795 Watertown○ 19,489	C2
06089 Weatogue 2,249	D1
06498 Westbrook○ 5,216	F3
06498 Westbrook 2,035	F3
06796 West Cornwall 425	B1
06090 West Granby 567	D1
06107 West Hartford○ 61,301	D1
06516 West Haven 53,184	D3
06388 West Mystic 3,364	H3
06883 Weston○ 8,284	B4
06880 Westport○ 25,290	B4
06896 West Redding 500	B3
06092 West Simsbury 2,140	D1
06109 Wethersfield○ 26,013	E2
06517 Whitneyville	D3
06226 Willimantic 14,652	G2
†06279 Willington○ 4,694	F1
06897 Wilton○ 15,351	B4
06094 Winchester○ 10,841	C1
06094 Winchester Center 350	C1
06280 Windham○ 21,062	G2
06095 Windsor○ 25,204	E1
06095 Windsor 17,517	E1
06096 Windsor Locks○ 12,190	E1
06097 Windsorville 450	E1
06098 Winsted 8,092	C1
†06417 Winthrop 750	E3
06716 Wolcott○ 13,008	D2
†06515 Woodbridge○ 7,761	D3
06798 Woodbury○ 6,942	C2
06798 Woodbury 1,290	C2
†06460 Woodmont 1,797	D4
06281 Woodstock○ 5,117	H1

OTHER FEATURES

Aspetuck (res.)	B4
Bantam (lake)	C2
Barkhamsted (res.)	D1
Bear (mt.)	B1
Byram (riv.)	A4
Candlewood (lake)	A2
Coast Guard Academy	G3

Colebrook River (lake)	C1
Congamond (lkes)	E1
Connecticut (riv.)	E2
Dennis (hill)	C1
Easton (res.)	B3
Eight Mile (riv.)	F3
Farmington (riv.)	D1
French (riv.)	H1
Frissell (mt.)	B1
Gaillard (lake)	D3
Gardner (lake)	G2
Hammonasset (pt.)	E3
Hammonasset (res.)	E3
Haystack (mt.)	C1
Highland (lake)	C1
Hockanum (riv.)	E1
Hop (riv.)	F1
Housatonic (riv.)	C2
Lillinonah (lake)	B3
Little (riv.)	G2
Long Island (sound)	C4
Mad (riv.)	C1
Mashapaug (lake)	G1
Mason (isl.)	H3
Mattabesset (riv.)	E2
Mianus (riv.)	A4
Mohawk (mt.)	B1
Moosup (riv.)	H2
Mount Hope (riv.)	G1
Mudge (pond)	B1
Mystic (riv.)	H3
Natchaug (riv.)	G1
Naugatuck (riv.)	C2
Nepaug (res.)	D1
Niantic (riv.)	G3
Norwalk (riv.)	B4
Pachaug (pond)	H2
Pawcatuck (riv.)	H3
Pequabuck (riv.)	D2
Pequonnock (riv.)	C3
Pocotopaug (lake)	E2
Quaddick (res.)	H1
Quinebaug (riv.)	H2
Quinnipiac (riv.)	D3
Rippowam (riv.)	A4
Sachem (head)	E4
Salmon (brook)	D1
Salmon (riv.)	F2
Saugatuck (res.)	B3
Scantic (riv.)	E1
Shenipsit (lake)	F1
Shepaug (riv.)	B2
Shetucket (riv.)	G2
Silvermine (riv.)	B4
Spectacle (lkes)	B2
Still (riv.)	B3
Still (riv.)	C1
Talcott (range)	D1
Thames (riv.)	G3
Thomaston (res.)	C2
Titicus (riv.)	A3
Trap Falls (res.)	C3
Twin (lkes)	B1
Wamgumbaug (lake)	F1
Waramaug (lake)	B2
West Rock Ridge (hills)	D3
Willimantic (riv.)	F1
Wononscopomuc (lake)	B1
Yantic (riv.)	G2

‡Population of metropolitan area.
○Population of town or township.
† Zip of nearest p.o.   * Multiple zips.

06424 East Hampton 2,152	E2
06108 East Hartford○ 52,563	E1
06027 East Hartland 900	D1
06512 East Haven 25,028	D3
06243 East Killingly 900	H1
06333 East Lyme○ 13,870	G3
†06763 East Morris 800	C2
06612 Easton○ 5,962	B4
†06088 East Windsor○ 8,925	E1
06028 East Windsor Hill 500	E1
06244 East Woodstock 400	H1
06029 Ellington○ 9,711	F1
06082 Enfield○ 42,695	E1
06082 Enfield 8,151	E1
06426 Essex○ 5,078	F3
06426 Essex 2,501	F3
06245 Fabyan 600	H1
06430 Fairfield○ 54,849	B4
06031 Falls Village 600	B1
06032 Farmington 16,407	D2
06334 Fitchville 400	G2
†06254 Franklin○ 1,592	G2
06335 Gales Ferry 1,191	G3
06755 Gaylordsville 960	A2
06829 Georgetown 1,834	B4
06336 Gilman 350	G2
06337 Glasgo 450	H2
06033 Glastonbury 24,327	E2
06033 Glastonbury 7,049	E2
06756 Goshen○ 1,706	C1
06035 Granby○ 7,956	D1
06035 Granby 1,912	D1
06830 Greenwich○ 59,578	A4
06246 Grosvenor Dale 700	H1
06340 Groton○ 41,062	G3
06340 Groton 10,086	G3
06437 Guilford○ 17,375	E3
06437 Guilford 2,555	E3
06438 Haddam○ 6,383	E2
06439 Hadlyme 450	F3
06514 Hamden○ 51,071	D3
06247 Hampton○ 1,322	G1
06350 Hanover 500	G2
*06101 Hartford (cap.) 136,392	E1
Hartford‡ 726,114	E1
†06091 Hartland○ 1,416	D1
06791 Harwinton○ 4,889	C1
06791 Harwinton 3,293	C1
06440 Hawleyville 600	B3
06082 Hazardville 5,436	E1
06248 Hebron○ 5,453	F2
06441 Higganum 1,660	E2
†06040 Highland Park 500	F1
06351 Jewett City 3,294	H2
06037 Kensington 7,502	D2
06757 Kent○ 2,505	B2
06241 Killingly○ 14,519	H1
†06413 Killingworth○ 3,976	E3
06424 Lake Pocotopaug 2,137	E2
06758 Lakeside 350	B2
06249 Lebanon○ 4,762	G2
06339 Ledyard○ 13,735	G3
†06437 Leetes Island 500	E3
†06039 Lime Rock 350	B1

Agriculture, Industry and Resources

DOMINANT LAND USE

- Specialized Dairy
- Dairy, Poultry, Mixed Farming
- Forests
- Urban Areas

MAJOR MINERAL OCCURRENCES

Cl Clay   Mi Mica

Major Industrial Areas

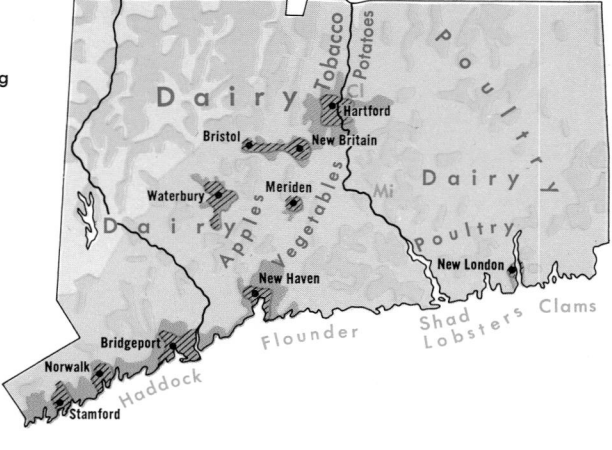

Florida

SCALE
State Capitals ⊛
County Seats ◉
Canals
Major Limited Access Hwys.
Scale 1:2,550,000

Western Part of Florida

Same scale as main map

© Copyright HAMMOND INCORPORATED, Maplewood, N.J.

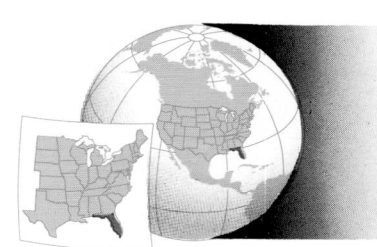

AREA 58,664 sq. mi. (151,940 sq. km.)
POPULATION 9,746,342
CAPITAL Tallahassee
LARGEST CITY Jacksonville
HIGHEST POINT (Walton County) 345 ft. (105 m.)
SETTLED IN 1565
ADMITTED TO UNION March 3, 1845
POPULAR NAME Sunshine State; Peninsula State
STATE FLOWER Orange Blossom
STATE BIRD Mockingbird

Topography

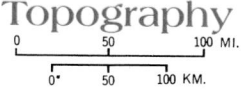

Zip	Name/Pop.	Key
32012	Crescent City 1,722	E2
32536	Crestview⊙ 7,617	C6
32628	Cross City⊙ 2,154	C2
32629	Crystal River 2,778	D3
33157	Cutler Ridge 20,886	F6
33880	Cypress Gardens 8,043	E3
†33472	Cypress Quarters 1,479	F4
33525	Dade City⊙ 4,923	D3
33004	Dania 11,811	B4
33837	Davenport 1,509	E3
33314	Davie 20,877	B4
*32014	Daytona Beach 54,176⊙	F2
	Daytona Beach‡ 258,762	F2
32016	Daytona Beach Shores 1,324	F2
32713	De Bary 4,980	E3
33441	Deerfield Beach 39,193	F5
32433	De Funiak Springs⊙ 5,563	C6
32720	De Land⊙ 15,354	E2
32028	De Leon Springs 1,669	E2
*33444	Delray Beach 34,325	F5
32725	Deltona 15,710	E3
32541	Destin 3,672	C6
33527	Dover 2,354	D4
33838	Dundee 2,227	E3
33528	Dunedin 30,203	B2
32630	Dunnellon 1,427	D2
33839	Eagle Lake 1,678	E4
†33601	East Lake-Orient Park 5,612	C2
†33940	East Naples 12,127	E5
32031	East Palatka 1,613	E2
32328	Eastpoint 1,246	B2
32751	Eatonville 2,185	E3
32437	Ebro 233	C6
32032	Edgewater 6,726	F3
†32801	Edgewood 1,034	E3
†33614	Egypt Lake 11,932	C2
33531	Elfers 11,396	D3
†33101	El Portal 1,819	B4
33533	Englewood 9,633	D5
32504	Ensley 14,422	B6
32425	Esto 304	C5
32726	Eustis 9,453	E3
33929	Everglades City 524	E6
32634	Fairfield 450	D2
†32693	Fanning Springs (Suwannee Riv.) 314	D2
32948	Fellsmere 1,161	F4
32034	Fernandina Beach⊙ 7,224	E1
32922	Five Points 1,691	D1
32036	Flagler Beach 2,208	E2
32636	Floral City 1,181	D3
33034	Florida City 6,174	F6
†32960	Florida Ridge 4,988	F4
†33472	Fort Drum 70	F4
*33301	Fort Lauderdale⊙ 153,279	C4
	Fort Lauderdale-Hollywood‡ 1,014,043	C4
33841	Fort Meade 5,546	E4
33842	Fort Ogden 900	E4
*33901	Fort Myers⊙ 36,638	E5
	Fort Myers-Cape Coral‡ 205,266	E5
33931	Fort Myers Beach 5,753	E5
33450	Fort Pierce⊙ 33,802	F4
32548	Fort Walton Beach 20,829	C6
	Fort Walton Beach‡ 109,920	C6
32038	Fort White 386	D2
32438	Fountain 900	D6
32439	Freeport 669	C6
33843	Frostproof 2,995	E4
32731	Fruitland Park 2,259	D3
33578	Fruitville 3,070	D4
*32601	Gainesville⊙ 81,371	D2
	Gainesville‡ 151,348	D2
32732	Geneva 1,120	E3
33534	Gibsonton 7,219	C3
32960	Gifford 6,240	F4
32040	Glen Saint Mary 462	D1
†33160	Golden Beach 612	C4
33999	Golden Gate 4,327	E5
†33444	Golf 110	F5
32560	Gonzalez 6,084	B6
33933	Goodland 600	E6
†32502	Goulding 5,352	B6
33170	Goulds 7,078	F6
32440	Graceville 2,918	D5
33463	Greenacres City 8,843	F5
32043	Green Cove Springs⊙ 4,154	E2
32330	Greensboro 562	B1
32331	Greenville 1,096	C1
32443	Greenwood 577	C1
32332	Gretna 1,448	B1
33533	Grove City 1,932	D5
32736	Groveland 1,992	E3
32561	Gulf Breeze 5,478	B6
33737	Gulfport 11,180	B3
33483	Gulf Stream 475	F5
†33301	Hacienda Village 126	B4
33009	Hallandale 36,517	B4
32044	Hampton 466	D2

Zip	Name/Pop.	Key
33440	Harlem 2,669	F5
32045	Hastings 636	E2
32333	Havana 2,782	B1
32640	Hawthorne 1,303	D2
32642	Hernando 1,653	D3
*33010	Hialeah 145,254	B4
†33010	Hialeah Gardens 2,700	B4
33431	Highland Beach 2,030	F5
33846	Highland City 1,555	E4
32401	Highland Park 184	E4
32643	High Springs 2,491	D2
32405	Hiland Park 4,763	C6
†33827	Hillcrest Heights 177	E4
32046	Hilliard 1,869	E1
†33060	Hillsboro Beach 1,554	F5
33455	Hobe Sound 6,822	F4
32047	Hollister 980	E2
32017	Holly Hill 9,953	E2
*33020	Hollywood 121,323	B4
33509	Holmes Beach 4,023	D4
*33030	Homestead 20,668	F6
32646	Homosassa 1,426	D3
32648	Horseshoe Beach 304	C2
32334	Hosford 750	B1
32737	Howey In The Hills 626	E3
33568	Hudson 5,799	D3
†33460	Hypoluxo 573	F5
33934	Immokalee 11,038	E5
32903	Indialantic 2,883	F3
†33139	Indian Creek 103	B4
†32901	Indian Harbour Beach 5,967	F3
32960	Indian River Shores 1,254	F4
33535	Indian Rocks Beach 3,717	B3
†33535	Indian Shores 984	B3
33456	Indiantown 3,383	F4
32649	Inglis 1,173	D2
32048	Interlachen 848	E2
32650	Inverness⊙ 4,095	D3
33036	Islamorada 1,441	F7
†33101	Islandia 12	F6
*32201	Jacksonville⊙ 540,920	E1
	Jacksonville‡ 737,519	E1
32250	Jacksonville Beach 15,462	E1
†33568	Jasmine Estates 11,995	D3
32052	Jasper⊙ 2,093	D1
32053	Jennings 749	C1
33457	Jensen Beach 6,639	F4
32901	June Park 4,051	F3
†33404	Juno Beach 1,142	F5
33458	Jupiter 9,868	F5
†33455	Jupiter Island 364	F4
33849	Kathleen 1,866	D3
33156	Kendall 73,758	B5
33709	Kenneth City 4,344	B3
33149	Key Biscayne 6,313	B5
33051	Key Colony Beach 977	F7
33037	Key Largo 7,447	F6
32656	Keystone Heights 1,056	E2
33040	Key West⊙ 24,382	E7
32741	Kissimmee⊙ 15,487	E3
33935	La Belle⊙ 2,287	E5
33537	Lacoochee 1,720	D3
32658	La Crosse 170	D2
32659	Lady Lake 1,193	E3
33850	Lake Alfred 3,134	E3
†32830	Lake Buena Vista 98	E3
32054	Lake Butler⊙ 1,830	D1
†33601	Lake Carroll 13,012	C2
32055	Lake City⊙ 9,257	D1
32744	Lake Helen 2,047	E3
*33801	Lakeland 47,406	D3
	Lakeland-Winter Haven‡ 321,652	D3
†33612	Lake Magdalene 13,331	D3
32746	Lake Mary 2,853	E3
33403	Lake Park 6,909	F5
33852	Lake Placid 963	E4
33853	Lake Wales 8,466	E4
*33460	Lake Worth 27,048	G5
33539	Land O'Lakes 4,515	D3
33462	Lantana 8,048	F5
*33540	Largo 58,977	B3
33308	Lauderdale-by-the-Sea 2,639	C3
†33313	Lauderdale Lakes 25,426	B3
33313	Lauderhill 37,271	B3
33545	Laurel 6,368	D4
32567	Laurel Hill 610	C5
32058	Lawtey 692	D1
†33050	Layton 88	F7
†33301	Lazy Lake 31	B3
32059	Lee 297	C1
32748	Leesburg 13,191	E3
33936	Lehigh Acres 9,404	E5
33033	Leisure City 17,905	F6
†33614	Leto 9,003	C2
32060	Live Oak⊙ 6,732	D1
32662	Lochloosa 450	E2
33548	Longboat Key 4,843	D4
32750	Longwood 10,029	E3
33549	Lutz 5,555	D3
32444	Lynn Haven 6,239	C6
32063	Macclenny⊙ 3,851	D1

(continued on following page)

33738 Madeira Beach 4,520 .... B3
32340 Madison⊙ 3,487 .... C1
32751 Maitland 8,763 .... E3
32950 Malabar 1,118 .... F3
32445 Malone 897 .... A1
33550 Mango 6,493 .... D4
33050 Marathon 7,568 .... E7
33937 Marco (Marco Island) 4,679 .... E6
33063 Margate 35,900 .... F5
32446 Marianna⊙ 7,006 .... A1
†32084 Marineland 31 .... E2
32569 Mary Esther 3,530 .... B6
32753 Mascotte 1,112 .... E3
32066 Mayo⊙ 891 .... C1
32664 McIntosh 404 .... D2
†33101 Medley 537 .... B4
*32901 Melbourne 46,536 .... F3
Melbourne-Titusville-Cocoa‡ 272,959 .... F3
32951 Melbourne Beach 2,713 .... F3
†33301 Melrose Park 5,672 .... B4
†33561 Memphis 5,501 .... D4
32952 Merritt Island 30,708 .... F3
32410 Mexico Beach 632 .... D6
*33101 Miami⊙ 346,931 .... B5
Miami‡ 1,625,979 .... B5
33139 Miami Beach 96,298 .... C5
†33101 Miami Lakes 9,809 .... B4
33153 Miami Shores 9,244 .... B4
33166 Miami Springs 12,350 ...... B5
32667 Micanopy 737 .... D2
†32960 Micco 3,585 .... F4
32343 Midway 950 .... B1
32570 Milton⊙ 7,206 .... B6
32754 Mims 7,583 .... F3
32755 Minneola 851 .... E3
33023 Miramar 32,813 .... B4
32577 Molino 1,456 .... B6
32344 Monticello⊙ 2,994 .... C1
32756 Montverde 397 .... E3
33471 Moore Haven⊙ 1,250 ...... E5
32757 Mount Dora 5,883 .... E3
33860 Mulberry 2,932 .... E4
33938 Murdock 272 .... D4
32506 Myrtle Grove 14,238 .... B6
*33940 Naples⊙ 17,581 .... E5
†33940 Naples Park 5,438 .... E5
33032 Naranja 10,381 .... F6
32233 Neptune Beach 5,248 .... E1
32669 Newberry 1,826 .... D2
*33552 New Port Richey 11,196 ... D3
32069 New Smyrna Beach 13,557 F2
32578 Niceville 8,543 .... C6
33555 Nokomis 3,108 .... D4
32452 Noma 113 .... C5
†33169 Norland 19,471 .... B4
33141 North Bay Village 4,920 .... B4
33903 North Fort Myers 22,808 ... E5
†33063 North Lauderdale 18,653 ... B3
33161 North Miami 42,566 .... B4
33161 North Miami Beach 36,481 C4
33940 North Naples 7,950 .... E5
33403 North Palm Beach 11,344 .. F5
33595 North Port 6,205 .... D4
†33708 North Redington Beach 1,156 .... B3
32759 Oak Hill 938 .... F3
32760 Oakland 658 .... E3
33334 Oakland Park 23,035 .... B3
*32670 Ocala⊙ 37,170 .... D2
Ocala‡ 122,488 .... D2
†33457 Ocean Breeze Park 469 ..... F4
33444 Ocean Ridge 1,355 .... F5
32761 Ocoee 7,803 .... E3
33163 Ojus 17,344 .... B4
32762 Okahumpka 900 .... D3
33472 Okeechobee⊙ 4,225 .... F4
33557 Oldsmar 2,608 .... B2
33558 Oneco 6,417 .... D4
33054 Opa Locka 14,460 .... B4
32763 Orange City 2,795 .... E3
32073 Orange Park 8,766 .... E1
†32970 Orchid 42 .... F4
*32801 Orlando⊙ 128,291 .... E3
Orlando‡ 700,699 .... E3
32074 Ormond Beach 21,378 ...... E2
32074 Ormond-by-the-Sea 7,665 . E2
33559 Osprey 1,660 .... D4
32683 Otter Creek 167 .... D2
32765 Oviedo 3,074 .... E3
32570 Pace 5,006 .... B6
33476 Pahokee 6,346 .... F5
†32036 Painters Hill 40 .... E2
32077 Palatka⊙ 10,175 .... E2
32905 Palm Bay 18,560 .... F3
33480 Palm Beach 9,729 .... G4
†33403 Palm Beach Gardens 14,407 .... F5
†33404 Palm Beach Shores 1,232 . G5
33490 Palm City 2,177 .... F4
32037 Palm Coast 2,837 .... E2
33561 Palmetto 8,637 .... D4
33563 Palm Harbor 5,215 .... D3
33619 Palm River-Clair Mel 14,447 .... C3
†32901 Palm Shores 77 .... F3
33460 Palm Springs 8,166 .... F5
*32401 Panama City⊙ 33,346 ...... C6
Panama City‡ 97,740 .... C6
32407 Panama City Beach 2,148 .. C6
32401 Parker 4,298 .... C6
†33441 Parkland 545 .... F5
32538 Paxton 659 .... C5
†33023 Pembroke Park 4,783 .... B4
33024 Pembroke Pines 35,776 .... B4
32079 Penney Farms 630 .... E2
†33010 Pennsuco 15 .... B4
*32501 Pensacola⊙ 57,619 .... B6
Pensacola‡ 289,782 .... B6
33157 Perrine 16,129 .... F6
32347 Perry⊙ 8,254 .... C1
32080 Pierson 1,085 .... E2
32808 Pine Hills 35,771 .... E3
33565 Pinellas Park 32,811 .... B3
33317 Plantation 48,653 .... B4
33566 Plant City 17,064 .... D3
33868 Polk City 576 .... E3
32081 Pomona Park 791 .... E2
*33060 Pompano Beach 52,618 .... F5
32455 Ponce de Leon 454 .... C6
†32019 Ponce Inlet 1,003 .... F2
33952 Port Charlotte 25,770 .... D5
32019 Port Orange 18,756 .... F2
33568 Port Richey 2,165 .... D3
32456 Port Saint Joe 4,027 .... D6
33452 Port Saint Lucie 14,690 ..... F4
33492 Port Salerno 4,511 .... F4
33032 Princeton 10,381 .... F6
*33950 Punta Gorda⊙ 6,797 .... E5
32351 Quincy⊙ 8,591 .... B1
32083 Raiford 259 .... D1
32686 Reddick 657 .... D2
33708 Redington Beach 1,708 ..... B3
†33708 Redington Shores 2,142 .... B3
†33158 Richmond Heights 8,577 ... F6
†33301 Riverland 5,919 .... B4
33404 Riviera Beach 26,489 .... G5
32955 Rockledge 11,877 .... F3
32957 Roseland 1,607 .... F4
33570 Ruskin 5,117 .... C3
33572 Safety Harbor 6,461 .... B2
32084 Saint Augustine⊙ 11,985 .. E2
32084 Saint Augustine Beach 1,289 .... E2
32769 Saint Cloud 7,840 .... E3
33956 Saint James City 1,298 ..... D5
33574 Saint Leo 917 .... D3
33452 Saint Lucie 593 .... F4
32355 Saint Marks 286 .... B1
*33701 Saint Petersburg 238,647 .. B3
33736 Saint Petersburg Beach 9,354 .... B3
†33508 Samoset 5,747 .... D4
†32069 Samsula 1,971 .... E2
33576 San Antonio 529 .... D3
32771 Sanford⊙ 23,176 .... E3
33957 Sanibel 3,363 .... D5
*33577 Sarasota⊙ 48,868 .... D4
Sarasota‡ 202,251 .... D4
†33577 Sarasota Springs 13,860 ... D4
32935 Satellite Beach 9,163 .... F3
32775 Scottsmoor 900 .... F3
†33301 Sea Ranch Lakes 584 .... C3
32958 Sebastian 2,831 .... F4
33870 Sebring⊙ 8,736 .... E4
33584 Seffner 6,493 .... D4
33542 Seminole 4,586 .... B3
†33457 Sewalls Point 1,187 .... F4
32579 Shalimar 390 .... C6
32959 Sharpes 4,149 .... F3
32688 Silver Springs 1,082 .... D2
32460 Sneads 1,690 .... B1
32358 Sopchoppy 444 .... B1
33493 South Bay 3,886 .... F5
32021 South Daytona 11,252 ...... F2
33143 South Miami 10,944 .... B5
†33157 South Miami Heights 23,559 .... F6
33707 South Pasadena 4,188 ...... B3
†32901 South Patrick Shores 9,816 .... F3
†32401 Southport 1,992 .... C6
33452 South Port Saint Lucie (Port Saint Lucie 14,690 ...... F4
33595 South Venice 8,075 .... D4
32690 Sparr 902 .... D2
32401 Springfield 7,220 .... D6
32091 Starke⊙ 5,306 .... D2
33494 Stuart⊙ 9,467 .... F4
33586 Sun City D4
†33570 Sun City Center 5,605 ...... C3
†33450 Sunland Gardens F4
33160 Sunny Isles 12,564 .... C4
33313 Sunrise 39,681 .... B4
33154 Surfside 3,763 .... B4
32692 Suwannee (Fanning Sprs.) 314 .... C2
†33144 Sweetwater 8,251 .... B5
†32043 Switzerland 3,906 .... E1
32809 Taft 900 .... E3
*32301 Tallahassee (cap.)⊙ 81,548 .... B1
Tallahassee‡ 159,542 .... B1
†33321 Tamarac 29,376 .... B3
*33601 Tampa⊙ 271,523 .... C2
Tampa-Saint Petersburg‡ 1,569,492 .. C2
*33589 Tarpon Springs 13,251 ..... D3
32778 Tavares⊙ 4,103 .... E3
33070 Tavernier 1,834 .... F6
33617 Temple Terrace 11,097 ..... C2
33458 Tequesta 3,685 .... F5
33905 Tice 6,645 .... E5
32780 Titusville⊙ 31,910 .... F3
33740 Treasure Island 6,316 ...... B3
32693 Trenton⊙ 1,131 .... D2
32784 Umatilla 1,872 .... E3
33620 University 24,514 .... C2
32580 Valparaiso 6,142 .... C6
*33595 Venice 12,153 .... D4
32462 Vernon 885 .... C6
32960 Vero Beach⊙ 16,176 .... F4
†33166 Virginia Gardens 2,098 ..... B5
32970 Wabasso 2,157 .... F4
†32327 Wakulla 225 .... B1
32694 Waldo 993 .... D2
†32456 Ward Ridge 104 .... D6
32507 Warrington 15,792 .... B6
†32055 Watertown 3,804 .... D1
33873 Wauchula⊙ 2,986 .... E4
32463 Wausau 347 .... D6
33877 Waverly 1,208 .... E4
33597 Webster 856 .... D3
†33512 Weeki Wachee 8 .... D3
32093 Welaka 492 .... E2
32935 West Eau Gallie 2,591 ...... F3
†32901 West Melbourne 5,078 ..... F3
†33101 West Miami 6,076 .... B5
*33401 West Palm Beach⊙ 63,305 F5
West Palm Beach-Boca Raton‡ 573,125 .... F5
†32502 West Pensacola 24,371 ..... B6
32464 Westville 343 .... C6
†33165 Westwood Lakes 11,478 .... B5
32465 Wewahitchka⊙ 1,742 .... D6
†32465 White City 4,110 .... F4
32096 White Springs 781 .... D1
32785 Wildwood 2,665 .... D3
32696 Williston 2,240 .... D2
33334 Wilton Manors 12,742 ...... B3
33598 Wimauma 1,477 .... D4
32786 Windermere 1,302 .... E3
33880 Winter Haven 21,119 .... E3
*32789 Winter Park 22,339 .... E3
†32801 Winter Springs 10,475 ..... E3
32362 Woodville 1,768 .... B1
32697 Worthington Springs 220 .. D2
32698 Yankeetown 600 .... D2
32097 Yulee 3,168 .... E1
32798 Zellwood 1,760 .... E3
33599 Zephyrhills 5,742 .... D3
33890 Zolfo Springs 1,495 .... E4

OTHER FEATURES

Alapaha (riv.) C1
Alligator (lake) E3
Amelia (isl.) E1
Anastasia (isl.) E2
Anclote (keys) D3
Apalachee (bay) B2
Apalachicola (bay) B2
Apalachicola (riv.) A1
Apopka (lake) E3
Arbuckle (lake) E4
Aucilla (riv.) C1
Banana (riv.) F3
Beresford (lake) E3
Big Cypress (swamp) E5
Big Cypress Nat'l Preserve E5
Biscayne (bay) F6
Biscayne (key) B5
Biscayne Nat'l Park F6
Blackwater (riv.) B6
Blue Cypress (lake) F4
Boca Chica (key) E7
Boca Ciega (bay) B3
Boca Grande (key) D7
Bryant (lake) E2
Caloosahatchee (riv.) E5
Captiva (isl.) D5
Casey (key) D4
Castillo de San Marcos Nat'l Mon. E2
Cecil Field Naval Air Sta. E1
Charlotte (harb.) D5
Chattahoochee (riv.) B1
Chipola (riv.) D6
Choctawhatchee (riv.) C6
Crescent (lake) E2
Cumberland Island Nat'l Seashore E1
Cypress (lake) E4
De Soto Nat'l Mem. D4
Dead (lake) D6
Dexter (lake) E2
Dog (isl.) B2
Dorr (lake) E2
Dry Tortugas (keys) D7
Dumfoundling (bay) C4
East (pt.) E6
Eglin A.F.B. 7,574 .... C6
Egmont (key) D4
Elliott (key) F6
Escambia (riv.) B6
Estero (isl.) E5
Eureka (res.) E2
Everglades, The (swamp) F6
Everglades Nat'l Park F6
Fenholloway (riv.) C1
Florida (bay) F6
Florida (cape) F6
Florida (keys) E7
Florida (strs) F7
Fort Caroline Nat'l Mem. E1
Fort Jefferson Nat'l Mon. C7
Fort Matanzas Nat'l Mon. E2
Gasparilla (isl.) D5
George (lake) E2
Grassy (key) F7
Gulf Island Nat'l Seashore B6
Harney (lake) F3
Hart (lake) E3
Hillsborough (bay) C3
Hillsborough (canal) F5
Hillsborough (riv.) C2
Homosassa (isls.) D3
Homestead A.F.B. 7,594 .... F6
Iamonia (lake) B1
Indian (riv.) F3
Iron (mt.) E4
Istokpoga (lake) E4
Jackson (lake) B1
Jackson (lake) E4
Jacksonville Naval Air Sta. E1
John F. Kennedy Space Center F3
June in Winter (lake) E4
Kennedy (Canaveral) (cape) F3
Kerr (lake) E2
Key Largo (key) F6
Key Vaca (key) E7
Key West Naval Air Sta. E7
Kissimmee (lake) E4
Kissimmee (riv.) E4
Largo (key) F6
Levy (lake) D2
Lochloosa (lake) D2
Long (key) B3
Long (key) F7
Longboat (key) D4
Lower Matecumbe (key) F7
Lowery (lake) E3
MacDill A.F.B. C3
Manatee (riv.) D4
Marco (isl.) E6
Marian (lake) E4
Marquesas (keys) D7
Matanzas (inlet) E2
Mayport Naval Air Sta. E1
McCoy A.F.B. E3
Merritt (isl.) F3
Mexico (gulf) C4
Miami (canal) F5
Miami (riv.) B5
Miccosukee (lake) B1
Monroe (lake) E3
Mosquito (lag.) F3
Mullet (key) D4
Myakka (riv.) D4
Nassau (riv.) E1
Nassau (sound) E1
New (riv.) B1
New (riv.) D1
Newnans (lake) D2
North Merritt (isl.) F3
North New River (canal) F5
Ochlockonee (riv.) B1
Okaloacoochee Slough (swamp) ... E5
Okeechobee (lake) F5
Okefenokee (swamp) D1
Oklawaha (riv.) E2
Old Rhodes (key) F6
Old Tampa (bay) B3
Olustee (riv.) D1
Orange (lake) D2
Patrick A.F.B. 2,843 .... F3
Peace (riv.) E4
Pensacola (bay) B6
Pensacola Naval Air Sta. B6
Perdido (riv.) B6
Pine (isl.) D5
Pine Island (sound) D5
Pine Log (creek) C6
Pinellas (pt.) C3
Piney (isl.) B1
Piney (pt.) C2
Placid (lake) E4
Plantation (key) F7
Poinsett (lake) F3
Ponce de Leon (bay) E6
Port Everglades (harb.) C4
Port Tampa (harb.) B3
Reedy (lake) E4
Romano (cape) E6
Sable (cape) E6
Saint Andrew (pt.) D6
Saint George (cape) A2
Saint George (isl.) B2
Saint George (sound) B2
Saint Johns (riv.) E2
Saint Joseph (bay) D6
Saint Joseph (pt.) D6
Saint Lucie (canal) F4
Saint Lucie (inlet) F4
Saint Marys (riv.) D1
Saint Marys Entrance (inlet) E1
Saint Vincent (isl.) D7
San Blas (cape) D7
Sand (key) B3
Sands (key) F6
Sanibel (isl.) D5
Santa Fe (lake) D2
Santa Fe (riv.) D2
Santa Rosa (isl.) B6
Santa Rosa (sound) B6
Sarasota (pt.) D4
Seminole (lake) B1
Seminole Ind. Res. E4
Seminole Ind. Res. F5
Shark (pt.) E6
Shoal (riv.) C6
Snake Creek (canal) B4
South New River (canal) F5
Stafford (lake) D2
Sugarloaf (key) E7
Suwannee (riv.) C2
Suwannee (sound) C2
Talbot (isl.) E1
Talquin (lake) B1
Tamiami (canal) E6
Tampa (bay) D4
Ten Thousand (isls.) E6
Torch (key) E7
Treasure (isl.) B3
Tsala Apopka (lake) D3
Tyndall A.F.B. 4,542 .... C6
Upper Matecumbe (key) F7
Vaca (key) E7
Virginia (key) B5
Waccasassa (bay) D2
Waccasassa (riv.) D2
Washington (lake) F3
Weir (lake) E2
Weohyakapka (lake) E4
West Palm Beach (canal) F5
Whitewater (bay) F6
Whiting Field Naval Air Sta. B6
Wimico (lake) A2
Winder (lake) F3
Withlacoochee (riv.) C1
Withlacoochee (riv.) D2
Yale (lake) E3
Yellow (riv.) B6

⊙County seat.
‡Population of metropolitan area.
† Zip of nearest p.o. * Multiple zips.

Agriculture, Industry and Resources

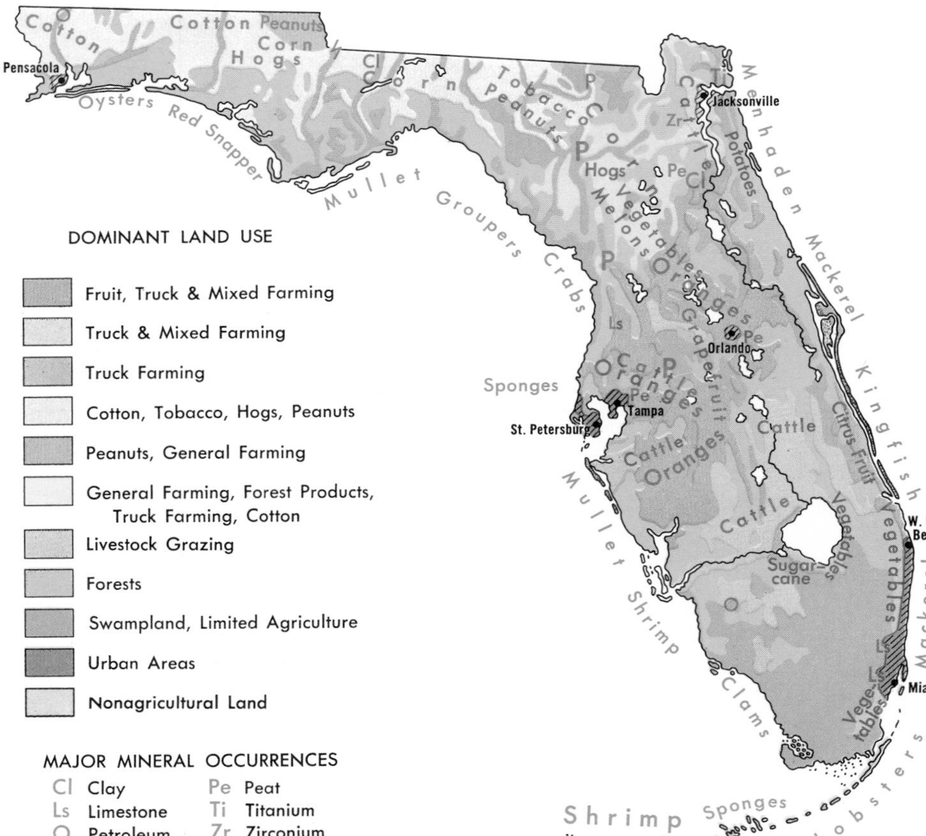
Cotton
Cotton Peanuts
Corn
Hogs
Pensacola
Oysters
Red Snapper
Mullet
Groupers
Crabs
Tobacco
Corn
Peanuts
Cattle
Potatoes
Jacksonville
Hogs
Melons
Vegetables
Oranges
Grapefruit
Menhaden
Mackerel
Orlando
Sponges
Tampa
St. Petersburg
Cattle
Oranges
Cattle
Citrus Fruit
Kingfish
Mullet
Vegetables
W. Palm Beach
Sugar-cane
Shrimp
Clams
Mackerel
Miami
Vegetables
Shrimp
Sponges
Lobsters
DOMINANT LAND USE
Fruit, Truck & Mixed Farming
Truck & Mixed Farming
Truck Farming
Cotton, Tobacco, Hogs, Peanuts
Peanuts, General Farming
General Farming, Forest Products, Truck Farming, Cotton
Livestock Grazing
Forests
Swampland, Limited Agriculture
Urban Areas
Nonagricultural Land
MAJOR MINERAL OCCURRENCES
Cl Clay
Ls Limestone
O Petroleum
P Phosphates
Pe Peat
Ti Titanium
Zr Zirconium
Water Power
Major Industrial Areas

AREA 58,910 sq. mi. (152,577 sq. km.)
POPULATION 5,463,105
CAPITAL Atlanta
LARGEST CITY Atlanta
HIGHEST POINT Brasstown Bald 4,784 ft.
   (1458 m.)
SETTLED IN 1733
ADMITTED TO UNION January 2, 1788
POPULAR NAME Empire State of the South;
   Peach State
STATE FLOWER Cherokee Rose
STATE BIRD Brown Thrasher

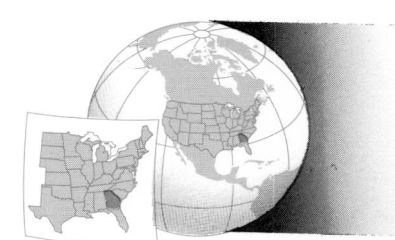

COUNTIES

County	Pop.	Key
Appling	15,565	H7
Atkinson	6,141	G8
Bacon	9,379	G7
Baker	3,808	D8
Baldwin	34,686	F4
Banks	8,702	E2
Barrow	21,293	E2
Bartow	40,760	C2
Ben Hill	16,000	F7
Berrien	13,525	F8
Bibb	151,085	E5
Bleckley	10,767	F6
Brantley	8,701	J8
Brooks	15,255	E9
Bryan	10,175	K6
Bulloch	35,785	J6
Burke	19,349	J4
Butts	13,665	E4
Calhoun	5,717	C7
Camden	13,371	J9
Candler	7,518	H6
Carroll	56,346	B3
Catoosa	36,991	B1
Charlton	7,343	H9
Chatham	202,226	K6
Chattahoochee	21,732	C6
Chattooga	21,956	B1
Cherokee	51,699	D2
Clarke	74,498	F3
Clay	3,553	B7
Clayton	150,357	D3
Clinch	6,660	G9
Cobb	297,694	C3
Coffee	26,894	G8
Colquitt	35,376	E8
Columbia	40,118	H3
Cook	13,490	F8
Coweta	39,268	C4
Crawford	7,684	E5
Crisp	19,489	E7
Dade	12,318	A1
Dawson	4,774	D2
Decatur	25,495	C9
De Kalb	483,024	D3
Dodge	16,955	F6
Dooly	10,826	E6
Dougherty	100,978	D7
Douglas	54,573	C3
Early	13,158	C8
Echols	2,297	G9
Effingham	18,327	K6
Elbert	18,758	G2
Emanuel	20,795	H5
Evans	8,428	J6
Fannin	14,748	D1
Fayette	29,043	C4
Floyd	79,800	B2
Forsyth	27,958	D2
Franklin	15,185	F2
Fulton	589,904	D3
Gilmer	11,110	D1
Glascock	2,382	G4
Glynn	54,981	J8
Gordon	30,070	C2
Grady	19,845	D9
Greene	11,391	F3
Gwinnett	166,903	D2
Habersham	25,020	E1
Hall	75,649	E2
Hancock	9,466	G4
Haralson	18,422	B3
Harris	15,464	C5
Hart	18,585	G2
Heard	6,520	B4
Henry	36,309	D4
Houston	77,605	E6
Irwin	8,988	F7
Jackson	25,343	E2
Jasper	7,553	E4
Jeff Davis	11,473	G7
Jefferson	18,403	H4
Jenkins	8,841	J5
Johnson	8,660	G5
Jones	16,579	E5
Lamar	12,215	D4
Lanier	5,654	F8
Laurens	36,990	G6
Lee	11,684	D7
Liberty	37,583	J7
Lincoln	6,949	H3
Long	4,524	J7
Lowndes	67,972	F9
Lumpkin	10,762	D1
Macon	14,003	D6
Madison	17,747	F2
Marion	5,297	C6
McDuffie	18,546	H4
McIntosh	8,046	K7
Meriwether	21,229	C4
Miller	7,038	C8
Mitchell	21,114	D8
Monroe	14,610	E4
Montgomery	7,011	G6
Morgan	11,572	F3
Murray	19,685	C1
Muscogee	170,108	C6
Newton	34,489	E3
Oconee	12,427	F3
Oglethorpe	8,929	F3
Paulding	26,042	C3
Peach	19,151	E5
Pickens	11,652	D2
Pierce	11,897	H8
Pike	8,937	D4
Polk	32,386	B3
Pulaski	8,950	E6
Putnam	10,295	F4
Quitman	2,357	B7
Rabun	10,466	F1
Randolph	9,599	C7
Richmond	181,629	H4
Rockdale	36,747	D3
Schley	3,433	D6
Screven	14,043	J5
Seminole	9,057	C9
Spalding	47,899	D4
Stephens	21,763	F1
Stewart	5,896	C6
Sumter	29,360	D6
Talbot	6,536	C5
Taliaferro	2,032	G3
Tattnall	18,134	J6
Taylor	7,902	D5
Telfair	11,445	G7
Terrell	12,017	D7
Thomas	38,098	E9
Tift	32,862	E7
Toombs	22,592	H6
Towns	5,638	E1
Treutlen	6,087	G6
Troup	50,003	B4
Turner	9,510	E7
Twiggs	9,354	F5
Union	9,390	E1
Upson	25,998	D5
Walker	56,470	B1
Walton	31,211	E3
Ware	37,180	H8
Warren	6,583	G4
Washington	18,842	G4
Wayne	20,750	J7
Webster	2,341	C6
Wheeler	5,155	G6
White	10,120	E1
Whitfield	65,780	B1
Wilcox	7,682	F7
Wilkes	10,951	G3
Wilkinson	10,368	F5
Worth	18,064	E8

CITIES and TOWNS

Zip	Name/Pop.	Key
31001	Abbeville⊙ 985	F7
30101	Acworth 3,648	C2
30103	Adairsville 1,739	C2
31620	Adel⊙ 5,592	F8
31002	Adrian 756	G5
30410	Ailey 579	G6
30411	Alamo⊙ 993	G6
31622	Alapaha 771	F8
*31701	Albany⊙ 74,550	D7
	Albany‡ 112,456	D7
†30204	Aldora 139	D4
31301	Allenhurst 606	J7
31003	Allentown 321	F5
31510	Alma⊙ 3,819	G7
30201	Alpharetta 3,128	D2
30412	Alston 111	H6
30510	Alto 618	E2
†30161	Alto Park	B2
31512	Ambrose 360	G7
31709	Americus⊙ 16,120	D6
31711	Andersonville 267	D6
30802	Appling⊙ 150	H3
31712	Arabi 376	E7
30104	Aragon 855	B2
†30549	Arcade 223	E2
†31520	Arco	J8
31623	Argyle 206	G8
31713	Arlington 1,572	C8
30619	Arnoldsville 187	F3
31714	Ashburn⊙ 4,766	E7
*30601	Athens⊙ 42,549	F3
	Athens‡ 130,015	F3
*30301	Atlanta (cap.)⊙ 425,022	K1
	Atlanta‡ 2,029,618	K1
31715	Attapulgus 623	D9
30203	Auburn 692	E2
*30901	Augusta⊙ 47,532	J4
	Augusta‡ 327,372	J4
30001	Austell 3,939	J1
†30557	Avalon 200	F1
30803	Avera 248	G4
30002	Avondale Estates 1,313	L1
31716	Baconton 763	D8
31717	Bainbridge⊙ 10,553	C9
30511	Baldwin 1,080	E2
30107	Ball Ground 640	D2
30204	Barnesville⊙ 4,887	D4
31625	Barney 146	E8
30413	Bartow 357	G5
31720	Barwick 413	E9
31513	Baxley⊙ 3,586	H7
†31554	Beach	G8
30414	Bellville 173	H6
31721	Benevolence 138	C7
†30136	Berkeley Lake 503	D3
31722	Berlin 538	E8
30620	Bethlehem 281	E3
†31901	Bibb City 667	B5
30621	Bishop 172	F3
31516	Blackshear⊙ 3,222	H8
30512	Blairsville⊙ 530	E1
31723	Blakely⊙ 5,880	C8
31302	Bloomingdale 1,855	K6
30513	Blue Ridge⊙ 1,376	D1
31724	Bluffton 132	C7
30805	Blythe 367	H4
30622	Bogart 819	E3
31626	Boston 1,424	E9
30623	Bostwick 357	E3
30108	Bowdon 1,743	B3
30516	Bowersville 318	G2
30624	Bowman 890	G2
30517	Braselton 308	E2
†30153	Braswell 282	C3
30110	Bremen 3,966	B3
31725	Brinson 274	C9
31726	Bronwood 524	D7
30415	Brooklet 1,035	J6
30205	Brooks 199	D4
31519	Broxton 1,117	G7
31520	Brunswick⊙ 17,605	K8
30113	Buchanan⊙ 1,019	B3
30625	Buckhead 219	F3
31803	Buena Vista⊙ 1,544	C6
30518	Buford 6,578	D2
31006	Butler⊙ 1,959	D5
31007	Byromville 567	E6
31008	Byron 1,661	E5
31009	Cadwell 353	G6
31728	Cairo⊙ 8,777	D9
30701	Calhoun⊙ 5,335	C1
30807	Camak 283	G4
31730	Camilla⊙ 5,414	D8
30520	Canon 704	F2
30114	Canton⊙ 3,601	C2
30203	Carl 239	E3
30627	Carlton 291	F2
30521	Carnesville⊙ 465	F2
30117	Carrollton⊙ 14,078	C3
30120	Cartersville⊙ 9,247	C2
30124	Cave Spring 883	B2
31627	Cecil 280	F8
30125	Cedartown⊙ 8,619	B2
†30601	Center 330	F2
31028	Centerville 2,622	E5
†30217	Centralhatchee 240	B4
†31816	Chalybeate Springs 265	C5
30341	Chamblee 7,137	K1
30705	Chatsworth⊙ 2,493	C1
31011	Chauncey 350	F6
31012	Chester 409	F6
30707	Chickamauga 2,232	B1
30523	Clarkesville⊙ 1,348	F1
30021	Clarkston 4,539	L1
30417	Claxton⊙ 2,694	J6
30525	Clayton⊙ 1,838	F1
30527	Clermont 300	E2
30528	Cleveland⊙ 1,578	E1
31734	Climax 407	D9
31735	Cobb	E7
30420	Cobbtown 494	H6
31014	Cochran⊙ 5,121	F6
30710	Cohutta 407	C1
30628	Colbert 498	F2
31736	Coleman 164	C7
30337	College Park 24,632	K2
30421	Collins 639	H6
31737	Colquitt⊙ 2,065	C8
*31901	Columbus⊙ 169,441	C6
	Columbus‡ 239,196	C6
30629	Comer 930	F2
30529	Commerce 4,092	E2
30206	Concord 317	D4
30209	Covington⊙ 10,586	E3
30711	Crandall	C1
30630	Crawford 498	F3
30631	Crawfordville⊙ 594	G3
†31771	Crosland	E8
31016	Culloden 281	D5
30130	Cumming⊙ 2,094	D2
31805	Cusseta⊙ 1,218	C6
31740	Cuthbert⊙ 4,340	C7
30211	Dacula 1,577	E3
30533	Dahlonega⊙ 2,844	D1
30423	Daisy 174	J6
30132	Dallas⊙ 2,440	C3
30720	Dalton⊙ 20,743	C1
31741	Damascus 403	C8
30633	Danielsville⊙ 354	F2
31017	Danville 529	F5
31305	Darien⊙ 1,731	K8
31601	Dasher 659	F9
31018	Davisboro 433	G5
31742	Dawson⊙ 5,699	D7
30534	Dawsonville⊙ 342	D2
30808	Dearing 539	H4
*30030	Decatur⊙ 18,404	K1
31501	Deenwood	H8
31082	Deepstep 120	G4
30535	Demorest 1,130	F1
31532	Denton 286	G7
31743	De Soto 248	D7
31019	Dexter 527	G6
30537	Dillard 238	F1
31629	Dixie 259	E9
†31520	Dock Junction (Arco)	J8
31744	Doerun 1,062	E8
31745	Donalsonville⊙ 3,320	C8
30340	Doraville 7,414	K1
31533	Douglas⊙ 10,980	G7
*30133	Douglasville⊙ 7,641	C3
31021	Dublin⊙ 16,083	G5
31022	Dudley 425	F5
30136	Duluth 2,956	D2
31630	Du Pont 267	G9
†31830	Durand 206	C5
31021	East Dublin 2,916	G5
30539	East Ellijay 469	C1

(continued on following page)

Agriculture, Industry and Resources

DOMINANT LAND USE

- Specialized Cotton
- Cotton, General Farming
- Cotton, Tobacco, Hogs, Peanuts
- Peanuts, General Farming
- General Farming, Livestock, Fruit, Tobacco
- General Farming, Forest Products, Cotton, Truck Farming
- Forests
- Swampland, Limited Agriculture
- Urban Areas

MAJOR MINERAL OCCURRENCES

- Al Bauxite
- Ba Barite
- C Coal
- Cl Clay
- Fe Iron Ore
- Gn Granite
- Mi Mica
- Mn Manganese
- Mr Marble
- Sl Slate
- Tc Talc
- Ti Titanium

⚡ Water Power
▨ Major Industrial Areas

†31046 East Juliette E4
31023 Eastman⊙ 5,330 .... F6
†30263 East Newnan C4
30344 East Point 37,486 .... K2
†30677 Eastville E3
31024 Eatonton⊙ 4,833 .... F4
31307 Eden 990 .... K6
31746 Edison 1,128 .... C7
30635 Elberton⊙ 5,686 .... G2
31806 Ellaville⊙ 1,684 .... D6
31747 Ellenton 277 .... E8
31807 Ellerslie 700 .... C5
30540 Ellijay⊙ 1,507 .... C1
30137 Emerson 1,110 .... C2
31749 Enigma 574 .... F8
†30217 Ephesus 184 .... B4
30724 Eton 301 .... C1
†30120 Euharlee 477 .... C2
30809 Evans H3
30212 Experiment D4
30213 Fairburn 3,466 .... J2
30139 Fairmount 842 .... C2
30214 Fayetteville⊙ 2,715 .... C4
†31071 Finleyson 101 .... F6
31750 Fitzgerald⊙ 10,187 .... F7
†31313 Flemington 440 .... K7
30216 Flovilla 458 .... E4
30542 Flowery Branch 755 .... E2
31537 Folkston⊙ 2,243 .... H9
30050 Forest Park 18,782 .... K2
31029 Forsyth⊙ 4,624 .... E4
31751 Fort Gaines⊙ 1,260 .... C7
30742 Fort Oglethorpe 5,443 .... B1
31030 Fort Valley⊙ 9,000 .... E5
30217 Franklin⊙ 711 .... B4
30639 Franklin Springs 797 .... F2
31753 Funston 337 .... E8
30501 Gainesville⊙ 15,280 .... E2
31408 Garden City 6,895 .... K6
30425 Garfield 222 .... H5
30218 Gay 175 .... C4
31810 Geneva 232 .... C5
31754 Georgetown⊙ 935 .... B7
30810 Gibson⊙ 730 .... G4
30426 Girard 225 .... J4
30427 Glennville 4,144 .... J7
30428 Glenwood 824 .... L1
30641 Good Hope 200 .... E3
31031 Gordon 2,768 .... F5
30220 Grantville 1,110 .... C4
31032 Gray⊙ 2,145 .... F4
30221 Grayson 464 .... E3
30726 Graysville 193 .... B1
30642 Greensboro⊙ 2,985 .... F3
30222 Greenville⊙ 1,213 .... C4
30223 Griffin⊙ 20,728 .... D4
30813 Grovetown 3,491 .... H4
31312 Guyton 749 .... K6
31033 Haddock 800 .... F4
30429 Hagan 880 .... J6

31632 Hahira 1,534 .... F9
31811 Hamilton⊙ 506 .... C5
30228 Hampton 2,059 .... D4
30354 Hapeville 6,166 .... K2
30229 Haralson 123 .... C4
31034 Hardwick F4
30814 Harlem 1,485 .... H4
31035 Harrison 456 .... G5
30643 Hartwell⊙ 4,855 .... G2
31036 Hawkinsville⊙ 4,372 .... E6
31539 Hazlehurst⊙ 4,249 .... G7
30545 Helen 265 .... E1
31037 Helena 1,390 .... G6
30815 Hephzibah 1,452 .... H4
30546 Hiawassee⊙ 491 .... E1
†30410 Higgston 152 .... G6
30467 Hilltonia 515 .... J5
31313 Hinesville⊙ 11,309 .... J7
30141 Hiram 711 .... C3
31542 Hoboken 514 .... H8
30230 Hogansville 3,362 .... C4
30142 Holly Springs 687 .... D2
†31537 Homeland 683 .... H9
30547 Homer⊙ 734 .... F2
31634 Homerville⊙ 3,112 .... G8
30548 Hoschton 490 .... E2
30646 Hull 188 .... F2
31041 Ideal 619 .... D6
30647 Ila 287 .... F2
†30705 Industrial City 1,054 .... C1
31759 Iron City 367 .... C8
31042 Irwinton⊙ 841 .... F5
†31031 Ivey 455 .... F5
30233 Jackson⊙ 4,133 .... E4
31544 Jacksonville 206 .... G7
31761 Jakin 194 .... C8
30143 Jasper⊙ 1,556 .... D2
30549 Jefferson⊙ 1,820 .... F2
31044 Jeffersonville⊙ 1,473 .... F5
30234 Jenkinsburg 360 .... E4
30235 Jersey 201 .... E3
31545 Jesup⊙ 9,418 .... J7
30236 Jonesboro⊙ 4,132 .... D4
31812 Junction City 254 .... C5
30144 Kennesaw 5,095 .... C2
31548 Kingsland 2,008 .... J9
30145 Kingston 733 .... C2
31049 Kite 328 .... G5
31050 Knoxville⊙ 75 .... E5
30728 La Fayette⊙ 6,517 .... B1
30240 La Grange⊙ 24,204 .... B4
30252 Lake 2,963 .... D3
31635 Lakeland⊙ 2,647 .... F8
31636 Lake Park 448 .... F9
30553 Lavonia 2,024 .... F2
30245 Lawrenceville⊙ 8,928 .... D3
31762 Leary 783 .... C8
30146 Lebanon 800 .... D2
31763 Leesburg⊙ 1,301 .... D7
31637 Lenox 965 .... F8

31764 Leslie 470 .... D7
30648 Lexington⊙ 278 .... F3
30247 Lilburn 3,765 .... D3
31051 Lilly 202 .... E6
†30286 Lincoln Park D5
30817 Lincolnton⊙ 1,406 .... G3
30147 Lindale B2
†30728 Linwood 417 .... B1
30058 Lithonia 2,637 .... D3
30248 Locust Grove 1,479 .... D4
30249 Loganville 1,841 .... E3
30433 Lollie G6
†30230 Lone Oak 119 .... C4
†30741 Lookout Mountain 1,505 ... B1
30434 Louisville⊙ 2,823 .... H4
30250 Lovejoy 205 .... D4
31316 Ludowici⊙ 1,286 .... J7
30554 Lula 857 .... E2
31549 Lumber City 1,426 .... G7
31815 Lumpkin⊙ 1,335 .... C6
30251 Luthersville 597 .... C4
30730 Lyerly 482 .... B2
30436 Lyons⊙ 4,203 .... H6
30059 Mableton J1
*31201 Macon⊙ 116,860 .... E5
Macon‡ 254,623 .... E5
30650 Madison⊙ 2,954 .... F3
30438 Manassas 116 .... H6
31816 Manchester 4,796 .... C5
30255 Mansfield 425 .... E4
*30060 Marietta⊙ 30,805 .... J1
31057 Marshallville 1,540 .... D6
30557 Martin 305 .... F2
30671 Maxeys 205 .... F3
30558 Maysville 619 .... E2
30555 McCaysville 1,219 .... D1
30253 McDonough⊙ 2,778 .... D4
31054 McIntyre 386 .... F5
31055 McRae⊙ 3,409 .... G6
30256 Meansville 303 .... D4
30040 Mechanicsville L1
31765 Meigs 1,231 .... D8
30731 Menlo 611 .... B2
†31792 Metcalf E9
30439 Metter⊙ 3,531 .... H6
30441 Midville 670 .... H5
31320 Midway 457 .... K7
31060 Milan 1,115 .... G6
31061 Milledgeville⊙ 12,176 .... F4
30442 Millen⊙ 3,988 .... J5
30257 Milner 320 .... D4
30207 Milstead D3
30559 Mineral Bluff 130 .... D1
30820 Mitchell 214 .... G4
30258 Molena 379 .... D4
30655 Monroe⊙ 8,854 .... E3
31063 Montezuma 4,830 .... E6
31064 Monticello⊙ 2,382 .... E4
31065 Montrose 170 .... F5
30259 Moreland 358 .... C4

31766 Morgan⊙ 364 .... C7
30560 Morganton 263 .... D1
30260 Morrow 3,791 .... K2
31638 Morven 471 .... E9
31768 Moultrie⊙ 15,708 .... E8
30562 Mountain City 701 .... F1
†30075 Mountain Park 378 .... D2
30563 Mount Airy 670 .... F1
30149 Mount Berry B2
30445 Mount Vernon⊙ 1,737 .... G6
30261 Mountville 168 .... C4
30150 Mount Zion 445 .... B3
31553 Nahunta⊙ 951 .... H8
31639 Nashville⊙ 4,831 .... F8
31641 Naylor 228 .... F9
30151 Nelson 562 .... D2
30262 Newborn 391 .... E3
30446 Newington 402 .... J5
30263 Newnan⊙ 11,449 .... C4
31770 Newton⊙ 711 .... D8
31554 Nicholls 1,114 .... G7
30565 Nicholson 491 .... F2
*30071 Norcross 3,317 .... D3
31771 Norman Park 757 .... E8
†30645 North High Shoals 256 .... F3
30821 Norwood 306 .... G4
30448 Nunez 168 .... H5
31772 Oakfield 113 .... E7
30732 Oakman 150 .... C1
31903 Oak Park 256 .... H6
30566 Oakwood 723 .... E2
31773 Ochlocknee 627 .... E9
31774 Ocilla⊙ 3,436 .... F7
31067 Oconee 306 .... G5
†30222 Odessadale 142 .... C5
31555 Odum 401 .... H7
31406 Oglethorpe⊙ 1,305 .... D6
30449 Oliver 239 .... J5
31821 Omaha 169 .... C6
31775 Omega 996 .... E8
30266 Orchard Hill 162 .... D4
30267 Oxford 1,750 .... E3
30268 Palmetto 2,086 .... C3
31777 Parrott 222 .... D7
31557 Patterson 763 .... H8
31778 Pavo 830 .... E9
†31201 Payne 196 .... E5
30269 Peachtree City 6,429 .... C4
31642 Pearson⊙ 1,827 .... G8
31779 Pelham 4,306 .... D8
31321 Pembroke⊙ 1,400 .... J6
30567 Pendergrass 302 .... E2
31069 Perry⊙ 9,453 .... E6
†31794 Phillipsburg E8
31070 Pinehurst 431 .... E6
30072 Pine Lake 901 .... D3
31822 Pine Mountain 984 .... C5
†31312 Pineora 387 .... K6
†31728 Pine Park D9
31071 Pineview 564 .... F6

31072 Pitts 384 .... E7
31073 Plainfield 128 .... F6
31780 Plains 651 .... D6
30733 Plainville 281 .... C2
31322 Pooler 2,543 .... K6
30450 Portal 694 .... J5
30270 Porterdale 1,451 .... E3
31407 Port Wentworth 3,947 .... K6
31781 Poulan 818 .... E8
30073 Powder Springs 3,381 .... C3
31824 Preston⊙ 429 .... C6
30451 Pulaski 257 .... J6
31643 Quitman⊙ 5,188 .... E9
30734 Ranger 171 .... C2
31645 Ray City 658 .... F8
30660 Rayle 177 .... G3
31783 Rebecca 272 .... E7
30453 Reidsville⊙ 2,296 .... H6
31601 Remerton 443 .... F9
31075 Rentz 337 .... G6
†30518 Rest Haven 231 .... E2
31076 Reynolds 1,298 .... D5
31077 Rhine 590 .... F7
31323 Riceboro 216 .... K7
31825 Richland 1,802 .... C6
31324 Richmond Hill 1,177 .... K7
†31018 Riddleville 154 .... G5
31326 Rincon 1,988 .... K6
30736 Ringgold⊙ 1,821 .... B1
*30274 Riverdale 7,121 .... K2
†31768 Riverside 99 .... E8
†30759 Riverside B2
31078 Roberta 859 .... D5
31079 Rochelle 1,626 .... F7
30153 Rockmart 3,645 .... B2
30455 Rocky Ford 223 .... J5
30161 Rome⊙ 29,654 .... B2
30170 Roopville 229 .... B4
30741 Rossville 3,851 .... B1
*30075 Roswell 23,337 .... D2
30662 Royston 2,404 .... F2
†30680 Russell 378 .... E3
30663 Rutledge 694 .... E3
31558 Saint Marys 3,596 .... J9
31522 Saint Simons Island K8
31784 Sale City 336 .... D8
31082 Sandersville⊙ 6,137 .... G5
†20436 Santa Claus 167 .... H6
30456 Sardis 1,180 .... J5
30275 Sargent 800 .... C4
31785 Sasser 407 .... D7
*31401 Savannah⊙ 141,634 .... L6
Savannah‡ 230,728 .... L6
31083 Scotland 222 .... G6
31095 Scott 139 .... G5
31560 Screven 872 .... H7
30276 Senoia 900 .... C4
31084 Seville 209 .... E7
31085 Shady Dale 155 .... E4
30172 Shannon B2
30664 Sharon 140 .... G3
30277 Sharpsburg 194 .... C4
31786 Shellman 1,254 .... C7
31826 Shiloh 392 .... C5
30665 Siloam 446 .... F3
31787 Smithville 867 .... D7
30080 Smyrna 20,312 .... K1
30278 Snellville 8,514 .... D3
30279 Social Circle 2,591 .... E3
30457 Soperton⊙ 2,981 .... G6
31647 Sparks 1,353 .... F8
31087 Sparta⊙ 1,754 .... F4
31329 Springfield⊙ 1,075 .... K6
†30705 Spring Place 246 .... C1
30823 Stapleton 388 .... H4
31648 Statenville⊙ 700 .... G9
30458 Statesboro⊙ 14,866 .... J6
30666 Statham 1,101 .... E3
30464 Stillmore 527 .... H6
30281 Stockbridge 2,103 .... D3
*30083 Stone Mountain 4,867 .... D3
†30518 Sugar Hill 2,473 .... E2
30746 Sugar Valley C1
30466 Summertown 215 .... H5
30747 Summerville⊙ 4,878 .... B2
31789 Sumner 213 .... E7
30284 Sunny Side 338 .... D4
31563 Surrency 368 .... H7
30174 Suwanee 1,026 .... D2
30401 Swainsboro⊙ 7,602 .... H5
31790 Sycamore 474 .... E7
30467 Sylvania⊙ 3,352 .... J5
31791 Sylvester⊙ 5,860 .... E7
31827 Talbotton⊙ 1,140 .... C5
30176 Tallapoosa 2,647 .... B3
30573 Tallulah Falls 162 .... F1
30575 Talmo E2
30470 Tarrytown 145 .... H6
30178 Taylorsville 266 .... C2
30179 Temple 1,520 .... B3
31089 Tennille 1,709 .... G5
30285 The Rock 78 .... D5
30286 Thomaston⊙ 9,682 .... D5
31792 Thomasville⊙ 18,463 .... E9
30824 Thomson⊙ 7,001 .... H4
†31404 Thunderbolt 2,165 .... K6
31794 Tifton⊙ 13,749 .... F8
30576 Tiger 299 .... F1
30668 Tignall 733 .... G3
30577 Toccoa⊙ 9,104 .... F1
31090 Toomsboro 673 .... F5
30752 Trenton⊙ 1,636 .... A1
30753 Trion 1,732 .... B1
30755 Tunnel Hill 867 .... C1
30289 Turin 260 .... C4
30471 Twin City 1,402 .... H5
31328 Tybee Island 2,240 .... L6
30290 Tyrone 1,038 .... C4
31795 Ty Ty 618 .... E8
31091 Unadilla 1,566 .... E6
30291 Union City 4,780 .... J2
30669 Union Point 1,750 .... F3
†31794 Unionville F8
30473 Uvalda 646 .... H6
31601 Valdosta⊙ 37,596 .... F9
30672 Vanna F2
†30153 Van Wert 303 .... B3

30756 Varnell 288 .... C1
†31401 Vernonburg 178 .... K7
30474 Vidalia 10,393 .... H6
†30830 Vidette H4
31092 Vienna⊙ 2,886 .... E6
30180 Villa Rica 3,420 .... C3
30182 Waco 471 .... B3
30477 Wadley 2,438 .... H5
30183 Waleska 450 .... D2
†30209 Walnut Grove 387 .... E3
31333 Walthourville 905 .... J7
31830 Warm Springs 425 .... C5
31093 Warner Robins 39,893 .... E5
30828 Warrenton⊙ 2,172 .... G4
31796 Warwick 488 .... E7
30673 Washington⊙ 4,662 .... G3
30677 Watkinsville⊙ 1,240 .... E3
31831 Waverly Hall 913 .... C5
31501 Waycross⊙ 19,371 .... H8
30830 Waynesboro⊙ 5,760 .... J4
31832 Weston 109 .... C7
31833 West Point 4,294 .... B5
31797 Whigham 507 .... D9
30184 White 501 .... C2
31568 White Oak 450 .... J8
30678 White Plains 231 .... F4
30185 Whitesburg 775 .... B4
31650 Willacoochee 1,166 .... G8
30292 Williamson 250 .... D4
31410 Wilmington Island L7
30680 Winder⊙ 6,705 .... E3
31406 Windsor Forest K7
30683 Winterville 621 .... F3
31569 Woodbine⊙ 910 .... J9
30293 Woodbury 1,738 .... C5
31836 Woodland 664 .... D5
30188 Woodstock 2,699 .... D2
30670 Woodville 455 .... F3
30833 Wrens 2,415 .... H4
31096 Wrightsville⊙ 2,526 .... G5
31097 Yatesville 390 .... D5
30582 Young Harris 687 .... E1
30295 Zebulon⊙ 995 .... D4

OTHER FEATURES

Alapaha (riv.) F7
Allatoona (lake) C2
Altamaha (riv.) H7
Andersonville Nat'l Hist. Site D6
Atlanta Nav. Air Sta. J1
Banks (lake) F9
Bartletts Ferry (dam) B5
Blackshear (lake) E7
Blue Ridge (mts.) D1
Brasstown Bald (mt.) E1
Burton (lake) E1
Carters (lake) C1
Chattahoochee (riv.) B8
Chattahoochee River Nat'l Rec. Area K1
Chattooga (riv.) A2
Chattooga (riv.) F1
Chatuge (lake) E1
Chickamauga and Chattanooga Nat'l Mil. Park B1
Coosa (riv.) A2
Coosawattee (riv.) C1
Cumberland (isl.) K9
Cumberland Island Nat'l Seashore K9
Dobbins A.F.B. J1
Doboy (sound) K8
Etowah (riv.) C2
Eufaula (Walter F. George Res.) (lake) B7
Flint (riv.) D8
Fort Benning B6
Fort Frederica Nat'l Mon. K8
Fort Gordon H4
Fort McPherson K1
Fort Pulaski Nat'l Mon. L6
Fort Stewart J7
Goat Rock (lake) B5
Harding (lake) B5
Hartwell (lake) G2
Jekyll (isl.) K8
Kennesaw Mtn. Nat'l Battlefield Park J1
Lawson A.A.F. B6
Martin Luther King, Jr., Nat'l Hist. Site K1
Moody A.F.B. F9
Nottely (lake) D1
Ochlockonee (riv.) C10
Ocmulgee (riv.) E5
Ocmulgee Nat'l Mon. E5
Oconee (riv.) F5
Ogeechee (riv.) J5
Okefenokee (swamp) H9
Oliver (lake) B5
Oostanaula (riv.) B2
Ossabaw (sound) K7
Rabun (lake) E1
Robins A.F.B. F5
Saint Andrew (sound) K9
Saint Catherines (isl.) K7
Saint Marys (riv.) J9
Saint Simons (isl.) K8
Sapelo (isl.) K8
Satilla (riv.) G8
Savannah (riv.) K5
Sea (isls.) K9
Seminole (lake) B9
Sidney Lanier (lake) D2
Sinclair (lake) F4
Skidaway (isl.) L7
Springer (mt.) D1
Strom Thurmond (lake) H3
Suwannee (riv.) G10
Tugaloo (riv.) F1
Walter F. George (res.) B7
Wassaw (sound) L7
Weiss (lake) A2
West Point (lake) B4

⊙County seat.
‡Population of metropolitan area.
† Zip of nearest p.o. * Multiple zips.

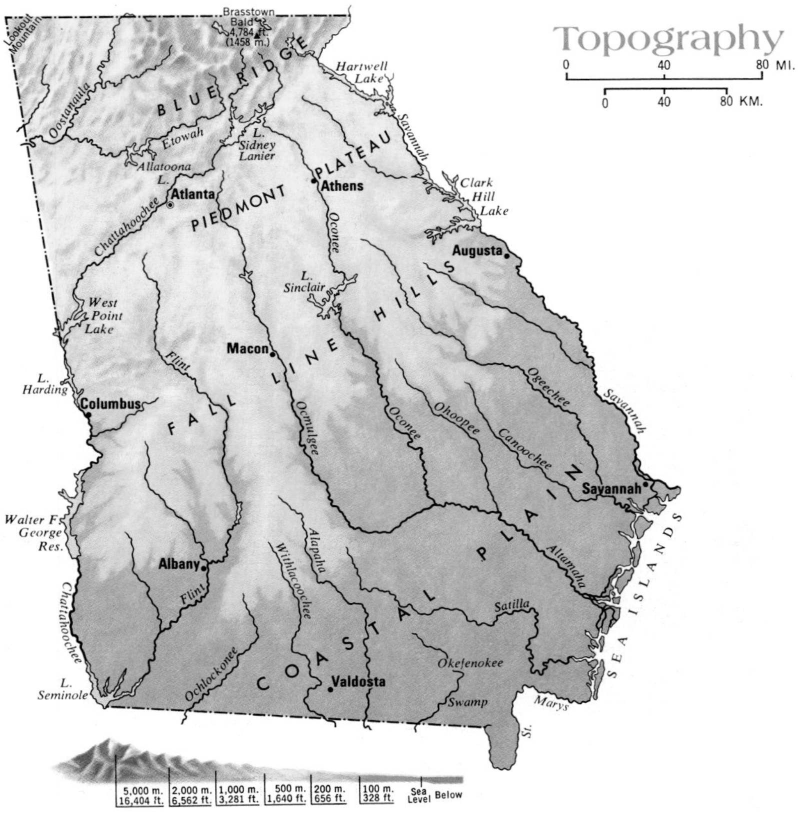

Topography
0 40 80 MI.
0 40 80 KM.
Brasstown Bald 4,784 ft. (1458 m.)
Lookout Mountain
BLUE RIDGE
Hartwell Lake
Oostanaula
Etowah
L. Sidney Lanier
Savannah
Allatoona L.
Atlanta
PIEDMONT
PLATEAU
Athens
Clark Hill Lake
Chattahoochee
Oconee
Augusta
L. Sinclair
HILLS
West Point Lake
Macon
FALL LINE
L. Harding
Columbus
Flint
Ocmulgee
Ogeechee
Ohoopee
Canoochee
Savannah
Walter F. George Res.
Albany
Alapaha
Withlacoochee
COASTAL PLAIN
Altamaha
SEA ISLANDS
Satilla
Okefenokee Swamp
Valdosta
Ochlockonee
L. Seminole
St. Marys
5,000 m. 16,404 ft.
2,000 m. 6,562 ft.
1,000 m. 3,281 ft.
500 m. 1,640 ft.
200 m. 656 ft.
100 m. 328 ft.
Sea Level
Below

Georgia

SCALE
0   5   10   20   30   40 MI.
0 5 10   20   30   40 KM.

State Capitals ⊛
County Seats ◉
Major Limited Access Hwys. ——

Scale 1:2,210,000

© Copyright HAMMOND INCORPORATED, Maplewood, N.J.

Topography

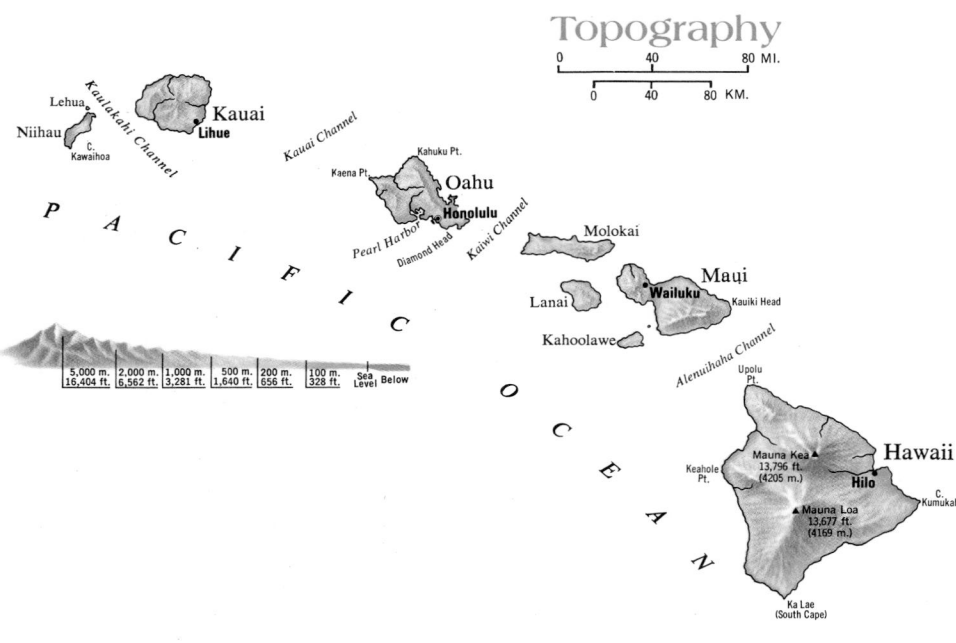

Agriculture, Industry and Resources

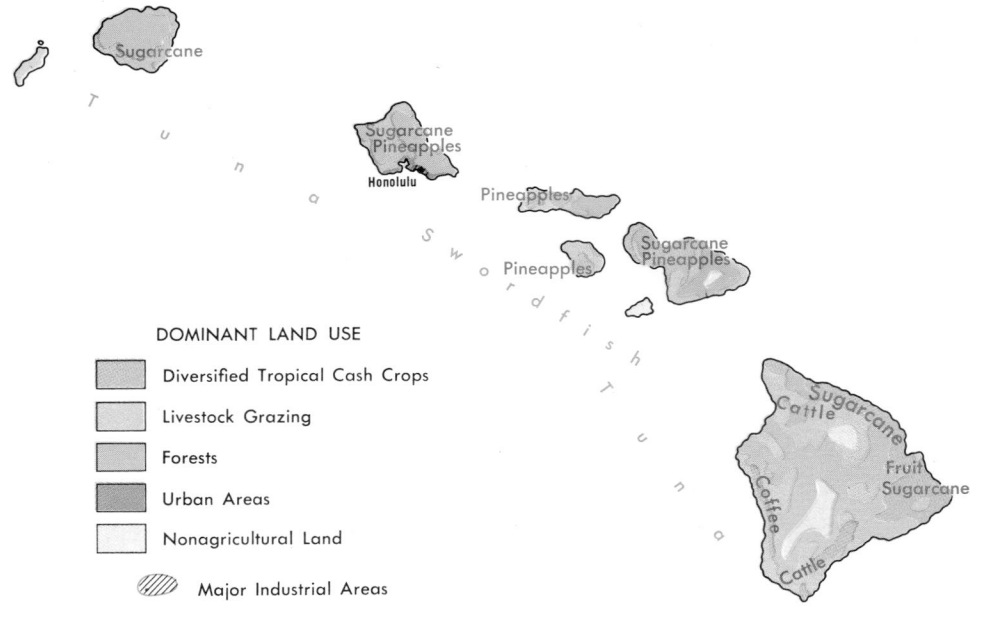

DOMINANT LAND USE

Diversified Tropical Cash Crops

Livestock Grazing

Forests

Urban Areas

Nonagricultural Land

Major Industrial Areas

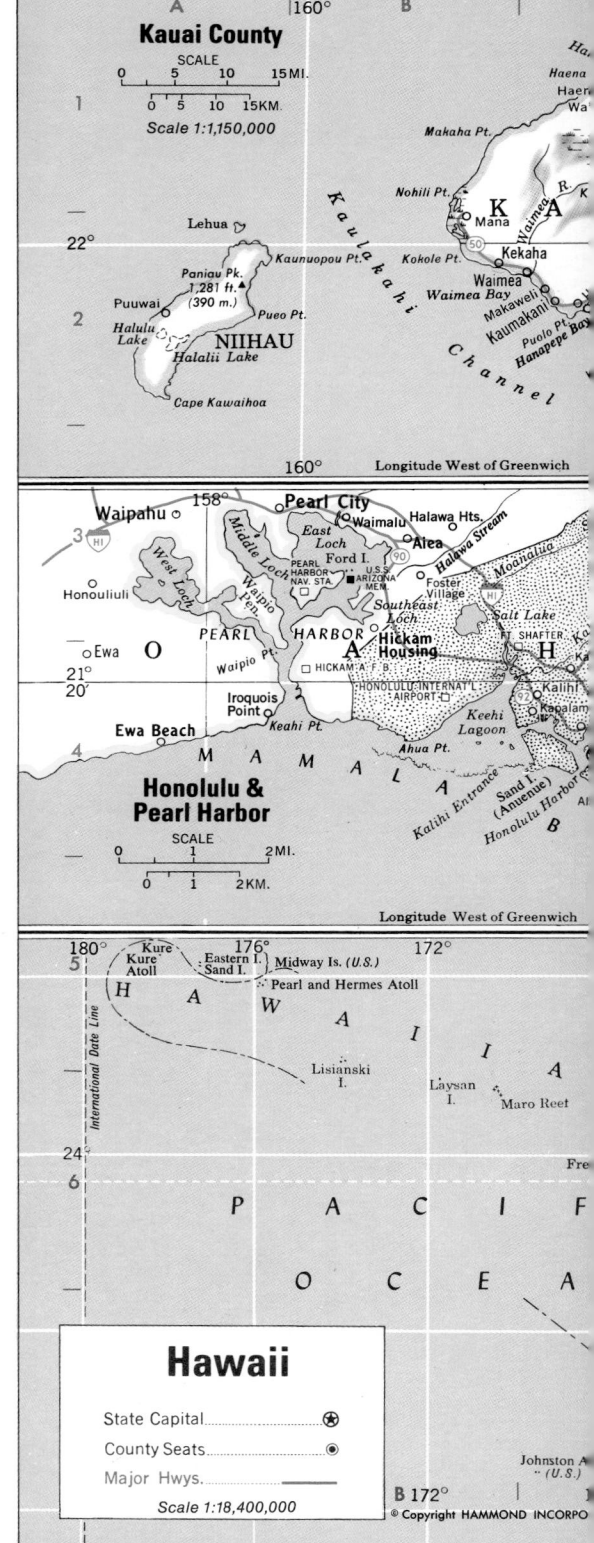

Kauai County

SCALE
0 5 10 15 MI.
0 5 10 15 KM.
Scale 1:1,150,000

Honolulu & Pearl Harbor

SCALE
0 1 2 MI.
0 1 2 KM.

Hawaii

State Capital .... ⊛
County Seats .... ⊙
Major Hwys. _____

Scale 1:18,400,000

© Copyright HAMMOND INCORPO

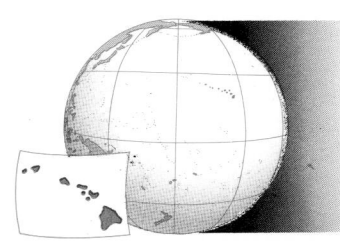

AREA 6,471 sq. mi. (16,760 sq. km.)
POPULATION 964,691
CAPITAL Honolulu
LARGEST CITY Honolulu
HIGHEST POINT Mauna Kea 13,796 ft. (4205 m.)
SETTLED IN —
ADMITTED TO UNION August 21, 1959
POPULAR NAME Aloha State
STATE FLOWER Hibiscus
STATE BIRD Nene (Hawaiian Goose)

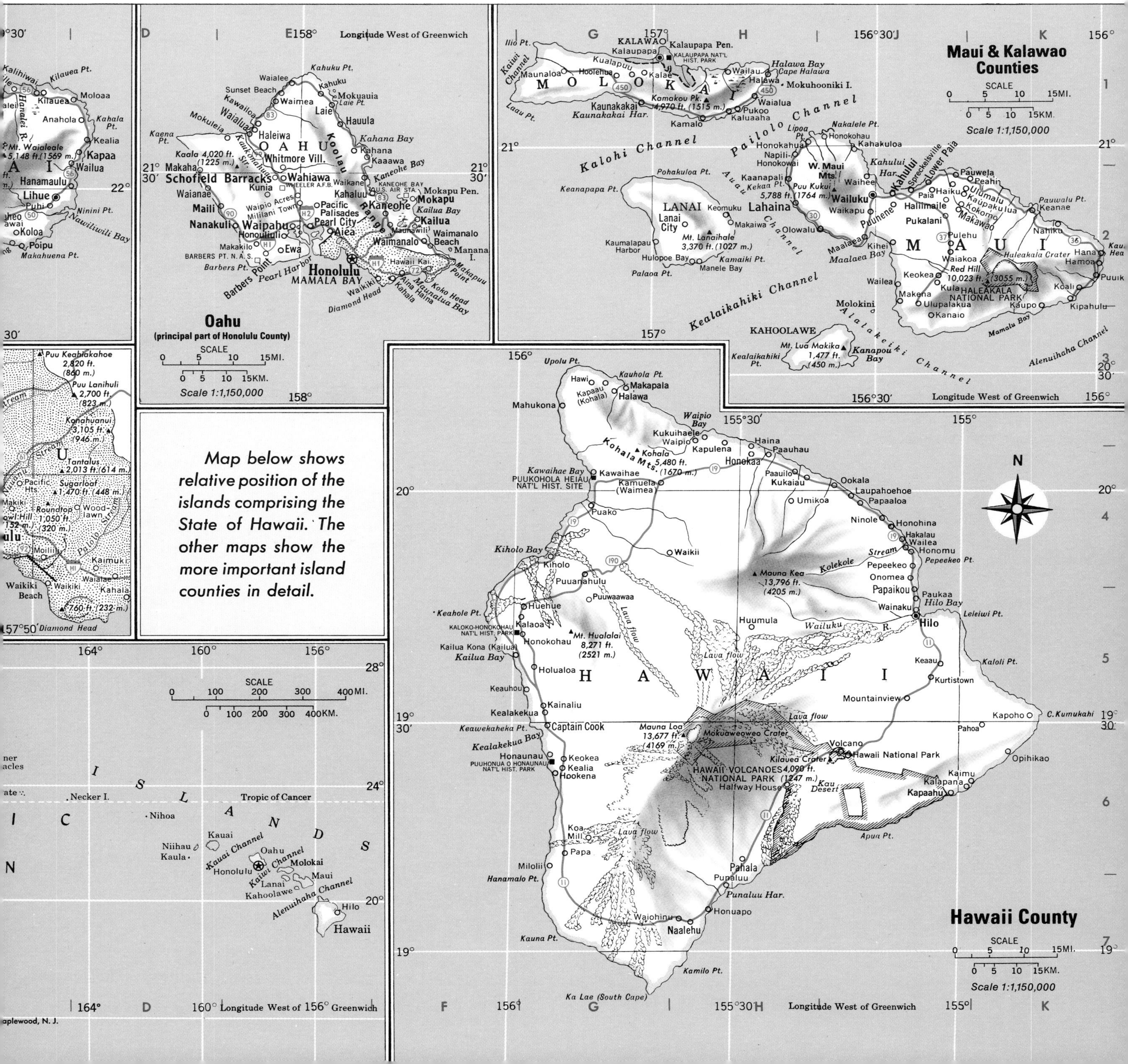

Maui & Kalawao Counties

Scale 1:1,150,000

Oahu
(principal part of Honolulu County)

SCALE

Scale 1:1,150,000

Map below shows relative position of the islands comprising the State of Hawaii. The other maps show the more important island counties in detail.

Hawaii County

Scale 1:1,150,000

Idaho

SCALE
0 5 10 20 30 40 50 MI.
0 5 10 20 30 40 50 KM.

State Capitals .... ⊛
County Seats .... ◉
Major Limited Access Hwys. ____

Scale 1:2,750,000

Topography

0   50   100 MI.
0   50   100 KM.

| Below Sea Level | 100 m. 328 ft. | 200 m. 656 ft. | 500 m. 1,640 ft. | 1,000 m. 3,281 ft. | 2,000 m. 6,562 ft. | 5,000 m. 16,404 ft. |

© Copyright HAMMOND INCORPORATED, Maplewood, N.J.

AREA 83,564 sq. mi. (216,431 sq. km.)
POPULATION 944,038
CAPITAL Boise
LARGEST CITY Boise
HIGHEST POINT Borah Pk. 12,662 ft. (3859 m.)
SETTLED IN 1842
ADMITTED TO UNION July 3, 1890
POPULAR NAME Gem State
STATE FLOWER Syringa
STATE BIRD Mountain Bluebird

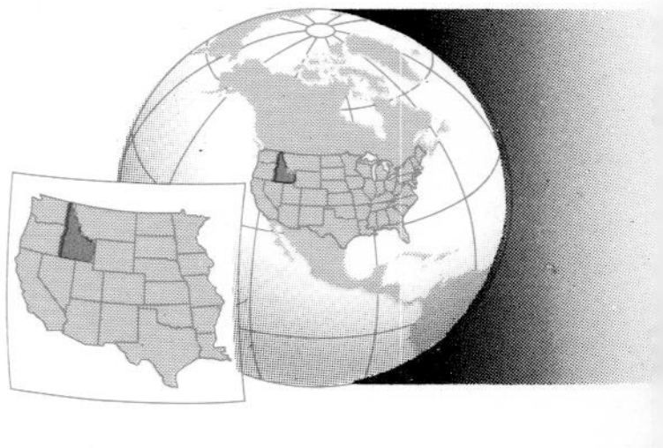

COUNTIES

Ada 173,036 B6
Adams 3,347 B5
Bannock 65,421 F7
Bear Lake 6,931 G7
Benewah 8,292 B2
Bingham 36,489 F6
Blaine 9,841 D6
Boise 2,999 C6
Bonner 24,163 B1
Bonneville 65,980 G6
Boundary 7,289 B1
Butte 3,342 E6
Camas 818 D6
Canyon 83,756 B6
Caribou 8,695 G7
Cassia 19,427 E7
Clark 798 F5
Clearwater 10,390 C3
Custer 3,385 D5
Elmore 21,565 C6
Franklin 8,895 G7
Fremont 10,813 G5
Gem 11,972 B6
Gooding 11,874 D6
Idaho 14,769 C4
Jefferson 15,304 F6
Jerome 14,840 D7
Kootenai 59,770 B2
Latah 28,749 B3
Lemhi 7,460 D4
Lewis 4,118 B3
Lincoln 3,436 D6
Madison 19,480 G6
Minidoka 19,718 E7
Nez Perce 33,220 B3
Oneida 3,258 F7
Owyhee 8,272 B7
Payette 15,825 B5
Power 6,844 F7
Shoshone 19,226 B2
Teton 2,897 G6
Twin Falls 52,927 D7
Valley 5,604 C5
Washington 8,803 B5

CITIES and TOWNS

Zip Name/Pop. Key
83210 Aberdeen 1,528 F7
83350 Acequia 100 E7
83311 Albion 286 E7
83211 American Falls⊙ 3,626 E7
†83401 Ammon 4,669 G6
83213 Arco⊙ 1,241 E6
83214 Arimo 338 F7
83420 Ashton 1,219 G5
83801 Athol 312 B2
83217 Bancroft 505 G7
83218 Basalt 414 F6
83313 Bellevue 1,016 D6
83221 Blackfoot⊙ 10,065 F6
83314 Bliss 208 D7
83223 Bloomington 212 G7
*83701 Boise (cap.)⊙ 102,160 B6
Boise‡ 173,036 B6
83805 Bonners Ferry⊙ 1,906 B1
83806 Bovill 289 B3
83316 Buhl 3,629 D7
83318 Burley⊙ 8,761 E7
83213 Butte City 93 E6
83605 Caldwell⊙ 17,699 B6
83610 Cambridge 428 B5
83611 Cascade⊙ 945 C5
83321 Castleford 191 C7
83226 Challis⊙ 758 D5
†83851 Chatcolet 181 B2
83202 Chubbuck 7,052 F7
83811 Clark Fork 449 B1
83227 Clayton 43 D5
83228 Clifton 208 F7
83814 Coeur d'Alene⊙ 20,054 B2
83522 Cottonwood 941 B3
83612 Council⊙ 917 B5
83523 Craigmont 617 B3
†83622 Crouch 69 B5
83524 Culdesac 261 B3
†83814 Dalton Gardens 1,795 B2
83232 Dayton 368 F7
83823 Deary 539 B3
83323 Declo 276 E7
83324 Dietrich 101 D7
83615 Donnelly 139 B5
83234 Downey 645 F7
83422 Driggs⊙ 727 G6
83423 Dubois⊙ 413 F5
83616 Eagle 2,620 B6
†83836 East Hope 258 B1
83325 Eden 355 D7
83827 Elk River 265 B3
83617 Emmett⊙ 4,605 B6
83327 Fairfield⊙ 404 D6
83526 Ferdinand 144 B3
†83814 Fernan Lake 178 B2
83328 Filer 1,645 D7
83236 Firth 460 F6
83203 Fort Hall 750 F6
83237 Franklin 423 G7
83619 Fruitland 2,456 B6
†83704 Garden City 4,571 B6
83832 Genesee 791 B3
83239 Georgetown 544 G7
83623 Glenns Ferry 1,374 C7
83330 Gooding⊙ 2,949 D7
83241 Grace 1,216 G7
83624 Grand View 366 B7
83530 Grangeville⊙ 3,666 B4
83626 Greenleaf 663 B6
83332 Hagerman 602 D7
83333 Hailey⊙ 2,109 D6
83425 Hamer 93 F6
83334 Hansen 1,078 D7
83833 Harrison 260 B2
†83854 Hauser 305 A2
†83835 Hayden 2,586 B2
83835 Hayden Lake 273 B2
83335 Hazelton 496 E7
83336 Heyburn 2,889 E7
†83301 Hollister 167 D7
83628 Homedale 2,078 A6
83836 Hope 106 B1
83629 Horseshoe Bend 700 B6
†83854 Huetter 65 B2
83631 Idaho City⊙ 300 C6
*83401 Idaho Falls⊙ 39,590 F6
83245 Inkom 800 F7
83427 Iona 1,072 G6
83428 Irwin 113 G6
83429 Island Park 154 G5
83338 Jerome⊙ 6,891 D7
83535 Juliaetta 522 B3
83536 Kamiah 1,478 B3
83837 Kellogg 3,417 B2
83537 Kendrick 395 B3
83340 Ketchum 2,200 D6
83341 Kimberly 2,307 D7
83539 Kooskia 784 C3
83840 Kootenai 280 B1
83634 Kuna 1,767 B6
83540 Lapwai 1,043 B3
83246 Lava Hot Springs 467 F7
83464 Leadore 114 E5
83501 Lewiston⊙ 27,986 A3
83431 Lewisville 502 F6
83251 Mackay 541 E6
83252 Malad City⊙ 1,915 F7
83342 Malta 196 E7
83639 Marsing 786 B6
83638 McCall 2,188 C5
83250 McCammon 770 F7
83641 Melba 276 B6
83434 Menan 605 F6
83642 Meridian 6,658 B6
83644 Middleton 1,901 B6
83645 Midvale 205 B5
83343 Minidoka 101 E7
83254 Montpelier 3,107 G7
83255 Moore 210 E6
83843 Moscow⊙ 16,513 B3
83647 Mountain Home⊙ 7,540 C6
83845 Moyie Springs 386 B1
†83450 Mud Lake 243 F6
83846 Mullan 1,269 C2
83650 Murphy⊙ 200 B6
83344 Murtaugh 114 D7
83651 Nampa 25,112 B6
83436 Newdale 329 G6
83654 New Meadows 576 B4
83655 New Plymouth 1,186 B6
83543 Nezperce⊙ 517 B3
83656 Notus 437 B6
83346 Oakley 663 D7
†99156 Oldtown 257 A1
†83855 Onaway 254 B3
83544 Orofino⊙ 3,711 B3
83849 Osburn 2,220 B2
†83263 Oxford 66 F7
83261 Paris⊙ 707 G7
83438 Parker 262 G6
83660 Parma 1,820 B6
83347 Paul 940 E7
83661 Payette⊙ 5,448 B5
83545 Peck 209 B3
83546 Pierce 1,060 C3
83850 Pinehurst 2,183 B2
83851 Plummer 634 B2
*83201 Pocatello⊙ 46,340 F7
83852 Ponderay 399 B1
83854 Post Falls 5,736 A2
83855 Potlatch 819 A3
83263 Preston⊙ 3,759 G7
83856 Priest River 1,639 A1
83858 Rathdrum 1,369 B2
83548 Reubens 87 B3
83440 Rexburg⊙ 11,559 G6
83349 Richfield 357 D6
83442 Rigby⊙ 2,624 F6
83549 Riggins 527 B4
83443 Ririe 555 G6
83444 Roberts 466 F6
83271 Rockland 283 F7
83445 Saint Anthony⊙ 3,212 G6
83272 Saint Charles 211 G7
83861 Saint Maries⊙ 2,794 B2
83467 Salmon⊙ 3,308 D4
83864 Sandpoint⊙ 4,460 B1
83274 Shelley 3,300 F6
83352 Shoshone⊙ 1,242 D7
†83650 Silver City 1 B6
83868 Smelterville 776 B2
83276 Soda Springs⊙ 4,051 G7
83869 Spirit Lake 834 A2
83278 Stanley 99 D5
83552 Stites 253 C3
83448 Sugar City 1,022 G6
83353 Sun Valley 545 D6
83449 Swan Valley 135 G6
83870 Tensed 113 B2
83451 Teton 559 G6
83452 Tetonia 191 G6
83871 Troy 820 B3
83301 Twin Falls⊙ 26,209 D7
83454 Ucon 833 F6
83455 Victor 323 G6
83873 Wallace⊙ 1,736 C2
†83837 Wardner 423 B2
83553 Weippe 828 C3
83672 Weiser⊙ 4,771 B5
83355 Wendell 1,974 D7
83286 Weston 310 F7
83554 White Bird 154 B4
83676 Wilder 1,260 A6
83555 Winchester 343 B3
83876 Worley 206 B2

OTHER FEATURES

Albeni Falls (dam) B1
Albion (mts.) E7
Allan (mt.) D4
American Falls (res.) F6
Anderson Ranch (res.) C6
Antelope (creek) E6
Arrowrock (res.) C6
Auger (falls) D7
Badger (peak) E7
Bald (mt.) D5
Bannock (creek) F7
Bannock (peak) F7
Bannock (range) F7
Bargamin (creek) C4
Battle (creek) B7
Bear (lake) G7
Bear (riv.) G7
Beaver (creek) F5
Beaverhead (mts.) E4
Big (creek) C4
Big Boulder (creek) B7
Big Elk (peak) G6
Big Hole (mts.) G6
Big Lost (riv.) E6
Big Southern (butte) E6
Big Wood (riv.) D6
Birch (creek) F5
Birch Creek (valley) E5
Bitterroot (range) D3
Blackfoot (res.) G7
Black Pine (mts.) E7
Blue Nose (mt.) D4
Boise (mts.) B6
Boise (riv.) B6
Borah (peak) E5
Boulder (mts.) D6
Brownlee (dam) B5
Bruneau (riv.) C7
Camas (creek) D5
Camas (creek) D6
Camas (creek) F5
Canyon (creek) C6
Cape Horn (mt.) C5
Caribou (mt.) G6
Caribou (range) G6
Cascade (res.) C5
Castle (creek) B7
Castle (peak) D5
Cedar Creek (peak) E7
Cedar Creek (res.) D7
Centennial (mts.) F5
Clearwater (mts.) C3
Clearwater (riv.) B3
Coeur d'Alene (lake) B2
Coeur d'Alene (mts.) C2
Coeur d'Alene (riv.) B2
Cottonwood (butte) C4
Craig (mts.) B4
Crane Creek (res.) B5
Craters of the Moon Nat'l Mon. E6
Deadwood (res.) C5
Deep (creek) B7
Deep (creek) F7
Deep Creek (mts.) F7
Diamond (peak) E5
Dworshak (res.) C3
East Sister (peak) C2
Eighteen Mile (peak) E5
Fish Creek (res.) E6
Fort Hall Ind. Res. F6
Goldstone (mt.) E4
Goose (creek) E7
Goose Creek (mts.) E7
Grand Canyon of the Snake River (canyon) B4
Grays (lake) G6
Grays Lake Outlet (creek) G6
Greylock (mt.) C6
Hayden (lake) B2
Hells (canyon) B4
Hells Canyon Nat'l Rec. Area B4
Henrys (lake) G5
Henrys Fork, Snake (riv.) G5
Hunter (peak) D3
Hyndman (peak) D6
Indian (creek) C5
Island Park (res.) G5
Jarbidge (riv.) C7
Johnson (creek) C5
Jordan (creek) A7
Kootenai (riv.) C1
Lemhi (pass) E5
Lemhi (range) E5
Lemhi (riv.) E5
Little Lost (riv.) E5
Little Owyhee (riv.) B7
Little Salmon (riv.) B4
Little Weiser (riv.) B5
Little Wood (riv.) D6
Lochsa (riv.) C3
Lolo (creek) C3
Lolo (pass) D3
Lone Pine (peak) D5
Lookout (mt.) D5
Lookout (mt.) F5
Lost River (range) E5
Lost Trail (pass) E4
Lowell (lake) B6
Lower Goose Creek (res.) D7
Lower Granite (lake) A3
Lucky Peak (lake) B6
Mackay (res.) E6
Magic (res.) D6
Malad (riv.) F7
Marsh (creek) F7
McGuire (mt.) D4
Meade (peak) G7
Meadow (creek) C4
Medicine Lodge (creek) F5
Middle Fork (peak) D5
Monument (peak) B4
Moose (creek) D3
Mores (creek) C6
Mormon (mt.) D4
Mountain Home (res.) C6
Mountain Home A.F.B. 6,403 C6
Moyie (riv.) B1
Mud (lake) F6
National Reactor Testing Sta. F6
Nez Perce Nat'l Hist. Park B-C3
North Fork (riv.) B7
Norton (peak) D6
Orofino (creek) C3
Owyhee (mts.) B6
Owyhee, East Fork (riv.) B7
Oxbow (dam) B5
Pack (riv.) B1
Pahsimeroi (riv.) E5
Palisades (res.) G6
Palouse (riv.) B3
Panther (creek) D4
Payette (lake) C4
Payette (mts.) B5
Payette (riv.) B6
Peale (mts.) G7
Pend Oreille (lake) B1
Pend Oreille (mt.) B1
Pend Oreille (riv.) A1
Pilot (peak) C4
Pilot (peak) C6
Pilot Knob (mt.) C4
Pinyon (peak) C5
Pioneer (mts.) D6
Portneuf (res.) F7
Pot (mt.) C3
Potlatch (riv.) B3
Priest (lake) B1
Priest (riv.) B1
Purcell (mts.) B1
Pyramid (peak) E4
Raft (riv.) E7
Rainbow (mt.) C4
Ranger (peak) D3
Rays (lake) F6
Red (riv.) C4
Redfish (lake) D5
Reynolds (creek) B6
Rhodes (peak) D3
Rocky (mts.) D1
Rocky Ridge (mt.) C3
Ryan (peak) D6
Saddle (mt.) D3
Saddle (mt.) F6
Sailor (creek) C7
Saint Joe (riv.) B2
Saint Maries (riv.) B2
Salmon (falls) C7
Salmon (riv.) B4
Salmon Falls (creek) D7
Salmon Falls Creek (res.) D7
Salmon River (mts.) C5
Sawtooth (range) C6
Sawtooth Nat'l Rec. Area D5
Secesh (riv.) C4
Selkirk (mts.) B1
Selway (riv.) C3
Seven Devils (mts.) B4
Shoshone (falls) D7
Sleeping Deer (mt.) D5
Smith (creek) B1
Smoky (mts.) D6
Snake (riv.) A3
Snake River (plain) D7
Snake River (range) G6
Spirit (lake) B2
Squaw (creek) B5
Squaw (peak) D4
Steamboat (mt.) C4
Steel (mt.) C6
Strike, C.J. (res.) C7
Sublett (mts.) E7
Sunset (peak) E6
Taylor (mt.) D5
Teton (riv.) G6
Thompson (peak) C5
Trinity (mt.) C6
Trout (creek) B1
Twin (falls) D7
Twin Peaks (mt.) D5
Walcott (lake) E7
Wasatch (range) G7
Waugh (mt.) D4
Weiser (riv.) B5
Western Shoshone Ind. Res. B7
White Knob (mts.) E6
Wickahoney (creek) C7
Willow (creek) G6
Wilson Lake (res.) D7
Yankee Fork, Salmon (riv.) D5
Yellowstone Nat'l Park G5

⊙County seat.
‡Population of metropolitan area.
† Zip of nearest p.o.
* Multiple zips.

Agriculture, Industry and Resources

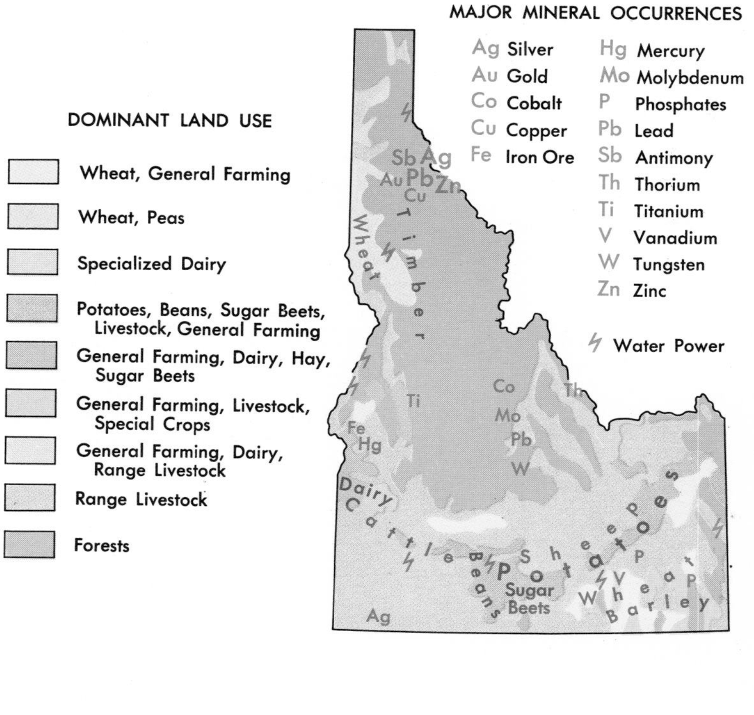
MAJOR MINERAL OCCURRENCES
Ag Silver
Au Gold
Co Cobalt
Cu Copper
Fe Iron Ore
Hg Mercury
Mo Molybdenum
P Phosphates
Pb Lead
Sb Antimony
Th Thorium
Ti Titanium
V Vanadium
W Tungsten
Zn Zinc
Water Power
DOMINANT LAND USE
Wheat, General Farming
Wheat, Peas
Specialized Dairy
Potatoes, Beans, Sugar Beets, Livestock, General Farming
General Farming, Dairy, Hay, Sugar Beets
General Farming, Livestock, Special Crops
General Farming, Dairy, Range Livestock
Range Livestock
Forests
Wheat
Timber
Dairy
Cattle
Sheep
Potatoes
Beans
Sugar Beets
Wheat
Barley

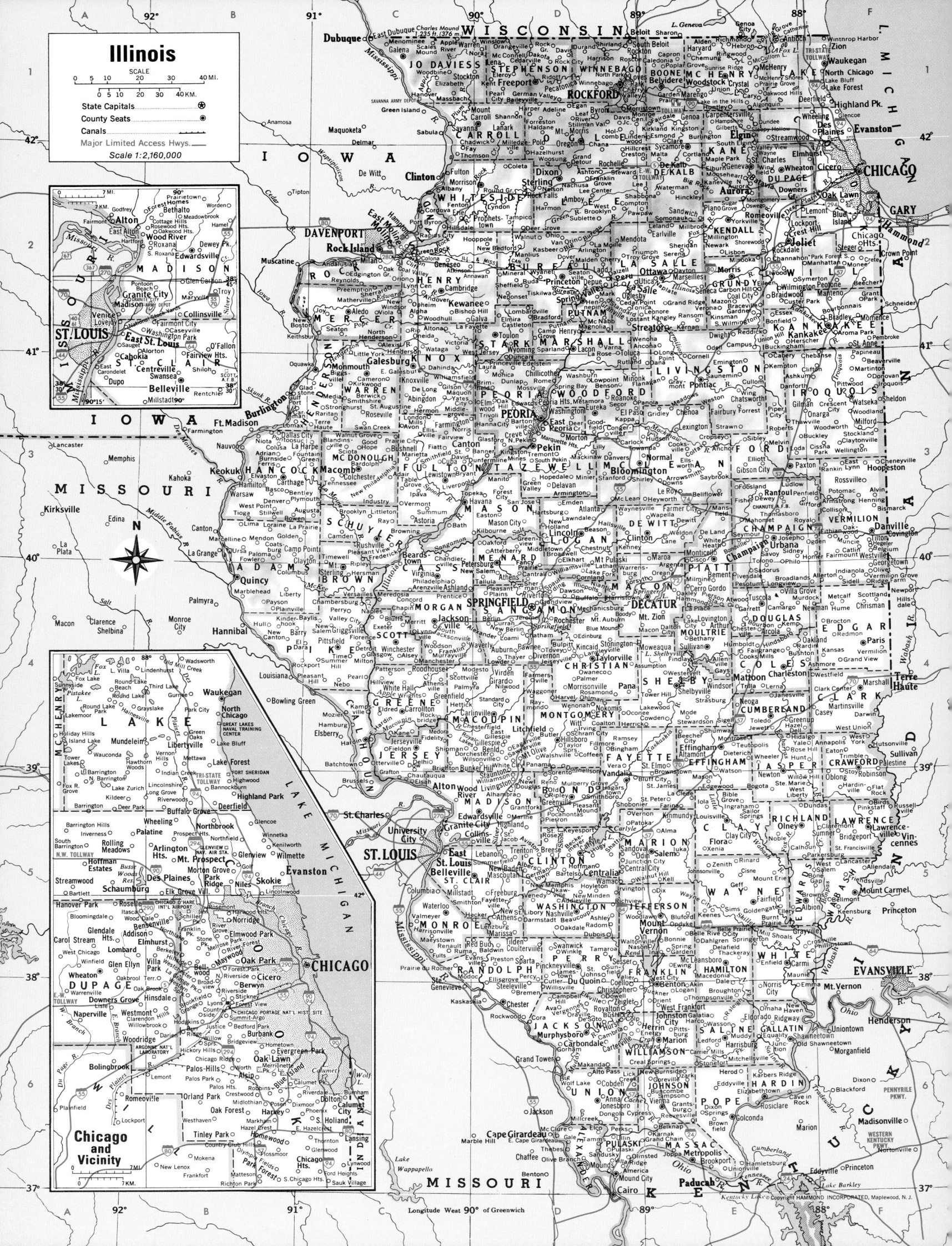

AREA 56,345 sq. mi. (145,934 sq. km.)
POPULATION 11,426,596
CAPITAL Springfield
LARGEST CITY Chicago
HIGHEST POINT Charles Mound 1,235 ft. (376 m.)
SETTLED IN 1720
ADMITTED TO UNION December 3, 1818
POPULAR NAME Prairie State; Land of Lincoln
STATE FLOWER Native Violet
STATE BIRD Cardinal

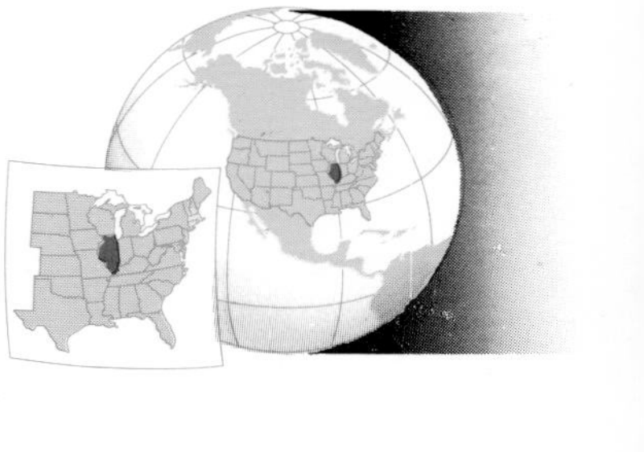

COUNTIES

Adams 71,622 B4
Alexander 12,264 D6
Bond 16,224 D5
Boone 28,630 E1
Brown 5,411 C4
Bureau 39,114 D2
Calhoun 5,867 C4
Carroll 18,779 D1
Cass 15,084 C4
Champaign 168,392 E3
Christian 36,446 D4
Clark 16,913 F4
Clay 15,283 E5
Clinton 32,617 D5
Coles 52,260 E4
Cook 5,253,655 F2
Crawford 20,818 F4
Cumberland 11,062 E4
De Kalb 74,624 E2
De Witt 18,108 E3
Douglas 19,774 E4
Du Page 658,835 E2
Edgar 21,725 F4
Edwards 7,961 E5
Effingham 30,944 E4
Fayette 22,167 D4
Ford 15,265 E3
Franklin 43,201 E5
Fulton 43,687 C3
Gallatin 7,590 E6
Greene 16,661 C4
Grundy 30,582 E2
Hamilton 9,172 E5
Hancock 23,877 B3
Hardin 5,383 E6
Henderson 9,114 C3
Henry 57,968 C2
Iroquois 32,976 F3
Jackson 61,522 D6
Jasper 11,318 E4
Jefferson 36,354 E5
Jersey 20,538 C4
Jo Daviess 23,520 C1
Johnson 9,624 E6
Kane 278,405 E2
Kankakee 102,926 F2
Kendall 37,202 E2
Knox 61,607 C3
Lake 440,372 E1
La Salle 112,033 E2
Lawrence 17,807 F5
Lee 36,328 D2
Livingston 41,381 E3
Logan 31,802 D3
Macon 131,375 E4
Macoupin 49,384 D4
Madison 247,691 D5
Marion 43,523 E5
Marshall 14,479 D2
Mason 19,492 D3
Massac 14,990 E6
McDonough 37,467 C3
McHenry 147,897 E1
McLean 119,149 E3
Menard 11,700 D3
Mercer 19,286 C2
Monroe 20,117 C5
Montgomery 31,686 D4
Morgan 37,502 C4
Moultrie 14,546 E4
Ogle 46,338 D1
Peoria 200,466 D3
Perry 21,714 D5
Piatt 16,581 E4
Pike 18,896 C4
Pope 4,404 E6
Pulaski 8,840 D6
Putnam 6,085 D2
Randolph 35,652 D5
Richland 17,587 E5
Rock Island 165,968 C2
Saint Clair 267,531 D5
Saline 28,448 E6
Sangamon 176,089 D4
Schuyler 8,365 C3
Scott 6,142 C4
Shelby 23,923 E4
Stark 7,389 D2
Stephenson 49,536 D1
Tazewell 132,078 D3
Union 17,765 D6
Vermilion 95,222 F3
Wabash 13,713 F5
Warren 21,943 C3
Washington 15,472 D5
Wayne 18,059 E5
White 17,864 E5
Whiteside 65,970 D2
Will 324,460 F2
Williamson 56,538 E6
Winnebago 250,884 D1
Woodford 33,320 D3

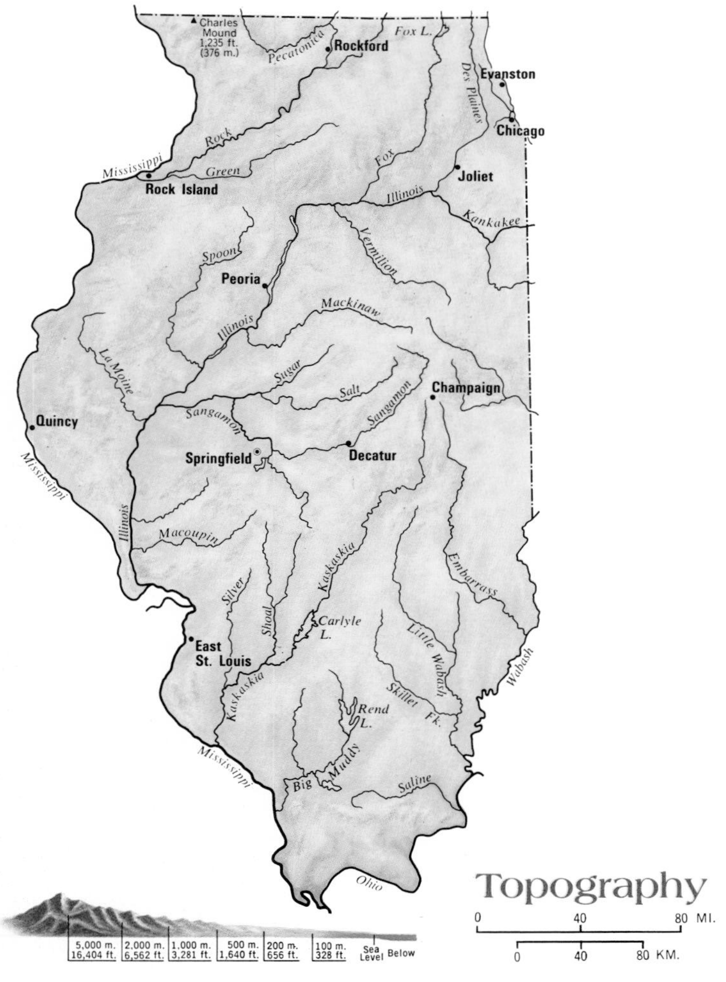

Charles Mound 1,235 ft. (376 m.)
Rockford
Pecatonica
Fox L.
Evanston
Des Plaines
Chicago
Rock
Mississippi
Green
Rock Island
Fox
Joliet
Illinois
Kankakee
Vermilion
Spoon
Peoria
Mackinaw
Illinois
La Moine
Sugar
Salt
Sangamon
Champaign
Quincy
Sangamon
Springfield
Decatur
Mississippi
Illinois
Macoupin
Embarrass
Silver
Shoal
Kaskaskia
Carlyle L.
Little Wabash
Wabash
East St. Louis
Kaskaskia
Skillet Fk.
Rend L.
Mississippi
Big Muddy
Saline
Ohio
5,000 m. 16,404 ft.
2,000 m. 6,562 ft.
1,000 m. 3,281 ft.
500 m. 1,640 ft.
200 m. 656 ft.
100 m. 328 ft.
Sea Level
Below
0 40 80 MI.
0 40 80 KM.

Topography

CITIES and TOWNS

Zip Name/Pop. Key

61410 Abingdon 4,210 C3
60101 Addison 29,826 B5
61230 Albany 1,014 C2
62806 Albion⊙ 2,285 E5
61231 Aledo⊙ 3,881 C2
61412 Alexis 1,076 C2
60102 Algonquin 5,834 E1
62207 Alorton 2,237 B2
61413 Alpha 815 C2
†60658 Alsip 17,134 B6
62411 Altamont 2,389 E4
62002 Alton 34,171 A2
61310 Amboy 2,377 D2
61232 Andalusia 1,238 C2
62906 Anna 5,408 D6
61234 Annawan 908 C2
60002 Antioch 4,419 E1
61910 Arcola 2,714 E4
62501 Argenta 994 E4
*60004 Arlington Heights 66,116 B5
61911 Arthur 2,122 E4
60911 Ashkum 735 E3
62612 Ashland 1,351 C4
62808 Ashley 658 D5
61912 Ashmore 883 F4
61006 Ashton 1,140 D2
62510 Assumption 1,283 E4
61501 Astoria 1,370 C3
62613 Athens 1,371 D4
61235 Atkinson 1,138 C2
61723 Atlanta 1,807 D3
61913 Atwood 1,464 E4
62615 Auburn 3,616 D4
62311 Augusta 764 C3
*60504 Aurora 81,293 E2
62907 Ava 811 D6
62216 Aviston 846 D5
61415 Avon 1,019 C3
†60015 Bannockburn 1,316 B5
60010 Barrington 9,029 A5
†60010 Barrington Hills 3,631 A5
62312 Barry 1,487 B4
60103 Bartlett 13,254 A5
61607 Bartonville 6,137 D3
60510 Batavia 12,574 E2
62618 Beardstown 6,338 C3
62219 Beckemeyer 1,119 D5
60401 Beecher 2,024 F2
*62220 Belleville⊙ 41,580 B3
60104 Bellwood 19,811 B5
61008 Belvidere⊙ 15,176 E1
61813 Bement 1,770 E4
62009 Benld 1,638 D4
60106 Bensenville 16,124 B5
62812 Benton⊙ 7,778 E6
60162 Berkeley 5,467 B5
60402 Berwyn 46,849 B6
62010 Bethalto 8,630 B2
61914 Bethany 1,550 E4
61420 Blandinsville 886 C3
60108 Bloomingdale 12,659 A5
61701 Bloomington⊙ 44,189 D3
Bloomington-Normal‡ 119,149 D3
60406 Blue Island 21,855 B6
62513 Blue Mound 1,338 D4
62621 Bluffs 821 C4
60439 Bolingbrook 37,261 A6
60914 Bourbonnais 13,280 F2
60407 Braceville 721 E2
61421 Bradford 924 D2
60915 Bradley 11,008 F2
60408 Braidwood 3,429 E2
62230 Breese 3,516 D5
62417 Bridgeport 2,281 F5
60455 Bridgeview 14,155 B6
62012 Brighton 2,364 C4
61517 Brimfield 890 D3
60153 Broadview 8,618 B6
60513 Brookfield 19,395 B6
†62059 Brooklyn (Lovejoy) 1,233 A2
62910 Brookport 1,128 E6
61314 Buda 668 D2
†60090 Buffalo Grove 22,230 B5
62014 Bunker Hill 1,700 D4
60459 Burbank 28,462 B6
†60601 Burnham 4,030 C6
†60558 Burr Ridge 3,833 B6
61422 Bushnell 3,811 C3
61010 Byron 2,035 D1
62206 Cahokia 18,904 A3
62914 Cairo⊙ 5,931 D6
60409 Calumet City 39,697 C6
†60643 Calumet Park 8,788 C6
62915 Cambria 1,090 D6
61238 Cambridge⊙ 2,217 C2
62320 Camp Point 1,285 B3
61520 Canton 14,626 C3
61239 Carbon Cliff 1,578 C2
62901 Carbondale 26,414 D6
62626 Carlinville⊙ 5,439 D4
62231 Carlyle⊙ 3,388 D5
62821 Carmi⊙ 6,264 E5
†60187 Carol Stream 15,472 A5
60110 Carpentersville 23,272 E1
62917 Carrier Mills 2,268 E6
62016 Carrollton⊙ 2,816 C4
62918 Carterville 3,445 D6
62321 Carthage⊙ 2,978 B3
60013 Cary 6,640 E1
62420 Casey 3,026 F4
62232 Caseyville 4,308 B2
61817 Catlin 2,226 F3
61013 Cedarville 766 D1
†62801 Central City 1,505 D5
62801 Centralia 15,126 D5
62206 Centreville 9,747 B3
61818 Cerro Gordo 1,553 E4
61820 Champaign 58,133 E3
Champaign-Urbana-Rantoul‡ 168,392 E3
62627 Chandlerville 842 C3
60410 Channahon 3,734 E2
61920 Charleston⊙ 19,355 E4
62629 Chatham 5,597 D4
60921 Chatsworth 1,187 E3
60922 Chebanse 1,191 F3
61726 Chenoa 1,847 E3
61016 Cherry Valley 946 D1
62233 Chester⊙ 8,401 D6
*60601 Chicago⊙ 3,005,072 C5
Chicago‡ 7,102,328 C5
60411 Chicago Heights 37,026 C6
60415 Chicago Ridge 13,473 B6
61523 Chillicothe 6,176 D3
61924 Chrisman 1,413 F4
62822 Christopher 3,086 D6
60650 Cicero 61,232 B5
60924 Cissna Park 825 F3
60514 Clarendon Hills 6,870 B6
62824 Clay City 1,038 E5
62324 Clayton 889 B3
60927 Clifton 1,390 F3
61727 Clinton⊙ 8,014 E3
60416 Coal City 3,028 E2
61240 Coal Valley 3,800 C2
62920 Cobden 1,210 D6
62017 Coffeen 842 D4
62326 Colchester 1,729 C3
61728 Colfax 920 E3
62234 Collinsville 19,613 B2
61241 Colona 2,172 C2
62236 Columbia 4,269 C5
60112 Cortland 1,019 E2
62018 Cottage Hills B2
62237 Coulterville 1,118 D5
†60525 Countryside 6,538 B6
62922 Creal Springs 845 E6
60431 Crest Hill 9,252 E2
†60445 Crestwood 10,852 B6
60417 Crete 5,417 F2
61611 Creve Coeur 6,851 D3
62827 Crossville 944 F5
60014 Crystal Lake 18,590 E1
61427 Cuba 1,648 C3
62330 Dallas City 1,408 B3
61320 Dalzell 824 D2
61732 Danvers 921 D3
61832 Danville⊙ 38,985 F3
†60559 Darien 14,536 B6
*62521 Decatur⊙ 94,081 E4
Decatur‡ 131,375 E4
60015 Deerfield 17,430 B5
†60010 Deer Park 1,368 A5
60115 De Kalb 33,099 E2
61734 Delavan 1,973 D3
61322 Depue 1,873 D2
62924 De Soto 1,589 D6
*60016 Des Plaines 53,568 B5
62530 Divernon 1,081 D4
†60469 Dixmoor 4,175 C6
61021 Dixon⊙ 15,701 D2
60419 Dolton 24,766 C6
62926 Dongola 886 D6
60515 Downers Grove 42,572 A6
60118 Dundee (East and West Dundee) 6,169 E1
61525 Dunlap 824 D3
62239 Dupo 3,039 A3
62832 Du Quoin 6,594 D5
61024 Durand 1,073 D1
60420 Dwight 4,146 E2
60518 Earlville 1,382 E2
62024 East Alton 7,096 A2
61025 East Dubuque 2,194 C1
†60118 East Dundee (Dundee) 2,618 E1
61430 East Galesburg 928 C3
†60429 East Hazelcrest 1,362 C6
61244 East Moline 20,907 C2
61611 East Peoria 22,385 D3
*62201 East Saint Louis 55,200 A2
62531 Edinburg 1,231 D4
62025 Edwardsville⊙ 12,480 B2
62401 Effingham⊙ 11,270 E4
60119 Elburn 1,224 E2
62930 Eldorado 5,198 E6
60120 Elgin 63,981 E1
61028 Elizabeth 772 C1
62931 Elizabethtown⊙ 478 E6
60007 Elk Grove Village 28,907 B5
62932 Elkville 973 D6
60126 Elmhurst 44,276 B5
61529 Elmwood 2,117 D3
60635 Elmwood Park 24,016 B5
61738 El Paso 2,676 D3
62028 Elsah 990 C5
60421 Elwood 814 E2
62933 Energy 1,138 E6
62835 Enfield 890 E5
62934 Equality 831 E6
61250 Erie 1,725 C2
61530 Eureka⊙ 4,306 D3
60201 Evanston 73,706 B5
62242 Evansville 863 D5
60642 Evergreen Park 22,260 B6
61739 Fairbury 3,544 E3
62837 Fairfield⊙ 5,954 E5
†62201 Fairmont City 2,313 B2
61841 Fairmount 851 F3
62208 Fairview Heights 12,414 B3
61842 Farmer City 2,252 E3
61531 Farmington 3,118 C3
62534 Findlay 868 E4
61843 Fisher 1,572 E3
61740 Flanagan 978 E3
62839 Flora 5,379 E5
60422 Flossmoor 8,423 B6
†60411 Ford Heights 5,347 C6
60130 Forest Park 15,177 B5
†60402 Forest View 764 B6
61741 Forrest 1,246 E3
61030 Forreston 1,384 D1
60020 Fox Lake 6,831 A4
60021 Fox River Grove 2,515 A5
60423 Frankfort 4,357 B6
61031 Franklin Grove 965 D2
60131 Franklin Park 17,507 B5
62243 Freeburg 2,989 D5
61032 Freeport⊙ 26,266 D1
61252 Fulton 3,936 C2
62935 Galatia 1,042 E6
61036 Galena⊙ 3,876 C1
61401 Galesburg⊙ 35,305 C3
61434 Galva 3,185 D2
60424 Gardner 1,322 E2
61254 Geneseo 6,373 C2
60134 Geneva⊙ 9,881 E2
60135 Genoa 3,276 E1
61846 Georgetown 4,220 F4
62245 Germantown 1,191 D5
60936 Gibson City 3,498 E3
61847 Gifford 848 E3
62033 Gillespie 3,740 D4
60938 Gilman 1,913 E3
62640 Girard 2,246 D4
61533 Glasford 1,201 D3
62034 Glen Carbon 5,197 B2
60022 Glencoe 9,200 B5
†60108 Glendale Heights 23,163 A5
60137 Glen Ellyn 23,717 A5
60025 Glenview 32,060 B5
60425 Glenwood 10,538 C6
62035 Godfrey A2
62938 Golconda⊙ 960 E6
62939 Goreville 978 E6
62037 Grafton 1,024 C5
62942 Grand Tower 748 D6
†62701 Grandview 1,794 D4
62040 Granite City 36,815 A2
60490 Grant Park 1,038 F2
61326 Granville 1,537 D2
60030 Grayslake 5,260 B4
62844 Grayville 2,313 B4
62044 Greenfield 1,090 C4
†60048 Green Oaks 1,415 B4
†61241 Green Rock 3,324 C2
62428 Greenup 1,655 E4
61534 Green Valley 768 D3
62642 Greenview 830 D3
62246 Greenville⊙ 5,271 D5
61744 Gridley 1,246 E3
62340 Griggsville 1,301 C4
60031 Gurnee 7,179 B4
62341 Hamilton 3,509 B3
60140 Hampshire 1,735 E1
61256 Hampton 1,873 C2
61536 Hanna City 1,361 D3
61041 Hanover 1,069 C1
60103 Hanover Park 28,719 A5
62047 Hardin⊙ 1,107 C4
62946 Harrisburg⊙ 10,410 E6
62537 Harristown 1,456 D4
62048 Hartford 1,887 A2
60033 Harvard 5,126 E1
60426 Harvey 35,810 B6
60656 Harwood Heights 8,228 B5
62644 Havana⊙ 4,277 D3
†60047 Hawthorn Woods 1,658 B5
60429 Hazel Crest 13,973 B6
60034 Hebron 786 E1
†61832 Hegeler 1,853 F3
61327 Hennepin⊙ 716 D2
61537 Henry 2,740 D2
62948 Herrin 10,708 E6
60941 Herscher 1,214 E2
61745 Heyworth 1,598 E3
60457 Hickory Hills 13,778 B6
62249 Highland 7,122 D5
60035 Highland Park 30,611 B5
60040 Highwood 5,452 B5
62049 Hillsboro⊙ 4,408 D4
60162 Hillside 8,279 B5
60520 Hinckley 1,447 E2
60521 Hinsdale 16,726 B6
60525 Hodgkins 2,005 B6
60195 Hoffman Estates 37,272 A5
61849 Homer 1,279 F3
60456 Hometown 5,324 B6
60430 Homewood 19,724 B6
60942 Hoopeston 6,411 F3
61747 Hohedale 913 D3
61748 Hudson 929 F3

(continued on following page)

Agriculture, Industry and Resources

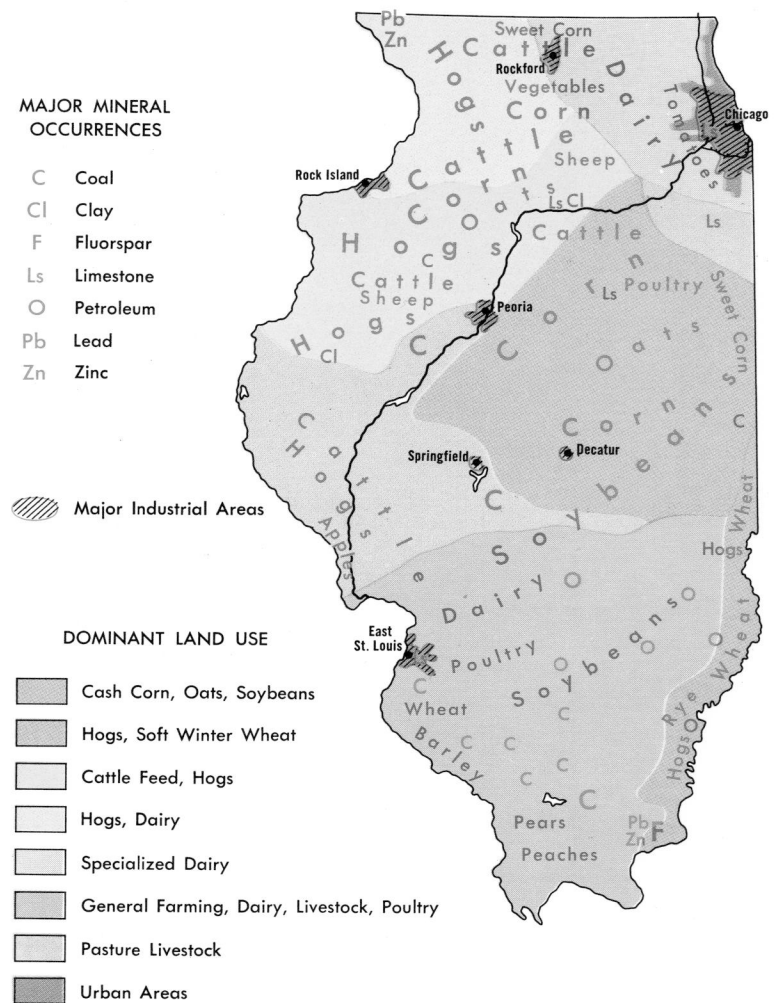

MAJOR MINERAL OCCURRENCES

C   Coal
Cl   Clay
F   Fluorspar
Ls   Limestone
⊙   Petroleum
Pb   Lead
Zn   Zinc

▨ Major Industrial Areas

DOMINANT LAND USE

- Cash Corn, Oats, Soybeans
- Hogs, Soft Winter Wheat
- Cattle Feed, Hogs
- Hogs, Dairy
- Specialized Dairy
- General Farming, Dairy, Livestock, Poultry
- Pasture Livestock
- Urban Areas

AREA 36,185 sq. mi. (93,719 sq. km.)
POPULATION 5,490,260
CAPITAL Indianapolis
LARGEST CITY Indianapolis
HIGHEST POINT 1,257 ft. (383 m.) (Wayne County)
SETTLED IN 1730
ADMITTED TO UNION December 11, 1816
POPULAR NAME Hoosier State
STATE FLOWER Peony
STATE BIRD Cardinal

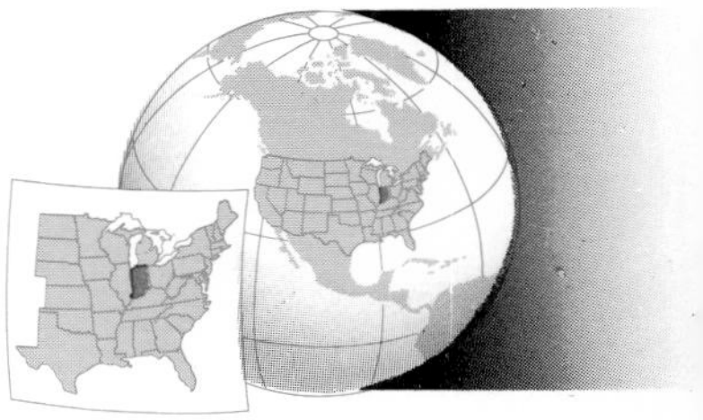

COUNTIES

Adams 29,619 H3
Allen 294,335 G2
Bartholomew 65,088 F6
Benton 10,218 C3
Blackford 15,570 G4
Boone 36,446 E4
Brown 12,377 E6
Carroll 19,722 D3
Cass 40,936 E3
Clark 88,838 F8
Clay 24,862 C6
Clinton 31,545 E4
Crawford 9,820 E8
Daviess 27,836 C7
Dearborn 34,291 H6
Decatur 23,841 G6
De Kalb 33,606 H2
Delaware 128,587 G4
Dubois 34,238 D8
Elkhart 137,330 F1
Fayette 28,272 G5
Floyd 61,169 F8
Fountain 19,033 C4
Franklin 19,612 G6
Fulton 19,335 E2
Gibson 33,156 B8
Grant 80,934 F3
Greene 30,416 D6
Hamilton 82,027 E4
Hancock 43,939 F5
Harrison 27,276 E8
Hendricks 69,804 D5
Henry 53,336 G5
Howard 86,896 E4
Huntington 35,596 G3
Jackson 36,523 E7
Jasper 26,138 C2
Jay 23,239 G4
Jefferson 30,419 G7
Jennings 22,854 F7
Johnson 77,240 E6
Knox 41,838 C7
Kosciusko 59,555 F2
Lagrange 25,550 G1
Lake 522,965 C2
LaPorte 108,632 D1
Lawrence 4,272 E7
Madison 139,336 F4
Marion 765,233 E5
Marshall 39,155 E2
Martin 11,001 D7
Miami 39,820 E3
Monroe 98,785 D6
Montgomery 35,501 D4
Morgan 51,999 E6
Newton 14,844 C3
Noble 35,443 G2
Ohio 5,114 H7
Orange 18,677 E7
Owen 15,841 D6
Parke 16,372 C5
Perry 19,346 D8
Pike 13,465 C8
Porter 119,816 C2
Posey 26,414 B8
Pulaski 13,258 D2
Putnam 29,163 D5
Randolph 29,997 G4
Ripley 24,398 G6
Rush 19,604 G5
Saint Joseph 241,617 E1
Scott 20,422 F7
Shelby 39,887 F5
Spencer 19,361 C9
Starke 21,997 D2
Steuben 24,694 G1
Sullivan 21,107 C6
Switzerland 7,153 G7
Tippecanoe 121,702 D4
Tipton 16,819 E4
Union 6,860 H5
Vanderburgh 167,515 B8
Vermillion 18,229 C5
Vigo 112,385 C6
Wabash 36,640 F3
Warren 8,976 C4
Warrick 41,474 C8
Washington 21,932 E7
Wayne 76,058 G5
Wells 25,401 G3
White 23,867 D3
Whitley 26,215 F2

CITIES and TOWNS

Zip Name/Pop. Key

47240 Adams 250 F6
†46947 Adamsboro 325 E3
46102 Advance 559 D5
46910 Akron 1,045 E2
47320 Albany 2,625 G4
46701 Albion⊙ 1,637 G2
†47283 Alert 102 F6
46001 Alexandria 6,028 F4
†46738 Altona 263 G2
47917 Ambia 274 C4
46911 Amboy 450 F3
†46131 Amity 200 E6
46103 Amo 444 D5
*46011 Anderson⊙ 64,695 F4
Anderson‡ 139,336 F4
†47024 Andersonville 225 G5
46702 Andrews 1,243 F3
46703 Angola⊙ 5,486 G1
46030 Arcadia 1,801 E4
46704 Arcola 300 G2
†46624 Ardmore 800 E1
46501 Argos 1,547 E2
46104 Arlington 500 F5
46031 Atlanta 657 E4
47918 Attica 3,841 C4
46502 Atwood 300 F2
46706 Auburn⊙ 8,122 G2
47001 Aurora 3,816 H6
47102 Austin 4,857 F7
46710 Avilla 1,272 G2
47420 Avoca 400 D7
46105 Bainbridge 644 D5
46106 Bargersville 1,647 E5
47006 Batesville 4,152 G6
47920 Battle Ground 812 D3
47421 Bedford⊙ 14,410 E7
46107 Beech Grove 13,196 E5
†46526 Benton 220 F2
46711 Berne 3,300 H3
†46111 Bethany 127 E5
46301 Beverly Shores 864 C1
47512 Bicknell 4,713 C7
46713 Bippus 300 F3
47513 Birdseye 533 D8
†46406 Black Oak C1
47831 Blanford 500 B5
47138 Blocher 400 F7
47424 Bloomfield⊙ 2,705 D6
47832 Bloomingdale 409 C5
47401 Bloomington⊙ 52,044 D6
Bloomington‡ 98,387 D6
†47360 Blountsville 213 G4
†46176 Blue Ridge 219 F5
46714 Bluffton⊙ 8,705 G3
46110 Boggstown 200 F5
46302 Boone Grove 220 C2
47601 Boonville⊙ 6,300 C8
47106 Borden 384 F8
47324 Boston 189 H5
47921 Boswell 810 C3
46504 Bourbon 1,522 E2
47833 Bowling Green 200 D6
47107 Bradford 350 E8
47834 Brazil⊙ 7,852 C5
46506 Bremen 3,565 E2
47836 Bridgeton 250 C5
†45030 Bright 450 H6
46720 Brimfield 292 G2
46913 Bringhurst 275 E3
46507 Bristol 1,203 F1
47922 Brook 926 C3
46111 Brooklyn 889 E5
†47250 Brooksburg 132 G7
47923 Brookston 1,701 D3
47012 Brookville⊙ 2,874 G6
46112 Brownsburg 6,242 E5
47220 Brownstown⊙ 2,704 F7
47325 Brownsville 250 H5
47516 Bruceville 646 C7
47326 Bryant 277 G3
47924 Buck Creek 225 D4
47647 Buckskin 200 C8
47925 Buffalo 500 D3
46914 Bunker Hill 984 E3
46508 Burket 260 F2
46915 Burlington 680 E4
47926 Burnettsville 496 D3
47222 Burney 300 F6
†46401 Burns Harbor 920 C1
46916 Burrows 250 E3
46721 Butler 2,509 H2
47223 Butlerville 300 F6
†46371 Byron 200 C5
†47362 Cadiz 180 G5
47327 Cambridge City 2,407 G5
46917 Camden 618 D3
47108 Campbellsburg 695 E7
47224 Canaan 90 G7
47519 Cannelburg 152 C7
47520 Cannelton⊙ 2,373 D9
47837 Carbon 307 C5
47838 Carlisle 717 C7
46032 Carmel 18,272 E5
46114 Cartersburg 300 E5
46115 Carthage 886 F5
47927 Cates 125 C4
47928 Cayuga 1,258 C5
47016 Cedar Grove 217 H6
46303 Cedar Lake 8,754 C2
47521 Celestine 150 D8
†47842 Centenary 150 B5
†46901 Center 310 E4
47840 Centerpoint 242 C6
46116 Centerton 250 E5
47330 Centerville 2,284 H5
47929 Chalmers 554 D3
47610 Chandler 3,043 C8
47111 Charlestown 5,596 F8
46117 Charlottesville 300 F5
†47138 Chelsea 200 F7
46017 Chesterfield 2,701 F4
46304 Chesterton 8,531 D1
47611 Chrisney 537 C8
46723 Churubusco 1,638 G2
46034 Cicero 2,557 E4
47225 Clarksburg 300 G6
47930 Clarks Hill 653 D4
47130 Clarksville 15,164 F8
47841 Clay City 883 C6
46510 Claypool 464 F2
46118 Clayton 703 D5
47426 Clear Creek 200 E6
†46737 Clear Lake 301 H1
47226 Clifford 310 F6
47842 Clinton 5,267 C5
46120 Cloverdale 1,357 D5
†47834 Cloverland 175 C6
47427 Coal City 225 D6
47845 Coalmont 450 C6
46121 Coatesville 474 D5
47931 Colburn 300 D3
46035 Colfax 823 D4
47978 Collegeville 1,059 C3
46725 Columbia City⊙ 5,091 G2
47201 Columbus⊙ 30,614 E6
47331 Connersville⊙ 17,023 G5
46919 Converse 1,279 F3
47228 Cortland 175 F7
46730 Corunna 304 G2
47112 Corydon⊙ 2,724 E8
47932 Covington⊙ 2,883 C4
†47302 Cowan 428 G4
47114 Crandall 176 E8
47522 Crane D7
47933 Crawfordsville⊙ 13,325 D4
46732 Cromwell 458 F2
47229 Crothersville 1,747 F7
46307 Crown Point⊙ 16,455 C2
46511 Culver 1,601 E2
46229 Cumberland 3,375 E5
47612 Cynthiana 874 B8
47523 Dale 1,693 D8
47334 Daleville F4
47847 Dana 803 C5
46122 Danville⊙ 4,220 D5
47940 Darlington 811 D4
47618 Darmstadt 1,280 B8
47941 Dayton 781 D4
46733 Decatur⊙ 8,649 H3
47524 Decker 256 B7
†46917 Deer Creek 250 E3
46923 Delphi⊙ 3,042 D3
46310 Demotte 2,559 C2
46926 Denver 589 E3
47230 Deputy 200 F7
47302 Desoto 385 G4
47018 Dillsboro 1,038 G6
46513 Donaldson 320 E2
†47118 Doolittle Mills 200 D8
47335 Dublin 979 G5
47525 Dubois 550 D8
47848 Dugger 1,118 C6
†46304 Dune Acres 291 C1
47336 Dunkirk 3,180 G4
†46514 Dunlap 5,397 F1
47337 Dunreith 184 F5
47231 Dupont 392 G7
46311 Dyer 9,555 C1
†46074 Eagletown 306 E4
47942 Earl Park 469 C3
46312 East Chicago 39,786 C1
47019 East Enterprise 250 H7
†47370 East Germantown (Pershing) 438 G5
47338 Eaton 1,804 G4
47116 Eckerty 108 D8
47339 Economy 237 G5
†46011 Edgewood 2,215 F4
46124 Edinburgh 4,856 E6
47528 Edwardsport 459 C7
†47150 Edwardsville 700 F8
47613 Elberfeld 640 C8
47117 Elizabeth 178 F8
47232 Elizabethtown 603 F6
46514 Elkhart 41,305 F1
Elkhart‡ 137,330 F1
47429 Ellettsville 3,328 D6
47529 Elnora 756 C7
†47018 Elrod 200 G6
†47901 Elston 500 D4
46036 Elwood 10,867 F4
46125 Eminence 200 D5
47118 English⊙ 633 E8
46524 Etna Green 522 E2
†47928 Eugene 400 B5
*47701 Evansville⊙ 130,496 C9
Evansville‡ 309,408 C9
†47331 Everton 500 G5
46126 Fairland 950 F5
46928 Fairmount 3,286 F4
†47842 Fairview Park 1,545 C5
47850 Farmersburg 1,240 C6
47340 Farmland 1,560 G4
†47421 Fayetteville 180 D7
47532 Ferdinand 2,192 D8
46128 Fillmore 550 D5
46129 Finly 400 F5
46038 Fishers 2,008 E5
47234 Flat Rock 323 F6
46929 Flora 2,303 E3
47119 Floyds Knobs 500 F8
47851 Fontanet 325 C5
46039 Forest 400 E4
47648 Fort Branch 2,504 B8
46040 Fortville 2,787 F5
*46801 Fort Wayne⊙ 172,028 G2
Fort Wayne‡ 382,961 G2
47341 Fountain City 839 H5
46130 Fountaintown 225 F5
47944 Fowler⊙ 2,319 C3
46930 Fowlerton 300 F4
47946 Francesville 944 D3
47649 Francisco 612 B8
46041 Frankfort⊙ 15,168 E4
46131 Franklin⊙ 11,563 E6
46044 Frankton 2,080 F4
47120 Fredericksburg 233 E8
47431 Freedom 100 D6
47535 Freelandville 600 C7
47235 Freetown 600 E7
46737 Fremont 1,180 H1
47432 French Lick 2,265 D7
46931 Fulton 393 E3
†47119 Galena 1,186 F8
46932 Galveston 1,822 E3
46738 Garrett 4,751 G2
*46401 Gary 151,953 C1
Gary-Hammond-East Chicago‡ 642,781 C1
46933 Gas City 6,370 F4
47342 Gaston 1,150 G4
46740 Geneva 1,430 H3
47537 Gentryville 299 C8
47122 Georgetown 1,494 F8
46133 Glenwood 370 G5
†47567 Glezen 300 C8
46045 Goldsmith 235 E4

(continued on following page)

Agriculture, Industry and Resources

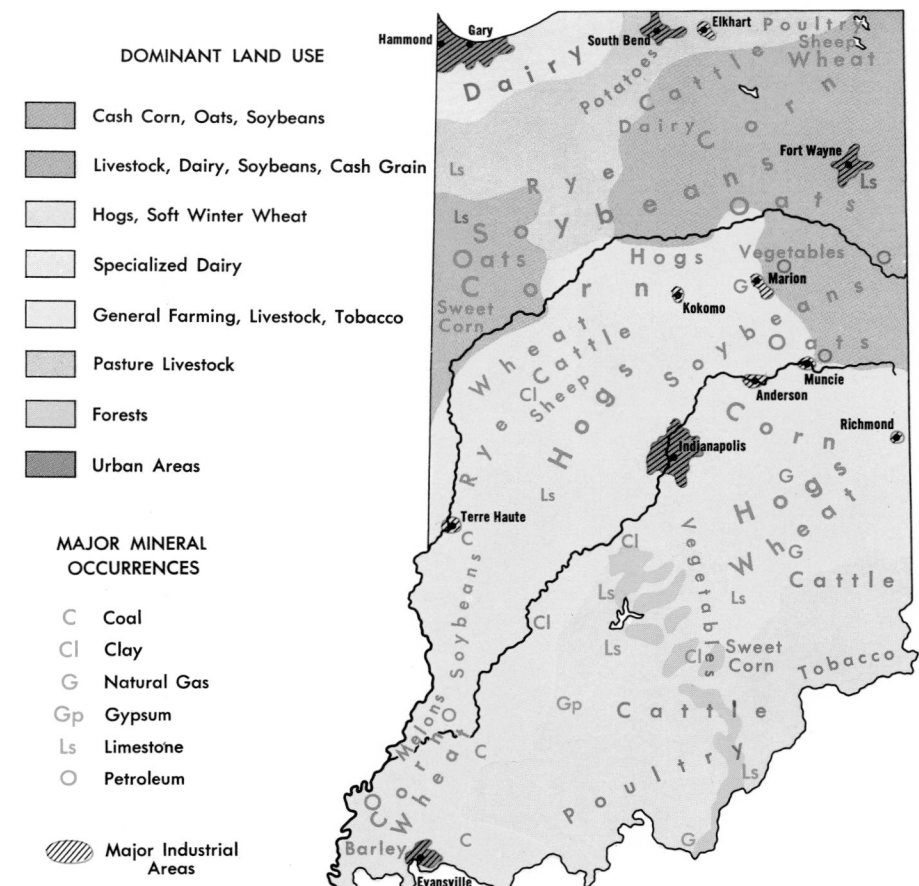

DOMINANT LAND USE

- Cash Corn, Oats, Soybeans
- Livestock, Dairy, Soybeans, Cash Grain
- Hogs, Soft Winter Wheat
- Specialized Dairy
- General Farming, Livestock, Tobacco
- Pasture Livestock
- Forests
- Urban Areas

MAJOR MINERAL OCCURRENCES

- C Coal
- Cl Clay
- G Natural Gas
- Gp Gypsum
- Ls Limestone
- O Petroleum

Major Industrial Areas

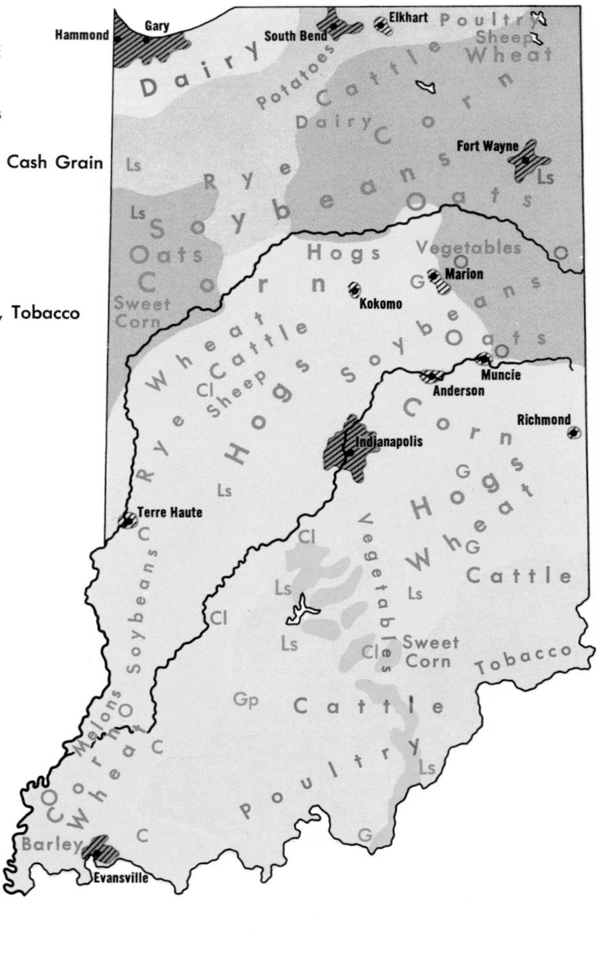

⊙County seat.
‡Population of metropolitan area.
† Zip of nearest p.o.   * Multiple zips.

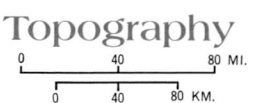

Topography

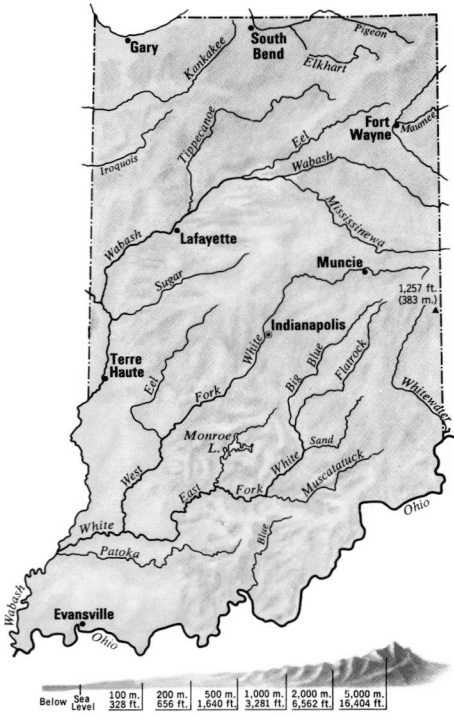

Indiana

SCALE

| 0 | 5 | 10 | 20 | 30 | 40 MI. |

| 0 | 5 | 10 | 20 | 30 | 40 KM. |

State Capitals .... ⍟

County Seats .... ◉

Major Limited Access Hwys. _____

Scale 1:1,570,000

© Copyright HAMMOND INCORPORATED, Maplewood, N.J.

228

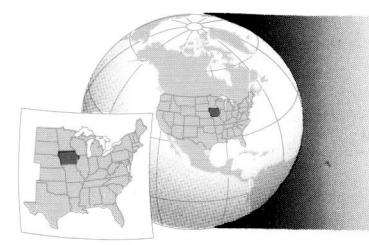

AREA 56,275 sq. mi. (145,752 sq. km.)
POPULATION 2,913,808
CAPITAL Des Moines
LARGEST CITY Des Moines
HIGHEST POINT (Osceola Co.) 1670 ft.
  (509 m.)
SETTLED IN 1788
ADMITTED TO UNION December 28, 1846
POPULAR NAME Hawkeye State
STATE FLOWER Wild Rose
STATE BIRD Eastern Goldfinch

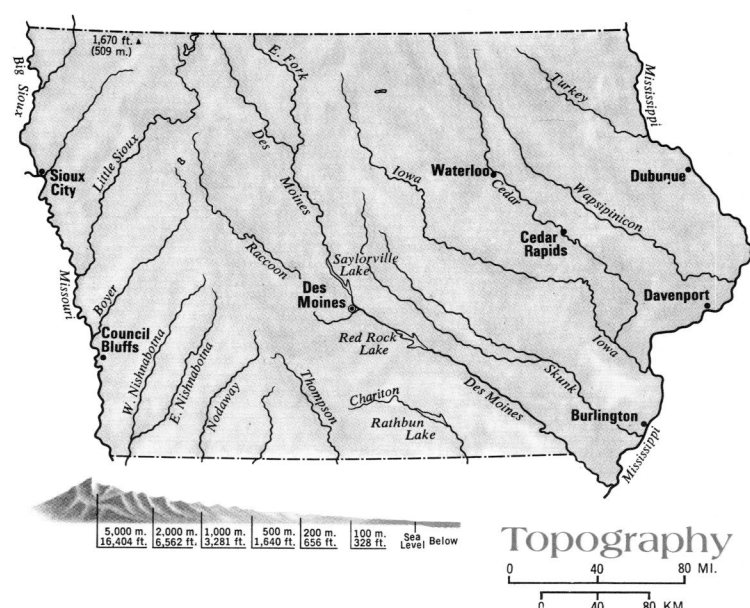

Topography

(continued on following page)

Agriculture, Industry and Resources

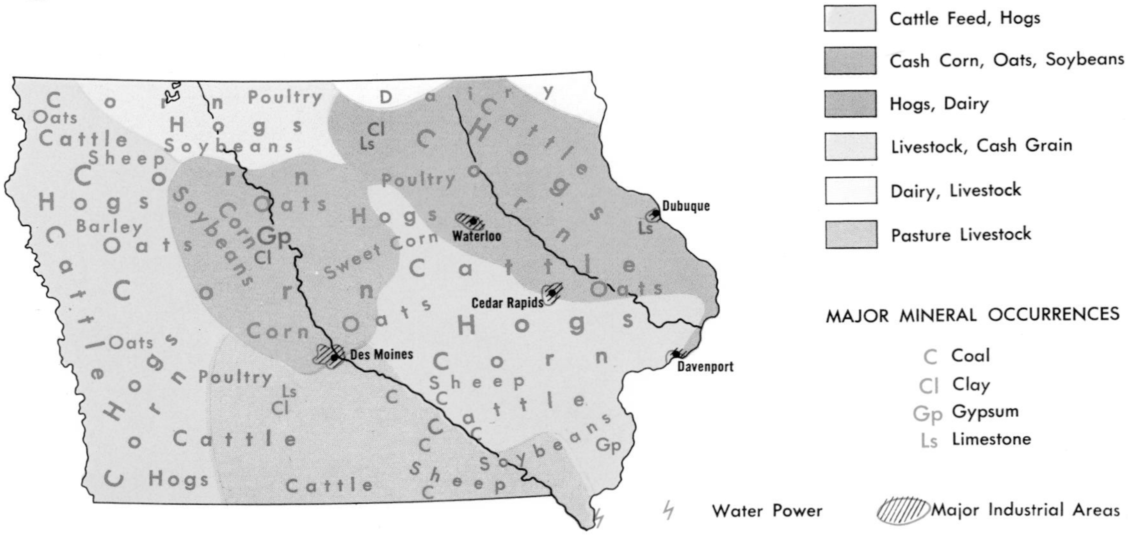
DOMINANT LAND USE
Cattle Feed, Hogs
Cash Corn, Oats, Soybeans
Hogs, Dairy
Livestock, Cash Grain
Dairy, Livestock
Pasture Livestock
MAJOR MINERAL OCCURRENCES
C Coal
Cl Clay
Gp Gypsum
Ls Limestone
Water Power
Major Industrial Areas
Dubuque
Waterloo
Cedar Rapids
Des Moines
Davenport

51535 Griswold 1,176 ..... C6
50638 Grundy Center⊙ 2,880 ..... H4
50115 Guthrie Center⊙ 1,713 ..... D5
52052 Guttenberg 2,428 ..... L3
51640 Hamburg 1,597 ..... B7
50441 Hampton⊙ 4,630 ..... G3
51536 Hancock 254 ..... C6
50544 Harcourt 347 ..... E4
51537 Harlan⊙ 5,357 ..... C5
52146 Harpers Ferry 258 ..... L2
50118 Hartford 761 ..... G6
51346 Hartley 1,700 ..... C2
50119 Harvey 275 ..... H6
50546 Havelock 279 ..... D3
51023 Hawarden 2,722 ..... A2
52147 Hawkeye 512 ..... J3
50641 Hazleton 877 ..... K3
52563 Hedrick 847 ..... J6
51541 Henderson 236 ..... B6
52233 Hiawatha 4,825 ..... K4
52235 Hills 547 ..... K5
52630 Hillsboro 208 ..... K7
51024 Hinton 659 ..... A3
50642 Holland 278 ..... H4
51025 Holstein 1,477 ..... B4
52053 Holy Cross 310 ..... L3
52237 Hopkinton 774 ..... L4
51026 Hornick 239 ..... A4
51238 Hospers 655 ..... B2
50122 Hubbard 852 ..... G4
50643 Hudson 2,267 ..... H4
51239 Hull 1,714 ..... A2
50548 Humboldt 4,794 ..... E3
50123 Humeston 671 ..... G7
50124 Huxley 1,884 ..... F5
51445 Ida Grove⊙ 2,285 ..... B4
50644 Independence⊙ 6,392 ..... K4
50125 Indianola⊙ 10,843 ..... F6
51240 Inwood 755 ..... A2
50645 Ionia 350 ..... J2
52240 Iowa City⊙ 50,508 ..... L5
Iowa City○‡ 81,717 ..... L5
50126 Iowa Falls 6,174 ..... G3
51027 Ireton 588 ..... A3
51446 Irwin 427 ..... C5
50128 Jamaica 275 ..... E5
50647 Janesville 840 ..... J3
50129 Jefferson⊙ 4,854 ..... E4
50648 Jesup 2,343 ..... J4
50130 Jewell 1,145 ..... F4
50131 Johnston 2,617 ..... F5
52247 Kalona 1,862 ..... K6
50447 Kanawha 756 ..... F3
50133 Kellerton 278 ..... E7
50134 Kelley 237 ..... F5
50135 Kellogg 654 ..... H5
50448 Kensett 360 ..... G2
52632 Keokuk⊙ 13,536 ..... L8
52565 Keosauqua⊙ 1,003 ..... J7
52248 Keota 1,034 ..... K6
50136 Keswick 300 ..... J6
52249 Keystone 618 ..... J5
51543 Kimballton 362 ..... D5
51028 Kingsley 1,209 ..... A3
51448 Kiron 317 ..... C4
50449 Klemme 620 ..... F3
50138 Knoxville⊙ 8,143 ..... G6
50139 Lacona 376 ..... G6
52251 Ladora 289 ..... J5
51449 Lake City 2,006 ..... D4
50450 Lake Mills 2,281 ..... F2
51347 Lake Park 1,123 ..... C2
50588 Lakeside 589 ..... C3
51450 Lake View 1,291 ..... C4
50451 Lakota 330 ..... E2
50140 Lamoni 2,705 ..... E7
50650 Lamont 554 ..... K3
52054 La Motte 322 ..... M4
52151 Lansing 1,181 ..... L2
50651 La Porte City 2,324 ..... J4
51241 Larchwood 701 ..... A2
50452 Latimer 441 ..... G3
50141 Laurel 278 ..... H5
50554 Laurens 1,606 ..... D3
52154 Lawler 534 ..... J2
51030 Lawton 447 ..... A4
52753 Le Claire 2,899 ..... N5
50142 Le Grand 921 ..... H5
50557 Lehigh 654 ..... E4
50453 Leland 274 ..... F2
51031 Le Mars⊙ 8,276 ..... A3
50851 Lenox 1,338 ..... D7
50144 Leon⊙ 2,094 ..... F7
51242 Lester 274 ..... A2
52754 Letts 473 ..... L6
51544 Lewis 497 ..... C6
52567 Libertyville 281 ..... K7
52155 Lime Springs 476 ..... J2
50146 Linden 264 ..... E5
50147 Lineville 319 ..... G7
52253 Lisbon 1,458 ..... L5
50148 Liscomb 296 ..... H4
51243 Little Rock 490 ..... B2
51545 Little Sioux 251 ..... B5
50558 Livermore 490 ..... E3
52635 Lockridge 271 ..... K7
51546 Logan⊙ 1,540 ..... B5
51453 Lohrville 521 ..... D4
52755 Lone Tree 1,014 ..... L6
52756 Long Grove 596 ..... M5
50149 Lorimor 405 ..... E6
52254 Lost Nation 524 ..... M5
50150 Lovilia 637 ..... H6
52255 Lowden 717 ..... L5
52757 Low Moor 346 ..... N5
52156 Luana 246 ..... K2
50151 Lucas 292 ..... G6
50560 Lu Verne 418 ..... E3
52056 Luxemburg 271 ..... L3
50153 Lynnville 406 ..... H5
50561 Lytton 377 ..... D4
51549 Macedonia 279 ..... C6
50156 Madrid 2,281 ..... F5
50157 Malcom 418 ..... H5
50562 Mallard 407 ..... D3
51551 Malvern 1,244 ..... B7
52057 Manchester⊙ 4,942 ..... L3
51454 Manilla 1,020 ..... C5
50456 Manly 1,496 ..... G2
51455 Manning 1,609 ..... C5
50563 Manson 1,924 ..... D3
51034 Mapleton 1,495 ..... B4
52060 Maquoketa⊙ 6,313 ..... M4
50565 Marathon 442 ..... C3
50653 Marble Rock 419 ..... H3
51035 Marcus 1,206 ..... B3
52301 Marengo⊙ 2,308 ..... J5
52302 Marion 19,474 ..... K4
52158 Marquette 528 ..... L2
50158 Marshalltown⊙ 26,938 ..... G4
52305 Martelle 316 ..... L4
50160 Martensdale 438 ..... F6
50401 Mason City⊙ 30,144 ..... G2
50853 Massena 518 ..... D6
51036 Maurice 288 ..... A3
50161 Maxwell 783 ..... G5
50655 Maynard 561 ..... K3
50154 McCallsburg 304 ..... G4
52758 McCausland 381 ..... M5
52157 McGregor 945 ..... L2
52306 Mechanicsville 1,166 ..... L5
52637 Mediapolis 1,685 ..... L6
50162 Melbourne 732 ..... G5
50163 Melcher 953 ..... G6
51350 Melvin 277 ..... B2
50164 Menlo 410 ..... E5
51037 Meriden 233 ..... B3
51038 Merrill 737 ..... A3
50457 Meservey 324 ..... G3
52307 Middle 335 ..... K5
52638 Middletown 487 ..... L7
52064 Miles 398 ..... N4
51351 Milford 2,076 ..... C2
50166 Milo 778 ..... G6
52570 Milton 567 ..... J7
50167 Minburn 390 ..... E5
51553 Minden 419 ..... C6
50168 Mingo 303 ..... G5
51555 Missouri Valley 3,107 ..... B5
50169 Mitchellville 1,530 ..... G5
51556 Modale 373 ..... B5
51557 Mondamin 423 ..... B5
52159 Monona 1,530 ..... L2
50170 Monroe 1,875 ..... G5
50171 Montezuma⊙ 1,485 ..... H5
52310 Monticello 3,641 ..... L4
50173 Montour 387 ..... H5
52759 Montpelier 250 ..... M6
52639 Montrose 1,038 ..... L7
51558 Moorhead 264 ..... B5
50566 Moorland 257 ..... E4
52571 Moravia 706 ..... H7
52640 Morning Sun 959 ..... L6
52760 Moscow 350 ..... L5
52572 Moulton 762 ..... H7
50854 Mount Ayr⊙ 1,938 ..... E7
52641 Mount Pleasant⊙ 7,322 ..... L7
52314 Mount Vernon 3,325 ..... K5
51039 Moville 1,273 ..... A4
50174 Murray 703 ..... F6
52761 Muscatine⊙ 23,467 ..... L6
52574 Mystic 665 ..... H7
50658 Nashua 1,846 ..... J3
51559 Neola 839 ..... B6
50201 Nevada⊙ 5,912 ..... G5
52160 New Albin 609 ..... L2
50568 Newell 913 ..... D3
52315 Newhall 899 ..... K5
50660 New Hartford 764 ..... H3
52645 New London 2,043 ..... L7
51646 New Market 554 ..... D7
50206 New Providence 249 ..... G4
50207 New Sharon 1,225 ..... H6
50208 Newton⊙ 15,292 ..... H5
52065 New Vienna 430 ..... L3
50210 New Virginia 512 ..... F6
52766 Nichols 375 ..... L6
50458 Nora Springs 1,572 ..... H2
52316 North English 990 ..... J5
52317 North Liberty 2,046 ..... K5
50459 Northwood⊙ 2,193 ..... G2
50211 Norwalk 2,676 ..... F6
52318 Norway 633 ..... K5
52319 Oakdale 300 ..... K5
51560 Oakland 1,552 ..... C6
52646 Oakville 470 ..... L6
51354 Ocheyedan 599 ..... B2
51458 Odebolt 1,299 ..... C4
50662 Oelwein 7,564 ..... K3
50212 Ogden 1,953 ..... E4
51355 Okoboji 559 ..... C2
52320 Olin 735 ..... L5
52576 Ollie 232 ..... J6
51040 Onawa⊙ 3,283 ..... A4
51041 Orange City⊙ 4,588 ..... A2
50858 Orient 416 ..... E6
†51360 Orleans 546 ..... C2
50461 Osage⊙ 3,718 ..... H2
50213 Osceola⊙ 3,750 ..... F6
52577 Oskaloosa⊙ 10,984 ..... H6
52161 Ossian 829 ..... K2
50569 Otho 692 ..... E4
52501 Ottumwa⊙ 27,381 ..... J6
52322 Oxford 676 ..... K5
52323 Oxford Junction 600 ..... M4
51561 Pacific Junction 511 ..... B6
50571 Palmer 288 ..... D3
52324 Palo 529 ..... K4
51562 Panama 229 ..... B5
50216 Panora 1,211 ..... E5
50665 Parkersburg 1,968 ..... H3
52325 Parnell 234 ..... J5
50217 Paton 291 ..... E4
51046 Paullina 1,224 ..... B3
50219 Pella 8,349 ..... H6
50220 Perry 7,053 ..... E5
50221 Pershing 325 ..... G6
51563 Persia 355 ..... B5
51047 Peterson 470 ..... C3
51048 Pierson 408 ..... B3
51564 Pisgah 307 ..... B5
50666 Plainfield 469 ..... J3
50225 Pleasantville 1,531 ..... G6
50464 Plymouth 463 ..... G2
50574 Pocahontas⊙ 2,352 ..... D3
50226 Polk City 1,658 ..... F5
50575 Pomeroy 895 ..... D3
51565 Portsmouth 240 ..... C5
52162 Postville 1,475 ..... K2
50228 Prairie City 1,278 ..... G5
50859 Prescott 349 ..... D6
52069 Preston 1,120 ..... N4
Primghar⊙ 1,050 ..... B2
52768 Princeton 965 ..... N5
52163 Protivin 368 ..... J2
52584 Pulaski 267 ..... J7
52326 Quasqueton 599 ..... K4
51049 Quimby 424 ..... B3
50230 Radcliffe 593 ..... G4
50465 Rake 283 ..... F2
50667 Raymond 655 ..... J4
50668 Readlyn 858 ..... J3
50232 Reasnor 277 ..... G5
50233 Redfield 959 ..... E5
51566 Red Oak⊙ 6,810 ..... C6
50669 Reinbeck 1,808 ..... H4
50576 Rembrandt 291 ..... C3
51050 Remsen 1,592 ..... B3
50577 Renwick 410 ..... E3
50234 Rhodes 367 ..... G5
50466 Riceville 919 ..... H2
52585 Richland 600 ..... K6
52165 Ridgeway 308 ..... K2
50578 Ringsted 557 ..... D2
50235 Rippey 304 ..... E5
†52722 Riverdale 462 ..... N5
52327 Riverside 826 ..... K6
51650 Riverton 342 ..... B7
52328 Robins 726 ..... K4
50468 Rockford 1,012 ..... H2
51246 Rock Rapids⊙ 2,693 ..... A2
51247 Rock Valley 2,706 ..... A2
50469 Rockwell 1,039 ..... G3
50579 Rockwell City⊙ 2,276 ..... D4
50236 Roland 1,005 ..... F4
50581 Rolfe 796 ..... D3
50470 Rowan 259 ..... F3
52329 Rowley 275 ..... K4
51357 Royal 522 ..... C2
50471 Rudd 460 ..... H2
50237 Runnells 377 ..... G5
50238 Russell 593 ..... G7
51358 Ruthven 769 ..... D2
52330 Ryan 390 ..... K4
52070 Sabula 824 ..... N4
50583 Sac City⊙ 3,000 ..... C4
†52001 Sageville 291 ..... M3
50472 Saint Ansgar 1,100 ..... H2
50240 Saint Charles 507 ..... F6
52649 Salem 463 ..... K7
51052 Salix 429 ..... A4
51248 Sanborn 1,398 ..... B2
51053 Schaller 832 ..... C4
51461 Schleswig 868 ..... B4
51462 Scranton 748 ..... D4
51054 Sergeant Bluff 2,416 ..... A4
52590 Seymour 1,036 ..... G7
50475 Sheffield 1,224 ..... G3
51570 Shelby 665 ..... C5
50243 Sheldahl 315 ..... F5
51201 Sheldon 5,003 ..... B2
50670 Shell Rock 1,478 ..... H3
52332 Shellsburg 771 ..... K4
51601 Shenandoah 6,274 ..... C7
†52401 Shueyville 287 ..... K5
51249 Sibley⊙ 3,051 ..... B2
51652 Sidney⊙ 1,308 ..... B7
52591 Sigourney⊙ 2,330 ..... J6
51571 Silver City 291 ..... B6
51250 Sioux Center 4,588 ..... A2
*51101 Sioux City⊙ 82,003 ..... A3
Sioux City‡ 117,457 ..... A3
50585 Sioux Rapids 897 ..... C3
50244 Slater 1,312 ..... F5
51055 Sloan 978 ..... A4
51056 Smithland 282 ..... B4
51572 Soldier 257 ..... B5
52333 Solon 969 ..... L5
51301 Spencer⊙ 11,726 ..... C2
52168 Spillville 415 ..... J2
51360 Spirit Lake⊙ 3,976 ..... C2
52336 Springville 1,165 ..... L4
50476 Stacyville 538 ..... H2
50246 Stanhope 492 ..... F4
51573 Stanton 747 ..... C7
52337 Stanwood 705 ..... L5
50247 State Center 1,292 ..... G5
50672 Steamboat Rock 387 ..... G4
52651 Stockport 272 ..... K7
52769 Stockton 240 ..... M5
50588 Storm Lake⊙ 8,814 ..... C3
50248 Story City 2,762 ..... F4
50249 Stratford 806 ..... F4
52076 Strawberry Point 1,463 ..... K3
50250 Stuart 1,650 ..... E6
50251 Sully 828 ..... H5
50674 Sumner 2,335 ..... J3
51058 Sutherland 897 ..... B3
50590 Swea City 813 ..... E2
52338 Swisher 654 ..... K5
51653 Tabor 1,088 ..... B7
52339 Tama 2,968 ..... H5
51463 Templeton 319 ..... D5
51364 Terril 420 ..... C2
50478 Thompson 668 ..... F2
50479 Thornton 442 ..... G3
52340 Tiffin 413 ..... K5
52772 Tipton⊙ 3,055 ..... L5
50480 Titonka 607 ..... E2
52342 Toledo⊙ 2,445 ..... H4
50675 Traer 1,703 ..... J4
51575 Treynor 981 ..... B6
50676 Tripoli 1,280 ..... J3
50257 Truro 407 ..... F6
51576 Underwood 448 ..... B6
50258 Union 515 ..... G4
†52240 University Heights 1,069 ..... K5
52595 University Park 645 ..... H6
52345 Urbana 574 ..... K4
50322 Urbandale 17,869 ..... F5
51060 Ute 479 ..... B4
51465 Vail 490 ..... C4
52346 Van Horne 682 ..... J4
50261 Van Meter 747 ..... E5
50262 Van Wert 245 ..... F7
50482 Ventura 614 ..... F2
52347 Victor 1,046 ..... J5
50864 Villisca 1,434 ..... C7
52349 Vinton⊙ 5,040 ..... J4
52077 Volga 310 ..... L3
52169 Wadena 230 ..... K3
†51360 Wahpeton 372 ..... C2
52773 Walcott 1,425 ..... M5
52351 Walford 285 ..... K5
52352 Walker 733 ..... K4
51365 Wallingford 256 ..... D2
51466 Wall Lake 892 ..... C4
51577 Walnut 897 ..... C6
52653 Wapello⊙ 2,011 ..... L6
52353 Washington⊙ 6,584 ..... K6
51061 Washta 320 ..... B3
*50701 Waterloo⊙ 75,985 ..... J4
Waterloo-Cedar Falls‡ 137,961 ..... J4
52171 Waucoma 308 ..... J2
50263 Waukee 2,227 ..... F5
52172 Waukon⊙ 3,983 ..... L2
50677 Waverly⊙ 8,444 ..... J3
52654 Wayland 720 ..... K6
52356 Wellman 1,125 ..... K6
50680 Wellsburg 761 ..... H4
50483 Wesley 598 ..... E2
50597 West Bend 941 ..... D3
52358 West Branch 1,867 ..... L5
52655 West Burlington 3,371 ..... L7
50318 West Des Moines 21,894 ..... F5
50681 Westgate 263 ..... K3
52776 West Liberty 2,723 ..... L5
†51351 West Okoboji 435 ..... C2
52656 West Point 1,133 ..... K7
51467 Westside 387 ..... C4
52175 West Union⊙ 2,783 ..... K3
50268 What Cheer 803 ..... J6
52777 Wheatland 840 ..... M5
51063 Whiting 734 ..... A4
50598 Whittemore 647 ..... E2
50271 Williams 410 ..... F3
52361 Williamsburg 2,033 ..... J5
52778 Wilton 2,502 ..... M5
50311 Windsor Heights 5,474 ..... F5
52659 Winfield 1,042 ..... L6
50273 Winterset⊙ 4,021 ..... E6
50682 Winthrop 767 ..... K4
50484 Woden 287 ..... F2
51579 Woodbine 1,463 ..... B5
50276 Woodward 1,212 ..... E5
50599 Woolstock 235 ..... F3
52078 Worthington 432 ..... L4
52362 Wyoming 702 ..... L4
50277 Yale 299 ..... E5
50278 Zearing 630 ..... G4

OTHER FEATURES

Big Sioux (riv.) A3
Boyer (riv.) B5
Cedar (riv.) K4
Chariton (riv.) G7
Clear (lake) G2
Eagle (lake) F2
East Nishnabotna (riv.) C6
Effigy Mounds Nat'l Mon. L2
Five Island (lake) D2
Floyd (riv.) A3
Herbert Hoover Nat'l Hist. Site L5
Iowa (riv.) H4
Little Sioux (riv.) B3
Lost Island (lake) D2
Mississippi (riv.) L7
Missouri (riv.) A4
Nodaway (riv.) D7
Palo Alto (lake) D2
Platte (riv.) D8
Raccoon (riv.) D4
Rathbun (lake) G7
Red Rock (lake) G6
Rock (riv.) A2
Sac and Fox Ind. Res. H5
Saylorville (lake) F5
Skunk (riv.) K6
Spirit (lake) C2
Storm (lake) C3
Thompson (riv.) E7
Trumbull (lake) C2
Turkey (riv.) K2
Upper Iowa (riv.) K2
Wapsipinicon (riv.) J3
West Nishnabotna (riv.) C6

⊙County seat.
‡Population of metropolitan area.
† Zip of nearest p.o. * Multiple zips.

COUNTIES

Allen 15,654 .... G4
Anderson 8,749 .... G3
Atchison 18,397 .... G2
Barber 6,548 .... D4
Barton 31,343 .... D3
Bourbon 15,969 .... H4
Brown 11,955 .... G2
Butler 44,782 .... F4
Chase 3,309 .... F3
Chautauqua 5,016 .... F4
Cherokee 22,304 .... H4
Cheyenne 3,678 .... A2
Clark 2,599 .... C4
Clay 9,802 .... E2
Cloud 12,494 .... E2
Coffey 9,370 .... G3
Comanche 2,554 .... C4
Cowley 36,824 .... F4
Crawford 37,916 .... H4
Decatur 4,509 .... B2
Dickinson 20,175 .... E3
Doniphan 9,268 .... G2
Douglas 67,640 .... G3
Edwards 4,271 .... C4
Elk 3,918 .... F4
Ellis 26,098 .... C3
Ellsworth 6,640 .... D3
Finney 23,825 .... B3
Ford 24,315 .... C4
Franklin 22,062 .... G3
Geary 29,852 .... F3
Gove 3,726 .... B3
Graham 3,995 .... C2
Grant 6,977 .... A4
Gray 5,138 .... B4
Greeley 1,845 .... A3
Greenwood 8,764 .... F4
Hamilton 2,514 .... A3
Harper 7,778 .... D4
Harvey 30,531 .... E3
Haskell 3,814 .... B4
Hodgeman 2,269 .... C3
Jackson 11,644 .... G2
Jefferson 15,207 .... G2
Jewell 5,241 .... D2
Johnson 270,269 .... H3
Kearny 3,435 .... A3
Kingman 8,960 .... D4
Kiowa 4,046 .... C4
Labette 25,682 .... G4
Lane 2,472 .... B3
Leavenworth 54,809 .... G2
Lincoln 4,145 .... D2
Linn 8,234 .... H3
Logan 3,478 .... A3
Lyon 35,108 .... F3
Marion 13,522 .... E3
Marshall 12,787 .... F2
McPherson 26,855 .... E3
Meade 4,788 .... B4
Miami 21,618 .... H3
Mitchell 8,117 .... D2
Montgomery 42,281 .... G4
Morris 6,419 .... F3
Morton 3,454 .... A4
Nemaha 11,211 .... F2
Neosho 18,967 .... G4
Ness 4,498 .... C3
Norton 6,689 .... C2
Osage 15,319 .... G3
Osborne 5,959 .... D2
Ottawa 5,971 .... E2
Pawnee 8,065 .... C3
Phillips 7,406 .... C2
Pottawatomie 14,782 .... F2
Pratt 10,275 .... D4
Rawlins 4,105 .... A2
Reno 64,983 .... D4
Republic 7,569 .... E2
Rice 11,900 .... D3
Riley 63,505 .... F2
Rooks 7,006 .... C2
Rush 4,516 .... C3
Russell 8,868 .... D3
Saline 48,905 .... E3
Scott 5,782 .... B3
Sedgwick 367,088 .... E4
Seward 17,071 .... B4
Shawnee 154,916 .... G2
Sheridan 3,544 .... B2
Sherman 7,759 .... A2
Smith 5,947 .... D2
Stafford 5,694 .... D3
Stanton 2,339 .... A4
Stevens 4,736 .... A4
Sumner 24,928 .... E4
Thomas 8,451 .... A2
Trego 4,165 .... C3
Wabaunsee 6,867 .... F3
Wallace 2,045 .... A3
Washington 8,543 .... E2
Wichita 3,041 .... A3
Wilson 12,128 .... G4
Woodson 4,600 .... G4
Wyandotte 172,335 .... H2

CITIES and TOWNS

Zip *Name/Pop.* *Key*

67510 Abbyville 123 .... D4
67410 Abilene⊙ 6,572 .... E3
66830 Admire 158 .... F3
66930 Agenda 106 .... E2
67621 Agra 321 .... C2
67511 Albert 236 .... C3
67512 Alden 214 .... D3
67513 Alexander 116 .... C3
66833 Allen 205 .... F3
66401 Alma⊙ 925 .... F2
67622 Almena 517 .... C2
67330 Altamont 1,054 .... G4
66834 Alta Vista 430 .... F3
67623 Alton 135 .... D2
66710 Altoona 564 .... G4
66835 Americus 915 .... F3
67001 Andale 538 .... E4
67002 Andover 2,801 .... E4
67003 Anthony⊙ 2,661 .... D4
66711 Arcadia 460 .... H4
67004 Argonia 587 .... E4
67005 Arkansas City 13,201 .... E4
67514 Arlington 631 .... D4
66712 Arma 1,676 .... H4
67831 Ashland⊙ 1,096 .... C4
67416 Assaria 414 .... E3
66002 Atchison⊙ 11,407 .... G2
66932 Athol 90 .... D2
67008 Atlanta 256 .... F4
67009 Attica 730 .... D4
67730 Atwood⊙ 1,665 .... B2
66402 Auburn 890 .... G3
67010 Augusta 6,968 .... F4
67417 Aurora 130 .... E2
66403 Axtell 470 .... F2
66404 Baileyville 130 .... F2
66006 Baldwin City 2,829 .... G3
67418 Barnard 163 .... D2
66933 Barnes 257 .... F2
67332 Bartlett 163 .... G4
66007 Basehor 1,483 .... G2
†66749 Bassett 31 .... G4
66713 Baxter Springs 4,730 .... H4
67516 Bazine 385 .... C3
66406 Beattie 316 .... F2
67013 Belle Plaine 1,706 .... E4
66935 Belleville⊙ 2,805 .... E2
67420 Beloit⊙ 4,367 .... D2
67519 Belpre 154 .... C4
66407 Belvue 212 .... F2
66714 Benedict 111 .... G4
67422 Bennington 579 .... E2
67016 Bentley 311 .... E4
67017 Benton 609 .... E4
66408 Bern 220 .... F2
67423 Beverly 171 .... E2
67731 Bird City 546 .... A2
67520 Bison 279 .... C3
66010 Blue Mound 319 .... H3
66411 Blue Rapids 1,280 .... F2
67018 Bluff City 95 .... E4
67625 Bogue 197 .... C2
66012 Bonner Springs 6,266 .... H2
67732 Brewster 327 .... A2
66716 Bronson 414 .... H4
67425 Brookville 259 .... E3
67521 Brownell 92 .... C3
67834 Bucklin 786 .... C4
66717 Buffalo 386 .... G4
67522 Buhler 1,188 .... E3
67626 Bunker Hill 124 .... D3
67019 Burden 518 .... F4
67523 Burdett 275 .... C3
66413 Burlingame 1,239 .... G3
66839 Burlington⊙ 2,901 .... G3
66840 Burns 224 .... F3
66936 Burr Oak 366 .... D2
67020 Burrton 976 .... E3
66841 Bushong 62 .... F3
67427 Bushton 388 .... D3
67021 Byers 47 .... D4
67022 Caldwell 1,401 .... E4
67023 Cambridge 113 .... F4
67333 Caney 2,284 .... G4
67428 Canton 926 .... E3
66414 Carbondale 1,518 .... G3
67429 Carlton 49 .... E3
66842 Cassoday 122 .... F3
67430 Cawker City 640 .... D2
67628 Cedar 53 .... D2
66843 Cedar Point 66 .... F3
67024 Cedar Vale 848 .... F4
66415 Centralia 486 .... F2
66720 Chanute 10,506 .... G4
67431 Chapman 1,255 .... E3
67524 Chase 753 .... D3
67334 Chautauqua 156 .... F4
67025 Cheney 1,404 .... E4
66724 Cherokee 775 .... H4
67335 Cherryvale 2,769 .... G4
67336 Chetopa 1,751 .... G4
67835 Cimarron⊙ 1,491 .... B4
66416 Circleville 164 .... G2
67525 Claflin 764 .... D3
67432 Clay Center⊙ 4,948 .... E2
67629 Clayton 102 .... B2
67026 Clearwater 1,684 .... E4
66937 Clifton 695 .... E2
67027 Climax 81 .... F4
66938 Clyde 909 .... E2
67028 Coats 153 .... D4
67337 Coffeyville 15,185 .... G4
67701 Colby⊙ 5,544 .... A2
67029 Coldwater⊙ 989 .... C4
67631 Collyer 151 .... B2
66015 Colony 474 .... G3
66725 Columbus⊙ 3,426 .... H4
67030 Colwich 935 .... E4
66901 Concordia⊙ 6,847 .... E2
67031 Conway Springs 1,313 .... E4
67836 Coolidge 82 .... A3
67837 Copeland 323 .... B4
66417 Corning 158 .... F2
66845 Cottonwood Falls⊙ 954 .... F3
66846 Council Grove⊙ 2,381 .... F3
66939 Courtland 377 .... E2
66727 Coyville 98 .... G4
66940 Cuba 286 .... E2
†67124 Cullison 154 .... D4
67435 Culver 167 .... E3
67035 Cunningham 540 .... D4
67632 Damar 204 .... C2
67036 Danville 71 .... E4
67340 Dearing 475 .... G4
67838 Deerfield 538 .... A4
66418 Delia 181 .... G2
67436 Delphos 570 .... E2
66419 Denison 231 .... G2
66017 Denton 156 .... G2
67037 Derby 9,786 .... E4
66018 De Soto 2,061 .... H3
67038 Dexter 366 .... F4
67839 Dighton⊙ 1,390 .... B3

AREA 82,277 sq. mi. (213,097 sq. km.)
POPULATION 2,364,236
CAPITAL Topeka
LARGEST CITY Wichita
HIGHEST POINT Mt. Sunflower 4,039 ft. (1231 m.)
SETTLED IN 1831
ADMITTED TO UNION January 29, 1861
POPULAR NAME Sunflower State
STATE FLOWER Sunflower
STATE BIRD Western Meadowlark

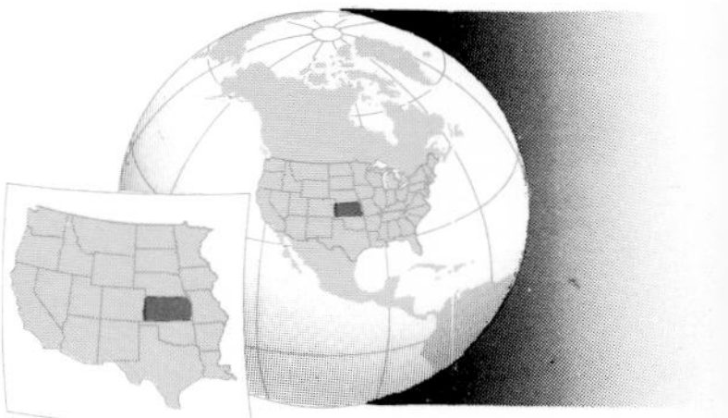

Agriculture, Industry and Resources

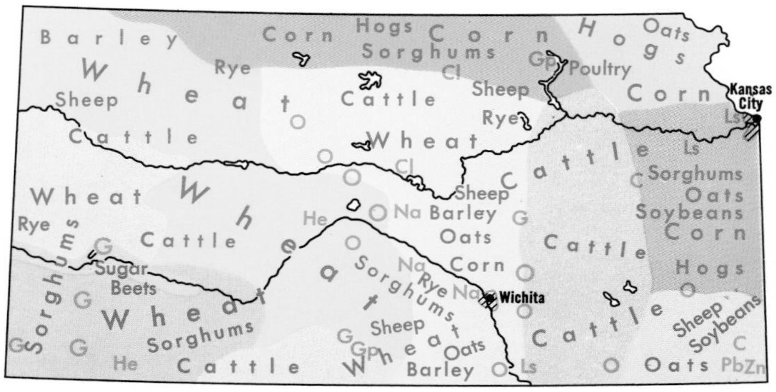

DOMINANT LAND USE

- Specialized Wheat
- Wheat, General Farming
- Wheat, Range Livestock
- Wheat, Grain Sorghums, Range Livestock
- Cattle Feed, Hogs
- Livestock, Cash Grain
- Livestock, Cash Grain, Dairy
- General Farming, Livestock, Cash Grain
- General Farming, Livestock, Special Crops
- Range Livestock

MAJOR MINERAL OCCURRENCES

C	Coal	Ls	Limestone
Cl	Clay	Na	Salt
G	Natural Gas	O	Petroleum
Gp	Gypsum	Pb	Lead
He	Helium	Zn	Zinc

Major Industrial Areas

67801 Dodge City⊙ 18,001 .... B4
67634 Dorrance 220 .... D3
67039 Douglass 1,450 .... F4
67437 Downs 1,324 .... D2
67635 Dresden 84 .... B2
66848 Dunlap 82 .... F3
67438 Durham 130 .... E3
66849 Dwight 320 .... F3
†66720 Earlton 79 .... G4
†67201 Eastborough 854 .... E4
66020 Easton 460 .... G2
66021 Edgerton 1,214 .... H3
67636 Edmond 56 .... C2
67342 Edna 537 .... G4
66113 Edwardsville 3,364 .... H2
66023 Effingham 634 .... G2
67041 Elbing 175 .... E3
67042 El Dorado⊙ 10,510 .... F4
†67361 Elgin 139 .... F4
67344 Elk City 404 .... G4
67345 Elk Falls 151 .... F4
67950 Elkhart⊙ 2,243 .... A4
67526 Ellinwood 2,508 .... D3
67637 Ellis 2,062 .... C3
67439 Ellsworth⊙ 2,465 .... D3
66850 Elmdale 109 .... F3
66732 Elsmore 104 .... G4
66024 Elwood 1,275 .... H2
66422 Emmett 223 .... F2
66801 Emporia⊙ 25,287 .... F3
67840 Englewood 111 .... C4
67841 Ensign 209 .... B4
67441 Enterprise 839 .... E3
66733 Erie⊙ 1,415 .... G4
66941 Esbon 234 .... D2
66423 Eskridge 603 .... F3
66025 Eudora 2,934 .... G3
67045 Eureka⊙ 3,425 .... F4
66424 Everest 331 .... G2
66425 Fairview 258 .... G2
†66101 Fairway 4,619 .... H2
67047 Fall River 173 .... G4
66851 Florence 729 .... E3
66026 Fontana 173 .... H3
67842 Ford 272 .... C4
66942 Formoso 166 .... D2
67843 Fort Dodge 400 .... C4
66027 Fort Leavenworth H2
66701 Fort Scott⊙ 8,893 .... H4
67844 Fowler 592 .... B4
66427 Frankfort 1,038 .... F2
66735 Franklin 400 .... H4
66736 Fredonia⊙ 3,047 .... G4
67049 Freeport 12 .... E4
66762 Frontenac 2,586 .... H4
66738 Fulton 194 .... H4
66739 Galena 3,587 .... H4
66740 Galesburg 181 .... G4
67443 Galva 651 .... E3
67846 Garden City⊙ 18,256 .... B4
67050 Garden Plain 775 .... E4
66030 Gardner 2,392 .... H3
67529 Garfield 277 .... C3
66032 Garnett⊙ 3,310 .... G3
66742 Gas 543 .... G4
67638 Gaylord 203 .... D2
67734 Gem 101 .... B2
67444 Geneseo 496 .... D3
67051 Geuda Springs 217 .... E4
66743 Girard⊙ 2,888 .... H4
67639 Glade 131 .... C2
67445 Glasco 710 .... E2
67446 Glen Elder 491 .... D2
67052 Goddard 1,427 .... E4
67053 Goessel 421 .... E3
66428 Goff 196 .... G2
67735 Goodland⊙ 5,708 .... A2
67640 Gorham 355 .... D3
67736 Gove⊙ 148 .... B3
67737 Grainfield 417 .... B2
†66441 Grandview Plaza 1,189 .... F2
66429 Grantville 220 .... G2
67530 Great Bend⊙ 16,608 .... D3
66033 Greeley 405 .... G3
67447 Green 155 .... E2
66943 Greenleaf 462 .... E2
67054 Greensburg⊙ 1,885 .... C4
67346 Grenola 335 .... F4
66852 Gridley 404 .... G3
67738 Grinnell 410 .... B2
67448 Gypsum 423 .... E3
66944 Haddam 239 .... E2
67056 Halstead 1,994 .... E4
66853 Hamilton 363 .... F4
66945 Hanover 802 .... F2
67849 Hanston 257 .... C3
67057 Hardtner 336 .... D4
67058 Harper 1,823 .... D4
66854 Hartford 551 .... F3
66431 Harveyville 280 .... F3
67347 Havana 169 .... G4
67543 Haven 1,125 .... E4
66432 Havensville 183 .... F2
67059 Haviland 770 .... C4

(continued on following page)

67601 Hays⊙ 16,301 .... C3
67060 Haysville 8,006 .... E4
67850 Healy 275 .... B3
67061 Hazelton 143 .... D4
66746 Hepler 165 .... H4
67449 Herington 2,930 .... E3
67739 Herndon 220 .... B2
67062 Hesston 3,013 .... E3
66434 Hiawatha⊙ 3,702 .... G2
†67880 Hickock 68 .... A4
66035 Highland 954 .... G2
67642 Hill City⊙ 2,028 .... C2
67063 Hillsboro 2,717 .... E3
67544 Hoisington 3,678 .... D3
67851 Holcomb 816 .... B3
66946 Hollenberg 57 .... F2
66436 Holton⊙ 3,132 .... G2
67450 Holyrood 567 .... D3
67451 Hope 468 .... E3
†67879 Horace 137 .... A3
66439 Horton 2,130 .... G2
67349 Howard⊙ 965 .... F4
67740 Hoxie⊙ 1,462 .... B2
66440 Hoyt 536 .... G2

67545 Hudson 157 .... D3
67951 Hugoton⊙ 3,165 .... A4
66748 Humboldt 2,230 .... G4
67452 Hunter 135 .... D2
66038 Huron 107 .... G2
67501 Hutchinson⊙ 40,284 .... D3
67301 Independence⊙ 10,598 .... G4
67853 Ingalls 274 .... B4
67546 Inman 947 .... E3
66749 Iola⊙ 6,938 .... G4
67065 Isabel 137 .... D4
67066 Iuka 235 .... D4
66948 Jamestown 440 .... E2
67643 Jennings 194 .... B2
67854 Jetmore⊙ 862 .... B3
66949 Jewell 589 .... D2
67855 Johnson⊙ 1,244 .... A4
66441 Junction City⊙ 19,305 .... E2
67454 Kanopolis 729 .... D3
67741 Kanorado 217 .... A2
*66101 Kansas City⊙ 161,148 .... H2
Kansas City‡ 1,327,020 .... H2
67067 Kechi 288 .... E4
66951 Kensington 681 .... C2

66039 Kincaid 192 .... G3
67068 Kingman⊙ 3,563 .... D4
67547 Kinsley⊙ 2,074 .... C4
67070 Kiowa 1,409 .... D4
67644 Kirwin 249 .... C2
67859 Kismet 368 .... B4
67350 Labette 123 .... G4
67548 La Crosse⊙ 1,618 .... C3
66040 La Cygne 1,025 .... H3
66751 La Harpe 687 .... G4
67860 Lakin⊙ 1,823 .... A4
66041 Lancaster 274 .... G2
66042 Lane 249 .... G3
67549 Langdon 84 .... D4
66043 Lansing 5,307 .... H2
67550 Larned⊙ 4,811 .... C3
67072 Latham 148 .... F4
66044 Lawrence⊙ 52,738 .... G3
Lawrence‡ 67,640 .... G3
66048 Leavenworth⊙ 33,656 .... H2
66206 Leawood 13,360 .... H3
66952 Lebanon 440 .... D2
66856 Lebo 966 .... G3
66050 Lecompton 576 .... G2

67073 Lehigh 189 .... E3
66215 Lenexa 18,639 .... H2
67645 Lenora 444 .... C2
67074 Leon 667 .... F4
66448 Leona 73 .... G2
66449 Leonardville 437 .... F2
67861 Leoti⊙ 1,869 .... A3
66857 Le Roy 701 .... G3
67552 Lewis 551 .... C4
67901 Liberal⊙ 14,911 .... B4
67351 Liberty 174 .... G4
67553 Liebenthal 163 .... C3
67455 Lincoln⊙ 1,599 .... D2
66858 Lincolnville 235 .... F3
67456 Lindsborg 3,155 .... E3
66953 Linn 483 .... E2
66052 Linwood 343 .... G2
67457 Little River 529 .... E3
67646 Logan 720 .... C2
67458 Longford 109 .... E2
67647 Long Island 187 .... C2
67352 Longton 396 .... F4
67459 Lorraine 157 .... D3
66859 Lost Springs 94 .... E3

66053 Louisburg 1,744 .... H3
66450 Louisville 207 .... F2
67648 Lucas 524 .... D2
67649 Luray 295 .... D2
66451 Lyndon⊙ 1,132 .... G3
67554 Lyons⊙ 4,134 .... D3
67557 Macksville 546 .... D4
66860 Madison 1,099 .... F3
66955 Mahaska 119 .... E2
67101 Maize 1,294 .... E4
67463 Manchester 98 .... E2
66502 Manhattan⊙ 32,644 .... F2
66956 Mankato⊙ 1,205 .... D2
67862 Manter 205 .... A4
66507 Maple Hill 381 .... F2
66754 Mapleton 121 .... H3
66861 Marion⊙ 1,951 .... F3
67464 Marquette 639 .... E3
66508 Marysville⊙ 3,670 .... F2
66862 Matfield Green 71 .... F3
66509 Mayetta 287 .... G2
67103 Mayfield 128 .... E4
67556 McCracken 292 .... C3
66753 McCune 528 .... G4

67745 McDonald 239 .... A2
66501 McFarland 242 .... F2
66054 McLouth 700 .... G2
67460 McPherson⊙ 11,753 .... E3
67864 Meade⊙ 1,777 .... B4
67104 Medicine Lodge⊙ 2,384 .... D4
66510 Melvern 481 .... G3
67746 Menlo 42 .... B2
66512 Meriden 707 .... G2
66203 Merriam 10,794 .... H3
67105 Milan 135 .... E4
66055 Mildred 64 .... G3
66514 Milford 465 .... F2
67466 Miltonvale 588 .... E2
67467 Minneapolis⊙ 2,075 .... E2
67865 Minneola 712 .... C4
66205 Mission 8,643 .... H2
67353 Moline 553 .... F4
67867 Montezuma 730 .... B4
66755 Moran 643 .... G4
67468 Morganville 261 .... E2
67650 Morland 223 .... B2
66515 Morrill 336 .... G2
66958 Morrowville 180 .... E2

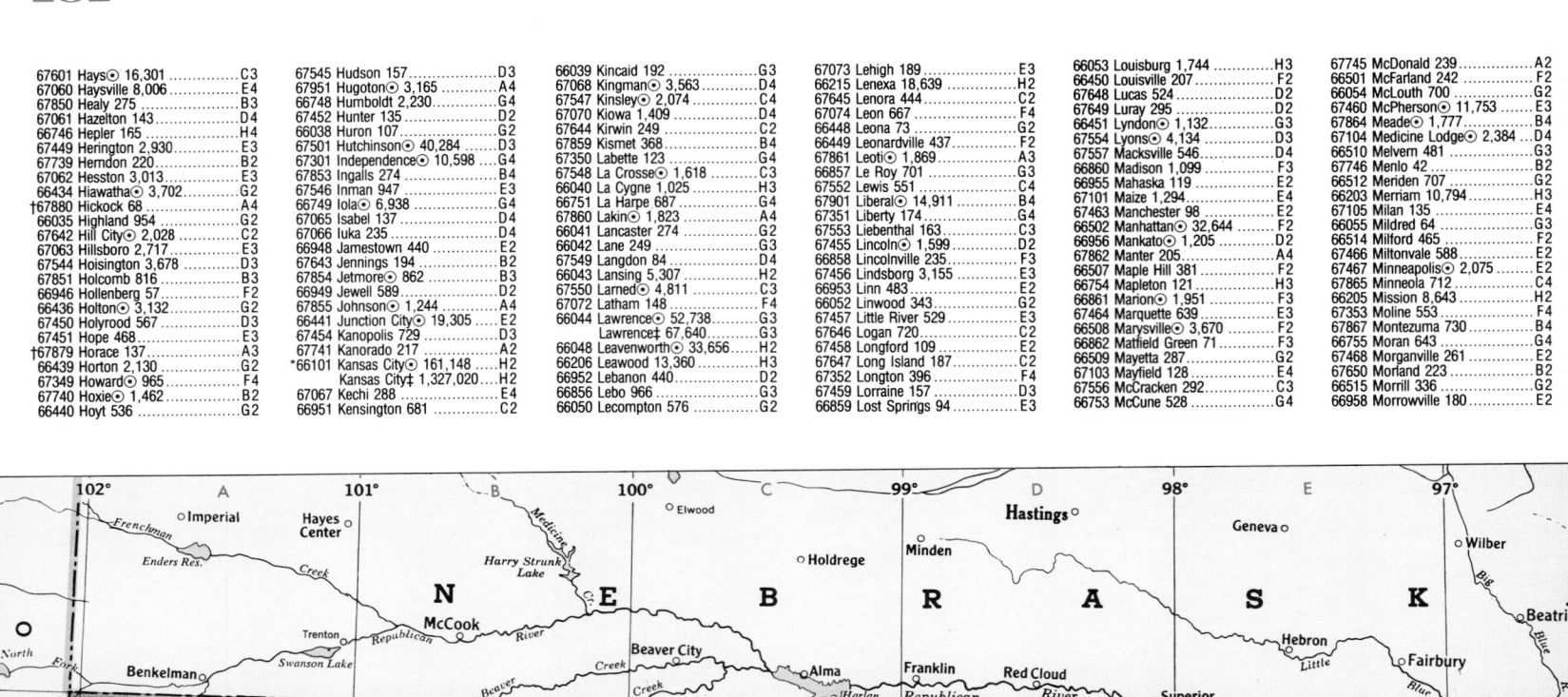

Kansas
SCALE
0 5 10 20 30 40 50 MI.
0 5 10 20 30 40 50 KM.
State Capitals
County Seats
Major Limited Access Hwys.
Scale 1:2,250,000
N E B R A S K A
O K L A
T E X A S
C O L O R A D O
Longitude
West of
Greenwich
© Copyright HAMMOND INCORPORATED, Maplewood, N. J.

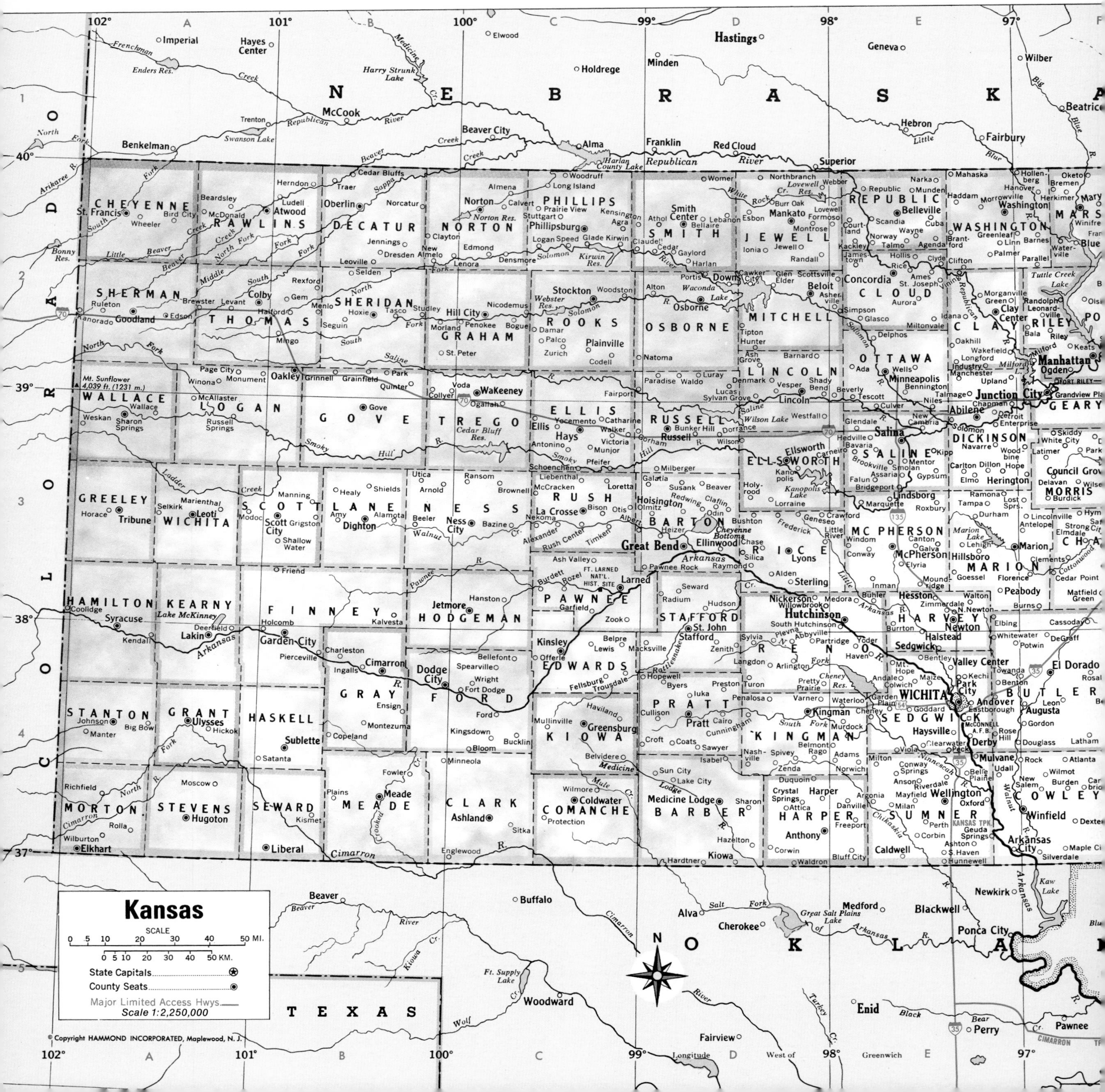

67952 Moscow 228	A4	
66056 Mound City⊙ 755	H3	
67107 Moundridge 1,453	E3	
67354 Mound Valley 381	G4	
67108 Mount Hope 791	E4	
66756 Mulberry 647	H4	
67109 Mullinville 339	C4	
67110 Mulvane 4,254	E4	
66959 Munden 152	E2	
66058 Muscotah 248	G2	
66960 Narka 120	E2	
67112 Nashville 127	D4	
67651 Natoma 515	D2	
66757 Neodesha 3,414	G4	
66758 Neosho Falls 157	G4	
66864 Neosho Rapids 289	F3	
67560 Ness City⊙ 1,769	C3	
66516 Netawaka 218	G2	
66759 New Albany 78	G4	
67470 New Cambria 175	D3	
66839 New Strawn (Strawn) 457	G3	
67114 Newton⊙ 16,332	E3	
67561 Nickerson 1,292	D3	
67355 Niotaze 104	F4	
67653 Norcatur 226	B2	
67117 North Newton 1,222	E3	
67654 Norton⊙ 3,400	C2	
66060 Nortonville 692	G2	
67472 Norwich 476	E4	
67472 Oakhill 35	E2	
67748 Oakley 2,343	B2	
67749 Oberlin⊙ 2,387	B2	
67563 Offerle 244	C4	
66517 Ogden 1,804	F2	
66518 Oketo 130	F2	
67564 Olathe⊙ 37,258	H3	
67564 Olmitz 140	D3	
66865 Olpe 477	F3	
66520 Olsburg 166	F2	
66521 Onaga 752	G2	
66522 Oneida 120	G2	
66523 Osage City 2,667	G3	
66064 Osawatomie 4,459	H3	
67473 Osborne⊙ 2,120	D2	
66066 Oskaloosa⊙ 1,092	G2	
66356 Oswego⊙ 2,218	G4	
67565 Otis 410	C3	
66067 Ottawa⊙ 11,016	G3	

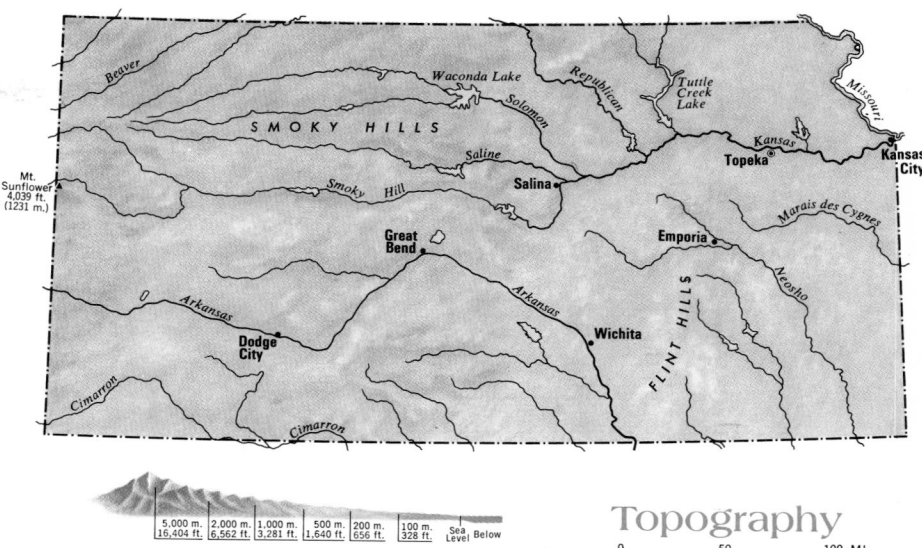

Topography

66524 Overbrook 930	G3	
66204 Overland Park 81,784	H3	
67119 Oxford 1,125	E4	
66070 Ozawkie 472	G2	
67657 Palco 329	C2	
66962 Palmer 149	E2	
66071 Paola⊙ 4,557	H3	
67658 Paradise 89	D2	
67751 Park 183	B2	
†67201 Park City 3,778	E4	
66072 Parker 270	H3	
67357 Parsons 12,898	G4	
67566 Partridge 268	D4	
67567 Pawnee Rock 409	D3	
66526 Paxico 125	F2	
66866 Peabody 1,474	E3	
67120 Peck 250	E4	
67121 Penalosa 31	D4	
66073 Perry 907	G2	
67360 Peru 286	F4	
67661 Phillipsburg⊙ 3,229	C2	
66762 Pittsburg 18,770	H4	
67869 Plains 1,044	B4	
67663 Plainville 2,458	C2	
66075 Pleasanton 1,303	H3	
67568 Plevna 115	D4	
66076 Pomona 868	G3	
67474 Portis 172	D2	
67123 Potwin 563	E4	
66527 Powhattan 95	G2	
67664 Prairie View 145	C2	
66208 Prairie Village 24,657	H2	
67124 Pratt⊙ 6,885	D4	
66767 Prescott 319	H3	
67569 Preston 227	D4	
67570 Pretty Prairie 655	D4	
66078 Princeton 244	G3	
67127 Protection 684	C4	
66528 Quenemo 413	G3	
67752 Quinter 931	B2	
67571 Radium 47	D3	
67475 Ramona 116	E3	
66963 Randall 154	D2	
66554 Randolph 131	F2	
67572 Ransom 448	C3	
66079 Rantoul 212	G3	
67573 Raymond 132	D3	
66868 Reading 244	F3	
66769 Redfield 185	H4	
66964 Republic 223	E2	
66529 Reserve 105	G2	
67753 Rexford 204	B2	
67953 Richfield 81	A4	
66080 Richmond 510	G3	
66531 Riley 829	F2	
66770 Riverton 650	H4	
66532 Robinson 324	G2	
†66205 Roeland Park 7,962	H2	
67954 Rolla 417	A4	
67133 Rose Hill 1,557	E4	
†66773 Roseland 119	H4	
66533 Rossville 1,045	G2	
67574 Rozel 219	C3	
67575 Rush Center 207	C3	
67665 Russell⊙ 5,427	D3	
67755 Russell Springs 56	A3	
66534 Sabetha 2,286	G2	
67535 Saint Francis⊙ 1,610	A2	
66535 Saint George 309	F2	
67576 Saint John⊙ 1,501	D3	
66536 Saint Marys 1,598	G2	
66771 Saint Paul 746	G4	
67401 Salina⊙ 41,843	E3	
67870 Satanta 1,117	B4	
66772 Savonburg 113	G4	
67134 Sawyer 213	D4	
66773 Scammon 501	H4	
66966 Scandia 480	E2	
67667 Schoenchen 209	C3	
67871 Scott City⊙ 4,154	B3	
67477 Scottsville 56	D2	
66537 Scranton 664	G3	
67361 Sedan⊙ 1,579	F4	
67135 Sedgwick 1,471	E4	
67757 Selden 266	B2	
66538 Seneca⊙ 2,389	F2	
66081 Severance 134	G2	
67137 Severy 447	E4	
67577 Seward 88	D3	
67138 Sharon 283	D4	
67758 Sharon Springs⊙ 982	A3	
*66202 Shawnee 29,653	H2	
66539 Silver Lake 1,350	G2	
67478 Simpson 123	E2	
66967 Smith Center⊙ 2,240	D2	
67479 Smolan 169	E3	
66540 Soldier 165	G2	
67480 Solomon 1,018	E3	
67140 South Haven 439	E4	
†67501 South Hutchinson 2,226	D3	
67876 Spearville 693	C4	
67142 Spivey 83	D4	
66083 Spring Hill 2,005	H3	
67578 Stafford 1,425	D4	
66775 Stark 143	G4	
67579 Sterling 2,312	D3	
67669 Stockton⊙ 1,825	C2	
66839 Strawn 457	G3	
66869 Strong City 675	F3	
67877 Sublette⊙ 1,293	B4	
66541 Summerfield 225	F2	
67143 Sun City 85	D4	
67481 Sylvan Grove 376	D2	
67581 Sylvia 353	D4	
67878 Syracuse⊙ 1,654	A3	
67483 Tampa 113	E3	
67484 Tescott 331	D3	
66542 Tecumseh 300	G2	
66776 Thayer 517	G4	
67582 Timken 99	C3	
67485 Tipton 321	D2	
66086 Tonganoxie 1,864	G2	
*66601 Topeka (cap.)⊙ 115,266	G2	
Topeka‡ 185,442	G2	
66777 Toronto 466	G4	
67144 Towanda 1,332	E4	
†66075 Trading Post 35	H3	
66778 Treece 194	H4	
67879 Tribune⊙ 955	A3	
66087 Troy⊙ 1,240	G2	
67583 Turon 481	D4	
67364 Tyro 289	G4	
67146 Udall 891	E4	
67880 Ulysses⊙ 4,653	A4	
66779 Uniontown 371	H4	
67584 Utica 275	B3	
67147 Valley Center 3,300	E4	
66088 Valley Falls 1,189	G2	
66544 Vermillion 191	F2	
67671 Victoria 1,328	C3	
†66937 Vining 85	E2	
67149 Viola 199	E4	
66870 Virgil 169	F4	
67672 WaKeeney⊙ 2,388	C2	
67487 Wakefield 803	E2	
67673 Waldo 75	D2	
67150 Waldron 29	D4	
66780 Wallace 86	A3	
66780 Walnut 308	G4	
67151 Walton 269	E3	
66547 Wamego 3,159	F2	
66968 Washington⊙ 1,488	F2	
66548 Waterville 694	F2	
66090 Wathena 1,418	H2	
66871 Waverly 671	G3	
66781 Weir 705	H4	
67152 Wellington⊙ 8,212	E4	
66092 Wellsville 1,612	G3	
66782 West Mineral 229	H4	
66549 Westmoreland⊙ 598	F2	
66093 Westphalia 204	G3	
67869 West Plains (Plains) 1,044	B4	
66550 Wetmore 376	G2	
66551 Wheaton 90	F2	
66872 White City 534	F3	
66094 White Cloud 234	G2	
67154 Whitewater 751	E4	
66552 Whiting 270	G2	
*67201 Wichita⊙ 279,835	E4	
Wichita‡ 411,313	E4	
†66601 Willard 128	G2	
66095 Williamsburg 362	G3	
66435 Willis 85	G2	
†67501 Willowbrook 109	D3	
66873 Wilsey 179	F3	
67490 Wilson 978	D3	
66097 Winchester 570	G2	
67491 Windom 160	E3	
67156 Winfield⊙ 10,736	F4	
67764 Winona 258	A2	
67492 Woodbine 172	E3	
67675 Woodston 157	C2	
66783 Yates Center⊙ 1,998	G4	
67159 Zenda 146	D4	
67676 Zurich 185	C2	

OTHER FEATURES

Arkansas (riv.)	D3	
Beaver (creek)	A2	
Big Blue (riv.)	F1	
Cedar Bluff (res.)	C3	
Cheney (res.)	E4	
Cheyenne Bottoms (lake)	D3	
Chikaskia (riv.)	E4	
Cimarron (riv.)	B4	
Cottonwood (riv.)	F3	
Council Grove (lake)	F3	
Crooked (creek)	B4	
Elk (riv.)	F4	
Fall (riv.)	G4	
Fall River (lake)	F4	
Fort Larned Nat'l Hist. Site	C3	
Fort Riley-Camp Whiteside 18,233	F2	
John Redmond (res.)	G3	
Hulah (lake)	F5	
Kanopolis (lake)	D3	
Kansas (riv.)	F2	
Kickapoo Ind. Res.	G2	
Kirwin (res.)	C2	
Little Arkansas (riv.)	E3	
Little Blue (riv.)	E1	
Lovewell (res.)	D2	
Marion (res.)	E3	
McConnell A.F.B.	E4	
McKinney (lake)	A3	
Medicine Lodge (riv.)	D4	
Milford (lake)	E2	
Missouri (riv.)	G1	
Mule (creek)	C4	
Nemaha (riv.)	G1	
Neosho (riv.)	G4	
Ninnescah (riv.)	E4	
Norton (res.)	C2	
Olathe Nav. Air Sta.	H3	
Pawnee (riv.)	B3	
Perry (lake)	G2	
Pomona (lake)	G3	
Potawatomi Ind. Res.	G2	
Rattlesnake (creek)	D4	
Republican (riv.)	E2	
Sac-Fox-Iowa Ind. Res.	G2	
Saline (riv.)	D3	
Sappa (creek)	B2	
Smoky Hill (riv.)	C3	
Solomon (riv.)	E2	
Sunflower (mt.)	A2	
Toronto (lake)	F4	
Tuttle Creek (lake)	F2	
Verdigris (riv.)	G5	
Walnut (riv.)	E4	
Webster (res.)	C2	
White Rock (creek)	D2	
Wilson (lake)	D3	

⊙County seat.
‡Population of metropolitan area.
† Zip of nearest p.o.
* Multiple zips.

KENTUCKY

COUNTIES

County	Key
Adair 15,233	L6
Allen 14,128	J7
Anderson 12,567	M5
Ballard 8,798	C6
Barren 34,009	K7
Bath 10,025	O4
Bell 34,330	O7
Boone 45,842	M3
Bourbon 19,405	N4
Boyd 55,513	R4
Boyle 25,066	M5
Bracken 7,738	N3
Breathitt 17,004	P5
Breckinridge 16,861	H5
Bullitt 43,346	K5
Butler 11,064	H6
Caldwell 13,473	F6
Calloway 30,031	E7
Campbell 83,317	N3
Carlisle 5,487	C7
Carroll 9,270	L3
Carter 25,060	P4
Casey 14,818	M6
Christian 66,878	F7
Clark 28,322	N4
Clay 22,752	O6
Clinton 9,321	L7
Crittenden 9,207	E6
Cumberland 7,289	L7
Daviess 85,949	G5
Edmonson 9,962	J6
Elliott 6,908	P4
Estill 14,495	O5
Fayette 204,165	N4
Fleming 12,323	O4
Floyd 48,764	R5
Franklin 41,830	M4
Fulton 8,971	C7
Gallatin 4,842	M3
Garrard 10,853	M5
Grant 13,308	M3
Graves 34,049	D7
Grayson 20,854	J5
Green 11,043	K6
Greenup 39,132	R3
Hancock 7,742	H5
Hardin 88,917	K5
Harlan 41,889	P7
Harrison 15,166	N4
Hart 15,402	K6
Henderson 40,849	F5
Henry 12,740	L4
Hickman 6,065	C7
Hopkins 46,174	F6
Jackson 11,996	N6
Jefferson 684,565	K4
Jessamine 26,065	M5
Johnson 24,432	R5
Kenton 137,058	M3
Knott 17,940	R6
Knox 30,239	O7
Larue 11,922	K5
Laurel 38,982	N6
Lawrence 14,121	R4
Lee 7,754	O5
Leslie 14,882	P6
Letcher 30,687	R6
Lewis 14,545	P3
Lincoln 19,053	M6
Livingston 9,219	E6
Logan 24,138	H7
Lyon 6,490	E6
Madison 53,352	N5
Magoffin 13,515	P5
Marion 17,910	L5
Marshall 25,637	E7
Martin 13,925	R5
Mason 17,765	O3
McCracken 61,310	D6
McCreary 15,634	N7
McLean 10,090	G5
Meade 22,854	J5
Menifee 5,117	O5
Mercer 19,011	M5
Metcalfe 9,484	K7
Monroe 12,353	K7
Montgomery 20,046	O4
Morgan 12,103	P5
Muhlenberg 32,238	G6
Nelson 27,584	K5
Nicholas 7,157	N4
Ohio 21,765	H6
Oldham 27,795	L4
Owen 8,924	M3
Owsley 5,709	O6
Pendleton 10,989	N3
Perry 33,763	P6
Pike 81,123	S6
Powell 11,101	O5
Pulaski 45,803	M6
Robertson 2,265	N3
Rockcastle 13,973	N6
Rowan 19,049	P4
Russell 13,708	L7
Scott 21,813	M4
Shelby 23,328	L4
Simpson 14,673	H7
Spencer 5,929	L4
Taylor 21,178	L6
Todd 11,874	G7
Trigg 9,384	F7
Trimble 6,253	L3
Union 17,821	F5
Warren 71,828	H6
Washington 10,764	L5
Wayne 17,022	M7
Webster 14,832	F5
Whitley 33,396	N7
Wolfe 6,698	O5
Woodford 17,778	M4

CITIES and TOWNS

Zip	*Name/Pop.*	*Key*
42202	Adairville 1,105	H7
42602	Albany⊙ 2,083	L7
41001	Alexandria⊙ 4,735	N3
41601	Allen 338	R5
42204	Allensville 170	G7
40223	Anchorage 1,726	L2
41101	Ashland 27,064	R4
	Ashland-Huntington‡ 311,350	R4
42206	Auburn 1,467	H7
†40201	Audubon Park 1,571	J2
41002	Augusta 1,455	N3
41602	Auxier 900	R5
†40222	Bancroft 725	K1
41603	Banner 950	R5
†40201	Barbourmeade 1,038	K1
40906	Barbourville⊙ 3,333	O7
40004	Bardstown⊙ 6,155	L5
42023	Bardwell⊙ 988	D7
42024	Barlow 746	D6
41311	Beattyville⊙ 1,068	O5
42320	Beaver Dam 3,185	H6
40006	Bedford⊙ 835	L3
40359	Beechwood Village 1,462	K2
†40201	Bellemeade 918	L2
41073	Bellevue 7,678	S1
40807	Benham 936	R7
42025	Benton⊙ 3,700	E7
40403	Berea 8,226	N5
41003	Berry 287	N3
41605	Betsy Layne 975	R5
41124	Blaine 358	R4
40008	Bloomfield 954	L5
†40201	Blue Ridge Manor 465	L2
42713	Bonnieville 372	K6
†40403	Boone 300	N5
41314	Booneville⊙ 191	O6
42101	Bowling Green⊙ 40,450	H7
40009	Bradfordsville 331	L6
40108	Brandenburg⊙ 1,831	J4
†42025	Briensburg	E7
†40201	Broadfields 311	K2
40409	Brodhead 686	N6
†41016	Bromley 844	S2
40109	Brooks 1,344	K4
41004	Brooksville⊙ 680	N3
†40201	Brownsboro Farm 790	L1
42210	Brownsville⊙ 674	J6
40218	Buechel 6,709	K2
40310	Burgin 1,008	M5
42717	Burkesville⊙ 2,051	L7
41005	Burlington⊙ 500	R2
42519	Burnside 775	M6
41006	Butler 663	N3
42211	Cadiz⊙ 1,661	F7
42327	Calhoun⊙ 1,080	G5
41007	California 135	N3
42029	Calvert City 2,388	E6
†40337	Camargo 1,301	K4
40011	Campbellsburg 714	L3
42718	Campbellsville⊙ 8,715	L6
41301	Campton⊙ 486	O5
42721	Caneyville 642	J6
40311	Carlisle⊙ 1,757	N4
41008	Carrollton⊙ 3,967	L3
42030	Carrsville 99	E6
†42459	Caseyville 43	E5
41129	Catlettsburg⊙ 3,005	R4
42127	Cave City 2,098	K6
†41522	Cedarville 81	S6
42328	Centertown 462	G6
42330	Central City 5,214	G6
42726	Clarkson 666	J6
42404	Clay 1,356	F6
40312	Clay City 1,276	O5
40313	Clearfield 1,250	P4
42031	Clinton⊙ 1,720	D7
40111	Cloverport 1,585	H5
†41501	Coal Run 348	R5
41076	Cold Spring 2,117	T2
42728	Columbia⊙ 3,710	L6
42032	Columbus 296	C7
41729	Combs 900	P6
41131	Concord 67	P3
40701	Corbin 8,075	N7
41010	Corinth 258	M3
42406	Corydon 874	F5
*41011	Covington 49,563	S2
40419	Crab Orchard 843	M6
†41016	Crescent Springs 1,951	R2
†41076	Crestview 528	S2
†41017	Crestview Hills 1,408	R2
40014	Crestwood 531	L4
41030	Crittenden 597	M3
42217	Crofton 823	G6
40823	Cumberland 3,712	R6
41031	Cynthiana⊙ 5,881	N4
40422	Danville⊙ 12,942	M5
42408	Dawson Springs 3,275	F6
41074	Dayton 6,979	T1
†40201	Devondale 1,164	K2
42036	Dexter	E7
42409	Dixon⊙ 533	F5
†40243	Douglass Hills 4,384	L2
41034	Dover 305	O3
42337	Drakesboro 798	H6
41035	Dry Ridge 1,250	M3
42037	Dycusburg 64	E6
42410	Earlington 2,011	F6
42038	Eddyville⊙ 1,949	E6
†41017	Edgewood 7,230	S2
42129	Edmonton⊙ 1,401	K7
40117	Ekron 239	J5
42701	Elizabethtown⊙ 15,380	K5
41522	Elkhorn City 1,446	S6
42220	Elkton⊙ 1,815	G7
†41018	Elsmere 7,203	R2
40019	Eminence 2,260	L4
40826	Eolia 875	R6
41018	Erlanger 14,433	R2
40827	Essie 650	P6
42567	Eubank 207	M6
40828	Evarts 1,234	P7
41039	Ewing 144	O4
40118	Fairdale 7,315	K4
40020	Fairfield 169	L5
†41101	Fairview 198	S2
41040	Falmouth⊙ 2,482	N3
41524	Fedscreek 950	S6
42533	Ferguson 1,009	M6
†40222	Fincastle 804	L1
41139	Flatwoods 8,354	R4
41816	Fleming-Neon 1,195	R6
41041	Flemingsburg⊙ 2,835	O4
41042	Florence 15,586	R2
42343	Fordsville 561	H5
41527	Forest Hills 502	L2
40121	Fort Knox 31,055	K5
41017	Fort Mitchell 7,297	S2
41075	Fort Thomas 16,012	S2
†41011	Fort Wright 4,481	S2
41043	Foster 80	N3
42133	Fountain Run 340	K7
40601	Frankfort (cap.)⊙ 25,973	M4
42134	Franklin⊙ 7,738	J7
42411	Fredonia 535	E6
40322	Frenchburg⊙ 550	O5
†41175	Fullerton 950	P3
42041	Fulton 3,137	D7
42140	Gamaliel 456	K7
40324	Georgetown⊙ 10,972	M4
41044	Germantown 347	O3
41045	Ghent 439	L3
42044	Gilbertsville	E7
42141	Glasgow⊙ 12,958	J7
41046	Glencoe 354	M3
†40222	Glenview 212	K1
†40222	Goose Creek 394	L1
42045	Grand Rivers 428	E7
†41005	Grant 150	M3
40327	Gratz 124	M4
†40201	Graymoor 1,167	K1
41143	Grayson⊙ 3,423	R4
42743	Greensburg⊙ 2,377	K6
41144	Greenup⊙ 1,386	R3
42345	Greenville⊙ 4,631	G6
42234	Guthrie 1,361	G7
42413	Hanson 485	G6
42048	Hardin 545	E7
40143	Hardinsburg⊙ 2,211	H5
41531	Hardy 900	S5
40831	Harlan⊙ 3,024	P7
40330	Harrodsburg⊙ 7,265	M5
42347	Hartford⊙ 2,512	H6
42348	Hawesville⊙ 1,036	H5
41701	Hazard⊙ 5,371	P6
42049	Hazel 465	E7
40949	Heidrick 400	O7
42420	Henderson⊙ 24,834	F5
42050	Hickman⊙ 2,894	C7
42051	Hickory	D7
41076	Highland Heights 4,435	T2
41822	Hindman⊙ 876	R6
42152	Hiseville 349	K6
42748	Hodgenville⊙ 2,531	K5
†40228	Hollow Creek 1,023	K4
†41018	Hopeful Heights	R2
42240	Hopkinsville⊙ 27,318	F7
42749	Horse Cave 2,045	K6
†40201	Houston Acres 608	K2
40437	Hustonville 339	M6
41749	Hyden⊙ 488	P6
41051	Independence⊙ 7,998	M3
†40201	Indian Hills 787	K1
41224	Inez⊙ 413	S5
40336	Irvine⊙ 2,889	O5
40146	Irvington 1,409	J5
42350	Island 532	G6
41642	Ivel 850	R5
41339	Jackson⊙ 2,651	P5
42629	Jamestown⊙ 1,441	L7
40299	Jeffersontown 15,795	L2
40337	Jeffersonville 1,528	O5
41537	Jenkins 3,271	R6
40440	Junction City 2,045	M5
40737	Keavy 900	N6
†41011	Kenton Vale 145	S2
42053	Kevil 382	D6
†40201	Kingsley 464	K2
42055	Kuttawa 560	E6
42056	La Center 1,044	C6
41643	Lackey	R6
42254	La Fayette 160	F7
40031	La Grange⊙ 2,971	L4
†41017	Lakeside Park 3,038	R2
40444	Lancaster⊙ 3,365	M5
40342	Lawrenceburg⊙ 5,167	M4
40033	Lebanon⊙ 6,590	L5
40150	Lebanon Junction 1,581	K5
42754	Leitchfield⊙ 4,533	J6
42256	Lewisburg 972	G6
42351	Lewisport 1,832	H5
*40501	Lexington⊙ 204,165	N4
	Lexington‡ 318,136	N4
42539	Liberty⊙ 2,206	M6
42352	Livermore 1,672	G5
40445	Livingston 334	N6
40036	Lockport 84	M4
40741	London⊙ 4,002	N6
42001	Lone Oak 443	D6
40037	Loretto 954	L5
41230	Louisa⊙ 1,832	R4
*40201	Louisville⊙ 298,840	J2
	Louisville‡ 906,240	J2
40854	Loyall 1,210	P7
41016	Ludlow 4,959	S2
40855	Lynch 1,614	R7
†40201	Lynnview 1,157	K4
40040	Mackville 229	L5
42431	Madisonville⊙ 16,979	F6
40962	Manchester⊙ 1,838	O6
42064	Marion⊙ 3,392	E6
41649	Martin 827	R5
42066	Mayfield⊙ 10,705	D7
41056	Maysville⊙ 7,983	O3
41543	McAndrews 975	S5
42354	McHenry 582	H6
40447	McKee⊙ 759	O6
41835	McRoberts 1,106	R6
†40201	Meadow Vale 1,008	L1
41059	Melbourne 628	T2
†41060	Mentor 169	N3
40965	Middlesboro 12,251	O7
40243	Middletown 414	L2
40347	Midway 1,445	M4
40348	Millersburg 987	N4
40045	Milton 718	L3
†40201	Minor Lane Heights 1,882	K4
†40359	Monterey 186	M4
42633	Monticello⊙ 5,677	M7
†40223	Moorland 513	L2
40351	Morehead⊙ 7,789	P4
42437	Morganfield⊙ 3,781	E5
42261	Morgantown⊙ 2,000	H6
42440	Mortons Gap 1,201	F6
41064	Mount Olivet⊙ 346	N3
†40437	Mount Salem 50	M6
40353	Mount Sterling⊙ 5,820	N4
40456	Mount Vernon⊙ 2,334	N6
40047	Mount Washington 3,997	K4
41548	Mouthcard 900	S6
40155	Muldraugh 1,752	J5
42765	Munfordville⊙ 1,783	J6
42071	Murray⊙ 14,248	E7
42441	Nebo 269	F6
41840	Neon-Fleming 1,195	R6
40050	New Castle⊙ 832	L4
40051	New Haven 926	K5
*41071	Newport 21,587	S2
40356	Nicholasville⊙ 10,319	N5
†40201	Northfield 906	K1
40357	North Middletown 637	N4
42442	Nortonville 1,336	G6
42262	Oak Grove 2,088	G7
42159	Oakland 264	J6
41238	Oil Springs 900	P5
40219	Okolona 20,039	K4
41164	Olive Hill 2,539	P4
42301	Owensboro⊙ 54,450	G5
	Owensboro‡ 85,949	G5
40359	Owenton⊙ 1,341	M3
40360	Owingsville⊙ 1,419	O4
42001	Paducah⊙ 29,315	D6
41240	Paintsville⊙ 3,815	R5
40361	Paris⊙ 7,935	N4
42160	Park City 614	J6
†41011	Park Hills 3,500	S2
†40201	Parkway Village 754	J2
42266	Pembroke 636	G7
40468	Perryville 841	M5
40056	Pewee Valley 982	L4
41553	Phelps 1,126	S6
41501	Pikeville⊙ 4,756	S6
42635	Pine Knot 1,389	M7
40977	Pineville⊙ 2,599	O7
†40201	Plantation 969	K1
40258	Pleasure Ridge Park 27,332	J4
40057	Pleasureville 837	L4
†42101	Plum Springs 393	J7
42367	Powderly 848	G6
41653	Prestonsburg⊙ 4,011	R5
†41008	Prestonville 205	L3
42445	Princeton⊙ 7,073	F6
40059	Prospect 1,981	K4
42450	Providence 4,434	F6
41169	Raceland 1,970	R3
40160	Radcliff 14,519	K5
40472	Ravenna 793	O5
40475	Richmond⊙ 21,705	N5
†40222	Riverwood 435	K1
42273	Rochester 289	H6

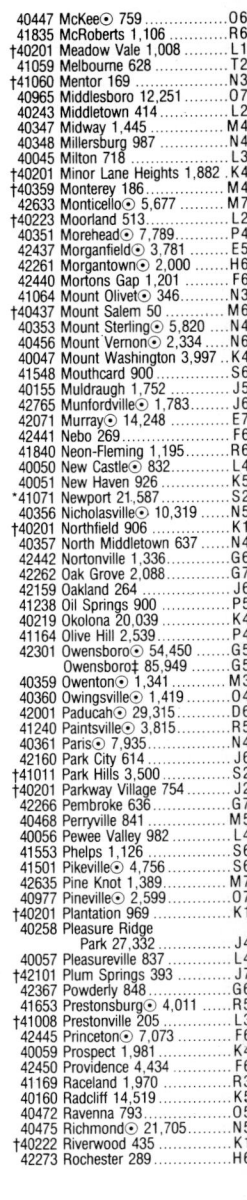

Agriculture, Industry and Resources

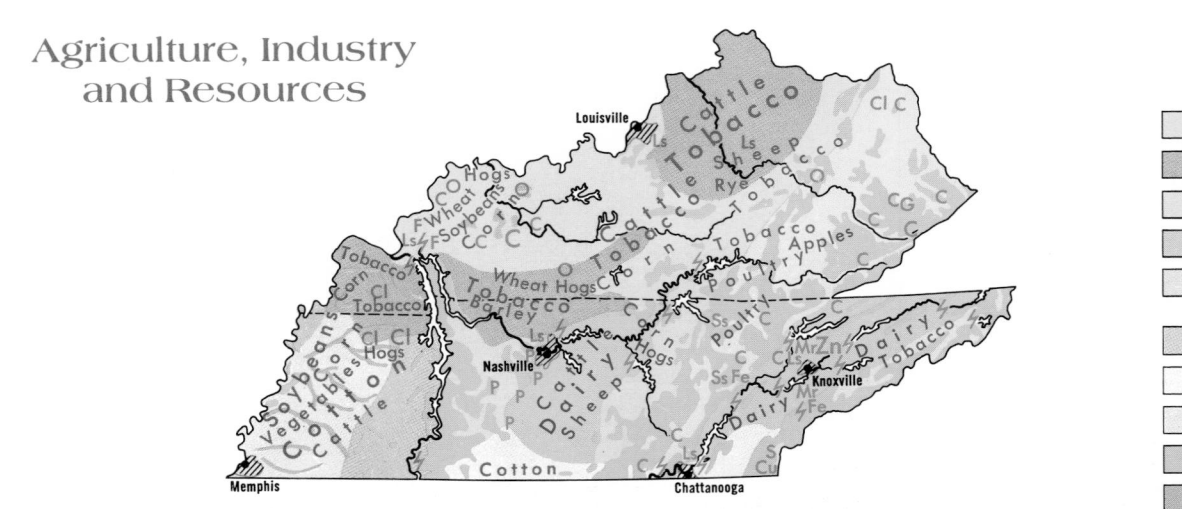

DOMINANT LAND USE

- Hogs, Soft Winter Wheat
- Tobacco, General Farming
- General Farming, Livestock, Tobacco
- General Farming, Livestock, Dairy
- General Farming, Livestock, Fruit, Tobacco
- Specialized Cotton
- Cotton, General Farming
- Cotton, Livestock
- Forests
- Swampland, Limited Agriculture

MAJOR MINERAL OCCURRENCES

C	Coal	G	Natural Gas	P	Phosphates
Cl	Clay	Ls	Limestone	S	Pyrites
Cu	Copper	Mr	Marble	Ss	Sandstone
F	Fluorspar	O	Petroleum	Zn	Zinc
Fe	Iron Ore				

Water Power

Major Industrial Areas

KENTUCKY

AREA 40,409 sq. mi. (104,659 sq. km.)
POPULATION 3,660,257
CAPITAL Frankfort
LARGEST CITY Louisville
HIGHEST POINT Black Mtn. 4,145 ft. (1263 m.)
SETTLED IN 1774
ADMITTED TO UNION June 1, 1792
POPULAR NAME Bluegrass State
STATE FLOWER Goldenrod
STATE BIRD Cardinal

TENNESSEE

AREA 42,144 sq. mi. (109,153 sq. km.)
POPULATION 4,591,120
CAPITAL Nashville
LARGEST CITY Memphis
HIGHEST POINT Clingmans Dome 6,643 ft. (2025 m.)
SETTLED IN 1757
ADMITTED TO UNION June 1, 1796
POPULAR NAME Volunteer State
STATE FLOWER Iris
STATE BIRD Mockingbird

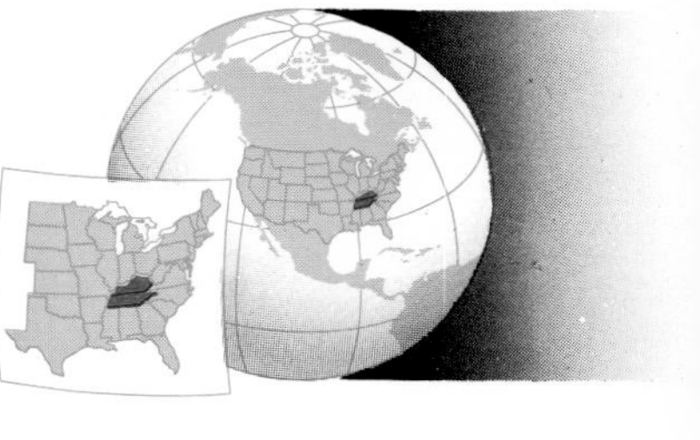

42369 Rockport 511 .... H6
†40201 Rolling Fields 731 .... K2
†40201 Rolling Hills 1,122 .... L1
41169 Russell 3,824 .... R3
42642 Russell Springs 1,831 .... L6
42276 Russellville⊙ 7,520 .... H7
†41015 Ryland Heights 252 .... M3
42372 Sacramento 538 .... G6
40370 Sadieville 253 .... M4
42453 Saint Charles 405 .... F6
40207 Saint Matthews 13,519 .... K2
†40201 Saint Regis Park 1,735 .... K2
42078 Salem 833 .... E6
40371 Salt Lick 347 .... O4
41465 Salyersville⊙ 1,352 .... P5
41083 Sanders 332 .... M3
41171 Sandy Hook⊙ 627 .... P4
41056 Sardis 198 .... O3
42553 Science Hill 655 .... M6
42164 Scottsville⊙ 4,278 .... J7
42455 Sebree 1,516 .... F5
†40201 Seneca Gardens 748 .... K2
40983 Sextons Creek 975 .... O6
40374 Sharpsburg 339 .... O4
40065 Shelbyville⊙ 5,329 .... L4
40165 Shepherdsville⊙ 4,454 .... K4
40216 Shively 16,819 .... K4
41085 Silver Grove 1,260 .... T2
40067 Simpsonville 642 .... L4
42456 Slaughters 269 .... F6
41764 Smilax 987 .... P6
40068 Smithfield 137 .... L4
42081 Smithland⊙ 512 .... E6
42171 Smiths Grove 767 .... J6
42501 Somerset⊙ 10,649 .... M6
42776 Sonora 416 .... K5
42374 South Carrollton 262 .... G6
41071 Southgate 2,833 .... T2
41174 South Portsmouth 900 .... P3
41175 South Shore 1,525 .... R3
25661 South Williamson 1,016 .... S5
41086 Sparta 192 .... M3
42458 Spottsville 914 .... G5
40069 Springfield⊙ 3,179 .... L5
†40201 Springlee 498 .... K2
40379 Stamping Ground 562 .... M4
40484 Stanford⊙ 2,764 .... M5
40380 Stanton⊙ 2,691 .... O5
42647 Stearns 1,557 .... N7
41567 Stone 900 .... S5
†40201 Strathmoor Village 466 .... J2
42459 Sturgis 2,293 .... F5
†41011 Taylor Mill 4,509 .... S2
40071 Taylorsville⊙ 801 .... L4
†40222 Thornhill 233 .... K1
41189 Tollesboro 808 .... O3
42167 Tompkinsville⊙ 4,366 .... K7
42286 Trenton 465 .... G7
41091 Union 601 .... M3
42461 Uniontown 1,169 .... F5
42784 Upton 731 .... K6
40272 Valley Station 24,474 .... K4
41179 Vanceburg⊙ 1,939 .... P3
41265 Van Lear 2,035 .... R5
†40828 Verda 1,133 .... P7
40383 Versailles⊙ 6,427 .... M4
41773 Vicco 456 .... P6
†41017 Villa Hills 4,402 .... R2
40175 Vine Grove 3,583 .... K5
†41063 Visalia 198 .... N3
40873 Wallins Creek 459 .... O7
41094 Walton 1,651 .... M3
41095 Warsaw⊙ 1,328 .... M3
41096 Washington 624 .... O3
42085 Water Valley 395 .... D7
42462 Waverly 434 .... F5
41666 Wayland 601 .... R6
41667 Weeksbury 850 .... R6
†40201 Wellington 653 .... K2
†40218 West Buechel 1,205 .... K2
41472 West Liberty⊙ 1,381 .... P5
40177 West Point 1,339 .... J4
42501 West Somerset 850 .... M6
41301 Westwood 5,973 .... R4
40207 Westwood 826 .... L1
42463 Wheatcroft 325 .... F5
41669 Wheelwright 865 .... R6
41390 Whick 280 .... P6
42464 White Plains 859 .... G6
41858 Whitesburg⊙ 1,525 .... R6
42378 Whitesville 788 .... H5
42653 Whitley City⊙ 1,683 .... N7
42087 Wickliffe⊙ 1,034 .... C7
41071 Wilders 633 .... S2
40769 Williamsburg⊙ 5,560 .... N7
41097 Williamstown⊙ 2,502 .... M3
40078 Willisburg 235 .... L5
40390 Wilmore 3,787 .... M5
40391 Winchester⊙ 15,216 .... N5
40201 Windy Hills 2,214 .... K1
42088 Wingo 606 .... D7
40771 Woodbine 900 .... N7
42170 Woodburn 330 .... J7
40201 Woodland Hills 839 .... L2
42001 Woodlawn-Oakdale 4,722 .... D6
41071 Woodlawn 331 .... T2
†40201 Woodlawn Park 1,052 .... K2
41183 Worthington 1,948 .... R3
41098 Worthville 272 .... L3
41144 Wurtland 1,301 .... R3

OTHER FEATURES

Abraham Lincoln Birthplace Nat'l Hist. Site K5
Barkley (dam) E6
Barkley (lake) F7
Barren (riv.) H6
Barren River (lake) J7
Beech Fork (riv.) L5
Big Sandy (riv.) R4
Black (mt.) R7
Buckhorn (lake) O6
Chaplin (riv.) L5
Clarks, East Fork (riv.) E7
Cove Run (lake) O4
Cumberland (lake) M7
Cumberland (mt.) P7
Cumberland (riv.) K8
Cumberland Gap Nat'l Hist. Park P7
Dale Hollow (lake) L7
Dewey (lake) R5
Dix (riv.) M5
Drakes (creek) J7
Dry (creek) R3
Eagle (creek) M3
Fishtrap (lake) S6
Fort Campbell G7
Grayson (lake) P4
Green (riv.) G6
Green River (lake) L6
Herrington (lake) M5
Hinkston (creek) N4
Kentucky (dam) E7
Kentucky (lake) E8
Kentucky (riv.) M3
Land Between The Lakes Rec. Area E7
Laurel River (lake) N6
Lexington Blue Grass Army Depot N5
Licking (riv.) N3
Mammoth Cave Nat'l Park J6
Mayfield (creek) C7
Mississippi (riv.) A10
Mud (riv.) H7
Nolin (lake) K6
Nolin (riv.) J6
Obion (creek) C7
Ohio (riv.) F5
Paint Lick (riv.) M5
Panther (creek) G5
Pine (mt.) O7
Pond (riv.) G6
Red (riv.) O5
Red (riv.) G7
Rockcastle (riv.) N6
Rolling Fork (riv.) L5
Rough (riv.) H5
Rough River (lake) J5
Salt (riv.) K5
Tennessee (riv.) D6
Tradewater (riv.) F6
Tug Fork (riv.) S5

TENNESSEE

COUNTIES

Anderson 67,346 .... N8
Bedford 27,916 .... J9
Benton 14,901 .... E8
Bledsoe 9,478 .... L9
Blount 77,770 .... O9
Bradley 67,547 .... M10
Campbell 34,923 .... N8
Cannon 10,234 .... J9
Carroll 28,285 .... E9
Carter 50,205 .... S8
Cheatham 21,616 .... G8
Chester 12,727 .... D10
Claiborne 24,595 .... O8
Clay 7,676 .... K7
Cocke 28,792 .... P9
Coffee 38,311 .... J9
Crockett 14,941 .... C9
Cumberland 28,676 .... L9
Davidson 477,811 .... H8
Decatur 10,857 .... E9
De Kalb 13,589 .... K9
Dickson 30,037 .... G8
Dyer 34,663 .... C8
Fayette 25,305 .... C10
Fentress 14,826 .... M8
Franklin 31,983 .... J10
Gibson 49,467 .... D9
Giles 24,625 .... G10
Grainger 16,751 .... O8
Greene 54,422 .... R8
Grundy 13,787 .... K10
Hamblen 49,300 .... P8
Hamilton 287,740 .... L10
Hancock 6,887 .... P7
Hardeman 23,873 .... C10
Hardin 22,280 .... E10
Hawkins 43,751 .... P8
Haywood 20,318 .... C9
Henderson 21,390 .... E9
Henry 28,656 .... E8
Hickman 15,151 .... G9
Houston 6,871 .... F8
Humphreys 15,957 .... F8
Jackson 9,398 .... K8
Jefferson 31,284 .... P8
Johnson 13,745 .... T7
Knox 319,694 .... O9
Lake 7,455 .... B8
Lauderdale 24,555 .... B9
Lawrence 34,110 .... G10
Lewis 9,700 .... F9
Lincoln 26,483 .... H10
Loudon 28,553 .... N9
Macon 15,700 .... J7
Madison 74,546 .... D9
Marion 24,416 .... K10
Marshall 19,698 .... H10
Maury 51,095 .... G9
McMinn 41,878 .... M10
McNairy 22,525 .... D10
Meigs 7,431 .... M9
Monroe 28,700 .... N10
Montgomery 83,342 .... G8
Moore 4,510 .... J10
Morgan 16,604 .... M8
Obion 32,781 .... C8
Overton 17,575 .... L8
Perry 6,111 .... F9
Pickett 4,358 .... M7
Polk 13,602 .... N10
Putnam 47,690 .... K8
Rhea 24,235 .... M9
Roane 48,425 .... M9
Robertson 37,021 .... H7
Rutherford 84,058 .... J9
Scott 19,259 .... M8
Sequatchie 8,605 .... L10
Sevier 41,418 .... O9
Shelby 777,113 .... B10
Smith 14,935 .... J8
Stewart 8,665 .... F7
Sullivan 143,968 .... S7
Sumner 85,790 .... J8
Tipton 32,930 .... B9
Trousdale 6,137 .... J8
Unicoi 16,362 .... S8
Union 11,707 .... O8
Van Buren 4,728 .... L9
Warren 32,653 .... K9
Washington 88,755 .... R8
Wayne 13,946 .... F10
Weakley 32,896 .... D8
White 19,567 .... L9
Williamson 58,108 .... H9
Wilson 56,064 .... J8

CITIES and TOWNS

Zip Name/Pop. Key

†38301 Adair 70 .... D9
37010 Adams 600 .... G7
38310 Adamsville 1,453 .... E10
38001 Alamo⊙ 2,615 .... C9
37701 Alcoa 6,870 .... N9
37012 Alexandria 689 .... J8
38501 Algood 2,406 .... K8
38504 Allardt 654 .... M8
37301 Altamont⊙ 679 .... K10
38449 Ardmore 835 .... H10
38002 Arlington 1,778 .... B10
37015 Ashland City⊙ 2,329 .... G8
37303 Athens⊙ 12,080 .... M10
38004 Atoka 691 .... B10
38220 Atwood 1,143 .... D9
37016 Auburntown 204 .... J9
37743 Baileyton 333 .... R8
†37650 Banner Hill 2,913 .... R8
38134 Bartlett 17,170 .... B10
38544 Baxter 1,411 .... K8
37305 Beersheba Springs 643 .... K10
37020 Bell Buckle 450 .... J9
37205 Belle Meade 3,182 .... H8
38006 Bells 1,571 .... C9
37307 Benton⊙ 1,115 .... M10
†37201 Berry Hill 1,113 .... H8
†37027 Berry's Chapel 2,703 .... H9
38315 Bethel Springs 873 .... D10
38221 Big Sandy 650 .... E8
37709 Blaine 1,147 .... O8
37660 Bloomingdale 12,088 .... R7
37617 Blountville⊙ 2,554 .... S7
37618 Bluff City 1,121 .... S8
38008 Bolivar⊙ 6,597 .... C10
38010 Braden 293 .... B10
38316 Bradford 1,146 .... D8
37027 Brentwood 9,431 .... H8
37710 Briceville 850 .... N8
38011 Brighton 976 .... B10
37620 Bristol 23,986 .... S7
38012 Brownsville⊙ 9,307 .... C9
38317 Bruceton 1,579 .... E8
37711 Bulls Gap 821 .... P8
38015 Burlison 386 .... B9
37029 Burns 777 .... G8
38549 Byrdstown⊙ 884 .... L7
37309 Calhoun 590 .... M10
38320 Camden⊙ 3,279 .... E8
37030 Carthage⊙ 2,672 .... K8
37714 Caryville 2,039 .... N8
37032 Cedar Hill 420 .... H7
38551 Celina⊙ 1,580 .... K7
†37110 Centertown 300 .... K9
37033 Centerville⊙ 2,824 .... G9
37034 Chapel Hill 861 .... H9
37310 Charleston 756 .... M10
37036 Charlotte⊙ 788 .... G8
*37401 Chattanooga⊙ 169,558 .... K10
Chattanooga‡ 426,540 .... K10
37642 Church Hill 4,110 .... R7
38324 Clarksburg 400 .... E9
37040 Clarksville⊙ 54,777 .... G7
Clarksville‡ 150,220 .... G7
37311 Cleveland⊙ 26,415 .... M10
38425 Clifton 773 .... F10
37716 Clinton⊙ 5,245 .... N8
37313 Coalmont 625 .... K10
37315 Collegedale 4,607 .... M10
38017 Collierville 7,839 .... B10
38450 Collinwood 1,064 .... F10
37663 Colonial Heights 6,744 .... R8
38401 Columbia⊙ 26,571 .... G9
37720 Concord 8,569 .... N9
38501 Cookeville⊙ 20,535 .... L8
37317 Copperhill 418 .... N10
37047 Cornersville 722 .... H10
38224 Cottage Grove 117 .... E8
38326 Counce 975 .... E10
38019 Covington⊙ 6,065 .... B9
37318 Cowan 1,790 .... K10
37723 Crab Orchard 1,065 .... M9
37049 Cross Plains 655 .... H7
38555 Crossville⊙ 6,394 .... L9
37050 Cumberland City 276 .... F8
37724 Cumberland Gap 263 .... O8
37725 Dandridge⊙ 1,383 .... O8
37321 Dayton⊙ 5,913 .... L9
37322 Decatur⊙ 1,069 .... M9
38329 Decaturville⊙ 1,004 .... E9
37324 Decherd 2,233 .... J10
38391 Denmark 51 .... D9
37055 Dickson 7,040 .... G8
37058 Dover⊙ 1,197 .... F8
37059 Dowelltown 341 .... K8
38559 Doyle 344 .... K9
38225 Dresden⊙ 2,256 .... D8
37326 Ducktown 583 .... N10
37327 Dunlap⊙ 3,681 .... L10
38330 Dyer 2,419 .... D8
38024 Dyersburg⊙ 15,856 .... C8
†37801 Eagleton Village 5,331 .... O9
37060 Eagleville 444 .... H9
37412 East Ridge 21,236 .... L11
†38367 Eastview 552 .... D10
37643 Elizabethton⊙ 12,431 .... S8
38455 Elkton 540 .... H10
38029 Ellendale 850 .... B10
37329 Englewood 1,840 .... M10
38332 Enville 287 .... E10
37061 Erin⊙ 1,614 .... F8
37650 Erwin⊙ 4,739 .... S8
37330 Estill Springs 1,324 .... J10
38456 Ethridge 548 .... G10
37331 Etowah 3,758 .... M10
37062 Fairview 3,648 .... G9
37656 Fall Branch 1,340 .... R8
37334 Fayetteville⊙ 7,559 .... H10
38334 Finger 245 .... D10
38030 Finley 1,014 .... B8
†37201 Forest Hills 4,516 .... H8
37064 Franklin⊙ 12,407 .... H9
38034 Friendship 763 .... C9
37737 Friendsville 694 .... N9
38337 Gadsden 683 .... D9
38562 Gainesboro⊙ 1,119 .... K8
37066 Gallatin⊙ 17,191 .... H8
38036 Gallaway 804 .... B10
†38019 Garland 301 .... B9
38037 Gates 729 .... C9
37738 Gatlinburg 3,210 .... O9
38138 Germantown 21,482 .... B10
38338 Gibson 458 .... D9
†38015 Gilt Edge 142 .... B9
38229 Gleason 1,335 .... D8
37072 Goodlettsville 8,327 .... H8
38563 Gordonsville 893 .... K8
38039 Grand Junction 360 .... C10
37338 Graysville 1,380 .... L10
37742 Greenback 546 .... N9
37073 Greenbrier 3,180 .... H8
37743 Greeneville⊙ 14,097 .... R8
38230 Greenfield 2,109 .... D8
37339 Gruetli 910 .... K10
38040 Halls 2,444 .... C9
37658 Hampton 2,236 .... S8
37748 Harriman 8,303 .... M9
37341 Harrison 6,206 .... L10
37752 Harrogate-Shawanee 2,530 .... O8
37074 Hartsville⊙ 2,674 .... J8
38340 Henderson⊙ 4,449 .... D10
37075 Hendersonville 26,561 .... H8
38041 Henning 638 .... B9
38231 Henry 295 .... E8
38042 Hickory Valley 252 .... C10
38462 Hohenwald⊙ 3,922 .... F9
38342 Hollow Rock 955 .... E8
38232 Hornbeak 452 .... C8
38044 Hornsby 401 .... D10
38343 Humboldt 10,209 .... D9
38344 Huntingdon⊙ 3,962 .... E8
37345 Huntland 983 .... J10
37756 Huntsville⊙ 519 .... N8
37078 Hurricane Mills 850 .... F9
38463 Iron City 482 .... F10
37757 Jacksboro⊙ 1,722 .... N8
38301 Jackson⊙ 49,131 .... D9
38556 Jamestown⊙ 2,364 .... M8
37347 Jasper⊙ 2,633 .... K10
37760 Jefferson City 5,612 .... P8
37762 Jellico 2,798 .... N7
37601 Johnson City 39,753 .... S8
Johnson City-Kingsport-Bristol‡ 433,638 .... S8
37659 Jonesboro⊙ 2,829 .... R8
37921 Karns 1,173 .... N9
38233 Kenton 1,551 .... C8
†37347 Kimball 1,220 .... K10
*37660 Kingsport 32,027 .... R7
37763 Kingston⊙ 4,441 .... N9
37082 Kingston Springs 1,017 .... G8
*37901 Knoxville⊙ 175,045 .... O9
Knoxville‡ 476,517 .... O9
37083 Lafayette⊙ 3,808 .... J7
37766 La Follette 8,198 .... N8
38046 La Grange 185 .... C10
37769 Lake City 2,335 .... N8
†38134 Lakeland 612 .... B10
†37379 Lakesite 651 .... L10
†37138 Lakewood 2,325 .... H8
37086 La Vergne 5,495 .... H9
38464 Lawrenceburg⊙ 10,184 .... G10
37087 Lebanon⊙ 11,872 .... J8
37771 Lenoir City 5,446 .... N9
37091 Lewisburg⊙ 8,760 .... H10
38351 Lexington⊙ 5,934 .... E9
37095 Liberty 365 .... K8
37096 Linden⊙ 1,087 .... F9
38570 Livingston⊙ 3,372 .... L8
37097 Lobelville 993 .... F9
37350 Lookout Mountain 1,886 .... L11
38469 Loretto 1,612 .... G10
37774 Loudon⊙ 3,943 .... N9
37779 Luttrell 962 .... O8
37352 Lynchburg⊙ 668 .... J10
38472 Lynnville 383 .... G10
37354 Madisonville⊙ 2,884 .... N9
37355 Manchester⊙ 7,250 .... J10
38237 Martin 8,898 .... D8
37801 Maryville⊙ 17,480 .... O9
37806 Mascot 2,203 .... O8
38049 Mason 471 .... B10
38050 Maury City 989 .... C9
37807 Maynardville⊙ 924 .... O8
37101 McEwen 1,352 .... F8
38201 McKenzie 5,405 .... E8
38235 McLemoresville 311 .... D9
37110 McMinnville⊙ 10,683 .... K9
38355 Medina 687 .... D9
38356 Medon 169 .... D10
*38101 Memphis⊙ 646,174 .... B10
Memphis‡ 912,887 .... B10
38357 Michie 530 .... E10
38052 Middleton 596 .... D10
38358 Milan 8,083 .... D9
38359 Milledgeville 392 .... E10
38053 Millington 20,236 .... B10
38473 Minor Hill 564 .... G10
37119 Mitchellville 209 .... J7
37356 Monteagle 1,126 .... K10
38574 Monterey 2,610 .... L8
37357 Morrison 587 .... K9
†37660 Morrison City 2,032 .... R7
37814 Morristown⊙ 19,683 .... P8
38057 Moscow 499 .... C10
37818 Mosheim 1,539 .... R8
37683 Mountain City⊙ 2,125 .... T8
37642 Mount Carmel 3,764 .... R8
37122 Mount Juliet 2,879 .... H8
38474 Mount Pleasant 3,375 .... G9
38058 Munford 2,336 .... B10
37130 Murfreesboro⊙ 32,845 .... J9
*37201 Nashville (cap.)⊙ 455,651 .... H8
Nashville-Davidson‡ 850,505 .... H8
38059 Newbern 2,794 .... C8
†37380 New Hope 681 .... K11
37134 New Johnsonville 1,824 .... E8
37820 New Market 1,216 .... O8
37821 Newport⊙ 7,580 .... P9
37825 New Tazewell 1,677 .... O8
37826 Niota 765 .... M9
37360 Normandy 118 .... J10
37828 Norris 1,374 .... N8
37829 Oakdale 323 .... M9
†37201 Oak Hill 4,609 .... H8
38060 Oakland 472 .... B10
37830 Oak Ridge 27,662 .... N8
38240 Obion 1,282 .... C8
37840 Oliver Springs 3,659 .... N8
37841 Oneida 3,717 .... N7
37363 Ooltewah 950 .... M10
†37660 Orebank 1,284 .... R7
37141 Orlinda 382 .... H7
35740 Orme 181 .... K10
37365 Palmer 1,027 .... K10
38242 Paris⊙ 10,728 .... E8
37843 Parrottsville 118 .... P8
38363 Parsons 2,422 .... E9
37143 Pegram 1,081 .... H8
37144 Petersburg 681 .... H10
37845 Petros 1,286 .... M8
37846 Philadelphia 507 .... M9
37863 Pigeon Forge 1,822 .... O9
37367 Pikeville⊙ 2,085 .... L9
†38017 Piperton 746 .... B10
†37738 Pittman Center 488 .... P9
38578 Pleasant Hill 371 .... L9
37148 Portland 4,030 .... H7
37849 Powell 7,220 .... N8
†37397 Powells Crossroads 918 .... L10
38478 Pulaski⊙ 7,184 .... G10
38251 Puryear 624 .... E8
38367 Ramer 429 .... D10
37415 Red Bank 13,299 .... L10
37150 Red Boiling Springs 1,173 .... K7
†37641 Rheatown R8
†37380 Richard City 87 .... K11
38080 Ridgely 1,932 .... B8
†37401 Ridgeside 417 .... L10
37152 Ridgetop 1,225 .... H8
38063 Ripley⊙ 6,366 .... B9
38253 Rives 386 .... C8
37687 Roan Mountain 1,108 .... S8
37853 Rockford 567 .... O9
37854 Rockwood 5,767 .... M9
37857 Rogersville⊙ 4,368 .... P8
38053 Rosemark 950 .... B10
38066 Rossville 379 .... B10
37860 Russellville 1,069 .... P8
38369 Rutherford 1,378 .... C8
37861 Rutledge⊙ 1,058 .... P8
38481 Saint Joseph 897 .... G10
37373 Sale Creek 900 .... L10
38370 Saltillo 434 .... E10
38254 Samburg 465 .... C8
38371 Sardis 301 .... E10
38067 Saulsbury 156 .... C10
38372 Savannah⊙ 6,992 .... E10
38374 Scotts Hill 668 .... E10
38375 Selmer⊙ 3,979 .... D10
37862 Sevierville⊙ 4,556 .... P9
37375 Sewanee 2,298 .... K10
38255 Sharon 1,134 .... D8
37160 Shelbyville⊙ 13,530 .... H10
37376 Sherwood 900 .... K10
37377 Signal Mountain 5,818 .... L10
38377 Silerton 100 .... D10
37165 Slayden 69 .... G8
37166 Smithville⊙ 3,839 .... K9
37167 Smyrna 8,839 .... H9
37869 Sneedville⊙ 1,110 .... P7
37319 Soddy-Daisy 8,388 .... L10
38068 Somerville⊙ 2,264 .... C10
†37030 South Carthage 1,004 .... K8
†37311 South Cleveland 4,360 .... M10
†37716 South Clinton 1,671 .... N8
†42041 South Fulton 2,735 .... D9
37380 South Pittsburg 3,636 .... K10
37171 Southside 800 .... G8
38583 Sparta⊙ 4,864 .... K9
38585 Spencer⊙ 1,126 .... L9
37381 Spring City 1,951 .... M9
37172 Springfield⊙ 10,814 .... H8
37174 Spring Hill 989 .... H9
38069 Stanton 540 .... C10
38379 Stantonville 271 .... E10
†37660 Sullivan Gardens 2,513 .... R8
38483 Summertown 850 .... G10
37873 Surgoinsville 1,536 .... R8
37874 Sweetwater 4,725 .... N9
37877 Talbott 975 .... P8
37879 Tazewell⊙ 2,090 .... O8
37385 Tellico Plains 698 .... N10
37178 Tennessee Ridge 1,325 .... F8
38079 Tiptonville⊙ 2,438 .... B8
38381 Toone 355 .... D10
37882 Townsend 351 .... O9
37387 Tracy City 1,356 .... K10
38382 Trenton⊙ 4,601 .... D9
38258 Trezevant 921 .... D8
38259 Trimble 722 .... C8
38260 Troy 1,093 .... C8
37388 Tullahoma 15,800 .... J10
37743 Tusculum 1,242 .... R8
38261 Union City⊙ 10,436 .... C8
37181 Vanleer 401 .... G8
†37397 Victoria 800 .... K10
37394 Viola 149 .... K9

(continued on following page)

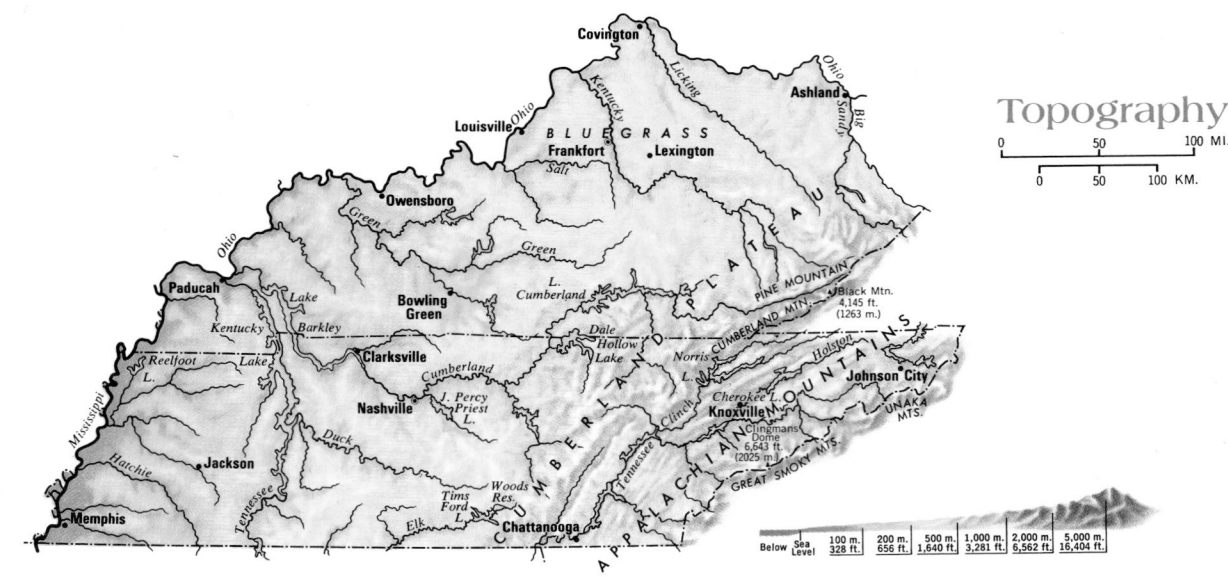

Topography

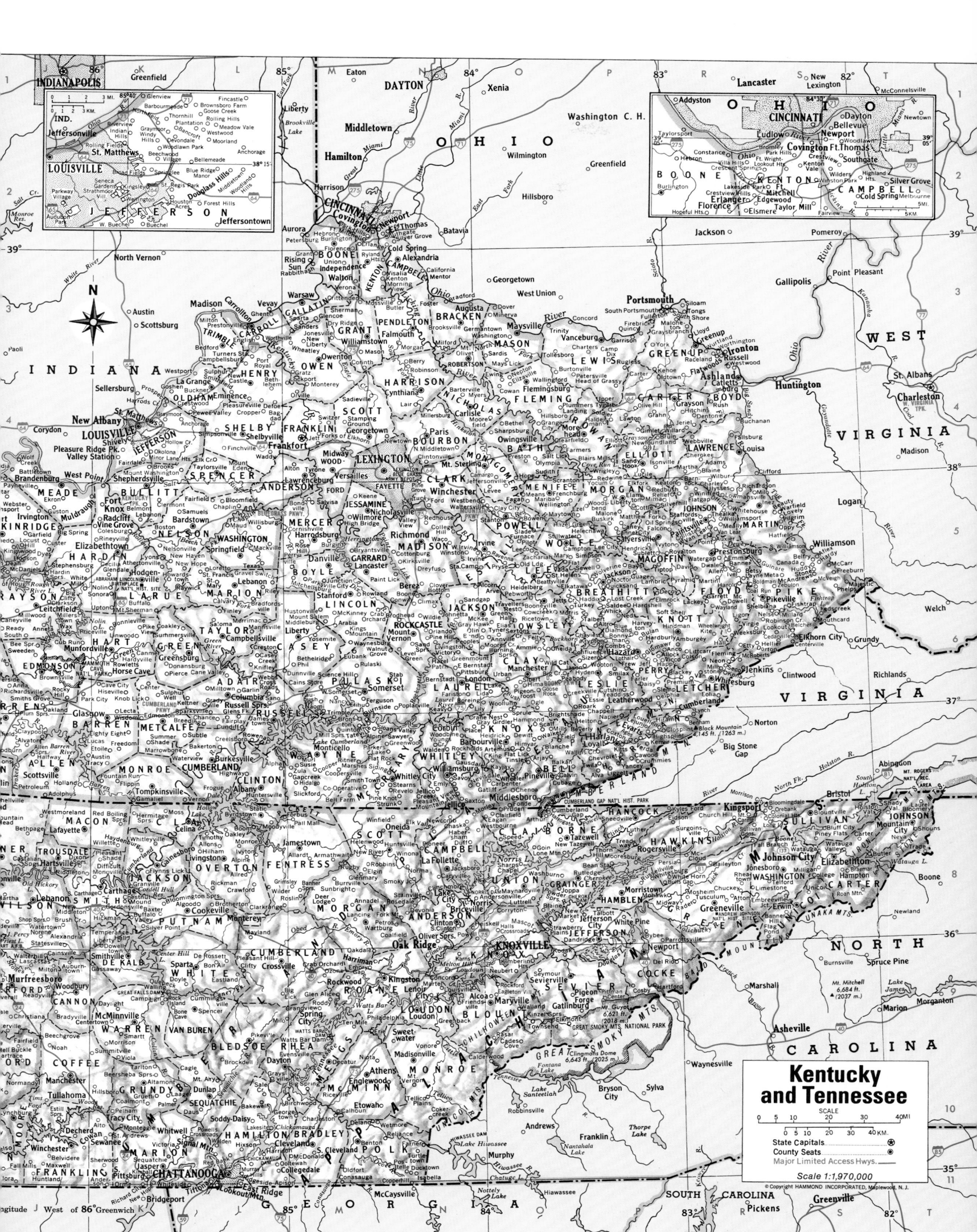

Kentucky and Tennessee

SCALE

0 5 10   20   30   40MI

0 5 10   20   30   40 KM.

State Capitals .... ⊛

County Seats .... ⊙

Major Limited Access Hwys. ——

Scale 1:1,970,000

© Copyright HAMMOND INCORPORATED, Maplewood, N.J.

Topography

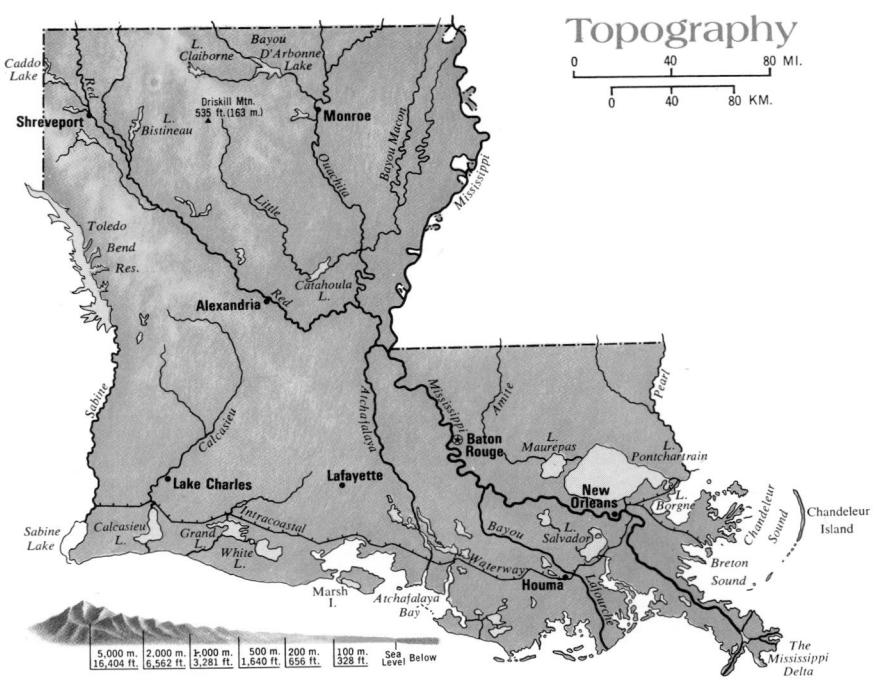

5,000 m. 2,000 m. 1,000 m. 500 m. 200 m. 100 m. Sea Below
16,404 ft. 6,562 ft. 3,281 ft. 1,640 ft. 656 ft. 328 ft. Level

PARISHES

Acadia 56,427 .... F6
Allen 21,390 .... E5
Ascension 50,068 .... J6
Assumption 22,084 .... H7
Avoyelles 41,393 .... G4
Beauregard 29,692 .... D5
Bienville 16,387 .... D2
Bossier 80,721 .... C1
Caddo 252,358 .... C1
Calcasieu 167,223 .... D6
Caldwell 10,761 .... F2
Cameron 9,336 .... D7
Catahoula 12,287 .... G3
Claiborne 17,095 .... D1
Concordia 22,981 .... G4
De Soto 25,727 .... C2
East Baton Rouge 366,191 .... K1
East Carroll 11,772 .... H1
East Feliciana 19,015 .... H5
Evangeline 33,343 .... F5
Franklin 24,141 .... G2
Grant 16,703 .... E3
Iberia 63,752 .... G7
Iberville 32,159 .... H6
Jackson 17,321 .... E2
Jefferson 454,592 .... K7
Jefferson Davis 32,168 .... E6
Lafayette 150,017 .... F6
Lafourche 82,483 .... K7
La Salle 17,004 .... F3
Lincoln 39,763 .... E1
Livingston 58,806 .... L2
Madison 15,975 .... H2
Morehouse 34,803 .... G1
Natchitoches 39,863 .... D3
Orleans 557,515 .... L6
Ouachita 139,241 .... F2
Plaquemines 26,049 .... L8
Pointe Coupee 24,045 .... G5
Rapides 135,282 .... E4
Red River 10,433 .... D2
Richland 22,187 .... G2
Sabine 25,280 .... C3
Saint Bernard 64,097 .... L7
Saint Charles 37,259 .... K7
Saint Helena 9,827 .... J5
Saint James 21,495 .... L3
Saint John the Baptist 31,924 .. M3
Saint Landry 84,128 .... G6
Saint Martin 40,214 .... G6
Saint Mary 64,253 .... H7
Saint Tammany 110,869 ... L6
Tangipahoa 80,698 .... K5
Tensas 8,525 .... H2
Terrebonne 94,393 .... J8
Union 21,167 .... F1
Vermilion 48,458 .... F7
Vernon 53,475 .... D4
Washington 44,207 .... K5
Webster 43,631 .... D1
West Baton Rouge 19,086 .. H6
West Carroll 12,922 .... H1
West Feliciana 12,186 ..... H5
Winn 17,253 .... E3

CITIES and TOWNS

Zip   Name/Pop.   Key

70510 Abbeville⊙ 12,391 .... F7
70420 Abita Springs 1,072 .... L6
71316 Acme 235 .... G4
70710 Addis 1,320 .... J2
71401 Aimwell 55 .... G3
70421 Akers 150 .... N2
71226 Chatham 714 .... F2
70344 Chauvin 3,338 .... J8
71325 Cheneyville 865 ...... F4
71412 Chopin 175 .... E4
71227 Choudrant 809 .... F1
70525 Church Point 4,599 .. F6
71414 Clarence 612 .... E3
71415 Clarks 931 .... F2
71326 Clayton 1,204 ...... H3
70722 Clinton⊙ 1,919 .... J5
71416 Cloutierville 100 .. E3
71417 Colfax⊙ 1,680 .... E3
71229 Collinston 439 .... G1
71418 Columbia⊙ 687 ... F2
70723 Convent⊙ 400 .... L3
71419 Converse 449 ..... C3
†71107 Cooper Road C1
71327 Cottonport 1,911 .. F5
71018 Cotton Valley 1,445 .. D1
71019 Coushatta⊙ 2,084 ... D2
70433 Covington⊙ 7,892 .. K5
†70510 Cow Island 200 .... F7
†70656 Cravens 200 ...... E5
71020 Creston 135 .... E3
70526 Crowley⊙ 16,036 .. F6
71230 Crowville 400 ..... G2
70345 Cut Off 5,049 .... K7
70046 Davant 600 ...... L7
70528 Delcambre 2,216 .. G7
71232 Delhi 3,290 ...... H2
71233 Delta 295 .... J2
70726 Denham Springs 8,563 .. L2
70633 De Quincy 3,966 .. D6
70634 De Ridder⊙ 11,057 .. D5
71421 Derry 75 .... E3
70030 Des Allemands 2,920 .. N4
70047 Destrehan 2,382 .. N4
†71055 Dixie Inn 453 .... D1
71422 Dodson 469 ...... E2
70346 Donaldsonville⊙ 7,901 .. K3
70352 Donner 500 ...... J7
71234 Downsville 213 ... F1
71023 Doyline 801 ...... D1
70637 Dry Creek 300 ... D5
71423 Dry Prong 526 ... E3
71235 Dubach 1,161 .... E1
71024 Dubberly 421 .... D1
70353 Dulac 675 .... J8
71236 Dunn 225 .... G2
70728 Duplessis 500 ... K2
70529 Duson 1,253 .... F6
†71247 East Hodge 439 .. F1
71025 East Point 100 .. D2
71330 Echo 525 .... F4
70049 Edgard⊙ 400 ... M3
†71019 Edgefield 312 ... D2
71331 Effie 300 ...... E4
70638 Elizabeth 454 .. E5
71424 Elmer 200 ..... E4
71051 Elm Grove 100 .. C2
70532 Elton 1,450 .... E6
71425 Enterprise 375 .. G3
71332 Eola 47 .... F5
71237 Epps 672 ...... G1
70533 Erath 2,133 .... F7
71238 Eros 158 ...... F2
70534 Estherwood 691 .. F6
70730 Ethel 250 ...... H5
70535 Eunice 12,479 .. F6
70639 Evans 500 ..... D5
71333 Evergreen 272 .. F5
71240 Fairbanks 300 .. F1
71241 Farmerville⊙ 3,768 .. F1
70640 Fenton 491 .... E6

70711 Albany 857 .... M1
71301 Alexandria⊙ 51,565 .... E4
      Alexandria‡ 151,985 .... E4
†70458 Alton 500 .... L6
70340 Amelia 3,617 .... H7
70422 Amite⊙ 4,301 .... K5
71403 Anacoco 820 .... D4
70426 Angie 311 .... L5
70712 Angola 600 .... G5
70032 Arabi 10,248 .... P4
71001 Arcadia⊙ 3,403 .... E1
71218 Archibald 425 .... G2
70512 Arnaudville 1,679 .... G6
71002 Ashland 307 .... D2
71003 Athens 419 .... E1
71404 Atlanta 127 .... E3
70513 Avery Island 500 .... G7
70714 Baker 12,865 .... K1
70514 Baldwin 2,644 .... H7
71405 Ball 3,405 .... F4
70036 Barataria 1,123 ...... K7
70515 Basile 2,635 .... E5
71219 Baskin 286 .... G2
71220 Bastrop⊙ 15,527 ... G1
70715 Batchelor 500 ...... G5
*70801 Baton Rouge
      (cap.)⊙ 219,419 ..... K2
      Baton Rouge‡ 493,973 .. K2
†70360 Bayou Cane 15,723 .. J7
†70380 Bayou Vista 5,805 .. H7
71004 Belcher 436 .... C1
70630 Bell City 400 ...... D6
70037 Belle Chasse 5,412 .. O4
71406 Belmont 350 .... C3
71407 Bentley 120 .... E3
71006 Benton⊙ 1,864 ... C1
†70558 Bermuda 50 .... D3
71222 Bernice 1,956 ..... E1
70342 Berwick 4,466 .... H7
71007 Bethany 300 ..... B2
71008 Bienville 249 .... D2
71009 Blanchard 1,128 .. C1
70427 Bogalusa 16,976 .. L5
†71064 Bolinger 200 ..... C1
71223 Bonita 503 ...... G1
71320 Bordelonville 350 .. G4
*71111 Bossier City 50,817 .. C1
70343 Bourg 2,073 ..... J7
71409 Boyce 1,198 .... E4
70040 Braithwaite 350 .. P4
70516 Branch 200 ..... F6
70517 Breaux Bridge 5,922 .. G6
70718 Brittany 475 .... L3
70518 Broussard 2,923 .. F6
70719 Brusly 1,762 .... J2
71014 Bryceland 94 .... E2
71321 Buckeye 280 .... F4
71322 Bunkie 5,364 .... F5
70041 Buras-Triumph 4,137 .. L8
70519 Cade 175 .... G6
71225 Calhoun 350 .... F2
71410 Calvin 263 ..... E3
71411 Campti 1,069 ... D3
†70584 Cankton 303 .... F6
70520 Carencro 3,712 .. G6
70042 Carlisle 975 .... L7
70721 Carville 1,037 ... K3
71015 Caspiana 50 .... C2
71016 Castor 195 ..... D2
70522 Centerville 600 .. H7
70043 Chalmette⊙ 33,847 .. P4
†70767 Chamberlin 20 .. J1
71324 Chase 200 ..... G2
70524 Chataignier 431 .. F5

(continued)

Louisiana

SCALE
0 5 10 20 30 40 MI.
0 5 10 20 30 40 KM.

State Capitals .... ⊛
Parish Seats .... ⊙
Canals ....
Major Limited Access Hwys. ____

Scale 1:2,000,000

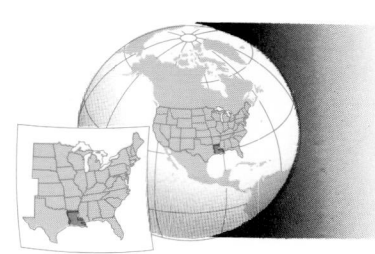

AREA   47,752 sq. mi. (123,678 sq. km.)
POPULATION   4,206,312
CAPITAL   Baton Rouge
LARGEST CITY   New Orleans
HIGHEST POINT   Driskill Mtn. 535 ft. (163 m.)
SETTLED IN   1699
ADMITTED TO UNION   April 30, 1812
POPULAR NAME   Pelican State
STATE FLOWER   Magnolia
STATE BIRD   Eastern Brown Pelican

New Orleans, Baton Rouge and Vicinity

© Copyright HAMMOND INCORPORATED, Maplewood, N.J.

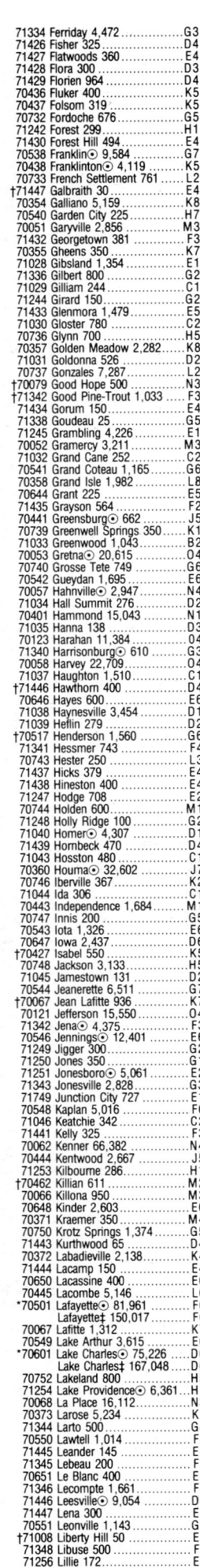

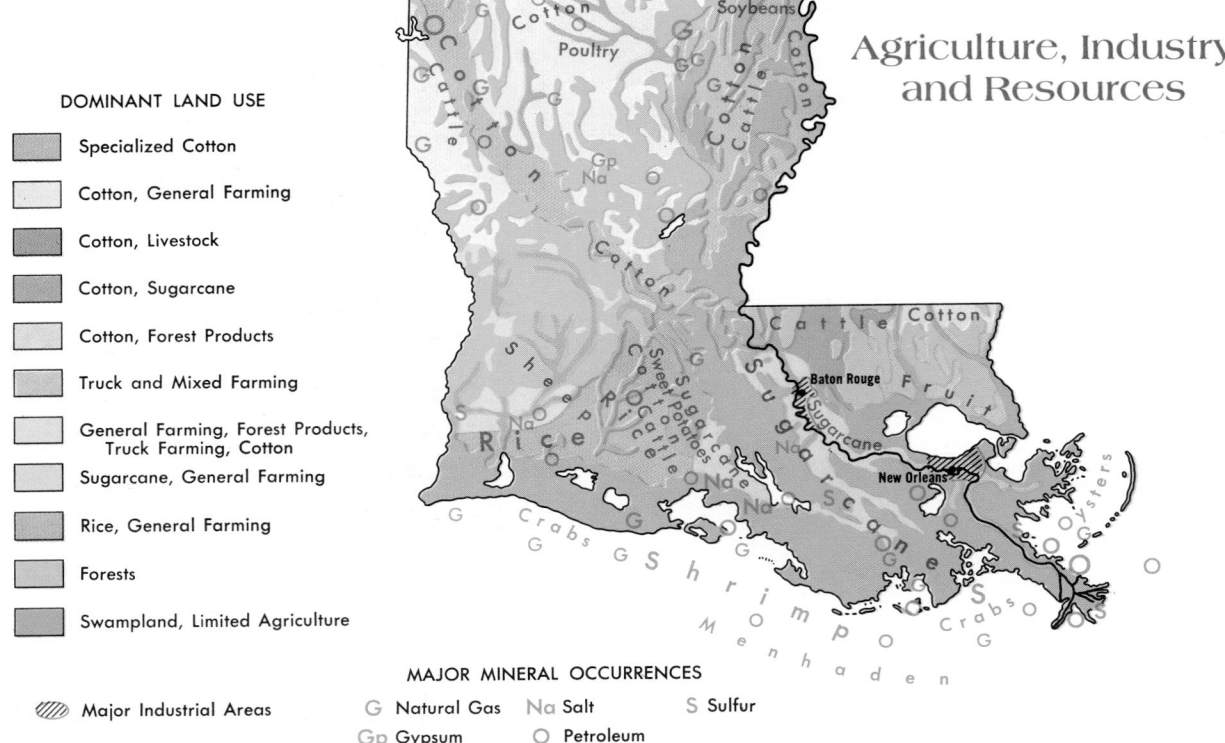

Agriculture, Industry and Resources

DOMINANT LAND USE

- Specialized Cotton
- Cotton, General Farming
- Cotton, Livestock
- Cotton, Sugarcane
- Cotton, Forest Products
- Truck and Mixed Farming
- General Farming, Forest Products, Truck Farming, Cotton
- Sugarcane, General Farming
- Rice, General Farming
- Forests
- Swampland, Limited Agriculture

MAJOR MINERAL OCCURRENCES

//// Major Industrial Areas   G Natural Gas   Na Salt   S Sulfur

Gp Gypsum   O Petroleum

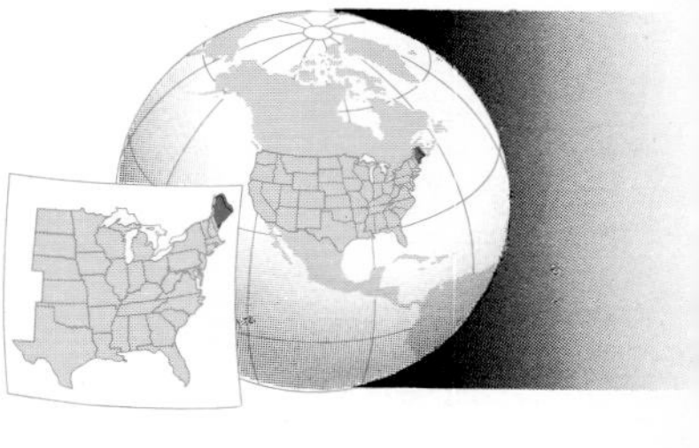

AREA 33,265 sq. mi. (86,156 sq. km.)
POPULATION 1,125,027
CAPITAL Augusta
LARGEST CITY Portland
HIGHEST POINT Katahdin 5,268 ft. (1606 m.)
SETTLED IN 1624
ADMITTED TO UNION March 15, 1820
POPULAR NAME Pine Tree State
STATE FLOWER White Pine Cone & Tassel
STATE BIRD Chickadee

COUNTIES

Androscoggin 99,657 .... C7
Aroostook 91,331 .... F2
Cumberland 215,789 .... C8
Franklin 27,098 .... B5
Hancock 41,781 .... G6
Kennebec 109,889 .... D7
Knox 32,941 .... E7
Lincoln 25,691 .... D7
Oxford 48,968 .... B7
Penobscot 137,015 .... F5
Piscataquis 17,634 .... E4
Sagadahoc 28,795 .... D7
Somerset 45,028 .... C4
Waldo 28,414 .... E6
Washington 34,963 .... H6
York 139,666 .... B9

CITIES and TOWNS

Zip Name/Pop. Key

04406 Abbot Village○ 576 .... D5
04001 Acton○ 1,228 .... B8
04606 Addison○ 1,061 .... H6
04910 Albion○ 1,551 .... E6
†04610 Alexander○ 385 .... H5
04002 Alfred○ 1,890 .... B9
†04774 Allagash○ 448 .... F1
†04938 Allens Mills 100 .... C6
04535 Alna○ 425 .... D7
†04468 Alton○ 468 .... F5
†04408 Amherst○ 203 .... G6
04216 Andover○ 850 .... B6
04911 Anson○ 2,226 .... D6
†04862 Appleton○ 818 .... E7
†04468 Argyle 225 .... F5
04732 Ashland○ 1,865 .... G2
04607 Ashville 36 .... G7
04912 Athens○ 802 .... D6
†04426 Atkinson○ 306 .... E5
04608 Atlantic 120 .... G7
04210 Auburn⊙ 23,128 .... C7
04330 Augusta (cap.)⊙ 21,819 .... D7
04408 Aurora○ 110 .... G6
04003 Bailey Island 500 .... D8
†04497 Bancroft○ 61 .... H4
04401 Bangor⊙ 31,643 .... F6
Bangor‡ 83,919 .... F6
04609 Bar Harbor○ 4,124 .... G7
04609 Bar Harbor 2,685 .... G7
†04619 Baring○ 308 .... J5
04004 Bar Mills 800 .... C8
04653 Bass Harbor 450 .... G7
04530 Bath⊙ 10,246 .... D8
†04915 Bayside F7
04611 Beals○ 695 .... H7
†04622 Beddington○ 36 .... H6
04915 Belfast⊙ 6,243 .... F7
04917 Belgrade○ 2,043 .... D7
†04915 Belmont○ 520 .... E7
04733 Benedicta○ 225 .... G4
†04937 Benton○ 2,188 .... D6
03901 Berwick○ 4,149 .... B9
03901 Berwick 2,378 .... B9
04217 Bethel○ 2,340 .... B7
04005 Biddeford 19,638 .... B9
04920 Bingham○ 1,184 .... D5
04920 Bingham 1,074 .... D5
04613 Birch Harbor 300 .... H7
04734 Blaine○ 922 .... H2
04734 Blaine-Mars Hill 1,921 .... H2
04614 Blue Hill○ 1,644 .... F7
04615 Blue Hill Falls 135 .... F7
04537 Boothbay○ 2,308 .... D8
04538 Boothbay Harbor 2,207 .... D8
04008 Bowdoinham○ 1,828 .... D7
†04481 Bowerbank○ 27 .... E5
04410 Bradford○ 888 .... F5
†04410 Bradford Center 105 .... F5
04411 Bradley○ 1,149 .... F6
04412 Brewer 9,017 .... F6
04735 Bridgewater○ 742 .... H3
04009 Bridgton○ 3,528 .... B7
04009 Bridgton 1,639 .... B7
†04990 Brighton○ 74 .... D5
04539 Bristol○ 2,095 .... D8
04616 Brooklin○ 619 .... F7
04921 Brooks○ 804 .... E6
04617 Brooksville○ 753 .... F7
04413 Brookton 175 .... H4
04010 Brownfield○ 767 .... B8
04414 Brownville○ 1,545 .... E5
04011 Brunswick○ 17,366 .... C8
04011 Brunswick 10,990 .... C8
04219 Bryant Pond 600 .... B7
†04232 Buckfield○ 1,333 .... C7
04618 Bucks Harbor 300 .... J6
04416 Bucksport○ 4,345 .... F6
04416 Bucksport 2,853 .... F6
04540 Burkettville 120 .... E7
04417 Burlington○ 322 .... G5
04922 Burnham○ 951 .... E6
†04093 Buxton○ 5,775 .... C8
†04275 Byron○ 114 .... B6
04619 Calais 4,262 .... J5
04923 Cambridge○ 445 .... E5
04843 Camden○ 4,584 .... F7
04843 Camden 3,743 .... F7
04924 Canaan○ 1,189 .... D6
04221 Canton○ 831 .... C7
03902 Cape Neddick 850 .... B9
04014 Cape Porpoise 500 .... C9
04736 Caribou 9,916 .... G2
04419 Carmel○ 1,695 .... E6
†04947 Carrabassett Valley○ 107 .... C5
†04487 Carroll○ 175 .... G5
†04224 Carthage○ 438 .... C6
†04465 Cary○ 229 .... H4
04015 Casco○ 2,243 .... B7
04421 Castine○ 1,304 .... F7
†04941 Center Montville 16 .... E7
†04623 Centerville○ 28 .... H6
†04757 Chapman○ 406 .... G2
04422 Charleston○ 1,037 .... F5
†04666 Charlotte○ 300 .... J5
04017 Chebeague Island 900 .... C8
†04345 Chelsea○ 2,522 .... D7
04622 Cherryfield○ 983 .... H6
†04458 Chester○ 434 .... F5
†04938 Chesterville○ 869 .... C6
†04478 Chesuncook 6 .... D3
04926 China○ 2,918 .... E7
†04239 Chisholm 1,796 .... C7
†04428 Clifton○ 462 .... G6
04927 Clinton○ 2,696 .... D6
04927 Clinton 1,305 .... D6
†04623 Columbia○ 275 .... H6
04623 Columbia Falls○ 517 .... H6
†04638 Cooper○ 105 .... H6
04624 Corea 375 .... H7
04928 Corinna○ 1,887 .... E6
04020 Cornish○ 1,047 .... B8
†04976 Cornville○ 838 .... D6
04625 Cranberry Isles○ 198 .... G7
†04610 Crawford○ 86 .... H5
†04015 Crescent Lake 325 .... C7
†04851 Criehaven 5 .... F8
04738 Crouseville 450 .... G2
†04747 Crystal○ 349 .... G4
04021 Cumberland Center○ 5,284 .... C8
04021 Cumberland Center 2,015 .... C8
04563 Cushing○ 795 .... E7
04626 Cutler○ 726 .... J6
04543 Damariscotta○ 1,493 .... E7
04543 Damariscotta-Newcastle
1,411 .... E7
04424 Danforth○ 826 .... H4
†04622 Deblois○ 44 .... H6
†04429 Dedham○ 841 .... F6
04627 Deer Isle○ 1,492 .... F7
04022 Denmark○ 672 .... B8
04628 Dennysville○ 296 .... J6
04929 Detroit○ 744 .... E6
04930 Dexter○ 4,286 .... E5
04930 Dexter 3,118 .... E5
04224 Dixfield○ 2,389 .... C6
04224 Dixfield 1,725 .... C6
04932 Dixmont○ 812 .... E6
04426 Dover-Foxcroft○ 4,323 .... E5
04426 Dover-Foxcroft⊙ 2,974 .... E5
†04426 Dover South Mills 54 .... E5
04342 Dresden○ 998 .... D7
†04747 Dyer Brook○ 275 .... G3
04739 Eagle Lake○ 1,019 .... F1
04226 East Andover 250 .... B6
04544 East Boothbay 800 .... D8
04427 East Corinth 525 .... F5
04227 East Dixfield 250 .... C6
04429 East Holden 600 .... F6
04027 East Lebanon 950 .... B9
04228 East Livermore 500 .... C7
04630 East Machias○ 1,233 .... J6
04430 East Millinocket○ 2,372 .... F4
04430 East Millinocket 2,361 .... F4
04740 Easton○ 1,305 .... H2
04028 East Parsonfield 400 .... B8
04229 East Peru 200 .... C7
†04210 East Poland 200 .... C7
04631 Eastport 1,982 .... K6
04231 East Stoneham 300 .... B7
†04607 East Sullivan 496 .... G6
†04220 East Sumner 120 .... C7
†04862 East Union 75 .... E7
†04428 Eddington○ 1,769 .... F6
†04556 Edgecomb○ 841 .... D8
03903 Eliot○ 4,948 .... B9
04605 Ellsworth⊙ 5,179 .... F6
04031 Emery Mills 100 .... B8
04433 Enfield○ 1,397 .... F5
04434 Etna○ 758 .... E6
04936 Eustis○ 582 .... B5
04435 Exeter○ 823 .... E6
†04938 Fairbanks 400 .... C6
04937 Fairfield○ 6,113 .... D6
04937 Fairfield 3,169 .... D6
04105 Falmouth○ 6,853 .... C8
04105 Falmouth 1,655 .... C8
†04345 Farmingdale○ 2,535 .... D7
†04345 Farmingdale 2,014 .... D7
04938 Farmington○ 6,730 .... C6
04938 Farmington⊙ 3,583 .... C6
04940 Farmington Falls 500 .... C6
†04349 Fayette○ 812 .... C7
04546 Five Islands 225 .... D8
04742 Fort Fairfield○ 4,376 .... H2
04742 Fort Fairfield 2,282 .... H2
04743 Fort Kent○ 4,826 .... F1
04743 Fort Kent 2,375 .... F1
04744 Fort Kent Mills 200 .... F1
04438 Frankfort○ 783 .... F6
04634 Franklin○ 979 .... G6
04941 Freedom○ 458 .... E7
04032 Freeport○ 5,863 .... C8
04032 Freeport 1,906 .... C8
04635 Frenchboro○ 43 .... G7
04745 Frenchville○ 1,450 .... G1
04547 Friendship○ 1,000 .... E7
04037 Fryeburg○ 2,715 .... A7
04037 Fryeburg 1,644 .... A7
04345 Gardiner 6,485 .... D7
04939 Garland○ 718 .... E5
04548 Georgetown○ 735 .... D8
†04217 Gilead○ 191 .... B7
†04401 Glenburn○ 2,319 .... F6
04846 Glen Cove 250 .... E7
04038 Gorham○ 10,101 .... C8
04038 Gorham 4,052 .... C8
†04607 Gouldsboro○ 1,574 .... H7
04746 Grand Isle○ 719 .... G1
04637 Grand Lake Stream○ 198 .... H5
04039 Gray○ 4,344 .... C8
†04408 Great Pond○ 45 .... G6
04236 Greene○ 3,037 .... C7
04441 Greenville○ 1,839 .... D5
04441 Greenville 1,640 .... D5
04442 Greenville Junction 650 .... D5
04443 Guilford○ 1,793 .... E5
04443 Guilford 1,235 .... E5
04347 Hallowell 2,502 .... D7
†04785 Hamlin○ 340 .... H1
04444 Hampden○ 5,250 .... F6
04444 Hampden 3,538 .... F6
04445 Hampden Highlands 950 .... F6
04640 Hancock○ 1,409 .... G6
04237 Hanover○ 256 .... B7
04942 Harmony○ 755 .... D6
†04011 Harpswell○ 3,796 .... D8
04643 Harrington○ 859 .... H6
04040 Harrison○ 1,667 .... B7
†04221 Hartford○ 480 .... C7
04943 Hartland○ 1,669 .... D6
04943 Hartland 1,041 .... D6
04446 Haynesville○ 169 .... G4
04238 Hebron○ 665 .... C7
†04401 Hermon○ 3,170 .... F6
04944 Hinckley 140 .... D6
04041 Hiram○ 1,067 .... B8
†04730 Hodgdon○ 1,084 .... H3
04042 Hollis Center○ 2,892 .... B8
04847 Hope○ 730 .... E7
04730 Houlton○ 6,766 .... H3
04730 Houlton⊙ 5,730 .... H3
04448 Howland○ 1,602 .... F5
04448 Howland 1,502 .... F5
04449 Hudson○ 797 .... F5
04644 Hulls Cove 200 .... G7
04747 Island Falls○ 981 .... G3
04645 Isle Au Haut○ 57 .... F7
04848 Islesboro○ 521 .... F7
04945 Jackman○ 1,003 .... C4
†04630 Jacksonville 200 .... J6
04239 Jay○ 5,080 .... C7
04348 Jefferson○ 1,616 .... D7
04648 Jonesboro○ 553 .... J6
04649 Jonesport○ 1,512 .... H6
04649 Jonesport 1,050 .... H6
04450 Kenduskeag○ 1,210 .... E6
04043 Kennebunk○ 6,621 .... B9
04043 Kennebunk 3,294 .... B9
†04043 Kennebunk Beach 200 .... C9
04046 Kennebunkport○ 2,952 .... C9
04046 Kennebunkport 1,685 .... C9
04349 Kents Hill 300 .... D7
04947 Kingfield○ 1,083 .... C6
04451 Kingman 281 .... G4
†04990 Kingsbury○ 4 .... D5
03904 Kittery○ 9,314 .... B9
03904 Kittery 5,465 .... B9
03905 Kittery Point 1,260 .... B9
†04986 Knox○ 558 .... E6
04453 La Grange○ 509 .... F5
†04463 Lake View○ 20 .... F5
†04605 Lamoine○ 953 .... G7
04455 Lee○ 688 .... G5
†04263 Leeds○ 1,463 .... C7
04456 Levant○ 1,117 .... F6
04240 Lewiston 40,481 .... C7
Lewiston-Auburn‡ 72,378 .... C7
04949 Liberty○ 694 .... E7
04749 Lille 300 .... G1
04048 Limerick○ 1,356 .... B8
04750 Limestone○ 8,719 .... H2
04750 Limestone 1,334 .... H2
04049 Limington○ 2,203 .... B8
04457 Lincoln○ 5,066 .... G5
04457 Lincoln 3,524 .... G5
04849 Lincolnville○ 1,414 .... E7
04850 Lincolnville Center 200 .... E7
†04730 Linneus○ 752 .... H3
04250 Lisbon○ 8,769 .... C7
04250 Lisbon-Lisbon
Center 1,865 .... C7
04252 Lisbon Falls 4,370 .... D7
04350 Litchfield○ 1,954 .... D7
†04627 Little Deer Isle 475 .... F7
04082 Little Falls-South
Windham 1,366 .... C8
†04760 Littleton○ 1,009 .... H3
04253 Livermore○ 1,826 .... C7
04254 Livermore Falls○ 3,572 .... C7
04254 Livermore Falls 2,441 .... C7
04255 Locke Mills 600 .... B7
04051 Lovell○ 767 .... B7
†04433 Lowell○ 194 .... F5
04652 Lubec○ 2,045 .... K6
†04730 Ludlow○ 403 .... G3
04654 Machias○ 2,458 .... J6
04654 Machias⊙ 1,277 .... J6
04655 Machiasport○ 1,108 .... H6
†04451 Macwahoc○ 126 .... G4
04756 Madawaska○ 5,282 .... G1
04756 Madawaska 4,165 .... G1
04950 Madison○ 4,367 .... D6
04950 Madison 2,788 .... D6
†04966 Madrid○ 178 .... B6
†04942 Mainstream 100 .... D6
04351 Manchester○ 1,949 .... D7
04757 Mapleton○ 1,895 .... G2
04758 Mars Hill○ 1,892 .... H2
04758 Mars Hill-Blaine 1,921 .... H2
04759 Masardis○ 328 .... G3
04851 Matinicus 66 .... F8
04459 Mattawamkeag○ 1,000 .... G5
04256 Mechanic Falls○ 2,616 .... C7
04256 Mechanic Falls 2,198 .... C7
04657 Meddybemps○ 110 .... J5
†04453 Medford○ 163 .... F5
†04453 Medford Center 100 .... F5
04460 Medway○ 1,871 .... G4
04957 Mercer○ 448 .... D6
04257 Mexico○ 3,698 .... B6
04257 Mexico 3,207 .... B6
†04216 Middledam 10 .... B6
04658 Milbridge○ 1,306 .... H6
04461 Milford○ 2,160 .... F6
04461 Milford 1,688 .... F6
04462 Millinocket○ 7,567 .... F4

(continued on following page)

Agriculture, Industry and Resources

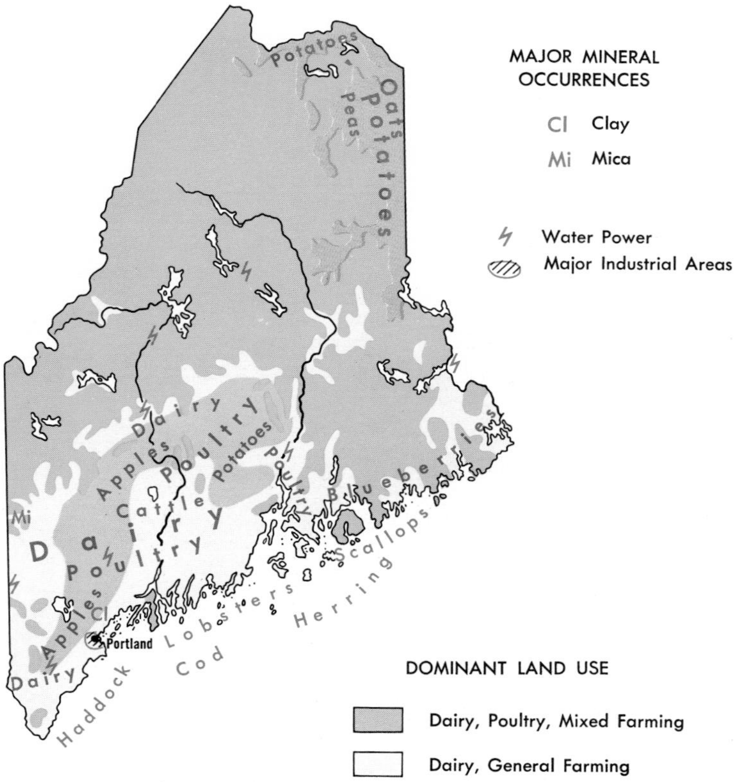
Potatoes
Oats
Peas
Potatoes
Dairy
Poultry
Potatoes
Apples
Cattle
Poultry
Blueberries
Dairy
Poultry
Apples
Scallops
Lobsters
Herring
Portland
Cod
Haddock
Dairy
Mi
Cl
MAJOR MINERAL OCCURRENCES
Cl Clay
Mi Mica
Water Power
Major Industrial Areas
DOMINANT LAND USE
Dairy, Poultry, Mixed Farming
Dairy, General Farming
Potatoes, General Farming
Forests

Topography

0   30   60 MI.

0   30   60 KM.

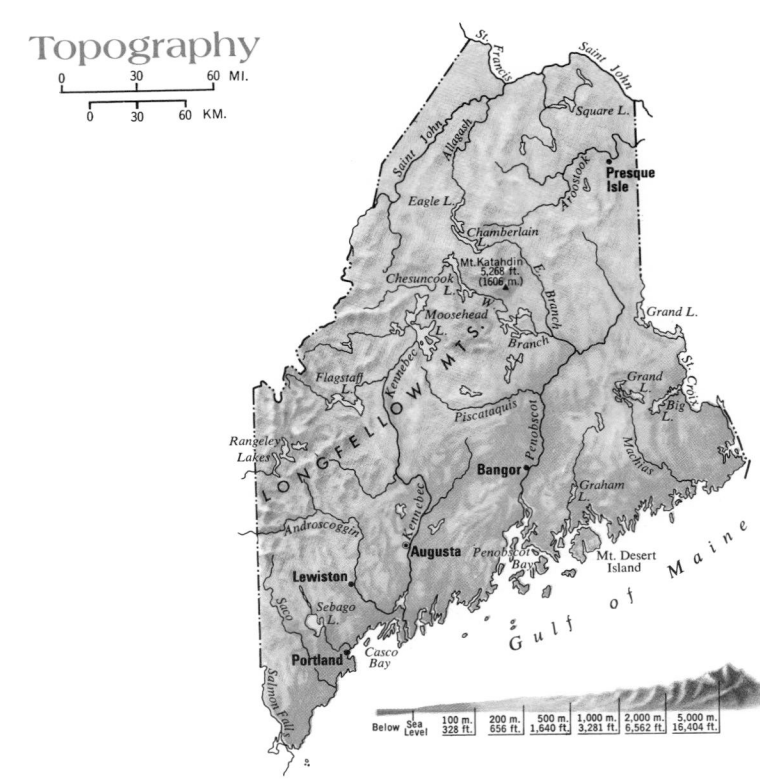

| Below Sea Level | 100 m. 328 ft. | 200 m. 656 ft. | 500 m. 1,640 ft. | 1,000 m. 3,281 ft. | 2,000 m. 6,562 ft. | 5,000 m. 16,404 ft. |

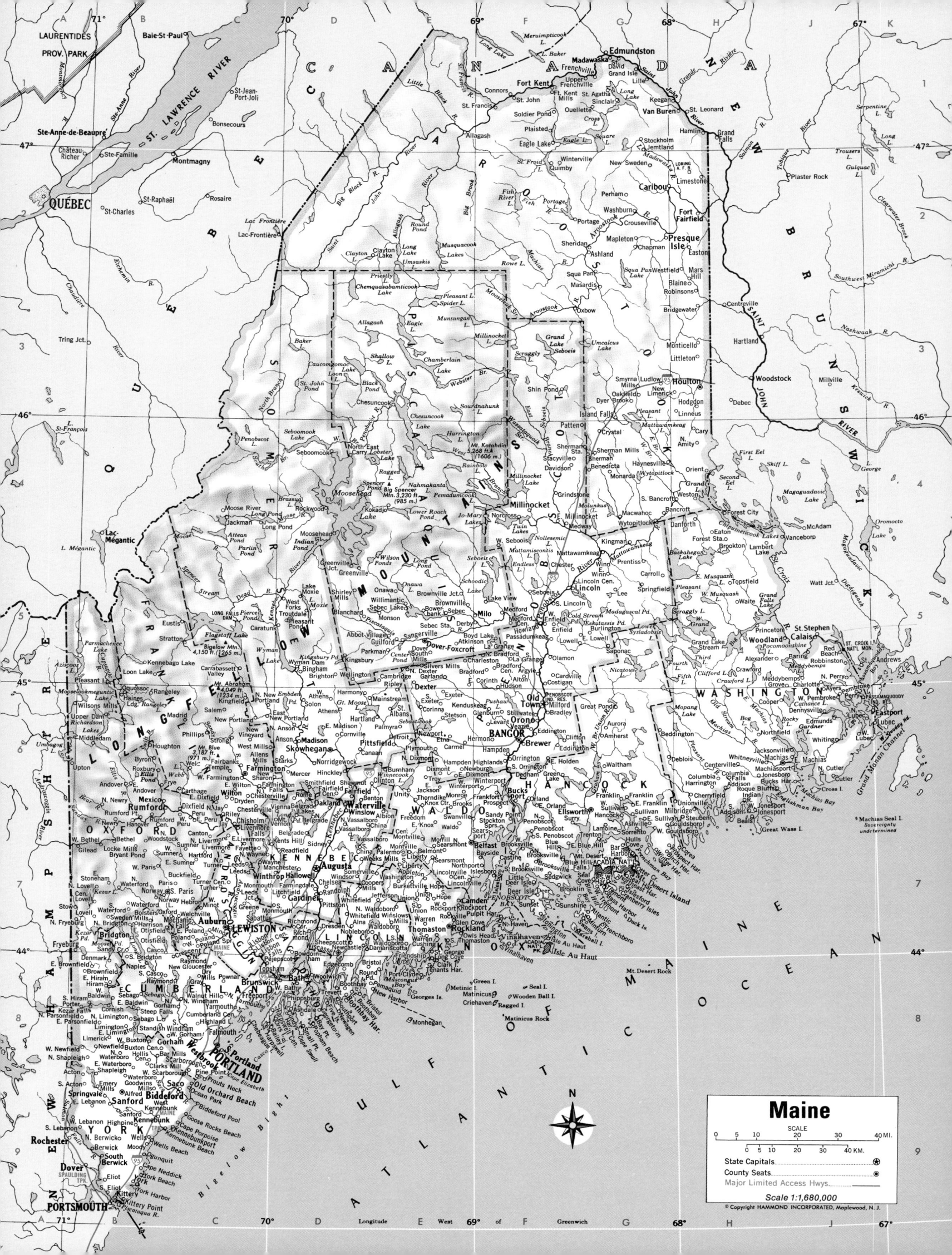

MARYLAND

COUNTIES

Allegany 80,548 ....C2
Anne Arundel 370,775 ....M4
Baltimore 655,615 ....M3
Baltimore (city county) 786,775 ...M3
Calvert 34,638 ....M6
Caroline 23,143 ....P5
Carroll 96,356 ....K2
Cecil 60,430 ....P2
Charles 72,751 ....K6
Dorchester 30,623 ....O7
Frederick 114,792 ....J3
Garrett 26,498 ....A2
Harford 145,930 ....N2
Howard 118,572 ....L4
Kent 16,695 ....O3
Montgomery 579,053 ....J4
Prince Georges 665,071 ....L5
Queen Annes 25,508 ....P4
Saint Marys 59,895 ....M7
Somerset 19,188 ....R8
Talbot 25,604 ....O5
Washington 113,086 ....G2
Wicomico 64,540 ....R7
Worcester 30,889 ....S8

CITIES and TOWNS

Zip   Name/Pop.   Key

21001 Aberdeen 11,533 ....O2
21009 Abingdon 500 ....N3
21520 Accident 246 ....A2
20607 Accokeek 3,894 ....L6
*21401 Annapolis (cap.)⊙ 31,740 M5
20701 Annapolis Junction 775 .....M4
20608 Aquasco 950 ....L6
†21227 Arbutus 20,163 ....M4
    Aspen Hill 47,455 ....K4
*21201 Baltimore 786,775 ....M3
    Baltimore‡ 2,174,023 ....M3
20610 Barstow 500 ....M6
21521 Barton 617 ....B2
21014 Bel Air⊙ 7,814 ....N2
20611 Bel Alton 800 ....L7
20705 Beltsville 12,760 ....G3
20612 Benedict 850 ....M6
21811 Berlin 2,162 ....T7
†20740 Berwyn Heights 3,135 ....G4
*20014 Bethesda 62,736 ....E4
21609 Bethlehem 500 ....P6
21610 Betterton 356 ....O3
20710 Bladensburg 7,691 ....G4
21523 Bloomington 486 ....B3
21713 Boonsboro 1,908 ....H2
†20027 Boulevard Heights 500 ...F5
20715 Bowie 33,695 ....L4
21612 Bozman 700 ....N5
20613 Brandywine 1,319 ....L6
20722 Brentwood 2,988 ....F4
21225 Brooklyn 11,508 ....M4
†21659 Brookview 78 ....P6
21716 Brunswick 4,572 ....H3
21717 Buckeystown 400 ....J3
21718 Burkittsville 202 ....H3
20618 Bushwood 750 ....L7
20731 Cabin
    John-Brookmont 5,135 .E4
20619 California 5,770 ....M7
†20705 Calverton 7,649 ....L4
21613 Cambridge⊙ 11,703 ....O6
20748 Camp Springs 16,118 .....G6
21401 Cape Saint Claire 6,022 ...N4
20743 Capitol Heights 3,271 .....G5
21024 Cardiff 475 ....N2
†20028 Carmody Hills-Pepper Mill
    Village 5,571 ....G5
†21034 Castleton 750 ....N2
†21788 Catoctin Furnace 516 .....J2
21228 Catonsville 33,208 ....M3
21720 Cavetown 1,533 ....H2
21913 Cecilton 508 ....P3
21617 Centreville⊙ 2,018 ....O4
21816 Chance 600 ....P8
21914 Charlestown 720 ....P2
20622 Charlotte Hall 1,901 ....M7
21027 Chase 900 ....N3
20623 Cheltenham 950 ....L6
20732 Chesapeake Beach 1,408 .N6
21915 Chesapeake City 899 ......P2
21619 Chester 950 ....N5
21620 Chestertown⊙ 3,300 ......O4
20785 Cheverly 5,751 ....G4
20815 Chevy Chase 12,232 .....E4
†20015 Chevy Chase Section
    Four 3,189 ....E4
20783 Chillum 32,775 ....F4
21622 Church Creek 124 ....O6
21623 Church Hill 319 ....O4
21028 Churchville 500 ....N2
20734 Clarksburg 400 ....J4
21029 Clarksville 500 ....L4
21722 Clear Spring 477 ....G2
20624 Clements 800 ....L7
20735 Clinton 16,438 ....G6
21030 Cockeysville 17,013 ......M3
20904 Colesville 14,359 ....K4
20740 College Park 23,614 ......G4
†20722 Colmar Manor 1,286 ....F4
20626 Coltons Point 600 ....M8
21043 Columbia 52,518 ....L4
20627 Compton 500 ....M7
21723 Cooksville 497 ....K3
†20027 Coral Hills 11,602 ....G5
21524 Corriganville 1,020 ....C2
†20722 Cottage City 1,122 ....F4
†20611 Cox Station (Bel
    Alton) 800 ....L7
21502 Cresaptown 4,645 ....C2
21817 Crisfield 2,924 ....P9
21114 Crofton 12,009 ....M4
21032 Crownsville 500 ....M4
21502 Cumberland⊙ 25,933 .....D2
    Cumberland‡ 107,782 .....D2

20750 Damascus 4,129 ....K3
20628 Dameron 759 ....N8
21034 Darlington 850 ....N2
†20760 Darnestown 950 ....J4
20751 Deale 3,008 ....M5
21821 Deal Island 800 ....P8
21550 Deer Park 486 ....A3
†20784 Defense Heights G4
21875 Delmar 1,232 ....R7
21629 Denton⊙ 1,927 ....P5
20855 Derwood 413 ....K4
20753 Dickerson 530 ....J4
20747 District Heights 6,799 ....G5
20630 Drayden 400 ....N8
21222 Dundalk 71,293 ....N3

†21659 Eldorado 93 ....P6
21920 Elk Mills 550 ....P2
†21901 Elk Neck 700 ....P2
21921 Elkton⊙ 6,468 ....P2
21529 Ellerslie 950 ....C2
21043 Ellicott City⊙ 21,784 .....L3
21727 Emmitsburg 1,552 ....J2
21824 Ewell 595 ....O9
†20027 Fairmount Heights 1,616 ..G5
21047 Fallston 5,572 ....N2
21632 Federalsburg 1,952 ....P6
21061 Ferndale 14,314 ....M4
21048 Finksburg 950 ....L3
21634 Fishing Creek 595 ....N7
21530 Flintstone 400 ....D2
20001 Forest Heights 2,999 .....F5
21050 Forest Hill 450 ....N2
†20022 Forestville 16,401 ....G5
20022 Fort Foote 700 ....F6
†20744 Fort Washington L6
†21740 Fountain Head 1,745 .....G2
21734 Funkstown 1,103 ....H2
20760 Gaithersburg 26,424 .....K4
21635 Galena 374 ....P3
†19973 Galestown 142 ....P6
20765 Galesville 600 ....M5
†21048 Gamber 500 ....L3
21054 Gambrills 460 ....M4
20766 Garrett Park 1,178 ....E3
21055 Garrison 950 ....L3
20767 Germantown 9,721 ....J4
†20801 Glenarden 4,993 ....G4
20031 Glen Burnie 37,263 ......M4
20768 Glen Echo 229 ....E4
21737 Glenelg 400 ....L3
21636 Goldsboro 188 ....P4
20636 Hughesville 1,208 ....L6
†21163 Granite 950 ....L3
21536 Grantsville 498 ....B2
21638 Grasonville 1,910 ....O5
20770 Greenbelt 17,332 ....G4

21053 Freeland 500 ....M2
20758 Friendship 600 ....M6
21531 Friendsville 511 ....A2
21532 Frostburg 7,715 ....C2
21826 Fruitland 2,694 ....R7
21734 Funkstown 1,103 ....H2
20760 Gaithersburg 26,424 .....K4
21635 Galena 374 ....P3
20765 Galesville 600 ....M5
†21048 Gamber 500 ....L3
21054 Gambrills 460 ....M4
20766 Garrett Park 1,178 ....E3
21055 Garrison 950 ....L3
20767 Germantown 9,721 ....J4
†20801 Glenarden 4,993 ....G4
20031 Glen Burnie 37,263 ......M4
20768 Glen Echo 229 ....E4
21737 Glenelg 400 ....L3
21636 Goldsboro 188 ....P4
20639 Huntingtown 450 ....M6
21643 Hurlock 1,690 ....P6
20640 Indian Head 1,381 ....L6

21122 Green Haven 6,577 ......M4
21639 Greensboro 1,253 ....P5
21740 Hagerstown⊙ 34,132 ....G2
    Hagerstown‡ 113,086 ....G2
†21740 Halfway 8,659 ....G2
21074 Hampstead 1,103 ....L2
21750 Hancock 1,887 ....F2
21201 Hanover 500 ....M4
21077 Harmans 400 ....M4
21078 Havre de Grace 8,763 ...O2
21830 Hebron 714 ....R7
21640 Henderson 156 ....P4
†21111 Hereford 680 ....M2
21753 Highfield-Cascade 1,096 ...J2
21401 Highland Beach 8 ....M5
†20903 Hillandale 9,686 ....G4
20031 Hillcrest Heights 17,021 ..F5
21641 Hillsboro 180 ....P5
20636 Hollywood 500 ....M7
20637 Hughesville 1,208 ....L6
20639 Huntingtown 450 ....M6
21643 Hurlock 1,690 ....P6
20640 Indian Head 1,381 ....L6

†20685 Island Creek 400 ....M7
21084 Jarrettsville 1,485 ....M2
†21085 Joppatowne 11,348 ......N3
21756 Keedysville 476 ....H3
†20901 Kemp Mill E4
20795 Kensington 1,822 ....E4
21087 Kingsville 2,824 ....N3
21538 Kitzmiller 387 ....A3
21758 Knoxville 500 ....H3
20785 Landover 5,374 ....G4
20784 Landover Hills 1,428 .....G4
20787 Langley Park 14,038 .....F4
20801 Lanham-Seabrook 15,814 ..G4
21227 Lansdowne-Baltimore
    Highlands 16,759 ....M3
20646 La Plata⊙ 2,484 ....L6
†20870 Largo 5,557 ....L4
*20810 Laurel 12,103 ....L4
21502 La Vale-Narrows
    Park 5,523 ....C2
20760 Laytonsville 195 ....K4
21761 Le Gore 500 ....J2
†20740 Leitersburg 350 ....H2
20650 Leonardtown⊙ 1,448 .....M7

(continued)

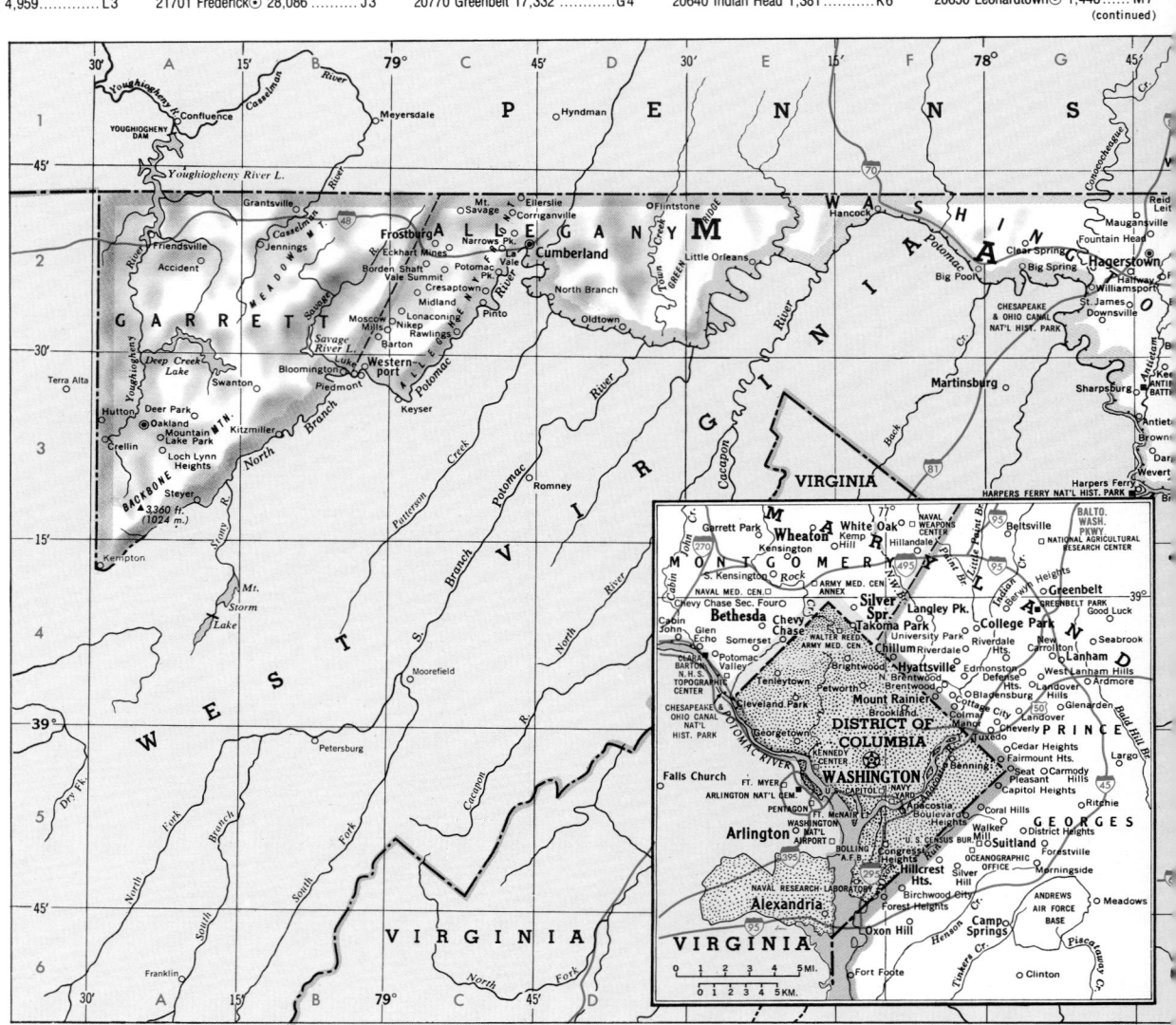

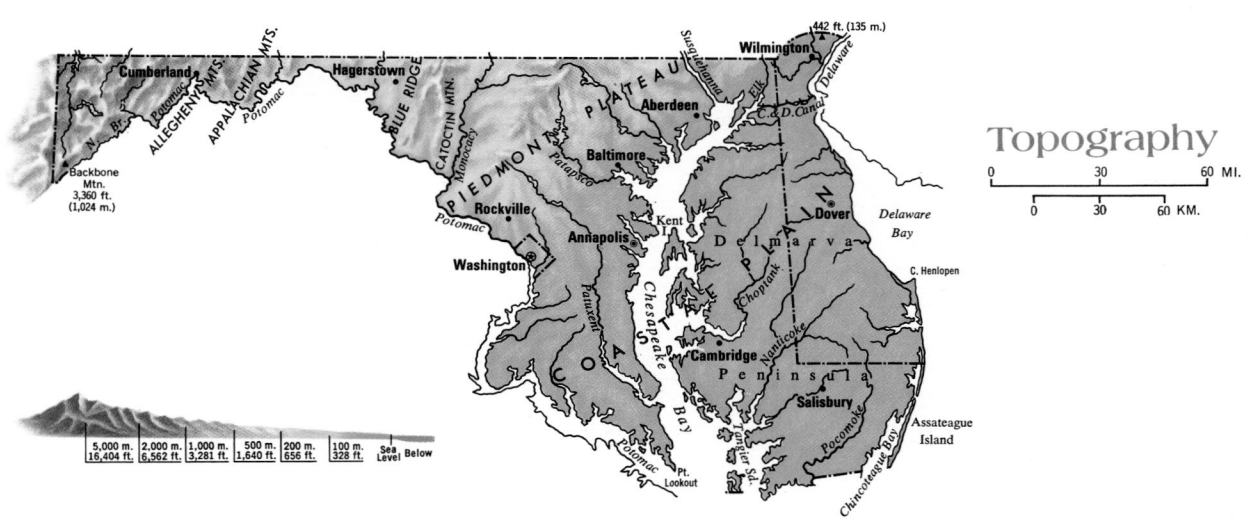

Topography

0   30   60 MI.

0   30   60 KM.

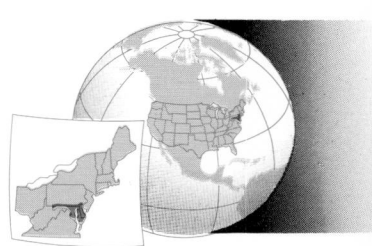

MARYLAND

AREA 10,460 sq. mi. (27,091 sq. km.)
POPULATION 4,216,975
CAPITAL Annapolis
LARGEST CITY Baltimore
HIGHEST POINT Backbone Mtn. 3,360 ft.
(1024 m.)
SETTLED IN 1634
ADMITTED TO UNION April 28, 1788
POPULAR NAME Old Line State; Free State
STATE FLOWER Black-eyed Susan
STATE BIRD Baltimore Oriole

DELAWARE

AREA 2,044 sq. mi. (5,294 sq. km.)
POPULATION 594,317
CAPITAL Dover
LARGEST CITY Wilmington
HIGHEST POINT Ebright Road 442 ft. (135 m.)
SETTLED IN 1627
ADMITTED TO UNION December 7, 1787
POPULAR NAME First State; Diamond State
STATE FLOWER Peach Blossom
STATE BIRD Blue Hen Chicken

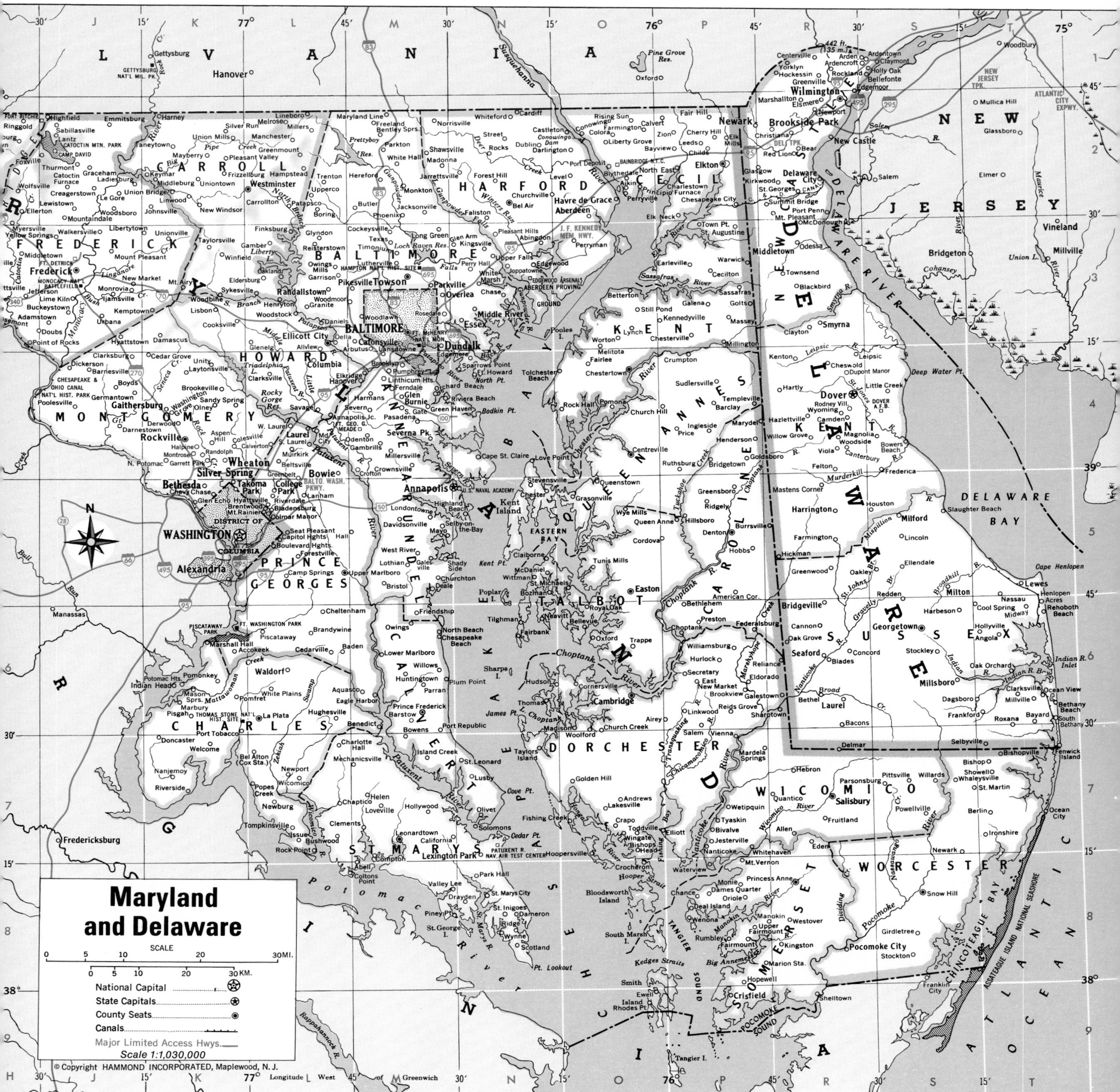

Maryland and Delaware

SCALE

0 5 10 20 30 MI.

0 5 10 20 30 KM.

National Capital .... ⊛
State Capitals .... ◉
County Seats .... ◎
Canals ....

Major Limited Access Hwys. ....
Scale 1:1,030,000

© Copyright HAMMOND INCORPORATED, Maplewood, N.J.

Agriculture, Industry and Resources

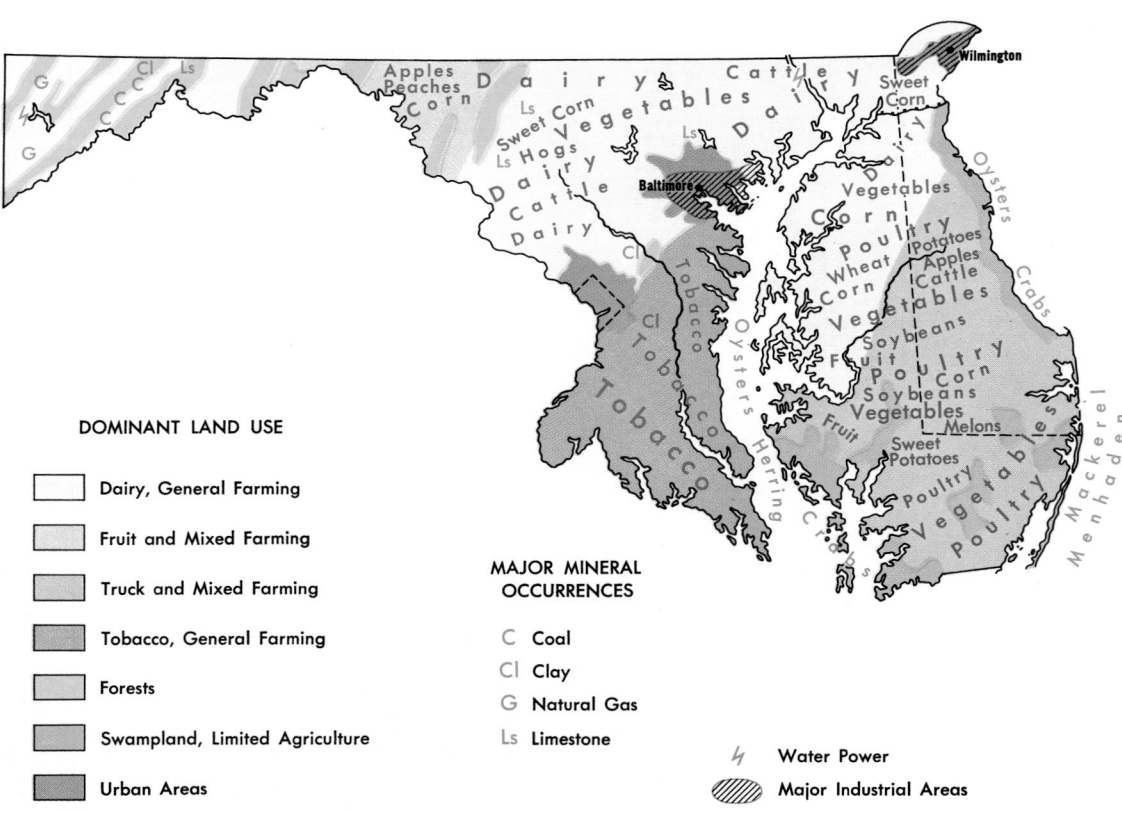

DOMINANT LAND USE

- Dairy, General Farming
- Fruit and Mixed Farming
- Truck and Mixed Farming
- Tobacco, General Farming
- Forests
- Swampland, Limited Agriculture
- Urban Areas

MAJOR MINERAL OCCURRENCES

- C Coal
- Cl Clay
- G Natural Gas
- Ls Limestone

⚡ Water Power

▨ Major Industrial Areas

MASSACHUSETTS

AREA 8,284 sq. mi. (21,456 sq. km.)
POPULATION 5,737,037
CAPITAL Boston
LARGEST CITY Boston
HIGHEST POINT Mt. Greylock 3,491 ft.
(1064 m.)
SETTLED IN 1620
ADMITTED TO UNION February 6, 1788
POPULAR NAME Bay State; Old Colony
STATE FLOWER Mayflower
STATE BIRD Chickadee

RHODE ISLAND

AREA 1,212 sq. mi. (3,139 sq. km.)
POPULATION 947,154
CAPITAL Providence
LARGEST CITY Providence
HIGHEST POINT Jerimoth Hill 812 ft.
(247 m.)
SETTLED IN 1636
ADMITTED TO UNION May 29, 1790
POPULAR NAME Little Rhody; Ocean State
STATE FLOWER Violet
STATE BIRD Rhode Island Red

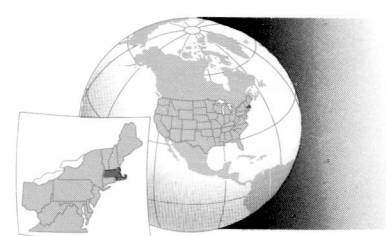

Agriculture, Industry and Resources

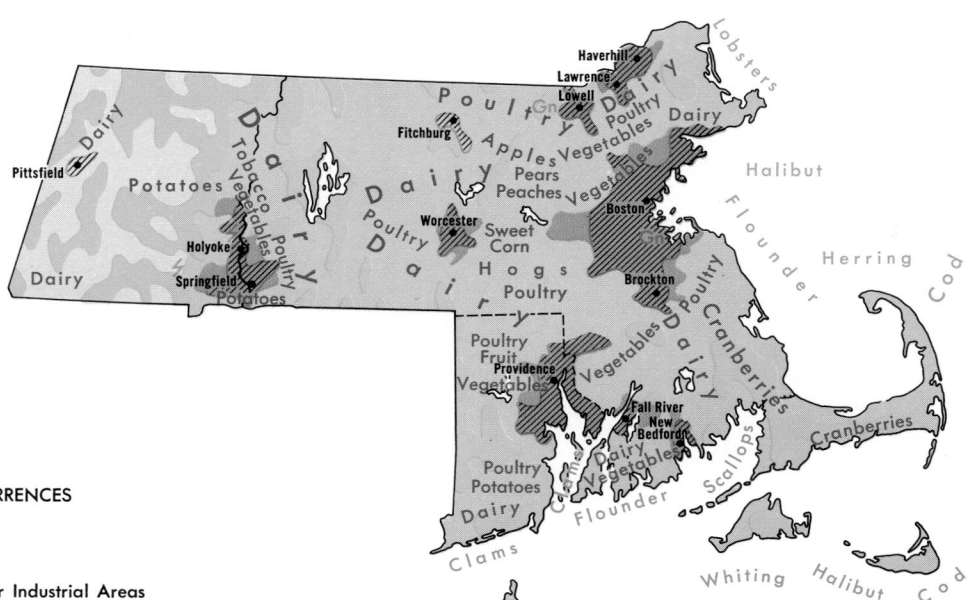

DOMINANT LAND USE

- Specialized Dairy
- Dairy, Poultry, Mixed Farming
- Forests
- Urban Areas

MAJOR MINERAL OCCURRENCES

Gn Granite

⚡ Water Power   ▨ Major Industrial Areas

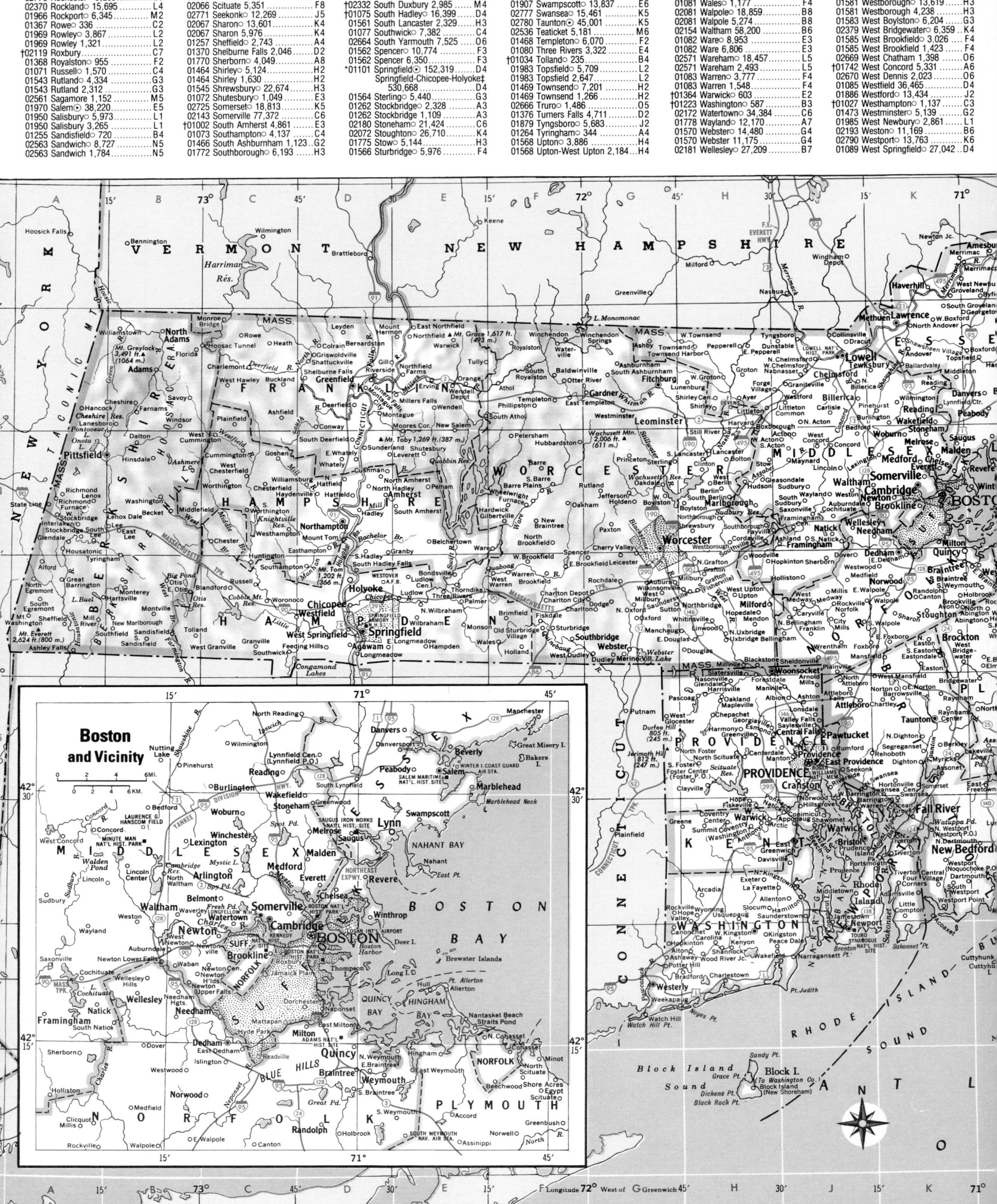

01266 West Stockbridge○ 1,280 ..A3	02152 Winthrop◦ 19,294 ....D6	Berkshire (hills) B4
02575 West Tisbury 1,010.......M7	01801 Woburn 36,626 ....C6	Big (pond) B4
01587 West Upton-Upton 2,184...H4	02543 Woods Hole 1,080 ....M6	Bigelow (bight) M1
02576 West Wareham 1,837.....L5	*01601 Worcester⊙ 161,799 ...H3	Blackstone (riv.) G3
02090 Westwood◦ 13,212 ....B8	Worcester‡ 372,940 .....H3	Blue (hills) C8
02673 West Yarmouth 3,852 ...N6	01098 Worthington◦ 932 ....C3	Boston (bay) E6
02188 Weymouth 55,601.........D8	02093 Wrentham◦ 7,580 ....J4	Boston (harb.) D7
01093 Whately◦ 1,341 ....D3	Yarmouth 18,449 ....O6	Boston Nat'l Hist. Park D6
01588 Whitinsville 5,379 ....H4	02675 Yarmouth Port 2,490 ....N6	Brewster (isls.) E7
02382 Whitman◦ 13,534 ....L4		Buel (lake) A4
01095 Wilbraham 12,053 ....E4	**OTHER FEATURES**	Buzzards (bay) L7
01095 Wilbraham 3,379 ....E4		Cambridge (res.) B6
01096 Williamsburg 2,237 ......C3	Adams Nat'l Hist. Site D7	Cape Cod (bay) N5
01267 Williamstown◦ 8,741 .....B2	Agawam (riv.) M5	Cape Cod (canal) N5
01267 Williamstown 4,798 ......B2	Allerton (pt.) E7	Cape Cod Nat'l Seashore P5
01887 Wilmington 17,471 ....C5	Ann (cape) M2	Chappaquiddick (isl.) N7
01475 Winchendon◦ 7,019 ......F2	Ashmere (lake) B3	Charles (riv.) C7
01475 Winchendon 4,030 ......F2	Assabet (riv.) H3	Chicopee (riv.) D4
01890 Winchester◦ 20,701 .....C6	Assawompset (pond) L5	Cobble Mountain (res.) C4
01270 Windsor◦ 598 ....B2	Bachelor (brook) D3	Cochituate (lake) A7

Cod (cape) O4	Otis A.F.B. M6	02822 Exeter◦ 4,453 ....H6
Concord (riv.) J2	Pasque (isl.) L7	02825 Foster◦ 3,370 ....H5
Congamond (lkes.) D4	Plum (isl.) L2	02828 Greenville 7,516 ....H5
Connecticut (riv.) D2	Plymouth (bay) M5	02830 Harrisville 1,224 ....H5
Cuttyhunk (isl.) L7	Poge (cape) N7	02832 Hope Valley 1,414 ......H6
Deer (isl.) E7	Pontoosuc (lake) A3	02833 Hopkinton◦ 6,406 ....H7
Deerfield (riv.) C2	Quabbin (res.) E3	02835 Jamestown◦ 4,040 ......J6
East (pt.) E6	Quaboag (riv.) F4	02835 Jamestown 2,156 ......J6
East Chop (pt.) M7	Quincy (bay) D7	02881 Kingston 5,479 ....J7
Eastern (pt.) M2	Quinebaug (riv.) F4	02837 Little Compton◦ 3,085 ...K6
Elizabeth (isls.) L7	Race (pt.) N4	02840 Middletown◦ 17,216 .....J7
Everett (mt.) A4	Salem Maritime Nat'l Hist.	02882 Narragansett 12,088 ....J7
Falls (riv.) D2	Site E5	02882 Narragansett 3,342 .....J7
Fort Devens H2	Saugus Iron Works Nat'l Hist.	02840 Newport⊙ 29,259 ....J7
Fort Rodman L6	Site D6	†02807 New Shoreham (Block
Fresh (pond) C6	Shawshine (riv.) K2	Island) 620 ....H8
Gammon (pt.) N6	Silver (lake) L4	02852 North Kingstown◦
Gay Head (prom.) L7	South (riv.) D2	21,938 ....J6
Grace (mt.) F2	Springfield Armory Nat'l Hist.	02908 North Providence◦
Great (pt.) O7	Site D4	29,188 ....J5
Green (riv.) B2	Squibnocket (pt.) M7	02859 Pascoag 3,807 ....H5
Greylock (mt.) B2	Stillwater (riv.) G3	*02860 Pawtucket 71,204 ......J5
Gurnet (pt.) M4	Stillwater (res.) H3	02883 Peace
Hingham (bay) E7	Sudbury (res.) A6	Dale-Wakefield 6,474 ...J7
Holyoke (range) D3	Sudbury (riv.) H3	02871 Portsmouth◦ 14,257 .....J6
Hoosac (mts.) B2	Swift (riv.) E4	*02901 Providence
Hoosic (riv.) A1	Taconic (mts.) A2	(cap.)⊙ 156,804 ....H5
Housatonic (riv.) A4	Taunton (riv.) K5	Providence-Warwick-
Ipswich (riv.) L2	Thompson (isl.) D7	Pawtucket‡ 919,216 ...H5
John F. Kennedy Nat'l Hist.	Toby (mt.) E3	02878 Tiverton◦ 13,526 ....K6
Site C7	Tom (mt.) D4	02878 Tiverton 7,653 ....K6
Knightville (res.) C3	Tuckernuck (isl.) N7	†02864 Valley Falls 10,892 .....J5
Laurence G. Hanscom Field ...B6	Vineyard (sound) L7	*02879 Wakefield-Peace
Little (riv.) C4	Wachusett (mt.) G3	Dale 6,474 ....J7
Logan Internat'l Airport D7	Wachusett (res.) G3	02885 Warren◦ 10,640 ....J6
Long (isl.) E7	Walden (pond) A6	*02886 Warwick 87,123 ....J6
Long (pt.) O4	Walden (pond) A6	02891 Westerly◦ 18,580 ....G7
Long (pond) L5	Ware (riv.) F3	02891 Westerly⊙ 14,093 ....G7
Lowell Nat'l Hist. Park J2	Watuppa (pond) K6	02893 West Warwick 27,026 ....H6
Maine (gulf) M2	Webster (lake) G4	02895 Woonsocket⊙ 45,914 ....J4
Manhan (riv.) D4	Wellfleet (harb.) O5	
Manomet (pt.) N5	West (riv.) H4	**OTHER FEATURES**
Marblehead (neck) F6	West Branch, Farmington	
Martha's Vineyard (isl.) M7	(riv.) B4	Black Rock (pt.) H8
Massachusetts (bay) M4	West Chop (pt.) M7	Block (isl.) H8
Merrimack (riv.) K1	Westfield (riv.) C3	Block Island (sound) H8
Mill (riv.) M3	Westover A.F.B. D4	Brenton (pt.) J6
Mill (riv.) D3	Weweantic (riv.) L5	Conanicut (isl.) J6
Millers (riv.) E2	Whitman (riv.) G2	Dickens (pt.) H8
Minute Man Nat'l Hist. Park ...B6	Winter I. Coast Guard Air Sta. ..E5	Durfee (hill) G5
Mishaum (pt.) L6		Grace (pt.) H8
Monomonac (lake) G2	**RHODE ISLAND**	Jerimoth (hill) G5
Monomoy (isl.) O6		Judith (pt.) J7
Monomoy (pt.) O6	**COUNTIES**	Mount Hope (bay) K6
Mount Hope (bay) K6		Narragansett (bay) J6
Muskeget (chan.) N7	Bristol 46,942 ....J6	Noyes (pt.) H7
Muskeget (isl.) N7	Kent 154,163 ....H6	Pawcatuck (riv.) G7
Mystic (lake) C6	Newport 81,383 ....K6	Prudence (isl.) J6
Mystic (riv.) C6	Providence 571,349 ....H5	Rhode Island (isl.) J6
Nahant (bay) E6	Washington 93,317 ....H7	Rhode Island (sound) J6
Nantucket (isl.) O8		Roger Williams Nat'l Mem. J5
Nantucket (sound) N6	**CITIES and TOWNS**	Sakonnet (pt.) K7
Nashawena (isl.) L7		Sakonnet (riv.) K7
Nashua (riv.) H3	*Zip* *Name/Pop.* *Key*	Sandy (pt.) H8
Naushon (isl.) L7	02804 Ashaway 1,747 ....G7	Scituate (res.) H5
Neponset (riv.) C8	02806 Barrington◦ 16,174 ......J6	Stillwater (res.) C2
Nomans Land (isl.) L7	02807 Block Island 620 ....H8	Touro Synagogue Nat'l Hist.
Nonamesset (isl.) M6	02808 Bradford 1,354 ....H7	Site J7
North (pt.) D2	02809 Bristol⊙ 20,128 ....J6	Watch Hill G7
North (riv.) L4	02863 Central Falls 16,995 .....J5	
Onota (lake) A3	02816 Coventry 27,065 ....H6	⊙County seat (Shire town).
Otis (res.) B4	02910 Cranston 71,992 ....J5	‡Population of metropolitan area.
	02818 East Greenwich⊙ 10,211 ..H6	◦Population of town or township.
	02914 East Providence 50,980 ...J5	† Zip of nearest p.o. * Multiple zips.

Massachusetts and Rhode Island

SCALE

0 5 10 15 20MI.

0 5 10 15 20KM.

State Capitals ....⍟

County Seats (Shire Towns) ....⊙

Canals ....

Major Limited Access Hwys. ____

Scale 1:970,000

ATLANTIC OCEAN

GULF OF MAINE

CAPE COD BAY

BARNSTABLE

NANTUCKET SOUND

ELIZABETH ISLANDS

Martha's Vineyard

Nantucket I.

© Copyright HAMMOND INCORPORATED, Maplewood, N.J.

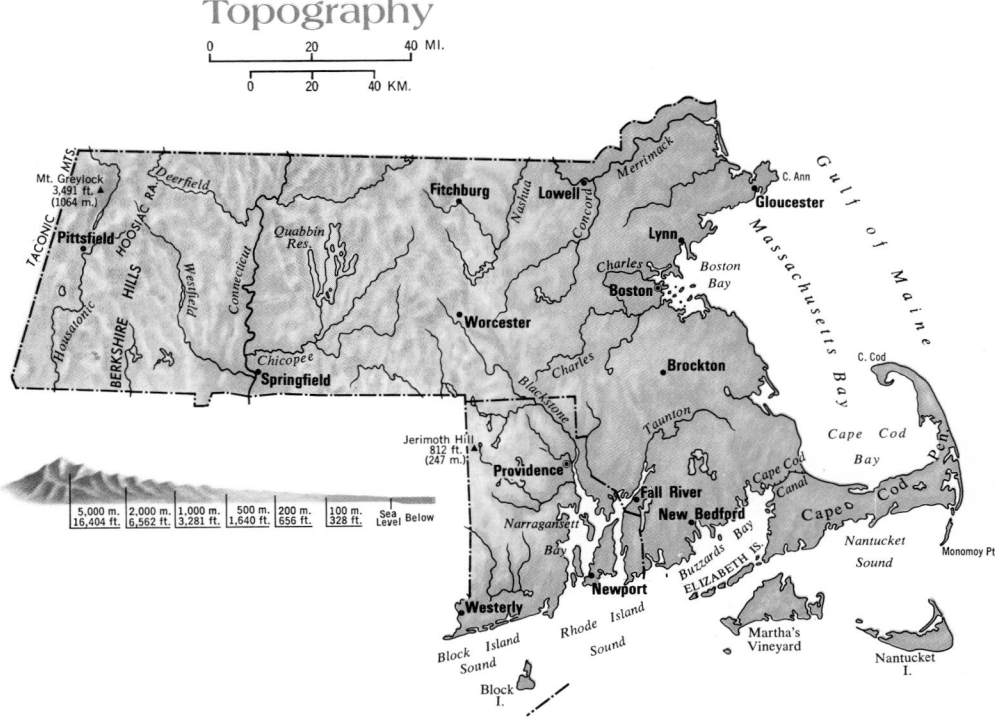

Topography

0 20 40 MI.

0 20 40 KM.

5,000 m. / 16,404 ft.   2,000 m. / 6,562 ft.   1,000 m. / 3,281 ft.   500 m. / 1,640 ft.   200 m. / 656 ft.   100 m. / 328 ft.   Sea Level   Below

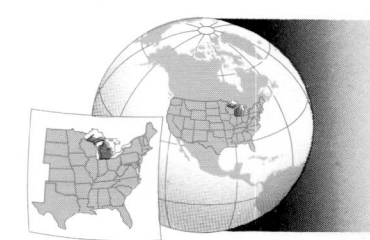

AREA 58,527 sq. mi. (151,585 sq. km.)
POPULATION 9,262,078
CAPITAL Lansing
LARGEST CITY Detroit
HIGHEST POINT Mt. Curwood 1,980 ft. (604 m.)
SETTLED IN 1650
ADMITTED TO UNION January 26, 1837
POPULAR NAME Wolverine State
STATE FLOWER Apple Blossom
STATE BIRD Robin

Topography

0   50   100 MI.

0   50   100 KM.

Below Sea Level	100 m. 328 ft.	200 m. 656 ft.	500 m. 1,640 ft.	1,000 m. 3,281 ft.	2,000 m. 6,562 ft.	5,000 m. 16,404 ft.

COUNTIES

Alcona 9,740 .... F4
Alger 9,225 .... C2
Allegan 81,555 .... D6
Alpena 32,315 .... F4
Antrim 16,194 .... D3
Arenac 14,706 .... F4
Baraga 8,484 .... A2
Barry 45,781 .... D6
Bay 119,881 .... E5
Benzie 11,205 .... C4
Berrien 171,276 .... C7
Branch 40,188 .... D7
Calhoun 141,557 .... D6
Cass 49,499 .... C7
Charlevoix 19,907 .... D3
Cheboygan 20,649 .... E3
Chippewa 29,029 .... E2
Clare 23,822 .... E5
Clinton 55,893 .... E6
Crawford 9,465 .... E4
Delta 38,947 .... C2
Dickinson 25,341 .... B2
Eaton 88,337 .... E6
Emmet 22,992 .... E3
Genesee 450,449 .... F5
Gladwin 19,957 .... E4
Gogebic 19,686 .... F2
Grand Traverse 54,899 .... D4
Gratiot 40,448 .... E5
Hillsdale 42,071 .... E7
Houghton 37,872 .... G1
Huron 36,459 .... F5
Ingham 275,520 .... E6
Ionia 51,815 .... D6
Iosco 28,349 .... F4
Iron 13,635 .... G2
Isabella 54,110 .... E5
Jackson 151,495 .... E6
Kalamazoo 212,378 .... D6
Kalkaska 10,952 .... D4
Kent 444,506 .... D5
Keweenaw 1,963 .... A1
Lake 7,711 .... D5
Lapeer 70,038 .... F5
Leelanau 14,007 .... D4
Lenawee 89,948 .... E7
Livingston 100,289 .... F6
Luce 6,659 .... D2
Mackinac 10,178 .... D2
Macomb 694,600 .... G6
Manistee 23,019 .... C4
Marquette 74,101 .... B2
Mason 26,365 .... C4
Mecosta 36,961 .... D5
Menominee 26,201 .... B3
Midland 73,578 .... E5
Missaukee 10,009 .... D4
Monroe 134,659 .... F7
Montcalm 47,555 .... D5
Montmorency 7,492 .... E3
Muskegon 157,589 .... C5
Newaygo 34,917 .... D5
Oakland 1,011,793 .... F6
Oceana 22,002 .... C5
Ogemaw 16,436 .... E4
Ontonagon 9,861 .... F1
Osceola 18,928 .... D5
Oscoda 6,858 .... E4
Otsego 14,993 .... E3
Ottawa 157,174 .... C6
Presque Isle 14,267 .... F3
Roscommon 16,374 .... E4
Saginaw 228,059 .... E5
Saint Clair 138,802 .... G6
Saint Joseph 56,083 .... D7
Sanilac 40,789 .... G5
Schoolcraft 8,575 .... C2
Shiawassee 71,140 .... E6
Tuscola 56,961 .... F5
Van Buren 66,814 .... C6
Washtenaw 264,748 .... F6
Wayne 2,337,891 .... F6
Wexford 25,102 .... D4

CITIES and TOWNS

Zip   Name/Pop.   Key

49220 Addison 655 .... E7
49221 Adrian⊙ 21,186 .... E7
48701 Akron 538 .... F5
†48763 Alabaster 46 .... F4
49224 Albion 11,059 .... E6
48001 Algonac 4,412 .... G6
49010 Allegan⊙ 4,576 .... D6
48101 Allen Park 34,196 ...... B7
48801 Alma 9,652 .... E5
48003 Almont 1,857 .... F6
49707 Alpena⊙ 12,214 .... F3
*48103 Ann Arbor⊙ 107,966 ... F6
    Ann Arbor‡ 264,748 .... F6
48005 Armada 1,392 .... G6
48806 Ashley 570 .... E5

49011 Athens 960 .... D6
49709 Atlanta⊙ 475 .... E3
48611 Auburn 1,921 .... F5
49012 Augusta 913 .... D6
†48750 Au Sable 1,240 .... F4
48413 Bad Axe⊙ 3,184 ...... G5
49304 Baldwin⊙ 674 .... D5
48414 Bancroft 618 .... E6
49013 Bangor 2,001 .... C6
49908 Baraga 1,055 .... G1
49101 Baroda 627 .... C7
*49014 Battle Creek 35,724 ... D6
    Battle Creek‡ 187,338 .. D6
48706 Bay City⊙ 41,593 .... F5
    Bay City‡ 119,881 ..... F5
48612 Beaverton 1,025 ..... E5
†49423 Beechwood 2,333 .... C6
48809 Belding 5,634 .... D5
49615 Bellaire⊙ 1,063 ...... D4
48111 Belleville 3,366 ...... F6
49021 Bellevue 1,289 .... E6
49022 Benton Harbor 14,707 . C6
    Benton Harbor‡ 171,276 . C6
†49022 Benton Heights 6,787 . C6
48072 Berkley 18,637 .... B6
49103 Berrien Springs 2,042 . C7
49911 Bessemer⊙ 2,553 .... F2
49617 Beulah⊙ 454 .... C4
†48010 Beverly Hills 11,598 .. B6
49307 Big Rapids⊙ 14,361 .. D5
48415 Birch Run 1,196 ...... F5
*48008 Birmingham 21,689 .. B6
49228 Blissfield 3,107 ...... F7
48013 Bloomfield Hills 3,985 . B6
49026 Bloomingdale 537 ... C6
49712 Boyne City 3,348 .... E3
48615 Breckenridge 1,495 .. E5
49106 Bridgman 2,235 ..... C7
48116 Brighton 4,268 ...... F6
49229 Britton 693 .... F6
49028 Bronson 2,271 .... D7
49230 Brooklyn 1,110 ...... E6
48416 Brown City 1,163 .... G5
49107 Buchanan 5,142 ..... C7
49030 Burr Oak 853 .... D7
48507 Burton 29,976 .... F5
48418 Byron 689 .... E6
49601 Cadillac⊙ 10,199 .... D4
49316 Caledonia 722 .... D6
49913 Calumet 1,013 .... A1
48014 Capac 1,377 .... G5
48117 Carleton 2,786 ...... F6
48723 Caro⊙ 4,317 .... F5
48724 Carrollton 7,482 ..... E5
48811 Carson City 1,229 ... E5
48419 Carsonville 622 ..... G5
48725 Caseville 851 .... F5
49915 Caspian 1,038 .... G2
48726 Cass City 2,258 ..... F5
49031 Cassopolis⊙ 1,933 ... C7
49319 Cedar Springs 2,615 . D6
49233 Cement City 539 .... E6
49622 Central Lake 895 .... D3
49032 Centreville⊙ 1,202 .. D7
49720 Charlevoix⊙ 3,296 .. D3
48813 Charlotte⊙ 8,251 ... E6
49721 Cheboygan⊙ 5,106 . E3
48118 Chelsea 3,816 .... F6
48616 Chesaning 2,656 .... E5
48617 Clare 3,300 .... E5
48016 Clarkston 968 .... F6
48017 Clawson 15,103 ..... B6
49034 Climax 619 .... D6
49236 Clinton 2,342 .... F6
48420 Clio 2,669 .... F5
49036 Coldwater⊙ 9,461 .. D7
48618 Coleman 1,429 ...... E5
49038 Coloma 1,833 .... C6
49040 Colon 1,190 .... D7
48421 Columbiaville 953 ... F5
49041 Comstock⊙ 11,162 . D6
49237 Concord 900 .... E6
49042 Constantine 1,680 .. D7
49404 Coopersville 2,889 .. C5
48817 Corunna⊙ 3,206 ... E6
48422 Croswell 2,073 ...... G5
49920 Crystal Falls⊙ 1,965 . A2
48423 Cutlerville 8,256 .... D6
48423 Davison 6,087 ...... F5
*48120 Dearborn 90,660 ... B7
48127 Dearborn Heights 67,706 . B7
49045 Decatur 1,915 ...... C6
48427 Deckerville 887 ..... G5
48239 Deerfield 957 .... F7
*48201 Detroit⊙ 1,203,339 . B7
    Detroit‡ 4,352,762 .... B7
†48161 Detroit Beach 2,112 . F7
48820 De Witt 3,165 ...... E6
48130 Dexter 1,524 .... F6
48821 Dimondale 1,008 ... E6
49406 Douglas 948 .... C6
49047 Dowagiac 6,307 .... D6
48020 Drayton Plains F6
49726 Drummond Island⊙ 746 . F3

48428 Dryden 650 .... F6
48131 Dundee 2,575 ...... F7
48429 Durand 4,241 ...... E6
49924 Eagle River⊙ 20 .... A1
48021 East Detroit 38,280 . B6
†49506 East Grand Rapids 10,914 . D6
49727 East Jordan 2,185 .. D3
†49801 East Kingsford A3
48823 East Lansing 51,392 . E6
48730 East Tawas 2,584 .. F4
49034 East Tawas 2,584 .. F4
48827 Eaton Rapids 4,510 . E6
49111 Eau Claire 573 ..... C6
48229 Ecorse 14,447 ...... B7
48829 Edmore 1,176 ...... E5
49112 Edwardsburg 1,135 . C7
49628 Elberta 556 .... C4
49629 Elk Rapids 1,504 ... D4
48731 Elkton 953 .... F5
48831 Elsie 1,022 .... E5
49829 Escanaba⊙ 14,355 . C3
48732 Essexville 4,378 .... F5
49631 Evart 1,945 .... D5
48733 Fairgrove 691 ...... F5
49022 Fair Plain 8,289 .... C6
*48024 Farmington 11,022 . F6
48024 Farmington Hills 58,056 . F6
48622 Farwell 804 .... E5
49408 Fennville 934 ...... C6
48430 Fenton 8,098 .... F6
48220 Ferndale 26,227 .... B6
49409 Ferrysburg 2,440 .. C5
48134 Flat Rock 6,853 .... F6
*48501 Flint⊙ 159,611 ..... F5
    Flint‡ 521,589 .... F5
48433 Flushing 8,624 ..... F5
48835 Fowler 1,021 .... E5
48836 Fowlerville 2,289 ... F6

48734 Frankenmuth 3,753 ... F5
49635 Frankfort 1,603 ..... C4
48025 Franklin 2,864 ...... B6
48026 Fraser 14,560 ...... B6
48623 Freeland 1,364 ..... E5
49412 Fremont 3,672 ..... D5
49415 Fruitport 1,143 ..... C5
49053 Galesburg 1,822 ... D6
49113 Galien 692 .... C7
48135 Garden City 35,640 . F6
49735 Gaylord⊙ 3,011 ... E3
48173 Gibraltar 4,458 .... F6
49837 Gladstone 4,533 ... C3
48624 Gladwin⊙ 2,479 .. E5
49055 Gobles 816 .... C6
48438 Goodrich 795 ...... F6
48439 Grand Blanc 6,848 . F6
49417 Grand Haven⊙ 11,763 . C5
48837 Grand Ledge 6,920 . E6
*49501 Grand Rapids⊙ ... D5
    Grand Rapids‡ 601,680 . D5
49418 Grandville 12,412 .. D6
49327 Grant 683 .... D5
49240 Grass Lake 962 .... E6
49738 Grayling⊙ 1,792 .. E4
48838 Greenville 8,019 ... D5
48138 Grosse Ile 9,320 ... B7
48236 Grosse Pointe 5,901 . B7
†48236 Grosse Pointe
    Farms 10,551 ...... B6
†48236 Grosse Pointe Park 13,639 B7
†48236 Grosse Pointe
    Shores 3,122 ...... B6
†48236 Grosse Pointe
    Woods 18,886 ..... B6
49841 Gwinn 1,408 ...... B2
48212 Hamtramck 21,300 . B6
49930 Hancock 5,122 .... G1

48441 Harbor Beach 2,000 ... G5
49740 Harbor Springs 1,567 .. D3
48225 Harper Woods 16,361 . B6
48625 Harrison⊙ 1,700 .. E4
48740 Harrisville⊙ 559 ... F4
49420 Hart⊙ 1,888 ...... C5
49057 Hartford 2,493 .... C6
48840 Haslett 7,025 ...... E6
49058 Hastings⊙ 6,418 .. D6
48626 Hemlock 1,362 .... E5
49421 Hesperia 876 ...... D5
49242 Hillsdale⊙ 7,432 .. E7
49423 Holland 26,281 .... C6
48842 Holt 10,097 .... E6
49245 Homer 1,791 ...... E6
49931 Houghton⊙ 7,512 . G1
48629 Houghton Lake 2,449 . E4
48630 Houghton Lake Heights . E4
49329 Howard City 1,118 . D5
48843 Howell⊙ 6,976 ... F6
49247 Hudson 2,545 ..... E7
49426 Hudsonville 4,844 . D6
48444 Imlay City 2,495 ... F5
48141 Inkster 35,190 ..... B7
49643 Interlochen 900 ... D4
48846 Ionia⊙ 5,920 ...... D6
49801 Iron Mountain⊙ 8,341 . B3
49935 Iron River 2,426 ... G2
49938 Ironwood 7,741 ... F2
49849 Ishpeming 7,538 .. B2
48847 Ithaca⊙ 2,950 .... E5
*49201 Jackson⊙ 39,739 . E6
    Jackson‡ 151,495 ... E6
49428 Jenison 16,330 .... D6
49250 Jonesville 2,172 ... E6

*49001 Kalamazoo⊙ 79,722 ... D6
    Kalamazoo-Portage‡
    279,192 .... D6
49646 Kalkaska⊙ 1,654 .. D4
49030 Keego Harbor 3,083 . F6
49330 Kent City 860 ..... D5
49508 Kentwood 30,438 . D6
48445 Kinde 600 .... G5
49801 Kingsford 5,290 ... A3
49649 Kingsley 664 ...... D4
48848 Laingsburg 1,145 .. E6
49651 Lake City⊙ 843 ... D4
49945 Lake Linden 1,181 . A1
†49039 Lake Michigan Beach 2,001 C6
48849 Lake Odessa 2,171 . D6
48035 Lake Orion 2,907 .. F6
48850 Lakeview 1,139 .... D5
†49440 Lakewood Club 695 . C5
48144 Lambertville 6,341 . F7
49946 L'Anse⊙ 2,500 .... G1
*48901 Lansing (cap.) 130,414 . E6
    Lansing-East
    Lansing‡ 468,482 ... E6
48446 Lapeer⊙ 6,198 .... F5
49913 Laurium 2,678 .... A1
49064 Lawrence 903 ..... C6
49065 Lawton 1,558 ..... D6
49654 Leland⊙ 776 ...... D3
48449 Lennon 600 .... E6
49251 Leslie 2,110 .... E6
48450 Lexington 765 ..... G5
48742 Lincoln 361 .... F4
48146 Lincoln Park 45,105 . B7
48451 Linden 2,174 ...... F6
49252 Litchfield 1,353 ... E6
*48150 Livonia 104,814 ... F6
49331 Lowell 3,707 ...... D6
49431 Ludington⊙ 8,937 . C5

(continued on following page)

48157 Luna Pier 1,443 F7
48851 Lyons 708 E6
49757 Mackinac Island 479 E3
49701 Mackinaw City 820 E3
48071 Madison Heights 35,375 B6
49659 Mancelona 1,432 E4
48158 Manchester 1,686 E6
49660 Manistee⊙ 7,566 C4
49854 Manistique⊙ 3,962 C3
49663 Manton 1,212 D4
48853 Maple Rapids 683 E5
49067 Marcellus 1,134 D6
48039 Marine City 4,414 G6
49665 Marion 816 D4
48453 Marlette 1,761 G5
49855 Marquette⊙ 23,288 B2
49068 Marshall⊙ 7,201 E6
49070 Martin 447 D6
48040 Marysville 7,345 G6
48854 Mason⊙ 6,019 E6
49071 Mattawan 2,143 D6
48744 Mayville 958 F5
49657 McBain 519 D4
48122 Melvindale 12,322 B7
48041 Memphis 1,171 G6
49072 Mendon 951 D7
49858 Menominee⊙ 10,099 B3
48637 Merrill 851 E5
48455 Metamora 552 F6
49254 Michigan Center 5,244 E6
49333 Middleville 1,797 D6
48640 Midland⊙ 37,250 E5
48160 Milan 4,182 F6
48042 Milford 5,041 F6
48746 Millington 1,237 F5
48647 Mio⊙ 975 E4
48161 Monroe⊙ 23,531 F7
49437 Montague 2,332 C5
48457 Montrose 1,706 F5
49256 Morenci 2,110 E7
49336 Morley 507 D5
48857 Morrice 733 E6
48043 Mount Clemens⊙ 18,806 G6
48458 Mount Morris 3,246 F5
48858 Mount Pleasant⊙ 23,746 E5
48860 Muir 698 D5
48861 Mulliken 550 E6
49862 Munising⊙ 3,083 C2
*49440 Muskegon⊙ 40,823 C5
Muskegon-Norton Shores-Muskegon Heights‡ 179,591 C5
49444 Muskegon Heights 14,611 C5
49261 Napoleon 1,400 E6
49073 Nashville 1,628 D6
49866 Negaunee 5,189 B2
49337 Newaygo 1,271 D5
48047 New Baltimore 5,439 G6
49868 Newberry⊙ 2,120 D2
48164 New Boston 1,200 F6
49117 New Buffalo 2,821 C7
48048 New Haven 1,871 G6
48460 New Lothrop 646 F5
49120 Niles 13,115 C7
49262 North Adams 565 E7
48461 North Branch 896 F5
49445 North Muskegon 4,024 C5
49670 Northport 611 D3
48167 Northville 5,698 F6
†49441 Norton Shores 22,025 C5
49870 Norway 2,919 B3
48050 Novi 22,525 F6
48237 Oak Park 31,537 B6
48864 Okemos 8,882 E6
49076 Olivet 1,604 E6
49765 Onaway 1,084 E3
49675 Onekama 582 C4
49265 Onsted 670 E6
49953 Ontonagon⊙ 2,182 F1
48033 Orchard Lake 1,798 F6
48462 Ortonville 1,190 F6
48750 Oscoda 2,431 F4
48463 Otisville 682 F5
49078 Otsego 3,802 D6
48866 Ovid 1,712 E5
48867 Owosso 16,455 E5
48051 Oxford 2,746 F6
49004 Parchment 1,817 D6
49269 Parma 873 E6
49079 Paw Paw⊙ 3,211 D6
†49038 Paw Paw Lake 4,193 C6
48052 Pearl Beach 3,430 G6
48466 Peck 606 G5
49769 Pellston 565 E3
49449 Pentwater 1,165 C5
48872 Perry 2,051 E6
49270 Petersburg 1,222 F7
49770 Petoskey⊙ 6,097 E3
48755 Pigeon 1,247 F5
48169 Pinckney 1,390 F6
48650 Pinconning 1,430 F5
49080 Plainwell 3,751 D6
48069 Pleasant Ridge 3,217 B6
*48170 Plymouth 9,986 F6
*48053 Pontiac⊙ 76,715 F6
49081 Portage 38,157 D6
48467 Port Austin 839 F4
48060 Port Huron⊙ 33,981 G6
48875 Portland 3,963 E6
48469 Port Sanilac 598 G5
49776 Posen 270 F3
48876 Potterville 1,502 E6
49082 Quincy 1,569 E7
49959 Ramsay F2
49451 Ravenna 951 D5
49274 Reading 1,203 E7
49677 Reed City⊙ 2,221 D5
48757 Reese 1,645 F5
48062 Richmond 3,536 G6
48218 River Rouge 12,912 B7
48192 Riverview 14,569 B7
48063 Rochester 7,203 F6
49341 Rockford 3,324 D5
48173 Rockwood 3,346 F6
49779 Rogers City⊙ 3,923 F3
48065 Romeo 3,509 F6
48174 Romulus 24,857 F6
49444 Roosevelt Park 4,015 C5
48653 Roscommon⊙ 834 E4
48654 Rose City 661 E4
48066 Roseville 54,311 B6
49452 Rothbury 522 C5
*48067 Royal Oak 70,893 B6
*48601 Saginaw⊙ 77,508 F5
Saginaw‡ 228,059 F5
48655 Saint Charles 2,276 E5
48079 Saint Clair 4,780 G6
*48080 Saint Clair Shores 76,210 B6
49781 Saint Ignace⊙ 2,632 E3
48879 Saint Johns⊙ 7,376 E6
49085 Saint Joseph⊙ 9,622 C6
48880 Saint Louis 4,107 E5
48176 Saline 6,483 F6
48471 Sandusky⊙ 2,216 G5
48657 Sanford 864 E5
48881 Saranac 1,421 D6
49453 Saugatuck 1,079 C6
49783 Sault Sainte Marie⊙ 14,448 E2
49087 Schoolcraft 1,359 D6
49454 Scottville 1,241 C5
48759 Sebewaing 2,046 F5
49455 Shelby 1,624 C5
48883 Shepherd 1,534 E5
48884 Sheridan 664 D5
†49085 Shoreham 742 C6
†49125 Shorewood 1,735 C7
*48034 Southfield 75,568 F6
48195 Southgate 32,058 F6
49090 South Haven 5,943 C6
48178 South Lyon 5,214 F6
†48161 South Monroe 4,232 F7
49963 South Range 861 G1
48179 South Rockwood 1,353 F7
†48060 Sparlingville 1,718 G6
49345 Sparta 3,373 D5
49283 Spring Arbor 2,101 E6
49015 Springfield 5,917 D6
49456 Spring Lake 2,731 C5
49284 Springport 675 E6
49964 Stambaugh 1,442 G2
48658 Standish⊙ 1,264 F5
48888 Stanton⊙ 1,315 D5
49887 Stephenson 967 B3
48659 Sterling 457 E4
48077 Sterling Heights 108,999 B6
49127 Stevensville 1,268 C6
49285 Stockbridge 1,213 E6
49091 Sturgis 9,468 D7
48890 Sunfield 591 D6
49682 Suttons Bay 504 D3
48473 Swartz Creek 5,013 F6
†48053 Sylvan Lake 1,949 F6
48763 Tawas City⊙ 1,967 F4
48180 Taylor 77,568 B7
49286 Tecumseh 7,320 E7
49092 Tekonsha 755 E6
49128 Three Oaks 1,774 C7
49093 Three Rivers 7,015 D7
49684 Traverse City⊙ 15,516 D4
48183 Trenton 22,762 B7
*48084 Troy 67,102 B6
48475 Ubly 862 G5
49094 Union City 1,667 D6
49129 Union Pier 1,039 C7
48767 Unionville 578 F5
*48087 Utica 5,282 F6
49095 Vandalia 447 D7
49795 Vanderbilt 525 E3
48768 Vassar 2,727 F5
49096 Vermontville 832 E6
48476 Vernon 1,008 F6
49097 Vicksburg 2,224 D6
49968 Wakefield 2,591 F2
49288 Waldron 570 E7
49504 Walker 15,088 D6
48088 Walled Lake 4,748 F6
*48089 Warren 161,134 B6
49098 Watervliet 1,867 C6
49348 Wayland 2,023 D6
48184 Wayne 21,159 F6
48892 Webberville 1,535 E6
49894 Wells B3
48661 West Branch⊙ 1,785 E4
48185 Westland 84,603 F6
48894 Westphalia 896 E6
49349 White Cloud⊙ 1,101 D5
49461 Whitehall 2,856 C5
49099 White Pigeon 1,478 D7
49971 White Pine 1,142 F1
48189 Whitmore Lake 2,920 F6
48770 Whittemore 438 F4
48895 Williamston 2,981 E6
48096 Wixom 6,705 F6
†49440 Wolf Lake 3,876 D5
49799 Wolverine 364 E3
†48183 Woodhaven 10,902 F6
48897 Woodland 431 D6
48192 Wyandotte 34,006 B7
49509 Wyoming 59,616 D6
48097 Yale 1,814 G5
48197 Ypsilanti 24,031 F6
49464 Zeeland 4,764 D6
†48601 Zilwaukee 2,201 F5

OTHER FEATURES

Abbaye (pt.) B2
Au Sable (pt.) C2
Au Sable (pt.) F4
Au Sable (riv.) E4
Au Train (bay) C2
Bad (riv.) E5
Barques (pt.) C3
Beaver (isl.) D3
Beaver (lake) F4
Belle (riv.) G6
Bete Grise (bay) B1
Betsy (riv.) D2
Big Bay (pt.) B2
Big Bay de Noc (bay) C3
Big Iron (riv.) F1
Big Sable (pt.) C4
Big Sable (riv.) C4
Big Star (lake) C5
Black (lake) E3
Black (riv.) E3
Black (riv.) G5
Blake (pt.) E1
Boardman (riv.) D4
Bois Blanc (isl.) E3
Bond Falls (res.) G2
Brevoort (lake) D3
Brule (riv.) A3
Burt (lake) E3
Cass (riv.) F5
Cedar (lake) F4
Charlevoix (lake) D3
Chippewa (riv.) E5
Crisp (pt.) D2
Crystal (lake) C4
Curwood (mt.) A2
Dead (riv.) B2
Deer (riv.) A2
De Tour (passage) E3
Detour (pt.) C3
Detroit (riv.) B7
Drummond (isl.) F2
Duck (lake) F4
Elk (lake) D4
Erie (lake) G7
Escanaba (riv.) B2
False Detour (chan.) F3
Fawn (riv.) D7
Fence (riv.) A2
Firesteel (riv.) G1
Fletcher (pond) F4
Flint (riv.) F5
Ford (riv.) B2
Forty Mile (pt.) F3
Fourteen Mile (pt.) F1
Garden (isl.) D3
Garden (pen.) C3
Glen (lake) C4
Gogebic (lake) F2
Good Harbor (bay) D3
Government (peak) F1
Grand (isl.) C2
Grand (lake) F3
Grand (riv.) D6
Grand Traverse (bay) D3
Granite (pt.) B2
Green (bay) B4
Gun (lake) D6
Hamlin (lake) C4
Higgins (lake) E4
High (isl.) D3
Hog (isl.) D3
Houghton (lake) E4
Hubbard (lake) F4
Huron (bay) A2
Huron (lake) G4
Huron (riv.) F6
Huron River (pt.) B2
Independence (lake) B2
Indian (lake) C2
Isle Royale Nat'l Park E1
Kalamazoo (riv.) C6
Keweenaw (bay) A1
Keweenaw (pt.) B1
K.I. Sawyer A.F.B. 7,345 B2
L'Anse Ind. Res. A2
Laughing Fish (pt.) B2
Leelanau (lake) D4
Light House (pt.) D3
Little Bay de Noc (bay) B3
Little Girl (pt.) E1
Little Sable (pt.) C5
Little Summer (isl.) C3
Little Traverse (bay) D3
Long (lake) F3
Lookingglass (riv.) E6
Mackinac (isl.) E3
Mackinac (str.) E3
Manistee (riv.) C4
Manistique (lake) D2
Manistique (riv.) C2
Manitou (isl.) B1
Maple (riv.) E5
Margrethe (lake) E4
Marquette (isl.) E3
Maumee (bay) F7
Menominee (riv.) B3
Michigamme (lake) A2
Michigamme (res.) B2
Michigamme (riv.) A2
Michigan (lake) B5
Mill (creek) G5
Millecoquins (lake) D2
Misery (bay) G1
Misery (riv.) G1
Montreal (riv.) F1
Mullett (lake) E3
Munuscong (lake) E2
Muskegon (riv.) C5
Neebish (isl.) E2
Net (riv.) G2
Ninemile (pt.) E3
North (chan.) F2
North (pt.) F3
North Fox (isl.) D3
North Manitou (isl.) C3
Oak (pt.) F5
Ontonagon (riv.) G1
Ontonagon Ind. Res. F1
Otsego (lake) E4
Paint (riv.) A2
Paradise (lake) E3
Passage (isl.) E1
Patterson (pt.) D3
Paw Paw (riv.) C6
Peninsula (pt.) C3
Perch (lake) G2
Perch (riv.) G2
Pere Marquette (riv.) D5
Pictured Rocks (cliff) C2
Pictured Rocks Nat'l Lakeshore C2
Pigeon (riv.) D7
Pigeon (riv.) E3
Pine (lake) F4
Pine (riv.) D4
Pine (riv.) E5
Platte (lake) C4
Porcupine (mts.) F1
Potagannissing (bay) F2
Poverty (isl.) C3
Prairie (riv.) D7
Presque Isle (riv.) F1
Rabbit (riv.) D6
Raisin (riv.) F7
Rapid (riv.) B2
Reedsburg (res.) E4
Rifle (riv.) E4
Royale (isl.) E1
Saginaw (bay) F5
Saginaw (riv.) F5
Saint Clair (lake) G6
Saint Clair (riv.) G6
Saint Joseph (riv.) C7
Saint Martin (bay) E3
Saint Martin (isl.) C3
Saint Marys (riv.) E2
Salt (pt.) E2
Sand (pt.) F5
Seul Choix (pt.) D3
Shiawassee (riv.) E5
Siskiwit (bay) E1
Sleeping Bear Dunes Nat'l Lakeshore C4
South (bay) C2
South (chan.) E3
South (pt.) F4
South Fox (isl.) D3
South Manitou (isl.) C3
Sturgeon (riv.) C2
Sugar (isl.) E2
Summer (isl.) C3
Superior (lake) C2
Tahquamenon (falls) D2
Tahquamenon (riv.) D2
Tawas (lake) F4
Tawas (pt.) F4
Thunder (bay) F4
Thunder Bay (riv.) F3
Tittabawassee (riv.) E5
Torch (lake) D3
Traverse (isl.) A1
Traverse (pt.) A1
Turtle (lake) F4
Two Hearted (riv.) D2
Vieux Desert (lake) G2
Walloon (lake) E3
White (riv.) C5
Whitefish (bay) E2
Whitefish (pt.) E2
Whitefish (riv.) C2
Wood (isl.) C2
Wurtsmith A.F.B. 5,166 F4
Yellow Dog (riv.) B2

⊙County seat.
‡Population of metropolitan area.
○Population of township.
† Zip of nearest p.o. * Multiple zips.

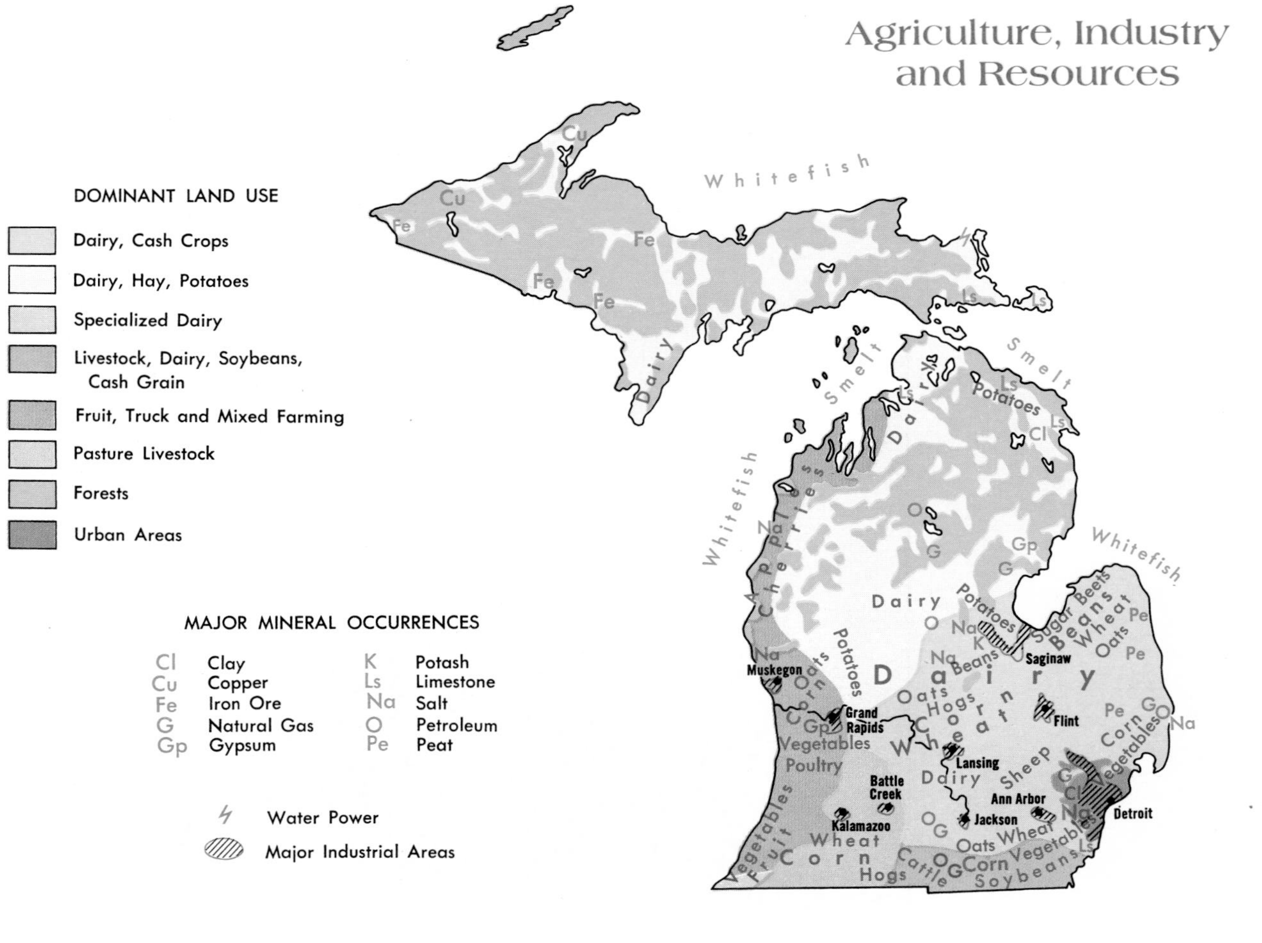
Agriculture, Industry and Resources
DOMINANT LAND USE
Dairy, Cash Crops
Dairy, Hay, Potatoes
Specialized Dairy
Livestock, Dairy, Soybeans, Cash Grain
Fruit, Truck and Mixed Farming
Pasture Livestock
Forests
Urban Areas
MAJOR MINERAL OCCURRENCES
Cl Clay
Cu Copper
Fe Iron Ore
G Natural Gas
Gp Gypsum
K Potash
Ls Limestone
Na Salt
O Petroleum
Pe Peat
Water Power
Major Industrial Areas
Whitefish
Smelt
Dairy
Potatoes
Cherries
Oats
Beans
Sugar Beets
Wheat
Corn
Hogs
Sheep
Vegetables
Poultry
Fruit
Cattle
Soybeans
Muskegon
Saginaw
Grand Rapids
Flint
Lansing
Battle Creek
Ann Arbor
Jackson
Kalamazoo
Detroit

AREA 84,402 sq. mi. (218,601 sq. km.)
POPULATION 4,075,970
CAPITAL St. Paul
LARGEST CITY Minneapolis
HIGHEST POINT Eagle Mtn. 2,301 ft. (701 m.)
SETTLED IN 1805
ADMITTED TO UNION May 11, 1858
POPULAR NAME North Star State; Gopher State
STATE FLOWER Pink & White Lady's-Slipper
STATE BIRD Common Loon

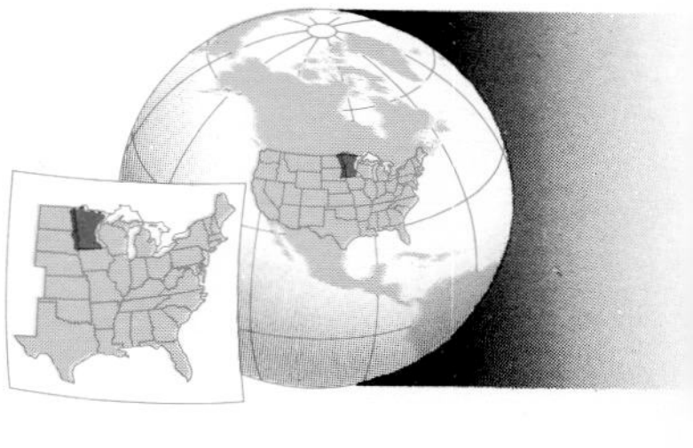

COUNTIES

Aitkin 13,404 ..... E4
Anoka 195,998 ..... E5
Becker 29,336 ..... C4
Beltrami 30,982 ..... C2
Benton 25,187 ..... D5
Big Stone 7,716 ..... B5
Blue Earth 52,314 ..... D6
Brown 28,645 ..... D6
Carlton 29,936 ..... F4
Carver 37,046 ..... E6
Cass 21,050 ..... D4
Chippewa 14,941 ..... C5
Chisago 25,717 ..... F5
Clay 49,327 ..... B4
Clearwater 8,761 ..... C3
Cook 4,092 ..... H3
Cottonwood 14,854 ..... C6
Crow Wing 41,722 ..... D4
Dakota 194,279 ..... E6
Dodge 14,773 ..... F7
Douglas 27,839 ..... C5
Faribault 19,714 ..... D7
Fillmore 21,930 ..... F7
Freeborn 36,329 ..... E7
Goodhue 38,749 ..... F6
Grant 7,171 ..... B5
Hennepin 941,411 ..... E5
Houston 18,382 ..... G7
Hubbard 14,098 ..... D3
Isanti 23,600 ..... E5
Itasca 43,069 ..... E3
Jackson 13,690 ..... C7
Kanabec 12,161 ..... E5
Kandiyohi 36,763 ..... C5
Kittson 6,672 ..... B2
Koochiching 17,571 ..... E2
Lac qui Parle 10,592 ..... B6
Lake 13,043 ..... G3
Lake of the Woods 3,764 ..... D2
Le Sueur 23,434 ..... E6
Lincoln 8,207 ..... B6
Lyon 25,207 ..... C6
Mahnomen 5,535 ..... C3
Marshall 13,027 ..... B2
Martin 24,687 ..... D7
McLeod 29,657 ..... D6
Meeker 20,594 ..... D5
Mille Lacs 18,430 ..... E5
Morrison 29,311 ..... D4
Mower 40,390 ..... F7
Murray 11,507 ..... C6
Nicollet 26,929 ..... D6
Nobles 21,840 ..... C7
Norman 9,379 ..... B3
Olmsted 92,006 ..... F7
Otter Tail 51,937 ..... C4
Pennington 15,258 ..... B2
Pine 19,871 ..... F4
Pipestone 11,690 ..... B6
Polk 34,844 ..... B3
Pope 11,657 ..... C5
Ramsey 459,784 ..... E5
Red Lake 5,471 ..... B3
Redwood 19,341 ..... C6
Renville 20,401 ..... C6
Rice 46,087 ..... E6
Rock 10,703 ..... B7
Roseau 12,574 ..... C2
Saint Louis 222,229 ..... F3
Scott 43,784 ..... E6
Sherburne 29,908 ..... E5
Sibley 15,448 ..... D6
Stearns 108,161 ..... D5
Steele 30,328 ..... E7
Stevens 11,322 ..... B5
Swift 12,920 ..... C5
Todd 24,991 ..... D4
Traverse 5,542 ..... B5
Wabasha 19,335 ..... F6
Wadena 14,192 ..... D4
Waseca 18,448 ..... E6
Washington 113,571 ..... F5
Watonwan 12,361 ..... D7
Wilkin 8,454 ..... B4
Winona 46,256 ..... G6
Wright 58,681 ..... D5
Yellow Medicine 13,653 ..... B6

CITIES and TOWNS

Zip *Name/Pop.* *Key*

56510 Ada⊙ 1,971 ..... B3
55909 Adams 797 ..... F7
56110 Adrian 1,336 ..... C7
55001 Afton 2,550 ..... F6
56430 Ah-Gwah-Ching 400 ..... D3
56431 Aitkin⊙ 1,770 ..... E4
56433 Akeley 486 ..... D3
56307 Albany 1,569 ..... D5
56207 Alberta 145 ..... B5
56007 Albert Lea⊙ 19,200 ..... E7
55301 Albertville 564 ..... E5
56009 Alden 687 ..... E7
56308 Alexandria⊙ 7,608 ..... C5
56111 Alpha 180 ..... D7
55910 Altura 354 ..... G6
56710 Alvarado 385 ..... B2
56010 Amboy 606 ..... D7
†55303 Andover 9,387 ..... E5
55302 Annandale 1,568 ..... D5
55303 Anoka⊙ 15,634 ..... E5
56208 Appleton 1,842 ..... C5
†55124 Apple Valley 21,818 ..... G6
56713 Argyle 741 ..... B2
55307 Arlington 1,779 ..... D6
56309 Ashby 486 ..... C4
55704 Askov 350 ..... F4
56209 Atwater 1,128 ..... D5
56511 Audubon 383 ..... C4
55705 Aurora 2,670 ..... F3
55912 Austin⊙ 23,020 ..... E7
56114 Avoca 201 ..... C7
56310 Avon 804 ..... D5
55706 Babbitt 2,435 ..... G3
56435 Backus 255 ..... D4
56714 Badger 320 ..... B2
56621 Bagley⊙ 1,321 ..... C3
56115 Balaton 752 ..... C6
56514 Barnesville 2,207 ..... B4
55707 Barnum 464 ..... F4
56311 Barrett 388 ..... B5
56515 Battle Lake 708 ..... C4
56623 Baudette⊙ 1,170 ..... D2
†56401 Baxter 2,625 ..... D4
55003 Bayport 2,932 ..... F5
56211 Beardsley 344 ..... B5
55601 Beaver Bay 283 ..... G3
56116 Beaver Creek 260 ..... B7
55308 Becker 601 ..... E5
56312 Belgrade 805 ..... C5
†55027 Bellechester 220 ..... F6
56011 Belle Plaine 2,754 ..... E6
56212 Bellingham 290 ..... B5
56214 Belview 438 ..... C6
56601 Bemidji⊙ 10,949 ..... D3
56626 Bena 153 ..... D3
56215 Benson⊙ 3,656 ..... C5
56437 Bertha 510 ..... C4
55005 Bethel 272 ..... E5
56117 Bigelow 249 ..... C7
56627 Big Falls 490 ..... E2
56628 Bigfork 457 ..... E3
55309 Big Lake 2,210 ..... E5
56118 Bingham Lake 222 ..... C7
55310 Bird Island 1,372 ..... D6
55708 Biwabik 1,428 ..... F3
56630 Blackduck 653 ..... D3
†55433 Blaine 28,558 ..... G5
56216 Blomkest 200 ..... D6
55917 Blooming Prairie 1,969 ..... E7
55420 Bloomington 81,831 ..... G6
56013 Blue Earth⊙ 4,132 ..... D7
56518 Bluffton 206 ..... C4
56519 Borup 160 ..... B3
55709 Bovey 813 ..... E3
56314 Bowlus 276 ..... D5
56218 Boyd 329 ..... C6
55006 Braham 1,015 ..... E5
56401 Brainerd⊙ 11,489 ..... D4
†55056 Branch 1,866 ..... F5
56315 Brandon 473 ..... C5
56520 Breckenridge⊙ 3,909 ..... B4
†56472 Breezy Point 384 ..... D4
56119 Brewster 559 ..... C7
56014 Bricelyn 487 ..... E7
55429 Brooklyn Center 31,230 ..... G5
†55444 Brooklyn Park 43,332 ..... G5
56715 Brooks 173 ..... B3
56316 Brooten 647 ..... C5
56438 Browerville 693 ..... D4
55918 Brownsdale 691 ..... F7
56219 Browns Valley 887 ..... B5
55919 Brownsville 418 ..... G7
55312 Brownton 697 ..... D6
56317 Buckman 171 ..... D5
55313 Buffalo⊙ 4,560 ..... E5
55314 Buffalo Lake 782 ..... D6
55713 Buhl 1,284 ..... F3
55337 Burnsville 35,674 ..... E6
56318 Burtrum 177 ..... D5
56120 Butterfield 634 ..... D7
55920 Byron 1,715 ..... F6
55921 Caledonia⊙ 2,691 ..... G7
56521 Callaway 238 ..... C3
55716 Calumet 469 ..... E3
55008 Cambridge⊙ 3,287 ..... E5
56522 Campbell 286 ..... B4
56220 Canby 2,143 ..... B6
55009 Cannon Falls 2,653 ..... F6
55922 Canton 386 ..... F7
56319 Carlos 364 ..... C5
55718 Carlton⊙ 862 ..... F4
55315 Carver 642 ..... E6
56633 Cass Lake 1,001 ..... D3
55012 Center City⊙ 458 ..... F5
†55038 Centerville 734 ..... E5
56121 Ceylon 543 ..... D7
55316 Champlin 9,006 ..... G5
56122 Chandler 344 ..... C7
55317 Chanhassen 6,359 ..... F6
55318 Chaska⊙ 8,346 ..... F6
55923 Chatfield 2,055 ..... F7
55013 Chisago City 1,634 ..... E5
55719 Chisholm 5,930 ..... E3
56221 Chokio 559 ..... B5
55014 Circle Pines 3,321 ..... G5
56222 Clara City 1,574 ..... C6
55924 Claremont 591 ..... E6
56440 Clarissa 663 ..... C4
56223 Clarkfield 1,171 ..... C6
56016 Clarks Grove 620 ..... E7
56634 Clearbrook 579 ..... C3
55319 Clear Lake 266 ..... E5
55320 Clearwater 379 ..... D5
56224 Clements 227 ..... D6
56017 Cleveland 699 ..... E6
56523 Climax 273 ..... B3
56225 Clinton 622 ..... B5
56226 Clontarf 196 ..... C5
55720 Cloquet 11,142 ..... F4
†55068 Coates 207 ..... E6
55321 Cokato 2,056 ..... D5
56320 Cold Spring 2,294 ..... D5
55722 Coleraine 1,116 ..... E3
55322 Cologne 545 ..... E6
55421 Columbia Heights 20,029 ..... G5
56019 Comfrey 548 ..... D6
56020 Conger 183 ..... E7
55723 Cook 800 ..... F3
55433 Coon Rapids 35,826 ..... G5
†55340 Corcoran 4,252 ..... F5
56228 Cosmos 571 ..... D6
55016 Cottage Grove 18,994 ..... F6
56229 Cottonwood 924 ..... C6
56021 Courtland 399 ..... D6
55726 Cromwell 229 ..... F4
56716 Crookston⊙ 8,628 ..... B3
56441 Crosby 2,218 ..... D4
56442 Crosslake 1,064 ..... E4
†55428 Crystal 25,543 ..... G5
55323 Crystal Bay (Orono) 6,845 ..... F5
56123 Currie 359 ..... C6
56323 Cyrus 334 ..... C5
55925 Dakota 350 ..... G7
56324 Dalton 248 ..... C4
56230 Danube 590 ..... C6
56231 Danvers 152 ..... C5
56022 Darfur 139 ..... D6
55324 Darwin 282 ..... D5
55325 Dassel 1,066 ..... D5
56232 Dawson 1,901 ..... B6
55327 Dayton 4,070 ..... E5
55391 Deephaven 3,716 ..... G5
56527 Deer Creek 392 ..... C4
56636 Deer River 907 ..... E3
56444 Deerwood 580 ..... E4
56233 De Graff 179 ..... C5
55328 Delano 2,480 ..... E5
56023 Delavan 262 ..... D7
†55110 Dellwood 751 ..... F5
56528 Dent 167 ..... C4
56501 Detroit Lakes⊙ 7,106 ..... C4
55926 Dexter 279 ..... F7
56529 Dilworth 2,585 ..... B4
55927 Dodge Center 1,816 ..... F6
56235 Donnelly 317 ..... B5
55929 Dover 312 ..... F7
*55801 Duluth⊙ 92,811 ..... F4
Duluth-Superior‡ 266,650 ..... F4
56236 Dumont 173 ..... B5
55019 Dundas 422 ..... E6
56127 Dunnell 216 ..... D7
55111 Eagan 20,700 ..... G6
56446 Eagle Bend 593 ..... D4
56024 Eagle Lake 1,470 ..... E6
†55005 East Bethel 6,626 ..... E5
56721 East Grand Forks 8,537 ..... B3
†56401 East Gull Lake 586 ..... D4
56025 Easton 283 ..... E7
56237 Echo 334 ..... C6
55344 Eden Prairie 16,263 ..... G6
55329 Eden Valley 763 ..... D5
56128 Edgerton 1,123 ..... B7
55424 Edina 46,073 ..... G5
55931 Eitzen 226 ..... G7
†55910 Elba 198 ..... F6
56531 Elbow Lake⊙ 1,358 ..... B5
55932 Elgin 667 ..... F6
56533 Elizabeth 195 ..... B4
55020 Elko 274 ..... E6
55330 Elk River⊙ 6,785 ..... E5
56026 Ellendale 555 ..... E7
56129 Ellsworth 629 ..... C7
56027 Elmore 882 ..... D7
56325 Elrosa 214 ..... C5
55731 Ely 4,820 ..... G3
56028 Elysian 454 ..... E6
56447 Emily 588 ..... E4
56029 Emmons 465 ..... E7
56534 Erhard 194 ..... B4
56535 Erskine 585 ..... B3
56326 Evansville 571 ..... C4
55734 Eveleth 5,042 ..... F3
55331 Excelsior 2,523 ..... E6
55934 Eyota 1,244 ..... F7
55332 Fairfax 1,405 ..... D6
56031 Fairmont⊙ 11,506 ..... D7
55113 Falcon Heights 5,291 ..... G5
55021 Faribault⊙ 16,241 ..... E6
55024 Farmington 4,370 ..... E6
56641 Federal Dam 192 ..... D3
56536 Felton 264 ..... B3
56537 Fergus Falls⊙ 12,519 ..... B4
56540 Fertile 869 ..... B3
56448 Fifty Lakes 263 ..... D4
55735 Finlayson 202 ..... F4
56723 Fisher 453 ..... B3
56328 Flensburg 256 ..... D5
55736 Floodwood 648 ..... E4
56329 Foley⊙ 1,606 ..... D5
†56308 Forada 191 ..... C5
55025 Forest Lake 4,596 ..... F5
56330 Foreston 283 ..... E5
56542 Fosston 1,599 ..... C3
55935 Fountain 327 ..... F7
56543 Foxhome 161 ..... B4
55333 Franklin 512 ..... D6
56544 Frazee 1,284 ..... C4
56032 Freeborn 323 ..... E7
56331 Freeport 563 ..... D5
55432 Fridley 30,228 ..... G5
56033 Frost 293 ..... D7
56131 Fulda 1,308 ..... C7
56332 Garfield 284 ..... C5
56450 Garrison 174 ..... E4
56132 Garvin 172 ..... C6
56545 Gary 241 ..... B3
55334 Gaylord⊙ 1,933 ..... D6
56035 Geneva 417 ..... E7
56239 Ghent 356 ..... C6
55335 Gibbon 787 ..... D6
55741 Gilbert 2,721 ..... F3
56333 Gilman 156 ..... E5
55336 Glencoe⊙ 4,396 ..... D6
56036 Glenville 851 ..... E7
56334 Glenwood⊙ 2,523 ..... C5
56547 Glyndon 882 ..... B4
55427 Golden Valley 22,775 ..... G5
56644 Gonvick 362 ..... C3
55027 Goodhue 657 ..... F6
56725 Goodridge 191 ..... C2
56037 Good Thunder 560 ..... D6
55027 Goodview 2,567 ..... G6
56240 Graceville 780 ..... B5
56039 Granada 377 ..... D7
55604 Grand Marais⊙ 1,289 ..... G2
55936 Grand Meadow 965 ..... F7
55744 Grand Rapids⊙ 7,934 ..... E3
56241 Granite Falls⊙ 3,451 ..... C6
55030 Grasston 123 ..... E5
56726 Greenbush 817 ..... B2
†55373 Greenfield 1,391 ..... F5
55338 Green Isle 357 ..... E6
56335 Greenwald 259 ..... D5
56336 Grey Eagle 338 ..... D5
56243 Grove City 596 ..... D5
56727 Grygla 216 ..... C2
56452 Hackensack 285 ..... D4
56728 Hallock⊙ 1,405 ..... A2
56548 Halstad 690 ..... B3
55339 Hamburg 475 ..... D6
55340 Hamel 2,623 ..... F5
55304 Ham Lake 7,832 ..... E5
55938 Hammond 178 ..... F6
55031 Hampton 299 ..... E6
56244 Hancock 877 ..... C5
56245 Hanley Falls 265 ..... C6
55341 Hanover 647 ..... E5
56041 Hanska 429 ..... D6
56134 Hardwick 279 ..... B7
55939 Harmony 1,133 ..... F7
55032 Harris 678 ..... F5
56042 Hartland 322 ..... E7
55033 Hastings⊙ 12,827 ..... F6
56549 Hawley 1,634 ..... B4
55940 Hayfield 1,243 ..... F7
56043 Hayward 294 ..... E7
55342 Hector 1,252 ..... D6
56044 Henderson 739 ..... E6
56136 Hendricks 737 ..... B6
56550 Hendrum 336 ..... B3
56551 Henning 832 ..... C4
56248 Herman 600 ..... B5
†55811 Hermantown 6,759 ..... F4
56137 Heron Lake 783 ..... C7
56453 Hewitt 299 ..... C4
55746 Hibbing 21,193 ..... F3
55748 Hill City 533 ..... E4
56138 Hills 598 ..... B7
55037 Hinckley 963 ..... E4
56552 Hitterdal 253 ..... B4

(continued on following page)

Agriculture, Industry and Resources

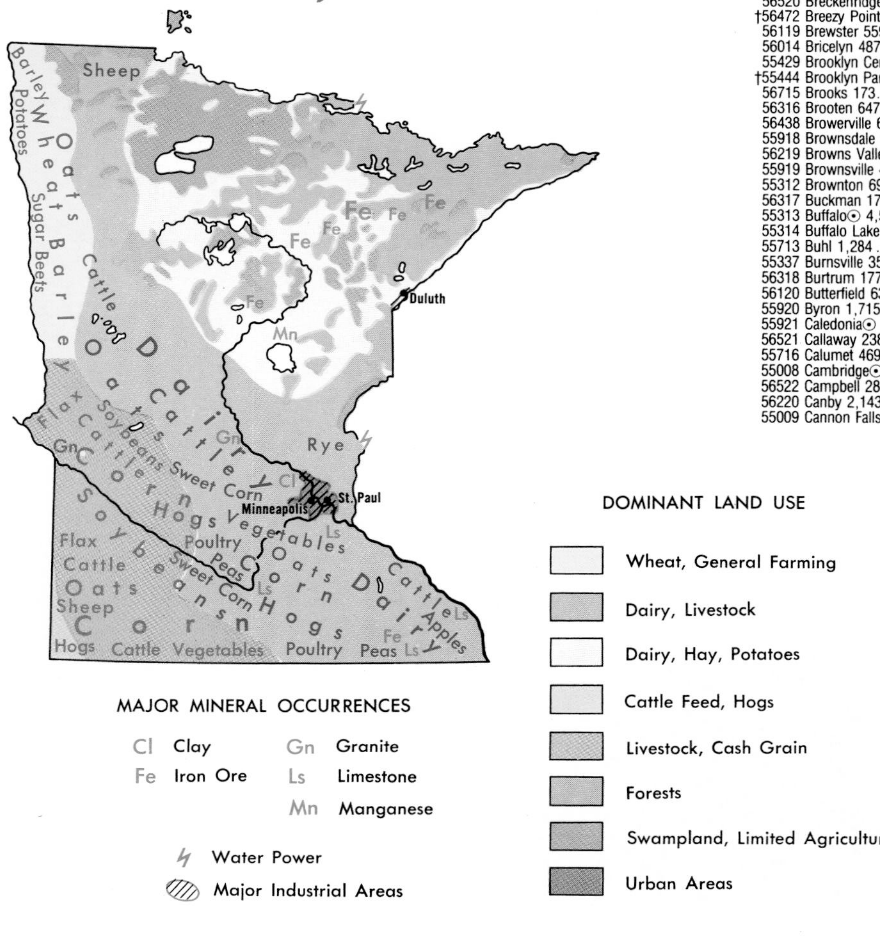

Sheep
Barley
Wheat
Potatoes
Oats
Sugar Beets
Cattle
Barley
Oats
Dairy
Cattle
Flax
Soybeans
Sweet Corn
Cattle
Corn
Hogs
Vegetables
Poultry
Peas
Corn
Oats
Dairy
Cattle
Apples
Flax
Cattle
Oats
Sheep
Soybeans
Sweet Corn
Hogs
Corn
Hogs
Cattle
Vegetables
Poultry
Peas
Rye
Fe
Mn
Gn
Cl
Ls
Duluth
St. Paul
Minneapolis
DOMINANT LAND USE
Wheat, General Farming
Dairy, Livestock
Dairy, Hay, Potatoes
Cattle Feed, Hogs
Livestock, Cash Grain
Forests
Swampland, Limited Agriculture
Urban Areas
MAJOR MINERAL OCCURRENCES
Cl Clay
Fe Iron Ore
Gn Granite
Ls Limestone
Mn Manganese
Water Power
Major Industrial Areas

Topography

Below Sea Level | 100 m. 328 ft. | 200 m. 656 ft. | 500 m. 1,640 ft. | 1,000 m. 3,281 ft. | 2,000 m. 6,562 ft. | 5,000 m. 16,404 ft.

0   50   100 MI.

0   50   100 KM.

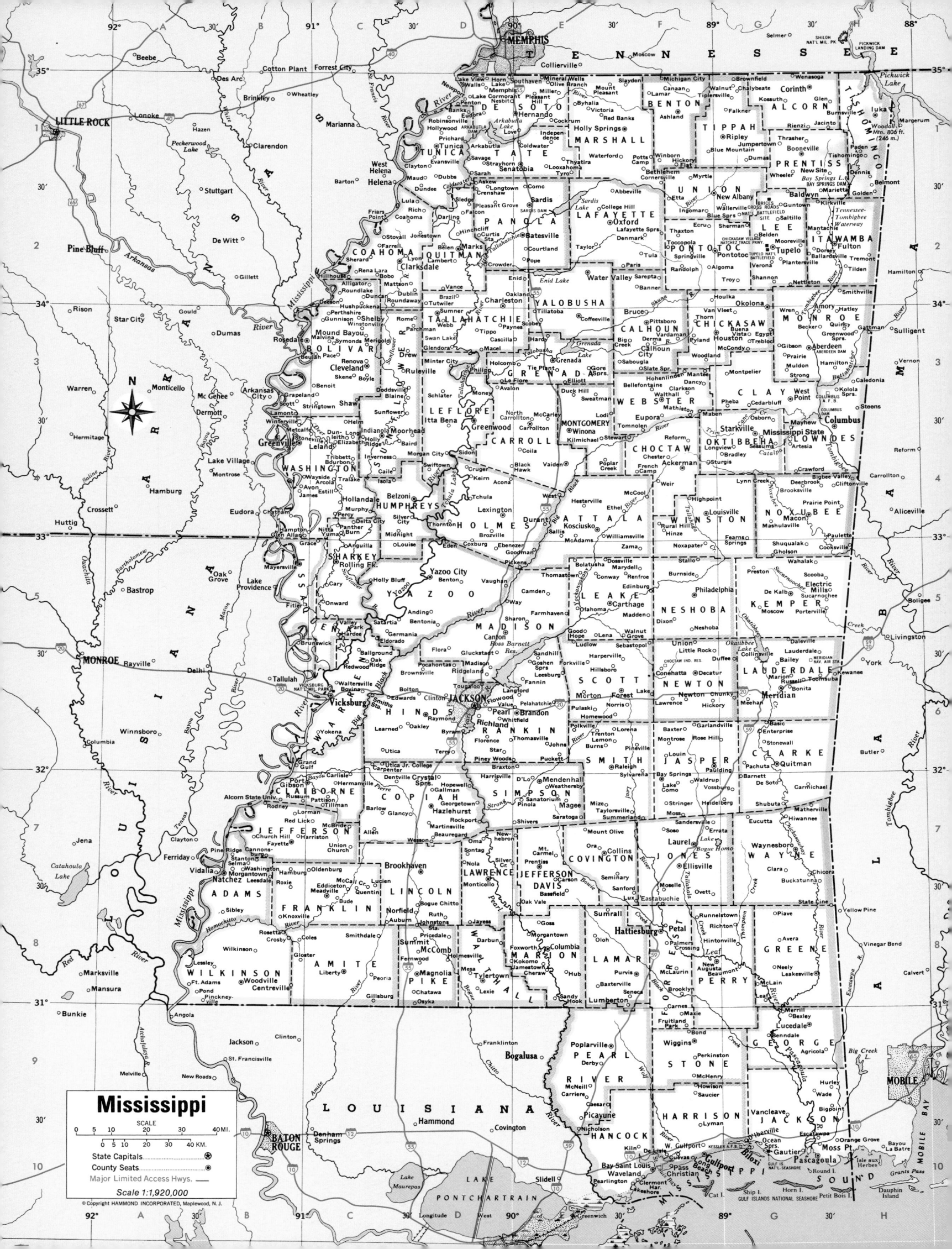

AREA 47,689 sq. mi. (123,515 sq. km.)
POPULATION 2,520,638
CAPITAL Jackson
LARGEST CITY Jackson
HIGHEST POINT Woodall Mtn. 806 ft. (246 m.)
SETTLED IN 1716
ADMITTED TO UNION December 10, 1817
POPULAR NAME Magnolia State
STATE FLOWER Magnolia
STATE BIRD Mockingbird

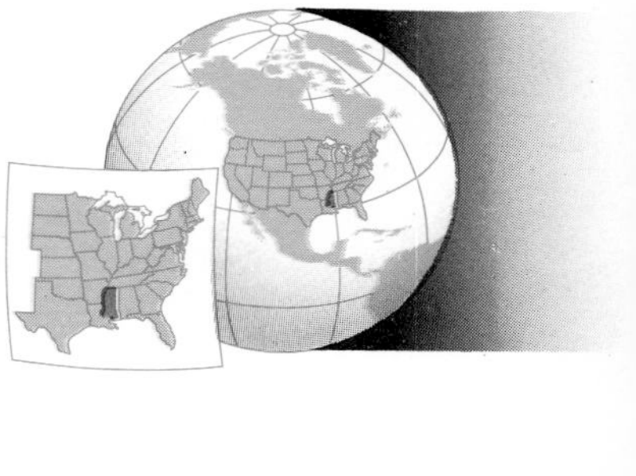

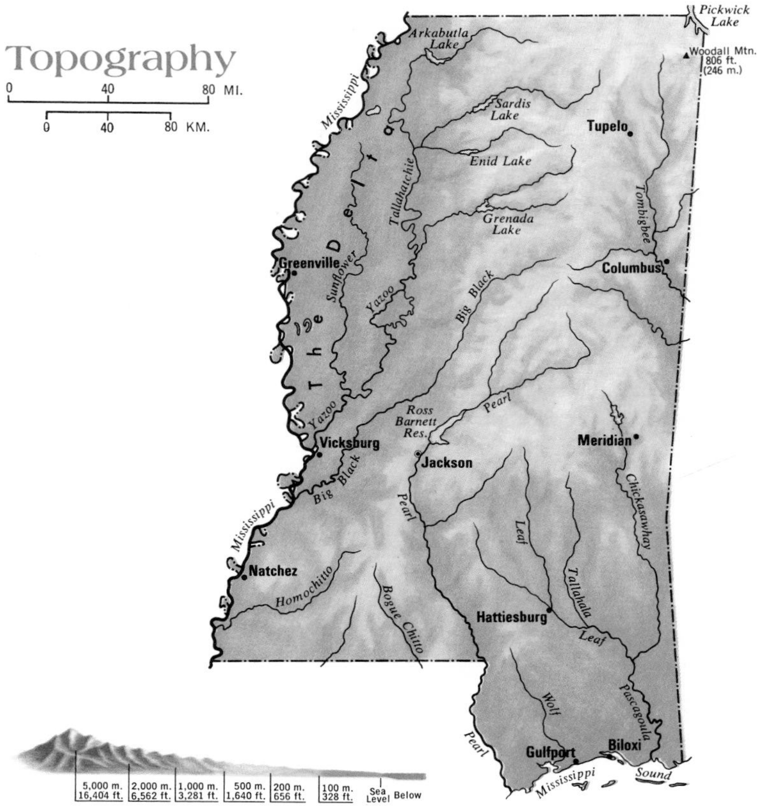

COUNTIES

Adams 38,035 .... B8
Alcorn 33,036 .... G1
Amite 13,369 .... C8
Attala 19,865 .... E4
Benton 8,153 .... F1
Bolivar 45,965 .... C3
Calhoun 15,664 .... F3
Carroll 9,776 .... E4
Chickasaw 17,853 .... G3
Choctaw 8,996 .... F4
Claiborne 12,279 .... C7
Clarke 16,945 .... G6
Clay 21,082 .... G3
Coahoma 36,918 .... C2
Copiah 26,503 .... D7
Covington 15,927 .... E7
De Soto 53,930 .... E1
Forrest 66,018 .... F8
Franklin 8,208 .... C8
George 15,297 .... G9
Greene 9,827 .... G8
Grenada 21,043 .... E3
Hancock 24,537 .... E10
Harrison 157,665 .... F10
Hinds 250,998 .... D6
Holmes 22,970 .... D4
Humphreys 13,931 .... C4
Issaquena 2,513 .... B5
Itawamba 20,518 .... H2
Jackson 118,015 .... G9
Jasper 17,265 .... F6
Jefferson 9,181 .... B7
Jefferson Davis 13,846 .... E7
Jones 61,912 .... F7
Kemper 10,148 .... G5
Lafayette 31,030 .... E2
Lamar 23,821 .... E8
Lauderdale 77,285 .... G6
Lawrence 12,518 .... D7
Leake 18,790 .... E5
Lee 57,061 .... G2
Leflore 41,525 .... D3
Lincoln 30,174 .... D8
Lowndes 57,304 .... H4
Madison 41,613 .... D5
Marion 25,708 .... E8
Marshall 29,296 .... E1
Monroe 36,404 .... H3
Montgomery 13,366 .... E4
Neshoba 23,789 .... F5
Newton 19,944 .... F6
Noxubee 13,212 .... G4
Oktibbeha 36,018 .... G4
Panola 28,164 .... E2
Pearl River 33,795 .... E9
Perry 9,864 .... G8
Pike 36,173 .... D8
Pontotoc 20,918 .... F2
Prentiss 24,025 .... G1
Quitman 12,636 .... D2
Rankin 69,427 .... E6
Scott 24,556 .... E6
Sharkey 7,964 .... C5
Simpson 23,441 .... E7
Smith 15,077 .... E6
Stone 9,716 .... F9
Sunflower 34,844 .... C3
Tallahatchie 17,157 .... D3
Tate 20,119 .... E1
Tippah 18,739 .... G1
Tishomingo 18,434 .... H1
Tunica 9,652 .... D1
Union 21,741 .... F2
Walthall 13,761 .... D8
Warren 51,627 .... C6
Washington 72,344 .... C4
Wayne 19,135 .... G7
Webster 10,300 .... F3
Wilkinson 10,021 .... B8
Winston 19,474 .... F4
Yalobusha 13,139 .... E2
Yazoo 27,349 .... D5

CITIES and TOWNS

Zip Name/Pop. Key

38601 Abbeville 448 .... F2
39730 Aberdeen⊙ 7,184 .... H3
39735 Ackerman⊙ 1,567 .... F4
39096 Alcorn State University B7
38820 Algoma 175 .... G2
†39083 Allen 15 .... C7
38720 Alligator 256 .... C2
38821 Amory 7,307 .... H3
38721 Anguilla 950 .... C5
38722 Arcola 588 .... C4
38602 Arkabutla 400 .... D1
39736 Artesia 526 .... G4
38603 Ashland⊙ 532 .... F1
38604 Askew 300 .... D1
†39664 Auburn 500 .... C8
38912 Avalon 100 .... D3
38723 Avon 400 .... B4
39320 Bailey 320 .... G6
38724 Baird 150 .... C4
38824 Baldwyn 3,427 .... G2
†39156 Ballground 30 .... C5
38913 Banner 120 .... F2
†39083 Barlow 20 .... C7
†39330 Basic 60 .... G6
39421 Bassfield 325 .... E8
38606 Batesville⊙ 4,692 .... E2
†39343 Baxter 75 .... F6
†39455 Baxterville 100 .... E8
39520 Bay Saint Louis⊙ 7,891 .... F10
39422 Bay Springs⊙ 1,884 .... F7
39423 Beaumont 1,112 .... G8
†39191 Beauregard 185 .... D7
38825 Becker 350 .... G3
38826 Belden 241 .... G2
38609 Belen 400 .... D2
39737 Bellefontaine 400 .... F3
38827 Belmont 1,420 .... H1
39038 Belzoni⊙ 2,982 .... C4
†39450 Benndale 500 .... G9
38725 Benoit 499 .... C3
39039 Benton 350 .... D5
39040 Bentonia 518 .... D5
†38659 Bethlehem 210 .... F1
38726 Beulah 431 .... B3
39738 Bigbee Valley 370 .... H4
38914 Big Creek 146 .... F3
†39567 Bigpoint 350 .... H9
*39530 Biloxi 49,311 .... G10
Biloxi-Gulfport‡ 191,918 .... G10
†38917 Black Hawk 41 .... E4
38727 Blaine 75 .... C3
38610 Blue Mountain 867 .... G1
38828 Blue Springs 131 .... G2
†38614 Bobo 200 .... C2
39629 Bogue Chitto 575 .... D8
39041 Bolton 664 .... D6
39550 Bond 350 .... F9
†39301 Bonita 300 .... G6
38829 Booneville⊙ 6,199 .... G1
†38756 Bourbon 200 .... C4
†39180 Bovina 50 .... C6
38730 Boyle 888 .... C3
39042 Brandon⊙ 9,626 .... E6
39044 Braxton 172 .... D6
38963 Brazil 229 .... D2
39601 Brookhaven⊙ 10,800 .... C7
39425 Brooklyn 450 .... F8
39739 Brooksville 1,038 .... G4
†38683 Brownfield 125 .... G1
38915 Bruce 2,208 .... F3
39322 Buckatunna 500 .... G7
39630 Bude 1,092 .... C8
38833 Burnsville 889 .... H1
38611 Byhalia 757 .... E1
†39205 Byram 250 .... D6
†38754 Caile 30 .... C4
39740 Caledonia 497 .... H3
38916 Calhoun City 2,033 .... F3
39045 Camden 150 .... E5
38612 Canaan 200 .... F1
39046 Canton⊙ 11,116 .... D5
39049 Carlisle 425 .... C7
†39360 Carmichael 75 .... G7
39050 Carpenter 200 .... C6
39426 Carriere 900 .... E9
38917 Carrollton⊙ 338 .... E4
39427 Carson 400 .... E7
39051 Carthage⊙ 3,453 .... E5
39054 Cary 470 .... C5
38920 Cascilla 230 .... D3
39741 Cedarbluff 175 .... G3
39631 Centreville 1,844 .... B8
38684 Chalybeate 350 .... G1
38921 Charleston⊙ 2,878 .... D2
39632 Chatawa 300 .... D8
38731 Chatham 150 .... B4
39323 Chunky 277 .... G6
39055 Church Hill 350 .... B7
39324 Clara 275 .... G7
38614 Clarksdale⊙ 21,137 .... D2
39551 Clermont Harbor 550 .... F10
38732 Cleveland⊙ 14,524 .... C3
39056 Clinton 14,660 .... D6
38617 Coahoma 350 .... C2
†38632 Cockrum 150 .... E1
38922 Coffeeville⊙ 1,129 .... E3
38923 Coila 75 .... E4
38618 Coldwater 1,505 .... E1
†39638 Coles 150 .... C8
†38655 College Hill 150 .... E2
39428 Collins⊙ 2,131 .... E7
39325 Collinsville 700 .... G6
39429 Columbia⊙ 7,733 .... E8
39701 Columbus⊙ 27,383 .... H3
38619 Como 1,378 .... E1
39057 Conehatta 200 .... F6
†39051 Conway 25 .... E5
38834 Corinth⊙ 13,839 .... G1
†38659 Cornersville 65 .... F1
38620 Courtland 381 .... E2
†39095 Coxburg 300 .... D5
39743 Crawford 495 .... G4
38621 Crenshaw 1,019 .... D2
39633 Crosby 349 .... B8
38622 Crowder 789 .... D2
38924 Cruger 540 .... D4
39059 Crystal Springs 4,902 .... D7
†38606 Curtis Station 350 .... D2
39326 Daleville 210 .... G5
†39643 Darbun 100 .... D8
38623 Darling 275 .... D2
39327 Decatur⊙ 1,148 .... F6
†39739 Deerbrook 30 .... G4
39328 De Kalb⊙ 1,159 .... G5
†39571 De Lisle 400 .... F10
39061 Delta City 310 .... C4
†38655 Denmark 40 .... F2
38838 Dennis 150 .... H1
†39059 Dentville 175 .... C7
†39470 Derby 298 .... E9
38839 Derma 793 .... F3
†39532 D'Iberville 13,369 .... G10
39062 D'Lo 463 .... E7
38736 Doddsville 232 .... C3
38737 Drew 2,528 .... C3
38739 Dublin 100 .... C2
38925 Duck Hill 706 .... E3
†39337 Duffee 175 .... G6
38625 Dumas 312 .... G1
38740 Duncan 501 .... C2
38626 Dundee 600 .... D1
39063 Durant 2,889 .... E4
39436 Eastabuchie 200 .... F8
39064 Ebenezer 200 .... D5
38841 Ecru 687 .... F2
39634 Eddiceton 65 .... C8
39065 Eden 150 .... D5
39066 Edwards 1,515 .... C6
†39156 Eldorado 20 .... C5
39329 Electric Mills 100 .... G5
38742 Elizabeth 500 .... C4
38926 Elliott 200 .... E3
39437 Ellisville⊙ 4,652 .... F7
38927 Enid E2
39330 Enterprise 607 .... G6
†39440 Errata 85 .... F7
39552 Escatawpa 5,367 .... G10
39067 Ethel 486 .... F4
38627 Etta 75 .... F2
39744 Eupora 2,048 .... F3
†38676 Evansville 60 .... D1
38628 Falcon 260 .... D2
38629 Falkner 251 .... G1
38630 Farrell 300 .... C2
39069 Fayette⊙ 2,033 .... B7
39635 Fernwood 500 .... D8
39070 Fitler 175 .... B5
39071 Flora 1,507 .... D5
39073 Florence 1,111 .... D6
†39201 Flowood 943 .... D6
39074 Forest⊙ 5,229 .... F6
39076 Forkville 185 .... E6
39636 Fort Adams 75 .... B8
39483 Foxworth 800 .... E8
39745 French Camp 306 .... F4
38631 Friars Point 1,400 .... C2
39577 Fruitland Park 75 .... F9
38843 Fulton⊙ 3,238 .... H2
39077 Gallman D7
38844 Gattman 151 .... H3
39553 Gautier 8,917 .... G10
39078 Georgetown 343 .... D7
†39354 Gholson 50 .... G5
†39083 Glancy 25 .... C7
38846 Glen 100 .... H1
38744 Glen Allan 650 .... B4
38928 Glendora 220 .... D3
39638 Gloster 1,726 .... B8
†39110 Gluckstadt 150 .... D5
38847 Golden 292 .... H2
39079 Goodman 1,285 .... E5
38929 Gore Springs 125 .... E3
38745 Grace 325 .... C5
†38725 Grapeland 200 .... B3
38701 Greenville⊙ 40,613 .... B4
38930 Greenwood⊙ 20,115 .... D4
38848 Greenwood Springs 170 .... H3
38901 Grenada⊙ 12,641 .... E3
*39501 Gulfport⊙ 39,676 .... F10
38746 Gunnison 708 .... C3
38849 Guntown 359 .... G2
†39661 Hamburg 150 .... B7
39746 Hamilton 500 .... H3
†38901 Hardy 45 .... E3
39080 Harperville 200 .... E6
39081 Harriston 500 .... C7
39082 Harrisville 500 .... D7
†38821 Hatley 497 .... H3
39401 Hattiesburg⊙ 40,829 .... F8
39083 Hazlehurst⊙ 4,437 .... D7
39439 Heidelberg 1,098 .... F7
39086 Hermanville 750 .... C7
38632 Hernando⊙ 2,969 .... E1
†39192 Hesterville 25 .... E4
39332 Hickory 670 .... F6
38633 Hickory Flat 458 .... F1
39087 Hillsboro 800 .... E6
†38646 Hinchcliff 60 .... D2
†39462 Hintonville 300 .... F8
†39108 Hinze 30 .... F4
†39751 Hohenlinden 96 .... F3
38940 Holcomb 50 .... D3
38748 Hollandale 4,336 .... C4
39088 Holly Bluff 700 .... C5
38749 Holly Ridge 350 .... C4
38635 Holly Springs⊙ 7,285 .... E1
†38676 Hollywood 80 .... D1
†39648 Holmesville 50 .... D8
38637 Horn Lake 4,326 .... D1
38850 Houlka 710 .... G2
38851 Houston⊙ 3,747 .... G3
†39574 Howison 300 .... F9
†39429 Hub 80 .... E8
39555 Hurley 500 .... H9
†38774 Hushpuckena 60 .... C2
38638 Independence 150 .... E1
38751 Indianola⊙ 8,221 .... C4
†38652 Ingomar 150 .... F2
38753 Inverness 1,034 .... C4
38754 Isola 834 .... C4
38941 Itta Bena 2,904 .... D4
38852 Iuka⊙ 2,846 .... H1
†38865 Jacinto 65 .... H1
*39201 Jackson (cap.)⊙ 202,895 .... D6
Jackson‡ 320,425 .... D6
39641 Jayess 200 .... D8
38639 Jonestown 1,231 .... D2
†38829 Jumpertown 472 .... G1
†38924 Keirn 3 .... D4
†39364 Kewanee 250 .... H6
39747 Kilmichael 906 .... E4
39556 Kiln 800 .... F10
†39661 Knoxville 65 .... B8
39643 Kokomo 250 .... E8
†39740 Kolola Springs 100 .... H3
39090 Kosciusko⊙ 7,415 .... E4
38834 Kossuth 190 .... G1
38640 Lafayette Springs 80 .... F2
39092 Lake 524 .... F6
38641 Lake Cormorant 300 .... D1
39558 Lakeshore 550 .... F10
38642 Lamar 200 .... F1
38643 Lambert 1,624 .... D2
38755 Lamont 400 .... B3
39335 Lauderdale 600 .... G5
39440 Laurel⊙ 21,897 .... F7
39336 Lawrence 250 .... F6
39450 Leaf 250 .... G8
39451 Leakesville⊙ 1,120 .... G8
39093 Learned 113 .... C6
38756 Leland 6,667 .... C4
39094 Lena 231 .... E5
†39667 Lexie 40 .... D8
39095 Lexington⊙ 2,628 .... D4
39645 Liberty⊙ 669 .... C8
39337 Little Rock 70 .... F6
39560 Long Beach 7,967 .... F10
†39759 Longview 800 .... G4
39096 Lorman 350 .... B7
39338 Louin 338 .... F6
39097 Louise 400 .... C5
39339 Louisville⊙ 7,323 .... G4
†38632 Love 50 .... D1
39452 Lucedale⊙ 2,429 .... G9
39646 Lucien 75 .... C7
39098 Ludlow 350 .... E5
38644 Lula 394 .... C2
39455 Lumberton 2,217 .... E8
†39501 Lyman 500 .... F10
†39739 Lynn Creek 20 .... G4
38645 Lyon 531 .... D2
39750 Maben 855 .... F3
39341 Macon⊙ 2,396 .... G4
39109 Madden 450 .... F5
39110 Madison 2,241 .... D6
39111 Magee 3,497 .... E7
39652 Magnolia⊙ 2,461 .... D8
†38769 Malvina 100 .... C3
38855 Mantachie 732 .... H2
39751 Mantee 158 .... F3
38856 Marietta 298 .... H2
39342 Marion 771 .... G6
38646 Marks⊙ 2,260 .... D2
†39083 Martinsville 30 .... D7
†39051 Marydell 99 .... F5
39752 Mathiston 632 .... F3
38758 Mattson 200 .... C2
†39458 Maxie 233 .... F9
39113 Mayersville⊙ 378 .... B5
39753 Mayhew 150 .... G4
39107 McAdams 350 .... E4
†39144 McBride 2 .... C7
39647 McCall Creek 250 .... C7
38943 McCarley 250 .... E3
39648 McComb 12,331 .... D8
38854 McCondy 150 .... G3
39108 McCool 203 .... F4
39561 McHenry 660 .... F9
39456 McLain 688 .... G8
39457 McNeill 800 .... E9
39653 Meadville⊙ 575 .... C8
39114 Mendenhall⊙ 2,533 .... E7
39301 Meridian⊙ 46,577 .... G6
38759 Merigold 574 .... C3
†39667 Mesa 30 .... D8
38760 Metcalfe 952 .... B4
38647 Michigan City 350 .... F1
39115 Midnight 500 .... C4
38648 Mineral Wells 250 .... E1
38944 Minter City 150 .... D3
39762 Mississippi State G4
39116 Mize 363 .... E7
38945 Money 350 .... D3
39654 Monticello⊙ 1,834 .... D7
39754 Montpelier 175 .... G3
†39338 Montrose 120 .... F6
38857 Mooreville 200 .... G2
38761 Moorhead 2,358 .... C4
38946 Morgan City 319 .... D4
39484 Morgantown 325 .... E8
†39120 Morgantown 3,445 .... B7
39117 Morton 3,303 .... E6
†39328 Moscow 30 .... G5
39459 Moselle 525 .... F8
39460 Moss 265 .... F7
39563 Moss Point 18,998 .... G10
38762 Mound Bayou 2,917 .... C3
†39474 Mount Carmel 30 .... E7
39119 Mount Olive 993 .... E7
38649 Mount Pleasant 250 .... E1
38650 Myrtle 402 .... F1
39120 Natchez⊙ 22,015 .... B7
39461 Neely 270 .... G8
38651 Nesbit 366 .... D1
39365 Neshoba 250 .... F5
38858 Nettleton 1,911 .... G2
38652 New Albany⊙ 7,072 .... G2
39462 New Augusta⊙ 589 .... F8
39140 Newhebron 470 .... D7
38850 New Houlka (Houlka) 710 .... G2
38859 New Site 100 .... H1
39345 Newton 3,708 .... F6
39463 Nicholson 400 .... E10
†38763 Nitta Yuma 150 .... C4
†39629 Norfield 75 .... C8
38947 North Carrollton 859 .... E3
39346 Noxapater 516 .... F5
38948 Oakland 540 .... E2
†39154 Oakley 133 .... D6
39656 Oak Vale E8
39564 Ocean Springs 14,504 .... G10
39141 Ofahoma 350 .... E5
38860 Okolona⊙ 3,409 .... G2
38654 Olive Branch 2,067 .... E1
†39482 Oloh 93 .... E8
†39654 Oma 200 .... D7
†39501 Orange Grove 13,476 .... H10
39657 Osyka 581 .... D8
39464 Ovett 600 .... F8
38655 Oxford⊙ 9,882 .... F2
38764 Pace 519 .... C3
39347 Pachuta 256 .... G6
38861 Paden 119 .... H1
†39401 Palmers Crossing 2,765 .... F8
38765 Panther Burn 300 .... C4
38738 Parchman 200 .... D3
38949 Paris 253 .... F2
39567 Pascagoula⊙ 29,318 .... G10
Pascagoula-Moss Point‡ 118,015 .... G10
39571 Pass Christian 5,014 .... F10
39144 Pattison 540 .... C7
39348 Paulding⊙ 630 .... F6
39349 Paulette 230 .... H4
†38920 Paynes 100 .... D3
39028 Pearl 18,580 .... D6
39572 Pearlington 500 .... E10
39145 Pelahatchie 1,445 .... E6
39573 Perkinston 950 .... F9
†38746 Perthshire 25 .... C3
39465 Petal 8,476 .... F8
39755 Pheba 280 .... G3
39350 Philadelphia⊙ 6,434 .... F5
38950 Philipp 975 .... D3
†39476 Piave 150 .... G8
39466 Picayune 10,361 .... E9
39146 Pickens 1,386 .... E5
39148 Piney Woods 450 .... D6
39149 Pinola E7

(continued on following page)

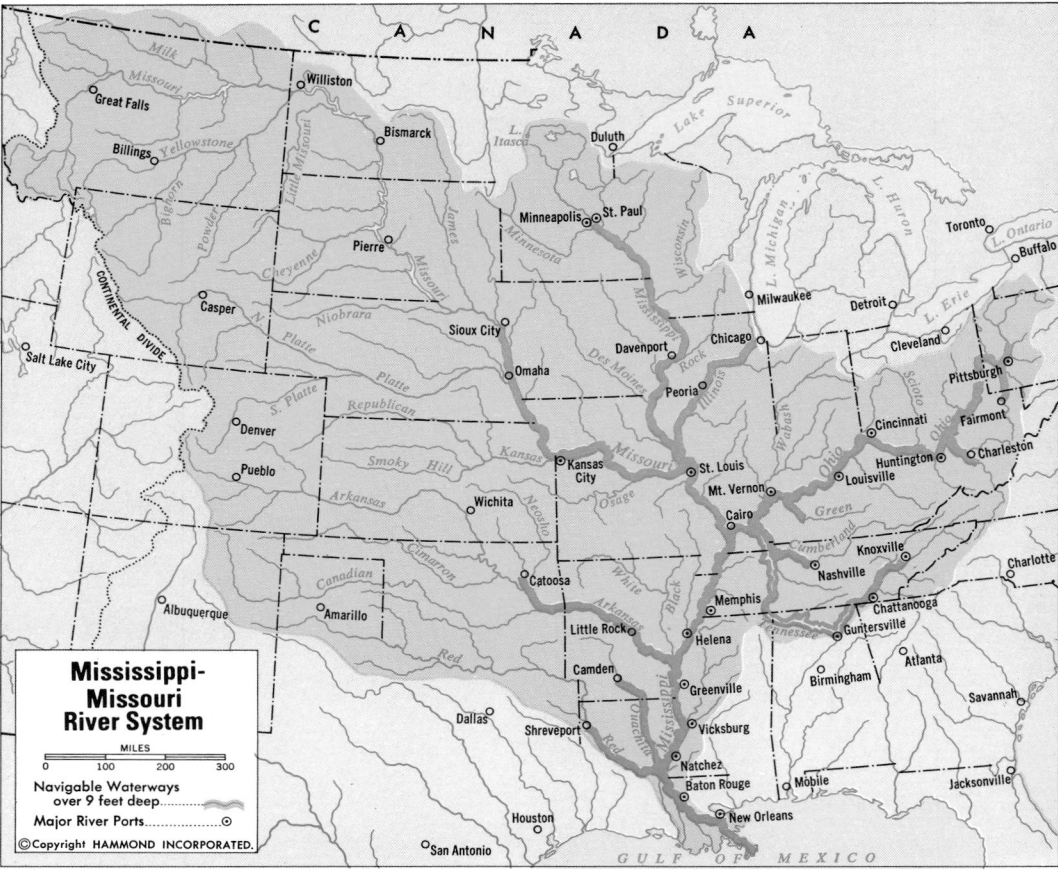

Mississippi-Missouri River System

MILES
0   100   200   300

Navigable Waterways over 9 feet deep
Major River Ports...........⊙

©Copyright HAMMOND INCORPORATED.

Agriculture, Industry and Resources

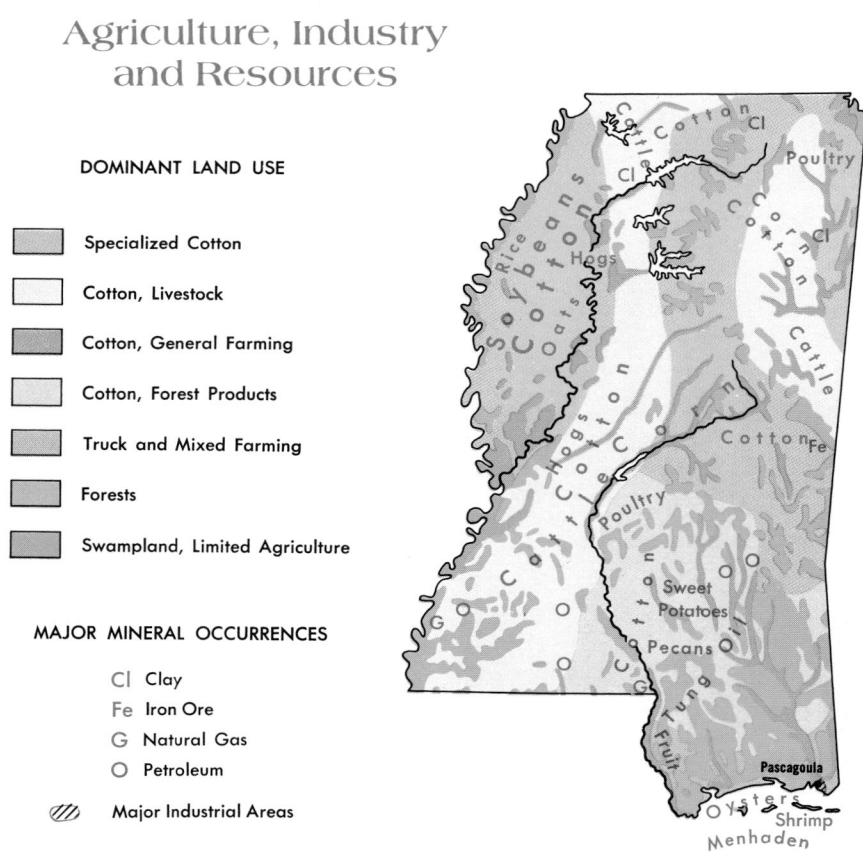

DOMINANT LAND USE

- Specialized Cotton
- Cotton, Livestock
- Cotton, General Farming
- Cotton, Forest Products
- Truck and Mixed Farming
- Forests
- Swampland, Limited Agriculture

MAJOR MINERAL OCCURRENCES

Cl Clay
Fe Iron Ore
G   Natural Gas
O   Petroleum

⫽ Major Industrial Areas

38951 Pittsboro⊙ 269 ....F3	38873 Tishomingo 387 ....H1
38862 Plantersville 920 ....G2	38874 Toccopola 184 ....F2
38657 Pleasant Grove 100 ....D2	39770 Tomnolen 200 ....F4
†38651 Pleasant Hill 400 ....E1	39364 Toomsuba 500 ....G6
39072 Pocahontas 80 ....D6	39174 Tougaloo 800 ....D6
39118 Polkville 129 ....E6	38757 Tralake 200 ....C4
38863 Pontotoc⊙ 4,723 ....G2	38875 Trebloc 100 ....G3
38568 Pope 208 ....E2	38876 Tremont 379 ....H2
39470 Poplarville⊙ 2,562 ....E9	38779 Tribbett 100 ....C4
39352 Porterville 150 ....G5	38675 Tula 140 ....F2
39150 Port Gibson⊙ 2,371 ....B7	38676 Tunica⊙ 1,361 ....D1
38659 Potts Camp 525 ....F1	38801 Tupelo⊙ 23,905 ....G2
39756 Prairie G3	38963 Tutwiler 1,174 ....C3
39353 Prairie Point 150 ....H4	39667 Tylertown⊙ 1,976 ....D8
39474 Prentiss⊙ 1,465 ....E7	39365 Union 1,931 ....F5
39354 Preston 500 ....F4	39668 Union Church 75 ....C7
†39666 Pricedale 400 ....D8	39175 Utica 865 ....C6
†38676 Prichard 50 ....D1	39175 Utica Junior College 40 ....C6
39151 Puckett 279 ....E6	39176 Vaiden⊙ 924 ....E4
39152 Pulaski 108 ....E6	39177 Valley Park 400 ....C5
39475 Purvis⊙ 2,256 ....F8	39178 Value 327 ....D6
39647 Quentin 40 ....C8	38964 Vance 200 ....D3
39355 Quitman⊙ 2,632 ....G6	†39564 Vancleave 1,330 ....G9
39153 Raleigh⊙ 998 ....F6	†38851 Van Vleet 400 ....G2
38864 Randolph F2	38878 Vardaman 1,009 ....F3
39154 Raymond⊙ 1,967 ....D6	39179 Vaughan 210 ....D5
38661 Red Banks 350 ....F1	38879 Verona 2,497 ....G2
†39096 Red Lick 100 ....B7	39180 Vicksburg⊙ 25,434 ....C6
39156 Redwood 80 ....C6	38679 Victoria 800 ....E1
39757 Reform 100 ....F4	39366 Vossburg 300 ....F6
38767 Rena Lara 350 ....C2	†39567 Wade 800 ....G9
†39051 Renfroe 32 ....F5	†39358 Wahalak 92 ....H5
†38732 Renova 659 ....C3	38680 Walls 50 ....D1
38662 Rich 72 ....D2	38683 Walnut 513 ....G1
†39218 Richland 3,955 ....D6	39189 Walnut Grove 439 ....F5
39476 Richton 1,205 ....G8	39771 Walthall⊙ 206 ....F3
39157 Ridgeland 5,461 ....D6	39190 Washington 250 ....B7
38865 Rienzi 423 ....G1	38685 Waterford 400 ....E1
38663 Ripley⊙ 4,271 ....G1	38965 Water Valley⊙ 4,147 ....E2
38664 Robinsonville 285 ....D1	39576 Waveland 4,186 ....F10
†39083 Rockport 30 ....D7	39367 Waynesboro⊙ 5,349 ....G7
†39096 Rodney 100 ....B7	38780 Wayside 500 ....C4
39159 Rolling Fork⊙ 2,590 ....C5	†39114 Weathersby D3
38768 Rome C3	38966 Webb 782 ....D3
38769 Rosedale⊙ 2,793 ....C3	39772 Weir 553 ....F4
39356 Rose Hill 500 ....F6	†38834 Wenasoga 175 ....G1
†39633 Rosetta 120 ....B8	39191 Wesson 1,313 ....D7
38661 Roxie 591 ....B8	39192 West 253 ....E5
38771 Ruleville 3,332 ....D3	†39501 West Gulfport (North
†39108 Rural Hill 25 ....E4	Gulfport) 6,660 ....F10
†39150 Russum 200 ....B7	39773 West Point⊙ 8,811 ....G3
39662 Ruth 400 ....D8	38880 Wheeler 600 ....G1
39160 Sallis 211 ....E4	39193 Whitfield 900 ....E6
38866 Saltillo 1,271 ....G2	39577 Wiggins⊙ 3,205 ....F9
39112 Sanatorium 400 ....F7	†38659 Winborn 70 ....F1
39161 Sandersville 800 ....F7	38967 Winona⊙ 6,177 ....E4
39161 Sandhill 100 ....E5	38781 Winstonville 486 ....C3
39478 Sandy Hook 70 ....E8	38782 Winterville 200 ....B4
*39479 Sanford 150 ....F8	39776 Woodland 135 ....F3
38665 Sarah 150 ....D1	†39730 Wren 150 ....G3
38666 Sardis⊙ 2,278 ....E2	39669 Woodville⊙ 1,512 ....A8
38867 Sarepta 120 ....F2	39194 Yazoo City⊙ 12,092 ....D5
39162 Satartia 73 ....C5	†39090 Zama 100 ....E5
39574 Saucier 100 ....F9	
38667 Savage 100 ....D1	**OTHER FEATURES**
38952 Schlater 429 ....D3	
38953 Scobey 100 ....E3	Amite (riv.) C9
39358 Scooba 511 ....G5	Arkabutla (lake) D1
38772 Scott 400 ....B3	Big Black (riv.) C6
39359 Sebastopol 314 ....F5	Black (creek) F8
39479 Seminary 327 ....E7	Bogue Chitto (riv.) D8
38668 Senatobia⊙ 5,013 ....E1	Bogue Homo (lake) F7
39758 Sessums 150 ....G4	Bowie (creek) F7
38868 Shannon 680 ....G2	Brices Cross Roads Nat'l Battlefield
39163 Sharon 200 ....E5	Site G2
38773 Shaw 2,461 ....C3	Buttahatchee (riv.) H3
38774 Shelby 2,540 ....C3	Cat (isl.) F10
38669 Sherard 150 ....C2	Catalpa (creek) G4
38869 Sherman 499 ....G2	Chickasaw Village, Natchez Trace
39164 Shivers 100 ....E7	Pkwy. G2
39360 Shubuta 626 ....G7	Chickasawhay (riv.) G7
39361 Shuqualak 554 ....G5	Coldwater (riv.) D1
39165 Sibley 350 ....B8	Columbus A.F.B. 3,650 ....H3
38954 Sidon 450 ....D4	Deer (creek) C4
39166 Silver City 378 ....C4	Enid (lake) E2
39663 Silver Creek 272 ....D7	Grenada (lake) E3
38775 Skene 250 ....C3	Gulf Islands Nat'l Seashore G10
38955 Slate Spring 102 ....F3	Homochitto (riv.) B8
38670 Sledge 699 ....D2	Horn (isl.) G10
39664 Smithdale 200 ....C8	Keesler A.F.B. G10
38870 Smithville 866 ....H2	Leaf (riv.) F8
39665 Sontag 200 ....D7	Little Tallahatchie (riv.) E2
39480 Soso 434 ....F7	Meridian Naval Air Sta. G5
38671 Southaven 16,071 ....E1	Mississippi (riv.) A8
39167 Star 600 ....D6	Mississippi (sound) G10
39759 Starkville⊙ 15,169 ....G4	Noxubee (riv.) G4
39362 State Line 484 ....G8	Okatibbee (lake) G5
39766 Steens 125 ....H3	Pascagoula (riv.) G9
39767 Stewart 350 ....F4	Pearl (riv.) D8
38776 Stoneville 250 ....C4	Petit Bois (isl.) H10
39363 Stonewall 1,345 ....G6	Pickwick (lake) H1
38672 Stovall 50 ....C2	Pierre (bayou) C7
†38665 Strayhorn 275 ....D1	Ross Barnett (res.) D6
39481 Stringer 350 ....F7	Round (isl.) G10
38777 Stringtown 300 ....C3	Saint Louis (bay) F10
39769 Sturgis 269 ....G4	Sardis (lake) E2
39666 Summit 1,753 ....D8	Ship (isl.) G10
38957 Sumner⊙ 452 ....D3	Skuna (riv.) F2
39482 Sumrall 1,197 ....E8	Strong (riv.) D7
38778 Sunflower 1,027 ....C3	Sucarnoochee (creek) G5
38958 Swan Lake 325 ....D3	Sunflower (riv.) C5
38959 Swiftown 320 ....D4	Tallahaga (creek) G5
39153 Sylvarena 102 ....F6	Tallahala (creek) F7
38673 Taylor 301 ....E2	Tallahatchie (riv.) D3
39168 Taylorsville 1,387 ....F7	Tchula (lake) D4
39169 Tchula 1,931 ....D4	Tennessee-Tombigbee Waterway H2
38871 Thaxton 404 ....F2	Thompson (creek) G8
39170 Terry 655 ....D6	Tombigbee (riv.) H4
39171 Thomastown 400 ....E5	Trim Cane (creek) G4
†39073 Thomasville 50 ....E6	Tupelo Nat'l Battlefield G2
39172 Thornton 135 ....D4	Vicksburg Nat'l Mil. Park C6
†38829 Thrasher 100 ....G1	Wolf (riv.) F9
38960 Tie Plant 500 ....E3	Woodall (mt.) H1
38961 Tillatoba 106 ....E3	Yalobusha (riv.) E3
†39150 Tillman 65 ....C7	Yazoo (riv.) D5
38674 Tiplersville 100 ....G1	Yockanookany (riv.) E5
38962 Tippo 200 ....D3	⊙County seat.
	‡Population of metropolitan area.
	† Zip of nearest p.o. * Multiple zips.

AREA 69,697 sq. mi. (180,515 sq. km.)
POPULATION 4,916,759
CAPITAL Jefferson City
LARGEST CITY St. Louis
HIGHEST POINT Taum Sauk Mtn. 1,772 ft. (540 m.)
SETTLED IN 1764
ADMITTED TO UNION August 10, 1821
POPULAR NAME Show Me State
STATE FLOWER Hawthorn
STATE BIRD Bluebird

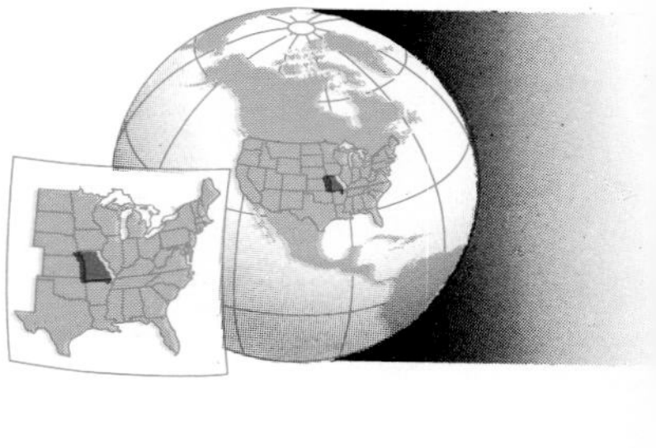

COUNTIES

Adair 24,870 .... G2
Andrew 13,980 .... C3
Atchison 8,605 .... B2
Audrain 26,458 .... J4
Barry 24,408 .... E9
Barton 11,292 .... D7
Bates 15,873 .... D6
Benton 12,183 .... F6
Bollinger 10,301 .... M8
Boone 100,376 .... H4
Buchanan 87,888 .... C3
Butler 37,693 .... M9
Caldwell 8,660 .... E3
Callaway 32,252 .... J5
Camden 20,017 .... G6
Cape Girardeau 58,837 .... N8
Carroll 12,131 .... F4
Carter 5,428 .... L9
Cass 51,029 .... D5
Cedar 11,894 .... E7
Chariton 10,489 .... F3
Christian 22,402 .... F9
Clark 8,493 .... J2
Clay 136,488 .... D4
Clinton 15,916 .... D3
Cole 56,663 .... H6
Cooper 14,643 .... G5
Crawford 18,300 .... K7
Dade 7,383 .... E8
Dallas 12,096 .... F7
Daviess 8,905 .... E3
De Kalb 8,222 .... D3
Dent 14,517 .... J7
Douglas 11,594 .... G9
Dunklin 36,324 .... M10
Franklin 71,233 .... K6
Gasconade 13,181 .... J6
Gentry 7,887 .... D2
Greene 185,302 .... F8
Grundy 11,959 .... E2
Harrison 9,890 .... E2
Henry 19,672 .... E6
Hickory 6,367 .... F7
Holt 6,882 .... B2
Howard 10,008 .... G4
Howell 28,807 .... J9
Iron 11,084 .... L7
Jackson 629,266 .... R5
Jasper 86,958 .... D8
Jefferson 146,183 .... L6
Johnson 39,059 .... E5
Knox 5,508 .... H2
Laclede 24,323 .... G7
Lafayette 29,925 .... E4
Lawrence 28,973 .... E8
Lewis 10,901 .... J2
Lincoln 22,193 .... L4
Linn 15,495 .... F3
Livingston 15,739 .... E3
Macon 16,313 .... G3
Madison 10,725 .... M8
Maries 7,551 .... J6
Marion 28,638 .... J3
McDonald 14,917 .... D9
Mercer 4,685 .... E2
Miller 18,532 .... H6
Mississippi 15,726 .... O9
Moniteau 12,068 .... G5
Monroe 9,716 .... H3
Montgomery 11,537 .... K5
Morgan 13,807 .... G6
New Madrid 22,945 .... N9
Newton 40,555 .... D9
Nodaway 21,996 .... C2
Oregon 10,238 .... K9
Osage 12,014 .... J6
Ozark 7,961 .... H9
Pemiscot 24,987 .... N10
Perry 16,784 .... N7
Pettis 36,378 .... F5
Phelps 33,633 .... J7
Pike 17,568 .... K4
Platte 46,341 .... C4
Polk 18,822 .... F7
Pulaski 42,011 .... H7
Putnam 6,092 .... F2
Ralls 8,984 .... J3
Randolph 25,460 .... G3
Ray 21,378 .... E4
Reynolds 7,230 .... L8
Ripley 12,458 .... L9
Saint Charles 144,107 .... M2
Saint Clair 8,622 .... E6
Sainte Genevieve 15,180 .... M7
Saint Francois 42,600 .... M7
Saint Louis 973,896 .... O3
Saint Louis (city county) 453,085 ... P3
Saline 24,919 .... F4
Schuyler 4,979 .... G2
Scotland 5,415 .... H2
Scott 39,647 .... N8
Shannon 7,885 .... K8
Shelby 7,826 .... H3
Stoddard 29,009 .... N9
Stone 15,587 .... F9
Sullivan 7,434 .... F2
Taney 20,467 .... F9
Texas 21,070 .... J8
Vernon 19,806 .... D7
Warren 14,900 .... K5
Washington 17,983 .... L7
Wayne 11,277 .... L8
Webster 20,414 .... G8
Worth 3,008 .... D2
Wright 16,188 .... H8

CITIES and TOWNS

Zip Name/Pop. Key

64720 Adrian 1,484 .... D6
63730 Advance 1,054 .... N8
63123 Affton 23,181 .... P4
64401 Agency 419 .... C3
64830 Alba 474 .... D8
64402 Albany⊙ 2,152 .... D2
63430 Alexandria 417 .... K2
64001 Alma 445 .... E4
65606 Alton⊙ 721 .... K9
64421 Amazonia 314 .... C3
64723 Amsterdam 231 .... D6
64831 Anderson 1,237 .... D9
63620 Annapolis 370 .... L8
63820 Anniston 320 .... O9
64724 Appleton City 1,257 .... D6
63821 Arbyrd 704 .... M10
63621 Arcadia 683 .... L7
64725 Archie 753 .... D5
65230 Armstrong 360 .... G4
63010 Arnold 19,141 .... M6
65604 Ash Grove 1,157 .... E8
65010 Ashland 1,021 .... H5
63530 Atlanta 441 .... H3
63332 Augusta 308 .... L5
65605 Aurora 6,437 .... E9
65231 Auxvasse 858 .... J4
65608 Ava⊙ 2,761 .... G9
64010 Avondale 612 .... P5
63011 Ballwin 12,656 .... N3
64011 Bates City 199 .... E5
†65619 Battlefield 1,227 .... F8
†63101 Bella Villa 758 .... R4
63735 Bell City 539 .... N8
65013 Belle 1,233 .... J6
†63137 Bellefontaine Neighbors 12,082 .... R2
63333 Bellflower 403 .... K4
†63101 Bel-Nor 2,047 .... P2
†63101 Bel-Ridge 3,682 .... P2
64012 Belton 12,708 .... C5
63736 Benton⊙ 674 .... O8
63134 Berkeley 15,922 .... P2
63822 Bernie 1,975 .... M9
63823 Bertrand 688 .... O9
64424 Bethany⊙ 3,095 .... E2
63532 Bevier 733 .... G3
65610 Billings 911 .... F8
65438 Birch Tree 622 .... K9
63624 Bismarck 1,625 .... L7
65321 Blackburn 314 .... F4
†63031 Black Jack 5,293 .... R1
65014 Bland 662 .... J6
63825 Bloomfield⊙ 1,795 .... M9
63627 Bloomsdale 397 .... M6
64015 Blue Springs 25,927 .... R6
†64101 Blue Summit R5
65613 Bolivar⊙ 5,919 .... F7
63628 Bonne Terre 3,797 .... L7
65233 Boonville⊙ 6,959 .... G5
64723 Bosworth 394 .... F4
65441 Bourbon 1,259 .... K6
63334 Bowling Green⊙ 3,022 .... K4
65616 Branson 2,550 .... F9
63533 Brashear 332 .... H2
64624 Braymer 986 .... E3
64625 Breckenridge 523 .... E3
†63114 Breckenridge Hills 5,666 .... O2
63144 Brentwood 8,209 .... P3
63044 Bridgeton 18,445 .... O2
†63044 Bridgeton Terrace 334 .... O2
64628 Brookfield 5,555 .... F3
64630 Browning 368 .... F2
65236 Brunswick 1,272 .... F4
64631 Bucklin 713 .... G3
64016 Buckner 2,848 .... R5
65622 Buffalo⊙ 2,217 .... F7
65237 Bunceton 419 .... G5
63629 Bunker 673 .... K8
64428 Burlington Junction 657 .... B2
64730 Butler⊙ 4,107 .... D6
65689 Cabool 2,090 .... H8
64632 Cainsville 496 .... E2
65239 Cairo 315 .... H4
65323 Calhoun 427 .... E6
65018 California⊙ 3,381 .... H5
63534 Callao 326 .... G3
†63101 Calverton Park 1,717 .... P2
65020 Camdenton⊙ 2,303 .... G6
64429 Cameron 4,519 .... D3
63933 Campbell 2,134 .... M9
63828 Canalou 369 .... N9
63435 Canton 2,435 .... J2
63701 Cape Girardeau 34,361 .... O8
63829 Cardwell 831 .... M10
64834 Carl Junction 3,937 .... C8
64633 Carrollton⊙ 4,700 .... E4
64835 Carterville 1,973 .... D8
64836 Carthage⊙ 11,104 .... D8
63830 Caruthersville⊙ 7,958 .... N10
65625 Cassville⊙ 2,091 .... E9
65022 Cedar City 427 .... H5
63436 Center 669 .... J3
65023 Centertown 304 .... H5
63633 Centerville⊙ 241 .... L8
65240 Centralia 3,537 .... H4
63740 Chaffee 3,241 .... N8
65024 Chamois 546 .... J5
†63101 Charlack 1,537 .... P2
63834 Charleston⊙ 5,230 .... O9
64733 Chilhowee 349 .... E5
64601 Chillicothe⊙ 9,089 .... E3
63437 Clarence 1,147 .... H3
65243 Clark 304 .... H4
65025 Clarksburg 352 .... G5
64430 Clarksdale 278 .... D3
†63017 Clarkson Valley 1,435 .... N3
63336 Clarksville 585 .... K4
63837 Clarkton 1,228 .... M10
†64119 Claycomo 1,671 .... P5
63105 Clayton⊙ 14,273 .... P3
64734 Cleveland 485 .... C5
65631 Clever 551 .... F8
64735 Clinton⊙ 8,366 .... E6
65325 Cole Camp 1,022 .... F6
65201 Columbia⊙ 62,061 .... H5
Columbia‡ 100,376 .... H5
†63128 Concord 20,896 .... P4
64020 Concordia 2,129 .... E5
65632 Conway 601 .... G7
†63101 Cool Valley 2,084 .... P2
63839 Cooter 479 .... N10
64021 Corder 483 .... E4
†64501 Country Club Village 1,234 .... C3
64437 Craig 379 .... B2
65633 Crane 1,185 .... E9
64739 Creighton 301 .... D6
†63126 Crestwood 12,815 .... O3
63141 Creve Coeur 11,757 .... O2
65452 Crocker 979 .... H7
63019 Crystal City 3,618 .... M6
†63101 Crystal Lake Park 496 .... O3
65453 Cuba 2,120 .... K6
63339 Curryville 323 .... K4
64439 Dearborn 547 .... C3
64740 Deepwater 475 .... E6
64440 De Kalb 245 .... C3
†63135 Dellwood 6,200 .... R2
63744 Delta 524 .... N8
63636 Des Arc 237 .... L8
63601 Desloge 3,481 .... M7
63020 De Soto 5,993 .... L6
63131 Des Peres 8,254 .... O3
63841 Dexter 7,043 .... N9
64840 Diamond 766 .... D9
65459 Dixon 1,402 .... H6
63935 Doniphan⊙ 1,921 .... L9
†65550 Doolittle 701 .... J7
63536 Downing 462 .... H2
64742 Drexel 908 .... C6
64841 Duenweg 703 .... D8
†64801 Duquesne 1,252 .... D8
64442 Eagleville 364 .... D2
64443 Easton 313 .... C3
63845 East Prairie 3,713 .... O9
64444 Edgerton 584 .... C3
63537 Edina⊙ 1,520 .... H2
†63101 Edmundson 1,374 .... O2
65026 Eldon 4,342 .... G6
64744 El Dorado Springs 3,868 .... E7
63638 Ellington 1,215 .... L8
†63011 Ellisville 6,233 .... M3
63937 Ellsinore 362 .... L9
63343 Elsberry 1,272 .... L4
63639 Elvins 1,548 .... L7
65466 Eminence⊙ 614 .... K8
63344 Eolia 401 .... L4
63846 Essex 545 .... N9
†63601 Esther 1,038 .... M7
63025 Eureka 3,862 .... M4
65646 Everton 317 .... E8
63440 Ewing 400 .... J2
64024 Excelsior Springs 10,424 .... R4
65647 Exeter 588 .... D9
64446 Fairfax 835 .... B2
65648 Fair Grove 863 .... F8
65649 Fair Play 384 .... E7
63345 Farber 503 .... J4
63640 Farmington⊙ 8,270 .... M7
65248 Fayette⊙ 2,983 .... G4
63026 Fenton 2,417 .... O4
63135 Ferguson 24,740 .... P2
64163 Ferrelview 447 .... O4
63028 Festus 7,574 .... M6
64449 Fillmore 265 .... C2
63940 Fisk 450 .... M9
63601 Flat River 4,443 .... M7
*63031 Florissant 55,372 .... P1
65652 Fordland 569 .... G8
64451 Forest City 387 .... B3
65653 Forsyth⊙ 1,010 .... F9
63441 Frankford 443 .... K4
63645 Fredericktown⊙ 4,036 .... M7
65035 Freeburg 554 .... J6
64746 Freeman 485 .... C5
†63101 Frontenac 3,654 .... O3
65251 Fulton⊙ 11,046 .... J5
65655 Gainesville⊙ 707 .... G9
65656 Galena⊙ 423 .... F9
64640 Gallatin⊙ 2,063 .... E3
64641 Galt 323 .... F2
64747 Garden City 1,021 .... D5
63037 Gerald 921 .... K6
63848 Gideon 1,240 .... N10
64642 Gilman City 414 .... D2
64118 Gladstone 24,990 .... P5
65254 Glasgow 1,336 .... G4
†64068 Glenaire 541 .... R5
63122 Glendale 6,035 .... P3
64748 Golden City 900 .... D8
63843 Goodman 1,030 .... C9
63543 Gorin H2
64454 Gower 1,276 .... C3
64029 Grain Valley 1,327 .... S6
64844 Granby 1,908 .... D9
64030 Grandview 24,502 .... P6
64456 Grant City⊙ 1,068 .... D2
†63155 Grantwood Village 1,002 .... O4
65037 Gravois Mills G6
63545 Green City 719 .... F2
65661 Greenfield⊙ 1,394 .... E8
65332 Green Ridge 488 .... F5
63546 Greentop 538 .... H2
63944 Greenville⊙ 393 .... M8
64034 Greenwood 1,315 .... R6
64643 Hale 529 .... F3
65255 Hallsville 624 .... H4
64644 Hamilton 1,582 .... E3
†63101 Hanley Hills 2,439 .... P2
63401 Hannibal 18,811 .... K3
64035 Hardin 688 .... E4
64701 Harrisonville⊙ 6,372 .... D5
65667 Hartville⊙ 576 .... G8
63945 Harviell M9
63349 Hawk Point 386 .... K5
63851 Hayti 3,964 .... N10
†63851 Hayti Heights 1,023 .... N10
†63736 Haywood City 425 .... N9
*63042 Hazelwood 12,935 .... P2
64036 Henrietta 424 .... E4
63048 Herculaneum 2,293 .... M6
65041 Hermann⊙ 2,695 .... K5
65668 Hermitage⊙ 384 .... F7
65257 Higbee 817 .... H4
64037 Higginsville 4,595 .... E4
63350 High Hill 254 .... K5
63050 Hillsboro⊙ 1,508 .... L6
†63101 Hillsdale 2,247 .... R2
63852 Holcomb 632 .... N10
64040 Holden 2,195 .... E5
63853 Holland 295 .... N10
65672 Hollister 1,439 .... F9
64048 Holt 276 .... D4
65043 Holts Summit 2,540 .... H5
†63879 Homestown 306 .... N10
64461 Hopkins 634 .... C1
63855 Hornersville 704 .... M10
65483 Houston⊙ 2,157 .... J8
65333 Houstonia 327 .... F5
†64152 Houston Lake 280 .... O5
†63869 Howardville 536 .... N9
65674 Humansville 907 .... E7
64752 Hume 315 .... C6
63443 Hunnewell 235 .... J3
†63101 Huntleigh 428 .... O3
65259 Huntsville⊙ 1,657 .... H4
63547 Hurdland 227 .... H2
65486 Iberia 852 .... H6
63754 Illmo 1.368 .... O8

(continued on following page)

Agriculture, Industry and Resources

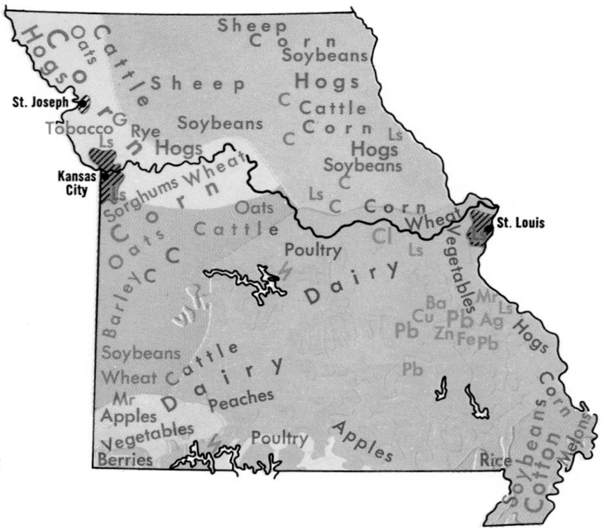

DOMINANT LAND USE

- Cattle Feed, Hogs
- Livestock, Cash Grain, Dairy
- Pasture Livestock
- Specialized Cotton
- General Farming, Dairy, Livestock, Poultry
- General Farming, Livestock, Truck Farming, Cotton
- Fruit and Mixed Farming
- Forests
- Urban Areas

MAJOR MINERAL OCCURRENCES

Ag	Silver	G	Natural Gas
Ba	Barite	Ls	Limestone
C	Coal	Mr	Marble
Cl	Clay	Pb	Lead
Cu	Copper	Zn	Zinc
Fe	Iron Ore		

Water Power — Major Industrial Areas

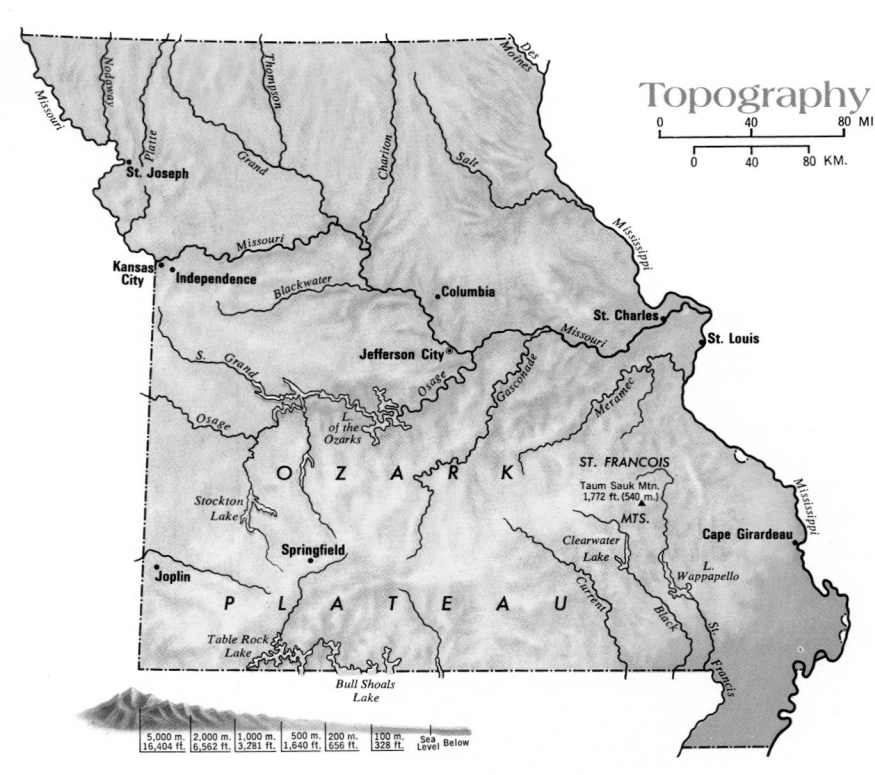

Topography

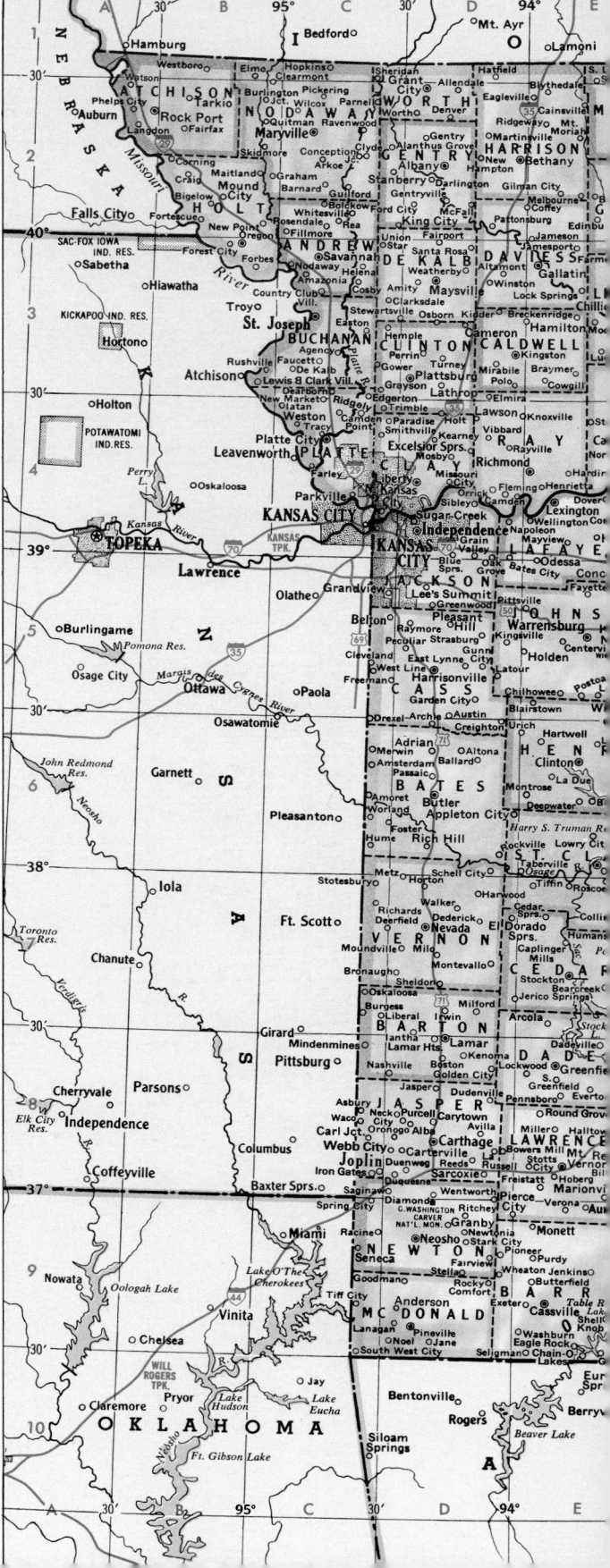

Agriculture, Industry and Resources

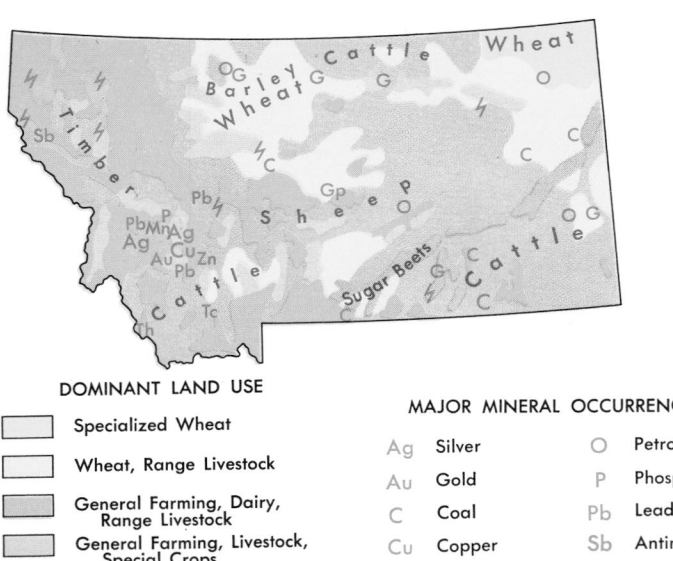

DOMINANT LAND USE

	Specialized Wheat
	Wheat, Range Livestock
	General Farming, Dairy, Range Livestock
	General Farming, Livestock, Special Crops
	Range Livestock
	Sugar Beets, Beans, Livestock, General Farming
	Forests

MAJOR MINERAL OCCURRENCES

Ag	Silver		O	Petroleum
Au	Gold		P	Phosphates
C	Coal		Pb	Lead
Cu	Copper		Sb	Antimony
G	Natural Gas		Tc	Talc
Gp	Gypsum		Th	Thorium
Mn	Manganese		Zn	Zinc

⚡ Water Power

COUNTIES

Beaverhead 8,186 ....C5
Big Horn 11,096 ....J5
Blaine 6,999 ....E4
Broadwater 3,267 ....G5
Carbon 8,099 ....H5
Carter 1,799 ....M5
Cascade 80,696 ....E3
Chouteau 6,092 ....F3
Custer 13,109 ....L4
Daniels 2,835 ....L2
Dawson 11,805 ....M3
Deer Lodge 12,518 ....C5
Fallon 3,763 ....M4
Fergus 13,076 ....G3
Flathead 51,966 ....B2
Gallatin 42,865 ....F5
Garfield 1,656 ....J3
Glacier 10,628 ....C2
Golden Valley 1,026 ....G4
Granite 2,700 ....C4
Hill 17,985 ....F2
Jefferson 7,029 ....D4
Judith Basin 2,646 ....F4
Lake 19,056 ....B3
Lewis and Clark 43,039 ....D2
Liberty 2,329 ....E2
Lincoln 17,752 ....A2
Madison 5,448 ....D5
McCone 2,702 ....L3
Meagher 2,154 ....F4
Mineral 3,675 ....B3
Missoula 76,016 ....C3
Musselshell 4,428 ....H4
Park 12,869 ....F5
Petroleum 655 ....H3
Phillips 5,367 ....J2
Pondera 6,731 ....D2
Powder River 2,520 ....L5
Powell 6,958 ....D4
Prairie 1,836 ....L4
Ravalli 22,493 ....B4
Richland 12,243 ....M3
Roosevelt 10,467 ....L2
Rosebud 9,899 ....K4
Sanders 8,675 ....A3
Sheridan 5,414 ....M2

Silver Bow 38,092 ....D5
Stillwater 5,598 ....G5
Sweet Grass 3,216 ....G5
Teton 6,491 ....D3
Toole 5,559 ....E2
Treasure 981 ....J4
Valley 10,250 ....K2
Wheatland 2,359 ....G4
Wibaux 1,476 ....M4
Yellowstone 108,035 ....H4
Yellowstone Nat'l Park 275 ...F6

CITIES and TOWNS

Zip — Name/Pop. — Key

59001 Absarokee 830 ....G5
59820 Alberton 368 ....B3
59710 Alder 120 ....D5
†59741 Amsterdam 130 ....E5
59711 Anaconda-Deer Lodge
      County⊙ 12,518 ....C4
59312 Angela 50 ....K4
59211 Antelope 83 ....M2
59821 Arlee 200 ....B3
59003 Ashland 600 ....K5
59410 Augusta 497 ....D3
59713 Avon 125 ....D4
59411 Babb 150 ....C2
59212 Bainville 245 ....M2
59313 Baker⊙ 2,354 ....M4
59006 Ballantine 380 ....J5
†59725 Bannack 2 ....C5
59613 Basin 350 ....D4
59008 Belfry 300 ....H5
59714 Belgrade 2,336 ....E5
59412 Belt 825 ....E3
59911 Bigfork 1,080 ....C2
59520 Big Sandy 835 ....G2
59910 Big Arm 250 ....B3
59011 Big Timber⊙ 1,690 ....G5
*59101 Billings⊙ 66,842 ....H5
      Billings‡ 108,035 .....H5
59012 Birney 100 ....K5
59414 Black Eagle 1,500 ....E3

59415 Blackfoot 100 ....D2
59823 Bonner-West
      Riverside 1,742 ......C4
59632 Boulder⊙ 1,441 ....E4
59521 Box Elder 300 ....F2
59715 Bozeman⊙ 21,645 .....E5
59416 Brady 450 ....E3
59014 Bridger 724 ....H5
59317 Broadus⊙ 712 ....L5
59015 Broadview 120 ....H4
59213 Brockton 374 ....M2
59417 Browning 1,226 ....C2
59016 Busby 700 ....J5
59701 Butte-Silver Bow
      County⊙ 37,205 ......D5
59720 Cameron 150 ....E5
59633 Canyon Creek 100 .....D4
†59347 Cartersville 115 .....K4
59421 Cascade 773 ....E3
59824 Charlo 250 ....B3
59522 Chester⊙ 963 ....E2
59523 Chinook⊙ 1,660 ....G2
59422 Choteau⊙ 1,798 ....D3
59215 Circle⊙ 931 ....L3
59634 Clancy 550 ....E4
59018 Clyde Park 283 ....F5
†59351 Coalwood 2 ....L5
59322 Cohagen 12 ....K3
59323 Colstrip 1,476 ....K5
59912 Columbia Falls 3,112 ..B2
59019 Columbus⊙ 1,439 ......G5
59826 Condon 300 ....C3
59827 Conner 420 ....C4
59425 Conrad⊙ 3,074 ....D2
59020 Cooke City 120 ....G5
59913 Coram 450 ....B2
59828 Corvallis 500 ....C4
59217 Crane 163 ....M3
59022 Crow Agency 975 ......J5
59218 Culbertson 887 ....M2
59024 Custer 300 ....J4
59427 Cut Bank⊙ 3,688 ......D2
59829 Darby 581 ....B3
59914 Dayton 140 ....B3
59830 De Borgia 300 ....A3
59025 Decker 150 ....K5
59722 Deer Lodge⊙ 4,023 ....D4
59430 Denton 356 ....G3

Montana

SCALE

0 5 10   20   40   60 MI.

0 5 10 20   40   60 KM.

State Capitals ....⊛
County Seats ....⊙
Major Limited Access Hwys.

Scale 1:3,450,000

© Copyright HAMMOND INCORPORATED, Maplewood, N.J.

Topography

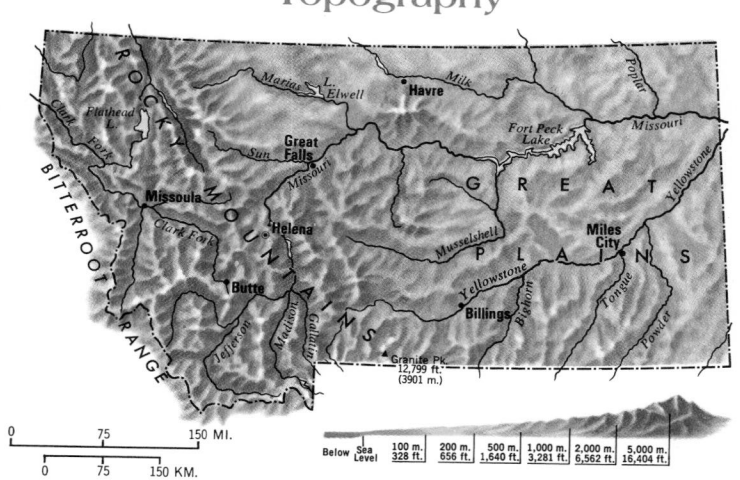

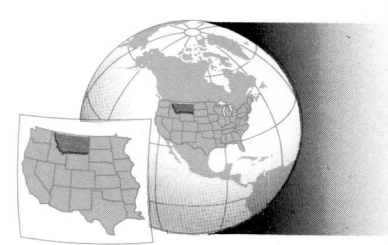

AREA 147,046 sq. mi. (380,849 sq. km.)
POPULATION 786,690
CAPITAL Helena
LARGEST CITY Billings
HIGHEST POINT Granite Pk. 12,799 ft. (3901 m.)
SETTLED IN 1809
ADMITTED TO UNION November 8, 1889
POPULAR NAME Treasure State; Big Sky Country
STATE FLOWER Bitterroot
STATE BIRD Western Meadowlark

59725 Dillon⊙ 3,976	D5	
59727 Divide 275	D5	
59831 Dixon 550	B3	
59524 Dodson 158	H2	
59832 Drummond 414	D4	
59432 Dupuyer 105	D2	
59433 Dutton 359	E3	
59434 East Glacier Park 475	C2	
59635 East Helena 1,647	E4	
59026 Edgar 220	H5	
59324 Ekalaka⊙ 620	M5	
59728 Elliston 250	D4	
59915 Elmo 250	B3	
59729 Ennis 660	E5	
59917 Eureka 1,119	B2	
59436 Fairfield 650	D3	
59221 Fairview 1,366	M3	
59326 Fallon 225	L4	
59222 Flaxville 142	L2	
59833 Florence 700	B4	
59441 Forestgrove 100	H3	
59327 Forsyth⊙ 2,553	K4	

†59526 Fort Belknap 185	H2
59442 Fort Benton⊙ 1,693	F3
59918 Fortine 250	A2
59223 Fort Peck 456	K2
59443 Fort Shaw 200	E3
†59075 Fort Smith 300	J5
59225 Frazer 200	K2
59834 Frenchtown 300	B3
59226 Froid 323	M2
59029 Fromberg 469	H5
59444 Galata 100	E2
59730 Gallatin Gateway 600	E5
59030 Gardiner 600	F5
59731 Garrison 300	D4
59031 Garryowen 200	J5
59446 Geraldine 305	F3
59447 Geyser 125	F3
59525 Gildford 250	F2
59230 Glasgow⊙ 4,455	K2
59330 Glendive⊙ 5,978	M3
59733 Goldcreek 100	D4
59835 Grantsdale 500	B4
59032 Grass Range 139	H3
59401 Great Falls⊙ 56,725	E3
Great Falls‡ 80,696	E3
59836 Greenough 120	C4
59837 Hall 130	C4
59840 Hamilton⊙ 2,661	B4
59034 Hardin⊙ 3,300	J5
59526 Harlem 1,023	H2
59036 Harlowton⊙ 1,181	F4
59735 Harrison 94	E5
59842 Haugan 90	A3
59501 Havre⊙ 10,891	G2
59527 Hays 400	H2
59448 Heart Butte 300	C2
59601 Helena (cap.)⊙ 23,938	E4
59843 Helmville 250	C4
59450 Highwood 150	F3
59528 Hingham 186	F2
59241 Hinsdale 260	K2
59452 Hobson 261	G4
59845 Hot Springs 601	B3
59919 Hungry Horse 700	C2
59037 Huntley 250	H5
59846 Huson 97	B3
59038 Hysham⊙ 449	J4
59530 Inverness 150	F2
59336 Ismay 31	M4
59736 Jackson 210	C5
59638 Jefferson City 162	E4
59041 Joliet 580	G5
59531 Joplin 300	F2
59337 Jordan⊙ 485	J3
59453 Judith Gap 213	G4
59901 Kalispell⊙ 10,648	B2
59454 Kevin 208	D2
59920 Kila 350	B2
59338 Kinsey 100	L4
†59072 Klein 250	H4
59532 Kremlin 304	F2
59922 Lakeside 663	B2
59243 Lambert 203	M3
59043 Lame Deer 460	K5
59044 Laurel 5,481	H5
59046 Lavina 164	H4
59457 Lewistown⊙ 7,104	G3
59923 Libby⊙ 2,748	A2
59739 Lima 200	D6
59639 Lincoln 473	D4
59047 Livingston⊙ 6,994	F5
59050 Lodge Grass 771	J5
†59524 Lodge Pole 292	H2
59847 Lolo 2,418	B4
†59847 Lolo Hot Springs 25	B4
59460 Loma 200	F3
59225 Lustre 25	K2
59538 Malta⊙ 2,367	J2
59741 Manhattan 988	E5
59925 Marion 450	B2
59052 McLeod 150	G5
59247 Medicine Lake 408	M2
59743 Melrose 350	D5
59054 Melstone 238	H4
59055 Melville 100	F4
59301 Miles City⊙ 9,602	L4
59851 Milltown 300	C4
*59801 Missoula⊙ 33,388	C4
59463 Monarch 120	F3

59464 Moore 229	G4
59059 Musselshell 117	H4
59248 Nashua 495	K2
59465 Neihart 91	F4
†59501 North Havre 1,230	G2
59853 Noxon 800	A3
59927 Olney 100	B2
59250 Opheim 210	K2
59252 Outlook 122	M2
59854 Ovando 300	C3
59855 Pablo 500	B3
59856 Paradise 400	B3
59063 Park City 800	H5
59253 Peerless 110	L2
59467 Pendroy 100	D2
59858 Philipsburg⊙ 1,138	C4
59859 Plains 1,116	B3
59254 Plentywood⊙ 2,476	M2
59344 Plevna 191	M4
59860 Polson⊙ 2,798	B3
59064 Pompeys Pillar 300	J5
59747 Pony 130	E5
59255 Poplar 995	L2
59468 Power 159	E3
59929 Proctor 150	B2
59066 Pryor 146	H5
59641 Radersburg 104	E4
59863 Ravalli 150	B3
59068 Red Lodge⊙ 1,896	G5
59069 Reedpoint 160	G5
59258 Reserve 80	M2
59930 Rexford 250	A2
59259 Richey 417	L3
59642 Ringling 102	F4
59070 Roberts 312	G5
59931 Rollins 200	B3
59864 Ronan 1,530	C3
59347 Rosebud 259	K4
59072 Roundup⊙ 2,119	H4
59471 Roy 200	H3
59540 Rudyard 450	F2
59074 Ryegate⊙ 273	G4
59261 Saco 252	J2
59865 Saint Ignatius 877	C3
59866 Saint Regis 500	A3
59075 Saint Xavier 200	J5
59867 Saltese 90	A3
59472 Sand Coulee 600	E3
59473 Santa Rita 120	D2
59262 Savage 300	M3
59263 Scobey⊙ 1,382	L2
59868 Seeley Lake 600	C3
59474 Shelby⊙ 3,142	E2
59079 Shepherd 200	H5
59749 Sheridan 646	D5
59270 Sidney⊙ 5,726	M3
59751 Silver Star 125	D5
59477 Simms 200	E3
59932 Somers 700	B2
59479 Stanford⊙ 595	F3
59870 Stevensville 1,207	C4
59480 Stockett 500	E3
59933 Stryker 96	B2
59871 Sula 200	B4
59482 Sunburst 476	E2
59483 Sun River 300	E3
59872 Superior⊙ 1,054	B3
59911 Swan Lake 100	C3
59484 Sweetgrass 250	E2
59349 Terry⊙ 929	L4
59873 Thompson Falls 1,478	A3
59752 Three Forks 1,247	E5
59644 Townsend⊙ 1,587	E4
59874 Trout Creek 300	A3
59935 Troy 1,088	A2
59542 Turner 150	H4
59754 Twin Bridges 437	D5
59085 Twodot 285	F4
59485 Ulm 450	E3
59486 Valier 640	D2
59487 Vaughn 2,270	E3
59875 Victor 700	B4
59755 Virginia City⊙ 192	E5
59351 Volborg 125	L5
59701 Walkerville 887	D4
59756 Warmsprings 500	D4
59275 Westby 291	M2
59936 West Glacier 150	C2
59758 West Yellowstone 735	E6

59937 Whitefish 3,703	B2
59759 Whitehall 1,030	D5
59645 White Sulphur Springs⊙ 1,302	E4
59276 Whitetail 150	L2
59544 Whitewater 100	J2
59353 Wibaux⊙ 782	M3
59760 Willow Creek 150	E5
59086 Wilsall 250	F5
59489 Winifred 155	G3
59087 Winnett⊙ 207	H4
59647 Winston 120	E4
59761 Wisdom 140	C5
59762 Wise River 150	C5
59648 Wolf Creek 500	D3
59201 Wolf Point⊙ 3,074	L2
59088 Worden 600	H5
59089 Wyola 350	J5

OTHER FEATURES

Absaroka (range)	F5
Allen (mt.)	C2
Arrow (creek)	F3
Ashley (lake)	B2
Battle (creek)	G1
Bearhat (mt.)	C2
Bearpaw (mts.)	G2
Beartooth (mts.)	G5
Beaver (creek)	J2
Beaverhead (riv.)	D5
Benton (lake)	E3
Big (lake)	G5
Big Belt (mts.)	E4
Big Dry (creek)	K3
Big Hole (riv.)	C5
Big Hole Nat'l Battlefield	C5
Bighorn (lake)	H5
Bighorn (riv.)	J5
Bighorn Canyon Nat'l Rec. Area	H5
Big Muddy (riv.)	M2
Big Porcupine (creek)	J4
Birch (creek)	D2
Birch Creek (res.)	D2
Bitterroot (range)	B4
Bitterroot (riv.)	B4
Blackfeet Ind. Res.	D2
Blackfoot (riv.)	C4
Blackmore (mt.)	F5
Bowdoin (lake)	J2
Boxelder (creek)	H3
Boxelder (creek)	M5
Bynum (res.)	D2
Cabinet (mts.)	A2
Canyon Ferry (lake)	E4
Clark Canyon (res.)	D6
Clark Fork (riv.)	A3
Clarks Fork, Yellowstone (riv.)	G6
Cottonwood (creek)	E2
Cow (creek)	G3
Crazy (peak)	F4
Crow Ind. Res.	H5
Custer Battlefield Nat'l Mon.	J5
Cut Bank (creek)	D2
Douglas (mt.)	F5
Earthquake (lake)	E6
Electric (peak)	F6
Elwell (lake)	E2
Emigrant (peak)	F5
Ennis (lake)	E5
Flathead (lake)	B2
Flathead (riv.)	B2
Flathead, North Fork (riv.)	B2
Flathead, South Fork (riv.)	C3
Flathead Ind. Res.	B3
Flatwillow (creek)	H4
Fort Belknap Ind. Res.	H2
Fort Peck (lake)	K3
Fort Union Trading Post Nat'l Hist. Site	N2
Frances (lake)	D2
Freezeout (lake)	D3
Frenchman (riv.)	J1
Fresno (res.)	F2
Gallatin (peak)	E5
Gallatin (riv.)	E5
Georgetown (lake)	C4
Gibson (res.)	D3
Glacier Nat'l Park	C2

Granite (peak)	F5
Grant-Kohrs Ranch Nat'l Hist. Site	D4
Hauser (lake)	E4
Haystack (peak)	A3
Hebgen (lake)	E6
Helena (lake)	E4
Holter (lake)	D4
Hungry Horse (res.)	C2
Hurricane (mt.)	D2
Hyalite (peak)	E5
Jackson (mt.)	C2
Jefferson (riv.)	D5
Judith (riv.)	G3
Koocanusa (lake)	A2
Kootenai (riv.)	A2
Lemhi (pass)	C6
Lewis (range)	C2
Lima (res.)	D6
Little Bighorn (riv.)	J5
Little Bitterroot (lake)	B2
Little Dry (creek)	K3
Little Missouri (riv.)	M5
Lockhart (mt.)	D3
Lodge (creek)	G1
Lolo (pass)	B4
Lone (mt.)	E5
Lost Trail (pass)	B5
Lower Red Rock (lake)	E6
Lower Saint Mary (lake)	C2
Madison (riv.)	E5
Malmstrom A.F.B. 6,675	E3
Marias (riv.)	D2
Martinsdale (res.)	F4
Mary Ronan (lake)	B3
McDonald (lake)	B2
McGloughlin (peak)	C4
McGregor (lake)	B3
Medicine (lake)	M2
Milk (riv.)	J2
Mission (range)	C3
Missouri (riv.)	L3
Musselshell (riv.)	J3
Nelson (res.)	J2
Ninepipe (res.)	C3
Northern Cheyenne Indian Reservation	K5
O'Fallon (creek)	L4
Pishkun (res.)	D3
Poplar (riv.)	L2
Porcupine (creek)	K2
Powder (riv.)	L4
Purcell (mts.)	A2
Railley (mt.)	F2
Red Rock (lkes)	E6
Red Rock (riv.)	D6
Redwater (riv.)	L3
Rock (creek)	C4
Rocky (mts.)	D4
Rocky Boy's Ind. Res.	G2
Rosebud (creek)	K4
Ruby (riv.)	D5
Ruby River (res.)	D5
Sage (creek)	F2
Saint Mary (lake)	C2
Saint Mary (riv.)	C1
Sandy (creek)	F2
Sheep (mt.)	F4
Shields (riv.)	F4
Siyeh (mt.)	C2
Smith (riv.)	E3
Sphinx (mt.)	E5
Stillwater (riv.)	G5
Stimson (mt.)	C2
Sun (riv.)	D3
Swan (lake)	C3
Teton (riv.)	D3
Tongue (riv.)	K5
Upper Red Rock (lake)	E6
Ward (peak)	A3
Waterton-Glacier Int'l Peace Park	C2
Whitefish (lake)	B2
Willow (creek)	E2
Willow Creek (res.)	D3
Yellowstone (riv.)	M3
Yellowstone National Park	F6

⊙County seat.
‡Population of metropolitan area.
† Zip of nearest p.o.   * Multiple zips.

264

COUNTIES

Adams 30,656		F4
Antelope 8,675		F2
Arthur 513		C3
Banner 918		A3
Blaine 867		E3
Boone 7,391		F3
Box Butte 13,696		A2
Boyd 3,331		F2
Brown 4,377		E2
Buffalo 34,797		E4
Burt 8,813		H3
Butler 9,330		G3
Cass 20,297		H4
Cedar 11,375		G2
Chase 4,758		C4
Cherry 6,758		C2
Cheyenne 10,057		A3
Clay 8,106		F4
Colfax 9,890		G3
Cuming 11,664		H3
Custer 13,877		E3
Dakota 16,573		H2
Dawes 9,609		A2
Dawson 22,304		E4
Deuel 2,462		B3
Dixon 7,137		H2
Dodge 35,847		H3
Douglas 397,038		H3
Dundy 2,861		C4
Fillmore 7,920		G4
Franklin 4,377		F4
Frontier 3,647		D4
Furnas 6,486		E4
Gage 24,456		H4
Garden 2,802		B3
Garfield 2,363		F3
Gosper 2,140		E4
Grant 877		C3
Greeley 3,462		F3
Hall 47,690		F4
Hamilton 9,301		F4
Harlan 4,292		E4
Hayes 1,356		C4
Hitchcock 4,079		C4
Holt 13,552		F2
Hooker 990		C3
Howard 6,773		F3
Jefferson 9,817		G4
Johnson 5,285		H4
Kearney 7,053		F4
Keith 9,364		C3
Keya Paha 1,301		E2
Kimball 4,882		A3
Knox 11,457		G2
Lancaster 192,884		H4
Lincoln 36,455		D4
Logan 983		D3
Loup 859		E3
Madison 31,382		G3
McPherson 593		C3
Merrick 8,945		F3
Morrill 6,085		A3
Nance 4,740		F3
Nemaha 8,367		J4
Nuckolls 6,726		F4
Otoe 15,183		H4
Pawnee 3,937		H4
Perkins 3,637		C4
Phelps 9,769		E4
Pierce 8,481		G2
Platte 28,852		G3
Polk 6,320		G3
Red Willow 12,615		D4
Richardson 11,315		J4
Rock 2,383		E2
Saline 13,131		G4
Sarpy 86,015		H3
Saunders 18,716		H3
Scotts Bluff 38,344		A3
Seward 15,789		G4
Sheridan 7,544		B2
Sherman 4,226		F3
Sioux 1,845		A2
Stanton 6,549		G3
Thayer 7,582		G4
Thomas 973		D3
Thurston 7,186		H2
Valley 5,633		E3
Washington 15,508		H3
Wayne 9,858		G2
Webster 4,858		F4
Wheeler 1,060		F3
York 14,798		G4

CITIES and TOWNS

Zip	Name/Pop.	Key
68301	Adams 395	H4
69210	Ainsworth⊙ 2,256	D2
68620	Albion⊙ 1,997	F3
68810	Alda 601	F4
68710	Allen 390	H2
69301	Alliance⊙ 9,920	A2
68920	Alma⊙ 1,369	E4
68304	Alvo 144	H4
68812	Amherst 269	E4
68814	Ansley 644	E3
68922	Arapahoe 1,107	E4
68815	Arcadia 412	F3
68002	Arlington 1,117	H3
69120	Arnold 813	D3
69121	Arthur⊙ 124	C3
68003	Ashland 2,274	H3
68713	Atkinson 1,521	F2
68305	Auburn⊙ 3,482	J4
68818	Aurora⊙ 3,717	F4
68924	Axtell 602	E4
68004	Bancroft 552	H2
68622	Bartlett⊙ 144	F3
69020	Bartley 342	D4
68714	Bassett⊙ 1,009	E2
68715	Battle Creek 948	G3
68310	Beatrice⊙ 12,891	H4
68926	Beaver City⊙ 775	E4
68313	Beaver Crossing 458	G4
68716	Beemer 853	H3
68005	Bellevue 21,813	J3
68624	Bellwood 407	G3
69021	Benkelman⊙ 1,235	C4
68317	Bennet 523	H4
68007	Bennington 631	H3
68927	Bertrand 775	E4
69122	Big Springs 505	B3
68928	Bladen 298	F4
68008	Blair⊙ 6,418	H3
68718	Bloomfield 1,393	G2
68930	Blue Hill 883	F4
68318	Blue Springs 521	H4
68010	Boys Town 622	H3
68319	Bradshaw 373	G4
69123	Brady 377	D3
68821	Brewster⊙ 46	E3
69336	Bridgeport⊙ 1,668	A3
68822	Broken Bow⊙ 3,979	E3
69127	Brule 438	C3
68823	Bruning 330	G4
68823	Brunswell⊙ 1,383	E3
68722	Butte⊙ 529	F2
68824	Cairo 737	F3
68825	Callaway 579	D3
69022	Cambridge 1,206	D4
68932	Campbell 441	F4
68015	Cedar Bluffs 632	H3
68016	Cedar Creek 311	H3
68627	Cedar Rapids 447	F3
68724	Center⊙ 123	G2
68826	Central City⊙ 3,083	F3
68017	Ceresco 836	H3
69337	Chadron⊙ 5,933	B2
68725	Chambers 390	F2
68827	Chapman 349	F3
68327	Chester 435	G4
68628	Clarks 445	G3
68629	Clarkson 817	G3
68328	Clatonia 273	H4
68933	Clay Center⊙ 962	F4
68726	Clearwater 409	F2
†69343	Clinton 80	B2
68727	Coleridge 673	G2
68601	Columbus⊙ 17,328	G3
68329	Cook 341	H4
68331	Cortland 403	H4
68730	Crofton 948	G2
69024	Culbertson 767	C4
69025	Curtis 1,014	D4
68731	Dakota City⊙ 1,440	H2
69131	Dalton 345	B3
68831	Dannebrog 356	F3
68335	Davenport 445	G4
68632	David City⊙ 2,514	G3
68020	Decatur 723	H3
68340	Deshler 997	G4
68341	De Witt 642	H4
68342	Diller 311	H4
69133	Dix 275	A3
68633	Dodge 815	H3
68832	Doniphan 696	F4
68343	Dorchester 611	G4
68634	Duncan 410	G3
68347	Eagle 832	H4
68935	Edgar 705	F4
68636	Elgin 807	F3
68022	Elkhorn 1,344	H3
68836	Elm Creek 862	E4
68349	Elmwood 598	H4
68937	Elwood⊙ 716	E4
68733	Emerson 874	H2
68350	Endicott 198	G4
69028	Eustis 460	D4
68735	Ewing 520	F2
68351	Exeter 807	G4
68352	Fairbury⊙ 4,885	G4
68938	Fairfield 543	F4
68354	Fairmont 767	G4
68355	Falls City⊙ 5,374	J4
69029	Farnam 268	D4
68358	Firth 384	H4
68023	Fort Calhoun 641	J3
68839	Franklin⊙ 1,167	E4
68025	Fremont⊙ 23,979	H3
68359	Friend 1,079	G4
68638	Fullerton⊙ 1,506	F3
68361	Geneva⊙ 2,400	G4
68640	Genoa 1,090	G3
69341	Gering⊙ 7,760	A3
68840	Gibbon 1,531	F4
68841	Giltner 400	F4
68941	Glenvil 363	F4
69343	Gordon 2,167	B2
69138	Gothenburg 3,479	D4
68801	Grand Island⊙ 33,180	F4
69140	Grant⊙ 1,270	C4
68842	Greeley⊙ 597	F3
68366	Greenwood 587	H3
68367	Gresham 320	G3
68028	Gretna 1,609	H3
68942	Guide Rock 344	F4
68738	Hadar 286	G2
68368	Hallam 290	H4
68843	Hampton 419	G4
69346	Harrison⊙ 361	A2
68739	Hartington⊙ 1,730	G2
68944	Harvard 1,217	F4
68901	Hastings⊙ 23,045	F4
69032	Hayes Center⊙ 231	C4
69347	Hay Springs 794	B2
68370	Hebron⊙ 1,906	G4
69348	Hemingford 1,023	A2
68371	Henderson 1,072	G4
68029	Herman 340	H3
69143	Hershey 633	D3
68372	Hickman 687	H4
68947	Hildreth 394	E4
68948	Holbrook 297	D4
68601	Holdrege⊙ 5,624	E4
68030	Homer 564	H2
68031	Hooper 932	H3
68740	Hoskins 306	G2
68641	Howells 677	H3
68376	Humboldt 1,176	J4
68642	Humphrey 799	G3
69350	Hyannis⊙ 336	C3
69033	Imperial⊙ 1,941	C4
69034	Indianola 856	D4
68743	Jackson 287	H2
68378	Johnson 341	J4
68955	Juniata 703	F4
68847	Kearney⊙ 21,158	E4
68956	Kenesaw 854	F4
68034	Kennard 372	H3
69145	Kimball⊙ 3,120	A3
68045	Oakland 1,393	H3
68415	Odell 322	H4
69153	Ogallala⊙ 5,638	C3
68763	O'Neill⊙ 4,049	F2
68764	Orchard 482	F2
68862	Ord⊙ 2,658	F3
68966	Orleans 527	E4
68651	Osceola⊙ 975	G3
68765	Osmond 871	G2
68863	Overton 633	E4
68967	Oxford 1,109	E4
69040	Palisade 401	C4
68046	Papillion⊙ 6,399	J3
68420	Pawnee City⊙ 1,156	H4
69155	Paxton 568	C3
68047	Pender⊙ 1,318	H2
68421	Peru 998	J4
68652	Petersburg 381	F3
68865	Phillips 405	F4
68767	Pierce⊙ 1,535	G2
68768	Pilger 400	G2
68769	Plainview 1,483	G2
68653	Platte Center 367	G3
68048	Plattsmouth⊙ 6,295	J3
68424	Plymouth 506	G4
68654	Polk 440	G3
68770	Ponca⊙ 1,057	H2
68867	Poole	F4
69156	Potter 369	A3
68050	Prague 285	H3
68771	Randolph 1,106	G2
68869	Ravenna 1,296	F3
68970	Red Cloud⊙ 1,300	F4
68658	Rising City 392	G3
69360	Rushville⊙ 1,217	B2
68660	Saint Edward 891	G3
68873	Saint Paul⊙ 2,094	F3
†68760	Santee 388	G2
68874	Sargent 828	E3
68661	Schuyler⊙ 4,151	G3
68875	Scotia 349	F3
69361	Scottsbluff 14,156	A3
68057	Scribner 1,011	H3
68434	Seward⊙ 5,713	H4
68662	Shelby 724	G3
68876	Shelton 1,046	E4
68436	Shickley 413	G4
69162	Sidney⊙ 6,010	B3
68663	Silver Creek 496	G3
68664	Snyder 387	H3
68776	South Sioux City 9,339	H2
68665	Spalding 645	F3
68777	Spencer 596	F2
68059	Springfield 1,483	J3
68778	Springview⊙ 326	E2
68779	Stanton⊙ 1,603	G3
68439	Staplehurst 306	G4
69163	Stapleton⊙ 340	D3
68442	Stella 289	J4
68443	Sterling 526	H4
69042	Stockville⊙ 45	D4
68436	Stromsburg 1,290	G3
68780	Stuart 641	E2
68978	Superior 2,502	F4
69165	Sutherland 1,238	C3
68979	Sutton 1,416	G4
68446	Syracuse 1,638	H4
68447	Table Rock 393	H4
69038	Maywood 332	D4
69001	McCook⊙ 8,404	D4
68401	McCool Junction 404	G4
68041	Mead 506	H3
68752	Meadow Grove 400	G2
68856	Merna 389	E3
68405	Milford 2,108	H4
68406	Milligan 332	G4
69356	Minatare 969	A3
68959	Minden⊙ 2,939	F4
69357	Mitchell 1,956	A3
68647	Monroe 380	G3
69358	Morrill 1,097	A3
69152	Mullen⊙ 720	C2
68409	Murray 465	J4
68410	Nebraska City⊙ 7,127	J4
68413	Nehawka 270	H4
68756	Neligh⊙ 1,893	G2
68961	Nelson⊙ 733	F4
68757	Newcastle 348	H2
68758	Newman Grove 930	G3
68760	Niobrara 419	G2
68962	Nora 24	F4
68701	Norfolk 19,449	G2
68649	North Bend 1,368	H3
68859	North Loup 405	F3
69101	North Platte⊙ 24,509	D3
68761	Oakdale 410	F2
68501	Lincoln (cap.)⊙ 171,932	H4
	Lincoln† 192,884	H4
68644	Lindsay 383	G3
69149	Lodgepole 413	B3
69217	Long Pine 521	E2
68958	Loomis 441	E4
68037	Louisville 1,022	H3
68853	Loup City⊙ 1,368	E3
69352	Lyman 551	A3
68746	Lynch 357	F2
68038	Lyons 1,214	H3
68748	Madison⊙ 1,950	G3
69150	Madrid 284	C4
68402	Malcolm 355	H4
68854	Marquette 303	G4
69151	Maxwell 410	D3
*68101	Omaha⊙ 313,911	J3
	Omaha† 570,399	J3
†68046	La Vista 9,588	J3
68957	Lawrence 350	F4
68643	Leigh 509	G3
69147	Lewellen 368	B3
*68501	Lexington⊙ 7,040	E4
69035	Lamar 60	C4
68745	Laurel 1,031	G2

Agriculture, Industry and Resources

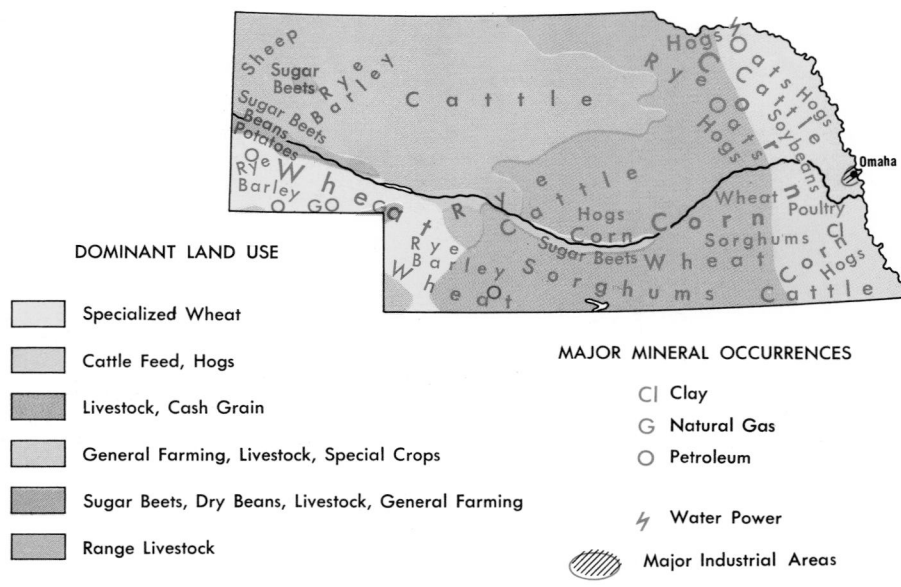

DOMINANT LAND USE

- Specialized Wheat
- Cattle Feed, Hogs
- Livestock, Cash Grain
- General Farming, Livestock, Special Crops
- Sugar Beets, Dry Beans, Livestock, General Farming
- Range Livestock

MAJOR MINERAL OCCURRENCES

- Cl Clay
- G Natural Gas
- O Petroleum
- Water Power
- Major Industrial Areas

Nebraska

SCALE
0 5 10 20 30 40 50 60 MI.
0 5 10 20 30 40 50 60 KM.

State Capitals ⊛
County Seats ⊙
Major Limited Access Hwys.
Scale 1:2,400,000

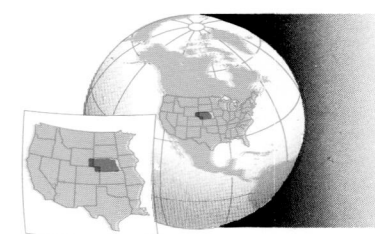

AREA 77,355 sq. mi. (200,349 sq. km.)
POPULATION 1,569,825
CAPITAL Lincoln
LARGEST CITY Omaha
HIGHEST POINT (Kimball Co.) 5,246 ft. (1654 n
SETTLED IN 1847
ADMITTED TO UNION March 1, 1867
POPULAR NAME Cornhusker State
STATE FLOWER Goldenrod
STATE BIRD Western Meadowlark

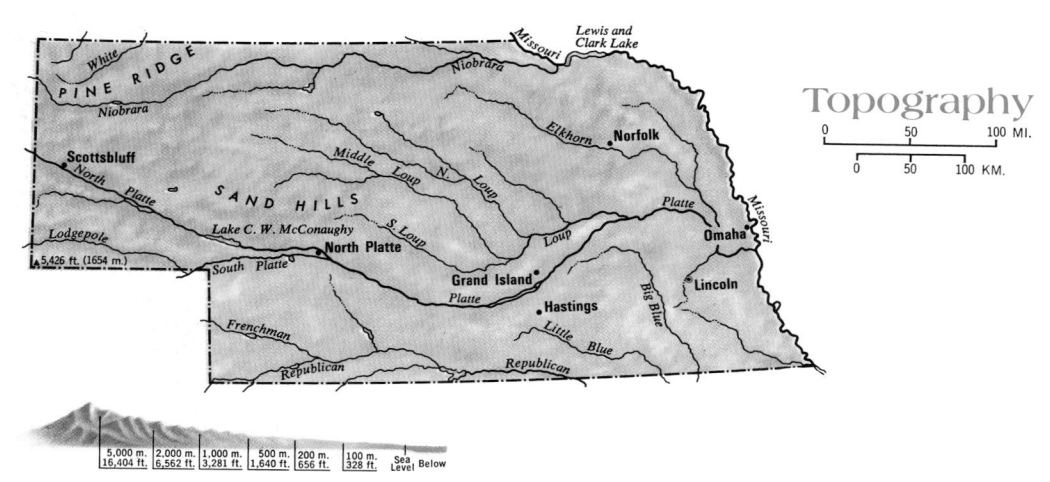

Topography

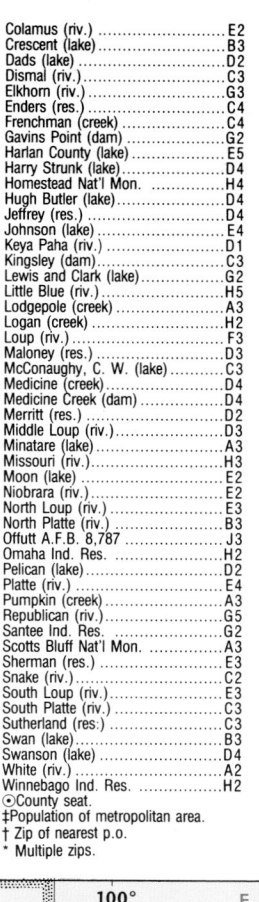

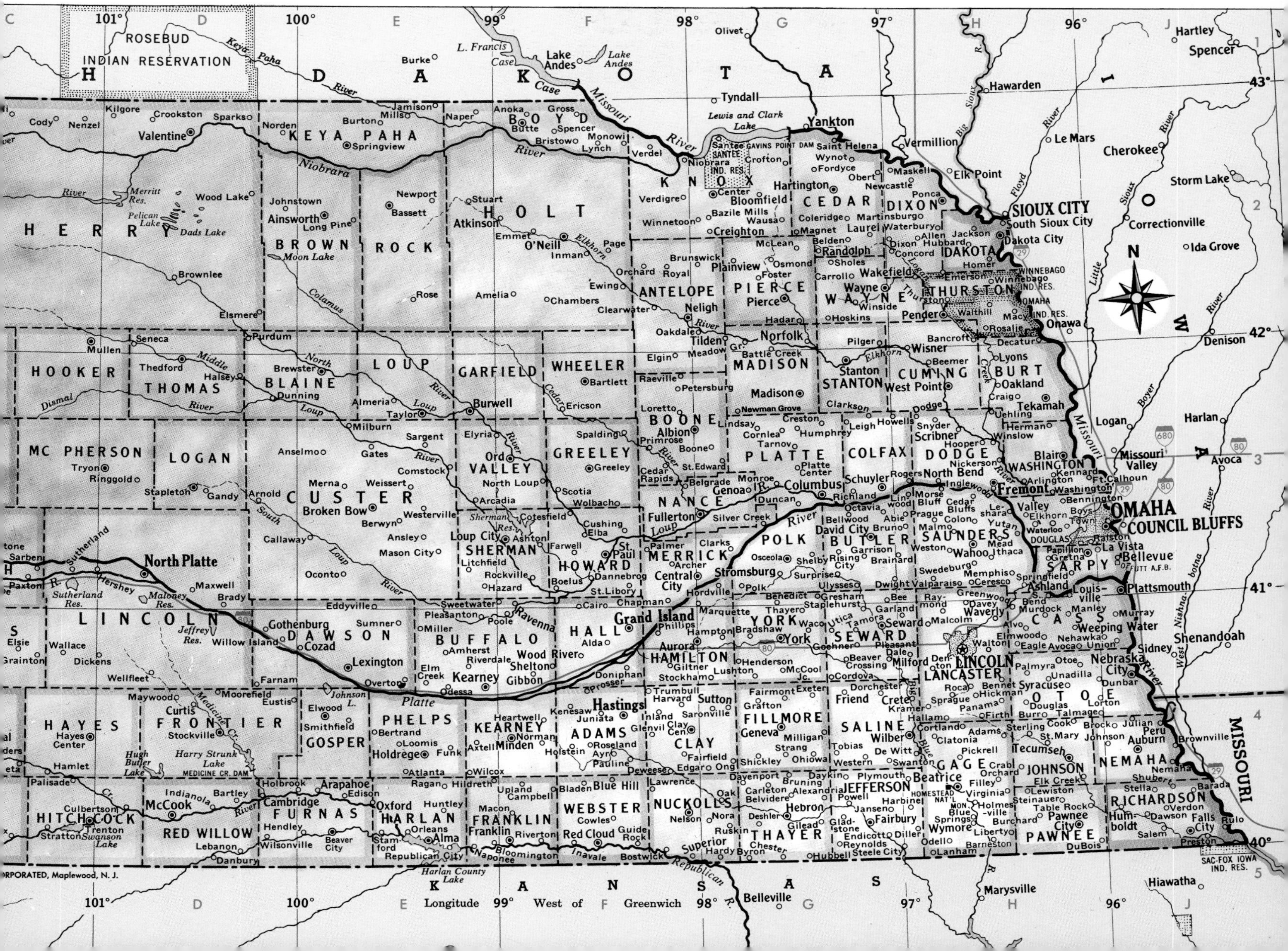

Nevada

SCALE
0 5 10 20 30 40 50 60 MI.
0 5 10 20 30 40 50 60 KM.

State Capitals ⊛
County Seats ◉
Major Limited Access Hwys.

Scale 1:2,740,000

© Copyright HAMMOND INCORPORATED, Maplewood, N.J.

Agriculture, Industry and Resources

AREA 110,561 sq. mi. (286,353 sq. km.)
POPULATION 800,493
CAPITAL Carson City
LARGEST CITY Las Vegas
HIGHEST POINT Boundary Pk. 13,143 ft.
(4006 m.)
SETTLED IN 1850
ADMITTED TO UNION October 31, 1864
POPULAR NAME Silver State; Sagebrush
State
STATE FLOWER Sagebrush
STATE BIRD Mountain Bluebird

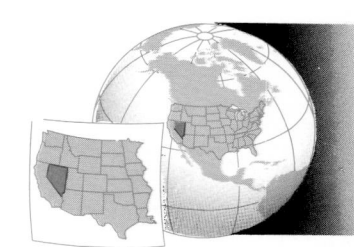

MAJOR MINERAL OCCURRENCES

Ag Silver
Au Gold
Ba Barite
Cu Copper
Gp Gypsum
Hg Mercury
Lt Lithium
Mg Magnesium
Mo Molybdenum
Na Salt
O Petroleum
Pb Lead
S Sulfur
W Tungsten
Zn Zinc

⚡ Water Power

DOMINANT LAND USE

General Farming, Dairy, Livestock
General Farming, Livestock, Special Crops
Range Livestock
Forests
Nonagricultural Land

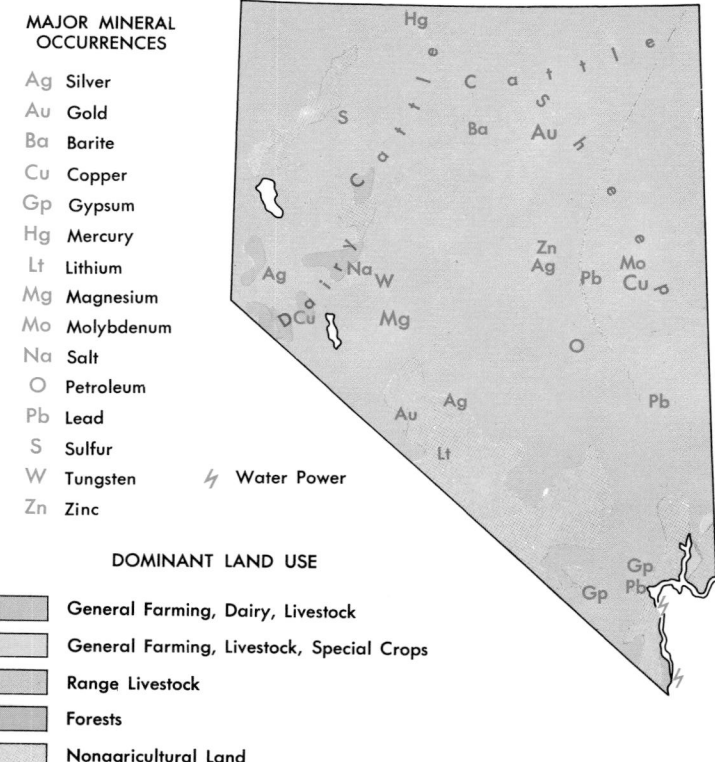

Topography

0   60   120 MI.
0   60   120 KM.

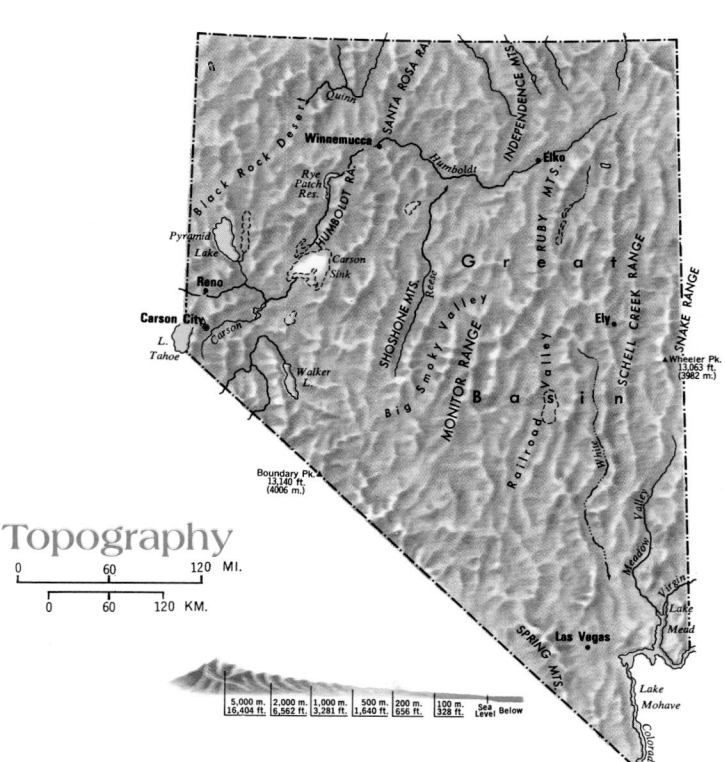

COUNTIES

Carson City (city) 32,022......B 3
Churchill 13,917..............C 3
Clark 463,087................F 6
Douglas 19,421..............B 4
Elko 17,269.................F 1
Esmeralda 777..............D 5
Eureka 1,198...............E 3
Humboldt 9,434.............C 1
Lander 4,076...............D 3
Lincoln 3,732..............F 5
Lyon 13,594................B 3
Mineral 6,217..............C 4
Nye 9,048..................E 4
Pershing 3,40R.............C 2
Storey 1,503...............B 3
Washoe 193,623.............B 2
White Pine 8,167...........F 3

CITIES and TOWNS

Zip	Name/Pop.	Key
89001	Alamo 300	F5
89310	Austin 300	E3
89416	Babbitt	C4
89311	Baker 140	G3
89820	Battle Mountain⊙ 2,749	E2
89003	Beatty 600	E6
89821	Beowawe 77	E2
†89508	Black Springs 180	B3
89005	Boulder City 9,590	G7
89007	Bunkerville 300	G6
89008	Caliente 982	G5
89822	Carlin 1,232	E2
†89008	Carp 30	G5
89701	Carson City (cap.) 32,022	B3
†89043	Caselton	G5
†99301	Cherry Creek 80	G3
89402	Crystal Bay 6,225	A3
89403	Dayton 350	B3
89823	Deeth 125	F1
89404	Denio 35	C1
89314	Duckwater 80	F4
89010	Dyer 56	C5
89315	East Ely	G3
89112	East Las Vegas 6,449	F6
89801	Elko⊙ 8,758	F2
89301	Ely⊙ 4,882	G3
89316	Eureka⊙ 300	E3
89406	Fallon⊙ 4,262	C3
89408	Fernley 750	B3
89409	Gabbs 811	D4
89410	Gardnerville 1,610	B4
89411	Genoa 250	B4
89412	Gerlach 400	B2
89413	Glenbrook 800	B3
89014	Golconda 275	D2
89013	Goldfield⊙ 500	D5
89019	Goodsprings 80	F7
89824	Halleck 68	F2
89415	Hawthorne⊙ 3,741	C4
89417	Hazen 76	C3
89015	Henderson 24,363	G6
89017	Hiko 210	F5
†89418	Humboldt 14	C2
89418	Imlay 250	C2
89018	Indian Springs 500	F6
†89310	Ione 20	D4
†89834	Jack Creek	E1
89825	Jackpot 400	G1
89826	Jarbidge 11	F1
89019	Jean 125	F7
89828	Lamoille 100	F2
*89101	Las Vegas⊙ 164,674	F6
	Las Vegas‡ 461,816	F6
89829	Lee 125	F2
89021	Logandale 410	G6
89419	Lovelock⊙ 1,680	C2
89317	Lund 380	F4
89420	Luning 90	C4
89022	Manhattan 93	E4
†89447	Mason 200	B4
89421	McDermitt 240	D1
89318	McGill 1,419	G3
89023	Mercury 900	E6
89024	Mesquite 500	G6
89422	Mina 450	C4
89423	Minden⊙ 1,029	B4
89025	Moapa 275	G6
89830	Montello 100	G1
89831	Mountain City 100	F1
†89046	Nelson 75	G7
89424	Nixon 400	B3
89030	North Las Vegas 42,739	F6
89425	Orovada 200	D1
89040	Overton 1,111	G6
89041	Pahrump 400	E6
89042	Panaca 650	G5
89119	Paradise Valley 84,818	F6
89426	Paradise Valley 115	D1
89043	Pioche⊙ 850	G5
*89501	Reno⊙ 100,756	B3
	Reno‡ 193,623	B3
†89003	Rhyolite (Ghost Town) 8	E6
89045	Round Mountain 400	E4
89833	Ruby Valley 150	F2
89319	Ruth 455	F3
89427	Schurz 800	C4
89046	Searchlight 500	F7
89428	Silver City 150	B3
89047	Silverpeak 100	D5
89430	Smith 200	B4
89431	Sparks 40,780	B3
†89406	Stillwater 150	C3
†89445	Sulphur	C2
†89110	Sunrise Manor 44,155	F6
†89431	Sun Valley 8,822	B3
†89835	Thousand Springs	G1
89049	Tonopah⊙ 1,952	D4
89834	Tuscarora 24	E1
89438	Valmy 200	D2
89121	Vegas Creek	G6
89440	Virginia City⊙ 750	B3
89442	Wadsworth 400	B3
89443	Weed Heights 8	B4
89444	Wellington 505	B4
89835	Wells 1,218	G1
†89109	Winchester 19,728	F6
89445	Winnemucca⊙ 4,140	D2
89447	Yerington⊙ 2,021	B4
89448	Zephyr Cove 1,316	A3

OTHER FEATURES

Alkali (lake)	B1
Antelope (range)	E3
Arc Dome (mt.)	D4
Arrow Canyon (range)	G6
Beaver Creek Fork, Humboldt (riv.)	F1
Belted (range)	E5
Berlin (mt.)	D4
Big (mt.)	B1
Big Smoky (valley)	D4
Bishop (creek)	F1
Black Rock (des.)	B2
Black Rock (range)	B1
Boundary (peak)	C5
Buffalo (creek)	B2
Butte (mts.)	F3
Cactus (range)	E5
Carson (lake)	C3
Carson (riv.)	B3
Carson (sink)	C3
Cedar (mt.)	D4
Charleston (peak)	F6
Clan Alpine (mts.)	D3
Columbus Salt (marsh)	C4
Cortez (mts.)	E2
Crescent (valley)	E2
Davis (dam)	G7
Death Valley Nat'l Mon.	E6
Delamar (mts.)	G5
Desatoya (mts.)	D3
Desert (range)	F6
Desert (valley)	C1
Devil's Hole (Death Valley Nat'l Mon.)	E6
Division (peak)	B1
Duck (creek)	G3
East (range)	D2
East Walker (riv.)	B4
Egan (range)	G4
Ely (range)	G4
Emigrant (peak)	C5
Excelsior (mts.)	C4
Fallon Ind. Res.	C3
Fallon Nav. Air Sta.	C3
Fish Creek (mts.)	D2
Fort McDermitt Ind. Res.	D1
Fort Mohave Ind. Res.	G7
Franklin (lake)	F2
Frenchman Flat (basin)	F6
Gillis (range)	C4
Golden Gate (range)	F5
Goshute (mts.)	G2
Goshute Ind. Res.	G3
Granite (peak)	B2
Granite (range)	B2
Grant (range)	F4
Great Basin Nat'l Pk.	G 4
Great Salt Lake (des.)	H 2
High Rock (creek)	B1
Highland (peak)	G 5
Hoover (dam)	G 7
Hot Creek (range)	E 4
Hot Creek (valley)	E 4
Humboldt (range)	C 2
Humboldt (riv.)	C 2
Humboldt (sink)	C 2
Humboldt Salt (marsh)	D 3
Huntington (creek)	F 2
Independence (mts.)	E 1
Jackson (mts.)	C 1
Job (peak)	C 3
Kawich (range)	E 5
Kelley (creek)	D 1
Kings (riv.)	C 1
Lahontan (res.)	B 3
Lake Mead Nat'l Rec. Area.	G 6
Las Vegas (range)	F 6
Little Humboldt (riv.)	D1
Little Smoky (valley)	E4
Lone (mt.)	D4
Long (valley)	B1
Marys (riv.)	F1
Mason (peak)	F1
Massacre (lake)	B1
Mead (lake)	G6
Meadow Valley Wash (riv.)	G5
Moapa River Ind. Res.	G6
Mohave (lake)	G7
Monitor (range)	E4
Monte Cristo (range)	D4
Mormon (mts.)	G5
Muddy (mts.)	G6
Nellis A.F.B. 7,476	F6
Nellis Air Force Range and Nuclear Testing Site	E5
Nelson (creek)	G2
New Pass (range)	D3
Nightingale (mts.)	B2
Owyhee (riv.)	E1
Pahranagat (range)	F5
Pahrock (range)	F5
Pah-rum (peak)	B2
Pahrump (valley)	F6
Pahute (mesa)	E5
Pancake (range)	F4
Pequop (mts.)	G2
Pilot (peak)	C4
Pine (creek)	E2
Pine Forest (range)	C1
Pintwater (range)	F6
Piper (peak)	D5
Potosi (mt.)	F7
Pyramid (lake)	B2
Pyramid Lake Ind. Res.	B2
Quinn (riv.)	D1
Quinn Canyon (range)	F4
Railroad (valley)	F4
Reese (riv.)	D3
Reveille (peak)	E5
Reveille (range)	E4
Ruby (lake)	F2
Ruby (mts.)	F3
Rye Patch (res.)	C2
Sand Springs (salt flat)	C3
Santa Rosa (range)	D1
Schell Creek (range)	G3
Sheep (range)	F6
Shoshone (mts.)	E6
Shoshone (mts.)	D3
Shoshone (range)	D2
Silver Peak (range)	D5
Simpson Park (mts.)	E3
Smith Creek (valley)	D3
Smoke Creek (des.)	B2
Snake (mts.)	F1
Snake (range)	G3
Snow Water (lake)	G2
Sonoma (range)	D2
Specter (range)	E6
Spotted (range)	F6
Spring (creek)	G2
Spring (mts.)	F6
Spring (valley)	G3
Stillwater (range)	C3
Sulphur Spring (range)	E3
Summit (lake)	C1
Summit Lake Ind. Res.	B1
Table (mt.)	E3
Tahoe (lake)	B3
Thousand Spring (creek)	G1
Timber (mt.)	F4
Timber (mt.)	E5
Timpahute (range)	F5
Toana (range)	G2
Toiyabe (range)	D3
Topaz (lake)	B4
Toquima (range)	E4
Trident (peak)	C1
Trinity (range)	C2
Truckee (riv.)	B3
Tule (des.)	G5
Tuscarora (mts.)	E1
Virgin (mts.)	G6
Virgin (peak)	G6
Virgin (riv.)	G6
Virginia (range)	B3
Walker (lake)	C4
Walker (riv.)	C3
Walker River Ind. Res.	C3
Washoe (lake)	B3
Wassuk (range)	C4
Western Shoshone Ind. Res.	E1
Wheeler (peak)	G4
White (riv.)	F4
White Pine (range)	F3
Wild Horse (res.)	E1
Winnemucca (lake)	B2
Winnemucca Ind. Res.	D2
Yerington Ind. Res.	B3
Yucca Flat (basin)	E6
⊙County seat.	
‡Population of metropolitan area.	
† Zip of nearest p.o.	
* Multiple zips.	

NEW HAMPSHIRE

AREA 9,279 sq. mi. (24,033 sq. km.)
POPULATION 920,610
CAPITAL Concord
LARGEST CITY Manchester
HIGHEST POINT Mt. Washington 6,288 ft. (1917 m.)
SETTLED IN 1623
ADMITTED TO UNION June 21, 1788
POPULAR NAME Granite State
STATE FLOWER Purple Lilac
STATE BIRD Purple Finch

VERMONT

AREA 9,614 sq. mi. (24,900 sq. km.)
POPULATION 511,456
CAPITAL Montpelier
LARGEST CITY Burlington
HIGHEST POINT Mt. Mansfield 4,393 ft. (1339 m.)
SETTLED IN 1764
ADMITTED TO UNION March 4, 1791
POPULAR NAME Green Mountain State
STATE FLOWER Red Clover
STATE BIRD Hermit Thrush

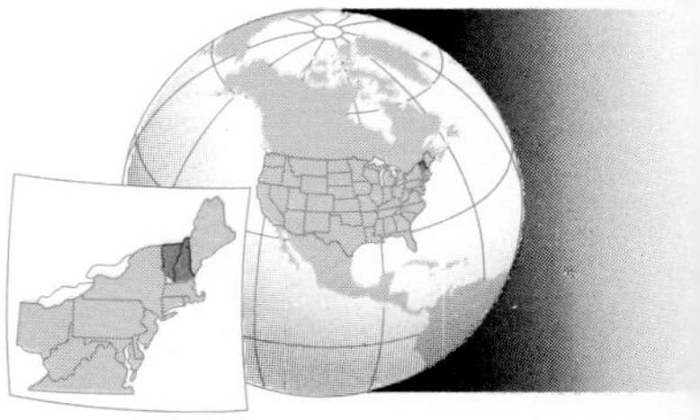

NEW HAMPSHIRE

COUNTIES

County	Key
Belknap 42,884	D4
Carroll 27,931	E4
Cheshire 62,116	C6
Coos 35,147	E2
Grafton 65,806	D4
Hillsborough 276,608	D6
Merrimack 98,302	D5
Rockingham 190,345	E5
Strafford 85,408	E5
Sullivan 36,063	C5

CITIES and TOWNS

Zip	Name/Pop.	Key
03601	Acworth○ 590	C5
†03864	Albany○ 383	E4
†03222	Alexandria○ 706	D4
†03275	Allenstown○ 4,398	E5
03602	Alstead○ 1,461	C5
03809	Alton○ 2,440	E5
03810	Alton Bay 500	E5
03031	Amherst○ 8,243	D6
03216	Andover○ 1,587	D5
03440	Antrim○ 2,208	D5
03440	Antrim 1,142	D5
03217	Ashland○ 1,807	D4
03217	Ashland 1,479	D4
03441	Ashuelot 810	C6
03811	Atkinson○ 4,397	E6
03032	Auburn○ 2,883	E5
03218	Barnstead○ 2,292	E5
†03825	Barrington○ 4,404	F5
03812	Bartlett○ 1,566	E3
03740	Bath○ 761	D3
03102	Bedford○ 9,481	D6
03220	Belmont○ 4,026	E5
03442	Bennington○ 890	D5
†03785	Benton○ 333	D3
03570	Berlin 13,084	E3
03574	Bethlehem○ 1,784	D3
03301	Boscawen○ 3,435	D5
03221	Bradford○ 1,115	D5
†03833	Brentwood○ 2,004	E6
†03222	Bridgewater○ 606	D4
03222	Bristol○ 2,198	D4
03222	Bristol 1,258	D4
†03872	Brookfield○ 385	E4
03033	Brookline○ 1,766	D6
03223	Campton○ 1,694	D4
03741	Canaan○ 2,456	C4
03034	Candia○ 2,989	E5
03224	Canterbury○ 1,410	D5
†03595	Carroll○ 647	D3
03813	Center Conway 558	E4
03226	Center Harbor○ 808	E4
03814	Center Ossipee 800	E4
03603	Charlestown○ 4,417	C5
03603	Charlestown 1,294	C5
†04037	Chatham○ 189	E3
03036	Chester○ 2,006	E6
03443	Chesterfield○ 2,561	C6
†03258	Chichester○ 1,492	E5
03817	Chocorua 575	E4
03743	Claremont 14,557	C5
†05902	Clarksville○ 262	E1
03576	Colebrook○ 2,459	E2
03576	Colebrook 1,131	E2
03301	Concord (cap.)⊙ 30,400	D5
03229	Contoocook 1,499	D5
03818	Conway○ 7,158	E4
03818	Conway 1,781	E4
03746	Cornish Flat 450	C4
†03753	Croydon○ 457	C5
†03598	Dalton○ 672	D3
03230	Danbury○ 680	D4
03819	Danville○ 1,318	E6
03037	Deerfield○ 1,979	E5
†03244	Deering○ 1,041	D5
03038	Derry○ 18,875	E6
03038	Derry 12,248	E6
†03266	Dorchester○ 244	D4
03820	Dover⊙ 22,377	F5
03444	Dublin○ 1,303	C6
†03588	Dummer○ 390	E2
†03301	Dunbarton○ 1,174	D5
03824	Durham○ 10,652	F5
03824	Durham 8,448	F5
03231	East Andover 500	D5
03826	East Hampstead 900	E6
03827	East Kingston○ 1,135	F6
†03580	Easton○ 124	D3
03446	East Swanzey 500	C6
03832	Eaton (Eaton Center)○ 256	E4
†03264	Ellsworth○ 53	D4
03748	Enfield○ 3,175	C4
03748	Enfield 1,581	C4
03042	Epping○ 3,460	E5
03042	Epping 1,384	E5
03234	Epsom○ 2,743	E5
03579	Errol○ 313	E2
03750	Etna 550	C4
03833	Exeter○ 11,024	F6
03833	Exeter⊙ 8,947	F6
03835	Farmington○ 4,630	E5
03835	Farmington 3,284	E5
03447	Fitzwilliam○ 1,795	C6
03043	Francestown○ 830	D6
03580	Franconia○ 743	D3
03235	Franklin 7,901	D5
03836	Freedom○ 720	E4
03044	Fremont○ 1,333	E6
†03246	Gilford○ 4,841	E4
03237	Gilmanton○ 1,941	E5
03448	Gilsum○ 652	C5
03838	Glen 600	E3
03045	Goffstown○ 11,315	D5
03581	Gorham○ 3,322	E3
03581	Gorham 2,180	E3
03752	Goshen○ 549	C5
03240	Grafton○ 739	D4
03753	Grantham○ 704	C5
03047	Greenfield○ 972	D6
03840	Greenland○ 2,129	F5
03048	Greenville○ 1,988	D6
03048	Greenville 1,447	D6
†03241	Groton○ 255	D4
03582	Groveton 1,389	D2
03754	Guild 500	C5
03841	Hampstead○ 3,785	E6
03842	Hampton○ 10,493	F6
03842	Hampton 6,779	F6
03844	Hampton Falls○ 1,372	F6
03449	Hancock○ 1,193	C6
03755	Hanover○ 9,119	C4
03755	Hanover 6,861	C4
03450	Harrisville○ 860	C6
03765	Haverhill○ 3,445	C3
03241	Hebron○ 349	D4
03242	Henniker○ 3,246	D5
03242	Henniker 1,538	D5
03243	Hill○ 736	D4
03244	Hillsboro○ 3,437	D5
03244	Hillsboro 1,797	D5
03451	Hinsdale○ 3,631	C6
03451	Hinsdale 1,546	C6
03245	Holderness○ 1,586	D4
03049	Hollis○ 4,679	D6
03106	Hooksett○ 7,303	E5
03106	Hooksett 1,868	E5
03301	Hopkinton○ 3,861	D5
03051	Hudson○ 14,022	E6
03051	Hudson 6,248	E6
03845	Intervale 725	E3
03846	Jackson○ 642	E3
03452	Jaffrey○ 4,349	C6
03452	Jaffrey 2,684	C6
03583	Jefferson○ 803	D3
03431	Keene⊙ 21,449	C6
03848	Kingston○ 4,111	E6
03246	Laconia⊙ 15,575	E4
03584	Lancaster○ 3,401	D3
03584	Lancaster⊙ 2,134	D3
†03585	Landaff○ 266	D3
†03602	Langdon○ 437	C5
03766	Lebanon 11,134	C4
†03857	Lee○ 2,111	F5
03606	Lempster○ 637	C5
03251	Lincoln○ 1,313	D3
03585	Lisbon○ 1,517	D3
03585	Lisbon 1,151	D3
†03051	Litchfield○ 4,150	E6
03561	Littleton○ 5,558	D3
03561	Littleton 4,480	D3
03053	Londonderry○ 13,598	E6
03301	Loudon○ 2,454	E5
†03585	Lyman○ 281	D3
03768	Lyme○ 1,289	C4
†03082	Lyndeborough○ 1,070	D6
†03820	Madbury○ 987	F5
03849	Madison○ 1,051	E4
*03101	Manchester 90,936	E6
	Manchester‡ 160,767	E6
03455	Marlborough○ 1,846	C6
03455	Marlborough 1,184	C6
03456	Marlow○ 542	C5
03850	Melvin Village 450	E4
03253	Meredith○ 4,646	D4
03253	Meredith 1,202	D4
03770	Meriden 800	C4
03054	Merrimack○ 15,406	D6
†03887	Middleton○ 734	E5
03588	Milan○ 1,013	E2
03055	Milford○ 8,685	D6
03055	Milford 6,269	D6
03851	Milton○ 2,438	F5
03852	Milton Mills 450	F4
03771	Monroe○ 619	C3
03057	Mont Vernon○ 1,444	D6
03254	Moultonboro○ 2,206	E4
03060	Nashua⊙ 67,865	D6
	Nashua‡ 114,221	D6
†03457	Nelson○ 442	C6
03070	New Boston○ 1,928	D6
03255	Newbury○ 961	C5
03854	New Castle○ 936	F5
03855	New Durham○ 1,183	E5
03856	Newfields○ 817	F5
03256	New Hampton○ 1,249	D4
†03801	Newington○ 716	F5
03071	New Ipswich○ 2,433	D6
03257	New London○ 2,935	D5
03257	New London 1,335	D5
03857	Newmarket○ 4,290	F5
03857	Newmarket 3,749	F5
03773	Newport○ 6,229	C5
03773	Newport⊙ 4,388	C5
03858	Newton○ 3,068	E6
03859	Newton Junction 450	E6
03860	North Conway 2,104	E3
†03276	Northfield○ 3,051	D5
†03276	Northfield-Tilton 2,574	D5
03862	North Hampton○ 3,425	F6
03590	North Stratford 600	D2
†03582	Northumberland○ 2,520	D2
03261	Northwood○ 2,175	E5
03262	North Woodstock 750	D3
03290	Nottingham○ 1,952	E5
†03741	Orange○ 197	D4
03777	Orford○ 928	C4
03864	Ossipee 2,465	E4
03076	Pelham○ 8,090	E6
†03275	Pembroke○ 4,861	E5
03458	Peterborough○ 4,895	D6
03458	Peterborough 2,568	D6
03779	Piermont○ 507	C4
03592	Pittsburg○ 780	E1
03263	Pittsfield○ 2,889	E5
03263	Pittsfield 1,584	E5
03781	Plainfield○ 1,749	C4
03865	Plaistow○ 5,609	E6
03264	Plymouth○ 5,094	D4
03264	Plymouth 3,628	D4
03801	Portsmouth 26,254	F5
	Portsmouth-Dover-Rochester‡ 163,880	F5
03593	Randolph○ 274	E3
03077	Raymond○ 5,453	E5
03077	Raymond 1,192	E5
†03470	Richmond○ 518	C6
03461	Rindge○ 3,375	C6
03867	Rochester 21,560	E5
†03431	Roxbury○ 190	C6
03266	Rumney○ 1,212	D4
03870	Rye○ 4,508	F5
03871	Rye Beach 600	F6
03079	Salem○ 24,124	E6
03268	Salisbury○ 781	D5
03269	Sanbornton○ 1,679	D5
03872	Sanbornville 750	F4
03873	Sandown○ 2,057	E6
03270	Sandwich○ 905	E4
03874	Seabrook○ 5,917	F6
†03458	Sharon○ 184	D6
†03581	Shelburne○ 318	E3
03878	Somersworth 10,350	F5
†01913	South Hampton○ 660	F6
03462	Spofford 750	C6
†03284	Springfield○ 532	C4
†03582	Stark○ 470	E2
†03576	Stewartstown○ 943	E2
03464	Stoddard○ 482	C5
03884	Strafford○ 1,663	E5
†03590	Stratford○ 989	D2
03885	Stratham○ 2,507	F5
03585	Sugar Hill○ 397	D3
†03445	Sullivan○ 585	C5
03782	Sunapee○ 2,312	C5
03275	Suncook 4,698	D5
03431	Surry○ 656	C5
†03260	Sutton○ 1,091	D5
†03431	Swanzey○ 5,183	C6
03886	Tamworth○ 1,672	E4
03084	Temple○ 692	D6
†03285	Thornton○ 952	D4
03276	Tilton○ 3,387	D5
03276	Tilton-Northfield 2,574	D5
03465	Troy○ 2,131	C6
03465	Troy 1,318	C6
†03816	Tuftonboro○ 1,500	E4
03595	Twin Mountain 500	D3
†03743	Unity○ 1,092	C5
†03872	Wakefield○ 2,237	F4
03608	Walpole○ 3,188	C5
03278	Warner○ 1,963	D5
03279	Warren○ 650	D4
03280	Washington○ 411	C5
03223	Waterville Valley○ 180	D4
03281	Weare○ 3,232	D5
†03301	Webster○ 1,095	D5
03282	Wentworth○ 527	D4
†03579	Wentworths Location○ 49	E2
†03242	West Henniker 500	D5
03784	West Lebanon	C4
03467	Westmoreland○ 1,452	C6
03597	West Stewartstown 700	E2
03469	West Swanzey 1,022	C6
03865	Westville 750	E6
03598	Whitefield○ 1,681	D3
03598	Whitefield 1,005	D3
†03287	Wilmot○ 725	D5
03287	Wilmot Flat 450	D5
03086	Wilton○ 2,669	D6
03086	Wilton 1,310	D6
03470	Winchester○ 3,465	C6
03470	Winchester 1,732	C6
03087	Windham○ 5,664	E6
03289	Winnisquam 500	E5
03894	Wolfeboro○ 3,968	E4
03894	Wolfeboro 2,271	E4
03896	Wolfeboro Falls 600	E4
03293	Woodstock○ 1,008	D4
03785	Woodsville⊙ 1,195	C3

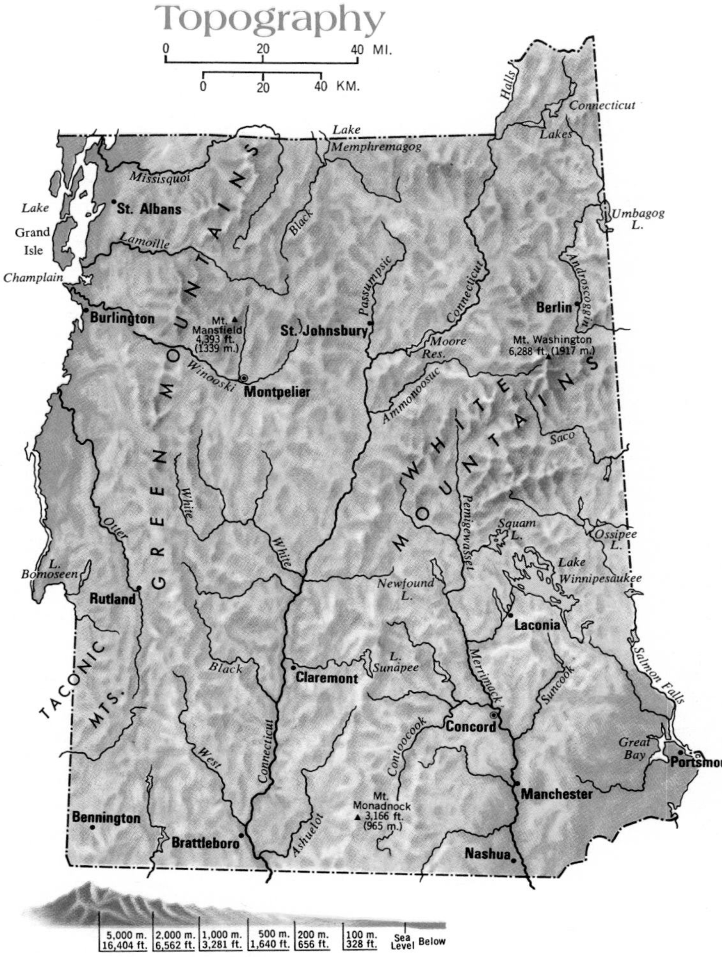
Topography
0 20 40 MI.
0 20 40 KM.
Lake Memphremagog
Missisquoi
St. Albans
Lake
Grand Isle
Champlain
Lamoille
Black
Passumpsic
Connecticut
Lakes
Halls
Umbagog L.
Androscoggin
Burlington
Mt. Mansfield 4,393 ft. (1339 m.)
St. Johnsbury
Moore Res.
Berlin
Mt. Washington 6,288 ft. (1917 m.)
Winooski
Montpelier
Ammonoosuc
GREEN MOUNTAINS
WHITE MOUNTAINS
Saco
White
Pemigewasset
Squam L.
Ossipee L.
Otter
L. Bomoseen
Lake Winnipesaukee
Newfound L.
Rutland
Laconia
Black
L. Sunapee
Claremont
Merrimack
Suncook
Salmon Falls
TACONIC MTS.
Concord
Contoocook
Great Bay
Portsmouth
West
Connecticut
Manchester
Mt. Monadnock 3,166 ft. (965 m.)
Bennington
Brattleboro
Ashuelot
Nashua
5,000 m. 16,404 ft.
2,000 m. 6,562 ft.
1,000 m. 3,281 ft.
500 m. 1,640 ft.
200 m. 656 ft.
100 m. 328 ft.
Sea Level
Below

OTHER FEATURES

Feature	Key
Adams (mt.)	E3
Ammonoosuc (riv.)	D3
Androscoggin (riv.)	E2
Ashuelot (riv.)	C6
Back (lake)	E1
Baker (riv.)	D4
Bearcamp (riv.)	E4
Beaver (brook)	E6
Belknap (mt.)	E5
Blackwater (res.)	D5
Blue (mt.)	E2
Bond (mt.)	E3
Bow (lake)	E5
Cabot (mt.)	E3
Cannon (mt.)	D3
Cardigan (mt.)	D4
Carrigain (mt.)	E3
Carter Dome (mt.)	E3
Chocorua (mt.)	E4
Cocheco (riv.)	E5
Cold (riv.)	C5
Comerford (dam)	D3
Connecticut (riv.)	B6
Contoocook (riv.)	D6
Conway (lake)	E4
Crawford Notch (pass)	E3
Croydon (peak)	C5
Croydon Branch, Sugar (riv.)	C5
Crystal (lake)	E5
Cube (mt.)	D4
Dixville (peak)	E2
Dixville Notch (pass)	E2
Edward MacDowell (res.)	D6
Ellis (riv.)	E3
Everett (dam)	D5
Exeter (riv.)	E6
First Connecticut (lake)	E1
Francis (lake)	E1
Franconia Notch (pass)	D3
Franklin Falls (res.)	D4
Gale (riv.)	D3
Great (bay)	F5
Halls (stream)	E1
Hancock (mt.)	D3
Highland (lake)	C5
Hutchins (mt.)	E2
Indian (stream)	E1
Jefferson (mt.)	E3
Kearsarge (mt.)	D5
Kinsman (mt.)	D3
Kinsman Notch (pass)	D3
Lafayette (mt.)	D3
Lamprey (riv.)	E5
Liberty (mt.)	D3
Lincoln (mt.)	D3
Long (mt.)	E2
Mad (riv.)	D4
Madison (mt.)	E3
Mascoma (lake)	C4
Massabesic (lake)	E6
Merrimack (riv.)	D5
Merrymeeting (lake)	E5
Mohawk (riv.)	E2
Monadnock (mt.)	C6
Monroe (mt.)	E3
Moore (dam)	D3
Moore (res.)	D3
Moosilauke (mt.)	D3
Nash (stream)	E2
Newfound (lake)	D4
North Carter (mt.)	E3
North Twin (mt.)	D3
Nubanusit (lake)	C5
Osceola (mt.)	E3
Ossipee (lake)	E4
Ossipee (mts.)	E4
Ossipee (riv.)	F4
Passaconaway (mt.)	E4
Pawtuckaway (pond)	E5
Pease A.F.B.	F5
Pemigewasset (riv.)	D4
Perry (stream)	E1
Pine (riv.)	E4
Pinkham Notch (pass)	E3
Piscataqua (riv.)	F5
Piscataquog (riv.)	D5
Presidential (range)	E3
Rice (mt.)	E2
Saco (riv.)	E3
Saint-Gaudens Nat'l Hist. Site	B4
Salmon Falls (riv.)	F5

(continued on following page)

Agriculture, Industry and Resources

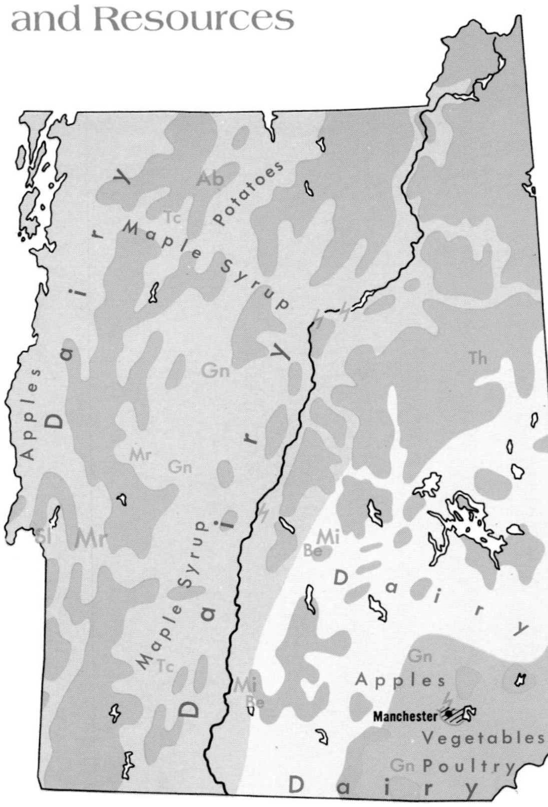

DOMINANT LAND USE

- Specialized Dairy
- Dairy, General Farming
- Dairy, Poultry, Mixed Farming
- Forests

- Water Power
- Major Industrial Areas

MAJOR MINERAL OCCURRENCES

Ab Asbestos
Be Beryl
Gn Granite
Mi Mica
Mr Marble
Sl Slate
Tc Talc
Th Thorium

Sandwich (mt.) ... E4
Sandwich (range) ... E4
Second (lake) ... E1
Shaw (mt.) ... E4
Shoals (isls.) ... F6
Smarts (mt.) ... C4
Souhegan (riv.) ... D6
South Twin (mt.) ... D3
Squam (lake) ... E4
Starr King (mt.) ... E3
Stub Hill (mt.) ... E1
Sugar (riv.) ... C5
Sunapee (lake) ... C5
Suncook (lkes) ... E5
Suncook (riv.) ... E5
Surry Mountain (lake) ... C5
Tarleton (lake) ... D4
Tecumseh (mt.) ... D4
Third (lake) ... E1
Tom (mt.) ... E3
Umbagog (lake) ... E2
Upper Ammonoosuc (riv.) ... E2
Warner (riv.) ... D5
Washington (mt.) ... E3
Waumbek (mt.) ... E3
Wentworth (lake) ... E4
White (isl.) ... F6
White (mts.) ... E3
Whiteface (mt.) ... E4
Wild Ammonoosuc (riv.) ... D3
Wilder (dam) ... C4
Winnipesaukee (lake) ... E4
Winnipesaukee (riv.) ... D5
Winnisquam (lake) ... D4

VERMONT

COUNTIES

Addison 29,406 ... A3
Bennington 33,345 ... A6
Caledonia 25,808 ... C2
Chittenden 115,534 ... A3
Essex 6,313 ... D2
Franklin 34,788 ... B2
Grand Isle 4,613 ... A2
Lamoille 16,767 ... B2
Orange 22,739 ... C3
Orleans 23,440 ... C2
Rutland 58,347 ... A4
Washington 52,393 ... B3
Windham 36,933 ... B5
Windsor 51,030 ... B4

CITIES and TOWNS

Zip *Name/Pop.* *Key*

05820 Albany○ 705 ... C2
05440 Alburg○ 1,352 ... A2
05440 Alburg 496 ... A2
†05143 Andover○ 350 ... B5
05250 Arlington○ 2,184 ... A5
05250 Arlington 1,309 ... A5
05441 Bakersfield○ 852 ... B2
05031 Barnard○ 790 ... B4
05821 Barnet○ 1,338 ... C3
05641 Barre 9,824 ... C3
05641 Barre○ 7,090 ... C3
05822 Barton○ 2,990 ... C2
05822 Barton 1,062 ... C2
05823 Beebe Plain 500 ... C2
05902 Beecher Falls 950 ... D2
05101 Bellows Falls 3,456 ... C5
05442 Belvidere○ 218 ... B2
05201 Bennington○ 15,815 ... A6
05201 Bennington⊙ 9,349 ... A6
05731 Benson○ 739 ... A4
†05476 Berkshire○ 1,116 ... B2
05032 Bethel○ 1,715 ... B4
05032 Bethel 1,016 ... B4
†03590 Bloomfield○ 188 ... D2
†05466 Bolton○ 715 ... B3
05732 Bomoseen 700 ... A4
05340 Bondville 500 ... B5
05033 Bradford○ 2,191 ... C3
05033 Bradford 831 ... C3
†05669 Braintree○ 1,065 ... B4
05733 Brandon○ 4,194 ... A4
05733 Brandon 1,925 ... A4
05301 Brattleboro○ 11,886 ... B6
05301 Brattleboro 8,596 ... B6
05034 Bridgewater○ 867 ... B4
05734 Bridport○ 997 ... A4
05443 Bristol○ 3,293 ... A3
05443 Bristol 1,793 ... A3
05036 Brookfield○ 959 ... B3
†05345 Brookline○ 310 ... B5
†05860 Brownington○ 708 ... C2
†05871 Burke○ 1,385 ... D2
05401 Burlington⊙ 37,712 ... A3
Burlington‡ 114,070 ... A3
05647 Cabot○ 958 ... C3
05647 Cabot 259 ... C3
05648 Calais○ 1,207 ... B3
05444 Cambridge○ 2,019 ... B2
05444 Cambridge 217 ... B2
05903 Canaan○ 1,196 ... D2
05735 Castleton○ 3,637 ... A4
05142 Cavendish○ 1,355 ... B5
05736 Center Rutland 465 ... A4
05445 Charlotte○ 2,561 ... A3
05038 Chelsea 1,091 ... C4
05143 Chester○ 2,791 ... B5
05143 Chester-Chester Depot 1,267 ... B5
05737 Chittenden○ 927 ... B4
†05759 Clarendon○ 2,372 ... A4
05446 Colchester○ 12,629 ... A2
05824 Concord○ 1,125 ... D3
05039 Corinth○ 904 ... C3
†05753 Cornwall○ 993 ... A4
05825 Coventry○ 674 ... C2
05826 Craftsbury○ 844 ... C2
05739 Danby○ 992 ... A5
05828 Danville○ 1,705 ... C3
05829 Derby○ 4,222 ... C2
05829 Derby (Derby Center) 598 ... C2
05830 Derby Line 874 ... C2
05251 Dorset○ 1,648 ... A5
†05676 Duxbury○ 877 ... B3
05252 East Arlington 600 ... A5
05649 East Barre-Graniteville 2,172 ... C3
05253 East Dorset 550 ... A5
05837 East Haven○ 280 ... D2
05740 East Middlebury 550 ... A4
05651 East Montpelier○ 2,205 ... B3
05741 East Poultney 450 ... A4
05742 East Wallingford 500 ... B5
05652 Eden○ 612 ... B2
05450 Enosburg Falls 1,207 ... B2
05451 Essex○ 14,392 ... A2
05452 Essex Junction 7,033 ... A3
05454 Fairfax○ 1,805 ... B2
05455 Fairfield○ 1,493 ... B2
05743 Fair Haven○ 2,819 ... A4
05743 Fair Haven 2,363 ... A4
05045 Fairlee○ 770 ... C4
05456 Ferrisburg○ 2,117 ... A3
†05444 Fletcher○ 626 ... B2
05745 Forest Dale 500 ... A4
05457 Franklin○ 1,006 ... B2
†05478 Georgia○ 2,818 ... A2
05904 Gilman 600 ... D3
05839 Glover○ 843 ... C2
05146 Grafton○ 604 ... B5
05840 Granby○ 70 ... D2
05458 Grand Isle○ 1,238 ... A2
05654 Graniteville-East Barre 2,172 ... C3
05747 Granville○ 288 ... B4
05841 Greensboro○ 677 ... C2
05046 Groton○ 667 ... C3
05905 Guildhall 202 ... D2
†05301 Guilford○ 1,532 ... B6
†05358 Halifax○ 488 ... B6
05748 Hancock○ 334 ... B4
05843 Hardwick○ 2,613 ... C2
05843 Hardwick 1,476 ... C2
05047 Hartford○ 7,963 ... C4
05048 Hartland○ 2,396 ... C4
†05459 Highgate○ 2,493 ... B2
05461 Hinesburg○ 2,690 ... A3
†05830 Holland○ 473 ... D2
05749 Hubbardton○ 490 ... A4
05462 Huntington○ 1,161 ... B3
05655 Hyde Park○ 2,021 ... B2
05655 Hyde Park⊙ 475 ... B2
05750 Hydeville 500 ... A4
†05777 Ira○ 354 ... A4
05845 Irasburg○ 870 ... C2
05846 Island Pond 1,216 ... D2
05463 Isle La Motte○ 393 ... A2
05342 Jacksonville 252 ... B6
05343 Jamaica○ 681 ... B5
†05859 Jay○ 302 ... C2
05464 Jeffersonville 491 ... B2
05465 Jericho○ 3,575 ... A2
05465 Jericho 1,340 ... A2
05656 Johnson○ 2,581 ... B2
05656 Johnson 1,393 ... B2
05751 Killington 700 ... B4
†05752 Leicester○ 803 ... A4
†03576 Lemington○ 108 ... D2
†05443 Lincoln○ 870 ... B3
05148 Londonderry○ 1,510 ... B5
05847 Lowell○ 573 ... C2
05149 Ludlow○ 2,414 ... B5
05149 Ludlow 1,352 ... B5
05906 Lunenburg○ 1,138 ... D3
05849 Lyndon○ 4,924 ... C2
05850 Lyndon Center ... C2
05851 Lyndonville 1,401 ... D2
†05905 Maidstone○ 100 ... D2
05254 Manchester○ 3,261 ... A5
05254 Manchester⊙ 563 ... A5
05255 Manchester Center 1,719 ... A5
05344 Marlboro○ 695 ... B6
05658 Marshfield○ 1,267 ... C3
05658 Marshfield 301 ... C3
†05701 Mendon○ 1,056 ... B4
05753 Middlebury○ 7,574 ... A3
05753 Middlebury⊙ 5,591 ... A3
†05602 Middlesex○ 1,235 ... B3
05757 Middletown Springs○ 603 ... A5
05468 Milton○ 6,829 ... A2
05468 Milton 1,411 ... A2
05469 Monkton○ 1,201 ... A3
05470 Montgomery○ 681 ... B2
05471 Montgomery Center 400 ... B2
05602 Montpelier (cap.)⊙ 8,241 ... B3
05660 Moretown○ 1,221 ... B3
05853 Morgan○ 460 ... D2
†05661 Morristown○ 4,448 ... B2
05661 Morrisville 2,074 ... B2
05758 Mount Holly○ 938 ... B5
†05739 Mount Tabor○ 211 ... B5
†05871 Newark○ 280 ... D2
05051 Newbury○ 1,699 ... C3
05051 Newbury 425 ... C3
05345 Newfane○ 1,129 ... B6
05345 Newfane⊙ 119 ... B6
05472 New Haven○ 1,217 ... A3
05855 Newport○ 1,319 ... C2
05855 Newport⊙ 4,756 ... C2
05257 North Bennington 1,685 ... A6
05663 Northfield○ 5,435 ... B3
05663 Northfield 2,033 ... B3
05664 Northfield Falls 600 ... B3
05052 North Hartland 500 ... C4
05474 North Hero 442 ... A2
05665 North Hyde Park 450 ... B2
05053 North Pomfret 400 ... B4
05260 North Pownal 700 ... A6
05150 North Springfield ... B5
05859 North Troy 717 ... C2
†05101 North Westminster 310 ... B5
05907 Norton○ 184 ... D2
05055 Norwich○ 2,398 ... C4
†05201 Old Bennington 353 ... A6
†05649 Orange○ 752 ... C3
05860 Orleans 983 ... C2
05760 Orwell○ 901 ... A4
†05491 Panton○ 537 ... A3
05761 Pawlet○ 1,244 ... A5
05862 Peacham○ 531 ... C3
05151 Perkinsville 187 ... B5
05152 Peru○ 312 ... B5
05762 Pittsfield○ 396 ... B4
05763 Pittsford○ 2,590 ... A4
05763 Pittsford 666 ... A4
05667 Plainfield○ 1,249 ... C3
05667 Plainfield 599 ... C3
05056 Plymouth○ 405 ... B4
†05067 Pomfret○ 856 ... B4
05058 Post Mills 500 ... C4
05764 Poultney○ 3,196 ... A4
05764 Poultney 1,554 ... A4
05261 Pownal○ 3,269 ... A6
05765 Proctor○ 1,998 ... A4
05153 Proctorsville 481 ... B5
05346 Putney○ 1,850 ... B6
05059 Quechee 900 ... C4
05060 Randolph○ 4,689 ... B4
05060 Randolph 2,217 ... B4
05062 Reading○ 647 ... B5
05350 Readsboro○ 638 ... B6
05350 Readsboro 402 ... B6
05476 Richford○ 2,206 ... B2
05476 Richford 1,471 ... B2
05477 Richmond○ 3,159 ... A3
05477 Richmond 865 ... A3
05766 Ripton○ 327 ... A4
05767 Rochester○ 1,054 ... B4
†05101 Rockingham○ 5,538 ... B5
05669 Roxbury○ 452 ... B3
†05068 Royalton○ 2,100 ... B4
05768 Rupert○ 605 ... A5
05701 Rutland○ 3,300 ... B4
05701 Rutland⊙ 18,436 ... B4
05042 Ryegate○ 1,000 ... C3
05478 Saint Albans○ 3,555 ... A2
05478 Saint Albans⊙ 7,308 ... A2
†05401 Saint George○ 677 ... A2
05819 Saint Johnsbury○ 7,938 ... D3
05819 Saint Johnsbury⊙ 7,150 ... D3
05863 Saint Johnsbury Center 400 ... D3
05769 Salisbury○ 881 ... A4
†05250 Sandgate○ 234 ... A5
05154 Saxtons River 593 ... B5
†05363 Searsburg○ 72 ... A6
05262 Shaftsbury○ 3,001 ... A6
05065 Sharon○ 828 ... C4
05866 Sheffield○ 435 ... C2
05482 Shelburne○ 5,000 ... A3
05483 Sheldon○ 1,618 ... B2
05770 Shoreham○ 972 ... A4
†05738 Shrewsbury○ 866 ... B4
05670 South Barre 1,301 ... B3
05401 South Burlington 10,679 ... A3
05486 South Hero○ 1,188 ... A2
05155 South Londonderry 500 ... B5
05068 South Royalton 700 ... C4
05069 South Ryegate 400 ... C3
05156 Springfield○ 10,190 ... B5
05156 Springfield 5,603 ... B5
05352 Stamford○ 773 ... A6
05487 Starksboro○ 1,336 ... A3
05772 Stockbridge○ 508 ... B4
05672 Stowe○ 2,991 ... B3
05672 Stowe 531 ... B3
05072 Strafford○ 731 ... C4
†05360 Stratton○ 122 ... B5
†05733 Sudbury○ 380 ... A4
†05250 Sunderland○ 768 ... A5
05867 Sutton○ 667 ... C2
05488 Swanton○ 5,141 ... A2
05488 Swanton 2,520 ... A2
05074 Thetford○ 2,188 ... C4
†05773 Tinmouth○ 406 ... A5
05076 Topsham○ 767 ... C3
05353 Townshend○ 849 ... B5
05868 Troy○ 1,498 ... C2
05077 Tunbridge○ 925 ... C4
05489 Underhill○ 2,172 ... B2
05490 Underhill Center 575 ... B2
05491 Vergennes 2,273 ... A3
05354 Vernon○ 1,175 ... B6
05079 Vershire○ 442 ... C4
05673 Waitsfield○ 1,300 ... B3
†05873 Walden○ 575 ... C3
05773 Wallingford○ 1,893 ... B5
05773 Wallingford 1,141 ... B5
†05491 Waltham○ 394 ... A3
05355 Wardsboro○ 505 ... B5
05674 Warren○ 956 ... B3
05675 Washington○ 855 ... C3
05676 Waterbury○ 4,465 ... B3
05676 Waterbury 1,892 ... B3
05492 Waterville○ 470 ... B2
05678 Websterville 700 ... B3
05774 Wells○ 815 ... A5
05081 Wells River 396 ... C3
05301 West Brattleboro 2,795 ... B6
05871 West Burke 338 ... C2
05356 West Dover 550 ... B6
05083 West Fairlee○ 427 ... C4
05874 Westfield○ 418 ... C2
05494 Westford○ 1,413 ... A2
05875 West Glover ... C2
†05743 West Haven○ 253 ... A4
05158 Westminster○ 2,493 ... C5
05158 Westminster 319 ... C5
†05860 Westmore○ 257 ... C2
05161 Weston○ 627 ... B5
05777 West Rutland○ 2,351 ... A4
05777 West Rutland 2,169 ... A4
05359 West Townshend 500 ... B5
†05753 Weybridge○ 667 ... A3
†05851 Wheelock○ 444 ... C2
05001 White River Junction 2,582 ... C4
05778 Whiting○ 379 ... A4
05361 Whitingham○ 1,043 ... B6
05088 Wilder 1,461 ... C4
05679 Williamstown○ 2,284 ... B3
05495 Williston○ 3,843 ... A3
05363 Wilmington○ 1,808 ... B6
†05359 Windham○ 223 ... B5
05089 Windsor○ 4,084 ... C5
05089 Windsor 3,478 ... C5
05404 Winooski 6,318 ... A2
05680 Wolcott○ 986 ... C2
05681 Woodbury○ 573 ... C3
†05201 Woodford○ 314 ... A6
05091 Woodstock○ 3,214 ... B4
05091 Woodstock⊙ 1,178 ... B4
05682 Worcester○ 727 ... B3

OTHER FEATURES

Abraham (mt.) ... B3
Arrowhead Mountain (lake) ... A2
Ascutney (mt.) ... C5
Bald (mt.) ... D2
Barton (riv.) ... C2
Batten Kill (riv.) ... A5
Belvidere (mt.) ... B2
Black (riv.) ... B5
Black (riv.) ... C2
Bloodroot (mt.) ... B4
Bolton (mt.) ... B3
Bomoseen (lake) ... A4
Brandon Gap (pass) ... B4
Bread Loaf (mt.) ... A3
Bromley (mt.) ... B5
Brown's (riv.) ... A2
Burke (mt.) ... D2
Camels Hump (mt.) ... B3
Carmi (lake) ... B2
Caspian (lake) ... C2
Champlain (lake) ... A2
Chittenden (res.) ... B4
Clyde (riv.) ... C2
Comerford (dam) ... D3
Connecticut (riv.) ... C4
Crystal (lake) ... C2
Dorset (peak) ... A5
Dunmore (lake) ... A4
Echo (lake) ... D2
Ellen (mt.) ... B3
Equinox (mt.) ... A5
Fairfield (pond) ... A2
Glastenbury (mt.) ... A6
Gore (mt.) ... D2
Green (mts.) ... B4
Green River (res.) ... B2
Groton (lake) ... C3
Hardwick (lake) ... C2
Harriman (res.) ... B6
Harveys (lake) ... C3
Haystack (mt.) ... B6
Hoosic (riv.) ... A6
Hortonia (lake) ... A4
Hunger (mt.) ... B3
Iroquois (lake) ... A3
Island (pond) ... D2
Jay (peak) ... B2
Joes (brook) ... C3
Killington (peak) ... B4
Lamoille (riv.) ... A2
Lewis (creek) ... A3
Lincoln Gap (pass) ... B3
Little (riv.) ... B3
Mad (riv.) ... B3
Maidstone (lake) ... D2
Mansfield (mt.) ... B2
Memphremagog (lake) ... C1
Mettawee (riv.) ... A5
Middlebury Gap (pass) ... B4
Mill (riv.) ... B4
Missisquoi (riv.) ... B2
Mollys Falls (pond) ... C3
Moore (dam) ... D3
Moore (res.) ... D3
Moose (riv.) ... D2
Norton (pond) ... D2
Nulhegan (riv.) ... D2
Ottauquechee (riv.) ... B4
Otter (creek) ... A3
Passumpsic (riv.) ... D2
Pico (peak) ... B4
Poultney (riv.) ... A4
Saint Catherine (lake) ... A5
Salem (lake) ... C2
Seymour (lake) ... D2
Shelburne (pond) ... A3
Smugglers Notch (pass) ... B2
Snow (mt.) ... B6
Somerset (res.) ... A5
Spruce (mt.) ... C3
Stratton (mt.) ... B5
Tabor (mt.) ... B5
Trout (riv.) ... B2
Waits (riv.) ... C3
Waterbury (res.) ... B3
Wells (riv.) ... C3
West (riv.) ... B5
White (riv.) ... C4
White Face (mt.) ... B2
Wilder (dam) ... C4
Willoughby (lake) ... D2
Winooski (riv.) ... B3

⊙County seat.
‡Population of metropolitan area.
○Population of town or township.
† Zip of nearest p.o. * Multiple zips.

AREA 7,787 sq. mi. (20,168 sq. km.)
POPULATION 7,364,823
CAPITAL Trenton
LARGEST CITY Newark
HIGHEST POINT High Point 1,803 ft. (550 m.)
SETTLED IN 1617
ADMITTED TO UNION December 18, 1787
POPULAR NAME Garden State
STATE FLOWER Purple Violet
STATE BIRD Eastern Goldfinch

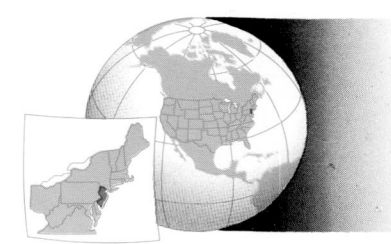

Agriculture, Industry and Resources

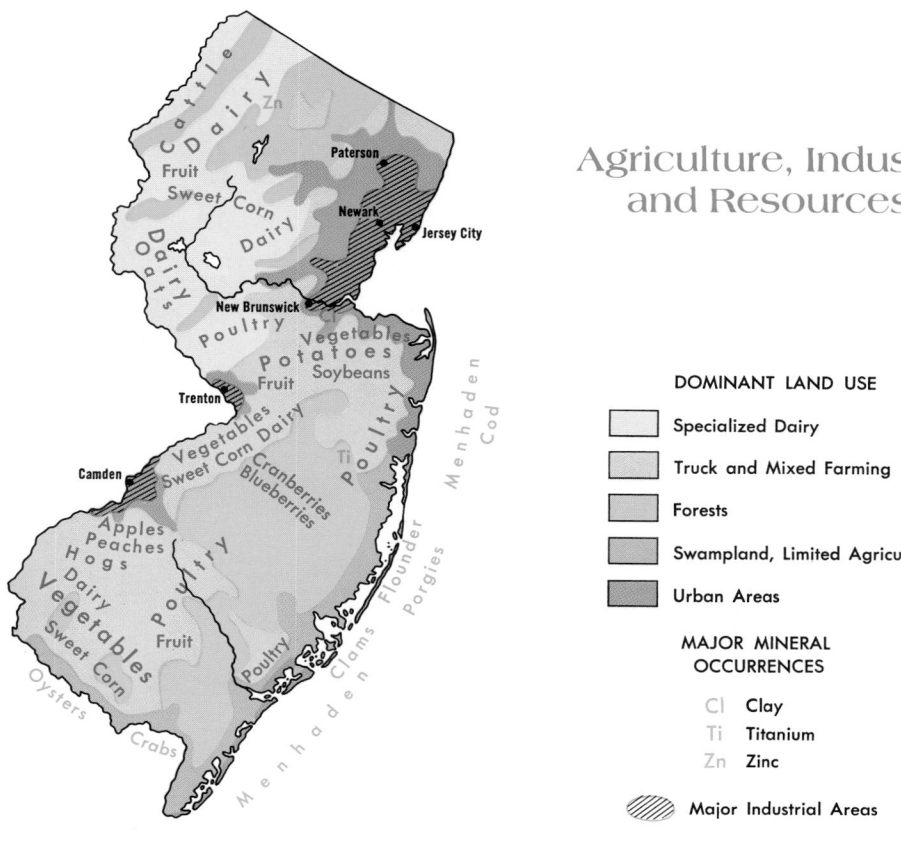

DOMINANT LAND USE

Specialized Dairy

Truck and Mixed Farming

Forests

Swampland, Limited Agriculture

Urban Areas

MAJOR MINERAL OCCURRENCES

Cl Clay

Ti Titanium

Zn Zinc

Major Industrial Areas

The Urban Northeast

- Urbanized Areas
- Places with more than 10,000 inhabitants
- Places with 5,000-10,000 inhabitants
- Places with 2,500-5,000 inhabitants

© Copyright HAMMOND INCORPORATED, Maplewood, N. J.

COUNTIES

Name/Pop.	Key
Atlantic 194,119	D5
Bergen 845,385	E2
Burlington 362,542	D4
Camden 471,650	D4
Cape May 82,266	D5
Cumberland 132,866	C5
Essex 851,116	E2
Gloucester 199,917	C4
Hudson 556,972	E2
Hunterdon 87,361	D2
Mercer 307,863	D3
Middlesex 595,893	E3
Monmouth 503,173	E3
Morris 407,630	D2
Ocean 346,038	E4
Passaic 447,585	E1
Salem 64,676	C4
Somerset 203,129	D2
Sussex 116,119	D1
Union 504,094	E2
Warren 84,429	C2

CITIES and TOWNS

Zip	Name/Pop.	Key
08201	Absecon 6,859	D5
07820	Allamuchy 600	D2
07401	Allendale 5,901	B1
07711	Allenhurst 912	F3
08501	Allentown 1,962	D3
08720	Allenwood	E3
08001	Alloway 1,370	C4
08865	Alpha 2,644	C2
07620	Alpine 1,549	C1
07821	Andover 892	D2
08801	Annandale 1,040	D2
07712	Asbury Park 17,015	F3
	Asbury Park-Long Branch‡	
	503,173	F3
†08033	Ashland	B3
08004	Atco	D4
*08401	Atlantic City 40,199	E5
	Atlantic City‡ 194,119	E5
07716	Atlantic Highlands 4,950	F3
08106	Audubon 9,533	B3
†08106	Audubon Park 1,274	B3
08202	Avalon 2,162	D5
07001	Avenel	E2
07717	Avon By The Sea 2,337	E3
08005	Barnegat 1,012	E4
08006	Barnegat Light 619	E4
08007	Barrington 7,418	B3
07920	Basking Ridge	D2
08742	Bay Head 1,340	E3
07002	Bayonne 65,047	B2
08008	Beach Haven 1,714	E4
08722	Beachwood 7,687	E4
07921	Bedminster○ 2,469	D2
08502	Belle Mead	D3
07109	Belleville 35,367	B2
08031	Bellmawr 13,721	B3
07719	Belmar 6,771	E3
07823	Belvidere⊙ 2,475	C2
07621	Bergenfield 25,568	C1
07922	Berkeley Heights○ 12,549	E2
08009	Berlin 5,786	D4
07924	Bernardsville 6,715	D2
08010	Beverly 2,919	D3
08012	Blackwood 5,219	C4
07825	Blairstown○ 4,360	C2
07003	Bloomfield 47,792	B2
07403	Bloomingdale 7,867	E1
08804	Bloomsbury 864	C2
07603	Bogota 8,344	B2
07005	Boonton 8,620	E2
08505	Bordentown 4,441	D3
08805	Bound Brook 9,710	D2
07720	Bradley Beach 4,772	F3
07826	Branchville 870	D1
08723	Breton Woods	E3
08723	Brick○ 53,629	E3
08014	Bridgeport 750	C4
08302	Bridgeton⊙ 18,795	C5
08807	Bridgewater○ 29,175	D2
08730	Brielle 4,068	E3
08203	Brigantine 8,318	E5
08030	Brooklawn 2,133	B3
08015	Browns Mills 10,568	D4
07828	Budd Lake 6,523	D2
08310	Buena 3,642	D4
08016	Burlington 10,246	D3
07405	Butler 7,616	E2
07006	Caldwell 7,624	B2
07830	Califon 1,023	D2
*08101	Camden⊙ 84,910	B3
†08701	Candlewood 6,750	E3
08204	Cape May 4,853	D6
08210	Cape May Court House⊙	
	3,597	D5
07072	Carlstadt 6,166	B2
08069	Carneys Point 7,574	C4
07008	Carteret 20,598	E2
07009	Cedar Grove○ 12,600	B2
†08723	Cedarwood Park	E3

Zip	Name/Pop.	Key
07928	Chatham 8,537	E2
08019	Chatsworth 700	D4
08879	Cheesequake	E3
*08034	Cherry Hill○ 68,785	B3
†08089	Chesilhurst 1,590	D4
07930	Chester 1,433	D2
†08505	Chesterfield○ 3,867	D3
†08077	Cinnaminson○ 16,072	B3
07066	Clark○ 16,699	A3
08020	Clarksboro	C4
08510	Clarksburg 800	E3
08312	Clayton 6,013	C4
08021	Clementon 5,764	D4
07010	Cliffside Park 21,464	C2
07721	Cliffwood	E3
*07011	Clifton 74,388	B2
08809	Clinton 1,910	D2
07624	Closter 8,164	C1
08108	Collingswood 15,838	B3
08213	Cologne 800	D4
07722	Colts Neck 950	E3
07832	Columbia 600	C2
08022	Columbus 800	D3
07961	Convent Station	E2
†08270	Corbin City 254	D5
†07821	Cranberry Lake 500	D2
08512	Cranbury 1,255	E3
07016	Cranford○ 24,573	E2
07626	Cresskill 7,609	C1
08515	Crosswicks 265	D3
07723	Deal 1,952	F3
08023	Deepwater 800	C4
08110	Delair	B3
08075	Delanco○ 3,730	D3
08075	Delran○ 14,811	B3
07627	Demarest 4,963	C1
08214	Dennisville 890	D5
07834	Denville○ 14,380	E2
08096	Deptford○ 23,473	B4
08317	Dorothy 900	D5
07801	Dover 14,681	D2
07628	Dumont 18,334	C1
08812	Dunellen 6,593	D2
08816	East Brunswick○ 37,711	E3
07936	East Hanover○ 9,319	E2
07734	East Keansburg	E3
08873	East Millstone 950	D3
†07100	East Newark 1,923	B2
*07017	East Orange 77,690	B2
07073	East Rutherford 7,849	B2
07724	Eatontown 12,703	E3
07020	Edgewater 4,628	C2
†08010	Edgewater Park○ 9,273	D3
*08817	Edison○ 70,193	E2
08215	Egg Harbor City 4,618	D4
07740	Elberon	F3
*07201	Elizabeth⊙ 106,201	B2
08318	Elmer 1,569	C4
†07407	Elmwood Park 18,377	B2
08217	Elwood 1,538	D4
07630	Emerson 7,793	B1
*07631	Englewood 23,701	C2
07632	Englewood Cliffs 5,698	C2
07726	Englishtown 976	E3
07021	Essex Fells 2,363	B2
08319	Estell Manor 848	D5
08025	Ewan 610	C4
07006	Fairfield○ 7,987	A2
07701	Fair Haven 5,679	E3
07410	Fair Lawn 32,229	B1
08320	Fairton 1,107	C5
07022	Fairview 10,519	C2
07023	Fanwood 7,767	E2
07931	Far Hills 677	D2
07727	Farmingdale 1,348	E3
†08505	Fieldsboro 597	D3
07836	Flanders	D2
08822	Flemington⊙ 4,132	D2
08518	Florence-Roebling 7,677	D3
07932	Florham Park 9,359	E2
†08037	Folsom 1,892	D4
08863	Fords	B2
08731	Forked River 900	E4
07024	Fort Lee 32,449	C2
07416	Franklin 4,486	D1
07417	Franklin Lakes 8,769	B1
†08823	Franklin Park○ 31,358	D3
08322	Franklinville	C4
07728	Freehold⊙ 10,020	E3
08825	Frenchtown 1,573	C2
07026	Garfield 26,803	B2
07027	Garwood 4,752	E2
08026	Gibbsboro 2,510	B4
08027	Gibbstown	C4
†08753	Gilford Park 6,528	E4
07933	Gillette	E2
08028	Glassboro 14,574	C4
08029	Glendora 5,632	B4
08826	Glen Gardner 834	D2
07028	Glen Ridge 7,855	B2
07452	Glen Rock 11,497	B1
08030	Gloucester City 13,121	B3
07435	Green Pond 800	E1
07935	Green Village 800	E2
08323	Greenwich○ 973	C5
08032	Grenloch 700	C4

(continued on following page)

07093 Guttenberg 7,340 .... C2
*07601 Hackensack⊙ 36,039 .... B2
07840 Hackettstown 8,850 .... D2
08033 Haddonfield 12,337 .... B3
08035 Haddon Heights 8,361 ...... B3
08036 Hainesport○ 3,236 .... D4
07508 Haledon 6,607 .... B1
07419 Hamburg 1,832 .... D1
08690 Hamilton Square-
Mercerville 25,446 .... D3
08037 Hammonton 12,298 .... D4
08827 Hampton 1,614 .... D2
07640 Harrington Park 4,532 ...... C1
07029 Harrison 12,242 .... B2
†08057 Hartford 650 .... D4
08008 Harvey Cedars 363 .... E4
07604 Hasbrouck Heights 12,166 . B2
07641 Haworth 3,509 .... C1
07507 Hawthorne 18,200 .... B2
07730 Hazlet 23,013 .... E3
08828 Helmetta 955 .... E3
07421 Hewitt 950 .... E1
08829 High Bridge 3,435 .... D2
07422 Highland Lakes 2,888 .... E1
08904 Highland Park 13,396 .... D2
07732 Highlands 5,187 .... F3
08520 Hightstown 4,581 .... D3
07642 Hillsdale 10,495 .... B1
07205 Hillside○ 21,440 .... B2
†08083 Hi-Nella 1,250 .... B4
07030 Hoboken 42,460 .... C2
07423 Ho Ho Kus 4,129 .... B1
07733 Holmdel○ 8,447 .... E3
07843 Hopatcong 15,531 .... D2
07844 Hope 310 .... D2
08525 Hopewell 2,001 .... D3
07731 Howell○ 25,065 .... E3
†07712 Interlaken 1,037 .... E3
07845 Ironia D2
07111 Irvington 61,493 .... B2
08830 Iselin E2
08732 Island Heights 1,575 .... E4
08527 Jackson○ 25,644 .... E3
08831 Jamesburg 4,114 .... E3
*07301 Jersey City⊙ 223,532 ...... B2
Jersey City‡ 556,972 .... B2
07734 Keansburg 10,613 .... E3
07032 Kearny 35,735 .... B2
08824 Kendall Park 7,419 .... D3
07033 Kenilworth 8,221 .... E2
07735 Keyport 7,413 .... E3
08528 Kingston D3
07405 Kinnelon 7,770 .... E2
07848 Lafayette 900 .... D1
07034 Lake Hiawatha E2
07849 Lake Hopatcong D2
08733 Lakehurst 2,908 .... E3
†07871 Lake Mohawk 8,498 .... D1
08701 Lakewood 22,863 .... E3
08530 Lambertville 4,044 .... D3
07850 Landing D2
08734 Lanoka Harbor E4
08021 Laurel Springs 2,249 .... B4
08879 Laurence Harbor 6,737 ..... E3
08735 Lavallette 2,072 .... E4
08045 Lawnside 3,042 .... B3
08648 Lawrenceville 19,724 .... D3
08833 Lebanon 820 .... D2
07852 Ledgewood D2
08327 Leesburg 700 .... D5
07737 Leonardo E3
07605 Leonia 8,027 .... C2
07938 Liberty Corner D2
07035 Lincoln Park 8,806 .... A1
07738 Lincroft E3
07036 Linden 37,836 .... A3
08021 Lindenwold 18,196 .... B4
08221 Linwood 6,144 .... D5
07424 Little Falls○ 11,496 .... B2
07643 Little Ferry 9,399 .... B2
07739 Little Silver 5,548 .... F3
07039 Livingston○ 28,040 .... E2
07644 Lodi 23,956 .... B2
07740 Long Branch 29,819 .... F3
Long Branch-Asbury Park‡
503,173 .... F3
08403 Longport 1,249 .... D5
07853 Long Valley 1,682 .... D2
08048 Lumberton 600 .... D4
07071 Lyndhurst○ 20,326 .... B2
07939 Lyons D2
07940 Madison 15,357 .... E2
08049 Magnolia 4,881 .... B3
07430 Mahwah○ 12,127 .... E1
08328 Malaga 950 .... C4
08050 Manahawkin 1,469 .... E4
08736 Manasquan 5,354 .... E3
08738 Mantoloking 433 .... E3
08051 Mantua○ 9,193 .... C4
08835 Manville 11,278 .... D2
08052 Maple Shade○ 20,525 ...... B3
07040 Maplewood○ 22,950 .... E2
08402 Margate City 9,179 .... E5
07746 Marlboro○ 17,560 .... E3
08053 Marlton 9,411 .... D4
08223 Marmora 650 .... D5
08836 Martinsville D2
07747 Matawan 8,837 .... E3
08330 Mays Landing⊙ 2,054 ..... D5
07607 Maywood 9,895 .... B2
07428 McAfee 800 .... D1
†08232 McKee City 950 .... D5
08055 Medford D4
08055 Medford Lakes 4,958 .... D4
07945 Mendham 4,899 .... D2
08837 Menlo Park E2
08619 Mercerville-Hamilton
Square 25,446 .... D3
08109 Merchantville 3,972 .... B3
08840 Metuchen 13,762 .... E2
08846 Middlesex 13,480 .... E2
07748 Middletown○ 62,574 .... E3
07432 Midland Park 7,381 .... B1
08848 Milford 1,368 .... C2
07041 Millburn○ 19,543 .... E2
07946 Millington 975 .... D2
†08876 Millstone 530 .... D2

08850 Milltown 7,136 .... E3
08332 Millville 24,815 .... C5
†07801 Mine Hill○ 3,325 .... D2
08342 Mizpah 900 .... D5
07750 Monmouth Beach 3,318 .... F3
08852 Monmouth Junction 2,579 . D3
07434 Monroe○ 15,858 .... E3
*07042 Montclair 38,321 .... B2
07645 Montvale 7,318 .... B1
07045 Montville○ 14,290 .... E2
†07070 Moonachie 2,706 .... B2
08057 Moorestown 13,695 .... B3
07950 Morris Plains 5,305 .... D2
07960 Morristown⊙ 16,614 .... D2
07046 Mountain Lakes 4,153 ..... E2
07092 Mountainside 7,118 .... E2
07856 Mount Arlington 4,251 ..... D2
08059 Mount Ephraim 4,863 ...... B3
07970 Mount Freedom D2
08060 Mount Holly 10,818 .... D4
†08054 Mount Laurel○ 17,614 ...... D4
†07828 Mount Olive○ 18,748 .... D2
08061 Mount Royal 900 .... C4
08062 Mullica Hill 1,050 .... C4
08087 Mystic Islands 4,929 .... E4
08063 National Park 3,552 .... B3
07752 Navesink E3
07753 Neptune○ 28,366 .... E3
07753 Neptune City 5,276 .... E3
07857 Netcong 3,557 .... D2
*07101 Newark⊙ 329,248 .... B2
Newark‡ 1,965,304 .... B2
*08901 New Brunswick⊙ 41,442 .. E3
New Brunswick-Perth
Amboy-Sayreville‡
595,893 ...... E3
08533 New Egypt 2,111 .... E3
08344 Newfield 1,563 .... D4
07435 Newfoundland 900 .... D1
08224 New Gretna 800 .... E4
07646 New Milford 16,876 .... B1
07974 New Providence 12,426 .... E2
07860 Newton⊙ 7,748 .... D1
08346 Newtonville 950 .... D4
07976 New Vernon D2
07032 North Arlington 16,587 ..... B2
07047 North Bergen○ 47,019 ...... B2
08876 North Branch 610 .... D2
08902 North Brunswick○ 22,220 .. D3
†07006 North Caldwell 5,832 .... B2
08204 North Cape May 4,029 ..... C6
08225 Northfield 7,795 .... D5
07508 North Haledon 8,177 .... B1
07060 North Plainfield 19,108 ..... E2
07647 Northvale 5,046 .... F1
08260 North Wildwood 4,714 ..... D6
07648 Norwood 4,413 .... C1
07110 Nutley 28,998 .... B2
07755 Oakhurst E3
07436 Oakland 13,443 .... B1
08107 Oaklyn 4,223 .... B3
08226 Ocean City 13,949 .... D5
08740 Ocean Gate 1,385 .... E4
07756 Ocean Grove F3
07757 Oceanport 5,888 .... F3
07439 Ogdensburg 2,737 .... D1
08857 Old Bridge 21,815 .... E3
07675 Old Tappan 4,168 .... C1
07649 Oradell 8,658 .... B1
*07050 Orange 31,136 .... B2
08723 Osbornsville E3
07863 Oxford 1,587 .... C2
07470 Packanack Lake B1
07650 Palisades Park 13,732 ...... C2
08065 Palmyra 7,085 .... B3
07652 Paramus 26,474 .... B1
07656 Park Ridge 8,515 .... B1
07054 Parsippany-Troy
Hills○ 49,868 .... E2
07055 Passaic 52,463 .... E2
*07501 Paterson⊙ 137,970 .... B2
Paterson-Clifton-Passaic‡
447,585 .... B2
08066 Paulsboro 6,944 .... C4
07977 Peapack-Gladstone 2,038 .. D2
08067 Pedricktown C4
08068 Pemberton 1,198 .... D4
08534 Pennington 2,109 .... D3
08110 Pennsauken○ 33,775 .... B3
08069 Penns Grove 5,760 .... C4
08070 Pennsville 12,467 .... C4
07440 Pequannock○ 13,776 .... B1
*08861 Perth Amboy 38,951 .... E2
08865 Phillipsburg 16,647 .... C2
08741 Pine Beach 1,796 .... E4
07058 Pine Brook E2
08021 Pine Hill 8,684 .... D4
08854 Piscataway○ 42,223 .... D2
08071 Pitman 9,744 .... C4
*07060 Plainfield 45,555 .... E2
08536 Plainsboro D3
08232 Pleasantville 13,435 .... D5
08742 Point Pleasant 17.747 ...... E3
08742 Point Pleasant Beach
5,415 .... E3
08240 Pomona 2,358 .... D5
07442 Pompton Lakes 10,660 ..... A1
07444 Pompton Plains B1
07758 Port Monmouth E3
†07850 Port Morris 616 .... D2
07865 Port Murray 250 .... D2
08349 Port Norris 1,730 .... C5
08241 Port Republic 837 .... D4
08540 Princeton 12,035 .... D3
08550 Princeton Junction 2,419 ... D3
†07885 Prospect Park 5,142 .... B1
08072 Quinton 750 .... C4
*07065 Rahway 26,723 .... E2
†08054 Ramblewood 6,475 .... D4
07446 Ramsey 12,899 .... B1
†07801 Randolph○ 17,828 .... D2
08869 Raritan 6,128 .... D2
07701 Red Bank 12,031 .... E3
07657 Ridgefield 10,294 .... B2
07660 Ridgefield Park 12,738 ..... B2
*07450 Ridgewood 25,208 .... B1
08551 Ringoes 682 .... D3

07456 Ringwood 12,625 .... E1
08242 Rio Grande 2,016 .... D5
07457 Riverdale 2,530 .... A1
07661 River Edge 11,111 .... B1
08075 Riverside○ 7,941 .... B3
08077 Riverton 3,068 .... B3
07675 River Vale○ 9,489 .... B1
07662 Rochelle Park○ 5,603 ...... B2
07866 Rockaway 6,852 .... D2
07647 Rockleigh 192 .... C1
08553 Rocky Hill 717 .... D3
08554 Roebling-Florence 7,677 .... D3
08555 Roosevelt 835 .... E3
07068 Roseland 5,330 .... A2
07203 Roselle 20,641 .... B2
07204 Roselle Park 13,377 .... A2
08352 Rosenhayn 950 .... C5
†07876 Roxbury○ 18,878 .... D2
07760 Rumson 7,623 .... F3
08078 Runnemede 9,461 .... B3
*07070 Rutherford 19,068 .... B2
07662 Saddle Brook○ 14,084 ...... B1
07458 Saddle River 2,763 .... B1
08079 Salem⊙ 6,959 .... C4
08872 Sayreville 29,969 .... E3
07076 Scotch Plains○ 20,774 ...... E2
07760 Sea Bright 1,812 .... F3
08302 Seabrook 1,411 .... C5
08750 Sea Girt 2,650 .... E3
08243 Sea Isle City 2,644 .... D5
08751 Seaside Heights 1,802 ...... E4
08752 Seaside Park 1,795 .... E4
07094 Secaucus 13,719 .... B2
07077 Sewaren E2
08080 Sewell C4
08353 Shiloh 604 .... C5
08008 Ship Bottom 1,427 .... E4
07078 Short Hills E2
07701 Shrewsbury 2,962 .... E3
08081 Sicklerville D4
08558 Skillman D3
08201 Smithville 70 .... E5
08083 Somerdale 5,900 .... B4
08244 Somers Point 10,330 .... D5
08876 Somerville⊙ 11,973 .... D2
08879 South Amboy 8,322 .... E3
†07719 South Belmar 1,566 .... E3
08880 South Bound Brook 4,331 . E2
†08852 South Brunswick○ 17,127 . E3
07079 South Orange○ 15,864 ..... A2
07080 South Plainfield 20,521 ..... E2
08882 South River 14,361 .... E3
08753 South Toms River 3,954 ... E4
07871 Sparta○ 13,333 .... D1
08884 Spotswood 7,840 .... E3
07081 Springfield○ 13,955 .... E2
07762 Spring Lake 4,215 .... F3
†07762 Spring Lake Heights 5,424 . E3
07874 Stanhope 3,638 .... D2
08886 Stewartsville 950 .... C2
07980 Stirling E2
07460 Stockholm D1
08559 Stockton 643 .... D3
08247 Stone Harbor 1,187 .... D5
08084 Stratford 8,005 .... B4
†07747 Strathmore E3
07876 Succasunna 10,931 .... D2
07901 Summit 21,071 .... E2
08008 Surf City 1,571 .... E4
07461 Sussex 2,418 .... D1
08085 Swedesboro 2,031 .... C4
07878 Tabor E2
07666 Teaneck○ 39,007 .... B2
07670 Tenafly 13,552 .... C1
07608 Teterboro 19 .... B2
08086 Thorofare B4
08887 Three Bridges 750 .... D2
07724 Tinton Falls 7,740 .... E3
08753 Toms River⊙ 7,465 .... E4
07512 Totowa 11,448 .... B1
07082 Towaco E2
*08601 Trenton (cap.)⊙ 92,124 ... D3
Trenton‡ 307,863 .... D3
08087 Tuckerton 2,472 .... E4
07083 Union○ 50,184 .... A2
07735 Union Beach 6,354 .... E3
07087 Union City 55,593 .... C2
†07421 Upper Greenwood
Lake 2,734 .... E1
†07458 Upper Saddle River 7,958 .. B1
08406 Ventnor City 11,704 .... E5
07462 Vernon 800 .... E1
07044 Verona 14,166 .... B2
08251 Villas 5,909 .... D5
08088 Vincentown 900 .... D4
08360 Vineland 53,753 .... C5
Vineland-Millville-Bridgeton‡
132,866 .... C5
†08043 Voorhees○ 12,919 .... B3
07463 Waldwick 10,802 .... B1
07719 Wall○ 18,952 .... E3
07057 Wallington 10,741 .... B2
†07712 Wanamassa E3
07465 Wanaque 10,025 .... B1
08758 Waretown 1,175 .... E4
†07060 Warren○ 9,805 .... D2
07882 Washington 6,429 .... D2
07060 Watchung 5,290 .... E2
07470 Wayne○ 46,474 .... A1
07087 Weehawken○ 13,168 .... C2
08090 Wenonah 2,303 .... C4
07006 West Caldwell 11,407 .... A2
†08204 West Cape May 1,091 ...... D6
08092 West Creek 827 .... E4
†08086 West Deptford○ 18,002 ..... B3
*07090 Westfield 30,447 .... E2
07764 West Long Branch 7,380 ... F3
07480 West Milford 950 .... E1
08108 Westmont 15,875 .... B3
07093 West New York 39,194 ..... C2
07052 West Orange 39,510 .... A2
07424 West Paterson 11,293 ...... B2
08628 West Trenton D3
08093 Westville 4,786 .... B3
†08260 West Wildwood 360 .... D6
07675 Westwood 10,714 .... B1
07885 Wharton 5,485 .... D2

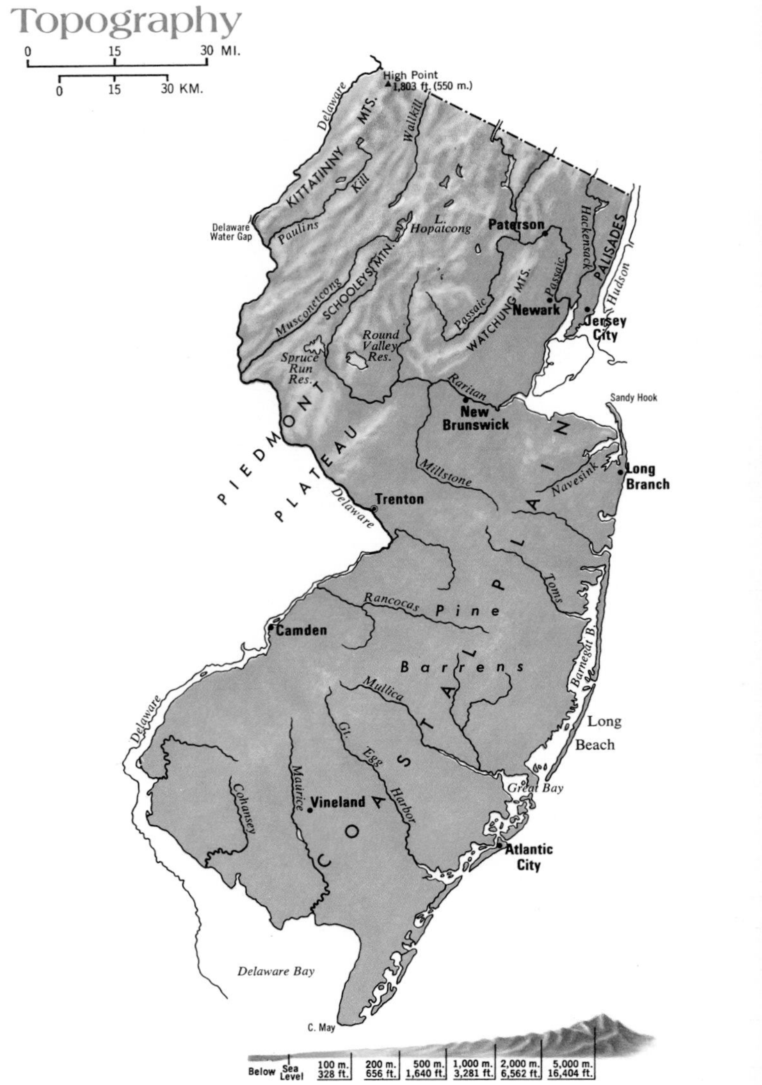
Topography
0 15 30 MI.
0 15 30 KM.
High Point 1,803 ft. (550 m.)
Delaware
KITTATINNY MTS.
Wallkill
Paulins Kill
Delaware Water Gap
L. Hopatcong
Paterson
Hackensack
PALISADES
Hudson
Musconetcong
SCHOOLEY'S MTN.
Passaic
WATCHUNG MTS.
Newark
Jersey City
Round Valley Res.
Spruce Run Res.
Raritan
Sandy Hook
New Brunswick
PIEDMONT PLATEAU
Millstone
Navesink
Long Branch
Trenton
Delaware
Toms
Rancocas
Pine
Camden
Barrens
COASTAL PLAIN
Barnegat B.
Mullica
Long Beach
Gt. Egg Harbor
Maurice
Cohansey
Vineland
Great Bay
Atlantic City
Delaware Bay
C. May
Below Sea Level
100 m. 328 ft.
200 m. 656 ft.
500 m. 1,640 ft.
1,000 m. 3,281 ft.
2,000 m. 6,562 ft.
5,000 m. 16,404 ft.

07981 Whippany E2
08889 White House Station D2
†07866 White Meadow Lake 8,429 D2
08252 Whitesboro 1,583 .... D5
07765 Wickatunk 950 .... E3
08260 Wildwood 4,913 .... D6
08260 Wildwood Crest 4,149 ...... D6
08094 Williamstown 5,768 .... D4
08046 Willingboro○ 39,912 .... D3
†07036 Winfield○ 1,785 .... B2
08270 Woodbine 2,809 .... D5
07095 Woodbridge○ 90,074 .... E2
08096 Woodbury⊙ 10,353 .... B4
08097 Woodbury Heights 3,460 ... B4
07675 Woodcliff Lake 5,644 .... B1
†08107 Wood-Lynne 2,578 .... B3
†07885 Woodport D2
07075 Wood-Ridge 7,929 .... B2
08098 Woodstown 3,250 .... C4
08562 Wrightstown 3,031 .... D3
07481 Wyckoff○ 15,500 .... B1
08620 Yardville 9,414 .... D3

OTHER FEATURES

Absecon (inlet) E5
Alloways (creek) C4
Arthur Kill (str.) B3
Atlantic Highlands (ridge) E3
Barnegat (bay) E4
Batsto (riv.) D4
Bayonne Military Ocean Terminal .. B2
Beach Haven (inlet) E4
Beaver (brook) C2
Ben Davis (pt.) C5
Big Flat (brook) D1
Big Timber (creek) C4
Boonton (res.) E2
Brigantine (inlet) E5
Budd (lake) D2
Canistear (res.) E1
Cedar (creek) E4
Clinton (res.) E1
Cohansey (riv.) C5
Cold Spring (inlet) D6
Cooper (riv.) B3
Corson (inlet) D5
Crosswicks (creek) D3
Culvers (lake) D1
Delaware (bay) C5
Delaware (riv.) D3
Delaware Water Gap Nat'l Rec.
Area C1
Earle Naval Weapons Sta. E3
Echo (lake) E1
Edison Nat'l Hist. Site A2
Egg Island (pt.) C5
Fort Dix 14,297 .... D3
Fort Hancock F3
Fort Monmouth E3
Gateway Nat'l Rec. Area E2
Great (bay) E4
Great Egg Harbor (inlet) E5
Greenwood (lake) E1
Hackensack (riv.) C1
Hereford (inlet) D5
High Point (mt.) D1
Hopatcong (lake) D2
Hudson (riv.) C1
Island (beach) E4
Kill Van Kull (str.) B2
Kittatinny (mts.) D1
Lakehurst Naval Air-Engineering
Center E3
Lamington (riv.) D2
Landing (creek) D4
Little Egg (harb.) E4
Lockatong (creek) C3
Long (beach) E4
Long Beach (isl.) E4
Lower New York (bay) E2
Manasquan (riv.) E3
Manumuskin (riv.) D5
Maurice (riv.) C4
May (cape) C6
McGuire A.F.B. 7,853 .... D3
Metedeconk (riv.) E3
Mill (creek) E4
Millstone (riv.) D3
Mohawk (lake) D1
Morristown Nat'l Hist. Park D2
Mullica (riv.) D4
Musconetcong (riv.) C2
Navesink (riv.) E3
Newark (bay) B2
Oak Ridge (res.) D1
Oldmans (creek) C4
Oradell (res.) B1
Oswego (riv.) E4
Owassa (lake) D1
Palisades C1
Passaic (riv.) E2
Paulins Kill (riv.) D1
Pennsauken (creek) B3
Pequest (riv.) D2
Picatinny Arsenal D2
Pohatcong (creek) C2
Pompton (lake) B1
Raccoon (creek) C4
Ramapo (riv.) E1
Rancocas (creek) D3
Raritan (bay) E3
Raritan (riv.) D2
Ridgeway Branch, Toms (riv.) E3
Round Valley (res.) D2
Saddle (riv.) B1
Salem (riv.) C4
Sandy Hook (spit) F3
Shoal Branch, Wading (riv.) D4
Spruce Run (res.) D2
Statue of Liberty Nat'l Mon. B2
Stony (brook) D3
Stow (creek) C5
Swartswood (lake) D1
Tappan (lake) C1
The Narrows (str.) E2
Toms (riv.) E3
Townsend (inlet) D5
Tuckahoe (riv.) D5
Union (lake) C5
Upper New York (bay) B2
Wading (riv.) D4
Wallkill (riv.) D1
Wanaque (res.) E1
Wawayanda (lake) E1

⊙County seat.
‡Population of metropolitan area.
○Population of town or township.
† Zip of nearest p.o. * Multiple zips.

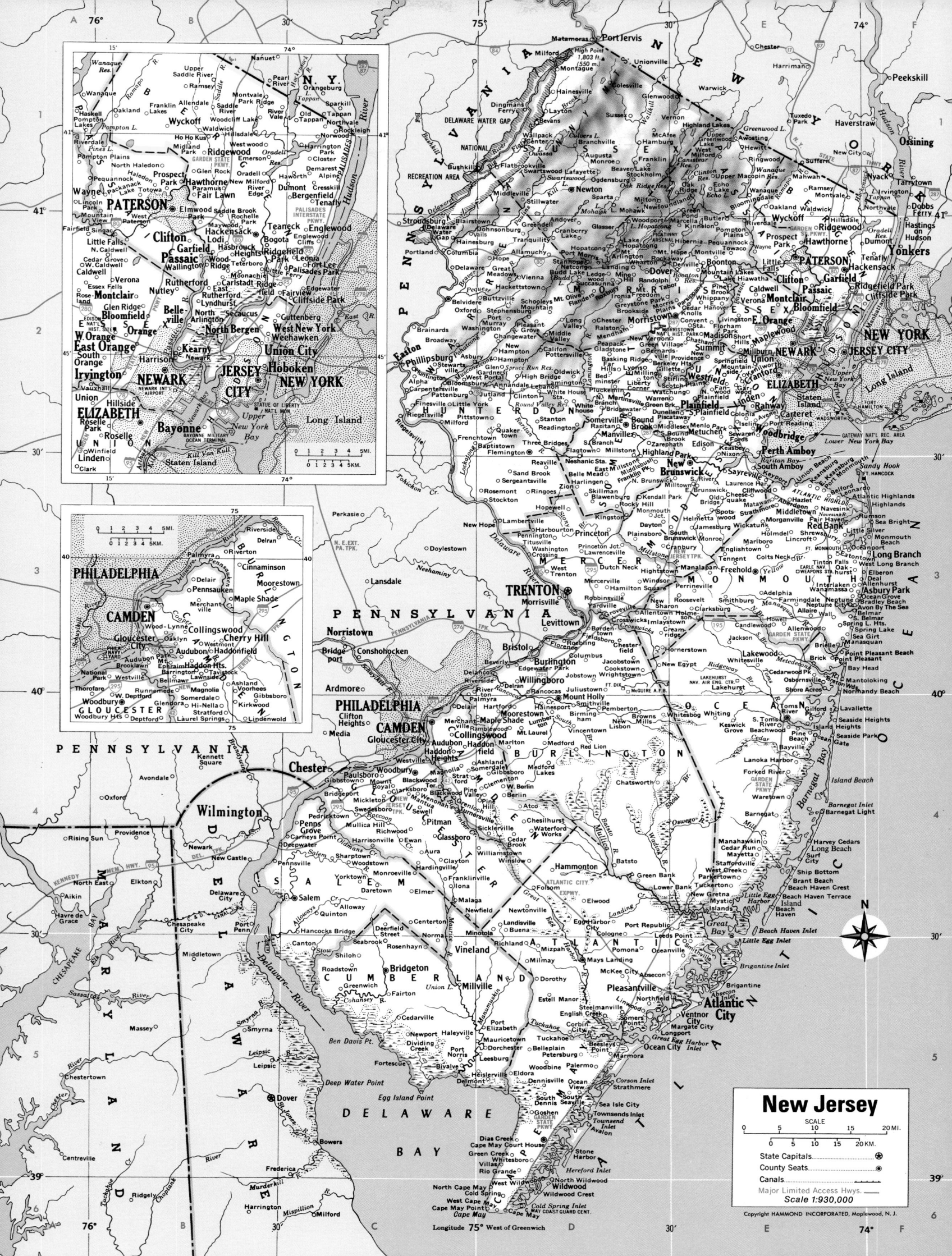

New Jersey

SCALE
0   5   10   15   20 MI.

0   5   10   15   20 KM.

State Capitals............⊛
County Seats.............⊙
Canals

Major Limited Access Hwys.
Scale 1:930,000

Copyright HAMMOND INCORPORATED, Maplewood, N.J.

Longitude 75° West of Greenwich

COUNTIES

Bernalillo 419,700 .... C4
Catron 2,720 .... A4
Chaves 51,103 .... E5
Cibola B3
Colfax 13,667 .... E2
Curry 42,019 .... F4
De Baca 2,454 .... E4
Dona Ana 96,340 .... C6
Eddy 47,855 .... E6
Grant 26,204 .... A5
Guadalupe 4,496 .... E4
Harding 1,090 .... F3
Hidalgo 6,049 .... A7
Lea 55,993 .... F6
Lincoln 10,997 .... D5

Los Alamos 17,599 .... C3
Luna 15,585 .... B6
McKinley 56,449 .... A3
Mora 4,205 .... E3
Otero 44,665 .... D6
Quay 10,577 .... F3
Rio Arriba 29,282 .... B2
Roosevelt 15,695 .... F4
Sandoval 34,799 .... C3
San Juan 81,433 .... A2
San Miguel
  22,751 .... D3
Santa Fe 75,360 .... C3
Sierra 8,454 .... B5
Socorro 12,566 .... C5
Taos 19,456 .... D2
Torrance 7,491 .... D4
Union 4,725 .... F2
Valencia 61,115 .... C4

CITIES and TOWNS

Zip   Name/Pop.   Key

87510 Abiquiu 500 .... C2
†87034 Acoma 150 .... B4
†87034 Acomita (Pueblo of
  Acoma) 975 .... B3
88310 Alamogordo⊙ 24,024 ..... C6
*87101 Albuquerque⊙ 331,767 ... C3
  Albuquerque‡ 454,499 ...... C3
87511 Alcalde 975 .... C2
87001 Algodones 195 .... C3
88312 Alto 285 .... D5
87512 Amalia 200 .... D2
88021 Anthony 3,285 .... C6
87711 Anton Chico 400 .... D3
87930 Arrey 367 .... B6
87513 Arroyo Hondo 400 .... D2

87514 Arroyo Seco 500 .... D2
88210 Artesia 10,385 .... E6
87410 Aztec⊙ 5,512 .... B2
88023 Bayard 3,036 .... A6
87002 Belen 5,617 .... C4
88314 Bent 294 .... D5
88024 Berino 600 .... A6
87004 Bernalillo⊙ 3,012 .... C3
87412 Blanco 200 .... A2
87413 Bloomfield 4,881 .... A2
87005 Bluewater 300 .... A3
87006 Bosque (Bosque
  Farms) 3,353 .... C4
87712 Buena Vista 178 .... D3
87515 Canjilon 380 .... C2
87516 Canones 300 .... C2
88316 Capitan 762 .... D5
88414 Capulin 100 .... F2
88220 Carlsbad⊙ 25,496 ...... E6

88301 Carrizozo⊙ 1,222 .... D5
87007 Casa Blanca 560 .... B4
88113 Causey 81 .... F5
87518 Cebolla 100 .... C2
87008 Cedar Crest 600 .... C3
88026 Central 1,968 .... A6
87010 Cerrillos 500 .... C3
87519 Cerro 400 .... D2
87713 Chacon 310 .... D2
87520 Chama 1,090 .... C2
88027 Chamberino 700 .... C6
87521 Chamisal 642 .... D2
87522 Chimayo 1,993 .... D3
87714 Cimarron 888 .... E2
88415 Clayton⊙ 2,968 .... F2
87715 Cleveland 450 .... D2
88028 Cliff 600 .... A6
88317 Cloudcroft 521 .... D6

88101 Clovis⊙ 31,194 .... F4
†87041 Cochiti 983 .... C3
88029 Columbus 414 .... B7
88416 Conchas Dam 240 ..... E3
87523 Cordova 750 .... D2
88318 Corona 236 .... D4
87048 Corrales 2,791 .... C3
87524 Costilla 400 .... D2
87313 Crownpoint 1,134 ..... A3
†86504 Crystal 200 .... A3
87013 Cuba 609 .... B2
87014 Cubero 300 .... B4
87821 Datil 150 .... C5
88030 Deming⊙ 9,964 .... B6
87933 Derry 175 .... B6
88418 Des Moines 178 ...... F2
88230 Dexter 882 .... E5
87527 Dixon 800 .... D2
88032 Dona Ana 800 .... C6

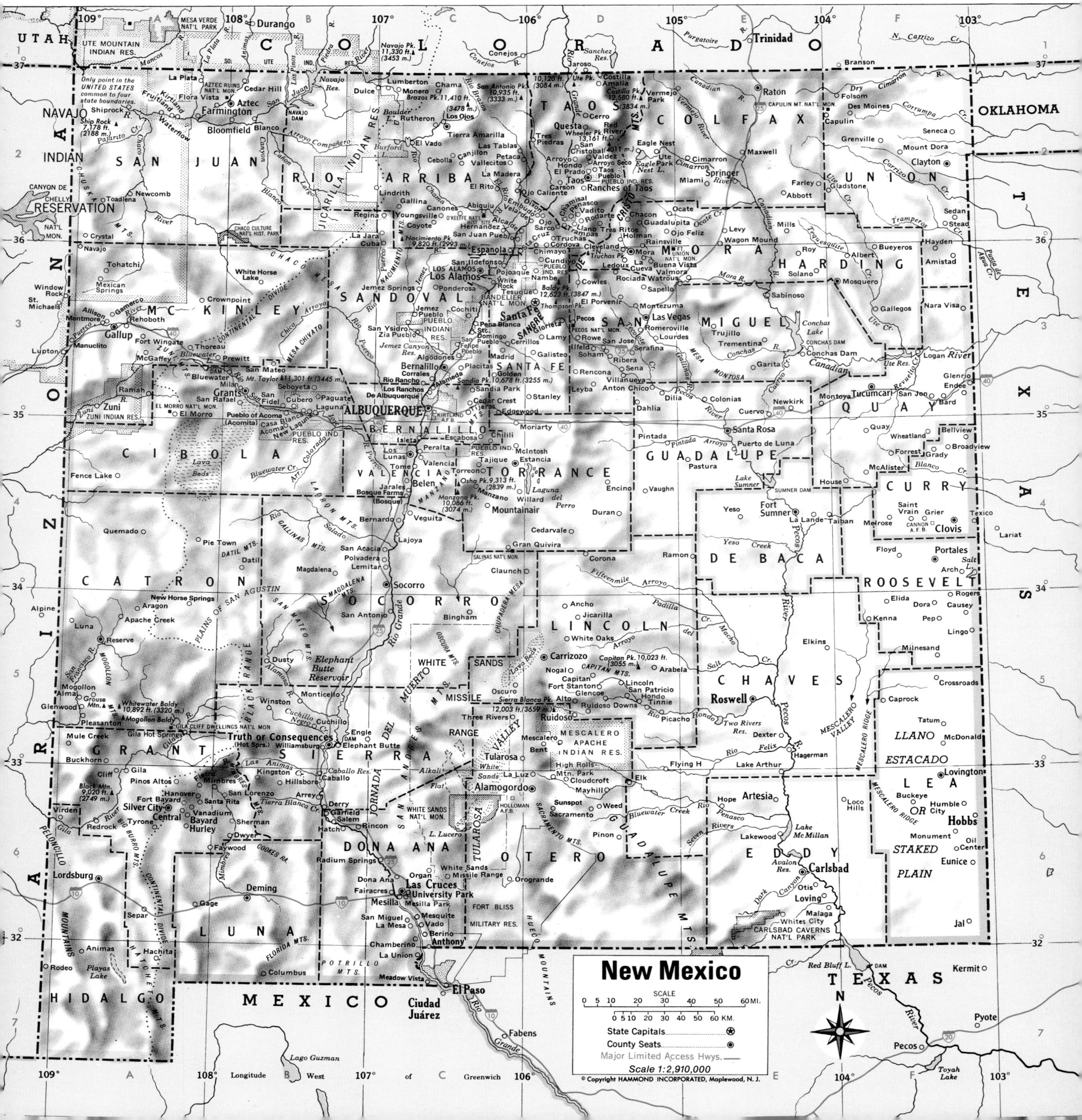

New Mexico

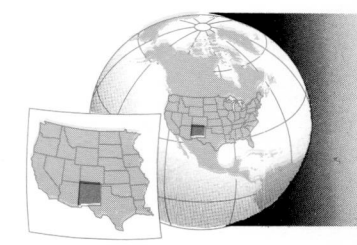

88115 Dora 168 ..... F5
87528 Dulce 1,648 ..... B2
88718 Eagle Nest 202 ..... D2
88116 Elida 202 ..... F5
87529 El Prado 200 ..... D2
87530 El Rito 475 ..... C2
87531 Embudo 400 ..... C2
88321 Encino 155 ..... D4
87532 Espanola 6,803 ..... C3
87016 Estancia⊙ 830 ..... D4
88231 Eunice 2,970 ..... F6
88033 Fairacres 700 ..... C6
87401 Farmington 31,222 ..... A2
†88041 Fierro 200 ..... A6
87415 Flora Vista 500 ..... A2
88118 Floyd 146 ..... F4
88419 Folsom 73 ..... F2
88036 Fort Bayard 400 ..... A6
87537 Fort Stanton 80 ..... D5
88119 Fort Sumner⊙ 1,421 ..... E4
87316 Fort Wingate 800 ..... A3
87416 Fruitland 800 ..... A2
†87540 Galisteo 125 ..... D3
87017 Gallina 420 ..... C2
87301 Gallup⊙ 18,167 ..... A3
87317 Gamerco 800 ..... A3
87936 Garfield 600 ..... B6
88038 Gila 350 ..... A6
88324 Glencoe 125 ..... D5
88039 Glenwood 220 ..... A5
87535 Glorieta 300 ..... D3
88120 Grady 122 ..... F4
87200 Grants 11,439 ..... B3
88424 Grenville 39 ..... F2
87722 Guadalupita 300 ..... D2
88232 Hagerman 936 ..... E5
88041 Hanover 300 ..... A6
87937 Hatch 1,028 ..... B6
87537 Hernandez 500 ..... C2
88325 High Rolls-Mountain Park 555 ..... D5
88042 Hillsboro 175 ..... B6
88240 Hobbs 29,153 ..... F6
87723 Holman 400 ..... D2
88336 Hondo 425 ..... D5
88250 Hope 111 ..... E6
87901 Hot Springs (Truth or Consequences)⊙ 5,219 ..... B5
88121 House 117 ..... F4
88043 Hurley 1,616 ..... A6
87022 Isleta 1,246 ..... C4
88252 Jal 2,675 ..... F6
87023 Jarales 700 ..... C4
87024 Jemez Pueblo 1,503 ..... C3
87025 Jemez Springs 316 ..... C3
87417 Kirtland 2,358 ..... A2
87026 Laguna 900 ..... B3
87027 La Jara 210 ..... B2
88253 Lake Arthur 327 ..... E5
88337 La Luz 1,194 ..... C6
87539 La Madera 200 ..... C2
88044 La Mesa 900 ..... C6
87418 La Plata 150 ..... A2
88001 Las Cruces⊙ 45,086 ..... C6
Las Cruces‡ 96,340 ..... C6
87701 Las Vegas⊙ 14,322 ..... D3
87725 Ledoux 300 ..... D3
87823 Lemitar 800 ..... B4
88338 Lincoln 100 ..... D5
87543 Llano 325 ..... D2
88255 Loco Hills 375 ..... F6
88426 Logan 735 ..... F3
88045 Lordsburg⊙ 3,195 ..... A6
87544 Los Alamos⊙ 11,039 ..... C3

87031 Los Lunas⊙ 3,525 ..... C4
†87101 Los Ranchos De Albuquerque 2,702 ..... C3
88256 Loving 1,355 ..... E6
88260 Lovington⊙ 9,727 ..... F6
87547 Lumberton 175 ..... C2
87824 Luna 200 ..... A5
87825 Magdalena 1,022 ..... B4
88263 Malaga 300 ..... E6
88728 Maxwell 316 ..... E2
88339 Mayhill 300 ..... D6
†79901 Meadow Vista 3,377 ..... C7
88124 Melrose 649 ..... F4
87319 Mentmore 315 ..... A3
88340 Mescalero 1,259 ..... D5
88046 Mesilla 2,029 ..... C6
88047 Mesilla Park C6
88048 Mesquite 500 ..... C6
87320 Mexican Springs 150 ..... A3
87729 Miami 112 ..... E2
87021 Milan 3,747 ..... B3
88049 Mimbres 300 ..... B6
88731 Montezuma 250 ..... D3
87939 Monticello 125 ..... B5
88265 Monument 300 ..... F6
87732 Mora⊙ D2
87035 Moriarty 1,276 ..... D4
87733 Mosquero⊙ 197 ..... F3
87036 Mountainair 1,170 ..... C4
†87501 Nambe 1,017 ..... C3
88430 Nara Visa 250 ..... F3
87328 Navajo 920 ..... A3
†87325 Newcomb 500 ..... A2
87038 New Laguna 250 ..... B4
88266 Oil Center 236 ..... F6
87549 Ojo Caliente 600 ..... D2
88735 Ojo Feliz 133 ..... E2
88550 Ojo Sarco 380 ..... D2
88052 Organ 300 ..... C6
87040 Paguate 500 ..... B3
87552 Pecos 885 ..... D3
87041 Pena Blanca 700 ..... C3
87553 Penasco 860 ..... D2
87042 Peralta 300 ..... C4
88343 Picacho 100 ..... D5
88053 Pinos Altos 250 ..... A6
87044 Ponderosa 300 ..... C3
88130 Portales⊙ 9,940 ..... F4
87045 Prewitt 300 ..... B3
88432 Puerto de Luna 175 ..... E4
87829 Quemado 450 ..... A4
87556 Questa 1,202 ..... D2
88054 Radium Springs 150 ..... B6
87736 Rainsville 350 ..... D2
87321 Ramah 574 ..... A3
87557 Ranches of Taos 1,411 ..... D2
87740 Raton⊙ 8,225 ..... E2
87558 Red River 332 ..... D2
87322 Rehoboth 200 ..... A3
87830 Reserve⊙ 439 ..... A5
87560 Ribera 84 ..... D3
87940 Rincon 300 ..... C6
87124 Rio Rancho 9,985 ..... C3
87561 Rodarte 650 ..... D2
88201 Roswell⊙ 39,676 ..... E5
87562 Rowe 290 ..... D3
87743 Roy 381 ..... E3
88345 Ruidoso 4,260 ..... D5
88346 Ruidoso Downs 949 ..... D5
87941 Salem 400 ..... B6
87831 San Acacia 286 ..... B4
87832 San Antonio 359 ..... B4
87564 San Cristobal 350 ..... D2
87047 Sandia Park 450 ..... C3

†87001 San Felipe Pueblo 1,465 ..... C3
†87501 San Ildefonso 232 ..... C3
88434 San Jon 341 ..... F3
87565 San Jose 150 ..... D3
87566 San Juan Pueblo 870 ..... C2
88041 San Lorenzo 200 ..... B6
87050 San Mateo 200 ..... B3
88058 San Miguel 400 ..... C6
88348 San Patricio 300 ..... D5
87051 San Rafael 300 ..... A3
87567 Santa Cruz 754 ..... D2
87501 Santa Fe (cap.)⊙ 48,953 ..... C3
†88041 Santa Rita 600 ..... B6
87052 Santa Rosa⊙ 2,469 ..... E4
87052 Santo Domingo Pueblo 2,082 ..... C3
87053 San Ysidro 199 ..... C3
87745 Sapello 600 ..... D3
87055 Seboyeta 125 ..... B3
87568 Sena 150 ..... D3
87569 Serafina 225 ..... D3
87420 Shiprock 7,237 ..... A2
88061 Silver City⊙ 9,887 ..... A6
87801 Socorro⊙ 7,173 ..... C4
†87565 Soham 104 ..... D3
87747 Springer 1,657 ..... E2
87057 Tajique 145 ..... C4
87571 Taos⊙ 3,369 ..... D2
†87571 Taos Pueblo 900 ..... D2
88267 Tatum 896 ..... F5
87574 Tesuque 1,014 ..... C3
88135 Texico 958 ..... F4
87323 Thoreau 1,099 ..... A3
87575 Tierra Amarilla⊙ 850 ..... C2
87059 Tijeras 311 ..... C3
87324 Toadlena 200 ..... A2
87325 Tohatchi 1,011 ..... A3
87060 Tome 500 ..... C4
87577 Tres Piedras 200 ..... D2
87578 Truchas 275 ..... D2
†87701 Trujillo 148 ..... E3
87901 Truth or Consequences⊙ 5,219 ..... B5
88401 Tucumcari⊙ 6,765 ..... F3
88352 Tularosa 2,536 ..... C5
88003 University Park 4,353 ..... C6
87579 Vadito 400 ..... D2
88072 Vado 325 ..... C6
87580 Valdez 300 ..... D2
†87031 Valencia 500 ..... C4
87581 Vallecitos 450 ..... C2
88073 Vanadium 150 ..... A6
88353 Vaughn 737 ..... D4
87582 Velarde 950 ..... C2
87583 Villanueva 500 ..... D3
†88055 Virden 246 ..... A6
87752 Wagon Mound 416 ..... E2
87421 Waterflow 475 ..... A2
87753 Watrous 75 ..... D3
87544 White Rock 6,560 ..... C3
88002 White Sands Missile Range 3,120 ..... C6
87063 Willard 166 ..... D4
87942 Williamsburg 433 ..... B5
88136 Yeso 200 ..... E4
87064 Youngsville 125 ..... C2
†87053 Zia Pueblo 500 ..... C3
87327 Zuni 5,551 ..... A3

OTHER FEATURES

Abiquiu (res.) C2
Alamosa (riv.) B5
Animas (riv.) B1
Avalon (res.) E6
Aztec Ruins Nat'l Mon. A2
Baldy (peak) D3
Bandelier Nat'l Mon. C3
Big Burro (mts.) A6
Black (mt.) A6
Black (range) B5
Blanco (creek) F4
Bluewater (creek) B4
Bluewater (creek) D6
Bluewater (lake) A3
Boulder (lake) C2
Brazos (peak) C2
Burford (lake) C2
Caballo (res.) B6
Canadian (riv.) F3
Cannon A.F.B. 3,798 ..... F4
Canyon Blanco (creek) D2
Capitan (mts.) D5
Capitan (peak) D5
Capulin Mountain Nat'l Mon. F2
Carlsbad Caverns Nat'l Park E6
Carrizo (creek) F2
Chaco (mesa) B3
Chaco (riv.) A2
Chaco Culture Nat'l Hist. Park B2
Chico Arroyo (creek) B3
Chivato (mesa) B3
Chupadera (mesa) C5
Chuska (mts.) A2
Cimarron (riv.) E2
Colorado, Arroyo (riv.) B4
Compañero, Arroyo (creek) B2
Conchas (lake) E3
Conchas (riv.) E3
Cookes (range) B6
Corrumpa (creek) F2
Costilla (peak) D2
Cuchillo Negro (creek) B5
Cuervo (creek) E3
Dark Canyon (creek) E6
Datil (mts.) B4
Dry Cimarron (riv.) F2
Eagle Nest (lake) D2
Elephant Butte (res.) B5
El Morro Nat'l Mon. A3
El Rito (creek) C2
Fifteenmile Arroyo (creek) D4
Florida (mts.) B7
Fort Bliss Mil. Res. C6
Fort Union Nat'l Mon. E3
Gallinas (mts.) E3
Gallinas (riv.) E3
Gila (riv.) A6
Gila Cliff Dwellings Nat'l Mon. A5
Grouse (mt.) A5
Guadalupe (mts.) D6
Hatchet (mts.) A7
Holloman A.F.B. 7,245 ..... C6
Hueco (mts.) D6
Jemez (riv.) C3
Jemez Canyon (res.) C3
Jicarilla Ind. Res. B2
Jornada del Muerto (valley) C5
Kirtland A.F.B. C3
Ladron (mts.) B4
La Plata (riv.) A1
Largo, Cañon (creek) B2
Las Animas (creek) B5
Llano Estacado (Staked) (plain) F5
Lucero (lake) C6
Macho, Arroyo del (creek) D5
Magdalena (mts.) B4
Manzano (mts.) C4
Manzano (peak) C4
McMillan (lake) E5
Mescalero (ridge) F6
Mescalero (valley) F5
Mescalero Apache Ind. Res. D5
Mimbres (mts.) B6
Mimbres (riv.) B6
Mogollon (mts.) A5
Mogollon Baldy (peak) A5
Montosa (mesa) E3
Mora (riv.) C3
Nacimiento (mts.) C3
Nacimiento (peak) C2
Navajo (res.) B2
Navajo Ind. Res. A2
North Truchas (peak) D3
Ocate (creek) E2
O'Keeffe Nat'l Hist. Site C2
Oscura (mts.) C4
Osha (peak) C4
Padilla (creek) D5
Pajarito (creek) A2
Pecos (riv.) E5
Pecos Nat'l Mon. D3
Peloncillo (mts.) A6
Perro (mts.) D4
Pinos, Rio de los (riv.) B2
Pintada Arroyo (creek) E4
Playas (lake) A7
Potrillo (mts.) B7
Pueblo Ind. Res. B4
Pueblo Ind. Res. D3
Pueblo Ind. Res. C4
Pueblo Ind. Res. D2
Puerco (riv.) A3
Red Bluff (lake) E7
Revuelto (creek) F3
Rio Brazos (riv.) C2
Rio Chama (riv.) C2
Rio Felix (riv.) E5
Rio Grande (riv.) C5
Rio Hondo (riv.) E5
Rio Penasco (riv.) E6
Rio Puerco (riv.) C4
Rio Salado (riv.) B4
Rocky (mts.) C1
Sacramento (mts.) D6
Salinas Nat'l Mon. C4
Salt (creek) E5
Salt (lake) F4
San Agustin (plains) B5
San Andres (mts.) C6
San Antonio (peak) C2
Sandia (peak) C3
San Francisco (riv.) A5
Sangre de Cristo (mts.) D3
San Jose (riv.) B3
San Juan (riv.) B2
San Mateo (mts.) B5
Seven Rivers (riv.) E6
Ship Rock (mt.) A2
Sierra Blanca (peak) C5
Staked (Llano Estacado) (plain) F5
Sumner (lake) E4
Taylor (mt.) B3
Tecolote (creek) D3
Tequesquite (creek) E2
Thompson (peak) E2
Tierra Blanca (creek) B6
Tramperos (creek) F2
Tularosa (valley) C6
Ute (creek) F2
Ute (peak) D2
Ute (res.) F3
Ute Mountain Ind. Res. A1
Vermejo (riv.) E2
Wheeler (peak) D2
White Sands (des.) C5
White Sands Missile Range C5
White Sands Nat'l Mon. C6
Whitewater Baldy (mt.) A5
Wingate Army Depot A3
Yeso (creek) E4
Zuni (mts.) A3
Zuni (riv.) A3
Zuni Ind. Res. A3

⊙County seat.
‡Population of metropolitan area.
† Zip of nearest p.o.   * Multiple zips.

AREA 121,593 sq. mi. (314,926 sq. km.)
POPULATION 1,302,981
CAPITAL Santa Fe
LARGEST CITY Albuquerque
HIGHEST POINT Wheeler Pk. 13,161 ft. (4011 m.)
SETTLED IN 1605
ADMITTED TO UNION January 6, 1912
POPULAR NAME Land of Enchantment
STATE FLOWER Yucca
STATE BIRD Road Runner

Topography

0   50   100 MI.
0   50   100 KM.

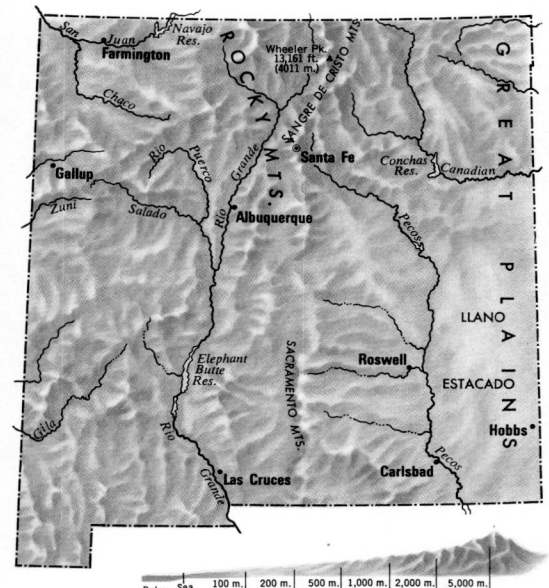

Agriculture, Industry and Resources

DOMINANT LAND USE

- Wheat, Grain Sorghums, Range Livestock
- General Farming, Livestock, Special Crops
- General Farming, Livestock, Cash Grain
- Dry Beans, General Farming
- Cotton, Forest Products
- Range Livestock
- Forests
- Nonagricultural Land

MAJOR MINERAL OCCURRENCES

Ag Silver
Au Gold
C Coal
Cu Copper
G Natural Gas
Gp Gypsum
K Potash
Mo Molybdenum
Mr Marble
Na Salt
O Petroleum
Pb Lead
U Uranium
V Vanadium
Zn Zinc
⚡ Water Power

New York

SCALE
0 5 10 20 30 40 MI.
0 5 10 20 30 40 KM.

State Capitals..............✪
County Seats...............⊙
Canals.........................
Major Limited Access Hwys._____

Scale 1:1,920,000

COUNTIES

Albany 285,909 .... M5
Allegany 51,742 .... D6
Bronx 1,168,972 .... N9
Broome 213,648 .... J6
Cattaraugus 85,697 .... C6
Cayuga 79,894 .... G4
Chautauqua 146,925 .... B6
Chemung 97,656 .... G6
Chenango 49,344 .... J6
Clinton 80,750 .... N1
Columbia 59,487 .... N6
Cortland 48,820 .... H5
Delaware 46,824 .... K6
Dutchess 245,055 .... N7
Erie 1,015,472 .... C5
Essex 36,176 .... N2
Franklin 44,929 .... M1
Fulton 55,153 .... M4
Genesee 59,400 .... D4
Greene 40,861 .... M6
Hamilton 5,034 .... L3
Herkimer 66,714 .... L4
Jefferson 88,151 .... J2
Kings 2,230,936 .... N9
Lewis 25,035 .... K3
Livingston 57,006 .... E5
Madison 65,150 .... J5
Monroe 702,238 .... E4
Montgomery 53,439 .... M5
Nassau 1,321,582 .... N9
New York 1,428,285 .... M9
Niagara 227,354 .... C4
Oneida 253,466 .... J4
Onondaga 463,920 .... H5
Ontario 88,909 .... F5
Orange 259,603 .... M8
Orleans 38,496 .... D4
Oswego 113,901 .... H4
Otsego 59,075 .... K5
Putnam 77,193 .... N8
Queens 1,891,325 .... N9
Rensselaer 151,966 .... O5
Richmond 352,121 .... M9
Rockland 259,530 .... M8
Saint Lawrence 114,254 .... K2
Saratoga 153,759 .... N4
Schenectady 149,946 .... M5
Schoharie 29,710 .... M5
Schuyler 17,686 .... G5
Seneca 33,733 .... G5
Steuben 99,217 .... F6
Suffolk 1,284,231 .... P9
Sullivan 65,155 .... L7
Tioga 49,812 .... H6
Tompkins 87,085 .... H6
Ulster 158,158 .... M7
Warren 54,854 .... N3
Washington 54,795 .... O4
Wayne 84,581 .... F4
Westchester 866,599 .... N8
Wyoming 39,895 .... D5
Yates 21,459 .... G5

CITIES and TOWNS

Zip   Name/Pop.   Key

13605 Adams 1,701 .... J3
14801 Addison 2,028 .... F6
14001 Akron 2,971 .... C4
*12201 Albany (cap.)⊙ 101,727 .... N5
   Albany-Schenectady-Troy‡
        795,019 .... N5
14411 Albion⊙ 4,897 .... D4

14004 Alden 2,488 .... C5
13607 Alexandria Bay 1,265 .... J2
14802 Alfred 4,967 .... E6
14706 Allegany 2,078 .... C6
12009 Altamont 1,292 .... M5
11930 Amagansett 2,188 .... R9
11701 Amityville 9,076 .... O9
12010 Amsterdam 21,872 .... M5
14006 Angola 2,292 .... C5
14009 Arcade 2,052 .... D5
10502 Ardsley 4,183 .... O6
12603 Arlington 11,305 .... N7
12015 Athens 1,738 .... N6
11509 Atlantic Beach 1,775 .... P7
14011 Attica 2,659 .... D5
13021 Auburn⊙ 32,548 .... G5
13026 Aurora 926 .... G5
12018 Averill Park 1,337 .... O5
14414 Avon 3,006 .... E5
11702 Babylon 12,388 .... O9
13733 Bainbridge 1,603 .... J6
11510 Baldwin 31,630 .... R7
13027 Baldwinsville 6,446 .... H4
12020 Ballston Spa⊙ 4,711 .... N5
†12550 Balmville 2,919 .... M7
14020 Batavia⊙ 16,703 .... D5
14810 Bath⊙ 6,042 .... F6
11706 Bay Shore 10,784 .... O9
11709 Bayport 7,034 .... R6
12508 Beacon 12,937 .... N7
11710 Bellmore 18,106 .... R7
11713 Bellport 2,809 .... P9
14813 Belmont⊙ 1,024 .... E6
14814 Big Flats 2,892 .... G6
*13901 Binghamton⊙ 55,860 .... J6
   Binghamton‡ 301,336 .... J6

13612 Black River 1,384 .... J3
14219 Blasdell 3,288 .... C5
14715 Bolivar 1,345 .... D6
13309 Boonville 2,344 .... K4
13613 Brasher
   Falls-Winthrop 1,454 .... L1
11717 Brentwood 44,321 .... O9
13029 Brewerton 2,472 .... H4
10509 Brewster 1,650 .... N8
11932 Bridgehampton 1,941 .... R9
†12524 Brinckerhoff 3,030 .... N7
12025 Broadalbin 1,415 .... M4
14420 Brockport 9,776 .... D4
14716 Brocton 1,416 .... B6
*10401 Bronx
   (borough)⊙ 1,168,972 .... N9
10708 Bronxville 6,267 .... O7
*11201 Brooklyn
   (borough)⊙ 2,230,936 .... N9
†11545 Brookville 3,290 .... R6
10511 Buchanan 2,041 .... N8
*14201 Buffalo⊙ 357,870 .... B5
   Buffalo‡ 1,242,573 .... B5
12413 Cairo 1,281 .... M6
14423 Caledonia 2,188 .... E5
12816 Cambridge 1,820 .... O4
13316 Camden 2,667 .... J4
13031 Camillus 1,298 .... H4
13317 Canajoharie 2,412 .... L5
14424 Canandaigua⊙ 10,419 .... F5
13032 Canastota 4,773 .... J4
14823 Canisteo 2,679 .... E6
13617 Canton⊙ 7,055 .... K1
10512 Carmel⊙ 27,948 .... N8
13619 Carthage 3,643 .... J3
12033 Castleton-on-Hudson 1,627 .... N5
12414 Catskill⊙ 4,718 .... N6
††14850 Cayuga Heights 3,170 .... H6

13035 Cazenovia 2,599 .... J5
11516 Cedarhurst 6,162 .... P7
14720 Celoron 1,405 .... B6
11720 Centereach 30,136 .... O9
11934 Center Moriches 5,703 .... P9
11722 Central Islip 19,734 .... O9
13036 Central Square 1,418 .... H4
10917 Central Valley 1,705 .... M8
12919 Champlain 1,410 .... N1
12037 Chatham 2,001 .... N6
14225 Cheektowaga 92,145 .... C5
10918 Chester 1,910 .... M8
13037 Chittenango 4,290 .... J4
14428 Churchville 1,399 .... E4
14031 Clarence 18,146 .... C5
†12118 Clifton Park 23,989 .... N5
14432 Clifton Springs 2,039 .... F4
13323 Clinton 2,107 .... K4
14433 Clyde 2,491 .... G4
12043 Cobleskill 5,272 .... L5
12047 Cohoes 18,144 .... N5
10516 Cold Spring 2,161 .... N8
11724 Cold Spring Harbor 5,336 .... R6
†12201 Colonie 8,869 .... N5
11725 Commack 34,719 .... O9
13326 Cooperstown⊙ 2,342 .... L5
11726 Copiague 20,132 .... O9
12822 Corinth 2,702 .... N4
14830 Corning 12,953 .... F6
12518 Cornwall On Hudson 3,164 .... M8
13045 Cortland⊙ 20,138 .... H5
12051 Coxsackie 2,659 .... N6
10520 Croton-on-Hudson 6,889 .... N8
14727 Cuba 1,739 .... D6
11935 Cutchogue-New
   Suffolk 2,788 .... P8
12929 Dannemora 3,770 .... N1

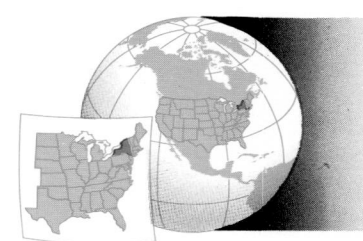

AREA 49,108 sq. mi. (127,190 sq. km.)
POPULATION 17,558,072
CAPITAL Albany
LARGEST CITY New York
HIGHEST POINT Mt. Marcy 5,344 ft. (1629 m.)
SETTLED IN 1614
ADMITTED TO UNION July 26, 1788
POPULAR NAME Empire State
STATE FLOWER Rose
STATE BIRD Bluebird

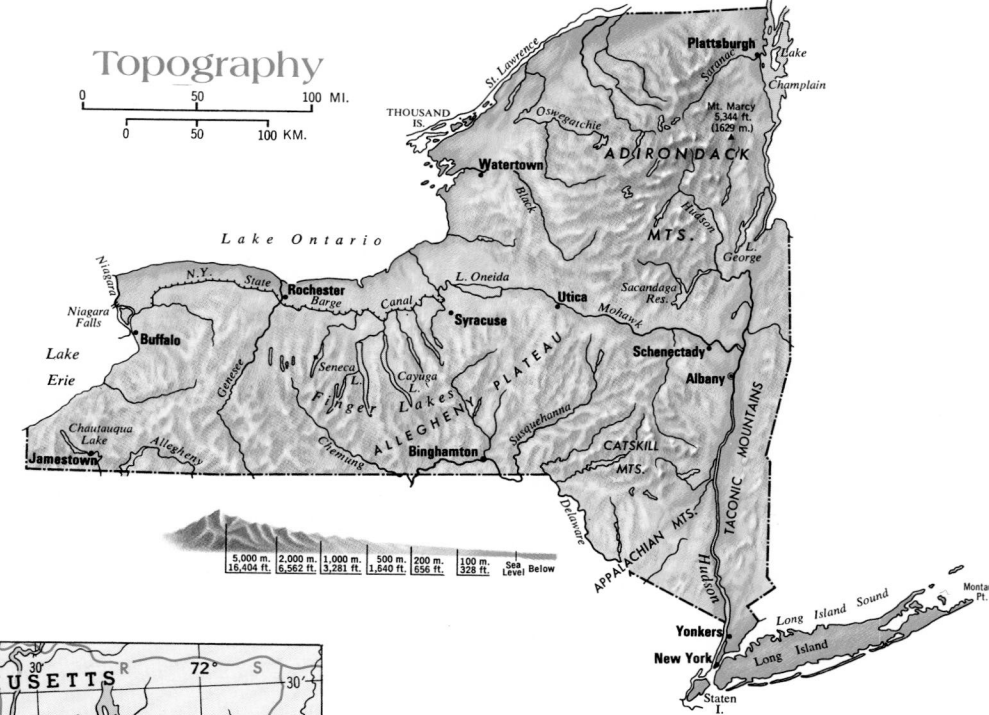

Topography

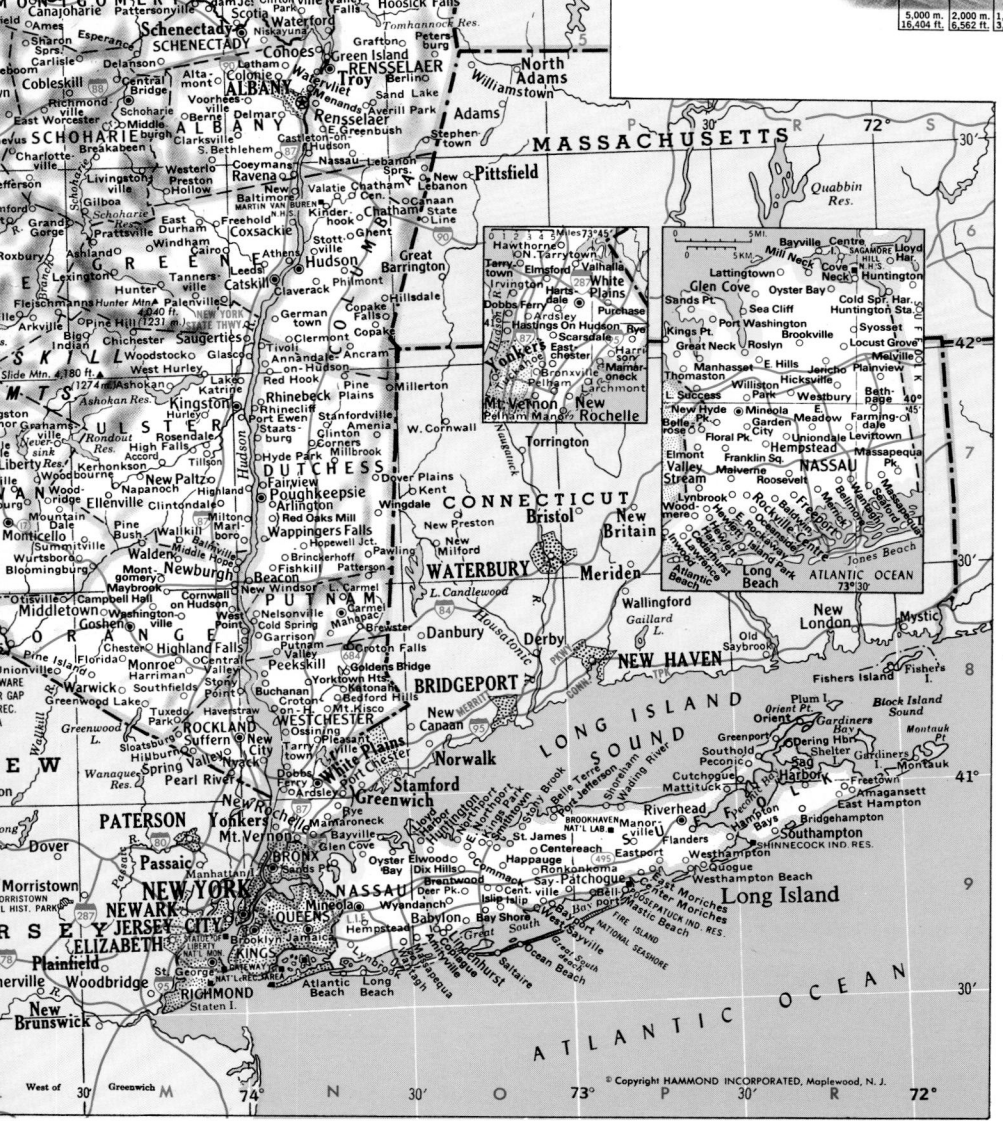

14437 Dansville 4,979	E5
11729 Deer Park 30,394	O9
13753 Delhi⊙ 3,374	L6
12054 Delmar 8,423	N5
14043 Depew 19,819	C5
13754 Deposit 1,897	K6
13214 DeWitt 9,024	H4
11746 Dix Hills 26,693	O9
10522 Dobbs Ferry 10,053	O6
13329 Dolgeville 2,602	L4
12522 Dover Plains 1,753	O7
14837 Dundee 1,556	F5
14048 Dunkirk 15,310	B5
14052 East Aurora 6,803	C5
10709 Eastchester 20,305	P6
11937 East Hampton 1,886	R9
11554 East Meadow 39,317	R7
11731 East Northport 20,187	O9
14445 East Rochester 7,596	F4
11518 East Rockaway 10,917	R7
13057 East Syracuse 3,412	H4
14057 Eden 3,000	C5
14058 Elba 750	D4
12932 Elizabethtown⊙ 659	N2
12428 Ellenville 4,405	M7
14059 Elma 2,459	C5
*14901 Elmira⊙ 35,327	G6
Elmira‡ 97,656	G6
14903 Elmira Heights 4,279	G6
11003 Elmont 27,592	P7
10523 Elmsford 3,361	O6
11731 Elwood 11,847	O9
13760 Endicott 14,457	H6
13760 Endwell 13,745	H6
14450 Fairport 5,970	F4
†12601 Fairview 5,852	N7
14733 Falconer 2,778	B6
11735 Farmingdale 7,946	R7
13066 Fayetteville 4,709	J4
†12801 Fernwood 3,640	N4
12524 Fishkill 1,555	N7
†11901 Flanders-Riverside 5,400	P9
*11001 Floral Park 16,805	P7
10921 Florida 1,947	M8
12068 Fonda⊙ 1,006	M5
12937 Fort Covington 1,804	M1
12828 Fort Edward 3,561	O4
13339 Fort Plain 2,376	L5
13340 Frankfort 2,995	K4
11010 Franklin Square 29,051	P7
14737 Franklinville 1,887	D6
14063 Fredonia 11,126	B6
11520 Freeport 38,272	R7
14738 Frewsburg 1,908	B6
14739 Friendship 1,461	D6
13069 Fulton 13,312	H4
11530 Garden City 22,927	R7
14067 Gasport 1,339	C4
14454 Geneseo⊙ 6,746	E5
14456 Geneva 15,133	G5
11542 Glen Cove 24,618	R6
12801 Glens Falls 15,897	N4
Glens Falls‡ 109,649	N4
12078 Gloversville 17,836	M4
10526 Golden's Bridge 1,367	N8
10924 Goshen⊙ 4,874	M8
13642 Gouverneur 4,285	K2
14070 Gowanda 2,713	B6
12832 Granville 2,696	O4
*11020 Great Neck 9,168	P6
14616 Greece 16,177	E4
13778 Greene 1,747	J6
12183 Green Island 2,696	N5
11944 Greenport 2,273	P8
12834 Greenwich 1,955	O4
10925 Greenwood Lake 2,809	M8
13073 Groton 2,313	H5
12835 Hadley-Lake Luzerne 1,988	N4
12086 Hagaman 1,331	M5
14075 Hamburg 10,582	C5
13346 Hamilton 3,725	J5
11946 Hampton Bays 7,256	R9
13783 Hancock 1,526	K7
10528 Harrison 23,046	P6
10530 Hartsdale 10,216	P6
10706 Hastings On Hudson 8,573	O6
11787 Hauppauge 20,960	O9
10927 Haverstraw 8,800	M8
10532 Hawthorne 5,010	O6
*11550 Hempstead 40,404	R7
13350 Herkimer⊙ 8,383	L4
11557 Hewlett 6,986	L7
†11557 Hewlett Harbor 1,331	P7
*11801 Hicksville 43,245	R7
12528 Highland 3,967	M7
10928 Highland Falls 4,187	M8
10931 Hillburn 926	M8
*10977 Hillcrest 5,733	K8
14468 Hilton 4,151	E4
14617 Irondequoit 57,648	O4
10533 Irvington 5,774	O6
11558 Island Park 4,847	R7
13077 Homer 3,635	H5
14472 Honeoye Falls 2,410	F5
12090 Hoosick Falls 3,609	O5
12533 Hopewell Junction 1,754	N7
14843 Hornell 10,234	E6
14845 Horseheads 7,348	G6
14744 Houghton 1,604	D6
12534 Hudson⊙ 7,986	N6
12839 Hudson Falls⊙ 7,419	O4
11743 Huntington 21,727	R6
11746 Huntington Station 28,769	R6
12443 Hurley 4,892	M7
12538 Hyde Park 2,550	N6
13357 Ilion 9,450	K5
11696 Inwood 8,228	P7

(continued on following page)

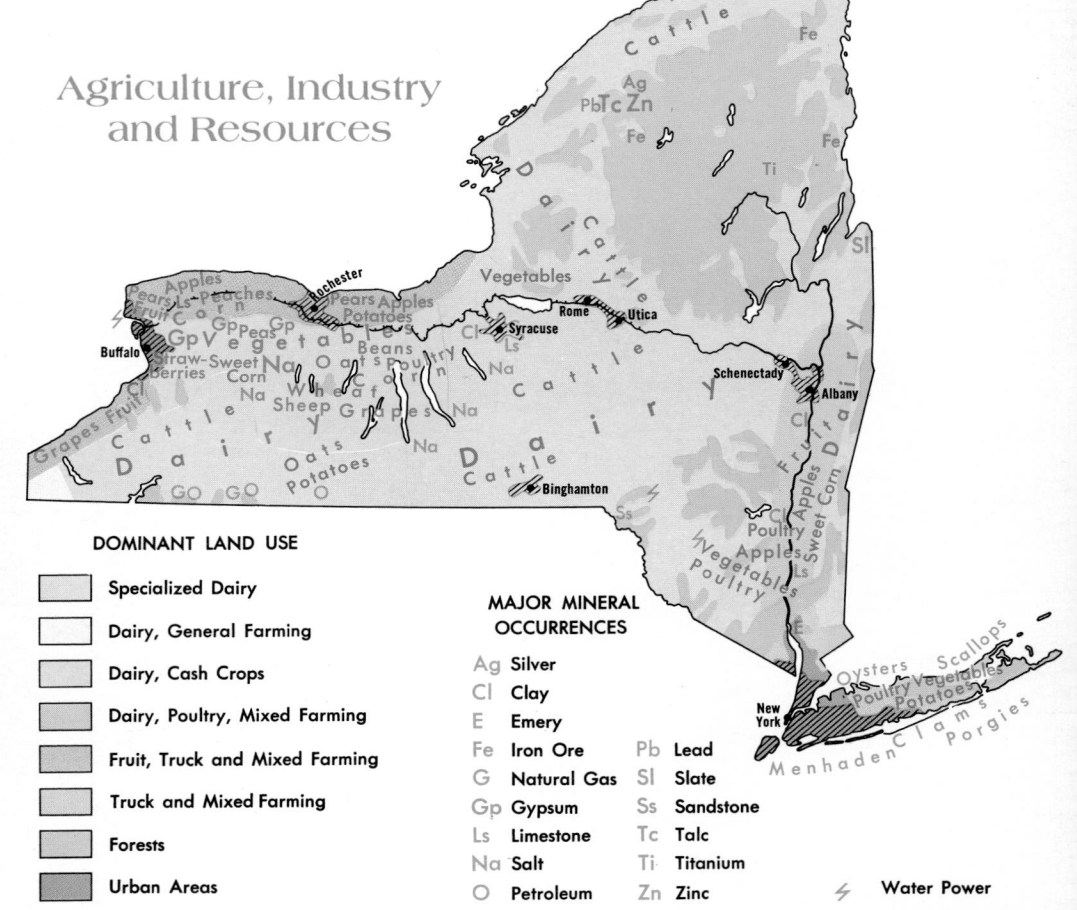

Agriculture, Industry and Resources

DOMINANT LAND USE

- Specialized Dairy
- Dairy, General Farming
- Dairy, Cash Crops
- Dairy, Poultry, Mixed Farming
- Fruit, Truck and Mixed Farming
- Truck and Mixed Farming
- Forests
- Urban Areas

MAJOR MINERAL OCCURRENCES

Ag Silver
Cl Clay
E Emery
Fe Iron Ore
G Natural Gas
Gp Gypsum
Ls Limestone
Na Salt
O Petroleum
Pb Lead
Sl Slate
Ss Sandstone
Tc Talc
Ti Titanium
Zn Zinc

⚡ Water Power
▨ Major Industrial Areas

AREA 52,669 sq. mi. (136,413 sq. km.)
POPULATION 5,881,813
CAPITAL Raleigh
LARGEST CITY Charlotte
HIGHEST POINT Mt. Mitchell 6,684 ft. (2037 m.)
SETTLED IN 1650
ADMITTED TO UNION November 21, 1789
POPULAR NAME Tarheel State
STATE FLOWER Flowering Dogwood
STATE BIRD Cardinal

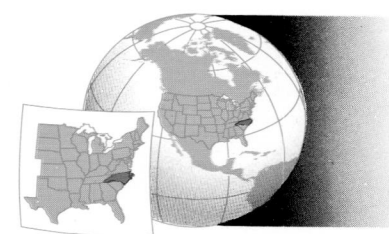

COUNTIES

Alamance 99,319 .... L3
Alexander 24,999 .... G3
Alleghany 9,587 .... G1
Anson 25,649 .... J4
Ashe 22,325 .... F2
Avery 14,409 .... F2
Beaufort 40,355 .... R4
Bertie 21,024 .... P2
Bladen 30,491 .... M5
Brunswick 35,777 .... N6
Buncombe 160,934 .... D3
Burke 72,504 .... F3
Cabarrus 85,895 .... H4
Caldwell 67,746 .... F3
Camden 5,829 .... S2
Carteret 41,092 .... R5
Caswell 20,705 .... L2
Catawba 105,208 .... G3
Chatham 33,415 .... L3
Cherokee 18,933 .... A4
Chowan 12,558 .... R2
Clay 6,619 .... B4
Cleveland 83,435 .... F4
Columbus 51,037 .... M6
Craven 71,043 .... P4
Cumberland 247,160 .... M4
Currituck 11,089 .... S2
Dare 13,377 .... T3
Davidson 113,162 .... J3
Davie 24,599 .... H3
Duplin 40,952 .... O5
Durham 152,785 .... M3
Edgecombe 55,988 .... O3
Forsyth 243,683 .... J2
Franklin 30,055 .... N2
Gaston 162,568 .... G4
Gates 8,875 .... R2
Graham 7,217 .... B4
Granville 34,043 .... M2
Greene 16,117 .... O3
Guilford 317,154 .... K3
Halifax 55,286 .... O2
Harnett 59,570 .... M4
Haywood 46,495 .... C3
Henderson 58,580 .... D4
Hertford 23,368 .... R2
Hoke 20,383 .... L4
Hyde 5,873 .... S3
Iredell 82,538 .... H3
Jackson 25,811 .... C4
Johnston 70,599 .... N4
Jones 9,705 .... P4

Lee 36,718 .... L4
Lenoir 59,819 .... O4
Lincoln 42,372 .... G3
Macon 20,178 .... B4
Madison 16,827 .... D3
Martin 25,948 .... P3
McDowell 35,135 .... E3
Mecklenburg 404,270 .... H4
Mitchell 14,428 .... E2
Montgomery 22,469 .... K4
Moore 50,505 .... L4
Nash 67,153 .... O2
New Hanover 103,471 .... O6
Northampton 22,584 .... P2
Onslow 112,784 .... P5
Orange 77,055 .... L2
Pamlico 10,398 .... R4
Pasquotank 28,462 .... S2
Pender 22,215 .... O5
Perquimans 9,486 .... S2
Person 29,164 .... M2
Pitt 90,146 .... P3
Polk 12,984 .... E4
Randolph 91,728 .... K3
Richmond 45,481 .... K4
Robeson 101,610 .... L5
Rockingham 83,426 .... L2
Rowan 99,186 .... H3
Rutherford 53,787 .... E4
Sampson 49,687 .... N4
Scotland 32,273 .... L5
Stanly 48,517 .... J4
Stokes 33,086 .... J2
Surry 59,449 .... H2
Swain 10,283 .... B3
Transylvania 23,417 .... D4
Tyrrell 3,975 .... S3
Union 70,380 .... H4
Vance 36,748 .... N2
Wake 301,327 .... M3
Warren 16,232 .... N2
Washington 14,801 .... R3
Watauga 31,666 .... F2
Wayne 97,054 .... N4
Wilkes 58,657 .... G2
Wilson 63,132 .... O3
Yadkin 28,439 .... H2
Yancey 14,934 .... E3

CITIES and TOWNS

Zip Name/Pop. Key

28315 Aberdeen 1,945 .... L4
27910 Ahoskie 4,887 .... P2
27201 Alamance 320 .... K2
28001 Albemarle⊙ 15,110 .... J4
†28043 Alexander Mills 643 .... F4
28509 Alliance 616 .... R4
28702 Almond 140 .... B4
28901 Andrews 1,621 .... B4
27501 Angier 1,709 .... M4
28007 Ansonville 794 .... J4
27502 Apex 2,847 .... M3
28510 Arapahoe 467 .... R4
27263 Archdale 5,326 .... K3
†28642 Arlington 872 .... L3
28420 Ash 150 .... N6
27203 Asheboro⊙ 15,252 .... K3
*28801 Asheville⊙ 53,583 .... D3
       Asheville‡ 177,761 .... D3
†27983 Askewville 227 .... R2
28421 Atkinson 298 .... N5
28512 Atlantic Beach 941 .... R5
27805 Aulander 1,214 .... P2
27806 Aurora 698 .... R4
28318 Autryville 228 .... M4

27915 Avon 500 .... U4
28513 Ayden 4,361 .... P4
27916 Aydlett 205 .... T2
28009 Badin 1,514 .... J4
27807 Bailey 685 .... N5
28705 Bakersville⊙ 373 .... E2
28706 Balfour 1,772 .... E4
28707 Balsam 200 .... C4
28604 Banner Elk 1,087 .... F2
†27030 Bannertown 1,028 .... H1
27008 Barber 155 .... H3
†28739 Barker Heights 1,267 .... D4
28710 Bat Cave 450 .... E4
27808 Bath 207 .... R4
27809 Battleboro 632 .... O2
28515 Bayboro⊙ 759 .... R4
†27892 Beargrass 82 .... P3
28516 Beaufort⊙ 3,826 .... R5
27810 Belhaven 2,430 .... R3
27811 Bellarthur 350 .... O3
28012 Belmont 4,607 .... H4
†28451 Belville 102 .... N6

†28090 Belwood 613 .... F4
27208 Bennett 254 .... K3
28504 Benson 2,792 .... N4
28016 Bessemer City 4,787 .... G4
27812 Bethel 1,825 .... P3
28518 Beulaville 1,060 .... O5
†28803 Biltmore Forest 1,499 .... E3
27209 Biscoe 1,334 .... K4
27813 Black Creek 523 .... O3
28711 Black Mountain 4,083 .... E3
28320 Bladenboro 1,428 .... M5
27212 Blanch 200 .... L2
28605 Blowing Rock 1,337 .... F2
28092 Boger City 2,252 .... G4
28461 Boiling Spring Lakes 998 .... N7
28017 Boiling Springs 2,381 .... F4
28422 Bolivia⊙ 252 .... N6
28423 Bolton 563 .... N6
27213 Bonlee 300 .... L3
28606 Boomer 250 .... G2
28607 Boone⊙ 10,191 .... F2
27011 Boonville 1,028 .... H2
28322 Bowdens 200 .... N4
28712 Brevard⊙ 5,323 .... D4
28519 Bridgeton 461 .... R4
27505 Broadway 908 .... L4
†28601 Brookford 467 .... G3
28424 Brunswick 223 .... M6
28713 Bryson City⊙ 1,556 .... C4
27506 Buies Creek 1,939 .... M4
27508 Bunn 505 .... N3
28425 Burgaw⊙ 1,738 .... N5
27215 Burlington 37,266 .... K2
       Burlington‡ 99,136 .... F2
28714 Burnsville⊙ 1,452 .... E3
27509 Butner 4,240 .... M2
27312 Bynum 350 .... L3
†29566 Calabash 128 .... M7
28325 Calypso 689 .... N4
27921 Camden⊙ 300 .... S2
28326 Cameron 225 .... L4
28229 Candor 868 .... K4
28716 Canton 4,631 .... D3
†28584 Cape Carteret 944 .... P5
28428 Carolina Beach 2,000 .... O6
27510 Carrboro 7,336 .... L3
28327 Carthage⊙ 925 .... K4
27511 Cary 21,763 .... M3
28020 Casar 346 .... F3
28717 Cashiers 553 .... C4
27816 Castalia 358 .... O2
28429 Castle Hayne 1,087 .... O6
†28461 Caswell Beach 110 .... N7
28609 Catawba 509 .... G3
27230 Cedar Falls 400 .... K3
27231 Cedar Grove 250 .... L2
28520 Cedar Island 310 .... S5
†27549 Centerville 135 .... N2
28430 Cerro Gordo 295 .... M6
28431 Chadbourn 1,975 .... M6
†28445 Chadwick Acres 15 .... P6
27514 Chapel Hill 32,421 .... L3
*28201 Charlotte⊙ 314,447 .... H4
       Charlotte-Gastonia‡
       637,218 .... H4
28021 Cherryville 4,844 .... G4
28023 China Grove 2,081 .... H3
28521 Chinquapin 280 .... O5
27817 Chocowinity 644 .... P4
28610 Claremont 880 .... G3
28433 Clarkton 664 .... M6
27520 Clayton 4,091 .... N3
27012 Clemmons 7,401 .... J2

27013 Cleveland 595 .... H3
28328 Clinton⊙ 7,552 .... N5
28721 Clyde 1,008 .... D3
27521 Coats 1,385 .... M4
27922 Cofield 465 .... R2
27924 Colerain 284 .... R2
27925 Columbia⊙ 758 .... S3
28722 Columbus⊙ 727 .... E4
28522 Comfort 325 .... O5
27818 Como 89 .... P1
28025 Concord⊙ 16,942 .... H4
28819 Conetoe 215 .... O3
28613 Conover 4,245 .... G3
27820 Conway 678 .... P2
27014 Cooleemee 1,448 .... H3
28031 Cornelius 1,460 .... H4
27927 Corolla 158 .... T2
28523 Cove City 500 .... P4
28032 Cramerton 1,869 .... G4
27522 Creedmoor 1,641 .... M2
27928 Creswell 426 .... S3
27852 Crisp 435 .... O3
28616 Crossnore 297 .... F2
28331 Cumberland 400 .... M5
27237 Cumnock 200 .... L3
27929 Currituck⊙ 700 .... T2
28034 Dallas 3,340 .... G4
27016 Danbury⊙ 140 .... J2
28036 Davidson 3,241 .... H4
28524 Davis 612 .... R5
27239 Denton 949 .... J3
28725 Dillsboro 179 .... C4
27017 Dobson⊙ 1,222 .... H2
†27801 Dortches 885 .... O2
28526 Dover 600 .... P4
28619 Drexel 1,392 .... F3
28332 Dublin 477 .... M5
28334 Dunn 8,962 .... M4
*27701 Durham⊙ 100,538 .... M2
       Durham-Raleigh‡ 530,673 .... M2
27242 Eagle Springs 280 .... K4
28038 Earl 206 .... F4
†28434 East Arcadia 461 .... N6
27018 East Bend 602 .... H2
28726 East Flat Rock 3,365 .... E4
†28723 East Laport 150 .... C4
28352 East Laurinburg 536 .... L5
†28752 East Marion 1,851 .... F3
28039 East Spencer 2,150 .... J3
27288 Eden 15,672 .... K1
27932 Edenton⊙ 5,357 .... R2
27909 Elizabeth City⊙ 14,004 .... S2
28337 Elizabethtown⊙ 3,551 .... M5
28621 Elkin 2,858 .... H2
28622 Elk Park 535 .... E2
28040 Ellenboro 565 .... F4
28338 Ellerbe 1,415 .... K4
27822 Elm City 1,561 .... O3
27244 Elon College 2,873 .... L2
†28557 Emerald Isle 865 .... P5
27823 Enfield 2,995 .... O2
28728 Enka 5,567 .... D3
28339 Erwin 2,828 .... M4
27247 Ether 425 .... K4
27935 Eure 300 .... R2
27830 Eureka 303 .... O3
27825 Everetts 213 .... P3
28438 Evergreen 310 .... M6
28439 Fair Bluff 1,095 .... M6
27826 Fairfield 900 .... S3
28340 Fairmont 2,658 .... L6
28730 Fairview 1,122 .... D3
28341 Faison 636 .... N4
28041 Faith 552 .... J3

(continued on following page)

Agriculture, Industry and Resources

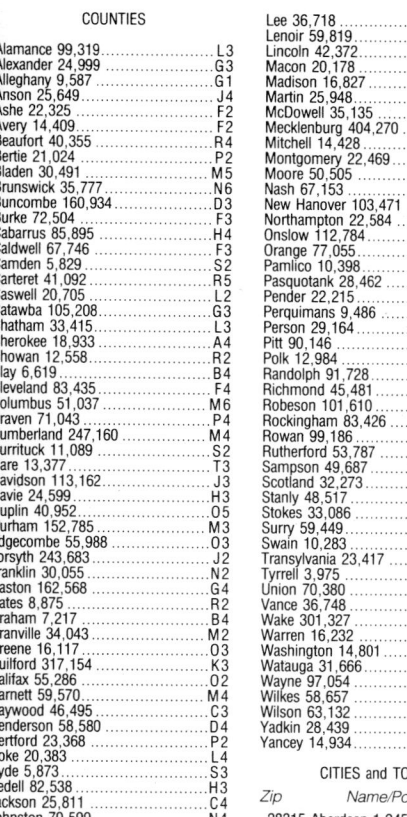

DOMINANT LAND USE

- Specialized Cotton
- Cotton, General Farming
- Cotton and Tobacco
- Tobacco, General Farming
- Peanuts, General Farming
- General Farming, Livestock, Fruit, Tobacco
- General Farming, Truck Farming, Tobacco, Livestock
- Forests
- Swampland, Limited Agriculture
- Nonagricultural Land

⚡ Water Power
▨ Major Industrial Areas

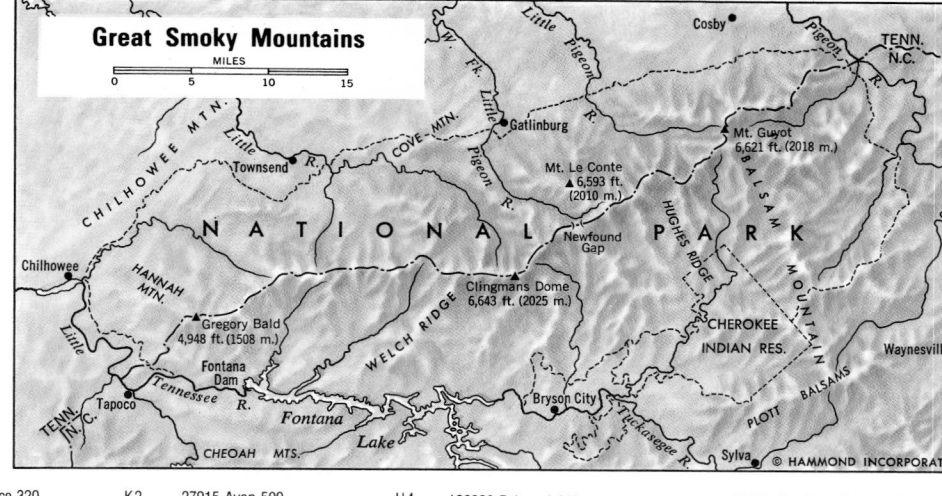

MAJOR MINERAL OCCURRENCES

Ab Asbestos
Au Gold
Cl Clay
Cu Copper
Gn Granite
Lt Lithium

Mi Mica
Mr Marble
P Phosphates
Tc Talc
W Tungsten

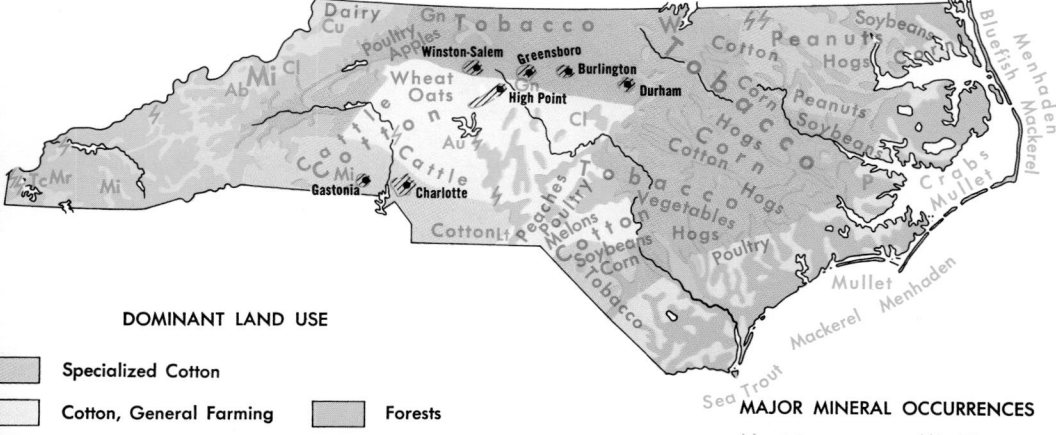

Topography

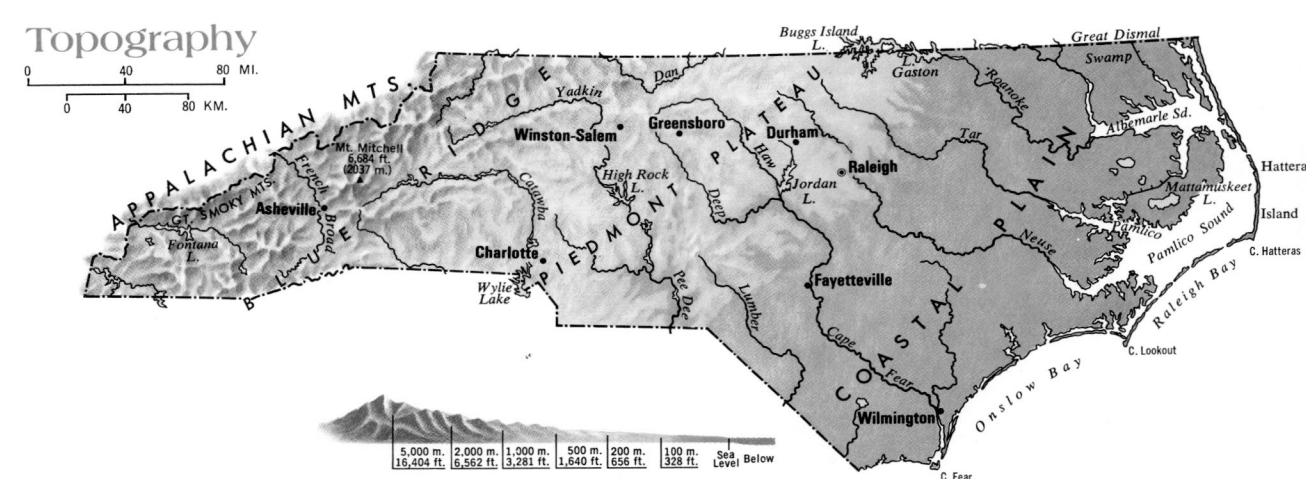

| 5,000 m. 16,404 ft. | 2,000 m. 6,562 ft. | 1,000 m. 3,281 ft. | 500 m. 1,640 ft. | 200 m. 656 ft. | 100 m. 328 ft. | Sea Level | Below |

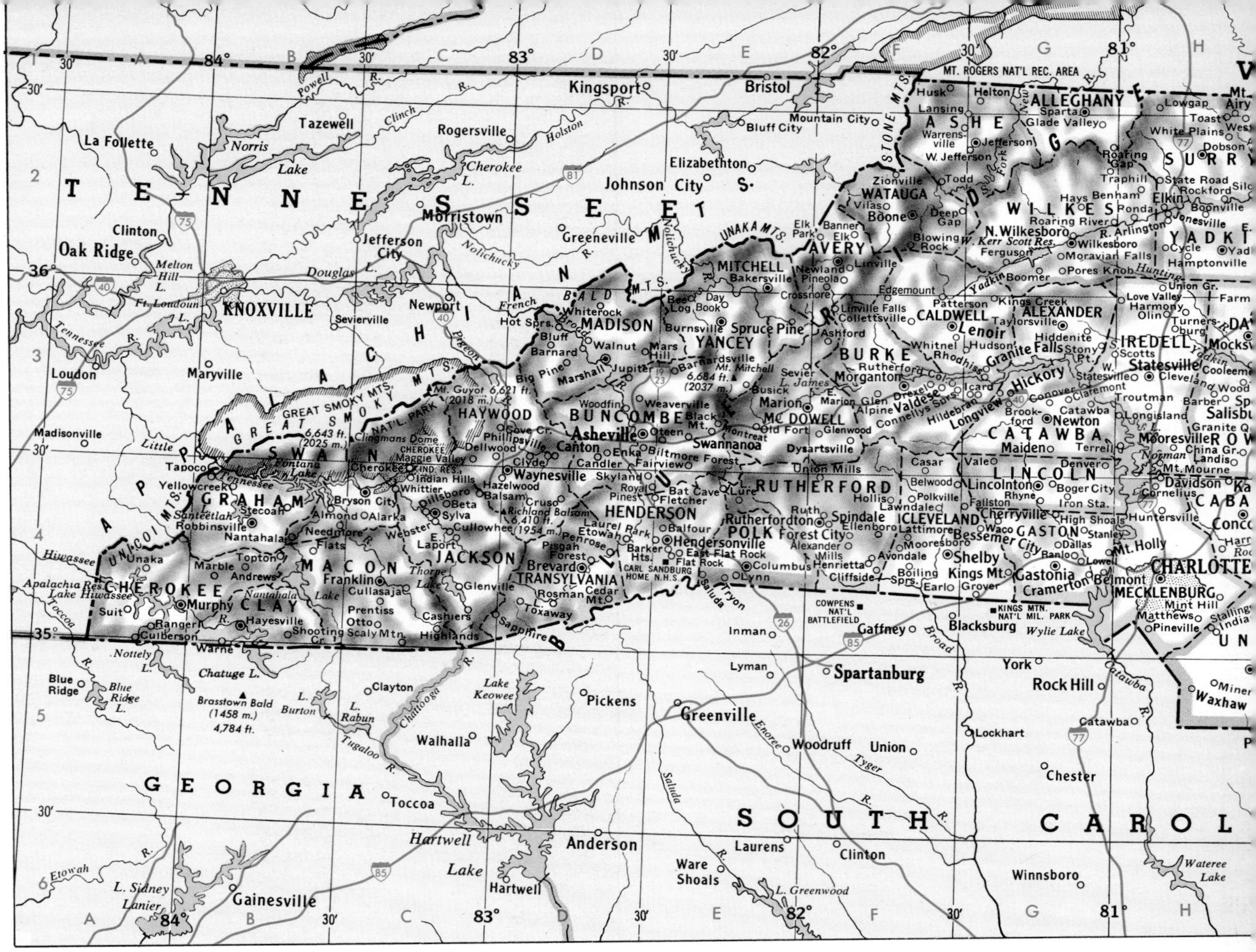

North Carolina

SCALE
0 5 10 20 30 40 50 MI.
0 5 10 20 30 40 50 KM.
State Capitals .... ⊛
County Seats .... ◉
Canals ....
Major Limited Access Hwys. ————

Scale 1:2,070,000

© Copyright HAMMOND INCORPORATED, Maplewood, N.J.

†28302 Rockfish 200...............L5	27530 South Goldsboro 2,531......N4
28379 Rockingham⊙ 8,300.....K5	28461 Southport 2,824..........N7
28138 Rockwell 1,339..........J3	†27890 South Weldon 1,801......O2
27801 Rocky Mount 41,283......O3	28675 Sparta⊙ 1,687..........G1
27571 Rolesville 381..........N3	27881 Speed 95..............P3
28670 Ronda 457..............H2	28159 Spencer 2,938..........H3
27970 Roper 795..............R3	28160 Spindale 4,246..........F4
28382 Roseboro 1,227..........N5	27882 Spring Hope 1,254........O3
28458 Rose Hill 1,508..........N5	28390 Spring Lake 6,273........M4
28772 Rosman 512..............D4	28777 Spruce Pine 2,282........E3
28383 Rowland 1,841..........L5	27355 Staley 204..............K3
27573 Roxboro⊙ 7,532..........M2	†28079 Stallings 1,826..........H4
28872 Roxobel 278............P2	28163 Stanfield 463............J4
27326 Ruffin 680..............K2	28164 Stanley 2,341............G4
27045 Rural Hall 1,336..........J2	†27045 Stanleyville 5,039........J2
†28139 Ruth 381..............E4	28396 Stantonsburg 920........O3
28671 Rutherford College 1,108..F3	27356 Star 816..............K4
28139 Rutherfordton⊙ 3,434....E4	28677 Statesville⊙ 18,622......H3
28384 Saint Pauls 1,639........M5	28391 Stedman 723............M4
28385 Salemburg 742..........N4	28582 Stella 700............P5
28144 Salisbury⊙ 22,677........H3	27581 Stem 222..............M2
Salisbury-Concord‡	27884 Stokes 450............P3
185,081............H3	27357 Stokesdale 1,070........K2
28773 Saluda 607............E4	27048 Stoneville 1,054........K2
27972 Salvo 150............U3	28583 Stonewall 360..........R4
27330 Sanford⊙ 14,773........L4	28678 Stony Point 1,150........G3
28774 Sapphire 350..........D4	27582 Stovall 417............M2
27340 Saxapahaw 500........L3	†28579 Straits 151............R5
28775 Scaly Mountain 250......C4	27978 Stumpy Point 250........T3
27874 Scotland Neck 2,834......P2	28906 Suit 350............A4
28699 Scotts 500............H3	27589 Warrenton⊙ 908..........N2
28875 Scranton 250..........S4	27358 Summerfield 1,680........K2
27876 Seaboard 687..........O1	27979 Sunbury 400............R2
27341 Seagrove 294..........K3	28459 Surf City 421............O6
27576 Selma 4,762............N3	28778 Swannanoa 5,586........E3
27343 Semora 500............L2	28584 Swansboro 976..........P5
28578 Seven Springs 166........O4	28779 Sylva⊙ 1,699............C4
27877 Severn 309............P2	28463 Tabor City 2,710........M6
28459 Shallotte 680..........N7	27886 Tarboro⊙ 8,634..........O3
27878 Sharpsburg 997........O3	28392 Tar Heel 118............M5
27973 Shawboro 300..........R2	28681 Taylorsville⊙ 1,103......G3
28150 Shelby⊙ 15,310........G4	28464 Teachey 373............N5
27344 Siler City 4,446........L3	27360 Thomasville 14,144......J3
27879 Simpson 407............P3	27887 Tillery 400............O2
27880 Sims 192..............N3	27583 Timberlake 500..........M2
27577 Smithfield⊙ 7,288........N3	27049 Toast 2,339............J2
28579 Smyrna 291............R5	28445 Topsail Beach 264........O6
28580 Snow Hill⊙ 1,374........O4	28685 Traphill 550............G2
27350 Sophia 350............K3	28585 Trenton⊙ 407..........P4
28387 Southern Pines 8,620.....L4	

†28560 Trent Woods 1,177........P4	Wilmington‡ 139,238........N6
28166 Troutman 1,360..........H3	27893 Wilson⊙ 34,424..........O3
27371 Troy⊙ 2,702............K4	27983 Windsor⊙ 2,126..........P2
28782 Tryon 1,796............E4	27985 Winfall 634............S2
28393 Turkey 417............N4	28174 Wingate 2,615..........J5
27980 Tyner 264............R2	*27101 Winston-Salem⊙ 131,885..J2
†27203 Ulah 546..............K3	28590 Winterville 2,052........P3
28689 Union Grove 614..........H2	27986 Winton⊙ 825............P2
28690 Valdese 3,364............F3	27594 Wise 550..............N1
28586 Vandemere 335..........R4	†28804 Woodfin 3,260..........D3
28587 Vandemere 335..........R4	28790 Woodland 861............P2
28394 Vass 828..............L4	27054 Woodleaf 550..........H3
28169 Waco 322..............G4	†27849 Woodville 212..........P2
28395 Wade 474..............M4	27378 Worthville 350..........K3
28170 Wadesboro⊙ 4,206......J5	28480 Wrightsville Beach 2,910..O6
28396 Wagram 617............L5	27055 Yadkinville⊙ 2,216......H2
27587 Wake Forest 3,780......M3	27379 Yanceyville⊙ 1,511......L2
28466 Wallace 2,903............N5	†28461 Yaupon Beach 569......N7
27373 Walburg 300............J3	27596 Youngsville 486..........N3
27052 Walnut Cove 1,147........J2	27597 Zebulon 2,055..........N3
†27530 Walnut Creek 343........O4	28698 Zionville 525............F2
28888 Walstonburg 181........O3	
27981 Wanchese 1,105..........T3	**OTHER FEATURES**
28909 Warne 200..............B5	
27589 Warrenton⊙ 908..........N2	Albemarle (sound)............S2
28398 Warsaw 2,910............N4	Alligator (lake)............S3
27889 Washington⊙ 8,418......R3	Alligator (riv.)............S3
†27889 Washington Park 514......R3	Angola (swamp)............O5
28471 Watha 196..............O5	Apalachia (res.)............A4
28173 Waxhaw 1,208..........H5	Appalachian (mts.)..........D2
28786 Waynesville⊙ 6,765......D4	Ashe (isl.)..............P6
28787 Weaverville 1,495........D3	Bald (mts.)..............D2
28788 Webster 200............C4	Black (riv.)..............N5
27909 Weeksville 500..........S2	Blue Ridge (mts.)............D2
27374 Welcome 3,243..........J3	Bodie (isl.)..............T3
27890 Weldon 1,844............O2	Broad (riv.)..............E4
27591 Wendell 2,822............N3	Buggs (isl.)..............M1
27375 Wentworth⊙ 150........K2	Camp Lejeune Marine Corps
27053 Westfield 450..........H2	Base 30,764............N6
28694 West Jefferson 822.......F2	Cape Fear (riv.)............M5
†28389 Whispering Pines 1,160...L4	Cape Hatteras Nat'l Seashore..T4
27891 Whitakers 935..........O2	Carl Sandburg Home Nat'l Hist.
28337 White Lake 968..........M5	Site............D4
27031 White Plains 200........H2	Catawba (lake)............G4
28472 Whiteville⊙ 5,565........M6	Catawba (riv.)............F4
28789 Whittier 200............C4	Catfish (lake)............O4
28697 Wilkesboro⊙ 2,335......G2	Chatuge (lake)............B5
†27536 Williamsboro 50........M2	Cherokee Ind. Res...........C3
27892 Williamston⊙ 6,159......R3	Cherry Point Marine Air Sta...R4
28401 Wilmington⊙ 44,000......N6	Chowan (riv.)............R2

Clingmans Dome (mt.)........C3	Neuse (riv.)..............R5
Contentnea (creek)..........N3	New (riv.)..............O5
Core (banks)............S5	New, South Fork (riv.)........G2
Core (sound)............S5	New River (inlet)............P6
Corncake (inlet)............O7	Nolichucky (riv.)............E2
Croatan (sound)............T3	Norman (lake)............H3
Currituck (sound)............T2	North East Cape Fear (riv.)....O4
Dan (riv.)..............L1	Ocracoke (inlet)............T5
Deep (riv.)..............K3	Ocracoke (isl.)............T4
Dismal (Great) (swamp)......S1	Onslow (bay)............P6
Drum (inlet)............S5	Oregon (inlet)............U3
Fear (cape)............O7	Pamlico (riv.)............R4
Fishing (creek)............O2	Pamlico (sound)............S4
Fontana (lake)............B4	Pee Dee (riv.)............J4
Fort Bragg 37,834..........M4	Phelps (lake)............S3
Fort Raleigh Nat'l Hist. Site...T3	Pigeon (riv.)............C3
French Broad (riv.)..........D3	Pope A.F.B...............L4
Gaston (res.)............O2	Portsmouth (isl.)............T5
Great (lake)............P5	Pungo (lake)............S3
Great Dismal (swamp)........S1	Pungo (riv.)............R4
Great Smoky (mts.)..........B3	Raleigh (bay)............S5
Great Smoky Mts. Nat'l Park...B3	Richland Balsam (mt.)........D4
Green (swamp)............N6	Roanoke (isl.)............T3
Guyot (mt.)............C3	Roanoke (riv.)............P2
Hatteras (cape)............U4	Rocky (riv.)............H4
Hatteras (inlet)............T4	Santeetlah (lake)............B4
Hatteras (isl.)............U4	Seymour Johnson A.F.B.......O4
Haw (riv.)..............K2	Six Run (creek)............N4
High Rock (lake)............J3	Smith (isl.)............O7
Hiwassee (lake)............A4	South (riv.)............M5
Hiwassee (riv.)............A4	South Yadkin (riv.)..........H3
Holly Shelter (swamp)........O6	Stone (mts.)............F2
Hunting (riv.)............H2	Sunny Point Mil. Ocean Term...O6
Hyco (riv.)..............L2	Tar (riv.)..............O3
James (lake)............E3	Thorpe (lake)............C4
Jordan, B. Everett (lake)......M3	Trent (riv.)............P4
Kerr, W. Scott (res.)........G2	Unaka (mts.)............E2
Lanes (creek)............J5	Unicoi (mts.)............A4
Little (creek)............N3	Waccamaw (lake)............N6
Little (riv.)..............L4	Waccamaw (riv.)............M7
Little Pee Dee (riv.)..........L6	Whiteoak (swamp)............P5
Little Tennessee (riv.)........B4	W. Scott Kerr (res.)..........G2
Long (lake)............P5	Wright Brothers Nat'l Mem.....T2
Lookout (cape)............S5	Yadkin (riv.)............J3
Lumber (riv.)............L6	
Mattamuskeet (lake)..........S3	⊙County seat.
Meherrin (riv.)............P1	‡Population of metropolitan area.
Mitchell (mt.)............E3	† Zip of nearest p.o.
Moores Creek Nat'l Battlefield..N6	* Multiple zips.
Nantahala (lake)............B4	

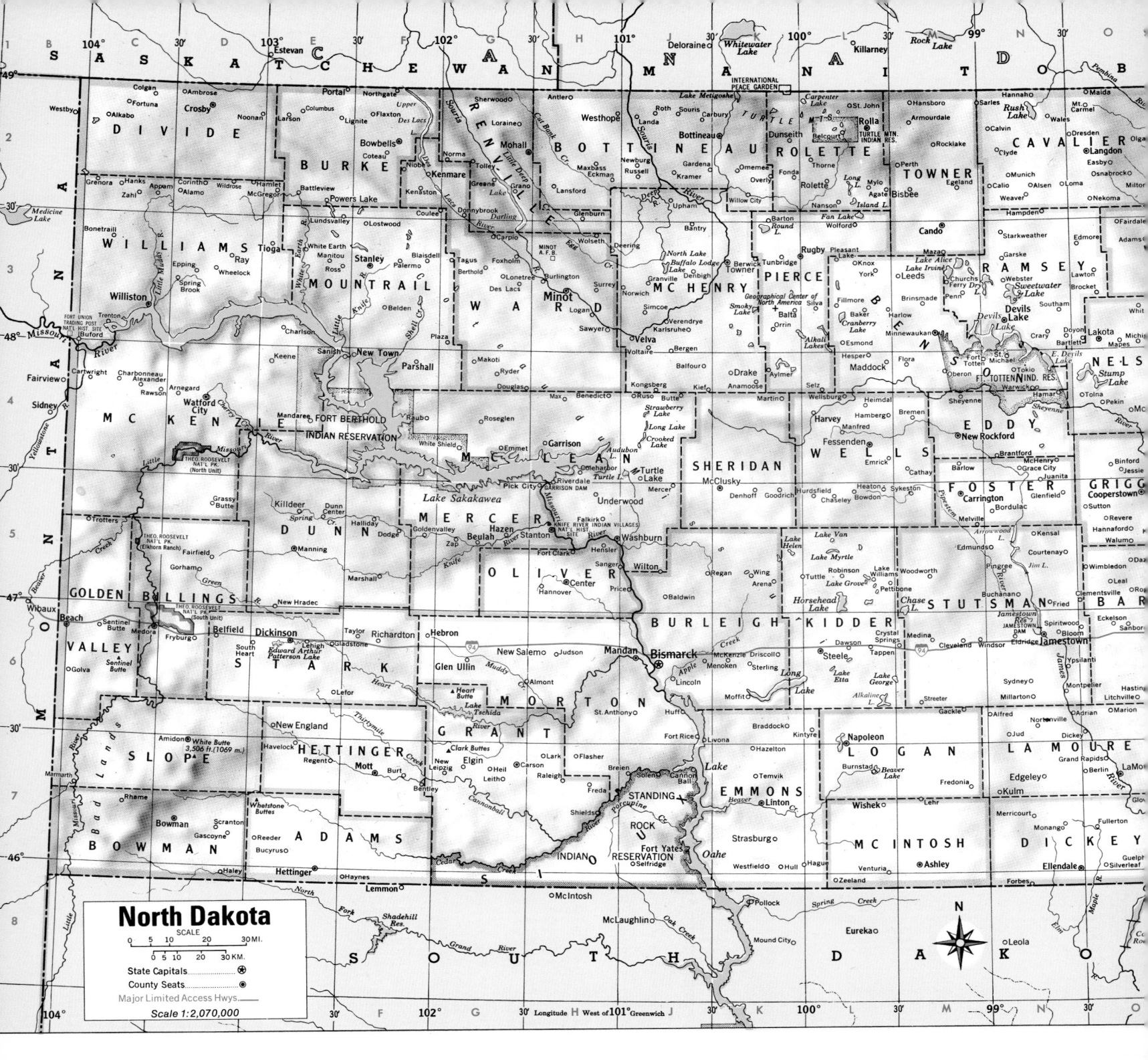

North Dakota

SCALE
0 5 10   20   30 MI.
0 5 10   20   30 KM.
State Capitals........⊛
County Seats..........⊙
Major Limited Access Hwys.
Scale 1:2,070,000

COUNTIES

Adams 3,584................F7
Barnes 13,960................O5
Benson 7,944................M3
Billings 1,138................D5
Bottineau 9,239................J2
Bowman 4,229................C7
Burke 3,822................E2
Burleigh 54,811................J6
Cass 88,247................R5
Cavalier 7,636................N2
Dickey 7,207................N7
Divide 3,494................C2
Dunn 4,627................E5
Eddy 3,554................N4
Emmons 5,877................K7
Foster 4,611................N5
Golden Valley 2,391................C5
Grand Forks 66,100................P3
Grant 4,274................G6
Griggs 3,714................O5
Hettinger 4,275................E7
Kidder 3,833................L6
LaMoure 6,473................N7
Logan 3,493................L7
McHenry 7,858................J3
McIntosh 4,800................L7
McKenzie 7,132................D4
McLean 12,383................G4
Mercer 9,404................G5
Morton 25,177................H6
Mountrail 7,679................E3

Nelson 5,233................O4
Oliver 2,495................H5
Pembina 10,399................P2
Pierce 6,166................K3
Ramsey 13,048................N3
Ransom 6,698................P7
Renville 3,608................G2
Richland 19,207................R7
Rolette 12,177................L2
Sargent 5,512................P7
Sheridan 2,819................K4
Sioux 3,620................H7
Slope 1,157................C7
Stark 23,697................E6
Steele 3,106................P4
Stutsman 24,154................M5
Towner 4,052................M2
Traill 9,624................R5
Walsh 15,371................P3
Ward 58,392................G3
Wells 6,979................L4
Williams 22,237................C3

CITIES and TOWNS

Zip   Name/Pop.   Key

58001 Abercrombie 260................S7
58210 Adams 303................O3
58831 Alexander 358................C4
58003 Alice 62................P6
58004 Amenia 93................R6
58620 Amidon⊙ 43................D7

58710 Anamoose 355................K4
58212 Aneta 341................P4
58213 Ardoch 78................R3
58835 Arnegard 193................D4
58006 Arthur 445................R5
58413 Ashley⊙ 1,192................M7
58007 Ayr 42................P5
58712 Balfour 51................J4
58008 Barney 70................S7
58216 Bathgate 67................P2
58621 Beach⊙ 1,381................C6
58316 Belcourt 1,803................L2
58622 Belfield 1,274................D6
58716 Benedict 68................H4
58415 Berlin 85................O7
58718 Berthold 485................G3
58523 Beulah 2,908................G5
58416 Binford 293................O4
58317 Bisbee 257................M2
58501 Bismarck (cap.)⊙ 44,485................J6
58318 Bottineau⊙ 2,829................J2
58721 Bowbells⊙ 587................F2
58623 Bowman⊙ 2,071................D7
58524 Braddock 86................K6
58320 Brinsmade 54................M3
58321 Brocket 74................O3
58722 Burlington 762................H3
58218 Buxton 336................R4
58322 Calio 60................N2
58323 Calvin 61................N2
58324 Cando⊙ 1,496................M3
†58241 Canton (Hensel) 68................P2
58725 Carpio 244................G3

58421 Carrington⊙ 2,641................M5
58529 Carson⊙ 469................H7
58012 Casselton 1,661................R6
58422 Cathay 66................M4
58220 Cavalier⊙ 1,505................P2
58013 Cayuga 75................R7
58530 Center⊙ 900................H5
58016 Clifford 51................R5
58017 Cogswell 227................P7
58727 Columbus 325................E2
58425 Cooperstown⊙ 1,308................O5
58730 Crosby⊙ 1,469................D2
58222 Crystal 256................P2
58021 Davenport 195................R6
58731 Deering 85................J3
58301 Devils Lake⊙ 7,442................N3
58431 Dickey 74................N6
58601 Dickinson⊙ 15,924................E6
58736 Drake 479................K4
58225 Drayton 1,082................R2
58329 Dunseith 625................K2
58024 Dwight 72................S7
58433 Edgeley 843................N7
58227 Edinburg 300................P3
58330 Edmore 416................O3
58533 Elgin 930................G7
58436 Ellendale⊙ 1,967................N7
58228 Emerado 596................R4
58027 Enderlin 1,151................P6
58332 Esmond 337................L3
58229 Fairdale 97................O3
58030 Fairmount 480................S7
58102 Fargo⊙ 61,383................S6

Fargo-Moorhead‡ 137,574 S6
58438 Fessenden⊙ 761................L4
58230 Finley⊙ 718................P4
58535 Flasher 410................H7
58439 Forbes 84................N8
58231 Fordville 326................P3
58032 Forman⊙ 629................P7
58844 Fortuna 98................C2
58538 Fort Yates⊙ 771................J7
58440 Fredonia 82................M7
58442 Gackle 456................M6
58739 Gardena 66................J2
58540 Garrison 1,830................H4
58235 Gilby 283................P3
58630 Gladstone 317................F6
58740 Glenburn 454................J2
58631 Glen Ullin 1,125................G6
58541 Goldenvalley 287................F5
58444 Goodrich 288................K5
58040 Gwinner 725................P7
58236 Halliday 355................F5
58041 Hankinson 1,158................S7
58239 Hannah 90................N2
58341 Harvey 2,527................L4
58042 Harwood 326................S6
58240 Hatton 787................R4

58637 Haynes 58................F8
58544 Hazelton 266................K7
58545 Hazen 2,365................G5
58638 Hebron 1,078................G6
58639 Hettinger⊙ 1,739................E8
58045 Hillsboro⊙ 1,600................S5
58243 Hoople 350................P2
58046 Hope 406................R5
58047 Horace 494................S6
58048 Hunter 369................R5
58244 Inkster 135................P3
58401 Jamestown⊙ 16,280................N6
58744 Karlsruhe 164................J3
58049 Kathryn 95................P6
58456 Kulm 570................N7
58344 Lakota⊙ 963................O3
58458 LaMoure⊙ 1,077................O7
58201 Grand Forks⊙ 43,765................R4
Grand Forks‡ 100,944................R4
58741 Granville 281................J3
58845 Grenora 362................C2
58040 Gwinner 725................P7
58631 Glen Ullin 1,125................G6
58343 Knox 69................L3
58748 Kramer 84................J2
58551 Leith 59................G7
58052 Leonard 289................R6
58053 Lidgerwood 971................R7
58752 Lignite 332................F2
58749 Landa 62................J2
58249 Langdon⊙ 2,335................O2
58750 Lansford 294................H2
58251 Larimore 1,524................P4
58459 Leal 45................O5
58346 Leeds 678................M3
58460 Lehr 254................M7

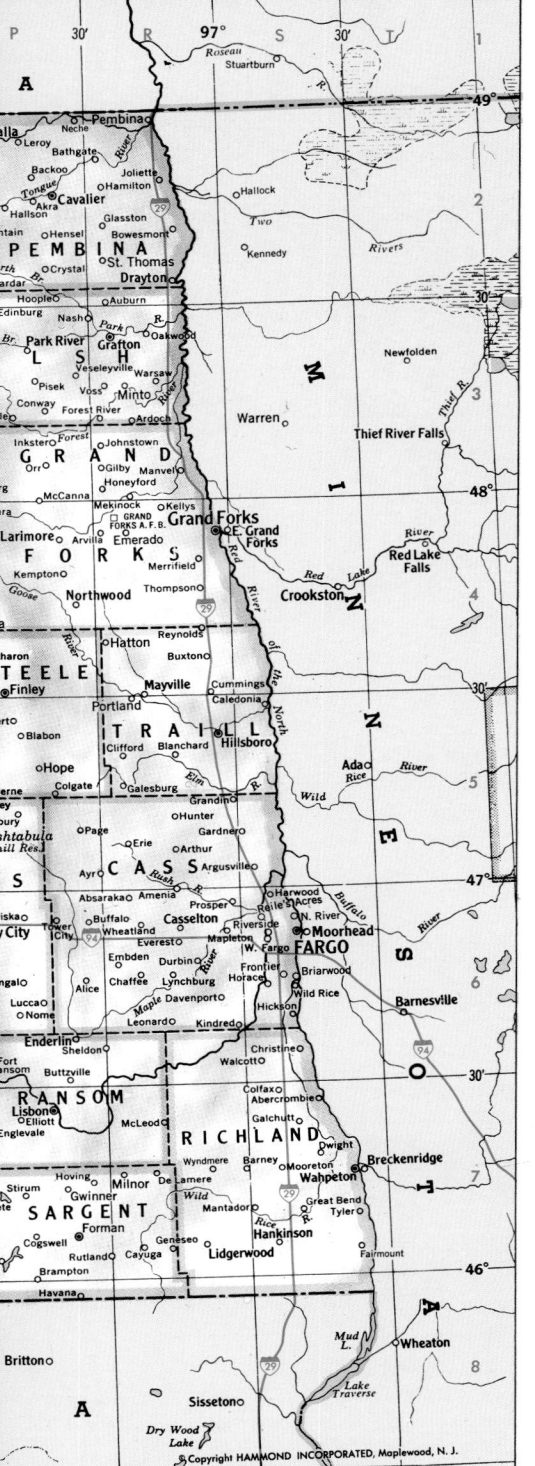

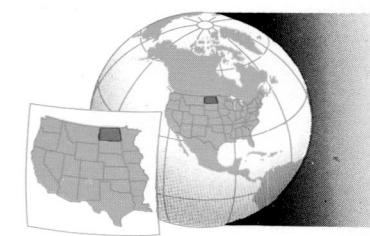

58276 Saint Thomas 528	R2
58780 Sanish	E4
58781 Sawyer 417	H3
58653 Scranton 415	D7
58568 Selfridge 273	J7
58654 Sentinel Butte 86	C6
58068 Sheldon 173	P6
58782 Sherwood 294	G2
58374 Sheyenne 307	M4
58655 South Heart 294	D6
58850 Spring Brook 52	D3
58784 Stanley⊙ 1,631	F3
58571 Stanton⊙ 623	H5
58482 Steele⊙ 796	L6
58573 Strasburg 623	K7
58483 Streeter 264	M6
58785 Surrey 999	H3
58487 Tappen 271	L6
58656 Taylor 239	F6
58278 Thompson 785	R4
58852 Tioga 1,597	E3
58380 Tolna 241	O4
58071 Tower City 293	P6
58788 Towner⊙ 867	K3
58575 Turtle Lake 802	J4
58576 Underwood 1,329	H5
58072 Valley City⊙ 7,774	P6
58790 Velva 1,101	J3
58792 Voltaire 65	J3
58075 Wahpeton⊙ 9,064	S7
58281 Wales 74	N2
58282 Walhalla 1,429	P2
58577 Washburn⊙ 1,767	J5
58854 Watford City⊙ 2,119	D4
58078 West Fargo 10,099	S6
58793 Westhope 741	H2
58794 White Earth 98	E3
58795 Wildrose 214	D2
58801 Williston⊙ 13,336	C3
58384 Willow City 329	K2
58579 Wilton 950	J5
58492 Wimbledon 330	O5
58495 Wishek 1,345	L7
58385 Wolford 76	L3
58081 Wyndmere 550	R7
58386 York 69	L3
58580 Zap 511	G5
58581 Zeeland 253	L8

AREA 70,702 sq. mi. (183,118 sq. km.)
POPULATION 652,717
CAPITAL Bismarck
LARGEST CITY Fargo
HIGHEST POINT White Butte 3,506 ft. (1069 m.)
SETTLED IN 1780
ADMITTED TO UNION November 2, 1889
POPULAR NAME Flickertail State; Sioux State
STATE FLOWER Wild Prairie Rose
STATE BIRD Western Meadowlark

Topography

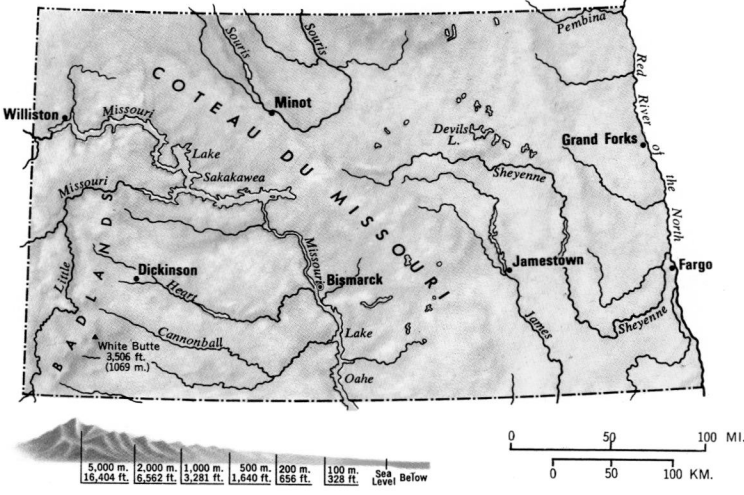

	5,000 m.	2,000 m.	1,000 m.	500 m.	200 m.	100 m.	Sea	Below
	16,404 ft.	6,562 ft.	3,281 ft.	1,640 ft.	656 ft.	328 ft.	Level	

0   50   100 MI.
0   50   100 KM.

OTHER FEATURES

Alkali (lke)	L3	Fan (lake)	L2	Little Missouri (riv.)	D4	Smoky (lake)	K3
Alkaline (lake)	L6	Forest (riv.)	P3	Little Muddy (riv.)	C3	Souris (riv.)	J2
Apple (creek)	J6	Fort Berthold Ind. Res.	E4	Long (lake)	J4	Spring (creek)	E5
Arrowwood (lake)	N5	Fort Totten Ind. Res.	N4	Long (lake)	K6	Standing Rock Ind. Res.	J7
Ashtabula (lake)	P5	Fort Union Trading Post Nat'l Hist.		Long (lake)	L2	Strawberry (lake)	J4
Audubon (lake)	H4	Site	B3	Maple (riv.)	O8	Stump (lake)	O4
Bad Lands (reg.)	C7	Garrison (dam)	H5	Maple (riv.)	R6	Sweetwater (lake)	N3
Baldhill (Ashtabula) (res.)	P5	George (lake)	L6	Metigoshe (lake)	K2	Theodore Roosevelt Nat'l Mem. Park
Bear (creek)	O7	Goose (riv.)	P4	Minot A.F.B. 9,880	H3		C5, D4,D6
Beaver (creek)	B5	Grand, North Fork (riv.)	E8	Missouri (riv.)	H5	Thirty Mile (creek)	F6
Beaver (creek)	K7	Grand Forks A.F.B. 9,390	R4	Muddy (creek)	G6	Tongue (riv.)	P2
Beaver (lake)	L7	Green (riv.)	D5	Myrtle (lake)	L5	Tschida (lake)	G6
Buffalo Lodge (lake)	J3	Grove (lake)	L5	North (lake)	J3	Turtle (lake)	H4
Cannonball (riv.)	G7	Heart (butte)	G6	Oahe (lake)	J7	Turtle (mts.)	K2
Carpenter (lake)	L2	Heart (riv.)	F6	Oak (creek)	J8	Turtle Mountain Ind. Res.	L2
Cedar (creek)	G7	Helen (lake)	K5	Park (riv.)	R3	Upper Des Lacs (lake)	F2
Chase (lake)	M5	Horsehead (lake)	L5	Patterson, Edward A. (lake)	R3	Van (lake)	L5
Cherry (creek)	D4	International Peace Garden	K1	Pembina (riv.)	O1	Whetstone (buttes)	E7
Clark (buttes)	G7	Irvine (lake)	M3	Pipestem (riv.)	M5	White (butte)	D7
Coteau du Missouri (plain)	G3	Island (lake)	L2	Porcupine (creek)	J7	White Butte (mt.)	D7
Cranberry (lake)	L3	James (riv.)	N6	Red River of the North (riv.)	S4	White Earth (riv.)	E3
Crooked (lake)	J4	Jamestown (res.)	N6	Round (lake)	K3	Wild Rice (riv.)	R7
Cut Bank (creek)	H2	Jim (riv.)	N5	Rush (lake)	N2	Yellowstone (riv.)	B4
Darling (lake)	G2	Knife (riv.)	G5	Rush (lake)	R5	
Deep (riv.)	J1	Knife R. Indian Villages Nat'l Hist.		Sakakawea (lake)	G5	⊙County seat.
Des Lacs (riv.)	G3	Site	H5	Sentinel (butte)	C6	‡Population of metropolitan area.
Devils (lake)	N3	Little Deep (creek)	G2	Shell (creek)	F3	† Zip of nearest p.o.
Dry (riv.)	M3	Little Knife (riv.)	F3	Sheyenne (riv.)	O6	* Multiple zips.
East Devils (lake)	N4					
Egg (creek)	H3					
Elm (riv.)	N8					
Elm (riv.)	R5					
Etta (lake)	L6					

†58501 Lincoln 656	J6	58563 New Salem 1,081	G6
58552 Linton⊙ 1,561	K7	58763 New Town 1,335	F4
58054 Lisbon⊙ 2,283	P7	58266 Niagara 76	P4
58461 Litchville 251	O6	58062 Nome 67	P6
58056 Luverne 65	P5	58765 Noonan 283	D2
58348 Maddock 677	L4	†58102 North River 65	S6
58554 Mandan⊙ 15,513	J6	58267 Northwood 1,240	P4
58642 Manning⊙ 75	E5	58474 Oakes 2,112	O7
58058 Mantador 76	R7	58063 Oriska 125	P6
58256 Manvel 308	R3	58064 Page 329	P5
58059 Mapleton 306	R6	58769 Palermo 97	F3
58643 Marmarth 190	B7	58270 Park River 1,844	P3
58759 Max 317	H4	58770 Parshall 1,059	F4
58257 Mayville 2,255	R4	58271 Pembina 673	R2
58463 McClusky⊙ 658	K4	58476 Pingree 88	N5
58254 McVille 626	O4	58772 Portal 238	E2
58467 Medina 521	M6	58274 Portland 627	R5
58645 Medora⊙ 94	C6	58773 Powers Lake 466	D3
58259 Michigan 502	O3	58849 Ray 766	D3
58060 Milnor 716	R7	58649 Reeder 355	E7
58351 Minnewaukan⊙ 461	M3	58477 Regan 71	K5
58701 Minot⊙ 32,843	H3	58650 Regent 297	E7
58261 Minto 592	R3	58275 Reynolds 309	R4
58761 Mohall⊙ 1,049	G2	58651 Rhame 222	C7
58471 Monango 59	N7	58652 Richardton 699	F6
58472 Montpelier 96	N6	†58078 Riverside 465	S6
58646 Mott⊙ 1,315	F7	58365 Rocklake 287	M2
58352 Munich 300	N2	58479 Rogers 68	O5
58561 Napoleon⊙ 1,103	L6	58366 Rolette 667	L2
58265 Neche 471	P2	58367 Rolla⊙ 1,538	L2
58647 New England 825	E6	58368 Rugby⊙ 3,335	L3
58562 New Leipzig 352	G7	58067 Rutland 250	P7
58356 New Rockford⊙ 1,791	N4	58369 Saint John 401	L2

Agriculture, Industry and Resources

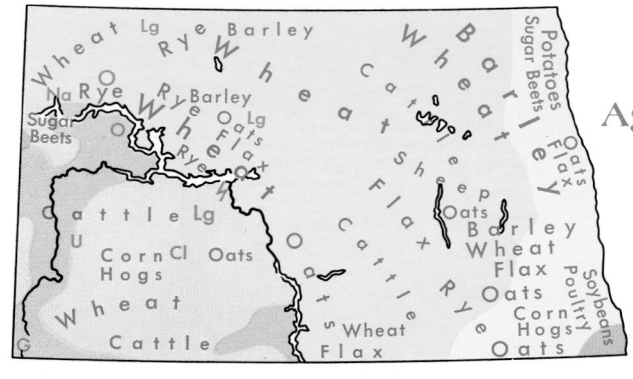

DOMINANT LAND USE

- Specialized Wheat
- Wheat, General Farming
- Wheat, Range Livestock
- Livestock, Cash Grain
- Sugar Beets, Dry Beans, Livestock, General Farming
- Range Livestock
- ⚡ Water Power

MAJOR MINERAL OCCURRENCES

Cl	Clay
G	Natural Gas
Lg	Lignite
Na	Salt
O	Petroleum
U	Uranium

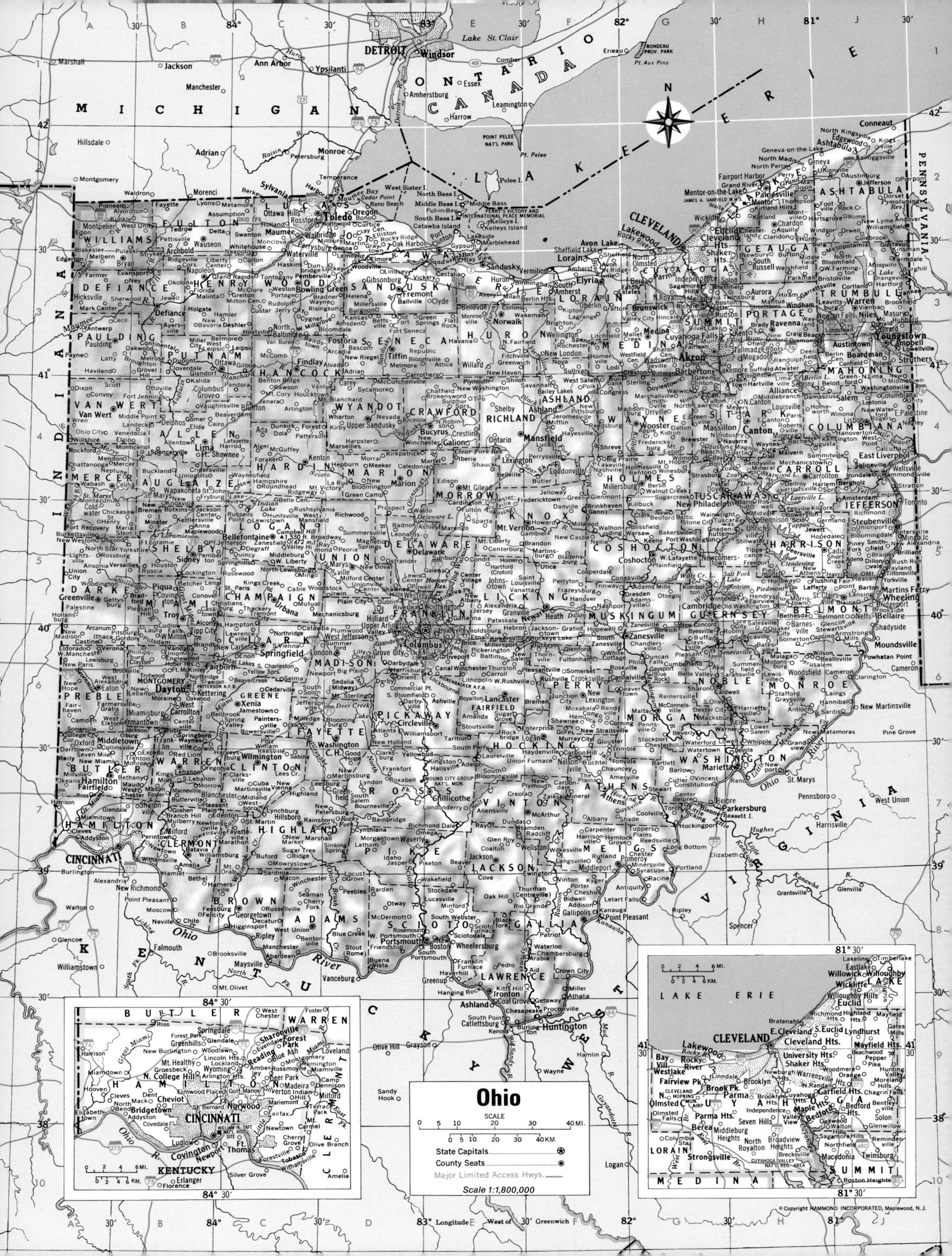

Ohio

SCALE

0 5 10   20   30   40 MI.

0 5 10   20   30   40 KM.

State Capitals .... ⊛

County Seats .... ◉

Major Limited Access Hwys. _____

Scale 1:1,800,000

© Copyright HAMMOND INCORPORATED, Maplewood, N.J.

Topography

0   40   80 MI.

0   40   80 KM.

5,000 m. | 2,000 m. | 1,000 m. | 500 m. | 200 m. | 100 m. | Sea Level | Below
16,404 ft. | 6,562 ft. | 3,281 ft. | 1,640 ft. | 656 ft. | 328 ft. | |

AREA 41,330 sq. mi. (107,045 sq. km.)
POPULATION 10,797,624
CAPITAL Columbus
LARGEST CITY Cleveland
HIGHEST POINT Campbell Hill 1,550 ft.
(472 m.)
SETTLED IN 1788
ADMITTED TO UNION March 1, 1803
POPULAR NAME Buckeye State
STATE FLOWER Scarlet Carnation
STATE BIRD Cardinal

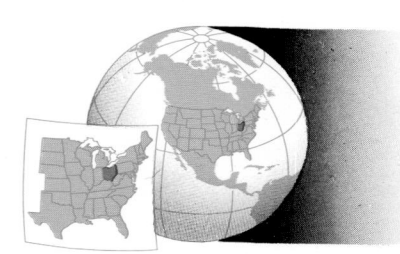

COUNTIES

Adams 24,328	D8
...llen 112,241	B4
...shland 46,178	F4
...shtabula 104,215	J2
...uglaize 42,554	B4
...rown 31,920	C8
...utler 258,787	A7
...arroll 25,598	H4
...hampaign 33,649	C5
...ark 150,236	C6
...lermont 128,483	B7
...linton 34,603	C7
...olumbiana 113,572	J4
...oshocton 36,024	G5
...rawford 50,075	E4
...uyahoga 1,498,400	G3
...efiance 39,987	A3
...elaware 53,840	D5
...ie 79,655	E3
...airfield 93,678	E6
...ayette 27,467	D6
...ranklin 869,126	E5
...ulton 37,751	B2
...allia 30,098	F8
...eauga 74,474	H3
...reene 129,769	C6
...uernsey 42,024	H5
...amilton 873,224	A7
...ancock 64,581	C4
...ardin 32,719	C4
...arrison 18,152	H5
...enry 28,383	B3
...ghland 33,477	C7
...ocking 24,304	F6
...olmes 29,416	G4
...uron 54,608	E3
...ackson 30,592	E7
...efferson 91,564	J5
...nox 46,304	F5
...ake 212,801	H2
...awrence 63,849	E8
...icking 120,981	F5
...ogan 39,155	C5
...orain 274,909	F3
...ucas 471,741	C2
...adison 33,004	D6
...ahoning 289,487	J4
...arion 67,974	D4
...edina 113,150	G3
...eigs 23,641	F7
...ercer 38,334	A4
...iami 90,381	B5
...onroe 17,382	H6
...ontgomery 571,697	B6
...organ 14,241	G6
...orrow 26,480	E4
...uskingum 83,340	G5
...oble 11,310	H6
...ttawa 40,076	D2
...aulding 21,302	A3
...erry 31,032	F6
Pickaway 43,662	D6
Pike 22,802	D7
Portage 135,856	H3
Preble 40,113	A6
Putnam 32,991	B3
Richland 131,205	E4
Ross 65,004	D7
Sandusky 63,267	D3
Scioto 84,545	D8
Seneca 61,901	D3
Shelby 43,089	B5
Stark 378,823	H4
Summit 524,472	G3
Trumbull 241,863	J3
Tuscarawas 84,614	H5
Union 29,536	D5
Van Wert 30,458	A4
Vinton 11,584	E7
Warren 99,276	B7
Washington 64,266	H7
Wayne 97,408	G4
Williams 36,369	A2
Wood 107,372	C3
Wyandot 22,651	D4

CITIES and TOWNS

Zip	Name/Pop.	Key
45101	Aberdeen 1,566	C8
45810	Ada 5,669	C4
45001	Addyston 1,195	B9
43101	Adelphi 472	E7
43901	Adena 1,062	J5
*44301	Akron⊙ 237,177	G3
	Akron‡ 660,328	G3
45710	Albany 905	F7
43001	Alexandria 489	E5
45812	Alger 992	C4
44601	Alliance 24,315	H4
43102	Amanda 720	E6
†45201	Amberley 3,442	C9
45102	Amelia 1,108	D10
44001	Amherst 10,638	F3
43903	Amsterdam 783	J5
44003	Andover 1,205	J2
45302	Anna 1,038	B5
45303	Ansonia 1,267	A5
45813	Antwerp 1,765	A3
44606	Apple Creek 741	G4
44804	Arcadia 580	D3
45304	Arcanum 2,002	A6
43502	Archbold 3,318	B2
45814	Arlington 1,187	C4
†45201	Arlington Heights 1,082	C9
44805	Ashland⊙ 20,326	F4
43003	Ashley 1,057	E5
44004	Ashtabula 23,449	J2
43103	Ashville 2,046	E6
45701	Athens⊙ 19,743	F7
44807	Attica 865	E3
44201	Atwater 975	H3
44202	Aurora 8,177	H3
44010	Austinburg 900	J2
44515	Austintown 33,636	J3
44011	Avon 7,241	F3
44012	Avon Lake 13,222	F2
†43512	Ayersville 950	B3
†44805	Bailey Lakes 397	F4
45612	Bainbridge 1,042	D7
43804	Baltic 563	G5
43105	Baltimore 2,689	E6
44203	Barberton 29,751	G4
43713	Barnesville 4,633	H6
43905	Barton 1,039	J5
45103	Batavia⊙ 1,896	B7
44140	Bay Village 17,846	G9
†44870	Bay View 804	E3
44608	Beach City 1,083	G4
44122	Beachwood 9,983	J9
43716	Beallsville 601	J6
45808	Beaverdam 492	C4
44146	Bedford 15,056	H9
†44146	Bedford Heights 13,214	J9
43906	Bellaire 8,241	J5
45305	Bellbrook 5,174	C6
44310	Belle Center 930	C4
43311	Bellefontaine⊙ 11,888	C5
44811	Bellevue 8,187	E4
44813	Bellville 1,714	E4
43718	Belmont 714	J5
44609	Beloit 1,093	J4
45714	Belpre 7,193	G7
44017	Berea 19,567	G10
43908	Bergholz 914	J4
44814	Berlin Heights 756	F3
45106	Bethel 2,231	B8
43719	Bethesda 1,429	H5
44815	Bettsville 752	D3
45715	Beverly 1,471	G6
43209	Bexley 13,405	E6
45107	Blanchester 3,202	B7
44817	Bloomdale 744	D3
43106	Bloomingburg 869	D6
44818	Bloomville 1,019	D3
†45242	Blue Ash 9,506	C9
45817	Bluffton 3,310	C4
44512	Boardman 39,161	J3
44612	Bolivar 989	G4
†44264	Boston Heights 781	J10
45306	Botkins 1,372	B5
44695	Bowerston 487	H5
43402	Bowling Green⊙ 25,728	C3
45308	Bradford 2,166	B5
43406	Bradner 1,175	C3
44211	Brady Lake 470	H3
†44101	Bratenahl 1,485	H9
44141	Brecksville 10,132	H10
43107	Bremen 1,432	F6
44613	Brewster 2,321	G4
43912	Bridgeport 2,642	J5
45211	Bridgetown 11,460	B9
43913	Brilliant 1,751	J5
43515	Delta 2,831	B2
44621	Dennison 3,398	H5
†45202	Dent 800	B9
43516	Deshler 1,870	C3
45750	Devola 2,708	H7
43917	Dillonvale 912	J5
44622	Dover 11,782	G4
44230	Doylestown 2,493	G4
43821	Dresden 1,646	G5
45309	Brookville 4,322	B6
44212	Brunswick 28,104	G3
43506	Bryan⊙ 7,879	A3
45716	Buchtel 585	F7
43008	Buckeye Lake 3,657	F6
44820	Bucyrus⊙ 13,433	E4
†45680	Burlington 900	F9
44021	Burton 1,401	H3
44822	Butler 991	F4
43723	Byesville 2,572	G6
45820	Cairo 596	B4
43907	Cadiz⊙ 4,058	J5
43920	Calcutta 1,121	J4
43724	Caldwell⊙ 1,935	G6
43314	Caledonia 759	D4
43725	Cambridge⊙ 13,573	G5
45311	Camden 1,971	A6
44405	Campbell 11,619	J3
45111	Camp Dennison 625	D9
44614	Canal Fulton 3,481	H4
43110	Canal Winchester 2,749	E6
44406	Canfield 5,535	J3
*44701	Canton⊙ 93,077	H4
	Canton‡ 404,421	H4
43315	Cardington 1,665	E5
43316	Carey 3,674	D4
45005	Carlisle 4,276	B6
43112	Carroll 641	E6
44615	Carrollton⊙ 3,065	J4
44824	Castalia 973	E3
45314	Cedarville 2,799	C6
45822	Celina⊙ 9,137	A4
43011	Centerburg 1,275	E5
45459	Centerville 18,886	B6
44022	Chagrin Falls 4,335	J9
†45631	Chambersburg	F8
44024	Chardon⊙ 4,434	H2
45719	Chauncey 1,050	F7
†45202	Cherry Grove 850	C10
45619	Chesapeake 1,370	E9
44026	Chesterland 2,301	H2
†45211	Cheviot 9,888	B9
45601	Chillicothe⊙ 23,420	E7
43009	Christiansburg 593	C5
45389	Bailey Lakes 397	F4
*45201	Cincinnati⊙ 385,457	B9
	Cincinnati‡ 1,401,403	B9
43113	Circleville⊙ 11,700	D6
43915	Clarington 558	J6
43115	Clarksburg 483	D7
45113	Clarksville 525	C7
45315	Clayton 752	B6
*44101	Cleveland⊙ 573,822	H9
	Cleveland‡ 1,898,720	H9
44118	Cleveland Heights 56,438	H9
44216	Clinton 1,277	G4
43410	Clyde 5,491	E3
45638	Coal Grove 2,602	E9
45621	Coalton 639	E7
45828	Coldwater 4,220	A5
†44034	Colebrook 700	J2
44028	Columbia Station 518	G10
44408	Columbiana 4,987	J4
*43201	Columbus (cap.)⊙ 565,032	E6
	Columbus‡ 1,093,293	E6
45830	Columbus Grove 2,313	B4
43811	Conesville 451	G5
44030	Conneaut 13,835	J2
45831	Continental 1,179	B3
45832	Convoy 1,140	A4
45723	Coolville 649	G7
43730	Corning 789	F6
44410	Cortland 5,011	J3
43812	Coshocton⊙ 13,405	G5
†45238	Covedale 5,830	B10
45318	Covington 2,610	B5
†44429	Craig Beach 1,657	H3
44827	Crestline 5,406	E4
44217	Creston 1,828	G3
45806	Cridersville 1,843	B4
43731	Crooksville 2,766	F6
45623	Crown City 513	F8
†45341	Crystal Lakes 1,463	C6
*44221	Cuyahoga Falls 43,890	G3
44101	Cuyahoga Heights 739	H9
43413	Cygnet 646	C3
44618	Dalton 1,357	G4
43014	Danville 1,127	F5
†43123	Darbydale 825	D6
*45401	Dayton⊙ 193,444	B6
	Dayton‡ 830,070	B6
44411	Deerfield 800	H3
45236	Deer Park 6,745	C9
43512	Defiance⊙ 16,810	B3
45304	Delaware⊙ 18,780	E5
45833	Delphos 7,314	B4
43017	Dublin 3,855	D5
43734	Duncan Falls 900	G6
45836	Dunkirk 954	C4
44730	East Canton 1,721	H4
44112	East Cleveland 36,957	H9
†44094	Eastlake 22,104	J8
43920	East Liverpool 16,687	J4
44413	East Palestine 5,306	J4
44626	East Sparta 868	H4
45320	Eaton⊙ 6,839	A6
†44035	Eaton Estates 1,806	G3
43517	Edgerton 1,813	A3
†44004	Edgewood 3,099	J2
43320	Edison 504	E4
43518	Edon 947	A2
45321	Eldorado 509	A6
45807	Elida 1,349	B4
43416	Elmore 1,271	D3
45216	Elmwood Place 2,840	B9
*44035	Elyria⊙ 57,538	F3
45322	Englewood 11,329	B6
45323	Enon 2,597	C6
44117	Euclid 59,999	J9
†45201	Evendale 1,954	C9
45042	Excello 900	B7
45324	Fairborn 29,702	B6
†45201	Fairfax 2,222	C9
45014	Fairfield 30,777	A7
44313	Fairlawn 6,100	G3
44077	Fairport Harbor 3,357	H2
44126	Fairview Park 19,311	G9
45325	Farmersville 950	A6
43521	Fayette 1,222	B2
45120	Felicity 929	B8
45840	Findlay⊙ 35,594	C3
45326	Fletcher 498	B5
43977	Flushing 1,266	J5
45843	Forest 1,633	C4
45405	Forest Park 18,675	B9
45230	Forestville 950	C10
45844	Fort Jennings 538	B4
45845	Fort Loramie 977	B5
†45426	Fort McKinley	B6
45846	Fort Recovery 1,370	A5
†45801	Fort Shawnee 4,541	B4
44830	Fostoria 15,743	D3
45628	Frankfort 1,008	D7
43915	Franklin 10,711	B6
45629	Franklin Furnace 1,093	E8
43822	Frazeysburg 1,025	F5
44627	Fredericksburg 511	G4
43019	Fredericktown 2,299	F5
43973	Freeport 525	H5
43420	Fremont⊙ 17,834	D3
45630	Friendship 900	D8
43230	Gahanna 18,001	E5
44833	Galion 12,391	E4
45631	Gallipolis⊙ 5,576	F8
43022	Gambier 2,056	F5
44125	Garfield Heights 34,938	J9
44231	Garrettsville 1,769	H3
44040	Gates Mills 2,236	J9
44041	Geneva 6,655	J2
44043	Geneva-on-the-Lake 1,634	H2
43430	Genoa 2,213	D3
45121	Georgetown⊙ 3,467	C8
45327	Germantown 5,015	B6
45328	Gettysburg 545	A5
43431	Gibsonburg 2,479	D3
44420	Girard 12,517	J3
45848	Glandorf 746	B3
45246	Glendale 2,368	C9
†44139	Glenwillow 492	J10
45732	Glouster 2,211	F6
44629	Gnadenhutten 1,320	G5
45122	Goshen	B8
†45201	Golf Manor 4,317	C9
44044	Grafton 2,231	F3
43522	Grand Rapids 962	C3
44045	Grand River 412	H2
†43212	Grandview Heights 7,420	D6
43023	Granville 3,851	E5
45330	Gratis 809	A6
43322	Green Camp 475	D4
45123	Greenfield 5,150	D7
45218	Greenhills 4,927	B9
44232	Greensburg 950	G4
44836	Green Springs 1,568	D3
44630	Greentown 300	H4
45331	Greenville⊙ 12,999	A5
44837	Greenwich 1,458	E3
43123	Grove City 16,816	D6
43125	Groveport 3,286	E6
45849	Grover Hill 486	B3
45634	Hamden 1,010	F7
44836	Hamersville 688	C8
*45011	Hamilton⊙ 63,189	A7
	Hamilton-Middletown‡ 258,787	A7
43524	Hamler 625	B3
43931	Hannibal 550	J6
†43055	Hanover 926	F5
43126	Harrisburg 363	D6
45030	Harrison 5,855	A9
45850	Harrod 506	C4
†44085	Hartgrove 200	J2
44632	Hartville 1,772	H4
43525	Haskins 568	C3
43127	Haydenville 395	F7
44838	Hayesville 518	F4
43055	Heath 6,969	F5
43025	Hebron 2,035	E6
43526	Hicksville 3,929	A3
†44143	Highland Heights 5,739	J9
43026	Hilliard 8,008	D5
45133	Hillsboro⊙ 6,356	C7
44234	Hiram 1,360	H3
43527	Holgate 1,315	B3
43528	Holland 1,048	C2
45033	Hooven 550	A9
43976	Hopedale 857	J5
44425	Hubbard 9,245	J3
45424	Huber Heights 35,480	B6
44236	Hudson 4,615	H3
†44022	Hunting Valley 786	J9
44839	Huron 7,123	E3
44131	Independence 6,607	H9
†45201	Indian Hill 5,521	C9
43932	Irondale 535	J4
45638	Ironton⊙ 14,290	E8
45640	Jackson⊙ 6,675	E7
45334	Jackson Center 1,310	B5
45740	Jacksonville 651	F7
45335	Jamestown 1,702	C6
44047	Jefferson⊙ 2,952	J2
†43162	Jefferson (West Jefferson) 4,448	D6
43128	Jeffersonville 1,252	C6
44840	Jeromesville 582	F4
43437	Jerry City 512	C3
43986	Jewett 972	H5
43031	Johnstown 3,158	E5
43748	Junction City 754	F6
45853	Kalida 1,019	B4
44240	Kent 26,164	H3
43326	Kenton⊙ 8,605	C4
45429	Kettering 61,186	B6
44637	Killbuck 930	G5
45034	Kings Mills 500	B7
45644	Kingston 1,208	E7
44048	Kingsville	J2
44428	Kinsman 900	J3
44033	Kirkersville 626	E6
†44094	Kirtland 5,969	H2
43951	Lafferty 855	H5
44050	Lagrange 1,258	F3
44250	Lakemore 2,744	H3
45140	Lakeside 850	E2
44331	Lakeview 1,089	C4
44107	Lakewood 61,963	G9
44130	Lancaster⊙ 34,953	E6
43934	Lansing 950	J5
44332	La Rue 861	D4
43135	Laurelville 591	E7
†45201	Lawrenceville 307	C6
45036	Lebanon⊙ 9,636	B7
45135	Leesburg 1,019	D7
44431	Leetonia 2,121	J4
45856	Leipsic 2,171	C3
45338	Lewisburg 1,450	A6
44904	Lexington 3,823	E4
43532	Liberty Center 1,111	B3
*45801	Lima⊙ 47,381	B4
	Lima‡ 218,244	B4
†45201	Lincoln Heights 5,259	C9
43442	Lindsey 591	D3
44432	Lisbon⊙ 3,159	J4
44253	Litchfield 650	F3
43136	Lithopolis 652	E6
45742	Little Hocking 800	G7
45215	Lockland 4,292	C9
44254	Lodi 2,942	F3
43138	Logan⊙ 6,557	F6
43140	London⊙ 6,958	C6
*44052	Lorain 75,416	F3
	Lorain-Elyria‡ 274,909	F3
†44481	Lordstown 3,280	J3
44842	Loudonville 2,945	F4
44641	Louisville 7,996	H4
45140	Loveland 9,106	D9
45744	Lowell 729	H6
44436	Lowellville 1,558	J3
44843	Lucas 753	F4
45648	Lucasville 3,349	E8
43443	Luckey 895	D3
45142	Lynchburg 1,205	C7
44124	Lyndhurst 18,092	J9
44533	Lyons 596	B2
44056	Macedonia 6,571	J10
†45202	Mack	B9
45243	Madeira 9,341	C9
44057	Madison 2,291	H2
44643	Magnolia 986	H4
43758	Malta 956	G6
44644	Malvern 1,032	H4
45144	Manchester 2,313	C8
*44901	Mansfield⊙ 53,927	F4
	Mansfield‡ 131,205	F4
44111	Mantua 1,043	H3
44137	Maple Heights 29,735	H9
†43440	Marblehead 679	E2
45860	Maria Stein 950	A5

(continued on following page)

Agriculture, Industry and Resources

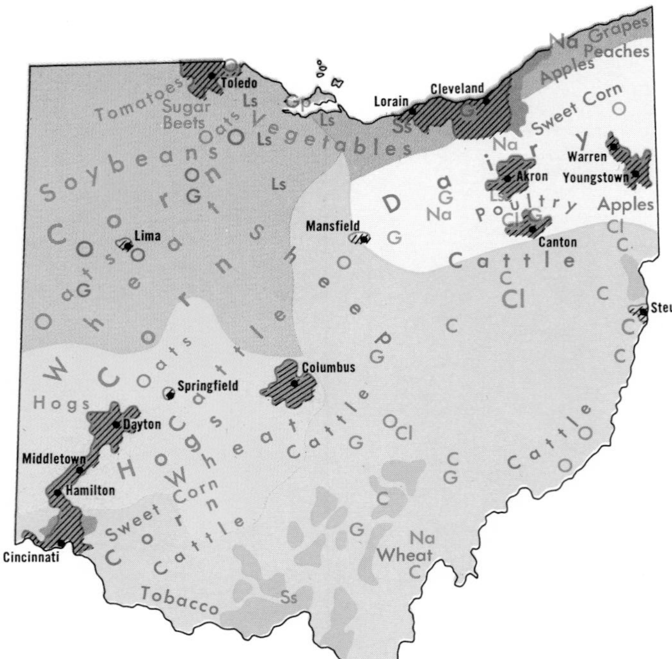

DOMINANT LAND USE

- Hogs, Soft Winter Wheat
- Livestock, Dairy, Soybeans, Cash Grain
- Dairy, General Farming
- General Farming, Livestock, Tobacco
- Fruit, Truck and Mixed Farming
- Forests
- Urban Areas

MAJOR MINERAL OCCURRENCES

- C Coal
- Cl Clay
- G Natural Gas
- Gp Gypsum
- Ls Limestone
- Na Salt
- O Petroleum
- Ss Sandstone
- Major Industrial Are

45227 Mariemont 3,295 ....C9
45750 Marietta⊙ 16,467 ....G7
43302 Marion⊙ 37,040............D4
44645 Marshallville 788 ....G4
43935 Martins Ferry 9,331 ....J5
45146 Martinsville 539 ....C7
43040 Marysville⊙ 7,414 ....D5
45040 Mason 8,692 ....B7
44646 Massillon 30,557 ....H4
44438 Masury 1,836 ....J3
†45069 Maud 800 ....B7
43537 Maumee 15,747 ....C2
44124 Mayfield 3,577 ....J9
44124 Mayfield Heights 21,550.... J9
45651 McArthur⊙ 1,912 ....F7
43534 McClure 694 ....C3
45858 McComb 1,608 ....C3
43756 McConnelsville⊙ 2,018.....G6
44437 McDonald 3,744 ....J3
45859 McGuffey 646 ....C4
43044 Mechanicsburg 1,792 ......D5
44256 Medina⊙ 15,268 ....G3
45862 Mendon 749 ....A4
44060 Mentor 42,065 ....H2
44060 Mentor-on-the-Lake 7,919 .G2
43540 Metamora 556............C2
45342 Miamisburg 15,304 ....B6
45041 Miamitown 800............A9
44652 Middlebranch 300............H4
†44017 Middleburg Heights 16,218G10
44062 Middlefield 1,997 ....H3
45863 Middle Point 709............B4
45760 Middleport 2,971 ....F7
45042 Middletown 43,719............A6
44653 Midvale 654............H5
44846 Milan 1,569............E3
45150 Milford 5,232............D9
43045 Milford Center 764............D5
43447 Millbury 955 ....D2
44654 Millersburg⊙ 3,247 ....F4
43046 Millersport 844 ....E6
†45011 Millville 809 ....A7
44656 Mineral City 884 ....H4
44657 Minerva 4,549............H4
†43201 Minerva Park 1,618 ....E5
43938 Mingo Junction 4,834 ...... J5
45865 Minster 2,557 ....B5
44260 Mogadore 4,190 ....H3
45050 Monroe 4,256 ....B7
44847 Monroeville 1,329 ....E3
45242 Montgomery 10,088 ....C9
43543 Montpelier 4,431............A2
†45439 Moraine 5,325............B6
†44022 Moreland Hills 3,083............J9
45152 Morrow 1,254 ....B7
43338 Mount Gilead⊙ 2,911 ......E4
45231 Mount Healthy 7,562............B9
45154 Mount Orab 1,573............C7
43939 Mount Pleasant 616............J5
43143 Mount Sterling 1,623 ....D6
43050 Mount Vernon⊙ 14,323 ... E5
43340 Mount Victory 667............D4
44262 Munroe Falls 4,731............H3
43144 Murray City 579............F6
43545 Napoleon⊙ 8,614 ....B3
44662 Navarre 1,343 ....H4
43940 Neffs 1,106 ....J5
44441 Negley 917............J4
45764 Nelsonville 4,567............F7
44849 Nevada 945 ....D4
43055 Newark⊙ 41,200 ....F5
Newark‡ 120,981............F5
45662 New Boston 3,188............E8
45869 New Bremen 2,393............B5
†44101 Newburgh Heights 2,678...H9
†45201 New Burlington 900 ....B9
45344 New Carlisle 6,498 ....C6
43832 Newcomerstown 3,986 .....G5
43762 New Concord 1,860............G6
43145 New Holland 783 ....D6
45871 New Knoxville 760............B5
45345 New Lebanon 4,501............B6
43764 New Lexington⊙ 5,179 .... F6
44851 New London 2,449............F3

45346 New Madison 1,008............A6
45767 New Matamoras............J6
45011 New Miami 2,980............A7
44442 New Middletown 2,195 ..... J4
45347 New Paris 1,709 ....A6
44663 New Philadelphia⊙ 16,883 G5
45768 Newport 975............H7
45157 New Richmond 2,769............B8
43766 New Straitsville 937 ....F6
44444 Newton Falls 4,960............J3
45244 Newtown 1,817 ....C10
45159 New Vienna 1,133 ....C7
44854 New Washington 1,213..... E4
44445 New Waterford 1,314 .... J4
44446 Niles 23,088 ....J3
45872 North Baltimore 3,127 ......C3
45052 North Bend 546 ....B9
44450 North Bloomfield 650 .... J3
44720 North Canton 14,228............H4
45239 North College Hill 11,114 ..B9
44855 North Fairfield 525............E3
44067 Northfield 3,913............J10
44707 North Industry............H4
44068 North Kingsville 2,939 ...... J2
43060 North Lewisburg 1,072 .....C5
44452 North Lima 800 ....J4
†44057 North Madison 8,741 ....H2
44070 North Olmsted 36,486 ......G9
†44081 North Perry 897............H2
†44101 North Randall 1,054............H9
45414 Northridge 9,720............B6
44039 North Ridgeville 21,522 .... F3
44133 North Royalton 17,671 ... H10
†43619 Northwood 5,495 ....D2
†43701 North Zanesville 2,166......G6
44203 Norton 12,242............G3
44857 Norwalk⊙ 14,358 ....E3
45212 Norwood 26,342............C9
43449 Oak Harbor 2,678 ....D2
45656 Oak Hill 1,713............E8
†45419 Oakwood 9,372 ....B6
†44146 Oakwood 3,786 ....H9
45873 Oakwood 886............B3
44074 Oberlin 8,660............F3
†43201 Obetz 3,095............E6
45874 Ohio City 881 ....A4
44138 Olmsted Falls 5,868............G9
44862 Ontario 4,123............E4
†44101 Orange 2,376............J9
43616 Oregon 18,675 ....D2
44667 Orrville 7,511 ....G4
44076 Orwell 1,067 ....J2
45875 Ottawa⊙ 3,874 ....B3
†43601 Ottawa Hills 4,065 ....C2
45876 Ottoville 833 ....B4
45160 Owensville 858 ....B7
45056 Oxford 17,655............A6
44077 Painesville⊙ 16,391 ....H2
45877 Pandora 977 ....C4
44080 Parkman 600 ....H3
44129 Parma 92,548 ....H9
†44130 Parma Heights 23,112......G9
43062 Pataskala 2,284 ....E5
45879 Paulding⊙ 2,754 ....A3
45880 Payne 1,399 ....A3
45660 Peebles 1,790 ....D8
43450 Pemberville 1,321 ....C3
44264 Peninsula 604 ....G3
†44124 Pepper Pike 6,177............J9
44081 Perry 961............H2
43551 Perrysburg 10,215............C2
44864 Perrysville 836............F4
45354 Phillipsburg 705............B6
43771 Philo 799 ....G6
43147 Pickerington 3,917 ....E6
45661 Piketon 1,726............E7
43554 Pioneer 1,133 ....A2
45356 Piqua 20,480 ....B5
43064 Plain City 2,102............D5
43772 Pleasant City 481 ....G6
45359 Pleasant Hill 1,051 ....B5
43148 Pleasantville 780 ....F6
44865 Plymouth 1,939............E4
44514 Poland 3,084 ....J3

45769 Pomeroy⊙ 2,728............G7
43452 Port Clinton⊙ 7,223 ....E2
45770 Portland 150............G7
45662 Portsmouth⊙ 25,943.......D8
43837 Port Washington 622 ....G5
43942 Powhatan Point 2,181 ...... J6
45669 Proctorville 975 ....F9
43342 Prospect 1,159............D5
43456 Put-in-Bay 146 ....E2
43773 Quaker City 698............H6
43343 Quincy 633............C5
45771 Racine 908............G8
44265 Randolph 900 ....H3
44266 Ravenna⊙ 11,987............H3
43943 Rayland 566 ....J5
45215 Reading 12,843 ....C9
†44202 Reminderville 1,960 ....J10
†45202 Remington 600............C9
45773 Reno 576............H7
†43412 Reno Beach D2
44867 Republic 656............D3
43068 Reynoldsburg 20,661 ....E6
44286 Richfield 3,437 ....G3
43944 Richmond 624............J5
†44045 Richmond (Grand River) 412 ....H2
45673 Richmond Dale 950 ....E7
44143 Richmond Heights 10,095 .H9
43344 Richwood 2,181 ....D5
45674 Rio Grande 864 ....F8
45167 Ripley 2,174 ....C8
43457 Risingsun 698 ....C3
44270 Rittman 6,063 ....G4
†43085 Riverlea 528 ....D5
44670 Robertsville 600 ....H4
44084 Rock Creek 652 ....J2
45882 Rockford 1,245 ....A4
44116 Rocky River 21,084 ....G9
44085 Rome 210............J2
44272 Rootstown 900 ....H3
†45662 Rosemount 1,747............D8
43777 Roseville 1,915............F6
45061 Ross 2,767 ....B9
43460 Rossford 5,978 ....C2
45236 Rossmoyne C9
†43943 Rush Run 560............J5
43347 Rushsylvania 610 ....C5
43348 Russells Point 1,156 ....C5
45775 Rutland 635............F7
45169 Sabina 2,799 ....C7
†44067 Sagamore Hills J10
45217 Saint Bernard 5,396............B9
43950 Saint Clairsville⊙ 5,452 .... J5
45883 Saint Henry 1,596 ....A5
45885 Saint Marys 8,414............B4
43072 Saint Paris 1,742 ....C5
44460 Salem 12,869 ....J4
43945 Salineville 1,629............J4
44870 Sandusky⊙ 31,360 ....E3
44671 Sandyville 500 ....H4
45171 Sardinia 826 ....C7
43946 Sardis 865 ....J6
43988 Scio 1,003 ....H5
†45662 Sciotodale 1,191 ....E8
45679 Seaman 1,039............C8
44672 Sebring 5,078 ....H4
†44131 Seven Hills 13,650 ....H9
45062 Seven Mile 841............A7
44273 Seville 1,568............G3
43947 Shadyside 4,315 ....J6
44120 Shaker Heights 32,487 .....H9
45241 Sharonville 10,108............C9
43782 Shawnee 924 ....F6
†44052 Sheffield 1,886 ....F3
44054 Sheffield Lake 10,484 .... F3
44875 Shelby 9,646 ....E4
43556 Sherwood 915............A3
44878 Shiloh 857 ....E4
44676 Shreve 1,608 ....F4
45365 Sidney⊙ 17,657 ....B5
†44221 Silver Lake 2,915 ....G3
†45201 Silverton 6,172............C9
43948 Smithfield 1,308 ....J5
44677 Smithville 1,467............G4

44139 Solon 14,341 ....J9
43783 Somerset 1,432............F6
†44001 South Amherst 1,848 .... F3
†43103 South Bloomfield 934 ....D6
45368 South Charleston 1,682 ....C6
44121 South Euclid 25,713 ....H9
45065 South Lebanon 2,700.......B7
45680 South Point 3,918 ....E9
†44022 South Russell 2,784............H3
45369 South Vienna 464............C6
45682 South Webster 886............E8
43701 South Zanesville 1,739 ..... F6
44275 Spencer 764 ....F3
45887 Spencerville 2,184 ....B4
45066 Springboro 4,962 ....B6
45246 Springdale 10,111 ....B9
*45501 Springfield⊙ 72,563 ....C6
Springfield‡ 183,885........C6
45370 Spring Valley 541 ....C6
44276 Sterling 600............G4
43952 Steubenville⊙ 26,400....... J5
Steubenville-Weirton‡ 163,099 ....J5
43787 Stockport 558 ....G6
43154 Stoutsville 537............E6
44224 Stow 25,303............H3
44680 Strasburg 2,091............G4
44240 Streetsboro 9,055 ....H3
44136 Strongsville 28,577 .... G10
44471 Struthers 13,624............J3
43557 Stryker 1,423............B3
†44260 Suffield 650 ....H3
44681 Sugarcreek 1,966............G5
43074 Sunbury 2,101 ....E5
43558 Swanton 3,424............C2
44882 Sycamore 1,059 ....D4
43560 Sylvania 15,527 ....C2
45779 Syracuse 946 ....G7
44278 Tallmadge 15,269............H3
†43771 Taylorsville (Philo) 799......G6
45174 Terrace Park 2,044 ....D9
45780 The Plains 2,044............F7
43076 Thornville 838 ....F6
44883 Tiffin⊙ 19,549 ....D3
43963 Tiltonsville 1,750............J5
†44094 Timberlake 885............J8
45371 Tipp City 5,595............B6
†45245 Tobasco 950 ....C10
*43601 Toledo⊙ 354,635 ....D2
Toledo‡ 791,599 ....D2
43964 Toronto 6,934 ....J5
45067 Trenton 6,401 ....B7
45782 Trimble 579............F7
45426 Trotwood 7,802............B6
45373 Troy⊙ 19,086............B5
44682 Tuscarawas 917............H5
44087 Twinsburg 7,632............J10
44683 Uhrichsville 6,130............H5
45322 Union 5,219 ....B6
†47390 Union City 1,716............A5
44685 Uniontown 875............H4
44118 University Heights 15,401 ..H9
43221 Upper Arlington 35,648.....D6
43351 Upper Sandusky⊙ 5,967 ..D4
43078 Urbana⊙ 10,762 ....C5
†43123 Urbancrest 880............D6
43080 Utica 2,238 ....F5
†43201 Valley View 730 ....D6
†44101 Valleyview 1,576 ....H9
45377 Vandalia 13,161 ....B6
45890 Vanlue 390............C4
45891 Van Wert⊙ 11,035............A4
44089 Vermilion 11,012 ....F3
45378 Verona 571............A6
45380 Versailles 2,384 ....A5
44473 Vienna 900............J3
44281 Wadsworth 15,166 ....G3
†44094 Waite Hill 529 ....H2
45687 Wakefield 300 ....E8
44889 Wakeman 906 ....F3
43465 Walbridge 2,900 ....C2
44687 Walnut Creek 550............G4
†44146 Walton Hills 2,199............J10
45895 Wapakoneta⊙ 8,402........B4

45785 Warner 250 ....H6
*44481 Warren⊙ 56,629 ....J3
44128 Warrensville Heights 16,565 ....H9
43844 Warsaw 765 ....G5
43160 Washington Court House⊙ 12,682............D6
44490 Washingtonville 865 .... J4
45786 Waterford 600............G6
43566 Waterville 3,884............C3
43567 Wauseon⊙ 6,173 ....B2
45690 Waverly⊙ 4,603 ....D7
43466 Wayne 894............C3
44688 Waynesburg 1,160 ....H4
45896 Waynesfield 826 ....C4
45068 Waynesville 1,796 ....B6
44090 Wellington 4,146............F3
45692 Wellston 6,016 ....F7
43968 Wellsville 5,095 ....J4
45381 West Alexandria 1,313......A6
45449 West Carrollton 13,148.....B6
43081 Westerville 23,414............D5
44491 West Farmington 563 .... J3
44251 Westfield Center 791 ....G3
43162 West Jefferson 4,448 ....D6
43845 West Lafayette 2,225 ....G5
44145 Westlake 19,483 ....G9
43357 West Liberty 1,653 ....C5
43358 West Mansfield 716 ....C5
45383 West Milton 4,119............B6
43569 Weston 1,708 ....C3
†45662 West Portsmouth 4,095 ....D8
44287 West Salem 1,357............F4
45693 West Union⊙ 2,791 ....C8
43570 West Unity 1,639............B2
45694 Wheelersburg 4,796............E8
43213 Whitehall 21,299............E6
43571 Whitehouse 2,137 ....C2
44092 Wickliffe 16,790............J9
44890 Willard 5,720 ....E3
45176 Williamsburg 1,952............B7
44093 Williamsfield 950............J2
43164 Williamsport 792............D6
44094 Willoughby 19,329 ....J8
†44094 Willoughby Hills 8,612...... J9
44094 Willowick 17,834 ....J8
45898 Willshire 564............A4
45177 Wilmington⊙ 10,431 ....C7
45697 Winchester 1,080............C8
44288 Windham 3,721 ....H3
43952 Wintersville 4,724............J5
45245 Withamsville 975............C10
†45201 Woodlawn 2,715............C9
†44101 Woodmere 877............J9
43793 Woodsfield⊙ 3,145 ....H6
43469 Woodville 2,050............D3
44691 Wooster⊙ 19,289 ....G4
43085 Worthington 15,016............E5
45215 Wyoming 8,282 ....C9
45385 Xenia⊙ 24,653 ....C6
45387 Yellow Springs 4,077 ....C6
43971 Yorkville 1,447 ....J5
*44501 Youngstown⊙ 115,436 .... J3
Youngstown-Warren‡ 531,350 ....J3
43701 Zanesville⊙ 28,655 ....G6
44697 Zoar 264............H4
44698 Zoarville 125 ....H4

OTHER FEATURES

Atwood (lake) H4
Auglaize (riv.) B4
Berlin (lake) H4
Big Walnut (creek) E5
Black (riv.)............F3
Black Fork, Mohican (riv.) F4
Blanchard (riv.) C4
Blennerhassett (isl.)............G7
Buckeye (lake) F6
Campbell (hill) C5
Captina (creek)............J6
Cedar (pt.)............
Chagrin (riv.)............
Clear Fork (res.)............
Clear Fork, Mohican (riv.) ....
Clendening (lake)............
Cleveland-Hopkins Mun. Airport ....
Cuyahoga (riv.) ....H
Darby (creek) ....
Deer (creek) ....
Delaware (lake) ....
Dillon (lake) ....
Dover (lake) ....
Duck (creek) ....
Erie (lake)............
Eufaula (res.)............
Grand (riv.)............
Great Miami (riv.) ....
Hocking (riv.) ....
Hoover (res.)............
Huron (riv.)............
Indian (lake) ....
James A. Garfield Nat'l Hist. Site ....
Kelleys (isl.)............
Keystone (res.) ....
Killbuck (creek) ....
Kokosing (riv.)............
Leesville (lake) ....
Licking (riv.) ....
Little Beaver (creek)............
Little Miami (riv.)............
Little Miami, East Fork (riv.) ....
Little Muskingum (riv.)............
Loramie (lake) ....
Mad (riv.)............
Maumee (bay) ....
Maumee (riv.)............
Middle Bass (isl.) ....
Mohican (riv.)............
Mosquito Creek (lake) ....
Mound City Group Nat'l Mon. ......
Muskingum (riv.)............
North Bass (isl.)............
Ohio (riv.) ....
Ohio Brush (creek)............
Olentangy (riv.) ....
Paint (creek)............
Perry's Victory and Int'l Peace Mem. ....
Piedmont (lake)............
Portage (riv.)............
Pymatuning (res.)............
Raccoon (creek) ....
Rattlesnake (creek)............
Rickenbacker Air Force Base 1,763.
Rocky (riv.)............
Rocky, West Branch (riv.)............ G
Rocky Fork (lake) ....
Saint Joseph (riv.) ....
Saint Marys (lake)............
Saint Marys (riv.) ....
Salt Fork (creek)............
Sandusky (bay) ....
Sandusky (riv.) ....
Scioto (riv.) ....
Senecaville (lake) ....
Sevenmile (creek) ....
South Bass (isl.) ....
Stillwater (riv.) ....
Symmes (creek) ....
Tappan (lake) ....
Tiffin (riv.) ....
Tuscarawas (riv.)............
Vermilion (riv.)............
Wabash (riv.) ....
West Sister (isl.) ....
Whiteoak (creek) ....
William H. Taft Nat'l Hist. Site ... C
Wills (creek)............
Wills Creek (lake)............
Wright-Patterson Air Force Base 9,155 ....
Yellow (creek)............

⊙County seat.
‡Population of metropolitan area.
† Zip of nearest p.o. * Multiple z

AREA 69,956 sq. mi. (181,186 sq. km.)
POPULATION 3,025,290
CAPITAL Oklahoma City
LARGEST CITY Oklahoma City
HIGHEST POINT Black Mesa 4,973 ft. (1516 m.)
SETTLED IN 1889
ADMITTED TO UNION November 16, 1907
POPULAR NAME Sooner State
STATE FLOWER Mistletoe
STATE BIRD Scissor-tailed Flycatcher

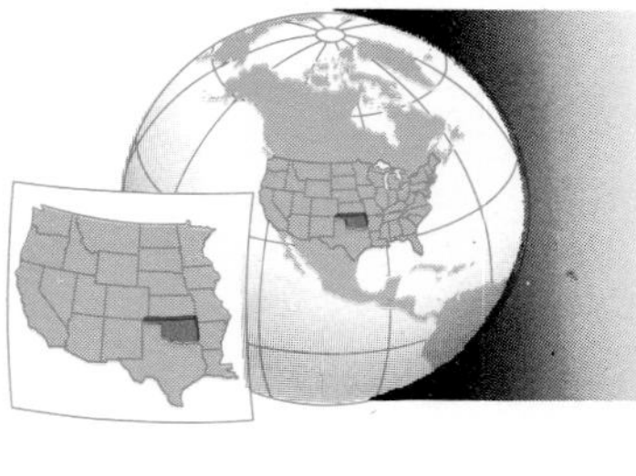

COUNTIES

County	Key
Adair 18,575	S3
Alfalfa 7,077	K1
Atoka 12,748	O6
Beaver 6,806	E1
Beckham 19,243	G4
Blaine 13,443	K3
Bryan 30,535	O7
Caddo 30,905	K4
Canadian 56,452	K3
Carter 43,610	M6
Cherokee 30,684	R3
Choctaw 17,203	P6
Cimarron 3,648	A1
Cleveland 133,173	M4
Coal 6,041	O5
Comanche 112,456	K5
Cotton 7,338	K6
Craig 15,014	R1
Creek 59,016	O3
Custer 25,995	H3
Delaware 23,946	S2
Dewey 5,922	H2
Ellis 5,596	G2
Garfield 62,820	L2
Garvin 27,856	M5
Grady 39,490	L5
Grant 6,518	L1
Greer 7,028	G5
Harmon 4,519	G5
Harper 4,715	G1
Haskell 11,010	R4
Hughes 14,338	O4
Jackson 30,356	H5
Jefferson 8,183	L6
Johnston 10,356	N6
Kay 49,852	M1
Kingfisher 14,187	L3
Kiowa 12,711	J5
Latimer 9,840	R5
Le Flore 40,698	S5
Lincoln 26,601	N3
Logan 26,881	M3
Love 7,469	M7
Major 8,772	K2
Marshall 10,550	N6
Mayes 32,261	R2
McClain 20,291	L5
McCurtain 36,151	S6
McIntosh 15,562	P4
Murray 12,147	M6
Muskogee 66,939	R3
Noble 11,573	M2
Nowata 11,486	P1
Okfuskee 11,125	O3
Oklahoma 568,933	M3
Okmulgee 39,169	P3
Osage 39,327	O1
Ottawa 32,870	S1
Pawnee 15,310	N2
Payne 62,435	N2
Pittsburg 40,524	P5
Pontotoc 32,598	N5
Pottawatomie 55,239	N4
Pushmataha 11,773	R6
Roger Mills 4,799	G3
Rogers 46,436	P2
Seminole 27,473	N4
Sequoyah 30,749	S3
Stephens 43,419	L6
Texas 17,727	C1
Tillman 12,398	J6
Tulsa 470,593	P2
Wagoner 41,801	P3
Washington 48,113	P1
Washita 13,798	J4
Woods 10,923	J1
Woodward 21,172	H2

CITIES and TOWNS

Zip	Name/Pop.	Key
74720	Achille 480	O7
74820	Ada⊙ 15,902	N5
74330	Adair 508	R2
73901	Adams 150	D1
73520	Addington 141	L6
74331	Afton 1,174	S1
74824	Agra 354	N3
74721	Albany 65	O7
73001	Albert 100	K4
74521	Albion 165	R5
74522	Alderson 366	P5
73002	Alex 769	L5
73716	Aline 313	K1
74825	Allen 998	O5
73521	Altus⊙ 23,101	H5
73717	Alva⊙ 6,416	J1
73004	Amber 416	L4
73718	Ames 314	K2
73719	Amorita 66	K1
73005	Anadarko⊙ 6,378	K4
74523	Antlers⊙ 2,989	P6
73006	Apache 1,560	K5
73620	Arapaho⊙ 851	H3
73401	Ardmore⊙ 23,689	M6
74901	Arkoma 2,175	T4
73832	Arnett⊙ 714	G2
74826	Asher 659	N5
74524	Ashland 72	O5
74525	Atoka⊙ 3,409	O6
74827	Atwood 225	O5
74001	Avant 461	O2
†73860	Avard 51	J1
73930	Baker 70	D1
74002	Barnsdall 1,501	O1
†74965	Baron 300	S3
74003	Bartlesville⊙ 34,568	O1
74722	Battiest 250	S6
73932	Beaver⊙ 1,939	F1
74421	Beggs 1,428	P3
†74966	Bengal 300	R5
74723	Bennington 302	P7
74331	Bernice 318	S1
73622	Bessie 245	H4
73008	Bethany 22,130	L3
74724	Bethel 350	S6
†74801	Bethel Acres 2,314	M4
74332	Big Cabin 252	R1
74630	Billings 632	M1
73009	Binger 791	K4
73720	Bison 103	L2
74008	Bixby 6,969	P3
74058	Blackburn 114	N2
74631	Blackwell 8,400	M1
73526	Blair 1,092	H5
73010	Blanchard 1,688	L4
74528	Blanco 215	P5
74529	Blocker 135	P4
†74701	Blue 150	O7
74333	Bluejacket 247	R1
73933	Boise City⊙ 1,761	B1
74726	Bokchito 628	O6
74930	Bokoshe 556	S4
74829	Boley 423	O4
74727	Boswell 702	P6
74830	Bowlegs 522	N4
74009	Bowring 115	O1
74422	Boynton 518	P3
73011	Bradley 284	L5
74423	Braggs 351	R3
74632	Braman 355	M1
73012	Bray 591	L5
73721	Breckinridge 261	L2
†73047	Bridgeport 115	K3
74010	Bristow 4,702	O3
74012	Broken Arrow 35,761	P2
74728	Broken Bow 3,965	S7
74530	Bromide 180	N6
†74873	Brooksville 46	M4
†74437	Bryant 74	P4
73834	Buffalo⊙ 1,381	G1
74931	Bunch 64	S3
74633	Burbank 161	N1
73722	Burlington 206	K1
73430	Burneyville 150	M7
73624	Burns Flat 2,431	H4
73625	Butler 388	H3
74831	Byars 353	N5
†74820	Byng 833	N5
73723	Byron 67	K1
73527	Cache 1,661	J5
74729	Caddo 923	O6
74730	Calera 1,390	O7
73014	Calumet 469	K3
74531	Calvin 315	O5
73835	Camargo 264	H2
74932	Cameron 365	T4
74425	Canadian 279	P4
74533	Caney 147	O6
73724	Canton 854	J2
73626	Canute 676	H4
73725	Capron 54	J1
74335	Cardin 500	S1
73726	Carmen 516	J1
73015	Carnegie 2,016	J4
74832	Carney 622	N3
73727	Carrier 259	K2
73627	Carter 367	H4
74934	Cartersville 79	S4
73016	Cashion 547	L3
74833	Castle 130	O4
74015	Catoosa 1,561	P2
73017	Cement 884	K5
74534	Centrahoma 166	O5
74834	Chandler⊙ 2,926	N3
73528	Chattanooga 403	J6
74426	Checotah 3,454	R4
74016	Chelsea 1,754	P1
73728	Cherokee⊙ 2,105	K1
73838	Chester 104	J2
73628	Cheyenne⊙ 1,207	G3
73018	Chickasha⊙ 15,828	L4
74635	Chilocco 400	M1
73020	Choctaw 7,520	M3
74337	Chouteau 1,559	R2
†74965	Christie 375	S3
73111	Cimarron	L3
74017	Claremore⊙ 12,085	R2
74535	Clarita 72	O6
74536	Clayton 833	R5
74835	Clearview 250	O4
73729	Cleo Springs 514	K2
74020	Cleveland 2,972	O2
73601	Clinton 8,796	H3
74538	Coalgate⊙ 2,001	O5
74733	Colbert 1,122	O7
74338	Colcord 530	S2
†73010	Cole 309	L5
73432	Coleman 200	O6
74021	Collinsville 3,556	P2
73021	Colony 185	J4
73529	Comanche 1,937	L6
74339	Commerce 2,556	R1
73022	Concho 300	L3
†73041	Cooperton 31	J5
74022	Copan 960	P1
73632	Cordell⊙ 3,301	H4
73024	Corn 542	J4
†73456	Cornish 115	L6
74428	Council Hill 141	P3
73025	Countyline 550	L6
73730	Covington 715	L2
74429	Coweta 4,554	P3
†74934	Cowlington 546	S4
73027	Coyle 345	M3
73638	Crawford 53	G3
73028	Crescent 1,651	L3
74837	Cromwell 337	N4
74430	Crowder 431	P4
†73446	Cumberland 100	N6
74023	Cushing 7,720	N3
73639	Custer City 530	J3
73029	Cyril 1,220	K5
73731	Dacoma 226	J1
74838	Dale 160	M4
74026	Davenport 974	N3
73530	Davidson 501	J6
73030	Davis 2,782	M5
74636	Deer Creek 174	L1
74027	Delaware 544	P1
73115	Del City 28,523	L4
74028	Depew 682	O3
73531	Devol 186	J6
74431	Dewar 1,048	P4
74029	Dewey 3,545	P1
73031	Dibble 348	L4
†73401	Dickson 996	M6
73641	Dill City 649	H4
74340	Disney 464	S2
73032	Dougherty 210	M6
73733	Douglas 89	L2
74341	Douthat 30	S1
73734	Dover 570	L3
73735	Drummond 482	L2
74030	Drumright 3,162	N3
73533	Duncan⊙ 22,517	L5
74701	Durant⊙ 11,972	O6
73642	Durham 30	G3
74839	Dustin 498	O4
74734	Eagletown 650	S6
73033	Eakly 452	K4
74840	Earlsboro 266	N4
†73532	East Duke 484	H5
73034	Edmond 34,637	M3
73537	Eldorado 688	G6
73538	Elgin 1,003	K5
73644	Elk City 9,579	G4
73539	Elmer 131	H6
73035	Elmore City 582	M5
73935	Elmwood 300	F1
73036	El Reno⊙ 15,486	K3
†73529	Empire City 13	L6
73701	Enid⊙ 50,363	L2
73645	Erick 1,375	G4
74342	Eucha 210	S2
74432	Eufaula⊙ 3,159	P4
74637	Fairfax 1,949	N1
74343	Fairland 1,073	S1
73736	Fairmont 419	L2
†74080	Fair Oaks 346	P2
73737	Fairview⊙ 3,370	J2
†74881	Fallis 22	M3
74935	Fanshawe 416	S5
73840	Fargo 409	G2
73540	Faxon 140	J6
73646	Fay 140	J3
73937	Felt 120	A1
74543	Finley 350	R6
74842	Fittstown 500	N5
74843	Fitzhugh 150	N5
†73569	Fleetwood 12	L7
73541	Fletcher 1,074	K5
74652	Foraker 34	Q1
†73101	Forest Park 1,148	M3
73938	Forgan 611	E1
73038	Fort Cobb 760	K4
74434	Fort Gibson 2,477	R3
73841	Fort Supply 559	G1
74735	Fort Towson 789	R7
73647	Foss 188	H4
73039	Foster 100	M5
73435	Fox 400	M6
74031	Foyil 191	R2
74844	Francis 365	N5
73542	Frederick⊙ 6,153	H6
73842	Freedom 339	H1
73843	Gage 667	G2
74936	Gans 346	S4
73738	Garber 1,215	M2
74736	Garvin 162	S7
73844	Gate 146	F1
73040	Geary 1,700	K3
73436	Gene Autry 178	N6
73543	Geronimo 726	K6
†74531	Gerty 149	O5
74032	Glencoe 490	M2
74033	Glenpool 2,706	P3
74737	Golden 300	S6
†73093	Goldsby 603	L4
73739	Goltry 305	K1
†74740	Goodwater 240	S7
73939	Goodwell 1,186	C1
74435	Gore 445	R3
73041	Gotebo 457	J4
73544	Gould 318	G5
74545	Gowen 75	R5
73042	Gracemont 503	K4
73545	Grady 85	L6
73437	Graham 200	M6
†74652	Grainola 67	N1
73546	Grandfield 1,445	J6
†74349	Grand Lake Towne 36	S1
73547	Granite 1,617	H5
†74437	Grayson 150	P3
73043	Greenfield 233	K3
74344	Grove 3,378	S1
73044	Guthrie⊙ 10,312	M3
73942	Guymon⊙ 8,492	D1
74546	Haileyville 832	P5
74034	Hallett 186	N2
†73069	Hall Park 577	M4
73650	Hammon 866	H3
74845	Hanna 157	P4
74846	Harden City 250	N5
73944	Hardesty 243	D1
73832	Harmon 27	G2
73045	Harrah 2,897	M4
†74740	Harris 192	S7
74547	Hartshorne 2,380	R5
74436	Haskell 1,953	P3
73548	Hastings 246	K6
74740	Haworth 341	S7
73549	Headrick 223	H5
73438	Healdton 3,769	M6
74937	Heavener 2,776	S5
73741	Helena 710	K1
74741	Hendrix 106	O7
73046	Hennepin 300	M5
73742	Hennessey 2,287	L2
74437	Henryetta 6,432	O4
†73086	Hickory 95	N5
73743	Hillsdale 110	K1
73047	Hinton 1,432	K4
73744	Hitchcock 172	K3
74438	Hitchita 126	P3
73651	Hobart⊙ 4,735	J5
74439	Hoffman 407	P4
74848	Holdenville⊙ 5,469	O4
73550	Hollis⊙ 2,958	G5
73551	Hollister 82	J6
74035	Hominy 3,130	O2
74549	Honobia 80	R5
73945	Hooker 1,788	D1
†74366	Hoot Owl 3	R2
73746	Hopeton 42	J1
74940	Howe 562	S5
74440	Hoyt 160	R4
74743	Hugo⊙ 7,172	P7
74441	Hulbert 633	R3
74640	Hunter 276	L1
73048	Hydro 938	J3
74745	Idabel⊙ 7,622	S7
73552	Indiahoma 364	J5
74442	Indianola 254	P4
74036	Inola 1,550	P2
73747	Isabella 113	K2
74346	Jay⊙ 2,100	S2
†73759	Jefferson 92	L1
74037	Jenks 5,876	P2
74038	Jennings 395	N2
73749	Jet 352	K1
73049	Jones 2,270	M3
74347	Kansas 491	S2
74641	Kaw City 283	N1
74039	Kellyville 960	O3

(continued on following page)

Agriculture, Industry and Resources

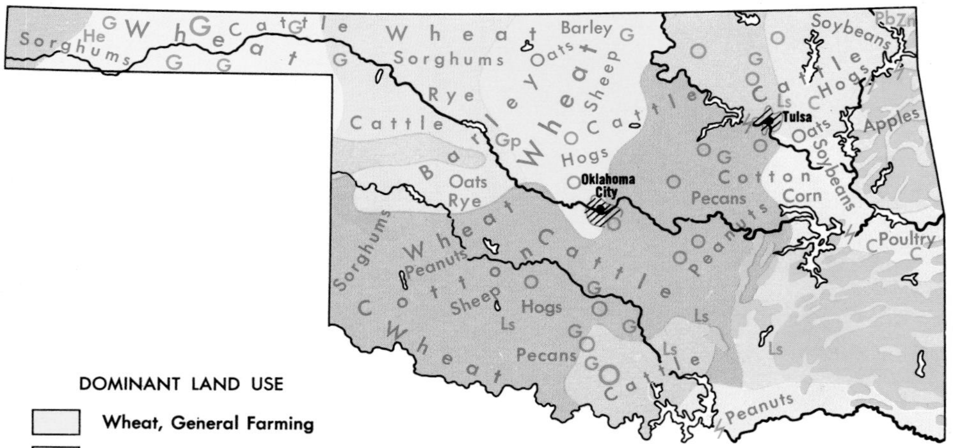

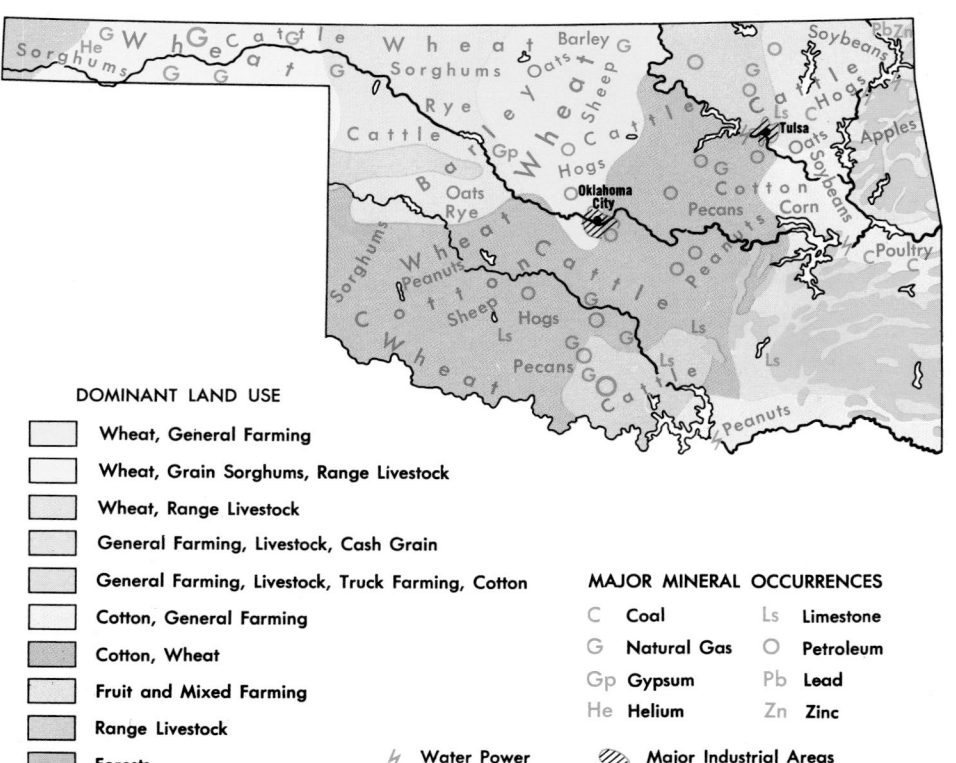

DOMINANT LAND USE

- Wheat, General Farming
- Wheat, Grain Sorghums, Range Livestock
- Wheat, Range Livestock
- General Farming, Livestock, Cash Grain
- General Farming, Livestock, Truck Farming, Cotton
- Cotton, General Farming
- Cotton, Wheat
- Fruit and Mixed Farming
- Range Livestock
- Forests

MAJOR MINERAL OCCURRENCES

C	Coal	Ls	Limestone
G	Natural Gas	O	Petroleum
Gp	Gypsum	Pb	Lead
He	Helium	Zn	Zinc

Water Power

Major Industrial Areas

Topography

74461 Stidham 60	P4	74653 Tonkawa 3,524	M1
74462 Stigler⊙ 2,630	R4	†74852 Tribbey 215	M4
74074 Stillwater⊙ 38,268	N2	†74856 Troy 92	N6
74960 Stilwell⊙ 2,369	S3	74875 Tryon 83	N3
74871 Stonewall 672	O5	74466 Tullahassee 145	P3
74367 Strang 126	R2	*74101 Tulsa⊙ 360,919	O2
74872 Stratford 1,459	M5	Tulsa‡ 689,628	O2
74569 Stringtown 1,047	P6	74572 Tupelo 542	O5
73665 Strong City 56	G4	73950 Turpin 450	E1
74079 Stroud 3,148	N3	74753 Tushka 358	O6
74570 Stuart 235	O5	74574 Tuskahoma 168	R5
†73565 Sugden 76	L6	73095 Wayne 621	M5
73086 Sulphur⊙ 5,516	N5	73088 Tussy 157	L6
74966 Summerfield 150	S5	73089 Tuttle 3,051	L4
73666 Sweetwater 85	G4	73090 Union City 558	L4
74463 Taft 489	R3	74763 Utica 38	O7
74464 Tahlequah⊙ 9,708	R3	†73101 Valley Brook 921	M4
74080 Talala 191	P1	74764 Valliant 927	R6
74571 Talihina 1,387	R4	†74820 Vanoss 130	N5
73667 Taloga⊙ 446	J2	73091 Velma 831	L6
†74462 Tamaha 145	R4	74082 Vera 182	P2
73087 Tatums 281	M6	73092 Verden 625	K4
74873 Tecumseh 5,123	N4	†74017 Verdigris 150	P2
73568 Temple 1,339	K6	74877 Vernon 100	P4
74081 Terlton 155	O2	74962 Vian 1,521	S4
73569 Terral 604	L7	73859 Vici 845	H2
73949 Texhoma 785	C1	74301 Vinita⊙ 6,740	R1
73668 Texola 106	G4	73571 Vinson 42	G5
73459 Thackerville 431	M7	74467 Wagoner⊙ 6,191	R3
73120 The Village 11,049	L3	74468 Wainwright 182	R3
73669 Thomas 1,515	J3	73771 Wakita 526	L1
†74017 Tiawah 125	P2	73572 Walters⊙ 2,778	K6
73570 Tipton 1,475	H6	74878 Wanette 473	M5
73460 Tishomingo⊙ 3,212	N6	74083 Wann 156	P1

73461 Wapanucka 472	N6	73801 Woodward⊙ 13,610	H2
74469 Warner 1,310	R4	74766 Wright City 1,168	R6
73132 Warr Acres 9,940	L3	74370 Wyandotte 336	S1
74834 Warwick 167	M3	73098 Wynnewood 2,615	M5
73093 Washington 477	L4	74084 Wynona 780	O1
73094 Watts 316	S2	74085 Yale 1,652	N2
73772 Watonga⊙ 4,139	K3	†74574 Yanush 123	R5
74964 Watts 316	S2	†74848 Yeager 138	O4
73773 Waukomis 1,551	K2	73099 Yukon 17,112	L3
73573 Waurika⊙ 2,258	L6		
73095 Wayne 621	M5	**OTHER FEATURES**	
73860 Waynoka 1,377	J1		
73096 Weatherford 9,640	J4	Altus (res.)	H5
74654 Webb City 157	N1	Altus A.F.B.	H5
74470 Webbers Falls 461	R3	Arbuckle Nat'l Rec. Area	N6
74369 Welch 697	R1	Arbuckles, Lake of the (lake)	M6
74880 Weleetka 1,195	O4	Arkansas (riv.)	S4
74471 Welling 115	S3	Atoka (res.)	P5
74881 Wellston 802	M3	Beaver (creek)	K6
74882 Welty 80	O3	Beaver (riv.)	F1
†74020 Westport 265	O2	Bird (creek)	O1
†72761 West Siloam Springs 431	S2	Black Bear (creek)	M2
74965 Westville 1,049	S2	Black Mesa (mt.)	A1
74883 Wetumka 1,725	O4	Blue (riv.)	O6
74884 Wewoka⊙ 5,480	O4	Bluestem (lake)	O1
74472 Whitefield 240	R4	Boston (mts.)	S3
74577 Whitesboro 450	S5	Broken Bow (lake)	S6
74578 Wilburton⊙ 2,996	R5	Cache (creek)	K6
†74932 Williams 110	T4	Canadian (riv.)	O4
73673 Willow 162	G4	Caney (riv.)	O1
73463 Wilson 1,585	M6	Canton (lake)	J2
74966 Wister 982	S5	Carl Blackwell (lake)	M2
†74868 Wolf 200	N4	Cherokees, Lake O'The (lake)	S1
73466 Woodville 94	N7	Chickasha (lake)	K4

Cimarron (riv.)	N2	North Canadian (riv.)	K3
Clear Boggy (creek)	O6	North Carrizo (riv.)	A1
Deep Fork, North Canadian (riv.)	N3	Oologah (lake)	P1
Denison (dam)	O7	Optima (lake)	D1
Elk (creek)	H4	Osage Ind. Res.	O1
Ellsworth (lake)	K5	Ouachita (mts.)	R5
Eucha (lake)	S2	Pine Creek (lake)	R6
Eufaula (lake)	P4	Platt Nat'l Park	N6
Fort Cobb (res.)	J4	Poteau (riv.)	S5
Fort Gibson (lake)	R2	Prairie Dog Town Fork, Red	
Fort Sill 15,924	K6	(riv.)	F5
Fort Supply (lake)	G1	Red (riv.)	R7
Foss (res.)	H3	Red, North Fork (riv.)	H4
Great Salt Plains (lake)	K1	Salt Fork, Arkansas (riv.)	J1
Heyburn (res.)	O3	Salt Fork, Red (riv.)	G5
Hudson (lake)	R2	Sans Bois (mts.)	R4
Hugo (lake)	R6	Scott (mt.)	K5
Hulah (lake)	O1	Spavinaw (lake)	S2
Illinois (riv.)	S3	Tenkiller Ferry (lake)	S3
Jackfork (mt.)	P5	Texoma (lake)	N7
Kaw (lake)	N1	Thunderbird (lake)	M4
Kerr, Robert S. (res.)	S4	Tinker A.F.B.	M4
Keystone (lake)	O2	Tom Steed (res.)	J5
Kiamichi (mts.)	R5	Vance A.F.B.	K2
Kiamichi (riv.)	R5	Verdigris (riv.)	P2
Kiowa (creek)	F1	Washita (riv.)	M5
Lawtonka (lake)	K5	Waurika (lake)	K6
Little (riv.)	R6	Webbers Falls (lake)	R3
McAlester (lake)	P4	Wichita (mts.)	J5
Mountain Fork (riv.)	S6	Wildhorse (creek)	L5
Mud (creek)	L6	Wister (lake)	S5
Muddy Boggy (creek)	O5	Wolf (creek)	G2
Murray (lake)	M6	
Neosho (riv.)	R1	⊙County seat.

‡Population of metropolitan area.
† Zip of nearest p.o. * Multiple zips.

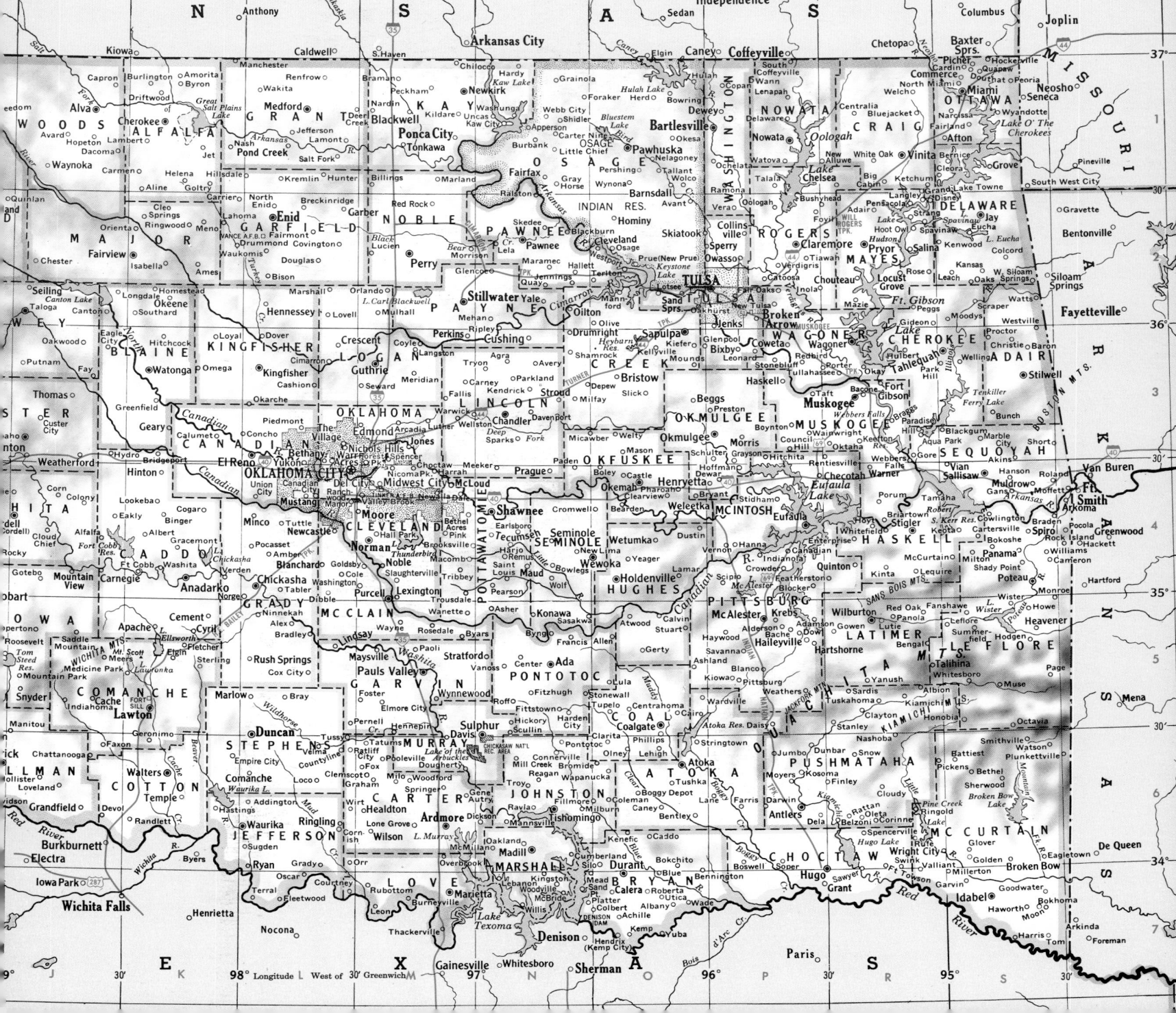

COUNTIES

Baker 16,134 .... K3
Benton 68,211 .... D3
Clackamas 241,911 .... E2
Clatsop 32,489 .... D1
Columbia 35,646 .... D2
Coos 64,047 .... C4
Crook 13,091 .... G3
Curry 16,992 .... C5
Deschutes 62,142 .... F4
Douglas 93,748 .... D4
Gilliam 2,057 .... G2
Grant 8,210 .... J3
Harney 8,314 .... H4
Hood River 15,835 .... F2
Jackson 132,456 .... E5
Jefferson 11,599 .... F3
Josephine 58,855 .... D5
Klamath 59,117 .... F5
Lake 7,532 .... G5
Lane 275,226 .... E4
Lincoln 35,264 .... D3
Linn 89,495 .... E3

Malheur 26,896 .... K4
Marion 204,692 .... E3
Morrow 7,519 .... H2
Multnomah 562,640 .... E2
Polk 45,203 .... D3
Sherman 2,172 .... F2
Tillamook 21,164 .... D2
Umatilla 58,861 .... J2
Union 23,921 .... K2
Wallowa 7,273 .... K2
Wasco 21,732 .... F2
Washington 245,860 .... D2
Wheeler 1,513 .... G3
Yamhill 55,332 .... D2

CITIES and TOWNS

Zip	Name/Pop.	Key
†97330	Adair Village 589	D3
97810	Adams 240	J2
97620	Adel 24	H5
97901	Adrian 162	K4
†97365	Agate Beach 975	C3
97406	Agness 150	C5
97321	Albany ⊙ 26,678	D3
97407	Allegany 300	D4
97005	Aloha 28,353	A2
97621	Alsea 125	D3
†97601	Altamont 19,805	F5
97409	Alvadore 800	D3
97101	Amity 1,092	D3
97001	Antelope 39	G3
97530	Applegate 150	D5
97458	Arago 200	C4
97812	Arlington 521	G2
97520	Ashland 14,943	E5
97103	Astoria ⊙ 9,998	D1
97325	Aumsville 1,432	E3
97002	Aurora 523	E2
97817	Austin 19	J3
97814	Baker ⊙ 9,471	K3
†97738	Ballston 120	D2
97411	Bandon 2,311	C4
97106	Banks 489	A1
†97013	Barlow 105	B2

†97009	Barton 100	B2
†97136	Bar View 170	C2
97420	Barview 1,462	C4
97817	Bates 56	J3
97107	Bay City 986	D2
97621	Beatty 350	F5
97108	Beaver 350	D2
97004	Beavercreek 708	B2
97005	Beaverton 30,582	A2
97701	Bend ⊙ 17,263	F3
97058	Biggs 50	F2
97412	Blachly 80	D3
97108	Blaine 38	D2
97326	Blodgett 250	D3
97413	Blue River 318	E3
97622	Bly 800	F5
97818	Boardman 1,261	H2
97623	Bonanza 270	F5
97008	Bonneville 80	C2
97009	Boring 150	E2
97010	Bridal Veil 20	E2
97458	Bridge 200	D4
†97136	Brighton 150	C2
97001	Brightwood 200	E2

97414	Broadbent 400	C4
97903	Brogan 130	K3
97415	Brookings 3,384	C5
97305	Brooks 490	A3
†97524	Brownsboro 150	E5
97327	Brownsville 1,261	E3
†97351	Buena Vista 130	D3
†97420	Bunker Hill 1,555	C4
97720	Burns ⊙ 3,579	H4
97522	Butte Falls 428	E5
†97002	Butteville 20	A2
97109	Buxton 450	D2
97416	Camas Valley 750	D4
97730	Camp Sherman 350	F3
†97493	Canary 23	D4
97013	Canby 7,659	B2
97110	Cannon Beach 1,187	D2
97820	Canyon City ⊙ 639	J3
97417	Canyonville 1,288	D5
97111	Carlton 1,302	D2
97014	Cascade Locks 838	E2
97329	Cascadia 250	E3
97523	Cave Junction 1,023	D5
97821	Cayuse 200	J2

97225	Cedar Hills 9,619	A2
97005	Cedar Mill 900	A2
†97058	Celilo 50	G2
97502	Central Point 6,357	D5
97420	Charleston 500	C4
97306	Chemawa 400	A3
†97731	Chemult 800	F4
†97119	Cherry Grove 350	A2
†97055	Cherryville 75	C2
97419	Cheshire 300	D3
97624	Chiloquin 778	F5
97015	Clackamas	A2
97016	Clatskanie 1,648	D1
97112	Cloverdale 260	C2
97401	Coburg 699	D3
97017	Colton 305	B3
97018	Columbia City 678	E2
97823	Condon ⊙ 783	G2
97420	Coos Bay 14,424	C4
97423	Coquille ⊙ 4,481	C4
97113	Cornelius 4,462	A2
97330	Corvallis ⊙ 40,960	D3
97424	Cottage Grove 7,148	D4

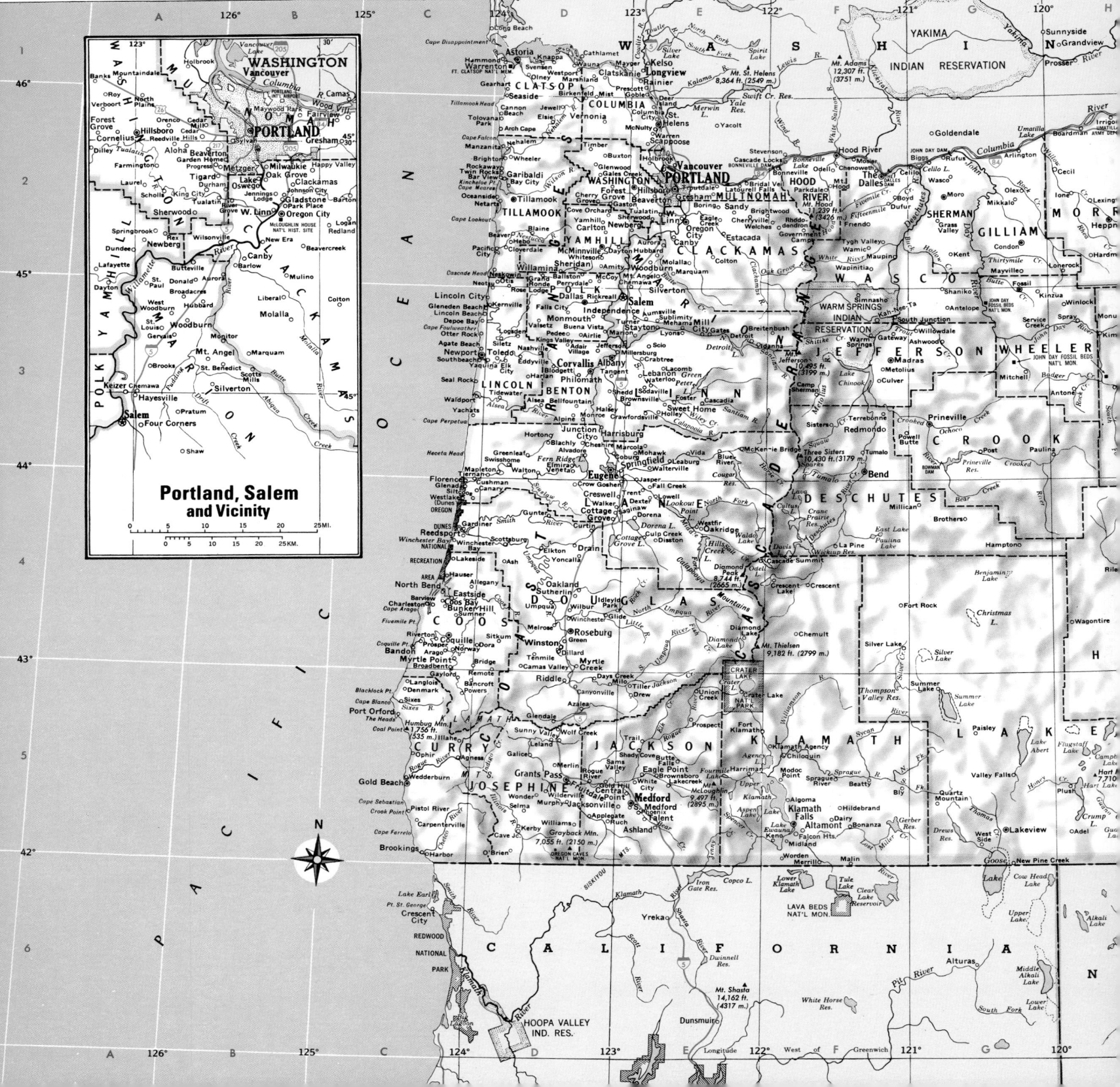

97824 Cove 451 ....K2
97335 Crabtree 200 ....E3
97732 Crane 84 ....J4
97336 Crawfordsville 350 ....E3
97733 Crescent 750 ....F4
97425 Crescent Lake 120 ....F4
97426 Creswell 1,770 ....D4
†97401 Crow 200 ....D4
97427 Culp Creek 600 ....E4
97734 Culver 514 ....F3
97428 Curtin 350 ....D4
†97439 Cushman 175 ....D4
97625 Dairy 80 ....F5
97338 Dallas⊙ 8,530 ....D3
97058 Dalles, The⊙ 10,820 ....F2
97429 Days Creek 550 ....D5
97114 Dayton 1,409 ....A3
97825 Dayville 199 ....H3
97054 Deer Island 225 ....E2
97341 Depoe Bay 723 ....C3
97342 Detroit 367 ....E3
97431 Dexter 500 ....E4
97432 Dillard 602 ....D4
†97116 Dilley 250 ....A2

†97427 Disston 123 ....E4
97020 Donald 267 ....A3
97434 Dorena 200 ....E4
97435 Drain 1,148 ....D4
97021 Dufur 560 ....F2
97115 Dundee 1,223 ....A2
†97493 Dunes (Westlake) 1,124 ...C4
97233 Durham 707 ....A2
97905 Durkee 158 ....K3
97022 Eagle Creek 250 ....E2
97524 Eagle Point 2,764 ....E5
97420 Eastside 1,601 ....C4
97826 Echo 624 ....H2
97343 Eddyville 564 ....D3
97827 Elgin 1,701 ....K2
97436 Elkton 155 ....D4
97437 Elmira 900 ....D3
97828 Enterprise⊙ 2,003 ....K2
97023 Estacada 1,419 ....E2
*97401 Eugene⊙ 105,624 ....D3
  Eugene-Springfield‡ 275,226 ...D3
97024 Fairview 1,749 ....B2
†97601 Falcon Heights F5

97344 Falls City 804 ....D3
97710 Fields 150 ....J5
97439 Florence 4,411 ....C4
97116 Forest Grove 11,499 ......A2
97626 Fort Klamath 200 ....E5
97735 Fort Rock 150 ....G4
97830 Fossil⊙ 535 ....G2
97345 Foster 850 ....E3
97301 Four Corners 11,331 ......A3
97831 Fox 30 ....H3
†97526 Fruitdale-Harbeck 4,733 ...D5
97117 Gales Creek 150 ....D2
97223 Garden Home-Whitford 6,926 ...A2
97441 Gardiner 750 ....C4
97118 Garibaldi 999 ....D2
97119 Gaston 471 ....D2
97346 Gates 455 ....E3
†97741 Gateway 108 ....F3
97458 Gaylord 80 ....C5
97138 Gearhart 967 ....C1
97026 Gervais 799 ....A3
†97810 Gibbon 100 ....J2
97027 Gladstone 9,500 ....B2

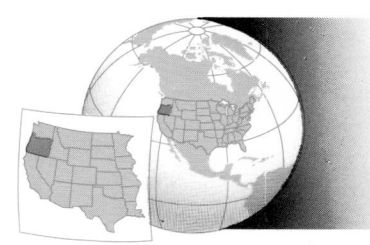

AREA 97,073 sq. mi. (251,419 sq. km.)
POPULATION 2,633,149
CAPITAL Salem
LARGEST CITY Portland
HIGHEST POINT Mt. Hood 11,239 ft. (3426 m.)
SETTLED IN 1810
ADMITTED TO UNION February 14, 1859
POPULAR NAME Beaver State
STATE FLOWER Oregon Grape
STATE BIRD Western Meadowlark

Topography

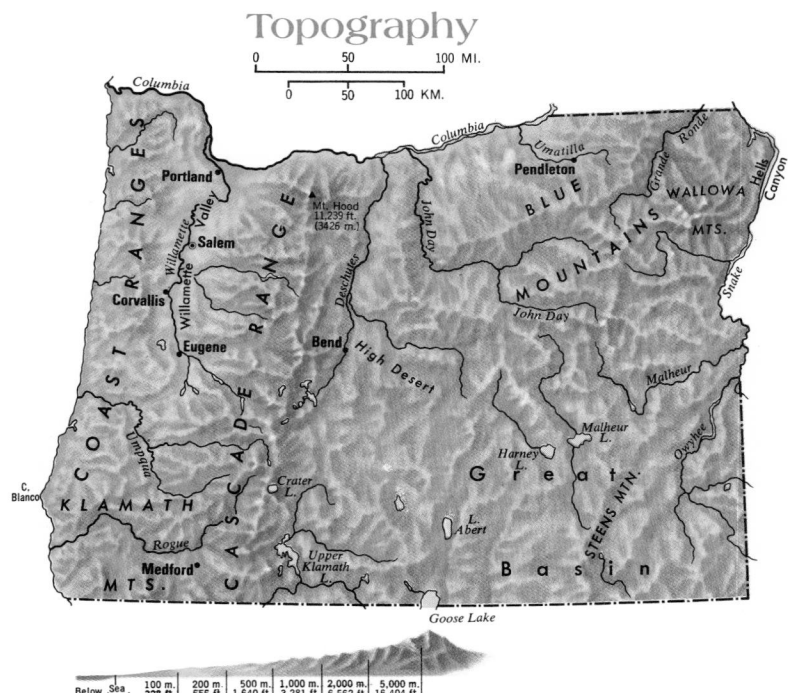

0 50 100 MI.
0 50 100 KM.

Below Sea Level | 100 m. 328 ft. | 200 m. 656 ft. | 500 m. 1,640 ft. | 1,000 m. 3,281 ft. | 2,000 m. 6,562 ft. | 5,000 m. 16,404 ft.

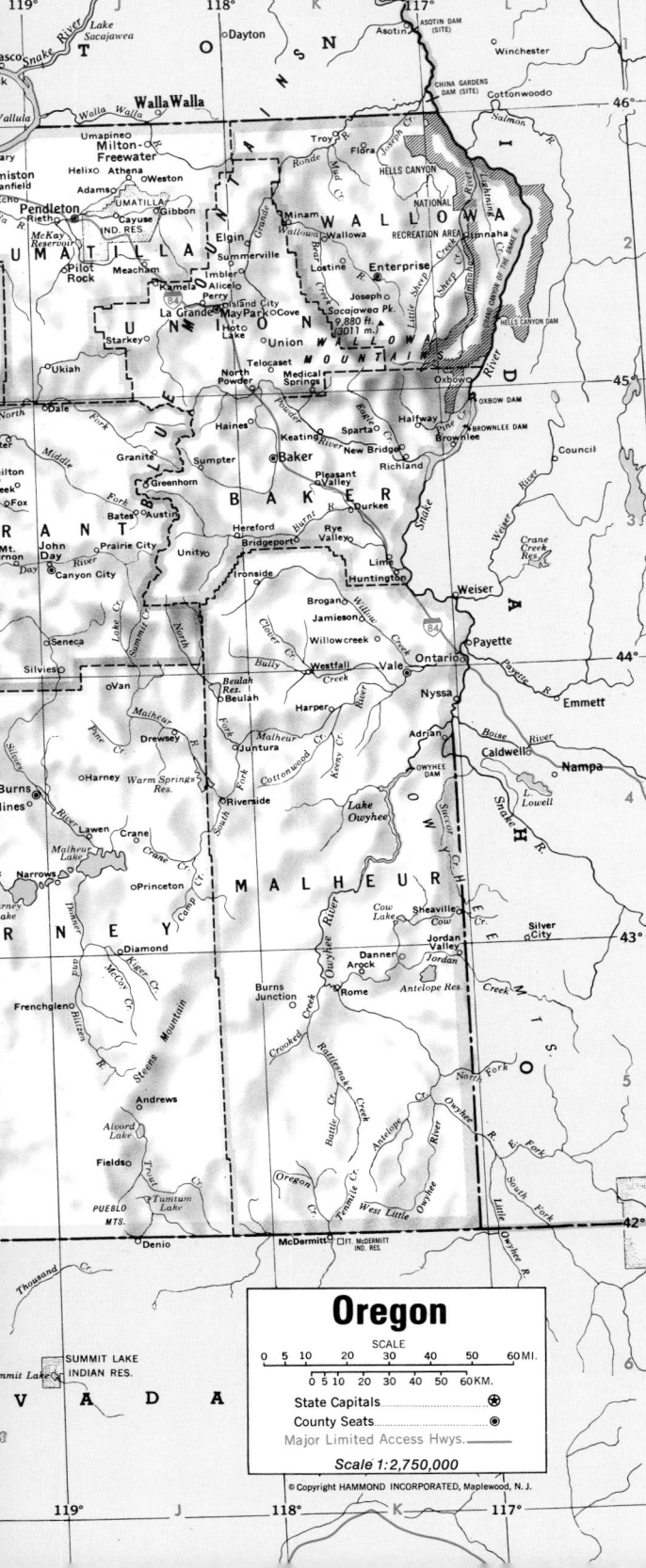

Oregon

SCALE
0 5 10 20 30 40 50 60 MI.
0 5 10 20 30 40 50 60 KM.
State Capitals .... ⊛
County Seats .... ⊙
Major Limited Access Hwys.
Scale 1:2,750,000
© Copyright HAMMOND INCORPORATED, Maplewood, N.J.

†97439 Glenada 300 ....C4
97442 Glendale 712 ....D5
97388 Gleneden Beach 400 ....C3
97120 Glenwood 225 ....D2
97443 Glide 470 ....D4
97048 Goble 108 ....E1
97444 Gold Beach⊙ 1,515 ....C5
97525 Gold Hill 904 ....D5
97401 Goshen 200 ....D4
97028 Government Camp 230 .....F2
97347 Grand Ronde 289 ....D2
†97877 Granite 17 ....J3
97526 Grants Pass⊙ 15,032 .....D5
97029 Grass Valley 164 ....G2
†97470 Green 3,897 ....D4
97030 Gresham 33,005 ....B2
97833 Haines 341 ....J3
97834 Halfway 380 ....K3
97348 Halsey 693 ....D3
97121 Hammond 516 ....C1
†97222 Happy Valley 1,499 ......B2
97415 Harbor 2,856 ....C5
97906 Harper 400 ....K4
†97601 Harriman 250 ....E5
97446 Harrisburg 1,881 ....D3
†97459 Hauser 400 ....C4
†97301 Hayesville 9,213 ....A3
97122 Hebo 400 ....D2
97835 Helix 155 ....J2
97836 Heppner⊙ 1,498 ....H2
97837 Hereford 128 ....K3
97838 Hermiston 9,408 ....H2
97123 Hillsboro⊙ 27,664 ....A2
97738 Hines 1,632 ....H4
†97208 Holbrook 494 ....A1
†97386 Holley 75 ....E3
97031 Hood River⊙ 4,329 ......F2
97448 Horton 175 ....D3
†97850 Hot Lake 4 ....K2
97032 Hubbard 1,640 ....A3
97907 Huntington 539 ....K3
97350 Idanha 319 ....E3
97447 Idleyld Park 300 ....D4
97841 Imbler 292 ....J2
97351 Independence 4,024 ......D3
97843 Ione 345 ....H2
97844 Irrigon 700 ....H2
97851 Island City 477 ....K2
97530 Jacksonville 2,030 ....D5
97909 Jamieson 120 ....K3
97401 Jasper 231 ....E3
97352 Jefferson 1,702 ....D3
†97201 Jennings Lodge B2
97845 John Day 2,012 ....J3
97027 Johnson City 378 ....B2
97910 Jordan Valley 473 ....K5
97846 Joseph 999 ....K2
97448 Junction City 3,320 ....D3
97911 Juntura K4
97303 Keizer 18,592 ....A3

97627 Keno 500 ....F5
97033 Kent 200 ....G2
97531 Kerby 650 ....D5
97223 King City 1,853 ....A2
†97361 Kings Valley 50 ....D3
97849 Kinzua 2 ....H3
97601 Klamath Falls⊙ 16,661 ...F5
97127 Lafayette 1,215 ....A2
97850 La Grande⊙ 11,354 ......J2
†97524 Lakecreek 160 ....E5
97034 Lake Oswego 22,527 .....B2
97449 Lakeside 1,453 ....C4
97630 Lakeview⊙ 2,770 ....G5
97450 Langlois 150 ....C5
97739 La Pine 850 ....F4
97401 Leaburg 150 ....E3
97355 Lebanon 10,413 ....E3
97839 Lexington 307 ....H2
†97042 Liberal 300 ....B3
†97341 Lincoln Beach 425 ....C3
97367 Lincoln City 5,469 ....C3
97405 Logan 450 ....B2
†97823 Lonerock 26 ....H2
97856 Long Creek 252 ....H3
97857 Lostine 250 ....K2
97452 Lowell 661 ....E4
97358 Lyons 877 ....E3
97741 Madras⊙ 2,235 ....F3
97632 Malin 539 ....F5
97130 Manzanita 443 ....C2
97453 Mapleton 950 ....C4
97454 Marcola 900 ....E3
97359 Marion 450 ....E3
97037 Maupin 495 ....F2
†97850 May Park J2
97220 Maywood Park 1,083 ....B2
97401 McKenzie Bridge 500 .....E3
97128 McMinnville⊙ 14,080 ....A2
97858 McNary 330 ....H2
†97053 McNulty 1,805 ....B2
97859 Meacham 150 ....J2
97501 Medford⊙ 39,603 ....E5
  Medford‡ 132,456 ....E5
97384 Mehama 250 ....E3
97532 Merlin 500 ....D5
97633 Merrill 500 ....F5
†97741 Metolius 451 ....F3
†97223 Metzger 5,544 ....A2
97634 Midland 520 ....F5
97360 Mill City 1,565 ....E3
97844 Milton-Freewater 5,086 ...J2
97222 Milwaukie 17,931 ....B2
97750 Mitchell 183 ....G3
97038 Molalla 2,992 ....B2
97361 Monmouth 5,594 ....D3
97456 Monroe 412 ....D3

97864 Monument 192 ....H3
97039 Moro⊙ 336 ....G2
97040 Mosier 340 ....F2
97362 Mount Angel 2,876 ....B3
97041 Mount Hood 200 ....F2
97042 Mulino 720 ....B2
97533 Murphy 500 ....D5
97457 Myrtle Creek 3,365 ....D4
97458 Myrtle Point 2,859 ....C4
97131 Nehalem 258 ....D2
97364 Neotsu 300 ....C2
97149 Neskowin 250 ....D2
97143 Netarts 975 ....C2
97132 Newberg 10,394 ....A2
97635 New Pine Creek 400 ......G5
97365 Newport⊙ 7,519 ....C3
97459 North Bend 9,779 ....C4
97133 North Plains 715 ....A2
97867 North Powder 430 ....K2
97460 Norway 150 ....C4
97913 Nyssa 2,862 ....K4
97268 Oak Grove 11,640 ....B2
97462 Oakland 886 ....D4
97463 Oakridge 3,729 ....E4
97534 O'Brien 850 ....D5
97134 Oceanside 300 ....C2
97044 Odell 450 ....F2
97914 Ontario 8,814 ....K3
97464 Ophir 275 ....C5
97045 Oregon City⊙ 14,673 .....B2
†97123 Orenco 220 ....A2
97368 Otis 200 ....D2
97369 Otter Rock 450 ....C3
97840 Oxbow 100 ....L2
97135 Pacific City 500 ....C2
97636 Paisley 343 ....G5
97041 Parkdale 350 ....F2
†97045 Park Place 500 ....B2
97801 Pendleton⊙ 14,521 ....J2
†97101 Perrydale 200 ....D2
97370 Philomath 2,673 ....D3
97535 Phoenix 2,309 ....E5
97868 Pilot Rock 1,630 ....J2
*97201 Portland⊙ 366,383 ......B2
  Portland‡ 1,242,187 ....B2
97465 Port Orford 1,061 ....C5
97753 Powell Butte 350 ....G3
97466 Powers 819 ....D5
97869 Prairie City 1,106 ....J3
97048 Prescott 73 ....D1
97721 Princeton 5 ....J4
97754 Prineville⊙ 5,276 ....G3
†97233 Progress 100 ....A2
97536 Prospect 200 ....E5
†97411 Prosper 110 ....C4
97048 Rainier 1,655 ....E1
†97045 Redland 700 ....B2
97756 Redmond 6,452 ....F3
97467 Reedsport 4,984 ....C4

(continued on following page)

Agriculture, Industry and Resources

DOMINANT LAND USE

- Specialized Wheat
- Wheat, Peas
- Specialized Dairy
- Dairy, Poultry, Mixed Farming
- Fruit and Mixed Farming
- Potatoes, General Farming
- General Farming, Dairy, Hay, Sugar Beets
- General Farming, Livestock, Special Crops
- Range Livestock
- Forests
- Nonagricultural Land

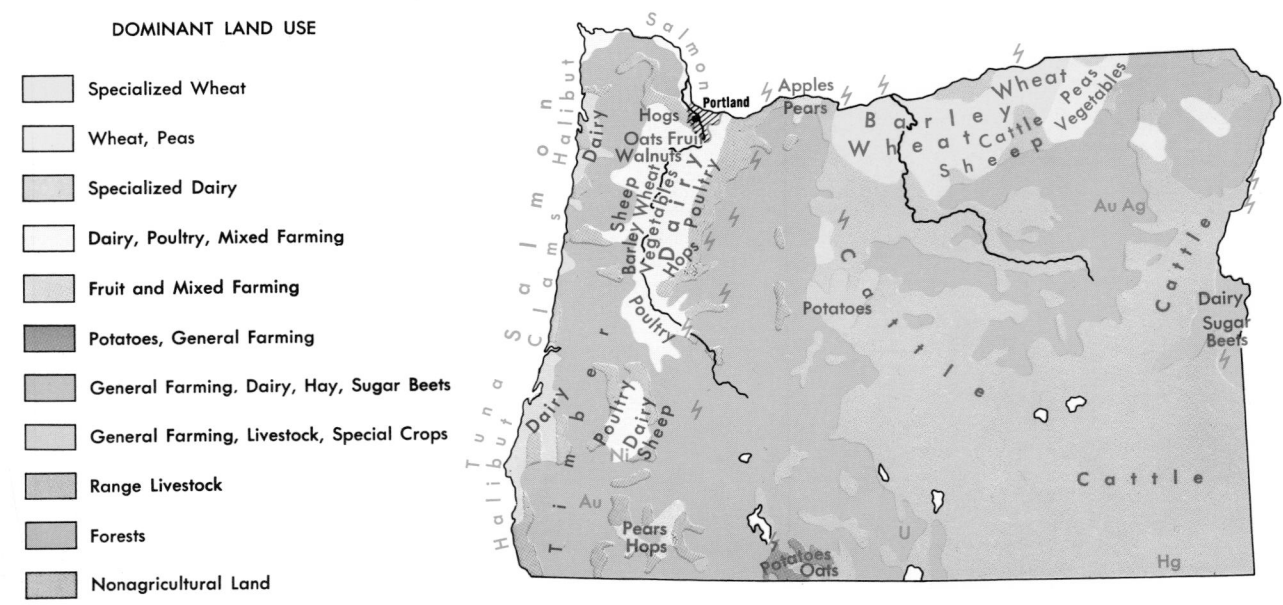

MAJOR MINERAL OCCURRENCES

Ag Silver   Hg Mercury

Au Gold   Ni Nickel

U Uranium

⚡ Water Power

▨ Major Industrial Areas

DOMINANT LAND USE

- Specialized Dairy
- Dairy, General Farming
- Fruit and Mixed Farming
- Fruit, Truck and Mixed Farming
- General Farming, Livestock, Tobacco
- General Farming, Livestock, Fruit, Tobacco
- Forests
- Urban Areas

AREA 45,308 sq. mi. (117,348 sq. km.)
POPULATION 11,863,895
CAPITAL Harrisburg
LARGEST CITY Philadelphia
HIGHEST POINT Mt. Davis 3,213 ft. (979 m.)
SETTLED IN 1682
ADMITTED TO UNION December 12, 1787
POPULAR NAME Keystone State
STATE FLOWER Mountain Laurel
STATE BIRD Ruffed Grouse

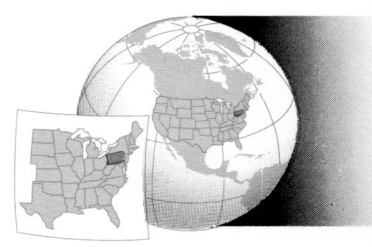

MAJOR MINERAL OCCURRENCES

C Coal	G Natural Gas	Sl Slate
Cl Clay	Ls Limestone	Ss Sandstone
Co Cobalt	O Petroleum	Zn Zinc
Fe Iron Ore		

⚡ Water Power
▨ Major Industrial Areas

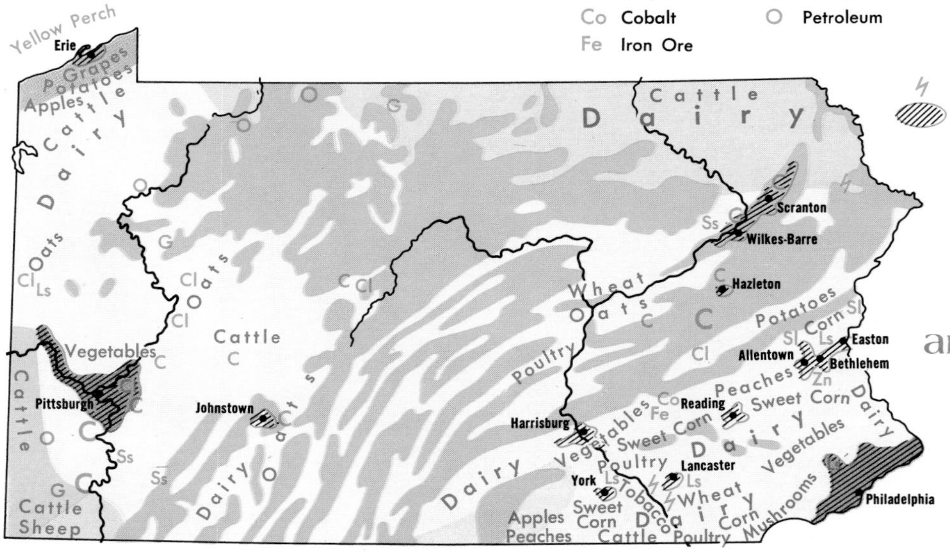

Agriculture, Industry and Resources

Map labels: Erie, Yellow Perch, Grapes, Potatoes, Apples, Cattle, Dairy, Oats, Cl, Ls, Clay, Vegetables, Pittsburgh, Cattle, Sheep, Cattle, Johnstown, Oats, Cattle, Dairy, Scranton, Wilkes-Barre, Hazleton, Wheat, Oats, Poultry, Potatoes, Corn, Sl, Easton, Allentown, Bethlehem, Peaches, Zn, Reading, Sweet Corn, Dairy, Harrisburg, Vegetables, Fe, Sweet Corn, Lancaster, Poultry, Dairy, York, Ls, Vegetables, Apples, Peaches, Sweet Corn, Tobacco, Cattle, Wheat, Corn, Dairy, Poultry, Mushrooms, Philadelphia

(continued on following page)

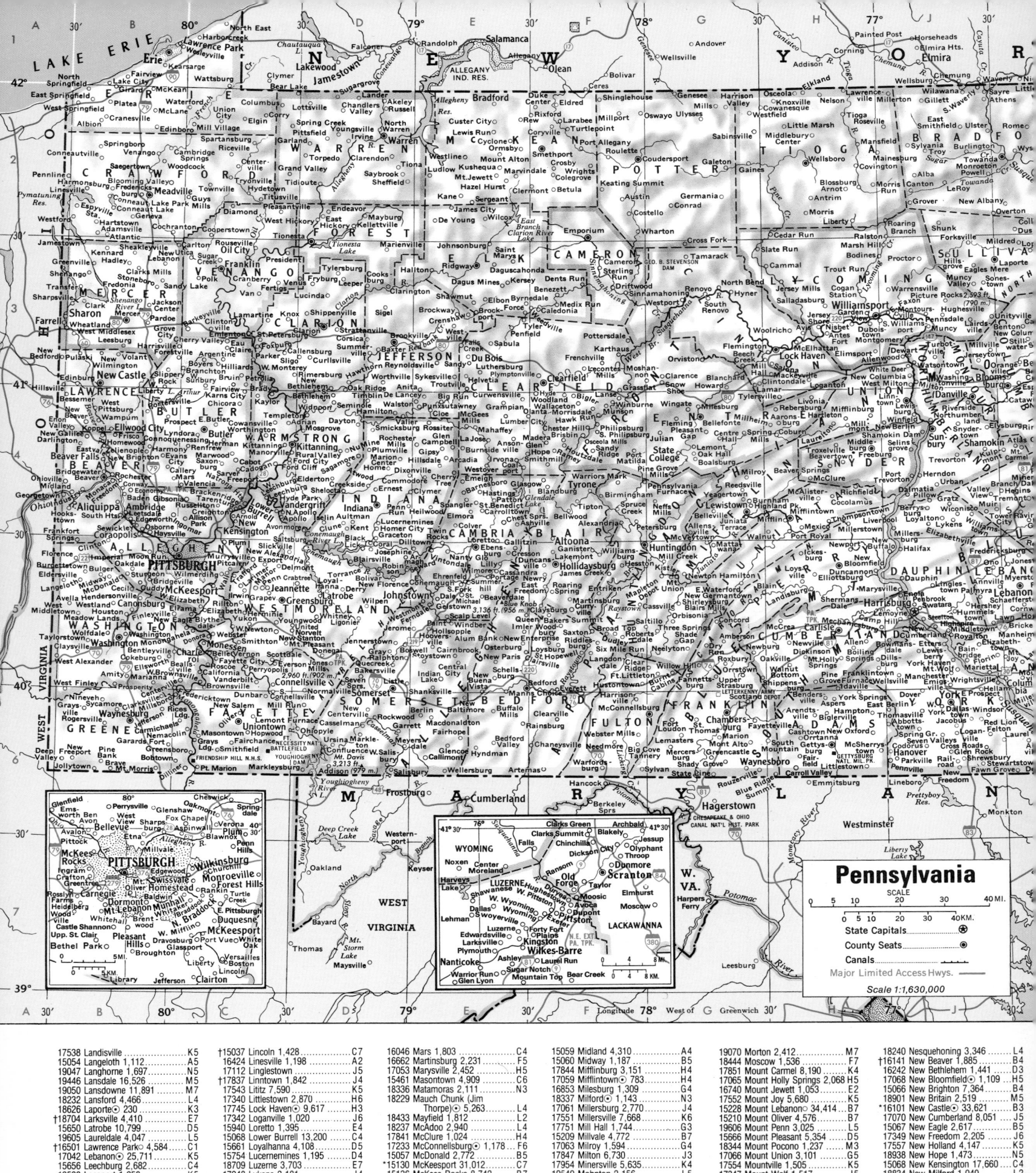

Pennsylvania

SCALE

0 5 10 20 30 40 MI.

0 5 10 20 30 40 KM.

⊗ State Capitals

⊙ County Seats

Canals

Major Limited Access Hwys. ———

Scale 1:1,630,000

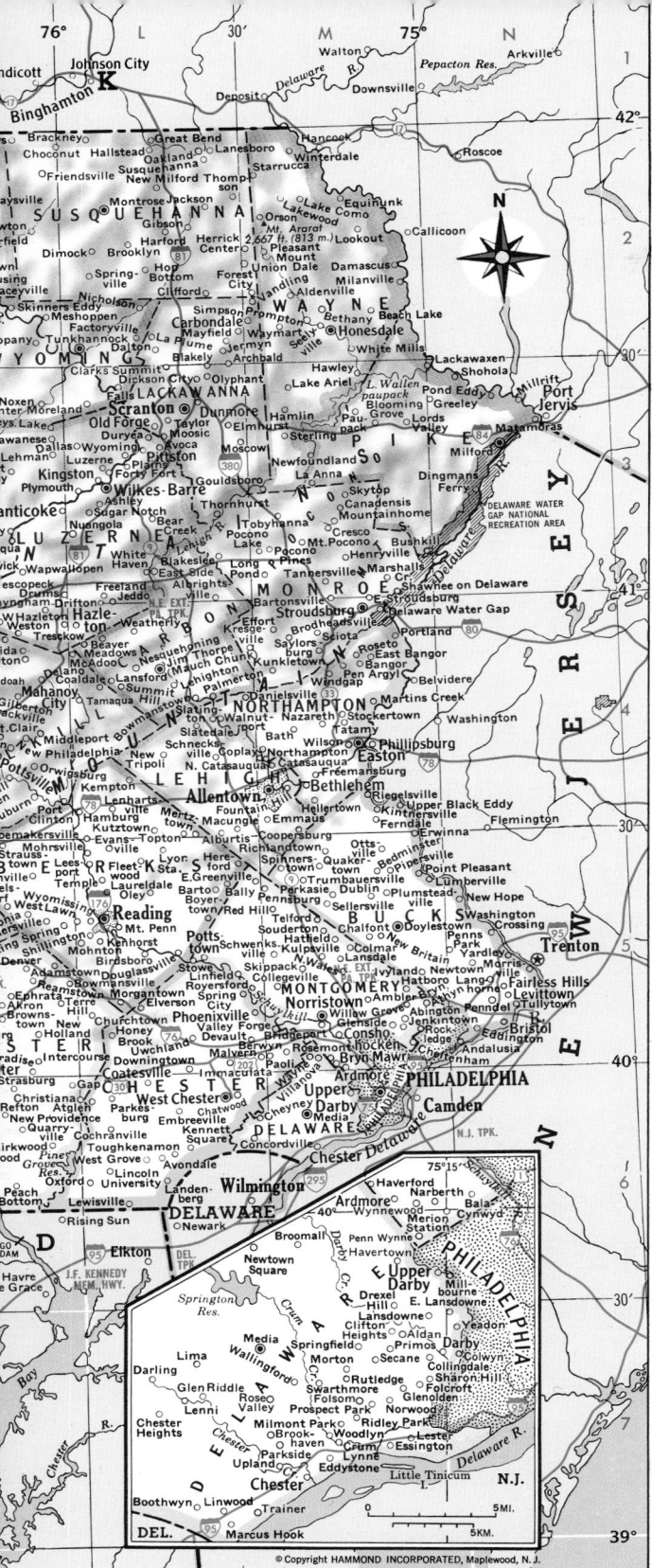

© Copyright HAMMOND INCORPORATED, Maplewood, N.J.

16823 Pleasant Gap 1,859 ....G4
15236 Pleasant Hills 9,676 ....B7
16341 Pleasantville 1,099 ....C2
15239 Plum 25,390 ....C5
18651 Plymouth 7,605 ....E7
15474 Point Marion 1,642 ....C6
16342 Polk 1,884 ....C3
15946 Portage 3,510 ....E5
16743 Port Allegany 2,593 ....F2
17965 Port Carbon 2,576 ....K4
††15133 Port Vue 5,316 ....C7
19464 Pottstown 22,729 ....L5
17901 Pottsville⊙ 18,195 ....K4
19076 Prospect Park 6,593 ....M7
15767 Punxsutawney 7,479 ....E4
18951 Quakertown 8,867 ....M5
17566 Quarryville 1,558 ....K6
††15104 Rankin 2,892 ....C7
*19601 Reading⊙ 78,686 ....L5
    Reading‡ 312,509 ....L5
17567 Reamstown 1,308 ....L5
18076 Red Hill 1,727 ....M5
17356 Red Lion 5,824 ....J6
17084 Reedsville 1,023 ....G4
17764 Renovo 1,812 ....G3
15851 Reynoldsville 3,016 ....D3
17087 Richland 1,470 ....L5
18955 Richlandtown 1,180 ....M5
15853 Ridgway 5,604 ....E3
19078 Ridley Park 7,889 ....M7
18077 Riegelsville 993 ....M4
16248 Rimersburg 1,096 ....D3
17868 Riverside 2,266 ....J4
16673 Roaring Spring 2,962 ....F5
19551 Robesonia 1,748 ....L5
15074 Rochester 4,759 ....B4
19101 Rockledge 2,538 ....M5
15557 Rockwood 1,058 ....D6
15477 Roscoe 1,123 ....C5
18013 Roseto 1,484 ....M4
††19065 Rose Valley 1,038 ....L7
17250 Rouzerville 1,371 ....G6
19468 Royersford 4,243 ....L5
16249 Rural Valley 1,033 ....D4
15076 Russellton 1,878 ....C4
17970 Saint Clair 4,037 ....K4
15857 Saint Marys 6,417 ....E3
15951 Saint Michael 1,445 ....E5
15681 Saltsburg 964 ....C4
††15801 Sandy 1,835 ....E3
16056 Saxonburg 1,336 ....C4
18840 Sayre 6,951 ....K2
††15963 Scalp Level 1,084 ....E5
17972 Schuylkill Haven 5,977 ....K4
19473 Schwenksville 1,041 ....L5
15683 Scottdale 5,833 ....C5
*18501 Scranton⊙ 88,117 ....F7
    Scranton (Northeast
    Pa.)‡ 640,396 ....F7
17870 Selinsgrove 5,227 ....J4
18960 Sellersville 3,143 ....M5
15143 Sewickley 4,778 ....B4
17872 Shamokin 10,357 ....J4
17876 Shamokin Dam 1,622 ....J4
16146 Sharon 19,057 ....B3
    Sharon‡ 128,299 ....B3
19079 Sharon Hill 6,221 ....N7
15215 Sharpsburg 4,351 ....B6
16150 Sharpsville 5,375 ....A3
16347 Sheffield 1,471 ....D2
17976 Shenandoah 7,589 ....K4
18655 Shickshinny 1,192 ....K3
19607 Shillington 5,601 ....K5
16748 Shinglehouse 1,310 ....F2
17257 Shippensburg 5,261 ....H5
19555 Shoemakersville 1,391 ....K4
17361 Shrewsbury 2,688 ....J6
19608 Sinking Spring 2,617 ....K5
18080 Slatington 4,277 ....L4
15684 Slickville 1,178 ....C5
16057 Slippery Rock 3,047 ....B3
16749 Smethport⊙ 1,797 ....F2
15478 Smithfield 1,084 ....C6
15501 Somerset⊙ 6,474 ....D6
18964 Souderton 6,657 ....M5
15425 South Connellsville 2,296 ....C6
15956 South Fork 1,401 ....E5
††18840 South Waverly 1,176 ....J2

17701 South Williamsport 6,581 ..J3
15775 Spangler 2,399 ....E4
19475 Spring City 3,389 ....L5
19064 Springfield 25,326 ....M7
17362 Spring Grove 1,832 ....J6
16801 State College 36,130 ....G4
    State College‡ 112,760 ....G4
17263 State Line 1,253 ....G6
17113 Steelton 6,484 ....J5
17363 Stewartstown 1,072 ....K6
16153 Stoneboro 1,177 ....B3
19464 Stowe 3,860 ....L5
17579 Strasburg 1,999 ....K6
18360 Stroudsburg⊙ 5,148 ....M4
15082 Sturgeon 1,312 ....B5
††16323 Sugar Creek 5,954 ....C3
18706 Sugar Notch 1,191 ....E7
18250 Summit Hill 3,418 ....L4
17801 Sunbury⊙ 12,292 ....J4
18847 Susquehanna 1,994 ....L2
19081 Swarthmore 5,950 ....M7
††17111 Swatara⊙ 18,796 ....J5
15218 Swissvale 11,345 ....C7
18704 Swoyersville 5,795 ....E7
15865 Sykesville 1,537 ....E3
18252 Tamaqua 8,843 ....L4
15084 Tarentum 6,419 ....C4
18517 Taylor 7,246 ....F7
18969 Telford 3,507 ....M5
19560 Temple 1,486 ....L5
17581 Terre Hill 1,217 ....L5
18512 Throop 4,166 ....F7
16351 Tidioute 844 ....D2
16353 Tionesta⊙ 659 ....C2
16684 Tipton 1,348 ....F4
16354 Titusville 6,884 ....C2
19562 Topton 1,818 ....L5
19374 Toughkenamon 1,111 ....L6
18848 Towanda⊙ 3,526 ....J2
17980 Tower City 1,667 ....J4
15085 Trafford 3,662 ....C5
*19013 Trainer 2,056 ....L7
17981 Tremont 1,796 ....K4
18254 Tresckow 1,128 ....K4
17881 Trevorton 2,192 ....J4
16947 Troy 1,381 ....J2
19007 Tullytown 2,277 ....N5
18657 Tunkhannock⊙ 2,144 ....L2
15145 Turtle Creek 6,959 ....C7
16686 Tyrone 6,346 ....F4
16438 Union City 3,623 ....C2
15401 Uniontown⊙ 14,510 ....C6
††19013 Upland 3,458 ....L7
*19082 Upper Darby⊙ 84,054 ...M6
15241 Upper Saint Clair⊙ 19,023 B7
19481 Valley Forge 400 ....L5
17983 Valley View 1,722 ....J4
15690 Vandergrift 6,823 ....D4
15147 Verona 3,179 ....C6
15132 Versailles 2,150 ....C7
19085 Villanova M6
18088 Walnutport 2,007 ....L4
16365 Warren⊙ 12,146 ....D2
15301 Washington⊙ 18,363 ....B5
16441 Waterford 1,568 ....B2
17777 Watsontown 2,366 ....J3
19087 Wayne M6
17268 Waynesboro 9,726 ....G6
15370 Waynesburg⊙ 4,482 ....B6
18255 Weatherly 2,891 ....L4
16901 Wellsboro⊙ 3,805 ....H2
19565 Wernersville 1,811 ....K5
16510 Wesleyville 3,998 ....C1
15417 West Brownsville 1,433 ...C5
19380 West Chester⊙ 17,435 ...L6
16950 Westfield 1,268 ....H2
19390 West Grove 1,820 ....L6
18201 West Hazleton 4,871 ....K4
††16201 West Kittanning 1,591 ...C4
††15656 West Leechburg 1,395 ...C4
16159 West Middlesex 1,064 ....B3
15122 West Mifflin 26,279 ....C7
††15905 Westmont 6,113 ....D5
15089 West Newton 3,387 ....C5
16160 West Pittsburg 1,133 ....B4
18643 West Pittston 5,980 ....F7
15229 West View 7,648 ....B6

18644 West Wyoming 3,288 ....E7
††17401 West York 4,526 ....J6
15120 Whitaker 1,615 ....C7
††15234 Whitehall 15,206 ....B7
18661 White Haven 1,921 ....L3
15131 White Oak 9,480 ....C7
17097 Wiconisco 1,321 ....J4
*18701 Wilkes-Barre⊙ 51,551 ....F7
15221 Wilkinsburg 23,669 ....C7
16693 Williamsburg 1,400 ....F5
17701 Williamsport⊙ 33,401 ....H3
    Williamsport‡ 118,416 ....H3
17098 Williamstown 1,664 ....J4
19090 Willow Grove M5
15148 Wilmerding 2,421 ....C5
15025 Wilson 7,564 ....M4
15963 Windber 5,585 ....E5
18091 Windgap 2,651 ....M4
19567 Womelsdorf 1,827 ....K5
19094 Woodlyn M7
17368 Wrightsville 2,365 ....J5
18644 Wyoming 3,655 ....E7
19610 Wyomissing 6,551 ....L5
19067 Yardley 2,533 ....N5
19050 Yeadon 11,727 ....N7
17099 Yeagertown 1,305 ....G4
*17401 York⊙ 44,619 ....J6
    York‡ 381,255 ....J6
16371 Youngsville 2,006 ....D2
15697 Youngwood 3,749 ....D5
16063 Zelienople 3,502 ....B4

OTHER FEATURES

Allegheny (res.) E2
Allegheny (riv.) E5
Allegheny Front (mts.) E5
Appalachian (mts.) H4
Ararat (mt.) M2
Arthur (lake) C4
Beaver (riv.) B5
Blue (mt.) G5
Blue Knob (mt.) E5
Casselman (riv.) D6
Clarion (riv.) D3
Conemaugh (riv.) D5
Conemaugh River (lake) D4
Conewango (creek) D1
Davis (mt.) D6
Delaware (riv.) N3
Delaware Water Gap Nat'l Rec.
    Area N3
Erie (lake) B1
Fort Necessity Nat'l
    Battlefield C6
George B. Stevenson (dam)...G3
Gettysburg Nat'l Mil. Park ...H6
Glendale (lake) F4
Juniata (riv.) G5
Laurel Hill (mt.) D5
Lehigh (riv.) L3
Letterkenny Army Depot F6
Licking (creek) F6
Little Tinicum (isl.) M7
Lycoming (creek) H3
Monongahela (riv.) C6
North (mt.) K3
Ohio (riv.) A4
Oil (creek) C3
Pine (creek) H2
Pine Grove (res.) K6
Pocono (mts.) M3
Pymatuning (res.) A2
Redbank (creek) E3
Schuylkill (riv.) M5
Shenango River (lake) B3
Sinnemahoning (creek) G3
South (mt.) H6
Susquehanna (riv.) J5
Tioga (riv.) H1
Tionesta Creek (lake) D3
Towanda (creek) J2
Tuscarora (mt.) G5
Wallenpaupack (lake) M3
Youghiogheny River (lake)...D6
⊙County seat.
‡Population of metropolitan area.
⊙Population of town or township.
† Zip of nearest p.o. * Multiple zips.

Topography

18067 Northampton 8,240 ....M4
15673 North Apollo 1,487 ....D4
15104 North Braddock 8,711 ....C7
††18032 North Catasauqua 2,554 ...L4
16428 North East 4,568 ....C1
17857 Northumberland 3,636 ....J4
19454 North Wales 3,391 ....M5
*16365 North Warren 1,232 ....D2
15674 Norvelt 2,541 ....D5
19074 Norwood 6,647 ....M7
15071 Oakdale 1,955 ....B5
15139 Oakmont 7,039 ....C6
††15059 Ohioville 4,217 ....B4
16301 Oil City 13,881 ....C3
18518 Old Forge 9,304 ....F7
15472 Oliver 3,777 ....C6
18447 Olyphant 5,204 ....F7
17961 Orwigsburg 2,700 ....K4
16666 Osceola Mills 1,466 ....F4
19363 Oxford 3,633 ....K6
††15963 Paint 1,177 ....E5
15201 Pittsburgh⊙ 423,938 ....B7
    Pittsburgh‡ 2,263,894 ....B7
*18640 Pittston 9,930 ....F7
††18701 Plains 5,455 ....F7

17562 Paradise 1,107 ....K5
19365 Parkesburg 2,578 ....L6
19013 Parkside 2,464 ....M7
††17331 Parkville 5,009 ....J6
16668 Patton 2,441 ....E4
18072 Pen Argyl 3,388 ....M4
17103 Penbrook 3,006 ....J5
19047 Penndel 2,703 ....N5
18073 Pennsburg 2,339 ....M5
††17331 Pennville 1,398 ....J6
††19151 Penn Wynne M6
18944 Perkasie 5,241 ....M5
15473 Perryopolis 2,139 ....C5
19101 Philadelphia⊙ 1,688,210...N6
    Philadelphia‡ 4,716,818...N6
16866 Philipsburg 3,533 ....F4
19460 Phoenixville 14,165 ....L5
17963 Pine Grove 2,244 ....K4
16868 Pine Grove Mills 1,030 ...G4
15140 Pitcairn 4,175 ....C5

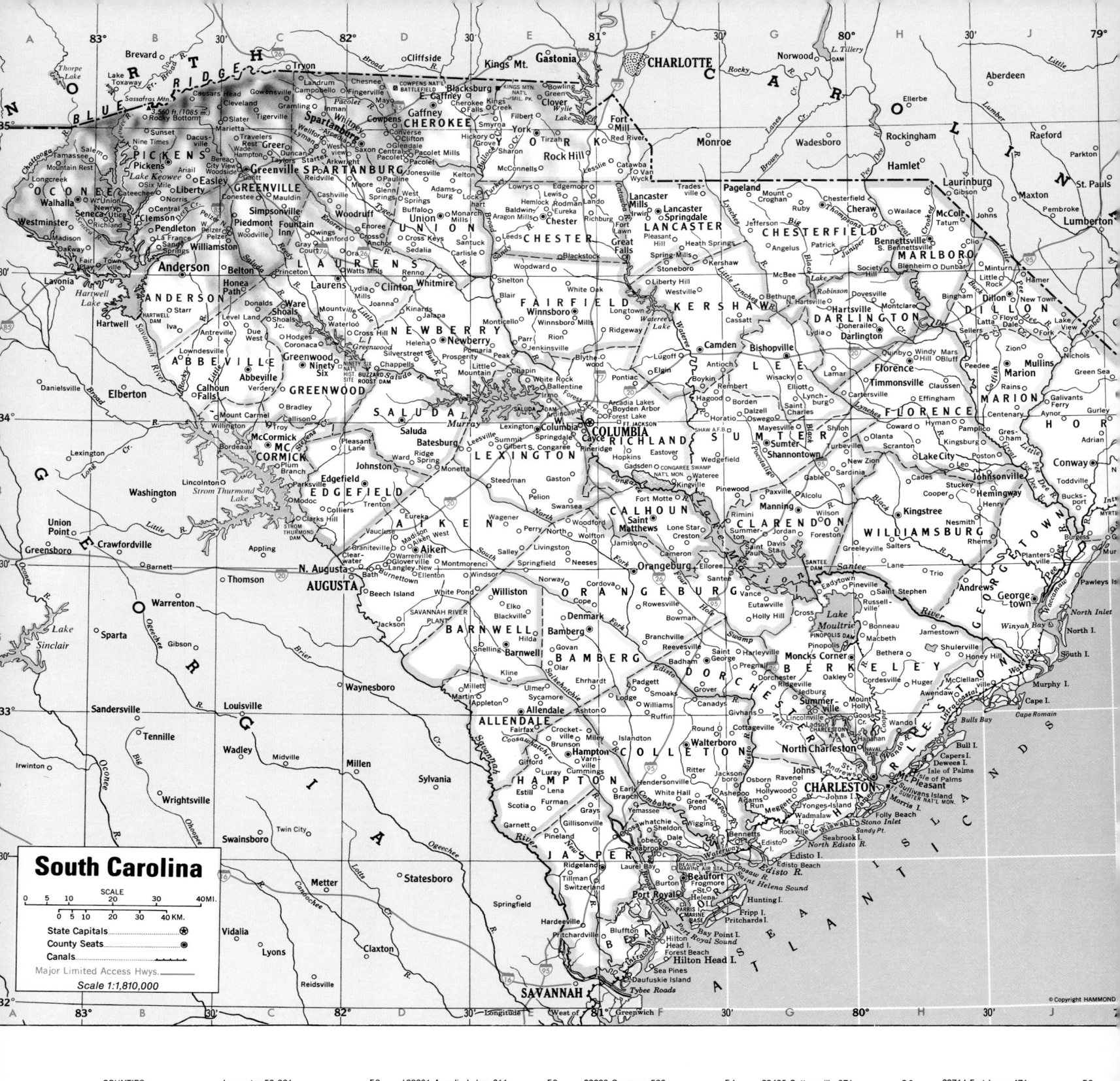

South Carolina

SCALE
0 5 10   20   30   40MI.
0 5 10 20   30 40 KM.

State Capitals........................⊛
County Seats..........................⊙
Canals...................................
Major Limited Access Hwys..........
Scale 1:1,810,000

© Copyright HAMMOND

COUNTIES

Abbeville 22,627	B3
Aiken 105,625	D4
Allendale 10,700	E6
Anderson 133,235	B2
Bamberg 18,118	E5
Barnwell 19,868	E5
Beaufort 65,364	F7
Berkeley 94,727	G5
Calhoun 12,206	F4
Charleston 276,974	H6
Cherokee 40,983	D1
Chester 30,148	E2
Chesterfield 38,161	G2
Clarendon 27,464	G4
Colleton 31,776	F6
Darlington 62,717	H3
Dillon 31,083	J3
Dorchester 58,761	G5
Edgefield 17,528	D4
Fairfield 20,700	E3
Florence 110,163	H3
Georgetown 42,461	J5
Greenville 287,913	C2
Greenwood 57,847	C3
Hampton 18,159	E6
Horry 101,419	J4
Jasper 14,504	E6
Kershaw 39,015	F3
Lancaster 53,361	F2
Laurens 52,214	D2
Lee 18,929	G3
Lexington 140,353	E4
Marion 34,179	J3
Marlboro 31,634	H2
McCormick 7,797	C4
Newberry 31,242	D3
Oconee 48,611	A2
Orangeburg 82,276	F5
Pickens 79,292	B2
Richland 269,735	F4
Saluda 16,150	D3
Spartanburg 201,861	D2
Sumter 88,243	G4
Union 30,764	D2
Williamsburg 38,226	H4
York 106,720	E2

CITIES and TOWNS

Zip	Name/Pop.	Key
29620	Abbeville ⊙ 5,833	C3
29801	Aiken ⊙ 14,978	D4
†29801	Aiken West 3,083	D4
29810	Allendale ⊙ 4,400	E5
*29621	Anderson ⊙ 27,965	B2
	Anderson‡ 133,235	B2
29510	Andrews 3,129	H5
29320	Arcadia 2,088	C2

Zip	Name/Pop.	Key
†29201	Arcadia Lakes 611	F3
†29640	Ariail 2,419	C2
†29301	Arkwright 2,623	C2
†29582	Atlantic Beach 289	K4
29511	Aynor 643	J3
29003	Bamberg ⊙ 3,672	E5
29812	Barnwell ⊙ 5,572	E5
29006	Batesburg 4,023	D4
29816	Bath 2,242	D5
29902	Beaufort ⊙ 8,634	F7
29627	Belton 5,312	C2
29512	Bennettsville ⊙ 8,774	H2
29611	Berea 13,164	C2
29009	Bethune 481	G3
29010	Bishopville ⊙ 3,429	G3
29702	Blacksburg 1,873	D1
29817	Blackville 2,840	E5
29516	Blenheim 202	H2
29910	Bluffton 541	F7
29016	Blythewood 92	F3
29431	Bonneau 401	H5
29018	Bowman 1,137	F5
29432	Branchville 1,769	F5
29911	Brunson 590	E6
29527	Bucksport 1,125	J4
29321	Buffalo 1,641	D2
29834	Burnettown 359	D5
29902	Burton 6,976	F7
29628	Calhoun Falls 2,491	B3
29020	Camden ⊙ 7,462	F3

Zip	Name/Pop.	Key
29030	Cameron 536	F4
29322	Campobello 472	C1
29031	Carlisle 503	D2
29169	Cayce 11,701	E4
29519	Centenary 700	J3
29630	Central 1,914	B2
†29372	Central Pacolet 315	D2
29036	Chapin 311	E3
29037	Chappells 109	D3
*29401	Charleston ⊙ 69,510	G6
	Charleston-North	
	Charleston‡ 430,301	G6
29520	Cheraw 5,654	H2
29323	Chesnee 1,069	D1
29706	Chesterfield ⊙ 1,432	G2
29611	City View 1,662	C2
29822	Clearwater 3,967	D4
29631	Clemson 8,118	B2
29635	Cleveland 800	C1
29324	Clifton 950	D2
29325	Clinton 8,596	D3
29525	Clio 1,031	H2
29710	Clover 3,451	E1
*29201	Columbia (cap.) ⊙ 100,385	F4
	Columbia‡ 408,176	F4
29329	Converse 1,173	D2
29526	Conway ⊙ 10,240	J4
29038	Cope 167	F5
29039	Cordova 202	F5

Zip	Name/Pop.	Key
29435	Cottageville 371	G6
29530	Coward 428	H4
29330	Cowpens 2,023	D1
29332	Cross Hill 604	D3
29532	Darlington ⊙ 7,989	H3
29042	Denmark 4,434	E5
29536	Dillon ⊙ 7,060	J3
29638	Donalds 366	C3
†29532	Doneraile 1,276	H3
29440	Georgetown ⊙ 10,144	J5
29334	Duncan 1,259	C2
29640	Easley 14,264	B2
†29340	East Gaffney 4,092	D1
29044	Eastover 899	F4
29824	Edgefield ⊙ 2,713	C4
29438	Edisto Beach 193	G7
29438	Edisto Island 900	G6
29081	Ehrhardt 353	E5
29045	Elgin 595	F3
29826	Elko 329	E5
29047	Elloree 909	F4
29335	Enoree 1,107	D2
29918	Estill 2,308	E6
†29706	Eureka 1,627	G2
29827	Fairfax 2,154	E6
29501	Florence ⊙ 29,176	H3
	Florence‡ 110,163	H3
29439	Folly Beach 1,478	H6
29206	Forest Acres 6,071	E3

Zip	Name/Pop.	Key
29714	Fort Lawn 471	F2
29715	Fort Mill 4,162	F1
29050	Fort Motte 700	F4
29644	Fountain Inn 4,226	C2
29921	Furman 348	E6
29340	Gaffney ⊙ 13,453	D1
†29609	Gantt 13,719	C2
29053	Gaston 960	E4
29440	Georgetown ⊙ 10,144	J5
29923	Gifford 385	E6
29054	Gilbert 211	E4
29346	Glendale 1,049	D2
29828	Gloverville 2,619	D4
29445	Goose Creek 17,811	H6
†29843	Govan 109	E5
29829	Graniteville 1,158	D4
29645	Gray Court 988	C2
29055	Great Falls 2,601	E2
29055	Greeleyville 593	H4
*29601	Greenville ⊙ 58,242	C2
	Greenville-Spartanburg‡	
	568,758	C2
29646	Greenwood ⊙ 21,613	C3
29651	Greer 10,525	C2
29924	Hampton ⊙ 3,143	E6
29410	Hanahan 13,224	H6
29927	Hardeeville 1,250	E7
29448	Harleyville 606	G5
29550	Hartsville 7,631	G3
29058	Heath Springs 979	F2

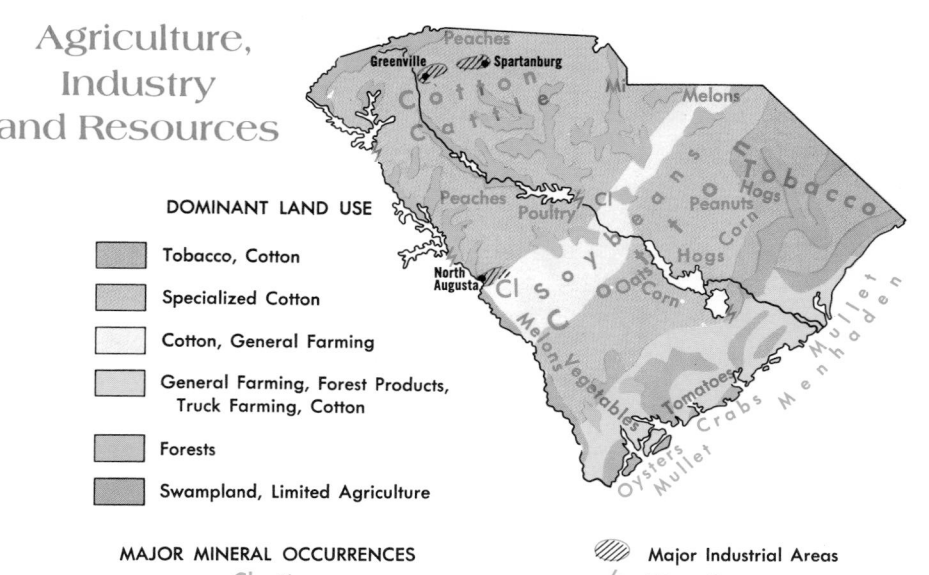

Agriculture, Industry and Resources

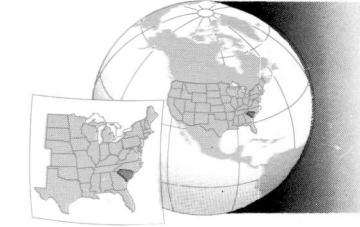

DOMINANT LAND USE

- Tobacco, Cotton
- Specialized Cotton
- Cotton, General Farming
- General Farming, Forest Products, Truck Farming, Cotton
- Forests
- Swampland, Limited Agriculture

MAJOR MINERAL OCCURRENCES

Cl Clay
Mi Mica

Major Industrial Areas
Water Power

AREA 31,113 sq. mi. (80,583 sq. km.)
POPULATION 3,121,833
CAPITAL Columbia
LARGEST CITY Columbia
HIGHEST POINT Sassafras Mtn. 3,560 ft. (1085 m.)
SETTLED IN 1670
ADMITTED TO UNION May 23, 1788
POPULAR NAME Palmetto State
STATE FLOWER Carolina (Yellow) Jessamine
STATE BIRD Carolina Wren

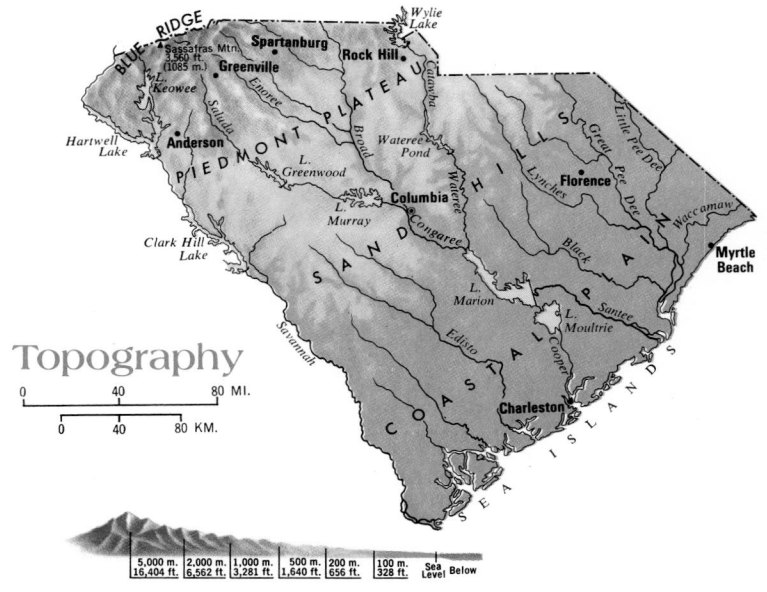

Topography

0 40 80 MI.
0 40 80 KM.

5,000 m. 2,000 m. 1,000 m. 500 m. 200 m. 100 m. Sea Below
16,404 ft. 6,562 ft. 3,281 ft. 1,640 ft. 656 ft. 328 ft. Level

ORATED, Maplewood, N.J.

COUNTIES

Aurora 3,628 ....M6
Beadle 19,195 ....N5
Bennett 3,044 ....F7
Bon Homme 8,059 ......O7
Brookings 24,332 ....R5
Brown 36,962 ....N2
Brule 5,245 ....L6
Buffalo 1,795 ....L5
Butte 8,372 ....B4
Campbell 2,243 ....J2
Charles Mix 9,680 .....M7
Clark 4,894 ....P4
Clay 13,689 ....P8
Codington 20,885 ......P4
Corson 5,196 ....G2
Custer 6,000 ....B6
Davison 17,820 ....N6
Day 8,133 ....O3

Deuel 5,289 ....R4
Dewey 5,366 ....G3
Douglas 4,181 ....N7
Edmunds 5,159 ....L3
Fall River 8,439 ....B7
Faulk 3,327 ....L3
Grant 9,013 ....R3
Gregory 6,015 ....L7
Haakon 2,794 ....F5
Hamlin 5,261 ....P4
Hand 4,948 ....L4
Hanson 3,415 ....O6
Harding 1,700 ....B2
Hughes 14,220 ....J5
Hutchinson 9,350 ......O7
Hyde 2,069 ....K4
Jackson 3,437 ....F6
Jerauld 2,929 ....M5
Jones 1,463 ....H6
Kingsbury 6,679 ....O5
Lake 10,724 ....P5
Lawrence 18,339 ....B5
Lincoln 13,942 ....R7

Lyman 3,864 ....J6
Marshall 5,404 ....O2
McCook 6,444 ....P6
McPherson 4,027 ......L2
Meade 20,717 ....D5
Mellette 2,249 ....H6
Miner 3,739 ....O5
Minnehaha 109,435 ...R6
Moody 6,692 ....R5
Pennington 70,361 .....C6
Perkins 4,700 ....D3
Potter 3,674 ....J3
Roberts 10,911 ....R2
Sanborn 3,213 ....N5
Shannon 11,323 ....D7
Spink 9,201 ....N4
Stanley 2,533 ....H5
Sully 1,990 ....J4
Todd 7,328 ....G7
Tripp 7,268 ....K7
Turner 9,255 ....P7
Union 10,938 ....R8
Walworth 7,011 ....J3

Yankton 18,952 ....P7
Ziebach 2,308 ....F4

CITIES and TOWNS

Zip	Name/Pop.	Key
57401	Aberdeen⊙ 25,851	M3
57310	Academy 10	M7
57520	Agar 139	J4
57420	Akaska 49	J3
57210	Albee 23	S3
57001	Alcester 885	R7
57311	Alexandria⊙ 588	O6
57714	Allen 300	F7
57312	Alpena 288	N5
57211	Altamont 58	R4
57421	Amherst 75	O2
57422	Andover 139	O3
57715	Ardmore 16	B7
57212	Arlington 991	P5
57313	Armour⊙ 819	N7
57423	Artas 43	K2
57314	Artesian 227	O6

57424	Ashton 154	N3
57213	Astoria 154	S4
57425	Athol 38	M3
57002	Aurora 507	R5
57315	Avon 576	N8
57214	Badger 99	P5
57003	Baltic 679	R6
57316	Bancroft 41	O4
57426	Barnard 65	N2
57716	Batesland 163	E7
57427	Bath 175	N3
57717	Belle Fourche⊙ 4,692	B4
57521	Belvidere 80	G6
57215	Bemis 37	R4
57004	Beresford 1,865	R7
57216	Big Stone City 672	S3
†57310	Bijou Hills 12	L6
57718	Black Hawk 1,608	C5
57522	Blunt 424	J4
57317	Bonesteel 358	M7
57428	Bowdle 644	K3
57719	Box Elder 3,186	D5

57217	Bradley 135	O3
57005	Brandon 2,589	R6
57218	Brandt 129	R4
57429	Brentford 91	N3
57319	Bridgewater 653	P6
57219	Bristol 445	O3
†57350	Broadland 49	N4
57006	Brookings⊙ 14,951	R5
57220	Bruce 254	R5
57221	Bryant 388	P4
57720	Buffalo⊙ 453	C6
57722	Buffalo Gap 186	G2
57621	Bullhead 400	G2
57010	Burbank 92	R8
57523	Burke⊙ 859	L7
†57276	Bushnell 76	R5
57222	Butler 22	O3
57724	Camp Crook 100	B2
57012	Canistota 626	P6
57321	Canova 194	O6
57013	Canton⊙ 2,886	R7
57725	Caputa 50	D5

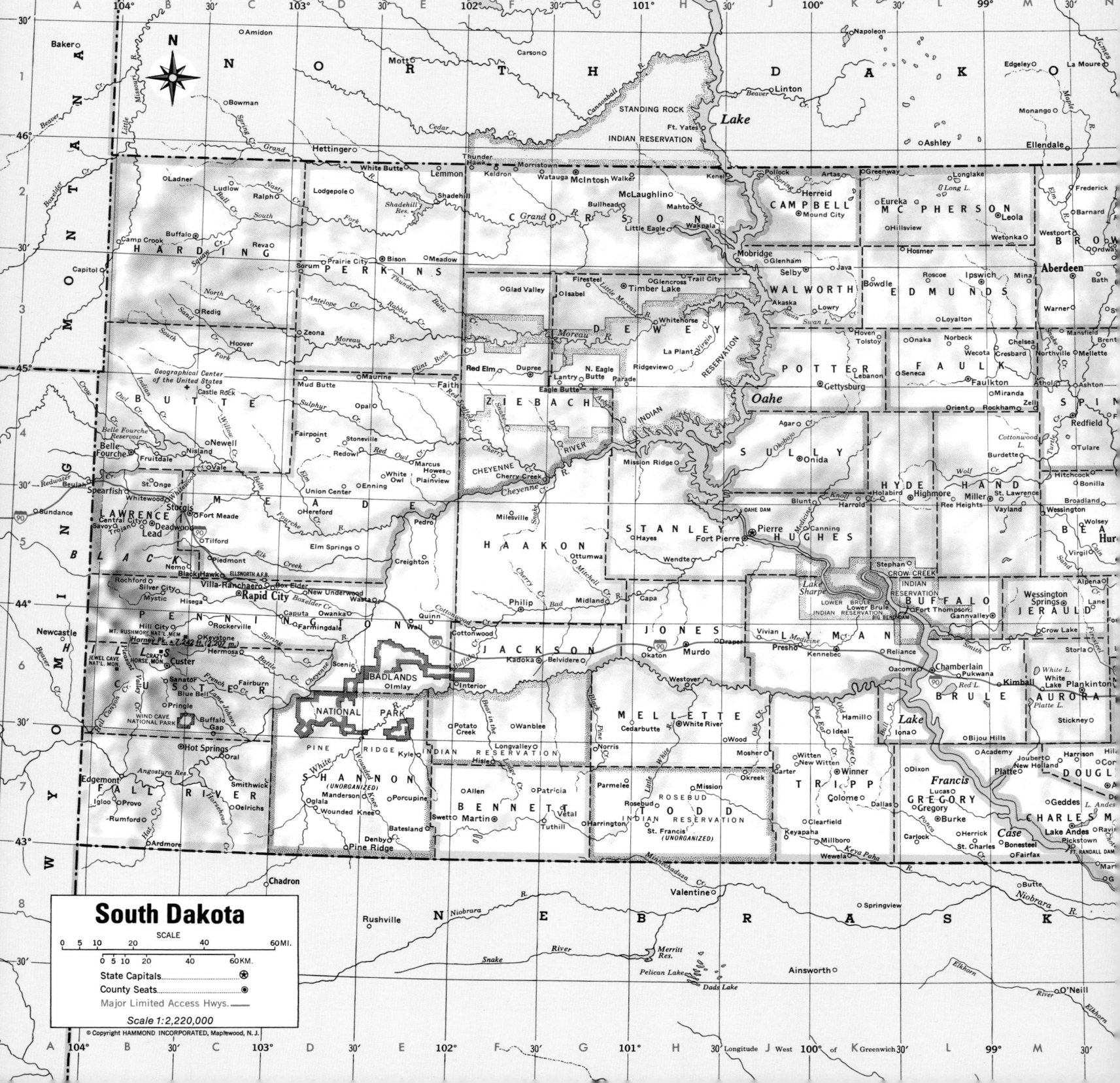

South Dakota

SCALE

0 5 10   20   40   60 MI.

0 5 10 20   40   60 KM.

State Capitals ....⊛

County Seats ....⊙

Major Limited Access Hwys. ————

Scale 1:2,220,000

© Copyright HAMMOND INCORPORATED, Maplewood, N.J.

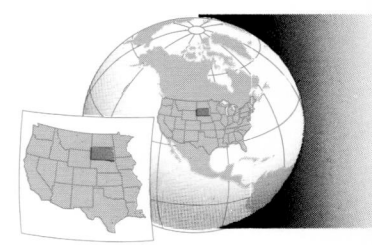

(continued on following page)

AREA 77,116 sq. mi. (199,730 sq. km.)
POPULATION 690,768
CAPITAL Pierre
LARGEST CITY Sioux Falls
HIGHEST POINT Harney Pk. 7,242 ft.
(2207 m.)
SETTLED IN 1856
ADMITTED TO UNION November 2, 1889
POPULAR NAME Coyote State; Sunshine
State
STATE FLOWER Pasqueflower
STATE BIRD Ring-necked Pheasant

Topography

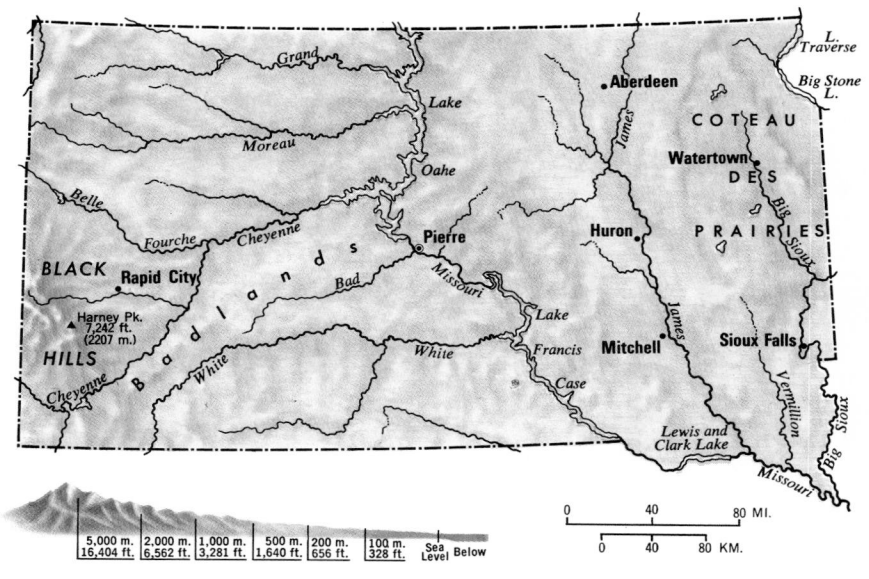

5,000 m.	2,000 m.	1,000 m.	500 m.	200 m.	100 m.	Sea	Below
16,404 ft.	6,562 ft.	3,281 ft.	1,640 ft.	656 ft.	328 ft.	Level	

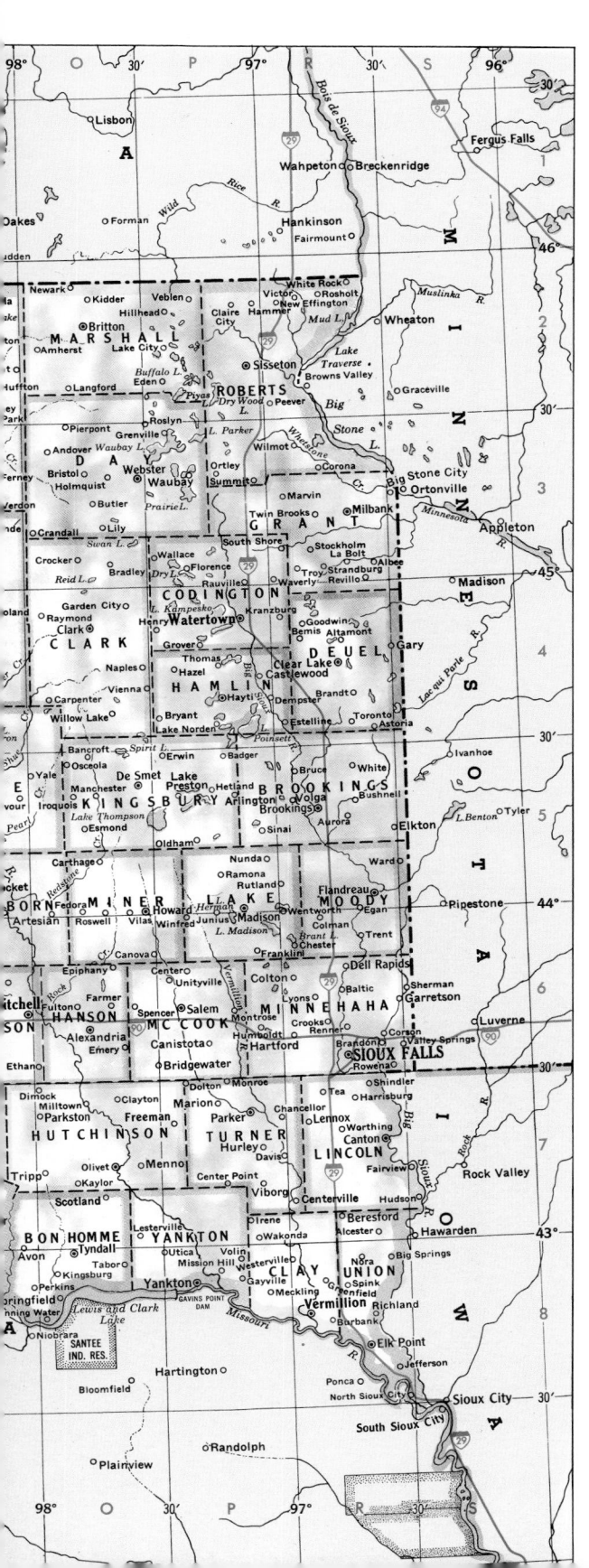

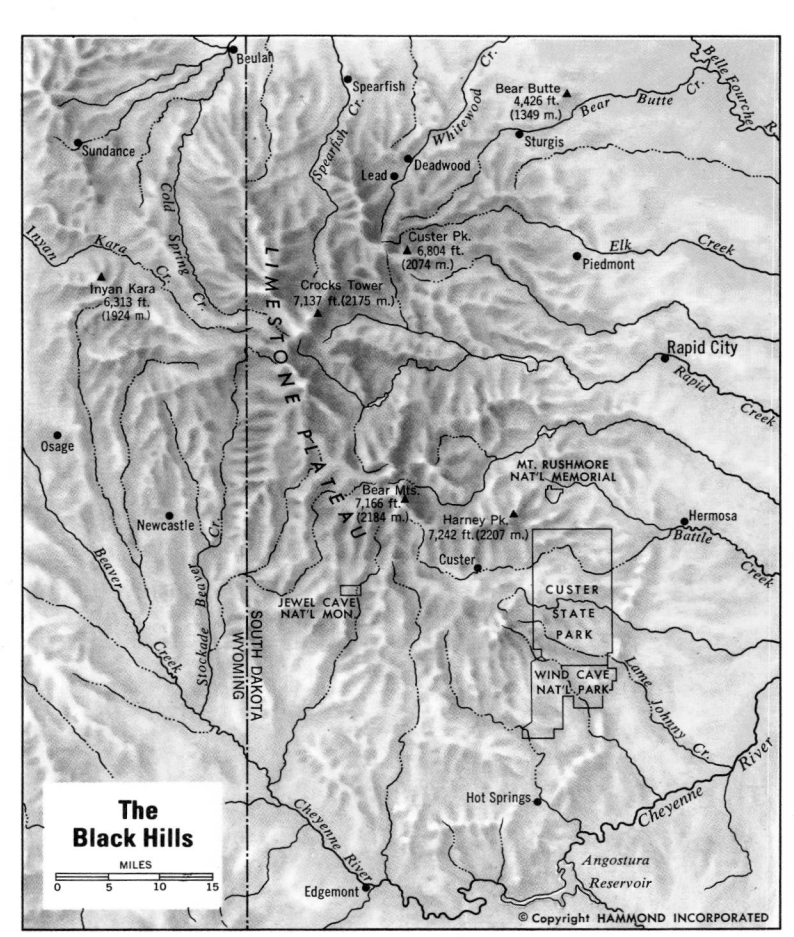

The Black Hills

MILES
0   5   10   15

Agriculture, Industry and Resources

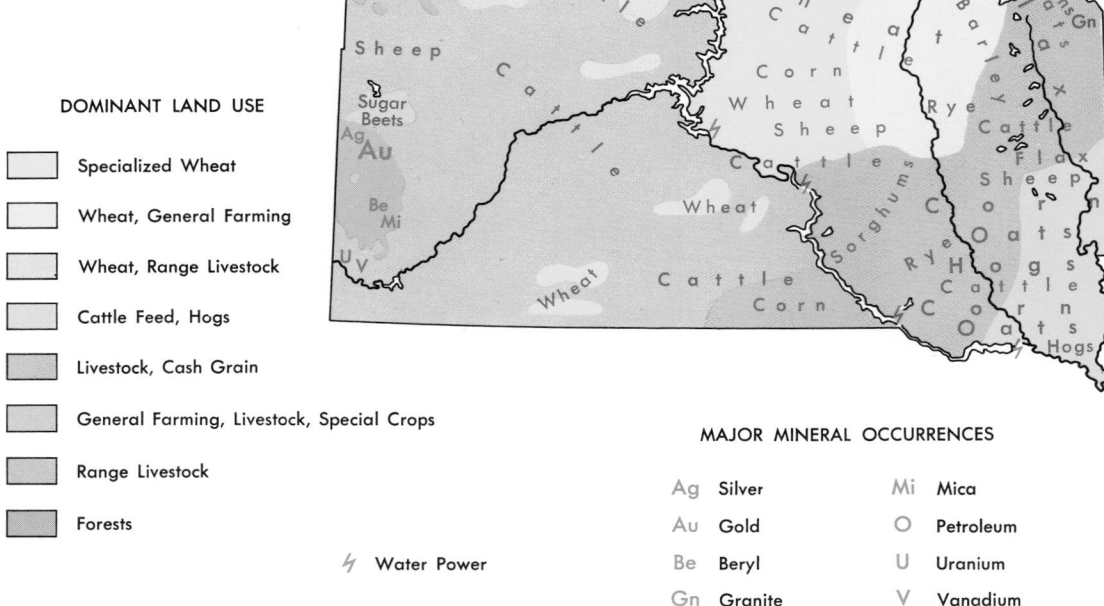

DOMINANT LAND USE

- Specialized Wheat
- Wheat, General Farming
- Wheat, Range Livestock
- Cattle Feed, Hogs
- Livestock, Cash Grain
- General Farming, Livestock, Special Crops
- Range Livestock
- Forests

⚡ Water Power

MAJOR MINERAL OCCURRENCES

Ag	Silver	Mi	Mica
Au	Gold	O	Petroleum
Be	Beryl	U	Uranium
Gn	Granite	V	Vanadium

AREA 266,807 sq. mi. (691,030 sq. km.)
POPULATION 14,229,288
CAPITAL Austin
LARGEST CITY Houston
HIGHEST POINT Guadalupe Pk. 8,749 ft. (2667 m.)
SETTLED IN 1686
ADMITTED TO UNION December 29, 1845
POPULAR NAME Lone Star State
STATE FLOWER Bluebonnet
STATE BIRD Mockingbird

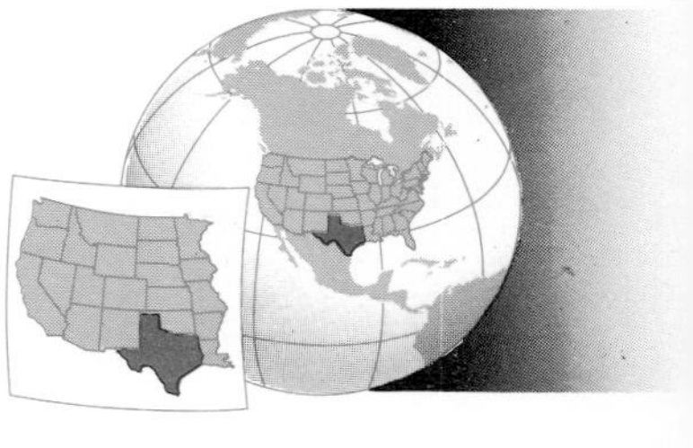

COUNTIES

Anderson 38,381 J6
Andrews 13,323 B5
Angelina 64,172 K6
Aransas 14,260 H10
Archer 7,266 F4
Armstrong 1,994 C3
Atascosa 25,055 F9
Austin 17,726 H8
Bailey 8,168 B3
Bandera 7,084 E8
Bastrop 24,726 G7
Baylor 4,919 E4
Bee 26,030 G9
Bell 157,820 G6
Bexar 988,798 F8
Blanco 4,681 F8
Borden 859 C5
Bosque 13,401 G6
Bowie 75,301 K4
Brazoria 169,587 J8
Brazos 93,588 H7
Brewster 7,573 A8
Briscoe 2,579 C3
Brooks 8,428 F11
Brown 33,057 F6
Burleson 12,313 H7
Burnet 17,803 F7
Caldwell 23,637 G8
Calhoun 19,574 H9
Callahan 10,992 E5
Cameron 209,727 G11
Camp 9,275 K5
Carson 6,672 C2
Cass 29,430 K4
Castro 10,556 B3
Chambers 18,538 K8
Cherokee 38,127 J6
Childress 6,950 D3
Clay 9,582 F4
Cochran 4,825 B4
Coke 3,196 D6
Coleman 10,439 E6
Collin 144,576 H4
Collingsworth 4,648 D3
Colorado 18,823 H8
Comal 36,446 F8
Comanche 12,617 F5
Concho 2,915 E6
Cooke 27,656 G4
Coryell 56,767 G6
Cottle 2,947 D3
Crane 4,600 B6
Crockett 4,608 C7
Crosby 8,859 C4
Culberson 3,315 C11
Dallam 6,531 B1
Dallas 1,556,390 H5
Dawson 16,184 C5
Deaf Smith 21,165 B3
Delta 4,839 J4
Denton 143,126 G4
De Witt 18,903 G9
Dickens 3,539 D4
Dimmit 11,367 E9
Donley 4,075 D2
Duval 12,517 F10
Eastland 19,480 F5
Ector 115,374 B6
Edwards 2,033 D7
Ellis 59,743 H5
El Paso 479,899 A10
Erath 22,560 F5
Falls 17,946 H6
Fannin 24,285 H4
Fayette 18,832 H8
Fisher 5,891 D5
Floyd 9,834 C3
Foard 2,158 E3
Fort Bend 130,846 J8
Franklin 6,893 J4
Freestone 14,830 H6
Frio 13,785 E9
Gaines 13,150 B5
Galveston 195,940 K8
Garza 5,336 C4
Gillespie 13,532 F7
Glasscock 1,304 C6
Goliad 5,193 G9
Gonzales 15,949 G8
Gray 26,386 D2
Grayson 89,796 H4
Gregg 99,495 K5
Grimes 13,580 J7
Guadalupe 46,708 G8
Hale 37,592 C3
Hall 5,594 D3
Hamilton 8,297 F6
Hansford 6,209 C1
Hardeman 6,368 E3
Hardin 40,721 K7
Harris 2,409,547 J8
Harrison 52,265 K5
Hartley 3,987 B2
Haskell 7,725 E4
Hays 40,594 F7
Hemphill 5,304 D2
Henderson 42,606 J5
Hidalgo 283,323 F11
Hill 25,024 G5
Hockley 23,230 B4
Hood 17,714 G5
Hopkins 25,247 J4
Houston 22,299 J6
Howard 33,142 C5
Hudspeth 2,728 B10
Hunt 55,248 H4
Hutchinson 26,304 C2
Irion 1,386 C6
Jack 7,408 F4
Jackson 13,352 H9
Jasper 30,781 K7
Jeff Davis 1,647 C11
Jefferson 250,938 K8
Jim Hogg 5,168 F11
Jim Wells 36,498 F10
Johnson 67,649 G5
Jones 17,268 E5
Karnes 13,593 G9
Kaufman 39,029 H5
Kendall 10,635 F8
Kenedy 543 G11
Kent 1,145 D4
Kerr 28,780 E7
Kimble 4,063 E7
King 425 D4
Kinney 2,279 D8
Kleberg 33,358 G10
Knox 5,329 E4
Lamar 42,156 J4
Lamb 18,669 B3
Lampasas 12,005 F6
La Salle 5,514 E9
Lavaca 19,004 H8
Lee 10,952 H7
Leon 9,594 J6
Liberty 47,088 K7
Limestone 20,224 H6
Lipscomb 3,766 D1
Live Oak 9,606 F9
Llano 10,144 F7
Loving 91 A6
Lubbock 211,651 C4
Lynn 8,605 C4
Madison 10,649 J6
Marion 10,360 K5
Martin 4,684 C5
Mason 3,683 E7
Matagorda 37,828 H9
Maverick 31,398 D9
McCulloch 8,735 E6
McLennan 170,755 G6
McMullen 789 F9
Medina 23,164 E8
Menard 2,346 E7
Midland 82,636 B6
Milam 22,732 H7
Mills 4,477 F6
Mitchell 9,088 D5
Montague 17,410 G4
Montgomery 128,487 J7
Moore 16,575 C2
Morris 14,629 K4
Motley 1,950 D3
Nacogdoches 46,786 K6
Navarro 35,323 H5
Newton 13,254 L7
Nolan 17,359 D5
Nueces 268,215 G10
Ochiltree 9,588 D1
Oldham 2,283 B2
Orange 83,838 L7
Palo Pinto 24,062 F5
Panola 20,724 K5
Parker 44,609 G5
Parmer 11,038 B3
Pecos 14,618 B7
Polk 24,407 K7
Potter 98,637 C2
Presidio 5,188 C12
Rains 4,839 J5
Randall 75,062 C2
Reagan 4,135 C6
Real 2,469 E8
Red River 16,101 J4
Reeves 15,801 D11
Refugio 9,289 G9
Roberts 1,187 D2
Robertson 14,653 H6
Rockwall 14,528 H5
Runnels 11,872 E6
Rusk 41,382 K5
Sabine 8,702 L6
San Augustine 8,785 K6
San Jacinto 11,434 J7
San Patricio 58,013 G10
San Saba 6,204 F6
Schleicher 2,820 D7
Scurry 18,192 D5
Shackelford 3,915 E5
Shelby 23,084 K6
Sherman 3,174 C1
Smith 128,366 J5
Somervell 4,154 G5
Starr 27,266 F11
Stephens 9,926 F5
Sterling 1,206 C6
Stonewall 2,406 D4
Sutton 5,130 D7
Swisher 9,723 C3
Tarrant 860,880 G5
Taylor 110,932 E5
Terrell 1,595 B7
Terry 14,581 B4
Throckmorton 2,053 E4
Titus 21,442 K4
Tom Green 84,784 D6
Travis 419,573 G7
Trinity 9,450 J6
Tyler 16,223 K7
Upshur 28,595 K5
Upton 4,619 B6
Uvalde 22,441 E8
Val Verde 35,910 C8
Van Zandt 31,426 J5
Victoria 68,807 H9
Walker 41,789 J7
Waller 19,798 J8
Ward 13,976 A6
Washington 21,998 H7
Webb 99,258 E10
Wharton 40,242 H8
Wheeler 7,137 D2
Wichita 121,082 F3
Wilbarger 15,931 E3
Willacy 17,495 G11
Williamson 76,507 G7
Wilson 16,756 F8
Winkler 9,944 A6
Wise 26,575 G4
Wood 24,697 J5
Yoakum 8,299 B4
Young 19,083 F4
Zapata 6,628 E11
Zavala 11,666 E9

CITIES and TOWNS

Zip Name/Pop. Key

*79601 Abilene⊙ 98,315 E5
Abilene‡ 139,192 E5
78516 Alamo 5,831 F11
78209 Alamo Heights 6,252 K10
76430 Albany⊙ 2,450 E5
78332 Alice⊙ 20,961 F10
75002 Allen 8,314 H1
79830 Alpine⊙ 5,465 D12
77511 Alvin 16,515 J3
*79101 Amarillo⊙ 149,230 C2
Amarillo‡ 173,699 C2
77514 Anahuac⊙ 1,840 K8
77830 Anderson⊙ 500 J7
79714 Andrews⊙ 11,061 B5
77515 Angleton⊙ 13,929 J8
79501 Anson⊙ 2,831 E5
78336 Aransas Pass 7,173 G10
76351 Archer City⊙ 1,862 F4
*76010 Arlington 160,123 F2
79502 Aspermont⊙ 1,357 D4
75751 Athens⊙ 10,197 J5
75551 Atlanta 6,272 K4
*78701 Austin (cap.)⊙ 345,496 G7
Austin‡ 536,450 G7
76020 Azle 5,822 E2
77518 Bacliff 4,851 K2
79504 Baird⊙ 1,696 E5
75180 Balch Springs 13,746 H2
†78201 Balcones Heights 2,511 J10
76821 Ballinger⊙ 4,207 E6
78003 Bandera⊙ 947 F8
77532 Barrett 3,183 K1
78602 Bastrop⊙ 3,789 G7
77414 Bay City⊙ 17,837 H9
77520 Baytown 56,923 L2
*77701 Beaumont⊙ 118,102 K7
Beaumont-Port Arthur-Orange‡ 375,497 K7
76021 Bedford 20,821 F2
78102 Beeville⊙ 14,574 G9
77401 Bellaire 14,950 J2
76704 Bellmead 7,569 H6
77418 Bellville⊙ 2,860 H8
76513 Belton⊙ 10,660 G7
76126 Benbrook 13,579 E2
79505 Benjamin⊙ 257 E4
76932 Big Lake⊙ 3,404 C6
79720 Big Spring⊙ 24,804 C5
78006 Boerne⊙ 3,229 J10
75418 Bonham⊙ 7,338 H4
79007 Borger 15,837 C2
75557 Boston⊙ 400 K4
76230 Bowie 5,610 G4
78832 Brackettville⊙ 1,676 D8
76825 Brady⊙ 5,969 E6
77422 Brazoria 3,025 J9
76024 Breckenridge⊙ 6,921 F5
77833 Brenham⊙ 10,966 H7
77611 Bridge City 7,667 L7
79316 Brownfield⊙ 10,387 B4
*78520 Brownsville⊙ 84,997 G12
Brownsville-Harlingen-San Benito‡ 209,680 G12
76801 Brownwood⊙ 19,396 F6
77801 Bryan⊙ 44,337 H7
Bryan-College Station‡ 93,588 H7
76354 Burkburnett 10,668 F3
76028 Burleson 11,734 F3
78611 Burnet⊙ 3,410 F7
77836 Caldwell⊙ 2,953 H7
76520 Cameron⊙ 5,721 H7
79014 Canadian⊙ 3,491 D2
75103 Canton⊙ 2,845 J5
79015 Canyon⊙ 10,724 C3
78834 Carrizo Springs⊙ 6,886 E9
*75006 Carrollton 40,595 G2
75633 Carthage⊙ 6,447 K5
†78213 Castle Hills 4,773 J10
75104 Cedar Hill 6,849 G3
75935 Center⊙ 5,827 K6
75833 Centerville⊙ 799 H6
77530 Channelview 17,471 K1
79018 Channing⊙ 304 B2
79201 Childress⊙ 5,817 D3
76437 Cisco 4,517 E5
79226 Clarendon⊙ 2,220 C3
75426 Clarksville⊙ 4,917 K4
79019 Claude⊙ 1,112 C2
†77565 Clear Lake Shores 755 K2
76031 Cleburne⊙ 19,218 G5
77327 Cleveland 5,977 K7
77531 Clute 9,577 J9
77331 Coldspring⊙ 569 J7
76834 Coleman⊙ 5,960 E6
77840 College Station 37,272 H7
76034 Colleyville 6,700 F2
79512 Colorado City⊙ 5,405 C5
78934 Columbus⊙ 3,923 H8
76442 Comanche⊙ 4,075 F6
75428 Commerce 8,136 J4
*77301 Conroe⊙ 18,034 J7
78109 Converse 5,150 K11
75432 Cooper⊙ 2,338 J4
76522 Copperas Cove 19,469 G6
*78401 Corpus Christi⊙ 231,999 G10
Corpus Christi‡ 326,228 G10
75110 Corsicana⊙ 21,712 H5
78014 Cotulla⊙ 3,912 E9
79731 Crane⊙ 3,622 B6
75835 Crockett⊙ 7,405 J6
79322 Crosbyton⊙ 2,289 C4
79227 Crowell⊙ 1,509 E4
76036 Crowley 5,852 E3
78839 Crystal City⊙ 8,334 E9
77954 Cuero⊙ 7,124 G8
75638 Daingerfield⊙ 3,030 K4
79022 Dalhart⊙ 6,854 B1
*75201 Dallas⊙ 904,078 G2
Dallas-Ft. Worth‡ 2,974,878 G2
77535 Dayton 4,908 J7
76234 Decatur⊙ 4,104 G4
77536 Deer Park 22,648 K2
76444 De Leon 2,478 F5
78840 Del Rio⊙ 30,034 D8
75020 Denison 23,884 H4
76201 Denton⊙ 48,063 G4

(continued on following page)

DOMINANT LAND USE

- Wheat, Grain Sorghums, Range Livestock
- Cotton, Wheat
- Specialized Cotton
- Cotton, General Farming
- Cotton, Forest Products
- Cotton, Range Livestock
- Rice, General Farming
- Peanuts, General Farming
- General Farming, Livestock, Cash Grain
- General Farming, Forest Products, Truck Farming, Cotton
- Fruit, Truck and Mixed Farming
- Range Livestock
- Forests
- Swampland, Limited Agriculture
- Nonagricultural Land
- Urban Areas

MAJOR MINERAL OCCURRENCES

At	Asphalt	He	Helium
Cl	Clay	Ls	Limestone
Fe	Iron Ore	Na	Salt
G	Natural Gas	O	Petroleum
Gn	Granite	S	Sulfur
Gp	Gypsum	Tc	Talc
Gr	Graphite	U	Uranium

ϟ Water Power
Major Industrial Areas

Agriculture, Industry and Resources

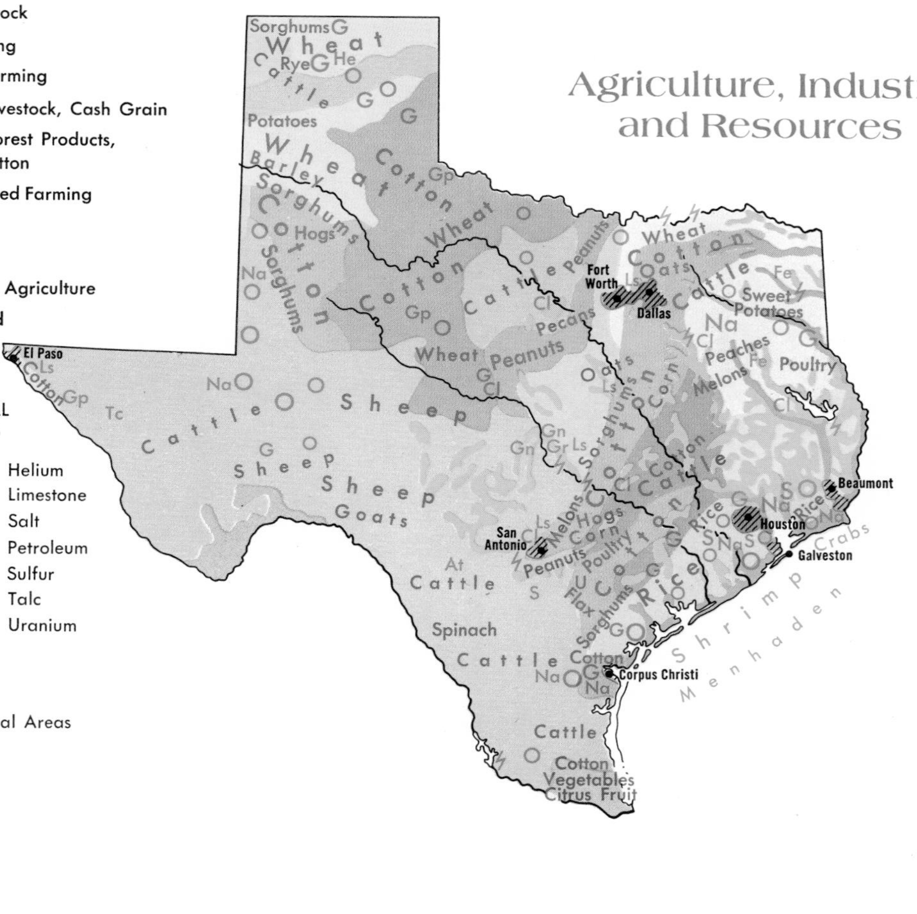
Sorghums
Wheat
Rye
Cattle
Potatoes
Barley
Cotton
Sorghums
Hogs
Peanuts
Fort Worth
Dallas
Pecans
Oats
Sweet Potatoes
Peaches
Poultry
Melons
Corn
El Paso
Sheep
Goats
San Antonio
Houston
Beaumont
Galveston
Rice
Flax
Shrimp
Crabs
Menhaden
Spinach
Corpus Christi
Vegetables
Citrus Fruit

79323 Denver City 4,704 ... B4
75115 De Soto 15,538 ... G3
78016 Devine 3,756 ... E8
75941 Diboll 5,227 ... K6
79229 Dickens⊙ 409 ... D4
77539 Dickinson 7,505 ... K3
79027 Dimmitt⊙ 5,019 ... B3
78537 Donna 9,952 ... F11
79029 Dumas⊙ 12,194 ... C2
75116 Duncanville 27,781 ... G3
78852 Eagle Pass⊙ 21,407 ... D9
76448 Eastland⊙ 3,747 ... F5
78539 Edinburg⊙ 24,075 ... F11
77957 Edna⊙ 5,650 ... H9
77437 El Campo 10,462 ... H8
76936 Eldorado⊙ 2,061 ... D7
78621 Elgin 4,535 ... G7
*79901 El Paso⊙ 425,259 ... A10
El Paso‡ 479,899 ... A10
78543 Elsa 5,061 ... G11
75440 Emory⊙ 813 ... J5
75119 Ennis 12,110 ... H5
76039 Euless 24,002 ... F2
76140 Everman 5,387 ... F3
79838 Fabens 4,285 ... B10
75840 Fairfield⊙ 3,505 ... H6
78355 Falfurrias⊙ 6,103 ... F10
75234 Farmers Branch 24,863 ... G2
79325 Farwell⊙ 1,354 ... A3
78114 Floresville⊙ 4,381 ... K11
†75067 Flower Mound 4,402 ... F1
79235 Floydada⊙ 4,193 ... C3
†76119 Forest Hill 11,684 ... F2
79734 Fort Davis⊙ 900 ... D11
79735 Fort Stockton⊙ 8,688 ... A7
*76101 Fort Worth⊙ 385,164 ... F2
77856 Franklin⊙ 1,349 ... H7
78624 Fredericksburg⊙ 6,412 ... E7
76842 Fredonia 50 ... E7
77541 Freeport 13,444 ... J9
77546 Friendswood 10,719 ... J2
79035 Friona 3,809 ... B3
75034 Frisco 3,499 ... H4
79738 Gail⊙ 171 ... C5
76240 Gainesville⊙ 14,081 ... G4
77547 Galena Park 9,879 ... J1
*77550 Galveston⊙ 61,902 ... L3
Galveston-Texas City‡ 195,940 ... L3
79739 Garden City⊙ 350 ... C6
*75040 Garland 138,857 ... H2
76528 Gatesville⊙ 6,260 ... G6
78626 Georgetown⊙ 9,468 ... G7
78022 George West⊙ 2,627 ... F9
78942 Giddings⊙ 3,950 ... H7
75644 Gilmer⊙ 5,167 ... J5
75647 Gladewater 6,548 ... K5
76043 Glen Rose⊙ 2,075 ... G5
76844 Goldthwaite⊙ 1,783 ... F6
77963 Goliad⊙ 1,990 ... G9
78629 Gonzales⊙ 7,152 ... G8
76046 Graham⊙ 9,170 ... F4
76048 Granbury⊙ 3,332 ... G5
*75050 Grand Prairie 71,462 ... G2
76051 Grapevine 11,801 ... F2
75401 Greenville⊙ 22,161 ... H4
76642 Groesbeck⊙ 3,373 ... H6
77619 Groves 17,090 ... L8
75845 Groveton⊙ 1,262 ... J7
79236 Guthrie⊙ 170 ... D4
77964 Hallettsville⊙ 2,865 ... G8
76117 Haltom City 29,014 ... F2
76531 Hamilton⊙ 3,189 ... G6
78550 Harlingen 43,543 ... G11
79521 Haskell⊙ 3,782 ... E4
77859 Hearne 5,418 ... H7
78361 Hebbronville⊙ 4,684 ... F10
75948 Hemphill⊙ 1,353 ... L6
77445 Hempstead⊙ 3,456 ... J7
75652 Henderson⊙ 11,473 ... K5
76365 Henrietta⊙ 3,149 ... F4
79045 Hereford⊙ 15,853 ... B3
†75201 Highland Park 8,909 ... G2
77562 Highlands 6,467 ... K1
76645 Hillsboro⊙ 7,397 ... G5
77563 Hitchcock 6,655 ... K3
78861 Hondo⊙ 6,057 ... E8
*77001 Houston⊙ 1,595,138 ... J2
Houston‡ 2,905,350 ... J2
*77338 Humble 6,729 ... J7
†77001 Hunters Creek Village 4,215 ... J1
77340 Huntsville⊙ 23,936 ... J7
76053 Hurst 31,420 ... F2
76367 Iowa Park 6,184 ... F4
*75061 Irving 109,943 ... G2
77029 Jacinto City 8,953 ... J1
76056 Jacksboro⊙ 4,000 ... F4
75766 Jacksonville 12,264 ... J5
75951 Jasper⊙ 6,959 ... L7
79528 Jayton⊙ 638 ... D4
75657 Jefferson⊙ 2,643 ... K5
†77001 Jersey Village 4,084 ... J1
78636 Johnson City⊙ 872 ... F7
78026 Jourdanton⊙ 2,743 ... F9
76849 Junction⊙ 2,593 ... E7
78118 Karnes City⊙ 3,296 ... G9
77450 Katy 5,660 ... J8
75142 Kaufman⊙ 4,658 ... H5
76248 Keller 4,156 ... F2
78119 Kenedy 4,356 ... G9
79745 Kermit⊙ 8,015 ... B6
78028 Kerrville⊙ 15,276 ... E7
75662 Kilgore 11,006 ... K5
76541 Killeen 46,296 ... G6
Killeen-Temple‡ 214,656 ... G6
78363 Kingsville⊙ 28,808 ... G10
†78109 Kirby 6,435 ... K11
77625 Kountze⊙ 2,716 ... K7
78945 La Grange⊙ 3,768 ... G8
77566 Lake Jackson 19,102 ... J8
76135 Lake Worth 4,394 ... E2
77568 La Marque 15,372 ... K3
79331 Lamesa⊙ 11,790 ... C5
76550 Lampasas⊙ 6,165 ... F6
*75146 Lancaster 14,807 ... G3
77571 La Porte 14,062 ... K2

*78040 Laredo⊙ 91,449 ... E10
Laredo‡ 99,258 ... E10
77573 League City 16,578 ... K2
78873 Leakey⊙ 468 ... E8
†78201 Leon Valley 9,088 ... J10
79336 Levelland⊙ 13,809 ... B4
*75067 Lewisville 24,273 ... G1
77575 Liberty⊙ 7,945 ... K7
75563 Linden⊙ 2,443 ... K4
79056 Lipscomb⊙ 52 ... D1
79339 Littlefield⊙ 7,409 ... B4
†78201 Live Oak 8,183 ... K10
77351 Livingston⊙ 4,928 ... K7
78643 Llano⊙ 3,071 ... F7
78644 Lockhart⊙ 7,953 ... G8
79241 Lockney 2,334 ... C3
*75601 Longview⊙ 62,762 ... K5
Longview-Marshall‡ 151,752 ... K5
*79401 Lubbock⊙ 173,979 ... C4
Lubbock‡ 211,651 ... C4
75901 Lufkin⊙ 28,562 ... K6
78648 Luling 5,039 ... G8
77864 Madisonville⊙ 3,660 ... J7
76063 Mansfield 8,092 ... F3
77578 Manvel 3,549 ... J3
79843 Marfa⊙ 2,466 ... C12
76661 Marlin⊙ 7,099 ... H6
75670 Marshall⊙ 24,921 ... K5
76856 Mason⊙ 2,153 ... E7
79244 Matador⊙ 1,052 ... D3
78368 Mathis 5,667 ... G9
78501 McAllen 66,281 ... F11
McAllen-Pharr-Edinburg‡ 283,229 ... F11
76657 McGregor 4,513 ... G6
75069 McKinney⊙ 16,256 ... H4
†77520 McNair ... K1
79245 Memphis⊙ 3,352 ... D3
76859 Menard⊙ 1,697 ... E7
79754 Mentone⊙ 50 ... D10
78570 Mercedes 11,851 ... F12
76665 Meridian⊙ 1,330 ... G6
76941 Mertzon⊙ 687 ... C6
*75149 Mesquite 67,053 ... H2
76667 Mexia 7,094 ... H6
79059 Miami⊙ 813 ... D2
*79701 Midland⊙ 70,525 ... C6
Midland‡ 82,636 ... C6
76065 Midlothian 3,219 ... G5
75773 Mineola 4,346 ... J5
76067 Mineral Wells 14,468 ... F5
78572 Mission 22,653 ... F11
77459 Missouri City 24,533 ... J2
79756 Monahans⊙ 8,397 ... B6
76251 Montague⊙ 1,253 ... G4
79346 Morton⊙ 2,674 ... B4
75455 Mount Pleasant⊙ 11,003 ... K4
75457 Mount Vernon⊙ 2,025 ... J4
79347 Muleshoe⊙ 4,842 ... B3
75961 Nacogdoches⊙ 27,149 ... J6
†77598 Nassau Bay 4,526 ... K2
77868 Navasota 5,971 ... J7
77627 Nederland 16,855 ... K8
75570 New Boston 4,628 ... K4
78130 New Braunfels⊙ 22,402 ... K10
75966 Newton⊙ 1,620 ... L7
76118 North Richland Hills 30,592 ... F2
79760 Odessa⊙ 90,027 ... B6
Odessa‡ 115,374 ... B6
76374 Olney 4,060 ... F4
77630 Orange⊙ 23,628 ... L7
76943 Ozona⊙ 3,766 ... C7
79248 Paducah⊙ 2,216 ... D4
76866 Paint Rock⊙ 256 ... E6
77465 Palacios 4,667 ... H9
75801 Palestine⊙ 15,948 ... J6
76072 Palo Pinto⊙ 350 ... F5
79065 Pampa⊙ 21,396 ... D2
79068 Panhandle⊙ 2,226 ... C2
75460 Paris⊙ 25,498 ... J4
*77501 Pasadena 112,560 ... J2
77581 Pearland 13,248 ... J2
78061 Pearsall⊙ 7,383 ... E9
79772 Pecos⊙ 12,855 ... D10
79070 Perryton⊙ 7,991 ... D1
78577 Pharr 21,381 ... F11
75686 Pittsburg⊙ 4,245 ... J4
79355 Plains⊙ 1,457 ... B4
79072 Plainview⊙ 22,187 ... C3
75074 Plano 72,331 ... G1
78064 Pleasanton 6,346 ... F9
77640 Port Arthur 61,251 ... K8
78578 Port Isabel 3,769 ... G11
78374 Portland 12,023 ... G10
77979 Port Lavaca⊙ 10,911 ... H9
77651 Port Neches 13,944 ... K7
79356 Post⊙ 3,961 ... C4
78065 Poteet 3,086 ... F8
77445 Prairie View 3,993 ... J7
79845 Presidio 1,723 ... C12
79252 Quanah⊙ 3,890 ... E3
76470 Ranger 3,142 ... F5
79778 Rankin⊙ 1,216 ... B6
78580 Raymondville⊙ 9,493 ... G11
78377 Refugio⊙ 3,898 ... G9
75080 Richardson 72,496 ... G2
76118 Richland Hills 7,977 ... F2
77469 Richmond⊙ 9,692 ... J8
78582 Rio Grande City⊙ 8,930 ... F11
77019 River Oaks 6,890 ... E2
76945 Robert Lee⊙ 1,202 ... D6
78380 Robstown 12,100 ... G10
79543 Roby⊙ 814 ... D5
76567 Rockdale 5,611 ... G7
78382 Rockport⊙ 3,686 ... H9
78880 Rocksprings⊙ 1,317 ... D8
75087 Rockwall⊙ 5,939 ... H5
78584 Roma-Los Saenz 3,384 ... E11
77471 Rosenberg 17,995 ... J8
78664 Round Rock 12,740 ... G7
75088 Rowlett 7,522 ... H2
75785 Rusk⊙ 4,681 ... J6
76179 Saginaw 5,736 ... E2
*76901 San Angelo⊙ 73,240 ... D6
San Angelo‡ 84,784 ... D6

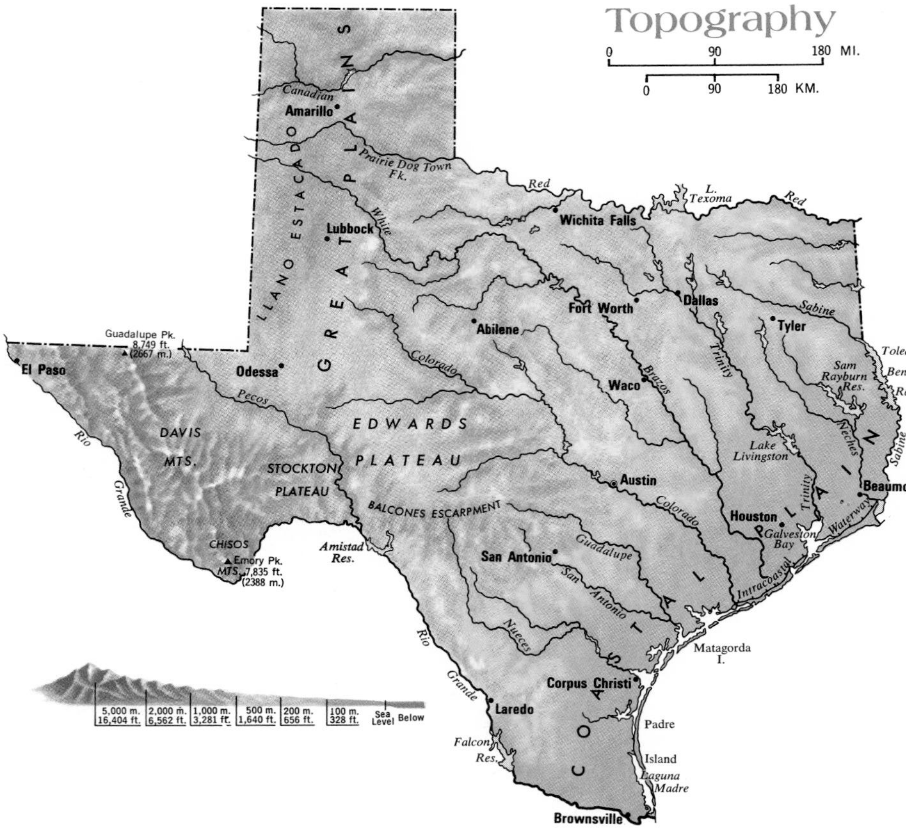

*78201 San Antonio⊙ 786,023 ... J11
San Antonio‡ 1,071,954 ... J11
75972 San Augustine⊙ 2,930 ... K6
78586 San Benito 17,988 ... G12
79848 Sanderson⊙ 1,241 ... B7
78384 San Diego⊙ 5,225 ... F10
76266 Sanger 2,574 ... G4
78589 San Juan 7,608 ... F11
78666 San Marcos⊙ 23,420 ... F8
76877 San Saba⊙ 2,847 ... F6
†76101 Sansom Park Village 3,921 ... E2
†77510 Santa Fe 6,172 ... K3
78385 Sarita⊙ 200 ... G10
78154 Schertz 7,262 ... K10
77586 Seabrook 4,670 ... K2
75159 Seagoville 7,304 ... H3
77474 Sealy 3,875 ... H8
78155 Seguin⊙ 17,854 ... G8
79360 Seminole⊙ 6,080 ... B5
†78357 Seven Sisters 2 ... F9
76380 Seymour⊙ 3,657 ... E4
75090 Sherman⊙ 30,413 ... H4
Sherman-Denison‡ 89,796 ... H4
79851 Sierra Blanca⊙ 800 ... B11
77656 Silsbee 7,684 ... K7
79257 Silverton⊙ 918 ... C3
78387 Sinton⊙ 6,044 ... G9
79364 Slaton 6,804 ... C4
78957 Smithville 3,470 ... G7
79549 Snyder⊙ 12,705 ... D5
76950 Sonora⊙ 3,856 ... D7
77587 South Houston 13,293 ... J2
79081 Spearman⊙ 3,413 ... C1
*77373 Spring ... J7
†77001 Spring Valley 3,353 ... J1
77477 Stafford 4,755 ... J2
79553 Stamford 4,542 ... E5
79782 Stanton⊙ 2,314 ... C5
76401 Stephenville⊙ 11,881 ... F5
76951 Sterling City⊙ 915 ... D6
79083 Stinnett⊙ 2,222 ... C2
79084 Stratford⊙ 1,917 ... C1
77478 Sugar Land 8,826 ... J8
75482 Sulphur Springs⊙ 12,804 ... J4
77480 Sweeny 3,538 ... J8
79556 Sweetwater⊙ 12,242 ... D5
78390 Taft 3,686 ... G9
79373 Tahoka⊙ 3,262 ... C4
76574 Taylor 10,619 ... G7
†77586 Taylor Lake Village 3,669 ... K2
75860 Teague 3,390 ... H6
76501 Temple 42,354 ... G6
79852 Terlingua 100 ... D12
75160 Terrell 13,269 ... H5
†78201 Terrell Hills 4,644 ... K11
*75501 Texarkana 31,271 ... L4
Texarkana, Tex.-Texarkana, Ark.‡ 27,019 ... L4
77590 Texas City 41,403 ... K3
73949 Texhoma 358 ... C1
The Colony 11,586 ... G1
76083 Throckmorton⊙ 1,174 ... F4
78072 Tilden⊙ 450 ... F9
77375 Tomball 3,996 ... J7
75862 Trinity 2,620 ... J7
79088 Tulia⊙ 5,033 ... C3
*75701 Tyler⊙ 70,508 ... J5
Tyler‡ 128,366 ... J5
78148 Universal City 10,720 ... K10
†75205 University Park 22,254 ... G2
78801 Uvalde⊙ 14,178 ... E8
75095 Van Alstyne 1,860 ... H4

79855 Van Horn⊙ 2,772 ... C11
79092 Vega⊙ 900 ... B2
76384 Vernon⊙ 12,695 ... E3
77901 Victoria⊙ 50,695 ... H9
Victoria‡ 68,807 ... H9
77662 Vidor 11,834 ... L7
*76701 Waco⊙ 101,261 ... G6
Waco‡ 170,755 ... G6
75501 Wake Village 3,865 ... K4
75165 Waxahachie⊙ 14,624 ... H5
76086 Weatherford⊙ 12,049 ... G5
79095 Wellington⊙ 3,043 ... D3
78596 Weslaco 19,331 ... F11
77486 West Columbia 4,109 ... J8
77630 West Orange 4,610 ... L7
†77005 West University Place 12,010 ... J2
†76101 Westworth 3,651 ... E2
77488 Wharton⊙ 9,033 ... J8
79096 Wheeler⊙ 1,584 ... D2
75693 White Oak 4,415 ... K5
76273 Whitesboro 3,197 ... H4
76108 White Settlement 13,508 ... E2
*76301 Wichita Falls⊙ 94,201 ... F4
Wichita Falls‡ 130,664 ... F4
†78201 Windcrest 5,332 ... K11
75494 Winnsboro 3,458 ... J5
79567 Winters 3,061 ... E6
75979 Woodville⊙ 2,821 ... K7
75098 Wylie 3,152 ... H1
78076 Zapata⊙ 3,831 ... E11

OTHER FEATURES

Amistad (res.) ... C8
Amistad Nat'l Rec. Area ... D8
Angelina (riv.) ... K6
Apache (mts.) ... C11
Aransas (passage) ... H10
Arlington (lake) ... F2
Baffin (bay) ... G10
Balcones Escarpment (plat.) ... E8
Beals (creek) ... C5
Benbrook (lake) ... E3
Bergstrom A.F.B. ... G7
Big Bend Nat'l Park ... A8
Bolivar (pen.) ... K8
Brazos (riv.) ... H7
Brownwood (lake) ... E6
Buchanan (lake) ... F7
Buck (creek) ... D3
Caddo (lake) ... L5
Canadian (riv.) ... D1
Carrizo (creek) ... A1
Carswell A.F.B. ... E2
Cathedral (mt.) ... D12
Cavallo (passage) ... H9
Cedar (lake) ... B5
Cerro Alto (mt.) ... B10
Chamizal Nat'l Mem. ... A10
Chase N.A.S. ... G9
Chinati (mts.) ... C12
Chinati (peak) ... C12
Chisos (mts.) ... A8
Cibolo (creek) ... K11
Clear Fork, Brazos (riv.) ... D5
Coldwater (creek) ... B1
Colorado (riv.) ... F7
Copano (bay) ... G9
Corpus Christi (lake) ... F9
Corpus Christi N.A.S. ... G10
Cottonwood Draw (dry riv.) ... C10
Davis (mts.) ... C11
Deep (creek) ... C5
Delaware (creek) ... C10
Delaware (mts.) ... C10
Denison (dam) ... H4
Devils (riv.) ... D7
Diablo, Sierra (mts.) ... C10
Double Mountain Fork, Brazos (riv.) ... C4
Dyess A.F.B. ... D5
Eagle (peak) ... C11
Eagle Mountain (lake) ... E2
Edwards (plat.) ... C7
Elephant (mt.) ... D12
Ellington A.F.B. ... K2
Elm Fork, Trinity (riv.) ... G2
Emory (peak) ... A8
Falcon (res.) ... E11
Finlay (mts.) ... B10
Fort Bliss 12,687 ... A10
Fort Davis Nat'l Hist. Site ... D11
Fort Hood 31,250 ... G6
Frio (riv.) ... E8
Galveston (bay) ... L2
Galveston (isl.) ... K8
Glass (mts.) ... A7
Goodfellow A.F.B. ... D6
Grapevine (lake) ... F2
Guadalupe (mts.) ... C10
Guadalupe (peak) ... B10
Guadalupe (riv.) ... G8
Guadalupe Mts. Nat'l Park ... C10
Houston (lake) ... J8
Houston Ship (chan.) ... K2
Howard (creek) ... C7
Hubbard Creek (lake) ... F5
Hueco (mts.) ... B10
Intracoastal Waterway ... J9
Johnson Draw (dry riv.) ... C7
Kelly A.F.B. ... J11
Kemp (lake) ... E4
Kingsville N.A.S. ... G10
Kiowa (creek) ... D1
Lackland A.F.B. 14,459 ... J11
Lake Meredith Nat'l Rec. Area ... C2
Lampasas (riv.) ... G6
Laughlin A.F.B. 2,994 ... D8
Lavon (lake) ... H1
Leon (riv.) ... F6
Livermore (mt.) ... C11
Livingston (lake) ... K7
Llano (riv.) ... D7
Llano Estacado (plain) ... B4
Locke (mt.) ... D11
Los Olmos (creek) ... F10
Los Olmos (creek) ... F11
Lyndon B. Johnson Nat'l Hist. Site ... F7
Lyndon B. Johnson Space Ctr. ... K2
Madre (lag.) ... G11
Maravillas (creek) ... A7
Matagorda (bay) ... H9
Matagorda (isl.) ... H9
Matagorda (pen.) ... J9
Matagorda Isl. Bombing and Gunnery Range ... H9
Medina (lake) ... E8
Medina (riv.) ... J11
Mexico (gulf) ... K9
Middle Concho (riv.) ... C6
Mountain Creek (lake) ... G2
Mustang (creek) ... A1
Mustang (isl.) ... G10
Mustang Draw (dry riv.) ... B5
Navasota (riv.) ... H7
Navidad (riv.) ... H8
Neches (riv.) ... K6
North Concho (riv.) ... C6
North Pease (riv.) ... D3
Nueces (riv.) ... F9
Padre (isl.) ... G10
Padre Island Nat'l Seashore ... G11
Palo Duro (creek) ... B2
Palo Duro (creek) ... C1
Pease (riv.) ... D3
Pecos (riv.) ... C7
Pedernales (riv.) ... F7
Possum Kingdom (lake) ... F5
Prairie Dog Town Fork, Red (riv.) ... C3
Quitman (mts.) ... B11
Red (riv.) ... F3
Red Bluff (lake) ... A6
Reese A.F.B. 1,934 ... B4
Rio Grande (riv.) ... D9
Rita Blanca (creek) ... B2
Sabine (riv.) ... L7
Salt Fork, Red (riv.) ... D3
Sam Rayburn (res.) ... K6
San Antonio (bay) ... H9
San Antonio (mt.) ... B10
San Antonio Missions Nat'l Hist. Park ... J11
San Francisco (creek) ... B8
San Luis (passage) ... K8
San Martine Draw (dry riv.) ... C11
San Saba (riv.) ... D7
Santa Isabel (creek) ... E10
Santiago (mts.) ... A8
Santiago (peak) ... D12
Sheppard A.F.B. ... F3
Sierra Diablo (mts.) ... C10
Sierra Vieja (mts.) ... C11
Staked (Llano Estacado) (plain) ... B4
Stamford (lake) ... E4
Stockton (plat.) ... B7
Sulphur (riv.) ... J4
Sulphur Draw (dry riv.) ... B4
Sulphur Springs (creek) ... B4
Tenmile (creek) ... G3
Terlingua (creek) ... D12
Texoma (lake) ... H3
Tierra Blanca (creek) ... B3
Toledo Bend (res.) ... L6
Toyah (creek) ... D11
Toyah (lake) ... A6
Travis (lake) ... G7
Trinity (bay) ... L2
Trinity (riv.) ... H5
Trinity, West Fork (riv.) ... G2
Trujillo (creek) ... A2
Vieja, Sierra (mts.) ... C11
Walnut (creek) ... F3
Washita (riv.) ... D2
West (bay) ... K3
White (riv.) ... C3
White River (lake) ... C4
White Rock (creek) ... G2
Wichita (riv.) ... F4
Wolf (creek) ... D1
Worth (lake) ... E2

⊙County seat.
‡Population of metropolitan area.
† Zip of nearest p.o. * Multiple zips.

Texas

State Capitals ....⊛
County Seats ....⊙
Major Limited Access Hwys. ————

Scale 1:4,600,000

Western Part of Texas

Same scale as main map

© Copyright HAMMOND INCORPORATED, Maplewood, N. J.

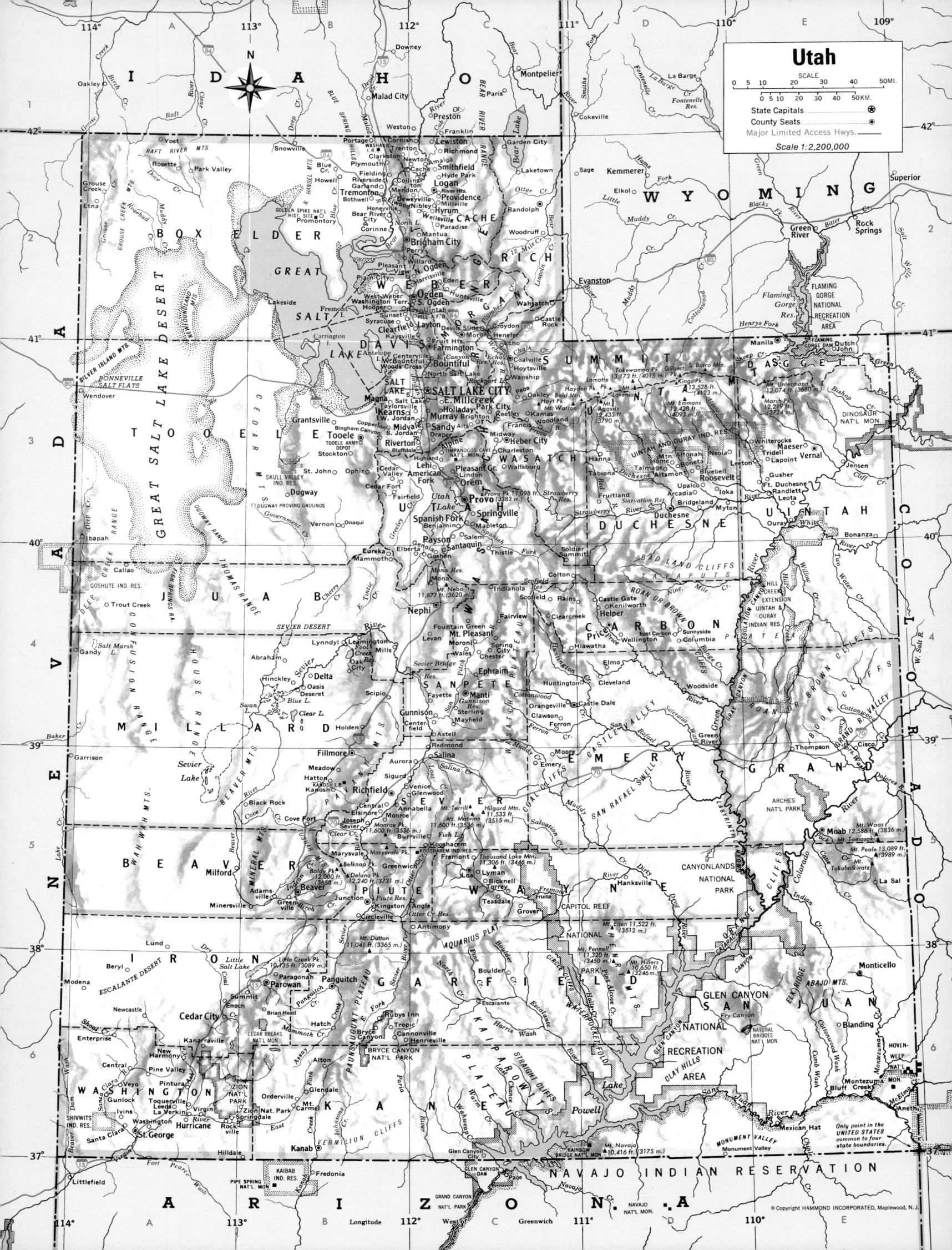

AREA 84,899 sq. mi. (219,888 sq. km.)
POPULATION 1,461,037
CAPITAL Salt Lake City
LARGEST CITY Salt Lake City
HIGHEST POINT Kings Pk. 13,528 ft. (4123 m.)
SETTLED IN 1847
ADMITTED TO UNION January 4, 1896
POPULAR NAME Beehive State
STATE FLOWER Sego Lily
STATE BIRD Sea Gull

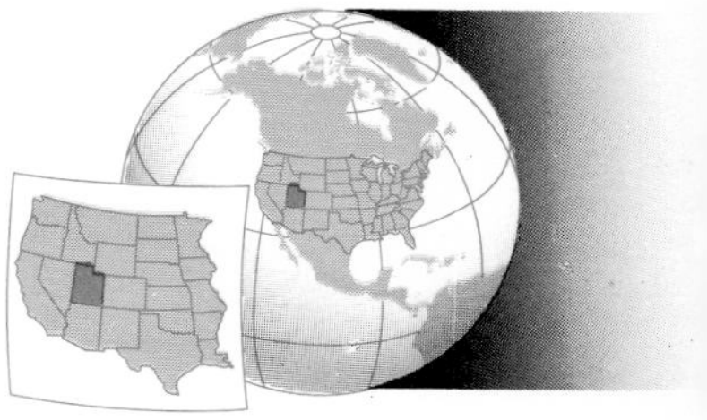

COUNTIES

- Beaver 4,378 A5
- Box Elder 33,222 A2
- Cache 57,176 C2
- Carbon 22,179 D4
- Daggett 769 E3
- Davis 146,540 B3
- Duchesne 12,565 D3
- Emery 11,451 D4
- Garfield 3,673 C6
- Grand 8,241 E5
- Iron 17,349 A6
- Juab 5,530 A4
- Kane 4,024 B6
- Millard 8,970 A4
- Morgan 4,917 C2
- Piute 1,329 B5
- Rich 2,100 C2
- Salt Lake 619,066 B3
- San Juan 12,253 E6
- Sanpete 14,620 C4
- Sevier 14,727 C5
- Summit 10,198 D3
- Tooele 26,033 A3
- Uintah 20,506 E3
- Utah 218,106 C3
- Wasatch 8,523 C3
- Washington 26,065 A6
- Wayne 1,911 C5
- Weber 144,616 B2

CITIES and TOWNS

Zip *Name/Pop.* *Key*

- †84003 Alpine 2,649 C3
- 84003 American Fork 12,693 C3
- 84713 Beaver⊙ 1,792 B5
- 84511 Blanding 3,118 E6
- †84065 Bluffdale 1,300 B3
- 84010 Bountiful 32,877 C3
- 84302 Brigham City⊙ 15,596 C2
- †84101 Brighton 150 C3
- 84513 Castle Dale⊙ 1,910 D4
- 84720 Cedar City 10,972 A6
- 84014 Centerville 8,069 C3
- 84015 Clearfield 17,982 B2
- 84017 Coalville⊙ 1,031 C3
- 84624 Delta 1,930 B4
- 84020 Draper 5,521 C3
- 84021 Duchesne⊙ 1,677 D3
- 84022 Dugway 1,646 B3
- 84520 East Carbon 1,942 D4
- 84109 East Millcreek 24,150 C3
- 84627 Ephraim 2,810 C4
- 84025 Farmington⊙ 4,691 C3
- 84523 Ferron 1,718 C4
- 84631 Fillmore⊙ 2,083 B5
- †84037 Fruit Heights 2,728 C2
- 84312 Garland 1,405 B2
- 84029 Grantsville 4,419 B3
- 84525 Green River 1,048 D4
- 84634 Gunnison 1,255 C4
- †84401 Harrisville 1,371 C2
- 84032 Heber City⊙ 4,362 C3
- 84526 Helper 2,724 D4
- †84043 Highland 2,435 C3
- †84767 Hilldale 1,009 A6
- 84117 Holladay 22,189 C3
- 84528 Huntington 2,316 C4
- 84737 Hurricane 2,361 A6
- 84318 Hyde Park 1,495 C2
- 84319 Hyrum 3,952 C2
- 84740 Junction⊙ 151 B5
- 84036 Kamas 1,064 C3
- 84741 Kanab⊙ 2,148 B6
- 84037 Kaysville 9,811 B2
- 84118 Kearns 21,353 B3
- 84745 La Verkin 1,174 A6
- 84041 Layton 22,862 C2
- 84043 Lehi 6,848 C3
- 84320 Lewiston 1,438 C2
- †84062 Lindon 2,796 C3
- 84747 Loa⊙ 364 C5
- 84321 Logan⊙ 26,844 C2
- †84078 Maeser 2,216 E3
- 84044 Magna 13,138 B3
- 84046 Manila⊙ 272 E3
- 84642 Manti⊙ 2,080 C4
- †84663 Mapleton 2,726 C3
- 84531 Mexican Hat 250 E6
- 84047 Midvale 10,146 B3
- 84049 Midway 1,194 C3
- 84751 Milford 1,293 A5
- 84532 Moab⊙ 5,333 E5
- 84754 Monroe 1,476 B5
- 84535 Monticello⊙ 1,929 E6
- 84050 Morgan⊙ 1,896 C2
- 84646 Moroni 1,086 C4
- 84647 Mount Pleasant 2,049 C4
- 84107 Murray 25,750 C3
- 84648 Nephi⊙ 3,285 C4
- †84321 Nibley 1,036 C2
- †84404 North Ogden 9,309 C2
- †84010 North Salt Lake 5,548 C3
- *84401 Ogden⊙ 64,407 C2
- Ogden-Salt Lake City‡ 936,255 C4
- 84537 Orangeville 1,309 C4
- 84057 Orem 52,399 C3
- Orem-Provo‡ 218,106 C3
- 84759 Panguitch⊙ 1,343 B6
- 84060 Park City 2,823 C3
- 84761 Parowan⊙ 1,836 B6
- 84651 Payson 8,246 C3
- †84302 Perry 1,084 C2
- †84401 Plain City 2,379 B2
- 84062 Pleasant Grove 10,833 C3
- †84401 Pleasant View 3,983 B2
- 84501 Price⊙ 9,086 D4
- 84332 Providence 2,675 C2
- 84601 Provo⊙ 74,108 C3
- Provo-Orem‡ 218,106 C3
- 84064 Randolph⊙ 659 C2
- 84701 Richfield⊙ 5,482 B5
- 84333 Richmond 1,705 C2
- †84321 River Heights 1,211 C2
- 84065 Riverton 7,293 B3
- 84066 Roosevelt 3,842 D3
- 84067 Roy 19,694 C2
- Saint George⊙ 11,350 A6
- 84653 Salem 2,233 C3
- 84654 Salina 1,992 C5
- *84101 Salt Lake City (cap)⊙ 163,697 C3
- Salt Lake City-Ogden‡ 936,255 C3
- *84070 Sandy 52,210 C3
- 84765 Santa Clara 1,091 A6
- 84655 Santaquin 2,175 C4
- 84335 Smithfield 4,993 C2
- †84065 South Jordan 7,492 B3
- †84403 South Ogden 11,366 C2
- 84115 South Salt Lake 9,884 C3
- 84660 Spanish Fork 9,825 C3
- 84663 Springville 12,101 C3
- †84015 Sunset 5,733 B2
- †84041 Syracuse 3,702 B2
- †84101 Taylorsville 17,448 B3
- 84074 Tooele⊙ 14,335 B3
- 84337 Tremonton 3,464 B2
- 84078 Vernal⊙ 6,600 E3
- 84780 Washington 3,092 A6
- †84403 Washington Terrace 8,212 B2
- 84542 Wellington 1,406 D4
- 84339 Wellsville 1,952 C2
- 84083 Wendover 1,099 A3
- †84087 West Bountiful 3,556 B3
- 84084 West Jordan 27,192 B3
- 84340 Willard 1,241 C2
- 84087 Woods Cross 4,263 B3

OTHER FEATURES

- Abajo (mts.) E6
- Agassiz (mt.) D3
- Antelope (isl.) B3
- Aquarius (plat.) C5
- Arches Nat'l Park E5
- Assay (creek) B6
- Bad Land (cliffs) D4
- Baldy (peak) B5
- Bear (lake) C2
- Bear (riv.) B2
- Beaver (mts.) A5
- Beaver (riv.) A5
- Beaver Dam Wash (creek) A6
- Birch (creek) B5
- Blue (creek) B2
- Bonneville (salt flats) A3
- Book (cliffs) E4
- Brown (Roan) (cliffs) E4
- Bryce Canyon Nat'l Park B6
- Canyonlands Nat'l Park D5
- Capitol Reef Nat'l Park C5
- Castle (valley) D4
- Cedar (mts.) B3
- Cedar Breaks Nat'l Mon. B6
- Chalk (creek) C3
- Chinle (creek) E6
- Clear (lake) B4
- Cliff (creek) E3
- Coal (cliffs) C5
- Colorado (riv.) E5
- Confusion (range) A4
- Cottonwood (creek) C4
- Cub (creek) C1
- Deep (creek) B1
- Deep Creek (range) A4
- Delano (peak) B5
- Desolation (canyon) E4
- Dinosaur Nat'l Mon. E3
- Dirty Devil (riv.) D5
- Dolores (riv.) E5
- Dry Coal (creek) A6
- Duchesne (riv.) D3
- Dugway (range) A3
- Dugway Proving Grounds B3
- Dutton (mt.) B5
- East Canyon (res.) C3
- Echo (res.) C3
- Elk (ridge) E6
- Ellen (mt.) D5
- Emmons (mt.) D3
- Escalante (des.) A6
- Escalante (riv.) C6
- Fish (lake) C5
- Fish Springs (range) A4
- Flaming Gorge (res.) E3
- Flaming Gorge Nat'l Rec. Area E2
- Fool Creek (res.) B4
- Fremont (isl.) B2
- Fremont (riv.) C5
- Glen Canyon Nat'l Rec. Area D6
- Golden Spike Nat'l Hist. Site B2
- Goshute Ind. Res. A4
- Government (creek) B3
- Gray (canyon) D4
- Great Salt (lake) B2
- Great Salt Lake (des.) A3
- Greeley (creek) B3
- Green (riv.) D4
- Grouse (creek) A2
- Grouse Creek (mts.) A2
- Gunnison (res.) C4
- Henry (mts.) D6
- Hilgard (mt.) C5
- Hill (creek) E4
- Hill A.F.B. C2
- Hill Creek Ext., Uintah and Ouray Ind. Res. E4
- Hillers (mt.) D6
- House (range) A4
- Hovenweep Nat'l Mon. E6
- Huntington (creek) C4
- Indian (creek) B5
- Jordan (riv.) C3
- Kaiparowits (plat.) C6
- Kanab (creek) B7
- Kanosh Ind. Res. B5
- Kings (peak) D3
- Koosharem Ind. Res. C5
- Little Creek (peak) B6
- Little Salt (lake) A6
- Malad (riv.) B1
- Marsh (peak) E3
- Marvine (mt.) C5
- Mineral (mts.) B5
- Mona (res.) C4
- Monroe (peak) B5
- Montezuma (creek) E6
- Monument (valley) D6
- Muddy (creek) C4
- Natural Bridges Nat'l Mon. E6
- Navajo (mt.) D6
- Navajo Ind. Res. D7
- Nebo (mt.) C4
- Newfoundland (mts.) A2
- Nine Mile (creek) D4
- North (lake) B2
- Orange (cliffs) D5
- Otter (creek) C5
- Otter Creek (res.) C5
- Paria (riv.) B6
- Paunsaugunt (plat.) B6
- Pavant (mts.) B5
- Peale (mt.) E5
- Pennell (mt.) D6
- Piute (res.) B5
- Plumber (creek) C2
- Powell (lake) D6
- Price (riv.) D4
- Provo (peak) C3
- Provo (riv.) C3
- Raft River (mts.) A2
- Rainbow Bridge Nat'l Mon. C6
- Roan (cliffs) E4
- Rockport (lake) C3
- Salvation (creek) C5
- San Juan (riv.) D6
- San Pitch (riv.) C4
- San Rafael (riv.) D4
- San Rafael Swell (mts.) D5
- Santa Clara (riv.) A6
- Sevier (des.) B4
- Sevier (lake) A5
- Sevier (riv.) B4
- Sevier Bridge (res.) C4
- Shivwits Ind. Res. A6
- Silver Island (mts.) A3
- Skull Valley Ind. Res. B3
- Spanish Fork (riv.) C3
- Strait (cliffs) C6
- Strawberry (res.) C3
- Strawberry (riv.) D3
- Swan (lake) B4
- Tavaputs (plat.) D4
- Thomas (range) A4
- Thousand Lake (mt.) C5
- Timpanogos Cave Nat'l Mon. C3
- Tokewamna (peak) D3
- Tooele Army Depot B3
- Two Water (creek) E4
- Uinta (mts.) D3
- Uinta (riv.) D3
- Uintah and Ouray Ind. Res. D3
- Utah (lake) C3
- Virgin (riv.) A6
- Waas (mt.) E5
- Wah Wah (mts.) A5
- Wahweap (creek) C6
- Wasatch (range) C3
- Washakie Ind. Res. B2
- Waterpocket Fold (cliffs) D6
- Weber (riv.) C3
- White (riv.) E3
- Willow (creek) E4
- Zion Nat'l Park A6

⊙County seat.
‡Population of metropolitan area.
† Zip of nearest p.o.
* Multiple zips.

Agriculture, Industry and Resources

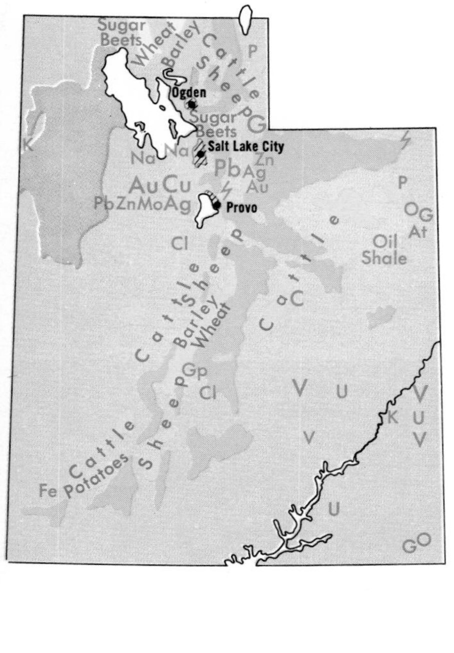
Sugar Beets
Wheat
Barley
Cattle
Sheep
P
G
Ogden
Sugar Beets
Salt Lake City
Na
Pb Ag
Zn
Au Cu
Au
PbZnMoAg
Provo
O
G
At
Oil Shale
Cl
Cattle
Sheep
Barley
Wheat
Cattle
C
Gp
Cl
V
U
K
Fe
Potatoes
GO

DOMINANT LAND USE

- Wheat, General Farming
- General Farming, Livestock, Special Crops
- Range Livestock
- Forests
- Nonagricultural Land

MAJOR MINERAL OCCURRENCES

Ag	Silver	Fe	Iron Ore	O	Petroleum
At	Asphalt	G	Natural Gas	P	Phosphates
Au	Gold	Gp	Gypsum	Pb	Lead
C	Coal	K	Potash	U	Uranium
Cl	Clay	Mo	Molybdenum	V	Vanadium
Cu	Copper	Na	Salt	Zn	Zinc

Water Power

Major Industrial Areas

Topography

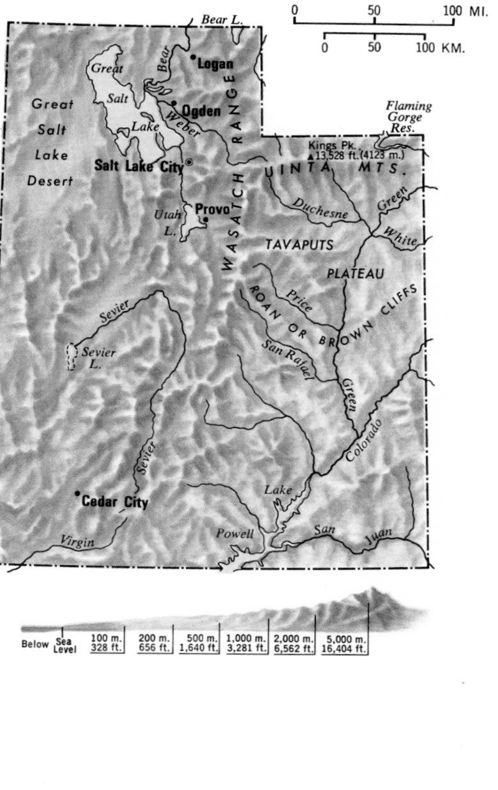
0 50 100 MI.
0 50 100 KM.
Bear L.
Logan
Great Salt Lake
Bear
Weber
Ogden
Great Salt Lake Desert
Salt Lake City
Flaming Gorge Res.
Kings Pk. ▲13,528 ft. (4123 m.)
UINTA MTS.
Utah L.
Provo
WASATCH RANGE
Duchesne
Green
White
TAVAPUTS PLATEAU
ROAN OR BROWN CLIFFS
Price
Sevier
Sevier L.
San Rafael
Green
Colorado
Sevier
Cedar City
Lake
Powell
San Juan
Virgin
Below Sea Level
100 m. 328 ft.
200 m. 656 ft.
500 m. 1,640 ft.
1,000 m. 3,281 ft.
2,000 m. 6,562 ft.
5,000 m. 16,404 ft.

Topography

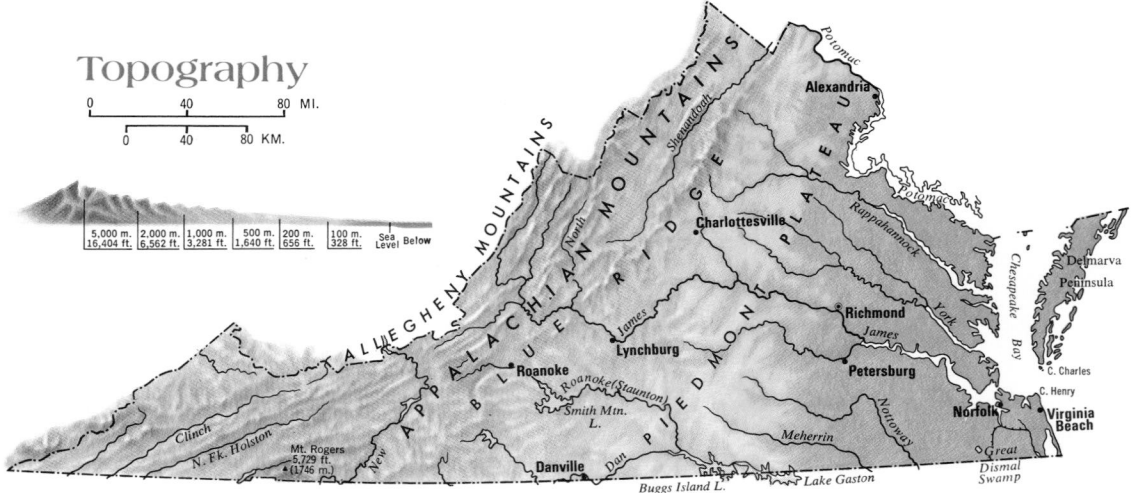

5,000 m. 2,000 m. 1,000 m. 500 m. 200 m. 100 m. Sea
16,404 ft. 6,562 ft. 3,281 ft. 1,640 ft. 656 ft. 328 ft. Level Below

COUNTIES

Accomack 31,268 .... S5
Albemarle 55,783 .... L5
Alleghany 14,333 .... H5
Amelia 8,405 .... M6
Amherst 29,122 .... K5
Appomattox 11,971 .... L6
Arlington 152,599 .... S2
Augusta 53,732 .... K4
Bath 5,860 .... J4
Bedford 34,927 .... J6
Bland 6,349 .... F6
Botetourt 23,270 .... J5
Brunswick 15,632 .... N7
Buchanan 37,989 .... D6
Buckingham 11,751 .... L5
Campbell 45,424 .... K6
Caroline 17,904 .... O4
Carroll 27,270 .... G7
Charles City 6,692 .... O6
Charlotte 12,266 .... L6
Chesterfield 141,372 .... N6
Clarke 9,965 .... M2
Craig 3,948 .... H6
Culpeper 22,620 .... M3
Cumberland 7,881 .... M6
Dickenson 19,806 .... D6
Dinwiddie 22,602 .... N6
Essex 8,864 .... P5
Fairfax 596,901 .... O3
Fauquier 35,889 .... N3
Floyd 11,563 .... H7
Fluvanna 10,244 .... M5
Franklin 35,740 .... J6
Frederick 34,150 .... M2
Giles 17,810 .... G6
Gloucester 20,107 .... P6
Goochland 11,761 .... N5
Grayson 16,579 .... F7
Greene 7,625 .... M4
Greensville 10,903 .... N7
Halifax 30,599 .... L7
Hanover 50,398 .... N5
Henrico 180,735 .... O6
Henry 57,654 .... J7
Highland 2,937 .... J4
Isle of Wight 21,603 .... P7
James City 22,763 .... P6
King and Queen 5,968 .... P5
King George 10,543 .... O4
King William 9,334 .... O5
Lancaster 10,129 .... R5
Lee 25,956 .... B7
Loudoun 57,427 .... N2
Louisa 17,825 .... N5
Lunenburg 12,124 .... M7
Madison 10,232 .... M4
Mathews 7,995 .... R6
Mecklenburg 29,444 .... M7
Middlesex 7,719 .... R5
Montgomery 63,516 .... H6
Nelson 12,204 .... L5
New Kent 8,781 .... P5
Northampton 14,625 .... S6
Northumberland 9,828 ...... R5
Nottoway 14,666 .... M6
Orange 18,063 .... M4
Page 19,401 .... M3
Patrick 17,647 .... H7
Pittsylvania 66,147 .... K7
Powhatan 13,062 .... N5
Prince Edward 16,456 .... M6
Prince George 25,733 .... O6
Prince William 144,703 ...... O3
Pulaski 35,229 .... G6
Rappahannock 6,093 .... M3
Richmond 6,952 .... P5
Roanoke 72,945 .... H6
Rockbridge 17,911 .... K5
Rockingham 57,038 .... L4
Russell 31,761 .... D7
Scott 25,068 .... C7
Shenandoah 27,559 .... L3
Smyth 33,366 .... E7
Southampton 18,731 .... O7
Spotsylvania 34,435 .... N4
Stafford 40,470 .... O4
Surry 6,046 .... P6
Sussex 10,874 .... O7
Tazewell 50,511 .... E6
Warren 21,200 .... M3

Washington 46,487 .... D7
Westmoreland 14,041 ...... P4
Wise 43,863 .... C6
Wythe 25,522 .... F7
York 35,463 .... P6

CITIES and TOWNS

Zip	Name/Pop.	Key

24210 Abingdon⊙ 4,318 ..... D7
23301 Accomac 522 .... S5
23001 Achilles 525 .... R6
22920 Afton 350 .... L4
23821 Alberta 394 .... N7
*22301 Alexandria (I.C.)⊙ 103,217 .. S3
24310 Allisonia 325 .... G7
24517 Altavista 3,849 ..... K6
24520 Alton 500 .... K7
23002 Amelia Court House⊙ 500 .. N6
24521 Amherst⊙ 1,135 .... K5
24601 Amonate 350 ...... E6
22003 Annandale 49,524 .. S3
24216 Appalachia 2,418 ... C7
24522 Appomattox⊙ 1,345 .. L6
24220 Ararat 500 .... G7
*22201 Arlington⊙ 152,599 .. T3
22922 Arrington 500 ...... L5

23004 Arvonia 500 .... M5
22011 Ashburn 345 ...... O2
23005 Ashland 4,640 ..... N5
24311 Atkins 1,352 ...... F7
24411 Augusta Springs 600 .. K4
24312 Austinville 750 ..... F7
24054 Axton 540 .... J7
22041 Bailey's
Crossroads 12,564 .... S3
24230 Banner 327 .... D7
22923 Barboursville 600 .. M4
24055 Bassett 2,034 ..... J7
24314 Bastian 500 .... F6
22924 Batesville 575 ..... L5
23015 Beaverdam 500 ... N5
24523 Bedford (I.C.)⊙ 5,991 .. J6
23306 Belle Haven 589 ... S5
24218 Ben Hur 400 ...... B7
22610 Bentonville 500 ... M3
22611 Berryville⊙ 1,752 ... M2
24526 Big Island 500 .... K5
24603 Big Rock 900 ..... D6
24219 Big Stone Gap 4,748 .. C7
24220 Birchleaf 650 ..... D6
23307 Birdsnest 736 ..... S6
24604 Bishop 600 .... E6
24060 Blacksburg 30,638 .. H6

23824 Blackstone 3,624 ..... N6
24527 Blairs 500 .... K7
24315 Bland⊙ 950 .... F6
23308 Bloxom 407 ...... S5
24605 Bluefield 5,946 .... F6
24064 Blue Ridge 2,347 .. J6
24606 Boissevain 975 ... F6
23235 Bon Air 16,224 ... N5
24065 Boones Mill 344 ... J6
22713 Boston 400 .... M3
22427 Bowling Green⊙ 665 .. O4
22620 Boyce 401 .... M2
23917 Boydton⊙ 486 .... M7
23827 Boykins 791 ...... O7
22714 Brandy Station 400 .. N4
24607 Breaks 550 .... D6
22812 Bridgewater 3,289 .. K4
24201 Bristol (I.C.)⊙ 19,042 .. D7
24316 Broadford 500 .... E7
22815 Broadway 1,234 ... L3
23920 Brodnax 492 ..... N7
22430 Brooke 245 ...... O4
24528 Brookneal 1,454 ... L6
24415 Brownsburg 300 .. K5
22610 Browntown 300 ... M3
22622 Brucetown 250 ... M2
24066 Buchanan 1,205 ... J5

23921 Buckingham⊙ 200 ..... L5
24416 Buena Vista
(I.C.)⊙ 6,717 ..... K5
24529 Buffalo Junction 300 .. L7
22015 Burke 33,835 ..... R3
24608 Burkes Garden 267 .. F6
23922 Burkeville 606 .... M6
22435 Callao 500 .... P5
24067 Callaway 225 ..... H7
22016 Calverton 500 .... N3
23310 Cape Charles 1,512 .. R6
23313 Capeville 325 ..... R6
23829 Capron 238 ...... O7
23315 Carrsville 300 .... P7
23830 Carson 200 ...... O6
22017 Casanova 300 .... N3
24069 Cascade 835 ..... J7
24224 Castlewood 2,420 .. D7
24070 Catawba 350 .... H6
22019 Catlett 500 ...... N3
24609 Cedar Bluff 1,550 .. E6
22437 Center Cross 360 .. P5
†22401 Chancellorsville 40 .. N4
22021 Chantilly 12,259 ... O3
23030 Charles City⊙ 5 ... O6
23923 Charlotte Court
House⊙ 568 ...... L6

*22901 Charlottesville
(I.C.)⊙ 39,916 ..... M4
Charlottesville‡ 113,568 .. M4
23924 Chase City 2,749 ..... M7
24531 Chatham⊙ 1,390 ... K7
23316 Cheriton 695 ...... R6
*23320 Chesapeake (I.C.)
114,486 .... R7
23831 Chester 11,728 .... N6
23832 Chesterfield⊙ 950 .. N6
22623 Chester Gap 400 ... M3
24319 Chilhowie 1,269 ... E7
23336 Chincoteague 1,607 .. T5
24073 Christiansburg 10,345 .. H6
23032 Church View 200 ... P5
23899 Claremont 380 .... P6
23927 Clarksville 1,468 ... L7
†23061 Clay Bank 200 ..... P6
23139 Clayville 200 ...... N6
22624 Clear Brook 300 ... M2
24225 Cleveland 360 .... D7
24422 Clifton Forge
(I.C.)⊙ 5,046 ..... J5
24321 Clinchburg 250 .... H5
24226 Clinchco 900 ...... D6
24244 Clinchport 89 ..... C7
24228 Clintwood⊙ 1,369 .. D6
24534 Clover 215 .... L7
24077 Cloverdale 850 .... J6
24535 Cluster Springs 350 .. L7
23035 Cobbs Creek 700 .. R6
24230 Coeburn 2,625 .... D7
24536 Coleman Falls 250 .. K6
†24450 Collierstown 200 ... K5
24078 Collinsville 7,517 ... J7
22443 Colonial Beach 2,474 .. P4
23834 Colonial Heights
(I.C.)⊙ 16,509 .... O6
23038 Columbia 111 ..... M5
24538 Concord 500 ..... K6
23837 Courtland⊙ 976 ... O7
22931 Covesville 475 .... L5
†24426 Covington (I.C.)⊙
9,063 .... H5
24430 Craigsville 845 .... J4
23930 Crewe 2,325 ..... M6
24431 Crimora 450 ..... L4
24322 Cripple Creek 200 .. F7
24323 Crockett 200 ..... F7
22932 Crozet 2,553 ..... L4
23039 Crozier 300 ...... N5
24539 Crystal Hill 475 ... L7
23934 Cullen 725 .... L6
22701 Culpeper⊙ 6,621 .. M4
23040 Cumberland⊙ 300 .. M6
22448 Dahlgren 350 .... O4
22193 Dale City 33,127 ... O3
24083 Daleville 450 ..... J6
24236 Damascus 1,330 ... E7
24237 Dante 1,083 ...... D7
*24540 Danville (I.C.)⊙ 45,642 .. J7
Danville‡ 111,789 .. J7

(continued on following page)

AREA 40,767 sq. mi. (105,587 sq. km.)
POPULATION 5,346,818
CAPITAL Richmond
LARGEST CITY Norfolk
HIGHEST POINT Mt. Rogers 5,729 ft. (1746 m.)
SETTLED IN 1607
ADMITTED TO UNION June 26, 1788
POPULAR NAME Old Dominion
STATE FLOWER Dogwood
STATE BIRD Cardinal

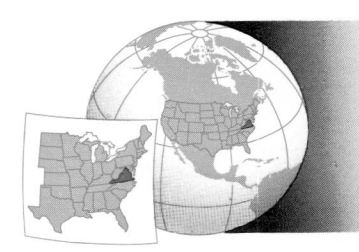

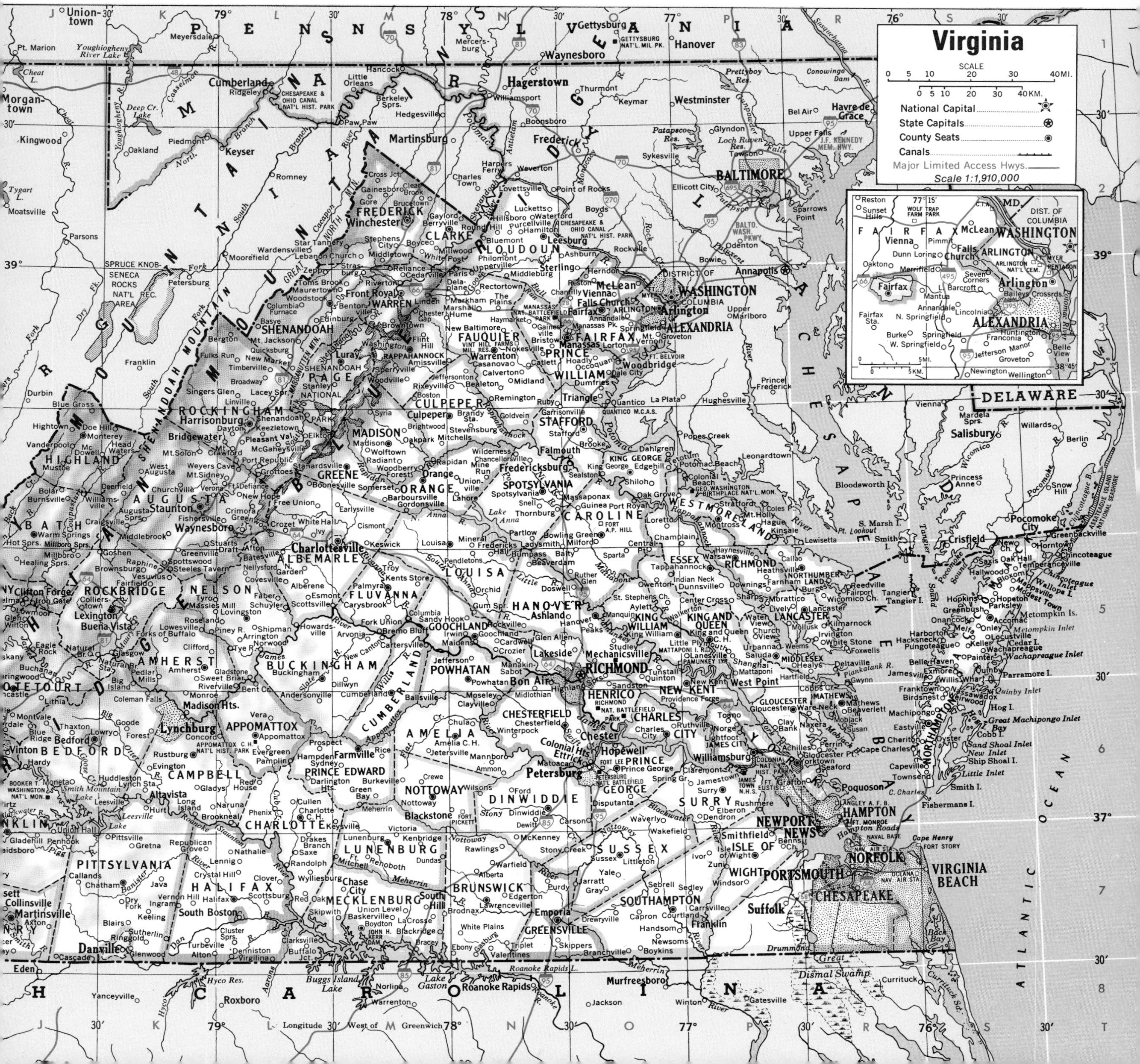

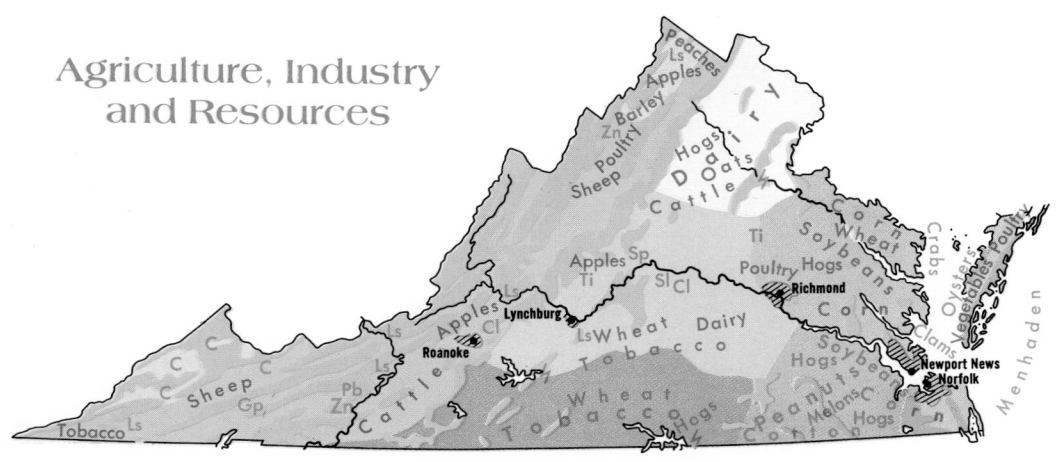

Agriculture, Industry and Resources

MAJOR MINERAL OCCURRENCES

C	Coal	Sl	Slate	⚡	Water Power
Cl	Clay	Sp	Soapstone		Major Industrial Areas
Gp	Gypsum	Ti	Titanium		
Ls	Limestone	Zn	Zinc		
Pb	Lead				

DOMINANT LAND USE

- Dairy, General Farming
- General Farming, Livestock, Dairy
- General Farming, Livestock, Tobacco
- General Farming, Livestock, Fruit, Tobacco
- General Farming, Truck Farming, Tobacco, Livestock
- Tobacco, General Farming
- Peanuts, General Farming
- Fruit and Mixed Farming
- Truck and Mixed Farming
- Forests
- Swampland, Limited Agriculture

AREA 68,139 sq. mi. (176,480 sq. km.)
POPULATION 4,132,180
CAPITAL Olympia
LARGEST CITY Seattle
HIGHEST POINT Mt. Rainier 14,410 ft. (4392 m.)
SETTLED IN 1811
ADMITTED TO UNION November 11, 1889
POPULAR NAME Evergreen State
STATE FLOWER Western Rhododendron
STATE BIRD Willow Goldfinch

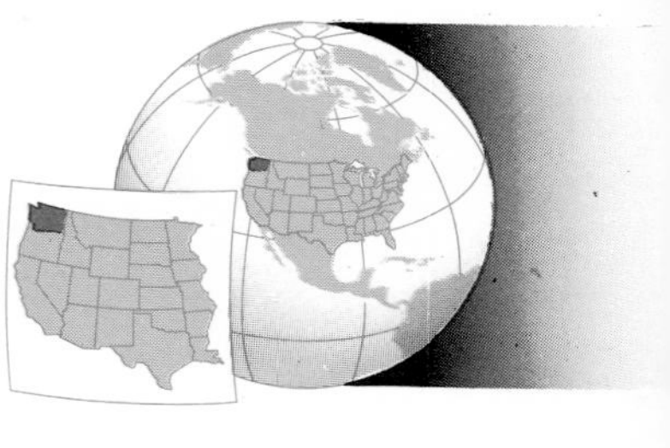

COUNTIES

Adams 13,267 G3
Asotin 16,823 H4
Benton 109,444 F4
Chelan 45,061 E3
Clallam 51,648 B2
Clark 192,227 C5
Columbia 4,057 H4
Cowlitz 79,548 C4
Douglas 22,144 F3
Ferry 5,811 G2
Franklin 35,025 G4
Garfield 2,468 H4
Grant 48,522 F3
Grays Harbor 66,314 B3
Island 44,048 C2
Jefferson 15,965 B3
King 1,269,749 D3
Kitsap 147,152 C3
Kittitas 24,877 E3
Klickitat 15,822 E5
Lewis 56,028 C4
Lincoln 9,604 G3
Mason 31,184 B3
Okanogan 30,639 F2
Pacific 17,237 B4
Pend Oreille 8,580 H2
Pierce 485,667 C3
San Juan 7,838 C2
Skagit 64,138 D2
Skamania 7,919 D5
Snohomish 337,720 D2
Spokane 341,835 H3
Stevens 28,979 H2
Thurston 124,264 C4
Wahkiakum 3,832 B4
Walla Walla 47,435 G4
Whatcom 106,701 D2
Whitman 40,103 H4
Yakima 172,508 E4

CITIES and TOWNS

Zip Name/Pop. Key

98520 Aberdeen 18,739 B3
98220 Acme 500 C2
99001 Airway Heights 1,730 H3
99102 Albion 631 H4
†98328 Alder 300 C4
98002 Algona 1,467 C3
98524 Allyn 850 C3
99103 Almira 330 G3
98526 Amanda Park 495 A3
98601 Amboy 480 C5
98221 Anacortes 9,013 C2
98603 Ariel 386 C5
98223 Arlington 3,282 C2
98304 Ashford 300 C4
99402 Asotin⊙ 943 H4
98002 Auburn 26,417 C3
98110 Bainbridge Island-Winslow (Winslow) 2,196 A2
98604 Battle Ground 2,774 C5
†98004 Beaux Arts Village 328 B2
98305 Beaver 450 A2
98528 Belfair 500 C3
*98004 Bellevue 73,903 B2
98225 Bellingham⊙ 45,794 C2
Bellingham‡ 106,701 C2
99320 Benton City 1,980 F4
98605 Bingen 644 D5
98010 Black Diamond 1,170 D3
98230 Blaine 2,363 C2
†98390 Bonney Lake 5,328 C3
98011 Bothell 7,943 B1
98310 Bremerton 36,208 A2
Bremerton‡ 146,609 A2
98812 Brewster 1,337 F2
98813 Bridgeport 1,174 F3
†98036 Brier 2,915 C3
98320 Brinnon 500 B3
†98101 Bryn Mawr-Skyway 11,754 B2
98321 Buckley 3,143 C3
98530 Bucoda 519 C4
98921 Buena 590 E4
98166 Burien 23,189 A2
98233 Burlington 3,894 C2
98013 Burton 650 C3
98607 Camas 5,681 C5
98323 Carbonado 456 D3
98324 Carlsborg 500 B2
98814 Carlton 410 F2
98014 Carnation 913 D3
98610 Carson 500 D5
98815 Cashmere 2,240 E3
98611 Castle Rock 2,162 B4
98612 Cathlamet⊙ 635 B4
98531 Centralia 11,555 C4
98520 Central Park 2,709 B3
98532 Chehalis⊙ 6,100 C4
98816 Chelan 2,802 E3
99004 Cheney 7,630 H3
99109 Chewelah 1,888 H2
98614 Chinook 928 B4
98326 Clallam Bay 600 A2
99403 Clarkston 6,903 H4
98235 Clearlake 750 C2
98922 Cle Elum 1,773 E3
98236 Clinton 900 C3
†98004 Clyde Hill 3,229 B2
†98055 Coalfield 500 B2
99111 Colfax⊙ 2,780 H4
99324 College Place 5,771 G4
99113 Colton 307 H4
†98632 Columbia Heights 2,515 C4
99114 Colville⊙ 4,510 H2
98819 Conconully 157 F2
98237 Concrete 592 D2
99326 Connell 1,981 G4
98535 Copalis Beach 600 A3
98536 Copalis Crossing 500 B3
98537 Cosmopolis 1,575 B4
99115 Coulee City 510 F3
99116 Coulee Dam 1,412 G3
98239 Coupeville⊙ 1,006 C2
99117 Creston 309 G3
99119 Cusick 246 H2
98240 Custer 300 C2
98617 Dallesport 600 D5
98241 Darrington 1,064 D2
99122 Davenport⊙ 1,559 G3
99328 Dayton⊙ 2,565 H4
98243 Deer Harbor 400 B2
99006 Deer Park 2,140 H3
98188 Des Moines 7,378 B2
99213 Dishman 10,169 H3
99329 Dixie 210 G4
98821 Dryden 500 E3
98327 Du Pont 559 C3
†98382 Dungeness 675 B2
98019 Duvall 729 D3
98245 Eastsound 800 B2
98801 East Wenatchee 1,640 E3
98328 Eatonville 998 C4
98020 Edmonds 27,679 C3
99123 Electric City 927 F3
98926 Ellensburg⊙ 11,752 E3
98541 Elma 2,720 B4
99124 Elmer City 312 G2
99125 Endicott 290 H4
†98310 Enetai 2,638 A2
98822 Entiat 445 E3
98022 Enumclaw 5,427 D3
98823 Ephrata⊙ 5,359 F3
†98310 Erlands Point 1,254 A2
*98201 Everett⊙ 54,413 C3
98247 Everson 898 C2
99012 Fairfield 582 H3
†98901 Fairview-Sumach 2,788 E4
98024 Fall City 1,528 D3
99128 Farmington 176 H3
98248 Ferndale 3,855 C2
98424 Fife 1,823 C3
98466 Fircrest 5,477 C3
†98531 Fords Prairie 2,582 B4
98331 Forks 3,060 A3
99014 Four Lakes 500 H3
98250 Friday Harbor⊙ 1,200 B2
†98901 Fruitvale 3,967 E4
99130 Garfield 599 H3
†99362 Garrett 1,134 G4
98824 George 261 F3
98335 Gig Harbor 2,429 C3
98336 Glenoma 500 C4
98619 Glenwood 626 D4
98251 Gold Bar 794 D3
98620 Goldendale⊙ 3,575 E5
98337 Gorst 750 C3
99133 Grand Coulee 1,180 G3
98930 Grandview 5,615 F4
98932 Granger 1,812 E4
98252 Granite Falls 911 D2
98547 Grayland 750 A4
98621 Grays River 350 B4
98253 Greenbank 600 C2
98339 Hadlock-Irondale 1,752 C2
98255 Hamilton 268 D2
†98366 Harper 300 A2
98933 Harrah 343 E4
99134 Harrington 507 G3
99135 Hartline 165 F3
99332 Hatton 81 G4
98025 Hobart 500 D3
98548 Hoodsport 500 B3
98550 Hoquiam 9,719 A3
†98004 Hunts Point 480 B2
98624 Ilwaco 604 A4
98256 Index 147 D3
98342 Indianola 800 A1
99139 Ione 594 H2
98027 Issaquah 5,536 C3
98343 Joyce 375 B2
98033 Juanita 17,232 B1
99335 Kahlotus 203 G4
98625 Kalama 1,216 C4
98344 Kapowsin 500 C4
98626 Kelso⊙ 11,129 C4
98028 Kenmore 7,281 B1
99336 Kennewick 34,397 F4
98031 Kent 23,152 C3
99141 Kettle Falls 1,087 H2
98345 Keyport 900 A2
98346 Kingston 950 C3
98033 Kirkland 18,779 B2
98934 Kittitas 782 E4
98628 Klickitat 750 D5
†98832 Krupp (Marlin) 83 F3
98629 La Center 439 C5
98503 Lacey 13,940 C3
98257 La Conner 633 C2
99143 Lacrosse 373 H4
†98101 Lake Forest Park 2,485 B1
98258 Lake Stevens 1,660 D3
99017 Lamont 101 H3
98260 Langley 650 C2
98350 La Push 500 A3
99018 Latah 155 H3
98826 Leavenworth 1,522 E3
99019 Liberty Lake 1,599 J3
98555 Lilliwaup 75 B3
99341 Lind 567 G4
98556 Littlerock 850 B4
98631 Long Beach 1,199 A4
98351 Longbranch 640 C3
98632 Longview 31,052 B4
99148 Loon Lake 500 H2
98262 Lummi Island 675 C2
98635 Lyle 580 D5
98263 Lyman 285 D2
98264 Lynden 4,022 C2
98036 Lynnwood 22,641 C3
98935 Mabton 1,248 E4
99149 Malden 200 H3
98829 Malott 350 F2
98353 Manchester 400 A2
98830 Mansfield 315 F3
98266 Maple Falls 300 D2
98038 Maple Valley 900 C3
99151 Marcus 174 H2
98268 Marietta-Alderwood 2,324 C2
98832 Marlin 83 F3
98270 Marysville 5,080 C2
99344 Mattawa 299 F4
98557 McCleary 1,419 B3
99022 Medical Lake 3,600 H3
98039 Medina 3,220 B2
98040 Mercer Island (city) 21,522 B2
99343 Mesa 278 G4
99152 Metaline 190 H2
99153 Metaline Falls 296 H2
†99210 Millwood 1,717 H3
98354 Milton 3,162 C3
98355 Mineral 550 C4
98562 Moclips 500 A3
98836 Monitor 650 E3
98272 Monroe 2,869 D3
98563 Montesano⊙ 3,247 B4
98356 Morton 1,264 C4
98837 Moses Lake 10,629 F3
98564 Mossyrock 463 C4
98043 Mountlake Terrace 16,534 B1
98273 Mount Vernon⊙ 13,009 C2
98936 Moxee City 687 E4
98275 Mukilteo 1,426 C3
98937 Naches 644 E4
98565 Napavine 611 C4
98638 Naselle 500 B4
†98310 Navy Yard City 2,594 A2
98357 Neah Bay 800 A2
99155 Nespelem 284 G2
†98283 Newhalem 350 D2
99156 Newport⊙ 1,665 H2
†98501 Nisqually 500 C3
98276 Nooksack 429 C2
98358 Nordland 706 C2
†98100 Normandy Park 4,268 A2
98045 North Bend 1,701 D3
98639 North Bonneville 394 C5
99157 Northport 368 H2
99158 Oakesdale 444 H3
98277 Oak Harbor 12,271 C2
98568 Oakville 537 B4
98569 Ocean City 350 A3
98640 Ocean Park 918 A4
98551 Ocean Shores 1,692 A3
†98520 Ocosta 369 B4
99159 Odessa 1,009 G3
98840 Okanogan⊙ 2,302 F2
98359 Olalla 500 A2
*98501 Olympia (cap.)⊙ 27,447 C3
Olympia‡ 124,264 C3
98841 Omak 4,007 F2
98570 Onalaska 600 C4
99214 Opportunity 21,241 H3
98662 Orchards 8,828 C5
98844 Oroville 1,483 F2
98360 Orting 1,787 C3
99344 Othello 4,454 F4
99027 Otis Orchards-East Farms 4,597 H3
98938 Outlook 300 E4
98047 Pacific 2,261 C3
98571 Pacific Beach 900 A3
98361 Packwood 800 D4
99161 Palouse 1,005 H4
98939 Parker 500 E4
98444 Parkland 23,355 C3
99301 Pasco⊙ 18,425 F4
98846 Pateros 555 E2
98572 Pe Ell 617 B4
98847 Peshastin 500 E3
98281 Point Roberts 500 B2
99347 Pomeroy⊙ 1,716 H4
98362 Port Angeles⊙ 17,311 B2
†98101 Port Blakely 600 A2
98366 Port Orchard⊙ 4,787 A2
98368 Port Townsend⊙ 6,067 C2
†98584 Potlach 100 B3
98370 Poulsbo 3,453 A1
99348 Prescott 341 G4
98050 Preston 500 D3
99350 Prosser⊙ 3,896 F4
99163 Pullman 23,579 H4
98371 Puyallup 18,251 C3
98376 Quilcene 900 B3
98575 Quinault 450 B3
98848 Quincy 3,525 F3
98576 Rainier 891 C4

(continued on following page)

Agriculture, Industry and Resources

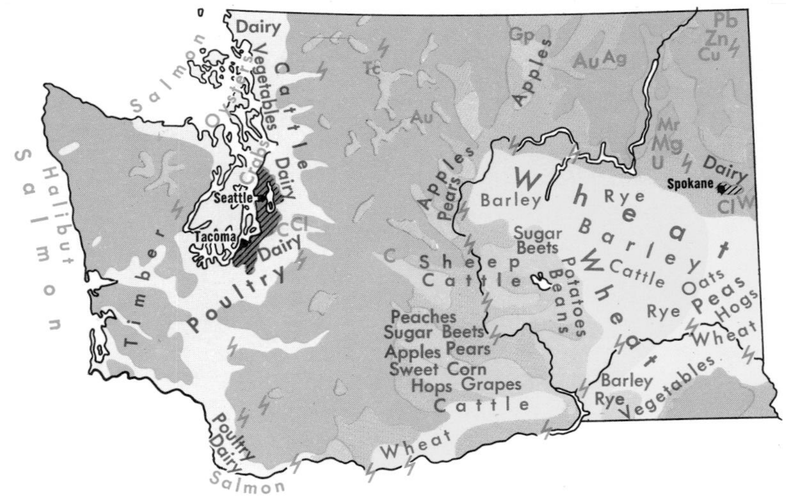

DOMINANT LAND USE

- Specialized Wheat
- Wheat, Peas
- Dairy, Poultry, Mixed Farming
- Fruit and Mixed Farming
- General Farming, Dairy, Range Livestock
- General Farming, Livestock, Special Crops
- Range Livestock
- Forests
- Urban Areas
- Nonagricultural Land

MAJOR MINERAL OCCURRENCES

Ag Silver
Au Gold
C Coal
Cl Clay
Cu Copper
Gp Gypsum
Mg Magnesium
Mr Marble
Pb Lead
Tc Talc
U Uranium
W Tungsten
Zn Zinc

Water Power
Major Industrial Areas

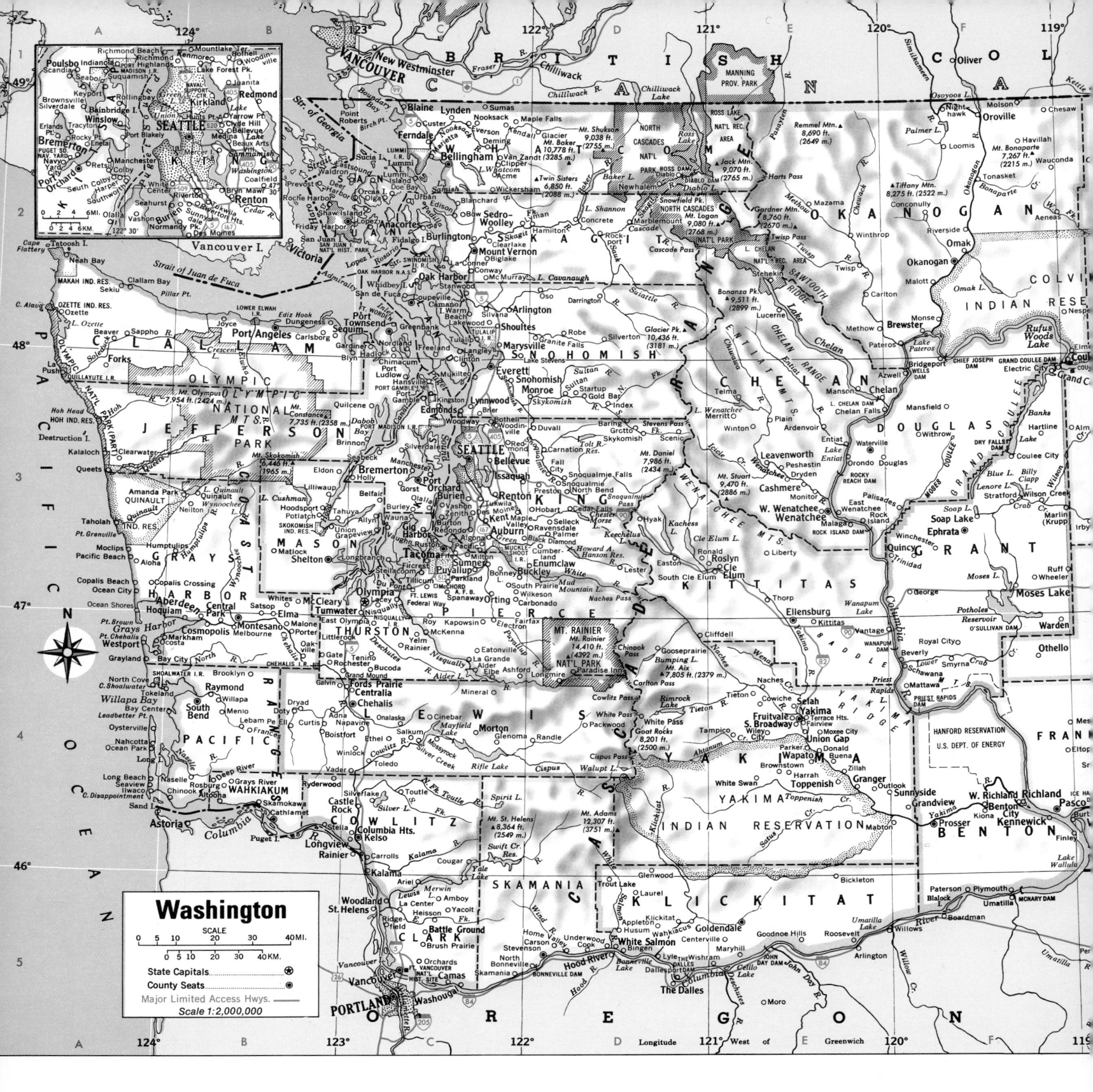

Washington

SCALE
0   5   10   20   30   40 MI.
0 5 10   20   30   40 KM.

State Capitals .... ⊛
County Seats .... ◉
Major Limited Access Hwys. ————
Scale 1:2,000,000

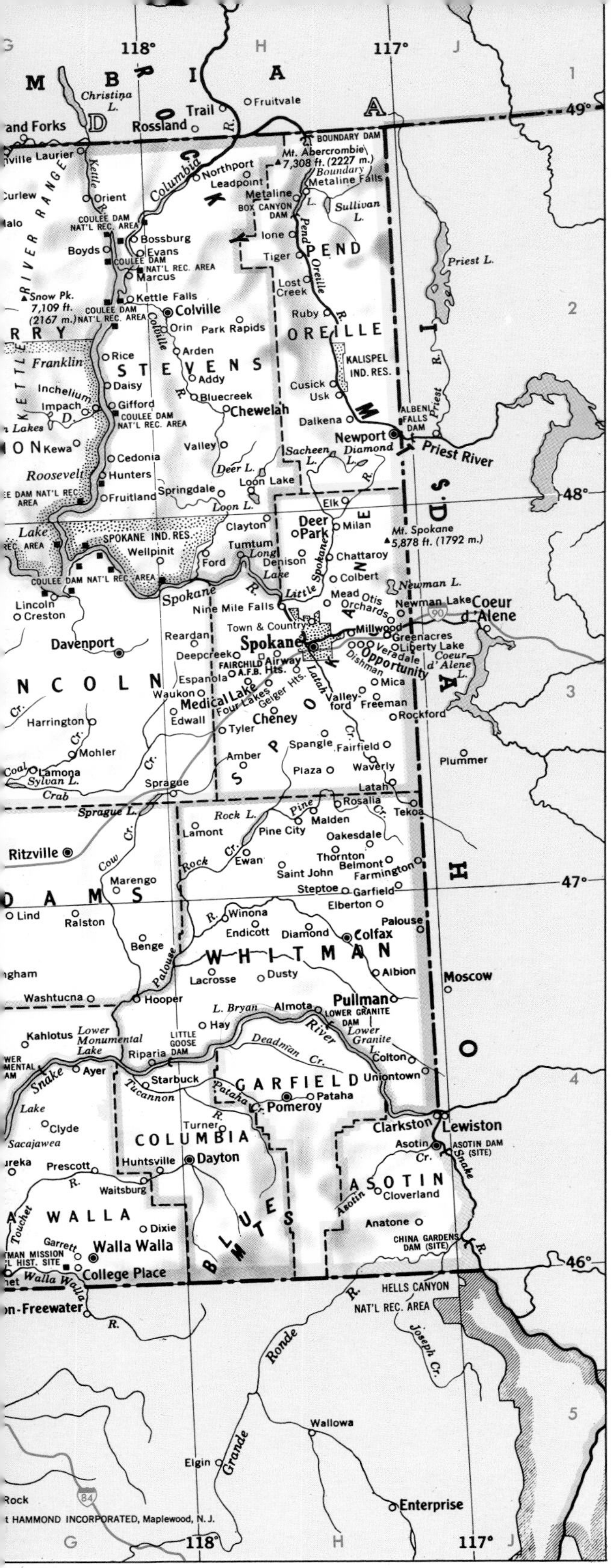

118°
117°
49°
48°
47°
46°
Trail
Fruitvale
Rossland
Northport
Leadpoint
Metaline
Metaline Falls
Mt. Abercrombie 7,308 ft. (2227 m.)
BOUNDARY DAM
BOX CANYON DAM
Sullivan L.
Orient
Bossburg
Evans
Marcus
Kettle Falls
Colville
Orin
Park Rapids
Arden
Rice
Daisy
Gifford
Addy
Bluecreek
Chewelah
Ione
Tiger
PEND OREILLE
Lost Creek
Ruby
Cusick
Usk
KALISPEL IND. RES.
Priest L.
Dalkena
Newport
Priest River
STEVENS
Kewa
Cedonia
Hunters
Fruitland
Springdale
Valley
Loon Lake
Deer Park
Milan
Clayton
Elk
Mt. Spokane 5,878 ft. (1792 m.)
SPOKANE IND. RES.
Wellpinit
Ford
Tumtum
Chattaroy
Colbert
Mead
Newman L.
Nine Mile Falls
Davenport
Reardan
Spokane
Millwood
Greenacres
Liberty Lake
Coeur d'Alene
Opportunity
Deepcreek
Medical Lake
Espanola
Waukon
Edwall
Cheney
Valleyford
Mica
Freeman
Rockford
Harrington
Mohler
Lamona
Tyler
Amber
Spangle
Fairfield
Plaza
Waverly
Plummer
Sprague
Latah
Rosalia
Tekoa
Ritzville
Lamont
Pine City
Malden
Oakesdale
Ewan
Thornton
Belmont
Farmington
Saint John
Steptoe
Garfield
Elberton
Marengo
Lind
Ralston
Winona
Endicott
Diamond
Colfax
Palouse
Benge
WHITMAN
Albion
Lacrosse
Dusty
Washtucna
Hooper
Pullman
Almota
Moscow
Kahlotus
Hay
Riparia
Ayer
Starbuck
Pataha
Pomeroy
GARFIELD
Colton
Uniontown
Clarkston
Lewiston
Asotin
Clyde
Turner
COLUMBIA
Huntsville
Dayton
Prescott
Waitsburg
ASOTIN
Cloverland
Anatone
WALLA
Dixie
Walla Walla
College Place
BLUE MTS.
HELLS CANYON NAT'L REC. AREA
Wallowa
Elgin
Enterprise
Moscow
IDAHO
HAMMOND INCORPORATED, Maplewood, N.J.

Topography

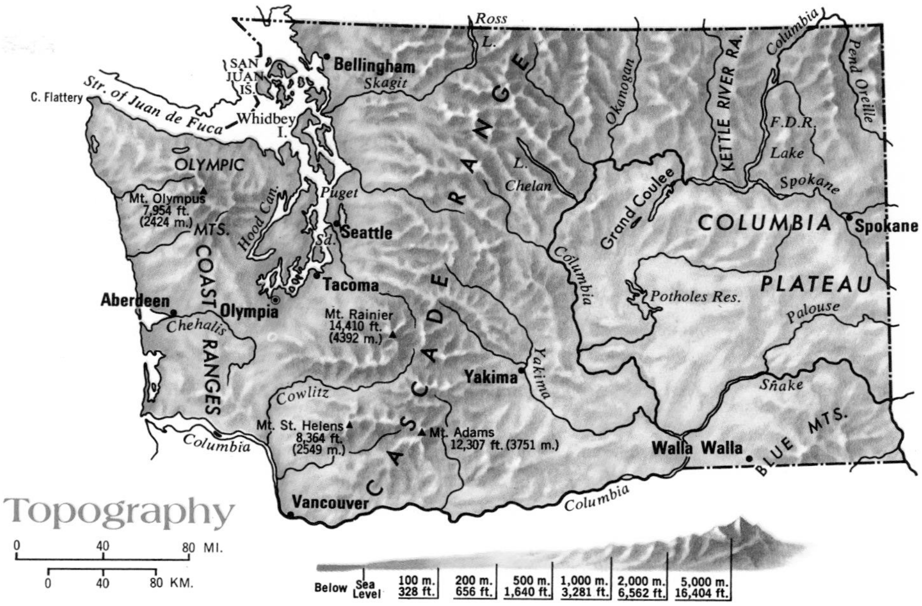

Ross L.
Columbia
Pend Oreille
SAN JUAN IS.
Bellingham
Skagit
C. Flattery
Str. of Juan de Fuca
Whidbey I.
KETTLE RIVER RA.
F.D.R. Lake
Okanogan
OLYMPIC
Mt. Olympus 7,954 ft. (2424 m.)
MTS.
Puget Sd.
L. Chelan
Grand Coulee
Spokane
COLUMBIA
Spokane
Seattle
Tacoma
Hood Can.
COAST RANGES
Aberdeen
Olympia
Chehalis
Mt. Rainier 14,410 ft. (4392 m.)
Potholes Res.
PLATEAU
Palouse
CASCADE RANGE
Yakima
Snake
Cowlitz
Mt. St. Helens 8,364 ft. (2549 m.)
Mt. Adams 12,307 ft. (3751 m.)
Walla Walla
BLUE MTS.
Vancouver
0 40 80 MI.
0 40 80 KM.
Below Sea Level
100 m. 328 ft.
200 m. 656 ft.
500 m. 1,640 ft.
1,000 m. 3,281 ft.
2,000 m. 6,562 ft.
5,000 m. 16,404 ft.

Adams (mt.) D4
Admiralty (inlet) B2
Ahtanum (creek) D4
Aix (mt.) D4
Alava (cape) A2
Alder (lake) C4
Asotin (creek) H4
Asotin (dam) J4
Bainbridge (isl.) A2
Baker (lake) D2
Baker (mt.) D2
Baker (riv.) D2
Banks (lake) F3
Birch (pt.) C2
Blalock (isl.) F5
Blue (lake) F3
Blue (mts.) H4
Bonanza (peak) E2
Bonaparte (creek) F2
Bonaparte (mt.) F2
Bonneville (dam) D5
Bonneville (lake) D5
Boundary (bay) C1
Boundary (dam) H2
Boundary (lake) H2
Box Canyon (dam) H2
Brown (pt.) A4
Bumping (lake) D4
Camano (isl.) C2
Carlton (pass) D4
Cascade (pass) D2
Cascade (range) D4
Cascade (riv.) D2
Cavanaugh (lake) D2
Cedar (riv.) B2
Celilo (lake) E5
Chehalis (pt.) A4
Chehalis (riv.) B4
Chehalis Ind. Res. B4
Chelan (lake) E2
Chelan (range) E2
Chester Morse (lake) D3
Chewack (riv.) E2
Chief Joseph (dam) F3
China Gardens (dam) J4
Chinook (pass) D4
Chiwawa (riv.) E2
Cispus (pass) D4
Cispus (riv.) D4
Cle Elum (lake) E3
Coal (creek) G3
Coast (ranges) B3
Columbia (riv.) B4
Colville (riv.) H2
Colville Ind. Res. G2
Constance (mt.) B3
Coulee Dam Nat'l Rec. Area G2
Cow (creek) G3
Cowlitz (pass) D4
Cowlitz (riv.) C4
Crab (creek) F3
Crescent (lake) B2
Curlew (lake) G2
Cushman (lake) B3
Dabob (bay) C3
Dalles, The (dam) D5
Daniel (mt.) D3
Deadman (creek) H4
Deer (lake) H2
Deschutes (riv.) C4
Destruction (isl.) A3
Diablo (lake) D2
Diamond (lake) H2
Disappointment (cape) A4
Dry Falls (dam) F3
Ediz Hook (pen.) B2
Elwha (riv.) B3
Entiat (lake) E3
Entiat (mts.) E2
Entiat (riv.) E3
Fairchild A.F.B. 5,353 H3
Fidalgo (isl.) C2
Flattery (cape) A2
Fort Lewis 23,761 C3
Fort Vancouver Nat'l Hist. Site C5
Fort Worden C2
Franklin D. Roosevelt (lake) G2
Gardner (mt.) E2
Georgia (str.) B2
Glacier (peak) D2
Goat Rocks (mt.) D4
Grand Coulee (canyon) F3
Grand Coulee (dam) F3
Grande Ronde (riv.) H5
Grays (harb.) A4
Green (lake) A2
Green (riv.) C3
Grenville (pt.) A3
Hanford Reservation-U.S. Dept. of Energy F4
Haro (str.) B2
Harts (pass) E2
Hells Canyon Nat'l Rec. Area H5
Hoh (head) A3
Hoh (riv.) A3
Hoh Ind. Res. A3
Hood (canal) B3
Howard A. Hanson (res.) D3
Humptulips (riv.) B3
Ice Harbor (dam) G4
Icicle (creek) E3
Jack (mt.) E2
John Day (dam) E5
Juan de Fuca (str.) A2
Kachess (lake) D3
Kalama (riv.) C4
Kalispel Ind. Res. H2
Keechelus (lake) D3
Kettle (riv.) G2
Kettle River (range) G2
Klickitat (riv.) D4
Lake (creek) G3
Lake Chelan Nat'l Rec. Area E2
Latah (creek) H3
Leadbetter (pt.) A4
Lenore (lake) F3
Lewis (riv.) C5
Little Goose (dam) G4
Little Spokane (riv.) H3
Logan (mt.) E2
Long (isl.) A4
Long (lake) H3
Loon (lake) H2
Lopez (isl.) C2
Lower Crab (creek) F4
Lower Elwah Ind. Res. B2
Lower Granite (lake) H4
Lower Monumental (lake) G4
Lummi (isl.) C2
Lummi Ind. Res. C2
Makah Ind. Res. A2
Mayfield (lake) C4
McChord A.F.B. 5,746 C3
McNary (dam) F5
Merwin (lake) C5
Methow (riv.) E2
Moses (lake) F3
Moses Coulee (canyon) F3
Mount Rainier Nat'l Park D4
Muckleshoot Ind. Res. C3
Mud Mountain (lake) D3
Naches (pass) D3
Naches (riv.) E4
Naselle (riv.) B4
Naval Support Ctr. B1
Newman (lake) H3
Nisqually (riv.) C4
Nisqually Ind. Res. C4
Nooksack (riv.) C2
North (riv.) B4
North Cascades Nat'l Park D2
Oak Harbor Naval Air Sta. C2
Okanogan (riv.) F2
Olympic (mts.) B3
Olympic Nat'l Park B3
Olympus (mt.) B3
Omak (lake) F2
Orcas (isl.) C2
Osoyoos (lake) F1
O'Sullivan (dam) F4
Ozette (lake) A2
Ozette Ind. Res. A2
Padilla (bay) C2
Palmer (lake) F2
Palouse (riv.) G4
Pasayten (riv.) E2
Pataha (creek) H4
Pateros (lake) F2
Pend Oreille (riv.) H2
Pillar (pt.) A2
Pine (creek) H3
Port Angeles Ind. Res. B2
Port Gamble Ind. Res. C3
Port Madison Ind. Res. A1
Potholes (res.) F3
Priest Rapids (lake) E4
Puget (isl.) B4
Puget (sound) C3
Puget Sound Navy Yard A2
Puyallup (riv.) C4
Queets (riv.) A3
Quillayute Ind. Res. A3
Quinault (lake) B3
Quinault (riv.) A3
Quinault Ind. Res. A3
Rainier (mt.) D4
Remmel (mt.) E2
Rifle (lake) C4
Rimrock (lake) D4
Rock (creek) H3
Rock (lake) H3
Rock Island (dam) E3
Rocky (mts.) H2
Rocky Reach (dam) E3
Rosario (str.) C2
Ross (dam) D2
Ross (lake) D2
Ross Lake Nat'l Rec. Area E2
Rufus Woods (lake) F2
Sacajawea (lake) G4
Sacheen (lake) H2
Saddle (mts.) E4
Saint Helens (mt.) C4
Samish (lake) C2
Sammamish (lake) B2
Sand (isl.) A4
San Juan (isl.) B2
San Juan Island Nat'l Hist. Park B2
Sanpoil (riv.) G2
Satus (creek) E4
Sauk (riv.) D2
Sawtooth (ridge) E2
Shannon (lake) D2
Shoalwater (cape) A4
Shoalwater Ind. Res. B4
Shuksan (mt.) D2
Silver (lake) C4
Similkameen (riv.) F1
Skagit (riv.) C2
Skokomish (mt.) B3
Skokomish Ind. Res. B3
Skykomish (riv.) D3
Snake (riv.) G4
Snohomish (riv.) C3
Snoqualmie (pass) D3
Snoqualmie (riv.) D3
Snow (peak) G2
Snowfield (peak) D2
Soap (lake) F3
Soleduck (riv.) A3
Spirit (lake) C4
Spokane (mt.) H3
Spokane (riv.) H3
Spokane Ind. Res. G3
Sprague (lake) G3
Stevens (pass) D3
Stuart (mt.) E3
Sucia (isl.) C2
Suiattle (riv.) D2
Sullivan (lake) H2
Sultan (riv.) D3
Swift Creek (res.) C4
Swinomish Ind. Res. C2
Sylvan (lake) G3
Tatoosh (isl.) A2
The Dalles (dam) D5
Tieton (riv.) D4
Tiffany (mt.) F2
Tolt River (res.) D3
Toppenish (creek) E4
Touchet (riv.) G4
Toutle, North Fork (riv.) C4
Toutle, South Fork (riv.) C4
Tucannon (riv.) G4
Tulalip Ind. Res. C2
Tule (lake) G3
Twin (lkes) G2
Twin Sisters (mt.) D2
Twisp (pass) E2
Twisp (riv.) E2
Umatilla (lake) E5
Union (lake) B2
Vancouver (lake) C5
Walla Walla (riv.) G4
Wallula (lake) F4
Walupt (lake) D4
Wanapum (lake) E3
Washington (lake) B2
Wells (dam) F3
Wenas (creek) E4
Wenatchee (lake) E3
Wenatchee (mts.) E3
Wenatchee (riv.) E3
Whatcom (lake) C2
Whidbey (isl.) C2
White (pass) D4
White (riv.) D3
White Salmon (riv.) D4
Whitman Mission Nat'l Hist. Site G4
Willapa (bay) A4
Wilson (creek) F3
Wind (riv.) D5
Wynoochee (lake) B3
Wynoochee (riv.) B3
Yakima (ridge) E4
Yakima (riv.) F4
Yakima Ind. Res. E4

⊙County seat.
‡Population of metropolitan area.
† Zip of nearest p.o. * Multiple zips.

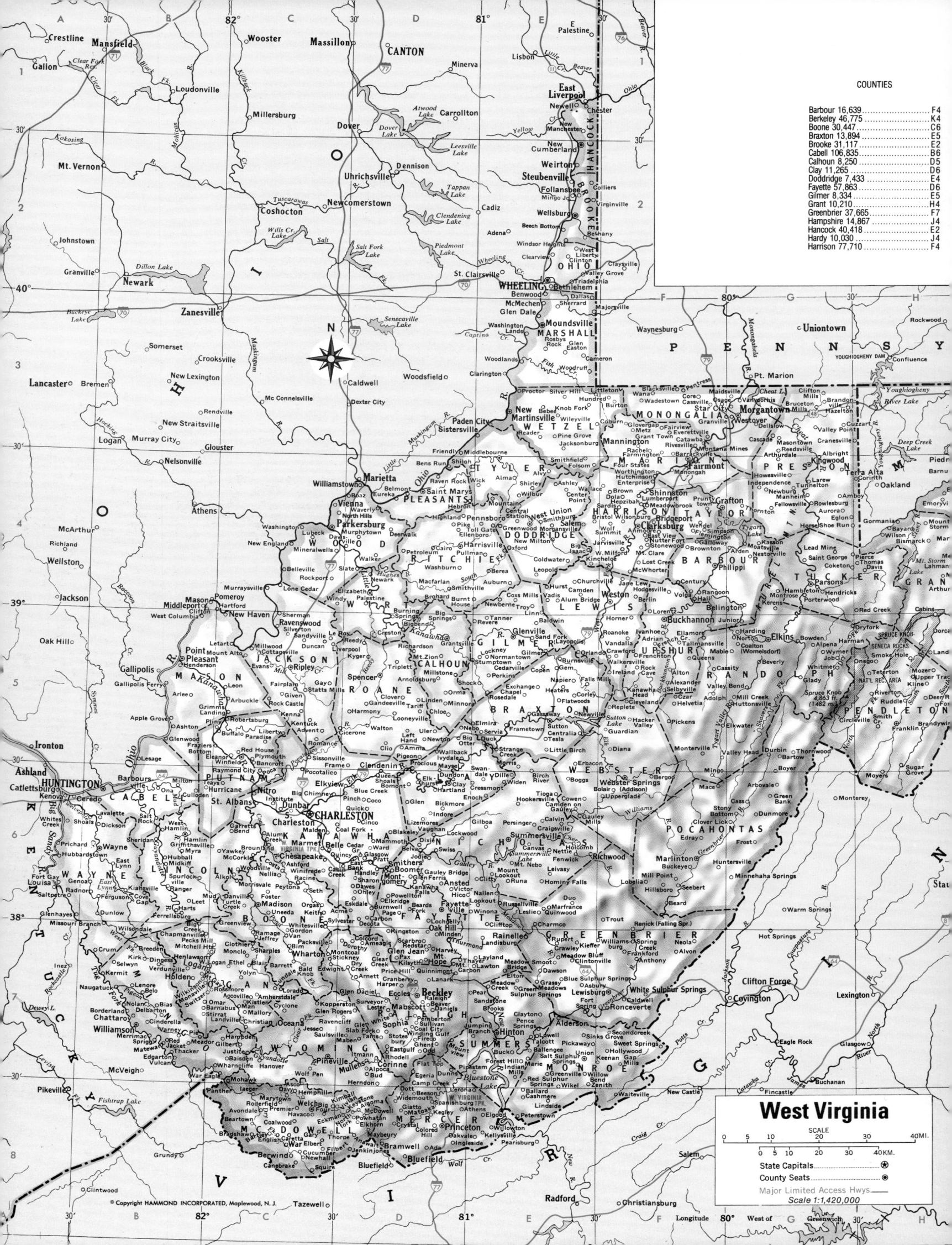

West Virginia

COUNTIES

Barbour 16,639 .... F4
Berkeley 46,775 .... K4
Boone 30,447 .... C6
Braxton 13,894 .... E5
Brooke 31,117 .... E2
Cabell 106,835 .... B6
Calhoun 8,250 .... D5
Clay 11,265 .... D6
Doddridge 7,433 .... E4
Fayette 57,863 .... D6
Gilmer 8,334 .... E5
Grant 10,210 .... H4
Greenbrier 37,665 .... F7
Hampshire 14,867 .... J4
Hancock 40,418 .... E2
Hardy 10,030 .... J4
Harrison 77,710 .... F4

SCALE
0   5   10   20   30   40MI.
0 5 10   20   30   40KM.

State Capitals .... ✪
County Seats .... ◉
Major Limited Access Hwys. _____
Scale 1:1,420,000

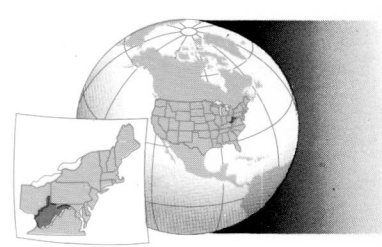

Jackson 25,794		C5
Jefferson 30,302		L4
Kanawha 231,414		C6
Lewis 18,813		E4
Lincoln 23,675		B6
Logan 50,679		C7
Marion 65,789		F4
Marshall 41,608		E3
Mason 27,045		B5
McDowell 49,899		C8
Mercer 73,942		D8
Mineral 27,234		J4
Mingo 37,336		B7
Monongalia 75,024		F3
Monroe 12,873		E7
Morgan 10,711		K3
Nicholas 28,126		E6
Ohio 61,389		E2
Pendleton 7,910		H5
Pleasants 8,236		D4
Pocahontas 9,919		F6
Preston 30,460		G4
Putnam 38,181		C6
Raleigh 86,821		D7
Randolph 28,734		G5
Ritchie 11,442		D4
Roane 15,952		D5
Summers 15,875		E7
Taylor 16,584		F4
Tucker 8,675		G4
Tyler 11,320		E4
Upshur 23,427		F5
Wayne 46,021		B6
Webster 12,245		F6
Wetzel 21,874		E3
Wirt 4,922		D4
Wood 93,648		D4
Wyoming 35,993		C7

CITIES and TOWNS

Zip	Name/Pop.	Key
25606	Accoville 975	C7
†26288	Addison (Webster Springs)⊙ 939	F6
26210	Adrian 510	F5
26519	Albright 357	G3
24910	Alderson 1,375	E7
24807	Algoma 200	D8
25501	Alkol 500	C6
26320	Alma 197	E4
24710	Alpoca 200	D7
26321	Alum Bridge 150	E4
25003	Alum Creek 900	C6
26322	Alvy 150	E4
25004	Ameagle 230	D7
25607	Amherstdale 1,075	C7
25005	Amma 200	D5
24808	Anawalt 652	D8

AREA 24,231 sq. mi. (62,758 sq. km.)
POPULATION 1,950,279
CAPITAL Charleston
LARGEST CITY Charleston
HIGHEST POINT Spruce Knob 4,863 ft. (1482 m.)
SETTLED IN 1774
ADMITTED TO UNION June 20, 1863
POPULAR NAME Mountain State
STATE FLOWER Big Rhododendron
STATE BIRD Cardinal

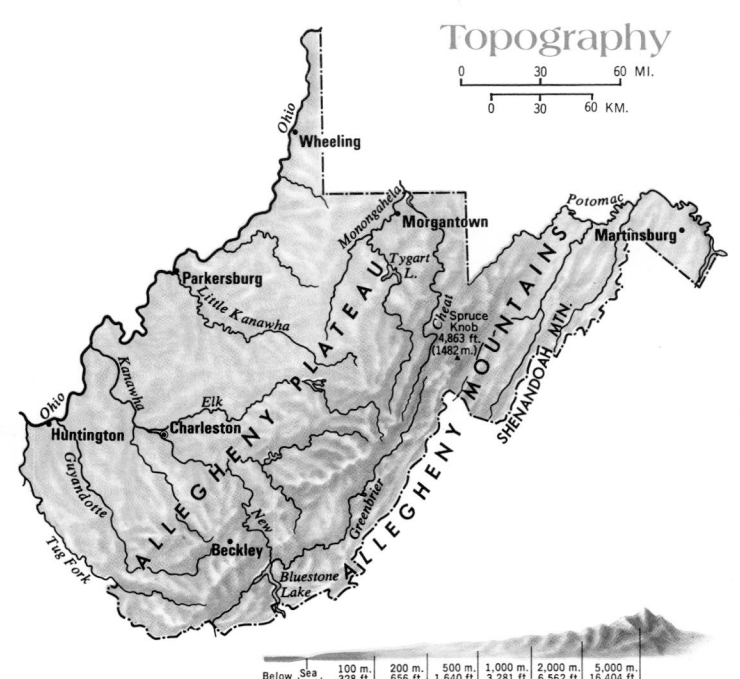

Topography

0 30 60 MI.
0 30 60 KM.

Below Sea Level | 100 m. 328 ft. | 200 m. 656 ft. | 500 m. 1,640 ft. | 1,000 m. 3,281 ft. | 2,000 m. 6,562 ft. | 5,000 m. 16,404 ft.

Zip	Name/Pop.	Key
26323	Anmoore 865	F4
25812	Ansted 1,952	D6
25502	Apple Grove 900	B5
24915	Arbovale 610	G6
26816	Arthur 350	H4
26520	Arthurdale 1,063	G3
24916	Asbury 280	E7
24809	Asco 175	C8
25009	Ashford 400	C6
25503	Ashton 259	B5
24712	Athens 1,147	E8
26325	Auburn 116	E4
26704	Augusta 750	J4
26705	Aurora 250	G4
24811	Avondale 250	C8
25608	Baisden 500	C7
26801	Baker 200	J4
25410	Bakerton 125	L4
25010	Bald Knob 356	C7
26520	Baldwin 92	E5
25011	Bancroft 528	C5
25609	Barnabus 750	C7
26559	Barrackville 1,815	F3
25013	Barrett 950	C7
24813	Bartley 900	C8
24920	Bartow 95	G5
25411	Bath (Berkeley Springs) 789	K3
26707	Bayard 540	H4
25014	Beards Fork 400	D6
25813	Beaver (Glen Hedrick) 1,122	D7
25801	Beckley⊙ 20,492	D7
26030	Beech Bottom 507	E2
24714	Beeson 300	D8
26250	Belington 2,038	F4
25015	Belle 1,621	C6
26133	Belleville 105	C4
26134	Belmont 887	D4
26656	Belva 275	D6
26135	Bens Run 85	D4
26031	Benwood 1,994	E2
26298	Bergoo 220	F6
25411	Berkeley Springs (Bath)⊙ 789	K3
24815	Berwind 615	C8
26032	Bethany 1,336	E2
†26003	Bethlehem 3,045	E2
26253	Beverly 475	G5
25019	Bickmore 300	D6
26136	Bigbend 120	D5
25302	Big Chimney 450	C6
25505	Big Creek 500	B7
26137	Big Springs 485	D5
25021	Bim 500	C7
26610	Birch River 650	E6
26521	Blacksville 248	F3
25022	Blair 800	C7
25026	Blue Creek 650	D6
24701	Bluefield 16,060	D8
26288	Bolair 450	F6
*25425	Bolivar 672	L4
25030	Bomont 170	D6
25031	Boomer 1,051	D6
24817	Bradshaw 1,002	C8
24715	Bramwell 989	D8
26523	Brandonville 92	G3
26802	Brandywine 300	H5
25666	Breeden 600	B7
26330	Bridgeport 6,604	F4
26138	Brohard 80	D4
25957	Brooks 196	E7
26334	Brownton 400	F4
26525	Bruceton Mills 296	G3
24924	Buckeye 125	F6
26201	Buckhannon⊙ 6,820	F5
24716	Bud 400	D7
25033	Buffalo 1,034	C5
25413	Bunker Hill 600	K4
26710	Burlington 300	J4
26335	Burnsville 531	E5
26336	Burnt House 175	D4
26562	Burton 200	F3
25035	Cabin Creek 900	C6
26337	Cairo 428	D4
24925	Caldwell 795	E7
26660	Calvin 400	E6
26208	Camden on Gauley 236	E6
26033	Cameron 1,474	E3
24819	Canebrake 300	C8
26662	Canvas 300	E6
26711	Capon Bridge 191	K4
26823	Capon Springs 580	K4
25037	Carbon 300	D6
24821	Caretta 650	C8
24927	Cass 148	G6
26527	Cassville 800	F3
25039	Cedar Grove 1,479	D6
26339	Center Point 250	E4
26612	Centralia 100	E5
26340	Central Station 200	D4
26214	Century 250	F4
25507	Ceredo 2,255	B6
25508	Chapmanville 1,164	B7

Zip	Name/Pop.	Key
*25301	Charleston (cap.)⊙ 63,968	C6
	Charleston‡ 269,595	C6
25414	Charles Town⊙ 2,857	L4
25958	Charmco 800	E6
25667	Chattaroy 1,383	B7
25418	Cherry Run 120	L3
†25301	Chesapeake 2,364	C6
26034	Chester 3,297	E1
26301	Clarksburg⊙ 22,371	F4
25043	Clay⊙ 940	D6
25044	Clear Creek 300	D7
25045	Clendenin 1,373	D5
26215	Cleveland 74	F5
25822	Clifftop 100	D6
25237	Clifton 325	B5
24928	Clintonville 250	E7
25046	Clio 300	D5
25047	Clothier 900	C7
25823	Coal City 2,324	D7
25306	Coal Fork 2,775	D6
26257	Coalton 306	G5
24824	Coalwood 650	C8
25048	Colcord 600	D7
26035	Colliers 864	E2
26615	Copen 50	E5
25826	Corinne 900	D7
25051	Costa 200	C6
25239	Cottageville 300	C5
25509	Cove Gap 650	B6
26206	Cowen 723	E6
26342	Coxs Mills 275	E4
26205	Craigsville 1,562	E6
25828	Cranberry 315	D7
24931	Crawley 395	E7
25669	Crum 500	B7
24826	Cucumber 274	C8
25510	Culloden 2,931	B6
24827	Cyclone 500	C7
26036	Dallas 450	E2
25832	Daniels 1,959	D7
25053	Danville 727	C6
25054	Dawes 800	D6
24932	Dawson 300	E7
25670	Delbarton 981	B7
26531	Dellslow 300	G3
26217	Diana 300	F5
26617	Dille 300	E6
25671	Dingess 600	B7
25059	Dixie 985	D6
25060	Dorothy 400	D7
24721	Dott 100	D8
25062	Dry Creek 441	D7
26263	Dryfork 425	H5
25063	Duck 500	E5
25064	Dunbar 9,285	C6
24934	Dunmore 280	G6
26264	Durbin 379	G5
25067	East Bank 1,155	D6
25835	Eastgulf 300	D7
25512	East Lynn 150	B6
†26301	East View 1,222	F4
25836	Eccles 1,162	D7
24829	Eckman 750	C8
25672	Edgarton 415	B7
26716	Eglon 70	G4
24830	Elbert 400	C8
25070	Eleanor 1,282	C5
26143	Elizabeth⊙ 856	D4
26717	Elk Garden 291	H4
26241	Elkins⊙ 8,536	G5
25071	Elkview 1,161	C6
26267	Ellamore 250	F5
26346	Ellenboro 357	D4
25965	Elton 200	E7
24832	English 500	C8
26568	Enterprise 1,110	F4
25075	Eskdale 400	D6
25076	Ethel 450	C7
26144	Eureka 125	D4
25241	Evans 400	C5
26533	Everettville 175	F3
26554	Fairmont 23,863	F4
26570	Fairview 759	F3
†24966	Falling Spring (Renick) 240	F6
26571	Farmington 583	F3
25840	Fayetteville⊙ 2,366	D6
26202	Fenwick 500	E6
24835	Filbert 130	D8
26818	Fisher 500	H4
25841	Flat Top 500	D7
26621	Flatwoods 405	E5
26347	Flemington 452	F4
26037	Follansbee 3,994	E2
26348	Folsom 360	E3
24935	Forest Hill 314	E7
26719	Fort Ashby 1,205	J4
25514	Fort Gay 886	A6
26806	Fort Seybert 200	H5
24936	Fort Spring 250	E7
25081	Foster 500	C6

Zip	Name/Pop.	Key
26572	Four States 500	F4
25071	Frame 76	C5
26623	Frametown 150	E5
26807	Franklin⊙ 780	H5
25082	Fraziers Bottom 250	B5
26219	Frenchton 102	F5
26146	Friendly 242	D3
25515	Gallipolis Ferry 325	B5
26349	Galloway 500	F4
25243	Gandeeville 150	D5
24941	Gap Mills 300	F7
24836	Gary 2,233	C8
26624	Gassaway 1,225	E5
25085	Gauley Bridge 1,177	D6
26240	Gauley Mills 165	E6
25244	Gay 300	C5
25420	Gerrardstown 240	K4
25843	Ghent 500	D7
25621	Gilbert 757	C7
26671	Gilboa 500	E6
26350	Gilmer 110	E5
26268	Glady 175	G5
25086	Glasgow 1,031	D6
25088	Glen 175	D6
26038	Glen Dale 1,875	E3
26039	Glen Easton 100	E3
25090	Glen Ferris 200	D6
25421	Glengary 250	K4
†25813	Glen Hedrick (Beaver) 1,122	D7
25846	Glen Jean	D7
25848	Glen Rogers 500	D7
26351	Glenville⊙ 2,155	E5
25849	Glen White 300	D7
25520	Glenwood 400	B5
†26585	Glovergap 100	F3
25093	Gordon 300	C7
26720	Gormania 100	H4
26354	Grafton⊙ 6,845	G4
26147	Grantsville⊙ 788	D5
26574	Grant Town 987	F3
26534	Granville 750	F3
24943	Grassy Meadows 100	E7
25422	Great Cacapon 750	K3
24944	Green Bank 115	G6
25966	Green Sulphur Springs 225	E7
24945	Greenville 125	E7
26360	Greenwood 750	E4
25095	Grimms Landing 350	B5
26221	Guardian 175	F5
26222	Hacker Valley 440	F5
25423	Halltown 375	L4
26269	Hambleton 403	G4
25523	Hamlin⊙ 1,219	B6
25623	Hampden 300	C7
25424	Hancock 175	K3
25102	Handley 633	D6
†26250	Harding 100	G5
26270	Harman 181	G5
25246	Harmony 600	D5
25851	Harper 400	D7
25425	Harpers Ferry 361	L4
26362	Harrisville⊙ 1,673	E4
25247	Hartford 556	C4
25524	Harts 400	B6
25852	Harvey 300	D7
24841	Havaco 350	C8
26627	Heaters 440	E5
25427	Hedgesville 217	K3
26224	Helvetia 130	F5
24842	Hemphill 700	C8
25106	Henderson 604	B5
26271	Hendricks 390	G4
25624	Henlawson 900	B7
26369	Hepzibah 600	F4
24726	Herndon 500	D7
25854	Hico 750	D6
24946	Hillsboro 276	F6
25951	Hinton⊙ 4,622	E7
25625	Holden 2,036	B7
26372	Horner 125	F5
26769	Horse Shoe Run 500	G4
†25506	Hubball 145	B6
26575	Hundred 485	E3
*25701	Huntington⊙ 63,684	A6
	Huntington-Ashland‡ 311,350	A6
25526	Hurricane 3,751	C6
26273	Huttonsville 242	G5
24844	Iaeger 833	C8
26374	Independence 200	G4
24949	Indian Mills 150	E7
25111	Indore 300	D6
25112	Institute	C6
25428	Inwood 1,159	K4
24847	Itmann 600	D7
25113	Ivydale 800	D5
26377	Jacksonburg 400	E3
26378	Jane Lew 406	F4
25114	Jeffrey 900	C7
24848	Jenkinjones 750	D8
24849	Jesse 400	C7
26674	Jodie 440	D6
25969	Jumping Branch 700	E7
26824	Junction 75	J4

(continued on following page)

DOMINANT LAND USE

- Dairy, General Farming
- General Farming, Livestock, Dairy
- General Farming, Livestock, Tobacco
- General Farming, Livestock, Fruit, Tobacco
- Fruit and Mixed Farming
- Forests

MAJOR MINERAL OCCURRENCES

- C   Coal
- Cl   Clay
- G   Natural Gas
- Ls   Limestone
- Na   Salt
- O   Petroleum
- ⚡   Water Power
- Major Industrial Areas

Agriculture, Industry and Resources

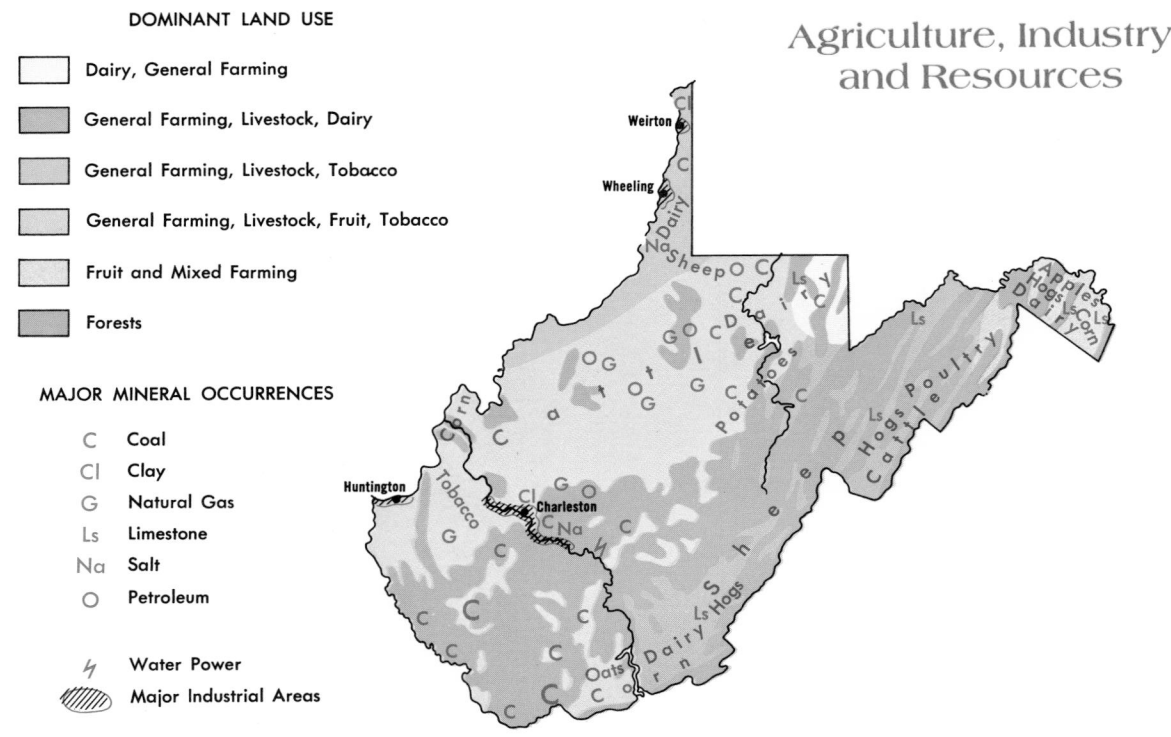

26275 Junior 591 ....G5	25678 Matewan 822 ....B7	25902 Odd 500 ....D7	24966 Renick 240 ....F6
24851 Justice 600 ....C7	24736 Matoaka 613 ....D8	25147 Ohley 450 ....D6	25915 Rhodell 472 ....D7
25115 Kanawha Falls 105 ....D6	24861 Maybeury 300 ....D8	25638 Omar 900 ....C7	26261 Richwood 3,568 ....F6
25430 Kearneysville 250 .....L4	26833 Maysville 150 ....H4	26886 Onego 400 ....H5	26753 Ridgeley 994 ....J3
24731 Kegley 900 ....D8	24858 McDowell 500 ....D8	25148 Orgas 500 ....C6	25440 Ridgeway 200 ....K4
24732 Kellysville 165 ....E8	26040 McMechen 2,402 ......E3	26412 Orlando 700 ....E5	26755 Rio 140 ....J4
25248 Kenna 150 ....C5	26401 McWhorter 150 ....F4	25268 Orma D5	25271 Ripley⊙ 3,464 ....C5
25530 Kenova 4,454 ....A6	24958 Meadow Bluff 250 .....E7	26543 Osage 285 ....F3	25441 Rippon 500 ....L4
25249 Kentuck 200 ....C5	25976 Meadow Bridge 530 ...E7	25151 Packsville 225 ....C7	26588 Rivesville 1,327 ....F3
25674 Kermit 705 ....B7	26404 Meadowbrook 500 .....F4	26159 Paden City 3,671 .....D3	26234 Rock Cave 400 ....F5
26726 Keyser⊙ 6,569 ....J4	25977 Meadow Creek 300 ....E7	25152 Page 600 ....D6	24881 Roderfield 900 ....C8
24852 Keystone 902 ....D8	26585 Metz 150 ....F3	26160 Palestine 110 ....D4	26757 Romney⊙ 2,094 ....J4
24950 Kieffer 135 ....E7	26149 Middlebourne⊙ 941 ...E3	24872 Panther 450 ....C8	24970 Ronceverte 2,312 ......F7
25859 Kilsyth 200 ....D7	25540 Midkiff 650 ....B6	26101 Parkersburg⊙ 39,967 ..D4	26636 Rosedale 400 ....E5
24853 Kimball 871 ....C8	26280 Mill Creek 801 ....G5	162,836 ....D4	25643 Rossmore 200 ....C7
25120 Kingston 189 ....D7	24959 Mill Point 148 ....F6	26287 Parsons⊙ 1,937 ......G4	26425 Rowlesburg 966 ....G4
26537 Kingwood⊙ 2,877 ......G4	25261 Millstone 850 ....D5	26746 Patterson Creek 157 ..J3	26688 Runa 150 ....E6
26729 Kirby 110 ....J4	25262 Millwood 800 ....C5	25434 Paw Paw 644 ....K3	26689 Russellville 280 ....E6
25628 Kistler 200 ....C7	25541 Milton 2,178 ....B6	25904 Pax 274 ....D7	25177 Saint Albans 12,402 ...C6
26579 Knob Fork 106 ....E3	25879 Minden 800 ....D7	25555† Pear 100 ....E7	26290 Saint George 150 ......G4
24854 Kopperston 700 ....C7	26150 Mineralwells 325 .,....D4	25547 Pecks Mill 350 ....B7	26170 Saint Marys⊙ 2,219 ...D4
26731 Lahmansville 200 ......H4	26281 Mingo 350 ....F5	25905 Pemberton 300 ....D7	26426 Salem 2,706 ....E4
25860 Lanark 559 ....D7	25263 Minnora 500 ....D5	24962 Pence Springs 300 ....E7	25559 Salt Rock 350 ....B6
25629 Landville 400 ....C7	26405 Moatsville 150 ....G4	26415 Pennsboro 1,652 ......E4	26430 Sand Fork 280 ....E5
24535 Lavalette 600 ....B6	25636 Monaville 950 ....B7	26554 Monongah 1,132 ......F4	25985 Sandstone 300 ....E7
25863 Lawton 100 ....E7	25537 Lesage 600 ....B5	26586 Montana Mines 200 ...F3	25275 Sandyville 500 ....C5
25864 Layland 500 ....E7	25972 Leslie 350 ....E6	25135 Montcoal 150 ....D7	25876 Saulsville 250 ....C7
26430† Layopolis (Sand Fork)	25865 Lester 626 ....D7	26282 Monterville 250 ....F5	25917 Scarbro 800 ....D7
280 ....E5	25253 Letart 350 ....C5	25136 Montgomery 3,104 ....D6	24975 Seebert 100 ....F6
25251 Left Hand 700 ....D5	25431 Levels 180 ....J4	26283 Montrose 129 ....G4	25181 Seth 950 ....D6
26676 Leivasy 200 ....E6	24901 Lewisburg⊙ 3,065 .....E7	26836 Moorefield⊙ 2,257 ....J4	26761 Shanks 500 ....J4
25676 Lenore 800 ....B7	26384 Linn 165 ....E4	26505 Morgantown⊙ 27,605 ..G3	25182 Sharon 450 ....D6
25123 Leon 228 ....C5	26629 Little Birch 400 ....E5	25542 Morrisvale 450 ....C6	25183 Sharples 250 ....C7
25971 Lerona 550 ....D8	26581 Littleton 335 ....F3	26041 Moundsville⊙ 12,419 ..E3	25443 Shepherdstown 1,791 ..L4
25537 Lesage 600 ....B5	25125 Lizemores 400 ....D6	25264 Mount Alto 200 ....C5	26173 Sherman 104 ....C5
25972 Leslie 350 ....E6	25866 Lochgelly 250 ....D6	25139 Mount Carbon 450 ....D7	26431 Shinnston 3,059 ......F4
25865 Lester 626 ....D7	25258 Lockney 190 ....E5	26408 Mount Clare 950 ......F4	26434 Shirley 275 ....E4
25253 Letart 350 ....C5	25601 Logan⊙ 3,029 ....B7	25637 Mount Gay 4,366 .....C7	25158 Shirley 250 ....B5
25431 Levels 180 ....J4	25630 Lorado 400 ....C7	25880 Mount Hope 1,849 ....D7	25159 Shock 200 ....D5
24901 Lewisburg⊙ 3,065 .....E7	26201† Lorentz 200 ....F4	26678 Mount Lookout 500 ...E6	26638 Shoals 150 ....B6
26384 Linn 165 ....E4	26810 Lost City 130 ....J5	26679 Mount Nebo 535 ......E6	25562 Shoals 150 ....B6
26629 Little Birch 400 ....E5	26385 Lost Creek 604 ....F4	26739 Mount Storm 500 .....H4	25286 Walton 550 ....D5
26581 Littleton 335 ....F3	26811 Lost River 500 ....J5	25882 Mullens 2,919 ....D7	26435 Simpson 250 ....E4
25125 Lizemores 400 ....D6	26101† Lubeck 1,356 ....C4	26680 Nallen 250 ....E6	24976 Sinks Grove 156 ......F7
25866 Lochgelly 250 ....D6	26386 Lumberport 939 ......F4	26631 Napier 158 ....E5	25320 Sissonville 450 ....C5
25258 Lockney 190 ....E5	26047 New Cumberland⊙ 1,752..E2	25685 Naugatuck 500 ....B7	26175 Sistersville 2,367 ......D3
25601 Logan⊙ 3,029 ....B7	26050 Newell 2,032 ....E1	25141 Nebo 200 ....D7	25920 Slab Fork 210 ....D7
25630 Lorado 400 ....C7	26154 New England 335 .....C4	25142 Nellis 600 ....C6	25444 Slanesville 250 ....K4
26201† Lorentz 200 ....F4	24866 Newhall 400 ....C8	24961 Neola 300 ....F7	26436 Smithburg 130 ....E4
26810 Lost City 130 ....J5	25265 New Haven 1,723 .....C5	26681 Nettie 500 ....E6	25186 Smithers 1,482 ....D6
26385 Lost Creek 604 ....F4	26056 New Manchester 800 ..E1	26410 Newburg 418 ....G4	26437 Smithfield 278 ....E4
26811 Lost River 500 ....J5	26155 New Martinsville⊙ 7,109..E3	26632 Newville 160 ....C6	26178 Smithville 200 ....D4
26101† Lubeck 1,356 ....C4	25266 Newton 390 ....D5	25143 Nitro 8,074 ....C6	24977 Smoot 350 ....D7
26386 Lumberport 939 ......F4	26632 Newville 160 ....C6	25687 Nolan 250 ....B7	26421 Pullman 196 ....D4
25870 Mabie 450 ....D7	25143 Nitro 8,074 ....C6	25267 Normantown 112 .....E5	26852 Purgitsville 450 ....J4
26278 Mabie 450 ....F5	25687 Nolan 250 ....B7	24868 Northfork 1,105 ......D8	25045 Quick 400 ....D6
25871 Mabscott 1,668 ....D7	25267 Normantown 112 .....E5	26101† North Hills 940 ......D4	25161 Powellton 1,339 ......D6
26148 Macfarlan 436 ....D4	24868 Northfork 1,105 ......D8	26285 Norton 400 ....G5	24877 Powhatan 400 ....D8
25130 Madison⊙ 3,228 ......C6	26101† North Hills 940 ......D4	26301 Nutter Fort 2,078 ....F4	25162 Pratt 821 ....D6
26541 Maidsville 500 ....F3	26285 Norton 400 ....G5	25901 Oak Hill 7,120 ....D6	24878 Premier 400 ....C8
25306 Malden 900 ....C6	26301 Nutter Fort 2,078 ....F4	24739 Oakvale 208 ....D8	26752 Price Hill 175 ....D7
25634 Mallory 1,330 ....C7	25901 Oak Hill 7,120 ....D6	24870 Oceana 2,143 ....C7	25880† Price Hill 175 ....D7
25132 Mammoth 563 ....D6	24739 Oakvale 208 ....D8		25555 Prichard 500 ....A6
25635 Man 1,333 ....C7	24870 Oceana 2,143 ....C7		24740 Princeton⊙ 7,493 ....D8

OTHER FEATURES

Big Sandy (riv.) A6
Bluestone (lake) E7
Buckhannon (riv.) F4
Cacapon (riv.) J4
Cheat (riv.) G4
Cherry (riv.) E6
Chesapeake and Ohio Canal Nat'l Hist.
    Pa J3
Clear Fork, Guyandotte (riv.) .C7
Coal (riv.) C6
Dry Fork (riv.) C8
Dry Fork (riv.) G5
East Lynn (lake) B6
Elk (riv.) D6
Fish (creek) E3
Gauley (riv.) D6
Greenbrier (riv.) E6
Guyandotte (riv.) B6
Harpers Ferry Nat'l Hist. Park .L4
Hughes (riv.) D4
Kanawha (riv.) C5
Little Kanawha (riv.) D5
Meadow (riv.) E6
Mill (creek) E5
Monongahela (riv.) G3
Mount Storm (lake) H4
Mud (riv.) B6
New (riv.) E7
North (riv.) J4
Ohio (riv.) B5
Patterson (creek) J4
Pigeon (creek) B7
Pocatalico (riv.) C6
Pond Fork (riv.) C6
Potomac (riv.) J3
Potts (creek) F7
Reedy (creek) D5
Shavers Fork (riv.) G5
Shenandoah (riv.) K4
Spruce Knob (mt.) G5
Spruce Knob-Seneca Rocks Nat'l Rec.
    Area G5
Stony (riv.) H4
Summersville (lake) E6
Sutton (lake) E5
Tug Fork (riv.) B7
Twelvepole (creek) A6
Tygart (riv.) G4
Tygart Valley (riv.) F5
West Fork (riv.) E4
Williams (riv.) F6

⊙ County seat.
‡ Population of metropolitan area.
† Zip of nearest p.o.   * Multiple zips.

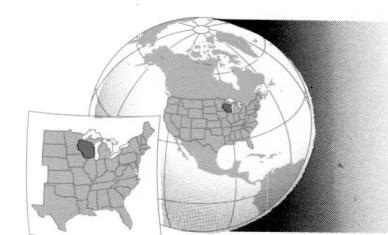

AREA 56,153 sq. mi. (145,436 sq. km.)
POPULATION 4,705,521
CAPITAL Madison
LARGEST CITY Milwaukee
HIGHEST POINT Timms Hill 1,951 ft. (595 m.)
SETTLED IN 1670
ADMITTED TO UNION May 29, 1848
POPULAR NAME Badger State
STATE FLOWER Wood Violet
STATE BIRD Robin

COUNTIES

Adams 13,457 ... G7
Ashland 16,783 ... E3
Barron 38,730 ... C5
Bayfield 13,822 ... D3
Brown 175,280 ... L7
Buffalo 14,309 ... C7
Burnett 12,340 ... B4
Calumet 30,867 ... K7
Chippewa 52,127 ... D5
Clark 32,910 ... E6
Columbia 43,222 ... H9
Crawford 16,556 ... E9
Dane 323,545 ... H9
Dodge 75,064 ... J9
Door 25,029 ... M6
Douglas 44,421 ... C3
Dunn 34,314 ... C6
Eau Claire 78,805 ... D6
Florence 4,172 ... K4
Fond du Lac 88,964 ... K8
Forest 9,044 ... J4
Grant 51,736 ... E10
Green 30,012 ... G10
Green Lake 18,370 ... H8
Iowa 19,802 ... F9
Iron 6,730 ... F3
Jackson 16,831 ... E7
Jefferson 66,152 ... J9
Juneau 21,039 ... F8
Kenosha 123,137 ... K10
Kewaunee 19,539 ... L6
La Crosse 91,056 ... D8
Lafayette 17,412 ... F10
Langlade 19,978 ... H5
Lincoln 26,555 ... G5
Manitowoc 82,918 ... L7
Marathon 111,270 ... G6
Marinette 39,314 ... K5
Marquette 11,672 ... H8
Menominee 3,373 ... J5
Milwaukee 964,988 ... L9
Monroe 35,074 ... E8
Oconto 28,947 ... K6
Oneida 31,216 ... G4
Outagamie 128,799 ... K7
Ozaukee 66,981 ... L9
Pepin 7,477 ... C6
Pierce 31,149 ... B6
Polk 32,351 ... B5
Portage 57,420 ... G6
Price 15,788 ... F4
Racine 173,132 ... K10
Richland 17,476 ... F9
Rock 139,420 ... H10
Rusk 15,589 ... D5
Saint Croix 43,262 ... B5
Sauk 43,469 ... G9
Sawyer 12,843 ... D4
Shawano 35,928 ... J6
Sheboygan 100,935 ... L8
Taylor 18,817 ... E5
Trempealeau 26,158 ... D7
Vernon 25,642 ... E8
Vilas 16,535 ... G3
Walworth 71,507 ... J10
Washburn 13,174 ... C4
Washington 84,848 ... K9
Waukesha 280,080 ... K9
Waupaca 42,831 ... J6
Waushara 18,526 ... H7
Winnebago 131,722 ... J8
Wood 72,799 ... F7

CITIES and TOWNS

Zip *Name/Pop.* *Key*

54405 Abbotsford 1,901 ... F6
53910 Adams 1,744 ... G8
53001 Adell 545 ... L8
53501 Afton 225 ... H10
53502 Albany 1,051 ... G10
†53534 Albion 300 ... H10
54201 Algoma 3,656 ... M6
53002 Allenton 915 ... K9
†54301 Allouez 14,882 ... L7
54610 Alma⊙ 876 ... C7
54611 Alma Center 454 ... E7
54805 Almena 526 ... B5
54909 Almond 477 ... G7
54720 Altoona 4,393 ... C6
54102 Amberg 875 ... K5
54001 Amery 2,404 ... B5
54406 Amherst 701 ... H7
54407 Amherst Junction 225 ... H7
54408 Aniwa 273 ... H6
54409 Antigo⊙ 8,653 ... H5
54911 Appleton⊙ 58,913 ... J7
Appleton-Oshkosh‡ 291,325 J7
†54568 Arbor Vitae 900 ... G4
54612 Arcadia 2,109 ... D7
53503 Arena 451 ... G9
54511 Argonne 600 ... J4
53504 Argyle 720 ... G10
54721 Arkansaw 400 ... B6
53911 Arlington 440 ... H9
54103 Armstrong Creek 615 ... K4
54410 Arpin 361 ... G6
53003 Ashippun 750 ... H1
54806 Ashland⊙ 9,115 ... E2
54304 Ashwaubenon 14,486 ... K7
54411 Athens 988 ... G5
54412 Auburndale 641 ... F6
54722 Augusta 1,560 ... D6
53506 Avoca 505 ... F9
†53520 Avon 120 ... H10
54413 Babcock 250 ... F7
53801 Bagley 317 ... D10
54202 Baileys Harbor 250 ... M5
54002 Baldwin 1,620 ... B6
54810 Balsam Lake⊙ 749 ... B5
54921 Bancroft 355 ... G7
54614 Bangor 1,012 ... E8
53913 Baraboo⊙ 8,081 ... G9
†54873 Barnes 225 ... D3
53507 Barneveld 579 ... F10
54812 Barron⊙ 2,595 ... C5
†53001 Batavia 125 ... K8
54723 Bay City 543 ... B6
54814 Bayfield 778 ... E2
†53201 Bayside 4,724 ... M1
54922 Bear Creek 454 ... J6
53916 Beaver Dam 14,149 ... J9
53802 Beetown 150 ... E10
53004 Belgium 892 ... L8
†54631 Bell Center 124 ... E9
53508 Belleville 1,302 ... G10
53510 Belmont 826 ... F10
53511 Beloit 35,207 ... H10
53803 Benton 983 ... F10
54923 Berlin 5,478 ... H8
†54410 Bethel 210 ... F6
†54440 Bevent 200 ... H6
53103 Big Bend 1,345 ... K2
54926 Big Falls 107 ... H6
54817 Birchwood 437 ... C4
54414 Birnamwood 688 ... H6
†54494 Biron 698 ... G7
54106 Black Creek 1,097 ... K7
53515 Black Earth 1,145 ... G9
54615 Black River Falls⊙ 3,434 ... E7
†54541 Blackwell 550 ... J4
54616 Blair 1,142 ... D7
53516 Blanchardville 803 ... G10
54617 Bloom City 167 ... E8
54724 Bloomer 3,342 ... D5
53804 Bloomington 743 ... E10
53517 Blue Mounds 387 ... G9
53518 Blue River 412 ... E9
†53581 Boaz 161 ... E9
†53105 Bohners Lake 1,507 ... K10
54107 Bonduel 1,160 ... K6
53805 Boscobel 2,662 ... E9
54512 Boulder Junction 780 ... G3
54416 Bowler 339 ... J6
54725 Boyceville 862 ... C5
54726 Boyd 660 ... E6
54203 Branch 300 ... L7
53919 Brandon 862 ... J8
54513 Brantwood 500 ... F4
53920 Briggsville 250 ... H8
54110 Brillion 2,907 ... L7
53520 Brodhead 3,153 ... G10
54417 Brokaw 298 ... G5
53005 Brookfield 34,035 ... K1
53521 Brooklyn 627 ... H10
53209 Brown Deer 12,921 ... L1
†53105 Brown's Lake 1,648 ... K3
53006 Brownsville 433 ... J8
53522 Browntown 284 ... G10
54819 Bruce 905 ... D5
54820 Brule 335 ... C2
54204 Brussels 500 ... L6
†54622 Buffalo 894 ... C7
53105 Burlington 8,385 ... K10
53922 Burnett 260 ... J9
53007 Butler 2,059 ... K1
54514 Butternut 438 ... E3
53009 Byron 40 ... K8
54821 Cable 227 ... D3
54727 Cadott 1,247 ... D6
53923 Cambria 680 ... H8
53523 Cambridge 844 ... H9
54822 Cameron 1,115 ... C5
†53019 Campbellsport 1,740 ... K8
54618 Camp Douglas 589 ... F8
53109 Camp Lake 2,060 ... K10
54823 Canton 100 ... C5
54928 Caroline 450 ... J6
53011 Cascade 615 ... K8
54205 Casco 484 ... L6
54619 Cashton 827 ... E8
53806 Cassville 1,270 ... E10
54620 Cataract 200 ... E7
54515 Catawba 205 ... E4
54206 Cato 85 ... L7
53924 Cazenovia 259 ... F8
54111 Cecil 445 ... K6
53012 Cedarburg 9,005 ... L9
53013 Cedar Grove 1,420 ... L8
54824 Centuria 711 ... A5
54621 Chaseburg 279 ... D8
54419 Chelsea 120 ... F5
†53029 Chenequa 532 ... J1
54728 Chetek 1,931 ... C5
54420 Chili 185 ... F6
53014 Chilton⊙ 2,965 ... K7
54729 Chippewa Falls⊙ 12,270 ... D6
54004 Clayton 425 ... B5
54005 Clear Lake 899 ... B5
53015 Cleveland 1,270 ... L8
53525 Clinton 1,751 ... J10
54929 Clintonville 4,567 ... J6
53016 Clyman 317 ... J9
53526 Cobb 409 ... F10
54622 Cochrane 512 ... C7
54421 Colby 1,496 ... F6
54112 Coleman 852 ... L5
54730 Colfax 1,149 ... C6
54930 Coloma 367 ... H7
53925 Columbus 4,049 ... H9
54113 Combined Locks 2,573 ... K7
†53147 Como 1,376 ... K10
54519 Conover 480 ... H3
54731 Conrath 86 ... E5
54623 Coon Valley 758 ... E8
54732 Cornell 1,583 ... D5
54827 Cornucopia 250 ... D2
54520 Crandon⊙ 1,969 ... H4
54114 Crivitz 1,041 ... L5
53528 Cross Plains 2,156 ... G9
53807 Cuba City 2,129 ... F10
53110 Cudahy 19,547 ... M2
54829 Cumberland 1,983 ... C4
54422 Curtiss 127 ... F6
54006 Cushing 150 ... A4
54931 Dale 410 ... J7
54733 Dallas 477 ... C5
53926 Dalton 300 ... H8
53529 Dane 518 ... G9
53114 Darien 1,152 ... J10
53530 Darlington⊙ 2,300 ... F10
53531 Deerfield 1,466 ... H9
54007 Deer Park 232 ... B5
53532 De Forest 3,367 ... H9
53018 Delafield 4,083 ... J1
53115 Delavan 5,684 ... J10
†53115 Delavan Lake 2,082 ... J10
†54856 Delta 35 ... D3
54208 Denmark 1,475 ... L7
54115 De Pere 14,892 ... K7
†54663 De Soto 318 ... D9
†54014 Diamond Bluff 100 ... A6
53808 Dickeyville 1,156 ... E10
54625 Dodge 185 ... D7
53533 Dodgeville⊙ 3,458 ... F10
54425 Dorchester 613 ... F5
53118 Dousman 1,153 ... J1
54734 Downing 242 ... B5
54735 Downsville 200 ... C6
53928 Doylestown 294 ... H9
54009 Dresser 670 ... A5
54832 Drummond 200 ... D3
54736 Durand⊙ 2,047 ... C6
53119 Eagle 1,008 ... H2
54521 Eagle River⊙ 1,326 ... H4
54626 Eastman 371 ... D9
53120 East Troy 2,385 ... J2
54701 Eau Claire⊙ 51,509 ... D6
Eau Claire‡ 130,507 ... D6
53019 Eden 534 ... K8
54426 Edgar 1,194 ... G6
53534 Edgerton 4,335 ... H10
54209 Egg Harbor 238 ... M5
54427 Eland 230 ... H6
54428 Elcho 500 ... H5
54429 Elderon 191 ... H6
54932 Eldorado 200 ... J8
54738 Eleva 593 ... D6
53020 Elkhart Lake 1,054 ... L8
53121 Elkhorn⊙ 4,605 ... J10
54739 Elk Mound 737 ... C6
54210 Ellison Bay 112 ... M5
54011 Ellsworth⊙ 2,143 ... A6
53122 Elm Grove 6,735 ... K1
54740 Elmwood 885 ... B6
†53401 Elmwood Park 483 ... M3
53929 Elroy 1,504 ... F8
54430 Elton 150 ... J5
54933 Embarrass 496 ... J6
53930 Endeavor 335 ... G8
54211 Ephraim 319 ... M5
54627 Ettrick 462 ... D7
53536 Evansville 2,835 ... H10
54835 Exeland 219 ... D4
54741 Fairchild 577 ... D6
53931 Fair Water 310 ... J8
54742 Fall Creek 1,148 ... D6
53932 Fall River 850 ... H9
†54840 Falun 95 ... A4
54120 Fence 200 ... K4
53809 Fennimore 2,212 ... E9
54431 Fenwood 165 ... F6
54628 Ferryville 227 ... D9
54524 Fifield 310 ... F4
54212 Fish Creek 119 ... M5
54121 Florence⊙ 780 ... K4
54935 Fond du Lac⊙ 35,863 ... K8
53125 Fontana 1,764 ... J10
53537 Footville 794 ... H10
54123 Forest Junction 140 ... K7
54213 Forestville 455 ... L6
53538 Fort Atkinson 9,785 ... J10
54629 Fountain City 963 ... C7
54836 Foxboro 360 ... B2
53933 Fox Lake 1,373 ... J8
†53117 Fox Point 7,649 ... M1
54214 Francis Creek 589 ... L7
53132 Franklin 16,871 ... L2
54837 Frederic 1,039 ... B4
53021 Fredonia 1,437 ... L8
54940 Fremont 510 ... J7
53934 Friendship⊙ 744 ... G8
53935 Friesland 267 ... H8
54630 Galesville 1,239 ... D7
54631 Gays Mills 627 ... E9
53127 Genesee Depot 350 ... J2
54632 Genoa 283 ... D8
53128 Genoa City 1,202 ... K11
53022 Germantown 10,729 ... K1
54124 Gillett 1,356 ... K6
54433 Gilman 436 ... E5
54743 Gilmanton 300 ... C7
54435 Gleason 200 ... G5
53023 Glenbeulah 423 ... L8
†53209 Glendale 13,882 ... M1
54526 Glen Flora 83 ... E4
53810 Glen Haven 160 ... E10
54013 Glenwood City 950 ... B5
54527 Glidden 940 ... E3
54125 Goodman 875 ... K4
54838 Gordon 600 ... C3
53540 Gotham 250 ... F9
53024 Grafton 8,381 ... L9
53936 Grand Marsh 725 ... G8
54839 Grand View 447 ... D3
54436 Granton 399 ... E6
54840 Grantsburg⊙ 1,153 ... A4
53541 Gratiot 280 ... F10
*54301 Green Bay⊙ 87,899 ... K6
Green Bay‡ 175,280 ... K6
53129 Greendale 16,928 ... L2
53220 Greenfield 31,467 ... L2
54941 Green Lake⊙ 1,208 ... H8
54126 Greenleaf 300 ... L7
54942 Greenville 900 ... J7
54437 Greenwood 1,124 ... E6
54128 Gresham 534 ... J6
54014 Hager City 110 ... A6
53130 Hales Corners 7,110 ... K2
54015 Hammond 991 ... A6
54943 Hancock 419 ... G7
54529 Harshaw 87 ... G4
53027 Hartford 7,046 ... K9
53029 Hartland 5,559 ... J1
54440 Hatley 300 ... H6
54841 Haugen 251 ... C4
54530 Hawkins 407 ... E4
54842 Hawthorne 200 ... C3
54843 Hayward⊙ 1,698 ... D3
53811 Hazel Green 1,282 ... F11
54531 Hazelhurst 630 ... G4
†53538 Hebron 450 ... J10
53137 Helenville 300 ... J10
54844 Herbster 100 ... D2
54441 Hewitt 470 ... F6
53543 Highland 860 ... F9
54129 Hilbert 1,176 ... K7
†54511 Hiles 350 ... J4

(continued on following page)

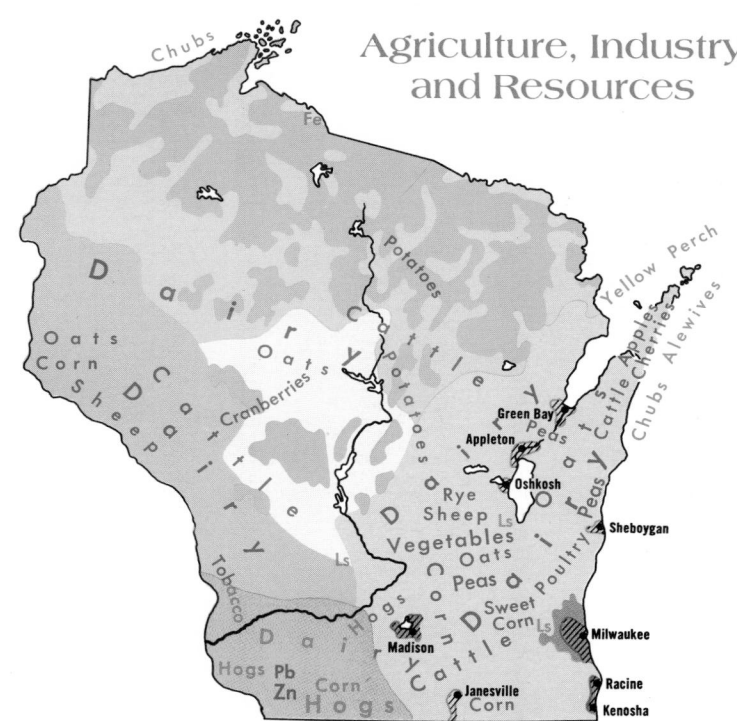

Agriculture, Industry and Resources

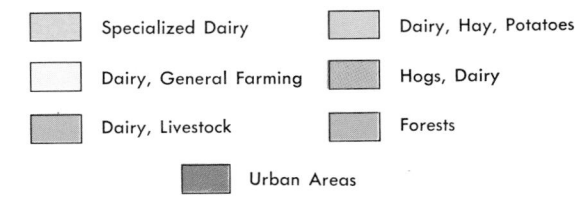

DOMINANT LAND USE

Specialized Dairy
Dairy, Hay, Potatoes
Dairy, General Farming
Hogs, Dairy
Dairy, Livestock
Forests
Urban Areas

MAJOR MINERAL OCCURRENCES

Fe Iron Ore
Pb Lead
Ls Limestone
Zn Zinc

Major Industrial Areas

Topography

0   40   80 MI.

0   40   80 KM.

Below Sea Level | 100 m. 328 ft. | 200 m. 656 ft. | 500 m. 1,640 ft. | 1,000 m. 3,281 ft. | 2,000 m. 6,562 ft. | 5,000 m. 16,404 ft.

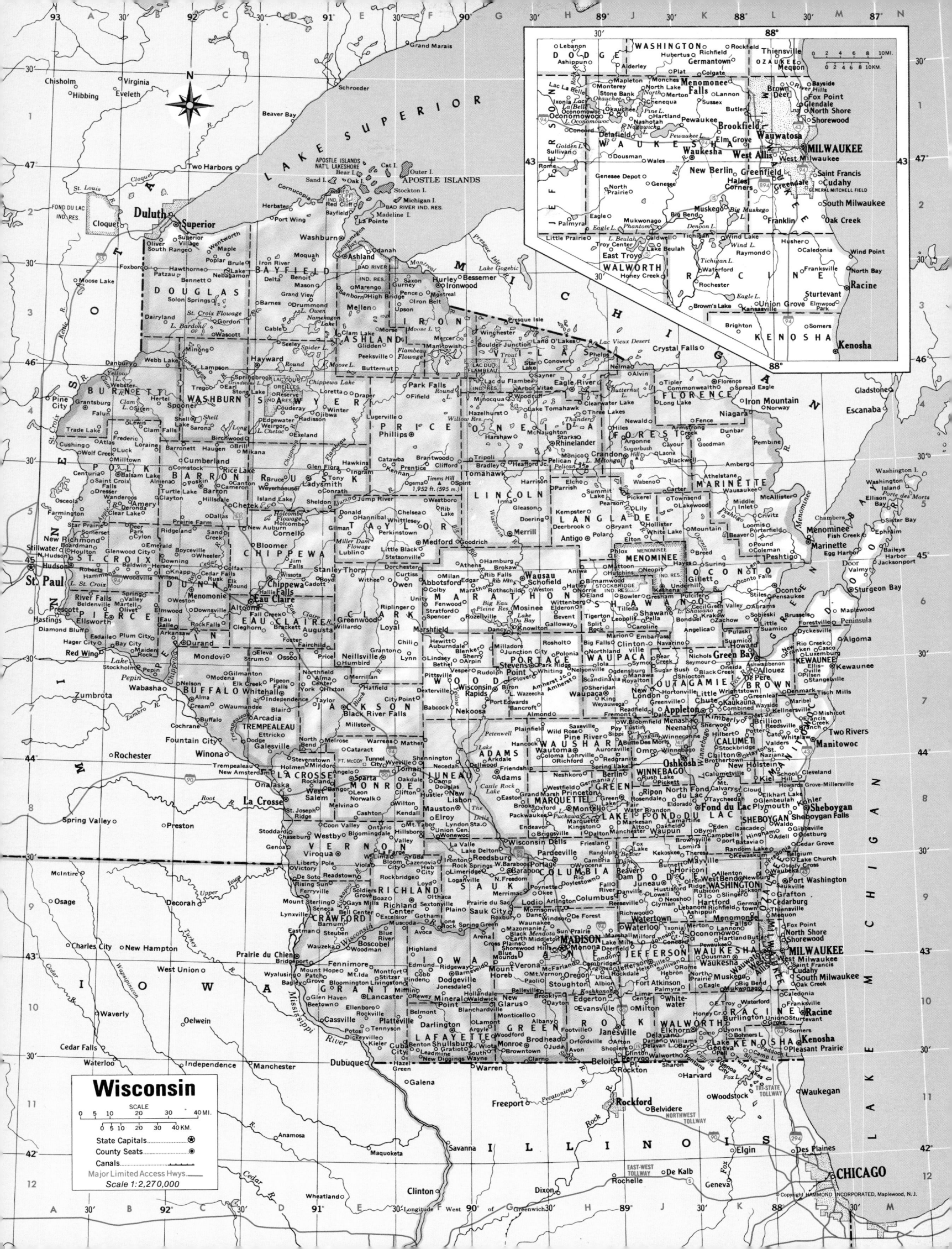

Wisconsin

SCALE
0 5 10 20 30 40 MI.
0 5 10 20 30 40 KM.

State Capitals ⊛
County Seats ◉
Canals
Major Limited Access Hwys
Scale 1:2,270,000

Copyright HAMMOND INCORPORATED, Maplewood, N.J.

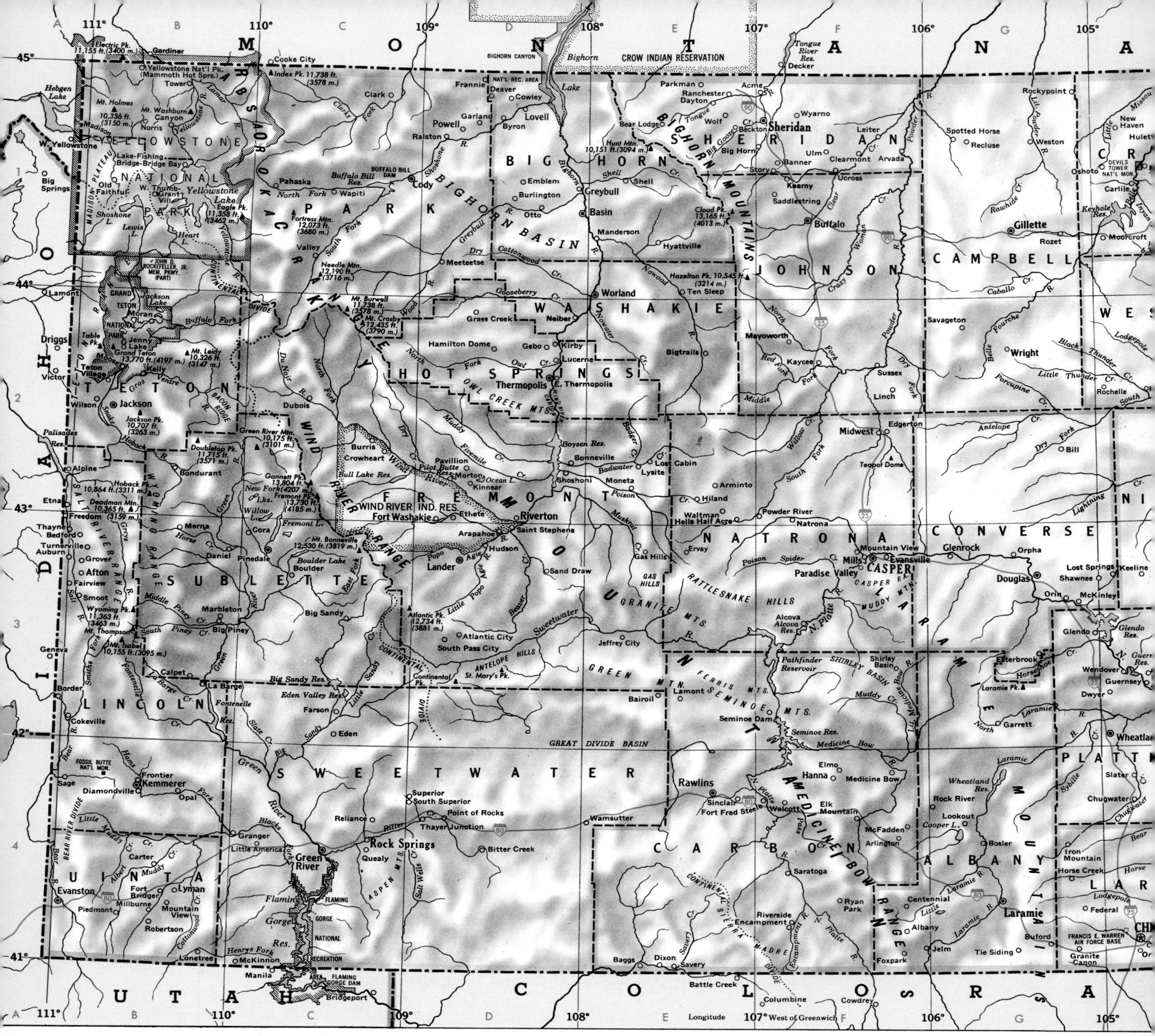

Agriculture, Industry and Resources

DOMINANT LAND USE

- Specialized Wheat
- Specialized Dairy
- General Farming, Livestock, Special Crops
- Sugar Beets, Dry Beans, Livestock, General Farming
- Range Livestock
- Forests
- Nonagricultural Land

MAJOR MINERAL OCCURRENCES

- **C** Coal
- **Cl** Clay
- **Fe** Iron Ore
- **G** Natural Gas
- **O** Petroleum
- **P** Phosphates
- **So** Soda Ash
- **U** Uranium
- **V** Vanadium
- ⚡ Water Power

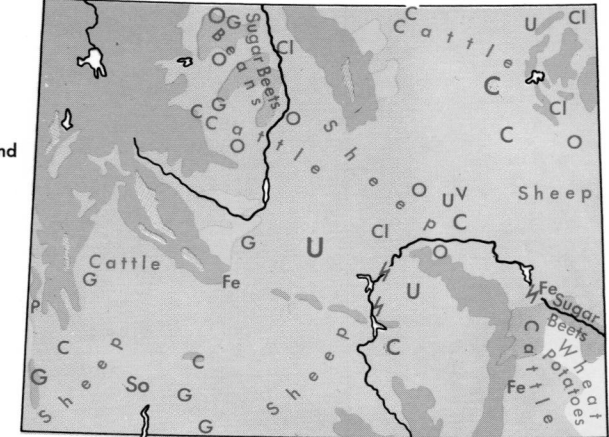

COUNTIES

Albany 29,062 .... G4
Big Horn 11,896 .... E1
Campbell 24,367 .... G1
Carbon 21,896 .... F4
Converse 14,069 .... G3
Crook 5,308 .... H1
Fremont 38,992 .... D2
Goshen 12,040 .... H4
Hot Springs 5,710 .... D2
Johnson 6,700 .... F1
Laramie 68,649 .... H4
Lincoln 12,177 .... B3
Natrona 71,856 .... F3
Niobrara 2,924 .... H2
Park 21,639 .... C1
Platte 11,975 .... H4
Sheridan 25,048 .... F1
Sublette 4,548 .... C3
Sweetwater 41,723 .... D4
Teton 9,355 .... B2
Uinta 13,021 .... B4
Washakie 9,496 .... E2
Weston 7,106 .... H2

CITIES and TOWNS

Zip	Name/Pop.	Key
83110	Afton 1,481	B3
82050	Albin 128	H4
82620	Alcova 275	F3

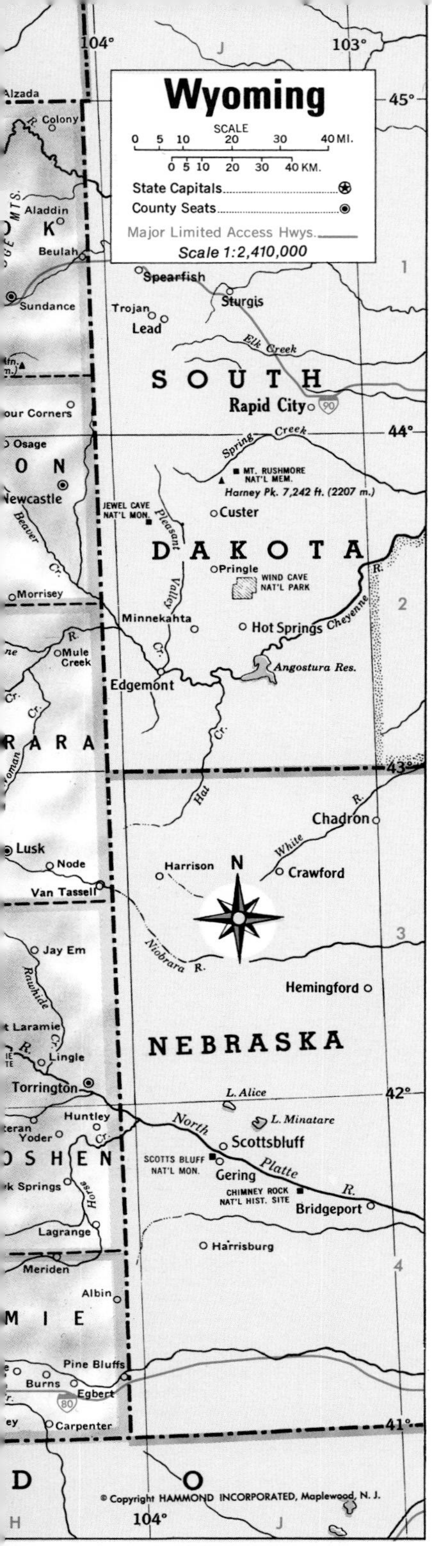

Wyoming
SCALE
0 5 10 20 30 40 MI.
0 5 10 20 30 40 KM.
State Capitals
County Seats
Major Limited Access Hwys.
Scale 1:2,410,000
SOUTH
DAKOTA
NEBRASKA
Spearfish
Sturgis
Lead
Rapid City
Custer
Pringle
Hot Springs
Edgemont
Chadron
Crawford
Harrison
Hemingford
Torrington
Scottsbluff
Gering
Bridgeport
Harrisburg
Lusk
Newcastle
Sundance
Beulah
Aladdin
Colony
Van Tassell
Lingle
Pine Bluffs
Burns
Egbert
Carpenter
Angostura Res.
Harney Pk. 7,242 ft. (2207 m.)
WIND CAVE NAT'L PARK
SCOTTS BLUFF NAT'L MON.
CHIMNEY ROCK NAT'L HIST. SITE
© Copyright HAMMOND INCORPORATED, Maplewood, N. J.

AREA 97,809 sq. mi. (253,325 sq. km.)
POPULATION 469,557
CAPITAL Cheyenne
LARGEST CITY Casper
HIGHEST POINT Gannett Pk. 13,804 ft. (4207 m.)
SETTLED IN 1834
ADMITTED TO UNION July 10, 1890
POPULAR NAME Equality State
STATE FLOWER Indian Paintbrush
STATE BIRD Meadowlark

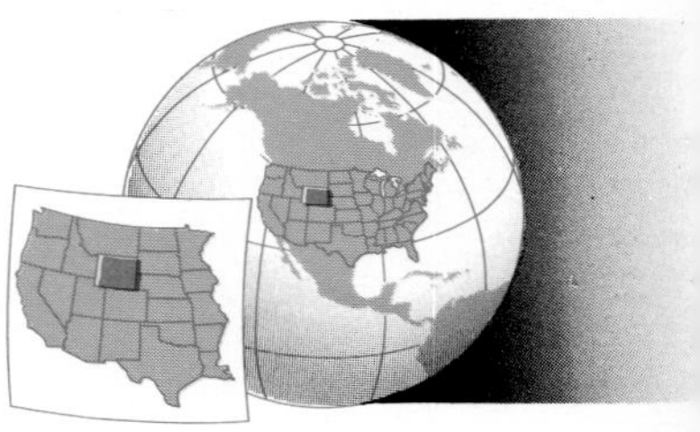

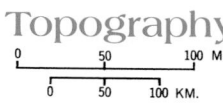

Topography

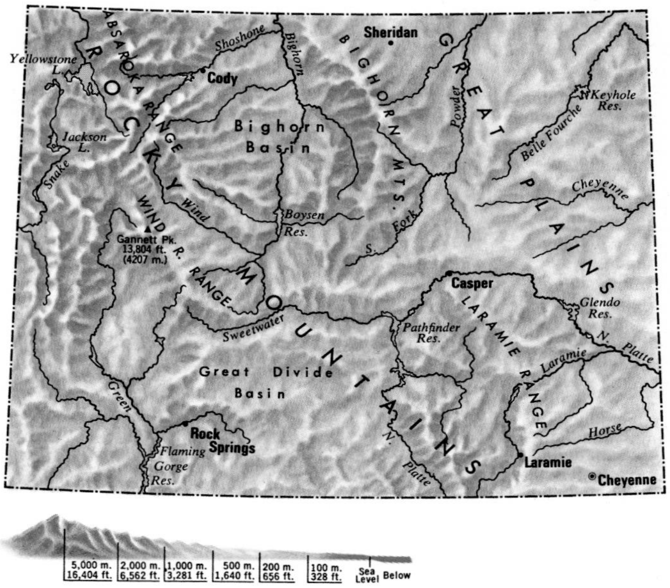

0 50 100 MI.
0 50 100 KM.
ROCKY MOUNTAINS
ABSAROKA RANGE
WIND R. RANGE
BIGHORN MTS.
GREAT PLAINS
LARAMIE RANGE
Bighorn Basin
Great Divide Basin
Sheridan
Cody
Casper
Rock Springs
Laramie
Cheyenne
Yellowstone L.
Jackson L.
Gannett Pk. 13,804 ft. (4207 m.)
Boysen Res.
Pathfinder Res.
Glendo Res.
Keyhole Res.
Flaming Gorge Res.
5,000 m. 16,404 ft.
2,000 m. 6,562 ft.
1,000 m. 3,281 ft.
500 m. 1,640 ft.
200 m. 656 ft.
100 m. 328 ft.
Sea Level
Below

82510 Arapahoe 682 .... D3
83111 Auburn 360 .... A3
82321 Baggs 433 .... E4
82322 Bairoil 300 .... E3
82410 Basin⊙ 1,349 .... E1
†82801 Beckton 110 .... E1
83112 Bedford 350 .... A3
82712 Beulah 184 .... H1
82833 Big Horn 350 .... E1
83113 Big Piney 530 .... B3
82051 Bosler 195 .... G4
82834 Buffalo⊙ 3,799 .... F1
82411 Burlington 300 .... D1
82053 Burns 268 .... H4
82412 Byron 633 .... D1
82601 Casper⊙ 51,016 .... F3
82055 Centennial 140 .... F4
82001 Cheyenne (cap.)⊙ 47,283 . H4
82210 Chugwater 282 .... H4
82835 Clearmont 191 .... F1
82414 Cody⊙ 6,790 .... D1
83114 Cokeville 515 .... B3
82420 Cowley 455 .... D1
82512 Crowheart 200 .... C2
83115 Daniel 130 .... B3
82836 Dayton 701 .... E1
82421 Deaver 178 .... D1
83116 Diamondville 1,000 .... B4
82323 Dixon 82 .... E4
82633 Douglas⊙ 6,030 .... G3
82513 Dubois 1,067 .... C2
†82443 East Thermopolis 359 .... D2
82926 Eden 198 .... C3
82635 Edgerton 510 .... F2
82324 Elk Mountain 338 .... F4
82325 Encampment 611 .... F4
83118 Etna 200 .... A2
82930 Evanston⊙ 6,421 .... B4
82636 Evansville 2,335 .... F3
83119 Fairview 150 .... B3
82932 Farson 350 .... C3
82933 Fort Bridger 300 .... B4
82212 Fort Laramie 356 .... H3
82514 Fort Washakie 400 .... C2
†82001 Fox Farm 2,850 .... H4
82423 Frannie 138 .... D1
83120 Freedom 400 .... B3
83121 Frontier 150 .... B4
82501 Gas Hills 150 .... E3
82716 Gillette⊙ 12,134 .... G1
82213 Glendo 367 .... G3
82637 Glenrock 2,736 .... G3
82934 Granger 177 .... C4
82425 Grass Creek 152 .... D2
82935 Green River⊙ 12,807 .... C4
82426 Greybull 2,277 .... E1
83122 Grover 425 .... B3
82214 Guernsey 1,512 .... H3
82327 Hanna 2,288 .... F4
82215 Hartville 149 .... H3
82060 Hillsdale 160 .... H4
82061 Horse Creek 225 .... G4
82515 Hudson 514 .... D3
82720 Hulett 291 .... H1
83001 Jackson⊙ 4,511 .... B2
82310 Jeffrey City 1,882 .... E3
82639 Kaycee 271 .... F2
83011 Kelly 100 .... B2
83101 Kemmerer⊙ 3,273 .... B4
82516 Kinnear 145 .... D2
82430 Kirby 129 .... D2
83123 La Barge 302 .... B3
82221 Lagrange 232 .... H4
82520 Lander⊙ 7,867 .... D3
82070 Laramie⊙ 24,410 .... G4
82640 Linch 187 .... F2
82223 Lingle 475 .... H3
82929 Little America 175 .... C4
†82642 Lost Cabin 25 .... E2
82224 Lost Springs 9 .... G3
82431 Lovell 2,447 .... D1
†82443 Lucerne 240 .... D2
82225 Lusk⊙ 1,650 .... H3
82937 Lyman 2,284 .... B4
82642 Lysite 175 .... E2
†82190 Mammoth Hot.Springs (Yellowstone Nat'l Park 350 .... B1
82432 Manderson 174 .... E1
82227 Manville 94 .... H3
†83113 Marbleton 537 .... B3
82938 McKinnon 135 .... C4
82329 Medicine Bow 953 .... F4
82433 Meeteetse 512 .... D1
82643 Midwest 638 .... F2
82644 Mills 2,139 .... F3
82721 Moorcroft 1,014 .... H1
83012 Moose 150 .... B2
83013 Moran 200 .... B2
†82601 Mountain View F3
82939 Mountain View 628 .... B4
82701 Newcastle⊙ 3,596 .... H2
82190 Old Faithful 75 .... B1
†82001 Orchard Valley 3,327 .... H4
82723 Osage 500 .... H2
†82601 Paradise Valley F3
82523 Pavillion 287 .... D2
82082 Pine Bluffs 1,077 .... H4
82941 Pinedale⊙ 1,066 .... C3
82942 Point of Rocks 425 .... D4
82435 Powell 5,310 .... D1
82839 Ranchester 655 .... E1
82301 Rawlins⊙ 11,547 .... E4
82725 Recluse 225 .... G1
82943 Reliance 325 .... C4
†82325 Riverside 55 .... F4
82501 Riverton 9,247 .... D2
82944 Robertson 142 .... B4
82083 Rock River 415 .... G4
82901 Rock Springs 19,458 .... C4
82331 Saratoga 2,410 .... F4
82801 Sheridan⊙ 15,146 .... F1
82615 Shirley Basin 400 .... F3
82649 Shoshoni 879 .... D2
82334 Sinclair 586 .... E4
83126 Smoot 310 .... B3
†82945 South Superior 586 .... D4
82842 Story 637 .... F1
82729 Sundance⊙ 1,087 .... H1
82945 Superior 500 .... D4
82442 Ten Sleep 407 .... E1
83127 Thayne 256 .... A3
82443 Thermopolis⊙ 3,852 .... D2
82240 Torrington⊙ 5,441 .... H3
82730 Upton 1,193 .... H1
82242 Van Tassell 10 .... H3
82335 Walcott 200 .... F4
82336 Wamsutter 681 .... E4
82201 Wheatland⊙ 5,816 .... H3
83014 Wilson 480 .... B2
82401 Worland⊙ 6,391 .... E1
82732 Wright 1,117 .... G2
82190 Yellowstone Nat'l Pk. 350 .. B1
82244 Yoder 110 .... H4

OTHER FEATURES

Absaroka (range) C1
Antelope (creek) G2
Antelope (hills) D3
Aspen (mts.) C4
Atlantic (peak) D3
Badwater (creek) E2
Bear (creek) H4
Bear (riv.) B4
Bear Lodge (mts.) H1
Bear River Divide (mts.) B4
Beaver (creek) D3
Beaver (creek) H2
Belle Fourche (riv.) H1
Big Goose (creek) E1
Bighorn (basin) D1
Bighorn (lake) D1
Bighorn (mts.) E1
Bighorn (riv.) D1
Bighorn Canyon Nat'l Rec. Area D1
Big Sandy (riv.) C3
Bitter (creek) C4
Blacks Fork, Green (riv.) C4
Black Thunder (creek) G2
Bonneville (mt.) C3
Boysen (res.) D2
Buffalo Bill (dam) C1
Buffalo Bill (res.) C1
Buffalo Fork, Snake (riv.) B2
Burwell (mt.) C2
Caballo (creek) G1
Casper (range) F3
Cheyenne (riv.) H2
Chugwater (creek) H4
Clarks Fork (riv.) C1
Clear (creek) F1
Cloud (peak) E1
Cottonwood (creek) B4
Crazy Woman (creek) F1
Crosby (mt.) C2
Crow (creek) H4
Deadman (mt.) B2
Devils Tower Nat'l Mon. H1
Doubletop (peak) B2
Dry (creek) C2
Dry Cottonwood (creek) D1
Eagle (peak) B1
Fivemile (creek) D2
Flaming Gorge (res.) C4
Flaming Gorge Nat'l Rec. Area C4
Fontenelle (creek) B3
Fontenelle (res.) B3
Fort Laramie Nat'l Hist. Site H3
Fortress (mt.) C1
Fossil Butte Nat'l Mon. B4
Francis E. Warren A.F.B. 3,627 .... G4
Fremont (lake) C3
Fremont (peak) C2
Gannett (peak) C2
Gas (hills) E3
Glendo (res.) H3
Gooseberry (creek) D1
Grand Teton (mt.) B2
Grand Teton Nat'l Park B2
Granite (mts.) E3
Great Divide (basin) E3
Green (mt.) E3
Green (riv.) C4
Green, East Fork (riv.) C3
Green River (mt.) C2
Greybull (riv.) D1
Greys (riv.) B3
Gros Ventre (riv.) B2
Guernsey (res.) H3
Hams Fork (riv.) B4
Hazelton (peak) E1
Henrys Fork, Green (riv.) C4
Hoback (peak) B2
Hoback (riv.) B2
Holmes (mt.) B1
Horse (creek) H4
Horseshoe (creek) G3
Hunt (mt.) E1
Index (peak) C1
Inyan Kara (creek) H1
Inyan Kara (mt.) H1
Isabel (mt.) B3
Jackson (lake) B2
Jackson (peak) B2
John D. Rockefeller, Jr., Mem. Pkwy. B1
Keyhole (res.) H1
Lamar (riv.) B1
Lance (creek) H2
Laramie (mts.) G3
Laramie (peak) G3
Laramie (riv.) G4
Leidy (mt.) B2
Lewis (lake) B1
Lightning (creek) G2
Little Missouri (riv.) H1
Little Muddy (creek) B4
Little Powder (riv.) G1
Little Sandy (creek) C3
Little Thunder (creek) G2
Lodgepole (creek) H2
Lodgepole (creek) H4
Madison (plat.) B1
Medicine Bow (range) F4
Medicine Bow (riv.) F3
Middle Piney (creek) B3
Muddy (creek) D2
Muskrat (creek) E2
Needle (mt.) C1
Niobrara (riv.) J3
North Laramie (riv.) G3
North Platte (riv.) H3
Nowater (creek) E2
Nowood (riv.) E1
Owl, North Fork (creek) D2
Owl Creek (mts.) D2
Palisades (res.) A2
Pass (creek) F4
Pathfinder (res.) F3
Poison (creek) E2
Poison Spider (creek) F3
Popo Agie (riv.) D3
Powder (riv.) F2
Rattlesnake (range) E3
Rawhide (creek) G1
Rawhide (creek) H3
Rocky (mts.) C1
Salt (riv.) B3
Salt River (range) B3
Salt Wells (creek) D4
Seminoe (mts.) E3
Seminoe (res.) F3
Shell (creek) E1
Shirley (basin) F3
Shoshone (lake) B1
Shoshone (riv.) D1
Sierra Madre (mts.) E4
Slate (creek) C3
Smiths Fork (riv.) B3
Snake (riv.) B2
South Cheyenne (riv.) H2
South Piney (creek) B3
Sweetwater (riv.) D3
Sybille (creek) G4
Teapot Dome (mt.) F2
Teton (range) B2
Tongue (riv.) E1
Washburn (mt.) B1
Wheatland (res.) G4
Willow (creek) F2
Wind (riv.) C2
Wind River (canyon) D2
Wind River (range) C2
Wind River Ind. Res. C2
Wood (riv.) C2
Wyoming (peak) B3
Wyoming (range) B2
Yellowstone (lake) B1
Yellowstone (riv.) B1
Yellowstone Nat'l Park B1

⊙County seat.
† Zip of nearest p.o. * Multiple zips.

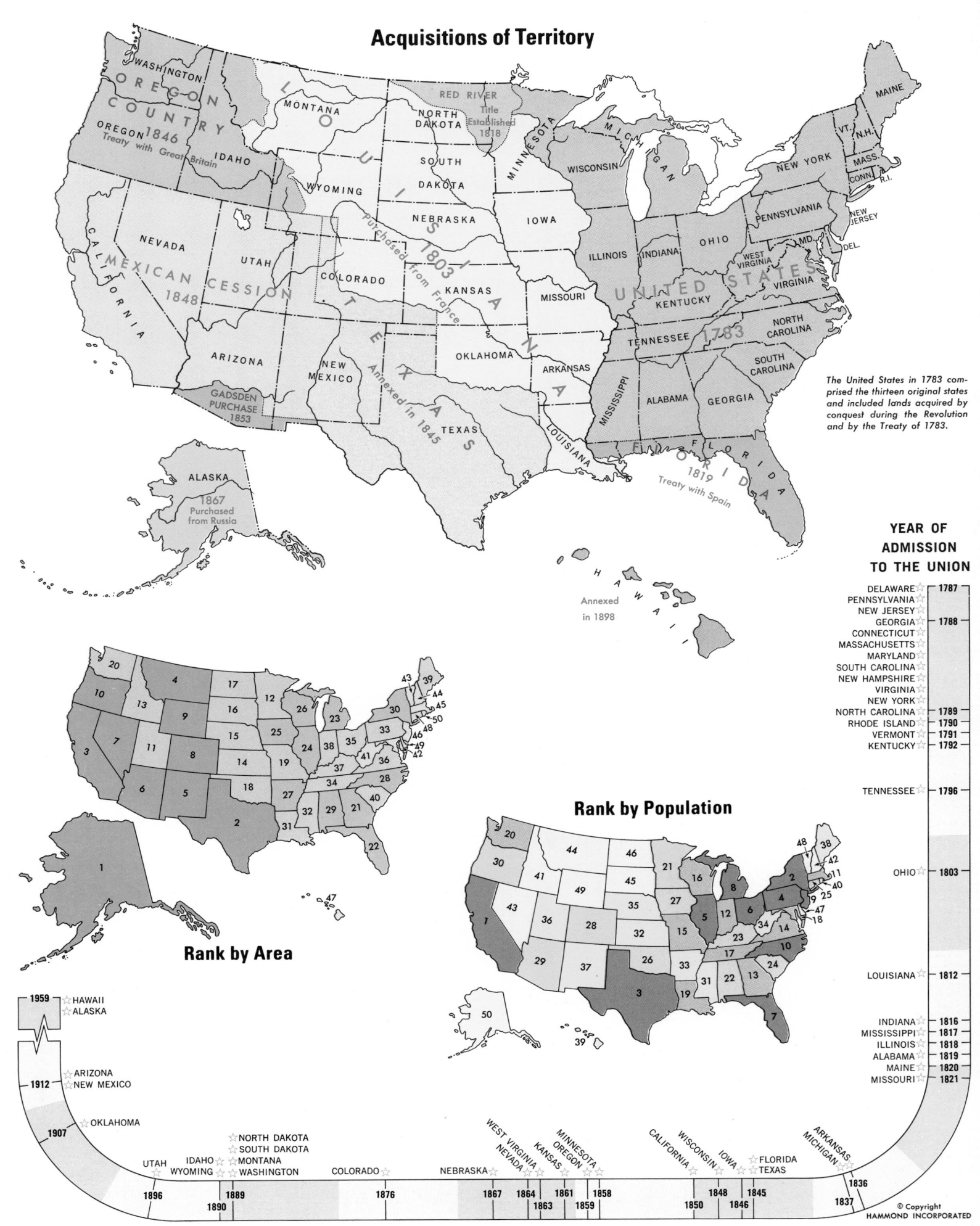

Acquisitions of Territory

WASHINGTON
OREGON COUNTRY
OREGON 1846
Treaty with Great Britain
IDAHO
MONTANA
NORTH DAKOTA
RED RIVER
Title Established 1818
MINNESOTA
MICHIGAN
MAINE
VT. N.H.
NEW YORK
MASS.
CONN. R.I.
CALIFORNIA
NEVADA
UTAH
WYOMING
SOUTH DAKOTA
NEBRASKA
IOWA
WISCONSIN
PENNSYLVANIA
NEW JERSEY
MEXICAN CESSION 1848
COLORADO
KANSAS
MISSOURI
ILLINOIS
INDIANA
OHIO
WEST VIRGINIA
MD.
DEL.
UNITED STATES
KENTUCKY
VIRGINIA
ARIZONA
NEW MEXICO
OKLAHOMA
ARKANSAS
TENNESSEE 1783
NORTH CAROLINA
SOUTH CAROLINA
GADSDEN PURCHASE 1853
Annexed in 1845
TEXAS
LOUISIANA
MISSISSIPPI
ALABAMA
GEORGIA
LOUISIANA
FLORIDA 1819
Treaty with Spain
Purchased from France
L O U I S I A N A 1803
ALASKA
1867 Purchased from Russia

HAWAII
Annexed in 1898

The United States in 1783 comprised the thirteen original states and included lands acquired by conquest during the Revolution and by the Treaty of 1783.

Rank by Area

20, 4, 17, 43, 39, 44, 45, 50, 10, 13, 16, 12, 26, 23, 30, 48, 46, 49, 42, 9, 7, 11, 15, 25, 38, 35, 33, 41, 36, 3, 8, 14, 19, 37, 28, 6, 5, 18, 34, 40, 32, 29, 21, 22, 2, 31, 1, 47

Rank by Population

20, 48, 38, 42, 30, 44, 46, 21, 11, 40, 41, 16, 8, 2, 25, 47, 1, 43, 49, 45, 27, 5, 12, 6, 4, 18, 36, 28, 35, 15, 23, 34, 14, 29, 32, 17, 10, 37, 26, 33, 31, 22, 13, 24, 3, 19, 7, 50, 39

YEAR OF ADMISSION TO THE UNION

DELAWARE ☆	1787
PENNSYLVANIA ☆	
NEW JERSEY ☆	
GEORGIA ☆	1788
CONNECTICUT ☆	
MASSACHUSETTS ☆	
MARYLAND ☆	
SOUTH CAROLINA ☆	
NEW HAMPSHIRE ☆	
VIRGINIA ☆	
NEW YORK ☆	
NORTH CAROLINA ☆	1789
RHODE ISLAND ☆	1790
VERMONT ☆	1791
KENTUCKY ☆	1792
TENNESSEE ☆	1796
OHIO ☆	1803
LOUISIANA ☆	1812
INDIANA ☆	1816
MISSISSIPPI ☆	1817
ILLINOIS ☆	1818
ALABAMA ☆	1819
MAINE ☆	1820
MISSOURI ☆	1821

1959 ☆HAWAII ☆ALASKA
1912 ☆ARIZONA ☆NEW MEXICO
1907 ☆OKLAHOMA
☆UTAH
☆WYOMING
☆IDAHO ☆WASHINGTON
☆NORTH DAKOTA
☆SOUTH DAKOTA
☆MONTANA
COLORADO ☆
WEST VIRGINIA
NEVADA
KANSAS
OREGON
MINNESOTA
NEBRASKA
CALIFORNIA
WISCONSIN
IOWA
☆FLORIDA
TEXAS
ARKANSAS
MICHIGAN
1896
1890
1889
1876
1867
1864
1863
1861
1859
1858
1850
1848
1846
1845
1836
1837

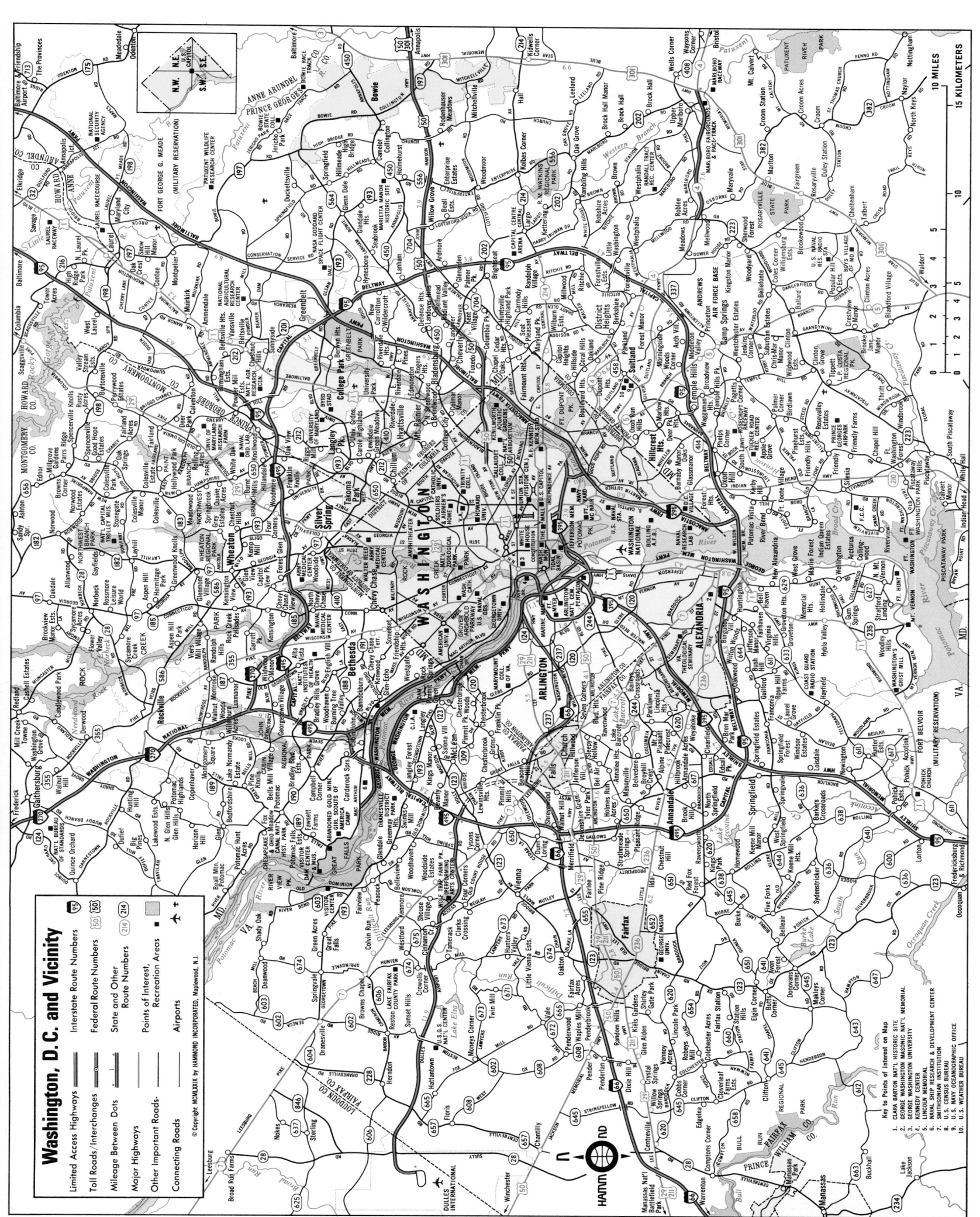

Washington, D.C. and Vicinity

Limited Access Highways	Interstate Route Numbers
Toll Roads/Interchanges	Federal Route Numbers
Mileage Between Dots	State and Other Route Numbers
Major Highways	Points of Interest, Recreation Areas
Other Important Roads	Airports
Connecting Roads	

© Copyright MCMLXXIV by HAMMOND INCORPORATED, Maplewood, N.J.

Key to Points of Interest on Map
1. Clark Barton Nat'l Historic Site
2. George Washington Masonic Memorial
3. George Washington University
4. Kennedy Center
5. Lincoln Memorial
6. Naval Ship Research & Development Center
7. Smithsonian Institution
8. U.S. Census Bureau
9. U.S. Naval Oceanographic Office
10. U.S. Weather Bureau

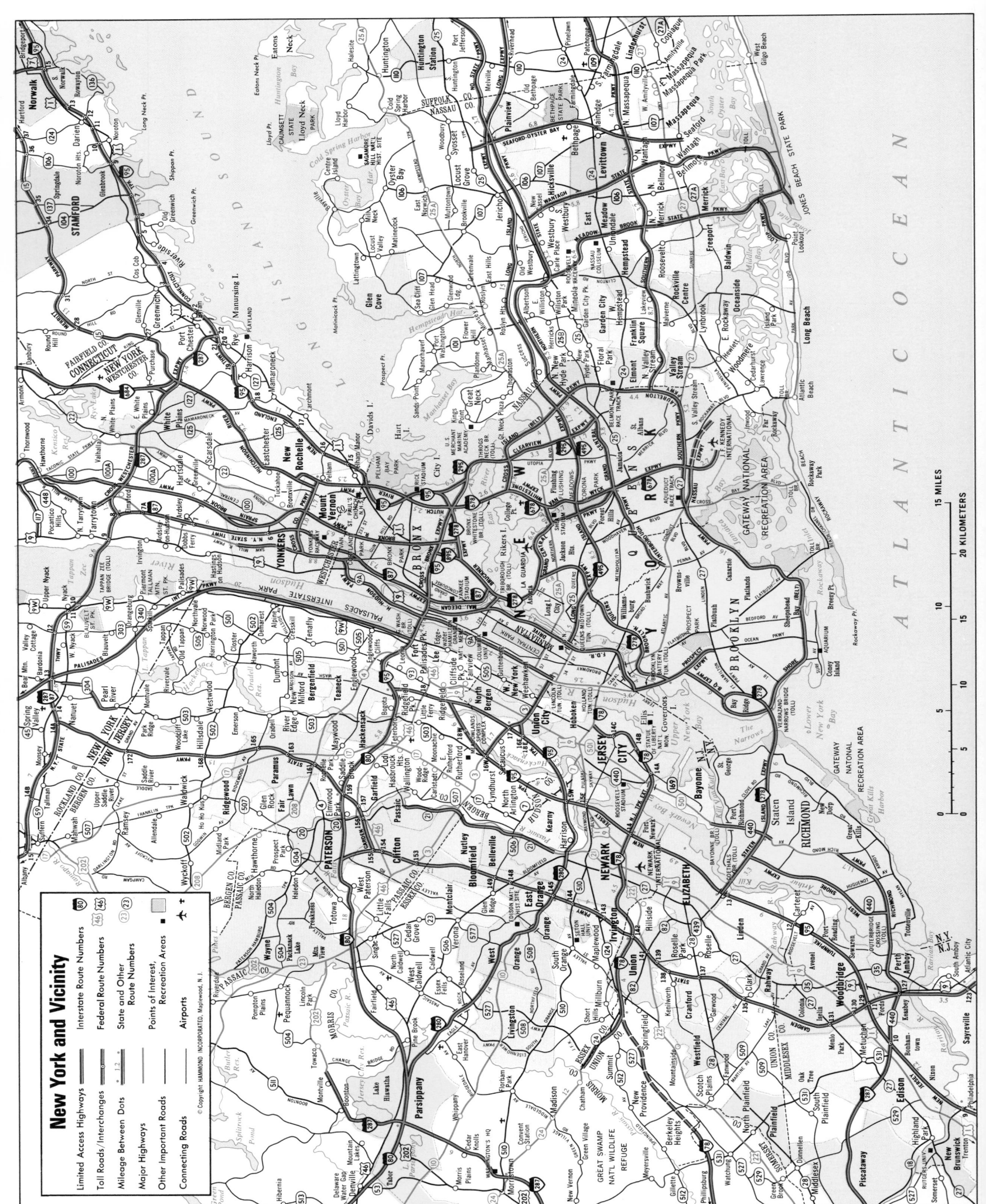

New York and Vicinity

Limited Access Highways	Interstate Route Numbers
Toll Roads/Interchanges	Federal Route Numbers
Mileage Between Dots	State and Other Route Numbers
Major Highways	Points of Interest, Recreation Areas
Other Important Roads	Airports
Connecting Roads	

© Copyright HAMMOND INCORPORATED, Maplewood, N.J.

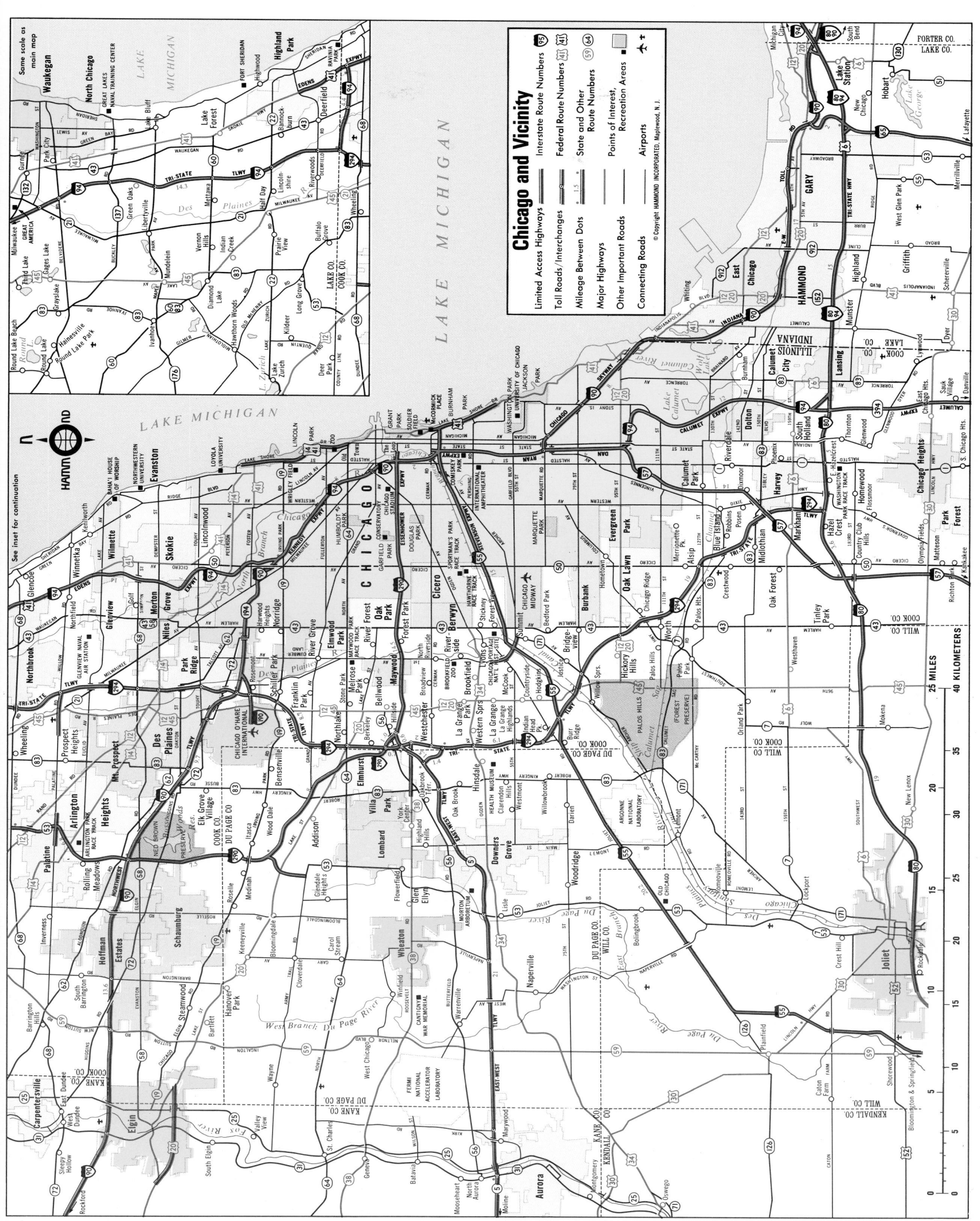

Chicago and Vicinity

Limited Access Highways	Interstate Route Numbers 95	State and Other Route Numbers 59 64
Toll Roads/Interchanges	Federal Route Numbers 41	Points of Interest, Recreation Areas
Mileage Between Dots *.5*		
Major Highways		Airports
Other Important Roads		
Connecting Roads		

© Copyright HAMMOND INCORPORATED, Maplewood, N.J.

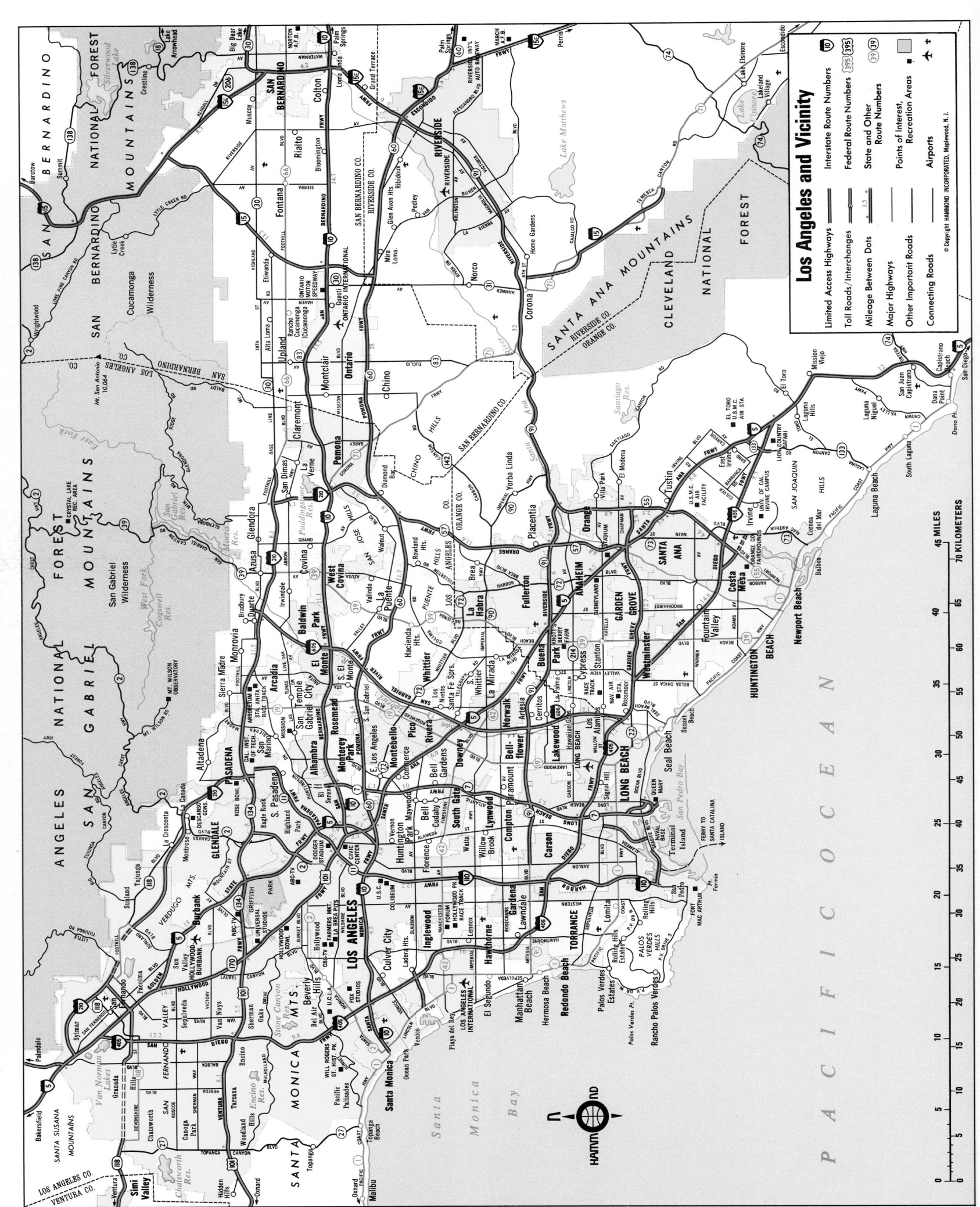

Los Angeles and Vicinity

10	Interstate Route Numbers
395	Federal Route Numbers
39	State and Other Route Numbers
	Points of Interest, Recreation Areas
	Airports

Limited Access Highways
Toll Roads/Interchanges
Mileage Between Dots
Major Highways
Other Important Roads
Connecting Roads

© Copyright HAMMOND INCORPORATED, Maplewood, N.J.

45 MILES
70 KILOMETERS

HAMMOND

INDEX OF THE WORLD

Introduction

This index is a directory to the atlas as a whole. It contains an alphabetical listing of the major political divisions (countries and administrative subdivisions, i.e., states, provinces, departments), principal cities and towns, and geographical features, such as mountains, rivers, bays, islands, shown on the maps contained in this atlas.

Entries are generally indexed to the map or inset having the largest scale, but in some cases, where the entry has equal coverage or is important to its surroundings on more than one map, more than one reference is given.

Each entry gives the political division in which it is located, or in the case of certain geographical features the appropriate continent or regional name, and the page number of the map on which the name will be found. The user who is unfamiliar with a place name will thus be able to identify the political division to which it belongs and to locate quickly the appropriate map or maps.

Once having found the map listed in this index, the user will easily find the place name on the map by first locating it in the accompanying map index. Here the user will find the necessary index key reference. When there is more than one place of the same name on the same map, only one reference is given. The individual map index will give the multiple listings of names and key references. A glance at adjacent pages will show whether there are additional maps on which the place name may be found, by referring to the accompanying index or by looking in the same relative location on the map.

The abbreviations for the political division names and geographical terms are explained in the glossary in the front of the atlas. In some cases place names have been shortened here. The full name will be found in the individual index accompanying the map itself.

A

Aa (river), Switz., 39
Aachen, W. Ger., 22
Aalen, W. Ger., 22
Aalst, Belg., 27
Äänekoski, Fin., 18
Aarau, Switz., 39
Aare (river), Switz., 39
Aargau (canton), Switz., 39
Aba, Nigeria, 106
Aba as Saud, Saudi Arabia, 59
Abacaxis (riv.), Brazil, 132
Abadan, Iran, 66
Abadeh, Iran, 66
Abadla, Algeria, 106
Abaetetuba, Brazil, 132
Abagnar, China, 77
Abaiang (atoll), Kiribati, 87
Abajo (mts.), Utah, 304
Abakan, U.S.S.R., 48
Abancay, Peru, 128
Abarqu, Iran, 66
Abashiri, Japan, 81
Abau, Papua N.G., 85
Abay (riv.), Ethiopia, 111
Abaya (lake), Ethiopia, 111
Abbe (lake), Africa, 111
Abbeville, Ala., 195
Abbeville, France, 28
Abbeville, La., 238
Abbeville, S.C., 296
Abbeyfeale, Ireland, 17
Abbottabad, Pakistan, 68
Abdulino, U.S.S.R., 52
Abéché, Chad, 111
Abemama (atoll), Kiribati, 87
Abengourou, Ivory Coast, 106
Åbenrå, Den., 21
Abeokuta, Nigeria, 106
Aberaeron, Wales, 13
Abercorn (Mbala), Zambia, 114
Aberdare, Wales, 13
Aberdeen, Md., 245
Aberdeen, Miss., 256
Aberdeen (lake), N.W. Terr., 187
Aberdeen (co.), Scotland, 15
Aberdeen, Scotland, 15
Aberdeen, S. Dak., 298
Aberdeen, Wash., 310
Aberfeldy, Scotland, 15
Abergavenny, Wales, 13
Abergele, Wales, 13
Abertillery, Wales, 13
Aberystwyth, Wales, 13
Abha, Saudi Arabia, 59
Abidjan (cap.), Ivory Coast, 106
Abilene, Kans., 232
Abilene, Texas, 303
Abingdon, England, 13
Abingdon, Ill., 222
Abingdon, Va., 307
Abington, Pa., 294
Abitibi (lake), Ontario, 175
Abitibi (riv.), Ontario, 177
Abkhaz A.S.S.R., U.S.S.R., 52
Abnûb, Egypt, 111
Åbo (Turku), Fin., 18
Abomey, Benin, 106
Abony, Hung., 41
Abor (hills), India, 68
Abqaiq, Saudi Arabia, 59
Abra (prov.), Phil., 82
Abraham Lincoln Birthplace Nat'l Hist. Site, Ky., 237
Abruzzi (reg.), Italy, 34
Absecon, N.J., 273
Abu 'Arish, Saudi Arabia, 59
Abu Dara, Ras (cape), Sudan, 111
Abu Dhabi (cap.), U.A.E., 59
Abu Hadriya, Saudi Arabia, 59
Abu Hamed, Sudan, 111
Abu Kemal, Syria, 63
Abu-Mad, Ras (cape), Saudi Arabia, 59
Abu Road, India, 68
Abu Shagara, Ras (cape), Sudan, 111
Abu Zabad, Sudan, 111
Abydos (ruins), Egypt, 111
Abydos (ruins), Turkey, 63
Acadia Nat'l Park, Maine, 243
Acadia Valley, Alberta, 182
Acajutla, El Salv., 154
Acámbaro, Mexico, 150
Acaponeta, Mexico, 150
Acapulco de Juarez, Mexico, 150
Acarai (mts.), Guyana, 131
Acarigua, Venez., 124
Acatlán de Osorio, Mexico, 150
Acatzingo de Hidalgo, Mexico, 150
Accra (cap.), Ghana, 106
Accrington, England, 10
Achacachi, Bolivia, 136
Achalpur, India, 68
Achill (isl.), Ireland, 17
Achnasheen, Scotland, 15
Acireale, Italy, 34
Acklins (isl.), Bahamas, 156
Aconcagua, Cerro (mt.), Arg., 143
Aconcagua (prov.), Chile, 138
Aconchi, Mexico, 150
Acoyapa, Nicaragua, 154
Acqui Terme, Italy, 34
Acre (state), Brazil, 132
Acre (riv.), Brazil, 132
Acre, Israel, 65
Acri, Italy, 34
Actopan, Mexico, 150
Ada, Minn., 255
Ada, Ohio, 284
Ada, Okla., 288
Adam, Oman, 59
Adamawa (reg.), Africa, 115
Adams, Mass., 249
Adam's (peak), Sri Lanka, 68
Adams (mt.), Wash., 310
Adam's Bridge (shoals), Asia, 68
Adams Nat'l Hist. Site, Mass., 249
Adamstown (cap.), Pitcairn Is., 87
Adana (prov.), Turkey, 63
Adana, Turkey, 63
Adapazarı, Turkey, 63
Adare (cape), Antarc., 5
Adda (riv.), Italy, 34
Addis Ababa (cap.), Ethiopia, 111
Addis Alam, Ethiopia, 111
Addison, Ill., 222
Ad Diwaniya, Iraq, 66
Adel, Ga., 217
Adelaide (isl.), Antarc., 5
Adelaide (pen.), N.W. Terr., 187
Adelaide (cap.), S. Australia, 94
Adelaide River, N. Terr., 93
Adélie Coast (reg.), Antarc., 5
Aden (gulf), 54
Aden (cap.), P.D.R. Yemen, 59
Adige (riv.), Italy, 34
Adilabad, India, 68
Adirondack (mts.), N.Y., 276
Adıyaman (prov.), Turkey, 63
Adjuntas, P. Rico, 161
Admiralty (isls.), Papua N.G., 87
Admiralty (gulf), W. Australia, 92
Ado, Nigeria, 106
Adoni, India, 68
Adour (riv.), France, 28
Adra, Spain, 33
Adrano, Italy, 34
Adrar, Algeria, 106
Adrar (reg.), Mauritania, 106
Adrar des Iforas (plat.), Africa, 106
Adria, Italy, 34
Adrian, Mich., 250
Adriatic (sea), Europe, 7
Adwa, Ethiopia, 111
Adygey Aut. Oblast, U.S.S.R., 52
Adzhar A.S.S.R., U.S.S.R., 52
Aegean (sea), 45
Aegean Islands (reg.), Greece, 45
Afghanistan, 68
Åfjord, Norway, 18
Afmadu, Somalia, 115
Africa, 102
Afton, Wyo., 319
Afyonkarahisar (prov.), Turkey, 63
Afyonkarahisar, Turkey, 63
Agadès, Niger, 106
Agadir, Mor., 106
Agaña (cap.), Guam, 87
Agartala, India, 68
Agate Fossil Beds Nat'l Mon., Nebr., 264
Agats, Indonesia, 85
Agatti (isl.), India, 68
Agboville, Ivory Coast, 106
Agdam, U.S.S.R., 52
Agde, France, 28
Agen, France, 28
Aginsk Buryat Aut. Okr., U.S.S.R., 48
Aginskoye, U.S.S.R., 48
Agiobampo (bay), Mexico, 150
Agira, Italy, 34
Agordat, Ethiopia, 111
Agra, India, 68
Ağrı (prov.), Turkey, 63
Ağrı (Karaköse), Turkey, 63
Agrigento (prov.), Italy, 34
Agrigento, Italy, 34
Agrihan (isl.), N. Marianas, 87
Agrinion, Greece, 45
Agryz, U.S.S.R., 52
Aguada, P. Rico, 161
Aguadilla (dist.), P. Rico, 161
Aguadilla, P. Rico, 161
Aguadulce, Panama, 154
Aguán (riv.), Honduras, 154
Aguanaval (riv.), Mexico, 150
Aguanus (riv.), Canada, 174
Agua Prieta, Mexico, 150
Aguarico (riv.), S. Amer., 128
Aguas Buenas, P. Rico, 161
Aguascalientes (state), Mexico, 150
Aguascalientes, Mexico, 150
Agueda, Portugal, 33
Aguilar, Colo., 208
Aguilar, Spain, 33
Aguilas, Spain, 33
Aguililla, Mexico, 150
Aguja (pt.), Peru, 128
Agulhas (cape), S. Africa, 118
Agusan del Norte (prov.), Phil., 82
Agusan del Sur (prov.), Phil., 82
Ahaggar (range), Algeria, 10
Ahau, Fiji, 87
Ahlen, W. Ger., 22
Ahmadabad, India, 68
Ahmadnagar, India, 68
Ahmadpur East, Pakistan, 68
Ahoskie, N.C., 281
Ahrensburg, W. Ger., 22
Ahuacatlán, Mexico, 150
Ahuachapán, El Salv., 154
Ahuás, Honduras, 154
Ahurei, Fr. Poly., 87
Åhus, Sweden, 18
Ahvaz (Ahwaz), Iran, 66
Ahvenanmaa (prov.), Fin., 18
Ahwar, P.D.R. Yemen, 59
Aibonito, P. Rico, 161
Aichi (pref.), Japan, 81
Aiea, Hawaii, 218
Aiguá, Uruguay, 145
Aihui (Heihe), China, 77
Aiken, S.C., 296
Ailinglapalap (atoll), Marshall Is., 87
Ailuk (atoll), Marshall Is., 87
Ain (dept.), France, 28
Ain (riv.), France, 28
Aina Haina, Hawaii, 218
'Ain al Mubarrak, Saudi Arabia, 59
Aïn Beïda, Algeria, 106
Aïn Sefra, Algeria, 106
Ainsworth, Nebr., 264
Aïn Temouchent, Algeria, 106
Aïon el Atrous, Mauritania, 106
Air (mts.), Niger, 106
Airdrie, Scotland, 15
Aire (riv.), England, 13
Air Force (isl.), N.W. Terr., 187
Air Force Acad., Colo., 208
Aisén del Geral. Carlos Ibáñez del Campo (prov.), Chile, 138
Aisne (dept.), France, 28
Aisne (riv.), France, 28
Aitape, Papua N.G., 85
Aitkin, Minn., 255
Aitutaki (atoll), Cook Is., 87
Aiud, Romania, 45
Aix-en-Provence, France, 28
Aix-les-Bains, France, 28
Aíyina, Greece, 45
Aíyion, Greece, 45
Aizuwakamatsu, Japan, 81
Aizwal, India, 68
Ajaccio, France, 28
Ajaccio (gulf), France, 28
Ajanta, India, 68
Ajax, Ontario, 177
Ajedabia, Libya, 111
Ajka, Hung., 41
'Ajlun (gov.), Jordan, 65
'Ajman, U.A.E., 59
Ajmer, India, 68
Ajo, Ariz., 198
Akashi, Japan, 81
Akdağ (mt.), Turkey, 63
Aken, E. Ger., 22
Akershus (co.), Norway, 18
Aketi, Zaire, 114
Akhaltsikhe, U.S.S.R., 52
Akhdar, Jebel (mts.), Libya, 111
Akhdar, Jebel (range), Oman, 59
Akhisar, Turkey, 63
Akhtopol, Bulg., 45
Akhtubinsk, U.S.S.R., 52
Akhtyrka, U.S.S.R., 52
Akita (pref.), Japan, 81
Akita, Japan, 81
Akjoujt, Mauritania, 106
Akkerman (Belgorod-Dnestrovskiy), U.S.S.R., 52
Aklan (prov.), Phil., 82
Aklavik, N.W. Terr., 187
Akmolinsk (Tselinograd), U.S.S.R., 48
Akobo (riv.), Africa, 111
Akola, India, 68
Akpatok (isl.), N.W. Terr., 187
Akritas (cape), Greece, 45
Akron, N.Y., 276
Akron, Ohio, 284
Akşehir, Turkey, 63
Aksu, China, 77
Aksum, Ethiopia, 111
Aktí (pen.), Greece, 45
Aktyubinsk, U.S.S.R., 48
Akureyri, Iceland, 21
Akyab (Sittwe), Burma, 72
Ål, Norway, 18
Alabama (riv.), Ala., 195
Alabama (state), U.S., 195
Alabat (isl.), Phil., 82
Alagir, U.S.S.R., 52
Alagoas (state), Brazil, 132
Alagoinhas, Brazil, 132
Alagón, Spain, 33
Al Ahqaf (Bahr es Safi) (des.), Saudi Arabia, 59
Alajuela, C. Rica, 154
Alakol' (lake), U.S.S.R., 48
Alameda, Calif., 204
Alamikamba, Nicaragua, 154
Alamo, Texas, 303
Alamogordo, N. Mex., 274
Alamo Hts., Texas, 303
Álamos, Mexico, 150
Alamosa, Colo., 208
Åland (isls.), Fin., 18
Alanje, Panama, 154
Alanya, Turkey, 63
Alaotra (lake), Madagascar, 118
Alaşehir, Turkey, 63
Alashan (Alxa Shamo) (des.), China, 77
Alaska (gulf), Alaska, 196
Alaska (pen.), Alaska, 196
Alaska (range), Alaska, 196
Alaska (state), U.S., 196
Alassio, Italy, 34
Alatri, Italy, 34
Alatyr', U.S.S.R., 52
Alausí, Ecuador, 128
Álava (prov.), Spain, 33
Alavus, Fin., 18
Alayor, Spain, 33
Al 'Aziziya, Iraq, 66
Alba, Italy, 34
Albacete (prov.), Spain, 33
Albacete, Spain, 33
Alba Iulia, Romania, 45
Albania, 45
Albano Laziale, Italy, 34
Albany, Calif., 204
Albany, Ga., 217
Albany (cap.), N.Y., 276
Albany (riv.), Ontario, 175
Albany, Oreg., 291
Albany, Pr. Edward I., 169
Albany, W. Australia, 92
Albay (prov.), Phil., 82
Albemarle (pt.), Ecuador, 128
Albemarle, N.C., 281
Alberni, Br. Col., 184
Albert (Mobutu Sese Seko) (lake), Africa, 115
Albert, France, 28
Alberta (mt.), Alberta, 182
Alberta (prov.), Canada, 182
Albert Lea, Minn., 255
Alberton, Pr. Edward I., 169
Alberton, S. Africa, 118
Albertville, Ala., 195
Albertville, France, 28
Albi, France, 28
Albia, Iowa, 229
Albina, Suriname, 131
Albino, Italy, 34
Albion, Mich., 250
Albion, Nebr., 264
Albion, N.Y., 276
Alborán (isl.), Spain, 33
Ålborg, Den., 21
Albox, Spain, 33
Albuquerque, N. Mex., 274
Alburquerque, Spain, 33
Albury, N.S. Wales, 97
Alcácer do Sal, Portugal, 33
Alcalá de Guadaira, Spain, 33
Alcalá de Henares, Spain, 33
Alcalá de los Gazules, Spain, 33
Alcalá la Real, Spain, 33
Alcamo, Italy, 34
Alcanar, Spain, 33
Alcañiz, Spain, 33
Alcântara, Portugal, 33
Alcántara, Spain, 33
Alcantarilla, Spain, 33
Alcaraz (range), Spain, 33
Alcaudete, Spain, 33
Alcázar de San Juan, Spain, 33
Alcira, Spain, 33
Alcoa, Tenn., 237
Alcobaça, Portugal, 33
Alcoy, Spain, 33
Alcudia (bay), Spain, 33
Aldabra (isls.), Seychelles, 118
Aldama, Mexico, 150
Aldan, Pa., 294
Aldan, U.S.S.R., 48
Aldan (plat.), U.S.S.R., 48
Aldeia Nova de São Bento, Portugal, 33
Alderney (isl.), Chan. Is., 13
Aldershot, England, 13
Aldershot, Nova Scotia, 168
Aldridge Brownhills, England, 10
Aledo, Ill., 222
Aleg, Mauritania, 106
Alegrete, Brazil, 132
'Aleih, Leb., 63
Aleksandriya, U.S.S.R., 52
Aleksandrovsk-Sakhalinskiy, U.S.S.R., 48
Alekseyevka, U.S.S.R., 52
Aleksin, U.S.S.R., 52
Aleksinac, Yugo., 45
Além Paraíba, Brazil, 135
Alençon, France, 28
Aleppo (prov.), Syria, 63
Aleppo, Syria, 63
Alert, N.W. Terr., 187
Alert Bay, Br. Col., 184
Alès, France, 28
Alessandria (prov.), Italy, 34
Alessandria, Italy, 34
Ålesund, Norway, 18
Aleutian (isls.), Alaska, 196
Alexander (arch.), Alaska, 196
Alexander (isl.), Antarc., 5
Alexander City, Ala., 195
Alexandra, N. Zealand, 100
Alexandra Land (isl.), U.S.S.R., 48
Alexandretta (Iskenderun), Turkey, 63
Alexandria, Egypt, 111
Alexandria, Ind., 227
Alexandria, La., 238
Alexandria, Minn., 255
Alexandria, Romania, 45
Alexandria, Scotland, 15
Alexandria, Va., 307
Alexandroúpolis, Greece, 45
Aleysk, U.S.S.R., 48
Al Falluja, Iraq, 66
Alfaro, Spain, 33
Alfatar, Bulg., 45
Alfeld, W. Ger., 22
Alfenas, Brazil, 135
Alford, Scotland, 15
Alfred, N.Y., 276
Alga, U.S.S.R., 48
Algeciras, Spain, 33
Algemesí, Spain, 33
Algeria, 106
Algés, Portugal, 33
Alghero, Italy, 34
Algiers (cap.), Algeria, 106
Algoa (bay), S. Africa, 118
Algoma, Wis., 317
Algona, Iowa, 229
Algonac, Mich., 250
Algonquin Prov. Park, Ontario, 177
Alhama de Granada, Spain, 33
Alhama de Murcia, Spain, 33
Alhambra, Calif., 204
Al Hawtah, P.D.R. Yemen, 59
Al Hoceima, Mor., 106
Alhos Vedros, Portugal, 33
Ali-Bayramly, U.S.S.R., 52
Alicante (prov.), Spain, 33
Alicante, Spain, 33
Alice, Texas, 303
Alice Arm, Br. Col., 184
Alice Springs, N. Terr., 93
Aliceville, Ala., 195
Aligarh, India, 68
Alingsås, Sweden, 18
Aliquippa, Pa., 294
Alivérion, Greece, 45
Aliwal North, S. Africa, 118
Aljezur, Portugal, 33
Aljojuca, Mexico, 150
Aljustrel, Portugal, 33
Alkmaar, Neth., 27
Al Kufa, Iraq, 66
Al Kuwait (cap.), Kuwait, 59
Allahabad, India, 68
Allakh-Yun', U.S.S.R., 48
Allanmyo, Burma, 72
Allegan, Mich., 250
Allen (lake), Ireland, 17
Allendale, N.J., 273
Allendale, S.C., 296
Allende, Mexico, 150
Allen Park, Mich., 250
Allentown, Pa., 294
Alleppey, India, 68
Aller (riv.), W. Ger., 22
Allgäu (reg.), W. Ger., 22
Alliance, Nebr., 264
Alliance, Ohio, 284
Allier (dept.), France, 28
Allinge-Sandvig, Den., 21
Allison Pk., Pa., 294
Al Lith, Saudi Arabia, 59
Alloa, Scotland, 15
All Saints, Ant. & Bar., 161
Alma, Ga., 217
Alma, Mich., 250
Alma, Nebr., 264
Alma, Québec, 172
Alma-Ata, U.S.S.R., 48
Almada, Portugal, 33
Almadén, Spain, 33
Almagro, Spain, 33
Almansa, Spain, 33
Almanzor (mt.), Spain, 33
Almanzora (riv.), Spain, 33
Almeirim, Portugal, 33
Almelo, Neth., 27
Almendralejo, Spain, 33
Almería (prov.), Spain, 33
Almería, Spain, 33
Almería (gulf), Spain, 33
Al'met'yevsk, U.S.S.R., 52
Almhult, Sweden, 18
Almirante, Panama, 154
Almirós, Greece, 45
Almodóvar del Campo, Spain, 33
Almoloya del Río, Mexico, 150
Almonte, Spain, 33
Almora, India, 68
Almuñecar, Spain, 33
Alofi (cap.), Niue, 87
Álora, Spain, 33
Alor Setar, Malaysia, 72
Alorton, Ill., 222
Alpena, Mich., 250
Alpes-de-Haute-Provence (dept.), France, 28
Alpes-Maritimes (dept.), France, 28
Alpiarça, Portugal, 33
Alpine, Texas, 303
Alps (mts.), Europe, 7
Al Qaiyara, Iraq, 66
Alsace (trad. prov.), France, 29
Alsask, Sask., 181
Alsdorf, W. Ger., 22
Alsek (riv.), Yukon, 187
Alsip, Ill., 222
Alsten (isl.), Norway, 18
Altaelv (riv.), Norway, 18
Altadena, Calif., 204
Alta Gracia, Arg., 143
Altagracia, La (prov.), Dom. Rep., 158
Altagracia, Venez., 124
Altai (mts.), Asia, 54
Altamira, Mexico, 150
Altamont, Oreg., 291
Altar, Mexico, 150
Altavista, Va., 307
Altay, Mong., 77
Altena, W. Ger., 22
Altenburg, E. Ger., 22
Altevatn (lake), Norway, 18
Altındağ, Turkey, 63
Altmark (reg.), E. Ger., 22
Alto Araguaia, Brazil, 132
Alton, Ill., 222
Altona, Manitoba, 179
Altona, W. Ger., 22
Altoona, Pa., 294
Alto Paraguay (dept.), Paraguay, 144
Alto Paraná (dept.), Paraguay, 144
Alto Park, Ga., 217
Alto Ritacuva (mt.), Colombia, 126
Altotonga, Mexico, 150
Altrincham, England, 10
Altun Shan (range), China, 77
Alturas, Calif., 204
Altus, Okla., 288
Alula, Somalia, 115
Alum Rock, Calif., 204
Alushta, U.S.S.R., 52
Alva, Okla., 288
Alva, Scotland, 15
Alvarado, Mexico, 150
Alvesta, Sweden, 18
Alvin, Texas, 303
Älvsborg (co.), Sweden, 18
Älvsbyn, Sweden, 18
Alwar, India, 68
Alxa Shamo (des.), China, 77
Alyth, Scotland, 15
Alz (riv.), W. Ger., 22
Alzey, W. Ger., 22
Amadeus (lake), N. Terr., 93
'Amadiya, Iraq, 66
Amadora, Portugal, 33
Amagasaki, Japan, 81
Amakusa (isls.), Japan, 81
Åmål, Sweden, 18
Amaliás, Greece, 45
Amalner, India, 68
Amambaí, Brazil, 132
Amambay (dept.), Paraguay, 144
Amami (isls.), Japan, 81
Amami-O-Shima (isl.), Japan, 81
Amanos (mts.), Turkey, 63
Amapá (terr.), Brazil, 132
Amapala, Honduras, 154
Amapari (riv.), Brazil, 132
'Amara, Iraq, 66
Amarante, Brazil, 132
Amarapura, Burma, 72
Amarillo, Texas, 303
Amasya (prov.), Turkey, 63
Amasya, Turkey, 63
Amatitlán, Guat., 154
Amatlán de los Reyes, Mexico, 150
Amazon (riv.), S. Amer., 120
Amazonas (state), Brazil, 132
Amazonas (comm.), Colombia, 126
Amazonas (dept.), Peru, 128
Amazonas (terr.), Venez., 124
Ambala, India, 68
Ambarchik, U.S.S.R., 48
Ambato, Ecuador, 128
Ambatondrazaka, Madagascar, 118
Amberg, W. Ger., 22
Ambergris (cay), Belize, 154
Ambérieu-en-Bugey, France, 28
Amberley, Ohio, 284
Ambler, Pa., 294
Amboise, France, 28
Ambon (Amboina), Indon., 85
Ambositra, Madagascar, 118
Ambridge, Pa., 294
Ambriz, Angola, 115
Ambrym (isl.), Vanuatu, 87
Ambunti, Papua N.G., 85
Amchitka (isl.), Alaska, 196
Amealco, Mexico, 150
Ameca, Mexico, 150
Amecameca de Juárez, Mexico, 150
Americana, Brazil, 135
American Falls, Idaho, 220
American Fork, Utah, 304
American Highland, Antarc., 5
American Samoa, 87
Americus, Ga., 217
Amersfoort, Neth., 27
Amery Ice Shelf, Antarc., 5
Ames, Iowa, 229
Amesbury, Mass., 249
Amfilokhía, Greece, 45
Amfissa, Greece, 45
Amherst, Burma, 72
Amherst, Mass., 249
Amherst, Nova Scotia, 169
Amherst, Ohio, 284
Amherstburg, Ontario, 177
Amiens, France, 28
Amindiri (isl.), India, 68
Amindivi (isls.), India, 68
Amini (Amindiri) (isl.), India, 68
Amisk (lake), Sask., 181
Amistad (res.), 150
Amistad Nat'l Rec. Area, Texas, 303
Amite, La., 238
Amityville, N.Y., 276
Amlwch, Wales, 13
Amman (gov.), Jordan, 65
Amman (cap.), Jordan, 65
Ammanford, Wales, 13
Ammersee (lake), W. Ger., 22
Amnat, Thai., 72
Amne Machin (A'nyêmaqên Shan) (mts.), China, 77
Amol, Iran, 66
Amorgós (isl.), Greece, 45
Amory, Miss., 256
Amos, Québec, 174
Amoy (Xiamen), China, 77
Amozoc de Mota, Mexico, 150
Amposta, Spain, 33
Amqui, Québec, 172
Amravati, India, 68
Amreli, India, 68
Amritsar, India, 68
Amsterdam (isl.), 3
Amsterdam (cap.), Neth., 27
Amsterdam, N.Y., 276
Amstetten, Austria, 41
Am-Timan, Chad, 111
Amuay, Venez., 124
Amudar'ya (riv.), Asia, 48
Amuku (mts.), Guyana, 131
Amund Ringnes (isl.), N.W. Terr., 187
Amundsen (bay), Antarc., 5
Amundsen (sea), Antarc., 5
Amundsen (gulf), N.W. Terr., 187
Amur (riv.), Asia, 48
Amya (pass), Asia, 72
'Ana, Iraq, 66
Anaa (atoll), Fr. Poly., 87
Anaco, Venez., 124
Anaconda, Mont., 262
Anacortes, Wash., 310
Anadarko, Okla., 288
Anadyr', U.S.S.R., 48
Anadyr' (gulf), U.S.S.R., 48
Anadyr' (range), U.S.S.R., 48
Anadyr' (riv.), U.S.S.R., 48
Anáfi (isl.), Greece, 45
Anaheim, Calif., 204
Anai Mudi (mt.), India, 68
'Anaiza, Saudi Arabia, 59
Anakapalle, India, 68
Anambas (isls.), Indon., 85
Anambra (state), Nigeria, 106
Anamosa, Iowa, 229
Anamur (cape), Turkey, 63
Anan, Japan, 81
Anantapur, India, 68
Anantnag, India, 68
Anapa, U.S.S.R., 52
Anápolis, Brazil, 132
Añasco, P. Rico, 161
Anatom (isl.), Vanuatu, 87
Añatuya, Arg., 143
Anauá (riv.), Brazil, 132
Anbar (gov.), Iraq, 66
Ancash (dept.), Peru, 128
Ancaster, Ontario, 177
Anchorage, Alaska, 196
Ancohuma, Nevado (mt.), Bolivia, 136
Ancona (prov.), Italy, 34
Ancona, Italy, 34
Ancón de Sardinas (bay), Ecuador, 128
Ancud, Chile, 138
Andalgalá, Arg., 143
Åndalsnes, Norway, 18
Andalusia, Ala., 195
Andalusia (reg.), Spain, 33
Andaman (sea), Asia, 54
Andaman (isls.), India, 68
Andaman and Nicobar Islands (terr.), India, 68
Anderlecht, Belg., 27
Andernach, W. Ger., 22
Anderson, Calif., 204
Anderson, Ind., 227
Anderson (riv.), N.W. Terr., 187
Anderson, S.C., 296
Andes (mts.), S. Amer., 120
Andheri, India, 68
Andhra Pradesh (state), India, 68
Andikíthira (isl.), Greece, 45
Andissa, Greece, 45
Andizhan, U.S.S.R., 48
Andkhvoy, Afghan., 68
Andong, S. Korea, 81
Andorra, 33
Andorra la Vella (cap.), Andorra, 33
Andover, England, 13
Andravídha, Greece, 45
Andreas (cape), Cyprus, 63
Andrew Johnson Nat'l Hist. Site, Tenn., 237
Andrews, S.C., 296
Andrews, Texas, 303
Andros (isl.), Bahamas, 156
Ándros, Greece, 45
Ándros (isl.), Greece, 45
Androth (isl.), India, 68
Andsfjorden (fjord), Norway, 18
Andújar, Spain, 33
Andulo, Angola, 115
Anécho, Togo, 106
Anegada (isl.), Virgin Is. (Br.), 156
Aneityum (Anatom) (isl.), Vanuatu, 87
'Aneiza, Jebel (mt.), Asia, 59
Aneto (peak), Spain, 33
Angara (riv.), U.S.S.R., 48
Angarsk, U.S.S.R., 48
Angaur (isl.), Belau, 87
Ånge, Sweden, 18
Angel (fall), Venez., 124
Angel de la Guarda (isl.), Mexico, 150
Angeles, Phil., 82
Ängelholm, Sweden, 18
Ångermanälven (riv.), Sweden, 18
Angermünde, E. Ger., 22
Angers, France, 28
Angikuni (lake), N.W. Terr., 187
Angkor Wat (ruins), Cambodia, 72
Anglesey (co.), Wales, 13
Angleton, Texas, 303
Angliers, Québec, 174
Angmagssalik, Greenl., 4
Ango, Zaire, 115
Angoche, Mozamb., 118
Angoche (isl.), Mozamb., 118
Angol, Chile, 138
Angola, 115
Angola, Ind., 227
Angoram, Papua N.G., 85
Angostura, Mexico, 150
Angoulême, France, 28
Angoumois (trad. prov.), France, 29
Angra do Heroismo, Portugal, 32
Anguilla (isl.), 156
Anguss (co.), Scotland, 15
Anholt (isl.), Den., 21
Anhui (Anhwei) (prov.), China, 77
Aniene (riv.), Italy, 34
Anina, Romania, 45
Anjou (trad. prov.), France, 29
Anjou, Québec, 172
Anjouan (isl.), Comoros, 118
Ankara (prov.), Turkey, 63
Ankara (cap.), Turkey, 63
Ankeny, Iowa, 229
Anker (riv.), England, 10
Anking (Anqing), China, 77
Anklam, E. Ger., 22
Ankober, Ethiopia, 111
An Loc (Binh Long), Vietnam, 72
Ann (cape), Mass., 249
Anna, Ill., 222
Annaba, Algeria, 106
Annaberg-Buchholz, E. Ger., 22
An Najaf (gov.), Iraq, 66
An Najaf, Iraq, 66
Annan, Scotland, 15
Annandale, Va., 307
Annapolis (cap.), Md., 245
Annapolis (basin), Nova Scotia, 169
Annapolis Royal, Nova Scotia, 169
Annapurna (mt.), Nepal, 68
Ann Arbor, Mich., 250
An Nasiriya, Iraq, 66
Annecy, France, 28
An Nhon, Vietnam, 72
Anniston, Ala., 195
Annobón (isl.), Eq. Guinea, 102
Annonay, France, 28
Annotto Bay, Jamaica, 158
Annville, Pa., 294
Anoka, Minn., 255
Áno Viánnos, Greece, 45
Anóyia, Greece, 45
Anqing, China, 77
Ansbach, W. Ger., 22
Anse la Raye, St. Lucia, 161
Anshan, China, 77
Anshun, China, 77
Ansŏng, S. Korea, 81
Ansonia, Conn., 210
Antakya, Turkey, 63
Antalaha, Madagascar, 118
Antalya (prov.), Turkey, 63
Antalya, Turkey, 63
Antalya (gulf), Turkey, 63
Antananarivo (prov.), Madagascar, 118
Antananarivo (cap.), Madagascar, 118
Antarctic (pen.), Antarc., 5
Antarctica, 5
Antequera, Spain, 33
Anthony, Kans., 232
Anthony, N. Mex., 274
Anti-Atlas (ranges), Mor., 106
Antibes, France, 28
Anticosti (isl.), Québec, 174
Antietam Nat'l Battlefield Site, Md., 245
Antigo, Wis., 317
Antigonish, Nova Scotia, 169
Antigua and Barbuda, 161
Antigua, Guat., 154
Antigua (riv.), Mexico, 150
Antilla, Cuba, 158
Antilles, Greater (isls.), W. Indies, 156, 158, 161
Antilles, Lesser (isls.), W. Indies, 156, 161
Antioch, Calif., 204
Antioch, Ill., 222
Antioquia (dept.), Colombia, 126
Antipodes (isls.), N. Zealand, 5
Antique (prov.), Phil., 82
Anti-Taurus (mts.), Turkey, 63
Antlers, Okla., 288
Antofagasta (reg.), Chile, 138
Antofagasta, Chile, 138
Antofagasta de la Sierra, Arg., 143
Antón, Panama, 154
Antongil (bay), Madagascar, 118
Antony, France, 28
Antrim (dist.), N. Ireland, 17
Antrim, N. Ireland, 17
Antsirabe, Madagascar, 118
Antsiranana (prov.), Madagascar, 118
Antsiranana, Madagascar, 118
Antwerp (prov.), Belg., 27
Antwerp, Belg., 27
An Uaimh, Ireland, 17
Anuradhapura, Sri Lanka, 68
Anyang, China, 77
A'nyêmaqên Shan (mts.), China, 77
Anzhero-Sudzhensk, U.S.S.R., 48
Anzoátegui (state), Venez., 124
Aomori (pref.), Japan, 81
Aomori, Japan, 81
Aosta (reg.), Italy, 34
Aosta (prov.), Italy, 34
Aosta, Italy, 34
Aoulef, Algeria, 106
Apa (riv.), S. Amer., 144
Apache Jct., Ariz., 198
Apalachee (bay), Fla., 212
Apalachicola, Fla., 212
Apan, Mexico, 150
Apaporis (riv.), Colombia, 126
Aparri, Phil., 82
Apataki, Fr. Poly., 87
Apatity, U.S.S.R., 52
Apatzingán de la Constitución, Mexico, 150
Apeldoorn, Neth., 27
Apennines (mts.), Italy, 34
Apennines, Central (range), Italy, 34
Apennines, Northern (range), Italy, 34
Apennines, Southern (range), Italy, 34
Apia (cap.), W. Samoa, 87
Apizaco, Mexico, 150
Ap Long Ha, Vietnam, 72
Apo (vol.), Phil., 82
Apolda, E. Ger., 22
Apollo, Pa., 294
Apopka, Fla., 212
Aporé (riv.), Brazil, 132
Appalachian (mts.), U.S., 188
Appenzell Ausser-Rhoden (canton), Switz., 39
Appenzell Inner-Rhoden (canton), Switz., 39
Appleton, Wis., 317
Appleton City, Mo., 261
Apple Valley, Calif., 204
Apple Valley, Minn., 255
Appomattox C.H. Nat'l Hist. Pk., Va., 307
Approuague (riv.), Fr. Guiana, 131
Apsheron (pen.), U.S.S.R., 52
Apsheronsk, U.S.S.R., 52
Apt, France, 28
Apulia (Puglia) (reg.), Italy, 34
Apure (state), Venez., 124
Apure (riv.), Venez., 124
Apurímac (dept.), Peru, 128
Apurímac (riv.), Peru, 128
Aqaba (gulf), Asia, 59
'Aqaba, Jordan, 65
Aquidauana, Brazil, 132
Aquiles Serdán, Mexico, 150
Aquin, Haiti, 158
Arab, Ala., 195
'Arab, Shatt-al (riv.), Asia, 66
'Araba, Wadi (valley), Asia, 65
Arabian (sea), Asia, 54
Arabian (des.), Egypt, 111
Aracaju, Brazil, 132
Aracati, Brazil, 132
Araçatuba, Brazil, 135
Aracena, Spain, 33
Arad, Romania, 45
'Arafat, Jebel (mt.), Saudi Arabia, 59
Arafura (sea), 85
Aragón (reg.), Spain, 33
Aragón (riv.), Spain, 33
Aragua (state), Venez., 124
Aragua de Barcelona, Venez., 124
Araguaia (riv.), Brazil, 132
Araguari, Brazil, 132
Araguari (riv.), Brazil, 132
Arak, Iran, 66
Arakan (state), Burma, 72
Arakan Yoma (mts.), Burma, 72
Araks (riv.), Asia, 59
Aral (sea), U.S.S.R., 48
Aral'sk, U.S.S.R., 48
Aramberri, Mexico, 150
Aran (isl.), Ireland, 17
Aran (isls.), Ireland, 17
Aranda de Duero, Spain, 33
Arandas, Mexico, 150
Aranjuez, Spain, 33
Aransas Pass, Texas, 303
Arapey Grande (riv.), Uruguay, 145
Arapkir, Turkey, 63
Araranguá, Brazil, 132
Araraquara, Brazil, 135
Araras, Brazil, 135
Ararat (mt.), Turkey, 63
Ararat, Victoria, 97
Arauca (inten.), Colombia, 126
Arauca, Colombia, 126
Arauca (riv.), S. Amer., 120
Arauco, Chile, 138
Arax (Araks) (riv.), Asia, 59
Araxá, Brazil, 132
Arbela (Erbil), Iraq, 66
Arboga, Sweden, 18
Arborfield, Sask., 181
Arborg, Manitoba, 179
Arbroath, Scotland, 15
Arcachon, France, 28
Arcadia, Calif., 204
Arcadia, Fla., 212
Arcadia, La., 238
Arcata, Calif., 204
Arcelia, Mexico, 150
Archangel, U.S.S.R., 52
Archbald, Pa., 294
Archena, Spain, 33
Arches Nat'l Park, Utah, 304
Archidona, Spain, 33
Arco, Ga., 217
Arco, Idaho, 220
Arcola, Sask., 181
Arcos de la Frontera, Spain, 33
Arcot, India, 68
Arcoverde, Brazil, 132
Arctic Circle, 4
Arctic Ocean, 4
Arctic Red River, N.W. Terr., 187
Arda (riv.), Europe, 45
Ardabil, Iran, 66
Ardahan, Turkey, 63
Ardchamich, Scotland, 15
Ardèche (dept.), France, 28
Ardee, Ireland, 17
Ardennes (plat.), Belg., 27
Ardennes (dept.), France, 28
Ardestan, Iran, 66
Ardhéa, Greece, 45
Ardino, Bulg., 45
Ardmore, Ind., 227
Ardmore, Okla., 288
Ardmore, Pa., 294
Ardrossan, Scotland, 15
Ards (dist.), N. Ireland, 17
Ardsley, N.Y., 276
Arecibo (dist.), P. Rico, 161
Arecibo, P. Rico, 161
Areia Branca, Brazil, 132
Arena (pt.), Mexico, 150
Arenas (cay), Mexico, 150
Arenas de San Pedro, Spain, 33
Arendal, Norway, 18
Arenys de Mar, Spain, 33
Arequipa (dept.), Peru, 128
Arequipa, Peru, 128
Arezzo (prov.), Italy, 34

E

F

H

Hudson (riv.), U.S., 276
Hudson, Wis., 317
Hudson Bay, Sask., 181
Hudson Falls, N.Y., 276
Hudsonville, Mich., 250
Hue, Vietnam, 72
Huehuetenango, Guat., 154
Huejotzingo, Mexico, 150
Huejutla, Mexico, 150
Huelva (prov.), Spain, 33
Huelva, Spain, 33
Huesca (prov.), Spain, 33
Huesca, Spain, 33
Huetamo, Mexico, 150
Hueytown, Ala., 195
Hugo, Okla., 288
Hugoton, Kans., 232
Huhehot (Hohhot), China, 77
Huíla (dist.), Angola, 115
Huila (dept.), Colombia, 126
Huila (mt.), Colombia, 126
Huimanguillo, Mexico, 150
Huitzuco de los Figueroa, Mexico, 150
Huixtla, Mexico, 150
Hull, England, 13
Hull (isl.), Kiribati, 87
Hull, Mass., 249
Hull, Québec, 172
Humacao (dist.), P. Rico, 161
Humacao, P. Rico, 161
Humber (riv.), England, 13
Humberside (co.), England, 13
Humboldt, Iowa, 229
Humboldt (riv.), Nev., 266
Humboldt, Sask., 181
Humboldt, Tenn., 237
Hume (lake), Australia, 97
Hummelstown, Pa., 294
Humphreys (peak), Ariz., 198
Húnaflói (bay), Iceland, 21
Hunan (prov.), China, 77
Hunchun, China, 77
Hunedoara, Romania, 45
Hungary, 41
Hŭngnam, N. Korea, 81
Hungtow (isl.), China, 77
Hunjiang, China, 77
Hunsrück (mts.), W. Ger., 22
Hunter (mts.), N. Zealand, 100
Hunter (isls.), Tasmania, 99
Hunters Hill, N.S. Wales, 97
Huntingburg, Ind., 227
Huntingdon, Pa., 294
Huntingdon, Québec, 172
Huntington, Ind., 227
Huntington, N.Y., 276
Huntington, W. Va., 313
Huntington Beach, Calif., 204
Huntington Park, Calif., 204
Huntington Sta., N.Y., 276
Huntly, Scotland, 15
Huntsville, Ala., 195
Huntsville, Ontario, 177
Huntsville, Texas, 303
Hunucmá, Mexico, 150
Hunza (Baltit), Pakistan, 68
Huon (isls.), New Cal., 87
Huon (gulf), Papua N.G., 85
Hupei (Hubei) (prov.), China, 77
Hurd (cape), Ontario, 177
Hureidha, P.D.R. Yemen, 59
Hurghada, Egypt, 111
Hurley, Wis., 317
Huron (lake), N. Amer., 188
Huron, Ohio, 284
Huron, S. Dak., 298
Hurstville, N.S. Wales, 97
Hürth, W. Ger., 22
Húsavík, Iceland, 21
Huşi, Romania, 45
Husum, W. Ger., 22
Hutchinson, Kans., 232
Hutchinson, Minn., 255
Huth, Yemen Arab Rep., 59
Hutt (Upper and Lower), N. Zealand, 100
Hüttental, W. Ger., 22
Hvar (isl.), Yugo., 45
Hvítá (river), Iceland, 21
Hwainan (Huainan), China, 77
Hwange (Wankie), Zimbabwe, 118
Hwang Ho (Huang He) (riv.), China, 77
Hyannis, Mass., 249
Hyargas Nuur (lake), Mong., 77
Hyattsville, Md., 245
Hyde, England, 10
Hyderabad, India, 68
Hyderabad, Pakistan, 68
Hyères, France, 28
Hyères (isls.), France, 28
Hyogo (pref.), Japan, 81
Hythe, England, 13
Hyvinkää, Fin., 18

I

Ia Drang (riv.), Asia, 72
Ialomiţa (riv.), Romania, 45
Iar Connacht (dist.), Ireland, 17
Iaşi, Romania, 45
Ibadan, Nigeria, 106
Ibagué, Colombia, 126
Ibar (riv.), Yugo., 45
Ibaraki (pref.), Japan, 81
Ibarra, Ecuador, 128
Ibb, Yemen Arab Rep., 59
Iberville, Québec, 172
Ibiza, Spain, 33
Ibiza (isl.), Spain, 33
'Ibri, Oman, 59
Içá (riv.), Brazil, 132
Ica (dept.), Peru, 128
Ica, Peru, 128
İçel (prov.), Turkey, 63
Iceland, 21
Ichang (Yichang), China, 77
Ichikawa, Japan, 81
Ichinomiya, Japan, 81
Ichinoseki, Japan, 81
Idabel, Okla., 288
Idaho (state), U.S., 220
Idaho Falls, Idaho, 220
Idar-Oberstein, W. Ger., 22
Idehan Ubari (des.), Africa, 111
Ider Gol (riv.), Mong., 77
Idfu, Egypt, 111
Idiofa, Zaire, 115
Idlib (prov.), Syria, 63
Idlib, Syria, 63
Ieper, Belg., 27
Ifalik (atoll), Micronesia, 87
Ife, Nigeria, 106
Iférouane, Niger, 106
Ifni, Morocco, 106
Ifugao (prov.), Phil., 82
Igarka, U.S.S.R., 48
Iglesias, Italy, 34
Igloolik, N.W. Terr., 187
Igualada, Spain, 33
Iguala de la Independencia, Mexico, 150
Iguazú (falls), S. Amer., 132
Iguidi, Erg (des.), Africa, 106
Ihosy, Madagascar, 118
Iida, Japan, 81
Iijoki (riv.), Fin., 18
Iisalmi, Fin., 18
Iizuka, Japan, 81
IJsselmeer (lake), Neth., 27
Ikaría (isl.), Greece, 45
Ikeda, Japan, 81
Ikela, Zaire, 115
Ikhtiman, Bulg., 45
Ilagan, Phil., 82
Ilam (gov.), Iran, 66
Ilanskiy, U.S.S.R., 48
Ilebo, Zaire, 115
Ile de France (trad. prov.), France, 29
Iles (lake), Québec, 172
Ilesha, Nigeria, 106
Ilhavo, Portugal, 33
Ilhéus, Brazil, 132
Ili (riv.), U.S.S.R., 48
Iliamna (lake), Alaska, 196
Iligan, Phil., 82
Ilion, N.Y., 276
Ilium (Troy) (ruins), Turkey, 63
Ilkeston, England, 13
Illampu (mt.), Bolivia, 136
Illapel, Chile, 138
Ille-et-Vilaine (dept.), France, 28
Iller (riv.), W. Ger., 22
Illimani (mt.), Bolivia, 136
Illinois (state), U.S., 222
Illizi, Algeria, 106
Illora, Spain, 33
Il'men' (lake), U.S.S.R., 52
Ilmenau, E. Ger., 22
Ilmenau (riv.), W. Ger., 22
Ilo, Peru, 128
Ilobasco, El Salv., 154
Ilocos Norte (prov.), Phil., 82
Ilocos Sur (prov.), Phil., 82
Iloilo (prov.), Phil., 82
Iloilo, Phil., 82
Ilorin, Nigeria, 106
Ilubabor (prov.), Ethiopia, 111
Imabari, Japan, 81
Imandra (lake), U.S.S.R., 48
Imari, Japan, 81
Imatra, Fin., 18
Imbâba, Egypt, 111
Imbabura (prov.), Ecuador, 128
Immenstadt im Allgäu, W. Ger., 22
Immokalee, Fla., 212
Imo (state), Nigeria, 106
Imola, Italy, 34
Imperia (prov.), Italy, 34
Imperia, Italy, 34
Imperial, Calif., 204
Imperial Beach, Calif., 204
Impfondo, Congo, 115
Imphal, India, 68
İmroz (Gökçeada) (isl.), Turkey, 63
Ina, Japan, 81
Inala, Queensland, 95
Inari (lake), Fin., 18
Inca, Spain, 33
İnce (cape), Turkey, 63
Inchiri (reg.), Mauritania, 106
Inch'ŏn, S. Korea, 81
Indawgyi (lake), Burma, 72
Independence, Iowa, 229
Independence, Kans., 232
Independence, Mo., 261
Independence (mts.), Nev., 266
Independence, Ohio, 284
Independencia (prov.), Dom. Rep., 158
India, 68
Indiana, Pa., 294
Indiana (state), U.S., 227
Indiana Dunes Nat'l Lakeshore, Ind., 227
Indianapolis (cap.), Ind., 227
Indian Head, Sask., 181
Indian Hill, Ohio, 284
Indian Ocean, 3
Indianola, Iowa, 229
Indianola, Miss., 256
Indigirka (riv.), U.S.S.R., 48
Indio, Calif., 204
Indochina (pen.), Asia, 72
Indonesia, 85
Indooroopilly, Queensland, 95
Indore, India, 68
Indramayu, Indon., 85
Indre (dept.), France, 28
Indre (riv.), France, 28
Indre-et-Loire (dept.), France, 28
Indus (riv.), Asia, 68
Indus, Mouths of the (delta), Pakistan, 68
İnebolu, Turkey, 63
Ingende, Zaire, 115
Ingersoll, Ontario, 177
Ingham, Queensland, 95
Inglewood, Calif., 204
Ingolstadt, W. Ger., 22
Ingonish, Nova Scotia, 168
Ingram, Pa., 294
Inhambane (prov.), Mozamb., 118
Inhambane, Mozamb., 118
Inharrime, Mozamb., 118
Iniesta, Spain, 33
Inírida, Colombia, 126
Inírida (riv.), Colombia, 126
Inishbofin (isl.), Ireland, 17
Inishturk (isl.), Ireland, 17
Inkster, Mich., 250
Inn (riv.), Europe, 41
Inner (sound), Scotland, 15
Inner Hebrides (isls.), Scotland, 15
Innerleithen, Scotland, 15
Inner Mongolia (Nei Monggol) (aut. reg.), China, 77
Innisfail, Alberta, 182
Innisfail, Queensland, 95
Innsbruck, Austria, 41
Inongo, Zaire, 115
Inoucdjouac, Québec, 174
Inowroclaw, Poland, 47
In Salah, Algeria, 106
Insein, Burma, 72
Inta, U.S.S.R., 52
Interlaken, Switz., 39
International Falls, Minn., 255
International Peace Garden, N. Amer., 179, 283
Intipucá, El Salv., 154
Inuvik, N.W. Terr., 187
Inveraray, Scotland, 15
Inverbervie, Scotland, 15
Invercargill, N. Zealand, 100
Inverell, N.S. Wales, 97
Invergordon, Scotland, 15
Inverkeithing, Scotland, 15
Inverness, Nova Scotia, 169
Inverness (trad. co.), Scotland, 15
Inverness, Scotland, 15
Inverurie, Scotland, 15
Investigator (str.), S. Australia, 94
Inwood, N.Y., 276
Ioánnina, Greece, 45
Iola, Kans., 232
Ioma, Papua N.G., 85
Iona (isl.), Scotland, 15
Ionia, Mich., 250
Ionian (sea), Europe, 7
Ionian Islands (reg.), Greece, 45
Ios (isl.), Greece, 45
Iowa (state), U.S., 229
Iowa City, Iowa, 229
Iowa Falls, Iowa, 229
Iowa Park, Texas, 303
Ipala, Guat., 154
Ipiales, Colombia, 126
Ipoh, Malaysia, 72
Ipperwash Prov. Park, Ontario, 177
Ippy, Cent. Afr. Rep., 115
Ipswich, England, 13
Ipswich, Mass., 249
Ipswich, Queensland, 95
Iquique, Chile, 138
Iquitos, Peru, 128
Iracoubo, Fr. Guiana, 131
Iráklion, Greece, 45
Iran, 66
Irapuato, Mexico, 150
Iraq, 66
Irazú (mt.), C. Rica, 154
Irbid, Jordan, 65
Ireland, 17
Ireland, Northern, 17
Ireland (isl.), Berm., 156
Ireng (riv.), S. Amer., 131
Iri, S. Korea, 81
Iriga, Phil., 82
Iringa (reg.), Tanz., 115
Iringa, Tanz., 115
Iriri (riv.), Brazil, 132
Irish (sea), Europe, 13
Irkutsk, U.S.S.R., 48
Irondale, Ala., 195
Irondequoit, N.Y., 276
Iron Mountain, Mich., 250
Iron River, Mich., 250
Ironton, Ohio, 284
Ironwood, Mich., 250
Iroquois, Ontario, 177
Iroquois Falls, Ontario, 175
Iroquois Point, Hawaii, 218
Irrawaddy (div.), Burma, 72
Irrawaddy (riv.), Burma, 72
Irrawaddy, Mouths of the (delta), Burma, 72
Irtysh (riv.), U.S.S.R., 48
Irún, Spain, 33
Irvine, Calif., 204
Irvine, Ky., 237
Irvine, Scotland, 15
Irving, Texas, 303
Irvington, N.J., 273
Irvington, N.Y., 276
Irwin, Pa., 294
Isabela (isl.), Ecuador, 128
Isabela (prov.), Phil., 82
Isabela, Phil., 82
Isabela, P. Rico, 158
Isabelia (range), Nicaragua, 154
Isabel Segunda, P. Rico, 161
Isachsen, N.W. Terr., 187
Isahaya, Japan, 81
Isangi, Zaire, 115
Isar (riv.), W. Ger., 22
Ischia (isl.), Italy, 34
Ise, Japan, 81
Iselin, N.J., 273
Isère (dept.), France, 28
Isère (riv.), France, 28
Iserlohn, W. Ger., 22
Iseyin, Nigeria, 106
Isfahan (prov.), Iran, 66
Isfahan, Iran, 66
Ishigaki, Japan, 81
Ishikawa (pref.), Japan, 81
Ishim, U.S.S.R., 48
Ishimbay, U.S.S.R., 52
Ishinomaki, Japan, 81
Ishpeming, Mich., 250
Isil'kul', U.S.S.R., 48
Isiolo, Kenya, 115
Isiro, Zaire, 115
İskenderun, Turkey, 63
Iskŭr (riv.), Bulg., 45
Isla Cristina, Spain, 33
Islamabad (dist.), Pakistan, 68
Islamabad (cap.), Pakistan, 68
Isla Mujeres, Mexico, 150
Island (lake), Manitoba, 179
Island Park, N.Y., 276
Islands (bay), Newf., 166
Islands (bay), N. Zealand, 100
Islay (isl.), Scotland, 15
Isle (riv.), France, 28
Isle of Man, 13
Isle of Purbeck (pen.), England, 13
Isle of Wight (co.), England, 13
Isle Royale Nat'l Park, Mich., 250
Islington, England, 10
Islip, N.Y., 276
Ismailia, Egypt, 111
Isna, Egypt, 111
Isparta (prov.), Turkey, 63
Isparta, Turkey, 63
Israel, 65
Issaouane, Erg (des.), Algeria, 106
Issoire, France, 28
Issoudun, France, 28
Issyk-Kul' (lake), U.S.S.R., 48
Issy-les-Moulineaux, France, 28
İstanbul (prov.), Turkey, 63
İstanbul, Turkey, 63
Isulan, Phil., 82
Itá, Paraguay, 144
Itabuna, Brazil, 132
Itajaí, Brazil, 132
Itajubá, Brazil, 135
Itala, Somalia, 115
Italy, 34
Itami, Japan, 81
Itanagar, India, 68
Itapecuru (riv.), Brazil, 132
Itapetininga, Brazil, 135
Itapicuru (riv.), Brazil, 132
Itapúa (dept.), Paraguay, 144
Itaqui, Brazil, 132
Itarsi, India, 68
Itasca, Ill., 222
Itasca (lake), Minn., 255
Itbayat (isl.), Phil., 82
Ithaca, Mich., 250
Ithaca, N.Y., 276
Itháki (Ithaca) (isl.), Greece, 45
Ito, Japan, 81
Itoman, Japan, 81
Ituiutaba, Brazil, 132
Ituri (forest), Zaire, 115
Itzehoe, W. Ger., 22
Ival (riv.), Brazil, 132
Ivalo, Fin., 18
Ivano-Frankovsk, U.S.S.R., 52
Ivanovo, U.S.S.R., 52
Ivory Coast, 106
Ivry-sur-Seine, France, 28
Iwaki, Japan, 81
Iwakuni, Japan, 81
Iwamizawa, Japan, 81
Iwata, Japan, 81
Iwate (pref.), Japan, 81
Iwo (isl.), Japan, 81
Iwo, Nigeria, 106
Ixtapalapa, Mexico, 150
Ixtenco, Mexico, 150
Ixtepec, Mexico, 150
Iyo (sea), Japan, 81
Izabal (lake), Guat., 154
Izhevsk, U.S.S.R., 52
Izmail, U.S.S.R., 52
İzmir (prov.), Turkey, 63
İzmir, Turkey, 63
İzmit, Turkey, 63
İznik (lake), Turkey, 63
Izu (isls.), Japan, 81
Izu (pen.), Japan, 81
Izúcar de Matamoros, Mexico, 150
Izumi, Japan, 81
Izumisano, Japan, 81
Izumo, Japan, 81
Izyum, U.S.S.R., 52

J

Jabalpur, India, 68
Jablonec nad Nisou, Czech., 41
Jacaltenango, Guat., 154
Jacarel, Brazil, 132
Jáchal, Arg., 143
Jacksboro, Texas, 303
Jackson, Ala., 195
Jackson, Ga., 217
Jackson, Mich., 250
Jackson, Minn., 255
Jackson (cap.), Miss., 256
Jackson, Mo., 261
Jackson, N.J., 273
Jackson, Ohio, 284
Jackson, Tenn., 237
Jackson, Wyo., 319
Jacksonville, Ala., 195
Jacksonville, Ark., 203
Jacksonville, Fla., 212
Jacksonville, Ill., 222
Jacksonville, N.C., 281
Jacksonville, Texas, 303
Jacksonville Beach, Fla., 212
Jacmel, Haiti, 158
Jacobabad, Pakistan, 68
Jacques-Cartier (mt.), Québec, 172
Jacques-Cartier (passage), Québec, 174
Jade (bay), W. Ger., 22
Jaén (prov.), Spain, 33
Jaén, Spain, 33
Jaffna, Sri Lanka, 68
Jafura (des.), Saudi Arabia, 59
Jagdalpur, India, 68
Jaghbub (Jarabub), Libya, 111
Jagtial, India, 68
Jahrom, Iran, 66
Jaipur, India, 68
Jakarta (cap.), Indon., 85
Jakobstad, Fin., 18
Jal, N. Mex., 274
Jalalabad, Afghan., 68
Jalapa, Guat., 154
Jalapa Enríquez, Mexico, 150
Jalgaon, India, 68
Jalisco (state), Mexico, 150
Jalna, India, 68
Jalo (oasis), Libya, 111
Jalón (riv.), Spain, 33
Jalpa, Mexico, 150
Jalpaiguri, India, 68
Jaluit (atoll), Marshall Is., 87
Jamaica, 158
Jamaica, N.Y., 276
Jamaica (chan.), W. Indies, 156
Jamalpur, Bang., 68
Jamalpur, India, 68
Jamama, Somalia, 115
Jambi, Indon., 85
Jambuair (cape), Indon., 85
James (bay), Canada, 174
James (riv.), U.S., 188
James (riv.), Va., 307
Jamesburg, N.J., 273
Jamestown, N.Y., 276
Jamestown, N. Dak., 283
Jamestown (res.), N. Dak., 283
Jamestown (cap.), St. Helena, 102
Jamestown, S. Australia, 94
Jammerbugt (bay), Den., 21
Jammu, India, 68
Jammu and Kashmir (state), India, 68
Jamnagar, India, 68
Jamshedpur, India, 68
Jämtland (co.), Sweden, 18
Jamursba (cape), Indon., 85
Janakpur, Nepal, 68
Janesville, Wis., 317
Jan Mayen (isl.), Norway, 4
Jánoshalma, Hung., 41
Jaora, India, 68
Japan, 81
Japan (sea), Asia, 81
Japurá (riv.), Brazil, 132
Jarabub, Libya, 111
Jarama (riv.), Spain, 33
Jardines de la Reina (arch.), Cuba, 158
Jarosław, Poland, 47
Jarrow, England, 13
Jars (plain), Laos, 72
Jarvis (isl.), Pacific, 87
Jasper, Ala., 195
Jasper, Alberta, 182
Jasper, Ind., 227
Jasper, Texas, 303
Jasper Nat'l Park, Alberta, 182
Jászberény, Hung., 41
Játiva, Spain, 33
Jaú, Brazil, 135
Jauf, Saudi Arabia, 59
Jauja, Peru, 128
Jaunjelgava, U.S.S.R., 53
Jaunpur, India, 68
Java (head), Indon., 85
Java (isl.), Indon., 85
Java (sea), Indon., 85
Javari (riv.), Brazil, 132
Jaworzno, Poland, 47
Jaya, Puncak (mt.), Indon., 85
Jayapura, Indon., 85
Jayawijaya (range), Indon., 85
Jeanerette, La., 238
Jeannette, Pa., 294
Jeble, Syria, 63
Jedburgh, Scotland, 15
Jeddah (Jidda), Saudi Arabia, 59
Jefferson, Iowa, 229
Jefferson, Ohio, 284
Jefferson (mt.), Oreg., 291
Jefferson, Pa., 294
Jefferson, Texas, 303
Jefferson, Wis., 317
Jefferson City (cap.), Mo., 261
Jefferson City, Tenn., 237
Jefferson Nat'l Expansion Mem. Nat'l Hist. Site, Mo., 261
Jeffersontown, Ky., 237
Jeffersonville, Ind., 227
Jēkabpils, U.S.S.R., 53
Jelenia Góra, Poland, 47
Jelgava, U.S.S.R., 53
Jena, E. Ger., 22
Jendouba, Tun., 106
Jenin, West Bank, 65
Jenison, Mich., 250
Jenkins, Ky., 237
Jenkintown, Pa., 294
Jennings, La., 238
Jennings, Mo., 261
Jennings Lodge, Oreg., 291
Jequié, Brazil, 132
Jequitinhonha (riv.), Brazil, 132
Jerablus, Syria, 63
Jérémie, Haiti, 158
Jerez de la Frontera, Spain, 33
Jerez de los Caballeros, Spain, 33
Jericho, N.Y., 276
Jericho, West Bank, 65
Jerome, Idaho, 220
Jersey (isl.), Chan. Is., 13
Jersey City, N.J., 273
Jersey Shore, Pa., 294
Jerseyville, Ill., 222
Jerusalem (dist.), Israel, 65
Jerusalem (cap.), Israel, 65
Jervis Bay, Aust. Cap. Terr., 97
Jesenice, Yugo., 45
Jesi, Italy, 34
Jessore, Bang., 68
Jesup, Ga., 217
Jette, Belg., 27
Jewel Cave Nat'l Mon., S. Dak., 298
Jewett City, Conn., 210
Jewish Aut. Oblast, U.S.S.R., 48
Jeypore, India, 68
Jhang Sadar, Pakistan, 68
Jhansi, India, 68
Jhelum (riv.), Asia, 68
Jhelum, Pakistan, 68
Jhunjhunu, India, 68
Jiamusi, China, 77
Ji'an, China, 77
Jiangmen, China, 77
Jiangsu (prov.), China, 77
Jiangxi (prov.), China, 77
Jian'ou, China, 77
Jianshui, China, 77
Jiao Xian, China, 77
Jiaozuo, China, 77
Jiaxing, China, 77
Jiayuguan, China, 77
Jibhalanta (Uliastay), Mong., 77
Jibsh, Ras (cape), Oman, 59
Jičín, Czech., 41
Jidda, Saudi Arabia, 59
Jiguero (pt.), P. Rico, 161
Jihlava, Czech., 41
Jihočeský (reg.), Czech., 41
Jihomoravský (reg.), Czech., 41
Jijel, Algeria, 106
Jilib, Somalia, 115
Jilin (prov.), China, 77
Jilin, China, 77
Jimbolia, Romania, 45
Jiménez, Mexico, 150
Jimma, Ethiopia, 111
Jim Thorpe, Pa., 294
Jinan, China, 77
Jind, India, 68
Jingdezhen, China, 77
Jingxi, China, 77
Jingyuan, China, 77
Jinhua, China, 77
Jining, China, 77
Jinja, Uganda, 115
Jinmen (isl.), China, 77
Jinotega, Nicaragua, 154
Jinotepe, Nicaragua, 154
Jinshi, China, 77
Jinzhou, China, 77
Jipijapa, Ecuador, 128
Jirgalanta (Hovd), Mong., 77
Jisr esh Shugur, Syria, 63
Jiu (riv.), Romania, 45
Jiujiang, China, 77
Jiuquan, China, 77
Jixi, China, 77
João Pessoa, Brazil, 132
Jódar, Spain, 33
Jodhpur, India, 68
Joe Batt's Arm, Newf., 166
Joensuu, Fin., 18
Jofra (oasis), Libya, 111
Jogjakarta (Yogyakarta), Indon., 85
Johannesburg, S. Africa, 118
John Day (riv.), Oreg., 291
John F. Kennedy Nat'l Hist. Site, Mass., 248
John Muir Nat'l Hist. Site, Calif., 204
John O'Groats, Scotland, 15
Johns (isl.), S.C., 296
Johnsonburg, Pa., 294
Johnson City, N.Y., 276
Johnson City, Tenn., 237
Johnston (atoll), Pacific, 87
Johnston City, Ill., 222
Johnstone, Scotland, 15
Johnstown, N.Y., 276
Johnstown, Ohio, 284
Johnstown, Pa., 294
Johor (Johore) (state), Malaysia, 72
Johor Baharu (Johore Bharu), Malaysia, 72
Johore (str.), Asia, 72
Joinville, Brazil, 132
Joinville (isl.), Antarc., 5
Jojutla de Juárez, Mexico, 150
Jokkmokk, Sweden, 18
Jökulsá (riv.), Iceland, 21
Joliet, Ill., 222
Joliette, Québec, 172
Jolo (isl.), Phil., 82
Jones (plain), Asia, 72
Jonesboro, Ark., 203
Jonesboro, Ga., 217
Jonesboro, La., 238
Jönköping (co.), Sweden, 18
Jönköping, Sweden, 18
Jonquière, Québec, 172
Joplin, Mo., 261
Jordan, 65
Jordan (riv.), Asia, 65
Jorhat, India, 68
Jorm, Afghan., 68
Jos, Nigeria, 106
Jose Panganiban, Phil., 82
Joseph (lake), Newf., 166
Joseph Bonaparte (gulf), Australia, 92, 93
Joshua Tree Nat'l Mon., Calif., 204
Jostedalsbreen (glac.), Norway, 18
Jost Van Dyke (isl.), Virgin Is. (Br.), 161
Jovellanos, Cuba, 158
Joyce's Country (dist.), Ireland, 17
Juan Aldama, Mexico, 150
Juan de Fuca (str.), N. Amer., 184
Juan de Nova (isl.), Réunion, 118
Juan Fernández (isls.), Chile, 120
Juani (isl.), Tanz., 115
Juanita, Wash., 310
Juan L. Lacaze, Uruguay, 145
Juazeiro do Norte, Brazil, 132
Juba, Sudan, 111
Jubail, Saudi Arabia, 59
Jubbada Hoose (prov.), Somalia, 115
Jubbulpore (Jabalpur), India, 68
Juby (cape), Mor., 106
Júcar (riv.), Spain, 33
Juchitán de Zaragoza, Mexico, 150
Judaea (reg.), Asia, 65
Juigalpa, Nicaragua, 154
Juiz de Fora, Brazil, 135
Jujuy (prov.), Arg., 143
Jujuy, Arg., 143
Juliaca, Peru, 128
Julian Alps (range), Italy, 34
Julianatop (mt.), Suriname, 131
Julianehåb, Greenl., 4
Jülich, W. Ger., 22
Jullundur, India, 68
Jumilla, Spain, 33
Jumna (riv.), India, 68
Junagadh, India, 68
Juncos, P. Rico, 161
Junction City, Kans., 232
Jundial, Brazil, 132
Juneau (cap.), Alaska, 196
Junee, N.S. Wales, 97
Jungfrau (mt.), Switz., 39
Junglei (prov.), Sudan, 111
Junín, Arg., 143
Junín (dept.), Peru, 128
Jun Xian, China, 77
Juojärvi (lake), Fin., 18
Jura (mts.), Europe, 28, 39
Jura (dept.), France, 28
Jura (isl.), Scotland, 15
Jura (sound), Scotland, 15
Jurmala, U.S.S.R., 53
Juruena (riv.), Brazil, 132
Justice, Ill., 222
Jutaí (riv.), Brazil, 132
Jüterbog, E. Ger., 22
Jutiapa, Guat., 154
Juticalpa, Honduras, 154
Jutland (pen.), Den., 21
Juventud (isl.), Cuba, 158
Juwara, Oman, 59
Jylland (Jutland) (pen.), Den., 21
Jyväskylä, Fin., 18

K

K2 (mt.), Pakistan, 68
Kabala, Sierra Leone, 106
Kabale, Uganda, 115
Kabalo, Zaire, 115
Kabambare, Zaire, 115
Kabardin-Balkar A.S.S.R., U.S.S.R., 52
Kabba, Nigeria, 106
Kabongo, Zaire, 115
Kabul (cap.), Afghan., 68
Kabul (riv.), Asia, 68
Kabwe, Zambia, 115
Kabylia (reg.), Algeria, 106
Kachin (state), Burma, 72
Kachug, U.S.S.R., 48
Kadayanallur, India, 68
Kadıköy, Turkey, 63
Kadiyevka (Stakhanov), U.S.S.R., 52
Kadoma, Japan, 81
Kadoma (Gatooma), Zimbabwe, 118
Kadugli, Sudan, 111
Kaduna (state), Nigeria, 106
Kaduna, Nigeria, 106
Kaédi, Mauritania, 106
Kaesŏng, N. Korea, 81
Kaf, Saudi Arabia, 59
Kaffa (prov.), Ethiopia, 111
Kafue (riv.), Zambia, 115
Kaga, Japan, 81
Kagan, U.S.S.R., 48
Kagawa (pref.), Japan, 81
Kağızman, Turkey, 63
Kagoshima (pref.), Japan, 81
Kagoshima, Japan, 81
Kagul, U.S.S.R., 52
Kahemba, Zaire, 115
Kahramanmaraş (prov.), Turkey, 63
Kahramanmaraş (Maraş), Turkey, 63
Kahului, Hawaii, 218
Kai (isls.), Indon., 85
Kaieteur (fall), Guyana, 131
Kaifeng, China, 77
Kaikoura (pen.), N. Zealand, 100
Kailua, Hawaii, 218
Kaimana, Indon., 85
Kainan (bay), Antarc., 5
Kainji (res.), Nigeria, 106
Kaipara (harb.), N. Zealand, 100
Kairouan, Tun., 106
Kairuku, Papua N.G., 85
Kaiserslautern, W. Ger., 22
Kaiserstuhl (mt.), W. Ger., 22
Kaizuka, Japan, 81
Kajaani, Fin., 18
Kakhovka, U.S.S.R., 52
Kakinada, India, 68
Kakogawa, Japan, 81
Kalaa-Kebira, Tun., 106
Kalach, U.S.S.R., 52
Kalachinsk, U.S.S.R., 48
Kaladan (riv.), Burma, 72
Kalahari (des.), Africa, 118
Kahalari Gemsbok Nat'l Park, S. Africa, 118
Kalajoki, Fin., 18
Kalajoki (riv.), Fin., 18
Kalakan, U.S.S.R., 48
Kalámai, Greece, 45
Kalamazoo, Mich., 250
Kalat, Pakistan, 68
Kalemie, Zaire, 115
Kalemyo, Burma, 72
Kalevala, U.S.S.R., 52
Kalgan (Zhangjiakou), China, 77
Kalgoorlie, W. Australia, 92
Kalianda, Indon., 85
Kalibo, Phil., 82
Kalimantan (reg.), Indon., 85
Kálimnos (isl.), Greece, 45
Kalinga-Apayao (prov.), Phil., 82
Kalinin, U.S.S.R., 52
Kaliningrad, U.S.S.R., 52
Kalinkovichi, U.S.S.R., 52
Kalispell, Mont., 262
Kalisz, Poland, 47
Kalixälv (riv.), Sweden, 18
Kallavesi (lake), Fin., 18
Kalmar (co.), Sweden, 18
Kalmar, Sweden, 18
Kalmarsund (sound), Sweden, 18
Kalmuck A.S.S.R., U.S.S.R., 52
Kalmunai, Sri Lanka, 68
Kalmykovo, U.S.S.R., 48
Kalomo, Zambia, 115
Kalpeni (isl.), India, 68
Kaluga, U.S.S.R., 52
Kalundborg, Den., 21
Kalutara, Sri Lanka, 68
Kalyan, India, 68
Kama, Burma, 72
Kama (riv.), U.S.S.R., 52
Kamaishi, Japan, 81
Kamakura, Japan, 81
Kamaran (isl.), P.D.R. Yemen, 59
Kamarhati, India, 68
Kambia, Sierra Leone, 106
Kambove, Zaire, 115
Kamchatka (pen.), U.S.S.R., 48
Kamenets-Podol'skiy, U.S.S.R., 52
Kamenjak (cape), Yugo., 45
Kamenka, U.S.S.R., 52
Kamenskoye, U.S.S.R., 48
Kamensk-Shakhtinskiy, U.S.S.R., 52
Kamensk-Ural'skiy, U.S.S.R., 48
Kamenz, E. Ger., 22
Kamet (mt.), India, 68
Kamina, Zaire, 115
Kamloops, Br. Col., 184
Kampala (cap.), Uganda, 115
Kampar, Malaysia, 72
Kampen, Neth., 27
Kamphaeng Phet, Thai., 72
Kampong Cham, Cambodia, 72
Kampong Chhnang, Cambodia, 72
Kampong Saom, Cambodia, 72
Kampong Spoe, Cambodia, 72
Kampong Thum, Cambodia, 72
Kampong Trabek, Cambodia, 72
Kampot, Cambodia, 72
Kamptee, India, 68
Kampuchea (Cambodia), 72
Kamsack, Sask., 181
Kamui (cape), Japan, 81
Kamyshin, U.S.S.R., 52
Kanaaupscow (riv.), Québec, 174
Kanab, Utah, 304
Kanagawa (pref.), Japan, 81
Kananga, Zaire, 115
Kanash, U.S.S.R., 52
Kanazawa, Japan, 81
Kanbalu, Burma, 72
Kanchanaburi, Thai., 72
Kanchenjunga (mt.), Asia, 68
Kanchipuram, India, 68
Kandahar (Qandahar), Afghan., 68
Kandalaksha, U.S.S.R., 52
Kandalaksha (gulf), U.S.S.R., 52
Kandavu (isl.), Fiji, 87
Kandi, Benin, 106
Kandy, Sri Lanka, 68
Kane (basin), N. Amer., 187
Kane, Pa., 294
Kanem (reg.), Chad, 111
Kaneohe, Hawaii, 218
Kangar, Malaysia, 72
Kangaroo (isl.), S. Australia, 94
Kangding, China, 77
Kangean (isls.), Indon., 85
Kangnŭng, S. Korea, 81
Kaniama, Zaire, 115
Kanin (pen.), U.S.S.R., 52
Kanjiža, Yugo., 45
Kankakee, Ill., 222
Kankan, Guinea, 106
Kankossa, Mauritania, 106
Kannapolis, N.C., 281
Kano (state), Nigeria, 106
Kano, Nigeria, 106
Kanoya, Japan, 81
Kanpur, India, 68
Kansas (riv.), Kans., 232
Kansas (state), U.S., 232
Kansas City, Kans., 232
Kansas City, Mo., 261
Kansk, U.S.S.R., 48
Kansu (Gansu) (prov.), China, 77
Kanturk, Ireland, 17
Kanuma, Japan, 81
Kanye, Botswana, 118
Kaohsiung, China, 77
Kaolack, Senegal, 106
Kaoma, Zambia, 115
Kaopao (Gaoyou Hu) (lake), China, 77
Kapaa, Hawaii, 218
Kapanga, Zaire, 115
Kapfenberg, Austria, 41
Kapingamarangi (atoll), Micronesia, 87
Kaplan, La., 238
Kaposvár, Hung., 41
Kapsukas, U.S.S.R., 53
Kapuas (riv.), Indon., 85
Kapuskasing, Ontario, 175
Kapydzhik (mt.), U.S.S.R., 52
Kara, U.S.S.R., 48
Kara (sea), U.S.S.R., 48
Kara-Bogaz-Gol (gulf), U.S.S.R., 48
Karabük, Turkey, 63
Karachay-Cherkess Aut. Oblast, U.S.S.R., 52
Karachi, Pakistan, 68
Karadeniz Boğazı (Bosporus) (strait), Turkey, 63
Karaganda, U.S.S.R., 48
Karaikudi, India, 68
Karakalpak A.S.S.R., U.S.S.R., 48
Karakhoto (ruins), China, 77
Karakoram (mts.), Asia, 68
Karakorum (ruins), Mong., 77
Karaköse (Ağri), Turkey, 63
Kara-Kum (canal), U.S.S.R., 48
Kara-Kum (des.), U.S.S.R., 48
Karaman, Turkey, 63
Karamay, China, 77
Karamea (bight), N. Zealand, 100
Kara Nor (Har Hu) (lake), China, 77
Karasburg, Namibia, 118
Karasu, Turkey, 63
Karasuk, U.S.S.R., 48
Karatsu, Japan, 81
Karawanken (range), Europe, 41
Karbala' (gov.), Iraq, 66
Karbala', Iraq, 66
Karcag, Hung., 41
Kardhítsa, Greece, 45
Karelian A.S.S.R., U.S.S.R., 52
Karema, Tanz., 115
Karen (state), Burma, 72
Kariba (lake), Africa, 118
Kariba, Zimbabwe, 118
Karibib, Namibia, 118
Karikal, India, 68
Karima, Sudan, 111
Karimata (arch.), Indon., 85
Karis (Karjaa), Fin., 18
Karisimbi (mt.), Africa, 115
Karkkila, Fin., 18
Karl-Marx-Stadt (dist.), E. Ger., 22
Karl-Marx-Stadt, E. Ger., 22
Karlovac, Yugo., 45
Karlovo, Bulg., 45
Karlovy Vary, Czech., 41
Karlshamn, Sweden, 18
Karlskoga, Sweden, 18
Karlskrona, Sweden, 18
Karlsruhe, W. Ger., 22
Karlstad, Sweden, 18
Karnal, India, 68
Karnataka (state), India, 68
Karnes City, Texas, 303
Karnobat, Bulg., 45
Karonga, Malawi, 115
Kárpathos (isl.), Greece, 45
Kars (prov.), Turkey, 63
Kars, Turkey, 63
Karshi, U.S.S.R., 48
Karşıyaka, Turkey, 63
Karskiye Vorota (strait), U.S.S.R., 52
Karun (riv.), Iran, 66
Karviná, Czech., 41
Kasai (riv.), Africa, 115
Kasai-Occidental (prov.), Zaire, 115
Kasai-Oriental (prov.), Zaire, 115
Kasama, Zambia, 115
Kasanga, Tanz., 115
Kasba (lake), N.W. Terr., 187
Kashan, Iran, 66

L

340

Samut Prakan, Thai., 72
Samut Sakhon, Thai., 72
Samut Songkhram, Thai., 72
San, Se (riv.), Asia, 72
San, Mali, 106
San (riv.), Poland, 47
Saña, Peru, 128
San'a (cap.), Yemen Arab Rep., 59
Sanaag (prov.), Somalia, 115
Sanae Sta., Antarc., 5
Sanaga (riv.), Cameroon, 115
San Agustín, Colombia, 126
San Agustin (cape), Phil., 82
San Ambrosio (isl.), Chile, 120
Sanana, Indon., 85
Sanandaj, Iran, 66
San Andrés (isl.), Colombia, 126
San Andrés Antioquan, Colombia, 126
San Andrés Tuxtla, Mexico, 150
San Andrés y Providencia (inten.), Colombia, 126
San Angelo, Texas, 303
San Anselmo, Calif., 204
San Antero, Colombia, 126
San Antonio (cape), Arg., 143
San Antonio, Chile, 138
San Antonio (cape), Cuba, 158
San Antonio, N. Mex., 274
San Antonio, Texas, 303
San Antonio de Areco, Arg., 143
San Antonio de los Baños, Cuba, 158
San Antonio del Táchira, Venez., 124
San Antonio Oeste, Arg., 143
Sanare, Venez., 124
San Augustine, Texas, 303
San Benito (isl.), Mexico, 150
San Benito, Texas, 303
San Bernardino, Calif., 204
San Bernardino (mts.), Calif., 204
San Bernardino (strait), Phil., 82
San Bernardino (pass), Switz., 39
San Bernardo, Chile, 138
San Blas, Mexico, 150
San Blas, Archipiélago de (arch.), Panama, 154
San Blas, Cordillera de (mts.), Panama, 154
San Blas, Golfo de (gulf), Panama, 154
San Bruno, Calif., 204
San Buenaventura, Mexico, 150
San Carlos, Arg., 143
San Carlos, Calif., 204
San Carlos, Chile, 138
San Carlos, Nicaragua, 154
San Carlos, Phil., 82
San Carlos, Uruguay, 145
San Carlos, Venez., 124
San Carlos de Bariloche, Arg., 143
San Casimiro, Venez., 124
San Cataldo, Italy, 34
Sánchez, Dom. Rep., 158
Sánchez Ramírez (prov.), Dom. Rep., 158
San Clemente, Calif., 204
San Clemente (isl.), Calif., 204
San Cristóbal, Arg., 143
San Cristóbal (prov.), Dom. Rep., 158
San Cristóbal, Dom. Rep., 158
San Cristóbal (isl.), Ecuador, 128
San Cristobal (isl.), Sol. Is., 87
San Cristóbal, Venez., 124
San Cristóbal de las Casas, Mexico, 150
Sancti Spíritus (prov.), Cuba, 158
Sancti Spíritus, Cuba, 158
Sandakan, Malaysia, 85
Sandalwood (Sumba) (isl.), Indon., 85
Sandanski, Bulg., 45
Sanday (isl.), Scotland, 15
Sandefjord, Norway, 18
Sanderson, Texas, 303
Sandersville, Ga., 217
Sandgate, Queensland, 95
Sandia (peak), N. Mex., 274
San Diego (cape), Arg., 143
San Diego, Calif., 204
San Diego, Texas, 303
San Dimas, Calif., 204
Sandnes, Norway, 18
Sandoa, Zaire, 115
Sandoná, Colombia, 126
Sandoway, Burma, 72
Sandown (bay), S. Africa, 118
Sandown-Shanklin, England, 13
Sandpoint, Idaho, 220
Sandringham, Victoria, 97
Sand Springs, Okla., 288
Sandston, Va., 307
Sandusky, Ohio, 284
Sandvika, Norway, 18
Sandviken, Sweden, 18
Sandwich, Ill., 222
Sandwich (bay), Newf., 166
Sandy (cape), Queensland, 95
Sandy, Utah, 304
Sandy Hook (spit), N.J., 273
Sandy Point, St. Chris.-Nevis, 161
San Estanislao, Paraguay, 144
San Felipe, Chile, 138
San Felipe (cays), Cuba, 158
San Felipe, Guat., 154
San Felipe, N. Mex., 274
San Felipe, Venez., 124
San Felipe Pueblo, Mex., 150
San Félix, (isl.), Chile, 120
San Fernando, Arg., 143
San Fernando, Calif., 204
San Fernando, Chile, 138
San Fernando, Mexico, 150
San Fernando, Spain, 33
San Fernando, Trin. & Tob., 161
San Fernando, Venez., 124
Sanford, Fla., 212
Sanford, Maine, 243
Sanford, N.C., 281
San Francisco, Arg., 143
San Francisco, Calif., 204
San Francisco (bay), Calif., 204
San Francisco de la Paz, Honduras, 154
San Francisco del Oro, Mexico, 150
San Francisco del Rincón, Mexico, 150
San Francisco de Macorís, Dom. Rep., 158
San Francisco Gotera, El Salv., 154
San Gabriel, Calif., 204
San Gabriel, Ecuador, 128
San Gabriel Chilac, Mexico, 150
Sangamner, India, 68
Sanger, Calif., 204
Sangerhausen, E. Ger., 22
San Germán, Cuba, 158
San Germán, P. Rico, 161
Sangha (riv.), Africa, 115
Sangihe (isls.), Indon., 85
San Gil, Colombia, 126
Sangju, S. Korea, 81
Sangli, India, 68
Sangmélima, Cameroon, 115
Sangolquí, Ecuador, 128
Sangre de Cristo (mts.), U.S., 208, 274
Sangre Grande, Trin. & Tob., 161
San Ignacio, Bolivia, 136
San Ignacio, Paraguay, 144
San Jacinto, Calif., 204
San Jacinto, Colombia, 126
San Javier, Arg., 143
San Javier, Chile, 138
San Joaquín, Bolivia, 136
San Joaquin (riv.), Calif., 204
San Jorge (gulf), Arg., 143
San Jorge (bay), Mexico, 150
San Jorge, Nicaragua, 154
San Jose, Calif., 204
San José (cap.), Costa Rica, 154
San José, Guat., 154
San José (isl.), Mexico, 150
San José, Paraguay, 144
San José (dept.), Uruguay, 145
San José, Venez., 124
San Jose de Buenavista, Phil., 82
San José de Chiquitos, Bolivia, 136
San José de las Lajas, Cuba, 158
San José del Cabo, Mexico, 150
San José de Mayo, Uruguay, 145
San José de Ocoa, Dom. Rep., 158
San Juan (prov.), Arg., 143
San Juan, Arg., 143
San Juan (riv.), Cent. Amer., 154
San Juan (prov.), Dom. Rep., 158
San Juan, Dom. Rep., 158
San Juan, Mexico, 150
San Juan (dist.), P. Rico, 161
San Juan (cap.), P. Rico, 161
San Juan, Texas, 303
San Juan, Trin. & Tob., 161
San Juan (riv.), U.S., 276, 304
San Juan (isl.), Wash., 310
San Juan Bautista, Paraguay, 144
San Juan de Flores, Honduras, 154
San Juan del Norte, Nicaragua, 154
San Juan de los Morros, Venez., 124
San Juan del Sur, Nicaragua, 154
San Juan Isl. Nat'l Hist. Park, Wash., 310
San Juan Nat'l Hist. Site, P. Rico, 161
San Juan Pueblo, N. Mex., 274
San Juan Xiutetelco, Mexico, 150
San Julián, Arg., 143
Sankt Anton am Neuwalde, Austria, 41
Sankt Gallen (canton), Switz., 39
Sankt Gallen, Switz., 39
Sankt Ingbert, W. Ger., 22
Sankt Pölten, Austria, 41
Sankt Veit an der Glan, Austria, 41
Sankt Vith, Belg., 27
Sankt Wolfgang im Salzkammergut, Austria, 41
Sankuru (riv.), Zaire, 115
San Lázaro (cape), Mexico, 150
San Leandro, Calif., 204
San Lorenzo, Arg., 143
San Lorenzo, Calif., 204
San Lorenzo, Paraguay, 144
San Lorenzo de El Escorial, Spain, 33
Sanlúcar de Barrameda, Spain, 33
San Lucas (cape), Mexico, 150
San Luis (prov.), Arg., 143
San Luis, Arg., 143
San Luis, Cuba, 158
San Luis, Honduras, 154
San Luis de la Paz, Mexico, 150
San Luis del Cordero, Mexico, 150
San Luis Jilotepeque, Guat., 154
San Luis Obispo, Calif., 204
San Luis Potosí (state), Mexico, 150
San Luis Potosí, Mexico, 150
San Luis Río Colorado, Mexico, 150
San Manuel, Ariz., 198
San Marcos, Colombia, 126
San Marcos, Guat., 154
San Marcos, Honduras, 154
San Marcos, Mexico, 150
San Marcos, Texas, 303
San Marino, 34
San Marino, Calif., 204
San Marino (cap.), San Marino, 34
San Martín, Colombia, 126
San Martín (dept.), Peru, 128
San Martín (lake), S. Amer., 143
San Martín Jilotepeque, Guat., 154
San Martín Texmelucan, Mexico, 150
San Mateo, Calif., 204
San Mateo Ixtatan, Guat., 154
San Matías (gulf), Arg., 143
San Miguel (riv.), Bolivia, 136
San Miguel, El Salv., 154
San Miguel (bay), Panama, 154
San Miguel Allende, Mexico, 150
San Miguel de Tucumán, Arg., 143
Sanming, China, 77
San Nicolás, Arg., 143
San Nicolas (isl.), Calif., 204
San Nicolás, Cuba, 158
San Nua, Laos, 72
San Onofre, Colombia, 126
San Pablo, Calif., 204
San Pablo, Phil., 82
San Pedro, Arg., 143
San Pedro, Calif., 204
San Pedro (riv.), Guat., 154
San Pedro (dept.), Paraguay, 144
San Pedro, Paraguay, 144
San Pedro Carchá, Guat., 154
San Pedro de las Colonias, Mexico, 150
San Pedro de Lloc, Peru, 128
San Pedro de Macorís (prov.), Dom. Rep., 158
San Pedro de Macorís, Dom. Rep., 158
San Pedro Pochutla, Mexico, 150
San Pedro Sula, Honduras, 154
Sanpoil (riv.), Wash., 310
Sanquhar, Scotland, 15
San Rafael, Arg., 143
San Rafael, Calif., 204
San Rafael (riv.), Utah, 304
San Rafael, Venez., 124
San Rafael del Sur, Nicaragua, 154
San Ramón, Bolivia, 136
San Ramón, C. Rica, 154
San Ramón, Uruguay, 145
San Ramón de la Nueva Orán, Arg., 143
San Remo, Italy, 34
San Roque, Colombia, 126
San Saba, Texas, 303
San Salvador (isl.), Bahamas, 156
San Salvador (isl.), Ecuador, 128
San Salvador (cap.), El Salv., 154
San Sebastián, P. Rico, 161
San Sebastián, Spain, 33
San Sebastián, Venez., 124
San Severo, Italy, 34
Sansom Park Vill., Texas, 303
Santa Ana, Bolivia, 136
Santa Ana, Calif., 204
Santa Ana, El Salv., 154
Santa Ana, Mexico, 150
Santa Ana, Venez., 124
Santa Barbara, Calif., 204
Santa Barbara (isls.), Calif., 204
Santa Bárbara, Colombia, 126
Santa Bárbara, Honduras, 154
Santa Bárbara, Mexico, 150
Santa Catalina (isl.), Calif., 204
Santa Catalina (isl.), Mexico, 150
Santa Catarina (state), Brazil, 132
Santa Catarina (isl.), Brazil, 132
Santa Clara, Calif., 204
Santa Clara, Cuba, 158
Santa Cruz (prov.), Arg., 143
Santa Cruz, Arg., 143
Santa Cruz (dept.), Bolivia, 136
Santa Cruz, Bolivia, 136
Santa Cruz, Calif., 204
Santa Cruz, Chile, 138
Santa Cruz, C. Rica, 154
Santa Cruz (isl.), Ecuador, 128
Santa Cruz, India, 68
Santa Cruz, Jamaica, 158
Santa Cruz (isl.), Mexico, 150
Santa Cruz (isls.), Sol. Is., 87
Santa Cruz, Venez., 124
Santa Cruz del Quiché, Guat., 154
Santa Cruz de Tenerife (prov.), Spain, 33
Santa Cruz de Tenerife, Spain, 33
Santa Cruz de Yojoa, Honduras, 154
Santa Cruz do Rio Pardo, Brazil, 135
Santa Elena (cape), Costa Rica, 154
Santa Elena, Ecuador, 128
Santa Eugenia (pt.), Mexico, 150
Santa Fe (prov.), Arg., 143
Santa Fe, Arg., 143
Santa Fé, Cuba, 158
Santa Fe (cap.), N. Mex., 274
Santa Fe Sprs., Calif., 204
Santai, China, 77
Santa Isabel, P. Rico, 161
Santa Isabel (isl.), Sol. Is., 87
Santa Lucía, Arg., 143
Santa Lucía, Uruguay, 145
Santa Maria (cape), Angola, 115
Santa Maria, Brazil, 132
Santa Maria, Calif., 204
Santa Maria, Cape Verde, 106
Santa María (isl.), Ecuador, 128
Santa María (riv.), Mexico, 150
Santa Maria (cape), Portugal, 33
Santa Maria (isl.), Portugal, 32
Santa Maria Capua Vetere, Italy, 34
Santa María del Río, Mexico, 150
Santa María del Tule, Mexico, 150
Santa María del Orinoco, Venez., 124
Santa Marta, Colombia, 126
Santa Monica, Calif., 204
Santana do Livramento, Brazil, 132
Santander (dept.), Colombia, 126
Santander, Colombia, 126
Santander (prov.), Spain, 33
Santander, Spain, 33
Sant'Antioco (isl.), Italy, 34
Santa Paula, Calif., 204
Santarém, Brazil, 132
Santarém, Portugal, 33
Santa Rita, Honduras, 154
Santa Rita, N. Mex., 274
Santa Rita, Venez., 124
Santa Rosa, Arg., 143
Santa Rosa, Calif., 204
Santa Rosa, Ecuador, 128
Santa Rosa (mts.), Nev., 266
Santa Rosa, N. Mex., 274
Santa Rosa, Paraguay, 144
Santa Rosa de Aguán, Honduras, 154
Santa Rosa de Copán, Honduras, 154
Santa Rosa de Lima, El Salv., 154
Santa Rosa de Osos, Colombia, 126
Santa Rosalía, Mexico, 150
Santa Teresa, Venez., 124
Santee, Calif., 204
Santee (riv.), S.C., 296
Santiago, Región Metropolitana de (met. reg.), Chile, 138
Santiago (cap.), Chile, 138
Santiago (prov.), Dom. Rep., 158
Santiago, Dom. Rep., 158
Santiago, Mexico, 150
Santiago, Panama, 154
Santiago, Spain, 33
Santiago (mts.), Texas, 303
Santiago de Chuco, Peru, 128
Santiago de Cuba (prov.), Cuba, 158
Santiago de Cuba, Cuba, 158
Santiago de las Vegas, Cuba, 158
Santiago del Estero (prov.), Arg., 143
Santiago del Estero, Arg., 143
Santiago Juxtlahuaca, Mexico, 150
Santiago Papasquiaro, Mexico, 150
Santiago Rodríguez (prov.), Dom. Rep., 158
Santiago Tuxtla, Mexico, 150
San Timoteo, Venez., 124
Santipur, India, 68
Santo Amaro, Brazil, 132
Santo André, Brazil, 135
Santo Ângelo, Brazil, 132
Santo Antão (isl.), Cape Verde, 106
Santo Domingo, C. Rica, 154
Santo Domingo (cap.), Dom. Rep., 158
Santo Domingo, Nicaragua, 154
Santo Domingo de los Colorados, Ecuador, 128
Santos, Brazil, 135
Santos Dumont, Brazil, 135
Santo Tomás, Nicaragua, 154
Santo Tomás de Castilla, Guat., 154
Santurce, P. Rico, 161
San Vicente, Peru, 128
San Vito, Italy, 34
São Bernardo do Campo, Brazil, 135
São Borja, Brazil, 132
São Carlos, Brazil, 135
São Francisco (riv.), Brazil, 132
São Francisco do Sul, Brazil, 132
São João da Bôa Vista, Brazil, 135
São João da Madeira, Portugal, 33
São João del Rei, Brazil, 135
São Joaquim da Barra, Brazil, 135
São Jorge (isl.), Portugal, 32
São José do Rio Pardo, Brazil, 135
São José do Rio Prêto, Brazil, 135
São José dos Campos, Brazil, 135
São Leopoldo, Brazil, 132
São Lourenço, Brazil, 135
São Luís, Brazil, 132
São Manuel, Brazil, 135
São Miguel (isl.), Portugal, 32
São Miguel Arcanjo, Brazil, 135
Saona (isl.), Dom. Rep., 158
Saône (riv.), France, 28
Saône-et-Loire (dept.), France, 28
São Paulo (state), Brazil, 132
São Paulo, Brazil, 135
São Roque (cape), Brazil, 132
São Sebastião (isl.), Brazil, 135
São Sebastião (pt.), Mozamb., 118
São Tiago (isl.), Cape Verde, 106
São Tomé (cape), Brazil, 132
São Tomé (cap.), São T. e Pr., 106
São Tomé (isl.), São T. e Pr., 106
São Tomé e Príncipe, 106
Saoura, Wadi (dry riv.), Algeria, 106
São Vicente, Brazil, 135
São Vincent (cape), Portugal, 32
Saparua, Indon., 85
Sapele, Nigeria, 106
Sapporo, Japan, 81
Sapucaí, Paraguay, 144
Sapulpa, Okla., 288
Saqqez, Iran, 66
Sara (riv.), Africa, 111
Sara Buri, Thai., 72
Saragossa (Zaragoza) (prov.), Spain, 33
Saragossa (Zaragoza), Spain, 33
Sarajevo, Yugo., 45
Saraland, Ala., 195
Saramacca (dist.), Suriname, 131
Saranac Lake, N.Y., 276
Sarandë, Alb., 45
Sarandí del Yí, Uruguay, 145
Sarandí Grande, Uruguay, 145
Sarangani (isls.), Phil., 82
Saransk, U.S.S.R., 52
Sarapul, U.S.S.R., 52
Sarare, Venez., 124
Sarasota, Fla., 212
Saraswati (riv.), India, 68
Saratoga, Calif., 204
Saratoga, Wyo., 319
Saratoga Nat'l Hist. Park, N.Y., 276
Saratoga Springs, N.Y., 276
Saratov, U.S.S.R., 52
Saravan, Laos, 72
Sarawak (state), Malaysia, 85
Sardarshahr, India, 68
Sardinata, Colombia, 126
Sardinia (reg.), Italy, 34
Sardinia (isl.), Italy, 34
Sardis (lake), Miss., 256
Sar-e Pol, Afghan., 68
Sargodha, Pakistan, 68
Sarh, Chad, 111
Sari, Iran, 66
Sarıkamış, Turkey, 63
Sariwŏn, N. Korea, 81
Sarıyer, Turkey, 63
Sark (isl.), Chan. Is., 13
Sarmi, Indon., 85
Sarnath, India, 68
Sarnen, Switz., 39
Sarnia, Ontario, 177
Saronic (gulf), Greece, 45
Saronno, Italy, 34
Saros (gulf), Turkey, 63
Sarpsborg, Norway, 18
Sarreguemines, France, 28
Sarstún (riv.), Cent. Amer., 154
Sarthe (dept.), France, 28
Sarthe (riv.), France, 28
Sartrouville, France, 28
Sasaram, India, 68
Sasebo, Japan, 81
Saskatchewan (prov.), Canada, 181
Saskatchewan (riv.), Canada, 162
Saskatoon, Sask., 181
Sassafras (riv.), Md., 245
Sassandra, Ivory Coast, 106
Sassari (prov.), Italy, 34
Sassari, Italy, 34
Satara, India, 68
Satawal (isl.), Micronesia, 87
Satluj (Sutlej) (riv.), Asia, 68
Satna, India, 68
Satpura (range), India, 68
Satu Mare, Romania, 45
Sauce (lagoon), Uruguay, 145
Saucillo, Mexico, 150
Saudhárkrókur, Iceland, 21
Saudi Arabia, 59
Sauer (riv.), Europe, 27
Sauerland (reg.), W. Ger., 22
Saugerties, N.Y., 276
Saugus, Mass., 249
Saugus Iron Works Nat'l Hist. Site, Mass., 249
Sauk Centre, Minn., 255
Sauk City, Wis., 317
Sauk Rapids, Minn., 255
Sauk Village, Ill., 222
Sault Sainte Marie, Mich., 250
Sault Sainte Marie, Ontario, 175, 177
Saumâtre (lake), Haiti, 158
Saumlaki, Indon., 85
Saumur, France, 28
Sauqira (bay), Oman, 59
Saurimo, Angola, 115
Sausalito, Calif., 204
Sauteurs, Grenada, 161
Sava (riv.), Yugo., 45
Savage (riv.), Md., 245
Savai'i (isl.), W. Samoa, 87
Savalou, Benin, 106
Savanna, Ill., 222
Savannah, Ga., 217
Savannah, Tenn., 237
Savannah (riv.), U.S., 217, 296
Savannakhét, Laos, 72
Savanna-la-Mar, Jamaica, 158
Savannes (bay), St. Lucia, 161
Savantvadi, India, 68
Savanur, India, 68
Savé, Benin, 106
Save (riv.), Mozamb., 118
Saveh, Iran, 66
Savoie (Savoy) (dept.), France, 28
Savona (prov.), Italy, 34
Savona, Italy, 34
Savonlinna, Fin., 18
Sävsjö, Sweden, 18
Sawahlunto, Indon., 85
Sawara, Japan, 81
Sawtooth (range), Idaho, 220
Sawu (isls.), Indon., 85
Sawu (sea), Indon., 85
Saxon, S.C., 296
Saxony (reg.), E. Ger., 22
Say, Niger, 106
Sayaboury (Muang Xaignabouri), Laos, 72
Sayama, Japan, 81
Sayan (mts.), U.S.S.R., 48
Saynshand, Mong., 77
Sayre, Okla., 288
Sayre, Pa., 294
Sayreville, N.J., 273
Sayula, Mexico, 150
Sayville, N.Y., 276
Sazan (isl.), Alb., 45
Scafell Pike (mt.), England, 13
Scandanavia, 18
Scapa Flow (chan.), Scotland, 15
Scarborough, England, 13
Scarborough, Ontario, 177
Scarborough, Trin. & Tob., 156
Scarsdale, N.Y., 276
Sceaux, France, 28
Schaan, Liecht., 39
Schaerbeek, Belg., 27
Schaffhausen (canton), Switz., 39
Schaffhausen, Switz., 39
Schaumburg, Ill., 222
Schefferville, Québec, 174
Scheldt (Schelde) (riv.), Europe, 27
Schell Creek (range), Nev., 266
Schenectady, N.Y., 276
Schererville, Ind., 227
Scheveningen, Neth., 27
Schiedam, Neth., 27
Schiller Park, Ill., 222
Schio, Italy, 34
Schleswig, W. Ger., 22
Schleswig-Holstein (state), W. Ger., 22
Schlieren, Switz., 39
Schneeberg, E. Ger., 22
Schnee Eifel (plat.), Belg., 27
Schoelcher, Mart., 161
Schofield, Wis., 317
Schofield Barracks, Hawaii, 218
Schoharie (res.), N.Y., 276
Schönebeck, E. Ger., 22
Schöneberg, W. Ger., 22
Schoten, Belg., 27
Schouten (isls.), Indon., 85
Schouten (isls.), Papua N.G., 85
Schouwen (isl.), Neth., 27
Schreiber, Ontario, 175
Schroon (lake), N.Y., 276
Schuyler, Nebr., 264
Schuylkill (riv.), Pa., 294
Schuylkill Haven, Pa., 294
Schwabach, W. Ger., 22
Schwäbisch Gmünd, W. Ger., 22
Schwäbisch Hall, W. Ger., 22
Schwaner (mts.), Indon., 85
Schwarzwald (Black) (for.), W. Ger., 22
Schwedt, E. Ger., 22
Schweinfurt, W. Ger., 22
Schwelm, W. Ger., 22
Schwerin (dist.), E. Ger., 22
Schwerin, E. Ger., 22
Schwerinersee (lake), E. Ger., 22
Schwyz (canton), Switz., 39
Schwyz, Switz., 39
Sciacca, Italy, 34
Scilly, Isles of (isls.), England, 13
Scioto (riv.), Ohio, 284
Scituate, Mass., 249
Scituate (res.), R.I., 249
Scobey, Mont., 262
Scone, N.S. Wales, 97
Scoresby (sound), Greenl., 4
Scoresbysund, Greenl., 4
Scotch Plains, N.J., 273
Scotia (sea), Antarc., 5
Scotia, N.Y., 276
Scotland, 15
Scotland Neck, N.C., 281
Scotlandville, La., 238
Scott (isl.), Antarc., 5
Scott City, Kans., 232
Scottdale, Pa., 294
Scottsbluff, Nebr., 264
Scotts Bluff Nat'l Mon., Nebr., 264
Scottsboro, Ala., 195
Scottsburg, Ind., 227
Scottsdale, Ariz., 198
Scottsdale, Tasmania, 99
Scranton, Pa., 294
Scunthorpe, England, 13
Scutari (lake), Europe, 45
Sea (isls.), U.S., 217, 296
Seabrook, Texas, 303
Sea Cliff, N.Y., 276
Seaford, Del., 245
Seaford, England, 13
Seaforth, Ontario, 177
Seagoville, Texas, 303
Seaham, England, 13
Seal (riv.), Manitoba, 179
Seal Beach, Calif., 204
Searcy, Ark., 203
Seaside, Calif., 204
Seaside, Oreg., 291
Seat Pleasant, Md., 245
Seattle, Wash., 310
Sebastián Vizcaíno (bay), Mexico, 150
Sebastopol, Calif., 204
Sebastopol, Victoria, 97
Sebha, Libya, 111
Seboruco, Venez., 124
Sebou (riv.), Mor., 106
Sebring, Fla., 212
Sebring, Ohio, 284
Sebuku (bay), Indon., 85
Secaucus, N.J., 273
Sechura (bay), Peru, 128
Secunderabad, India, 68
Security, Colo., 208
Sedalia, Mo., 261
Sedan, France, 28
Sedhiou, Senegal, 106
Sedro-Wooley, Wash., 310
Seeheim, Namibia, 118
Sefrou, Mor., 106
Segamat, Malaysia, 72
Ségou, Mali, 106
Segovia (Coco) (riv.), Cent. Amer., 154
Segovia, Colombia, 126
Segovia (prov.), Spain, 33
Segovia, Spain, 33
Segre (riv.), Spain, 33
Séguéla, Ivory Coast, 106
Seguin, Texas, 303
Segura (riv.), Spain, 33
Sehore, India, 68
Seibo, El (prov.), Dom. Rep., 158
Sein (isl.), France, 28
Seinäjoki, Fin., 18
Seine (bay), France, 28
Seine (riv.), France, 28
Seine-et-Marne (dept.), France, 28
Seine-Saint-Denis (dept.), France, 28
Seiyun, P.D.R. Yemen, 59
Sekondi, Ghana, 106
Selah, Wash., 310
Selangor (state), Malaysia, 72
Selaphum, Thai., 72
Selatan (cape), Indon., 85
Selayar (isl.), Indon., 85
Selemiya, Syria, 63
Selenge (prov.), Mong., 77
Selenge Mörön (Selenga) (riv.), Asia, 77
Sélibaby, Mauritania, 106
Selima (oasis), Sudan, 111
Selinsgrove, Pa., 294
Selkirk (mts.), Br. Col., 184
Selkirk, Manitoba, 179
Selkirk (trad. co.), Scotland, 15
Selkirk, Scotland, 15
Selle (peak), Haiti, 158
Sellersburg, Ind., 227
Selma, Ala., 195
Selma, Calif., 204
Selma, N.C., 281
Selmont, Ala., 195
Selsey Bill (pt.), England, 13
Selukwe, Zimbabwe, 118
Selwyn (lake), Canada, 187
Selwyn (mts.), Canada, 187
Semarang, Indon., 85
Semeru (mt.), Indon., 85
Seminoe (res.), Wyo., 319
Seminole, Okla., 288
Seminole, Texas, 303
Semipalatinsk, U.S.S.R., 48
Semirara (isls.), Phil., 82
Semmering (pass), Austria, 41
Semnan (gov.), Iran, 66
Semnan, Iran, 66
Sempach (lake), Switz., 39
Semporna, Malaysia, 85
Sen, Stoeng (riv.), Cambodia, 72
Senanga, Zambia, 115
Senatobia, Miss., 256
Sendai, Japan, 81
Seneca (lake), N.Y., 276
Seneca, S.C., 296
Seneca Falls, N.Y., 276
Senegal, 106
Senegal (riv.), Africa, 106
Senftenberg, E. Ger., 22
Senhor do Bonfim, Brazil, 132
Senigallia, Italy, 34
Senja (isl.), Norway, 18
Sennar, Sudan, 111
Sennar (dam), Sudan, 111
Sennestadt, W. Ger., 22
Senneterre, Québec, 174
Sens, France, 28
Sensuntepeque, El Salv., 154
Senta, Yugo., 45
Senyavin (isls.), Micronesia, 87
Seoni, India, 68
Seoul (cap.), S. Korea, 81
Sepik (riv.), Papua N.G., 85
Sept-Îles, Québec, 174
Septimer (pass), Switz., 39
Sequoia Nat'l Park, Calif., 204
Seraing, Belg., 27
Serampore, India, 68
Serang, Indon., 85
Serangoon, Sing., 72
Serbia (rep.), Yugo., 45
Serdobsk, U.S.S.R., 52
Seremban, Malaysia, 72
Serengeti Nat'l Park, Tanz., 115
Serenje, Zambia, 115
Sergipe (state), Brazil, 132
Sérifos (isl.), Greece, 45
Seringapatam, India, 68
Serov, U.S.S.R., 48
Serowe, Botswana, 118
Serpa, Portugal, 33
Serpents Mouth (passage), 124
Serpukhov, U.S.S.R., 52
Sérrai, Greece, 45
Serrinha, Brazil, 132
Serui, Indon., 85
Sesimbra, Portugal, 33
Sesto, Italy, 34
Sète, France, 28
Sétif, Algeria, 106
Settat, Mor., 106
Setté-Cama, Gabon, 115
Setúbal, Portugal, 33
Setúbal (bay), Portugal, 33
Seul (lake), Ontario, 175
Sevan (lake), U.S.S.R., 52
Sevastopol', U.S.S.R., 52
Seven Hills, Ohio, 284
Seven Islands (bay), Newf., 166
Seven Islands (Sept-Îles), Québec, 174
Sevenoaks, England, 10
Severn (riv.), Md., 245
Severn (riv.), Ontario, 177
Severn (riv.), U.K., 13
Severna Park, Md., 245
Severnaya Zemlya (isls.), U.S.S.R., 48
Severočeský (reg.), Czech., 41
Severodonetsk, U.S.S.R., 52
Severodvinsk, U.S.S.R., 52
Severo-Kuril'sk, U.S.S.R., 48
Severomoravský (reg.), Czech., 41
Severomorsk, U.S.S.R., 52
Severoural'sk, U.S.S.R., 48
Sevier (lake), Utah, 304
Sevier (riv.), Utah, 304
Sevierville, Tenn., 237
Sevilla, Colombia, 126
Sevilla (prov.), Spain, 33
Seville, Spain, 33
Sèvres, France, 28
Seward, Alaska, 196
Seward (pen.), Alaska, 196
Seward, Nebr., 264
Sewickley, Pa., 294
Sexsmith, Alberta, 182
Seychelles, 118
Seydhisfjördhur, Iceland, 21
Seyhan (riv.), Turkey, 63
Seymour, Conn., 210
Seymour, Ind., 227
Seymour, Texas, 303
Seymour (lake), Vt., 268
Seymour, Victoria, 97
Sfax, Tun., 106
's Gravenhage (The Hague) (cap.), Neth., 27
Shaanxi (prov.), China, 77
Shaba (prov.), Zaire, 115
Shabani, Zimbabwe, 118
Shabeellaha Dhexe (prov.), Somalia, 115
Shabeellaha Hoose (prov.), Somalia, 115
Shabunda, Zaire, 115
Shache, China, 77
Shackleton Ice Shelf, Antarc., 5
Shadehill (res.), S. Dak., 298
Shadrinsk, U.S.S.R., 48
Shadyside, Ohio, 284
Shafter, Calif., 204
Shahat, Libya, 111
Shahdol, India, 68
Shahi, Iran, 66
Shahjahanpur, India, 68
Shah Juy, Afghan., 68
Shahreza, Iran, 66
Shahrud, Iran, 66
Shaikh Shu'aib (isl.), Iran, 66
Shajapur, India, 68
Shaker Hts., Ohio, 284
Shakhty, U.S.S.R., 52
Shaki, Nigeria, 106
Shakopee, Minn., 255
Sham, Jebel (mt.), Oman, 59
Shammar, Jebel (plat.), Saudi Arabia, 59
Shamo, Mu Us (Gobi) (des.), Asia, 77
Shamokin, Pa., 294
Shan (state), Burma, 72
Shan (plat.), Burma, 72
Shandong (prov.), China, 77
Shangani (riv.), Zimbabwe, 118
Shanghai, China, 77
Shangqui (Shangkiu), China, 77
Shangrao (Shangjao), China, 77
Shangshui, China, 77
Shang Xian, China, 77
Shangzhi, China, 77
Shannon (riv.), Ireland, 17
Shannon Airport, Ireland, 17
Shanshan, China, 77
Shantou, China, 77
Shantung (Shandong) (prov.), China, 77
Shanxi (Shansi) (prov.), China, 77
Shaoguan, China, 77
Shaoxing (Shaohing), China, 77
Shaoyang, China, 77
Shari (riv.), Africa, 111
Sharjah, U.A.E., 59
Shark (bay), W. Australia, 92
Sharon, Mass., 249
Sharon, Pa., 294
Sharon Hill, Pa., 294
Sharonville, Ohio, 284
Sharpsburg, Pa., 294
Sharpsville, Pa., 294
Shar'ya, U.S.S.R., 52
Shashe (riv.), Africa, 118
Shashi (Shasi), China, 77
Shasta (lake), Calif., 204
Shasta (mt.), Calif., 204
Shatra, Iraq, 66
Shatt-al-'Arab (riv.), Iraq, 66
Shaunavon, Sask., 181
Shawano, Wis., 317
Shawinigan, Québec, 172
Shawnee, Kans., 232
Shawnee, Okla., 288
Sheberghan, Afghan., 68
Sheboygan, Wis., 317
Sheboygan Falls, Wis., 317
Shediac, New Bruns., 170
Sheffield, Ala., 195
Sheffield, England, 13
Sheffield Lake, Ohio, 284
Sheikh Sa'id, Yemen Arab Rep., 59
Sheki, U.S.S.R., 52
Shelagskiy (cape), U.S.S.R., 48
Shelburne, Nova Scotia, 169
Shelby, Mont., 262
Shelby, N.C., 281
Shelby, Ohio, 284
Shelbyville, Ill., 222
Shelbyville, Ind., 227
Shelbyville, Ky., 237
Shelbyville, Tenn., 237
Sheldon, Iowa, 229
Shelekhov (gulf), U.S.S.R., 48
Shellbrook, Sask., 181
Shelley, Idaho, 220
Shellharbour, N.S. Wales, 97
Shelton, Conn., 210
Shelton, Wash., 310
Shenandoah, Iowa, 229
Shenandoah, Pa., 294
Shenandoah (mt.), U.S., 307
Shenandoah (riv.), U.S., 307, 313
Shenandoah Nat'l Park, Va., 307
Shendi, Sudan, 111
Shensi (Shaanxi) (prov.), China, 77
Shenyang, China, 77
Sheopur, India, 68
Shepetovka, U.S.S.R., 52
Shepparton, Victoria, 97
Sheppey (isl.), England, 13
Sherbro (isl.), Sierra Leone, 106
Sherbrooke (lake), Nova Scotia, 169
Sherbrooke, Québec, 172
Sheridan, Colo., 208
Sheridan, Wyo., 319
Sherman (inlet), N.W. Terr., 187
Sherman, Texas, 303
Sherridon, Manitoba, 179
Sherrill, N.Y., 276
's Hertogenbosch, Neth., 27
Sherwood, Pr. Edward I., 169
Sherwood Park, Alberta, 182
Shetland (isls.), Scotland, 15
Shevchenko, U.S.S.R., 48
Sheyenne (riv.), N. Dak., 283
Shibam, P.D.R. Yemen, 59
Shibata, Japan, 81
Shibetsu, Japan, 81
Shibin el Kom, Egypt, 111
Shiel (lake), Scotland, 15
Shiga (pref.), Japan, 81
Shigatse (Xigazê), China, 77
Shihezi, China, 77
Shihr, P.D.R. Yemen, 59
Shijak, Alb., 45
Shijiazhuang (Shihkiachwang), China, 77
Shikoku (isl.), Japan, 81
Shikotan (isl.), Japan, 81
Shildon, England, 13
Shillington, Pa., 294
Shillong, India, 68
Shiloh Nat'l Mil. Park, Tenn., 237
Shimabara, Japan, 81
Shimane (pref.), Japan, 81
Shimizu, Japan, 81
Shimoda, Japan, 81
Shimoga, India, 68
Shimonoseki, Japan, 81
Shin (lake), Scotland, 15
Shinano (riv.), Japan, 81
Shindand, Afghan., 68
Shingu, Japan, 81
Shinjo, Japan, 81
Shinko (riv.), Cent. Afr. Rep., 115
Shinnston, W. Va., 313

GEOGRAPHICAL TERMS

A. = Arabic Burm. = Burmese Camb. = Cambodian Ch. = Chinese Czech. = Czechoslovakian Dan. = Danish Du. = Dutch Finn. = Finnish Fr. = French Ger. = German Ice. = Icelandic It. = Italian Jap. = Japanese Mong. = Mongol Nor. = Norwegian Per. = Persian Port. = Portuguese Russ. = Russian Sp. = Spanish Sw. = Swedish Turk. = Turkish

Å	Nor., Sw.	Stream
Aas	Dan., Nor.	Hills
Abajo	Sp.	Lower
Ada, Adasi	Turk.	Island
Altipiano	It.	Plateau
Altiplano	Sp.	Plateau
Alv, Alf, Elf	Sw.	River
Arrecife	Sp.	Reef
Asa	Nor., Sw.	Hill
Asaga	Turk.	Lower
Austral	Sp.	Southern
Baai	Du.	Bay
Bab	Arabic	Gate or Strait
Bahia	Sp.	Bay
Bahr	Arabic	Marsh, Lake, Sea, River
Baia	Port.	Bay
Baie	Fr.	Bay, Gulf
Baizo	Port.	Low
Bakke	Dan.	Hill
Bana	Jap.	Cape
Bañados	Sp.	Marshes
Band	Per.	Mt. Range
Bandao	Ch.	Peninsula
Bandar	Per.	Harbor
Barra	Sp.	Reef
Bel	Turk.	Pass
Belt	Ger.	Strait
Ben	Gaelic	Mountain
Bera	Du.	Mountain
Berg	Ger., Du.	Mountain
Bir	Arabic	Well
Boca	Sp.	Gulf, Inlet
Boğhaz	Turk.	Strait
Bolshoi, Bolshaya	Russ.	Big
Bolson	Sp.	Depression
Bong	Korean	Mountain
Boreal	Sp.	Northern
Breen	Nor.	Glacier
Bro	Dan., Nor., Sw.	Bridge
Bucht	Ger.	Bay
Bugt	Dan.	Bay
Bukhta	Russ.	Bay
Bukit	Malay	Hill, Mountain
Bukt	Nor., Sw.	Bay, Gulf
Burnu, Burun	Turk.	Cape, Point
By	Dan., Nor., Sw.	Town
Cabo	Port., Sp.	Cape
Campos	Port.	Plains
Canal	Port., Sp.	Channel
Cap, Capo	Fr., It.	Cape
Cataratas	Sp.	Falls
Catena	It.	Mt. Range
Catingas	Port.	Open Woodlands
Cayos	Sp.	Islands
Central, Centrale	Fr., It.	Middle
Cerrito, Cerro	Sp.	Hill
Cerros	Sp.	Hills, Mountains
Chai	Turk.	River
Chott	Arabic	Salt Lake
Ciénaga	Sp.	Swamp
Ciudad	Sp.	City
Col	Fr.	Pass
Cordillera	Sp.	Mt. Range, Mts.
Côte	Fr.	Coast
Csatoria	Magyar	Canal
Cuchilla	Sp.	Mt. Range
Curiche	Sp.	Swamp
Dağ, Dağı	Turk.	Mountain, Peak
Dağlari	Turk.	Mt. Range
Dal	Nor., Sw.	Valley
Dar	Arabic	Land
Dar'ya	Russ.	River
Daryacheh	Per.	Marshy Lake
Dasht	Per.	Desert, Plain
Deniz, Denizi	Turk.	Sea, Lake
Desierto	Sp.	Desert
Détroit	Fr.	Strait
Djeziret	Arabic, Turk.	Island
Do	Korean	Island
Doi	Thai	Mountain
Eiland	Du.	Island
Elv	Dan., Nor.	River
Embalse	Sp.	Reservoir
Emi	Berber	Mountain
Erg	Arabic	Dune, Desert
Eski	Turk.	Old
Est, Este	Fr., Port., Sp.	East
Estero	Sp.	Estuary, Creek
Estrecho, Estreito	Sp., Port.	Strait
Etang	Fr.	Pond, Lagoon, Lake
Feng	Ch.	Mountain
Fiume	It.	River
Fjäll	Sw.	Mountain
Fjeld, Fjell	Nor.	Hills, Mountain
Fjord	Dan., Nor., Sw.	Fiord
Fleuve	Fr.	River
Fljót	Ice.	Stream
Fluss	Ger.	River
Fors	Sw.	Waterfall
Fos, Foss	Dan., Nor.	Waterfall
Gamla	Nor.	Old
Gamle	Dan.	Old
Gata	Jap.	Lake
Gawa	Jap.	River
Gebel	Arabic	Mountain
Gebergte	Du.	Mt. Range
Gebirge	Ger.	Mt. Range
Gobi	Mongol	Desert
Goe	Jap.	Pass
Gol	Mongol, Turk.	Lake, Stream
Golf	Ger., Du.	Gulf
Golfe	Fr.	Gulf
Golfo	Sp., It., Port.	Gulf
Gölü	Turk.	Lake
Gora	Russ.	Mountain
Grand, Grande	Fr., Sp.	Big
Groot	Du.	Big
Gross	Ger.	Big
Grosso	It., Port.	Big
Guba	Russ.	Bay, Gulf
Gunto	Jap.	Archipelago
Gunung	Malay	Mountain
Hai	Ch.	Sea
Haixia	Ch.	Strait
Halbinsel	Ger.	Peninsula
Hamáda, Hammada	Arabic	Rocky Plateau
Hamn	Sw.	Harbor
Hamún	Per.	Marsh
Hanto	Jap.	Peninsula
Has, Hassi	Arabic	Well
Hav	Dan., Nor., Sw.	Sea, Ocean
Havet	Nor.	Bay
Havn	Dan., Nor.	Harbor
Havre	Fr.	Harbor
He	Ch.	River, Stream
Higashi, Higasi	Jap.	East
Hochebene	Ger.	Plateau
Hoek	Du.	Cape
Hoku	Jap.	North
Holm	Dan., Nor., Sw.	Island
Hory	Czech	Mountains
Hoved	Dan., Nor.	Cape, Promontory
Hu	Ch.	Lake
Huang	Ch.	Yellow
Huk	Dan., Nor., Sw.	Point
Hus, Huus	Dan., Nor., Sw.	House
Idehan	Arabic	Desert
Ile	Fr.	Island
Ilet	Fr.	Islet
Ilot	Fr.	Islet
Indre	Dan., Nor.	Inner
Inferieur, Inferiore	Fr., It.	Lower
Inner, Inre	Sw.	Inner
Insel	Ger.	Island
Irmak	Turk.	River
Isla	Sp.	Island
Isola	It.	Island
Jabal, Jebel	Arabic	Mountains
Järvi	Finn.	Lake
Jaure	Sw.	Lake
Jiang	Ch.	River, Stream
Jima	Jap.	Island
Joki	Finn.	River
Kaap	Du.	Cape
Kabir, Kebir	Arabic	Big
Kai	Jap.	Sea
Kaikyo	Jap.	Strait
Kami	Turk.	Upper
Kanaal	Du.	Canal
Kanal	Russ., Ger.	Canal, Channel
Kao	Thai	Mountain
Kap, Kapp	Nor., Sw., Ice.	Cape
Kaupunki	Finn.	Town
Kawa	Jap.	River
Khao	Thai	Mountain
Khrebet	Russ.	Mt. Range
Kita	Jap.	North
Klein	Du., Ger.	Small
Klint	Dan	Promontory
Kô	Jap.	Lake
Ko	Thai	Island
Koh	Camb., Khmer	Island
Kop	Du.	Peak, Head
Köping	Sw.	Market, Borough
Körfez, Körfezi	Turk.	Gulf
Kosa	Russ	Spit
Kosui	Jap.	Lake
Kraal	Du.	Native Village
Kuchuk	Turk.	Small
Kuh, Kuhha	Per.	Mt. Range, Mts.
Kul	Sinkiang Turki	Lake
Kum	Turk.	Desert
Kuro	Jap.	Black
Laag	Du.	Low
Lac	Fr.	Lake
Lago	Port., Sp., It.	Lake
Lagoa	Port.	Lagoon
Laguna	Sp.	Lagoon
Lagune	Fr.	Lagoon
Lahti	Finn.	Bay, Bight
Län	Sw.	County
Liedao	Ch.	Islands, Archipelago
Lilla	Sw.	Small
Lille	Dan., Nor.	Small
Ling	Ch.	Mountain
Llanos	Sp.	Plains
Mae Nam	Thai	River
Mali, Malaya	Russ.	Small
Man	Korean	Bay
Mar	Sp., Port.	Sea
Mare	It.	Sea
Medio	Sp.	Middle
Meer	Du.	Lake
Meer	Ger.	Sea
Mer	Fr.	Sea
Meridionale	It.	Southern
Meseta	Sp.	Plateau
Middelst, Midden	Du.	Middle
Minami	Jap.	Southern
Mis	Russ.	Cape
Misaki	Jap.	Cape
Mittel	Ger.	Middle
Mont	Fr.	Mountain
Montagne	Fr.	Mountain
Montaña	Sp.	Mountains
Monte	Sp., It., Port.	Mountain
More	Russ.	Sea
Mörön	Mong.	Stream
Morro	Port., Sp.	Mountain, Promontory
Morue	Fr.	Hill
Moyen	Fr.	Middle
Muang	Siamese	Town
Mui	Vietnamese	Cape, Point
Mys	Russ.	Cape
Nada	Jap.	Sea
Naka	Jap.	Middle
Nam	Burm., Lao	River
Namakzar	Per.	Salt Waste
Nan	Jap.	South
Nes	Nor.	Cape, Point
Nevado	Sp.	Snow-covered Peak
Nieder	Ger.	Lower
Nishi, Nisi	Jap.	West
Nizhni, Nizhnyaya	Russ.	Lower
Njarga	Finn.	Peninsula, Promontory
Nong	Thai	Lake
Noord	Du.	North
Nord	Fr., Ger.	North
Norte	Sp., It., Port.	North
Nos	Russ.	Cape
Novi, Novaya	Russ.	New
Nur, Nuur	Ch., Mong.	Lake
Nuruu	Mong.	Mountains
Nusa	Malay	Island
Ny, Nya	Nor., Sw.	New
O	Jap.	Big
Ö	Nor., Sw.	Island
Ober	Ger.	Upper
Occidental, Occidentale	Sp., It.	Western
Odde	Dan.	Point
Oeste	Port.	West
Ooster	Du.	Eastern
Opper, Over	Du.	Upper
Oriental	Sp., Fr.	Eastern
Orientale	It.	Eastern
Orta	Turk.	Middle
Ost	Ger.	East
Ostrov	Russ.	Island
Ouest	Fr.	West
Öy	Nor.	Island
Ozero	Russ.	Lake
Pampa	Sp.	Plain
Pas	Fr.	Channel, Strait
Paso	Sp.	Pass
Passo	It., Port.	Pass
Peña	Sp.	Rock, Mountain
Pendi	Ch.	Basin
Penisola	It.	Peninsula
Pequeño	Sp.	Small
Pereval	Russ.	Pass
Peski	Russ.	Desert
Petit, Petite	Fr.	Small
Phu	Lao, Annamese	Mtn.
Pic	Fr.	Mountain
Piccolo	It.	Small
Pico	Port., Sp.	Mountain, Peak
Pik	Russ.	Mountain, Peak
Piton	Fr.	Mountain, Peak
Planalto	Port.	Plateau
Plato	Russ.	Plateau
Pointe	Fr.	Point
Poluostrov	Russ.	Peninsula
Ponta	Port.	Point
Presa	Sp.	Reservoir
Presqu'île	Fr.	Peninsula
Proliv	Russ.	Strait
Pulou, Pulo	Malay	Island
Punt	Du.	Point
Punta	Sp., It., Port.	Point
Qiryat	Hebrew	City, Settlement
Qum	Turk.	Desert
Qundao	Ch.	Islands
Rada	Sp.	Inlet
Rade	Fr.	Bay, Inlet
Ras	Arabic	Cape
Reka	Russ.	River
Retto	Jap.	Archipelago
Ria	Sp.	Estuary
Río	Sp.	River
Rivier, Rivière	Du., Fr.	River
Rud	Per.	River
Sai	Jap.	West
Saki	Jap.	Cape
Salar, Salina	Sp.	Salt Deposit
Salto	Sp., Port.	Falls
San	Jap., Korean	Hill
Sanmaek	Korean	Mt. Range
Schiereiland	Du.	Peninsula
Se	Camb., Khmer	River
See	Ger.	Sea, Lake
Selvas	Sp., Port.	Woods, Forest
Seno	Sp.	Bay, Gulf
Serra	Port.	Mts.
Serranía	Sp.	Mts.
Seto	Jap.	Strait
Settentrionale	It.	Northern
Severni, Severnaya	Russ.	North
Shamo	Ch.	Desert
Shan	Ch., Jap.	Hill, Mts.
Shankou	Ch.	Pass
Shatt	Arabic	River
Shima	Jap.	Island
Shimo	Jap.	Lower
Shin	Jap.	Land
Shiro	Jap.	White
Shoto	Jap.	Islands
Si	Ch.	West
Sierra	Sp.	Mt. Range, Mts.
Sjö	Nor., Sw.	Lake, Sea
Sok, Suk, Souk	Arabic	Market
Song	Annamese	River
Sopka	Russ.	Volcano
Spitze	Ger.	Mt. Peak
Sredni, Srednyaya	Russ.	Middle
Stad	Dan., Nor., Sw.	City
Stari, Staraya	Russ.	Old
Step	Russ.	Treeless Plain
Straat	Du.	Strait
Strasse	Ger.	Strait
Stretto	It.	Strait
Ström	Dan., Nor., Sw.	Sound
Stung	Camb., Khmer	River
Su	Turk.	River
Sud, Süd	Sp., Fr., Ger.	South
Suido	Jap.	Strait, Channel
Sul	Port.	South
Sund	Dan., Nor., Sw.	Sound
Sungei	Malay	River
Supérieur	Fr.	Upper
Superior, Superiore	Sp., It.	Upper
Sur	Sp.	South
Suyu	Turk.	River
Ta	Ch.	Big
Tafelland	Du.	Plateau
Tagh	Turk.	Mt. Range
Take	Jap.	Peak, Ridge
Takht	Arabic	Lower
Tal	Ger.	Valley
Tanjung	Malay	Cape, Point
Tell	Arabic	Hill
Thale	Thai	Sea, Lake
Tind	Nor.	Peak
Tō	Jap.	East
To	Jap.	Island
Toge	Jap.	Pass
Trask	Finn.	Lake
Tugh	Somali	Dry River
Ujung	Malay	Point
Umi	Jap.	Bay
Unter	Ger.	Lower
Ura	Jap.	Inlet
Uul	Mong.	Mountain
Val	Fr.	Valley
Vatn	Nor.	Lake
Vecchio	It.	Old
Veld	Du.	Plain, Field
Velho	Port.	Old
Verkhni	Russ.	Upper
Vesi	Finn.	Lake
Viejo	Sp.	Old
Vik	Nor., Sw.	Bay
Vishni, Vishnyaya	Russ.	High
Vodokhranilishche	Russ.	Reservoir
Volcán	Sp.	Volcano
Vostochni, Vostochnaya	Russ.	East, Eastern
Wadi	Arabic	Dry River
Wald	Ger.	Forest
Wan	Jap.	Bay
Westersch	Du.	Western
Wüste	Ger.	Desert
Yama	Jap.	Mountain
Yug, Yuzhni, Yuzhnaya	Russ.	South, Southern
Zaki	Jap.	Cape
Zaliv	Russ.	Bay, Gulf
Zangbo	Tibetan	River, Stream
Zapadni, Zapadnaya	Russ.	Western
Zee	Du.	Sea
Zemlya	Russ.	Land
Zizhiqu	Ch.	Autonomous Region
Zuid	Du.	South

Between Principal Cities in the United States

FROM/TO	Albuquerque, N. Mex.	Atlanta, Ga.	Baltimore, Md.	Boise, Idaho	Boston, Mass.	Brownsville, Tex.	Buffalo, N. Y.	Chicago, Ill.	Cincinnati, Ohio	Cleveland, Ohio
Albuquerque, N. Mex.	....	1273	1670	774	1967	838	1577	1126	1248	1417
Atlanta, Ga	1273	....	575	1830	933	960	695	583	368	550
Baltimore, Md	1670	575	....	2055	358	1525	273	603	423	305
Boise, Idaho	774	1830	2055	....	2266	1610	1872	1453	1663	1754
Boston, Mass	1967	933	358	2266	....	1881	398	849	737	550
Brownsville, Tex	838	960	1525	1610	1881	....	1575	1234	1184	1402
Buffalo, N. Y	1577	695	273	1872	398	1575	....	454	392	175
Chicago, Ill	1126	583	603	1453	849	1234	454	....	249	307
Cincinnati, Ohio	1248	368	423	1663	737	1184	392	249	....	218
Cleveland, Ohio	1417	550	305	1754	550	1402	175	307	218	....
Denver, Colo	332	1208	1505	637	1766	1047	1368	918	1090	1223
Des Moines, Iowa	833	738	913	1155	1159	1102	762	310	509	617
Detroit, Mich	1360	595	398	1671	613	1398	218	236	234	94
El Paso, Tex	228	1293	1750	969	2067	682	1690	1249	1333	1521
Fargo, N. Dak	968	1112	1143	975	1304	1445	923	571	818	838
Fort Worth, Tex	561	750	1239	1263	1574	471	1221	820	839	1046
Galveston, Tex	803	688	1245	1538	1598	287	1289	954	897	1116
Hastings, Nebr	588	901	1154	934	1415	1013	1019	566	742	871
Hot Springs, Ark	773	498	964	1384	1302	650	956	585	569	787
Houghton, Mich	1252	947	808	1367	922	1543	560	367	589	518
Jacksonville, Fla	1492	286	682	2098	1015	1025	880	861	628	768
Kansas City, Mo	717	675	962	1158	1250	923	862	413	541	700
Los Angeles, Calif	663	1935	2313	663	2590	1370	2195	1741	1892	2044
Louisville, Ky	1174	317	498	1623	823	1093	483	268	92	309
Memphis, Tenn	938	335	792	1506	1133	777	802	481	410	627
Miami, Fla	1710	610	958	2368	1258	1100	1184	1190	957	1088
Minneapolis, Minn	980	905	948	1140	1125	1335	733	356	603	632
Missoula, Mont	895	1790	1947	252	2124	1706	1740	1348	1578	1640
Nashville, Tenn	1117	218	597	1631	941	952	626	394	239	456
New Orleans, La	1030	427	1001	1713	1359	536	1087	831	708	922
New York, N. Y	1810	747	170	2153	188	1695	291	711	568	404
Norfolk, Va	1696	507	167	2137	467	1465	435	696	474	429
Oklahoma, Okla	518	753	1173	1138	1490	659	1117	689	755	946
Omaha, Nebr	718	815	1026	1044	1280	1061	883	432	620	738
Philadelphia, Pa	1748	663	90	2113	268	1614	278	664	501	343
Phoenix, Ariz	330	1592	2002	733	2295	1023	1904	1451	1578	1745
Pittsburgh, Pa	1498	520	194	1863	478	1424	178	411	258	115
Portland, Me	2015	1022	446	2282	100	1961	438	892	802	603
Portland, Oreg	1107	2172	2367	349	2553	1944	2167	1765	1987	2063
Richmond, Va	1628	470	128	2060	471	1428	375	618	399	353
St. Louis, Mo	938	467	731	1389	1036	975	662	259	308	490
Salt Lake City, Utah	483	1580	1858	292	2099	1317	1701	1260	1450	1567
San Francisco, Calif	893	2133	2451	516	2696	1675	2298	1855	2037	2163
Schenectady, N. Y	1823	840	278	2120	150	1770	249	702	605	408
Seattle, Wash	1178	2180	2341	405	2508	2015	2130	1743	1974	2035
Shreveport, La	764	548	1064	1433	1410	510	1080	725	688	904
Spokane, Wash	1028	1960	2110	290	2279	1852	1900	1514	1746	1804
Springfield, Mass	1889	863	282	2196	79	1805	325	774	659	473
Vermillion, S. Dak	742	917	1083	973	1314	1161	916	479	694	785
Washington, D. C	1648	542	33	2045	392	1493	290	594	403	303

FROM/TO	Denver, Colo.	Des Moines, Iowa	Detroit, Mich.	El Paso, Tex.	Fargo, N. Dak.	Fort Worth, Tex.	Galveston, Tex.	Hastings, Nebr.	Hot Springs, Ark.	Houghton, Mich.
Albuquerque, N. Mex.	332	833	1360	228	968	561	803	588	773	1252
Atlanta, Ga	1208	738	595	1293	1112	750	688	901	498	947
Baltimore, Md	1505	913	398	1750	1143	1239	1245	1154	964	808
Boise, Idaho	637	1155	1671	969	975	1263	1538	934	1384	1367
Boston, Mass	1766	1159	613	2067	1304	1574	1598	1415	1302	922
Brownsville, Tex	1047	1102	1398	682	1445	471	287	1013	650	1543
Buffalo, N. Y	1368	762	218	1690	923	1221	1289	1019	956	560
Chicago, Ill	918	310	236	1249	571	820	954	566	585	367
Cincinnati, Ohio	1090	509	234	1333	818	839	897	742	569	589
Cleveland, Ohio	1223	617	94	1521	838	1046	1116	871	787	518
Denver, Colo	....	607	1153	554	642	643	925	353	749	970
Des Moines, Iowa	607	....	545	980	397	640	851	256	488	458
Detroit, Mich	1153	545	....	1475	745	1018	1111	800	761	427
El Paso, Tex	554	980	1475	....	1161	543	723	757	802	1422
Fargo, N. Dak	642	397	745	1161	....	973	1218	440	875	393
Fort Worth, Tex	643	640	1018	543	973	....	283	544	273	1093
Galveston, Tex	925	851	1111	723	1218	283	....	808	375	1277
Hastings, Nebr	353	256	800	757	440	544	808	....	513	666
Hot Springs, Ark	749	488	761	802	875	273	375	513	....	901
Houghton, Mich	970	458	427	1422	393	1093	1277	666	901	....
Jacksonville, Fla	1468	1024	832	1481	1400	943	799	1178	728	1216
Kansas City, Mo	555	180	643	836	548	460	677	226	326	633
Los Angeles, Calif	828	1433	1976	702	1426	1212	1423	1177	1437	1787
Louisville, Ky	1035	477	315	1253	818	751	807	693	480	636
Memphis, Tenn	878	485	621	978	882	448	492	591	176	830
Miami, Fla	1732	1338	1156	1662	1721	1150	941	1468	983	1545
Minneapolis, Minn	699	235	542	1156	219	870	1087	399	722	272
Missoula, Mont	670	1074	1552	1115	819	1312	1595	891	1385	1208
Nashville, Tenn	1018	523	468	1169	900	643	666	697	370	760
New Orleans, La	1079	825	938	986	1221	470	288	870	358	1187
New York, N. Y	1628	1023	483	1902	1213	1398	1415	1275	1125	849
Norfolk, Va	1562	983	522	1755	1258	1226	1195	1216	955	946
Oklahoma, Okla	503	469	905	578	786	188	456	357	260	926
Omaha, Nebr	485	122	666	875	390	590	828	135	490	547
Philadelphia, Pa	575	972	444	1834	1186	1324	1335	1222	1051	827
Phoenix, Ariz	585	1154	1685	347	1225	858	1065	901	1094	1550
Pittsburgh, Pa	1320	718	208	1592	952	1097	1140	967	825	530
Portland, Me	1803	1197	657	2126	1313	1642	1678	1454	1371	924
Portland, Oreg	985	1479	1975	1286	1248	1612	1885	1271	1733	1638
Richmond, Va	1488	905	445	1695	1180	1170	1154	1142	897	870
St. Louis, Mo	793	270	452	1033	658	568	697	455	325	591
Salt Lake City, Utah	372	952	1490	689	865	977	1249	708	1116	1242
San Francisco, Calif	946	1547	2087	993	1447	1454	1693	1297	1648	1833
Schenectady, N. Y	1618	1012	467	1930	1157	1445	1487	1267	1175	776
Seattle, Wash	1020	1470	1945	1373	1206	1658	1938	1288	1759	1588
Shreveport, La	799	624	891	752	1002	209	233	615	142	1043
Spokane, Wash	827	1243	1715	1238	976	1470	1753	1061	1552	1360
Springfield, Mass	1692	1085	540	1990	1240	1495	1524	1340	1224	860
Vermillion, S. Dak	468	187	705	920	284	689	938	167	605	510
Washington, D. C	1490	895	397	1726	1141	1210	1214	1139	936	813

FROM/TO	Jacksonville, Fla.	Kansas City, Mo.	Los Angeles, Calif.	Louisville, Ky.	Memphis, Tenn.	Miami, Fla.	Minneapolis, Minn.	Missoula, Mont.	Nashville, Tenn.	New Orleans, La.
Albuquerque, N. Mex.	1492	717	663	1174	938	1710	980	895	1117	1030
Atlanta, Ga	286	675	1935	317	335	610	905	1790	218	427
Baltimore, Md	682	962	2313	498	792	958	948	1947	597	1001
Boise, Idaho	2098	1158	663	1623	1506	2368	1140	252	1631	1713
Boston, Mass	1015	1250	2590	823	1133	1258	1125	2124	941	1359
Brownsville, Tex	1025	923	1370	1093	777	1100	1335	1706	952	536
Buffalo, N. Y	880	862	2195	483	802	1184	733	1740	626	1087
Chicago, Ill	861	413	1741	268	481	1190	356	1348	394	831
Cincinnati, Ohio	628	541	1892	92	410	957	603	1578	239	708
Cleveland, Ohio	768	700	2044	309	627	1088	632	1640	456	922
Denver, Colo	1468	555	828	1035	878	1732	699	670	1018	1079
Des Moines, Iowa	1024	180	1433	477	485	1338	235	1074	523	825
Detroit, Mich	832	643	1976	315	621	1156	542	1552	468	938
El Paso, Tex	1481	836	702	1253	978	1662	1156	1115	1169	986
Fargo, N. Dak	1400	548	1426	818	882	1721	219	819	900	1221
Fort Worth, Tex	943	460	1212	751	448	1150	870	1312	643	470
Galveston, Tex	799	677	1423	807	492	941	1087	1595	666	288
Hastings, Nebr	1178	226	1177	693	591	1468	399	891	697	870
Hot Springs, Ark	728	326	1437	480	176	983	722	1385	370	358
Houghton, Mich	1216	633	1787	636	830	1545	272	1208	760	1187
Jacksonville, Fla	....	952	2153	595	591	328	1192	2070	502	511
Kansas City, Mo	952	....	1352	480	370	1247	413	1117	472	678
Los Angeles, Calif	2153	1352	....	1825	1602	2355	1522	910	1777	1675
Louisville, Ky	595	480	1825	....	319	923	605	1550	153	623
Memphis, Tenn	591	370	1602	319	....	878	700	1483	195	358
Miami, Fla	328	1247	2355	923	878	....	1516	2359	821	681
Minneapolis, Minn	1192	413	1522	605	700	1516	....	1010	695	1050
Missoula, Mont	2070	1117	910	1550	1483	2359	1010	....	1582	1733
Nashville, Tenn	502	472	1777	153	195	821	695	1582	....	470
New Orleans, La	511	678	1675	623	358	681	1050	1733	470	....
New York, N. Y	838	1097	2446	650	953	1095	1019	2030	758	1173
Norfolk, Va	548	1009	2352	528	778	802	1047	2045	586	932
Oklahoma, Okla	988	293	1182	675	422	1233	692	1162	602	575
Omaha, Nebr	1098	165	1312	579	529	1402	291	978	604	845
Philadelphia, Pa	758	1037	2388	580	878	1023	985	1997	683	1090
Phoenix, Ariz	1800	1045	357	1512	1264	1998	1279	932	1445	1318
Pittsburgh, Pa	703	784	2135	345	660	1014	745	1754	472	923
Portland, Me	1113	1300	2631	892	1205	1357	1145	2133	1015	1445
Portland, Oreg	2442	1397	825	1953	1852	2716	1435	430	1970	2063
Richmond, Va	953	937	2283	457	722	831	968	1967	526	899
St. Louis, Mo	755	238	1585	242	242	1067	464	1331	253	599
Salt Lake City, Utah	1840	922	577	1400	1250	2098	988	435	1390	1433
San Francisco, Calif	2375	1500	345	1983	1800	2603	1585	762	1958	1923
Schenectady, N. Y	960	1107	2445	695	1010	1229	975	1978	820	1259
Seattle, Wash	2450	1505	956	1945	1867	2740	1403	395	1973	2098
Shreveport, La	733	326	1420	598	279	950	859	1457	470	280
Spokane, Wash	2239	1286	939	1720	1652	2528	1173	170	1752	1898
Springfield, Mass	957	1173	2515	745	1055	1210	1056	2060	863	1287
Vermillion, S. Dak	1203	280	1291	663	642	1510	238	887	704	960
Washington, D. C	647	943	2295	473	763	927	936	1940	567	968

FROM/TO	New York, N. Y.	Norfolk, Va.	Oklahoma, Okla.	Omaha, Nebr.	Philadelphia, Pa.	Phoenix, Ariz.	Pittsburgh, Pa.	Portland, Me.
Albuquerque, N. Mex.	1810	1696	518	718	1748	330	1498	2015
Atlanta, Ga	747	507	753	815	663	1592	520	1022
Baltimore, Md	170	167	1173	1026	90	2002	194	446
Boise, Idaho	2153	2137	1138	1044	2113	733	1863	2282
Boston, Mass	188	467	1490	1280	268	2295	478	100
Brownsville, Tex	1695	1465	659	1061	1614	1023	1424	1961
Buffalo, N. Y	291	435	1117	883	278	1904	178	438
Chicago, Ill	711	696	689	432	664	1451	411	892
Cincinnati, Ohio	568	474	755	620	501	1578	258	802
Cleveland, Ohio	404	429	946	738	343	1745	115	603
Denver, Colo	1628	1562	503	485	1575	585	1320	1803
Des Moines, Iowa	1023	983	469	122	972	1154	718	1197
Detroit, Mich	483	522	905	666	444	1685	208	657
El Paso, Tex	1902	1755	578	875	1834	347	1592	2126
Fargo, N. Dak	1213	1258	786	390	1186	1225	952	1313
Fort Worth, Tex	1398	1226	188	590	1324	858	1097	1642
Galveston, Tex	1415	1195	456	828	1336	1065	1140	1078
Hastings, Nebr	1275	1216	357	135	1222	901	967	1454
Hot Springs, Ark	1125	955	260	490	1051	1094	825	1371
Houghton, Mich	849	946	926	547	827	1550	630	924
Jacksonville, Fla	838	548	988	1098	758	1800	703	1113
Kansas City, Mo	1097	1009	293	165	1037	1045	784	1300
Los Angeles, Calif	2446	2352	1182	1312	2388	357	2135	2631
Louisville, Ky	650	528	675	579	580	1512	345	892
Memphis, Tenn	953	778	422	529	878	1264	660	1205
Miami, Fla	1095	802	1233	1402	1023	1998	1014	1357
Minneapolis, Minn	1019	1047	692	291	985	1279	745	1145
Missoula, Mont	2030	2045	1162	978	1997	932	1754	2133
Nashville, Tenn	758	586	602	604	683	1445	472	1015
New Orleans, La	1173	932	575	845	1090	1318	923	1445
New York, N. Y	....	293	1324	1144	83	2142	313	277
Norfolk, Va	293	....	1186	1095	220	2027	316	565
Oklahoma, Okla	1324	1186	....	405	1256	843	1013	1550
Omaha, Nebr	1144	1095	405	....	1094	1032	837	1318
Philadelphia, Pa	83	220	1256	1094	....	2079	254	360
Phoenix, Ariz	2142	2027	843	1032	2079	....	1829	2345
Pittsburgh, Pa	313	316	1013	837	254	1829	....	545
Portland, Me	277	565	1550	1318	360	2345	545	....
Portland, Oreg	2455	2458	1488	1373	2419	1007	2174	2563
Richmond, Va	287	79	1122	1020	205	1960	242	565
St. Louis, Mo	873	771	456	352	808	1270	561	1094
Salt Lake City, Utah	1972	1925	862	833	1923	504	1670	2127
San Francisco, Calif	2568	2510	1386	1425	2518	652	2264	2725
Schenectady, N. Y	142	426	1354	1133	205	2152	350	197
Seattle, Wash	2419	2440	1523	1372	2388	1112	2145	2513
Shreveport, La	1230	1037	297	617	1153	1067	939	1484
Spokane, Wash	2190	2211	1324	1149	2159	1020	1918	2285
Springfield, Mass	120	411	1412	1205	201	2220	400	159
Vermillion, S. Dak	1189	1166	502	115	1143	1043	891	1345
Washington, D. C	204	145	1150	1012	122	1980	188	480

Between Principal Cities of Europe

	Amsterdam	Athens	Baku	Barcelona	Belgrade	Berlin	Brussels	Bucharest	Budapest	Cologne	Copenhagen	Istanbul	Dresden	Dublin	Frankfort
Amsterdam	....	1340	2218	770	875	365	105	1100	710	128	381	1360	385	468	228
Athens	1340	....	1395	1160	500	1112	1292	460	698	1200	1320	350	1022	1765	1113
Baku	2218	1395	....	2427	1487	1867	2240	1220	1562	2127	1980	1070	1837	2490	2055
Barcelona	770	1160	2427	....	998	925	658	1210	924	692	1085	1380	860	919	665
Belgrade	875	500	1487	998	....	618	850	295	205	750	840	502	530	1327	652
Berlin	365	1112	1867	925	618	....	401	798	425	300	225	1068	95	815	268
Brussels	105	1292	2240	658	850	401	....	1110	700	110	475	1345	407	480	198
Bucharest	1100	460	1220	1210	295	798	1110	....	295	982	970	272	725	1560	890
Budapest	710	698	1562	924	205	425	700	295	....	590	629	650	345	1176	504
Cologne	128	1200	2127	692	750	300	110	982	590	....	400	1240	292	585	93
Copenhagen	381	1320	1960	1085	840	225	475	970	629	400	....	1240	315	768	412
Istanbul	1360	350	1070	1380	502	1068	1345	272	650	1240	1240	....	995	1830	1150
Dresden	385	1022	1837	860	530	95	407	725	345	292	315	995	....	852	236
Dublin	468	1765	2490	919	1327	815	480	1560	1176	585	768	1830	852	....	671
Frankfort	228	1113	2055	665	652	268	198	890	504	93	412	1150	236	671	....
Hamburg	232	1250	2020	910	760	165	301	950	572	228	180	1222	238	668	250
Leningrad	1090	1535	1570	1740	1165	815	1175	1080	965	1090	708	1292	885	1440	1075
Lisbon	1140	1770	3050	610	1555	1410	998	1842	1515	1126	1520	2005	1380	1015	1160
London	220	1476	2435	707	1040	575	202	1285	900	308	590	1540	592	300	392
Lyon	458	1100	2238	327	752	601	352	1025	680	370	760	1238	540	720	350
Madrid	912	1463	2742	316	1235	1149	807	1518	1214	875	1272	1690	1100	902	888
Marseilles	627	1025	2238	211	750	730	521	1020	718	528	906	1205	655	875	492
Milan	517	900	2028	450	540	570	435	819	476	390	720	1030	435	880	323
Moscow	1325	1388	1175	1852	1160	995	1392	920	965	1285	970	1180	1200	1728	1240
Munich	415	925	1912	648	475	310	372	725	350	282	520	975	227	855	193
Oslo	568	1610	2118	1330	1112	520	672	1245	920	635	303	1505	620	786	675
Paris	257	1300	2335	518	890	540	170	1152	770	250	634	1390	523	480	295
Riga	820	1310	1590	1440	855	520	900	870	685	805	453	1115	585	1210	780
Rome	808	650	1900	530	440	730	730	700	500	675	948	840	630	1175	698
Sofia	1073	335	1360	1072	231	810	945	194	395	945	1010	315	730	1525	860
Stockholm	695	1495	1862	1410	1005	503	793	1080	820	722	330	1340	598	1010	730
Toulouse	625	1215	2425	156	930	815	515	1210	883	875	962	1400	762	761	560
Warsaw	673	990	1555	1150	510	320	720	580	342	602	415	852	325	1130	550
Vienna	580	795	1700	830	300	322	568	520	128	460	538	790	235	1040	370
Zurich	375	1000	2050	513	590	410	312	855	498	259	595	1090	342	768	193

	Hamburg	Leningrad	Lisbon	London	Lyon	Madrid	Marseilles	Milan	Moscow	Munich	Oslo	Paris	Riga	Rome	Sofia	Stockholm	Toulouse	Warsaw	Vienna	Zurich
Amsterdam	232	1090	1140	220	458	912	627	517	1325	415	568	257	820	808	1073	695	625	673	580	375
Athens	1250	1535	1770	1476	1100	1463	1025	900	1388	925	1610	1300	1310	650	335	1495	1215	990	795	1000
Baku	2020	1570	3050	2435	2238	2742	2238	2028	1175	1912	2118	2335	1590	1900	1360	1862	2425	1555	1700	2050
Barcelona	910	1740	610	707	327	316	211	450	1852	648	1330	518	1440	530	1072	1410	156	1150	830	513
Belgrade	760	1165	1555	1040	752	1235	750	540	1160	475	1112	890	855	440	231	1005	930	510	300	590
Berlin	165	815	1410	575	601	1149	730	570	995	310	520	540	520	730	810	503	815	320	322	410
Brussels	301	1175	998	202	352	807	521	435	1392	372	672	170	900	730	945	793	515	720	568	312
Bucharest	950	1080	1842	1285	1025	1518	1020	819	920	725	1245	1152	870	700	194	1080	1210	580	520	855
Budapest	572	965	1515	900	680	1214	718	476	965	350	920	770	685	500	395	820	883	342	128	498
Cologne	228	1090	1126	308	370	875	528	390	1285	282	635	250	805	675	945	722	875	602	460	259
Copenhagen	180	708	1520	590	760	1272	906	720	970	520	303	634	453	948	1010	330	962	415	538	595
Istanbul	1222	1292	2005	1540	1238	1690	1205	1030	1180	975	1505	1390	1115	840	315	1340	1400	852	790	1090
Dresden	238	885	1380	592	540	1100	655	435	1200	227	620	523	585	630	730	598	762	325	235	342
Dublin	668	1440	1015	300	720	902	875	880	1728	855	786	480	1210	1175	1525	1010	761	1130	1040	768
Frankfort	250	1075	1160	392	350	888	492	323	1240	193	675	295	780	698	860	730	560	550	370	193
Hamburg	....	880	1301	448	580	1098	730	570	1100	378	445	459	600	810	954	502	780	462	460	432
Leningrad	880	....	2235	1300	1420	1980	1540	1315	391	1100	670	1335	300	1440	1218	435	1635	640	975	1225
Lisbon	1301	2235	....	975	850	313	810	1350	430	1208	1690	890	1940	1150	1685	1848	640	1700	1415	1058
London	448	1300	975	....	455	777	620	595	1540	526	720	210	1035	890	1235	885	550	890	762	480
Lyon	580	1420	850	455	....	577	170	210	1560	352	1005	248	1122	462	928	1080	228	850	562	206
Madrid	1098	1980	313	777	557	....	394	728	2120	910	1474	645	1670	840	1385	1598	344	1410	1110	765
Marseilles	730	1540	810	620	170	394	....	238	1642	445	1165	410	1238	372	895	1225	196	950	620	318
Milan	570	1315	1350	595	210	728	238	....	1408	215	1000	400	1010	295	715	1020	400	705	385	137
Moscow	1100	391	430	1540	1560	2120	1642	1408	....	1220	1030	1538	520	1462	1100	770	1770	710	1028	1350
Munich	378	1100	1208	526	352	910	445	215	1220	....	810	425	800	430	672	811	570	500	222	158
Oslo	445	670	1690	720	1005	1474	1165	1000	1030	810	....	830	531	1242	1295	267	1140	653	835	869
Paris	459	1335	890	210	248	645	410	400	1538	425	830	....	1050	690	1080	950	431	845	770	295
Riga	600	300	1940	1035	1122	1670	1238	1010	520	800	531	1050	....	1155	985	276	1335	350	685	930
Rome	810	1440	1150	890	462	840	372	295	1462	430	1242	690	1155	....	545	1220	569	810	470	421
Sofia	954	1218	1685	1235	928	1385	895	715	1100	672	1295	1080	985	545	....	1170	1080	662	500	780
Stockholm	502	435	1848	885	1080	1598	1225	1020	770	811	267	950	276	1220	1170	....	1281	500	770	908
Toulouse	780	1635	640	550	228	344	196	400	1770	570	1140	431	1335	569	1080	1281	....	1062	725	425
Warsaw	462	640	1700	890	850	1410	950	705	710	500	653	845	350	810	662	500	1062	....	345	640
Vienna	460	975	1415	762	562	1110	620	385	1028	222	835	770	685	470	500	770	725	345	....	365
Zurich	432	1225	1058	480	206	765	318	137	1350	158	869	295	930	421	780	908	425	640	365	....

Portland, Oreg.	Richmond, Va.	St. Louis, Mo.	Salt Lake City, Utah	San Francisco, Calif.	Schenectady, N. Y.	Seattle, Wash.	Shreveport, La.	Spokane, Wash.	Springfield, Mass.	Vermillion, S. Dak.	Washington, D.
1107	1628	938	483	893	1823	1178	764	1028	1889	742	1648
2172	470	467	1580	2133	840	2180	548	1960	863	917	542
2367	128	731	1858	2451	278	2341	1064	2110	282	1083	33
349	2060	1389	292	516	2120	405	1433	290	2196	973	2045
2553	471	1036	2099	2696	150	2508	1410	2279	79	1314	392
1944	1428	975	1317	1675	1770	2015	510	1852	1805	1161	1493
2167	375	662	1701	2298	249	2130	1080	1900	325	916	290
1765	618	259	1260	1855	702	1743	725	1514	774	479	594
1987	399	308	1450	2037	605	1974	688	1746	659	694	403
2063	353	490	1567	2163	408	2035	904	1804	478	785	303
985	1488	793	372	946	1618	1020	799	827	1692	468	1490
1479	905	270	952	1547	1012	1470	624	1243	1085	187	895
1975	445	452	1490	2087	467	1945	891	1715	540	705	397
1286	1695	1033	689	993	1930	1373	752	1238	1990	920	1726
1248	1180	658	865	1447	1157	1206	1002	976	1240	284	1141
1612	1170	568	977	1454	1445	1658	209	1470	1495	689	1210
1885	1154	697	1249	1693	1487	1938	233	1753	1524	938	1214
1271	1142	455	708	1297	1267	1288	615	1061	1340	167	1139
1733	897	325	1116	1648	1175	1759	142	1552	1224	605	936
1638	870	591	1242	1833	776	1588	1043	1360	860	510	813
2442	953	755	1840	2375	960	2450	733	2239	957	1203	647
1397	937	238	922	1500	1107	1505	326	1286	1173	280	943
825	2283	1585	577	345	2445	956	1420	939	2515	1291	2295
1953	457	242	1400	1983	695	1945	598	1720	745	663	473
1852	722	242	1250	1800	1010	1867	279	1652	1055	642	763
2716	831	1067	2098	2603	1229	2740	950	2528	1210	1510	927
1435	968	464	988	1585	975	1403	859	1173	1056	238	936
430	1967	1331	435	762	1978	395	1457	170	2060	887	1940
1970	526	253	1390	1958	820	1973	470	1752	863	704	567
2063	899	599	1433	1923	1259	2098	280	1898	1287	960	968
2455	287	873	1972	2568	142	2419	1230	2190	120	1189	204
2458	79	771	1925	2510	426	2440	1037	2211	411	1166	145
1488	1122	456	862	1386	1354	1523	297	1324	1412	502	1150
1373	1020	352	833	1425	1133	1372	617	1149	1205	115	1012
2419	205	808	1923	2518	205	2388	1153	2159	201	1143	122
1007	1960	1270	504	652	2152	1112	1067	1020	2220	1043	1980
2174	242	561	1670	2264	350	2145	939	1918	400	891	188
2563	565	1094	2127	2725	197	2513	1484	2285	159	1345	480
....	2381	1723	636	536	2405	143	1783	295	2488	1293	2360
2381	....	699	1850	2436	406	2362	985	2133	407	1089	96
1723	699	....	1158	1738	898	1722	466	1500	958	450	710
636	1850	1158	....	592	1950	697	1155	548	2027	785	1845
536	2436	1738	592	....	2548	680	1655	730	2625	1383	2437
2405	406	898	1950	2548	....	2363	1290	2139	86	1165	313
143	2362	1722	697	680	2363	....	1820	229	2445	1282	2335
1783	985	466	1155	1655	1290	1820	....	1621	1333	726	1035
295	2133	1500	548	730	2139	229	1621	....	2216	1055	2105
2488	407	958	2027	2625	86	2445	1333	2216	....	1242	321
1293	1089	450	785	1383	1165	1282	726	1055	1242	....	1073
2360	96	710	1845	2437	313	2335	1035	2105	321	1073	....

New York to	Miles	San Francisco to	Miles	Seattle to	Miles	Washington to	Miles
Buenos Aires	5,295	Buenos Aires	6,487	Buenos Aires	6,956	Buenos Aires	5,205
Bogota	2,474	Bogota	3,863	Bogota	4,166	Bogota	2,344
Caracas	2,100	Caracas	3,900	Caracas	4,100	Caracas	2,040
Guatemala City	2,060	Guatemala City	2,525	Guatemala City	2,930	Guatemala City	1,835
Havana	1,302	Havana	2,600	Havana	2,805	Havana	1,110
La Paz	3,905	La Paz	5,080	La Paz	5,110	La Paz	3,780
Panama	2,211	Panama	3,349	Panama	3,680	Panama	2,020
Para	3,281	Para	5,430	Para	5,550	Para	3,270
Managua	2,100	Managua	2,860	Managua	3,240	Managua	1,920
Rio de Janeiro	4,810	Rio de Janeiro	6,655	Rio de Janeiro	6,945	Rio de Janeiro	4,710
San Jose	2,200	San Jose	3,070	San Jose	3,430	San Jose	2,030
Santiago	5,134	Santiago	5,960	Santiago	6,466	Santiago	4,965
Tampico	1,880	Tampico	1,790	Tampico	2,200	Tampico	1,665

Between Representative Cities of the United States and Latin America

Chicago to	Miles	Denver to	Miles	Los Angeles to	Miles	New Orleans to	Miles
Buenos Aires	5,598	Buenos Aires	5,935	Buenos Aires	6,148	Buenos Aires	4,902
Bogota	2,691	Bogota	3,100	Bogota	3,515	Bogota	1,996
Caracas	2,480	Caracas	3,105	Caracas	3,610	Caracas	1,990
Guatemala City	1,870	Guatemala City	1,935	Guatemala City	2,190	Guatemala City	1,050
Havana	1,315	Havana	1,760	Havana	2,320	Havana	672
La Paz	4,130	La Paz	4,445	La Paz	4,805	La Paz	3,480
Panama	2,320	Panama	2,620	Panama	3,025	Panama	1,600
Para	3,820	Para	4,580	Para	5,110	Para	3,470
Managua	2,060	Managua	2,230	Managua	2,540	Managua	1,250
Rio de Janeiro	5,320	Rio de Janeiro	5,900	Rio de Janeiro	6,330	Rio de Janeiro	4,798
San Jose	2,100	San Jose	2,420	San Jose	2,725	San Jose	1,425
Santiago	5,320	Santiago	5,495	Santiago	5,595	Santiago	4,553
Tampico	1,460	Tampico	1,240	Tampico	1,470	Tampico	720

TABLES OF AIRLINE DISTANCES

All Distances in Statute Miles

Between Principal Cities of the World

FROM/TO	Azores	Bagdad	Berlin	Bombay	Buenos Aires	Callao	Cairo	Cape Town	Chicago	Istanbul	Guam	Honolulu	Juneau	London	Los Angeles
Azores	....	3906	2148	5930	5385	4825	3325	5670	3305	2880	8985	7421	4715	1562	5034
Bagdad	3906	....	2040	2022	8215	8618	785	4923	6490	1085	6380	8445	6180	2568	7695
Berlin	2148	2040	....	3947	7411	6937	1823	5949	4458	1068	7158	7384	4638	575	5849
Bombay	5930	2022	3947	....	9380	10530	2698	5133	8144	3043	4831	8172	6992	4526	8810
Buenos Aires	5385	8215	7411	9380	....	1982	7428	4332	5598	7638	10516	7653	7964	6919	6148
Callao	4825	8618	6937	10530	1982	....	7870	6195	3765	7666	9760	5993	5806	6376	4155
Cairo	3325	785	1823	2698	7428	7870	....	4476	6231	780	7175	8925	6352	2218	7675
Cape Town	5670	4923	5949	5133	4332	6195	4476	....	8551	5210	8918	11655	10382	5975	10165
Chicago	3305	6490	4458	8144	5598	3765	6231	8551	....	5530	7510	4315	2310	4015	1741
Istanbul	2880	1085	1068	3043	7638	7666	780	5210	5530	....	7015	8200	5665	1540	6895
Guam	8985	6380	7158	4831	10516	9760	7175	8918	7510	7015	....	3896	5225	7605	6255
Honolulu	7421	8445	7384	8172	7653	5993	8925	11655	4315	8200	3896	....	2825	7320	2620
Juneau	4715	6180	4638	6992	7964	5806	6352	10382	2310	5665	5225	2825	....	4496	1835
London	1562	2568	575	4526	6919	6376	2218	5975	4015	1540	7605	7320	4496	....	5496
Los Angeles	5034	7695	5849	8810	6148	4155	7675	10165	1741	6895	6255	2620	1835	5496	....
Melbourne	12190	8150	9992	6140	7336	8196	8720	6510	9837	9189	3497	5581	8162	10590	8098
Mexico City	4584	8155	6119	9818	4609	2619	7807	8620	1690	7160	7690	3846	3210	5605	1445
Montreal	2548	5814	3776	7582	5619	3954	5502	7975	750	4825	7840	4992	2647	3370	2468
New Orleans	3718	7212	5182	8952	4902	2990	6862	8390	827	6220	7895	4305	2860	4656	1695
New York	2604	6066	4026	7875	5295	3633	5701	7845	727	5060	8115	5051	2874	3500	2466
Panama	3918	7807	5902	9832	3319	1450	7230	7090	2320	6797	9220	5347	4456	5310	3025
Paris	1617	2385	540	4391	6891	6455	2020	5762	4219	1390	7675	7525	4700	210	5711
Rio de Janeiro	4312	7012	6246	8438	1230	2400	6242	3850	5320	6420	11710	8400	7611	5747	6330
San Francisco	5114	7521	5744	8523	6487	4500	7554	10340	1875	6770	5952	2407	1530	5440	345
Santiago	5718	8876	7842	10127	731	1548	8100	5080	5325	8230	9946	6935	7320	7275	5595
Seattle	4720	6848	5121	7830	6956	4964	6915	10305	1753	6124	5785	2707	870	4850	961
Shanghai	7324	4468	5323	3219	12295	10760	5290	8179	7155	5084	1945	5009	4968	5841	6598
Singapore	8338	4443	6226	2425	9940	11700	5152	6025	9475	5440	2990	6874	7375	6818	8955
Tokyo	7370	5242	5623	4247	11601	9740	6005	9234	6410	5649	1596	3940	4117	6050	5600
Wellington	11475	9782	11384	7752	6341	6696	10360	7149	8465	10790	4206	4676	7501	11790	6806

FROM/TO	Melbourne	Mexico City	Montreal	New Orleans	New York	Panama	Paris	Rio de Janeiro	San Francisco	Santiago	Seattle	Shanghai	Singapore	Tokyo	Wellington
Azores	12190	4584	2548	3718	2604	3918	1617	4312	5114	5718	4720	7324	8338	7370	11475
Bagdad	8150	8155	5814	7212	6066	7807	2385	7012	7521	8876	6848	4468	4443	5242	9782
Berlin	9992	6119	3776	5182	4026	5902	540	6246	5744	7842	5121	5323	6226	5623	11384
Bombay	6140	9818	7582	8952	7875	9832	4391	8438	8523	10127	7830	3219	2425	4247	7752
Buenos Aires	7336	4609	5619	4902	5295	3319	6891	1230	6487	731	6956	12295	9940	11601	6341
Callao	8196	2619	3954	2990	3633	1450	6455	2400	4500	1548	4964	10760	11700	9740	6696
Cairo	8720	7807	5502	6862	5701	7230	2020	6242	7554	8100	6915	5290	5152	6005	10360
Cape Town	6510	8620	7975	8390	7845	7090	5732	3850	10340	5080	10305	8179	6025	9234	7149
Chicago	9837	1690	750	827	727	2320	4219	5320	1875	5325	1753	7155	9475	6410	8465
Istanbul	9189	7160	4825	6220	5060	6797	1390	6420	6770	8230	6124	5084	5440	5649	10790
Guam	3497	7690	7840	7895	8115	9220	7675	11710	5952	9946	5785	1945	2990	1596	4206
Honolulu	5581	3846	4992	4305	5051	5347	7525	8400	2407	6935	2707	5009	6874	3940	4676
Juneau	8162	3210	2647	2860	2874	4456	4700	7611	1530	7320	870	4968	7375	4117	7501
London	10590	5605	3370	4656	3500	5310	210	5747	5440	7275	4850	5841	6818	6050	11790
Los Angeles	8098	1445	2468	1695	2466	3025	5711	6330	345	5595	961	6598	8955	5600	6806
Melbourne	....	8599	10553	9455	10541	9211	10500	8340	7970	7130	8330	4967	3768	5172	1655
Mexico City	8599	....	2247	940	2110	1532	5800	4810	1870	4122	2339	8120	10495	7190	7003
Montreal	10553	2247	....	1390	340	2545	3490	5110	2557	5461	2309	7141	9280	6546	9206
New Orleans	9455	940	1390	....	1161	1600	4846	4798	1960	4553	2137	7830	10255	6993	7950
New York	10541	2110	340	1161	....	2211	3600	4810	2606	5134	2440	7460	9617	6846	9067
Panama	9211	1532	2545	1600	2211	....	5440	3311	3349	3000	3680	9430	11800	8560	7580
Paris	10500	5800	3490	4846	3600	5440	....	5710	5680	7300	5080	5855	6730	6132	11865
Rio de Janeiro	8340	4810	5110	4798	4810	3311	5710	....	6655	1852	6945	11510	9875	11600	7510
San Francisco	7970	1870	2557	1960	2606	3349	5680	6655	....	5960	692	6245	8440	5250	6800
Santiago	7130	4122	5461	4553	5134	3000	7300	1852	5960	....	6466	11850	10270	10850	5925
Seattle	8330	2339	2309	2137	2440	3680	5080	6945	692	6466	....	5780	8200	4863	7310
Shanghai	4967	8120	7141	7830	7460	9430	5855	11510	6245	11850	5780	....	2395	1095	6080
Singapore	3768	10495	9280	10255	9617	11800	6730	9875	8440	10270	8200	2395	....	3350	5360
Tokyo	5172	7190	6546	6993	6846	8560	6132	11600	5250	10850	4863	1095	3350	....	5730
Wellington	1655	7003	9206	7950	9067	7580	11865	7510	6800	5925	7310	6080	5360	5730	......

WORLD STATISTICAL TABLES

Elements of the Solar System

	Mean Distance from Sun: in Miles	in Kilometers	Period of Revolution around Sun	Period of Rotation on Axis	Equatorial Diameter: in Miles	in Kilometers	Surface Gravity (Earth = 1)	Mass (Earth = 1)	Mean Density (Water = 1)	Number of Satellites
MERCURY	35,990,000	57,900,000	87.97 days	59 days	3,032	4,880	0.38	0.055	5.5	0
VENUS	67,240,000	108,200,000	224.70 days	243 days†	7,523	12,106	0.90	0.815	5.25	0
EARTH	93,000,000	149,700,000	365.26 days	23h 56m	7,926	12,755	1.00	1.00	5.5	1
MARS	141,730,000	228,100,000	687.00 days	24h 37m	4,220	6,790	0.38	0.107	4.0	2
JUPITER	483,880,000	778,700,000	11.86 years	9h 50m	88,750	142,800	2.87	317.9	1.3	16
SATURN	887,130,000	1,427,700,000	29.46 years	10h 14m	74,580	120,020	1.32	95.2	0.7	17
URANUS	1,783,700,000	2,870,500,000	84.01 years	10h 49m†	31,600	50,900	0.93	14.6.	1.3	5
NEPTUNE	2,795,500,000	4,498,800,000	164.79 years	15h 48m	30,200	48,600	1.23	17.2	1.8	3
PLUTO	3,667,900,000	5,902,800,000	247.70 years	6.39 days (?)	1,500	2,400	0.03 (?)	0.01(?)	0.7(?)	1

†Retrograde motion

Facts About the Sun

Equatorial diameter	865,000 miles	1,392,000 kilometers
Period of rotation on axis	25-35 days*	
Orbit of galaxy	every 225 million years	
Surface gravity (Earth = 1)	27.8	
Mass (Earth = 1)	333,000	
Density (Water = 1)	1.4	
Mean distance from Earth	93,000,000 miles	149,700,000 kilometers

*Rotation of 25 days at Equator, decreasing to about 35 days at the poles.

Facts About the Moon

Equatorial diameter	2,160 miles	3,476 kilometers
Period of rotation on axis	27 days, 7 hours, 43 minutes	
Period of revolution around Earth (sidereal month)	27 days, 7 hours, 43 minutes	
Phase period between new moons (synodic month)	29 days, 12 hours, 44 minutes	
Surface gravity (Earth = 1)	0.16	
Mass (Earth = 1)	0.0123	
Density (Water = 1)	3.34	
Maximum distance from Earth	252,710 miles	406,690 kilometers
Minimum distance from Earth	221,460 miles	356,400 kilometers
Mean distance from Earth	238,860 miles	384,400 kilometers

Dimensions of the Earth

	Area in Sq. Miles	Sq. Kilometers
Superficial area	197,751,000	512,175,090
Land surface	57,970,000	150,142,300
Water surface	139,781,000	362,032,790

	Miles	Kilometers
Equatorial circumference	24,902	40,075
Polar circumference	24,860	40,007
Equatorial diameter	7,926.68	12,756.4
Polar diameter	7,899.99	12,713.4
Equatorial radius	3,963.34	6,378.2
Polar radius	3,949.99	6,356.7

Volume of the Earth	2.6×10^{11} cubic miles	10.84×10^{11} cubic kilometers
Mass or weight	6.6×10^{21} short tons	6.0×10^{21} metric tons
Maximum distance from Sun	94,600,000 miles	152,000,000 kilometers
Minimum distance from Sun	91,300,000 miles	147,000,000 kilometers

The Continents

	Area in: Sq. Miles	Sq. Km.	Percent of World's Land
Asia	17,128,500	44,362,815	29.5
Africa	11,707,000	30,321,130	20.2
North America	9,363,000	24,250,170	16.2
South America	6,875,000	17,806,250	11.8
Antarctica	5,500,000	14,245,000	9.5
Europe	4,057,000	10,507,630	7.0
Australia	2,966,136	7,682,300	5.1

Oceans and Major Seas

	Area in: Sq. Miles	Sq. Km.	Greatest Depth in: Feet	Meters
Pacific Ocean	64,186,000	166,241,700	36,198	11,033
Atlantic Ocean	31,862,000	82,522,600	28,374	8,648
Indian Ocean	28,350,000	73,426,500	25,344	7,725
Arctic Ocean	5,427,000	14,056,000	17,880	5,450
Caribbean Sea	970,000	2,512,300	24,720	7,535
Mediterranean Sea	969,000	2,509,700	16,896	5,150
Bering Sea	875,000	2,266,250	15,800	4,800
Gulf of Mexico	600,000	1,554,000	12,300	3,750
Sea of Okhotsk	590,000	1,528,100	11,070	3,370
East China Sea	482,000	1,248,400	9,500	2,900
Sea of Japan	389,000	1,007,500	12,280	3,740
Hudson Bay	317,500	822,300	846	258
North Sea	222,000	575,000	2,200	670
Black Sea	185,000	479,150	7,365	2,245
Red Sea	169,000	437,700	7,200	2,195
Baltic Sea	163,000	422,170	1,506	459

Major Ship Canals

	Length in: Miles	Kms.	Minimum Feet	Depth in: Meters
Volga-Baltic, U.S.S.R.	225	362	—	—
Baltic-White Sea, U.S.S.R.	140	225	16	5
Suez, Egypt	100.76	162	42	13
Albert, Belgium	80	129	16.5	5
Moscow-Volga, U.S.S.R.	80	129	18	6
Volga-Don, U.S.S.R.	62	100	—	—
Göta, Sweden	54	87	10	3
Kiel (Nord-Ostsee), W. Ger.	53.2	86	38	12
Panama Canal, Panama	50.72	82	41.6	13
Houston Ship, U.S.A.	50	81	36	11

Largest Islands

	Area in: Sq. Mi.	Sq. Km.		Area in: Sq. Mi.	Sq. Km.		Area in: Sq. Mi.	Sq. Km.
Greenland	840,000	2,175,600	South I., New Zealand	58,393	151,238	Hokkaido, Japan	28,983	75,066
New Guinea	305,000	789,950	Java, Indonesia	48,842	126,501	Banks, Canada	27,038	70,028
Borneo	290,000	751,100	North I., New Zealand	44,187	114,444	Ceylon, Sri Lanka	25,332	65,610
Madagascar	226,400	586,376	Newfoundland, Canada	42,031	108,860	Tasmania, Australia	24,600	63,710
Baffin, Canada	195,928	507,454	Cuba	40,533	104,981	Svalbard, Norway	23,957	62,049
Sumatra, Indonesia	164,000	424,760	Luzon, Philippines	40,420	104,688	Devon, Canada	21,331	55,247
Honshu, Japan	88,000	227,920	Iceland	39,768	103,000	Novaya Zemlya (north isl.), U.S.S.R.	18,600	48,200
Great Britain	84,400	218,896	Mindanao, Philippines	36,537	94,631	Marajó, Brazil	17,991	46,597
Victoria, Canada	83,896	217,290	Ireland	31,743	82,214	Tierra del Fuego, Chile & Argentina	17,900	46,360
Ellesmere, Canada	75,767	196,236	Sakhalin, U.S.S.R.	29,500	76,405	Alexander, Antarctica	16,700	43,250
Celebes, Indonesia	72,986	189,034	Hispaniola, Haiti & Dom. Rep.	29,399	76,143			

Principal Mountains of the World

	Feet	Meters		Feet	Meters		Feet	Meters
Everest, Nepal-China	29,028	8,848	Pissis, Argentina	22,241	6,779	Kazbek, U.S.S.R.	16,512	5,033
Godwin Austen (K2),			Mercedario, Argentina	22,211	6,770	Puncak Jaya, Indonesia	16,503	5,030
Pakistan-China	28,250	8,611	Huascarán, Peru	22,205	6,768	Tyree, Antarctica	16,289	4,965
Kanchenjunga, Nepal-India	28,208	8,598	Llullaillaco, Chile-Argentina	22,057	6,723	Blanc, France	15,771	4,807
Lhotse, Nepal-China	27,923	8,511	Nevada Ancohuma, Bolivia	21,489	6,550	Klyuchevskaya Sopka, U.S.S.R.	15,584	4,750
Makalu, Nepal-China	27,824	8,481	Illampu, Bolivia	21,276	6,485	Fairweather (Br. Col., Canada)	15,300	4,663
Dhaulagiri, Nepal	26,810	8,172	Chimborazo, Ecuador	20,561	6,267	Dufourspitze (Mte. Rosa), Italy-		
Nanga Parbat, Pakistan	26,660	8,126	McKinley, Alaska	20,320	6,194	Switzerland	15,203	4,634
Annapurna, Nepal	26,504	8,078	Logan, Canada (Yukon)	19,524	5,951	Ras Dashan, Ethiopia	15,157	4,620
Gasherbrum, Pakistan-China	26,740	8,068	Cotopaxi, Ecuador	19,347	5,897	Matterhorn, Switzerland	14,691	4,478
Nanda Devi, India	25,645	7,817	Kilimanjaro, Tanzania	19,340	5,895	Whitney, California, U.S.A.	14,494	4,418
Rakaposhi, Pakistan	25,550	7,788	El Misti, Peru	19,101	5,822	Elbert, Colorado, U.S.A.	14,433	4,399
Kamet, India	25,447	7,756	Pico Cristóbal Colón, Colombia	19,029	5,800	Rainier, Washington, U.S.A.	14,410	4,392
Gurla Mandhada, China	25,355	7,728	Huila, Colombia	18,865	5,750	Shasta, California, U.S.A.	14,162	4,350
Kongur Shan, China	25,325	7,719	Citlaltépetl (Orizaba), Mexico	18,855	5,747	Pikes Peak, Colorado, U.S.A.	14,110	4,301
Tirich Mir, Pakistan	25,230	7,690	El'brus, U.S.S.R.	18,510	5,642	Finsteraarhorn, Switzerland	14,022	4,274
Gongga Shan, China	24,790	7,556	Damavand, Iran	18,376	5,601	Mauna Kea, Hawaii, U.S.A.	13,796	4,205
Muztagata, China	24,757	7,546	St. Elias, Alaska-Canada			Mauna Loa, Hawaii, U.S.A.	13,677	4,169
Communism Peak, U.S.S.R.	24,599	7,498	(Yukon)	18,008	5,489	Jungfrau, Switzerland	13,642	4,158
Pobeda Peak, U.S.S.R.	24,406	7,439	Vilcanota, Peru	17,999	5,486	Cameroon, Cameroon	13,350	4,069
Chomo Lhari, Bhutan-China	23,997	7,314	Popocatépetl, Mexico	17,887	5,452	Grossglockner, Austria	12,457	3,797
Muztag, China	23,891	7,282	Dykhtau, U.S.S.R.	17,070	5,203	Fuji, Japan	12,389	3,776
Cerro Aconcagua, Argentina	22,831	6,959	Kenya, Kenya	17,058	5,199	Cook, New Zealand	12,349	3,764
Ojos del Salado, Chile-Argentina	22,572	6,880	Ararat, Turkey	16,946	5,165	Etna, Italy	11,053	3,369
Bonete, Chile-Argentina	22,541	6,870	Vinson Massif, Antarctica	16,864	5,140	Kosciusko, Australia	7,310	2,228
Tupungato, Chile-Argentina	22,310	6,800	Margherita (Ruwenzori), Africa	16,795	5,119	Mitchell, North Carolina, U.S.A.	6,684	2,037

Longest Rivers of the World

	Length in: Miles	Kms.		Length in: Miles	Kms.		Length in: Miles	Kms.
Nile, Africa	4,145	6,671	São Francisco, Brazil	1,811	2,914	Ohio-Allegheny, U.S.A.	1,306	2,102
Amazon, S. Amer.	3,915	6,300	Indus, Asia	1,800	2,897	Kama, U.S.S.R.	1,262	2,031
Chang Jiang (Yangtze), China	3,900	6,276	Danube, Europe	1,775	2,857	Red, U.S.A.	1,222	1,966
Mississippi-Missouri-Red Rock, U.S.A.	3,741	6,019	Salween, Asia	1,770	2,849	Don, U.S.S.R.	1,222	1,967
Ob'Irtysh-Black Irtysh, U.S.S.R.	3,362	5,411	Brahmaputra, Asia	1,700	2,736	Columbia, U.S.A.-Canada	1,214	1,953
Yenisey-Angara, U.S.S.R.	3,100	4,989	Euphrates, Asia	1,700	2,736	Saskatchewan, Canada	1,205	1,939
Huang He (Yellow), China	2,877	4,630	Tocantins, Brazil	1,677	2,699	Peace-Finlay, Canada	1,195	1,923
Amur-Shilka-Onon, Asia	2,744	4,416	Xi (Si), China	1,650	2,655	Tigris, Asia	1,181	1,901
Lena, U.S.S.R.	2,734	4,400	Amudar'ya, Asia	1,616	2,601	Darling, Australia	1,160	1,867
Congo (Zaire), Africa	2,718	4,374	Nelson-Saskatchewan, Canada	1,600	2,575	Angara, U.S.S.R.	1,135	1,827
Mackenzie-Peace-Finlay, Canada	2,635	4,241	Orinoco, S. Amer.	1,600	2,575	Sungari, Asia	1,130	1,819
Mekong, Asia	2,610	4,200	Zambezi, Africa	1,600	2,575	Pechora, U.S.S.R.	1,124	1,809
Missouri-Red Rock, U.S.A.	2,564	4,125	Paraguay, S. Amer.	1,584	2,549	Snake, U.S.A.	1,000	1,609
Niger, Africa	2,548	4,101	Kolyma, U.S.S.R.	1,562	2,514	Churchill, Canada	1,000	1,609
Paraná-La Plata, S. Amer.	2,450	3,943	Ganges, Asia	1,550	2,494	Pilcomayo, S. Amer.	1,000	1,609
Mississippi, U.S.A.	2,348	3,778	Ural, U.S.S.R.	1,509	2,428	Magdalena, Colombia	1,000	1,609
Murray-Darling, Australia	2,310	3,718	Japurá, S. Amer.	1,500	2,414	Uruguay, S. Amer.	994	1,600
Volga, U.S.S.R.	2,194	3,531	Arkansas, U.S.A.	1,450	2,334	Platte-N. Platte, U.S.A.	990	1,593
Madeira, S. Amer.	2,013	3,240	Colorado, U.S.A.-Mexico	1,450	2,334	Ohio, U.S.A.	981	1,578
Purus, S. Amer.	1,995	3,211	Negro, S. Amer.	1,400	2,253	Pecos, U.S.A.	926	1,490
Yukon, Alaska-Canada	1,979	3,185	Dnieper, U.S.S.R.	1,368	2,202	Oka, U.S.S.R.	918	1,477
St. Lawrence, Canada-U.S.A.	1,900	3,058	Orange, Africa	1,350	2,173	Canadian, U.S.A.	906	1,458
Rio Grande, Mexico-U.S.A.	1,885	3,034	Irrawaddy, Burma	1,325	2,132	Colorado, Texas, U.S.A.	894	1,439
Syrdar'ya-Naryn, U.S.S.R.	1,859	2,992	Brazos, U.S.A.	1,309	2,107	Dniester, U.S.S.R.	876	1,410

Principal Natural Lakes

	Area in: Sq. Miles	Sq. Km.	Max. Depth in: Feet	Meters		Area in: Sq. Miles	Sq. Km.	Max. Depth in: Feet	Meters
Caspian Sea, U.S.S.R.-Iran	143,243	370,999	3,264	995	Lake Eyre, Australia	3,500-0	9,000-0	—	—
Lake Superior, U.S.A.-Canada	31,820	82,414	1,329	405	Lake Titicaca, Peru-Bolivia	3,200	8,288	1,000	305
Lake Victoria, Africa	26,724	69,215	270	82	Lake Nicaragua, Nicaragua	3,100	8,029	230	70
Aral Sea, U.S.S.R.	25,676	66,501	256	78	Lake Athabasca, Canada	3,064	7,936	400	122
Lake Huron, U.S.A.-Canada	23,010	59,596	748	228	Reindeer Lake, Canada	2,568	6,651	—	—
Lake Michigan, U.S.A.	22,400	58,016	923	281	Lake Turkana (Rudolf), Africa	2,463	6,379	240	73
Lake Tanganyika, Africa	12,650	32,764	4,700	1,433	Issyk-Kul', U.S.S.R.	2,425	6,281	2,303	702
Lake Baykal, U.S.S.R.	12,162	31,500	5,316	1,620	Lake Torrens, Australia	2,230	5,776	—	—
Great Bear Lake, Canada	12,096	31,328	1,356	413	Vänern, Sweden	2,156	5,584	328	100
Lake Nyasa (Malawi), Africa	11,555	29,928	2,320	707	Nettilling Lake, Canada	2,140	5,543	—	—
Great Slave Lake, Canada	11,031	28,570	2,015	614	Lake Winnipegosis, Canada	2,075	5,374	38	12
Lake Erie, U.S.A.-Canada	9,940	25,745	210	64	Lake Mobutu Sese Seko (Albert),				
Lake Winnipeg, Canada	9,417	24,390	60	18	Africa	2,075	5,374	160	49
Lake Ontario, U.S.A.-Canada	7,540	19,529	775	244	Kariba Lake, Zambia-Zimbabwe	2,050	5,310	295	90
Lake Ladoga, U.S.S.R.	7,104	18,399	738	225	Lake Nipigon, Canada	1,872	4,848	540	165
Lake Balkhash, U.S.S.R.	7,027	18,200	87	27	Lake Mweru, Zaire-Zambia	1,800	4,662	60	18
Lake Maracaibo, Venezuela	5,120	13,261	100	31	Lake Manitoba, Canada	1,799	4,659	12	4
Lake Chad, Africa	4,000-	10,360-			Lake Taymyr, U.S.S.R.	1,737	4,499	85	26
	10,000	25,900	25	8	Lake Khanka, China-U.S.S.R.	1,700	4,403	33	10
Lake Onega, U.S.S.R.	3,710	9,609	377	115	Lake Kioga, Uganda	1,700	4,403	25	8

MAP PROJECTIONS

by Erwin Raisz

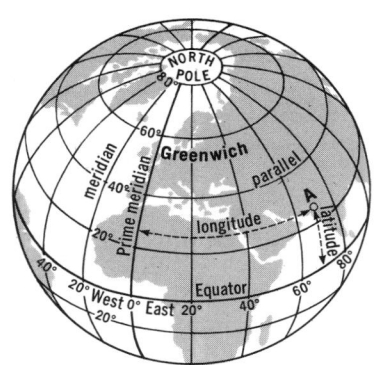

Our earth is rotating around its *axis* once a day. The two end points of its axis are the *poles;* the line circling the earth midway between the poles is the *equator.* The arc from either of the poles to the equator is divided into 90 *degrees.* The distance, expressed in degrees, from the equator to any point is its *latitude* and circles of equal latitude are the *parallels.* On maps it is customary to show parallels of evenly-spaced degrees such as every fifth or every tenth.

The equator is divided into 360 degrees. Lines circling from pole to pole through the degree points on the equator are called *meridians.* They are all equal in length but by international agreement the meridian passing through the Greenwich Observatory in London has been chosen as *prime meridian.* The distance, expressed in degrees, from the prime meridian to any point is its *longitude.* While meridians are all equal in length, parallels become shorter and shorter as they approach the poles. Whereas one degree of latitude represents everywhere approximately 69 miles, one degree of longitude varies from 69 miles at the equator to nothing at the poles.

Each degree is divided into 60 minutes and each minute into 60 seconds. One minute of latitude equals a nautical mile.

The map is flat but the earth is nearly spherical. Neither a rubber ball nor any part of a rubber ball may be flattened without stretching or tearing unless the part is very small. To present the curved surface of the earth on a flat map is not difficult as long as the areas under consideration are small, but the mapping of countries, continents, or the whole earth requires some kind of *projection.* Any regular set of parallels and meridians upon which a map can be drawn makes a map projection. Many systems are used.

In any projection only the parallels or the meridians or some other set of lines can be *true* (the same length as on the globe of corresponding scale); all other lines are too long or too short. Only on a globe is it possible to have both the parallels and the meridians true. The scale given on a flat map cannot be true everywhere. The construction of the various projections begins usually with laying out the parallels or meridians which have true lengths.

RECTANGULAR PROJECTION — This is a set of evenly-placed meridians and horizontal parallels. The central or *standard parallel* and all meridians are true. All other parallels are either too long or too short. The projection is used for simple maps of small areas, as city plans, etc.

MERCATOR PROJECTION — In this projection the meridians are evenly-spaced vertical lines. The parallels are horizontal, spaced so that their length has the same relation to the meridians as on a globe. As the meridians converge at higher latitudes on the globe, while on the map they do not, the parallels have to be drawn also farther and farther apart to maintain the correct relationship. When every very small area has the same shape as on a globe we call the projection *conformal.* The most interesting quality of this projection is that all *compass directions* appear as straight lines. For this reason it is generally used for marine charts. It is also frequently used for world maps in spite of the fact that the high latitudes are very much exaggerated in size. Only the equator is true to scale; all other parallels and meridians are too long. The Mercator projection did *not* derive from projecting a globe upon a cylinder.

SINUSOIDAL PROJECTION — The parallels are truly-spaced horizontal lines. They are divided truly and the connecting curves make the meridians. It does not make a good world map because the outer regions are distorted, but the

Rectangular Projection

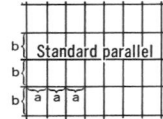

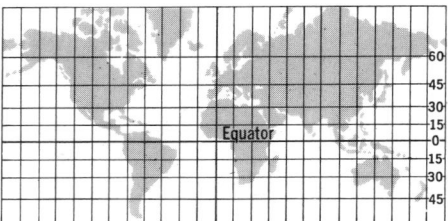

Mercator Projection

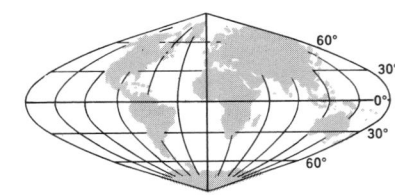

Sinusoidal Projection

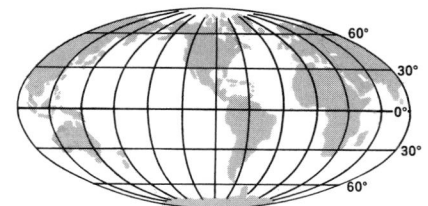

Mollweide Projection

central portion is good and this part is often used for maps of Africa and South America. Every part of the map has the same area as the corresponding area on the globe. It is an *equal-area* projection.

MOLLWEIDE PROJECTION — The meridians are equally-spaced ellipses; the parallels are horizontal lines spaced so that every belt of latitude should have the same area as on a globe. This projection is popular for world maps, especially in European atlases.

GOODE'S INTERRUPTED PROJECTIONS—Only the good central part of the Mollweide or sinusoidal (or both) projection is used and the oceans are cut. This makes an equal-area map with little distortion of shape. It is commonly used for world maps.

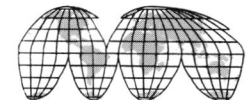

Goode's Interrupted Projection

Eckert Projection

ECKERT PROJECTIONS — These are similar to the sinusoidal or the Mollweide projections, but the poles are shown as lines half the length of the equator. There are several variants; the meridians are either sine curves or ellipses; the parallels are horizontal and spaced either evenly or so as to make the projection equal area. Their use for world maps is increasing. The figure shows the elliptical equal-area variant.

CONIC PROJECTION — The original idea of the conic projection is that of capping the globe by a cone upon which both the parallels and meridians are projected from the center of the globe. The cone is then cut open and laid flat. A cone can be made tangent to any chosen *standard parallel*.

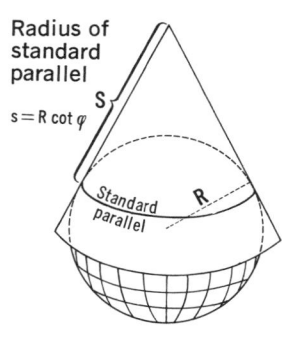

Radius of standard parallel

$s = R \cot \varphi$

Conic Projection

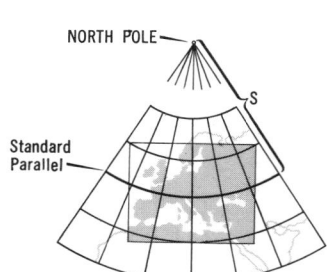

The actually-used conic projection is a modification of this idea. The radius of the standard parallel is obtained as above. The meridians are straight radiating lines spaced truly on the standard parallel. The parallels are concentric circles spaced at true distances. All parallels except the standard are too long. The projection is used for maps of countries in middle latitudes, as it presents good shapes with small scale error.

There are several variants: The use of *two standard parallels,* one near the top, the other near the bottom of the map, reduces the scale error. In the *Albers projection* the parallels are spaced unevenly, to make the projection equal-area. This is a good projection for the United States. In the *Lambert conformal conic projection* the parallels are spaced so that any small quadrangle of the grid should have the same shape as on the globe. This is the best projection for air-navigation charts as it has relatively straight azimuths.

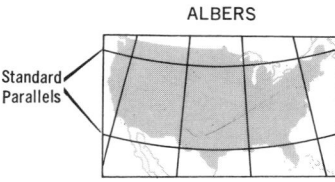

Albers Projection

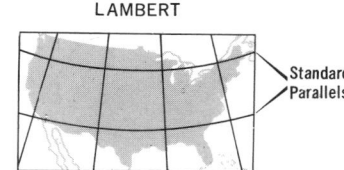

Lambert Conformal Conic Projection

An *azimuth* is a great-circle direction reckoned clockwise from north. A *great-circle direction* points to a place along the shortest line on the earth's surface. This is not the same as compass direction. The center of a great circle is the center of the globe.

BONNE PROJECTION — The parallels are laid out exactly as in the conic projection. All parallels are divided truly and the connecting curves make the meridians. It is an equal-area projection. It is used for maps of the northern continents, as Asia, Europe, and North America.

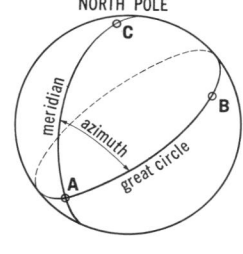

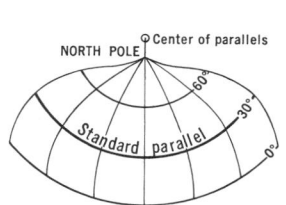

Bonne Projection

POLYCONIC PROJECTION — The central meridian is divided truly. The parallels are non-concentric circles, the radii of which are obtained by drawing tangents to the globe as though the globe were covered by several cones rather than by only one. Each parallel is divided truly and the connecting curves make the meridians. All meridians except the central one are too long. This projection is used for large-scale topographic sheets — less often for countries or continents.

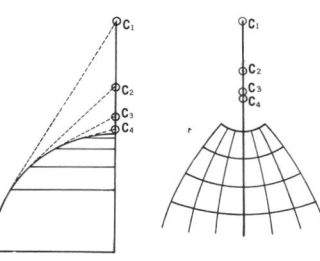

Polyconic Projection

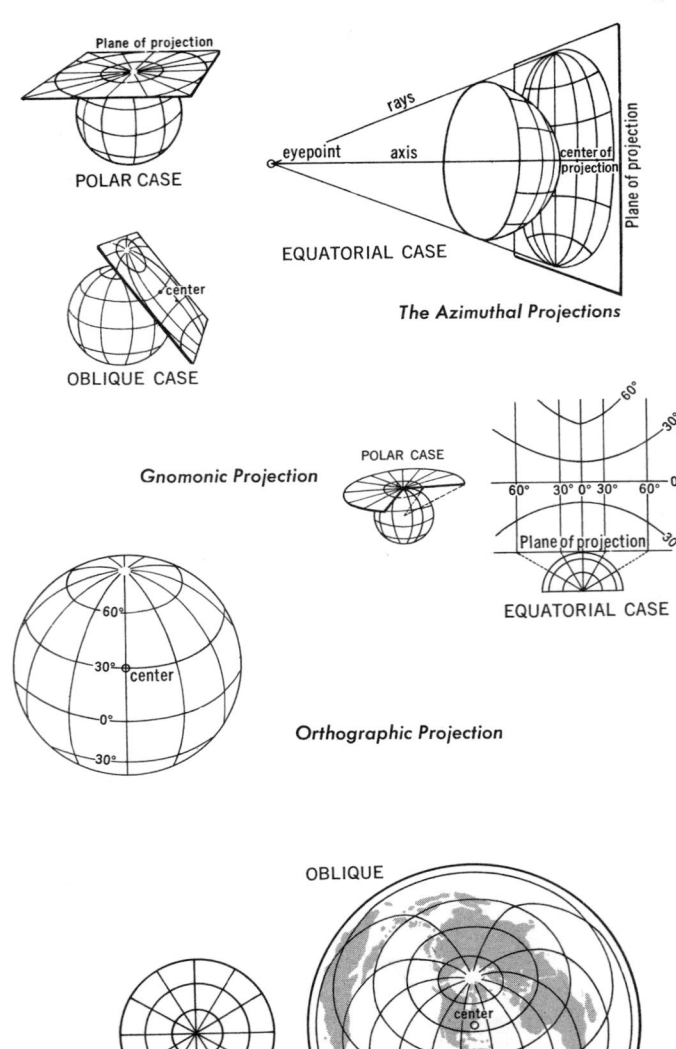

POLAR CASE

EQUATORIAL CASE

The Azimuthal Projections

OBLIQUE CASE

POLAR CASE

Gnomonic Projection

EQUATORIAL CASE

Plane of projection

Orthographic Projection

OBLIQUE

POLAR CASE

Azimuthal Equidistant Projection

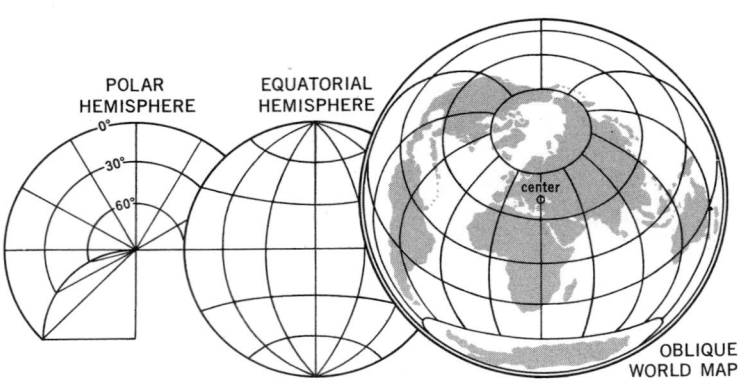

POLAR HEMISPHERE   EQUATORIAL HEMISPHERE

OBLIQUE WORLD MAP

Lambert Azimuthal Equal-Area Projection

THE AZIMUTHAL PROJECTIONS — In this group a part of the globe is projected from an eyepoint onto a plane. The eyepoint can be at different distances, making different projections. The plane of projection can be tangent at the equator, at a pole, or at any other point on which we want to focus attention. The most important quality of all azimuthal projections is that they show every point at its true direction (azimuth) from the center point, and all points equally distant from the center point will be equally distant on the map also.

GNOMONIC PROJECTION — This projection has the eyepoint at the center of the globe Only the central part is good; the outer regions are badly distorted. Yet the projection has one important quality, all great circles being shown as straight lines. For this reason it is used for laying out the routes for long range flying or trans-oceanic navigation.

ORTHOGRAPHIC PROJECTION — This projection has the eyepoint at infinite distance and the projecting rays are parallel. The polar or equatorial varieties are rare but the oblique case became very popular on account of its visual quality. It looks like a picture of a globe. Although the distortion on the peripheries is extreme, we see it correctly because the eye perceives it not as a map but as a picture of a three-dimensional globe. Obviously only a hemisphere (half globe) can be shown.

Some azimuthal projections do not derive from the actual process of projecting from an eyepoint, but are arrived at by other means:

AZIMUTHAL EQUIDISTANT PROJECTION — This is the only projection in which every point is shown both at true great-circle direction and at true distance from the center point, but all other directions and distances are distorted. The principle of the projection can best be understood from the polar case. Most polar maps are in this projection. The oblique case is used for radio direction finding, for earthquake research, and in long-distance flying. A separate map has to be constructed for each central point selected.

LAMBERT AZIMUTHAL EQUAL-AREA PROJECTION—The construction of this projection can best be understood from the polar case. All three cases are widely used. It makes a good polar map and it is often extended to include the southern continents. It is the most common projection used for maps of the Eastern and Western Hemispheres, and it is a good projection for continents as it shows correct areas with relatively little distortion of shape. Most of the continent maps in this atlas are in this projection.

IN THIS ATLAS, on almost all maps, parallels and meridians have been marked because they are useful for the following:

(a) They show the north-south and east-west directions which appear on many maps at oblique angles especially near the margins.

(b) With the help of parallels and meridians every place can be exactly located; for instance, New York City is at 41° N and 74° W on any map.

(c) They help to measure distances even in the distorted parts of the map. The scale given on each map is true only along certain lines which are specified in the foregoing discussion for each projection. One degree of latitude equals nearly 69 statute miles or 60 nautical miles. The length of one degree of longitude varies (1° long. = 1° lat. × cos lat.).